World Cars
1978

ISBN 0-910714-10-X
LC 74-643381
Published in the English language
edition throughout the world in 1978
by
HERALD BOOKS
Pelham, New York

WORLD CARS
1978

Published annually by
THE AUTOMOBILE CLUB OF ITALY

Edited by
L'EDITRICE DELL'AUTOMOBILE LEA

Management
ARNOLDO MONDADORI EDITORE
OFFICINE GRAFICHE

HERALD BOOKS, PELHAM, NEW YORK

Cover pictures

Pininfarina Ferrari 308 GTB (front)
Stutz Blackhawk VI (back)

Cover and layout:
Ovidio Ricci, Francesco Ricciardi

Editor

Annamaria Lösch

**Contributors and
correspondents**

Alberto Bellucci
Mario Bilancioni
Gianni Costa (China, India)
John Crawford (Australia)
Filippo Crispolti
Antonio Di Fazio
Flora Di Giovanni
Alan Langley (Great Britain)
Antonio Lioy
Hilmar Schmitt (Germany)
L.J.K. Setright
Bob Tripolsky (USA)
Jack K. Yamaguchi (Japan)

Language consultant

Jean Gribble

Editorial offices

L'Editrice dell'Automobile LEA
Viale Regina Margherita 279
00198 Rome, Italy

Composition and printing

Arnoldo Mondadori Editore
Stabilimento Grafico di Roma, Italy

Illustrations

Riproduzioni-Lith
Rome, Italy

SUMMARY

6 Editor's note

7 Motor racing - A triumph of tactics
by Filippo Crispolti

SPECIAL BODIES

14 Illustrations and technical information

ELECTRIC VEHICLES

40 Illustrations and technical information

WORLD AUTOMOBILE PRODUCTION

53 Europe - Back from the abyss
by L.J.K. Setright

59 Japan - Successes - Excesses
by Jack K. Yamaguchi

66 USA - A new dimension for a new generation
by Bob Tripolsky

EUROPE

74 Austria

74 Czechoslovakia

76 France

103 Germany (DDR)

104 Germany (FR)

145 Great Britain

198 Greece

199 Holland

200 Italy

226 Poland

227 Rumania

228 Spain

236 Sweden

EUROPE

242 Switzerland

246 USSR

250 Yugoslavia

THE AMERICAS

252 Canada

255 USA

313 Mexico

313 Brazil

323 Argentina

MIDDLE EAST AFRICA ASIA AUSTRALASIA

330 Turkey

331 Israel

332 Egypt

332 Nigeria

333 South Africa

342 Iran

342 India

343 China (People's Republic)

344 South Korea

345 Taiwan

346 Japan

392 Malaysia

394 Philippines

394 Australia

CAR MANUFACTURERS AND COACHBUILDERS

402 History, structure and activities

INDEXES

414 Name of car

416 Maximum speed

420 Makes, models and prices

Editor's note

The aim of *World Cars* is to present accurate information that is as complete as possible and to present it in a concise form. It is not always easy to reconcile the search for accuracy and completeness, for clarity and uniformity, and one or two preliminary remarks may help readers consulting this reference book.

The technical data is based on questionnaires completed by motor manufacturers throughout the world, and only when this information was incomplete or not made available has it been supplemented from other reliable sources.

Different cultures have always used different formulae to express maximum power and torque. DIN and SAE standards are familiar to most readers, while Japan alone uses the Japanese Industrial Standard (JIS). Expressed in DIN, power or torque is 20% lower than when expressed in SAE, while JIS ratings roughly correspond to SAE gross ratings. Horsepower in Anglo-Saxon countries expresses slightly higher power than the horsepower used by other countries (1.0139:1).

The innovation that marks recent editions of *World Cars* stems from the new units of measurement established by the Système Internationale d'Unites (SI). These are the kilowatt (kW), which replaces horsepower (hp), and the Newton metre (Nm), which replaces lb/ft. The conversion ratios are:

1 hp = 0.736 kW or 1 kW = 1.360 hp
1 kg m = 7 lb ft = 9.807 Nm or 1 Nm = 0.714 lb ft = 0.012 kg m

Fuel consumption, indicated by figures that are inevitably only a rough calculation, is based on a medium load and a cruising speed of about 60% of the car's maximum speed on a varied run. By dry weight is meant the fully-equipped car ready for the road (plus water, oil and petrol).

Since two valves per cylinder are now the norm and dual braking circuits are prevalent, only exceptions to the two have been indicated. Again, since the cylinders of all American V8 engines are slanted at 90°, this indication has been omitted for United States production. The technical information is grouped in descriptions of basic models, and similar models differing only in price and some details refer back to these descriptions.

Quite often a model is available with engines differing both in size and power. For the production of the United States, Canada, South Africa, and Australia, and some German, British and Japanese makes, each of these engines is described separately. In this case, whenever they are not given, the measurements and weight are the same as in the standard version. When the power-weight ratio is given, this usually refers to the 4-door sedan version. For other countries, the various engines have been listed under "Variations" at the foot of the basic description and — except when otherwise specifically indicated — should be taken as being available for all the models that refer back to the basic description. The "Optional Accessories" also apply to all the models that refer back to the basic description, except when otherwise specified. Some accessories may become "standard" or not be available, and others may be added, but this is always specified.

Editorial problems have prevented us from making certain corrections to the prices in the main body of the volume after the end of 1977 and so the reader is advised to refer to the price index for more recent prices of models, many of which may be raised in the course of the year. When prices are shown in the currency of the country of origin, these should be taken as ex-factory and therefore subject to revision if the car is imported into another country. Asterisked prices include VAT (value added tax) or its equivalent in other European countries, and in Great Britain also SCT (special car tax). The prices for American cars refer to models equipped with a standard engine of the lowest power listed (generally a four- or six-cylinder engine). Any surcharge for higher power standard engines is indicated at the foot of the list of models and prices. For cars imported into the United States, asterisked figures denote prices ex-showroom. In view of the requirements of Federal legislation, cars imported into the United States differ from the ones on sale in the respective countries of origin.

Technical and photographic coverage is given to over 1,500 models at present in production. It has sometimes been necessary to exclude models produced in very small numbers or visually almost identical to others illustrated, and also models that, even if built or assembled under another name outside the country of origin, are to all purposes a repetition of the model presented as part of the maker's standard range.

A TRIUMPH OF TACTICS

by Filippo Crispolti

There are not many fields of sport than can match the vitality shown over the last few years by motor racing at its highest level, that is to say in the 17 Formula 1 competitions. For some seasons now, the World Championship has not known the meaning of the word monotony. It is no longer followed just by an élite but is rather moving triumphantly towards wider and wider popularity. There is, too, a tendency among the major motor manufacturers to take a growing interest in Formula 1. At present only Ferrari, Lotus, Renault, Alfa Romeo and Matra count for something both in the field of mass production and that of motor racing, but a renewal of interest is in the air. Constructors who in the past have been involved in racing activities but today confine their efforts to the minor formulas and others tempted to take the great step in order to capture a more dynamic and younger image are finding it contagious. We shall have to wait and see whether vague intentions will crystallize into reality but there is no doubt that the trend is a positive one, not least because it will give less elbow-room to extra-sectorial sponsors, blamed by many for a certain economic pollution that has often damaged Formula 1 instead of ensuring its progress and vitality. While we are on the subject of sponsors, it is worth noting how, all over the world, antagonism is hardening towards cigarette advertising. In Germany the McLaren, Lotus and Ligier teams have for some years been obliged to cover up their advertising slogans and in other countries direct television coverage has been denied. In this atmosphere, it is very likely that there will be a growing flight from tobacco sponsors who

will make way for other backers on the Formula 1 waiting list.

But let us come to the events that characterized the 1977 season and saw the great come-back of Niki Lauda and the Ferrari who together had already taken the 1975 title. To some, the vicissitudes by which they regained the title were not particularly exalting, but I believe the detractors are mistaken. The fact that the Ferrari came home first in only four Grands Prix (three with Lauda and one with Reutemann) as compared with the five chalked up by the Lotus team (four with Andretti and one with Nilsson) and that the latter closed

Niki Lauda intelligently exploited his own driving skill and the Ferrari's reliability and endurance to take the Championship.

the encounter so far behind points-wise does not mean much. As long as the regulations are written in a certain way — awarding the championship not to the man who wins most often but to the one who notches up most points — it is only right that whoever best adapts himself to them should carry off the prize. Some people would like to see the regulations modified, protesting that the title did not go to the fastest, but it must be admitted that Lauda nearly always based his racing tactics on the objective need to score points and not so much on an atempt to lead the field home. There is no knowing how he would have behaved had the rules been different.

This is the controversial point. Last season Niki Lauda was accused of having too often played safe, backed up by his Ferrari which demonstrated exceptional reliability or at any rate much greater reliability than its chief rival, the Lotus. The fact is that the Ferrari team started out the 1977 season with a hangover of the problems that had dogged it in the second half of the 1976 season, or after Nürburgring. Its roadholding was not up to the mark and could not rival that of the keenest competition, the Lotuses, McLarens and the Wolf, and even the flat-12 power unit could no longer match up to the progress made by the best Cosworth eight-cylinders. The Ferrari boxer was still markedly superior to the British engine but it had to expend that superiority in compensating for the flaws of the chassis and suspension. Under those circumstances it was absurd to demand that either Lauda or Reutemann should drive an attacking race. It was much better tactics to play a waiting game and that is just what Lauda did with marked success. In my opinion, the fact that the tactics paid dividends fully justifies the methods used even if at times they were not particularly exalting ones. Carlos Reutemann in fact, who had a name to make, took greater risks and often had to pay for his daring with collisions or running off the track.

At this point it should be pointed out that in the second half of the season, the progressive deterioration of the relations between Lauda and his team led certain circles and journalists to express severe criticisms of the Austrian driver, not merely for the fireworks at the end of the season but also for the way he had driven earlier in the season and for some of his earlier attitudes.

But let us run through the main stages of the season in due order.

When the Championship got under way on 9 January at Buenos Aires, there were many questions left unanswered after the uncertain result of the 1976 season. James Hunt, who had taken the World Championship with an advantage of only one point over Niki Lauda, who had had to miss three races and was almost miraculously once more on the track, had not convinced everyone. A return match between the McLaren and the Ferrari was what everyone was waiting for. On the other side of the fence, in the Ferrari stable, there were serious doubts about the validity of their number one driver, especially after his declaring forfeit in Japan. As a result, there is a tendency to rely more — at least in these opening races — on the new boy, Carlos Reutemann, who had driven a Ferrari in only one Grand Prix, and was deeply engaged in testing on the magnificent Fiorano track, equipped with every kind of electronic apparatus for the measurement of partial times. The Argentine had lapped the miles of a fair number of Grands Prix while Lauda was rather lackadaisically concluding the 1976 season in America and it seemed only right that great faith should be placed in Reutemann. So the starter's flag dropped on the Argentine Grand Prix with the two members of the Ferrari team eager to shine — Lauda to shake off the shades of Fuji and Reutemann to win (if he could) his place as number one driver. James Hunt, on the other hand, was called upon to live up to his new title, while all the others were coming to grips with the innovations to their machines made during the brief winter pause.

James Hunt in pole position looked set to dominate the race with his McLaren but then incredibly the race went to the brand-new Wolf driven by Jody Scheckter who, with a fine instinct, had turned his back on the 6-wheeled Tyrrell for the more conventional four-wheeler ordered by the Austro-Canadian millionaire Wolf with no regard to cost. To win a race when you are making your debut is an achievement worthy of Jim Clark and the unforgettable revolutionary Lotus 25, and the Wolf hardly seemed to be in the same class. Nevertheless, its victory — facilitated by numerous retirements, brought the Scheckter-Wolf pairing to the attention of the spectators and, what is more, encouraged the team's " patron " not to spare his pocket in buying, for instance, the costly carbonium fibre for the shell and whatever else was necessary to let them fulfil their promise. For James Hunt the first championship competition was a complete flop, for his McLaren ran off the track ingloriously. It was a black day too for the Martini-Brabham Alfa Romeos which had seemed to be in fine form. The Anglo-Italian monocoque was often

Having to walk home too often when his McLaren M26 broke down meant that Hunt was out of the running for the title.

to come tantalizingly close to victory. For the Ferraris, the race was inconclusive, seeing that Niki Lauda retired with mechanical trouble and Reutemann was third.

The teams remained in South America to dispute the second Grand Prix of the season at Interlagos in Brazil, where Reutemann covered himself with glory by winning his first race for Ferrari thanks to the miraculous wing which paid off immediately.

Meanwhile Lauda inaugurates the waiting tactics which over the whole arc of the season are to prove to be the right ones for reconquering the title and for the moment bring him in a third place. Finishing between the two Ferraris is the McLaren of the reigning champion, James Hunt, while both Scheckter's Wolf and Andretti's Lotus were brought to a halt by engine failure, another of last year's dominating motifs which was to cost both of them dear. In South Africa, Niki Lauda matches Carlos Reutemann's Interlagos win. The Austrian drives a magnificent race while on his heels Scheckter confirms that the Wolf is a competitor to be reckoned with in the championship race. James Hunt upholds his reputation as the fastest driver in practice but is once again afflicted by endless problems during the race, partly because he is obliged to use the old McLaren M23 as the new, revolutionary M26 is not yet ready to assume the responsibility of representing the McLaren colours. Another breakdown for Andretti's Lotus and now, with hindsight, we can see how much the Ferrari's reliability counted against adversaries who were often more brilliant, but in fits and snatches.

At this point, some of the main themes of the 1977 season were already clear. It was obvious that Niki Lauda had fully recovered from the physical consequences of his Nürburgring smash and the potentially equally serious hangover of his withdrawal from the Japanese Grand Prix. The presence of Reutemann in the team and an ill-disguised lack of faith in Lauda that contaminates the highest levels of the Ferrari team merely stimulate the Austrian ace and enhance his determination to show that he is as great as ever — if anything, greater than ever.

The last race on the American side of the Atlantic, before the F 1 circus finally returns to the old continent, is at Long Beach in California on the second town circuit at present in use. Only the most superficial of observers are ready to assert that the two victories that the Ferrari team has already carried off are enough to demonstrate beyond all doubt that the Italian car has established its supremacy. The Ferrari has its problems, above all ones of roadholding on medium speed tracks, the very type of circuit that is most favourable to the Lotus. At Long Beach the clash between the two marques comes to the fore, and in the final analysis Mario Andretti had the better of Lauda thanks to the superior handling and braking qualities of the Lotus. Once again the Wolf shone and in fact, Jody Scheckter failed to win this race only because of engine trouble. At the start of the California G.P. Reutemann committed a ghastly mistake on coming into the first extremely difficult bend on the downward slope. Luckily the escape road prevents a disaster because behind the Argentine driver there are collisions involving Regazzoni and Brambilla, and Watson and Hunt. This leit motiv of accidents at the start is a dangerous trend that is gaining ground, due to the fact that on many circuits a good start is of enormous importance as it pays to conquer a handy position at the start rather than laboriously work your way up through the field during the race.

After a month's pause comes the Spanish Grand Prix where this year, too, there is no lack of drama. In fact, at the last minute Lauda cries off because of a painful ribcage. The X-rays fail to show up anything, but this is often the case. And so Mario Andretti drives his Lotus to a trouble-free victory, partly because Jacques Laffite is put out of the race by the failure to tighten up a wheel of his Ligier-Matra properly and Reutemann can do no better than second place. The Martini-Brabham Alfa Romeos, in the limelight at the beginning of the season, fail to shine here. The series of slower circuits — all roadholding and traction — do not suit this machine either and all the forecasts are for the brightest of futures for Andretti and his Lotus, with the main danger coming from the business-like Wolf-Scheckter pairing. Meanwhile the world champion has to come to grips with the problems of getting the new McLaren M 26 up to scratch.

Monte Carlo, the society circuit par excellence, has always been more of a meeting place for the jet set than a scene for a hard-fought race. Anyone who happened to be present just at this race, or watch it on television, would get a rather distorted idea of the world of Formula 1 racing, for many of the most important elements of motor racing at its highest level are here relegated to a secondary position. It is a show rather than a competition. It is won in 1977

James Hunt, frequently the fastest in practice, was let down by the unreliability of the Cosworth engines, pushed beyond the limit.

by an up-and-coming Scheckter thanks to a fine get-away, while James Watson in the pole position completely fails to take advantage of it. The driving wheels of the Irishman's Brabham are slap on the painted stripes of a pedestrian crossing and when the flag goes down the great rear tyres spin desperately but vainly. After that, given the narrowness of the... track, there is no question of overtaking Scheckter's Wolf. In fact, in his repeated attempts to remedy his initial error, Watson sacrifices the brakes of his Brabham and the second place goes to Lauda, followed home by his team-companion Reutemann. James Hunt

makes it clear once more that town circuits are not for him. For the Cosworth engine, this is the hundredth victory, an historic event and a record that is unlikely ever to be surpassed.

From now on, the season takes on a frenzied rhythm which, on the technical level, makes most of the ritual and sometimes indispensable mechanical adjustments out of the question. There is only fifteen days between races and, for testing the tyres above all, the time flies. At Zolder, in Belgium, the cards are shuffled once more. In practice Mario Andretti demonstrates untouchable superiority, outclassing the man with the second fastest lap time — James Watson — by no less than a second and a half on a circuit of 4,262 metres. Here, not only the streamlining but also a differential in controlled skidding plays in favour of the Lotus. At the moment of the race, down comes the rain and Andretti with dual caliper brakes at the front as well runs into Watson's Brabham from the back, eliminating him and putting himself out of the race as well. But even so it is a Lotus that is first past the chequered flag, for Gunnar Nilsson manages to get the better of a Lauda whom some would accuse of being too cautious on a wet track but who in fact completes a race that is a masterpiece of intelligence and positive prudence. This is more than Reutemann, who runs off the track, can do or Scheckter for that matter, while Hunt's McLaren is penalized from the outset by his choice of tyres for a dry surface.

Scheckter and the Wolf, or the 1977 phenomena. It rarely happens that a debutant car and team can get within sight of the world championship.

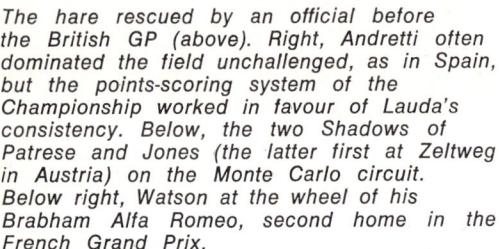

The hare rescued by an official before the British GP (above). Right, Andretti often dominated the field unchallenged, as in Spain, but the points-scoring system of the Championship worked in favour of Lauda's consistency. Below, the two Shadows of Patrese and Jones (the latter first at Zeltweg in Austria) on the Monte Carlo circuit. Below right, Watson at the wheel of his Brabham Alfa Romeo, second home in the French Grand Prix.

(photos by Filippo Crispolti)

Above, two 12-cylinders, the Matra and Alfa, during the Monte Carlo GP. Below Niki Lauda, 1977 World Champion.

In Sweden, the next race on the calendar, the loser-out is Mario Andretti who has to cede the race to Laffite's Ligier Matra, the first Formula 1 win for a French car, because he runs out of petrol. Anderstorp has never been a circuit to favour the Ferraris and this year Niki Lauda spins off the road while Reutemann earns a good third place. Scheckter is let down by his engine and Hunt is badly hampered by his tyres.

In France, at Dijon, Andretti takes his revenge for the Swedish defeat by winning in the final lap a race that had been dominated by Watson and his Brabham. For the two Ferrari men a fifth (Lauda) and a sixth (Reutemann) place. It is not much to crow over but it is in this race that Niki Lauda regains the top position in the championship table, a position he was never to lose.

On his home circuit, Silverstone, it is James Hunt who achieves the best result. Although this is not a sign of things to come, the retirement of Andretti and Scheckter due to engine failure is very worrying for the future for the Lotus and Wolf teams. On fast circuits the Cosworth engine is proving extremely unreliable both in the updated version prepared by Nicholson and in the "official" version called the "development" engine with a wide use of magnesium. In the British G.P. Lauda is second and, although Reutemann is only 14th, the come-back of the Ferraris continues, favoured to some extent by fast circuits that exalt the power and new and improved aerodynamics of the Italian machine.

In Germany, this time at Hockenheim after the veto against Nürburgring, Lauda wins and Reutemann is fourth, while Hunt and Andretti and Scheckter are out of the race due to engine trouble. Disa-

ster, in fact, seems to have struck the eight-cylinder engine and the phenomenon is destined to repeat itself in Austria where, because of the rain, the winner is the outsider Alan Jones with the Shadow. But Lauda cannot be deprived of second place (Reutemann is fourth) and leaps well into the lead in the championship table.

In Holland, the Austrian triumphs once more on a favourable track but here the way is laid for the Ferrari's success by the mess-up between Hunt and Andretti. The latter, attempting an impossible overtaking manoeuvre, collides with Hunt, and for the Lotus and the best-placed McLaren one of the crucial races of the season is over. Andretti duly wins in Italy when for once he is not harassed by mechanical difficulties but by now it is too late, for Lauda comes second to him and chalks up all the points he needs.

But on the eve of the Monza race the bombshell of the season explodes. Lauda declares that, as there is no more reason for him to remain with the Ferrari team, he is leaving. It is a shock for everyone in the Ferrari stable. The only one to benefit from it is Reutemann who, had Lauda remained, would probably have switched teams himself. Then, a few days after the first announcement, the second. Lauda is moving over to the Brabham-Alfa Romeo team which in its turn is divorcing from its Italian vermouth sponsor to pair up with another backer —another Italian but this time specializing in less inebriating drinks — milk and other dairy products. Once again, it is Lauda the half-hearted on the scene, for after competing at Watkins Glen in the United States and taking a second place behind James Hunt and thus making mathematically certain of

the World Championship title, he deserts both the Canadian and the Japanese Grands Prix, won respectively by Scheckter and Hunt. For the last two Grands Prix, Lauda's place in the Ferrari team is taken by the Canadian Gilles Villeneuve whose only previous F 1 experience has been a British Grand Prix at the wheel of a McLaren. Villeneuve runs off the track both at Mosport and Fuji. On the latter occasion, after running into Peterson's Tyrrell, the greenhorn's Ferrari lands on top of a group of spectators in an unauthorized position, killing two of them. This was a bitter close to what had been a thrilling championship season.

Lauda's change of stable is certainly one of the motifs that will lend interest to the present season, just as it will be interesting to see how the Ferraris will get on without the driver who has given them the greatest number of outright victories in Formula one — fourteen in three years. And all the more so since Villeneuve seems remarkably accident-prone.

The other major 1978 theme is likely to be the Michelin challenge to Goodyear. After dominating the scene for so long, Goodyear are clearly worried after the success of the Michelin tyres mounted by Reutemann in his Brazil walkover.

The surprise of the early part of the 1978 season is Emerson Fittipaldi's Copersugar. Driving the team's spare car, he brought the Rio crowd to its feet as he closed the gap on Andretti whose 3rd gear packed up, costing him what might have been, with his Argentina win, a useful lead in the Championship. It seems that the John Player Lotus specials may once more be envying the Ferraris' reliability in spite of an all-new Lotus transmission.

It must be said that the 1977 season was particularly generous with Italian colours. Not only was the World Championship won at the wheel of a Ferrari, but in the rallies, too, there was a come-back on the international scene by Fiat who with the 131 Abarth had the better of the Ford Escort. In Formula 2 the Frenchman Arnoux made good use of his experience which gave him the edge over the nineteen-year-old "Roman American", Eddie Cheever, but in the Formula 3 European Championship it was once again an Italian, the rising star Piercarlo Ghinzani, who carried off the laurels. Finally, there was the World Makers Championship won by Alfa Romeo which really had no competitors due to ill-chosen regulations which led at times to races where there were only eight or ten starters.

The Fiat 131 Abarth led the Ford Escort home in the World Rally Championship, with Waldegaard coming second to Munari.

Special bodies

Illustrations and technical information

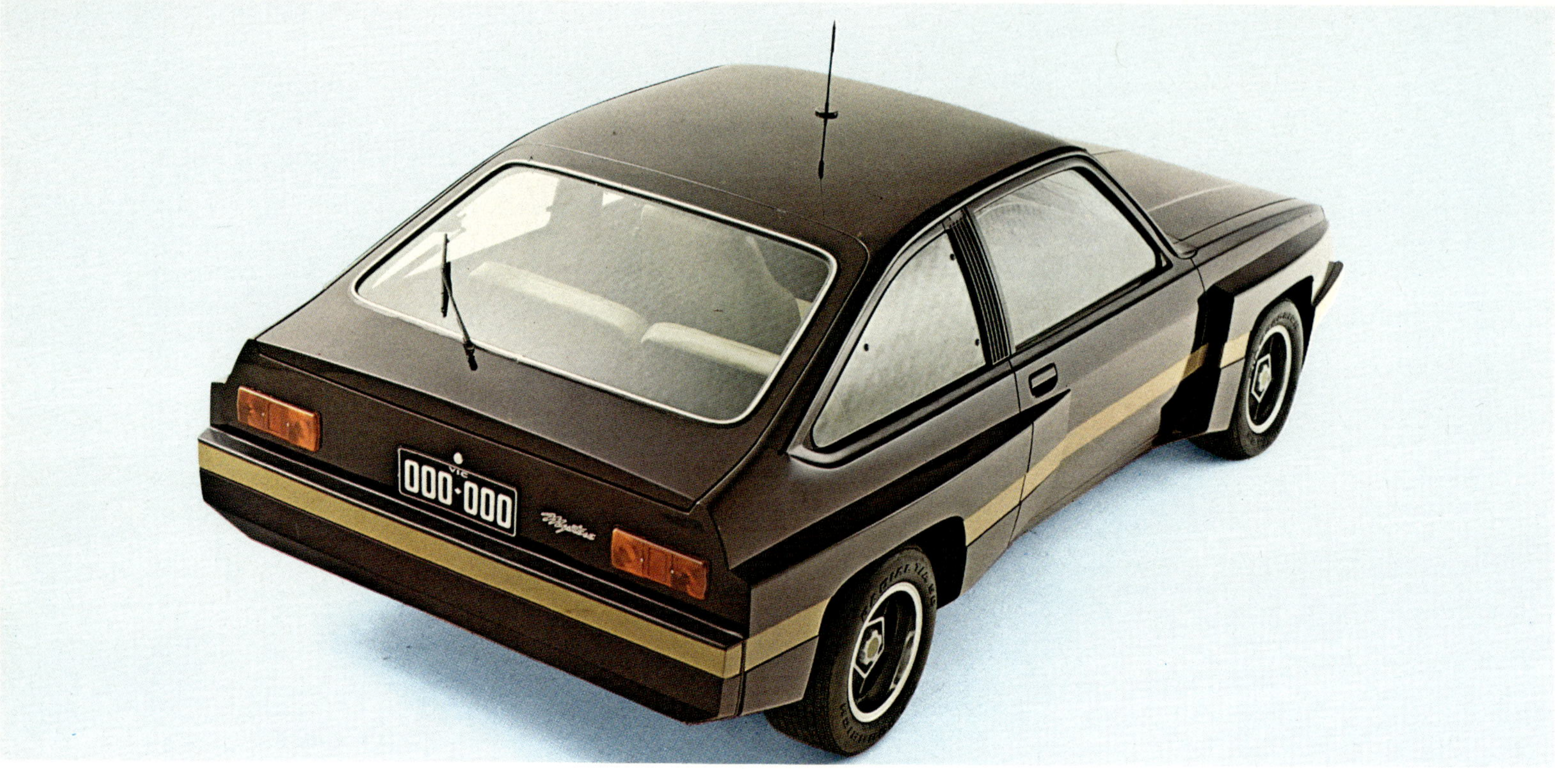

Simple, economical maintenance, availability of spare parts from all Holden dealers and low price distinguish this sports coupé completely restyled around the original Tornana Hatchback. The tail has been sectioned and shortened by 14 in and the front has a new nose-cone and aerodynamical wind-dam.

BERTONE   Ascot   ITALY

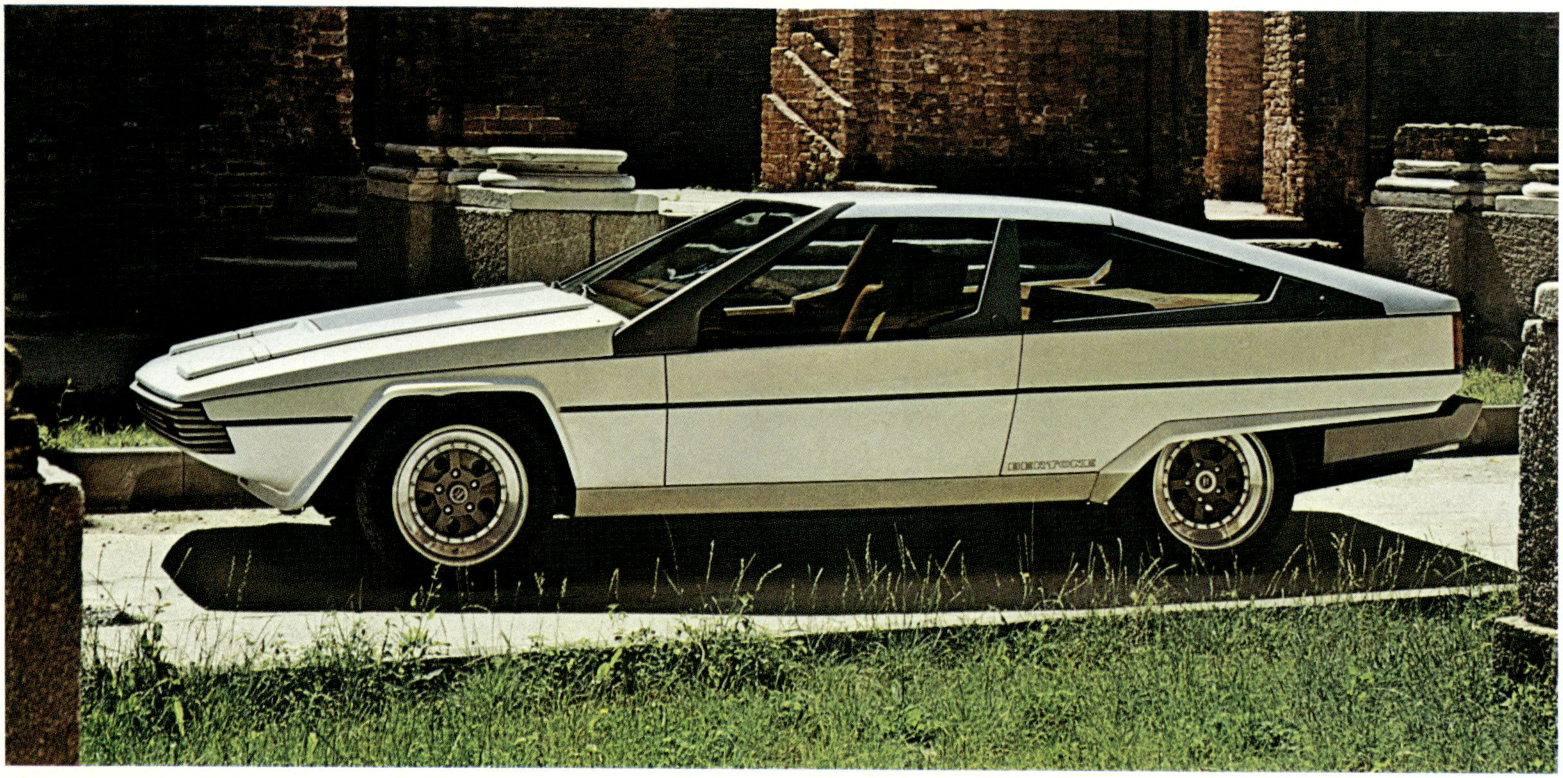

The lure of the XJS's 12 cylinders led Bertone to design this refined and harmonious 3-door sports car. Great ingenuity marks the solution for the air filter which has its own housing, separate from the rest of the bonnet, making it look lower although it is 20 cm shorter than the original.

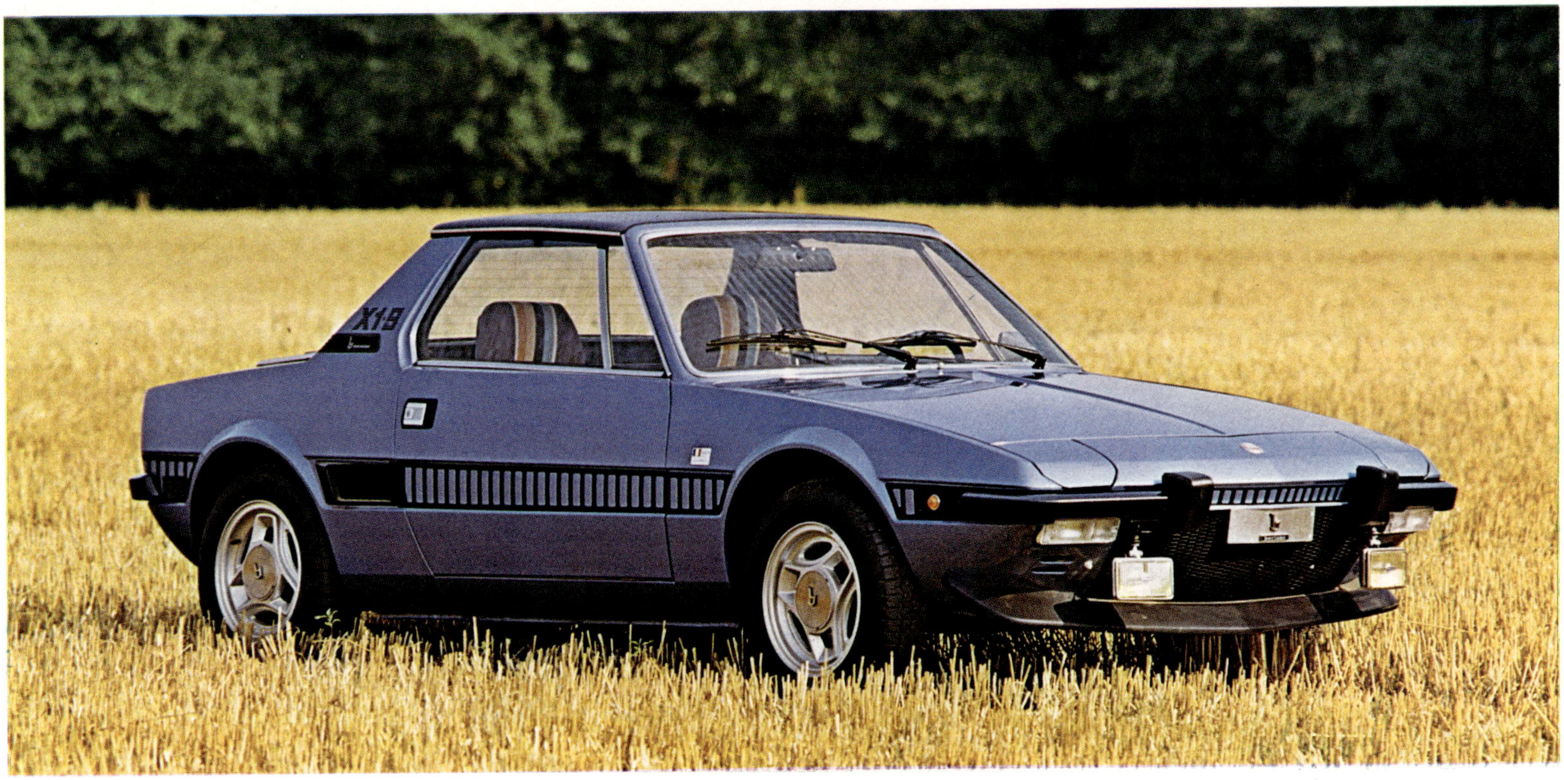

The marked success enjoyed by the standard version of the X 1/9 led to the realization of this " Series Speciale "
in which both the body and the interior have undergone modifications. On the flank of each car sold figures the flag
of the owner's country with a progressive number and the signature of the coachbuilder.

This extremely sporty saloon aimed at an élite of enthusiasts is homologated for Group 4-Special GT.
The cars entered for competitions will be prepared by Abarth who hope to confirm the success of the Rally
in winning the 1977 Rally championship. The Rally exploits Fiat experimental research on a safety car.

BERTONE — Volvo 264 TE — ITALY

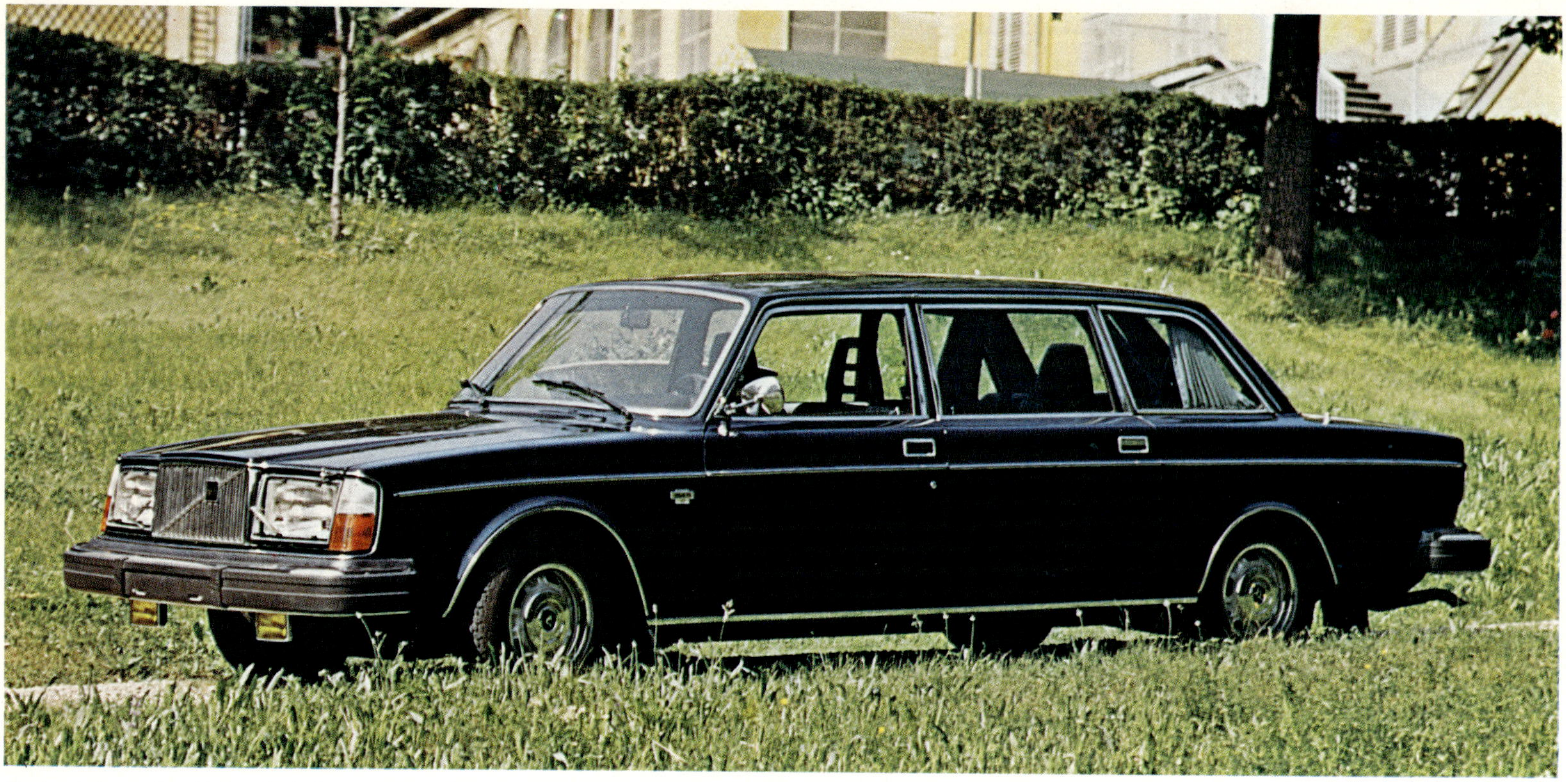

Derived from the Volvo 264 GL saloon, this elegant limousine is destined for diplomats and the like. The hull has been reinforced and lengthened by the insertion of new doors, windows, roof and various other elements. The sumptuous equipment includes a radio telephone and refrigerator. Overall length 220.47 in (560 cm), height 56.69 in (144 cm).

BERTONE — Volvo 262C — ITALY

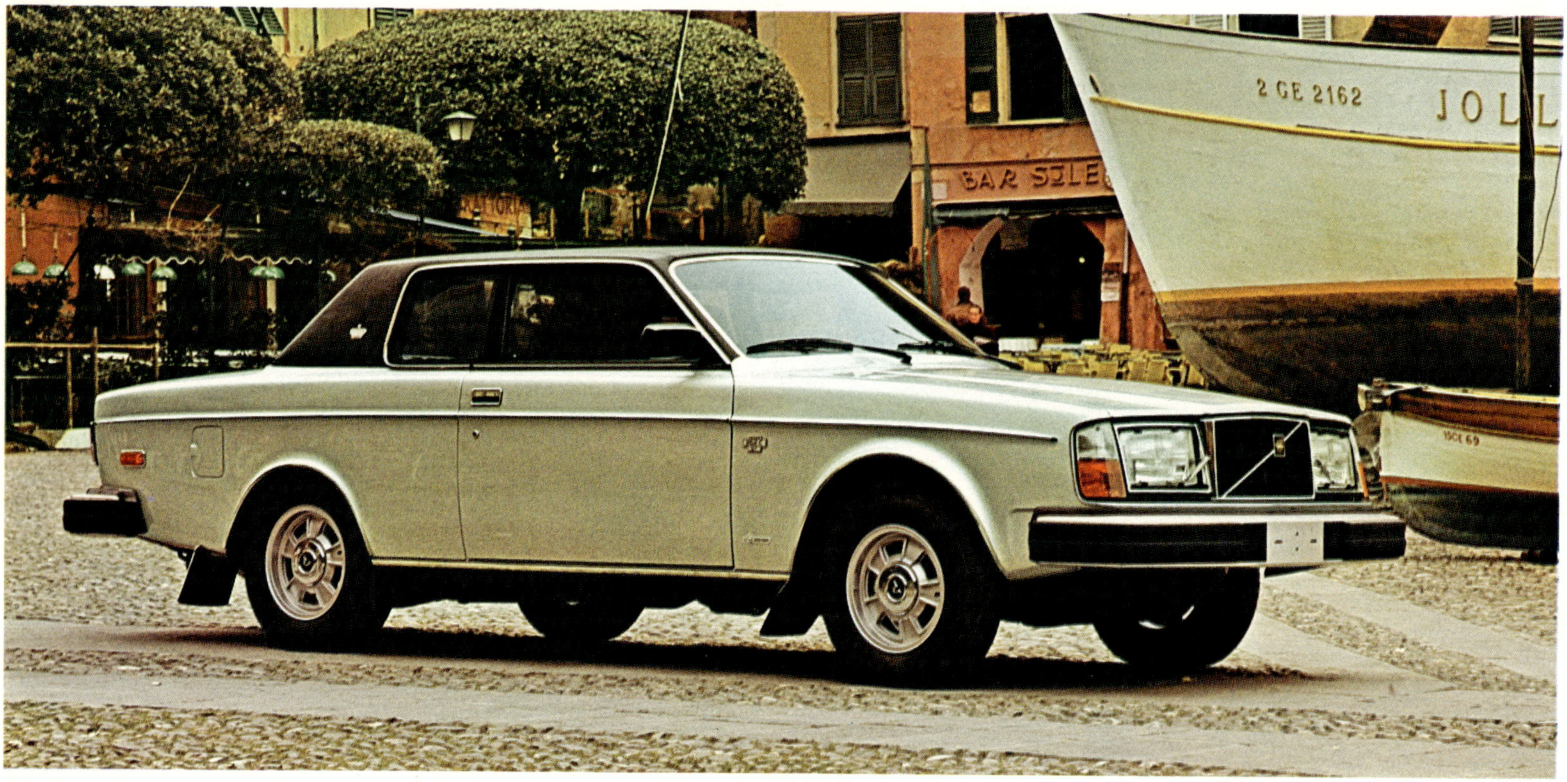

Bertone is building the 262C to Volvo specifications aimed at providing maximum comfort and low noise levels in a 4-seater coupé for an exclusive clientèle. The spare tyre is stowed flat in the boot, to be blown up with a compressed air cylinder when needed.

Simple, pleasing lines characterize this 2+2 coupé with Turbo-Hydramatic 3-speed automatic gearbox.
Its dimensions are: 190.94 in (485 cm) long, 72.44 in (184 cm) wide, weight 4,443 lb (2,015 kg).
The 8-cylinder 5,354 cc engine develops 230 bhp (DIN) at 4,700 rpm, with a maximum speed in the region of 137 mph (220 km/h).

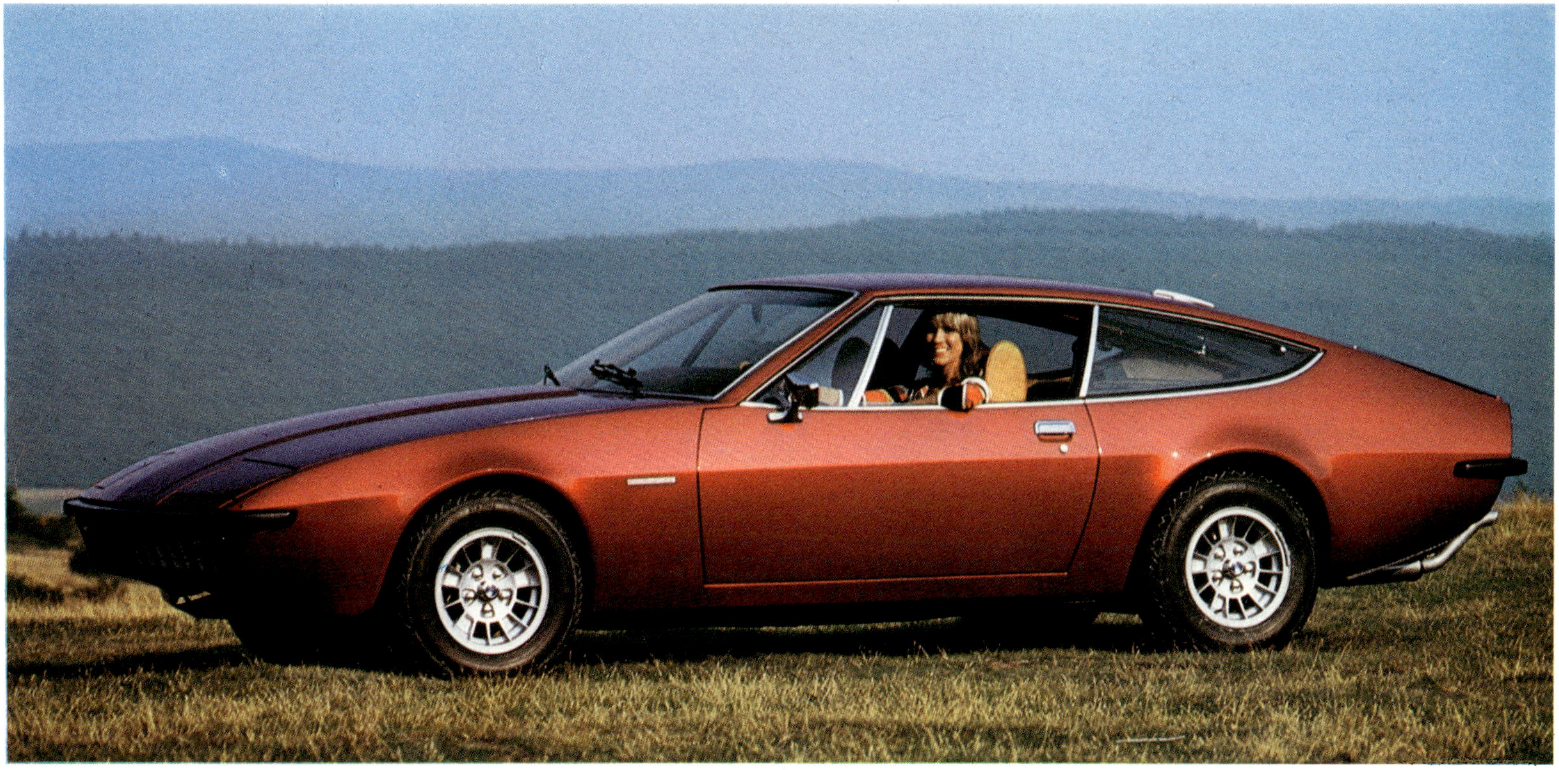

USA   Rolls-Royce Silver Shadow Estate Pickup   CLYDE CASSADY

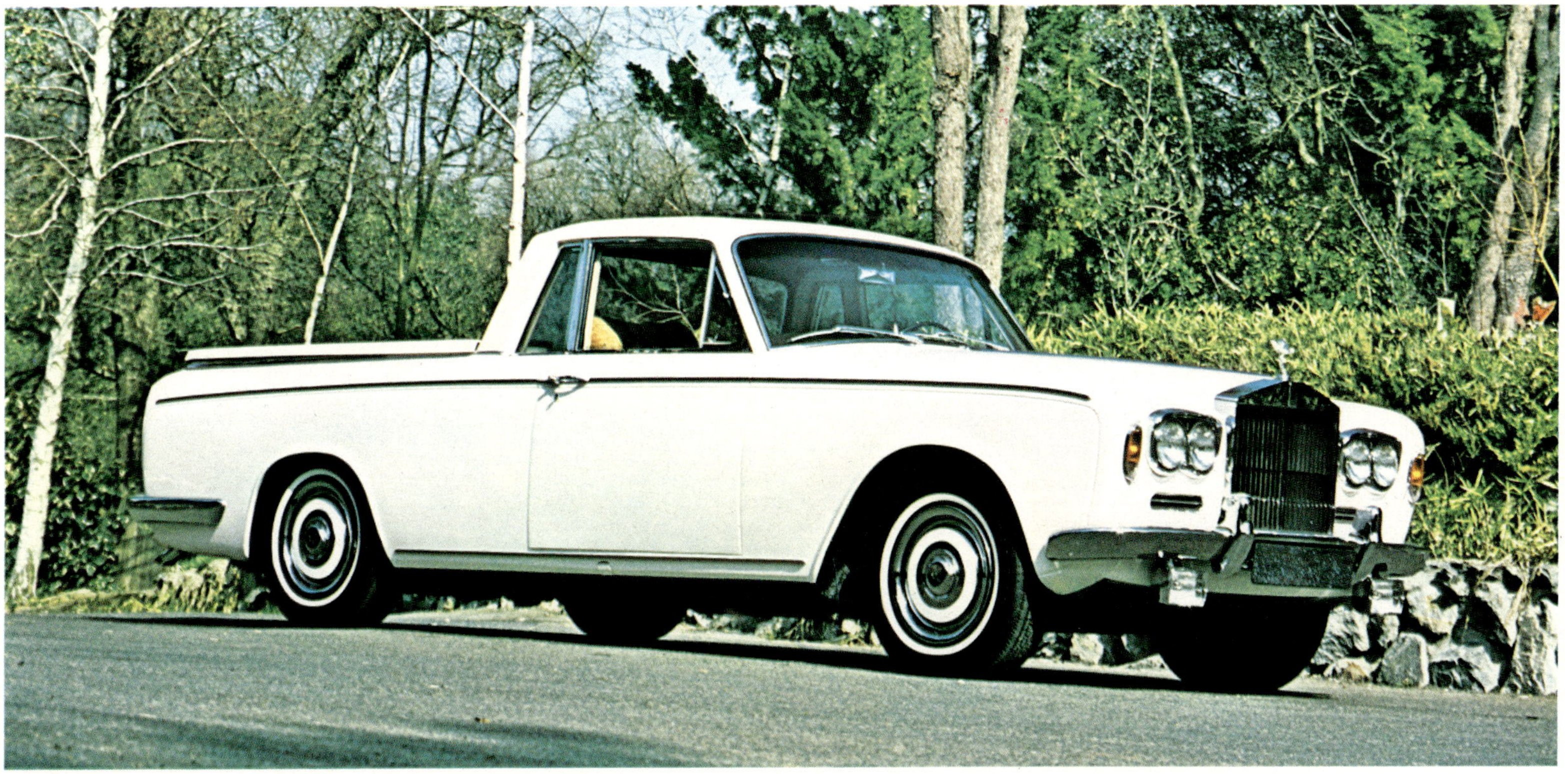

The body of a 1967 Silver Shadow has been modified only at the rear where the pickup section continues the original lines.
Two electric syneoids with a reverse type shock automatically lift the cargo cover, while the tailgate lowers conventionally.
Tinted glass and an electronically controlled bar drawer are other features.

This running prototype with 70 hp DIN diesel engine has a righthand sliding passenger door, electrically controlled by the driver, A safety bar with adjustable height gives rear seat protection, while for the driver there is the bullet-proof partition and a seat specially designed for long driving hours.

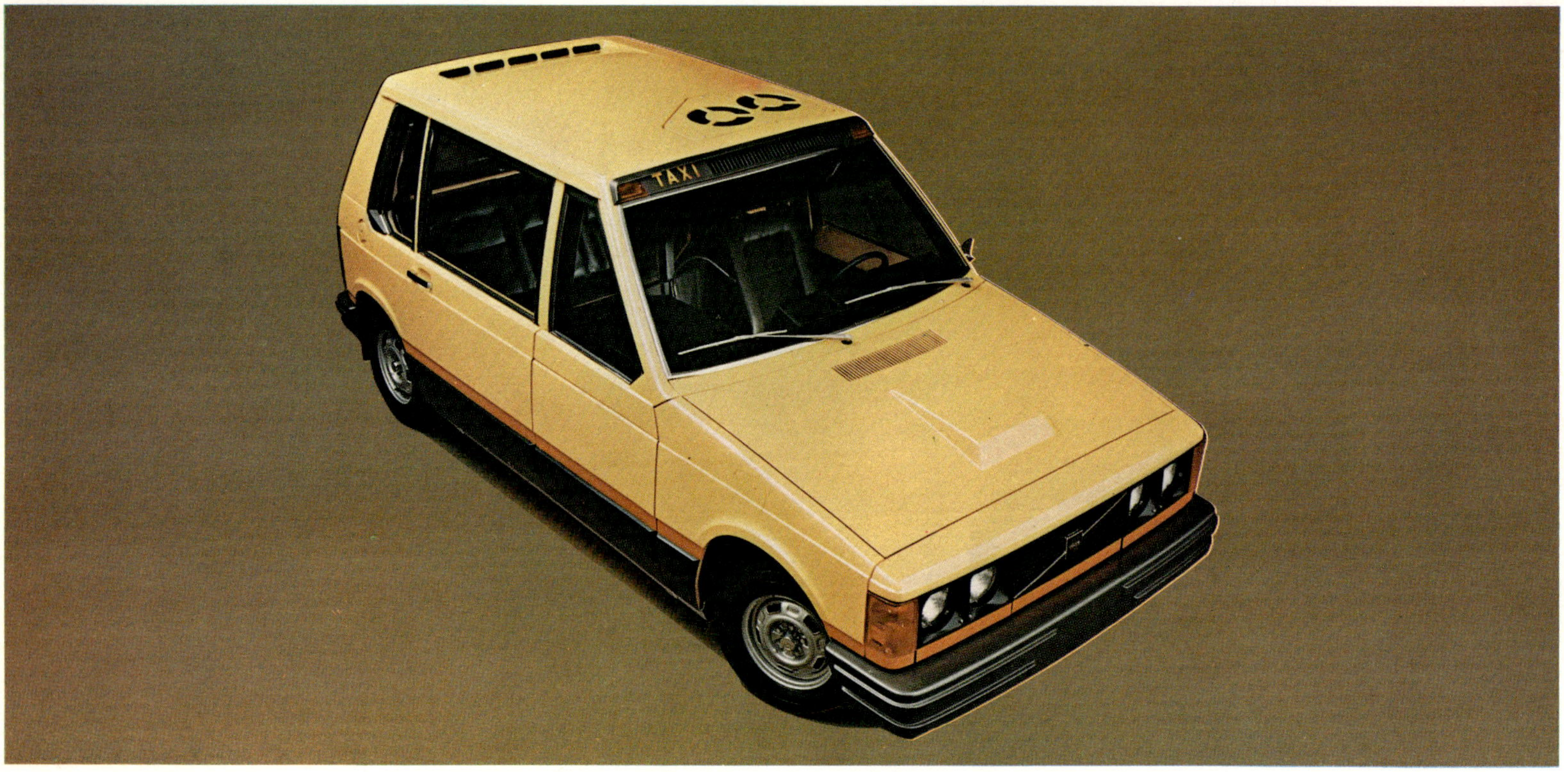

COLEMAN - MILNE Minster **GREAT BRITAIN**

An extra 10 in (25 cm) of rear compartment leg room is built into the Minster derived from the 2.8 litre Ford Granada. The designers cut the body in half and weld in additional bodywork, fitting larger rear doors and a distinctive front end. Air-conditioning and electric windows and partition are among the extras.

*This luxury convertible is the most advanced and sophisticated convertible
Crayford has yet made. It confirms that a market still exists for an elegant,
powerful convertible even if few major manufacturers are prepared to cater for it.*

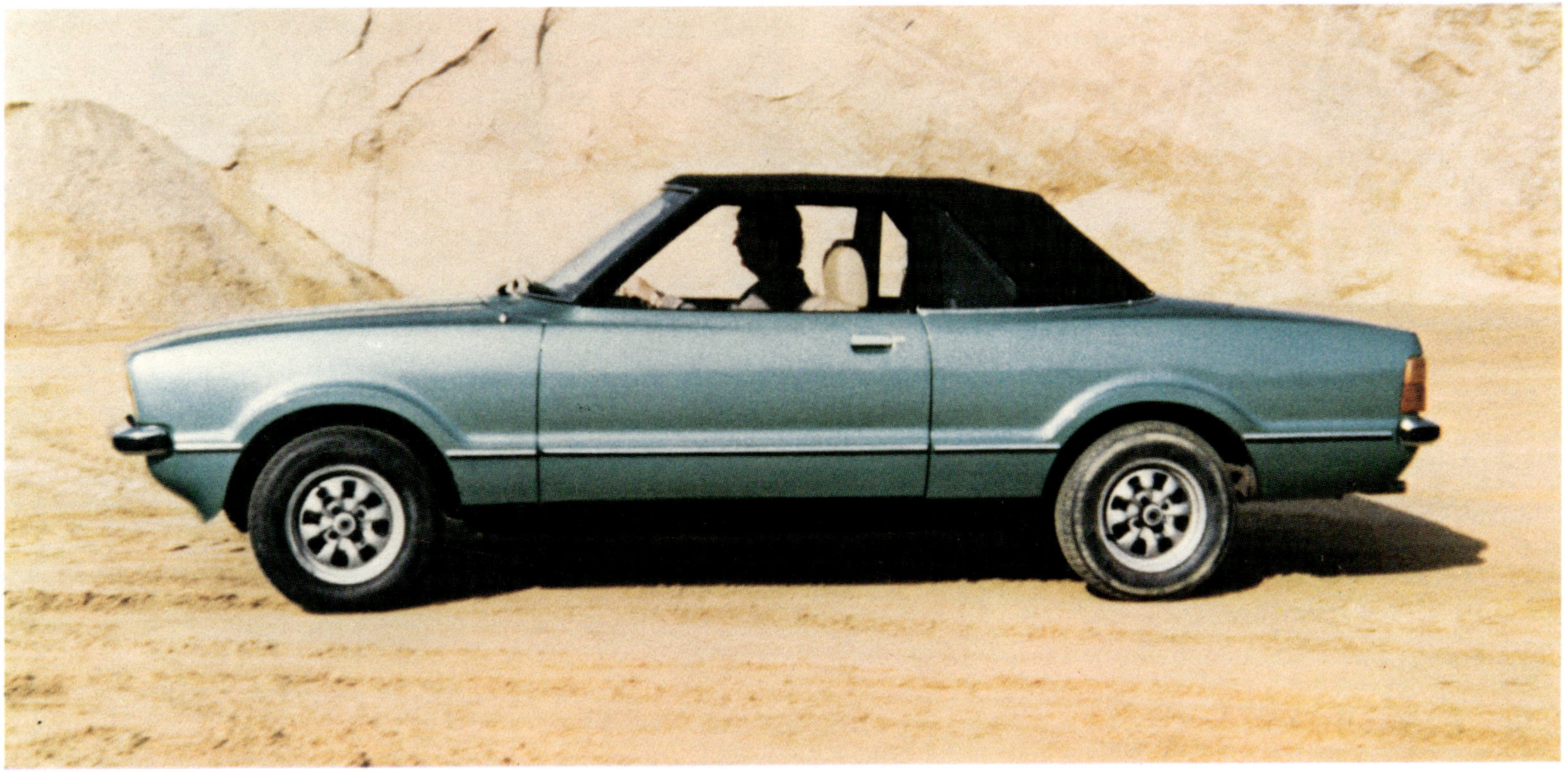

GREAT BRITAIN   Mercedes-Benz 450 SEL Estate   CRAYFORD

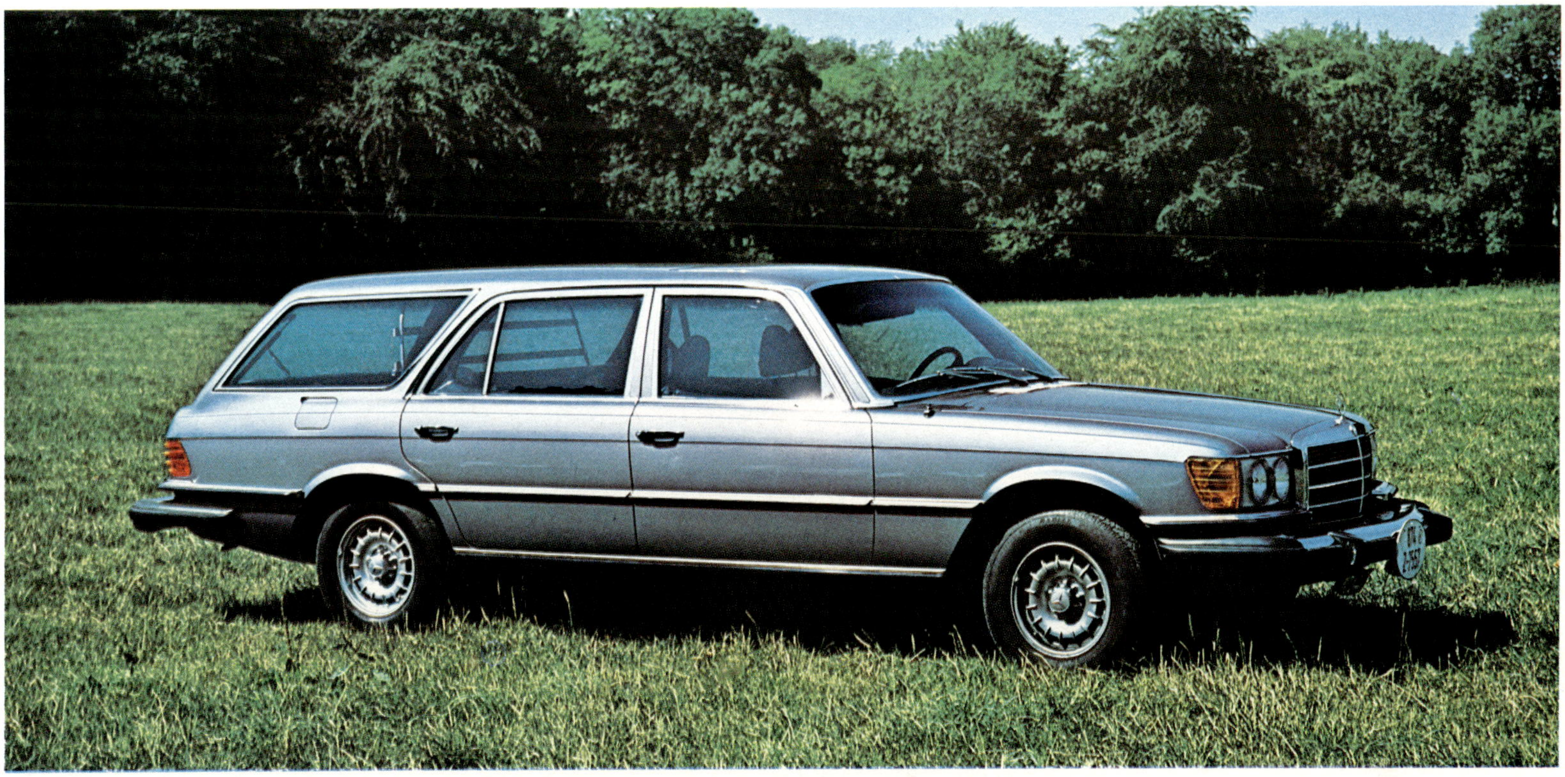

*A station wagon that retains the elegant lines of the 450 S limousine, the Crayford Mercedes
has a 4,520 cc engine that guarantees a very respectable top speed - 130 mph (210 km/h). The conversion entails a longer roof,
tailgate and large side windows for the luggage area. It is now built under licence in Australia and the U.S.A..*

DELOREAN **DMC - 12** **USA**

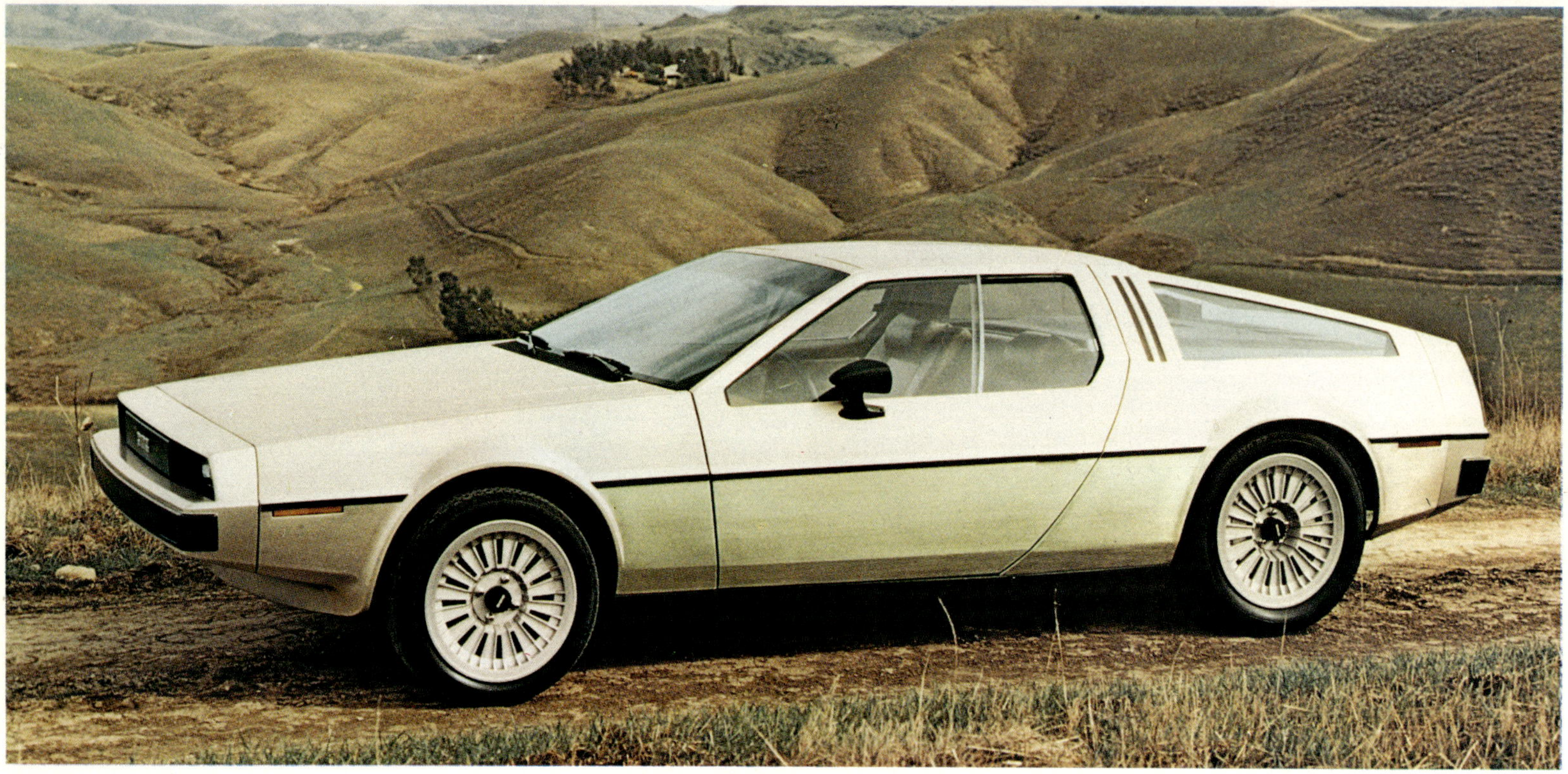

Giugiaro's futuristic 2-seater has crisp, aggressive lines in which the 10 mph (16 km/h) safety bumpers are smoothly integrated into the whole design. The chassis-body will be in Elastic Reservoir Molding, which is much lighter than steel. Safety and low consumption are emphasized.

FISSORE **Scout 127** **ITALY**

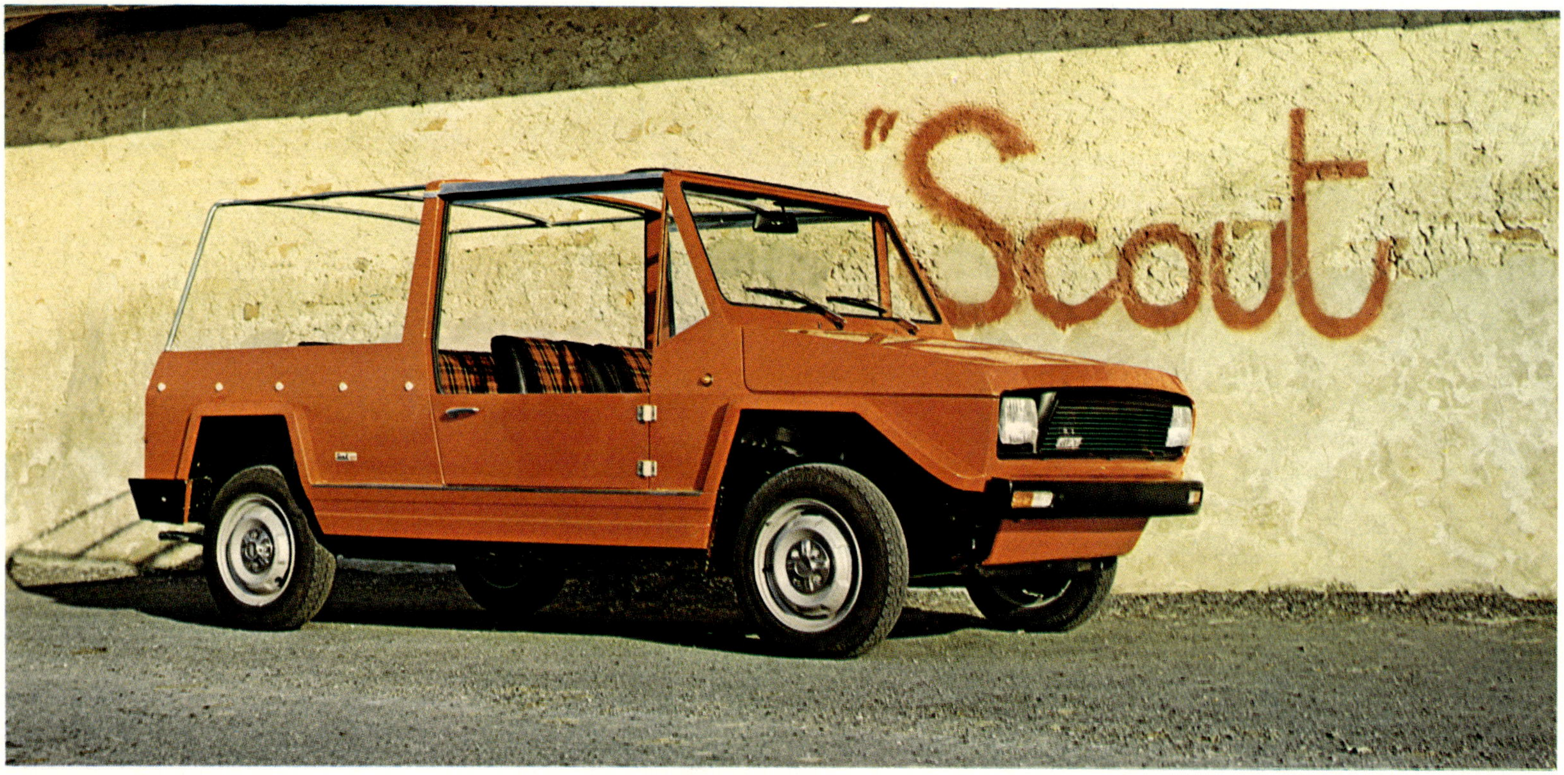

Based on the chassis and mechanics of the Fiat 127 903 cc, the Scout is built in four versions, basic, pick-up, hard-top and removable roof. The overall length is 138.98 in (353 cm), width 57.87 in (147 cm) and curb weight without driver 1,510 lb (685 kg).

BMW GT Coupé

FRUA

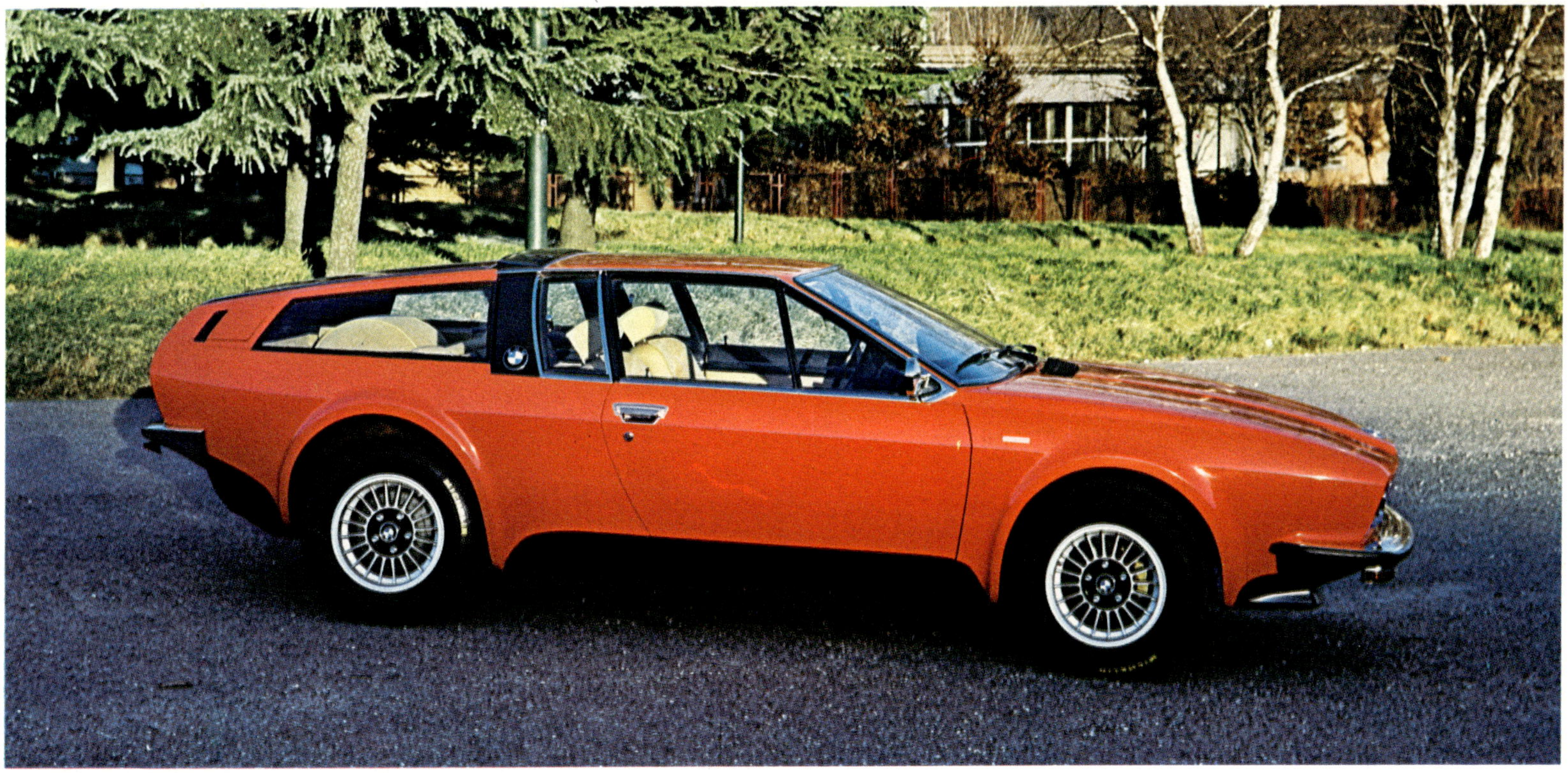

On the chassis of the Series 5, Frua has created this snappy coupé with wheelbase shortened to 94.49 in (240 cm). BMW 520 I mechanics with a 1,990 cc injection engine and 5-speed gearbox are used. The belt line is low to increase lateral vision and a tailgate gives access to the luggage area. Overall length 167.32 in (425 cm) and width 69.68 in (177 cm).

ITALY

Maserati Kyalami

FRUA

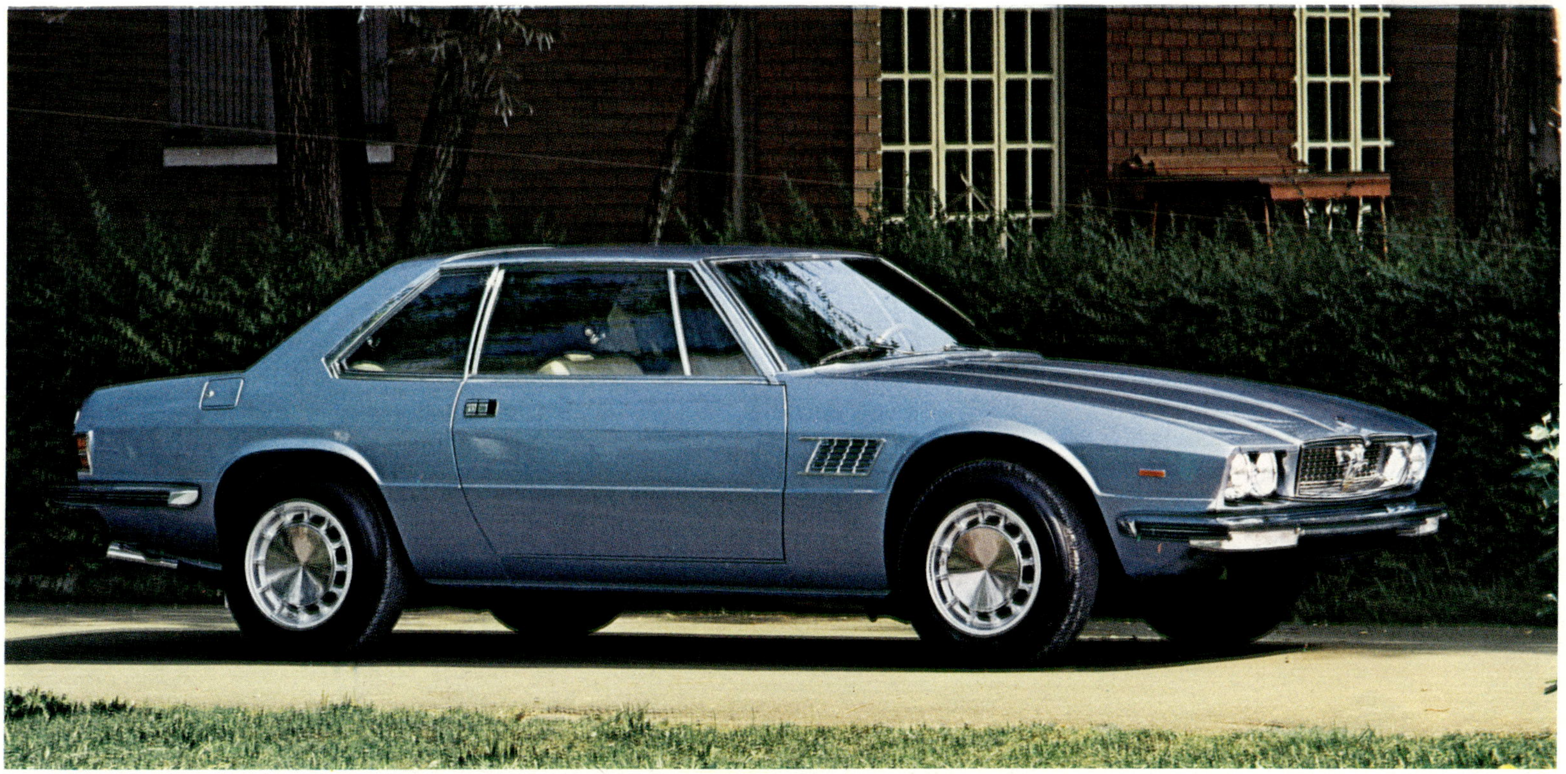

This 2+2 coupé is called Kyalami, after the famous South African Grand Prix track near Johannesburg. The mechanical parts are by Maserati, with the V8 4,136 cc 265 bhp engine developing a maximum speed in the region of 150 mph (240 km/h).

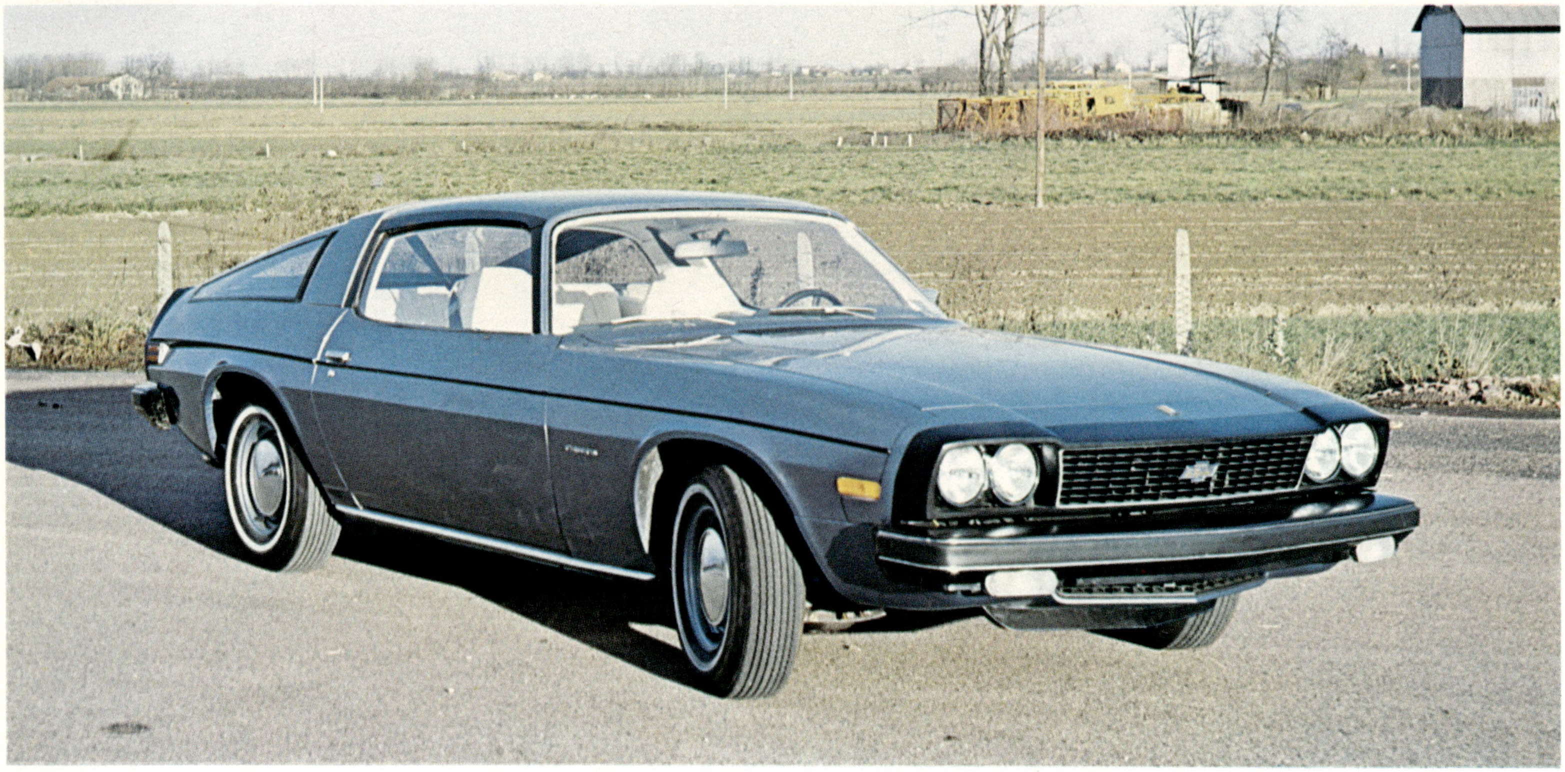

While respecting American legislation on safety, Frua has modified the lines of the standard Camaro and given the body
a truly Italian air, with an upward opening tailgate-rear window affording access to the luggage. The 5,700 cc V8 engine is
more than ample for a 4-seater coupé. Overall length 196.46 in (499 cm), width 74.80 in (190 cm) and height 49.21 in (125 cm).

GHIA Ford Urban Car ITALY

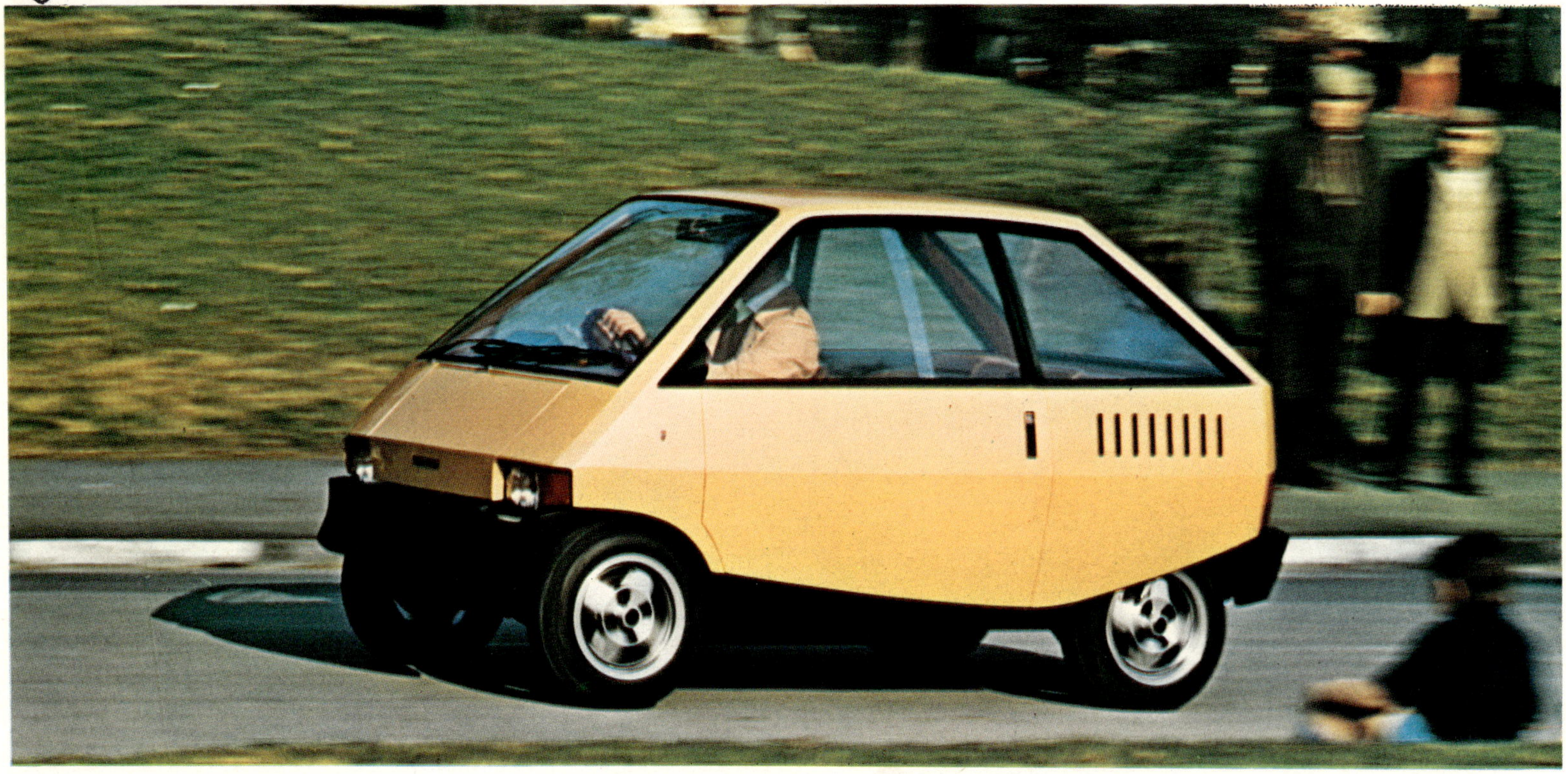

This lively little car is the search for a solution, for the immediate future, to personal transport
problems in the great metropolitan areas. Despite its compactness (the overall length is a mere 113.39 in,
288 cm), the prototype can carry four comfortably thanks to the adoption of a rear-mounted Fiesta engine.

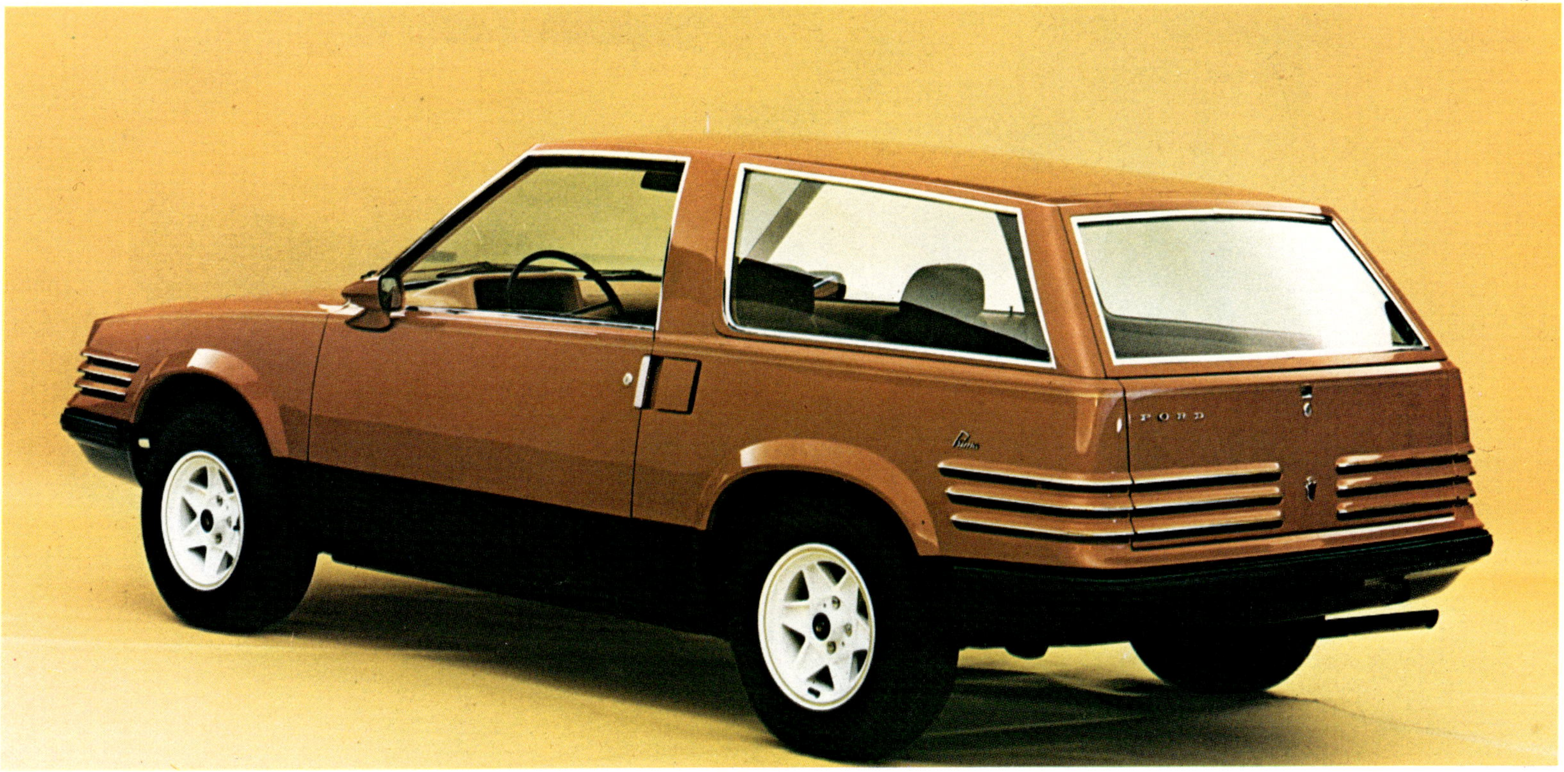

On the chassis of the Ford Fiesta and in collaboration with the Ford Design Studio in Dearborn, Ghia has prepared this prototype, the most versatile of the ones built up to now and with the widest range of uses. The estate car illustrated above is one of the four different cars into which the Prima can be transformed in a few minutes.

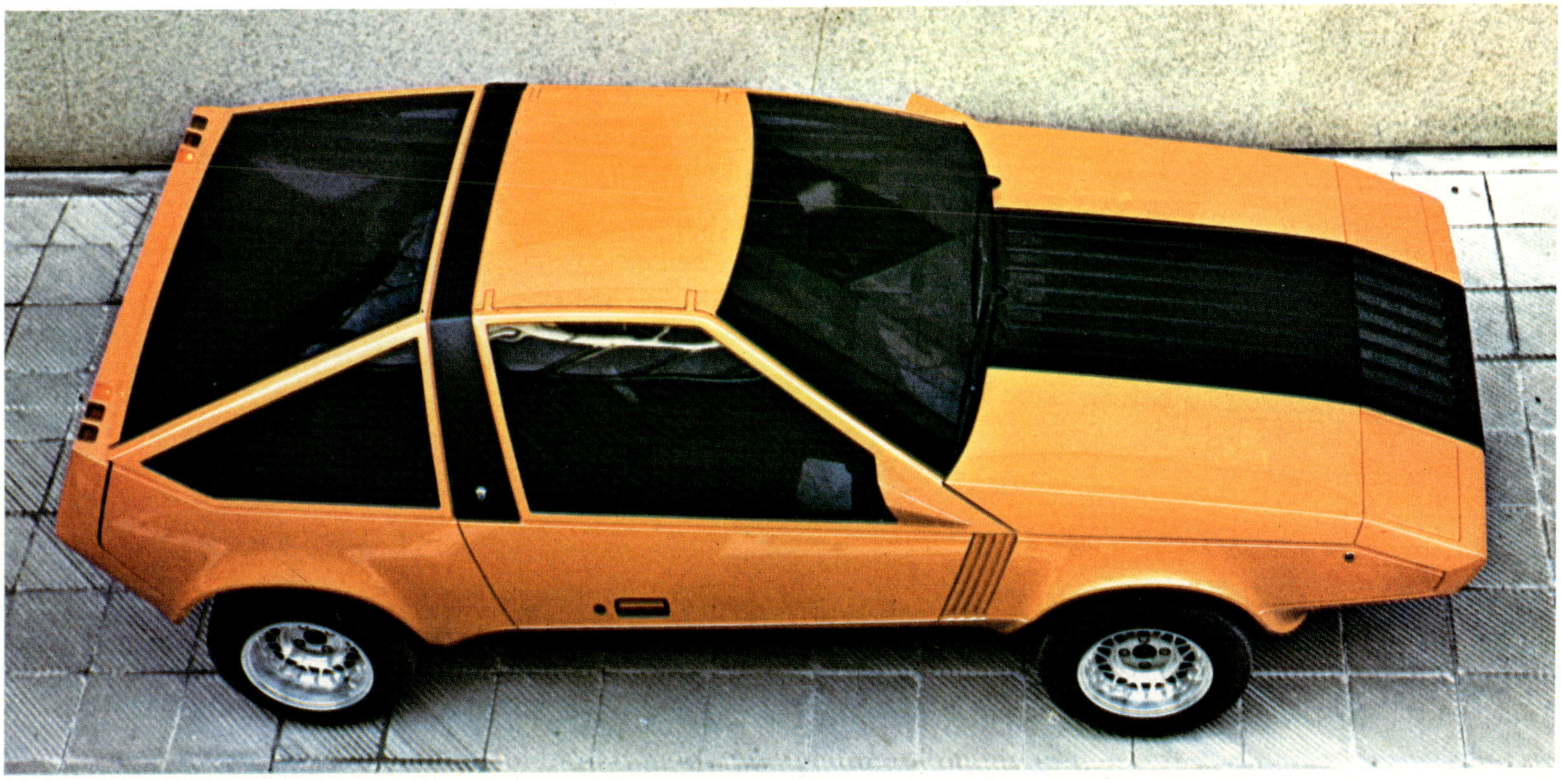

This one-off prototype based on the Fiesta chassis and mechanics is a proposal for a car with markedly sporting characteristics enhanced by solutions that guarantee the passengers' safety. The gull's wing doors are in two segments and the rear door is bottom-hinged to increase the luggage space. The headlamps are retractable. Overall length 151.57 in (385 cm).

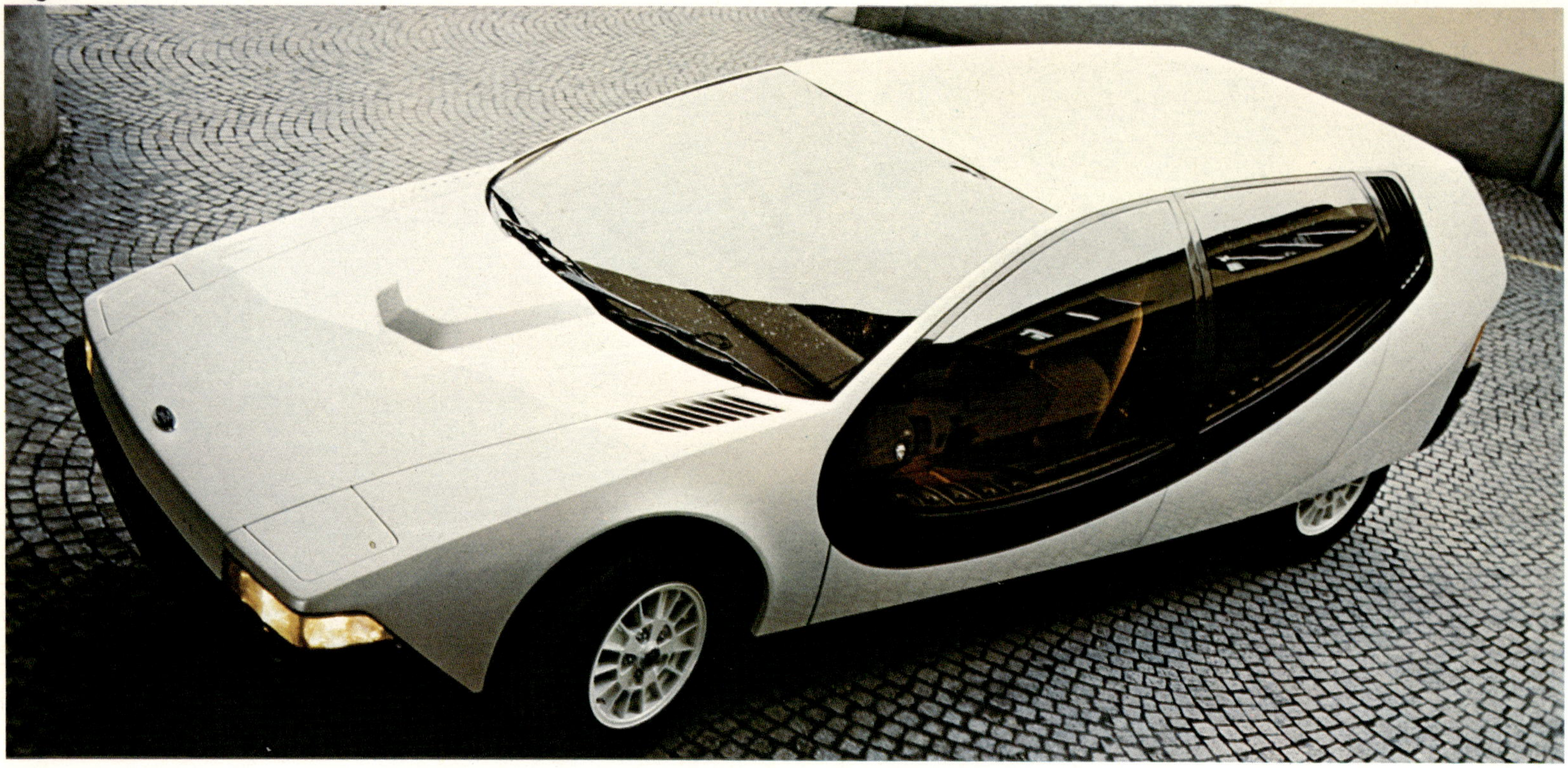

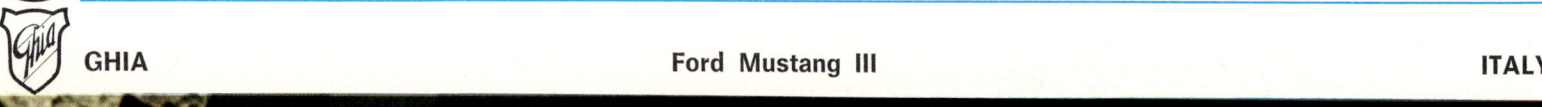

This concept car based on the Ford Granada 3-litre 4-door sedan is designed for energy conservation and performance. 80% of the area of the front doors and 60% of the rear doors is glass. The louvred air intake speeds up air flow at low speeds and decreases it at high speeds.

GHIA   Ford Mustang III   **ITALY**

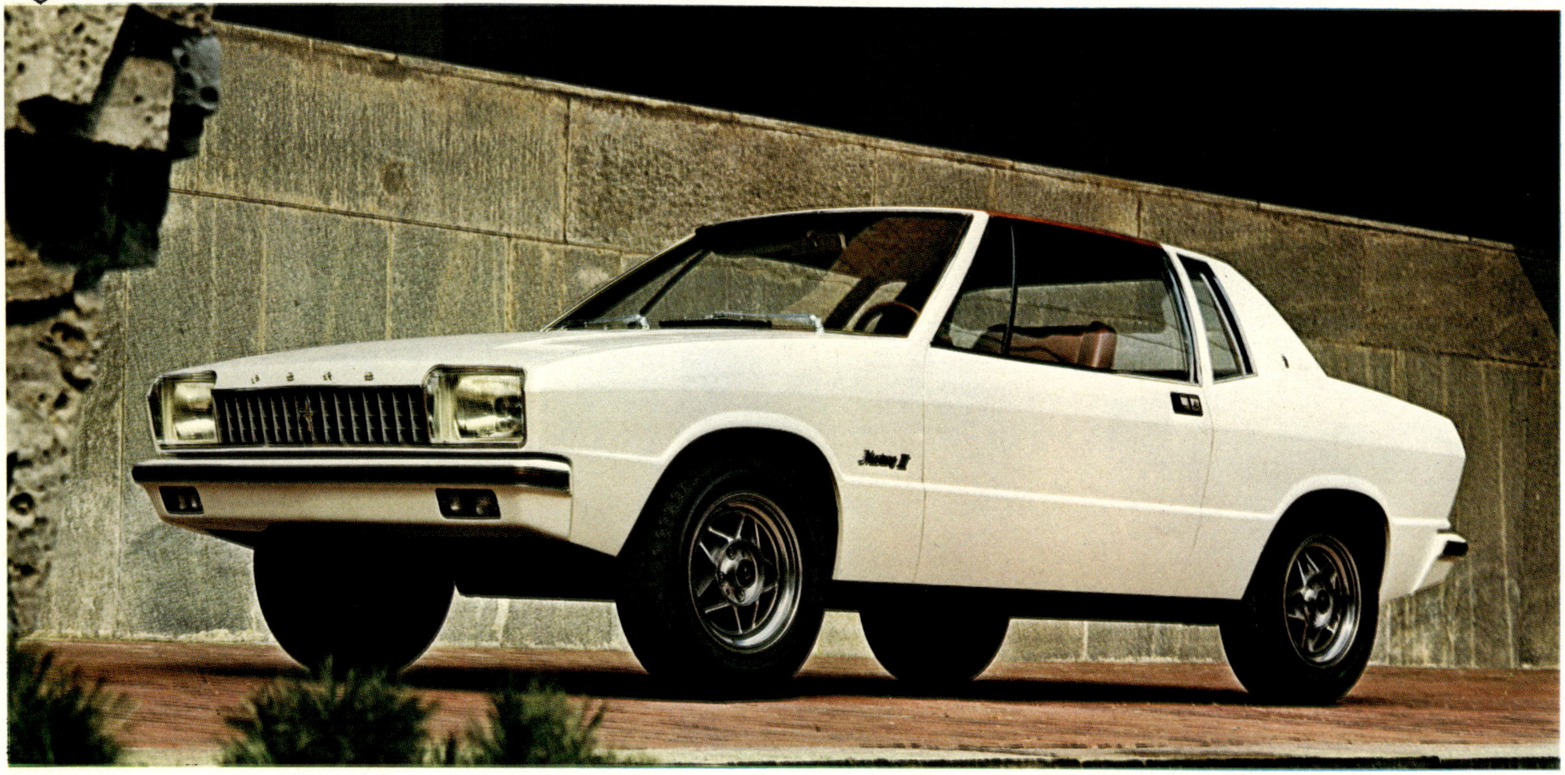

Ghia's 2+2 coupé-spider version of Ford America's famous Mustang has European dimensions and decidedly Italian lines. The mechanics are taken from the Ford Fiesta. This high-tailed coupé is 157.48 in (400 cm) shorter than the original and has a removable roof that can be stowed in the luggage boot.

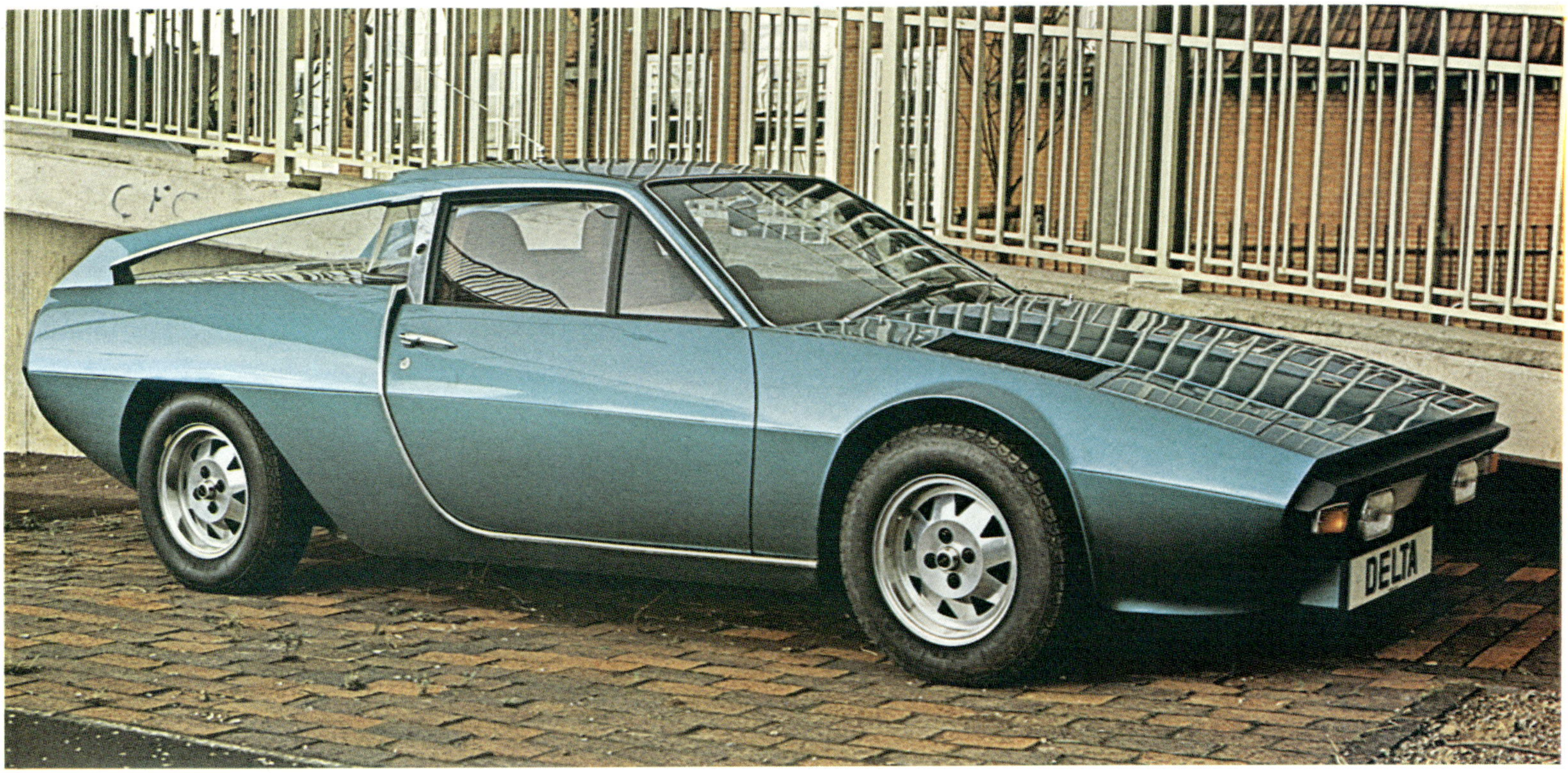

An aluminium coachbuilt body, tubular steel chassis and safety bumpers ensure a high level of safety. The luxuriously appointed interior is complete with air-conditioning and electrically controlled windows. The mid-engine configuration ensures good handling.

GREAT BRITAIN   **Alfa Romeo Sextet**   **HUMBERSTONE**

Sponsored by Triplex, the Sextet was first seen at the Geneva Motor Show in 1977 as the TTS. Based on the Alfasud, this six-seater is a practical demonstration of safety glass advances, including the sharply raked laminated windscreen and removable bronze glass roof.

ITAL DESIGN — **Maserati Quattroporte** — **ITALY**

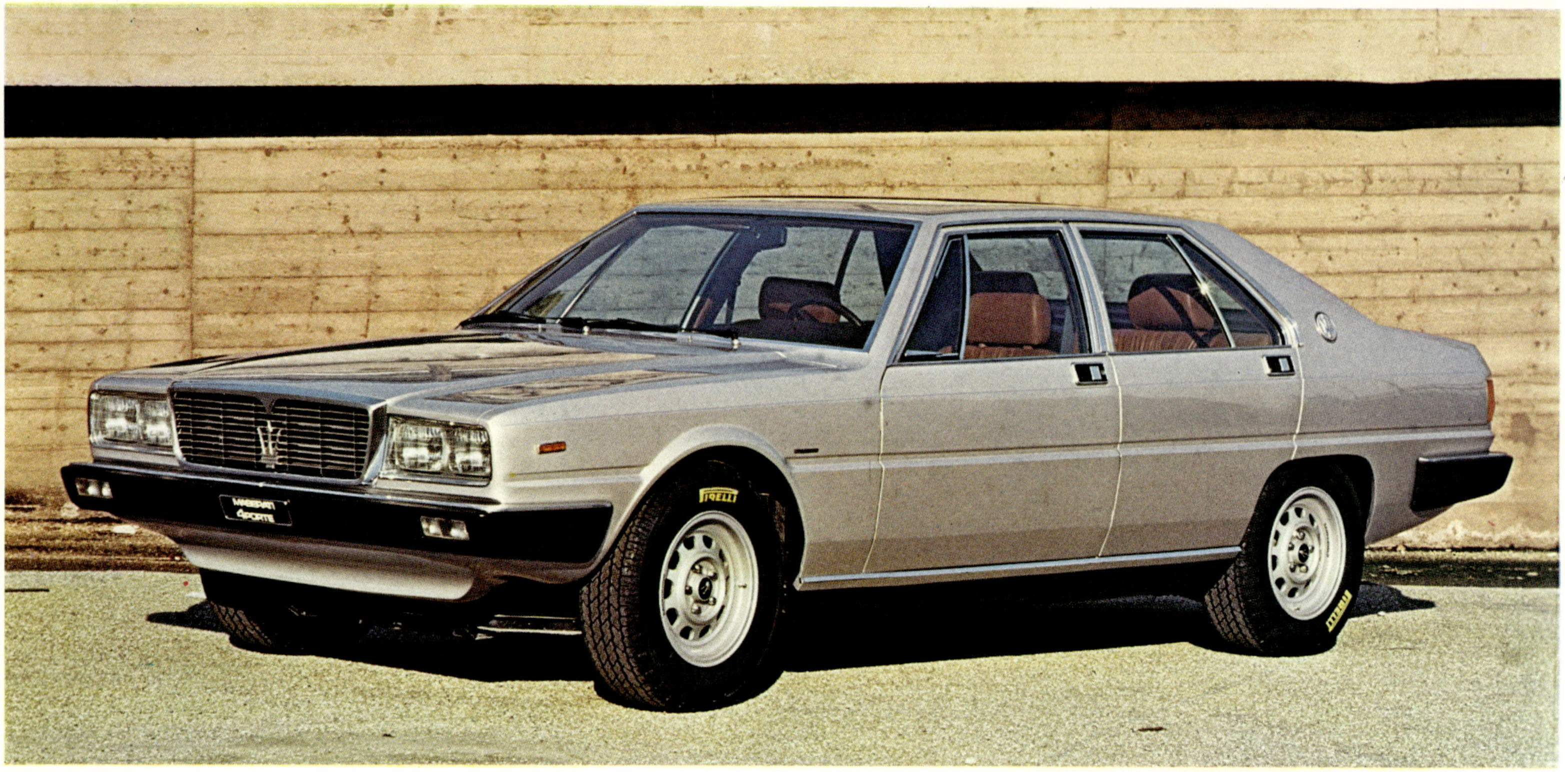

In close collaboration with Maserati, Ital Design has created a thoroughbred high-performance 4-seater beautifully finished throughout. The side lines are upswept with respect to the belt line and the rear quarter lights set well forward to give the rear seat passengers privacy. Overall length 192.13 in (488 cm), width 66.54 in (169 cm) and height 52.76 in (134 cm).

ITAL DESIGN — **Maserati Medici** — **ITALY**

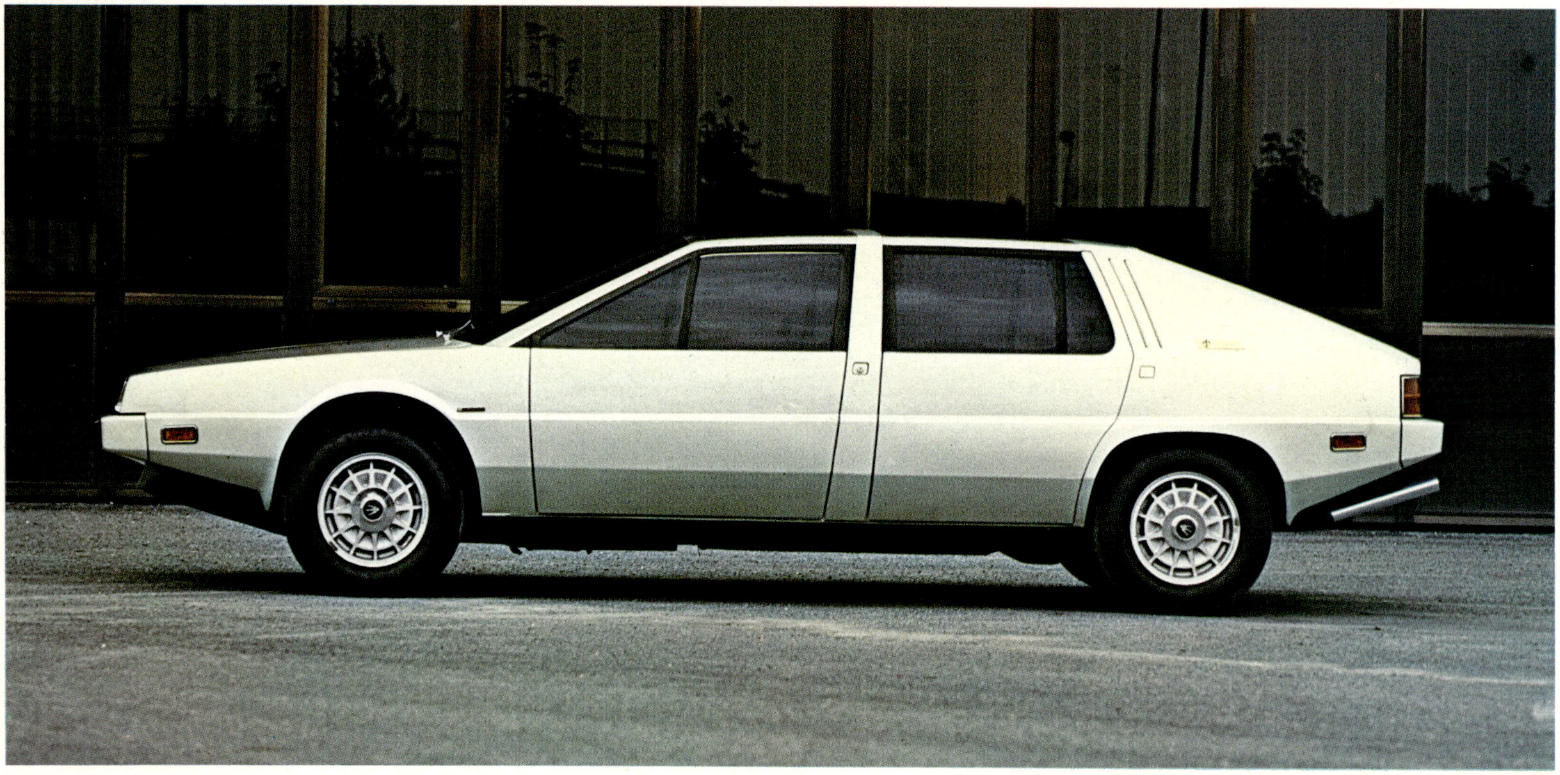

The starting point of Giugiaro's new version of the Medici with Maserati Indy 8-cylinder 4,930 cc engine is the prototype exhibited at Turin in 1974. Bar, radio-telephone and television take the place of the rear-facing seats. Overall length 205.51 in (522 cm), height 53.94 in (137 cm).

GERMANY/ITALY — BMW Karo-As — KARMANN - ITAL DESIGN

KARMANN

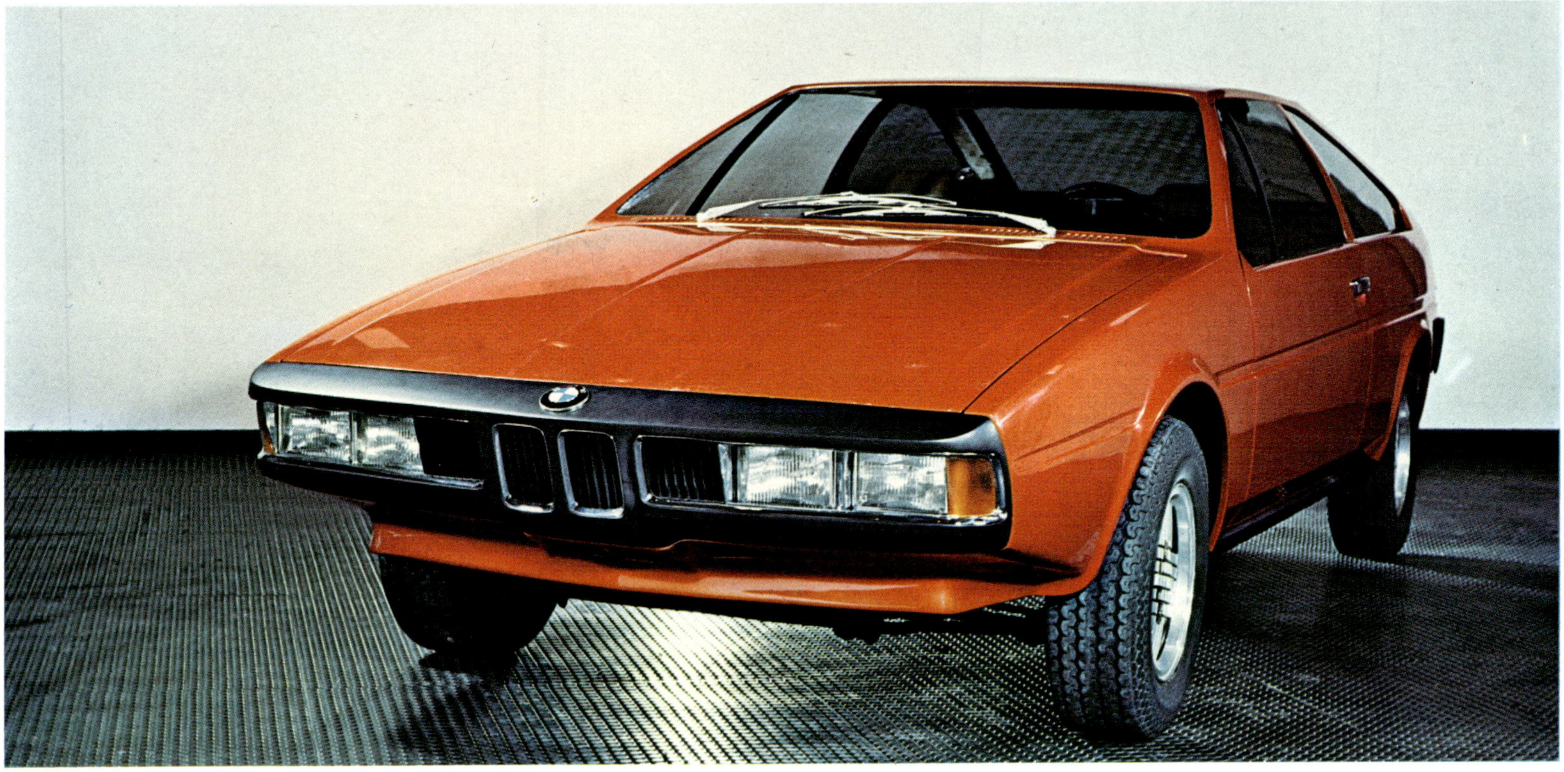

On behalf of Karmann, Ital Design has created this aesthetically advanced sports car. The wedge-shaped bonnet and reduced length (64.96 in, 165 cm), plus the elimination of the rear window, chrome windscreen frame, water channels, etc. have ensured low drag. The windows are all mounted from inside, thus conforming with US security norms.

GREAT BRITAIN — Centaur — MAGRAW

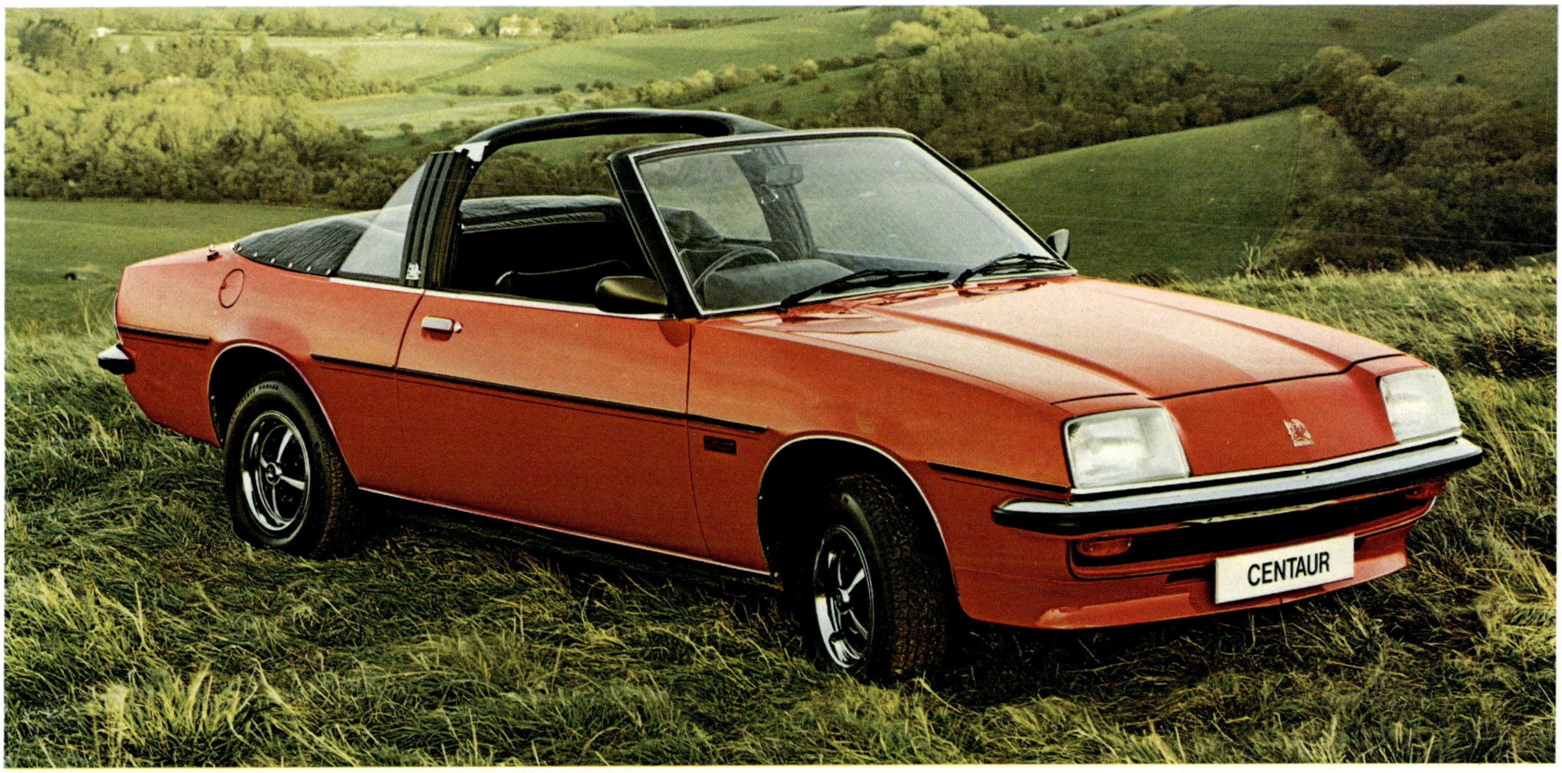

An immensely strong T-bar for maximum rigidity, and the original upper safety belt mounting points give this 4-seater convertible based on the Cavalier Coupé exceptional safety qualities. The hood mechanism is trouble-free to the point that it is hoped to make it hydraulic in the near future.

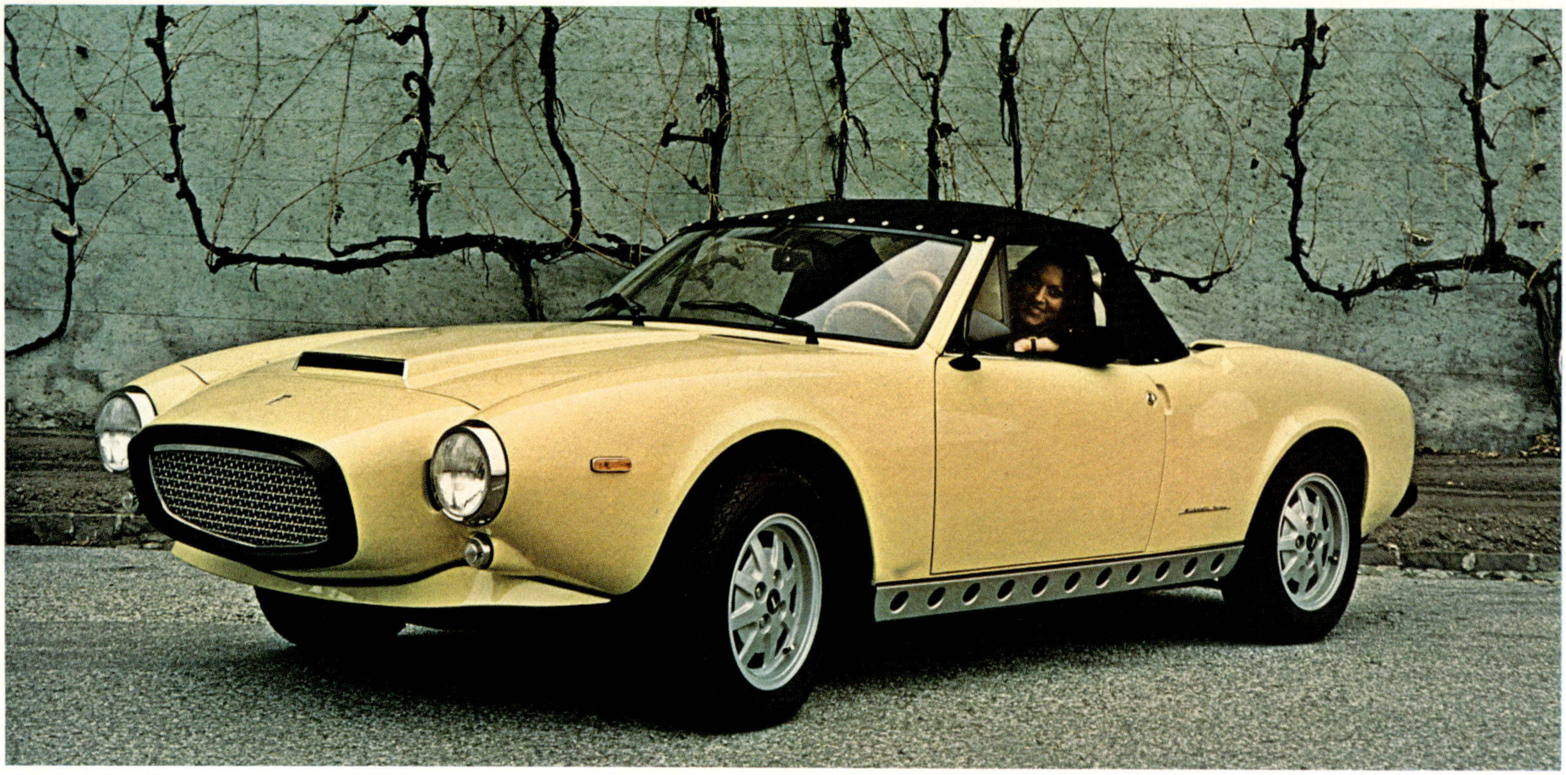

Following the current trend of reproposing old-style bodies with modern mechanics, Michelotti has designed this spider that vaguely recalls the Lancia D24 Carrera. The mechanics of the Beta Coupé are used and thus front-wheel drive and 5-speed gearbox. The alloy wheels mount 175 HR x 14 tyres. Overall length 159.05 in (404 cm).

MINICARS   **RSV Eagle II**   **USA**

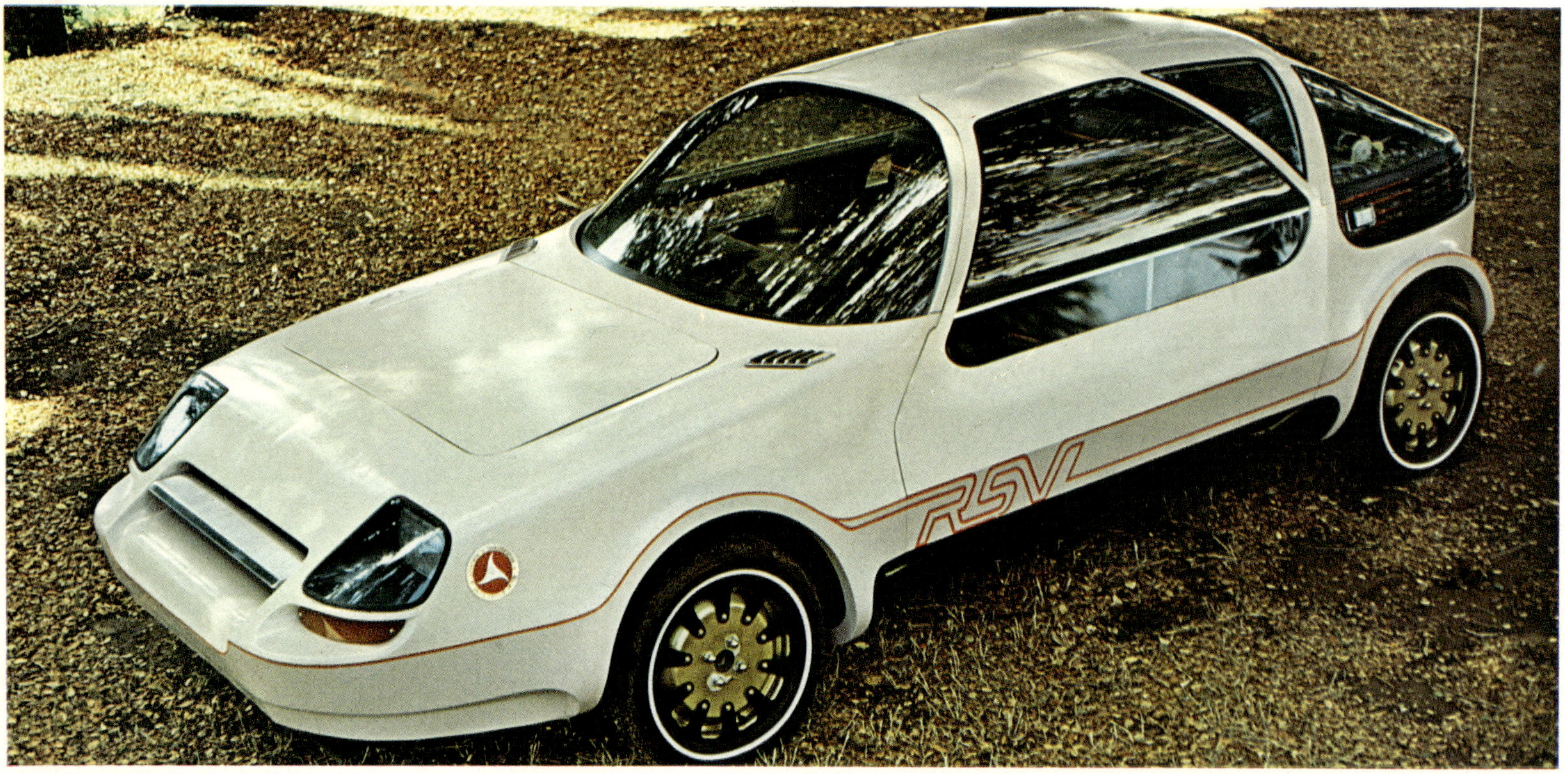

Dual-chambered air-cushion restraints at the front and force limiters combined with 3-point harnesses at the rear afford excellent protection for the occupants of this safety car in a frontal collision. Resilient plastic covers the energy-absorbent, foam-filled steel structure.

USA **Royale Cadillac Limousine** **PHAETON**

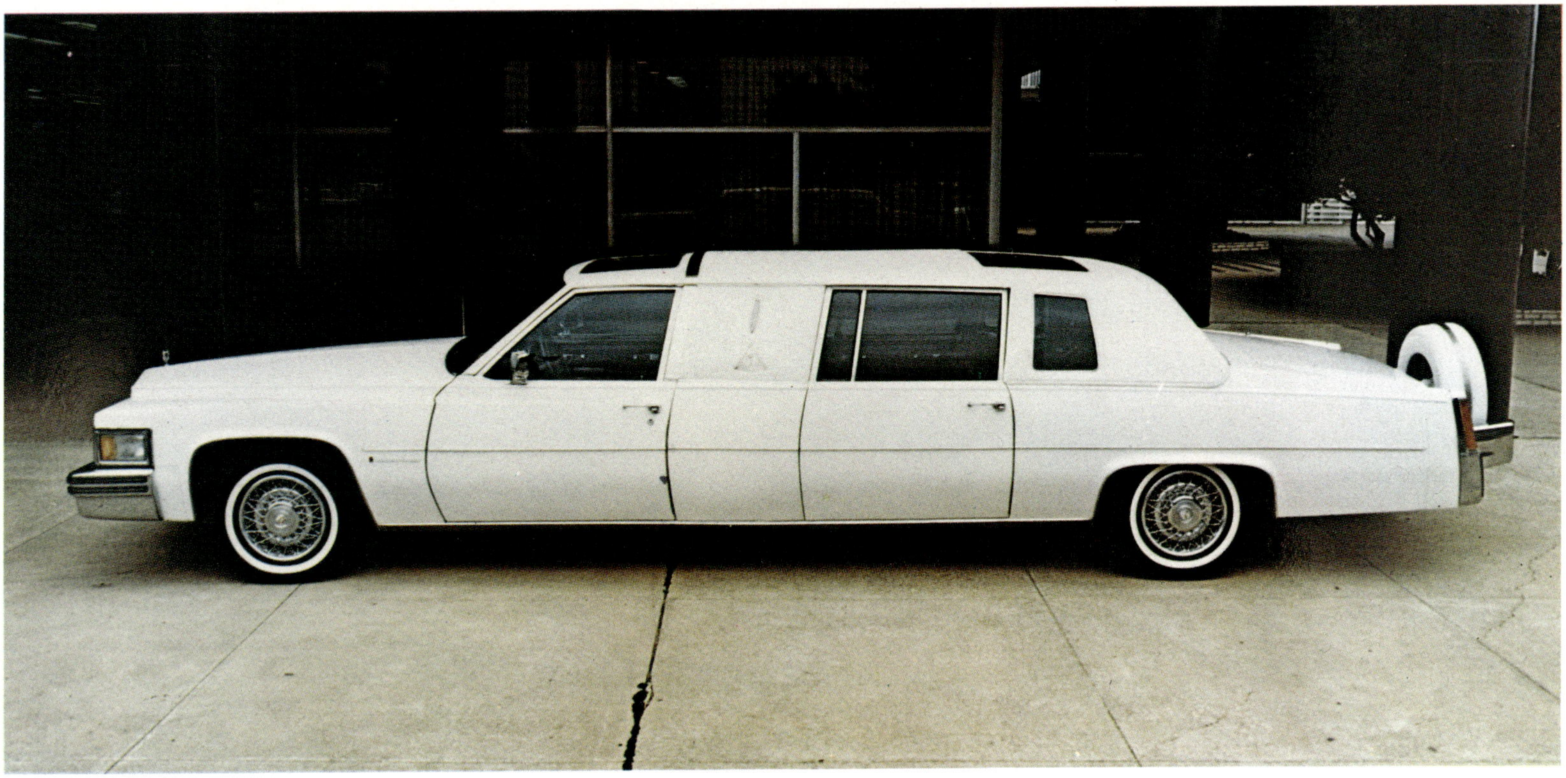

Custom-made for the Saudi Arabia royal family, the Fleetwood-based Phaeton features colour TV with video cassettes, a walnut Moroccan-design divider window, and two sunshine roofs. A love-seat design is adopted for the passenger seating and the entire limousine is carpeted in fur. It is 264 in (670 cm) long.

ITALY **Ferrari 308 GTB** **PININFARINA**

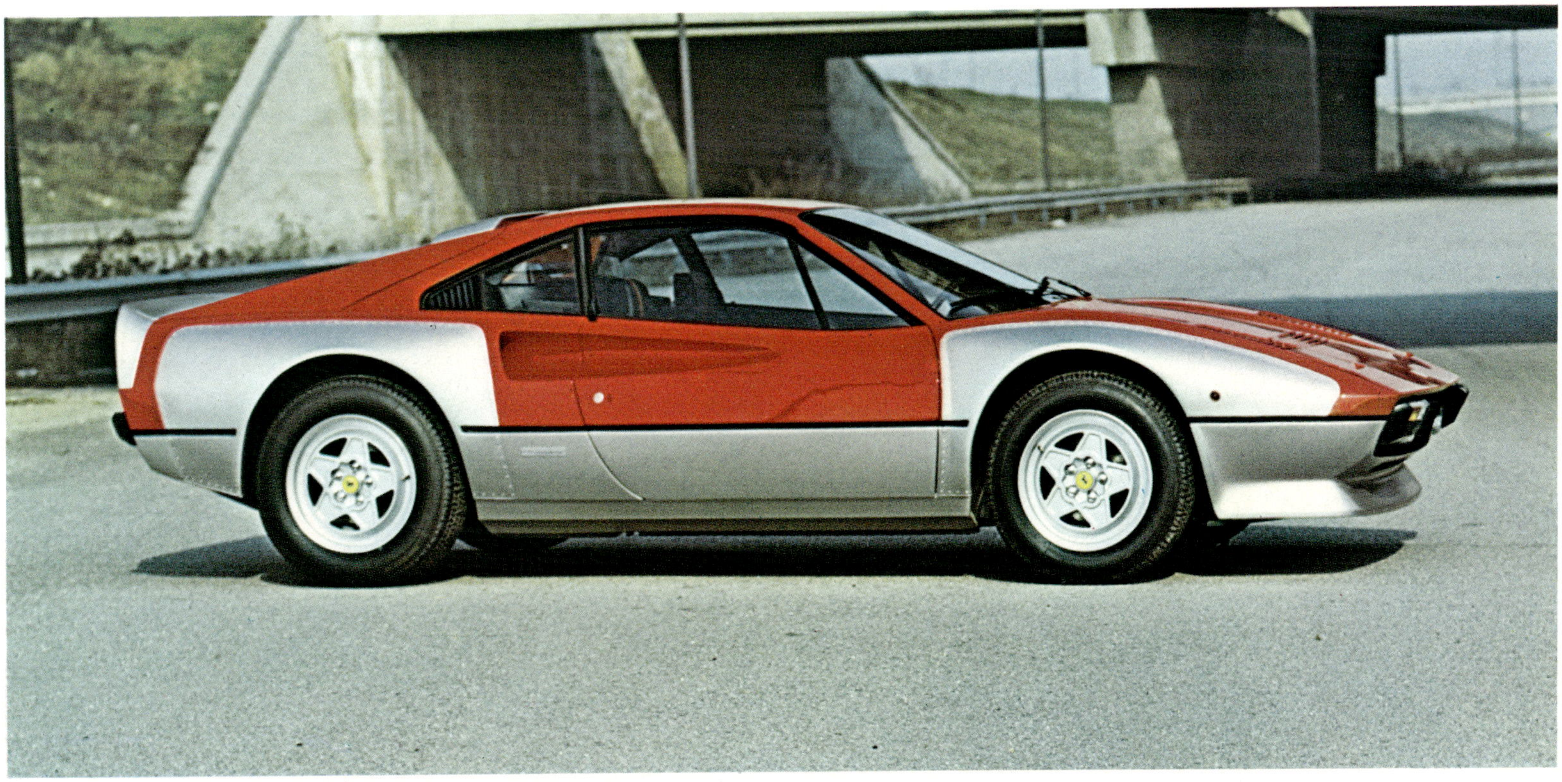

Pininfarina used his wind gallery to ensure more markedly aerodynamic lines for the 308 GTB. It features large spoilers and a wing set behind the passenger area. The choice and distribution of the colours emphasize its sporting personality.

Derived from the Ferrari 308 GTB berlinetta, this comfortable spider with modern lines and marked sporting characteristics does not fail to respect the contemporary demand for safety features and reliability. It is produced by Ferrari and the Carrozzeria Scaglietti.

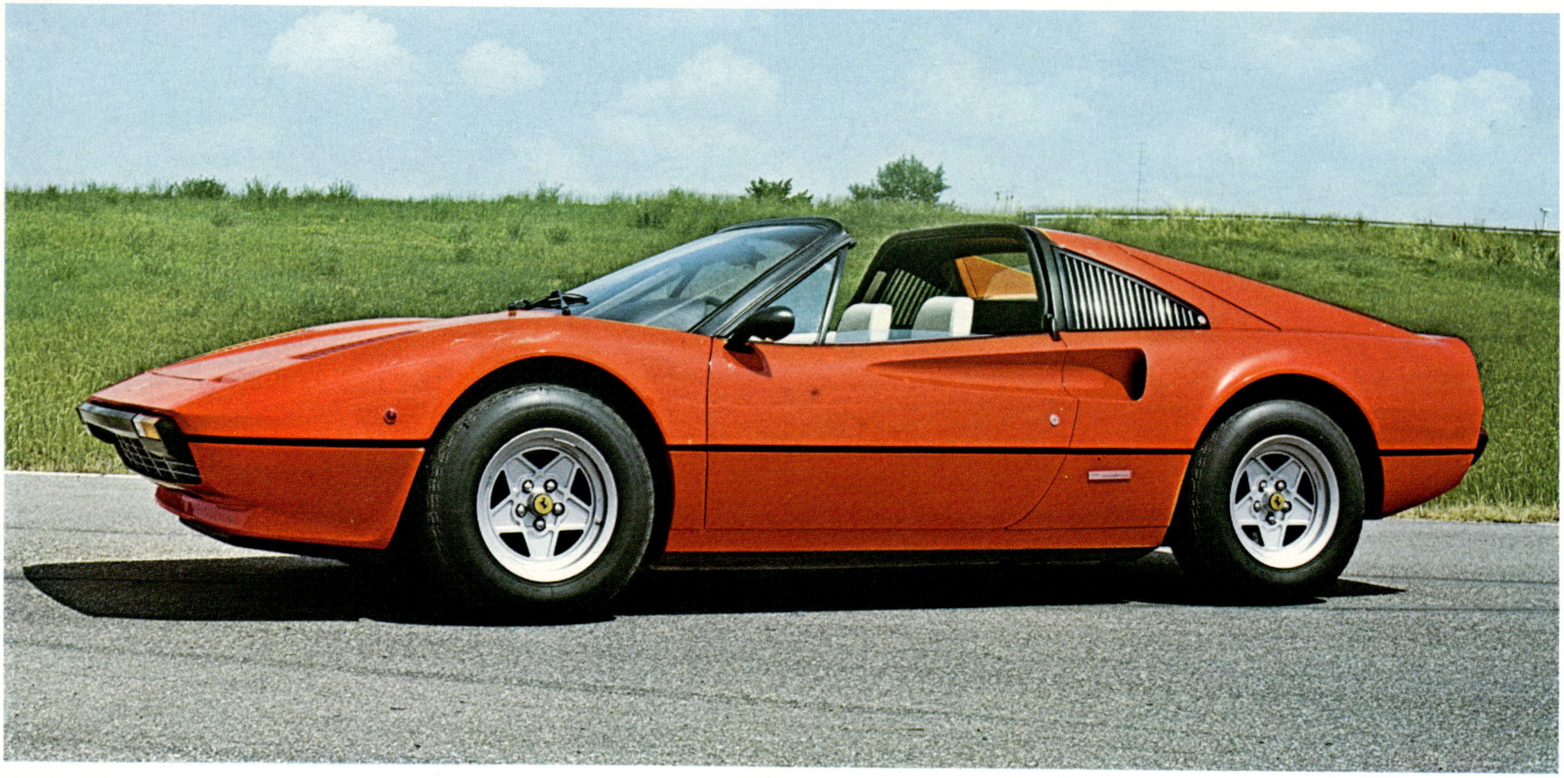

PININFARINA   Ferrari 400 Automatic   **ITALY**

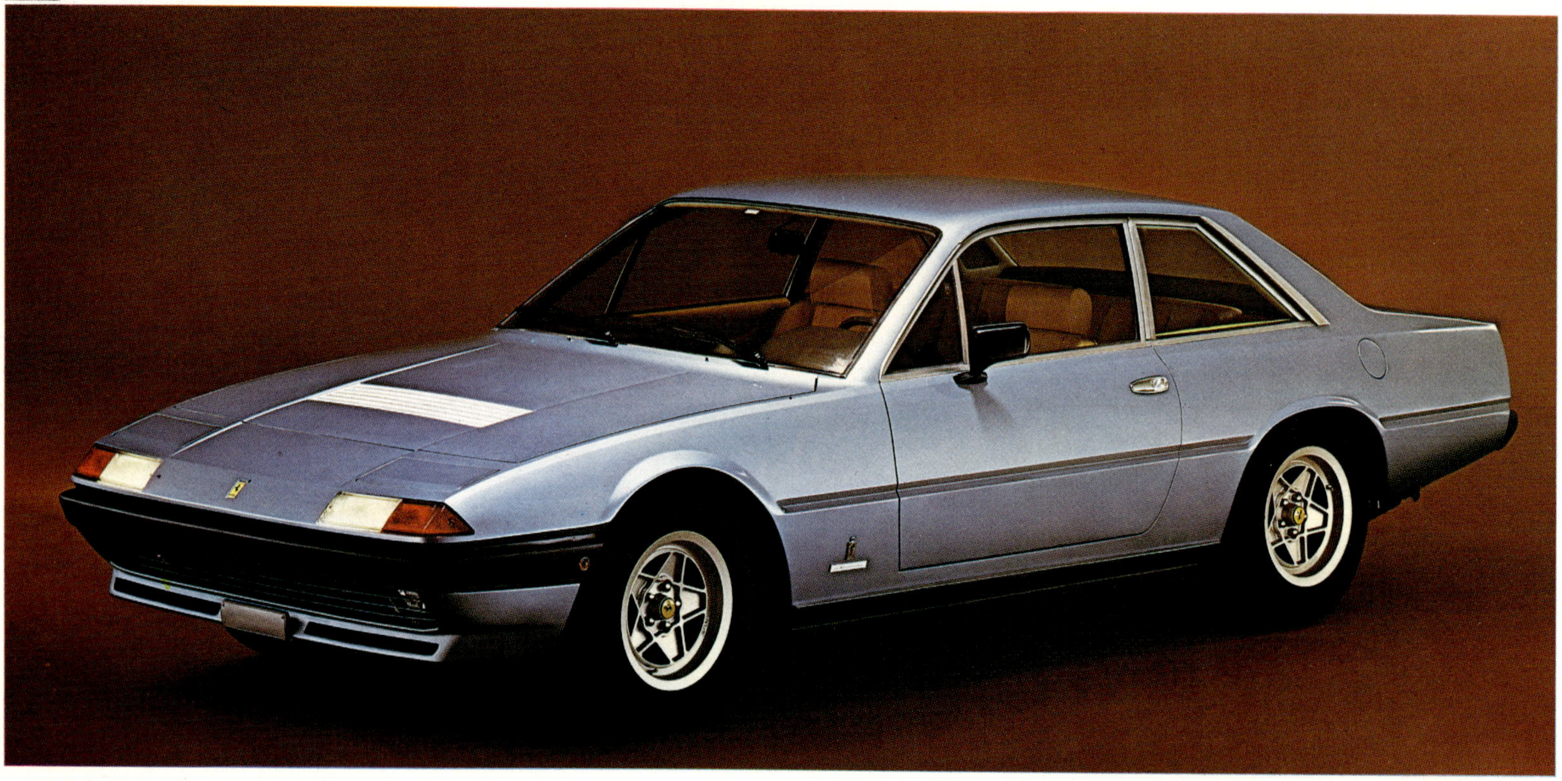

This Ferrari, which is the evolution of the 365 GT4, whose lines it retains unchanged, is notable for the innovations in the mechanics and the interior. It is in fact the first Ferrari with automatic transmission but this has meant no loss of its traditional high performance characteristics. Space has been found in the interior for four comfortable seats.

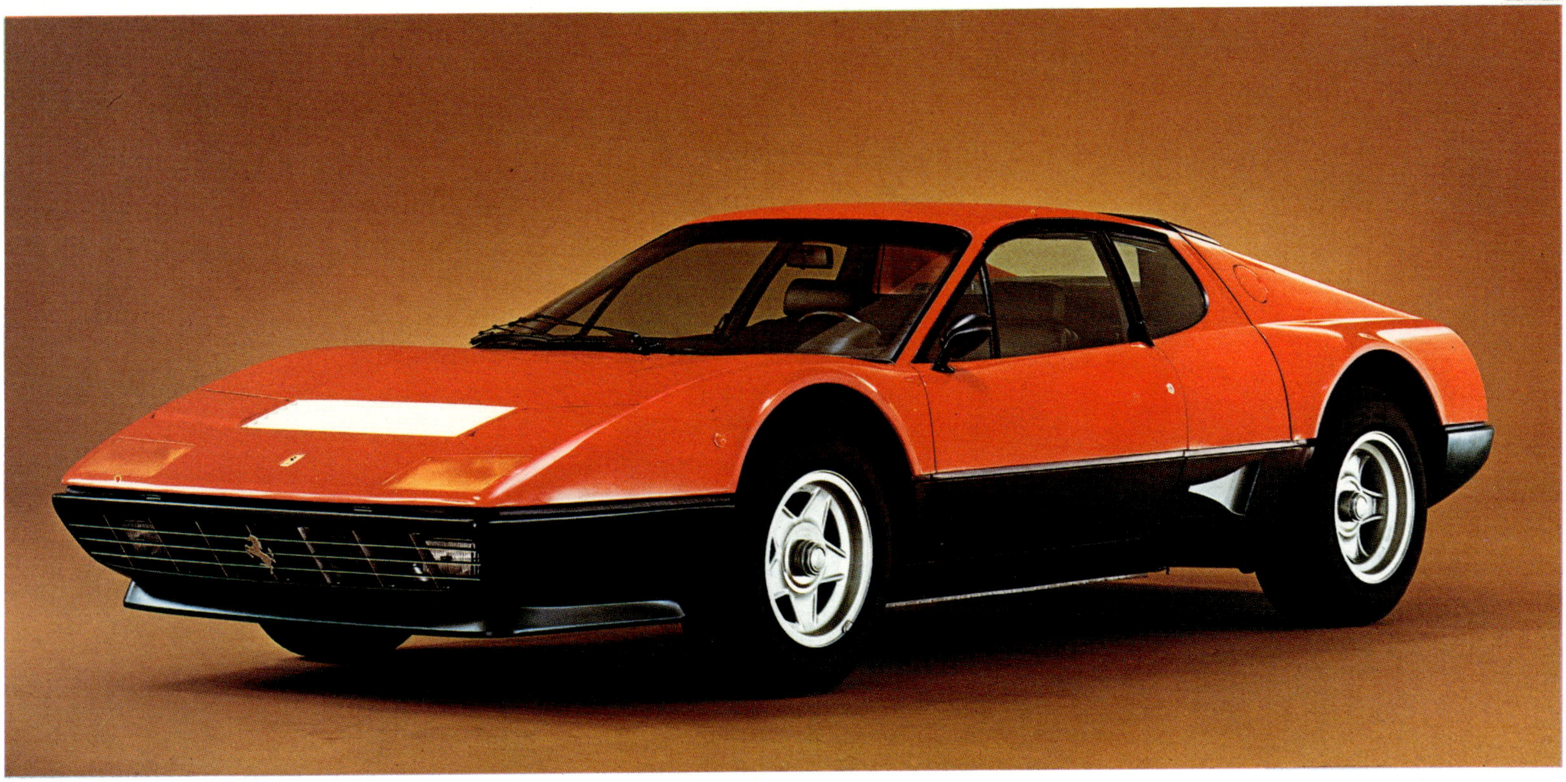

The fascination of this car, typical of all the others of the marque of the rampant horse does not lie merely in its high performance figures. The great attraction is the smooth, clean lines, studied specially to allow the powerful 12-cylinder engine developing 360 bhp (DIN) to top 300 km/h (186 mph).

Low, wide and aggressive at the same time, this car has original lines and several stylistic innovations. The central-rear engine geometry, typical of modern sports cars, makes comfortable and safe seating possible. The arrangement of the various instruments is rational and they are in easy reach.

More compact than the saloon version, this coupé, besides being easier to handle, has the advantage of a lower drag coefficient with higher performance at the same power. The high level of the finishings and the great comfort can be further enhanced by the adoption of the optional accessories offered, including hide upholstery and air-conditioning.

PININFARINA   Peugette 104 Corsa   **ITALY**

In this new interpretation, the versatile Peugette, with the adoption of a tonneau-cover, is transformed into a single-seater designed for racing. Engines with various capacities can be adopted, and the Corsa can only enhance Peugeot's racing reputation.

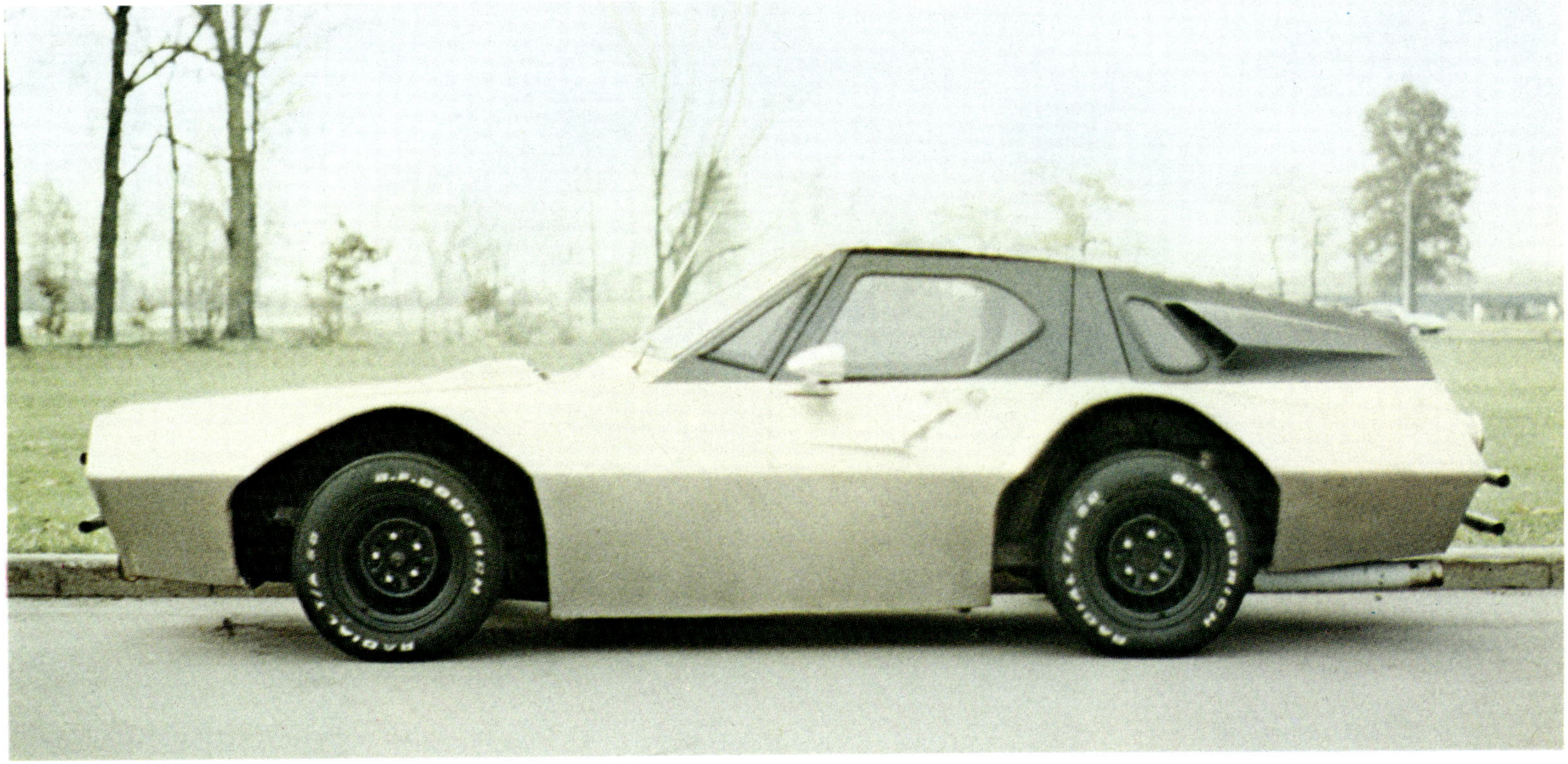

Experiments with scale models in a wind tunnel influenced the final design of this streamlined coupé, the brain-child of Sam Tafoya. Based of Chevrolet Monza 2800 mechanics, it seeks the optimum in terms of handling and down force while braking and cornering. The latest version mounts special 13'' x 8½'' wheels and BR 50-13 tyres which improve its stability.

CANADA　　　　　　　GT Turbo　　　　　**TREBRON**

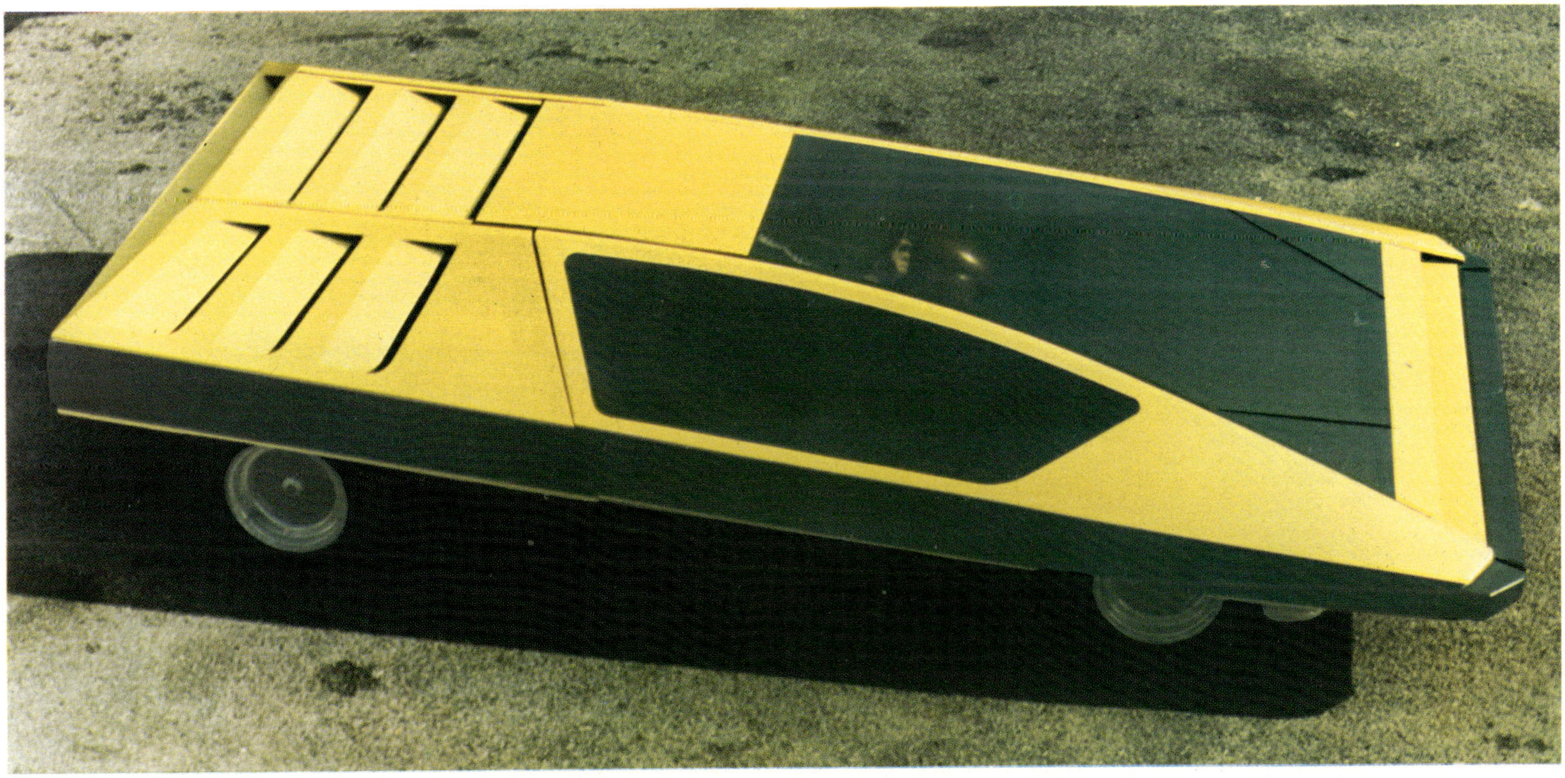

Based on the styling of the Concordia I, another Trebron design, the GT Turbo has a 1:7 power-weight ratio resulting from a conservative 320 bhp, promising phenomenal acceleration and top-speed performance. Its unique Double Roll Suspension is patented by Trebron.

VEHICLE DESIGN FORCE — Vector W2 — USA

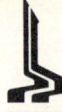

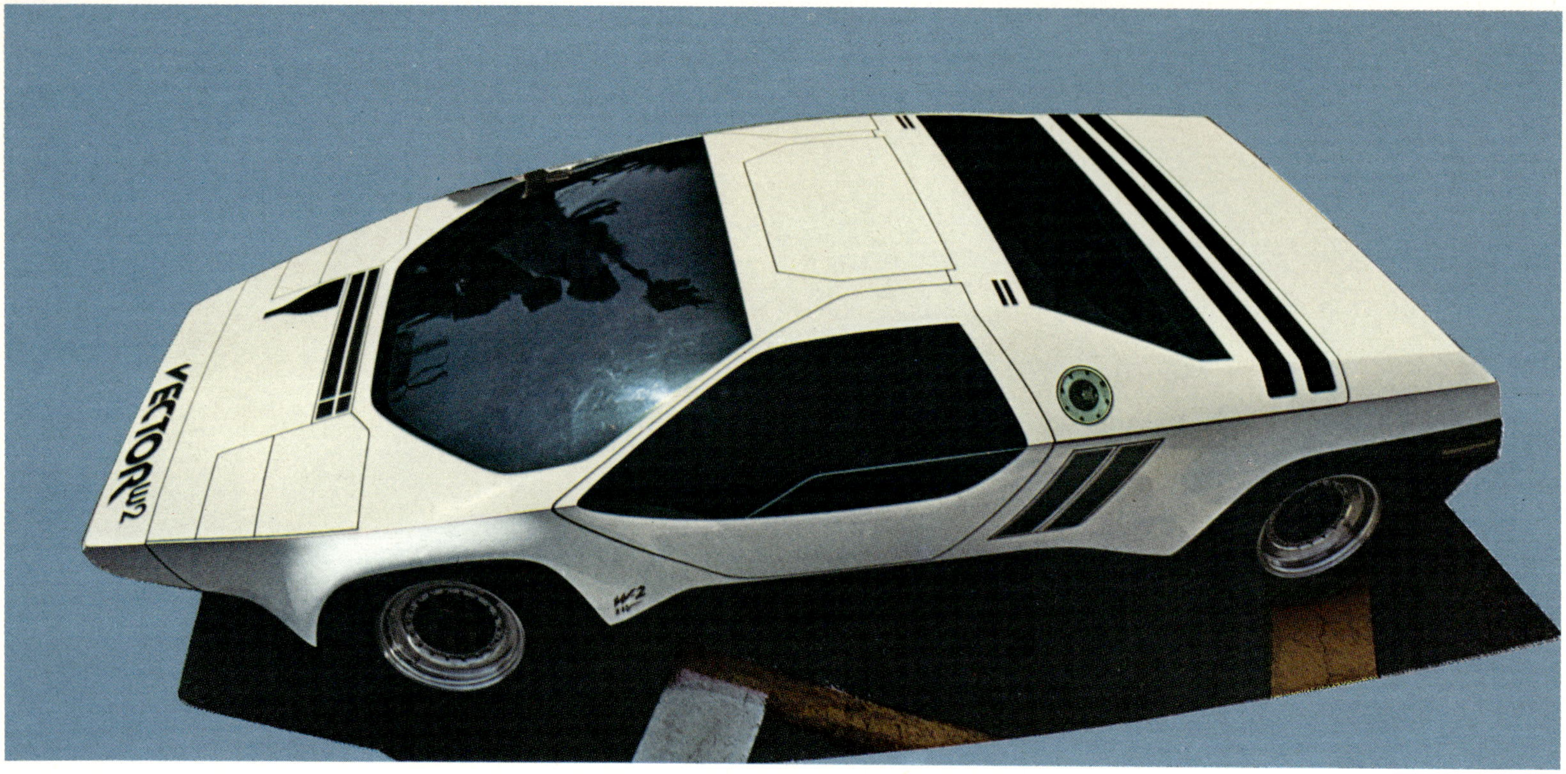

The first running prototype of the Vector W2, a blend of aerospace and sports racing technology, is expected any day now. Urethane foam sandwich allows its front and rear panels to double as bumpers. The engine is based on a compact GM V8 block with Moser DOHC head. It is designed to produce 500 bhp.

ZAGATO — Z 80 — ITALY

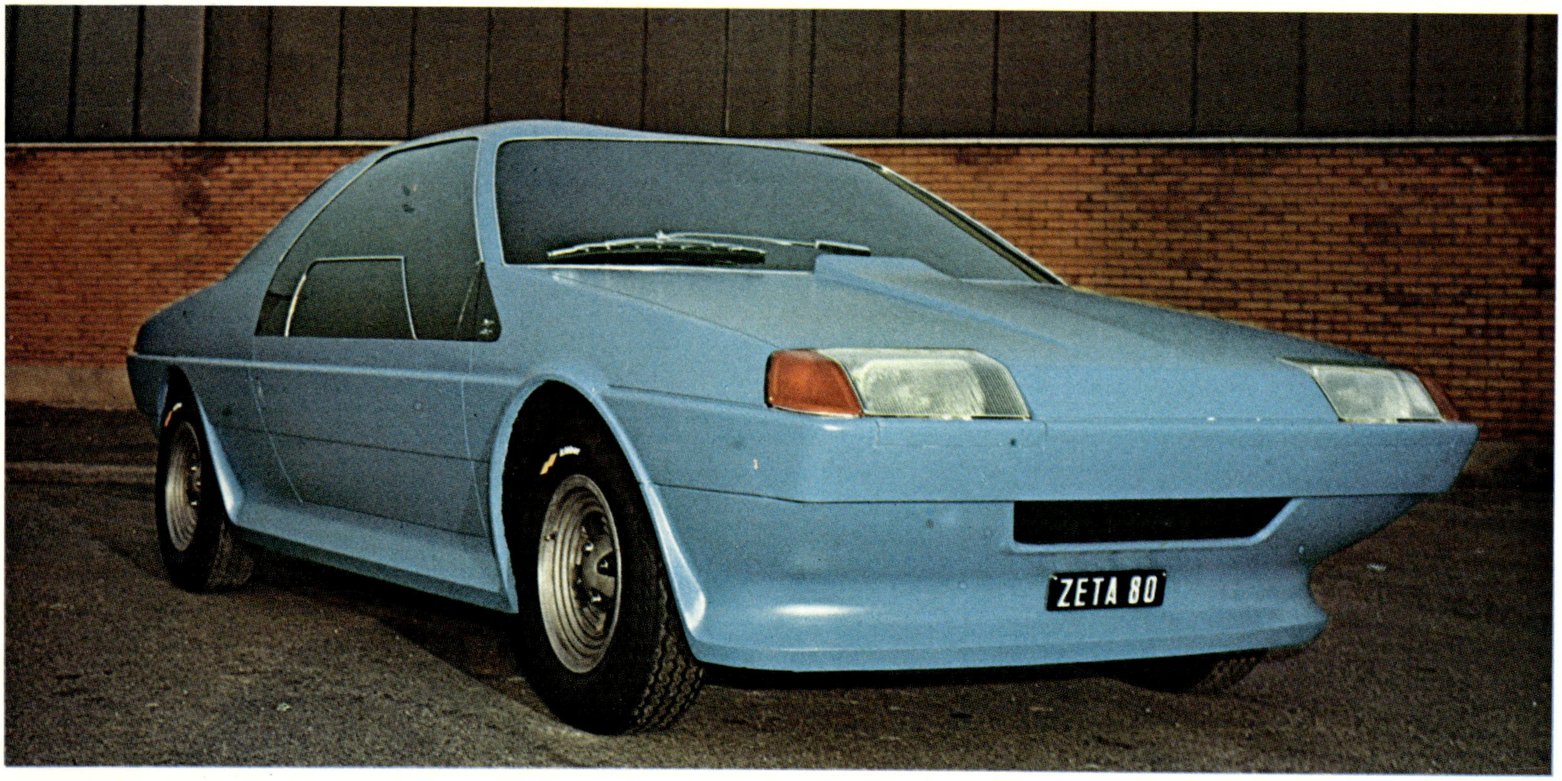

This is Zagato's proposal for a spacious 4-seater sports car of the future, the 'eighties, as the name suggests. To reduce consumption to the minimum, great attention has been paid to the aerodynamics, above all wind resistance. Overall length 166.14 in (422 cm).

AMC

Concept II   USA

The Concept vehicles blend styling and function in a smaller energy-saving design that
represents American Motors' ideas of trends
in small cars for the 1980s. In the Concept II,
the centre structural roof band adds strength
to the roof area and unifies the lower and
upper body sections. Integrated soft bumpers
provide front and rear damage protection. All-
round visibility is excellent.

AMC

Concept Grand Touring   USA

Designed as a 4-seater sporty hatchback, the
Grand Touring has the detailed excellence of
a prestige car. The luxurious leather upholstery and bucket seats are set off by deep-
pile carpeting. Opera-styled recessed quarter
windows, wire wheels and rally-type road lights
within the Venturi grille contribute to the theme
of elegance and performance. It is 169 in
(429 cm) long, 71 in (180 cm) wide and 52 in
(132 cm) high.

AMC

Concept AM Van   USA

The AM Van is a go-anywhere vehicle that
opens up new recreational possibilities. The
unusual styling includes full front and rear
wheel flares and a front air dam, and the
rectangular headlamps project from the sharply
canted hood. Dual off-road lights are mounted
under the chromed bumpers.

ISUZU

A hatchback Gemini — née GM T car coupé — is an interesting and inviting proposition. Isuzu designers rigged this one-off prototype to a small camping trailer. When a soft top is erected, the combination turns to a comfortable and spacious living quarters.

Gemini Hatchback JAPAN

LAMBORGHINI

The Cheetah is a 4-wheel drive off-road vehicle with exceptional performance (167 mph - 268 km/h) and adaptability to all terrains and gradients. The water-cooled V8 Chrysler engine is mounted centrally at the rear and a turbocharger can be installed. The tubular steel frame has an integral safety cage surrounding the occupants.

Cheetah ITALY

NISSAN

Nissan's interpretation of an inter-city luxury 6-seater is this 4-door sedan with large greenhouse. Nose airdam theme is carried to the lower side of the body which is flared outward and acts as a splash-guard. The large wraparound rear window offers excellent visibility. The AD-2 is 185.04 in (470 cm) long, 70.87 in (180 cm) wide and 50 in (127 cm) high with a 104.72 in (266 cm) wheelbase and 59.06 in (150 cm) front and rear tracks. The power unit is Nissan's 2.8 liter electronic fuel injection inline six, and the rear suspension appears to be straight from the company's Laurel sedan with rigid axle located by four links.

Datsun AD-2 JAPAN

36

TOYOTA

"CAL" is short for California where a vehicle of this type should prove popular. The CAL-1 is based on the updated and lengthened Celica sedan chassis, whose rear end is cut off to make room for a pickup-bed. There is a folding rumble seat on the truck bed: the windshield for this is normally the rear window.

TOYOTA

This experimental 6-seater sedan features an unique asymmetrical door arrangement; one large sliding door on the driver's side, and a swinging front and a sliding rear door on the other side, as well as a large tailgate. Originally intended as a front-wheel drive, transverse-engined car, the prototype has a conventionally-placed engine driving, by a separately-mounted (under the front seat) gearbox, the independently sprung rear wheels. Inboard disc brakes are used at the rear.

TOYOTA

This project was undertaken by a private research laboratory sponsored by Toyota. This lightweight coupé is 140.16 in (356 cm) long, 58.66 in (149 cm) wide and 45.67 in (116 cm) high and scales a mere 992 lb (450 kg). The Daihatsu Max type AB10 547 cc 2-cylinder engine drives the front wheels. The interconnecting of the front and rear suspensions is interesting. A top speed of 70 mph (110 km/h) is claimed and it boasts a fuel consumption of 35 km (22 miles) per litre at a steady 60 km/h (37 mph).

Electric vehicles

Illustrations and technical information

AMC   Concept Electron

Based on a previous development of the American Motors Amitron, a vehicle powered by a lightweight lithium battery system, the wedge-nosed Electron anticipates further advances in electronic technology in the 1980s. This unusually shaped three-seater electric commuter car is designed for short-trip urban transportation. It has a clam-shell roof that swings back on rear-mounted pivots for easy entry and exit. No parking problems are presented by the Electron for it is a mere 85 inches (216 cm) long, 69.50 in (176 cm) wide and 46 in (117 cm) high.

AM GENERAL   Electruck DJ-5E

Derived from the classic Jeep, the Electruck retains its appearance and most of its dimensions but with rear wheel drive only. The 54 V 30 bhp d.c. motor has electronic regulation. Top speed is 40 mph (64 km/h) and town autonomy with frequent stops 30 miles (50 km). The chassis and body are all of steel construction. Dimensions: wheelbase 81 in (206 cm), front track 51.50 in (131 cm), rear track 50 in (127 cm), overall length 136 in (345 cm), width 59.88 in (152 cm), height 69.49 in (176 cm), dry weight 3,618 lb (1,641 kg), maximum weight 4,304 lb (1,952 kg), weight of batteries 1,301 lb (590 kg). Three hundred and fifty-two have been ordered for U.S. postal deliveries in urban areas with pollution problems.

BATTRONIC   Minivan

This little utilitarian vehicle for mixed transport purposes is built in plastic on a steel frame. The d.c. electric motor has a separate exciting field — voltage is 112 volt and power 42 bhp with a maximum of 6,000 rpm. The two-speed constant-mesh transmission is completed by an electronic regulator. The batteries are interchangeable according to the usage and autonomy required. A maximum speed of up to 60 mph (96 km/h) is possible. Dimensions: wheelbase 94.49 (in (240 cm), front track 61.02 in (155 cm), rear track 63.39 in (161 cm), overall length 145 in (368 cm), width 74 in (188 cm), height 92 in (234 cm), maximum weight with batteries and full load 6,800 lb (2,902 kg). It features sliding doors.

BILLINGS   Hybrid Cadillac Seville

Hydrogen and gasoline are the two fuels that give this car, which first appeared in President Jimmy Carter's inaugural parade, its name. The two hydride tanks mounted in the trunk add only 300 lb (136 kg) to the weight. The battery is safe and easy to recharge and energy is extracted by electrolysis. Simply by flicking a switch, the driver can change over from hydrogen to gasoline while the car is in motion. When operated on hydrogen, the range of the Billings Seville is 30-40 miles (48-64 km), depending upon driving conditions, and with engine power and performance matching those of the standard Cadillac it is based on. The dimensions are of course those of the conventional Seville.

B&Z   PFS 123 and PFS 125

The PFS 123 is a small three-wheeler two-seater also built in a four-wheeler version. Different motors adapt it to various purposes. Overall width is 45 in (114 cm), height 60 in (152 cm) and length 101 in (256 cm). The four-wheeler weighs 1,100 lb (500 kg) and the three-wheeler 990 lb (450 kg). Top speed varies between 16 and 22 mph (25 and 35 km/h) with a 1 bhp or 2 bhp motor and a maximum of 29 mph (47 km/h) with a 3½ bhp motor. Six 6 V 170 Ah batteries each weighing 56 lb (25 kg) give a range of not over 30 miles (50 km), according to motor and usage. Single lever hand control and tiller steering are optional extras.

CHW   886 and 887

CHW has based both a saloon version and an estate car on the DAF 44 converted for electric traction. In both versions there are 16 6 V batteries in two groups, one at the front and one at the rear, connected in parallel to drive the motor at 48 V in direct current. Speed regulation is by a three-stage electro-mechanical controller. The maximum speed is 45 mph (72 km/h) with a 50 mile (80 km) range that can be raised to 80 miles (130 km) by mounting an additional group of batteries. Both versions have an overall width of 61 in (155 cm) and a wheelbase of 89 in (226 cm). The overall length of the saloon is 152 in (386 cm) while the estate car is slightly longer at 153 in (389 cm).

CHW   952

C.H. Waterman Industries, Inc. has added another model to its fleet of little electric cars based on European-designed conventional cars. The 952, as can clearly be seen, is based on the Renault R-5. In the electric version, sixteen six volt traction batteries provide power to the motor through a two-stage electromechanical speed controller in conjunction with a four-speed manual transmission. As in the 886 and 887, the maximum speed is 45 mph (72 km/h) with a range between charges in excess of 75 miles (120 km). The chief dimensions are: overall length 141.50 in (359 cm), overall width 60 in (152 cm), overall height 55 in (140 cm) and wheelbase 95.20 in (242 cm).

COPPER   Town Car

This two-seater hatchback is the fourth prototype electric vehicle built by the Copper Development Association using existing components and innovative technology aimed at ensuring exceptional range. In fact, this economical car's range is just over 100 miles (160 km) at 40 mph (64 km/h) and 69 miles (111 km) in stop-and-go city driving. The 18 6 V batteries may be recharged in the user's garage overnight and it is hoped to cut their weight — 1,200 lb (544 kg) — down significantly in the future. They power a specially wound, separately excited motor with a matched control system. The unusual doors swing outward until they clear the car's body and then travel rearward parallel to the body.

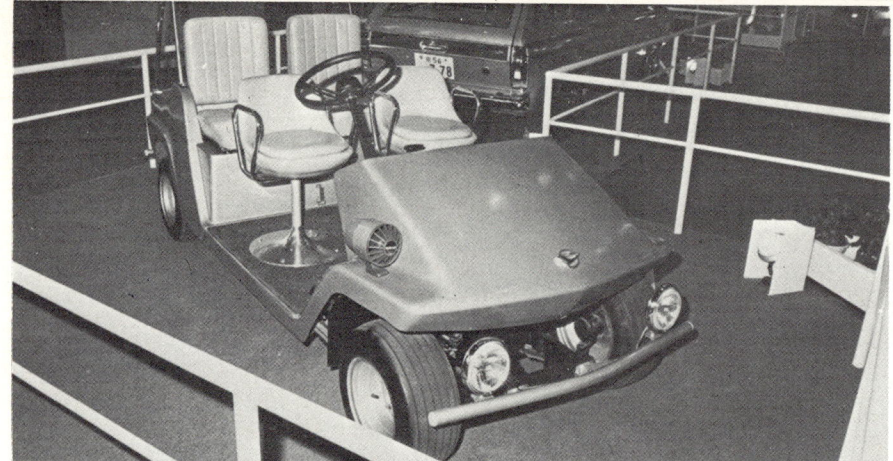

DAIHATSU Masters L

Daihatsu, a longstanding protagonist in the relatively recent field of electric passenger vehicles, markets this charming and adaptable little runabout built for a variety of uses and errands, such as on golf courses, in hotel grounds and amusement parks and for resort use in general. It is powered by a 2.3 kW motor running on three 150 Ah lead-acid batteries stowed well away out of sight. It can reach a maximum speed of 10 mph (16 km/h) and has a maximum range between charges of about 18 miles (30 km). The price in Japan is 950,000 yen, the equivalent of approximately 4,000 US dollars.

DIE MESH Spider

The successful Fiat 850 Sport Spider body ensures a sportier appearance than usual for this electric car. The top speed, too, is well above the average at 55 mph (88 km/h) and the car's autonomy is quite adequate for commuting — 42 miles (67 km). The 18 lead batteries are divided into three separate battery packs, supplying the power for three 3.2 hp electric motors. The curb weight (batteries included) is slightly greater than the original model at 2,850 lb (1,292 kg) but the overall length — 150.55 in (382 cm) — and height — 48.03 in (122 cm) are the same as in the Fiat from which it is derived. The wheelbase is 77.80 in (203 cm), the front track 46.06 in (117 cm) and the rear track 48.11 in (122 cm).

EFP Transformer I

Electric Fuel Propulsion has designed this elegant 2-door 4-seater coupé with semi-automatic transmission, power steering and brakes, tinted glass and swivel bucket seats. A top speed of 70 mph (112 km/h) with a cruising speed of 55 mph (88 km/h) on motorways is allied to a range of up to 100 miles (160 km) and makes it ideal for commuting. To recharge the 180 V tripolar lead-cobalt battery takes 45 minutes for an 80% charge from an external fast charger or 8 hours using the on-board charger. The Transformer has a 32 hp direct current motor and solid state electronic control. Overall length is 212 in (538 cm), width 76.60 in (195 cm) and wheelbase 112 in (284 cm).

ELECTRACTION Rickshaw

The Rickshaw is an ideal car for leisure resorts. It is one of a series of vehicles planned by ElecTraction as a ready-made mobile test bed for organizations involved in the development of electric vehicle components and systems. The 7.5 hp electric motor is powered by 12 6 V lightweight traction batteries and has a thyristor controller. It is capable of 30 mph (50 km/h) and has a range between charges at that speed on level ground of 55-65 miles (88-105 km). The Rickshaw has a shower-proof 'Surrey' top and ample picnic basket space. It fits radial tyres. The overall length is 133 in (332 cm), width 62 in (158 cm), height 61 in (155 cm) and approximate weight 2,244 lb (1,020 kg).

ELECTRACTION   Tropicana

Electraction's open 2/3-seater sports vehicle has a durable glass fibre body on a galvanised steel tubular chassis, which absorbs energy in the event of an accident through a safety bumper at the rear. It has disc brakes and the rack and pinion steering gives a small turning circle. The 12 6 V lightweight traction batteries are housed in easily removable sliding trays. The motor, control system and transmission are identical to the Rickshaw's. The Tropicana is however slightly shorter at 128 in (325 cm) and lower at 49 in (163 cm) and weighs only 2,156 lb (980 kg). Top speed is 36 mph (58 km/h) and its range is 50-60 miles (80-96 km).

ELECTRACTION   EVR-1 Precinct

Aerodynamic in shape, with a low drag coefficient, the prototype EVR-1 "Precinct" is styled by Haynes Automotive International. A gearless 7.5 hp motor with thyristor type controller is powered by heavy duty lead-acid traction batteries with a 153 Ah capacity at a 5-hour rate. The makers claim a range of 100 miles (160 km) at 40 mph (64 km/h). The GRP body and electrically welded 146 steel tubing section chassis is available either with front wishbones, coil springs and electric dampers or with heavy duty suspension. The steering is rack and pinion and the EVR-1 has hydraulic dual-line brakes. Overall length 126 in (320 cm), width 65 in (165 cm), height 54 in (137 cm), wheelbase 76 in (193 cm).

ELECTRIC AUTO   Silver Volt

This 3-door hatchback 2-seater with fully automatic transmission and many safety features is a 1978 novelty. Like many American electric cars, it is aimed at the man commuting 50 to 100 miles (80 to 160 km) a day. With a cruising speed of 50 mph (80 km/h), it is capable of a top speed of 70 mph (112 km/h). It mounts a 30 hp d.c. 240 V motor acting as a generator on deceleration, and the combination field control ensures smooth starting. The 240 V tripolar lead cobalt battery develops 136 Ah. It can be recharged in 45 minutes from an EFP mobile power plant or an electrically powered charge station and has an onboard charger. Overall length is 153 in (225 cm), width 61 in (154 cm) and curb weight 3,500 lb (1,590 kg).

EPC   Hummingbird Hybrid Mk I

Based on the Volkswagen Rabbit, the Hummingbird built by Electric Passenger Cars Inc. of California is available in 2-door and 4-door versions. With its 10 hp Balder motor driven by 36 2 V sealed high energy batteries through an EVC solid state controller, it has a top speed of 60 mph (96 km/h). At the recommended cruising speed of 45-50 mph (72-80 km/h), its range is 40 miles (64 km), but with a 10 hp gasoline generator especially designed for the car, the range is doubled. The Hummingbird Hybrid Mk I has a curb weight of 2,740 lb (1,242 kg), and the other chief dimensions are: overall length 155.30 in (394 cm), overall width 63.40 in (161 cm), and overall height 55.50 in (141 cm).

EVA   Delta Pacer

EVA's neat four-seater is based on an AMC Pacer chassis. The 15 kW d.c. series motor is powered by 18 6 V traction batteries weighing 76 lb (34 kg), each in a 108 V system with 3-speed automatic transmission using motor-speed to motor-current logic. The Delta Pacer has a range of 54 miles (87 km) at 25 mph (40 km/h) or 32 miles (50 km) at its top speed of 50 mph (80 km/h). Consumption is 0.62 kW/h in an urban situation and charging takes 12-20 hours at 110 V or 6-8 hours at 220 V. The dimensions are those of the AMC Pacer but with an increase in weight due to the batteries. The curb weight of the Delta is 4,100 lb (1,859 kg). It accelerates from 0-50 mph (0-80 km/h) in 70 seconds.

EXXON   Experimental Electric Vehicle

The striking gull-wing door body of this proto-type is based on a Bradley GT design but incorporates graphite fiber reinforced plastics. A proprietary direct current system is powered by twelve 6 V batteries weighing 750 lb (340 kg). The propulsion unit allows a top speed of 55 mph (88 km/h) to be reached, while a cruising speed of 45 mph (72 km/h) is recommended. Range between charges varies according to how the car is driven but is roughly 30 miles (48 km). The Exxon is not a small car as can be seen from the dimensions: overall length 177 in (450 cm), width 69 in (175 cm), height 43.50 in (110 cm), wheelbase 95 in (241 cm) and curb weight 2,350 lb (1,066 kg).

FIAT   X 1/23

The Fiat X 1/23 is a little two-seater experimental car for town use. It was presented some years ago at the Turin Motor Show minus power unit and in 1976 it was fitted with a 14 kW electric motor with separate exciting field and lead-acid batteries. The traditional brakes are supplemented by a regenerating brake. Cooling is by a fan driven by an auxiliary electric motor. An electronic impulse traction regulator adjusts the speed of the vehicle continuously from zero to top speed, ensures that it functions in a regular manner at all speeds and provides for energy-recovery braking. The X 1/23 has front wheel drive while the batteries are housed at the rear. Top speed is 45 mph (75 km/h) and the range about 50 miles (80 km).

FIAT   900 T Elettrico

Fiat's experimental electric van is derived from their standard '900 T commercial vehicle and is powered by a Fiat electric motor weighing 121 lb (55 kg) and developing a nominal power of 14 kW at 3,200 rpm. The 12 V batteries are connected in series and housed in a single central tray. An electronic traction regulator adjusts the speed and provides electric braking with recovery of kinetic energy. The van has a top speed of 37 mph (60 km/h) and a range between charges of 30 miles (50 km). The chief dimensions are: overall length 146.85 in (373 cm), overall width 58.66 in (149 cm), and overall height 65.35 in (166 cm). The curb weight is 4,095 lb (1,857 kg).

ITALY

FIAT 242 Electric Van Prototype

The Fiat Research Centre has derived this electric van from the 242, retaining the same geometry of the traction organs. The d.c. series excited motor with 24 kW nominal power and the electronic controller with energy-recovery braking are front-mounted under the bonnet, while the batteries are housed in two compartments along the sides of the van, leaving ample cargo space. They are accessible from the exterior for easy removal by means of a fork-lift truck. In an alternative version, the batteries are stowed under the floor. The maximum speed is 50 mph (80 km/h) and the range in normal town conditions 40-50 miles (65-81 km). The curb weight is 7,720 lb (3,500 kg) and the payload capacity 1,918 lb (870 kg).

AUSTRALIA

FLINDERS Investigator Mk II

The Flinders University team has spent five years developing its twin-module motor electric version of a Fiat 127. A practical and viable propulsion system is linked to advanced battery developments to give exceptional acceleration and hill-climbing and a range of up to 50 miles (80 km) at 37-47 mph (60-75 km/h). The novelty is a printed circuit motor and a method of matching impedance with a series-pass transistor. The motor and control system is designed as a modular assembly and the Flinders linear current control system (FLCC) allows infinitely variable power control of both output and regenerative power. There are plans to add a third motor module to the two 5 kW motors.

POLAND

FSM Polski-Fiat 126

The FSM (Fabryka Samochodów Malolitrazowych), which builds cars derived from Italian Fiat models in Poland, has also prepared an experimental electric version of the 126. The body is unchanged but the petrol engine has been replaced by an a.c. electric motor with a power of 5 kw (about 7 bhp). A current invertor is used to transform the d.c. current of the lead batteries into alternating current. The car has a top speed of roughly 43 mph (70 km/h) and an autonomy of 25 miles (40 km). But forthcoming improvements should more than double the autonomy, making it adequate for city use. An air-zinc battery is also being studied giving an energy-weight ratio that is five times better than the lead batteries and would greatly improve the autonomy.

USA

GARRETT ERDA Passenger Vehicle

Sponsored by the Energy Research and Development Administration, this commuter vehicle prototype with FRP body panels and a new hybrid regenerative power system powered by standard lead-acid batteries emphasizes performance, reliability and passenger safety. Flywheel stored energy provides high transient power for acceleration and recovering vehicle kinetic energy during braking, while the battery pack weighing 1,040 lb (471 kg) merely supplies the average sustaining power. The range is 70 miles (112 km) with a cruising speed of 55 mph (88 km/h) and a top speed of 70 mph (112 km/h). The overall length is 158 in (401 cm), width 70 in (178 cm), height 57 in (145 cm) and curb weight 2,566 lb (1,164 kg).

GENERAL MOTORS XP512E

Since 1968, General Motor's engineering staff has been experimenting with a prototype special purpose 2-passenger electric vehicle for short-range personal transportation with some package-carrying capability behind the passenger compartment. Front-wheel drive allows room for the 12 lead-acid traction batteries stored under the seat between the rear wheels. The XP512E will cruise 50 miles (80 km) at 30 mph (50 km/h) and reach a top speed of 40 mph (64 km/h). The 16.8 kW coaxial d.c. motor is rear-mounted and there is a solid state controller. Overall length is 116.90 in (297 cm), overall height 55.50 in (141 cm), and wheelbase (74.80 in (190 cm). Curb weight is 1,779 lb (807 kg).

GLOBE-UNION Endura

This one-off prototype was built by the McKee Engineering Corporation to serve as a vehicle for Globe Union's technology in batteries, power systems and electric components. Built in fiberglass, the 4-seater body can be transformed into a 2+2 coupé or a station wagon simply by removing the hatchback. Powered by 20 Globe Union high energy density advanced lead-acid batteries, it has a range between charges of 115 miles (184 km) under controlled 35 mph (56 km/h) driving conditions and a top speed of 60 mph (96 km/h). Overall length is 184 in (467 cm), overall width 72 in (183 cm) and wheelbase 108 in 274 cm). The weight, including the batteries, is 1,300 lb (589 kg).

JET INDUSTRIES Electra Van

The Electra is a multi-purpose 2-door vehicle specially designed for the economical smooth delivery of passengers and cargo. It features a traction forced air motor developing 15 bhp at 3,800 rpm with electronic pulse controller and on-board charger for the 220 Ah 84 V lead-acid EV batteries. Rack and pinion steering, hydraulic brakes and radial tyres ensure good road-holding qualities at the van's top speed of 55 mph (88 km/h). At its cruising speed of 38 mph (61 km/h), a range of 60-100 miles (96-160 km) is possible. The chief dimensions are: overall length 120 in (305 cm), width 53 in (135 cm), height 64 in (162 cm) wheelbase 68 in (173 cm) and gross weight 2,352 lb (1,066 kg).

LUCAS CF Electric Van

In the early spring of 1978, between 25 and 30 of these vehicles are going into service in the London area in a government sponsored electric vehicle trial. Based, like the Limousine on a Bedford van, they are undergoing exhaustive tests partly aimed at obtaining data on operating costs and operators' reactions. Lucas is also facing problems such as the possible inhibition of cardiac pacemakers, the possible hazards from the evolution of hydrogen from lead-acid batteries and the dangers represented by the vehicles' very silence. The latter problem has been solved by using a warning buzzer for reverse and solutions to the others are expected. The van is 169 in (430 cm) long, 88 in (223 cm) wide and 76 in (193 cm) high.

LUCAS   Taxi II

A prototype taxi built for Lucas by Ogle Design set up the first lap record for electric vehicles at Brands Hatch 47.99 mph (77 km/h). Carrying four plus driver, they are even more compact and roomier than the London taxi. The body is a fully floating monocoque of sheet steel and bonded grp mounted on a box-steel perimeter chassis housing the battery tray. A 50 bhp 216 V motor, Lucas-developed SCR chopper type control gear and improved polypropylene SLI lead-acid batteries allow a top speed of nearly 60 mph (96 km/h) with a projected range of 100 miles (160 km). Overall length 140.50 in (357 cm), width 69.50 in (177 cm), height 70 in (178 cm), wheelbase 94 in (239 cm), front track 60.50 in (154 cm) and rear 59.50 in (151 cm).

LUCAS   Limousine

The body of this sophisticated luxury personnel carrier is based on the Bedford CG 35 cwt van, modified to house a 50 hp 216 V CAV motor at the rear and an underslung battery pack. As in the Lucas taxi, the motor drives the rear wheels through a 2-stage reduction Morse HY-Vo chain transmission and conventional differential gear set. The regenerative motor braking system is supplemented by servo-assisted hydraulic brakes. Even with a top speed of over 50 mph (80 km/h), the working range is 70 miles (112 km), rising to 140 miles (225 km) at 30 mph (48 km/h). Curb weight is 5,513 lb (2,500 kg) and payload 2,205 lb (1,000 kg). Overall length is 189 in (481 cm), width 88 in (223 cm) and height 82 in (208 cm).

MARATHON   C.300

Marathon, which traditionally builds golf buggies, has designed a multiple-purpose vehicle with fiberglass or steel body and soft top on a welded tubular steel frame. An 8 hp d.c. motor with variable speed transmission is powered by twelve 6 V 225 Ah batteries plus an auxiliary battery, with on-board charger which can be charged from any 110 V a.c. outlet. With a payload capacity of 500 lb (227 kg), top speed is 50 mph (80 km/h) and the recommended cruising speed 35 mph (56 km/h). On one charge the range is 50 miles (80 km). The overall length is 150 in (381 cm), overall width 62 in (157 cm), overall height 53 in (135 cm) and weight including batteries 2,200-2,600 lb (998-1,179 kg).

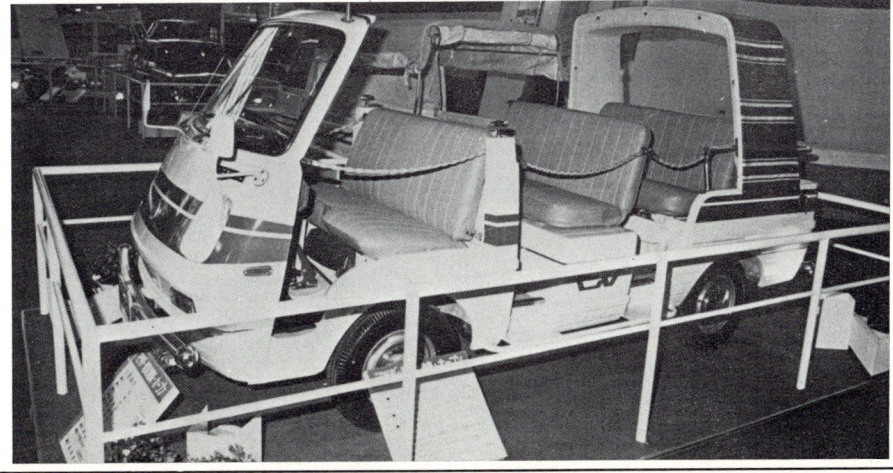

MAZDA   Bongo

This 5-seater minibus is a limited production model based on the Mazda Bongo van. Instead of the normal 1,000 cu cm piston engine, the electric version is powered by a 19.2 kW 2,560 rpm d.c. motor drawing electricity from eight 12 V lead-acid batteries. Conventional 4-speed mechanical transmission is retained for the drive train. The vehicle is 148.40 in (377 cm) long, 59.10 in (150 cm) wide and 66.10 in (168 cm) high on a 78.70 in (200 cm) wheelbase and weighs 2,789 lb (1,265 kg). It can reach a maximum speed of 20 mph (32 km/h), and has a range of 37 miles (60 km). The rear seat folds down for luggage. An open-bodied 8-seater has also been developed on the Bongo chassis for recreational purposes.

McKEE MK-16 Commuter Car

McKee Engineering claims to have designed, built and tested more on-road electric vehicles than any other American company. In its latest MK-16, 12 6 V batteries plus an auxiliary battery fit into a battery tray which can be rolled out and replaced in 5 minutes. The tray is housed in the backbone frame pioneered by McKee, because this battery location ensures a low centre of gravity and isolation from the car's occupants. The 8 hp motor allows a top speed of 60 mph (96 km/h) and a range of 120 miles (193 km) at 30 mph (48 km/h), or 75-85 miles (120-136 km) of city driving. Curb weight, complete with batteries, is 1,614 lb (732 kg), and the car has a wheelbase of 72 in (183 cm).

MELEX WGF-2

This 2-passenger delivery truck will also be available in a 4-passenger WGD version. A 48 V d.c. motor developing 1.54 kW at 2,800 rpm is mounted in front of the rear axle and powered by eight 6 V 240 Ah Varta batteries. Alternatively, six batteries power a 36 V motor. The four gears are engaged by briefly taking the foot off the acelerator. The rear-wheels only disc brakes are supplemented by a handbrake actioned automatically when there is no load on the driving seat. Maximum speed is a mere 15 mph (25 km/h) but the range is about 65 miles (100 km) and the vehicle carries a one year guarantee. Overall length 89 in (226 cm), width 46.90 in (119 cm) and height 67.70 in (172 cm).

MERCEDES-BENZ OE 305 Elektrobus

Daimler-Benz are researching into a variety of theoretically feasible propulsion systems. One example is its OE 305 hybrid bus powered by two 3.5 ton traction batteries. The batteries are recharged when the 100 hp Diesel engine is started up — for instance on reaching the outskirts of towns or at the end of the line. The 100-seater bus has a range of up to 186 miles (300 km), that is to say a whole day's operation. The derated Diesel engine operates at a constant speed and is encapsulated for noise abatement. Maximum speed is about 43 mph (70 km/h). Fifty electro-transporters with battery changing system are being field-tested in collaboration with the Association for Electric Road Transport.

NISSAN-DATSUN Electric

Nissan-Datsun has built a fleet of these electric runabouts and finds the open body ideal for carrying visitors around on visits to its factories. It has room for six to eight passengers besides the driver and is capable of reaching 30 mph (50 km/h). It has a range between charges of 43 miles (70 km) at a constant cruising speed of 25 mph (40 km/h) under normal driving conditions. The bodywork of this fine-weather vehicle is reinforced fiberglass. The electric motor is powered by high performance lead batteries. The chief dimensions are: overall length 150.79 in (383 cm) and overall width 62.99 in (160 cm), while the curb weight is 2,249 lb (1,020 kg).

P.G.E.   3 P

Designed as a town car, the 3 P is built for three passengers and luggage weighing 110 lb (50 kg). The sides of the body and the doors are molded sheet and the roof and bonnet fiberglass. The motor, which weighs 132 lb (60 kg), has a continuous power of 9 kW. The nominal tension of the batteries is 72 V. Speed regulation is by means of a thyristor control shutter, complete with static circuit for energy recovery during braking and an excitation circuit controlled by a transistor control shutter. Maximum speed is 37 mph (60 km/h) with a range of 47 miles (75 km). The main dimensions are: overall length 104.32 in (265 cm), overall width 60.24 in (153 cm), overall height 60.63 in (154 cm). The curb weight is 2,161 lb (980 kg).

P.G.E.   Taxi Bimotore

The success of the Lucas taxi may have inspired this Italian electric taxi which can also be fitted with an internal combustion engine. It carries four passengers in addition to the driver and 154 lb (70 kg) of luggage. The 9 kW d.c. motor weights 132 lb (60 kg). The batteries have a nominal tension of 96 V. Transmission is by means of a mitre wheel gearing set at an angle with a magnetic clutch acting on the countershaft of the gearbox. The top speed is roughly 30 mph (50 km/h) with a range of 46 miles (75 km) in normal town driving. A 20% slope can be tackled at 12 mph (20 km/h). Overall length 136.11 in (347 cm), overall width 59.06 in (150 cm), overall height 62.20 in (158 cm) and curb weight 2,646 lb (1,200 kg).

P.G.E.   6 P

This snub-nosed little open runabout, built of light alloy flat panels riveted and framed with square section steel, can carry six passengers in addition to the driver. The motor, which weighs 99 lb (45 kg), develops a continuous power of 5 kW. The nominal tension of the batteries, which are housed in a central tray, is 72 V. The instruments provided include an ammeter for the armature current, a voltmeter for the tension of the batteries, a tachometer and an instrument indicating the state of charge of the batteries. The maximum speed that can be reached by the 6 P is about 37 mph (60 km/h) and it has a range between charges of about 62 miles (100 km) when driven in normal town conditions.

PIAGGIO   Ape Elettrocar

Piaggio's electric van, derived from the 3-wheeled Ape running on petroil mixture fits a Bosch rear-mounted electric motor developing 8 kW at 2,400 rpm. Transmission is by reduction gears with a built-in differential. The twelve batteries are connected in series with 6 V tension and are divided into three groups. A Bosch electronic group looks after speed adjustment. Top speed is a respectable 28 mph (45 km/h) and the van has a range between charges of 30 miles (50 km). The chief dimensions are: overall length 128,74 in (327 cm), overall width 57.09 in (145 cm) and overall height 68.11 in (173 cm). The total weight is 2,796 lb (1,268 kg).

PILCAR   4-seater

A three-year guarantee or unlimited mileage is the main selling point of this handy little 4-seater with three doors. The body is reinforced polyester with independent suspension all round. The 22 hp (DIN) 8/16 kW motor has an output of 84 V and is powered by improved batteries with a 40 W/kg capacity that can be completely recharged in 8 hours. There is an onboard charger. Automatic transmission and hydraulic brakes on all four wheels with electric braking on the rear wheels are features of the Pilcar. Top speed is 55 mph (90 km/h), cruising speed 37-43 mph (60-70 km/h) and the range as much as 74 miles (120 km). The overall length is 120.47 in (306 cm), and the overall width 61.02 in (155 cm).

SAAB   Prototype

Saab-Scania is cooperating with AGA Innovation and the Swedish Post Office on the development of an electric van based on Saab components. Field trials are now in progress and two vans are being used in mail deliveries in one of Stockholm's satellite towns. The van is powered by modified AGA/Tudor lead batteries with an output of 144 V. A Bosch motor provides feedback current when braking and it is estimated that this system offers a feedback of 10-15% of the energy. With the current capacity of the batteries, the van's range is roughly 25 miles (40 km) with 300 stops and starts or, in normal urban traffic 43-50 miles (70-80 km). Front-wheel drive and excellent weight distribution make for good handling.

SEBRING VANGUARD   CitiCar II

The experience of over 2,000 users of the Citi-Car I has led to the design of the improved CitiCar II, potentially for the Energy Research and Development arm of the U.S. Department of Energy. All Federal Motor Safety Standards will be met and the interior will be roomier. Full hatchback is standard. A new solid state control system gives infinite speeds and smooth and rapid acceleration. A new high speed switch offers a top speed of 44 mph (71 km/h) and a cruising speed of 38 mph (61 km/h). The electric traction consists, as in the CitiCar I, of a group of eight 6 V lead-acid batteries and a series-wound d.c. 6 hp motor with electromechanical regulator. There is a built-in charging device and various extras are available.

SEBRING VANGUARD   CitiVan

Sebring has developed a highly manoeuverable van with 28 cu ft (793 dm³) of carrying space claimed to cost only a penny a mile. The serieswound 6 hp d.c. motor is powered by 6 V lead-acid batteries with a rated voltage of 48 V. The CitiVan cruises at 35-38 mph (56-61 km/h) and accelerates from 0-20 mph (0-32 km/h) in 5 seconds. The maximum range per charge is 40-50 miles (64-80 km), depending on driving conditions, and the maximum daily range is 100 miles (160 km) with intermittent charging. The chief dimensions are: overall length 110 in (279 cm), overall width 54.75 in (139 cm), overall height 59.50 in (151 cm) and wheelbase 76 in (193 mm). The curb weight is 1,360 lb (618 kg).

SRF   Flywheel Combi

As its name suggests, the novelty of this vehicle is the use of a small flywheel which supplies all the power necessary for acceleration. High battery current peaks are thus eliminated and the usable capacity of the battery and the vehicle's range greatly increased. During deceleration, kinetic energy is returned to the flywheel. No armature controller is used. Vehicle speed is controlled by high efficiency continuously variable transmission over a 16:1 range. The General Electric 19 kW motor, separately excited and shunt wound, is powered by a Varta MD 750-V3 144 V battery housed on the floor of the truck. Curb weight is 6,174 lb (2,800 kg) and gross weight 7,718 lb (3,500 kg). Top speed is about 45 mph (70 km/h).

TEILHOL   Messagette

The successful Messagette is now available in various versions — the 2-seater Series B, Series D with canvas hood, 4-seater beach buggy, golf buggy with no lighting and space for clubs, and Series P for industrial use. All have stratified polyester bodies and welded steel tubing frames and are powered by a 2 kW motor driving the rear wheel through a two-stage helicoidal pinion reduction gear. There is a built-in charger for the 8 143 Ah batteries which weigh 441 lb (200 kg) and allow a maximum speed in the Series B of 15 mph (25 km/h) and autonomy of about 55 miles (90 km). The overall length is 90.55 in (230 cm), width 54.33 in (138 cm), height 61.02 in (155 cm), dry weight minus batteries 882 lb (400 kg). No driving licence is needed in France.

TEILHOL   Handicar

This 4-wheeler is primarily intended for the disabled or invalids using a wheel-chair. By pressing a button the floor descends to ground level allowing simple access in a wheel-chair by the rear door. The floor is then raised again. The rear door can be opened from the driving seat by pressing a button. The 2-seater stratified polyester body is mounted on a steel frame and has lateral boxes for the eight 12 V Ah batteries. The Handicar has a 4 kW motor, independent wheels and hydraulic drum brakes on all 4 wheels. Dimensions: overall length 95.28 in (242 cm), width 53.15 in (135 cm), height 61.02 in (155 cm), dry weight with batteries 1,389 lb (630 kg). Top speed is 30 mph (50 km/h) and autonomy about 43 miles (70 km).

TEILHOL   Citacome K 5 and K 10

Teilhol's economical new Citacome comes in two versions, the K 10 being the more powerful. For both, the body is reinforced polyester and the chassis steel tubes. They are powered by a 96 V 4 kW motor connected in series and have an onboard charger. The 8 12 V batteries weighing 452 lb (205 kg) of the model K 5 develop 105 Ah and allow a range of 30 miles (50 km), while the 16 10 V batteries weighing 970 lb (440 kg) of the K 10 develop 105 Ah with a range of 62 miles (100 km). For both versions, the top speed is 30 mph (50 km/h). They are identical in overall length, width and height at 112.99 in (287 cm), 54.33 in (138 cm), and 66.93 in (170 cm) respectively. The K 5 weighs 1,411 lb (640 kg) and the K 10 1,962 lb (890 kg).

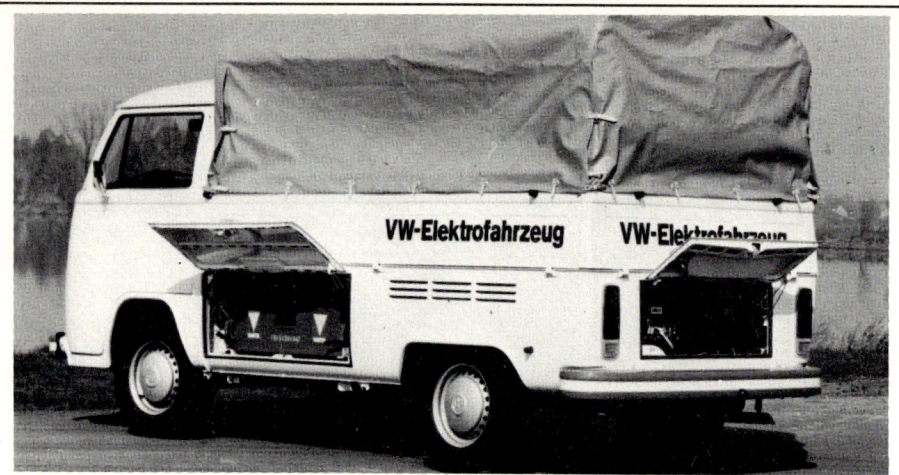

VOLKSWAGEN   Elektrotransporter

The trend in Germany seems to be towards large-scale electric vehicles, not runabouts. The explanation is simple: in a heavy vehicle, the weight of the batteries and the complexity of the electrical equipment pose fewer problems. The VW truck presented at the 1977 Frankfurt Motor Show mounts a 45 hp separately excited motor connected in parallel with thyristor control. The electric current is automatically reduced should the motor overheat or the minimum value of the battery voltage fall. Maximum speed is 43 mph (70 km/h) and the range between charges is 30-50 miles (50-80 km). The batteries weigh 1,874 lb (850 kg) and a load of 1,763 lb (800 kg) can be carried. The curb weight with driver is 5,016 lb (2,275 kg).

VOLVO   Prototype

To gain know-how about electric cars while waiting for developments in batteries, Volvo has built two prototypes which are narrower and higher than the smallest Volvo production model but weigh 2,205 lb (1,000 kg). Rear-wheel drive, button selection of forward or reverse and an electronically actuated transmission make for easy driving. Thyristors aid starting and slow running, making them jerk-free. The 4-seater passenger car has a 8 kW 11 hp motor and the 2-seater van with sliding door mounts a 9.5 kW 13 hp motor. The 12 batteries of the 4-seater provide 72 V and the 10 batteries of the van 60 V. The battery container allows swift replacement.

ZAGATO   Zele 1000 and 2000

Various versions of the Zele are produced, the 1000 and the 2000, and the Van and Golf, carrying two plus luggage, with bodywork in reinforced polyester. They are driven by accumulator traction in four 12 V groups of 160 Ah batteries. Suspension is independent at the front and drum brakes are used all round. Dimensions: overall length 76.77 in (195 cm), width 53.15 in (135 cm), height 63.39 in (161 cm), curb weight 1,091 lb (495 kg), wheelbase 51.18 in (130 cm), front track 43.31 in (110 cm), rear track 42.52 in (108 cm), turning circle about 11,5 ft (3,5 m). For the 1000 version top speed is 25 mph (40 km/h) and range about 43 miles (70 km), and for the 2000 34 mph (55 km/h) and 31 miles (50 km).

ZAGATO   Zele Van

In view of the success of the Zeles, Zagato presented a new electric Van at the Chicago International Electric Vehicle Show. The range, top speed and battery recharging and replacement have been improved. Eight 6 V 215 Ah batteries power a 48 V d.c. motor which allows a top speed of over 30 mph (50 km/h) and a range of about 37 miles (60 km). It is expected that a more powerful motor and improved batteries will shortly be adopted. The batteries are housed under the car's floor in an independent sliding tray. The chief dimensions are: overall length 81.89 in (208 cm), overall width 55.12 in (140 cm), height 60.63 in (154 cm) and wheelbase 53.15 in (135 cm). The compact reinforced glass fibre body is designed by the Zagato styling centre.

Europe

BACK FROM THE ABYSS

by L.J.K. Setright

They had stopped telling us that happiness was just around the corner; but they have started again. There was still the implied suggestion that nobody has any right to consume happiness without producing it, but the car industry at least has been doing its best: 1977 was an exceptionally fruitful year for interesting and impressive new models, and if their regular 90-day rises in price may discourage some consumers from buying the things, very few commentators have dared to criticise what the industry produces as being unlikely to bring happiness. Maybe it is because of some great international brainwashing conspiracy designed to persuade everybody that contentment depends on having the car that everybody else, from the legislators to the advertisers, insists we should enjoy; or maybe it is because the increasingly international nature of the motor industry must needs impose a correspondingly international uniformity upon products that were once full of national, social, or similarly inherited local characteristics. It is getting a bit hard to stomach, though: it takes more than a cursory look at the shovel-nose of the new Opel Rekord to distinguish it from the similar noses of the new Ford Granada, the new Chrysler Sunbeam, the fairly new Audi 100, and what not. They all talk glibly of aerodynamic efficiency, so maybe they all hire the same wind-tunnel experts — or are they simply all trying to catch up with the late lamented NSU Ro80 in which such things were so properly done 10 years ago?

If happiness, motoring or otherwise, is truly just around the corner, it comes as something of a surprise after what we have been told in previous years. The astonishing thing about 1977 is not what happened but what did not: all the crises, all the conceptual upsets, the rocketing price of oil, the shrinking of the market and of the cars intended for it, the confinements of the battery electric vehicle or of liquefied petroleum gas, the air bags and 50 mph barrier tests and the demise of the high-performance car — all the nasty things that had been promised to us after the oil crisis of 1973 have somehow failed to materialise. Even the speed limits have grown no worse; indeed some of them have grown better — by a process of simplification and levelling up in Britain, and by a more cunning process of complication and tax gathering in Italy.

If any one car can best express this new optimism, it must be the Porsche 928. Its manufacturers have been very brave about it, if only because it con-stitutes a denial of all their own long-established traditions (though these live on in the latest expanded versions of the 911), and because it is an entirely new car from stem to stern, inheriting nothing from previous production. That is brave enough, but the real courage of Porsche shows in the fact that the 928 is not only an expensive car but also a big one and, most of all, a fast one. It is in fact a magnificent tribute to man's conviction that he should not trouble himself unduly to fare well, but be content to fare forward and let the moralists pass judgement when they are good and ready. Technically the car is full of interest, from the constructional details of the big light-alloy V8 engine to the disposition of the transmission with its major masses concentrated at the rear. The suspension of that posterior includes a new device to counter an increasingly familiar handl-

With the Granada, the company's flagship, Ford too launches into the diesel sector. It is the first diesel to start up as easily as a petrol-engined car.

A huge 4.5-litre V8 engine in light alloy, a highly sophisticated chassis - these are the characteristics of the Porsche 928, elected car of the year.

ing deficiency, which is the intrusion of oversteer when closing the throttle in mid-corner; and what Porsche have chosen to call the Weissach axle is in fact a pair of semi-trailing wishbones with spring-loaded pivots that affect an automatic variation of rear wheel alignment as tractive effort is altered. Up to a point it works well, but as the car's limits are approached it fails and the old oversteer returns, albeit controllably and almost pleasantly. What matters more is that those limits are so high because of the formidable performance of the Pirelli P7 tyres which are standard equipment on the 928. All these technicalities, not to mention a top speed of 143 mph and an impressive quality of manufacture, may have sufficed to persuade the majority of my fellow judges, as I was persuaded, that the Porsche 928 deserved to be voted the Car of

the Year; but it was the sheer courage of the venture that did most to earn my approval, including the stylistic bravery that promised a return to curves in place of the rectilinear boxes that have served as car bodywork since the mid-1960s.

If the P7, the most advanced road tyre on the market, plays an important part in making the 928 what it is, it is not without competition from Michelin, whose new TRX has been long awaited. It made its appearance at last as a production option for the new refined

The restyled Ford Capri II S. Five engines are offered: 1.6-litre (68 and 72 hp), 2-litre 90 hp, 2.3-litre 108 hp and 3-litre 138 hp.

The new Renault 18 is available with a 1,397 cc engine developing 64 hp or a 79 hp 1,647 cc engine.

and improved 2-litre version of the Fiat 132. Alas, trials showed that the TRX was disastrous on the Fiat, while Pirelli's big surprise, the P6 (a sort of poor man's version of the P7, and soon to be accompanied by the even more humble P8 to complete the new family of ultra-low profile nylon-bandaged steel-belted radials) made the Fiat so much better that Michelin's reputation never seemed in greater danger. Fortunately they were redeemed by the magnificent showing of the TRX on the top-of-the-range version of the new Ford Granada. For the rest, the Granada in its various guises amounts to a handsome and appropriately sumptuous new body enclosing fairly well established machinery, though the 2.3 and 2.8 litre German built V6 engines are now standardised for all markets and the bigger and more ponderous V6 engines made by Ford

in England will survive only in the new Capri.

Six-cylinder engines were quite a feature of 1977 in Europe, as they were (for different reasons) in the USA. The most interesting of them were the new 2.3 and 2.6 litre power units which began what will doubtless be a varied career in assorted Leyland models during the forthcoming decade, in some lower-priced versions of the attractive Rover 3500. The nicest feature to emerge from a generally impressive if simple specification for this new engine is that its beautiful crankshaft is carried in only four main bearings, a feature recognised by the discerning (such as Daimler-Benz a year earlier) as contributing to torsional stiffness at high speeds and fuel economy at all speeds. Yet the Rover six-cylinder engine is not to be dismissed as a mere economy device:

the 2.6 litre version makes the car practically as quick as the bigger V8, and does it with an altogether crisper and more patrician character.

BMW have been banging the six-cylinder drum too, getting rid of all but the smallest of their four-cylinder engines and creating a new, if depressingly conservative, family of small in-line sixes that will be shared by the 3 and 5 Series saloons. Their bigger sixes continue in new shells, the 7 Series saloon emerging during the year as a curiously reactionary, not to say downright old-fashioned, challenger in the luxury tourer category. All its mechanical features seem terribly long in the tooth and do little to justify the high price being asked for the car, but it must be admitted that the thing does go well, and around corners it goes very well indeed.

In both respects the most impressive BMW by a very long way will be the new mid-engined coupé, engineered and built for them by Lamborghini. It is not yet in production, but plenty of prototypes have been seen around, all of them behaving very impressively. The high performance of the car, secured by a 24 valve version of the 3.3 litre six-cylinder engine, is rendered exceptionally manageable by suspension calculated to make the most of the P7 tyre. Most of the expertise required for doing this was derived from Lamborghini's work on their own Countach, now revealed in a modified P7-tyred S version that is faster than ever — which means that it is fastest of all.

The Countach S is not going unchallenged, though that may change when the 5-litre engine comes along. The gauntlet has been thrown down by Panther, who stole the limelight from everybody else in the autumn with their new six-wheeler. With its layout, suspension and steering ostensibly aping those of the now defunct Tyrrell Grand Prix six-wheeler, the Panther in fact does not pretend to its six wheels for any technical reasons, but rather for the sake of distinctiveness. It is aided in this by a beautiful — and exceptionally beautifully made — open 2/3 seater body, in the tail of which sits a Cadillac Eldorado engine and transmission. With 190 bhp available from this in standard form, which is all that American and certain other customers will ever be allowed, the Panther may prove

Above, the Opel Monza, a new 3-door hatchback coupé, uses the mechanics of the Senator saloon (below) with a 2.8 or a 3-litre 6-cylinder injection engine both with automatic transmission as an optional.

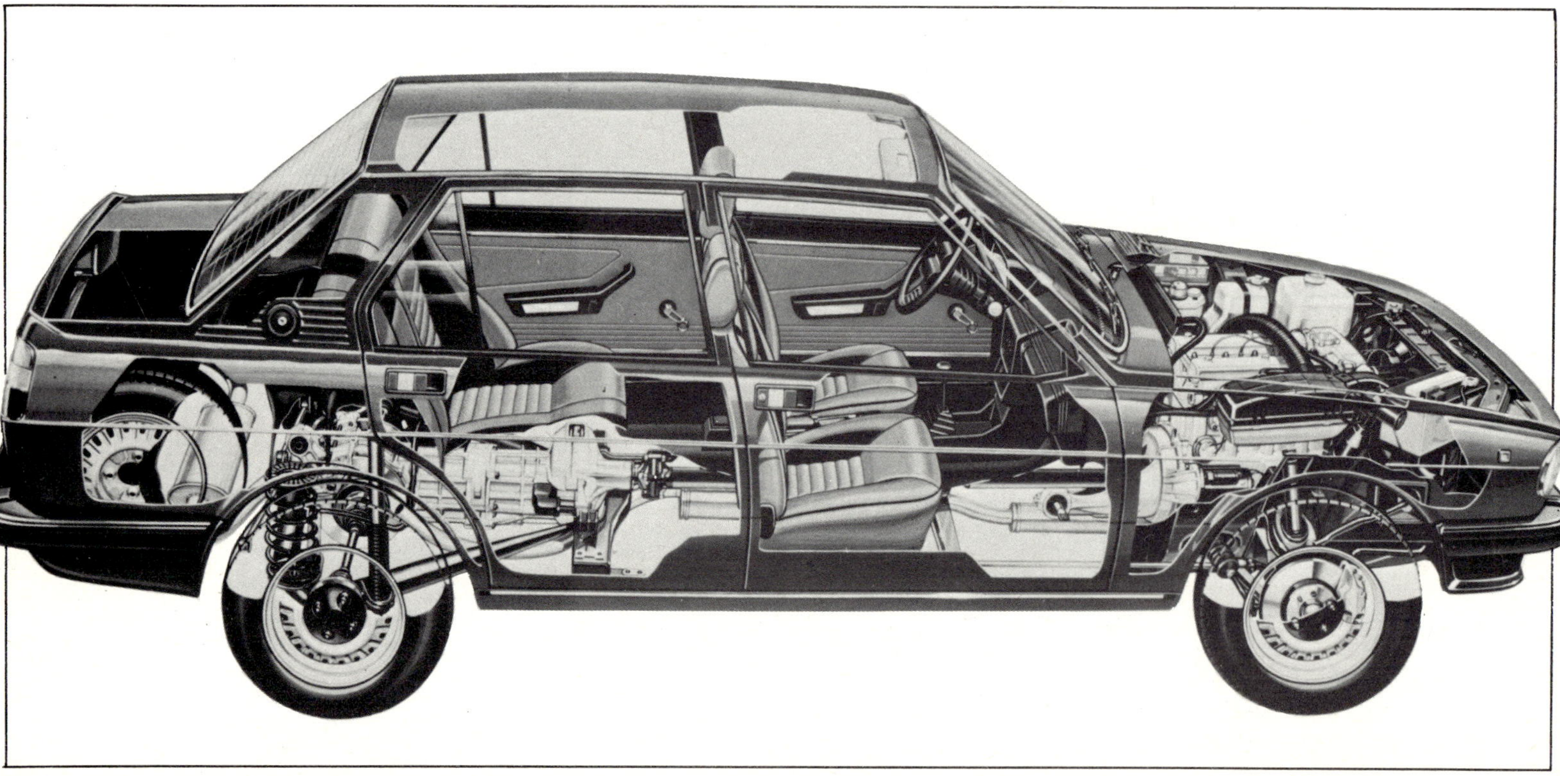

capable of 150 mph; but for other less inhibited markets, the car enjoys a pair of turbochargers which raise its power output to 600 bhp and should elevate its maximum speed to something in excess of 200 mph.

There has been a lot of talk about turbochargers lately, but most of the action has been in the USA. Europeans seem principally concerned about its application to the diesel engine, which undoubtedly needs it more and equally suits it better; but Saab have tacked a turbocharger onto their 2-litre model 99, and have not unnaturally improved the car's performance considerably. Technically the most interesting feature of this car is, however, the primary transmission from the engine to the gearbox, an ingeniously engineered triple row of Renold's chains taking the place of the previous train of gears and entraining improvements in quietness, smoothness, efficiency and ease of maintenance. Several other transverse-engined front-wheel-drive cars may enjoy similar treatment before long, but the most impressive front-drivers of the year have had their engines arranged longitudinally. The Renault R20 TS is indeed remarkable only for its engine, the rest of the car closely resembling the ordinary R20 and the earlier R30, the levels of mechanical sophistication and bodily furnishing being approximately mid-way between those two. The 2-litre engine of the TS is however a beautiful job apart from the old-fashioned ignition distributor (which also rather let down

To the rennovated Fiat 131 range has been added the Supermirafiori version, equipped with either a 1,301 or 1,585 cc twin overhead cam engine. The interior is particularly well finished and a vast series of accessories is available.

After 12 years' absence Alfa Romeo's Giulietta is back. Either a 1,357 cc 95 bhp (DIN) or a 1,570 cc 109 bhp engine is mounted, both with twin overhead camshafts. The Giulietta takes the place of the Giulia and slots into the intermediate position between the Alfasud and Alfetta range.

the Rover sixes), powerful, crisp, and uncommonly efficient. A competition version of it is under development for Formula 3 racing, but it is likely to encounter a fair amount of opposition, for several other manufacturers have also grown tired or resentful of Toyota's domination of this category.

Another nice new front drive car is the Audi Avant, but really it amounts to nothing more than an Audi 100 with the notch-back body replaced by a hatch-back affair very closely resembling that of the smaller (and itself improved during 1977) Volkswagen Passat. Although the Avant is in fact a very fine piece of work with exceptionally precise steering, there is perhaps more of interest in the transverse engined front-wheel drive Simca Horizon. Chrysler launched this in France as a gap-filler, meant to be inserted into the marketing slot between the Simca 1100 and the 1307/1308 or Alpine. Their claim is

not easy to justify, except on the grounds that the Horizon is about the same length as the 1100 and the same width as the Alpine, and it is more likely that the 1100 is due for the axe. There is not much new in the engine and drive-line, the suspension or the running gear, but of course the new Horizon is more crashable and stylistically more fashionable. What makes it most interesting is that in the USA Chrysler market an essentially similar car called the Plymouth Horizon, but with the important difference that the engine is made for Chrysler in the USA by Volkswagen, and the rear suspension looks as though it might have been. In Simca or Plymouth form, the Horizon offers an interesting contrast to Chrysler's Scottish built Sunbeam, which looks very similar but is in fact a front-engined, rear-wheel-drive car, the chassis pan, engine and running gear all being inherited from the now rather old Avenger. For what it is, the Sunbeam is a quite nice little car, but the smoothest and sweetest-running version of it, the smallest-engined economy model, gets its good manners from an enlarged version of the old Hillman Imp engine, which in turn was based on the Coventry Climax sports-car unit, which was originally derived from a portable fire pump. The trouble with this smallest-engined Sunbeam is that, sweetly though it behaves, its performance is no better than that of the Morris Minor 1000 of ancient if precious memory. Maybe that will not matter: the Minor endeared itself to multitudes, and the Sunbeam is capable in the right social conditions of doing the same.

Much more certain to enjoy popular acceptance is the new Opel Rekord. This is very much a car of its times, refined, comfortable, well handling, with exceptionally sweet ride, and with a well-appointed body that is really rather beautiful and should — given sufficient time and practice — be distinguishable from the Ford, the Audi, and all the other identicars. Family likenesses are all very well, but the whole European motor industry seems to be getting incestuous, and the arrival of new 1200 and 1500 saloons and estate cars from Russia does not make it any easier than it was before to tell the difference between a Lada and a Fiat 124.

No such difficulties are likely to obscure recognition of the tolerably pretty new Skoda Estelle. It is particularly easy to identify when it is coming round a corner, for if driven with any zeal, it will probably come around sideways or even backwards. The typical oversteer engendered by swinging half-axles at the rear is redolent of a happily bygone age — so much so that, in answer to the outcry that arose in Britain when the car was introduced there, the importers were forced to cobble together a modified version with stiffer suspension, more generous wheels and tyres, and other alterations calculated to improve its handling and roadholding. It was really rather a pity that the car should have been so misunderstood, for its virtues are of a special and now rather rare kind. It is a simple sensible workaday saloon, designed so that even major maintenance jobs can easily be undertaken without elaborate servicing facilities. There are still plenty of places in the world, and not only in the Eastern Bloc whence the Skoda comes, where such a car is worth its weight in mechanics. In any case the present Estelle is admitted to be a transitional model; having already had its nose enlarged and the cooling system removed there from the tail, it will in due course have the engine transplanted there as well and should eventually emerge as a front wheel drive car with all its present undeniable virtues and fewer of its avoidable vices.

How much better to begin life without any vices — which brings us happily to the new Alfa Romeo Giulietta. The latest in a long and little changed line of attractive and deservedly popular little sporting saloons, the new Giulietta features an engine drive-line and suspension simliar in design but superior in behaviour to those of the Alfetta, all wrapped up in a new wedge-based saloon body that is astonishingly roomy in the right places without being too big in the wrong ones. There is no need to await the happiness that is supposed to lie just around the corner: this car's behaviour is so faultless that happiness can be found in the middle of the corner, and no moralist whether good or ready will find in it cause for complaint.

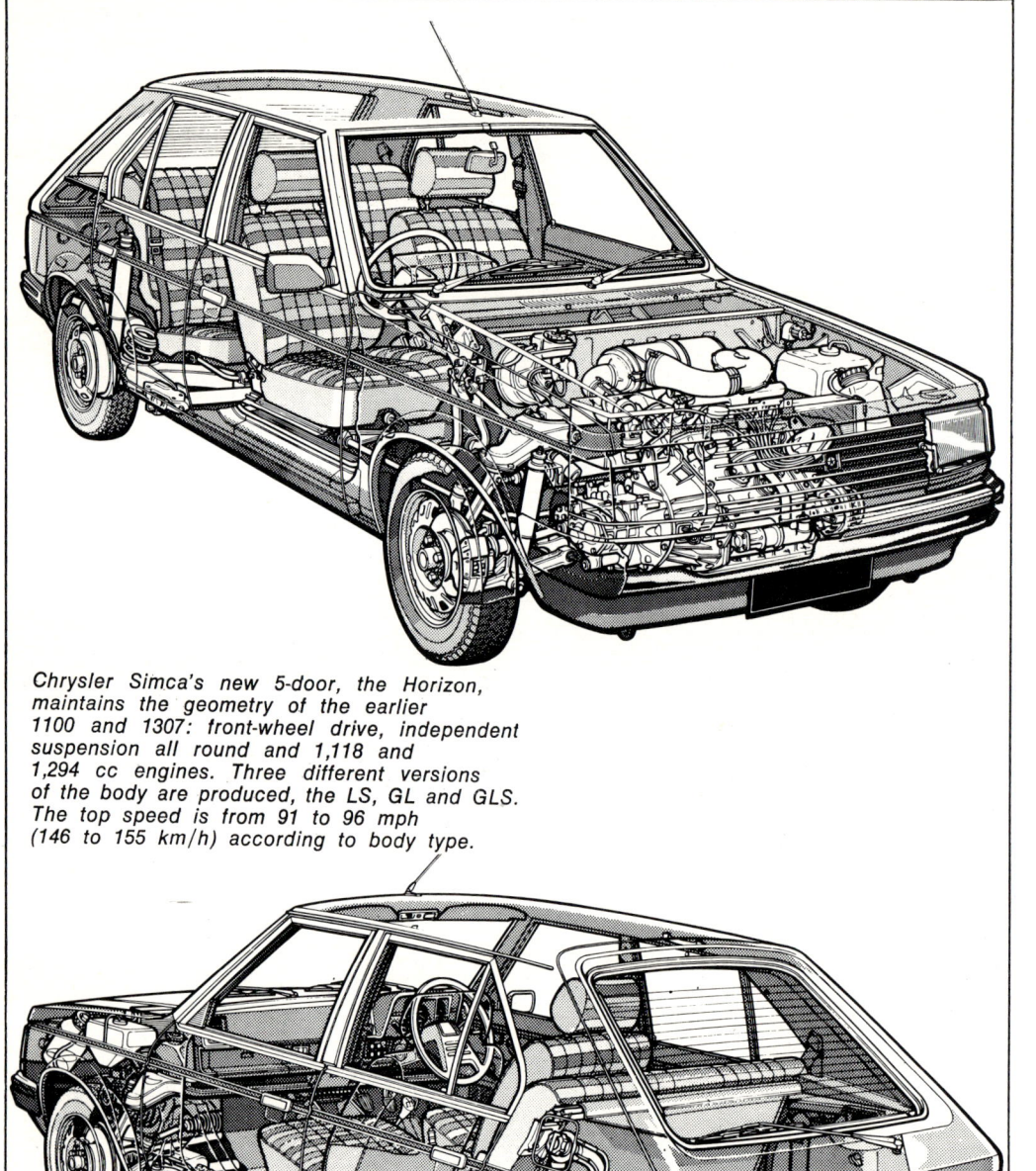

Chrysler Simca's new 5-door, the Horizon, maintains the geometry of the earlier 1100 and 1307: front-wheel drive, independent suspension all round and 1,118 and 1,294 cc engines. Three different versions of the body are produced, the LS, GL and GLS. The top speed is from 91 to 96 mph (146 to 155 km/h) according to body type.

Japan

SUCCESSES - EXCESSES

by Jack K. Yamaguchi

The President of the Toyota Motor Sales Company, the dynamic and shrewd commercial half of the mighty empire, regrets that his company failed to attain the projected domestic sales target of 1.5 million motor vehicles for the 1977 calender year, missing it by nearly 200,000 units. On the other side of the corporate coin, however, the company surpassed its wildest export expectations and shipped out 1.41 million vehicles. The aggregate was an impressive 9% gain over the previous year's record, thus pouring all-time high profits into the general coffers of the group. Wherefore rejoice, reflects the honourable and sober president nonetheless, when wealth was not shared with his faithful local distributors and dealers?

The paradox and predicament apply equally tó other members of the Japanese motor industry. On the home front, Nissan could do no better than the bleak 1976 season but more than offset the loss by thriving exports. The smaller members have done considerably better in the domestic market, notably Mitsubishi and Toyo Kogyo, marking up 13.4% and 8.0% gains respectively. But again their true growth area is overseas. In fact, while the Big Two's domestic-export ratio is held at a healthy 50:50, the Third Power members rely more heavily on exports, their ratios hovering around 30:70. For example, with its potent merchandise, Honda could lure only 246,000 domestic buyers, while the same products were appreciated by 445,000 foreign customers. These represent a fall of 1.3% and a whopping 44.8% rise over the previous year.

The industry's total performance for

Nissan outdoes them all. This is the striking A10 with Auster face.

1977 is approximately 8.5 million motor vehicles produced, including light vehicles, 4.2 millions of them consumed domestically and the remainder exported.

1977 was to be the year of the active home market, reversing the 1976 trend. The major powers expected and tried strenuously to attain two digit growth rates in domestic sales. It didn't work quite that way. The 1976 mid-year pause of the Japanese economy wasn't a pause after all. It lingered on into the new year, worsened in the spring with every evil symptom of a proper recession, and indeed developed into one in the autumn. The stagnant economy alarmed the motoring public, many of whom shied away from new car purchases, or turned to used cars instead. The used car market, by the

way, was very active indeed throughout the year. The nine passenger car manufacturers weren't exactly sitting idle. On the contrary, the season saw an unprecedented onrush of new and revamped car releases. They were invariably sales successes, to varying degrees depending on their manufacturers' marketing and financing capabilities. But very few provided what was hoped for in the overall buyer traffic; the new cars did not generate slipstream effects that would attract buyers to other existing models. Not only that, their own worth was precarious. New car effects were less magnetic and longlasting than had been the case a few years ago.

The aforementioned president of the Toyota sales organization most aptly described 1977 as the year of the Third

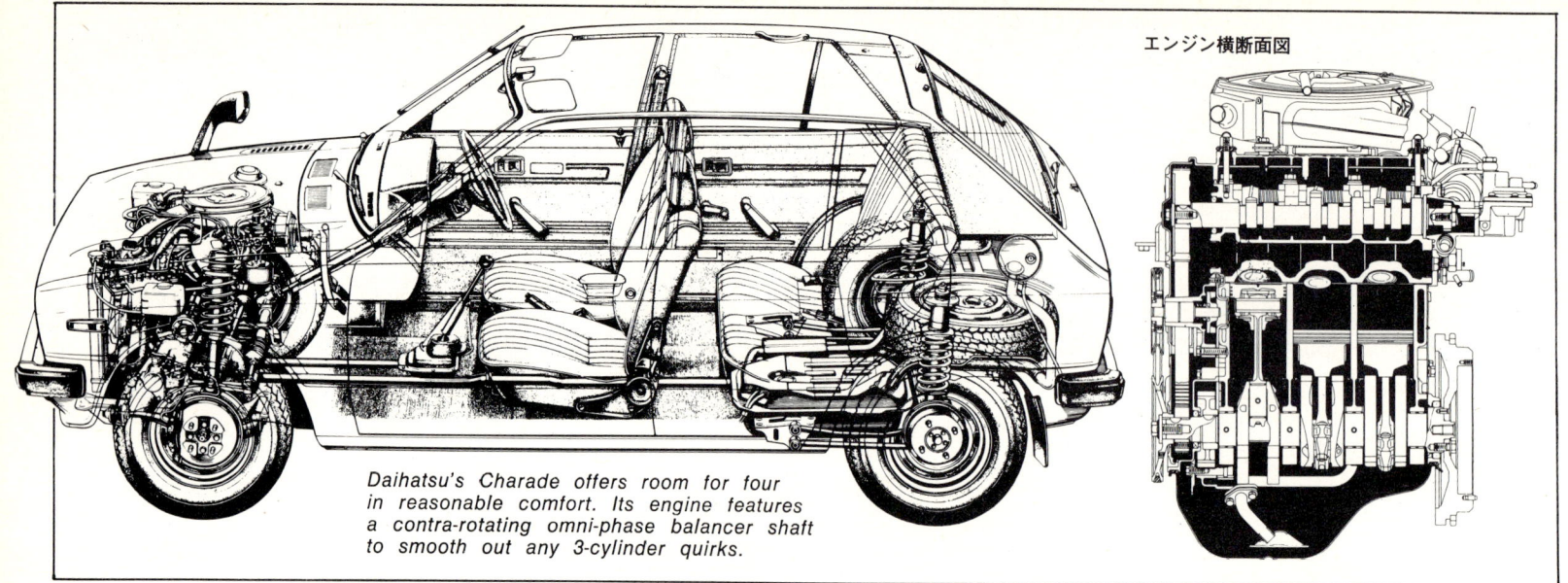

エンジン横断面図

Daihatsu's Charade offers room for four in reasonable comfort. Its engine features a contra-rotating omni-phase balancer shaft to smooth out any 3-cylinder quirks.

Shock. The first was by courtesy of former President Richard Nixon, who chilled Japan's economy of the early '70s with a freezing glance. The second was brought about by those Arab sheiks who had suddenly decided to shut off the oil valves. The Japanese cannot entirely blame third parties for the third crisis, or the "Yen Shock" as it was referred to, which was due to the country's own, though certainly not voluntary, doings. Japan's, and West Germany's, trade performance had been spectacular, in sharp contrast to the U.S. which was dipped deep into red ink. The extraordinary contrast could not escape the hawk eyes of the international money men. The value of the yen shot skywards. In a single year it rose by 20%. Again to quote President Kato of Toyota, the pains of the Third Shock weren't so swift and acute as those of the First and Second crises, but more of a duller and more progressive variety. Their effects were nevertheless as deadly, and are already showing up on vulnerable sectors of the Japanese scene. In the meantime, exports held on strongly. The strength of the yen hiked Japanese car prices up considerably in major export markets, as much as $600 on a popularly-priced small car in the competitive U.S. market, but demand did not seem to recede. Even in November-December last year, when U.S. domestic car sales turned soft, the Japanese Big Two went on to set sales records. Toyota, the top seller, sold 493,048 cars in 1977, followed by the runner-up, Nissan, with 388,378. And Honda was breathing down the neck of VW in third place with 223,633 unit sales. On all other export fronts the Japanese gained precious ground, recording an estimated growth rate of

Above, Nissan's best-selling Sunny dons new clothing. This is the hatchback coupé version. Below, Toyota has revamped the Celica. This is a 2000 GT Liftback coupé powered by a potent twin cam 2-litre four.

14.3% over the 1976 statistics, or a total of 4.24 million vehicles exported. Industry sources do not want the hefty gain to be construed as an uncontrolled avalanche of more cars pouring onto foreign shores, lest it may spark off a series of trade battles. Their forecast for the present year is both restrained and conservative; it is to be a year of no growth. But two of the smaller automakers have revealed their plans to expand export programs. Mitsubishi Motor Corp. intends to export

360,000 cars in 1978, or 5% more than 1977, many of which fall in the "captive import" category, being marketed through Chrysler's dealer network in America. Ambitious Daihatsu Motor Company of Osaka also aims to increase its exports to 70,000 units. It has high hopes for its brand new Charade small hatchback.

Like people, cars are products of their natural environment. Bred in a country with narrow and congested roads, and low and strictly enforced

TABLE 1. TOTAL MOTOR VEHICLE PRODUCTION, CALENDAR YEAR 1977

	1976 (% to previous year)	1977 estimate
PASSENGER CAR		
Normal	4,860,063 (110.3%)	5,250,000 (108.0%)
Light	167,726 (104.7%)	180,000 (107.3%)
TOTAL	5,027,792 (110.1%)	5,430,000 (108.0%)
COMMERCIAL VEHICLE		
Normal (large)	448,141 (155.5%)	609,000 (135.9%)
Small	1,830,522 (113.7%)	1,831,000 (100.0%)
Light	492,853 (112.3%)	598,000 (121.3%)
TOTAL	2,771,516 (118.6%)	3,038,000 (109.6%)
BUS	42,139 (116.7%)	49,000 (116.3%)
GRAND TOTAL	7,841,447 (113.0%)	8,517,000 (108.6%)

speed limits, Japanese cars have never been renowned for their dynamic qualities. But not all Germans are autobahn stormers, nor do all French men yearn to be grand prix bravados. To them, Japanese cars sold themselves by their static appeal, reliability and durability, economy, superb finish and generous standard equipment. There were exceptions, like Honda's delightful Civic and sophisticated Accord, and Nissan's masculine Z coupé, but they were a minority. All this is now changing. The signs are here that Japanese cars are improving quickly and dynamically now that the nine manufacturers have all licked the toughest engineering obstacle that stood in their way so long

— the most stringent exhaust emission standards in the world. The Japanese government has methodically and without the slightest hesitation tightened up the standards. The 1978 set of rules is the final one of several installments, which over five years required the reduction of the unregulated level. Specifically, mean limits for carbon monoxides, unburned hydrocarbon and oxides of nitrogen are set at 2.1, 0.25 and 0.25 grams per kilometer respectively. These are in essence a metric translation of Senator Muskie's original Clean Air Act of 1970, though measured on a different test cycle mode with emphasis on low speed city driving.

There seem to be more things in

heaven and earth than are dreamt of in our limited philosophy of internal combustion, as is proved by several Japanese manufacturers. Their varied approaches include the already famous Honda CVCC stratified chargé engine in its refined form, a number of lean-burn engines, combinations of engine modifications and catalytic converters, a Wankel rotary system and even a 2-stroke engine. Of the lean-burn school, Mitsubishi's MCA-Jet conversion has a third valve in the combustion chamber which injects a powerful airstream that creates turbulence, in turn ensuring proper mixing of the lean charge. Toyota's TTC-L system has a tiny dead-end auxiliary chamber atop the combustion chamber, officially called Turbulence Generating Pot. It is now used in conjunction with a small capacity catalyst, and performance and fuel economy have been greatly improved. Daihatsu twisted the Toyota method, and hung the TGP directly under the sparking plug. Three element catalysts are now widely employed, on more expensive models with Bosch patented and licensed L-jetronic electronic fuel injection. Mazda uses the catalyst but has done away with an expensive electronic oxygen sensor, and instead has an ingenious self-adjusting carburetter. Subaru's system is an anti-climax in its utter simplicity, a very normal looking flat four with a dash of exhaust gas recirculation but

TABLE 2. PASSENGER CAR PRODUCTION BY MAKES, JANUARY THROUGH NOVEMBER 1977 (11 mos).

Toyota	1,726,979
Nissan	1,476,411
Honda	519,964
Toyo Kogyo (Mazda)	458,555
Mitsubishi	435,355
Fuji Heavy Industries (Subaru)	143,492
Daihatsu	71,904
Isuzu	67,125
Suzuki	51,770
TOTAL	4,951,555

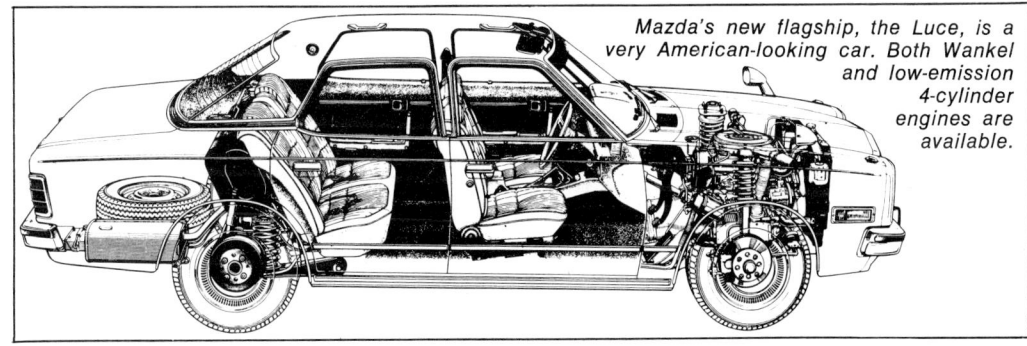

Mazda's new flagship, the Luce, is a very American-looking car. Both Wankel and low-emission 4-cylinder engines are available.

TABLE 3. HOME REGISTRATION BY MAKES

	1976 (% to previous year)	1977 (%) estimate	1978 (%) forecast *
PASSENGER CAR			
Normal cars	2,270,521 (88.3%)	2,329,000 (102.6%)	2,320,000 (99.6%)
Light cars	178,057 (113.3%)	165,000 (92.7%)	134,000 (81.2%)
TOTAL	2,448,578 (89.7%)	2,494,000 (101.9%)	2,454,000 (98.4%)
COMMERCIAL VEHICLE			
Normal (large)	129,272 (104.8%)	135,000 (104.4%)	141,000 (104.4%)
Small	1,043,493 (103.9%)	1,034,000 (99.1%)	1,059,000 (102.4%)
Light	459,455 (106.6%)	513,000 (111.7%)	512,000 (99.8%)
TOTAL	1,632,220 (104.7%)	1,682,000 (103.0%)	1,712,000 (101.8%)
BUS	23,309 (108.3%)	23,000 (98.7%)	24,000 (104.3%)
GRAND TOTAL	4,104,107 (95.2%)	4,199,000 (102.3%)	4,190,000 (99.8%)

none of those add-on devices. Suzuki has also mastered the art of tailoring its 2-stroke engine to the stringent standards with a clever two-stage catalyst. A welcome bonus in the clean air regulations is the Government's requirement of fuel consumption estimates based on the emission test cycle mode, rather like that of the U.S. city model. The 10-mode consumption, as it is called, is far more realistic than the previous one measured at a steady 60 km/h.

And now the engineering chieftains' attention and the efforts of their vast armies of engineers and technicians are being directed to other important matters pending, such as styling refine-

ment and chassis improvement. No Gallic revolution or Teutonic innovations overnight — that's not in the character of the cautious Japanese whose forte will still be relatively inexpensive volume productions cars. A recent crop of Datsun cars, made by the country's Number Two manufacturer, are good examples of the new evolution. Nissan released the long awaited replacement for the Skyline series, to be called the Datsun 240KC GT for export. The Skyline is unique in the export-minded Nissan camp in that nearly 95% of its production has hitherto been consumed in the domestic market. The car has been so popular here and the factory is quite happy to keep it that way. It is also unique among Japanese cars in that for three generations it has been the responsibility of a single chief en-

Above, Mitsubishi's sleek Mirage frontwheel drive hatchback is another to join the fierce battle in the small car class. Below, diesels are in. This is Toyota's Crown 2200 Diesel with a brand-new 4-cylinder engine.

TABLE 4. **EXPORT SALES BY MAKE**

	1976 (% to previous year)	1977 (%) estimate	1978 (%) forecast *
PASSENGER CAR			
Normal cars	2,534,458 (139.1%)	2,900,000 (114.4%)	2,888,000 (99.6%)
Light cars	4,659 (85.5%)	10,000 (214.6%)	11,000 (110 %)
TOTAL	2,539,117 (139.0%)	2,910,000 (114.6%)	2,899,000 (99.6%)
COMMERCIAL VEHICLE			
Normal (large)	194,412 (115.5%)	259,000 (133.2%)	250,000 (96.5%)
Small	888,223 (138.1%)	971,000 (109.3%)	987,000 (101.6%)
Light	69,974 (317.1%)	76,000 (108.6%)	80,000 (105.3%)
TOTAL	1,152,609 (138.3%)	1,306,000 (113.3%)	1,317,000 (100.8%)
BUS	17,882 (107.4%)	24,000 (134.2%)	24,000 (100 %)
GRAND TOTAL	3,709,608 (138.5%)	4,240,000 (114.3%)	4,240,000 (100 %)

* Based on Nissan Motor Company's forecast.

gineer, the respected Shinichiro Sakurai, formerly the racing director of the giant company. The new series 210 Skyline still borrows heavily from the corporate parts bins, but its racing heritage is obvious. For export to certain European countries, the 240KC GT will be powered by a 2.4 litre fuel-injected six and have an all-independent suspension. The stylish coupé is capable of reaching 192 km/h, and can give a fast run for their money to many of Europe's better sporting sedans and coupés. Four-cylinder Skyline models, redesignated TI, have finally foresaken leaf springs in the rear suspension for a more sophisticated four-link and coil-spring system. Nissan is now spreading the four-

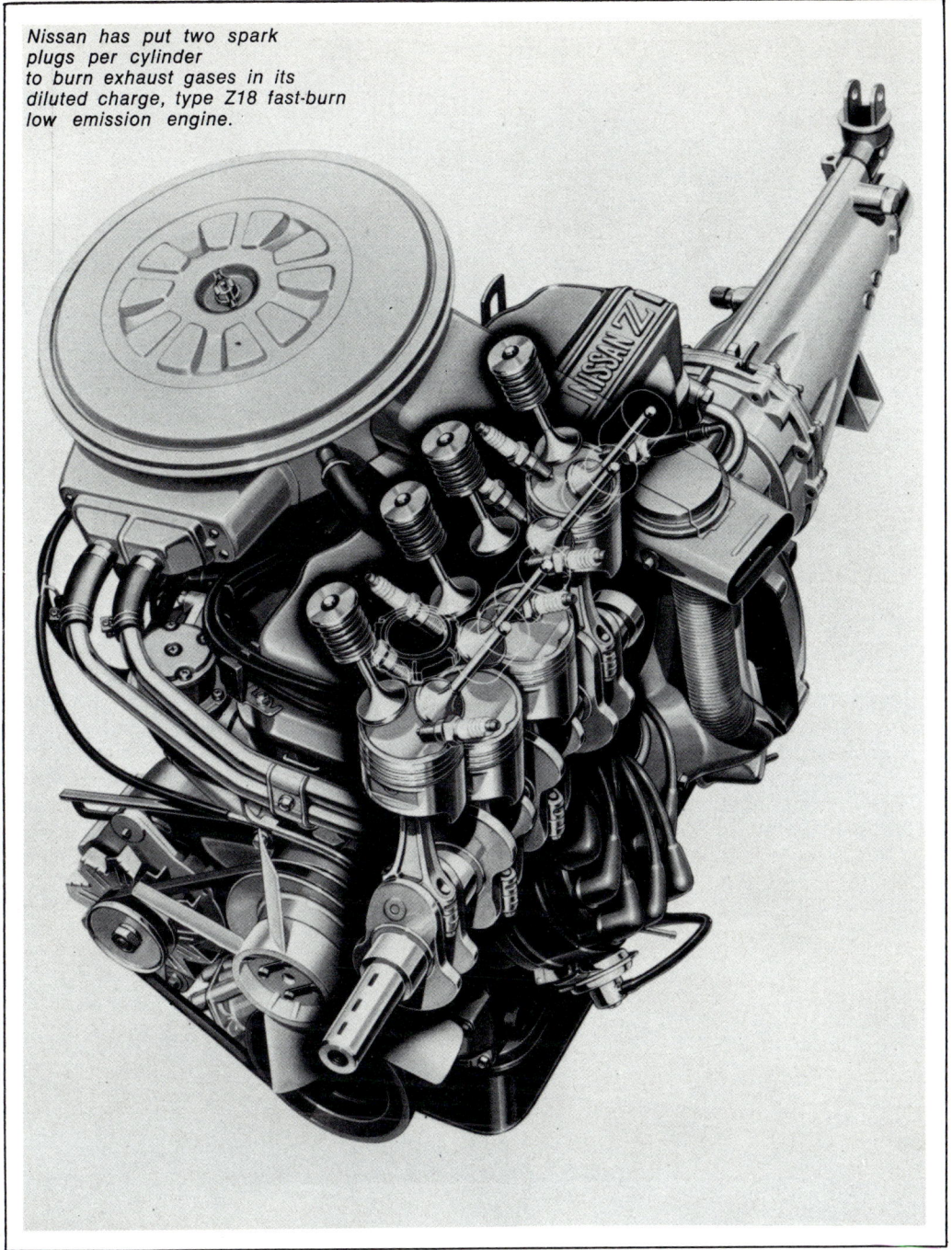

Nissan has put two spark plugs per cylinder to burn exhaust gases in its diluted charge, type Z18 fast-burn low emission engine.

TABLE 5. DOMESTIC SALES, PASSENGER CARS, DECEMBER 1976 THROUGH NOVEMBER 1977 (12 mos) (Passenger Cars except Light Cars).

Toyota	891,672
Nissan (Datsun)	751,156
Mitsubishi	186,907
Toyo Kogyo (Mazda)	175,495
Honda	164,517
Fuji Heavy Ind. (Subaru)	49,237
Daihatsu	28,065
Isuzu	36,291
Import	41,299

TABLE 6. DOMESTIC CAR SALES, LIGHT CLASS, JANUARY THROUGH DECEMBER 1977 (12 mos).

Mitsubishi	33,490
Daihatsu	34,801
Suzuki	50,771
Fuji Heavy Ind. (Subaru)	46,004

variant, which is basically the same car with a wider grin, or grille. Like the Mark II, top models feature a type M fuel-injected inline six combined with a three-element catalyst, all-independent, and four-wheel disc brakes. Toyota carried out a major change on the popular Celica range and its twin chassis sedan, the Carina. As before, there are two body styles for the Celica, a 2-door coupé and an up-to-date liftback. The latter is rather Euro-American in its looks, or should I call it GMish (compare the new Opel Monza)? It is said that the original design concept for the car came from Toyota's California R&D studio, whose chief stylist had come from Warren, Michigan. The chassis of the twins remains basically the same as before but the high performance versions have gained rear disc brakes. Toyota has revived its potent twin cam engines in two sizes, a carburetted 2000 and an electronically injected 1600, both produced by Yamaha of motorcycle fame.

Toyota has introduced two important technical innovations, an automatic transmission with an overdrive fourth ratio and a brand new 2.2. litre diesel, both in Crown shells (the overdrive automatic is offered in the U.S. Cressida). Their obvious aim — fuel economy. The expanding diesel market is thus no longer the monopoly of Nissan, whose big Cedric/Gloria (260C) Diesels are now being well received. Another compression ignition engine proponent is Isuzu who is second to none in its accumulation of experience and knowledge of diesel power units through wide application in commercial vehicles. Isuzu, too, developed a new 2-litre diesel, and now offers it in the aging

link suspension on a wholesale scale to new and revamped models, among them the A10 Violet/Auster/Stanza triplets, the B310 Sunny series and the 4-cylinder 810 Bluebird. The Violet and company are products of Nissan's badge-engineering, which it is pushing vigorously to increase shares in the domestic market. The A10 in an American uniform is called "510", the designation of the first successful Datsun marketed in the U.S.A. The new 510 bears strong visual resemblance to the old one, which Datsun describes as being purely coincidental and accidental. It is still kilometres better than the curiously curvy 710 series. Likewise, the new B310 Sunny (120/140Y for other export

markets) has inherited the code B210 for the American market. Mechanically it follows the same evolutionary steps as the A10 but it now has a proper rear suspension, a rigid axle located by four links and sprung by coils. Again styling is a conventional threebox shape for the sedan, which is accompanied by coupé and station wagon variants. The Sunny is a vast improvement over the B210 in its road manners. And that's all it needs to make another giant sales leap.

Toyota is an old hand at badge engineering. It followed the successful Mark II (live-axled versions, 6-cylinder for the U.S. and 4-cylinder for Europe, are called Cressidas) with the Chaser

Florian sedan. It is an open secret that Mitsubishi is not too far behind, and Honda is said to be working on a high performance diesel, turbocharged!

Daihatsu is a member of the Toyota group of companies but hasn't lost its individual thinking. The new Charade mini is a happy manifestation of technical rebellion against the staid Establishment. To achieve super economy Daihatsu designers thought small and came up with a mini 346 cm long and 151 cm wide on a 230 cm wheelbase. It can seat four adults in reasonable comfort with usable luggage space which can be increased by folding down the rear seat. The 650 kg 4-door hatchback is powered by a unique water-cooled SOHC inline three cylinder engine with 120 degree crank throws. A contra-rotating harmonic balancer shaft is included in the engine to offset inherent inbalancing forces. The cylinder head incorporates a Toyota inspired and Daihatsu refined lean-burn system which reduces the three major pollutants to 1978 standard levels, and attains outstanding fuel economy. The Charade is a pleasant and peppy runabout with an incredibly flexible engine and good road manners. This car was chosen as the Japanese Car of the Year by a panel of technical professors and motoring journalists.

The Charade will soon be joined by another transverse-engined frontwheel drive mini, the Mitsubishi Mirage. At the time of writing, very little is known about this car, except its handsome styling. It is a contemporary FWD car with 1200/1400 cc engine mounted sideways driving the front wheels. Suspension is all independent. Noteworthy is the fact that the Mirage, at least the top models, will have an auxiliary gearbox, rather like the Jeep's (Mitsubishi produces Jeeps under license) with two ratios, in addition to the normal 4-speed gearbox. Obviously this is not a 4WD vehicle, so the auxiliary gearbox could only mean a very high cruise ratio, to conserve precious and expensive fuel ($1.70 per U.S. gallon).

Honda, the undisputed leader of the FWD movement, has two variants of the existing themes. A 1500 cc 4-door hatchback was added to the Civic, and the Accord coupé was joined by a new 4-door sedan. The latter is mechanically similar to the successful coupé, riding on the same wheelbase with a stretched rear overhang to accommodate a cavernous luggage space. The already commendable ride of the Accord is further refined in the 4-door sedan. A more powerful 1750 cc CVCC engine expected to be added soon should make this

Honda has added a 4-door saloon, a suave car, to the popular Accord range.

car even more attractive. The 4-door Accord was, by the way, originally called the Accord Saloon with a capital "S", but no sooner had the car hit the showroom than the company flabbergasted journalists by dropping the suffix. Apparently Honda was nudged by an official elbow, reminding it that the 4-door version had been granted roadworthiness certification as an extention of the Accord line. As such it should not assume a different designation. Mazda received a similar reprimand. It wanted to call the new Luce (the replacement for the Wankel RX4 and piston 929 the "Legato". Sales brochures and posters were printed to proclaim the arrival of the Luce Legato. Again the government must have delivered its administrative guidance (it's not an of-

This is Isuzu's new QD2000 4-cylinder diesel engine for the Florian sedan.

Toyota's Mark II, née Cressida. With a wider grin, the Mark II becomes the Chaser.

ficial veto, so it doesn't show on paper). Hey presto, all the "Legatos" were crudely blacked out. The Japanese government controls more than the names of cars. Mazda's pending problem is how to obtain certification for the new RX7 Savanna "Speciality Car". An authoritative bureaucrat is said to have remarked, shaking his head, "This car looks too much like a super car". Super cars and sports cars are dirty words in the official language book. Mazda's job is to convince him that it's a specialty car. For all its purpose and intent, the RX7 looks like a proper ...., and a very good one at that with the fabulous Wankel rotary power pushing it to unholy velocities and handling to match.

Not only the government, but the Japanese automakers must match their wits with other political elements. A recent debate between a Ministry of Transportation official and an opposition member of the Diet (parliament) blew the lid off the Big Two's 1978 new car release schedules. The staggering disclosure named car after car. The list included Toyota's 170B which would replace the current Publica/Starlet range, a long-nose Celina powered by the company's SOHC Six, a brand new front-wheel drive hatchback 30B, the revamped Corona, the facelifted Corolla/Sprinter twins, and so on. Nissan suffered almost as badly: the current Cherry F10 FWD range would be replaced by a new series in three installments, first a sedan, a couple of months later wagon and coupé, and finally a new hatchback sedan; the famous Z

would don new clothing; the Silvia 200SX would be completely new; facelifting on the Bluebird, Laurel...

In 1976, a total of 42,541 imported cars were sold in Japan. The number for last year was about the same. It is a tiny droplet of new car sales in this 2.5 million car market. The foreign contingents are now certainly trying much harder. Ford, ably aided by a Honda-owned distributor, is now pushing its international lines of small and medium-sized cars, which include hybrid Fiestas (European body with U.S. detoxined engine) and the Cortina 2000 Ghia as well as Granadas, Monarchs, Zephyrs. The wandering British Leyland must finally have planted its feet onto Japanese soil, by going into partnership with the established trading house of Mitsui. It intends to market such specialty products as Jaguars, Rovers, Triumph and MG sports cars. Even the staid GM is becoming active. With renewed and new efforts by importers, will the situation improve? The Japanese industry would be delighted if they could make positive inroads into the market. After all, what better way could there be to improve strained trade relations than for Japan to buy more foreign goods?

The prediction by the most authoritative prophet in the country, one Jiro Yanase, "Mr. Success" of the import trade, who handles VW, Daimler Benz and GM products, or more than half total imports is far from optimistic. Given all possible concessions in tariffs, which were already below the interna-

tional level and have recently been completely eliminated, and safety and emission regulations, he would consider 100,000 cars per annum as the absolute maximum attainable in the eighties — and that would be his life-long dream come true. This is a tough market with discriminating buyers. Here the renowned Japanese quality might work against imports. Yanase would have to spend as much as US $4000 on a luxury American car to correct manufacturing faults and shipping damage, and add and modify safety and emission control equipment. The hefty hike in cost could be absorbed in a large high-priced car, which the Japanese motor industry cannot rival. Incidentally, Japan consumes more American cars than all the EEC countries put together, according to Mr. Yanase. But how a US $6000 Fiesta or a $10,000 Cortina could compete in the volume market remains to be shown.

The Japanese motor industry would certainly like to repeat its past successes, but would have to correct its excesses. The domestic market will see more competition, while the exporters will tread more gently on foreign soils. President Ishihara of Nissan feels that a 20% penetration in the U.S. market is a danger line, after which the Japanese may have to consider production in that country. Already Honda is establishing a factory in Ohio, initially to produce motorcycles, but which may spread to car production. Exports to Europe may have to level off, while developing countries may become key markets for the industry's future growth.

A NEW DIMENSION FOR A NEW GENERATION

by Bob Tripolsky

During the last few decades Americans have viewed the existence and function of the automobile in diverse ways. For many, these pieces of rolling machinery have been to provide transportation — nothing more. For others, status symbols and ego-extenders. For still others, living breathing beings with personalities — to be loved and treasured.

No matter how they regarded the automobile, in the past most people believed that a heavier car meant a better handling one; that the vast supply of natural resources would never be depleted or even questioned; that engine emissions were unimportant if they were considered at all. Near the close of the 1960s questions were raised about the social responsibilities of the manufacturers. Demand called for a safer and less-polluting vehicle. Lawmakers around the country scurried to take positive action and, in the process, assumed direction of the industry. Today both emission legislation and fuel economy laws have drawn the automakers into a state of total vehicle re-evaluation and re-development.

Last year with the introduction of downsized (now referred to as "resized") standard cars from General Motors the cornerstone was laid for a new generation. A more compact exterior helped to eliminate excess pounds yet offered equal or better interior roominess. Smaller-displacement engines provided a more fuel-efficient package. In the Battle of the Titans as it was called by some between the all-new models from GM and the carry-over versions of Ford and Chrysler, the buying public was to make the final decision. It was a battle, incidentally, that everybody won.

Named "Car of the Year" by a major U.S. auto magazine, the Plymouth Horizon/Dodge Omni is the first front-wheel-drive small car built in America. Available only as a four-door sedan it offers ample seating and cargo space.

Buick's all-new Century has the "aero" design with its sloping rear deck. As with all other '78 GM intermediates the rear door windows are stationary with ventilation provided by opening the triangular-shaped pillar window. The sedan is now 18 inches shorter and 600 pounds lighter than its 1977 counterpart.

The nation's economy and business climate were in considerably better shape during the 1977 model year than in 1976 with an increase in the real gross national product. Inflation was kept to a rate around 6% — still high — but in sharp contrast to the earlier double-digit figure. Such promising reports and an upsurge in buyer confidence enabled the industry to ring up sales of 11,178,554 million passenger cars, the second highest total in history.

The public's acceptance of GM's new trend was a great relief to the world's largest automaker and also to its competitors. The gamble had been a proven success, thus validating the decision to continue with the scaledown program. For 1978 the plot had become thicker.

Even before model start-up Detroit was uncertain if any '78 cars would roll off the assembly lines. All the auto makers were bucking the government's red tape in the Clean Air Bill calling for stringent emission standards they felt could not be met. Industry said that if the requirements were not postponed at least one more year mass production would become economically prohibitive. Thankfully, a compromise was reached which delayed implementation of the new standards for the next two years.

Ford is building for national consumption a limited number of 302 cu in V8's equipped with Electronic Engine Control to control spark timing and exhaust gas recirculation. An ingenious solid-state device determines such essential facts as air intake temperature, manifold pressure, throttle position and coolant temperatures, and then calcu-

lates the necessary spark advance. With tighter requirements in California, the Pinto and Bobcat series, powered by the 140 cu in 4-cylinder, utilize a three-way catalytic converter. Again for the California market they are equipped with an Electronically Controlled Carburetor that provides an ideal air/ fuel mixture. Both engines are cleaner-burning than ever before.

Of more concern at this time is the heavy emphasis on energy conservation aimed at forcing the so-called "gas guzzlers" from the American highways by 1985. Starting this year each ma-

nufacturer must meet the established Corporate Average Fuel Economy (CAFE) guidelines.

For the '78 model year the figure was set at a fleet average of 184 miles per gallon and has thus far been met with ease. The sales-weighted figures for '79 and '80 are 19 and 20 mpg respectively. Farther down the road, 1985 models are expected to yield a 27.5 mpg fleet average.

To comply with this law, each corporation must sell enough small cars to balance sales of the intermediate and large ones. It's going to take a

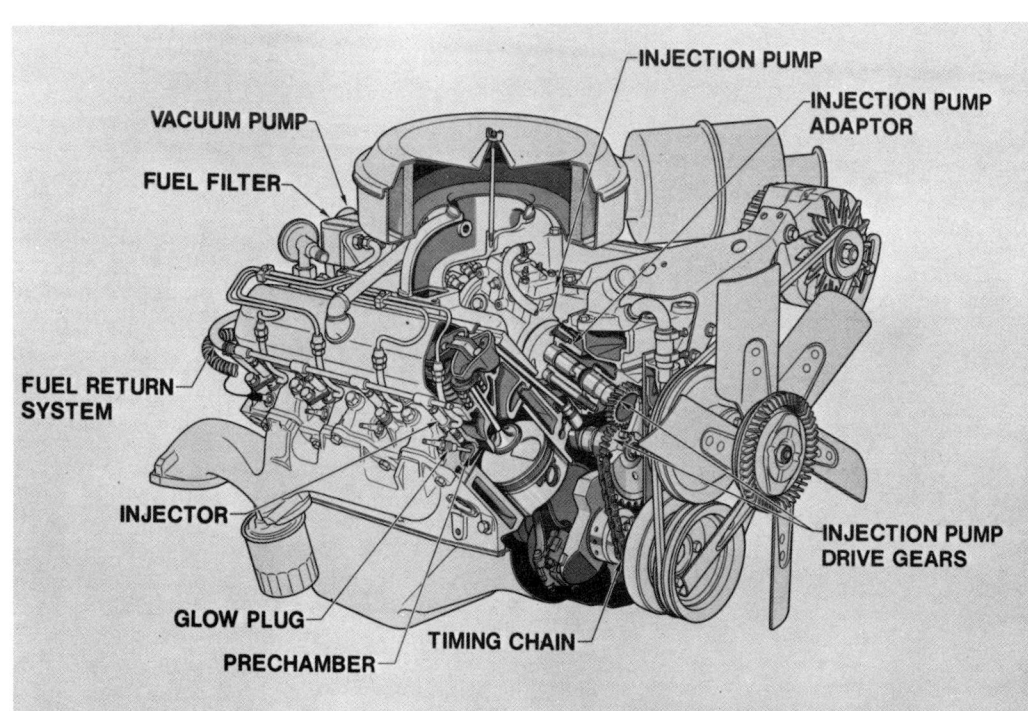

This cutaway reveals the components needed to convert the 5.7 litre V8 to diesel. An option on the Olds Delta 88 and Ninety-Eight series and GMC pickups, it produces 120 hp and 220 ft/lb torque.

VACUUM PUMP
FUEL FILTER
INJECTION PUMP
INJECTION PUMP ADAPTOR
FUEL RETURN SYSTEM
INJECTOR
GLOW PLUG
PRECHAMBER
TIMING CHAIN
INJECTION PUMP DRIVE GEARS

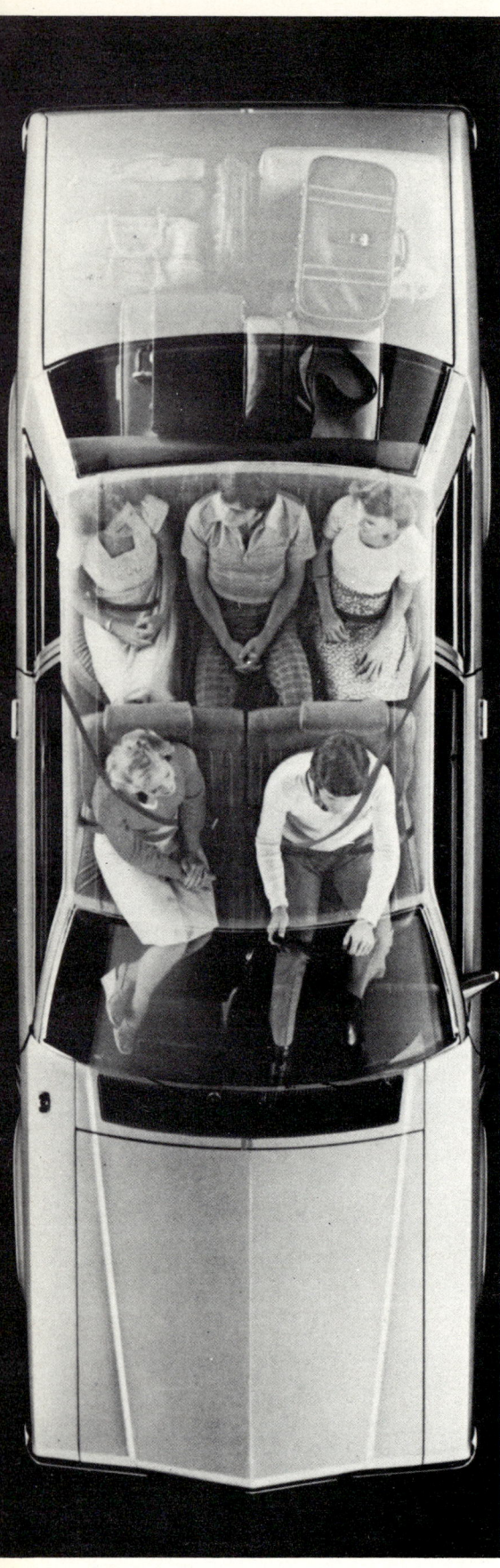

Although about the same size as the Maverick and Comet they replace, the Ford Fairmont and Mercury Zephyr are nearly 300 lb lighter with more passenger and luggage room. A 2.3 litre Four engine is standard, 3.3 litre V6 optional and 5.0 litre V8 a supplement.

perfect combination of marketing wizardry, production flexibility and product design to meet the goal. At the same time, the law of the marketplace cannot be overlooked. Small cars are not in demand by all buyers. Many still want and/or need the comfort, carrying capacity and luxury of the larger models. The penalty for coming up one mpg short of the CAFE requirement is a fine of $50 levied against each car and there is an additional $50 fine for every mpg thereafter which the buyer will obviously have to pay as part of the purchase price.

Following the master plan closely, this year GM has taken its intermediates down a step in weight and exterior dimensions — as much as 700 lb per car and from 6 to 12 inches in length — much like what was done in '77. And since last year's battle was victorious there is little reason to fear this one will be less successful.

GM buyers have been given the choice between two distinct body styles among the four divisions which share the same body shells. Chevrolet's Malibú and Pontiac's LeMans are offered as notchbacks while the Oldsmobile Cutlass and Buick Century/Regal buyers can choose a unique new 'aero' design. In essence, the 'aero' is of full fastback configuration which increases rear seating comfort and glass area. Early in this model year public acceptance was lower than originally anticipated but there are indications this controversial design will gain favor during the remainder of this and following years.

The last time such a design was offered in the showrooms of America (including Chevrolet's) was during the early 1950s. Yet another resurrection from that era is the Nomad-type rear door on the intermediate wagons. The upper glass section hinges up via gas-filled struts while the lower body portion folds downward in conventional fashion. Weight-conscious engineers were thus able to save a goodly amount of weight and mechanicals. A pound of material means little to the buyer but to designers a mere ounce is noteworthy.

Interior roominess has always been a top priority in the resizing program and, as with last year's B-bodies, passengers are indeed pleased with the final results. Improved accommodations are the net result of thinner and lighter seat assemblies which provide a more upright position for the occupants. Rooflines are higher, featuring a one-piece molded headliner which allows for a greater expanse of glass area and

enables one to see and be seen with ease.

Such advances in design help to retain the desired big-car feel and flair so common among the vehicles of days gone by. Detroit's move to redimension their vehicles (often called the 'Great Disappearing Act') was accompanied by vigorous concentration on materials substitution in the '78s. Stepping up the major trends of recent years, more pounds of plastics, aluminum and high-strength steel are to be found.

Dimensional reductions have, of course, been a move in the right direction. For example, the new Olds Cutlass is 15 inches shorter than its '77 counterpart thus removing about 450 lb, mostly by eliminating excessive body overhang. Thanks to a generous use of aluminum, another 112 lb has been pared off: the aluminum hood saves 32 lb, bumper reinforcements 37 lb, rear brake drums another 13 crucial lb and a cast-aluminum intake manifold on the V8 engine slices off the last 30 lb.

Plastics, although a derivative of our diminishing petroleum supplies, are gaining increasing favor with manufacturers as they are less expensive than steel and easier to form. Pontiac's new LeMans and Grand Am now feature resilient plastic front and rear bumper systems. These soft facias reduce weight by about 110 total pounds, replacing the former chrome-plated steel bumpers. Buyers are also elated over the corrosion protection afforded by use of plastics. Inner fender liners are fiberglass-reinforced on all GM mid-size cars except the LeMans.

Besides vehicle weight tipping the scales at a lower figure than ever, sweeping changes have also taken place in powerplants. Last year GM neglected to inform the public that certain Olds, Buick and Pontiac models were equipped with Chevrolet engines. The reason for using these engines, from the Corporation's point of view, was to reduce the number of different but similar engines and cut costs. A buyer discovered the "engine swapping" and the matter received wide-spread national attention. As a consequence, a great many lawsuits were brought against GM. For the '78 models the giant automaker, feeling it had nothing to hide, waged a campaign in the media and in dealer showrooms clearly indicating the source of the engines. This year GM is marketing 28 different powerplants produced by five passenger car divisions.

The workhorse units for '78 are the Buick 231 cu in V6 and the Chevrolet 305 cu in V8. Each is being offered on 18 car lines, mostly for the A-bodies.

*The Mercury Zephyr family of compacts includes (top to bottom)
a station wagon, sedan and Z-7 sports coupé. Along with the Ford Fairmont
they have already become the best-selling series of Ford Motor Co. to date.*

Largest of all GM engines is still the 425 cu in in the Cadillac line, with fuel-injection as an option.

Buick's Regal and Century coupés are bolstered in the highly-competitive youth market by offering a mass-produced turbocharged V6. Neither the 150 hp 2V nor the 165 hp 4V produce blinding acceleration like Porsche's Turbo and were not meant to. In theory and practice, during normal operations these GM coupés achieve the fuel economy inherent in the V6 yet deliver V8 performance when desired. A Turbo Control Center monitors the detonation level and then adjusts the spark to keep detonation at an acceptable level during acceleration. Fuel efficiency has been in-

creased by one mpg and the general public learns that diesel trucks aren't the only turbos worthy of running the highways.

Speaking of diesels, Oldsmobile expects to sell all the 55,000 diesel passenger units planned for the year. An equal number of diesels will be found in Chevy and GMC pickup trucks. This prechamber 350 cu in version is the product of an extended research and development program that has solved several of the problems associated with the diesel. The wait-to-start period has been reduced and, thanks to large amounts of sound-deadening material, noise is minimal. Testing shows that the fuel economy of this engine is 25%

better than the gasoline version. Cadillac's Seville may also use it as a mid-year option.

Demand called for dropping the problem-plagued aluminum four-cylinder in favor of a cast-iron block pushrod Four similar to Pontiac's Iron Duke 151 CID. Buick, too, has been responsive in taking the shakes out of their 231 cu in V6 with the change to an even-firing system. By offsetting crankpin journals 30 degrees, two cylinders are fired every 120 degrees of crank rotation providing V8 smoothness.

More han ever, the specialty and sports-oriented cars have increased their market share. For GM, the Corvette, America's only true sports car,

Power for the Omni/Horizon comes from a 1.7 litre, transverse mounted, 4-cylinder. Both the cast iron block and aluminum head are purchased from VW as is the four-speed manual gearbox. A 3-speed automatic transaxle is an option.

The Trans Am version of Pontiac's Firebird, powered by a 6.6 litre V8, ranks as one of the fastest selling and best performing cars.

In its last year as a large "full size" family car is the Mercury Grand Marquis. Its great expanse of interior and trunk area suits those who want or need those big car features.

celebrates its silver anniversary while sales of the fast-looking and fast-performing Firebird soar upward. The Monte Carlo and Grand Prix also reflect the new A-body changeover.

With the addition of a four-door hatchback, the subcompact Chevette is gathering impetus. Still without the aid of front wheel drive, more options have become standard features and the price has been dropped several hundred dollars with the public liking every minute of it. A needed shot in the arm for Chevy; a shot in the back for the imports. In mid-'79 GM will be going into Step Three with the introduction of their resized, front-wheel-drive compacts.

During the past two years, though, there has been renewed interest in standard-size and intermediate cars. Market penetration of the mid-size segment reached its highest peak during 1976 and declared the Olds Cutlass the undisputed champion. Last year the market was split more evenly among the standard, mid-range and small models and where this breakdown is headed remains an open question.

Will the new A-cars gather a larger share of the market this season just as they did two years before? So far the answer is in the affirmative and in GM's favor. What can be expected from the large and compact segments? Quite a bit, especially from Ford Motor Company. Ford is now the undisputed leader in large cars. Its Ford LTD and Mercury Marquis continue to chalk up more high-figure sales than most other models. However, they will go by the board in '79 as they, too, receive the size-chopping routine this fall.

Most of Ford's high-dollar advertising budget is concentrated on its new Fairmont and Zephyr compacts which have replaced the aged Maverick and Comet lines. Fairmont sales thus far continue to outpace the original '65 Mustang as the industry's hottest-selling nameplate in history. In fact it's about 40% ahead of the Mustang's sales for the first six months.

Corporate strategy in the matter of sizing seems uncertain to those outside the industry. Peering through the massive piles of paperwork, we see that GM is redimensioning from the large to the small. Ford, on the other hand, elected to start its program from the middle of its range and its new entries have placed GM's antiquated compacts in a very tenuous competitive position. The fight with Ford for market supremacy comes mostly from the Chrysler camp in the form of its proven Aspen and Volare series.

Buick offers buyers of its Regal and Century Sport Coupés two versions of the Turbo V6. Both the 150 and 165 horsepower engines provide the economy of a six-cylinder during normal driving conditions yet give the performance of a V8 when needed. About 5,000 units are expected to be sold during the '78 model year.

Ford's exterior styling is heavily influenced by its international operations as can be seen in the fresh and clean shell with high rooflines and areas. Optimism abounds within the corporation as it forecasts a combined total of 585,000 units offered in two- and four-door sedans and wagons and two-door sporty coupés.

Playing the semantics game, Fairmont and Zephyr are relegated to the "compact" tag, yet aren't noticeably smaller than the current crop of GM intermediates. One can see this comparing wheelbase, height and overall length. The Ford's compact dimensions are respectively, 105.5, 53.5 and 193.8 inches; GM's intermediates are 108.1, 54.2 and 192.7 inches. Checking the weight scales, the Ford gets the featherweight title as it registers 365 lb less (2,748 lb to GM's 3,113 lb) in

basic four-door sedan packages.

Standard Ford powerplant is the 140 CID inline-four mated to a four-speed manual gearbox. Most buyers seem to be opting for either the 200 cu in six-cylinder or the more peppy 302 V8 with automatic transmission, the former being the best compromise for performance and economy with the latter favored by those in the sporty crowd.

Henry Ford II has predicted that the U.S. auto industry will "push the import cars right to the shores of the country. When our industry gets into that market full steam, imports are going to have a hard time". Foreign models currently account for about 18% of all cars sold in the U.S. In an apparent contradiction, Mr. Ford is importing the Fiesta, a captive import. Within the first full month of sales this mini was ranked fourth best-selling import in the country.

Expected to be a walk-away winner, the forecast is for importation of 100,000 Fiestas this year. A price rise from the initial $3,680, due in part to increased production costs and fluctuation in the value of the Deutschmark has had little effect on overall sales.

The Fiesta may not be fun and games for its maker in the long term, since from 1980 on captive imports cannot be included in the CAFE fleet for purposes of the average mpg. Next year, the small domestic Mustang will be redone and Mercury's Capri, formerly imported from across the waters, will be reborn within our own boundaries. Various sources in the Motor City speculate that these may spell the early departure of the Fiesta from the American market. Officially, no decision has

The convertible look is back with a "Carriage Roof" offered as an option on the Continental Mark V. The non-retractable top is white vinyl embossed with a canvas weave and where other Mark Vs have opera windows, this roof has oval mirrors inside.

This TURBINE CONCEPT car was built for the U.S. Department of Energy by Chrysler Corporation. Based on a LeBaron, it was dramatically restyled and equipped with a polyurethane "soft" front end, retractable headlight covers and T-bar roof.

been announced but most say that this is highly probable.

A roundup of the sub-compact category shows a new Chevy Chevette four-door, equipped with more options as standard; Fairmont/Zephyr will take a bite out of the Pinto/Bobcat sales; Pontiac drops the forlorn Astre nameplate but continues some models under the Sunbird tag; Chevy, too, places the Vega name in their 'dead' files and retrieves some features for use in their Monza series. Not until January did the subcompact class get a needed addition — and from Chrysler.

The third-largest manufacturer beat all others to the punch by introducing America's first mass-produced front-wheel-drive cars. Dubbed the Dodge Omni and Plymouth Horizon, they are referred to as vehicles of import-fight-ing caliber "built in America, by Americans, for the American market". Another new dimension for a new generation.

Lo and behold, they are not based heavily on the great Simca 1307/1308 as many outsiders predicted. Actually a combination of European styling and engine components, Japanese-type names and American assembly, some call them re-furred Rabbits. The overall length of 164.8 inches and wheelbase of 99.2 inches exceed, but are very close to, the dimensions of their competitors.

Biggest news of all is that the Omni and Horizon are propelled by basic engines consisting of assembled block and cylinder head purchased, like the standard four-speed transmission, from VW. They are good sellers but may fall a bit short of the predicted 200,000 units for '78. In successive years, they are expected to reach a goal of 300,000 combined sales.

Afficionados find a wide choice in specialty cars within the Chrysler ranks. The uniquely-styled Dodge Magnum XE, a spinoff from the Charger SE, with its clear headlight covers, tight suspension, and big engine will find many a happy home. Aerodynamics are a major factor in the design, leading many to believe that numerous NASCAR racing teams will choose the Magnum and win with it.

Some buyers are also tending to lean towards the lower-production Aspen and Volare "Super Coupés" with their "Muscle Car" appeal. Matte-black body panels, high-horsepower engines, and wide tires still draw sales and create a sensation.

A new direction at American Motors was taken last fall when Roy Chapin, Jr., Chairman of the Board and President, relinquished the latter title to the talented up-and-coming Gerald Meyers. Using the authority delegated to him by the move, Meyers flatly denied rumors that the No. 4 auto maker will cease passenger car production and concentrate on its more lucrative Jeep and AM General (which builds buses and government vehicles).

Prior to the change of command, AMC introduced its new Concord luxury compact, successor to the Hornet. Further plans for the Concord call for an optional economical Audi-based 4-cylinder engine, and a new model in the lineup. Other developments are an addition to the Gremlin series in the form of a GT version, a youth-appealing van based on the Pacer wagon which presently has an optional 304 CID engine, and the "super luxury in a four-wheel-drive vehicle" offered by Jeep Wagoneer Limited. AMC is also committed to the development of a new car line for 1979.

Already the reigning president has been able to reveal good news for the company by announcing increased sales figures and has moved to beef up the management team. A package display of six advanced design AMC prototypes, tagged "Concept 80", toured the country to quiet the doomsayers and assure both dealers and the public that AMC will still be producing passenger cars in the 1980s.

With the success so far of the new GM, Ford and Chrysler products, sources close to the industry are forecasting another record year. With a sparkle in their eyes, optimists are proud of that prediction; pessimists, little to talk about.

Europe

Models now in production

Illustrations and technical information

CUSTOCA   AUSTRIA

Hurrycane

PRICE EX WORKS: 29,400 schillings (body only)

ENGINE Volkswagen, rear, 4 stroke; 4 cylinders, horizontally opposed; 96.7 cu in, 1,584 cc (3.37 x 2.72 in, 85.5 x 69 mm); max power (DIN): 50 hp (36.8 kW) at 4,000 rpm; max torque (DIN): 78 lb ft, 10.8 kg m (105.9 Nm) at 2,800 rpm; 31.6 hp/l (23.2 kW/l).

PERFORMANCE max speeds: (I) 22 mph, 35 km/h; (II) 47 mph, 75 km/h; (III) 68 mph, 110 km/h; (IV) 96 mph, 155 km/h; power-weight ratio: 30.9 lb/hp (41.9 lb/kW), 14 kg/hp (19 kg/kW); acceleration: standing ¼ mile 12.5 sec; consumption: 23.5 m/imp gal, 19.6 m/US gal, 12 l x 100 km.

STEERING turns lock to lock: 2.50.

ELECTRICAL EQUIPMENT 12 V; 4 headlamps.

DIMENSIONS AND WEIGHT wheel base: 94.49 in, 240 cm; tracks: 55.12 in, 140 cm front, 55.91 in, 142 cm rear; length: 171.26 in, 435 cm; width: 67.72 in, 172 cm; height: 44.09 in, 112 cm; ground clearance: 6.30 in, 16 cm; weight: 1,544 lb, 700 kg; weight distribution: 46% front, 54% rear; turning circle (between walls): 41 ft, 12.5 m; fuel tank: 9.2 imp gal, 11.1 US gal, 42 l.

BODY coupé in plastic material; 2 doors; 2 + 2 seats.

PRACTICAL INSTRUCTIONS tyre pressure: front 19 psi, 1.2 atm, rear 22 psi, 1.5 atm.

For further data, see Volkswagen.

Strato ES

See Hurrycane, except for:

PRICE EX WORKS: 29,980 schillings (body only)

PERFORMANCE power-weight ratio: 30 lb/hp (40.7 lb/kW), 13.6 kg/hp (18.5 kg/kW).

DIMENSIONS AND WEIGHT length: 164.57 in, 418 cm; width: 62.99 in, 160 cm; weight: 1,499 lb, 680 kg.

ŠKODA   CZECHOSLOVAKIA

105 S

PRICE IN GB: £ 1,549*

ENGINE rear, 4 stroke; 4 cylinders slanted 30° to right, in line; 63.8 cu in, 1,046 cc (2.68 x 2.83 in, 68 x 72 mm); compression ratio: 8.5:1; max power (DIN): 46 hp (33.9 kW) at 4,800 rpm; max torque (DIN): 55 lb ft, 7.6 kg m (74.5 Nm) at 3,000 rpm; max engine rpm: 5,200; 43.2 hp/l (31.8 kW/l); light alloy block, cast iron head, wet liners; 3 crankshaft bearings; valves: overhead, in line, push-rods and rockers; camshafts: 1, side; lubrication: gear pump, cartridge on by-pass, 7 imp pt, 8.5 US pt, 4 l; 1 Jikov EDS R downdraught carburettor; fuel feed: mechanical pump; water-cooled, front radiator, 22 imp pt, 26.4 US pt, 12.5 l.

TRANSMISSION driving wheels: rear; clutch: single dry plate, hydraulically-controlled; gearbox: mechanical; gears: 4, fully synchronized; ratios: I 3.800, II 2.120, III 1.410, IV 0.960, rev 3.270; lever: central; final drive: spiral bevel; axle ratio: 4.444; width of rims: 4.5''; tyres: 155 SR x 14.

PERFORMANCE max speeds: (I) 20 mph, 32 km/h; (II) 34 mph, 55 km/h; (III) 53 mph, 85 km/h; (IV) 81 mph, 130 km/h; power-weight ratio: 41 lb/hp (55.6 lb/kW), 18.6 kg/hp (25.2 kg/kW); carrying capacity: 882 lb, 400 kg; speed in top at 1,000 rpm: 15.5 mph, 25 km/h; consumption: 40.4 m/imp gal, 33.6 m/US gal, 7 l x 100 km.

CHASSIS integral; front suspension: independent, wishbones, coil springs, anti-roll bar, telescopic dampers; rear: independent, swinging semi-axles, swinging longitudinal leading arms, coil springs, telescopic dampers.

STEERING screw and nut; turns lock to lock: 2.50.

BRAKES front disc (diameter 9.92 in, 25.2 cm), rear drum; lining area: front 11.8 sq in, 76 sq cm, rear 59.7 sq in, 385 sq cm, total 71.5 sq in, 461 sq cm.

CUSTOCA Strato ES

ŠKODA 120 L

ELECTRICAL EQUIPMENT 12 V; 35 Ah battery; 490 W alternator; Pal distributor; 2 headlamps.

DIMENSIONS AND WEIGHT wheel base: 94.49 in, 240 cm; tracks: 50.39 in, 128 cm front, 49.21 in, 125 cm rear; length: 163.78 in, 416 cm; width: 62.60 in, 159 cm; height: 55.12 in, 140 cm; ground clearance: 6.69 in, 17 cm; weight: 1,885 lb, 855 kg; turning circle (between walls): 36.1 ft, 11 m; fuel tank: 8.4 imp gal, 10 US gal, 38 l.

BODY saloon/sedan; 4 doors; 5 seats, separate front seats.

PRACTICAL INSTRUCTIONS fuel: 90 oct petrol; oil: engine 7 imp pt, 8.5 US pt, 4 l, SAE 20W (winter) 40W (summer), change every 3,100 miles, 5,000 km - gearbox and final drive 4.4 imp pt, 5.3 US pt, 2.5 l, SAE 90, change every 12,400 miles, 20,000 km; greasing: every 6,200 miles, 10,000 km, 4 points; tyre pressure: front 21 psi, 1.4 atm, rear 23 psi, 1.6 atm.

VARIATIONS

(only for export).
ENGINE max power (DIN) 45 hp (33.1 kW) at 4,800 rpm, 43 hp/l (31.6 kW/l).
PERFORMANCE power-weight ratio 41.9 lb/hp (56.9 lb/kW), 19 kg/hp (25.8 kg/kW).

OPTIONAL ACCESSORIES 4.666 axle ratio; servo brake.

ŠKODA 105 S

105 L

See 105 S, except for:

PRICE IN GB: £ 1,625*

PERFORMANCE power-weight ratio: 41.9 lb/hp (56.9 lb/kW), 19 kg/hp (25.8 kg/kW).

DIMENSIONS AND WEIGHT weight: 1,929 lb, 875 kg.

120 L

See 105 S, except for:

PRICE IN GB: £ 1,699*

ENGINE 71.6 cu in, 1,174 cc (2.83 x 2.83 in, 72 x 72 mm); max power (DIN): 52 hp (38.3 kW) at 5,000 rpm; max torque (DIN): 63 lb ft, 8.7 kg m (85.2 Nm) at 3,000 rpm; max engine rpm: 5,400; 44.3 hp/l (32.6 kW/l).

PERFORMANCE max speed: 87 mph, 140 km/h; power-weight ratio: 37.1 lb/hp (50.4 lb/kW), 16.8 kg/hp (22.8 kg/kW); consumption: 35.8 m/imp gal, 29.8 m/US gal, 7.9 l x 100 km.

ELECTRICAL EQUIPMENT 4 headlamps.

DIMENSIONS AND WEIGHT weight: 1,929 lb, 875 kg.

VARIATIONS

None.

120 LS

See 120 L, except for:

PRICE IN GB: £ 1,799*

ENGINE compression ratio: 9.5:1; max power (DIN): 58 hp (42.7 kW) at 5,200 rpm; max torque (DIN): 67 lb ft, 9.2 kg m (90.2 Nm) at 3,250 rpm; max engine rpm: 5,500; 49.4 hp/l (36.2 kW/l); lubrication: oil cooler, 8.1 imp pt, 9.7 US pt, 4.6 l.

PERFORMANCE max speed: 93 mph, 150 km/h; power-weight ratio: 33.7 lb/hp (45.6 lb/kW), 15.3 kg/hp (20.7 kg/kW); consumption: 32.8 m/imp gal, 27.3 m/US gal, 8.6 l x 100 km.

BRAKES servo (standard).

DIMENSIONS AND WEIGHT weight: 1,951 lb, 885 kg.

PRACTICAL INSTRUCTIONS fuel: 95 oct petrol; oil: engine 8.1 imp pt, 9.7 US pt, 4.6 l.

110 R Coupé

PRICE IN GB: £ 1,600*

ENGINE rear, 4 stroke; 4 cylinders slanted 30° to right, in line; 67.5 cu in, 1,107 cc (2.83 x 2.68 in, 72 x 68 mm); compression ratio: 9.5:1; max power (DIN): 52 hp (38.3 kW) at 4,650 rpm; max torque (DIN): 59 lb ft, 8.1 kg m (79.4 Nm) at 3,500 rpm; max engine rpm: 5,800; 47 hp/l (34.6 kW/l); light alloy block, cast iron head, wet liners; 3 crankshaft bearings; valves: overhead, in line, push-rods and rockers; camshafts: 1, side; lubrication: gear pump, cartridge on by-pass, oil cooler, 8.1 imp pt, 9.7 US pt, 4.6 l; 1 Jikov 32 EDS R downdraught twin barrel carburettor; fuel feed: mechanical pump; water-cooled, front radiator, 13 imp pt, 15.6 US pt, 7.4 l.

TRANSMISSION driving wheels: rear; clutch: single dry plate, hydraulically-controlled; gearbox: mechanical; gears: 4, fully synchronized; ratios. I 3.800, II 2.120, III 1.410, IV 0.960, rev 3.270; lever: central; final drive: spiral bevel; axle ratio: 4.444; width of rims: 4.5''; tyres: 155 SR x 14.

PERFORMANCE max speeds: (I) 20 mph, 32 km/h; (II) 35 mph, 56 km/h; (III) 54 mph, 87 km/h; (IV) 90 mph, 145 km/h; power-weight ratio: 35.4 lb/hp (48.1 lb/kW), 16 kg/hp (21.8 kg/kW); carrying capacity: 805 lb, 365 kg; speed in top at 1,000 rpm: 15.5 mph, 25 km/h; consumption: 33.2 m/imp gal, 27.7 m/US gal, 8.5 l x 100 km.

CHASSIS integral; front suspension: independent, wishbones, coil springs, anti-roll bar, telescopic dampers; rear: independent, swinging semi-axles, swinging longitudinal leading arms, coil springs, telescopic dampers.

STEERING screw and nut; turns lock to lock: 2.50.

BRAKES front disc (diameter 9.92 in, 25.2 cm), rear drum; lining area: front 11.8 sq in, 76 sq cm, rear 59.7 sq in, 385 sq cm, total 71.5 sq in, 461 sq cm.

ŠKODA 120 LS

ŠKODA 110 R Coupé

ELECTRICAL EQUIPMENT 12 V; 35 Ah battery; 35 A alternator; Pal distributor; 4 headlamps (2 halogen).

DIMENSIONS AND WEIGHT wheel base: 94.49 in, 240 cm; tracks: 50.39 in, 128 cm front, 49.21 in, 125 cm rear; length: 163.39 in, 415 cm; width: 63.78 in, 162 cm; height: 52.76 in, 134 cm; ground clearance: 6.89 in, 17.5 cm; weight: 1,841 lb, 835 kg; turning circle (between walls): 33.5 ft, 10.2 m; fuel tank: 8.4 imp gal, 10 US gal, 38 l.

BODY coupé; 2 doors; 2+2 seats, built-in headrests.

PRACTICAL INSTRUCTIONS fuel: 95 oct petrol; oil: engine 8.1 imp pt, 9.7 US pt, 4.6 l, SAE 20W (winter) 40W (summer), change every 3,100 miles, 5,000 km - gearbox and final drive 4.4 imp pt, 5.3 US pt, 2.5 l, SAE 90, change every 12,400 miles, 20,000 km; greasing: every 6,200 miles, 10,000 km, 4 points; valve timing: 18° 49° 53° 14°; tyre pressure: front 21 psi, 1.4 atm, rear 23 psi, 1.6 atm.

OPTIONAL ACCESSORIES 4.666 axle ratio; servo brake.

TATRA CZECHOSLOVAKIA

T 613

ENGINE rear, 4 stroke; 8 cylinders, Vee-slanted at 90°; 213.3 cu in, 3,495 cc (3.35 x 3.03 in, 85 x 77 mm); compression ratio: 9.2:1; max power (DIN): 165 hp (121.4 kW) at 5,200 rpm; max torque (DIN): 196 lb ft, 27 kg m (264.8 Nm) at 2,500 rpm; max engine rpm: 5,600; 47.2 hp/l (34.7 kW/l); cast iron block, light alloy head; 5 crankshaft bearings; valves: overhead, Vee-slanted, rockers; camshafts: 2 per block, overhead; lubrication: gear pump, full flow filter (cartridge), oil cooler, 16.7 imp pt, 20.1 US pt, 9.5 l; 2 Jikov DDSR 32/34 downdraught twin barrel carburettors; fuel feed: mechanical pump; air-cooled.

TRANSMISSION driving wheels: rear; clutch: single dry plate, hydraulically controlled; gearbox: mechanical; gears: 4, fully synchronized; ratios: I 3.394, II 1.889, III 1.165, IV 0.862, rev 3.243; lever: central; final drive: hypoid bevel; axle ratio: 3.909; width of rims: 6''; tyres: 215/70 HR x 14.

PERFORMANCE max speeds: (I) 29 mph, 47 km/h; (II) 53 mph, 85 km/h; (III) 86 mph, 138 km/h; (IV) 116 mph, 186 km/h; power-weight ratio: 21.4 lb/hp (29.1 lb/kW), 9.7 kg/hp (13.2 kg/kW); carrying capacity: 1,036 lb, 470 kg; speed in top at 1,000 rpm: 22.2 mph, 35.8 km/h; consumption: 15.7 m/imp gal, 13.1 m/US gal, 18 l x 100 km.

CHASSIS integral; front suspension: independent (by McPherson), wishbones, coil springs, anti-roll bar, telescopic dampers; rear: independent, swinging semi-axles, swinging longitudinal trailing arms, coil springs, telescopic dampers.

STEERING rack-and-pinion, damper; turns lock to lock: 4.25.

BRAKES disc, servo; lining area: front 30.7 sq in, 198 sq cm, rear 21.1 sq in, 136 sq cm, total 51.8 sq in, 334 sq cm.

TATRA T 613

T 613

ELECTRICAL EQUIPMENT 12 V; 75 Ah 2 x 6 V batteries; 55 A alternator; PAL Magneton distributor; electronic ignition; 4 headlamps, 2 iodine fog lamps.

DIMENSIONS AND WEIGHT wheel base: 117.32 in, 298 cm; tracks: 60 in, 152 cm front, 60 in, 152 cm rear; length: 198 in, 503 cm; width: 71 in, 180 cm; height: 59.25 in, 151 cm; ground clearance: 6.30 in, 16 cm; weight: 3,528 lb, 1,600 kg; weight distribution: 43% front, 57% rear; turning circle (between walls): 41 ft, 12.5 m; fuel tank: 15.8 imp gal, 19 US gal, 72 l.

BODY saloon/sedan; 4 doors; 5 seats, separate front seats, reclining backrests, built-in headrests.

PRACTICAL INSTRUCTIONS fuel: 96 oct petrol; oil: engine 16.7 imp pt, 20.1 US pt, 9.5 l, SAE 20W-50, change every 6,200 miles, 10,000 km - gearbox 3.5 imp pt, 4.2 US pt, 2 l, SAE 90, change every 18,600 miles, 30,000 km - final drive 1.8 imp pt, 2.1 US pt, 1 l, SAE 90, change every 6,200 miles, 10,000 km; greasing: none; sparking plug: 200°; tappet clearances: inlet 0.004 in, 0.10 mm, exhaust 0.004 in, 0.10 mm; valve timing: 0° 30° 30° 0°; tyre pressure (max load): front 24 psi, 1.7 atm, rear 33 psi, 2.3 atm.

ALPINE   FRANCE

ALPINE A 310 V6

A 310 V6

PRICE EX WORKS: 80,600* francs

ENGINE Renault, rear, 4 stroke; 6 cylinders, Vee-slanted at 90°; 162.6 cu in, 2,664 cc (3.46 x 2.87 in, 88 x 73 mm); compression ratio: 10.1:1; max power (DIN): 150 hp (110.4 kW) at 6,000 rpm; max torque (DIN): 151 lb ft, 20.8 kg m (204 Nm) at 3,500 rpm; max engine rpm: 6,400; 56.3 hp/l (41.4 kW/l); light alloy block and head, wet liners, hemispherical combustion chambers; 4 crankshaft bearings; valves: overhead, Vee-slanted, rockers; camshafts: 1 per block, overhead; lubrication: gear pump, full flow filter, 10.6 imp pt, 12.7 US pt, 6 l; 1 Solex 34 TBIA downdraught single barrel carburettor and 1 Solex 35 CEEI downdraught twin barrel carburettor; fuel feed: mechanical pump; sealed circuit cooling, expansion tank, 21.1 imp pt, 25.4 US pt, 12 l, viscous coupling thermostatic fan.

TRANSMISSION driving wheels: rear; clutch: single dry plate (diaphragm), hydraulically controlled; gearbox: mechanical; gears: 4, fully synchronized; ratios: I 3.364, II 2.059, III 1.318, IV 0.931, rev 3.182; lever: central; final drive: hypoid bevel; axle ratio: 3.444; width of rims: 7''; tyres: 185/70 VR x 13 front. 205/70 VR x 13 rear.

PERFORMANCE max speeds: (I) 39 mph, 62 km/h; (II) 63 mph, 102 km/h; (III) 99 mph, 159 km/h; (IV) 137 mph, 220 km/h; power-weight ratio: 14.4 lb/hp (19.6 lb/kW), 6.5 kg/hp (8.9 kg/kW); carrying capacity: 794 lb, 360 kg; acceleration: standing ¼ mile 15.4 sec; speed in top at 1,000 rpm: 22 mph, 35.4 km/h; consumption: 30.7 m/imp gal, 25.6 m/US gal, 9.2 l x 100 m at 75 mph, 120 km/h.

CHASSIS integral, central steel backbone; front suspension: independent, wishbones, rubber elements, coil springs, anti-roll bar, telescopic dampers; rear: independent, wishbones, coil springs, anti-roll bar, telescopic dampers.

STEERING rack-and-pinion; turns lock to lock: 3.70.

BRAKES disc, front internal radial fins, servo; lining area: total 22.5 sq in, 145 sq cm.

ELECTRICAL EQUIPMENT 12 V; 50 Ah battery; 50 A alternator; Ducellier distributor; 4 headlamps.

DIMENSIONS AND WEIGHT wheel base: 89.37 in, 227 cm; tracks: 55.28 in, 140 cm front, 56.30 in, 143 cm rear; length: 164.57 in, 418 cm; width: 64.57 in, 164 cm; height: 45.28 in, 115 cm; ground clearance: 6.30 in, 16 cm; weight: 2,161 lb, 980 kg; turning circle (between walls): 32.5 ft, 9.9 m; fuel tank: 12.3 imp gal, 14.8 US gal, 56 l.

BODY coupé in plastic material; 2 doors; 2+2 seats; separate front seats, reclining backrests; electrically-controlled windows; heated rear window.

PRACTICAL INSTRUCTIONS fuel: 98-100 oct petrol; oil: engine 10.6 imp pt, 12.7 US pt, 6 l, SAE 10W-30, change every 4,650 miles, 7,500 km - gearbox and final drive 6.5 imp pt, 7.8 US pt, 3.7 l, SAE 80, change every 9,300 miles, 15,000 km; tappet clearances: inlet 0.004-0.006 in, 0.10-0.15 mm, exhaust 0.010-0.012 in, 0.25-0.30 mm; valve timing: 9° 45° 45° 9° (left), 7° 43° 43° 7° (right); tyre pressure: front 22 psi, 1.5 atm, rear 38 psi, 2.7 atm.

OPTIONAL ACCESSORIES tinted glass; leather upholstery; metallic spray.

ALPINE A 310 V6

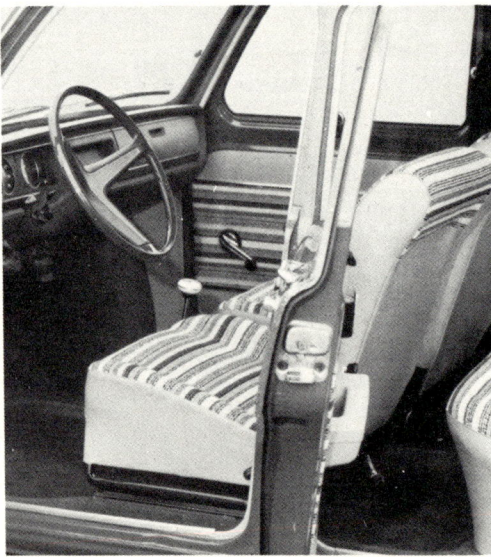

CHRYSLER FRANCE Simca 1006 GLS

CHRYSLER FRANCE   FRANCE

Simca 1000 Series

PRICES IN GB AND EX WORKS:	£	francs
1 Simca 1005 LS	1,893*	15,490*
2 Simca 1006 GLS	2,085*	18,300*
3 Simca Rallye 1	—	18,900*
4 Simca Rallye 2	—	23,800*

Power team:	Standard for:	Optional for:
40 hp	1	—
55 hp	2	—
60 hp	3	—
86 hp	4	—

40 hp power team

ENGINE rear, slanted 15° to left, 4 stroke; 4 cylinders, in line; 57.6 cu in, 944 cc (2.68 x 2.56 in, 68 x 65 mm); compression ratio: 9.4:1; max power (DIN): 40 hp (29.4 kW) at 5,800 rpm; max torque (DIN): 46 lb ft, 6.4 m (62.8 Nm) at 2,200 rpm; max engine rpm: 6,000; 42.4 hp/l (31.1 kW/l); cast iron block, light alloy head; 5 crankshaft bearings; valves: overhead, in line, push-rods and rockers; camshafts: 1, side; lubrication: gear pump, centrifugal filter, 5.3 imp pt, 6.3 US pt, 3 l; 1 Solex 32 BICSA 4A downdraught single barrel carburettor; fuel feed: mechanical pump; water-cooled, 9.7 imp pt, 11.6 11.6 US pt, 5.5 l.

TRANSMISSION driving wheels: rear; clutch: single dry plate (diaphragm), hydraulically controlled; gearbox: mechanical; gears: 4, fully synchronized; ratios: I 3.545, II 2.118, III 1.409, IV 0.963, rev 3.429; lever: central; final drive: hypoid bevel; axle ratio: 4.375; width of rims: 4''; tyres: 145 SR x 13.

PERFORMANCE max speeds: (I) 24 mph, 38 km/h; (II) 40 mph, 64 km/h; (III) 60 mph, 96 km/h; (IV) 83 mph, 133 km/h; power-weight ratio: 43.8 lb/hp (59.6 lb/kW), 19.9 kg/hp (27 kg/kW); carrying capacity: 882 lb, 400 kg; acceleration: standing ¼ mile 22 sec; speed in top at 1,000 rpm: 15 mph, 24.1 km/h; consumption: 38.2 m/imp gal, 31.8 m/US gal, 7.4 l x 100 km.

CHASSIS integral; front suspension: independent, wishbones, transverse leafspring lower arms, anti-roll bar, telescopic dampers; rear: independent, semi-trailing arms, coil springs, telescopic dampers.

STEERING rack-and-pinion; turns lock to lock: 3.17.

BRAKES drum; swept area: front 84.2 sq in, 543 sq cm, rear 73.8 sq in, 476 sq cm, total 158 sq in, 1,019 sq cm.

ELECTRICAL EQUIPMENT 12 V; 36 Ah battery; 35 A alternator; Ducellier distributor; 2 headlamps.

DIMENSIONS AND WEIGHT wheel base: 87.40 in, 222 cm; tracks: 49.61 in, 126 cm front, 50 in, 127 cm rear; length: 150 in, 381 cm; width: 58.27 in, 148 cm; height: 53.54 in, 136 cm; ground clearance: 5.51 in, 14 cm; weight: 1,753 lb, 795 kg; turning circle (between walls): 30.8 ft, 9.4 m; fuel tank: 7.9 imp gal, 9.5 US gal, 36 l.

BODY saloon/sedan; 4 doors; 5 seats, separate front seats, reclining backrests; heated rear window; back seat folding down to luggage table.

PRACTICAL INSTRUCTIONS fuel: 98 oct petrol; oil: engine 5.3 imp pt, 6.3 US pt, 3 l, SAE 20W-40, change every 4,650 miles, 7,500 km - gearbox and final drive 2.6 imp pt, 3.2 US pt, 1.5 l, SAE 90 EP, change every 9,300 miles, 15,000 km; greasing: none; tappet clearances (hot): inlet 0.014 in, 0.35 mm, exhaust 0.016 in, 0.40 mm; valve timing: 16°30' 58° 60°30' 14°; tyre pressure: front 20 psi, 1.4 atm, rear 27 psi, 1.9 atm.

OPTIONAL ACCESSORIES Ferodo 3-speed semi-automatic transmission, hydraulic torque converter (I 2.532, II 1.524, III 0.963, rev 3.463), max ratio of converter at stall 2, possible manual selection; tinted glass; metallic spray.

55 hp power team

See 40 hp power team, except for:

ENGINE 68.2 cu in, 1,118 cc (2.91 x 2.56 in, 74 x 65 mm); compression ratio: 9.6:1; max power (DIN): 55 hp (40.5 kW) at 5,800 rpm; max torque (DIN): 58 lb ft, 8 kg m (78.5 Nm) at 2,600 rpm; 49.2 hp/l (36.2 kW/l).

TRANSMISSION axle ratio: 4.111; width of rims: 5''.

PERFORMANCE max speeds: (I) 25 mph, 40 km/h; (II) 42 mph, 68 km/h; (III) 64 mph, 103 km/h; (IV) 90 mph, 145 km/h; power-weight ratio: 32.5 lb/hp (44.1 lb/kW), 14.7 kg/hp (20 kg/kW); acceleration: standing ¼ mile 20.2 sec; speed in top at 1,000 rpm: 16.1 mph, 25.9 km/h; consumption: 34.4 m/imp gal, 28.7 m/US gal, 8.2 l x 100 km.

BRAKES front disc (diameter 9.21 in, 23.4 cm), rear drum; swept area: front 147.6 sq in, 952 sq cm, rear 73.8 sq in, 476 sq cm, total 221.4 sq in, 1.428 sq cm.

DIMENSIONS AND WEIGHT weight: 1,786 lb, 810 kg.

PRACTICAL INSTRUCTIONS gearbox and final drive oil: 3.2 imp pt, 3.8 US pt, 1.8 l.

OPTIONAL ACCESSORIES iodine long-distance lights; back seat folding down to luggage table; Ferodo 3-speed semi-automatic transmission not available.

60 hp power team

See 40 hp power team, except for:

ENGINE 79 cu in, 1,294 cc (3.02 x 2.76 in, 76.7 x 70 mm); compression ratio: 9.5:1; max power (DIN): 60 hp (44.2 kW) at 5,800 rpm; max torque (DIN): 72 lb ft, 10 kg m (98.1 Nm) at 2,200 rpm; 46.4 hp/l (34.2 kW/l); 1 Solex 34 BICSA 4A downdraught single barrel carburettor; cooling system: 11.3 imp pt, 13.5 US pt, 6.4 l.

TRANSMISSION axle ratio: 4.111; width of rims: 5''.

PERFORMANCE max speed: 93 mph, 150 km/h; power-weight ratio: 29.9 lb/hp (40.7 lb/kW), 13.6 kg/hp (18.4 kg/kW); acceleration: standing ¼ mile 19.3 sec; speed in top at 1,000 rpm: 16.1 mph, 25.9 km/h; consumption: 30.4 m/imp gal, 25.3 m/US gal, 9.3 l x 100 km.

BRAKES front disc (diameter 9.21 in, 23.4 cm), rear drum; swept area: front 147.6 sq in, 952 sq cm, rear 73.8 sq in, 476 sq cm, total 221.4 sq in, 1,428 sq cm.

ELECTRICAL EQUIPMENT iodine long-distance lights.

DIMENSIONS AND WEIGHT weight: 1,797 lb, 815 kg.

BODY built-in headrests on front seats.

PRACTICAL INSTRUCTIONS gearbox and final drive oil: 3.2 imp pt, 3.8 US pt, 1.8 l.

OPTIONAL ACCESSORIES Ferodo semi-automatic transmission not available.

86 hp power team

See 60 hp power team, except for:

ENGINE max power (DIN): 86 hp (63.3 kW) at 6,200 rpm; max torque (DIN): 78 lb ft, 10.8 kg m (105.9 Nm) at 4,600 rpm; 66.5 hp/l (48.9 kW/l); lubricating system: 7 imp pt, 8.5 US pt, 4 l; 2 Solex 35 PHHE twin barrel carburettors; water-cooled, radiator on front, expansion tank, electric thermostatic fan, 18.5 imp pt, 22.2 US pt, 10.5 l.

TRANSMISSION axle ratio: 3.888; tyres: 145 HR x 13.

PERFORMANCE max speed: 106 mph, 170 km/h; power-weight ratio: 22 lb/hp (29.9 lb/kW), 10 kg/hp (13.6 kg/kW); acceleration: standing ¼ mile 18.3 sec; consumption: 31.7 m/imp gal, 26.4 m/US gal, 8.9 l x 100 km.

CHRYSLER FRANCE Simca Rallye 2

BRAKES disc (front diameter 9.37 in, 23.8 cm, rear 8.70 in, 22.1 cm), rear compensator; swept area: front 160.6 sq in, 1,036 sq cm, rear 131.5 sq in, 848 sq cm, total 292.1 sq in, 1,884 sq cm.

ELECTRICAL EQUIPMENT 40 Ah battery.

DIMENSIONS AND WEIGHT rear track: 50.39 in, 128 cm; height: 53.10 in, 135 cm; ground clearance: 4.72 in, 12 cm; weight: 1,896 lb, 860 kg; fuel tank: 11 imp gal, 13.2 US gal, 50 l.

PRACTICAL INSTRUCTIONS oil: engine 7 imp pt, 8.5 US pt, 4 l.

Simca 1100 Series

PRICES IN GB AND EX WORKS:	£	francs
1 Simca 1100 LE 2-door Berline	2,296*	18,980*
2 Simca 1100 LE 4-door Berline	2,366*	20,400*
3 Simca 1100 LE Break	—	22,650*
4 Simca 1100 GLX 4-door Berline	2,569*	23,300*
5 Simca 1100 GLS Break	2,762*	24,300*
6 Simca 1100 ES 4-door Berline	2,691*	24,230*
7 Simca 1100 TI 4-door Berline	—	27,500*

Power team:	Standard for:	Optional for:
50 hp	1,2	3,4
58 hp	3 to 6	—
82 hp	7	—

50 hp power team

ENGINE front, transverse, slanted 41° to rear, 4 stroke; 4 cylinders, in line; 68.2 cu in, 1,118 cc (2.91 x 2.56 in, 74 x 65 mm); compression ratio: 8.8:1; max power (DIN): 50 hp (36.8 kW) at 5,800 rpm; max torque (DIN): 57 lb ft, 7.8 kg m (76.5 Nm) at 3,000 rpm; max engine rpm: 6,000; 44.7 hp/l (32.9 kW/l); cast iron block, light alloy head; 5 crankshaft bearings; valves: overhead, in line, push-rods and rockers; camshafts: 1, side; lubrication: gear pump, full flow filter, 5.3 imp pt, 6.3 US pt, 3 l; 1 Solex 32 BISA downdraught single barrel carburettor; fuel feed: mechanical pump; sealed circuit cooling, liquid, expansion tank, 10.6 imp pt, 12.7 US pt, 6 l, electric thermostatic fan.

TRANSMISSION driving wheels: front; clutch: single dry plate (diaphragm), hydraulically controlled; gearbox: mechanical, in unit with final drive; gears: 4, fully synchronized; ratios: I 3.900, II 2.312, III 1.524, IV 1.080, rev 3.769; lever: central; final drive: cylindrical gears; axle ratio: 3.937; width of rims: 4.5'' or 5''; tyres: 145 SR x 13 or 155 SR x 13.

PERFORMANCE max speeds: (I) 25 mph, 40 km/h; (II) 42 mph, 68 km/h; (III) 64 mph, 103 km/h; (IV) 87 mph, 140 km/h; power-weight ratio: 4-dr. 41 lb/hp (55.7 lb/kW), 18.6 kg/hp (25.3 kg/kW) - 2-dr. 40.1 lb/hp (54.5 lb/kW), 18.2 kg/hp (24.7 kg/kW); carrying capacity: 882 lb, 400 kg; speed in top at 1,000 rpm: 15 mph, 24 km/h; consumption: 30.1 m/imp gal, 25 m/US gal, 9.4 l x 100 km.

CHASSIS integral; front suspension: independent, wishbones, longitudinal torsion bars, anti-roll bar, telescopic dampers; rear: independent, longitudinal trailing arms, transverse torsion bars, anti-roll bar, telescopic dampers.

STEERING rack-and-pinion; turns lock to lock: 3.25.

BRAKES front disc (diameter 9.21 in, 23.4 cm), rear drum, rear compensator, servo; swept area: front 146.2 sq in, 943 sq cm, rear 73.8 sq in, 476 sq cm, total 220 sq in, 1,419 sq cm.

ELECTRICAL EQUIPMENT 12 V; 36 Ah battery; 40 A alternator; Ducellier distributor; 2 headlamps.

DIMENSIONS AND WEIGHT wheel base: 99.21 in, 252 cm; front track: 53.94 in, 137 cm - 2-dr. 54.33 in, 138 cm; rear track: 51.57 in, 131 cm - 2-dr. 52.36 in, 133 cm; length: 155.12 in, 394 cm; width: 62.60 in, 159 cm; height: 57.48 in, 146 cm; ground clearance: 5.12 in, 13 cm; weight: 2,051 lb, 930 kg - 2-dr. 2,007 lb, 910 kg; turning circle (between walls): 34.1 ft, 10.4 m; fuel tank: 9.2 imp gal, 11.1 US gal, 42 l.

BODY 5 seats, separate front seats; back seat folding down to luggage table; heated rear window.

PRACTICAL INSTRUCTIONS fuel: 85 oct petrol; oil: engine 5.3 imp pt, 6.3 US pt, 3 l, SAE 20W-40, change every 4,650 miles, 7,500 km - gearbox and final drive 1,9 imp pt, 2.3 US pt, 1.1 l, SAE 90 EP, change every 9,300 miles, 15,000 km; greasing: none; tyre pressure: front 25 psi, 1.7 atm, rear 26 psi, 1.8 atm.

OPTIONAL ACCESSORIES sunshine roof; tinted glass; headlamps with wiper-washers; rear window wiper-washer.

CHRYSLER FRANCE Simca Rallye 2

58 hp power team

See 50 hp power team, except for:

ENGINE compression ratio: 9.6:1; max power (DIN): 58 hp (42.7 kW) at 6,000 rpm; max torque (DIN): 62 lb ft, 8.6 kg m (84.3 Nm) at 3,000 rpm; 51.9 hp/l (38.2 kW/l).

PERFORMANCE max speed: 91 mph, 146 km/h - breaks 87 mph, 140 km/h; power-weight ratio: 35.4 lb/hp (48 lb/kW), 16 kg/hp (21.8 kg/kW); carrying capacity: breaks 992 lb, 450 kg.

DIMENSIONS AND WEIGHT tracks: GLX 54.33 in, 138 cm front, 52.36 in, 133 cm rear; length: breaks 154.72 in, 393 cm; height: breaks 58.27 in, 148 cm; ground clearance: breaks 5.51 in, 14 cm; weight: 2,051 lb, 930 kg.

BODY built-in headrests on front seats (except for breaks).

PRACTICAL INSTRUCTIONS fuel: 98-100 oct petrol.

OPTIONAL ACCESSORIES Ferodo 3-speed semi-automatic transmission, hydraulic torque converter (I 2.469, II 1.650, III 1.080, rev 3.774), max ratio of converter at stall 2, possible manual selection, max speeds (I) 40 mph, 64 km/h, (II) 59 mph, 95 km/h, (III) 91 mph, 146 km/h (breaks 87 mph, 140 km/h).

82 hp power team

See 50 hp power team, except for:

ENGINE 79 cu in, 1,294 cc (3.02 x 2.76 in, 76.7 x 70 mm); compression ratio: 9.5:1; max power (DIN): 82 hp (60.3 kW) at 6,000 rpm; max torque (DIN): 77 lb ft, 10.6 kg m (104 Nm) at 3,200 rpm; max engine rpm: 6,400; 63.4 hp/l (46.6 kW/l); 2 Weber 36 DCNF downdraught twin barrel carburettors.

TRANSMISSION axle ratio: 3.706; width of rims: 5''; tyres: 145 HR x 13.

PERFORMANCE max speeds: (I) 27 mph, 43 km/h; (II) 45 mph, 72 km/h; (III) 68 mph, 109 km/h; (IV) 103 mph, 165 km/h; power-weight ratio: 26.5 lb/hp (36 lb/kW), 12 kg/hp (16.3 kg/kW); acceleration: standing ¼ mile 18.4 sec; speed in top at 1,000 rpm: 16 mph, 25.8 km/h; consumption: 28.8 m/imp gal, 24 m/US gal, 9.8 l x 100 km.

BRAKES front disc (diameter 9.37 in, 23.8 cm), rear drum, servo; swept area: front 160 sq in, 1,032 sq cm, rear 90.2 sq in, 582 sq cm, total 250.2 sq in, 1,614 sq cm.

ELECTRICAL EQUIPMENT 40 Ah battery; 6 headlamps, iodine long-distance lights.

DIMENSIONS AND WEIGHT tracks: 54.33 in, 138 cm front, 52.36 in, 133 cm rear; weight: 2,172 lb, 985 kg.

BODY built-in headrests on front seats; light alloy wheels; rear window wiper-washer.

OPTIONAL ACCESSORIES headlamps with wiper-washers; Ferodo semi-automatic transmission not available.

Simca Horizon Series

PRICES EX WORKS:

1 Simca Horizon LS	**24,400* francs**
2 Simca Horizon GL	**25,500* francs**
3 Simca Horizon GLS	**27,500* francs**

Power team:	Standard for:	Optional for:
60 hp	1,2	—
68 hp	3	—

60 hp power team

ENGINE front, transverse, slanted 41° to rear, 4 stroke; 4 cylinders, in line; 68.2 cu in, 1,118 cc (2.91 x 2.56 in, 74 x 65 mm); compression ratio: 9.6:1; max power (DIN): 60 hp (44.2 kW) at 5,600 rpm; max torque (DIN): 65 lb ft, 9 kg m (88.3 Nm) at 3,000 rpm; max engine rpm: 5,800; 53.7 hp/l (39.5 kW/l); cast iron block, light alloy head; 5 crankshaft bearings; valves: overhead, push-rods and rockers, thimble tappets; camshafts: 1, side; lubrication: gear pump, full flow filter, 5.3 imp pt, 6.3 US pt, 3 l; 1 Solex 32 BISA 6 single barrel carburettor; fuel feed: mechanical pump; sealed circuit cooling, expansion tank, liquid, 10.6 imp pt, 12.7 US pt, 6 l, electric thermostatic fan.

TRANSMISSION driving wheels: front; clutch: single dry plate (diaphragm), hydraulically controlled; gearbox: mechanical; gears: 4, fully synchronized; ratios: I 3.900, II 2.312, III 1.524, IV 1.080; final drive: cylindrical gears; axle ratio: 3.705; width of rims: 4.5''; tyres: 145 SR x 13.

PERFORMANCE max speed: 92 mph, 148 km/h; power-weight ratio: 35.3 lb/hp (47.8 lb/kW), 16 kg/hp (21.7 kg/kW); carrying capacity: 882 lb, 400 kg; acceleration:

CHRYSLER FRANCE Simca 1100 LE 2-door Berline

CHRYSLER FRANCE Simca Horizon GLS

CHRYSLER FRANCE Simca Horizon GLS

standing ¼ mile 20.4 sec; consumption: 32.5 m/imp gal, 27 m/US gal, 8.7 l x 100 km.

CHASSIS integral; front suspension: independent, longitudinal torsion bars, wishbones, anti-roll bar, telescopic dampers; rear: independent, swinging longitudinal trailing arms, coil springs, anti-roll bar, telescopic dampers.

STEERING rack-and-pinion; turns lock to lock: 4.35.

BRAKES front disc (diameter 9.45 in, 24 cm), rear drum, rear compensator, servo; swept area: front 155 sq in, 1,000 sq cm, rear 89 sq in, 574 sq cm, total 244 sq in, 1,574 sq cm.

ELECTRICAL EQUIPMENT 12 V; 40 Ah battery; 40 A alternator; Chrysler transistorized ignition; 2 headlamps.

DIMENSIONS AND WEIGHT wheel base: 99.21 in, 252 cm; tracks: 55.91 in, 142 cm front, 53.94 in, 137 cm rear; length: 155.91 in, 396 cm; width: 66.14 in, 168 cm; height: 55.51 in, 141 cm; ground clearance: 7.48 in, 19 cm; weight: 2,117 lb, 960 kg; weight distribution: 59.4% front, 40.6% rear; turning circle (between walls): 33.5 ft, 10.2 m; fuel tank: 10.3 imp gal, 12.4 US gal, 47 l.

BODY saloon/sedan; 4 + 1 doors; 5 seats, separate front seats, reclining backrests; heated rear window; folding rear seat.

PRACTICAL INSTRUCTIONS fuel: 98-100 oct petrol; oil: engine 5.3 imp pt, 6.3 US pt, 3 l, SAE 20W-40, change every 4,650 miles, 7,500 km - gearbox and final drive 1.9 imp pt, 2.3 US pt, 1.1 l, SAE 90 EP, change every 9,300 miles, 15,000 km; greasing: none.

OPTIONAL ACCESSORIES metallic spray; headlamps with wiper-washers; rear window wiper-washer (for GL only).

68 hp power team

See 60 hp power team, except for:

ENGINE 79 cu in, 1,294 cc (3.02 x 2.76 in, 76.7 x 70 mm); compression ratio: 9.5:1; max power (DIN): 68 hp (50 kW) at 5,600 rpm; max torque (DIN): 78 lb ft, 10.8 kg m (105.9 Nm) at 2,800 rpm; 52.6 hp/l (38.7 kW/l).

TRANSMISSION axle ratio: 3.588.

PERFORMANCE max speed: 96 mph, 155 km/h; power-weight ratio: 31.5 lb/hp (43 lb/kW), 14.3 kg/hp (19.5 kg/kW); acceleration: standing ¼ mile 19.6 sec; consumption: 33.2 m/imp gal, 27.7 m/US gal, 8.5 l x 100 km.

ELECTRICAL EQUIPMENT iodine headlamps.

DIMENSIONS AND WEIGHT weight: 2,150 lb, 975 kg; weight distribution: 59.5% front, 40.5% rear.

BODY adjustable headrests.

Simca 1307 GLS

PRICE EX WORKS: 26,990* francs

ENGINE front, transverse, slanted 41° to rear, 4 stroke; 4 cylinders, in line; 79 cu in, 1,294 cc (3.02 x 2.76 in, 76.7 x 70 mm); compression ratio: 9.5:1; max power (DIN): 68 hp (50 kW) at 5,600 rpm; max torque (DIN): 78 lb ft, 10.7 kg m (104.9 Nm) at 2,800 rpm; max engine rpm: 5,800; 52.6 hp/l (38.6 kW/l); cast iron block, light alloy head; 5 crankshaft bearings; valves: overhead, in line, push-rods and rockers; camshafts: 1, side; lubrication: gear pump, full flow filter, 5.3 imp pt, 6.3 US pt, 3 l; 1 Solex 32 BISA 5 A or Weber 32 IBSA 9 downdraught single barrel carburettor; fuel feed: mechanical pump; sealed circuit cooling, expansion tank, liquid, 11.4 imp pt, 13.7 US pt, 6.5 l, electric thermostatic fan.

TRANSMISSION driving wheels: front; clutch: single dry plate (diaphragm), hydraulically controlled; gearbox: mechanical; gears: 4, fully synchronized; ratios: I 3.900, II 2.312, III 1.524, IV 1.080, rev 3.769; lever: central; final drive: cylindrical gears; axle ratio: 3.706; width of rims: 5''; tyres: 155 SR x 13.

PERFORMANCE max speed: 94 mph, 152 km/h; power-weight ratio: 34 lb/hp (46.3 lb/kW), 15.4 kg/hp (21 kg/kW); carrying capacity: 882 lb, 400 kg; acceleration: standing ¼ mile 19.8 sec, 0-50 mph (0-80 km/h) 10.7 sec; speed in top at 1,000 rpm: 16.3 mph, 26.2 km/h; consumption: 31 m/imp gal, 25.8 m/US gal, 9.1 l x 100 km.

CHASSIS integral; front suspension: independent, wishbones, longitudinal torsion bars, anti-roll bar, telescopic dampers; rear: independent, swinging longitudinal trailing arms, coil springs, anti-roll bar, telescopic dampers.

STEERING rack-and-pinion; turns lock to lock: 4.15.

BRAKES front disc (diameter 9.45 in, 24 cm), rear drum, rear compensator, servo; swept area: front 169.3 sq in, 1,092 sq cm, rear 90.2 sq in, 582 sq cm, total 259.5 sq in, 1,674 sq cm.

ELECTRICAL EQUIPMENT 12 V; 40 Ah battery; 40 A alternator; Chrysler transistorized ignition; 2 headlamps.

DIMENSIONS AND WEIGHT wheel base: 102.36 in, 260 cm; tracks: 55.51 in, 141 cm front, 54.72 in, 139 cm rear; length: 166.93 in, 424 cm; width: 66.14 in, 168 cm; height: 54.72 in, 139 cm; ground clearance: 5.12 in, 13 cm; weight: 2,315 lb, 1,050 kg; turning circle (between walls): 36.1 ft, 11 m; fuel tank: 13.2 imp gal, 15.8 US gal, 60 l.

BODY saloon/sedan; 4 doors; 5 seats, separate front seats, reclining backrests; electrically-heated rear window; back seat folding down to luggage table.

PRACTICAL INSTRUCTIONS fuel: 98-100 oct petrol; oil: engine 5.3 imp pt, 6.3 US pt, 3 l, SAE 20W-40, change every 4,650 miles, 7,500 km - gearbox and final drive 1.9 imp pt, 2.3 US pt, 1.1 l, SAE 90 EP, change every 9,300 miles, 15,000 km; greasing: none.

OPTIONAL ACCESSORIES iodine long-distance lights; headrests on front seats; tinted glass; headlamps with wiper-washers; rear window wiper-washer.

Simca 1307 S

See Simca 1307 GLS, except for:

PRICE EX WORKS: 29,950* francs

ENGINE max power (DIN): 82 hp (60.3 kW) at 6,000 rpm; max torque (DIN): 79 lb ft, 10.9 kg m (106.9 Nm) at 3,000

CHRYSLER FRANCE Simca 1307 S

rpm; max engine rpm: 6,200; 63.4 hp/l (46.6 kW/l); 2 Weber 36 DCNF A downdraught twin barrel carburettors.

PERFORMANCE max speed: 101 mph, 163 km/h; power-weight ratio: 28.8 lb/hp (39.1 lb/kW), 13 kg/hp (17.7 kg/kW); acceleration: standing ¼ mile 18.9 sec, 0-50 mph (0-80 km/h) 9 sec; consumption: 29.7 m/imp gal, 22.4 m/US gal, 10.5 l x 100 km.

ELECTRICAL EQUIPMENT iodine long-distance lights (standard).

DIMENSIONS AND WEIGHT weight: 2,359 lb, 1,070 kg.

OPTIONAL ACCESSORIES electrically-controlled windows.

Simca 1308 GT

See Simca 1307 GLS, except for:

PRICE EX WORKS: 32,100* francs

ENGINE 88 cu in, 1,442 cc (3.02 x 3.07 in, 76.7 x 78 mm); max power (DIN): 85 hp (62.6 kW) at 5,600 rpm; max torque (DIN): 92 lb ft, 12.7 kg m (124.5 Nm) at 3,000 rpm; max engine rpm: 6,000; 58.9 hp/l (43.4 kW/l); 1 Weber 36 DCNVA downdraught twin barrel carburettor.

TRANSMISSION axle ratio: 3.588.

CHRYSLER FRANCE Simca 1307 S

PERFORMANCE max speed: 102 mph, 164 km/h; power-weight ratio: 27.9 lb/hp (37.9 lb/kW), 12.6 kg/hp (17.2 kg/kW); acceleration: standing ¼ mile 19 sec, 0-50 mph (0-80 km/h) 8.9 sec; speed in top at 1,000 rpm: 16.8 mph, 27.1 km/h; consumption: 26.2 m/imp gal, 21.8 m/US gal, 10.8 l x 100 km.

ELECTRICAL EQUIPMENT iodine long-distance lights (standard).

DIMENSIONS AND WEIGHT weight: 2,370 lb, 1,075 kg.

BODY (standard) tinted glass, headlamps with wiper-washers, electrically-controlled windows.

Chrysler Simca 1610

PRICE EX WORKS: 30,500* francs

ENGINE front, slanted 15° to right, 4 stroke; 4 cylinders, in line; 110.6 cu in, 1,812 cc (3.45 x 2.95 in, 87.7 x 75 mm); compression ratio: 9.45:1; max power (DIN): 100 hp (73.6 kW) at 5,800 rpm; max torque (DIN): 107 lb ft, 14.7 kg m (144.2 Nm) at 3,800 rpm; max engine rpm: 5,800; 55.2 hp/l (40.6 kW/l); cast iron block, light alloy head; 5 crankshaft bearings; valves: overhead, rockers; camshafts: 1, overhead; lubrication: gear pump, full flow filter, 7 imp pt, 8.5 US pt, 4 l; 1 Weber 34 ADS-D downdraught twin barrel carburettor; fuel feed: mechanical pump; water-cooled, 17.6 imp pt, 21.1 US pt, 10 l, electric thermostatic fan.

TRANSMISSION driving wheels: rear; clutch: single dry plate (diaphragm), hydraulically controlled; gearbox: mechanical; gears: 4, fully synchronized; ratios: I 3.546, II 2.175, III 1.418, IV 1, rev 3.226; lever: central; final drive: hypoid bevel; axle ratio: 3.909; width of rims: 5.5''; tyres: 175 SR x 14.

PERFORMANCE max speeds: (I) 27 mph, 44 km/h; (II) 45 mph, 73 km/h; (III) 70 mph, 113 km/h; (IV) 106 mph, 170 km/h; power-weight ratio: 24.3 lb/hp (33 lb/kW), 11 kg/hp (14.9 kg/kW); carrying capacity: 915 lb, 415 kg; acceleration: standing ¼ mile 18.1 sec; speed in direct drive at 1,000 rpm: 18 mph, 29 km/h; consumption: 22.2 m/imp gal, 18.5 m/US gal, 12.7 l x 100 km.

CHASSIS integral; front suspension: independent, by McPherson, coil springs/telescopic damper struts, lower wishbones, anti-roll bar; rear: rigid axle, lower longitudinal trailing arms, upper torque arms, transverse linkage bar, coil springs, anti-roll bar, telescopic dampers.

STEERING rack-and-pinion; turns lock to lock: 4.

BRAKES disc (front diameter 9.80 in, 24.9 cm, rear 9.02 in, 22.9 cm), rear compensator, servo; swept area: front 186 sq in, 1,200 sq cm, rear 145.1 sq in, 936 sq cm, total 331.1 sq in, 2,136 sq cm.

ELECTRICAL EQUIPMENT 12 V; 36 Ah battery; 35 A alternator; Chrysler transistorized ignition; 2 headlamps, iodine long-distance lights.

DIMENSIONS AND WEIGHT wheel base: 105.12 in, 267 cm; tracks: 55.12 in, 140 cm front, 55.12 in, 140 cm rear; length: 178.35 in, 453 cm; width: 68.11 in, 173 cm; height: 56.69 in, 144 cm; ground clearance: 5.71 in, 14.5 cm; weight:

CHRYSLER SIMCA 1610

2,426 lb, 1,100 kg; weight distribution: 53.8% front, 46.2% rear; turning circle (between walls): 33.8 ft, 10.3 m; fuel tank: 14.3 imp gal, 17.2 US gal, 65 l.

BODY saloon/sedan; 4 doors; 5 seats, separate front seats; built-in headrests; heated rear window.

PRACTICAL INSTRUCTIONS fuel: 98-100 oct petrol; oil: engine 7 imp pt, 8.5 US pt, 4 l, SAE 10 W-50, change every 4,650 miles, 7,500 km - gearbox 2.6 imp pt, 3.2 US pt, 1.5 l, SAE 90 EP, change every 12,400 miles, 20,000 km - final drive 2.3 imp pt, 2.7 US pt, 1.3 l, SAE 90 EP, change every 12,400 miles, 20,000 km; greasing: none; sparking plug: 225°; tappet clearances: inlet 0.010 in, 0.25 mm, exhaust 0.014 in, 0.35 mm; tyre pressure: front 24 psi, 1.7 atm, rear 27 psi, 1.9 atm.

OPTIONAL ACCESSORIES tinted glass.

Chrysler Simca 2 L Automatic

See Chrysler Simca 1610, except for:

PRICE IN GB: £ 4,109*
PRICE EX WORKS: 33,400* francs

ENGINE 120.9 cu in, 1,981 cc (3.61 x 2.95 in, 91.7 x 75 mm); max power (DIN): 110 hp (81 kW) at 5,800 rpm; max torque (DIN): 117 lb ft, 16.1 kg m (157.9 Nm) at 3,400 rpm; 55.5 hp/l (40.9 kW/l).

TRANSMISSION gearbox: Chrysler A904 automatic transmission, hydraulic torque converter and planetary gears with 3 ratios + reverse, max ratio of converter at stall 2.2, possible manual selection; ratios: I 2.450, II 1.450, III 1, rev 2.200; lever: central; axle ratio: 3.727.

PERFORMANCE max speed: 106 mph, 170 km/h; power-weight ratio: 22.6 lb/hp (30.6 lb/kW), 10.2 kg/hp (13.9 kg/kW); carrying capacity: 904 lb, 410 kg; acceleration: standing ¼ mile 18.7 sec; speed in direct drive at 1,000 rpm: 18.3 mph, 29.5 km/h; consumption: 23.7 m/imp gal, 19.8 m/US gal, 11.9 l x 100 km.

STEERING turns lock to lock: 4.50.

DIMENSIONS AND WEIGHT weight: 2,481 lb, 1,125 kg.

CITROËN   FRANCE

2 CV Spécial

PRICE EX WORKS: 12,700* francs

ENGINE front, 4 stroke; 2 cylinders, horizontally opposed; 26.5 cu in, 435 cc (2.70 x 2.32 in, 68.5 x 59 mm); compression ratio: 8.5:1; max power (DIN): 24 hp (17.7 kW) at 6,750 rpm; max torque (DIN): 21 lb ft, 2.9 kg m (28.4 Nm) at 4,500 rpm; max engine rpm: 6,750; 55.2 hp/l (40.7 kW/l); cast iron block, light alloy head, dry liners, light alloy sump, hemispherical combustion chambers; 2 crankshaft bearings; valves: overhead, Vee-slanted at 70°, push-rods and rockers; camshafts: 1, central, lower; lubrication: rotary pump, filter in sump, oil cooler, 3.5 imp pt, 4.2 US pt, 2 l; 1 Solex 34 PICS 6 downdraught carburettor; fuel feed: mechanical pump; air-cooled.

TRANSMISSION driving wheels: front (double homokinetic joints); clutch: single dry plate; gearbox: mechanical; gears: 4, II, III and IV synchronized; ratios: I 6.961, II 3.554, III 2.134, IV 1.474, rev 6.961; lever: on facia; final drive: spiral bevel; axle ratio: 4.125; width of rims: 4''; tyres: 125 x 15.

PERFORMANCE max speeds: (I) 16 mph, 25 km/h; (II) 30 mph, 49 km/h; (III) 52 mph, 83 km/h; (IV) 63 mph, 102 km/h; power-weight ratio: 51.4 lb/hp (69.8 lb/kW), 23.3 kg/hp (31.6 kg/kW); carrying capacity: 739 lb, 335 kg; acceleration: standing ¼ mile 24.3 sec; speed in top at 1,000 rpm: 11 mph, 17.7 km/h; consumption: 48.7 m/imp gal, 40.6 m/US gal, 5.8 l x 100 km at 56 mph, 90 km/h.

CHASSIS platform; front suspension: independent, swinging leading arms, 2 friction dampers, 2 inertia-type patter dampers; rear: independent, swinging longitudinal trailing arms linked to front suspension by longitudinal coil springs, 2 inertia-type patter dampers, 2 telescopic dampers.

STEERING rack-and-pinion; turns lock to lock: 3.25.

BRAKES drum, single circuit; lining area: front 30.4 sq in, 196 sq cm, rear 30.4 sq in, 196 sq cm, total 60.8 sq in, 392 sq cm.

CHRYSLER FRANCE Simca 1610

ELECTRICAL EQUIPMENT 12 V; 25 Ah battery; 390 W alternator; 2 headlamps, height adjustable from driving seat.

DIMENSIONS AND WEIGHT wheel base: 94.49 in, 240 cm; tracks: 49.61 in, 126 cm front, 49.61 in, 126 cm rear; length: 150.79 in, 383 cm; width: 58.27 in, 148 cm; height: 62.99 in, 160 cm; ground clearance: 5.91 in, 15 cm; weight: 1,235 lb, 560 kg; turning circle (between walls): 36.7 ft, 11.2 m; fuel tank: 4.4 imp gal, 5.3 US gal, 20 l.

BODY saloon/sedan; 4 doors; 4 seats, bench front seats; back seat folding down to luggage table; fully opening canvas sunshine roof.

PRACTICAL INSTRUCTIONS fuel: 80-85 oct petrol; oil: engine 3.5 imp pt, 4.2 US pt, 2 l, SAE 20W-50, change every 3,100 miles, 5,000 km - gearbox and final drive 1.6 imp pt, 1.9 US pt, 0.9 l, SAE 80, change every 12,400 miles, 20,000 km; greasing: every 1,900 miles, 3,000 km, 4 points; tyre pressure: front 20 psi, 1.4 atm, rear 26 psi, 1.8 atm.

2 CV 4

See 2 CV Spécial, except for:

PRICE EX WORKS: 13,600* francs

OPTIONAL ACCESSORIES centrifugal clutch; separate front seats.

2 CV 6

See 2 CV 4, except for:

PRICE IN GB: 1,579*
PRICE EX WORKS: 14,400* francs

ENGINE 36.7 cu in, 602 cc (2.91 x 2.76 in, 74 x 70 mm); max power (DIN): 26 hp (19.1 kW) at 5,500 rpm; max torque (DIN): 29 lb ft, 4 kg m (39.2 Nm) at 3,500 rpm; max engine rpm: 6,000; 43.2 hp/l (31.7 kW/l); lubricating system: 3.9 imp pt, 4.7 US pt, 2.2 l.

TRANSMISSION gearbox ratios: I 5.203, II 2.656, III 1.786, IV 1.316, rev 5.203.

PERFORMANCE max speeds: (I) 19 mph, 30 km/h; (II) 37 mph, 59 km/h; (III) 55 mph, 88 km/h; (IV) 68 mph, 110 km/h; power-weight ratio: 47.5 lb/hp (64.7 lb/kW), 21.5 kg/hp (29.3 kg/kW); acceleration: standing ¼ mile 22.7 sec; speed in top at 1,000 rpm: 12.4 mph, 19.9 km/h; consumption: 49.6 m/imp gal, 41.3 m/US gal, 5.7 l x 100 km at 56 mph, 90 km/h.

Mehari 2 + 2

See 2 CV 6, except for:

PRICE EX WORKS: 17,260* francs

TRANSMISSION gearbox ratios: I 6.051, II 3.089, III 1.923, IV 1.421, rev 6.051; axle ratio: 3.875; tyres: 135 x 15.

CITROËN 2 CV Spécial

PERFORMANCE max speed: 62 mph, 100 km/h; power-weight ratio: 47.1 lb/hp (64.1 lb/kW), 21.3 kg/hp (29 kg/kW); carrying capacity: 838 lb, 380 kg; acceleration: standing ¼ mile 23.6 sec; speed in top at 1,000 rpm: 12.4 mph, 20 km/h; consumption: 38.7 m/imp gal, 32.2 m/US gal, 7.3 l x 100 km at 56 mph, 90 km/h.

BRAKES front disc (diameter 9.61 in, 24.4 cm), rear drum; lining area: front 13 sq in, 84 sq cm, rear 34.7 sq in, 224 sq cm, total 47.7 sq in, 308 sq cm.

DIMENSIONS AND WEIGHT length: 138.58 in, 352 cm; width: 60.24 in, 153 cm; height: 64.17 in, 163 cm; ground clearance: 6.89 in, 17.5 cm; weight: 1,224 lb, 555 kg; turning circle (between walls): 36.1 ft, 11 m; fuel tank: 5.5 imp gal, 6.6 US gal, 25 l.

BODY open in plastic material; no doors; 2 + 2 seats, separate front seats.

OPTIONAL ACCESSORIES only tonneau cover.

Dyane 6

PRICE IN GB: £ 1,737*
PRICE EX WORKS: 15,200* francs

ENGINE front, 4 stroke; 2 cylinders, horizontally opposed; 36.7 cu in, 602 cc (2.91 x 2.76 in, 74 x 70 mm); compression ratio 9:1; max power (DIN): 32 hp (23.6 kW) at 5,750 rpm; max torque (DIN): 30 lb ft, 4.2 kg m (41.2 Nm) at 4,000 rpm; max engine rpm: 6,000; 53.3 hp/l (39.2 kW/l); cast iron block, light alloy head, dry liners, light alloy sump, hemispherical combustion chambers; 2 crankshaft bearings; valves: overhead, Vee-slanted at 70°, push-rods and rockers; camshafts: 1, central, lower; lubrication: rotary pump, filter in sump, oil cooler, 3.9 imp pt, 4.7 US pt, 2.2 l; 1 Solex 26 35 CSIC downdraught twin barrel carburettor; fuel feed: mechanical pump; air-cooled.

TRANSMISSION driving wheels: front (double homokinetic joints); clutch: single dry plate; gearbox: mechanical; gears: 4, fully synchronized; ratios: I 5.749, II 2.935, III 1.923, IV 1.350, rev 5.749; lever: on facia; final drive: spiral bevel; axle ratio: 3.875; width of rims: 4''; tyres: 125 x 15.

PERFORMANCE max speeds: (I) 18 mph, 29 km/h; (II) 35 mph, 57 km/h; (III) 54 mph, 87 km/h; (IV) 75 mph, 120 km/h; power-weight ratio: 41.3 lb/hp (56.1 lb/kW), 18.7 kg/hp (25.4 kg/kW); carrying capacity: 728 lb, 330 kg; acceleration: standing ¼ mile 22 sec; speed in top at 1,000 rpm: 12.8 mph, 20.6 km/h; consumption: 49.6 m/imp gal, 41.3 m/US gal, 5.7 l x 100 km at 56 mph, 90 km/h.

CHASSIS platform; front suspension: independent, swinging leading arms, 2 friction dampers, 2 inertia-type patter dampers; rear: independent, swinging longitudinal trailing arms linked to front suspension by longitudinal coil springs, 2 inertia-type patter dampers, 2 telescopic dampers.

STEERING rack-and-pinion; turns lock to lock: 3.25.

BRAKES front disc (diameter 9.61 in, 24.4 cm), rear drum, single circuit; lining area: front 13 sq in, 84 sq cm, rear 34.7 sq in, 224 sq cm, total 47.7 sq in, 308 sq cm.

ELECTRICAL EQUIPMENT 12 V; 25 Ah battery; 390 W alternator; 2 headlamps, height adjustable from driving seat.

DIMENSIONS AND WEIGHT wheel base: 94.49 in, 240 cm; front and rear tracks: 49.16 in, 126 cm; length: 152.36 in, 387 cm; width: 59.06 in, 150 cm; height: 60.63 in, 154 cm; ground clearance: 6.10 in, 15.5 cm; weight: 1,323 lb, 600 kg; turning circle (between walls): 36.4 ft, 11.1 m; fuel tank: 5.5 imp gal, 6.6 US gal, 25 l.

BODY saloon/sedan; 4+1 doors; 4 seats, bench front seats; fully opening canvas sunshine roof.

PRACTICAL INSTRUCTIONS fuel: 80-85 oct petrol; oil: engine 3.9 imp pt, 4.7 US pt, 2.2 l, SAE 20W-50 change every 3,100 miles, 5.000 km - gearbox and final drive 1.6 imp pt, 1.9 US pt, 0.9 l, SAE 80, change every 12,400 miles, 20,000 km; greasing: every 1,900 miles, 3,000 km, 4 points; tyre pressure: front 20 psi, 1.4 atm, rear 26 psi, 1.8 atm.

OPTIONAL ACCESSORIES centrifugal clutch; back seat folding down to luggage table; separate front seats.

Ami 8 Berline Confort

PRICE IN GB: £ 1,881*
PRICE EX WORKS: 17,000* francs

ENGINE front, 4 stroke; 2 cylinders, horizontally opposed; 36.7 cu in, 602 cc (2.91 x 2.76 in, 74 x 70 mm); compression ratio 9:1; max power (DIN): 32 hp (23.6 kW) at 5,750 rpm; max torque (DIN): 30 lb ft, 4.2 kg m (41.2 Nm) at 4,000 rpm; max engine rpm: 6,000; 53.3 hp/l (39.2 kW/l); cast iron block, light alloy head, dry liners, light alloy sump, hemispherical combustion chambers; 2 crankshaft bearings;

CITROËN Dyane 6

CITROËN Mehari 2 + 2

CITROËN Ami 8 Break Confort

valves: overhead, Vee-slanted at 70°; camshafts: 1, central; lubrication: gear pump, filter in sump, oil cooler, 3.9 imp pt, 4.7 US pt, 2.2 l; 1 Solex 26 35 CSIC downdraught twin barrel carburettor; fuel feed: mechanical pump; air-cooled.

TRANSMISSION driving wheels: front (double homokinetic joints); clutch: single dry plate; gearbox: mechanical; gears: 4, fully synchronized; ratios: I 5.749, II 2.935, III 1.923, IV 1.350, rev 5.749; lever: on facia; final drive: spiral bevel; axle ratio: 3.875; width of rims: 4''; tyres: 125 x 15.

PERFORMANCE max speeds: (I) 18 mph, 29 km/h; (II) 35 mph, 57 km/h; (III) 54 mph, 87 km/h; (IV) 76 mph, 123 km/h; power-weight ratio: 50 lb/hp (67.8 lb/kW), 22.7 kg/hp (30.7 kg/kW); carrying capacity: 717 lb, 325 kg; acceleration: standing ¼ mile 23.2 sec; speed in top at 1,000 rpm: 12.8 mph, 20.6 km/h; consumption: 49.6 m/imp gal, 41.3 m/US gal, 5.7 l x 100 km at 56 mph, 90 km/h.

CHASSIS platform; front suspension: independent, swinging leading arms, 2 telescopic dampers, 2 inertia-type patter dampers, anti-roll bar; rear: independent, swinging longitudinal trailing arms linked to front suspension by longitudinal coil springs, 2 telescopic dampers, 2 inertia-type patter dampers.

STEERING rack-and-pinion; turns lock to lock: 3.25.

BRAKES front disc (diameter 9.61 in, 24.4 cm), rear drum, single circuit; lining area: front 13 sq in, 84 sq cm, rear 34.7 sq in, 224 sq cm, total 47.7 sq in, 308 sq cm.

ELECTRICAL EQUIPMENT 12 V; 25 Ah battery; 390 W alternator; 2 headlamps, height adjustable from driving seat.

DIMENSIONS AND WEIGHT wheel base: 94.49 in, 240 cm; tracks: 49.61 in, 126 cm front, 48.03 in, 122 cm rear; length: 157.09 in, 399 cm; width: 59.84 in, 152 cm; height: 58.66 in, 149 cm; ground clearance: 5.12 in, 13 cm; weight: 1,599 lb, 725 kg; turning circle (between walls): 37.4 ft, 11.4 m; fuel tank: 7 imp gal, 8.4 US gal, 32 l.

BODY saloon/sedan; 4 doors; 4 seats, separate front seats, reclining backrests.

PRACTICAL INSTRUCTIONS fuel: 98 oct petrol; oil: engine 3.9 imp pt, 4.7 US pt, 2.2 l, SAE 10W-30, change every 3,100 miles, 5,000 km - gearbox and final drive 1.6 imp pt, 1.9 US pt, 0.9 l, SAE 80, change every 12,400 miles, 20,000 km; greasing: every 1,900 miles, 3,000 km, 4 points; tyre pressure: front 26 psi, 1.8 atm, rear 26 psi, 1.8 atm.

OPTIONAL ACCESSORIES centrifugal clutch; metallic spray.

Ami 8 Break Confort

See Ami 8 Berline Confort, except for:

PRICE IN GB: £ 1,986*
PRICE EX WORKS: 18,100* francs

TRANSMISSION tyres: 135 x 15.

PERFORMANCE max speed: 75 mph, 120 km/h; carrying capacity: 827 lb, 375 kg; speed in top at 1,000 rpm: 13.3 mph, 21.4 km/h.

CHASSIS reinforced suspension.

AMI 8 BREAK CONFORT

DIMENSIONS AND WEIGHT height: 59.84 in, 152 cm.

BODY estate car/station wagon; 4+1 doors; 4-5 seats; back seat folding down to luggage table.

PRACTICAL INSTRUCTIONS tyre pressure: front 20 psi, 1.4 atm.

LN

PRICE EX WORKS: 17,500* francs

ENGINE front, 4 stroke; 2 cylinders, horizontally opposed; 36.7 cu in, 602 cc (2.91 x 2.76 in, 74 x 70 mm); compression ratio: 9:1; max power (DIN): 32 hp (23.6 kW) at 5,750 rpm; max torque (DIN): 30 lb ft, 4.2 kg m (41.2 Nm) at 3,500 rpm; max engine rpm: 6,000; 53.3 hp/l (39.2 kW/l); cast iron block, light alloy head, dry liners, light alloy sump, hemispherical combustion chambers; 2 crankshaft bearings; valves: overhead, Vee-slanted at 70º, push-rods and rockers; camshafts: 1, central, lower; lubrication: rotary pump, filter in sump, oil cooler, 3.9 imp pt, 4.7 US pt, 2.2; 1 Solex 26 35 CSIC downdraught twin barrel carburettor; fuel feed: mechanical pump; air-cooled.

TRANSMISSION driving wheels: front (double homokinetic joints); clutch: single dry plate (diaphragm); gearbox: mechanical; gears: 4, fully synchronized; ratios: I 4.545, II 2.500, III 1.601, IV 1.350, rev 4.184; lever: central; final drive: spiral bevel; axle ratio: 4.375; width of rims: 4''; tyres: 135 x 13.

PERFORMANCE max speeds: (I) 19 mph, 31 km/h; (II) 32 mph, 52 km/h; (III) 49 mph, 79 km/h; (IV) 75 mph, 120 km/h; power-weight ratio: 48.6 lb/hp (70 lb/kW), 22.1 kg/hp (29.9 kg/kW); carrying capacity: 728 lb, 320 kg; acceleration: standing ¼ mile 23.2 sec; speed in top at 1,000 rpm: 12 mph, 20 km/h; consumption: 47.9 m/imp gal, 39.9 m/US gal, 5.9 l x 100 km at 56 mph, 90 km/h.

CHASSIS integral; front suspension: independent, by McPherson, coil springs/telescopic damper struts, lower wishbones (trailing links), anti-roll bar; rear: independent, swinging longitudinal trailing arms, coil springs, telescopic dampers.

STEERING rack-and-pinion; turns lock to lock: 3.33.

BRAKES front disc (diameter 9.49 in, 24.1 cm), rear drum, rear compensator; lining area: front 22.3 sq in, 144 sq cm, rear 32.9 sq in, 212 sq cm, total 55.2 sq in, 356 sq cm.

ELECTRICAL EQUIPMENT 12 V; 25 Ah battery; 390 W alternator; 2 headlamps, height adjustable from driving seat.

DIMENSIONS AND WEIGHT wheel base: 87.80 in, 223 cm; tracks: 50.79 in, 129 cm front, 48.82 in, 124 cm rear; length: 133.07 in, 338 cm; width: 59.84 in, 152 cm; height: 53.94 in, 137 cm; ground clearance: 4.72 in, 12 cm; weight: 1,557 lb, 706 kg; turning circle (between walls): 30.8 ft, 9.4 m; fuel tank: 8.8 imp gal, 10.6 US gal, 40 l.

BODY coupé; 2 + 1 doors; 4 seats, separate front and rear seats, reclining driver's seat, back seats folding down to luggage table.

PRACTICAL INSTRUCTIONS fuel: 80-85 oct petrol; oil: engine 3.9 imp pt, 4.7 US pt, 2.2 l, SAE 20W-50, change every 3,100 miles, 5,000 km - gearbox and final drive 2.5 imp pt, 3 US pt, 1.4 l, SAE 80 EP, change every 12,400 miles, 20,000 km; greasing: every 3,100 miles, 5,000 km, 1 point; tyre pressure: front 23 psi, 1.6 atm, rear 27 psi, 1.9 atm.

OPTIONAL ACCESSORIES centrifugal clutch; metallic spray; heated rear window.

GSpecial Berline

PRICE IN GB: £ 2,490*
PRICE EX WORKS: 21,800* francs

ENGINE front, 4 stroke; 4 cylinders, horizontally opposed; 68.9 cu in, 1,129 cc (2.91 x 2.58 in, 74 x 65.6 mm); compression ratio: 9:1; max power (DIN): 56 hp (41.2 kW) at 5,750 rpm; max torque (DIN): 59 lb ft, 8.1 kg m (79.4 Nm) at 3,500 rpm; max engine rpm: 6,000; 49.6 hp/l (36.5 kW/l); light alloy block, head with cast iron liners, light alloy fins, hemispherical combustion chambers; 3 crankshaft bearings; valves: overhead, Vee-slanted; camshafts: 1, per block, overhead, cogged belt; lubrication: gear pump, full flow filter, oil cooler, 7 imp pt, 8.5 US pt, 4 l; 1 Solex 28 CIC 2 or Weber 30 DGS 9 downdraught twin barrel carburettor; fuel feed: mechanical pump; air-cooled.

TRANSMISSION driving wheels: front; clutch: single dry plate (diaphragm); gearbox: mechanical; gears: 4, fully synchronized; ratios: I 3.818, II 2.294, III 1.500, IV 1.031, rev 4.182; lever: central; final drive: spiral bevel; axle ratio: 4.125; width of rims: 4.5''; tyres: 145 SR x 15.

CITROËN LN

CITROËN GSpecial Berline

CITROËN GS Club Berline

PERFORMANCE max speeds: (I) 28 mph, 45 km/h; (II) 45 mph, 73 km/h; (III) 71 mph, 114 km/h; (IV) 93 mph, 149 km/h; power-weight ratio: 36.4 lb/hp (49.5 lb/kW), 16.5 kg/hp (22.4 kg/kW); carrying capacity: 904 lb, 410 kg; acceleration: standing ¼ mile 20.7 sec; speed in top at 1,000 rpm: 16.4 mph, 26.4 km/h; consumption: 44.1 m/imp gal, 36.8 m/US gal, 6.4 l x 100 km at 56 mph, 90 km/h.

CHASSIS integral; front suspension: independent, wishbones, hydropneumatic suspension, anti-roll bar, automatic levelling control; rear: independent, swinging trailing arms, hydropneumatic suspension, anti-roll bar, automatic levelling control.

STEERING rack-and-pinion; turns lock to lock: 3.80.

BRAKES disc (front diameter 10.63 in, 27 cm, rear diameter 7.01 in, 17.8 cm), servo; lining area: front 22.6 sq in, 146 sq cm, rear 10.5 sq in, 68 sq cm, total 33.1 sq in, 214 sq cm.

ELECTRICAL EQUIPMENT 12 V; 35 Ah battery; 490 W alternator; Sev distributor; 2 headlamps.

DIMENSIONS AND WEIGHT wheel base: 100.39 in, 255 cm; tracks: 54.33 in, 138 cm front, 52.36 in, 133 cm rear; length: 162.20 in, 412 cm; width: 63.39 in, 161 cm; constant height: 53.15 in, 135 cm; ground clearance (variable): 6.06 in, 15.4 cm; weight: 2,040 lb, 925 kg; weight distribution: 62.5% front, 37.5% rear; turning circle (between walls): 33.5 ft, 10.2 m; fuel tank: 9.5 imp gal, 11.4 US gal, 43 l.

BODY saloon/sedan; 4 doors; 5 seats, separate front seat, reclining backrests.

PRACTICAL INSTRUCTIONS fuel: 98 oct petrol; oil: engine 7 imp pt, 8.5 US pt, 4 l, SAE 20W-50, change every 3,100 miles, 5,000 km - gearbox and final drive 2.5 imp pt, 3 US pt, 1.4 l, SAE 90, change every 12,400 miles, 20,000 km - hydropneumatic suspension 5.8 imp pt, 7 US pt, 3.3 l; greasing: none; tappet clearances: inlet 0.008 in, 0.20 mm, exhaust 0.008 in, 0.20 mm; valve timing: 2°20' 34° 34°20 2°; tyre pressure: front 26 psi, 1.8 atm, rear 27 psi, 1.9 atm.

OPTIONAL ACCESSORIES heated rear window; tinted glass; sunshine roof; metallic spray.

GS X

See GSpecial Berline, except for:

PRICE EX WORKS: 22,800* francs

TRANSMISSION axle ratio: 4.375.

PERFORMANCE power-weight ratio: 36.8 lb/hp (50 lb/kW), 16.7 kg/hp (22.7 kg/kW); acceleration: standing ¼ mile 20.3 sec; speed in top at 1,000 rpm: 15.5 mph, 24.9 km/h; consumption: 43.5 m/imp gal, 36.2 m/US gal, 6.5 l x 100 km at 56 mph, 90 km/h.

ELECTRICAL EQUIPMENT 45 Ah battery.

DIMENSIONS AND WEIGHT weight: 2,062 lb, 935 kg.

BODY built-in headrests on front seats; luxury equipment.

GSpecial Break

See GSpecial Berline, except for:

PRICE IN GB: 2,699*
PRICE EX WORKS: 23,400* francs

PERFORMANCE max speed: 91 mph, 146 km/h; power-weight ratio: 36.8 lb/hp (50 lb/kW), 16.7 kg/hp (22.7 kg/kW); acceleration: standing ¼ mile 20.9 sec; speed in top at 1,000 rpm: 16.4 mph, 26.4 km/h; consumption: 43.5 m/imp gal, 36.2 m/US gal, 6.5 l x 100 km at 56 mph, 90 km/h.

BODY estate car/station wagon; 4+1 doors; back seat folding down to luggage table; wiper and washer on rear window.

OPTIONAL ACCESSORIES sunshine roof not available.

GS Club Berline

See GSpecial Berline, except for:

PRICE IN GB: £ 2,700*
PRICE EX WORKS: 24,100* francs

ENGINE 74.6 cu in, 1,222 cc (3.03 x 2.58 in, 77 x 65.6 mm); compression ratio: 8.2:1; max power (DIN): 59 hp (43.4 kW) at 5,750 rpm; max torque (DIN): 64 lb ft, 8.9 kg m (87.3 Nm) at 3,250 rpm; max engine rpm: 6,500; 48.3 hp/l (35.5 kW/l); 1 Solex 28 CIC or Weber 30 DGS1 downdraught twin barrel carburettor.

TRANSMISSION gearbox ratios: I 3.812, II 2.294, III 1.500, IV 1.096, rev 4.182.

PERFORMANCE max speeds: (I) 29 mph, 46 km/h; (II) 48 mph, 77 km/h; (III) 72 mph, 116 km/h; (IV) 94 mph, 151 km/h; power-weight ratio: 34.8 lb/hp (47.3 lb/kW), 15.8 kg/hp (21.4 kg/kW); acceleration: standing ¼ mile 19.7 sec; speed in top at 1,000 rpm: 15.4 mph, 24.8 km/h; consumption: 41.5 m/imp gal, 34.6 m/US gal, 6.8 l x 100 km at 56 mph, 90 km/h.

DIMENSIONS AND WEIGHT weight: 2,051 lb, 930 kg.

PRACTICAL INSTRUCTIONS valve timing: 4°10' 31°50' 36°10' 0°10'.

OPTIONAL ACCESSORIES semi-automatic transmission, hydraulic torque converter and planetary gears with 3 ratios (I 2.786, II 1.700, III 1.120, rev 2.500), max ratio of converter at stall 2, max speed 92 mph, 148 km/h, consumption 38.2 m/imp gal, 31.8 m/US gal, 7.4 l x 100 km at 56 mph, 90 km/h.

GS Club Break

See GS Club Berline, except for:

PRICE IN GB: £ 2,898*
PRICE EX WORKS: 25,700* francs

PERFORMANCE max speed: 93 mph, 149 km/h; power-weight ratio: 35.1 lb/hp (47.8 lb/kW), 15.9 kg/hp (21.6 kg/kW); acceleration: standing ¼ mile 20.9 sec; speed

CITROËN GS Pallas

CITROËN GS Series

CITROËN GS X 2

in top at 1,000 rpm: 15.4 mph, 24.8 km/h; consumption: 41.5 m/imp gal, 34.6 m/US gal, 6.8 l x 100 km at 56 mph, 90 km/h.

ELECTRICAL EQUIPMENT iodine headlamps.

DIMENSIONS AND WEIGHT weight: 2,073 lb, 940 kg.

BODY estate car/station wagon; 4 + 1 doors; heated rear window (standard); wiper and washer on rear window; luxury equipment; back seat folding down to luggage table.

OPTIONAL ACCESSORIES semi-automatic transmission and sunshine roof not available.

GS Pallas

See GS Club Berline, except for:

PRICE IN GB: £ 2,978*
PRICE EX WORKS: 26,000* francs

PERFORMANCE power-weight ratio: 35.3 lb/hp (48 lb/kW), 16 kg/hp (21.8 kg/kW).

DIMENSIONS AND WEIGHT weight: 2,084 lb, 945 kg.

BODY luxury equipment; heated rear window (standard).

GS X 2

See GS Club Berline, except for:

PRICE IN GB: £ 2,940*
PRICE EX WORKS: 24,700* francs

ENGINE compression ratio: 8.7:1; max power (DIN): 64 hp (47.1 kW/l) at 5,750 rpm; max torque (DIN): 67 lb ft, 9.3 kg m (91.2 Nm) at 3,500 rpm; 52.4 hp/l (38.5 kW/l); 1 Solex CIC or Weber 30 DGS 2 downdraught twin barrel carburettor.

PERFORMANCE max speed: 98 mph, 156 km/h; power-weight ratio: 32.4 lb/hp (44 lb/kW), 14.7 kg/hp (20 kg/kW); acceleration: standing ¼ mile 19.3 sec.

ELECTRICAL EQUIPMENT 45 Ah battery.

DIMENSIONS AND WEIGHT weight: 2,073 lb, 940 kg.

BODY heated rear window (standard); built-in headrests on front seats.

OPTIONAL ACCESSORIES semi-automatic transmission not available.

CX 2000 Confort

PRICE IN GB: £ 4,461*
PRICE EX WORKS: 33,860* francs

ENGINE front, transverse, slanted 30° to front, 4 stroke; 4 cylinders, in line; 121.1 cu in, 1,985 cc (3.39 x 3.37 in,

CITROËN CX 2400 Break Super

CX 2000 CONFORT

86 x 85.5 mm); compression ratio: 9:1; max power (DIN): 102 hp (75.1 kW) at 5,500 rpm; max torque (DIN): 112 lb ft, 15.5 kg m (152 Nm) at 3,000 rpm; max engine rpm: 6,000; 51.4 hp/l (37.8 kW/l); cast iron block, light alloy head; 5 crankshaft bearings; valves: overhead, Vee-slanted at 60°, push-rods and rockers; camshafts: 1, side; lubrication: gear pump, full flow filter, 9.3 imp pt, 11.2 US pt, 5.3 l; 1 Weber 34 DMTR 25 downdraught twin barrel carburettor; fuel feed: mechanical pump; water-cooled, 19.4 imp pt, 23.3 US pt, 11 l, electric thermostatic fan.

TRANSMISSION driving wheels: front; clutch: single dry plate (diaphragm); gearbox: mechanical; gears: 4, fully synchronized; ratios: I 3.166, II 1.833, III 1.133, IV 0.800, rev 3.153; lever: central; final drive: spiral bevel; axle ratio: 4.769; width of rims: 5.5''; tyres: 185 SR x 14 front, 175 SR x 14 rear.

PERFORMANCE max speeds: (I) 29 mph, 47 km/h; (II) 50 mph, 81 km/h; (III) 81 mph, 131 km/h; (IV) 108 mph, 174 km/h; power-weight ratio: 27.3 lb/hp (37.1 lb/kW), 12.4 kg/hp (16.8 kg/kW); carrying capacity: 1,047 lb, 475 kg; acceleration: standing ¼ mile 18.3 sec; speed in top at 1,000 rpm: 19.3 mph, 31 km/h; consumption: 27.7 m/imp gal, 23.1 m/US gal, 10.2 l x 100 km at 75 mph, 120 km/h.

CHASSIS integral with front and rear subframes; front suspension: independent, wishbones, hydropneumatic suspension, anti-roll bar, automatic levelling control; rear independent, swinging trailing arms, hydropneumatic suspension, anti-roll bar, automatic levelling control.

STEERING rack-and-pinion; turns lock to lock: 4.50.

BRAKES disc (front diameter 10.24 in, 26 cm, rear diameter 9.17 in, 23.3 cm), internal radial fins, rear compensator, servo; lining area: front 34.1 sq in, 220 sq cm, rear 14.9 sq in, 96 sq cm, total 49 sq in, 316 sq cm.

ELECTRICAL EQUIPMENT 12 V; 50 Ah battery; 1,008 W alternator; Ducellier distributor; 2 halogen headlamps.

DIMENSIONS AND WEIGHT wheel base: 111.81 in, 284 cm; tracks: 57.87 in, 147 cm front, 53.54 in, 136 cm rear; length: 183.46 in, 466 cm; width: 68.11 in, 173 cm; height: 53.54 in, 136 cm; ground clearance: 6.10 in, 15.5 cm; weight: 2,789 lb, 1,265 kg; weight distribution: 66.8% front, 33.2% rear; turning circle (between walls): 38.7 ft, 11.8 m; fuel tank: 15 imp gal, 18 US gal, 68 l.

BODY saloon/sedan; 4 doors; 5 seats, separate front seats, reclining backrests, built-in headrests, heated rear window.

PRACTICAL INSTRUCTIONS fuel: 95 oct petrol; oil: engine 8.1 imp pt, 9,7 US pt, 4.6 l, SAE 20W-50, change every 3,100 miles, 5,000 km - gearbox and final drive 2.8 imp pt, 3.4 US pt, 1.6 l, SAE 80, change every 19,000 miles, 30,000 km - hydraulic suspension 7 imp pt, 8.5 US pt, 4 l; greasing: none; tyre pressure: front 27 psi, 2 atm, rear 30 psi, 2.1 atm.

OPTIONAL ACCESSORIES power steering; tinted glass; metallic spray; air-conditioning.

CITROËN CX 2400 Break Super

CITROËN CX 2200 Diesel

CX 2000 Break Confort

See CX 2000 Confort, except for:

PRICE /EX WORKS: 38,560* francs

TRANSMISSION tyres: 185 SR x 14 front and rear.

PERFORMANCE max speed: 106 mph, 171 km/h; power-weight ratio: 29.9 lb/hp (40.7 lb/kW), 13.6 kg/hp (18.4 kg/kW); carrying capacity: 1,510 lb, 685 kg; acceleration: standing ¼ mile 19.3 sec; consumption: 26.2 m/imp gal, 21.8 m/US gal, 10.8 l x 100 km at 75 mph, 120 km/h.

CHASSIS reinforced suspension.

BRAKES lining area: front 34.1 sq in, 220 sq cm, rear 22.5 sq in, 145 sq cm, total 56.6 sq in, 365 sq cm.

DIMENSIONS AND WEIGHT wheel base: 121.65 in, 309 cm; tracks: 57.87 in, 147 cm front, 54.72 in, 139 cm rear; length: 193.70 in, 492 cm; height: 57.48 in, 146 cm; weight: 3,054 lb, 1,385 kg; turning circle (between walls): 40 ft, 12.2 m.

BODY estate car/station wagon; 4+1 doors; back seat folding down to luggage table; heated rear window with wiper-washer.

PRACTICAL INSTRUCTIONS tyre pressure: front 31 psi, 2.2 atm, rear 31 psi, 2.2 atm.

CX 2000 Super

See CX 2000 Confort, except for:

PRICE EX WORKS: 35,760* francs

PERFORMANCE power-weight ratio: 27.7 lb/hp (37.6 lb/kW), 12.6 kg/hp (17 kg/kW).

DIMENSIONS AND WEIGHT weight: 2,822 lb, 1,280 kg.

BODY luxury equipment; electrically-controlled front windows.

CX 2200 Diesel

See CX 2000 Confort, except for:

PRICE /EX WORKS: 39,260* francs

ENGINE 132.7 cu in, 2,175 cc (3.54 x 3.37 in, 90 x 85.5 mm); compression ratio: 22.25:1; max power (DIN): 66 hp (48.6 kW) at 4,500 rpm; max torque (DIN): 93 lb ft, 12.8 kg m (125.5 Nm) at 2,750 rpm; max engine rpm: 4,700; 30.3 hp/l (22.3 kW/l); Bosch PVA ignition system: sealed circuit cooling, liquid, 22 imp pt, 26.4 US pt, 12.5 l, 2 electric thermostatic fans.

PERFORMANCE max speeds: (I) 22 mph, 35 km/h; (II) 38 mph, 61 km/h; (III) 62 mph, 99 km/h; (IV) 91 mph, 146 km/h; power-weight ratio: 44.8 lb/hp (60.8 lb/kW), 20.3 kg/hp (27.6 kg/kW); carrying capacity: 1,074 lb, 487 kg; acceleration: standing ¼ mile 21.8 sec; consumption: 44.8 m/imp gal, 37.3 m/US gal, 6.3 l x 100 km at 56 mph, 90 km/h.

ELECTRICAL EQUIPMENT 88 Ah battery.

DIMENSIONS AND WEIGHT weight: 2,955 lb, 1,340 kg.

PRACTICAL INSTRUCTIONS fuel: Diesel oil; tyre pressure: front 30 psi, 2.1 atm.

CX 2200 Break Confort Diesel

See CX 2200 Diesel Confort, except for:

PRICE EX WORKS: 43,960* francs

TRANSMISSION tyres: 185 SR x 14 front and rear.

PERFORMANCE max speed: 89 mph, 144 km/h; power-weight ratio: 48.3 lb/hp (65.6 lb/kW), 21.9 kg/hp (29.7 kg/kW); carrying capacity: 1,466 lb, 665 kg; acceleration: standing ¼ mile 22.8 sec; consumption: 44.1 m/imp gal, 36.8 m/US gal, 6.4 l x 100 km at 56 mph, 90 km/h.

CHASSIS reinforced suspension.

BRAKES lining area: front 34.1 sq in, 220 sq cm, rear 22.5 sq in, 145 sq cm, total 56.6 sq in, 365 sq cm.

DIMENSIONS AND WEIGHT wheel base: 121.65 in, 309 cm; tracks: 57.87 in, 147 cm front, 54.72 in, 139 cm rear; length: 193.70 in, 492 cm; height: 57.48 in, 146 cm; weight: 3,186 lb, 1,445 kg; turning circle (between walls): 40 ft, 12.2 m.

BODY estate car/station wagon; 4 + 1 doors; back seat folding down to luggage table; heated rear window with wiper-washer.

PRACTICAL INSTRUCTIONS tyre pressure: front 33 psi, 2.3 atm, rear 31 psi, 2.2 atm.

CX 2400 Super

See CX 2000 Confort, except for:

PRICE IN GB: £ 4,529*
PRICE EX WORKS: 37,860* francs

ENGINE 143.2 cu in, 2,347 cc (3.68 x 3.37 in, 93.5 x 85.5 mm); compression ratio: 8.75:1; max power (DIN): 115 hp (84.6 kW) at 5,500 rpm; max torque (DIN): 133 lb ft, 18.3 kg m (179.5 Nm) at 2,750 rpm; max engine rpm: 5,750; 49 hp/l (36 kW/l); 1 Weber 34 DMTR 25 downdraught twin barrel carburettor; cooling system: 18.7 imp pt, 22.4 US pt, 10.6 l.

TRANSMISSION tyres: 185 HR x 14 front, 175 HR x 14 rear.

PERFORMANCE max speeds: (I) 30 mph, 49 km/h; (II) 53 mph, 85 km/h; (III) 85 mph, 136 km/h; (IV) 112 mph, 181 km/h; power-weight ratio: 24.6 lb/hp (33.5 lb/kW), 11.2 kg/hp (15.2 kg/kW); acceleration: standing ¼ mile 17.8 sec; consumption: 26.9 m/imp gal, 22.4 m/US gal, 10.5 l x 100 km at 75 mph, 120 km/h.

DIMENSIONS AND WEIGHT weight: 2,833 lb, 1,285 kg; weight distribution: 66.9% front, 33.1% rear.

OPTIONAL ACCESSORIES semi-automatic transmission, hydraulic torque converter and planetary gears with 3 ratios (I 1.944, II 1.133, III 0.800, rev 2.389), max speeds (I) 45 mph, 72 km/h, (II) 77 mph, 124 km/h, (III) 110 mph, 177 km/h, acceleration standing ¼ mile 19.3 sec, consumption 24.6 m/imp gal, 20.5 m/US gal, 11.5 l x 100 km at 75 mph, 120 km/h; 5-speed fully synchronized mechanical gearbox (I 3.166, II 1.833, III 1.250, IV 0.939, V 0.733, rev 3.153), 4.357 axle ratio, max speed 112 mph, 180 km/h, acceleration standing ¼ mile 17.9 sec, speed in top at 1,000 rpm 23 mph, 37 km/h, consumption 30.1 m/imp gal, 25 m/US gal, 9.4 l x 100 km at 75 mph, 120 km/h.

CX 2400 Break Super

See CX 2400 Super, except for:

PRICE EX WORKS: 42,560* francs

TRANSMISSION tyres: 185 SR x 14 front and rear.

PERFORMANCE max speed: 106 mph, 171 km/h; power-weight ratio: 28 lb/hp (38 lb/kW), 12.7 kg/hp (17.3 kg/kW); carrying capacity: 1,510 lb, 685 kg; acceleration: standing ¼ mile 19.3 sec; consumption: 24.6 m/imp gal, 20.5 m/US gal, 11.5 l x 100 km at 75 mph, 120 Km/h.

CHASSIS reinforced suspension.

BRAKES lining area: front 34.1 sq in, 220 sq cm, rear 22.5 sq in, 145 sq cm, total 56.6 sq in, 365 sq cm.

DIMENSIONS AND WEIGHT wheel base: 121.65 in, 309 cm; tracks: 57.87 in, 147 cm front, 54.72 in, 139 cm rear; length: 193.70 in, 492 cm; height: 57.48 in, 146 cm; weight: 3,219 lb, 1,460 kg.

BODY estate car/station wagon; 4 + 1 doors; back seat folding down to luggage table; heated rear window with wiper-washer.

PRACTICAL INSTRUCTIONS tyre pressure: front 31 psi, 2.2 atm, rear 34 psi, 2.4 atm.

OPTIONAL ACCESSORIES automatic transmission not available.

CX 2400 Familiale Super

See CX 2400 Break Super, except for:

PRICE EX WORKS: 43,560* francs

BODY 7 seats.

CX 2400 Pallas

See CX 2400 Super, except for:

PRICE IN GB: £ 4,940*
PRICE EX WORKS: 39,860* francs

PERFORMANCE power-weight ratio: 24.9 lb/hp (33.9 lb/kW), 11.3 kg/kW (15.4 kg/kW).

DIMENSIONS AND WEIGHT weight: 2,867 lb, 1,300 kg.

BODY luxury equipment.

OPTIONAL ACCESSORIES leather upholstery.

CITROËN CX 2400 GTI

CITROËN CX Prestige

CX 2400 GTI

See CX 2400 Super, except for:

PRICE EX WORKS: 53,560* francs

ENGINE max power (DIN): 128 hp (94.2 kW) at 4,800 rpm; max torque (DIN): 146 lb ft, 20.1 kg m (197.1 Nm) at 3,600 rpm; max engine rpm: 5,500; 54.5 hp/l (40.1 kW/l); Bosch L-Jetronic fuel injection system; cooling system: 21.6 imp pt, 26 US pt, 12.3 l.

TRANSMISSION gears: 5, fully synchronized; ratios: I 3.166, II 1.833, III 1.290, IV 0.939, V 0.733, rev 3.153; axle ratio: 4.769; tyres: 185 HR x 14.

PERFORMANCE max speed: 117 mph, 189 km/h; power-weight ratio: 23.7 lb/hp (32.2 lb/kW), 10.7 kg/hp (14.6 kg/kW); acceleration: standing ¼ mile 17.1 sec; speed in top at 1,000 rpm: 16.4 mph, 26.4 km/h; consumption: 28 m/imp gal, 23.3 m/US gal, 10.1 l x 100 km at 75 mph, 120 km/h.

STEERING servo, variable ratio (standard); turns lock to lock: 2.50.

ELECTRICAL EQUIPMENT 60 Ah battery; 1,120 W alternator.

DIMENSIONS AND WEIGHT weight: 3,032 lb, 1,375 kg.

BODY leather upholstery.

OPTIONAL ACCESSORIES semi-automatic transmission not available.

CX Prestige

See CX 2400 Super, except for:

PRICE IN GB: £ 7,770*
PRICE EX WORKS: 56,000* francs

ENGINE max power (DIN): 128 hp (94.2 kW) at 4,800 rpm; max torque (DIN): 146 lb ft, 20.1 kg/m (197.1 Nm) at 3,600 rpm; max engine rpm: 5,500; 54.5 hp/l (40.1 kW/l); Bosch L-Jetronic fuel injection system; cooling system: 21.6 imp pt, 26 US pt, 12.3 l.

TRANSMISSION gears: 5, fully synchronized; ratios: I 3.166, II 1.833, III 1.290, IV 0.939, V 0.733, rev 3.153; axle ratio: 4.357; tyres: 185 HR x 14.

PERFORMANCE max speed: 118 mph, 190 km/h; power-weight ratio: 25.4 lb/hp (34.5 lb/kW), 11.5 kg/hp (15.6 kg/kW); acceleration: standing ¼ mile 17.6 sec; speed in top at 1,000 rpm: 18 mph, 28.9 km/h; consumption: 29.1 m/imp gal, 24.2 m/US gal, 9.7 l x 100 km at 75 mph, 120 km/h.

STEERING servo, variable ratio (standard); turns lock to lock: 2.50.

ELECTRICAL EQUIPMENT 70 Ah battery; 1,120 W alternator.

DIMENSIONS AND WEIGHT wheel base: 121.65 in, 309 cm; length: 193.31 in, 491 cm; weight: 3,252 lb, 1,475 cm; turning circle (between walls): 40 ft, 12.2 m.

CX PRESTIGE

BODY limousine; 4 seats; luxury equipment; headrests on front and rear seats; electrically-controlled windows; vinyl roof; air-conditioning (standard).

VARIATIONS

ENGINE max power (DIN) 115 hp (84.6 kW) at 5,500 rpm, max torque (DIN) 133 lb ft, 18.3 kg m (179.5 Nm) at 2,750 rpm, max engine rpm 5,750, 49 hp/l (36 kW/l), 1 Weber 34 DMTR 35 downdraught twin barrel carburettor.
TRANSMISSION semi-automatic transmission, hydraulic torque converter and planetary gears with 3 ratios (I 1.944, II 1.133, III 0.800, rev 2.389).
PERFORMANCE max speed 109 mph, 176 km/h, power-weight ratio 28.3 lb/hp (38.4 lb/kW), 12.8 kg/hp (17.4 kg/kW), acceleration standing ¼ mile 19.5 sec, speed in top at 1,000 rpm 19.3 mph, 31 km/h, consumption 24.1 m/imp gal, 20.1 m/US gal, 11.7 l x 100 km at 75 mph, 120 km/h.

OPTIONAL ACCESSORIES tinted glass; glass partition.

MATRA   FRANCE

MATRA Simca Rancho

Simca Rancho

PRICE EX WORKS: 35,995* francs

ENGINE Simca, front, transverse, slanted 41° to rear, 4 stroke; 4 cylinders, in line; 88 cu in, 1,442 cc (3.02 x 3.07 in, 76.7 x 78 mm); compression ratio: 9.5:1; max power (DIN) 80 hp (58.9 kW) at 5,600 rpm; max torque (DIN) 87 lb ft, 12 kg m (117.7 Nm) at 3,000 rpm; max engine rpm: 6,000; 55.5 hp/l (40.8 kW/l); cast iron block, light alloy head; 5 crankshaft bearings; valves: overhead, in line, push-rods and rockers; camshafts: 1, side; lubrication: gear pump, full flow filter, 5.3 imp pt, 6.3 US pt, 3 l; 1 Weber 36 DCNVA downdraught twin barrel carburettor; fuel feed: mechanical pump; sealed circuit cooling, expansion tank, liquid, 10.6 imp pt, 12.7 US pt, 6 l, electric thermostatic fan.

TRANSMISSION driving wheels: front; clutch: single dry plate (diaphragm), hydraulically controlled; gearbox: mechanical; gears: 4, fully synchronized; ratios: I 3.900, II 2.312, III 1.524, IV 1.080, rev 3.769; lever: central; final drive: cylindrical gears; axle ratio: 3.706; width of rims: 5.5''; tyres: 185/70 SR x 14.

PERFORMANCE max speed: 90 mph, 145 km/h; power-weight ratio: 31.1 lb/hp (42.3 lb/kW), 14.1 kg/hp (19.2 kg/kW); carrying capacity: 1,103 lb, 500 kg; speed in top at 1,000 rpm: 17.6 mph, 28.4 km/h; consumption: 24.6 m/imp gal, 20.5 m/US gal, 11.5 l x 100 km at 75 mph, 120 km/h.

CHASSIS integral; front suspension: independent, wishbones, longitudinal torsion bars, anti-roll bar, telescopic dampers; rear: independent, swinging longitudinal trailing arms, transverse torsion bars, anti-roll bar, telescopic dampers.

STEERING rack-and-pinion; turns lock to lock: 3.75.

BRAKES front disc (diameter 9.37 in, 23.8 cm), rear drum, rear compensator, servo; swept area: front 158.8 sq in, 1,024 sq cm, rear 90.2 sq in, 582 sq cm, total 249 sq in, 1,606 sq cm.

ELECTRICAL EQUIPMENT 12 V; 40 Ah battery; 40 A alternator; Ducellier distributor; 4 iodine headlamps.

DIMENSIONS AND WEIGHT wheel base: 99.21 in, 252 cm; tracks: 55.51 in, 141 cm front, 53.15 in, 135 cm rear; length: 169.68 in, 431 cm; width: 65.35 in, 166 cm; height: 68.11 in, 173 cm; ground clearance: 6.57 in, 16.7 cm front, 6.69 in, 17 cm rear; weight: 2,492 lb, 1,130 kg; turning circle (between walls): 36.1 ft, 11 m; fuel tank: 13.2 imp gal, 15.8 US gal, 60 l.

BODY estate car/station wagon; 2 + 1 doors; 5 seats, separate front seats, reclining backrests with built-in headrests; back seat folding down to luggage table; heated rear window with wiper-washer.

PRACTICAL INSTRUCTIONS fuel: 95 oct petrol; oil: engine 5.3 imp pt, 6.3 US pt, 3 l, SAE 20W-40, change every 3,100 miles, 5,000 km - gearbox and final drive 1.9 imp pt, 2.3 US pt, 1.1 l, SAE 90 EP, change every 6,200 miles, 10,000 km; greasing: none.

OPTIONAL ACCESSORIES light alloy wheels; metallic spray; tinted glass.

Simca Bagheera

PRICE EX WORKS: 39,300* francs

ENGINE Simca, central, transverse, slanted 41° to rear, 4 stroke; 4 cylinders, in line; 79 cu in, 1,294 cc (3.02 x 2.76 in, 76.7 x 70 mm); compression ratio: 9.5:1; max power (DIN): 84 hp (61.8 kW) at 6,000 rpm; max torque (DIN): 78 lb ft, 10.8 kg m (105.9 Nm) at 3,200 rpm; max engine rpm: 6,000; 64.9 hp/l (47.8 kW/l); cast iron block, light alloy head; 5 crankshaft bearings; valves: overhead, push-rods and rockers; camshafts: 1, side; lubrication: gear pump, full flow filter, 5.3 imp pt, 6.3 US pt, 3 l; 2 Weber 36 DCNF downdraught twin barrel carburettors; fuel feed: mechanical pump; sealed circuit cooling, expansion tank, radiator on front, electric thermostatic fan, 17.6 imp pt, 21.1 US pt, 10 l.

TRANSMISSION driving wheels: rear; clutch: single dry plate (diaphragm), hydraulically controlled; gearbox: mechanical; gears: 4, fully synchronized; ratios: I 3.900, II 2.312, III 1.524, IV 1.080, rev 3.769; lever: central; final drive: cylindrical gears; axle ratio: 3.588; width of rims: 5.5''; tyres: 155 HR x 13 front, 185 HR x 13 rear.

PERFORMANCE max speeds: (I) 33 mph, 53 km/h; (II) 53 mph, 85 km/h; (III) 81 mph, 130 km/h; (IV) 102 mph, 164 km/h; power-weight ratio: 25.7 lb/hp (35 lb/kW), 11.7 kg/hp (15.9 kg/kW); acceleration: standing ¼ mile 18.7 sec; speed in top at 1,000 rpm: 17.7 mph, 28.5 km/h; consumption: 31 m/imp gal, 25.8 m/US gal, 9.1 l x 100 km.

CHASSIS integral, box-type reinforced platform; front suspension: independent, wishbones, longitudinal torsion bars, anti-roll bar, telescopic dampers; rear: independent, swinging longitudinal trailing arms, transverse torsion bars, anti-roll bar, telescopic dampers.

STEERING rack-and-pinion; turns lock to lock: 3.25.

BRAKES disc (front diameter 9.37 in, 23.8 cm, rear 9.21 in, 23.4 cm), rear compensator, servo; swept area: front 158.8 sq in, 1,024 sq cm, rear 161.6 sq in, 1,042 sq cm, total 320.4 sq in, 2,066 sq cm.

ELECTRICAL EQUIPMENT 12 V; 40 Ah battery; 40 A alternator; Ducellier distributor; 4 headlamps, 2 retractable iodine long-distance lights.

DIMENSIONS AND WEIGHT wheel base: 93.31 in, 237 cm; tracks: 55.12 in, 140 cm front, 57.48 in, 146 cm rear; length: 157.87 in, 401 cm; width: 68.39 in, 174 cm; height: 48.03 in, 122 cm; ground clearance: 6.73 in, 17.1 cm front, 7.48 in, 19 cm rear; weight: 2,161 lb, 980 kg; weight distribution: 41% front, 59% rear; turning circle (between walls): 32.8 ft, 10 m; fuel tank: 12.3 imp gal, 14.8 US gal, 56 l.

BODY coupé in plastic material; 3 front seats in a row, separate driving seat, built-in headrests; heated rear window.

MATRA Simca Bagheera X

PRACTICAL INSTRUCTIONS fuel: 98-100 oct petrol; oil: engine 5.3 imp pt, 6.3 US pt, 3 l, SAE 20W-40, change every 3,100 miles, 5,000 km - gearbox and final drive 1.9 imp pt, 2.3 US pt, 1.1 l, SAE 90 EP, change every 6,200 miles, 10,000 km; greasing: none; tyre pressure: front 20 psi, 1.4 atm, rear 28 psi, 2 atm.

OPTIONAL ACCESSORIES light alloy wheels; electrically-controlled windows; tinted glass; sunshine roof.

Simca Bagheera S

See Simca Bagheera, except for:

PRICE EX WORKS: 43,100* francs

ENGINE 88 cu in, 1,442 cc (3.02 x 3.07 in, 76.7 x 78 mm); max power (DIN): 90 hp (66.2 kW) at 5,800 rpm; max torque (DIN): 88 lb ft, 12.2 kg m (119.6 Nm) at 3,200 rpm; 62.4 hp/l (45.9 kW/l).

TRANSMISSION axle ratio: 3.470.

PERFORMANCE max speeds: (I) 34 mph, 55 km/h; (II) 54 mph, 87 km/h; (III) 83 mph, 133 km/h; (IV) 115 mph, 185 km/h; power-weight ratio: 24.9 lb/hp (33.8 kW/kW), 11.3 kg/hp (15.3 kg/kW); acceleration: standing ¼ mile 17.7 sec; speed in top at 1,000 rpm: 18.3 mph, 29.4 km/h; consumption: 22.2 m/imp gal, 18.5 m/US gal, 12.7 l x 100 km.

ELECTRICAL EQUIPMENT 48 Ah battery; 50 A alternator.

DIMENSIONS AND WEIGHT weight: 2,238 lb, 1,015 kg.

BODY electrically-controlled tinted glass (standard).

Simca Bagheera X

See Simca Bagheera S, except for:

PRICE EX WORKS: 46,930* francs

TRANSMISSION light alloy wheels.

BODY luxury equipment; heated rear window with wiper-washer.

PEUGEOT   FRANCE

104 GL Berline

PRICE IN GB: £ 2,287*
PRICE EX WORKS: 21,100* francs

ENGINE front, transverse, slanted 72° to rear, 4 stroke; 4 cylinders, in line; 58.2 cu in, 954 cc (2.76 x 2.44 in, 70 x 62 mm); compression ratio: 8.8:1; max power (DIN): 44 hp (32.4 kW) at 6,000 rpm; max torque (DIN): 45 lb ft, 6.2 kg m (61.3 Nm) at 3,000 rpm; max engine rpm: 6,250; 46.1 hp/l (34 kW/l); light alloy block and head, wet liners, bi-hemispherical combustion chambers; 5 crankshaft bearings; valves: overhead, Vee-slanted, rockers; camshafts: 1, overhead; lubrication: gear pump, full flow filter, 7.9 imp pt, 9.5 US pt, 4.5 l; 1 Solex 32 HSA2 horizontal single barrel carburettor; fuel feed: mechanical pump; water-cooled, 9.9 imp pt, 11.8 US pt, 5.6 l, electric thermostatic fan.

TRANSMISSION driving wheels: front; clutch: single dry plate (diaphragm); gearbox: mechanical, in unit with engine and final drive; gears: 4, fully synchronized; ratios: I 3.882, II 2.296, III 1.501, IV 1.042, rev 3.568; lever: central; final drive: spiral bevel; axle ratio: 4.067; width of rims: 4''; tyres: 135 SR x 13.

PERFORMANCE max speeds: (I) 28 mph, 45 km/h; (II) 47 mph, 76 km/h; (III) 72 mph, 116 km/h; (IV) 84 mph, 135 km/h; power-weight ratio: 43.8 lb/hp (54.1 lb/kW), 19.9 kg/hp (24.5 kg/kW); carrying capacity: 882 lb, 400 kg; acceleration: standing ¼ mile 20.5 sec; speed in top at 1,000 rpm: 14.7 mph, 23.6 km/h; consumption: 33.2 m/imp gal, 27.7 m/US gal, 8.5 l x 100 km.

CHASSIS integral; front suspension: independent, by McPherson, coil springs/telescopic damper struts, lower wishbones (trailing links), anti-roll bar; rear: independent, swinging longitudinal trailing arms, coil springs, telescopic dampers.

STEERING rack-and-pinion; turns lock to lock: 3.33.

BRAKES front disc (diameter 9.49 in, 24.1 cm), rear drum, rear compensator; swept area: front 176.1 sq in, 1,136 sq cm, rear 68.4 sq in, 441 sq cm, total 244.5 sq in, 1,577 sq cm.

MATRA Simca Bagheera X

ELECTRICAL EQUIPMENT 12 V; 30 Ah battery; 500 W alternator; Ducellier or Paris-Rhone distributor; 2 headlamps.

DIMENSIONS AND WEIGHT wheel base: 95.28 in, 242 cm; tracks: 50.79 in, 129 cm front, 48.82 in, 124 cm rear; length: 140.94 in, 358 cm; width: 59.84 in, 152 cm; height: 55.12 in, 140 cm; ground clearance: 5.04 in, 12.8 cm; weight: 1,753 lb, 795 kg; turning circle (between walls): 33.1 ft, 10.1 m; fuel tank: 8.8 imp gal, 10.6 US gal, 40 l.

BODY saloon/sedan; 4 + 1 doors; 4 seats, separate front seats; back seat folding down to luggage table.

PRACTICAL INSTRUCTIONS fuel: 88 oct petrol; oil: engine, gearbox and final drive 7 imp pt, 8.5 US pt, 4 l, SAE 10W-50, change every 3,100 miles, 5,000 km; greasing: every 3,100 miles, 5,000 km, 1 point; valve timing: -2° 32° 33°30' -2°; tyre pressure: front 26 psi, 1.8 atm, rear 28 psi, 2 atm.

OPTIONAL ACCESSORIES heated rear window; sunshine roof.

104 GL6 Berline

See 104 GL Berline, except for:

PRICE EX WORKS: 22,650* francs

ENGINE 68.6 cu in, 1,124 cc (2.83 x 2.72 in, 72 x 69 mm); compression ratio: 9.2:1; max power (DIN): 57 hp (42 kW)

at 6,000 rpm; max torque (DIN): 59 lb ft, 8.2 kg m (80.4 Nm) at 3,000 rpm; max engine rpm: 6,500; 50.7 hp/l (37.4 kW/l); lubricating system: 8.8 imp pt, 10.6 US pt, 5 l; 1 Solex 32 PBISA7 downdraught twin barrel carburettor.

TRANSMISSION axle ratio: 3.867.

PERFORMANCE max speed: 90 mph, 145 km/h; power-weight ratio: 31.1 lb/hp (42.3 lb/kW), 14.1 kg/hp (19.2 kg/kW); acceleration: standing ¼ mile 20 sec; speed in top at 1,000 rpm: 15.5 mph, 24.9 km/h; consumption: 33.6 m/imp gal, 28 m/US gal, 8.4 l x 100 km.

DIMENSIONS AND WEIGHT length: 142.36 in, 362 cm; height: 55.35 in, 141 cm; ground clearance: 4.80 in, 12.2 cm; weight: 1,775 lb, 805 kg.

PRACTICAL INSTRUCTIONS fuel: 95 oct petrol; oil: engine, gearbox and final drive 7.9 imp pt, 9.5 US pt, 4.5 l; valve timing: 5°20' 36°50' 36°50' 5°20'.

104 SL Berline

See 104 GL6 Berline, except for:

PRICE IN GB: £ 2,600*
PRICE EX WORKS: 23,700* francs

TRANSMISSION axle ratio: 4.067; width of rims: 4.5''; tyres: 145 SR x 13.

PERFORMANCE power-weight ratio: 31.5 lb/hp (42.8 lb/kW), 14.3 kg/hp (19.4 kg/kW); speed in top at 1,000 rpm: 14.5 mph, 24.3 km/h.

DIMENSIONS AND WEIGHT weight: 1,797 lb, 815 kg.

BODY heated rear window (standard).

OPTIONAL ACCESSORIES metallic spray; tinted glass; rear window wiper-washer.

104 ZL Coupé

See 104 GL Berline, except for:

PRICE EX WORKS: 21,350* francs

PERFORMANCE max speed: over 84 mph, 135 km/h; carrying capacity: 706 lb, 320 kg; consumption: 35.2 m/imp gal, 27 m/US gal, 8.7 l x 100 km.

DIMENSIONS AND WEIGHT wheel base: 87.80 in, 223 cm; length: 128.92 in, 330 cm; height: 52.76 in, 134 cm; ground clearance: 4.72 in, 12 cm; turning circle (between walls): 30.8 ft, 9.4 m.

BODY coupé; 2 + 1 doors.

OPTIONAL ACCESSORIES tinted glass with rear window wiper-washer.

PEUGEOT 104 GL Berline

104 ZS Coupé

See 104 ZL Coupé, except for:

PRICE IN GB: £ 2,704*
PRICE EX WORKS: 24,400* francs

ENGINE 68.6 cu in, 1,124 cc (2.83 x 2.72 in, 72 x 69 mm); compression ratio: 9.2:1; max power (DIN): 66 hp (48.6 kW) at 6,200 rpm; max torque (DIN): 62 lb ft, 8.5 kg m (83.4 Nm) at 4,000 rpm; max engine rpm: 6,500; 58.5 hp/l (43.2 kW/l); lubricating system: 8.8 imp pt, 10.6 US pt, 5 l; 1 Solex 32 PBISA7 downdraught twin barrel carburettor.

TRANSMISSION axle ratio: 3.867; width of rims: 4.5''; tyres: 145 SR x 13.

PERFORMANCE max speed: over 96 mph, 155 km/h; power-weight ratio: 26.1 lb/hp (35.4 lb/kW), 11.8 kg/hp (16 kg/kW); acceleration: standing ¼ mile 19 sec; speed in top at 1,000 rpm: 15.9 mph, 25.6 km/h; consumption: 34.9 m/imp gal, 29 m/US gal, 8.1 l x 100 km.

CHASSIS rear suspension: anti-roll bar.

BRAKES servo.

ELECTRICAL EQUIPMENT halogen headlamps.

DIMENSIONS AND WEIGHT weight: 1,720 lb, 780 kg.

BODY (standard) reclining backrests with built-in headrests, heated rear window, rev counter.

PRACTICAL INSTRUCTIONS fuel: 95 oct petrol; oil: engine, gearbox and final drive 7.9 imp pt, 9.5 US pt, 4.5 l; valve timing: 5º20' 36º50' 36º50' 5º20'.

OPTIONAL ACCESSORIES metallic spray; tinted glass; rear window wiper-washer.

304 GL Berline

PRICE IN GB: £ 2,810*
PRICE EX WORKS: 24,450* francs

ENGINE front, transverse, slanted 20º to front, 4 stroke; 4 cylinders, in line; 78.7 cu in, 1,290 cc (3.07 x 2.66 in, 78 x 67.5 mm); compression ratio: 8.8:1; max power (DIN): 65 hp (47.8 kW) at 6,000 rpm; max torque (DIN): 70 lb ft, 9.6 kg m (9.41 Nm) at 3,750 rpm; max engine rpm: 6,100; 50.4 hp/l (37.1 kW/l); light alloy block and head. wet liners, bi-hemispherical combustion chambers; 5 crankshaft bearings; valves: overhead, Vee-slanted, rockers; cam'shafts: 1 overhead; lubrication: rotary pump, cartridge on by-pass, 7 imp pt, 8.5 US pt, 4 l; 1 Solex 34 PBISA4 downdraught single barrel carburettor; fuel feed: mechanical pump; water-cooled, 10.2 imp pt, 12.3 US pt, 5.8 l, electromagnetically-operated fan.

TRANSMISSION driving wheels: front; clutch: single dry plate (diaphragm), hydraulically controlled; gearbox: mechanical; gears: 4, fully synchronized; ratios: I 3.650, II 2.217, III 1.451, IV 0.986, rev 3.953; lever: steering column; final drive: helical spur gears; axle ratio: 4.065; width of rims: 4.5''; tyres: 145 SR x 14.

PERFORMANCE max speeds: (I) 27 mph, 44 km/h; (II) 45 mph, 73 km/h; (III) 69 mph, 111 km/h; (IV) 93 mph, 150 km/h; power-weight ratio: 31.6 lb/hp (42.9 lb/kW), 14.3 kg/hp (19.5 kg/kW); carrying capacity: 882 lb, 400 kg; acceleration: standing ¼ mile 19.5 sec; speed in top at 1,000 rpm: 16.7 mph, 26.9 km/h; consumption: 31.7 m/imp gal, 26.4 m/US gal, 8.9 l x 100 km.

CHASSIS integral; front suspension: independent, by McPherson, coil springs/telescopic dampers, lower wishbones, anti-roll bar; rear: independent, swinging longitudinal trailing arms, anti-roll bar, coil springs/telescopic dampers.

STEERING rack-and-pinion; turns lock to lock: 3.75.

BRAKES front disc (diameter 10.08 in, 25.6 cm), rear drum, rear compensator, servo; swept area: front 192.2 sq in, 1,240 sq cm, rear 89.1 sq in, 575 sq cm, total 281.3 sq in, 1,815 sq cm.

ELECTRICAL EQUIPMENT 12 V; 44 Ah battery; 500 W alternator; Ducellier distributor; 2 headlamps.

DIMENSIONS AND WEIGHT wheel base: 101.97 in, 259 cm; tracks: 51.97 in, 132 cm front, 50.79 in, 129 cm rear; length: 162.99 in, 414 cm; width: 61.81 in, 157 cm; height: 55.51 in, 141 cm; ground clearance: 4.72 in, 12 cm; weight: 2,051 lb, 930 kg; turning circle (between walls): 34.8 ft, 10.6 m; fuel tank: 9.2 imp gal, 11.1 US gal, 42 l.

BODY saloon/sedan; 4 doors; 5 seats, separate front seats, reclining backrests; heated rear window.

PRACTICAL INSTRUCTIONS fuel: 95 oct petrol; oil: engine, gearbox and final drive 7 imp pt, 8.5 US pt, 4 l, SAE

PEUGEOT 104 ZS Coupé

PEUGEOT 304 SL Break

PEUGEOT 304 SLS Berline

20W-40, change every 3,100 miles, 5,000 km; greasing: every 3,100 miles, 5,000 km, 5 points; tyre pressure: front 23 psi, 1.6 atm, rear 27 psi, 1.9 atm.

OPTIONAL ACCESSORIES sunshine roof; metallic spray.

304 GL Break

See 304 GL Berline, except for:

PRICE IN GB: £ 2,827*
PRICE EX WORKS: 24,500* francs

ENGINE 68.8 cu in, 1,127 cc (3.07 x 2.32 in, 78 x 59 mm); max power (DIN) 59 hp (43.4 kW) at 6,250 rpm; max torque (DIN): 59 lb ft, 8.2 kg m (80.4 Nm) at 3,750 rpm; 52.3 hp/l (38.5 kW/l).

PERFORMANCE max speed: 87 mph, 140 km/h; power-weight ratio: 35.5 lb/hp (48.3 lb/kW), 16.1 kg/hp (21.9 kg/kW); carrying capacity: 1,014 lb, 460 kg; acceleration: standing ¼ mile 21.1 sec; speed in top at 1,000 rpm: 16.3 mph, 26.2 km/h.

DIMENSIONS AND WEIGHT length: 157.87 in, 401 cm; height: 56 in, 142 cm; weight: 2,095 lb, 950 kg.

BODY estate car/station wagon; 4 + 1 doors; back seat folding down to luggage table.

304 GLD Berline

See 304 GL Berline, except for:

PRICE EX WORKS: 28,700* francs

ENGINE Diesel; 82.8 cu in, 1,357 cc (3.07 x 2.80 in, 78 x 71 mm); compression ratio: 23.3:1; max power (DIN): 45 hp (33.1 kW) at 5,000 rpm; max torque (DIN): 57 lb ft, 7.8 kg m (76.5 Nm) at 2,500 rpm; max engine rpm: 5,450 rpm; 33.2 hp/l (24.4 kW/l); lubricating system: 8.8 imp pt, 10.6 US pt, 5 l; heating plugs on head; Bosch injection pump; cooling system: 11.4 imp pt, 13.7 US pt, 6.5 l.

PERFORMANCE max speed: 81 mph, 130 km/h; power-weight ratio: 45.6 lb/hp (62 lb/kW), 20.7 kg/hp (28.1 kg/kW); acceleration: standing ¼ mile 22.5 sec; consumption: 34.4 m/imp gal, 28.7 m/US gal, 8.2 l x 100 km.

ELECTRICAL EQUIPMENT 60 Ah battery.

PRACTICAL INSTRUCTIONS fuel: Diesel oil; oil: engine, gearbox and final drive 8.8 imp pt, 10.6 US pt, 5 l, change every 1,600 miles, 2,500 rpm; tyre pressure: front 24 psi, 1.7 atm.

304 GLD Break

See 304 GLD Berline, except for:

PRICE EX WORKS: 28,750* francs

PERFORMANCE power-weight ratio: 46.6 lb/hp (63.3 lb/kW), 21.1 kg/hp (28.7 kg/kW); carrying capacity: 1,014 lb, 460 kg.

ELECTRICAL EQUIPMENT 65 Ah battery.

DIMENSIONS AND WEIGHT length: 157.87 in, 401 cm; height: 56.30 in, 143 cm; weight: 2,095 lb, 950 kg.

BODY estate car/station wagon; 4 + 1 doors; back seat folding down to luggage table.

304 SL Berline

See 304 GL Berline, except for:

PRICE EX WORKS: 25,800* francs

TRANSMISSION lever: central.

ELECTRICAL EQUIPMENT halogen headlamps.

BODY built-in headrests; metallic spray and sunshine roof (standard).

OPTIONAL ACCESSORIES tinted glass.

304 SL Break

See 304 SL Berline, except for:

PRICE IN GB: £ 3,051*
PRICE EX WORKS: 26,550* francs

PERFORMANCE power-weight ratio: 32.2 lb/hp (43.8 lb/kW), 14.6 kg/hp (19.9 kg/kW); carrying capacity: 1,014 lb, 460 kg.

DIMENSIONS AND WEIGHT length: 157.87 in, 401 cm; weight: 2,095 lb, 950 kg.

BODY estate car/station wagon; 4 + 1 doors; back seat folding down to luggage table.

PRACTICAL INSTRUCTIONS tyre pressure: rear 35 psi, 2.5 atm.

OPTIONAL ACCESSORIES rear window wiper-washer.

304 SLS Berline

See 304 GL Berline, except for:

PRICE IN GB: 3,151* (with sunshine roof)
PRICE EX WORKS: 26,950* francs

ENGINE max power (DIN): 74.5 hp (54.9 kW) at 6,000 rpm; max torque (DIN): 75 lb ft, 10.3 kg m (101 Nm) at 3,750 rpm; 57.8 hp/l (42.6 kW/l); 1 Solex 35 EEISA downdraught twin barrel carburettor; cooling system: 11.8 imp pt, 14.2 US pt, 6.7 l.

TRANSMISSION lever: central.

PERFORMANCE max speed: 99 mph, 160 km/h; power-weight ratio: 27.5 lb/hp (37.4 lb/kW), 12.5 kg/hp (16.9 kg/kW); acceleration: standing ¼ mile 18.6 sec; consumption: 32.1 m/imp gal, 26.7 m/US gal, 8.8 l x 100 km.

ELECTRICAL EQUIPMENT halogen headlamps.

BODY built-in headrests; metallic spray and sunshine roof (standard).

OPTIONAL ACCESSORIES tinted glass.

305 GL/305 GR

PRICES EX WORKS: 305 GL: 26,300* francs
305 GR: 27,900* francs

ENGINE front, transverse, slanted 20° to front, 4 stroke; 4 cylinders, in line; 78.7 cu in, 1,290 cc (3.07 x 2.66 in, 78 x 67.5 mm); compression ratio: 8.8:1; max power (DIN): 65 hp (47.8 kW) at 6,000 rpm; max torque (DIN): 70 lb ft, 9.6 kg m (94.1 Nm) at 3,750 rpm; max engine rpm: 6,500; 50.4 hp/l (37.1 kW/l); light alloy block and head, wet liners, bi-hemispherical combustion chambers; 5 crankshaft bearings; valves: overhead, Vee-slanted; rockers; camshafts: 1, overhead; lubrication: rotary pump, cartridge on by-pass, 7 imp pt, 8.5 US pt, 4 l; 1 Solex 34 PBISA5 downdraught single barrel carburettor; fuel feed: mechanical pump; water-cooled, 10.2 imp pt, 12.3 US pt, 5.8 l, electro-magnetically-operated fan.

TRANSMISSION driving wheels: front; clutch: single dry plate (diaphragm); gearbox: mechanical; gears: 4, fully synchronized; ratios: I 3.650, II 2.217, III 1.451, IV 0.986, rev 3.952; lever: central; final drive: helical spur gears; axle ratio: 4.065; width of rims: 4.5''; tyres: 165 SR x 13.

PERFORMANCE max speed: 91 mph, 147 km/h; power-weight ratio: 31.3 lb/hp (42.7 lb/kW), 14.2 kg/hp (19.4 kg/kW); carrying capacity: 915 lb, 415 kg; acceleration: standing ¼ mile 19.9 sec; speed in top at 1,000 rpm: 16.7 mph, 26.9 km/h; consumption: 31.4 m/imp gal, 26.1 m/US gal, 9 l x 100 km.

CHASSIS integral; front suspension: independent, by McPherson, coil springs/telescopic dampers, lower wishbones, anti-roll bar; rear: independent, coil springs, anti-roll bar, telescopic dampers.

STEERING rack-and-pinion; turns lock to lock: 3.60.

BRAKES front disc (diameter 10.35 in, 26.3 cm), rear drum, rear compensator, servo; swept area: total 275.2 sq in, 1,775 sq cm.

ELECTRICAL EQUIPMENT 12 V; 45 Ah battery; 500 W alternator; Ducellier distributor; 2 headlamps.

DIMENSIONS AND WEIGHT wheel base: 103.15 in, 262 cm; tracks: 53.94 in, 137 cm front, 51.97 in, 132 cm rear; length: 166.93 in, 424 cm; width: 64.17 in, 163 cm; height: 55.12 in, 140 cm; ground clearance: 4.96 in, 12.6 cm; weight: 2,040 lb, 925 kg; turning circle (betwen walls): 35.4 ft, 10.8 m; fuel tank: 9.5 imp gal, 11.4 US gal, 43 l.

BODY saloon/sedan; 4 doors; 5 seats, separate front seats, reclining backrests, heated rear window.

PRACTICAL INSTRUCTIONS fuel: 97 oct petrol; oil: engine, gearbox and final drive 7 imp pt, 8.5 US pt, 4 l, SAE 10W-40, change every 4,750 miles, 7,500 km; valve timing: 6° 38° 45° 1°; tyre pressure: front 26 psi, 1.8 atm, rear 30 psi, 2.1 atm.

OPTIONAL ACCESSORIES sunshine roof.

305 SR

See 305 GL/305 GR, except for:

PRICE EX WORKS: 29,600* francs

ENGINE 89.8 cu in, 1,472 cc (3.07 x 3.03 in, 78 x 77 mm); compression ratio: 9.2:1; max power (DIN): 74 hp (54.5 kW) at 6,000 rpm; max torque (DIN): 86 lb ft, 11.8 kg m (115.7 Nm) at 3,000 rpm; 50.3 hp/l (37 kW/l); 1 Solex 35 PBISA9 downdraught single barrel carburettor.

TRANSMISSION gearbox ratios: I 3.344, II 1.930, III 1.312, IV 0.929, rev 3.436.

PERFORMANCE max speed: 95 mph, 153 km/h; power-weight ratio: 28 lb/hp (38 lb/kW), 12.7 kg/hp (17.2 kg/kW); acceleration: standing ¼ mile 18.5 sec; speed in top at 1,000 rpm: 17.8 mph, 28.6 km/h; consumption: 34 m/imp gal, 28.3 m/US gal, 8.3 l x 100 km.

DIMENSIONS AND WEIGHT ground clearance: 4.72 in, 12 cm; weight: 2,073 lb, 940 kg.

PRACTICAL INSTRUCTIONS valve timing: 3° 41° 42° 2°.

PEUGEOT 305 SR

PEUGEOT 305 SR

PEUGEOT 504 GL Berline

504 L Berline

PRICE IN GB: £ 3,730*
PRICE IN USA: $ 7,490*

ENGINE front, slanted 45° to right, 4 stroke; 4 cylinders, in line; 109.6 cu in, 1,796 cc (3.31 x 3.19 in, 84 x 81 mm); compression ratio: 7.5:1; max power (DIN): 79 hp (58.1 kW) at 5,100 rpm; max torque (DIN): 105 lb ft, 14.5 kg m (142.2 Nm) at 2,500 rpm; max engine rpm: 5,500; 44 hp/l (32.3 kW/l); cast iron block, wet liners, light alloy head, hemispherical combustion chambers; 5 crankshaft bearings; valves: overhead, Vee-slanted, push-rods and rockers; camshafts: 1, side; lubrication: gear pump, metal gauze filter, 7 imp pt, 8.5 US pt, 4 l; 1 Solex 34 PBICA-9 downdraught single barrel carburettor; fuel feed: mechanical pump; water-cooled, 13.7 imp pt, 16.5 US pt, 7.8 l, electromagnetic thermostatic fan.

TRANSMISSION driving wheels: rear; clutch: single dry plate (diaphragm), hydraulically controlled; gearbox: mechanical; gears: 4, fully synchronized; ratios: I 3.663, II 2.169, III 1.408, IV 1, rev 3.636; lever: steering column; final drive: hypoid bevel; axle ratio: 3.888; width of rims: 4.5''; tyres: 165 SR x 14.

PERFORMANCE max speeds: (I) 25 mph, 40 km/h; (II) 43 mph, 70 km/h; (III) 65 mph, 105 km/h; (IV) 96 mph, 154 km/h; power-weight ratio: 31 lb/hp (42.1 lb/kW), 14.1 kg/hp (19.1 kg/kW); carrying capacity: 1,169 lb, 530 kg; acceleration: standing ¼ mile 19.3 sec, 0-50 mph (0-80 km/h) 10.6 sec; speed in direct drive at 1,000 rpm: 18.1 mph, 29.1 km/h; consumption: 26.9 m/imp gal, 22.4 m/US gal, 10.5 l x 100 km.

CHASSIS integral; front suspension: independent, by McPherson, coil springs/telescopic damper struts, lower wishbones, anti-roll bar; rear: rigid axle, trailing lower radius arms, upper oblique torque arms, coil springs, anti-roll bar, telescopic dampers.

STEERING rack-and-pinion; turns lock to lock: 4.50.

BRAKES front disc (diameter 10.75 in, 27.3 cm), rear drum, rear compensator, servo; swept area: total 400.5 sq in, 2,583 sq cm.

ELECTRICAL EQUIPMENT 12 V; 60 Ah battery; 500 W alternator; Ducellier distributor; 2 headlamps.

DIMENSIONS AND WEIGHT wheel base: 107.87 in, 274 cm; tracks: 55.91 in, 142 cm front, 53.54 in, 136 cm rear; length: 176.77 in, 449 cm; width: 66.54 in, 169 cm; height: 57.48 in, 146 cm; ground clearance: 6.30 in, 16 cm; weight: 2,448 lb, 1,110 kg; turning circle (between walls): 35.8 ft, 10.9 m; fuel tank: 12.3 imp gal, 14.8 US gal, 56 l.

BODY saloon/sedan; 4 doors; 5 seats, separate front seats, reclining backrests; heated rear window.

PRACTICAL INSTRUCTIONS fuel: 85 oct petrol; oil: engine 7 imp pt, 8.5 US pt, 4 l, SAE 20W-40, change every 3,100 miles, 5,000 km - gearbox 1.9 imp pt, 2.3 US pt, 1.1 l, SAE 20W-40, change every 6,200 miles, 10,000 km - final drive 2.1 imp pt, 1.5 US pt, 1.2 l, GP 90, change every 6,200 miles, 10,000 km; greasing: every 3,100 miles, 5,000 km, 6 points; tappet clearances: inlet 0.004 in, 0.10 mm, exhaust 0.010 in, 0.25 mm; tyre pressure: front 21 psi, 1.5 atm, rear 26 psi, 1.8 atm.

VARIATIONS

ENGINE Diesel, slanted 20°, 118.9 cu in, 1,948 cc (3.36 x 3.15 in, 88 x 80 mm), 21.8:1 compression ratio, max power (DIN) 55 hp (40 kW) at 4,500 rpm, max torque (DIN) 80 lb ft, 11 kg m (107.9 Nm) at 2,000 rpm, max engine rpm 4,750, 28.2 hp/l (20.5 kW/l), Bosch injection pump.
PERFORMANCE max speed 83 mph, 133 km/h, power-weight ratio 46.5 lb/hp (63.9 lb/kW), 21.1 kg/hp (29 kg/kW), consumption 30.4 m/imp gal, 25.3 m/US gal, 9.3 l x 100 km.
ELECTRICAL EQUIPMENT 90 Ah battery.
DIMENSIONS AND WEIGHT weight 2,558 lb, 1,160 kg.

504 L Break

See 504 L Berline, except for:

PRICE IN GB: £ 4,107*
PRICE IN USA: $ 7,990*

ENGINE max power (DIN): 73 hp (53.7 kW) at 5,000 rpm; max torque (DIN): 101 lb ft, 14 kg m (137.7 Nm) at 2,500 rpm; 40.6 hp/l (29.9 kW/l); 1 downdraught twin barrel carburettor.

TRANSMISSION axle ratio: 4.222; width of rims: 5''; tyres: 185 SR x 14.

PERFORMANCE max speed: 91 mph, 146 km/h; power-weight ratio: 37.9 lb/hp (51.5 lb/kW), 17.2 kg/hp (23.4 kg/kW);

PEUGEOT 504 GL Break

carrying capacity: 1,477 lb, 670 kg; speed in direct drive at 1,000 rpm: 16.5 mph, 26.5 km/h; consumption: 23.5 m/imp gal, 19.6 m/US gal, 12 l x 100 km.

CHASSIS rear suspension: rigid axle, 4 coil springs.

DIMENSIONS AND WEIGHT wheel base: 114.17 in, 290 cm; length: 118.98 in, 480 cm; height: 61.02 in, 155 cm; ground clearance: 6.50 in, 16.5 cm; weight: 2,767 lb, 1,255 kg; turning circle (between walls): 37.4 ft, 11.4 m; fuel tank: 13.2 imp gal, 15.8 US gal, 60 l.

BODY estate car/station wagon; 4 + 1 doors; back seat folding down to luggage table.

VARIATIONS

ENGINE Diesel, 128.9 cu in, 2,112 cc (3.54 x 3.27 in, 90 x 83 mm), 22.2:1 compression ratio, max power (DIN) 59 hp (43 kW) at 4,500 rpm, max torque (DIN) 86 lb ft, 11.9 kg m (116.7 Nm) at 2,500 rpm, 27.9 hp/l (20.3 kW/l).
PERFORMANCE max speed 78 mph, 126 km/h, power-weight ratio 46.9 lb/hp (64.3 lb/kW), 21.3 kg/hp (29.2 kg/kW), consumption 31 m/imp gal, 25.8 m/US gal, 9.1 l x 100 km.

504 GL Berline

See 504 L Berline, except for:

PRICE IN GB: £ 4,210*
PRICE IN USA: $ 8,790

ENGINE 120.3 cu in, 1,971 cc (3.46 x 3.19 in, 88 x 81 mm); compression ratio: 8.8:1; max power (DIN): 96 hp (70.7 kW) at 5,200 rpm; max torque (DIN): 119 lb ft, 16.4 kg m (160.8 Nm) at 3,000 rpm; 48.7 hp/l (35.9 kW/l); 1 Zenith downdraught twin barrel carburettor.

TRANSMISSION gearbox ratios: I 3.558, II 2.105, III 1.366, IV 1, rev 3.636; lever: central; width of rims: 5''; tyres: 175 SR x 14.

PERFORMANCE max speed: 102 mph, 164 km/h; power-weight ratio: 28.2 lb/hp (38.4 lb/kW), 12.8 kg/hp (17.4 kg/kW); carrying capacity: 1,058 lb, 480 kg; acceleration: standing ¼ mile 18.3 sec; consumption: 27.7 m/imp gal, 23.1 m/US gal, 10.2 l x 100 km.

CHASSIS rear suspension: independent, oblique semi-trailing arms, coil springs/telescopic dampers, anti-roll bar.

BRAKES disc (diameter 10.75 in, 27.3 cm), rear compensator, servo; swept area: front 236.9 sq in, 1,528 sq cm, rear 201.6 sq in, 1,300 sq cm, total 438.5 sq in, 2,828 sq cm.

ELECTRICAL EQUIPMENT halogen headlamps.

DIMENSIONS AND WEIGHT weight: 2,712 lb, 1,230 kg.

BODY built-in adjustable headrests.

VARIATIONS

ENGINE Diesel, slanted 20°, 140.6 cu in, 2,304 cc (3.70 x 3.27 in, 94 x 83 mm), 22.2:1 compression ratio, max power (DIN) 70 hp (51.5 kW) at 4,500 rpm, max torque (DIN) 97 lb ft, 13.4 kg m (131.4 Nm) at 2,200 rpm, 30.4 hp/l (22.4 kW/l). Bosch injection pump.
PERFORMANCE max speed 88 mph, 141 km/h, power-weight ratio 40.3 lb/hp (54.8 lb/kW), 18.3 kg/hp (24.9 kg/kW), consumption 32.8 m/imp gal, 27.3 m/US gal, 8.6 l x 100 km.
ELECTRICAL EQUIPMENT 90 Ah battery.
DIMENSIONS AND WEIGHT weight 2,822 lb, 1,280 kg.

OPTIONAL ACCESSORIES ZF automatic transmission, hydraulic torque converter and planetary gears with 3 ratios (I 2.564, II 1.520, III 1, rev 2), max ratio of converter at stall 2.3, max speed 91 mph, 146 km/h; leather upholstery; sunshine roof; tinted glass; metallic spray.

504 GL Break

See 504 GL Berline, except for:

PRICE IN GB: £ 4,578*
PRICE IN USA: $ 9,290

TRANSMISSION lever: steering column; axle ratio: 4.222; tyres: 185 SR x 14.

PERFORMANCE max speed: 101 mph, 162 km/h; power-weight ratio: 30.6 lb/hp (41.5 lb/kW), 13.9 kg/hp (18.8 kg/kW); carrying capacity: 1,411 lb, 640 kg; speed in direct drive at 1,000 rpm: 17 mph, 28 km/h; consumption: 26.6 m/imp gal, 22.2 m/US gal, 10.6 l x 100 km.

CHASSIS rear suspension: rigid axle, 4 coil springs.

BRAKES rear drum; swept area: total 400.5 sq in, 2,583 sq cm.

DIMENSIONS AND WEIGHT wheel base: 114.17 in, 290 cm; length: 188.98 in, 480 cm; height: 61.02 in, 155 cm; ground clearance: 6.50 in, 16.5 cm; weight: 2,933 lb, 1,330 kg; turning circle (between walls): 37.4 ft, 11.4 m; fuel tank: 13.2 imp gal, 15.8 US gal, 60 l.

BODY estate car/station wagon; 4+1 doors; back seat folding down to luggage table.

VARIATIONS

(with Diesel engine).
PERFORMANCE max speed 81 mph, 130 km/h, power-weight ratio 44.2 lb/hp (60.1 lb/kW), 20.1 kg/hp (27.3 kg/kW), consumption 31.4 m/imp gal, 26.1 m/US gal, 9 l x 100 km.
ELECTRICAL EQUIPMENT 90 Ah battery.
DIMENSIONS AND WEIGHT weight 3,098 lb, 1,405 kg.

OPTIONAL ACCESSORIES ZF automatic transmission, 4.110 axle ratio, max speed 96 mph, 154 km/h; tinted glass; metallic spray; rear window wiper-washer.

504 Break Familial

See 504 GL Berline, except for:
PRICE IN GB: £ 4,610*
PRICE EX WORKS: 35,100* francs

TRANSMISSION lever: steering column; axle ratio: 4.222; tyres: 185 SR x 14.

PERFORMANCE max speed: 101 mph, 162 km/h; power-weight ratio: 30.6 lb/hp (41.5 lb/kW), 13.9 kg/hp (18.8 kg/kW); carrying capacity: 1,411 lb, 640 kg; speed in direct drive at 1,000 rpm: 17 mph, 28 km/h; consumption: 26.6 m/imp gal, 22.2 m/US gal, 10.6 l x 100 km.

CHASSIS rear suspension: rigid axle, 4 coil springs.

BRAKES rear drum; swept area: total 400.5 sq in, 2,583 sq cm.

DIMENSIONS AND WEIGHT wheel base: 114.17 in, 290 cm; length: 188.98 in, 480 cm; height: 61.02 in, 155 cm; ground clearance: 6.50 in, 16.5 cm; weight: 2,933 lb, 1,330 kg; turning circle (between walls): 37.4 ft, 11.4 m; fuel tank: 13.2 imp gal, 15.8 US gal, 60 l.

BODY estate car/station wagon; 4 + 1 doors; 7 seats; back seat folding down to luggage table.

VARIATIONS

(with Diesel engine).
PERFORMANCE max speed 81 mph, 130 km/h, power-weight ratio 44.4 lb/hp (60.4 lb/kW), 20.1 kg/hp (27.4 kg/kW), consumption 31.4 m/imp gal, 26.1 m/US gal, 9 l x 100 km.
ELECTRICAL EQUIPMENT 90 Ah battery.
DIMENSIONS AND WEIGHT weight 3,109 lb, 1,410 kg.

OPTIONAL ACCESSORIES tinted glass; metallic spray; wiper and washer on rear window; ZF automatic transmission not available.

504 TI Berline

See 504 L Berline, except for:
PRICE IN GB: £ 4,623*
PRICE EX WORKS: 36,550* francs

ENGINE 120.3 cu in, 1,971 cc (3.46 x 3.19 in, 88 x 81 mm); compression ratio: 8.8:1; max power (DIN): 106 hp (78 kW) at 5,200 rpm; max torque (DIN): 125 lb ft, 17.2 kg m (168.7 Nm) at 3,000 rpm; 53.8 hp/l (39.6 kW/l); 4-cylinder injection pump in inlet pipes (Kugelfischer system); fuel feed: electric pump.

TRANSMISSION gearbox ratios: I 3.558, II 2.105, III 1.366, IV 1, rev 3.636; lever: central; axle ratio: 3.777; width of rims: 5''; tyres: 175 HR x 14.

PERFORMANCE max speeds: (I) 29 mph, 46 km/h; (II) 48 mph, 78 km/h; (III) 75 mph, 121 km/h; (IV) 107 mph, 173 km/h; power-weight ratio: 25.6 lb/hp (34.8 lb/kW), 11.6 kg/hp (15.8 kg/kW); carrying capacity: 1,058 lb, 480 kg; acceleration: standing ¼ mile 17.8 sec; speed in direct drive at 1,000 rpm: 19 mph, 30.6 km/h; consumption: 28.2 m/imp gal, 23.5 m/US gal, 10 l x 100 km.

CHASSIS rear suspension: independent, oblique semi-trailing arms, coil springs/telescopic dampers, anti-roll bar.

BRAKES disc (diameter 10.75 in, 27.3 cm), rear compensator, servo; swept area: front 236.9 sq in, 1,528 sq cm, rear 201.6 sq in, 1,300 sq cm, total 438.5 sq in, 2,828 sq cm.

PEUGEOT 504 Break Familial

PEUGEOT 504 Cabriolet

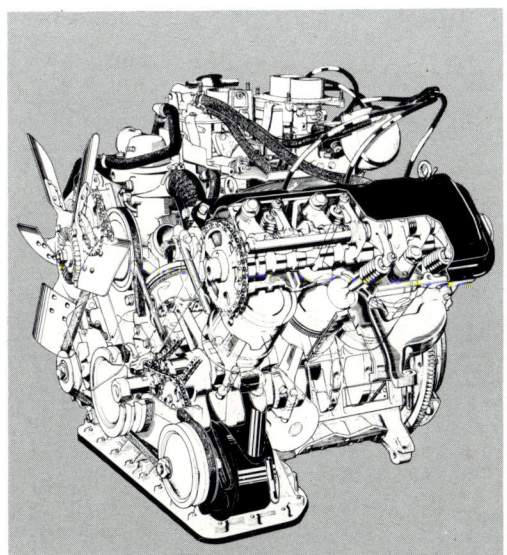

PEUGEOT 504 V6 Coupé

ELECTRICAL EQUIPMENT halogen headlamps.

DIMENSIONS AND WEIGHT weight: 2,712 lb, 1,230 kg.

BODY sunshine roof; built-in adjustable headrests; electrically-controlled front windows.

VARIATIONS

None.

OPTIONAL ACCESSORIES ZF automatic transmission, hydraulic torque converter and planetary gears with 3 ratios (I 2.564, II 1.520, III 1, rev 2), max ratio of converter at stall 2.3, max speed 104 mph, 167 km/h; leather upholstery; tinted glass; metallic spray.

504 Cabriolet

PRICE EX WORKS: 50,500* francs

ENGINE front, slanted 45° to right, 4 stroke; 4 cylinders, in line; 120.3 cu in, 1,971 cc (3.46 x 3.19 in, 88 x 81 mm); compression ratio: 8.8:1; max power (DIN): 106 hp (78 kW) at 5,200 rpm; max torque (DIN): 125 lb ft, 17.2 kg m (168.7 Nm) at 3,000 rpm; max engine rpm: 5,500; 53.8 hp/l (39.6 kW/l); cast iron block, wet liners, light alloy head, hemispherical combustion chambers; 5 crankshaft bearings; valves: overhead, Vee-slanted, push-rods and rockers; camshafts: 1, side; lubrication: gear pump, metal gauze filter, 7 imp pt, 8.5 US pt, 4 l; 4 cylinder injection pump in inlet pipes (Kugelfischer system); fuel feed: electric pump; water-cooled, 13.7 imp pt, 16.5 US pt, 7.8 l, electromagnetic thermostatic fan.

TRANSMISSION driving wheels: rear; clutch: single dry plate (diaphragm), hydraulically controlled; gearbox: mechanical; gears: 4, fully synchronized; ratios: I 3.460, II 2.062, III 1.406, IV 1, rev 3.496; lever: central; final drive: hypoid bevel; axle ratio: 3.700; width of rims: 5.5''; tyres: 175 HR x 14.

PERFORMANCE max speed: 111 mph, 179 km/h; power-weight ratio: 22.7 lb/hp (34.9 lb/kW), 11.6 kg/hp (15.8 kg/kW); carrying capacity: 706 lb, 320 g; speed in direct drive at 1,000 rpm: 20.2 mph, 32.5 km/h; consumption: 28.2 m/imp gal, 23.5 m/US gal, 10 l x 100 km.

CHASSIS integral; front suspension: independent, by McPherson, coil springs/telescopic damper struts, lower wishbones, anti-roll bar; rear: independent, oblique semi-trailing arms, coil springs/telescopic damper struts, anti-roll bar.

STEERING rack-and-pinion, servo; turns lock to lock: 3.50.

BRAKES disc (diameter 10.75 in, 27.3 cm), front internal radial fins, rear compensator, servo; lining area: front 22.9 sq in, 148 sq cm, rear 16.7 sq in, 108 sq cm, total 39.6 sq in, 256 sq cm.

ELECTRICAL EQUIPMENT 12 V; 60 Ah battery; 500 W alternator; Ducellier distributor; 4 halogen headlamps.

DIMENSIONS AND WEIGHT wheel base 100.39 in, 255 cm; tracks: 58.66 in, 149 cm front, 56.30 in, 143 cm rear;

504 CABRIOLET

length: 171.65 in, 436 cm; width: 66.93 in, 170 cm; height: 53.34 in, 136 cm; ground clearance: 4.72 in, 12 cm; weight: 2,723 lb, 1,235 kg; turning circle (between walls): 34.8 ft, 10.6 m; fuel tank: 12.3 imp gal, 14.8 US gal, 56 l.

BODY convertible; 2 doors; 2 + 2 seats, separate front seats, reclining backrests with built-in-headrests; electrically-controlled windows; tinted glass.

PRACTICAL INSTRUCTIONS fuel: 85 oct petrol; oil: engine 7 imp pt, 8.5 US pt, 4 l, SAE 20W-40, change every 3,100 miles, 5,000 km - gearbox 2.3 imp pt, 2.7 US pt, 1.3 l, SAE 20W-40, change every 6,200 miles, 10,000 km - final drive 2.6 imp pt, 3.2 US pt, 1.5 l, SAE 80, change every 6,200 miles, 10,000 km; greasing every 3,100 miles, 5,000 km, 6 points.

OPTIONAL ACCESSORIES metallic spray.

504 Coupé

See 504 Cabriolet, except for:

PRICE EX WORKS 50,500* francs

PERFORMANCE power-weight ratio: 26 lb/hp (35.3 lb/kW), 11.8 kg/hp (16 kg/kW).

PEUGEOT 604 SL

PEUGEOT 504 V6 Coupé

DIMENSIONS AND WEIGHT height: 53.15 in, 135 cm; weight: 2,756 lb, 1,250 kg.

BODY coupé; 4 seats; heated rear window.

504 V6 Coupé

See 504 Coupé, except for:

PRICE EX WORKS: 61,500* francs

ENGINE 6 cylinders, Vee-slanted at 90°; 162.6 cu in, 2,664 cc (3.46 x 2.87 in, 88 x 73 mm); compression ratio: 8.65:1; max power (DIN): 114 hp (106 kW) at 5,500 rpm; max torque (DIN): 160 lb ft, 22.1 kg m (216.7 Nm) at 3,200 rpm; max engine rpm: 6,000; 54 hp/l (39.8 kW/l); light alloy block and head, wet liners, bi-hemispherical combustion chambers; 4 crankshaft bearings; valves: overhead, Vee-slanted, rockers; camshafts: 1 per block, overhead; lubrication: gear pump, full flow filter, 10.6 imp pt, 12.7 US pt, 6 l; 1 Solex 34 TBIA downdraught single barrel carburettor and 1 Solex 35 CEEI downdraught twin barrel carburettor; fuel feed: mechanical pump; water-cooled, expansion tank, 18.1 imp pt, 21.8 US pt, 10.3 l, viscous coupling thermostatic fan.

TRANSMISSION gears: 5, fully synchronized; tyres: 190/65 HR x 390.

PERFORMANCE max speed: 117 mph, 189 km/h; power-weight ratio: 19.8 lb/hp (26.9 lb/kW), 9 kg/hp (12.2 kg/kW); speed in direct drive at 1,000 rpm: 19.6 mph, 31.5 km/h; consumption: 25 m/imp gal, 20.8 m/US gal, 11.3 l x 100 km.

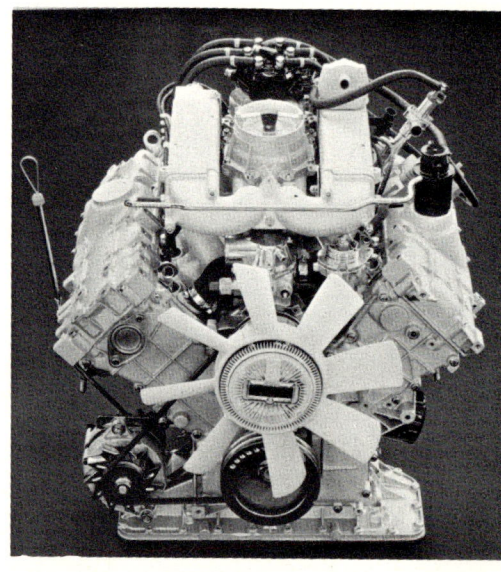

PEUGEOT 604 TI

ELECTRICAL EQUIPMENT 750 W alternator.

DIMENSIONS AND WEIGHT height: 52.76 in, 134 cm; weight: 2,855 lb, 1,295 kg; fuel tank: 13.2 imp gal, 15.8 US gal, 60 l.

PRACTICAL INSTRUCTIONS oil: engine 10.6 imp pt, 12.7 US pt, 6 l, SAE 10W-50; tappet clearances: inlet 0.006 in, 0.15 mm, exhaust 0.012 in, 0.30 mm; xalxe timing: 32° 72° 20° 32°.

604 SL

PRICE IN GB: £ 6,695
PRICE IN USA: $ 10,990*

ENGINE front, 4 stroke; 6 cylinders, Vee-slanted at 90°; 162.6 cu in, 2,664 cc (3.46 x 2.87 in, 88 x 73 mm); compression ratio: 8.65:1; max power (DIN): 136 hp (100.1 kW) at 5,750 rpm; max torque (DIN): 153 lb ft, 21.1 kg m (207 Nm) at 3,500 rpm; max engine rpm: 6,000; 51 hp/l (37.6 kW/l); light alloy block and head, wet liners, bi-hemispherical combustion chambers; 4 crankshaft bearings; valves: overhead, Vee-slanted, rockers; camshafts: 1 per block, overhead; lubrication: gear pump, full flow filter, 10.6 imp pt, 12.7 US pt, 6 l; 1 Solex 34 TBIA downdraught single barrel carburettor and 1 Solex 35 CEEI downdraught twin barrel carburettor; fuel feed: mechanical pump; water-cooled, expansion tank, 18.1 imp pt, 21.8 US pt, 10.3 l, viscous coupling thermostatic fan.

TRANSMISSION driving wheels: rear; clutch: single dry plate (diaphragm), hydraulically controlled; gearbox: mechanical; gears: 4, fully synchronized; ratios: I 3.460, II 2.062, III 1.406, IV 1, rev 3.496; lever: central; final drive: hypoid bevel; axle ratio: 3.700; width of rims: 5.5''; tyres: 175 HR x 14.

PERFORMANCE max speeds: (I) 32 mph, 52 km/h; (II) 55 mph, 88 km/h; (III) 80 mph, 129 km/h; (IV) 113 mph, 182 km/h; power-weight ratio: 22.5 lb/hp (30.6 lb/kW), 10.2 kg/hp (13.9 kg/kW); carrying capacity: 1,257 lb, 570 kg; acceleration: standing ¼ mile 17.2 sec; speed in direct drive at 1,000 rpm: 19.4 mph, 31.3 km/h; consumption: 24.6 m/imp gal, 20.5 m/US gal, 11.5 l x 100 km.

CHASSIS integral; front suspension: independent, by McPherson, coil springs/telescopic damper struts, lower wishbones, anti-roll bar; rear: independent, oblique semi-trailing arms, coil springs, anti-roll bar, telescopic dampers.

STEERING rack-and-pinion, servo; turns lock to lock: 3.50.

BRAKES disc (diameter 10.75 in, 27.3 cm), front internal radial fins, rear compensator, servo; swept area: front 223 sq in, 1,438 sq cm, rear 192 sq in, 1,239 sq cm, total 415 sq in, 2,677 sq cm.

ELECTRICAL EQUIPMENT 12 V; 60 Ah battery; 750 W alternator; Ducellier distributor; 4 halogen headlamps.

DIMENSIONS AND WEIGHT wheel base: 110.24 in, 280 cm; tracks: 58.66 in, 149 cm front, 56.30 in, 143 cm rear; length: 185.83 in, 472 cm; width: 69.68 in, 177 cm; height: 56.30 in, 143 cm; ground clearance: 5.91 in, 15 cm; weight: 3,065 lb, 1,390 kg; turning circle (between walls): 37.7 ft, 11.5 m; fuel tank: 15.4 imp gal, 18.5 US gal, 70 l.

BODY saloon/sedan; 4 doors, 5 seats, separate front seats, reclining backrests with built-in headrests; electrically-controlled windows; heated rear window.

PRACTICAL INSTRUCTIONS fuel: 85 oct petrol; oil: engine 10.6 imp pt, 12.7 US pt, 6 l, SAE 10W-50, change every 3,100 miles, 5,000 km - gearbox 2.3 imp pt, 2.7 US pt, 1.3 l, SAE 20W-40, change every 6,200 miles, 10,000 km - final drive 2.6 imp pt, 3.2 US pt, 1.5 l, SAE 80, change every 6,200 miles, 10,000 km; greasing: every 3,100 miles, 5,000 km; tappet clearances: inlet 0.006 in, 0.15 mm, exhaust 0.012 in, 0.30 mm; valve timing: 32° 72° 20° 32°.

OPTIONAL ACCESSORIES automatic transmission with 3 ratios (I 2.400, II 1.480, III 1, rev 1.920), max ratio of converter at stall 2.3, possible manual selection, max speed 111 km/h, 178 km/h, acceleration standing ¼ mile 18.3 sec, consumption 21.7 m/imp gal, 18.1 m/US gal, 13 l x 100 km; electrically-controlled sunshine roof; leather upholstery; metallic spray.

604 TI

See 604 SL, except for:

PRICE EX WORKS: 52,500* francs

ENGINE max power (DIN): 144 hp (106 kW) at 5,500 rpm; max torque (DIN): 160 lb ft, 22.1 kg m (216.7 Nm) at 3,200 rpm; 54 hp/l (39.8 kW/l); Bosch K-Jetronic fuel injection system; fuel feed: electric pump.

TRANSMISSION gears: 5, fully synchronized.

PERFORMANCE max speed: 115 mph, 185 km/h; power-weight ratio: 22 lb/hp (29.9 lb/kW), 10 kg/hp (13.6 kg/kW); consumption: 25.9 m/imp gal, 21.6 m/US gal, 10.9 l x 100 km.

DIMENSIONS AND WEIGHT weight: 3,175 lb, 1,440 kg.

RENAULT   FRANCE

4

(for France only)

PRICE EX WORKS: 15,980* francs

ENGINE front, 4 stroke; 4 cylinders, vertical, in line; 47.7 cu in, 782 cc (2.20 x 3.15 in, 55.8 x 80 mm); compression ratio: 8.5:1; max power (DIN): 27 hp (19.9 kW) at 5,000 rpm; max torque (DIN): 38 lb ft, 5.2 kg m (51 Nm) at 2,500 rpm; max engine rpm: 5,000; 34.5 hp/l (25.4 kW/l); cast iron block, wet liners, light alloy head; 3 crankshaft bearings; valves: overhead, in line, push-rods and rockers; camshafts: 1, side; lubrication: gear pump, filter in sump, 4.4 imp pt, 5.3 US pt, 2.5 l; 1 Zenith 28 IF downdraught single barrel carburettor; fuel feed: mechanical pump; sealed circuit cooling, liquid, expansion tank, 8.4 imp pt, 10.1 US pt, 4.8 l.

TRANSMISSION driving wheels: front; clutch: single dry plate (diaphragm); gearbox: mechanical; gears: 4, fully synchronized; ratios: I 3.833, II 2.235, III 1.458, IV 1.026, rev 3.545; lever: on facia; final drive: spiral bevel; axle ratio: 4.125; width of rims: 4''; tyres: 135 SR x 13.

PERFORMANCE max speeds: (I) 21 mph, 33 km/h; (II) 34 mph 54 km/h; (III) 52 mph, 83 km/h; (IV) 68 mph, 110 km/h; power-weight ratio: 56.7 lb/hp (77 lb/kW), 25.7 kg/hp (34.9 kg/kW); carrying capacity: 728 lb, 330 kg; acceleration: standing ¼ mile 27.1 sec, 0-50 mph (0-80 km/h) 34.2 sec; speed in top at 1,000 rpm: 14.7 mph, 23.7 km/h; consumption: 34 m/imp gal, 28.3 m/US gal, 8.3 l x 100 km.

CHASSIS platform; front suspension: independent, wishbones, longitudinal torsion bars, anti-roll bar, telescopic dampers; rear: independent, swinging longitudinal trailing arms, transverse torsion bars, telescopic dampers.

STEERING rack-and-pinion; turns lock to lock: 3.75.

BRAKES drum (front diameter 7.87 in, 20 cm, rear 6.30 in, 16 cm), rear compensator; lining area: front 36.4 sq in, 235 sq cm, rear 17.4 sq in, 112 sq cm, total 53.8 sq in, 347 sq cm.

ELECTRICAL EQUIPMENT 12 V; 28 Ah battery; 35 A alternator; 2 headlamps.

DIMENSIONS AND WEIGHT wheel base: 96.46 in, 245 cm (right), 94.49 in, 240 cm (left); tracks: 50.39 in, 128 cm front, 48.82 in, 124 cm rear; length: 144.49 in, 367 cm; width: 58.27 in, 148 cm; height: 61.02 in, 155 cm; ground clearance: 6.89 in, 17.5 cm; weight: 1,532 lb, 695 kg; weight distribution: 56.1% front, 43.9% rear; turning circle (between walls): 33.1 ft, 10.1 m; fuel tank: 7.5 imp gal, 9 US gal, 34 l.

BODY estate car/station wagon; 4 + 1 doors; 4 seats, bench front seats; back seat folding down to luggage table; heated rear window.

PRACTICAL INSTRUCTIONS fuel: 85 oct petrol; oil: engine 4.4 imp pt, 5.3 US pt, 2.5 l, SAE 10W-40, change every 4,650 miles, 7,500 km - gearbox and final drive 3.2 imp pt, 3.8 US pt, 1.8 l, SAE 80 EP, change every 9,300 miles, 15,000 km; greasing: none; tappet clearances: inlet 0.006-0.007 in, 0.15-0.18 mm, exhaust 0.007-0.009 in, 0.18-0.22 mm; valve timing: 10° 34° 49° 11°; tyre pressure: front 20 psi, 1.4 atm, rear 24 psi, 1.7 atm.

OPTIONAL ACCESSORIES luxury interior.

4 TL

(for France only)

See 4, except for:

PRICE EX WORKS: 18,280* francs

BODY separate front seats.

OPTIONAL ACCESSORIES sunshine roof; metallic spray; reclining backrests.

PEUGEOT 604 TI

RENAULT 4 Rodeo

RENAULT 4 TL

4 Safari

(for France only)

See 4 TL, except for:

PRICE EX WORKS: 17,280* francs

BODY separate front seats with built-in headrests.

OPTIONAL ACCESSORIES metallic spray not available.

4 Rodeo

See 4, except for:

PRICE EX WORKS: 22,100* francs

ENGINE 51.6 cu in, 845 cc (2.28 x 3.15 in, 58 x 80 mm); compression ratio: 8:1; max power (DIN): 34 hp (25 kW) at 5,000 rpm; max torque (DIN): 43 lb ft, 5.9 kg m (57.9 Nm) at 2,500 rpm; 40.2 hp/l (29.6 kW/l); water-cooled, 9.7 imp pt, 11.6 US pt, 5.5 l.

TRANSMISSION tyres: 145 SR x 13.

PERFORMANCE max speeds: (I) 21 mph, 34 km/h; (II) 35 mph, 56 km/h; (III) 53 mph, 86 km/h; (IV) 68 mph, 110 km/h; power-weight ratio: 43.4 lb/hp (59.1 kg/kW), 19.7 kg/hp (26.8 kg/kW); speed in top at 1,000 rpm: 15.2 mph, 24.4 km/h.

4 RODEO

CHASSIS reinforced platform; rear suspension: anti-roll bar.

BRAKES drum (front diameter 8.98 in, 22.8 cm, rear 6.30 in, 16 cm), rear compensator; lining area: front 44.8 sq in, 289 sq cm, rear 17.4 sq in, 112 sq cm, total 62.2 sq in, 401 sq cm.

ELECTRICAL EQUIPMENT 30/40 A alternator.

DIMENSIONS AND WEIGHT length: 146.85 in, 373 cm; width: 60.79 in, 154 cm; height: 62.99 in, 160 cm; ground clearance: 5.51 in, 14 cm; weight: 1,477 lb, 670 kg.

BODY open, in plastic material; 2 doors; 2 or 4 seats.

PRACTICAL INSTRUCTIONS valve timing: 16° 52° 52° 16°; tyre pressure: front 18 psi, 1.3 atm, rear 24 psi, 1.7 atm.

OPTIONAL ACCESSORIES 4-wheel drive; « Evasion » version; « Chantier » version; « Coursière » version; « Quatre saisons » version; « Artisane » version.

6 Rodeo

See 4 Rodeo, except for:

PRICE EX WORKS: 23,667* francs

ENGINE 67.6 cu in, 1,108 cc (2.76 x 2.83 in, 70 x 72 mm); compression ratio: 9.5:1; max power (DIN): 47 hp (34.6 kW) at 5,300 rpm; max torque (DIN): 57 lb ft, 7.9 kg m (77.5 Nm) at 3,000 rpm; max engine rpm: 5,400; 42.4 hp/l (31.2 kW/l); lubricating system: 5.3 imp pt, 6.3 US pt, 3 l; 1 Zenith 32 IF 8 downdraught single barrel carburettor; water-cooled, 11.1 imp pt, 13.3 US pt, 6.3 l.

PERFORMANCE max speeds: (I) 23 mph, 37 km/h; (II) 37 mph, 60 km/h; (III) 58 mph, 93 km/h; (IV) 81 mph, 130 km/h; power-weight ratio: 35 lb/hp (47.5 lb/kW), 15.8 kg/hp (21.5 kg/kW).

BRAKES front disc (diameter 8.98 in, 22.8 cm), rear drum, rear compensator; lining area: front 19.8 sq in, 128 sq cm, rear 22.2 sq in, 143 sq cm, total 42 sq in, 271 sq cm.

DIMENSIONS AND WEIGHT tracks: 50.63 in, 129 cm front, 49.13 in, 125 cm rear; length: 148.62 in, 377 cm; height: 61.18 in, 155 cm; ground clearance: 5.71 in, 14.5 cm; weight: 1,643 lb, 745 kg; turning circle (between walls): 35.4 ft, 10.8 m; fuel tank: 8.8 imp gal, 10.6 US gal, 40 l.

BODY 2 seats.

PRACTICAL INSTRUCTIONS oil: engine 5.3 imp pt, 6.3 US pt, 3 l; tappet clearances: inlet 0.006 in, 0.15 mm, exhaust 0.008 in, 0.20 mm; valve timing: 18° 54° 53° 23°; tyre pressure: front 20 psi, 1.4 atm, rear 24 psi, 1.7 atm.

RENAULT 5

5

PRICE IN GB: £ 2,057*
PRICE EX WORKS: 19,050* francs

ENGINE front, 4 stroke; 4 cylinders, vertical, in line: 51.6 cu in, 845 cc (2.28 x 3.15 in, 58 x 80 mm); compression ratio: 8:1; max power (DIN): 36 hp (26.5 kW) at 5,500 rpm; max torque (DIN): 42 lb ft, 5.8 kg m (56.9 Nm) at 2,500 rpm; max engine rpm: 6,000; 42.6 hp/l (31.4 kW/l); cast iron block, wet liners, light alloy head; 3 crankshaft bearings; valves: overhead, in line, push-rods and rockers; camshafts: 1, side; lubrication: gear pump, filter in sump (cartridge), 4.4 imp pt, 5.3 US pt, 2.5 l; 1 Solex 32 DIS downdraught single barrel carburettor; fuel feed: mechanical pump; sealed circuit cooling, liquid, expansion tank, 10.2 imp pt, 12.3 US pt, 5.8 l.

TRANSMISSION driving wheels: front; clutch: single dry plate (diaphragm); gearbox: mechanical; gears: 4, fully synchronized; ratios: I 3.833, II 2.235, III 1.458, IV 1.026, rev 3.545; lever: central; final drive: spiral bevel; axle ratio: 4.125; width of rims: 4''; tyres: 135 SR x 13.

PERFORMANCE max speeds: (I) 24 mph, 38 km/h; (II) 39 mph, 63 km/h; (III) 60 mph, 97 km/h; (IV) 76 mph, 123 km/h; power-weight ratio: 44.7 lb/hp (60.7 lb/kW), 20.3 kg/hp (27.5 kg/kW); carrying capacity: 728 lb, 330 kg; speed in top at 1,000 rpm: 14.7 mph, 23.7 km/h; consumption: 34.9 m/imp gal, 29 m/US gal, 8.1 l x 100 km.

CHASSIS integral; front suspension: independent, wishbones, longitudinal torsion bar, anti-roll bar, telescopic dampers; rear: independent, swinging longitudinal trailing arms, transverse torsion bars, telescopic dampers.

STEERING rack-and-pinion; turns lock to lock: 3.75.

BRAKES drum (diameter 7.87 in, 20 cm front, 6.30 in, 16 cm rear), rear compensator; lining area: front 68.2 sq in, 440 sq cm, rear 38.9 sq in, 251 sq cm, total 107.1 sq in, 691 sq cm.

ELECTRICAL EQUIPMENT 12 V; 28 Ah battery; 35 A alternator; R 220 distributor; 2 headlamps.

DIMENSIONS AND WEIGHT wheel base: 94.49 in, 240 cm (right), 95.67 in, 243 cm (left); tracks: 50.39 in, 128 cm front, 48.82 in, 124 cm rear; length: 138.19 in, 351 cm; width: 59.84 in, 152 cm; height: 55.12 in, 140 cm; ground clearance: 7.87 in, 20 cm; weight: 1,610 lb, 730 kg; weight distribution: 58.2% front, 41.8% rear; turning circle (between walls): 33.1 ft, 10.1 m; fuel tank: 8.4 imp gal, 10 US gal, 38 l.

BODY saloon/sedan; 2 + 1 doors; 4 seats, separate front seats; heated rear window; back seat folding down to luggage table.

PRACTICAL INSTRUCTIONS fuel: 98-100 oct petrol; oil: engine 4.4 imp pt, 5.3 US pt, 2.5 l, SAE 20W-40, change every 4,650 miles, 7,500 km - gearbox and final drive 3.2 imp pt, 3.8 US pt, 1.8 l, SAE 80 EP, change every 9,300 miles, 15,000 km; greasing: none; tappet clearances: inlet 0.006-0.007 in, 0.15-0.18 mm, exhaust 0.007-0.009 in, 0.18-0.22 mm; valve timing: 20° 56° 53° 23°; tyre pressure: front 24 psi, 1.7 atm, rear 28 psi, 1.9 atm.

OPTIONAL ACCESSORIES luxury interior; metallic spray.

5 TL

See 5, except for:

PRICE IN GB: £ 2,324*
PRICE IN USA: $ 3,345*

ENGINE 58.3 cu in, 956 cc (2.56 x 2.83 in, 65 x 72 mm); compression ratio: 9.25:1; max power (DIN): 44 hp (32.4 kW) at 5,500 rpm; max torque (DIN): 48 lb ft, 6.4 kg m (62.8 Nm) at 3,500 rpm; 46 hp/l (33.9 kW/l); 5 crankshaft bearings; lubricating system: 5.3 imp pt, 6.3 US pt, 3 l; sealed circuit cooling, liquid, electric thermostatic fan, 11.1 imp pt, 13.3 US pt, 6.3 l.

PERFORMANCE max speeds: (I) 24 mph, 39 km/h; (II) 40 mph, 64 km/h; (III) 62 mph, 100 km/h; (IV) 85 mph, 136 km/h; power-weight ratio: 38.8 lb/hp (52.7 lb/kW), 17.6 kg/hp (23.9 kg/kW); carrying capacity: 882 lb, 400 kg; consumption: 31.4 m/imp gal, 26.1 m/US gal, 9 l x 100 km.

BRAKES front disc (diameter 8.98 in, 22.8 cm), rear drum, rear compensator; swept area: front 157.2 sq in, 1,014 sq cm, rear 52.6 sq in, 339 sq cm, total 209.8 sq in, 1,353 sq cm.

ELECTRICAL EQUIPMENT 30/40 A alternator; R 248 C 33 distributor.

RENAULT 5 TL

DIMENSIONS AND WEIGHT front track: 50.71 in, 129 cm; weight: 1,709 lb, 775 kg; weight distribution: 60% front, 40% rear.

BODY 5 seats, reclining backrests.

PRACTICAL INSTRUCTIONS oil: engine 5.3 imp pt, 6.3 US pt, 3 l; tappet clearances: inlet 0.006 in, 0.15 mm, exhaust 0.008 in, 0.20 mm; valve timing: 18° 54° 53° 23°.

OPTIONAL ACCESSORIES tinted glass; sunshine roof; rear window wiper-washer.

5 GTL

See 5 TL, except for:

PRICE IN GB: £ 2,499*
PRICE IN USA: $ 3,495*

ENGINE 78.7 cu in, 1,289 cc (2.87 x 3.03 in, 73 x 77 mm); compression ratio: 9.5:1; max power (DIN): 42 hp (30.9 kW) at 5,000 rpm; max torque (DIN): 61 lb ft, 8.4 kg m (82.4 Nm) at 2,500 rpm; max engine rpm: 5,000; 32.6 hp/l (24 kW/l).

TRANSMISSION axle ratio: 3.100.

PERFORMANCE max speeds: (I) 26 mph, 42 km/h; (II) 45 mph, 72 km/h; (III) 68 mph, 110 km/h; (IV) 85 mph.

RENAULT 5 Alpine

RENAULT 5 Alpine

136 km/h; power-weight ratio: 41.2 lb/hp (56 lb/kW), 18.7 kg/hp (25.4 kg/kW); speed in top at 1,000 rpm: 19.6 mph, 31.5 km/h; consumption: 32.5 m/imp gal, 27 m/US gal, 8.7 l x 100 km.

BRAKES servo.

DIMENSIONS AND WEIGHT width: 61.02 in, 155 cm; weight: 1,731 lb, 785 kg.

PRACTICAL INSTRUCTIONS valve timing: 22° 62° 65° 25°.

5 TS

See 5 TL, except for:

PRICE IN GB: £ 2,797*
PRICE EX WORKS: 25,490* francs

ENGINE 78.7 cu in, 1,289 cc (2.87 x3.03 in, 73 x 77 mm); compression ratio: 9.5:1; max power (DIN): 64 hp (47.1 kW) at 6,000 rpm; max torque (DIN): 70 lb ft, 9.6 kg m (94.1 Nm) at 3,500 rpm; 49.6 hp/l (36.5 kW/l); 1 Weber 32 DIR 11 downdraught twin barrel carburettor.

TRANSMISSION ratios: I 3.833, II 2.375, III 1.522, IV 1.026, rev 3.545; axle ratio: 3.625; width of rims: 4.5''; tyres: 145 SR x 13.

PERFORMANCE max speeds: (I) 29 mph, 47 km/h; (II) 45 mph, 73 km/h; (III) 70 mph, 113 km/h; (IV) 94 mph,

RENAULT 6

151 km/h; power-weight ratio: 27.6 lb/hp (37.4 lb/kW), 12.5 kg/hp (17 kg/kW); speed in top at 1,000 rpm: 17.2 mph, 27.7 km/h; consumption: 28.2 m/imp gal, 23.5 m/US gal, 10 l x 100 km.

CHASSIS rear suspension: anti-roll bar.

BRAKES servo.

ELECTRICAL EQUIPMENT 36 Ah battery; 50 A alternator; iodine headlamps.

DIMENSIONS AND WEIGHT weight: 1,764 lb, 800 kg.

BODY rear window wiper-washer (standard).

PRACTICAL INSTRUCTIONS valve timing: 22° 62° 65° 25°; tyre pressure: front 23 psi, 1.6 atm, rear 27 psi, 1.9 atm.

5 Alpine

See 5 TL, except for:

PRICE EX WORKS: 35,160* francs

ENGINE 85.2 cu in, 1,397 cc (2.99 x 3.03 in, 76 x 77 mm); compression ratio: 10:1; max power (DIN): 93 hp (68.4 kW) at 6,400 rpm; max torque (DIN): 86 lb ft, 11.8 kg m (115.7 Nm) at 4,000 rpm; max engine rpm: 6,500; 66.6 hp/l (49 kW/l); 1 Weber 32 DIR 11 downdraught twin barrel carburettor.

TRANSMISSION gears: 5 fully synchronized; ratios: I 3.818, II 2.235, III 1.478, IV 1.036, V 0.861, rev 3.083; axle ratio: 3.875; width of rims: 4.5''; tyres: 155/70 HR x 13.

PERFORMANCE max speeds: (I) 27 mph, 44 km/h; (II) 46 mph, 74 km/h; (III) 70 mph, 113 km/h; (IV) 100 mph, 161 km/h; (V) 109 mph, 175 km/h; power-weight ratio: 20.1 lb/hp (27.4 lb/kW), 9.1 kg/hp (12.4 kg/kW); carrying capacity: 992 lb, 450 kg; speed in top at 1,000 rpm: 18.8 mph, 30.2 km/h; consumption: 26.4 m/imp gal, 22 m/US gal, 10.7 l x 100 km.

CHASSIS rear suspension: anti-roll bar.

BRAKES servo.

ELECTRICAL EQUIPMENT 36 Ah battery; 50 A alternator; iodine headlamps.

DIMENSIONS AND WEIGHT wheel base: 94.96 in, 241 cm (right), 96.14 in, 244 cm (left); tracks: 50.94 in, 129 cm front, 50 in, 127 cm rear; length: 139.49 in, 354 cm; height: 54.17 in, 138 cm; ground clearance: 4.72 in, 12 cm; weight: 1,874 lb, 850 kg.

BODY tinted glass, rear window wiper-washer (standard).

PRACTICAL INSTRUCTIONS gearbox and final drive oil: 3 imp pt, 3.6 US pt, 1.7 l; tappet clearances: inlet 0.008-0.009 in, 0.20-0.22 mm, exhaust 0.010-0.011 in, 0.25-0.27 mm; valve timing: 30° 72° 72° 30°; tyre pressure: front 23 psi, 1.6 atm, rear 28 psi, 2 atm.

OPTIONAL ACCESSORIES luxury equipment; metallic spray.

6

PRICE EX WORKS: 20,050* francs

ENGINE front, 4 stroke; 4 cylinders, vertical, in line; 51.6 cu in, 845 cc (2.28 x 3.15 in, 58 x 80 mm); compression ratio: 8:1; max power (DIN): 34 hp (25 kW) at 5,000 rpm; max torque (DIN): 42 lb ft, 5.8 kg m (56.9 Nm) at 3,000 rpm; max engine rpm: 5,200: 40.2 hp/l (29.6 kW/l); cast iron block, wet liners, light alloy head; 3 crankshaft bearings; valves : overhead, in line, push-rods and rockers; camshafts: 1, side; lubrication: gear pump, filter in sump, 4.4 imp pt 5.3 US pt, 2.5 l; 1 Solex 32 DIS downdraught carburettor; fuel feed: mechanical pump; sealed circuit cooling, liquid, expansion tank, 9.7 imp pt, 11.6 US pt, 5.5 l.

TRANSMISSION driving wheels: front; clutch: single dry plate (diaphragm); gearbox: mechanical; gears: 4, fully synchronized; ratios: I 3.833, II 2.235, III 1.458, IV 1.026, rev 3.545; lever: on facia; final drive: spiral bevel; axle ratio: 4.125; width of rims: 4''; tyres: 135 SR x 13.

PERFORMANCE max speeds: (I) 24 mph, 39 km/h; (II) 39 mph, 63 km/h; (III) 60 mph, 97 km/h; (IV) 73 mph, 118 km/h; power-weight ratio: 50.9 lb/hp (69.2 lb/kW), 23.1 kg/hp (31.4 kg/kW); carrying capacity: 816 lb, 370 kg; speed in top at 1,000 rpm: 14.7 mph, 23.7 km/h; consumption: 32.1 m/imp gal, 26.7 m/US gal, 8.8 l x 100 km.

CHASSIS platform; front suspension: independent, wishbones, longitudinal torsion bars, anti-roll bar, telescopic dampers; rear: independent, swinging longitudinal trailing arms, transverse torsion bars, telescopic dampers.

STEERING rack-and-pinion; turns lock to lock: 3.75.

6

BRAKES drum (diameter 8.98 in, 22.8 cm front, 6.30 in, 16 cm rear), rear compensator; lining area: front 44.8 sq in, 289 sq cm, rear 17.4 sq cm, 112 sq cm, total 62.2 sq in, 401 sq cm.

ELECTRICAL EQUIPMENT 12 V; 28 Ah battery; 35 A alternator; Lucas distributor; 2 headlamps.

DIMENSIONS AND WEIGHT wheel base: 96.46 in, 245 cm (right), 94.49 in, 240 cm (left); tracks: 50.39 in, 128 cm front, 48.82 in, 124 cm rear; length: 151.97 in, 386 cm; width: 59.06 in, 150 cm; height: 57.87 in, 147 cm; ground clearance: 4.92 in, 12.5 cm; weight: 1,731 lb, 785 kg; weight distribution: 56.5% front, 43.5% rear; turning circle (between walls): 34.1 ft, 10.4 m; fuel tank: 8.6 imp gal, 10.3 US gal, 39 l.

BODY saloon/sedan; 4 + 1 doors; 4 seats, separate front seats; back seat folding down to luggage table; heated rear window.

PRACTICAL INSTRUCTIONS fuel: 90 oct petrol; oil: engine 4.4 imp pt, 5.3 US pt, 2.5 l, SAE 10 or 20W-40, change every 4,650 miles, 7,500 km - gearbox and final drive 3.2 imp pt, 3.8 US pt, 1.8 l, SAE 80 EP, change every 9,300 miles, 15,000 km; greasing: none; tappet clearances: inlet 0.006-0.007 in, 0.15-0.18 mm, exhaust 0.007-0.009 in, 0.18-0.22 mm; valve timing: 16° 52° 52° 22°; tyre pressure: front 21 psi, 1.5 atm, rear 24 psi, 1.7 atm.

OPTIONAL ACCESSORIES reclining backrests; luxury interior; metallic spray.

6 TL

See 6, except for:

PRICE IN GB: £ 2,520*
PRICE EX WORKS: 21,570* francs

ENGINE 67.6 cu in, 1,108 cc (2.76 x 2.83 in, 70 x 72 mm); compression ratio: 9.5:1; max power (DIN): 47 hp (34.6 kW) at 5,300 rpm; max torque (DIN): 57 lb ft, 7.9 kg m (77.5 Nm) at 3,000 rpm; max engine rpm: 5,700; 42.4 hp/l (31.2 kW/l); 5 crankshaft bearings; valves: slanted; lubrication: full flow filter, 5.3 imp pt, 6.3 US pt, 3 l; 1 Zenith 32 IF 8 or Solex 32 SEIA downdraught carburettor; cooling system: 11.1 imp pt, 13.3 US pt, 6.3 l, electric thermostatic fan.

TRANSMISSION tyres: 145 SR x 13.

PERFORMANCE max speeds: (I) 22 mph, 35 km/h; (II) 39 mph, 63 km/h; (III) 60 mph, 97 km/h; (IV) 84 mph, 135 km/h; power-weight ratio: 38.5 lb/hp (52.2 lb/kW), 17.4 kg/hp (23.7 kg/kW); carrying capacity: 882 lb, 400 kg; speed in top at 1,000 rpm: 15.2 mph, 24.4 km/h; consumption: 30.7 m/imp gal, 25.6 m/US gal, 9.2 l x 100 km.

CHASSIS rear suspension: anti-roll bar.

BRAKES front disc (diameter 8.98 in, 22.8 cm), rear drum, rear compensator; lining area: front 19.8 sq in, 128 sq cm, rear 52.6 sq in, 339 sq cm, total 72.4 sq in, 467 sq cm.

RENAULT 6 TL

ELECTRICAL EQUIPMENT 30/40 A alternator.

DIMENSIONS AND WEIGHT tracks: 50.79 in, 129 cm front, 49.21 in, 125 cm rear; weight: 1,808 lb, 820 kg; weight distribution: 56.1% front, 43.9% rear.

BODY 5 seats; reclining backrests (standard).

PRACTICAL INSTRUCTIONS oil: engine 5.3 imp pt, 6.3 US pt, 3 l; tappet clearances: inlet 0.006 in, 0.15 mm, exhaust 0.009 in, 0.22 mm; valve timing: 18° 54° 53° 23°; tyre pressure: front 20 psi, 1.4 atm.

OPTIONAL ACCESSORIES tinted glass.

14

PRICE EX WORKS: 25,690* francs

ENGINE front, transverse, slanted 72° to rear, 4 stroke; 4 cylinders, vertical, in line; 74.3 cu in, 1,218 cc (2.95 x 2.72 in, 75 x 69 mm); compression ratio: 9.3:1; max power (DIN): 57 hp (41.9 kW) at 6,000 rpm; max torque (DIN): 68 lb ft, 9.4 kg m (92.2 Nm) at 3,000 rpm; max engine rpm: 6,000; 46.8 hp/l (34.4 kW/l); light alloy block and head, wet liners, hemispherical combustion chambers; 5 crankshaft bearings; valves: overhead, Vee-slanted, rockers; camshafts: 1, overhead; lubrication: gear pump, full flow filter, 7 imp pt, 8.3 US pt, 4 l; 1 Solex 32 SHA

RENAULT 6 TL

downdraught single barrel carburettor; sealed circuit cooling, liquid, expansion tank, 10.6 imp pt, 12.7 US pt, 6 l, electric thermostatic fan.

TRANSMISSION driving wheels: front; clutch: single dry plate (diaphragm); gearbox: mechanical, in unit with engine and final drive; gears: 4, fully synchronized; ratios: I 3.883, II 2.296, III 1.501, IV 1.042, rev 3.568; lever: central; final drive: spiral bevel; axle ratio: 3.867; width of rims: 4.5''; tyres: 145 SR x 13.

PERFORMANCE max speeds: (I) 26 mph, 42 km/h; (II) 43 mph, 70 km/h; (III) 66 mph, 107 km/h; (IV) 89 mph, 143 km/h; power-weight ratio: 33.4 lb/hp (45.5 lb/kW), 15.2 kg/hp (20.6 kg/kW); carrying capacity: 882 lb, 400 kg; acceleration: standing ¼ mile 20.3 sec; speed in top at 1,000 rpm: 15.9 mph, 25.6 km/h; consumption: 31 m/imp gal, 25.8 m/US gal, 9.1 l x 100 km.

CHASSIS integral; front suspension: independent, by McPherson, coil springs/telescopic damper struts, lower wishbones; rear: independent, swinging longitudinal trailing arms, transverse torsion bars, telescopic dampers.

STEERING rack-and-pinion; turns lock to lock: 4.

BRAKES front disc (diameter 9.49 in, 24.1 cm), rear drum, rear compensator; lining area: front 22.2 sq in, 143 sq cm, rear 35.2 sq in, 227 sq cm, total 57.4 sq in, 370 sq cm.

ELECTRICAL EQUIPMENT 12 V; 32 Ah battery; 40 A alternator; 2 headlamps.

DIMENSIONS AND WEIGHT wheel base: 98.35 in, 250 cm (right), 99.61 in, 253 cm (left); tracks: 53.23 in, 135 cm front, 54.25 in, 138 cm rear; length: 158.46 in, 402 cm; width: 63.94 in, 162 cm; height: 55.31 in, 140 cm; ground clearance: 5.91 in, 15 cm; weight: 1,907 lb, 865 kg; turning circle (between walls): 34.8 ft, 10.6 m; fuel tank: 10.6 imp gal, 12.7 US gal, 48 l.

BODY saloon/sedan; 4 doors; 5 seats, separate front seats; back seat folding down to luggage table; heated rear window.

PRACTICAL INSTRUCTIONS fuel: 98-100 oct petrol; oil: engine, gearbox and final drive 7 imp pt, 8.3 US pt, 4 l, change every 4,650 miles, 7,500 km; tappet clearances: inlet 0.004-0.006 in, 0.10-0.15 mm, exhaust 0.009-0.011 in, 0.23-0.28 mm; valve timing: 15° 45° 46° 15°; tyre pressure: front 24 psi, 1.7 atm, rear 27 psi, 1.9 atm.

OPTIONAL ACCESSORIES luxury interior; metallic spray.

14 TL

See 14, except for:

PRICE IN GB: £ 2,829*
PRICE EX WORKS: 27,290* francs

BRAKES servo.

BODY luxury interior (standard); reclining backrests on front seats.

OPTIONAL ACCESSORIES tinted glass; sunshine roof.

12 Berline

PRICE IN GB: £ 2,429*
PRICE EX WORKS: 24,890* francs

ENGINE front, 4 stroke; 4 cylinders, vertical, in line; 78.7 cu in, 1,289 cc (2.87 x 3.03 in, 73 x 77 mm); compression ratio: 8.5:1; max power (DIN): 50 hp (36.8 kW) at 5,000 rpm; max torque (DIN): 64 lb ft, 8.8 kg m (86.3 Nm) at 3,000 rpm; max engine rpm: 5,200; 38.8 hp/l (28.5 kW/l); cast iron block, wet liners, light alloy head; 5 crankshaft bearings; valves: overhead, slanted, push-rods and rockers; camshafts: 1, side; lubrication: gear pump, filter in sump, 5.3 imp pt, 6.3 US pt, 3 l; 1 Solex 32 SEIA or Zenith 32 IF 8 downdraught carburettor; fuel feed: mechanical pump; sealed circuit cooling, liquid, expansion tank, 8.8 imp pt, 10.6 US pt, 5 l.

TRANSMISSION driving wheels: front; clutch: single dry plate (diaphragm); gearbox: mechanical; gears: 4, fully synchronized; ratios: I 3.818, II 2.235, III 1.478, IV 1.036, rev 3.083; lever: central; final drive: hypoid bevel; axle ratio: 3.778; width of rims: 4.5''; tyres: 145 SR x 13.

PERFORMANCE max speeds: (I) 23 mph, 37 km/h; (II) 40 mph, 64 km/h; (III) 60 mph, 96 km/h; (IV) 87 mph, 140 km/h; power-weight ratio: 39.7 lb/hp (53.9 lb/kW), 18 kg/hp (24.4 kg/kW); carrying capacity: 882 lb, 400 kg; speed in top at 1,000 rpm: 16.4 mph, 26.4 km/h; consumption: 27.4 m/imp gal, 22.8 m/US gal, 10.3 l x 100 km.

CHASSIS integral; front suspension: independent, wishbones, anti-roll bar, coil springs/telescopic dampers; rear: rigid

RENAULT 12 Berline

axle, trailing arms, A-bracket, anti-roll bar, coil springs/telescopic dampers.

STEERING rack-and-pinion; turns lock to lock: 3.50.

BRAKES front disc (diameter 8.98 in, 22.8 cm), rear drum, rear compensator; lining area: front 22.2 sq in, 143 sq cm, rear 33.2 sq in, 214 sq cm, total 55.4 sq in, 357 sq cm.

ELECTRICAL EQUIPMENT 12 V; 36 Ah battery; 38 A alternator; 2 headlamps.

DIMENSIONS AND WEIGHT wheel base: 96.06 in, 244 cm; front and rear tracks: 51.57 in, 131 cm; length: 171.26 in, 435 cm; width: 63.78 in, 162 cm; height: 56.30 in, 143 cm; ground clearance: 4.41 in, 11.2 cm; weight: 1,985 lb, 900 kg; weight distribution: 58.3% front, 41.7% rear; turning circle (between walls): 35.4 ft, 10.8 m; fuel tank: 10.3 imp gal, 12.4 US gal, 47 l.

BODY saloon/sedan; 4 doors; 5 seats, separate front seats; heated rear window.

PRACTICAL INSTRUCTIONS fuel: 92 oct petrol; oil: engine 5.3 imp pt, 6.3 US pt pt, 3 l, SAE 10W-40, change every 4,650 miles, 7,500 km - gearbox and final drive 3.5 imp pt, 4.2 US pt, 2 l, SAE 80 EP, change every 9,300 miles, 15,000 km; greasing: none; tappet clearances: inlet 0.006 in, 0.15 mm, exhaust 0.008 in, 0.20 mm; valve timing: 22° 62° 60° 20°; tyre pressure: front 23 psi, 1.6 atm, rear 26 psi, 1.8 atm.

OPTIONAL ACCESSORIES luxury interior; metallic spray.

RENAULT 12 Break

RENAULT 12 Break TL

12 Break

See 12 Berline, except for:

PRICE EX WORKS: 26,290* francs

TRANSMISSION tyres: 155 SR x 13.

PERFORMANCE max speeds: (I) 24 mph, 38 km/h; (II) 40 mph, 65 km/h; (III) 61 mph, 98 km/h; (IV) 87 mph, 140 km/h; power-weight ratio: 42.3 lb/hp (57.5 lb/kW), 19.2 kg/hp (26.1 kg/kW); carrying capacity: 937 lb, 425 kg; speed in top at 1,000 rpm: 16.8 mph, 27 km/h.

BRAKES front disc, rear drum, servo; lining area: front 22.2 sq in, 143 sq cm, rear 38.3 sq in, 247 sq cm, total 60.5 sq cm, 390 sq cm.

DIMENSIONS AND WEIGHT length: 172.09 in, 437 cm; height: 57.09 in, 145 cm; ground clearance: 5.12 in, 13 cm; weight: 2,117 lb, 960 kg.

BODY estate car/station wagon; 4 + 1 doors; back seat folding down to luggage table.

12 TL Berline

See 12 Berline, except for:

PRICE IN GB: £ 2,689*
PRICE EX WORKS: 26,490* francs

ENGINE compression ratio: 9.5:1; max power (DIN): 54 hp (39.7 kW) at 5,250 rpm; max torque (DIN): 65 lb ft, 9 kg m (88.3 Nm) at 3,500 rpm; max engine rpm: 5,500; 41.9 hp/l (30.8 kW/l).

PERFORMANCE power-weight ratio: 36.8 lb/hp (50 lb/kW), 16.7 kg/hp (22.7 kg/kW); consumption: 28.8 m/imp gal, 24 m/US gal, 9.8 l x 100 km.

BRAKES front disc, rear drum, servo.

BODY reclining backrests, luxury equipment.

PRACTICAL INSTRUCTIONS fuel: 98-100 oct petrol.

OPTIONAL ACCESSORIES tinted glass.

12 Break TL

See 12 TL Berline, except for:

PRICE IN GB: £ 3,022*
PRICE EX WORKS: 27,790* francs

TRANSMISSION tyres: 155 SR x 13.

PERFORMANCE power-weight ratio: 39.2 lb/hp (53.3 lb/kW), 17.8 kg/hp (24.2 kg/kW); carrying capacity: 937 lb, 425 kg; speed in top at 1,000 rpm: 16.8 mph, 27 km/h.

BRAKES lining area: front 22.2 sq in, 143 sq cm, rear 38.3 sq in, 247 sq cm, total 60.5 sq in, 390 sq cm.

DIMENSIONS AND WEIGHT length: 172.09 in, 437 cm; height: 57.09 in, 145 cm; ground clearance: 5.12 in, 13 cm; weight: 2,117 lb, 960 kg.

BODY estate car/station wagon; 4 + 1 doors; back seat folding down to luggage table.

12 TS Berline

See 12 Berline, except for:

PRICE IN GB: £ 2,941*
PRICE EX WORKS: 27,990* francs

ENGINE compression ratio: 9.5:1; max power (DIN): 60 hp (44.2 kW) at 5,500 rpm; max torque (DIN): 67 lb ft, 9.3 kg m (91.2 Nm) at 3,500 rpm; max engine rpm: 5,700; 46.5 hp/l (34.3 kW/l); 1 Weber 32 DIR 21 downdraught carburettor.

PERFORMANCE max speeds: (I) 27 mph, 43 km/h; (II) 43 mph, 69 km/h; (III) 72 mph, 116 km/h; (IV) 92 mph, 148 km/h; power weight ratio: 33.8 lb/hp (45.9 lb/kW), 15.3 kg/hp (20.8 kg/kW); carrying capacity: 948 lb, 430 kg; consumption: 26.6 m/imp gal, 22.2 m/US gal, 10.6 l x 100 km.

BRAKES servo.

ELECTRICAL EQUIPMENT 50 A alternator; R 24C 34 distributor; iodine long-distance lights.

DIMENSIONS AND WEIGHT weight: 2,029 lb, 920 kg; weight distribution: 59.4% front, 40.6% rear.

BODY reclining backrests with built-in headrests.

12 TS BERLINE

PRACTICAL INSTRUCTIONS fuel: 98-100 oct petrol; valve timing: 22° 62° 65° 25°.

OPTIONAL ACCESSORIES luxury interior; metallic spray; tinted glass.

12 Break TS

See 12 TS Berline, except for:

PRICE EX WORKS: 29,790* francs

TRANSMISSION tyres: 155 SR x 13.

PERFORMANCE max speeds: (I) 29 mph, 47 km/h; (II) 45 mph, 72 km/h; (III) 68 mph, 110 km/h; (IV) 92 mph, 148 km/h; power-weight ratio: 36 lb/hp (48.9 lb/kW), 16.3 kg/hp (22.2 kg/kW); carrying capacity: 937 lb, 425 kg; speed in top at 1,000 rpm: 16.8 mph, 27 km/h.

BRAKES lining area: front 22.2 sq in, 143 sq cm, rear 38.3 sq in, 247 sq cm, total 60.5 sq in, 390 sq cm.

DIMENSIONS AND WEIGHT length: 172.09 in, 437 cm; height: 57.09 in, 145 cm; ground clearance: 5.12 in, 13 cm; weight: 2,161 lb, 980 kg.

BODY estate car/station wagon; 4 + 1 doors; back seat folding down to luggage table; rear window wiper-washer.

PRACTICAL INSTRUCTIONS tyre pressure: front 23 psi, 1.6 atm, rear 26 psi, 1.8 atm.

12 Berline Automatic

See 12 TS Berline, except for:

PRICE IN GB: £ 3,148*
PRICE EX WORKS: 29,990* francs

ENGINE 1 Weber 32 DIR 39 downdraught carburettor.

TRANSMISSION gearbox: automatic transmission, hydraulic torque converter and planetary gears with 3 ratios, max ratio of converter at stall 2.3, possible manual selection; ratios: I 2.600, II 1.609, III 1.114, rev 2.229; axle ratio: 3.556.

PERFORMANCE max speeds: (I) 37 mph, 60 km/h; (II) 60 mph, 97 km/h; (III) 89 mph, 144 km/h; power-weight ratio: 34.9 lb/hp (47.4 lb/kW), 15.8 kg/hp (21.5 kg/kW); carrying capacity: 882 lb, 400 kg; speed in top at 1,000 rpm: 16.2 mph, 26.1 km/h; consumption: 27.2 m/imp gal, 22.6 m/US gal, 10.4 l x 100 km.

STEERING turns lock to lock: 3.25.

DIMENSIONS AND WEIGHT weight: 2,095 lb, 950 kg; turning circle (between walls): 34.8 ft, 11.7 m.

RENAULT 12 Berline Automatic

PRACTICAL INSTRUCTIONS oil: automatic transmission and final drive 8.8 imp pt, 10.6 US pt, 5 l, change every 18,600 miles, 30,000 km.

12 Break Automatic

See 12 Berline Automatic, except for:

PRICE EX WORKS: 30,990* francs

TRANSMISSION tyres: 155 SR x 13.

PERFORMANCE power-weight ratio: 36 lb/hp (48.9 lb/kW), 16.3 kg/hp (22.2 kg/kW); carrying capacity: 937 lb, 425 kg; speed in top at 1,000 rpm: 16.6 mph, 26.7 km/h.

BRAKES lining area: front 22.2 sq in, 143 sq cm, rear 38.3 sq in, 247 sq cm, total 60.5 sq in, 390 sq cm.

DIMENSIONS AND WEIGHT length: 172.09 in, 437 cm; height: 57.09 in, 145 cm; ground clearance: 5.12 in, 13 cm; weight: 2,161 lb, 980 kg.

BODY estate car/station wagon; 4 + 1 doors; back seat folding down to luggage table.

PRACTICAL INSTRUCTIONS tyre pressure: front 23 psi, 1.6 atm, rear 26 psi, 1.8 atm.

15 TL

PRICE EX WORKS: 29,290* francs

ENGINE front, 4 stroke; 4 cylinders, vertical, in line; 78.7 cu in, 1,289 cc (2.87 x 3.03 in, 73 x 77 mm); compression ratio: 9.5:1; max power (DIN): 60 hp (44.2 kW) at 5,500 rpm; max torque (DIN): 67 lb ft, 9.3 kg m (91.2 Nm) at 3,500 rpm; max engine rpm: 6,000; 46.5 hp/l (34.2 kW/l); cast iron block, light alloy head, wet liners; 5 crankshaft bearings; valves: overhead, in line, slanted, push-rods and rockers; camshafts: 1, side; lubrication: gear pump, full flow filter, 5.3 imp pt, 6.3 US pt, 3 l; 1 Weber 32 DIR Z.I.T. downdraught twin barrel carburettor; fuel feed: mechanical pump; sealed circuit cooling, liquid, expansion tank, 8.8 imp pt, 10.6 US pt, 5 l, electric thermostatic fan.

TRANSMISSION driving wheels: front; clutch: single dry plate (diaphragm); gearbox: mechanical; gears: 4, fully syinchronized; ratios: I 3.818, II 2.235, III 1.478, IV 1.036, rev. 3.083; lever: central; final drive: hypoid bevel; axle ratio: 3.778; width of rims: 4.5''; tyres: 145 SR x 13.

PERFORMANCE max speeds: (I) 29 mph, 46 km/h; (II) 46 mph, 74 km/h; (III) 70 mph, 113 km/h; (IV) 92 mph, 148 km/h; power-weight ratio: 35.5 lb/hp (48.1 lb/kW), 16.1 kg/hp (21.8 kg/kW); carrying capacity: 761 lb, 345 kg; speed in top at 1,000 rpm: 16.4 mph, 26.4 km/h; consumption: 26.6 m/imp gal, 22.2 m/US gal, 10.6 l x 100 km.

CHASSIS integral; front suspension: independent, wishbones, anti-roll bar, coil springs/telescopic dampers; rear: rigid axle, trailing arms, A-bracket, anti-roll bar, coil springs/telescopic dampers.

STEERING rack-and-pinion; turns lock to lock: 3.50.

BRAKES front disc, rear drum, rear compensator, servo; swept area: front 157.2 sq in, 1,014 sq cm, rear 70.1 sq in, 452 sq cm, total 227.3 sq in, 1,466 sq cm.

ELECTRICAL EQUIPMENT 12 V; 36 Ah battery; 50 A alternator; 2 iodine headlamps.

DIMENSIONS AND WEIGHT wheel base: 96.06 in, 244 cm; front and rear tracks: 51.57 in, 131 cm; length: 167.72 in, 426 cm; width: 64.17 in, 163 cm; height: 51.57 in, 131 cm; ground clearance: 4.45 in, 11.3 cm; weight: 2,128 lb, 965 kg; weight distribution: 60.6% front, 39.4% rear; turning circle (between walls): 36.1 ft, 11 m; fuel tank: 12.1 imp gal, 14.5 US gal, 55 l.

BODY coupé; 2 doors; 4 seats, separate front seats, reclining backrests; heated rear window.

PRACTICAL INSTRUCTIONS fuel: 98-100 oct petrol; oil: engine 5.3 imp pt, 6.3 US pt, 3 l, change every 4,650 miles, 7,500 km - gearbox and final drive 3.5 imp pt, 4.2 US pt, 2 l, change every 9,300 miles, 15,000 km; greasing: none; tappet clearances: inlet 0.006-0.007 in, 0.15-0.18 mm, exhaust 0.007-0.009 in, 0.18-0.22 mm; valve timing: 22° 62° 65° 25°; tyre pressure: front 26 psi, 1.8 atm, rear 27 psi, 1.9 atm.

OPTIONAL ACCESSORIES luxury interior; metallic spray.

15 GTL

See 15 TL, except for:

PRICE IN GB: £ 3,429*
PRICE EX WORKS: 31,390* francs

BODY luxury equipment.

OPTIONAL ACCESSORIES luxury interior; metallic spray; tinted glass; electrically-controlled front windows.

15 GTL Automatic

See 15 GTL, except for:

PRICE IN GB: £ 3,724*
PRICE EX WORKS: 35,690* francs

TRANSMISSION gearbox: automatic transmission, hydraulic torque converter and planetary gears with 3 ratios, max ratio of converter at stall 2.3, possible manual selection; ratios: I 2.600, II 1.609, III 1.114, rev 2.229; axle ratio: 3.556.

PERFORMANCE max speeds: (I) 37 mph, 60 km/h; (II) 60 mph, 98 km/h; (III) 89 mph, 144 km/h; power-weight ratio: 36.4 lb/hp (49.4 lb/kW), 16.5 kg/hp (22.4 kg/kW); speed in top at 1,000 rpm: 16.2 mph, 26.1 km/h; consumption: 27.2 m/imp gal, 22.6 m/US gal, 10.4 l x 100 km.

STEERING turns lock to lock: 3.25.

DIMENSIONS AND WEIGHT weight: 2,183 lb, 990 kg; turning circle (between walls): 38.4 ft, 11.7 m.

RENAULT 15 GTL

PRACTICAL INSTRUCTIONS oil: automatic transmission and final drive 8.8 imp pt, 10.6 US pt, 5 l, change every 18,600 miles, 30,000 km.

OPTIONAL ACCESSORIES luxury interior; metallic spray.

16 TL (55 hp)

PRICE IN GB: £ 3,254*
PRICE EX WORKS: 28,980* francs

ENGINE front, 4 stroke; 4 cylinders, vertical, in line; 95.5 cu in, 1,565 cc (3.03 x 3.31 in, 77 x 84 mm); compression ratio: 8:1; max power (DIN): 55 hp (40.5 kW) at 5,000 rpm; max torque (DIN): 79 lb ft, 10.9 kg m (106.9 Nm) at 2,500 rpm; max engine rpm: 5,200; 35.1 hp/l (25.9 kW/l); light alloy block and head, wet liners; 5 crankshaft bearings; valves: overhead, in line, slanted at 20°, push-rods and rockers; camshafts: 1, side; lubrication: eccentric pump, filter in sump, 7 imp pt, 8.5 US pt, 4 l; 1 Solex MIMAT downdraught carburettor; fuel feed: mechanical pump; sealed circuit cooling, liquid, expansion tank, 10.9 imp pt, 13.1 US pt, 6.2 l, electric thermostatic fan.

TRANSMISSION driving wheels: front; clutch: single dry plate (diaphragm); gearbox: mechanical; gears: 4, fully synchronized; ratios: I 3.818, II 2.235, III 1.478, IV 1.036, rev 3.083; lever: steering column; final drive: hypoid bevel; axle ratio: 3.778; width of rims: 4.5''; tyres: 145 SR x 14.

RENAULT 15 TL - 15 GTL

PERFORMANCE max speeds: (I) 24 mph, 39 km/h; (II) 41 mph, 66 km/h; (III) 63 mph, 101 km/h; (IV) 87 mph, 140 km/h; power-weight ratio: 40.5 lb/hp (55 lb/kW), 18.4 kg/hp (24.9 kg/kW); carrying capacity: 882 lb, 400 kg; speed in top at 1,000 rpm: 17.1 mph, 27.6 km/h; consumption: 27.4 m/imp gal, 22.8 m/US gal, 10.3 l x 100 km.

CHASSIS platform; front suspension: independent, wishbones, longitudinal torsion bars, anti-roll bar, telescopic dampers; rear: independent, swinging longitudinal trailing arms, transverse torsion bar, anti-roll bar, telescopic dampers.

STEERING rack-and-pinion; turns lock to lock: 4.11.

BRAKES front disc, rear drum, rear compensator, servo; lining area: front 22.2 sq in, 143 sq cm, rear 42.3 sq in, 273 sq cm, total 64.5 sq in, 416 sq cm.

ELECTRICAL EQUIPMENT 12 V; 36 Ah battery; 30/40 A alternator; 2 headlamps.

DIMENSIONS AND WEIGHT wheel base: 104.33 in, 265 cm (right), 107.09 in, 272 cm (left); tracks: 52.76 in, 134 cm front, 50.79 in, 129 cm rear; length: 166.93 in, 424 cm; width: 64.17 in, 163 cm; height: 57.09 in, 145 cm; ground clearance: 4.13 in, 10.5 cm; weight: 2,227 lb, 1,010 kg; weight distribution: 55.9% front, 44.1% rear; turning circle (between walls): 36.1 ft, 11 m; fuel tank: 11 imp gal, 13.2 US gal, 50 l.

BODY saloon/sedan; 4 + 1 doors; 5 seats, separate front seats, reclining backrests; back seat folding down to luggage table; heated rear window.

PRACTICAL INSTRUCTIONS fuel: 85 oct petrol; oil: engine 7 imp pt, 8.5 US pt, 4 l, SAE 10W-40, change every 4,650 miles, 7,500 km - gearbox and final drive 2.8 imp pt, 3.4 US pt, 1.6 l, SAE 80 EP, change every 9,300 miles, 15,000 km; greasing: none; tappet clearances: inlet 0.008 in, 0.20 mm, exhaust 0.010 in, 0.25 mm; valve timing: 18° 54° 58° 18°; tyre pressure: front 23 psi, 1.6 atm, rear 28 psi, 2 atm.

OPTIONAL ACCESSORIES luxury interior; metallic spray.

RENAULT 16 TL

16 TL (66 hp)

See 16 TL (55 hp), except for:

PRICE EX WORKS: 29,680* francs

ENGINE compression ratio: 8.6:1; max power (DIN): 66 hp (48.6 kW) at 5,000 rpm; max torque (DIN): 82 lb ft, 11.3 kg m (110.8 Nm) at 3,000 rpm; max engine rpm: 5,500; 42.2 hp/l (31 kW/l).

PERFORMANCE max speeds: (I) 25 mph, 41 km/h; (II) 43 mph, 70 km/h; (III) 66 mph, 106 km/h; (IV) 92 mph, 148 km/h; power-weight ratio: 33.7 lb/hp (45.8 lb/kW), 15.3 kg/hp (20.8 kg/kW); consumption: 26.9 m/imp gal, 22.4 m/US gal, 10.5 l x 100 km.

PRACTICAL INSTRUCTIONS fuel: 98-100 oct petrol.

OPTIONAL ACCESSORIES tinted glass; electrically-controlled sunshine roof.

16 TL Automatic

See 16 TL (55 hp), except for:

PRICE IN GB: £ 3,549*
PRICE EX WORKS: 32,200* francs

ENGINE 100.5 cu in, 1,647 cc (3.11 x 3.31 in, 79 x 84 mm); compression ratio: 8.6:1; max power (DIN): 68 hp (50 kW) at 5,000 rpm; max torque (DIN): 87 lb ft, 12 kg m (117.7 Nm) at 3,000 rpm; 41.3 hp/l (30.3 kW/l); valves: Vee-slanted.

TRANSMISSION gearbox: automatic transmission, hydraulic torque converter and planetary gears with 3 ratios, max ratio of converter at stall 2.3, possible manual selection; ratios: I 2.396, II 1.484, III 1.027, rev 2.054.

PERFORMANCE max speeds: (I) 37 mph, 59 km/h; (II) 60 mph, 96 km/h; (III) 90 mph, 145 km/h; power-weight ratio: 33.9 lb/hp (46.1 lb/kW), 15.4 kg/hp (20.9 kg/kW); speed in top at 1,000 rpm: 17.2 mph, 27.7 km/h; consumption: 26.4 m/imp gal, 22 m/US gal, 10.7 l x 100 km.

ELECTRICAL EQUIPMENT 50 A alternator.

DIMENSIONS AND WEIGHT weight: 2,304 lb, 1,045 kg; weight distribution: 56.9% front, 43.1% rear.

PRACTICAL INSTRUCTIONS fuel: 98-100 oct petrol; oil: automatic transmission and final drive 10.6 imp pt, 12.7 US pt, 6 l, change every 18,600 miles, 30,000 km; tyre pressure: front 24 psi, 1.7 atm.

OPTIONAL ACCESSORIES tinted glass; electrically-controlled sunshine roof.

RENAULT 16 TL Automatic

16 TX

See 16 TL (55 hp), except for:

PRICE IN GB: £ 3,970*
PRICE EX WORKS: 34,380* francs

ENGINE 100.5 cu in, 1,647 cc (3.11 x 3.31 in, 79 x 84 mm); compression ratio: 9.25:1; max power (DIN): 90 hp (66.2 kW) at 6,000 rpm; max torque (DIN): 95 lb ft, 13.1 kg m (128.5 Nm) at 4,000 rpm; max engine rpm: 6,300; 54.6 hp/l (40.2 kW/l); valves: Vee-slanted; lubrication: eccentric pump, full flow filter; 1 Weber 32 DAR 7 twin barrel carburettor; cooling system: 12 imp pt, 14.4 US pt, 6.8 l.

TRANSMISSION gears: 5, fully synchronized; ratios: I 3.818, II 2.235, II 1.478, IV 1.036, V 0.861, rev 3.083; axle ratio: 3.875; tyres: 155 SR x 14.

PERFORMANCE max speeds: (I) 28 mph, 45 km/h; (II) 48 mph, 77 km/h; (III) 72 mph, 116 km/h; (IV) 103 mph, 166 km/h; (V) 106 mph, 170 km/h; power-weight ratio: 26.1 lb/hp (58.4 lb/kW), 11.8 kg/hp (26.5 kg/kW); carrying capacity: 937 lb, 425 kg; acceleration: 0-50 mph (0-80 km/h) 8.1 sec; speed in top at 1,000 rpm: 20.7 mph, 33.3 km/h; consumption: 26.4 m/imp gal, 22 m/US gal, 10.7 l x 100 km.

ELECTRICAL EQUIPMENT 50 A alternator; 4 iodine headlamps.

DIMENSIONS AND WEIGHT ground clearance: 4.13 in, 10.5 cm; weight: 2,348 lb, 1,065 kg; weight distribution: 56.6% front, 43.4% rear.

BODY reclining backrests with built-in headrests; electrically-controlled windows; rear window wiper-washer.

PRACTICAL INSTRUCTIONS fuel: 98-100 oct petrol; oil: gearbox and final drive 3 imp pt, 3.6 US pt, 1.7 l; valve timing: 24° 68° 68° 24°; tyre pressure: front 24 psi, 1.7 atm.

OPTIONAL ACCESSORIES luxury interior; metallic spray; leather upholstery; tinted glass; electrically-controlled sunshine roof; air-conditioning.

16 TX Automatic

See 16 TX, except for:

PRICE IN GB: £ 4,265*
PRICE EX WORKS: 27,480* francs

ENGINE max torque (DIN): 96 lb ft, 13.2 kg m (129.5 Nm) at 3,500 rpm; 1 Weber 32 DAR 8 twin barrel carburettor.

TRANSMISSION gearbox: automatic transmission, hydraulic torque converter and planetary gears with 3 ratios, max ratio of converter at stall 2.3, possible manual selection; ratios: I 2.459, II 1.523, III 1.054, rev 2.108; axle ratio: 3.556.

PERFORMANCE max speeds: (I) 47 mph, 76 km/h; (II) 76 mph, 123 km/h; (III) 103 mph, 165 km/h; power-weight ratio: 26.7 lb/hp (36.3 lb/kW), 12.1 kg/hp (16.5 kg/kW); carrying capacity: 882 lb, 400 kg; speed in top at 1,000 rpm: 18.5 mph, 29.7 km/h; consumption: 25.2 m/imp gal, 21 m/US gal, 11.2 l x 100 km.

DIMENSIONS AND WEIGHT weight: 2,403 lb, 1,090 kg.

PRACTICAL INSTRUCTIONS oil: automatic transmission and final drive 10.6 imp pt, 12.7 US pt, 6 l, change every 18,600 miles, 30,000 km; valve timing: 21° 59° 59° 21°.

17 TS Cabriolet

PRICE IN GB: £ 4,166*
PRICE EX WORKS: 39,980* francs

ENGINE front, 4 stroke; 4 cylinders, vertical, in line; 100.5 cu in, 1,647 cc (3.11 x 3.31 in, 79 x 84 mm); compression ratio: 9.25:1; max power (DIN): 98 hp (72.1 kW) at 5,750 rpm; max torque (DIN): 98 lb ft, 13.5 kg m (132.4 Nm) at 3,500 rpm; max engine rpm: 6,000; 59.5 hp/l (43.8 kW/l); light alloy block and head, wet liners; 5 crankshaft bearings; valves: overhead, Vee-slanted, push-rods and rockers; camshafts: 1, side; lubrication: rotary pump, full flow filter, 7.9 imp pt, 9.5 US pt, 4.5 l; 1 Weber 32 DARA downdraught twin barrel carburettor; fuel feed: mechanical pump; sealed circuit cooling, liquid, expansion tank, 9.7 imp pt, 11.6 US pt, 5.5 l, electric thermostatic fan.

TRANSMISSION driving wheels: front; clutch: single dry plate (diaphragm); gearbox: mechanical; gears: 5, fully synchronized; ratios: I 3.818, II 2.235, III 1.478, IV 1.036, V 0.861, rev 3.083; lever: central; final drive: hypoid bevel; axle ratio: 3.778; width of rims: 4.5"; tyres: 155 SR x 13.

PERFORMANCE max speeds: (I) 26 mph, 42 km/h; (II) 45 mph, 72 km/h; (III) 68 mph, 109 km/h; (IV) 96 mph, 155 km/h; (V) 106 mph, 170 km/h; power-weight ratio: 24.3 lb/hp (30.3 lb/kW), 11 kg/hp (15 kg/kW); carrying ca-

RENAULT 16 TX

RENAULT 17 TS Cabriolet Automatic

pacity: 761 lb, 345 kg; speed in top at 1,000 rpm: 20.2 mph, 32.5 km/h; consumption: 26.2 m/imp gal, 21.8 m/US gal, 10.8 l x 100 km.

CHASSIS platform; front suspension: independent, wishbones, longitudinal torsion bars, anti-roll bar, telescopic dampers; rear: independent, swinging longitudinal trailing arms, transverse torsion bar, anti-roll bar, telescopic dampers.

STEERING rack-and-pinion; turns lock to lock: 3.50.

BRAKES front disc (diameter 8.98 in, 22.8 cm), internal radial fins, rear drum, servo; swept area: front 157.2 sq in, 1,014 sq cm, rear 89 sq in, 574 sq cm, total 246.2 sq in, 1,588 sq cm.

ELECTRICAL EQUIPMENT 12 V; 36 Ah battery; 50 A alternator; 4 headlamps.

DIMENSIONS AND WEIGHT wheel base: 96.06 in, 244 cm; tracks: 52.76 in, 134 cm front, 51.57 in, 131 cm rear; length: 167.72 in, 426 cm; width: 64.17 in, 163 cm; height: 51.57 in, 131 cm; ground clearance: 4.72 in, 12 cm; weight: 2,381 lb, 1,080 kg; turning circle (between walls): 36.1 ft, 11 m; fuel tank: 12.1 imp gal, 14.5 US gal, 55 l.

BODY convertible; 2 doors; 4 seats, separate front seats, reclining backrests; heated rear window; electrically-controlled tinted glass.

PRACTICAL INSTRUCTIONS fuel: 98-100 oct petrol; oil:

RENAULT 17 TS Cabriolet

engine 7 imp pt, 8.5 US pt, 4 l, change every 4,650 miles, 7,500 km - gearbox and final drive 3.5 imp pt, 4.2 US pt, 2 l, change every 9,300 miles, 15,000 km; greasing: none; tappet clearances: inlet 0.008 in, 0.20 mm, exhaust 0.010 in, 0.25 mm; valve timing: 30° 72° 72° 30°; tyre pressure: front 26 psi, 1.8 atm, rear 27 psi, 1.9 atm.

OPTIONAL ACCESSORIES luxury interior; metallic spray; power steering; air-conditioning.

17 TS Cabriolet Automatic

See 17 TS Cabriolet, except for:

PRICE EX WORKS: 42,500* francs

TRANSMISSION gearbox: automatic transmission, hydraulic torque converter and planetary gears with 3 ratios, max ratio of converter at stall 2.3, possible manual selection; ratios: I 2.396, II 1.484, III 1.027, rev 2.054; axle ratio: 3.556.

PERFORMANCE max speeds: (I) 45 mph, 72 km/h; (II) 73 mph, 117 km/h; (III) 103 mph, 165 km/h; power-weight ratio: 24.9 lb/hp (33.8 lb/kW), 11.3 kg/hp (15.3 kg/kW); speed in top at 1,000 rpm: 18 mph, 28.9 km/h; consumption: 26.9 m/imp gal, 22.4 m/US gal, 10.5 l x 100 km.

STEERING turns lock to lock: 3.25.

DIMENSIONS AND WEIGHT weight: 2,437 lb, 1,105 kg; turning circle (between walls): 38.4 ft, 11.7 m.

PRACTICAL INSTRUCTIONS oil: automatic transmission and final drive 10.6 imp pt, 12.7 US pt, 6 l, change every 18,600 miles, 30,000 km; tyre pressure: front 27 psi, 1.9 atm.

20 TL

PRICE IN GB: £ 3,833*
PRICE EX WORKS: 35,380* francs

ENGINE front, 4 stroke; 4 cylinders, vertical, in line; 100.5 cu in, 1,647 cc (3.11 x 3.31 in, 79 x 84 mm); compression ratio: 9.3:1; max power (DIN): 96 hp (70.7 kW) at 5,750 rpm; max torque (DIN): 99 lb ft, 13.6 kg m (133.4 Nm) at 3,500 rpm; max engine rpm: 6,000 58.3 hp/l (42.9 kW/l); light alloy block and head, wet liners, hemispherical combustion chambers; 5 crankshaft bearings; valves: overhead. Vee-slanted, push-rods and rockers; camshafts: 1, side; lubrication: gear pump, full flow filter, 7 imp pt, 8.5 US pt, 4 l; 1 Weber 32 DARA downdraught twin barrel carburettor; sealed circuit cooling, liquid, expansion tank, 12.3 imp pt, 14.8 US pt, 7 l, electric thermostatic fan.

TRANSMISSION driving wheels: front; clutch: single dry plate (diaphragm), hydraulically controlled; gearbox: mechanical, in unit with engine and final drive; gears: 4, fully synchronized; ratios: I 3.818, II 2.235, III 1.478, IV 1.036, rev 3.083; lever: central; final drive: hypoid bevel; axle ratio: 3.778; width of rims: 5.5''; tyres: 165 SR x 13.

PERFORMANCE max speeds: (I) 28 mph, 45 km/h; (II) 48 mph, 77 km/h; (III) 73 mph, 117 km/h; (IV) 102 mph, 164 km/h; power-weight ratio: 27 lb/hp (36.8 lb/kW), 12.2 kg/hp (16.6 kg/kW); carrying capacity: 882 lb, 400 kg; speed in top at 1,000 rpm: 17.2 mph, 27.7 km/h; consumption: 25.7 m/imp gal, 21.4 m/US gal, 11 l x 100 km.

CHASSIS integral; front suspension: independent, by McPherson, coil springs/telescopic damper struts, lower wishbones, anti-roll bar; rear: independent, oblique semi-trailing arms, coil springs, anti-roll bar, telescopic dampers.

STEERING rack-and-pinion; turns lock to lock: 4.

BRAKES front disc, internal radial fins, rear drum, rear compensator, servo; lining area: front 22.2 sq in, 143 sq cm, rear 42.3 sq in, 273 sq cm, total 64.5 sq in, 416 sq cm.

ELECTRICAL EQUIPMENT 12 V; 40 Ah battery; 50 A alternator; 2 headlamps.

DIMENSIONS AND WEIGHT wheel base: 104.68 in, 266 cm; tracks: 56.85 in, 144 cm front, 56.61 in, 144 cm rear; length: 177.95 in, 452 cm; width: 67.95 in, 173 cm; height: 56.50 in, 143 cm; weight: 2,591 lb, 1,175 kg; turning circle (between walls): 36.7 ft, 11.2 m; fuel tank: 13.2 imp gal, 15.8 US gal, 60 l.

BODY saloon/sedan; 4 doors; 5 seats, separate front seats, reclining backrests; heated rear window.

PRACTICAL INSTRUCTIONS fuel: 98-100 oct petrol; oil: engine 7 imp pt, 8.5 US pt, 4 l, SAE 10W-50, change every 4,650 miles, 7,500 km - gearbox 3.5 imp pt, 4.2 US pt, 2 l, SAE 20W-40, change every 9,300 miles, 15,000 km - final drive 2.8 imp pt, 3.4 US pt, 1.6 l, SAE 80, change every 9,300 miles, 15,000 km; tappet clearances: inlet 0.008 in, 0.20 mm, exhaust 0.010 in, 0.25 mm; valve timing: 30° 72° 72° 30°; tyre pressure: front and rear 27 psi, 1.9 atm.

OPTIONAL ACCESSORIES luxury interior; metallic spray; tinted glass; electrically-controlled sunshine roof.

RENAULT 20 - 30 Series

RENAULT 20 GTL

20 TL Automatic

See 20 TL, except for:

PRICE IN GB: £ 4,161*
PRICE EX WORKS: 37,900* francs

TRANSMISSION gearbox: automatic transmission, hydraulic torque converter and planetary gears with 3 ratios, max ratio of converter at stall 2.3, possible manual selection; ratios: I 2.222, II 1.370, III 0.925, rev 1.777; axle ratio: 4.125.

PERFORMANCE max speeds: (I) 44 mph, 71 km/h; (II) 71 mph, 115 km/h; (III) 98 mph, 157 km/h; power-weight ratio: 27.9 lb/hp (37.9 lb/kW), 12.6 kg/hp (17.2 kg/kW); speed in top at 1,000 rpm: 17 mph, 27.4 km/h; consumption: 24.1 m/imp gal, 20.1 m/US gal, 11.7 l x 100 km.

DIMENSIONS AND WEIGHT weight: 2,679 lb, 1,215 kg.

PRACTICAL INSTRUCTIONS oil: automatic transmission 10.6 imp pt, 12.7 US pt, 6 l, change every 18,600 miles, 30,000 km.

20 GTL

See 20 TL, except for:

PRICE EX WORKS: 38,880* francs

STEERING servo; turns lock to lock: 3.

DIMENSIONS AND WEIGHT turning circle (between walls): 38 ft, 11.6 m.

BODY luxury equipment; electrically-controlled windows.

OPTIONAL ACCESSORIES air-conditioning.

20 GTL Automatic

See 20 GTL, except for:

PRICE EX WORKS: 41,980* francs

TRANSMISSION gearbox: automatic transmission, hydraulic torque converter and planetary gears with 3 ratios, max ratio of converter at stall 2.3, possible manual selection; ratios: I 2.222, II 1.370, III 0.925, rev. 1.777; axle ratio: 4.125.

PERFORMANCE max speeds: (I) 44 mph, 71 km/h; (II) 71 mph, 115 km/h; (III) 98 mph, 157 km/h; power-weight ratio: 27.9 lb/hp (37.9 lb/kW), 12.6 kg/hp (17.2 kg/kW); speed in top at 1,000 rpm: 17 mph, 27.4 km/h; consumption: 24.1 m/imp gal, 20.1 m/US gal, 11.7 l x 100 km.

DIMENSIONS AND WEIGHT weight: 2,679 lb, 1,215 kg.

PRACTICAL INSTRUCTIONS oil: automatic transmission 10.6 imp pt, 12.7 US pt, 6 l, change every 18,600 miles, 30,000 km.

RENAULT 20 TL

20 TS

See 20 TL, except for:

PRICE EX WORKS: 40,320* francs

ENGINE 121.7 cu in, 1,995 cc (3.46 x 3.23 in, 88 x 82 mm); compression ratio: 9.2:1; max power (DIN): 110 hp (81 kW) at 5,500 rpm; max torque (DIN): 123 lb ft, 17 kg m (166.7 Nm) at 3,000 rpm; 55.1 hp/l (40.6 kW/l); camshafts: 1, overhead, cogged belt.

TRANSMISSION gearbox ratios: I 3.364, II 2.059, III 1.318, IV 0.931, rev 3.182; axle ratio: 4.125; tyres: 165 SR x 14.

PERFORMANCE max speed: 106 mph, 170 km/h; power-weight ratio: 25.2 lb/hp (34.3 lb/kW), 11.4 kg/hp (15.6 kg/kW); speed in top at 1,000 rpm: 13 mph, 20.9 km/h; consumption: 22.8 m/imp gal, 19 m/US gal, 12.4 l x 100 km.

STEERING servo; turns lock to lock: 3.25.

BRAKES lining area: front 27.3 sq in, 176 sq cm, rear 42.3 sq in, 273 sq cm, total 69.6 sq in, 449 sq cm.

DIMENSIONS AND WEIGHT weight: 2,778 lb, 1,260 kg; turning circle (between walls): 37.4 ft, 11.4 m.

BODY luxury equipment; electrically-controlled windows.

PRACTICAL INSTRUCTIONS tappet clearances: inlet 0.010-0.012 in, 0.15-0.18 mm, exhaust 0.006-0.008 in, 0.25-0.30 mm; valve timing: 20° 60° 60° 20°; tyre pressure: front 27 psi, 1.9 atm, rear 28 psi, 2 atm.

OPTIONAL ACCESSORIES air-conditioning.

20 TS Automatic

See 20 TS, except for:

PRICE EX WORKS: 32,000* francs

TRANSMISSION gearbox: automatic transmission, hydraulic torque converter and planetary gears with 3 ratios, max ratio of converter at stall 2.3, possible manual selection; ratios: I 2.222, II 1.370, III 0.926, rev 1.777.

PERFORMANCE max speed: 103 mph, 165 km/h; power-weight ratio: 25.6 lb/hp (34.8 lb/kW), 11.6 kg/hp (15.8 kg/kW); speed in top at 1,000 rpm: 18.5 mph, 29.7 km/h; consumption: 24.8 m/imp gal, 20.6 m/US gal, 11.4 l x 100 km.

DIMENSIONS AND WEIGHT weight: 2,822 lb, 1,280 kg.

PRACTICAL INSTRUCTIONS oil: automatic transmission 10.6 imp pt, 12.7 US pt, 6 l, change every 18,600 miles, 30,000 km; tyre pressure: front and rear 28 psi, 2 atm.

30 TS

PRICE IN GB: £ 5,834*
PRICE EX WORKS: 45,000* francs

ENGINE front, 4 stroke; 6 cylinders, Vee-slanted at 90°; 162.6 cu in, 2,664 cc (3.46 x 2.87 in, 88 x 73 mm); compression ratio: 8.65:1; max power (DIN): 125 hp (92 kW) at 5,000 rpm; max torque (DIN): 151 lb ft, 20.8 kg m (204 Nm) at 2,500 rpm; max engine rpm: 6,000; 49.2 hp/l (34.5 kW/l); light alloy block and head, wet liners, hemispherical combustion chambers; 4 crankshaft bearings; valves: overhead, Vee-slanted, rockers; camshafts: 1 per block, overhead; lubrication: gear pump, full flow filter, 10.6 imp pt, 12.7 US pt, 6 l; 1 Weber 38-38 DGAR downdraught twin barrel carburettor; fuel feed: mechanical pump; water-cooled, expansion tank, 17.2 imp pt, 20.7 US pt, 9.8 l, viscous coupling thermostatic fan.

TRANSMISSION driving wheels: front; clutch: single dry plate (diaphragm), hydraulically controlled; gearbox: mechanical; gears: 4, fully synchronized; ratios: I 3.364, II 2.059, III 1.318, IV 0.931, rev 3.182; lever: central; final drive: hypoid bevel; axle ratio: 3.889; width of rims: 5.5''; tyres: 175 HR x 14.

PERFORMANCE max speeds: (I) 31 mph, 50 km/h; (II) 50 mph, 81 km/h; (III) 79 mph, 127 km/h; (IV) 114 mph, 183 km/h; power-weight ratio: 23.3 lb/hp (31.6 lb/kW), 10.6 kg/hp (14.3 kg/kW); carrying capacity: 926 lb, 420 kg; acceleration: standing ¼ mile 17.1 sec, 0-50 mph (0-80 km/h) 6.8 sec; speed in top at 1,000 rpm: 19.9 mph, 32 km/h; consumption: 16.3 m/imp gal, 13.6 m/US gal, 17.3 l x 100 km.

CHASSIS integral; front suspension: independent, by McPherson, coil springs/telescopic damper struts, lower wishbones, anti-roll bar; rear: independent, oblique semi-trailing arms, coil springs, anti-roll bar, telescopic dampers.

RENAULT 20 TS Automatic

RENAULT 20 TS

STEERING rack-and-pinion, servo; turns lock to lock: 3.50.

BRAKES disc (front diameter 9.92 in, 25.2 cm, rear 10 in, 25.4 cm), front internal radial fins, rear compensator, servo; lining area: front 29.8 sq in, 192 sq cm, rear 22.2 sq in, 143 sq cm, total 52 sq in, 335 sq cm.

ELECTRICAL EQUIPMENT 12 V; 50 Ah battery; 50 A alternator; dual ignition; 4 iodine headlamps, height adjustable from driving seat.

DIMENSIONS AND WEIGHT wheel base: 105.12 in, 267 cm; tracks: 56.89 in, 144.5 cm front, 56.69 in, 144 cm rear; length: 177.95 in, 452 cm; width: 68.11 in, 173 cm; height: 56.30 in, 143 cm; weight: 2,911 lb, 1,320 kg; turning circle (between walls): 35.8 ft, 10.9 m; fuel tank: 14.7 imp gal, 17.7 US gal, 67 l.

BODY saloon/sedan; 4 doors; 5 seats, separate front seats, reclining backrests with adjustable built-in headrests; electrically-controlled front windows; heated rear window; headlamps with wiper-washers; tinted glass.

PRACTICAL INSTRUCTIONS fuel: 98-100 oct petrol; oil: engine 9.7 imp pt, 11.6 US pt, 5.5 l, SAE 10W-50, change every 4,650 miles, 7,500 km - gearbox 6 imp pt, 7.2 US pt, 3.4 l, SAE 20W-40, change every 9,300 miles, 15,000 km - final drive 2.8 imp pt, 3.4 US pt, 1.6 l, SAE 80, change every 9,300 miles, 15,000 km; tappet clearances: inlet 0.004-0.006 in, 0.10-0.15 mm, exhaust 0.010-0.012 in, 0.25-0.30 mm; valve timing: 9° 45° 45° 9° (left), 7° 43° 43° 7° (right); tyre pressure: front 26 psi, 1.8 atm, rear 28 psi, 2 atm.

RENAULT 30 TS

OPTIONAL ACCESSORIES metallic spray; electrically-controlled sunshine roof; leather upholstery; air-conditioning.

30 TS Automatic

See 30 TS, except for:

PRICE IN GB: £ 6,185*
PRICE EX WORKS: 48,200* francs

TRANSMISSION gearbox: automatic transmission, hydraulic torque converter and planetary gears with 3 ratios, max ratio of converter at stall 2.3, possible manual selection; ratios: I 2.307, II 1.423, III 0.961, rev 1.846.

PERFORMANCE max speeds: (I) 45 mph, 72 km/h; (II) 70 mph, 113 km/h; (III) 110 mph, 177 km/h; power-weight ratio: 23.6 lb/hp (32.1 lb/kW), 10.7 kg/hp (14.6 kg/kW); carrying capacity: 882 lb, 400 kg; speed in top at 1,000 rpm: 19.3 mph, 31 km/h; consumption: 17.1 m/imp gal, 14.3 m/US gal, 16.5 l x 100 km.

STEERING turns lock to lock: 3.25.

DIMENSIONS AND WEIGHT weight: 2,955 lb, 1,340 kg, turning circle (between walls): 37.4 ft, 11.4 m.

PRACTICAL INSTRUCTIONS oil: automatic transmission 13.4 imp pt, 16.1 US pt, 7.6 l; tyre pressure: front 27 psi, 1.9 atm

---

SCORA   FRANCE

Coupé

ENGINE Renault, rear, transverse, 4 stroke; 4 cylinders, vertical, in line; 109.6 cu in, 1,796 cc (3.25 x 3.31 in, 82.5 x 84 mm); compression ratio: 11.2:1; max power (DIN): 183 hp (134.7 kW); max torque (DIN): 145 lb ft, 20 kg m (196.1 Nm) at 5,200 rpm; max engine rpm: 7,500; 101.8 hp/l (75 kW/l); light alloy block and head, wet liners; 5 crankshaft bearings; valves: overhead, Vee-slanted, push-rods and rockers; camshafts: 1, side; lubrication: eccentric pump, full flow filter, oil cooler, 8.4 imp pt, 10.1 US pt, 4.8 l; electronic injection; fuel feed: electric pump; water-cooled, 9.9 imp pt, 11.8 US pt, 5.6 l.

TRANSMISSION driving wheels: rear; clutch: single dry plate (diaphragm); gearbox: mechanical; gears: 5, fully synchronized; ratios: I 3.455, II 2.235, III 1.609, IV 1.214, V 0.35, rev 3.080; lever: central; final drive: spiral bevel; axle ratio: 3.083; tyres: front 19 x 13, rear 25 x 13.

PERFORMANCE not declared.

CHASSIS tubular; front suspension: independent, wishbones, longitudinal torsion bars, coil springs, anti-roll bar, telescopic dampers; rear: independent, wishbones (trailing links), coil springs, anti-roll bar, telescopic dampers.

SCORA Coupé

TRABANT 601 Limousine

STEERING rack-and-pinion.

BRAKES disc.

ELECTRICAL EQUIPMENT 12 V; 36 Ah battery; 50 A alternator; 4 headlamps (2 retractable).

DIMENSIONS AND WEIGHT wheel base: 87.80 in, 223 cm; length: 141.73 in, 360 cm; width: 66.14 in, 168 cm; height: 40.16 in, 102 cm; weight: 1,345 lb, 610 kg; fuel tank: 13.2 imp gal, 15.8 US gal, 60 l.

BODY coupé, in plastic material; 2 doors; 2 seats.

PRACTICAL INSTRUCTIONS fuel: 98-100 oct petrol; oil: engine 7 imp pt, 8.5 US pt, 4 l, change every 4,650 miles, 7,500 km - gearbox and final drive 3.5 imp pt, 4.2 US pt, 2 l, change every 9,300 miles, 15,000 km.

VARIATIONS

ENGINE Renault, 97.9 cu in, 1,605 cc (3.07 x 3.31 in, 78 x 84 mm), 10.25:1 compression ratio, max power (DIN) 108 hp (79.5 kW) at 6,000 rpm, max torque (DIN) 99 lb ft, 13.7 kg m (134.4 Nm) at 5,500 rpm, 63.7 hp/l (49.5 kW/l).

ENGINE Renault, 109.6 cu in, 1,796 cc (3.25 x 3.31 in, 82.5 x 84 mm), max power (DIN) 178 hp (131 kW), 99.1 hp/l (72.9 kW/l), 1 downdraught twin barrel carburettor.

For further data, see Renault.

TRABANT   GERMANY DDR

601 Limousine

ENGINE front, transverse, 2 stroke; 2 cylinders, in line; 36.2 cu in, 594.5 cc (2.83 x 2.87 in, 72 x 73 mm); compression ratio: 7.6:1; max power (DIN): 26 hp (19.1 kW) at 4,200 rpm; max torque (DIN): 40 lb ft, 5.5 kg m (53.9 Nm) at 3,000 rpm; max engine rpm: 4,500; 43.7 hp/l (32.1 kW/l); light alloy block and head, dry liners; 3 crankshaft bearings; valves: 1, per cylinder, rotary; lubrication: mixture; 1 BVF type 28 HB 2-8 horizontal single barrel carburettor; fuel feed: gravity; air-cooled.

TRANSMISSION driving wheels: front; clutch: single dry plate; gearbox: mechanical; gears: 4, fully synchronized; ratios: I 4.080, II 2.320, III 1.520, IV 1.103, rev 3.830; lever: on facia; final drive: conic bevel; axle ratio: 3.950; width of rims: 4''; tyres: 5.20 or 145 SR x 13.

PERFORMANCE max speeds: (I) 16 mph, 25 km/h; (II) 28 mph, 45 km/h; (III) 43 mph, 70 km/h; (IV) 62 mph, 100 km/h; power-weight ratio: 52.1 lb/hp (71 lb/kW), 23.6 kg/hp (32.2 kg/kW); carrying capacity: 849 lb, 385 kg; acceleration: 0-50 mph (0-80 km/h) 22.5 sec; speed in top at 1,000 rpm: 14.6 mph, 23.5 km/h; consumption: 40.4 m/imp gal, 33.6 m/US gal, 7 l x 100 km.

CHASSIS integral; front suspension: independent, wishbones, transverse leafspring upper arms, telescopic dampers; rear: independent, swinging semi-axles, transverse semi-elliptic leafspring, telescopic dampers.

STEERING rack-and-pinion; turns lock to lock: 2.60.

BRAKES drum, single circuit; swept area: front 38.9 sq in, 251 sq cm, rear 34.1 sq in, 220 sq cm, total 73 sq in, 471 sq cm.

ELECTRICAL EQUIPMENT 6 V; 56 Ah battery; 220 W dynamo; AKA distributor; 2 headlamps.

DIMENSIONS AND WEIGHT wheel base: 79.53 in, 202 cm; tracks: 47.64 in, 121 cm front, 49.21 in, 125 cm rear; length: 139.76 in, 355 cm; width: 59.06 in, 150 cm; height: 56.69 in, 144 cm; ground clearance: 6.10 in, 15.5 cm; weight: 1,356 lb, 615 kg; weight distribution: 45% front, 55% rear; turning circle (between walls): 32.8 ft, 10 m; fuel tank: 5.7 imp gal, 6.9 US gal, 26 l.

BODY saloon/sedan; 2 doors; 4 seats, separate front seats, reclining backrests.

PRACTICAL INSTRUCTIONS fuel: mixture 1:50, 88 oct petrol, SAE 20; oil: gearbox and final drive 2.6 imp pt, 3.2 US pt, 1.5 l, SAE 10W-30, change every 9,300 miles, 15,000 km; greasing: every 3,100 miles, 5,000 km, 9 points; sparking plug: 260°; valve timing: 45° 45° 72°5' 72°5'; tyre pressure: front 20 psi, 1.4 atm, rear 20 psi, 1.4 atm.

OPTIONAL ACCESSORIES Hycomat automatic clutch.

601 Universal

See 601 Limousine, except for:

PERFORMANCE power-weight ratio: 55.1 lb/hp (75 lb/kW), 25 kg/hp (34 kg/kW); carrying capacity: 860 lb, 390 kg.

DIMENSIONS AND WEIGHT length: 140.16 in, 356 cm; width: 59.45 in, 151 cm; height: 57.87 in, 147 cm; weight: 1,433 lb, 650 kg; weight distribution: 44% front, 56% rear.

BODY estate car/station wagon; 2 + 1 doors; back seat folding down to luggage table.

WARTBURG   GERMANY DDR

353 W

ENGINE front, 2 stroke; 3 cylinders, vertical, in line; 60.5 cu in, 992 cc (2.89 x 3.07 in, 73.5 x 78 mm); compression ratio: 7.5:1; max power (DIN): 50 hp (36.8 kW) at 4,250 rpm; max torque (DIN): 72 lb ft, 10 kg m (98.1 Nm) at 3,000 rpm; max engine rpm: 4,250; 50.4 hp/l (37.1 kW/l); cast iron block, light alloy head; 4 crankshaft bearings; lubrication: mixture 1:50; 1 BVF 40F1-11 single barrel carburettor; fuel feed: mechanical pump; sealed circuit cooling, liquid, 13.2 imp pt, 15.9 US pt, 7.5 l.

TRANSMISSION driving wheels: front; clutch: single dry plate; gearbox: mechanical; gears: 4, fully synchronized; ratios: I 3.769, II 2.160, III 1.347, IV 0.906, rev 3.385; lever: steering column; final drive: spiral bevel; axle ratio: 4.222; width of rims: 4.5''; tyres: 6.00 x 13 or 165 SR x 13.

PERFORMANCE max speeds: (I) 20 mph, 32 km/h; (II) 35 mph, 57 km/h; (III) 56 mph, 90 km/h; (IV) 81 mph, 130 km/h; power-weight ratio: 40.6 lb/hp (55.1 lb/kW), 18.4 kg/hp (25 kg/kW); carrying capacity: 882 lb, 400 kg; acceleration: 0-50 mph (0-80 km/h) 14.5 sec; speed in top at 1,000 rpm: 17.4 mph, 28 km/h; consumption: 28.8 m/imp gal, 24 m/US gal, 9.8 l x 100 km.

CHASSIS box-type ladder frame; front suspension: independent, wishbones, coil springs, rubber elements, telescopic dampers; rear: independent, semi-trailing arms, coil springs, rubber elements, anti-roll bar, telescopic dampers.

STEERING rack-and-pinion; turns lock to lock: 3.50.

BRAKES front disc, rear drum, rear compensator; lining area: front 20 sq in, 129 sq cm, rear 61.4 sq in, 396 sq cm, total 81.4 sq in, 525 sq cm.

ELECTRICAL EQUIPMENT 12 V; 42 Ah battery; 588 W alternator; FEK distributor; 2 headlamps.

DIMENSIONS AND WEIGHT wheel base: 96.46 in, 245 cm; tracks: 50.39 in, 128 cm front, 51.18 in, 130 cm rear; length: 166.14 in, 422 cm; width: 64.57 in, 164 cm; height: 58.66 in, 149 cm; ground clearance: 6.10 in, 15.5 cm; weight: 2,029 lb, 920 kg; weight distribution: 51.5% front, 48.5% rear; turning circle (between walls): 33.5 ft, 10.2 m; fuel tank: 9.7 imp gal, 11.6 US gal, 44 l.

BODY saloon/sedan; 4 doors; 5 seats, separate front seats, reclining backrests.

PRACTICAL INSTRUCTIONS fuel: mixture 1:50, SAE 20-40; oil: gearbox and final drive 3.2 imp pt, 3.8 US pt, 1.8 l, SAE 80 EP, change every 31,100 miles, 50,000 km; greasing: every 6,200 miles, 10,000 km, 3 points; sparking plug: 175°; opening timing: 62°17' 62°17' 78°2' 78°2'; tyre pressure: front 23 psi, 1.6 atm, rear 24 psi, 1.7 atm.

OPTIONAL ACCESSORIES central lever; halogen headlamps; sunshine roof; luxury version.

353 W Tourist

See 353 W, except for:

PERFORMANCE max speed: 78 mph, 125 km/h; power-weight ratio: 42.8 lb/hp (58.1 lb/kW), 19.4 kg/hp (26.4 kg/kW); carrying capacity: 970 lb, 440 kg; consumption: 28.2 m/imp gal, 23.5 m/US gal, 10 l x 100 km.

DIMENSIONS AND WEIGHT length: 172.44 in, 438 cm; weight: 2,139 lb, 970 kg.

BODY estate car/station wagon; 4 + 1 doors; back seat folding down to luggage table.

PRACTICAL INSTRUCTIONS tyre pressure: rear 27 psi, 1.9 atm.

WARTBURG 353 W De Luxe

AUDI 50 LS

AUDI NSU   GERMANY FR

Audi 50 LS

PRICE EX WORKS: 9,915* marks

ENGINE front, transverse, slanted 15° to front, 4 stroke; 4 cylinders, in line; 66.7 cu in, 1,093 cc (2.74 x 2.83 in, 69.5 x 72 mm); compression ratio: 8:1; max power (DIN): 50 hp (36.8 kW) at 5,800 rpm; max torque (SAE): 56 lb ft, 7.7 kg m (75.5 Nm) at 3,500 rpm; max engine rpm: 5,800; 45.7 hp/l (33.7 kW/l); cast iron block, light alloy head; 5 crankshaft bearings; valves: overhead, in line, thimble tappets; camshafts: 1, overhead, cogged belt; lubrication: gear pump, full flow filter, 5.3 imp pt, 6.3 US pt, 3 l; 1 Solex 35 PICT-5 downdraught single barrel carburettor; fuel feed: mechanical pump; water-cooled, 11.4 imp pt, 13.7 US pt, 6.5 l, electric thermostatic fan.

TRANSMISSION driving wheels: front; clutch: single dry plate gearbox: mechanical; gears: 4, fully synchronized; ratios: I 3.454, II 2.050, III 1.347, IV 0.963, rev 3.384; lever: central; final drive: hypoid bevel; axle ratio: 4.266; width of rims: 4.5''; tyres: 145 SR x 13.

PERFORMANCE max speeds: (I) 26 mph, 42 km/h; (II) 44 mph, 71 km/h; (III) 67 mph, 108 km/h; (IV) 88 mph, 142 km/h; power-weight ratio: 30.2 lb/hp (41 lb/kW), 13.7

AUDI 50 LS

kg/hp (18.6 kg/kW); acceleration: 0-50 mph (0-80 km/h) 9.6 sec; speed in top at 1,000 rpm: 15.1 mph, 24.3 km/h; consumption: 37.2 m/imp gal, 30.9 m/US gal, 7.6 l x 100 km.

CHASSIS integral; front suspension: independent, by Mc-Pherson, lower wishbones, anti-roll bar, coil springs/telescopic damper struts; rear: independent, longitudinal trailing radius arms, coil spring/telescopic damper struts.

STEERING rack-and-pinion; turns lock to lock: 3.50.

BRAKES front disc (diameter 9.43 in, 23.9 cm), rear drum, 2 K circuits, servo; lining area: front 16.3 sq in, 105 sq cm, rear 29.3 sq in, 189 sq cm, total 45.6 sq in, 294 sq cm.

ELECTRICAL EQUIPMENT 12 V; 36 Ah battery; 35 A alternator; Bosch distributor; 2 headlamps.

DIMENSIONS AND WEIGHT wheel base: 91.93 in, 233 cm; tracks: 51.18 in, 130 cm front, 51 in, 131 cm rear; length: 139.28 in, 354 cm; width: 61.42 in, 156 cm; height: 52.90 in, 134 cm; ground clearance: 4.17 in, 10.6 cm; weight: 1,510 lb, 685 kg; turning circle (between walls): 31.5 ft, 9.6 m; fuel tank: 7.9 imp gal, 9.5 US gal, 36 l.

BODY saloon/sedan; 2 doors; 4 seats, separate front seats with built-in headrests; back seat folding down to luggage table; heated rear window.

PRACTICAL INSTRUCTIONS fuel: 91 oct petrol; oil: engine 5.3 imp pt, 6.3 US pt, 3 l, SAE 20W-30, change every 4,700 miles, 7,500 km - gearbox and final drive 3.2 imp pt, 3.8 US pt, 1.8 l, SAE 80 or 90; greasing: none.

VARIATIONS

ENGINE 77.6 cu in, 1,272 cc (2.95 x 2.83 in, 75 x 72 mm), 8.2:1 compression ratio, max power (DIN) 60 hp (44.2 kW) at 5,600 rpm, max torque (DIN) 69 lb ft, 9.5 kg m (93.2 Nm) at 3,400 rpm, 47.2 hp/l (34.8 kW/l).
PERFORMANCE max speeds (I) 28 mph, 45 km/h, (II) 47 mph, 76 km/h, (III) 71 mph, 115 km/h, (IV) 94 mph, 152 km/h, power-weight ratio 25.2 lb/hp (34.2 lb/kW), 11.4 kg/hp (15.5 kg/kW), acceleration 0-50 mph (0-80 km/h) 8.3 sec, consumption 34 m/imp gal, 28.3 m/US gal, 8.3 l x 100 km.

OPTIONAL ACCESSORIES 155/70 SR x 13 tyres; halogen headlamps; sunshine roof; metallic spray; rear window wiper-washer.

Audi 50 GLS

See Audi 50 LS, except for:

PRICE EX WORKS: 10,405* marks

BODY luxury equipment.

Audi 80 Series

PRICES IN GB, IN USA AND EX WORKS:

	£	$	DM
1 Audi 80 2-door Limousine	—	—	11,580*
2 Audi 80 4-door Limousine	—	—	12,130*
3 Audi 80 L 2-door Limousine	—	—	12,385*
4 Audi 80 L 4-door Limousine	—	—	12,935*
5 Audi 80 GLS 2-door Limousine	—	5,895*	13,695*
6 Audi 80 GLS 4-door Limousine	4,358*	6,045*	14,245*
7 Audi 80 GTE 2-door Limousine	—	—	15,815*
8 Audi 80 GTE 4-door Limousine	—	—	16,365*

Power team:	Standard for:	Optional for:
55 hp	1 to 4	—
75 hp	5,6	1 to 4
85 hp	—	3 to 6
110 hp	7,8	—

55 hp power team

ENGINE front, 4 stroke; 4 cylinders, in line; 79.1 cu in, 1,297 cc (2.95 x 2.89 in, 75 x 73.4 mm); compression ratio: 8.5:1; max power (DIN): 55 hp (40.5 kW) at 5,500 rpm; max torque (DIN): 68 lb ft, 9.4 kg m (92.2 Nm) at 2,500 rpm; max engine rpm: 5,500; 42.4 hp/l (31.2 kW/l); cast iron block, light alloy head; 5 crankshaft bearings; valves: overhead, in line, thimble tappets; camshafts: 1, overhead, cogged belt; lubrication: gear pump, full flow filter, 5.3 imp pt, 6.3 US pt, 3 l; 1 Solex 30-35 PDSIT downdraught single barrel carburettor; fuel feed: mechanical pump; watercooled, 11.4 imp pt, 13.7 US pt, 6.5 l, electric thermostatic fan.

TRANSMISSION driving wheels: front; clutch: single dry plate (diaphragm); gearbox: mechanical; gears: 4, fully synchronized; ratios: I 3.454, II 1.940, III 1.290, IV 0.909, rev 3.166; lever: central; final drive: hypoid bevel; axle ratio: 4.556; width of rims: 5''; tyres: 155 SR x 13.

PERFORMANCE max speeds: (I) 25 mph, 41 km/h; (II) 42 mph, 68 km/h; (III) 68 mph, 110 km/h; (IV) 90 mph, 145 km/h; power-weight ratio: 33.9 lb/hp (46 lb/kW), 15.4 kg/hp (20.9 kg/kW); carrying capacity: 948 lb, 430 kg;

AUDI 80 GLS 4-door Limousine

AUDI 80 GTE Series

acceleration: 0-50 mph (0-80 km/h) 10.5 sec; speed in top at 1,000 rpm: 14.9 mph, 24 km/h; consumption: 32.1 m/imp gal, 26.7 m/US gal, 8.8 l x 100 km.

CHASSIS integral, front auxiliary subframe; front suspension: independent, by McPherson, lower wishbones, anti-roll bar, coil springs/telescopic damper struts; rear: rigid axle, trailing radius arms, transverse linkage bar, telescopic damper struts.

STEERING rack-and-pinion; turns lock to lock: 3.94.

BRAKES front disc (diameter 9.43 in, 23.9 cm), rear drum, servo.

ELECTRICAL EQUIPMENT 12 V; 36 Ah battery; 35 A alternator; Bosch distributor; 2 headlamps.

DIMENSIONS AND WEIGHT wheel base: 96.69 in, 246 cm; tracks: 52.76 in, 134 cm front, 53.15 in, 135 cm rear; length: 167.13 in, 424 cm; width: 62.99 in, 160 cm; height: 53.54 in, 136 cm; ground clearance: 4.21 in, 10.7 cm; weight: 1,863 lb, 845 kg; turning circle (between walls): 33.8 ft, 10.3 m; fuel tank: 9.9 imp gal, 11.9 US gal, 45 l.

BODY saloon/sedan; 5 seats, separate front seats.

PRACTICAL INSTRUCTIONS fuel: 91 oct petrol; oil: engine 5.3 imp pt, 6.3 US pt, 3 l, SAE 20W-30, change every 4,700 miles, 7,500 km - gearbox and final drive 3.2 imp pt, 3.8 US pt, 1.8 l, SAE 80 or 90; greasing: none: sparking plug: 175°; tappet clearances: inlet 0.008-0.012 in, 0.20-0.30 mm, exhaust 0.016-0.020 in, 0.40-0.50 mm; tyre pressure: front 26 psi, 1.8 atm, rear 26 psi, 1.8 atm.

OPTIONAL ACCESSORIES 175/70 SR x 13 tyres; halogen headlamps; sunshine roof; vinyl roof.

75 hp power team

See 55 hp power team, except for:

ENGINE 96.9 cu in, 1,588 cc (3.13 x 3.15 in, 79.5 x 80 mm); compression ratio: 8.2:1; max power (DIN): 75 hp (55.2 kW) at 5,600 rpm; max torque (DIN): 88 lb ft, 12.1 kg m (118.7 Nm) at 3,200 rpm; max engine rpm: 5,600; 47.2 hp/l (34.8 kW/l).

TRANSMISSION gearbox ratios: I 3.455, II 1.940, III 1.290, IV 0.909, rev 3.166; axle ratio: 4.111.

PERFORMANCE max speeds: (I) 27 mph, 44 km/h; (II) 47 mph, 75 km/h; (III) 70 mph, 112 km/h; (IV) 99 mph, 160 km/h; power-weight ratio: 24.8 lb/hp (33.7 lb/kW), 11.3 kg/hp (15.3 kg/kW); acceleration: 0-50 mph (0-80 km/h) 8.5 sec; speed in top at 1,000 rpm: 16.2 mph, 26 km/h; consumption: 31.7 m/imp gal, 26.4 m/US gal, 8.9 l x 100 km.

PRACTICAL INSTRUCTIONS sparking plug: 200°; valve timing: 3° 47° 43° 7°.

OPTIONAL ACCESSORIES automatic transmission, hydraulic torque converter and planetary gears with 3 ratios (I 2.550, II 1.450, III 1, rev 2.460), max ratio of converter at stall 2.2, possible manual selection, 3.910 axle ratio, 5'' wide rims, max speed 97 mph, 156 km/h, consumption 29.7 m/imp gal, 24.8 m/US gal, 9.5 l x 100 km.

AUDI 80 GTE 2-door Limousine

AUDI 100 GL 4-door Limousine

85 hp power team

See 55 hp power team, except for:

ENGINE 96.9 cu in, 1,588 cc (3.13 x 3.15 in, 79.5 x 80 mm); compression ratio: 8.2:1; max power (DIN): 85 hp (62.6 kW) at 5,600 rpm; max torque (DIN): 92 lb ft, 12.7 kg m (124.5 Nm) at 3,200 rpm; max engine rpm: 5,600; 53.5 hp/l (39.4 kW/l); 1 Solex 32-35 TDID downdraught carburettor.

TRANSMISSION gearbox ratios: I 3.455, II 1.940, III 1.290, IV 0.909, rev 3.166; axle ratio: 4.111; tyres: 175/70 SR x 13.

PERFORMANCE max speeds: (I) 29 mph, 46 km/h; (II) 48 mph, 78 km/h; (III) 73 mph, 117 km/h; (IV) 106 mph, 170 km/h; power-weight ratio: 21.9 lb/hp (29.8 lb/kW), 9.9 kg/hp (13.5 kg/kW); acceleration: 0-50 mph (0-80 km/h) 7.9 sec; speed in top at 1,000 rpm: 17.4 mph, 28 km/h; consumption: 32.5 m/imp gal, 27 m/US gal, 8.7 l x 100 km.

ELECTRICAL EQUIPMENT 45 Ah battery; 55 A alternator; halogen headlamps.

PRACTICAL INSTRUCTIONS sparking plug: 225°; valve timing: 3° 47° 43° 7°.

OPTIONAL ACCESSORIES automatic transmission with 3 ratios (I 2.550, II 1.450, III 1, rev 2.460), 3.909 axle ratio, 5'' wide rims, max speed 103 mph, 166 km/h, consumption 30.4 m/imp gal, 25.3 m/US gal, 9.3 l x 100 km; air-conditioning.

110 hp power team

See 55 hp power team, except for:

ENGINE 96.9 cu in, 1,588 cc (3.13 x 3.15 in, 79.5 x 80 mm); compression ratio: 9.5:1; max power (DIN): 110 hp (81 kW) at 6,100 rpm; max torque (DIN): 101 lb ft, 14 kg m (137.3 Nm) at 5,000 rpm; max engine rpm: 6,100; 69.3 hp/l (51 kW/l); lubricating system: 6.2 imp pt, 7.4 US pt, 3.5 l; Bosch K-Jetronic fuel injection system; fuel feed: electric pump.

TRANSMISSION gearbox ratios: I 3.455, II 1.940, III 1.290, IV 0.909, rev 3.166; axle ratio: 3.889; tyres: 175/70 HR x 13.

PERFORMANCE max speeds: (I) 31 mph, 50 km/h; (II) 52 mph, 83 km/h; (III) 80 mph, 128 km/h; (IV) 112 mph, 181 km/h; power-weight ratio: 16.9 lb/hp (23 lb/kW), 7.7 kg/hp (10.4 kg/kW); acceleration: 0-50 mph (0-80 km/h) 6.2 sec; speed in top at 1,000 rpm: 17.5 mph, 28.2 km/h; consumption: 34.4 m/imp gal, 28.7 m/US gal, 8.2 l x 100 km.

BRAKES lining area: front 16.3 sq in, 105 sq cm, rear 34.6 sq in, 223 sq cm, total 50.9 sq in, 328 sq cm.

ELECTRICAL EQUIPMENT 45 Ah battery; 55 A alternator; halogen headlamps.

BODY built-in headrests (standard).

PRACTICAL INSTRUCTIONS fuel: 97 oct petrol; oil: engine 6.2 imp pt, 7.4 US pt, 3.5 l, SAE 20W-30, change every 4,700 miles, 7,500 km; sparking plug: 225°; valve timing: 4° 46° 44° 6°.

Audi 100 Series

PRICES IN GB, IN USA AND EX WORKS:

	£	$	DM
Audi 100 2-door Limousine	—	—	14,955*
Audi 100 4-door Limousine	—	—	15,535*
Audi 100 L 2-door Limousine	—	—	15,820*
Audi 100 L 4-door Limousine	4,269*	—	16,400*
Audi 100 GL 4-door Limousine	4,659*	8,450*	17,710*

Power team:	Standard for:	Optional for:
85 hp	all	—
115 hp	—	all
136 hp	—	all

85 hp power team

ENGINE front, 4 stroke; 4 cylinders, in line; 96.9 cu in, 1,588 cc (3.13 x 3.15 in, 79.5 x 80 mm); compression ratio: 8.2:1; max power (DIN): 85 hp (62.6 kW) at 5,600 rpm; max torque (DIN): 90 lb ft, 12.4 kg m (121.6 Nm) at 3,200 rpm; max engine rpm: 5.600; 53.5 hp/l (39.4 kW/l); cast iron block, light alloy head; 5 crankshaft bearings; valves: overhead, in line, rockers; camshafts: 1, overhead, cogged belt; lubrication: gear pump, full flow filter, 6.2 imp pt, 7.4 US pt, 3.5 l; 1 Solex 2 B2 downdraught carburettor; fuel feed: mechanical pump; water-cooled, 12.3 imp pt, 14.8 US pt, 7 l.

TRANSMISSION driving wheels: front; clutch: single dry plate (diaphragm); gearbox: mechanical; gears: 4, fully synchronized; ratios: I 3.454, II 1.944, III 1.286, IV 0.909, rev 3.166; lever: central; final drive: hypoid bevel; axle ratio: 4.444; width of rims: 5.5''; tyres: 165 SR x 14.

PERFORMANCE max speeds: (I) 29 mph, 46 km/h; (II) 52 mph, 83 km/h; (III) 77 mph, 124 km/h; (IV) 99 mph, 160 km/h; power-weight ratio: 28.8 lb/hp (39.1 lb/kW), 13.1 kg/hp (17.7 kg/W); carrying capacity: 1,014 lb, 460 kg; acceleration: 0-50 mph (0-80 m/h) 8.6 sec; speed in top at 1,000 rpm: 17.6 mph, 28.3 km/h; consumption: 31.7 m/imp gal, 26.4 m/US gal, 8.9 l x 100 km.

CHASSIS integral, front auxiliary subframe; front suspension: independent, by McPherson, lower wishbones, anti-roll bar, coil springs/telescopic damper struts; rear: rigid axle, swinging longitudinal trailing radius arms, transverse linkage bar, anti-roll bar, telescopic dampers.

STEERING rack-and-pinion.

BRAKES front disc (diameter 10.24 in, 26 cm), rear drum, servo; lining area: front 20.2 sq in, 130 sq cm, rear 39.7 sq in, 256 sq cm, total 59.9 sq in, 386 sq cm.

ELECTRICAL EQUIPMENT 12 V; 45 Ah battery; 55 A alternator; Bosch distributor; 2 headlamps.

DIMENSIONS AND WEIGHT wheel base: 105.40 in, 268 cm; tracks: 57.90 in, 147 cm front, 56.90 in, 144 cm rear; length: 184.30 in, 468 cm - GL 185 in, 470 cm; width: 69.60 in, 177 cm; height: 54.80 in, 139 cm; ground clearance: 5.10 in, 13 cm; weight: 2,448 lb, 1,110 kg; weight distribution: 49% front, 51% rear; turning circle (between walls): 37.1 ft, 11.3 m; fuel tank: 13.2 imp gal, 15.8 US gal, 60 l.

BODY saloon/sedan; 5 seats, separate front seats, reclining backrests, heated rear window.

PRACTICAL INSTRUCTIONS fuel: 91 oct petrol; oil: engine 5.3 imp pt, 6.3 US pt, 3 l, SAE 10W-30, change every 4,700 miles, 7,500 km - gearbox and final drive 3 imp pt, 3.6 US pt, 1.7 l, SAE 80; greasing: none; tyre pressure: front 28 psi, 2 atm, rear 28 psi, 2 atm.

OPTIONAL ACCESSORIES automatic transmission, hydraulic torque converter and planetary gears with 3 ratios (I 2.550, II 1.440, III 1, rev 4.090), max speed 97 mph, 156 km/h, acceleration 0-50 mph ((0-80 km/h) 11.5 sec, consumption 29.7 m/imp gal, 24.8 m/US gal, 9.5 l x 100 km, 54 Ah battery; 185/70 HR x 14 tyres; sunshine roof; metallic spray; halogen headlamps (except for L and GL models).

115 hp power team

See 85 hp power team, except for:

ENGINE 115.6 cu in, 1,984 cc (3.41 x 3.32 in, 86.5 x 84.4 mm); compression ratio: 9.3:1; max power (DIN): 115 hp (84.6 kW) at 5,500 rpm; max torque (DIN): 122 lb ft, 16.8 kg m (164.8 Nm) at 3,500 rpm; max engine rpm: 5,500; 58 hp/l (42.6 kW/l); lubricating system: 8.8 imp pt, 10.6 US pt, 5 l; 1 Solex 2 B3 downdraught carburettor; cooling system: 13.2 imp pt, 15.9 US pt, 7.5 l.

TRANSMISSION gearbox ratios: I 3.600, II 2.125, III 1.360, IV 0.956, rev 3.500; axle ratio: 3.888.

AUDI 100 Avant L 5-door Limousine

PERFORMANCE max speed: 111 mph, 179 km/h; power-weight ratio: 22 lb/hp ((30 lb/kW), 10 kg/hp (13.6 kg/kW); acceleration: 0-50 mph (0-80 km/h) 7.2 sec; consumption: 29.4 m/imp gal, 24.5 m/US gal, 9.6 l x 100 km.

BRAKES lining area: front 20.2 sq in, 130 sq cm, rear 44.5 sq in, 287 sq cm, total 64.7 sq in, 417 sq cm.

ELECTRICAL EQUIPMENT 54 Ah battery.

DIMENSIONS AND WEIGHT weight: 2,536 lb, 1,150 kg; weight distribution: 50% front, 50% rear.

PRACTICAL INSTRUCTIONS fuel: 98 oct petrol; oil: engine 7.9 imp pt, 9.5 US pt, 4.5 l.

OPTIONAL ACCESSORIES automatic transmission with 3 ratios, max speed 109 mph, 175 km/h, acceleration 0-50 mph (0-80 km/h) 8.5 sec, consumption 27.7 m/imp gal, 23.1 m/US gal, 10.2 l x 100 km; power steering; air-conditioning.

136 hp power team

See 85 hp power team, except for:

ENGINE 5 cylinders, in line; 130.8 cu in, 2,144 cc (3.13 x 3.40 in, 79.5 x 86.4 mm); compression ratio: 9.3:1; max power (DIN): 136 hp (100.1 kW) at 5,700 rpm; max torque (DIN): 134 lb ft, 18.5 kg m (181.4 Nm) at 4,200 rpm; max engine rpm: 5,700; 63.4 hp/l (46.7 kW/l); 6 crankshaft bearings; lubricating system: 8.8 imp pt, 10.6 US pt, 5 l; Bosch K-Jetronic injection system; cooling system: 14.3 imp pt, 17.1 US pt, 8.1 l.

TRANSMISSION gearbox ratios: I 3.600, II 2.125, III 1.360, IV 0.956, rev 3.500; axle ratio: 3.777; tyres: 185/70 HR x 14.

PERFORMANCE max speed: 118 mph, 190 km/h; power-weight ratio: 19 lb/hp (25.8 lb/kW), 8.6 kg/hp (11.7 kg/kW); consumption: 26.9 m/imp gal, 22.4 m/US gal, 10.5 l x 100 km.

BRAKES lining area: front 20.2 sq in, 130 sq cm, rear 44.5 sq in, 287 sq cm, total 64.7 sq in, 417 sq cm.

ELECTRICAL EQUIPMENT 63 Ah battery.

DIMENSIONS AND WEIGHT weight 2,580 lb, 1,170 kg.

PRACTICAL INSTRUCTIONS fuel: 98 oct petrol; oil: engine 7.9 imp pt, 9.5 US pt. 4.5 l.

OPTIONAL ACCESSORIES automatic transmission with 3 ratios, max speed 115 mph, 185 km/h, consumption 25.4 m/imp gal, 21.2 m/US gal, 11.1 l x 100 km; power steering; air-conditioning.

Audi 100 Avant Series

PRICES IN GB AND EX WORKS:	£	DM
Audi 100 Avant L 5-door Limousine	4,235*	16,995*
Audi 100 Avant GL 5-door Limousine	—	18,305*

Power team:	Standard for:	Optional for:
85 hp	both	—
115 hp	—	both
136 hp	—	both

85 hp power team

ENGINE front, 4 stroke; 4 cylinders, in line; 96.9 cu in, 1,588 cc (3.13 x 3.15 in, 79.5 x 80 mm); compression ratio: 8.2:1; max power (DIN): 85 hp (62.6 kW) at 5,600 rpm; max torque (DIN): 90 lb ft, 12.4 kg m (121.6 Nm) at 3,200 rpm; max engine rpm: 5,600; 53.5 hp/l (39.4 kW/l); cast iron block, light alloy head; 5 crankshaft bearings; valves: overhead, in line, rockers; camshafts: 1, overhead, cogged belt; lubrication: gear pump, full flow filter, 6.2 imp pt, 7.4 US pt, 3.5 l; 1 Solex 2 B2 downdraught carburettor; fuel feed: mechanical pump; water-cooled, 12.3 imp pt, 14.8 US pt, 7 l, electric thermostatic fan.

TRANSMISSION driving wheels: front; clutch: single dry plate (diaphragm); gearbox: mechanical; gears: 4, fully synchronized; ratios: I 3.454, II 1.944, III 1.286, IV 0.909, rev 3.166; lever: central; final drive: hypoid bevel; axle ratio: 4.444; width of rims: 5.5''; tyres: 165 SR x 14.

PERFORMANCE max speeds: (I) 29 mph, 46 km/h; (II) 52 mph, 83 km/h; (III) 77 mph, 124 km/h; (IV) 99 mph, 160 km/h; power-weight capacity: 1,014 lb, 460 kg; acceleration: 0-50 mph (0-80 km/h) 8.6 sec; speed in top at 1,000 rpm: 17.6 mph, 28.3 km/h; consumption: 31.7 m/imp gal, 26.4 m/US gal, 8.9 l x 100 km.

CHASSIS integral, front auxiliary subframe; front suspension: independent, by Mc-Pherson, lower wishbones, anti-roll bar, coil springs/telescopic damper struts; rear: rigid axle, swinging longitudinal trailing radius arms, transverse linkage bar, anti-roll bar, telescopic dampers.

STEERING rack-and-pinion.

AUDI 100 GL 4-door Limousine

AUDI 100 Avant GL 5E (136 hp)

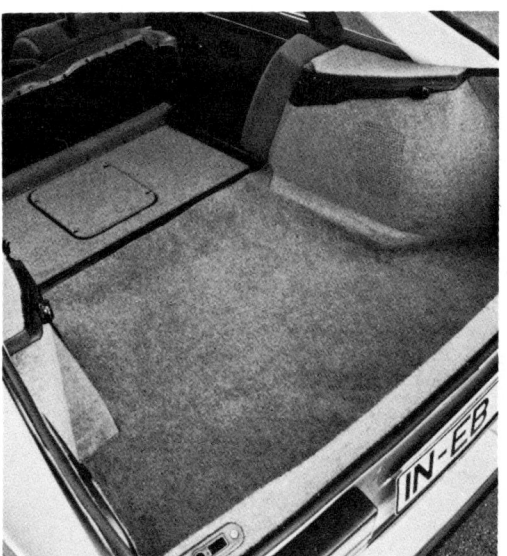

AUDI 100 Avant Series

BRAKES front disc (diameter 10.24 in, 26 cm), rear drum, 2 X circuits, servo; lining area: front 20.2 sq in, 130 sq cm, rear 39.7 sq in, 256 sq cm, total 59.9 sq in, 386 sq cm.

ELECTRICAL EQUIPMENT 12 V; 45 Ah battery; 55 A alternator; Bosch distributor; 2 headlamps.

DIMENSIONS AND WEIGHT wheel base: 105.40 in, 268 cm; tracks: 57.90 in, 147 cm front, 56.90 in, 144 cm rear; length: 180.59 in, 459 cm - GL 181.38 in, 461 cm; width: 69.60 in, 177 cm; height: 54.80 in, 139 cm; ground clearances: 5.10 in, 13 cm; weight: 2,448 lb, 1,110 kg; turning circle (between walls): 37.1 ft, 11.3 m; fuel tank: 13.2 imp gal, 15.8 US gal, 60 l.

BODY 5 seats, separate seats, reclining backrests; heated rear window; folding rear seat.

PRACTICAL INSTRUCTIONS fuel: 91 oct petrol; oil: engine 5.3 imp pt, 6.3 US pt, 3 l, SAE 10W-30, change every 4,700 miles, 7,500 km - gearbox and final drive 3 imp pt, 3.6 US pt, 1.7 l, SAE 80; greasing: none; tyre pressure: front 28 psi, 2 atm, rear 28 psi, 2 atm.

OPTIONAL ACCESSORIES automatic transmission, hydraulic torque converter and planetary gears with 3 ratios (I 2.552, II 1.448, III 1, rev 2.462), 4.091 axle ratio, max speed 97 mph, 156 km/h, acceleration 0-50 mph (0-80 km/h) 11.5 sec, consumption 29.7 m/imp gal, 24.8 m/US gal, 9.5 l x 100 km, 54 Ah battery; 185/70 HR x 14 tyres; sunshine roof; metallic spray; rear window wiper-washer.

115 hp power team

See 85 hp power team, except for:

ENGINE 115.6 cu in, 1,984 cc (3.41 x 3.32 in, 86.5 x 84.4 mm); compression ratio: 9.3:1; max power (DIN): 115 hp (84.6 kW) at 5,500 rpm; max torque (DIN): 122 lb ft, 16.8 kg m (164.8 Nm) at 3,500 rpm; max engine rpm: 5,500; 58 hp/l (42.6 kW/l); lubricating system: 8.8 imp pt, 10.6 US pt, 5 l; cooling system: 13.2 imp pt, 15.9 US pt, 7.5 l.

TRANSMISSION gearbox ratios: I 3.600, II 2.125, III 1.360, IV 0.966, rev 3.500; axle ratio: 3.889.

PERFORMANCE max speed: 111 mph, 179 km/h; power-weight ratio: 22 lb/hp (30 lb/kW), 10 kg/hp (13.6 kg/kW); acceleration: 0-50 mph (0-80 km/h) 7.2 sec; consumption: 29.4 m/imp gal, 24.5 m/US gal, 9.6 l x 100 km.

BRAKES lining area: front 20.2 sq in, 130 sq cm, rear 44.5 sq in, 287 sq cm, total 64.7 sq in, 417 sq cm.

ELECTRICAL EQUIPMENT 54 Ah battery.

DIMENSIONS AND WEIGHT weight: 2,536 lb, 1,150 kg.

PRACTICAL INSTRUCTIONS fuel: 98 oct petrol; oil: engine 7.9 imp pt, 9.5 US pt, 4.5 l.

OPTIONAL ACCESSORIES automatic transmission with 3 ratios, 3.727 axle ratio, max speed 109 mph, 175 km/h, acceleration 0-50 mph (0-80 km/h) 8.5 sec, consumption 27.7 m/imp gal, 23.1 m/US gal, 10.2 l x 100 km; 63 Ah battery; power steering; air-conditioning.

136 hp power team

See 85 hp power team, except for:

ENGINE 5 cylinders, in line; 130.8 cu in, 2,144 cc (3.13 x 3.40 in, 79.5 x 86.4 mm); compression ratio: 9.3:1; max power (DIN): 136 hp (100.1 kW) at 5,700 rpm; max torque (DIN): 134 lb ft, 18.5 kg m (181.4 Nm) at 4,200 rpm; max engine rpm: 5,700; 63.4 hp/l (46.7 kW/l); 6 crankshaft bearings; lubricating system: 8.8 imp pt, 10.6 US pt, 5 l; Bosch K-Jetronic system; cooling system: 14.3 imp pt, 17.1 US pt, 8.1 l.

TRANSMISSION gearbox ratios: I 3.600, II 2.125, III 1.360, IV 0.966, rev 3.500; axle ratio: 3.889; tyres: 185/70 HR x 14 (standard).

PERFORMANCE max speed: 118 mph, 190 km/h; power-weight ratio: 19 lb/hp (25.8 lb/kW), 8.6 kg/hp (11.7 kg/kW); acceleration: 0-50 mph (0-80 km/h) 6.3 sec; consumption: 26.9 m/imp gal, 22.4 m/US gal, 10.5 l x 100 km.

BRAKES lining area: front 20.2 sq in, 130 sq cm, rear 44.5 sq in, 287 sq cm, total 64.7 sq in, 417 sq cm.

ELECTRICAL EQUIPMENT 63 Ah battery; 75 A alternator.

DIMENSIONS AND WEIGHT weight: 2,580 lb, 1,170 kg.

PRACTICAL INSTRUCTIONS fuel: 98 oct petrol; oil: engine 7.9 imp pt, 9.5 US pt, 4.5 l.

OPTIONAL ACCESSORIES automatic transmission with 3 ratios, 3.727 axle ratio, max speed 115 mph, 185 km/h, acceleration 0-50 mph (0-80 km/h) 7.8 sec, consumption 25.4 m/imp gal, 21.2 m/US gal, 11.1 l x 100 km; power steering; air-conditioning.

BMW 316 - 318

BMW   GERMANY FR

(For cars imported into the USA and Canada, exhaust system with thermal reactor and lower compression ratio).

316

PRICE IN GB: £ 3,929*
PRICE EX WORKS: 14,980* marks

ENGINE front, 4 stroke; 4 cylinders, slanted at 30°, in line; 96 cu in, 1,573 cc (3.31 x 2.80 in, 84 x 71 mm); compression ratio: 8.3:1; max power (DIN): 90 hp (66.2 kW) at 6,000 rpm; max torque (DIN): 91 lb ft, 12.5 kg m (122.6 Nm) at 4,000 rpm; max engine rpm: 6,000; 57.2 hp/l (42.1 kW/l); cast iron block, light alloy head, hemispherical combustion chambers; 5 crankshaft bearings; valves: overhead, Vee-slanted at 52°, rockers; camshafts: 1, overhead; lubrication: gear pump, full flow filter, 7.4 imp pt, 8.9 US pt, 4.2 l; 1 Solex DIDTA 32/32 downdraught twin barrel carburettor; fuel feed: mechanical pump; water-cooled, 12.3 imp pt, 14.8 US pt, 7 l.

TRANSMISSION driving wheels: rear; clutch: single dry plate (diaphragm), hydraulically controlled; gearbox: mecha-

BMW 320

nical; gears: 4, fully synchronized; ratios: I 3.764, II 2.022, III 1.320, IV 1, rev 4.096; lever: central; final drive: hypoid bevel; axle ratio: 4.100; width of rims: 5''; tyres: 165 SR x 13.

PERFORMANCE max speeds: (I) 26 mph, 42 km/h; (II) 49 mph, 79 km/h; (III) 75 mph, 121 km/h; (IV) 99 mph, 160 km/h; power-weight ratio: 25 lb/hp (34 lb/kW), 11.3 kg/hp (15.4 kg/kW); carrying capacity: 926 lb, 420 kg; acceleration: standing ¼ mile 18.8 sec, 0-50 mph (0-80 km/h) 8.7 sec; speed in direct drive at 1,000 rpm: 16.3 mph, 26.3 km/h; consumption: 28.5 m/imp gal, 23.8 m/US gal, 9.9 l x 100 km.

CHASSIS integral; front suspension: independent, by McPherson, coil springs/telescopic damper struts, auxiliary rubber springs, lower wishbones, lower trailing links, anti-roll bar; rear: independent, oblique semi-trailing arms, auxiliary rubber springs, coil springs, telescopic dampers.

STEERING ZF, rack-and-pinion; turns lock to lock: 4.05.

BRAKES front disc (diameter 10.04 in, 25.5 cm), rear drum, servo; lining area: front 23.9 sq in, 154 sq cm, rear 51.5 sq in, 332 sq cm, total 75.4 sq in, 486 sq cm.

ELECTRICAL EQUIPMENT 12 V; 45 Ah battery; 630 W alternator; Bosch distributor; 2 headlamps.

DIMENSIONS AND WEIGHT wheel base: 100.79 in, 256 cm; tracks: 54.60 in, 139 cm front, 55.10 in, 140 cm rear; length: 171.26 in, 435 cm; width: 63.39 in, 161 cm; height: 54.33 in, 138 cm; ground clearance: 5.51 in, 14 cm; weight: 2,249 lb, 1,020 kg; turning circle (between walls): 33.5 ft, 10.2 m; fuel tank: 12.8 imp gal, 15.3 US gal, 58 l.

BODY saloon/sedan; 2 doors; 5 seats, separate front seats, reclining backrests, built-in adjustable headrest, heated rear window.

PRACTICAL INSTRUCTIONS fuel: 92 oct petrol; oil: engine 7.4 imp pt, 8.9 US pt, 4.2 l, SAE 20W-50, change every 3,700 miles, 6,000 km - gearbox 1.8 imp pt, 2.1 US pt, 1 l, SAE 80, change every 14,800 miles, 24,000 km - final drive 1.6 imp pt, 1.9 US pt, 0.9 l, SAE 90, no change recommended; greasing: none; sparking plug: 145°.

OPTIONAL ACCESSORIES limited slip differential; headlamps with wiper-washers; anti-roll bar on rear suspension; halogen headlamps; fog lamps; 55 Ah battery; 185/70 HR x 13 tyres; light alloy wheels; sunshine roof; metallic spray.

318

See 316, except for:

PRICE EX WORKS: 15,980* marks

ENGINE 107.8 cu in, 1,766 cc (3.50 x 2.80 in, 89 x 71 mm); max power (DIN): 98 hp (72.1 kW) at 5,800 rpm; max torque (DIN): 105 lb ft, 14.5 kg m (142.2 Nm) at 4,000 rpm; 55.5 hp/l (40.8 kW/l).

PERFORMANCE max speed: 103 mph, 165 km/h; power-weight ratio: 23.2 lb/hp (31.5 lb/kW), 10.5 kg/hp (14.3 kg/kW); acceleration: standing ¼ mile 17.9 sec, 0-50 mph (0-80 km/h) 7.6 sec; speed in direct drive at 1,000 rpm: 17.2 mph, 27.7 km/h.

ELECTRICAL EQUIPMENT halogen headlamps.

BMW 320

DIMENSIONS AND WEIGHT weight: 2,271 lb, 1,030 kg.

OPTIONAL ACCESSORIES ZF HP 22 automatic transmission, hydraulic torque converter and planetary gears with 3 ratios (I 2.478, II 1.478, III 1, rev 2.090), 3.640 axle ratio, max ratio of converter at stall 2, possible manual selection, max speed 99 mph, 160 km/h, consumption 26.4 m/imp gal, 22 m/US gal, 10.7 l x 100 km.

320

See 316, except for:

PRICE IN GB: £ 4,649*
PRICE EX WORKS: 17,980* marks

ENGINE 6 cylinders, in line; 121.4 cu in, 1,990 cc (3.15 x 2.60 in, 80 x 66 mm); compression ratio: 9.2:1; max power (DIN): 122 hp (89.8 kW) at 6,000 rpm; max torque (DIN): 118 lb ft, 16.3 kg m (159.8 Nm) at 4,000 rpm; max engine rpm: 6,000; 61.3 hp/l (45.1 kW/l); 7 crankshaft bearings; valves: overhead, Vee-slanted, rockers; lubricating system: 10 imp pt, 12 US pt, 5.7 l; 1 Solex 4A1 downdraught 4-barrel carburettor; cooling system: 21.1 imp pt, 25.4 US pt, 12 l.

TRANSMISSION axle ratio: 3.640; width of rims: 5.5''; tyres: 185/70 HR x 13.

PERFORMANCE max speed: 112 mph, 181 km/h; power-weight ratio: 20.1 lb/hp (27.4 lb/kW), 9.1 kg/hp (12.4 kg/kW); acceleration: standing ¼ mile 17.4 sec, 0-50 mph (0-80 km/h) 7.2 sec; speed in direct drive at 1,000 rpm: 18.8 mph, 30.2 km/h; consumption: 29.7 m/imp gal, 24.8 m/US gal, 9.5 l x 100 km.

ELECTRICAL EQUIPMENT 65 A alternator; 4 halogen head-lamps.

DIMENSIONS AND WEIGHT weight: 2,459 lb, 1,115 kg.

PRACTICAL INSTRUCTIONS fuel: 98 oct petrol; oil: engine 10 imp pt, 12 US pt, 5.7 l.

OPTIONAL ACCESSORIES ZF HP 22 automatic transmission, hydraulic torque converter and planetary gears with 3 ratios (I 2.478, II 1.478, III 1, rev 2.090), 3.640 axle ratio, max ratio of converter at stall 2, possible manual selection, max speed 109 mph, 176 km/h, consumption 27.2 m/imp gal, 22.6 m/US gal, 10.4 l x 100 km.

323 i

See 316, except for:

PRICE EX WORKS: 20,350* marks

ENGINE 6 cylinders, in line; 141 cu in, 2,315 cc (3.15 x 3.02 in, 80 x 76.8 mm); compression ratio: 9.5:1; max power (DIN): 143 hp (105.2 kW) at 6,000 rpm; max torque (DIN): 141 lb ft, 19.4 kg m (190.3 Nm) at 4,500 rpm; max engine rpm: 6,000; 61.8 hp/l (45.4 kW/l); 7 crankshaft bearings; valves: overhead, Vee-slanted, rockers; lubricating system: 10 imp pt, 12 US pt, 5.7 l; Bosch K-Jetronic injection system; cooling system: 21.1 imp pt, 25.4 US pt, 12 l.

TRANSMISSION axle ratio: 3.450; width of rims: 5.5''; tyres: 185/70 HR x 13.

BMW 316 - 318 - 320

BMW 323 i

BMW 5-Series

PERFORMANCE max speed: 118 mph, 190 km/h; power-weight ratio: 17.5 lb/hp (23.8 lb/kW), 7.9 kg/hp (10.8 kg/kW); acceleration: standing ¼ mile 16.7 sec, 0-50 mph (0-80 km/h) 6.4 sec; speed in direct drive at 1,000 rpm: 19.7 mph, 31.7 km/h; consumption: 30.7 m/imp gal, 25.6 m/US gal, 9.2 l x 100 km.

ELECTRICAL EQUIPMENT 55 Ah battery; 65 A alternator; transistorized ignition; 4 halogen headlamps.

DIMENSIONS AND WEIGHT weight: 2,503 lb, 1,135 kg.

PRACTICAL INSTRUCTIONS fuel: 98 oct petrol; oil: engine 10 imp pt, 12 US pt, 5.7 l.

518

PRICE IN GB: £ 4,979*
PRICE EX WORKS: 17,980* marks

ENGINE front, 4 stroke; 4 cylinders, in line; 107.8 cu in, 1,766 cc (2.80 x 3.50 in, 71 x 89 mm); compression ratio: 8.3:1; max power (DIN): 90 hp (66.2 kW) at 5,500 rpm; max torque (DIN): 104 lb ft, 14.3 kg m (140.2 Nm) at 3,500 rpm; max engine rpm: 6,300; 51 hp/l (37.5 kW/l); cast iron block, light alloy head, hemispherical combustion chambers; 5 crankshaft bearings; valves: overhead, Vee-slanted at 52°, rockers; camshafts: 1, overhead; lubrication: rotary pump, full flow filter, 7.4 imp pt, 8.9 US pt, 4.2 l; 1 Solex DIDTA 32/32 downdraught twin barrel carburettor; fuel feed: mechanical pump; water-cooled, 12.3 imp pt, 14.8 US pt, 7 l.

TRANSMISSION driving wheels: rear; clutch: single dry plate; gearbox: mechanical; gears: 4, fully synchronized; ratios: I 3.764, II 2.022, III 1.320, IV 1, rev 4.096; lever: central; final drive: hypoid bevel; axle ratio: 4.440; width of rims: 5.5''; tyres: 175 SR x 14.

PERFORMANCE max speeds: (I) 27 mph, 43 km/h; (II) 49 mph, 79 km/h; (III) 76 mph, 122 km/h; (IV) 99 mph, 160 km/h; power-weight ratio: 30.4 lb/hp (41.3 lb/kW), 13.8 kg/hp (18.7 kg/kW); carrying capacity: 1,036 lb, 470 kg; speed in direct drive at 1,000 rpm: 15.8 mph, 25.5 km/h; consumption: 28.8 m/imp gal, 24 m/US gal, 9.8 l x 100 km.

CHASSIS integral; front suspension: independent, by Mc-Pherson, coil springs/telescopic damper struts, auxiliary rubber springs, lower wishbones, lower trailing links, anti-roll bar; rear: independent, oblique semi-trailing arms, auxiliary rubber springs, coil springs, telescopic dampers.

STEERING ZF, worm and roller.

BRAKES front disc (diameter 11 in, 28 cm), rear drum, rear compensator, servo.

ELECTRICAL EQUIPMENT 12 V; 36 Ah battery; 630 W alternator; 4 halogen headlamps.

DIMENSIONS AND WEIGHT wheel base: 103.94 in, 264 cm; tracks: 56 in, 142 cm front, 57.70 in, 147 cm rear; length: 181.89 in, 462 cm; width: 66.54 in, 169 cm; height: 55.91 in, 142 cm; ground clearance: 5.51 in, 14 cm; weight: 2,734 lb, 1,240 kg; turning circle (between walls): 34.4 ft, 10.5 m; fuel tank: 15.4 imp gal, 18.5 US gal, 70 l.

BODY saloon/sedan; 4 doors; 5 seats, separate front seats, reclining backrest; heated rear window.

PRACTICAL INSTRUCTIONS fuel: 90 oct petrol; oil: engine 7.4 imp pt, 8.9 US pt, 4.2 l, SAE 20W-50, change every 3,700 miles, 6,000 km - gearbox 1.8 imp pt, 2.1 US pt, 1 l, SAE 80, change every 14,900 miles, 24,000 km - final drive 1.6 imp pt, 1.9 US pt, 0.9 l, SAE 90, no change recommended; greasing: none.

OPTIONAL ACCESSORIES limited slip differential; 195/70 HR x 14 tyres; light alloy wheels; power steering; manually- or electrically-controlled sunshine roof; fog lamps; metallic spray; 55 Ah battery; 770 W alternator; ZF 3 HP 22 automatic transmission, hydraulic torque converter and planetary gears with 3 ratios (I 2.478, II 1.478, III 1, rev 2.090), max ratio of converter at stall 2, possible manual selection, max speed 96 mph, 155 km/h, consumption 26.4 m/imp gal, 22 m/US gal, 10.7 l x 100 km.

520

See 518, except for:

PRICE IN GB: £ 5,729*
PRICE EX WORKS: 20,200* marks

ENGINE 6 cylinders, in line; 121.4 cu in, 1,990 cc (3.15 x 2.60 in, 80 x 66 mm); compression ratio: 9.2:1; max power (DIN): 122 hp (89.8 kW) at 6,000 rpm; max torque (DIN): 118 lb ft, 16.3 kg m (159.8 Nm) at 4,000 rpm; max engine rpm: 6,000; 61.3 hp/l (45.1 kW/l); 7 crankshaft bearings; valves: overhead, Vee-slanted, rockers; lubricating system: 10 imp pt, 12 US pt, 5.7 l; 1 Solex 4A1 downdraught 4-barrel carburettor; cooling system: 21.1 imp pt, 25.4 US pt, 12 l.

TRANSMISSION axle ratio: 3.900; tyres: 175 HR x 14.

PERFORMANCE max speed: 112 mph, 180 km/h; power-weight ratio: 23.7 lb/hp (32.2 lb/kW), 10.7 kg/hp (14.6 kg/kW); speed in direct drive at 1,000 rpm: 18.8 mph,

520

30.2 km/h; consumption: 27.4 m/imp gal, 22.8 m/US gal, 10.3 l x 100 km.

ELECTRICAL EQUIPMENT 44 Ah battery; 55 A alternator.

DIMENSIONS AND WEIGHT weight: 2,889 lb, 1,310 kg.

PRACTICAL INSTRUCTIONS fuel: 98 oct petrol; oil: engine 10 imp pt, 12 US pt, 5.7 l.

OPTIONAL ACCESSORIES ZF 3 HP 22 automatic transmission, hydraulic torque converter and planetary gears with 3 ratios (I 2.478, II 1.478, III 1, rev 2.090), max ratio of converter at stall 2, possible manual selection, 3.900 axle ratio, max speed 108 mph, 174 km/h, consumption 25.2 m/imp gal, 21 m/US gal, 11.2 l x 100 km.

525

See 520, except for:

PRICE IN GB: £ 6,999*
PRICE EX WORKS: 22,800* marks

ENGINE 152.2 cu in, 2,494 cc (3.39 x 2.82 in, 86 x 71.6 mm); compression ratio: 9:1; max power (DIN): 150 hp (110.4 kW) at 6,000 rpm; max torque (DIN): 154 lb ft, 21.2 kg m (207.9 Nm) at 4,000 rpm; 60.1 hp/l (44.2 kW/l).

TRANSMISSION gearbox ratios: I 3.855, II 2.203, III 1.402, IV 1, rev 4.300; axle ratio: 3.640.

PERFORMANCE max speeds: (I) 32 mph, 51 km/h; (II) 57 mph, 91 km/h; (III) 87 mph, 140 km/h; (IV) 120 mph, 193 km/h; power-weight ratio: 19.8 lb/hp (26.9 lb/kW), 9 kg/hp (12.2 kg/kW); carrying capacity: 1,014 lb, 460 kg; acceleration: standing ¼ mile 17.1 sec; consumption: 26.9 m/imp gal, 22.4 m/US gal, 10.5 l x 100 km.

CHASSIS front and rear suspension: anti-roll bar.

BRAKES rear disc (diameter 10.71 in, 27.2 cm).

ELECTRICAL EQUIPMENT 55 Ah battery.

DIMENSIONS AND WEIGHT weight: 2,977 lb, 1,350 kg.

OPTIONAL ACCESSORIES ZF 3 HP 22 automatic transmission, max speed 115 mph, 185 km/h, consumption 24.8 m/imp gal, 20.6 m/US gal, 11.4 l x 100 km.

528 i

See 525, except for:

PRICE IN USA: $ 11,250*
PRICE EX WORKS: 26,850* marks

ENGINE 170.1 cu in, 2,788 cc (3.39 x 3.15 in, 86 x 80 mm); max power (DIN): 177 hp (130 kW) at 5,800 rpm; max torque (DIN): 174 lb ft, 24 kg m (235.4 Nm) at 4,300 rpm; max engine rpm: 6,500; 63.5 hp/l (46.6 kW/l); Bosch L-Jetronic injection system.

TRANSMISSION width of rims: 6''; tyres: 195/70 VR x 14.

PERFORMANCE max speed: 129 mph, 208 km/h; power-weight ratio: 17.6 lb/hp (23.9 lb/kW), 8 kg/hp (10.8 kg/kW); consumption: 26.6 m/imp gal, 22.2 m/US gal, 10.6 l x100 km.

STEERING servo (standard).

DIMENSIONS AND WEIGHT weight: 3,109 lb, 1,410 kg.

OPTIONAL ACCESSORIES ZF 3 HP 22 automatic transmission, max speed 124 mph, 200 km/h, consumption 24.4 m/imp gal, 20.3 m/US gal, 11.6 l x 100 km.

530 i

(For USA and Canada only).

See 520, except for:

PRICE IN USA: $ 13,620*

ENGINE 6 cylinders, in line; 182 cu in, 2,982 cc (3.50 x 3.15 in, 89 x 80 mm); compression ratio: 8:1; max power (DIN): 175 hp (128.8 kW) at 5,500 rpm; max torque (DIN): 185 lb ft, 25.5 kg m (250.1 Nm) at 4,500 rpm; max engine rpm: 6,500; 58.7 hp/l (43.2 kW/l); cast iron block, light alloy head, polyspherical combustion chambers; 7 crankshaft bearings; valves: overhead, Vee-slanted, rockers; Bosch electronic injection; exhaust thermal reactor; electric thermostatic fan.

TRANSMISSION ratios: I 3.855, II 2.203, III 1.402, IV 1, rev 4.030; axle ratio: 3.640; width of rims: 6''; tyres: 195/70 HR x 14.

PERFORMANCE max speed: 124 mph, 200 km/h; power-weight ratio: 18.5 lb/hp (25.1 lb/kW), 8.4 kg/hp (11.4

BMW 528 i

BMW 525

BMW 728 - 730 - 733 i

kg/kW); consumption: 19.6 m/imp gal, 16.3 m/US gal, 14.4 l x 100 km.

CHASSIS rear suspension: anti-roll bar.

STEERING adjustable steering wheel.

BRAKES disc (diameter 10.71 in, 27.2 cm), dual servo.

ELECTRICAL EQUIPMENT 55 Ah battery; 770 W alternator.

DIMENSIONS AND WEIGHT wheel base: 103.8 in, 264 cm; tracks: 55.9 in, 142 cm front, 57.9 in, 147 cm rear; length: 189.9 in, 482 cm; width: 67.2 in, 171 cm; height: 55.9 in, 142 cm; weight: 3,230 lb, 1,465 kg; turning circle (between walls): 35.2 ft, 10.7 m; fuel tank: 15.4 imp gal, 18.5 US gal, 70 l.

PRACTICAL INSTRUCTIONS fuel: 91 oct petrol.

OPTIONAL ACCESSORIES automatic gearbox; limited slip differential.

728

PRICE IN GB: £ 8,950*
PRICE EX WORKS: 29,300* marks

ENGINE front, 4 stroke; 6 cylinders, in line; 170.1 cu in, 2,788 cc (3.39 x 3.15 in, 86 x 80 mm); compression ratio: 9:1; max power (DIN): 170 hp (125.1 kW) at 5,800 rpm; max torque (DIN): 172 lb ft, 23.8 kg m (233.4 Nm) at 4,000 rpm; max engine rpm: 6,500; 61 hp/l (44.9 kW/l); cast iron block, light alloy head, polyspherical combustion chambers; 7 crankshaft bearings; valves: overhead, Vee-slanted, rockers; camshafts: 1, overhead; lubrication: rotary pump, full flow filter, 10 imp pt, 12 US pt, 5.7 l; 1 Solex 4A1 downdraught 4-barrel carburettor; fuel feed: mechanical pump; water-cooled, 21.1 imp pt, 25.4 US pt, 12 l.

TRANSMISSION driving wheels: rear; clutch: single dry plate (diaphragm), hydraulically controlled; gearbox: mechanical; gears: 4, fully synchronized; ratios: I 3.855, II 2.203, III 1.402, IV 1, rev 4.300; lever: central; final drive: hypoid bevel; axle ratio: 3.640; width of rims: 6''; tyres: 195/70 HR x 14.

PERFORMANCE max speed: 119 mph, 192 km/h; power-weight ratio: 19.8 lb/hp (27 lb/kW), 9 kg/hp (12.2 kg/kW); carrying capacity: 1,036 lb, 470 kg; speed in direct drive at 1,000 rpm: 18.4 mph, 29.6 km/h; consumption: 24.6 m/imp gal, 20.5 m/US gal, 11.5 l x 100 km.

CHASSIS integral; front suspension: independent, by McPherson, coil springs/telescopic damper struts, auxiliary rubber springs, lower wishbones (trailing links), anti-roll bar; rear: independent, semi-trailing arms, auxiliary rubber springs, coil springs, telescopic dampers.

STEERING recirculating ball, servo; turns lock to lock: 3.80.

BRAKES disc (diameter 11 in, 28 cm), front internal radial fins, 2 X circuits, servo.

ELECTRICAL EQUIPMENT 12 V; 55 Ah battery; 55 A alternator; Bosch distributor; 4 halogen headlamps.

DIMENSIONS AND WEIGHT wheel base: 110 in, 279 cm; tracks: 59.45 in, 151 cm front, 59.84 in, 152 cm rear; length: 191.30 in, 486 cm; width: 70.90 in, 180 cm; height: 56.30

in, 143 cm; weight: 3,374 lb, 1,530 kg; turning circle (between walls): 37.4 ft, 11.4 m; fuel tank: 18.7 imp gal, 22.4 US gal, 85 l.

BODY saloon/sedan; 4 doors; 5 seats, separate front seats, reclining backrests, adjustable built-in headrests, heated rear window.

PRACTICAL INSTRUCTIONS fuel: 98 oct petrol; oil: engine 10 imp pt, 12 US pt, 5.7 l, SAE 20W-50, change every 3,700 miles, 6,000 km - gearbox 2.1 imp pt, 2.5 US pt, 1.2 l, SAE 20W-50, change every 14,800 miles, 24,000 km - final drive 2.6 imp pt, 3.2 US pt, 1.5 l, SAE 90, no change recommended; greasing: none.

OPTIONAL ACCESSORIES limited slip differential; ZF automatic transmission, hydraulic torque converter and planetary gears with 3 ratios (I 2.478, II 1.478, III 1, rev 2.090), max ratio of converter at stall 2, possible manual selection, 3.640 axle ratio, max speed 116 mph, 186 km, consumption 22.6 m/imp gal, 18.8 m/US gal, 12.5 l x 100 km; light alloy wheels; sunshine roof; air-conditioning.

730

See 728, except for:

PRICE IN GB: £ 10,540*
PRICE EX WORKS: 33,600* marks

ENGINE 182 cu in, 2,986 cc (3.50 x 3.15 in, 89 x 80 mm); max power (DIN): 184 hp (135.4 kW) at 5,800 rpm; max torque (DIN): 188 lb ft, 26 kg m (255 Nm) at 3,500 rpm; 61.6 hp/l (45.4 kW/l).

TRANSMISSION axle ratio: 3.450; width of rims: 6.5''; tyres: 205/70 HR x 14.

PERFORMANCE max speed: 124 mph, 200 km/h; power-weight ratio: 18.9 lb/hp (25.7 lb/kW), 8.6 kg/hp (11.6 kg/kW); speed in direct drive at 1,000 rpm: 19.1 mph, 30.8 km/h; consumption: 23.7 m/imp gal, 19.8 m/US gal, 11.9 l x 100 km.

DIMENSIONS AND WEIGHT weight: 3,484 lb, 1,580 kg.

OPTIONAL ACCESSORIES ZF automatic transmission, 3.450 axle ratio, max speed 121 mph, 194 km/h, consumption 21.9 m/imp gal, 18.2 m/US gal, 12.9 l x 100 km.

733 i

See 728, except for:

PRICE IN GB: £ 11,550*
PRICE EX WORKS: 38,600* marks

ENGINE 195.81 cu in, 3,210 cc (3.50 x 3.39 in, 89 x 86 mm); max power (DIN): 197 hp (145 kW) at 5,500 rpm; max torque (DIN): 207 lb ft, 28.5 kg m (279.5 Nm) at 4,300 rpm; 61.4 hp/l (45.2 kW/l); Bosch L-Jetronic electronic fuel injection system.

TRANSMISSION axle ratio: 3.450; width of rims: 6.5''; tyres: 205/70 VR x 14.

PERFORMANCE max speed: 127 mph, 205 km/h; power-weight ratio: 17.9 lb/hp (24.3 lb/kW), 8.1 kg/hp (11 kg/kW); speed in direct drive at 1,000 rpm: 19.6 mph, 31.5 km/h; consumption: 23.9 m/imp gal, 19.9 m/US gal, 11.8 l x 100 km.

BMW 733 i

ELECTRICAL EQUIPMENT 65 A alternator.

DIMENSIONS AND WEIGHT weight: 3,528 lb, 1,600 kg.

OPTIONAL ACCESSORIES ZF automatic transmission, 3.450 axle ratio, max speed 123 mph, 198 km/h, consumption 22.1 m/imp gal, 18.4 m/US gal, 12.8 l x 100 km.

630 CS

PRICE EX WORKS: 42,300* marks

ENGINE front, 4 stroke; 6 cylinders, in line; 182 cu in, 2,986 cc (3.50 x 3.15 in, 89 x 80 mm); compression ratio 9:1; max power (DIN): 185 hp (136.2 kW) at 5,800 rpm; max torque (DIN): 188 lb ft, 26 kg m (255 Nm) at 3,500 rpm; max engine rpm: 6,200; 62 h/l (45.6 kW/l); cast iron block, light alloy head, polispherical combustion chambers; 7 crankshaft bearings; valves: overhead, Vee-slanted at 52°, rockers; camshafts: 1, overhead, chain-driven; lubrication: rotary pump, full flow filter, 10 imp pt, 12 US pt, 5.7 l; 1 Solex 4A1 4-barrel carburettor with automatic choke and thermostatic by-pass starting device; fuel feed: electric pump; water-cooled, 21.1 imp pt, 25.4 US pt, 12 l.

TRANSMISSION driving wheels: rear; clutch: single dry plate (diaphragm), hydraulically controlled; gearbox: mechanical; gears: 4, fully synchronized; ratios: I 3.855, II 2.203, III 1.402, IV 1, rev 4.300; lever: central; final drive: hypoid bevel; axle ratio: 3.450; width of rims: 6''; tyres: 195/70 VR x 14.

PERFORMANCE max speeds: (I) 34 mph, 54 km/h; (II) 59 mph, 95 km/h; (III) 93 mph, 150 km/h; (IV) 130 mph, 210 km/h; power-weight ratio: 17.3 lb/hp (23.4 lb/kW), 7.8 kg/hp (10.6 kg/kW); carrying capacity: 838 lb, 380 kg; acceleration: standing ¼ mile 16.3 sec, 0-50 mph (0-80 km/h) 5.9 sec; speed in direct drive at 1,000 rpm: 20.9 mph, 33.7 km/h; consumption: 24.8 m/imp gal, 20.6 m/US gal, 11.4 l x 100 km.

CHASSIS integral; front suspension: independent, by McPherson, coil springs/telescopic damper struts, auxiliary rubber springs, anti-roll bar, lower wishbones; rear: independent, semi-trailing arms, auxiliary rubber springs, coil springs, telescopic dampers.

STEERING ZF, recirculating ball, variable ratio servo; turns lock to lock: 3.50.

BRAKES ventilated discs (diameter 11 in, 28 cm), twin dual-circuit system, servo, rear compensator.

ELECTRICAL EQUIPMENT 12 V; 66 Ah battery; 770 W alternator; Bosch distributor, 4 halogen headlamps.

DIMENSIONS AND WEIGHT wheel base: 103.15 in, 262 cm; tracks: 55.91 in, 142 cm front, 58.27 in, 148 cm rear; length: 187.01 in, 475 cm; width: 67.72 in, 172 cm; height: 53.54 in, 136 cm; ground clearance: 5.51 in, 14 cm; weight: 3,197 lb, 1,450 kg; turning circle (between walls): 36.7 ft, 11.2 m; fuel tank: 15.4 imp gal, 18.5 US gal, 70 l.

BODY coupé; 2 doors; 4 seats, separate front seats, reclining backrests; tinted glass; heated rear window.

PRACTICAL INSTRUCTIONS fuel: 98 oct petrol; oil: engine 10 imp pt, 12 US pt, 5.7 l, change every 3,700 miles, 6,000 km - gearbox 2.1 imp pt, 2.5 US pt, 1.2 l, SAE 20W-50, change every 14,800 miles, 24,000 km - final drive 2.6 imp pt, 3.2 US pt, 1.5 l, SAE 90, no change recommended; greasing: none; sparking plug: 175° T30; tappet clearances: inlet 0.010 in, 0.25 mm, exhaust 0.012 in, 0.30 mm; valve timing: 6° 50° 50° 6°; tyre pressure: front 28 psi, 2 atm, rear 27 psi, 1.9 atm.

OPTIONAL ACCESSORIES ZF 3 HP 22 automatic transmission, hydraulic torque converter and planetary gears with 3 ratios + reverse (I 2.478, II 1.478, III 1, rev 2.090), max ratio of converter at stall 2, possible manual selection, max speed 126 mph, 202 km/h, consumption 22.8 m/imp gal, 19 m/US gal, 12.4 l x 100 km; limited slip differential; tyres with 7'' wide rims.

633 CSi

See 630 CS, except for:

PRICE IN GB: £ 14,799*
PRICE EX WORKS: 44,900* marks

ENGINE 195.81 cu in, 3,210 cc (3.50 x 3.39 in, 89 x 86 mm); max power (DIN): 200 hp (147.2 kW) at 5,500 rpm; max torque (DIN): 210 lb ft, 29 kg m (284.4 Nm) at 4,250 rpm; max engine rpm: 6,000; 62.3 hp/l (45.9 kW/l); Bosch L-Jetronic intermittent injection pump in inlet pipes and automatic starting device.

TRANSMISSION axle ratio: 3.250.

PERFORMANCE max speeds: (I) 35 mph, 56 km/h; (II) 61 mph, 98 km/h; (III) 95 mph, 153 km/h; (IV) 134 mph, 215 km/h; power-weight ratio: 16.1 lb/hp (22 lb/kW), 7.3 kg/hp (10 kg/kW); carrying capacity: 838 lb, 380 kg; acceleration: standing ¼ mile 15.8 sec, 0-50 mph (0-80 km/h) 5.6 sec; speed in direct drive at 1,000 rpm: 22.2 mph, 35.8

BMW 630 CS - 633 CSi

633 CSi

km/h; consumption: 28.2 m/imp gal, 23.5 m/US gal, 10 l x 100 km.

ELECTRICAL EQUIPMENT 910 W alternator.

DIMENSIONS AND WEIGHT weight: 3,241 lb, 1,470 kg.

OPTIONAL ACCESSORIES ZF 3 HP 22 automatic transmission, max speed 129 mph, 207 km/h, consumption 25.7 m/imp gal, 21.4 m/US gal, 11 l x 100 km.

EL-KG　　　　　　　　GERMANY FR

Bugatti 35 B

PRICE EX WORKS: 10,650* marks

ENGINE Volkswagen, rear, 4 stroke; 4 cylinders, horizontally opposed; 96.7 cu in, 1,584 cc (3.37 x 2.72 in, 85.5 x 69 mm); compression ratio: 7.5:1; max power (DIN): 50 hp (36.8 kW) at 4,000 rpm; max torque (DIN): 78 lb ft, 10.8 kg m (105.9 Nm) at 2,800 rpm; max engine rpm: 4,500; 31.6 hp/l (23.2 kW/l); block with cast iron liners and light alloy fins, light alloy head; 4 crankshaft bearings; valves: overhead, push-rods and rockers; camshafts: 1, central, lower; lubrication: gear pump, filter in sump, oil cooler, 5.3 imp pt, 6.3 US pt, 3 l; 1 Solex 34 PICT 2 downdraught carburettor; fuel feed: mechanical pump; air-cooled.

TRANSMISSION driving wheels: rear; clutch: single dry plate; gearbox: mechanical; gears: 4, fully synchronized; ratios: I 3.780, II 2.060, III 1.260, IV 0.930, rev 4.010; lever: central; final drive: spiral bevel; axle ratio: 4.375; width of rims: 4.5''; tyres: 185/70 SR x 15.

PERFORMANCE max speed: about 100 mph, 161 km/h; power-weight ratio: 35 lb/hp (47.6 lb/kW), 15.9 kg/hp (21.5 kg/kW); carrying capacity: 442 lb, 200 kg; speed in top at 1,000 rpm: 21.7 mph, 35 km/h; consumption: 30.7 m/imp gal, 25.6 m/US gal, 9.2 l x 100 km.

CHASSIS backbone platform; front suspension: independent, twin swinging longitudinal trailing arms, transverse laminated torsion bars, anti-roll bar, telescopic dampers; rear: independent, semi-trailing arms, transverse compensating torsion bar, telescopic dampers.

STEERING worm and roller, telescopic damper; turns lock to lock: 2.60.

BRAKES front disc (diameter 10.91 in, 27.7 cm), rear drum; lining area: front 12.4 sq in, 80 sq cm, rear 55.5 sq in, 358 sq cm, total 67.9 sq in, 438 sq cm.

ELECTRICAL EQUIPMENT 12 V; 36 Ah battery; 50 A alternator; Bosch distributor; 2 headlamps.

DIMENSIONS AND WEIGHT wheel base: 94.50 in, 240 cm; tracks: 56 in, 142 cm front, 57 in, 144 cm rear; length: 154 in, 391 cm; height: 58 in, 147 cm; ground clearance: 9 in, 22.9 cm; weight: 1,750 lb, 793 kg; fuel tank: 8.8 imp gal, 10.6 US gal, 40 l.

BODY sports in plastic material; no doors; 2 seats.

PRACTICAL INSTRUCTIONS fuel: 87 oct petrol; oil: engine 4.4 imp pt, 5.3 US pt, 2.5 l, SAE 10W-20 (winter) 20W-30 (summer), change every 3,100 miles, 5,000 km - gearbox and final drive 5.3 imp pt, 6.3 US pt, 3 l, SAE 90, change every 31,000 miles, 50,000 km; greasing: every 6,200 miles, 10,000 km, 4 points; sparking plug: 175°; tappet clearances: inlet 0.004 in, 0.10 mm, exhaust 0.004 in, 0.10 mm; valve timing: 7°30' 37° 44°30' 4°.

OPTIONAL ACCESSORIES tonneau cover; wire wheels.

FIBERFAB　　　　　　GERMANY FR

Bonito

ENGINE Volkswagen, rear, 4 stroke; 4 cylinders, horizontally opposed; 72.7 cu in, 1,192 cc (3.03 x 2.52 in, 77 x 64 mm); compression ratio: 7:1; max power (DIN): 34 hp (25 kW) at 3,600 rpm; max torque (DIN): 61 lb ft, 8.4 kg m (82.4 Nm) at 2,000 rpm; max engine rpm: 4,500; 28.5 hp/l (21 kW/l).

TRANSMISSION width of rims: 4'' or 6''; tyres: 165 x 15 or 175 x 14.

DIMENSIONS AND WEIGHT wheel base: 94.49 in, 240 cm; tracks: 51.18 in, 130 cm front, 53.54 in, 136 cm rear; length: 171.26 in, 435 cm; width: 66.14 in, 168 cm; height: 45.28 in, 115 cm; ground clearance: 5.91 in, 15 cm; weight: 1,499 lb, 680 kg; fuel tank: 9.2 imp gal, 11.1 US gal, 42 l.

BODY coupé in plastic material; 2 doors; 2 + 2 seats, separate front seats.

VARIATIONS

ENGINE Volkswagen, 78.4 cu in, 1,285 cc (3.03 x 2.72 in, 77 x 69 mm).
ENGINE Volkswagen, 91.1 cu in, 1,493 cc (3.27 x 2.72 in, 83 x 69 mm).
ENGINE Volkswagen, 96.7 cu in, 1,584 cc (3.37 x 2.72 in, 85.5 x 69 mm).

For further data, see Volkswagen.

Sherpa

ENGINE Citroën, front, 4 stroke; 2 cylinders, horizontally opposed; 26.5 cu in, 435 cc (2.70 x 2.32 in, 68.5 x 59 mm); compression ratio: 8.5:1; max power (DIN): 24 hp (17.7 kW) at 6,750 rpm; max torque (DIN): 21 lb ft, 2.9 kg m (28.4 Nm) at 4,500 rpm; max engine rpm: 6,750; 55.2 hp/l (40.7 kW/l); cast iron block, light alloy head, dry liners, light alloy sump, hemispherical combustion chambers; 2 crankshaft bearings; valves: overhead, Vee-slanted at 70°, push-rods and rockers; camshafts: 1, central, lower; lubrication: rotary pump, filter in sump, oil cooler, 3.5 imp pt, 4.2 US pt, 2 l; 1 Solex 34 PICS 6 downdraught carburettor; fuel feed: mechanical pump; air-cooled.

TRANSMISSION driving wheels: front (double homokinetic joints); clutch: single dry plate; gearbox: mechanical.

PERFORMANCE carrying capacity: 717 lb, 325 kg.

CHASSIS platform; front suspension: independent, swinging leading arms, 2 friction dampers, 2 inertia-type patter dampers; rear: independent, swinging longitudinal trailing arms linked to front suspension by longitudinal coil springs, 2 inertia-type patter dampers, 2 telescopic dampers.

DIMENSIONS AND WEIGHT wheel base: 94.49 in, 240 cm; tracks: 49.61 in, 126 cm front, 49.61 in, 126 cm rear; length: 138.58 in, 352 cm; width: 59.84 in, 152 cm; height: 55.51 in, 141 cm; ground clearance: 7.09 in, 18 cm; weight: 1,257 lb, 570 kg; turning circle (between walls): 35.1 ft, 10.7 m; fuel tank: 4.4 imp gal, 5.3 US gal, 20 l.

BODY open in plastic material; 2 doors; 4 seats, separate front seats; built-in headrests on front seats.

VARIATIONS

ENGINE Citroën, front, 4 stroke, 2 cylinders, horizontally opposed, 36.7 cu in, 602 cc (2.91 x 2.76 in, 74 x 70 mm), max power (DIN) 26 hp (19.1 kW) at 5,500 rpm, max torque (DIN) 29 lb ft, 4 kg m (39.2 Nm) at 3,500 rpm, max engine rpm 6,000, 43.2 hp/l (31.7 kW/l), lubricating system 3.9 imp pt, 4.7 US pt, 2.2 l.
ENGINE Citroën, front, 4 stroke, 2 cylinders, horizontally opposed, 36.7 cu in, 602 cc (2.91 x 2.76 in, 74 x 70 mm), 9:1 compression ratio, max power (DIN) 32 hp (23.6 kW) at 5,750 rpm, max torque (DIN) 30 lb ft, 4.2 kg m (41.2 Nm) at 4,000 rpm, max engine rpm 6,000, 53.3 hp/l (39.2 kW/l), lubricating system 3.9 imp pt, 4.7 US pt, 2.2 l.

For further data, see Citroën.

EL-KG Bugatti 35 B

FIBERFAB Bonito

FIBERFAB Sherpa

FORD Fiesta L 3-door Limousine

FORD GERMANY FR

Fiesta Series

PRICES EX WORKS:

1 Fiesta 3-door Limousine	DM	8,735*
2 Fiesta L 3-door Limousine	DM	9,340*
3 Fiesta S 3-door Limousine	DM	10,510*
4 Fiesta Ghia 3-door Limousine	DM	11,220*

Power team:	Standard for:	Optional for:
40 hp	1,2,4	—
45 hp	—	1,2,4
53 hp	3	1,2,4
66 hp	—	3,4

40 hp power team

ENGINE front, transverse, 4 stroke; 4 cylinders, vertical, in line; 57.1 cu in, 935 cc (2.91 x 2.19 in, 74 x 55.7 mm); compression ratio: 8.3:1; max power (DIN): 40 hp (29.4 kW) at 5,500 rpm; max torque (DIN): 47 lb ft, 6.5 kg m (63.7 Nm) at 2,700 rpm; max engine rpm: 5,700; 42.8 hp/l (31.4 kW/l); cast iron block and head; 3 crankshaft bearings; valves: overhead, in line, push-rods and rockers; camshafts: 1, side, chain-driven; lubrication: gear pump, full flow filter (cartridge), 5.6 imp pt, 6.8 US pt, 3.2 l; 1 Ford downdraught single barrel carburettor; fuel feed: mechanical pump; semi-sealed circuit cooling expansion tank, 8.8 imp pt, 10.6 US pt, 5 l, electric fan.

TRANSMISSION driving wheels: front; clutch: single dry plate (diaphragm); gearbox: mechanical, in unit with final drive; gears: 4, fully synchronized; ratios: I 3.583, II 2.050, III 1.346, IV 0.959, rev 3.769; lever: central; final drive: spiral bevel; axle ratio: 4.060; width of rims: 4'' - Ghia 4.5''; tyres: 145 SR x 12.

PERFORMANCE max speed: 81 mph, 130 km/h; power-weight ratio: 40.2 lb/hp (54.7 lb/kW), 18.2 kg/hp (24.8 kg/kW); carrying capacity: 948 lb, 430 kg; acceleration: 0-50 mph (0-80 km/h) 14.2 sec; speed in top at 1,000 rpm: 15.8 mph, 25.4 km/h; consumption: 41.5 m/imp gal, 34.6 m/US gal, 6.8 l x 100 km.

CHASSIS integral; front suspension: independent, by McPherson, coil springs/telescopic damper struts, lower wishbones (trailing links); rear: rigid axle, swinging longitudinal trailing arms, upper oblique torque arms, Panhard rod, coil springs, telescopic dampers.

STEERING rack-and-pinion; turns lock to lock: 3.40.

BRAKES front disc (diameter 8.71 in, 22.1 cm), rear drum, rear compensator; lining area: front 18.6 sq in, 120 sq cm, rear 26.4 sq in, 169.9 sq cm, total 45 sq in, 289.9 sq cm.

ELECTRICAL EQUIPMENT 12 V; 35 Ah battery; 45 A alternator; Motorcraft distributor; 2 headlamps.

DIMENSIONS AND WEIGHT wheel base: 90.16 in, 229 cm; tracks: 52.36 in, 133 cm front, 51.97 in, 132 cm rear; length: 140.16 in, 356 cm; width: 61.81 in, 157 cm; height: 53.54 in, 136 cm; weight: ground clearance: 5.51 in, 14 cm; weight: 1,610 lb, 730 kg; turning circle (between walls): 32.1 ft, 9.8 m; fuel tank: 7.5 imp gal, 9 US gal, 34 l.

FORD Fiesta Ghia 3-door Limousine

FORD Fiesta S 3-door Limousine

BODY saloon/sedan; 3 doors; 5 seats, separate front seats; back seat folding down to luggage table; 4.5'' wide rims, light alloy wheels (standard for Ghia only).

PRACTICAL INSTRUCTIONS fuel: 90 oct petrol; oil: engine 4.8 imp pt, 5.7 US pt, 2.7 l, change every 6,200 miles, 10,000 km - gearbox and final drive 3.9 imp pt, 4.7 US pt, 2.2 l, change every 6,200 miles, 10,000 km; valve timing: 21° 55° 70° 22°.

OPTIONAL ACCESSORIES 155 SR x 12 tyres with 4.5'' wide rims; servo brake; headrests on front seats; tinted glass; light alloy wheels; sunshine roof; rear window wiper-washer; headlamps with wiper-washers; halogen headlamps; fog lamps; metallic spray; Touring equipment (except for Ghia).

45 hp power team

See 40 hp power team, except for:

ENGINE compression ratio: 9:1; max power (DIN): 45 hp (33.1 kW) at 6,000 rpm; max torque (DIN): 48 lb ft, 6.6 kg m (64.7 Nm) at 3,300 rpm; max engine rpm: 6,500; 48.1 hp/l (35.4 kW/l).

TRANSMISSION axle ratio: 4.290.

PERFORMANCE max speed: 85 mph, 137 km/h; power-weight ratio: 35.8 lb/hp (48.6 lb/kW), 16.2 kg/hp (22 kg/kW); speed in top at 1,000 rpm: 14.9 mph, 24 km/h; consumption: 37.7 m/imp gal, 31.4 m/US gal, 7.5 l x 100 km.

PRACTICAL INSTRUCTIONS fuel: 97 oct petrol.

53 hp power team

See 40 hp power team, except for:

ENGINE 66.3 cu in, 1,087 cc (2.91 x 2.56 in, 74 x 65 mm); compression ratio: 9:1; max power (DIN): 53 hp (39 kW) at 5,700 rpm; max torque (DIN): 59 lb ft, 8.2 kg m (80.4 Nm) at 3,000 rpm; max engine rpm: 6,000; 48.8 hp/l (35.9 kW/l); semi-sealed circuit cooling, expansion tank, 8.8 imp pt, 10.6 US pt, 5 l, electric thermostatic fan.

TRANSMISSION width of rims: 4.5''.

PERFORMANCE max speed: 90 mph, 145 km/h; power-weight ratio: 30.4 lb/hp (41.3 lb/kW), 13.8 kg/hp (18.7 kg/kW); consumption: 35.8 m/imp gal, 29.8 m/US gal, 7.9 l x 100 km.

CHASSIS rear suspension: anti-roll bar.

PRACTICAL INSTRUCTIONS fuel: 97 oct petrol.

66 hp power team

See 40 hp power team, except for:

ENGINE 77.1 cu in, 1,263 cc (3.19 x 2.48 in, 81 x 63 mm); compression ratio: 9.2:1; max power (DIN): 66 hp (48.6 kW) at 5,600 rpm; max torque (DIN): 70 lb ft, 9.6 kg m (94.1 Nm) at 3,250 rpm; max engine rpm: 6,000; 52.2 hp/l (38.5 kW/l); 1 Weber downdraught single barrel carburettor; semi-sealed circuit cooling, expansion tank, 10.9 imp pt, 13.1 US pt, 6.2 l, electric thermostatic fan.

TRANSMISSION axle ratio: 3.840; width of rims: 4.5''; tyres: 155 SR x 12.

PERFORMANCE max speed: 98 mph, 158 km/h; power-weight ratio: 25.9 lb/hp (35.2 lb/kW), 11.7 kg/hp (15.9 kg/kW); speed in top at 1,000 rpm: 16.3 mph, 26.3 km/h; consumption: 36.2 m/imp gal, 30.2 m/US gal, 7.8 l x 100 km.

CHASSIS rear suspension: anti-roll bar.

DIMENSIONS AND WEIGHT weight: 1,709 lb, 775 kg.

PRACTICAL INSTRUCTIONS fuel: 97 oct petrol.

Escort Series

PRICES EX WORKS:

1 Escort 2-door Limousine	DM	9,240*
2 Escort 4-door Limousine	DM	9,760*
3 Escort Turnier	DM	9,995*
4 Escort L 2-door Limousine	DM	9,865*
5 Escort L 4-door Limousine	DM	10,385*
6 Escort L Turnier	DM	10,620*
7 Escort GL 2-door Limousine	DM	10,865*
8 Escort GL 4-door Limousine	DM	11,385*
9 Escort GL Turnier	DM	11,620*
10 Escort Ghia 2-door Limousine	DM	12,825*
11 Escort Ghia 4-door Limousine	DM	13,345*
12 Escort Sport 2-door Limousine	DM	11,280*
13 Escort Sport 4-door Limousine	DM	11,800*
14 Escort RS 2000 2-door Limousine	DM	14,400*

Power team:	Standard for:	Optional for:
44 hp	—	1 to 9
54 hp	1 to 9	10,11
57 hp	—	1 to 11
70 hp	10,11	all except 3,6,9,14
84 hp	12,13	10,11
110 hp	14	—

FORD Escort GL 4-door Limousine

44 hp power team

ENGINE front, 4 stroke; 4 cylinders, vertical, in line; 65.4 cu in, 1,071 cc (3.19 x 2.10 in, 81 x 53.3 mm); compression ratio: 8:1; max power (DIN): 44 hp (32.4 kW) at 5,500 rpm; max torque (DIN): 52 lb ft, 7.2 kg m (70.6 Nm) at 3,000 rpm; max engine rpm: 6,000; 41.1 hp/l (30.2 kW/l); cast iron block and head; 5 crankshaft bearings; valves: overhead, in line, push-rods and rockers; camshafts: 1, side; lubrication: gear pump, full flow filter (cartridge), 5.6 imp pt, 6.8 US pt, 3.2 l; 1 Ford downdraught single barrel carburettor; fuel feed: mechanical pump; water-cooled, 8.8 imp pt, 10.6 US pt, 5 l.

TRANSMISSION driving wheels: rear; clutch: single dry plate (diaphragm); gearbox: mechanical; gears: 4, fully synchronized; ratios: I 3.656, II 2.185, III 1.425, IV 1, rev 4.235; lever: central; final drive: hypoid bevel; axle ratio: 4.110; width of rims: 4.5''; tyres: 155 SR x 13.

PERFORMANCE max speeds: (I) 24 mph, 38 km/h; (II) 41 mph, 66 km/h; (III) 62 mph, 100 km/h; (IV) 79 mph, 127 km/h; power-weight ratio: 4-dr. limousines 44.1 hp/l (61.9 lb/kW), 20 kg/hp (28.1 kg/kW); carrying capacity: 970 lb, 440 kg; speed in direct drive at 1,000 rpm: 16 mph, 25.7 km/h; consumption: 35.3 m/imp gal, 29.4 m/US gal, 8 l x 100 km (Turnier 35.8 m/imp gal, 29.8 m/US gal, 7.9 l x 100 km).

CHASSIS integral; front suspension: independent, by McPherson, coil springs/telescopic damper struts, anti-roll bar; rear: rigid axle, semi-elliptic leafsprings, torque trailing links, anti-roll bar, telescopic dampers.

STEERING rack-and-pinion; turns lock to lock: 3.50.

BRAKES front disc (diameter 9.72 in, 24.7 cm), rear drum; lining area: front 23.4 sq in, 151.2 sq cm, rear 36.4 sq in, 235 sq cm, total 59.8 sq in, 386.2 sq cm.

ELECTRICAL EQUIPMENT 12 V; 35 Ah battery; 35 A alternator (45 A for GL only); Motorcraft distributor; 2 headlamps.

DIMENSIONS AND WEIGHT wheel base: 94.88 in, 241 cm; tracks: 50 in, 127 cm front, 51.18 in, 130 cm rear; length: 159.84 in, 406 cm - Turnier 162.99 in, 414 cm; width: 62.99 in, 160 cm - Turnier 61.42 in, 156 cm; height: 55.12 in, 140 cm - Turnier 55.51 in, 141 cm; ground clearance: 4.72 in, 12 cm; weight: 2-dr. limousines 1,940 lb, 880 kg - 4-dr. limousines 2,007 lb, 910 kg - Turnier 2,029 lb, 920 kg; turning circle (between walls): 31.2 ft, 9.5 m; fuel tank: 9 imp gal, 10.8 US gal, 41 l.

BODY 4-5 seats, separate front seats.

PRACTICAL INSTRUCTIONS fuel: 90 oct petrol; oil: engine 4.8 imp pt, 5.7 US pt, 2.7 l, SAE 10W-30, change every 6,200 miles, 10,000 km - gearbox 1.6 imp pt, 1.9 US pt, 0.9 l, SAE 80, no change recommended - final drive 2.6 imp pt, 3.2 US pt, 1.5 l, SAE 90, no change recommended; greasing: none; tappet clearances: inlet 0.010 in, 0.25 mm, exhaust 0.017 in, 0.43 mm; valve timing: 17° 51° 51° 17°; tyre pressure: front 24 psi, 1.7 atm, rear 24 psi, 1.7 atm.

OPTIONAL ACCESSORIES 165 SR x 13 tyres 5'' wide rims except for Turnier; servo brake; heated rear window; halogen headlamps; metallic spray.

54 hp power team

See 44 hp power team, except for:

ENGINE 77.1 cu in, 1,263 cc (3.19 x 2.48 in, 81 x 63 mm); max power (DIN): 54 hp (39.7 kW) at 5,500 rpm; max torque (DIN): 63 lb ft, 8.7 kg m (85.3 Nm) at 3,000 rpm; 42.8 hp/l (31.4 kW/l).

TRANSMISSION axle ratio: 3.890; width of rims: Ghia 5''.

PERFORMANCE max speed: 85 mph, 137 km/h; power-weight ratio: 4-dr. limousines 37.4 lb/hp (50.8 lb/kW), 16.9 kg/hp (23 kg/kW) - Ghia 4-dr. Limousine 38.4 lb/hp (52.2 lb/kW), 17.4 kg/hp (23.7 kg/kW); carrying capacity: Ghia 937 lb, 425 kg; speed in direct drive at 1,000 rpm: 16.9 mph, 27.2 km/h; consumption: 33.2 m/imp gal, 27.7 m/US gal, 8.5 l x 100 km.

BRAKES servo (standard).

DIMENSIONS AND WEIGHT weight: 2-dr. limousines 1,951 lb, 885 kg - 4-dr. limousines 2,018 lb, 915 kg - Turnier 2,029 lb, 920 kg - Ghia 2-dr. Limousine 2,007 lb, 910 kg - 4-dr. Limousine 2,073 lb, 940 kg.

BODY heated rear window (standard for Ghia only).

FORD Escort Ghia 4-door Limousine

57 hp power team

See 54 hp power team, except for:

ENGINE compression ratio: 9.2:1; max power (DIN): 57 hp (41.9 kW) at 5,500 rpm; max torque (DIN): 67 lb ft, 9.3 kg m (91.2 Nm) at 3,000 rpm; 45.1 hp/l (33.2 kW/l).

TRANSMISSION gearbox: Ford C3 automatic transmission, hydraulic torque converter and planetary gears with 3 ratios, max ratio of converter at stall 2, possible manual selection; ratios: I 2.474, II 1.474, III 1, rev 2.111; axle ratio: 3.890.

PERFORMANCE max speed 84 mph, 135 km/h; power-weight ratio: 4-dr. limousines 35.4 lb/hp (48.2 lb/kW), 16 kg/hp (21.8 kg/kW) - Ghia 4-dr. Limousine 36.4 lb/hp (49.5 lb/kW), 16.5 kg/hp (22.4 kg/kW); speed in direct drive at 1,000 rpm: 15.3 mph, 24.6 km/h; 30.7 m/imp gal, 25.6 m/US gal, 9.2 l x 100 km.

ELECTRICAL EQUIPMENT 55 Ah battery.

PRACTICAL INSTRUCTIONS fuel: 97 oct petrol.

70 hp power team

See 44 hp power team, except for:

ENGINE 77.1 cu in, 1,263 cc (3.19 x 2.48 in, 81 x 63 mm); compression ratio: 9.2:1; max power (DIN): 70 hp (51.5 kW) at 5,500 rpm; max torque (DIN): 68 lb ft, 9.4 kg m (92.2 Nm) at 4,000 rpm; 55.4 hp/l (40.8 kW/l); 1 Weber downdraught twin barrel carburettor.

TRANSMISSION gearbox ratios: I 3.337, II 1.995, III 1.418, IV 1, rev 3.867; width of rims: 5''; tyres: Sport 175/70 SR x 13.

PERFORMANCE max speed: 93 mph, 150 km/h; power-weight ratio: Ghia 4-dr. Limousine 30.1 lb/hp (40.9 lb/kW), 13.6 kg/hp (18.5 kg/kW) - Sport 4-dr. Limousine 28.8 lb/hp (39.2 lb/kW), 13.1 kg/hp (17.8 kg/kW); carrying capacity: Ghia 937 lb, 425 kg - Sport 970 lb, 440 kg; consumption: 29.7 m/imp gal, 24.8 m/US gal, 9.5 l x 100 km.

BRAKES servo (standard); lining area: front 23.4 sq in, 151.2 sq cm, rear 47.3 sq in, 305.2 sq cm, total 70.7 sq in, 456.4 sq cm.

ELECTRICAL EQUIPMENT 45 A alternator.

DIMENSIONS AND WEIGHT length: Sport 160.63 in, 408 cm; height: Sport 54.33 in, 138 cm; weight: Ghia 2-dr. Limousine 2,040 lb, 925 kg - 4-dr. Limousine 2,106 lb, 955 kg - Sport 2-dr. Limousine 1,951 lb, 885 kg - 4-dr. Limousine 2,018 lb, 915 kg.

PRACTICAL INSTRUCTIONS fuel: 97 oct petrol.

OPTIONAL ACCESSORIES 175/70 SR x 13 tyres (for Ghia only).

84 hp power team

See 70 hp power team, except for:

ENGINE 95.6 cu in, 1,566 cc (3.19 x 3.06 in, 81 x 77.6 mm); compression ratio: 9:1; max power (DIN) 84 hp (61.8 kW) at 5,500 rpm; max torque (DIN): 92 lb ft, 12.7 kg m (124.5 Nm) at 3,500 rpm; 53.6 hp/l (39.5 kW/l); cooling system: 9.5 imp pt, 11.4 US pt, 5.4 l.

TRANSMISSION axle ratio: 3.540.

PERFORMANCE max speed: 101 mph, 162 km/h; power-weight ratio: Sport 4-dr. Limousine 24.4 lb/hp (33.2 lb/kW), 11.1 kg/hp (15 kg/kW) - Ghia 4-dr. Limousine 25.1 lb/hp (34.1 lb/kW), 11.4 kg/hp (15.4 kg/kW); speed in direct drive at 1,000 rpm: 18.5 mph, 29.8 km/h; consumption: 31 m/imp gal, 25.8 m/US gal, 9.1 l x 100 km.

DIMENSIONS AND WEIGHT weight: Sport 2-dr. Limousine 1,985 lb, 900 kg - 4-dr. Limousine 2,051 lb, 930 kg - Ghia 2-dr. Limousine 2,040 lb, 925 kg - 4-dr. Limousine 2,106 lb, 955 kg.

OPTIONAL ACCESSORIES Ford C3 automatic transmission, hydraulic torque converter and planetary gears with 3 ratios (I 2.474, II 1.474, III 1, rev. 2.111), max ratio of converter at stall 2, possible manual selection, 3.540 axle ratio, max speed 98 mph, 157 km/h, consumption 28.2 m/imp gal, 23.5 m/US gal, 10 l x 100 km, 55 Ah battery.

110 hp power team

See 44 hp power team, except for:

ENGINE 119.3 cu in, 1,955 cc (3.57 x 3.03 in, 90.8 x 76.9 mm); compression ratio: 9.2:1; max power (DIN): 110 hp (81 kW) at 5,500 rpm; max torque (DIN): 119 lb ft, 16.4 kg m (160.8 Nm) at 3,750 rpm; max engine rpm: 6,500; 56.3 hp/l (41.4 kW/l); valves; overhead, Vee-slanted, rockers; camshafts: 1, overhead, cogged belt; lubricating system: 6.7 imp pt, 8 US pt, 3.8 l; 1 Weber downdraught twin barrel carburettor; water-cooled, 10.7 imp pt, 12.9 US pt, 6.1 l, electric thermostatic fan.

TRANSMISSION gearbox ratios: I 3.656, II 1.970, III 1.370, IV 1, rev 3.660; axle ratio: 3.540; width of rims: 5.5''; tyres: 175/70 HR x 13.

PERFORMANCE max speed: 112 mph, 180 km/h; power-weight ratio: 18.6 lb/hp (25.2 lb/kW), 8.4 kg/hp (11.4 kg/kW); carrying capacity: 882 lb, 400 kg; consumption: 32.5 m/imp gal, 27 m/US gal, 8.7 l x 100 km.

BRAKES front disc, rear drum, servo (standard); lining area: front 23.4 sq in, 151.2 sq cm, rear 47.3 sq in, 305.2 sq cm, total 70.07 sq in, 456.4 sq cm.

ELECTRICAL EQUIPMENT 55 Ah battery; 55 A alternator; 4 halogen headlamps.

DIMENSIONS AND WEIGHT tracks: 50.79 in, 129 cm front, 51.57 in, 131 cm rear; length: 163.39 in, 415 cm; height: 54.72 in, 139 cm; ground clearance: 5.51 in, 14 cm; weight: 2,040 lb, 925 kg; turning circle (between walls): 32.1 ft, 9.8 m.

BODY built-in headrests; heated rear window (standard).

PRACTICAL INSTRUCTIONS fuel: 97 oct petrol; oil: engine 5.8 imp pt, 7 US pt, 3.3 l.

FORD Escort RS 2000 2-door Limousine

Taunus Series

PRICES EX WORKS:

1 Taunus 2-door Limousine	DM 10,945*
2 Taunus 4-door Limousine	DM 11,490*
3 Taunus Turnier	DM 12,095*
4 Taunus L 2-door Limousine	DM 11,555*
5 Taunus L 4-door Limousine	DM 12,100*
6 Taunus L Turnier	DM 12,705*
7 Taunus GL 2-door Limousine	DM 13,395*
8 Taunus GL 4-door Limousine	DM 13,940*
9 Taunus GL Turnier	DM 14,545*
10 Taunus Ghia 2-door Limousine	DM 15,775*
11 Taunus Ghia 4-door Limousine	DM 16,320*
12 Taunus S 2-door Limousine	DM 14,660*
13 Taunus S 4-door Limousine	DM 15,205*

Power team:	Standard for:	Optional for:
55 hp	1 to 6	—
68 hp	—	1 to 9
72 hp	7 to 11	1 to 6
90 hp	—	4 to 11
98 hp	12, 13	—
108 hp	—	10 to 13

55 hp power team

ENGINE front, 4 stroke; 4 cylinders, vertical, in line; 78.4 cu in, 1,285 cc (3.11 x 2.60 in, 79 x 66 mm); compression ratio: 8:1; max power (DIN): 55 hp (40.5 kW) at 5,500 rpm; max torque (DIN): 67 lb ft, 9.3 kg m (91.2 Nm) at 3,000 rpm; max engine rpm: 6,000; 42.8 hp/l (31.5 kW/l); cast iron block and head; 5 crankshaft bearings; valves: overhead, Vee-slanted, rockers; camshafts: 1, overhead, cogged belt; lubrication: gear pump, full flow filter (cartridge), 6.5 imp pt, 7.8 US pt, 3.7 l; 1 Ford downdraught carburettor; fuel feed: mechanical pump; water-cooled, 10.2 imp pt, 12.3 US pt, 5.8 l.

TRANSMISSION driving wheels: rear; clutch: single dry plate (diaphragm); gearbox: mechanical; gears: 4, fully synchronized; ratios: I 3.660, II 2.190, III 1.430, IV 1, rev 4.240; lever: central; final drive: hypoid bevel; axle ratio: 4.110 - Turniers 4.440; width of rims: 4.5''; tyres: 165 SR x 13.

PERFORMANCE max speed: 85 mph, 137 km/h; power-weight ratio: 4-dr. limousines 41.7 lb/hp (56.6 lb/kW), 18.9 kg/hp (25.7 kg/kW); speed in direct drive at 1,000 rpm: 14.2 mph, 22.8 km/h; consumption: 29.7 m/imp gal, 24.8 m/US gal, 9.5 l x 100 km - Turniers 28.5 m/imp gal, 23.8 m/US gal, 9.9 l x 100 km.

CHASSIS integral; front suspension: independent, wishbones (lower trailing links), coil springs/telescopic dampers, anti-roll bar; rear: rigid axle, lower trailing arms, upper oblique torque arms, coil springs, anti-roll bar, telescopic dampers.

STEERING rack-and-pinion.

BRAKES front disc (diameter 9.72 in, 24.7 cm), rear drum, rear compensator, servo; lining area: front 23.4 sq in, 151.2

FORD Taunus Series

sq cm, rear 40.9 sq in, 264.5 sq cm, total 64.3 sq in, 415.7 sq cm.

ELECTRICAL EQUIPMENT 12 V; 44 Ah battery; 45 A alternator; Bosch distributor; 2 headlamps (4 halogen headlamps standard for GL only).

DIMENSIONS AND WEIGHT wheel base: 102.57 in, 258 cm; front and rear tracks: 55.91 in, 142 cm; length: 172.44 in, 438 cm - Turniers 176.38 in, 448 cm; width: 66.93 in, 170 cm; height: 53.54 in, 136 cm - Turniers 53.94 in, 137 cm; ground clearance: 3.82 in, 9.7 cm; weight: 2-dr. limousines 2,249 lb, 1,020 kg - 4-dr. limousines 2,293 lb, 1,040 kg - Turniers 2,437 lb, 1,105 kg; turning circle (between walls): 34.8 ft, 10.6 m; fuel tank: 11.9 imp gal, 14.3 US gal, 54 l.

BODY 5 seats, separate front seats, separate front seats; heated rear window.

PRACTICAL INSTRUCTIONS fuel: 90 oct petrol; oil: engine 5.6 imp pt, 6.8 US pt, 3.2 l, SAE 10W-40, change every 6,200 miles, 10,000 km - gearbox 1.4 imp pt, 1.7 US pt, 0.8 l, SAE 80 EP, change every 12,400 miles, 20,000 km - final drive 1.8 imp pt, 2.1 US pt, 1 l, SAE 90, change every 12,400 miles, 20,000 km; greasing: every 31,100 miles, 50,000 km, 2 points; tyre pressure: front 24 psi, 1.7 atm, rear 24 psi, 1.7 atm.

OPTIONAL ACCESSORIES 4.440 axle ratio; 185/70 SR x 13 tyres with 5.5'' wide rims; halogen headlamps; built-in headrests on front seats; fog lamps; metallic spray; sunshine roof except for Turniers.

68 hp power team

See 55 hp power team, except for:

ENGINE 96.2 cu in, 1,576 cc (3.45 x 2.60 in, 87 x 66 mm); compression ratio: 8.2:1; max power (DIN): 68 hp (50 kW) at 5,200 rpm; max torque (DIN): 85 lb ft, 11.7 kg m (114.7 Nm) at 2,700 rpm; 43.1 hp/l (31.7 kW/l).

TRANSMISSION gearbox ratios: I 3.580, II 2.010, III 1.400, IV 1, rev 3.320; axle ratio: 3.890 - Turniers 4.110; width of rims: GL 5''.

PERFORMANCE max speed: 91 mph, 147 km/h; power-weight ratio: 4-dr. limousines 34.2 lb/hp (46.5 lb/kW), 15.5 kg/hp (21.1 kg/kW); speed in direct drive at 1,000 rpm: 15.2 mph, 24.5 km/h; consumption: 26.4 m/imp gal, 22 m/US gal, 10.7 l x 100 km.

DIMENSIONS AND WEIGHT weight: 2-dr. limousines 2,282 lb, 1,035 kg - 4-dr. limousines 2,326 lb, 1,055 kg - Turniers 2,459 lb, 1,115 kg.

OPTIONAL ACCESSORIES 4.110 axle ratio; Ford C3 automatic transmission, hydraulic torque converter and planetary gears with 3 ratios (I 2.474, II 1.474, III 1, rev 2.111), max ratio of converter at stall 2, possible manual selection, 55 Ah battery, max speed 88 mph, 142 km/h, consumption 24.6 m/imp gal, 20.5 m/US gal, 11.5 l x 100 km (Turniers 24.4 m/imp gal, 20.3 m/US gal, 11.6 l x 100 km).

72 hp power team

See 55 hp power team, except for:

ENGINE 96.2 cu in, 1,576 cc (3.45 x 2.60 in, 87.7 x 66 mm); compression ratio: 9.2:1; max power (DIN): 72 hp (53 kW) at 5,000 rpm; max torque (DIN): 87 lb ft, 12 kg m (117.7 Nm) at 2,700 rpm; 45.7 hp/l (33.6 kW/l).

TRANSMISSION gearbox ratios: I 3.580, II 2.010, III 1.400, IV 1, rev 3.320; axle ratio: 3.890 - Turniers 4.110; width of rims GL and Ghia 5.5''; tyres: Ghia 185/70 SR x 13.

PERFORMANCE max speed: 94 mph, 152 km/h; power-weight ratio: 4-dr. limousines 32.3 lb/hp (43.9 lb/kW), 14.7 kg/hp (19.9 kg/kW); speed in direct drive at 1,000 rpm: 15.7 mph, 25.3 km/h; consumption: 28.2 m/imp gal, 23.5 m/US gal, 10 l x 100 km - Turniers 28 m/imp gal, 23.3 m/US gal, 10.1 l x 100 km.

ELECTRICAL EQUIPMENT halogen headlamps (standard for GL and Ghia only).

DIMENSIONS AND WEIGHT weight: 2-dr. limousines 2,282 lb, 1,035 kg - 4-dr. limousines 2,326 lb, 1,055 kg - Turniers 2,459 lb, 1,115 kg.

PRACTICAL INSTRUCTIONS fuel: 97 oct petrol.

OPTIONAL ACCESSORIES 4.110 axle ratio; Ford C3 automatic transmission, hydraulic torque converter and planetary gears with 3 ratios (I 2.474, II 1.474, III 1, rev 2.111), max ratio of converter at stall 2, possible manual selection, 55 Ah battery, max speed 91 mph, 147 km/h, consumption 25.9 m/imp gal, 21.6 m/US gal, 10.9 l x 100 km (Turniers 25.7 m/imp gal, 21.4 m/US gal, 11 l x 100 km).

90 hp power team

See 55 hp power team, except for:

ENGINE 6 cylinders, Vee-slanted at 60°; 120.9 cu in, 1,981 cc (3.31 x 2.37 in, 84 x 60.1 mm); compression ratio: 8.75:1; max power (DIN): 90 hp (66.2 kW) at 5,000 rpm; max torque (DIN): 110 lb ft, 15.2 kg m at 3,000 rpm; 45.4 hp/l (33.4 kW/l); 4 crankshaft bearings; camshafts: 1, at centre of Vee; lubricating system: 7.4 imp pt, 8.9 US pt, 4.2 l; 1 Solex 32/32 EEIT downdraught twin barrel carburettor; cooling system: 12.1 imp pt, 14.6 US pt, 6.9 l.

TRANSMISSION gearbox ratios: I 3.650, II 1.970, III 1.370, IV 1, rev 3.660; axle ratio: 3.440; width of rims: 4.5'' - GL and Ghia 5.5''; tyres: Ghia 185/70 SR x 13.

PERFORMANCE max speed: 101 mph, 163 km/h; power-weight ratio: 4-dr. limousines 27.7 lb/hp (37.6 lb/kW), 12.6 kg/hp (17.1 kg/kW); speed in direct drive at 1,000 rpm: 16.9 mph, 27.2 km/h; consumption: 27.7 m/imp gal, 23.1 m/US gal, 10.2 l x 100 km - Turniers 28.5 m/imp gal, 23.8 m/US gal, 9.9 l x 100 km.

BRAKES lining area: front 23.4 sq in, 151.2 sq cm, rear 58.6 sq in, 377.6 sq cm, total 82 sq in, 528.8 sq cm.

ELECTRICAL EQUIPMENT halogen headlamps (standard for GL and Ghia only).

DIMENSIONS AND WEIGHT weight: 2-dr. limousines 2,448 lb, 1,110 kg - 4-dr. limousines 2,492 lb, 1,130 kg - Turniers 2,591 lb, 1,175 kg.

PRACTICAL INSTRUCTIONS fuel: 97 oct petrol; oil: engine 7 imp pt, 8.5 US pt, 4 l.

OPTIONAL ACCESSORIES Ford C3 automatic transmission, hydraulic torque converter and planetary gears with 3 ratios (I 2.474, II 1.474, III 1, rev 2.111), max ratio of converter at stall 2, possible manual selection, 55 Ah battery, max speed 98 mph, 158 km/h, consumption 25.2 m/imp gal, 21 m/US gal, 11.2 l x 100 km (Turniers 25.9 m/imp gal, 21.6 m/US gal, 10.9 l x 100 km).

98 hp power team

See 55 hp power team, except for:

ENGINE 119.3 cu in, 1,955 cc (3.57 x 3.03 in, 90.8 x 76.9 mm); compression ratio: 9.2:1; max power (DIN): 98 hp (72.1 kW) at 5,200 rpm; max torque (DIN): 112 lb ft, 15.4 kg m (151 Nm) at 3,500 rpm; 50.1 hp/l (36.9 kW/l); 1 Weber 32/36 DGAV downdraught twin barrel carburettor; cooling system: 10.7 imp pt, 12.9 US pt, 6.1 l.

TRANSMISSION gearbox ratios: I 3.650, II 1.970, III 1.370, IV 1, rev 3.660; axle ratio: 3.750; width of rims: 5.5''; tyres: 185/70 SR x 13.

PERFORMANCE max speed: 104 mph, 167 km/h; power-weight ratio: 4-dr. Limousine 24.3 lb/hp (33 lb/kW), 11 kg/hp (15 kg/kW); speed in direct drive at 1,000 rpm: 17.3 mph, 27.8 km/h; consumption: 26.6 m/imp gal, 22.2 m/US gal, 10.6 l x 100 km.

FORD Taunus Ghia 4-door Limousine

FORD Taunus S 2-door Limousine

BRAKES lining area: front 23.4 sq in, 151.2 sq cm, rear 58.6 sq in, 377.6 sq cm, total 82 sq in, 528.8 sq cm.

ELECTRICAL EQUIPMENT 4 halogen headlamps (standard).

DIMENSIONS AND WEIGHT weight: 2-dr. Limousine 2,337 lb, 1,060 kg - 4-dr. Limousine 2,381 lb, 1,080 kg.

PRACTICAL INSTRUCTIONS fuel: 97 oct petrol.

OPTIONAL ACCESSORIES Ford C3 automatic transmission, hydraulic torque converter and planetary gears with 3 ratios (I 2.474, II 1.474, III 1, rev 2.111), max ratio of converter at stall 2, possible manual selection, 55 Ah battery, max speed 101 mph, 162 km/h, consumption 24.1 m/imp gal, 20.1 m/US gal, 11.7 l x 100 km.

108 hp power team

See 55 hp power team, except for:

ENGINE 6 cylinders, Vee-slanted at 60°; 138.8 cu in, 2,274 cc (3.54 x 2.37 in, 90 x 60.1 mm); compression ratio: 8.75:1; max power (DIN): 108 hp (79.5 kW) at 5,000 rpm; max torque (DIN): 130 lb ft, 18 kg m (176.5 Nm) at 3,000 rpm; 47.5 hp/l (35 kW/l); 4 crankshaft bearings; camshafts: 1, at centre of Vee; lubricating system: 7.4 imp pt, 8.9 US pt, 4.2 l; 1 Solex 35/35 EEIT downdraught twin barrel carburettor; cooling system: 12.1 imp pt, 14.6 US pt 6.9 l.

TRANSMISSION gearbox ratios: I 3.650, II 1.970, III 1.370, IV 1, rev 3.660; axle ratio: 3.440; width of rims: 5.5''; tyres: 185/70 SR x 13.

PERFORMANCE max speed: 107 mph, 173 km/h; power-weight ratio: 4-dr. limousines 23.1 lb/hp (31.3 lb/kW), 10.5 kg/hp (14.2 kg/kW); speed in direct drive at 1,000 rpm: 17.9 mph, 28.8 km/h; consumption: 28 m/imp gal, 23.3 m/US gal, 10.1 l x 100 km.

BRAKES lining area: front 23.4 sq in, 151.2 sq cm, rear 58.6 sq in, 377.6 sq cm, total 82 sq in, 528.8 sq cm.

ELECTRICAL EQUIPMENT 4 headlamps (standard).

DIMENSIONS AND WEIGHT weight: 2-dr. limousines 2,448 lb, 1,110 kg - 4-dr. limousines 2,492 lb, 1,130 kg.

PRACTICAL INSTRUCTIONS fuel: 97 oct petrol; oil: engine 7 imp pt, 8.5 US pt, 4 l.

OPTIONAL ACCESSORIES Ford C3 automatic transmission, hydraulic torque converter and planetary gears with 3 ratios (I 2.474, II 1.474, III 1, rev 2.111), max ratio of converter at stall 2, possible manual selection, 55 Ah battery, max speed 104 mph, 168 km/h, consumption 26.2 m/imp gal, 21.8 m/US gal, 10.8 l x 100 km.

Capri II Series

PRICES IN USA AND EX WORKS:	$	DM
1 Capri II L Coupé	—	11,690*
2 Capri II GL Coupé	—	13,545*
3 Capri II S Coupé	4,361	15,305*
4 Capri II Ghia Coupé	4,984	18,280*

Power team:	Standard for:	Optional for:
54 hp	1	—
68 hp	—	1,2
72 hp	2	1
90 hp	3,4	2
108 hp	—	3,4
138 hp	—	3,4

54 hp power team

ENGINE front, 4 stroke; 4 cylinders, vertical, in line; 77.1 cu in, 1,263 cc (3.19 x 2.48 in, 81 x 63 mm); compression ratio: 8:1; max power (DIN): 54 hp (39.7 kW) at 5,500 rpm; max torque (DIN): 63 lb ft, 8.7 kg m (85.3 Nm) at 3,000 rpm; max engine rpm: 6,000; 42.8 hp/l (31.4 kW/l); cast iron block and head; 5 crankshaft bearings; valves: overhead, in line, push-rods and rockers; camshafts: 1, side; lubrication: rotary pump, full flow filter (cartridge), 5.8 imp pt, 7 US pt, 3.3 l; 1 Ford downdraught carburettor; fuel feed: mechanical pump; water-cooled, 8.3 imp pt, 9.9 US pt, 4.7 l.

TRANSMISSION driving wheels: rear; clutch: single dry plate (diaphragm); gearbox: mechanical; gears: 4, fully synchronized; ratios: I 3.580, II 2.010, III 1.397, IV 1, rev 3.324; lever: central; final drive: hypoid bevel; axle ratio: 4.125; width of rims: 5''; tyres: 165 SR x 13.

PERFORMANCE max speeds: (I) 27 mph, 44 km/h; (II) 53 mph, 85 km/h; (III) 69 mph, 111 km/h; (IV) 87 mph, 140 km/h; power-weight ratio: 41.2 lb/hp (56.1 lb/kW), 18.7 kg/hp (25.4 kg/kW); carrying capacity: 750 lb, 340 kg; speed in direct drive at 1,000 rpm: 16.3 mph, 26.2 km/h; consumption: 30.4 m/imp gal, 25.3 m/US gal, 9.3 l x 100 km.

FORD Taunus GL 4-door Limousine

CHASSIS integral; front suspension: independent, by Mc-Pherson, coil springs/telescopic damper struts, lower transverse arms, anti-roll bar; rear: rigid axle, semi-elliptic leafsprings, rubber springs, anti-roll bar, telescopic dampers.

STEERING rack-and-pinion.

BRAKES front disc (diameter 9.49 in, 24.1 cm), rear drum; lining area: front 17.4 sq in, 112.3 sq cm, rear 35 sq in, 226 sq cm, total 52.4 sq in, 338.3 sq cm.

ELECTRICAL EQUIPMENT 12 V; 35 Ah battery; 45 A alternator; Bosch distributor; 2 headlamps.

DIMENSIONS AND WEIGHT wheel base: 100.79 in, 256 cm; tracks: 53.15 in, 135 cm front, 54.33 in, 138 cm rear; length: 170.87 in, 434 cm; width: 66.93 in, 170 cm; height: 53.54 in, 136 cm; ground clearance: 4.92 in, 12.5 cm; weight: 2,227 lb, 1,010 kg; turning circle (between walls): 35.4 ft, 10.8 m; fuel tank: 12.8 imp gal, 15.3 US gal, 58 l.

BODY coupé; 2 + 1 doors; 5 seats, separate front seats, reclining backrests; back seats folding down to luggage table.

PRACTICAL INSTRUCTIONS fuel: 90 oct petrol; oil: engine 4.8 imp pt, 5.7 US pt, 2.7 l, SAE 20W-40, change every 6,200 miles, 10,000 km - gearbox 2.3 imp pt, 2.7 US pt, 1.3 l, SAE 80, change every 12,400 miles, 20,000 km - final drive 1.9 imp pt, 2.3 US pt, 1.1 l, SAE 90, change every 12,400 miles, 20,000 km; greasing: none.

FORD Capri II Ghia Coupé

FORD Capri II Ghia Coupé

OPTIONAL ACCESSORIES servo brake; heated rear window with 55 A alternator; wiper on rear window; headrests on front seats; sunshine roof; vinyl roof; halogen headlamps; metallic spray; 185/70 SR x 13 tyres.

68 hp power team

See 54 hp power team, except for:

ENGINE 96.2 cu in, 1,576 cc (3.45 x 2.60 in, 87.7 x 66 mm); compression ratio: 8.2:1; max power (DIN): 68 hp (50 kW) at 5,200 rpm; max torque (DIN): 85 lb ft, 11.7 kg m (114.7 Nm) at 2,700 rpm; 43.1 hp/l (31.7 kW/l); valves: overhead, Vee-slanted, rockers; camshafts: 1, overhead, cogged belt; lubricating system: 6.5 imp pt, 7.8 US pt, 3.7 l; cooling system: 10.2 imp pt, 12.3 US pt, 5.8 l.

TRANSMISSION gearbox ratios: I 3.650, II 1.970, III 1.370, IV 1, rev 3.660; axle ratio: 3.770.

PERFORMANCE max speed: 95 mph, 153 km/h; power-weight ratio: 33.7 lb/hp (45.9 lb/kW), 15.3 kg/hp (20.8 kg/kW); carrying capacity: 816 lb, 370 kg; speed in direct drive at 1,000 rpm: 17.8 mph, 28.6 km/h; consumption: 29.1 m/imp gal, 24.2 m/US gal, 9.7 l x 100 km.

BRAKES front disc (diameter 9.61 in, 24.4 cm), rear drum, servo (standard); lining area: front 17.4 sq in, 151.2 sq cm, rear 45.4 sq in, 293.4 sq cm, total 62.8 sq in, 444.6 sq cm.

ELECTRICAL EQUIPMENT 44 Ah battery; 45 A (55 A for GL) alternator.

DIMENSIONS AND WEIGHT weight: 2,293 lb, 1,040 kg.

PRACTICAL INSTRUCTIONS oil: engine 5.6 imp pt, 6.8 US pt, 3.2 l.

OPTIONAL ACCESSORIES Ford C-3 automatic transmission, hydraulic torque converter and planetary gears with 3 ratios (I 2.474, II 1.474, III 1, rev 2.111), max ratio of converter at stall 2, possible manual selection, oil cooler, 55 Ah battery, max speed 92 mph, 148 km/h, consumption 26.2 m/imp gal, 21.8 m/US gal, 10.8 l x 100 km.

72 hp power team

See 68 hp power team, except for:

ENGINE compression ratio: 9.2:1; max power (DIN): 72 hp (53 kW) at 5,200 rpm; max torque (DIN): 87 lb ft, 12 kg m (117.7 Nm) at 2,700 rpm; 45.7 hp/l (33.6 kW/l).

PERFORMANCE max speed: 97 mph, 156 km/h; power-weight ratio: 31.8 lb/hp (43.3 lb/kW), 14.4 kg/hp (19.6 kg/kW); consumption: 30.4 m/imp gal, 25.3 m/US gal, 9.3 l x 100 km.

PRACTICAL INSTRUCTIONS fuel: 97 oct petrol.

OPTIONAL ACCESSORIES with Ford C-3 automatic transmission, max speed 94 mph, 151 km/h, consumption 27.7 m/imp gal, 23.1 m/US gal, 10.2 l x 100 km.

90 hp power team

See 54 hp power team, except for:

ENGINE 6 cylinders, Vee-slanted at 60°; 120.9 cu in, 1,981 cc (3.31 x 2.37 in, 84 x 60.1 mm); compression ratio: 8.75:1; max power (DIN): 90 hp (66.2 kW) at 5,000 rpm; max torque (DIN): 110 lb ft, 15.2 kg m (149.1 Nm) at 3,000 rpm; 45.4 hp/l (33.4 kW/l); 4 crankshaft bearings; valves: overhead, push-rods and rockers; camshafts: 1, at centre of Vee; lubricating system: 7.4 imp pt, 8.9 US pt, 4.2 l; 1 Solex 32/32 EEIT downdraught twin barrel carburettor; cooling system: 13.7 imp pt, 16.5 US pt, 7.8 l.

TRANSMISSION gearbox ratios: I 3.650, II 1.970, III 1.370, IV 1, rev 3.660; axle ratio: 3.440; width of rims: 5.5''.

PERFORMANCE max speed: 104 mph, 168 km/h - Capri S 106 mph, 171 km/h; power-weight ratio: 27.4 lb/hp (37.3 lb/kW), 12.4 kg/hp (16.9 kg/kW); consumption: 29.4 m/imp gal, 24.5 m/US gal, 9.6 l x 100 km - Capri S 30.4 m/imp gal, 25.3 m/US gal, 9.3 l x 100 km.

BRAKES front disc (diameter 9.61 in, 24.4 cm), rear drum, servo (standard); lining area: front 17.4 sq in, 151.2 sq cm, rear 45.4 sq in, 293.4 sq cm, total 62.8 sq in, 444.6 sq cm.

ELECTRICAL EQUIPMENT 44 Ah battery; 55 A alternator.

DIMENSIONS AND WEIGHT weight: 2,470 lb, 1,120 kg.

PRACTICAL INSTRUCTIONS fuel: 97 oct petrol; oil: engine 7 imp pt, 8.5 US pt, 4 l.

OPTIONAL ACCESSORIES Ford C-3 automatic transmission, hydraulic torque converter and planetary gears with 3 ratios (I 2.474, II 1.474, III 1, rev 2.111), max ratio of converter at stall 2, possible manual selection, oil cooler, 55 Ah battery, max speed 101 mph, 163 km/h (Capri S 103 mph, 166 km/h), consumption 26.6 m/imp gal, 22.2 m/US gal, 10.6 l x 100 km (Capri S 27.4 m/imp gal, 22.8 m/US gal, 10.3 l x 100 km); power steering.

108 hp power team

See 54 hp power team, except for:

ENGINE 6 cylinders, Vee-slanted at 60°; 138.8 cu in, 2,274 cc (3.54 x 2.37 in, 90 x 60.1 mm); compression ratio: 8.75:1; max power (DIN): 108 hp (79.5 kW) at 5,000 rpm; max torque (DIN): 130 lb ft, 18 kg m (176.5 Nm) at 3,000 rpm; max engine rpm: 5,600; 47.5 hp/l (35 kW/l); 4 crankshaft bearings; valves: overhead, push-rods and rockers; camshafts: 1, at centre of Vee; lubricating system: 7.4 imp pt, 8.9 US pt, 4.2 l; 1 Solex 35/35 EEIT downdraught twin barrel carburettor; cooling system: 13.7 imp pt, 16.5 US pt, 7.8 l.

TRANSMISSION gearbox ratios: I 3.650, II 1.970, III 1.370 IV 1, rev 3.660; axle ratio: 3.220; width of rims: 5.5''; tyres: 185/70 HR x 13.

PERFORMANCE max speed: 111 mph, 178 km/h - Capri S 113 mph, 181 km/h; power-weight ratio: 22.9 lb/hp (31.1 lb/kW), 10.4 kg/hp (14.1 kg/kW); speed in direct drive at 1,000 rpm: 20.8 mph, 33.4 km/h; consumption: 30.1 m/imp gal, 25 m/US gal, 9.4 l x 100 km - Capri S 31 m/imp gal, 25.8 m/US gal, 9.1 l x 100 km.

BRAKES front disc (diameter 9.61 in, 24.4 cm), rear drum, servo (standard); lining area: front 17.4 sq in, 151.2 sq cm, rear 45.4 sq in, 293.4 sq cm, total 62.8 sq in, 444.6 sq cm.

ELECTRICAL EQUIPMENT 44 Ah battery; 55 A alternator; halogen headlamps and fog lamps (standard).

DIMENSIONS AND WEIGHT weight: 2,470 lb, 1,120 kg.

BODY light alloy wheels, headrests on front seats and heated rear window (standard).

PRACTICAL INSTRUCTIONS fuel: 97 oct petrol; oil: engine 7 imp pt, 8.5 US pt, 4 l.

OPTIONAL ACCESSORIES Ford C-3 automatic transmission, hydraulic torque converter and planetary gears with 3 ratios (I 2.474, II 1.474, III 1, rev 2.111), max ratio of converter at stall 2, possible manual selection, oil cooler, 55 Ah battery, max speed 107 mph, 172 km/h (Capri S 109 mph, 175 km/h), consumption 27.4 m/imp gal, 22.8 m/US gal, 10.3 l x 100 km (Capri S 28.2 m/imp gal, 23.5 m/US gal, 10 l x 100 km); power steering.

138 hp power team

See 54 hp power team, except for:

ENGINE 6 cylinders, Vee-slanted at 60°; 179.7 cu in, 2,945 cc (3.69 x 2.85 in, 93.7 x 72.4 mm); compression ratio: 9:1; max power (DIN): 138 hp (101.6 kW) at 5,000 rpm; max torque (DIN): 174 lb ft, 24 kg m (235.4 Nm) at 3,000 rpm; 46.9 hp/l (34.5 kW/l); 4 crankshaft bearings; valves: overhead, push-rods and rockers; camshafts: 1, at centre of Vee; lubricating system: 8.8 imp pt, 10.6 US pt, 5 l; 1

138 HP POWER TEAM

Weber 38/38 EGAS downdraught twin barrel carburettor; cooling system: 16.4 imp pt, 19.7 US pt, 9.3 l.

TRANSMISSION gearbox ratios: I 3.163, II 1.940, III 1.412, IV 1, rev 3.346; axle ratio: 3.090; width of rims: 5.5''; tyres: 185/70 HR x 13.

PERFORMANCE max speed: 121 mph, 195 km/h - Capri S 123 mph, 198 km/h; power-weight ratio: 18.7 lb/hp (25.4 lb/kW), 8.5 kg/hp (11.5 kg/kW); speed in direct drive at 1,000 rpm: 21.8 mph, 35.1 km/h; consumption: 25.9 m/imp gal, 21.6 m/US gal, 10.9 l x 100 km - Capri S 26.4 m/imp gal, 22 m/US gal, 10.7 l x 100 km; weight ratio: 18.7 lb/hp, 8.5 kg/hp; speed in direct drive at 1,000 rpm: 21.8 mph, 35.1 km/h; consumption: 25.9 m/imp gal, 21.6 m/US gal, 10.9 l x 100 km - Capri S 26.4 m/imp gal, 22 m/US gal, 10.7 l x 100 km.

BRAKES front disc (diameter 9.72 in, 24.7 cm), rear drum, servo (standard); lining area: front 17.4 sq in, 151.2 sq cm, rear 59.5 sq in, 384.4 sq cm, total 76.9 sq in, 535.6 sq cm.

ELECTRICAL EQUIPMENT 44 Ah battery; 55 A alternator; halogen headlamps and fog lamps (standard).

DIMENSIONS AND WEIGHT weight: 2,580 lb, 1,170 kg.

BODY light alloy wheels, tinted glass, headrests on front seats and heated rear window (standard).

PRACTICAL INSTRUCTIONS fuel: 97 oct petrol; oil: engine 7.4 imp pt, 8.9 US pt, 4.2 l.

OPTIONAL ACCESSORIES Ford C-3 automatic transmission, hydraulic torque converter and planetary gears with 3 ratios (I 2.474, II 1.474, III 1, rev 2.111), max ratio of converter at stall 2, possible manual selection, oil cooler, 55 Ah battery, max speed 118 mph, 190 km/h (Capri S 120 mph, 193 km/h), consumption 23.9 m/imp gal, 19.9 m/US gal, 11.8 l x 100 km (Capri S 24.6 m/imp gal, 20.5 m/US gal, 11.5 l x 100 km); power steering.

Granada Series

PRICES EX WORKS:

1 Granada 2-door Limousine	DM	13,875*
2 Granada 4-door Limousine	DM	14,445*
3 Granada Turnier	DM	14,995*
4 Granada L 2-door Limousine	DM	14,620*
5 Granada L 4-door Limousine	DM	15,100*
6 Granada L Turnier	DM	15,990*
7 Granada GL 2-door Limousine	DM	18,635*
8 Granada GL 4-door Limousine	DM	19,205*
9 Granada GL Turnier	DM	20,220*
10 Granada Ghia 4-door Limousine	DM	23,250*

Power team:	Standard for:	Optional for:
70 hp	1 to 6	—
73 hp	—	1 to 6
90 hp	7 to 9	1 to 6
108 hp	10	all except 10
135 hp	—	all except 1,2,3,6
160 hp	—	all except 1,2,3,6

70 hp power team

ENGINE front, 4 stroke; 4 cylinders, Vee-slanted at 60°; 102.5 cu in, 1,680 cc (3.54 x 2.63 in, 90 x 66.8 mm); compression ratio: 7.75:1; max power (DIN): 70 hp (51.5 kW) at 5,000 rpm; max torque (DIN): 88 lb/ft, 12.2 kg m (119.6 Nm) at 3,000 rpm; max engine rpm: 5,500; 41.7 hp/l (30.6 kW/l); cast iron block and head; 3 crankshaft bearings; valves: overhead, in line, rockers; camshafts: 1, at centre of Vee; lubrication: gear pump, full flow filter, 6.5 imp pt, 7.8 US pt, 3.7 l; 1 Solex 32 TDID downdraught carburettor; fuel feed: mechanical pump; water-cooled, 10.6 imp pt, 12.7 US pt, 6 l.

TRANSMISSION driving wheels: rear; clutch: single dry plate (diaphragm); gearbox: mechanical; gears: 4, fully synchronized; ratios: I 3.650, II 1.970, III 1.370, IV 1, rev 3.660; lever: central; final drive: hypoid bevel; axle ratio: 4.110 - Turniers 4.440; width of rims: 5.5''; tyres: 175 SR x 14 - Turniers 185 SR x 14.

PERFORMANCE max speed: 89 mph, 144 km/h; power-weight ratio: 4-dr. limousines 39 lb/hp (53.1 lb/kW), 17.7 kg/hp (24.1 kg/kW); speed in direct drive at 1,000 rpm: 16.8 mph, 27.1 km/h; consumption: 26.4 m/imp gal, 22 m/US gal, 10.7 l x 100 km - Turniers 25.7 m/imp gal, 21.4 m/US gal, 11 l x 100 km.

CHASSIS integral, front and rear auxiliary frames; front suspension: independent, wishbones (lower trailing links), coil springs, anti-roll bar, telescopic dampers; rear: independent, semi-trailing arms, coil springs, telescopic dampers.

STEERING rack-and-pinion.

BRAKES front disc (diameter 10.31 in, 26.2 cm), rear drum, servo; lining area: front 23.4 sq in, 151.2 sq cm, rear 58

sq in, 374.6 sq cm, total 81.4 sq in, 528.5 sq cm - Turniers rear 83.4 sq in, 538.5 sq cm, total 106.8 sq in, 689.7 sq cm.

ELECTRICAL EQUIPMENT 12 V; 35 Ah battery; 45 A (55 A for L limousines) alternator; Ford distributor; 2 headlamps.

DIMENSIONS AND WEIGHT wheel base: 109.05 in, 277 cm; tracks: 59.45 in, 151 cm front, 60.24 in, 153 cm rear; length: 185.83 in, 472 cm - Turniers 189.76 in, 482 cm; width: 70.47 in, 179 cm; height: 55.91 in, 142 cm; weight: 2-dr. limousines 2,701 lb, 1,225 kg - 4-dr. limousines 2,734 lb, 1,240 kg - Turniers 2,889 lb, 1,310 kg; turning circle (between walls): 36.7 ft, 11.2 m; fuel tank: 14.5 imp gal, 17.4 US gal, 66 l - Turniers 13.6 imp gal, 16.4 US gal, 62 l.

BODY 5 seats, separate front seats, reclining backrests; heated rear window.

PRACTICAL INSTRUCTIONS fuel: 90 oct petrol; oil: engine 5.6 imp pt, 6.8 US pt, 3.2 l, SAE 10W-40, change every 6,200 miles, 10,000 km - gearbox 3 imp pt, 3.6 US pt, 1.8 l, SAE 80, no change recommended - final drive 3.2 imp pt, 3.8 US pt, 1.8 l, SAE 90, no change recommended; greasing: none; tappet clearances: inlet 0.014 in, 0.35 mm, exhaust 0.016 in, 0.40 mm; valve timing: 24° 84° 65° 42°; tyre pressure: front 20 psi, 1.4 atm, rear 23 psi, 1.6 atm.

OPTIONAL ACCESSORIES 4.440 axle ratio; 185 SR x 14 tyres with 6'' wide rims; 66 Ah battery; 55 A alternator; halogen headlamps; power steering; built-in headrests; heated rear window sunshine roof; metallic spray; S equipment with 190/65 HR 390 TRX tyres; rear window wiper-washer; headlamps with wiper-washers.

FORD Granada 2-door Limousine

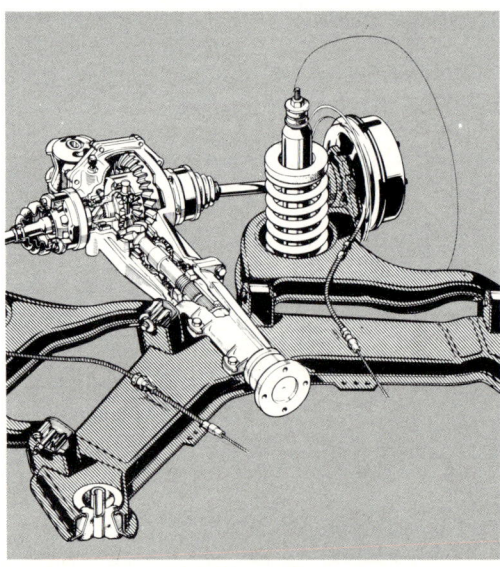

FORD Granada Series

73 hp power team

See 70 hp power team, except for:

ENGINE compression ratio: 8.75:1; max power (DIN): 73 hp (53.7 kW) at 5,000 rpm; max Torque (DIN): 93 lb ft, 12.8 kg m (125.5 Nm) at 3,000 rpm; 43.4 hp/l (32 kW/l).

PERFORMANCE max speed: 92 mph, 147 km/h; power-weight ratio: 4-dr. limousines 37.4 lb/hp (50.9 lb/kW), 17 kg/hp (23.1 kg/kW).

PRACTICAL INSTRUCTIONS fuel: 97 oct petrol.

OPTIONAL ACCESSORIES Ford C-3 automatic transmission, hydraulic torque converter and planetary gears with 3 ratios (I 2.474, II 1.474, III 1, rev 2.111), max ratio of converter at stall 2, possible manual selection, oil cooler, max speed 87 mph, 140 km/h, consumption 25.9 m/imp gal, 21.6 m/US gal, 10.9 l x 100 km - Turniers 25.4 m/imp gal, 21.2 m/US gal, 11.1 l x 100 km, 55 Ah battery.

90 hp power team

See 70 hp power team, except for:

ENGINE 6 cylinders, Vee-slanted at 60°; 120.9 cu in, 1,981 cc (3.31 x 2.37 in, 84 x 60.1 mm); compression ratio: 8.75:1; max power (DIN): 90 hp (66.2 kW) at 5,000 rpm; max

torque (DIN): 110 lb ft, 15.2 kg m (149.1 Nm) at 3,000 rpm; 45.4 hp/l (33.4 kW/l); 4 crankshaft bearings; lubricating system: 7.4 imp pt, 8.9 US pt, 4.2 l; 1 Solex 32/32 EEIT downdraught twin barrel carburettor; cooling system: 12.1 imp pt, 14.6 US pt, 6.9 l.

TRANSMISSION axle ratio: 3.890; width of rims: GL limousines 6''; tyres: 185 SR x 14.

PERFORMANCE max speed: 98 mph, 158 km/h; power-weight ratio: GL 4-dr. Limousine 33.2 lb/hp (45.1 lb/kW), 15 kg/hp (20.5 kg/kW); speed in direct drive at 1,000 rpm: 17.3 mph, 27.9 km/h; consumption: 25.9 m/imp gal, 21.6 m/US gal, 10.9 l x 100 km - GL models 25.4 m/imp gal, 21.2 m/US gal, 11.1 l x 100 km.

STEERING servo (standard for GL only).

BRAKES lining area (except for Turniers): front 23.4 sq in, 151.2 sq cm, rear 75.3 sq in, 486 sq cm, total 98.7 sq in, 637.2 sq cm.

ELECTRICAL EQUIPMENT 44 Ah battery.

DIMENSIONS AND WEIGHT weight: GL 2-dr. Limousine 2,955 lb, 1,340 kg - GL 4-dr. Limousine 2,988 lb, 1,355 kg - GL Turnier 3,131 lb, 1,420 kg.

PRACTICAL INSTRUCTIONS fuel: 97 oct petrol; oil: engine 7 imp pt, 8.5 US pt, 4 l.

OPTIONAL ACCESSORIES Ford C-3 automatic transmission, hydraulic torque converter and planetary gears with 3 ratios (I 2.474, II 1.474, III 1, rev 2.111), max ratio of converter at stall 2, possible manual selection, 3.890 axle ratio, max speed 94 mph, 152 km/h, consumption 23.9 m/imp gal, 19.9 m/US gal, 11.8 l x 100 km - GL Limousines 23.5 m/imp gal, 19.6 m/US gal, 12 l x 100 km - GL Turnier 23.3 m/imp gal, 19.4 m/US gal, 12.1 l x 100 km, 55 Ah battery.

108 hp power team

See 70 hp power team, except for:

ENGINE 6 cylinders, Vee-slanted at 60°; 138.8 cu in, 2,274 cc (3.54 x 2.37 in, 90 x 60.1 mm); compression ratio: 8.75:1; max power (DIN): 108 hp (79.5 kW) at 5,000 rpm; max torque (DIN): 130 lb ft, 18 kg m (176.5 Nm) at 3,000 rpm; max engine rpm: 5,600; 47.5 hp/l (35 kW/l); 4 crankshaft bearings; lubricating system: 7.4 imp pt, 8.9 US pt, 4.2 l; 1 Solex 35/35 EEIT downdraught twin barrel carburettor; cooling system: 12.1 imp pt, 14.6 US pt, 6.9 l.

TRANSMISSION gearbox ratios (only for Turniers): I 3.360, II 1.810, III 1.260, IV 1, rev 3.370; axle ratio: 3.640; width of rims: Ghia and GL limousines 6''; tyres 185 SR x 14.

PERFORMANCE max speed: 104 mph, 167 km/h; power-weight ratio: Ghia 28.4 lb/hp (38.6 lb/kW), 12.9 kg/hp (17.5 kg/kW); speed in direct drive at 1,000 rpm: 18.5 mph, 29.8 km/h; consumption: 26.6 m/imp gal, 22.2 m/US gal, 10.6 l x 100 km - GL models 26.4 m/imp gal, 22 m/US gal, 10.7 l x 100 km - Ghia 26.2 m/imp gal, 21.8 m/US gal, 10.8 l x 100 km.

STEERING servo (standard only for GL and Ghia).

BRAKES lining area (except for Turniers): front 23.4 sq in, 151.2 sq cm, rear 75.3 sq in, 486 sq cm, total 98.7 sq in, 637.2 sq cm.

ELECTRICAL EQUIPMENT 44 Ah battery.

DIMENSIONS AND WEIGHT weight: L 2-dr. Limousine 2,889 lb, 1,310 kg - L 4-dr. Limousine 2,922 lb, 1,325 kg - L Turnier 3,076 lb, 1,395 kg - GL 2-dr. Limousine 2,988 lb, 1,355 kg - GL 4-dr. Limousine 3,021 lb, 1,370 kg - GL Turnier 3,131 lb, 1,420 kg - Ghia 4-dr. Limousine 3,065 lb, 1,390 kg.

BODY heated rear window (standard).

PRACTICAL INSTRUCTIONS fuel: 97 oct petrol; oil: engine 7 imp pt, 8.5 US pt, 4 l.

OPTIONAL ACCESSORIES Ford C-3 automatic transmission, hydraulic torque converter and planetary gears with 3 ratios (I 2.474, II 1.474, III 1, rev 2.111), max ratio of converter at stall 2, possible manual selection, oil cooler, max speed 100 mph, 161 km/h, consumption 25.4 m/imp gal, 21.2 m/US gal, 11.1 l x 100 km - GL and Ghia 24.8 m/imp gal, 20.6 m/US gal, 11.4 l x 100 km, 55 Ah battery; air-conditioning.

135 hp power team

See 70 hp power team, except for:

ENGINE 6 cylinders, Vee-slanted at 60°; 169.1 cu in, 2,772 cc (3.66 x 2.70 in, 93 x 68.5 mm); compression ratio: 9.2:1; max

FORD Granada GLS Turnier

FORD Granada Ghia 4-door Limousine

power (DIN): 135 hp (99.4 kW) at 5,200 rpm; max torque (DIN): 159 lb ft, 22 kg m (215.8 Nm) at 3,000 rpm; 48.7 hp/l (35.8 kW/l); 4 crankshaft bearings; lubricating system: 8.8 imp pt, 10.6 US pt, 5 l; 1 Solex downdraught twin barrel carburettor; cooling system: 18 imp pt, 21.6 US pt, 10.2 l.

TRANSMISSION gearbox ratios: I 3.160, II 1.940, III 1.410, IV 1, rev 3.350; axle ratio: 3.450; width of rims: GL and Ghia limousines 6''; tyres: 185 HR x 14.

PERFORMANCE max speed: 114 mph, 183 km/h; power-weight ratio: GL 4-dr. Limousine 22.8 lb/hp (31 lb/kW), 10.4 kg/hp (14.1 kg/kW) - Ghia 23.2 lb/hp (31.5 lb/kW), 10.5 kg/hp (14.3 kg/kW); speed in top at 1,000 rpm: 20.7 mph, 33.3 km/h; consumption: GL 25.7 m/imp gal, 21.4 m/US gal, 11 l x 100 km - Ghia 25.4 m/imp gal, 21.2 m/US gal, 11.1 l x 100 km.

STEERING servo (standard for GL and Ghia).

BRAKES front disc with internal radial fins; lining area (except for Turniers): front 29.3 sq in, 188.8 sq cm, rear 75.3 sq in, 486 sq cm, total 104.6 sq in, 674.8 sq cm.

ELECTRICAL EQUIPMENT 44 Ah battery.

DIMENSIONS AND WEIGHT (see 108 hp power team) weight: plus 66 lb, 30 kg - 2-dr. limousines plus 110 lb, 50 kg.

BODY heated rear window (standard).

PRACTICAL INSTRUCTIONS fuel: 97 oct petrol; oil: engine 7.4 imp pt, 8.9 US pt, 4.2 l.

OPTIONAL ACCESSORIES Ford C-3 automatic transmission, hydraulic torque converter and planetary gears with 3 ratios (I 2.474, II 1.474, III 1, rev 2.111), max ratio of converter at stall 2, possible manual selection, oil cooler, 3.450 axle ratio, max speed 109 mph, 176 km/h, consumption 23.9 m/imp gal, 19.9 m/US gal, 11.8 l x 100 km (GL 24.1 m/imp gal, 20.1 m/US gal, 11.7 l x 100 km); 55 Ah battery; air-conditioning.

160 hp power team

See 135 hp power team, except for:

ENGINE max power (DIN): 160 hp (117.8 kW) at 5,700 rpm; max torque (DIN): 163 lb ft, 22.5 kg m (220.7 Nm) at 4,300 rpm; max engine rpm: 5,700; 57.7 hp/l (42.5 kW/l); Bosch K-Jetronic fuel injection system.

PERFORMANCE max speed: 120 mph, 193 km/h; power-weight ratio: GL 4-dr. Limousine 19.3 lb/hp (26.2 lb/kW), 8.7 kg/hp (11.9 kg/kW) - Ghia 19.6 lb/hp (26.6 lb/kW), 8.9 kg/hp (12 kg/kW); speed in direct drive at 1,000 rpm: 21.1 mph, 33.9 km/h; consumption: GL 25.4 m/imp gal, 21.2 m/US gal, 11.1 l x 100 km - Ghia 25.2 m/imp gal, 21 m/US gal, 11.2 l x 100 km.

ELECTRICAL EQUIPMENT 70 A alternator.

OPTIONAL ACCESSORIES with Ford C-3 automatic transmission, max speed 117 mph, 188 km/h, consumption GL 23.7 m/imp gal, 19.8 m/US gal, 11.9 l x 100 km (Ghia 23.5 m/imp gal, 19.6 m/US gal, 12 l x 100 km).

FORD Granada Ghia 4-door Limousine

MERCEDES-BENZ GERMANY FR

200

PRICE IN GB: £ 5,650*
PRICE EX WORKS: 19,025* marks

ENGINE front, 4 stroke; 4 cylinders, vertical, in line; 121.3 cu in, 1,988 cc (3.43 x 3.29 in, 87 x 83.6 mm); compression ratio: 9:1; max power (DIN): 94 hp (69.2 kW) at 4,800 rpm; max torque (DIN): 117 lb ft, 16.1 kg m (157.9 Nm) at 3,000 rpm; max engine rpm: 6,000; 47.3 hp/l (34.8 kW/l); cast iron block, light alloy head; 5 crankshaft bearings; valves: overhead, in line, finger levers; camshafts: 1, overhead; lubrication: gear pump, oil-water heat exchanger, full flow filter (cartridge), 8.8 imp pt, 10.6 US pt, 5 l; 1 Stromberg 175 CD horizontal carburettor; fuel feed: mechanical pump; water-cooled, 18.8 imp pt, 22.6 US pt, 10.7 l.

TRANSMISSION driving wheels: rear; clutch: single dry plate, hydraulically controlled; gearbox: mechanical; gears: 4, fully synchronized; ratios: I 3.900, II 2.300, III 1.410, IV 1, rev 3.660; lever: steering column or central; final drive: hypoid bevel; axle ratio: 3.920; width of rims: 5.5''; tyres: 175 SR x 14.

PERFORMANCE max speeds: (I) 28 mph, 45 km/h; (II) 47 mph, 75 km/h; (III) 78 mph, 125 km/h; (IV) 99 mph, 160 km/h; power-weight ratio: 31.4 lb/hp (42.7 lb/kW), 14.3 kg/hp (19.4 kg/kW); carrying capacity: 1,145 lb, 520 kg; consumption: 25.4 m/imp gal, 21.2 m/US gal, 11.1 l x 100 km.

CHASSIS integral, front auxiliary frame; front suspension: independent, wishbones, coil springs, auxiliary rubber springs, anti-roll bar, telescopic dampers; rear: independent, oblique semi-trailing arms, coil springs, auxiliary rubber springs, anti-roll bar, telescopic dampers.

STEERING recirculating ball, damper.

BRAKES disc (front diameter 10.75 in, 27.3 cm, rear 10.98 in, 27.9 cm), servo; swept area: front 225.4 sq in, 1,454 sq cm, rear 195.8 sq in, 1,263 sq cm, total 421.2 sq in, 2.717 sq cm.

ELECTRICAL EQUIPMENT 12 V; 55 Ah battery; 490 W alternator; Bosch distributor; 4 headlamps.

DIMENSIONS AND WEIGHT wheel base: 110.04 in, 279 cm; tracks: 58.58 in, 149 cm front, 56.93 in, 145 cm rear; length: 186.02 in, 472 cm; width: 70.31 in, 179 cm; height: 56.69 in, 144 cm; ground clearance: 6.50 in, 16.5 cm; weight: 2,955 lb, 1,340 kg; turning circle (between walls): 36.7 ft, 11.2 m; fuel tank: 14.3 imp gal, 17.2 US gal, 65 l.

BODY saloon/sedan; 4 doors; 5 seats, separate front seats, reclining backrests.

PRACTICAL INSTRUCTIONS fuel: 98 oct petrol; oil: engine 7.9 imp pt, 9.5 US pt, 4.5 l, SAE 20W-30, change every 6,200 miles, 10,000 km - gearbox 2.8 imp pt, 3.4 US pt, 1.6 l, ATF, change every 12,400 miles, 20,000 km - final drive 1.9 imp pt, 2.3 US pt, 1.1 l, SAE 90, change every 12,400 miles, 20,000 km; greasing: none; tappet clearances: inlet 0.003 in, 0.08 mm, exhaust 0.008 in, 0.20 mm; valve timing: 11° 47° 48° 16°; tyre pressure: front 21 psi, 1.5 atm, rear 26 psi, 1.8 atm.

OPTIONAL ACCESSORIES MB automatic transmission, hydraulic torque converter and planetary gears with 4 ratios (I 3.980, II 2.390, III 1.460, IV 1, rev 5.480), possible manual selection, max speeds (I) 23 mph, 38 km/h, (II) 47 mph, 75 km/h, (III) 78 mph, 125 km/h, (IV) 96 mph, 155 km/h; automatic levelling control on rear suspension; power steering; halogen headlamps; fog lamps; electrically- or manually-controlled sunshine roof; heated rear window; heated seats; electrically-controlled windows; tinted glass; headrests; air-conditioning; light alloy wheels; metallic spray.

230

See 200, except for:

PRICE IN GB: £ 6,990*
PRICE IN USA: $ 12,880*
PRICE EX WORKS: 19,980* marks

ENGINE 140.8 cu in, 2,307 cc (3.69 x 3.29 in, 93.7 x 83.6 mm); max power (DIN): 109 hp (80.2 kW) at 4,800 rpm; max torque (DIN): 137 lb ft, 18.9 kg m (185.4 Nm) at 3,000 rpm; 47.2 hp/l (34.8 kW/l).

TRANSMISSION axle ratio: 3.690.

PERFORMANCE max speeds (I) 30 mph, 48 km/h; (II) 50 mph, 80 km/h; (III) 83 mph, 134 km/h; (IV) 106 mph, 170 km/h; power-weight ratio: 27.3 lb/hp (37.1 lb/kW), **12.4**

MERCEDES-BENZ 200

MERCEDES-BENZ 200

MERCEDES-BENZ 250

kg/hp (16.8 kg/kW); consumption: 24.1 m/imp gal, 20.1 m/US gal, 11.7 l x 100 km.

DIMENSIONS AND WEIGHT weight: 2,977 lb, 1,350 kg.

OPTIONAL ACCESSORIES with MB automatic transmission, max speeds (I) 25 mph, 40 km/h, (II) 50 mph, 80 km/h, (III) 83 mph, 134 km/h, (IV) 103 mph, 165 km/h.

230 C

See 230, except for:

PRICE EX WORKS: 25,064* marks

TRANSMISSION width of rims: 6''; tyres: 195/70 HR x 14.

PERFORMANCE power-weight ratio: 27.8 lb/hp (37.8 lb/kW), 12.6 kg/hp (17.1 kg/kW).

DIMENSIONS AND WEIGHT wheel base: 106.69 in, 271 cm; length: 182.68 in, 464 cm; height: 54.72 in, 139 cm; weight: 3,032 lb, 1,375 kg; turning circle (between walls): 36.1 ft, 11 m.

BODY coupé; 2 doors.

OPTIONAL ACCESSORIES 195/70 SR x 14 tyres.

230 T

See 230, except for:

PRICE EX WORKS: 23,976* marks

TRANSMISSION width of rims: 6''; tyres: 195/70 SR x 14.

PERFORMANCE power-weight ratio: 29.3 lb/hp (39.9 lb/kW), 13.3 kg/hp (18.1 kg/kW); carrying capacity: 1,235 lb, 560 kg.

CHASSIS rear suspension: automatic levelling control.

DIMENSIONS AND WEIGHT rear track: 57.20 in, 145 cm; height: 56.10 in, 142 cm; weight: 3,197 lb, 1,450 kg; fuel tank: 15.4 imp gal, 18.5 US gal, 70 l.

BODY estate car/station wagon; 4+1 doors; back seat folding down to luggage table; rear window wiper-washer.

OPTIONAL ACCESSORIES 175 HR x 15 tyres.

250

See 200, except for:

PRICE IN GB: £ 7,750*
PRICE EX WORKS: 22,755* marks

ENGINE 6 cylinders; 154.1 cu in, 2,525 cc (3.39 x 2.85 in, 86 x 72.4 mm); compression ratio: 8.7:1; max power (DIN): 129 hp (94.9 kW) at 5,500 rpm; max torque (DIN): 145 lb ft, 20 kg m (196.1 Nm) at 3,500 rpm; 51.1 hp/l (37.3 kW/l); 4 crankshaft bearings; lubricating system: 10.6 imp pt, 12.7 US pt, 6 l; 1 Solex 4 A 1 downdraught twin barrel carburettor.

TRANSMISSION axle ratio: 3.690.

MERCEDES-BENZ 300 D

PERFORMANCE max speeds: (I) 30 mph, 48 km/h; (II) 50 mph, 80 km/h; (III) 83 mph, 134 km/h; (IV) 112 mph, 180 km/ h; power-weight ratio: 23.2 lb/hp (31.8 lb/kW), 10.5 kg/hp (14.4 kg/kW); consumption: 23.9 m/imp gal, 19.9 m/US gal, 11.8 l x 100 km.

ELECTRICAL EQUIPMENT 770 W alternator.

DIMENSIONS AND WEIGHT weight: 2,999 lb, 1,360 kg.

PRACTICAL INSTRUCTIONS oil: engine 9.7 imp pt, 11.6 US pt, 5.5 l.

OPTIONAL ACCESSORIES with MB automatic transmission, max speeds (I) 25 mph, 40 km/h, (II) 50 mph, 80 km/h, (III) 83 mph, 134 km/h, (IV) 109 mph, 175 km/h.

250 Long Wheelbase

See 250, except for:

PRICE EX WORKS: 34,798* marks

TRANSMISSION tyres: 185 SR x 15.

PERFORMANCE power-weight ratio: 26.3 lb/hp (36 lb/kW), 11.9 kg/hp (16.3 kg/kW); carrying capacity: 1,466 lb, 665 kg.

DIMENSIONS AND WEIGHT wheel base: 134.65 in, 342 cm; tracks: 58.27 in, 148 cm front, 56.30 in, 143 cm rear; length: 210.36 in, 535 cm; height: 58.27 in, 148 cm; weight: 3,396 lb, 1,540 kg; turning circle (between walls): 43.6 ft, 13.3 m.

250 T

See 250, except for:

PRICE EX WORKS: 26,751 marks

TRANSMISSION width of rims: 6''; tyres: 195/70 HR x 14.

PERFORMANCE power-weight ratio: 24.9 lb/hp (34.2 lb/kW), 11.3 kg/hp (15.5 kg/kW); carrying capacity: 1,235 lb, 560 kg.

CHASSIS rear suspension: automatic levelling control.

DIMENSIONS AND WEIGHT rear track: 57.20 in, 145 cm; height: 56.10 in, 142 cm; weight: 3,219 lb, 1,460 kg; fuel tank: 15.4 imp gal, 18.5 US gal, 70 l.

BODY estate car/station wagon; 4+1 doors; back seat folding down to luggage table; rear window wiper-washer.

OPTIONAL ACCESSORIES 185 HR x 15 tyres.

200 D

See 200, except for:

PRICE IN GB: £ 5,795*
PRICE EX WORKS: 19,536* marks

ENGINE Diesel; compression ratio: 21:1; max power (DIN): 55 hp (40.5 kW) at 4,200 rpm; max torque (DIN): 83 lb

MERCEDES-BENZ 300 D

ft, 11.5 kg m (112.8 Nm) at 2,400 rpm; max engine rpm: 5,200; 27.7 hp/l (20.4 kW/l); cast iron block and head; lubrication: gear pump, full flow (cartridge) and by-pass filters, 10.6 imp pt, 12.7 US pt, 6 l; 4-cylinder Bosch indirect injection pump.

PERFORMANCE max speeds: (I) 21 mph, 33 km/h; (II) 35 mph, 56 km/h; (III) 57 mph, 92 km/h; (IV) 81 mph, 130 km/h; power-weight ratio: 55.1 lb/hp (74.9 lb/kW), 25 kg/hp (33.9 kg/kW); consumption: 34 m/imp gal, 28.3 m/US gal, 8.3 l x 100 km.

ELECTRICAL EQUIPMENT 66 Ah battery.

DIMENSIONS AND WEIGHT weight: 3,032 lb, 1,375 kg.

PRACTICAL INSTRUCTIONS fuel: Diesel oil; oil: engine 10.6 imp pt, 12.7 US pt, 6 l; tappet clearances: inlet 0.008 in, 0.10 mm, exhaust 0.016 in, 0.40 mm; valve timing: 12°30' 41°30' 45° 9°.

OPTIONAL ACCESSORIES with MB automatic transmission, max speeds (I) 20 mph, 32 km/h, (II) 35 mph, 56 km/h, (III) 57 mph, 92 km/h, (IV) 78 mph, 125 km/h.

220 D

See 200 D, except for:

PRICE EX WORKS: 20,346* marks

ENGINE 134.1 cu in, 2,197 cc (3.43 x 3.64 in, 87 x 92.4 mm);

max power (DIN): 60 hp (44.2 kW) at 4,200 rpm; max torque (DIN): 93 lb ft, 12.8 kg m (125.5 Nm) at 2,400 rpm; 27.3 hp/l (20.1 kW/l).

PERFORMANCE max speeds: (I) 21 mph, 33 km/h; (II) 35 mph, 56 km/h; (III) 57 mph, 92 km/h; (IV) 84 mph, 135 km/h; power-weight ratio: 50.7 lb/hp (68.8 lb/kW), 23 kg/hp (31.2 kg/kW); consumption: 31.4 m/imp gal, 26.1 m/US gal, 9 l x 100 km.

ELECTRICAL EQUIPMENT 88 Ah battery.

DIMENSIONS AND WEIGHT weight: 3,043 lb, 1,380 kg.

OPTIONAL ACCESSORIES with MB automatic transmission, max speeds (I) 20 mph, 32 km/h, (II) 35 mph, 56 km/h, (III) 57 mph, 92 km/h, (IV) 81 mph, 130 km/h.

240 D

See 200 D, except for:

PRICE IN GB: £ 7,196*
PRICE IN USA: $ 11,920*
PRICE EX WORKS: 21,057* marks

ENGINE 146.7 cu in, 2,404 cc (3.58 x 3.64 in, 91 x 92.4 mm); max power (DIN): 65 hp (47.8 kW) at 4,200 rpm; max torque (DIN): 101 lb ft, 14 kg m (137.3 Nm) at 2,400 rpm; 27 hp/l (19.9 kW/l); oil cooler; cooling system: 17.6 imp pt, 21.1 US pt, 10 l.

TRANSMISSION axle ratio: 3.690.

PERFORMANCE max speeds: (I) 22 mph, 35 km/h; (II) 37 mph, 60 km/h; (III) 61 mph, 98 km/h; (IV) 86 mph, 138 km/h; power-weight ratio: 47 lb/hp (63.9 lb/kW), 21.3 kg/hp (29 kg/kW); consumption: 29.7 m/imp gal, 24.8 m/US gal, 9.5 l x 100 km.

ELECTRICAL EQUIPMENT 88 Ah battery.

DIMENSIONS AND WEIGHT weight: 3,054 lb, 1,385 kg.

OPTIONAL ACCESSORIES with MB automatic transmission, max speeds (I) 21 mph, 34 km/h, (II) 37 mph, 60 km/h, (III) 61 mph, 98 km/h, (IV) 83 mph, 133 km/h.

240 D Long Wheelbase

See 240 D, except for:

PRICE EX WORKS: 33,100* marks

TRANSMISSION tyres: 185 SR x 15.

PERFORMANCE power-weight ratio: 53.1 lb/hp (72.2 lb/kW), 24.1 kg/hp (32.7 kg/kW); carrying capacity: 1,466 lb, 665 kg.

DIMENSIONS AND WEIGHT wheel base: 134.65 in, 342 cm; tracks: 58.27 in, 148 cm front, 56.30 in, 143 cm rear; length: 210.63 in, 535 cm; height: 58.27 in, 148 cm; weight: 3,451 lb, 1,565 kg; turning circle (between walls): 43.6 ft, 13.3 m.

240 TD

See 240 D, except for:

PRICE EX WORKS: 25,053* marks

TRANSMISSION width of rims: 6''; tyres: 195/70 SR x 14.

PERFORMANCE power-weight ratio: 50.4 lb/hp (68.5 lb/kW), 22.8 kg/hp (31.1 kg/kW); carrying capacity: 1,235 lb, 560 kg.

CHASSIS rear suspension: automatic levelling control.

DIMENSIONS AND WEIGHT rear track: 57.20 in, 145 cm; height: 56.10 in, 142 cm; weight: 3,274 lb, 1,485 kg; fuel tank: 15.4 imp gal, 18.5 US gal, 70 l.

BODY estate car/station wagon; 4+1 doors; back seat folding down to luggage table; rear window wiper-washer.

OPTIONAL ACCESSORIES 185 HR x 15 tyres.

300 D

See 200 D, except for:

PRICE IN GB: £ 8,395*
PRICE IN USA: $ 16,590*
PRICE EX WORKS: 23,321* marks

ENGINE 5 cylinders, in line; 183.4 cu in, 3,005 cc (3.58 x 3.64 in, 91 x 92.4 mm); max power (DIN): 80 hp (58.9 kW) at 4,000 rpm; max torque (DIN): 127 lb ft, 17.5 kg m (171.6 Nm) at 2,400 rpm; max engine rpm: 5,100; 26.6 hp/l (19.6

300 D

kW/l); 6 crankshaft bearings; oil cooler; 5-cylinders Bosch indirect injection pump; cooling system: 19 imp pt, 22.8 US pt, 10.8 l.

TRANSMISSION axle ratio: 3.460.

PERFORMANCE max speed: (I) 24 mph, 38 km/h; (II) 40 mph, 64 km/h; (III) 65 mph, 104 km/h; (IV) 92 mph, 148 km/h; power-weight ratio: 39.8 lb/hp (54.1 lb/kW), 18.1 kg/hp (24.5 kg/kW); consumption: 26.2 m/imp gal, 21.8 m/US gal, 10.8 l x 100 km.

STEERING servo (standard).

ELECTRICAL EQUIPMENT 88 Ah battery.

DIMENSIONS AND WEIGHT weight: 3,186 lb, 1,445 kg.

OPTIONAL ACCESSORIES with MB automatic transmission, max speeds (I) 22 mph, 36 km/h, (II) 40 mph, 64 km/h, (III) 65 mph, 104 km/h, (IV) 89 mph, 143 km/h.

300 D Long Wheelbase

See 300 D, except for:

PRICE EX WORKS: 34,699* marks

TRANSMISSION tyres: 185 SR x 15.

PERFORMANCE power-weight ratio: 44.5 lb/hp (60.4 lb/kW), 20.2 kg/hp (27.4 kg/kW); carrying capacity: 1,466 lb, 665 kg.

DIMENSIONS AND WEIGHT wheel base: 134.65 in, 342 cm; tracks: 58.27 in, 148 cm front, 56.30 in, 143 cm rear; length: 210.63 in, 535 cm; height: 58.27 in, 148 cm; weight: 3,561 lb, 1,615 kg; turning circle (between walls): 43.6 ft, 13.3 m.

300 TD

See 300 D, except for:

PRICE EX WORKS: 27,319* marks

TRANSMISSION width of rims: 6''; tyres: 195/70 SR x 14.

PERFORMANCE power-weight ratio: 42.6 lb/hp (57.8 lb/kW), 19.3 kg/hp (26.2 kg/kW); carrying capacity: 1,235 lb, 560 kg.

CHASSIS rear suspension: automatic levelling control.

DIMENSIONS AND WEIGHT rear track: 57.20 in, 145 cm; height: 56.10 in, 142 cm; weight: 3,407 lb, 1,545 kg; fuel tank: 15.4 imp gal, 18.5 US gal, 70 l.

BODY estate car/station wagon; 4+1 doors; back seat folding down to luggage table; rear window wiper-washer.

OPTIONAL ACCESSORIES 185 HR x 15 tyres.

300 SD

(only for USA).

See 300 D, except for:

ENGINE 182.9 cu in, 2,998 cc (3.58 x 3.64 in, 90.9 x 92.4 mm); compression ratio: 21.5:1; max power (DIN): 115 hp (84.6 kW) at 4,200 rpm; max torque (DIN): 168 lb ft, 23.2 kg m (227.5 Nm) at 2,400 rpm; 38.3 hp/l (28.2 kW/l); lubricating system: 15.1 imp pt, 18.2 US pt, 8.6 l; 5-cylinders Bosch indirect injection pump with turbocharger.

TRANSMISSION width of rims: 6''; tyres: 185 HR x 14.

PERFORMANCE max speed: 103 mph, 165 km/h; power-weight ratio: 33.8 lb/hp (46 lb/kW), 15.3 kg/hp (20.9 kg/kW); carrying capacity: 992 lb, 450 kg; speed in direct drive at 1,000 rpm: 20.1 mph, 32.3 km/h; consumption: 26.6 m/imp gal, 22.2 m/US gal, 10.6 l x 100 km.

STEERING servo (standard).

ELECTRICAL EQUIPMENT 770 W alternator.

DIMENSIONS AND WEIGHT wheel base: 112.80 in, 286 cm; tracks: 59.88 in, 152 cm front, 59.25 in, 150 cm rear; length: 205.51 in, 522 cm; width: 73.62 in, 187 cm; height: 56.10 in, 142 cm; weight: 3,892 lb, 1,765 kg; turning circle (between walls): 38 ft, 11.6 m; fuel tank: 18 imp gal, 21.6 US gal, 82 l.

PRACTICAL INSTRUCTIONS oil: engine 15.1 imp pt, 18.2 US pt, 8.6 l.

MERCEDES-BENZ 280 - 280 E

MERCEDES-BENZ 300 SD

MERCEDES-BENZ 300 SD

280

PRICE EX WORKS: 26,129* marks

ENGINE front, 4 stroke; 6 cylinders, vertical, in line; 167.6 cu in, 2,746 cc (3.39 x 3.10 in, 86 x 78.8 mm); compression ratio: 8.7:1; max power (DIN): 156 hp (114.8 kW) at 5,500 rpm; max torque (DIN): 164 lb ft, 22.7 kg m (222.6 Nm) at 4,000 rpm; max engine rpm: 6,500; 56.8 hp/l (41.8 kW/l); cast iron block, light alloy head; 7 crankshaft bearings; valves: overhead, Vee-slanted at 54°, finger levers; camshafts: 2, overhead; lubrication: gear pump, oil-water heat exchanger, filter (cartridge) on by-pass, oil cooler, 10.6 imp pt, 12.7 US pt, 6 l; 1 Solex 4 A 1 downdraught twin barrel carburettor; fuel feed: mechanical pump; water-cooled, 17.1 imp pt, 20.5 US pt, 9.7 l, magnetically-controlled fan.

TRANSMISSION driving wheels: rear; clutch: single dry plate, hydraulically controlled; gearbox: mechanical; gears: 4, fully synchronized; ratios: I 3.900, II 2.300, III 1.410, IV 1, rev 3.660; lever: steering column or central; final drive: hypoid bevel; axle ratio: 3.540; width of rims: 6''; tyres: 195/70 HR x 14.

PERFORMANCE max speeds: (I) 34 mph, 55 km/h; (II) 55 mph, 88 km/h; (III) 90 mph, 145 km/h; (IV) 118 mph, 190 km/h; power-weight ratio: 20.6 lb/hp (27.9 lb/kW), 9.3 kg/hp (12.7 kg/kW); carrying capacity: 1,147 lb, 520 kg; consumption: 22.6 m/imp gal, 18.8 m/US gal, 12.5 l x 100 km.

CHASSIS integral, front auxiliary frame; front suspension: independent, wishbones, coil springs, auxiliary rubber springs, anti-roll bar, telescopic dampers; rear: independent, oblique semi-trailing arms, coil springs, auxiliary rubber springs, anti-roll bar, telescopic dampers.

STEERING recirculating ball, dampers, servo.

BRAKES disc (front diameter 10.94 in, 27.8 cm, rear 10.98 in, 27.9 cm), rear compensator, servo; swept area: front 255.5 sq in, 1,648 sq cm, rear 195.8 sq in, 1,263 sq cm, total 451.3 sq in, 2,911 sq cm.

ELECTRICAL EQUIPMENT 12 V; 55 Ah battery; 770 W alternator; Bosch distributor; 4 halogen headlamps.

DIMENSIONS AND WEIGHT wheel base: 110.04 in, 279 cm; tracks: 58.58 in, 149 cm front, 56.93 in, 145 cm rear; length: 186.02 in, 472 cm; width: 70.31 in, 179 cm; height: 56.69 in, 144 cm; ground clearance: 6.50 in, 16.5 cm; weight: 3,208 lb, 1,455 kg; turning circle (between walls): 36.7 ft, 11.2 m; fuel tank: 17.6 imp gal, 21.1 US gal, 80 l.

BODY saloon/sedan; 4 doors; 5 seats, separate front seats, reclining backrests with built-in headrests.

PRACTICAL INSTRUCTIONS fuel: 98 oct petrol; oil: engine 10.6 imp pt, 12.7 US pt, 6 l, SAE 20W-30, change every 3,600 miles, 6,000 km - gearbox 3.2 imp pt, 3.8 US pt, 1.8 l, ATF, change every 12,400 miles, 20,000 km - final drive 4.4 imp pt, 5.3 US pt, 2.5 l, SAE 90, change every 12,400 miles, 20,000 km; greasing: every 3,100 miles, 5,000 km, 20 points; tyre pressure: front 22 psi, 1.6 atm, rear 28 psi, 1.9 atm.

OPTIONAL ACCESSORIES MB automatic transmission hydraulic torque converter and planetary gears with 4 ratios (I 3.980, II 2.390, III 1.460, IV 1, rev 5.470), possible manual selection, max speeds (I) 26 mph, 42 km/h, (II) 55 mph, 88 km/h, (III) 90 mph, 145 km/h, (IV) 115 km/h; automatic levelling control on rear suspension; fog lamps; electrically-or manually-controlled sunshine roof; heated rear window; heated seats; electrically-controlled windows; tinted glass; air-conditioning; light alloy wheels; metallic spray.

280 C

See 280, except for:

PRICE EX WORKS: 29,848* marks

PERFORMANCE power-weight ratio: 20.4 lb/hp (27.7 lb/kW), 9.3 kg/hp (12.6 kg/kW).

DIMENSIONS AND WEIGHT wheel base: 106.69 in, 271 cm; length: 182.68 in, 464 cm; height: 54.72 in, 139 cm; weight: 3,186 lb, 1,445 kg; turning circle (between walls): 36.1 ft, 11 m.

BODY coupé; 2 doors.

280 E

See 280, except for:

PRICE IN GB: £ 8,951*
PRICE IN USA: $ 17,114*
PRICE EX WORKS: 28,116* marks

ENGINE max power (DIN): 177 hp (130.3 kW) at 6,000 rpm; max torque (DIN): 172 lb ft, 23.8 kg m (233.4 Nm) at 4,500 rpm; 64.4 hp/l (47.4 kW/l); Bosch K-Jetronic indirect injection system.

TRANSMISSION axle ratio: 3.550.

PERFORMANCE max speeds: (I) 34 mph, 55 km/h; (II) 55 mph, 88 km/h; (III) 90 mph, 145 km/h; (IV) 124 mph, 200 km/h; power-weight ratio: 18.2 lb/hp (24.7 lb/kW), 8.3 kg/hp (11.2 kg/kW).

DIMENSIONS AND WEIGHT weight: 3,219 lb, 1,460 kg.

OPTIONAL ACCESSORIES with MB automatic transmission, max speeds (I) 26 mph, 42 km/h, (II) 55 mph, 88 km/h, (III) 90 mph, 145 km/h, (IV) 121 mph, 195 km/h.

280 CE

See 280 E, except for:

PRICE EX WORKS: 31,835* marks

PERFORMANCE power-weight ratio: 18.1 lb/hp (24.5 lb/kW), 8.2 kg/hp (11.1 kg/kW).

DIMENSIONS AND WEIGHT wheel base: 106.69 in, 271 cm; length: 182.68 in, 464 cm; height: 54.72 in, 139 cm; weight: 3,197 lb, 1,450 kg; turning circle (between walls): 36.1 ft, 11 m.

BODY coupé; 2 doors.

MERCEDES-BENZ 280 - 280 E

280 TE

See 280 E, except for:

PRICE EX WORKS: 32,057* marks

PERFORMANCE power-weight ratio: 19 lb/hp (25.8 lb/kW), 8.6 kg/hp (11.7 kg/kW); carrying capacity: 1,235 lb, 560 kg.

CHASSIS rear suspension: automatic levelling control.

DIMENSIONS AND WEIGHT rear track: 57.20 in, 145 cm; height: 56.10 in, 142 cm; weight: 3,363 lb, 1,525 kg; fuel tank: 15.4 imp gal, 18.5 US gal, 70 l.

BODY estate car/station wagon; 4+1 doors; back seat folding down to luggage table; rear window wiper-washer.

OPTIONAL ACCESSORIES 185 HR x 15 tyres.

280 S

PRICE EX WORKS: 30,159* marks

ENGINE front, 4 stroke; 6 cylinders, vertical, in line; 167.6 cu in, 2,746 cc (3.39 x 3.10 in, 86 x 78.8 mm); compression ratio: 8.7:1; max power (DIN): 156 hp (114.8 kW) at 5,500 rpm; max torque (DIN): 164 lb ft, 22.7 kg m (222.6 Nm) at 4,000 rpm; max engine rpm: 6,500; 54.6 hp/l (41.8 kW/l);

MERCEDES-BENZ 280 SL - 280 SLC

cast iron block, light alloy head; 7 crankshaft bearings; valves: overhead, Vee-slanted at 54º, finger levers; camshafts: 2, overhead; lubrication: gear pump, full flow filter, oil cooler, 10.6 imp pt, 12.7 US pt, 6 l; 1 Solex, 4 A 1 downdraught twin barrel carburettor; fuel feed: mechanical pump; water-cooled, 19.4 imp pt, 23.3 US pt, 11 l, thermostatic fan.

TRANSMISSION driving wheels: rear; clutch: single dry plate, hydraulically controlled; gearbox: mechanical; gears: 4, fully synchronized; ratios: I 3.900, II 2.380, III 1.410, IV 1, rev 3.660; lever: central; final drive: hypoid bevel; axle ratio: 3.690; width of rims: 6''; tyres: 185 HR x 14.

PERFORMANCE max speeds: (I) 32 mph, 52 km/h; (II) 55 mph, 88 km/h; (III) 90 mph, 145 km/h; (IV) 118 mph, 190 km/h; power-weight ratio: 22.7 lb/hp (30.9 lb/kW), 10.3 kg/hp (14 kg/kW); carrying capacity: 1,147 lb, 520 kg; speed in direct drive at 1,000 rpm: 19.8 mph, 31.8 km/h; consumption: 22.6 m/imp gal, 18.9 m/US gal, 12.5 l x 100 km.

CHASSIS integral; front suspension: independent, upper wishbones with single transverse rod, longitudinal leading arm in one with anti-roll bar, coil springs, telescopic dampers; rear: independent, oblique semi-trailing arms, coil springs, anti-roll bar, auxiliary rubber springs, telescopic dampers.

STEERING recirculating ball, dampers, servo.

BRAKES disc (front diameter 10.94 in, 27.8 cm, rear 10.98 in, 27.9 cm), rear compensator, servo; swept area: front 255.5 sq in, 1,648 sq cm, rear 195.8 sq in, 1,263 sq cm, total 451.3 sq in, 2,911 sq cm.

ELECTRICAL EQUIPMENT 12 V; 55 Ah battery; 770 W alternator; Bosch distributor; 4 headlamps.

DIMENSIONS AND WEIGHT wheel base: 112.60 in, 286 cm; tracks: 59.84 in, 152 cm front, 59.05 in, 150 cm rear; length: 195.28 in, 496 cm; width: 73.62 in, 187 cm; height: 55.90 in, 142 cm; ground clearance: 5.91 in, 15 cm; weight: 3,550 lb, 1,610 kg; turning circle (between walls): 37.4 ft, 11.4 m; fuel tank: 21.1 imp gal, 25.3 US gal, 96 l.

BODY saloon/sedan; 4 doors; 5 seats, separate front seats, reclining backrests.

PRACTICAL INSTRUCTIONS fuel: 98 oct petrol; oil: engine 10.6 imp pt, 12.7 US pt, 6 l, SAE 20W-30, change every 3,600 miles, 6,000 km - gearbox 3.2 imp pt, 3.8 US pt, 1.8 l, AFT, change every 12,400 miles, 20,000 km - final drive 4.4 imp pt, 5.3 US pt, 2.5 l, SAE 90, change every 12,400 miles, 20,000 km; tyre pressure: front 22 psi, 1.6 atm, rear 28 psi, 1.9 atm.

OPTIONAL ACCESSORIES MB automatic transmission, hydraulic torque converter and planetary gears with 4 ratios (I 3.980, II 2.390, III 1.460, IV 1, rev 5.480), max ratio of converter at stall 2.2, possible manual selection, steering column or central lever, max speeds (I) 25 mph, 40 km/h, (II) 55 mph, 88 km/h, (III) 90 mph, 145 km/h, (IV) 115 mph, 185 km/h; automatic levelling control; electrically-controlled sunshine roof; heated rear window; electrically-controlled windows; headrests; metallic spray; light alloy wheels; tinted glass; air-conditioning.

280 SE

See 280 S, except for:

PRICE IN GB: £ 10,851*
PRICE IN USA: $ 19,993*
PRICE EX WORKS: 32,290* marks

ENGINE max power (DIN): 177 hp (130.3 kW) at 6,000 rpm; max torque (DIN): 172 lb ft, 23.8 kg m (233.4 Nm) at 4,500 rpm; 64.4 hp/l (47.4 kW/l); 6-cylinder Bosch electronic injection, injectors in inlet pipes; fuel feed: electric pump.

PERFORMANCE max speed: 124 mph, 200 km/h; power-weight ratio: 20 lb/hp (27.2 lb/kW), 9.1 kg/hp (12.4 kg/kW).

ELECTRICAL EQUIPMENT transistorized ignition.

OPTIONAL ACCESSORIES with MB automatic transmission, max speeds (I) 26 mph, 42 km/h, (II) 55 mph, 88 km/h, (III) 90 mph, 145 km/h, (IV) 121 mph, 195 km/h; rev counter.

280 SEL

See 280 SE, except for:

PRICE EX WORKS: 34,854* marks

PERFORMANCE power-weight ratio: 20.5 lb/hp (27.8 lb/kW), 9.3 kg/hp (12.6 kg/kW).

DIMENSIONS AND WEIGHT wheel base: 116.73 in, 296 cm; length: 199.21 in, 506 cm; height: 56.30 in, 143 cm; weight: 3,627 lb, 1,645 kg; turning circle (between walls): 38.7 ft, 11.8 m.

MERCEDES-BENZ 280 TE

280 SL

Se 280 SE, except for:

PRICE EX WORKS: 35,620* marks

TRANSMISSION width of rims: 6.5''.

PERFORMANCE power-weight ratio: 18.6 lb/hp (25.4 lb/kW), 8.5 kg/hp (11.5 kg/kW); carrying capacity: 926 lb, 420 kg.

DIMENSIONS AND WEIGHT wheel base 96.85 in, 246 cm; tracks: 57.09 in, 145 cm front, 56.69 in, 144 cm rear; length: 172.83 in, 439 cm; width: 70.47 in, 179 cm; height: 51.18 in, 130 cm; ground clearance: 5.31 in, 13.5 cm; weight: 3,308 lb, 1,500 kg; turning circle (between walls): 33.8 ft, 10.3 m; fuel tank: 19.8 imp gal, 23.8 US gal, 90 l.

BODY convertible; 2 doors; 2 seats.

OPTIONAL ACCESSORIES hardtop.

280 SLC

See 280 SL, except for:

PRICE EX WORKS: 41,170* marks

PERFORMANCE power-weight ratio: 19.3 lb/hp (26.2 lb/kW), 8.8 kg/hp (11.9 kg/kW); carrying capacity: 1,080 lb, 490 kg.

DIMENSIONS AND WEIGHT wheel base 111.02 in, 282 cm; length: 187.01 in, 475 cm; height: 52.36 in, 133 cm; weight: 3,418 lb, 1,550 kg; turning circle (between walls): 37.7 ft, 11.5 m.

BODY coupé; 5 seats.

350 SE

See 280 S, except for:

PRICE IN GB: £ 12,100*
PRICE EX WORKS: 36,430* marks

ENGINE 8 cylinders, Vee-slanted at 90º; 213.5 cu in, 3,499 cc (3.62 x 2.59 in, 92 x 65.8 mm); compression ratio: 9:1; max power (DIN): 195 hp (143.5 kW) at 5,500 rpm; max torque (DIN): 203 lb ft, 28 kg m (274.6 Nm) at 4,000 rpm; max engine rpm: 6,300; 55.7 hp/l (41 kW/l); 57.1 hp/l (42.1 kW/l); 5 crankshaft bearings; valves: overhead, finger levers; camshafts: 1 per block, overhead; lubricating system: 13.2 imp pt, 15.9 US pt, 7.5 l; Bosch electronic injection, injectors in inlet pipes; fuel feed: electric pump; cooling system: 23.8 imp pt, 28.5 US pt, 13.5 l.

TRANSMISSION gearbox ratios: I 3.960, II 2.340, III 1.430, IV 1, rev 3.720; axle ratio: 3.460; width of rims: 6.5''; tyres: 205/70 HR x 14.

PERFORMANCE max speeds: (I) 34 mph, 54 km/h; (II) 56 mph, 90 km/h; (III) 93 mph, 150 km/h; (IV) 127 mph, 205 km/h; power-weight ratio: 18.9 lb/hp (25.7 lb/kW), 8.6 kg/hp (11.7 kg/kW); speed in direct drive at 1,000 rpm: 21.1 mph, 33.9 km/h; consumption: 21.7 m/imp gal, 18.1 m/US gal, 13 l x 100 km.

ELECTRICAL EQUIPMENT 66 Ah battery; transistorized ignition.

DIMENSIONS AND WEIGHT weight: 3,693 lb, 1,675 kg.

PRACTICAL INSTRUCTIONS oil: engine 13.2 imp pt, 15.9 US pt, 7.5 l.

OPTIONAL ACCESSORIES MB automatic transmission, hydraulic torque converter and planetary gears with 3 ratios (I 2.310, II 1.460, III 1, rev 1.840), max ratio of converter at stall 2.2, possible manual selection, steering column or central lever, max speeds (I) 56 mph, 90 km/h, (II) 93 mph, 150 km/h, (III) 124 mph, 200 km/h; rev counter.

350 SEL

See 350 SE, except for:

PRICE EX WORKS: 38,550* marks

PERFORMANCE power-weight ratio: 19.2 lb/hp (26.1 lb/kW), 8.7 kg/hp (11.8 kg/kW).

DIMENSIONS AND WEIGHT wheel base 116.73 in, 296 cm; length: 199.21 in, 506 cm; height: 56.30 in, 143 cm; weight: 3,749 lb, 1,700 kg; turning circle (between walls): 38.7 ft, 11.8 m.

350 SL

PRICE IN GB: £ 11,236*
PRICE EX WORKS: 39,361* marks

ENGINE front, 4 stroke; 8 cylinders, Vee-slanted at 90º; 213 cu in, 3,499 cc (3.62 x 2.59 in, 92 x 65.8 mm); compression ratio: 9:1; max power (DIN): 195 hp (143.5 kW) at 5,500 rpm; max torque (DIN): 203 lb ft, 28 kg m (274.6 Nm) at 4,000 rpm; max engine rpm: 6,300; 55.7 hp/l (41 kW/l); cast iron block, light alloy head; 5 crankshaft bearings; valves: overhead, finger levers; camshafts: 1 per block, overhead; lubrication: gear pump, full flow filter, oil cooler, 13.2 imp pt, 15.9 US pt, 7.5 l; Bosch electronic injection; fuel feed: electric pump; water-cooled, fan with revolution limiting device (1,900 rpm), 25.2 imp pt, 30.2 US pt, 14.3 l.

TRANSMISSION driving wheels: rear; clutch: single dry plate, hydraulically controlled; gearbox: mechanical; gears: 4, fully synchronized; ratios: I 3.960, II 2.340, III 1.430, IV 1, rev 3.720; lever: central; final drive: hypoid bevel; axle ratio: 3.460; width of rims: 6.5''; tyres: 205/70 VR x 14.

PERFORMANCE max speeds: (I) 34 mph, 54 km/h; (II) 56 mph, 90 km/h; (III) 93 mph, 150 km/h; (IV) 127 mph, 205 km/h; power-weight ratio: 17.4 lb/hp (23.7 lb/kW), 7.9 kg/hp (10.7 kg/kW); carrying capacity: 926 lb, 420 kg; consumption: 21.7 m/imp gal, 18.1 m/US gal, 13 l x 100 km.

CHASSIS backbone platform with box-type ladder frame; front suspension: independent, wishbones, coil springs, auxiliary rubber springs, anti-roll bar, telescopic dampers; rear: independent, oblique semi-trailing arms, coil springs, auxiliary rubber springs, anti-roll bar, telescopic dampers.

STEERING recirculating ball, damper, servo.

BRAKES disc (front diameter 10.75 in, 27.3 cm, rear 10.98 in, 27.9 cm), front internal radial fins, rear compensator, servo.

ELECTRICAL EQUIPMENT 12 V; 66 Ah battery; 770 W alternator; Bosch (transistorized) distributor; 2 iodine headlamps.

DIMENSIONS AND WEIGHT wheel base: 96.85 in, 246 cm; tracks: 57.08 in, 145 cm front, 56.69 in, 144 cm rear; length: 172.83 in, 439 cm; width: 70.47 in, 179 cm; height: 51.18 in, 130 cm; ground clearance: 5.12 in, 13 cm; weight: 3,396 lb, 1,540 kg; turning circle (between walls): 33.8 ft, 10.3 m; fuel tank: 19.8 imp gal, 23.8 US gal, 90 l.

BODY convertible; 2 doors; 2 seats, reclining backrests.

PRACTICAL INSTRUCTIONS fuel: 96 oct petrol; oil: engine 13.2 imp pt, 15.9 US pt, 7.5 l, SAE 20W-40, change every 3,700 miles, 6,000 km - gearbox 9.5 imp pt, 11.4 US pt, 5.4 l; sparking plug: 215º; tyre pressure: front 30 psi, 2.1 atm, rear 34 psi, 2.4 atm.

OPTIONAL ACCESSORIES MB automatic transmission, hydraulic torque converter and planetary gears with 3 ratios (I 2.310, II 1.460, III 1, rev 1.840), central lever, max speed 124 mph, 200 km/h; limited slip differential; hardtop; air-conditioning; electrically-controlled windows.

MERCEDES-BENZ 280 TE

350 SLC

See 350 SL, except for:

PRICE EX WORKS: 44,911* marks

TRANSMISSION axle ratio: 3.640.

PERFORMANCE max speed: 130 mph, 210 km/h; power-weight ratio: 18 lb/hp (24.4 lb/kW), 8.2 kg/hp (11.1 kg/kW); carrying capacity: 1,080 lb, 490 kg.

DIMENSIONS AND WEIGHT wheel base: 111.02 in, 282 cm; length: 187.01 in, 475 cm; height: 52.36 in, 133 cm; weight: 3,506 lb, 1,590 kg; turning circle (between walls): 37.7 ft, 11.5 m.

BODY coupé; 5 seats.

OPTIONAL ACCESSORIES with MB automatic transmission, max speed 127 mph, 205 km/h.

450 SE

PRICE IN GB: £ 13,776*
PRICE EX WORKS: 40,926* marks

ENGINE front, 4 stroke; 8 cylinders, Vee-slanted at 90°; 275.8 cu in, 4,520 cc (3.62 x 3.35 in, 92 x 85 mm); compression ratio: 8.8:1; max power DIN: 217 hp (159.7 kW) at 5,000 rpm; max torque (DIN): 266 lb ft, 36.7 kg m (359.9 NM) at 3,250 rpm; max engine rpm: 5,800; 48 hp/l (35.3 kW/l); cast iron block, light alloy head; 5 crankshaft bearings; valves: overhead, finger levers; camshafts: 1 per block, overhead; lubrication: gear pump, full flow filter, oil cooler, 13.2 imp pt, 15.9 US pt, 7.5 l; Bosch electronic injection; fuel feed: electric pump; water-cooled, viscous coupling thermostatic fan, 26.4 imp pt, 31.7 US pt, 15 l.

TRANSMISSION driving wheels: rear; gearbox: MB automatic transmission, hydraulic torque converter and planetary gears with 3 ratios, max ratio of converter at stall 2.5, possible manual selection; ratios: I 2.310, II 1.460, III 1, rev 1.840; lever: central or steering column; final drive: hypoid bevel; axle ratio: 3.070; width of rims: 6.5''; tyres: 205/70 VR x 14.

PERFORMANCE max speeds: (I) 59 mph, 95 km/h; (II) 96 mph, 155 km/h; (III) 130 mph, 210 km/h; power-weight ratio: 17.6 lb/hp (23.9 lb/kW), 8 kg/hp (10.8 kg/kW); carrying capacity: 1,147 lb, 520 kg; speed in direct drive at 1,000 rpm: 21.9 mph, 35.3 km/h; consumption: 19.5 m/imp gal, 16.2 m/US gal, 14.5 l x 100 km.

CHASSIS integral, front auxiliary frame (welded to body); front suspension: independent, wishbones, coil springs, anti-roll bar, telescopic dampers; rear: independent, oblique semi-trailing arms, coil springs, anti-roll bar, auxiliary rubber springs, telescopic dampers.

STEERING recirculating ball, servo; turns lock to lock: 2.70.

BRAKES disc (front diameter 10.94 in, 27.8 cm, rear 10.98 in, 27.9 cm), servo; swept area: front 255.5 sq in, 1,648 sq cm, rear 195.8 sq in, 1,263 sq cm, total 451.3 sq in, 2,911 sq cm.

ELECTRICAL EQUIPMENT 12 V; 66 Ah battery; 770 W alternator; Bosch (transistorized) distributor; 2 iodine headlamps.

DIMENSIONS AND WEIGHT wheel base: 112.60 in, 286 cm; tracks: 59.84 in, 152 cm front, 59.06 in, 150 cm rear; length: 195.28 in, 496 cm; width: 73.62 in, 187 cm; height: 55.91 in, 142 cm; ground clearance: 5.31 in, 13.5 cm; weight: 3,815 lb, 1,730 kg; turning circle (between walls): 37.4 ft, 11.4 m; fuel tank: 21.1 imp gal, 25.3 US gal, 96 l.

BODY saloon/sedan; 4 doors; 5 seats, separate front seats; reclining backrests, headrests; automatic safety belts.

PRACTICAL INSTRUCTIONS fuel: 98 oct petrol; oil: engine 13.2 imp pt, 15.9 US pt, 7.5 l, SAE 20W-40, change every 3,700 miles, 6,000 km - automatic transmission 15.7 imp pt, 18.8 US pt, 8.9 l, ATF, change every 12,400 miles, 20,000 km - final drive 2.3 imp pt, 2.7 US pt, 1.3 l, SAE 90, change every 12,400 miles, 20,000 km; sparking plug: 200°; tappet clearances (cold): inlet 0.003 in, 0.08 mm, exhaust 0.008 in, 0.20 mm; valve timing: 5° 21° 25° 5°.

VARIATIONS

(only for USA).
ENGINE 8:1 compression ratio, max power (DIN) 190 hp (139.8 kW) at 5,000 rpm, max torque (DIN) 280 lb ft, 38.6 kg m (378.6 Nm) at 3,200 rpm, 42 hp/l (30.9 kW/l).
PERFORMANCE power-weight ratio 20.1 lb/hp (27.3 lb/kW), 9.1 kg/hp (12.4 kg/kW).
PRACTICAL INSTRUCTIONS 91 oct petrol.

OPTIONAL ACCESSORIES electrically-controlled sunshine roof; electrically-controlled windows; rev counter; heated rear window; headrests; metallic spray; light alloy wheels; automatic levelling control; tinted glass; air-conditioning.

MERCEDES-BENZ 350 SL

450 SEL

See 450 SE, except for:

PRICE IN GB: £ 14,895*
PRICE IN USA: $ 25,241*
PRICE EX WORKS: 45,799* marks

PERFORMANCE power-weight ratio: 17.9 lb/hp (24.4 lb/kW), 8.1 kg/hp (11 kg/kW).

DIMENSIONS AND WEIGHT wheel base: 116.54 in, 296 cm; length: 199.21 in, 506 cm; height: 56.30 in, 143 cm; weight: 3,892 lb, 1,765 kg; turning circle (between walls): 38.7 ft, 11.8 m.

BODY electrically-controlled windows (standard).

VARIATIONS

PERFORMANCE power-weight ratio 20.5 lb/hp (27.8 lb/kW), 9.3 kg/hp (12.6 kg/kW).

450 SL

See 450 SE, except for:

PRICE IN GB: £ 12,195*
PRICE IN USA: $ 22,601*
PRICE EX WORKS: 43,856* marks

PERFORMANCE power-weight ratio: 16 lb/hp (21.8 lb/kW), 7.3 kg/hp (9.9 kg/kW); carrying capacity: 926 lb, 420 kg.

MERCEDES-BENZ 350 SL

STEERING turns lock to lock: 3.

DIMENSIONS AND WEIGHT wheel base: 96.46 in, 245 cm; tracks: 57.09 in, 145 cm front, 56.69 in, 144 cm rear; length: 177.83 in, 439 cm; width: 70.47 in, 179 cm; height: 51.18 in, 130 cm; weight: 3,484 lb, 1,580 kg; turning circle (between walls): 33.8 ft, 10.3 m; fuel tank: 19.8 imp gal, 23.8 US gal, 90 l.

BODY convertible; 2 doors; 2 seats.

VARIATIONS

PERFORMANCE 18.3 lb/hp (24.9 lb/kW), 8.3 kg/hp (11.3 kg/kW).

OPTIONAL ACCESSORIES hardtop.

450 SLC

See 450 SE, except for:

PRICE IN GB: £ 14,750*
PRICE IN USA: $ 27,903*
PRICE EX WORKS: 49,406* marks

PERFORMANCE power-weight ratio: 16.6 lb/hp (22.5 lb/kW), 7.5 kg/hp (10.2 kg/kW); carrying capacity: 1,080 lb, 490 kg.

STEERING turns lock to lock: 3.

DIMENSIONS AND WEIGHT wheel base: 110.63 in, 281 cm; tracks: 57.09 in, 145 cm front, 56.69 in, 144 cm rear; length: 187.01 in, 475 cm; width: 70.47 in, 179 cm; height: 52.36 in, 133 cm; weight: 3,594 lb, 1,630 kg; turning circle (between walls): 37.7 ft, 11.5 m; fuel tank: 19.8 imp gal, 23.8 US gal, 90 l.

BODY coupé; 2 doors; 4-5 seats.

VARIATIONS

PERFORMANCE power-weight ratio 18.9 lb/hp (25.7 lb/kW), 8.6 kg/hp (11.7 kg/kW).

450 SLC 5.0

See 450 SLC, except for:

PRICE EX WORKS: 58,841* marks

ENGINE 304.5 cu in, 4,990 cc (3.82 x 3.35 in, 97 x 85 mm); max power (DIN): 240 hp (176.6 kW) at 5,000 rpm; max torque (DIN): 297 lb ft, 41 kg m (402.1 Nm) at 3,200 rpm; 48.1 hp/l (35.4 kW/l); light alloy block and head; lubricating system: 14.1 imp pt, 16.9 US pt, 8 l.

PERFORMANCE max speed: 140 mph, 225 km/h; power-weight ratio: 13.9 lb/hp (18.9 lb/kW), 6.3 kg/hp (8.6 kg/kW); speed in direct drive at 1,000 rpm: 24.1 mph, 38.8 km/h.

DIMENSIONS AND WEIGHT weight: 3,341 lb, 1,515 kg.

PRACTICAL INSTRUCTIONS oil: engine 14.1 imp pt, 16.9 US pt, 8 l.

450 SEL 6.9

See 450 SE, except for:

PRICE IN GB: £ 23,850*
PRICE IN USA: $ 39,377*
PRICE EX WORKS: 73,093* marks

ENGINE 417 cu in, 6,834 cc (4.21 x 3.74 in, 107 x 95 mm); max power (DIN): 286 hp (210.5 kW) at 4,250 rpm; max torque (DIN): 406 lb ft, 56 kg m (549.2 Nm) at 3,000 rpm; max engine rpm: 5,300; 41.8 hp/l (30.8 kW/l); lubrication: gear pump, full flow filter, dry sump, oil cooler, 21.1 imp pt, 25.4 US pt, 12 l; Bosch K-Jetronic injection.

TRANSMISSION final drive: limited slip differential; axle ratio: 2.650; tyres: 215/70 VR x 14.

PERFORMANCE max speeds: (I) 59 mph, 95 km/h; (II) 96 mph, 155 km/h; (III) 140 mph, 225 km/h; power-weight ratio: 14.9 lb/hp (20.3 lb/kW), 6.8 kg/hp (9.2 kg/kW); carrying capacity: 1,069 lb, 485 kg; speed in direct drive at 1,000 rpm: 28.3 mph, 45.5 km/h; consumption: 17.7 m/imp gal, 14.7 m/US gal, 16 l x 100 km.

CHASSIS front suspension: independent, wishbones, hydropneumatic suspension, anti-roll bar, automatic levelling control, hydropneumatic telescopic dampers; rear: independent, oblique semi-trailing arms, hydropneumatic suspension, anti-roll bar, automatic levelling control, hydropneumatic telescopic dampers.

ELECTRICAL EQUIPMENT 88 Ah battery; 1,050 W alternator.

DIMENSIONS AND WEIGHT wheel base: 116.54 in, 296 cm; length: 199.21 in, 506 cm; height: 56.69 in, 144 cm; weight: 4,267 lb, 1,935 kg; turning circle (between walls): 39.7 ft, 12.1 m.

BODY headrests, tinted glass with air-conditioning, heated rear window, electrically-controlled windows, headlamps wiper-washers.

PRACTICAL INSTRUCTIONS oil: engine 17.6 imp pt, 21.1 US pt, 10 l.

VARIATIONS

None.

600

PRICE EX WORKS: 133,422* marks

ENGINE front, 4 stroke; 8 cylinders, Vee-slanted at 90°; 386.4 cu in, 6,332 cc (4.06 x 3.74 in, 103 x 95 mm); compression ratio: 9:1; max power (DIN): 250 hp (184 kW) at 4,000 rpm; max torque (DIN): 370 lb ft, 51 kg m (500.2 Nm) at 4,800 rpm; max engine rpm: 4,800; 39.5 hp/l (29 kW/l); cast iron block, light alloy head; 5 crankshaft bearings; valves: overhead, finger levers; camshafts: 1 per block, overhead; lubrication: gear pump, full flow and by-pass filters, 12.3 imp pt, 14.8 US pt, 7 l; 8-cylinder Bosch intermittent injection pump in inlet pipes; fuel feed: electric pump; water-cooled, 40.5 imp pt, 48.6 US pt, 23 l, thermostatic fan.

TRANSMISSION driving wheels: rear; gearbox: MB automatic transmission, hydraulic coupling and twin planetary gears with 4 ratios; ratios: I 3.980, II 2.460, III 1.580, IV 1, rev 4.150; lever: steering column; final drive: hypoid bevel, limited slip differential; axle ratio: 3.230; width of rims: 6.5''; tyres: 9.00 H x 15.

PERFORMANCE max speeds: (I) 31 mph, 50 km/h; (II) 50 mph, 80 km/h; (III) 81 mph, 130 km/h; (IV) 127 mph, 205 km/h; power-weight ratio: 21.8 lb/hp (29.6 lb/kW), 9.9 kg/hp (13.4 kg/kW); carrying capacity: 1,297 lb, 580 kg; acceleration: 0-50 mph (0-80 km/h) 6.9 sec; speed in direct drive at 1,000 rpm: 26.4 mph, 42.5 km/h; consumption: 15.9 m/imp gal, 13.2 m/US gal, 17.8 l x 100 km.

CHASSIS integral, front auxiliary frame; front suspension: independent, wishbones, air rubber springs, auxiliary rubber springs, automatically- and manually-controlled levelling system, anti-roll bar, telescopic dampers adjustable while running; rear: independent, single joint low pivot, swinging semi-axles, trailing lower radius arms, air rubber springs, auxiliary rubber springs, automatically- and manually-controlled levelling system, anti-roll bar, telescopic dampers adjustable while running.

STEERING recirculating ball, damper, servo, adjustable height of steering wheel; turns lock to lock: 3.30.

MERCEDES-BENZ 450 SLC 5.0

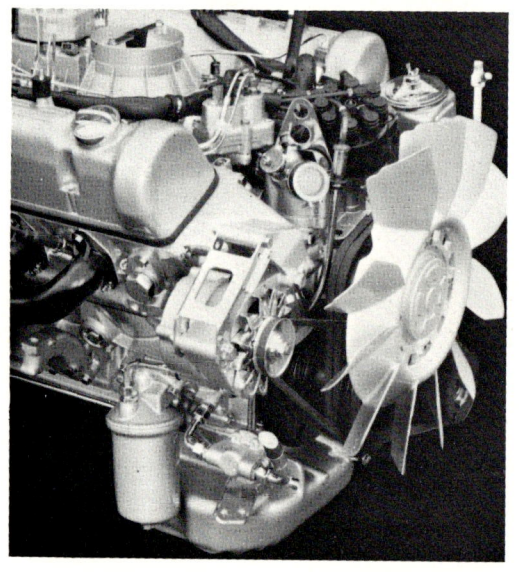

BRAKES disc [front diameter (twin calipers) 11.46 in, 29.1 cm, rear 11.57 in, 29.4 cm], rear compensator, servo; lining area: front 31.6 sq in, 204 sq cm, rear 24.7 sq in, 159 sq cm, total 56.3 sq in, 363 sq cm.

ELECTRICAL EQUIPMENT 12 V; 88 Ah battery; 2 490 W alternators; Bosch distributor; 2 headlamps.

DIMENSIONS AND WEIGHT wheel base: 125.98 in, 320 cm; tracks: 62.60 in, 159 cm front, 62.20 in, 158 cm rear; length: 218.11 in, 554 cm; width: 76.77 in, 195 cm; height: 58.26 in, 148 cm; ground clearance: 6.30 in, 16 cm; weight: 5,457 lb, 2,475 kg; weight distribution: 50.6% front, 49.4% rear; turning circle (between walls): 41.7 ft, 12.7 m; fuel tank: 24.6 imp gal, 29.6 US gal, 112 l.

BODY limousine; 4 doors; 6 seats, bench front seats; windows, locks, glass partition and front and rear seats (shifting horizontally and vertically) hydraulically controlled.

PRACTICAL INSTRUCTIONS fuel: 96 oct petrol; oil: engine 12.3 imp pt, 14.8 US pt, 7 l, SAE 20W-20, change every 3,700 miles, 6,000 km - automatic transmission 13.6 imp pt, 16.3 US pt, 7.7 l, ATF, change every 12,400 miles, 20,00 km - final drive 5.6 imp pt, 6.8 US pt, 3.2 l, SAE 90, change every 12,400 miles, 20,000 km; greasing: none; sparking plug: 215°; tappet clearances: inlet 0.004 in, 0.10 mm, exhaust 0.010 in, 0.25 mm; valve timing: 2°30' 52°30' 37°30' 18°; tyre pressure: front 28 psi, 2 atm, rear 33 psi, 2.3 atm.

OPTIONAL ACCESSORIES air-conditioning; sunshine roof.

MERCEDES-BENZ 600

600 Pullman

See 600, except for:

PRICE EX WORKS: 153,180* marks

PERFORMANCE power-weight ratio: 23.4 lb/hp (31.7 lb/kW), 10.6 kg/hp (14.4 kg/kW); carrying capacity: 1,544 lb, 700 kg.

DIMENSIONS AND WEIGHT wheel base: 153.54 in, 390 cm; length: 245.67 in, 624 cm; height: 59.06 in, 150 cm; weight: 5,843 lb, 2,650 kg; weight distribution: 51.5% front, 48.5% rear; turning circle (between walls): 49.2 ft, 15 m.

BODY 4 doors; 7-8 seats.

VARIATIONS

BODY 6 doors.

OPEL   GERMANY FR

City Series

PRICES IN GB AND EX WORKS:	£	DM
1 City Hatchback Coupé	—	9,500*
2 City L Hatchback Coupé	2,307*	10,045*
3 City « Berlina » Hatchback Coupé	2,566*	10,720*

For 60 hp engine add DM 180; for 75 hp engine add DM 835.

Power team:	Standard for:	Optional for:
40 hp	—	all
48 hp	—	all
55 hp	all	—
60 hp	—	all
75 hp	—	2,3

40 hp power team

ENGINE front, 4 stroke; 4 cylinders, in line; 60.6 cu in, 993 cc (2.83 x 2.40 in, 72 x 61 mm); compression ratio: 7.9:1; max power (DIN): 40 hp (29.4 kW) at 5,400 rpm; max torque (DIN): 51 lb ft, 7 kg m (68.6 Nm) at 2,600-3,000 rpm; max engine rpm: 5,800; 40.3 hp/l (29.7 kW/l); cast iron block and head; 3 crankshaft bearings; valves: overhead, push-rods and rockers; camshafts: 1, side, chain-driven; lubrication: gear pump, full flow filter, 4.8 imp pt, 5.7 US pt, 2.7 l; 1 Solex 30 PDSI downdraught single barrel carburettor; fuel feed: mechanical pump; anti-freeze liquid cooled, 8.6 imp pt, 10.4 US pt, 4.9 l.

TRANSMISSION driving wheels: rear; clutch: single dry plate (diaphragm); gearbox: mechanical; gears: 4, fully synchronized; ratios: I 3.733, II 2.243, III 1.432, IV 1, rev 3.939; lever: central; final drive: hypoid bevel; axle ratio: 4.110; width of rims: 5''; tyres: 155 SR x 13.

PERFORMANCE max speed: 76 mph, 122 km/h; power-weight ratio: 43.8 lb/hp (59.6 lb/kW), 19.9 kg/hp (27 kg/kW); carrying capacity: 882 lb, 410 kg; acceleration: 0-50 mph (0-80 km/h) 15 sec; speed in direct drive at 1,000 rpm: 15.5 mph, 25 km/h; consumption: 36.7 m/imp gal, 30.5 m/US gal, 7.7 l x 100 km.

CHASSIS integral; front suspension: independent, wishbones, coil springs, anti-roll bar, telescopic dampers; rear: rigid axle (torque tube), longitudinal trailing radius arms, coil springs, transverse linkage bar, telescopic dampers.

STEERING rack-and-pinion; turns lock to lock: 3.75.

BRAKES front disc, rear drum; lining area: total 49.2 sq in, 317 sq cm.

ELECTRICAL EQUIPMENT 12 V; 36 Ah battery; 45 A alternator; Bosch distributor; 2 headlamps.

DIMENSIONS AND WEIGHT wheel base: 94.09 in, 239 cm; tracks: 51.18 in, 130 cm front, 51.18 in, 130 cm rear; length: 153.27 in, 389 cm; width: 62.20 in, 158 cm; height: 54.13 in, 137 cm; ground clearance: 5.91 in, 15 cm; weight: 1,753 lb, 795 kg; turning circle (between walls): 32.6 ft, 9.9 m; fuel tank: 8.1 imp gal, 9.8 US gal, 37 l.

MERCEDES-BENZ 600 Pullman

OPEL City « Berlina » Hatchback Coupé

BODY hatchback coupé; 2 + 1 doors; 5 seats, separate front seats.

PRACTICAL INSTRUCTIONS fuel: 91 oct petrol; oil: engine 4.8 imp pt, 5.7 US pt, 2.7 l, SAE 20W-30, change every 3,100 miles, 5,000 km - gearbox 1.2 imp pt, 1.5 US pt, 0.7 l, SAE 80, no change recommended - final drive 1.2 imp pt, 1.5 US pt, 0.7 l, SAE 90, no change recommendend; greasing: none; sparking plug: 200°; tappet clearances: inlet 0.006 in, 0.15 mm, exhaust 0.010 in, 0.25 mm; valve timing: 39° 93° 65° 45°.

OPTIONAL ACCESSORIES limited slip differential; 175/70 SR x 13 tyres with 5.5'' wide rims; anti-roll bar on rear suspension; servo brake; 44 Ah battery; halogen headlamps; headrests; sunshine roof; heated rear window; metallic spray; SR equipment for City L and City « Berlina ».

48 hp power team

(only for export).

See 40 hp power team, except for:

ENGINE compression ratio: 8.8:1; max power (DIN): 48 hp (35.3 kW) at 5,600 rpm; max torque (DIN): 52 lb ft, 7.2 kg m (70.6 Nm) at 3,400 rpm; max engine rpm: 6,000; 48.3 hp/l (35.5 kW/l); cooling system: 8.1 imp pt, 9.7 US pt, 4.6 l.

TRANSMISSION axle ratio: 4.375.

PERFORMANCE max speed: 80 mph, 128 km/h; power-weight ratio: 36.5 lb/hp (49.7 lb/kW), 16.6 kg/hp (22.5 kg/kW); acceleration: 0-50 mph (0-80 km/h) 13 sec; speed in direct drive at 1,000 rpm: 14.6 mph, 23.5 km/h.

PRACTICAL INSTRUCTIONS fuel: 98 oct petrol; valve timing: 44° 88° 78° 40°.

55 hp power team

See 40 hp power team, except for:

ENGINE 76 cu in, 1,196 cc (3.11 x 2.40 in, 79 x 61 mm); compression ratio: 7.8:1; max power (DIN): 55 hp (40.5 kW) at 5,400 rpm; max torque (DIN): 62 lb ft, 8.5 kg m (83.4 Nm) at 3,400 rpm; max engine rpm: 6,000; 46 hp/l (33.9 kW/l); 1 Solex 35 PDSI downdraught single barrel carburettor; cooling system: 8.1 imp pt, 9.7 US pt, 4.6 l.

PERFORMANCE max speed: 84 mph, 136 km/h; power-weight ratio: 31.9 lb/hp (43.3 lb/kW), 14.4 kg/hp (19.6 kg/kW); acceleration: 0-50 mph (0-80 km/h) 12.5 sec; consumption: 31.4 m/imp gal, 26.1 m/US gal, 9 l x 100 km.

PRACTICAL INSTRUCTIONS valve timing: 46° 90° 70° 90°.

OPEL City « Berlina » Hatchback Coupé

OPEL Kadett 2-door Limousine

60 hp power team

See 40 hp power team, except for:

ENGINE 76 cu in, 1,196 cc (3.11 x 2.40 in, 79 x61 mm); compression ratio: 9:1; max power (DIN): 60 hp (44.2 kW) at 5,400 rpm; max torque (DIN): 65 lb ft, 9 kg m (88.3 Nm) at 2,600-3,400 rpm; max engine rpm: 6,000; 50.2 hp/l (32.5 kW/l); 1 Solex 35 PDSI downdraught single barrel carburettor; cooling system: 8.1 imp pt, 9.7 US pt, 4.6 l.

PERFORMANCE max speed: 87 mph, 140 km/h; power-weight ratio: 29.7 lb/hp (40.4 lb/kW), 13.5 kg/hp (18.3 kg/kW); acceleration: 0-50 mph (0-80 km/h) 11.5 sec; consumption: 31.4 m/imp gal, 26.1 m/US gal, 9 l x 100 km.

CHASSIS rear suspension: anti-roll bar (standard).

DIMENSIONS AND WEIGHT weight: 1,786 lb, 810 kg.

PRACTICAL INSTRUCTIONS fuel: 98 oct petrol; valve timing: 46° 90° 70° 30°.

OPTIONAL ACCESSORIES Opel automatic transmission with 3 ratios (I 2.400, II 1.480, III 1, rev 1.920), max ratio of converter at stall 2.2, possible manual selection, central lever, 4.110 axle ratio, max speed 84 mph, 135 km/h, consumption 29.1 m/imp gal, 24.2 m/US gal, 9.7 l x 100 km.

OPEL Kadett 2-door Limousine

OPEL Kadett GT/E Coupé

75 hp power team

See 40 hp power team, except for:

ENGINE 96.7 cu in, 1,584 cc (3.35 x 2.75 in, 85 x 69.8 mm); compression ratio: 8.8:1; max power (DIN): 75 hp (55.2 kW) at 5,200 rpm; max torque (DIN): 83 lb ft, 11.5 kg m (112.8 Nm) at 3,800-4,200 rpm; 47.3 hp/l (34.8 kW/l); 5 crankshaft bearings; lubricating system: 6.7 imp pt, 8 US pt, 3.8 l; 1 Solex 32/32 DIDTA-4 downdraught single barrel carburettor; cooling system: 11.6 imp pt, 14 US pt, 6.6 l.

TRANSMISSION gearbox ratios: I 3.640, II 2.120, III 1.336, IV 1, rev 3.522; axle ratio: 3.890.

PERFORMANCE max speed: 97 mph, 155 km/h; power-weight ratio: 26.8 lb/hp (36.3 lb/kW), 12.1 kg/hp (16.5 kg/kW); speed in direct drive at 1,000 rpm: 16.2 mph, 26 km/h; consumption: 26.9 m/imp gal, 22.4 m/US gal, 10.5 l x 100 km.

CHASSIS rear suspension: anti-roll bar (standard).

BRAKES lining area: total 85.7 sq in, 553 sq cm.

ELECTRICAL EQUIPMENT 44 Ah battery.

DIMENSIONS AND WEIGHT: 2,007 lb, 910 kg.

PRACTICAL INSTRUCTIONS fuel: 98 oct petrol; oil: engine 6.7 imp pt, 8 US pt, 3.8 l; tappet clearances: inlet 0.012 in, 0.30 mm, exhaust 0.012 in, 0.30 mm; valve timing: 44° 86° 84° 46°.

OPTIONAL ACCESSORIES Opel automatic transmission with 3 ratios (I 2.400, II 1.480, III 1, rev 1.920), max ratio of converter at stall 2.2, possible manual selection, central lever, 3.670 axle ratio, max speed 93 mph, 150 km/h, consumption 25.7 m/imp gal, 21.4 m/US gal, 11 l x 100 km.

Kadett Series

PRICES IN GB AND EX WORKS:	£	DM
1 Kadett 2-door Limousine	2,058*	9,395*
2 Kadett 4-door Limousine	—	9,915*
3 Kadett Caravan	—	10,155*
4 Kadett L 2-door Limousine	2,249*	9,940*
5 Kadett L 4-door Limousine	—	10,460*
6 Kadett L Coupé	2,861*	10,640*
7 Kadett L Caravan	—	10,700*
8 Kadett « Berlina » 2-door Limousine	2,479*	10,615*
9 Kadett « Berlina » 4-door Limousine	2,572*	11,045*
10 Kadett « Berlina » Caravan	2,739*	12,285*
11 Kadett Aero Cabriolet	—	14,500*
12 Kadett GT/E Coupé	3,866*	16,700*

For 60 hp engine add DM 180; for 75 hp engine add DM 835.

Power team:	Standard for:	Optional for:
40 hp	—	1 to 10
48 hp	—	1 to 10
55 hp	1 to 10	—
60 hp	11	1 to 10
75 hp	—	4 to 11
115 hp	12	—

40 hp power team

ENGINE front, 4 stroke; 4 cylinders, in line; 60.6 cu in, 993 cc (2.83 x 2.40 in, 72 x 61 mm); compression ratio: 7.9:1; max power (DIN): 40 hp (29.4 kW) at 5,400 rpm; max torque (DIN): 51 lb ft, 7 kg (68.6 Nm) at 2,600-3,000 rpm; max engine rpm: 5,800; 40.3 hp/l (29.7 kW/l); cast iron block and head; 3 crankshaft bearings; valves: overhead, push-rods and rockers; camshafts: 1, side, chain-driven; lubrication: gear pump, full flow filter, 4.8 imp pt, 5.7 US pt, 2.7 l; 1 Solex 30 PDSI downdraught single barrel carburettor; fuel feed: mechanical pump; anti-freeze liquid cooled, 8.6 imp pt, 10.4 US pt, 4.9 l.

TRANSMISSION driving wheels: rear; clutch: single dry plate (diaphragm); gearbox: mechanical; gears: 4, fully synchronized; ratios: I 3.733, II 2.243, III 1.432, IV 1, rev 3.939; lever: central; final drive: hypoid bevel; axle ratio: 4.111; width of rims: 5''; tyres: 155 SR x 13.

PERFORMANCE max speed: 76 mph, 122 km/h - Coupé 78 mph, 125 km/h; power-weight ratio: 4-dr. limousines 44.4 lb/hp (60.4 lb/kW), 20.1 kg/hp (27.4 kg/kW); acceleration: 0-50 mph (0-80 km/h) 15 sec; speed in direct drive at 1,000 rpm: 15.5 mph, 25 km/h; consumption: 36.7 m/imp gal, 30.5 m/US gal, 7.7 l x 100 km.

CHASSIS integral; front suspension: independent, wishbones, coil springs, anti-roll bar, telescopic dampers; rear: rigid axle (torque tube), longitudinal trailing radius arms, coil springs, transverse linkage bar, telescopic dampers (anti-roll bar only for st. wagons).

STEERING rack-and-pinion; turns lock to lock: 3.75.

BRAKES front disc, rear drum; lining area: front 16.3 sq in, 105 sq cm, rear 32.9 sq in, 212 sq cm, total 49.2 sq in, 317 sq cm.

ELECTRICAL EQUIPMENT 12 V; 36 Ah battery; 45 A alternator; Bosch distributor; 2 headlamps.

DIMENSIONS AND WEIGHT wheel base: 94.09 in, 239 cm; tracks: 51.18 in, 130 cm front, 51.18 in, 130 cm rear; length: 162.36 in, 412 cm - Coupé, L and « Berlina » models 162.60 in, 413 cm - Caravan 162.91 in, 414 cm; width: 62.20 in, 158 cm; height: 54.13 in, 137 cm - Coupé 52.76 in, 134 cm, Caravan 54.33 in, 138 cm; ground clearance: 5.91 in, 15 cm; weight: 2-dr. limousines 1,731 lb, 785 kg - 4-dr. limousines 1,775 lb, 805 kg - Coupé 1,742 lb, 790 kg - Caravan 1,808 lb, 820 kg; turning circle (between walls): 32.6 ft, 9.9 m; fuel tank: 9.5 imp gal, 11.4 US gal. 43 l.

BODY 5 seats, separate front seats.

PRACTICAL INSTRUCTIONS fuel: 92 oct petrol; oil: engine 4.8 imp pt, 5.7 US pt, 2.7 l, SAE 20W-30, change every 3,100 miles, 5,000 km - gearbox 1.2 imp pt, 1.5 US pt, 0.7 l, SAE 80, no change recommended - final drive 1.2 imp pt, 1.5 US pt, 0.7 l, SAE 90, no change recommended; greasing: none; sparking plug: 200°; tappet clearances: inlet 0.006 in, 0.15 mm, exhaust 0.010 in, 0.25 mm; valve timing: 39° 93° 65° 45°.

OPTIONAL ACCESSORIES limited slip differential; 175/70 SR x 13 tyres with 5.5'' wide rims except for st. wagons; anti-roll bar on rear suspension; 44 Ah battery; halogen headlamps; headrests; heated rear window; sunshine roof except for st. wagons; metallic spray; rear window wiperwasher for st. wagons only.

48 hp power team

(only for export).

See 40 hp power team, except for:

ENGINE compression ratio: 8.8:1; max power (DIN): 48 hp (35.3 kW) at 5,600 rpm; max torque (DIN): 52 lb ft, 7.2 kg m (70.6 Nm) at 3,400 rpm; max engine rpm: 6,000; 48.3 hp/l (35.5 kW/l); cooling system: 8.1 imp pt. 9.7 US pt, 4.6 l.

TRANSMISSION axle ratio: 4.375.

PERFORMANCE max speed: 80 mph, 128 km/h - Coupé 82 mph, 132 km/h; power-weight ratio: 4-dr. limousines 37 lb/hp (50.3 lb/kW), 16.8 kg/hp (22.8 kg/kW); acceleration: 0-50 mph (0-80 km/h) 13 sec; speed in direct drive at 1,000 rpm: 14.6 mph, 23.5 km/h.

PRACTICAL INSTRUCTIONS fuel: 98 oct petrol; valve timing: 44° 88° 78° 40°.

55 hp power team

See 40 hp power team, except for:

ENGINE 76 cu in, 1,196 cc (3.11 x 2.40 in, 79 x 61 mm); compression ratio: 7.8:1; max power (DIN): 55 hp (40.5 kW) at 5,600 rpm; max torque (DIN): 62 lb ft, 8.5 kg m (83.4 Nm) at 3,400 rpm; max engine rpm: 6,000; 46 hp/l (33.9 kW/l); 1 Solex 35 PDSI downdraught single barrel carburettor; cooling system: 8.1 imp pt, 9.7 US pt, 4.6 l.

PERFORMANCE max speed: 86 mph, 138 km/h - Coupé 88 mph, 142 km/h; power-weight ratio: 4-dr. limousines 32.2 lb/hp (43.9 lb/kW), 14.6 kg/hp (19.9 kg/kW); acceleration: 0-50 mph (0-80 km/h) 12.5 sec; consumption: 31.4 m/imp gal, 26.1 m/US gal, 9 l x 100 km - Coupé 32.2 m/imp gal, 27.7 m/US gal, 8.5 l x 100 km.

PRACTICAL INSTRUCTIONS valve timing: 46° 90° 70° 30°.

60 hp power team

See 40 hp power team, except for:

ENGINE 76 cu in, 1,196 cc (3.11 x 2.40 in, 79 x 61 mm); compression ratio: 9:1; max power (DIN): 60 hp (44.2 kW) at 5,400 rpm; max torque (DIN): 65 lb ft, 9 kg m (88.3 Nm) at 2,600-3,400 rpm; max engine rpm: 6,000; 50.2 hp/l (32.5 kW/l); 1 Solex 35 PDSI downdraught single barrel carburettor; cooling system: 8.1 imp pt, 9.7 US pt, 4.6 l.

TRANSMISSION (Kadett Aero only) width of rims: 5.5''; tyres: 175/70 SR x 13.

PERFORMANCE max speed: 88 mph, 142 km/h - Coupé 91 mph, 146 km/h; power-weight ratio: Kadett Aero and 4-dr. limousines 30.1 lb/hp (41 lb/kW), 13.6 kg/hp (18.6 kg/kW); acceleration: 0-50 mph (0-80 km/h) 11.5 sec; consumption: 33.2 m/imp gal, 27.7 m/US gal, 8.5 l x 100 km - Coupé 34.4 m/imp gal, 28.7 m/US gal, 8.2 l x 100 km.

CHASSIS rear suspension: anti-roll bar (standard).

OPEL Kadett « Berlina » 4-door Limousine

OPEL Kadett « Berlina » 4-door Limousine Automatic

OPEL Kadett L 1.2

DIMENSIONS AND WEIGHT weight: plus 33 lb, 15 kg - Coupé plus 66 lb, 30 kg.

PRACTICAL INSTRUCTIONS fuel: 98 oct petrol; valve timing: 46° 90° 70° 30°.

OPTIONAL ACCESSORIES Opel automatic transmission with 3 ratios (I 2.400, II 1.480, III 1, rev 1.920), max ratio of converter at stall 2.2, 4.110 axle ratio, max speed 85 mph, 137 km/h (Coupé 88 mph, 141 km/h), consumption 30.7 m/imp gal, 25.6 m/US gal, 9.2 l x 100 km - Coupé 31.4 m/imp gal, 26.1 m/US gal, 9 l x 100 km; SR equipment with 175/70 SR x 13 tyres except for st. wagons.

75 hp power team

See 40 hp power team, except for:

ENGINE 96.7 cu in, 1,584 cc (3.35 x 2.75 in, 85 x 69.8 mm); compression ratio: 8.8:1; max power (DIN): 75 hp (55.2 kW) at 5,200 rpm; max torque (DIN): 83 lb ft, 11.5 kg m (112.8 Nm) at 3,800-4,200 rpm; 47.3 hp/l (34.8 kW/l); 5 crankshaft bearings; lubricating system: 6.7 imp pt, 8 US pt, 3.8 l; 1 Solex 32/32 DIDTA-4 downdraught single barrel carburettor; cooling system: 11.6 imp pt, 14 US pt, 6.6 l.

TRANSMISSION gearbox ratios: I 3.640, II 2.120, III 1.336, IV 1, rev 3.522; axle ratio: 3.890; width of rims: Kadett Aero 5.5''; tyres: Kadett Aero 175/70 SR x 13.

PERFORMANCE max speed: 98 mph, 157 km/h - Coupé 99 mph, 160 km/h; power-weight ratio: 4-dr. limousines 27 lb/hp (36.7 lb/kW), 12.3 kg/hp (16.7 kg/kW); speed in direct drive at 1,000 rpm: 16.2 mph, 26 km/h; consumption: 27.7 m/imp gal, 23.1 m/US gal, 10.2 l x 100 km - Coupé 28.2 m/imp gal, 23.5 m/US gal, 10 l x 100 km.

CHASSIS rear suspension: anti-roll bar (standard).

BRAKES lining area: total 85.7 sq in, 553 sq cm.

ELECTRICAL EQUIPMENT 44 Ah battery.

DIMENSIONS AND WEIGHT weight: plus 253 lb, 115 kg - Coupé plus 286 lb, 130 kg.

PRACTICAL INSTRUCTIONS fuel: 98 oct petrol; oil: engine 6.7 imp pt, 8 US pt, 3.8 l; tappet clearances: inlet 0.012 in, 0.30 mm, exhaust 0.012 in, 0.30 mm; valve timing: 44° 86° 84° 46°.

OPTIONAL ACCESSORIES Opel automatic transmission with 3 ratios (I 2.400, II 1.480, III 1, rev 1.920), max ratio of converter at stall 2.2, possible manual selection, central lever, 3.670 axle ratio, max speed 94 mph, 152 km/h (Coupé 96 mph, 155 km/h), consumption 26.4 m/imp gal, 22 m/US gal, 10.7 l x 100 km - Coupé 27.7 m/imp gal, 23.1 m/US gal, 10.2 l x 100 km.

115 hp power team

See 40 hp power team, except for:

ENGINE 120.8 cu in, 1,979 cc (3.74 x 2.75 in, 95 x 69.8 mm); compression ratio: 9.6:1; max power (DIN): 115 hp (84.6 kW) at 5,600 rpm; max torque (DIN): 117 lb ft, 16.2 kg m (158.9 Nm) at 3,000 rpm; max engine rpm: 6,000; 58.1 hp/l (42.7 kW/l); 5 crankshaft bearings; valves: overhead, in line,

115 HP POWER TEAM

rockers, hydraulic tappets; camshafts: 1, overhead; lubricating system: 6.7 imp pt, 8 US pt, 3.8 l; Bosch L-Jetronic electronic injection; fuel feed: electric pump; cooling system: 12 imp pt, 14.4 US pt, 6.8 l.

TRANSMISSION gears: 5, fully synchronized; ratios: I 2.991, II 1.763, III 1.301, IV 1, V 0.874, rev 3.663; axle ratio: 3.890; width of rims: 6''; tyres: 175/70 HR x 13.

PERFORMANCE max speed: 118 mph, 190 km/h; power-weight ratio: 17.6 lb/hp (24 lb/kW), 8 kg/hp (10.9 kg/kW); carrying capacity: 827 lb, 375 kg; speed in top at 1,000 rpm: 19.7 mph, 31.7 km/h; consumption: 32.1 m/imp gal, 26.7 m/US gal, 8.8 l x 100 km.

CHASSIS rear suspension: anti-roll bar (standard).

STEERING turns lock to lock: 3.50

BRAKES front disc, rear drum, rear compensator, servo; lining area: total 85.7 sq in, 553 sq cm.

ELECTRICAL EQUIPMENT 55 Ah battery; halogen headlamps (standard).

DIMENSIONS AND WEIGHT tracks: 51.97 in, 132 cm front, 51.57 in, 131 cm rear; height: 52.76 in, 134 cm; ground clearance: 5 in, 12.7 cm; weight: 2,029 lb, 920 kg.

BODY coupé; 2 doors; 5 seats, separate front seats, built-in headrests, heated rear window.

PRACTICAL INSTRUCTIONS fuel: 98 oct petrol; oil: engine 6.7 imp pt, 8 US pt, 3.8 l - gearbox 1.9 imp pt, 2.3 US pt, 1.1 l - final drive 1.9 imp pt, 2.3 US pt, 1.1 l; tappet clearances: inlet 0.012 in, 0.30 mm, exhaust 0.012 in, 0.30 mm; valve timing: 44° 88° 84° 48°; tyre pressure: front 24 psi, 1.7 atm, rear 24 osi, 1.7 atm.

OPTIONAL ACCESSORIES 4.750 axle ratio; light alloy wheels.

Rallye Series

PRICES EX WORKS:

1 Rallye 1.6 Coupé	DM 11,900*
2 Rallye E Coupé	DM 13,475*

Power team:	Standard for:	Optional for:
75 hp	1	—
110 hp	2	—

75 hp power team

ENGINE front, 4 stroke; 4 cylinders, in line; 96.7 cu in, 1,584 cc (3.35 x 2.75 in, 85 x 69.8 mm); compression ratio: 8.8:1; max power (DIN): 75 hp (55.2 kW) at 5,200 rpm; max torque (DIN): 83 lb ft, 11.5 kg m (112.8 Nm) at 3,800-4,200 rpm; max engine rpm: 5,800; 47.3 hp/l (34.8 kW/l); cast iron block and head; 5 crankshaft bearings; valves: over-

OPEL Kadett L Caravan

head, push-rods and rockers; camshafts: 1, side chain-driven; lubrication: gear pump, full flow filter, 6.7 imp pt, 8 US pt, 3.8 l; 1 Solex 32/32 DIDTA-4 downdraught single barrel carburettor; fuel feed: mechanical pump; antifreeze liquid cooled, 11.6 imp pt, 14 US pt, 6.6 l.

TRANSMISSION driving wheels: rear; clutch: single dry plate (diaphragm); gearbox: mechanical; gears: 4, fully synchronized; ratios: I 3.640, II 2.120, III 1.336, IV 1, rev 3.522; lever: central; final drive: hypoid bevel; axle ratio: 3.890; width of rims: 5.5''; tyres 175/70 SR x 13.

PERFORMANCE max speed: 99 mph, 160 km/h; power-weight ratio: 26.6 lb/hp (36.1 lb/kW), 12.1 kg/hp (16.4 kg/kW); carrying capacity: 805 lb, 365 kg; speed in direct drive at 1,000 rpm: 17.1 mph, 27.6 km/h; consumption: 28.2 m/imp gal, 23.5 m/US gal, 10 l x 100 km.

CHASSIS integral; front suspension: independent, wishbones, coil springs, anti-roll bar, telescopic dampers; rear: rigid axle (torque tube), longitudinal trailing radius arms, coil springs, transverse linkage bar, anti-roll bar, telescopic dampers.

STEERING rack-and-pinion.

BRAKES front disc, rear drum; lining area: total 85.7 sq in, 553 sq cm.

ELECTRICAL EQUIPMENT 12 V; 44 Ah battery; 45 A alternator; Bosch distributor; 2 halogen headlamps.

DIMENSIONS AND WEIGHT wheel base: 94.09 in, 239 cm; tracks: 51.18 in, 130 cm front, 51.18 in, 130 cm rear; length: 162.36 in, 412 cm; width: 62.20 in, 158 cm; height: 52.76 in, 134 cm; ground clearance: 5.91 in, 15 cm; weight: 1,996 lb, 905 kg; turning circle (between walls): 32.6 ft, 9.9 m; fuel tank: 9.5 imp gal, 11.4 US gal, 43 l.

BODY coupé; 2 doors; 5 seats, separate front seats, reclining backrests with built-in headrests.

PRACTICAL INSTRUCTIONS fuel: 98 oct petrol; oil: engine 6.7 imp pt, 8 US pt, 3.8 l, SAE 20W-30, change every 3,100 miles, 5,000 km - gearbox 1.9 imp pt, 2.3 US pt, 1.1 l, SAE 80, no change recommended - final drive 1.9 imp pt, 2.3 US pt, 1.1 l, SAE 90, no change recommended; greasing: none; tappet clearances: inlet 0.012 in, 0.30 mm, exhaust 0.012 in, 0.30 mm; valve timing: 46° 90° 70° 30°; tyre pressure: front 24 psi, 1.7 atm, rear 24 psi, 1.7 atm.

OPTIONAL ACCESSORIES limited slip differential; 3.670 axle ratio; light alloy wheels; heated rear window.

110 hp power team

See 75 hp power team, except for:

ENGINE 120.8 cu in, 1,979 cc (3.74 x 2.75 in, 95 x 69.8 mm); compression ratio: 9.4:1; max power (DIN): 110 hp (81 kW) at 5,400 rpm; max torque (DIN): 117 lb ft, 16.2 kg m (158.9 Nm) at 3,400 rpm; max engine rpm: 6,000; 55.6 hp/l (40.9 kW/l); valves: idraulic tappets; Bosch L-Jetronic electronic injection; fuel feed: electric pump; cooling system: 12 imp pt, 14.4 US pt, 6.8 l.

TRANSMISSION axle ratio: 3.440; tyres: 175/70 HR x 13.

PERFORMANCE max speed: 117 mph, 189 km/h; power-weight ratio: 18.3 lb/hp (24.9 lb/kW), 8.3 kg/hp (11.3 kg/kW); carrying capacity: 827 lb, 375 kg; speed in direct drive at 1,000 rpm: 19.6 mph, 31.5 km/h; consumption: 29.7 m/imp gal, 24.8 m/US gal, 9.5 l x 100 km.

DIMENSIONS AND WEIGHT weight: 2,018 lb, 915 kg.

PRACTICAL INSTRUCTIONS valve timing: 34° 88° 74° 48°.

OPTIONAL ACCESSORIES 5-speed fully synchronized mechanical gearbox (I 3.875, II 2.400, III 1.760, IV 1.260, V 1, rev 3.670).

Ascona Series

PRICES IN GB AND EX WORKS:	£	DM
1 Ascona 1.2 2-door Limousine	—	10,945*
2 Ascona 1.2 4-door Limousine	—	11,475*
3 Ascona 1.2 L 2-door Limousine	—	11,770*
4 Ascona 1.2 L 4-door Limousine	—	12,300*
5 Ascona 1.2 « Berlina » 2-door Limousine	—	12,552*
6 Ascona 1.2 « Berlina » 4-door Limousine	—	12,940*
7 Ascona 1.6 2-door Limousine	2,828*	11,365*
8 Ascona 1.6 4-door Limousine	2,925*	11,895*
9 Ascona 1.6 L 2-door Limousine	3,163*	12,190*
10 Ascona 1.6 L 4-door Limousine	3,257*	12,720*
11 Ascona 1.6 « Berlina » 2-door Limousine	—	12,972*
12 Ascona 1.6 « Berlina » 4-door Limousine	3,656*	13,360*

OPEL Rallye 1.6 Coupé

For 75 hp engine add DM 262; for 90 hp engine add DM 472; for 100 hp engine add DM 608.

Power team:	Standard for:	Optional for:
55 hp	—	1 to 6
60 hp	1 to 6	—
60 hp (1,584 cc)	7 to 12	—
75 hp	—	7 to 12
90 hp	—	7 to 12
100 hp	—	7 to 12

55 hp power team

ENGINE front, 4 stroke; 4 cylinders, in line; 76 cu in, 1,196 cc (3.11 x 2.40 in, 79 x 61 mm); compression ratio: 7.8:1; max power (DIN) 55 hp (40.5 kW) at 5,400 rpm; max torque (DIN): 62 lb ft, 8.5 kg m (83.4 Nm) at 3,400 rpm; max engine rpm: 5,800; 50.2 hp/l (36.9 kW/l); cast iron block and head; 3 crankshaft bearings; valves: overhead, push-rods and rockers; camshafts: 1, side, chain-driven; lubrication: gear pump, full flow filter, 4.8 imp pt, 5.7 US pt. 2.7 l; 1 Solex 35 PDSI downdraught single barrel carburettor; fuel feed: mechanical pump; anti-freeze liquid cooled, 9.3 imp pt, 11.2 US pt, 5.3 l.

TRANSMISSION driving wheels: rear; clutch: single dry plate (diaphragm); gearbox: mechanical; gears: 4, fully synchronized; ratios: I 3.733, II 2.243, III 1.432, IV 1, rev 3.939; lever: central; final drive: hypoid bevel; axle ratio: 4.110; width of rims: 5''; tyres: 165 SR x 13.

PERFORMANCE max speed: 86 mph, 138 km/h; power-weight ratio: 4-dr. limousines 36.6 lb/hp (49.8 lb/kW), 16.6 kg/hp (22.6 kg/kW); carrying capacity: 937 lb, 425 kg - 4-dr. limousines 893 lb, 405 kg; acceleration: standing ¼ mile 21 sec, 0-50 mph (0-80 km/h) 12 sec; speed in direct drive at 1,000 rpm: 23.7 mph, 38.1 km/h; consumption: 31.4 m/imp gal, 26.1 m/US gal, 9 l x 100 km.

CHASSIS integral; front suspension: independent, wishbones, coil springs, anti-roll bar, telescopic dampers; rear: rigid axle (torque tube), trailing radius arms, transverse linkage bar, coil springs, anti-roll bar, telescopic dampers.

STEERING rack-and-pinion; turns lock to lock: 4.

BRAKES front disc, rear drum, servo; lining area: front 22.9 sq in, 148 sq cm, rear 47.1 sq in, 304 sq cm, total 70 sq in, 452 sq cm.

ELECTRICAL EQUIPMENT 12 V; 36 Ah battery; 45 A alternator; Bosch or Delco Remy distributor; 2 headlamps.

DIMENSIONS AND WEIGHT wheel base: 99.21 in, 252 cm; front and rear tracks: 54.13 in, 137 cm; length: 170.12 in, 432 cm; width: 65.75 in, 167 cm; height: 54.33 in, 138 cm; ground clearance: 5.12 in, 13 cm; weight: 2-dr. limousines 1,973 lb, 895 kg - 4-dr. limousines 2,018 lb, 915 kg; turning circle (between walls): 33.1 ft, 10.1 m; fuel tank: 11 imp gal, 13.2 US gal, 50 l.

BODY 5 seats, separate front seats, adjustable backrests.

PRACTICAL INSTRUCTIONS fuel: 98 oct petrol; oil: engine 4.8 imp pt, 5.7 US pt, 2.7 l, SAE 20W-30, change every 6,200 miles, 10,000 km - gearbox 1.1 imp pt, 1.3 US pt, 0.6 l, SAE 80, no change recommended - final drive 1.1 imp pt, 1.3 US pt, 0.6 l, SAE 90, no change recommended; greasing: none; sparking plug: 200°; tappet clearances (hot): inlet 0.006 in, 0.15 mm, exhaust 0.010 in, 0.25 mm; valve timing: 46° 90° 70° 30°; tyre pressure: front 24 psi, 1.7 atm, rear 24 psi, 1.7 atm.

OPTIONAL ACCESSORIES 185/70 SR x 13 tyres with 5.5'' wide rims; 44 Ah battery; 55 Ah battery; sunshine roof; heated rear window; headrests; halogen headlamps; vinyl roof; headlamps with wiper-washers; metallic spray; SR equipment.

60 hp power team

See 55 hp power team, except for:

ENGINE compression ratio: 9:1; max power (DIN): 60 hp (44.2 kW) at 5,400 rpm; max torque (DIN): 65 lb ft, 9 kg m (88.3 Nm) at 2,600-3,400 rpm; 50.2 hp/l (36.9 kW/l).

PERFORMANCE max speed: 88 mph, 142 km/h; power-weight ratio: 4-dr. limousines 33.5 lb/hp (45.6 lb/kW), 15.2 kg/hp (20.7 kg/kW); consumption: 33.2 m/imp gal, 27.7 m/US gal, 8.5 l x 100 km.

60 hp (1,584 cc) power team

See 55 hp power team, except for:

ENGINE 96.7 cu in, 1,584 cc (3.35 x 2.75 in, 85 x 69.8 mm); compression ratio: 8:1; max power (DIN): 60 hp (44.2 kW) at 5,000 rpm; max torque (DIN): 76 lb ft, 10.5 kg m (103 Nm) at 3,000-3,400 rpm; max engine rpm: 6,000; 37.9 hp/l

OPEL Rallye 1.6 Coupé

(27.9 kW/l); 5 crankshaft bearings; valves: overhead, in line, rockers; camshafts: 1, overhead; lubricating system: 6.7 imp pt, 8 US pt, 3.8 l; cooling system: 11.1 imp pt, 13.3 US pt, 6.3 l.

TRANSMISSION gearbox ratios: I 3.640, II 2.120, III 1.366, IV 1, rev 3.522; axle ratio: 3.700.

PERFORMANCE max speed: 90 mph, 145 km/h; power-weight ratio: 4-dr. limousines 35.6 lb/hp (48.3 lb/kW), 16.1 kg/hp (21.9 kg/kW); acceleration: standing ¼ mile 20 sec, 0-50 mph (0-80 km/h) 11 sec; speed in direct drive at 1,000 rpm: 21.3 mph, 34.3 km/h; consumption: 26.4 m/imp gal, 22 m/US gal, 10.7 l x 100 km.

DIMENSIONS AND WEIGHT weight: 2-dr. limousines 2,095 lb, 950 kg - 4-dr. limousines 2,139 lb, 970 kg.

PRACTICAL INSTRUCTIONS fuel: 92 oct petrol; oil: engine 6.7 imp pt, 8 US pt, 3.8 l, SAE 20W-30, change every 6,200 miles, 10,000 km - gearbox 1.9 imp pt, 2.3 US pt, 1.1 l, SAE 80, no change recommended - final drive 1,9 imp pt, 2.3 US pt, 1.1 l, SAE 90, no change recommended; tappet clearances (hot): inlet 0.012 in, 0.30 mm, exhaust 0.012 in, 0.30 mm; valve timing: 44° 86° 84° 46°.

OPTIONAL ACCESSORIES Opel automatic transmission with 3 ratios (I 2.400, II 1.480, III 1, rev 1.920), max ratio of converter at stall 2.5, 3.670 axle ratio, max speed 87 mph, 140 km/h, consumption 24.6 m/imp gal, 20.5 m/US gal, 11.5 l x 100 km; 55 A alternator; air-conditioning.

OPEL Ascona 4-door Limousine

OPEL Ascona L 2-door Limousine

OPEL Ascona « Berlina » 4-door Limousine

75 hp power team

See 60 hp (1,584 cc) power team, except for:

ENGINE 115.8 cu in, 1,897 cc (3.66 x 2.75 in, 93 x 69.8 mm); compression ratio: 7.9:1; max power (DIN): 75 hp (55.2 kW) at 4,800 rpm; max torque (DIN): 98 lb ft, 13.5 kg m (132.4 Nm) at 2,200-3,400 rpm; max engine rpm: 5,200; 39.5 hp/l (29.1 kW/l); cooling system: 10.4 imp pt, 12.5 US pt, 5.9 l.

TRANSMISSION axle ratio: 3.670.

PERFORMANCE max speed: 98 mph, 157 km/h; power-weight ratio: 4-dr. limousines 29.4 lb/hp (39.9 lb/kW), 13.3 kg/hp (18.1 kg/kW).

ELECTRICAL EQUIPMENT 44 Ah battery.

DIMENSIONS AND WEIGHT weight: 2-dr. limousines 2,161 lb, 980 kg - 4-dr. limousines 2,205 lb, 1,000 kg.

OPTIONAL ACCESSORIES with Opel automatic transmission, max speed 95 mph, 152 km/h.

90 hp power team

See 60 hp (1,584 cc) power team, except for:

ENGINE 115.8 cu in, 1,897 cc (3.66 x 2.75 in, 93 x 69.8 mm); compression ratio: 8.8:1; max power (DIN): 90 hp (66.2 kW) at 4,800 rpm; max torque (DIN): 109 lb ft, 15 kg m (147.1 Nm) at 3,800 rpm; 47.4 hp/l (34.9 kW/l); 1 Zenith 35/40 INAT downdraught carburettor; cooling system: 10.4 imp pt, 12.5 US pt, 5.9 l.

TRANSMISSION axle ratio: 3.670.

PERFORMANCE max speed: 104 mph, 167 km/h; power-weight ratio: 4-dr. limousines 24.5 lb/hp (33.3 lb/kW), 11.1 kg/hp (15.1 kg/kW); carrying capacity: 970 lb, 400 kg - 4-dr. limousines 926 lb, 420 kg; acceleration: standing ¼ mile 18 sec, 0-50 mph (0-80 km/h) 8 sec; speed in direct drive at 1,000 rpm: 21.1 mph, 34 km/h; consumption: 28.2 m/imp gal, 23.5 m/US gal, 10 l x 100 km.

BRAKES rear compensator; lining area: front 22.9 sq in, 148 sq cm, rear 62.8 sq in, 405 sq cm, total 85.7 sq in, 553 sq cm.

ELECTRICAL EQUIPMENT 44 Ah battery.

DIMENSIONS AND WEIGHT weight: 2-dr. limousines 2,161 lb, 980 kg - 4-dr. limousines 2,205 lb, 1,000 kg.

PRACTICAL INSTRUCTIONS fuel: 98 oct petrol.

OPTIONAL ACCESSORIES with Opel automatic transmission, max speed 101 mph, 162 km/h, consumption 26.4 m/imp gal, 22 m/US gal, 10.7 l x 100 km; limited slip differential.

100 hp power team

See 60 hp (1,584 cc) power team, except for:

ENGINE 120.8 cu in, 1,979 cc (3.74 x 2.75 in, 95 x 69.8 mm); compression ratio: 9:1; max power (DIN): 100 hp (73.6 kW) at 5,400 rpm; max torque (DIN): 111 lb ft, 15.3 kg m (150 Nm) at 3,800 rpm; 50.5 hp/l (37.2 kW/l); valves: hydraulic tappets; 1 GMF Varajet II downdraught single barrel carburettor; cooling system: 10.9 imp pt, 13.1 US pt, 6.2 l.

OPEL Manta « Berlinetta » Coupé

TRANSMISSION axle ratio: 3.440.

PERFORMANCE max speed: 109 mph, 175 km/h; power-weight ratio: 4-dr. limousines 22 lb/hp (29.9 lb/kW), 10 kg/hp (13.6 kg/kW); speed in direct drive at 1,000 rpm: 18.1 mph, 29.2 km/h; consumption: 28.2 m/imp gal, 23.5 m/US gal, 10 l x 100 km.

BRAKES rear compensator; lining area: front 22.9 sq in, 148 sq cm, rear 62.8 sq in, 405 sq cm, total 85.7 sq in, 553 sq cm.

ELECTRICAL EQUIPMENT 44 Ah battery.

DIMENSIONS AND WEIGHT weight: 2-dr. limousines 2,161 lb, 980 kg - 4-dr. limousines 2,205 lb, 1,000 kg.

PRACTICAL INSTRUCTIONS fuel: 98 oct petrol; valve timing: 32° 90° 72° 50°.

OPTIONAL ACCESSORIES with Opel automatic transmission, max speed 106 mph, 170 km/h, consumption 26.4 m/imp gal, 22 m/US gal, 10.7 l x 100 km.

Manta Series

PRICES IN GB AND EX WORKS:

1 Manta 1.2 Coupé	DM	12,060*
2 Manta 1.2 L Coupé	DM	12,875*
3 Manta 1.2 « Berlinetta » Coupé	DM	13,657*
4 Manta 1.6 Coupé	DM	12,480*
5 Manta 1.6 L Coupé	DM	13,295*
6 Manta 1.6 « Berlinetta » Coupé	DM	14,077*
7 Manta E Coupé	DM	15,520*
8 Manta E « Berlinetta » Coupé	DM	16,271*
9 Manta GT/E Coupé	DM	15,520*

For 75 hp engine add DM 262; for 90 hp engine add DM 472; for 100 hp engine add DM 985 (DM 859 for Manta 1.6 L, DM 828 for Manta 1.6 « Berlinetta »).

Power team:	Standard for:	Optional for:
55 hp	—	1 to 3
60 hp	1 to 3	
60 hp (1,584 cc)	4 to 6	—
75 hp	—	4 to 6
90 hp	—	4 to 6
100 hp	—	4 to 6
110 hp	7 to 9	—

55 hp power team

ENGINE front, 4 stroke; 4 cylinders, in line; 76 cu in, 1,196 cc (3.11 x 2.40 in, 79 x 61 mm); compression ratio: 7.8:1; max power (DIN): 55 hp (40.5 kW) at 5,400 rpm; max torque (DIN): 62 lb ft, 8.5 kg m (83.4 Nm) at 3,400 rpm; max engine rpm: 5,800; 50.2 hp/l (36.9 kW/l); cast iron block and head; 3 crankshaft bearings; valves: overhead, push-rods and rockers; camshafts: 1, side, chain-driven; lubrication: gear pump, full flow filter, 4.8 imp pt, 5.7 US pt, 2.7 l; 1 Solex 35 PDSI downdraught single barrel carburettor; fuel feed: mechanical pump; antifreeze liquid cooled, 9 imp pt, 10.8 US pt, 5.1 l.

TRANSMISSION driving wheels: rear; clutch: single dry plate (diaphragm); gearbox: mechanical; gears: 4, fully

OPEL Manta E « Berlinetta » Coupé

synchronized; ratios: I 3.733, II 2.243, III 1.432, IV 1, rev 3.939; lever: central; final drive: hypoid bevel; axle ratio: 4.110; width of rims: 5''; tyres: 165 SR x 13.

PERFORMANCE max speed: 89 mph, 143 km/h; power-weight ratio: 37.1 lb/hp (50.4 lb/kW), 16.8 kg/hp (22.8 kg/kW); carrying capacity: 816 lb, 370 kg; acceleration: standing ¼ mile 21 sec, 0-50 mph (0-80 km/h) 12 sec; speed in direct drive at 1,000 rpm: 23.7 mph, 38.1 km/h; consumption: 32.5 m/imp gal, 27 m/US gal, 8.7 l x 100 km.

CHASSIS integral; front suspension: independent, wishbones (lower trailing links), coil springs, anti-roll bar, telescopic dampers; rear: rigid axle (torque tube), trailing radius arms, transverse linkage bar, coil springs, anti-roll bar, telescopic dampers.

STEERING rack-and-pinion; turns lock to lock: 4.

BRAKES front disc, rear drum, rear compensator, servo; lining area: front 22.9 sq in, 148 sq cm, rear 47.1 sq in, 304 sq cm, total 70 sq in, 452 sq cm.

ELECTRICAL EQUIPMENT 12 V; 36 Ah battery; 45 A alternator; Bosch or Delco Remy distributor; 2 headlamps.

DIMENSIONS AND WEIGHT wheel base: 99.13 in, 252 cm; front and rear tracks: 54.13 in, 137 cm; length: 175.39 in, 444 cm; width: 65.75 in, 167 cm; height: 52.36 in, 133 cm; ground clearance: 5.12 in, 13 cm; weight: 2,040 lb, 925 kg; turning circle (between walls): 33.8 ft, 10.3 m; fuel tank: 11 imp gal, 13.2 US gal, 50 l.

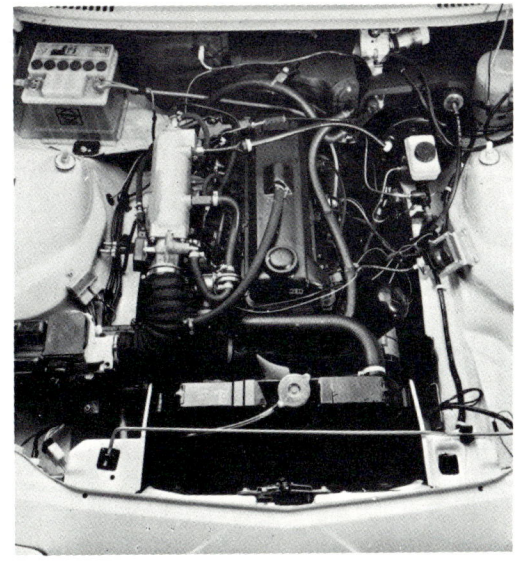

OPEL Manta GT/E Coupé

OPEL Manta GT/E Coupé

BODY coupé; 2 doors: 5 seats, separate front seats, adjustable backrests.

PRACTICAL INSTRUCTIONS fuel: 91 oct petrol; oil: engine 4.8 imp pt, 5.7 US pt, 2.7 l, SAE 20W-30, change every 6,200 miles, 10,000 km - gearbox 1.1 imp pt, 1.3 US pt, 0.6 l, SAE 80, no change recommended - final drive 1.1 imp pt, 1.3 US pt, 0.6 l, SAE 90, no change recommended; greasing: none; sparking plug: 200°; tappet clearances (hot): inlet 0.006 in, 0.15 mm, exhaust 0.010 in, 0.25 mm; valve timing: 46° 90° 70° 30°; tyre pressure: front 24 psi, 1.7 atm, rear 24 psi, 1.7 atm.

OPTIONAL ACCESSORIES 185/70 SR x 13 tyres with 5.5'' wide rims; 44 or 55 Ah battery; heated rear window; sunshine roof; headrests; metallic spray; halogen headlamps; vinyl roof; headlamps with wiper-washers; air-conditioning; SR equipment.

60 hp power team

See 55 hp power team, except for:

ENGINE compression ratio: 9:1; max power (DIN): 60 hp (44.2 kW) at 5,400 rpm; max torque (DIN): 65 lb ft, 9 kg m (88.3 Nm) at 2,600-3,400 rpm; 50.2 hp/l (36.9 kW/l).

PERFORMANCE max speed: 91 mph, 147 km/h; power-weight ratio: 35 lb/hp (46.1 lb/kW), 15.9 kg/hp (20.9 kg/kW); consumption: 33.2 m/imp gal, 27.7 m/US gal, 8.5 l x 100 km.

PRACTICAL INSTRUCTIONS fuel: 98 oct petrol.

60 hp (1,584 cc) power team

See 55 hp power team, except for:

ENGINE 96.7 cu in, 1,584 cc (3.35 x 2.75 in, 85 x 69.8 mm); compression ratio: 8:1; max power (DIN): 60 hp (44.2 kW) at 5,000 rpm; max torque (DIN): 76 lb ft, 10.5 kg m (103 Nm) at 3,000-3,400 rpm; max engine rpm: 6,000; 37.9 hp/l (27.9 kW/l); 5 crankshaft bearings; valves: overhead, in line, rockers; camshafts: 1, overhead; lubricating system: 6.7 imp pt, 8 US pt, 3.8 l; cooling system: 11.4 imp pt, 13.7 US pt, 6.5 l.

TRANSMISSION gearbox ratios: I 3.640, II 2.120, III 1.336, IV 1, rev 3.522; axle ratio: 3.700.

PERFORMANCE max speed: 93 mph, 150 km/h; power-weight ratio: 36 lb/hp (48.9 lb/kW), 16.3 kg/hp (22.2 kg/kW); acceleration: standing ¼ mile 20 sec, 0-50 mph (0-80 km/h) 11 sec; speed in direct drive at 1,000 rpm: 21.3 mph, 34.3 km/h; consumption: 28.2 m/imp gal, 23.5 m/US gal, 10 l x 100 km.

DIMENSIONS AND WEIGHT weight: 2,161 lb, 980 kg.

PRACTICAL INSTRUCTIONS oil: engine 6.7 imp pt, 8 US pt, 3.8 l, SAE 20W-30, change every 6,200 miles, 10,000 km - gearbox 1.9 imp pt, 2.3 US pt, 1.1 l, SAE 90, no change recommended; tappet clearances (hot): inlet 0.012 in, 0.30 mm, exhaust 0.012 in, 0.30 mm; valve timing: 44° 86° 84° 46°.

OPTIONAL ACCESSORIES Opel automatic transmission with 3 ratios (I 2.400, II 1.480, III 1, rev 1.920), max ratio of converter at stall 2.5, 3.670 axle ratio, max speed 90 mph, 145 km/h, consumption 26.4 m/imp gal, 22 m/US gal, 10.7 l x 100 km.

75 hp power team

See 60 hp (1,584 cc) power team, except for:

ENGINE 115.8 cu in, 1,897 cc (3.66 x 2.75 in, 93 x 69.8 mm); compression ratio: 7.9:1; max power (DIN): 75 hp (55.2 kW) at 4,800 rpm; max torque (DIN): 98 lb ft, 13.5 kg m (132.4 Nm) at 2,200-3,400 rpm; max engine rpm: 5,200; 39.5 hp/l (29.1 kw/l); cooling system: 11.3 imp pt, 13.5 US pt, 6.4 l.

TRANSMISSION axle ratio: 3.670.

PERFORMANCE max speed: 101 mph, 162 km/h; power-weight ratio: 29.4 lb/hp (39.9 lb/kW), 13.3 kg/hp (18.1 kg/kW); consumption: 27.7 m/imp gal, 23.1 m/US gal, 10.2 l x 100 km.

BRAKES lining area: front 22.9 sq in, 148 sq cm, rear 62.8 sq in, 405 sq cm, total 85.7 sq in, 553 sq cm.

ELECTRICAL EQUIPMENT 44 Ah battery.

DIMENSIONS AND WEIGHT weight: 2,205 lb, 1,000 kg.

OPTIONAL ACCESSORIES with Opel automatic transmission, max speed 97 mph, 157 km/h, consumption 25.7 m/imp gal, 21.4 m/US gal, 11 l x 100 km.

OPEL Manta E « Berlinetta » Coupé

90 hp power team

See 60 hp (1,584 cc) power team, except for:

ENGINE 115.8 cu in, 1,897 cc (3.66 x 2.75 in, 93 x 69.8 mm); compression ratio: 8.8:1; max power (DIN): 90 hp (66.2 kW) at 4,800 rpm; max torque (DIN): 109 lb ft, 15 kg m (147.1 Nm) at 2,600-3,800 rpm; 47.7 hp/l (34.9 kW/l); 1 Zenith 35/40 INAT downdraught carburettor; cooling system: 11.3 imp pt, 13.5 US pt, 6.4 l.

TRANSMISSION axle ratio: 3.670.

PERFORMANCE max speed: 107 mph, 172 km/h; power weight ratio: 24.5 lb/hp (33.3 lb/kW), 11.1 kg/hp (15.1 kg/kW); acceleration: standing ¼ mile 18 sec, 0-50 mph (0-80 km/h) 8 sec; speed in direct drive at 1,000 rpm: 21.1 mph, 34 km/h; consumption: 31.4 m/imp gal, 26.1 m/US gal, 9 l x 100 km.

BRAKES lining area: front 22.9 sq in, 148 sq cm, rear 62.8 sq in, 405 sq cm, total 85.7 sq in, 553 sq cm.

ELECTRICAL EQUIPMENT 44 Ah battery.

DIMENSIONS AND WEIGHT weight: 2,205 lb, 1,000 kg.

PRACTICAL INSTRUCTIONS fuel: 98 oct petrol.

OPTIONAL ACCESSORIES with Opel automatic transmission, max speed 104 mph, 167 km/h, consumption 29.1 m/imp gal, 24.2 m/US gal, 9.7 l x 100 km; limited slip differential.

100 hp power team

See 60 hp (1,584 cc) power team, except for:

ENGINE 120.8 cu in, 1,979 cc (3.74 x 2.75 in, 95 x 69.8 mm); compression ratio: 9:1; max power (DIN): 100 hp (73.6 kW) at 5,400 rpm; max torque (DIN): 111 lb ft, 15.3 kg m (150 Nm) at 3,800 rpm; 50.5 hp/l (37.2 kW/l); valves: hydraulic tappets; 1 GMF Varajet II downdraught single barrel carburettor; cooling system: 10.9 imp pt, 13.1 US pt, 6.2 l.

TRANSMISSION axle ratio: 3.440; tyres: 165 HR x 13.

PERFORMANCE max speed: 112 mph, 180 km/h; power-weight ratio: 22 lb/hp (29.9 lb/kW), 10 kg/hp (13.6 kg/kW); speed in direct drive at 1,000 rpm: 20.7 mph, 33.3 km/h; consumption: 31.4 m/imp gal, 26.1 m/US gal, 9 l x 100 km.

BRAKES lining area: front 22.9 sq in, 148 sq cm, rear 62.8 sq in, 405 sq cm, total 85.7 sq in, 553 sq cm.

ELECTRICAL EQUIPMENT 44 Ah battery.

DIMENSIONS AND WEIGHT weight: 2,205 lb, 1,000 kg.

PRACTICAL INSTRUCTIONS fuel: 98 oct petrol; valve timing: 32° 90° 72° 50°.

OPEL Rekord 2-door Limousine

OPEL Rekord L

OPTIONAL ACCESSORIES with Opel automatic transmission, max speed 109 mph, 175 km/h, consumption 29.1 m/imp gal, 24.2 m/US gal, 9.7 l x 100 km; 185/70 HR x 13 tyres with 5.5'' wide rims.

110 hp power team

See 60 hp (1,584 cc) power team, except for:

ENGINE 120.8 cu in, 1,979 cc (3.74 x 2.75 in, 95 x 69.8 mm); compression ratio: 9.4:1; max power (DIN): 110 hp (81 kW) at 5,400 rpm; max torque (DIN): 117 lb ft, 16.2 kg m (158.9 Nm) at 3,400 rpm; max engine rpm: 6,000; 55.6 hp/l (40.9 kW/l); valves: hydraulic tappets; Bosch L-Jetronic electronic injection; cooling system: 10.9 imp pt, 13.1 US pt, 6.2 l.

TRANSMISSION axle ratio: 3.440; width of rims: 5.5'' - Manta GT/E 6''; tyres: 185/70 HR x 13.

PERFORMANCE max speed: 116 mph, 187 km/h; power-weight ratio: 20 lb/hp (27.2 lb/kW) 9.1 kg/hp (12.3 kg/kW) - Manta GT/E 20.2 lb/hp (27.5 lb/kW), 9.2 kg/hp (12.5 kg/kW); speed in direct drive at 1,000 rpm: 19.6 mph, 31.5 km/h; consumption: 31.4 m/imp gal, 26.1 m/US gal, 9 l x 100 km.

BRAKES lining area: front 22.9 sq in, 148 sq cm, rear 62.8 sq in, 405 sq cm, total 85.7 sq in, 553 sq cm.

ELECTRICAL EQUIPMENT 44 Ah battery.

DIMENSIONS AND WEIGHT weight: Manta E 2,205 lb, 1,000 kg - Manta GT/E 2,227 lb, 1,010 kg.

PRACTICAL INSTRUCTIONS fuel: 98 oct petrol; valve timing: 34° 88° 74° 48°.

OPTIONAL ACCESSORIES with Opel automatic transmission, max speed 113 mph, 182 km/h, consumption 29.1 m/imp gal, 24.2 m/US gal, 9.7 l x 100 km; 195/70 HR x 13 tyres.

Rekord Series

PRICES EX WORKS:

1 Rekord 2-door Limousine	DM	13,640*
2 Rekord 4-door Limousine	DM	14,205*
3 Rekord 3-door Caravan	DM	14,195*
4 Rekord 5-door Caravan	DM	14,760*
5 Rekord L 2-door Limousine	DM	14,450*
6 Rekord L 4-door Limousine	DM	14,865*
7 Rekord L 5-door Caravan	DM	15,565*
8 Rekord « Berlina » 2-door Limousine	DM	15,175*
9 Rekord « Berlina » 4-door Limousine	DM	15,590*

For 90 hp engine add DM 472; for 100 hp engine add DM 608; for 110 hp engine add DM 2,068; for 60 hp Diesel engine add DM 2,935.

Power team:	Standard for:	Optional for:
60 hp	—	all
75 hp	all	—
90 hp	—	all
100 hp	—	all
110 hp	—	all
60 hp (Diesel)	—	all

OPEL Rekord L 4-door Limousine

60 hp power team

ENGINE front, 4 stroke; 4 cylinders, in line; 103.6 cu in, 1,698 cc (3.46 x 2.75 in, 88 x 69.8 mm); compression ratio: 8:1; max power (DIN): 60 hp (44.2 kW) at 4,800 rpm; max torque (DIN): 83 lb ft, 11.4 kg m (111.8 Nm) at 2,200-3,000 rpm; max engine rpm: 5,000; 35.3 hp/l (26 kW/l); cast iron block and head; 5 crankshaft bearings; valves: overhead, in line, rockers; camshafts: 1, overhead; lubrication: gear pump, full flow filter, 6.7 imp pt, 8 US pt, 3.8 l; 1 Solex 35 PDSI downdraught carburettor; fuel feed: mechanical pump; anti-freeze liquid cooled, 11.1 imp pt, 13.3 US pt, 6.3 l.

TRANSMISSION driving wheels: rear; clutch: single dry plate (diaphragm); gearbox: mechanical; gears: 4, fully synchronized; ratios: I 3.640, II 2.120, III 1.336, IV 1, rev 3.522; lever: central; final drive: hypoid bevel; axle ratio: 3.890; width of rims: 5.5''; tyres: 175 SR x 14.

PERFORMANCE max speed: 91 mph, 146 km/h; st. wagons 89 mph, 143 km/h; power-weight ratio: 4-dr. limousines 41 lb/hp (55.6 lb/kW), 18.6 kg/hp (25.2 kg/kW); speed in direct drive at 1,000 rpm: 18.3 mph, 29.4 km/h; consumption: 26.9 m/imp gal, 22.4 m/US gal, 10.5 l x 100 km - st. wagons 24.6 m/imp gal, 20.5 m/US gal, 11.5 l x 100 km.

CHASSIS integral; front suspension: independent, wishbones, lower trailing links, coil springs, anti-roll bar, telescopic dampers; rear: rigid axle, trailing lower radius

OPEL Rekord L 5-door Caravan

OPTIONAL ACCESSORIES 185/70 SR x 14 tyres with 5.5'' wide rims; sunshine roof; headrests: 55 Ah battery; 55 A alternator; halogen headlamps; heated rear window; metallic spray; headlamps with wiper-washers; rear window wiper-washer for st. Wagons only.

75 hp power team

See 60 hp power team, except for:

ENGINE 115.8 cu in, 1,897 cc (3.66 x 2.75 in, 93 x 69.8 mm); compression ratio: 7.9:1; max power (DIN): 75 hp (55.2 kW) at 4,800 rpm; max torque (DIN): 98 lb ft, 13.5 kg m (132.4 Nm) at 2,200-3,400 rpm; 39.5 hp/l (29.1 kW/l); cooling system: 10.9 imp pt, 13.1 US pt, 6.2 l.

TRANSMISSION axle ratio: 3.890.

PERFORMANCE max speed: 96 mph, 155 km/h - st. wagons 94 mph, 152 km/h; power-weight ratio: 4-dr. limousines 32.8 lb/hp (44.5 lb/kW), 14.9 kg/hp (20.2 kg/kW); speed in direct drive at 1,000 rpm: 19.4 mph, 31.2 km/h; consumption: 25.7 m/imp gal, 21.4 m/US gal, 11 l x 100 km - st. wagons 24.6 m/imp gal, 20.5 m/US gal, 11.5 l x 100 km.

OPTIONAL ACCESSORIES Opel automatic transmission with 3 ratios (I 2.400, II 1.480, III 1, rev 1.920), max ratio of converter at stall 2.5, possible manual selection, max speed 93 mph, 150 km/h (st. wagons 91 mph, 147 km/h), consumption 24.6 m/imp gal, 20.5 m/US gal, 11.5 l x 100 km - st. wagons 23.5 m/imp gal, 19.6 m/US gal, 12 l x 100 km.

90 hp power team

See 75 hp power team, except for:

ENGINE compression ratio: 8:1; max power (DIN): 90 hp (66.2 kW) at 5,200 rpm; max torque (DIN): 105 lb ft, 14.5 kg m (142.2 Nm) at 3,000-3,800 rpm; 47.4 hp/l (34.9 kW/l); valves: hydraulic tappets; 1 Varajet II downdraught carburettor; cooling system: 11.1 imp pt, 13.3 US pt, 6.3 l.

PERFORMANCE max speed: 103 mph, 165 km/h - st. wagons 101 mph, 162 km/h; power-weight ratio: 4-dr. limousines 27.3 lb/hp (37 lb/kW), 12.4 kg/hp (16.8 kg/kW); speed in direct drive at 1,000 rpm: 20.4 mph, 32.8 km/h; consumption: 24.6 m/imp gal, 20.5 m/US gal, 11.5 l x 100 km - st. wagons 23.5 m/imp gal, 19.6 m/US gal, 12 l x 100 km.

BRAKES rear compensator (for st. wagons only).

PRACTICAL INSTRUCTIONS valve timing: 32° 90° 72° 50°.

OPTIONAL ACCESSORIES with Opel automatic transmission, max speed 99 mph, 160 km/h - st. wagons 97 mph, 157 km/h, consumption 23.2 m/imp gal, 19.3 m/US gal, 12.2 l x 100 km - st. wagons 22.2 m/imp gal, 18.5 m/US gal, 12.7 l x 100 km; limited slip differential.

OPEL Rekord L 5-door Caravan

arms, upper torque arms, transverse linkage bar, coil springs, anti-roll bar, telescopic dampers.

STEERING recirculating ball; turns lock to lock: 4.

BRAKES front disc (diameter 9.37 in, 23.8 cm), rear drum, servo; lining area: total 85.7 sq in, 553 sq cm.

ELECTRICAL EQUIPMENT 12 V; 44 Ah battery; 45 A alternator; Bosch distributor; 2 headlamps.

DIMENSIONS AND WEIGHT wheel base: 105.04 in, 267 cm; tracks: 56.34 in, 143 cm front, 55.59 in, 141 cm rear; length: 108.75 in, 459 cm - st. wagons 181.81 in, 462 cm; width: 68.03 in, 173 cm; height: 55.71 in, 141 cm - st. wagons 56.69 in, 144 cm; ground clearance: 5.12 in, 13 cm; weight: 2-dr. limousines 2,414 lb, 1,095 kg - 4-dr. limousines 2,459 lb, 1,115 kg - 3-dr. Caravan 2,514 lb, 1,140 kg - 5-dr. Caravan 2,569 lb, 1,165 kg; turning circle (between walls): 37.4 ft, 11.4 m; fuel tank: 15.4 imp gal, 18.5 US gal, 70 l.

BODY 5 seats, separate front seats, reclining backrests.

PRACTICAL INSTRUCTIONS fuel: 92 oct petrol; oil: engine 6.7 imp pt, 8 US pt, 3.8 l, SAE 20W-30, change every 6,200 miles, 10,000 km - gearbox 1.9 imp pt, 2.3 US pt, 1.1 l, SAE 80, no change recommended - final drive 1.9 imp pt, 2.3 US pt, 1.1 l, SAE 90, no change recommended; greasing: none; sparking plug: 200°; tappet clearances (hot): inlet 0.012 in, 0.30 mm, exhaust 0.012 in, 0.30 mm; valve timing: 44° 86° 84° 46°; tyre pressure: front 24 psi, 1.7 atm, rear 25 psi, 1.8 atm.

OPEL Rekord E « Berlina » Diesel

100 hp power team

See 75 hp power team, except for:

ENGINE 120.8 cu in, 1,979 cc (3.74 x 2.75 in, 95 x 69.8 mm): compression ratio: 9:1; max power (DIN): 100 hp (73.6 kW) at 5,200 rpm; max torque (DIN): 114 lb ft, 15.8 kg m (155 Nm) at 3,400-3,800 rpm; max engine rpm: 5,500; 50.5 hp/l (37.2 kW/l); valves; hydraulic tappets; 1 Zenith 35/40 INAT downdraught carburettor; cooling system: 11.1 imp pt, 13.3 US pt, 6.3 l.

PERFORMANCE max speed: 107 mph, 173 km/h - st. wagons 106 mph, 170 km/h; power-weight ratio: 4-dr. limousines 24.6 lb/hp (33.3 lb/kW), 11.1 kg/hp (15.1 kg/kW): speed in direct drive at 1,000 rpm: 19.8 mph, 31.8 km/h; consumption: 27.7 m/imp gal, 23.1 m/US gal, 10.2 l x 100 km - st. wagons 26.4 m/imp gal, 22 m/US gal, 10.7 l x 100 km.

BRAKES rear compensator (for st. wagons only).

PRACTICAL INSTRUCTIONS fuel: 98 oct petrol; valve timing: 32° 90° 72° 50°.

OPTIONAL ACCESSORIES with Opel automatic transmission, max speed 104 mph, 168 km/h - st. wagons 103 mph, 165 km/h, consumption 25.7 m/imp gal, 21.4 m/US gal, 11 l x 100 km - st. wagons 24.6 m/imp gal, 20.5 m/US gal. 11.5 l x 100 km; limited slip differential.

110 hp power team

See 75 hp power team, except for:

ENGINE 120.8 cu in, 1,979 cc (3.74 x 2.75 in, 95 x 69.8 mm); compression ratio: 9.4:1; max power (DIN): 110 hp (81 kW) at 5,400 rpm; max torque (DIN): 117 lb ft, 16.2 kg m (158.9 Nm) at 3,000 rpm; max engine rpm: 6,000; 55.6 hp/l (40.9 kW/l); valves: hydraulic tappets; Bosch L-Jetronic electronic injection; cooling system: 16 imp pt, 19.2 US pt, 9.1 l.

PERFORMANCE max speed: 111 mph, 179 km/h - st. wagons 109 mph, 176 km/h; power-weight ratio: 4-dr. limousines 22.3 lb/hp (30.3 lb/kW), 10.1 kg/hp (13.8 kg/kW); speed in direct drive at 1,000 rpm: 18.6 mph, 30 km/h; consumption: 27.7 m/imp gal, 23.1 m/US gal, 10.2 l x 100 km - st. wagons 26.4 m/imp gal, 22 m/US gal, 10.7 l x 100 km.

BRAKES rear compensator (for st. wagons only).

PRACTICAL INSTRUCTIONS fuel: 98 oct petrol; valve timing: 34° 88° 74° 48°.

OPTIONAL ACCESSORIES with Opel automatic transmission, max speed 108 mph, 174 km/h - st. wagons 106 mph, 171 km/h, consumption 25.7 m/imp gal, 21.4 m/US gal, 11 l x 100 km - st. wagons 24.6 m/imp gal, 20.5 m/US gal. 11.5 l x 100 km; limited slip differential.

60 hp (Diesel) power team

See 60 hp power team, except for:

ENGINE Diesel; 126.2 cu in, 2,068 cc (3.46 x 3.35 in, 88 x 85 mm); compression ratio: 22:1; max power (DIN): 60 hp (44.2 kW) at 4,400 rpm; max torque (DIN) 12 kg m (117.7 Nm) at 2,500 rpm; max engine rpm: 4,600; 29 hp/l (21.3 kW/l); lubricating system: 9.7 imp pt, 11.6 US pt, 5.5 l; Bosch injection system; cooling system: 20.2 imp pt, 24.3 US pt, 11.5 l.

TRANSMISSION axle ratio: 3.670.

PERFORMANCE max speed: 84 mph, 135 km/h; power-weight ratio: 4-dr. limousines 45.9 lb/hp (62.4 lb/kW), 20.8 kg/hp (28.3 kg/kW); speed in direct drive at 1,000 rpm: 18 mph, 29 km/h; consumption: 31.4 m/imp gal, 26.1 m/US gal, 9 l x 100 km.

ELECTRICAL EQUIPMENT 88 Ah battery; 55 A alternator.

DIMENSIONS AND WEIGHT height: 56.50 in, 143 cm; weight: 2-dr. limousine 2,712 lb, 1,230 kg - 4-dr. limousines 2,756 lb, 1,250 kg - 3-dr. Caravan 2,789 lb, 1,265 kg - 5-dr. Caravan 2,844 lb, 1,290 kg.

PRACTICAL INSTRUCTIONS fuel: Diesel oil; oil: engine 9.7 imp pt, 11.6 US pt, 5.5 l; tappet clearances (hot): inlet 0.008 in, 0,20 mm, exhaust 0.008 in, 0,20 mm; valve timing: 24° 76° 48° 27°; tyre pressure: front 28 psi, 2 atm, rear 28 psi, 2 atm.

VARIATIONS

(only for Italy).
ENGINE 121.9 cu in, 1,998 cc (3.41 x 3.35 in, 86.5 x 85 mm), max power (DIN) 57 hp (42 kW) at 4,400 rpm, max torque (DIN) 83 lb ft, 11.5 kg m (112.8 Nm) at 2,200 rpm, 28.5 hp/l (21 kW/l).

OPEL Rekord (Diesel engine)

PORSCHE 924

PERFORMANCE max speed 81 mph, 130 km/h, power-weight ratio 4-dr. limousines 48.3 lb/hp (65.7 lb/kW), 21.9 kg/hp (29.8 kg/kW), consumption 37.7 m/imp gal, 31.4 m/US gal, 7.5 l x 100 km.

OPTIONAL ACCESSORIES with Opel automatic transmission, max speed 81 mph, 130 km/h, consumption 29.1 m/imp gal, 24.2 m/US gal, 9.7 l x 100 km; power steering; 185/70 SR x 14 tyres not available.

PORSCHE
GERMANY FR

924

PRICE IN GB: £ 7,530*
PRICE IN USA: $ 11,325*

ENGINE front, 4 stroke; 4 cylinders, vertical, in line; 121.1 cu in, 1,984 cc (3.41 x 3.32 in, 86.5 x 84.4 mm); compression ratio: 9.3:1; max power (DIN): 125 hp (92 kW) at 5,800 rpm; max torque (DIN): 122 lb ft, 16.8 kg m (164.8 Nm) at 3,500 rpm; max engine rpm: 6,500; 63 hp/l (46.3 kW/l); cast iron block, light alloy head: 5 crankshaft bearings; valves: overhead, in line, thimble tappets; camshafts: 1, overhead, cogged belt; lubrication: gear pump, full flow filter, 8.8 imp pt, 10.6 US pt, 5 l; Bosch K-Jetronic injection system; fuel feed: electric pump; water-cooled, 14.1 imp pt, 16.9 US pt, 8 l, electric thermostatic fan.

TRANSMISSION driving wheels: rear; clutch: single dry plate; gearbox: mechanical, in unit with differential; gears: 4, fully synchronized; ratios: I 3.600, II 2.125, III 1.360, IV 0.966, rev 3.500; lever: central; final drive: hypoid bevel; axle ratio: 3.444; width of rims: 5.5''; tyres: 165 HR x 14.

PERFORMANCE max speeds: (I) 35 mph, 56 km/h; (II) 60 mph, 96 km/h; (III) 93 mph, 150 km/h; (IV) 125 mph, 200 km/h; power-weight ratio: 19 lb/hp (26 lb/kW), 8.6 kg/hp (11.7 kg/kW); carrying capacity: 706 lb, 320 kg; speed in top at 1,000 rpm: 19.5 mph, 31.4 km/h; consumption: 36.7 m/imp gal, 30.5 m/US gal, 7.7 l x 100 km.

CHASSIS integral; front suspension: independent, by McPherson, lower wishbones, coil springs/telescopic damper struts; rear: independent, semi-trailing radius arms, transverse guide by oblique rods, transverse torsion bars, coil springs/telescopic damper struts.

STEERING rack-and-pinion.

BRAKES front disc, rear drum, 2 X circuits, servo; lining area: front 20.2 sq in, 130 sq cm, rear 37.2 sq in, 240 sq cm, total 57.4 sq in, 370 sq cm.

ELECTRICAL EQUIPMENT 12 V; 45 Ah battery; 1,050 W alternator; Bosch electronic ignition; 4 headlamps (2 retractable).

PORSCHE 924

DIMENSIONS AND WEIGHT wheel base: 94.49 in, 240 cm; tracks: 55.83 in, 142 cm front, 54.02 in, 137 cm rear; length: 165.35 in, 420 cm; width: 66.34 in, 168 cm; height: 50 in, 127 cm; weight: 2,381 lb, 1,080 kg; fuel tank: 13.6 imp gal, 16.4 US gal, 62 l.

BODY coupé; 2 doors; 2 + 2 seats, separate front seats, reclining backrests with built-in headrests; heated rear window.

PRACTICAL INSTRUCTIONS fuel: 98 oct petrol; oil: engine 8.8 imp pt, 10.6 US pt, 5 l, SAE 30W (summer), 20W (winter), Change every 6,100 miles, 10,000 km - gearbox and final drive 4.6 imp pt, 5.5 US pt, 2.6 l, SAE 80; greasing: none; sparking plug: 225°.

OPTIONAL ACCESSORIES automatic transmission, hydraulic torque converter and planetary gears with 3 ratios (I 2.551, II 1.448, III 1, rev 2.461), max ratio of converter at stall 2.1, possible manual selection, 3.454 axle ratio, max speed 121 mph, 195 km/h, consumption 29.7 m/imp gal, 24.8 m/US gal, 9.5 l x 100 km; 5-speed fully synchronized mechanical gearbox (I 2.780, II 1.720, III 1.210, IV 0.930, V 0.700, rev 2.500), 4.714 axle ratio; anti-roll bar on front and rear suspensions; 6'' wide rims light alloy wheels with 185/70 HR x 14 tyres: air-conditioning; sunshine roof; fog lamps; 63 Ah battery.

911 SC Coupé

PRICE IN GB: £ 12,600*
PRICE IN USA: $ 17,950*

ENGINE rear, 4 stroke; 6 cylinders, horizontally opposed; 182.7 cu in, 2,994 cc (3.74 x 2.77 in, 95 x 70.4 mm); compression ratio: 8.5:1; max power (DIN) 180 hp (132.5 kW) at 5,500 rpm; max torque (DIN): 196 lb ft, 27 kg m (264.8 Nm) at 4,200 rpm; max engine rpm: 7,000; 60.1 hp/l (42.3 kW/l); light alloy block with cast iron liners, light alloy head; 8 crankshaft bearings; valves: overhead, Vee-slanted, rockers; camshafts: 1 per block, overhead, double cogged belt; lubrication: gear pump, full flow filter, dry sump, thermostatically-controlled oil cooler, 22.9 imp pt, 27.5 US pt, 13 l; Bosch K-Jetronic fuel injection system; fuel feed: electric pump; air-cooled.

TRANSMISSION driving wheels: rear; clutch: single dry plate; gearbox: mechanical; gears: 5, fully synchronized; ratios: I 3.181, II 1.833, III 1.261, IV 1, V 0.821, rev 3.325; lever: central; final drive: spiral bevel; axle ratio: 3.875; width of rims: 6'' front, 7'' rear; tyres: 185/70 VR x 15 front, 215/60 VR x 15 rear.

PERFORMANCE max speed: over 136 mph, 220 km/h; power-weight ratio: 14.2 lb/hp (19.3 lb/kW), 6.4 kg/hp (8.7 kg/kW); carrying capacity: 750 lb, 340 kg; speed in top at 1,000 rpm: 25 mph, 40 km/h; consumption: 25.7 m/imp gal, 21.4 m/US gal, 11 l x 100 km.

CHASSIS integral; front suspension: independent, by McPherson, coil springs/telescopic damper struts, longitudinal torsion bars, lower wishbones, anti-roll bar; rear: independent, semi-trailing radius arms, transverse guide by oblique rods, transverse torsion bars, anti-roll bar, telescopic dampers.

STEERING ZF rack-and-pinion; turns lock to lock: 3.10.

PORSCHE 911 SC Coupé

PORSCHE Turbo Coupé

BRAKES disc (front diameter 9.25 in, 23.5 cm, rear 9.61 in, 24.4 cm), internal radial fins; lining area: total 47.1 sq in, 304 sq cm.

ELECTRICAL EQUIPMENT 12 V; 66 Ah battery; 980 W alternator; Bosch electronic ignition; 2 iodine headlamps.

DIMENSIONS AND WEIGHT wheel base: 89.41 in, 227 cm; tracks: 54.02 in, 137 cm front, 54.33 in, 138 cm; length: 168.90 in, 429 cm; width: 64.96 in, 165 cm; height: 51.97 in, 132 cm; ground clearance: 4.72 in, 12 cm; weight: 2,558 lb, 1,160 kg; turning circle (between walls): 35.8 ft, 10.9 m; fuel tank: 17.6 imp gal, 21.1 US gal, 80 l.

BODY coupé; 2 doors; 2 + 2 seats, separate front seats, adjustable backrests, built-in headrests; heated rear window; light alloy wheels.

PRACTICAL INSTRUCTIONS fuel: 91 oct petrol; oil: engine 17.6 imp pt, 21.1 US pt, 10 l, SAE 30 (summer) 20 (winter), change every 6,200 miles, 10,000 km - gearbox and final drive 5.3 imp pt, 6.3 US pt, 3 l, SAE 90, change every 6,200 miles, 10,000 km; greasing: none; sparking plug: 225°; tappet clearances: inlet 0.004 in, 0.10 mm, exhaust 0.004 in, 0.10 mm; valve timing: 35° 50° 40° 20°; tyre pressure: front 29 psi, 2 atm, rear 34 psi, 2.4 atm.

OPTIONAL ACCESSORIES Sportomatic semi-automatic transmission with 3 ratios (I 2.400, II 1.429, III 0.926, rev 2.534), single dry plate clutch automatically operated by gear lever, hydraulic torque converter, max ratio of converter at stall 2.18, 3.375 axle ratio; Sportomatic transmission clutch; ZF limited slip differential (only with mechanical gearbox); independent heating; air-conditioning; electric sunshine roof; electric windows; rear window wiper-washer; tinted glass; 88 Ah battery; 205/55 VR x 16 front tyres; 225/50 VR x 16 rear tyres; metallic spray.

911 SC Targa

See 911 SC Coupé, except for:

PRICE IN GB: £ 14,100*
PRICE EX WORKS: 42,700* marks

BODY convertible; roll bar, detachable roof.

Turbo Coupé

See 911 SC Coupé, except for:

PRICE IN GB: £ 23,200*
PRICE IN USA: $ 34,000*

ENGINE 201.3 cu in, 3,299 cc (3.82 x 2.93 in, 97 x 74.4 mm); compression ratio: 7:1; max power (DIN): 300 hp (220.1 kW) at 5,500 rpm; max torque (DIN): 304 lb ft, 42 kg m (411.9 Nm) at 4,000 rpm; max engine rpm: 6,800; 90.9 hp/l (66.7 kW/l); Bosch K-Jetronic fuel injection system with KKK 3 LDZ centrifugal compressor, mounted co-axially with exhaust driven turbine; fuel feed: 2 electric pumps.

TRANSMISSION gearbox ratios: I 2.250, II 1.304, III 0.893, IV 0.656, rev 3.325; axle ratio: 4.222; width of rims: 7'' front, 8'' rear; tyres: 205/55 VR x 16 front, 225/50 VR x 16 rear.

PORSCHE Turbo Coupé

TURBO COUPÉ

PERFORMANCE max speed: over 162 mph, 260 km/h; power-weight ratio: 9.6 lb/hp (13 lb/kW), 4.3 kg/hp (5.9 kg/kW); carrying capacity: 838 lb, 380 kg; speed in top at 1,000 rpm: 29.3 mph, 47.2 km/h; consumption: 26.9 m/imp gal, 22.4 m/US gal, 10.5 l x 100 km.

DIMENSIONS AND WEIGHT tracks: 56.30 in, 143 cm front, 59.06 in, 150 cm rear; width: 69.68 in, 177 cm; height: 51.57 in, 131 cm; weight: 2,867 lb, 1,300 kg; turning circle (between walls): 35.1 ft, 10.7 m.

BODY rear window wiper-washer (standard).

PRACTICAL INSTRUCTIONS fuel: 96 oct petrol; oil: gearbox and final drive 6.5 imp pt, 7.8 US pt, 3.7 l; sparking plug: 280°.

OPTIONAL ACCESSORIES only limited slip differential, electric sunshine roof and air-conditioning.

928

PRICE IN USA: $ 24,880*
PRICE EX WORKS: 55,000* marks

ENGINE front, 4 stroke; 8 cylinders, Vee-slanted at 90°; 273 cu in, 4,474 cc (3.74 x 3.11 in, 95 x 78.9 mm); compression ratio: 8.5:1; max power (DIN): 240 hp (176.6 kW) at 5,250 rpm; max torque (DIN): 268 lb ft, 37 kg m (362.9 Nm) at 3,600 rpm; 53.6 hp/l (39.5 kW/l); light alloy block and head; 5 crankshaft bearings; valves: overhead, in line, hydraulic tappets; camshafts: 1 per block, overhead, cogged belt; lubrication: gear pump, full flow filter, 11.4 imp pt, 13.7 US pt, 6.5 l; Bosch K-Jetronic electronic injection; fuel feed: 2 electric pumps; water-cooled, 28.2 imp pt, 33.8 US pt, 16 l.

TRANSMISSION driving wheels: rear; clutch: single dry plate; gearbox: mechanical, in unit with differential; gears: 5, fully synchronized; ratios: I 3.601, II 2.466, III 1.819, IV 1.343, V 1, rev 3.162; lever: central; final drive: hypoid bevel; axle ratio: 2.750; width of rims: 7''; tyres: 225/50 VR x 16.

PERFORMANCE max speed: over 143 mph, 230 km/h; power-weight ratio: 13.3 lb/hp, (18.1 lb/kW), 6 kg/hp (8.2 kg/kW); carrying capacity: 926 lb, 420 kg; speed in direct drive at 1,000 rpm: 26.5 mph, 42.6 km/h; consumption: 21.7 m/imp gal, 18.1 m/US gal, 13 l x 100 km.

CHASSIS integral; front suspension: independent, wishbones, coil springs/telescopic damper struts, anti-roll bar; rear: independent, Weissach axle, wishbones, semi-trailing radius arms, transverse guide by oblique rods, transverse torsion bars, coil springs/telescopic damper struts.

STEERING rack-and-pinion.

BRAKES disc (front diameter 11.10 in, 28.2 cm, rear 11.38 in, 28.9 cm), internal radial fins, servo; lining area: total 49.3 sq in, 318 sq cm.

PORSCHE 928

PORSCHE 928

ELECTRICAL EQUIPMENT 12 V; 66 Ah battery; 1,260 W alternator; electronic ignition; 2 retractable headlamps.

DIMENSIONS AND WEIGHT wheel base: 98.43 in, 250 cm; tracks: 60.63 in, 154 cm front, 59.45 in, 151 cm rear; length: 175.20 in, 445 cm; width: 72.44 in, 184 cm; height: 51.57 in, 131 cm; weight: 3,197 lb, 1,450 kg; fuel tank: 18.9 imp gal, 22.7 US gal, 86 l.

BODY coupé; 2 doors; 2 + 2 seats, separate front seats, reclining backrests with built-in headrests.

PRACTICAL INSTRUCTIONS fuel: 91 oct petrol; oil: engine 11.4 imp pt, 13.7 US pt, 6.5 l - gearbox and final drive 6.7 imp pt, 8 US pt, 3.8 l.

OPTIONAL ACCESSORIES automatic transmission with 3 ratios (I 2.310, II 1.460, III 1, rev 1.840), max ratio of converter at stall 2, possible manual selection; limited slip differential; 88 Ah battery; air-conditioning; metallic spray; rear window wiper-washer.

VOLKSWAGEN   GERMANY FR

Polo Series

PRICES IN GB AND EX WORKS:	£	DM
1 Polo 2-door Limousine	2,198*	8,620*
2 Polo L 2-door Limousine	2,487*	9,255*
3 Polo S 2-door Limousine	—	8,925*
4 Polo LS 2-door Limousine	2,699*	9,560*
5 Polo GLS 2-door Limousine	—	10,255*

For 60 hp engine add DM 570 (GLS add DM 265).

Power team:	Standard for:	Optional for:
40 hp	1,2	—
50 hp	3 to 5	—
60 hp	—	4,5

40 hp power team

ENGINE front, transverse, slanted 15° to front, 4 stroke; 4 cylinders, in line; 54.6 cu in, 895 cc (2.74 x 2.32 in, 69.5 x 59 mm); compression ratio: 8:1; max power (DIN): 40 hp (29.4 kW) at 5,900 rpm; max torque (DIN): 45 lb ft, 6.2 kg m (60.8 Nm) at 3,500 rpm; max engine rpm; 6,000: 44.7 hp/l (32.8 kW/l); cast iron block, light alloy head; 5 crankshaft bearings; valves: overhead, in line, thimble tappets; camshafts: 1, overhead, cogged belt; lubrication: gear pump, full flow filter, 6.2 imp pt, 7.4 US pt, 3.5 l; 1 Solex 31 PICT-5 downdraught single barrel carburettor; fuel feed: mechanical pump; water-cooled, 8.8 imp pt, 10.6 US pt, 5 l, electric thermostatic fan.

TRANSMISSION driving wheels: front; clutch: single dry plate; gearbox: mechanical; gears: 4, fully synchronized; ratios: I 3.454, II 2.050, III 1.347, IV 0.963, rev 3.384; lever: central; final drive: spiral bevel; axle ratio: 4.571; width of rims: 4.5''; tyres: 135 SR x 13.

VOLKSWAGEN Polo 2-door Limousine

PERFORMANCE max speeds: (I) 27 mph, 43 km/h; (II) 46 mph, 74 km/h; (III) 62 mph, 110 km/h; (IV) 82 mph, 132 km/h; power-weight ratio: 37.7 lb/hp (51.4 lb/kW), 17.1 kg/hp (23.3 kg/kW); carrying capacity: 915 lb, 415 kg; acceleration: 0-50 mph (0-80 km/h) 12.7 sec; speed in top at 1,000 rpm: 14.2 mph, 22.8 km/h; consumption: 38.7 m/imp gal, 32.2 m/US gal, 7.3 l x 100 km.

CHASSIS integral; front suspension: independent, by McPherson, lower wishbones, anti-roll bar, coil springs/telescopic damper struts; rear: independent, longitudinal trailing radius arms, coil springs/telescopic damper struts.

STEERING rack-and-pinion; turns lock to lock: 3.25.

BRAKES front disc, rear drum, 2 X circuits.

ELECTRICAL EQUIPMENT 12 V; 36 Ah battery; 35 A alternator; Bosch distributor; 2 headlamps.

DIMENSIONS AND WEIGHT wheel base: 91.93 in, 233 cm; tracks: 51.02 in, 130 cm front, 51.65 in, 131 cm rear: length: 139.37 in, 354 cm; width: 61.38 in, 156 cm; height: 52.91 in, 134 cm; ground clearance: 4.72 in, 12 cm; weight: 1,510 lb, 685 kg; turning circle (between walls): 31.5 ft, 9.6 m; fuel tank: 7.9 imp gal, 9.5 US gal, 36 l.

BODY saloon/sedan; 2 + 1 doors; 4-5 seats, separate front seats, reclining backrests with built-in headrests; heated rear window; folding rear seat.

VOLKSWAGEN Polo 2-door Limousine

VOLKSWAGEN Derby LS 2-door Limousine

PRACTICAL INSTRUCTIONS fuel: 91 oct petrol; oil: engine 5.3 imp pt, 6.3 US pt, 3 l, SAE 20W-30, change every 4,700 miles, 7,500 km - gearbox and final drive 4 imp pt, 4.9 US pt, 2.3 l, SAE 80 or 90; greasing: none; sparking plug: 175º; tyre pressure: front 26 psi, 1.8 atm, rear 28 psi, 2 atm.

OPTIONAL ACCESSORIES rear window wiper-washer; halogen headlamps; 155/70 SR x 13 tyres; sunshine roof; metallic spray.

50 hp power team

See 40 hp power team, except for:

ENGINE 66.7 cu in, 1,093 cc (2.74 x 2.83 in, 69.5 x 72 mm); max power (DIN): 50 hp (36.8 kW) at 5,900 rpm; max torque (DIN): 56 lb ft, 7.7 kg m (75.5 Nm) at 3,500 rpm; 47.5 hp/l (33.7 kW/l); cooling system: 10.9 imp pt, 13.1 US pt, 6.2 l.

TRANSMISSION tyres: 145 SR x 13.

PERFORMANCE max speed: 88 mph, 142 km/h; power-weight ratio: 30.2 lb/hp (41 lb/kW), 13.7 kg/hp (18.6 kg/kW); acceleration: 0-50 mph (0-80 km/h) 9.6 sec; consumption: 37.2 m/imp gal, 30.9 m/US gal, 7.6 l x 100 km.

BRAKES servo.

VOLKSWAGEN Derby LS 2-door Limousine

60 hp power team

See 40 hp power team, except for:

ENGINE 77.6 cu in, 1,272 cc (2.95 x 2.83 in, 75 x 72 mm); compression ratio: 8.2:1; max power (DIN): 60 hp (44.2 kW) at 5,600 rpm; max torque (DIN): 70 lb ft, 9.7 kg m (95.1 Nm) at 3,400 rpm; 47.2 hp/l (34.7 kW/l); cooling system: 10.9 imp pt, 13.1 US pt, 6.2 l.

TRANSMISSION axle ratio: 4.063; tyres: 145 SR x 13.

PERFORMANCE max speed: 94 mph, 152 km/h; power-weight ratio: 25.2 lb/hp (34.2 lb/kW), 11.4 kg/hp (15.5 kg/kW); acceleration: 0-50 mph (0-80 km/h) 8.3 sec; consumption: 34 m/imp gal, 28.3 m/US gal, 8.3 l x 100 km.

CHASSIS rear suspension: anti-roll bar.

BRAKES rear compensator, servo.

Derby Series

PRICES EX WORKS:

1 Derby 2-door Limousine	DM	9,055*
2 Derby L 2-door Limousine	DM	9,690*
3 Derby S 2-door Limousine	DM	9,360*
4 Derby LS 2-door Limousine	DM	9,995*
5 Derby GLS 2-door Limousine	DM	10,535*

For 60 hp engine add DM 570 (for GLS add DM 265).

Power team:	Standard for:	Optional for:
40 hp	1,2	—
50 hp	3 to 5	—
60 hp	—	4,5

40 hp power team

ENGINE front, transverse, slanted 15º to front, 4 stroke; 4 cylinders, in line; 54.6 cu in, 895 cc (2.74 x 2.32 in, 69.5 x 59 mm); compression ratio: 8:1; max power (DIN): 40 hp (29.4 kW) at 5,900 rpm; max torque (DIN): 45 lb ft, 6.2 kg m (60.8 Nm) at 3,500 rpm; max engine rpm: 6,000; 44.7 hp/l (32.8 kW/l); cast iron block, light alloy head; 5 crankshaft bearings; valves: overhead, in line, thimble tappets; camshafts: 1, overhead, cogged belt; lubrication: gear pump, full flow filter, 6.2 imp pt, 7.4 US pt, 3.5 l; 1 Solex 35 PICT-5 downdraught single barrel carburettor; fuel feed: mechanical pump; water-cooled, 8.8 imp pt, 10.6 US pt, 5 l, electric thermostatic fan.

TRANSMISSION driving wheels: front; clutch: single dry plate; gearbox: mechanical; gears: 4, fully synchronized; ratios: I 3.454, II 2.050, III 1.347, IV 0.963, rev 3.384; lever: central; final drive: spiral bevel; axle ratio: 4.571; width of rims: 4.5''; tyres: 145 SR x 13.

PERFORMANCE max speeds: (I) 27 mph, 43 km/h; (II) 46 mph, 74 km/h; (III) 62 mph, 110 km/h; (IV) 82 mph, 132 km/h; power-weight ratio: 38.6 lb/hp (52.5 lb/kW), 17.5 kg/hp (23.8 kg/kW); carrying capacity: 948 lb, 430 kg; acceleration: 0-50 mph (0-80 km/h) 12.7 sec; speed in top at 1,000 rpm: 14.2 mph, 22.8 km/h; consumption: 38.7 m/imp gal, 32.2 m/US gal, 7.3 l x 100 km.

CHASSIS integral; front suspension: independent, by McPherson, lower wishbones, anti-roll bar, coil springs/telescopic damper struts; rear: independent, longitudinal trailing radius arms, coil springs/telescopic damper struts.

STEERING rack-and-pinion; turns lock to lock: 3.25.

BRAKES front disc (diameter 9.41 in, 23.9 cm), rear drum, 2 x circuits; lining area: front 16.3 sq in, 105 sq cm, rear 45.6 sq in, 189 sq cm, total 61.9 sq in, 294 sq cm.

ELECTRICAL EQUIPMENT 12 V; 36 Ah battery; 35 A alternator; Bosch distributor; 2 headlamps.

DIMENSIONS AND WEIGHT wheel base: 91.93 in, 233 cm; tracks: 51.02 in, 130 cm front, 51.65 in, 131 cm rear; length: 152.20 in, 387 cm; width: 61.38 in, 156 cm; height: 53.23 in, 135 cm; ground clearance: 3.74 in, 9.5 cm; weight: 1,544 lb, 700 kg; turning circle (between walls): 31.5 ft, 9.6 m; fuel tank: 7.9 imp gal, 9.5 US gal, 36 l.

BODY saloon/sedan; 2 doors; 4-5 seats, separate front seats, reclining backrests with built-in headrests; heated rear window.

PRACTICAL INSTRUCTIONS fuel: 91 oct petrol; oil: engine 5.3 imp pt, 6.3 US pt, 3 l, SAE 20W-30, change every 4,700 miles, 7,500 km - gearbox and final drive 4 imp pt, 4.9 US pt, 2.3 l, SAE 80 or 90; greasing: none; sparking plug: 175º; tyre pressure: front 26 psi, 1.8 atm, rear 28 psi, 2 atm.

OPTIONAL ACCESSORIES 155/70 SR x 13 tyres; metallic spray; sunshine roof; halogen headlamps.

50 hp power team

See 40 hp power team, except for:

ENGINE 66.7 cu in, 1,093 cc (2.74 x 2.83 in, 69.5 x 72 mm); max power (DIN): 50 hp (36.8 kW) at 5,800 rpm; max torque (DIN): 56 lb ft, 7.7 kg m (75.5 Nm) at 3,500 rpm; 47.5 hp/l (33.7 kW/l); cooling system: 10.9 imp pt, 13.1 US pt, 6.2 l.

TRANSMISSION axle ratio: 4.267.

PERFORMANCE max speed: 88 mph, 142 km/h; power-weight ratio: 30.9 lb/hp (41.9 lb/kW), 14 kg/hp (19 kg/kW); acceleration: 0-50 mph (0-80 km/h) 9.6 sec; speed in top at 1,000 rpm: 15.7 mph, 25.2 km/h; consumption: 37.2 m/imp gal, 30.9 m/US gal, 7.6 l x 100 km.

BRAKES servo.

60 hp power team

See 40 hp power team, except for:

ENGINE 77.6 cu in, 1,272 cc (2.95 x 2.83 in, 75 x 72 mm); compression ratio: 8.2:1; max power (DIN): 60 hp (44.2 kW) at 5,600 rpm; max torque (DIN): 70 lb ft, 9.7 kg m (95.1 Nm) at 3,400 rpm; 47.2 hp/l (34.7 kW/l); cooling system: 10.9 imp pt, 13.1 US pt, 6.2 l.

TRANSMISSION axle ratio: 4.063.

VOLKSWAGEN Golf LS 2-door Limousine

50 hp power team

ENGINE front, transverse, slanted 15° to front, 4 stroke; 4 cylinders, vertical, in line; 66.7 cu in, 1,093 cc (2.74 x 2.83 in, 69.5 x 72 mm); compression ratio: 8:1; max power (DIN): 50 hp (36.8 kW) at 6,000 rpm; max torque (DIN): 57 lb ft, 7.9 kg m (77.5 Nm) at 3,000 rpm; 45.7 hp/l (33.7 kW/l); cast iron block, light alloy head; 5 crankshaft bearings; valves: overhead, in line, thimble tappets; camshafts: 1, overhead, cogged belt; lubrication: gear pump, full flow filter, 5.3 imp pt, 6.3 US pt, 3 l; 1 Solex 35 PICT-5 downdraught single barrel carburettor; fuel feed: mechanical pump; liquid-cooled, expansion tank, 10.9 imp pt, 13.1 US pt, 6.2 l, electric thermostatic fan.

TRANSMISSION driving wheels: front; clutch: single dry plate, hydraulically controlled; gearbox: mechanical; gears: 4, fully synchronized; ratios: I 3.454, II 2.055, III 1.350, IV 0.960, rev 3.390; lever: central; final drive: spiral bevel; axle ratio: 4.570; width of rims: 4.5''; tyres: 145 SR x 13.

PERFORMANCE max speed: 87 mph, 140 km/h; power-weight ratio: 2-dr. limousines 33 lb/hp (44.9 lb/kW), 15 kg/hp (20.4 kg/kW) - 4-dr. limousines 34.2 lb/hp (46.4 lb/kW), 15.5 kg/hp (21.1 kg/kW); carrying capacity: 2-dr. limousines 992 lb, 450 kg - 4-dr. limousines 937 lb, 425 kg; acceleration: 0-50 mph (0-80 km/h) 10 sec; speed in top at 1,000 rpm: 14.9 mph, 24 km/h; consumption: 34 m/imp gal, 28.3 m/US gal, 8.3 l x 100 km.

CHASSIS integral; front suspension: independent, by McPherson, lower wishbones, coil springs/telescopic damper struts; rear: independent, swinging longitudinal trailing arms linked by a T-section cross-beam, coil springs/telescopic damper struts.

STEERING rack-and-pinion.

BRAKES front disc, rear drum, 2 X circuits.

ELECTRICAL EQUIPMENT 12 V; 36 Ah battery; 36 A alternator; Bosch distributor; 2 headlamps.

DIMENSIONS AND WEIGHT wheel base: 94.49 in, 240 cm; tracks: 54.72 in, 139 cm front, 53.46 in, 136 cm rear; length: 146.65 in, 372 cm; width: 63.39 in, 161 cm; height: 55.51 in, 141 cm; ground clearance: 4.92 in, 12.5 cm; weight: 2-dr. limousines 1,654 lb, 750 kg - 4-dr. limousines 1,709 lb, 775 kg; turning circle (between walls): 33.8 ft, 10.3 m; fuel tank: 8.8 imp gal, 10 US gal, 40 l.

BODY saloon/sedan; 5 seats, separate front seats; folding rear seat; heated rear window.

PRACTICAL INSTRUCTIONS fuel: 90 oct petrol; oil: engine 5.3 imp pt, 6.3 US pt, 3 l, SAE 20W-30, change every 4,700 miles, 7,500 km - gearbox and final drive 3.2 imp pt, 3.8 US pt, 1.8 l, SAE 80 or 90; sparking plug: 175°; tyre pressure: front 26 psi, 1.8 atm, rear 26 psi, 1.8 atm.

OPTIONAL ACCESSORIES 5'' rim sports wheels; 175/70 SR x 13 tyres with 5'' wide rims; 155 SR x 13 tyres with 4.5'' wide rims; servo brake; halogen headlamps; sunshine roof; built-in headrests on front seats; metallic spray; rear window wiper-washer.

VOLKSWAGEN Golf 4-door Limousine

PERFORMANCE max speed: 94 mph, 152 km/h; power-weight ratio: 25.7 lb/hp (34.9 lb/kW), 11.7 kg/hp (15.8 kg/kW); acceleration: 0-50 mph (0-80 km/h) 8.3 sec; speed in top at 1,000 rpm: 16.4 mph, 26.4 km/h; consumption: 34 m/imp gal, 28.3 m/US gal, 8.3 l x 100 km.

CHASSIS rear suspension: anti-roll bar.

BRAKES rear compensator, servo.

Golf Series

PRICES IN GB, IN USA AND EX WORKS:

	£	$	DM
1 Golf 2-door Limousine	2,487*	4,030*	9,540*
2 Golf 4-door Limousine	2,699*	—	10,075*
3 Golf L 2-door Limousine	2,799*	4,509*	10,250*
4 Golf L 4-door Limousine	2,959*	4,649*	10,785*
5 Golf GL 2-door Limousine	—	4,845*	11,030*
6 Golf GL 4-door Limousine	—	4,985*	11,565*
7 Golf S 2-door Limousine	—	—	10,360*
8 Golf S 4-door Limousine	—	—	10,895*
9 Golf LS 2-door Limousine	3,019*	—	11,070*
10 Golf LS 4-door Limousine	—	—	11,605*
11 Golf GLS 2-door Limousine	—	—	11,850*
12 Golf GLS 4-door Limousine	3,292*	—	12,385*
13 Golf GTI 2-door Limousine	3,986*	—	14,435*

Power team:	Standard for:	Optional for:
50 hp	1 to 6	—
70 hp	7 to 12	—
110 hp	13	—

VOLKSWAGEN Golf GTI 2-door Limousine

70 hp power team

See 50 hp power team, except for:

ENGINE front, transverse, slanted 15° to rear; 88.9 cu in, 1,457 cc (3.13 x 2.89 in, 79.5 x 73.4 mm); compression ratio: 8.2:1; max power (DIN): 70 hp (51.5 kW) at 5,600 rpm; max torque (DIN): 81 lb ft, 11.2 kg m (109.8 Nm) at 2,500 rpm; 48 hp/l (35.3 kW/l); 1 Solex 34 PICT-5 downdraught single barrel carburettor.

TRANSMISSION gearbox ratios: I 3.454, II 1.960, III 1.370, IV 0.970, rev 3.170; axle ratio: 3.900; width of rims: 5''; tyres: 155 SR x 13 (standard).

PERFORMANCE max speed: 98 mph, 158 km/h; power-weight ratio: 2-dr. limousines 24.6 lb/hp (33.4 lb/kW), 11.1 kg/hp (15.1 kg/kW) - 4-dr. limousines 25.4 lb/hp (34.5 lb/kW), 11.5 kg/hp (15.6 kg/kW); acceleration: 0-50 mph (0-80 km/h) 8.2 sec; speed in top at 1,000 rpm: 17.3 mph, 27.8 km/h; consumption: 32.8 m/imp gal, 27.3 m/US gal, 8.6 l x 100 km.

BRAKES front disc, rear drum, servo (standard).

ELECTRICAL EQUIPMENT halogen headlamps (standard).

DIMENSIONS AND WEIGHT weight: 2-dr. limousines 1,720 lb, 780 kg - 4-dr. limousines 1,775 lb, 805 kg.

OPTIONAL ACCESSORIES automatic transmission, hydraulic torque converter and planetary gears with 3 ratios (I 2.550, II 1.450, III 1, rev 2.410), max ratio of converter at stall 2.44, possible manual selection, central lever, 3.760 axle ratio, max speed 95 mph, 153 km/h, acceleration 0-50 mph (0-80 km/h) 9.4 sec, consumption 30.7 m/imp gal, 25.6 m/US gal, 9.2 l x 100 km.

110 hp power team

See 50 hp power team, except for:

ENGINE front, transverse, slanted 20° to rear; 96.9 cu in, 1,588 cc (3.13 x 3.15 in, 79.5 x 80 mm); compression ratio: 9.5:1; max power (DIN): 110 hp (81 kW) at 6,100 rpm; max torque (DIN): 101 lb ft, 14 kg m (137.3 Nm) at 5,000 rpm; max engine rpm: 6,900; 69.3 hp/l (51 kW/l); Bosch K-Jetronic electronic injection; fuel feed: electric pump.

TRANSMISSION gearbox ratios: I 3.454, II 1.960, III 1.370, IV 0.970, rev 3.170; axle ratio: 3.900; width of rims: 5.5''; tyres: 175/70 HR x 13 (standard).

PERFORMANCE max speed: 113 mph, 182 km/h; power-weight ratio: 16.2 lb/hp (22 lb/kW), 7.4 kg/hp (10 kg/kW); carrying capacity: 926 lb, 420 kg; acceleration: 0-50 mph (0-80 km/h) 6.1 sec; speed in top at 1,000 rpm: 18.5 mph, 29.8 km/h; consumption: 35.3 m/imp gal, 29.4 m/US gal, 8 l x 100 km.

BRAKES front disc, rear drum, rear compensator, servo (standard).

ELECTRICAL EQUIPMENT 55 A alternator; 2 halogen headlamps (standard).

DIMENSIONS AND WEIGHT tracks: 55.28 in, 140 cm front, 54.02 in, 137 cm rear; width: 64.09 in, 163 cm; height: 54.72 in, 139 cm; weight: 1,786 lb, 810 kg.

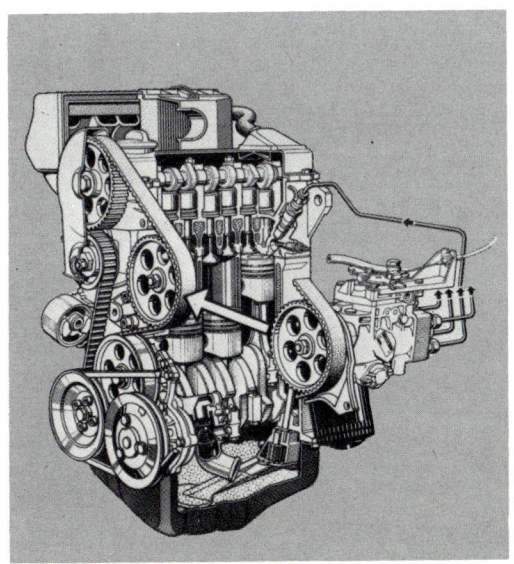

VOLKSWAGEN Golf D

VOLKSWAGEN Golf

4, fully synchronized; ratios: I 3.454, II 2.055, III 1.350, IV 0.960, rev 3.390; lever: central; final drive: spiral bevel; axle ratio: 4.570; width of rims: 4.5''; tyres: 145 SR x 13.

PERFORMANCE max speed: 87 mph, 140 km/h; power-weight ratio: 2-dr. limousines 35.5 lb/hp (48.2 lb/hp), 16.1 kg/hp (21.9 kg/kW) - 4-dr. limousines 36.6 lb/hp (49.7 lb/hp), 16.6 kg/hp (22.6 kg/kW); carrying capacity: 2-dr. limousines 981 lb, 445 kg - 4-dr. limousines 926 lb, 420 kg; acceleration: 0-50 mph (0-80 km/h) 11.5 sec; speed in top at 1,000 rpm: 17.4 mph, 28 km/h; consumption: 43.5 m/imp gal, 36.2 m/US gal, 6.5 l x 100 km.

CHASSIS integral; front suspension: independent, by McPherson, lower wishbones, coil springs/telescopic damper struts; rear: independent, swinging longitudinal trailing arms linked by a T-section cross-beam, coil springs/telescopic damper struts.

STEERING rack-and-pinion.

BRAKES front disc, rear drum, 2 X circuits.

ELECTRICAL EQUIPMENT 12 V; 36 Ah battery; 35 A alternator; 2 headlamps.

DIMENSIONS AND WEIGHT wheel base: 94.49 in, 240 cm; tracks: 54.72 in, 139 cm front, 53.46 in, 136 cm rear; length: 146.65 in, 372 cm; width: 63.39 in, 161 cm; height: 55.51 in, 141 cm; ground clearance: 4.92 in, 12.5 cm; weight: 2-dr. limousines 1,775 lb, 805 kg - 4-dr. limousines 1,830 lb, 830 kg; turning circle (between walls): 33.8 ft, 10.3 m; fuel tank: 8.8 imp gal, 10.6 US gal, 40 l.

VOLKSWAGEN Golf L D 4-door Limousine

BODY built-in headrests on front seats (standard).

PRACTICAL INSTRUCTIONS fuel: 98-100 oct petrol.

Golf Diesel Series

PRICES IN USA AND EX WORKS:	$	DM
Golf D 2-door Limousine	—	10.950*
Golf D 4-door Limousine	—	11.485*
Golf L D 2-door Limousine	4,704	11.660*
Golf L D 4-door Limousine	4,844*	12.195*
Golf GL D 2-door Limousine	5.040*	12.440*
Golf GL D 4-door Limousine	5,180*	12.975*

50 hp power team

ENGINE Diesel, front, transverse, 4 stroke; 4 cylinders, vertical, in line; 89.8 cu in, 1,471 cc (3.01 x 3.15 in, 76.5 x 80 mm); compression ratio: 23.5:1; max power (DIN): 50 hp (36.8 kW) at 5,000 rpm; max torque (DIN): 59 lb ft, 8.2 kg m (80.4 Nm) at 3,000 rpm; max engine rpm: 5,000; 34 hp/l (25 kW/l); cast iron block, light alloy head; 5 crankshaft bearings; valves: overhead, in line, thimble tappets; camshafts: 1, overhead, cogged belt; lubrication: gear pump, full flow filter, 6.2 imp pt, 7.4 US pt, 3.5 l; indirect injection pump; fuel feed: mechanical pump; liquid-cooled, expansion tank, 10.9 imp pt, 13.1 US pt, 6.2 l, electric thermostatic fan.

TRANSMISSION driving wheels: front; clutch: single dry plate, hydraulically controlled; gearbox: mechanical; gears:

BODY saloon/sedan; 5 seats, separate front seats; built-in headrests; folding rear seat; heated rear window.

PRACTICAL INSTRUCTIONS fuel: Diesel oil; oil: engine 5.3 imp pt, 6.3 US pt, 3 l - gearbox and final drive 3.2 imp pt, 3.8 US pt, 1.8 l, SAE 80 or 90; tyre pressure: front 26 psi, 1.8 atm, rear 26 psi, 1.8 atm.

OPTIONAL ACCESSORIES 175/70 SR x 13 or 155 SR x 13 tyres with 5'' wide rims; servo brake; halogen headlamps; sunshine roof; metallic spray; rear window wiper-washer.

Scirocco Series

PRICES EX WORKS:	
1 Scirocco Coupé	DM 12,460*
2 Scirocco L Coupé	DM 13,430*
3 Scirocco S Coupé	DM 12,990*
4 Scirocco LS Coupé	DM 13,960*
5 Scirocco GT Coupé	DM 14,460*
6 Scirocco GL Coupé	DM 15,160*
7 Scirocco GTI Coupé	DM 16,780*
8 Scirocco GLI Coupé	DM 17,480*

For USA prices, see price index

Power team:	Standard for:	Optional for:
50 hp	1,2	—
70 hp	3 to 6	—
110 hp	7,8	

50 hp power team

ENGINE front, transverse, slanted 15° to front, 4 stroke; 4 cylinders, vertical, in line; 66.7 cu in, 1,093 cc (2.74 x 2.83 in, 69.5 x 72 mm); compression ratio: 8:1; max power (DIN): 50 hp (36.8 kW) at 6,000 rpm; max torque (DIN): 57 lb ft, 7.9 kg m (77.5 Nm) at 3,000 rpm; 45.7 hp/l (33.7 kW/l); cast iron block, light alloy head; 5 crankshaft bearings; valves: overhead, in line, thimble tappets; camshafts: 1, overhead, cogged belt; lubrication: gear pump, full flow filter, 6.2 imp pt, 7.4 US pt, 3.5 l; 1 Solex 35 PICT-5 downdraught single barrel carburettor; fuel feed: mechanical pump; liquid cooled, expansion tank, 10.9 imp pt, 13.1 US pt, 6.2 l, electric thermostatic fan.

TRANSMISSION driving wheels: front; clutch: single dry plate, hydraulically controlled; gearbox: mechanical; gears: 4, fully synchronized; ratios: I 3.454, II 2.055, III 1.370, IV 0.939, rev 3.166; lever: central; final drive: spiral bevel; axle ratio: 4.570; width of rims: 5''; tyres: 155 SR x 13.

PERFORMANCE max speed: 89 mph, 144 km/h; power-weight ratio: 34.4 lb/hp (46.7 lb/kW), 15.6 kg/hp (21.2 kg/kW); carrying capacity: 860 lb, 390 kg; acceleration: 0-50 mph (0-80 km/h) 9.9 sec; speed in top at 1,000 rpm: 14.9 mph, 24 km/h; consumption: 35.3 m/imp gal, 29.4 m/US gal, 8 l x 100 km.

CHASSIS integral; front suspension: independent, by McPherson, lower wishbones, coil springs/telescopic damper struts; rear: independent, swinging longitudinal trailing arms linked by a T-section cross beam, coil springs/telescopic damper struts.

STEERING rack-and-pinion.

BRAKES front disc (diameter 9.41 in, 23.9 cm), rear drum, servo; swept area: front 160 sq in, 1,032 sq cm, rear 90.9 sq in, 586 sq cm, total 250.9 sq in, 1,618 sq cm.

ELECTRICAL EQUIPMENT 12 V; 36 Ah battery; 35 A alternator; Bosch distributor; 2 headlamps.

DIMENSIONS AND WEIGHT wheel base: 94.49 in, 240 cm; tracks: 54.72 in, 139 cm front, 53.46 in, 136 cm rear; length: 152.95 in, 388 cm; width: 63.78 in, 162 cm; height: 50.98 in, 129 cm; ground clearance: 4.92 in, 12.5 cm; weight: 1,720 lb, 780 kg; turning circle (between walls): 33.8 ft, 10.3 m; fuel tank: 8.8 imp pt, 10.6 US pt, 40 l.

BODY coupé; 2+1 doors; 4 seats, separate front seats; electrically-heated rear window; folding rear seat; built-in headrests on front seats (standard for L only).

PRACTICAL INSTRUCTIONS fuel: 90 oct petrol; oil: engine 5.3 imp pt, 6.3 US pt, 3 l, SAE 20W-30, change every 4,700 miles, 7,500 km - gearbox and final drive 3.2 imp pt, 3.8 US pt, 1.8 l, SAE 80 or 90; sparking plug: 175°; tyre pressure: front 26 psi, 1.8 atm, rear 26 psi, 1.8 atm.

OPTIONAL ACCESSORIES 5'' rim sports wheels; 175/70 SR x 13 tyres; halogen headlamps; built-in headrests on front seats; reclining front seats; rear window wiper-washer; metallic spray.

VOLKSWAGEN Scirocco L Coupé

70 hp power team

See 50 hp power team, except for:

ENGINE front, transverse, slanted 20° to rear; 88.9 cu in, 1,457 cc (3.13 x 2.89 in, 79.5 x 73.4 mm); compression ratio: 8.2:1; max power (DIN): 70 hp (51.5 kW) at 5,600 rpm; max torque (DIN): 81 lb ft, 11.2 kg m (109.8 Nm) at 2,500 rpm; 48 hp/l (35.3 kW/l); 1 Solex 34 PICT-5 downdraught single barrel carburettor.

TRANSMISSION gearbox ratios: I 3.454, II 1.960, III 1.370, IV 0.970, rev 3.170; axle ratio: 3.900.

PERFORMANCE max speed: 101 mph, 162 km/h; power-weight ratio: 25.2 lb/hp (34.2 lb/kW), 11.4 kg/hp (15.5 kg/kW); acceleration: 0-50 mph (0-80 km/h) 8.1 sec; speed in top at 1,000 rpm: 17.3 mph, 27.9 km/h; consumption: 34 m/imp gal, 28.3 m/US gal, 8.3 l x 100 km.

ELECTRICAL EQUIPMENT 4 halogen headlamps.

DIMENSIONS AND WEIGHT weight: 1,764 lb, 800 kg.

BODY built-in headrests on front seats (standard); tinted glass.

OPTIONAL ACCESSORIES automatic transmission, hydraulic torque converter and planetary gears with 3 ratios (I 2.550, II 1.450, III 1, rev 2.410), max ratio of converter at stall 2.44, possible manual selection, central lever,

VOLKSWAGEN Scirocco L Coupé

3.760 axle ratio, max speed 98 mph, 157 km/h, acceleration 0-50 mph (0-80 km/h) 9.3 sec, carrying capacity 849 lb, 385 kg, consumption 31.7 m/imp gal, 26.4 m/US gal, 8.9 l x 100 km.

110 hp power team

See 50 hp power team, except for:

ENGINE front, transverse, slanted 20° to rear; 96.9 cu in, 1,588 cc (3.13 x 3.15 in, 79.5 x 80 mm); compression ratio: 9.5:1; max power (DIN): 110 hp (81 kW) at 6,100 rpm; max torque (DIN): 101 lb ft, 14 kg m (137.3 Nm) at 5,000 rpm; max engine rpm: 6,900; 69.3 hp/l (51 kW/l); Bosch K-Jetronic electronic injection; fuel feed: electric pump.

TRANSMISSION gearbox ratios: I 3.450, II 1.960, III 1.370, IV 0.970, rev 3.170; axle ratio: 3.900; width of rims: 5.5''; tyres: 175/70 HR x 13.

PERFORMANCE max speed: 115 mph, 185 km/h; power-weight ratio: 16 lb/hp (21.8 lb/kW), 7.3 kg/hp (9.9 kg/kW); carrying capacity: 904 lb, 410 kg; acceleration: 0-50 mph (0-80 km/h) 6 sec; speed in top at 1,000 rpm: 18.8 mph, 30.3 km/h; consumption: 36.2 m/imp gal, 30.2 m/US gal, 7.8 l x 100 km.

CHASSIS front and rear suspension: anti-roll bar.

ELECTRICAL EQUIPMENT 55 A alternator; 4 halogen headlamps.

VOLKSWAGEN Scirocco GTI Coupé

DIMENSIONS AND WEIGHT tracks: 55.28 in, 140 cm front, 54.02 in, 137 cm rear; weight: 1,764 lb, 800 kg.

BODY built-in headrests on front seats (standard); tinted glass.

PRACTICAL INSTRUCTIONS fuel: 98-100 oct petrol.

Passat Series

PRICES IN GB, IN USA AND EX WORKS:

	£	$	DM
1 Passat 2-door Limousine	3,194*	—	11,192*
2 Passat 4-door Limousine	—	—	11,745*
3 Passat Variant	3,438*	—	12,105*
4 Passat L 2-door Limousine	—	—	11,945*
5 Passat L 4-door Limousine	3,538*	—	12,495*
6 Passat L Variant	—	—	12,855*
7 Passat GL 2-door Limousine	—	—	12,855*
8 Passat GL 4-door Limousine	—	—	13,405*
9 Passat GL Variant	—	—	13,765*
10 Passat S 2-door Limousine	—	—	11,675*
11 Passat S 4-door Limousine	—	—	12,225*
12 Passat S Variant	—	—	12,585*
13 Passat LS 2-door Limousine	—	5,749	12,425*
14 Passat LS 4-door Limousine	3,729*	5,849	12,975*
15 Passat LS Variant	3,866*	6,149	13,335*
16 Passat GLS 2-door Limousine	—	—	13,335*
17 Passat GLS 4-door Limousine	3,988*	—	13,885*
18 Passat GLS Variant	—	—	14,245*

For 85 hp engine add DM 830.

Power team:	Standard for:	Optional for:
55 hp	1 to 9	—
75 hp	10 to 18	—
85 hp	—	13 to 18

VOLKSWAGEN Passat LS 4-door Limousine

55 hp power team

ENGINE front, slanted 20º to right, 4 stroke; 4 cylinders, in line; 79.1 cu in, 1,297 cc (2.95 x 2.89 in, 75 x 73.4 mm); compression ratio: 8.5:1; max power (DIN): 55 hp (40.5 kW) at 5,500 rpm; max torque (DIN): 68 lb ft, 9.4 kg m (92.2 Nm) at 2,500 rpm; max engine rpm: 6,500; 42.4 hp/l (31.2 kW/l); cast iron block, light alloy head; 5 crankshaft bearings; valves: overhead, in line, thimble tappets; camshafts: 1, overhead, cogged belt; lubrication: gear pump, full flow filter, 5.3 imp pt, 6.3 US pt, 3 l; 1 Solex 30-35 PDSI (T) downdraught single barrel carburettor; fuel feed: mechanical pump; water-cooled, 10.9 imp pt, 13.1 US pt, 6.2 l, electric thermostatic fan.

TRANSMISSION driving wheels: front; clutch: single dry plate (diaphragm); gearbox: mechanical; gears: 4, fully synchronized; ratios: I 3.454, II 2.055, III 1.370, IV 0.968, rev 3.166; lever: central; final drive: spiral bevel; axle ratio: 4.555; width of rims: 5''; tyres: 155 SR x 13.

PERFORMANCE max speeds: (I) 25 mph, 41 km/h; (II) 42 mph, 68 km/h; (III) 68 mph, 110 km/h; (IV) 93 mph, 150 km/h; power-weight ratio: 2-dr. limousines 34.4 lb/hp (46.8 lb/kW), 15.6 kg/hp (21.2 kg/kW); carrying capacity:

2-dr. limousines 1,036 lb, 470 kg - 4-dr. limousines 981 lb, 445 kg; acceleration: 0-50 mph (0-80 km/h) 10.5 sec; speed in top at 1,000 rpm: 14.9 mph, 24 km/h; consumption: 32.1 m/imp gal, 26.7 m/US gal, 8.8 l x 100 km.

CHASSIS integral, front auxiliary subframe; front suspension: independent, by McPherson, lower wishbones, anti-roll bar, coil springs/telescopic damper struts; rear: rigid axle, trailing radius arms, transverse linkage bar, coil springs, anti-roll bar, telescopic dampers.

STEERING rack-and-pinion, damper.

BRAKES front disc (diameter 9.41 in, 23.9 cm), rear drum; servo.

ELECTRICAL EQUIPMENT 12 V; 36 Ah battery; 35 A alternator; Bosch distributor; 2 headlamps.

DIMENSIONS AND WEIGHT wheel base: 97.24 in, 247 cm; tracks: 52.76 in, 134 cm front, 53.15 in, 135 cm rear; length: 168.90 in, 429 cm - Variants 167.91 in, 426 cm; width: 63.58 in, 161 cm; height: 53.54 in, 136 cm; ground clearance: 7.09 in, 18 cm; weight: 2-dr. limousines 1,896 lb, 860 kg - 4-dr. limousines 1,951 lb, 885 kg - Variants 2,029 lb, 920 kg; turning circle (between walls): 33.8 ft, 10.3 m; fuel tank: 9.9 imp gal, 11.9 US gal, 45 l.

BODY 5 seats, separate front seats, reclining backrests with built-in headrests; heated rear window; folding rear seat (for Variant only).

PRACTICAL INSTRUCTIONS fuel: 86 oct petrol; oil: engine 4.4 imp pt, 5.3 US pt, 2.5 l, SAE 20W-30, change every 9,000 miles, 15,000 km - gearbox and final drive 3.2 imp pt, 3.8 US pt, 1.8 l, SAE 80 or 90, no change recommended; greasing: none; sparking plug: 175º; tappet clearances inlet 0.008-0.012 in, 0.20-0.30 mm, exhaust 0.016-0.020 in, 0.40-0.50 mm; tyre pressure: front 24 psi, 1.7 atm, rear 24 psi, 1.7 atm.

OPTIONAL ACCESSORIES 175/70 SR x 13 tyres; sport wheels; sunshine roof; halogen headlamps; metallic spray; tinted glass; tailgate with folding rear seat (for limousines only); rear window wiper-washer (for Variant only).

75 hp power team

See 55 hp power team, except for:

ENGINE 96.9 cu in, 1,588 cc (3.13 x 3.15 in, 79.5 x 80 mm); compression ratio: 8.2:1; max power (DIN): 75 hp (55.2 kW) at 5,600 rpm; max torque (DIN): 88 lb ft, 12.1 kg m (118.7 Nm) at 3,200 rpm; 47.2 hp/l (34.8 kW/l); 1 Solex PDSIT downdraught single barrel carburettor.

TRANSMISSION axle ratio: 4.111.

PERFORMANCE max speed: 102 mph, 164 km/h; power-weight ratio: 2-dr. limousines 25.4 lb/hp (34.3 lb/kW), 11.5 kg/hp (15.6 kg/kW); acceleration: 0-50 mph (0-80 km/h) 8.4 sec; speed in top at 1,000 rpm: 16.3 mph, 26.3 km/h.

ELECTRICAL EQUIPMENT 4 halogen headlamps (standard for GLS only).

DIMENSIONS AND WEIGHT length: GLS 166.14 in, 422 cm.

OPTIONAL ACCESSORIES automatic transmission, hydraulic torque converter and planetary gears with 3 ratios (I 2.650, II 1.580, III 1, rev 1.800), max ratio of converter at stall 2.2, possible manual selection, 4.091 axle ratio, max speed 99 mph, 159 km/h, acceleration 0-50 mph (0-80 km/h) 9.6 sec, consumption 30.1 m/imp gal, 25 m/US gal, 9.4 l x 100 km.

85 hp power team

See 75 hp power team, except for:

ENGINE max power (DIN): 85 hp (62.6 kW) at 5,600 rpm; max torque (DIN): 92 lb ft, 12.7 kg m (124.5 Nm) at 3,200 rpm; 53.5 hp/l (39.4 kW/l); 1 Solex 32/35 TDID downdraught twin barrel carburettor.

TRANSMISSION tyres: 175/70 SR x 13.

PERFORMANCE max speed: 107 mph, 173 km/h; power-weight ratio 2-dr. limousines 22.3 lb/hp (30.3 lb/kW), 10.1 kg/hp (13.7 kg/kW); acceleration: 0-50 mph (0-80 km/h) 7.9 sec; speed in top at 1,000 rpm: 16.5 mph, 26.6 km/h; consumption: 32.8 m/imp gal, 27.3 m/US gal, 8.6 l x 100 km.

ELECTRICAL EQUIPMENT 45 Ah battery; 55 A alternator.

OPTIONAL ACCESSORIES automatic transmission with 3 ratios (I 2.590, II 1.590, III 1, rev 1.800), 3.909 axle ratio, max speed 104 mph, 168 km/h, acceleration 0-50 mph (0-80 km) 9.1 sec, consumption 30.7 m/imp gal, 25.6 m/US gal, 9.2 l x 100 km.

VOLKSWAGEN Passat LS 4-door Limousine

1303 Cabriolet

PRICE IN GB: £ 4,231*
PRICE IN USA: $ 5,495*

ENGINE rear, 4 stroke; 4 cylinders, horizontally opposed; 96.7 cu in, 1,584 cc (3.37 x 2.72 in, 85.5 x 69 mm); compression ratio: 7.5:1; max power (DIN): 50 hp (36.8 kW) at 4,000 rpm; max torque (DIN): 78 lb ft, 10.8 kg m (105.9 Nm) at 2,800 rpm; max engine rpm: 4,600; 31.6 hp/l (23.2 kW/l); block with cast iron liners and light alloy fins, light alloy head; 4 crankshaft bearings; valves: overhead, push-rods and rockers; camshafts: 1, central, lower; lubrication: gear pump, filter in sump, oil cooler, 4.4 imp pt, 5.3 US pt, 2.5 l; 1 Solex 34 PICT 2 downdraught carburettor; fuel feed: mechanical pump; air-cooled.

TRANSMISSION driving wheels: rear; clutch: single dry plate; gearbox: mechanical; gears: 4, fully synchronized; ratios: I 3.780, II 2.060, III 1.260, IV 0.930, rev 4.010; lever: central; final drive: spiral bevel; axle ratio: 3.875; width of rims: 4''; tyres: 5.60 x 15.

PERFORMANCE max speeds: (I) 19 mph, 31 km/h; (II) 35 mph, 57 km/h; (III) 58 mph, 94 km/h; (IV) 81 mph, 130 km/h; weight ratio: 41.7 lb/hp, (55.7 lb/kW), 18.6 kg/hp (25.3 kg/kW); carrying capacity: 794 lb, 360 kg; acceleration: 0-50 mph (0-80 km/h) 13 sec; speed in top at 1,000 rpm: 18,6 mph, 30 km/h; consumption: 30.7 m/imp gal, 25.6 m/US gal, 9.2 l x 100 km.

VOLKSWAGEN 1303 Cabriolet

VOLKSWAGEN 1303 Cabriolet

CHASSIS backbone platform; front suspension: independent, by McPherson, coil springs/telescopic damper struts, anti-roll bar, lower swinging trailing arms; rear: independent, semi-trailing arms, transverse compensating torsion bar, telescopic dampers.

STEERING rack-and-pinion; turns lock to lock: 2.60.

BRAKES front disc (diameter 10.91 in, 27.7 cm), rear drum; lining area: front 12.4 sq in, 80 sq cm, rear 55.5 sq in, 358 sq cm, total 67.9 sq in, 438 sq cm.

ELECTRICAL EQUIPMENT 12 V; 36 Ah battery; 50 A alternator; Bosch distributor; 2 headlamps.

DIMENSIONS AND WEIGHT wheel base: 95.28 in, 242 cm; tracks: 54.72 in, 139 cm front, 53.15 in, 135 cm rear; length: 162.99 in, 414 cm; width: 62.20 in, 158 cm; height: 59.06 in, 150 cm; ground clearance: 5.90 in, 15 cm; weight: 2,051 lb, 930 kg; turning circle (between walls): 31.5 ft, 9.6 m; fuel tank: 9.2 imp gal, 11.1 US gal, 42 l.

BODY convertible; 2 doors; 4 seats, reclining backrests.

PRACTICAL INSTRUCTIONS fuel: 87 oct petrol; oil: engine 4.4 imp pt, 5.3 US pt, 2.5 l, SAE 10W-20 (winter) 20W-30 (summer), change every 3,100 miles, 5,000 km; gearbox and final drive 5.3 imp pt, 6.3 US pt, 3 l, SAE 90, change every 31,000 miles, 50,000 km; greasing: every 6,200 miles, 10,000 km, 4 points; sparking plug: 175°; tappet clearances: inlet 0.004 in, 0.10 mm, exhaust 0.004 in, 0.10 mm; valve timing: 7°30' 37° 44°30' 4°; tyre pressure: front 16 psi, 1.1 atm, rear 24 psi, 1.7 atm.

OPTIONAL ACCESSORIES 6.00 x 15 or 155 SR x 15 tyres; limited slip differential; independent heating; halogen headlamps; heated rear window; built-in headrests.

181

PRICE EX WORKS: 13,730* marks

ENGINE rear, 4 stroke; 4 cylinders, horizontally opposed; 96.7 cu in, 1,584 cc (3.37 x 2.72 in, 85.5 x 69 mm); compression ratio: 7.5:1; max power (DIN): 48 hp (35.3 kW) at 4,000 rpm; max torque (DIN): 74 lb ft, 10.2 kg m (100 Nm) at 2,000 rpm; max engine rpm: 4,600; 30.3 hp/l (22.3 kW/l); block with cast iron liners and light alloy fins, light alloy head; 4 crankshaft bearings; valves: overhead, push-rods and rockers; camshafts: 1, central, lower; lubrication: gear pump, filter in sump, oil cooler, 4.4 imp pt, 5.3 US pt, 2.5 l; 1 Solex 30 PICT 2 downdraught carburettor; fuel feed: mechanical pump; air-cooled.

TRANSMISSION driving wheels: rear; clutch: single dry plate; gearbox: mechanical; gears: 4, fully synchronized; ratios: I 3.800, II 2.060, III 1.220, IV 0.820, rev 3.610; transfer box; lever: central; final drive: spiral bevel; axle ratio: 4.880; width of rims: 5''; tyres: 185 SR x 14.

PERFORMANCE max speeds: (I) 15 mph, 24 km/h; (II) 28 mph, 45 km/h; (III) 47 mph, 76 km/h; (IV) 71 mph, 115 km/h; power-weight ratio: 41.3 lb/hp, (56.2 lb/kW), 18.7 kg/hp (25.5 kg/kW); carrying capacity: 970 lb, 440 kg; acceleration: 0-50 mph (0-80 km/h) 14.5 sec; speed in top at 1,000 rpm: 18.3 mph, 29.5 m/h; consumption: 29.7 m/imp gal, 24.8 m/US gal, 9.5 l x 100 km.

CHASSIS backbone platform; front suspension: independent, by McPherson, coil springs/telescopic damper struts, anti-roll bar, lower swinging trailing arms, rubber cone springs; rear: independent, semi-trailing arms, transverse compensating torsion bar, telescopic dampers.

STEERING worm and roller.

BRAKES drum; lining area: total 125.3 sq in, 808 sq cm.

ELECTRICAL EQUIPMENT 12 V; 36 Ah battery; 30 A alternator; Bosch distributor; 2 headlamps.

DIMENSIONS AND WEIGHT wheel base: 94.49 in, 240 cm; tracks: 53.35 in, 135 cm front, 54.53 in, 138 cm rear; length: 148.82 in, 378 cm; width: 64.57 in, 164 cm; height: 63.78 in, 162 cm; ground clearance: 8.07 in, 20.5 cm; weight: 1,985 lb, 900 kg; turning circle (between walls): 36.1 ft, 11 m; fuel tank: 8.8 imp gal, 10.6 US gal, 40 l.

BODY convertible; 4 doors; 5 seats, separate front seats.

PRACTICAL INSTRUCTIONS fuel: 87 oct petrol; oil: engine 4.4 imp pt, 5.3 US pt, 2.5 l, SAE 10W-30 (winter) 20W-30 (summer), change every 3,100 miles, 5,000 km; gearbox and final drive 4.4 imp pt, 5.3 US pt, 2.5 l, SAE 90, change every 31,000 miles, 50,000 km; greasing: every 6,200 miles, 10,000 km, 4 points; sparking plug: 175°; tappet clearances: inlet 0.004 in, 0.10 mm, exhaust 0.004 in, 0.10 mm; valve timing: 7°30' 37° 44°30' 4°; tyre pressure: front 16 psi, 1.1 atm, rear 24 psi, 1.7 atm.

OPTIONAL ACCESSORIES limited slip differential; 6.00 x 15 or 155 SR x 15 tyres.

VOLKSWAGEN 181

AC   GREAT BRITAIN

ME 3000

ENGINE Ford, rear, central, transverse, 4 stroke; 6 cylinders, Vee-slanted at 60°; 182.7 cu in 2,994 cc (3.69 x 2.85 in, 93.7 x 72.4 mm); compression ratio: 9:1; max power (DIN): 140 hp (103 kW) at 5,500 rpm; max torque (DIN): 174 lb ft, 24 kg m (235.4 Nm) at 3,000 rpm; max engine rpm: 5,750; 46.8 hp/l (34.4 kW/l); cast iron block and head; 4 crankshaft bearings; valves: overhead, push-rods and rockers; camshafts: 1, at centre of Vee; lubrication: rotary pump, full flow filter, oil cooler, 10.9 imp pt, 13.1 US pt, 6.2 l; 1 Weber 38/38 EGAS downdraught twin barrel carburettor; fuel feed: mechanical pump; water-cooled, 18 imp pt, 21.6 US pt, 10.2 l, electric thermostatic fan.

TRANSMISSION driving wheels: rear; clutch: single dry plate; gearbox: mechanical; gears: 5, fully synchronized; ratios: I 2.966, II 1.947, III 1.403, IV 1, V 0.835, rev 2.901; lever: central; final drive: hypoid bevel; axle ratio: 3.167; width of rims: 6.5''; tyres: 205/60 VR x 14.

PERFORMANCE max speed: 135 mph, 217 km/h; power-weight ratio: 13.6 lb/hp (18.4 lb/kW), 6.2 kg/hp (8.4 kg/kW); speed in top at 1,000 rpm: 25.3 mph, 40.7 km/h; consumption: 26.9 m/imp gal, 22.4 m/US gal, 10.5 l x 100 km.

CHASSIS perimeter box-type frame; front suspension: independent, wishbones, coil springs, anti-roll bar, telescopic dampers; rear: independent, wishbones (lower reversed), lower radius arms, coil springs, anti-roll bar, telescopic dampers.

STEERING rack-and-pinion, adjustable steering wheel; turns lock to lock: 2.70.

BRAKES disc (front diameter 10 in, 25.4 cm, rear 9.41 in, 23.9 cm); swept area: front 200.8 sq in, 1,295 sq cm, rear 172.1 sq in, 1,110 sq cm, total 372.9 sq in, 2,405 sq cm.

ELECTRICAL EQUIPMENT 12 V; 55 Ah battery; 35 A alternator; Lucas distributor; 2 retractable headlamps.

DIMENSIONS AND WEIGHT wheel base: 90.50 in, 230 cm; tracks: 55 in, 140 cm front, 56 in, 142 cm rear; length: 157 in, 399 cm; width: 65 in, 165 cm; height: 45 in, 114 cm; ground clearance: 5.25 in, 13.3 cm; weight: 1,900 lb, 862 kg; weight distribution: 45% front, 55% rear; turning circle (between walls): 32 ft, 9.8 m; fuel tank: 12 imp gal, 14.5 US gal, 55 l.

BODY coupé in plastic material; 2 doors; 2 seats with built-in headrests; detachable roof; electric windows.

PRACTICAL INSTRUCTIONS fuel: 97 oct petrol; oil: engine 9.7 imp pt, 11.6 US pt, 5.5 l, SAE 20W-50, change every 6,200 miles, 10,000 km; greasing: every 6,200 miles, 10,000 km, 4 points; tappet clearances: inlet 0.012 in, 0.30 mm, exhaust 0.012 in, 0.30 mm; valve timing: 20° 56° 62° 14°.

OPTIONAL ACCESSORIES servo brake; 7'' wide rims.

AC ME 3000

ARGYLL   GREAT BRITAIN

Turbo GT

PRICES EX WORKS: £ 9,500 (turbocharged engine)
                      £ 8,300

ENGINE Rover, turbocharged, central, transverse, 4 stroke; 8 cylinders, Vee-slanted at 90°; 215 cu in, 3,528 cc (3.50 x 2.80 in, 88.9 x 71.1 mm); compression ratio: 8.5:1; max power (DIN): 250 hp (184 kW) at 5,200-6,200 rpm; max torque (DIN): 310 lb ft, 42.8 kg m (419.7 Nm) at 3,500-4,500 rpm; max engine rpm: 6,200; 70.9 hp/l (52.2 kW/l); light alloy block and head, dry liners; 5 crankshaft bearings; valves: overhead, in line, push-rods and rockers, hydraulic tappets; camshafts: 1, at centre of Vee; lubrication: gear pump, full flow filter, oil cooler, 15 imp pt, 18 US pt, 8.5 l; 1 Minnow Fish TM7 carburettor; turbocharger; fuel feed: electric pump; water-cooled, 30 imp pt, 35.9 US pt, 17 l.

TRANSMISSION driving wheels: rear; clutch: single dry plate; gearbox: ZF mechanical; gears: 5, fully synchronized; ratios: I 2.580, II 1.520, III 1.040, IV 0.850, V 0.740, rev 2.860; lever: central; final drive: hypoid bevel, limited slip differential; width of rims: 7'' front, 8'' rear; tyres: 205 x 15.

PERFORMANCE max speed: over 150 mph, 241 km/h; power-weight ratio: 9.3 lb/hp (12.6 lb/kW), 4.2 kg/hp (5.7 kg/kW); carrying capacity: 353 lb, 160 kg; consumption: not declared.

CHASSIS box-section with integral roll cage; front suspension: independent, by McPherson, coil springs/telescopic damper struts, lower wishbones (leading arms), anti-roll bar; rear: independent, semi-trailing arms, coil springs, telescopic dampers.

STEERING rack-and-pinion; turns lock to lock: 2.50.

BRAKES disc (diameter 10.30 in, 26 cm).

ELECTRICAL EQUIPMENT 12 V; 60 Ah battery; alternator; Lucas distributor; 4 headlamps.

DIMENSIONS AND WEIGHT wheel base: 118 in, 300 cm; tracks: 59.50 in, 151 cm front, 59.50 in, 151 cm rear; length: 183 in, 465 cm; width: 72 in, 183 cm; height: 48 in, 122 cm; ground clearance: 6 in, 15 cm; weight: 2,300 lb, 1,043 kg; weight distribution: 48% front, 52% rear; fuel tank: 20 imp gal, 24 US gal, 91 l.

BODY coupé, in plastic material; 2 doors; 2 seats.

PRACTICAL INSTRUCTIONS fuel: 97 oct petrol; oil: engine 15 imp pt, 18 US pt, 8.5 l, SAE 20W-30, change every 3,100 miles, 5,000 km - gearbox and final drive 5.8 imp pt, 7 US pt, 3.3 l, SAE 90, change every 12,400 miles, 20,000 km; tyre pressure: front 22 psi, 1.5 atm, rear 24 psi, 1.7 atm.

VARIATIONS

ENGINE 4 cylinders, in line, 121.1 cu in, 1,985 cc (3.54 x 3.07 in, 90 x 78 mm), 7.5:1 compression ratio, max power (DIN) 175 hp (128.8 kW) at 5,500-6,500 rpm, max torque (DIN) 220 lb ft, 30.3 kg m (297.2 Nm) at 3,500-4,500 rpm, max engine rpm 6,500, 88.2 hp/l (64.9 kW/l), cast iron block, light alloy head, 1 overhead camshafts, 1 Minnow Fish TB7 carburettor.
TRANSMISSION 4-speed fully synchronized mechanical gearbox, 185 x 15 tyres.
PERFORMANCE max speed 130 mph, 209 km/h, power-weight ratio 13.2 lb/hp (17.9 lb/kW), 6 kg/hp (8.1 kg/kW), carrying capacity 706 lb, 320 kg.
ELECTRICAL EQUIPMENT Bosch distributor.
BODY 4 seats.

OPTIONAL ACCESSORIES power steering; servo brake.

ARKLEY   GREAT BRITAIN

SS

PRICE EX WORKS: £ 2,658

ENGINE Triumph, front, 4 stroke; 4 cylinders, vertical, in line; 91.1 cu in, 1,493 cc (2.90 x 3.44 in, 73.7 x 87.5 mm); compression ratio: 9:1; max power (DIN): 65 hp (47.8 kW) at 5,500 rpm; max torque (DIN): 84 lb ft, 11.6 kg m (113.8 Nm) at 3,000 rpm; max engine rpm: 6,000; 43.5 hp/l (32 kW/l); cast iron block and head; 3 crankshaft bearings; valves: overhead, in line, push-rods and rockers; camshafts: 1, side; lubrication: eccentric pump, full flow filter, 7 imp pt, 8.5 US pt, 4 l; 2 SU type HS4 horizontal carburettors; fuel feed: electric pump; sealed circuit cooling, water, 6 imp pt, 7.2 US pt, 3.4 l.

TRANSMISSION driving wheels: rear; clutch: single dry plate (diaphragm); gearbox: mechanical; gears: 4, fully synchronized; ratios: I 3.412, II 2.112, III 1.433, IV 1, rev

ARGYLL Turbo GT

SS

3.753; lever: central; final drive: hypoid bevel; axle ratio: 3.900; width of rims: 7''; tyres: 195/70 x 13.

PERFORMANCE max speeds: (I) 35 mph, 57 km/h; (II) 59 mph, 96 km/h; (III) 85 mph, 137 km/h; (IV) 110 mph, 177 km/h; power-weight ratio: 19.8 lb/hp (26.9 lb/kW), 9 kg/hp (12.2 kg/kW); carrying capacity: 353 lb, 160 kg; acceleration: standing ¼ mile 17.5 sec, 0-50 mph (0-80 km/h) 8.2 sec; speed in direct drive at 1,000 rpm: 19.8 mph, 31.8 km/h; consumption: 38 m/imp gal, 31.8 m/US gal, 7.4 l x 100 km.

CHASSIS integral; front suspension: independent, wishbones, coil springs, anti-roll bar, telescopic dampers; rear: rigid axle, semi-elliptic leafsprings, telescopic dampers.

STEERING rack-and-pinion; turns lock to lock: 2.25.

BRAKES front disc (diameter 8.25 in, 21 cm), rear drum.

ELECTRICAL EQUIPMENT 12 V; 40 Ah battery; 34 A alternator; Lucas distributor; 2 headlamps.

DIMENSIONS AND WEIGHT wheel base: 79.92 in, 203 cm; tracks: 46.46 in, 118 cm front, 44.88 in, 114 cm rear; length: 123 in, 312 cm; width: 60 in, 152 cm; height: 47.50 in, 121 cm; ground clearance: 4.50 in, 10.3 cm; weight: 1,288 lb, 584 kg; weight distribution: 52.4% front, 47.6% rear; turning circle (between walls): 32 ft, 9.8 m; fuel tank: 7 imp gal, 8.4 US gal, 32 l.

BODY convertible; 2 doors; 2 seats, reclining backrests with built-in headrests.

PRACTICAL INSTRUCTIONS fuel: 98 oct petrol; oil: engine 6.5 imp pt, 7.8 US pt, 3.7 l, CAE 10W-30 (winter) 20W-50 (summer), change every 6,000 miles, 9,700 km - gearbox 2.3 imp pt, 2.7 US pt, 1.3 l, SAE 10W-30 (winter) 20W-50 (summer) - final drive 1.4 imp pt, 1.7 US pt, 0.8 l, SAE 90, change every 6,000 miles, 9,700 km; greasing: every 3,000 miles, 4,800 km, 8 points; tappet clearances: inlet 0.010 in, 0.25 mm, exhaust 0.010 in, 0.25 mm, exhaust 0.010 in, 0.25 mm; valve timing: 18° 58° 58° 18°; tyre pressure: front 18 psi, 1.3 atm, rear 20 psi, 1.4 atm.

ARKLEY SS

ASTON MARTIN   GREAT BRITAIN

V8

PRICE IN USA: $ 37,680*
PRICE EX WORKS: £ 19,999*

ENGINE front, 4 stroke; 8 cylinders, Vee-slanted at 90°; 325.8 cu in, 5,340 cc (3.94 x 3.35 in, 100 x 85 mm); compression ratio: 9:1; max engine rpm: 6,000; light alloy block and head, wet liners, hemispherical combustion chambers; 5 crankshaft bearings; valves: overhead, Vee-slanted at 64°, thimble tappets; camshafts: 2 per block, overhead; lubrication: rotary pump, full flow filter, 2 oil coolers, 24 imp pt, 28.8 US pt, 13.6 l; 4 Weber 42 DCNF downdraught twin barrel carburettors; fuel feed; 2 electric pumps; water-cooled, 32 imp pt, 38.5 US pt, 18.2 l, viscous coupling fan drive.

TRANSMISSION driving wheels: rear; clutch: single dry plate (diaphragm), hydraulically controlled; gearbox: mechanical; gears: 5, fully synchronized; ratios: I 2.900, II 1.780, III 1.220, IV 1, V 0.845, rev 2.630; lever: central; final drive: hypoid bevel, limited slip differential; axle ratio: 3.310; width of rims: 7''; tyres: GR 70 VR x 15.

PERFORMANCE max speeds: (I) 47 mph, 75 km/h; (II) 77 mph, 124 km/h; (III) 112 mph, 180 km/h; (IV) 136 mph, 219; (V) 160 mph, 257 km/h; acceleration: standing ¼ mile 14 sec, 0-50 mph (0-80 km/h) 4.5 sec; speed in top at 1,000 rpm: 27 mph, 43.5 km/h; consumption: 15 m/imp gal, 12.5 m/US gal, 18.8 l x 100 km.

CHASSIS box-type platform; front suspension: independent, wishbones, coil springs, anti-roll bar, telescopic dampers; rear: de Dion rigid axle, parallel trailing arms, transverse Watt linkage, coil springs, telescopic dampers.

STEERING rack-and-pinion, adjustable height and tilt of steering wheel, servo; turns lock to lock: 2.90.

BRAKES disc (front diameter 11.50 in, 29.2 cm, rear 10.80 in, 27.4 cm), internal radial fins, rear compensator, servo; swept area: front 259 sq in, 1,670 sq cm, rear 209 sq in, 1,348 sq cm, total 468 sq in, 3,018 sq cm.

ELECTRICAL EQUIPMENT 12 V; 73 Ah battery; 75 A alternator; Lucas transistorized ignition; 2 halogen headlamps.

DIMENSIONS AND WEIGHT wheel base: 102.75 in, 261 cm; front and rear tracks: 59 in, 150 cm; length: 182 in, 462 cm; width: 72 in, 183 cm; height: 52.25 in, 133 cm; ground clearance: 5.50 in, 14 cm; weight: 3,900 lb, 1,769 kg; weight distribution: 52% front, 48% rear; turning circle (between walls): 43 ft, 13.1 m; fuel tank: 25 imp gal, 30.1 US gal, 114 l.

ASTON MARTIN V8 Vantage

ASTON MARTIN V8 Vantage

BODY coupé; 2 doors; 4 seats, separate front seats, reclining backrests; adjustable two-position clutch, brake and accelerator pedals; leather upholstery; heated rear window; electric windows; air-conditioning.

PRACTICAL INSTRUCTIONS fuel: 97 oct petrol; oil: engine 22 imp pt, 26.4 US pt, 12.5 l, SAE 10W-50, change every 5,000 miles, 8,000 km; greasing: every 5,000 miles, 8,000 km, 6 points; tappet clearances: inlet 0.010 in, 0.25 mm, exhaust 0.012 in, 0.30 mm; valve timing: 30° 66° 68° 28°; tyre pressure: front 35 psi, 2.4 atm, rear 35 psi, 2.4 atm.

OPTIONAL ACCESSORIES Chrysler-Torqueflite automatic transmission, hydraulic torque converter and planetary gears with 3 ratios (I 2.450, II 1.450, III 1, rev 2.200), max ratio of converter at stall 2.1; possible manual selection, 3.070 axle ratio; sunshine roof; headlamps with wiper-washers.

V8 Vantage

See V8, except for:

PRICE EX WORKS: £ 22,999*

ENGINE compression ratio: 9.3:1; max engine rpm: 6,500; 4 Weber 48IDF downdraught twin barrel carburettors.

TRANSMISSION tyres: 255/60 VR x 15.

PERFORMANCE max speeds: (I) 46 mph, 74 km/h; (II) 75 mph, 120 km/h; (III) 109 mph, 175 km/h; (IV) 133 mph, 214 km/h; (V) 170 mph, 273 km/h; acceleration: 0-50 mph (0-80 km/h) 3.8 sec.

ELECTRICAL EQUIPMENT 4 headlamps.

Lagonda

PRICE EX WORKS: £ 32,620*

ENGINE front, 4 stroke; 8 cylinders, Vee-slanted at 90°; 325.8 cu in, 5,340 cc (3.94 x 3.35 in, 100 x 85 mm); compression ratio: 9:1; max engine rpm: 6,000; light alloy block and head; 5 crankshaft bearings; valves: overhead, Vee-slanted at 64°, thimble tappets; camshafts: 2 per block, overhead; lubrication: rotary pump, full flow filter, 2 oil coolers, 24 imp pt, 28.8 US pt, 13.6 l; 4 Weber 42 DCNF downdraught twin barrel carburettors; fuel feed: 2 electric pumps; water-cooled, 32 imp pt, 38.5 US pt, 18.2 l, viscous coupling fan drive.

TRANSMISSION driving wheels: rear; gearbox: Chrysler Torqueflite automatic transmission, hydraulic torque converter and planetary gears with 3 ratios, max ratio of converter at stall 2.1, possible manual selection; ratios: I 2.450, II 1.450, III 1, rev 2.200; lever: central; final drive: hypoid bevel, limited slip differential; axle ratio: 3.070; width of rims: 7''; tyres: 235/250 x 15.

PERFORMANCE max speed: 155 mph, 250 km/h; speed in direct drive at 1,000 rpm: 24.4 mph, 39.3 km/h; consumption: 15 m/imp gal, 12.5 m/US gal, 18.8 l x 100 km.

CHASSIS box-type platform; front suspension: independent, wishbones, coil springs, anti-roll bar, telescopic dampers; rear: de Dion rigid axle, parallel trailing arms, transverse Watt linkage, coil springs, telescopic dampers, self-levelling system.

STEERING rack-and-pinion, variable ratio servo; turns lock to lock: 2.

BRAKES disc, internal radial fins, servo.

ELECTRICAL EQUIPMENT 12 V; 73 Ah battery; 75 A alternator; Lucas transistorized ignition; 4 halogen headlamps.

DIMENSIONS AND WEIGHT wheel base: 114.02 in, 290 cm; tracks: 58.27 in, 148 cm front, 59.06 in, 150 cm rear; length: 207.99 in, 528 cm; width: 70 in, 178 cm; height: 50.98 in, 129 cm; ground clearance: 9.84 in, 25 cm; weight: 3,800 lb, 1,723 kg; weight distribution: 52% front, 48% rear; turning circle (between walls): 38 ft, 11.6 m; fuel tank: 28 imp gal, 33.8 US gal, 128 l.

BODY saloon/sedan; 4 doors; 4 seats, separate front seats, reclining backrests, headrests; adjustable two-position clutch, brake and accelerator pedals; leather upholstery; heated rear window; electric windows; air-conditioning; cruise control; laminated windscreen; glass panel in roof above rear compartment.

PRACTICAL INSTRUCTIONS fuel: 97 oct petrol; oil: engine 22 imp pt, 26.4 US pt, 12.5 l, SAE 10W-50, change every 5,000 miles, 8,000 km; greasing: every 5,000 miles, 8,000 km, 6 points; tappet clearances: inlet 0.010 in, 0.25 mm, exhaust 0.012 in, 0.30 mm; valve timing: 30° 66° 68° 28°; tyre pressure: front 35 psi, 2.4 atm, rear 35 psi, 2.4 atm.

ASTON MARTIN Lagonda

TRANSMISSION driving wheels: front; clutch: single dry plate (diaphragm); gearbox: mechanical; gears: 4, fully synchronized; ratios: I 3.525, II 2.218, III 1.433, IV 1, rev 3.544; lever: central; final drive: helical spur gears; axle ratio: 4.130; width of rims: 4'' or 4.5''; tyres: 145 x 13.

PERFORMANCE max speeds: (I) 26 mph, 42 km/h; (II) 41 mph, 66 km/h; (III) 64 mph, 103 km/h; (IV) 80 mph, 129 km/h; power-weight ratio: 4-dr. Saloon 41 lb/hp (55.8 lb/kW), 18.6 kg/hp (25.3 kg/kW); carrying capacity: 710 lb, 320 kg; acceleration: standing ¼ mile 22.1 sec; speed in direct drive at 1,000 rpm: 15.5 mph, 24.9 km/h; consumption: 38.2 m/imp gal, 31.8 m/US gal, 7.4 l x 100 km.

CHASSIS integral; front suspension: independent, wishbones, hydragas (liquid and gas) rubber cone springs, hydraulic connecting pipes to rear wheels; rear, independent, swinging longitudinal trailing arms, hydragas (liquid and gas) rubber cone springs, hydraulic connecting pipes to front wheels.

STEERING rack-and-pinion; turns lock to lock: 3.50.

BRAKES front disc (diameter 9.68 in, 24.6 cm), rear drum; swept area: front 178 sq in, 1,148 sq cm, rear 75.6 sq in, 487 sq cm, total 253.6 sq in, 1,635 sq cm.

ELECTRICAL EQUIPMENT 12 V; 40 Ah battery; 34 A alternator; Lucas distributor; 2 headlamps.

DIMENSIONS AND WEIGHT wheel base: 96.14 in, 244 cm; tracks: 54.33 in, 138 cm front, 54.41 in, 138 cm rear; length: 151.67 in, 385 cm; width: 63.52 in, 161 cm; height: 54.75 in.

ASTON MARTIN Lagonda

AUSTIN   GREAT BRITAIN

Allegro Series

PRICES EX WORKS:

1 Allegro 1100 De Luxe 2-door Saloon	£	2,221*
2 Allegro 1100 De Luxe 4-door Saloon	£	2,310*
3 Allegro 1300 Super 2-door Saloon	£	2,435*
4 Allegro 1300 Super 4-door Saloon	£	2,524*
5 Allegro 1300 Super Estate Car	£	2,702*
6 Allegro 1500 Super 4-door Saloon	£	2,659*
7 Allegro 1500 Super Estate Car	£	2,868*
8 Allegro 1500 Special 4-door Saloon	£	2,913*
9 Allegro 1750 HL 4-door Saloon	£	3,091*

Power team:	Standard for:	Optional for:
45 hp	1,2	—
54 hp	3 to 5	—
68 hp	6 to 8	—
90 hp	9	—

45 hp power team

ENGINE front, transverse, 4 stroke, in unit with gearbox and final drive; 4 cylinders, vertical, in line; 67 cu in, 1,098 cc (2.54 x 3.29 in, 64.4 x 83.5 mm); compression ratio: 8.5:1; max power (DIN): 45 hp (33.1 kW) at 5,250 rpm; max torque (DIN): 57 lb ft, 7.9 kg m (77.5 Nm) at 2,600 rpm; max engine rpm: 6,000; 41 hp/l (30.1 kW/l); cast iron block and head; 3 crankshaft bearings; valves: overhead, in line, push-rods and rockers; camshafts: 1, side; lubrication: rotary pump, full flow filter by cartridge, 8.5 imp pt, 10.1 US pt, 4.8 l; 1 SU type HS4 single barrel carburettor; fuel feed: mechanical pump; sealed circuit cooling, liquid, 7.2 imp pt, 8.7 US pt, 4.1 l, electric thermostatic fan.

AUSTIN Allegro 1500 Super Estate Car

147

45 HP POWER TEAM

139 cm; ground clearance: 7.48 in, 19 cm; weight: 2-dr. Saloon 1,815 lb, 823 kg - 4-dr. Saloon 1,847 lb, 838 kg; turning circle (between walls): 33.2 ft, 10.1 m; fuel tank: 10.5 imp gal, 12.7 US gal, 48 l.

BODY saloon/sedan; 4-5 seats, separate front seats, reclining backrests; heated rear window.

PRACTICAL INSTRUCTIONS fuel: 97 oct petrol; oil: engine, gearbox and final drive 8.5 imp pt, 10.1 US pt, 4.8 l, SAE 20W-50, change every 6,000 miles, 9,700 km; greasing: every 6,000 miles, 9,700 km, 4 points; tappet clearances (cold): inlet 0.012 in, 0.30 mm, exhaust 0.012 in, 0.30 mm; valve timing: 5° 45° 51° 21°; tyre pressure: front 26 psi, 1.8 atm, rear 24 psi, 1.7 atm.

OPTIONAL ACCESSORIES servo brake.

54 hp power team

See 45 hp power team, except for:

ENGINE 77.8 cu in, 1,275 cc (2.78 x 3.20 in, 70.5 x 81.2 mm); compression ratio: 8.8:1; max power (DIN): 54 hp (39.7 kW) at 5,250 rpm; max torque (DIN): 68 lb ft, 9.4 kg m (92.2 Nm) at 2,700 rpm; max engine rpm: 6,000; 42.3 hp/l (31.1 kW/l).

TRANSMISSION axle ratio: 3.940.

PERFORMANCE max speeds: (I) 30 mph, 48 km/h; (II) 48 mph, 77 km/h; (III) 74 mph, 119 km/h; (IV) 87 mph, 140 km/h; power-weight ratio: 4-dr. Saloon 35.1 lb/hp (47.8 lb/kW), 15.9 kg/hp (21.7 kg/kW); acceleration: standing ¼ mile 21.4 sec, 0-50 mph (0-80 km/h) 14 sec; speed in direct drive at 1,000 rpm: 16.4 mph, 26.4 km/h; consumption: 37 m/imp gal, 30.9 m/US gal, 7.6 l x 100 km.

DIMENSIONS AND WEIGHT length: Estate Car 155.22 in, 394 cm; height: Estate Car 55.80 in, 141 cm; weight: 2-dr. Saloon 1,830 lb, 830 kg - 4-dr. Saloon 1,896 lb, 860 kg - Estate Car 1,929 lb, 875 kg.

BODY rear window wiper-washer (Estate Car only).

OPTIONAL ACCESSORIES servo brake (except for Estate Car); metallic spray.

68 hp power team

See 45 hp power team, except for:

ENGINE 90.6 cu in, 1,485 cc (3 x 3.20 in, 76.1 x 81.2 mm); compression ratio: 9:1; max power (DIN): 68 hp (50 kW) at 5,500 rpm; max torque (DIN): 80 lb ft, 11.1 kg m (108.9 Nm) at 3,100 rpm; max engine rpm: 6,500; 45.8 hp/l (33.7 kW/l); 5 crankshaft bearings; valves: overhead, Vee-slanted, thimble tappets; camshafts: 1, overhead, chain-driven; lubricating system: 9.7 imp pt, 11.6 US pt, 5.5 l; 1 SU type HS6 carburettor; cooling system: 9.7 imp pt, 11.6 US pt, 5.5 l.

AUSTIN Allegro 1300 Super 2-door Saloon

AUSTIN Allegro 1750 HL 4-door Saloon

TRANSMISSION gears: 5, fully synchronized; ratios: I 3.202, II 2.004, III 1.372, IV 1, V 0.869, rev 3.467; axle ratio: 3.647.

PERFORMANCE max speeds: (I) 33 mph, 53 km/h; (II) 54 mph, 87 km/h; (III) 78 mph, 125 km/h; (IV) 92 mph, 148 km/h; (V) 90 mph, 145 km/h; power-weight ratio: 4-dr. saloons 28.2 lb/hp (38.4 lb/kW), 12.8 kg/hp (17.4 kg/kW); acceleration: standing ¼ mile 20 sec, 0-50 mph (0-80 km/h) 10 sec; speed in top at 1,000 rpm: 19 mph, 30.5 km/h; consumption: 32.1 m/imp gal, 26.7 m/US gal, 8.8 l x 100 km.

BRAKES servo (standard).

DIMENSIONS AND WEIGHT length: Estate Car 155.22 in, 394 cm; height: Estate Car 55.80 in, 141 cm; weight: 4-dr. saloons 1,918 lb, 870 kg - Estate Car 1,996 lb, 905 kg.

BODY vinyl roof (1500 Special only); rear window wiper-washer (Estate Car only).

PRACTICAL INSTRUCTIONS oil: engine, gearbox and final drive 9.7 imp pt, 11.6 US pt, 5.5 l; tappet clearances: inlet 0.012-0.018 in, 0.30-0.45 mm, exhaust 0.012-0.022 in, 0.30-0.55 mm; valve timing: 9° 50° 48° 11°.

OPTIONAL ACCESSORIES automatic transmission with 4 ratios (I 2.612, II 1.807, III 1.446, IV 1, rev 2.612), max ratio of converter at stall 2, possible manual selection, 3.800 axle ratio, max speed 87 mph, 140 km/h; metallic spray.

90 hp power team

See 45 hp power team, except for:

ENGINE 106.7 cu in, 1,748 cc (3 x 3.77 in, 76.1 x 95.7 mm); compression ratio: 9.5:1; max power (DIN): 90 hp (66.2 kW) at 5,500 rpm; max torque (DIN): 104 lb ft, 14.3 kg m (140.2 Nm) at 3,100 rpm; max engine rpm: 6,500; 51.5 hp/l (37.9 kW/l); 5 crankshaft bearings; valves: overhead, Vee-slanted, thimble tappets; camshafts: 1, overhead, chain-driven; lubricating system: 9.7 imp pt, 11.6 US pt, 5.5 l; 2 Su type HS6 carburettors; cooling system: 9.7 imp pt, 11.6 US pt, 5.5 l.

TRANSMISSION gears: 5, fully synchronized; ratios: I 3.202, II 2.004, III 1.372, IV 1, V 0.869, rev 3.467; axle ratio: 3.647; tyres: 155 x 13.

PERFORMANCE max speeds: (I) 34 mph, 54 km/h; (II) 54 mph, 87 km/h; (III) 80 mph, 128 km/h; (IV) 94 mph, 151 km/h; (V) 94 mph, 151 km/h; power-weight ratio: 22.7 lb/hp (30.8 lb/kW), 10.3 kg/hp (14 kg/kW); acceleration: standing ¼ mile 19.1 sec, 0-50 mph (0-80 km/h) 9.2 sec; speed in top at 1,000 rpm: 19.4 mph, 31.2 km/h; consumption: 32 m/imp gal, 27.3 m/US gal, 8.6 l x 100 km.

BRAKES servo (standard).

ELECTRICAL EQUIPMENT 50 Ah battery; fog lamps.

DIMENSIONS AND WEIGHT weight: 2,040 lb, 925 kg.

BODY built-in headrests.

AUSTIN Maxi 1750 HL Saloon

PRACTICAL INSTRUCTIONS oil: engine, gearbox and final drive 9.7 imp pt, 11.6 US pt, 5.5 l; tappet clearances: inlet 0.012-0.018 in, 0.30-0.45 mm, exhaust 0.012-0.022 in, 0.30-0.55 mm; valve timing: 9° 51° 49° 11°.

OPTIONAL ACCESSORIES metallic spray; laminated windscreen.

Maxi Series

PRICES EX WORKS:

1 Maxi 1500 Saloon	£ 2,939*
2 Maxi 1750 Saloon	£ 3,047*
3 Maxi 1750 HL Saloon	£ 3,378*

Power team:	Standard for:	Optional for:
68 hp	1	—
72 hp	2	—
91 hp	3	—

68 hp power team

ENGINE front, transverse, 4 stroke, in unit with gearbox and final drive; 4 cylinders, in line; 90.6 cu in, 1,485 cc (3 x 3.20 in, 76.2 x 81.3 mm); compression ratio: 9:1; max power (DIN): 68 hp (50 kW) at 5,500 rpm; max torque (DIN): 82 lb/ft, 11.3 kg m (110.8 Nm) at 3,200 rpm; max engine rpm: 6,000; 45.8 hp/l (33.7 kW/l); cast iron block and head; 5 crankshaft bearings; valves: overhead, Vee-slanted, thimble tappets; camshafts: 1, overhead, chain-driven; lubrication: rotary pump, full flow filter, 9.5 imp pt, 11.4 US pt, 5.4 l; 1 SU type HS6 horizontal carburettor; fuel feed: mechanical pump; water-cooled, 9.5 imp pt, 11.4 US pt, 5.4 l.

TRANSMISSION driving wheels: front; clutch: single dry plate (diaphragm), hydraulically controlled; gearbox: mechanical; gears: 5, fully synchronized; ratios: I 3.202, II 2.004; III 1.372, IV 1, V 0.795, rev 3.467; lever: central; final drive: helical spur gears; axle ratio: 3.938; width of rims: 4.5''; tyres: 155 x 13.

PERFORMANCE max speeds: (I) 30 mph, 48 km/h; (II) 50 mph, 80 km/h; (III) 70 mph, 112 km/h; (IV) 90 mph, 145 km/h; (V) 85 mph, 136 km/h; power-weight ratio: 32.4 lb/hp (44.1 lb/kW), 14.7 kg/hp (20 kg/kW);* carrying capacity: 882 lb, 400 kg; speed in 4th gear at 1,000 rpm: 15.6 mph, 25.2 km/h; consumption: 32.1 m/imp gal, 26.7 m/US gal, 8.8 l x 100 km.

CHASSIS integral; front suspension: independent, wishbones, hydrolastic (liquid) rubber cone springs, hydraulic connecting pipes to rear wheels; rear: independent, swinging longitudinal trailing arms, hydraulic (liquid) rubber cone springs, hydraulic connecting pipes to front wheels.

STEERING rack-and-pinion; turns lock to lock: 3.90.

BRAKES front disc (diameter 9.68 in, 24.6 cm), rear drum, servo; swept area: front 182 sq in, 1,174 sq cm, rear 75.3 sq in, 486 sq cm, total 257.3 sq in, 1,660 sq cm.

ELECTRICAL EQUIPMENT 12 V; 40 Ah battery; 34 A alternator; Lucas distributor; 2 headlamps.

DIMENSIONS AND WEIGHT wheel base: 104 in, 264 cm; tracks: 53.80 in, 137 cm front, 53.20 in, 135 cm rear; length: 158.33 in, 402 cm; width: 64.12 in, 163 cm; height: 55.28 in, 140 cm; ground clearance: 5.50 in, 14 cm; weight: 2,204 lb, 999 kg; weight distribution: 62.3% front, 37.7% rear; turning circle (between walls): 33.9 ft, 10.3 m; fuel tank: 9 imp gal, 10.8 US gal, 41 l.

BODY saloon/sedan; 4 + 1 doors; 4-5 seats, separate front seats, reclining backrests; heated rear window.

PRACTICAL INSTRUCTIONS fuel: 98-100 oct petrol; oil: engine, gearbox and final drive 9.5 imp pt, 11.4 US pt, 5.4 l, SAE 10W-30 (winter) 20W-50 (summer), change every 6,000 miles, 9,700 km; greasing: none; tappet clearances: inlet 0.016-0.018 in, 0.40-0.45 mm, exhaust 0.020-0.022 in, 0.50-0.55 mm; valve timing: 9°4' 50°56' 48°56' 11°4'; tyre pressure: front 26 psi, 1.8 atm, rear 24 psi, 1.7 atm.

72 hp power team

See 68 hp power team, except for:

ENGINE 106.7 cu in, 1,748 cc (3 x 3.77 in, 76.2 x 95.7 mm); compression ratio: 8.75:1; max power (DIN): 72 hp (53 kW) at 4,900 rpm; max torque (DIN): 97 lb ft, 13.4 kg m (131.4 Nm) at 2,600 rpm; 41.2 hp/l (30.3 kW/l).

AUSTIN Maxi 1750 HL Saloon

TRANSMISSION gearbox ratio: V 0.869; axle ratio: 3.647.

PERFORMANCE max speeds: (I) 34 mph, 54 km/h; (II) 56 mph, 90 km/h; (III) 78 mph, 125 km/h; (IV) 92 mph, 148 km/h; (V) 86 mph, 138 km/h; power-weight ratio: 30.6 lb/hp (41.6 lb/kW), 13.9 kg/hp (18.8 kg/kW); speed in 4th gear at 1,000 rpm: 16.8 mph, 27 km/h; consumption: 24.6 m/imp gal, 20.5 m/US gal, 11.5 l x 100 km.

PRACTICAL INSTRUCTIONS tappet clearances: inlet 0.012 in, 0.30 mm, exhaust 0.012 in, 0.30 mm; valve timing: 9° 51° 49° 11°.

OPTIONAL ACCESSORIES AP automatic transmission, hydraulic torque converter with 2 conic bevel gears (twin concentric differential-like gear clusters) with 4 ratios (I 2.612, II 1.807, III 1.446, IV 1, rev 2.612), operated by 3 brake bands and 2 multi-disc clutches, max ratio of converter at stall 2, possible manual selection, max speeds (I) 41 mph, 66 km/h, (II) 59 mph, 95 km/h, (III) 73 mph, 118 km/h, (IV) 88 mph, 141 km/h.

91 hp power team

See 68 hp power team, except for:

ENGINE 106.7 cu in, 1,748 cc (3 x 3.77 in, 76.2 x 95.7 mm); compression ratio: 9.5:1; max power (DIN): 91 hp (67 kW) at 5,250 rpm; max torque (DIN): 104 lb ft, 14.4 kg m (141.2 Nm) at 3,400 rpm; 52.1 hp/l (38.3 kW/l); 2 SU type HS6 semi-downdraught carburettors.

TRANSMISSION gearbox ratio: V 0.869; axle ratio: 3.647; tyres: 165 x 13.

PERFORMANCE max speeds: (I) 35 mph, 56 km/h; (II) 56 mph, 90 km/h; (III) 82 mph, 132 km/h; (IV) 98 mph, 158 km/h; (V) 96 mph, 155 km/h; power-weight ratio: 24.3 lb/hp (33.1 lb/kW), 11 kg/hp (15 kg/kW); speed in top at 1,000 rpm: 19.9 mph, 32 km/h; consumption: 23.2 m/imp gal, 19.3 m/US gal, 12.2 l x 100 km.

STEERING turns lock to lock: 4.20.

DIMENSIONS AND WEIGHT weight: 2,216 lb, 1,005 kg.

PRACTICAL INSTRUCTIONS tappet clearances: inlet 0.012 in, 0.30 mm, exhaust 0.012 in, 0.30 mm; valve timing: 9° 51° 49° 11°.

OPTIONAL ACCESSORIES metallic spray.

BENTLEY   GREAT BRITAIN

T2 Saloon

PRICE EX WORKS: £ 25,992*

ENGINE front, 4 stroke; 8 cylinders, Vee-slanted at 90°; 441.9 cu in, 6,750 cc (4.10 x 3.90 in, 104.1 x 99.1 mm); compression ratio: 8:1; aluminium alloy block and head, cast iron wet liners; 5 crankshaft bearings; valves: overhead, in line, slanted, push-rods and rockers, hydraulic tappets; camshafts: 1, at centre of Vee; lubrication: gear pump, full flow filter (cartridge), 14.5 imp pt, 17.5 US pt, 8.3 l; 2 SU type HIF7 horizontal carburettors; fuel feed: 2 electric pumps; sealed circuit cooling, expansion tank, 28.5 imp pt, 34.2 US pt, 16.2 l, viscous coupling thermostatic fan.

TRANSMISSION driving wheels: rear; gearbox: Turbo-Hydramatic 400 automatic transmission, hydraulic torque converter and planetary gears with 3 ratios, max ratio of converter at stall 2, possible manual selection; ratios: I 2.500, II 1.500, III 1, rev 2; lever: steering column; final drive: hypoid bevel; axle ratio: 3.080; width of rims: 6''; tyres: 235/70 HR x 15.

PERFORMANCE max speeds: (I) 47 mph, 76 km/h; (II) 79 mph, 126 km/h; (III) 118 mph, 190 km/h; carrying capacity: 1,014 lb, 460 kg; speed in direct drive at 1,000 rpm: 26.2 mph, 42.2 km/h; consumption: 14.1 m/imp gal, 11.8 m/US gal, 20 l x 100 km.

CHASSIS integral, front and rear auxiliary frames; front suspension: independent, lower wishbones, coil springs, anti-roll bar, automatic levelling control, telescopic dampers; rear: independent, semi-trailing arms, coil springs, anti-roll bar, automatic levelling control, telescopic dampers.

STEERING rack-and-pinion, progressive servo, right-hand drive; turns lock to lock: 3.20.

BRAKES disc (diameter 11 in, 27.9 cm), front internal radial fins, servo; swept area: front 227 sq in, 1,464 sq cm, rear 286 sq in, 1,845 sq cm, total 513 sq in, 3,309 sq cm.

BENTLEY T2 Saloon

T2 SALOON

ELECTRICAL EQUIPMENT 12 V; 68 Ah battery; 75 A alternator; Lucas transistorized distributor; 4 headlamps.

DIMENSIONS AND WEIGHT wheel base: 120.10 in, 305 cm; tracks: 60 in, 152 cm front, 59.60 in, 151 cm rear; length: 204.50 in, 519 cm; width: 71 in, 180 cm; height: 59.75 in, 152 cm; ground clearance 6.50 in, 16.5 cm; weight: 4,930 lb, 2,236 kg; turning circle (between walls): 38.5 ft, 11.7 m; fuel tank: 23.5 imp gal, 28.2 US gal, 107 l.

BODY saloon/sedan; 4 doors; 5 seats, separate front seats, adjustable and reclining backrests; headrests; air-conditioning; heated rear window, electric windows.

PRACTICAL INSTRUCTIONS fuel: 98 oct petrol; oil: engine 14.5 imp pt, 17.5 US pt, 8.3 l, SAE 20W-50, change every 6,000 miles, 9,700 km - automatic transmission 18.6 imp pt, 22.2 US pt, 10.5 l, Dexron, change every 24,000 miles, 38,600 km - final drive 4.5 imp pt, 5.3 US pt, 2.5 l, SAE 90 EP, change every 24,000 miles, 38,600 km - power steering and automatic levelling control change every 20,000 miles, 32,000 km; greasing: every 12,000 miles, 19,300 km, 5 points; valve timing: 26° 52° 68° 10°; tyre pressure: front 28 psi, 2 atm, rear 28 psi, 2 atm.

OPTIONAL ACCESSORIES iodine headlamps; tinted glass.

Corniche Saloon

See T2 Saloon, except for:

PRICE EX WORKS: £ 37,785*

ENGINE 2 Solex 4A1 4-barrel carburettors.

DIMENSIONS AND WEIGHT width: 72 in, 183 cm; height: 58.75 in, 149 cm; ground clearance: 6 in, 15.2 cm; weight: 5,045 lb, 2,288 kg.

ELECTRICAL EQUIPMENT 55 A alternator.

BODY 2 doors; 4 seats.

Corniche Convertible

See T2 Saloon, except for:

PRICE EX WORKS: £ 40,131*

ENGINE 2 Solex 4A1 4-barrel carburettors.

DIMENSIONS AND WEIGHT width: 72 in, 183 cm; ground clearance: 6 in, 15.2 cm; weight: 5,200 lb, 2,358 kg.

ELECTRICAL EQUIPMENT 55 A alternator.

BODY convertible; 2 doors; 4 seats.

BENTLEY T2 Saloon

BRISTOL 603 E - 603 S2

BRISTOL 412 S2 Convertible-Saloon

BRISTOL   GREAT BRITAIN

603 E

PRICE EX WORKS: £ 25,992*

ENGINE Chrysler, front, 4 stroke; 8 cylinders, Vee-slanted at 90°; 318 cu in, 5,211 cc (3.91 x 3.31 in, 99.3 x 84.1 mm); compression ratio: 8.5:1; cast iron block and head; 5 crankshaft bearings; valves: overhead, push-rods and rockers, hydraulic tappets; camshafts: 1, at centre of Vee, chain driven; lubrication: rotary pump, full flow filter, 8.3 imp pt, 9.9 US pt, 4.7 l; 1 Carter downdraught twin barrel carburettor; cleaner air system; fuel feed: mechanical pump; water-cooled, 29 imp pt, 34.9 US pt, 16.5 l, 2 thermostatically-controlled electric fans.

TRANSMISSION driving wheels: rear; gearbox: Chrysler Torqueflite automatic transmission, hydraulic torque converter and planetary gears with 3 ratios, max ratio of converter at stall 2.07, possible manual selection: ratios: I 2.450, II 1.450, III 1, rev 2.200; lever: central; automatic speed control; final drive: hypoid bevel, limited slip differential; axle ratio: 2.880; width of rims: 6''; tyres: 205 VR x 15.

PERFORMANCE max speed: about 118 mph, 190 km/h; speed in direct drive at 1,000 rpm: 28.2 mph, 45.4 km/h; consumption: 20 m/imp gal, 16.7 m/US gal, 14.1 l x 100 km at 70 mph, 112 km/h.

CHASSIS box-type ladder frame with cross members; front suspension: independent, wishbones, coil springs, anti-roll bar, adjustable telescopic dampers; rear: rigid axle, longitudinal torsion bars, trailing lower radius arms, upper torque arms, transverse Watt linkage, automatic levelling control, adjustable telescopic dampers.

STEERING recirculating ball, servo.

BRAKES disc (front diameter 10.91 in, 27.7 cm, rear 10.60 in, 26.9 cm), servo; swept area: front 224 sq in, 1,445 sq cm, rear 196 sq in, 1,264 sq cm, total 420 sq in, 2,709 sq cm.

ELECTRICAL EQUIPMENT 12 V; 71 Ah battery; 60 A alternator; Chrysler electronic ignition; 4 halogen headlamps.

DIMENSIONS AND WEIGHT wheel base: 114 in, 290 cm; tracks: 54.33 in, 138 cm front, 54.72 in, 139 cm rear; length: 193.31 in, 491 cm; width: 69.68 in, 177 cm; height: 56.69 in, 144 cm; ground clearance: 5 in, 12.7 cm; weight: 3,936 lb, 1,785 kg; turning circle (between walls): 39.4 ft. 12 m; fuel tank: 18 imp gal, 21.6 US gal, 82 l.

BODY saloon/sedan; 2 doors; 4 seats, electrically-controlled separate front seats; reclining backrests with built-in headrests; electric windows; heated rear window; laminated windscreen.

PRACTICAL INSTRUCTIONS fuel: 87 oct petrol; oil: engine 8.3 imp pt, 9.9 US pt, 4.7 l, SAE 10W-50, change every 4,000 miles, 6,500 km - automatic transmission 13 imp pt, 15.6 US pt, 7.4 l, Dexron, change every 32,000 miles, 51,500 km - final drive 3.5 imp pt, 4.2 US pt, 2 l, SAE 90 EP, change every 20,000 miles, 32,200 km; greasing: every 8,000 miles, 13,000 km, 4 points.

OPTIONAL ACCESSORIES 3.070 axle ratio; air-conditioning.

603 S2

See 603 E, except for:

PRICE EX WORKS: £ 27,995*

ENGINE 360 cu in, 5,900 cc (4 x 3.58 in, 101.6 x 90.9 mm); compression ratio: 8.4:1; 1 Carter downdraught 4-barrel carburettor.

TRANSMISSION gearbox: Chrysler Torqueflite automatic transmission with max ratio of converter at stall 2.23.

PERFORMANCE max speed: about 124 mph, 200 km/h.

412 S2 Convertible-Saloon

PRICE EX WORKS: £ 24,874*

ENGINE Chrysler, front, 4 stroke; 8 cylinders, Vee-slanted at 90°; 360 cu in, 5,900 cc (4 x 3.58 in, 101.6 x 90.9 mm); compression ratio: 8.4:1; cast iron block and head; 5 crankshaft bearings; valves: overhead, push-rods and rockers, hydraulic tappets; camshafts: 1, at centre of Vee, chain driven; lubrication: rotary pump, full flow filter, 10.4 imp pt, 12.5 US pt, 5.9 l; 1 Carter Thermoquad downdraught 4-barrel car-

BRISTOL 603 E - 603 S2

BRISTOL 412 S2 Convertible-Saloon

CHRYSLER Alpine S

burettor; cleaner air system; fuel feed: mechanical pump; water-cooled, 29 imp pt, 34.9 US pt, 16.5 l, 2 thermostatically-controlled electric fans.

TRANSMISSION driving wheels: rear; gearbox: Torqueflite automatic transmission, hydraulic torque converter and planetary gears with 3 ratios, max ratio of converter at stall 2, possible manual selection; ratios: I 2.450, II 1.450, III 1, rev 2.200; lever: central; automatic speed control; final drive: hypoid bevel, limited slip differential; axle ratio: 3.070; width of rims: 6''; tyres: 205 VR x 15.

PERFORMANCE max speeds: (I) 50 mph, 80 km/h; (II) 90 mph, 145 km/h; (III) 140 mph, 225 km/h; carrying capacity: 1,125 lb, 510 kg; acceleration: 0-50 mph (0-80 km/h) 6 sec; speed in direct drive at 1,000 rpm: 28.2 mph, 45.4 km/h; consumption: 14 m/imp gal, 11.6 m/US gal, 20.2 l x 100 km.

CHASSIS box-type ladder frame with cross members; front suspension: independent, wishbones, coil springs, anti-roll bar, adjustable telescopic dampers; rear: rigid axle, longitudinal torsion bars, trailing lower radius arms, upper torque arms, transverse Watt linkage, automatic levelling control, adjustable telescopic dampers.

STEERING recirculating ball, servo; turns lock to lock: 3.

BRAKES disc (front diameter 10.91 in, 27.7 cm, rear 10.60 in, 26.9 cm), servo; swept area: front 224 sq in, 1,445 sq cm, rear 196 sq in, 1,264 sq cm, total 420 sq in, 2,709 sq cm.

ELECTRICAL EQUIPMENT 12 V; 71 Ah battery; 55 A alternator; Chrysler electronic ignition; 2 headlamps.

DIMENSIONS AND WEIGHT wheel base: 114 in, 290 cm; tracks: 54.33 in, 138 cm front, 54.72 in, 139 cm rear; length: 194.49 in, 494 cm; width: 69.68 in, 177 cm; height: 56.69 in, 144 cm; ground clearance: 5 in, 12.7 cm; weight: 3,780 lb, 1,714 kg; weight distribution: 53% front, 47% rear; turning circle (between walls): 40 ft, 12.2 m; fuel tank: 18 imp gal, 21.6 US gal, 82 l.

BODY convertible; 2 doors; 4 seats, separate front seats, reclining backrests, detachable headrests; roll bar; detachable roof; electric windows; heated rear window; leather upholstery; Avon light alloy safety wheels; laminated windscreen.

PRACTICAL INSTRUCTIONS fuel: 92 oct petrol; oil: engine 10.4 imp pt, 12.5 US pt, 5.9 l, SAE 20W-50, change every 4,000 miles, 6,400 km - gearbox 13 imp pt, 15.6 US pt, 7.4 l, Dexron, change every 32,000 miles, 51,500 km - final drive 3.5 imp pt, 4.2 US pt, 2 l, SAE 90 EP, change every 20,000 miles, 32,200 km; greasing: every 20,000 miles, 32,200 km, 4 points; valve timing: 21° 67° 79° 25°; tyre pressure: front 28 psi, 2 atm, rear 28 psi, 2 atm.

OPTIONAL ACCESSORIES air-conditioning.

CHRYSLER   **GREAT BRITAIN**

Alpine GL

PRICE EX WORKS: £ 3,072*

ENGINE front, transverse, slanted 45° to rear, 4 stroke, 4 cylinders, in line; 79 cu in, 1,294 cc (3.02 x 2.76 in, 76.7 x 70 mm); compression ratio: 9.5:1; max power (DIN): 68 hp (50 kW) at 5,600 rpm; max torque (DIN): 78 lb ft, 10.7 kg m (104.9 Nm) at 2,800 rpm; max engine rpm: 5,800; 52.6 hp/l (38.6 kW/l); cast iron block, light alloy head; 5 crankshaft bearings; valves: overhead, in line, push-rods and rockers; camshafts: 1, side; lubrication: gear pump, full flow filter, 5.3 imp pt, 6.1 US pt, 3 l; 1 Solex 32 BISA downdraught single barrel carburettor; fuel feed: mechanical pump; sealed circuit cooling, expansion tank, liquid, 11.4 imp pt, 13.7 US pt, 6.5 l, electric thermostatic fan.

TRANSMISSION driving wheels: front; clutch: single dry plate (diaphragm), hydraulically controlled; gearbox: mechanical; gears: 4, fully synchronized; ratios: I 3.900, II 2.312, III 1.524, IV 1.080, rev 3.769; lever: central; final drive: cylindrical gears; axle ratio: 3.706; width of rims: 5''; tyres: 155 SR x 13.

PERFORMANCE max speed: 94 mph, 151 km/h; power-weight ratio: 33.5 lb/hp (45.6 lb/kW) 15.2 kg/hp (20.7 kg/kW); carrying capacity: 882 lb, 400 kg; speed in top at 1,000 rpm: 16.3 mph, 26.2 km/h; consumption: about 38.5 m/imp gal, 32.2 m/US gal, 7.3 l x 100 km.

CHASSIS integral; front suspension: independent, wishbones, longitudinal torsion bars, anti-roll bar, telescopic dampers; rear: independent, swinging longitudinal trailing arms, coil springs, anti-roll bar, telescopic dampers.

STEERING rack-and-pinion; turns lock to lock: 4.15.

BRAKES front disc (diameter 9.45 in, 24 cm), rear drum, rear compensator, servo; swept area: front 169.3 sq in,

ALPINE GL

1,092 sq cm, rear 90.2 sq in, 582 sq cm, total 259.5 sq in, 1,674 sq cm.

ELECTRICAL EQUIPMENT 12 V; 40 Ah battery; 35 A alternator; Chrysler transistorized ignition; 2 headlamps.

DIMENSIONS AND WEIGHT wheel base: 102.36 in, 260 cm; tracks: 55.51 in, 141 cm front, 54.72 in, 139 cm rear; length: 166.93 in, 424 cm; width: 66.14 in, 168 cm; height: 54.72 in, 139 cm; ground clearance: 7.87 in, 20 cm; weight: 2,282 lb, 1,035 kg; turning circle (between walls): 36.1 ft, 11 m; fuel tank: 13.2 imp gal, 15.8 US gal, 60 l.

BODY saloon/sedan; 4 doors; 5 seats, separate front seats, reclining backrests; heated rear window; folding rear seat.

PRACTICAL INSTRUCTIONS fuel: 98-100 oct petrol; oil: engine 5.3 imp pt, 6.3 US pt, 3 l, SAE 20W-50, change every 5,000 miles, 8,000 km - gearbox and final drive 1.9 imp pt, 2.3 US pt, 1.1 l, SAE 90 EP, no change recommended; greasing: none.

VARIATIONS

ENGINE 88 cu in, 1,442 cc (3.02 x 3.07 in, 76.7 x 78 mm); max power (DIN) 85 hp (62.6 kW) at 5,600 rpm, max torque (DIN) 92 lb ft, 12.7 kg m (124.5 Nm) at 3,000 rpm, 6,000 max engine rpm, 58.9 hp/l (43.4 kW/l), 1 Weber 36 DCNV downdraught twin barrel carburettor.
TRANSMISSION 3.588 axle ratio.
PERFORMANCE max speed 102 mph, 164 km/h, power-weight ratio 26.9 lb/hp (36.4 lb/kW), 12.2 kg/hp (16.5 kg/kW), speed in top at 1,000 rpm 16.8 mph, 27.1 km/h, consumption about 37.5 m/imp gal, 31.4 m/US gal, 7.5 l x 100 m.

OPTIONAL ACCESSORIES halogen headlamps; headrests on front seats; tinted glass; headlamps with wiper-washers; metallic spray.

Alpine S

See Alpine GL, except for:

PRICE EX WORKS: £ 3,477*

ENGINE 88 cu in, 1,442 cc (3.02 x 3.07 in, 76.7 x 78 mm); max power (DIN) 85 hp (62.6 kW) at 5,600 rpm; max torque (DIN) 92 lb ft, 12.7 kg m (124.5 Nm) at 3,000 rpm; max engine rpm: 6,000; 58.9 hp/l (43.4 kW/l); 1 Weber 36 DCNV downdraught twin barrel carburettor.

TRANSMISSION axle ratio: 3.588.

PERFORMANCE max speed: 102 mph, 164 km/h; power-weight ratio: 27.2 lb/hp (36.8 lb/kW), 12.3 kg/hp (16.7 kg/kW); speed in top at 1,000 rpm: 16.8 mph, 27.1 km/h; consumption: about 37.5 m/imp gal, 31.4 m/US gal, 7.5 l x 100 km.

ELECTRICAL EQUIPMENT halogen headlamps.

DIMENSIONS AND WEIGHT weight: 2,304 lb, 1,045 kg.

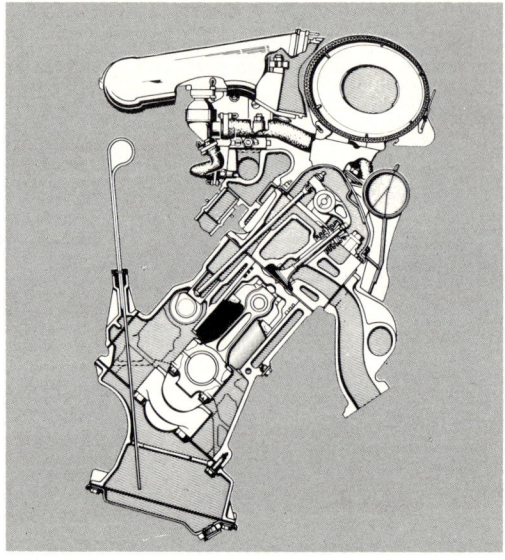

CHRYSLER Alpine GLS

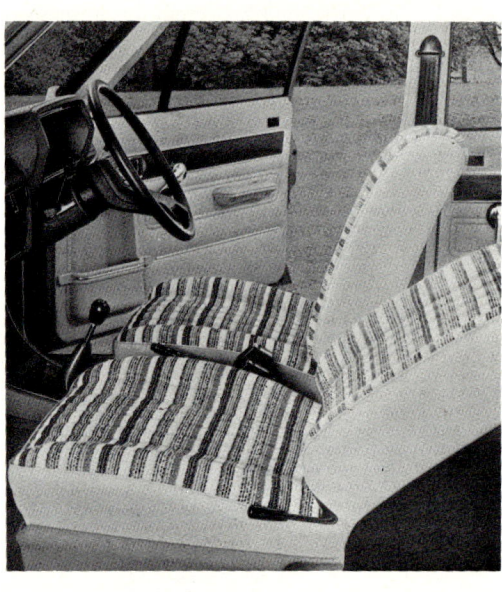

CHRYSLER Avenger GLS

Alpine GLS

See Alpine S, except for:

PRICE EX WORKS: £ 3,984*

PERFORMANCE power-weight ratio: 27.6 lb/hp (37.3 lb/kW), 12.5 kg/hp (16.9 kg/kW).

DIMENSIONS AND WEIGHT weight: 2,335 lb, 1,059 kg.

BODY laminated windscreen; headlamps with wiper-washers; electric windows; tinted glass.

Avenger Series

PRICES EX WORKS:

1 LS 1.3 2-door Saloon	£	2,315*
2 LS 1.3 4-door Saloon	£	2,437*
3 LS 1.3 Estate Car	£	2,716*
4 GL 1.3 2-door Saloon	£	2,652*
5 GL 1.3 4-door Saloon	£	2,776*
6 GL 1.3 Estate Car	£	3,072*
7 LS 1.6 4-door Saloon	£	2,541*
8 LS 1.6 Estate Car	£	2,820*
9 GL 1.6 4-door Saloon	£	2,881*
10 GL 1.6 Estate Car	£	3,177*
11 GLS 1.6 4-door Saloon	£	3,317*

Power team:	Standard for:	Optional for:
59 hp	1 to 6	—
69 hp	7 to 10	—
80 hp	11	—

59 hp power team

ENGINE front, 4 stroke; 4 cylinders, in line; 79 cu in, 1,295 cc (3.09 x 2.62 in, 78.6 x 66.7 mm); compression ratio: 8.8:1; max power (DIN): 59 hp (43.4 kW) at 5,000 rpm; max torque (DIN): 69 lb ft, 9.5 kg m (93.2 Nm) at 2,600 rpm; max engine rpm: 5,900; 45.6 hp/l (33.5 kW/l); cast iron block and head; 5 crankshaft bearings; valves: overhead, in line, push-rods and rockers; camshafts: 1, side chain driven; lubrication: rotary pump, full flow filter, 7 imp pt, 8.5 US pt, 4 l; 1 Zenith-Stromberg 150 CD3 horizontal carburettor; fuel feed: mechanical pump; water-cooled, 12.9 imp pt, 15.4 US pt, 7.3 l, thermostatically-controlled electric fan.

TRANSMISSION driving wheels: rear; clutch: single dry plate (diaphragm); gearbox: mechanical; gears: 4, fully synchronized; ratios: I 3.894, II 2.382, III 1.527, IV 1, rev 4.050; lever: central; final drive: hypoid bevel; axle ratio: saloons 3.700 - station wagons 3.890; width of rims: 4.5''; tyres: 155 SR x 13.

PERFORMANCE max speed: (I) 27 mph, 43 km/h; (II) 43 mph, 69 km/h; (III) 68 mph, 109 km/h; (IV) 89 mph, 143 km/h; power-weight ratio: LS 13 4-dr. Saloon 34.6 lb/hp (47 lb/kW), 15.7 kg/hp (21.3 kg/kW) - GL 1.3 4-dr. Saloon 35.3 lb/hp (48.1 lb/kW), 16 kg/hp (21.8 kg/kW); carrying capacity: 948 lb, 430 kg; acceleration: 0-50 mph (0-80 km/h) 11.6 sec; speed in direct drive at 1,000 rpm: 17.6 mph, 28.3 km/h; consumption: 41 m/imp gal, 34.1 m/US gal, 6.9 l x 100 km.

CHASSIS integral; front suspension: independent, by McPherson, coil springs/telescopic damper struts, wishbones, anti-roll bar; rear: rigid axle, swinging longitudinal trailing arms, upper oblique torque arms, coil springs, telescopic dampers (transverse linkage bar for station wagons only).

STEERING rack-and-pinion; turns lock to lock: 3.66.

BRAKES front disc (diameter 9.50 in, 24.1 cm), rear drum, servo; swept area: front 177.8 sq in, 1,147 sq cm, rear 74 sq in, 477 sq cm, total 251.8 sq in, 1,624 sq cm.

ELECTRICAL EQUIPMENT 12 V; 40 Ah battery; 34 A alternator; Lucas distributor; 2 headlamps.

DIMENSIONS AND WEIGHT wheel base: 98 in, 248 cm; tracks: 51.80 in, 132 cm front, 51.30 in, 130 cm rear; length: 164 in, 416 cm - LS saloons 163.10 in, 414 cm; width: 63.50 in, 161 cm; height: 55.30 in, 140 cm - station wagons 55.60 in, 141 cm; ground clearance: 5.60 in, 14.4 cm - station wagons 6.75 in, 17.2 cm; weight: LS 1.3 2-dr. Saloon 2,030 lb, 920 kg - 4-dr. Saloon 2,041 lb, 925 kg - Estate Car 2,142 lb, 971 kg - GL 1.3 2-dr. Saloon 2,072 lb, 940 kg - 4-dr. Saloon 2,083 lb, 944 kg - Estate Car 2,204 lb, 999 kg; turning circle (between walls): 31.9 ft, 9.7 m; fuel tank: 9.8 imp gal, 11.6 US gal, 44 l.

BODY 4-5 seats, separate front seats (reclining backrests on GL models); heated rear window.

PRACTICAL INSTRUCTIONS fuel: 97 oct petrol; oil: engine 7 imp pt, 8.5 US pt, 4 l, SAE 20W-50, change every 5,000

CHRYSLER Avenger GLS

CHRYSLER Avenger GL Estate Car

miles, 8,000 km - gearbox 3 imp pt, 3.6 US pt, 1.7 l, SAE 20W-50, no change recommended - final drive 1.5 imp pt, 1.9 US pt, 0.9 l, SAE 90 EP, no change recommended; greasing: none; tappet clearances: inlet 0.008 in, 0.20 mm, exhaust 0.016 in, 0.40 mm; valve timing: 38° 66° 72° 20°; tyre pressure: front 24 psi, 1.7 atm, rear 24 psi, 1.7 atm.

OPTIONAL ACCESSORIES sports road wheels; tinted glass; metallic spray; reclining backrests (on LS models); vinyl roof (on saloons).

69 hp power team

See 59 hp power team, except for:

ENGINE 97.5 cu in, 1,598 cc (3.44 x 2.62 in, 87.3 x 66.5 mm); max power (DIN): 69 hp (50.8 kW) at 4,800 rpm; max torque (DIN): 91 lb ft, 12.6 kg m (123.6 Nm) at 2,900 rpm; 43.2 hp/l (31.8 kW/l).

TRANSMISSION gearbox ratios: I 3.538, II 2.165, III 1.387, IV 1, rev 3.680; axle ratio: 3.540.

PERFORMANCE max speeds: (I) 30 mph, 48 km/h; (II) 48 mph, 77 km/h; (III) 75 mph, 120 km/h; (IV) 95 mph, 153 km/h; acceleration: 0-50 mph (0-80 km/h) 9 sec; speed in direct drive at 1,000 rpm: 18.5 mph, 29.8 km/h; consumption: 39.2 m/imp gal, 32.7 m/US gal, 7.2 l x 100 km.

CHRYSLER Avenger LS Estate Car

CHRYSLER Hunter De Luxe

OPTIONAL ACCESSORIES Borg-Warner 45 automatic transmission, hydraulic torque converter and planetary gears with 4 ratios (I 3, II 1.937, II 1.351, IV 1, rev 4.692), max ratio of converter at stall 2.43, possible manual selection, max speed 90 mph, 145 km/h, acceleration 0-50 mph (0-80 km/h) 10.3 sec, consumption 33.5 m/imp gal, 28 m/US gal, 8.4 l x 100 km.

80 hp power team

See 59 hp power team, except for:

ENGINE 97.5 cu in, 1,598 cc (3.44 x 2.62 in, 87.3 x 66.5 mm); max power (DIN): 80 hp (58.9 kW) at 5,400 rpm; max torque (DIN): 86 lb ft, 11.9 kg m (116.7 Nm) at 4,400 rpm; max engine rpm: 6,500; 50 hp/l (36.9 kW/l); 1 Zenith-Stromberg 175 CD3 VX horizontal carburettor.

TRANSMISSION axle ratio: 3.700.

PERFORMANCE max speeds: (I) 30 mph, 48 km/h; (II) 51 mph, 82 km/h; (III) 79 mph, 127 km/h; (IV) 100 mph, 161 km/h; power-weight ratio: 26.7 lb/hp (36.2 lb/kW), 12.1 kg/hp (16.4 kg/kW); acceleration: 0-50 mph (0-80 km/h) 8.5 sec; speed in direct drive at 1,000 rpm: 17.7 mph, 28.5 km/h; consumption: 36.2 m/imp gal, 30.2 m/US gal, 7.8 l x 100 km.

DIMENSIONS AND WEIGHT weight: 2,134 lb, 968 kg.

BODY reclining backrests; vinyl roof (standard).

PRACTICAL INSTRUCTIONS tappet clearances: inlet 0.010 in, 0.25 mm; valve timing: 44° 78° 69° 23°

OPTIONAL ACCESSORIES Borg-Warner 45 automatic transmission, hydraulic torque converter and planetary gears with 4 ratios (I 3, II 1.937, III 1.351, IV 1, rev 4.692), max ratio of converter at stall 2.43, possible manual selection, max speed 95 mph, 153 km/h, acceleration 0-50 mph (0-80 km/h) 10 sec, consumption 33.5 m/imp gal, 28 m/US gal, 8.4 l x 100 km.

Hunter Series

PRICES EX WORKS:

1 De Luxe	£ 2,779*
2 Super	£ 3,258*

Power team:	Standard for:	Optional for:
61 hp	1	—
74 hp	2	—

61 hp power team

ENGINE front, 4 stroke; 4 cylinders, in line; 105.2 cu in, 1,725 cc (3.21 x 3.25 in, 81.5 x 82.5 mm); compression ratio: 8.4:1; max power (DIN): 61 hp (44.9 kW) at 4,700 rpm; max torque (DIN): 85 lb ft, 11.8 kg m (115.7 Nm) at 2,600 rpm; max engine rpm: 5,500; 35.4 hp/l (26 kW/l); cast iron block and head; 5 crankshaft bearings; valves: overhead, in line, push-rods and rockers; camshafts: 1, side, chain-driven; lubrication: rotary pump, full flow filter, 7.5 imp pt, 8.9 US pt, 4.2 l; 1 Zenith-Stromberg 150 CD3 horizontal carburettor; fuel feed: mechanical pump; water-cooled, 12.6 imp pt, 15 US pt, 7.1 l.

TRANSMISSION driving wheels: rear; clutch: single dry plate (diaphragm), hydraulically controlled; gearbox: mechanical; gears: 4, fully synchronized; ratios: I 3.353, II 2.142, III 1.393, IV 1, rev 3.569; lever: central; final drive: hypoid bevel; axle ratio: 3.890; width of rims: 4.5''; tyres: 155 x 13.

PERFORMANCE max speeds: (I) 29 mph, 46 km/h; (II) 45 mph, 72 km/h; (III) 69 mph, 111 km/h; (IV) 89 mph, 143 km/h; power-weight ratio: 31.9 lb/hp (43.3 lb/kW), 14.5 kg/hp (19.6 kg/kW); carrying capacity: 960 lb, 435 kg; acceleration: 0-50 mph (0-80 km/h) 11 sec; speed in direct drive at 1,000 rpm: 16.8 mph, 27 km/h; consumption: 36.2 m/imp gal, 30.2 m/US gal, 7.8 l x 100 km.

CHASSIS integral; front suspension: independent, coil springs/telescopic damper struts, lower wishbones (trailing links), anti-roll bar; rear: rigid axle, semi-elliptic leaf-springs, telescopic dampers.

STEERING recirculating ball; turns lock to lock: 3.36.

BRAKES front disc (diameter 9.60 in, 24.4 cm), rear drum, servo; swept area: front 179 sq in, 1,155 sq cm, rear 99 sq in, 639 sq cm, total 278 sq in, 1,794 sq cm.

ELECTRICAL EQUIPMENT 12 V; 40 Ah battery; 34 A alternator; Lucas distributor; 4 headlamps.

61 HP POWER TEAM

DIMENSIONS AND WEIGHT wheel base: 98.50 in, 250 cm; tracks: 52 in, 132 cm front, 52 in, 132 cm rear; length: 171 in, 434 cm; width: 63.50 in, 161 cm; height: 56 in, 142 cm; ground clearance: 5.75 in, 14.6 cm; weight: 1,945 lb, 882 kg; turning circle (between walls): 34 ft, 10.4 m; fuel tank: 10 imp gal, 11.9 US gal, 45 l.

BODY saloon/sedan; 4 doors; 4-5 seats, separate front seats; heated rear window.

PRACTICAL INSTRUCTIONS fuel: 97 oct petrol; oil: engine 7.5 imp pt, 8.9 US pt, 4.2 l, SAE 20W-50, change every 5,000 miles, 8,000 km - gearbox 3.5 imp pt, 4.2 US pt, 2 l, SAE 20W-50, no change recommended - final drive 1.8 imp pt. 2.1 US pt, 1 l, SAE 90 EP, no change recommended; greasing: none; tappet clearances: inlet 0.012 in, 0.30 mm, exhaust 0.014 in, 0.36 mm; valve timing: 47° 86° 82° 36°; tyre pressure: front 24 psi, 1.7 atm, rear 24 psi, 1.7 atm.

OPTIONAL ACCESSORIES Borg-Warner 45 automatic transmission, hydraulic torque converter and planetary gears width 4 ratios (I 3, II 1.937, III 1.351, IV 1, rev 4.692), max ratio of converter at stall 2.26, possible manual selection, 3.890 axle ratio; sports wheels; reclining backrests; vinyl roof; metallic spray; tinted glass.

74 hp power team

See 61 hp power team, except for:

ENGINE compression ratio: 9.2:1; max power (DIN): 74 hp (54.5 kW) at 5,100 rpm; max torque (DIN): 95 lb ft, 13.1 kg m (128.5 Nm) at 2,500 rpm; max engine rpm: 6,000; 42.9 hp/l (31.6 kW/l); cast iron block, light alloy head; viscous coupling thermostatic fan.

TRANSMISSION axle ratio: 3.700.

PERFORMANCE max speeds: (I) 33 mph, 53 km/h; (II) 52 mph, 84 km/h; (III) 76 mph, 122 km/h; (IV) 93 mph, 149 km/h; power-weight ratio: 26.7 lb/hp (36.3 lb/kW), 12.1 kg/hp (16.4 kg/kW); acceleration: 0-50 mph (0-80 km/h) 9.4 sec; speed in direct drive at 1,000 rpm: 17.7 mph, 28.5 km/h; consumption: 36.7 m/imp gal, 30.5 m/US gal, 7.7 l x 100 km.

DIMENSIONS AND WEIGHT weight: 1,976 lb, 896 kg.

BODY (standard) reclining backrests; vinyl roof.

PRACTICAL INSTRUCTIONS tappet clearances: inlet 0.013 in, 0.32 mm, exhaust 0.013 in, 0.32 mm; valve timing: 44° 66° 78° 32°.

OPTIONAL ACCESSORIES Borg-Warner 45 automatic transmission, hydraulic torque converter and planetary gears with 4 ratios (I 3, II 1.937, III 1.351, IV 1, rev 4.692), max ratio of converter at stall 2.26, possible manual selection, 3.700 axle ratio.

Sunbeam Series

PRICES EX WORKS:

1 Sunbeam LS Hatchback Saloon	£ 2,324*
2 Sunbeam GL Hatchback Saloon	£ 2,512*
3 Sunbeam S Hatchback Saloon	£ 2,985*

For 59 hp engine add £ 76; for 69 hp engine add £ 180.

Power team:	Standard for:	Optional for:
42 hp	1,2	—
59 hp	—	1,2
69 hp	3	2
70 hp	—	1,2

42 hp power team

ENGINE front, 4 stroke; 4 cylinders, in line; 56.6 cu in, 928 cc (2.76 x 2.37 in, 70 x 60.3 mm); compression ratio: 9:1; max power (DIN): 42 hp (30.9 kW) at 5,000 rpm; max torque (DIN): 51 lb ft, 7 kg m (68.6 Nm) at 2,600 rpm; max engine rpm: 6,000; 45.3 hp/l (33.3 kW/l); light alloy block and head; 3 crankshaft bearings; valves: overhead; camshafts: 1, overhead; lubrication: rotary pump, full flow filter, 5.3 imp pt, 6.3 US pt, 3 l; 1 Zenith 150 DC3 downdraught single barrel carburettor; fuel feed: mechanical pump; water-cooled, 8 imp pt, 9.5 US pt, 4.5 l, electric thermostatic fan.

TRANSMISSION driving wheels: rear; clutch: single dry plate (diaphragm); gearbox: mechanical; gears: 4, fully synchronized; ratios: I 3.894, II 2.382, III 1.527, IV 1, rev 4.050; lever: central; final drive: hypoid bevel; axle ratio: 4.375; width of rims: 4.5''; tyres: 145 x 13.

CHRYSLER Hunter Super

PERFORMANCE max speeds: (I) 22.6 mph, 36 km/h; (II) 37 mph, 60 km/h; (III) 57.6 mph, 93 km/h; (IV) 80 mph, 129 km/h; power-weight ratio: LS 40.7 lb/hp (55.3 lb/kW), 18.4 kg/hp (25 kg/kW) - GL 41 lb/hp (55.8 lb/kW), 18.6 kg/hp (25.3 kg/kW); carrying capacity: 980 lb, 445 kg; acceleration: 0-50 mph (0-80 km/h) 14.3 sec; speed in direct drive top at 1,000 rpm: 14.7 mph, 23.6 km/h; consumption: 50.4 m/imp gal, 42 m/US gal, 5.6 l x 100 km.

CHASSIS integral; front suspension: independent, by McPherson, coil springs/telescopic damper struts, wishbones, anti-roll bar; rear: rigid axle, swinging longitudinal trailing arms, upper oblique torque arms, coil springs, telescopic dampers.

STEERING rack-and-pinion; turns lock to lock: 3.66.

BRAKES front disc (diameter 9.50 in, 24.1 cm), rear drum, servo; swept area: front 177.8 sq in, 1,147 sq cm, rear 74 sq in, 477 sq cm, total 251.8 sq in, 1,624 sq cm.

ELECTRICAL EQUIPMENT 12 V; 40 Ah battery; 35 A alternator; Lucas distributor; 2 headlamps.

DIMENSIONS AND WEIGHT wheel base: 95 in, 241 cm; tracks: 51.80 in, 132 cm front, 51.30 in, 130 cm rear; length: 150.70 in, 383 cm; width: 63.10 in, 160 cm; height: 54.90 in, 139 cm; ground clearance: 6.50 in, 16.6 cm; weight: LS 1,709 lb, 775 kg - GL 1,725 lb, 782 kg; weight distribution: 52% front, 48% rear; turning circle (between walls): 33.5 ft, 10.2 m; fuel tank: 9 imp gal, 10.8 US gal, 41 l.

BODY hatchback saloon; 2+1 doors; 4 seats, separate front seats; reclining backrests; folding rear seat; heated rear window.

PRACTICAL INSTRUCTIONS fuel: 97 oct petrol; oil: engine 5.3 imp pt, 6.3 US pt, 3 l, SAE 20W-50, change every 5,000 miles, 8,000 km - gearbox 3 imp pt, 3.6 US pt, 1.7 l, SAE 20W-50, no change recommended; final drive 1.5 imp pt, 1.9 US pt, 0.9 l, SAE 90 EP, no change recommended; greasing: none; tappet clearances: inlet 0.007 in, 0.17 mm, exhaust 0.009 in, 0.22 mm; valve timing: 27° 61° 55° 9°; tyre pressure: front 21 psi, 1.5 atm, rear 26 psi, 1.8 atm.

OPTIONAL ACCESSORIES tinted glass; laminated windscreen; halogen headlamps; metallic spray; rear window wiper-washer.

59 hp power team

See 42 hp power team, except for:

ENGINE 79 cu in, 1,295 cc (3.09 x 2.62 in, 78.6 x 66.7 mm); compression ratio: 8.8:1; max power (DIN): 59 hp (43.4 kW) at 5,000 rpm; max torque (DIN): 69 lb ft, 9.5 kg m (93.2 Nm) at 2,600 rpm; max engine rpm: 5,900; 45.5 hp/l (33.5 kW/l); cast iron block and head; 5 crankshaft bearings; valves: overhead, push-rods and rockers; camshafts: 1, side; lubricating system: 7 imp pt, 8.5 US pt, 4 l; cooling system: 12.8 imp pt, 15.4 US pt, 7.3 l.

CHRYSLER Sunbeam GL Hatchback Saloon

TRANSMISSION axle ratio: 3.700; tyres: 155 x 13.

PERFORMANCE max speeds: (I) 27 mph, 43 km/h; (II) 44 mph, 71 km/h; (II) 69 mph, 111 km/h; (IV) 89 mph, 143 km/h; power-weight ratio: LS 31.4 lb/hp (42.7 lb/kW), 14.3 kg/hp (19.4 kg/kW) - GL 31.7 lb/hp (43 lb/kW), 14.4 kg/hp (19.5 kg/kW);carrying capacity: 960 lb, 435 kg; acceleration: 0-50 mph (0-80 km/h) 12.6 sec; speed in direct drive at 1,000 rpm: 17.6 mph, 28.4 km/h; consumption: 41.5 m/imp gal, 34.6 m/US gal, 6.8 l x 100 km.

DIMENSIONS AND WEIGHT weight: LS 1,853 lb, 840 kg - GL 1,868 lb, 847 kg; weight distribution: 55.5% front, 44.5% rear.

PRACTICAL INSTRUCTIONS oil: engine 7 imp pt, 8.5 US pt, 4 l; tappet clearances: inlet 0.008 in, 0.20 mm, exhaust 0.016 in, 0.40 mm; valve timing: 38° 66° 72° 20°; tyre pressure: front 22 psi, 1.6 atm, rear 22 psi, 1.6 atm.

69 hp power team

See 42 hp power team, except for:

ENGINE 97.5 cu in, 1,598 cc (3.44 x 2.62 in, 87.3 x 66.7 mm); compression ratio: 8.8:1; max power (DIN): 69 hp (50.8 kW) at 4,800 rpm; max torque (DIN): 91 lb ft, 12.5 kg m (122.6 Nm) at 2,900 rpm; max engine rpm: 5,700; 43.2 hp/l (31.8 kW/l); cast iron block and head; 5 crankshaft bearings; valves: overhead, push-rods and rockers; camshafts: 1, side;

CHRYSLER Sunbeam LS Saloon

CHRYSLER Sunbeam S Hatchback Saloon

lubricating system: 7 imp pt, 8.5 US pt, 4 l; cooling system: 12.9 imp pt, 15.6 US pt, 7.4 l.

TRANSMISSION gearbox ratios: I 3.538, II 2.165, III 1.387, IV 1, rev 3.680; axle ratio: 3.540; tyres: 155 x 13.

PERFORMANCE max speeds: (I) 30 mph, 48 km/h; (II) 49 mph, 79 km/h; (III) 76 mph, 122 km/h; (IV) 95 mph, 153 km/h; power-weight ratio: GL 27 lb/hp (36.8 lb/kW), 12.3 kg/hp (16.7 kg/kW) - S 27.6 lb/hp (37.6 lb/kW), 12.5 kg/hp (17 kg/kW); carrying capacity: 920 lb, 416 kg; acceleration: 0-50 mph (0-80 km/h) 10.3 sec; speed in direct drive at 1,000 rpm: 18.4 mph, 29.6 km/h; consumption: 40.9 m/imp gal, 34.1 m/US gal, 6.9 l x 100 km.

ELECTRICAL EQUIPMENT (standard on S model) halogen headlamps.

DIMENSIONS AND WEIGHT weight: GL 1,868 lb, 847 kg - S 1,910 lb, 866 kg; weight distribution: 55% front, 45% rear.

BODY (standard on S model) tinted glass and rear window wiper-washer.

PRACTICAL INSTRUCTIONS oil: engine 7 imp pt, 8.5 US pt, 4 l; tappet clearances: inlet 0.008 in, 0.20 mm, exhaust 0.016 in, 0.40 mm; valve timing: 38° 66° 72° 20°; tyre pressure: front 22 psi, 1.6 atm, rear 22 psi, 1.6 atm.

OPTIONAL ACCESSORIES Borg-Warner 65 automatic transmission with 4 ratios.

70 hp power team

(only for export).

See 59 hp power team, except for:

ENGINE max power (DIN): 70 hp (51.5 kW) at 5,600 rpm; max torque (DIN): 71 lb ft, 9.8 kg m (96.1 Nm) at 4,800 rpm; 54 hp/l (39.8 kW/l).

PERFORMANCE power-weight ratio: LS 26.5 lb/hp (36 lb/kW), 12 kg/hp (16.3 kg/kW) - GL 26.7 lb/hp (36.3 lb/kW), 12 kg/hp (16.4 kg/kW).

CONCEPT   GREAT BRITAIN

Centaur Mk II

PRICE EX WORKS: £ 1,990

ENGINE rear, 4 stroke; 4 cylinders, slanted at 45°, in line; 53.4 cu in, 875 cc (2.68 x 2.38 in, 68 x 60.4 mm); compression ratio: 10.1; max power (DIN): 37 hp (27.2 kW) at 4,800 rpm; max torque (DIN): 49 lb ft, 6.7 kg m (65.7 Nm) at 2,600 rpm; max engine rpm: 5,600; 42.3 hp/l (31.2 kW/l); light alloy block and head, dry liners; 3 crankshaft bearings; valves: overhead, slanted, thimble tappets; camshafts: 1, overhead, chain driven; lubrication: eccentric pump, full flow filter, 5.5 imp pt, 6.6 US pt, 3.1 l; 1 Solex 30 PIH-5 semi-downdraught single barrel carburettor; fuel feed: mechanical pump; water-cooled, 11.1 imp pt, 13.3 US pt, 6.3 l.

TRANSMISSION driving wheels: rear; clutch: single dry plate (diaphragm), hydraulically controlled; gearbox: mechanical; gears: 4, fully synchronized; ratios: I 3.417, II 1.833, III 1.174, IV 0.852, rev 2.846; lever: central; final drive: hypoid bevel; axle ratio: 4.857.

PERFORMANCE max speed: about 110 mph, 177 km/h; power-weight ratio: 33.3 lb/hp (45.4 lb/kW), 15.1 kg/hp (20.6 kg/kW); consumption: 50 m/imp gal, 42 m/US gal, 5.6 l x 100 km.

CHASSIS integral; front suspension: independent, U-shaped swinging semi-axles, coil springs, telescopic dampers; rear: independent, semi-trailing arms, coil springs, telescopic dampers.

STEERING rack-and-pinion.

BRAKES drum, 2 front leading shoes.

ELECTRICAL EQUIPMENT 12 V; 32 Ah battery; alternator; Lucas distributor; 2 headlamps.

DIMENSIONS AND WEIGHT wheel base: 92 in, 234 cm; tracks: 53 in, 135 cm front, 50 in, 127 cm rear; length: 156 in, 396 cm; width: 66 in, 168 cm; height: 41 in, 104 cm; ground clearance: 5 in, 12.7 cm; weight: 1,233 lb, 559 kg; weight distribution: 60% front, 40% rear; fuel tank: 10 imp gal, 11.9 US gal, 45 l.

BODY sports, in plastic material; 2 doors; 2 seats.

CONCEPT Centaur Mk II

DAIMLER   GREAT BRITAIN

Sovereign 3.4

PRICE EX WORKS: £ 8,830*

ENGINE front, 4 stroke; 6 cylinders, vertical, in line; 210 cu in, 3,442 cc (3.28 x 4.17 in, 83 x 106 mm); compression ratio: 8.5:1; max power (DIN): 161 hp (118.5 kW) at 5,250 rpm; max torque (DIN): 184 lb ft, 25.4 kg m (249.1 Nm) at 4,000 rpm; max engine rpm: 5,500; 46.8 hp/l (34.4 kW/l); cast iron block, dry liners, light alloy head, hemispherical combustion chambers; 7 crankshaft bearings; valves: overhead, Vee-slanted, thimble tappets; camshafts: 2, overhead; lubrication: rotary pump, full flow filter, oil cooler, 14.5 imp pt, 17.3 US pt, 8.2 l; 2 SU type HS8 horizontal carburettors; fuel feed: 2 electric pumps; water-cooled, 31.7 imp pt, 38.1 US pt, 18 l, viscous coupling thermostatic fan.

TRANSMISSION driving wheels: rear; clutch: single dry plate (diaphragm), hydraulically controlled; gearbox: mechanical; gears: 4 + overdrive/top, fully synchronized; ratios: I 3.238, II 1.905, III 1.389, IV 1, overdrive 0.779, rev 3.428; lever: central; final drive: hypoid bevel; axle ratio: 3.540; width of rims: 6''; tyres: E70 VR x 15.

PERFORMANCE max speeds: (I) 36 mph, 58 km/h; (II) 62 mph, 99 km/h; (III) 85 mph, 136 km/h; (IV) 117 mph, 188 km/h; power-weight ratio: 23.1 lb/hp (31.3 lb/kW), 10.5 kg/hp (14.2 kg/kW); carrying capacity: 904 lb, 410 kg; acceleration: standing ¼ mile 18 sec, 0-50 mph (0-80 km/h) 8.7 sec; speed in direct drive at 1,000 rpm: 21.4 mph, 34.4 km/h; consumption: 21.7 m/imp gal, 18.1 m/US gal, 13 l x 100 km.

CHASSIS integral, front and rear auxiliary frames; front suspension: independent, wishbones, lower trailing links, coil springs, anti-roll bar, telescopic dampers; rear: independent, lower wishbones, semi-axles as upper arms, trailing lower radius arms, 4 coil springs, 4 telescopic dampers.

STEERING rack-and-pinion, adjustable steering wheel, servo; turns lock to lock: 3.30.

BRAKES disc (front diameter 11.18 in, 28.4 cm, rear 10.38 in, 26.4 cm), front internal radial fins, servo; swept area: front 234.5 sq in, 1,512 sq cm, rear 213.7 sq in, 1,378 sq cm, total 448.2 sq in, 2,890 sq cm.

ELECTRICAL EQUIPMENT 12 V; 66 Ah battery: 45 A alternator; Lucas distributor; 4 halogen headlamps.

DIMENSIONS AND WEIGHT wheel base: 112.80 in, 286 cm; tracks: 57.99 in, 147 cm front, 58.58 in, 149 cm rear; length: 194.68 in, 494 cm; width: 69.68 in, 177 cm; height: 54.13 in, 137 cm; ground clearance: 7.09 in, 18 cm; weight: 3,715 lb, 1,685 kg; turning circle (between walls): 40 ft, 12.2 m; fuel tank: 20 imp gal, 24 US gal, 91 l (2 separate tanks).

BODY saloon/sedan; 4 doors; 5 seats, separate front seats, reclining backrests; heated rear window.

PRACTICAL INSTRUCTIONS fuel: 97 oct' petrol; oil: engine 14.5 imp pt, 17.3 US pt, 8.2 l, SAE 20W-50, change every 6,000 miles, 9,700 km - gearbox 4.5 imp pt, 6.3 US pt, 2.5 l, SAE 90 EP, change every 12,000 miles, 19,400 km - final drive 2.7 imp pt, 3.2 US pt, 1.5 l, SAE 90 EP, change every 12,000 miles, 19,400 km; greasing: every 6,000 miles, 9,700 km, 17 points; tappet clearances: inlet 0.012-0.014 in, 0.30-0.35 mm, exhaust 0.012-0.014 in, 0.30-0.35 mm; tyre pressure: front 25 psi, 1.7 atm, rear 26 psi, 1.8 atm.

OPTIONAL ACCESSORIES Borg-Warner 65 automatic transmission, hydraulic torque converter and planetary gears with 3 ratios (I 2.400, II 1.460, III 1, rev 2), max ratio of converter at stall 2, possible manual selection, 3.070 or 3.310 axle ratio, 60 A alternator, max speed 115 mph, 185 km/h, acceleration ¼ mile 18.6 sec, consumption 19 m/imp gal, 15.8 m/US gal, 14.9 l x 100 km; headrests; tinted glass; fog lamps; light alloy wheels.

Sovereign 4.2

See Sovereign 3.4, except for:

PRICE EX WORKS: £ 9,065*

ENGINE 258.4 cu in, 4,235 cc (3.63 x 4.17 in, 92 x 106 mm); compression ratio: 7.8:1; max power (DIN): 166 hp (122.2 kW) at 4,750 rpm; max torque (DIN): 222 lb ft, 30.7 kg m (301.1 Nm) at 3,000 rpm; 39.2 hp/l (28.9 kW/l).

TRANSMISSION axle ratio: 3.310.

DAIMLER Double-Six - Vanden Plas

PERFORMANCE max speeds: (I) 40 mph, 64 km/h; (II) 62 mph, 99 km/h; (III) 85 mph, 136 km/h; (IV) 121 mph, 195 km/h; power-weight ratio: 23.8 lb/hp (32.3 lb/kW), 10.8 kg/hp (14.6 kg/kW); acceleration: standing ¼ mile 16.4 sec; speed in direct drive at 1,000 rpm: 22 mph, 35.4 km/h; consumption: 16 m/imp gal, 13.4 m/US gal, 17.6 l x 100 km.

DIMENSIONS AND WEIGHT weight: 3,947 lb, 1,790 kg.

BODY electric windows; headrests (standard).

OPTIONAL ACCESSORIES Borg-Warner 65 automatic transmission, 3.540 axle ratio, max speed 118 mph, 190 km/h, acceleration standing ¼ mile 17.5 sec, consumption 15.3 m/imp gal, 12.7 m/US gal, 18.5 l x 100 km; air-conditioning.

Vanden Plas 4.2

See Sovereign 4.2, except for:

PRICE EX WORKS: £ 12,420*

TRANSMISSION gearbox: Borg-Warner 65 automatic transmission (standard), hydraulic torque converter and planetary gears with 3 ratios, max ratio of converter at stall 2, possible manual selection; ratios: I 2.400, II 1.460, III 1, rev 2; axle ratio: 3.540.

PERFORMANCE max speed: 118 mph, 190 m/h; power-weight ratio: 28.7 lb/hp (39 lb/kW), 13 kg/hp (17.7 kg/kW); acceleration: standing ¼ mile 17.5 sec; consumption: 15.3 m/imp gal, 12.7 m/US gal, 18.5 l x 100 km.

ELECTRICAL EQUIPMENT halogen headlamps (standard).

DIMENSIONS AND WEIGHT weight: 4,763 lb, 2,160 kg.

BODY electric windows; headrests; tinted glass; vinyl roof and air-conditioning (standard).

Double-Six

PRICE EX WORKS: £ 11,102*

ENGINE front, 4 stroke; 12 cylinders, Vee-slanted at 60°; 326 cu in, 5,343 cc (3.54 x 2.76 in, 90 x 70 mm); compression ratio: 9:1; max power (DIN): 284 hp (209 kW) at 5,750 rpm; max torque (DIN): 294 lb ft, 40.7 kg m (399.1 Nm) at 3,500 rpm; max engine rpm: 6,500; 53.2 hp/l (39.1 kW/l); light alloy block and head, wet liners, hemispherical combustion chambers; 7 crankshaft bearings; valves: overhead, in line, thimble tappets; camshafts: 1 per block, overhead; lubrication: rotary pump, full flow filter, oil cooler, 19 imp pt, 22.8 US pt, 10.8 l; Lucas-Bosch electronic injection; fuel feed: electric pump; water-cooled, 36 imp pt, 43.3 US pt, 20.5 l, 1 viscous coupling thermostatic and 1 electric thermostatic fan.

TRANSMISSION driving wheels: rear; gearbox: Turbo-Hydramatic 400 automatic transmission, hydraulic torque converter and planetary gears with 3 ratios, max ratio of converter at stall 2, possible manual selection; ratios: I 2.480, II 1.480, III 1, rev 2.070; lever: central; final drive: hypoid bevel, limited slip differential; axle ratio: 3.310; width of rims: 6''; tyres: 205/70 VR x 15.

DAIMLER Vanden Plas 4.2

PERFORMANCE max speeds: (I) 58 mph, 94 km/h; (II) 96 mph, 155 km/h; (III) 140 mph, 225 km/h; power-weight ratio: 14.6 lb/hp (20 lb/kW), 6.6 kg/hp (9 kg/kW); carrying capacity: 904 lb, 410 kg; acceleration: standing ¼ mile 15.7 sec, 0-50 mph (0-80 km/h) 6.1 sec; speed in direct drive at 1,000 rpm: 24.3 mph, 39.1 km/h; consumption: 14.1 m/imp gal, 11.8 m/US gal, 20 l x 100 km.

CHASSIS integral, front and rear auxiliary frames; front suspension: independent, wishbones, lower trailing links, coil springs, anti-roll bar, telescopic dampers; rear: independent, wishbones, semi-axles as upper arms, trailing lower radius arms, 4 coil springs, 4 telescopic dampers.

STEERING rack-and-pinion, adjustable steering wheel, servo; turns lock to lock: 3.30.

BRAKES disc (front diameter 11.18 in, 28.4 cm, rear 10.38 in, 26.4 cm), front internal radial fins, servo; swept area: front 234.5 sq in, 1,512 sq cm, rear 213.7 sq in, 1,378 sq cm, total 448.2 sq in, 2,890 sq cm.

ELECTRICAL EQUIPMENT 12 V; 68 Ah battery; 60 A alternator; Lucas electronic distributor; 4 halogen headlamps.

DIMENSIONS AND WEIGHT wheel base: 112.80 in, 286 cm; tracks: 57.99 in, 147 cm front, 58.58 in, 149 cm rear; length: 194.68 in, 494 cm; width: 69.68 in, 177 cm; height: 54.13 in, 137 cm; ground clearance: 7.09 in, 18 cm; weight: 4,156 lb, 1,885 kg; turning circle (between walls): 40 ft, 12.2 m; fuel tanks: 20 imp gal, 24 US gal, 91 l (2 separate tanks).

BODY saloon/sedan; 4 doors; 5 seats, separate front seats, reclining backrests with built-in headrests; heated rear window; electric windows.

PRACTICAL INSTRUCTIONS fuel: 97 oct petrol; oil: engine 19 imp pt, 22.8 US pt, 10.8 l, SAE 10W-40 (winter) 20W-50 (summer), change every 6,000 miles, 9,700 km; final drive 2.7 imp pt, 3.2 US pt, 1.5 l, SAE 90 EP, change every 12,000 miles, 19,400 km; greasing: every 6,000 miles, 9,700 km, 17 points; tappet clearances: inlet 0.012-0.014 in, 0.30-0.35 mm, exhaust 0.012-0.014 in, 0.30-0.35 mm; tyre pressure: front 25 psi, 1.7 atm, rear 26 psi, 1.8 atm.

OPTIONAL ACCESSORIES air-conditioning; fog lamps; light alloy wheels.

Double-Six - Vanden Plas

See Double-Six, except for:

PRICE EX WORKS: £ 14,583*

PERFORMANCE power-weight ratio: 14.5 lb/hp (19.7 lb/kW), 6.6 kg/hp (8.9 kg/kW).

DIMENSIONS AND WEIGHT weight: 4,116 lb, 1,866 kg.

BODY luxury equipment; air-conditioning, vinyl roof and tinted glass (standard).

DAIMLER Sovereign Saloon

bar, telescopic dampers; rear: independent, wishbones, semi-axle as upper arm, trailing lower radius arms, 4 coil springs, 4 telescopic dampers.

STEERING recirculating ball, adjustable steering wheel, variable ratio gearing servo; turns lock to lock: 2.75.

BRAKES disc (front diameter 10.90 in, 27.7 cm, rear 10.30 in, 26.1 cm), internal radial fins, servo; swept area: front 234 sq in, 1,509 sq cm, rear 212 sq in, 1,367 sq cm, total 446 sq in, 2,876 sq cm.

ELECTRICAL EQUIPMENT 12 V; 60 Ah battery: 45 A alternator; Lucas distributor; 4 headlamps.

DIMENSIONS AND WEIGHT wheel base: 141 in, 358 cm; front and rear tracks: 58 in, 147 cm; length: 226 in, 574 cm; width: 77.56 in, 197 cm; height: 63.39 in, 161 cm; ground clearance: 7.09 in, 18 cm; weight: 4,705 lb, 2,134 kg; turning circle (between walls): 46 ft, 14 m; fuel tanks: 20 imp gal, 24 US gal, 91 l (2 separate tanks).

BODY limousine; 4 doors; 8 seats, bench front seats; glass partition.

PRACTICAL INSTRUCTIONS fuel: 97 oct petrol; oil: engine 12 imp pt, 14.4 US pt, 6.8 l, multigrade, change every 3,000 miles, 5,000 km; tappet clearances: inlet 0.012-0.014 in, 0.31-0.36 mm, exhaust 0.012-0.014 in, 0.31-0.36 mm.

OPTIONAL ACCESSORIES air-conditioning; electric glass partition; electric windows; tinted glass; heated rear window; halogen headlamps.

DAIMLER Limousine

Limousine

PRICE EX WORKS: £ 13,572*

ENGINE front, 4 stroke; 6 cylinders, vertical, in line; 258.4 cu in, 4,235 cc (3.63 x 4.17 in, 92.1 x 106 mm); compression ratio: 7.5:1; max power (DIN): 162 hp (119.2 kW) at 4,250 rpm; max torque (DIN): 222 lb ft, 30.7 kg m (301.1 Nm) at 3,000 rpm; max engine rpm: 5,500; 38.2 hp/l (28.1 kW/l); cast iron block, dry liners, light alloy head, hemispherical combustion chambers; 7 crankshaft bearings; valves: overhead, Vee-slanted at 70°, thimble tappets; camshafts: 2, overhead; lubrication: mechanical pump, full flow filter, 12 imp pt, 14.4 US pt, 6.8 l; 2 SU type HD8 horizontal carburettors; fuel feed: 2 electric pumps; water-cooled, 25.5 imp pt, 30.7 US pt, 14.5 l, viscous coupling thermostatic fan.

TRANSMISSION driving wheels: rear; gearbox: Borg-Warner automatic transmission, hydraulic torque converter and planetary gears with 3 ratios, max ratio of converter at stall 2, possible manual selection; ratios: I 2.401, II 1.458, III 1, rev 2; lever: steering column; final drive: hypoid bevel; axle ratio: 3.540; tyres 205/70 HR x 15.

PERFORMANCE max speeds: (I) 48 mph, 78 km/h; (II) 79 mph, 127 km/h; (III) 115 mph, 185 km/h; power-weight ratio: 29 lb/hp (39.7 lb/kW), 13.2 kg/hp (17.9 kg/kW); carrying capacity: 1,235 lb, 560 kg; acceleration: standing ¼ mile 19.5 sec; speed in direct drive at 1,000 rpm: 20.9 mph, 33.6 km/h; consumption: 17.6 m/imp gal, 14.7 m/US gal, 16 l x 100 km.

CHASSIS integral, front and rear auxiliary frames; front suspension: independent, wishbones, coil springs, anti-roll

DAIMLER Double-Six - Vanden Plas

DAIMLER Limousine

DAVRIAN Imp

DAVRIAN   GREAT BRITAIN

Imp

ENGINE Hillman Imp, rear, 4 stroke; 4 cylinders, slanted at 45º, in line; 53.4 cu in, 875 cc (2.68 x 2.38 in, 68 x 60.4 mm); compression ratio: 10:1; max power (DIN): 39 hp (28.7 kW) at 5,000 rpm; max torque (DIN): 52 lb ft, 7.2 kg m (70.6 Nm) at 2,800 rpm; max engine rpm: 5,600; 44.6 hp/l (32.8 kW/l); light alloy block and head, dry liners; 3 crankshaft bearings; valves: overhead, slanted, thimble tappets; camshafts: 1, overhead, chain driven; lubrication: eccentric pump, full flow filter, 5.5 imp pt, 6.6 US pt, 3.1 l; 1 Solex 30 PIH-5 semi-downdraught single barrel carburettor; fuel feed: mechanical pump; water-cooled, 11.4 imp pt, 13.7 US pt, 6.5 l.

TRANSMISSION driving wheels: rear; clutch: single dry plate (diaphragm), hydraulically controlled; gearbox: mechanical; gears: 4, fully synchronized; ratios: I 3.417, II 1.833, III 1.174, IV 0.852, rev 2.846; lever: central; final drive: hypoid bevel; axle ratio: 4.857; width of rims: 4.5''; tyres: 155 x 12.

PERFORMANCE max speed: 95 mph, 153 km/h; power-weight ratio: 26 lb/hp (35.3 lb/kW), 11.8 kg/hp (16 kg/kW); carrying capacity: 353 lb, 160 kg; acceleration: standing ¼ mile 16.8 sec, 0-50 mph (0-80 km/h) 6.1 sec; consumption: 45.6 m/imp gal, 37.9 m/US gal, 6.2 l x 100 km.

CHASSIS integral; front suspension: independent, U-shaped swinging semi-axles, coil springs, telescopic dampers; rear: independent, semi-trailing arms, coil springs, telescopic dampers.

STEERING rack-and-pinion.

BRAKES drum, 2 front leading shoes; swept area: total 150 sq in, 967 sq cm.

ELECTRICAL EQUIPMENT 12 V; 32 Ah battery; 297 W dynamo; Lucas distributor; 2 retractable headlamps.

DIMENSIONS AND WEIGHT wheel base: 83.86 in, 213 cm; tracks: 48.03 in, 122 cm front, 48.03 in, 122 cm rear; length: 140.94 in, 358 cm; width: 59.84 in, 152 cm; height: 39.76 in, 101 cm; ground clearance: 6.30 in, 16 cm; weight: 1,014 lb, 460 kg; fuel tanks: 8 imp gal, 9.5 US gal, 36 l (2 separate tanks).

BODY coupé, in plastic material; 2 doors; 2 seats.

PRACTICAL INSTRUCTIONS fuel: 98-100 oct petrol; oil: engine 5.5 imp pt, 6.6 US pt, 3.1 l, SAE 30W-50, change every 5,000 miles, 8,000 km - gearbox and final drive 4.5 imp pt, 5.3 US pt, 2.5 l, SAE 80 EP, no change recommended; greasing: none; tappet clearances: inlet 0.007 in, 0.18 mm, exhaust 0.014 in, 0.36 mm; valve timing: 67º 93º 63º 13º; tyre pressure: front 18 psi, 1.3 atm, rear 30 psi, 2.1 atm.

VARIATIONS

ENGINE Sunbeam Sport, max power (DIN) 50 hp (36.8 kW) at 5,800 rpm, max torque (DIN) 52 lb ft, 7.2 kg m (70.6 Nm)

DAVRIAN Imp

at 4,300 rpm, 57.1 hp/l (42.1 kW/l), lubricating system 6 imp pt, 7.2 US pt, 3.4 l, oil cooler, 2 Zenith-Stromberg 125 CD horizontal carburettors.
PERFORMANCE max speed 110 mph, 177 km/h, power-weight ratio 20.3 lb/hp (27.6 lb/kW), 9.2 kg/hp (12.5 kg/kW), consumption 39.2 m/imp gal, 32.7 m/US gal, 7.2 l x 100 km.

OPTIONALS Mini, Volkswagen and Ford engines; front radiator; sunshine roof.

DUTTON   GREAT BRITAIN

Malaga

PRICE EX WORKS: £ 295* (body and chassis)

ENGINE Ford Cortina 1600, front, 4 stroke; 4 cylinders, vertical, in line; 97.2 cu in, 1,593 cc (3.45 x 2.60 in, 87.6 x 66 mm); compression ratio: 9:1; max power (DIN): 72 hp (53 kW) at 5,500 rpm; max torque (DIN): 87 lb ft, 12 kg m (117.7 Nm) at 3,000 rpm; max engine rpm: 6,000; 45.2 hp/l (33.3 kW/l); cast iron block and head; 5 crankshaft bearings; valves: overhead; camshafts: 1, overhead; lubrication: rotary pump, full flow filter, 6 imp pt, 7.2 US pt, 3.4 l; 1 Weber downdraught twin barrel carburettor; fuel feed: mechanical pump; water-cooled, 11.4 imp pt, 13.7 US pt, 6.5 l.

TRANSMISSION driving wheels: rear; clutch: single dry plate (diaphragm); gearbox: mechanical; gears: 4, fully synchronized; ratios: I 3.580, II 2.010, III 1.400, IV 1, rev 3.320; lever: central; final drive: hypoid bevel; axle ratio: 3.700; width of rims: 5.5'' or 6''.

PERFORMANCE power-weight ratio: 15.6 lb/hp (21.2 lb/kW), 7.1 kg/hp (9.6 kg/kW).

CHASSIS multi-tubular space frame; front suspension: independent, lower wishbones, coil springs/telescopic damper units, anti-roll bar; rear: rigid axle, twin trailing radius arms, A-bracket, coil springs/telescopic damper units.

STEERING rack-and-pinion; turns lock to lock: 3.50.

BRAKES front disc, rear drum.

ELECTRICAL EQUIPMENT 12 V; 2 headlamps.

DIMENSIONS AND WEIGHT wheel base: 86 in, 218 cm; tracks: 52 in, 132 cm front, 52 in, 132 cm rear; length: 138 in, 351 cm; width: 61 in, 155 cm; height: 42.50 in, 108 cm; ground clearance: 6 in, 15 cm; weight: about 1,125 lb, 510 kg.

BODY roadster, in plastic material; 2 seats; 2 side screens; roll bar.

DUTTON Malaga

VARIATIONS

ENGINE Ford Capri II 3000 GT, 6 cylinders, Vee-slanted at 60°, 182.7 cu in, 2,994 cc (3.69 x 2.85 in, 93.7 x 72.4 mm), max power (DIN) 142 hp (104.5 kW) at 5,100 rpm, max torque (DIN) 174 lb ft, 24 kg m (235.4 Nm) at 3,000 rpm, 47.4 hp/l (34.9 kW/l).
PERFORMANCE power-weight ratio 7.9 lb/hp (10.8 lb/kW), 3.6 kg/hp (4.9 kg/kW).

B Plus

PRICE EX WORKS: £ 295* (body and chassis)

ENGINE Ford Cortina 1600, front, 4 stroke; 4 cylinders, vertical, in line; 97.2 cu in, 1,593 cc (3.45 x 2.60 in, 87.6 x 66 mm); compression ratio: 9:1; max power (DIN): 72 hp (53 kW) at 5,500 rpm; max torque (DIN): 87 lb ft, 12 kg m (117.7 Nm) at 3,000 rpm; max engine rpm: 6,000; 45.2 hp/l (33.3 kW/l); cast iron block and head; 5 crankshaft bearings; valves: overhead; camshafts: 1, overhead; lubrication: rotary pump, full flow filter, 6 imp pt, 7.2 US pt, 3.4 l; 1 Weber downdraught twin barrel carburettor; fuel feed: mechanical pump; water-cooled, 11.4 imp pt, 13.7 US pt, 6.5 l.

TRANSMISSION driving wheels: rear; clutch: single dry plate (diaphragm); gearbox: mechanical; gears: 4, fully synchronized; ratios: I 3.580, II 2.010, III 1.400, IV 1, rev 3.320; lever: central; final drive: hypoid bevel; axle ratio: 3.700; width of rims: 5.5'' or 6''.

PERFORMANCE power-weight ratio: 15.6 lb/hp (21.2 lb/kW), 7.1 kg/hp (9.6 kg/kW).

CHASSIS multi-tubular space frame; front suspension: independent, lower wishbones, coil springs/telescopic damper units, anti-roll bar; rear: rigid axle, twin trailing radius arms, A-bracket, coil springs/telescopic damper units.

STEERING rack-and-pinion; turns lock to lock: 3.50.

BRAKES front disc, rear drum.

ELECTRICAL EQUIPMENT 12 V; 2 headlamps.

DIMENSIONS AND WEIGHT wheel base: 86 in, 218 cm; tracks: 52 in, 132 cm front, 52 in, 132 cm rear; length: 135 in, 343 cm; width: 61 in, 155 cm; height: 42.50 in, 108 cm; ground clearance: 6 in, 15 cm; weight: about 1,125 lb, 510 kg.

BODY roadster, in plastic material; 2 seats; 2 side screens; roll bar.

VARIATIONS

ENGINE Ford Capri II 3000 GT, 6 cylinders, Vee-slanted at 60°, 182.7 cu in, 2,994 cc (3.69 x 2.85 in, 93.7 x 72.4 mm), max power (DIN) 142 hp (104.5 kW) at 5,100 rpm, max torque (DIN) 174 lb ft, 24 kg m (235.4 Nm) at 3,000 rpm, 47.4 hp/l (34.9 kW/l).
PERFORMANCE power-weight ratio 7.9 lb/hp (10.8 lb/kW), 3.6 kg/hp (4.9 kg/kW).

DUTTON B Plus

FAIRTHORPE TX 1500 - 2000

FAIRTHORPE GREAT BRITAIN

TX 1500

PRICE EX WORKS: £ 2,754*

ENGINE front, 4 stroke; 4 cylinders, in line; 91.1 cu in, 1,493 cc (2.90 x 3.44 in, 73.7 x 87.5 mm); compression ratio: 9.5:1; max power (SAE): 71 hp (52.3 kW) at 5,000 rpm; max torque (SAE): 82 lb ft, 11.3 kg m (110.8 Nm) at 3,000 rpm; max engine rpm: 6,000; 47.6 hp/l (35 kW/l); cast iron block and head; 5 crankshaft bearings; valves: overhead, in line, push-rods and rockers; camshafts: 1, side; lubrication: gear pump, full flow filter, 8 imp pt, 9.5 US pt, 4.5 l; 2 SU type HS 4 semi-downdraught carburettors; fuel feed: mechanical pump; water-cooled, 6 imp pt, 7.2 US pt, 3.4 l.

TRANSMISSION driving wheels: rear; clutch: single dry plate (diaphragm), hydraulically controlled; gearbox: mechanical; gears: 4, fully synchronized; ratios: I 3.500, II 2.160, III 1.390, IV 1, rev 3.990; lever: central; final drive: hypoid bevel; axle ratio: 3.890; width of rims: 5''; tyres: 165 SR x 13.

PERFORMANCE max speed: 105 mph, 169 km/h; power-weight ratio: 21.3 lb/hp (28.9 lb/kW), 9.6 kg/hp (13.1

kg/kW); carrying capacity: 672 lb, 304 kg; speed in direct drive at 1,000 rpm: 17.2 mph, 27.7 km/h; consumption: 33 m/imp gal, 27.7 m/US gal, 8.5 l x 100 km.

CHASSIS double backbone, box section with outriggers; front suspension: independent, wishbones, coil springs, telescopic dampers; rear: independent, wishbones, transverse leafspring as upper arms, lower trailing links, telescopic dampers.

STEERING rack-and-pinion; turns lock to lock: 3.50.

BRAKES front disc (diameter 9 in, 22.3 cm), rear drum; swept area: front 197 sq in, 1,270 sq cm, rear 63 sq in, 406 sq cm, total 260 sq in, 1,676 sq cm.

ELECTRICAL EQUIPMENT 12 V; 52 Ah battery; 17 A alternator; Lucas distributor; 2 headlamps.

DIMENSIONS AND WEIGHT wheel base: 83 in, 211 cm; tracks: 49.50 in, 126 cm front, 49.50 in, 126 cm rear; length: 146.46 in, 372 cm; width: 58 in, 147 cm; height: 44.49 in, 113 cm; ground clearance: 5 in, 12.7 cm; weight: 1,512 lb, 685 kg; turning circle (between walls): 25.3 ft, 7.7 m; fuel tank: 9.7 imp gal, 11.6 US gal, 44 l.

BODY coupé, in reinforced plastic material; 2 doors; 2 seats.

PRACTICAL INSTRUCTIONS fuel: 97 oct petrol; oil: engine 6.5 imp pt, 7.8 US pt, 3.7 l, SAE 20W-30, change every 6,000 miles, 9,700 km - gearbox 1.4 imp pt, 1.7 US pt, 0.8 l, SAE 90, no change recommended - final drive 1.6 imp pt, 1.9 US pt, 0.9 l, SAE 90, no change recommended;

greasing: every 6,000 miles, 9,700 km, 3 points; tappet clearances: inlet 0.010 in, 0.25 mm, exhaust 0.010 in, 0.25 mm; valve timing: 18° 58° 58° 18°; tyre pressure: front 23 psi, 1.6 atm, rear 23 psi, 1.6 atm.

TX 2000

See TX 1500, except for:

PRICE EX WORKS: £ 3,453*

ENGINE 121.9 cu in, 1,998 cc (3.56 x 3.07 in, 90.3 x 78 mm); max power (SAE): 127 hp (93.5 kW) at 5,700 rpm; max torque (SAE): 122 lb ft, 16.8 kg m (164.8 Nm) at 4,500 rpm; 63.6 hp/l (46.8 kW/l); cast iron block, light alloy head; valves: overhead, in line, thimble tappets; camshafts: 1, overhead; 2 Stromberg 175 CD SEV horizontal carburettors; cooling system: 12.8 imp pt, 15.4 US pt, 7.3 l.

PERFORMANCE max speed: 118 mph, 190 km/h; power-weight ratio: 12.8 lb/hp (17.4 lb/kW), 5.8 kg/hp (7.9 kg/kW); carrying capacity: 728 lb, 330 kg; speed in direct drive at 1,000 rpm: 19.7 mph, 31.7 km/h; consumption: 24 m/imp gal, 19.9 m/US gal, 11.8 l x 100 km.

DIMENSIONS AND WEIGHT weight: 1,624 lb, 736 kg.

PRACTICAL INSTRUCTIONS tappet clearances: inlet 0.008 in, 0.20 mm, exhaust 0.008 in, 0.20 mm; valve timing: 16° 56° 56° 16°.

FORD   GREAT BRITAIN

Fiesta Series

PRICES EX WORKS:

1 Fiesta 3-door Saloon	£ 2,114*
2 Fiesta L 3-door Saloon	£ 2,329*
3 Fiesta S 3-door Saloon	£ 2,680*
4 Fiesta Ghia 3-door Saloon	£ 3,107*

Power team:	Standard for:	Optional for:
40 hp	1,2	—
45 hp	—	1,2
53 hp	3,4	2

40 hp power team

ENGINE front, transverse, 4 stroke; 4 cylinders, vertical, in line; 58.4 cu in, 957 cc ,2.91 x 2.19 in, 74 x 55.7 mm); compression ratio: 8.3:1; max power (DIN): 40 hp (29.4 kW) at 5,500 rpm; max torque (DIN): 47 lb ft, 6.5 kg m (63.7 Nm) at 2,700 rpm; max engine rpm: 5,700; 41.8 hp/l (30.7 kW/l); cast iron block and head; 3 crankshaft bearings; valves: overhead, in line, push-rods and rockers; camshafts: 1, side, chain driven; lubrication: gear pump, full flow filter (cartridge), 6.2 imp pt, 7.4 US pt, 3.5 l; 1 Ford downdraught single barrel carburettor; fuel feed: mechanical pump; semi-sealed circuit cooling, expansion tank, 8.8 imp pt, 10.6 US pt, 5 l, electric fan.

TRANSMISSION driving wheels: front; clutch: single dry plate (diaphragm); gearbox: mechanical, in unit with final drive; gears: 4, fully synchronized; ratios: I 3.583, II 2.050, III 1.346, IV 0.959, rev 3.769; lever: central; final drive: spiral bevel; axle ratio: 4.060; width of rims: 4''; tyres: 145 SR x 12.

PERFORMANCE max speed: 81 mph, 130 km/h; power-weight ratio: 38.6 lb/hp (52.5 lb/kW), 17.5 kg/hp (23.8 kg/kW); carrying capacity: 948 lb, 430 kg; acceleration: 0-50 mph, 0-80 km/h) 14.2 sec; speed in top at 1,000 rpm: 15.8 mph, 25.4 km/h; consumption: 41.5 m/imp gal, 34.5 m/US gal, 6.8 l x 100 km.

CHASSIS integral; front suspension: independent, by McPherson, coil springs/telescopic damper struts, lower wishbones (trailing links); rear: rigid axle, swinging longitudinal trailing arms, upper oblique torque arms, Panhard rod, coil springs, telescopic dampers.

STEERING rack-and-pinion; turns lock to lock: 3.40.

BRAKES front disc (diameter 8.71 in, 22.1 cm), rear drum, rear compensator; lining area: front 18.6 sq in, 120 sq cm, rear 26.4 sq in, 169.9 sq cm, total 45 sq in, 289.9 sq cm.

ELECTRICAL EQUIPMENT 12 V; 35 Ah battery; 45 A alternator; Motorcraft distributor; 2 headlamps.

DIMENSIONS AND WEIGHT wheel base: 90.16 in, 229 cm; tracks: 52.36 in, 133 cm front, 51.97 in, 132 cm rear; length: 140.16 in, 356 cm; width: 61.81 in, 157 cm; height: 53.54 in, 136 cm; ground clearance: 5.51 in, 14 cm; weight: 1,544 lb, 700 kg - L 1,561 lb, 708 kg; turning circle (between walls): 32.1 ft, 9.8 m; fuel tank: 7.5 imp gal, 9 US gal, 34 l.

BODY saloon/sedan; 3 doors; 5 seats, separate front seats; folding rear seat.

PRACTICAL INSTRUCTIONS fuel: 90 oct petrol; oil: engine 4.8 imp pt, 5.7 US pt, 2.7 l, change every 6,200 miles, 10,000 km - gearbox and final drive 3.9 imp pt, 4.7 US pt, 2.2 l, change every 6,200 miles, 10,000 km; valve timing: 21° 55° 70° 22°.

OPTIONAL ACCESSORIES 155 SR x 12 tyres with 4.5'' wide rims; servo brake; headrests on front seats; tinted glass; ligth alloy wheels; sunshine roof; rear window wiper-washer; headlamps washers; halogen headlamps; fog lamps; metallic spray; Touring equipment.

45 hp power team

See 40 hp power team, except for:

ENGINE compression ratio: 9:1; max power (DIN): 45 hp (33.1 kW) at 6,000 rpm; max torque (DIN): 48 lb ft, 6.6 kg ·m (64.7 Nm) at 3,300 rpm; max engine rpm: 6,500; 47 hp/l (34.6 kW/l).

TRANSMISSION axle ratio: 4.290.

PERFORMANCE max speed: 85 mph, 137 km/h; power-weight ratio: 34.3 lb/hp (46.6 lb/kW), 15.6 kg/hp (21.1 kg/kW); speed in top at 1,000 rpm: 14.9 mph, 24 km/h; consumption: 37.7 m/imp gal, 31.4 m/US gal, 7.5 l x 100 km.

PRACTICAL INSTRUCTIONS fuel: 97 oct petrol.

FORD Fiesta Ghia 3-door Saloon

FORD Fiesta S 3-door Saloon

53 hp power team

See 40 hp power team, except for:

ENGINE 68.2 cu in, 1,117 cc (2.91 x 2.56 in, 74 x 65 mm); compression ratio: 9:1; max power (DIN): 53 hp (39 kW) at 5,700 rpm; max torque (DIN): 59 lb ft, 8.2 kg m (80.4 Nm) at 3,000 rpm; max engine rpm: 6,000; 47.4 hp/l (34.9 kW/l); electric thermostatic fan.

TRANSMISSION width of rims: 4.5''.

PERFORMANCE max speed: 90 mph, 145 km/h; power-weight ratio: S 30.1 lb/hp (40.9 lb/kW), 13.6 kg/hp (18.5 kg/kW) - Ghia 30.4 lb/hp (41.2 lb/kW), 13.8 kg/hp (18.7 kg/kW); consumption: 35.8 m/imp gal, 29.8 m/US gal, 7.9 l x 100 km.

CHASSIS rear suspension: anti-roll bar.

DIMENSIONS AND WEIGHT weight: S 1,594 lb, 723 kg - Ghia 1,610 lb, 730 kg.

BODY Ghia light alloy wheels.

PRACTICAL INSTRUCTIONS fuel: 97 oct petrol.

Escort Series

PRICES EX WORKS:

1 Escort Popular 1100 2-door Saloon	£ 2,023*
2 Escort Popular 1100 Plus 2-door Saloon	£ 2,148*
3 Escort Popular 1100 Plus 4-door Saloon	£ 2,243*
4 Escort 1100 Estate Car	£ 2,312*
5 Escort 1100 L 2-door Saloon	£ 2,342*
6 Escort 1100 L 4-door Saloon	£ 2,437*
7 Escort Popular 1300 2-door Saloon	£ 2,121*
8 Escort Popular 1300 Plus 2-door Saloon	£ 2,229*
9 Escort Popular 1300 Plus 4-door Saloon	£ 2,323*
10 Escort 1300 Estate Car	£ 2,434*
11 Escort 1300 L 2-door Saloon	£ 2,410*
12 Escort 1300 L 4-door Saloon	£ 2,505*
13 Escort 1300 L Estate Car	£ 2,704*
14 Escort 1300 GL 2-door Saloon	£ 2,636*
15 Escort 1300 GL 4-door Saloon	£ 2,730*
16 Escort 1300 GL Estate Car	£ 2,930*
17 Escort 1300 Sport 2-door Saloon	£ 2,798*
18 Escort 1300 Ghia 2-door Saloon	£ 3,182*
19 Escort 1300 Ghia 4-door Saloon	£ 3,276*
20 Escort 1600 Sport 2-door Saloon	£ 2,883*
21 Escort 1600 Ghia 4-door Saloon	£ 3,361*
22 Escort RS Mexico 2-door Saloon	£ 3,281*
23 Escort RS 1800 2-door Saloon	£ 4,275*
24 Escort RS 2000 2-door Saloon	£ 3,973*

Power team:	Standard for:	Optional for:
41 hp	1 to 6	—
57 hp	7 to 16	—
70 hp	17 to 19	—
84 hp	20,21	—
95 hp	22	—
110 hp	24	—
115 hp	23	—

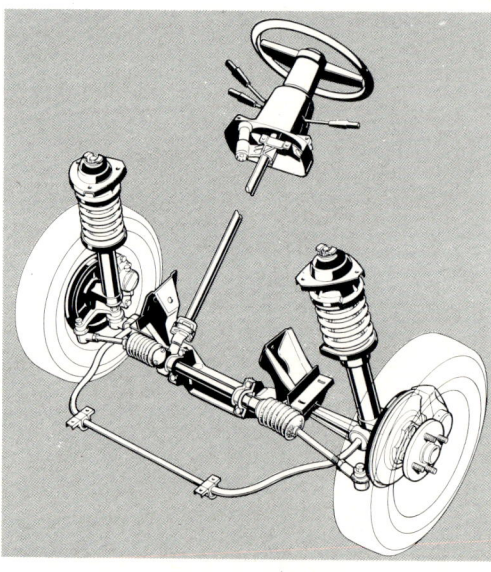

FORD Escort Series

41 hp power team

ENGINE front, 4 stroke; 4 cylinders, vertical, in line; 67 cu in, 1,098 cc (3.19 x 2.10 in, 81 x 53.3 mm); compression ratio: 9:1; max power (DIN): 41 hp (30.2 kW) at 5,300 rpm; max torque (DIN): 52 lb ft, 7.2 kg m (70.6 Nm) at 3,000 rpm; max engine rpm: 6,000: 37.3 hp/l (27.5 kW/l); cast iron block and head; 5 crankshaft bearings; valves: overhead, in line, push-rods and rockers; camshafts: 1, side, chain driven; lubrication: rotary or vane-type pump, full flow filter, 5.7 imp pt, 6.8 US pt, 3.2 l; 1 Ford GPD downdraught single barrel carburettor; fuel feed: mechanical pump; water-cooled, 8.8 imp pt, 10.6 US pt, 5 l.

TRANSMISSION driving wheels: rear; clutch: single dry plate (diaphragm); gearbox: mechanical; gears: 4, fully synchronized; ratios: I 3.656, II 2.185, III 1.425, IV 1, rev 4.235; lever: central; final drive: hypoid bevel; axle ratio: 3.890; width of rims: 4.5''; tyres: 155 SR x 12 - Popular models 6.00 x 12.

PERFORMANCE max speed: 76 mph, 122 km/h; power-weight ratio: 43.9 lb/hp (59.6 lb/kW), 19.9 kg/hp (27 kg/kW); carrying capacity: 939 lb, 426 kg; speed in direct drive at 1,000 rpm: 16 mph, 25.8 km/h; consumption: 43.7 m/imp gal, 36.2 m/US gal, 6.5 l x 100 km.

CHASSIS integral; front suspension: independent, by McPherson, coil springs/telescopic damper struts, anti-roll bar; rear: rigid axle, semi-elliptic leafsprings, telescopic dampers.

FORD Escort Popular

57 hp power team

See 41 hp power team, except for:

ENGINE 79.2 cu in, 1,298 cc (3.19 x 2.48 in, 81 x 63 mm); compression ratio: 9.2:1; max power (DIN): 57 hp (41.9 kW) at 5,500 rpm; max torque (DIN): 67 lb ft, 9.3 kg m (91.2 Nm) at 3,000 rpm; max engine rpm: 5,700; 43.9 hp/l (32.3 kW/l).

TRANSMISSION tyres: 155 SR x 13.

PERFORMANCE max speed: 88 mph, 141 km/h; power-weight ratio: Escort 1300 GL saloons 32.6 lb/hp (44.4 lb/kW), 14.8 kg/hp (20.1 kg/kW); acceleration: 0-50 mph (0-80 km/h) 16.5 sec; consumption: 37.8 m/imp gal, 31.4 m/US gal, 7.5 l x 100 km.

CHASSIS rear suspension: anti-roll bar.

ELECTRICAL EQUIPMENT halogen headlamps (standard for GL models only).

DIMENSIONS AND WEIGHT length: Escort 1300 GL saloons 159.50 in, 405 cm; weight: Escort 1300 GL saloons 1,859 lb, 843 kg.

OPTIONAL ACCESSORIES Ford C3 automatic transmission, hydraulic torque converter and planetary gears with 3 ratios (I 2.474, II 1.474, III 1, rev 2.111), max ratio of converter at stall 2.3, possible manual selection, max speed 84 mph, 135 km/h.

70 hp power team

See 41 hp power team, except for:

ENGINE 79.2 cu in, 1,298 cc (3.19 x 2.48 in, 81 x 63 mm); compression ratio: 9.2:1; max power (DIN): 70 hp (51.5 kW) at 5,500 rpm; max torque (DIN): 68 lb ft, 9.4 kg m (92.2 Nm) at 4,000 rpm; max engine rpm: 6,500; 53.9 hp/l (39.7 kW/l); 1 Weber 32/32 DGV downdraught twin barrel carburettor.

TRANSMISSION ratios: I 3.337, II 1.995, III 1.418, IV 1, rev 3.876; axle ratio: 4.125; width of rims: 5''; tyres: 155 SR x 13 - 1300 Sport 175/70 SR x 13.

PERFORMANCE max speed: 94 mph, 151 km/h - 1300 Ghia saloons 95 mph, 153 km/h; power-weight ratio: 1300 Sport 27.1 lb/hp (36.8 lb/kW), 12.3 kg/hp (16.7 kg/kW) - 1300 Ghia saloons 27.7 lb/hp (37.7 lb/kW), 12.6 kg/hp (17.1 kg/kW); consumption: 35.5 m/imp gal, 29.4 m/US gal, 8 l x 100 km.

CHASSIS rear suspension: anti-roll bar.

BRAKES servo.

ELECTRICAL EQUIPMENT halogen headlamps.

DIMENSIONS AND WEIGHT weight: 1300 Sport 1,896 lb, 860 kg - 1300 Ghia saloons 1,940 lb, 880 kg.

PRACTICAL INSTRUCTIONS valve timing: 29° 63° 71° 21°.

FORD Escort Popular 1100 Plus 2-door Saloon

STEERING rack-and-pinion; turns lock to lock: 3.50.

BRAKES front disc (diameter 9.60 in, 24.4 cm), rear drum (drum front and rear on Popular models).

ELECTRICAL EQUIPMENT 12 V; 38 Ah battery; 35 A alternator; Motorcraft distributor; 2 headlamps.

DIMENSIONS AND WEIGHT wheel base: 94.50 in, 240 cm; tracks: 49.50 in, 126 cm front, 50.60 in, 128 cm rear; length: 156.80 in, 398 cm; width: 61.80 in, 157 cm; height: 54.50 in, 138 cm; ground clearance: 4.92 in, 12.5 cm; weight: 1,799 lb, 816 kg; turning circle (between walls): 29.2 ft, 8.9 m; fuel tank: 9 imp gal, 10.8 US gal, 41 l.

BODY 5 seats, separate front seats; reclining backrests and heated rear window (standard for L models only).

PRACTICAL INSTRUCTIONS fuel: 97 oct petrol; oil: engine 5.8 imp pt, 7 US pt, 3.3 l, SAE 10W-30, change every 6,000 miles, 9,700 km - gearbox 1.6 imp pt, 1.9 US pt, 0.9 l, SAE 80, no change recommended - final drive 1.7 imp pt, 2.1 US pt, 1 l, SAE 90, no change recommended; greasing: none; tappet clearances: inlet 0.010 in, 0.25 mm; exhaust 0.017 in, 0.43 mm; valve timing: 21° 55° 70° 22'; tyre pressure: front 24 psi, 1.7 atm, rear 24 psi, 1.7 atm.

OPTIONAL ACCESSORIES laminated windscreen; heated rear window; halogen headlamps; rear fog lamps; headrests; metallic spray; servo brake (for Estate Car only); reclining backrests; 155 SR x 12 tyres (for L models only); tinted glass; vinyl roof; sports road wheels.

FORD Escort 1600 Sport 2-door Saloon

84 hp power team

See 41 hp power team, except for:

ENGINE 95.6 cu in, 1,599 cc (3.19 x 3.06 in, 81 x 77.6 mm); max power (DIN): 84 hp (61.8 kW) at 5,500 rpm; max torque (DIN): 92 lb ft, 12.7 kg m (124.5 Nm) at 3,500 rpm; max engine rpm: 6,600; 52.5 hp/l (38.6 kW/l); 1 Weber 32/32 DGV downdraught twin barrel carburettor; cooling system: 9.5 imp pt, 11.4 US pt, 5.4 l.

TRANSMISSION ratios: I 3.337, II 1.995, III 1.418, IV 1, rev 3.876; axle ratio: 3.540; width of rims: 5''; tyres: 155 SR x 13 - 1600 Sport 175/70 SR x 13.

PERFORMANCE max speed: 101 mph, 162 km/h; power-weight ratio: Sport 23.6 lb/hp (32 lb/kW), 10.7 kg/hp (14.5 kg/kW) - Ghia 24.2 lb/hp (32.9 lb/kW), 11 kg/hp (14.9 kg/kW); speed in direct drive at 1,000 rpm: 18.5 mph, 29.7 km/h; consumption: 36.7 m/imp gal, 30.5 m/US gal, 7.7 l x 100 km.

CHASSIS rear suspension: anti-roll bar.

BRAKES servo.

ELECTRICAL EQUIPMENT halogen headlamps.

DIMENSIONS AND WEIGHT weight: Sport 1,980 lb, 898 kg - Ghia 2,035 lb, 923 kg.

BODY reclining backrests with built-in headrests; sports road wheels; heated rear window.

PRACTICAL INSTRUCTIONS valve timing: 29° 63° 71° 21°.

OPTIONAL ACCESSORIES (for Ghia only) Ford C3 automatic transmission, hydraulic torque converter and planetary gears with 3 ratios (I 2.474, II 1.474, III 1, rev 2.111), max ratio of converter at stall 2.3, possible manual selection.

95 hp power team

See 41 hp power team, except for:

ENGINE 97.2 cu in, 1,593 cc (3.45 x 2.60 in, 87.6 x 66 mm); compression ratio: 9.2:1; max power (DIN): 95 hp (69.9 kW) at 5,750 rpm; max torque (DIN): 92 lb ft, 12.7 kg m (124.5 Nm) at 4,000 rpm; max engine rpm: 6,600; 59.6 hp/l (43.9 kW/l); valves: overhead, Vee-slanted, rockers; camshafts: 1, overhead, cogged belt; lubrication: rotary or vane-type pump, full flow filter, oil cooler, 6.7 imp pt, 8 US pt, 3.8 l; 1 Weber 32/36 DGAV downdraught twin barrel carburettor; cooling system: 12.5 imp pt, 15 US pt, 7.1 l, electric thermostatic fan.

TRANSMISSION ratios: I 3.656, II 1.970, III 1.370, IV 1, rev 3.656; axle ratio: 3.540; width of rims: 5.5''; tyres: 175/70 SR x 13.

PERFORMANCE max speeds: (I) 32 mph, 52 km/h; (II) 60 mph, 96 km/h; (III) 86 mph, 138 km/h; (IV) 106 mph, 170 km/h; power-weight ratio: 21.4 lb/hp (29 lb/kW), 9.7 kg/hp (13.2 kg/kW); speed in direct drive at 1,000 rpm: 18.6 mph, 29.9 km/h; consumption: 31.5 m/imp gal, 26.1 m/US gal, 9 l x 100 km.

FORD Escort RS Mexico 2-door Saloon

FORD Escort RS 1800 2-door Saloon

FORD Escort RS 1800 2-door Saloon

CHASSIS rear suspension: trailing radius arms.

STEERING turns lock to lock: 3.30.

BRAKES front disc (diameter 9.60 in, 24.4 cm), rear drum, servo; swept area: front 195 sq in, 1,258 sq cm, rear 99 sq in, 639 sq cm, total 294 sq in, 1,897 sq cm.

ELECTRICAL EQUIPMENT 55 Ah battery; 45 A alternator; halogen headlamps.

DIMENSIONS AND WEIGHT wheel base: 94 in, 239 cm; tracks: 50.30 in, 128 cm front, 51.10 in, 130 cm rear; length: 155.20 in, 394 cm; width: 61.60 in, 156 cm; height: 55 in, 140 cm; weight: 2,029 lb, 920 kg; weight distribution: 54% front, 46% rear.

PRACTICAL INSTRUCTIONS oil: engine 6.7 imp pt, 8 US pt, 3.8 l, SAE 10W-30, change every 6,000 miles, 9,700 km - gearbox 2.4 imp pt, 2.7 US pt, 1.3 l - final drive 2 imp pt, 2.3 US pt, 1.1 l; tappet clearances: inlet 0.008 in, 0.20 mm, exhaust 0.010 in, 0.25 mm; valve timing: 18° 70° 64° 24°.

OPTIONAL ACCESSORIES 6'' light alloy road wheels; rear fog lamp; vinyl roof; tinted glass with laminated windscreen; reclining backrests with built-in headrests; metallic spray.

110 hp power team

See 41 hp power team, except for:

ENGINE 121.6 cu in, 1,993 cc (3.57 x 3.03 in, 90.8 x 76.9 mm); compression ratio: 9.2:1; max power (DIN): 110 hp (81 kW) at 5,500 rpm; max torque (DIN): 118 lb ft, 16.3 kg m (159.8 Nm) at 3,750 rpm; max engine rpm: 6,600; 55.2 hp/l (40.6 kW/l); valves: overhead, Vee-slanted, rockers; camshafts: 1, overhead, cogged belt; lubrication: gear or vane-type pump, full flow filter, oil cooler, 6.7 imp pt, 8 US pt, 3.8 l; 1 Weber 32/36 DGAV downdraught twin barrel carburettor; cooling system: 12.5 imp pt, 15 US pt, 7.1 l, electric thermostatic fan.

TRANSMISSION ratios: I 3.656, II 1.970, III 1.370, IV 1, rev 3.660; axle ratio: 3.540; width of rims: 6''; tyres: 175/70 HR x 13.

PERFORMANCE max speeds: (I) 32 mph, 52 km/h; (II) 60 mph, 96 km/h; (III) 86 mph, 138 km/h; (IV) 110 mph, 177 km/h; power-weight ratio: 18.7 lb/hp (25.5 lb/kW), 8.5 kg/hp (11.5 kg/kW); speed in direct drive at 1,000 rpm: 18.6 mph, 29.9 km/h; consumption: 27.6 m/imp gal, 23.1 m/US gal, 10.2 l x 100 km.

CHASSIS rear suspension: trailing radius arms.

STEERING turns lock to lock: 3.30.

BRAKES front disc (diameter 9.60 in, 24.4 cm), rear drum, servo; swept area: front 195 sq in, 1,258 sq cm, rear 99 sq in, 639 sq cm, total 294 sq in, 1,897 sq cm.

ELECTRICAL EQUIPMENT 55 Ah battery; 45 A alternator; halogen headlamps.

DIMENSIONS AND WEIGHT wheel base: 94 in, 239 cm; tracks: 50.30 in, 128 cm front, 51.10 in, 130 cm rear; length: 161.80 in, 411 cm; width: 61.60 in, 156 cm; height: 55 in, 140 cm; weight: 2,062 lb, 935 kg; weight distribution: 54% front, 46% rear.

PRACTICAL INSTRUCTIONS oil: engine 6.7 imp pt, 8 US pt, 3.8 l, SAE 10W-30, change every 6,000 miles, 9,700 km - gearbox 2.4 imp pt, 2.7 US pt, 1.3 l - final drive 2 imp pt, 2.3 US pt, 1.1 l; tappet clearances: inlet 0.008 in, 0.20 mm, exhaust 0.010 in, 0.25 mm; valve timing: 18° 70° 64° 24°.

OPTIONAL ACCESSORIES competition equipment; sports road wheels; metallic spray; tinted glass with laminated windscreen; vinyl roof.

115 hp power team

See 41 hp power team, except for:

ENGINE 111.9 cu in, 1,834 cc (3.41 x 3.06 in, 86.7 x 77.6 mm); max power (DIN): 115 hp (84.6 kW) at 6,000 rpm; max torque (DIN): 126 lb ft, 17.4 kg m (170.6 Nm) at 3,750 rpm; max engine rpm: 7,000; 62.7 hp/l (46.1 kW/l); light alloy block and head; valves: 4 per cylinder, overhead, Vee-slanted, rockers; camshafts: 2, overhead, cogged belt; lubrication: gear pump, full flow filter, oil cooler, 6.7 imp pt, 8 US pt, 3.8 l; 1 Weber 32/36 DGAV carburettor; cooling system: 12.5 imp pt, 15 US pt, 7.1 l, electric thermostatic fan.

TRANSMISSION ratios: I 3.360, II 1.810, III 1.260, IV 1, rev 3.370; axle ratio: 3.540; width of rims: 5.5''; tyres: 175/70 HR x 13.

PERFORMANCE max speed: 115 mph, 185 km/h; power-weight ratio: 17.4 lb/hp (23.8 lb/kW), 7.9 kg/hp (10.8 kg/kW); acceleration: standing ¼ mile 16.7 sec, 0-50 mph (0-80 km/h) 6.8 sec; speed in direct drive at 1,000 rpm: 18.6 mph, 29.9 km/h; consumption: 29.6 m/imp gal, 24.8 m/US gal, 9.5 l x 100 km.

CHASSIS rear suspension: trailing radius arms.

STEERING turns lock to lock: 3.60.

BRAKES front disc (diameter 9.60 in, 24.4 cm), rear drum, servo; swept area: front 195 sq in, 1,258 sq cm, rear 99 sq in, 639 sq cm, total 294 sq in, 1,897 sq cm.

ELECTRICAL EQUIPMENT 55 Ah battery; 55 A alternator; halogen headlamps.

DIMENSIONS AND WEIGHT wheel base: 94 in, 239 cm; tracks: 50.30 in, 128 cm front, 51.10 in, 130 cm rear; length: 155.20 in, 394 cm; width: 61.60 in, 156 cm; height: 55 in, 140 cm; ground clearance: 5.79 in, 15 cm; weight: 2,015 lb, 914 kg; turning circle (between walls): 29.7 ft, 9.1 m.

BODY 2 bucket seats.

PRACTICAL INSTRUCTIONS oil: engine 6.7 imp pt, 8 US pt, 3.8 l, SAE 10W-30, change every 2,500 miles, 4,000 km - gearbox 1.8 imp pt, 2.1 US pt, 1 l; tappet clearances: inlet 0.005-0.007 in, 0.20-0.17 mm; exhaust 0.006-0.008 in, 0.15-0.20 mm; valve timing: 29° 63° 71° 21°; tyre pressure: front 28 psi, 2 atm, rear 28 psi, 2 atm.

OPTIONAL ACCESSORIES light alloy wheels with 6'' wide rims; rear fog lamp; tinted glass with laminated windscreen; vinyl roof.

FORD Cortina 1600 L Estate Car

Cortina Series

PRICES EX WORKS:

1	Cortina 1300 2-door Saloon	£ 2,523*
2	Cortina 1300 4-door Saloon	£ 2,625*
3	Cortina 1300 L 2-door Saloon	£ 2,716*
4	Cortina 1300 L 4-door Saloon	£ 2,818*
5	Cortina 1600 4-door Saloon	£ 2,782*
6	Cortina 1600 Estate Car	£ 3,103*
7	Cortina 1600 L 4-door Saloon	£ 2,975*
8	Cortina 1600 L Estate Car	£ 3,325*
9	Cortina 1600 GL 4-door Saloon	£ 3,263*
10	Cortina 1600 GL Estate Car	£ 3,614*
11	Cortina 1600 Ghia 4-door Saloon	£ 3,884*
12	Cortina 1600 Ghia Estate Car	£ 4,234*
13	Cortina 2000 GL 4-door Saloon	£ 3,452*
14	Cortina 2000 GL Estate Car	£ 3,803*
15	Cortina 2000 S 4-door Saloon	£ 3,678*
16	Cortina 2000 Ghia 4-door Saloon	£ 3,997*
17	Cortina 2000 Ghia Estate Car	£ 4,347*
18	Cortina 2300 GL 4-door Saloon	£ 3,900*
19	Cortina 2300 GL Estate Car	£ 4,251*
20	Cortina 2300 S 4-door Saloon	£ 4,126*
21	Cortina 2300 Ghia 4-door Saloon	£ 4,445*
22	Cortina 2300 Ghia Estate Car	£ 4,795*

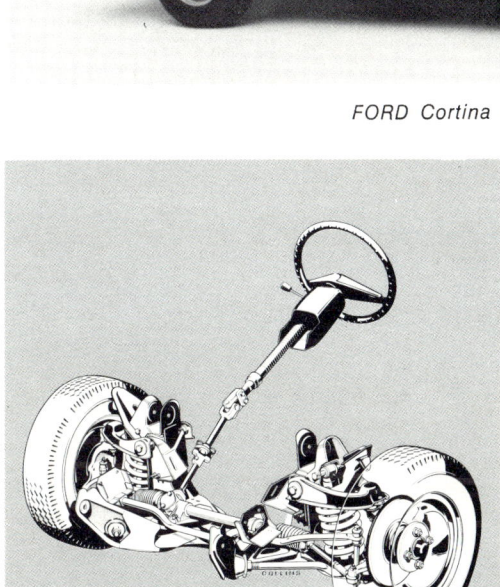

FORD Cortina Series

Power team:	Standard for:	Optional for:
50 hp	1 to 4	—
59 hp	5,6	7,8
72 hp	7 to 10	—
88 hp	11,12	—
98 hp	13 to 17	—
108 hp	18 to 22	—

50 hp power team

ENGINE front, 4 stroke; 4 cylinders, vertical, in line; 79.2 cu in, 1,298 cc (3.19 x 2.48 in, 81 x 63 mm); compression ratio: 9.2:1; max power (DIN): 50 hp (36.8 kW) at 5,000 rpm; max torque (DIN): 64 lb ft, 8.8 kg m (86.3 Nm) at 3,000 rpm; max engine rpm: 6,000; 38.6 hp/l (28.4 kW/l); cast iron block and head; 5 crankshaft bearings; valves: overhead, push-rods and rockers; camshafts: 1, side, chain driven; lubrication: rotary pump, full flow filter, 6 imp pt, 7.2 US pt, 3.4 l; 1 Motorcraft GPD downdraught single barrel carburettor; fuel feed: mechanical pump; water-cooled, 8.7 imp pt, 10.4 US pt, 4.9 l.

TRANSMISSION driving wheels: rear; clutch: single dry plate (diaphragm); gearbox: mechanical; gears: 4, fully synchronized; ratios: I 3.580, II 2.010, III 1.400, IV 1, rev 3.320; lever: central; final drive: hypoid bevel; axle ratio: 4.110; width of rims: 4.5''; tyres: 165 SR x 13.

PERFORMANCE max speeds: (I) 24 mph, 38 km/h; (II) 37 mph, 59 km/h; (III) 63 mph, 101 km/h; (IV) 82 mph, 132 km/h; power-weight ratio: 44.1 lb/hp (59.9 lb/kW), 20 kg/hp (27.2 kg/kW); carrying capacity: 1,049 lb, 475 kg; speed in direct drive at 1,000 rpm: 16.3 mph, 26.2 km/h; consumption: 41.5 m/imp gal, 34.6 m/US gal, 6.8 l x 100 km.

CHASSIS integral, front auxiliary frame; front suspension: independent, wishbones, anti-roll bar, coil springs/telescopic dampers; rear: rigid axle, lower longitudinal trailing arms, upper oblique torque arms, coil springs, anti-roll bar, telescopic dampers.

STEERING rack-and-pinion; turns lock to lock: 3.70.

BRAKES front disc (diameter 9.72 in, 24.7 cm), rear drum, servo.

ELECTRICAL EQUIPMENT 12 V; 38 Ah battery; 35 A alternator; Ford distributor; 2 headlamps.

DIMENSIONS AND WEIGHT wheel base: 101.50 in, 258 cm; tracks: 56.90 in, 144 cm front, 56 in, 142 cm rear; length: 170.35 in, 433 cm; width: 66.90 in, 170 cm; height: 52 in, 132 cm; ground clearance: 5.12 in, 13 cm; weight: 2,205 lb, 1,000 kg; weight distribution: 53% front, 47% rear; turning circle (between walls): 32 ft, 9.8 m; fuel tank: 12 imp gal, 14.3 US gal, 54 l.

BODY saloon/sedan; 5 seats, separate front seats.

PRACTICAL INSTRUCTIONS fuel: 97 oct petrol; oil: engine 6 imp pt, 7.2 US pt, 3.4 l, SAE 10W-30, change every 6,000 miles, 9,700 km - gearbox 1.6 imp pt, 1.9 US pt, 0.9 l, SAE 80 EP, no change recommended - final drive 1.8 imp pt, 2.1 US pt, 1 l, SAE 90 EP, no change recommended; greasing: none; tappet clearances: inlet 0.004 in, 0.10 mm, exhaust 0.007 in, 0.17 mm; valve timing: 21° 55° 70° 22°; tyre pressure: front 24 psi, 1.7 atm, rear 24 psi, 1.7 atm.

OPTIONAL ACCESSORIES laminated windscreen; metallic spray; rear fog lamp; reclining backrests; headrests (for **L** models only); sunshine roof; tinted glass; vinyl roof; 185/70 SR x 13 tyres only with sports road wheels.

FORD Cortina 1600 GL 4-door Saloon

59 hp power team

See 50 hp power team, except for:

ENGINE 97.2 cu in, 1,593 cc (3.45 x 2.60 in, 87.6 x 66 mm); max power (DIN): 59 hp (43.4 kW) at 4,500 rpm; max torque (DIN): 82 lb ft, 11.7 kg m (114.7 Nm) at 2,600 rpm; max engine rpm: 5,200; 37 hp/l (27.2 kW/l); valves: overhead, Vee-slanted, rockers; camshafts: 1, overhead, cogged belt.

TRANSMISSION axle ratio: 3.780.

PERFORMANCE max speed: 88 mph, 141 km/h; power-weight ratio: 39.4 lb/hp (53.6 lb/kW), 17.9 kg/hp (24.3 kg/kW); speed in direct drive at 1,000 rpm: 17.8 mph, 28.6 km/h; consumption: 37.2 m/imp gal, 30.9 m/US gal, 7.6 l x 100 km.

DIMENSIONS AND WEIGHT length: station wagons 174.30 in, 443 cm; height: station wagons 52.10 in, 132 cm; weight: 2,326 in, 1,055 kg; weight distribution: 54% front, 46% rear.

OPTIONAL ACCESSORIES rear window wiper-washer for Cortina 1600 L Estate Car only.

72 hp power team

See 59 hp power team, except for:

ENGINE max power (DIN): 72 hp (53 kW) at 5,000 rpm; max torque (DIN): 87 lb ft, 12 kg m (117.7 Nm) at 2,700 rpm; max engine rpm: 5,500; 45.2 hp/l (33.3 kW/l).

TRANSMISSION axle ratio: 3.890.

PERFORMANCE max speed: 94 mph, 151 km/h; power-weight ratio: 32.3 lb/hp (43.9 lb/kW), 14.6 kg/hp (19.9 kg/kW); carrying capacity: 977 lb, 443 kg; speed in direct drive at 1,000 rpm: 17.3 mph, 27.8 km/h; consumption: 34.4 m/imp gal, 28.7 m/US gal, 8.2 l x 100 km.

OPTIONAL ACCESSORIES Ford C3 automatic transmission, hydraulic torque converter and planetary gears with 3 ratios (I 2.474, II 1.474, III 1, rev 2.111), max ratio of converter at stall 2, possible manual selection, max speed 89 mph, 143 km/h, consumption 29.8 m/imp gal, 24.8 m/US gal, 9.5 l x 100 km - station wagons 29.1 m/imp gal, 24.2 m/US gal, 9.7 l x 100 km.

88 hp power team

See 59 hp power team, except for:

ENGINE max power (DIN): 88 hp (64.8 kW) at 5,700 rpm; max torque (DIN): 92 lb ft, 12.7 kg m (124.5 Nm) at 4,000 rpm; max engine rpm: 6,000; 55.2 hp/l (40.7 kW/l).

TRANSMISSION axle ratio: 3.890.

PERFORMANCE max speed: 101 mph, 163 km/h; power-weight ratio: 26.5 lb/hp (35.9 lb/kW), 12 kg/hp (16.3 kg/kW); carrying capacity: 977 lb, 443 kg; speed in direct drive at 1,000 rpm: 17.3 mph, 27.8 km/h; consumption: 31 m/imp gal, 25.8 m/US gal, 9.1 l x 100 km.

OPTIONAL ACCESSORIES Ford C3 automatic transmission, hydraulic torque converter and planetary gears with 3 ratios (I 2.474, II 1.474, III 1, rev 2.111), max ratio of converter at stall 2, possible manual selection, max speed 94 mph, 151 km/h, consumption 26.9 m/imp gal, 22.4 m/US gal, 10.5 l x 100 km.

98 hp power team

See 59 hp power team, except for:

ENGINE 121.6 cu in, 1,993 cc (3.89 x 3.03 in, 90.8 x 76.9 mm); max power (DIN): 98 hp (72.1 kW) at 5,200 rpm; max torque (DIN): 112 lb ft, 15.4 kg m (151 Nm) at 3,500 rpm; max engine rpm: 6,500; 49.2 hp/l (36.2 kW/l); 1 Weber 32/36 DGAV downdraught carburettor; cooling system: 13.7 imp pt, 16.5 US pt, 7.8 l.

TRANSMISSION ratios: I 3.650, II 1.970, III 1.370, IV 1, rev 3.660; axle ratio: 3.750; width of rims: 5.5''.

PERFORMANCE max speed: 103 mph, 166 km/h; power-weight ratio: 24.2 lb/hp (33 lb/kW), 11 kg/hp (15 kg/kW); carrying capacity: 977 lb, 443 kg; speed in direct drive at 1,000 rpm: 18.3 mph, 29.5 km/h; consumption: 30.7 m/imp gal, 25.6 m/US gal, 9.2 l x 100 km.

DIMENSIONS AND WEIGHT weight: 2,381 lb, 1,080 kg.

BODY sports road wheels; reclining backrests; light alloy wheels and headrests (except for GL models); tinted glass and vinyl roof (for Ghia models only); rear window wiper-washer (for station wagons only).

FORD Cortina GL Series

PRACTICAL INSTRUCTIONS tappet clearances: inlet 0.008 in, 0.20 mm, exhaust 0.010 in, 0.25 mm; valve timing: 18° 70° 64° 24°.

OPTIONAL ACCESSORIES Ford C3 automatic transmission, hydraulic torque converter and planetary gears with 3 ratios (I 2.474, II 1.474, III 1, rev 2.111), max ratio of converter at stall 2, possible manual selection, max speed 100 mph, 161 km/h; 66 Ah battery; sunshine roof; 185/70 SR x 13 tyres (for S and Ghia models only).

108 hp power team

See 59 hp power team, except for:

ENGINE 140.1 cu in, 2,296 cc (3.54 x 2.37 in, 90 x 60.1 mm); max power (DIN): 108 hp (79.5 kW) at 5,000 rpm; max torque (DIN): 138 lb ft, 19 kg m (186.3 Nm) at 3,000 rpm; max engine rpm: 5,500; 47 hp/l (34.6 kW/l); 1 Solex 35/35 downdraught carburettor; cooling system: 13.7 imp pt, 16.5 US pt, 7.8 l.

TRANSMISSION ratios: I 3.650, II 1.970, III 1.370, IV 1, rev 3.660; axle ratio: 3.440; width of rims: 5.5''.

PERFORMANCE max speed: 106 mph, 171 km/h; power-weight ratio: 23.1 lb/hp (31.3 lb/kW), 10.5 kg/hp (14.2 kg/kW); carrying capacity: 977 lb, 443 kg; speed in direct drive

at 1,000 rpm: 19.6 mph, 31.6 km/h; consumption: 29.7 m/imp gal, 24.8 m/US gal, 9.5 l x 100 km.

DIMENSIONS AND WEIGHT weight: 2,496 lb, 1,132 kg.

BODY sports road wheels; reclining backrests; light alloy wheels and headrests (except for GL models); tinted glass and vinyl roof (for Ghia models only); rear window wiper-washer (for station wagons only).

PRACTICAL INSTRUCTIONS tappet clearances: inlet 0.014 in, 0.35 mm, exhaust 0.016 in, 0.40 mm; valve timing: 20° 56° 62° 14°.

OPTIONAL ACCESSORIES Ford C3 automatic transmission, hydraulic torque converter and planetary gears with 3 ratios (I 2.474, II 1.474, III 1, rev 2.111), max ratio of converter at stall 2, possible manual selection, max speed 103 mph, 166 km/h; 66 Ah battery; sunshine roof; 185/70 SR x 13 tyres (for S and Ghia models only).

Capri II Series

PRICES EX WORKS:

1 Capri II 1300 Coupé	£	2,662*
2 Capri II 1300 L Coupé	£	2,791*
3 Capri II 1600 L Coupé	£	2,956*
4 Capri II 1600 GL Coupé	£	3,205*
5 Capri II 1600 S Coupé	£	3,643*
6 Capri II 2000 GL Coupé	£	3,394*
7 Capri II 2000 S Coupé	£	3,756*
8 Capri II 2000 Ghia Coupé	£	4,478*
9 Capri II 3000 S Coupé	£	4,125*
10 Capri II 3000 Ghia Coupé	£	5,088*

Power team:	Standard for:	Optional for:
50 hp	1,2	—
72 hp	3,4	—
88 hp	5	—
98 hp	6 to 8	—
138 hp	9,10	—

50 hp power team

ENGINE front, 4 stroke; 4 cylinders, vertical, in line; 79.2 cu in, 1,298 cc (3.19 x 2.48 in, 81 x 63 mm); compression ratio: 9.2:1; max power (DIN): 50 hp (36.8 kW) at 5,000 rpm; max torque (DIN): 64 lb ft, 8.8 kg m (86.3 Nm) at 3,000 rpm; max engine rpm: 6,000; 38.5 hp/l (28.4 kW/l); cast iron block and head; 5 crankshafts bearings; valves: overhead, in line, push-rods and rockers; camshafts: 1, side, chain driven; lubrication: rotary or vane-type pump, full flow filter, 5.7 imp pt, 6.8 US pt, 3.2 l; 1 Motorcraft GPD downdraught single barrel carburettor; fuel feed: mechanical pump; water-cooled, 8.2 imp pt, 9.7 US pt, 4.6 l.

TRANSMISSION driving wheels: rear; clutch: single dry plate (diaphragm); gearbox: mechanical; gears: 4, fully synchronized; ratios: I 3.580, II 2.010, III 1.400, IV 1, rev 3.320; lever: central; final drive: hypoid bevel; axle ratio: 3.890; width of rims: 5''; tyres: 165 x 13.

FORD Cortina 2000 S 4-door Saloon

FORD Capri II 1300 Coupé

FORD Capri II 1600 GL Coupé

PERFORMANCE max speeds: (I) 27 mph, 43 km/h; (II) 33 mph, 53 km/h; (III) 69 mph, 111 km/h; (IV) 85 mph, 136 km/h; power-weight ratio: 44.5 lb/hp (60.5 lb/kW), 20.2 kg/hp (27.4 kg/kW); carrying capacity: 750 lb, 340 kg; speed in direct drive at 1,000 rpm: 17.3 mph, 27.9 km/h; consumption: 40.9 m/imp gal, 34.1 m/US gal, 6.9 l x 100 km.

CHASSIS integral; front suspension: independent, by McPherson, coil springs/telescopic damper struts, lower wishbones (trailing arms), anti-roll bar; rear: rigid axle, semi-elliptic leafsprings, anti-roll bar (acting as torque radius arms), telescopic dampers.

STEERING rack-and-pinion.

BRAKES front disc (diameter 9.60 in, 24.4 cm), rear drum, servo.

ELECTRICAL EQUIPMENT 12 V; 38 Ah battery; 28 A alternator; Motorcraft distributor; 2 headlamps.

DIMENSIONS AND WEIGHT wheel base: 100.80 in, 256 cm; tracks: 53.30 in, 135 cm front, 54.40 in, 138 cm rear; length: 168 in, 427 cm; width: 66.90 in, 170 cm; height: 51.10 in, 130 cm; ground clearance: 4.50 in, 11 cm; weight: 2,227 lb, 1,010 kg; weight distribution: 52.5% front, 47.5% rear; turning circle (between walls): 32 ft, 9.8 m; fuel tank: 12.7 imp gal, 15.3 US gal, 58 l.

BODY coupé; 2 doors; 4 seats, separate front seats, reclining backrests.

PRACTICAL INSTRUCTIONS fuel: 97 oct petrol; oil: engine 5.3 imp pt, 6.3 US pt, 3 l, SAE 10W-30, change every 6,000

FORD Capri II Ghia Coupé

miles, 9,700 km - gearbox 1.7 imp pt, 1.9 US pt, 0.9 l, SAE 80, no change recommended - final drive 2 imp pt, 2.3 US pt, 1.1 l, SAE 90, no change recommended; greasing: none; tappet clearances: inlet 0.010 in, 0.25 mm, exhaust 0.017 in, 0.44 mm; valve timing: 21° 55° 70° 22°; tyre pressure: front 24 psi, 1.7 atm, rear 27 psi, 1.9 atm.

OPTIONAL ACCESSORIES 4.444 axle ratio; 35 A alternator; sunshine roof; vinyl roof; sports road wheels; tinted glass with laminated windscreen; halogen headlamps; metallic spray; rear window wiper-washer.

72 hp power team

See 50 hp power team, except for:

ENGINE 97.2 cu in, 1,593 cc (3.45 x 2.60 in, 87.6 x 66 mm); max power (DIN): 72 hp (53 kW) at 5,200 rpm; max torque (DIN): 87 lb ft, 12 kg m (117.7 Nm) at 2,700 rpm; 45.2 hp/l (33.3 kW/l); valves: overhead, Vee-slanted, rockers; camshafts: 1, overhead, cogged belt; lubrication: 6.5 imp pt, 7.8 US pt, 3.7 l.

TRANSMISSION axle ratio: 3.770.

PERFORMANCE max speed: 98 mph, 157 km/h; power-weight ratio: 31.7 lb/hp (43.3 lb/kW), 14.4 kg/hp (19.6 kg/kW); acceleration: standing ¼ mile 18.9 sec, 0-50 mph (0-80 km/h) 9 sec; speed in direct drive at 1,000 rpm: 17.8 mph, 28.6 km/h; consumption: 28.9 m/imp gal, 26.7 m/US gal, 9.8 l x 100 km.

DIMENSIONS AND WEIGHT weight: 2,293 lb, 1,040 kg; weight distribution: 52.6% front, 47.4% rear.

PRACTICAL INSTRUCTIONS oil: engine 6.5 imp pt, 7.8 US pt, 3.7 l.

OPTIONAL ACCESSORIES Ford C3 automatic transmission, hydraulic torque converter and planetary gears with 3 ratios (I 2.474, II 1.474, II 1, rev 2.111), max ratio of converter at stall 2.3, possible manual selection, max speed 95 mph, 153 km/h, 55 Ah battery.

88 hp power team

See 50 hp power team, except for:

ENGINE 97.2 cu in, 1,593 cc (3.45 x 2.60 in, 87.6 x 66 mm); max power (DIN): 88 hp (64.8 kW) at 5,700 rpm; max torque (DIN): 92 lb ft, 12.7 kg m (124.5 Nm) at 4,000 rpm; max engine rpm: 6,500; 55.2 hp/l (40.7 kW/l); valves: overhead, Vee-slanted, rockers; camshafts: 1, overhead, cogged belt; lubrication: 6.5 imp pt, 7.8 US pt, 3.7 l; 1 Weber 32/36 DGV downdraught twin barrel carburettor.

TRANSMISSION axle ratio: 3.750.

PERFORMANCE max speed: 106 mph, 170 km/h; power-weight ratio: 26.5 lb/hp (35.8 lb/kW), 12 kg/hp (16.3 kg/kW); speed in direct drive at 1,000 rpm: 18 mph, 28.9 km/h; consumption: 30.7 m/imp gal, 25.6 m/US gal, 9.2 l x 100 km.

ELECTRICAL EQUIPMENT 44 Ah battery.

DIMENSIONS AND WEIGHT weight: 2,326 lb, 1,055 kg; weight distribution: 52.6% front, 47.4% rear.

PRACTICAL INSTRUCTIONS oil: engine 6.5 imp pt, 7.8 US pt, 3.7 l; tappet clearances: inlet 0.008 in, 0.20 mm, exhaust 0.010 in, 0.25 mm; valve timing: 18° 70° 69° 24°.

OPTIONAL ACCESSORIES Ford C3 automatic transmission, hydraulic torque converter and planetary gears with 3 ratios (I 2.474, II 1.474, III 1, rev 2.111), max ratio of converter at stall 2.3, possible manual selection, max speed 102 mph, 164 km/h, 55 Ah battery; sports equipment.

98 hp power team

See 50 hp power team, except for:

ENGINE 121.6 cu in, 1,993 cc (3.89 x 3.03 in, 90.8 x 76.9 mm); max power (DIN): 98 hp (72.1 kW) at 5,200 rpm; max torque (DIN): 112 lb ft, 15.4 kg m (151 Nm) at 3,500 rpm; max engine rpm: 6,500; 49.2 hp/l (36.2 kW/l); valves: overhead, Vee-slanted, rockers; camshafts: 1, overhead, cogged belt; 1 Weber 32/36 DGAV downdraught carburettor; cooling system: 13.7 imp pt, 16.5 US pt, 7.8 l.

TRANSMISSION ratios: I 3.650, II 1.970, III 1.370, IV 1, rev 3.160; axle ratio: 3.440.

PERFORMANCE max speed: 108 mph, 174 km/h; power-weight ratio: 22.5 lb/hp (30.4 lb/kW), 10.2 kg/hp (13.8 kg/kW); acceleration: standing ¼ mile 18.2 sec, 0-50 mph

98 HP POWER TEAM

(0-80 km/h) 7.5 sec; speed in direct drive at 1,000 rpm: 19.5 mph, 31.4 km/h; consumption: 24.6 m/imp gal, 20.5 m/US gal, 11.5 l x 100 km.

ELECTRICAL EQUIPMENT 44 Ah battery.

DIMENSIONS AND WEIGHT weight: 2,194 lb, 995 kg; weight distribution: 55.1% front, 44.9% rear.

PRACTICAL INSTRUCTIONS tappet clearances: inlet 0.008 in, 0.20 mm, exhaust 0.010 in, 0.25 mm; valve timing: 18° 70° 64° 24°.

OPTIONAL ACCESSORIES Ford C3 automatic transmission, hydraulic torque converter and planetary gears with 3 ratios (I 2.474, II 1.474, III 1, rev 2.111), max ratio of converter at stall 2, possible manual selection, max speed 105 mph, 169 km/h, 55 Ah battery; sports equipment.

138 hp power team

See 50 hp power team, except for:

ENGINE 6 cylinders, Vee-slanted at 60°; 182.7 cu in, 2,994 cc (3.69 x 2.85 in, 93.7 x 72.4 mm); compression ratio: 9:1; max power (DIN): 138 hp (101.6 kW) at 5,000 rpm; max torque (DIN): 174 lb ft, 24 kg m (235.4 Nm) at 3,000 rpm; max engine rpm: 5,500; 46.1 hp/l (33.9 kW/l); 4 crankshaft bearings; camshafts: 1, at centre of Vee; lubrication: 7.6 imp pt, 9.1 US pt, 4.3 l; 1 Weber 38/38 EGAS downdraught twin barrel carburettor; cooling system: 16.4 imp pt, 19.7 US pt, 9.3 l.

TRANSMISSION ratios: I 3.160, II 1.940, III 1.412, IV 1, rev 3.346; axle ratio: 3.090; tyres: 185/70 HR x 13.

PERFORMANCE max speed: 122 mph, 196 km/h; power-weight ratio: 18.7 lb/hp (25.4 lb/kW), 8.5 kg/hp (11.5 kg/kW); acceleration: standing ¼ mile 16.6 sec, 0-50 mph (0-80 km/h) 6 sec; speed in direct drive at 1,000 rpm: 21.9 mph, 35.2 km/h; consumption: 20.7 m/imp gal, 17.2 m/US gal, 13.7 l x 100 km.

BRAKES front disc (diameter 9.72 in, 24.7 cm), rear drum, servo.

DIMENSIONS AND WEIGHT weight: 2,580 lb, 1,170 kg.

PRACTICAL INSTRUCTIONS oil: engine 6.7 imp pt, 8 US pt, 3.8 l - gearbox 3.2 imp pt, 3.8 US pt, 1.8 l; tappet clearances: inlet 0.012 in, 0.30 mm, exhaust 0.012 in, 0.30 mm; valve timing: 20° 56° 62° 14°.

OPTIONAL ACCESSORIES Ford C3 automatic transmission, hydraulic torque converter and planetary gears with 3 ratios (I 2.474, II 1.474, III 1, rev 2.111), max ratio of converter at stall 2.2, possible manual selection, max speed 118 mph, 190 km/h, 55 Ah battery.

Granada Series

PRICES EX WORKS:

1 Granada 2000 L Saloon	£ 4,144*
2 Granada 2000 L Estate Car	£ 4,850*
3 Granada 2300 GL Saloon	£ 5,261*
4 Granada 2800 S Saloon	£ 5,910*
5 Granada 2800 GL Saloon	£ 5,636*
6 Granada 2800 GL Estate Car	£ 6,303*
7 Granada 2800 Ghia Saloon	£ 6,747*

Power team:	Standard for:	Optional for:
98 hp	1,2	—
108 hp	3	1,2
135 hp	5 to 7	—
160 hp	4	5 to 7

98 hp power team

ENGINE front, 4 stroke; 4 cylinders, vertical, in line; 121.6 cu in, 1,993 cc (3.89 x 3.03 in, 90.8 x 76.9 mm); compression ratio: 9.2:1; max power (DIN): 98 hp (72.1 kW) at 5,200 rpm; max torque (DIN): 111 lb ft, 15.3 kg m (150 Nm) at 3,500 rpm; max engine rpm: 6,500; 49.2 hp/l (36.1 kW/l); cast iron block and head; 5 crankshaft bearings; valves: overhead, Vee-slanted, rockers; camshafts: 1, overhead, cogged belt; lubrication: rotary pump, full flow filter, 6.6 imp pt, 7.8 US pt, 3.7 l; 1 Weber 32/36 DGAV downdraught carburettor; fuel feed: mechanical pump; water-cooled, 10.8 imp pt, 12.9 US pt, 6.1 l.

TRANSMISSION driving wheels: rear; clutch: single dry plate (diaphragm); gearbox: mechanical; gears: 4, fully synchronized; ratios: I 3.650, II 1.970, III 1.370, IV 1, rev 3.660; lever: central; final drive: hypoid bevel; axle ratio: 3.890; width of rims: 5''; tyres: 175 x 14.

PERFORMANCE max speeds: (I) 29 mph, 47 km/h; (II) 54 mph, 87 km/h; (III) 78 mph, 125 km/h; (IV) 103 mph, 165 km/h; power-weight ratio: 26.7 lb/hp (36.2 lb/kW), 12.1 kg/hp (16.4 kg/kW); speed in direct drive at 1,000 rpm: 18 mph, 29 km/h; consumption: 26.2 m/imp gal, 21.8 m/US gal, 10.8 l x 100 km.

CHASSIS integral, front and rear auxiliary frames; front suspension: independent, wishbones (lower trailing links), coil springs, anti-roll bar, telescopic dampers; rear: independent, semi-trailing arms, coil springs, telescopic dampers.

STEERING rack-and-pinion; turns lock to lock: 4.39.

BRAKES front disc (diameter 10.31 in, 26.2 cm), rear drum, servo.

ELECTRICAL EQUIPMENT 12 V; 44 Ah battery; 28 A alternator; Motorcraft distributor; 2 halogen headlamps.

DIMENSIONS AND WEIGHT wheel base: 109.05 in, 277 cm; tracks: 59.45 in, 151 cm front, 60.63 in, 154 cm rear; length: 182.28 in, 463 cm; width: 70.47 in, 179 cm; height: 53.94 in, 137 cm; ground clearance: 5.12 in, 13 cm; weight: 2,613 lb, 1,185 kg; turning circle (between walls): 34.1 ft, 10.4 m; fuel tank: 14.3 imp gal, 17.2 US gal, 65 l.

BODY 4 doors; 5 seats, separate front seats, reclining backrests.

FORD Granada 2000 L Saloon

FORD Granada 2000 L Saloon

FORD Granada 2800 Ghia Saloon

FORD Granada 2800 Ghia Saloon

PERFORMANCE max speed: 113 mph, 182 km/h; power-weight ratio: 21.2 lb/hp (28.7 lb/kW), 9.6 kg/hp (13 kg/kW); speed in direct drive at 1,000 rpm: 20.8 mph, 33.4 km/h; consumption: 25.7 m/imp gal, 21.4 m/US gal, 11 l x 100 km.

STEERING servo.

BRAKES lining area: front 23.3 sq in, 150 sq cm, rear 75 sq in, 484 sq cm; total 98.3 sq in, 634 sq cm.

ELECTRICAL EQUIPMENT 55 Ah battery.

DIMENSIONS AND WEIGHT weight: 2,855 lb, 1,295 kg.

PRACTICAL INSTRUCTIONS oil: engine 7 imp pt, 8.5 US pt, 4 l.

160 hp power team

See 135 hp power team, except for:

ENGINE max power (DIN): 160 hp (117.8 kW) at 5,700 rpm; max torque (DIN): 162 lb ft, 22.4 kg m (219.7 Nm) at 4,300 rpm; max engine rpm: 6,000; 57.3 hp/l (42.2 kW/l); Bosch K-Jetronic fuel injection system.

PERFORMANCE max speed: 120 mph, 193 km/h; power-weight ratio: 17.9 lb/hp (24.3 lb/kW), 8.1 kg/hp (11 kg/kW); consumption: 25.2 m/imp gal, 21 m/US gal, 11.2 l x 100 km.

PRACTICAL INSTRUCTIONS fuel: 97 oct petrol; oil: engine 6 imp pt, 7.2 US pt, 3.4 l, SAE 20W-50, change every 6,200 miles, 10,000 km - gearbox 3 imp pt, 3.6 US pt, 1.7 l, SAE 80, no change recommended - final drive 3.2 imp pt, 3.8 US pt, 1.8 l, SAE 90, no change recommended; greasing: none; tappet clearances: inlet 0.008 in, 0.20 mm, exhaust 0.010 in, 0.25 mm; valve timing: 18° 70° 64° 24°; tyre pressure: front 24 psi, 1.7 atm, rear 26 psi, 1.8 atm.

OPTIONAL ACCESSORIES Ford C3 automatic transmission, hydraulic torque converter and planetary gears with 3 ratios (I 2.474, II 1.474, III 1, rev 2.111), max ratio of converter at stall 2.34, possible manual selection, max speed 95 mph, 153 m/h, consumption 25.7 m/imp gal, (21.4 m/US gal, 11 l x 100 km; 185 SR x 14 tyres with 6'' wide rims; sunshine roof.

108 hp power team

See 98 hp power team, except for:

ENGINE 6 cylinders, Vee-slanted at 60°; 139.9 cu in, 2,293 cc (3.54 x 2.37 in, 90 x 60.1 mm); compression ratio: 8.75:1; max power (DIN): 108 hp (79.5 kW) at 5,000 rpm; max torque (DIN): 130 lb ft, 18 kg m (176.5 Nm) at 3,000 rpm; max engine rpm: 5,600; 47.1 hp/l (34.7 kW/l); 4 crankshaft bearings; lubrication: 7.4 imp pt, 8.9 US pt, 4.2 l; 1 Solex 35/35 EEIT downdraught twin barrel carburettor; cooling system: 15.3 imp pt, 18.4 US pt, 8.7 l.

PERFORMANCE max speed: 105 mph, 169 km/h; power-weight ratio: 26.5 lb/hp (35.9 lb/kW), 12 kg/hp (16.3 kg/kW); speed in direct drive at 1,000 rpm: 19.6 mph, 31.6 km/h; consumption: 26.6 m/imp gal, 22.2 m/US gal, 10.6 l x 100 km.

STEERING servo.

BRAKES lining area: front 23.3 sq in, 150 sq cm, rear 75 sq in, 484 sq cm, total 98.3 sq in, 634 sq cm.

ELECTRICAL EQUIPMENT 55 Ah battery.

DIMENSIONS AND WEIGHT weight: 2,855 lb, 1,295 kg.

PRACTICAL INSTRUCTIONS oil: engine 7 imp pt, 8.5 US pt, 4 l.

135 hp power team

See 98 hp power team, except for:

ENGINE 6 cylinders, Vee-slanted at 60°; 170.4 cu in, 2,792 cc (3.66 x 2.70 in, 93 x 68.5 mm); max power (DIN): 135 hp (99.4 kW) at 5,200 rpm; max torque (DIN): 159 lb ft, 22 kg m (215.8 Nm) at 3,000 rpm; max engine rpm: 5,600; 48.4 hp/l (35.6 kW/l); 4 crankshaft bearings; lubrication: 7.4 imp pt, 8.9 US pt, 4.2 l; 1 Solex 35/35 EEIT downdraught twin barrel carburettor; cooling system: 15.3 imp pt, 18.4 US pt, 8.7 l.

TRANSMISSION ratios: I 3.160, II 1.950, III 1.410, IV 1, rev 3.350; axle ratio: 3.450; width of rims: Ghia 6''; tyres: Ghia 185 SR x 14.

G21

PRICE EX WORKS: £ 4,500

ENGINE Ford, front, 4 stroke; 6 cylinders, Vee-slanted at 60°; 182.7 cu in, 2,994 cc (3.69 x 2.85 in, 93.7 x 72.4 mm); compression ratio: 8.9:1; max power (DIN): 128 hp (94.2 kW) at 4,750 rpm; max torque (DIN): 174 lb ft, 24 kg m (235.4 Nm) at 3,000 rpm; max engine rpm: 5,500; 42.7 hp/l (31.5 kW/l); cast iron block and head; 4 crankshaft bearings; valves: overhead, in line, push-rods and rockers; camshafts: 1, at centre of Vee; lubrication: eccentric or vane-type pump, full flow filter, 10 imp pt, 12 US pt, 5.7 l; 1 Weber DFA 2 downdraught twin barrel carburettor; fuel feed: mechanical pump; water-cooled, 12.5 imp pt, 15 US pt, 7.1 l.

TRANSMISSION driving wheels: rear; clutch: single dry plate; gearbox: mechanical; gears: 4, fully synchronized; ratios: I 3.163, II 2.214, III 1.412, IV 1, rev 3.346; lever: central; final drive: hypoid bevel, limited slip differential; axle ratio: 2.880; width of rims: 5.5''; tyres: 165 x 13.

PERFORMANCE max speeds: (I) 45 mph, 72 km/h; (II) 61 mph, 98 km/h; (III) 98 mph, 157 km/h; (IV) 128 mph, 206 km/h; power-weight ratio: 15 lb/hp (20.4 lb/kW), 6.8 kg/hp (9.3 kg/kW); acceleration: standing 1/4 mile 14.9 sec, 0-50 mph (0-80 km/h) 5.5 sec; speed in direct drive at 1,000 rpm: 23.4 mph, 37.6 km/h; consumption: 26 m/imp gal, 21.6 m/US gal, 10.9 l x 100 km.

CHASSIS tubular; front suspension: independent, wishbones, coil springs, anti-roll bar, telescopic dampers; rear: independent, wishbones, semi-axles as upper arms, twin trailing longitudinal radius arms, coil springs, telescopic dampers.

STEERING rack-and-pinion; turns lock to lock: 2.75.

BRAKES disc; swept area: front 196.9 sq in, 1,270 sq cm, rear 193.2 sq in, 1,246 sq cm, total 390.1 sq in, 2,516 sq cm.

ELECTRICAL EQUIPMENT 12 V; 36 Ah battery; 516 W alternator; Autolite distributor; 2 headlamps.

DIMENSIONS AND WEIGHT wheel base: 91 in, 231 cm; tracks: 50.75 in, 129 cm front, 51 in, 129 cm rear; length: 156.50 in, 397 cm; width: 63 in, 160 cm; height: 46 in, 117 cm; ground clearance: 4.75 in, 12.1 cm; weight: 1,920 lb, 871 kg; weight distribution: 49% front, 51% rear; turning circle (between walls): 35 ft, 10.7 m; fuel tank: 10 imp gal, 11.9 US gal, 45 l.

BODY coupé, in plastic material; 2 doors; 2 seats, separate front seats, reclining backrests.

PRACTICAL INSTRUCTIONS fuel: 96 oct petrol; oil: engine 9.5 imp pt, 11.4 US pt, 5.4 l, SAE 20W-50, change every 10,000 miles, 16,100 km - gearbox 3.2 imp pt, 3.8 US pt, 1.8 l, SAE 80 EP, change every 10,000 miles, 16,100 km - final drive 2.8 imp pt, 3.4 US pt, 1.6 l, SAE 90 EP, change every 10,000 miles, 16,100 km; tappet clearances: inlet 0.012 in, 0.30 mm, exhaust 0.018 in, 0.45 mm; valve timing: 20° 56° 62° 14°; tyre pressure: front 22 psi, 1.6 atm, rear 24 psi, 1.7 atm.

GINETTA G21

G21

VARIATIONS

ENGINE Sunbeam Rapier, 4 cylinders, slanted at 10°, in line, 105.3 cu in, 1,725 cc (3.21 x 3.25 in, 81.5 x 82.5 mm), max power (DIN) 79 hp (58.1 kW) at 5,200 rpm, max torque (DIN) 91 lb ft, 12.5 kg m (122.6 Nm) at 3,800 rpm, 9.2:1 compression ratio, max engine rpm 6,200, 45.8 hp/l (33.7 kW/l), light alloy head, 5 crankshaft bearings, 1 side camshaft, lubrication 7.5 imp pt, 8.9 US pt, 4.2 l, 2 Zenith-Stromberg semi-downdraught carburettors, cooling system 13.7 imp pt, 16.5 US pt, 7.8 l.
TRANSMISSION 3.700 axle ratio.
PERFORMANCE max speed 112 mph, 180 km/h; power-weight ratio 24.3 lb/hp (33 lb/kW), 11 kg/hp (15 kg/kW), speed in direct drive at 1,000 rpm 19.3 mph, 31 km/h, consumption 25.7 m/imp gal, 21.4 m/US gal, 11 l x 100 km.
CHASSIS rear suspension: rigid axle, longitudinal trailing arms, transverse linkage bar.
DIMENSIONS AND WEIGHT rear track 50.50 in, 128 cm.

OPTIONAL ACCESSORIES Laycock-de Normanville overdrive/top (0.820 ratio); automatic transmission, hydraulic torque converter and planetary gears with 3 ratios (I 2.460, II 1.460, III 1, rev 2.200), max ratio of converter at stall 2; headrests; heated rear window; sunshine roof.

GINETTA G21

CHASSIS backbone platform; front suspension: independent, twin swinging longitudinal trailing arms, transverse laminated torsion bars, anti-roll bar, telescopic dampers; rear: independent, swinging semi-axles, swinging longitudinal trailing arms, transverse torsion bars, telescopic dampers.

STEERING worm and roller, telescopic damper; turns lock to lock: 2.60.

BRAKES drum.

ELECTRICAL EQUIPMENT 12 V; 36 Ah battery; 270 W dynamo; Bosch distributor; 2 headlamps.

DIMENSIONS AND WEIGHT length: 156.69 in, 398 cm; width: 61.42 in, 156 cm; weight: 1,568 lb, 711 kg; fuel tank: 8.8 imp gal, 10.6 US gal, 40 l.

BODY coupé, in plastic material; 2 doors; 2 seats.

PRACTICAL INSTRUCTIONS fuel: 87 oct petrol; oil: engine 4.4 imp pt, 5.3 US pt, 2.5 l, SAE 10W-20 (winter) 20W-30 (summer), change every 3,100 miles, 5,000 km - gearbox and final drive 5.3 imp pt, 6.3 US pt, 3 l, SAE 90, change every 31,000 miles, 50,000 km; greasing: every 6,200 miles, 10,000 km, 4 points; sparking plug: 175°; tappet clearances: inlet 0.004 in, 0.10 mm, exhaust 0.004 in, 0.10 mm; valve timing: 6° 35°5' 42°5' 3°.

VARIATIONS

ENGINE Volkswagen, 91.1 cu in, 1,493 cc (3.27 x 2.72 in, 83 x 69 mm), max power (DIN) 42 hp (30.9 kW) at 4,000 rpm, max torque (DIN) 69 lb ft, 9.5 kg m (93.2 Nm) at 2,200 rpm, 28.1 hp/l (20.7 kW/l).
PERFORMANCE max speed 100 mph, 161 km/h, power-weight ratio 37.3 lb/hp (50.7 lb/kW), 16.9 kg/hp (23 kg/kW), consumption 35 m/imp gal, 29 m/US gal, 8.1 l x 100 km.

ENGINE Volkswagen, 96.7 cu in, 1,584 cc (3.37 x 2.72 in, 85.5 x 69 mm), 7.5:1 compression ratio, max power (DIN) 50 hp (36.8 kW) at 4,000 rpm, max torque (DIN) 78 lb ft, 10.8 kg m (105.9 Nm) at 2,800 rpm, 31.6 hp/l (23.2 kW/l), 1 Solex 34 PICT 2 downdraught carburettor.
PERFORMANCE max speed 110 mph, 177 km/h, power-weight ratio 31.4 lb/hp (42.6 lb/kW), 14.2 kg/hp (19.3 kg/kW), consumption 30.7 m/imp gal, 25.6 m/US gal, 9.2 l x 100 km.

ENGINE Volkswagen, tuned, 134.2 cu in, 2,200 cc, max power (DIN) 110 hp (81 kW), 50 hp/l (36.8 kW/l).
PERFORMANCE max speed 125 mph, 201 km/h, power-weight ratio 14.3 lb/hp (19.8 lb/kW), 6.5 kg/hp (8.8 kg/kW).

ENGINE Volkswagen, tuned, 134.2 cu in, 2,200 cc, max power (DIN) 145 hp (106.7 kW), 65.9 hp/l (48.5 kW/l).
PERFORMANCE max speed 135 mph, 217 km/h, power-weight ratio 10.8 lb/hp (14.7 lb/kW), 4.9 kg/hp (6.7 kg/kW).

OPTIONAL ACCESSORIES light alloy wheels; tuned exhaust systems; sunshine roof; rally instruments; rally equipment; front disc brakes.

G.P. Centron II

G.P. GREAT BRITAIN

Centron II

PRICE EX WORKS: £ 950* (kit only)

ENGINE Volkswagen, rear, 4 stroke; 4 cylinders, horizontally opposed; 72.7 cu in, 1,192 cc (3.03 x 2.52 in, 77 x 64 mm); compression ratio: 7.3:1; max power (DIN): 34 hp (25 kW) at 3,800 rpm; max torque (DIN): 55 lb ft, 7.6 kg m (74.5 Nm) at 1,700 rpm; max engine rpm: 4,500; 28.5 hp/l (21 kW/l); block with cast iron liners and light alloy fins, light alloy head; 4 crankshaft bearings; valves: overhead, push-rods and rockers; camshafts: 1, central, lower; lubrication: gear pump, filter in sump, oil cooler, 4.4 imp pt, 5.3 US pt, 2.5 l; 1 Solex 30 PICT downdraught single barrel carburettor; fuel feed: mechanical pump; air-cooled.

TRANSMISSION driving wheels: rear; clutch: single dry plate; gearbox: mechanical; gears: 4, fully synchronized; ratios: I 3.780, II 2.060, III 1.260, IV 0.890, rev 4.010; lever: central; final drive: spiral bevel; axle ratio: 4.375; width of rims: 6'' front, 7'' rear; tyres: 185/70 x 15 front, 205/70 x 15 rear.

PERFORMANCE max speed: 90 mph, 145 km/h; power-weight ratio: 46.1 lb/hp (62.7 lb/kW), 20.9 kg/hp (28.4 kg/kW); consumption: 43 m/imp gal, 35.6 m/US gal, 6.6 l x 100 km.

JAGUAR XJ 3.4

JAGUAR GREAT BRITAIN

XJ 3.4

PRICE EX WORKS: £ 8,174*

ENGINE front, 4 stroke; 6 cylinders, vertical, in line; 210 cu in, 3,442 cc (3.28 x 4.17 in, 83 x 106 mm); compression ratio: 8.5:1; max power (DIN): 161 hp (118.5 kW) at 5,250 rpm; max torque (DIN): 184 lb ft, 25.4 kg m (249.1 Nm) at 4,000 rpm; max engine rpm: 5,500; 46.8 hp/l (34.4 kW/l); cast iron dry liners, light alloy head, hemispherical combustion chambers; 7 crankshaft bearings; valves: overhead, Vee-slanted 2, thimble tappets; camshafts: 2, overhead; lubrication: rotary pump, full flow filter, oil cooler, 14.5 imp pt, 17.3 US pt, 8.2 l; 2 SU type HS8 horizontal carburettors; fuel feed: 2 electric pumps; water-cooled, 32.5 imp pt, 38.9 US pt, 18.4 l, viscous coupling thermostatic fan.

TRANSMISSION driving wheels: rear; clutch: single dry plate (diaphragm), hydraulically controlled; gearbox: mechanical; gears: 4 + overdrive/top, fully synchronized; ratios: I 3.238, II 1.905, III 1.389, IV 1, overdrive 0.779, rev 3.428; lever: central; final drive: hypoid bevel; axle ratio: 3.540; width of rims: 6''; tyres: E70 VR x 15.

PERFORMANCE max speeds: (I) 36 mph, 58 km/h; (II) 62 mph, 99 km/h; (III) 85 mph, 136 km/h; (IV) 117 mph, 188 km/h; power-weight ratio: 23.1 lb/hp (31.5 lb/kW), 10.5 kg/hp (14.2 kg/kW); carrying capacity: 904 lb, 410 kg; acceleration: standing ¼ mile 18 sec, 0-50 mph (0-80 km/h) 8.7 sec; speed in direct drive at 1,000 rpm: 21.4 mph, 34.4 km/h; consumption: 21.7 m/imp gal, 18.1 m/US gal, 13 l x 100 km.

CHASSIS integral, front and rear auxiliary frames; front suspension: independent, wishbones, lower trailing links, coil springs, anti-roll bar, telescopic dampers; rear: independent, lower wishbones, semi-axles as upper arms, trailing lower radius arms, 4 coil springs, 4 telescopic dampers.

STEERING rack-and-pinion, adjustable steering wheel, servo; turns lock to lock: 3.30.

BRAKES disc (front diameter 11.18 in, 28.4 cm, rear 10.36 in, 26.4 cm); front internal radial fins, servo; swept area: front 234.5 sq in, 1,512 sq cm, rear 213.7 sq in, 1,378 sq cm, total 448.2 sq in, 2,890 sq cm.

ELECTRICAL EQUIPMENT 12 V; 66 Ah battery; 45 A alternator; Lucas distributor; 4 halogen headlamps.

DIMENSIONS AND WEIGHT wheel base: 112.83 in, 287 cm; tracks: 57.99 in, 147 cm front, 58.58 in, 149 cm rear; length: 194.68 in, 494 cm; width: 69.68 in, 177 cm; height: 54.13 in, 137 cm; ground clearance: 7.09 in, 18 cm; weight: 3,715 lb, 1,685 kg; turning circle (between walls): 40 ft, 12.2 m; fuel tanks: 20 imp gal, 24 US gal, 91 l (2 separate tanks).

BODY saloon/sedan; 4 doors; 5 seats, separate front seats, reclining backrests; heated rear window.

PRACTICAL INSTRUCTIONS fuel: 97 oct petrol; oil: engine 14.5 imp pt, 17.3 US pt, 8.2 l, SAE 20W-50, change every 6,000 miles, 9,700 km - gearbox 4.5 imp pt, 6.3 US pt, 2.5 l, SAE 90 EP, change every 12,000 miles, 19,400 km - final drive 2.7 imp pt, 3.2 US pt, 1.5 l, SAE 90 EP, change every 12,000 miles, 19,400 km; greasing: every 6,000 miles, 9,700 km, 17 points; tappet clearances: inlet 0.012-0.014 in, 0.30-0.35 mm, exhaust 0.012-0.014 in, 0.30-0.35 mm; tyre pressure: front 25 psi, 1.7 atm, rear 26 psi, 1.8 atm.

OPTIONAL ACCESSORIES Borg-Warner 65 automatic transmission, hydraulic torque converter and planetary gears with 3 ratios (I 2.400, II 1.460, III 1, rev 2), max ratio of converter at stall 2, possible manual selection, 3.070 or 3.310 axle ratio, 60 A alternator, max speed 115 mph, 185 km/h, acceleration standing ¼ mile 18.6 sec, consumption 19 m/imp gal, 15.8 m/US gal, 14.9 l x 100 km; headrests; tinted glass; fog lamps; light alloy wheels.

XJ 4.2

See XJ 3.4, except for:

PRICE IN USA: $ 16,500*
PRICE EX WORKS: £ 8,651*

ENGINE 258.4 cu in, 4,235 cc (3.63 x 4.17 in, 92 x 106 mm); compression ratio: 7.8:1; max power (DIN): 166 hp (122.2 kW) at 4,750 rpm; max torque (DIN): 222 lb ft, 30.7 kg m (301.1 Nm) at 3,000 rpm; 39.2 hp/l (28.9 kW/l).

TRANSMISSION axle ratio: 3.310.

PERFORMANCE max speeds: (I) 40 mph, 64 km/h; (II) 62 mph, 99 km/h; (III) 85 mph, 136 km/h; (IV) 121 mph, 195 km/h; power-weight ratio: 23.8 lb/hp (32.3 lb/kW), 10.8 kg/hp (14.6 kg/kW); acceleration: standing ¼ mile 16.4 sec;

JAGUAR XJ 4.2

JAGUAR XJ 5.3

speed in direct drive at 1,000 rpm: 22 mph, 35.4 km/h; consumption: 16 m/imp gal, 13.4 m/US gal, 17.6 l x 100 km.

DIMENSIONS AND WEIGHT weight: 3,947 lb, 1,790 kg.

BODY 4 doors; electric windows; headrests (standard).

OPTIONAL ACCESSORIES Borg-Warner 65 automatic transmission, 3.540 axle ratio, max speed 118 mph, 190 km/h, acceleration standing ¼ mile 17.5 sec, consumption 15.3 m/imp gal, 12.7 m/US gal, 18.5 l x 100 km; air-conditioning.

XJ 5.3

PRICE IN USA: $ 17,750*
PRICE EX WORKS: £ 10,668*

ENGINE front, 4 stroke; 12 cylinders, Vee-slanted at 60°; 326 cu in, 5,343 cc (3.54 x 2.76 in, 90 x 70 mm); compression ratio: 9:1; max power (DIN): 284 hp (209 kW) at 5,750 rpm; max torque (DIN): 294 lb ft, 40.7 kg m (399.1 Nm) at 4,500 rpm; max engine rpm: 6,500; 53.2 hp/l (39.1 kW/l); light alloy block and head, wet liners, hemispherical combustion chambers; 7 crankshaft bearings; valves: overhead, in line, thimble tappets; camshafts: 1 per block, overhead; lubrication: rotary pump, full flow filter, oil cooler, 19 imp pt, 22.8 US pt, 10.8 l; Lucas-Bosch electronic injection; fuel feed: electric pump; water-cooled, 36 imp pt, 43.3 US pt, 20.5 l, 1 viscous coupling thermostatic fan and 1 electric thermostatic fan.

JAGUAR XJ 5.3

XJ 5.3

TRANSMISSION driving wheels: rear; gearbox: Turbo-Hydra-matic 400 automatic transmission, hydraulic torque converter and planetary gears with 3 ratios, max ratio of converter at stall 2, possible manual selection; ratios: I 2.480, II 1.480, III 1, rev 2.070; lever: central; final drive: hypoid bevel, limited slip differential; axle ratio: 3.310; width of rims: 6''; tyres: 205/70 VR x 15.

PERFORMANCE max speeds: (I) 58 mph, 94 km/h; (II) 96 mph, 155 km/h; (III) 140 mph, 225 km/h; power-weight ratio: 14.6 lb/hp (20 lb/kW), 6.6 kg/hp (9 kg/kW); carrying capacity: 904 lb, 410 kg; acceleration: standing ¼ mile 15.7 sec, 0-50 mph (0-80 km/h) 6.1 sec; speed in direct drive at 1,000 rpm: 24.3 mph, 39.1 km/h; consumption: 14.1 m/imp gal, 11.8 m/US gal, 20 l x 100 km.

CHASSIS integral, front and rear auxiliary frames; front suspension: independent, wishbones, lower trailing links, coil springs, anti-roll bar, telescopic dampers; rear: independent, wishbones, semi-axles as upper arms, trailing lower radius arms, 4 coil springs, 4 telescopic dampers.

STEERING rack-and-pinion, adjustable steering wheel, servo; turns lock to lock: 3.30.

BRAKES disc (front diameter 11.18 in, 28.4 cm, rear 10.38 in, 26.4 cm), front internal radial fins, servo; swept area: front 234.5 sq in, 1,512 sq cm, rear 213.7 sq in, 1,378 sq cm, total 448.2 sq in, 2,890 sq cm.

ELECTRICAL EQUIPMENT 12 V; 68 Ah battery; 60 A alternator; Lucas electronic distributor; 4 halogen headlamps.

DIMENSIONS AND WEIGHT wheel base: 112.83 in, 287 cm; tracks: 57.99 in, 147 cm front, 58.27 in, 148 cm rear; length: 194.68 in, 494 cm; width: 69.68 in, 177 cm; height: 54.13 in, 137 cm; ground clearance: 7.09 in, 18 cm; weight: 4,156 lb, 1,885 kg; turning circle (between walls): 40 ft, 12.2 m; fuel tanks: 20 imp gal, 24 US gal, 91 l (2 separate tanks).

BODY saloon/sedan; 4 doors; 5 seats, separate front seats, reclining backrests with built-in headrests; heated rear window; electric windows; vinyl roof; tinted glass.

PRACTICAL INSTRUCTIONS fuel: 97 oct petrol; oil: engine 19 imp pt, 22.8 US pt, 10.8 l, SAE 10W-40 (winter) 20W-50 (summer), change every 6,000 miles, 9,700 km - final drive 2.7 imp pt, 3.2 US pt, 1.5 l, SAE 90 EP, change every 12,000 miles, 19,400 km; greasing: every 6,000 miles, 9,700 km, 17 points; tappet clearances: inlet 0.012-0.014 in, 0.30-0.35 mm, exhaust 0.012-0.014 in, 0.30-0.35 mm; tyre pressure: front 25 psi, 1.7 atm, rear 26 psi, 1.8 atm.

OPTIONAL ACCESSORIES air-conditioning; fog lamps; light alloy wheels.

XJ-S

PRICE IN USA: $ 21,700*
PRICE EX WORKS: £ 13,200*

ENGINE front, 4 stroke; 12 cylinders, Vee-slanted at 60°; 326 cu in, 5,343 cc (3.54 x 2.76 in, 90 x 70 mm); compression ratio: 9:1; max power (DIN): 284 hp (209 kW) at 5,750 rpm; max torque (DIN): 294 lb ft, 40.7 kg m (399.1 Nm) at 4,500 rpm; max engine rpm: 6,500; 53.2 hp/l (39.1 kW/l); light alloy block and head, wet liners, hemispherical combustion chambers; 7 crankshaft bearings; valves: overhead, in line, thimble tappets; camshafts: 1 per block, overhead; lubrication: rotary pump, full flow filter, oil cooler, 19 imp pt, 22.8 US pt, 10.8 l; Lucas-Bosch electronic injection; fuel feed: electric pump; water-cooled, 37.5 imp pt, 47.2 US pt, 21.3 l, 1 viscous coupling thermostatic fan and 1 electric thermostatic fan.

TRANSMISSION driving wheels: rear; clutch: single dry plate (diaphragm), hydraulically controlled; gearbox: mechanical; gears: 4, fully synchronized; ratios: I 3.238, II 1.905, III 1.389, IV 1, rev 3.428; lever: central; final drive: hypoid bevel, limited slip differential; axle ratio: 3.070; width of rims: 6''; tyres: 205/70 VR x 15.

PERFORMANCE max speeds: (I) 50 mph, 80 km/h; (II) 80 mph, 128 km/h; (III) 103 mph, 165 km/h; (IV) 150 mph, 241 km/h; power-weight ratio: 13.6 lb/hp (18.5 lb/kW), 6.2 kg/hp (8.4 kg/kW); carrying capacity: 990 lb, 408 kg; acceleration: standing ¼ mile 14.5 sec, 0-50 mph (0-80 km/h) 4.8 sec; speed in direct drive at 1,000 rpm: 24.8 mph, 39.9 km/h; consumption: 14 m/imp gal, 11.6 m/US gal, 20.2 l x 100 km.

CHASSIS integral, front and rear auxiliary frames; front suspension: independent, wishbones, lower trailing links, coil springs, anti-roll bar, telescopic dampers; rear: independent, lower wishbones, semi-axles as upper arms, trailing lower radius arms, 4 coil springs, 4 telescopic dampers, anti-roll bar.

JAGUAR XJ-S

JAGUAR XJ-S

JAGUAR XJ-S

STEERING rack-and-pinion, servo; turns lock to lock: 3.25.

BRAKES disc (front diameter 11.18 in, 28.4 cm, rear 10.38 in, 26.4 cm), front internal radial fins, servo; swept area: front 252 sq in, 1,624 sq cm, rear 148 sq in, 956 sq cm, total 400 sq in, 2,580 sq cm.

ELECTRICAL EQUIPMENT 12 V; 68 Ah battery; 60 A alternator; Lucas electronic distributor; 2 halogen headlamps.

DIMENSIONS AND WEIGHT wheel base: 102 in, 259 cm; tracks: 58 in, 147 cm front, 58.60 in, 149 cm rear; length: 191.70 in, 487 cm; width: 70.60 in, 179 cm; height: 49.65 in, 126 cm; ground clearance: 5.50 in, 14 cm; weight: 3,859 lb, 1,750 kg; turning circle (between walls): 36 ft, 11 m; fuel tanks: 20 imp gal, 24 US gal, 91 l (2 separate tanks)

BODY coupé; 2 doors; 4 seats, separate front seats, reclining backrests with built-in headrests; heated rear window; leather upholstery; tinted glass; air-conditioning.

PRACTICAL INSTRUCTIONS fuel: 98 oct petrol; oil: engine 16 imp pt, 19.2 US pt, 9.1 l, SAE 20W-50, change every 6,000 miles, 9,700 km - gearbox 2.8 imp pt, 3.4 US pt, 1.6 l - final drive 1.7 imp pt, 2.1 US pt, 1 l; greasing: every 12,000 miles, 19,400 km, 17 points; tappet clearances: inlet 0.014-0.016 in, 0.36-0.38 mm, exhaust 0.014-0.016 in, 0.36-0.38 mm; valve timing: 17° 59° 59° 17°; tyre pressure: front 26 psi, 1.8 atm, rear 24 psi, 1.7 atm.

VARIATIONS

(for USA only).
ENGINE 7.8:1 compression ratio, max power (DIN) 247 hp (181.8 kW) at 5,250 rpm, max torque (DIN) 270 lb ft, 37.2 kg m (364.8 Nm) at 4,500 rpm, 46.2 hp/l (34 kW/l).
TRANSMISSION 3.310 axle ratio.
PERFORMANCE power-weight ratio 15 lb/hp (20.5 lb/kW), 6.8 kg/hp (9.3 kg/kW).
PRACTICAL INSTRUCTIONS 91 oct petrol.

OPTIONAL ACCESSORIES Turbo-Hydramatic 400 automatic transmission, hydraulic torque converter and planetary gears with 3 ratios (I 2.480, II 1.480, III 1, rev 2.070), max ratio of converter at stall 2, possible manual selection, 3.070 axle ratio (3.310 for USA only).

JOHNARD VINTAGE CAR
GREAT BRITAIN

Bentley Donington

PRICE EX WORKS: $ 15,500*

ENGINE Rolls-Royce or Bentley, front, 4 stroke; 8 cylinders, Vee-slanted at 90°; 380.2 cu in, 6,230 cc (4.10 x 3.60 in, 104.1 x 91.4 mm); compression ratio: 9:1; light alloy block and head, cast iron wet liners; 5 crankshaft bearings; valves: overhead, in line, slanted, push-rods and

JOHNARD VINTAGE CAR Bentley Donington

52 in, 132 cm; weight: 2,271 lb, 1,030 kg; fuel tank: 20 imp gal, 24 US gal, 91 l.

BODY sports, in plastic material; no doors; 2 seats.

PRACTICAL INSTRUCTIONS fuel: 98-100 oct petrol; oil: engine 14.1 imp pt, 16.9 US pt, 8 l, SAE 20W-50, change every 6,000 miles, 9,700 km.

VARIATIONS

ENGINE 6 cylinders, in line, 262.4 cu in, 4,300 cc.

ENGINE 6 cylinders, in line, 280.7 cu in, 4,600 cc.

ENGINE 6 cylinders, in line 299 cu in, 4,900 cc.

ENGINE 8 cylinders, Vee-slanted at 90°, 441.9 cu in, 6,750 cc.

OPTIONAL ACCESSORIES 3.770, 3.310 or 3.540 axle ratio; Turbo-Hydramatic 400 automatic transmission, hydraulic torque converter and planetary gears with 3 ratios (I 2.480, II 1.480, III 1, rev 2.080), max ratio of converter at stall 2.1, possible manual selection; servo brake; left-hand drive; adjustable clutch, brake and accelerator pedals.

rockers, hydraulic tappets; camshafts: 1, at centre of Vee; lubrication: gear pump, full flow filter (cartridge), 14.4 imp pt, 17.3 US pt, 8.2 l; 2 SU type HD8 horizontal carburettors; fuel feed: mechanical pump; sealed circuit cooling, expansion tank, 28.2 imp pt, 33.8 US pt, 16 l, viscous coupling thermostatic fan.

TRANSMISSION driving wheels: rear; clutch: single dry plate; gearbox: mechanical; gears: 4, II, III and IV synchronized; ratios: I 2.990, II 2.050, III 1.330, IV 1; lever: central; final drive: hypoid bevel, limited slip differential; axle ratio: 2.880; width of rims: 7.5''; tyres: ER 70 VR x 15.

PERFORMANCE max speed: 140 mph, 225 km/h; speed in direct drive at 1,000 rpm: 28 mph, 45 km/h; consumption: 12 m/imp gal, 10 m/US gal, 23.5 l x 100 km.

CHASSIS channel section ladder frame; front suspension: independent, wishbones, coil springs, anti-roll bar, telescopic dampers; rear: rigid axle, semi-elliptic leafsprings, radius arms, adjustable telescopic dampers.

STEERING cam and roller, adjustable height.

BRAKES drum.

ELECTRICAL EQUIPMENT 12 V; 71 Ah battery; 55 A alternator; Lucas distributor; 2 headlamps.

DIMENSIONS AND WEIGHT wheel base: 109 in, 277 cm; tracks: 58 in, 147 cm front, 58 in, 147 cm rear; height:

JOHNARD VINTAGE CAR Bentley Donington

K.M.B.   **GREAT BRITAIN**

GTM Mk 1-3

PRICES EX WORKS: £ 2,800 or £ 1,350 (kit form)

ENGINE British Leyland, central, transverse, 4 stroke; 4 cylinders, vertical, in line; 77.8 cu in, 1,275 cc (2.78 x 3.20 in, 70.7 x 81.4 mm); compression ratio: 9.9:1; max power (SAE): 90 hp (66.2 kW) at 5,800 rpm; max torque (SAE): 83 lb ft, 11.4 kg m (111.8 Nm) at 3,200 rpm; max engine rpm: 7,600; 70.6 hp/l (51.9 kW/l); cast iron block and head; 3 crankshaft bearings; valves: overhead, in line, push-rods and rockers; camshafts: 1, side; lubrication: rotary pump, full flow filter, oil cooler, 8 imp pt, 9.5 US pt, 4.5 l; 2 SU carburettors; fuel feed: electric pump; water-cooled, 7 imp pt, 8.5 US pt, 4 l, rear mounted radiator.

TRANSMISSION driving wheels: rear; clutch: single dry plate (diaphragm); gearbox: mechanical; gears: 4, fully synchronized; ratios: I 3.203, II 1.919, III 1.358, IV 1, rev 3.350; lever: central; final drive: helical spur gears; axle ratios: from 2.900 to 4.300; width of rims: 5''; tyres: 145 x 10 or 165 x 10.

PERFORMANCE max speeds: (I) 39 mph, 62 km/h; (II) 61 mph, 98 km/h; (III) 90 mph, 145 km/h; (IV) 120 mph, 193 km/h; power-weight ratio: 13 lb/hp (17.9 lb/kW), 5.9 kg/hp (8.1 kg/hp); carrying capacity: 953 lb, 432 kg; acceleration: standing ¼ mile 17.5 sec, 0-50 mph (0-80 km/h) 7 sec; speed in direct drive at 1,000 rpm: 16 mph, 25.7 km/h; consumption: 38 m/imp gal, 31.8 m/US gal, 7.4 l x 100 km.

CHASSIS integral with front and rear tubular frame sections; front suspension: independent, wishbones, coil springs, telescopic dampers; rear: independent, wishbones, rubber elements, telescopic dampers.

STEERING rack-and-pinion; turns lock to lock: 3.20.

BRAKES front disc, rear drum, servo.

ELECTRICAL EQUIPMENT 12 V; 75 Ah battery; dynamo or alternator; Lucas distributor; 2 headlamps.

DIMENSIONS AND WEIGHT wheel base: 84 in, 213 cm; front and rear tracks: 48 in, 122 cm; length: 128 in, 325 cm; width: 56 in, 142 cm; height: 43 in, 109 cm; ground clearance: 5 in, 13 cm; weight: 1,175 lb, 533 kg; weight distribution: 45% front, 55% rear; fuel tank: 10 imp gal, 11.9 US gal, 45 l.

BODY coupé in plastic material; 2 doors; 2 seats.

PRACTICAL INSTRUCTIONS oil: engine, gearbox and final drive 8 imp pt, 9.5 US pt, 4.5 l, SAE 20W-50, change every 6,000 miles, 9,600 km; greasing: every 6,000 miles, 9,600 km, 12 points; tyre pressure: front 20 psi, 1.3 atm, rear 30 psi, 2.1 atm.

VARIATIONS

ENGINE 51.7 cu in, 848 cc.

K.M.B. GTM Mk 1-3

LOTUS Esprit

LOTUS   GREAT BRITAIN

Esprit

PRICE IN USA: $ 17,440*
PRICE EX WORKS: £ 9,138*

ENGINE central, longitudinal, 4 stroke; 4 cylinders, in line; 120.4 cu in, 1,973 cc (3.75 x 2.72 in, 95.2 x 69.2 mm); compression ratio: 9.5:1; max power (DIN): 160 hp (117.8 kW) at 6,200 rpm; max torque (DIN): 140 lb ft, 19.3 kg m (189.3 Nm) at 4,900 rpm; max engine rpm: 7,300; 81.1 hp/l (59.7 kW/l); light alloy block and head, wet liners; 5 crankshaft bearings; valves: 4 per cylinder, overhead, slanted at 38°, thimble tappets; camshafts: 2, overhead, cogged belt; lubrication: rotary pump, full flow filter, 10.5 imp pt, 12.5 US pt, 5.9 l; 2 Dell'Orto DHLA 45 horizontal twin barrel carburettors; fuel feed: electric pump; water-cooled, 15.8 imp pt, 19 US pt, 9 l, front radiator, electric thermostatic fans.

TRANSMISSION driving wheels: rear; clutch: single dry plate (diaphragm), hydraulically controlled; gearbox: mechanical; gears: 5, fully synchronized; ratios: I 2.920, II 1.940, III 1.320, IV 0.970, V 0.760, rev 4.375; lever: central; final drive: hypoid bevel, in unit with gearbox; axle ratio: 4.375; width of rims: 6'' front, 7'' rear; tyres: 195/70 HR x 14 front, 205/70 HR x 14 rear.

PERFORMANCE max speeds: (I) 36 mph, 58 km/h; (II) 54 mph, 87 km/h; (III) 79 mph, 127 km/h; (IV) 108 mph, 174 km/h; (V) 138 mph, 222 km/h; power-weight ratio: 12.4 lb/hp (16.8 lb/kW), 5.6 kg/hp (7.6 kg/kW); carrying capacity: 500 lb, 227 kg; acceleration: standing ¼ mile 15 sec, 0-50 mph (0-80 km/h) 4.9 sec; speed in top at 1,000 rpm: 21.8 mph, 35.1 km/h; consumption: 28 m/imp gal, 23.3 m/US gal, 10.1 l x 100 km.

CHASSIS box type backbone with space-frame section; front suspension: independent, wishbones, coil springs, anti-roll bar, telescopic dampers; rear: independent, wishbones, diagonal trailing arm and lateral link with fixed length driveshaft, coil springs, telescopic dampers.

STEERING rack-and-pinion.

BRAKES disc (front diameter 9.7 in, 24.6 cm, rear 10.6 in, 25.6 cm).

ELECTRICAL EQUIPMENT 12 V; 48 Ah battery; 45 A alternator; Lucas distributor; 4 retractable headlamps.

DIMENSIONS AND WEIGHT wheel base: 96 in, 244 cm; front and rear tracks: 59.50 in, 151 cm; length: 165 in, 419 cm; width: 73.25 in, 186 cm; height: 43.70 in, 111 cm; ground clearance: 5.50 in, 14 cm; weight: 1,980 lb, 898 kg; fuel tank: 15 imp gal, 18 US gal, 68 l.

BODY coupé, in reinforced plastic material; 2 doors; 2 seats with built-in headrests; electric windows; light alloy wheels; heated rear window.

PRACTICAL INSTRUCTIONS fuel: 98 oct petrol; oil: engine 10.5 imp pt, 12.5 US pt, 5.9 l, SAE 20W-50, change every 3,000 miles, 4,800 km - gearbox and final drive 4.4 imp pt, 5.3 US pt, 2.5 l, SAE 80 EP, change every 12,000 miles,

20,000 km; greasing: every 3,000 miles, 4,800 km, 4 points; tappet clearances: inlet 0.004-0.006 in, 0.11-0.14 mm, exhaust 0.008-0.10 in, 0.20-0.25 mm; valve timing: 30° 50° 50° 30°; tyre pressure: front 18 psi, 1.3 atm, rear 28 psi, 2 atm.

Eclat 520

PRICE IN USA: $ 15,350*
PRICE EX WORKS: £ 8,537*

ENGINE front, 4 stroke; 4 cylinders, in line; 120.4 cu in, 1,973 cc (3.75 x 2.72 in, 95.2 x 69.2 mm); compression ratio: 9.5:1; max power (DIN): 160 hp (117.8 kW) at 6,200 rpm; max torque (DIN): 140 lb ft, 19.3 kg m (189.3 Nm) at 4,900 rpm; max engine rpm: 7,300; 81.1 hp/l (59.7 kW/l); light alloy block and head, wet liners; 5 crankshaft bearings; valves: 4 per cylinder, overhead, slanted at 38°, thimble tappets; camshafts: 2, overhead, cogged belt; lubrication: rotary pump, full flow filter, 10.5 imp pt, 12.5 US pt, 5.9 l; 2 Dell'Orto DHLA 45E horizontal twin barrel carburettors; fuel feed: electric pump; water-cooled, 12 imp pt, 14.4 US pt, 6.8 l, electric thermostatic fan.

TRANSMISSION driving wheels: rear; clutch: single dry plate (diaphragm); gearbox: mechanical; gears: 4, fully synchronized; ratios: I 3.160, II 1.950, III 1.410, IV 1, rev 3.350; lever: central; final drive: hypoid bevel; axle ratio: 3.730; width of rims: 5.5''; tyres: 185/70 HR x 13.

PERFORMANCE max speeds: (I) 40 mph, 65 km/h; (II) 66 mph, 106 km/h; (III) 92 mph, 148 km/h; (IV) 130 mph, 210 km/h; power-weight ratio: 13.5 lb/hp (18.3 lb/kW).

LOTUS Eclat 520

6.1 kg/hp (8.3 kg/kW); carrying capacity: 706 lb, 320 kg; acceleration: standing ¼ mile 15.8 sec, 0-50 mph (0-80 km/h) 6 sec; speed in direct drive at 1,000 rpm: 17.9 mph, 28.8 km/h; consumption: 28 m/imp gal, 23.3 m/US gal, 10.1 l x 100 km.

CHASSIS box-type backbone; front suspension: independent, wishbones, coil springs, anti-roll bar, telescopic dampers; rear: independent, lower wide-based wishbones, semi-axles as upper arms, coil springs, telescopic dampers.

STEERING rack-and-pinion; turns lock to lock: 3.50.

BRAKES front disc, rear drum, servo.

ELECTRICAL EQUIPMENT 12 V; 48 Ah battery; 45 A alternator; Lucas distributor; 2 retractable headlamps.

DIMENSIONS AND WEIGHT wheel base: 97.75 in, 248 cm; tracks: 58.50 in, 149 cm front, 59 in, 150 cm rear; length: 175.50 in, 446 cm; width: 71.50 in, 182 cm; height: 47.25 in, 120 cm; ground clearance: 5.40 in, 13.7 cm; weight: 2,160 lb, 979 kg; fuel tank: 14.7 imp gal, 17.7 US gal, 67 l.

BODY coupé, in reinforced plastic material; 2 doors; 2+2 seats, separate front seats, reclining backrests with built-in headrests; electric windows; heated rear window.

PRACTICAL INSTRUCTIONS fuel: 98 oct petrol; oil: engine 10.5 imp pt, 12.5 US pt, 5.9 l, SAE 20W-50, change every 3,000 miles, 4,800 km - gearbox 2 imp pt, 2.3 US pt, 1.1 l,

LOTUS Esprit

SAE 80 EP, change every 6,000 miles, 9,700 km - final drive 2 imp pt, 2.3 US pt, 1.1 l, SAE 90 EP, change every 12,000 miles, 20,000 km; greasing: every 3,000 miles, 4,800 km, 4 points; tappet clearances: inlet 0.004-0.006 in, 0.11-0.14 mm, exhaust 0.008-0.10 in, 0.20-0.25 mm; valve timing: 30° 50° 50° 30°; tyre pressure: front 20 psi, 1.4 atm, rear 22 psi, 1.6 atm.

OPTIONAL ACCESSORIES 4.100 axle ratio.

Eclat 521

See Eclat 520, except for:

PRICE IN USA: $ 16,698*
PRICE EX WORKS: £ 9,107*

TRANSMISSION gears: 5, fully synchronized; ratios: I 3.200, II 2.010, III 1.370, IV 1, V 0.800, rev 3.467; width of rims: 7''; tyres: 205/60 VR x 14.

PERFORMANCE max speeds: (I) 42 mph, 67 km/h; (II) 66 mph, 106 km/h; (III) 97 mph, 156 km/h; (IV) 105 mph, 169 km/h; (V) 132 mph, 212 km/h; acceleration: standing ¼ mile 16 sec, 0-50 mph (0-80 km/h) 6.1 sec; speed in top at 1,000 rpm: 22.9 mph, 36.8 km/h.

BODY light alloy wheels.

OPTIONAL ACCESSORIES power steering; automatic transmission, hydraulic torque converter and planetary gears with 3 ratios (I 2.390, II 1.450, III 1, rev 2.090), max ratio of converter at stall 2, possible manual selection.

LOTUS Eclat 520

Eclat 522

See Eclat 521, except for:

PRICE IN USA: $ 17,688*
PRICE EX WORKS: £ 10,046*

ELECTRICAL EQUIPMENT halogen headlamps.

BODY air-conditioning; tinted glass.

Eclat 523

See Eclat 522, except for:

PRICE IN USA: $ 18,250*
PRICE EX WORKS: £ 10,363*

STEERING servo (standard).

Eclat 524

See Eclat 523, except for:

PRICE IN USA: $ 18,755*
PRICE EX WORKS: £ 10,584*

TRANSMISSION gearbox: automatic transmission (standard), hydraulic torque converter and planetary gears with 3 ratios, max ratio of converter at stall 2, possible manual selection; ratios: I 2.390, III 1.450, III 1, rev 2.090.

Elite 501

PRICE IN USA: $ 15,548*
PRICE EX WORKS: £ 9,612*

ENGINE front, 4 stroke; 4 cylinders, in line, slanted 45° to left; 120.4 cu in, 1,973 cc (3.75 x 2.72 in, 95.2 x 69.2 mm); compression ratio: 9.5:1; max power (DIN) 155 hp (114.1 kW) at 6,500 rpm; max torque (DIN): 135 lb ft, 18.6 kg m (182.4 Nm) at 5,000 rpm; max engine rpm: 7,000; 78.6 hp/l (57.8 kW/l); light alloy block and head, wet liners; 5 crankshaft bearings; valves: 4 per cylinder, overhead, slanted at 38°, thimble tappets; camshafts: 2, overhead, cogged belt; lubrication: rotary pump, full flow filter, 10 imp pt, 12 US pt, 5.7 l; 2 Dell'Orto DHLA 45E horizontal twin barrel carburettors; fuel feed: electric pump; water-cooled, 12 imp pt, 14.4 US pt, 6.8 l, electric thermostatic fan.

TRANSMISSION driving wheels: rear; clutch: single dry plate (diaphragm); gearbox: mechanical; gears: 5, fully synchronized; ratios: I 3.200, II 2.010, III 1.370, IV 1, V 0.800, rev 3.467; lever: central; final drive: hypoid bevel; axle ratio: 3.730; width of rims: 7''; tyres: 205/60 VR x 14.

PERFORMANCE max speeds: (I) 40 mph, 64 km/h; (II) 64 mph, 103 km/h; (II) 93 mph, 149 km/h; (IV) 128 mph, 206 km/h; (V) 125 mph, 201 km/h; power-weight ratio: 15 lb/hp (20.5 lb/kW), 6.8 kg/hp (9.3 kg/kW); carrying capacity: 860 lb, 390 kg; speed in top at 1,000 rpm: 20.7 mph, 33.3 km/h; consumption: 26.4 m/imp gal, 22 m/US gal. 10.7 l x 100 km.

CHASSIS box-type backbone; front suspension: independent, wishbones, coil springs, anti-roll bar, telescopic dampers; rear: independent, lower wide-based wishbones, semi-axles as upper arms, coil springs/telescopic struts.

STEERING rack-and-pinion; turns lock to lock: 3.50.

BRAKES disc (diameter 10.40 in, 26.4 cm), rear drum, servo.

ELECTRICAL EQUIPMENT 12 V; 50 Ah battery; 60 A alternator; Lucas distributor; 2 retractable headlamps .

DIMENSIONS AND WEIGHT wheel base: 97.64 in, 248 cm; tracks: 58.50 in, 149 cm front, 58.50 in, 149 cm rear; length: 175.50 in, 446 cm; width: 71.50 in, 182 cm; height: 47.65 in, 121 cm; ground clearance: 5.50 in, 14 cm; weight: 2,338 lb, 1,060 kg; turning circle (between walls): 34.5 ft, 10.5 m; fuel tank: 14.7 imp gal, 17.7 US gal, 67 l.

BODY coupé, in reinforced plastic material; 2 doors; 4 seats, separate front seats, reclining backrests, built-in headrests; electric windows; heated rear window; light alloy wheels; rear window wiper-washer.

PRACTICAL INSTRUCTIONS fuel: 98-100 oct petrol; oil: engine 9.2 imp pt, 11 US pt, 5.2 l, SAE 20W-50, change every 3,000 miles, 4,800 km - gearbox 2 imp pt, 2.3 US pt, 1.1 l, SAE 80 EP, change every 6,000 miles, 9,700 km - final drive 2 imp pt, 2.3 US pt, 1.1 l, SAE 90 EP, change every 12,000 miles, 20,000 km; greasing: every 3,000 miles, 4,800 km, 2 points; tappet clearances: inlet 0.010 in, 0.25

mm, exhaust 0.010 in, 0.25 mm; valve timing: 25° 65° 65° 25°; tyre pressure: front 22 psi, 1.6 atm, rear 22 psi, 1.6 atm.

VARIATIONS

(for USA only).
ENGINE 8.4:1 compression ratio, max power (DIN) 142 hp (104.5 kW) at 6,500 rpm, max torque (DIN) 130 lb ft, 18 kg m (176.5 Nm) at 5,000 rpm, 72 hp/l (53 kW/l), 2 Zenith-Stromberg 175 CD 2SE horizontal carburettors.
PERFORMANCE power-weight ratio 16.1 lb/hp (22.4 lb/kW), 7.3 kg/hp (10.1 kg/kW).
PRACTICAL INSTRUCTIONS valve timing 26° 66° 66° 26°.

OPTIONAL ACCESSORIES power steering; automatic transmission, hydraulic torque converter and planetary gears with 3 ratios (I 2.390, II 1.450, III 1, rev 2.090), max ratio of converter at stall 2, possible manual selection; 4.100 axle ratio: vinyl roof; metallic spray.

Elite 502

See Elite 501, except for:

PRICE IN USA: $ 16,417*
PRICE EX WORKS: £ 10,643*

ELECTRICAL EQUIPMENT halogen headlamps.

BODY tinted glass; air-conditioning.

Elite 503

See Elite 501, except for:

PRICE IN USA: $ 19,090*
PRICE EX WORKS: £ 10,961*

STEERING servo (standard).

ELECTRICAL EQUIPMENT halogen headlamps.

BODY tinted glass; air-conditioning.

Elite 504

See Elite 501, except for:

PRICE IN USA: $ 19,615*
PRICE EX WORKS: £ 11,191*

TRANSMISSION gearbox: automatic transmission (standard), hydraulic torque converter and planetary gears with 3 ratios, max ratio of converter at stall 2, possible manual selection; ratios: I 2.390, II 1.450, III 1, rev 2.090.

STEERING servo (standard).

ELECTRICAL EQUIPMENT halogen headlamps.

BODY tinted glass; air-conditioning.

LOTUS Elite 501

LYNX   GREAT BRITAIN

D Type

PRICES EX WORKS: £ 15,000 or £ 8,500 (kit form)

ENGINE Jaguar XKE front, 4 stroke; 6 cylinders, in line; 258.4 cu in, 4,235 cc (3.63 x 4.17 in, 92.1 x 106 mm); compression ratio: 9:1; max power (DIN): 171 hp (125.9 kW) at 4,500 rpm; max torque (DIN): 230 lb ft, 31.8 kg m (311.9 Nm) at 2,500 rpm; max engine rpm: 5,500; 40.4 hp/l (29.7 kW/l); block with chrome iron dry liners, head with aluminium alloy hemispherical combustion chambers; 7 crankshaft bearings; valves: overhead, Vee-slanted at 70°, thimble tappets; camshafts: 2, overhead; lubrication: rotary pump, full flow filter, 15 imp pt, 18 US pt, 8.5 l; 2 Weber semi-downdraught carburettors; fuel feed: electric pump; water-cooled, 32.9 imp pt, 39.5 US pt, 18.7 l, automatic thermostatic fan.

TRANSMISSION driving wheels: rear; clutch: single dry plate (diaphragm), hydraulically controlled; gearbox: mechanical; gears: 4, fully synchronized; ratios: I 2.933, II 1.905, III 1.389, IV 1, rev 3.378; lever: central; final drive: hypoid bevel, limited slip differential; axle ratio: 3.070; width of rims: 6''; tyres: E70 VR x 15.

PERFORMANCE max speeds: (I) 48 mph, 77 km/h; (II) 73 mph, 117 km/h; (III) 108 mph, 174 km/h; (IV) 150 mph, 241 km/h; power-weight ratio: 12.8 lb/hp (17.4 lb/kW), 5.8 kg/hp (7.9 kg/kW); carrying capacity: 408 lb, 185 kg; acceleration: standing ¼ mile 16 sec, 0-50 mph (0-80 km/h) 5.4 sec; consumption: 18.8 m/imp gal, 15.7 m/US gal, 15 l x 100 km.

CHASSIS integral, front and rear tubular auxiliary frames; front suspension: independent, wishbones, swinging longitudinal torsion bars, anti-roll bar, telescopic dampers; rear: independent, wide-based wishbones, semi-axles as upper arms, trailing lower radius arms, 4 coil springs, 4 telescopic dampers.

STEERING rack-and-pinion.

BRAKES disc (front diameter 11.18 in, 28.4 cm, rear 10.38 in, 26.4 cm), servo; swept area: front 234.5 sq in, 1,512 sq cm, rear 213.7 sq in, 1,378 sq cm, total 448.2 sq in, 2,890 sq cm.

ELECTRICAL EQUIPMENT 12 V; 68 Ah battery; 60 A alternator; Lucas distributor; 2 headlamps.

DIMENSIONS AND WEIGHT wheel base: 90.50 in, 230 cm; tracks: 50.25 in, 128 cm front, 51 in, 129 cm rear; length: 159 in, 404 cm; width: 63 in, 160 cm; height: 45.50 in, 116 cm; ground clearance: 5 in, 12.7 cm; weight: 2,184 lb, 990 kg; weight distribution: 51% front, 49% rear; turning circle (between walls): 32 ft, 9.8 m; fuel tank: 21 imp gal, 25.1 US gal, 95 l.

BODY sports; 2 doors; 2 seats.

PRACTICAL INSTRUCTIONS fuel: 97 oct petrol; oil: engine 15 imp pt, 18 US pt, 8.5 l, SAE 20W-50, change every 6,000 miles, 9,700 km - gearbox 2.5 imp pt, 3 US pt, 1.4 l, SAE 90 EP, change every 12,000 miles, 19,300 km - final drive 2.7 imp pt, 3.2 US pt, 1.5 l, SAE 90 EP, change every 12,000

LYNX D Type

LYNX D Type

miles, 19,300 km; greasing: every 6,000-12,000 miles, 9,700-19,300 km; tappet clearances: inlet 0.012-0.014 in, 0.30-0.35 mm, exhaust 0.012-0.014 in, 0.30-0.35 mm; valve timing: 17° 59° 59° 17°; tyre pressure: front 24 psi, 1.7 atm, rear 28 psi, 2 atm.

VARIATIONS

ENGINE Jaguar, tuned, max power (DIN) 285 hp (209.8 kW).
ENGINE Jaguar, tuned, max power (DIN) 320 hp (234.8 kW).

OPTIONAL ACCESSORIES 8:1 compression ratio; XKSS model; short nose body-work; dry sump lubrication with oil tank; oil cooler; light alloy wheels; 6.50L x 15 tyres; modified suspension; headrests; side exit exhaust; weather equipment.

MG   GREAT BRITAIN

Midget

PRICE IN USA: $ 4,150*
PRICE EX WORKS: £ 2,095*

ENGINE front, 4 stroke; 4 cylinders, vertical, in line; 91 cu in, 1,491 cc (2.90 x 3.44 in, 73.7 x 87.4 mm); compression ratio: 9:1; max power (DIN): 65 hp (47.8 kW) at 5,500 rpm; max torque (DIN): 84 lb ft, 10.6 kg m (104 Nm) at 3,000 rpm; max engine rpm: 6,000; 43.6 hp/l (32.1 kW/l); cast iron block and head; 3 crankshaft bearings; valves: overhead, push-rods and rockers; camshafts: 1, side; lubrication: eccentric pump, full flow filter, 7 imp pt, 8.5 US pt, 4 l; 2 SU type HS4 semi-downdraught carburettors; fuel feed: electric pump; water-cooled, 6 imp pt, 7.2 US pt, 3.4 l.

TRANSMISSION driving wheels: rear; clutch: single dry plate (diaphragm), hydraulically controlled; gearbox: mechanical; gears: 4, fully synchronized; ratios: I 3.412, II 2.112, III 1.433, IV 1, rev 3.753; lever: central; final drive: hypoid bevel; axle ratio: 3.720; width of rims: 4''; tyres: 145 x 13.

PERFORMANCE max speeds: (I) 29 mph, 46 km/h; (II) 47 mph, 75 km/h; (III) 69 mph, 111 km/h; (IV) 95 mph, 153 km/h; power-weight ratio: 27.3 lb/hp (37.1 lb/kW), 12.4 kg/hp (16.8 kg/kW); carrying capacity: 353 lb, 160 kg; speed in direct drive at 1,000 rpm: 16.4 mph, 26.4 km/h; consumption: 35.3 m/imp gal, 29.4 m/US gal, 8 l x 100 km.

CHASSIS integral; front suspension: independent, wishbones, coil springs, anti-roll bar, telescopic dampers; rear: rigid axle, semi-elliptic leafsprings, telescopic dampers.

STEERING rack-and-pinion; turns lock to lock: 2.25.

BRAKES front disc (diameter 8.25 in, 21 cm), rear drum.

ELECTRICAL EQUIPMENT 12 V; 40 Ah battery; 34 A alternator; Lucas distributor; 2 headlamps.

DIMENSIONS AND WEIGHT wheel base: 79.92 in, 203 cm; tracks: 46.46 in, 118 cm front, 44.88 in, 114 cm rear; length: 141 in, 358 cm; width: 60.24 in, 153 cm; height: 48.23 in, 123 cm; ground clearance: 5.12 in, 13 cm; weight: 1,774 lb, 804 kg; weight distribution: 52.4% front, 47.6% rear; turn-

MG Midget

ing circle (between walls): 32 ft, 9.8 m; fuel tank: 7 imp gal, 8.4 US gal, 32 l.

BODY convertible; 2 doors; 2 seats, built-in headrests; tonneau cover.

PRACTICAL INSTRUCTIONS fuel: 97 oct petrol; oil: engine 6.5 imp pt, 7.8 US pt, 3.7 l, SAE 20W-50, change every 6,000 miles, 9,700 km - gearbox 2 imp pt, 2.3 US pt, 1.1 l, SAE 90, change every 3,000 miles, 4,800 km - final drive 1.7 imp pt, 1.9 US pt, 0,9 l, SAE 90, change every 3,000 miles, 4,800 km; greasing: every 3,000 miles, 4,800 km, 8 points; tappet clearances: inlet 0.010 in, 0.25 mm, exhaust 0.010 in, 0.25 mm; valve timing: 18° 58° 58° 18°; tyre pressure: front 22 psi, 1.5 atm, rear 24 psi, 1.7 atm.

VARIATIONS

ENGINE 8:1 compression ratio.
TRANSMISSION (only for export) 5.20 x 13 tyres.

OPTIONAL ACCESSORIES oil cooler; wire wheels; hardtop.

MGB GT

PRICE EX WORKS: £ 3,576*

ENGINE front, 4 stroke; 4 cylinders, in line; 109.7 cu in, 1,798 cc (3.16 x 3.50 in, 80.3 x 88.9 mm); compression ratio: 9:1; max power (DIN): 97 hp (71.4 kW) at 5,500 rpm; max torque (DIN): 104 lb ft, 14.5 kg m (142.2 Nm) at 2,500 rpm; max engine rpm: 6,200; 53.9 hp/l (39.7 kW/l); cast iron block and head; 5 crankshaft bearings; valves: overhead, push-rods and rockers; camshafts: 1, side; lubrication: eccentric pump, full flow filter (cartridge), oil cooler, 6.5 imp pt, 7.8 US pt, 3.7 l; 2 SU type HIFA semi-downdraught carburettors; fuel feed: electric pump; sealed circuit cooling, liquid, expansion tank, 10 imp pt, 12 US pt, 5.7 l, thermostatically-controlled electric fan.

TRANSMISSION driving wheels: rear; clutch: single dry plate (diaphragm), hydraulically controlled; gearbox: mechanical; gears: 4, fully synchronized, and Laycock-de Normanville overdrive on III and IV; ratios: I 3.036, II 2.166, III 1.381 (overdrive 1.132), IV 1 (overdrive 0.820); rev 3.095; lever: central; final drive: hypoid bevel; axle ratio: 3.909; width of rims: 5''; tyres: 165 SR x 14.

PERFORMANCE max speeds: (I) 32 mph, 51 km/h; (II) 51 mph, 82 km/h; (III) 81 mph, 130 km/h; (IV) 107 mph, 173 km/h; power-weight ratio: 24.4 lb/hp (33.2 lb/kW), 11.1 kg/hp (15 kg/kW); carrying capacity: 529 lb, 240 kg; speed in direct drive at 1,000 rpm: 18 mph, 28.9 km/h; consumption: 25.4 m/imp gal, 21.2 m/US gal, 11.1 l x 100 km.

CHASSIS integral; front suspension: independent, wishbones, coil springs, anti-roll bar, lever dampers as upper arms; rear: rigid axle, semi-elliptic leafsprings, anti-roll bar, lever dampers.

STEERING rack-and-pinion; turns lock to lock: 3.57.

BRAKES front disc (diameter 10.75 in, 27.3 cm), rear drum, servo; lining area: front 20 sq in, 129 sq cm, rear 67.3 sq in, 434 sq cm, total 87.3 sq in, 563 sq cm.

ELECTRICAL EQUIPMENT 12 V; 66 Ah battery; 45 A alternator; Lucas distributor; 2 halogen headlamps.

DIMENSIONS AND WEIGHT wheel base: 91 in, 231 cm; tracks: 49 in, 124 cm front, 49.25 in, 125 cm rear; length: 158.25 in, 402 cm; width: 61.75 in, 157 cm; height: 50.79 in, 129 cm; ground clearance: 4.19 in, 10.6 cm; weight: 2,370 lb, 1,075 kg; turning circle (between walls): 32.6 ft, 9.9 m; fuel tank: 12 imp gal, 14.5 US gal, 55 l.

BODY coupé; 2 doors; 2+2 seats, separate front seats; built-in headrests; tinted glass; heated rear window.

PRACTICAL INSTRUCTIONS fuel: 98-100 oct petrol; oil: engine 6 imp pt, 7.2 US pt, 3.4 l, SAE 10W-30 (winter) 20W-50 (summer), change every 3,000 miles, 4,800 km - gearbox 4.6 imp pt, 5.5 US pt, 2.6 l, SAE 20W-50 - final drive 1.5 imp pt, 1.9 US pt, 0.9 l, SAE 90; greasing: every 3,000 miles, 4,800 km, 8 points; tappet clearances: inlet 0.015 in, 0.38 mm, exhaust 0.015 in, 0.38 mm; valve timing: 16° 56° 51° 21°; tyre pressure: front 21 psi, 1.5 atm, rear 24 psi, 1.7 atm.

OPTIONAL ACCESSORIES wire wheels.

MGB Sports

See MGB GT, except for:

PRICE IN USA: $ 5,150*
PRICE EX WORKS: £ 2,854*

PERFORMANCE power-weight ratio: 23.8 lb/hp (32.3 lb/kW), 10.8 kg/hp (14.7 kg/kW).

DIMENSIONS AND WEIGHT weight: 2,310 lb, 1,047 kg.

BODY sports; 2 seats; tonneau cover; tinted glass and heated rear window not available.

OPTIONAL ACCESSORIES hardtop.

MG MGB GT

MG MGB

MINI (BRITISH LEYLAND)
GREAT BRITAIN

850 Saloon

PRICE EX WORKS: £ 1,893*

ENGINE front, transverse, in unit with gearbox and final drive, 4 stroke; 4 cylinders, vertical, in line; 51.7 cu in, 848 cc (2.48 x 2.69 in, 62.9 x 68.2 mm); compression ratio: 8.3:1; max power (DIN): 33 hp (24.3 kW) at 5,300 rpm; max torque (DIN): 40 lb ft, 5.5 kg m (53.9 Nm) at 2,500 rpm; max engine rpm: 5,500; 38.9 hp/l (28.7 kW/l); cast iron block and head; 3 crankshaft bearings; valves: overhead, in line, push-rods and rockers; camshafts: 1, side; lubrication: rotary pump, full flow filter by cartridge, 8.4 imp pt, 10.1 US pt, 4.8 l; 1 SU type HS4 semi-downdraught carburettor; fuel feed: mechanical pump; water-cooled, 6.2 imp pt, 7.4 US pt, 3.5 l.

TRANSMISSION driving wheels: front; clutch: single dry plate (diaphragm), hydraulically controlled; gearbox: mechanical; gears: 4, fully synchronized; ratios: I 3.525, II 2.218, III 1.433, IV 1, rev 3.544; lever: central; final drive: helical spur gears; axle ratio: 3.765; width of rims: 3.5''; tyres: 145 SR x 10 (5.20 x 10 only for export).

MINI (British Leyland) 1000 Saloon

850 SALOON

PERFORMANCE max speeds: (I) 22 mph, 35 km/h; (II) 35 mph, 56 km/h; (III) 54 mph, 87 km/h; (IV) 73 mph, 177 km/h; power-weight ratio: 39.9 lb/hp (54.2 lb/kW), 18.1 kg/hp (24.6 kg/kW); carrying capacity: 706 lb, 320 kg; acceleration: standing ¼ mile 23.6 sec. 0-50 mph (0-80 km/h) 18.3 sec; speed in direct drive at 1,000 rpm: 15.9 mph, 25.6 km/h; consumption: 42.8 m/imp gal, 35.6 m/US gal, 6.6 l x 100 km.

CHASSIS integral, front and rear auxiliary frames; front suspension: independent, wishbones, rubber cone springs, telescopic dampers; rear: independent, swinging longitudinal trailing arms, rubber cone springs, telescopic dampers.

STEERING rack-and-pinion; turns lock to lock: 2.33.

BRAKES drum, single circuit, 2 front leading shoes; swept area: front 66 sq in, 426 sq cm, rear 55 sq in, 355 sq cm, total 121 sq cm, 781 sq cm.

ELECTRICAL EQUIPMENT 12 V; 30 Ah battery; 34 A alternator; Lucas distributor; 2 headlamps.

DIMENSIONS AND WEIGHT wheel base: 80.16 in, 204 cm; tracks: 47.82 in, 121 cm front, 46.40 in, 118 cm rear; length: 120.25 in, 305 cm; width: 55.50 in, 141 cm; height: 53 in, 135 cm; ground clearance: 5.75 in, 14.7 cm; weight: 1,318 lb, 598 kg; weight distribution: 61% front, 39% rear; turning circle (between walls): 29.5 ft, 9 m; fuel tank: 7.5 imp gal, 9 US gal, 34 l.

BODY saloon/sedan; 2 doors; 4 seats, separate front seats; heated rear window.

PRACTICAL INSTRUCTIONS fuel: 94 oct petrol; oil: engine, gearbox and final drive 9 imp pt, 10.8 US pt, 5.1 l, SAE 20W-50, change every 6,000 miles, 9,700 km; greasing: every 6,000 miles, 9,700 km, 8 points; tappet clearances: inlet 0.012 in, 0.30 mm, exhaust 0.012 in, 0.30 mm; valve timing: 5° 45° 40° 10°; tyre pressure: front 24 psi, 1.7 atm, rear 21 psi, 1.5 atm.

1000 Saloon

See 850 Saloon, except for:

PRICE EX WORKS: £ 1,964*

ENGINE 60.9 cu in, 998 cc (2.54 x 3 in, 64.6 x 76.2 mm); max power (DIN): 39 hp (28.7 kW) at 4,750 rpm; max torque (DIN): 51 lb ft, 7.1 kg m (69.6 Nm) at 2,000 rpm; 39 hp/l (28.8 kW/l).

TRANSMISSION axle ratio: 3.444.

PERFORMANCE max speeds: (I) 26 mph, 42 km/h; (II) 49 mph, 79 km/h; (III) 62 mph, 100 km/h; (IV) 77 mph, 123 km/h; power-weight ratio: 33.8 lb/hp (45.9 lb/kW), 15.3 kg/hp (20.8 kg/kW).

OPTIONAL ACCESSORIES AP automatic transmission, hydraulic torque converter with 2 conic bevel gears (twin concentric differential-like gear clusters) with 4 ratios (I 2.690, II 1.845, III 1.460, IV 1.269, rev 2.690), operated by 3 brake bands and 2 multi-disc clutches, max ratio of converter at stall 2, possible manual selection.

Clubman Saloon

See 1000 Saloon, except for:

PRICE EX WORKS: £ 2,177*

ENGINE 67 cu in, 1,098 cc (2.54 x 3.29 in, 64.4 x 83.5 mm); compression ratio: 8.5:1; max power (DIN): 45 hp (33.1 kW) at 5,250 rpm; max torque (DIN): 56 lb ft, 7.7 kg m (75.5 Nm) at 2,700 rpm; 41 hp/l (30.1 kW/l).

PERFORMANCE max speed: 81 mph, 130 km/h; power-weight ratio: 31.6 lb/hp (43 lb/kW), 14.4 kg/hp (19.5 kg/kW); consumption: 48.7 m/imp gal, 40.6 m/US gal, 5.8 l x 100 km at steady 50 mph, 80 km/h.

DIMENSIONS AND WEIGHT wheel base: 80.20 in, 204 cm; tracks: 48.77 in, 124 cm front, 47.43 in, 120 cm rear; length: 124.64 in, 317 cm; ground clearance: 6.55 in, 16.6 cm; weight: 1,424 lb, 646 kg; turning circle (between walls): 30 ft, 9.2 m.

BODY tinted glass; heated rear window.

PRACTICAL INSTRUCTIONS fuel: 97 oct petrol; valve timing: 5° 45° 51° 21°.

OPTIONAL ACCESSORIES metallic spray (only with 998 cc engine); AP automatic transmission, hydraulic torque converter with 2 conic bevel gears (twin concentric differential-like gear clusters) with 4 ratios (I 2.690, II 1.845, III 1.460, IV 1.269, rev 2.690), operated by 3 brake bands and 2 multi-disc clutches, max ratio of converter at stall 2, possible manual selection.

MINI (British Leyland) Clubman Estate Car

MINI (British Leyland) 1000 Saloon

MINI (British Leyland) 1275 GT

Clubman Estate Car

See Clubman Saloon, except for:

PRICE EX WORKS: £ 2,333*

PERFORMANCE power-weight ratio: 32.4 lb/hp (44 lb/kW), 14.7 kg/hp (20 kg/kW).

ELECTRICAL EQUIPMENT 36 Ah battery.

DIMENSIONS AND WEIGHT wheel base: 84.20 in, 214 cm; tracks: 47.82 in, 121 cm front, 46.40 in, 118 cm rear; length: 133.92 in, 340 cm; height: 53.50 in, 136 cm; ground clearance: 6.30 in, 16 cm; weight: 1,458 lb, 661 kg; turning circle (between walls): 30.5 ft, 9.3 m; fuel tank: 6 imp gal, 7.1 US gal, 27 l.

BODY estate car/station wagon; 2 + 2 doors; folding rear seat; heated rear window not available.

OPTIONAL ACCESSORIES metallic spray not available.

1275 GT

See 850 Saloon, except for:

PRICE EX WORKS: £ 2,429*

ENGINE 77.8 cu in, 1,275 cc (2.78 x 3.20 in, 70.6 x 81.3 mm); compression ratio: 8.8:1; max power (DIN): 54 hp (39.7 kW) at 5,250 rpm; max torque (DIN): 67 lb ft, 9.2 kg m (90.2 Nm) at 2,500 rpm; 42.4 hp/l (31.1 kW/l).

TRANSMISSION ratios: I 3.330, II 2.090, III 1.350, IV 1, rev 3.350; axle ratio: 3.440; width of rims: 4.5''; tyres: 155/65 R x 310.

PERFORMANCE max speeds: (I) 28 mph, 45 km/h; (II) 44 mph, 71 km/h; (III) 68 mph, 110 km/h; (IV) 87 mph, 140 km/h; power-weight ratio: 26.4 lb/hp (35.9 lb/kW), 12 kg/hp (16.3 kg/kW); acceleration: 0-50 mph (0-80 km/h) 9.5 sec; speed in direct drive at 1,000 rpm: 16.8 mph, 27 km/h; consumption: 40.4 m/imp gal, 33.6 m/US gal, 7 l x 100 km.

BRAKES front disc (diameter 8.50 in, 21.6 cm), rear drum, servo; swept area: front 134.5 sq in, 867 sq cm, rear 55 sq in, 355 sq cm, total 189.5 sq in, 1,222 sq cm.

ELECTRICAL EQUIPMENT 40 Ah battery.

DIMENSIONS AND WEIGHT wheel base: 80.20 in, 204 cm; tracks: 48.77 in, 124 cm front, 47.43 in, 120 cm rear; length: 124.64 in, 317 cm; height: 53.55 in, 136 cm; ground clearance: 6.55 in, 16.6 cm; weight: 1,424 lb, 646 kg; turning circle (between walls): 30 ft, 9.1 m; fuel tank: 7.5 imp gal, 9 US gal, 34 l.

BODY heated rear window.

PRACTICAL INSTRUCTIONS fuel: 97 oct petrol.

OPTIONAL ACCESSORIES metallic spray.

MORGAN   GREAT BRITAIN

4/4 1600 2-seater

PRICE EX WORKS: £ 3,990*

ENGINE front, 4 stroke; 4 cylinders, vertical, in line; 97.6 cu in, 1,599 cc (3.19 x 3.06 in, 81 x 77.6 mm); compression ratio: 9:1; max power (DIN): 84 hp (61.8 kW) at 5,500 rpm; max torque (DIN): 92 lb ft, 12.7 kg m (124.5 Nm) at 3,500 rpm; max engine rpm: 6,000; 52.5 hp/l (38.6 kW/l); cast iron block and head; 5 crankshaft bearings; valves: overhead, push-rods and rockers; camshafts: 1, side; lubrication: rotary pump, full flow filter, 7.5 imp pt, 8.9 US pt, 4.2 l; 1 Weber 32/36 downdraught twin barrel carburettor; fuel feed: mechanical pump; water-cooled, 12 imp pt, 14.4 US pt, 6.8 l.

TRANSMISSION driving wheels: rear; clutch: single dry plate, hydraulically controlled; gearbox: mechanical; gears: 4, fully synchronized; ratios: I 2.976, II 2.024, III 1.390, IV 1, rev 3.317; lever: central; final drive: hypoid bevel; axle ratio: 4.100; tyres: 165 x 15.

PERFORMANCE max speeds: (I) 37 mph, 59 km/h; (II) 55 mph, 88 km/h; (III) 80 mph, 128 km/h; (IV) 105 mph, 169 km/h; power-weight ratio: 19.3 lb/hp (26.3 lb/kW), 8.8 kg/hp (11.9 kg/kW); carrying capacity: 353 lb, 160 kg; speed in direct drive at 1,000 rpm: 18.5 mph, 29.7 km/h; consumption: 35.3 m/imp gal, 29.4 m/US gal, 8 l x 100 km.

CHASSIS ladder frame, Z-section long members, tubular and box-type cross members; front suspension: independent, vertical sliding pillars, coil springs, telescopic dampers; rear: rigid axle, semi-elliptic leafsprings, lever dampers.

STEERING cam and peg; turns lock to lock: 2.25.

BRAKES front disc (diameter 11 in, 27.9 cm), rear drum; swept area: total 325.1 sq in, 2,097 sq cm.

ELECTRICAL EQUIPMENT 12 V; 38 Ah battery; alternator; 2 headlamps.

DIMENSIONS AND WEIGHT wheel base: 96 in, 244 cm; tracks: 47 in, 119 cm front, 49 in, 124 cm rear; length: 144 in, 366 cm; width: 56 in, 142 cm; height: 51 in, 129 cm; ground clearance: 7 in, 17.8 cm; weight: 1,624 lb, 736 kg; weight distribution: 48% front, 52% rear; turning circle (between walls): 32 ft, 9.8 m; fuel tank: 8.5 imp gal, 10.3 US gal, 39 l.

BODY roadster; 2 doors; 2 seats.

PRACTICAL INSTRUCTIONS fuel: 98 oct petrol; oil: engine 7 imp pt, 8.5 US pt, 4 l, SAE 10W-30, change every 6,000 miles, 9,700 km - gearbox 1.8 imp pt, 2.1 US pt, 1 l, SAE 80 - final drive 1.9 imp pt, 2.3 US pt, 1.1 l, SAE 90; greas-

MORGAN 4/4 1600 2-seater

MORGAN 4/4 1600 (front suspension)

ing: every 3,000 and 9,000 miles, 4,800 and 14,500 km, 10 points; tyre pressure: front 17 psi, 1.2 atm, rear 17 psi, 1.2 atm.

OPTIONAL ACCESSORIES wire wheels.

4/4 1600 4-seater

See 4/4 1600 2-seater, except for:

PRICE EX WORKS: £ 4,387*

PERFORMANCE power-weight ratio: 20 lb/hp (27.2 lb/kW), 9.1 kg/hp (12.3 kg/kW).

DIMENSIONS AND WEIGHT weight: 1,680 lb, 762 kg; fuel tank: 10 imp gal, 12.1 US gal, 46 l.

BODY 4 seats.

Plus 8

See 4/4 1600 2-seater, except for:

PRICE EX WORKS: £ 5,961

ENGINE 8 cylinders, Vee-slanted at 90°; 215.3 cu in, 3,528 cc (3.50 x 2.80 in, 89 x 71 mm); compression ratio: 9.35:1; max power (DIN): 155 hp (114.1 kW) at 5,250 rpm; max torque (DIN): 199 lb, 27.5 kg m (269.7 Nm) at 2,500 rpm; max engine rpm: 5,800; 43.9 hp/l (32.3 kW/l); light alloy block and head; valves: hydraulic tappets; camshafts: 1, at centre of Vee; lubrication: gear pump, full flow filter, 9.5 imp pt, 11.4 US pt, 5.4 l; 2 SU type HIF6 semi-downdraught carburettors; water-cooled, 15 imp pt, 18 US pt, 8.5 l, electric thermostatic fan.

TRANSMISSION clutch: single dry plate (diaphragm), hydraulically controlled; gears: 5, fully synchronized; ratios: I 3.320, II 2.080, III 1.390, IV 1, V 0.860, rev 3.110; final drive: hypoid bevel, limited slip differential; axle ratio: 3.310; width of rims: 6''; tyres: 195 x 14.

PERFORMANCE max speeds: (I) 40 mph, 64 km/h; (II) 64 mph, 103 km/h; (III) 95 mph, 153 km/h; (IV) 132 mph, 212 km/h; (V) 150 mph, 241 km/h; power-weight ratio: 11.8 lb/hp (16 lb/kW), 5.3 kg/hp (7.3 kg/kW); acceleration: standing ¼ mile 14.5 sec, 0-50 mph (0-80 km/h) 5.1 sec; speed in direct drive at 1,000 rpm: 27.4 mph, 44.1 km/h; consumption: 24 m/imp gal, 20.1 m/US gal, 11.7 l x 100 km.

BRAKES servo.

ELECTRICAL EQUIPMENT 58 Ah battery; 4 headlamps.

DIMENSIONS AND WEIGHT wheel base: 98 in, 249 cm; tracks: 52 in, 132 cm front, 53 in, 135 cm rear; length: 147 in, 373 cm; width: 62 in, 158 cm; height: 52 in, 132 cm; weight: 1,826 lb, 828 kg; turning circle (between walls): 35 ft, 10.6 m; fuel tank: 13.5 imp gal, 16.1 US gal, 61 l.

MORGAN Plus 8

MORRIS

GREAT BRITAIN

Marina Series

PRICES EX WORKS:

1 Marina 1.3 De Luxe 2-door Saloon	£	2,381*
2 Marina 1.3 De Luxe 4-door Saloon	£	2,483*
3 Marina 1.3 De Luxe Estate Car	£	2,840*
4 Marina 1.3 Super 2-door Saloon	£	2,503*
5 Marina 1.3 Super 4-door Saloon	£	2,604*
6 Marina 1.8 Super 2-door Saloon	£	2,725*
7 Marina 1.8 Super 4-door Saloon	£	2,827*
8 Marina 1.8 Super Estate Car	£	3,185*
9 Marina 1.8 Special 2-door Saloon	£	3,007*
10 Marina 1.8 Special 4-door Saloon	£	3,109*
11 Marina 1.8 GT 2-door Saloon	£	3,213*
12 Marina 1.8 HL 4-door Saloon	£	3,315*

Power team:	Standard for:	Optional for:
57 hp	1 to 5	—
72 hp	6 to 10	—
85 hp	11,12	—

57 hp power team

ENGINE front, 4 stroke; 4 cylinders, in line; 77.8 cu in, 1,275 cc (2.78 x 3.20 in, 70.6 x 81.3 mm); compression ratio: 8.8:1; max power (DIN): 57 hp (41.9 kW) at 5,500 rpm; max torque (DIN): 68 lb ft, 9.5 kg m (93.2 Nm) at 2,450 rpm; max engine rpm: 6,500; 44.7 hp/l (32.9 kW/l); cast iron block and head; 3 crankshaft bearings; valves: overhead, in line, push-rods and rockers; camshafts: 1, side, chain-driven; lubrication: rotary pump, full flow filter, 7 imp pt, 8.5 US pt, 4 l; 1 SU type HS4 semi-downdraught carburettor; fuel feed: mechanical pump; water-cooled, 7.4 imp pt, 8.9 US pt, 4.2 l.

TRANSMISSION driving wheels: rear; clutch: single dry plate (diaphragm), hydraulically controlled; gearbox: mechanical; gears: 4, fully synchronized; ratios: I 3.412, II 2.112, III 1.433, IV 1, rev 3.753; lever: central; final drive: hypoid bevel; axle ratio: 4.111; width of rims: 4.5''; tyres: 145 SR x 13 - Estate Car 155 SR x 13.

PERFORMANCE max speeds: (I) 30 mph, 48 km/h; (II) 49 mph, 79 km/h; (III) 72 mph, 116 km/h; (IV) 82 mph, 132 km/h; power-weight ratio: 4-dr. saloons 34 lb/hp (46.3 lb/kW), 15.4 kg/hp (21 kg/kW); carrying capacity: 706 lb, 320 kg; acceleration: standing ¼ mile 21 sec, 0-50 mph (0-80 km/h) 12.1 sec; speed in direct drive at 1,000 rpm: 15.7 mph, 25.2 km/h; consumption: 34 m/imp gal, 28.3 m/US gal, 8.3 l x 100 km.

CHASSIS integral; front suspension: independent, wishbones, lower trailing links, longitudinal torsion bars, lever dampers as upper arms, telescopic dampers, anti-roll bar; rear: rigid axle, semi-elliptic leafsprings, telescopic dampers, anti-roll bar.

STEERING rack-and-pinion; turns lock to lock: 4.

BRAKES front disc (diameter 9.78 in, 24.8 cm), rear drum (servo on Estate Car only); swept area: front 182.9 sq in, 1,180 sq cm, rear 76 sq in, 490 sq cm, total 258.9 sq in, 1,670 sq cm.

ELECTRICAL EQUIPMENT 12 V; 40 Ah battery; 34 A alternator; Lucas distributor; 2 headlamps.

DIMENSIONS AND WEIGHT wheel base: 96.16 in, 244 cm; front and rear tracks: 52 in, 132 cm; length: 2-dr. saloons 165.75 in, 421 cm - 4-dr. saloons 169 in, 429 cm - Estate Car 170.09 in, 432 cm; width: 64.57 in, 164 cm; height: 2-dr. saloons 55.51 in, 141 cm - 4-dr. saloons 55.91 in, 142 cm - Estate Car 56.60 in, 144 cm; ground clearance: 5.60 in, 14.2 cm; weight: 2-dr. saloons 1,907 lb, 865 kg - 4-dr. saloons 1,940 lb, 880 kg - Estate Car 2,040 lb, 925 kg; turning circle (between walls): 31 ft, 9.5 m; fuel tank: 11.5 imp gal, 13.7 US gal, 52 l.

BODY 5 seats, separate front seats, reclining backrests; heated rear window.

PRACTICAL INSTRUCTIONS fuel: 97 oct petrol; oil: engine 7 imp pt, 8.5 US pt, 4 l, SAE 20W-50, change every 6,000 miles, 9,700 km - gearbox 2.2 imp pt, 2.5 US pt, 1.2 l, change every 6,000 miles, 9,700 km - final drive 1.2 imp pt, 1.5 US pt, 0.7 l, change every 6,000 miles, 9,700 km; greasing: every 3,000 miles, 4,800 km, 4 points; sparking plug: 225°; tappet clearances: inlet 0.012 in, 0.30 mm, exhaust 0.012 in, 0.30 mm; valve timing: 5° 45° 51° 21°; tyre pressure: front 26 psi, 1.8 atm, rear 28 psi, 2 atm.

MORRIS Marina 1.3 De Luxe Estate Car

MORRIS Marina 1.3 De Luxe Estate Car

OPTIONAL ACCESSORIES (only for 1.3 Super 4-dr. Saloon) Borg-Warner 65 automatic transmission, hydraulic torque converter and planetary gears with 3 ratios (I 2.393, II 1.450, III 1, rev 2.094), max ratio of converter at stall 2, possible manual selection; servo brake.

72 hp power team

See 57 hp power team, except for:

ENGINE 109.7 cu in, 1,798 cc (3.16 x 3.50 in, 80.3 x 89 mm); compression ratio: 9:1; max power (DIN): 72 hp (53 kW) at 4,750 rpm; max torque (DIN): 96 lb ft, 13.2 kg m (129.5 Nm) at 2,900 rpm; max engine rpm: 5,600; 40 hp/l (29.5 kW/l); 5 crankshaft bearings.

TRANSMISSION ratios: I 3.111, II 1.926, III 1.307, IV 1, rev 3.422; axle ratio: 3.640; tyres: 155 SR x 13.

PERFORMANCE max speeds: (I) 33 mph, 53 km/h; (II) 53 mph, 85 km/h; (III) 78 mph, 125 km/h; (IV) 95 mph, 153 km/h; power-weight ratio: 4-dr. saloons 28.6 lb/hp (38.9 lb/kW), 13 kg/hp (17.6 kg/kW); acceleration: standing ¼ mile 20 sec, 0-50 mph (0-80 km/h) 9.5 sec; speed in direct drive at 1,000 rpm: 18.1 mph, 29.2 km/h; consumption: 23.7 m/imp gal, 19.8 m/US gal, 11.9 l x 100 km.

BRAKES servo (standard).

MORRIS Marina 1.8 HL 4-door Saloon

ELECTRICAL EQUIPMENT 55 Ah battery.

DIMENSIONS AND WEIGHT weight: 2-dr. saloons 2,040 lb, 925 kg - 4-dr. saloons 2,062 lb, 935 kg - Estate Car 2,172 lb, 985 kg.

BODY headrests (Special models only); rear window wiper-washer (Estate Car only).

OPTIONAL ACCESSORIES (only for 4-dr. saloons and 1.8 Super Estate Car) Borg-Warner 65 automatic transmission; metallic spray.

85 hp power team

See 72 hp power team, except for:

ENGINE max power (DIN): 85 hp (62.6 kW) at 5,500 rpm; max torque (DIN): 100 lb ft, 13.8 kg m (135.3 Nm) at 3,000 rpm; 47.3 hp/l (34.8 kW/l); 2 SU type HS4 semi-downdraught carburettors.

PERFORMANCE max speeds: (I) 35 mph, 56 km/h; (II) 57 mph, 91 km/h; (III) 84 mph, 135 km/h; (IV) 100 mph, 161 km/h; power-weight ratio: GT 24.4 lb/hp (33.1 lb/kW), 11 kg/hp (15 kg/kW) - HL 25 lb/hp (34 lb/kW), 11.3 kg/hp (15.4 kg/kW).

ELECTRICAL EQUIPMENT 4 headlamps.

DIMENSIONS AND WEIGHT length: GT 166.81 in, 424 cm - HL 169.80 in, 431 cm; width: GT 65.04 in, 165 cm - HL 65.16 in, 166 cm; height: GT 55.51 in, 141 cm - HL 56.10 in, 143 cm; weight: GT 2,073 lb, 940 kg - HL 2,128 lb, 965 kg.

OPTIONAL ACCESSORIES metallic spray; laminated wind-screen; Borg-Warner 65 automatic transmission (except for GT).

MORRIS Marina 1.8 Special 4-door Saloon

PANTHER   GREAT BRITAIN

Rio

PRICE EX WORKS: £ 8,397*

ENGINE Triumph, front, 4 stroke; 4 cylinders, slanted at 45°, in line; 113.2 cu in, 1,854 cc (3.42 x 3.07 in, 87 x 78 mm); compression ratio: 9:1; max power (DIN): 91 hp (67 kW) at 5,200 rpm; max torque (DIN): 105 lb ft, 14.5 kg m (142.2 Nm) at 3,500 rpm; max engine rpm: 6,000; 49.1 hp/l (36.1 kW/l); cast iron block, light alloy head; 5 crankshaft bearings; valves: overhead, in line, thimble tappets; camshafts: 1, overhead; lubrication: rotary pump, full flow filter, 8 imp pt, 9.5 US pt, 4.5 l; 2 Stromberg 150 CDS (E) V carburettors; fuel feed: mechanical pump; water-cooled, 9.5 imp pt, 11.4 US pt, 5.4 l.

TRANSMISSION driving wheels: rear; clutch: single dry plate (diaphragm), hydraulically controlled; gearbox: mechanical; gears: 4, fully synchronized; ratios: I 2.646, II 1.779, III 1.254, IV 1, rev 3.011; lever: central; final drive: hypoid bevel; axle ratio: 3.640; width of rims: 4.5''; tyres: 155 SR x 13.

PERFORMANCE max speeds: (I) 41 mph, 66 km/h; (II) 61 mph, 98 km/h; (III) 86 mph, 139 km/h; (IV) 100 mph, 161 km/h; power-weight ratio: 31.4 lb/hp (42.6 lb/kW), 14.2 kg/hp (19.3 kg/kW); carrying capacity: 706 lb, 320 kg; acceleration: standing ¼ mile 19 sec, 0-50 mph (0-80 km/h) 8.5 sec; speed in direct drive at 1,000 rpm: 18 mph, 29 km/h; consumption: 35 m/imp gal, 29.8 m/US gal, 7.9 l x 100 km.

CHASSIS integral; front suspension: independent, wishbones (trailing links), coil springs, anti-roll bar, telescopic dampers; rear: rigid axle, lower trailing arms, upper oblique torque arms, coil springs, anti-roll bar, telescopic dampers.

STEERING rack-and-pinion, adjustable height of steering wheel.

BRAKES front disc (diameter 8.7 in, 22.2 cm), rear drum, servo; swept area: front 165 sq in, 1,065 sq cm, rear 75.5 sq in, 487 sq cm, total 240.5 sq in, 1,552 sq cm.

ELECTRICAL EQUIPMENT 12 V; 40 Ah battery; 36 A alternator; Lucas distributor; 2 headlamps.

DIMENSIONS AND WEIGHT wheel base: 96.46 in, 245 cm; tracks: 53.15 in, 135 cm front, 50 in, 127 cm rear; length: 162.60 in, 413 cm; width: 63.39 in, 161 cm; height: 53.15 in, 135 cm; weight: 2,855 lb, 1,295 kg; fuel tank: 12.5 imp gal, 15 US gal, 57 l.

BODY saloon/sedan; 4 doors; 4 seats, separate front seats; heated rear window; electric windows.

PRACTICAL INSTRUCTIONS fuel: 97 oct petrol; oil: engine 8 imp pt, 9.5 US pt, 4.5 l, SAE 20W-50, change every 6,000 miles, 9,700 km - gearbox 3.5 imp pt, 4.2 US pt, 2 l, SAE 90 EP, change every 6,000 miles, 9,700 km - final drive 2 imp pt, 2.5 US pt, 1.2 l, SAE 90 EP, change every 6,000 miles, 9,700 km, 1 point; greasing: every 6,000 miles, 9,700 km, 1 point; tappet clearances: inlet 0.008 in, 0.20 mm, exhaust 0.018 in, 0.45 mm; valve timing: 16° 56° 56° 16°; tyre pressure: front 22 psi, 1.6 atm, rear 24 psi, 1.7 atm.

OPTIONAL ACCESSORIES automatic transmission; electric sunshine roof; air-conditioning.

Rio Especial

See Rio, except for:

PRICE EX WORKS: £ 9,445*

ENGINE 122 cu in, 1,998 cc (3.56 x 3.07 in, 90.3 x 78 mm); compression ratio: 9.5:1; max power (DIN): 127 hp (93.5 kW) at 5,700 rpm; max torque (DIN): 124 lb ft, 17.1 kg m (167.7 Nm) at 4,500 rpm; max engine rpm: 6,500; 61 hp/l (46.8 kW/l); valves: 4 per cylinder; 2 SU type HS6 semi-downdraught carburettors.

TRANSMISSION gears: 4, fully synchronized, with overdrive on III and IV; ratios: I 2.990, II 2.100, III 1.390 (overdrive 1.110 ratio), IV 1 (overdrive 0.797 ratio), rev 3.370; axle ratio: 3.450; width of rims: 5.5''; tyres: 165 SR x 13.

PERFORMANCE max speeds: (I) 41 mph, 66 km/h; (II) 58 mph, 94 km/h; (III) 88 mph, 141 km/h (overdrive 109 mph, 175 km/h); (IV) 118 mph, 190 km/h (overdrive 109 mph, 175 km/h); power-weight ratio: 22.5 lb/hp (30.5 lb/kW), 10.2 kg/hp (13.8 kg/kW); acceleration: standing ¼ mile 16.5 sec, 0-50 mph (0-80 km/h) 6.2 sec; speed in direct drive at 1,000 rpm: 18.9 mph, 30.4 km/h; consumption: 23.6 m/imp gal, 19.8 m/US gal, 11.9 l x 100 km.

BRAKES swept area: front 165 sq in, 1,064 sq cm, rear 99 sq in, 639 sq cm, total 264 sq in, 1,703 sq cm.

DIMENSIONS AND WEIGHT tracks: 53.54 in, 136 cm front, 50.79 in, 129 cm rear.

BODY light alloy wheels.

PRACTICAL INSTRUCTIONS tappet clearances: inlet 0.018 in, 0.45 mm, exhaust 0.018 in, 0.45 mm; valve timing: 14° 50° 50° 14°.

PANTHER Rio Especial

PANTHER Rio Especial

Lima

PRICE EX WORKS: £ 5,564*

ENGINE Vauxhall, front, slanted at 45°, 4 stroke; 4 cylinders, in line; 139.2 cu in, 2,279 cc (3.84 x 3 in, 97.5 x 76.2 mm); compression ratio: 8.5:1; max power (DIN): 108 hp (79.5 kW) at 5,000 rpm; max torque (DIN): 138 lb ft, 19 kg m (186.3 Nm) at 3,000 rpm; max engine rpm: 5,500; 47.4 hp/l (34.9 kW/l); cast iron block and head; 5 crankshaft bearings; valves: overhead, in line, push-rods; camshafts: 1, overhead, cogged belt; lubrication: gear pump, full flow filter, 8.5 imp pt, 10.1 US pt, 4.8 l; 1 Zenith - Stromberg 175 CD2 downdraught single barrel carburettor; fuel feed: mechanical pump; water-cooled, 13.5 imp pt, 16.1 US pt, 7.6 l, viscous coupling thermostatic fan.

TRANSMISSION driving wheels: rear; clutch: single dry plate (diaphragm); gearbox: mechanical; gears: 4, fully synchronized; ratios: I 3.300, II 2.145, III 1.414, IV 1, rev 3.063; lever: central; final drive: hypoid bevel; axle ratio: 3.730; width of rims: 5.5''; tyres: 175/70 HR x 13.

PERFORMANCE max speed: 110 mph, 177 km/h; power-weight ratio: 16.7 lb/hp (22.6 lb/kW), 7.6 kg/hp (10.3 kg/kW); carrying capacity: 353 lb, 160 kg; speed in direct drive at 1,000 rpm: 18.9 mph, 30.4 km/h; consumption: 25 m/imp gal, 20.8 m/US gal, 11.3 l x 100 km.

CHASSIS integral; front suspension: independent, wishbones, coil springs, anti-roll bar, telescopic dampers; rear: rigid axle, twin trailing radius arms, transverse linkage bar, coil springs, anti-roll bar, telescopic dampers.

STEERING rack-and-pinion; turns lock to lock: 3.16.

BRAKES disc (front diameter 10.03 in, 25.5 cm, rear 9 in, 22.9 cm), servo.

ELECTRICAL EQUIPMENT 12 V; 39 Ah battery; 28 A alternator; Lucas distributor; 2 headlamps.

DIMENSIONS AND WEIGHT wheel base: 97 in, 246 cm; tracks: 52.30 in, 133 cm front, 52 in, 132 cm rear; length: 142.13 in, 361 cm; width: 63.39 in, 161 cm; height: 48.03 in, 122 cm; ground clearance: 4.53 in, 11.5 cm; weight: 1,800 lb, 816 kg; weight distribution: 50% front, 50% rear; turning circle (between walls): 32.2 ft, 9.8 m; fuel tank: 10 imp gal, 12.1 US gal, 46 l.

BODY roadster, in plastic material; 2 doors; 2 seats; leather upholstery.

PRACTICAL INSTRUCTIONS fuel: 98 oct petrol; oil: engine 8.5 imp pt, 10.1 US pt, 4.8 l, SAE 20W-50, change every 6,000 miles, 9,700 km - gearbox and final drive 2.5 imp pt, 3 US pt, 1.4 l, SAE 90 EP; greasing: none; tappet clearances: inlet 0.007-0.010 in, 0.17-0.25 mm, exhaust 0.015-0.019 in, 0.37-0.45 mm; valve timing: 31°36' 63°36' 63°36' 31°36'; tyre pressure: front 24 psi, 1.7 atm, rear 24 psi, 1.7 atm.

OPTIONAL ACCESSORIES ZF 5-speed fully synchronized mechanical gearbox (I 2.990, II 1.760, III 1.300, IV 1, V

PANTHER Lima

0.870); automatic transmission, hydraulic torque converter and planetary gears with 3 ratios (I 2.400, II 1.480, III 1, rev 1.920), max ratio of converter at stall 2.25, possible manual selection; wire wheels; laminated glass; metallic spray; tonneau cover; front spoiler; tuned engine with max speed 125 mph, 200 km/h.

J 72 4.2-Litre

PRICE EX WORKS: £ 14,918*

ENGINE Jaguar, front, 4 stroke; 6 cylinders, vertical, in line; 258.4 cu in, 4,235 cc (3.63 x 4.17 in, 92 x 106 mm); compression ratio: 8:1; max power (DIN): 190 hp (139.8 kW) at 5,000 rpm; max torque (DIN): 200 lb ft, 27.6 kg m (270.7 Nm) at 2,000 rpm; max engine rpm: 6,000; 44.9 hp/l (33 kW/l); cast iron block, light alloy head, hemispherical combustion chambers; 7 crankshaft bearings; valves: overhead, Vee-slanted at 70°, thimble tappets; camshafts: 2, overhead; lubrication: rotary pump, full flow filter, 14.5 imp pt, 17.3 US pt, 8.2 l; 2 SU type AED horizontal carburettors; fuel feed: 2 electric pumps; water-cooled, 20 imp pt, 23.9 US pt, 11.3 l.

TRANSMISSION driving wheels: rear; clutch: single dry plate (diaphragm); gearbox: mechanical; gears: 4, fully synchronized with overdrive/top; ratios: I 3.040, II 1.970, III 1.330, IV 1, overdrive 0.780, rev 3.490; lever: central;

final drive: hypoid bevel, limited slip differential; axle ratio: 3.540; width of rims: 6''; tyres: 225/70VR x 15.

PERFORMANCE max speeds: (I) 43 mph, 69 km/h; (II) 66 mph, 106 km/h; (III) 94 mph, 151 km/h; (IV) 114 mph, 183 km/h; power-weight ratio: 13.6 lb/hp (18.4 lb/kW), 6.2 kg/hp (8.3 kg/kW); carrying capacity: 420 lb, 190 kg; acceleration: standing 1/4 mile 15.3 sec; speed in direct drive at 1,000 rpm: 20.2 mph, 32.5 km/h; consumption: 15 m/imp gal, 12.5 m/US gal, 18.8 l x 100 km.

CHASSIS square section ladder frame; front suspension: independent, wishbones, coil springs, anti-roll bar, telescopic dampers; rear: rigid axle, trailing arms, Panhard rod, adjustable coil springs/telescopic damper units.

STEERING recirculating ball; turns lock to lock: 2.8.

BRAKES front disc, rear drum, servo.

ELECTRICAL EQUIPMENT 12 V; 57 Ah battery; 45 A alternator; Lucas distributor; 2 headlamps.

DIMENSIONS AND WEIGHT wheel base: 111 in, 282 cm; tracks: 58.50 in, 149 cm front, 58.50 in, 149 cm rear; length: 165 in, 419 cm; width: 68.50 in, 174 cm; height: 49 in, 124 cm; ground clearance: 5 in, 12.7 cm; weight: 2,576 lb, 1,166 kg; weight distribution: 53.5% front, 46.5% rear; turning circle (between walls): 40 ft, 9.3 m; fuel tank: 26 imp gal, 31.2 US gal, 118 l.

BODY roadster in light alloy; 2 doors; 2 seats; leather upholstery; laminated windscreen.

PRACTICAL INSTRUCTIONS fuel: 98 oct petrol; oil: engine 13 imp pt, 15.6 US pt, 7.4 l, SAE 20W-50, change every 6,000 miles, 9,700 km - gearbox and overdrive 4 imp pt, 4.9 US pt, 2.3 l, SAE 90 EP, change every 12,000 miles, 20,000 km - final drive 2.7 imp pt, 3.2 US pt, 1.6 l, SAE 90, change every 12,000 miles, 20,000 km; greasing: every 6,000 miles, 10,000 km, 4 points; tyre pressure: front 22 psi, 1.5 atm, rear 19 psi, 1.3 atm.

OPTIONAL ACCESSORIES Borg-Warner 65 automatic transmission, hydraulic torque converter and planetary gears with 3 ratios (I 2.400, II 1.450, III 1, rev 2.100), max ratio of converter at stall 2, possible manual selection; headrests; air-conditioning; metallic spray; tonneau cover; power steering; hardtop.

De Ville Saloon

PRICE EX WORKS: £ 39,049*

ENGINE Jaguar, front, 4 stroke; 12 cylinders, Vee-slanted at 60°; 326 cu in, 5,343 cc (3.54 x 2.76 in, 90 x 70 mm); compression ratio: 9:1; cast iron block with light alloy wet liners, aluminium alloy head with hemisperical combustion chambers; 7 crankshaft bearings; valves: overhead, in line, thimble tappets; camshafts: 1 per block, overhead; lubrication: rotary pump, full flow filter, 17.6 imp pt, 21.1 US pt, 10 l; electronic fuel injection; fuel feed: 2 electric pumps; water-cooled, 36 imp pt, 43.3 US pt, 20.5 l.

TRANSMISSION driving wheels: rear; gearbox: Borg-Warner 12 automatic transmission, hydraulic torque converter

PANTHER J 72 4.2-Litre

and planetary gears with 3 ratios, max ratio of converter at stall 2, possible manual selection; ratios: I 2.460, II 1.460, III 1, rev 2.090; lever: central; final drive: hypoid bevel, limited slip differential; axle ratio: 3.310; width of rims: 6''; tyres: 235/70 HR x 15.

PERFORMANCE max speed: 128 mph, 206 km/h; carrying capacity: 925 lb, 419 kg; acceleration: speed in direct drive at 1,000 rpm: 21.1 mph, 31.7 km/h; consumption: not declared.

CHASSIS ladder tube; front suspension: independent, wishbones, coil springs, anti-roll bar, telescopic dampers; rear: independent, wishbones (trailing links), 4 coil springs, transverse linkage bar, 4 telescopic dampers.

STEERING rack-and-pinion, servo.

BRAKES disc (front diameter 11.2 in, 28.4 cm, rear 10.4 in, 26.4 cm), front internal radial fins, servo; swept area: total 448 sq in, 2,890 sq cm.

ELECTRICAL EQUIPMENT 12 V; 68 Ah battery; 67 A alternator; Lucas distributor; 2 headlamps.

DIMENSIONS AND WEIGHT wheel base: 142 in, 361 cm; tracks: 58 in, 147 cm front, 58 in, 147 cm rear; length: 204 in, 519 cm; width: 71 in, 180 cm; height: 61 in, 155 cm; weight: 4,360 lb, 1,973 kg; fuel tank: 22 imp gal, 26.4 US gal, 100 l.

BODY saloon/sedan; 4 doors; 4 seats; separate front seats, reclining backrests with built-in headrests; leather upholstery tinted glass; heated rear window; electric windows; air-conditioning; laminated windscreen; light alloy wheels.

PRACTICAL INSTRUCTIONS fuel: 97 oct petrol; oil: engine 16 imp pt, 19.2 US pt, 9.1 l, SAE 20W-50, change every 6,000 miles, 9,700 km - automatic transmission 16 imp pt, 19.2 US pt, 9.1 l, TQF no change recommended - final drive 2.7 imp pt, 3.4 US pt, 1.6 l, SAE 90, change every 12,000 miles, 20,000 km; greasing: every 6,000 miles, 9,700 km, 17 points; tappet clearances: inlet 0.012-0.014 in, 0.30-0.35 mm, exhaust 0.012-0.014 in, 0.30-0.35 mm; type pressure: front 30 psi, 2.1 atm, rear 32 psi, 2.2 atm.

VARIATIONS

ENGINE Jaguar, 6 cylinders, vertical, in line, 258.4 cu in, 4,235 cc (3.63 x 4.17 in, 92 x 106 mm), 8:1 compression ratio, 7 crankshaft bearings, Vee-slanted valves, 2 overhead camshafts, lubricating system 14.5 imp pt, 17.3 US pt, 8.2 l, 2 SU type AED horizontal carburettors, cooling system 20 imp pt, 23.9 US pt, 11.3 l.
TRANSMISSION Borg-Warner 65 automatic transmission, hydraulic torque converter and planetary gears with 3 ratios (I 2.390, II 1.450, III 1, rev 2.090).

OPTIONAL ACCESSORIES 4-speed fully synchronized mechanical gearbox; electric sunshine roof; metallic spray.

De Ville Convertible

See De Ville Saloon, except for:

PRICE EX WORKS: £ 44,321*

BODY convertible; 2 doors; tonneau cover.

OPTIONAL ACCESSORIES detachable hardtop; electric sunshine roof not available.

Ferrari F.F.

ENGINE front, 4 stroke; 12 cylinders, Vee-slanted at 60°; 242.1 cu in, 3,967 cc (3.03 x 2.80 in, 77 x 71 mm); compression ratio: 8.8:1; max power (DIN): 300 hp (220.1 kW) at 7,000 rpm; max torque (DIN): 241 lb ft, 33.2 kg m (325.6 Nm) at 5,000 rpm; max engine rpm: 7,000; 75.6 hp/l (55.5 kW/l); light alloy block with wet liners, light alloy head with hemispherical combustion chambers; 7 crankshaft bearings; valves: overhead, Vee-slanted at 54°, roller rockers; camshafts: 1, overhead, per block; lubrication: gear pump, filter on by-pass, 17.6 imp pt, 21.1 US pt, 10 l; 2 Weber 40 DCN downdraught twin barrel carburettors; fuel feed: 1 mechanical and 1 electric pump; water-cooled, 24.6 imp pt, 29.6 US pt, 14 l, electric automatic fan.

TRANSMISSION driving wheels: rear; clutch: single dry plate; gearbox: mechanical, in unit with limited slip differential; gears: 5, fully synchronized; ratios: I 3.077, II 2.119, III 1.582, IV 1.250 V 0.961, rev 2.674; lever: central; final drive: spiral bevel, limited slip differential; axle ratio: 3.444; width of rims: 7''; tyres: 205 x 14.

PERFORMANCE max speeds: (I) 50 mph, 80 km/h; (II) 72 mph, 116 km/h; (III) 96 mph, 155 km/h; (IV) 122 mph, 197 km/h; (V) 160 mph, 257 km/h; power-weight ratio: 9.3 lb/hp (12.7 lb/kW), 4.2 kg/hp (5.8 kg/kW); carrying ca-

PANTHER *De Ville Convertible*

PANTHER *De Ville Saloon*

pacity: 529 lb, 240 kg; speed in top at 1,000 rpm: 22.7 mph, 36.5 km/h; consumption: 14.9 m/imp gal, 12.4 m/US gal, 19 l x 100 km.

CHASSIS tubular; front and rear suspensions: independent, wishbones, coil springs, anti-roll bar, telescopic dampers.

STEERING worm and roller; turns lock to lock: 3.50.

BRAKES disc (front diameter 12.36 in, 31.4 cm, rear 11.73 in, 29.8 cm), servo.

ELECTRICAL EQUIPMENT 12 V; 57 Ah battery; alternator; Marelli distributors; 2 headlamps.

DIMENSIONS AND WEIGHT wheel base: 94.50 in, 240 cm; tracks: 55.15 in, 140 cm front, 55.80 in, 142 cm rear; length: 160 in, 406 cm; height: 48 in, 122 cm; ground clearance: 5.50 in, 14 cm; weight: 2,800 lb, 1,270 kg; fuel tank: 18 imp gal, 21.6 US gal, 82 l.

BODY sports; no doors; 2 seats.

PRACTICAL INSTRUCTIONS fuel: 98-100 oct petrol; oil: engine 17.6 imp pt, 21.4 US pt, 10 l, SAE 20W-30 (winter) 40 (summer), change every 6,200 miles, 10,000 km - gearbox and final drive 7.9 imp pt, 9.5 US pt, 4.5 l, change every 6,200 miles, 10,000 km; greasing: every 3,100 miles, 5,000 km; tappet clearances: inlet 0.006 in, 0.15 mm, exhaust 0.008 in, 0.20 mm; tyre pressure: front 34 psi, 2.4 atm, rear 37 psi, 2.6 atm.

PANTHER *Ferrari F.F.*

6

PRICE EX WORKS: £ 39,950*

ENGINE Cadillac, central, 4 stroke; 8 cylinders, Vee-slanted at 90°; 500 cu in, 8,194 cc (4.30 x 4.30 in, 109.1 x 109.1 mm); compression ratio: 8.5:1; cast iron block and head; 5 crankshaft bearings; valves: overhead, in line, push-rods and rockers, hydraulic tappets; camshafts: 1, at centre of Vee; lubrication: gear pump, full flow filter, oil cooler, 10 imp pt, 12 US pt, 5.7 l; 2 Airesearch TO4 turbochargers with 1 Holley downdraught 4-barrel carburettor; water-cooled, 43.1 imp pt, 51.8 US pt, 24.5 l, 2 electric fans.

TRANSMISSION driving wheels: rear; gearbox: Turbo-Hydramatic 425 automatic transmission, hydraulic torque converter and planetary gears with 3 ratios, max ratio of converter at stall 2, possible manual selection; ratios: I 2.480, II 1.480, III 1, rev 2.090; lever: steering column; final drive: spiral bevel; axle ratio: 1.800; width of rims: 6'' front, 9'' rear; tyres: P7 205/40 VR x 13 front, P7 265/50 VR x 16 rear.

PERFORMANCE max speed: over 200 mph, 322 km/h.

CHASSIS tubular; front suspension: independent, wishbones, coil springs, anti-roll bar, telescopic dampers; rear: independent, wishbones, coil springs, anti-roll bar, telescopic dampers.

STEERING rack-and-pinion, servo; turns lock to lock: 2.80.

BRAKES disc (front diameter 10 in, 25.4 cm, rear 11 in, 27.9 cm), 3 circuits; swept area: front 400 sq in, 2,580 sq cm, rear 224 sq in, 1,445 sq cm, total 624 sq in, 4,025 sq cm.

ELECTRICAL EQUIPMENT 12 V; 66 Ah battery; 100 A alternator; 4 halogen headlamps.

DIMENSIONS AND WEIGHT wheel base: 105 in, 267 cm; tracks: 61.50 in, 156 cm front, 64.50 in, 164 cm rear; length: 192 in, 487 cm; width: 80 in, 203 cm; height: 48 in, 122 cm; ground clearance: 7 in, 17.8 cm; weight: 2,870 lb, 1,302 kg; fuel tank: 30 imp gal, 36.2 US gal, 137 l (2 separate tanks).

BODY convertible; 2 doors; 3 seats; leather upholstery, air-conditioning, tinted glass.

PRACTICAL INSTRUCTIONS fuel: 98 oct petrol; oil: engine; 10 imp pt, 12 US pt, 5.7 l, - automatic transmission 10.3 imp pt, 12.3 US pt, 5.8 l - final drive 3.3 imp pt, 4 US pt, 1.9 l.

OPTIONAL ACCESSORIES hardtop; metallic spray.

PANTHER 6

PRINCESS 2200 HLS Saloon

PRINCESS   GREAT BRITAIN

1800 - 2200 Series

PRICES EX WORKS:

1 1800 Saloon	£	3,297*
2 1800 HL Saloon	£	3,564*
3 2200 HL Saloon	£	3,846*
4 2200 HLS Saloon	£	4,320*

Power team:	Standard for:	Optional for:
82 hp	1,2	—
110 hp	3,4	—

82 hp power team

ENGINE front, transverse, in unit with gearbox and final drive, 4 stroke; 4 cylinders, vertical, in line; 109.7 cu in, 1,798 cc (3.16 x 3.50 in, 80.3 x 89 mm); compression ratio: 9:1; max power (DIN): 82 hp (60.3 kW) at 5,250 rpm; max torque (DIN): 102 lb ft, 14.1 kg m (138.3 Nm) at 2,800 rpm; max engine rpm: 5,600, 45.6 hp/l (33.5 kW/l); cast iron block and head; 5 crankshaft bearings; valves: overhead, push-rods and rockers; camshafts: 1, side, chain-driven; lubrication: rotary pump, magnetic metal gauze filter in sump and full flow, 10.2 imp pt, 12.3 US pt, 5.8 l; 1 SU type HS6 semi-downdraught carburettor; fuel feed: mechanical pump; sealed circuit cooling, liquid, expansion tank, 14.5 imp pt, 17 US pt, 8.2 l, thermostatically-controlled electric fan.

TRANSMISSION driving wheels: front; clutch: single dry plate (diaphragm), hydraulically controlled; gearbox: mechanical, in unit with engine; gears: 4, fully synchronized; ratios: I 3.292, II 2.059, III 1.384, IV 1, rev 3.075; lever: central; final drive: spiral bevel; axle ratio: 3.720; width of rims: 4.5''; tyres: 185/70 SR x 14.

PERFORMANCE max speeds: (I) 35 mph, 56 km/h; (II) 55 mph, 88 km/h; (III) 82 mph, 132 km/h; (IV) 98 mph, 157 km/h; power-weight ratio: 31.2 lb/hp (42.4 lb/kW), 14.1

PRINCESS 1800 HL Saloon

kg/hp (19.2 kg/kW); carrying capacity: 882 lb, 400 kg; acceleration: standing ¼ mile 18.6 sec, 0-50 mph (0-80 km/h) 8.8 sec; speed in direct drive at 1,000 rpm: 17.5 mph, 28.1 km/h; consumption: 25.9 m/imp gal, 21.6 m/US gal, 10.9 l x 100 km.

CHASSIS integral; front suspension: independent, wishbones, hydragas (liquid and gas) rubber cone springs, hydraulic connecting pipes to rear wheels; rear: independent, swinging longitudinal trailing arms, hydragas (liquid and gas) rubber cone springs, hydraulic connecting pipes to front wheels.

STEERING rack-and-pinion; turns lock to lock: 4.57.

BRAKES front disc (diameter 10.63 in, 27 cm), rear drum, servo; lining area: total 74.3 sq in, 479 sq cm.

ELECTRICAL EQUIPMENT 12 V; 55 Ah battery; 45 A alternator; Lucas distributor; 4 headlamps.

DIMENSIONS AND WEIGHT wheel base: 105.24 in, 267 cm; tracks: 58 in, 147 cm front, 57.36 in, 146 cm rear; length: 175.41 in, 445 cm; width: 68.11 in, 173 cm; height: 55.48 in, 141 cm; ground clearance: 6.45 in, 16.4 cm; weight: 2,558 lb, 1,160 kg; weight distribution: 63.5% front, 36.5% rear; turning circle (between walls): 37.1 ft, 11.3 m; fuel tank: 16 imp gal, 19.3 US gal, 73 l.

BODY saloon/sedan; 4 doors; 4-5 seats, separate front seats, reclining backrests; heated rear window.

PRACTICAL INSTRUCTIONS fuel: 96-98 oct petrol; oil: engine, gearbox and final drive 10.2 imp pt, 12.3 US pt,

5.8 I, SAE 20W-50, change every 6,000 miles, 9,700 km; greasing: every 6,000 miles, 9,700 km; tappet clearances: inlet 0.015 in, 0.38 mm, exhaust 0.015 in, 0.38 mm; valve timing: 5° 45° 40° 10°; tyre pressure: front 23 psi, 1.6 atm, rear 21 psi, 1.5 atm.

OPTIONAL ACCESSORIES Borg-Warner automatic transmission, hydraulic torque converter and planetary gears with 3 ratios (I 2.388, II 1.449, III 1, rev 2.388), max ratio of converter at stall 2, 3.940 axle ·ratio, max speed 95 mph, 153 km/h; power steering; tinted glass; headrests; laminated windscreen; Denovo wheels and tyres.

110 hp power team

See 82 hp power team, except for:

ENGINE 6 cylinders; 135.9 cu in, 2,227 cc (3 x 3.20 in, 76.2 x 81.3 mm); max power (DIN): 110 hp (81 kW) at 5,250 rpm; max torque (DIN): 124 lb ft, 17.1 kg m (167.7 Nm) at 3,500 rpm; 49.4 hp/l (36.4 kW/l); 7 crankshaft bearings; camshafts: 1, overhead; lubricating system: 13 imp pt, 15.6 US pt, 7.4 l; 2 SU type HIF6 carburettors.

PERFORMANCE max speed: 106 mph, 170 km/h; power-weight ratio: 24 lb/hp (32.7 lb/kW), 10.9 kg/hp (14.8 kg/kW); consumption: 24.6 m/imp gal, 20.5 m/US gal, 11.5 l x 100 km.

STEERING servo (standard).

ELECTRICAL EQUIPMENT 2 headlamps.

DIMENSIONS AND WEIGHT length: HLS 176.37 in, 448 cm; weight: 2,646 lb, 1,200 kg.

BODY tinted glass (standard HLS only).

PRACTICAL INSTRUCTIONS oil: engine, gearbox and final drive 13 imp pt, 15.6 US pt, 7.4 l; tappet clearances: inlet 0.015-0.016 in, 0.38-0.40 mm, exhaust 0.015-0.016 in, 0.38-0.40 mm.

RELIANT   GREAT BRITAIN

Kitten DL Saloon

PRICE EX WORKS: £ 2,139*

ENGINE front, 4 stroke; 4 cylinders, in line; 51.7 cu in, 848 cc (2.46 x 2.72 in, 62.5 x 69.1 mm); compression ratio: 9.5:1; max power (DIN): 40 hp (29.4 kW) at 5,500 rpm; max torque (DIN): 46 lb ft, 6.3 kg m (61.8 Nm) at 3,500 rpm; max engine rpm: 5,500; 47.2 hp/l (34.7 kW/l); light alloy block and head, wet liners; 3 crankshaft bearings; valves: overhead, in line, push-rods and rockers; camshafts: 1, side; lubrication: rotary pump, full flow filter, 5.5 imp pt, 6.6 US pt, 3.1 l; 1 SU HS2 1¼ semi-downdraught single barrel carburettor; sealed circuit cooling, anti-freeze liquid, 6.5 imp pt, 7.8 US pt, 3.7 l.

TRANSMISSION driving wheels: rear; clutch: single dry plate; gearbox: mechanical; gears: 4, fully synchronized; ratios: I 3.876, II 2.046, III 1.319, IV 1, rev 3.250; lever: central; final drive: spiral bevel; axle ratio: 3.230; width of rims: 3.5''; tyres: 145 x 10.

PERFORMANCE max speeds: (I) 24 mph, 39 km/h; (II) 45 mph, 73 km/h; (III) 71 mph, 114 km/h; (IV) 93 mph, 149 km/h; power-weight ratio: 29.4 lb/hp (40 lb/kW), 13.3 kg/hp (18.1 kg/kW); carrying capacity: 700 lb, 317 kg; acceleration: standing ¼ mile 20.4 sec, 0-50 mph (0-80 km/h) 11.1 sec; speed in direct drive at 1,000 rpm: 17 mph, 27.3 km/h; consumption: 60 m/imp gal, 50 m/US gal, 4.7 l x 100 km.

CHASSIS box-section side members and channel section diagonal reinforcements; front suspension: independent, wishbones, anti-roll bar, coil springs/telescopic damper units; rear: rigid axle, semi-elliptic leafsprings, telescopic dampers.

STEERING rack-and-pinion; turns lock to lock: 3.50.

BRAKES drum (diameter 7 in, 17.8 cm); swept area: front 66 sq in, 426 sq cm, rear 55 sq in, 355 sq cm, total 121 sq in, 781 sq cm.

ELECTRICAL EQUIPMENT 12 V; 35 Ah battery; 35 A alternator; Lucas distributor; 2 headlamps.

DIMENSIONS AND WEIGHT wheel base: 84.50 in, 215 cm; front and rear tracks: 49 in, 124 cm; length: 131 in, 333 cm; width: 56 in, 142 cm; height: 55 in, 140 cm; ground clearance: 5 in, 12.7 cm; weight: 1,175 lb, 533 kg; turning circle (between walls): 24 ft, 7.3 m; fuel tank: 6 imp gal, 7.1 US gal, 27 l.

RELIANT Kitten DL Saloon

RELIANT Kitten DL Estate Car

BODY saloon/sedan in plastic material; 2 doors; 4 seats, separate front seats, reclining driver's seat; heated rear window; folding rear seat.

PRACTICAL INSTRUCTIONS fuel: 97 oct petrol; oil: engine 5.5 imp pt, 6.6 US pt, 3.1 l, SAE 20W-50, change every 6,000 miles, 9,700 km - gearbox 1.1 imp pt, 1.3 US pt, 0.6 l, SAE 80 EP, change every 12,000 miles, 19,400 km - final drive 2.2 imp pt, 2.5 US pt, 1.2 l, change every 6,000 miles, 9,700 km; greasing: every 6,000 miles, 9,700 km, 7 points; tappet clearances: inlet 0.010 in, 0.25 mm, exhaust 0.010 in, 0.25 mm; valve timing: 13° 72° 54° 29°; tyre pressure: front 20 psi, 14 atm, rear 22 psi, 1.6 atm.

OPTIONAL ACCESSORIES light alloy wheels; laminated windscreen.

Kitten DL Estate Car

See Kitten DL Saloon, except for:

PRICE EX WORKS: £ 2,251*

PERFORMANCE power-weight ratio: 29.7 lb/hp (40.4 lb/kW), 13.5 kg/hp (18.3 kg/kW).

DIMENSIONS AND WEIGHT length: 131.75 in, 335 cm; weight: 1,189 lb, 539 kg.

BODY estate car/station wagon; 2+1 doors.

OPTIONAL ACCESSORIES rear window wiper-washer.

Robin 850 Saloon

PRICE EX WORKS: £ 1,719*

ENGINE front, 4 stroke; 4 cylinders, in line; 51.7 cu in, 848 cc (2.46 x 2.72 in, 62.5 x 69.1 mm); compression ratio: 9.5:1; max power (DIN): 40 hp (29.4 kW) at 5,500 rpm; max torque (DIN): 46 lb ft, 6.3 kg m (61.8 Nm) at 3,500 rpm; max engine rpm: 5,500; 47.2 hp/l (34.7 kW/l); light alloy block and head; 3 crankshaft bearings; valves: overhead, push-rods and rockers; camshafts: 1, side; lubrication: rotary pump, full flow filter, 5.5 imp pt, 6.6 US pt, 3.1 l; 1 SU type HS2 1¼ semi-downdraught carburettor; fuel feed: mechanical pump; water-cooled, 5 imp pt, 5.9 US pt, 2.8 l.

TRANSMISSION driving wheels: rear; clutch: single dry plate; gearbox: mechanical; gears: 4, fully synchronized; ratios: I 3.880, II 2.050, III 1.320, IV 1, rev 3.250; lever: central; final drive: spiral bevel; axle ratio: 3.230; width of rims: 3.5''; tyres: 5.20 x 10.

PERFORMANCE max speeds: (I) 25 mph, 40 km/h; (II) 47 mph, 75 km/h; (III) 73 mph, 117 km/h; (IV) 96 mph, 154 km/h; power-weight ratio: 24 lb/hp (32.7 lb/kW), 10.9 kg/hp (14.8 kg/kW); carrying capacity: 788 lb, 357 kg; acceleration: standing ¼ mile 20.9 sec, 0-50 mph (0-80 km/h) 11.4 sec; speed in direct drive at 1,000 rpm: 17 mph, 27.3 km/h; consumption: 60 m/imp gal, 50 m/US gal, 4.7 l x 100 km.

CHASSIS box-section ladder frame, tubular cross members; front suspension: single wheel, swinging leading arm, coil spring, telescopic damper; rear: rigid axle, semi-elliptic leafsprings, anti-roll bar, telescopic dampers.

STEERING worm and peg; turns of steering wheel lock to lock: 2.25.

BRAKES drum, single circuit; swept area: front 33 sq in, 213 sq cm, rear 55 sq in, 355 sq cm, total 88 sq in, 568 sq cm.

ELECTRICAL EQUIPMENT 12 V; 22 Ah battery; 28 A alternator; Lucas distributor; 4 headlamps.

DIMENSIONS AND WEIGHT wheel base: 85 in, 216 cm; rear track: 49 in, 124 cm; length: 131 in, 333 cm; width: 56 in, 142 cm; height: 54 in, 137 cm; ground clearance: 5 in, 12.7 cm; weight: 962 lb, 436 kg; weight distribution: 44% front, 56% rear; turning circle (between walls): 27 ft, 8.2 m; fuel tank: 6 imp gal, 7.1 US gal, 27 l.

BODY saloon/sedan in plastic material; 2 doors; 4 seats, separate front seats.

PRACTICAL INSTRUCTIONS fuel: 97 oct petrol; oil: engine 5.5 imp pt, 6.6 US pt, 3.1 l, SAE 20W-50, change every 6,000 miles, 9,700 km - gearbox 1.1 imp pt, 1.3 US pt, 0.6 l, SAE 80 EP, change every 12,000 miles, 19,400 km - final drive 2.2 imp pt, 2.5 US pt, 1.2 l, SAE 90 EP, change every 6,000 miles, 9,700 km; greasing: every 6,000 miles, 9,700 km, 4 points; tappet clearances: inlet 0.010 in, 0.25 mm hot, exhaust 0.010 in, 0.25 mm hot; valve timing: 13° 72° 54° 29°; tyre pressure: front 30 psi, 2.1 atm, rear 24 psi, 1.7 atm.

OPTIONAL ACCESSORIES heated rear window.

RELIANT Robin 850 Saloon

Robin 850 Estate Car

See Robin 850 Saloon, except for:

PRICE EX WORKS: £ 1,845*

BODY estate car/station wagon; 2 + 1 doors.

OPTIONAL ACCESSORIES rear window wiper-washer.

Super Robin 850 Saloon

See Robin 850 Saloon, except for:

PRICE EX WORKS: £ 1,968*

OPTIONAL ACCESSORIES light alloy wheels.

Super Robin 850 Estate Car

See Robin 850 Saloon, except for:

PRICE EX WORKS: £ 2,043*

BODY estate car/station wagon; 2 + 1 doors.

OPTIONAL ACCESSORIES rear window wiper-washer; light alloy wheels.

Robin 850 GBS Saloon

See Robin 850 Saloon, except for:

PRICE EX WORKS: £ 1,983*

BODY luxury equipment.

OPTIONAL ACCESSORIES light alloy wheels.

Scimitar GTE

PRICE EX WORKS: £ 6,333*

ENGINE front, 4 stroke; 6 cylinders, Vee-slanted at 60°; 182.7 cu in, 2,994 cc (3.69 x 2.85 in, 93.7 x 72.4 mm); compression ratio: 8.9:1; max power (DIN): 135 hp (99.4 kW) at 5,500 rpm; max torque (DIN): 172 lb ft, 23.7 kg m (232.4 Nm) at 3,000 rpm; max engine rpm: 6,400; 45.1 hp/l (33.2 kW/l); cast iron block and head; 4 crankshaft bearings; valves: overhead, push-rods and rockers; camshafts: 1, at centre of Vee; lubrication: rotary pump, full flow filter, 8.8 imp pt, 10.6 US pt, 5 l; 1 Weber 38 DGAS/3A downdraught twin barrel carburettor; fuel feed: mechanical pump; water-cooled, 21.5 imp pt, 26 US pt, 12.2 l, electric thermostatic fan.

TRANSMISSION driving wheels: rear; clutch: single dry plate (diaphragm); gearbox: mechanical; gears: 4+overdrive on III and IV; ratios: I 3.163, II 1.950, III 1.412 (overdrive 1.160), IV 1 (overdrive 0.780), rev 3.350; lever: central; final drive: hypoid bevel; axle ratio: 3.310; width of rims: 5.5''; tyres: 135 HR x 14.

BODY coupé in plastic material; 2 doors; 4 seats, separate front seats, reclining backrests with built-in headrests; folding rear seat; heated rear window.

PRACTICAL INSTRUCTIONS fuel: 97 oct petrol; oil: engine 8.8 imp pt, 10.6 US pt, 5 l, SAE 20W-50, change every 6,000 miles, 9,700 km - gearbox 5 imp pt, 6 US pt, 2.8 l, SAE 80, change every 6,000 miles, 9,700 km - final drive 3.5 imp pt, 4.2 US pt, 2 l, SAE 90, change every 6,000 miles, 9,700 km; greasing: every 6,000 miles, 9,700 km, 4 points; tappet clearances: inlet 0.012 in, 0.30 mm, exhaust 0.020 in, 0.50 mm; valve timing: 29° 67° 70° 14°; tyre pressure: front 24 psi, 1.6 atm, rear 24 psi, 1.6 atm.

OPTIONAL ACCESSORIES Ford C3 automatic transmission, hydraulic torque converter and planetary gears with 3 ratios (I 2.474, II 1.474, III 1, rev. 2.111), max ratio of converter at stall 2, possible manual selection, oil cooler, 3.310 axle ratio; power steering; light alloy wheels; electric windows; rear window wiper-washer; laminated windscreen; tinted glass; fog lamps; leather upholstery.

PERFORMANCE max speeds: (I) 38 mph, 6. km/h; (II) 62 mph, 100 km/h; (III) 85 mph, 136 km/h; (IV) 120 mph, 193 km/h; (overdrive/top) 112 mph, 180 km/h; power-weight ratio: 20.7 lb/hp (28.1 lb/kW), 9.4 kg/hp (12.8 kg/kW); carrying capacity: 850 lb, 385 kg; speed in direct drive at 1,000 rpm: 21.9 mph, 35.2 km/h; consumption: 25 m/imp gal, 20.8 m/US gal, 11.3 l x 100 km.

CHASSIS box-type ladder frame, tubular cross members; front suspension: independent, wishbones, anti-roll bar, coil springs/telescopic damper units; rear: rigid axle, twin trailing arms, transverse Watt linkage, coil springs/telescopic damper units.

STEERING rack-and-pinion; turns lock to lock: 4.30.

BRAKES front disc (diameter 10.51 in, 26.6 cm), rear drum, rear compensator, servo; swept area: front 237 sq in, 1,529 sq cm, rear 110 sq in, 710 sq cm, total 347 sq in, 2,239 sq cm.

ELECTRICAL EQUIPMENT 12 V; 55 Ah battery; 36 A alternator; Motorcraft distributor; 4 headlamps.

DIMENSIONS AND WEIGHT wheel base: 103.81 in, 264 cm; tracks: 58.14 in, 148 cm front, 56.13 in, 143 cm rear; length: 174.50 in, 443 cm; width: 67.25 in, 171 cm; height: 52 in, 132 cm; ground clearance: 5.50 in, 14 cm; weight: 2,797 lb, 1,269 kg; turning circle (between walls): 38.5 ft, 11.7 m; fuel tank: 20 imp gal, 24 US gal, 91 l.

ROLLS-ROYCE   GREAT BRITAIN

Silver Shadow II

PRICE IN USA: $ 48,600*
PRICE EX WORKS: £ 25,992*

ENGINE front, 4 stroke; 8 cylinders, Vee-slanted at 90°; 411.9 cu in, 6,750 cc (4.10 x 3.90 in, 104.1 x 99.1 mm); compression ratio: 8:1; aluminium alloy block and head, cast iron wet liners; 5 crankshaft bearings; valves: overhead, in line, slanted, push-rods and rockers, hydraulic tappets; camshafts: 1, at centre of Vee; lubrication: gear pump, full flow filter (cartridge), 14.5 imp pt, 17.5 US pt, 8.3 l; 2 SU type HIF7 horizontal carburettors; fuel feed: 2 electric pumps; sealed circuit cooling, expansion tank, 28.5 imp pt, 34.2 US pt, 16.2 l, viscous coupling thermostatic fan.

TRANSMISSION driving wheels: rear; gearbox: Turbo-Hydramatic 400 automatic transmission, hydraulic torque converter and planetary gears with 3 ratios, max ratio of converter at stall 2, possible manual selection; ratios: I 2.500, II 1.500, III 1, rev 2; lever: steering column; final drive: hypoid bevel; axle ratio: 3.080; width of rims: 6''; tyres: 235/70 HR x 15.

PERFORMANCE max speeds: (I) 47 mph, 76 km/h; (II) 79 mph, 126 km/h; (III) 118 mph, 190 km/h; carrying capacity: 1,014 lb, 460 kg; speed in direct drive at 1,000 rpm: 26.2 mph, 42.2 km/h; consumption: 14.1 m/imp gal, 11.8 m/US gal, 20 l x 100 km.

CHASSIS integral, front and rear auxiliary frames; front suspension: independent, lower wishbones, coil springs, anti-roll bar, automatic levelling control, telescopic dampers; rear: independent, semi-trailing arms, coil springs, anti-roll bar, automatic levelling control, telescopic dampers.

RELIANT Scimitar GTE

STEERING rack-and-pinion, progressive servo, right-hand drive; turns lock to lock: 3.20.

BRAKES disc (diameter 11 in, 27.9 cm), front internal radial fins, servo; swept area: front 227 sq in, 1,464 sq cm, rear 286 sq in, 1,845 sq cm, total 513 sq in, 3,309 sq cm.

ELECTRICAL EQUIPMENT 12 V; 68 Ah battery; 75 A alternator; Lucas transistorized distributor; 4 headlamps, 2 rear fog lamps.

DIMENSIONS AND WEIGHT wheel base: 120.10 in, 305 cm; tracks: 60 in, 152 cm front, 59.60 in, 151 cm rear; length: 204.50 in, 519 cm; width: 71 in, 180 cm; height: 59.75 in, 152 cm; ground clearance: 6.50 in, 16.5 cm; weight: 4,930 lb, 2,236 kg; turning circle (between walls): 38.5 ft, 11.7 m; fuel tank: 23.5 imp gal, 28.2 US gal, 107 l.

BODY saloon/sedan; 4 doors; 5 seats, separate front seats, adjustable and reclining backrests; headrests; air-conditioning; heated rear window; electric windows.

PRACTICAL INSTRUCTIONS fuel: 98 oct petrol; oil: engine 14.5 imp pt, 17.5 US pt, 8.3 l, SAE 20W-50, change every 6,000 miles, 9,700 km - automatic transmission 18.6 imp pt, 22.2 US pt, 10.5 l, Dexron, change every 24,000 miles, 38,600 km - final drive 4.5 imp pt, 5.3 US pt, 2.5 l, SAE 90 EP, change every 24,000 miles, 38,600 km - power steering and automatic levelling control change every 20,000 miles, 32,000 km; greasing: every 12,000 miles 19,300 km, 5 points; valve timing: 26° 52° 68° 10°; tyre pressure: front 28 psi, 2 atm, rear 28 psi, 2 atm.

OPTIONAL ACCESSORIES iodine headlamps; tinted glass.

ROLLS-ROYCE Silver Wraith II

Silver Wraith II

See Silver Shadow II, except for:

PRICE IN USA: $ 55,400*
PRICE EX WORKS: £ 30,501*

DIMENSIONS AND WEIGHT wheel base: 124.10 in, 315 cm; length: 208.50 in, 530 cm; weight: 5,020 lb, 2,277 kg; turning circle (between walls): 40 ft, 12.2 m.

PRACTICAL INSTRUCTIONS tyre pressure: rear 30 psi, 2.1 atm.

Silver Wraith II with division

See Silver Shadow II, except for:

PRICE EX WORKS: £ 31,918*

DIMENSIONS AND WEIGHT wheel base: 124.10 in, 315 cm; length: 208.50 in, 530 cm; weight: 5,260 lb, 2,386 kg; turning circle (between walls): 40 ft, 12.2 m.

BODY glass partition.

PRACTICAL INSTRUCTIONS tyre pressure: rear 30 psi, 2.1 atm.

ROLLS-ROYCE Silver Shadow II

Corniche Saloon

See Silver Shadow II, except for:

PRICE IN USA: $ 79,200*
PRICE EX WORKS: £ 37,785*

ENGINE 2 Solex 4A1 4-barrel carburettors.

DIMENSIONS AND WEIGHT width: 72 in, 183 cm; height: 58.75 in, 149 cm; ground clearance: 6 in, 15.2 cm; weight: 5,045 lb, 2,285 kg.

ELECTRICAL EQUIPMENT 55 A alternator.

BODY 2 doors; 4 seats.

Corniche Convertible

See Silver Shadow II, except for:

PRICE IN USA: $ 84,500*
PRICE EX WORKS: £ 40,131*

ENGINE 2 Solex 4A1 4-barrel carburettors.

DIMENSIONS AND WEIGHT width: 72 in, 183 cm; ground clearance: 6 in, 15.2 cm; weight: 5,200 lb, 2,358 kg.

ELECTRICAL EQUIPMENT 55 A alternator.

BODY convertible; 2 doors; 4 seats.

Phantom VI

PRICE EX WORKS: quotation on request.

ENGINE front, 4 stroke; 8 cylinders, Vee-slanted at 90°; 380 cu in, 6,230 cc (4.10 x 3.60 in, 104.1 x 91.4 mm); compression ratio: 9:1; aluminium alloy block and head, cast iron wet liners; 5 crankshaft bearings; valves: overhead, in line, slanted, push-rods and rockers, hydraulic tappets; camshafts: 1, at centre of Vee; lubrication: gear pump, full flow filter (cartridge), 14.5 imp pt, 17.5 US pt, 8.3 l; 2 SU type HD8 horizontal carburettors; fuel feed: 2 electric pumps; sealed circuit cooling, expansion tank, 28.5 imp pt, 34.2 US pt, 16.2 l, viscous coupling thermostatic fan.

TRANSMISSION driving wheels: rear; gearbox: Rolls-Royce automatic transmission, hydraulic coupling and planetary gears with 4 ratios, possible manual selection; ratios: I 3.820, II 2.630, III 1.450, IV 1, rev 4.300; lever: steering column; final drive: hypoid bevel; axle ratio: 3.890; width of rims: 6''; tyres: 8.90 x 15.

PERFORMANCE max speeds: (I) 29 mph, 47 km/h; (II) 42 mph, 68 km/h; (III) 77 mph, 124 km/h; (IV) 112 mph, 180 km/h; carrying capacity: 1,235 lb, 560 kg; acceleration: standing ¼ mile 19.4 sec, 0-50 mph (0-80 km/h) 9.7 sec; speed in direct drive at 1,000 rpm: 22.5 mph, 36.2 km/h; consumption: 14 m/imp gal, 11.6 m/US gal, 20.2 l x 100 km.

CHASSIS box-type ladder frame; front suspension: independent, wishbones, coil springs, anti-roll bar, lever dampers; rear: rigid axle, asymmetrical semi-elliptic leafsprings,

ROLLS-ROYCE Phantom VI

PHANTOM VI

Z-type transverse linkage bar, electrically-adjustable lever dampers.

STEERING worm and roller, progressive servo (50%-80%); turns lock to lock: 4.25.

BRAKES drum, 2 independent hydraulic circuits, mechanical servo; swept area: front 211.92 sq in, 1,361 sq cm, rear 211.92 sq in, 1,361 sq cm, total 423.84 sq in, 2,722 sq cm.

ELECTRICAL EQUIPMENT 12 V; 68 Ah battery; 75 A alternator; AC Delco distributor; 4 headlamps.

DIMENSIONS AND WEIGHT wheel base: 145 in, 368 cm; tracks: 60.87 in, 155 cm front, 64 in, 162 cm rear; length: 238 in, 604 cm; width: 79 in, 201 cm; height: 69 in, 175 cm; ground clearance: 7.25 in, 18.4 cm; weight: 5,994 lb, 2,718 kg; weight distribution: 48% front, 52% rear; turning circle (between walls): 48.7 ft, 14.9 m; fuel tank: 23 imp gal, 27.5 US gal, 104 l.

BODY limousine; 4 doors; 7 seats, separate front seats; glass partition; automatic air-conditioning; electric windows; heated rear window.

PRACTICAL INSTRUCTIONS fuel: 100 oct petrol; oil: engine 14.5 imp pt, 17.5 US pt, 8.3 l, SAE 20W-50, change every 6,000 miles, 9,700 km - automatic transmission 21 imp pt, 25.2 US pt, 11.9 l, change every 24,000 miles, 38,600 km - final drive 1.7 imp pt, 1.9 US pt, 0.9 l, SAE 90 EP, change every 24,000 miles, 38,600 km; greasing: every 12,000 miles, 19,300 km, 21 points; valve timing: 20° 61° 62° 19°; tyre pressure: front 24 psi, 1.7 atm, rear 30 psi, 2.1 atm.

OPTIONAL ACCESSORIES Landaulette version.

Camargue

PRICE IN USA: $ 104,000*
PRICE EX WORKS: £ 46,034*

ENGINE front, 4 stroke; 8 cylinders, Vee-slanted at 90°; 411.9 cu in, 6,750 cc (4.10 x 3.90 in, 104.1 x 99.1 mm); compression ratio: 8:1; aluminium alloy block and head, cast iron wet liners; 5 crankshaft bearings; valves: overhead, in line, push-rods and rockers, hydraulic tappets; camshafts: 1, at centre of Vee; lubrication: gear pump, full flow filter (cartridge), 14.5 imp pt, 17.5 US pt, 8.3 l; 1 Solex 4A1 horizontal 4-barrel carburettor; dual exhaust system; fuel feed: 2 electric pumps; sealed circuit cooling, expansion tank, 28.5 imp pt, 34.2 US pt, 16.2 l, viscous coupling thermostatic fan.

TRANSMISSION driving wheels: rear; gearbox: Turbo-Hydramatic 400 automatic transmission, hydraulic torque converter and planetary gears with 3 ratios, max ratio of converter at stall 2, possible manual selection; ratios: I 2.500, II 1.500, III 1, rev 2; lever: steering column; final drive: hypoid bevel; axle ratio: 3.080; width of rims: 6''; tyres HR70 x 15 or 235/70 HR x 15.

PERFORMANCE max speeds: (I) 47 mph, 76 km/h; (II) 79 mph, 127 km/h; (III) 118 mph, 190 km/h; carrying

ROLLS-ROYCE Carmargue

capacity: 882 lb, 400 kg; speed in direct drive at 1,000 rpm: 26.2 mph, 42.2 km/h; consumption: 14.1 m/imp gal, 11.8 m/US gal, 20 l x 100 km.

CHASSIS integral, front and rear auxiliary frame; front suspension: independent, lower wishbones, coil springs, anti-roll bar, automatic levelling control, telescopic dampers; rear: independent, semi-trailing arms, coil springs, anti-roll bar, automatic levelling control, telescopic dampers.

STEERING rack-and-pinion, servo; turns lock to lock: 3.20.

BRAKES disc [diameter (twin calipers) 11 in, 27.9 cm], front internal radial fins, servo; swept area: front 227 sq in, 1,464 sq cm, rear 286 sq in, 1,845 sq cm, total 513 sq in, 3,309 sq cm.

ELECTRICAL EQUIPMENT 12 V; 68 Ah battery; 75 A alternator; Lucas Opus electronic ignition; 4 headlamps, 2 rear fog lamps.

DIMENSIONS AND WEIGHT wheel base: 120.10 in, 305 cm; tracks: 60 in, 152 cm front, 59.60 in, 151 cm rear; length: 203.50 in, 517 cm; width: 75.59 in, 192 cm; height: 57.87 in, 147 cm; ground clearance: 6.50 in, 16.5 cm; weight: 5,135 lb, 2,329 kg; turning circle (between walls): 38.5 ft, 11.7 m; fuel tank: 23.5 imp gal, 28.2 US gal, 107 l.

BODY saloon/sedan; 2 doors; 5 seats, separate front seats, adjustable and reclining backrests; built-in headrests; leather upholstery; automatic air-conditioning; electric windows; heated rear window.

PRACTICAL INSTRUCTIONS fuel: 98 oct petrol; oil: engine 14.5 imp pt, 17.5 US pt, 8.3 l, SAE 20W-50, change every 6,000 miles, 9,700 km - automatic transmission 18.6 imp pt, 10.5 US pt, 22.2 l, Dexron, change every 24,000 miles, 38,600 km - final drive 4.5 imp pt, 5.3 US pt, 2.5 l, SAE 90 EP, change every 24,000 miles, 38,600 km - automatic levelling control 4 imp pt, 4.9 US pt, 2.3 l - power steering 3 imp pt, 3.6 US pt, 1.7 l; greasing: every 12,000 miles, 19,300 km; type pressure: front 28 psi, 2 atm, rear 28 psi, 2 atm.

VARIATIONS

(for USA and Japan only).
ENGINE 7.3:1 compression ratio, 2 SU type HD8 horizontal carburettors, single exhaust system, catalytic converter (except for Japan).

ROVER   GREAT BRITAIN

3500

PRICE EX WORKS: £ 6,800*

ENGINE front, 4 stroke; 8 cylinders, Vee-slanted at 90°; 215 cu in, 3,528 cc (3.50 x 2.80 in, 88.9 x 71.1 mm); compression ratio: 9.25:1; max power (DIN): 155 hp (114.1 kW) at 5,250 rpm; max torque (DIN): 198 lb ft, 27.3 kg m (267.7 Nm) at 2,500 rpm; max engine rpm: 6,000; 43.9 hp/l (32.3 kW/l); light alloy block and head, dry liners; 5 crankshaft bearings; valves: overhead, in line, push-rods and rockers, hydraulic tappets; camshafts: 1, at centre of Vee; lubrication: gear pump, full flow filter, 9.5 imp pt, 11.4 US pt, 5.4 l; 2 SU type HIF6 semi-downdraught carburettors; fuel feed: electric pump; water-cooled, 19.5 imp pt, 23.5 US pt, 11.1 l, viscous-coupling thermostatic fan.

TRANSMISSION driving wheels: rear; clutch: single dry plate (diaphragm), hydraulically controlled; gearbox: mechanical; gears: 5, fully synchronized; ratios: I 3.321, II 2.087, III 1.396, IV 1, V 0.833, rev 3.428; lever: central; final drive: hypoid bevel; axle ratio: 3.080; width of rims: 6''; tyres: 185 HR x 14.

PERFORMANCE max speed: 126 mph, 203 km/h; power-weight ratio: 18.7 lb/hp (25.4 lb/kW), 8.5 kg/hp (11.5 kg/kW); carrying capacity: 1,235 lb, 560 kg; acceleration: 0-50 mph (0-80 km/h) 6.4 sec; speed in top at 1,000 rpm: 28.8 mph, 46.4 km/h; consumption: 26 m/imp gal, 21.6 m/US gal, 10.9 l x 100 km.

CHASSIS integral with front cross members; front suspension: independent, by McPherson, wishbones (lower trailing links), coil spring/telescopic damper struts, anti-roll bar; rear: rigid axle (torque tube), coil springs with combined telescopic dampers and self-levelling struts, transverse Watt linkage.

STEERING rack-and-pinion, adjustable steering column, servo; turns lock to lock: 2.70.

BRAKES front disc (diameter 10.15 in, 25.8 cm), rear drum, rear compensator, servo.

ELECTRICAL EQUIPMENT 12 V; 68 Ah battery; 55 A alternator; Lucas electronic ignition; 2 halogen headlamps, plus 2 fog lamps.

DIMENSIONS AND WEIGHT wheel base: 111 in, 282 cm; tracks: 59 in, 150 cm front, 59 in, 150 cm rear; length: 165 in, 469 cm; width: 69.60 in, 177 cm; height: 53 in, 135 cm; weight: 2,895 lb, 1,313 kg; turning circle (between walls): 34.2 ft, 10.4 m; fuel tank: 14.5 imp gal, 17.4 US gal, 66 l.

BODY saloon/sedan; 5 doors; 5 seats, separate front seats, reclining backrests with adjustable built-in headrests; laminated windscreen with tinted glass; heated rear window; metallic spray; folding rear seat.

PRACTICAL INSTRUCTIONS fuel: 100 oct petrol; oil: engine 8.2 imp pt, 9.9 US pt, 4.7 l, SAE 20W-30, change every 6,000 miles, 9,700 km - gearbox 2.8 imp pt, 3.4 US pt, 1.6 l, SAE 90 EP, change every 6,000 miles, 9,700 km - final drive 1.6 imp pt, 1.9 US pt, 0.9 l, SAE 90 EP, change every 6,000 miles, 9,700 km; valve timing: 10° 75° 68° 37°; tyre pressure: front 26 psi, 1.8 atm, rear 26 psi, 1.8 atm.

OPTIONAL ACCESSORIES Borg-Warner 65 automatic transmission, hydraulic torque converter and planetary gears with 3 ratios (I 2.390, II 1.450, III 1, rev 2.090), max ratio of converter at stall 2.1, possible manual selection, 3.080 axle ratio; max speed 123 mph, 198 km/h, speed in direct drive at 1,000 rpm 23.5 mph, 37.8 km/h, consumption 24 m/imp gal, 19.9 m/US gal, 11.8 l x 100 km; Dunlop Denovo wheels and tyres; 195/70 HR tyres with light alloy wheels; electric windows; sunshine roof.

ROLLS-ROYCE Camargue

ROVER 3500

ROVER 2600 - 2300

2600

See 3500, except for:

PRICE EX WORKS: £ 5,800*

ENGINE 6 cylinders, in line; 158.3 cu in, 2,597 cc (3.19 x 3.31 in, 81 x 84 mm); max power (DIN): 136 hp (100.1 kW) at 5,000 rpm; max torque (DIN): 152 lb ft, 21 kg m (206 Nm) at 3,750 rpm; 52.4 hp/l (38.5 kW/l); cast iron block, light alloy head; 4 crankshaft bearings; valves: overhead, Vee-slanted, thimble tappets; camshafts: 1, overhead, cogged belt; lubrication: rotary pump, full flow filter, 11.1 imp pt, 13.3 US pt, 6.3 l; 2 SU type HS6 horizontal carburettors; cooling system: 15.5 imp pt, 18.6 US pt, 8.8 l.

TRANSMISSION axle ratio: 3.450; width of rims: 5.5''; tyres: 175 HR x 14.

PERFORMANCE max speed: 117 mph, 189 km/h; power-weight ratio: 21.8 lb/hp (29.8 lb/kW), 9.9 kg/hp (13.5 kg/kW); speed in top at 1,000 rpm: 25 mph, 40.2 km/h; consumption: 27.4 m/imp gal, 22.8 m/US gal, 10.3 l x 100 km.

STEERING rack-and-pinion; turns lock to lock: 4.50.

DIMENSIONS AND WEIGHT weight: 2,978 lb, 1,351 kg.

PRACTICAL INSTRUCTIONS fuel: 97 oct petrol; oil: engine 11.1 imp pt, 13.3 US pt, 6.3 l.

OPTIONAL ACCESSORIES power steering; fog lamps; tinted glass; metallic spray.

2300

See 3500, except for:

PRICE EX WORKS: £ 5,350*

ENGINE 6 cylinders, in line; 143.4 cu in, 2,350 cc (3.19 x 2.99 in, 81 x 76 mm); max power (DIN): 123 hp (90.5 kW) at 5,000 rpm; max torque (DIN): 134 lb ft, 18.5 kg m (181.4 Nm) at 4,000 rpm; 52.3 hp/l (38.5 kW/l); cast iron block, light alloy head; 4 crankshaft bearings; valves: overhead, Vee-slanted, thimble tappets; camshafts: 1, overhead, cogged belt; lubrication: rotary pump, full flow filter, 11.1 imp pt, 13.3 US pt, 6.3 l; 2 SU type HS6 horizontal carburettors; cooling system: 15.5 imp pt, 18.6 US pt, 8.8 l.

TRANSMISSION gears: 4, fully synchronized; ratios: I 3.321, II 2.087, III 1.396, IV 1, rev 3.428; axle ratio: 3.450; width of rims: 5.5''; tyres: 175 HR x 14.

PERFORMANCE max speed: 114 mph, 183 km/h; power-weight ratio: 22.7 lb/hp (30.8 lb/kW), 10.3 kg/hp (14 kg/kW); speed in direct drive at 1,000 rpm: 21 mph, 33.8 km/h; consumption: 25.4 m/imp gal, 21.2 m/US gal, 11.1 l x 100 km.

STEERING rack-and-pinion; turns lock to lock: 4.50.

DIMENSIONS AND WEIGHT weight: 2,787 lb, 1,264 kg.

PRACTICAL INSTRUCTIONS fuel: 97 oct petrol; oil: engine 11.1 imp pt, 13.3 US pt, 6.3 l; tappet clearances: inlet

0.018 in, 0.46 mm, exhaust 0.018 in, 0.46 mm; valve timing: 16° 56° 56° 16°; tyre pressure: front 26 psi, 1.8 atm, rear 28 psi, 2 atm.

OPTIONAL ACCESSORIES Borg-Warner 65 automatic transmission with 3.450 axle ratio; 5-speed fully synchronized mechanical gearbox (I 3.321, II 2.087, III 1.396, IV 1, V 0.833, rev 3.428), 3.450 axle ratio; power steering; halogen headlamps; fog lamps; tinted glass; metallic spray.

Land Rover 88" Regular

PRICE EX WORKS: £ 3,606*

ENGINE front, 4 stroke; 4 cylinders, vertical, in line; 139.5 cu in, 2,286 cc (3.56 x 3.50 in, 90.5 x 88.9 mm); compression ratio: 8:1; max power (DIN): 70 hp (51.5 kW) at 4,000 rpm; max torque (DIN): 120 lb ft, 16.5 kg m (161.8 Nm) at 1,500 rpm; max engine rpm: 5,000; 30.6 hp/l (22.5 kW/l); cast iron block and head; 3 crankshaft bearings; valves: overhead, in line, roller tappets, push-rods and rockers; camshafts: 1, side; lubrication: gear pump, full flow filter, 12.5 imp pt, 14.8 US pt, 7 l; 1 Zenith 36 IV downdraught single barrel carburettor; fuel feed: mechanical pump; water-cooled, 15.2 imp pt, 18.3 US pt, 8.7 l.

TRANSMISSION driving wheels: front (automatically engaged with transfer box low ratio) and rear; clutch: single dry plate, hydraulically controlled; gearbox: mechanical; gears: 4, fully synchronized and 2-ratio transfer box (high 1.150, low 2.350); ratios: I 3.680, II 2.220, III 1.500, IV 1, rev 4.020; gear and transfer levers: central; final drive: spiral bevel; axle ratio: 4.700; width of rims: 5''; tyres: 6.00 x 16.

PERFORMANCE max speeds: (I) 21 mph, 33 km/h; (II) 34 mph, 54 km/h; (III) 50 mph, 80 km/h; (IV) 66 mph, 106 km/h; power-weight ratio: 42.2 lb/hp (57.3 lb/kW), 19.1 kg/hp (26 kg/kW); carrying capacity: 1,499 lb, 680 kg; acceleration: 0-50 mph (0-80 km/h) 16.3 sec; speed in direct drive at 1,000 rpm: 15 mph, 24.1 km/h; consumption: 19.1 m/imp gal, 15.9 m/US gal, 14.8 l x 100 km.

CHASSIS box-type ladder frame; front suspension: rigid axle, semi-elliptic leafsprings, telescopic dampers; rear: rigid axle, semi-elliptic leafsprings, telescopic dampers.

STEERING recirculating ball; turns lock to lock: 3.35.

BRAKES drum; swept area: total 189 sq in, 1,219 sq cm.

ELECTRICAL EQUIPMENT 12 V; 58 Ah battery; 408 W alternator; Lucas distributor; 2 headlamps.

DIMENSIONS AND WEIGHT wheel base: 88 in, 223 cm; front and rear tracks: 51.50 in, 131 cm; length: 142.35 in, 362 cm; width: 66 in, 168 cm; height: 77.85 in, 198 cm; ground clearance: 7 in, 17.8 cm; weight: 2,953 lb, 1,339 kg; weight distribution: 52.5% front, 47.5% rear; turning circle (between walls): 38 ft, 11.6 m; fuel tank: 10 imp gal, 12 US gal, 45 l.

BODY estate car/station wagon; 2+1 doors; 7-8 seats; separate front seats.

PRACTICAL INSTRUCTIONS fuel: 91 oct petrol; oil: engine 12.5 imp pt, 14.8 US pt, 7 l, SAE 20W, change every 6,200 miles, 10,000 km - gearbox 2.5 imp pt, 3 US pt, 1.4 l - transfer box 4.4 imp pt, 5.3 US pt, 2.5 l, SAE 90 EP, change every 24,000 miles, 39,000 km - final drive 3 imp pt, 3.6 US pt, 1.7 l, SAE 90 EP, change every 24,000 miles, 39,000 km; greasing: every 6,200 miles, 10,000 km, 1 point; tappet clearances: inlet 0.010 in, 0.25 mm, exhaust 0.010 in, 0.25 mm; valve timing: 6° 52° 34° 24°; tyre pressure: front 25 psi, 1.7 atm, rear 25 psi, 1.7 atm.

VARIATIONS

ENGINE Diesel, 23:1 compression ratio, max power (DIN) 62 hp (45.6 kW) at 4,000 rpm, max torque (DIN) 103 lb ft, 14.2 kg m (139.3 Nm) at 1,800 rpm, max engine rpm 4,000, 27.1 hp/l (19.9 kW/l), cast iron head with precombustion chambers.
PERFORMANCE power-weight ratio 47.6 lb/hp (64.8 lb/kW), 21.6 kg/hp (29.4 kg/kW).

OPTIONAL ACCESSORIES oil cooler; front and rear power take-off; 7/7.50 x 16 tyres; servo brake; 45 A alternator; special equipment.

Land Rover 109" Estate Car

See Land Rover 88'' Regular, except for:

PRICE EX WORKS: £ 4,229*

TRANSMISSION width of rims: 5.5''; tyres: 7.50 x 16.

PERFORMANCE power-weight ratio: 53.6 lb/hp (72.9 lb/kW), 24.3 kg/hp (33 kg/kW).

ROVER Range Rover

Series III

PRICE EX WORKS: £ 3,711*

ENGINE Lotus front, 4 stroke; 4 cylinders, vertical, in line; 95.1 cu in, 1,558 cc (3.25 x 2.87 in, 82.6 x 72.8 mm); compression ratio: 10.3:1; max power (DIN): 126 hp (92.7 kW) at 6,500 rpm; max torque (DIN): 113 lb ft, 15.6 kg m (153 Nm) at 5,500 rpm; max engine rpm: 6,800; 80.9 hp/l (59.5 kW/l); cast iron block, light alloy head; 5 crankshaft bearings; valves: overhead, Vee-slanted, thimble tappets; camshafts: 2, overhead; lubrication: rotary pump, full flow filter by cartridge, 7.5 imp pt, 8.9 US pt, 4.2 l; 2 Dell'Orto 40 DHLA twin barrel carburettors; fuel feed: mechanical pump; water-cooled, 12 imp pt, 14.4 US pt, 6.8 l.

TRANSMISSION driving wheels: rear; clutch: single dry plate (diaphragm), hydraulically controlled; gearbox: mechanical; gears: 4, fully synchronized; ratios: I 2.972, II 2.010, III 1.400, IV 1, rev 3.325; lever: central; final drive: hypoid bevel; axle ratio: 3.890; width of rims: 5.5''; tyres: 165 SR x 13.

PERFORMANCE max speeds: (I) 38 mph, 61 km/h; (II) 60 mph, 96 km/h; (III) 81 mph, 130 km/h; (IV) 114 mph, 183 km/h; power-weight ratio: 8.7 lb/hp (11.9 lb/kW), 4 kg/hp (5.4 kg/kW); carrying capacity: 450 lb, 204 kg; acceleration: standing 1/4 mile 14.9 sec, 0-50 mph (0-80 km/h)

LAND ROVER 109'' ESTATE CAR

DIMENSIONS AND WEIGHT wheel base: 109 in, 277 cm; length: 175 in, 444 cm; height: 81.35 in, 207 cm; ground clearance: 8.25 in, 21 cm; weight: 3,752 lb, 1,702 kg; weight distribution: 46.5% front, 53.5% rear; turning circle (between walls): 48 ft, 14.6 m; fuel tank: 16 imp gal, 19.3 US gal, 73 l.

BODY 10-12 seats.

VARIATIONS

ENGINE Diesel (62 hp).

ENGINE 6 cylinders, 160.2 cu in, 2,625 cc (3.06 x 3.63 in, 77.8 x 92.1 mm), 7.8:1 compression ratio, max power (DIN) 86 hp (63.3 kW) at 4,500 rpm, max torque (DIN) 132 lb ft, 18.2 kg m (178.5 Nm) at 1,500 rpm, 32.8 hp/l (24.1 kW/l), 1 Zenith 175-CD2S carburettor.
PERFORMANCE max speed 72 mph, 116 km/h, power-weight ratio 45.5 lb/hp (61.8 lb/kW), 20.6 kg/hp (28 kg/kW).
DIMENSIONS AND WEIGHT weight 3,910 lb, 1,774 kg.

Range Rover

PRICE EX WORKS: £ 8,008*

ENGINE front, 4 stroke; 8 cylinders, Vee-slanted at 90°; 215 cu in, 3,528 cc (3.50 x 2.80 in, 88.9 x 71.1 mm); compression ratio: 8.13:1; max power (DIN): 132 hp (97.1 kW) at 5,000 rpm; max torque (DIN): 186 lb ft, 25.6 kg m (251.1 Nm) at 2,500 rpm; max engine rpm: 5,200; 37.4 hp/l (27.5 kw/l); light alloy block and head, dry liners; 5 crankshaft bearings; valves: overhead, in line, push-rods and rockers, hydraulic tappets; camshafts: 1, at centre of Vee; lubrication: gear pump, full flow filter, 10 imp pt, 12 US pt, 5.7 l; 2 Zenith-Stromberg CD2 semi-downdraught carburettors; fuel feed: electric pump; water-cooled, 20 imp pt, 23.9 US pt, 11.3 l.

TRANSMISSION driving wheels: 4, with lockable differential in transfer box; clutch: single dry plate (diaphragm), hydraulically controlled; gearbox: mechanical; gears: 4, fully synchronized, and 2-ratio transfer box (high 1.174, low 3.321); ratios: I 4.069, II 2.448, III 1.505, IV 1, rev 3.664; gear and transfer levers: central; final drive: spiral bevel; axle ratio: 3.540; width of rims: 6''; tyres: 205 x 16.

PERFORMANCE max speeds: (I) 24 mph, 39 km/h; (II) 41 mph, 66 km/h; (III) 68 mph, 109 km/h; (IV) 96 mph, 154 km/h; power-weight ratio: 28.8 lb/hp (39.1 lb/kW), 13.1 kg/hp (17.8 kg/kW); carrying capacity: 1,720 lb, 780 kg; acceleration: standing 1/4 mile 19.3 sec, 0-50 mph (0-80 km/h) 11.1 sec; speed in direct drive at 1,000 rpm: 20 mph, 32.2 km/h; consumption: 18.2 m/imp gal, 15.1 m/US gal, 15.5 l x 100 km.

CHASSIS box-type ladder frame; front suspension: rigid axle, longitudinal radius arms, transverse linkage bar, coil springs/dampers units; rear: rigid axle, longitudinal radius arms, upper A bracket, Boge Hydromat self-energizing levelling device, coil springs, telescopic dampers.

STEERING Burman, recirculating ball, worm and nut; turns lock to lock: 4.75.

SEVEN Series III

BRAKES disc (front diameter 11.75 in, 29.8 cm, rear 11.42 in, 29 cm); swept area: front 261 sq in, 1,683 sq cm, rear 235 sq in, 1,516 sq cm, total 496 sq in, 3,199 sq cm.

ELECTRICAL EQUIPMENT 12 V; 60 Ah battery; 540 W alternator; Lucas distributor; 2 headlamps.

DIMENSIONS AND WEIGHT wheel base: 100 in, 254 cm; front and rear tracks: 58.50 in, 149 cm; length: 175.98 in, 447 cm; width: 70 in, 178 cm; height: 70 in, 178 cm; ground clearance: 7.50 in, 19 cm; weight: 3,800 lb, 1,724 kg; weight distribution: 50% front, 50% rear; turning circle (between walls): 37 ft, 11.3 m; fuel tank: 18 imp gal, 21.6 US gal, 82 l.

BODY estate car/station wagon; 2 + 1 doors; 5 seats, separate front seats, reclining backrests; heated rear window with wiper-washer.

PRACTICAL INSTRUCTIONS fuel: 91-93 oct petrol; oil: engine 10 imp pt, 12 US pt, 5.7 l, SAE 20W, change every 6,200 miles, 10,000 km - gearbox 4.5 imp pt, 5.5 US pt, 2.6 l, SAE 80 EP, change every 24,000 miles, 39,000 km - transfer box 5.5 imp pt, 6.6 US pt, 3.1 l, SAE 80 EP, change every 6,200 miles, 10,000 km - final drive rear 2.7 imp pt, 3.2 US pt, 1.5 l, SAE 80 EP, change every 24,000 miles, 39,000 km, front 3 imp pt, 3.6 US pt, 1.7 l, SAE 80 EP, change every 24,000 miles, 39,000 km; greasing: every 6,200 miles, 10,000 km, 6 points; valve timing: 30° 75° 68° 37°; tyre pressure: front 25 psi, 1.7 atm, rear 25 psi, 1.7 atm.

OPTIONAL ACCESSORIES power steering; headrests; tinted glass.

4.5 sec; speed in direct drive at 1,000 rpm: 17.4 mph, 28 km/h; consumption: 25 m/imp gal, 20.8 m/US gal, 11.3 l x 100 km.

CHASSIS tubular space-frame with aluminium panels; front suspension: independent, lower wishbones, anti-roll bar, coil springs/telescopic dampers units; rear: rigid axle, twin trailing radius arms, A-bracket, coil spring/telescopic dampers units.

STEERING rack-and-pinion; turns lock to lock: 2.75.

BRAKES front disc, rear drum.

ELECTRICAL EQUIPMENT 12 V; 39 Ah battery; dynamo; Lucas distributor; 2 headlamps.

DIMENSIONS AND WEIGHT wheel base: 88 in, 223 cm; tracks: 49 in, 124 cm front, 51.50 in, 131 cm rear; length: 133 in, 338 cm; width: 65.50 in, 159 cm; height: 43.50 in, 110 cm; ground clearance: 4 in, 10 cm; weight: 1,100 lb, 499 kg; turning circle (between walls): 29.6 ft, 9 m; fuel tank: 8 imp gal, 9.5 US gal, 36 l.

BODY sports; no doors; 2 seats.

PRACTICAL INSTRUCTIONS fuel: 98-100 oct petrol; oil: engine 6.5 imp pt, 7.8 US pt, 3.7 l, SAE 20W-50, change every 6,000 miles, 9,700 km - gearbox 2 imp pt, 2.3 US pt, 1.1 l, SAE 80 EP, no change recommended - final drive 2 imp pt, 2.3 US pt, 1.1 l, SAE 90 EP, no change recommended; greasing: every 6,000 miles, 9,700 km, 5 points; tappet clearances: inlet 0.005-0.007 in, 0.12-0.17 mm, exhaust 0.009-0.011 in, 0.22-0.27 mm; valve timing: 26° 66° 66° 26°; tyre pressure: front 20 psi, 1.4 atm, rear 20 psi, 1.4 atm.

SPARTAN CARS 2-seater Sports

SPARTAN CARS   GREAT BRITAIN

2-seater Sports

PRICE EX WORKS: £ 3,391*

ENGINE Ford, front, 4 stroke; 4 cylinders, vertical, in line; 97.5 cu in, 1,598 cc (3.19 x 3.06 in, 81 x 77.6 mm); compression ratio: 9:1; max power (DIN): 84 hp (61.8 kW) at 5,500 rpm; max torque (DIN): 92 lb ft, 12.7 kg m (124.5 Nm) at 3,500 rpm; max engine rpm: 6,600; 52.6 hp/l (38.7 kW/l); cast iron block and head; 5 crankshaft bearings; valves: overhead, in line, push-rods and rockers; camshafts: 1, side, chain-driven; lubrication: rotary or vane-type pump, full flow filter, 5.7 imp pt, 6.8 US pt, 3.2 l; 1 Weber 32/32 DGV downdraught twin barrel carburettor; fuel feed: mechanical pump; water-cooled, 9.5 imp pt, 11.4 US pt, 5.4 l.

TRANSMISSION driving wheels: rear; clutch: single dry plate (diaphragm); gearbox: mechanical; gears: 4, fully synchronized; ratios: I 3.337, II 1.995, III 1.418, IV 1, rev 3.876; lever: central; final drive: hypoid bevel; axle ratio: 3.770; width of rims: 5.5''; tyres: 175/70 SR x 13.

PERFORMANCE max speed: 108 mph, 174 km/h; power-weight ratio: 18.7 lb/hp (25.4 lb/kW), 8.5 kg/hp (11.5 kg/kW); carrying capacity: 353 lb, 160 kg; acceleration: standing ¼ mile 17.3 sec; consumption: 33 m/imp gal, 27.7 m/US gal, 8.5 l x 100 km.

CHASSIS tubular space-frame with aluminium panels; front suspension: independent, by McPherson, coil springs/telescopic damper struts, anti-roll bar; rear: rigid axle, trailing lower radius arms, upper oblique torque arms, coil springs, telescopic dampers.

STEERING rack-and-pinion, turns lock to lock: 3.50.

BRAKES front disc (diameter 9.60 in, 24.4 cm), rear drum.

ELECTRICAL EQUIPMENT 12 V; 38 Ah battery; 35 A alternator; Motorcraft distributor; 2 headlamps.

DIMENSIONS AND WEIGHT length: 150 in, 381 cm; width: 62.60 in, 159 cm; height: 49.61 in, 126 cm; weight: 1,568 lb, 711 kg; fuel tank: 9 imp gal, 10.8 US gal, 41 l.

BODY sports; 2 doors; 2 seats; built-in headrests.

PRACTICAL INSTRUCTIONS fuel: 97 oct petrol; oil: engine 5.8 imp pt, 7 US pt, 3.3 l, SAE 10W-30, change every 6,000 miles, 9,700 km - gearbox 1.6 imp pt, 1.9 US pt, 0.9 l, SAE 80, no change recommended - final drive 1.7 imp pt, 2.1 US pt, 1 l, SAE 90, no change recommended; greasing: every 6,000 miles, 9,700 km, 2 points; tappet clearances: inlet 0.010 in, 0.25 mm, exhaust 0.017 in, 0.43 mm; valve timing: 29° 63° 71° 21°; tyre pressure: front 24 psi, 1.7 atm, rear 24 psi, 1.7 atm.

OPTIONAL ACCESSORIES light alloy wheels; reclining backrests; leather upholstery; halogen headlamps; rear fog lamps; tonneau cover; metallic spray.

2+2-seater Sports

See 2-seater Sports, except for:

PRICE EX WORKS: £ 3,649*

PERFORMANCE power-weight ratio: 20.2 lb/hp (27.5 lb/kW), 9.2 kg/hp (12.5 kg/kW); carrying capacity: 706 lb, 320 kg.

DIMENSIONS AND WEIGHT length: 156 in, 396 cm; height: 52.11 in, 132 cm; weight: 1,700 lb, 771 kg.

BODY 2+2 seats.

STEVENS   GREAT BRITAIN

Sienna

PRICE EX WORKS: £ 2,700

ENGINE Reliant, front, 4 stroke; 4 cylinders, in line; 51.7 cu in, 848 cc (2.46 x 2.72 in, 62.5 x 69.1 mm); compression ratio: 9.5:1; max power (DIN): 40 hp (29.4 kW) at 5,500 rpm; max torque (DIN): 46 lb ft, 6.3 kg m (61.8 Nm) at 3,500 rpm; max engine rpm: 5,500; 47.2 hp/l (34.7 kW/l); light alloy block and head, wet liners; 3 crankshaft bearings; valves: overhead, in line, push-rods and rockers; camshafts: 1, side; lubrication: rotary pump, full flow filter, 5.5 imp pt, 6.6 US pt, 3.1 l; 1 SU HS2 1 ¼ semi-downdraught single barrel carburettor; fuel feed: mechanical pump; sealed circuit cooling, anti-freeze liquid, 6.5 imp pt, 7.8 US pt, 3.7 l.

TRANSMISSION driving wheels: rear; clutch: single dry plate; gearbox: mechanical; gears: 4, fully synchronized; ratios: I 3.876, II 2.046, III 1.319, IV 1, rev 3.250; lever: central; final drive: spiral bevel; axle ratio: 3.560; width of rims: 5.5''; tyres: 5.50 x 13.

PERFORMANCE max speed: 80 mph, 129 km/h; power-weight ratio: 28.7 lb/hp (39 lb/kW), 13 kg/hp (17.7 kg/kW); acceleration: 0-50 mph (0-80 km/h) 11.4 sec; speed in direct drive at 1,000 rpm: 17 mph, 27.3 km/h; consumption: 56 m/imp gal, 47 m/US gal, 5 l x 100 km.

CHASSIS box section side members and channel section diagonal reinforcements; front suspension: independent, wishbones, anti-roll bar, coil sptings/telescopic damper units; rear: rigid axle, semi-elliptic leafsprings, telescopic dampers.

STEERING rack-and-pinion; turns lock to lock: 3.50.

BRAKES drum (diameter 7 in, 17.8 cm); swept area: front 66 sq in, 426 sq cm, rear 55 sq in, 355 sq cm, total 121 sq in, 781 sq cm.

ELECTRICAL EQUIPMENT 12 V; 35 Ah battery; 35 A alternator; Lucas distributor; 2 headlamps.

DIMENSIONS AND WEIGHT wheel base: 83 in, 211 cm; tracks: 49 in, 124 cm front, 49 in, 124 cm rear; length: 123 in, 312 cm; width: 59 in, 150 cm; height: 45 in, 114 cm; ground clearance: 7 in, 17.8 cm; weight: 1,148 lb, 520 kg; weight distribution: 50% front, 50% rear; turning circle (between walls): 25 ft, 7.6 m; fuel tank: 6 imp gal, 7.1 US gal, 27 l.

BODY convertible in plastic material; 2 doors; 2+2 seats, separate front seats, laminated windscreen; light alloy wheels.

PRACTICAL INSTRUCTIONS fuel: 97 oct petrol; oil: engine 5.5 imp pt, 6.6 US pt, 3.1 l, SAE 20W-50, change every 6,000 miles, 9,700 km - gearbox 1.1 imp pt, 1.3 US pt, 0.6 l, SAE 80 EP, change every 12,000 miles, 19,400 km - final drive 2.2 imp pt, 2.5 US pt, 1.2 l, SAE 90 EP, change every 6,000 miles, 9,700 km; greasing: every 6,000 miles, 9,700 km, 7 points; tappet clearances: inlet 0.010 in, 0.25 mm, exhaust 0.010 in, 0.25 mm; valve timing: 13° 72° 54° 29°; tyre pressure: front 22 psi, 1.6 atm, rear 22 psi, 1.6 atm.

SYD LAWRENCE   GREAT BRITAIN

Mk 2 Sports

PRICE EX WORKS: £ 15,000

ENGINE front, 4 stroke; 6 cylinders, in line; 259.8 cu in, 4,257 cc (3.50 x 4.50 in, 88.9 x 114.3 mm); compression ratio: 6.4:1; max engine rpm: 4,750; cast iron block, light alloy head; 7 crankshaft bearings; valves: overhead inlet, side exhaust, push-rods and rockers; camshafts: 1, lateral; lubrication: gear pump, full flow filter, 20 imp pt, 23.9 US pt, 11.3 l; 4 SU type H1-F carburettors; fuel feed: electric pump; water-cooled, 46 imp pt, 56 US pt, 26 l.

TRANSMISSION driving wheels: rear; clutch: single dry plate; gearbox: mechanical; gears: 4, II, III and IV synchronized; ratios: I 2.981, II 2.018, III 1.342, V 1, rev 3.155; lever: at driver's right; final drive: hypoid bevel; axle ratio: 3.727; width of rims: 6''; tyres: 8.15 x 15.

PERFORMANCE max speed: 120 mph, 193 km/h; speed in direct drive at 1,000 rpm: 30 mph, 48.2 km/h; consumption: about 17 m/imp gal, 14.2 m/US gal, 16.6 l x 100 km.

CHASSIS box-type ladder frame; front suspension: independent, wishbones, coil springs, lever dampers; rear: rigid axle, semi-elliptic leafsprings, telescopic dampers.

STEERING worm and roller; turns lock to lock: 3.

BRAKES drum, servo; lining area: total 186.6 sq in, 1,203 sq cm.

ELECTRICAL EQUIPMENT 12 V; 77 Ah battery; dynamo; Delco-Remy distributor; 2 headlamps.

DIMENSIONS AND WEIGHT wheel base: 114 in, 289 cm; tracks: 55.75 in, 144 cm front, 58.62 in, 149 cm rear; length: 165 in, 419 cm; width: 67 in, 170 cm; height: 43 in, 109 cm; ground clearance: 6 in, 15 cm; weight: 2,549 lb, 1,156 kg; fuel tank: 12 imp gal, 14.3 US gal, 54 l.

STEVENS Sienna

SYD LAWRENCE Mk 2 Sports

MK 2 SPORTS

BODY sports, in fibreglass material; 2 doors; 2 seats; leather upholstery.

PRACTICAL INSTRUCTIONS fuel: 98-100 oct petrol; oil: engine 16 imp pt, 19.2 US pt, 9.1 l, SAE 20W-50, change every 5,000 miles, 8,000 km - gearbox 6 imp pt, 7.2 US pt, 3.4 l, SAE 20W-50, change every 10,000 miles, 16,100 km - final drive 1.7 imp pt, 2.1 US pt, 1 l, SAE 90, change every 10,000 miles, 16,100 km; greasing: every 5,000 miles, 8,000 km, 10 points; tappet clearances (cold): inlet 0.006 in, 0.15 mm, exhaust 0.012 in, 0.30 mm; valve timing: 3° 43° 40° 1°; tyre pressure: front 23 psi, 1.6 atm, rear 25 psi, 1.7 atm.

OPTIONALS 8.15 x 16 tyres; long wheelbase 120 in, 305 cm.

TECHNICAL EXPONENTS
GREAT BRITAIN

TX Tripper 1500/De Luxe

PRICES EX WORKS: 1500: £ 2,923*
1500 De Luxe: £ 3,122*

ENGINE Triumph, front, 4 stroke; 4 cylinders, vertical, in line; 91.1 cu in, 1,493 cc (2.90 x 3.44 in, 73.7 x 87.5 mm); compression ratio: 9:1; max power (DIN): 71 hp (52.3 kW) at 5,500 rpm; max torque (DIN): 82 lb ft, 11.3 kg m (110.8 Nm) at 3,000 rpm; max engine rpm: 6,000; 47.6 hp/l (35 kW/l); cast iron block and head; 5 crankshaft bearings; valves: overhead, in line, push-rods and rockers; camshafts: 1, side; lubrication: gear pump, full flow filter, 8 imp pt, 9.5 US pt, 4.5 l; 2 SU type HS 4 semi-downdraught carburettors; fuel feed: mechanical pump; water-cooled, 6 imp pt, 7.2 US pt, 3.4 l.

TRANSMISSION driving wheels: rear; clutch: single dry plate (diaphragm); gearbox: mechanical; gears: 4, II, III and IV synchronized; ratios: I 3.750, II 2.160, III 1.390, IV 1, rev 3.750; lever: central; final drive: hypoid bevel; axle ratio: 3.690; width of rims: 5.5''; tyres: 165 x 13.

PERFORMANCE max speeds: (I) 35 mph, 56 km/h; (II) 52 mph, 83 km/h; (III) 81 mph, 130 km/h; (IV) 108 mph, 174 km/h; power-weight ratio: 15 lb/hp (20.4 lb/kW), 6.8 kg/hp (9.3 kg/kW); carrying capacity: 784 lb, 356 kg; acceleration: standing ¼ mile 7.6 sec; speed in direct drive at 1,000 rpm: 18.5 mph, 29.7 km/h; consumption: 40 m/imp gal, 33.1 m/US gal, 7.1 l x 100 km.

CHASSIS box-type double backbone with outriggers; front suspension: independent, wishbones, coil springs, telescopic dampers; rear: independent, wishbones, transverse leafspring as upper arms, telescopic dampers.

STEERING rack-and-pinion; turns lock to lock: 3.50.

BRAKES front disc (diameter 9 in, 22.9 cm), rear drum; swept area: total 197 sq in, 1,271 sq cm.

ELECTRICAL EQUIPMENT 12 V; 45 Ah battery; 15 W alternator; Lucas distributor; 2 headlamps.

DIMENSIONS AND WEIGHT wheel base: 83.07 in, 211 cm; tracks: 50.12 in, 127 cm front, 49.61 in, 126 cm rear; length: 145.08 in, 368 cm; width: 57.05 in, 145 cm; height: 47.17 in, 120 cm; ground clearance: 6.50 in, 16.5 cm; weight: 1,067 lb, 484 kg; weight distribution: 52% front, 48% rear; turning circle (between walls): 25.3 ft, 7.7 m; fuel tank: 8.2 imp gal, 9.8 US gal, 37 l.

BODY open, in plastic material; no doors; 2 seats; De Luxe: luxury equipment, folding rear seat.

PRACTICAL INSTRUCTIONS fuel: 97-100 oct petrol; oil: engine 7 imp pt, 8.5 US pt, 4 l, SAE 20, change every 6,000 miles, 9,700 km - gearbox 1.5 imp pt, 1.9 US pt, 0.9 l, SAE 90 - final drive 1.1 imp pt, 1.3 US pt, 0.6 l, SAE 90; greasing: every 6,000 miles, 9,700 km, 3 points, every 12,000 miles, 19,300 km, 2 points; tappet clearances: inlet 0.010 in, 0.25 mm; valve timing: 18° 58° 58° 18°; tyre pressure: front 21 psi, 1.5 atm, rear 26 psi, 1.8 atm.

OPTIONAL ACCESSORIES 3.270 or 4.110 axle ratio; overdrive, 0.797 ratio; oil cooler; left-hand drive; servo brake; larger fuel tank; halogen headlamps; laminated windscreen; hardtop with heated rear window; tonneau cover; reclining backrests with built-in headrests.

TX Tripper 2000 Sprint

See TX Tripper 1500, except for:

PRICE EX WORKS: £ 3,800*

ENGINE Triumph, front, 4 stroke; 121.9 cu in, 1,998 cc (3.56 x 3.07 in, 90.3 x 78 mm); compression ratio: 9.5:1; max power (DIN): 127 hp (93.5 kW) at 5,700 rpm; max torque (DIN): 122 lb ft, 16.9 kg m (165.7 Nm) at 4,500 rpm; max engine rpm: 6,500; 63.6 hp/l (46.8 kW/l); cast iron block, light alloy head; valves: 4 per cylinder, overhead, in line, thimble tappets; camshafts: 1, overhead; 2 SU type HS 6 horizontal carburettors.

TRANSMISSION gearbox ratios: I 2.995, II 2.100, III 1.386, IV 1 (overdrive 1.100), IV 1 (overdrive 0.797), rev 3.370; axle ratio: 3.450; width of rims: 5.5''; tyres: 175/70 HR x 13.

PERFORMANCE max speed: 125 mph, 200 km/h; power-weight ratio: 8.4 lb/hp (11.4 lb/kW), 3.8 kg/hp (5.2 kg/kW); speed in direct drive at 1,000 rpm: 20.6 mph, 33.1 km/h; consumption: 30 m/imp gal, 25 m/US gal, 9.4 l x 100 km.

CHASSIS anti-roll bar on front and rear suspension.

BRAKES servo.

PRACTICAL INSTRUCTIONS tappet clearances: inlet 0.018 in, 0.45 mm, exhaust 0.018 in, 0.45 mm; valve timing: 10° 50° 50° 10°.

TRIDENT   GREAT BRITAIN

Venturer V6

PRICE EX WORKS: £ 5,616

ENGINE Ford, front, 4 stroke; 6 cylinders, Vee-slanted at 60°; 182.7 cu in, 2,994 cc (3.69 x 2.85 in, 93.7 x 72.4 mm); compression ratio: 8.9:1; max power (DIN): 138 hp (101.6 kW) at 5,000 rpm; max torque (DIN): 175 lb ft, 24.1 kg m (236.3 Nm) at 3,000 rpm; max engine rpm: 6,000; 46.1 hp/l (33.9 kW/l); cast iron block and head; 4 crankshaft bearings; valves: overhead, in line, push-rods and rockers; camshafts: 1, at centre of Vee; lubrication: eccentric pump, full flow filter, 9.5 imp pt, 11.4 US pt, 5.4 l; 1 Weber DFA-1 downdraught twin barrel carburettor; fuel feed: mechanical pump; water-cooled, 14.4 imp pt, 17.3 US pt, 8.2 l.

TRANSMISSION driving wheels: rear; clutch: single dry plate (diaphragm), hydraulically controlled; gearbox: mechanical; gears: 4, fully synchronized; ratios: I 3.163, II 2.214, III 1.412, IV 1, rev 3.346; lever: central; final drive: hypoid bevel; axle ratio: 3.450; width of rims: 6''; tyres: 185 x 15.

PERFORMANCE max speed: 125 mph, 200 km/h; power-weight ratio: 19.2 lb/hp (26 lb/kW), 8.7 kg/hp (11.8 kg/kW); carrying capacity: 706 lb, 320 kg; acceleration: standing ¼ mile 15.5 sec; speed in direct drive at 1,000 rpm: 22.4 mph, 36 km/h; consumption: 25 m/imp gal, 20.8 m/US gal, 11.3 l x 100 km.

CHASSIS box-type ladder frame, X cross members; front suspension: independent, wishbones, coil springs, anti-roll bar, telescopic dampers; rear: independent, swinging lon-

TECHNICAL EXPONENTS TX Tripper 1500 - 2000 Sprint

gitudinal trailing arms, upper oblique semi-trailing arms, coil springs, telescopic dampers.

STEERING rack-and-pinion.

BRAKES front disc (diameter 10.87 in, 27.6 cm), rear drum, servo.

ELECTRICAL EQUIPMENT 12 V; 53 Ah battery; 516 W alternator; Autolite distributor; 4 headlamps.

DIMENSIONS AND WEIGHT wheel base: 93 in, 236 cm; tracks: 53.54 in, 136 cm front, 52.36 in, 133 cm rear; length: 161.81 in, 411 cm; width: 64.96 in, 165 cm; height: 52.36 in, 133 cm; ground clearance: 6 in, 15 cm; weight: 2,646 lb, 1,200 kg; turning circle (between walls): 34.1 ft, 10.4 m; fuel tank: 15.4 imp gal, 18.5 US gal, 70 l.

BODY coupé; 2 doors; 2 + 2 seats; reclining backrests with built-in headrests; electric windows; heated rear window; light alloy wheels; folding rear seat.

PRACTICAL INSTRUCTIONS fuel: 94 oct petrol; tappet clearances: inlet 0.012 in, 0.30 mm, exhaust 0.012 in, 0.30 mm; valve timing: 20º 56º 62º 14º.

OPTIONAL ACCESSORIES overdrive on III (1.158 ratio) and IV (0.820 ratio); automatic transmission, hydraulic torque converter and planetary gears with 3 ratios (I 2.460, II 1.460, III 1, rev 2.200), max ratio of converter at stall 2, possible manual selection; fog lamps; halogen headlamps; vinyl roof; sunshine roof; leather upholstery; metallic spray; 2-colour spray; air-conditioning.

TRIUMPH   GREAT BRITAIN

Dolomite 1300

PRICE EX WORKS: £ 2,773*

ENGINE front, 4 stroke; 4 cylinders, vertical, in line; 79.2 cu in, 1,296 cc (2.90 x 2.99 in, 73.7 x 76 mm); compression ratio: 8.5:1; max power (DIN): 58 hp (42.7 kW) at 5,500 rpm; max torque (DIN): 68 lb ft, 9.4 kg m (92.2 Nm) at 3,300 rpm; max engine rpm: 6,000; 44.8 hp/l (32.9 kW/l); cast iron block and head; 3 crankshaft bearings; valves: overhead, in line, push-rods and rockers; camshafts: 1, side; lubrication: rotary pump, full flow filter, 7.5 imp pt, 8.9 US pt, 4.2 l; 1 SU type HS4 E semi-downdraught carburettor; fuel feed: mechanical pump; water-cooled, 9.5 imp pt, 11.4 US pt, 5.4 l.

TRANSMISSION driving wheels: rear; clutch: single dry plate (diaphragm), hydraulically controlled; gearbox: mechanical; gears: 4, fully synchronized; ratios: I 3.504, II 2.158, III 1.394, IV 1, rev 3.988; lever: central; final drive: hypoid bevel; axle ratio: 4.110; width of rims: 4''; tyres: 155 SR x 13.

PERFORMANCE max speed: 84 mph, 135 km/h; power-weight ratio: 35.8 lb/hp (48.7 lb/kW), 16.3 kg/hp (22.1

---

kg/kW); carrying capacity: 882 lb, 400 kg; speed in direct drive at 1,000 rpm: 16.5 mph, 26.5 km/h; consumption: 41.5 m/imp gal, 34.6 m/US gal, 6.8 l x 100 km at steady 50 mph, 80 km/h.

CHASSIS integral; front suspension: independent, wishbones, lower trailing links, coil springs, anti-roll bar, telescopic dampers; rear: rigid axle, lower trailing arms, upper oblique torque arms, coil springs, telescopic dampers.

STEERING rack-and-pinion; turns lock to lock: 3.25.

BRAKES front disc (diameter 8.75 in, 22.2 cm), rear drum, servo; swept area: total 240.6 sq in, 1,552 sq cm.

ELECTRICAL EQUIPMENT 12 V; 40 Ah battery; alternator; Lucas distributor; 2 headlamps.

DIMENSIONS AND WEIGHT wheel base: 96.61 in, 245 cm; tracks: 53 in, 135 cm front, 50 in, 127 cm rear; length: 162.20 in, 411 cm; width: 62.50 in, 159 cm; height: 54 in, 137 cm; ground clearance: 4.25 in, 10.8 cm; weight: 2,079 lb, 943 kg; weight distribution: 48% front, 52% rear; turning circle (between walls). 30 ft, 9.1 m; fuel tank: 12.5 imp gal, 15 US gal, 57 l.

BODY saloon/sedan; 4 doors; 4-5 seats, separate front seats, reclining backrests with built-in headrests; laminated windscreen; heated rear window.

PRACTICAL INSTRUCTIONS fuel: 97 oct petrol; oil: engine 7.5 imp pt, 8.9 US pt, 4.2 l, SAE 20W-50, change every 6,000 miles, 9,700 km - gearbox 1.3 imp pt, 1.7 US pt, 0.8 l, SAE 90, change every 6,000 miles, 9,700 km - final drive 1.5 imp pt, 1.9 US pt, 0.9 l, SAE 90, change every 6,000 miles, 9,700 km; tappet clearances: inlet 0.010 in, 0.25 mm, exhaust 0.010 in, 0.25 mm; valve timing: 10º 58º 58º 10º; tyre pressure: front 22 psi, 1.5 atm, rear 26 psi, 1.8 atm.

OPTIONAL ACCESSORIES tinted glass.

Dolomite 1500

See Dolomite 1300, except for:

PRICE EX WORKS: £ 2,983*

ENGINE 91.1 cu in, 1,493 cc (2.90 x 3.44 in, 73.7 x 87.5 mm); compression ratio: 9:1; max power (DIN): 71 hp (52.3 kW) at 5,500 rpm; max torque (DIN): 82 lb ft, 11.3 kg m (110.8 Nm) at 3,000 rpm; 47.6 hp/l (35 kW/l); 2 SU type HS4 E semi-downdraught carburettors.

TRANSMISSION gearbox ratios: I 3.500, II 2.160, III 1.390, IV 1, rev 3.990; axle ratio: 3.630.

PERFORMANCE max speed: 91 mph, 146 km/h; power-weight ratio: 29.3 lb/hp (39.7 lb/kW), 13.3 kg/hp (18 kg/kW); speed in direct drive at 1,000 rpm: 16.9 mph, 27.2 km/h; consumption: 37 m/imp gal, 30.9 m/US gal, 7.6 l x 100 km at steady 50 mph, 80 km/h.

OPTIONAL ACCESSORIES tinted glass; overdrive.

TRIDENT Clipper V8

Clipper V8

See Venturer V6, except for:

PRICE EX WORKS: £ 8,371

ENGINE Chrysler, front, 4 stroke; 8 cylinders, Vee-slanted at 90º; 360 cu in, 5,900 cc (4.02 x 3.58 in, 102 x 91 mm); compression ratio: 8.4:1; max power (DIN): 230 hp (169.3 kW) at 4,800 rpm; max torque (DIN): 297 lb ft, 41 kg m (402.1 Nm) at 3,600 rpm; 39 hp/l (28.7 kW/l); 5 crankshaft bearings; valves: hydraulic tappets; lubrication: gear pump, full flow filter, 8.4 imp pt, 10.1 US pt, 4.8 l; 1 Carter Thermoquad downdraught 4-barrel carburettor; dual exhaust system.

TRANSMISSION gearbox: Torqueflite automatic transmission, hydraulic torque converter and planetary gears with 3 ratios, max ratio of converter at stall 2.16, possible manual selection; ratios: I 2.450, II 1.450, III 1, rev 2.200; axle ratio: 2.760; width of rims: 6.5''; tyres: 225 HR x 15.

PERFORMANCE max speed: about 140 mph, 225 km/h; power-weight ratio: 11.5 lb/hp (15.6 lb/kW), 5.2 kg/hp (7.1 kg/kW); speed in direct drive at 1,000 rpm: 23.3 mph, 37.5 km/h; consumption: 15.7 m/imp gal, 13.1 m/US gal, 18 l x 100 km.

ELECTRICAL EQUIPMENT halogen headlamps (standard).

BODY impact-absorbing bumpers; air-conditioning (standard).

OPTIONAL ACCESSORIES 4-speed fully synchronized mechanical gearbox (I 3.163, II 2.214, III 1.412, IV 1, rev 3.346).

TRIUMPH Dolomite 1300

Dolomite 1500 HL

See Dolomite 1500, except for:

PRICE EX WORKS: £ 3,382*

ELECTRICAL EQUIPMENT 4 headlamps.

BODY luxury equipment.

OPTIONAL ACCESSORIES automatic transmission with 3 ratios (I 2.390, II 1.430, III 1, rev 2.100).

Dolomite 1850 HL

See Dolomite 1300, except for:

PRICE EX WORKS: £ 3,772*

ENGINE 4 cylinders, slanted at 45°, in line; 113.2 cu in, 1,854 cc (3.42 x 3.07 in, 87 x 78 mm); compression ratio: 9:1; max power (DIN): 91 hp (67 kW) at 5,200 rpm; max torque (DIN): 105 lb ft, 14.5 kg m (142.2 Nm) at 3,500 rpm; 49.1 hp/l (36.1 kW/l); cast iron block, light alloy head; 5 crankshaft bearings; valves: overhead, in line, thimble tappets; camshafts: 1, overhead; lubricating system: 8 imp pt, 9.5 US pt, 4.5 l; 2 SU type HS6 horizontal carburettors; fuel feed: electric pump; water-cooled, 9.5 imp pt, 11.4 US pt, 5.4 l.

TRANSMISSION gearbox ratios: I 2.646, II 1.779, III 1.254, IV 1, rev 3.011; axle ratio: 3.630; width of rims: 4.5".

PERFORMANCE max speed: 100 mph, 161 km/h; power-weight ratio: 23.4 lb/hp (31.8 lb/kW), 10.6 kg/hp (14.4 kg/kW); speed in direct drive at 1,000 rpm: 18 mph, 29 km/h; consumption: 45 m/imp gal, 37.3 m/US gal, 6.3 l x 100 km at steady 50 mph, 80 km/h.

CHASSIS integral, front subframe; rear suspension: anti-roll bar.

STEERING rack-and-pinion, adjustable steering wheel; turns lock to lock: 3.

BRAKES lining area: front 17.4 sq in, 112 sq cm, rear 38 sq in, 245 sq cm, total 55.4 sq in, 357 sq cm.

ELECTRICAL EQUIPMENT 28 A alternator; AC Delco distributor; 4 headlamps.

DIMENSIONS AND WEIGHT tracks: 53.25 in, 135 cm front, 49.90 in, 127 cm rear; ground clearance: 4.37 in, 11 cm; weight: 2,128 lb, 965 kg.

BODY tinted glass (standard).

PRACTICAL INSTRUCTIONS oil: engine 8 imp pt, 9.5 US pt, 4.5 l, SAE 20W-30, change every 6,000 miles, 9,700 km - gearbox 1.5 imp pt, 1.9 US pt, 0.9 l, SAE 90, change every 6,000 miles, 9,700 km - final drive 1.5 imp pt, 1.9 US pt, 0.9 l, SAE 90, change every 6,000 miles, 9,700 km; greasing: every 6,000 miles, 9,700 km, 3 points; tappet clearances: inlet 0.008-0.010 in, 0.21-0.25 mm, exhaust 0.016-0.018 in, 0.40-0.45 mm; valve timing: 11° 56° 56° 11°; tyre pressure: front 26 psi, 1.8 atm, rear 30 psi, 2.1 atm.

OPTIONAL ACCESSORIES overdrive; automatic transmission.

Dolomite Sprint

See Dolomite 1850 HL, except for:

PRICE EX WORKS: £ 4,643*

ENGINE 121.9 cu in, 1,998 cc (3.56 x 3.07 in, 90.3 x 78 mm); compression ratio: 9.5:1; max power (DIN): 127 hp (93.5 kW) at 5,700 rpm; max torque (DIN): 122 lb ft, 16.9 kg m (165.7 Nm) at 4,500 rpm; max engine rpm: 6,500; 63.6 hp/l (46.8 kW/l); valves: 4 per cylinder.

TRANSMISSION gearbox ratios: I 2.995, II 2.100, III 1.386 (overdrive 1.110), IV 1 (overdrive 0.797), rev 3.370; axle ratio: 3.450; width of rims: 5.5"; tyres: 175/70 HR x 13.

PERFORMANCE max speed: 113 mph, 182 km/h; power-weight ratio: 17.6 lb/hp (23.9 lb/kW), 8 kg/hp (10.9 kg/kW); consumption: 34 m/imp gal, 28.3 m/US gal, 8.3 l x 100 km at steady 50 mph, 80 km/h.

STEERING steering wheel adjustable in height and distance; turns lock to lock: 3.75

BRAKES lining area: front 17.4 sq in, 112 sq cm, rear 49.5 sq in, 319 sq cm, total 66.9 sq in, 431 sq cm.

ELECTRICAL EQUIPMENT 36 A alternator.

DIMENSIONS AND WEIGHT tracks: 53.35 in, 135.5 cm front, 50 in, 127 cm rear; weight: 2,238 lb, 1,015 kg.

BODY vinyl roof; light alloy wheels.

TRIUMPH Dolomite Sprint

TRIUMPH Dolomite Sprint

PRACTICAL INSTRUCTIONS tappet clearances: inlet 0.018 in, 0.45 mm, exhaust 0.018 in, 0.45 mm; valve timing: 10° 50° 50° 10°; tyre pressure: front 22 psi, 1.5 atm, rear 24 psi, 1.7 atm.

OPTIONAL ACCESSORIES limited slip differential; automatic transmission.

Spitfire 1500

PRICE IN USA: $ 4,500*
PRICE EX WORKS: £ 2,383*

ENGINE front, 4 stroke; 4 cylinders, vertical, in line; 91.1 cu in, 1,493 cc (2.90 x 3.44 in, 73.7 x 87.5 mm); compression ratio: 9:1; max power (DIN): 71 hp (52.3 kW) at 5,500 rpm; max torque (DIN): 82 lb ft, 11.3 kg m (110.8 Nm) at 3,000 rpm; max engine rpm: 6,000; 47.6 hp/l (35 kW/l); cast iron block and head; 3 crankshaft bearings; valves: overhead, in line, push-rods and rockers; camshafts: 1, side; lubrication: rotary pump, full flow filter, 8 imp pt, 9.5 US pt, 4.5 l; 2 SU type HS4 horizontal carburettors; fuel feed: mechanical pump; sealed circuit cooling, liquid, 8 imp pt, 9.5 US pt, 4.5 l, viscous coupling thermostatic fan.

TRANSMISSION driving wheels: rear; clutch: single dry plate (diaphragm), hydraulically controlled; gearbox: mechanical; gears: 4, fully synchronized; ratios: I 3.500, II 2.160, III 1.390, IV 1, rev 3.990; lever: central; final drive: hypoid bevel; axle ratio: 3.630; width of rims: 4.5"; tyres: 155 SR x 13.

TRIUMPH Spitfire 1500

TRIUMPH TR 7

PERFORMANCE max speeds: (I) 28 mph, 45 km/h; (II) 45 mph, 73 km/h; (III) 71 mph, 114 km/h; (IV) 100 mph, 161 km/h; power-weight ratio: 26.1 lb/hp (35.4 lb/kW), 11.8 kg/hp (16.1 kg/kW); carrying capacity: 432 lb, 196 kg; speed in direct drive at 1,000 rpm: 18 mph, 29 km/h; consumption: 43.5 m/imp gal, 36.2 m/US gal, 6.5 l x 100 km at 50 mph, 80 km/h.

CHASSIS double backbone, channel section with outriggers; front suspension: independent, wishbones, coil springs, anti-roll bar; rear: independent, swinging semi-axles, transverse leafspring swinging longitudinal trailing arms, telescopic dampers.

STEERING rack-and-pinion; turns lock to lock: 3.75.

BRAKES front disc (diameter 9 in, 22.9 cm), rear drum; lining area: front 14.7 sq in, 95 sq cm, rear 34.1 sq in, 220 sq cm, total 48.8 sq in, 315 sq cm.

ELECTRICAL EQUIPMENT 12 V; 40 Ah battery; 34 A alternator; Delco distributor; 2 headlamps.

DIMENSIONS AND WEIGHT wheel base: 83 in, 211 cm; tracks: 49 in, 124 cm front, 50 in, 127 cm rear; length: 149 in, 378 cm; width: 58.58 in, 149 cm; height: 45.80 in, 116 cm; ground clearance: 5 in, 12.7 cm; weight: 1,852 lb, 840 kg; weight distribution: 56% front, 44% rear; turning circle (between walls): 23.9 ft, 7.3 m; fuel tank: 7.2 imp gal, 8.7 US gal, 33 l.

BODY convertible; 2 doors; 2 seats; built-in headrests; laminated windscreen.

PRACTICAL INSTRUCTIONS fuel: 97-100 oct petrol; oil: engine 7 imp pt, 8.5 US pt, 4 l, SAE 20, change every 6,000 miles, 9,700 km - gearbox 1.5 imp pt, 1.9 US pt, 0.9 l, SAE 90 - final drive 1.1 imp pt, 1.3 US pt, 0.6 l, SAE 90; greasing: every 6,000 miles, 9,700 km, 3 points, every 12,000 miles, 19,300 km, 2 points; tappet clearances: inlet 0.010 in, 0.25 mm, exhaust 0.010 in, 0.25 mm; valve timing: 18° 58° 58° 18°; tyre pressure: front 21 pi, 1.5 atm, rear 26 psi, 1.8 atm.

VARIATIONS

(optional for USA only).
ENGINE 8:1 compression ratio, max power (DIN) 58 hp (42.7 kW) at 5,000 rpm, max torque (DIN) 73 lb ft, 10.1 kg m (99.1 Nm) at 3,000 rpm, 38.8 hp/l (28.6 kW/l).
PERFORMANCE power-weight ratio 31.9 lb/hp (43.4 lb/kW), 14.5 kg/hp (19.7 kg/kW).
PRACTICAL INSTRUCTIONS 94 oct petrol.

OPTIONAL ACCESSORIES Laycock-de Normanville overdrive on III and IV, 0.797 ratio; hardtop.

TR 7

PRICE IN USA: $ 5,849*
PRICE EX WORKS: £ 3,371*

ENGINE front, slanted at 45°, 4 stroke; 4 cylinders, vertical, in line; 121.9 cu in, 1,998 cc (3.56 x 3.07 in, 90.3 x 78 mm); compression ratio: 9.25:1; max power (DIN): 105 hp (77.3 kW) at 5,500 rpm; max torque (DIN): 119 lb ft, 16.4 kg m (160.8 Nm) at 3,500 rpm; max engine rpm: 6,000; 52.6 hp/l

(38.7 kW/l); cast iron block, light alloy head; 5 crankshaft bearings; valves: overhead, in line, thimble tappets; camshafts: 1, overhead; lubrication: rotary pump, full flow filter, 8 imp pt, 9.5 US pt, 4.5 l; 2 SU type HS6 carburettors; fuel feed: electric pump; water-cooled, 12.8 imp pt, 15.4 US pt, 7.3 l.

TRANSMISSION driving wheels: rear; clutch: single dry plate (diaphragm), hydraulically controlled; gearbox: mechanical; gears: 4, fully synchronized; ratios: I 2.646, II 1.779, III 1.254, IV 1, rev 3.050; lever: central; final drive: hypoid bevel; axle ratio: 3.630; width of rims: 5.5''; tyres: 175/70 SR x 13.

PERFORMANCE max speed: 109 mph, 175 km/h; power-weight ratio: 20.5 lb/hp (27.8 lb/kW), 9.3 kg/hp (12.6 kg/kW); consumption: 26.4 m/imp gal, 22 m/US gal, 10.7 l x 100 km.

CHASSIS integral, front subframe; front suspension: independent, by McPherson, coil springs/telescopic damper struts, lower wishbones (leading arm), anti-roll bar; rear: rigid axle, lower trailing arms, upper oblique torque arms, coil springs, anti-roll bar, telescopic dampers.

STEERING rack-and-pinion; turns lock to lock: 3.87.

BRAKES front disc (diameter 9.75 in, 24.8 cm), rear drum, servo; swept area: front 183.5 sq in, 1,183 sq cm, rear 75.4 sq in, 487 sq cm, total 258.9 sq in, 1,670 sq cm.

ELECTRICAL EQUIPMENT 12 V; 40 Ah battery; 36 A alternator; Lucas electronic ignition; 2 retractable headlamps.

DIMENSIONS AND WEIGHT wheel base: 85.04 in, 216 cm; tracks: 55.47 in, 141 cm front, 55.28 in, 140 cm rear; length: 160 in, 406 cm; width: 66.20 in, 168 cm; height: 49.40 in, 125 cm; ground clearance: 4.50 in, 11.4 cm; weight: 2,148 lb, 974 kg; weight distribution: 53% front, 47% rear; turning circle (between walls): 29 ft, 8.8 m; fuel tank: 14.5 imp gal, 17.4 US gal, 66 l.

BODY coupé; 2 doors; 2 seats; reclining backrests with built-in headrests; laminated windscreen; heated rear window.

PRACTICAL INSTRUCTIONS fuel: 97 oct petrol; oil: engine 8 imp pt, 9.5 US pt, 4.5 l, SAE 20W-30, change every 6,000 miles, 9,700 km - gearbox 2.1 imp pt, 2.5 US pt, 1.2 l, SAE 90, no change recommended - final drive 2.2 imp pt, 2.7 US pt, 1.3 l, SAE 90, no change recommended; greasing: none; tappet clearances: inlet 0.008 in, 0,20 mm, exhaust 0.008 in, 0.20 mm; valve timing: 16° 56° 56° 16°; tyre pressure: front 24 psi, 1.7 atm, rear 28 psi, 2 atm.

OPTIONAL ACCESSORIES oil cooler; Borg-Warner automatic transmission, hydraulic torque converter and planetary gears with 3 ratios (I 2.390, II 1.450, III 1, rev 2.090), max ratio of converter at stall 1.9, possible manual selection, 3.270 axle ratio; 5-speed fully synchronized mechanical gearbox with 185 HR x 13 tyres and medium duty axle ratio; sunshine roof.

TVR   **GREAT BRITAIN**

3000 M

PRICE EX WORKS: £ 5,131*

ENGINE Ford, front, 4 stroke; 6 cylinders, Vee-slanted at 60°; 182.7 cu in, 2,994 cc (3.70 x 2.85 in, 94 x 72.4 mm); compression ratio: 8.9:1; max power (DIN): 142 hp (104.5 kW) at 5,000 rpm; max torque (DIN): 172 lb ft, 23.7 kg m (232.4 Nm) at 3,000 rpm; max engine rpm: 6,000; 47.4 hp/l (34.9 kW/l); cast iron block and head; 4 crankshaft bearings; valves: overhead, in line, push-rods and rockers; camshafts: 1, at centre of Vee; lubrication: eccentric pump, full flow filter, 9.8 imp pt, 11.6 US pt, 5.5 l; 1 Weber 40 DFA-1 downdraught twin barrel carburettor; fuel feed: mechanical pump; water-cooled, 19.9 imp pt, 23.9 US pt, 11.3 l, thermostatically-controlled electric fan.

TRANSMISSION driving wheels: rear; clutch: single dry plate (diaphragm), hydraulically-controlled; gearbox: mechanical; gears: 4, fully synchronized; ratios: I 3.163, II 1.950, III 1.412, IV 1, rev 3.346; lever: central; final drive: hypoid bevel; axle ratio: 3.450; width of rims: 6''; tyres: 185 HR x 14.

PERFORMANCE max speeds: (I) 41 mph, 66 km/h; (II) 66 mph, 106 km/h; (III) 91 mph, 146 km/h; (IV) 130 mph, 209 km/h; power-weight ratio: 15.5 lb/hp (21 lb/kW), 7 kg/hp (9.6 kg/kW); carrying capacity: 620 lb, 281 kg; acceleration: standing ¼ mile 16 sec, 0-50 mph (0-80 km/h) 5.6 sec; speed in direct drive at 1,000 rpm: 21.6 mph, 34.7 km/h; consumption: 22 m/imp gal, 18.4 m/US gal, 12.8 l x 100 km.

TVR Turbo

3000 M

CHASSIS multi-tubular backbone with outriggers; front suspension: independet, wishbones, coil springs, anti-roll bar, telescopic dampers; rear: independent, wishbones, coil springs, anti-roll bar, 4 telescopic dampers.

STEERING rack-and-pinion.

BRAKES front disc (diameter 10.87 in, 27.6 cm), rear drum, servo; swept area: front 233 sq in, 1,503 sq cm, rear 99 sq in, 639 sq cm, total 332 sq in, 2,142 sq cm.

ELECTRICAL EQUIPMENT 12 V; 58 Ah battery; 34 A alternator; 2 headlamps.

DIMENSIONS AND WEIGHT wheel base: 90 in, 229 cm; front and rear tracks: 53.75 in, 136 cm; length: 155.12 in, 394 cm; width: 63.78 in, 162 cm; height: 44.88 in, 114 cm; ground clearance: 5 in, 12.7 cm; weight: 2,200 lb, 998 kg; turning circle (between walls): 35.7 ft, 10.9 m; fuel tank: 12 imp gal, 14.5 US gal, 55 l.

BODY coupé, in plastic material; 2 doors; 2 seats, reclining backrests with built-in headrests; laminated windows; heated rear window; aluminium alloy wheels.

PRACTICAL INSTRUCTIONS fuel: 98 oct petrol; oil: engine 9.8 imp pt, 11.6 US pt, 5.5 l, SAE 20W-50, change every 6,000 miles, 9,700 km - gearbox 2.5 imp pt, 3 US pt, 1.4 l, SAE 90, change every 6,000 miles, 9,700 km - final drive 2 imp pt, 2.5 US pt, 1.2 l, SAE 90, change every 6,000 miles, 9,700 km; greasing: every 6,000 miles, 9,700 km, 10 points; tappet clearances: inlet 0.013 in, 0.32 mm, exhaust 0.020 in, 0.50 mm; valve timing: 29° 67° 70° 14°; tyre pressure: front 22 psi, 1.6 atm, rear 24 psi, 1.7 atm.

OPTIONAL ACCESSORIES Laycock-de Normanville overdrive on III (1.160 ratio) and IV (0.821 ratio); electric windows; halogen headlamps; sunshine roof; vinyl roof; leather upholstery; light alloy wheels.

Turbo

See 3000 M, except for:

PRICE EX WORKS: £ 8,150*

ENGINE with Holset 3LD turbocharger; compression ratio: 8:1; max power (DIN): 230 hp (169.3 kW) at 5,500 rpm; max torque (DIN): 273 lb ft, 37.7 kg m (369.7 Nm) at 3,500 rpm; max engine 76.8 hp/l (56.5 kW/l).

TRANSMISSION final drive: limited slip differential; tyres: 195 VR x 14.

PERFORMANCE max speeds: (I) 45 mph, 72 km/h; (II) 72 mph, 116 km/h; (III) 105 mph, 169 km/h; (IV) 140 mph, 225 km/h; power-weight ratio: 10.1 lb/hp (13.8 lb/kW), 4.6 kg/hp (6.2 kg/kW); speed in direct drive at 1,000 rpm: 25 mph, 40.2 km/h.

DIMENSIONS AND WEIGHT weight: 2,333 lb, 1,058 kg.

OPTIONAL ACCESSORIES Laycock-de Normanville overdrive not available.

TVR Taimar Turbo

Taimar

See 3000 M, except for:

PRICE EX WORKS: £ 5,814*

PERFORMANCE power-weight ratio: 16.1 lb/hp (21.9 lb/kW), 7.3 kg/hp (9.9 kg/kW).

DIMENSIONS AND WEIGHT weight: 2,293 lb, 1,040 kg.

BODY hatchback coupé; 2 + 1 doors.

Taimar Turbo

See Taimar, except for:

PRICE EX WORKS: £ 8,832*

ENGINE with Holset 3LD turbocharger; compression ratio: 8:1; max power (DIN): 230 hp (169.3 kW) at 5,500 rpm; max torque (DIN): 273 lb ft, 37.7 kg m (369.7 Nm) at 3,500 rpm; 76.8 hp/l (56.5 kW/l).

TRANSMISSION final drive: limited slip differential; tyres: 195 VR x 14.

PERFORMANCE max speeds: (I) 45 mph, 72 km/h; (II) 72 mph, 116 km/h; (III) 105 mph, 169 km/h; (IV) 140 mph, 225 km/h; power-weight ratio: 10.5 lb/hp (14.3 lb/kW), 4.8 kg/hp (6.5 kg/kW); speed in direct drive at 1,000 rpm: 25 mph, 40.2 km/h.

DIMENSIONS AND WEIGHT weight: 2,426 lb, 1,100 kg.

VANDEN PLAS

1500

PRICE EX WORKS: £ 3,510*

ENGINE front, transverse, in unit with gearbox and final drive, 4 stroke; 4 cylinders, vertical, in line; 90.6 cu in, 1,485 cc (3 x 3.20 in, 76.2 x 81.3 mm); compression ratio: 9:1; max power (DIN): 68 hp (50 kW) at 5,500 rpm; max torque (DIN): 80 lb ft, 11.1 kg m (108.9 Nm) at 2,900 rpm; max engine rpm: 5,900; 45.8 hp/l (33.7 kW/l); cast iron block and head; 5 crankshaft bearings; valves: overhead, Vee-slanted, thimble tappets; camshafts: 1, overhead, chain-driven; lubrication: mechanical pump, full flow filter (cartridge), 9.7 imp pt, 11.6 US pt, 5.5 l; 1 SU type HS6 single barrel carburettor; fuel feed: mechanical pump; sealed circuit cooling, liquid, expansion tank, 11.5 imp pt, 13.7 US pt, 6.5 l, electric thermostatic fan.

TRANSMISSION driving wheels: front; clutch: single dry plate (diaphragm); gearbox: mechanical; gears: 5, fully synchronized; ratios: I 3.202, II 2.004, III 1.372, IV 1, V 0.869, rev 3.467; lever: central; final drive: helical spur gears; axle ratio: 3.647; width of rims: 4''; tyres 155 SR x 13.

PERFORMANCE max speeds: (I) 33 mph, 53 km/h; (II) 54 mph, 87 km/h; (III) 78 mph, 125 km/h; (IV) 92 mph, 148 km/h; (V) 90 mph, 145 km/h; power-weight ratio: 29.2 lb/hp (39.7 lb/kW), 13.2 kg/hp (18 kg/kW); carrying capacity: 710 lb, 320 kg; acceleration: standing ¼ mile 20.2 sec, 0-50 mph (0-80 km/h) 10.4 sec; speed in top at 1,000 rpm: 20.1 mph, 32.3 km/h; consumption: 28.2 m/imp gal, 23.5 m/US gal, 10 l x 100 km.

CHASSIS integral; front suspension: independent, wishbones, hydragas (liquid and gas) rubber cone springs, hydraulic connecting pipes to rear wheels; rear: independent, swinging longitudinal trailing arms, hydragas (liquid and gas) rubber cone springs, hydraulic connecting pipes to front wheels.

STEERING rack-and-pinion; turns lock to lock: 3.50.

BRAKES front disc (diameter 9.68 in, 24.6 cm), rear drum, servo; swept area: front 178 sq in, 1,148 sq cm, rear 75.6 sq in, 487 sq cm, total 253.6 sq in, 1,635 sq cm.

ELECTRICAL EQUIPMENT 12 V; 40 Ah battery; 34 A alternator; Lucas distributor; 4 headlamps (2 fog lamps).

DIMENSIONS AND WEIGHT wheel base: 96.14 in, 244 cm; tracks: 54.33 in, 138 cm front, 54.41 in, 138 cm rear; length: 154.25 in, 392 cm; width: 63.52 in, 161 cm; height: 54.75 in, 139 cm; ground clearance: 7.48 in, 19 cm; weight: 1,984 lb, 900 kg; turning circle (between walls): 33.2 ft, 10.1 m; fuel tank: 10.5 imp gal, 12.7 US gal, 48 l.

BODY saloon/sedan; 4 doors; 4-5 seats, separate front seats, reclining backrests; picnic tables behind front seats; heated rear window.

PRACTICAL INSTRUCTIONS fuel: 97 oct petrol; oil: engine, gearbox and final drive 9.7 imp pt, 11.6 US pt, 5.5 l, SAE 20W-50, change every 6,000 miles, 9,700 km; greasing: every 6,000 miles, 9,700 km, 4 points; tappet clearances: inlet 0.012-0.018 in, 0.30-0.45 mm, exhaust 0.012-0.022 in, 0.30-0.55 mm; valve timing: 9° 51° 49° 11°; tyre pressure: front 26 psi, 1.8 atm, rear 24 psi, 1.7 atm.

OPTIONAL ACCESSORIES headrests; automatic transmission with 4 ratios (I 2.612, II 1.807, III 1.446, IV 1, rev 2.612), 3.800 axle ratio; metallic spray.

VANDEN PLAS 1500

VAUXHALL   GREAT BRITAIN

Chevette Series

PRICES EX WORKS:

Chevette E 2-door Saloon	£ 2,110*
Chevette E 4-door Saloon	£ 2,238*
Chevette E 3-door Hatchback	£ 2,182*
Chevette L 2-door Saloon	£ 2,359*
Chevette L 4-door Saloon	£ 2,452*
Chevette L 3-door Hatchback	£ 2,396*
Chevette L Estate Car	£ 2,641*
Chevette GL 3-door Hatchback	£ 2,526*
Chevette GLS 4-door Saloon	£ 2,781*
Chevette GLS 3-door Hatchback	£ 2,725*

57.7 hp power team

ENGINE front, 4 stroke; 4 cylinders, vertical, in line; 76.6 cu in, 1,256 cc (3.19 x 2.40 in, 81 x 61 mm); compression ratio: 9.2:1; (7.3:1 only for export); max power (DIN): 57.7 hp (42.7 kW) at 5,600 rpm; max torque (DIN): 66.5 lb ft, 9.1 kg m (89.2 Nm) at 2,600 rpm; max engine rpm: 6,000; 45.9 hp/l (34 kW/l); chromium cast iron block and head; 3 crankshaft bearings; valves: overhead, in line, push-rods and rockers; camshafts: 1, side; lubrication: gear pump, full flow filter, 5.5 imp pt, 6.6 US pt, 3.1 l; 1 Zenith-Stromberg 150 CDS downdraught single barrel carburettor; fuel feed: mechanical pump; water-cooled, 10.2 imp pt, 12.3 US pt, 5.8 l, viscous coupling fan.

TRANSMISSION driving wheels: rear; clutch: single dry plate (diaphragm); gearbox: mechanical; gears: 4, fully synchronized; ratios: I 3.460, II 2.213, III 1.404, IV 1, rev 3.707; lever: central; final drive: hypoid bevel; axle ratio: 4.111; width of rims: 5''; tyres: 5.60 x 13 - L and GL models 155 SR x 13 - GLS 175 SR x 13.

PERFORMANCE max speeds: (I) 31 mph, 50 km/h; (II) 49 mph, 79 km/h; (III) 77 mph, 124 km/h; (IV) 91 mph, 146 km/h; power-weight ratio: E 4-dr. Saloon 32.7 lb/hp (44.1 lb/kW), 14.8 kg/hp (20 kg/kW) - L 4-dr. Saloon 33 lb/hp (44.6 lb/kW), 15 kg/hp (20.2 kg/kW) - GLS 4-dr. Saloon 33.4 lb/hp (45.2 lb/kW), 15.2 kg/hp (20.5 kg/kW); carrying capacity: 906 lb, 411 kg; acceleration: standing ¼ mile 19.6 sec, 0-50 mph (0-80 km/h) 14.5 sec; speed in direct drive at 1,000 rpm: 15.9 mph, 25.6 km/h; consumption: 30.3 m/imp gal, 25.3 m/US gal, 9.3 l x 100 km.

CHASSIS integral; front suspension: independent, wishbones, coil springs, anti-roll bar, telescopic dampers; rear: rigid axle (torque tube), longitudinal trailing radius arms, coil springs, Panhard rod, anti-roll bar, telescopic dampers.

STEERING rack-and-pinion; turns lock to lock: 3.50.

BRAKES front disc (diameter 9.37 in, 23.8 cm), self-adjusting rear drum, rear compensator, servo; swept area: front 157.5 sq in, 1,016 sq cm, rear 73.8 sq in, 476 sq cm, total 231.3 sq in, 1,492 sq cm.

ELECTRICAL EQUIPMENT 12 V; 40 Ah battery; 444 W alternator; AC Delco distributor; 2 headlamps.

DIMENSIONS AND WEIGHT wheel base: 94.30 in, 239 cm; front and rear tracks: 51.20 in, 130 cm; length: 164.40 in, 417 cm - hatchbacks 155.20 in, 394 cm; width: 61.80 in, 157 cm - hatchbacks 62.20 in, 158 cm; height: saloons 51.70 in, 131 cm - Estate Car 52.10 in, 132 cm - hatchbacks 51.90 in, 132 cm; ground clearance: 4.70 in, 11.9 cm; weight: E 2-dr. Saloon 1,821 lb, 826 kg - E 4-dr. Saloon 1,885 lb, 855 kg - E Hatchback 1,865 lb, 846 kg - L 2-dr. Saloon 1,841 lb, 835 kg - L 4-dr. Saloon 1,903 lb, 863 kg - L Hatchback 1,885 lb, 855 kg - L Estate Car 1,951 lb, 885 kg - GL Hatchback 1,916 lb, 869 kg - GLS 4-dr. Saloon 1,929 lb, 875 kg - GLS Hatchback 1,960 lb, 889 kg; turning circle (between walls): 30.2 ft, 9.2 m; fuel tank: saloons 9.9 imp gal, 11.9 US gal, 45 l - Estate Car 9.5 imp gal, 11.4 US gal, 43 l - hatchbacks 8.4 imp gal, 10 US gal, 38 l.

BODY 5 seats, separate front seats.

PRACTICAL INSTRUCTIONS fuel: 98 oct petrol; oil: engine 4.9 imp pt, 5.9 US pt, 2.8 l, SAE 10W-30, change every 6,000 miles, 9,700 km - gearbox 0.9 imp pt, 1.1 US pt, 0.5 l, SAE 90, change every 6 months - final drive 1.2 imp pt, 1.5 US pt, 0.7 l, SAE 90, no change recommended; greasing: every 6 months, 4 points; tappet clearances: inlet 0.008 in, 0.20 mm, exhaust 0.008 in, 0.20 mm; valve timing: 39° 73° 71° 41°; tyre pressure: front 21 psi, 1.5 atm, rear 24 psi, 1.7 atm.

OPTIONAL ACCESSORIES headrests; metallic spray except for E models.

Viva Series

PRICES EX WORKS:

1	Viva E 2-door Saloon	£ 2,197*
2	Viva E 4-door Saloon	£ 2,291*
3	Viva 1300 L 2-door Saloon	£ 2,411*
4	Viva 1300 L 4-door Saloon	£ 2,505*
5	Viva 1300 L Estate Car	£ 2,693*
6	Viva 1300 GLS 2-door Saloon	£ 2,740*
7	Viva 1300 GLS 4-door Saloon	£ 2,834*
8	Viva 1300 GLS Estate Car	£ 3,022*
9	Viva 1800 L 2-door Saloon	£ 2,565*
10	Viva 1800 L 4-door Saloon	£ 2,658*
11	Viva 1800 L Estate Car	£ 2,847*

Power team:	Standard for:	Optional for:
57.7 hp	1 to 8	—
88 hp	9 to 11	—

57.7 hp power team

ENGINE front, 4 stroke; 4 cylinders, vertical, in line; 76.6 cu in, 1,256 cc (3.19 x 2.40 in, 81 x 61 mm); compression ratio: 9.2:1 (7.3:1 only for export); max power (DIN): 57.7 hp (42.7 kW) at 5,600 rpm; max torque (DIN): 66.5 lb ft, 9.1 kg m (89.2 Nm) at 2,600 rpm; max engine rpm: 6,000; 45.9 hp/l (34 kW/l); chromium cast iron block and head; 3 crankshaft bearings; valves: overhead, in line, push-rods and rockers; camshafts: 1, side; lubrication: gear pump, full flow filter, 5.5 imp pt, 6.6 US pt, 3.1 l; 1 Zenith-Stromberg 150 CDS downdraught single barrel carburettor; fuel feed: mechanical pump; water-cooled, 10.2 imp pt, 12.3 US pt, 5.8 l, viscous coupling fan.

TRANSMISSION driving wheels: rear; clutch: single dry plate (diaphragm); gearbox: mechanical; gears: 4, fully synchronized; ratios: I 3.460, II 2.213, III 1.404, IV 1, rev 3.707; lever: central; final drive: hypoid bevel; axle ratio: 4.125; width of rims: 4.5'' - GLS 5''; tyres: 5.60 x 13 - Viva 1300 L and Viva 1300 GLS models 155 SR x 13.

PERFORMANCE max speeds: (I) 27 mph, 43 km/h; (II) 43 mph, 70 km/h; (III) 74 mph, 119 km/h; (IV) 82 mph, 132 km/h; power-weight ratio: Viva 1300 L 4-dr. Saloon 34 lb/hp (46 lb/kW), 15.4 kg/hp (21 kg/kW) - 1300 GLS 4-dr. Saloon 34.8 lb/hp (47 lb/kW), 15.8 kg/hp (21.3 kg/kW); speed in direct drive at 1,000 rpm: 16.1 mph, 25.9 km/h; consumption: 33 m/imp gal, 27.7 m/US gal, 8.5 l x 100 km.

CHASSIS integral; front suspension: independent, wishbones, coil springs, telescopic dampers; rear: rigid axle, trailing lower radius arms, upper oblique radius arms, coil springs, telescopic dampers.

STEERING rack-and-pinion; turns lock to lock: 3.16.

BRAKES front disc (diameter 8.50 in, 33.5 cm), self-adjusting rear drum, servo; swept area: front 154.6 sq in, 997

VAUXHALL Chevette GL Hatchback

VAUXHALL Chevette L Estate Car

57.7 HP POWER TEAM

sq cm, rear 62.9 sq in, 405 sq cm, total 217.5 sq in, 1,402 sq cm.

ELECTRICAL EQUIPMENT 12 V; 33 Ah battery; 336 W alternator; AC Delco distributor; 2 headlamps (4 on GLS models).

DIMENSIONS AND WEIGHT wheel base: 97 in, 246 cm; tracks: 51.80 in, 13.2 cm front, 51.50 in, 131 cm rear; length: 162.90 in, 414 cm; width: 64.70 in, 164 cm; height: 53.20 in, 135 cm; ground clearance: 5.40 in, 13.7 cm; weight: E 2-dr. and 1300 L 2-dr. 1,927 lb, 828 kg - E 4-dr. 1,951 lb, 885 kg - 1300 L Estate Car 1,964 lb, 891 kg - 1300 L 4-dr. 1,964 lb, 891 kg - 1300 L Estate Car 2,030 lb, 920 kg - 1300 GLS 2-dr. 1,969 lb, 893 kg - 1300 GLS 4-dr. 2,006 lb, 910 kg - 1300 GLS Estate Car 2,072 lb, 940 kg; turning circle (between walls): 32.2 ft, 9.8 m; fuel tank: 8 imp gal, 9.5 US gal, 36 l.

BODY 4-5 seats, separate front seats, reclining backrests; heated rear window (except for Viva E models); luxury equipment (only for GLS models).

PRACTICAL INSTRUCTIONS fuel: 98 oct petrol; oil: engine 4.9 imp pt, 5.9 US pt, 2.8 l, SAE 10W-30, change every 6,000 miles, 9,700 km - gearbox 0.9 imp pt, 1.1 US pt. 0.5 l, SAE 90, change every 6 months - final drive 1.2 imp pt, 1.5 US pt, 0.7 l, SAE 90, no change recommended; greasing: every 6 months, 4 points; tappet clearances: inlet 0.008 in, 0.20 mm, exhaust 0.008 in, 0.20 mm; valve timing: 39° 73° 71° 41°; tyre pressure: front 24 psi, 1.7 atm, rear 24 psi, 1.7 atm.

OPTIONAL ACCESSORIES 155 SR x 13 tyres and heated rear window (only for Viva E); metallic spray (except for Viva E); vinyl roof (only for GLS saloons).

88 hp power team

See 57.7 hp power team, except for:

ENGINE 107.3 cu in, 1,759 cc (3.37 x 3 in, 85.7 x 76.1 mm); compression ratio: 8.5:1; max power (DIN): 88 hp (64.8 kW) at 5,800 rpm; max torque (DIN): 99 lb ft, 13.7 kg m (134.4 Nm) at 3,500 rpm; max engine rpm: 6,250; 50 hp/l (36.8 kW/l); 5 crankshaft bearings; valves: overhead, in line; camshafts: 1, overhead, cogged belt; lubricating system: 8.5 imp pt, 10.1 US pt, 4.8 l; 1 Zenith 36 IV downdraught single barrel carburettor; cooling system: 14 imp pt, 16.9 US pt, 8 l.

TRANSMISSION gearbox ratios: I 3.300, II 2.145, III 1.414, IV 1, rev 3.063; axle ratio: 3.727.

PERFORMANCE max speed: 93 mph, 149 km/h; power-weight ratio: 1800 L 4-dr. Saloon 25.3 lb/hp (34.4 lb/kW), 11.5 kg/hp (15.6 kg/kW); speed in direct drive at 1,000 rpm: 17.8 mph, 28.6 km/h; consumption: 26.2 m/imp gal, 21.8 m/US gal, 10.8 l x 100 km.

CHASSIS front suspension: anti-roll bar.

BRAKES front disc (diameter 10.03 in, 25.5 cm).

VAUXHALL Viva 1300 GLS 4-door Saloon

DIMENSIONS AND WEIGHT weight: 1800 L 2-dr. 2,193 lb, 994 kg - 1800 L 4-dr. 2,229 lb, 1,011 kg - 1800 L Estate Car 2,299 lb, 1,042 kg; fuel tank: 12 imp gal, 14.5 US gal, 55 l.

PRACTICAL INSTRUCTIONS oil: engine 8 imp pt, 9.5 US pt, 4.5 l; tappet clearances: inlet 0.005-0.010 in, 0.12-0.25 mm, exhaust 0.015-0.018 in, 0.37-0.45 mm; valve timing: 33°26' 65°26' 65°26' 33°26'.

OPTIONAL ACCESSORIES G.M. automatic transmission, hydraulic torque converter and planetary gears with 3 ratios (I 2.390, II 1.480, III 1, rev 1.920), max ratio of converter at stall 2, possible manual selection.

Magnum Series

PRICES EX WORKS:

1 Magnum 1800 2-door Saloon	£	2,893*
2 Magnum 1800 4-door Saloon	£	2,987*
3 Magnum 1800 Estate Car	£	3,175*
4 Magnum 2300 2-door Saloon	£	3,047*
5 Magnum 2300 4-door Saloon	£	3,140*
6 Magnum 2300 Estate Car	£	3,329*

Power team:	Standard for:	Optional for:
88 hp	1 to 3	—
108 hp	4 to 6	—

88 hp power team

ENGINE front, 4 stroke; 4 cylinders, in line, slanted at 45°; 107.3 cu in, 1,759 cc (3.37 x 3 in, 85.7 x 76.1 mm); compression ratio: 8.5:1; max power (DIN): 88 hp (64.8 kW) at 5,800 rpm; max torque (DIN): 99 lb ft, 13.7 kg m (134.4 Nm) at 3,500 rpm; max engine rpm: 6,250; 50 hp/l (36.8 kW/l); chromium cast iron block and head; 5 crankshaft bearings; valves: overhead, in line; camshafts: 1, overhead, cogged belt; lubrication: gear pump, full flow filter, 8.5 imp pt, 10.1 US pt, 4.8 l; 1 Zenith-Stromberg 175 single barrel carburettor; fuel feed: mechanical pump; water-cooled, 14 imp pt, 16.9 US pt, 8 l, viscous coupling fan.

TRANSMISSION driving wheels: rear; clutch: single dry plate (diaphragm); gearbox: mechanical; gears: 4, fully synchronized; ratios: I 3.300, II 2.145, III 1.414, IV 1, rev 3.063; lever: central; final drive: hypoid bevel; axle ratio: 3.727; width of rims: 5''; tyres: 175 SR x 13.

PERFORMANCE max speed: 94 mph, 151 km/h; power-weight ratio: 4-dr. Saloon 25.8 lb/hp (35.1 lb/kW), 11.7 kg/hp (15.9 kg/kW); speed in direct drive at 1,000 rpm: 17.8 mph, 28.6 km/h; consumption: 26.2 m/imp gal, 21.8 m/US gal, 10.8 l x 100 km.

CHASSIS integral; front suspension: independent, wishbones, coil springs, anti-roll bar, telescopic dampers; rear: rigid axle, trailing lower radius arms, upper oblique radius arms, coil springs, anti-roll bar (except for Estate Car), telescopic dampers.

STEERING rack-and-pinion; turns lock to lock: 3.16.

BRAKES front disc (diameter 10.03 in, 25.5 cm), self-adjusting rear drum, servo; swept area: front 197 sq in, 1,271 sq cm, rear 99 sq in, 638 sq cm, total 296 sq in, 1,909 sq cm.

ELECTRICAL EQUIPMENT 12 V; 39 Ah battery; 336 W alternator; AC Delco distributor; 4 halogen headlamps.

DIMENSIONS AND WEIGHT wheel base: 97 in, 246 cm; tracks: 52.30 in, 133 cm front, 52 in, 132 cm rear; length: 163.50 in, 420 cm; width: 64.70 in, 164 cm; height: 52.60 in, 134 cm; ground clearance: 5.40 in, 13.7 cm; weight: 2-dr. Saloon 2,238 lb, 1,015 kg - 4-dr. Saloon 2,273 lb, 1,031 kg - Estate Car 2,343 lb, 1,062 kg; turning circle (between walls): 34.1 ft, 10.4 m; fuel tank: 12 imp gal, 14.3 US gal, 54 l.

BODY 4-5 seats, separate front seats, reclining backrests; heated rear window; luxury equipment.

PRACTICAL INSTRUCTIONS fuel: 98 oct petrol; oil: engine 8 imp pt, 9.5 US pt, 4.5 l, SAE 10W-40, change every 6,000 miles, 9,700 km - gearbox and final drive 2.5 imp pt, 3 US pt, 1.4 l, SAE 90 EP, no change recommended; greasing: every 6 months, 4 points; tappet clearances: inlet 0.007-0.010 in, 0.18-0.25 mm, exhaust 0.015-0.018 in, 0.32-0.46 mm; valve timing: 31°36' 63°36' 63°36' 31°36'; tyre pressure: front 24 psi, 1.7 atm, rear 24 psi, 1.7 atm.

OPTIONAL ACCESSORIES G.M. automatic transmission, hydraulic torque converter and planetary gears with 3 ratios (I 2.390, II 1.480, III 1, rev 1.920), max ratio of converter at stall 2, possible manual selection; vinyl roof (except for Estate Car).

VAUXHALL Magnum 2300 2-door Saloon

108 hp power team

See 88 hp power team, except for:

ENGINE 139.1 cu in, 2,279 cc (3.84 x 3 in, 97.5 x 76.2 mm); max power (DIN): 108 hp (79.5 kW) at 5,000 rpm; max torque (DIN): 138 lb ft, 19 kg m (186.61 Nm) at 3,000 rpm; max engine rpm: 5,500; 47.4 hp/l (34.9 kW/l); 1 Zenith-Stromberg 175 CD downdraught carburettor.

TRANSMISSION axle ratio: 3.455.

PERFORMANCE max speed: 103 mph, 165 km/h; power-weight ratio: 4-dr. Saloon 21.3 lb/hp (29 lb/kW), 9.7 kg/hp (13.1 kg/kW); speed in direct drive at 1,000 rpm: 18.9 mph, 30.4 km/h; consumption: 25.3 m/imp gal, 21 m/US gal, 11.2 l x 100 km.

DIMENSIONS AND WEIGHT weight 2-dr. Saloon 2,269 lb, 1,029 kg - 4-dr. Saloon 2,304 lb, 1,045 kg - Estate Car 2,374 lb, 1,076 kg.

Cavalier Series

PRICES EX WORKS:

1 Cavalier 1300 L 2-door Saloon	£	2,746*
2 Cavalier 1300 L 4-door Saloon	£	2,840*
3 Cavalier 1600 L 4-door Saloon	£	2,899*
4 Cavalier 1600 L 4-door Saloon	£	2,993*
5 Cavalier 1600 GL 4-door Saloon	£	3,288*
6 Cavalier 1900 GL 4-door Saloon	£	3,441*
7 Cavalier 1900 GLS Coupé	£	4,072*

Power team:	Standard for:	Optional for:
57.7 hp	1,2	—
75 hp	3 to 5	—
90 hp	6,7	—

57.7 hp power team

ENGINE front, 4 stroke; 4 cylinders, vertical, in line; 76.6 cu in, 1,256 cc (3.19 x 2.40 in, 81 x 61 mm); compression ratio: 9.2:1; max power (DIN): 57.7 hp (42.7 kW) at 5,600 rpm; max torque (DIN): 66.5 lb ft, 9.1 kg m (89.2 Nm) at 2,600 rpm; max engine rpm: 6,000; 45.9 hp/l (34 kW/l); chromium cast iron block and head; 3 crankshaft bearings; valves: overhead, in line, push-rods and rockers; camshafts: 1, side; lubrication: gear pump, full flow filter, 5.5 imp pt, 6.6 US pt, 3.1 l; 1 Zenith-Stromberg 150 CDS downdraught single barrel carburettor; fuel feed: mechanical pump; water-cooled, 10.2 imp pt, 12.3 US pt, 5.8 l, viscous coupling thermostatic fan.

TRANSMISSION driving wheels: rear; clutch: single dry plate (diaphragm); gearbox: mechanical; gears: 4, fully synchronized; ratios: I 3.460, II 2.213, III 1.404, IV 1, rev 3.707; lever: central; final drive: hypoid bevel; axle ratio: 4.111; width of rims: 5''; tyres: 165 SR x 13.

PERFORMANCE max speed: (I) 31 mph, 50 km/h; (II) 49 mph, 79 km/h; (III) 77 mph, 124 km/h; (IV) 91 mph, 146 km/h; power-weight ratio: 4-dr. Saloon 37.5 lb/hp (50.7 lb/kW), 17 kg/hp (23 kg/kW); carrying capacity: 906 lb, 411 kg; acceleration: standing ¼ mile 19.6 sec, 0-50 mph (0-80 km/h) 14.5 sec; speed in direct drive at 1,000 rpm: 15.9 mph, 25.6 km/h; consumption: 30.3 m/imp gal, 25.3 m/US gal, 9.3 l x 100 km.

CHASSIS integral; front suspension: independent, wishbones, coil springs, anti-roll bar, telescopic dampers; rear: rigid axle (torque tube), trailing radius arms, transverse linkage bar, coil springs, anti-roll bar, telescopic dampers.

STEERING rack-and-pinion; turns lock to lock: 4.

BRAKES front disc (diameter 9.21 in, 23.4 cm), rear drum, rear compensator, servo.

ELECTRICAL EQUIPMENT 12 V; 36 Ah battery; 45 A alternator; Bosch or Delco-Remy distributor; 2 headlamps.

DIMENSIONS AND WEIGHT wheel base: 99.10 in, 252 cm; tracks: 54.10 in, 137 cm front, 54.10 in, 137 cm rear; length: 175 in, 444 cm; width: 64.70 in, 164 cm; height: 52 in, 132 cm; ground clearance: 5 in, 12.7 cm; weight: 2-dr. Saloon 1,989 lb, 902 kg - 4-dr. Saloon 2,163 lb, 981 kg; turning circle (between walls): 33.1 ft, 10.1 m; fuel tank: 11 imp gal, 13.2 US gal, 50 l.

BODY saloon/sedan; 5 seats, separate front seats, reclining backrests, heated rear window.

PRACTICAL INSTRUCTIONS fuel 98 oct petrol; oil: engine 4.9 imp pt, 5.9 US pt, 2.8 l, SAE 10W-30, change every 6,000 miles, 9,700 km - gearbox 0.9 imp pt, 1.1 US pt, 0.5 l, SAE 90, change every 6 months - final drive 1.2 imp pt, 1.5 US pt, 0.7 l, SAE 90, no change recommended; greasing: none; tappet clearances: inlet 0.008 in, 0.20 mm, exhaust 0.008 in, 0.20 mm; valve timing: 39° 73° 71° 41°; tyre pressure: front 28 psi, 2 atm, rear 28 psi, 2 atm.

75 hp power team

See 57.7 hp power team, except for:

ENGINE 96.7 cu in, 1,584 cc (3.35 x 2.75 in, 85 x 69.8 mm); compression ratio: 8.8:1; max power (DIN): 75 hp (55.2 kW) at 5,000 rpm; max torque (DIN): 81 lb ft, 11.2 kg m (109.8 Nm) at 3,800 rpm; max engine rpm: 6,000; 47.3 hp/l (34.8 kW/l); cast iron block, chromium cast iron head; 5 crankshaft bearings; camshafts: 1, overhead; lubricating system: 8.7 imp pt, 10.4 US pt, 4.9 l; 1 Solex 32 DIDTA-4 downdraught single barrel carburettor; fuel feed: electric pump; cooling system: 13.8 imp pt, 16.5 US pt, 7.8 l.

TRANSMISSION gearbox ratios: I 3.428, II 2.156, III 1.366, IV 1, rev 3.317; axle ratio: 3.670.

PERFORMANCE max speed: 98 mph, 158 km/h; power-weight ratio: 1600 L 4-dr. Saloon 29.4 lb/hp (40 lb/kW), 13.4 kg/hp (18.2 kg/kW) - 1600 GL 4-dr. Saloon 29.6 lb/hp (40.2 lb/kW), 13.4 kg/hp (18.2 kg/kW); carrying capacity: 937 lb, 425 kg; speed in direct drive at 1,000 rpm: 18.3 mph, 29.4 km/h; consumption: 30.7 m/imp gal, 25.6 m/US gal, 9.2 l x 100 km.

ELECTRICAL EQUIPMENT 44 Ah battery.

DIMENSIONS AND WEIGHT weight: 1600 L 2-dr. Saloon 2,165 lb, 982 kg - 4-dr. Saloon 2,209 lb, 1,002 kg - 1600 GL 4-dr. Saloon 2,220 lb, 1,007 kg.

VAUXHALL Cavalier GLS Coupé

BODY saloon/sedan; 5 seats, separate front seats, reclining backrests; heated rear window.

PRACTICAL INSTRUCTIONS oil: engine 6.7 imp pt, 8 US pt, 3.8 l, SAE 20W-30, change every 6,000 miles, 9,700 km - gearbox 2.3 imp pt, 2.7 US pt, 1.3 l, SAE 80, no change recommended - final drive 2.3 imp pt, 2.7 US pt, 1.3 l, SAE 90, no change recommended; tappet clearances: inlet 0.012 in, 0.30 mm, exhaust 0.012 in, 0.30 mm; valve timing: 44° 86° 84° 46°.

OPTIONAL ACCESSORIES G.M. automatic transmission, hydraulic torque converter and planetary gears with 3 ratios (I 2.400, II 1.480, III 1, rev 1.920), max ratio of converter at stall 2.5, possible manual selection, 3.670 axle ratio, max speed 95 mph, 153 km/h, consumption 27.7 m/imp gal, 23.1 m/US gal, 10.2 l x 100 km; metallic spray.

90 hp power team

See 75 hp power team, except for:

ENGINE 115.8 cu in, 1,897 cc (3.66 x 2.75 in, 93 x 69.8 mm); max power (DIN): 90 hp (66.2 kW) at 4,800 rpm; max torque (DIN): 105 lb ft, 14.5 kg m (142.2 Nm) at 3,800 rpm; 47.4 hp/l (34.9 kW/l); cooling system: 12.8 imp pt, 15.4 US pt, 7.3 l.

TRANSMISSION width of rims: Coupé 5.5''; tyres: Coupé 185 SR x 13.

PERFORMANCE max speed: 104 mph, 167 km/h - Coupé 107 mph, 172 km/h; power-weight ratio: 4-dr. Saloon 24.7 lb/hp (33.5 lb/kW), 11.2 kg/hp (15.2 kg/kW) - Coupé 24.7 lb/hp (33.6 lb/kW), 11.2 kg/hp (15.3 kg/kW); consumption: 30.1 m/imp gal, 25 m/US gal, 9.4 l x 100 km - Coupé 32.8 m/imp gal, 27.3 m/US gal, 8.6 l x 100 km.

DIMENSIONS AND WEIGHT length: Coupé 177 in, 450 cm; height: Coupé 50 in, 127 cm; weight: 4-dr. Saloon 2,220 lb, 1,007 kg - Coupé 2,227 lb, 1,010 kg; turning circle (between walls): Coupé 33.8 ft, 10.3 m.

BODY luxury equipment; sports wheels and instruments (for Coupé only).

OPTIONAL ACCESSORIES with G.M. automatic, max speed 101 mph, 162 km/h - Coupé 104 mph, 167 km/h, consumption 27.2 m/imp gal, 22.6 m/US gal, 10.4 l x 100 km - Coupé 29.1 m/imp gal, 24.2 m/US gal, 9.7 l x 100 km.

VX Series

PRICES EX WORKS:

1 VX 1800 Saloon	£	3,433*
2 VX 1800 Estate Car	£	3,715*
3 VX 2300 Saloon	£	3,586*
4 VX 2300 Estate Car	£	3,868*
5 VX 2300 GLS Saloon	£	4,564*
6 VX 4/90 Saloon	£	4,261*

Power team:	Standard for:	Optional for:
88 hp	1,2	—
108 hp	3 to 5	—
116 hp	6	—

VAUXHALL Cavalier 1300 L 4-door Saloon

88 hp power team

ENGINE front, 4 stroke; 4 cylinders, in line, slanted at 45°; 107.3 cu in, 1,759 cc (3.37 x 3 in, 85.7 x 76.2 mm); compression ratio: 8.5:1; max power (DIN): 88 hp (64.8 kW) at 5,800 rpm; max torque (DIN): 99 lb ft, 13.7 kg m (134.4 Nm) at 3,500 rpm; max engine rpm: 6,000; 46.6 hp/l (34.2 kW/l); cast iron block and head; 5 crankshaft bearings; valves: overhead, in line; camshafts: 1, overhead, cogged belt; lubrication: gear pump, full flow filter, 8.5 imp pt, 10.1 US pt, 4.8 l; 1 Zenith-Stromberg 175 CD-2 carburettor; fuel feed: mechanical pump; water-cooled, 14.4 imp pt, 17.3 US pt, 8.2 l, viscous coupling fan.

TRANSMISSION driving wheels: rear; clutch: single dry plate (diaphragm); gearbox: mechanical; gears: 4, fully synchronized; ratios: I 3.607, II 2.345, III 1.545, IV 1, rev 3.350; lever: central; final drive: hypoid bevel; axle ratio: 3.727; width of rims: 5''; tyres: 175 SR x 13.

PERFORMANCE max speeds: (I) 32 mph, 52 km/h; (II) 49 mph, 79 km/h; (III) 75 mph, 120 km/h; (IV) 100 mph, 161 km/h; power-weight ratio: Saloon 29.2 lb/hp (39.6 lb/kW), 13.2 kg/hp (18 kg/kW) - Estate Car 30.2 lb/hp (41 lb/kW), 13.7 kg/hp (18.6 kg/kW); carrying capacity: 1,091 lb, 495 kg; acceleration: standing ¼ mile 19.2 sec, 0-50 mph (0-80 km/h) 9.6 sec; speed in direct drive at 1,000 rpm: 18.5 mph, 29.8 km/h; consumption: 20.8 m/imp gal, 25.1 m/US gal, 11.3 l x 100 km.

CHASSIS integral; front suspension: independent, wishbones coil springs, anti-roll bar, telescopic dampers; rear: rigid axle, twin trailing radius arms, transverse linkage bar, coil springs, telescopic dampers.

STEERING rack-and-pinion; turns lock to lock: 4.

BRAKES front disc (diameter 9.37 in, 23.8 cm), rear drum, servo; swept area: front 202.2 sq in, 1,304 sq cm, rear 60 sq in, 387 sq cm, total 262.2 sq in, 1,691 sq cm.

ELECTRICAL EQUIPMENT 12 V; 39 Ah battery; 336 W alternator; AC Delco distributor; 2 halogen headlamps.

DIMENSIONS AND WEIGHT wheel base: 104.08 in, 264 cm; tracks: 56.20 in, 143 cm front, 55.40 in, 141 cm rear; length: 180 in, 457 cm; width: 66.90 in, 170 cm; height: 53.50 in, 135 cm; ground clearance: 4.90 in, 12.5 cm; weight: Saloon 2,569 lb, 1,165 kg - Estate Car 2,658 lb, 1,205 kg; weight distribution: 48% front, 52% rear; turning circle (between walls): 37.6 ft, 11.4 m; fuel tank: 14.3 imp gal, 17.2 US gal, 65 l.

BODY 4-5 seats, separate front seats, reclining backrests; heated rear window; folding rear seat (for Estate Car only).

PRACTICAL INSTRUCTIONS fuel: 97 oct petrol; oil: engine 8.5 imp pt, 10.1 US pt, 4.8 l, SAE 20W-50, change every 6,000 miles, 9,700 km - gearbox 2.5 imp pt, 3 US pt, 1.4 l, SAE 90 EP, change every 6,000 miles, 9,700 km - final drive 3.6 imp pt, 4.2 US pt, 2 l, SAE 90, change every 6,000 miles, 9,700 km; greasing: none; tappet clearances: inlet 0.007-0.010 in, 0.18-0.25 mm, exhaust 0.015-0.018 in, 0.38-0.46 mm; valve timing: 31°36' 63°36' 63°36' 31°36'; tyre pressure: front 24 psi, 1.7 atm, rear 24 psi, 1.7 atm.

OPTIONAL ACCESSORIES G.M. automatic transmission, hydraulic torque converter and planetary gears with 3 ratios (I 2.390, II 1.480, III 1, rev 1.920), max ratio of converter at stall 2, possible manual selection; metallic spray.

108 hp power team

See 88 hp power team, except for:

ENGINE 139.1 cu in, 2,279 cc (3.84 x 3 in, 97.5 x 76.2 mm); max power (DIN): 108 hp (79.5 kW) at 5,000 rpm; max torque (DIN): 138 lb ft, 19 kg m (186.3 Nm) at 3,000 rpm; 47.4 hp/l (34.9 kW/l).

TRANSMISSION axle ratio: 3.455 (GLS only); width of rims: 6''; tyres: 185 SR x 14.

PERFORMANCE max speeds: (I) 35 mph, 56 km/h; (II) 53 mph, 86 km/h; (III) 81 mph, 130 km/h; (IV) 103 mph, 165 km/h; power-weight ratio: Saloon 24.1 lb/hp (32.8 lb/kW), 10.9 kg/hp (14.9 kg/kW) - Estate Car 24.9 lb/hp (33.8 lb/kW), 11.3 kg/hp (15.3 kg/kW) - GLS 25.7 lb/hp (34.9 lb/kW), 11.7 kg/hp (15.8 kg/kW); acceleration: standing ¼ mile 18.3 sec, 0-50 mph (0-80 km/h) 8.1 sec; speed in direct drive at 1,000 rpm: 19.9 mph, 32.1 km/h - GLS 20.1 mph, 32.3 km/h; consumption: 25.2 m/imp gal, 21 m/US gal, 11.2 l x 100 km.

STEERING (GLS only) servo; turns lock to lock: 2.80.

VAUXHALL VX 2300 GLS

BRAKES (GLS only) swept area: total 297.8 sq in, 1,921 sq cm.

ELECTRICAL EQUIPMENT (GLS only) heavy-duty alternator; 4 halogen headlamps.

DIMENSIONS AND WEIGHT length: GLS 180.60 in, 459 cm; ground clearance: GLS 3.90 in, 9.9 cm; weight: Saloon 2,604 lb, 1,181 kg - Estate Car 2,689 lb, 1,220 kg - GLS 2,778 lb, 1,260 kg; turning circle (between walls): GLS 39.3 ft, 12 m.

BODY (GLS only) luxury equipment; sports instruments; vinyl roof.

116 hp power team

See 88 hp power team, except for:

ENGINE 139.1 cu in, 2,279 cc (3.84 x 3 in, 97.5 x 76.2 mm); max power (DIN): 116 hp (85.4 kW) at 5,000 rpm; max torque (DIN): 145 lb ft, 20 kg m (196.1 Nm) at 3,000 rpm; 50.9 hp/l (37.5 kW/l); lubrication: gear pump, full flow filter, oil cooler; 2 Zenith CD horizontal carburettors.

TRANSMISSION gears: 5, fully synchronized; ratios: I 3.370, II 2.160, III 1.580, IV 1.240, V 1, rev 4; axle ratio: 3.700; width of rims: 6''; tyres: 185/70 SR x 14.

PERFORMANCE max speeds: 106 mph, 170 km/h; power-weight ratio: 23.7 lb/hp (32.1 lb/kW), 10.7 kg/hp (14.6 kg/kW); speed in direct drive at 1,000 rpm: 18.9 mph, 30.4 km/h; consumption: 23.5 m/imp gal, 19.6 m/US gal, 12 l x 100 km.

CHASSIS rear suspension: anti-roll bar.

BRAKES front disc (diameter 10.70 in, 27.3 cm).

ELECTRICAL EQUIPMENT 40 Ah battery.

DIMENSIONS AND WEIGHT wheel base: 104.60 in, 266 cm; length: 180.60 in, 459 cm; width: 67.60 in, 172 cm; height: 51.60 in, 131 cm; weight: 2,745 lb, 1,245 kg; turning circle (between walls): 39.3 ft, 12 m.

DIM   **GREECE**

Dim

ENGINE Fiat 126, rear, 4 stroke; 2 cylinders, vertical, in line; 36.2 cu in, 594 cc (2.89 x 2.76 in, 73.5 x 70 mm); compression ratio: 7.5:1; max power (DIN): 23 hp (16.9 kW) at 4,700 rpm; max torque (DIN): 29 lb ft, 4 kg m (39.2 Nm) at 3,400 rpm; max engine rpm: 5,200; 38.7 hp/l (28.5 kW/l); 2 crankshaft bearings; valves: overhead, in line, push-rods and rockers; camshafts: 1, side; lubrication: gear pump, centrifugal filter, 4.8 imp pt, 5.7 US pt, 2.7 l; 1 Weber 28 IMB downdraught carburettor; fuel feed: mechanical pump; air-cooled.

TRANSMISSION driving wheels: rear; clutch: single dry plate; gearbox: mechanical; gears: 4, II, III and IV silent claw coupling; ratios: I 3.250, II 2.067, III 1.300, IV 0.872, rev 4.024; lever: central; final drive: spiral bevel; axle ratio: 4.875; width of rims: 4''; tyres: 135 SR x 12.

PERFORMANCE max speeds: (I) 19 mph, 30 km/h; (II) 31 mph, 50 km/h; (III) 50 mph, 80 km/h; (IV) over 65 mph, 105 km/h; power-weight ratio: 50.3 lb/hp, (68.6 lb/kW), 22.8 kg/hp (31.1 kg/kW); carrying capacity: 750 lb, 340 kg; speed in top at 1,000 rpm: 14 mph, 22.6 km/h; consumption: 52.3 m/imp gal, 43.6 m/US gal, 5.4 l x 100 km.

CHASSIS integral; front suspension: independent, wishbones, transverse leafspring lower arms, telescopic dampers; rear: independent, oblique semi-trailing arms, coil springs, telescopic dampers.

STEERING screw and sector; turns lock to lock: 2.90.

BRAKES drum; lining area: front 33.5 sq in, 216 sq cm, rear 33.5 sq in, 216 sq cm, total 67 sq in, 432 sq cm.

ELECTRICAL EQUIPMENT 12 V; 34 Ah battery; 33 A alternator; Marelli distributor; 2 headlamps.

DIMENSIONS AND WEIGHT wheel base: 77.95 in, 198 cm; tracks: 46.46 in, 118 cm front, 47.24 in, 120 cm rear; length: 125.98 in, 320 cm; width: 59.06 in, 150 cm; height: 52.36 in, 133 cm; ground clearance: 7.09 in, 18 cm; weight: 1,158 lb, 525 kg; turning circle (between walls): 28.2 ft, 8.6 m; fuel tank: 4.6 imp gal, 5.5 US gal, 21 l.

BODY saloon/sedan, in plastic material; 2 doors; 4 seats, separate front seats.

VAUXHALL VX 2300 GLS Saloon

DIM 2-door Sedan

PRACTICAL INSTRUCTIONS fuel: 80.85 oct petrol; oil: engine 4.4 imp pt, 5.3 US pt, 2.5 l, SAE 30W (summer) 20W (winter), change every 6,200 miles, 10,000 km - gearbox and final drive 1.9 imp pt, 2.3 US pt, 1.1 l, Fiat ZC 90, change every 18,600 miles, 30,000 km; greasing: none; tappet clearances: inlet 0.008 in, 0.20 mm, exhaust 0.010 in, 0.25 mm; valve timing: 26° 56° 66° 16°; tyre pressure: front 22 psi, 1.4 atm, rear 28 psi, 2 atm.

VOLVO   HOLLAND

66 DL 2-door

PRICE EX WORKS: 13,480* florins

ENGINE front, 4 stroke; 4 cylinders, vertical, in line; 67.6 cu in, 1,108 cc (2.76 x 2.83 in, 70 x 72 mm); compression ratio: 8.5:1; max power (DIN): 47 hp (34.6 kW) at 5,000 rpm; max torque (DIN): 54 lb ft, 7.6 kg m (74.5 Nm) at 2,700 rpm; max engine rpm: 6,200; 42.4 hp/l (31.2 kW/l); cast iron block, light alloy head; 5 crankshaft bearings; valves: overhead, in line, push-rods and rockers; camshafts: 1, side; lubrication: gear pump, full flow filter, 5.6 imp pt, 6.8 US pt, 3.2 l; 1 Solex 32 EHSAREN 577 carburettor; fuel feed: mechanical pump; water-cooled, 8.4 imp pt, 10.1 US pt, 4.8 l.

TRANSMISSION driving wheels: rear; clutch: automatic, centrifugal; transmission: C.V.T./transaxle automatic; gears: continuously variable ratio between 14.22:1 and 3.86:1; lever: central; width of rims: 4''; tyres: 135 SR x 14.

PERFORMANCE max speed: 85 mph, 136 km/h; power-weight ratio: 38.1 lb/hp (51.9 lb/kW), 17.3 kg/hp (23.6 kg/kW); carrying capacity: 849 lb, 385 kg; acceleration: 0-50 mph (0-80 km/h) 12.9 sec; consumption: 31.4 m/imp gal, 26.1 m/US gal, 9 l x 100 km.

CHASSIS integral; front suspension: independent, longitudinal torsion bars, telescopic damper struts, lower wishbones (trailing links), anti-roll bar; rear: de Dion rigid axle, semi-elliptic leafsprings, upper torque arms, telescopic dampers.

STEERING rack-and-pinion; turns lock to lock: 3.40.

BRAKES front disc, rear drum, servo; swept area: front 151.9 sq in, 980 sq cm, rear 74.4 sq in, 480 sq cm, total 226.3 sq in, 1,460 sq cm.

ELECTRICAL EQUIPMENT 12 V; 36 Ah battery; 500 W alternator; Ducellier distributor; 2 headlamps.

DIMENSIONS AND WEIGHT wheel base: 88.58 in, 225 cm; tracks: 51.57 in, 131 cm front, 48.82 in, 124 cm rear; length: 153.54 in, 390 cm; width: 59.84 in, 152 cm; height: 56.69 in, 144 cm; ground clearance: 4.72 in, 12 cm; weight: 1,797 lb, 815 kg; weight distribution: 56.2% front, 43.8% rear; turning circle (between walls): 32.1 ft, 9.8 m; fuel tank: 9.2 imp gal, 11.1 US gal, 42 l.

BODY saloon/sedan; 2 doors; 4-5 seats, separate front seats, reclining backrests, built-in headrests.

VOLVO 66 DL 2-door

PRACTICAL INSTRUCTIONS fuel: 98 oct petrol; oil: engine 5.6 imp pt, 6.8 US pt, 3.2 l, SAE 10W-30 (summer) 20W-40 (winter), change every 3,100 miles, 5,000 km - C.V.T. automatic transmission 1.4 imp pt, 1.7 US pt, 0.8 l, SAE 80 EP, change every 12,400 miles, 20,000 km; greasing: none; tappet clearances: 0.006 in, 0.15 mm, exhaust 0.008 in, 0.20 mm; valve timing: 0°30' 36° 38°30' 5°; tyre pressure: front 22 psi, 1.6 atm, rear 26 psi, 1.8 atm.

OPTIONAL ACCESSORIES 155 SR x 13 tyres only with 4.5'' wide rims; sunshine roof.

66 DL 3-door

See 66 DL 2-door, except for:

PRICE EX WORKS: 14,480* florins

BODY 2+1 doors.

66 GL 2-door

See 66 DL 2-door, except for:

PRICE IN GB: £ 2,757*
PRICE EX WORKS: 14,180* florins

ENGINE 78.7 cu in, 1,289 cc (2.87 x 3.03 in, 73 x 77 mm); max power (DIN): 57 hp (41.9 kW) at 5,200 rpm; max torque (DIN): 61 lb ft, 9.6 kg m (94.1 Nm) at 2,800 rpm; 44.2 hp/l (32.5 kW/l); 1 Solex 32 EHSAREN 596 carburettor.

TRANSMISSION width of rims: 4.5''; tyres: 155 SR x 13.

PERFORMANCE max speed: 90 mph, 145 km/h; power-weight ratio: 32.5 lb/hp (44.1 lb/kW), 14.7 kg/hp (20 kg/kW); carrying capacity: 915 lb, 415 kg; acceleration: 0-50 mph (0-80 km/h) 10.8 sec; consumption: 28.2 m/imp gal, 23.5 m/US gal, 10 l x 100 km.

ELECTRICAL EQUIPMENT 4 headlamps, 2 halogen.

DIMENSIONS AND WEIGHT width: 60.63 in, 154 cm; height: 54.33 in, 138 cm; weight: 1,846 lb, 837 kg; weight distribution: 56.3% front, 43.7% rear; turning circle (between walls): 31.2 ft, 9.5 m.

PRACTICAL INSTRUCTIONS tyre pressure: front 20 psi, 1.4 atm, rear 23 psi, 1.6 atm.

OPTIONAL ACCESSORIES metallic spray.

66 GL 3-door

See 66 GL 2-door, except for:

PRICE IN GB: £ 2,890*
PRICE EX WORKS: 15,180* florins

BODY 2+1 doors.

VOLVO 66 GL 3-door

343 L

PRICE EX WORKS: 16,900* florins

ENGINE front, 4 stroke; 4 cylinders, vertical, in line; 85.2 cu in, 1,397 cc (2.99 x 3.03 in, 76 x 77 mm); compression ratio: 9.5:1; max power (DIN): 70 hp (51.5 kW) at 5,500 rpm; max torque (DIN): 80 lb ft, 11 kg m (107.9 Nm) at 3,500 rpm; max engine rpm: 6,000; 50.1 hp/l (36.9 kW/l); cast iron block, wet liners, light alloy head; 5 crankshaft bearings; valves: overhead, in line, slanted, push-rods and rockers; camshafts: 1, side; lubrication: gear pump, full flow filter, 6.2 imp pt, 7.4 US pt, 3.5 l; 1 Weber 32 DIR 57-8400 downdraught carburettor; fuel feed: mechanical pump; sealed circuit cooling, 10.6 imp pt, 12.7 US pt, 6 l, electric fan.

TRANSMISSION driving wheels: rear; clutch: automatic, centrifugal; gearbox: C.V.T./transaxle automatic; gears: continuously variable ratio between 14.22:1 and 3.86:1; lever: central; width of rims: 5''; tyres: 155 SR x 13.

PERFORMANCE max speed: 90 mph, 145 km/h; power-weight ratio: 30.8 lb/hp (41.9 lb/kW), 14 kg/hp (19 kg/kW); carrying capacity: 931 lb, 422 kg; acceleration: 0-50 mph (0-80 km/h) 10.5 sec; consumption: 31.4 m/imp gal, 26.1 m/US gal, 9 l x 100 km.

CHASSIS integral; front suspension: independent, by McPherson, lower wishbones, coil springs/telescopic damper struts, anti-roll bar; rear: De Dion rigid axle, single leaf

VOLVO 343 DL

semi-elliptic springs, swinging longitudinal trailing arm, telescopic dampers.

STEERING rack-and-pinion; turns lock to lock: 4.10.

BRAKES front disc, rear drum, servo; lining area: front 17.4 sq in, 112 sq cm, rear 37.7 sq in, 243 sq cm, total 55.1 sq in, 355 sq cm.

ELECTRICAL EQUIPMENT 12 V; 36 Ah battery; 700 W alternator; Ducellier distributor; 2 headlamps.

DIMENSIONS AND WEIGHT wheel base: 94.09 in, 239 cm; tracks: 53.15 in, 135 cm front, 54.33 in, 138 cm rear; length: 164.96 in, 419 cm; width: 65.35 in, 166 cm; height: 54.72 in, 139 cm; ground clearance: 5.31 in, 13.5 cm; weight: 2,156 lb, 978 kg; weight distribution: 54.4% front, 45.6% rear; turning circle (between walls): 30.2 ft, 9.2 m; fuel tank: 9.9 imp gal, 11.9 US gal, 45 l.

BODY saloon/sedan; 2 + 1 doors; 4-5 seats, separate front seats, reclining backrests with built-in headrests; detachable back seat.

PRACTICAL INSTRUCTIONS fuel: 98 oct petrol; oil: engine 6.2 imp pt, 7.4 US pt, 3.5 l, SAE 10W-30 (summer) SAE 20W-40 (winter), change every 6,200 miles, 10,000 km - C.V.T. automatic transmission 1.4 imp pt, 1.7 US pt, 0.8 l, SAE 80 EP, change every 12,400 miles, 20,000 km; greasing: none; tappet clearances: inlet 0.006 in, 0.15 mm, exhaust 0.006 in, 0.15 mm; tyre pressure: front 24 psi, 1.7 atm, rear 28 psi, 2 atm.

OPTIONAL ACCESSORIES heated rear window.

343 DL

See 343 L, except for:

PRICE IN GB: £ 3,455*
PRICE EX WORKS: 17,900* florins

BODY folding rear seat; heated rear window (standard).

OPTIONAL ACCESSORIES 175/70 SR x 13 tyres; sunshine roof; tinted glass; metallic spray; halogen headlamps; headlamps with wiper/washers; vinyl upholstery.

VOLVO 343 DL

ALFA ROMEO   ITALY

Alfasud Series

PRICES IN GB AND EX WORKS:

	£	liras
1 Alfasud 4-door Berlina	—	3,836,000*
2 Alfasud Super 4-door Berlina	—	4,740,000*
3 Alfasud Super 1.3 4-door Berlina	—	4,846,000*
4 Alfasud Giardinetta 1.3 3-door S. W.	—	4,834,000*
5 Alfasud ti 1.3 2-door Berlina	3,000*	4,872,000*
6 Alfasud Sprint 2-door Coupé	—	6,219,000*

Power team:	Standard for:	Optional for:
63 hp	1,2	—
68 hp	3,4	—
76 hp	5,6	—

63 hp power team

ENGINE front, 4 stroke; 4 cylinders, horizontally opposed; 72.4 cu in, 1,186 cc (3.15 x 2.32 in, 80 x 59 mm); compression ratio: 8.8:1; max power (DIN): 63 hp (46.4 kW) at 6,000 rpm; max torque (DIN): 65 lb ft, 9 kg m (88.3 Nm) at 3,200 rpm; max engine rpm: 6,000; 53.1 hp/l (39.1 kW/l); cast iron block, light alloy head; 3 crankshaft bearings; valves: overhead, in line, thimble tappets, new valve adjustment patented by Alfa Romeo; camshafts: 2 per cylinder block, overhead, cogged belt; lubrication: gear pump, full flow filter (cartridge), 7 imp pt, 8.5 US pt, 4 l; 1 Solex C32 DISA/21 or Dell'Orto FRDA 32E downdraught single barrel carburettor; fuel feed: mechanical pump; water-cooled, 12.8 imp pt, 15.4 US pt, 7.3 l, electric thermostatic fan.

TRANSMISSION driving wheels: front; clutch: single dry plate (diaphragm), hydraulically controlled; gearbox: mechanical; gears: 4 (for Super 5), fully synchronized; ratios: I 3.545, II 1.941, III 1.292, IV 0.966, rev 3.091 (for Super I 3.545, II 2.062, III 1.434, IV 1.115, V 0.931, rev 3.091); lever: central; final drive: hypoid bevel; axle ratio: 4.111; width of rims: 5''; tyres: 165/70 SR x 13.

PERFORMANCE max speeds: (I) 26 mph, 42 km/h; (II) 48 mph, 77 km/h; (III) 71 mph, 115 km/h; (IV) over 93

ALFA ROMEO Alfasud Super 1.3 4-door Berlina

ALFA ROMEO Alfasud Super

mph, 150 km/h; power-weight ratio: 30.1 lb/hp (40.8 lb/kW), 13.6 kg/hp (18.5 kg/kW); carrying capacity: 882 lb, 400 kg; speed in top at 1,000 rpm: 16 mph, 25.7 km/h; consumption: 39.2 m/imp gal, 32.7 m/US gal, 7.2 l x 100 km.

CHASSIS integral; front suspension: independent, by McPherson, coil springs/telescopic damper struts, lower trailing links, anti-roll bar; rear: rigid axle, longitudinal Watt linkage, transverse linkage bar, coil springs, telescopic dampers.

STEERING rack-and-pinion, adjustable height of steering wheel; turns lock to lock: 3.40.

BRAKES disc (front diameter 10.16 in, 25.8 cm, rear 9.17 in, 23.3 cm), rear compensator, servo; swept area: front 193 sq in, 1,245 sq cm, rear 155.5 sq in, 1,003 sq cm, total 348.5 sq in, 2,248 sq cm.

ELECTRICAL EQUIPMENT 12 V; 43 Ah battery; 600 W alternator; 2 headlamps.

DIMENSIONS AND WEIGHT wheel base: 96.65 in, 245 cm; tracks: 54.49 in, 138 cm front, 53.19 in, 135 cm rear; length: 153.15 in, 389 cm; width: 62.48 in, 159 cm; height: 53.15 in, 137 cm; ground clearance: 5.91 in, 15 cm; weight: 1,896 lb, 860 kg; turning circle (between walls): 30.8 ft, 9.4 m; fuel tank: 11 imp gal, 13.2 US gal, 50 l.

BODY 5 seats, separate front seats, reclining backrests; heated rear window.

PRACTICAL INSTRUCTIONS fuel: 98-100 oct petrol; oil: engine 7 imp pt, 8.5 US pt, 4 l, SAE 20W-50, change every 6,200 miles, 10,000 km - gearbox and final drive 6 imp pt, 7.2 US pt, 3.4 l, SAE 90, change every 24,900 miles, 40,000 km; greasing: none; tappet clearances: inlet 0.014-0.016 in, 0.35-0.40 mm, exhaust 0.018-0.020 in, 0.45-0.50 mm; valve timing: 12° 48° 45° 7°; tyre pressure: front 28 psi, 1.9 atm, rear 21 psi, 1.5 atm.

OPTIONAL ACCESSORIES antitheft.

68 hp power team

See 63 hp power team, except for:

ENGINE 78.3 cu in, 1,286 cc (3.15 x 2.52 in, 80 x 64 mm); compression ratio: 9:1; max power (DIN): 68 hp (50 kW) at 6,000 rpm; max torque (DIN): 74 lb ft, 10.2 kg m (100 Nm) at 3,500 rpm; 52.9 hp/l (38.9 kW/l).

TRANSMISSION gearbox: mechanical; gears: 5, fully synchronized; ratios: I 3.545, II 2.062, III 1.434, IV 1.115, V 0.931, rev 3.091.

PERFORMANCE max speed: over 96 mph, 155 km/h; power-weight ratio: Super 28.2 lb/hp (38.4 lb/kW), 12.8 kg/hp (17.4 kg/kW) - Giardinetta 29.8 lb/hp (40.3 lb/kW), 13.5 kg/hp (18.3 kg/kW); speed in top at 1,000 rpm: 17 mph, 27.3 km/h; consumption: Super 40.9 m/imp gal, 34.1 m/US gal,

6.9 l x 100 km - Giardinetta 40.4 m/imp gal, 33.6 m/US gal, 7 l x 100 km.

DIMENSIONS AND WEIGHT length: Super 154.72 in, 393 cm - Giardinetta 156.30 in, 397 cm; weight: Super 1,918 lb, 870 kg - Giardinetta 2,018 lb, 915 kg.

OPTIONAL ACCESSORIES (for Super only) light alloy wheels; metallic spray.

76 hp power team

See 63 hp power team, except for:

ENGINE 78.3 cu in, 1,286 cc (3.15 x 2.52 in, 80 x 64 mm); compression ratio: 9:1; max power (DIN): 76 hp (55.9 kW) at 6,000 rpm; max torque (DIN): 76 lb ft, 10.5 kg m (103 Nm) at 3,500 rpm; 59 hp/l (43.4 kW/l); ti 1.3 1 Weber 32 DIR 61/250 downdraught twin barrel carburettor - Sprint 1 Solex C32 DISA/21 or Dell'Orto FRDA 32E downdraught twin barrel carburettor.

TRANSMISSION gearbox: mechanical; gears: 5, fully synchronized; ratios: I 3.545, II 2.062, III 1.434, IV 1.115, V 0.931, rev 3.091.

PERFORMANCE max speed: ti 1.3 99 mph, 160 km/h - Sprint 103 mph, 165 km/h; power-weight ratio: ti 1.3 23.6 lb/hp (32 lb/kW), 10.7 kg/hp (14.5 kg/kW) - Sprint 24.3 lb/hp (33.1 lb/kW), 11 kg/hp (15 kg/kW); speed in top at 1,000 rpm: Sprint 16.8 mph, 27 km/h; consumption: ti 1.3 32.8 m/imp gal, 27.3 m/US gal, 8.6 l x 100 km.

ELECTRICAL EQUIPMENT 4 iodine headlamps.

DIMENSIONS AND WEIGHT length: ti 1.3 154.72 in, 393 cm - Sprint 157.87 in, 401 cm; width: Sprint 63.39 in, 161 cm; height: Sprint 49.61 in, 126 cm; ground clearance: Sprint 6.30 in, 16 cm; weight: ti 1.3 1,786 lb, 810 kg - Sprint 1,848 lb, 838 kg.

OPTIONAL ACCESSORIES antitheft; light alloy wheels; metallic spray; adjustable headrests.

Spider Junior 1300

PRICE EX WORKS: 6,596,000* liras

ENGINE front, 4 stroke; 4 cylinders, vertical, in line; 78.7 cu in, 1,290 cc (2.91 x 2.95 in, 74 x 75 mm); compression ratio: 9:1; max power (SAE): 103 hp (75.8 kW) at 6,000 rpm; max torque (SAE): 101 lb ft, 14 kg m (137.3 Nm) at 3,200 rpm; max engine rpm: 6,000; 79.8 hp/l (58.7 kW/l); light alloy block and head, wet liners, hemispherical combustion chambers; 5 crankshaft bearings; valves: overhead, Vee-slanted at 80°, thimble tappets: camshafts: 2, overhead; lubrication: gear pump, full flow filter (cartridge), 12.7 imp pt, 15.2 US pt, 7.2 l; 2 Weber (or Solex or Dell'Orto) 40 DCOE 28 horizontal twin barrel carburettors; fuel feed: mechanical pump; water-cooled, 13.2 imp pt, 15.9 US pt, 7.5 l.

TRANSMISSION driving wheels: rear; clutch: single dry plate (diaphragm), hydraulically controlled; gearbox: mechanical; gears: 5, fully synchronized; ratios: I 3.300, II 1.990, III 1.350, IV 1, V 0.860, rev 3.010; lever: central; final drive: hypoid bevel; axle ratio: 4.555; width of rims: 4.5''; tyres: 155 SR x 15.

PERFORMANCE max speeds: (I) 27 mph, 44 km/h; (II) 46 mph, 74 km/h; (III) 67 mph, 108 km/h; (IV) 91 mph, 146 km/h; (V) over 106 mph, 170 km/h; power-weight ratio: 21.2 lb/hp (28.9 lb/kW), 9.6 kg/hp (13.1 kg/kW); carrying capacity: 706 lb, 320 kg; acceleration: standing ¼ mile 19.1 sec; speed in top at 1,000 rpm: 18.2 mph, 29.3 km/h; consumption: 28.5 m/imp gal, 23.8 m/US gal, 9.9 l x 100 km.

CHASSIS integral; front suspension: independent, wishbones, coil springs, anti-roll bar, telescopic dampers; rear: rigid axle, trailing lower radius arms, upper transverse Vee radius arms, coil springs, anti-roll bar, telescopic dampers.

STEERING recirculating ball or worm and roller; turns lock to lock: 3.70.

BRAKES disc (diameter 10.51 in, 26.7 cm), rear compensator, servo; swept area: front 184.5 sq in, 1,190 sq cm, rear 167.1 sq in, 1,078 sq cm, total 351.6 sq in, 2,268 sq cm.

ELECTRICAL EQUIPMENT 12 V; 50 Ah battery; 540 W alternator; Bosch distributor; 2 headlamps.

DIMENSIONS AND WEIGHT wheel base: 88.58 in, 225 cm; tracks: 52.13 in, 132 cm front, 50.16 in, 127 cm rear; length: 162.20 in, 412 cm; width: 64.17 in, 163 cm; height: 50.79 in, 129 cm; ground clearance: 4.72 in, 12 cm; weight: 2,183 lb, 990 kg; turning circle (between walls): 34.4 ft, 10.5 m; fuel tank: 10.1 imp gal, 12.1 US gal, 46 l.

BODY convertible; 2 doors; 2+2 seats, separate front seats.

ALFA ROMEO Alfasud Sprint

SPIDER JUNIOR 1300

PRACTICAL INSTRUCTIONS fuel: 98-100 oct petrol; oil: engine 12.7 imp pt, 15.2 US pt, 7.2 l, SAE 20W-40, change every 6,200 miles, 10,000 km - gearbox 3.2 imp pt, 3.8 US pt, 1.8 l, SAE 90 EP, change every 18,600 miles, 30,000 km - final drive 2.5 imp pt, 3 US pt, 1.4 l, SAE 90 EP, change every 18,600 miles, 30,000 km; greasing: every 7,500 miles, 12,000 km, 1 point; tappet clearances: inlet 0.019-0.020 in, 0.48-0.50 mm, exhaust 0.021-0.022 in, 0.53-0.55 mm; valve timing: 36°50' 60°50' 54°10' 30°10'; tyre pressure: front 24 psi, 1.7 atm, rear 26 psi, 1.8 atm.

OPTIONAL ACCESSORIES 165 SR x 14 tyres with 5'' wide rims; adjustable headrests; hardtop; metallic spray; sport steering wheel.

Spider Junior 1600

See Spider Junior 1300, except for:

PRICE EX WORKS: 6,789,000* liras

ENGINE 95.8 cu in, 1,570 cc (3.07 x 3.28 in, 78 x 82 mm); max power (SAE): 116 hp (85.4 kW) at 5,500 rpm; max torque (SAE): 120 lb ft, 16.5 kg m (161.8 Nm) at 2,900 rpm; 73.8 hp/l (54.3 kW/l); 2 Weber (or Solex or Dell'Orto) 40 DCOE 33 horizontal twin barrel carburettors.

PERFORMANCE max speed: over 109 mph, 175 km/h; power-weight ratio: 19.4 lb/hp (26.2 lb/kW), 8.8 kg/hp (11.9 kg/kW); acceleration: standing ¼ mile 18 sec; speed in top at 1,000 rpm: 19.8 mph, 31.8 km/h; consumption: 33.2 m/imp gal, 27.7 m/US gal, 8.5 l x 100 km.

DIMENSIONS AND WEIGHT weight: 2,249 lb, 1,020 kg.

Giulietta 1.3

PRICE EX WORKS: 6,337,000* liras

ENGINE front, 4 stroke; 4 cylinders, vertical, in line; 82.8 cu in, 1,357 cc (3.15 x 2.66 in, 80 x 67.5 mm); compression ratio: 9:1; max power (DIN): 95 hp (69.9 kW) at 6,000 rpm; max torque (DIN): 89 lb ft, 12.3 kg m (120.6 Nm) at 4,500 rpm; max engine rpm: 6,100; 70 hp/l (51.5 kW/l); light alloy block and head, wet liners, hemispherical combustion chambers; 5 crankshaft bearings; valves: overhead, Vee-slanted at 80°; camshafts: 2, overhead, chain driven; lubrication: gear pump, full flow filter (cartridge), 11.4 imp pt, 13.7 US pt, 6.5 l; 2 Solex Cho ADDHE downdraught twin barrel carburettors; fuel feed: mechanical pump; water-cooled, 14.1 imp pt, 16.9 US pt, 8 l.

TRANSMISSION driving wheels: rear; clutch: single dry plate (diaphragm); gearbox: mechanical; gears: 5, fully synchronized; ratios: I 3.307, II 1.956, III 1.345, IV 1.026, V 0.833, rev 2.615; lever: central; final drive: hypoid bevel; axle ratio: 4.778; width of rims: 5''; tyres: 165 SR x 13.

PERFORMANCE max speed: (I) 25 mph, 41 km/h; (II) 43 mph, 70 km/h; (III) 63 mph, 101 km/h; (IV) 83 mph, 133 km/h; (V) 103 mph, 165 km/h; power-weight ratio: 24.9

ALFA ROMEO Giulietta 1.3 - 1.6

lb/hp (33.7 lb/kW), 11.3 kg/hp (15.3 kg/kW); carrying capacity: 882 lb, 400 kg; acceleration: standing ¼ mile 18.8 sec; speed in top at 1,000 rpm: 16.9 mph, 27.2 km/h; consumption: 37.7 m/imp gal, 31.4 m/US gal, 7.5 l x 100 km.

CHASSIS integral; front suspension: independent, wishbones (upper trailing links), torsion bars, anti-roll bar, telescopic dampers; rear: de Dion rigid axle, oblique trailing arms, transverse Watt linkage, coil springs, anti-roll bar, telescopic dampers.

STEERING rack-and-pinion, adjustable height of steering wheel; turns lock to lock: 3.50

BRAKES disc (diameter 9.84 in, 25 cm), rear compensator, servo; swept area: front 173.3 sq in, 1,118 sq cm, rear 156.6 sq in, 1,010 sq cm, total 329.9 sq in, 2,128 sq cm.

ELECTRICAL EQUIPMENT 12 V; 50 Ah battery; 540 W alternator; Bosch or Marelli distributor; 2 iodine headlamps.

DIMENSIONS AND WEIGHT wheel base: 98.82 in, 251 cm; front and rear track: 53.54 in, 136 cm; length: 165.75 in, 421 cm; width: 64.96 in, 165 cm; height: 55.12 in, 140 cm; ground clearance: 5.51 in, 14 cm; weight: 2,359 lb, 1,070 kg; weight distribution: 50% front, 50% rear; turning circle (between walls): 35.8 ft, 10.9 m; fuel tank: 11 imp gal, 13.2 US gal, 50 l.

BODY saloon/sedan; 4 doors; 5 seats, separate front seats, reclining backrests, adjustable headrests; heated rear window.

ALFA ROMEO Giulietta 1.3 - 1.6

PRACTICAL INSTRUCTIONS fuel: 98 oct petrol; oil: engine 11.4 imp pt, 13.7 US pt, 6.5 l, SAE 10W-50, change every 6,200 miles, 10,000 km - gearbox 4.9 imp pt, 5.9 US pt, 2.8 l, SAE 90, change every 24,900 miles, 40,000 km; tappet clearances: inlet 0.019-0.020 in, 0.47-0.50 mm, exhaust 0.020-0.022 in, 0.52-0.55 mm; valve timing: 33°54' 57°54' 51°14' 21°14'; tyre pressure: front 26 psi, 1.8 atm, rear 28 psi, 2 atm.

OPTIONAL ACCESSORIES metallic spray; light alloy wheels; tinted glass; air-conditioning.

Giulietta 1.6

See Giulietta 1.3, except for:

PRICE EX WORKS: 6,561,000* liras

ENGINE 95.8 cu in, 1,570 cc (3.07 x 3.23 in, 78 x 82 mm); max power (DIN): 109 hp (80.2 kW) at 5,600 rpm; max torque (DIN): 105 lb ft, 14.5 kg m (142.2 Nm) at 4,300 rpm; max engine rpm: 5,800; 69.4 hp/l (51.1 kW/l); 2 Dell'Orto DHLA 40H downdraught twin barrel carburettors.

TRANSMISSION axle ratio: 4.300.

PERFORMANCE max speeds: (I) 26 mph, 42 km/h; (II) 45 mph, 72 km/h; (III) 65 mph, 105 km/h; (IV) 86 mph, 138 km/h; (V) 109 mph, 175 km/h; power-weight ratio: 21.6 lb/hp (29.3 lb/kW), 9.8 kg/hp (13.3 kg/kW); acceleration: standing ¼ mile 17.6 sec; speed in top at 1,000 rpm: 18.8 mph, 30.2 km/h; consumption: 36.2 m/imp gal, 30.2 m/US gal, 7.8 l x 100 km.

ALFA ROMEO Giulietta 1.3 - 1.6

Alfetta 1.6

PRICE EX WORKS: 7,133,000* liras

ENGINE front, 4 stroke; 4 cylinders, vertical, in line; 95.8 cu in, 1,570 cc (3.07 x 3.23 in, 78 x 82 mm); compression ratio: 9:1; max power (DIN): 108 hp (79.5 kW) at 5,600 rpm; max torque (DIN): 105 lb ft, 14.5 kg m (142.2 Nm) at 4,300 rpm; max engine rpm: 5,600; 68.8 hp/l (50.6 kW/l); light alloy block and head, wet liners, hemispherical combustion chambers; 5 crankshaft bearings; valves: overhead, Vee-slanted at 80°, thimble tappets; camshafts: 2, overhead; lubrication: gear pump, full flow filter (cartridge), 11.4 imp pt, 13.7 US pt, 6.5 l; 2 Dell'Orto DHLA 40F horizontal twin barrel carburettors; fuel feed: mechanical pump; water-cooled, 14.1 imp pt, 16.9 US pt, 8 l, electric thermostatic fan.

TRANSMISSION driving wheels: rear; clutch: single dry plate (diaphragm), hydraulically controlled; gearbox: mechanical, in unit with differential; gears: 5, fully synchronized; ratios: I 3.300, II 2.000, III 1.370, IV 1.040, V 0.830, rev 2.620; lever: central; final drive: hypoid bevel; axle ratio: 4.300; width of rims: 5.5''; tyres: 165 SR x 14.

PERFORMANCE max speeds: (I) 28 mph, 45 km/h; (II) 47 mph, 75 km/h; (III) 68 mph, 109 km/h; (IV) 90 mph, 145 km/h; (V) 109 mph, 175 km/h; power-weight ratio: 21.2 lb/hp (28.9 lb/kW), 9.6 kg/hp (13.1 kg/kW); carrying capacity: 882 lb, 400 kg; acceleration: standing ¼ mile 18 sec; speed in top at 1,000 rpm: 19.4 mph, 31.2 km/h; consumption: 33.6 m/imp gal, 28 m/US gal, 8.4 l x 100 km.

CHASSIS integral; front suspension: independent, wishbones (upper trailing links), torsion bars, anti-roll bar, telescopic dampers; rear: de Dion rigid axle, oblique trailing arms, transverse Watt linkage, coil springs, anti-roll bar, telescopic dampers.

STEERING rack-and-pinion, adjustable height of steering wheel; turns lock to lock: 3.50.

BRAKES disc, rear compensator, servo; swept area: front 182.3 sq in, 1,176 sq cm, rear 156.6 sq in, 1,010 sq cm, total 338.9 sq in, 2,186 sq cm.

ELECTRICAL EQUIPMENT 12 V; 50 Ah battery; 540 W alternator; Bosch or Marelli distributor; 4 iodine headlamps.

DIMENSIONS AND WEIGHT wheel base: 98.82 in, 251 cm; tracks: 53.54 in, 136 cm front, 53.15 in, 135 cm rear; length: 168.50 in, 428 cm; width: 63.78 in, 162 cm; height: 56.30 in, 143 cm; ground clearance: 4.92 in, 12.5 cm; weight: 2,293 lb, 1,040 kg; turning circle (between walls): 33.1 ft, 10.1 m; fuel tank: 10.8 imp gal, 12.9 US gal, 49 l.

BODY saloon/sedan; 4 doors; 5 seats, separate front seats, reclining backrests; heated rear window.

PRACTICAL INSTRUCTIONS fuel: 98 oct petrol; oil: engine 10.4 imp pt, 12.5 US pt, 5.9 l, SAE 20W-50, change every 6,200 miles, 10,000 km - gearbox and final drive 4.9 imp pt, 5.9 US pt, 2.8 l, SAE 90, change every 18,600 miles, 30,000 km; greasing: none; tappet clearances: inlet 0.019-0.020 in, 0.47-0.50 mm, exhaust 0.020-0.022 in, 0.52-0.55 mm; valve timing: 41°20' 60°20' 62°40' 25°40'; tyre pressure: front 22 psi, 1.6 atm, rear 26 psi, 1.8 atm.

OPTIONAL ACCESSORIES adjustable headrests; Texalfa interior; light alloy wheels; metallic spray; tinted glass; air-conditioning with tinted glass.

Alfetta GT 1.6

See Alfetta 1.6, except for:

PRICE IN GB: £ 4,999*
PRICE EX WORKS: 7,682,000* liras

PERFORMANCE max speeds: 112 mph, 180 km/h; power-weight ratio: 20.3 lb/hp (27.6 lb/kW), 9.2 kg/hp (12.5 kg/kW); consumption: 34 m/imp gal, 28.3 m/US gal, 8.3 l x 100 km.

DIMENSIONS AND WEIGHT wheel base: 94.49 in, 240 cm; rear track: 53.54 in, 136 cm; length: 164.96 in, 419 cm; width: 65.35 in, 166 cm; height: 52.36 in, 133 cm; ground clearance: 4.80 in, 12 cm; weight: 2,183 lb, 990 kg.

BODY coupé; 2 doors; 4 seats, separate front seats, reclining backrests.

Alfetta 1.8

See Alfetta 1.6, except for:

PRICE IN GB: £ 4,300*
PRICE EX WORKS: 7,357,000* liras

ENGINE 108.6 cu in, 1,779 cc (3.15 x 3.48 in, 80 x 88.5 mm); compression ratio: 9.5:1; max power (DIN): 118 hp (86.8 kW) at 5,300 rpm; max torque (DIN): 123 lb ft, 17 kg m

ALFA ROMEO Alfetta 2000

(166.7 Nm) at 4,400 rpm; max engine rpm: 5,300; 66.3 hp/l (48.8 kW/l); 2 Dell'Orto DHLA 40 (or Solex C40 DDHE or Weber 40 DCOE 32) horizontal twin barrel carburettors.

TRANSMISSION axle ratio: 4.100.

PERFORMANCE max speeds: (I) 29 mph, 46 km/h; (II) 48 mph, 77 km/h; (III) 70 mph, 112 km/h; (IV) 92 mph, 148 km/h; (V) 112 mph, 180 km/h; power-weight ratio: 19.8 lb/hp (26.9 lb/kW), 9 kg/hp (12.2 kg/kW); acceleration: standing ¼ mile 17.3 sec; speed in top at 1,000 rpm: 20.8 mph, 33.5 km/h; consumption: 32.1 m/imp gal, 26.7 m/US gal, 8.8 l x 100 km.

DIMENSIONS AND WEIGHT weight: 2,337 lb, 1,060 kg.

Alfetta 2000

See Alfetta 1.6 except for:

PRICE IN USA: $ 7,235
PRICE EX WORKS: 8,490,000* liras

ENGINE 119.7 cu in, 1,962 cc (3.31 x 3.48 in, 84 x 88.5 mm); max power (DIN): 122 hp (89.8 kW) at 5,300 rpm; max torque (DIN): 130 lb ft, 17.9 kg m (175.5 Nm) at 4,000 rpm; 62.2 hp/l (45.8 kW/l); 2 Dell'Orto DHLA 40G or Solex C40 ADDHE twin barrel carburettors.

ALFA ROMEO Alfetta 2000

ALFA ROMEO Alfetta GTV 2000

ALFETTA 2000

TRANSMISSION axle ratio: 4.100; tyres: 165 HR x 14.

PERFORMANCE max speeds: (I) 28 mph, 45 km/h; (II) 46 mph, 74 km/h; (III) 68 mph, 109 km/h; (IV) 89 mph, 143 km/h; (V) 115 mph, 185 km/h; power-weight ratio: 19.6 lb/hp (26.7 lb/kW), 8.9 kg/hp (12.1 kg/kW); acceleration: standing ¼ mile 16.8 sec; speed in top at 1,000 rpm: 20.6 mph, 33.2 km/h; consumption: 24.6 m/imp gal, 20.5 m/US gal, 11.5 l x 100 km.

ELECTRICAL EQUIPMENT 60 Ah battery.

DIMENSIONS AND WEIGHT rear track: 53.46 in, 136 cm; length: 172.64 in, 438 cm; width: 64.57 in, 164 cm; ground clearance: 5.51 in, 14 cm; weight: 2,403 lb, 1,090 kg; weight distribution: 50% front axle, 50% rear axle.

PRACTICAL INSTRUCTIONS oil: engine 11.4 imp pt, 13.7 US pt, 6.5 l, SAE 10W-50, change every 6,200 miles, 10,000 km; gearbox and final drive 4.9 imp pt, 5.9 US pt, 2.8 l, SAE 90, change every 24,900 miles, 40,000 km; valve timing: 33°54' 57°54' 57°14' 21°14'; tyre pressure: front 26 psi, 1.8 atm, rear 26 psi, 1.8 atm.

OPTIONAL ACCESSORIES light alloy wheels; metallic spray; air-conditioning.

Alfetta GTV 2000

See Alfetta 1.6, except for:

PRICE IN GB: £ 5,499*
PRICE IN USA: $ 8,515

ENGINE 119.7 cu in, 1,962 cc (3.31 x 3.48 in, 84 x 88.5 mm); max power (DIN): 122 hp (89.8 kW) at 5,300 rpm; max torque (DIN): 130 lb ft, 17.9 kg m (175.5 Nm) at 4000 rpm; max engine rpm: 5,500; 62.1 hp/l (45.7 kW/l).

PERFORMANCE max speed: 121 mph, 194 km/h; power-weight ratio: 17.9 lb/hp (24.3 lb/kW), 8.1 kg/hp (11 kg/kW); speed in top at 1,000 rpm: 20.8 mph, 33.5 km/h; consumption: 31.4 m/imp gal, 26.1 m/US gal, 9 l x 100 km.

DIMENSIONS AND WEIGHT wheel base: 94.49 in, 240 cm; rear track: 53.54 in, 136 cm; length: 165.35 in, 420 cm; width: 65.35 in, 166 cm; height: 52.36 in, 133 cm; ground clearance: 4.80 in, 12 cm; weight: 2,183 lb, 990 kg.

BODY coupé; 2 doors; 4 seats, separate front seats, reclining backrests.

2000 Spider Veloce

PRICE IN GB: £ 5,499*
PRICE IN USA: $ 8,895

ENGINE front, 4 stroke; 4 cylinders, vertical, in line; 119.7 cu in, 1,962 cc (3.31 x 3.48 in, 84 x 88.5 mm); compression ratio: 9:1; max power (SAE): 147 hp (108.2 kW) at 5,300 rpm; max torque (SAE): 151 lb ft, 20.9 kg m (205 Nm) at 4,400 rpm; max engine rpm: 5,300; 74.9 hp/l (55.1 kW/l); light alloy block and head, wet liners, hemispherical combustion chambers; 5 crankshaft bearings; valves: overhead, Vee-slanted at 80°, thimble tappets; camshafts: 2, overhead; lubrication: gear pump, full flow filter (cartridge), 12.7 imp pt, 15.2 US pt, 7.2 l; 2 Solex C 40 DDH5 or Dell'Orto DHLA 40 horizontal twin barrel carburettors; fuel feed: mechanical pump; water-cooled, 17.1 imp pt, 20.5 US pt, 9.7 l.

TRANSMISSION driving wheels: rear; clutch: single dry plate, hydraulically controlled; gearbox: mechanical; gears: 5, fully synchronized; ratios: I 3.300, II 1.990, III 1.350, IV 1, V 0.790, rev 3.010; lever: central; final drive: hypoid bevel, limited slip differential; axle ratio: 4.100; width of rims: 5.5''; tyres: 165 HR x 14.

PERFORMANCE max speeds: (I) 29 mph, 47 km/h; (II) 48 mph, 77 km/h; (III) 71 mph, 114 km/h; (IV) 96 mph, 154 km/h; (V) over 121 mph, 195 km/h; power-weight ratio: 15.7 lb/hp (21.2 lb/kW), 7.1 kg/hp (9.6 kg/kW); carrying capacity: 772 lb, 350 kg; acceleration: standing ¼ mile 16.8 sec; speed in top at 1,000 rpm: 20.9 mph, 33.7 km/h; consumption: 23.7 m/imp gal, 19.8 m/US gal, 11.9 l x 100 km.

CHASSIS integral; front suspension: independent, wishbones (lower trailing links), coil springs, anti-roll bar, telescopic dampers; rear: rigid axle, trailing lower radius arms, upper transverse Vee radius arm, coil springs, anti-roll bar, telescopic dampers.

STEERING recirculating ball or worm and roller; turns lock to lock: 3.70.

BRAKES disc, rear compensator, servo; swept area: front 229.8 sq in, 1,482 sq cm, rear 167.1 sq in, 1,078 sq cm, total 396.9 sq in, 2,560 sq cm.

ELECTRICAL EQUIPMENT 12 V; 50 Ah battery; 540 W alternator; Bosch or Marelli distributor; 4 iodine headlamps.

ALFA ROMEO Alfetta GTV 2000

AUTOBIANCHI A 112 Elegant

DIMENSIONS AND WEIGHT wheel base: 88.58 in, 225 cm; tracks: 52.13 in, 132 cm front, 50.16 in, 127 cm rear; length: 162.20 in, 412 cm; width: 64.17 in, 163 cm; height: 50.79 in, 129 cm; ground clearance: 4.72 in, 12 cm; weight: 2,293 lb, 1,040 kg; turning circle (between walls): 34.4 ft, 10.5 m; fuel tank: 11.2 imp gal, 13.5 US gal, 51 l.

BODY convertible; 2 doors; 2 + 2 seats, separate front seats, reclining backrests; heated rear window.

PRACTICAL INSTRUCTIONS fuel: 98-100 oct petrol; oil: engine 11.8 imp pt, 14.2 US pt, 6.7 l, SAE 20W-50, change every 6,200 miles, 10,000 km - gearbox 3.2 imp pt, 3.8 US pt, 1.8 l, SAE 90 EP, change every 11,200 miles, 18,000 km - final drive 2.5 imp pt, 3 US pt, 1.4 l, SAE 90 EP, change every 11,200 miles, 18,000 km; greasing: every 18,600 miles, 30,000 km, 1 point; tappet clearances: inlet 0.019-0.020 in, 0.47-0.50 mm, exhaust 0.020-0.022 in, 0.52-0.55 mm; valve timing: 41°20' 62°20' 53°40' 34°40'; tyre pressure: front 24 psi, 1.7 atm, rear 26 psi, 1.8 atm.

OPTIONAL ACCESSORIES hardtop; headrests; light alloy wheels; metallic spray; leather upholstery.

AUTOBIANCHI ITALY

A 112 Normale

PRICE EX WORKS: 2,280,000 liras

ENGINE front, transverse, 4 stroke; 4 cylinders, in line; 55.1 cu in, 903 cc (2.56 x 2.68 in, 65 x 68 mm); compression ratio: 9:1; max power (DIN): 42 hp (30.9 kW) at 5,400 rpm; max torque (DIN): 51 lb ft, 7 kg m (68.6 Nm) at 2,800 rpm; 46.5 hp/l (34.2 kW/l); cast iron cylinder block, light alloy head; 3 crankshaft bearings; valves: overhead, push-rods and rockers; camshafts: 1, side; lubrication: gear pump, cartridge filter, 6.0 imp pt, 8.2 US pt, 3.9 l; 1 Weber 32 IBA 23 downdraught single barrel carburettor; fuel feed: mechanical pump; water-cooled, 8.8 imp pt, 10.6 US pt, 5 l, electric thermostatic fan.

TRANSMISSION driving wheels: front; clutch: single dry plate; gearbox: mechanical; gears: 4, fully synchronized; ratios: I 3.909, II 2.055, III 1.348, IV 0.963, rev 3.615; lever: central; final drive: cylindrical gears; axle ratio: 4.460; width of rims: 4''; tyres: 135 SR x 13.

PERFORMANCE max speeds: (I) 23 mph, 37 km/h; (II) 43 mph, 70 km/h; (III) 66 mph, 107 km/h; (IV) 84 mph, 135 km/h; power-weight ratio: 34.4 lb/hp (46.7 lb/kW), 15.6 kg hp (21.2 kg/kW); carrying capacity: 882 lb, 400 kg; speed in top at 1,000 rpm: 13.8 mph, 22.2 km/h; consumption: 43.5 m/imp gal, 36.2 m/US gal, 6.5 l x 100 km.

CHASSIS integral; front suspension: independent, by McPherson, coil springs/telescopic damper struts, lower wishbones (trailing links), anti-roll bar; rear: independent, wishbones, transverse anti-roll leafspring lower arms, telescopic dampers.

AUTOBIANCHI A 112 Elegant

AUTOBIANCHI A 112 Abarth

STEERING rack-and-pinion; turns lock to lock: 3.40.

BRAKES front disc, rear drum, dual circuit, rear compensator; lining area: front 19.2 sq in, 124 sq cm, rear 33.5 sq in, 216 sq cm, total 52.7 sq in, 340 sq cm.

ELECTRICAL EQUIPMENT 12 V; 34 Ah battery; 400 W alternator; Marelli distributor; 2 headlamps.

DIMENSIONS AND WEIGHT wheel base: 80.24 in, 204 cm; tracks: 49.21 in, 125 cm front, 48.03 in, 122 cm rear; length: 125.98 in, 320 cm; width: 58.27 in, 148 cm; height: 53.54 in, 136 cm; ground clearance: 5.59 in, 14.2 cm; weight: 1,444 lb, 655 kg; weight distribution: 60% front, 40% rear; turning circle (between walls): 29.2 ft, 8.9 m; fuel tank: 6.6 imp gal, 7.9 US gal, 30 l.

BODY saloon/sedan; 2 + 1 doors; 5 seats, separate front seats, reclining backrests; folding rear seat.

PRACTICAL INSTRUCTIONS fuel: 98 oct petrol; oil: engine 6.2 imp pt, 7.4 US pt, SAE 10W-20 (winter) 30W-40 (summer), change every 6,200 miles, 10,000 km - gearbox and final drive 4.2 imp pt, 5.1 US pt, 2.4 l, ZC 90, change every 18,600 miles, 30,000 km; greasing: none; tappet clearances: inlet 0.006 in, 0.15 mm, exhaust 0.008 in, 0.20 mm; valve timing: 11° 43° 43° 11°; tyre pressure: front 24 psi, 1.7 atm, rear 27 psi, 1.9 atm.

OPTIONAL ACCESSORIES heated rear window; antitheft; adjustable front seats; front vents; rear opening vents.

AUTOBIANCHI A 112 Abarth

DE TOMASO Pantera GTS

A 112 Elegant

See A 112 Normale, except for:

PRICE EX WORKS: 2,500,000 liras

ENGINE 58.9 cu in, 965 cc (2.65 x 2.68 in, 67.2 x 68 mm); compression ratio: 9.2:1; max power (DIN): 48 hp (35.3 kW) at 5,600 rpm; max torque (DIN): 53 lb ft, 7.3 kg m (71.6 Nm) at 3,300 rpm; 49.7 hp/l (36.5 kW/l); 1 Weber 32 IBA 22 downdraught single barrel carburettor.

PERFORMANCE max speed: 87 mph, 140 km/h; power-weight ratio: 30 lb/hp (40.9 lb/kW), 13.6 kg/hp (18.5 kg/kW); consumption: 40.9 m/imp gal, 34.1 m/US gal, 6.9 l x 100 km.

BODY special luxury interior.

PRACTICAL INSTRUCTIONS tappet clearances: inlet 0.006 in, 0.15 mm, exhaust 0.006 in, 0.15 mm; valve timing: 17° 43° 57° 3°.

OPTIONAL ACCESSORIES 2-colour spray; light alloy wheels; tinted glass; metallic spray; built-in headrests; rev counter; heated rear window.

A 112 Abarth

See A 112 Berlina Normale, except for:

PRICE EX WORKS: 2,790,000 liras

ENGINE 64.1 cu in, 1,050 cc (2.65 x 2.91 in, 67.2 x 74 mm); compression ratio: 10.4:1; max power (DIN): 70 hp (51.5 kW) at 6,660 rpm; max torque (DIN): 63 lb ft, 8.7 kg m (85.3 Nm) at 4,200 rpm; 66.7 hp/l (49.1 kW/l); lubricating system: 7.9 imp pt, 9.5 US pt, 4.5 l; 1 Weber 32 DMTR 3 vertical twin barrel carburettor.

PERFORMANCE max speed: 99 mph, 160 km/h; power-weight ratio: 22.1 lb/hp (30 lb/kW), 10 kg/hp (13.6 kg/kW); consumption: 39.2 m/imp gal, 32.7 m/US gal, 7.2 l x 100 km.

BRAKES servo.

DIMENSIONS AND WEIGHT weight: 1,544 lb, 700 kg; weight distribution: 62% front, 38% rear.

BODY built-in headrests; rev counter (standard).

PRACTICAL INSTRUCTIONS oil: engine 7.9 imp pt, 9.5 US pt, 4.5 l; tappet clearances: inlet 0.010 in, 0.25 mm, exhaust 0.012 in, 0.30 mm; valve timing: 16° 56° 56° 16°.

DE TOMASO　　　　　　　　　　**ITALY**

Pantera L

PRICE IN GB: £ 13,280*
PRICE EX WORKS: 14,850,000* liras

ENGINE Ford, central, 4 stroke; 8 cylinders, Vee-slanted at 90°; 351.7 cu in, 5,763 cc (4 x 3.50 in, 101.6 x 89 mm); compression ratio: 8.5:1; max power (SAE): 330 hp (243 kW) at 5,400 rpm; max torque (SAE): 326 lb ft, 45 kg m (441.3 Nm) at 3,400 rpm; max engine rpm: 6,000; 53.8 hp/l (42.2 kW/l); cast iron block and head; 5 crankshaft bearings; valves: overhead, slanted, push-rods and rockers, hydraulic tappets; camshafts: 1, at centre of Vee; lubrication: rotary pump, full flow filter, 9.7 imp pt, 11.6 US pt, 5.5 l; 1 Motorcraft downdraught 4-barrel carburettor; fuel feed: mechanical pump; water-cooled, 42.2 imp pt, 50.7 US pt, 24 l, electric fan.

TRANSMISSION driving wheels: rear; clutch: single dry plate, hydraulically controlled; gearbox: ZF mechanical; gears: 5, fully synchronized; ratios: I 2.230, II 1.475, III 1.040, IV 0.846, V 0.705, rev 2.865; lever: central; final drive: spiral bevel, limited slip differential; axle ratio: 4.220; width of rims: 7" front, 8" rear; tyres: 185/70 VR x 15 front, 215/70 VR x 15 rear.

PERFORMANCE max speed: 158 mph, 254 km/h; power-weight ratio: 9.5 lb/hp (12.9 lb/kW), 4.3 kg/hp (5.8 kg/kW); speed in top at 1,000 rpm: 27 mph, 43.5 km/h; consumption: 14.1 m/imp gal, 11.8 m/US gal, 20 l x 100 km.

CHASSIS integral; front and rear suspension: independent, wishbones, coil springs, anti-roll bar, telescopic dampers.

STEERING rack-and-pinion; turns lock to lock: 3.40.

BRAKES disc (front diameter 11.18 in, 28.4 cm, rear 11.10 in, 28.2 cm), dual circuit, internal radial fins, servo.

ELECTRICAL EQUIPMENT 12 V; 72 Ah battery; 55 A alternator; 4 iodine headlamps.

PANTERA L

DIMENSIONS AND WEIGHT wheel base: 98.82 in, 251 cm; tracks: 57.09 in, 145 cm front, 57.48 in, 146 cm rear; length: 168.11 in, 427 cm; width: 72.05 in, 183 cm; height: 43.31 in, 110 cm; ground clearance: 4.72 in, 12 cm; dry weight: 3,131 lb, 1,420 kg; turning circle (between walls): 39.4 ft, 12 m; fuel tank: 17.6 imp gal, 21.1 US gal, 80 l.

BODY coupé; 2 doors; 2 seats, built-in headrests; electric windows; tinted glass; heated rear window; air-conditioning; light alloy wheels.

PRACTICAL INSTRUCTIONS fuel: 98-100 oct petrol; oil: engine 9.2 imp pt, 11 US pt, 5.2 l, SAE 10W-40 (winter) 20W-50 (summer), change every 3,100 miles, 5,000 km - gearbox and final drive 6 imp pt, 7.2 US pt, 3.4 l, SAE 90, change every 3,700 miles, 6,000 km; greasing: every 3,700 miles, 6,000 km, 2 points; valve timing: 14° 72° 70° 20°.

OPTIONAL ACCESSORIES right-hand drive; metallic spray.

Pantera GTS

See Pantera L, except for:

PRICE IN GB: £ 13,631*
PRICE EX WORKS 15,525,000* liras

ENGINE max power (SAE): 350 hp (257.6 kW) at 6,000 rpm; max torque (SAE): 333 lb ft, 46 kg m (451 Nm) at 3,800 rpm; 60.7 hp/l (44.7 kW/l).

PERFORMANCE max speed: about 174 mph, 280 km/h; power-weight ratio: 9 lb/hp (12.2 lb/kW), 4.1 kg/hp (5.5 kg/kW).

Deauville

See Pantera L, except for:

PRICE IN GB: £ 16,357*
PRICE EX WORKS: 19,450,000* liras

ENGINE front; cooling system capacity: 31.7 imp pt, 38.1 US pt, 18 l.

TRANSMISSION gearbox: Select-Shift Cruise-o-matic automatic transmission, hydraulic torque converter and planetary gears with 3 ratios + reverse, max ratio of converter at stall 2.05, possible manual selection; ratios: I 2.460, II 1.460, III 1, rev 2.100; axle ratio: 3.070; width of rims: 7''; tyres: 215/70 VR x 15.

PERFORMANCE max speed: over 150 mph, 241 km/h; power-weight ratio: 13 lb/hp (17.6 lb/kW), 5.9 kg/hp (8 kg/kW); carrying capacity: 1,169 lb, 530 kg; acceleration: standing ¼ mile 16 sec; speed in direct drive at 1,000 rpm: 23.9 mph, 38.4 km/h; fuel consumption: 16 m/imp gal, 13.4 m/US gal, 17.6 l x 100 km.

CHASSIS rear suspension: trailing radius arms, 4 coil springs, 4 telescopic dampers.

DE TOMASO Deauville

DE TOMASO Deauville

STEERING servo.

DIMENSIONS AND WEIGHT wheel base: 109.05 in, 277 cm; tracks: 59.84 in, 152 cm front, 59.84 in, 152 cm rear; length: 195.52 in, 489 cm; width: 73.94 in, 188 cm; height: 53.86 in, 137 cm; ground clearance: 5.12 in, 13 cm; dry weight: 4,278 lb, 1,940 kg; turning circle (between walls): 42.6 ft, 13 m; fuel tank: 26.4 imp gal, 31.7 US gal, 120 l.

BODY saloon/sedan; 4 doors; 5 seats, separate front seats, reclining backrests.

PRACTICAL INSTRUCTIONS oil: engine 7 imp pt, 8.5 US pt, 4 l - automatic transmission 17.6 imp pt, 21.1 US pt, 10 l - final drive 3.2 imp pt, 3.8 US pt, 1.8 l.

OPTIONAL ACCESSORIES oil cooler.

Longchamp 2 + 2

See Deauville, except for:

PRICE IN GB: £ 16,123*
PRICE EX WORKS: 18,500,000* liras

PERFORMANCE max speed: 149 mph, 240 km/h; power-weight ratio: 11.6 lb/hp (16.3 lb/kW), 5.3 kg/hp (7.2 kg/kW); speed in direct drive at 1,000 rpm: 24.9 mph, 40 km/h; consumption: 16.6 m/imp gal, 13.8 m/US gal, 17 l x 100 km.

ELECTRICAL EQUIPMENT 61 A alternator.

DIMENSIONS AND WEIGHT wheel base: 102.36 in, 260 cm; length: 177.95 in, 452 cm; width: 72.44 in, 184 cm; height: 50.79 in, 129 cm; ground clearance: 5.91 in, 15 cm; dry weight: 3,859 lb, 1,750 kg; turning circle (between walls): 37.7 ft, 11.5 m; fuel tank: 22 imp gal, 26.4 US gal, 100 l.

BODY coupé; 2 doors; 2 + 2 seats.

ENNEZETA   **ITALY**

Nuova Lele Iso Rivolta

PRICE EX WORKS: 15,000,000* liras

ENGINE Ford, front, 4 stroke; 8 cylinders, Vee-slanted at 90°; 351.6 cu in, 5,762 cc (4 x 3.50 in, 101.6 x 88.9 mm); compression ratio: 8.6:1; max power (SAE): 325 hp (239.2 kW) at 5,800 rpm; max torque (SAE): 349 lb ft, 48.3 kg m (473.7 Nm) at 3,800 rpm; max engine rpm: 5,800; 56.4 hp/l (82.2 kW/l); cast iron block and head; 5 crankshaft bearings; valves: 8, overhead, in line, push-rods and rockers, hydraulic tappets; camshafts: 1, at centre of Vee; lubrication: gear pump, full flow filter (cartridge), 11.4 imp pt, 13.7 US pt, 6.5 l; fuel feed: electric pump; water-cooled, 31.7 imp pt, 38.1 US pt, 18 l.

TRANSMISSION driving wheels: rear; automatic transmission, hydraulic torque converter and planetary gears with 3 ratios, max ratio of converter at stall 2.10, possible

ENNEZETA Nuova Lele Iso Rivolta

manual selection; ratios: I 2.460, II 1.460, III 1, rev 2.180; lever: central; final drive: hypoid bevel, limited slip differential; axle ratio: 3.310; width of rims: 7''; tyres: 215/70 VR x 15.

PERFORMANCE max speeds: (I) 57 mph, 91 km/h; (II) 95 mph, 153 km/h; (III) 149 mph, 240 km/h; power-weight ratio: 11.7 lb/hp (16.1 lb/kW), 5.3 kg/hp (7.3 kg/kW); carrying capacity: 882 lb, 400 kg; acceleration: standing ¼ mile 13.8 sec, 0-50 mph (0-80 km/h) 6 sec; speed in direct drive at 1,000 rpm: 26.1 mph, 42 km/h; consumption: 14.9 m/imp gal, 12.4 m/US gal, 19 l x 100 km.

CHASSIS integral; front suspension: independent, wishbones, coil springs, anti-roll bar, telescopic dampers; rear: De Dion rigid axle, twin trailing radius arms, transverse linkage bar, coil springs, telescopic dampers.

STEERING recirculating ball, servo; turns lock to lock: 4.

BRAKES disc, servo; lining area: front 36.7 sq in, 237 sq cm, rear 21.1 sq in, 136 sq cm, total 57.8 sq in, 373 sq cm.

ELECTRICAL EQUIPMENT 12 V; 80 Ah battery; 630 W alternator; Motorcraft distributor; electronic ignition; 4 iodine headlamps.

DIMENSIONS AND WEIGHT wheel base: 106.30 in, 270 cm; front and rear track: 56.69 in, 144 cm; length: 183.58 in, 466 cm; width: 69.90 in, 175 cm; height: 52.36 in, 133 cm; ground clearance: 4.72 in, 12 cm; weight: 3,837 lb, 1,740 kg; weight distribution: 55% front, 45% rear; turning circle (between walls): 39.4 ft, 12 m; fuel tank: 24.6 imp gal, 22 US gal, 100 l.

BODY saloon/sedan; 2 doors; 5 seats; built-in headrests; rear window.

PRACTICAL INSTRUCTIONS fuel: 88-100 oct petrol; oil: engine 11.4 imp pt, 13.7 US pt, 6.5 l, SAE 20W-50, change every 6,200 miles, 10,000 km - gearbox 16.7 imp pt, 4.6 US pt, 9.5 l, Castrol TQF - final drive 3.2 imp pt, 3.8 US pt, 1.8 l, SAE 90, change every 12,400 miles, 20,000 km; greasing: every 9,300 miles, 15,000 km, 12 points; tyre pressure: front 31 psi, 2.2 atm, rear 34 psi, 2.4 atm.

OPTIONAL ACCESSORIES leather upholstery; tinted glass; electric windows; adjustable steering wheel; adjustable speed wiper; brake warning light; electromagnetic bonnet and boot clips.

FERRARI   ITALY

Dino 208 GT 4

PRICE EX WORKS: 15,000,000 liras

ENGINE central, transverse, 4 stroke; 8 cylinders, Vee-slanted at 90°; 121.5 cu in, 1,991 cc (2.63 x 2.80 in, 66.8 x 71 mm); compression ratio: 9:1; max power (DIN) 170 hp (125.1 kW) at 7,700 rpm; max torque (DIN): 138 lb ft, 19 kg m (186.3 Nm) at 4,900 rpm; max engine rpm: 7,700; 85.4 hp/l (62.8 kW/l); light alloy block and head, wet liners; 5 crankshaft bearings; valves: overhead, Vee-slanted, thimble tappets; camshafts: 2 per cylinder block, overhead, cogged belt; lubrication: gear pump, full flow filter, oil cooler; 4 Weber 40 DCNF downdraught twin barrel carburettors; fuel feed: electric pump; water-cooled, front radiator, 2 electric automatic fans.

TRANSMISSION driving wheels: rear; clutch: single dry plate; gearbox: mechanical; gears: 5, fully synchronized; ratios: I 3.425, II 2.353, III 1.695, IV 1.245, V 0.882, rev 3; lever: central; final drive: hypoid bevel, limited slip differential; axle ratio: 4.600; width of rims: 6.5''; tyres: 195/70 VR x 14 DX.

PERFORMANCE max speeds: (I) 35 mph, 57 km/h; (II) 52 mph, 83 km/h; (III) 71 mph, 115 km/h; (IV) 98 mph, 157 km/h; (V) 138 mph, 222 km/h; power-weight ratio: 14.9 lb/hp (20.2 lb/kW), 6.8 kg/hp (9.1 kg/kW); acceleration: standing ¼ mile 16 sec; speed in top at 1,000 rpm: 17.9 mph, 28.8 km/h; consumption: 17.7/15.7 m/imp gal, 14.7/13.1 m/US gal, 16/18 l x 100 km.

CHASSIS tubular; front suspension: independent, wishbones, anti-roll bar, coil springs/telescopic dampers; rear: independent, wishbones, anti-roll bar, coil springs/telescopic dampers.

STEERING rack-and-pinion.

BRAKES disc, internal radial fins, dual circuit, servo.

ELECTRICAL EQUIPMENT 12 V; alternator; 2 Marelli distributors; electronic ignition; 4 retractable iodine headlamps.

DIMENSIONS AND WEIGHT wheel base: 100.39 in, 255 cm; front and rear track: 57.48 in, 146 cm; length: 169.29 in,

430 cm; width: 70.87 in, 180 cm; height: 46.46 in, 118 cm; ground clearance: 4.72 in, 12 cm; weight: 2,536 lb, 1,150 kg; turning circle (between walls): 41 ft, 12.5 m; fuel tank: 17.6 imp gal, 21.1 US gal, 80 l (2 separate tanks).

BODY coupé; 2 doors; 2 + 2 seats, separate front seats, reclining backrests; built-in headrests; tinted glass; heated rear window; light alloy wheels; quartz clock.

PRACTICAL INSTRUCTIONS fuel: 98-100 oct petrol.

OPTIONAL ACCESSORIES electric windows; air-conditioning.

Dino 308 GT 4

See Dino 208 GT 4, except for:

PRICE IN GB: £ 13,499*
PRICE IN USA: $ 27,650*

ENGINE 178.5 cu in, 2,926 cc (3.19 x 2.80 in, 81 x 71 mm); compression ratio: 8.8:1; max power (DIN): 255 hp (187.8 kW) at 7,600 rpm; max power: 87.1 hp/l (64.1 kW/l).

TRANSMISSION ratios: I 3.230, II 2.235, III 1.619, IV 1.200, V 0.897, rev 3; axle ratio: 3.500; tyres: 205/70 VR x 14.

PERFORMANCE max speeds: (I) 43 mph, 70 km/h; (II) 63 mph, 101 km/h; (III) 87 mph, 140 km/h; (IV) 119 mph, 191 km/h; (V) 155 mph, 250 km/h; power-weight ratio: 9.9 lb/hp (13.4 lb/kW), 4.5 kg/hp (6.1 kg/kW); acceleration:

standing ¼ mile 14.4 sec; speed in top at 1,000 rpm: 22.7 mph, 36.5 km/h; consumption: 14.9 m/imp gal, 12.4 m/US gal, 19 l x 100 km.

OPTIONAL ACCESSORIES leather upholstery; metallic spray; factory fitted sun-roof; air-conditioning.

308 GTB

See Dino 308 GT 4, except for:

PRICE IN GB: £ 14,500*
PRICE IN USA: $ 30,920*

ENGINE lubrication: dry sump.

TRANSMISSION axle ratio: 3.700.

PERFORMANCE max speeds: (I) 41 mph, 66 km/h; (II) 59 mph, 95 km/h; (III) 83 mph, 133 km/h; (IV) 112 mph, 180 km/h; (V) 157 mph, 252 km/h; power-weight ratio: 9.5 lb/hp (12.8 lb/kW), 4.3 kg/hp (5.8 kg/kW).

DIMENSIONS AND WEIGHT wheel base: 92.13 in, 234 cm; front and rear track: 57.48 in, 146 cm; length: 166.54 in, 423 cm; width: 67.72 in, 172 cm; height: 44.09 in, 112 cm; weight: 2,403 lb, 1,090 kg; turning circle (between walls): 39.4 ft, 12 m.

BODY 2 seats; built-in headrests; light alloy wheels; electronic speedometer; electronic rev counter; safety belts.

FERRARI Dino 208 GT 4

FERRARI 308 GTB

308 GTS

See 308 GTS, except for:

PRICE EX WORKS: 18,500,000 liras

BODY spider; 2 doors; 2 + 2 seats; built-in headrests; light alloy wheels; electronic speedometer; electronic rev counter; safety belts.

400 Automatic

PRICE IN GB: £ 23,999*
PRICE EX WORKS: 27,400,000 liras

ENGINE front, 4 stroke; 12 cylinders, Vee-slanted at 60°; 294.3 cu in, 4,823 cc (3.19 x 3.07 in, 81 x 78 mm); compression ratio: 8.8:1; max power (DIN): 340 hp (250.2 kW) at 6,500 rpm; max torque (DIN): 312 lb ft, 43 kg m (421.7 Nm) at 4,600 rpm; max engine rpm: 6,800; 70.5 hp/l (51.9 kW/l); light alloy block and head, wet liners; 7 crankshaft bearings; valves: overhead, Vee-slanted at 46°, thimble tappets; camshafts: 4 per cylinder block, overhead; lubrication: gear pump (cartridge), 31.7 imp pt, 38.1 US pt, 18 l; 6 Weber 38 DCOE 59/60 carburettors; fuel feed: 2 electric pumps; water-cooled, 22.9 imp pt, 27.5 US pt, 13 l, 2 electric automatic fans.

TRANSMISSION driving wheels: rear; gearbox: GM automatic transmission, hydraulic torque converter and planetary gears with 3 ratios, max ratio of converter at stall 2.20, possible manual selection; gears: ratios: I 2.520, II 1.520, III 1, rev 1.940; lever: central; final drive: spiral bevel, limited slip differential; axle ratio: 3.250; width of rims: 7.5''; tyres: 215/70 VR x 15.

PERFORMANCE max speeds: (I) 61 mph, 98 km/h; (II) 101 mph, 164 km/h; (III) 149 mph, 240 km/h; power-weight ratio: 11 lb/hp (15 lb/kW), 5 kg/hp (6.8 kg/kW); speed in direct drive at 1,000 rpm: 22.7 mph, 36.6 km/h; consumption: 14.1 m/imp gal, 11.8 m/US gal, 20 l x 100 km.

CHASSIS tubular; front suspension: independent, wishbones, anti-roll bar, coil springs/telescopic dampers; rear: independent, wishbones, anti-roll bar, coil springs/telescopic dampers.

STEERING recirculating ball, ZF servo; turns lock to lock: 3.20.

BRAKES discs (front diameter 11.34 in, 28.8 cm, rear 11.69 in, 29.7 cm), internal radial fins, dual circuit, servo; lining area: front 28.8 sq in, 186 sq cm, rear 19.5 sq in, 126 sq cm, total 48.3 sq in, 312 sq cm.

ELECTRICAL EQUIPMENT 12 V; 77 Ah battery; 960 W alternator; Marelli S 129 E distributor; 4 retractable iodine headlamps.

DIMENSIONS AND WEIGHT wheel base: 106.30 in, 270 cm; tracks: 57.87 in, 147 cm front, 59.06 in, 150 cm rear; length: 189.37 in, 481 cm; width: 70.87 in, 180 cm; height: 51.57 in, 131 cm; ground clearance: 5.12 in, 13 cm; weight: 3,749 lb, 1,700 kg; turning circle (between walls): 41.7 ft, 12.7 m; fuel tank: 26 imp gal, 31 US gal, 118 l.

BODY coupé; 2 doors; 2 + 2 seats, separate front seats, reclining backrests with built-in headrests; folding rear seat; air-conditioning; electric windows; heated rear window.

PRACTICAL INSTRUCTIONS fuel: 98-100 oct petrol; oil: engine 31.7 imp pt, 38.1 US pt, 18 l, SAE 20W-40, change every 6,200 miles, 10,000 km - gearbox 7.9 imp pt, 9.5 US pt, 4.5 l, SAE 80 EP, change every 6,200 miles, 10,000 km - final drive 4.4 imp pt, 5.3 US pt, 2.5 l, change every 6,200 miles, 10,000 km; greasing: every 6,200 miles, 10,000 km, 8 points; tappet clearances: inlet 0.004-0.006 in, 0.10-0.15 mm, exhaust 0.010-0.012 in, 0.25-0.30 mm; tyre pressure: front 34 psi, 2.4 atm, rear 38 psi, 2.7 atm.

OPTIONAL ACCESSORIES 5 speed mechanical gearbox, ratios (I 2.590, II 1.706, III 1.254, IV 1, V 0.815, rev 2.240), axle ratio 4.300.

BB 512

PRICE IN GB: £ 26,000*
PRICE EX WORKS: 29,500,000 liras

ENGINE rear, central, 4 stroke; 12 cylinders, horizontally opposed; 301.6 cu in, 4,942 cc (3.23 x 3.07 in, 82 x 78 mm); compression ratio: 9.2:1; max power (DIN): 360 hp (265 kW) at 6,800 rpm; max engine rpm: 6,800; 72.8 hp/l (53.6 kW/l); light alloy block and head, cast iron liners; 7 crankshaft bearings; valves: overhead, Vee-slanted, thimble tappets; camshafts: 4 overhead per cylinder block, cogged belt; lubrication: gear pump, full flow filter, dry sump, oil water heat exchanger, 17.6 imp pt, 21.1 US pt, 10 l; 4 Weber 40 IF3 C three-barrel carburettors; fuel feed: 2 electric pumps; water-cooled, 24.6 imp pt, 29.6 US pt, 14 l, 2 electric automatic fans.

TRANSMISSION driving wheels: rear; clutch: single dry plate; gearbox: mechanical, in unit with final drive; gears: 5, fully synchronized; ratios: I 3.075, II 2.120, III 1.572, IV 1.250, V 0.964, rev 2.670; lever: central; final drive: hypoid bevel, limited slip differential; axle ratio: 3.300.

width of rims: 7.5'' front, 9'' rear; tyres: 215/70 VR x 15 front, 225/70 VR x 15 rear.

PERFORMANCE max speeds: (I) 58 mph, 93 km/h; (II) 81 mph, 130 km/h; (III) 107 mph, 173 km/h; (IV) 141 mph, 227 km/h; (V) 188 mph, 302 km/h; power-weight ratio: 8.6 lb/hp (11.7 lb/kW), 3.9 kg/hp (5.3 kg/kW); speed in top at 1,000 rpm: 26.4 mph, 42.5 km/h; consumption: 13.5 m/imp gal, 11.2 m/US gal, 21 l x 100 km.

CHASSIS tubular; front suspension: independent, wishbones, anti-roll bar, coil springs/telescopic dampers; rear: independent, wishbones, coil springs, anti-roll bar, 4 telescopic dampers.

STEERING worm and roller.

BRAKES discs, internal radial fins, servo.

ELECTRICAL EQUIPMENT 12 V; 74 Ah battery; 660 W alternator; Marelli distributor; electronic ignition; 2 retractable headlamps.

DIMENSIONS AND WEIGHT wheel base: 98.43 in, 250 cm; tracks: 59.06 in, 150 cm front, 61.42 in, 156 cm rear; length: 173.23 in, 440 cm; width: 72.05 in, 183 cm; height: 44.09 in, 112 cm; ground clearance: 4.92 in, 12.5 cm; weight: 3,087 lb, 1,400 kg; turning circle (between walls): 40 ft, 12.2 m; fuel tank: 19.8 imp gal, 24.7 US gal, 90 l.

BODY coupé; 2 doors; 2 seats; light alloy wheels; electric windows; air-conditioning.

PRACTICAL INSTRUCTIONS fuel: 98-100 oct petrol.

FERRARI 308 GTS

126 Berlina Base

PRICE IN GB: £ 1,424*
PRICE EX WORKS: 2,283,000* liras

ENGINE rear, 4 stroke; 2 cylinders, vertical, in line; 39.8 cu in, 652 cc (3.03 x 2.76 in, 77 x 70 mm); compression ratio: 7.5:1; max power (DIN): 24 hp (17.7 kW) at 4,500 rpm; max torque (DIN): 30 lb ft, 4.2 kg m (41.2 Nm) at 3,000 rpm; max engine rpm: 5,200; 36.8 hp/l (27.1 kW/l); light alloy cylinder block and head; 2 crankshaft bearings; valves: overhead, in line, push-rods and rockers; camshafts: 1, side; lubrication: gear pump, centrifugal filter, 4.4 imp pt, 5.3 US pt, 2.5 l; 1 Weber 28 IMB downdraught carburettor; fuel feed: mechanical pump; air-cooled.

TRANSMISSION driving wheels: rear; clutch: single dry plate; gearbox: mechanical; gears: 4, II, III and IV silent claw coupling; ratios: I 3.250, II 2.067, III 1.300, IV 0.872, rev 4.024; lever: central; final drive: spiral bevel, axle ratio: 4.875; width of rims: 4''; tyres: 135 SR x 12.

PERFORMANCE max speeds: (I) 19 mph, 30 km/h; (II) 31 mph, 50 km/h; (III) 50 mph, 80 km/h; (IV) over 65 mph, 105 km/h; power-weight ratio: 53.3 lb/hp (72.2 lb/kW), 24.2 kg/hp (33.4 kg/kW); carrying capacity: 706 lb, 320 kg; speed in top at 1,000 rpm: 14 mph, 22.6 km/h; consumption: 52.3 m/imp gal, 43.6 m/US gal, 5.4 l x 100 km.

CHASSIS integral; front suspension: independent, wishbones, transverse leafspring lower arms, telescopic dampers; rear: independent, oblique semi-trailing arms, coil springs, telescopic dampers.

STEERING screw and sector; turns lock to lock: 2.90.

BRAKES drum; lining area: front 33.3 sq in, 215 sq cm, rear 33.3 sq in, 215 sq cm, total 66.6 sq in, 430 sq cm.

ELECTRICAL EQUIPMENT 12 V; 34 Ah battery; 230 W dynamo; Marelli distributor; 2 headlamps.

DIMENSIONS AND WEIGHT wheel base: 72.44 in, 184 cm; tracks: 44.96 in, 114 cm front, 47.36 in, 120 cm rear; length: 120.24 in, 305 cm; width: 54.21 in, 138 cm; height: 52.56 in, 133 cm; ground clearance: 4.92 in, 12.5 cm; weight: 1,279 lb, 580 kg; weight distribution: 40% front, 60% rear; turning circle (between walls): 28.2 ft, 8.6 m; fuel tank: 4.6 imp gal, 5.5 US gal, 21 l.

BODY saloon/sedan; 2 doors; 4 seats, separate front seats.

PRACTICAL INSTRUCTIONS fuel: 80-85 oct petrol; oil: engine 4.4 imp pt, 5.3 US pt, 2.5 l, SAE 30W (summer)

FERRARI 400 Automatic

20W (winter), change every 6,200 miles, 10,000 km - gearbox and final drive 1.9 imp pt, 2.3 US pt, 1.1 l, FIAT ZC 90, change every 18,600 miles, 30,000 km; greasing: every 3,100 miles, 5,000 km, 2 points; tappet clearances: inlet 0.008 in, 0.20 mm, exhaust 0.010 in, 0.25 mm; valve timing: 26° 57° 66° 17°; tyre pressure: front 22 psi, 1.4 atm, rear 28 psi, 2 atm.

OPTIONAL ACCESSORIES reclining backrests; luxury interior; opening rear windows; sunshine roof; folding rear seat; antitheft.

126 Personal

See 126 Berlina Base, except for:

PRICE IN GB: £ 1,595*
PRICE EX WORKS: 2,443,000* liras

PERFORMANCE power-weight ratio: 53.7 lb/hp (72.8 lb/kW), 24.4 kg/hp (33 kg/kW).

ELECTRICAL EQUIPMENT 33 A alternator.

DIMENSIONS AND WEIGHT length: 123.19 in, 313 cm; width: 54.33 in, 138 cm; weight: 1,289 lb, 585 kg.

FIAT 126 Personal

FIAT 127 CL 3-door Berlina

127 Series

PRICES IN GB AND EX WORKS:

		£	liras
1	127 L 2-door Berlina	1,865*	3,245,000*
2	127 L 3-door Berlina	—	3,363,000*
3	127 C 2-door Berlina	—	3,446,000*
4	127 C 3-door Berlina	2,126*	3,564,000*
5	127 CL 2-door Berlina	—	3,693,000*
6	127 CL 3-door Berlina	2,239*	3,811,000*

Power team:	Standard for:	Optional for:
45 hp	1 to 4	—
50 hp	5,6	—

45 hp power team

ENGINE front, transverse, 4 stroke; 4 cylinders, vertical, in line; 55.1 cu in, 903 cc (2.56 x 2.68 in, 65 x 68 mm); compression ratio: 9:1; max power (DIN): 45 hp (33.1 kW) at 5,600 rpm; max torque (DIN): 47 lb ft, 6.5 kg m (63.7 Nm) at 3,000 rpm; max engine rpm: 6,400; 49.8 hp/l (36.7 kW/l); cast iron cylinder block, light alloy head; 3 crankshaft bearings; valves: overhead, in line, push-rods and rockers; camshafts: 1, side; lubrication: gear pump, full flow filter (cartridge), 7.7 imp pt, 9.3 US pt, 4.4 l; 1 Weber 30 IBA 22 single barrel carburettor; fuel feed: mechanical pump; water-cooled, 8.8 imp pt, 10.6 US pt, 5 l, electric thermostatic fan.

TRANSMISSION driving wheels: front; clutch: single dry plate; gearbox: mechanical; gears: 4, fully synchronized; ratios: I 3.910, II 2.055, III 1.348, IV 0.963, rev 3.615; lever: central; final drive: cylindrical gears; axle ratio: 4.071; width of rims: 4''; tyres: 135 SR x 13.

PERFORMANCE max speeds: (I) 25 mph, 40 km/h; (II) 43 mph, 70 km/h; (III) 65 mph, 105 km/h; (IV) about 84 mph, 135 km/h; power-weight ratio: 33.7 lb/hp (45.8 lb/kW), 15.3 kg/hp (20.8 kg/kW); carrying capacity: 882 lb, 400 kg; acceleration: standing ¼ mile 20 sec; speed in top at 1,000 rpm: 15.8 mph, 25.4 km/h; consumption: 37.7 m/imp gal, 31.4 m/US gal, 7.5 l x 100 km.

CHASSIS integral; front suspension: independent, by McPherson, coil springs/telescopic damper struts, lower wishbones, anti-roll bar; rear: independent, single wide-based wishbone, transverse anti-roll leafspring, telescopic dampers.

STEERING rack-and-pinion; turns lock to lock: 3.40.

BRAKES front disc (diameter 8.94 in, 22.7 cm), rear drum, dual circuit, rear compensator; lining area: front 19.2 sq in, 124 sq cm, rear 33.5 sq in, 216 sq cm, total 52.7 sq in, 340 sq cm.

ELECTRICAL EQUIPMENT 12 V; 34 Ah battery; 33 A alternator; Marelli S 146 A distributor; 2 headlamps.

DIMENSIONS AND WEIGHT wheel base: 87.60 in, 222 cm; front and rear tracks: 50.38 in, 128 cm; length: 143.5 in, 364 cm; width: 60.12 in, 153 cm; height: 53.54 in, 136 cm; ground clearance: 5.12 in, 13 cm; weight: 1,517 lb, 688 kg; turning circle (between walls): 31.5 ft, 9.6 m; fuel tank: 6.6 imp gal, 7.9 US gal, 30 l.

BODY saloon/sedan; 5 seats, separate front seats; folding rear seat (for 3-dr. models only).

PRACTICAL INSTRUCTIONS fuel: 98 oct petrol; oil: engine 6.3 imp pt, 7.6 US pt, 3.6 l, SAE 20 W (winter) 30 (summer), change every 6,200 miles, 10,000 km - gearbox and final drive 4.2 imp pt, 5.1 US pt, 2.4 l, SAE 90, change every 18,600 miles, 30,000 km; greasing: homokinetic joints, every 18,600 miles, 30,000 km; sparking plug: 260°; tappet clearances: inlet 0.006 in, 0.15 mm, exhaust 0.008 in, 0.20 mm; valve timing: 17° 43° 57° 3°; tyre pressure: front 24 psi, 1.7 atm, rear 27 psi, 1.9 atm.

OPTIONAL ACCESSORIES headrests; reclining backrests; luxury interior; opening rear windows; heated rear window; antitheft; metallic spray.

50 hp power team

See 45 hp power team, except for:

ENGINE 64 cu in, 1,049 cc (2.99 x 2.27 in, 76 x 57.8 mm); compression ratio: 9.3:1; max power (DIN): 50 hp (36.8 kW) at 5,600 rpm; max torque (DIN): 57.2 lb ft, 7.9 kg m (77.4 Nm) at 4,000 rpm; 55.4 hp/l (40.7 kW/l); 5 crankshaft bearings; lubrication: four-lobe rotary pump; 1 Weber 32 ICEV 16 or Solex C32 TDI/4 downdraught carburettor.

PERFORMANCE max speed: 87 mph, 140 km/h; power-weight ratio: 31.2 lb/hp (42.4 lb/kW), 14.2 kg/hp (19.2 kg/kW); consumption: 35.3 m/imp gal, 29.4 m/US gal, 8 l x 100 km.

DIMENSIONS AND WEIGHT weight: 1,561 lb, 708 kg.

128 Series

PRICES IN GB, IN USA AND EX WORKS:

		£	$	liras
1	128 1100 Base 2-door Berlina	2,069*	—	3,611,000*
2	128 1100 Base 4-door Berlina	—	3,149	3,811,000*
3	128 1100 Base Panorama	—	—	3,941,000*
4	128 1100 Confort 4-door Berlina	2,250*	—	4,012,000*
5	128 1100 CL 2-door Berlina	—	—	3,923,000*
6	128 1100 CL 4-door Berlina	—	—	4,124,000*
7	128 1100 CL Panorama	—	—	4,254,000*
8	128 1300 Base 4-door Berlina	—	—	3,941,000*
9	128 1300 Confort 4-door Berlina	—	—	4,142,000*
10	128 1300 CL 4-door Berlina	2,390*	—	4,254,000*

Power team:	Standard for:	Optional for:
55 hp	1 to 7	—
60 hp	8 to 10	—

55 hp power team

ENGINE front, transverse, 4 stroke; 4 cylinders, in line; 68.1 cu in, 1,116 cc (3.15 x 2.19 in, 80 x 55.5 mm); compression ratio: 9.2:1; max power (DIN): 55 hp (40.4 kW) at 6,000 rpm; max torque (DIN): 60 lb ft, 8.3 kg m (81.4 Nm) at 2,800 rpm; max engine rpm: 6,500; 49.3 hp/l (36.2 kW/l); cast iron block, light alloy head; 5 crankshaft bearings; valves: overhead, thimble tappets; camshafts: 1, overhead, cogged belt; lubrication: gear pump, cartridge filter, 8.8 imp pt, 10.6 US pt, 5 l; 1 Weber 32 ICEV 14 or Solex C 32 DISA 41 downdraught carburettor; fuel feed: mechanical pump; water-cooled, 11.4 imp pt, 13.7 US pt, 6.5 l, electric thermostatic fan.

TRANSMISSION driving wheels: front; clutch: single dry plate; gearbox: mechanical; gears: 4, fully synchronized; ratios: I 3.583, II 2.235, III 1.454, IV 1.042, rev 3.714; lever: central; final drive: cylindrical gears; axle ratio: 3.765 - Panorama models 4.077; width of rims: 4.5''; tyres: 145 SR x 13.

PERFORMANCE max speeds: (I) 31 mph, 50 km/h; (II) 50 mph, 80 km/h; (III) 75 mph, 120 km/h; (IV) 87 mph, 140 km/h; power-weight ratio: 2-dr. models 30 lb/hp (40.9 lb/kW), 13.6 kg/hp (18.6 kg/kW); carrying capacity: 882 lb, 400 kg - Panorama models 948 lb, 430 kg; acceleration: standing 1/4 mile 19.7 sec; speed in top at 1,000 rpm: 16.3 mph, 26.3 km/h - Panorama models 15.1 mph, 24.3 km/h; consumption: 37.2 m/imp gal, 30.9 m/US gal, 7.6 l x 100 km.

CHASSIS integral; front suspension: independent, by McPherson, coil springs/telescopic damper struts, lower wishbones, anti-roll bar; rear: independent, single wide-based wishbones, transverse anti-roll leafspring, telescopic dampers.

STEERING rack-and-pinion; turns lock to lock: 3.40.

BRAKES front disc (diameter 8.94 in, 22.7 cm), rear drum, dual circuit, rear compensator, servo; lining area: front 19.2 sq in, 124 sq cm, rear 33.5 sq in, 216 sq cm, total 52.7 sq in, 340 sq cm.

ELECTRICAL EQUIPMENT 12 V; 34 Ah battery; 33 A alternator; Marelli distributor; 2 headlamps.

DIMENSIONS AND WEIGHT wheel base: 96.38 in, 245 cm; tracks: 51.50 in, 131 cm front, 51.69 in, 131 cm rear; length: 151.18 in, 384 cm - Panorama models 151.18 in, 384 cm; width: 62.60 in, 159 cm; height: 55.91 in, 142 cm; ground clearance: 5.71 in, 14.5 cm; weight: 2-dr. models 1,653 lb, 750 kg - 4-dr. models 1,698 lb, 770 kg - Panorama models 1,742 lb, 790 kg; weight distribution: 61.5% front, 38.5% rear (Panorama models 60% front, 40% rear); turning circle (between walls): 33.8 ft, 10.3 m; fuel tank: 8.4 imp gal, 10 US gal, 38 l.

BODY 5 seats, separate front seats; folding rear seat (for Panorama models only); reclining backrests.

PRACTICAL INSTRUCTIONS fuel: 98 oct petrol; oil: engine 7.4 imp pt, 8.9 US pt, 4.2 l, SAE 20W (winter) 30 (summer), change every 6,200 miles, 10,000 km - gearbox and final drive 5.5 imp pt, 6.6 US pt, 3.1 l, SAE 90, change every 18,600 miles, 30,000 km; greasing: homokinetic joints, every 18,600 miles, 30,000 km; sparking plug: 240°; tappet

FIAT 128 1100 CL 4-door Berlina

clearances: inlet 0.012 in, 0.30 mm, exhaust 0.016 in, 0.40 mm; valve timing: 12° 52° 52° 12°; tyre pressure: front 26 psi, 1.8 atm, rear 24 psi, 1.7 atm (Panorama models front 27 psi, 1.9 atm, rear 28 psi, 2 atm).

OPTIONAL ACCESSORIES reclining backrests; headrests; tinted glass with heated rear window; antitheft; opening rear windows (for 2-dr. models only); light alloy wheels; heated rear window; metallic spray (except for Panorama models).

60 hp power team

See 55 hp power team, except for:

ENGINE 78.7 cu in, 1,290 cc (3.39 x 2.19 in, 86 x 55.5 mm); max power (DIN): 60 hp (44.2 kW) at 6,000 rpm; max torque (DIN): 72 lb ft, 9.9 kg m (97.1 Nm) at 3,200 rpm; 46.5 hp/l (34.3 kW/l); 1 Weber 32 ICEV 18 or Solex C 32 DISA 40 downdraught carburettor.

PERFORMANCE max speed: 90 mph, 145 km/h; power-weight ratio: 4-dr. models 28.2 lb/hp (38.4 lb/kW), 12.8 kg/hp (17.4 kg/kW); acceleration: standing 1/4 mile 19 sec; consumption: 32.5 m/imp gal, 27 m/US gal, 8.7 l x 100 km.

ELECTRICAL EQUIPMENT 45 Ah battery.

PRACTICAL INSTRUCTIONS tappet clearances: inlet 0.016 in, 0.40 mm, exhaust 0.018 in, 0.45 mm; valve timing: 20° 44° 60° 4°.

128 3P 1100

PRICE EX WORKS: 4,036,000* liras

ENGINE front, transverse, 4 stroke; 4 cylinders, vertical, in line; 68.1 cu in, 1,116 cc (3.15 x 2.19 in, 80 x 55.5 mm); compression ratio: 9.2:1; max power (DIN): 65 hp (47.8 kW) at 6,000 rpm; max torque (DIN): 64 lb ft, 8.9 kg m (87.3 Nm) at 4,100 rpm; max engine rpm: 6,800; 58.2 hp/l (42.8 kW/l); cast iron block, light alloy head; 5 crankshaft bearings; valves: overhead, thimble tappets; camshafts: 1, overhead, cogged belt; lubrication: gear pump, full flow filter (cartridge), 8.8 imp pt, 10.6 US pt, 5 l; 1 Weber 32 DMTR 32 downdraught twin barrel carburettor; fuel feed: mechanical pump; water-cooled, 11.4 imp pt, 13.7 US pt, 6.5 l, electric thermostatic fan.

TRANSMISSION driving wheels: front; clutch: single dry plate (diaphragm); gearbox: mechanical; gears: 4, fully synchronized; ratios: I 3.583, II 2.235, III 1.454, IV 1.042, rev 3.714; lever: central; final drive: cylindrical gears; axle ratio: 4.077; width of rims: 4.5''; tyres: 145 SR x 13.

PERFORMANCE max speeds: (I) 31 mph, 50 km/h; (II) 50 mph, 80 km/h; (III) 75 mph, 120 km/h; (IV) about 93 mph, 150 km/h; power-weight ratio: 27.4 lb/hp (37.3 lb/kW), 12.4 kg/hp (16.9 kg/kW); carrying capacity: 706 lb, 320 kg; acceleration: standing 1/4 mile 18.5 sec; speed in top at 1,000 rpm: 15.1 mph, 24.3 km/h; consumption: 36.2 m/imp gal, 30.2 m/US gal, 7.8 l x 100 km.

CHASSIS integral; front suspension: independent, by McPherson, coil springs/telescopic damper struts, lower wishbones, anti-roll bar; rear: independent, single wide-based wishbones, transverse anti-roll leafspring, telescopic dampers.

STEERING rack-and-pinion; turns lock to lock: 3.40.

BRAKES front disc (diameter 8.94 in, 22.7 cm), rear drum, rear compensator, servo; lining area: front 19.2 sq in, 124 sq cm, rear 33.5 sq in, 216 sq cm, total 52.7 sq in, 340 sq cm.

ELECTRICAL EQUIPMENT 12 V; 45 Ah battery; 33 A alternator; Marelli distributor; 4 headlamps.

DIMENSIONS AND WEIGHT wheel base: 87.52 in, 222 cm; tracks: 52.17 in, 132 cm front, 52.48 in, 133 cm rear; length: 150.79 in, 383 cm; width: 61.42 in, 156 cm; height: 51.57 in, 131 cm; ground clearance: 5.12 in, 13 cm; weight: 1,782 lb, 808 kg; turning circle (between walls): 32.1 ft, 9.8 m; fuel tank: 11 imp gal, 13.2 US gal, 50 l.

BODY fastback coupé; 3 doors; 4 seats, separate front seats, reclining backrests; folding rear seat.

PRACTICAL INSTRUCTIONS fuel: 98 oct petrol; oil: engine 7.4 imp pt, 8.9 US pt, 4.2 l, SAE 20W (winter) 30 (summer), change every 6,200 miles, 10,000 km - gearbox and final drive 5.5 imp pt, 6.6 US pt, 3.1 l, SAE 90, change every 18,600 miles, 30,000 km; greasing: homokinetic joints, every 18,600 miles, 30,000 km; sparking plug: 240°; tappet clearances: inlet 0.016 in, 0.40 mm, exhaust 0.018 in, 0.45 mm; valve timing: 20° 44° 60° 4°; tyre pressure: front 26 psi, 1.8 atm, rear 24 psi, 1.7 atm.

OPTIONAL ACCESSORIES headrests on front seats; light alloy wheels; heated rear window; antitheft; tinted glass with heated rear window.

FIAT 128 3P 1100 - 1300

128 3P 1300

See 128 3P 1100, except for:

PRICE IN GB: £ 2,727*
PRICE IN USA: $ 3,828

ENGINE 78.7 cu in, 1,290 cc (3.39 x 2.19 in, 86 x 55.5 mm); max power (DIN): 73 hp (53.7 kW) at 6,000 rpm; max torque (DIN): 74 lb ft, 10.2 kg m (100 Nm) at 3,900 rpm; 56.6 hp/l (100 hp/l).

PERFORMANCE max speed: 99 mph, 160 km/h; power-weight ratio: 24.5 lb/hp (33.1 lb/kW), 11.1 kg/hp (15 kg/kW); acceleration: standing 1/4 mile 18 sec; consumption: 34.4 m/imp gal, 28.7 m/US gal, 8.2 l x 100 km.

PRACTICAL INSTRUCTIONS valve timing: 12° 52° 52° 12°.

X 1/9

PRICE IN GB: £ 3,627*
PRICE IN USA: $ 5,195

ENGINE central, rear, transverse, 4 stroke; 4 cylinders, vertical, in line; 78.7 cu in, 1,290 cc (3.39 x 2.19 in, 86 x 55.5 mm); compression ratio: 9.2:1; max power (DIN): 73 hp (53.7 kW) at 6,000 rpm; max torque (DIN): 74 lb ft, 10.3 kg m (101 Nm) at 3,400 rpm; max engine rpm: 6,900; 56.6 hp/l (41.6 kW/l); cast iron block, light alloy head; 5 crankshaft bearings; valves: overhead, in line, thimble tappets; camshafts: 1, overhead, cogged belt; lubrication: gear pump, full flow filter (cartridge), 7.4 imp pt, 8.9 US pt, 4.2 l; 1 Weber 32 DMTR-34 downdraught twin barrel carburettor; fuel feed: mechanical pump; water-cooled, 18.5 imp pt, 22.2 US pt, 10.5 l, electric thermostatic fan.

TRANSMISSION driving wheels: rear; clutch: single dry plate (diaphragm), hydraulically controlled; gearbox: mechanical; gears: 4, fully synchronized; ratios: I 3.583, II 2.235, III 1.454, IV 0.959, rev 3.714; lever: central; final drive: cylindrical gears; axle ratio: 4.077; width of rims: 4.5''; tyres: 145 SR x 13 or 145 HR x 13.

PERFORMANCE max speeds: (I) 31 mph, 50 km/h; (II) 50 mph, 80 km/h; (III) 75 mph, 120 km/h; (IV) over 106 mph, 170 km/h; power-weight ratio: 25.2 lb/hp (34.3 lb/kW), 11.4 kg/hp (15.5 kg/kW); carrying capacity: 441 lb, 200 kg; acceleration: standing 1/4 mile 17.9 sec; speed in top at 1,000 rpm: 16.4 mph, 26.4 km/h; consumption: 36.7 m/imp gal, 30.5 m/US gal, 7.7 l x 100 km.

CHASSIS integral; front suspension: independent, by McPherson (lower trailing links), coil springs/telescopic damper struts, lower wishbones; rear: independent, lower wishbones, each with articulated transverse control bar, coil springs/telescopic damper struts.

STEERING rack-and-pinion; turns lock to lock: 3.05.

BRAKES disc (diameter 8.94 in, 22.7 cm), dual circuit, servo; lining area: front 19.2 sq in, 124 sq cm, rear 19.2 sq in, 124 sq cm, total 38.4 sq in, 248 sq cm.

FIAT 128 1100 CL 4-door Berlina

FIAT 128 3P 1300

FIAT X 1/9

ELECTRICAL EQUIPMENT 12 V; 45 Ah battery; 33 A alternator; Marelli distributor; 2 retractable headlamps.

DIMENSIONS AND WEIGHT wheel base: 86.69 in, 220 cm; tracks: 52.56 in, 133 cm front, 52.87 in, 134 cm rear; length: 150.79 in, 383 cm; width: 61.81 in, 157 cm; height: 46.06 in, 117 cm; ground clearance: 4.92 in, 12.5 cm; weight: 1,841 lb, 835 kg; weight distribution: 41% front, 59% rear; turning circle (between walls): 32.8 ft, 10 m; fuel tank: 10.8 imp gal, 12.9 US gal, 49 l.

BODY sports; 2 doors; 2 seats, reclining backrests, built-in headrests; roll bar; detachable roof.

PRACTICAL INSTRUCTIONS fuel: 98-100 oct petrol; oil: engine 6.7 imp pt, 8 US pt, 3.8 l, SAE 30W (summer) 20W (winter), change every 6,200 miles, 10,000 km - gearbox and final drive 4.9 imp pt, 5.9 US pt, 2.8 l, FIAT ZC 90, change every 18,600 miles, 30,000 km; tappet clearances: inlet 0.016 in, 0.40 mm, exhaust 0.018 in, 0.45 mm; valve timing: 12° 52° 52° 12°; tyre pressure: front 26 psi, 1.8 atm, rear 28 psi, 2 atm.

OPTIONAL ACCESSORIES light alloy wheels; heated rear window; tinted glass with heated rear window.

131 Mirafiori Series

PRICES IN GB, IN USA AND EX WORKS:

		£	$	liras
1	131 1300 2-door Berlina	2,457*	—	4,242,000*
2	131 1300 4-door Berlina	2,542*	—	4,484,000*
3	131 1300 5-door Familiare	—	—	4,861,000*
4	131 1300 Special 2-door Berlina	—	—	4,725,000*
5	131 1300 Special 4-door Berlina	—	—	4,968,000*
6	131 1500 5-door Familiare	—	—	5,003,000*
7	131 1600 Special 4-door Berlina	2,962*	4,640	5,109,000*
8	131 1600 Special 4-door Familiare	3,196*	4,998	5,487,000*

Power team:	Standard for:	Optional for:
65 hp	1 to 5	—
75 hp	6 to 8	—

65 hp power team

ENGINE front, 4 stroke; 4 cylinders, vertical, in line; 79.1 cu in, 1,297 cc (2.99 x 2.81 in, 76 x 71.5 mm); compression ratio: 9.2:1; max power (DIN): 65 hp (47.8 kW) at 5,400 rpm; max torque (DIN): 75 lb ft, 10.4 kg m (102 Nm) at 3,000 rpm; 50.2 hp/l (36.9 kW/l); cast iron block, light alloy head; 5 crankshafts bearings; valves: overhead, in line, slanted at 10°, push-rods and rockers; camshafts: 1, side, in crankcase, cogged belt; lubrication: gear pump, full flow filter (cartridge), 7 imp pt, 8.4 US pt, 4 l; 1 Weber 32 ADF1 downdraught twin barrel carburettor; fuel feed: mechanical pump; water-cooled, 13.4 imp pt, 16.1 US pt, 7.6 l, electric thermostatic fan (for Special models only).

TRANSMISSION driving wheels: rear; clutch: single dry plate (diaphragm); gearbox: mechanical; gears: 4, fully synchronized; ratios: I 3.612, II 2.045, III 1.357, IV 1, rev 3.244; lever: central; final drive: hypoid bevel; axle ratio: 4.100; width of rims: 4.5'' - Familiare 5''; tyres: 155 SR x 13 - Familiare 165 SR x 13.

PERFORMANCE max speed: 93 mph, 150 km/h; power-weight ratio: 2-dr. Berlina 31.4 lb/hp (42.7 lb/kW), 14.2 kg/hp (19.3 kg/kW); carrying capacity: 882 lb, 400 kg - Familiare 948 lb, 430 kg; acceleration: standing 1/4 mile 19.2 sec; speed in direct drive at 1,000 rpm: 16.3 mph, 26.3 km/h - Familiare 15.1 mph, 24.3 km/h; consumption: 31.7 m/imp gal, 26.4 m/US gal, 8.9 l x 100 km.

CHASSIS integral; front suspension: independent, by McPherson, coil springs/telescopic damper struts, lower wishbones, anti-roll bar; rear: rigid axle, twin trailing lower radius arms, transverse linkage bar, coil springs, telescopic dampers.

STEERING rack-and-pinion, adjustable height of steering wheel (for Special models only); turns lock to lock: 3.40.

BRAKES front disc (diameter 8.94 in, 22.7 cm), rear drum (diameter 8.97 in, 22.8 cm), dual circuit, rear compensator, servo.

ELECTRICAL EQUIPMENT 12 V; 45 Ah battery; 44 A alternator; Marelli distributor; headlamps: 2 - Special models 4.

DIMENSIONS AND WEIGHT wheel base: 98.03 in, 249 cm; front track: 53.94 in, 137 cm - Familiare 53.54 in, 136 cm; rear track: 51.57 in, 131 cm - Familiare 51.18 in, 130 cm; length: 166.93 in, 424 cm - Special models 167.72 in, 426 cm; width: 64.17 in, 163 cm - Special models 64.57 in, 164 cm; height: 55.12 in, 140 cm - Familiare 55.51 in, 141 cm; weight: 2-dr. Berlina 2,020, 916 kg - 4-dr. Berlina 2,064 lb, 936 kg - Familiare 2,150 lb, 975 kg - Special 2-dr. Berlina 2,041 lb, 926 kg - Special 4-dr. Berlina 2,086 lb, 946 kg; turning circle (between walls): 34.8 ft, 10.6 m; fuel tank: 11 imp gal, 13.2 US gal, 50 l.

65 HP POWER TEAM

BODY 5 seats, separate front seats; folding rear seat (for Familiare only); reclining backrests (standard for Special models only).

PRACTICAL INSTRUCTIONS fuel: 98-100 oct petrol; oil: engine 6.5 imp pt, 7.8 US pt, 3.7 l, SAE 10W-30 (winter) 20W-40 (summer), change every 6,200 miles, 10,000 km - gearbox 3.2 imp pt, 3.8 US pt, 1.8 l, SAE 90 EP, change every 18,600 miles, 30,000 km - final drive 1.8 imp pt, 2.1 US pt, 1 l, SAE 90 EP, change every 18,600 miles, 30,000 km; sparking plug: 200°; valve timing: 3° 45° 43° 5°; tyre pressure: front 26 psi, 1.8 atm, rear 28 psi, 2 atm (Familiare 31 psi, 2.2 atm).

OPTIONAL ACCESSORIES 5-speed fully synchronized mechanical gearbox (I 3.612, II 2.045, III 1.357, IV 1, V 0.870, rev 3.244), speed in top at 1,000 rpm 18 mph, 29 km/h (Familiare 18.9 mph, 30.4 km/h), consumption 32.8 m/imp gal, 27.3 m/US gal, 8.6 l x 100 km; light alloy wheels; heated rear window; tinted glass with heated rear window; reclining backrests; reclining backrests with built-in headrests; antitheft; shock absorbing bumpers; opening rear windows (for 2-dr. models only); metallic spray; vinyl roof (for Special models only).

75 hp power team

See 65 hp power team, except for:

ENGINE 96.7 cu in, 1,585 cc (3.31 x 2.81 in, 84 x 71.5 mm); max power (DIN): 75 hp (55.2 kW) at 5,400 rpm; max torque (DIN): 91 lb ft, 12.6 kg m (123.6 Nm) at 3,000 rpm; 47.4 hp/l (34.8 kW/l); 1 Weber 32ADF3 downdraught twin barrel carburettor; cooling system: electric thermostatic fan.

TRANSMISSION axle ratio: 3.900.

PERFORMANCE max speed: 99 mph, 160 km/h; power-weight ratio: 4-dr. Berlina 27.8 lb/hp (37.7 lb/kW), 12.6 kg/hp (17.1 kg/kW); acceleration: standing ¼ mile 17.9 sec; speed in direct drive at 1,000 rpm: 16.5 mph, 26.6 km/h - Familiare models 17.3 mph, 27.8 km/h; consumption: 29.7 m/imp gal, 24.8 m/US gal, 9.5 l x 100 km.

DIMENSIONS AND WEIGHT weight 4-dr. Berlina 2,086 lb, 946 kg.

PRACTICAL INSTRUCTIONS valve timing: 10° 49° 50° 9°.

OPTIONAL ACCESSORIES limited slip differential; with 5-speed fully synchronized mechanical gearbox, 3.900 axle ratio, speed in top at 1,000 rpm 19 mph, 30.6 km/h (Familiare models 19.9 mph, 32 km/h), consumption 31.7 m/imp gal, 26.4 m/US gal, 8.9 l x 100 km; G.M.S. automatic transmission, hydraulic torque converter and planetary gears with 3 ratios (I 2.400, II 1.480, III 1, rev 1.920), max ratio of converter at stall 2.4, possible manual selection, 3.900 axle ratio, acceleration standing ¼ mile 19 sec, consumption 28 m/imp gal, 23.3 m/US gal, 10.1 l x 100 km; electronic rev counter and air-conditioning (for Special models only).

131 Fiat-Abarth Rally

ENGINE front, 4 stroke; 4 cylinders, in line; 121.7 cu in, 1,995 cc (3.31 x 3.54 in, 84 x 90 mm); compression ratio: 10:1; max power (DIN): 140 hp (103 kW) at 6,400 rpm; max torque (DIN): 130 lb ft, 18 kg m (176.5 Nm) at 3,800 rpm; max engine rpm: 6,500; 70.2 hp/l (51.6 kW/l); cast iron block, light alloy head; 5 crankshaft bearings; valves: overhead, Vee-slanted at 46°; camshafts: 2, overhead; lubrication: gear pump, full flow filter (cartridge), 7.4 imp pt, 8.9 US pt, 4.2 l; 1 Weber 34 ADF downdraught twin barrel carburettor; fuel feed: mechanical pump; water-cooled, 13.4 imp pt, 16.1 US pt, 7.6 l, electric thermostatic fan.

TRANSMISSION driving wheels: rear; clutch: single dry plate (diaphragm); gearbox: mechanical; gears: 5, fully synchronized; ratios: I 3.612, II 2.045, III 1.357, IV 1, V 0.870, rev 3.244; lever: central; final drive: hypoid bevel; axle ratio: 3.900; width of rims: 7''; tyres: Pirelli P7 195/50 VR15.

PERFORMANCE max speeds: (I) 31 mph, 50 km/h; (II) 56 mph, 90 km/h; (III) 84 mph, 135 km/h; (IV) 115 mph, 185 km/h; (V) 118 mph, 190 km/h; power-weight ratio: 15.4 lb/hp (20.9 lb/kW), 7 kg/hp (9.5 kg/kW); acceleration: standing ¼ mile 16 sec; speed in top at 1,000 rpm: 19.2 mph, 30.9 km/h; consumption: 25.4 m/imp gal, 21.2 m/US gal, 11.1 l x 100 km.

CHASSIS integral; front suspension: independent, by McPherson, coil springs/telescopic damper struts, anti-roll bar; rear: independent, by McPherson, coil springs/telescopic damper struts, semi-trailing arms, anti-roll bar.

STEERING rack-and-pinion; turns lock to lock: 3.40.

BRAKES disc, diameter 8.94 in, 22.7 cm, servo.

ELECTRICAL EQUIPMENT 12 V; 55 Ah battery; 44 A alternator; 4 iodine headlamps, 2 fog lamps.

DIMENSIONS AND WEIGHT wheel base: 98.03 in, 249 cm; tracks: 57.48 in, 146 cm front, 57.09 in, 145 cm rear; length: 163.39 in, 415 cm; width: 67.72 in, 172 cm; height: 54.33 in, 138 cm; weight: 2,161 lb, 980 kg; turning circle (between walls): 34.8 ft, 10.6 m; fuel tank: 11 imp gal, 13.2 US gal, 50 l.

BODY saloon/sedan; 2 doors; 4 seats.

PRACTICAL INSTRUCTIONS fuel: 98-100 oct petrol; oil: engine 7 imp pt, 8.5 US pt, 4 l, SAE 10W-30 (winter) 20W-40 (summer); sparking plug: Champion Ney or Marelli CW 8 LP; tyre pressure: front and rear 28 psi, 2 atm.

VARIATIONS

(Competition version).

ENGINE 10.7:1 compression ratio, max power (DIN) 215 hp (158 kW) at 7,000 rpm, max torque (DIN) 167 lb ft, 23 kg m (225.5 Nm) at 5,600 rpm, 107.8 hp/l (79.2 kW/l), injection pump, cleaner air system.

TRANSMISSION gearbox ratios I 2.170, II 1.600, III 1.270, IV 1, V 0.820 or I 2.020, II 1.510, III 1.205, IV 1, V 0.865, from 3.640 to 6.140 axle ratio, width of rims front 10'', rear 11'', 185/70 VR x 15 or 285/35 VR x 15 tyres.

PERFORMANCE max speed 143 mph, 230 km/h, power-weight ratio 10.1 lb/hp (13.7 lb/kW), 4.6 kg/hp (6.2 kg/kW).

FIAT 131 Mirafiori Special 4-door Berlina

ELECTRICAL EQUIPMENT 24 V, 150 Ah battery, 70 A alternator.
DIMENSIONS AND WEIGHT tracks 59.84 in, 152 cm front, 58.66 in, 149 cm rear.

132 1600 Berlina

PRICE EX WORKS: 6,337,000* liras

ENGINE front, 4 stroke; 4 cylinders, vertical, in line; 96.7 cu in, 1,585 cc (3.31 x 2.81 in, 84 x 71.5 mm); compression ratio: 9:1; max power (DIN): 98 hp (72.1 kW) at 5,600 rpm; max torque (DIN): 97 lb ft, 13.4 kg m (131.4 Nm) at 4,000 rpm; max engine rpm: 6,500; 61.8 hp/l (45.5 kW/l); cast iron block, light alloy head; 5 crankshaft bearings; valves: overhead, Vee-slanted at 63°30', thimble tappets; camshafts: 2, overhead, cogged belt; lubrication: gear pump, full flow filter (cartridge), 8.3 imp pt, 9.9 US pt, 4.7 l; 1 Weber 32 ADF2 downdraught twin barrel carburettor; fuel feed: mechanical pump; water-cooled, 14.1 imp pt, 16.9 US pt, 8 l, electric thermostatic fan.

TRANSMISSION driving wheels: rear; clutch: single dry plate; gearbox: mechanical; gears: 4, fully synchronized; ratios: I 3.612, II 2.045, III 1.357, IV 1, rev 3.244; lever: central; final drive: hypoid bevel; axle ratio: 3.727; width of rims: 5.5''; tyres: 175 SR x 14.

PERFORMANCE max speeds: (I) 28 mph, 45 km/h; (II) 50 mph, 80 km/h; (III) 78 mph, 125 km/h; (IV) 103 mph, 165 km/h; power-weight ratio: 23.9 lb/hp (32.5 lb/kW), 10.8

FIAT 131 Fiat-Abarth Rally

kg/hp (14.8 kg/kW); carrying capacity: 882 lb, 400 kg: acceleration: standing ¼ mile 18 sec; speed in direct drive at 1,000 rpm: 18.4 mph, 29.6 km/h; consumption: 29.4 m/imp gal, 24.5 m/US gal, 9.6 l x 100 km.

CHASSIS integral; front suspension: independent, wishbones (lower trailing links), coil springs, anti-roll bar, telescopic dampers; rear: rigid axle, lower longitudinal trailing radius arms, upper oblique torque arms, coil springs, telescopic dampers.

STEERING worm and roller; turns lock to lock: 3.05.

BRAKES front disc (diameter 9.88 in, 25.1 cm), rear drum, dual circuit, servo; swept area: total 165.1 sq in, 1,065 sq cm.

ELECTRICAL EQUIPMENT 12 V; 45 Ah battery; 45 A alternator; Marelli distributor; 4 headlamps.

DIMENSIONS AND WEIGHT wheel base: 100.67 in, 256 cm; tracks: 51.97 in, 132 cm front, 52.36 in, 133 cm rear; length: 172.83 in, 439 cm; width: 64.21 in, 163 cm; height: 5.91 in, 142 cm; ground clearance: 4.92 in, 12.5 cm; weight: 2,348 lb, 1,065 kg; weight distribution: 53% front, 47% rear; turning circle (between walls): 35.4 ft, 10.8 m; fuel tank: 12.1 imp gal, 14.5 US gal, 55 l.

BODY saloon/sedan; 4 doors; 5 seats, separate front seats, reclining backrests.

PRACTICAL INSTRUCTIONS fuel: 98-100 oct petrol; oil: engine 7 imp pt, 8.5 US pt, 4 l, SAE 30W (summer) 20W (winter), change every 6.200 miles, 10,000 km - gearbox 2.8 imp pt, 3.4 US pt, 1.6 l, FIAT ZC 90, change every 18,600 miles, 30,000 km - final drive 2.5 imp pt, 3 US pt, 1.4 l, FIAT W90/M, change every 18,600 miles, 30,000 km; greasing: every 18,600 miles, 30,000 km, 4 points; tappet clearances: inlet 0.018 in, 0.45 mm, exhaust 0.024 in, 0.60 mm; valve timing: 12° 53° 54° 11°; tyre pressure: front 26 psi, 1.8 atm, rear 27 psi, 1.9 atm.

OPTIONAL ACCESSORIES 5-speed fully synchronized mechanical gearbox (I 3.612, II 2.045, III 1.357, IV 1, V 0.870, rev 3.244), max speeds (I) 28 mph, 45 km/h, (II) 50 mph, 80 km/h, (III) 78 mph, 125 km/h, (IV) about 103 mph, 165 km/h, (V) about 99 mph, 160 km/h, consumption 27.7 m/imp gal, 23.1 m/US gal, 10.2 l x 100 km, gearbox oil 2.6 imp pt, 3.2 US pt, 1.5 l; G.M. automatic transmission with 3 ratios (I 2.400, II 1.480, III 1, rev 1.920), hydraulic torque converter and planetary gears, possible manual selection, max speeds (I) 43 mph, 70 km/h, (II) 71 mph, 115 km/h, (III) about 99 mph, 160 km/h, power-weight ratio 24.7 lb/hp (33.3 lb/kW), 11.2 kg/hp (15.1 kg/kW), acceleration standing ¼ mile 19.2 sec, consumption 25.4 m/imp gal, 21.2 m/US gal, 11.1 l x 100 km, weight 2,403 lb, 1,090 kg, gearbox oil 4.9 imp pt, 5.9 US pt, 2.8 l; limited slip differential; light alloy wheels; electronic ignition; headrests; heated rear window; tinted glass with heated rear window; rev counter; air-conditioning; metallic spray; antitheft.

132 2000 Berlina

See 132 1600 Berlina except for:

PRICE IN GB: £ 3,950*
PRICE EX WORKS: 7,316,000*ti liras

ENGINE 121.7 cu in, 1,995 cc (3.31 x 3.54 in, 84 x 90 mm); compression ratio: 8.9:1; max power (DIN): 112 hp (82.4 kW) at 5,600 rpm; max torque (DIN): 117 lb ft, 16.1 kg m (157.9 Nm) at 3,000 rpm; 56.1 hp/l (41.3 kW/l); 1 Weber 34 ADF downdraught twin barrel carburettor.

TRANSMISSION gears: 5, fully synchronized; ratios: I 3.612, II 2.045, III 1.357, IV 1, V 0.870, rev 3.244.

PERFORMANCE max speed: 105 mph, 170 km/h; power-weight ratio: 21.6 lb/hp (29.4 lb/kW), 9.8 kg/hp (13.3 kg/kW); acceleration: standing ¼ mile 17.2 sec; speed in top at 1,000 rpm: 20 mph, 32.2 km/h; consumption: 17.2 m/imp gal, 20.7 m/US gal, 9.8 l x 100 km.

DIMENSIONS AND WEIGHT weight: 2,425 lb, 1,100 kg.

124 Sport Spider 1800

(Only for USA).

PRICE IN USA: $ 6,299

ENGINE front, 4 stroke; 4 cylinders, vertical, in line; 107.2 cu in, 1,756 cc (3.31 x 3.12 in, 84 x 79.2 mm); compression ratio: 9.8:1; max power (DIN): 118 hp (86.8 kW) at 6,000 rpm; max torque (DIN): 113 lb ft, 15.6 kg m (153 Nm) at 4,000 rpm; max engine rpm: 6,600; 67.2 hp/l (49.4 kW/l); cast iron block, light alloy head; 5 crankshaft bearings; valves: overhead, Vee-slanted at 63°30', thimble tappets; camshafts: 2, overhead, cogged belt; lubrication: gear pump, full flow filter (cartridge), 8.3 imp pt, 9.9 US pt, 4.7 l; 1 Weber 34 DMS or Solex C 34 EIES 5 carburettor; fuel feed: electric pump; water-cooled, 14.1 imp pt, 16.9 US pt, 8 l, electric thermostat fan.

FIAT 132 2000 Berlina

TRANSMISSION driving wheels: rear; clutch: single dry plate; gearbox: mechanical; gears: 4, fully synchronized; ratios: I 3.797, II 2.175, III 1.410, IV 1, rev 3.650; lever: central; final drive: hypoid bevel; axle ratio: 3.900; width of rims: 5''; tyres: 165 HR x 13.

PERFORMANCE max speeds: (I) 28 mph, 45 km/h; (II) 53 mph, 85 km/h; (III) 81 mph, 130 km/h; (IV) 115 mph, 185 km/h; power-weight ratio: 17.9 lb/hp (24.5 lb/kW), 8.1 kg/hp (11.1 kg/kW); carrying capacity: 706 lb, 320 kg; acceleration: standing ¼ mile 16.5 sec; speed in direct drive at 1,000 rpm: 17.3 mph, 27.8 km/h; consumption: 34 m/imp gal, 28.3 m/US gal, 8.3 l x 100 km.

CHASSIS integral; front suspension: independent, wishbones, coil springs, anti-roll bar, telescopic dampers; rear: rigid axle, twin trailing radius arms, transverse linkage bar, coil springs, telescopic dampers.

STEERING worm and roller; turns lock to lock: 2.75.

BRAKES disc (diameter 8.94 in, 22.7 cm), dual circuit, servo; lining area: total 38.4 sq in, 248 sq cm.

ELECTRICAL EQUIPMENT 12 V; 45 Ah battery; 42 A alternator; Marelli distributor; 2 halogen headlamps.

DIMENSIONS AND WEIGHT wheel base: 89.76 in, 228 cm; tracks: 52.99 in, 135 cm front, 51.82 in, 132 cm rear; length: 156.34 in, 397 cm; width: 65.30 in, 161 cm; height: 49.21 in, 125 cm; ground clearance: 4.92 in, 12.5 cm;

weight: 2,117 lb, 960 kg; weight distribution; 56% front, 44% rear; turning circle (between walls): 34.1 ft, 10.4 m; fuel tank: 9.9 imp gal, 11.9 US gal, 45 l.

BODY sports; 2 doors; 2+2 seats, separate front seats, reclining backrests.

PRACTICAL INSTRUCTIONS fuel: 98 oct petrol; oil: engine 7 imp pt, 8.5 US pt, 4 l, SAE 30W (summer) 20W (winter), change every 6,200 miles, 10,000 km - gearbox 2.3 imp pt, 2.7 US pt, 1.3 l, FIAT ZC 90, change every 18,600 miles, 30,000 km - final drive 2.5 imp pt, 3 US pt, 1.4 l, FIAT W90/W, change every 18,600 miles, 30,000 km; greasing: every 18,600 miles, 30,000 km, 4 points; tappet clearances: inlet 0.018 in, 0.45 mm, exhaust 0.024 in, 0.60 mm; valve timing: 15° 55° 55° 15°; tyre pressure: front 26 psi, 1.8 atm, rear 26 psi, 1.8 atm.

OPTIONAL ACCESSORIES 5-speed fully synchronized mechanical gearbox (I 3.667, II 2.100, III 1.361, IV 1, V 0.881, rev 3.526), max power (DIN) 118 hp (86.8 kW) at 6,000 rpm, 67.2 hp/l (49.5 kW/l), dual exhaust system, 4.300 axle ratio, max speeds (I) 28 mph, 45 km/h, (II) 50 mph, 80 km/h, (III) 75 mph, 120 km/h, (IV) over 103 mph, 165 km/h, (V) 115 mph, 185 km/h, power-weight ratio 17.9 lb/hp (24.5 lb/kW), 8.1 kg/hp (11.1 kg/kW), speed in top at 1,000 rpm 15.7 mph, 25.3 km/h, consumption 35.3 m/imp gal, 29.4 m/US gal, 8 l x 100 km, gearbox oil 2.6 imp pt, 3.2 US pt, 1.5 l; headrests; limited slip differential; light alloy wheels; electronic ignition; metallic spray; hardtop.

FIAT 132 2000 Berlina

Campagnola

PRICE EX WORKS: 8,767,000* liras

ENGINE front, 4 stroke; 4 cylinders, vertical, in line; 121.7 cu in, 1,995 cc (3.31 x 3.54 in, 84 x 90 mm); compression ratio: 8.6:1; max power (DIN): 80 hp (58.9 kW) at 4,600 rpm; max torque (DIN): 112 lb ft, 15.4 kg m (151 Nm) at 2,800 rpm; 40.1 hp/l (29.5 kW/l); cast iron block, light alloy head; 5 crankshaft bearings; valves: overhead, slanted at 10°, push-rods and rockers; camshafts: 1, side, cogged belt; lubrication: gear pump, full flow filter (cartridge), 8.4 imp pt, 10.1 US pt, 4.8 l; 1 Solex C 32 PHHE-1 horizontal twin barrel carburettor; fuel feed: mechanical pump; water-cooled, 15.7 imp pt, 18.8 US pt, 8.9 l.

TRANSMISSION driving wheels: front and rear; clutch: single dry plate; gearbox: mechanical, in unit with engine; gears: 4, fully synchronized; high ratios: I 3.667, II 2.100, III 1.361, IV 1, rev 3.444; low ratios: I 1.120, rev 3.333; gear and transfer levers: central; final drive: hypoid bevel; axle ratio: 5.375; width of rims: 5Ke 5.00F; tyres: 6.50 x 16 C (PRB).

PERFORMANCE max speed: over 71 mph, 115 km/h; power-weight ratio: 44.3 lb/hp (60.2 lb/kW), 20.1 kg/hp (27.3 kg/kW); carrying capacity: 1,103 lb, 500 kg; speed in direct drive at 1,000 rpm: 14 mph, 22.5 km/h.

CHASSIS integral; front suspension: independent, by McPherson, coil springs/telescopic damper struts, lower wishbones, anti-roll bar; rear: independent, by McPherson, coil springs, 4 telescopic dampers, lower wishbones, anti-roll bar.

STEERING worm and roller; turns lock to lock: 4.60.

BRAKES drum, dual circuit; swept area: front 91.5 sq in, 590 sq cm, rear 91.5 sq in, 590 sq cm, total 183 sq in, 1,180 sq cm.

ELECTRICAL EQUIPMENT 12 V; 45 Ah battery; 44 A alternator; Marelli distributor; 2 headlamps.

DIMENSIONS AND WEIGHT wheel base: 90.55 in, 230 cm; tracks: 53.54 in, 136 cm front, 55.91 in, 142 cm rear; length: 148.42 in, 377 cm; width: 62.20 in, 158 cm; height: 76.77 in, 195 cm; ground clearance: 10.16 in, 25.8 cm; weight: 3,550 lb, 1,610 kg; turning circle (between walls): 35.4 ft, 10.8 m; fuel tank: 12.5 imp gal, 15 US gal, 57 l.

BODY open; 2 doors; 7 seats, separate front seats.

PRACTICAL INSTRUCTIONS fuel: 99 oct petrol; oil: engine 7.4 imp pt, 8.9 US pt, 4.2 l, SAE 10W-40, change every 3,100 miles, 5,000 km - gearbox 2.5 imp pt, 3 US pt, 1.4 l, SAE 90 EP, change every 12,400 miles, 20,000 km - transfer box 3.9 imp pt, 4.7 US pt, 2.2 l, SAE 90 EP, change every 12,400 miles, 20,000 km - final drive 3.2 imp pt, 3.8 US pt, 1.8 l front, 3.2 imp pt, 3.8 US pt, 1.8 l rear, SAE 90 EP, change every 12,400 miles, 20,000 km; valve timing: 10° 49° 50° 9°; tyre pressure: front 26 psi, 1.8 atm, rear 36 psi, 2.5 atm.

OPTIONAL ACCESSORIES long wheel base; hardtop; 7.00 x 16 tyres; 6.50 x 16 tyres; limited slip differential; front and rear limited slip differential; independent heating.

FIAT Campagnola

GIANNINI   ITALY

Fiat Giannini 126 Series

PRICES EX WORKS:

1 126 GP Base	2,470,000* liras
2 126 GP Personal	2,625,000* liras
3 126 GP S Base	2,615,000* liras
4 126 GP S Personal	2,765,000* liras
5 126 Sport Base DC	2,800,000* liras
6 126 Sport Personal DC	2,955,000* liras

Power team:	Standard for:	Optional for:
30 hp	1,2	—
35 hp	3,4	—
36.8 hp	5,6	—

30 hp power team

ENGINE rear, 4 stroke; 2 cylinders, vertical in line; 39.8 cu in, 652 cc (3.03 x 2.76 in, 77 x 70 mm); compression ratio: 8.8:1; max power (DIN): 30 hp (22 kW) at 5,000 rpm; max torque (DIN): 34 lb ft, 4.87 kg m (47.7 Nm) at 3,850 rpm; max engine rpm: 5,300; 46 hp/l (33.7 kW/l); light alloy block and head; 2 crankshaft bearings; valves: overhead, in line, push-rods and rockers; camshafts: 1, side; lubrication: gear pump, centrifugal filter, 6.2 imp pt, 7.4 US pt, 3.5 l; 1 Weber 28 IMB downdraught carburettor; fuel feed: mechanical pump; air-cooled.

TRANSMISSION driving wheels: rear; clutch: single dry plate; gearbox: mechanical; gears: 4, II, III and IV silent claw coupling; ratios: I 3.250, II 2.067, III 1.300, IV 0.872, rev 4.024; lever: central; final drive: spiral bevel; axle ratio: 4.875; width of rims: 4''; tyres: 135 SR x 12.

PERFORMANCE max speed: 75 mph, 120 km/h; power-weight ratio: 43 lb/hp (58.6 lb/kW), 19.5 kg/hp (26.5 kg/kW); carrying capacity: 706 lb, 320 kg; speed in top at 1,000 rpm: 14.3 mph, 23 km/h; consumption: 56.5 m/imp gal, 47 m/US gal, 5 l x 100 km.

CHASSIS integral; front suspension: independent, wishbones, transverse leafspring lower arms, telescopic dampers; rear: independent, oblique semi-trailing arms, coil springs, telescopic dampers.

STEERING screw and sector; turns lock to lock: 2.90.

BRAKES drum; lining area: front 33.5 sq in, 216 sq cm, rear 33.5 sq in, 216 sq cm, total 67 sq in, 432 sq cm.

ELECTRICAL EQUIPMENT 12 V; 34 Ah battery; 230 W alternator; Marelli distributor; 2 headlamps.

DIMENSIONS AND WEIGHT wheel base: 72.44 in, 184 cm; tracks: 44.96 in, 114 cm front, 47.36 in, 120 cm rear; length: 120.24 in, 305 cm; width: 54.21 in, 138 cm; height: 52.56 in, 133 cm; ground clearance: 5.51 in, 14 cm; weight: 1,290 lb, 585 kg; weight distribution: 40% front, 60% rear; turning circle (between walls): 28.2 ft, 8.6 m; fuel tank: 4.6 imp gal, 5.5 US gal, 21 l.

BODY saloon/sedan; 2 doors; 4 seats, separate front seats.

PRACTICAL INSTRUCTIONS fuel: 98-100 oct petrol; oil: engine 6.2 imp pt, 7.4 US pt, 3.5 l, SAE 20W-50, change every 3,700 miles, 6,000 km - gearbox and final drive 1.9 imp pt, 2.3 US pt, 1.1 l, Fiat ZC 90, change every 18,600 miles, 30,000 km; greasing: every 3,100 miles, 5,000 km, 2 points; sparking plug: 240°; tappet clearances: inlet 0.008 in, 0.20 mm, exhaust 0.010 in, 0.25 mm; valve timing: 28° 72° 66° 32°; tyre pressure: front 22 psi, 1.4 atm, rear 28 psi, 2 atm.

OPTIONAL ACCESSORIES light alloy wheels; electronic injection; roll-bar; twin barrel carburettor.

35 hp power team

See 30 hp power team, except for:

ENGINE 42.3 cu in, 694 cc (3.13 x 2.76 in, 79.5 x 70 mm); compression ratio: 9.5:1; max power (DIN): 35 hp (25.7 kW) at 5,400 rpm; max torque (DIN): 37 lb ft, 5.1 kg m (49.8 Nm) at 3,500 rpm; max engine rpm: 5,800; 50.4 hp/l (37 kW/l).

PERFORMANCE max speed: 81 mph, 130 km/h; power-weight ratio: 41.5 lb hp (56.6 lb/kW), 18.8 kg/hp (25.6 kg/kW); consumption: 52.3 m/imp gal, 43.6 m/US gal, 5.4 l x 100 km.

DIMENSIONS AND WEIGHT weight: 1,455 lb, 660 kg.

GIANNINI Fiat 126 GP Personal

GIANNINI Fiat 127 NP 2-door Berlina

GIANNINI Fiat 128 Series

36.8 hp power team

See 35 hp power team, except for:

ENGINE compression ratio: 8.8:1; max power (DIN): 36.8 hp (27.1 kW) at 5,400 rpm; max torque (DIN): 41 lb ft, 5.7 kg m (55.8 Nm) at 4,000 rpm; max engine rpm: 6,000; 53 hp/l (39 kW/l); 1 Weber 28 IMB downdraught`twin barrel carburettor.

PERFORMANCE max speed: 84 mph, 135 km/h; power-weight ratio: 35.9 lb hp (48.7 lb/kW), 16.3 kg/hp (22.1 kg/kW); consumption: 51.4 m/imp gal(42.8 m/US gal, 5.5 l x 100 km.

DIMENSIONS AND WEIGHT weight: 1,323 lb, 600 kg.

Fiat Giannini 127 Series

PRICES EX WORKS:

127 NP 2-door Berlina Base	3,515,000* liras
127 NP 3-door Berlina Base	3,640,000* liras
127 NP 2-door Berlina Confort	3,710,000* liras
127 NP 3-door Berlina Confort	3,835,000* liras

58 hp power team

ENGINE front, transverse, 4 stroke; 4 cylinders, vertical, in line; 55.1 cu in, 903 cc (2.56 x 2.68 in, 65 x 68 mm); compression ratio: 9.6:1; max power (DIN): 58 hp (42.6 kW) at 6,400 rpm; max torque (DIN): 49 lb ft, 6.8 kg m (66.6 Nm)

at 4,600 rpm; max engine rpm: 7,000; 64.2 hp/l (47.1 kW/l); cast iron block, light alloy head; 3 crankshaft bearings; valves: overhead, in line, push-rods and rockers; camshafts: 1, side; lubrication: gear pump, full flow filter (cartridge), 7.7 imp pt, 9.3 US pt, 4.4 l; 1 Weber 30 DIC twin barrel carburettor; fuel feed: mechanical pump; water-cooled, 8.8 imp pt, 10.6 US pt, 5 l, electric thermostatic fan.

TRANSMISSION driving wheels: front; clutch: single dry plate; gearbox: mechanical; gears: 4, fully synchronized; ratios: I 3.910, II 2.055, III 1.348, IV 0.963, rev 3.615; lever: central; final drive: cylindrical gears; axle ratio: 4.071; width of rims: 4''; tyres: 135 SR x 13.

PERFORMANCE max speed: 93 mph, 150 km/h; power-weight ratio: 26.5 lb/hp (35.6 lb/kW), 11.8 kg/hp (16.1 kg/kW); carrying capacity: 882 lb, 400 kg; speed in top at 1,000 rpm: 14 mph, 22 km/h; consumption: 44.8 m/imp gal, 37.3 m/US gal, 6.3 l x 100 km.

CHASSIS integral; front suspension: independent, by Mc-Pherson, coil springs/telescopic damper struts, lower wishbones, anti-roll bar; rear: independent, single wide-based wishbone, transverse anti-roll leafspring, telescopic dampers.

STEERING rack-and-pinion; turns lock to lock: 3.50.

BRAKES front disc (diameter 8.94 in, 22.7 cm), rear drum, dual circuit, rear lining compensator; area: front 19.2 sq in, 124 sq cm, rear 33.5 sq in, 216 sq cm, total 52.7 sq in, 340 sq cm.

ELECTRICAL EQUIPMENT 12 V; 34 Ah battery; 33 A alternator; Marelli distributor; 2 headlamps.

DIMENSIONS AND WEIGHT wheel base: 87.60 in, 222 cm; tracks: 50.39 in, 128 cm front, 50.98 in, 129 cm rear; length: 142.91 in, 363 cm; width: 60.12 in, 153 cm; height: 53.94 in, 137 cm; ground clearance: 5.12 in, 13 cm; weight: 1,517 lb, 688 kg; turning circle (between walls): 31.5 ft, 9.6 m; fuel tank: 6.6 imp gal, 7.9 US gal, 30 l.

BODY saloon/sedan; 5 seats, separate front seat; folding rear seat (for 3-door models only).

PRACTICAL INSTRUCTIONS fuel: 98 oct petrol; oil: engine 6.9 imp pt, 8.2 US pt, 3.9 l, SAE 20 W (winter) 30 (summer), change every 6,200 miles, 10,000 km - gearbox and final drive 4.2 imp pt, 5.1 US pt, 2.4 l, SAE 90, change every 18,600 miles, 30,000 km; greasing: every 18,600 miles, 30,000 km; sparking plug: 260°; tappet clearances: inlet 0.006 in, 0.15 mm, exhaust 0.008 in, 0.20 mm; valve timing: 25° 51° 64° 12°; tyre pressure: front 24 psi, 1.7 atm, rear 27 psi, 1.9 atm.

OPTIONAL ACCESSORIES light alloy wheels; iodine fog lamps; electronic injection; special instrument panel with rev counter.

Fiat Giannini 128 Series

PRICES EX WORKS:

1	128 NP 2-door Berlina Base	3,835,000* liras
2	128 NP 4-door Berlina Base	4,055,000* liras
3	128 NP 2-door Berlina Confort L	4,115,000* liras
4	128 NP 4-door Berlina Confort L	4,335,000* liras
5	128 NP S 2-door Berlina Base	4,055,000* liras
6	128 NP S 4-door Berlina Base	4,275,000* liras
7	128 NP S 2-door Berlina Confort L	4,335,000* liras
8	128 NP S 4-door Berlina Confort L	4,555,000* liras
9	128 5M 2-door Autostrada Base	4,525,000* liras
10	128 5M 4-door Autostrada Base	4,745,000* liras
11	128 5M 2-door Autostrada Confort L	4,835,000* liras
12	128 5M 4-door Autostrada Confort L	5,035,000* liras

Power team:	Standard for:	Optional for:
66.2 hp	1 to 4	—
80 hp	5 to 12	—

66.2 hp power team

ENGINE front, transverse, 4 stroke; 4 cylinders, vertical, in line; 68.1 cu in, 1,116 cc (3.15 x 2.19 in, 80 x 55.5 mm); compression ratio: 9.8:1; max power (DIN): 66.2 hp (48.7 kW) at 6,500 rpm; max torque (DIN): 62 lb ft, 8.6 kg m (84.3 Nm) at 4,000 rpm; max engine rpm: 6,500; 59.3 hp/l (43.6 kW/l); cast iron block, light alloy head; 5 crankshaft bearings; valves: overhead, thimble tappets; camshafts: 1, overhead, cogged belt; lubrication: gear pump, cartridge, 8.8 imp pt, 10.6 US pt, 5 l; 1 Weber 32 ICEV downdraught carburettor; fuel feed: mechanical pump; water-cooled, 11.4 imp pt, 13.7 US pt, 6.5 l, electric thermostatic fan.

TRANSMISSION driving wheels: front; clutch: single dry plate; gearbox: mechanical; gears: 4, fully synchronized; ratios: I 3.583, II 2.235, III 1.454, IV 1.042, rev 3.714; lever: central; final drive: cylindrical gears; axle ratio: 3.764; width of rims: 4.5''; tyres: 145 SR x 13.

PERFORMANCE max speed: 96 mph, 155 km/h; power-weight ratio: 2-dr. models 25 lb/hp (34.1 lb/kW), 11.3 kg/hp (15.4 kg/kW); carrying capacity: 882 lb, 400 kg; speed in top at 1,000 rpm: 15.1 mph, 24.3 km/h; consumption: 31 m/imp gal, 25.8 m/US gal, 9.1 l x 100 km.

CHASSIS integral; front suspension: independent, by Mc-Pherson, coil springs/telescopic damper struts, lower wishbones, anti-roll bar; rear: independent, single wide-based wishbones, transverse anti-roll leafspring, telescopic dampers.

STEERING rack-and-pinion; turns lock to lock: 3.50.

BRAKES front disc (diameter 8.94 in, 22.7 cm), rear drum, dual circuit, rear compensator, servo; lining area: front 19.2 sq in, 124 sq cm, rear 33.5 sq in, 216 sq cm, total 52.7 sq in, 340 sq cm.

ELECTRICAL EQUIPMENT 12 V; 34 Ah battery; 33 A alternator; Marelli distributor; 2 headlamps.

DIMENSIONS AND WEIGHT wheel base: 96.38 in, 245 cm; tracks: 51.50 in, 131 cm front, 51.69 in, 131 cm rear; length: 151.18 in, 384 cm; width: 62.60 in, 159 cm; height: 55.91 in, 142 cm; ground clearance: 5.71 in, 14.5 cm; weight: 2-dr. models 1,654 lb, 750 kg - 4-dr. models 1,698 lb, 770 kg; weight distribution: 61.5% front, 38.5% rear; turning circle (between walls): 33.8 ft, 10.3 m; fuel tank: 8.4 imp gal, 10 US gal, 38 l.

BODY saloon/sedan; 5 seats, separate front seats, reclining backrests.

PRACTICAL INSTRUCTIONS fuel: 98 oct petrol; oil: engine 7.4 imp pt, 8.9 US pt, 4.2 l, SAE 20W (winter) 30 (summer), change every 6,200 miles, 10,000 km - gearbox and final drive 5.5 imp pt, 6.6 US pt, 3.1 l, SAE 90, change every 18,600

66.2 HP POWER TEAM

miles, 30,000 km; greasing: every 18,600 miles, 30,000 km; sparking plug: 240°; tappet clearances: inlet 0.012 in, 0.30 mm, exhaust 0.016 in, 0.40 mm; valve timing: 12° 52° 52° 12°; tyre pressure: front 26 psi, 1.8 atm, rear 24 psi, 1.7 atm.

OPTIONAL ACCESSORIES 5-speed fully synchronized mechanical gearbox; light alloy wheels; iodine fog lamps; electronic injection.

80 hp power team

See 66.2 hp power team, except for:

ENGINE max power (DIN): 80 hp (58 kW) at 6,800 rpm; max torque (DIN): 67 lb ft, 9.2 kg m (90.2 Nm) at 4,800 rpm; max engine rpm: 7,200; 71.7 hp/l (52 kW/l); electronic injection (only for Autostrada models); 2 Weber 40 DCNF twin barrel carburettors.

TRANSMISSION (only for Autostrada models) 5-speed fully synchronized mechanical gearbox.

PERFORMANCE max speed: 103 mph, 165 km/h - Autostrada models about 109 mph, 175 km/h; power-weight ratio: 2-dr. models 20.6 lb/hp (28.5 lb/kW), 9.3 kg/hp (12.9 kg/kW).

LAMBORGHINI   ITALY

Urraco P 200

PRICE EX WORKS: 14,400,000 liras

ENGINE rear, central, transverse, 4 stroke; 8 cylinders, Vee-slanted at 90°; 121.7 cu in, 1,994 cc (3.05 x 2.09 in, 77.4 x 53 mm); compression ratio: 9.8:1; max power (DIN): 182 hp (134 kW) at 7,500 rpm; max torque (DIN): 109 lb ft, 15 kg m (147.1 Nm) at 3,800 rpm; max engine rpm: 7,900; 91.3 hp/l (67.2 kW/l); light alloy block and head, wet liners; 5 crankshaft bearings; valves: overhead, Vee-slanted at 45°, thimble tappets; camshafts: 2 per cylinder block, Vee-slanted at 70°, overhead, cogged belt; lubrication: gear pump, full flow filter, 13.2 imp pt, 15.9 US pt, 7.5 l; 4 Weber IDF 40 downdraught twin barrel carburettors; fuel feed: electric pump; water-cooled, 21.1 imp pt, 25.4 US pt, 12 l, 2 front fans, 1 electric and 1 thermostatic fan.

TRANSMISSION driving wheels: rear; clutch: single dry plate (diaphragm), hydraulically controlled; gearbox: mechanical; gears: 5, fully synchronized; ratios: I 2.935, II 2.105, III 1.565, IV 1.185, V 0.900, rev 2.540; lever: central; final drive: helical spur gears; axle ratio: 4.350; width of rims: 7.5''; tyres: 205/70 VR x 14.

PERFORMANCE max speed: 127 mph, 205 km/h; power-weight ratio: 15.1 lb/hp (20.6 lb/kW), 6.9 kg/hp (9.3 kg/kW); carrying capacity: 882 lb, 400 kg; speed in top at 1,000 rpm: 18.8 mph, 30.2 km/h; consumption: 20.5 m/imp gal, 17 m/US gal, 13.8 l x 100 km.

CHASSIS integral, rear auxiliary frame; front suspension: independent, by McPherson, coil springs/telescopic damper struts, lower wishbones (trailing links), anti-roll bar; rear: independent, by McPherson, coil springs/telescopic damper struts, lower wishbones, anti-roll bar.

STEERING rack-and-pinion; turns lock to lock: 4.25.

BRAKES disc (diameter 10.94 in, 27.8 cm), internal radial fins.

ELECTRICAL EQUIPMENT 12 V; 55 Ah battery; 770 W alternator; Marelli distributor; 2 iodine retractable headlamps.

DIMENSIONS AND WEIGHT wheel base: 96.46 in, 245 cm; front and rear track: 57.48 in, 146 cm; length: 168.50 in, 428 cm; width: 68.50 in, 174 cm; height: 44.88 in, 114 cm; ground clearance: 4.72 in, 12 cm; weight: 2,756 lb, 1,250 kg; turning circle (between walls): 35.1 ft, 10.7 m; fuel tank: 17.6 imp gal, 21.1 US gal, 80 l.

BODY coupé; 2 doors; 4 seats, separate front seats.

PRACTICAL INSTRUCTIONS fuel: 98-100 oct petrol; oil: engine 13.2 imp pt, 15.9 US pt, 7.5 l, SAE 20W-50, change every 2,500 miles, 4,000 km - gearbox and final drive 10.6 imp pt, 12.7 US pt, 6 l, SAE 90, change every 6,200 miles, 10,000 km; sparking plug: 235°; tappet clearances: inlet 0.018 in, 0.45 mm, exhaust 0.018 in, 0.45 mm; valve timing: 40° 60° 58° 38°; tyre pressure: front 28 psi, 2 atm, rear 31 psi, 2.2 atm.

OPTIONAL ACCESSORIES leather upholstery; metallic spray; electric tinted windows; air-conditioning.

LAMBORGHINI Urraco P 250

LAMBORGHINI Urraco P 300

Urraco P 250

See Urraco P 200, except for:

PRICE EX WORKS: 14,400,000 liras

ENGINE 150 cu in, 2,463 cc (3.39 x 2.09 in, 86 x 53 mm); compression ratio: 10.4:1; max power (DIN): 220 hp (161.9 kW) at 7,500 rpm; max torque (DIN): 167 lb ft, 23 kg m (225.6 Nm) at 5,600 rpm; 89.3 hp/l (65.7 kW/l).

PERFORMANCE max speed: over 149 mph, 240 km/h; power-weight ratio: 13.7 lb/hp (18.6 lb/kW), 6.2 kg/hp (8.5 kg/kW); speed in top at 1,000 rpm: 19.2 mph, 30.9 km/h; consumption: 18.8 m/imp gal, 15.7 m/US gal, 15 l x 100 km.

DIMENSIONS AND WEIGHT weight: 3,021 lb, 1,370 kg.

BODY (standard) leather upholstery, metallic spray, electric tinted windows.

Urraco P 300

See Urraco P 200, except for:

PRICE IN GB: £ 14,560*
PRICE EX WORKS: 15,700,000 liras

ENGINE 128.8 cu in, 2,996 cc (3.39 x 2.54 in, 86 x 64.5 mm); compression ratio: 10.1:1; max power (DIN): 265 hp (195 kW) at 7,800 rpm; max torque (DIN): 203 lb ft, 28 kg m (274.6 Nm) at 3,400 rpm; 88.5 hp/l (65.1 kW/l); 4 Weber 40 DCNF downdraught twin barrel carburettors.

PERFORMANCE max speed: 165 mph, 265 km/h; power-weight ratio: 10.8 lb/hp (14.7 lb/kW), 4.9 kg/hp (67 kg/kW); speed in top at 1,000 rpm: 19.9 mph, 32 km/h; consumption: 17.7 m/imp gal, 14.7 m/US gal, 16 l x 100 km.

DIMENSIONS AND WEIGHT weight: 2,867 lb, 1,300 kg.

PRACTICAL INSTRUCTIONS valve timing: 32° 60° 60° 32°.

Urraco Silhouette P 300

See Urraco P 200, except for:

PRICE IN GB: £ 17,798*
PRICE EX WORKS: 19,500,000 liras

ENGINE 182.8 cu in, 2,996 cc (3.39 x 2.54 in, 86 x 64.5 mm); compression ratio: 10.1:1; max power (DIN): 265 hp (195 kW) at 7,800 rpm; max torque (DIN): 203 lb ft, 28 kg m (274.6 Nm) at 3,400 rpm; 88.5 hp/l (65.1 kW/l); 4 Weber 40 DCNF downdraught twin barrel carburettors.

TRANSMISSION axle ratio: 4; width of rims: 8'' front, 11'' rear; tyres: 195/70 VR x 15 front, 285/40 VR x 15 rear.

PERFORMANCE max speeds: (I) 47 mph, 75 km/h; (II) 62 mph, 100 km/h; (III) 89 mph, 143 km/h; (IV) 111 mph, 178 km/h; (V) over 155 mph, 250 km/h; power-weight ratio: 9.9 lb/hp (14.8 lb/kW), 4.5 kg/hp (6.7 kg/kW); speed in top at 1,000 rpm: 19.9 mph, 32 km/h; consumption: 17.7 m/imp gal, 14.7 m/US gal, 16 l x 100 km.

DIMENSIONS AND WEIGHT tracks: 58.66 in, 149 cm front, 61.02 in, 155 cm rear; length: 170.08 in, 432 cm; width: 74.02 in, 188 cm; height: 44.09 in, 112 cm; ground clearance: 5.51 in, 14 cm; weight: 2,867 lb, 1,300 kg.

BODY sports; 2 seats.

PRACTICAL INSTRUCTIONS oil: engine 21.1 imp pt, 25.4 US pt, 12 l - gearbox and final drive 6.7 imp pt, 8 US pt. 3.8 l; valve timing: 32° 60° 60° 32°; tyre pressure: front 36 psi, 2.5 atm, rear 40 psi, 2.8 atm.

Espada 400 GT

PRICE IN GB: £ 22,990*
PRICE EX WORKS: 25,500,000 liras

ENGINE front, 4 stroke; 12 cylinders, Vee-slanted at 60°; 239.7 cu in, 3,929 cc (3.23 x 2.44 in, 82 x 62 mm); compression ratio: 9.55:1; max power (DIN): 350 hp (257.6 kW) at 7,500 rpm; max torque (DIN): 290 lb ft, 40 kg m (392.3 Nm) at 5,500 rpm; max engine rpm: 7,900; 89.1 hp/l (65.6 kW/l); light alloy block and head, wet liners; 7 crankshaft bearings; valves: overhead, Vee-slanted at 70°, thimble tappets; camshafts: 2 per cylinder block, overhead, cogged belts; lubrication: gear pump, full flow filter, 25.2 imp pt, 30.2 US pt, 14.3 l; 6 Weber 40 DCOE 20/21 horizontal twin barrel carburettors; fuel feed: electric pump; water-cooled, 24.6 imp pt, 29.6 US pt, 14 l, 2 electric thermostatic fans.

TRANSMISSION driving wheels: rear; clutch: single dry plate (diaphragm), hydraulically controlled; gearbox: mechanical; gears: 5, fully synchronized; ratios: I 2.520, II 1.735, III 1.225, IV 1, V 0.815, rev 2.765; lever: central; final drive: hypoid bevel; axle ratio: 4.100; width of rims: 7''; tyres: 205 VR x 15.

PERFORMANCE max speeds: (I) 47 mph, 75 km/h; (II) 68 mph, 110 km/h; (III) 93 mph, 150 km/h; (IV) 124 mph, 200 km/h; (V) 155 mph, 250 km/h; power-weight ratio: 10.3 lb/hp (13.1 lb/kW), 4.7 kg/hp (6.3 kg/kW); carrying capacity: 937 lb, 425 kg; acceleration: standing ¼ mile 15.5 sec; speed in top at 1,000 rpm: 21.6 mph, 34.8 km/h; consumption: 14.9 m/imp gal, 12.4 m/US gal, 19 l x 100 km.

CHASSIS integral; front suspension: independent, wishbones, coil springs, anti-roll bar, telescopic dampers; rear: independent, wishbones, coil springs, anti-roll bar, telescopic dampers.

STEERING ZF screw and sector; turns lock to lock: 3.80.

BRAKES disc (front diameter 11.81 in, 30 cm, rear 11.02 in, 28 cm), internal radial fins, dual circuit, each with servo; swept area: front 285.3 sq in, 1,840 sq cm, rear 206.2 sq in, 1,330 sq cm, total 491.5 sq in, 3,170 sq cm.

ELECTRICAL EQUIPMENT 12 V; 72 Ah battery; 2 x 770 W alternators; Marelli distributor; 2 iodine headlamps; 2 iodine fog lamps.

LAMBORGHINI Urraco Silhouette P 300

LAMBORGHINI Espada 400 GT

DIMENSIONS AND WEIGHT wheel base: 104.33 in, 265 cm; tracks: 58.66 in, 149 cm front, 58.66 in, 149 cm rear; length: 186.54 in, 474 cm; width: 73.23 in, 186 cm; height: 46.65 in, 118 cm; ground clearance: 4.92 in, 12.5 cm; weight: 3,605 lb, 1,635 kg; weight distribution: 49.5% front, 50.5% rear; turning circle (between walls): 39.4 ft. 12 m; fuel tank: 20.9 imp gal, 25.1 US gal, 95 l (2 separate tanks).

BODY coupé; 2 doors; 4 seats, separate front seats, reclining backrests; leather upholstery; air-conditioning; tinted glass; electric windows; heated rear window.

PRACTICAL INSTRUCTIONS fuel: 98-100 oct petrol; oil: engine 25.2 imp pt, 30.2 US pt, 14.3 l, SAE 20W-50, change every 2,500 miles, 4,000 km - gearbox 7 imp pt, 8.5 US pt, 4 l, SAE 90, change every 6,200 miles, 10,000 km - final drive 2.6 imp pt, 3.2 US pt, 1.5 l, SAE 90, change every 6,200 miles, 10,000 km; greasing: every 6,200 miles, 10,000 km, 2 points, every 12,400 miles, 20,000 km, 2 points; sparking plug: 235°; tappet clearances: inlet 0.010 in, 0.25 mm, exhaust 0.010 in, 0.25 mm; valve timing: 32° 76° 64° 32°; tyre pressure: front 34 psi, 2.4 atm, rear 37 psi, 2.6 atm.

OPTIONAL ACCESSORIES automatic transmission; right-hand drive; 4.090 axle ratio; power steering; metallic spray; special spray.

Countach LP 400 S

PRICE IN USA: $ 41,000*
PRICE EX WORKS: 35,000,000 liras

ENGINE rear, central, longitudinal, 4 stroke; 12 cylinders, Vee-slanted at 60°; 239.7 cu in, 3,929 cc (3.23 x 2.44 in, 82 x 62 mm); compression ratio: 10.5:1; max power (DIN): 353 hp (259.8 kW) at 7,500 rpm; max torque (DIN): 267 lb ft, 36.8 kg m (360.9 Nm) at 5,500 rpm; max engine rpm: 8,000; 89.8 hp/l (66.1 kW/l); light alloy block and head, wet liners; 7 crankshaft bearings; valves: overhead, Vee-slanted at 70°, thimble tappets; camshafts: 2 per cylinder block, overhead, cogged belts; lubrication: gear pump, full flow filter, oil cooler, 30.8 imp pt, 37 US pt. 17.5 l; 6 Weber 45 DCOE 104-105 horizontal twin barrel carburettors; fuel feed: 2 electric pumps; water-cooled, 29.9 imp pt, 35.9 US pt, 17 l, 2 radiators, 2 electric fans (1 thermostat).

TRANSMISSION driving wheels: rear; clutch: single dry plate (diaphragm), hydraulically controlled; gearbox: mechanical; gears: 5, fully synchronized; ratios: I 2.256, II 1.769, III 1.310, IV 0.990, V 0.755, rev 2.134; lever: central; final drive: hypoid bevel, limited slip differential; axle ratio: 4.090; width of rims: 8.5'' front, 12'' rear; tyres: 205/70 VR x 14 front, 345/35 VR x 15 rear.

PERFORMANCE max speeds: (I) 58 mph, 94 km/h; (II) 75 mph, 120 km/h; (III) 100 mph, 161 km/h; (IV) 132 mph, 213 km/h; (V) 174 mph, 280 km/h; power-weight ratio: 7.7 lb/hp (10.6 lb/kW), 3.5 kg/hp (4.8 kg/kW); carrying capacity: 397 lb, 180 kg; acceleration: 0-50 mph (0-80 km/h) 6 sec; speed in top at 1,000 rpm: 23.2 mph, 37.3 km/h; consumption: 19.8 m/imp gal, 16.4 m/US gal, 14.3 l x 100 km.

CHASSIS tubular; front suspension: independent, wishbones, coil springs, anti-roll bar, telescopic dampers; rear:

LAMBORGHINI Espada 400 GT

COUNTACH LP 400 S

independent, wishbones (trailing links), coil springs, anti-roll bar, telescopic dampers.

STEERING rack-and-pinion; turns lock to lock: 3.

BRAKES disc (diameter 10.51 in, 26.7 cm), internal radial fins, servo; lining area: front 27.9 sq in, 180 sq cm, rear 26.5 sq in, 171 sq cm, total 54.4 sq in, 351 sq cm.

ELECTRICAL EQUIPMENT 12 V; 72 Ah battery; 840 W alternator; 2 Marelli distributors; 4 iodine retractable headlamps.

DIMENSIONS AND WEIGHT wheel base: 96.46 in, 245 cm; tracks: 58.66 in, 149 cm front, 63.39 in, 161 cm rear; length: 162.99 in, 414 cm; width: 78.74 in, 200 cm; height: 42.13 in, 107 cm; ground clearance: 4.92 in, 12.5 cm; weight: 2,778 lb, 1,260 kg; weight distribution: 42% front axle, 58% rear axle; turning circle (between walls): 42.6 ft, 13 m; fuel tank: 26.4 imp gal, 31.7 US gal, 120 l.

BODY coupé; 2 doors; 2 seats; leather upholstery; tinted glass; heated rear window; light alloy wheels.

PRACTICAL INSTRUCTIONS fuel: 98-100 oct petrol; oil: engine 30.8 imp pt, 37 US pt, 17.5 l, SAE 20W-50, change every 3,100 miles, 5,000 km - gearbox 5.6 imp pt, 6.8 US pt, 3.2 l, SAE 90, change every 9,300 miles, 15,000 km - final drive 11.3 imp pt, 13.5 US pt, 6.4 l, SAE 90, change every 9,300 miles, 15,000 km; greasing: none; sparking plug: 235º; tappet clearances: inlet 0.010 in, 0.25 mm, exhaust 0.010 in, 0.25 mm; valve timing: 42º 70º 64º 40º; tyre pressure: front 34 psi, 2.4 atm, rear 34 psi, 2.4 atm.

OPTIONAL ACCESSORIES right-hand drive; air-conditioning.

Countach LP 400

See Countach LP 400 S, except for:

PRICE IN GB: £ 29,950*
PRICE EX WORKS: 30,300,000 liras

ENGINE max power (DIN) 375 hp (276 kW) at 8,000 rpm; 95.4 hp/l (70.2 kW/l); lubrication: 26.4 imp pt, 31.7 US pt, 15 l; 6 Weber 45 ACOE 96-97 horizontal twin barrel carburettors.

TRANSMISSION width of rims: 7.5'' front, 9.5'' rear; tyres: 205/70 VR x 14 front, 215/70 VR x 14 rear.

PERFORMANCE max speed: 196 mph, 315 km/h; power-weight ratio: 6.3 lb/hp (8.6 lb/kW), 2.8 kg/hp (3.9 kg/kW); speed in top at 1,000 rpm: 18.6 mph, 29.9 km/h; consumption: 12.8 m/imp gal, 10.7 m/US gal, 22 l x 100 km.

BRAKES lining area: total 68.2 sq in, 440 sq cm.

ELECTRICAL EQUIPMENT 70 A alternator.

DIMENSIONS AND WEIGHT tracks: 59.06 in, 150 cm front, 59.84 in, 152 cm rear; width: 74.41 in, 189 cm; weight: 2,348 lb, 1,065 kg.

LAMBORGHINI Countach LP 400

Beta Berlina 1300

PRICE IN GB: £ 3,175*
PRICE EX WORKS: 6,608,000* liras

ENGINE front, transverse, slanted 20º to rear, 4 stroke; 4 cylinders, in line; 79.1 cu in, 1,297 cc (2.99 x 2.81 in, 76 x 71.5 mm); compression ratio: 8.9:1; max power (DIN): 82 hp (60.3 kW) at 5,800 rpm; max torque (DIN): 80 lb ft, 11 kg m (107.8 Nm) at 3,300 rpm; max engine rpm: 6,400; 63.2 hp/l (46.5 kW/l); cast iron block, light alloy head, hemispherical combustion chambers; 5 crankshaft bearings; valves: overhead, Vee-slanted at 65º, thimble tappets; camshafts: 2, overhead, cogged belt; lubrication: gear pump, full flow filter, 7.4 imp pt, 8.9 US pt, 4.2 l; 1 Weber 32 DATR 3/250 31 downdraught twin barrel carburettor; fuel feed: mechanical pump; liquid-cooled, 13.4 imp pt, 16.1 US pt, 7.6 l, electric thermostatic fan.

TRANSMISSION driving wheels: front; clutch: single dry plate; gearbox: mechanical; gears: 5, fully synchronized; ratios: I 3.500, II 2.235, III 1.522, IV 1.152, V 0.925, rev 3.071; lever: central; final drive: cylindrical gears, in unit with gearbox; axle ratio: 4.466; width of rims: 5''; tyres: 155 SR x 14.

PERFORMANCE max speeds: (I) 28 mph, 45 km/h; (II) 44 mph, 71 km/h; (III) 64 mph, 105 km/h; (IV) 85 mph, 137 km/h; (V) 99 mph, 160 km/h; power-weight ratio: 29 lb/hp (39.5 lb/kW), 13.2 kg/hp (17.9 kg/kW); carrying capacity: 992 lb, 450 kg; acceleration: standing ¼ mile 19 sec; speed in top at 1,000 rpm: 16.7 mph, 26.8 km/h; consumption: 33.6 m/imp gal, 28 m/US gal, 8.4 l x 100 km.

CHASSIS integral; front suspension: independent, lower wide-based wishbones, coil springs, telescopic damper struts, anti-roll bar; rear: independent, wishbones, coil springs, telescopic dampers struts, anti-roll bar acting as longitudinal torque arm.

STEERING rack-and-pinion; turns lock to lock: 3.80.

BRAKES disc (diameter 9.88 in, 25.1 cm), rear compensator, servo; lining area: front 24.8 sq in, 160 sq cm, rear 22 sq in, 142 sq cm, total 46.8 sq in, 302 sq cm.

ELECTRICAL EQUIPMENT 12 V; 45 Ah battery; 600 W alternator; Marelli or Bosch distributor; 4 iodine headlamps.

DIMENSIONS AND WEIGHT wheel base: 100 in, 254 cm; tracks: 55.35 in, 141 cm front, 54.80 in, 139 cm rear; length: 168.90 in, 429 cm; width: 66.93 in, 170 cm; height: 55.12 in, 140 cm; ground clearance: 5.51 in, 14 cm; weight: 2,381 lb, 1,080 kg; turning circle (between walls): 34.8 ft, 10.6 m; fuel tank: 10.8 imp gal, 12.9 US gal, 49 l.

BODY saloon/sedan; 4 doors; 5 seats, separate front seats, reclining backrests; heated rear window.

PRACTICAL INSTRUCTIONS fuel: 98-100 oct petrol; oil: engine 7.4 imp pt, 8.9 US pt, 4.2 l, SAE 10W-50, change every 3,100 miles, 5,000 km - gearbox and final drive 3 imp pt, 3.6 US pt, 1.7 l, SAE 90, change every 18,600 miles, 30,000 km; greasing: none; tappet clearances: inlet 0.015-0.018 in, 0.39-0.45 mm, exhaust 0.018-0.020 in, 0.45-0.51 mm; valve timing: 17º 37º 48º 6º; tyre pressure: front 24 psi, 1.7 atm, rear 24 psi, 1.7 atm.

OPTIONAL ACCESSORIES L.P.G. fuel system; light alloy wheels with 175/70 SR x 14 tyres; fog lamps; manually-controlled sunshine roof; tinted glass; electric windows; leather upholstery; metallic spray; headrests; headlamps with automatically adjustable height.

Coupé 1300

See Beta Berlina 1300, except for:

PRICE IN GB: £ 3,643*
PRICE EX WORKS: 6,891,000* liras

PERFORMANCE max speed: over 103 mph, 165 km/h; power-weight ratio: 26.5 lb/hp (35.9 lb/kW), 12 kg/hp (16.3 kg/kW); carrying capacity: 794 lb, 360 kg; acceleration: standing ¼ mile 18 sec; consumption: 34.4 m/imp gal, 28.7 m/US gal, 8.2 l x 100 km.

DIMENSIONS AND WEIGHT wheel base: 92.52 in, 235 cm; length: 157.09 in, 399 cm; width: 64.96 in, 165 cm; height: 50.39 in, 128 cm; ground clearance: 5.31 in, 13.5 cm; weight: 2,161 lb, 980 kg; turning circle (between walls): 33.5 ft, 10.2 m.

BODY coupé; 2 doors; 4 seats.

OPTIONAL ACCESSORIES light alloy wheels with 175 SR x 14 tyres; tinted glass; electric windows; rear red fog lamp.

LANCIA Coupé 1300

Beta Berlina 1600

See Beta Berlina 1300, except for:

PRICE IN GB: £ 3,642
PRICE IN USA: $ 6,995

ENGINE 96.7 cu in, 1,585 cc (3.31 x 2.81 in, 84 x 71.5 mm); compression ratio: 9.4:1; max power (DIN): 100 hp (73.6 kW) at 5,800 rpm; max torque (DIN): 99 lb ft, 13.7 kg m (134.4 Nm) at 3,000 rpm; 63.1 hp/l (46.4 kW/l); 1 Weber 34 DATR 1/250 downdraught twin barrel carburettor.

TRANSMISSION axle ratio: 4.071; width of rims: 5.5''; tyres: 175/70 SR x 14 (standard).

PERFORMANCE max speeds: (I) 31 mph, 50 km/h; (II) 48 mph, 78 km/h; (III) 71 mph, 114 km/h; (IV) 94 mph, 151 km/h; (V) 106 mph, 170 km/h; power-weight ratio: 24.3 lb/hp (32.8 lb/kW), 11 kg/hp (14.9 kg/kW); acceleration: standing ¼ mile 18 sec; speed in top at 1,000 rpm: 18.2 mph, 29.3 km/h; consumption: 34 m/imp gal, 28.3 m/US gal, 8.3 l x 100 km.

ELECTRICAL EQUIPMENT 4 iodine headlamps with automatic adjustable height.

DIMENSIONS AND WEIGHT weight: 2,420 lb, 1,097 kg.

BODY luxury interior; built-in headrests (standard).

OPTIONAL ACCESSORIES L.P.G. fuel system and sunshine roof not available.

Beta Coupé 1600

See Beta Berlina 1600, except for:

PRICE IN GB: £ 4,168*
PRICE IN USA: $ 7,930

PERFORMANCE max speed: 111 mph, 178 km/h; power-weight ratio: 21.8 lb/hp (29.6 lb/kW), 9.9 kg/hp (13.4 kg/kW); carrying capacity: 794 lb, 360 kg; acceleration: standing ¼ mile 17.1 sec; consumption: 35.3 m/imp gal, 29.4 m/US gal, 8 l x 100 km.

STEERING turns lock to lock: 3.75.

ELECTRICAL EQUIPMENT 4 iodine headlamps.

DIMENSIONS AND WEIGHT wheel base: 92.52 in, 235 cm; length: 157.09 in, 399 cm; width: 64.96 in, 165 cm; height: 50.39 in, 128 cm; ground clearance: 5.31 in, 13.5 cm; weight: 2,180 lb, 988 kg; weight distribution: 61% front, 39% rear; turning circle (between walls): 33.5 ft, 10.2 m.

BODY coupé; 2 doors; 4 seats.

OPTIONAL ACCESSORIES heated rear window; L.P.G. fuel system and sunshine roof not available.

Beta HPE 1600

See Beta Coupé 1600, except for:

PRICE IN GB: £ 4,785*
PRICE IN USA: $ 8,995

PERFORMANCE max speed: 108 mph, 174 km/h; power-weight ratio: 23.4 lb/hp (31.7 lb/kW), 10.6 kg/hp (14.4 kg/kW); carrying capacity: 992 lb, 450 kg; acceleration: standing ¼ mile 17.5 sec; consumption: 34 m/imp gal, 28.3 m/US gal, 8.3 l x 100 km.

STEERING turns lock to lock: 4.

DIMENSIONS AND WEIGHT wheel base: 100 in, 254 cm; length: 168.50 in, 428 cm; height: 51.57 in, 131 cm; weight: 2,337 lb, 1,060 kg.

BODY 5 seats; wiper on rear window.

OPTIONAL ACCESSORIES sunshine roof.

Beta 1600 Spider

See Beta Coupé 1600, except for:

PRICE IN GB: £ 4,723*
PRICE EX WORKS: 7,932,000* liras

PERFORMANCE power-weight ratio: 23.1 lb/hp (31.4 lb/kW), 10.5 kg/hp (14.2 kg/kW); acceleration: standing ¼ mile 17.3 sec.

DIMENSIONS AND WEIGHT length: 159.05 in, 404 cm; height: 49.61 in, 126 cm; weight: 2,315 lb, 1,050 kg.

BODY convertible; detachable roof; heated rear window not available.

LANCIA Beta 1600 Spider

Beta Berlina 2000

See Beta Berlina 1300, except for:

PRICE IN GB: £ 3,887*
PRICE EX WORKS: 7,346,000* liras

ENGINE 121.7 cu in, 1,995 cc (3.31 x 3.54 in, 84 x 90 mm); max power (DIN): 115 hp (84.6 kW) at 5,500 rpm; max torque (DIN): 129 lb ft, 17.8 kg m (174.6 Nm) at 2,800 rpm; 57.6 hp/l (42.4 kW/l); lubrication: 7.9 imp pt, 9.5 US pt, 4.5 l; 1 Weber 34 DATR 2/250 downdraught twin barrel carburettor.

TRANSMISSION axle ratio: 3.785; width of rims: 5.5''; tyres: 175/70 SR x 14 (standard).

PERFORMANCE max speeds: (I) 33 mph, 53 km/h; (II) 52 mph, 83 km/h; (III) 76 mph, 123 km/h; (IV) 101 mph, 162 km/h; (V) 112 mph, 180 km/h; power-weight ratio: 21.2 lb/hp (28.7 lb/kW), 9.6 kg/hp (13 kg/kW); acceleration: standing ¼ mile 17 sec; speed in top at 1,000 rpm: 19.6 mph, 31.5 km/h; consumption: 32.8 m/imp gal, 27.3 m/US gal, 8.6 l x 100 km.

ELECTRICAL EQUIPMENT 4 iodine headlamps with automatically adjustable height (standard).

DIMENSIONS AND WEIGHT weight: 2,426 lb, 1,100 kg.

BODY luxury interior; built-in headrests (standard).

PRACTICAL INSTRUCTIONS valve timing: 13° 45° 49° 9°.

OPTIONAL ACCESSORIES light alloy wheels; air-conditioning with tinted glass.

Beta 2000 Coupé

See Beta Berlina 2000, except for:

PRICE IN GB: £ 4,513*
PRICE EX WORKS: 7,776,000* liras

TRANSMISSION tyres: 175/70 HR x 14.

PERFORMANCE max speed: 117 mph, 188 km/h; power-weight ratio: 19 lb/hp (25.8 lb/kW), 8.6 kg/hp (11.7 kg/kW); carrying capacity: 794 lb, 360 kg; acceleration: standing ¼ mile 16.2 sec; consumption: 33.6 m/imp gal, 28.6 m/US gal, 8.4 l x 100 km.

STEERING turns lock to lock: 3.75.

DIMENSIONS AND WEIGHT wheel base: 92.52 in, 235 cm; length: 157.09 in, 399 cm; width: 64.96 in, 165 cm; height: 50.39 in, 128 cm; ground clearance: 5.31 in, 13.5 cm; weight: 2,180 lb, 988 kg; weight distribution: 61% front, 39% rear; turning circle (between walls): 33.5 ft, 10.2 m.

BODY coupé; 2 doors; 4 seats.

OPTIONAL ACCESSORIES L.P.G. fuel system and sunshine roof not available.

LANCIA Beta Berlina 2000

Beta HPE 2000

See Beta 2000 Coupé, except for:

PRICE IN GB: £ 5,132
PRICE EX WORKS: 8,048,000 liras

TRANSMISSION tyres: 175/70 SR x 14.

PERFORMANCE max speed: 112 mph, 180 km/h; power-weight ratio: 20.3 lb/hp (27.6 lb/kW), 9.2 kg/hp (12.5 kg/kW); carrying capacity: 992 lb, 450 kg; acceleration: standing ¼ mile 16.8 sec; consumption: 32.8 m/imp gal, 27.3 m/US gal, 8.6 l x 100 km.

STEERING turns lock to lock: 4.

DIMENSIONS AND WEIGHT wheel base: 100 in, 254 cm; length: 168.50 in, 428 cm; height: 51.57 in, 131 cm; weight: 2,337 lb, 1,060 kg.

BODY 5 seats; heated rear window (standard); wiper on rear window.

OPTIONAL ACCESSORIES sunshine roof.

Beta Spider 2000

See Beta 2000 Coupé, except for:

PRICE IN GB: £ 4,884*
PRICE EX WORKS: 8,366,000* liras

PERFORMANCE max speed: 116 mph, 186 km/h; power-weight ratio: 20.1 lb/hp (27.3 lb/kW), 9.1 kg/hp (12.4 kg/kW); acceleration: standing ¼ mile 16.4 sec.

DIMENSIONS AND WEIGHT length: 159.05 in, 404 cm; height: 49.61 in, 126 cm; weight: 2,315 lb, 1,050 kg.

BODY convertible; detachable roof.

Beta ES 2000

(only for Great Britain).

See Beta Berlina 2000, except for:

PRICE IN GB: £ 4,197*

BODY (standard) manually-controlled sunshine roof, electric windows, tinted glass, built-in headrests and light alloy wheels.

Beta Montecarlo

PRICE IN GB: £ 5,927*
PRICE IN USA: S 9,995

ENGINE rear, central, transverse, in unit with gearbox and final drive, 4 stroke; 4 cylinders, in line; 121.7 cu in, 1,995 cc (3.31 x 3.54 in, 84 x 90 mm); compression ratio: 9.35:1; max power (DIN): 120 hp (88.3 kW) at 6,000 rpm;

LANCIA Beta HPE 2000

LANCIA Beta 2000 Coupé

max torque (DIN): 126 lb ft, 17.4 kg m (170.6 Nm) at 3,400 rpm; max engine rpm: 6,200; 60.1 hp/l (44.3 kW/l); cast iron block, light alloy head, hemispherical combustion chambers; 5 crankshaft bearings; valves: overhead, Vee-slanted at 65°, thimble tappets; camshafts: 2, overhead, cogged belt; lubrication: gear pump, full flow filter (cartridge), 7.9 imp pt, 9.5 US pt, 4.5 l; 1 Weber 34 DATR 4/250 downdraught twin barrel carburettor; fuel feed: mechanical pump; liquid-cooled, 13.4 imp pt, 16.1 US pt, 7.6 l, electric thermostatic fan.

TRANSMISSION driving wheels: rear; clutch: single dry plate (diaphragm), hydraulically controlled; gearbox: mechanical; gears: 5, fully synchronized; ratios: I 3.750, II 2.235, III 1.522, IV 1.152, V 0.925, rev 3.071; lever: central; final drive: helical spur gears; axle ratio: 3.714; width of rims: 5.5''; tyres: 185/70 HR x 13.

PERFORMANCE max speeds: (I) 30 mph, 49 km/h; (II) 52 mph, 84 km/h; (III) 80 mph, 128 km/h; (IV) 101 mph, 162 km/h; (V) over 118 mph, 190 km/h; power-weight ratio: 17.9 lb/hp (24.3 lb/kW), 8.1 kg/hp (11 kg/kW); carrying capacity: 463 lb, 210 kg; acceleration: standing ¼ mile 16 sec; speed in top at 1,000 rpm: 19.6 mph, 31.6 km/h; consumption: 29.7 m/imp gal, 24.8 m/US gal, 9.5 l x 100 km.

CHASSIS integral; front suspension: independent, by McPherson, coil springs/telescopic damper struts, lower wishbones, anti-roll bar; rear: independent, by McPherson, coil springs/telescopic damper struts, lower wishbones, anti-roll bar.

STEERING rack-and-pinion.

BRAKES disc (diameter 8.94 in, 22.7 cm), servo.

ELECTRICAL EQUIPMENT 12 V; 45 Ah battery; 460 W alternator; Marelli distributor; 2 iodine headlamps.

DIMENSIONS AND WEIGHT wheel base: 90.55 in, 230 cm; tracks: 55.59 in, 141 cm front, 57.32 in, 146 cm rear; length: 150.12 in, 381 cm; width: 66.77 in, 170 cm; height: 46.85 in, 119 cm; ground clearance: 5.20 in, 13.2 cm; weight: 2,139 lb, 970 kg; turning circle (between walls): 34.1 ft, 10.4 m; fuel tank: 13 imp gal, 15.6 US gal, 59 l.

BODY coupé; 2 doors; 2 seats; detachable roof; built-in headrests.

PRACTICAL INSTRUCTIONS fuel: 98 oct petrol; oil: engine 10.9 imp pt, 13.1 US pt, 6.2 l, SAE 10W-50, change every 3,100 miles, 5,000 km - gearbox and final drive 3 imp pt, 3.6 US pt, 1.7 l, SAE 90, change every 18,600 miles, 30,000 km; greasing: none; sparking plug: 200°; tappet clearances: inlet 0.016-0.020 in, 0.40-0.50 mm, exhaust 0.022-0.026 in, 0.55-0.65 mm; valve timing: 15° 55° 57° 13°; tyre pressure: front 24 psi, 1.7 atm, rear 27 psi, 1.9 atm.

OPTIONAL ACCESSORIES metallic spray; leather upholstery; heated rear window; tinted glass with heated rear window; electric windows.

Gamma Berlina 2000

PRICE EX WORKS: 10,478,000* liras

ENGINE front, 4 stroke; 4 cylinders, horizontally opposed; 122 cu in, 1,999 cc (3.60 x 2.99 in, 91.5 x 76 mm); compression ratio: 9:1; max power (DIN): 120 hp (88.3 kW) at 5,500 rpm; max torque (DIN): 127 lb ft, 17.5 kg m (171.6

LANCIA Beta Montecarlo

Nm) at 3,500 rpm; max engine rpm: 6,200; 60 hp/l (44.2 kW/l); 3 crankshaft bearings; valves: overhead; camshafts: 2, overhead; lubrication: rotary pump, full flow filter (cartridge), 10.7 imp pt, 12.9 US pt, 6.1 l; 1 Weber 36 ADLD/150 twin barrel carburettor, automatic starter; fuel feed: electric pump; liquid, 15.8 imp pt, 19 US pt, 9 l.

TRANSMISSION driving wheels: front; clutch: single dry plate (diaphragm); gearbox: mechanical; gears: 5, fully synchronized; ratios: I 3.462, II 2.105, III 1.458, IV 1.129, V 0.897, rev 3.214; lever: central; final drive: hypoid bevel; axle ratio: 4.100; width of rims: 6''; tyres: 185/70 HR x 14 tubeless.

PERFORMANCE max speeds: (I) 31 mph, 50 mph; (II) 51 mph, 82 km/h; (III) 73 mph, 118 km/h; (IV) 94 mph, 152 km/h; (V) 115 mph, 185 km/h; power-weight ratio: 24 lb/hp (32.9 lb/kW), 11 kg/hp (14.9 kg/kW); carrying capacity: 992 lb, 450 kg; acceleration: standing ¼ mile 17.4 sec; consumption: 30.1 m/imp gal, 25 m/US gal, 9.4 l x 100 km.

CHASSIS integral; front and rear suspension: independent, wishbones, coil springs, telescopic damper struts, anti-roll bar.

STEERING rack-and-pinion; turns lock to lock: 3.

BRAKES ventilated discs, servo.

ELECTRICAL EQUIPMENT 12 V; 60 Ah battery; 770 W alternator; electronic ignition; 4 iodine headlamps with automatically adjustable height.

DIMENSIONS AND WEIGHT wheel base: 105.12 in, 267 cm; tracks: 57.09 in, 145 cm front, 56.69 in, 144 cm rear; length: 180.31 in, 458 cm; width: 68.11 in, 173 cm; height: 55.51 in, 141 cm; weight: 2,911 lb, 1,320 kg; fuel tank: 13.9 imp gal, 16.6 US gal, 63 l.

BODY saloon/sedan; 4 doors; 5 seats, separate front seats, 4 built-in headrests, reclining backrest; front electric windows; adjustable height and tilt of steering wheel.

PRACTICAL INSTRUCTIONS fuel: 98 oct petrol; oil: engine 10.7 imp pt, 12.9 US pt, 6.1 l, 15W-50, change every 6,200 miles, 10,000 km - gearbox 5.8 imp pt, 7 US pt, 3.3 l, 85W-90, change every 18,600 miles, 30,000 km; greasing: none; sparking plug: Bosch W200 T 30 OV Champion N 7 y; tappet clearances: inlet 0.016 in, 0.40 mm, exhaust 0.014 in, 0.35 mm; valve timing: 15° 47° 53° 9°; front and rear tyre pressure: 28 psi, 2 atm.

OPTIONAL ACCESSORIES metallic spray; air-conditioning; tinted glass; rear electric windows; leather upholstery; light alloy wheels; front and rear (wrap-round) belts; rear red fog lamp; electric external rear mirror; engine oil level warning light; check lamps.

Gamma Coupé 2000

See Gamma Berlina 2000, except for:

PRICE EX WORKS: 13,440,000* liras

DIMENSIONS AND WEIGHT wheel base: 100.59 in, 255 cm; length: 176.38 in, 448 cm; height: 52.36 in, 133 cm.

BODY coupé; 2 doors; 4 seats.

Gamma Berlina 2500

See Gamma Berlina 2000, except for:

PRICE EX WORKS: 12,555,000* liras

ENGINE 151.6 cu in, 2,484 cc (4.02 x 2.99 in, 102 x 76 mm); max power (DIN): 140 hp (103 kW) at 5,400 rpm; max torque (DIN): 154 lb ft, 21.2 kg m (208 Nm) at 3,000 rpm; max engine rpm: 6,000; 56.4 hp/l (41.5 kW/l); 1 Weber 38 ADLD/150 twin barrel carburettor.

TRANSMISSION axle ratio: 3.700.

PERFORMANCE max speeds: (I) 33 mph, 53 km/h; (II) 55 mph, 88 km/h; (III) 79 mph, 127 km/h; (IV) 101 mph, 163 km/h; (V) 121 mph, 195 km/h; power-weight ratio: 20.7 lb/hp (28.2 lb/kW), 9.4 kg/hp (12.8 kg/kW); consumption: 29.4 m/imp gal, 24.5 m/US gal, 9.6 l x 100 km.

BODY light alloy wheels (standard).

Gamma Coupé 2500

See Gamma Berlina 2500, except for:

PRICE EX WORKS: 15,944,000* liras

PERFORMANCE max speed: over 121 mph, 195 km/h.

LANCIA Gamma Berlina 2000 - 2500

DIMENSIONS AND WEIGHT wheel base: 100.59 in, 255 cm; length: 176.38 in, 448 cm; height: 52.36 in, 133 cm.

BODY coupé; 2 doors; 4 seats.

Stratos

PRICE EX WORKS: 16,200,000* liras

ENGINE rear, central, transverse, in unit with gearbox and final drive, 4 stroke; 6 cylinders, Vee-slanted at 65°; 147.5 cu in, 2,418 cc (3.64 x 2.36 in, 92.5 x 60 mm); compression ratio: 9:1; max power (DIN): 190 hp (139.8 kW) at 7,000 rpm; max torque (DIN): 167 lb ft, 23 kg m (225.6 Nm) at 4,000 rpm; max engine rpm: 7,800; 78.6 hp/l (57.8 kW/l); light alloy block and head, wet liners; 4 crankshaft bearings; valves: overhead, Vee-slanted at 47°, thimble tappets; camshafts: 2 per cylinder block, overhead; lubrication: gear pump, full flow filter, 14.3 imp pt, 17.1 US pt, 8.1 l; 3 Weber 40 IDF 28 (left and central) 40 IDF 29 (right) downdraught twin barrel carburettors; fuel feed: 2 electric pumps, water-cooled, 26.4 imp pt, 31.7 US pt, 15 l, 2 electric thermostatic fans.

TRANSMISSION driving wheels: rear; clutch: single dry plate, hydraulically controlled; gearbox: mechanical; gears: 5, fully synchronized; ratios: I 3.554, II 2.459, III 1.781, IV 1.320, V 0.986, rev 3.300; lever: central; final drive: hypoid bevel, limited slip differential; axle ratio: 3.824; width of rims: 7.5''; tyres: 205/70 VR x 14 tubeless.

PERFORMANCE max speed: over 143 mph, 230 km/h; power-weight ratio: 11.5 lb/hp (15.4 lb/kW), 5.2 kg/hp (7 kg/kW); carrying capacity: 353 lb, 160 kg; consumption: 27.4 m/imp gal, 22.8 m/US gal, 10.3 l x 100 km.

CHASSIS integral; front suspension: independent, wishbones (lower trailing links), coil springs, anti-roll bar, telescopic dampers; rear: independent, wishbones, coil springs, anti-roll bar, telescopic dampers.

STEERING rack-and-pinion.

BRAKES disc, internal radial fins.

ELECTRICAL EQUIPMENT 12 V; 45 Ah battery; 830 W alternator; Marelli electronic ignition; 2 iodine retractable headlamps.

DIMENSIONS AND WEIGHT wheel base: 85.83 in, 218 cm; tracks: 56.30 in, 143 cm front, 57.48 in, 146 cm rear; length: 146.08 in, 371 cm; width: 68.90 in, 175 cm; height: 43.70 in, 111 cm; weight: 2,161 lb, 980 kg; fuel tank: 17.6 imp gal, 21.1 US gal, 80 l.

BODY coupé; 2 doors; 2 seats, built-in headrests.

PRACTICAL INSTRUCTIONS fuel: 98-100 oct petrol; oil: engine, gearbox and final drive 14.3 imp pt, 17.1 US pt, 8.1 l, SAE 20W-50, change every 6,200 miles, 10,000 km; greasing: every 3,100 miles, 5,000 km, 4 points; tappet clearances: inlet 0.006-0.008 in, 0.15-0.20 mm, exhaust 0.010-0.012 in, 0.25-0.30 mm.

LANCIA Stratos

LAWIL   ITALY

S3 Varzina

PRICE EX WORKS: 1,853,000* liras

ENGINE front, 2 stroke; 2 cylinders, in line; 15 cu in, 246 cc (2.05 x 2.28 in, 52 x 58 mm); compression ratio: 7.5:1; max power (SAE): 14 hp (10.3 kW) at 4,400 rpm; max torque (SAE): 14 lb ft, 1.9 kg m (18.6 Nm) at 3,000 rpm; max engine rpm: 4,500; 56.9 hp/l (41.8 kW/l); cast iron block, light alloy head; 3 crankshaft bearings; lubrication: mixture; 1 Dell'Orto WHB horizontal carburettor; fuel feed: gravity; air-cooled.

TRANSMISSION driving wheels: rear; clutch: single dry plate; gearbox: mechanical; gears: 4, silent claw coupling; ratios: I 2.449, II 1.492, III 0.986, IV 0.674, rev 2.760; lever: central; final drive: spiral bevel; axle ratio: 3.083; width of rims: 3''; tyres: 4.00 x 10.

PERFORMANCE max speeds: (I) 12 mph, 20 km/h; (II) 19 mph, 30 km/h; (III) 29 mph, 47 km/h; (IV) 39 mph, 63 km/h; power-weight ratio: 50.5 lb/hp (68.6 lb/kW), 22.9 kg/hp (31.1 kg/kW); carrying capacity: 353 lb, 160 kg; consumption: 70.6 m/imp gal, 58.8 m/US gal, 4 l x 100 km.

CHASSIS tubular; front suspension: independent, wishbones, transverse semi-elliptic leafsprings, telescopic dampers;

LAWIL A4 City

rear: rigid axle, semi-elliptic leafsprings, telescopic dampers.

STEERING rack-and-pinion; turns lock to lock: 3.50.

BRAKES drum, single circuit.

ELECTRICAL EQUIPMENT 12 V; 35 Ah battery; 160 W alternator; Ducati (electronic) distributor; 2 headlamps.

DIMENSIONS AND WEIGHT wheel base: 46.06 in, 117 cm; tracks: 40.94 in, 104 cm front, 42.32 in, 107 cm rear; length: 81.50 in, 207 cm; width: 50 in, 127 cm; height: 53.54 in, 136 cm; ground clearance: 4.72 in, 12 cm; weight: 706 lb, 320 kg; weight distributor: 55% front, 45% rear; turning circle (between walls): 19.7 ft, 6 m; fuel tank: 2.4 imp gal, 2.9 US gal, 11 l.

BODY sport; 2 doors; 2 seats, bench front seats.

PRACTICAL INSTRUCTIONS fuel: mixture 1:50; oil: gearbox 1.8 imp pt, 2.1 US pt, 1 l, SAE 90 EP, change every 3,100 miles, 5,000 km - final drive 1.1 imp pt, 1.3 US pt, 0.6 l, SAE 90 EP, change every 6,200 miles, 10,000 km; greasing: every 3,100 miles, 5,000 km, 3 points; sparking plug: 240°; tyre pressure: front 18 psi, 1.3 atm, rear 20 psi, 1.4 atm.

OPTIONAL ACCESSORIES tonneau cover; roll-bar.

A4 City

See S3 Varzina, except for:

PRICE EX WORKS: 1,829,000* liras

PERFORMANCE power-weight ratio: 55.1 lb/hp (75 lb/kW), 25 kg/hp (34 kg/kW).

DIMENSIONS AND WEIGHT length: 80.71 in, 205 cm; width: 50.39 in, 128 cm; height: 56.69 in, 144 cm; weight: 772 lb, 350 kg.

BODY saloon/sedan.

OPTIONAL ACCESSORIES none.

MASERATI   ITALY

Merak 2000

PRICE EX WORKS: 16,520,000* liras

ENGINE central, 4 stroke; 6 cylinders, Vee-slanted at 90°; 122 cu in, 1,999 cc (3.15 x 2.61 in, 80 x 66.3 mm); compression ratio: 9:1; max power (DIN): 170 hp (125.1 kW) at 7,000 rpm; max torque (DIN): 138 lb ft, 19 kg m (186.3 Nm) at 5,000 rpm; max engine rpm: 7,300; 86 hp/l (93.2 kW/l); light alloy block and head, wet liners, hemispherical combustion chambers; 4 crankshaft bearings; valves: overhead, Vee-slanted, thimble tappets; camshafts: 2 per cylinder block, overhead, chain driven; lubrication: gear pump, full flow filter, oil cooler, 13 imp pt, 16 US pt, 7 l; 3 Weber 44 DCNF downdraught twin barrel carburettors; fuel feed: 1 electric pump; water-cooled, 23 imp pt, 28 US pt, 14 l, front radiator, 2 electrically-controlled fans.

TRANSMISSION driving wheels: rear; clutch: single dry plate (diaphragm), hydraulically controlled; gearbox: mechanical; gears: 5, fully synchronized; ratios: I 2.920, II 1.940, III 1.320, IV 0.940, V 0.730, rev 3.150; lever: central; final drive: hypoid bevel, limited slip differential; axle ratio: 5.500; width of rims: 7.5''; tyres: 185/70 VR x 15 front, 205/70 VR x 15 rear.

PERFORMANCE max speed: 137 mph, 220 km/h; power-weight ratio: 15 lb/hp (18.2 lb/kW), 6.8 kg/hp (9.3 kg/kW); carrying capacity: 706 lb, 320 kg; speed in top at 1,000 rpm: 18.7 mph, 29.7 km/h; consumption: 30.7 m/imp gal, 25.6 m/US gal, 9.2 l x 100 km.

CHASSIS integral; front and rear suspension: independent, wishbones, coil springs, anti-roll bar, telescopic dampers.

STEERING rack-and-pinion, adjustable tilt and height, turns lock to lock: 3.

BRAKES ventilated discs, hydraulic servo, independent circuit for each axle; swept area: front 244.2 sq in, 1,575 sq cm, rear 209 sq in, 1,348 sq cm, total 453.2 sq in, 2,923 sq cm.

ELECTRICAL EQUIPMENT 12 V; 60 Ah battery; 780 W alternator; Bosch distributor; 2 retractable iodine headlamps.

DIMENSIONS AND WEIGHT wheel base: 102.30 in, 260 cm; front and rear track: 58 in, 147.40 cm; length: 170 in, 433 cm; width: 69.60 in, 177 cm; height: 44.60 in, 113 cm; ground clearance: 5.12 in, 13 cm; weight: 2,550 lb, 1,160 kg; turning circle (between walls): 34.4 ft, 10.5 m; fuel tank: 18.6 imp gal, 22.4 US gal, 85 l.

MASERATI Merak 2000

MASERATI Merak SS

BODY coupé; 2 doors; 2 + 2 seats, separate front seats, reclining backrests, headrests; tinted glass; electric windows; heated rear window; air-conditioning; light alloy wheels.

PRACTICAL INSTRUCTIONS fuel: 98-100 oct petrol; oil: engine 12.3 imp pt, 14.8 US pt, 7 l, SAE 10W/50, change every 3,100 miles, 5,000 km - gearbox 1.8 imp pt, 2.3 US pt, 1.1 l, SAE 90, change every 12,400 miles, 20,000 km - final drive 2.5 imp pt, 3 US pt, 1.4 l, change every 12,400 miles, 20,000 km; greasing: 2 points, every 3,100 miles, 5000 km; sparking plug type: Bosch 200 T 30; tappet clearances: inlet 0.011 in, 0.25 mm, exhaust 0.024 in, 0.50 mm; valve timing: 42° 80° 56° 20°; tyre pressure: front 31 psi, 2.5 atm, rear 34 psi, 2.4 atm.

Merak SS

See Merak 2000, except for:

PRICE IN GB: £ 12,390*
PRICE IN USA: $ 25,800*

ENGINE 108.9 cu in, 2,965 cc (3.61 x 2.95 in, 91.6 x 75 mm); max power (DIN): 220 hp (162 kW) at 6,500 rpm; max torque (DIN): 199 lb ft, 27.5 kg m (269.7 Nm) at 4,500 rpm; max engine rpm: 7,000; 74.2 hp/l (54.6 kW/l).

TRANSMISSION axle ratio: 4.370; tyres: 195/70 VR x 15 front, 215/70 VR x 15 rear.

PERFORMANCE max speed: 154 mph, 250 km/h; power-weight ratio: 11.8 lb/hp (16 lb/kW), 5.4 kg/hp (7.3 kg/kW); speed in top at 1,000 rpm: 24 mph, 38.5 km/h; consumption: 26.6 m/imp gal, 22.2 m/US gal, 10.6 l x 100 km.

BRAKES swept area: front 244.2 sq in, 1,575 sq cm, rear 254.3 sq in, 1,640 sq cm, total 498.5 sq in, 3,215 sq cm.

DIMENSIONS AND WEIGHT weight: 2,601 lb, 1,180 kg.

PRACTICAL INSTRUCTIONS oil: gearbox and final drive 4.3 imp pt, 5.5 US pt, 2.5 l.

OPTIONAL ACCESSORIES right-hand drive; leather upholstery.

Quattroporte

ENGINE front, 4 stroke; 8 cylinders, Vee-slanted at 90°; 252.3 cu in, 4,136 cc (3.46 x 3.35 in, 88 x 85 mm); compression ratio: 8.5:1; max power (DIN): 270 hp (198.7 kW) at 6,000 rpm; max torque (DIN): 289 lb ft, 40 kg m (392.3 Nm) at 3,800 rpm; max engine rpm: 6,000; 65 hp/l (48 kW/l); light alloy block and head, wet liners, hemispherical combustion chambers; 5 crankshaft bearings; valves: overhead; camshafts: 2 per cylinder block, overhead, chain driven; lubrication: gear pump, full flow filter, 17 imp pt, 21 US pt, 9 l; 4 Weber 42 DCNF downdraught twin barrel carburettors; fuel feed: electric pump; water-cooled, 28 imp pt, 33.5 US pt, 16 l, 2 electrically-controlled fans.

TRANSMISSION driving wheels: rear; clutch: single dry plate (diaphragm), hydraulically controlled; gearbox: ZF mechanical; gears: 5, fully synchronized; ratios: I 2.990, II 1.900, III 1.320, IV 1, V 0.890, rev 2.500; lever: central; final drive: hypoid bevel, limited slip differential; axle ratio: 3.540; width of rims: 7''; tyres: 215/70 VR x 15 XDX tubeless.

PERFORMANCE max speed: 143 mph, 230 km/h; power-weight ratio: 14.5 lb/hp (19.7 lb/kW), 6.6 kg/hp (8.9 kg/kW); carrying capacity: 1,103 lb, 500 kg; speed in top at 1,000 rpm: 24.2 mph, 39.5 km/h; consumption: 22.1 m/imp gal, 18.4 m/US gal, 12.8 l x 100 km.

CHASSIS integral; front and rear suspension: independent, wishbones, coil springs, anti-roll bar, telescopic dampers.

STEERING rack-and-pinion, steering wheel adjustable in height and distance, servo; turns lock to lock: 2.50.

BRAKES ventilated discs; swept area: front 245.4 sq in, 1,583 sq cm, rear 188.5 sq in, 1,216 sq cm, total 433.9 sq in, 2,799 sq cm.

ELECTRICAL EQUIPMENT 12 V; 60 Ah battery; 650 W alternator; Bosch distributor (transistorized); 4 iodine headlamps.

DIMENSIONS AND WEIGHT wheel base: 110.20 in, 280 cm; front and rear track: 60.03 in, 152 cm; length: 196 in, 498 cm; width: 70.47 in, 179 cm; height: 53.14 in, 135 cm; ground clearance: 5.55 in, 14 cm; weight: 3,924 lb, 1,780 kg; turning circle (between walls): 35 ft, 11.5 m; fuel tank: 22 imp gal, 26.4 US gal, 100 l.

MASERATI Quattroporte

BODY saloon/sedan; 4 doors; 5 seats, separate and reclining front seats; air-conditioning; tinted glass; electric windows; heated rear window; leather upholstery.

PRACTICAL INSTRUCTIONS fuel: 98-100 oct petrol; oil: engine 17.6 imp pt, 21.1 US pt, 10 l, SAE 10W/50, change every 3,000 miles, 5,000 km - gearbox and final drive 2.5 imp pt, 3 US pt, 1.4 l, SAE 90, change every 12,400 miles, 20,000 km; greasing: every 3,100 miles, 5,000 km; sparking plug type: Bosch 200 T 30; tappet clearances: inlet 0.011 in, 0.25 mm, exhaust 0.024 in, 0.50 mm; valve timing: 40° 80° 55° 25°; tyre pressure: front 31 psi, 2.2 atm, rear 34 psi, 2.4 atm.

OPTIONAL ACCESSORIES automatic transmission; right-hand drive.

Kyalami

See Quattroporte, except for:

PRICE IN GB: £ 16,673*
PRICE EX WORKS: 28,285,000* liras

ENGINE max engine rpm: 6,300.

TRANSMISSION width of rims: 7.5''; tyres: 205/70 VR x 15, tubeless.

PERFORMANCE max speed: 150 mph, 240 km/h; power-weight ratio: 126 lb/hp (17.2 lb/kW), 5.7 kg/hp (7.8 kg/kW); speed in top at 1,000 rpm: 24.5 mph, 39.7 km/h.

STEERING turns lock to lock: 2.

DIMENSIONS AND WEIGHT wheel base: 102.30 in, 260 cm; front and rear track: 60.20 in, 153 cm; length: 180 in, 458 cm; width: 72.80 in, 185 cm; height: 50 in, 127 cm; weight: 3,421 lb, 1,550 kg.

BODY coupé; 2 doors; 4 seats.

Bora 4900

PRICE IN GB: £ 17,960*
PRICE IN USA: $ 33,775

ENGINE front, 4 stroke; 8 cylinders, Vee-slanted at 90°; 308.8 cu in, 4930 cc (3.70 x 3.50 in, 93.9 x 89 mm); compression ratio: 8.5:1; max power (DIN): 320 hp (235.5 kW) at 5,500 rpm; max torque (DIN): 335 lb ft, 49 kg m (480.5 Nm) at 4,000 rpm; max engine rpm: 6,000; 64.9 hp/l (47.8 kW/l); light alloy block and head, wet liners, hemispherical combustion chambers; 5 crankshaft bearings; valves: overhead, Vee-slanted at 30°, thimble tappets; camshafts: 2 per cylinder block, overhead, driven by chain; lubrication: gear pump, full flow filter, dry sump, separate oil tank, 21 imp pt, 25.4 US pt, 12 l; 4 Weber 42 DCNF 6 downdraught twin barrel carburettors; fuel feed: 2 electric pumps; water-cooled, 28.2 imp pt, 33.8 US pt, 16 l, 2 electrically-controlled fans.

TRANSMISSION driving wheels: rear; clutch: single dry plate (diaphragm), hydraulically controlled; gearbox: mechanical; gears: 5, fully synchronized; ratios: I 2.580, II 1.520, III 1.040, IV 0.850, V 0.740, rev 2.860; lever: central; final drive: hypoid bevel, limited slip differential; axle ratio: 3.770; width of rims: 7.5''; tyres: 215/70 x 15.

MASERATI Kyalami

BORA 4900

PERFORMANCE max speeds: (I) 49 mph, 79 km/h; (II) 83 mph, 133 km/h; (III) 121 mph, 194 km/h; (IV) 148 mph, 238 km/h; (V) 174 mph, 280 km/h; power-weight ratio: 9.5 lb/hp (13.5 lb/kW), 4.4 kg/hp (6.1 kg/kW); carrying capacity: 662 lb, 300 kg; acceleration: standing ¼ mile 14.4 sec, 0-50 mph (0-80 km/h) 4.4 sec; speed in top at 1,000 rpm: 28.9 mph, 46.5 km/h; fuel consumption: 13.5 m/imp gal, 11.2 m/US gal, 21 l x 100 km.

CHASSIS integral; front suspension: independent, wishbones, coil springs, anti-roll bar, telescopic dampers; rear: independent, wishbones, coil springs, anti-roll bar, telescopic dampers.

STEERING rack-and-pinion, steering wheel adjustable in height and distance; turns lock to lock: 3.

BRAKES disc (front diameter 9.45 in, 24 cm, rear 9.76 in, 24.8 cm), internal radial fins, rear compensator, servo; swept area: front 244.2 sq in, 1,575 sq cm, rear 209 sq in, 1,348 sq cm, total 453.2 sq in, 2,923 sq cm.

ELECTRICAL EQUIPMENT 12 V; 66 Ah battery; 650 W alternator; Bosch distributor (transistorized); 2 retractable iodine headlamps.

DIMENSIONS AND WEIGHT wheel base: 102.36 in, 260 cm; tracks: 58.03 in, 147 cm front, 53.03 in, 145 cm rear; length: 170.67 in, 433 cm; width: 69.61 in, 177 cm; height: 44.49 in, 113 cm; ground clearance: 5.12 in, 13 cm; dry weight: 3,087 lb, 1,400 kg; distribution of weight: 42% front, 58% rear; turning circle (between walls): 36.1 ft, 11 m; fuel tank: 22 imp gal, 26.4 US gal, 100 l.

BODY coupé; 2 doors; 2 seats; adjustable pedals; air-conditioning; tinted glass; electric windows; heated rear window; leather upholstery.

PRACTICAL INSTRUCTIONS fuel: 98-100 oct petrol; oil: engine 17.6 imp pt, 21.1 US pt, 10 l, SAE 20W-50, change every 3,100 miles, 5,000 km - gearbox and final drive 5.8 imp pt, 7 US pt, 3.3 l, SAE 90, change every 12,400 miles, 20,000 km; greasing: every 3,100 miles, 5,000 km, 5 points; sparking plug: 240°; tappet clearances: inlet 0.011-0.012 in, 0.28-0.30 mm, exhaust 0.019-0.020 in, 0.47-0.50 mm; valve timing: 40° 80° 54° 22°; tyre pressure: front 36 psi, 2.5 atm, rear 38 psi, 2.7 atm.

OPTIONAL ACCESSORIES right-hand drive.

Khamsin

PRICE IN GB: £ 17,960*
PRICE IN USA: $ 35,945

ENGINE front, 4 stroke; 8 cylinders, Vee-slanted at 90°; 300.8 cu in, 4,930 cc (3.70 x 3.50 in, 93.9 x 89 mm); compression ratio: 8.5:1; max power (DIN): 320 hp (235.5 kW) at 5,500 rpm; max torque (DIN): 355 lb ft, 49 kg m (480.5 Nm) at 4,000 rpm; max engine rpm: 6,000; 64.9 hp/l (47.8 kW/l); light alloy cylinder block and head, wet liners,

MASERATI Bora 4900

hemispherical combustion chambers; 5 crankshaft bearings; valves: overhead, Vee-slanted at 30°, thimble tappets; camshafts: 2 per cylinder block, overhead, driven by chain; lubrication: gear pump, full flow filter, dry sump, separate oil tank, 21.1 imp pt, 25.4 US pt, 12 l; 4 Weber 42 DCNF 6 downdraught twin barrel carburettors; fuel feed: 2 electric pumps; water-cooled, 28.2 imp pt, 33.8 US pt, 16 l, 2 electrically-controlled fans.

TRANSMISSION driving wheels: rear; clutch: single dry plate, hydraulically controlled; gearbox: ZF mechanical; ratios: I 2.990, II 1.900, III 1.320, IV 1, V 0.890, rev 2.500; lever: central; final drive: hypoid bevel; axle ratio: 3.310; width of rims: 7.5''; tyres: 215/70 VR x 15.

PERFORMANCE max speed: 171 mph, 275 km/h; power-weight ratio: 10.4 lb/hp (14.3 lb/kW), 4.7 kg/hp (6.5 kg/kW); carrying capacity: 706 lb, 320 kg; speed in top at 1,000 rpm: 26.1 mph, 42 km/h; fuel consumption: 13.5 m/imp gal, 11.2 m/US gal, 21 l x 100 km.

CHASSIS tubular; front suspension: independent, wishbones, coil springs, anti-roll bar, telescopic dampers; rear: independent, wishbones, coil springs, anti-roll bar, 4 telescopic dampers.

STEERING rack-and-pinion, steering wheel adjustable in height and distance, variable ratio, servo; turns lock to lock: 2.

BRAKES disc (front diameter 10.75 in, 27.3 cm, rear 10.28 in, 26.1 cm), internal radial fins, servo; swept area: front

MASERATI Bora 4900

245.4 sq in, 1,583 sq cm, rear 188.5 sq in, 1,216 sq cm, total 423.9 sq in, 2,799 sq cm.

ELECTRICAL EQUIPMENT 12 V; 72 Ah battery; 650 W alternator; Bosch distributor (transistorized); 4 retractable iodine headlamps.

DIMENSIONS AND WEIGHT wheel base: 100.39 in, 255 cm; tracks: 56.69 in, 144 cm front, 57.87 in, 147 cm rear; length: 173.23 in, 440 cm; width: 70.87 in, 180 cm; height: 44.88 in, 114 cm; ground clearance: 5.51 in, 14 cm; dry weight: 3,374 lb, 1,530 kg; turning circle (between walls): 34.4 ft, 10.5 m; fuel tank: 19.8 imp gal, 23.8 US gal, 90 l.

BODY coupé; 2 doors; 2 + 2 seats, separate front seats, reclining backrests, built-in headrests; heated rear window; tinted glass; electric windows; leather upholstery; light alloy wheels; air-conditioning.

PRACTICAL INSTRUCTIONS fuel: 98-100 oct petrol; oil: engine 21.1 imp pt, 25.4 US pt, 12 l, SAE 20W-50, change every 3,100 miles, 5,000 km - gearbox 2.5 imp pt, 3 US pt, 1.4 l, SAE 90, change every 12,400 miles, 20,000 km - final drive 2.5 imp pt, 3 US pt, 1.4 l, SAE 90, change every 12,400 miles, 20,000 km; greasing: every 3,100 miles, 5,000 km, 4 points; sparking plug: 240°; tappets clearances: inlet 0.010 in, 0.25 mm, exhaust 0.020 in, 0.50 mm; valve timing: 40° 80° 55° 25°; tyre pressure: front 31 psi, 2.2 atm, rear 34 psi, 2.4 atm.

OPTIONAL ACCESSORIES right-hand drive; limited slip differential; Borg-Warner automatic transmission, hydraulic torque converter and planetary gears with 3 ratios (I 2.400, II 1.470, III 1, rev 2.700), max ratio of converter at stall 2.75, possible manual selection.

MASERATI Khamsin

NUOVA INNOCENTI   ITALY

Mini 90N/90L

PRICES EX WORKS: Mini 90N: 2,920,000* liras
Mini 90L: 3,046,000* liras

ENGINE front, transverse, 4 stroke; 4 cylinders, vertical, in line; 60.9 cu in, 998 cc (2.54 x 3 in, 64.6 x 76.2 mm); compression ratio: 9:1; max power (DIN): 49 hp (36.1 kW) at 5,600 rpm; max torque (DIN): 51 lb ft, 7 kg m (68.6 Nm) at 2,600 rpm; max engine rpm: 6,000; 49.1 hp/l (36.2 kW/l); cast iron block and head; 3 crankshaft bearings; valves: overhead, in line, push-rods and rockers; camshafts: 1, side; lubrication: eccentric pump, full flow filter (cartridge), 8.8 imp pt, 10.6 US pt, 5 l; 1 SU type HS 4 semi-downdraught carburettor; fuel feed: mechanical pump; water-cooled, 6.7 imp pt, 8 US pt, 3.8 l, electric thermostatic fan.

TRANSMISSION driving wheels: front; clutch: single dry plate (diaphragm), hydraulically controlled; gearbox: mechanical, in unit with engine; gears: 4, fully synchronized; ratios: I 3.525, II 2.217, III 1.433, IV 1, rev 3.544; lever: central; final drive: spiral bevel; axle ratio: 3.937; width of rims: 4.5''; tyres: 135/70 SR x 12 - (only for 90L) 145/70 SR x 12.

PERFORMANCE max speeds: (I) 25 mph, 40 km/h; (II) 39 mph, 63 km/h; (III) 61 mph, 98 km/h; (IV) about

5 l, SAE 20W-50, change every 3,100 miles, 5,000 km; greasing: every 3,100 miles, 5,000 km, 7 points; sparking plug: 175°; tappet clearances: inlet 0.012 in, 0.30 mm, exhaust 0.012 in, 0.30 mm; valve timing: 5° 45° 51° 21°; tyre pressure: front 30 psi, 2.1 atm, rear 28 psi, 2 atm.

OPTIONAL ACCESSORIES headrests; heated rear window; metallic spray.

Mini 90SL

See Mini 90N/90L, except for:

PRICE EX WORKS: 3,276,000* liras

ELECTRICAL EQUIPMENT 43 Ah battery; 385 W alternator.

BODY tinted glass; headrests; rear window wiper-washer.

Mini 120L/120SL

See Mini 90N/90L, except for:

PRICES EX WORKS: Mini 120L: 3,350,000* liras
Mini 120SL: 3,535,000* liras

ENGINE 77.8 cu in, 1,275 cc (2.78 x 3.20 in, 70.6 x 81.3 mm); compression ratio: 9.75:1; max power (DIN): 65 hp (47.8

kW) at 5,600 rpm; max torque (DIN): 72 lb ft, 10 kg m (98.1 Nm) at 2,600 rpm; 51 hp/l (37.5 kW/l); oil cooler; 1 SU type HS 6 semi-downdraught carburettor; fuel feed: electric pump.

TRANSMISSION gearbox ratios: I 3.329, II 2.094, III 1.353, IV 1, rev 3.347; axle ratio: 3.647; tyres: 155/70 SR x 12.

PERFORMANCE max speeds: (I) 29 mph, 46 km/h; (II) 45 mph, 73 km/h; (III) 70 mph, 113 km/h; (IV) about 96 mph, 155 km/h; power-weight ratio: 24.8 lb/hp (33.7 lb/kW), 11.2 kg/hp (15.3 kg/kW); speed in direct drive at 1,000 rpm: 16 mph, 25.7 km/h; consumption: 33.6 m/imp gal, 28 m/US gal, 8.4 l x 100 km.

ELECTRICAL EQUIPMENT 43 Ah battery; 385 W alternator; iodine headlamps.

DIMENSIONS AND WEIGHT weight: 1,610 lb, 730 kg.

BODY rear window wiper-washer; tinted glass; headrests.

PRACTICAL INSTRUCTIONS tappet clearances: inlet 0.014 in, 0.35 mm, exhaust 0.014 in, 0.35 mm; valve timing: 10° 50° 51° 21°.

Mini De Tomaso

See Mini 90N/90L, except for:

PRICE EX WORKS: 3,835,000* liras

ENGINE 77.8 cu in, 1,275 cc (2.78 x 3.20 in, 70.6 x 81.3 mm); compression ratio: 9.75:1; max power (SAE): 77 hp (56.7 kW) at 6,050 rpm; max torque (SAE): 77 lb ft, 10.6 kg m (104 Nm) at 3,200 rpm; max engine rpm: 6,100; 60.4 hp/l (44.5 kW/l); oil cooler; 1 SU type HS 6 semi-downdraught carburettor; fuel feed: electric pump.

TRANSMISSION gearbox ratios: I 3.329, II 2.094, III 1.353, IV 1, rev 3.347; axle ratio: 3.647; tyres: 155/70 SR x 12.

PERFORMANCE max speeds: (I) 30 mph, 48 km/h; (II) 47 mph, 76 km/h; (III) 73 mph, 118 km/h; (IV) over 99 mph, 160 km/h; power-weight ratio: 21.4 lb/hp (29.1 lb/kW), 9.7 kg/hp (13.2 kg/kW); consumption: 33.6 m/imp gal, 28 m/US gal, 8.4 l x 100 km.

ELECTRICAL EQUIPMENT 43 Ah battery; 385 W alternator; iodine headlamps.

DIMENSIONS AND WEIGHT length: 123.23 in, 313 cm; width: 59.84 in, 152 cm; height: 54.33 in, 138 cm; ground clearance: 5.12 in, 12 cm; weight: 1,654 lb, 750 kg.

BODY headrests; tinted glass; halogen fog lamps; rear window wiper-washer; light alloy wheels.

PRACTICAL INSTRUCTIONS tappet clearances: inlet 0.014 in, 0.35 mm, exhaust 0.014 in, 0.35 mm; valve timing: 10° 50° 51° 21°.

NUOVA INNOCENTI Mini 90N

87 mph, 140 km/h; power-weight ratio: 32.4 lb/hp (44 lb/kW), 14.7 kg/hp (20 kg/kW); carrying capacity: 882 lb, 400 kg; speed in direct drive at 1,000 rpm: 14.6 mph, 23.5 km/h; consumption: 36.7 m/imp gal, 30.5 m/US gal, 7.7 l x 100 km.

CHASSIS integral, front and rear auxiliary frames; front suspension: independent, wishbones (lower trailing links) rubber cone springs, telescopic dampers; rear: independent, swinging longitudinal trailing arms, rubber cone springs, telescopic dampers.

STEERING rack-and-pinion; turns lock to lock: 2.75.

BRAKES front disc (diameter 8.38 in, 21.3 cm), rear drum; lining area: front 17.7 sq in, 114 sq cm, rear 33.8 sq in, 218 sq cm, total 51.5 sq in, 332 sq cm.

ELECTRICAL EQUIPMENT 12 V; 35 Ah battery; 350 D dynamo; Lucas or Bosch distributor; 2 headlamps.

DIMENSIONS AND WEIGHT wheel base: 80.16 in, 204 cm; front and rear tracks: 49.21 in, 125 cm; length: 122.83 in, 312 cm; width: 59.06 in, 150 cm; height: 54.33 in, 138 cm; ground clearance: 4.92 in, 12.5 cm; weight: 1,588 lb, 720 kg; turning circle (between walls): 28.2 ft, 8.6 m; fuel tank: 8.4 imp gal, 10 US gal, 38 l.

BODY saloon/sedan; 2 + 1 doors; 5 seats, separate front seats, reclining backrests; heated rear window; folding rear seat.

PRACTICAL INSTRUCTIONS fuel: 98-100 oct petrol; oil: engine, gearbox and final drive 8.8 imp pt, 10.6 US pt,

NUOVA INNOCENTI Mini De Tomaso

POLSKI-FIAT   POLAND

126 P

ENGINE rear, 4 stroke; 2 cylinders, vertical, in line; 36.2 cu in, 594 cc (2.89 x 2.76 in, 73.5 x 70 mm); compression ratio: 7.5:1; max power (DIN): 23 hp (16.9 kW) at 4,800 rpm; max torque (DIN): 29 lb ft, 4 kg m (39.2 Nm) at 3,400 rpm; max engine rpm: 5,400; 38.7 hp/l (28.4 kW/l); light alloy block and head; 2 crankshaft bearings; valves: overhead, in line, push-rods and rockers; camshafts: 1, side, chain-driven; lubrication: gear pump, centrifugal filter, 4.8 imp pt, 5.7 US pt, 2.7 l; 1 Fos 28 IMB 3 downdraught carburettor; fuel feed: mechanical pump; air-cooled.

TRANSMISSION driving wheels: rear; clutch: single dry plate (diaphragm); gearbox: mechanical; gears: 4, II, III and IV silent claw coupling; ratios: I 3.250, II 2.067, III 1.300, IV 0.872, rev 4.024; lever: central; final drive: spiral bevel; axle ratio: 4.875; width of rims: 4''; tyres: 135 SR x 12.

PERFORMANCE max speeds: (I) 19 mph, 30 km/h; (II) 31 mph, 50 km/h; (III) 50 mph, 80 km/h; (IV) 68 mph, 110 km/h; power-weight ratio: 55.6 lb/hp (75.7 lb/kW), 25.2 kg/hp (34.3 kg/kW); carrying capacity: 750 lb, 340 kg; speed in direct drive at 1,000 rpm: 14.7 mph, 23.6 km/h; consumption: 51.4 m/imp gal, 42.8 m/US gal, 5.5 l x 100 km.

CHASSIS integral; front suspension: independent, wishbones, transverse leafspring lower arms, telescopic dampers; rear: independent, semi-trailing arms, coil springs, telescopic dampers.

STEERING screw and sector; turns lock to lock: 2.9.

BRAKES drum; lining area: front 17.2 sq in, 111 sq cm, rear 17.2 sq in, 111 sq cm, total 34.4 sq in, 222 sq cm.

ELECTRICAL EQUIPMENT 12 V; 34 Ah battery; 230 W dynamo; Zelmot distributor; 2 headlamps.

DIMENSIONS AND WEIGHT wheel base: 72.44 in, 184 cm; tracks: 44.88 in, 114 cm front, 47.24 in, 120 cm rear; length: 120.08 in, 305 cm; width: 54.33 in, 138 cm; height: 51.18 in, 130 cm; ground clearance: 5.51 in, 14 cm; weight: 1,279 lb, 580 kg; weight distribution: 39.5% front, 60.5% rear; turning circle (between walls): 28.2 ft, 8.6 m; fuel tank: 4.6 imp gal, 5.5 US gal, 21 l.

BODY saloon/sedan; 2 doors; 4 seats, separate front seats.

PRACTICAL INSTRUCTIONS fuel: 94 oct petrol; oil: engine 4.4 imp pt, 5.3 US pt, 2.5 l, SAE 10W-30, change every 6,200 miles, 10,000 km - gearbox and final drive 1.9 imp pt, 2.3 US pt, 1.1 l, SAE 90, change every 18,600 miles, 30,000 km; greasing: every 6,200 miles, 10,000 km, 2 points; tappet clearances: inlet 0.008 in, 0.20 mm, exhaust 0.010 in, 0.25 mm; valve timing: 26° 56° 66° 16°; tyre pressure: front 22 psi, 1.4 atm, rear 29 psi, 2 atm.

125 P 1300

ENGINE front, 4 stroke; 4 cylinders, in line; 79 cu in, 1,295 cc (2.83 x 3.13 in, 72 x 79.5 mm); compression ratio: 9:1; max power (DIN): 65 hp (47.8 kW) at 5,200 rpm; max torque (DIN): 69 lb ft, 9.5 kg m (93.2 Nm) at 4,000 rpm; max engine rpm: 6,000; 50.2 hp/l (36.9 kW/l); cast iron block, light alloy head, polispherical combustion chambers; 3 crankshaft bearings; valves: overhead, push-rods and rockers; camshafts: 1, side, in crankcase; lubrication: gear pump, centrifugal filter (cartridge), 6.2 imp pt, 7.4 US pt, 3.5 l; 1 Weber 34 DCHD 1-17 downdraught twin barrel carburettor; fuel feed: mechanical pump; water-cooled, 11.8 imp pt, 14.2 US pt, 6.7 l.

TRANSMISSION driving wheels: rear; clutch: single dry plate, hydraulically controlled; gearbox: mechanical; gears: 4, fully synchronized; ratios: I 3.750, II 2.300, III 1.490, IV 1, rev 3.870; lever: central; final drive: hypoid bevel; axle ratio: 4.100; width of rims: 4.5''; tyres: 165 SR x 13.

PERFORMANCE max speeds: (I) 25 mph, 40 km/h; (II) 40 mph, 65 km/h; (III) 62 mph, 100 km/h; (IV) over 90 mph, 145 km/h; power-weight ratio: 32.9 lb/hp (44.7 lb/kW), 14.9 kg/hp (20.3 kg/kW); carrying capacity: 882 lb, 400 kg; acceleration: 0-50 mph (0-80 km/h) 13 sec; speed in direct drive at 1,000 rpm: 15.8 mph, 25.9 km/h; consumption: 29.7 m/imp gal, 24.8 m/US gal, 9.5 l x 100 km.

CHASSIS integral; front suspension: independent, wishbones, coil springs, anti-roll bar acting as lower trailing arms, telescopic dampers; rear: rigid axle, semi-elliptic leaf-springs, telescopic dampers.

STEERING worm and roller; turns lock to lock: 3.

BRAKES disc (diameter 8.94 in, 22.7 mm), servo; lining area: total 38.4 sq in, 248 sq cm.

ELECTRICAL EQUIPMENT 12 V; 45 Ah battery; 1,500 W alternator; Marelli distributor; 4 headlamps.

DIMENSIONS AND WEIGHT wheel base: 98.62 in, 250 cm; tracks: 51.10 in, 130 cm front, 50.39 in, 128 cm rear; length: 166.65 in, 423 cm; width: 63.98 in, 162 cm; height: 56.69

POLSKI-FIAT 126 P

in, 144 cm; ground clearance: 5.51 in, 14 cm; weight: 2,139 lb, 970 kg; turning circle (between walls): 35.4 ft, 10.8 m; fuel tank capacity: 9.9 imp gal, 11.9 US gal, 45 l.

BODY saloon/sedan; 4 doors; 5 seats, separate front seats, reclining backrests, built-in headrests.

PRACTICAL INSTRUCTIONS fuel: 92 oct petrol; oil: engine 6.2 imp pt, 7.4 US pt, 3.5 l, SAE 20W-30, change every 6,200 miles, 10,000 km - gearbox 2.3 imp pt, 2.7 US pt, 1.3 l, SAE 90 EP, change every 18,600 miles, 30,000 km - final drive 3.5 imp pt, 4.2 US pt, 2 l, SAE 90 EP, change every 18,600 miles, 30,000 km; greasing: none; sparking plug: 240°; tappet clearances: inlet 0.008 in, 0.20 mm, exhaust 0.010 in, 0.25 mm; valve timing: 5° 44° 47° 2°; tyre pressure: front 23 psi, 1.6 atm, rear 27 psi, 1.9 atm.

OPTIONAL ACCESSORIES luxury interior; sunshine roof.

125 P 1300 Combi

See 125 P 1300, except for:

PERFORMANCE power-weight ratio: 36.1 lb/hp (49.1 lb/kW), 16.4 kg/hp (22.3 kg/kW); carrying capacity: 992 lb, 450 kg.

DIMENSIONS AND WEIGHT width: 66.34 in, 168 cm; height: 57.99 in, 147 cm; ground clearance: 6.06 in, 15.4 cm; weight: 2,348 lb, 1,065 kg.

BODY estate car/station wagon; 4 + 1 doors; back seat folding down to luggage table.

POLSKI-FIAT 125 P 1300 - 1500

POLSKI-FIAT 125 P 1500 Combi

125 P 1500

See 125 P 1300, except for:

PRICE IN GB: £ 1,849*

ENGINE 90,4 cu in, 1,481 cc (3.03 x 3.13 in, 77 x 79.5 mm); max power (DIN): 75 hp (55.2 kW) at 5,400 rpm; max torque (DIN): 83 lb ft, 11.5 kg m (112.8 Nm) at 3,800 rpm; max engine rpm: 6,000; 50.6 hp/l (37.2 kW/l); electric thermostatic fan.

PERFORMANCE max speed: 96 mph, 155 km/h; power-weight ratio: 28.4 lb/hp (38.8 lb/kW), 12.9 kg/hp (17.6 kg/kW); acceleration: 0-50 mph (0-80 km/h) 11 sec; consumption: 26.9 m/imp gal, 22.4 m/US gal, 10.5 l x 100 km.

125 P 1500 Combi

See 125 P 1300 Combi, except for:

PRICE IN GB: £ 2,019*

ENGINE 90.4 cu in, 1,481 cc (3.03 x 3.13 in, 77 x 79.5 mm); max power (DIN): 75 hp (55.2 kW) at 5,400 rpm; max torque (DIN): 83 lb ft, 11.5 kg m (112.8 Nm) at 3,800 rpm; max engine rpm: 6,000; 50.6 hp/l (37.2 kW/l); electric thermostatic fan.

PERFORMANCE max speed: 96 mph, 155 km/h; power-weight ratio: 31.3 lb/hp (42.6 lb/kW), 14.2 kg/hp (19.3 kg/kW); acceleration: 0-50 mph (0-80 km/h) 12 sec; consumption: 26.9 m/imp gal, 22.4 m/US gal, 10.5 l x 100 km.

SYRENA POLAND

105

ENGINE front, 2 stroke; 3 cylinders, vertical, in line; 51.4 cu in, 842 cc (2.76 x 2.87 in, 70 x 73 mm); compression ratio: 7-7.2:1; max power (DIN): 40 hp (29.4 kW) at 4,300 rpm; max torque (DIN): 58 lb ft, 8 kg m (78.5 Nm) at 2,750 rpm; max power rpm: 5,200; 47.5 hp/l (34.9 kW/l); cast iron block, dry liners, light alloy head; 4 crankshaft bearings on ball bearings; lubrication: mixture; 1 Jikov 35POH/048 horizontal carburettor; fuel feed: mechanical pump; water-cooled, 12.3 imp pt, 14.8 US pt, 7 l.

TRANSMISSION driving wheels: front; clutch: single dry plate; gearbox: mechanical; gears: 4, free wheel, fully synchronized; ratios: I 3.900, II 2.357, III 1.474, IV 0.958, rev 3.273; lever: steering column; final drive: spiral bevel; axle ratio: 4.875; width of rims: 4''; tyres: 5.60 x 15.

PERFORMANCE max speeds: (I) 19 mph, 31 km/h; (II) 32 mph, 51 km/h; (III) 50 mph, 81 km/h; (IV) 75 mph, 120 km/h; power-weight ratio: 47.8 lb/hp (65 lb/kW), 21.7 kg/hp (29.5 kg/kW); carrying capacity: 706 lb, 320 kg; acceleration: 0-50 mph (0-80 km/h) 21 sec; speed in top at 1,000 rpm: 14.9 mph, 24 km/h; consumption: 32.1 m/imp gal, 26.7 m/US gal, 8.8 l x 100 km.

CHASSIS box-type ladder frame; front suspension: independent, wishbones, tranverse leafspring lower arms, telescopic dampers; rear: rigid axle, transverse upper leafspring, trailing radius arms, telescopic dampers.

STEERING worm and roller; turns lock to lock: 2.80.

BRAKES drum; swept area: front 76.3 sq in, 492 sq cm, rear 45 sq in, 290 sq cm, total 121.3 sq in, 782 sq cm.

ELECTRICAL EQUIPMENT 12 V; 42 Ah battery; 300 W dynamo; 2 headlamps.

DIMENSIONS AND WEIGHT wheel base: 90.55 in, 230 cm; tracks: 47.24 in, 120 cm front, 48.82 in, 124 cm rear; length: 159.05 in, 404 cm; width: 61.42 in, 156 cm; height: 59.65 in, 151 cm; ground clearance: 7.87 in, 20 cm; weight: 1,912 lb, 867 kg; weight distribution: 48% front, 52% rear; turning circle (between walls): 34.1 ft, 10.4 m; fuel tank: 7 imp gal, 9.2 US gal, 35 l.

BODY saloon/sedan; 2 doors; 5 seats, separate front seats.

PRACTICAL INSTRUCTIONS fuel: mixture 1:30; oil: gearbox and final drive 4 imp pt, 4.9 US pt, 2.3 l, SAE 90, change every 7,500 miles, 12,000 km; greasing: every 7,500 miles, 12,000 km, 29 points; sparking plug: 175° or 225°; tyre pressure: front 23 psi, 1.6 atm, rear 23 psi, 1.6 atm.

SYRENA 105

ARO DACIA 240

ARO DACIA RUMANIA

M-461-C

ENGINE front, 4 stroke; 4 cylinders, vertical, in line; 153.3 cu in, 2,512 cc (3.82 x 3.35 in, 97 x 85 mm); compression ratio: 7.2:1; max power (DIN): 77 hp (56.7 kW) at 4,000 rpm; max torque (DIN): 116 lb ft, 16 kg m (156.9 Nm) at 2,700 rpm; max engine rpm: 4,500; 30.6 hp/l (22.6 kW/l); cast iron block, light alloy head; 4 crankshaft bearings; valves: overhead, Vee-slanted, push-rods and rockers; camshafts: 1, side; lubrication: gear pump, full flow filter, 9.7 imp pt, 11.6 US pt, 5.5 l; 1 K-22D downdraught single barrel carburettor; fuel feed: mechanical pump; water-cooled, 21.1 imp pt, 25.4 US pt, 12 l.

TRANSMISSION driving wheels; front (automatically engaged with transfer box low ratio) and rear; clutch: single dry plate; gearbox: mechanical; gears: 4, II, III and IV synchronized; ratios: I 4.788, II 2.680, III 1.653, IV 1, rev 1.585; lever: central; final drive: spiral bevel; axle ratio: 5.140; width of rims: 4.5''; tyres: 6.50 x 16 or 7.50 x 16.

PERFORMANCE max speed: 79 mph, 127 km/h; power-weight ratio: 46.3 lb/hp (63 lb/kW), 21 kg/hp (28.6 kg/kW); carrying capacity: 1,279 lb, 580 kg; consumption: 21.7 m/imp gal, 18.1 m/US gal, 13 l x 100 km.

CHASSIS box-type ladder frame; front and rear suspension: rigid axle, semi-elliptic leafsprings, telescopic dampers.

STEERING worm and roller; turns lock to lock: 3.50.

BRAKES drum; lining area: total 153.5 sq in, 990 sq cm.

ELECTRICAL EQUIPMENT 12 V; 64 Ah battery; 450 W dynamo; 2 headlamps.

DIMENSIONS AND WEIGHT wheel base: 91.73 in, 233 cm; tracks: 57.48 in, 146 cm front, 56.30 in, 143 cm rear; length: 151.97 in, 386 cm; width: 67.72 in, 172 cm; height: 79.13 in, 201 cm; ground clearance: 8.27 in, 21 cm; weight: 3,572 lb, 1,620 kg; weight distribution: 50.6% front, 49.4% rear; turning circle (between walls): 37.7 ft, 11.5 m; fuel tank: 15.4 imp gal, 18.5 US gal, 70 l.

BODY open; 2 doors; 8 seats, separate front seats.

PRACTICAL INSTRUCTIONS fuel: 72 oct petrol; oil: engine 9 imp pt, 10.8 US pt, 5.1 l, SAE 20W-30, change every 1,900 miles, 3,000 km - gearbox 1.4 imp pt, 1.7 US pt, 0.8 l, SAE 80-90, change every 7,000 miles, 12,000 km - final drive 1.4 imp pt, 1.7 US pt, 0.8 l, SAE 80-90, change every 7,000 miles, 12,000 km; greasing: every 1,200 miles, 2,000 km, 20 points; tyre pressure: front 28 psi, 2 atm, rear 31 psi, 2.2 atm.

VARIATIONS

ENGINE Peugeot Diesel, 128.9 cu in, 2,112 cc (3.54 x 3.27 in, 90 x 83 mm), 22.8:1 compression ratio, max power (DIN) 65 hp (47.8 kW) at 4,500 rpm, max torque (DIN) 89 lb ft, 12.3 kg m (120.6 Nm) at 2,200 rpm, max engine rpm 4,750, 30.8 hp/l.
PERFORMANCE max speed 62 mph, 100 km/h, power-weight ratio 54.9 lb/hp (74.5 lb/kW), 24.9 kg/hp (33.9 kg/kW), consumption 31.7 m/imp gal, 26.4 m/US gal, 8.9 l x 100 km.

ENGINE Perkins Diesel, 154 cu in, 2,523 cc (3.50 x 4 in, 88.9 x 101.6 mm), max power (DIN) 70 hp (51.5 kW) at 3,600 rpm, max torque (DIN) 112 lb ft, 15.6 kg m (153 Nm) at 2,000 rpm, 27.7 hp/l.
PERFORMANCE max speed 56 mph, 90 km/h, power-weight ratio 50.9 lb/hp (69.2 lb/kW), 23.1 kg/hp (31.4 kg/kW); consumption 30.4 m/imp gal, 25.3 m/US gal, 9.3 l x 100 km.

240/244

See M-461-C, except for:

ENGINE 152.2 cu in, 2,495 cc (3.82 x 3.32 in, 97 x 84.4 mm); compression ratio: 8:1; max power (DIN): 80 hp (58.9 kW) at 4,200 rpm; max torque (DIN): 123 lb ft, 17 kg m (167 Nm) at 2,800 rpm; 32.1 hp/l (23.6 kW/l); 1 Weber twin barrel carburettor; sealed circuit cooling, liquid.

TRANSMISSION gears: 4, fully synchronized; ratios: I 4.921, II 2.781, III 1.654, IV 1, rev 5.080; axle ratio: 4.700; tyres: 7.50 x 16.

PERFORMANCE max speed: 68 mph, 110 km/h; power-weight ratio: 41.2 lb/hp (53.9 lb/kW), 18.7 kg/hp (25.4 kg/kW); carrying capacity: 1,544 lb, 700 kg; consumption: 18.8 m/imp gal, 15.7 m/US gal, 15 l x 100 km.

CHASSIS front suspension: independent, wishbones, coil springs, telescopic dampers.

ELECTRICAL EQUIPMENT 56 Ah battery; 500 W alternator.

DIMENSIONS AND WEIGHT wheel base: 92.52 in, 235 cm; front and rear track: 56.69 in, 144 cm; length: 158.86 in, 403 cm; width: 70.08 in, 178 cm; height: 74.02 in, 188 cm; weight: 3,308 lb, 1,500 kg; turning circle (between walls): 39.4 ft, 12 m; fuel tank: 20.9 imp gal, 25.1 US gal, 95 l.

BODY estate car/station wagon; 3/5 doors; 5 seats.

DACIA 1300

DACIA   RUMANIA

1300 Saloon

ENGINE front, 4 stroke; 4 cylinders, vertical, in line; 78.7 cu in, 1,289 cc (2.87 x 3.03 in, 73 x 77 mm); compression ratio: 8.5:1; max power (DIN): 54 hp (39.7 kW) at 5,250 rpm; max torque (DIN): 65 lb ft, 9 kg m (88.3 Nm) at 3,500 rpm; max engine rpm: 5,500; 41.8 hp/l (30.8 kW/l); cast iron block, wet liners, light alloy head; 5 crankshaft bearings; valves: overhead, slanted, push-rods and rockers; camshafts: 1, side; lubrication: gear pump, filter in sump, 5.3 imp pt, 6.3 US pt, 3 l; 1 Solex 32 EISA downdraught carburettor; fuel feed: mechanical pump; sealed circuit cooling, liquid, 8.8 imp pt, 10.6 US pt, 5 l.

TRANSMISSION driving wheels: front; clutch: single dry plate (diaphragm); gearbox: mechanical; gears: 4, fully synchronized; ratios: I 3.615, II 2.263, III 1.480, IV 1.030, rev 3.080; lever: central; final drive: hypoid bevel; axle ratio: 3.780; width of rims: 4.5''; tyres: 155 SR x 13.

PERFORMANCE max speeds: (I) 30 mph, 48 km/h; (II) 45 mph, 73 km/h; (III) 68 mph, 110 km/h; (IV) 90 mph, 145 km/h; power-weight ratio: 36.8 lb/hp (50 lb/kW), 16.7 kg/hp (22.7 kg/kW); carrying capacity: 882 lb, 400 kg; speed in top at 1,000 rpm: 16.8 mph, 27 km/h; consumption: 33.2 m/imp gal, 27.7 m/US gal, 8.5 l x 100 km.

CHASSIS integral; front suspension: independent, wishbones, anti-roll bar, coil springs, telescopic dampers; rear: rigid axle, trailing arms, A-bracket, anti-roll bar, coil springs, telescopic dampers.

STEERING rack-and-pinion; turns lock to lock: 3.50.

BRAKES front disc (diameter 8.98 in, 22.8 cm), rear drum, rear compensator; swept area: front 157.2 sq in, 1,014 sq cm, rear 70.1 sq in, 452 sq cm, total 241.3 sq in, 1,466 sq cm.

ELECTRICAL EQUIPMENT 12 V; 36 Ah battery; 30-40 A alternator; 2 headlamps.

DIMENSIONS AND WEIGHT wheel base: 96.06 in, 244 cm; front and rear track: 51.57 in, 131 cm; length: 170.87 in, 434 cm; width: 64.57 in, 164 cm; height: 56.30 in, 143 cm; ground clearance: 4.33 in, 11 cm; weight: 1,985 lb, 900 kg; weight distribution: 58.3% front, 41.7% rear; turning circle (between walls): 35.4 ft, 10.8 m; fuel tank: 11 imp gal, 13.2 US gal, 50 l.

BODY saloon/sedan; 4 doors; 4-5 seats, separate front seats.

1300 Break

See 1300 Saloon, except for:

ENGINE 1 Zenith 32 IF8 downdraught carburettor.

PERFORMANCE power-weight ratio: 39.2 lb/hp (53.4 lb/kW), 17.8 kg/hp (24.2 kg/kW).

DIMENSIONS AND WEIGHT length: 173.23 in, 440 cm; height: 57.28 in, 145 cm; weight: 2,117 lb, 960 kg.

CHRYSLER   SPAIN

Simca 1200 Series

PRICES EX WORKS:

1 L	251,000	pesetas
2 LS	263,000	pesetas
3 LS Break	298,100	pesetas
4 LX	274,600	pesetas
5 GLS	284,900	pesetas
6 GLS Confort	295,600	pesetas
7 Special TI	320,400	pesetas
8 Special TI Break	334,300	pesetas

Power team:	Standard for:	Optional for:
52 hp	1 to 3	—
65 hp	4 to 6	—
85 hp	7,8	—

52 hp power team

ENGINE front, transverse, 4 stroke; 4 cylinders, in line; 68.2 cu in, 1,118 cc (2.91 x 2.56 in, 74 x 65 mm); compression ratio: 8.2:1; max power (DIN): 52 hp (38.2 kW) at 5,900 rpm; max torque (DIN): 55 lb ft, 7.6 kg m (74.5 Nm) at 3,000 rpm; max engine rpm: 6,000; 46.5 hp/l (34.2 kW/l); 5 crankshaft bearings; valves: overhead, in line, push-rods and rockers; camshafts: 1, side; lubrication: gear pump, full flow filter, 5.3 imp pt, 6.3 US pt, 3 l; 1 Bressel 32 IBS 7 downdraught single barrel carburettor; fuel feed: mechanical pump; sealed circuit cooling, liquid, expansion tank, 10.6 imp pt, 12.7 US pt, 6 l, electric thermostatic fan.

TRANSMISSION driving wheels: front; clutch: single dry plate (diaphragm), hydraulically controlled; gearbox: mechanical; gears: 4, fully synchronized; ratios: I 3.900, II 2.312, III 1.524, IV 1.080, rev 3.769; lever: central; final drive: cylindrical gears; axle ratio: 3.937; width of rims: 4.5''; tyres: 145 SR x 13 - LS Break 155 SR x 13.

PERFORMANCE max speed: 86 mph, 138 km/h; power-weight ratio: 39.4 lb/hp, (53.7 lb/kW), 17.9 kg/hp (24.3 kg/kW) - L 38.1 lb/hp (51.9 lb/kW), 17.3 kg/hp (23.5 kg/kW); carrying capacity: L 882 lb, 400 kg - LS 948 lb, 430 kg - LS Break 1,058 lb, 480 kg; speed in top at 1,000 rpm: 15 mph, 24 km/h; consumption: 37.6 m/imp gal, 31.3 m/US gal, 7.5 l x 100 km.

CHASSIS integral; front suspension: independent, wishbones, longitudinal torsion bars, anti-roll bar, telescopic dampers; rear: independent, longitudinal trailing arms, transverse torsion bars, anti-roll bar, telescopic dampers.

STEERING rack-and-pinion; turns lock to lock: 3.25.

BRAKES front disc (diameter 9.21 in, 23.4 cm), rear drum, dual circuit, rear compensator, servo; swept area: front 146.2 sq in, 943 sq cm, rear 73.8 sq in, 476 sq cm, total 220 sq in, 1,419 sq cm.

ELECTRICAL EQUIPMENT 12 V; 36 Ah battery; 35 A alternator; 2 headlamps.

DIMENSIONS AND WEIGHT wheel base: 99.21 in, 252 cm; tracks: 54.33 in, 138 cm front, 52.36 in, 133 cm rear; length: 155.12 in, 394 cm; width: 62.60 in, 159 cm; height: 57.48 in, 146 cm - LS Break 58.26 in, 148 cm; ground clearance: 5.50 in, 14 cm; weight: 2,051 lb, 930 kg - L 1,984 lb, 900 kg; turning circle (between walls): 34.1 ft, 10.4 m; fuel tank: 9.2 imp gal, 11.1 US gal, 42 l.

BODY saloon/sedan - LS Break estate car/station wagon; 4 doors - LS Break 4+1 doors; 5 seats, separate front seats; folding rear seat.

65 hp power team

See 52 hp power team, except for:

ENGINE 79 cu in, 1,294 cc (3.02 x 2.76 in, 76.7 x 70 mm); compression ratio: 9.5:1; max power (DIN): 65 hp (47.8 kW) at 6,000 rpm; max torque (DIN): 78 lb ft, 10.7 kg m (104.9 Nm) at 2,800 rpm; max engine rpm: 6,300; 50.2 hp/l (36.9 kW/l); 1 Bresel 32 IBS 6 downdraught single barrel carburettor.

TRANSMISSION width of rims: for LX only 5.5''.

PERFORMANCE max speed: 93 mph, 150 km/h; power-weight ratio: 31.5 lb/hp (42.9 lb/kW), 14.3 kg/hp (19.4 kg/kW) - LX 30.8 lb/hp (41.9 lb/kW), 14 kg/hp (19 kg/kW); carrying capacity: 904 lb, 410 kg - LX 926 lb, 420 kg; consumption: 35.3 m/imp gal, 29.4 m/US gal, 8 l x 100 km.

DIMENSIONS AND WEIGHT weight: LX 2,006 lb, 910 kg - GLS and GLS Confort 2,051 lb, 930 kg.

BODY LX 2 + 1 doors; GLS Confort heated rear window.

85 hp power team

See 52 hp power team, except for:

ENGINE 88 cu in, 1,442 cc (3.02 x 3.07 in, 76.7 x 78 mm); max power (DIN): 85 hp (62.6 kW) at 5,600 rpm; max torque (DIN): 92 lb ft, 12.7 kg m (124.5 Nm) at 3,000 rpm; max engine rpm: 7,200; 58.9 hp/l (43.4 kW/l); 1 Weber DCNVA downdraught twin barrel carburettor.

TRANSMISSION axle ratio: 3.588; width of rims: 5''; tyres: Special TI 155 SR x 13.

PERFORMANCE max speed: 106 mph, 170 km; power-weight ratio: 25.5 lb/hp (34.7 lb/kW), 11.6 kg/hp (15.7 kg/kW); carrying capacity: Special TI 1,058 lb, 480 kg; consumption: 24.6 m/imp gal, 20.5 m/US gal, 11.5 l x 100 km.

ELECTRICAL EQUIPMENT 2 halogen headlamps.

DIMENSIONS AND WEIGHT length: 154.70 in, 393 cm; height: 58.20 in, 148 cm; weight: 2,172 lb, 985 kg.

BODY Special TI 4 + 1 doors; heated rear window.

CHRYSLER Simca 1200 Special TI Break

CHRYSLER Diesel De Lujo

Chrysler Diesel

PRICE EX WORKS: 428,900 pesetas

ENGINE Diesel front, 4 stroke; 4 cylinders; 122.4 cu in, 2,007 cc (3.23 x 3.74 in, 82 x 95 mm); compression ratio: 21:1; max power (DIN): 65 hp (47.8 kW) at 4,000 rpm; max torque (DIN): 95.6 lb ft, 13.2 kg m (129 Nm) at 2,100 rpm; 32.3 hp/l (23.8 kW/l); lubrication: 10.9 imp pt, 13.1 US pt, 6.2 l; water-cooled, 14.9 imp pt, 17.9 US pt, 8.5 l.

TRANSMISSION driving wheels: rear; clutch: single dry plate (diaphragm), hydraulically controlled; gearbox: mechanical; gears: 4, fully synchronized; ratios: I 3.546, II 2.175, III 1.418, IV 1, rev 3.226; lever: central; final drive: hypoid bevel; axle ratio: 3.909; width of rims: 5.5''; tyres: 175 SR x 14.

PERFORMANCE max speed: 81 mph, 130 km/h; power-weight ratio: 41.4 lb/hp (56.4 lb/kW), 18.8 kg/hp (25.6 kg/kW); carrying capacity: 882 lb, 400 kg; consumption: 35.3 m/imp gal, 29.4 m/US gal, 8 l x 100 km.

CHASSIS integral; front suspension: independent, by Mc-Pherson, coil springs/telescopic damper struts, lower wishbones, anti-roll bar; rear: rigid axle, lower longitudinal trailing arms, upper torque arms, transverse linkage bar, coil springs, anti-roll bar, telescopic dampers.

STEERING rack-and-pinion; turns lock to lock: 4.

DODGE 3700 GT

BRAKES disc (front diameter 9.80 in, 24.9 cm, rear 9.02 in, 22.9 cm), dual circuit, rear compensator, servo; swept area: front 186 sq in, 1,200 sq cm, rear 141.1 sq in, 936 sq cm, total 331.1 sq in, 2,136 sq cm.

ELECTRICAL EQUIPMENT 12 V; 90 Ah battery; alternator: 2 headlamps.

DIMENSIONS AND WEIGHT wheel base: 105.12 in, 267 cm; front and rear track: 55.12 in, 140 cm; length: 178.35 in, 453 cm; width: 60.11 in, 173 cm; height: 57.09 in, 145 cm; ground clearance: 5.71 in, 14 cm; weight: 2,701 lb, 1,225 kg; turning circle (between walls): 36 ft, 11 m; fuel tank: 14.3 imp gal, 17.2 US gal, 65 l.

BODY saloon/sedan; 4 doors; 5 seats, separate front seats.

Chrysler Diesel De Lujo

See Chrysler Diesel, except for:

PRICE EX WORKS: 556,100 pesetas

ELECTRICAL EQUIPMENT 2 halogen headlamps.

BODY built-in headrests; luxury equipment.

DODGE   SPAIN

3700 Nuevo

PRICE EX WORKS: 505,560 pesetas

ENGINE front, slanted at 30° to right, 4 stroke; 6 cylinders, vertical, in line; 225 cu in, 3,687 cc (3.40 x 4.13 in, 86.4 x 104.8 mm); compression ratio: 8.4:1; max power (SAE): 165 hp (121.4 kW) at 4,200 rpm; max torque (SAE): 239 lb ft, 33 kg m (323.6 Nm) at 2,400 rpm; max engine rpm: 4,800; 44.7 hp/l (32.9 kW/l); cast iron block and head; 4 crankshaft bearings; valves: overhead, in line, push-rods and rockers; camshafts: 1, side; lubrication: rotary pump, full flow filter, 8.4 imp pt, 10.1 US pt, 4.8 l; 1 Carter BBD-4300S downdraught twin barrel carburettor; fuel feed: mechanical pump; water-cooled, 23.2 imp pt, 27.9 US pt, 13.2 l.

TRANSMISSION driving wheels: rear; clutch: single dry plate; gearbox: mechanical; gears: 3, II and III synchronized; ratios: I 2.950, II 1.830, III 1, rev 3.800; lever: steering column; final drive: hypoid bevel; axle ratio: 3.230; tyres: 185 SR x 14.

PERFORMANCE max speeds: (I) 38 mph, 61 km/h; (II) 60 mph, 97 km/h; (III) 111 mph, 179 km/h; power-weight ratio: 18.9 lb/hp (25.6 lb/kW), 8.6 kg/hp (11.6 kg/kW); carrying capacity: 1,069 lb, 485 kg; speed in direct drive at 1,000 rpm: 23.1 mph, 37.2 km/h; consumption: 20.2 m/imp gal, 16.8 m/US gal, 14 l x 100 km.

CHASSIS integral; front suspension: independent, wishbones (lower trailing links), longitudinal torsion bars, anti-roll bar, telescopic dampers; rear: rigid axle, semi-elliptic leafsprings, telescopic dampers.

STEERING recirculating ball, servo; turns lock to lock: 3.90.

BRAKES front disc (diameter 11 in, 27.8 cm), internal radial fins, rear drum, servo; lining area: total 102.3 sq in, 660 sq cm.

ELECTRICAL EQUIPMENT 12 V; 48 Ah battery; 40 A alternator; Femsa DE6-3 distributor; 4 headlamps.

DIMENSIONS AND WEIGHT wheel base: 110.98 in, 282 cm; tracks: 56.38 in, 143 cm front, 58.39 in, 148 cm rear; length: 196.61 in, 499 cm; width: 74.02 in, 188 cm; height: 54.92 in, 139 cm; ground clearance: 8.70 in, 22 cm; weight: 3,113 lb, 1,412 kg; weight distribution: 59.8% front, 40.2% rear; turning circle (between walls): 38.7 ft, 11.8 m; fuel tank: 15 imp gal, 18 US gal, 68 l.

BODY saloon/sedan; 4 doors; 5-6 seats, bench front seats; vinyl roof.

OPTIONAL ACCESSORIES 4-speed fully synchronized mechanical gearbox (I 3.090, II 1.920, III 1.400, IV 1, rev 3) with central lever and separate front seats.

3700 GT

See 3700 Nuevo, except for:

PRICE EX WORKS: 452,600 pesetas

TRANSMISSION gears: 4, fully synchronized; ratios: I 3.090, II 1.920, III 1.400, IV 1, rev 3; lever: central.

PERFORMANCE max speeds: (I) 36 mph, 58 km/h; (II) 58 mph, 93 km/h; (III) 78 mph, 126 km/h; (IV) 111 mph, 179 km/h.

BODY 5 seats, separate front seats.

DODGE 3700 Nuevo

FASA-RENAULT   SPAIN

4

PRICE EX WORKS: 172,000 pesetas

ENGINE front, 4 stroke; 4 cylinders, vertical, in line; 52 cu in, 852 cc (2.42 x 2.83 in, 61.4 x 72 mm); compression ratio: 8:1; max power (DIN): 32 hp (23.5 kW) at 5,000 rpm; max torque (DIN): 40.6 lb ft, 5.6 kg m (54.9 Nm) at 2,750 rpm; 37.5 hp/l (27.6 kW/l); 5 crankshaft bearings; valves: overhead, in line, push-rods and rockers; camshafts: 1, side; lubrication: gear pump, filter in sump, 5.3 imp pt, 6.3 US pt, 3 l; 1 Zenith 28 downdraught single barrel carburettor; fuel feed: mechanical pump; sealed circuit cooling, liquid, expansion tank, 10.2 imp pt, 12.2 US pt, 5.8 l.

TRANSMISSION driving wheels: front; clutch: single dry plate (diaphragm); gearbox: mechanical; gears: 4, fully synchronized; ratios: I 3.833, II 2.235, III 1.458, IV 1.026, rev 3.545; lever: on facia; final drive: spiral bevel; axle ratio: 4.125; width of rims: 4''; tyres: 135 SR x 13.

PERFORMANCE max speed: 71 mph, 115 km/h; power-weight ratio: 46.8 lb/hp (63.8 lb/kW), 21.2 kg/hp (28.9 kg/kW); carrying capacity: 860 lb, 390 kg; speed in top at 1,000 rpm: 14.7 mph, 23.7 km/h; consumption: 43.5 m/imp gal, 36.2 m/US gal, 6.5 l x 100 km.

CHASSIS platform; front suspension: independent, wishbones, longitudinal torsion bars, anti-roll bar, telescopic dampers; rear: independent, swinging longitudinal trailing arms, transverse torsion bars, telescopic dampers.

STEERING rack-and-pinion.

BRAKES drum, rear compensator; lining area: front 44.5 sq in, 287 sq cm, rear 19.4 sq in, 125 sq cm, total 63.9 sq in, 412 sq cm.

ELECTRICAL EQUIPMENT 12 V; 30 Ah battery; dynamo; 2 headlamps.

DIMENSIONS AND WEIGHT wheel base: 94.46 in, 245 cm (right), 94.49 in, 240 cm (left); tracks: 50.39 in, 128 cm front, 48.82 in, 124 cm rear; length: 144.49 in, 367 cm; width: 58.27 in, 148 cm; height: 61.02 in, 155 cm; weight: 1,499 lb, 680 kg; turning circle (between walls): 31.8 ft, 9.7 m; fuel tank: 5.7 imp gal, 6.8 US gal, 26 l.

BODY estate car/st. wagon; 4+1 doors; 4 seats, bench front seats; folding rear seat.

OPTIONAL ACCESSORIES metallic spray; luxury interior; heated rear window.

4 TL

See 4, except for:

PRICE EX WORKS: 191,500 pesetas

PERFORMANCE power-weight ratio 48.2 lb/hp (65.6 lb/kW), 21.8 kg/hp (29.8 kg/kW).

DIMENSIONS AND WEIGHT weight: 1,543 lb, 700 kg.

BODY luxury interior.

OPTIONAL ACCESSORIES sunshine roof; separate front seats with reclining backrests.

5 Series

PRICES EX WORKS:

1 5	—	
2 5 TL	235,200	pesetas
3 5 GTL	294,400	pesetas
4 5 TS	272,600	pesetas
5 5 Copa		

Power team:	Standard for:	Optional for:
44 hp	1,2	—
50 hp	3	—
64 hp	4	—
93 hp	5	—

44 hp power team

ENGINE front, 4 stroke; 4 cylinders, vertical, in line; 58.3 cu in, 956 cc (2.56 x 2.83 in, 65 x 72 mm); compression ratio: 9.25:1; max power (DIN): 44 hp (32.4 kW) at 5,500 rpm; max torque (DIN): 47.8 lb ft, 6.6 kg m (64.7 Nm) at 3,500 rpm; max engine rpm: 5,800; 46 hp/l (33.9 kW/l); cast iron block, wet liners, light alloy head; 5 crankshaft bearings; valves: overhead, in line, push-rods and rockers; camshafts: 1, side; lubrication: gear pump, 5.3 imp pt, 6.3 US pt, 3 l; 1 Solex 32 SEIA downdraught single barrel carburettor; fuel feed: mechanical pump; sealed circuit cooling, liquid, expansion tank, 11 imp pt, 13.3 US pt, 6.3 l.

TRANSMISSION driving wheels: front; clutch: single dry plate (diaphragm); gearbox: mechanical; gears: 4, fully synchronized; ratios: I 3.383, II 2.235, III 1.458, IV 1.026, rev

FASA-RENAULT 4

3.545; lever: central; final drive: spiral bevel; axle ratio: 4.125; width of rims: 4''; tyres: 135 SR x 13.

PERFORMANCE max speeds: (I) 24 mph, 39 km/h; (II) 40 mph, 64 km/h; (III) 62 mph, 100 km/h; (V) 84 mph, 135 km/h; power-weight ratio: 38.8 lb/hp (52.7 lb/kW), 17.6 kg/hp (23.9 kg/kW); carrying capacity: 882 lb, 400 kg; speed in top at 1,000 rpm: 14.6 mph, 23.6 km/h; consumption: 31.4 m/imp gal, 26.1 m/US gal, 9 l x 100 km.

CHASSIS integral; front suspension: independent, wishbones, longitudinal torsion bar, anti-roll bar, telescopic dampers; rear: independent, swinging longitudinal trailing arms, transverse torsion bars, telescopic dampers.

STEERING rack-and-pinion.

BRAKES front disc, rear drum, rear compensator; lining area: front 78.6 sq in, 507 sq cm, rear 26.2 sq in, 169 sq cm, total 104.8 sq in, 676 sq cm.

ELECTRICAL EQUIPMENT 12 V; 28 Ah battery; dynamo - TL alternator; 2 headlamps.

DIMENSIONS AND WEIGHT wheel base: 94.49 in, 240 cm (right), 95.67 in, 243 cm (left); tracks: 50.71 in, 129 cm front, 48.82 in, 124 cm rear; length: 138.19 in, 351 cm; width: 59.84 in, 152 cm; height: 55.12 in, 140 cm; weight: 1,709 lb, 775 kg; turning circle (between walls): 32.1 ft, 9.8 m; fuel tank: 8.4 imp gal, 10 US gal, 38 l.

BODY saloon/sedan; 2+1 doors; 4 seats, separate front seats.

50 hp power team

See 44 hp power team, except for:

ENGINE 63.27 cu in, 1,037 cc (2.66 x 2.83 in, 67.7 x 72 mm); compression ratio: 9.5:1; max power (DIN): 50 hp (36.7 kW) at 5,500 rpm; max torque (DIN): 54 lb ft, 7.4 kg m (72.5 Nm) at 3,000 rpm; max engine rpm: 6,000; 48.2 hp/l (35.4 kW/l).

PERFORMANCE max speed: 86 mph, 138 km/h; power-weight ratio: 34.6 lb/hp (47.1 lb/kW), 15.7 kg/hp (21.4 kg/hp).

CHASSIS rear suspension: anti-roll bar.

ELECTRICAL EQUIPMENT alternator.

DIMENSIONS AND WEIGHT weight: 1,730 lb, 785 kg.

BODY reclining front seats; built-in headrests.

64 hp power team

See 44 hp power team, except for:

ENGINE 78.7 cu in, 1,289 cc (2.87 x 3.03 in, 73 x 77 mm); compression ratio: 9.5:1; max power (DIN): 64 hp (47.1 kW) at 5,500 rpm; max torque (DIN): 70 lb ft, 9.6 kg m (94.1 Nm) at 3,500 rpm; 49.6 hp/l (36.5 kW/l); 1 Weber 32 DIR II downdraught twin barrel carburettor.

TRANSMISSION ratios: I 3.833, II 2.375, III 1.522, IV 1.026, rev 3.545; axle ratio: 3.625; width of rims: 4.5''; tyres: 145 SR x 13.

PERFORMANCE max speed: 93 mph, 150 km/h; power-weight ratio: 27.6 lb/hp (37.4 lb/kW), 12.5 kg/hp (17 kg/kW); speed in top at 1,000 rpm: 17.2 mph, 27.7 km/h; consumption: 28.2 m/imp gal, 23.5 m/US gal, 10 l x 100 km.

CHASSIS rear suspension: anti-roll bar, telescopic dampers.

BRAKES servo.

ELECTRICAL EQUIPMENT 36 Ah battery; 50 A alternator; iodine headlamps.

DIMENSIONS AND WEIGHT weight: 1,764 lb, 800 kg.

BODY rear window wiper-washer.

93 hp power team

See 44 hp power team, except for:

ENGINE 85.2 cu in, 1,397 cc (2.99 x 3.03 in, 76 x 77 mm); compression ratio: 10:1; max power (DIN): 93 hp (68.3 kW) at 6,400 rpm; max torque (DIN): 84 lb ft, 11.6 kg m (113.7 Nm) at 4,000 rpm; max engine rpm: 6,400; 66.5 hp/l (48.9 kW/l); 1 Weber 32 DIR 58 T twin barrel carburettor.

TRANSMISSION ratios: I 3.810, II 2.230, III 1.470, IV 1.030, rev 3.500; axle ratio: 4.125; width of rims: 5.5''; tyres: 175 SR x 13.

FASA-RENAULT 5 TS

PERFORMANCE max speed: 106 mph, 170 km/h; power-weight ratio: 20.1 lb/hp (27.4 lb/kW), 9.1 kg/hp (12.4 kg/kW); speed in top at 1,000 rpm: 17.5 mph, 28.2 km/h; consumption: 28.2 m/imp gal, 23.5 m/US gal, 10 l x 100 km.

CHASSIS rear suspension: anti-roll bar, telescopic dampers.

BRAKES servo.

ELECTRICAL EQUIPMENT 36 Ah battery; 55 A alternator; 2 halogen headlamps.

DIMENSIONS AND WEIGHT length: 139.30 in, 354 cm; weight: 1,874 lb, 850 kg.

BODY heated rear window; rear window wiper-washer.

6

ENGINE front, 4 stroke; 4 cylinders, vertical, in line; 58.3 cu in, 956 cc (2.56 x 2.83 in, 65 x 72 mm); compression ratio: 9.25:1; max power (DIN): 44 hp (32.3 kW) at 5,500 rpm; max torque (DIN): 47.8 lb ft, 6.6 kg m (64.7 Nm) at 3,500 rpm; max engine rpm: 5,800; 46 hp/l (33.8 kW/l); cast iron block, wet liners, light alloy head; 5 crankshaft bearings; valves: overhead, push-rods and rockers; camshafts: 1, side, chain driven; lubrication: gear pump, 5.3 imp pt, 6.3 US pt, 3 l; fuel feed: mechanical pump; sealed circuit cooling, liquid, 11.1 imp pt, 13.3 US pt, 6.3 l.

TRANSMISSION driving wheels: front; clutch: single dry plate; gearbox: mechanical; gears: 4, fully synchronized; ratios: I 3.660, II 2.230, III 1.450, IV 1.030, rev 3.230; lever: on facia; final drive: spiral bevel; axle ratio: 4.125; width of rims: 4''; tyres: 145 SR x 13.

PERFORMANCE max speed: 81 mph, 130 km/h; power-weight ratio: 41.6 lb/hp (56.6 lb/kW), 18.8 kg/hp (25.7 kg/kW); carrying capacity: 860 lb, 390 kg; speed in top at 1,000 rpm: 14.1 mph, 22.7 km/h; consumption: 43.4 m/imp gal, 36.2 m/US gal, 6.5 l x 100 km.

CHASSIS integral; front suspension: independent, swinging arms, longitudinal torsion bars, anti-roll bar, telescopic dampers; rear independent, swinging longitudinal leading arms, transverse torsion bars, anti-roll bar, telescopic dampers.

STEERING rack-and-pinion.

BRAKES front disc, rear drum, rear compensator; lining area: front 78.6 sq in, 507 sq cm, rear 26.3 sq in, 169 sq cm, total 104.9 sq in, 676 sq cm.

ELECTRICAL EQUIPMENT 12 V; 28 Ah battery; 35 A alternator; 2 headlamps.

DIMENSIONS AND WEIGHT wheel base: 96.46 in, 245 cm (right), 94.49 in, 240 cm (left); tracks: 50.39 in, 128 cm front, 48.82 in, 124 cm rear; length: 151.97 in, 386 cm; width: 59.06 in, 150 cm; height: 56.69 in, 144 cm; ground clearance: 4.92 in, 12.5 cm; weight: 1,830 lb, 830 kg; turning circle (between walls): 32.5 ft, 9.9 m; fuel tank: 8.8 imp gal, 10.5 US gal, 40 l.

BODY saloon/sedan; 4+1 doors; 4 seats, separate front seats, folding rear seat.

FASA-RENAULT 5 Copa

6 TL

See 6, except for:

PRICE EX WORKS: 240,900 pesetas

ENGINE 63.3 cu in, 1,037 cc (2.66 x 2.83 in, 67.7 x 72 mm); compression ratio: 9.5:1; max power (DIN): 50 hp (36.7 kW) at 5,500 rpm; max torque (DIN): 54 lb ft, 7.4 kg m (72.6 Nm) at 3,000 rpm; max engine rpm: 6,000; 48.2 hp/l (35.4 kW/l); 1 Zenith 32 IF or Solex 32 DIS downdraught carburettor.

TRANSMISSION width of rims: 4.5''.

PERFORMANCE max speed: 83 mph, 133 km/h; power-weight ratio: 36.6 lb/hp (49.8 lb/kW), 16.6 kg/hp (22.6 kg/kW).

Siete/Siete TL

See 6 TL, except for:

PRICE EX WORKS: Siete TL: 246,500 pesetas

TRANSMISSION ratios: I 3.830, II 2.230, III 1.450, IV 1.020, rev 3.540.

PERFORMANCE power-weight ratio: 35.9 lb/hp (48.9 lb/kW), 16.3 kg/hp (22.2 kg/kW); speed in top at 1,000 rpm: 15.2 mph, 24.4 km/h; consumption: 40.3 m/imp gal, 33.5 m/US gal, 7 l x 100 km.

FASA-RENAULT Siete TL

ELECTRICAL EQUIPMENT dynamo - Siete TL 38 A alternator.

DIMENSIONS AND WEIGHT wheel base: 99.60 in, 253 cm (right), 98.40 in, 250 cm (left); tracks: 50.78 in, 129 cm front, 49.21 in, 125 cm rear; length: 153.15 in, 389 cm; width: 59.80 in, 152 cm; height: 55 in, 140 cm; ground clearance: 5.50 in, 14 cm; weight: 1,797 lb, 815 kg; turning circle (between walls): 32.8 ft, 10 m; fuel tank: 8.4 imp gal, 10 US gal, 38 l.

12 Series

PRICES EX WORKS:

1 12	281,000	pesetas
2 12 Familiar	301,500	pesetas
3 12 TL	298,800	pesetas
4 12 TL Familiar	316,700	pesetas
5 12 TS	330,100	pesetas
6 12 TS Familiar	346,000	pesetas

Power team	Standard for:	Optional for:
57 hp	1 to 4	—
70 hp	5,6	—

57 hp power team

ENGINE front, 4 stroke; 4 cylinders, vertical, in line; 78.7 cu in, 1,289 cc (2.87 x 3.03 in, 73 x 77 mm); compression ratio: 8.5:1; max power (DIN): 57 hp (41.9 kW) at 5,300 rpm; max torque (DIN): 69 lb ft, 9.5 kg m (93.2 Nm) at 3,000 rpm; max engine rpm: 5,300; 44.2 hp/l (32.5 kW/l); cast iron block, wet liners, light alloy head; 5 crankshaft bearings; valves: overhead, slanted, push-rods and rockers; camshafts: 1, side; lubrication: gear pump, filter in sump, 5.3 imp pt, 6.3 US pt, 3 l; 1 Solex 32 downdraught single barrel carburettor; fuel feed: mechanical pump; sealed cooling, liquid, 3.5 imp pt, 4.2 US pt, 2 l.

TRANSMISSION driving wheels: front; clutch: single dry plate; gearbox: mechanical; gears: 4, fully synchronized; ratios: I 3.818, II 2.235, III 1.478, IV 1.036, rev 3.083; lever: central; final drive: hypoid bevel; axle ratio: 3.778; width of rims: 5''; tyres: 155 x 330.

PERFORMANCE max speed: 87 mph, 140 km/h; power-weight ratio: saloons 35 lb/hp (47.6 lb/kW), 15.8 kg/hp (21.6 kg/kW) - station wagons 37.1 lb/hp (50.5 lb/kW), 16.8 kg/hp (22.9 kg/kW); carrying capacity: saloons 882 lb, 400 kg - station wagons 937 lb, 425 kg; speed in top at 1,000 rpm: 16.6 mph, 26.7 km/h; consumption: 35.3 m/imp gal, 29.4 m/US gal, 8 l x 100 km.

CHASSIS integral; front suspension: independent, wishbones, anti-roll bar, coil springs/telescopic dampers; rear: rigid axle, trailing arms, A-bracket, anti-roll bar, coil springs/telescopic dampers.

STEERING rack-and-pinion.

BRAKES front disc, rear drum, rear compensator - 12 TL and station wagons servo; lining area: front 78.6 sq in, 507 sq cm, rear 35 sq in, 226 sq cm, total 113.6 sq in, 733 sq cm.

ELECTRICAL EQUIPMENT 12 V; dynamo - TL models alternator; 36 Ah battery; 2 headlamps.

DIMENSIONS AND WEIGHT wheel base: 96.06 in, 244 cm; front and rear track: 51.96 in, 132 cm; length: saloons 172.44 in, 438 cm - station wagons 173.23 in, 440 cm; width: 63.78 in, 162 cm; height: saloons 55.90 in, 142 cm - station wagons 57.08 in, 145 cm; ground clearance: 5.12 in, 13 cm; weight: saloons 1,995 lb, 905 kg - station wagons 2,117 lb, 960 kg; turning circle (between walls): 33 ft, 10.1 m; fuel tank: 11 imp gal, 13.2 US gal, 50 l.

BODY saloons 5 seats - station wagons 5/7 seats, separate front seats; heated rear window (for TL models only).

70 hp power team

See 57 hp power team, except for:

ENGINE 85.2 cu in, 1,397 cc (2.99 x 3.03 in, 76 x 77 mm); compression ratio: 9.2:1; max power (DIN): 70 hp (51.5 kW) at 5,500 rpm; max torque (DIN): 80 lb ft, 11 kg m (107.8 Nm) at 3,500 rpm; max engine rpm: 5,600; 50.1 hp/l (36.9 kW/l); 1 Weber 32 DIR 40 T downdraught twin barrel carburettor.

PERFORMANCE max speed: 92 mph, 148 km/h; power-weight ratio: 28.9 lb/hp (39.3 lb/kW), 13.1 kg/hp (17.8 kg/kW) - Familiar 30.7 lb/hp (41.7 lb/kW), 13.9 kg/hp (18.9 kg/kW).

BRAKES servo.

ELECTRICAL EQUIPMENT alternator; 4 headlamps, 2 iodine.

DIMENSIONS AND WEIGHT weight: 2,028 lb, 920 kg - Familiar 2,149 lb, 975 kg.

BODY built-in headrests.

MALLORCA   SPAIN

1800

PRICE EX WORKS: 650,000 pesetas

ENGINE Seat; front, 4 stroke; 4 cylinders, vertical, in line; 107.2 cu in, 1,756 cc (3.31 x 3.12 in, 84 x 79.2 mm); max power (DIN): 118 hp (86.7 kW) at 6,000 rpm; max torque (DIN): 104 lb ft, 14.4 kg m (141.2 Nm) at 4,000 rpm; max engine rpm: 6,300; 67.2 hp/l (49.3 kW/l); cast iron block, light alloy head; 5 crankshaft bearings; valves: overhead, Vee-slanted at 65°, thimble tappets; camshafts: 2, overhead, cogged belt; lubrication: gear pump, full flow filter (cartridge), 7.7 imp pt, 9.3 US pt, 4.4 l; 1 Weber 34 DMS downdraught twin barrel carburettor; fuel feed: mechanical pump; sealed circuit cooling, anti-freeze liquid, 14.1 imp pt, 16.9 US pt, 8 l, electric thermostatic fan.

TRANSMISSION driving wheels: front; clutch: single dry plate; gearbox: mechanical; gears: 4, fully synchronized; ratios: I 3.583, II 2.235, III 1.454, IV 1.042, rev 3.714; lever: central; final drive: hypoid bevel; axle ratio: 3.727; width of rims: 5''; tyres: 165/70 SR x 13.

PERFORMANCE max speed: about 106 mph, 170 km/h; power-weight ratio: 12.1 lb/hp (16.5 lb/kW), 5.5 kg/hp (7.5 kg/kW); carrying capacity: 551 lb, 250 kg.

CHASSIS reinforced platform; front suspension: independent, coil springs; rear: rigid axle, 4 trailing longitudinal arms, transverse linkage bar.

STEERING rack-and-pinion.

BRAKES disc, dual circuit.

ELECTRICAL EQUIPMENT 2 halogen headlamps.

DIMENSIONS AND WEIGHT length: 146.45 in, 372 cm; width: 60.62 in, 154 cm; height: 41.30 in, 105 cm; weight: 1,433 lb, 650 kg.

BODY coupé, in fibreglass material; no doors; 2 seats; detachable hardtop.

SEAT   SPAIN

133/133 Lujo

**PRICES EX WORKS: 133:   171,720* pesetas
133 Lujo: 188,000* pesetas**

ENGINE rear, longitudinal, 4 stroke; 4 cylinders, vertical, in line; 51.4 cu in, 843 cc (2.56 x 2.50 in, 65 x 63.5 mm); compression ratio: 8:1; max power (DIN): 34 hp (25 kW) at 4,800 rpm; max torque (DIN): 40 lb ft, 5.5 kg m (53.9 Nm) at 3,200 rpm; max engine rpm: 5,500; 40.3 hp/l (29.7 kW/l); cast iron block, light alloy head; 3 crankshaft bearings; valves: overhead, in line, push-rods and rockers; camshafts: 1, side; lubrication: gear pump, full flow filter, 6 imp pt, 7.2 US pt, 3.4 l; 1 Bressel 30 ICF-3 or Solex 30 PIB-5 downdraught single barrel carburettor; fuel feed: mechanical pump; sealed circuit cooling, liquid, 13.2 imp pt, 15.9 US pt, 7.5 l.

TRANSMISSION driving wheels: rear; clutch: single dry plate; gearbox: mechanical; gears: 4, fully synchronized; ratios: I 3.636, II 2.055, III 1.409, IV 0.963, rev 3.615; lever: central; final drive: hypoid bevel; axle ratio: 4.625; width of rims: 4''; tyres: 5.50 x 12.

PERFORMANCE max speeds: (I) 20 mph, 32 km/h; (II) 35 mph, 56 km/h; (III) 52 mph, 83 km/h; (IV) about 75 mph, 120 km/h; power-weight ratio: 44.7 lb/hp (60.8 lb/kW), 20.3 kg/hp (27.6 kg/kW); carrying capacity: 706 lb, 320 kg; speed in top at 1,000 rpm: 13.7 mph, 22.1 km/h; consumption: 40.9 m/imp gal, 34.1 m/US gal, 6.9 l x 100 km.

CHASSIS integral; front suspension: independent, wishbones, transverse leafspring lower arms, transverse torsion bar, telescopic dampers; rear: independent, semi-trailing arms, coil springs, torsion bar, telescopic dampers.

STEERING rack-and-pinion; turns lock to lock: 2.80.

BRAKES drum, dual circuit; lining area: front 33.5 sq in, 216 sq cm, rear 33.5 sq in, 216 sq cm, total 67 sq in, 432 sq cm.

ELECTRICAL EQUIPMENT 12 V; 34 Ah battery; 230 W dynamo; Femsa DI 4-7 distributor; 2 headlamps.

DIMENSIONS AND WEIGHT wheel base: 79.92 in, 203 cm; tracks: 45.28 in, 115 cm front, 48.03 in, 122 cm rear; length: 135.83 in, 345 cm; width: 55.91 in, 142 cm; height: 52.36 in, 133 cm; ground clearance: 5.30 in, 13 cm; weight: 1,521 lb, 690 kg; weight distribution: 39% front,

MALLORCA 1800

61% rear; turning circle (between walls): 31.5 ft, 9.6 m; fuel tank: 6.6 imp gal, 7.9 US gal, 30 l.

BODY saloon/sedan; 2 doors; 4-5 seats, separate front seats; for 133 Lujo luxury equipment.

PRACTICAL INSTRUCTIONS fuel: 85 oct petrol; oil: engine 5.8 imp pt, 7 US pt, 3.3 l, SAE 40W (winter) 30 (summer), change every 6,200 miles, 10,000 km - gearbox and final drive 3.7 imp pt, 4.4 US pt, 2.1 l, SAE 90 EP, change every 18,600 miles, 30,000 km; greasing: every 1,600 miles, 2,500 km, 2 points; sparking plug: 175°; tappet clearances: inlet 0.006 in, 0.15 mm, exhaust 0.006 in, 0.15 mm; valve timing: 16° 56° 56° 16°; tyre pressure: front 20 psi, 1.4 atm, rear 28 psi, 2 atm.

133 Especial/133 Especial Lujo

See 133/133 Lujo, except for:

**PRICES EX WORKS: 133 Especial: 154,000* pesetas
133 Especial Lujo: 194,246* pesetas**

ENGINE compression ratio: 9:1; max power (DIN): 44 hp (32.4 kW) at 6,400 rpm; max torque (DIN): 41 lb ft, 5.6 kg m (54.9 Nm) at 3,700 rpm; max engine rpm: 6,400; 52.2 hp/l (38.4 kW/l); 1 Bressel 30 DIC-10 downdraught twin barrel carburettor.

TRANSMISSION axle ratio: 5.125; tyres: 145 SR x 13.

PERFORMANCE max speeds: (I) 22 mph, 36 km/h; (II) 40 mph, 64 km/h; (III) 58 mph, 94 km/h; (IV) about 84 mph, 135 km/h; power-weight ratio: 35.1 lb/hp (47.7 lb/kW), 15.9 kg/hp (21.6 kg/kW); carrying capacity: 882 lb, 400 kg.

BRAKES front disc (diameter 8.94 in, 22.7 cm), rear drum; lining area: front 19.2 sq in, 124 sq cm, rear 33.5 sq in, 216 sq cm, total 52.7 sq in, 340 sq cm.

DIMENSIONS AND WEIGHT rear track: 47.91 in, 122 cm; length: 136.81 in, 347 cm; weight: 1,544 lb, 700 kg.

BODY for 133 Especial Lujo luxury equipment.

PRACTICAL INSTRUCTIONS fuel: 96 oct petrol; tappet clearances: inlet 0.006-0.008 in, 0.15-0.20 mm, exhaust 0.008-0.010 in, 0.20-0.25 mm; valve timing: 25° 51° 64° 12°.

127 2 Puertas/127 2 Puertas Confort Lujo

**PRICES EX WORKS: 127 2 Puertas: 225,867* pesetas
Confort Lujo: 256,997* pesetas**

ENGINE front, transverse, 4 stroke; 4 cylinders, vertical, in line; 55.1 cu in, 903 cc (2.56 x 2.68 in, 65 x 68 mm); compression ratio: 9:1; max power (DIN): 45 hp (33.1 kW) at 5,600 rpm; max torque (DIN): 47 lb ft, 65 kg m (63.7 Nm) at 3,000 rpm; max engine rpm: 6,200; 49.8 hp/l (36.7 kW/l); cast iron block, light alloy head; 3 crankshaft bear-

SEAT 133 Lujo

ings; valves: overhead, in line, push-rods and rockers; camshafts: 1, side; lubrication: gear pump, full flow filter (cartridge), 6 imp pt, 7.2 US pt, 3.4 l; 1 Bressel 32 IBA 20 downdraught single barrel carburettor; fuel feed: mechanical pump; water-cooled, 8.8 imp pt, 10.6 US pt, 5 l.

TRANSMISSION driving wheels: front; clutch: single dry plate; gearbox: mechanical; gears: 4, fully synchronized; ratios: I 3.909, II 2.055, III 1.348, IV 0.963, rev 3.615; lever: central; final drive: cylindrical gears; axle ratio: 4.692; width of rims: 4''; tyres: 135 SR x 13.

PERFORMANCE max speeds: (I) 21.7 mph, 35 km/h; (II) 40 mph, 65 km/h; (III) 62 mph, 100 km/h; (IV) over 84 mph, 135 km/h; power-weight ratio: 34.5 lb/hp (47 lb/kW), 15.6 kg/hp (21.3 kg/kW); carrying capacity: 882 lb, 400 kg; speed in top at 1,000 rpm: 13.7 mph, 22.1 km/h; consumption: 43.4 m/imp gal, 36.2 m/US gal, 6.5 l x 100 km.

CHASSIS integral; front suspension: independent, by Mc-Pherson, coil springs/telescopic damper struts, lower wishbones, anti-roll bar; rear: independent, single wide-based wishbone, transverse anti-roll leafsprings, telescopic dampers.

STEERING rack-and-pinion; turns lock to lock: 3.40.

BRAKES front disc (diameter 8.94 in, 22.7 cm), rear drum, rear compensator, dual circuit; lining area: front 19.2 sq in, 124 sq cm, rear 33.5 sq cm, 216 sq cm, total 52.7 sq in, 340 sq cm.

ELECTRICAL EQUIPMENT 12 V; 34 Ah battery; 33 A alternator; Femsa distributor; 2 headlamps.

DIMENSIONS AND WEIGHT wheel base: 87.40 in, 222 cm; tracks: 50.39 in, 128 cm front, 50.79 in, 129 cm rear; length: 142.90 in, 363 cm; width: 60.24 in, 153 cm; height: 53.50 in, 136 cm; ground clearance: 5.12 in, 13 cm; weight: 1,555 lb, 705 kg; weight distribution: 48% front, 52% rear; turning circle (between walls): 31.5 ft, 9.6 m; fuel tank: 6.6 imp gal, 7.9 US gal, 30 l.

BODY saloon/sedan; 2 doors; 5 seats, separate front seats; for 127 2 Puertas Confort Lujo luxury equipment.

PRACTICAL INSTRUCTIONS fuel: 96 oct petrol; oil: engine 6.9 imp pt, 8.2 US pt, 3.9 l, SAE 30W-40, change every 6,200 miles, 10,000 km - gearbox and final drive 4.2 imp pt, 5.1 US pt, 2.4 l, SAE 50, change every 18,600 miles, 30,000 km; greasing: every 3,100 miles, 5,000 km, 7 points; tappet clearances: inlet 0.006 in, 0.15 mm, exhaust 0.008 in, 0.20 mm; valve timing: 25° 51° 64° 12°; tyre pressure: front 24 psi, 1.7 atm, rear 27 psi, 1.9 atm.

127 3 Puertas/127 3 Puertas Confort Lujo

See 127 2 Puertas/127 2 Puertas Confort Lujo, except for:

PRICES EX WORKS: 127 3 Puertas: 234,827* pesetas
Confort Lujo: 265,957* pesetas

PERFORMANCE power-weight ratio: 34.8 lb/hp (47.4 lb/kW), 15.8 kg/hp (21.5 kg/kW).

DIMENSIONS AND WEIGHT weight: 1,566 lb, 710 kg.

SEAT 127 3 Puertas

BODY 2+1 doors; folding rear seat; for 127 3 Puertas Confort Lujo luxury equipment.

OPTIONAL ACCESSORIES Comercial version.

127 4 Puertas/127 4 Puertas Confort Lujo

See 127 2 Puertas/127 2 Puertas Confort Lujo, except for:

PRICES EX WORKS: 127 4 Puertas: 240,634* pesetas
Confort Lujo: 271,763* pesetas

PERFORMANCE max speed: 87 mph, 140 km/h; power-weight ratio: 35.3 lb/hp (48.1 lb/kW), 16 kg/hp (21.8 kg/kW).

DIMENSIONS AND WEIGHT weight: 1,588 lb, 720 kg.

BODY 4 doors; for 127 4 Puertas Confort Lujo luxury equipment.

128/3P 1200

PRICE EX WORKS: 324,852* pesetas

ENGINE front, transverse, slanted at 16°, 4 stroke; 4 cylinders, vertical, in line; 73 cu in, 1,197 cc (2.87 x 2.81 in, 73 x 71.5 mm); compression ratio: 8.8:1; max power

(DIN): 67 hp (49.3 kW) at 5,600 rpm; max torque (DIN): 67 lb ft, 9.2 kg m (90.2 Nm) at 3,700 rpm; max engine rpm: 5,600; 56 hp/l (41.2 kW/l); cast iron block, light alloy head; 5 crankshaft bearings; valves: overhead, push-rods and rockers; camshafts: 1, side, in crankcase; lubrication: gear pump, full flow filter (cartridge), 7.7 imp pt, 9.3 US pt, 4.4 l; 1 Bressel 32 DMTR downdraught twin barrel carburettor; fuel feed: mechanical pump; water-cooled, 13.2 imp pt, 15.9 US pt, 7.5 l.

TRANSMISSION driving wheels: front; clutch: single dry plate; gearbox: mechanical; gears: 4, fully synchronized; ratios: I 3.583, II 2.235, III 1.454, IV 1.042, rev 3.714; lever: central; final drive: cylindrical gears; axle ratio: 3.765; width of rims: 4.5''; tyres: 145 SR x 13.

PERFORMANCE max speeds: (I) 25 mph, 40 km/h; (II) 47 mph, 75 km/h; (III) 71 mph, 115 km/h; (IV) 99 mph, 160 km/h; power-weight ratio: 27.9 lb/hp (38 lb/kW), 12.7 kg/hp (17.2 kg/kW); carrying capacity: 794 lb, 360 kg; acceleration: standing 1/4 mile 19 sec; speed in top at 1,000 rpm: 17.8 mph, 28.6 km/h; consumption: 35.3 m/imp gal, 29.4 m/US gal, 8 l x 100 km.

CHASSIS integral; front suspension: independent, by Mc-Pherson, coil springs/telescopic damper struts, lower wishbones, anti-roll bar; rear: independent, single wide-based wishbone, transverse anti-roll leafsprings, telescopic dampers.

STEERING rack-and-pinion; turns lock to lock: 3.50.

BRAKES front disc (diameter 8.94 in, 22.7 cm), rear drum, dual circuit; lining area: front 19.2 sq in, 124 sq cm, rear 33.5 sq cm, 216 sq cm, total 52.7 sq in, 340 sq cm.

ELECTRICAL EQUIPMENT 12 V; 45 Ah battery; 480 W alternator; Femsa distributor; 4 headlamps.

DIMENSIONS AND WEIGHT wheel base: 87.60 in, 222 cm; front and rear track: 52.36 in, 133 cm front, 50.78 in, 383 cm; width: 61.18 in, 155 cm; height: 51.57 in, 131 cm; ground clearance: 5.12 in, 13 cm; weight: 1,874 lb, 850 kg; weight distribution: 51.7% front, 48.3% rear; turning circle (between walls): 31.5 ft, 9.6 m; fuel tank: 11 imp gal, 13.2 US gal, 50 l.

BODY coupé; 2 doors; 4 seats, separate front seats.

PRACTICAL INSTRUCTIONS fuel: 96 oct petrol; oil: engine 6.5 imp pt, 7.8 US pt, 3.7 l, SAE 40W (winter) 30 (summer), change every 6,200 miles, 10,000 km - gearbox and final drive 2.3 imp pt, 2.7 US pt, 1.3 l, SAE 90 EP, change every 12,400 miles, 20,000 km; greasing: homokinetic joints, every 18,600 miles, 30,000 km; sparking plug: 145°; tappet clearances: inlet and exhaust 0.010-0.012 in, 0.25-0.30 mm; valve timing: 10° 49° 50° 9°; tyre pressure: front 27 psi, 1.9 atm, rear 26 psi, 1.8 atm.

Sport 1200

See 128/3 P 1200, except for:

PRICE EX WORKS: 344,758* pesetas

ENGINE max engine rpm: 5,800.

TRANSMISSION tyres: 165/70 SR x 13.

PERFORMANCE max speed: over 102 mph, 165 km/h; power-weight ratio: 26.7 lb/hp (36.2 lb/kW), 12.1 kg/hp (16.4 kg/kW); consumption: 40 m/imp gal, 33.6 m/US gal, 7 l x 100 km.

CHASSIS swinging leading arms on front and rear suspension.

ELECTRICAL EQUIPMENT 2 headlamps.

DIMENSIONS AND WEIGHT tracks: 50.78 in, 129 cm front, 51.57 in, 131 cm rear; length: 144.49 in, 367 cm; height: 49.21 in, 125 cm; weight: 1,786 lb, 810 kg.

BODY built-in headrests.

128/3P 1430

See 128/3 P 1200, except for:

PRICE EX WORKS: 339,597* pesetas

ENGINE 87.74 cu in, 1,438 cc (3.15 x 2.81 in, 80 x 71.5 mm); compression ratio: 9:1; max power (DIN): 77 hp (56.6 kW) at 5,600 rpm; max torque (DIN): 82 lb ft, 11.3 kg m (110 Nm) at 2,800 rpm; 53.5 hp/l (39.3 kW/l).

PERFORMANCE max speeds: (I) 28 mph, 45 km/h; (II) 46 mph, 75 km/h; (III) 71 mph, 115 km/h; (IV) over 99 mph, 160 km/h; power-weight ratio: 24.5 lb/hp (33.3 lb/kW), 11.1 kg/hp (15.1 kg/kW); carrying capacity: 882 lb, 400 kg.

DIMENSIONS AND WEIGHT weight: 1,885 lb, 855 kg.

SEAT 127 4 Puertas

SEAT Sport 1430

Sport 1430

See 128/3 P 1430, except for:

PRICE EX WORKS: 359,504* pesetas

ENGINE max engine rpm: 5,800.

TRANSMISSION tyres: 165/70 SR x 13.

PERFORMANCE max speed: over 102 mph, 165 km/h; power-weight ratio: 23.2 lb/hp (31.5 lb/kW), 10.5 kg/hp (14.3 kg/kW); consumption: 40 m/imp gal, 33.6 m/US gal, 7 l x 100 km.

CHASSIS swinging leading arms on front and rear suspension.

ELECTRICAL EQUIPMENT 2 headlamps.

DIMENSIONS AND WEIGHT tracks: 50.78 in, 129 cm front, 51.57 in, 131 cm rear; length: 144.49 in, 367 cm; height: 49.21 in, 125 cm; weight: 1,786 lb, 810 kg.

BODY built-in headrests.

124-D/124-D LS

PRICES EX WORKS: 124-D: 274,758* pesetas
124-D LS: 305,263* pesetas

ENGINE front, 4 stroke; 4 cylinders, in line; 73 cu in, 1,197 cc (2.87 x 2.81 in, 73 x 71.5 mm); compression ratio: 8.8:1; max power (DIN): 65 hp (47.8 kW) at 5,600 rpm; max torque (DIN): 65 lb ft, 9 kg m (88.3 Nm) at 3,400 rpm; max engine rpm: 5,600; 54.3 hp/l (39.9 kW/l); cast iron block, light alloy head; 5 crankshaft bearings; valves: overhead, push-rods and rockers; camshafts: 1, side, in crankcase; lubrication: gear pump, full flow filter (cartridge), 7.7 imp pt, 9.3 US pt, 4.4 l; 1 Bressel 32 DHS-20 downdraught twin barrel carburettor; fuel feed: mechanical pump; water-cooled, 13.2 imp pt, 15.9 US pt, 7.5 l.

TRANSMISSION driving wheels: rear; clutch: single dry plate; gearbox: mechanical; gears: 4, fully synchronized; ratios: I 3.750, II 2.300, III 1.490, IV 1, rev 3.870; lever: central; final drive: hypoid bevel; axle ratio: 4.300; width of rims: 4.5''; tyres: 150 SR x 13 or 155 SR x 13.

PERFORMANCE max speeds: (I) 22 mph, 35 km/h; (II) 37 mph, 60 km/h; (III) 59 mph, 95 km/h; (IV) about 93 mph, 150 km/h; power-weight ratio: 29.7 lb/hp (40.3 lb/kW), 13.4 kg/hp (18.3 kg/kW); carrying capacity: 882 lb, 400 kg; speed in direct drive at 1,000 rpm: 16.7 mph, 26.8 km/h; consumption: 35.3 m/imp gal, 29.4 m/US gal, 8 l x 100 km.

CHASSIS integral; front suspension: independent, wishbones, coil springs, anti-roll bar, telescopic dampers; rear: rigid axle, twin trailing radius arms, transverse linkage bar, coil springs, telescopic dampers.

STEERING worm and roller; turns lock to lock: 2.75.

BRAKES disc (diameter 8.94 in, 22.7 cm), rear compensator, servo; lining area: front 19.2 sq in, 124 sq cm, rear 19.2 sq in, 124 sq cm, total 38.4 sq in, 248 sq cm.

ELECTRICAL EQUIPMENT 12 V; 45 Ah battery; 540 W alternator; Femsa DI 4-8 distributor; 2 headlamps.

DIMENSIONS AND WEIGHT wheel base: 95.28 in, 242 cm; tracks: 52.36 in, 133 cm front, 51.18 in, 130 cm rear; length: 159.05 in, 404 cm; width: 63.39 in, 161 cm; height: 55.91 in, 142 cm; ground clearance: 5.12 in, 13 cm; weight: 1,929 lb, 875 kg; weight distribution: 43% front, 57% rear; turning circle (between walls): 35.1 ft, 10.7 m; fuel tank: 8.6 imp gal, 10.3 US gal, 39 l.

BODY saloon/sedan; 4 doors; 5 seats, separate front seats; heated rear window; for 124-D LS tinted glass, built-in headrests and luxury equipment.

PRACTICAL INSTRUCTIONS fuel: 96 oct petrol; oil: engine 6.5 imp pt, 7.8 US pt, 3.7 l, SAE 30W (summer) 40 (winter), change every 6,200 miles, 10,000 km - gearbox 2.3 imp pt, 2.7 US pt, 1.3 l, ZC 90, change every 12,400 miles, 20,000 km - final drive 2.3 imp pt, 2.7 US pt, 1.3 l, SAE 90, change every 12,400 miles, 20,000 km; greasing: every 3,100 miles, 5,000 km, 4 points; sparking plug: 145º; tappet clearances: inlet and exhaust 0.010-0.012 in, 0.25-0.30 mm; valve timing: 10º 49º 50º 9º; tyre pressure: front 24 psi, 1.7 atm, rear 26 psi, 1.8 atm.

124-D Especial

See 124-D/124-D LS, except for.

PRICE EX WORKS: 324,719* pesetas

ENGINE 87.7 cu in, 1,438 cc (3.15 x 2.81 in, 80 x 71.5 mm); compression ratio: 9:1; max power (DIN): 75 hp (55.2 kW) at 5,400 rpm; max torque (DIN): 82 lb ft, 11.3 kg m (110.8 Nm) at 3,400 rpm; max engine rpm: 6,000; 52.2 hp/l (38.4 kW/l); 1 Bressel 32 DHS-21 downdraught twin barrel carburettor.

TRANSMISSION gearbox ratios: I 3.797, II 2.175, III 1.410, IV 1, rev 3.655.

PERFORMANCE max speeds: (I) 25 mph, 40 km/h; (II) 43 mph, 70 km/h; (III) 68 mph, 110 km/h; (IV) about 96 mph, 155 km/h; power-weight ratio: 26.8 lb/hp (36.4 lb/kW), 12.1 kg/hp (16.5 kg/kW); speed in direct drive at 1,000 rpm: 16 mph, 25.8 km/h; consumption: 32.1 m/imp gal, 26.7 m/US gal, 8.8 l x 100 km.

DIMENSIONS AND WEIGHT weight: 2,007 lb, 910 kg; weight distribution: 44% front, 56% rear.

PRACTICAL INSTRUCTIONS sparking plug: 175º.

OPTIONAL ACCESSORIES 5-speed mechanical gearbox (I 3.667, II 2.100, III 1.361, IV 1, V 0.881).

131-L

PRICE EX WORKS: 346,059* pesetas

ENGINE front, 4 stroke; 4 cylinders, vertical, in line; 87.7 cu in, 1,438 cc (3.15 x 2.81 in, 80 x 71.5 mm); compression ratio: 9:1; max power (DIN): 75 hp (55.2 kW) at 5,400 rpm; max torque (DIN): 82 lb ft, 11.3 kg m (110.8 Nm) at 3,400 rpm; max engine rpm: 6,300; 52.2 hp/l (38.4 kW/l); cast iron block, light alloy head; 5 crankshaft bearings; valves: overhead, push-rods and rockers; camshafts: 1, side, in crankcase; lubrication: gear pump, full flow filter (cartridge), 7.7 imp pt, 9.3 US pt, 4.4 l; 1 Bressel 32 DHS-26 or Solex 32EIES-4 downdraught twin barrel carburettor; fuel feed: mechanical pump; sealed circuit cooling, anti-freeze liquid, 13.2 imp pt, 15.9 US pt, 7.5 l.

TRANSMISSION driving wheels: rear; clutch: single dry plate; gearbox: mechanical; gears: 4, fully synchronized; ratios: I 3.667, II 2.100, III 1.361, IV 1, rev 3.526; lever: central; final drive: hypoid bevel; axle ratio: 3.900; width of rims: 4.5''; tyres: 155 SR x 13.

PERFORMANCE max speeds: (I) 28 mph, 45 km/h; (II) 47 mph, 75 km/h; (III) 75 mph, 120 km/h; (IV) about 96 mph, 155 km/h; power-weight ratio: 28.5 lb/hp (38.7 lb/kW), 12.9 kg/hp (17.6 kg/kW); carrying capacity: 882 lb, 400 kg; acceleration: standing ¼ mile 19 sec; speed in direct drive at 1,000 rpm: 16.8 mph, 27.1 km/h; consumption: 36 m/imp gal, 30 m/US gal, 7.8 l x 100 km.

CHASSIS integral; front suspension: independent, by McPherson, coil springs/telescopic damper struts, lower wishbones, anti-roll bar; rear: rigid axle, twin trailing lower

SEAT 124-D Especial

radius arms, transverse linkage bar, coil springs, telescopic dampers.

STEERING rack-and-pinion; turns lock to lock: 3.40.

BRAKES front disc (diameter 8.94 in, 22.7 cm), rear drum, rear compensator, servo; lining area: front 19.2 sq in, 124 sq cm, rear 41.7 sq in, 269 sq cm, total 60.9 sq in, 393 sq cm.

ELECTRICAL EQUIPMENT 12 V, 45 Ah battery; 540 W alternator; Femsa distributor; 2 headlamps.

DIMENSIONS AND WEIGHT wheel base: 98.03 in, 249 cm; tracks: 53.94 in, 137 cm front, 51.57 in, 131 cm rear; length: 166.93 in, 424 cm; width: 64.17 in, 163 cm; height: 53.54 in, 136 cm; weight: 2,139 lb, 970 kg; weight distribution: 44.4% front, 55.6% rear; turning circle (between walls): 34.8 ft, 10.6 m; fuel tank: 11 imp gal, 13.2 US gal, 50 l.

BODY saloon/sedan; 4 doors; 5 seats, separate front seats, reclining backrests.

PRACTICAL INSTRUCTIONS fuel: 96 oct petrol; oil: engine 6.7 imp pt, 8 US pt, 3.8 l, SAE 30W (winter) 40 (summer), change every 6,200 miles, 10,000 km - gearbox and final drive 1.6 imp pt, 1.9 US pt, 0.9 l, SAE 50 VS type ZC; greasing: none; sparking plug: 175°; tappet clearances: inlet and exhaust 0.010-0.012 in, 0.25-0.30 mm; valve timing: 10° 49° 50° 9°; tyre pressure: front 24 psi, 1.7 atm, rear 26 psi, 1.8 atm.

131-L 5 Puertas

See 131-L, except for:

PRICE EX WORKS: 382,083* pesetas

TRANSMISSION axle ratio: 4.100; tyres: 165 SR x 13.

PERFORMANCE max speeds: (I) 25 mph, 40 km/h; (II) 43 mph, 70 km/h; (III) 71 mph, 115 km/h; (IV) about 93 mph, 150 km/h; power-weight ratio: 29.5 lb/hp (40.1 lb/kW), 13.4 kg/hp (18.2 kg/kW); carrying capacity: 1,058 lb, 480 kg; acceleration: standing ¼ mile 19.1 sec.

DIMENSIONS AND WEIGHT tracks: 54.17 in, 138 cm front, 51.93 in, 132 cm rear; height: 55.12 in, 140 cm; weight: 2,216 lb, 1,005 kg.

BODY estate car/station wagon; 4 + 1 doors; folding rear seat.

PRACTICAL INSTRUCTIONS tyre pressure: front 26 psi, 1.8 atm, rear 31 psi, 2.2 atm.

131-E

See 131-L, except for:

PRICE EX WORKS: 391,883* pesetas

ENGINE 97.1 cu in, 1,592 cc (3.15 x 3.12 in, 80 x 79.2 mm); compression ratio: 8.98:1; max power (DIN): 95 hp (69.9 kW) at 6,000 rpm; max torque (DIN): 93 lb ft, 12.8 kg m (125.5 Nm) at 4,000 rpm; max engine rpm: 6,700; 59.7 hp/l (43.9 kW/l); valves: overhead, Vee-slanted at 65°15', thimble tappets; camshafts: 2, overhead, cogged belt; 1 Bressel 34 DMS-1 downdraught twin barrel carburettor; sealed circuit cooling, anti-freeze liquid, 13.4 imp pt, 16.1 US pt, 7.6 l, electric thermostatic fan.

TRANSMISSION gears: 5, fully synchronized; ratios: I 3.667, II 2.100, III 1.361, IV 1, V 0.881, rev 3.526; tyres: 160 SR x 13.

PERFORMANCE max speeds: (I) 31 mph, 50 km/h; (II) 56 mph, 90 km/h; (III) 84 mph, 135 km/h; (IV) 106 mph, 170 km/h; (V) 103 mph, 165 km/h; power-weight ratio: 23.2 lb/hp (31.5 lb/kW), 10.5 kg/hp (14.3 kg/kW); acceleration: standing ¼ mile 17.4 sec; speed in top at 1,000 rpm: 19.1 mph, 30.8 km/h; consumption: 31.7 m/imp gal, 26.4 m/US gal, 8.9 l x 100 km.

STEERING adjustable height of steering wheel.

BRAKES dual circuit.

ELECTRICAL EQUIPMENT 4 headlamps.

DIMENSIONS AND WEIGHT length: 167.72 in, 426 cm; width: 64.57 in, 164 cm; weight: 2,205 lb, 1,000 kg; weight distribution: 44.6% front, 55.4% rear.

BODY reclining backrests with built-in headrests.

PRACTICAL INSTRUCTIONS sparking plug: 215°; tappet clearances: inlet 0.018-0.020 in, 0.45-0.50 mm, exhaust 0.024-0.026 in, 0.60-0.65 mm; valve timing: 12° 53° 52° 13°; front tyre pressure 23 psi, 1.6 atm.

SEAT 131-E Automatic

OPTIONAL ACCESSORIES G.M.S. type Z. M. automatic transmission, hydraulic torque converter and planetary gears with 3 ratios (I 2.400, II 1.480, III 1, rev 1.920), max ratio of converter at stall 2.4, possible manual selection, 3.700 axle ratio; air-conditioning.

131-E 5 Puertas

See 131-E, except for:

PRICE EX WORKS: 419,193* pesetas

TRANSMISSION tyres: 165 SR x 13.

PERFORMANCE max speeds: (I) 31 mph, 50 km/h; (II) 56 mph, 90 km/h; (III) 84 mph, 135 km/h; (IV) about 103 mph, 165 km/h; (V) about 99 mph, 160 km/h; power-weight ratio: 24 lb/hp (32.6 lb/kW), 10.9 kg/hp (14.8 kg/kW); carrying capacity: 1,058 lb, 480 kg; acceleration: standing ¼ mile 17.7 sec.

DIMENSIONS AND WEIGHT tracks: 54.17 in, 138 cm front, 51.93 in, 132 cm rear; height: 55.12 in, 140 cm; weight: 2,282 lb, 1,035 kg.

BODY estate car/station wagon; 4 + 1 doors; folding rear seat.

PRACTICAL INSTRUCTIONS valve timing: 12° 53° 54° 11°; tyre pressure: front 26 psi, 1.8 atm, rear 31 psi, 2.2 atm.

132-L

PRICE EX WORKS: 501,318* pesetas

ENGINE front, 4 stroke; 4 cylinders, vertical, in line; 107.2 cu in, 1,756 cc (3.31 x 3.12 in, 84 x 79.2 mm); compression ratio: 8.9:1; max power (DIN): 107 hp (78.8 kW) at 6,000 rpm; max torque (DIN): 104 lb ft, 14.4 kg m (141.2 Nm) at 4,000 rpm; max engine rpm: 6,300; 60.9 hp/l (44.9 kW/l); cast iron block, light alloy head; 5 crankshaft bearings; valves: overhead, Vee-slanted at 65°, thimble tappets; camshafts: 2, overhead, cogged belt; lubrication: gear pump, full flow filter (cartridge), 7.7 imp pt, 9.3 US pt, 4.4 l; 1 Weber 34 DMS downdraught twin barrel carburettor; fuel feed: mechanical pump; sealed circuit cooling, anti-freeze liquid, 14.1 imp pt, 16.9 US pt, 8 l, electric thermostatic fan.

TRANSMISSION driving wheels: rear; clutch: single dry plate; gearbox: mechanical; gears: 5, fully synchronized; ratios: I 3.544, II 2.175, III 1.410, IV 1, V 0.913, rev 3.650; lever: central; final drive: hypoid bevel; axle ratio: 4.100; width of rims: 5.5''; tyres: 185 SR x 13.

PERFORMANCE max speeds: (I) 28 mph, 45 km/h; (II) 50 mph, 80 km/h; (III) 78 mph, 125 km/h; (IV) 106 mph, 170 km/h; (V) 103 mph, 165 km/h; power-weight ratio: 22 lb/hp (29.9 lb/kW), 10 kg/hp (13.6 kg/kW); carrying capacity: 882 lb, 400 kg; speed in top at 1,000 rpm: 16.8 mph, 27 km/h; consumption: 30.4 m/imp gal, 25.3 m/US gal, 9.3 l x 100 km.

CHASSIS integral; front suspension: independent, wishbones (lower trailing links), coil springs, anti-roll bar, telescopic dampers; rear: rigid axle, lower longitudinal trailing radius arms, upper oblique torque arms, coil springs, telescopic dampers.

STEERING worm and roller, adjustable height of steering wheel; turns lock to lock: 3.05.

BRAKES disc (diameter 8.94 in, 22.7 cm), rear compensator, dual circuit servo; lining area: front 19.2 sq in, 124 sq cm, rear 19.2 sq in, 124 sq cm, total 38.4 sq in, 248 sq cm.

ELECTRICAL EQUIPMENT 12 V; 45 Ah battery; 540 W alternator; Femsa distributor; 4 headlamps.

DIMENSIONS AND WEIGHT wheel base: 100.67 in, 256 cm; tracks: 51.97 in, 132 cm front, 52.36 in, 133 cm rear; length: 172 in, 437 cm; width: 64.57 in, 164 cm; height: 55.91 in, 142 cm; ground clearance: 4.72 in, 12 cm; weight: 2,359 lb, 1,070 kg; turning circle (between walls): 36.1 ft, 11 m; fuel tank: 12.3 imp gal, 14.8 US gal, 56 l.

BODY saloon/sedan; 4 doors; 5 seats, separate front seats, reclining backrest with built-in headrests.

PRACTICAL INSTRUCTIONS fuel: 96 oct petrol; oil: engine 7 imp pt, 8.5 US pt, 4 l, SAE 30W (summer) 40 (winter), change every 6,200 miles, 10,000 km - gearbox 2.3 imp pt, 2.7 US pt, 1.3 l, ZC 90, change every 18,600 miles, 30,000 km - final drive 2.8 imp pt, 3.4 US pt, 1.6 l, SAE 90 EP, change every 18,600 miles, 30,000 km; greasing: every 18,600 miles, 30,000 km, 4 points; tappet clearances: inlet 0.018 in, 0.45 mm, exhaust 0.024 in, 0.60 mm; valve timing: 12° 53° 52° 13°; tyre pressure: front 26 psi, 1.8 atm, rear 27 psi, 1.9 atm.

OPTIONAL ACCESSORIES air-conditioning.

SEAT 132-L

SEAT 132 Diesel

132 Automatic

See 132-L, except for:

PRICE EX WORKS: 540,875* pesetas

ENGINE 1 Bressel 34 DMS-2/201 or Solex C-34 EIES-9 downdraught twin barrel carburettor.

TRANSMISSION gearbox: G.M.S. type Z.M. automatic transmission, hydraulic torque converter and planetary gears with 3 ratios, max ratio of converter at stall 2.4, possible manual selection; ratios: I 2.400, II 1.480, III 1, rev 1.920; axle ratio: 3.700.

PERFORMANCE max speeds: (I) 47 mph, 75 km/h; (II) 78 mph, 125 km/h; (III) 103 mph, 165 km/h; power-weight ratio: 23 lb/hp (31.2 lb/kW), 10.4 kg/hp (14.1 kg/kW).

DIMENSIONS AND WEIGHT weight: 2,459 lb, 1,115 kg.

132 Diesel

See 132-L, except for:

PRICE EX WORKS: 586,074* pesetas

ENGINE Mercedes-Benz, Diesel, front, 4 stroke; 121.3 cu in, 1,988 cc (3.43 x 3.29 in, 87 x 83.6 mm); compression ratio: 21:1; max power (DIN): 55 hp (40.5 kW) at 4,200 rpm; max torque (DIN): 83 lb ft, 11.5 kg m (112.8 Nm) at 2,200 rpm; max engine rpm: 4,350; 27.6 hp/l (20.4 kW/l); valves: overhead, in line, finger levers; camshafts: 1, overhead; lubrication: gear pump, oil-water heat exchanger, full flow filter, 9.7 imp pt, 11.6 US pt, 5.5 l; Bosch injection pump; cooling system: 18.8 imp pt, 22.6 US pt, 10.7 l.

TRANSMISSION width of rims: 5''; tyres: 175 SR x 13 or 170 SR x 13.

PERFORMANCE max speeds: (I) 22 mph, 35 km/h; (II) 37 mph, 60 km/h; (III) 56 mph, 90 km/h; (IV) 81 mph, 130 km/h; (V) 87 mph, 140 km/h; power-weight ratio: 47.9 lb/hp (65.1 lb/kW), 21.7 kg/hp (29.5 kg/kW); acceleration: standing ¼ mile 25 sec; speed in top at 1,000 rpm: 19.3 mph, 30 km/h; consumption: 34.9 m/imp gal, 29 m/US gal, 8.1 l x 100 km.

ELECTRICAL EQUIPMENT 66 Ah battery.

DIMENSIONS AND WEIGHT weight: 2,635 lb, 1,195 kg; weight distribution: 50% front, 50% rear; turning circle (between walls): 35.4 ft, 10.8 m.

PRACTICAL INSTRUCTIONS fuel: Diesel oil; oil: engine 7.9 imp pt, 9.5 US pt, 4.5 l, SAE 20W-50, change every 6,200 miles, 10,000 km; tappet clearances: inlet 0.008 in, 0.10 mm, exhaust 0.016 in, 0.40 mm; valve timing: 12°30' 41°30' 45° 9°; tyre pressure: front 27 psi, 1.9 atm, rear 28 psi, 2 atm.

SAAB 96 GL

SAAB   SWEDEN

96 GL

ENGINE Ford, front, 4 stroke; 4 cylinders, Vee-slanted at 60°; 91.4 cu in, 1,498 cc (3.54 x 2.32 in, 90 x 58.9 mm); compression ratio: 9:1; max power (DIN): 68 hp (50 kW) at 5,500 rpm; max torque (DIN): 72 lb ft, 10 kg m (98.1 Nm) at 2,700 rpm; max engine rpm: 5,500; 45.4 hp/l (33.4 kW/l); cast iron block and head, 3 crankshaft bearings; valves: overhead, push-rods and rockers; camshafts: 1, at centre of Vee; lubrication: rotary pump, full flow filter, 5.8 imp pt, 7 US pt, 3.3 l; 1 Solex 77 TF 9510 SA downdraught carburettor; fuel feed: mechanical pump; liquid-cooled, expansion tank, 10.2 imp pt, 12.3 US pt, 5.8 l.

TRANSMISSION driving wheels: front; clutch: single dry plate, hydraulically controlled; gearbox: mechanical, in unit with differential; gears: 4, fully synchronized; ratios: I 3.479, II 2.088, III 1.296, IV 0.838, rev 3.182; lever: steering column; final drive: spiral bevel; axle ratio: 4.875; width of rims: 4.5''; tyres: 155 SR x 15.

PERFORMANCE max speeds: (I) 23 mph, 37 km/h; (II) 39 mph, 62 km/h; (III) 62 mph, 99 km/h; (IV) 93 mph, 150 km/h; power-weight ratio: 30.2 lb/hp (41 lb/kW), 13.7 kg/hp (18.6 kg/kW); carrying capacity: 925 lb, 420 kg; acceleration: standing ¼ mile 19.5 sec, 0-50 mph (0-80 km/h) 10.5 sec; speed in top at 1,000 rpm: 17.3 mph, 27.9 km/h; consumption: 32.1 m/imp gal, 26.7 m/US gal, 8.8 l x 100 km.

CHASSIS integral; front suspension: independent, wishbones, coil springs, telescopic dampers; rear: U-shaped tubular rigid axle (swept-back ends), swinging trailing lower radius levers, coil springs, telescopic dampers.

STEERING rack-and-pinion; turns lock to lock: 2.60.

BRAKES front disc (diameter 10.51 in, 26.7 cm), rear drum, 2 separate X hydraulic circuits, servo; swept area: front 182.2 sq in, 1,175 sq cm, rear 73.6 sq in, 475 sq cm, total 255.8 sq in, 1,650 sq cm.

ELECTRICAL EQUIPMENT 12 V; 60 Ah battery; 55 A alternator; Bosch distributor; 2 halogen headlamps.

DIMENSIONS AND WEIGHT wheel base: 98.35 in, 250 cm; tracks: 48.82 in, 124 cm front, 48.50 in, 123 cm rear; length: 169.29 in, 430 cm; width: 62.60 in, 159 cm; height: 57.87 in, 147 cm; ground clearance: 5.90 in, 15 cm; weight: 2,050 lb, 930 kg; weight distribution: 61.7% front, 38.3% rear; turning circle (between kerbs): 36.1 ft, 11 m; fuel tank: 8.4 imp gal, 10 US gal, 38 l.

BODY saloon/sedan; 2 doors; 5 seats, separate front seats, adjustable backrests, built-in headrest; heated rear window; heated driving seat; impact-absorbing bumpers; headlamps with wiper-washers.

PRACTICAL INSTRUCTIONS fuel: 97 oct petrol; oil: engine 5.8 imp pt, 7 US pt, 3.3 l, SAE 10W-30 (winter) 10W-40 (summer), change every 6,200 miles, 10,000 km - gearbox

SAAB 96 GL

SAAB 95 GL

and final drive 3 imp pt, 3.6 US pt, 1.7 l, SAE 80 EP, change every 12,400 miles, 20,000 km; greasing: none; tappet clearances: inlet 0.014 in, 0.35 mm, exhaust 0.016 in, 0.40 mm; valve timing: 21° 82° 63° 40°; tyre pressure: front 24 psi, 1.7 atm, rear 24 psi, 1.7 atm.

95 GL

See 96 GL, except for:

PERFORMANCE max speed: 90 mph, 145 km/h; power-weight ratio: 31.7 lb/hp (43.2 lb/kW), 14.4 kg/hp (19.6 kg/kW); carrying capacity: 1,230 lb, 558 kg; consumption: 30.7 m/imp gal, 25.6 m/US gal, 9.2 l x 100 km.

CHASSIS rear suspension: lever dampers.

DIMENSIONS AND WEIGHT length: 173.62 in, 441 cm; height: 58.66 in, 149 cm; weight: 2,160 lb, 980 kg; weight distribution: 57.9% front, 42.1% rear.

BODY estate car/st. wagon; 2 + 1 doors; 7 seats.

PRACTICAL INSTRUCTIONS tyre pressure (max load): front 27 psi, 1.9 atm, rear 30 psi, 2.1 atm.

99 GL 2-door

PRICE IN GB: £ 4,275*

ENGINE front, 4 stroke; 4 cylinders, slanted at 45°, in line; 121.1 cu in, 1,985 cc (3.54 x 3.07 in, 90 x 78 mm); compression ratio: 9.2:1; max power (DIN): 100 hp (73.6 kW) at 5,200 rpm; max torque (DIN): 120 lb ft, 16.5 kg m (161.8 Nm) at 3,500 rpm; max engine rpm: 6,000; 50.4 hp/l (37.1 kW/l); cast iron block, light alloy head; 5 crankshaft bearings; valves: overhead, thimble tappets; camshafts: 1, overhead, driven by double chain; lubrication: rotary pump, full flow filter, 6.2 imp pt, 7.4 US pt, 3.5 l; 1 Zenith-Stromberg 175 CDSEVX horizontal carburettor; fuel feed: mechanical pump; liquid-cooled, expansion tank, 14.1 imp pt, 16.9 US pt, 8 l, thermostatic fan.

TRANSMISSION driving wheels: front; clutch: single dry plate, hydraulically controlled; gearbox: mechanical, in unit with differential and engine, transfer train in front of engine ratio 0.968:1; gears: 4, fully synchronized; ratios: I 3.438, II 2.073, III 1.391, IV 1, rev 3.781; lever: central; final drive: spiral bevel; axle ratio: 3.889; width of rims: 5''; tyres: 165 SR x 15.

PERFORMANCE max speeds: (I) 34 mph, 55 km/h; (II) 57 mph, 91 km/h; (III) 84 mph, 135 km/h; (IV) 102 mph, 164 km/h; power-weight ratio: 25.1 lb/hp (34.2 lb/kW), 11.4 kg/hp (15.5 kg/kW); carrying capacity: 970 lb, 440 kg; speed in direct drive at 1,000 rpm: 19.3 mph, 31 km/h; consumption: 26.6 m/imp gal, 22.2 m/US gal, 10.6 l x 100 km.

CHASSIS integral; front suspension: independent, wishbones, coil springs, telescopic dampers; rear: rigid axle, twin longitudinal leading arms, twin swinging trailing radius arms, transverse linkage bar, coil springs, telescopic dampers.

STEERING rack-and-pinion; turns lock to lock: 4.11.

BRAKES disc (front diameter 11.02 in, 28 cm, rear 10.61 in, 27 cm), 2 separate X hydraulic circuits, servo; swept area: front 222 sq in, 1,432 sq cm, rear 169.8 sq in, 1,095 sq cm, total 391.8 sq in, 2,527 sq cm.

ELECTRICAL EQUIPMENT 12 V; 60 Ah battery; 55 A alternator; Bosch distributor; 2 halogen headlamps with wiper-washers.

DIMENSIONS AND WEIGHT wheel base: 97.36 in, 247 cm; tracks: 55.12 in, 140 cm front, 55.91 in, 142 cm rear; length: 174.02 in, 442 cm; width: 66.54 in, 169 cm; height: 57 in, 144 cm; ground clearance: 6.90 in, 17.5 cm; weight: 2,514 lb, 1,140 kg; weight distribution: 61.1% front, 38.9% rear; turning circle (between kerbs): 34.4 ft, 10.5 m; fuel tank: 12.1 imp gal, 14.5 US gal, 55 l.

BODY saloon/sedan; 2 doors; 5 seats, separate front seats, adjustable backrests; heated driving seat; folding rear seat; impact-absorbing bumpers.

PRACTICAL INSTRUCTIONS fuel: 97 oct petrol; oil: engine 6.2 imp pt, 7.4 US pt, 3.5 l, SAE 10W-40, change every 6,200 miles, 10,000 km - gearbox 4.4 imp pt, 5.3 US pt, 2.5 l, SAE 10W-30/40, change every 18,600 miles, 30,000 km; greasing: every 6,200 miles, 10,000 km; tappet clearances: inlet 0.006-0.012 in, 0.15-0.30 mm, exhaust 0.014-0.020 in, 0.35-0.50 mm; valve timing: 10° 54° 54° 10°; tyre pressure (max load): front 31 psi, 2.2 atm, rear 34 psi, 2.4 atm.

99 L 2-door

See 99 GL 2-door, except for:

PRICE IN GB: £ 4,150*

TRANSMISSION tyres: 155 SR x 15 or 165 SR x 15.

PERFORMANCE (with 155 SR x 15 tyres) max speeds: (I) 34 mph, 54 km/h; (II) 55 mph, 88 km/h; (III) 81 mph, 131 km/h; (IV) 102 mph, 164 km/h; power-weight ratio: 24.9 lb/hp (34 lb/kW), 11.3 kg/hp (15.4 kg/kW); speed in direct drive at 1,000 rpm: 19 mph, 30.5 km/h.

ELECTRICAL EQUIPMENT 60 Ah battery; conventional headlamp bulbs.

DIMENSIONS AND WEIGHT weight: 2,492 lb, 1,130 kg; weight distribution: 61.2% front, 38.8% rear.

PRACTICAL INSTRUCTIONS tyre pressure (max load): front 30 psi, 2.1 atm, rear 31 psi, 2.2 atm.

99 GL 4-door

See 99 GL 2-door, except for:

PRICE IN GB: £ 4,575*

PERFORMANCE power-weight ratio: 25.8 lb/hp (35.1 lb/kW), 11.7 kg/hp (15.9 kg/kW).

DIMENSIONS AND WEIGHT weight: 2,580 lb, 1,170 kg; weight distribution: 60.4% front, 39.6% rear.

BODY 4 doors.

99 GLE

See 99 GL 2-door, except for:

PRICE IN GB: £ 6,595*
PRICE IN USA: $ 7,298

ENGINE max power (DIN): 118 hp (86.8 kW) at 5,500 rpm; max torque (DIN): 123 lb ft, 17 kg m (166.7 Nm) at 3,700 rpm; 59.4 hp/l (43.7 kW/l); Bosch CI injection system; fuel feed: electric pump.

TRANSMISSION gearbox: Borg-Warner 35 automatic transmission, hydraulic torque converter and planetary gears with 3 ratios, max ratio of converter at stall 1.91, possible manual selection; ratios: I 2.390, II 1.450, III 1, rev 2.090.

PERFORMANCE max speed: 106 mph, 171 km/h; power-weight ratio: 23.4 lb/hp (31.7 lb/kW), 10.6 kg/hp (14.4 kg/kW).

STEERING servo; turns lock to lock: 3.60.

SAAB 99 GLE

237

99 GLE

DIMENSIONS AND WEIGHT weight: 2,756 lb, 1,250 kg; weight distribution: 59.1% front, 40.9% rear.

BODY 4 doors; luxury equipment; tinted glass; electric rear windows.

VARIATIONS

(only for USA and Canada).
ENGINE 9.2:1 compression ratio, max power (DIN) 115 hp (84.6 kW) at 5,500 rpm, max torque (DIN) 123 lb ft, 17 kg m (166.7 Nm) at 3,500 rpm, 57.9 hp/l (42.6 kW/l).
PERFORMANCE power-weight ratio 25 lb/hp (32.6 lb/kW), 10.9 kg/hp (14.8 kg/kW).
DIMENSIONS AND WEIGHT length: 175.20 in, 445 cm; weight distribution: 59.3% front, 40.7% rear.
OPTIONAL ACCESSORIES sunshine roof, 4-speed fully synchronized mechanical gearbox.

(only for California).
ENGINE 8.7:1 compression ratio, max power (DIN) 110 hp (81 kW) at 5,500 rpm, max torque (DIN) 119 lb ft, 16.4 kg m (160.8 Nm) at 3,500 rpm, 55.4 hp/l (40.8 kW/l).
PERFORMANCE power-weight ratio 25.1 lb/hp (34 lb/kW), 11.4 kg/hp (15.4 kg/kW).

99 GL Combi Coupé 3-door

See 99 GL 2-door, except for:

PRICE IN GB: £ 4,785*

PERFORMANCE max speed: 103 mph, 166 km/h; power-weight ratio: 26 lb/hp (35.3 lb/kW), 11.8 kg/hp (16 kg/kW).

DIMENSIONS AND WEIGHT length: 178.35 in, 453 cm; weight: 2,600 lb, 1,180 kg; weight distribution: 58.4% front, 41.6% rear.

BODY 2+1 doors.

99 GL Super 2-door

See 99 GL 2-door, except for:

ENGINE max power (DIN): 108 hp (79.5 kW) at 5,200 rpm; max torque (DIN): 121 lb ft, 16.7 kg m (163.8 Nm) at 3,300 rpm; 54.4 hp/l (40 kW/l); 2 Zenith-Stromberg 150 CDSEVX carburettors.

PERFORMANCE max speed: 106 mph, 171 km/h; power-weight ratio: 23.4 lb/hp (31.5 lb/kW), 10.6 kg/hp (14.3 kg/kW); consumption: 28.2 m/imp gal, 23.5 m/US gal, 10 l x 100 km.

OPTIONAL ACCESSORIES (for Norway only) Borg-Warner 35 automatic transmission, hydraulic torque converter and planetary gears with 3 ratios (I 2.390, II 1.450, III 1, rev 2.090), max ratio of converter at stall 1.91, max speed 102 mph, 164 km/h, power-weight ratio 23.6 lb/hp (32.2 lb/kW), 10.7 kg/hp (14.6 kg/kW), consumption 26.2 m/imp gal, 21.8 m/US gal, 10.8 l x 100 km, weight 2,558 lb, 1,160 kg, weight distribution 62.2% front, 37.8% rear.

99 GL Super 4-door

See 99 GL Super 2-door, except for:

PRICE IN GB: £ 4,575*

PERFORMANCE power-weight ratio: 23.8 lb/hp (32.4 lb/kW), 10.8 kg/hp (14.7 kg/kW).

DIMENSIONS AND WEIGHT weight: 2,580 lb, 1,170 kg; weight distribution: 60.5% front, 39.5% rear.

BODY 4 doors.

OPTIONAL ACCESSORIES with Borg-Warner 35 automatic transmission, power-weight ratio 24.3 lb/hp (33.1 lb/kW), 11 kg/hp (15 kg/kW), weight 2,624 lb, 1,190 kg, weight distribution 61.6% front, 38.4% rear.

99 GL Super Combi Coupé 3-door

See 99 GL Super 2-door, except for:

PRICE IN GB: £ 5,175* (automatic gearbox)

PERFORMANCE max speed: 106 mph, 171 km/h; power-weight ratio: 24.1 lb/hp (32.7 lb/kW), 10.9 kg/hp (14.8 kg/kW); carrying capacity: 970 lb, 440 kg.

SAAB 99 EMS 2-door

DIMENSIONS AND WEIGHT length: 178.35 in, 453 cm; weight: 2,600 lb, 1,179 kg; weight distribution: 58.5% front, 41.5% rear.

BODY 2+1 doors.

OPTIONAL ACCESSORIES with Borg-Warner 35 automatic transmission, max speed 103 mph, 166 km/h, power-weight ratio 24.5 lb/hp (33.3 lb/kW), 11.1 kg/hp (15.1 kg/kW), weight 2,640 lb, 1,197 kg, weight distribution 59.5% front, 40.5% rear.

99 GL Super Combi Coupé 5-door

See 99 GL Super Combi Coupé 3-door, except for:

PRICE IN GB: £ 5,155*

PERFORMANCE power-weight ratio: 24.9 lb/hp (33.8 lb/kW), 11.3 kg/hp (15.3 kg/kW).

DIMENSIONS AND WEIGHT weight: 2,690 lb, 1,220 kg; weight distribution: 57.7% front, 42.3% rear.

BODY 4 + 1 doors.

OPTIONAL ACCESSORIES with Borg-Warner 35 automatic transmission, max speed 103 mph, 166 km/h, power-weight ratio 25.3 lb/hp (34.4 lb/kW), 11.5 kg/hp (15.6 kg/kW), weight 2,740 lb, 1,242 kg; weight distribution 58.7% front, 41.3% rear.

99 GL Injection 2-door

(only for USA and Canada).

See 99 GL 2-door, except for:

PRICE IN USA: $ 6,698

ENGINE compression ratio: 9.2:1; max power (DIN): 115 hp (84.6 kW) at 5,500 rpm; max torque (DIN): 123 lb ft, 17 kg m (166.7 Nm) at 3,500 rpm; 57.9 hp/l (42.6 kW/l); Bosch CI injection system; fuel feed: electric pump.

PERFORMANCE max speed: 108 mph, 174 km/h; power-weight ratio: 22 lb/hp (30 lb/kW), 10 kg/hp (13.6 kg/kW); carrying capacity: 930 lb, 422 kg.

DIMENSIONS AND WEIGHT length: 175.20 in, 445 cm; weight: 2,536 lb, 1,150 kg; weight distribution: 61.4% front, 38.6% rear.

VARIATIONS

(for California only).
ENGINE 8.7:1; compression ratio, max power (DIN) 110 hp (81 kW) at 5,500 rpm, max torque (DIN) 119 lb ft, 16.4 kg m (160.8 Nm) at 3,500 rpm, 55.4 hp/l (40.8 kW/l).
PERFORMANCE power-weight ratio 22.9 lb/hp (31.3 lb/kW), 10.4 kg/hp (14.2 kg/kW).

OPTIONAL ACCESSORIES Borg-Warner 35 automatic transmission, hydraulic torque converter and planetary gears with 3 ratios (I 2.390, II 1.450, III 1, rev 2.090), max ratio of converter at stall 1.91, max speed 105 mph, 169 km/h, power steering, 3.60 turns of steering wheel lock to lock; sunshine roof.

99 GL Injection 4-door

(for Canada only).

See 99 GL Injection 2-door, except for:

PERFORMANCE power-weight ratio 22.7 lb/hp (30.6 lb/kW), 10.3 kg/hp (13.9 kg/kW).

DIMENSIONS AND WEIGHT weight: 2,602 lb, 1,180 kg; weight distribution: 60.8% front, 39.2% rear.

BODY 4 doors.

99 GL Injection Combi Coupé 3-door

(only for USA and Canada).

See 99 GL Injection 2-door, except for:

PRICE IN USA: $ 6,848

PERFORMANCE power-weight ratio 22.7 lb/hp (30.6 lb/kW), 10.3 kg/hp (13.9 kg/kW).

DIMENSIONS AND WEIGHT length: 179.10 in, 455 cm; weight: 2,602 lb, 1,180 kg; weight distribution: 59% front, 41% rear.

BODY 2 + 1 doors.

SAAB Turbo

99 GL Injection Combi Coupé 5-door

(only for USA and Canada).

See 99 GL Injection 2-door, except for:

PRICE IN USA: $ 7,248

ENGINE compression ratio: 8.7:1.

PERFORMANCE power-weight ratio: 23.4 lb/hp (31.7 lb/kW), 10.6 kg/hp (14.4 kg/kW).

DIMENSIONS AND WEIGHT length: 179.10 in, 455 cm; weight: 2,690 lb, 1,220 kg; weight distribution: 58.2% front, 41.8% rear.

BODY 4 + 1 doors.

VARIATIONS

(for California only).
ENGINE max power (DIN) 110 hp (81 kW) at 5,500 rpm, max torque (DIN) 119 lb ft, 16.4 kg m (160.8 Nm) at 3,500 rpm, 55.4 hp/l (40.8 kW/l).
PERFORMANCE power-weight ratio 24.5 lb/hp (33.3 lb/kW), 11.1 kg/hp (15.1 kg/kW).

99 EMS 2-door

See 99 GL 2-door, except for:

PRICE IN GB: £ 6,275*
PRICE IN USA: $ 7,198

ENGINE max power (DIN): 118 hp (86.8 kW) at 5,500 rpm; max torque (DIN): 123 lb ft, 17 kg m (166.7 Nm) at 3,700 rpm; 59.4 hp/l (43.7 kW/l); Bosch CI injection system; fuel feed: electric pump.

TRANSMISSION tyres: 175/70 HR x 15.

PERFORMANCE max speed: 108 mph, 174 km/h; power-weight ratio: 21.4 lb/hp (29.1 lb/kW), 9.7 kg/hp (13.2 kg/kW); consumption: 26.2 m/imp gal, 21.8 m/US gal, 10.8 l x 100 km.

STEERING turns lock to lock: 3.40.

DIMENSIONS AND WEIGHT weight: 2,536 lb, 1,150 kg; weight distribution: 60.9% front, 39.1% rear.

BODY luxury equipment; rev counter; light alloy wheels; front spoiler.

VARIATIONS

(only for USA, Canada and Finland).
ENGINE max power (DIN): 115 hp (84.6 kW) at 5,500 rpm, max torque (DIN) 123 lb ft, 17 kg m (166.7 Nm) at 3,500 rpm, 57.9 hp/l (42.6 kW/l).

SAAB Turbo

PERFORMANCE power-weight ratio 22.7 lb/hp (30.6 lb/kW), 10.3 kg/hp (13.9 kg/kW), carrying capacity 930 lb, 422 kg.
DIMENSIONS AND WEIGHT length 179.53 in, 456 cm, weight 2,602 lb, 1,180 kg, weight distribution 59.1% front, 40.9% rear.

(for California only).
ENGINE 8.7:1 compression ratio, max power (DIN) 110 hp (81 kW) at 5,500 rpm, max torque (DIN) 119 lb ft, 16.4 kg m (160.8 Nm) at 3,500 rpm, 55.4 hp/l (40.8 kW/l).
PERFORMANCE power-weight ratio 23.6 lb/hp (32.2 lb/kW), 10.7 kg/hp (14.6 kg/kW), carrying capacity 930 lb, 422 kg.
DIMENSIONS AND WEIGHT length 179.53 in, 456 cm, weight 2,602 lb, 1,180 kg, weight distribution 59.1% front, 40.9% rear.

OPTIONAL ACCESSORIES sunshine roof.

---

99 EMS Combi Coupé 3-door

See 99 EMS 2-door, except for:

PERFORMANCE power-weight ratio: 22.3 lb/hp (30.2 lb/kW), 10.1 kg/hp (13.7 kg/kW).

DIMENSIONS AND WEIGHT weight: 2,624 lb, 1,190 kg.

BODY 2 + 1 doors.

Turbo

ENGINE front, 4 stroke; 4 cylinders, slanted at 45°, in line; 121.1 cu in, 1,985 cc (3.54 x 3.07 in, 90 x 78 mm); compression ratio: 7.2:1; max power (DIN): 145 hp (106.7 kW) at 5,000 rpm; max torque (DIN): 174 lb ft, 24 kg m (235.4 Nm) at 3,000 rpm; max engine rpm: 6,000; 73 hp/l (53.8 kW/l); cast iron block, light alloy head; 5 crankshaft bearings; valves: overhead, thimble tappets; camshafts: 1, overhead, driven by double chain; lubrication: rotary pump, full flow filter, 6.2 imp pt, 7.4 US pt, 3.5 l; Bosch CI fuel injection system with centrifugal compressor, mounted coaxially with exhaust driven garrett airresearch turbine; fuel feed: electric pump; water-cooled, 14.1 imp pt, 16.9 US pt, 8 l, thermostatic fan (for USA 2 thermostatic fans).

TRANSMISSION driving wheels: front; clutch: single dry plate, hydraulically controlled; gearbox: mechanical, in unit with differential and engine, transfer train in front of engine ratio 0.900:1; gears: 4, fully synchronized; ratios: I 3.438, II 2.073, III 1.391, IV 1, rev 3.781; lever: central; final drive: spiral bevel; axle ratio: 3.889; width of rims: 5.5''; tyres: 175/70 HR x 15.

PERFORMANCE max speeds: (I) 36 mph, 58 km/h; (II) 59 mph, 95 km/h; (III) 88 mph, 142 km/h; (IV) 123 mph, 198 km/h; power-weight ratio: 18.3 lb/hp (24.9 lb/kW), 8.3 kg/hp (11.3 kg/kW); speed in direct drive at 1,000 rpm: 20.5 mph, 33 km/h; consumption: 25.7 m/imp gal, 21.4 m/US gal, 11 l x 100 km.

CHASSIS integral; front suspension: independent, wishbones, coil springs, telescopic dampers; rear: rigid axle, twin longitudinal leading arms, twin swinging trailing radius arms, transverse linkage bar, coil springs, telescopic dampers.

STEERING rack-and-pinion; turns lock to lock: 4.10 - for Canada and USA 3.60.

BRAKES disc (front diameter 11.02 in, 28 cm, rear 10.61 in, 27 cm), 2 separate X hydraulic circuits, servo; swept area: front 222 sq in, 1,432 sq cm, rear 169.8 sq in, 1,095 sq cm, total 391.8 sq in, 2,527 sq cm.

ELECTRICAL EQUIPMENT 12 V; 60 Ah battery; 65 A alternator; Bosch distributor; 2 halogen headlamps with wiper-washers - for Canada and USA 4 headlamps.

DIMENSIONS AND WEIGHT wheel base: 97.36 in, 247 cm; tracks: 55.51 in, 141 cm front, 56.30 in, 143 cm rear; length: 178.35 in, 453 cm - for USA 179.53 in, 456 cm; width: 66.54 in, 169 cm; height: 57 in, 144 cm; ground clearance: 6.90 in, 17.5 cm; weight: 2,668 lb, 1,210 kg; weight distribution: 59.1% front, 40.9% rear; turning circle (between kerbs): 34.4 ft, 10.5 m; fuel tank: 12.1 imp gal, 14.5 US gal, 55 l.

BODY hatchback; 2 + 1 doors; 5 seats, separate front seats, adjustable backrests; heated driving seat; front and rear spoilers.

PRACTICAL INSTRUCTIONS fuel: 97 oct petrol; oil: engine 6.2 imp pt, 7.4 US pt, 3.5 l, SAE 10W-40, change every 6,200 miles, 10,000 km - gearbox 4.4 imp pt, 5.3 US pt, 2.5 l, SAE 10W-30/40, change every 18,600 miles, 30,000 km; greasing: every 6,200 miles, 10,000 km; tappet clearances: inlet 0.006-0.012 in, 0.15-0.30 mm, exhaust 0.014-0.020 in, 0.35-0.50 mm; valve timing: 12° 40° 62° 2°; tyre pressure (max load): front 31 psi, 2.2 atm, rear 34 psi, 2.4 atm.

VOLVO   SWEDEN

242 L/244 L

ENGINE front, 4 stroke; 4 cylinders, in line; 121.2 cu in, 1,986 cc (3.50 x 3.15 in, 88.9 x 80 mm); compression ratio: 8.5:1; max power (DIN): 90 hp (66.2 kW) at 5,000 rpm; max torque (DIN): 112 lb ft, 15.5 kg m (152 Nm) at 2,500 rpm; max engine rpm: 6,000; 45.3 hp/l (33.3 kW/l); cast iron block, light alloy head; 5 crankshaft bearings; valves: overhead, push-rods and rockers; camshafts: 1, side, lubrication: gear pump, full flow filter, 6.5 imp pt, 7.8 US pt, 3.7 l; 1 SU type HIF 6 horizontal carburettor; fuel feed: mechanical pump; sealed circuit cooling, liquid, 16.7 imp pt, 20.1 US pt, 9.5 l.

TRANSMISSION driving wheels: rear; clutch: single dry plate (diaphragm); gearbox: mechanical; gears: 4, fully synchronized; ratios: I 3.790, II 2.160, III 1.370, IV 1, rev 3.680; lever: central; final drive: hypoid bevel; axle ratio: 3.910; width of rims: 5''; tyres: 165 SR x 14.

PERFORMANCE max speeds: (I) 28 mph, 45 km/h; (II) 50 mph, 80 km/h; (III) 75 mph, 121 km/h; (IV) 94 mph, 151 km/h; power-weight ratio: 30.4 lb/hp (41.3 lb/KW), 13.8 kg/hp (18.7 kg/kW); carrying capacity: 1,191 lb, 540 kg; consumption: 31.4 m/imp gal, 26.1 m/US gal, 9 l x 100 km.

VOLVO 244 DL

242 L/244 L

CHASSIS integral; front suspension: independent, lower wishbones, coil springs, damper struts, anti-roll bar; rear: rigid axle, twin trailing radius arms, transverse linkage bar, coil springs, anti-roll bar, telescopic dampers.

STEERING rack-and-pinion; turns lock to lock: 4.30.

BRAKES disc (front diameter 10.71 in, 27.2 cm, rear 11.61 in, 29.5 cm), dual circuit, rear compensator, servo.

ELECTRICAL EQUIPMENT 12 V; 60 Ah battery; 55 A alternator; Bosch distributor; 2 halogen headlamps.

DIMENSIONS AND WEIGHT wheel base: 103.94 in, 264 cm; tracks: 55.91 in, 142 cm front, 53.15 in, 135 cm rear; length: 192.91 in, 490 cm; width: 67.32 in, 171 cm; height: 56.30 in, 143 cm; ground clearance: 5.51 in, 14 cm; weight: 2,734 lb, 1,240 kg; turning circle (between walls): 32.1 ft, 9.8 m; fuel tank: 13.2 imp gal, 15.8 US gal, 60 l.

BODY saloon/sedan; 2 doors - 244 L 4 doors; 5 seats, separate front seats, reclining backrests, built-in adjustable headrests; heated rear window.

PRACTICAL INSTRUCTIONS fuel: 93 oct petrol; oil: engine 5.6 imp pt, 6.8 US pt, 3.2 l, SAE 10W-40, change every 6,200 miles, 10,000 km - gearbox 1.2 imp pt, 1.5 US pt, 0.7 l, SAE 80-90, change every 24,900 miles, 40,000 km - final drive 2.3 imp pt, 2.7 US pt, 1.3 l, SAE 90; greasing: none; sparking plug: 175°; tappet clearances: inlet and exhaust 0.016-0.018 in, 0.40-0.45 mm; tyre pressure: front 26 psi, 1.8 atm, rear 28 psi, 1.9 atm.

OPTIONAL ACCESSORIES limited slip differential; Borg-Warner 35 automatic transmission, hydraulic torque converter and planetary gears with 3 ratios (I 2.390, II 1.450, III 1, rev 2.090), max ratio of converter at stall 2.

242 DL

See 242 L/244 L, except for:

PRICE IN USA: $ 6,645

TRANSMISSION tyres: 175 SR x 14.

BODY luxury model.

VARIATIONS

ENGINE 129.8 cu in, 2,127 cc (3.62 x 3.15 in, 92 x 80 mm), 8.5:1 compression ratio, max power (DIN) 100 hp (73.6 kW) at 5,250 rpm, max torque (DIN) 125 lb ft, 17.3 kg m (169.7 Nm) at 3,000 rpm, 47 hp/l (34.6 kW/l), 1 overhead camshaft, lubrication 6.7 imp pt, 8 US pt, 3.8 l, 1 Zenith-Stromberg 175 CD2 SE carburettor.
PERFORMANCE max speed 101 mph, 162 km/h, power-weight ratio 27.3 lb/hp (37.2 lb/kW), 12.4 kg/hp (16.9 kg/kW).
DIMENSIONS AND WEIGHT weight 2,739 lb, 1,242 kg.
PRACTICAL INSTRUCTIONS oil engine 5.8 imp pt, 7 US pt, 3.3 l, tappet clearances inlet and exhaust 0.012-0.020 in, 0.30-0.50 mm.

OPTIONAL ACCESSORIES power steering (only with 2,127 cc); air-conditioning.

244 DL

See 242 L/244 L, except for:

PRICE IN GB: £ 4,769* (with 100 hp engine)
PRICE IN USA: $ 7,145

TRANSMISSION tyres: 175 SR x 14.

BODY 4 doors; luxury model.

VARIATIONS

ENGINE 129.8 cu in, 2,127 cc (3.62 x 3.15 in, 92 x 80 mm), 8.5:1 compression ratio, max power (DIN) 100 hp (73.6 kW) at 5,250 rpm, max torque (DIN) 125 lb ft, 17.3 kg m (169.7 Nm) at 3,000 rpm, 47 hp/l (34.6 kW/l), 1 overhead camshaft, lubrication 6.7 imp pt, 8 US pt, 3.8 l, 1 Zenith-Stromberg 175 CD2 SE carburettor.
PERFORMANCE max speed 101 mph, 162 km/h, power-weight ratio 27.9 lb/hp (38 lb/kW), 12.7 kg/hp (17.2 kg/kW).
DIMENSIONS AND WEIGHT weight 2,794 lb, 1,267 kg.
PRACTICAL INSTRUCTIONS oil engine 5.8 imp pt, 7 US pt, 3.3 l, tappet clearances inlet and exhaust 0.012-0.020 in, 0.30-0.50 mm.

OPTIONAL ACCESSORIES power steering (only with 2,127 cc); air-conditioning.

VOLVO 245 DL

244 GL

See 242 L/244 L, except for:

PRICE IN GB: £ 6,231* (with overdrive)

ENGINE 129.8 cu in, 2,127 cc (3.62 x 3.15 in, 92 x 80 mm); compression ratio: 9.3:1; max power (DIN): 123 hp (90.5 kW) at 5,500 rpm; max torque (DIN): 125 lb ft, 17.3 kg m (169.7 Nm) at 3,500 rpm; 57.8 hp/l (42.5 kW/l); camshafts: 1, overhead; Bosch CI fuel injection system.

TRANSMISSION width of rims: 5.5''; tyres: 185/70 SR x 14.

PERFORMANCE max speeds: (I) 35 mph, 56 km/h; (II) 55 mph, 88 km/h; (III) 80 mph, 128 km/h; (IV) 109 mph, 175 km/h; power-weight ratio: 22.7 lb/hp (30.9 lb/kW), 10.3 kg/hp (14 kg/kW).

STEERING servo.

ELECTRICAL EQUIPMENT transistorized Bosch ignition.

DIMENSIONS AND WEIGHT tracks: 56.30 in, 143 cm front, 53.54 in, 136 cm rear; weight: 2,794 lb, 1,267 kg.

BODY 4 doors; luxury model; metallic spray; sunshine roof; tinted glass; heated driver's seat.

PRACTICAL INSTRUCTIONS oil: engine 5.8 imp pt, 7 US pt, 3.3 l; tappet clearances: inlet and exhaust 0.012-0.020 in, 0.30-0.50 mm; front tyre pressure: 28 psi, 1.9 atm.

OPTIONAL ACCESSORIES overdrive; air-conditioning.

242 GT

See 244 GL, except for:

PRICE IN USA: $ 8,071

ELECTRICAL EQUIPMENT 2 fog headlamps.

BODY coupé; 2 doors; light alloy wheels.

245 L

See 242 L/244 L, except for:

TRANSMISSION axle ratio: 4.300; width of rims: 5.5''; tyres: 185/70 SR x 14.

PERFORMANCE max speeds: (I) 29 mph, 46 km/h; (II) 45 mph, 73 km/h; (III) 66 mph, 107 km/h; (IV) 90 mph, 145 km/h; power-weight ratio: 32.4 lb/hp (44 lb/kW), 14.7 kg/hp (20 kg/kW); carrying capacity: 1,257 lb, 570 kg.

CHASSIS rear suspension without anti-roll bar.

DIMENSIONS AND WEIGHT tracks: 56.30 in, 143 cm front, 53.54 in, 136 cm rear; height: 57.48 in, 146 cm; weight: 2,915 lb, 1,322 kg.

BODY estate car/st. wagon; 4 + 1 doors; heated rear window with wiper-washer.

VOLVO 242 GT

245 DL

See 245 L, except for:

PRICE IN GB: £ 5,357* (with 100 hp engine)
PRICE IN USA: $ 7,495

TRANSMISSION tyres: 185 3R x 14.

PERFORMANCE power-weight ratio: 32.1 lb/hp (43.7 lb/kW), 14.6 kg/hp (19.8 kg/kW).

DIMENSIONS AND WEIGHT weight: 2,893 lb, 1,312 kg.

BODY luxury model.

VARIATIONS

ENGINE 129.8 cu in, 2,127 cc (3.62 x 3.15 in, 92 x 80 mm), max power (DIN) 100 hp (73.6 kW) at 5,250 rpm, max torque (DIN) 125 lb ft, 17.3 kg m (169.7 Nm) at 3,000 rpm, 47 hp/l (34.6 kW/l), 1 overhead camshaft, lubrication 6.7 imp pt, 8 US pt, 3.8 l, 1 Zenith-Stromberg 175 CD2 SE carburettor.
PERFORMANCE max speed 101 mph, 162 km/h, power-weight ratio 29.3 lb/hp (39.8 lb/kW), 13.3 kg/hp (18.1 kg/kW).
DIMENSIONS AND WEIGHT weight 2,930 lb, 1,329 kg.
PRACTICAL INSTRUCTIONS oil engine 5.8 imp pt, 7 US pt, 3.3 l, tappet clearances inlet and exhaust 0.012-0.020 in, 0.30-0.50 mm.

OPTIONAL ACCESSORIES power steering (only with 2,127 cc); air-conditioning.

245 DLE

See 245 L, except for:

PRICE IN GB: £ 6,251*

ENGINE 129.8 cu in, 2,127 cc (3.62 x 3.15 in, 92 x 80 mm); compression ratio: 9.3:1; max power (DIN): 123 hp (90.5 kW) at 5,500 rpm; max torque (DIN): 125 lb ft, 17.3 kg m (169.7 Nm) at 3,500 rpm; 57.8 hp/l (42.5 kW/l); camshafts: 1, overhead; Bosch CI fuel injection system.

TRANSMISSION tyres: 185 SR x 14.

PERFORMANCE max speed: about 105 mph, 170 km/h; power-weight ratio: 23.7 lb/hp (32.2 lb/kW), 10.7 kg/hp (14.6 kg/kW).

BODY luxury model; tinted glass; metallic spray.

264 DL

PRICE IN GB: £ 6,270*

ENGINE front, 4 stroke; 6 cylinders, Vee-slanted at 90°; 162.6 cu in, 2,664 cc (3.46 x 2.87 in, 88 x 73 mm); compression ratio: 8.7:1; max power (DIN): 125 hp (92 kW) at 5,250 rpm; max torque (DIN): 145 lb ft, 20 kg m (196.1 Nm) at 3,500 rpm; max engine rpm: 6,000; 46.9 hp/l (34.5 kW/l); light alloy block and head; 4 crankshaft bearings; valves: overhead, rockers; camshafts: 1, per cylinder block, overhead; lubrication: gear pump, full flow filter, oil cooler, 11.4 imp pt, 13.7 US pt, 6.5 l; 1 SU type HIF 6 horizontal carburettor; fuel feed: electric pump; sealed circuit cooling, liquid, 19.2 imp pt, 23 US pt, 10.9 l.

TRANSMISSION driving wheels: rear; clutch: single dry plate (diaphragm); gearbox: mechanical; gears: 4, fully synchronized; ratios: I 3.710, II 2.160, III 1.370, IV 1, rev 4.300; lever: central; final drive: hypoid bevel; axle ratio: 3.910; width of rims: 5''; tyres: 175 HR x 14.

PERFORMANCE max speed: 117 mph, 188 km/h; power-weight ratio: 23.6 lb/hp (32 lb/kW), 10.7 kg/hp (14.5 kg/kW); carrying capacity: 1,103 lb, 500 kg; consumption: not declared.

CHASSIS integral; front suspension: independent, lower wishbones, coil springs, telescopic damper struts, anti-roll bar; rear; rigid axle, twin trailing radius arms, transverse linkage bar, coil springs, telescopic dampers, anti-roll bar.

STEERING rack-and-pinion, servo; turns lock to lock: 4.30.

BRAKES disc, servo.

ELECTRICAL EQUIPMENT 12 V; 70 Ah battery; 770 W alternator; Bosch transistorized ignition; 2 halogen headlamps.

DIMENSIONS AND WEIGHT wheel base: 103.94 in, 264 cm; tracks: 56.30 in, 143 cm front, 53.54 in, 136 cm rear; length: 192.91 in, 490 cm; width: 67.32 in, 171 cm; height: 56.30 in, 143 cm; ground clearance: 5.51 in, 14 cm; weight: 2,948 lb, 1,337 kg; turning circle (between walls): 32.1 ft, 9.8 m; fuel tank: 13.2 imp gal, 15.8 US gal, 60 l.

BODY saloon/sedan; 4 doors; 5 seats, separate front seats, reclining backrests, built in adjustable headrests; heated rear window and driver's seat.

PRACTICAL INSTRUCTIONS fuel: 93 oct petrol; oil: engine 10.6 imp pt, 12.7 US pt, 6 l, SAE 10W-40, change every 6,200 miles, 10,000 km - gearbox 1.9 imp pt, 2.3 US pt, 1.1 l, SAE 90, change every 24,900 miles, 40,000 km - final drive 2.8 imp pt, 3.4 US pt, 1.6 l, SAE 90 EP, change every 24,900 miles, 40,000 km; greasing: none; tappet clearances: inlet 0.006 in, 0.15 mm, exhaust 0.012 in, 0.30 mm; valve timing: 32° 72° 20° 32°; tyre pressure: front 26 psi, 1.8 atm, rear 27 psi, 1.9 atm.

OPTIONAL ACCESSORIES limited slip differential; 5-speed mechanical gearbox; Borg-Warner 55 automatic transmission, hydraulic torque converter and planetary gears with 3 ratios (I 2.390, II 1.450, III 1, rev 2.090), max ratio of converter at stall 2; air-conditioning.

264 GL

See 264 DL, except for:

PRICE IN GB: £ 6,799*
PRICE IN USA: $ 10,245

ENGINE max power (DIN): 140 hp (103 kW) at 6,000 rpm; max torque (DIN): 151 lb ft, 20.8 kg m (204 Nm) at 3,000 rpm; 52.6 hp/l (38.7 kW/l); Bosch electronically-controlled injection system.

TRANSMISSION ratios: I 3.710, II 2.220, III 1.400, IV 1, rev 4.300; axle ratio: 3.730; width of rims: 5.5''; tyres: 185/70 HR x 14.

PERFORMANCE power-weight ratio: 21.4 lb/hp (29 lb/kW), 9.7 kg/hp (13.2 kg/kW); carrying capacity: 1,058 lb, 480 kg.

DIMENSIONS AND WEIGHT weight: 2,992 lb, 1,357 kg.

BODY luxury model; headlamps with wiper-washers.

264 GLE

See 264 GL, except for:

PRICE IN GB: £ 7,948*

TRANSMISSION Borg-Warner 55 automatic transmission, hydraulic torque converter and planetary gears; ratios: I 2.450, II 1.450, III 1, rev 2.120; axle ratio: 3.540.

BODY electric windows; air-conditioning; sunshine roof.

264 TE

See 264 GL, except for:

TRANSMISSION Borg-Warner 55 automatic transmission, hydraulic torque converter and planetary gears; ratios: I 2.450, II 1.450, III 1, rev 2.120; axle ratio: 3.540.

PERFORMANCE power-weight ratio: 25.7 lb/hp (35 lb/kW), 11.7 kg/hp (15.8 kg/kW).

DIMENSIONS AND WEIGHT wheel base: 131.50 in, 334 cm; length: 220 in, 560 cm; weight: 3,605 lb, 1,635 kg.

BODY 6 seats; electric windows; air-conditioning; sunshine roof.

OPTIONAL ACCESSORIES telephone.

262 C

See 264 GL, except for:

PRICE IN USA: $ 14,776

TRANSMISSION Borg-Warner 55 automatic transmission, hydraulic torque converter and planetary gears; ratios: I 2.450, II 1.450, III 1, rev 2.120; axle ratio: 3.540.

BODY coupé by Bertone; 2 doors; heated driver's seat; electric windows; air-conditioning.

265 DL

See 264 DL, except for:

PRICE IN GB: £ 7,066*

TRANSMISSION tyres: 185 SR x 14.

PERFORMANCE power-weight ratio: 26.4 lb/hp (35.9 lb/kW), 12 kg/hp (16.3 kg/kW).

DIMENSIONS AND WEIGHT height: 57.48 in, 146 cm; weight: 3,305 lb, 1,499 kg.

BODY estate car/st. wagon; 4 + 1 doors; rear window with wiper-washer.

265 GL

See 264 GL, except for:

PRICE IN GB: £ 6,898*
PRICE IN USA: $ 10,495

TRANSMISSION power-weight ratio: 23.9 lb/hp (32.5 lb/kW), 10.8 kg/hp (14.7 kg/kW).

DIMENSIONS AND WEIGHT height: 57.48 in, 146 cm; weight: 3,351 lb, 1,520 kg.

BODY estate car/st. wagon; 4 + 1 doors; rear window with wiper-washer.

VOLVO 264 GLE

265 GLE

See 264 GL, except for:

PRICE IN GB: £ 7,748*

TRANSMISSION Borg-Warner 55 automatic transmission, hydraulic torque converter and planetary gears; ratios: I 2.450, II 1.450, III 1, rev 2.120; axle ratio: 3.540; tyres: 185 SR x 14.

PERFORMANCE power-weight ratio: 23.9 lb/hp (32.5 lb/kW), 10.8 kg/hp (14.7 kg/kW).

DIMENSIONS AND WEIGHT height: 57.48 in, 146 cm; weight: 3,351 lb, 1,520 kg.

BODY estate car/st. wagon; 4 + 1 doors; rear window with wiper washer; electric windows; air-conditioning.

FELBER   SWITZERLAND

FF Lancia 1600 Roadster

PRICE EX WORKS: $ 43,000 francs

ENGINE Lancia, front, 4 stroke; 4 cylinders, in line; 96.7 cu in, 1,585 cc (3.31 x 2.81 in, 84 x 71.5 mm); compression ratio: 9.4:1; max power (DIN): 100 hp (73.5 kW) at 5,800 rpm; max torque (DIN): 99 lb ft, 13.6 kg m (133 Nm) at 3,000 rpm; max engine rpm: 6,300; 63.1 hp/l (46.4 kW/l); 5 crankshaft bearings; valves: overhead, Vee-slanted at 65°, thimble tappets; camshafts: 2, overhead, cogged belt; lubrication: gear pump, full flow filter, 7.9 imp pt, 9.5 US pt, 4.5 l; 1 Weber 34 DATRI/200 or Solex C34 TCIC/1 downdraught twin barrel carburettor; fuel feed: mechanical pump; water-cooled, 14.4 imp pt, 17.3 US pt, 8.2 l, electric thermostatic fan.

TRANSMISSION driving wheels: front; clutch: single dry plate (diaphragm); gearbox: mechanical; gears: 5, fully synchronized; ratios: I 3.500, II 2.235, III 1.522, IV 1.152, V 0.925, rev 3.071; lever: central; final drive: cylindrical gears, in unit with gearbox; axle ratio: 4.071; width of rims: 5.5''; tyres: 175 HR x 14.

PERFORMANCE max speed: 112 mph, 180 km/h; power-weight ratio: 19.1 lb/hp (26 lb/kW), 8.7 kg/hp (11.8 kg/kW); carrying capacity: 706 lb, 320 kg; speed in top at 1,000 rpm: 18.3 mph, 29.5 km/h; consumption: 34 m/imp gal, 28.3 m/US gal, 8.3 l x 100 km.

CHASSIS integral; front suspension: independent, lower wide-based wishbones, coil springs, telescopic damper struts, anti-roll bar; rear: independent, wishbones, coil springs, telescopic damper struts, anti-roll bar acting as longitudinal torque arm.

STEERING worm and roller; turns lock to lock: 3.75.

BRAKES disc (diameter 9.85 in, 25.1 cm), rear compensator, servo; lining area: front 28.8 sq in, 192 sq cm, rear 16.1 sq in, 104 sq cm, total 44.9 sq in, 296 sq cm.

FELBER FF Lancia Michelotti

ELECTRICAL EQUIPMENT 12 V; 45 Ah battery; 750 W alternator; Marelli distributor; 2 headlamps.

DIMENSIONS AND WEIGHT wheel base: 94.49 in, 240 cm; tracks: 55.35 in, 141 cm front, 54.80 in, 139 cm rear; length: 158.27 in, 402 cm; width: 66.54 in, 169 cm; height: 45.28 in, 115 cm; ground clearance: 5.31 in, 13.5 cm; weight: 1,918 lb, 870 kg; turning circle (between walls): 33.5 ft, 10.2 m; fuel tank: 11.2 imp gal, 13.5 US gal, 51 l.

BODY sports; 2 doors; 2 seats.

PRACTICAL INSTRUCTIONS fuel: 98-100 oct petrol; oil: engine 7.9 imp pt, 9.5 US pt, 4.5 l, SAE 10W-40 or 10W-50, change every 3,100 miles, 5,000 km - gearbox and final drive 3.2 imp pt, 3.8 US pt, 1.8 l, SAE 90, change every 18,600 miles, 30,000 km; tappet clearances: inlet 0.015-0.018 in, 0.39-0.45 mm, exhaust 0.018-0.020 in, 0.45-0.51 mm; valve timing: 13° 45° 49° 9°; tyre pressure: front and rear 24 psi, 1.7 atm.

FF Lancia 2000 Roadster

See FF Lancia 1600 Roadster, except for:

PRICE EX WORKS: 45,000 francs

ENGINE 121.7 cu in, 1,995 cc (3.31 x 3.54 in, 84 x 90 mm); compression ratio: 8.9:1; max power (DIN): 119 hp (87.5 kW) at 5,500 rpm; max torque (DIN): 128 lb ft, 17.7 kg m

FELBER FF Ferrari

(174 Nm) at 2,800 rpm; 59.6 hp/l (43.9 kW/l); 1 Weber 34 DATR 2/200 or Solex C34 TCIC/1 downdraught twin barrel carburettor.

TRANSMISSION axle ratio: 3.785.

PERFORMANCE max speed: 121 mph, 195 km/h; power-weight ratio: 16.1 lb/hp (21.9 lb/kW), 7.3 kg/hp (9.9 kg/kW); speed in top at 1,000 rpm: 20 mph, 31.6 km/h; consumption: 28.2 m/imp gal, 23.5 m/US gal, 10 l x 100 km.

FF Lancia Michelotti

PRICE EX WORKS: 36,200 francs

ENGINE Lancia, front, transverse, slanted 20° to rear; 4 cylinders, in line; 107.2 cu in, 1,756 cc (3.31 x 3.12 in, 84 x 79.2 mm); compression ratio: 9.8:1; max power (DIN): 120 hp (88.3 kW) at 6,200 rpm; max torque (DIN): 111 lb ft, 15.3 kg m (150 Nm) at 4,500 rpm; max engine rpm: 6,400; 68.3 hp/l (50.3 kW/l); 5 crankshaft bearings; valves: overhead Vee-slanted at 65°, thimble tappets; camshafts: 2, overhead, cogged belt; lubrication: gear pump, full flow filter, 7.9 imp pt, 9.5 US pt, 4.5 l; 1 Weber 32 DMTR 24 or Solex C 32 CIC-1 downdraught twin barrel carburettor; water-cooled, 14.4 imp pt, 17.3 US pt, 8.2 l.

TRANSMISSION driving wheels: front; clutch: single dry plate (diaphragm); gearbox: mechanical; gears: 5, fully synchronized; ratios: I 3.500, II 2.235, III 1.522, IV 1.152, V 0.925, rev 3.071; lever: central; final drive: cylindrical gears, in unit with gearbox; axle ratio: 3.929; width of rims: 5.5''; tyres: 175 HR x 14.

PERFORMANCE max speeds: (I) 32 mph, 52 km/h; (II) 50 mph, 81 km/h; (III) 74 mph, 119 km/h; (IV) 98 mph, 157 km/h; (V) 118 mph, 190 km/h; power-weight ratio: 18 lb/hp (26.2 lb/kW), 8.2 kg/hp (11.9 kg/kW); carrying capacity: 706 lb, 320 kg; speed in top at 1,000 rpm: 19 mph, 30.5 km/h; consumption: 34 m/imp gal, 28.3 m/US gal, 8.3 l x 100 km.

CHASSIS integral, front suspension: independent, lower wide-based wishbones, coil springs, telescopic damper struts, anti-roll bar; rear: independent, wishbones, coil springs, telescopic damper struts, anti-roll bar acting as longitudinal torque arm.

STEERING worm and roller; turns lock to lock: 3.75.

BRAKES disc (diameter 9.85 in, 25.1 cm), rear compensator, servo; lining area: front 28.8 sq in, 192 sq cm, rear 16.1 sq in, 104 sq cm, total 44.9 sq in, 296 sq cm.

ELECTRICAL EQUIPMENT 12 V; 45 Ah battery; 750 W alternator; Marelli distributor; 2 headlamps.

DIMENSIONS AND WEIGHT wheel base: 92.52 in, 235 cm; tracks: 55.35 in, 141 cm front, 54.80 in, 139 cm rear; length: 159.05 in, 404 cm; width: 66.54 in, 169 cm; height: 55.12 in, 140 cm; ground clearance: 5.31 in, 13.5 cm; weight: 2,315 lb, 1,050 kg; turning circle (between walls): 33.5 ft, 10.2 m; fuel tank: 11.2 imp gal, 13.5 US gal, 51 l.

BODY sports; 2 doors; 2 seats.

PRACTICAL INSTRUCTIONS fuel: 98-100 oct petrol; oil: engine 7.9 imp pt, 9.5 US pt, 4.5 l, SAE 10W-40 or 10W-50, change every 3,100 miles, 5,000 km - gearbox and final drive 3.2 imp pt, 3.8 US pt, 1.8 l, SAE 90, change every 18,600 miles, 30,000 km; tappet clearances: inlet 0.015-0.018 in, 0.39-0.45 mm, exhaust 0.018-0.020 in, 0.45-0.51 mm; valve timing: 13° 45° 49° 9°; tyre pressure: front and rear 24 psi, 1.7 atm.

FF Ferrari

PRICE EX WORKS: 92,000 francs

ENGINE Ferrari, front, 4 stroke; 12 cylinders, Vee-slanted at 60°; 242.1 cu in, 3,967 cc (3.03 x 2.80 in, 77 x 71 mm); compression ratio: 8.8:1; max power (DIN): 300 hp (220.8 kW) at 7,000 rpm; max torque (DIN): 241 lb ft, 33.2 kg m (325.6 Nm) at 5,000 rpm; max engine rpm: 7,000; 75.6 hp/l (55.6 kW/l); light alloy block with wet liners, light alloy head with hemispherical combustion chambers; 7 crankshaft bearings; valves: overhead, Vee-slanted at 54°, roller rockers; camshafts: 1 per cylinder block, overhead; lubrication: gear pump, filter on by-pass, 17.6 imp pt, 21.1 US pt, 10 l; 3 Weber 40 DFI downdraught twin barrel carburettors; fuel feed: mechanical and electric pumps; water-cooled, 24.6 imp pt, 29.6 US pt, 14 l, electric thermostatic fans.

TRANSMISSION driving wheels: rear; clutch: single dry plate; gearbox: mechanical, in unit with limited slip final drive; gears: 5, fully synchronized; ratios: I 3.075, II 2.120, III 1.572, IV 1.250, V 0.964, rev 2.675; lever: central; final drive: spiral bevel, limited slip differential; axle ratio: 3.444; width of rims: 7''; tyres 205 VR x 14.

PERFORMANCE max speeds: (I) 50 mph, 80 km/h; (II) 72 mph, 116 km/h; (III) 98 mph, 157 km/h; (IV) 122 mph, 197 km/h; (V) 152 mph, 245 km/h; power-weight ratio:

7.2 lb/hp (9.7 lb/kW), 3.3 kg/hp (4.4 kg/kW); carrying capacity: 353 lb, 160 kg; speed in top at 1,000 rpm: 21.9 mph, 35.2 km/h; consumption: 14.9 m/imp gal, 12.4 m/US gal, 19 l x 100 km.

CHASSIS tubular; front suspension: independent, wishbones, coil springs, anti-roll bar, telescopic dampers; rear: independent, wishbones, coil springs, anti-roll bar, telescopic dampers.

STEERING ZF worm and roller; turns lock to lock: 3.50.

BRAKES disc (front diameter 10.71 in, 27.2 cm, rear 10.79 in, 27.4 cm), servo; lining area: total 40.5 sq in, 261 sq cm.

ELECTRICAL EQUIPMENT 12 V; 74 Ah battery; 600 W alternator; Marelli distributor; 2 headlamps.

DIMENSIONS AND WEIGHT wheel base: 94.49 in, 240 cm; tracks: 55.16 in, 140 cm front, 55.79 in, 142 cm rear; length: 155.51 in, 395 cm; width: 64.96 in, 165 cm; height: 46.46 in, 118 cm; ground clearance: 4.72 in, 12 cm; weight: 2,161 lb, 980 kg; turning circle (between walls): 44 ft, 13.4 m; fuel tank: 19.8 imp gal, 23.8 US gal, 90 l.

BODY sports; 2 doors; 2 seats.

PRACTICAL INSTRUCTIONS fuel: 98-100 oct petrol; oil: engine 17.6 imp pt, 21.1 US pt, 10 l, SAE 20W-30 (winter) 40 (summer), change every 6,200 miles, 10,000 km - gearbox and final drive 7.9 imp pt, 9.5 US pt, 4.5 l, change every 6,200 miles, 10,000 km; greasing: every 3,100 miles, 5,000 km; tappet clearances: inlet 0.006 in, 0.15 mm, exhaust 0.008 in, 0.20 mm; tyre pressure: front 34 psi, 2.4 atm, rear 37 psi, 2.6 atm.

MONTEVERDI Sierra

MONTEVERDI   SWITZERLAND

Sierra

PRICE EX WORKS: 69,000 francs

ENGINE Chrysler, front, 4 stroke; 8 cylinders, Vee-slanted at 90°; 359.9 cu in, 5,898 cc (4 x 3.58 in, 101.6 x 90.9 mm); compression ratio: 8.5:1; max power (SAE): 180 hp (132.5 kW) at 4,000 rpm; max torque (SAE): 287 lb ft, 39.6 kg m (388 Nm) at 2,400 rpm; 30.5 hp/l (22.5 kW/l); 5 crankshaft bearings; valves: overhead, in line, hydraulic tappets; camshafts: 1, at centre of Vee; lubrication: rotary pump, full flow filter, 13.2 imp pt, 15.8 US pt, 7.5 l; 1 Carter downdraught twin barrel carburettor; fuel feed: mechanical pump; water-cooled, 28.2 imp pt, 33.8 US pt, 16 l.

TRANSMISSION driving wheels: rear; gearbox: Torqueflite automatic transmission, hydraulic torque converter and planetary gears with 3 ratios, max ratio of converter at stall 2.3, possible manual selection; ratios: I 2.450, II 1.450, III 1, rev 2.200; lever: central; final drive: hypoid bevel; axle ratio: 2.710; width of rims: 6''; tyres: 215/70 VR x 14.

PERFORMANCE max speed: about 124 mph, 200 km/h; power-weight ratio: 19.6 lb/hp (26.6 lb/kW), 8.9 kg/hp (12 kg/kW); carrying capacity: 1,554 lb, 750 kg; speed in direct drive at 1,000 rpm: 28.6 mph, 46 km/h; consumption: 20.2 m/imp gal, 16.8 m/US gal, 14 l x 100 km.

CHASSIS integral; front suspension: upper wishbones and lower horizontal arms combined with trailing radius rods, coil springs, anti-roll bar, adjustable telescopic dampers; rear: de Dion rigid axle, semi-elliptic leafsprings, adjustable telescopic dampers.

STEERING worm and roller, servo.

BRAKES front disc (diameter 11.8 in, 30 cm), rear drum, dual circuit, servo; lining area: total 139.5 sq in, 900 sq cm.

ELECTRICAL EQUIPMENT 12 V; 65 Ah battery; 55 A alternator; 4 halogen headlamps.

DIMENSIONS AND WEIGHT wheel base: 112.20 in, 285 cm; tracks: 59.44 in, 151 cm front, 58.66 in, 149 cm rear; length: 192.12 in, 488 cm; width: 71.65 in, 182 cm; height: 55.12 in, 140 cm; ground clearance: 5.9 in, 15 cm; weight: 3,528 lb, 1,600 kg; turning circle (between walls): 41.9 ft, 12.8 m; fuel tank: 18 imp gal, 21.6 US gal, 82 l.

BODY saloon/sedan; 4 doors; 5 seats, separate front seats; air-conditioning; automatic speed control.

VARIATIONS

ENGINE 317.9 cu in, 5,210 cc (3.91 x 3.31 in, 99.3 x 84.1 mm), max power (DIN) 160 hp (117.8 kW) at 3,500 rpm, max torque (DIN) 287 lb ft, 39.6 kg m (388.4 Nm) at 2,000 rpm, 30.7 hp/l (22.6 kW/l).
PERFORMANCE power-weight ratio 22 lb/hp (30 lb/kW), 10 kg/hp (13.6 kg/hp).

High Speed 375 L

PRICE EX WORKS: 98,000 francs

ENGINE Chrysler, front, 4 stroke; 8 cylinders, Vee-slanted at 90°; 439.7 cu in, 7,206 cc (4.32 x 3.75 in, 109.7 x 95.2 mm); compression ratio: 8.2:1; max power (DIN): 304 hp (223 kW) at 4,200 rpm; max torque (DIN): 450 lb ft, 62.1 kg m (609 Nm) at 3,300 rpm; max engine rpm: 5,600; 42.2 hp/l (30.9 kW/l); cast iron block and head; 5 crankshaft bearings; valves: overhead, in line, push-rods and rockers; camshafts: 1, at centre of Vee; lubrication: rotary pump, full flow filter, 12.3 imp pt, 14.8 US pt, 7 l; 1 Carter downdraught 4-barrel carburettor; fuel feed: mechanical pump; sealed circuit cooling, liquid, 45.8 imp pt, 55 US pt, 26 l, 2 electric fans.

TRANSMISSION driving wheels: rear; gearbox: Torqueflite automatic transmission, hydraulic torque converter and planetary gears with 3 ratios, max ratio of converter at stall 2.16, possible manual selection; ratios: I 2.450, II 1.450, III 1, rev 2.200; lever: central; final drive: hypoid bevel, limited slip differential; axle ratio: 2.880; width of rims: 7''; tyres: GR 70 VR x 15.

PERFORMANCE max speed: 149 mph, 240 km/h; power-weight ratio: 13.2 lb/hp (18 lb/kW), 6 kg/hp (8.2 kg/kW); carrying capacity: 706 lb, 320 kg; speed in direct drive at 1,000 rpm: 26.4 mph, 42.5 km/h; consumption: 15.7 m/imp gal, 13.1 m/US gal, 18 l x 100 km.

CHASSIS box-section space frame type; front suspension: independent, wishbones, coil springs, anti-roll bar, adjustable telescopic dampers; rear: de Dion rigid axle, Watt transverse linkage bar, twin trailing radius arms, coil springs, anti-roll bar, adjustable telescopic dampers.

STEERING ZF worm and roller.

BRAKES disc (front diameter 11.81 in, 30 cm, rear 11.22 in, 28.5 cm), internal radial fins, dual circuit, each with servo; swept area: total 504.8 sq in, 3,256 sq cm.

ELECTRICAL EQUIPMENT 12 V; 70 Ah battery; 60 A alternator; 4 halogen headlamps.

DIMENSIONS AND WEIGHT wheel base: 105.51 in, 268 cm; tracks: 59.06 in, 150 cm front, 57.48 in, 146 cm rear; length: 190.94 in, 485 cm; width: 70.67 in, 179 cm; height: 50.78 in, 129 cm; ground clearance: 5.91 in, 15 cm; weight: 4,013 lb, 1,820 kg; turning circle (between walls): 39 ft, 11.9 m; fuel tank: 27.5 imp gal, 33 US gal, 125 l.

BODY coupé; 2 doors; 4 seats, separate front seats, reclining backrests; electric windows; heated rear window.

MONTEVERDI High Speed 375/4 Limousine

HIGH SPEED 375 L

VARIATIONS

ENGINE (Hemi) 425.6 cu in, 6,974 cc (4.25 x 3.75 in, 107.9 x 95.2 mm), 10.25:1 compression ratio, max power (DIN) 390 hp (286.3 kW) at 5,000 rpm, max torque (DIN) 432 lb ft, 59.6 kg m (584.5 Nm) at 4,000 rpm, max engine rpm 6,200, 55.9 hp/l (41 kW/l), cast iron block and head, hemispherical combustion chambers, Vee-slanted valves with hydraulic tappets, lubrication 19.4 imp pt, 23.3 US pt, 11 l, 2 Carter downdraught 4-barrel carburettors.
PERFORMANCE max speed 162 mph, 260 km/h, power-weight ratio 10.4 lb/hp (14.2 lb/kW), 4.7 kg/hp (6.4 kg/kW).
DIMENSIONS AND WEIGHT weight 4,057 lb, 1,840 kg.

OPTIONAL ACCESSORIES oil cooler; 4-speed fully synchronized mechanical gearbox; sunshine roof; air-conditioning; tinted glass; power steering with variable ratio.

High Speed 375/4 Limousine

See High Speed 375 L, except for:

PRICE EX WORKS: 114,000 francs

TRANSMISSION gearbox: max ratio of converter at stall 2; tyres: 205 VR x 15 or GR 70 VR x 15.

PERFORMANCE max speed: 140 mph, 225 km/h; power-weight ratio: 13.9 lb/hp (19 lb/kW), 6.3 kg/hp (8.6 kg/kW); carrying capacity: 1,160 lb, 530 kg.

BRAKES disc (front diameter 11.81 in, 30 cm, rear 10.63 in, 27 cm); swept area: front 280.3 sq in, 1,808 sq cm, rear 179.2 sq in, 1,156 sq cm, total 459.5 sq in, 2,964 sq cm.

DIMENSIONS AND WEIGHT wheel base: 125.20 in, 318 cm; length: 209.05 in, 531 cm; width: 70.47 in, 179 cm; height: 52.36 in, 133 cm; weight: 4,234 lb, 1,920 kg.

BODY saloon/sedan; 4 doors; 5 seats, separate front seats, built-in headrests.

VARIATIONS

(with Hemi engine)
PERFORMANCE power-weight ratio 10.9 lb/hp (14.9 lb/kW), 4.9 kg/hp (6.8 kg/kW).
DIMENSIONS AND WEIGHT weight 4,278 lb, 1,940 kg.

Palm Beach

(only on special request).

See High Speed 375 L, except for:

PRICE EX WORKS: 124,000 francs

TRANSMISSION tyres: 215 VR x 15 or GR 70 x 15.

PERFORMANCE power-weight ratio: 10.4 lb/hp (14.1 lb/kW), 4.7 kg/hp (6.4 kg/kW).

STEERING servo (standard); turns lock to lock: 3.50.

ELECTRICAL EQUIPMENT 65 A alternator; 2 halogen headlamps.

DIMENSIONS AND WEIGHT wheel base: 98.43 in, 250 cm; tracks: 59.45 in, 151 cm front, 57.87 in, 147 cm rear; length: 181.50 in, 461 cm; height: 49.21 in, 125 cm; weight: 3,153 lb, 1,430 kg; weight distribution: 50% front, 50% rear; fuel tank: 28.6 imp gal, 34.3 US gal, 130 l.

BODY convertible; 2 doors; 3 seats, separate front seats, tonneau cover.

VARIATIONS

(with Hemi engine)
PERFORMANCE power-weight ratio 8.1 lb/hp (11 lb/kW), 3.7 kg/hp (5 kg/kW).

Hai 450 GTS

(only on special request).

PRICE EX WORKS: 140,000 francs

ENGINE Chrysler, central, 4 stroke; 8 cylinders, Vee-slanted at 90°; 439.7 cu in, 7,206 cc (4.24 x 3.75 in, 107.7 x 95.2 mm); compression ratio: 9.6:1; max power (DIN) 340 hp

MONTEVERDI Palm Beach

(250 kW) at 4,400 rpm; max torque (DIN) 467.4 lb ft, 64.5 kg m (632.7 Nm) at 3,400 rpm; max engine rpm: 6,200; 47.2 hp/l (34.7 kW/l); cast iron block and head, hemispherical combustion chambers; 5 crankshaft bearings; valves: overhead, Vee-slanted, push-rods and rockers, hydraulic tappets; camshafts: 1, at centre of Vee; lubrication: rotary pump, full flow filter, 19.4 imp pt, 23.3 US pt, 11 l; 2 Carter downdraught 4-barrel carburettors; fuel feed; mechanical pump; sealed circuit cooling, liquid, 44 imp pt, 52.9 US pt, 25 l, 2 electric fans.

TRANSMISSION driving wheels: rear; clutch: single dry plate, hydraulically controlled; gearbox: mechanical; gears: 5, fully synchronized; ratios: I 2.470, II 1.470, III 1.090, IV 0.958, V 0.845, rev 2.800; lever: central; final drive: spiral bevel, limited slip differential; axle ratio: 3.200; width of rims: 7''; tyres: GR 70 VR x 15.

PERFORMANCE max speed: 180 mph, 290 km/h; power-weight ratio: 8.7 lb/hp (11.9 lb/kW), 4 kg/hp (5.4 kg/kW); carrying capacity: 397 lb, 180 kg; speed in top at 1,000 rpm: 29.5 mph, 47.5 km/h; consumption: 14.9 m/imp gal, 12.4 m/US gal, 19 l x 100 km.

CHASSIS tubular; front suspension: independent, wishbones, coil springs, anti-roll bar, adjustable telescopic dampers; rear: de Dion rigid axle, Watt transverse linkage bar, twin trailing arms, coil springs, anti-roll bar, adjustable telescopic dampers.

STEERING ZF worm and roller.

BRAKES disc (front diameter 12.99 in, 33 cm, rear 11.81 in, 30 cm), internal radial fins, dual circuit, each with servo; swept area: front 280.3 sq in, 1,808 sq cm, rear 179.2 sq in, 1,156 sq cm, total 459.5 sq in, 2,964 sq cm.

ELECTRICAL EQUIPMENT 12 V; 70 Ah battery; 60 A alternator; 2 retractable halogen headlamps.

DIMENSIONS AND WEIGHT wheel base: 102.76 in, 261 cm; tracks: 59.06 in, 150 cm front, 57.48 in, 146 cm rear; length: 172.05 in, 437 cm; width: 70.47 in, 179 cm; height: 40.2 in, 102 cm; ground clearance: 5.12 in, 13 cm; weight: 2,976 lb, 1,350 kg; turning circle (between walls): 36.7 ft, 11.2 m; fuel tank: 27.5 imp gal, 33 US gal, 125 l.

BODY coupé; 2 doors; 2 seats; heated rear window.

OPTIONAL ACCESSORIES tinted glass; air-conditioning.

Safari

PRICE EX WORKS: 39,000 francs

ENGINE Chrysler, front, 4 stroke; 8 cylinders, Vee-slanted at 90°; 318 cu in, 5,210 cc (3.91 x 3.31 in, 99.3 x 84.1 mm); compression ratio: 8.5:1; max power (DIN): 152 hp (111.9 kW) at 4,000 rpm; max torque (DIN): 256 lb ft, 35.3 kg

MONTEVERDI Hai 450 GTS

MONTEVERDI Safari

m (346.2 Nm) at 1,600 rpm; 29.2 hp/l (21.5 kW/l); cast iron block and head; 5 crankshaft bearings; valves: overhead, in line, push-rods and rockers, hydraulic tappets; camshafts: 1, at centre of Vee; lubrication: rotary pump, full flow filter, 13.2 imp pt, 15.9 US pt, 7.5 l; 1 Holley downdraught twin barrel carburettor; fuel feed: mechanical pump; water-cooled, 34.3 imp pt, 41.2 US pt, 19.5 l.

TRANSMISSION driving wheels: front and rear with lockable front differential in transfer box; gearbox: Torqueflite automatic transmission, hydraulic torque converter and planetary gears with 3 ratios, max ratio of converter at stall 2.16, possible manual selection; ratios: I 2.450, II 1.450, III 1 (transfer box 2.030 ratio), rev 2.200; lever: central; final drive: hypoid bevel, limited slip differential; axle ratio: 3.070; width of rims: 6''; tyres: HR78 x 15.

PERFORMANCE max speed: about 93 mph, 150 km/h; power-weight ratio: 27.5 lb/hp (37.4 lb/kW), 12.5 kg/hp (16.9 kg/kW); carrying capacity: 1,632 lb, 740 kg; consumption: 17.7 m/imp gal, 14.7 m/US gal, 16 l x 100 km.

CHASSIS box-type perimeter frame; front and rear suspension: rigid axle, semi-elliptic leafsprings, anti-roll bar, adjustable telescopic dampers.

STEERING ZF, recirculating ball, servo.

BRAKES front disc (diameter 11.81 in, 30 cm), front internal radial fins, rear drum, servo.

ELECTRICAL EQUIPMENT 12 V; 65 Ah battery; 55 A alternator; 4 headlamps.

DIMENSIONS AND WEIGHT wheel base: 100 in, 254 cm; front and rear track: 58.27 in, 148 cm; length: 179.50 in, 456 cm; width: 70.87 in, 180 cm; height: 68.50 in, 174 cm; ground clearance: 7.48 in, 19 cm; weight: 4,189 lb, 1,900 kg; turning circle (between walls): 35.8 in, 10.9 m; fuel tank: 18 imp gal, 21.6 US gal, 82 l.

BODY estate car/station wagon; 2 + 1 doors; 5 seats, separate front seats, reclining backrests; built-in headrests on front and rear seats; folding rear seat; air-conditioning.

PRACTICAL INSTRUCTIONS fuel: 91 oct petrol.

VARIATIONS

ENGINE 439.7 cu in, 7,206 cc (4.32 x 3.75 in, 109.7 x 95.2 mm), 9.7:1 compression ratio, max power (DIN) 305 hp (224.5 kW) at 4,200 rpm, max torque (DIN) 450 lb ft, 62.1 kg m (609 Nm) at 3,300 rpm, 42.3 hp/l (31.2 kW/l).
PERFORMANCE max speed 124 mph, 200 km/h, power-weight ratio 13.7 lb/hp (18.6 lb/kW), 6.2 kg/hp (8.5 kg/kW), consumption 11.3 m/imp gal, 9.4 m/US gal, 25 l x 100 km.

OPTIONAL ACCESSORIES 3.310 3.730 4.270 axle ratios.

Replica BMW 328 Standard

PRICE EX WORKS: 33,000 francs

ENGINE BMW, front, 4 stroke; 4 cylinders, slanted at 30°, in line; 96 cu in, 1,573 cc (3.31 x 2.80 in, 84 x 71 mm); compression ratio: 8.3:1; max power (DIN): 90 hp (66.2 kW) at 6,000 rpm; max torque (DIN): 91 lb ft, 12.5 kg m (122.6 Nm) at 4,000 rpm; max engine rpm: 6,200; 57.2 hp/l (42.1 kW/l); cast iron block, light alloy head, hemispherical combustion chambers; 5 crankshaft bearings; valves: overhead, Vee-slanted at 52°, rockers; camshafts: 1, overhead; lubrication: gear pump, full flow filter, 7.4 imp pt, 8.9 US pt, 4.2 l; 1 Solex DIDTA 32/32 downdraught twin barrel carburettor; fuel feed: mechanical pump; water-cooled, 12.3 imp pt, 14.8 US pt, 7 l.

TRANSMISSION driving wheels: rear; clutch: single dry plate (diaphragm), hydraulically controlled; gearbox: mechanical; gears: 4, fully synchronized; ratios: I 3.764, II 2.022, III 1.320, IV 1, rev 4.096; lever: central; final drive: hypoid bevel; axle ratio: 4.100; width of rims: 5''.

PERFORMANCE max speeds: (I) 30 mph, 48 km/h; (II) 55 mph, 89 km/h; (III) 85 mph, 136 km/h; (IV) 112 mph, 180 km/h; power-weight ratio: 18.3 lb/hp (24.9 lb/kW), 8.3 kg/hp (11.3 kg/kW); carrying capacity: 353 lb, 160 kg; speed in direct drive at 1,000 rpm: 18 mph, 29 km/h; consumption: 29.4 m/imp gal, 24.5 m/US gal, 9.6 l x 100 km.

CHASSIS integral, box-type reinforced platform; front suspension: independent, coil springs/telescopic damper struts, auxiliary rubber springs, lower wishbones, lower links; rear: independent, oblique semi-trailing arms, auxiliary rubber springs, coil springs, telescopic dampers.

STEERING rack-and-pinion.

BRAKES disc (diameter 10.71 in, 27.2 cm), servo.

ELECTRICAL EQUIPMENT 12 V; 36 Ah battery; 630 W alternator; Bosch distributor; 2 headlamps.

DIMENSIONS AND WEIGHT wheel base: 99.21 in, 252 cm; tracks: 63.78 in, 162 cm front, 61.02 in, 155 cm rear; length: 145.67 in, 370 cm; width: 61.42 in, 156 cm; ground clearance: 7.90 in, 18 cm; weight: 1,654 lb, 750 kg; turning circle (between walls): 29.5 ft, 9 m; fuel tank: 11 imp gal, 13.2 US gal, 50 l.

BODY roadster, in plastic material; 2 doors; 2 seats.

PRACTICAL INSTRUCTIONS fuel: 92 oct petrol; oil: engine 7.4 imp pt, 8.9 US pt, 4.2 l, SAE 20W-50, change every 3,700 miles, 6,000 km - gearbox 1.8 imp pt, 2.1 US pt, 1 l, SAE 80, change every 14,800 miles, 24,000 km - final drive 1.6 imp pt, 1.9 US pt, 0.9 l, SAE 90, no change recommended; greasing: none; sparking plug: 145°.

VARIATIONS

ENGINE BMW, 107.8 cu in, 1,766 cc (3.50 x 2.80 in, 89 x 71 mm), max power (DIN) 98 hp (72.1 kW) at 5,800 rpm, max torque (DIN) 105 lb ft, 14.5 kg m (142.2 Nm) at 4,000 rpm, 55.5 hp/l (40.8 kW/l).
TRANSMISSION 3.900 axle ratio.
PERFORMANCE power-weight ratio 17 lb/hp (22.9 lb/kW), 7.7 kg/hp (10.4 kg/kW), consumption 28.5 m/imp gal, 23.8 m/US gal, 9.9 l x 100 km.

ENGINE BMW, 121.4 cu in, 1,990 cc (3.50 x 3.15 in, 89 x 80 mm), 8.1:1 compression ratio, max power (DIN) 109 hp (80.2 kW) at 5,800 rpm, max torque (DIN) 116 lb ft, 16 kg m (156.9 Nm) at 3,700 rpm, 54.8 hp/l (40.3 kW/l).
TRANSMISSION 3.900 axle ratio.
PERFORMANCE power-weight ratio 15.2 lb/hp (20.7 lb/kW), 6.9 kg/hp (9.4 kg/kW), consumption 28.2 m/imp gal, 23.5 m/US gal, 10 l x 100 km.

ENGINE BMW, 121.4 cu in, 1,990 cc (3.50 x 3.15 in, 89 x 80 mm), 9.3:1 compression ratio, max power (DIN) 125 hp (92 kW) at 5,700 rpm, max torque (DIN) 127 lb ft, 17.5 kg m (171.6 Nm) at 4,350 rpm, 62.8 hp/l (46.2 kW/l), Bosch K-Jetronic injection system, electric pump.
TRANSMISSION 3.640 axle ratio.
PERFORMANCE max speed 137 mph, 220 km/h, power-weight ratio 13.2 lb/hp (18.1 lb/kW), 6 kg/hp (8.2 kg/kW), consumption 32.1 m/imp gal, 26.7 m/US gal, 8.8 l x 100 km.

OPTIONAL ACCESSORIES 5-speed fully synchronized mechanical gearbox (I 3.368, II 2.160, III 1.579, IV 1.241, V 1, rev 4); 3.640 or 3.450 axle ratio; 6'' or 7'' wide rims.

SBARRO Replica BMW 328 Standard

Replica BMW 328 America

See Replica BMW 328 Standard, except for:

PRICE EX WORKS: 42,000 francs

ENGINE 6 cylinders, in line; 152.2 cu in, 2,494 cc (3.39 x 2.82 in, 86 x 71.6 mm); compression ratio: 9:1; max power (DIN): 150 hp (110.4 kW) at 6,000 rpm; max torque (DIN): 154 lb ft, 21.2 kg m (207.9 Nm) at 4,000 rpm; 60.1 hp/l (44.2 kW/l); polispherical combustion chambers; 7 crankshaft bearings; lubrication: 10 imp pt, 12 US pt, 5.7 l; 1 Solex 4A1 downdraught twin barrel carburettor; cooling system: 21.1 imp pt, 25.4 US pt, 12 l.

PERFORMANCE max speed: 132 mph, 212 km/h; power-weight ratio: 13.3 lb/hp (18 lb/kW), 6 kg/hp (8.2 kg/kW); speed in direct drive at 1,000 rpm: 21.3 mph, 34.2 km/h; consumption: 25.9 m/imp gal, 21.6 m/US gal, 10.9 l x 100 km.

ELECTRICAL EQUIPMENT 55 Ah battery; 770 W alternator.

DIMENSIONS AND WEIGHT wheel base: 100.39 in, 255 cm; front and rear track: 64.17 in, 163 cm; length: 149.61 in, 380 cm; width: 67.32 in, 171 cm; weight: 1,989 lb, 902 kg.

PRACTICAL INSTRUCTIONS oil: engine 10 imp pt, 12 US pt, 5.7 l; tappet clearances: inlet 0.010 in, 0.25 mm, exhaust 0.012 in, 0.30 mm; valve timing: 6° 50° 50° 6°.

VARIATIONS

ENGINE 170.1 cu in, 2,788 cc (3.39 x 3.15 in, 86 x 80 mm); 8.3:1 compression ratio, max power (DIN) 170 hp (125.1 kW) at 5,800 rpm, max torque (DIN) 172 lb ft, 23.8 kg m (223.4 Nm) at 4,000 rpm, 6,500 max engine rpm, 61 hp/l (44.9 kW/l).
PERFORMANCE power-weight ratio 11.7 lb/hp (15.9 lb/kW), 5.3 kg/hp (7.2 kg/kW), consumption 25.7 m/imp gal, 21.4 m/US gal, 11 l x 100 km.

ENGINE 182 cu in, 2,982 cc (3.50 x 3.15 in, 89 x 80 mm), 8:1 compression ratio, max power (DIN) 175 hp (128.8 kW) at 5,500 rpm, max torque (DIN) 185 lb ft, 25.5 kg m (250.1 Nm) at 4,500 rpm, 6,500 max engine rpm, 58.7 hp/l (43.2 kW/l), Bosch electronic injection, exhaust thermal reactor, electric thermostatic fan.
PERFORMANCE power-weight ratio 11.5 lb/hp (15.4 lb/kW), 5.2 kg/hp (7 kg/kW), consumption 24.8 m/imp gal, 20.6 m/US gal, 11.4 l x 100 m.
PRACTICAL INSTRUCTIONS valve timing 14° 54° 54° 14°.

ENGINE 195.6 cu in, 3,205 cc (3.50 x 3.39 in, 89 x 86 mm), max power (DIN) 200 hp (147.2 kW) at 5,500 rpm, max torque (DIN) 210 lb ft, 29 kg m (284.4 Nm) at 4,250 rpm, 62.4 hp/l (45.9 kW/l), Bosch L-Jetronic electronic injection, electric pump.
PERFORMANCE power-weight ratio 9.9 lb/hp (13.4 lb/kW), 4.5 kg/hp (6.1 kg/kW).

AZLK   USSR

Moskvich 2138

ENGINE front, 4 stroke; 4 cylinders, in line; 82.8 cu in, 1,357 cc (2.99 x 2.95 in, 76 x 75 mm); compression ratio: 7:1; max power (DIN) 50 hp (36.8 kW) at 4,750 rpm; max torque (DIN) 67 lb ft, 9.3 kg m (91.2 Nm) at 2,750 rpm; max engine rpm: 4,750; 36.8 hp/l (27.1 kW/l); cast iron block, light alloy head; 3 crankshaft bearings; valves: overhead; camshafts: 1, side; lubrication: gear pump, filter on by-pass, 7.9 imp pt, 9.5 US pt, 4.5 l; 1 downdraught twin barrel carburettor; fuel feed: mechanical pump; water-cooled, 12.3 imp pt, 14.8 US pt, 7 l.

TRANSMISSION driving wheels: rear; clutch: single dry plate, hydraulically controlled; gearbox: mechanical; gears: 4, II, III and IV synchronized; ratios: I 3.810, II 2.242, III 1.450, IV 1, rev 4.710; lever: steering column; final drive: hypoid bevel; axle ratio: 4.220; width of rims: 4''; tyres: 5.90/6.00 x 13.

PERFORMANCE max speed: 75 mph, 120 km/h; power-weight ratio: 46.7 lb/hp (63.5 lb/kW), 21.2 kg/hp (28.8 kg/kW); carrying capacity: 882 lb, 400 kg; speed in direct drive at 1,000 rpm: 16.2 mph, 26 km/h; consumption: 26.9 m/imp gal, 22.4 m/US gal, 10.5 l x 100 km.

CHASSIS integral; front suspension: independent, wishbones, coil springs, anti-roll bar, telescopic dampers; rear: rigid axle, semi-elliptic leafsprings, telescopic dampers.

STEERING worm and roller.

BRAKES drum; lining area: front 59.5 sq in, 384 sq cm, rear 59.5 sq in, 384 sq cm, total 119 sq in, 768 sq cm.

ELECTRICAL EQUIPMENT 12 V; 42 or 55 Ah battery; 250 W dynamo; R 107 distributor; 2 headlamps.

DIMENSIONS AND WEIGHT wheel base: 94.49 in, 240 cm; tracks: 48.82 in, 124 cm front, 48.43 in, 123 cm rear; length: 167.32 in, 425 cm; width: 61.02 in, 155 cm; height: 58.27 in, 148 cm; ground clearance: 7.09 in, 18 cm; weight: 2,337 lb, 1,060 kg; turning circle (between walls): 37.7 ft, 11.5 m; fuel tank: 10.1 imp gal, 12.1 US gal, 46 l.

BODY saloon/sedan; 4 doors; 5 seats.

PRACTICAL INSTRUCTIONS fuel: 85 oct petrol; sparking plug: 175°.

OPTIONAL ACCESSORIES 4.5'' wide rims; front disc brakes; front and rear track 50 in, 127 cm.

Moskvich 2136

See Moskvich 2138, except for:

TRANSMISSION tyres: 6.40 x 13.

PERFORMANCE power-weight ratio: 48.5 lb/hp (65.9 lb/kW), 22 kg/hp (29.9 kg/kW).

DIMENSIONS AND WEIGHT height: 59.45 in, 151 cm; weight: 2,426 lb, 1,100 kg.

BODY estate car/st. wagon; 4 + 1 doors.

Moskvich 2140/Moskvich 2140 IZh

ENGINE front, slanted at 20°, 4 stroke; 4 cylinders, in line; 90.2 cu in, 1,479 cc (3.23 x 2.76 in, 82 x 70 mm); compression ratio: 8.8:1; max power (DIN) 75 hp (55.2 kW) at 5,800 rpm; max torque (DIN) 83 lb ft, 11.4 kg m (111.8 Nm) at 3,400 rpm; max engine rpm: 6,500; 50.7 hp/l (37.3 kW/l); light alloy block and head, wet liners; 5 crankshaft bearings; valves: overhead, Vee-slanted at 52°, rockers; camshafts: 1, overhead, chain driven; lubrication: gear pump, full flow filter, 8.8 imp pt, 10.6 US pt, 5 l; 1 K-126 H downdraught twin barrel carburettor; fuel feed: mechanical pump; sealed circuit cooling, liquid, 13.2 imp pt, 15.9 US pt, 7.5 l.

TRANSMISSION driving wheels: rear; clutch: single dry plate (diaphragm), hydraulically controlled; gearbox: mechanical; gears: 4, fully synchronized; ratios: I 3.490, II 2.040, III 1.330, IV 1, rev 3.390; lever: central; final drive: hypoid bevel; axle ratio: 4.220; width of rims: 4.5''; tyres: 6.45/6.95 x 13.

PERFORMANCE max speeds: (I) 27 mph, 43 km/h; (II) 45 mph, 73 km/h; (III) 70 mph, 113 km/h; (IV) 93 mph, 150 km/h; power-weight ratio: 31.7 lb/hp (43.2 lb/kW), 14.4 kg/hp (19.6 kg/kW); carrying capacity: 882 lb, 400 kg; speed in direct drive at 1,000 rpm: 16.9 mph, 27.2 km/h; consumption: 32.1 m/imp gal, 26.7 m/US gal, 8.8 l x 100 km.

CHASSIS integral; front suspension: independent, wishbones, coil springs, anti-roll bar, telescopic dampers; rear: rigid axle, semi-elliptic leafsprings, telescopic dampers.

STEERING worm and double roller; turns lock to lock: 3.50.

BRAKES front disc, rear drum, servo.

ELECTRICAL EQUIPMENT 12 V; 42 Ah battery; 40 A alternator; R 107 distributor; 2 headlamps.

DIMENSIONS AND WEIGHT wheel base: 94.49 in, 240 cm; tracks: 48.82 in, 124 cm front, 48.43 in, 123 cm rear; length: 167.32 in, 425 cm; width: 61.02 in, 155 cm; height: 58.27 in, 148 cm; ground clearance: 7.87 in, 20 cm; weight: 2,381 lb, 1,080 kg; turning circle (between walls): 37.7 ft, 11.5 m; fuel tank: 10.1 imp gal, 12.1 US gal, 46 l.

BODY saloon/sedan; 4 doors; 5 seats, separate front seats, reclining backrests with adjustable headrest; headlamps with wiper-washers.

OPTIONAL ACCESSORIES 165/175 SR x 13 tyres; cooling system 17.6 imp pt, 21.1 US pt, 10 l; front and rear track 50 in, 127 cm.

Moskvich 2137/Moskvich 2140 Combi IZh

See Moskvich 2140/Moskvich 2140 IZh, except for:

TRANSMISSION axle ratio: 4.550; tyres: 6.40 x 13.

PERFORMANCE max speed: 84 mph, 135 km/h; power-weight ratio: 32.8 lb/hp (44.8 lb/kW), 14.9 kg/hp (20.3 kg/kW).

DIMENSIONS AND WEIGHT height: 59.45 in, 151 cm; weight: 2,470 lb, 1,120 kg.

BODY estate car/st. wagon; 4 + 1 doors.

AZLK Moskvich 2140

AZLK Moskvich 2140 Combi IZh

GAZ   USSR

Volga 24

ENGINE front, 4 stroke; 4 cylinders, in line; 149.3 cu in, 2,446 cc (3.62 x 3.62 in, 92 x 92 mm); compression ratio: 8.2:1; max power (SAE): 110 hp (80.9 kW) at 4,500 rpm; max torque (SAE): 152 lb ft, 21 kg m (205.9 Nm) at 2,400 rpm; max engine rpm: 4,500; 45 hp/l (33 kW/l); light alloy block and head, wet liners; 5 crankshaft bearings; valves: overhead, in line, push-rods and rockers; camshafts: 1, side; lubrication: gear pump, filter on by-pass, 10.4 imp pt, 12.5 US pt, 5.9 l; 1 K-126 G downdraught twin barrel carburettor; fuel feed: mechanical pump; water-cooled, 20.2 imp pt, 24.3 US pt, 11.5 l.

TRANSMISSION driving wheels: rear; clutch: single dry plate, hydraulically controlled; gearbox: mechanical; gears: 4, fully synchronized; ratios: I 3.500, II 2.260, III 1.450, IV 1, rev 3.540; lever: central; final drive: hypoid bevel; axle ratio: 4.100; width of rims: 5''; tyres: 7.35/185 x 14.

PERFORMANCE max speeds: (I) 25 mph, 41 km/h; (II) 40 mph, 64 km/h; (III) 62 mph, 100 km/h; (IV) 90 mph, 145 km/h; power-weight ratio: 29.1 lb/hp (39.7 lb/kW), 13.2 kg/hp (18 kg/kW); carrying capacity: 1,058 lb, 480 kg; speed in direct drive at 1,000 rpm: 18 mph, 29 km/h; fuel consumption: 22.6 m/imp gal, 18.8 m/US gal, 12.5 l x 100 km.

CHASSIS integral; front suspension: independent, wishbones, coil springs, anti-roll bar, telescopic dampers; rear: rigid axle, semi-elliptic leafsprings, telescopic dampers.

STEERING worm and roller; turns lock to lock: 3.50.

BRAKES drum, servo; swept area: front 87.6 sq in, 565 sq cm, rear 87.6 sq in, 565 sq cm, total 175.2 sq in, 1,130 sq cm.

ELECTRICAL EQUIPMENT 12 V; 54 Ah battery; 40 A alternator; R 119-B distributor; 2 headlamps.

DIMENSIONS AND WEIGHT wheel base: 110.24 in, 280 cm; tracks: 57.87 in, 147 cm front, 55.91 in, 142 cm rear; length: 186.22 in, 473 cm; width: 70.87 in, 180 cm; height: 58.66 in, 149 cm; ground clearance: 7.09 in, 18 cm; weight: 3,208 lb, 1,455 kg; turning circle (between walls): 40.7 ft, 12.4 m; fuel tank: 12.1 imp gal, 14.5 US gal, 55 l.

BODY saloon/sedan; 4 doors; 5-6 seats, separate front seats, reclining backrest.

PRACTICAL INSTRUCTIONS fuel: 94 oct petrol; oil: engine 10.4 imp pt, 12.5 US pt, 5.9 l - gearbox 1.6 imp pt, 1.9 US pt, 0.9 l - final drive 0.2 imp pt, 0.2 US pt, 0.1 l; greasing: 9 points; sparking plug: 175°; tappet clearances: inlet 0.014 in, 0.35 mm, exhaust 0.014 in, 0.35 mm; tyre pressure: front 24 psi, 1.7 atm, rear 24 psi, 1.7 atm.

VARIATIONS

ENGINE 6.7:1 compression ratio, max power (SAE) 95 hp (69.9 kW) at 4,700 rpm, max torque (SAE) 141 lb ft, 19.5 kg m (191.2 Nm) at 2,400 rpm, 38.8 hp/l (28.5 kW/l).

GAZ Volga 24

PERFORMANCE power-weight ratio 33.7 lb/hp (45.9 lb/kW), 15.3 kg/hp (20.8 kg/kW).
ENGINE 7.8:1 compression ratio, max power (SAE) 105 hp (77.3 kW) at 4,700 rpm, max torque (SAE) 145 lb ft, 20 kg m (196.1 Nm) at 2,400 rpm, 43 hp/l (31.6 kW/l).
PERFORMANCE power-weight ratio 30.6 lb/hp (41.4 lb/kW), 13.9 kg/hp (18.8 kg/kW).

Volga 24-02

See Volga 24, except for:

PERFORMANCE power-weight ratio 31.5 lb/hp (43 lb/kW), 14.3 kg/hp (19.5 kg/kW); carrying capacity: 1,235 lb, 550 kg.

DIMENSIONS AND WEIGHT height: 60.63 in, 154 cm; weight: 3,473 lb, 1,575 kg.

BODY estate car/st. wagon; 4 + 1 doors; 7 seats; folding rear seat.

Volga 24 Indenor Diesel

See Volga 24, except for:

ENGINE Diesel; 4 cylinders, in line, slanted at 20° to right; 128.9 cu in, 2,112 cc (3.54 x 3.27 in, 90 x 83 mm); compression ratio: 22.2:1; max power (DIN): 59 hp (43.4

kW) at 4,500 rpm; max torque (DIN): 86 lb ft, 11.9 kg m (116.7 Nm) at 2,500 rpm; 27.9 hp/l (20.5 kW/l); injection pump.

PERFORMANCE max speed: 84 mph, 135 km/h; power-weight ratio: 54.5 lb/hp (73.9 lb/kW), 24.7 kg/hp (33.5 kg/kW); consumption: 35.3 m/imp gal, 29.4 m/US gal, 8 l x 100 km.

ELECTRICAL EQUIPMENT 65 Ah battery.

PRACTICAL INSTRUCTIONS fuel: Diesel oil.

VARIATIONS

ENGINE 118.9 cu in, 1,948 cc (3.46 x 3.15 in, 88 x 80 mm); 21.8:1 compression ratio, max power (DIN) 50 hp (36.8 kW) at 4,500 rpm, max torque (DIN) 79 lb ft, 10.9 kg m (106.9 Nm) at 2,250 rpm, 25.7 hp/l (18.9 kW/l).
PERFORMANCE power-weight ratio 64.2 lb/hp (87.1 lb/kW), 29.1 kg/hp (39.5 kg/kW).

Chaika

ENGINE front, 4 stroke; 8 cylinders, Vee-slanted at 80°; 337 cu in, 5,522 cc (3.94 x 3.46 in, 100 x 88 mm); compression ratio: 8.5:1; max power (DIN): 207 hp (152.4 kW) at 4,000 rpm; max torque (DIN): 297 lb ft, 41 kg m (402.1 Nm) at 2,300 rpm; max engine rpm: 4,400; 37.5 hp/l (27.6 kW/l); cast iron block, light alloy head; 5 crankshaft bearings; valves: overhead, in line; camshafts: 1, side; lubrication: gear pump, full flow filter, 11.4 imp pt, 13.7 US pt, 6.5 l; 2 LK3 type K113 downdraught 4-barrel carburettors; fuel feed: mechanical pump; water-cooled, thermostatic fan.

TRANSMISSION driving wheels: rear; gearbox: automatic transmission, hydraulic torque converter and planetary gears with 3 ratios; ratios: I 2.840, II 1.680, III 1; lever: push-button control; final drive: hypoid bevel; axle ratio: 3.540; tyres: 8.20 x 15.

PERFORMANCE max speed: about 112 mph, 180 km/h; power-weight ratio: 27.6 lb/hp (37.5 lb/kW), 12.5 kg/hp (17 kg/kW); carrying capacity: 1,235 lb, 560 kg; consumption: about 14.1 m/imp gal, 11.8 m/US gal, 20 l x 100 km.

CHASSIS integral; front suspension: independent, wishbones, coil springs, anti-roll bar, telescopic dampers; rear: rigid axle, semi-elliptic springs, telescopic dampers.

STEERING roller and sector, servo.

BRAKES front disc, rear drum, servo.

ELECTRICAL EQUIPMENT 12 V; 68 Ah battery; 300 W dynamo; P13 distributor; 4 headlamps.

DIMENSIONS AND WEIGHT wheel base: 135.80 in, 345 cm; tracks: 60.65 in, 154 cm front, 60.25 in, 153 cm rear; length: 240.70 in, 611 cm; width: 79.50 in, 202 cm; height: 60 in, 152 cm; ground clearance: 7.10 in, 18 cm; weight: 5,698 lb, 2,584 kg; turning circle (between walls): 26.2 ft, 8 m; fuel tank: 17.6 imp gal, 21.1 US gal, 80 l.

BODY saloon/sedan; 4 doors; 7 seats; folding rear seat; headlamps with wiper-washers.

GAZ Chaika

UAZ   USSR

469 B

ENGINE front, 4 stroke; 4 cylinders, vertical, in line; 149.2 cu in, 2,445 cc (3.62 x 3.62 in, 92 x 92 mm); compression ratio: 6.7:1; max power (SAE): 78 hp (57.4 kW) at 4,000 rpm; max torque (SAE): 125 lb ft, 17.2 kg m (168.6 Nm) at 2,200-2,500 rpm; max engine rpm: 4,500; 31.9 hp/l (23.4 kW/l); cast iron block and head; 4 crankshaft bearings; valves: overhead, in line, push-rods and rockers; camshafts: 1, side; lubrication: gear pump, full flow filter, oil cooler, 10.6 imp pt, 12.7 US pt, 6 l; 1 downdraught 4-barrel carburettor; fuel feed: mechanical pump; water-cooled, 22.9 imp pt, 27.5 US pt, 13 l.

TRANSMISSION driving wheels: front (automatically engaged with transfer box low ratio) and rear; clutch: single dry plate; gearbox: mechanical; gears: 4, III and IV synchronized; ratios: I 4.120, II 2.640, III 1.580, IV 1, rev 3.738; lever: central; final drive: spiral bevel; axle ratio: 5.125; tyres: 8.40 x 15.

PERFORMANCE max speed: about 71 mph, 115 km/h; power-weight ratio: 43.5 lb/hp (59.2 lb/kW), 19.7 kg/hp (26.8 kg/kW); carrying capacity: 1,654 lb, 750 kg; speed in direct drive at 1,000 rpm: 15.9 mph, 25.6 km/h; consumption: 23.5 m/imp gal, 19.6 m/US gal, 12 l x 100 km.

CHASSIS box-type ladder frame; front and rear suspension: rigid axle, semi-elliptic leafsprings, telescopic dampers.

STEERING worm and double roller.

BRAKES drum; lining area: total 153.5 sq in, 990 sq cm.

ELECTRICAL EQUIPMENT 12 V; 54 Ah battery; 350 W alternator; 2 headlamps.

DIMENSIONS AND WEIGHT wheel base: 93.70 in, 238 cm; front and rear track: 56.69 in, 144 cm; length: 158.27 in, 402 cm; width: 70.08 in, 178 cm; height: 79.13 in, 201 cm; ground clearance: 8.66 in, 22 cm; weight: 3,396 lb, 1,540 kg; turning circle (between walls): 39.4 ft, 12 m; fuel tank: 15.8 imp gal, 19 US gal, 72 l (2 separate tanks).

BODY open; 4 doors; 7 seats, separate front seats.

PRACTICAL INSTRUCTIONS fuel: 72 oct petrol.

VARIATIONS

ENGINE Peugeot Diesel, 128.9 cu in, 2,112 cc (3.54 x 3.27 in, 90 x 83 mm), 22.8:1 compression ratio, max power (DIN) 65 hp (47.8 kW) at 4,500 rpm, max torque (DIN) 89 lb ft, 12.3 kg m (120.6 Nm) at 2,200 rpm, max engine rpm 4,750, 30.8 hp/l (22.6 kW/l).
PERFORMANCE max speed 62 mph, 100 km/h, power-weight ratio 55.2 lb/hp (71 lb/kW), 23.7 kg/hp (32.2 kg/kW); consumption 31.7 m/imp gal, 26.4 m/US gal, 8.9 l x 100 km.

OPTIONAL ACCESSORIES independent heating; hardtop; fabric top.

UAZ 469 B

VAZ Lada 1500 4-door Sedan

VAZ Niva 2121 3-door Combi

VAZ   USSR

Lada Series

PRICES IN GB:

1 1200 4-door Sedan	£	1,867*
2 1200 5-door Combi	£	2,142*
3 1300 ES 4-door Sedan	£	2,148*
4 1500 4-door Sedan	£	2,376*
5 1500 5-door Combi	£	2,259*
6 1500 ES 5-door Combi	£	2,481*
7 1600 4-door Sedan	—	
8 Niva 2121 3-door Combi	—	

Power team:	Standard for:	Optional for:
60 hp	1,2	—
68 hp	3	—
75 hp	4 to 6	—
78 hp	7	—
80 hp	8	—

60 hp power team

ENGINE Fiat, front, 4 stroke; 4 cylinders, in line; 73.1 cu in, 1,198 cc (2.99 x 2.60 in, 76 x 66 mm); compression ratio: 8.8:1; max power (DIN): 60 hp (44.2 kW) at 5,600 rpm; max torque (DIN): 64 lb ft, 8.9 kg m (87.3 Nm) at 3,400 rpm; max engine rpm: 6,000; 50.1 hp/l (36.9 kW/l); cast iron cylinder block, light alloy head; 5 crankshaft bearings; valves: overhead, in line, rockers; camshafts: 1, overhead, chain driven; lubrication: gear pump, full flow filter, 6.5 imp pt, 7.8 US pt, 3.7 l; 1 Weber 32 DCR downdraught twin barrel carburettor; fuel feed: mechanical pump; sealed circuit cooling, liquid, 15 imp pt, 18 US pt, 8.5 l.

TRANSMISSION driving wheels: rear; clutch: single dry plate (diaphragm), hydraulically controlled; gearbox: mechanical; gears: 4, fully synchronized; ratios: I 3.753, II 2.303, III 1.493, IV 1, rev 3.867; lever: central; final drive: hypoid bevel; axle ratio: saloon 4.300, station wagon 4.440; width of rims: 4.5''; tyres: saloon 155 SR/6.15 x 13 - station wagon 165 SR/6.45 x 13.

PERFORMANCE max speeds: (I) 25 mph, 40 km/h; (II) 40 mph, 65 km/h; (III) 62 mph, 100 km/h; (IV) 87 mph, 140 km/h; power-weight ratio: saloon 35.7 lb/hp (48.3 lb/kW), 16.2 kg/hp (21.9 kg/kW) - station wagon 37 lb/hp (50.5 lb/kW), 16.8 kg/hp (22.9 kg/kW); carrying capacity: 882 lb, 400 kg; acceleration: 0-50 mph (0-80 km/h) 12 sec; speed in direct drive at 1,000 rpm: 15.2 mph, 24.5 km/h; consumption: 31.4 m/imp gal, 26.1 m/US gal, 9 l x 100 km.

CHASSIS integral; front suspension: independent, wishbones, coil springs, anti-roll bar, telescopic dampers; rear: rigid axle, twin trailing radius arms, transverse linkage bar, coil springs, telescopic dampers.

STEERING worm and roller; turns lock to lock: 3.

BRAKES front disc (diameter 9.96 in, 25.3 cm), rear drum, rear compensator; lining area: front 20.9 sq in, 135 sq cm, rear 76.9 sq in, 496 sq cm, total 97.8 sq in, 631 sq cm.

ELECTRICAL EQUIPMENT 12 V; 55 Ah battery; 40 A alternator; R 125 distributor; 2 headlamps.

ZAZ 968-A

DIMENSIONS AND WEIGHT wheel base: 95.47 in, 242 cm; tracks: 52.76 in, 134 cm front, 51.38 in, 130 cm rear; length: saloon 160.43 in, 407 cm - station wagon 159.84 in, 406 cm; width: 63.43 in, 161 cm; height: saloon 54.33 in, 138 cm - station wagon 57.48 in, 146 cm; ground clearance: 6.69 in, 17 cm; weight: saloon 2,139 lb, 970 kg - station wagon 2,227 lb, 1,010 kg; turning circle (between walls): 37.4 ft, 11.4 m; fuel tank: saloon 8.6 imp gal, 10.3 US gal, 39 l - station wagon 9.9 imp gal, 11.9 US gal, 45 l.

BODY 5 seats, separate front seats, reclining backrests.

68 hp power team

See 60 hp power team, except for:

ENGINE 79 cu in, 1,294 cc (3.11 x 2.60 in, 79 x 66 mm); max power (SAE): 68 hp (50 kW) at 5,400 rpm; max torque (SAE): 78 lb ft, 10.8 kg m (105.9 Nm) at 3,500 rpm; 52.6 hp/l (38.6 kW/l).

TRANSMISSION tyres: 155 x 13.

PERFORMANCE max speed: 92 mph, 148 km/h; power-weight ratio: 31.5 lb/hp (42.8 lb/kW), 14.3 kg/hp (19.4 kg/kW).

75 hp power team

See 60 hp power team, except for:

ENGINE 88.6 cu in, 1,452 cc (2.99 x 3.15 in, 76 x 80 mm); max power (DIN): 75 hp (55.2 kW) at 5,600 rpm; max torque (DIN): 78 lb ft, 10.8 kg m (105.9 Nm) at 3,500 rpm; max engine rpm: 6,500; 51.6 hp/l (38 kW/l).

TRANSMISSION axle ratio: 4.100; width of rims: 5''; tyres: 165 SR x 13.

PERFORMANCE max speed: 93 mph, 150 km/h; power-weight ratio: 30.2 lb/hp (41.2 lb/kW), 13.7 kg/hp (18.7 kg/kW); acceleration: 0-50 mph (0-80 km/h) 10.7 sec.

BRAKES servo.

ELECTRICAL EQUIPMENT 53 A alternator; 4 headlamps.

DIMENSIONS AND WEIGHT wheel base: 94.88 in, 241 cm; tracks: 52.95 in, 135 cm front, 50.79 in, 129 cm rear; length: saloon 162.20 in, 412 cm; height: station wagons 55.12 in, 140 cm; ground clearance: 6.89 in, 17.5 cm; weight: 2,271 lb, 1,030 kg; turning circle (between walls): 34.1 ft, 10.4 m.

BODY for 1500 ES 5-door Combi only heated rear window wiper-washer and vinyl roof.

78 hp power team

See 60 hp power team, except for:

ENGINE 95.7 cu in, 1,568 cc (3.11 x 3.15 in, 79 x 80 mm); max power (DIN): 78 hp (57.4 kW) at 5,200 rpm; max engine (DIN): 91 lb ft, 12.5 kg m (122.6 Nm) at 3,400 rpm; max engine rpm: 6,500; 49.7 hp/l (36.6 kW/l).

TRANSMISSION axle ratio: 4.100; width of rims: 5''; tyres: 165 SR x 13.

PERFORMANCE max speed: 96 mph, 155 km/h; power-weight ratio: 29.1 lb/hp (39.5 lb/kW), 13.2 kg/hp (17.9 kg/kW).

BRAKES servo.

ELECTRICAL EQUIPMENT 53 A alternator; 4 headlamps.

DIMENSIONS AND WEIGHT tracks: 53.54 in, 136 cm front, 51.97 in, 132 cm rear; length: 161.81 in, 411 cm; ground clearance: 6.88 in, 17.5 cm; weight: 2,271 lb, 1,030 kg; turning circle (between walls): 38.7 ft, 11.8 m.

80 hp power team

See 78 hp power team, except for:

TRANSMISSION driving wheels: front and rear; tyres: 6.40 x 15.

PERFORMANCE max speed: 82 mph, 132 km/h; power-weight ratio: 32.4 lb/hp (44.1 lb/kW), 14.7 kg/hp (20 kg/kW).

BRAKES front and rear drum.

DIMENSIONS AND WEIGHT wheel base: 110.24 in, 220 cm; length: 148 in, 376 cm; width: 66.14 in, 168 cm; height: 64.17 in, 164 cm; ground clearance: 10 in, 25.4 cm; weight: 2,536 lb, 1,150 kg; turning circle (between walls): 18 ft, 5.5 m; fuel tank: 9 imp gal, 10.8 US gal, 41 l.

BODY folding rear seat.

968-A

ENGINE rear, 4 stroke; 4 cylinders, Vee-slanted at 90°; 73 cu in, 1,196 cc (2.99 x 2.60 in, 76 x 66 mm); compression ratio: 8.4:1; max power (DIN): 45 hp (33.1 kW) at 4,500 rpm; max torque (DIN): 59 lb ft, 8.2 kg m (80.4 Nm) at 3,200 rpm; max engine rpm: 4,000; 37.6 hp/l (27.6 kW/l); cast iron block, light alloy head; 3 crankshaft bearings; valves: overhead, push-rods and rockers; camshafts: 1, at centre of Vee; lubrication: gear pump, full flow filter, 5.8 imp pt, 7 US pt, 3.3 l; 1 K 127 downdraught carburettor; fuel feed: mechanical pump; air-cooled.

TRANSMISSION driving wheels: rear; clutch: single dry plate, hydraulically controlled; gearbox: mechanical; gears: 4, II, III and IV synchronized; ratios: I 3.800, II 2.120, III 1.410, V 0.964, rev 4.165; lever: central; final drive: hypoid bevel; axle ratio: 4.125; tyres: 6.15 x 13 or 5.20/5.60 x 13 or 145 SR x 13.

PERFORMANCE max speed: 78 mph, 125 km/h; power-weight ratio: 38.7 lb/hp (52.6 lb/kW), 17.5 kg/hp (23.9 kg/kW); carrying capacity: 706 lb, 320 kg; speed in top at 1,000 rpm: 16.5 mph, 26.5 km/h; consumption: 35.3 m/imp gal, 29.4 m/US gal, 8 l x 100 km.

CHASSIS integral; front suspension: independent, swinging longitudinal trailing arms, transverse torsion bars, telescopic dampers; rear: independent, semi-trailing arms, coil springs, telescopic dampers.

STEERING worm and double roller.

BRAKES drum, dual circuit; lining area: total 78.9 sq in, 509 sq cm.

ELECTRICAL EQUIPMENT 12 V; 42 Ah battery; 250 W alternator; 2 headlamps.

DIMENSIONS AND WEIGHT wheel base: 85.04 in, 216 cm; tracks: 48.03 in, 122 cm front, 47.24 in, 120 cm rear; length: 146.85 in, 373 cm; width: 61.81 in, 157 cm; height: 55.12 in, 140 cm; ground clearance: 7.48 in, 19 cm; weight: 1,742 lb, 790 kg; turning circle (between walls): 36.1 ft, 11 m; fuel tank: 6.6 imp gal, 7.9 US gal, 30 l.

BODY saloon/sedan; 2 doors; 4 seats, separate front seats, reclining backrests; independent heating.

OPTIONAL ACCESSORIES 155 SR x 13 tyres.

114 Limousine

ENGINE front, 4 stroke; 8 cylinders, Vee-slanted at 90°; 424.8 cu in, 6,962 cc (4.25 x 3.74 in, 108 x 95 mm); compression ratio: 9:1; max power (SAE): 300 hp (220.8 kW) at 4,400 rpm; max torque (SAE): 420 lb ft, 58 kg m (568.8 Nm) at 2,900 rpm; max engine rpm: 4,500; 43.1 hp/l (31.7 kW/l); cast iron block, light alloy head; 7 crankshaft bearings; valves: overhead, push-rods and rockers; camshafts: 1, at centre of Vee; lubrication: gear pump, full flow filter, 12.3

ZIL 114 Limousine

114 LIMOUSINE

imp pt, 14.8 US pt, 7 l; 1 K 85 downdraught 4-barrel car-burrettor; fuel feed: electric pump; water-cooled, 39.9 imp pt, 48 US pt, 22.7 l.

TRANSMISSION driving wheels: rear; gearbox: automatic transmission, hydraulic torque converter and planetary gears with 2 ratios, max ratio of converter at stall 2.5; ratios: I 1.720, II 1, rev 2.930; lever: push button control; final drive: hypoid bevel; axle ratio: 3.540; width of rims: 6.5''; tyres: 8.90 x 15 or 9.35 x 15.

PERFORMANCE max speed: 124 mph, 200 km/h; power-weight ratio: 23.4 lb/hp (31.7 lb/kW), 10.6 kg/hp (14.4 kg/kW); carrying capacity: 1,411 lb, 640 kg; consumption: 9.4 m/imp gal, 7.8 m/US gal, 30 l x 100 km.

CHASSIS box-type ladder frame and X cross members; front suspension: independent, wishbones, coil springs, anti-roll bar, lever dampers; rear: rigid axle, semi-elliptic leafsprings, telescopic dampers.

STEERING recirculating ball, servo; turns lock to lock: 4.30.

BRAKES disc, servo.

ELECTRICAL EQUIPMENT 12 V; 2 x 54 Ah batteries; 500 W dynamo; R-4 distributor; 4 headlamps; 2 fog lamps.

DIMENSIONS AND WEIGHT wheel base: 148.03 in, 376 cm; tracks: 61.81 in, 157 cm front, 63.78 in, 162 cm rear; length: 247.44 in, 628 cm; width: 81.50 in, 207 cm; height: 59.45 in, 151 cm; ground clearance: 7.09 in, 18 cm; weight: 7,001 lb, 3,175 kg; turning circle (between walls): 52.4 ft, 16 m; fuel tank: 26.4 imp gal, 31.7 US gal, 120 l.

BODY limousine; 4 doors; 7 seats, separate front seats; air-conditioning; electric windows.

117 Limousine

See 114 Limousine, except for:

PERFORMANCE power-weight ratio: 21.4 lb/hp (28.9 lb/kW), 9.7 kg/hp (13.1 kg/kW).

DIMENSIONS AND WEIGHT wheel base: 128.35 in, 326 cm; length: 227.56 in, 578 cm; weight: 6,395 lb, 2,900 kg; turning circle (between walls): 45.9 ft, 14 m.

BODY 5 seats.

ZCZ   YUGOSLAVIA

Zastava 750 M/750 Luxe

ENGINE rear, 4 stroke; 4 cylinders, vertical, in line; 46.8 cu in, 767 cc (2.44 x 2.50 in, 62 x 63.5 mm); compression ratio: 7.5:1; max power (DIN): 25 hp (18.4 kW) at 4,600 rpm; max torque (DIN): 37 lb ft, 5.1 kg m (50 Nm) at 2,500 rpm; max engine rpm: 4,800; 32.6 hp/l (23.9 kW/l); cast iron block, light alloy head; 3 crankshaft bearings; valves: overhead, in line, push-rods and rockers; camshafts: 1, side; lubrication: gear pump, centrifugal filter, 6.5 imp pt, 7.8 US pt, 3.7 l; 1 Weber 28 ICP 6 or Solex C28PIB 3 or Holley 28 ICP 6 downdraught single barrel carburettor; fuel feed: mechanical pump; water-cooled, 7.9 imp pt, 9.5 US pt, 4.5 l.

TRANSMISSION driving wheels: rear; clutch: single dry plate; gearbox: mechanical; gears: 4, II, III and IV synchronized; ratios: I 3.385, II 2.055, III 1.333, IV 0.896, rev 4.275; lever: central; final drive: spiral bevel; axle ratio: 4.875; width of rims: 3.5''; tyres: 5.20 x 12.

PERFORMANCE max speeds: (I) 19 mph, 30 km/h; (II) 28 mph, 45 km/h; (III) 43 mph, 70 km/h; (IV) about 68 mph, 110 km/h; power-weight ratio: 54.2 lb/hp (73.7 lb/kW), 24.6 kg/hp (33.4 kg/kW); carrying capacity: 706 lb, 320 kg; acceleration: standing ¼ mile 26.7 sec, 0-50 mph (0-80 km/h) 24 sec; speed in top at 1,000 rpm: 14.1 mph, 22.7 km/h; consumption: 48.7 m/imp gal, 40.6 m/US gal, 5.8 l x 100 km.

CHASSIS integral; front suspension: independent, wishbones, transverse leafspring lower arms, telescopic dampers; rear: independent, oblique semi-trailing arms, coil springs, telescopic dampers.

STEERING screw and sector; turns lock to lock: 2.12.

BRAKES drum, single circuit; lining area: front 33.5 sq in, 216 sq cm, rear 33.5 sq in, 216 sq cm, total 67 sq in, 432 sq cm.

ELECTRICAL EQUIPMENT 12 V; 32 Ah battery; 230 W dynamo; Marelli distributor: 2 headlamps.

DIMENSIONS AND WEIGHT wheel base: 78.74 in, 200 cm; tracks: 45.28 in, 115 cm front, 45.67 in, 116 cm rear; length: 129.72 in, 329 cm; width: 54.25 in, 138 cm; height: 55.12 in, 140 cm; ground clearance: 5.71 in, 14.5 cm; weight: 1,356 lb, 615 kg; weight distribution: 46% front, 54% rear; turning circle (between walls): 30.5 ft, 9.3 m; fuel tank: 6.6 imp gal, 7.9 US gal, 30 l.

BODY saloon/sedan; 2 doors; 4 seats, separate front seats; folding rear seat; for Zastava 750 Luxe only reclining backrests and luxury interior.

Zastava 101

ENGINE front, transverse, slanted 20° to front, 4 stroke; 4 cylinders, in line; 68.1 cu in, 1,116 cc (3.15 x 2.19 in, 80 x 55.5 mm); compression ratio: 8.8:1; max power (DIN): 55 hp (40.4 kW) at 6,000 rpm; max torque (DIN): 57 lb ft, 7.9 kg m (77.4 Nm) at 3,000 rpm; max engine rpm: 6,000; 49.3 hp/l (36.2 kW/l); cast iron block, light alloy head; 5 crankshaft bearings; valves: overhead, thimble tappets; camshafts: 1, overhead; lubrication: gear pump, cartridge filter, 8.8 imp pt, 10.6 US pt, 5 l; 1 Weber 32

ZCZ Zastava 750 Luxe

ZCZ Zastava 1300

ICEV or Solex C 32 DISA downdraught carburettor; fuel feed: mechanical pump; water-cooled, 11.4 imp pt, 13.7 US pt, 6.5 l, electric thermostatic fan.

TRANSMISSION driving wheels: front; clutch: single dry plate; gearbox: mechanical; gears: 4, fully synchronized; ratios: I 3.583, II 2.235, III 1.454, IV 1.042, rev 3.714; lever: central; final drive: cylindrical gears; axle ratio: 4.077; width of rims: 4.5''; tyres: 145 SR x 13.

PERFORMANCE max speeds: (I) 28 mph, 45 km/h; (II) 47 mph, 75 km/h; (III) 71 mph, 115 km/h; (IV) 84 mph, 140 km/h; power-weight ratio: 32.6 lb/hp (44.5 lb/kW), 14.8 kg/hp (20.2 kg/kW); carrying capacity: 882 lb, 400 kg; acceleration: standing ¼ mile 21 sec, 0-50 mph (0-80 km/h) 12.7 sec; speed in top at 1,000 rpm: 15.2 mph, 24.4 km/h; consumption: 35.3 m/imp gal, 29.4 m/US gal, 8 l x 100 km.

CHASSIS integral; front suspension: independent, by McPherson, coil springs/telescopic damper struts, lower wishbones, anti-roll bar; rear: independent, single wide-based wishbone, transverse leafspring, telescopic dampers.

STEERING rack-and-pinion; turns lock to lock: 3.50.

BRAKES front disc (diameter 8.94 in, 22.7 cm), rear drum, rear compensator; lining area: front 19.2 sq in, 124 sq cm, rear 33.5 sq in, 216 sq cm, total 52.7 sq in, 340 sq cm.

ELECTRICAL EQUIPMENT 12 V; 34 Ah battery; 400 W alternator; Marelli distributor; 2 headlamps.

DIMENSIONS AND WEIGHT wheel base: 96.42 in, 245 cm; front and rear track: 51.34 in, 130 cm; length: 151.02 in, 384 cm; width: 62.60 in, 159 cm; height: 54.02 in, 137 cm; ground clearance: 5.71 in, 14.5 cm; weight: 1,797 lb, 815 kg; weight distribution: 61.5% front, 38.5% rear; turning circle (between walls): 35.8 ft, 10.9 m; fuel tank: 8.4 imp gal, 10 US gal, 38 l.

BODY saloon/sedan; 4 + 1 doors; 5 seats, separate front seats.

OPTIONAL ACCESSORIES reclining backrests; luxury interior; heated rear window.

Zastava 1300/1300 Luxe

ENGINE front, 4 stroke; 4 cylinders, vertical, in line; 79 cu in, 1,295 cc (2.83 x 3.13 in, 72 x 79.5 mm); compression ratio: 9:1; max power (DIN): 60 hp (44.1 kW) at 5,400 rpm; max torque (DIN): 69 lb ft, 9.5 kg m (93.1 Nm) at 3,200 rpm; max engine rpm: 6,000; 46.3 hp/l (34 kW/l); cast iron block, light alloy head, 3 crankshaft bearings; valves: overhead, Vee-slanted, push-rods and rockers; camshafts: 1, side; lubrication: gear pump, centrifugal filter, cartridge on by-pass, 7.6 imp pt, 9.1 US pt, 4.3 l; 1 Weber 34 DCHD or Solex C 34 PAIA 2 downdraught twin barrel carburettor; fuel feed: mechanical pump; water-cooled, 11.8 imp pt, 14.2 US pt, 6.7 l.

TRANSMISSION driving wheels: rear; clutch: single dry plate, hydraulically controlled; gearbox: mechanical; gears: 4, fully synchronized; ratios: I 3.750, II 2.300, III 1.490, IV 1, rev 3.870; lever: central; final drive: hypoid bevel; axle ratio: 4.100; width of rims: 4.5''; tyres: 5.60 S x 13.

PERFORMANCE max speeds: (I) 25 mph, 40 km/h; (II) 40 mph, 65 km/h; (III) 62 mph, 100 km/h; (IV) over 87 mph, 140 km/h; power-weight ratio: 1300 35.3 lb/hp (40 lb/kW), 16 kg/hp (21.8 kg/kW) - 1300 Luxe 35.5 lb/hp (48.5 lb/kW), 16.1 kg/hp (22 kg/kW); carrying capacity: 882 lb, 400 kg; acceleration: standing ¼ mile 23.1 sec, 0-50 mph (0-80 km/h) 13.9 sec; speed in direct drive at 1,000 rpm: 16.1 mph, 25.9 km/h; consumption: 32.8 m/imp gal, 27.3 m/US gal, 8.6 l x 100 km.

CHASSIS integral; front suspension: independent, wishbones, lower trailing links, coil springs, anti-roll bar, telescopic dampers; rear: rigid axle, semi-elliptic leaf-springs, telescopic dampers.

STEERING worm and roller; turns lock to lock: 3.

BRAKES disc, servo.

ELECTRICAL EQUIPMENT 12 V; 48 Ah battery; 400 W dynamo; Marelli distributor; 4 headlamps.

DIMENSIONS AND WEIGHT wheel base: 95.37 in, 242 cm; tracks: 50.98 in, 129 cm front, 50.08 in, 127 cm rear; length: 158.66 in, 403 cm; width: 60.83 in, 154 cm; height: 56.69 in, 144 cm; ground clearance: 5.12 in, 13 cm; weight: 1300 2,117 lb, 960 kg - 1300 Luxe 2,139 lb, 970 kg; weight distribution: 56% front, 44% rear; turning circle (between walls): 33.5 ft, 10.2 m; fuel tank: 9.9 imp gal, 11.9 US gal, 45 l.

BODY saloon/sedan; 4 doors; 5 seats, separate front seats, reclining backrests; for 1300 Luxe only luxury interior.

The Americas

Models now in production

Illustrations and technical information

CHEVROLET   CANADA

Bel Air Series

PRICES EX WORKS (Canadian $):

1 Bel Air 2-door Sport Coupé	$ 5,912
2 Bel Air 4-door Sedan	$ 5,980
3 Bel Air 6-pass. Station Wagon	$ 6,578
4 Bel Air 9-pass. Station Wagon	$ 6,723

Power team:	Standard for:	Optional for:
110 hp	1,2	—
145 hp	3,4	1,2
170 hp	—	all

110 hp power team

ENGINE front, 4 stroke; 6 cylinders, vertical, in line; 250 cu in, 4,097 cc (3.87 x 3.53 in, 98.2 x 89.6 mm); compression ratio: 8.1:1; max power (DIN): 110 hp at 3,800 rpm; max torque (DIN): 190 lb ft, 26.2 kg m at 1,600 rpm; max engine rpm: 4,400; 26.8 hp/l; cast iron block and head; 7 crankshaft bearings; valves: overhead, in line, push-rods and rockers, hydraulic tappets; camshafts: 1, side; lubrication: gear pump, full flow filter, 8.3 imp pt, 9.9 US pt, 4.7 l; 1 Rochester 17058014 downdraught single barrel carburettor; cleaner air system; exhaust system with catalytic converter; fuel feed: mechanical pump; water-cooled, 24.3 imp pt, 29.2 US pt, 13.8 l.

TRANSMISSION driving wheels: rear; gearbox: Turbo-Hydramatic automatic transmission, hydraulic torque converter and planetary gears with 3 ratios, max ratio of converter at stall 2, possible manual selection; ratios: I 2.520, II 1.520, III 1, rev 1.940; lever: steering column; final drive: hypoid bevel; axle ratio: 2.730; width of rims: 6''; tyres: FR78 x 15.

PERFORMANCE max speed: about 99 mph, 160 km/h; power-weight ratio: Sedan 35.3 lb/hp, 16 kg/hp; speed in direct drive at 1,000 rpm: 24.9 mph, 40 km/h; consumption: 22.8 m/imp gal, 19 m/US gal, 12.4 l x 100 km.

CHASSIS perimeter box-type with cross members; front suspension: independent, wishbones, coil springs, anti-roll bar, telescopic dampers; rear: rigid axle, lower trailing radius arms, upper oblique torque arms, coil springs, anti-roll bar, telescopic dampers.

STEERING recirculating ball, servo; turns lock to lock: 3.16.

BRAKES front disc (diameter 11 in, 27.9 cm), front internal radial fins, rear drum, servo; swept area: total 329.8 sq in, 2,127 sq cm.

ELECTRICAL EQUIPMENT 12 V; 2,500 W battery; 37 A alternator; Delco-Relmy high energy ignition system; 4 headlamps.

DIMENSIONS AND WEIGHT wheel base: 116 in, 295 cm; tracks: 61.80 in, 157 cm front, 60.80 in, 154 cm rear; length: 212.10 in, 538 cm; width: 76 in, 193 cm; height: Coupé 55.30 in, 141 cm - Sedan 56 in, 142 cm; ground clearance: 5.80 in, 14.7 cm; weight: Coupé 3,510 lb, 1,592 kg - Sedan 3,530 lb, 1,601 kg; turning circle (between walls): 44.6 ft, 13.6 m; fuel tank: 17.6 imp gal, 21 US gal, 80 l.

OPTIONALS central lever; limited slip differential; electric windows; heavy-duty front suspension; GR78 x 15 or GR70 x 15 tyres with 7'' wide rims; tilt of steering wheel; speed control device; heated rear window; vinyl roof; air-conditioning.

145 hp power team

See 110 hp power team, except for:

ENGINE 8 cylinders; 305 cu in, 4,998 cc (3.74 x 3.48 in, 94.9 x 88.3 mm); compression ratio: 8.4:1; max power (DIN): 145 hp at 3,800 rpm; max torque (DIN): 245 lb ft, 33.8 kg m at 2,400 rpm; max engine rpm: 4,000; 29 hp/l; camshafts: 1, at centre of Vee; 1 Rochester 17058108 downdraught twin barrel carburettor; cooling system: 29.9 imp pt, 35.9 US pt, 17 l.

TRANSMISSION automatic transmission ratios: I 2.740, II 1.570, III 1, rev 2.070; max ratio of converter at stall 2.35; axle ratio: 2.410 - st. wagons 2.560; width of rims: st. wagons 7''; tyres: st. wagons HR78 x 15.

PERFORMANCE max speed: about 106 mph, 170 km/h; power-weight ratio: 28.1 lb/hp, 12.7 kg/hp; speed in direct drive at 1,000 rpm: 26.2 mph, 42 km/h; consumption: 22.8 m/imp gal, 18 m/US gal, 12.4 l x 100 km.

STEERING turns lock to lock: st. wagons 3.30.

CHEVROLET Bel Air 2-door Sport Coupé

CHEVROLET Bel Air 4-door Sedan

BRAKES (st. wagons) front disc (diameter 11.86 in, 30.1 cm); swept area: total 375.14 sq in, 2,420 sq cm.

ELECTRICAL EQUIPMENT 3,200 W battery.

DIMENSIONS AND WEIGHT tracks: st. wagons 62.20 in, 158 cm front, 64.10 in, 163 cm rear; length: st. wagons 214.70 in, 545 cm; width: st. wagons 79.10 in, 201 cm; height: st. wagons 58 in, 147 cm; ground clearance: st. wagons 5.90 in, 15 cm; weight: 4,079 lb, 1,850 kg; turning circle (between walls): st. wagons 45.1 ft, 13.7 m; fuel tank: st. wagons 18.3 imp gal, 22 US gal, 83 l.

170 hp power team

See 145 hp power team, except for:

ENGINE 350 cu in, 5,736 cc (4 x 3.48 in, 101.6 x 88.3 mm); compression ratio: 8.2:1; max power (DIN): 170 hp at 3,800 rpm; max torque (DIN): 270 lb ft, 37.2 kg m at 2,400 rpm; 29.6 hp/l; 1 Rochester 17058202 downdraught 4-barrel carburettor.

PERFORMANCE max speed: about 109 mph, 175 km/h; power-weight ratio: Sedan 21.1 lb/hp, 9.6 kg/hp; consumption: 20.5 m/imp gal, 17 m/US gal, 13.8 l x 100 km.

DIMENSIONS AND WEIGHT weight: plus 53 lb, 24 kg.

OPTIONALS 3.080 axle ratio.

FORD   CANADA

Granada Special Edition Series

PRICES EX WORKS (Canadian $):

Granada Special Edition 2-door Sedan	$ 4,657
Granada Special Edition 4-door Sedan	$ 4,776

Power team:	Standard for:	Optional for:
97 hp	both	—
139 hp	—	both

97 hp power team

ENGINE front, 4 stroke; 6 cylinders, in line; 250 cu in, 4,097 cc (3.68 x 3.91 in, 93.5 x 99.3 mm); compression ratio: 8.5:1; max power (DIN): 97 hp at 3,200 rpm; max torque (DIN): 210 lb ft, 29 kg m at 1,400 rpm; max engine rpm: 3,800; 23.7 hp/l; cast iron block and head; 7 crankshaft bearings; valves: overhead, in line, push-rods and rockers, hydraulic tappets; camshafts: 1, side; lubrication: rotary pump, full flow filter, 8.3 imp pt, 9.9 US pt, 4.7 l; 1 Carter YFA 9510 D8DE-BB downdraught single barrel carburettor; cleaner air system; exhaust system with catalytic converter; fuel feed: mechanical pump; water-cooled, 17.4 imp pt, 21 US pt, 9.9 l.

TRANSMISSION driving wheels: rear; clutch: single dry plate, semi-centrifugal; gearbox: mechanical; gears: 4, fully synchronized with overdrive/top; ratios: I 3.290, II 1.840, III 1, IV 0.810, rev 3.290; lever: central; final drive: hypoid bevel; axle ratio: 3.000; width of rims: 6''; tyres: DR78 x 14.

PERFORMANCE max speed: about 93 mph, 150 km/h; power-weight ratio: 4-dr. 32 lb/hp, 14.5 kg/hp; speed in direct drive at 1,000 rpm: 25.5 mph, 41 km/h; consumption: 25.2 m/imp gal, 21 m/US gal, 11.2 l x 100 km.

CHASSIS integral; front suspension: independent, wishbones (lower trailing links), coil springs, anti-roll bar, telescopic dampers; rear: rigid axle, semi-elliptic leafsprings, telescopic dampers.

STEERING recirculating ball; turns lock to lock: 5.18.

BRAKES front disc (diameter 11.03 in, 28 cm), rear drum; swept area: front 222.5 sq in, 1,435 sq cm, rear 125.6 sq in, 810 sq cm, total 348.1 sq in, 2,245 sq cm.

ELECTRICAL EQUIPMENT 12 V; 36 Ah battery; 40 A alternator; Motorcraft transistorized ignition; 4 headlamps.

DIMENSIONS AND WEIGHT wheel base: 109.90 in, 279 cm; tracks: 59 in, 150 cm front, 57.70 in, 146 cm rear; length: 197.70 in, 502 cm; width: 74 in, 188 cm; height: 53.20 in, 135 cm - 4-dr. 53.30 in, 135 cm; ground clearance: 4.84 in, 12.3 cm; weight: 2-dr. 3,070 lb, 1,392 kg - 4-dr. 3,105 lb, 1,408 kg; fuel tank: 15 imp gal, 18 US gal, 68 l.

BODY saloon/sedan; 4-5 seats, separate front seats, reclining backrests.

FORD Custom 500 2-door Pillared Hardtop

OPTIONALS limited slip differential; Select-Shift Cruise-O-Matic automatic transmission with 3 ratios (I 2.460, II 1.460, III 1, rev 2.190), max ratio of converter at stall 2.29, possible manual selection, steering column or central lever, 2.470 or 2.500 axle ratio; aluminum wheels; ER78 x 14 or FR78 x 14 tyres; tilt of steering wheel; power-steering; servo brake; disc brakes (front diameter 11.03 in, 28 cm, rear 10.66 in, 27.1 cm), total swept area 433.7 sq in, 2,797 sq cm; 54 Ah battery; electric windows; heated rear window; tinted glass; vinyl roof; sunshine roof; air-conditioning.

139 hp power team

See 97 hp power team, except for:

ENGINE 8 cylinders; 302 cu in, 4,950 cc (4 x 3 in, 101.6 x 76.2 mm); compression ratio: 8.4:1; max power (DIN): 139 hp at 3,600 rpm; max torque (DIN): 250 lb ft, 34.5 kg m at 1,600 rpm; max engine rpm: 4,000; 28.1 hp/l; 5 crankshaft bearings; camshafts: 1, at centre of Vee; 1 Ford 2150A 9510 D8DE-HA downdraught twin barrel carburettor; cooling system: 24.3 imp pt, 29.2 US pt, 13.8 l.

PERFORMANCE max speed: about 103 mph, 165 km/h; power-weight ratio: 4-dr. 23 lb/hp, 10.4 kg/hp; consumption: 22.8 m/imp gal, 19 m/US gal, 12.4 l x 100 km.

DIMENSIONS AND WEIGHT weight: plus 90 lb, 41 kg.

Custom 500 Series

PRICE EX WORKS (Canadian $):

1 Custom 500 2-door Pillared Hardtop	$ 5,970
2 Custom 500 4-door Pillared Hardtop	$ 6,038
3 Custom 500 Station Wagon	$ 6,442

Power team:	Standard for:	Optional for:
134 hp	1,2	—
144 hp	—	1,2
145 hp	3	1,2
160 hp	—	all
202 hp	—	all

134 hp power team

ENGINE front, 4 stroke; 8 cylinders; 302 cu in, 4,950 cc (4 x 3 in, 101.6 x 76.2 mm); compression ratio: 8.4:1; max power (DIN): 134 hp at 3,400 rpm; max torque (DIN): 248 lb ft, 34.2 kg m at 1,600 rpm; max engine rpm: 4,000; 27.1 hp/l; cast iron block and head; 5 crankshaft bearings; valves: overhead, in line, push-rods and rockers, hydraulic tappets; camshafts: 1, at centre of Vee; lubrication: rotary pump, full flow filter, 8.3 imp pt, 9.9 US pt, 4.7 l; 1 Ford 2150A DBOE-EA downdraught twin barrel carburettor; cleaner air system; exhaust system with catalytic converter; fuel feed: mechanical pump; water-cooled, 22.5 imp pt, 27.1 US pt, 12.8 l.

TRANSMISSION driving wheels: rear; gearbox: Select-Shift Cruise-O-Matic automatic transmission, hydraulic torque converter and planetary gears with 3 ratios, max ratio of converter at stall 2.14, possible manual selection; ratios: I 2.460, II 1.460, III 1, rev 2.220; lever: steering column; final drive: hypoid bevel; axle ratio: 2.750; width of rims: 6''; tyres: 2-dr. GR78 x 15 - 4-dr. HR78 x 15.

PERFORMANCE max speed: about 96 mph, 155 km/h; power-weight ratio: 4-dr. 31.8 lb/hp, 14.4 kg/hp; speed in direct drive at 1,000 rpm: 25.4 mph, 40.8 km/h; consumption: 20.5 m/imp gal, 17 m/US gal, 13.8 l x 100 km.

CHASSIS perimeter box-type; front suspension: independent, wishbones (lower trailing links), coil springs, anti-roll bar, telescopic dampers; rear: rigid axle, lower trailing radius arms, upper oblique torque arms, transverse linkage bar, coil springs, telescopic dampers.

STEERING recirculating ball, servo; turns lock to lock: 3.99.

BRAKES front disc (diameter 11.80 in, 30 cm), front internal radial fins, rear drum, servo; swept area: front 242 sq in, 1,561 sq cm, rear 173.3 sq in, 1,117 sq cm, total 415.3 sq in, 2,678 sq cm.

ELECTRICAL EQUIPMENT 12 V; 36 Ah battery; 40 A alternator; Motorcraft transistorized ignition; 4 headlamps.

DIMENSIONS AND WEIGHT wheel base: 121 in, 307 cm; tracks: 64.10 in, 162 cm front, 64.30 in, 163 cm rear; length: 224.10 in, 569 cm; width: 79.50 in, 202 cm; height: 54.80 in, 139 cm - 2-dr. 53.80 in, 136 cm; ground clearance: 5.50 in, 14 cm; weight: 2-dr. 4,221 lb, 1,914 kg - 4-dr. 4,261 lb,

1,932 kg; turning circle (between walls): 45.3 ft, 13.8 m; fuel tank: 20.2 imp gal, 24.2 US gal, 92 l.

OPTIONALS limited slip differential; JR78 x 15 tyres; LR78 x 15 tyres with 6.5'' wide rims; tilt of steering wheel; disc brakes, total swept area 365.9 sq in, 2,360 sq cm; heavy-duty battery; heated rear window; electric windows; electric sunshine roof; reclining front seats; speed control; air-conditioning.

144 hp power team

See 134 hp power team, except for:

ENGINE 351 cu in, 5,732 cc (4 x 3.50 in, 101.6 x 88.8 mm); compression ratio: 8.3:1; max power (DIN): 144 hp at 3,200 rpm; max torque (DIN): 277 lb ft, 38.2 kg m at 1,600 rpm; 25.1 hp/l; 1 Ford 2150A D8WE-DA downdraught twin barrel carburettor; cooling system: 28.5 imp pt, 34.2 US pt, 16.2 l.

TRANSMISSION automatic transmission ratios: I 2.400, II 1.470, III 1, rev 2; max ratio of converter at stall 2; axle ratio: 2.470.

PERFORMANCE max speed: about 103 mph, 165 km/h; power-weight ratio: 4-dr. 29.6 lb/hp, 13.4 kg/hp; speed in direct drive at 1,000 rpm: 28.5 mph, 45.8 km/h; consumption: 19.2 m/imp gal, 16 m/US gal, 14.7 l x 100 km.

ELECTRICAL EQUIPMENT 45 Ah battery.

OPTIONALS 2.500 axle ratio.

145 hp power team

See 144 hp power team, except for:

ENGINE compression ratio: 8:1; max power (DIN): 145 hp at 3,400 rpm; max torque (DIN): 273 lb ft, 37.8 kg m at 1,800 rpm; 25.3 hp/l; 1 Ford 2150A TBD downdraught twin barrel carburettor.

TRANSMISSION width of rims: St. Wagon 6.5''; tyres St. Wagon JR78 x 15.

PERFORMANCE max speed: about 99 mph, 160 km/h; power-weight: St. Wagon 31.5 lb/hp, 14.3 kg/hp.

DIMENSIONS AND WEIGHT length: St. Wagon 225.70 in, 573 cm; width: St. Wagon 79.70 in, 202 cm; height: St. Wagon 56.70 in, 114 cm; weight: St. Wagon 4,573 lb, 2,074 kg; fuel tank: St. Wagon 17.6 imp gal, 21 US gal, 80 l.

160 hp power team

See 145 hp power team, except for:

ENGINE 400 cu in, 6,555 cc (4 x 4 in, 101.6 x 101.6 mm); compression ratio: 8:1; max power (DIN): 160 hp at 3,800 rpm; max torque (DIN): 314 lb ft, 43.3 kg m at 1,800 rpm; max engine rpm: 4,400; 24.4 hp/l; cooling system: 28.5 imp pt, 34.2 US pt, 16.2 l.

TRANSMISSION automatic transmission ratios: I 2.460, II 1.460, III 1, rev 2.180; max ratio of converter at stall 2.18; axle ratio: 2.470.

PERFORMANCE max speed: about 109 mph, 175 km/h; power-weight ratio: 4-dr. 26.6 lb/hp, 12 kg/hp; speed in direct drive at 1,000 rpm: 24.7 mph, 39.8 km/h; consumption: 18 m/imp gal, 15 m/US gal, 15.7 l x 100 km.

ELECTRICAL EQUIPMENT 50 Ah battery.

202 hp power team

See 160 hp power team, except for:

ENGINE 460 cu in, 7,539 cc (4.36 x 3.85 in, 110.7 x 97.8 mm); max power (DIN): 202 hp at 4,000 rpm; max torque (DIN): 348 lb ft, 48 kg m at 2,000 rpm; 26.8 hp/l; 1 Motorcraft TBD downdraught 4-barrel carburettor; cooling system: 32 imp pt, 38.5 US pt, 18.2 l.

TRANSMISSION automatic transmission ratios: I 2.460, II 1.460, III 1, rev 2.180; max ratio of converter at stall 1.87; axle ratio: 2.500.

PERFORMANCE max speed: about 112 mph, 180 km/h; power-weight ratio: 4-dr. 21.8 lb/hp, 9.9 kg/hp; speed in direct drive at 1,000 rpm: 28 mph, 45 km/h; consumption: 16.8 m/imp gal, 14 m/US gal, 16.8 l x 100 km.

ELECTRICAL EQUIPMENT 68 Ah battery.

DIMENSIONS AND WEIGHT weight: plus 137 lb, 62 kg.

OPTIONALS 2.750 axle ratio.

FORD Granada Special Edition Series

MERCURY   CANADA

Marquis Meteor Series

PRICES EX WORKS: (Canadian $):

Marquis Meteor 2-door Hardtop	$ 6,511
Marquis Meteor 4-door Hardtop	$ 6,586
Marquis Meteor Station Wagon	$ 6,805

Power team:	Standard for:	Optional for:
145 hp	all	—
160 hp	—	all
202 hp	—	all

145 hp power team

ENGINE front, 4 stroke; 8 cylinders; 351 cu in, 5,732 cc (4 x 3.50 in, 101.6 x 88.8 mm); compression ratio: 8:1; max power (DIN): 145 hp at 3,400 rpm; max torque (DIN): 273 lb ft, 37.7 kg m at 1,800 rpm; max engine rpm: 4,400; 25.3 hp/l; cast iron block and head; 5 crankshaft bearings; valves: overhead, in line, push-rods and rockers, hydraulic tappets; camshafts: 1, at centre of Vee; lubrication: rotary pump, full flow filter, 8.3 imp pt, 9.9 US pt, 4.7 l; 1 Ford 2150A downdraught twin barrel carburettor; cleaner air system; exhaust system with catalytic converter; fuel feed: mechanical pump; water-cooled, 28.2 imp pt, 33.8 US pt, 16 l.

TRANSMISSION driving wheels: rear; gearbox: Select-Shift Merc-O-Matic automatic transmission, hydraulic torque converter and planetary gears with 3 ratios, max ratio of converter at stall 2.17, possible manual selection; ratios: I 2.400, II 1.470, III 1, rev 2; lever: steering column; final drive: hypoid bevel; axle ratio: 2.470; width of rims: 6'' - St. Wagon 6.5''; tyres: HR78 x 15 - St. Wagon JR78 x 15.

PERFORMANCE max speed: about 103 mph, 165 km/h; power-weight ratio: 4-dr. Hardtop 29.8 lb/hp, 13.5 kg/hp; speed in direct drive at 1,000 rpm: 30.1 mph, 48.5 km/h; consumption: 19.2 m/imp gal, 16 m/US gal, 14.7 l x 100 km.

CHASSIS perimeter box-type; front suspension: independent, wishbones (lower trailing links), coil springs, anti-roll bar, telescopic dampers; rear: rigid axle, lower trailing radius arms, upper torque arms, transverse linkage bar, coil springs, telescopic dampers.

STEERING recirculating ball, servo; turns lock to lock: 3.99.

BRAKES front disc (diameter 11.80 in, 30 cm), front internal radial fins, rear drum, rear compensator, servo; swept area: front 242 sq in, 1,561 sq cm, rear 173.2 sq in, 1,117 sq cm, total 415.2 sq in, 2,678 sq cm.

ELECTRICAL EQUIPMENT 12 V; 45 Ah battery; 40 A alternator; Motorcraft transistorized ignition; 4 headlamps.

DIMENSIONS AND WEIGHT wheel base: 124 in, 315 cm - St. Wagon 121 in, 307 cm; tracks: 64.10 in, 163 cm front, 64.30 in, 163 cm rear; length: 229 in, 582 cm - St. Wagon 227.10 in, 577 cm; width: 79.60 in, 202 cm - St. Wagon 79.70 in, 202 cm; height: 2-dr. 54.80 in, 139 cm - 4-dr. 53.80 in, 137 cm - St. Wagon 56.90 in, 144 cm; ground clearance: 5.50 in, 14 cm; weight: 2-dr. 4,296 lb, 1,948 kg - 4-dr. 4,328 lb, 1,963 kg - St. Wagon 4,578 lb, 2,076 kg; turning circle (between walls): 46.5 ft, 14.2 m; fuel tank: 20.2 imp gal, 24.2 US gal, 92 l - St. Wagon 17.6 imp gal, 21 US gal, 80 l.

OPTIONALS limited slip differential; 2.500 axle ratio; automatic levelling control; J78 x 15 or JR78 x 15 tyres; LR78 x 15 tyres with 6.5'' wide rims; aluminum wheels; speed control device; tilt of steering wheel; 4-wheel disc brakes, total swept area 465.9 sq in, 3,005 sq cm; anti-skid brakes; heavy-duty battery; heated rear window; electric windows; reclining backrests; Colony Park equipment for St. Wagon; vinyl roof; air-conditioning.

160 hp power team

See 145 hp power team, except for:

ENGINE 400 cu in, 6,555 cc (4 x 4 in, 101.6 x 101.6 mm); max power (DIN): 160 hp at 3,800 rpm; max torque (DIN): 314 lb ft, 43.3 kg m at 1,800 rpm; 24.4 hp/l; 1 Ford 2150A downdraught twin barrel carburettor; cooling system: 31 imp pt, 37.2 US pt, 17.6 l.

TRANSMISSION gearbox: Select-Shift Merc-O-Matic automatic transmission with max ratio of converter at stall 1.94; ratios: I 2.460, II 1.460, III 1, rev 2.180.

PERFORMANCE max speed: about 106 mph, 170 km/h; power-weight ratio: 4-dr. Hardtop 27.1 lb/hp, 12.3 kg/hp; speed in direct drive at 1,000 rpm: 27.8 mph, 44.7 km/h; consumption: 18 m/imp gal, 15 m/US gal, 15.7 l x 100 km.

ELECTRICAL EQUIPMENT 54 Ah battery.

DIMENSIONS AND WEIGHT weight: plus 11 lb, 5 kg.

OPTIONALS 2.750 or 3.000 axle ratio.

MERCURY Marquis Meteor Station Wagon

202 hp power team

See 145 hp power team, except for:

ENGINE 460 cu in, 7,539 cc (4.36 x 3.85 in, 110.7 x 97.8 mm); max power (DIN): 202 hp at 4,000 rpm; max torque (DIN): 348 lb ft, 48 kg m at 2,000 rpm; 26.8 hp/l; 1 Motorcraft downdraught 4-barrel carburettor; cooling system: 32.7 imp pt, 39.3 US pt, 18.6 l.

TRANSMISSION gearbox: Select-Shift Merc-O-Matic automatic transmission with max ratio of converter at stall 1.94; ratios: I 2.460, II 1.460, III 1, rev 2.180; axle ratio: 2.500.

PERFORMANCE max speed: about 109 mph, 175 km/h; power-weight ratio: 4-dr. Hardtop 22 lb/hp, 10 kg/hp; speed in direct drive at 1,000 rpm: 27.2 mph, 43.7 km/h; consumption: 16.8 m/imp gal, 14 m/US gal, 16.8 l x 100 km.

ELECTRICAL EQUIPMENT 68 Ah battery.

DIMENSIONS AND WEIGHT weight: plus 114 lb, 52 kg.

OPTIONALS 2.750 axle ratio.

PONTIAC   CANADA

Acadian Series

PRICES EX WORKS (Canadian $):

Acadian S Hatchback Coupé	$ 3,458
Acadian Hatchback Coupé	$ 3,836
Acadian Hatchback Sedan	$ 3,962

Power team:	Standard for:	Optional for:
63 hp	all	—
68 hp	—	all

63 hp power team

ENGINE front, 4 stroke; 4 cylinders, vertical, in line; 97.6 cu in, 1,599 cc (3.23 x 2.98 in, 82 x 75.6 mm); compression ratio: 8.6:1; max power (DIN): 63 hp at 4,800 rpm; max torque (DIN): 82 lb ft, 11.3 kg m at 3,200 rpm; max engine rpm: 5,500; 39.4 hp/l; cast iron block and head; 5 crankshaft bearings; valves: overhead, hydraulic tappets; camshafts: 1, overhead, cogged belt; lubrication: gear pump, full flow filter, 8.3 imp pt, 9.9 US pt, 4.7 l; 1 Rochester 17058035 downdraught single barrel carburettor; cleaner air system; exhaust system with catalytic converter; fuel feed: mechanical pump; water-cooled, 15 imp pt, 18 US pt, 8.5 l.

TRANSMISSION driving wheels: rear; clutch: single dry plate (diaphragm); gearbox: mechanical; gears: 4, fully synchronized; ratios: I 3.750, II 2.160, III 1.380, IV 1, rev 3.820; lever: central; final drive: hypoid bevel; axle ratio: 3.700; width of rims: 5''; tyres: P155/80 x 13.

PERFORMANCE max speed: about 87 mph, 140 km/h; power-weight ratio: Hatchback Sedan 32.4 lb/hp, 14.7 kg/hp; speed in direct drive at 1,000 rpm: 16.8 mph, 27 km/h; consumption: 40.9 m/imp gal, 34 m/US gal, 6.9 l x 100 km.

CHASSIS / right column

CHASSIS integral with cross member reinforcements; front suspension: independent, wishbones, coil springs, anti-roll bar, telescopic dampers; rear: rigid axle (torque tube), longitudinal trailing radius arms, coil springs, transverse linkage bar, anti-roll bar, telescopic dampers.

STEERING rack-and-pinion; turns lock to lock: 3.60.

BRAKES front disc (diameter 9.68 in, 24.6 cm), rear drum; swept area: total 297.7 sq in, 1,920 sq cm.

ELECTRICAL EQUIPMENT 12 V; 2,500 W battery; 32 A alternator; Delco-Remy high energy ignition system; 2 headlamps.

DIMENSIONS AND WEIGHT wheel base: 94.30 in, 239 cm - Hatchback Sedan 97.30 in, 247 cm; tracks: 51.20 in, 130 cm front, 51.20 in, 130 cm rear; length: 159.70 in, 406 cm - Hatchback Sedan 162.60 in, 413 cm; width: 61.80 in, 157 cm; height: 52.30 in, 133 cm; ground clearance: 5.30 in, 13.5 cm; weight: Acadian S Hatchback Coupé 1,933 lb, 877 kg - Chevette Hatchback Coupé 1,969 lb, 893 kg - Hatchback Sedan 2,044 lb, 927 kg; turning circle (between walls): 34.3 ft, 10.5 m - Hatchback Sedan 34.9 ft, 10.6 m; fuel tank: 40.3 imp gal, 12.5 US gal, 47 l.

OPTIONALS Turbo-Hydramatic automatic transmission, hydraulic torque converter and planetary gears with 3 ratios (I 2.400, II 1.480, III 1, rev 1.920), max ratio of converter at stall 2.20, possible manual selection, central lever, 4.110 axle ratio; heavy-duty battery; servo brake; vinyl roof; heated rear window; air-conditioning.

68 hp power team

See 63 hp power team, except for:

ENGINE max power (DIN): 68 hp at 5,000 rpm; max torque (DIN): 84 lb ft, 11.6 kg m at 3,200 rpm; 42.5 hp/l; 1 Rochester 17058039 downdraught single barrel carburettor.

PERFORMANCE max speed: about 93 mph, 150 km/h; power-weight ratio: Hatchback Sedan 30 lb/hp, 13.6 kg/hp.

Laurentian-Parisienne Series

PRICES EX WORKS (Canadian $):

1 Laurentian Coupé	$ 6,090
2 Laurentian Sedan	$ 6,129
3 Laurentian Safari Station Wagon	$ 6,722
4 Parisienne Coupé	$ 6,660
5 Parisienne Sedan	$ 6,776

Power team:	Standard for:	Optional for:
110 hp	1,2,4,5	—
145 hp	3	1,2,4,5
170 hp	—	all

110 hp power team

ENGINE front, 4 stroke; 6 cylinders, vertical, in line; 250 cu in, 4,097 cc (3.87 x 3.53 in, 98.2 x 89.6 mm); compression ratio: 8.1:1; max power (DIN): 110 hp at 3,800 rpm; max torque (DIN): 190 lb ft, 26.2 kg m at 1,600 rpm; max engine rpm: 4,400; 26.8 hp/l; cast iron block and head; 7 crankshaft bearings; valves: overhead, in line, push-rods and rockers, hydraulic tappets; camshafts: 1, side; lubrication: gear pump, full flow filter, 8.3 imp pt, 9.9 US pt, 4.7 l; 1 Rochester 17058014 downdraught single barrel carburettor; cleaner air system; exhaust system with catalytic converter; fuel feed: mechanical pump; water-cooled, 24.3 imp pt, 29.2 US pt, 13.8 l.

TRANSMISSION driving wheels: rear; gearbox: Turbo-Hydramatic automatic transmission, hydraulic torque converter and planetary gears with 3 ratios, max ratio of converter at stall 2, possible manual selection; ratios: I 2.520, II 1.520, III 1, rev 1.940; lever: steering column; final drive: hypoid bevel; axle ratio: 2.730; width of rims: 6''; tyres: FR78 x 15.

PERFORMANCE max speed: about 99 mph, 160 km/h; speed in direct drive at 1,000 rpm: 24.9 mph, 40 km/h; consumption: 22.8 m/imp gal, 19 m/US gal, 12.4 l x 100 km.

CHASSIS perimeter box-type cross members; front suspension: independent, wishbones, coil springs, anti-roll bar, telescopic dampers; rear: rigid axle, lower trailing radius arms, upper oblique torque arms, coil springs, anti-roll bar, telescopic dampers.

STEERING recirculating ball, servo; turns lock to lock: 3.16

BRAKES front disc (diameter 11 in, 27.9 cm), front internal radial fins, rear drum, servo; swept area: total 329.8 sq in, 2,127 sq cm.

ELECTRICAL EQUIPMENT 12 V; 2,500 W battery; 37 A alternator; Delco-Remy high energy ignition system; 4 headlamps.

DIMENSIONS AND WEIGHT wheel base: 115.90 in, 294 cm; tracks: 61.70 in, 157 cm front, 60.70 in, 154 cm rear; length: 214.30 in, 544 cm; width: 75.70 in, 192 cm; height: coupés 55.30 in, 141 cm - sedans 56 in, 142 cm; ground clearance: 5.60 in, 14.2 cm; turning circle (between walls): 41.6 ft, 12.7 m; fuel tank: 17.6 imp gal, 21 US gal, 80 l.

OPTIONALS central lever; limited slip differential; electric windows; heavy-duty suspension; GR78 x 15 or GR70 x 15 tyres with 7'' wide rims; tilt of steering wheel; speed control device; heated rear window; electric sunshine roof; automatic levelling control; heavy-duty radiator; aluminum wheels; air-conditioning.

145 hp power team

See 110 hp power team, except for:

ENGINE 8 cylinders; 305 cu in; 4,998 cc (3.74 x 3.48 in, 94.9 x 88.3 mm); compression ratio: 8.4:1; max power (DIN): 145 hp at 3,800 rpm; max torque (DIN): 245 lb ft, 33.8 kg m at 2,400 rpm; 29 hp/l; 5 crankshaft bearings; camshafts: 1, at centre of Vee; 1 Rochester 17058108 downdraught twin barrel carburettor; cooling system: 29.9 imp pt, 35.9 US pt, 17 l.

TRANSMISSION automatic transmission ratios: I 2.740, II 1.570, III 1, rev 2.070; max ratio of converter at stall 2.35; axle ratio: 2.410 - St. Wagon 2.560; width of rims: St. Wagon 7''; tyres: St. Wagon HR78 x 15.

PERFORMANCE max speed: about 106 mph, 170 km/h; speed in direct drive at 1,000 rpm: 26.2 mph, 42 km/h; consumption: 22.8 m/imp gal, 19 m/US gal, 12.4 l x 100 km.

PONTIAC Parisienne Sedan

STEERING turns lock to lock: St. Wagon 3.30.

BRAKES (St. Wagon) front disc (diameter 11.86 in, 30.1 cm); swept area: total 375.14 sq in, 2,420 sq cm.

ELECTRICAL EQUIPMENT 3,200 W battery.

DIMENSIONS AND WEIGHT tracks: St. Wagon 62.10 in, 158 cm front, 64.10 in, 163 cm rear; length: St. Wagon 214.70 in, 545 cm; width: St. Wagon 75.70 in, 192 cm; height: St. Wagon 58 in, 147 cm; ground clearance: St. Wagon 5.90 in, 15 cm; turning circle (between walls): St. Wagon 45.1 ft, 13.7 m; fuel tank: St. Wagon 18.3 imp gal, 22 US gal, 83 l.

170 hp power team

See 145 hp power team, except for:

ENGINE 350 cu in, 5,736 cc (4 x 3.48 in, 101.6 x 88.3 mm); compression ratio: 8.2:1; max power (DIN): 170 hp at 3,800 rpm; max torque (DIN): 270 lb ft, 37.2 kg m at 2,400 rpm; 29.6 hp/l; 1 Rochester 17058202 downdraught 4-barrel carburettor.

PERFORMANCE max speed: about 109 mph, 175 km/h; consumption: 20.5 m/imp gal, 17 m/US gal, 13.8 l x 100 km.

OPTIONALS 3.080 axle ratio.

AMERICAN MOTORS USA

Gremlin

PRICE EX WORKS: $ 3,299

80 hp power team

(optional).

ENGINE front, 4 stroke; 4 cylinders, in line; 121 cu in, 1,983 cc (3.41 x 3.32 in, 86.5 x 84.4 mm); compression ratio: 8.2:1; max power (DIN): 80 hp at 5,000 rpm; max torque (DIN): 105 lb ft, 14.5 kg m at 2,800 rpm; max engine rpm: 5,400; 40.3 hp/l; cast iron block and head; 5 crankshaft bearings; valves: overhead, in line, push-rods and rockers; camshafts: 1, side; lubrication: gear pump, full flow filter, 7.6 imp pt, 9.1 US pt, 4.3 l; 1 Holley 5210 downdraught twin barrel carburettor; cleaner air system; exhaust system with catalytic converter; fuel feed: mechanical pump; water-cooled, 10.7 imp pt, 12.9 US pt, 6.1 l.

TRANSMISSION driving wheels: rear; clutch: single dry plate; gearbox: mechanical; gears: 4, fully synchronized; ratios: I 3.650, II 1.970, III 1.370, IV 1, rev 3.660; lever: central; final drive: hypoid bevel; axle ratio: 3.080 (3.310 California only); width of rims: 4.5''; tyres: B78 x 14.

PERFORMANCE max speed: about 85 mph, 136 km/h; power-weight ratio: 31.7 lb/hp, 14.4 kg/hp; speed in direct drive at 1,000 rpm: 16.9 mph, 27.2 km/h; consumption: 31.4 m/imp gal, 26 m/US gal, 9 l x 100 km.

CHASSIS integral; front suspension: independent, wishbones, coil springs, telescopic dampers; rear: rigid axle, torque tube, semi-elliptic leafsprings, telescopic dampers.

STEERING recirculating ball; turns lock to lock: 6.

BRAKES front disc (diameter 10.27 in, 27.4 cm), front internal radial fins, rear drum; swept area: total 265.28 sq in, 1,711 sq cm.

ELECTRICAL EQUIPMENT 12 V; 305 A battery; 37 A alternator; Bosch distributor; 2 headlamps.

DIMENSIONS AND WEIGHT wheel base: 96 in, 244 cm; tracks: 58.22 in, 148 cm front, 57.50 in, 146 cm rear; length: 166.56 in, 423 cm; width: 71.12 in, 181 cm; height: 51.49 in, 131 cm; ground clearance: 3.91 in, 9.9 cm; weight: 2,544 lb, 1,154 kg; turning circle (between walls): 35.3 ft, 10.7 m; fuel tank: 11 imp gal, 13 US gal, 50 l.

BODY saloon/sedan; 2 doors; 4 seats, separate front seats, reclining backrests; folding rear seat; rear lift gate window.

OPTIONALS Torque-Command automatic transmission with 3 ratios (I 2.450, II 1.450, III 1, rev 2.200), max ratio of converter at stall 2.58, possible manual selection, steering column or central lever, 3.310 axle ratio; limited slip differential; C78 x 14 or D78 x 14 tyres with 5'' wide rims; DR78 x 14 tyres with 6'' wide rims; anti-roll bar on front suspension; heavy-duty cooling system; heavy-duty battery; power steering; servo brake; heated rear window; sports steering wheel; tinted glass; aluminum wheels; Levi's interior; X equipment; air-conditioning.

AMERICAN MOTORS Gremlin X 2-door Sedan

90 hp power team

(standard, not available in California).

See 80 hp power team, except for:

ENGINE 6 cylinders, in line; 232 cu in, 3,802 cc (3.75 x 3.50 in, 95.2 x 88.8 mm); compression ratio: 8:1; max power (DIN): 90 hp at 3,400 rpm; max torque (DIN): 168 lb ft, 23.2 kg m at 1,600 rpm; max engine rpm: 3,800; 23.7 hp/l; 7 crankshaft bearings; valves: hydraulic tappets; lubricating system: 8.3 imp pt, 9.9 US pt, 4.7 l; 1 Carter YF 7229 downdraught single barrel carburettor; cooling system: 18.3 imp pt, 22 US pt, 10.4 l.

TRANSMISSION gears: 3, fully synchronized; ratios: I 2.990, II 1.750, III 1, rev 3.170; axle ratio: 2.730.

PERFORMANCE max speed: about 90 mph, 145 km/h; power-weight ratio: 31.9 lb/hp, 14.5 kg/hp; speed in direct drive at 1,000 rpm: 23.7 mph, 38.2 km/h; consumption: 27.7 m/imp gal, 23 m/US gal, 10.2 l x 100 km.

BRAKES front disc (diameter 10.80 in, 27.4 cm), rear drum; swept area: total 310.65 sq in, 2,004 sq cm.

ELECTRICAL EQUIPMENT 50 Ah battery; Motorcraft electronic distributor.

DIMENSIONS AND WEIGHT weight: 2,874 lb, 1,303 kg; fuel tank: 17.6 imp gal, 21 US gal, 80 l.

OPTIONALS Torque-Command automatic transmission with max ratio of converter at stall 2.10, 2.530 axle ratio; 4-speed fully synchronized mechanical gearbox (I 3.500, II 2.210, III 1.430, IV 1, rev 3.390), 2.530 axle ratio.

120 hp power team

(optional, not available in California).

See 80 hp power team, except for:

ENGINE 6 cylinders, in line; 258 cu in, 4,228 cc (3.75 x 3.90 in, 95.2 x 99 mm); compression ratio: 8:1; max power (DIN): 120 hp at 3,600 rpm; max torque (DIN): 201 lb ft, 27.7 kg m at 1,800 rpm; max engine rpm: 4,000; 28.4 hp/l; 7 crankshaft bearings; valves: hydraulic tappets; lubricating system: 8.3 imp pt, 9.9 US pt, 4.7 l; 1 Carter BBD 8129 downdraught twin barrel carburettor; cooling system: 18.3 imp pt, 22 US pt, 10.4 l.

TRANSMISSION gearbox ratios: I 3.500, II 2.210, III 1.430, IV 1, rev 3.390; axle ratio: 2.530.

PERFORMANCE max speed: about 99 mph, 160 km/h; power-weight ratio: 23.1 lb/hp, 10.5 kg/hp; speed in direct drive at 1,000 rpm: 24.9 mph, 40 km/h; consumption: 22.8 m/imp gal, 19 m/US gal, 12.4 l x 100 km.

BRAKES front disc (diameter 10.80 in, 27.4 cm), rear drum; swept area: total 310.65 sq in, 2,004 sq cm.

ELECTRICAL EQUIPMENT 50 Ah battery; Motorcraft electronic distributor.

DIMENSIONS AND WEIGHT weight: 2,772 lb, 1,257 kg; fuel tank: 17.6 imp gal, 21 US gal, 80 l.

OPTIONALS Torque-Command automatic transmission with max ratio of converter at stall 2.10, 2.530 axle ratio.

100 hp power team

(optional, for California only).

See 120 hp power team, except for:

ENGINE max power (DIN): 100 hp at 3,400 rpm; max torque (DIN): 200 lb ft, 27.6 kg m at 1,600 rpm; max engine rpm: 3,800; 23.6 hp/l; 1 Carter YF 7235 downdraught single barrel carburettor.

TRANSMISSION axle ratio: 2.730.

PERFORMANCE max speed: about 93 mph, 150 km/h; power-weight ratio: 27.8 lb/hp, 12.6 kg/hp; speed in direct drive at 1,000 rpm: 24.5 mph, 39.4 km/h; consumption: 19.2 m/imp gal, 16 m/US gal, 14.7 l x 100 km.

OPTIONALS Torque-Command automatic transmission with max ratio of converter at stall 2.10, 3.080 axle ratio.

AMERICAN MOTORS Pacer D/L Sedan

AMERICAN MOTORS Pacer D/L Station Wagon

Pacer Series

PRICES EX WORKS:

Pacer Sedan	$ 3,998
Pacer Station Wagon	$ 4,143

For 120 hp engine add $ 120 (for 130 hp engine add $ 233). For prices in GB, see price index.

Power team:	Standard for:	Optional for:
90 hp	both	—
120 hp	—	both
100 hp	both	—
130 hp	—	both

90 hp power team

(not available in California).

ENGINE front, 4 stroke; 6 cylinders, in line; 232 cu in, 3,802 cc (3.75 x 3.50 in, 95.2 x 88.8 mm); compression ratio: 8:1; max power (DIN): 90 hp at 3,400 rpm; max torque (DIN): 168 lb ft, 23.2 kg m at 1,600 rpm; max engine rpm: 3,800; 23.7 hp/l; cast iron block and head; 7 crankshaft bearings; valves: overhead, in line, push-rods and rockers, hydraulic tappets; camshafts: 1, side; lubrication: gear pump, full flow filter, 8.3 imp pt, 9.9 US pt, 4.7 l; 1 Carter YF 7229 downdraught single barrel carburettor; cleaner air system; with catalytic converter; fuel feed: mechanical pump; water-cooled, 23.2 imp pt, 27.9 US pt, 13.2 l.

TRANSMISSION driving wheels: rear; clutch: single dry plate; gearbox: mechanical; gears: 3, fully synchronized; ratios: I 2.990, II 1.750, III 1, rev 3.170; lever: central; final drive: hypoid bevel; axle ratio: 2.730; width of rims: 5''; tyres: D78 x 14.

PERFORMANCE max speed: about 85 mph, 136 km/h; power-weight ratio: Sedan 34.8 lb/hp, 15.8 kg/hp - St. Wagon 35.5 lb/hp, 16.1 kg/hp; speed in direct drive at 1,000 rpm: 22.1 mph, 35.6 km/h; consumption: 26.4 m/imp gal, 22 m/US gal, 10.7 l x 100 km.

CHASSIS integral; front suspension: independent, wishbones, coil springs, telescopic dampers; rear: rigid axle, semi-elliptic leafsprings, telescopic dampers.

STEERING rack-and-pinion; turns lock to lock: 5.30.

BRAKES front disc (diameter 10.80 in, 27.4 cm), front internal radial fins, rear drum; swept area: total 310.65 sq in, 2,004 sq cm.

ELECTRICAL EQUIPMENT 12 V; 50 Ah battery; 37 A alternator; Motorcraft electronic distributor; 2 headlamps.

DIMENSIONS AND WEIGHT wheel base: 100 in, 254 cm; tracks: 61.36 in, 153 cm front, 60 in, 152 cm rear; length: Sedan 172.10 in, 437 cm - St. Wagon 177 in, 450 cm; width: 77 in, 196 cm; height: Sedan 52.81 in, 134 cm - St. Wagon 53.16 in, 135 cm; ground clearance: Sedan 4.68 in, 11.9 cm - St. Wagon 4.93 in, 12.5 cm; weight: Sedan 3,142 lb, 1,425 kg - St. Wagon 3,189 lb, 1,446 kg; turning circle (between walls): 39 ft, 11.9 m; fuel tank: 16.7 imp gal, 20 US gal, 76 l.

OPTIONALS 4-speed fully synchronized mechanical gearbox (I 3.500, II 2.210, III 1.430, IV 1, rev 3.390), central lever, 2.530 axle ratio; Torque-Command automatic transmission, hydraulic torque converter and planetary gears with 3 ratios (I 2.450, II 1.450, III 1, rev 2.200), max ratio of converter at stall 2.10, possible manual selection, central lever, 2.730 axle ratio; limited slip differential; DR78 x 14 tyres with 6'' wide rims; anti-roll bar on front suspension; heavy-duty cooling system; heavy-duty battery; tilt of steering wheel; power steering; servo brake; heated rear window; reclining backrests; tinted glass; rear window wiper-washer; vinyl roof; D/L equipment; air-conditioning.

120 hp power team

(not available in California).

See 90 hp power team, except for:

ENGINE 258 cu in, 4,228 cc (3.75 x 3.90 in, 95.2 x 99 mm); max power (DIN): 120 hp at 3,600 rpm; max torque (DIN): 201 lb ft, 27.7 kg m at 1,800 rpm; max engine rpm: 4,000; 28.4 hp/l; 1 Carter BBD 8129 downdraught twin barrel carburettor.

TRANSMISSION gears: 4, fully synchronized; ratios: I 3.500, II 2.210, III 1.430, IV 1, rev 3.390; axle ratio: 2.530.

PERFORMANCE max speed: about 93 mph, 150 km/h; power-weight ratio: Sedan 26.2 lb/hp, 11.9 kg/hp - St. Wagon 26.7 lb/hp, 12.1 kg/hp; speed in direct drive at 1,000 rpm: 23.5 mph, 37.5 km/h; consumption: 22.8 m/imp gal, 19 m/US gal, 12.4 l x 100 km.

DIMENSIONS AND WEIGHT weight: plus 12 lb, 6 kg.

100 hp power team

(for California only).

See 120 hp power team, except for:

ENGINE max power (DIN): 100 hp at 3,400 rpm; max torque (DIN): 200 lb ft, 27.6 kg m at 1,600 rpm; max engine rpm: 3,800; 23.6 hp/l; 1 Carter YF 7235 downdraught single barrel carburettor.

TRANSMISSION axle ratio: 3.080.

PERFORMANCE max speed: about 90 mph, 145 km/h; power-weight ratio: Sedan 31.5 lb/hp, 14.3 kg/hp - St. Wagon 32 lb/hp, 14.5 kg/hp; speed in direct drive at 1,000 rpm: 24.5 mph, 39.4 km/h; consumption: 19.2 m/imp gal, 16 m/US gal, 14.7 l x 100 km.

OPTIONALS Torque-Command automatic transmission with 3.080 axle ratio.

130 hp power team

See 90 hp power team, except for:

ENGINE 8 cylinders; 304 cu in, 4,982 cc (3.75 x 3.44 in, 95.2 x 87.3 mm); compression ratio: 8.4:1; max power (DIN): 130 hp at 3,200 rpm; max torque (DIN): 238 lb ft, 32.8 kg m at 2,000 rpm; max engine rpm: 3,600; 26.1 hp/l; 5 crankshaft bearings; camshafts: 1, at centre of Vee; 1 Ford 2V 8DA2 downdraught twin barrel carburettor; cooling system: 29.9 imp pt, 35.9 US pt, 17 l.

TRANSMISSION gearbox: Torque-Command automatic transmission (standard), max ratio of converter at stall 2, possible manual selection; ratios: I 2.450, II 1.450, III 1, rev 2.200; lever: central or steering column; axle ratio: 2.870; width of rims: 6''; tyres: E78 x 14.

PERFORMANCE max speed: about 99 mph, 160 km/h; power-weight ratio: 25.8 lb/hp, 11.7 kg/hp - St. Wagon 26.2 lb/hp, 11.9 kg/hp; speed in direct drive at 1,000 rpm: 27.6 mph, 44.4 km/h; consumption: 19.2 m/imp gal, 16 m/US gal, 14.7 l x 100 km.

ELECTRICAL EQUIPMENT 40 A alternator.

DIMENSIONS AND WEIGHT weight: plus 217 lb, 98 kg.

OPTIONALS 3.150 or 2.560 axle ratio; ER78 x 14 tyres with 6'' wide rims.

Concord Series

PRICES EX WORKS:

Concord 2-door Sedan	$ 3,699
Concord 4-door Sedan	$ 3,799
Concord Hatchback	$ 3,799
Concord Station Wagon	$ 3,999

For 120 hp engine add $ 120 (for 130 hp engine add $ 233).

Power team:	Standard for:	Optional for:
90 hp	all	—
120 hp	—	all
100 hp	—	all
130 hp	—	all

90 hp power team

(not available in California).

ENGINE front, 4 stroke; 6 cylinders, in line; 232 cu in, 3,802 cc (3.75 x 3.50 in, 95.2 x 88.8 mm); compression ratio: 8:1; max power (DIN): 90 hp at 3,400 rpm; max torque (DIN): 168 lb ft, 23.2 kg m at 1,600 rpm; max engine rpm: 3,800; 23.7 hp/l; cast iron block and head; 7 crankshaft bearings; valves: overhead, in line, push-rods and rockers, hydraulic tappets; camshafts: 1, side; lubrication: gear pump, full flow filter, 8.3 imp pt, 9.9 US pt, 4.7 l; 1 Carter YF 7229 downdraught single barrel carburettor; cleaner air system with catalytic converter; fuel feed: mechanical pump; water-cooled, 18.3 imp pt, 22 US pt, 10.4 l.

TRANSMISSION driving wheels: rear; clutch: single dry plate; gearbox: mechanical; gears: 3, fully synchronized; ratios: I 2.990, II 1.750, III 1, rev 3.170; lever: central; final drive: hypoid bevel; axle ratio: 2.730; width of rims: 5''; tyres: C78 x 14.

PERFORMANCE max speed: about 85 mph, 136 km/h; power-weight ratio: 4-dr. Sedan 33.7 lb/hp, 15.3 kg/hp; speed in direct drive at 1,000 rpm: 22.1 mph, 35.6 km/h; consumption: 26.4 m/imp gal, 22 m/US gal, 10.7 l x 100 km.

CHASSIS integral; front suspension: independent, wishbones, coil springs, anti-roll bar, telescopic dampers; rear: rigid axle, torque tube, semi-elliptic leafsprings, telescopic dampers.

STEERING recirculating ball; turns lock to lock: 6.

AMERICAN MOTORS Concord D/L 2-door Sedan

BRAKES front disc (diameter 10.80 in, 27.4 cm), front internal radial fins, rear drum; swept area: total 310.65 sq in, 2,004 sq cm.

ELECTRICAL EQUIPMENT 12 V; 50 Ah battery; 37 A alternator; Motorcraft electronic distributor; 2 headlamps.

DIMENSIONS AND WEIGHT wheel base: 108 in, 274 cm; front track: 57.78 in, 147 cm; rear track: 57.06 in, 145 cm - sedans 57.50 in, 146 cm; length: 183.56 in, 466 cm; width: 71.12 in, 181 cm; height: 51.70 in, 131 cm - 4-dr. Sedan and St. Wagon 51.30 in, 130 cm; ground clearance: 4.08 in, 10.4 cm - 4-dr. Sedan and Station Wagon 3.65 in, 9.3 cm; weight: 2-dr. Sedan 2,961 lb, 1,343 kg - 4-dr. Sedan 3,031 lb, 1,375 kg - Hatchback 2,983 lb, 1,353 kg - St. Wagon 3,064 lb, 1,390 kg; turning circle (between walls): 38.6 ft, 11.8 m; fuel tank: 18.3 imp gal, 22 US gal, 83 l.

OPTIONALS 4-speed fully synchronized mechanical gearbox (I 3.500, II 2.210, III 1.430, IV 1, rev 3.390), central lever, 2.530 axle ratio; Torque-Command automatic transmission, hydraulic torque converter and planetary gears with 3 ratios (I 2.450, II 1.450, III 1, rev 2.200), max ratio of converter at stall 2.10, possible manual selection, steering column or central lever, 2.730 axle ratio; limited slip differential; D78 x 14 tyres with 5'' wide rims; DR78 x 14 tyres with 6'' wide rims; heavy-duty suspension; heavy-duty cooling system; heavy-duty battery; sports steering wheel; tilt of steering wheel; power steering; servo brake; heated rear window; reclining backrests; tinted glass; heated rear window; aluminum wheels; Sports equipment; D/L equipment; air-conditioning.

120 hp power team

(not available in California).

See 90 hp power team, except for:

ENGINE 258 cu in, 4,228 cc (3.75 x 3.90 in, 95.2 x 99 mm); max power (DIN): 120 hp at 3,600 rpm; max torque (DIN): 201 lb ft, 27.7 kg m at 1,800 rpm; max engine rpm: 4,000; 28.4 hp/l; 1 Carter BBD 8129 downdraught twin barrel carburettor.

TRANSMISSION gears: 4, fully synchronized; ratios: I 3.500, II 2.210, III 1.430, IV 1, rev 3.390; axle ratio: 2.530.

PERFORMANCE max speed: about 93 mph, 150 km/h; power-weight ratio: 4-dr. Sedan 25.4 lb/hp, 11.5 kg/hp; speed in direct drive at 1,000 rpm: 23.5 mph, 37.5 km/h; consumption: 22.8 m/imp gal, 19 m/US gal, 12.4 l x 100 km.

DIMENSIONS AND WEIGHT weight: plus 12 lb, 6 kg.

OPTIONALS Torque-Command automatic transmission with 2.530 or 2.730 axle ratio.

100 hp power team

(for California only).

See 120 hp power team, except for:

ENGINE max power (DIN): 100 hp at 3,400 rpm; max torque (DIN): 200 lb ft, 27.6 kg m at 1,600 rpm; max engine rpm: 3,800; 23.6 hp/l; 1 Carter YF 7235 downdraught single barrel carburettor.

TRANSMISSION axle ratio: 2.730.

PERFORMANCE max speed: about 90 mph, 145 km/h; power-weight ratio: 4-dr. Sedan 30.6 lb/hp, 13.9 kg/hp; speed in direct drive at 1,000 rpm: 24.5 mph, 39.4 km/h; consumption: 19.2 m/imp gal, 16 m/US gal, 14.7 l x 100 km.

DIMENSIONS AND WEIGHT weight: plus 12 lb, 6 kg.

OPTIONALS Torque-Command automatic transmission with 3.080 axle ratio.

130 hp power team

See 90 hp power team, except for:

ENGINE 8 cylinders; 304 cu in, 4,982 cc (3.75 x 3.44 in, 95.2 x 87.3 mm); compression ratio: 8.4:1; max power (DIN): 130 hp at 3,200 rpm; max torque (DIN): 238 lb ft, 32.8 kg m at 2,000 rpm; max engine rpm: 3,600; 26.1 hp/l; 5 crankshaft bearings; camshafts: 1, at centre of Vee; 1 Ford 2V 8DA2 downdraught twin barrel carburettor; cooling system: 29.9 imp pt, 35.9 US pt, 17 l.

TRANSMISSION gearbox: Torque-Command automatic transmission (standard), max ratio of converter at stall 2, possible manual selection; ratios: I 2.450, II 1.450, III 1, rev 2.200; lever: steering column or central; axle ratio: 2.870; tyres: D70 x 14.

AMERICAN MOTORS Concord D/L 2-door Sedan

130 HP POWER TEAM

PERFORMANCE max speed: about 99 mph, 160 km/h; power-weight ratio: 4-dr. Sedan 25.1 lb/hp, 11.4 kg/hp; speed in direct drive at 1,000 rpm: 27.6 mph, 44.4 km/h; consumption: 19.2 m/imp gal, 16 m/US gal, 14.7 l x 100 km.

ELECTRICAL EQUIPMENT 40 A alternator.

DIMENSIONS AND WEIGHT weight: plus 227 lb, 103 kg.

OPTIONALS 4-speed fully synchronized mechanical gearbox not available; DR x 14 tyres with 6'' wide rims.

AMX

PRICE EX WORKS: $ 4,599

120 hp power team

(standard, not available in California).

ENGINE front, 4 stroke; 6 cylinders, in line; 258 cu in, 4,228 cc (3.75 x 3.90 in, 95.2 x 99 mm); compression ratio: 8:1; max power (DIN): 120 hp at 3,600 rpm; max torque (DIN): 201 lb ft, 27.7 kg m at 1,800 rpm; max engine rpm: 4,000; 28.4 hp/l; cast iron block and head; 7 crankshaft

AMERICAN MOTORS AMX Hatchback

bearings; valves: overhead, in line, push-rods and rockers, hydraulic tappets; camshafts: 1, side; lubrication: gear pump, full flow filter, 8.3 imp pt, 9.9 US pt, 4.7 l; 1 Carter BBD 8129 downdraught twin barrel carburettor; cleaner air system; exhaust system with catalytic converter; fuel feed: mechanical pump; water-cooled, 18.3 imp pt, 22 US pt, 10.4 l.

TRANSMISSION driving wheels: rear; clutch: single dry plate; gearbox: mechanical; gears: 4, fully synchronized; ratios: I 3.500, II 2.210, III 1.430, IV 1, rev 3.390; lever: central; final drive: hypoid bevel; axle ratio: 2.530; width of rims: 6''; tyres: DR78 x 14.

PERFORMANCE max speed: about 93 mph, 150 km/h; power-weight ratio: 25.8 lb/hp, 11.7 kg/hp; speed in direct drive at 1,000 rpm: 23.5 mph, 37.5 km/h; consumption: 22.8 m/imp gal, 19 m /US gal, 12.4 l x 100 km.

CHASSIS integral; front suspension: independent, wishbones, coil springs, anti-roll bar, telescopic dampers; rear: rigid axle, torque tube, semi-elliptic leafsprings, telescopic dampers.

STEERING recirculating ball; turns lock to lock: 6.

BRAKES front disc (diameter 10.80 in, 27.4 cm), front internal radial fins, rear drum; swept area: total 310.65 sq in, 2,004 sq cm.

ELECTRICAL EQUIPMENT 12 V; 50 Ah battery; 37 A alternator; Motorcraft electronic distributor.

DIMENSIONS AND WEIGHT wheel base: 108 in, 274 cm; tracks: 57.78 in, 147 cm front, 57.06 in, 145 rear; length:

184.26 in, 468 cm; width: 71 in, 180 cm; height: 52.06 in, 132 cm; ground clearance: 4.08 in, 10.4 cm; weight: 3,090 lb, 1,402 kg; turning circle (between walls): 38.6 ft, 11.8 m; fuel tank: 18.3 imp gal, 22 US gal, 83 l.

BODY hatchback; 2 doors; 4 seats, separate front seats.

OPTIONALS limited slip differential; Torque-Command automatic transmission with 3 ratios (I 2.450, II 1.450, III 1, rev 2.200), max ratio of converter at stall 2.10, possible manual selection, central lever, 2.530 axle ratio; Levi's interior; heavy-duty suspension; heavy-duty cooling system; heavy-duty battery; tilt of steering wheel; power steering; servo brake; heated rear window; tinted glass; air-conditioning.

100 hp power team

(standard, for California only).

See 120 hp power team, except for:

ENGINE max power (DIN): 100 hp at 3,400 rpm; max torque (DIN): 200 lb ft, 27.6 kg m at 1,600 rpm; max engine rpm: 3,800; 23.6 hp/l; 1 Carter YF 7235 downdraught single barrel carburettor.

TRANSMISSION axle ratio: 2.730.

PERFORMANCE max speed: about 90 mph, 145 km/h; power-weight ratio: 30.9 lb/hp, 14 kg/hp; speed in direct drive

AMERICAN MOTORS Matador Station Wagon

at 1,000 rpm: 24.5 mph, 39.4 km/h; consumption: 19.2 m/imp gal, 16 m/US gal, 14.7 l x 100 km.

OPTIONALS Torque-Command automatic transmission with 3.080 axle ratio.

130 hp power team

(optional).

See 120 hp power team, except for:

ENGINE 8 cylinders; 304 cu in, 4,982 cc (3.75 x 3.44 in, 95.2 x 87.3 mm); compression ratio: 8.4:1; max power (DIN): 130 hp at 3,200 rpm; max torque (DIN): 238 lb ft, 32.8 kg m at 2,000 rpm; max engine rpm: 3,600; 26.1 hp/l; 5 crankshaft bearings; camshafts: 1, at centre of Vee; 1 Ford 2V 8DA2 downdraught twin barrel carburettor; cooling system: 29.9 imp pt, 35.9 US pt, 17 l.

TRANSMISSION gearbox: Torque-Command automatic transmission (standard), max ratio of converter at stall 2, possible manual selection; ratio: I 2.450, II 1.450, III 1, rev 2.200; lever: central; axle ratio: 2.870.

PERFORMANCE max speed: about 99 mph, 160 km/h; power-weight ratio: 25.6 lb/hp, 11.6 kg/hp; speed in direct drive at 1,000 rpm: 27.6 mph, 44.4 km/h; consumption: 19.2 m/imp gal, 16 m/US gal, 14.7 l x 100 km.

ELECTRICAL EQUIPMENT 40 A alternator.

DIMENSIONS AND WEIGHT weight: plus 227 lb, 103 kg.

Matador Series

PRICES EX WORKS:

1 Matador Coupé	$ 4,799
2 Matador Sedan	$ 4,849
3 Matador Station Wagon	$ 5,299

For V8 engine add $ 190.

Power team:	Standard for:	Optional for:
120 hp	1,2	—
140 hp	3	1,2

120 hp power team

(not available in California).

ENGINE front, 4 stroke; 6 cylinders, in line; 258 cu in, 4,228 cc (3.75 x 3.90 in, 95.2 x 99 mm); compression ratio: 8:1; max power (DIN): 120 hp at 3,600 rpm; max torque (DIN): 201 lb ft, 27.7 kg m at 1,800 rpm; max engine rpm: 4,000; 28.4 hp/l; cast iron block and head; 7 crankshaft bearings; valves: overhead, in line, push-rods and rockers, hydraulic tappets; camshafts: 1, side; lubrication: gear pump, full flow filter, 8.3 imp pt, 9.9 US pt, 4.7 l; 1 Carter BBD 8128 downdraught twin barrel carburettor; cleaner air system; exhaust system with catalytic converter; fuel feed: mechanical pump; water-cooled, 19.2 imp pt, 23 US pt, 10.9 l - Coupé 22.5 imp pt, 27.1 US pt, 12.8 l.

TRANSMISSION driving wheels: rear; gearbox: Torque-Command automatic transmission, hydraulic torque converter and planetary gears with 3 ratios, max ratio of converter at stall 2, possible manual selection; ratios: I 2.450, II 1.450, III 1, rev 2.200; lever: steering column; final drive: hypoid bevel; axle ratio: 3.150; width of rims; Sedan 5''- Coupé 6''; tyres: F78 x 14.

PERFORMANCE max speed: about 90 mph, 145 km/h; power-weight ratio: 30.2 lb/hp, 13.7 kg/hp; speed in direct drive at 1,000 rpm: 22.5 mph, 36.2 km/h; consumption: 19.2 m/imp gal, 16 m/US gal, 14.7 l x 100 km.

CHASSIS integral; front suspension: independent, wishbones, coil springs, anti-roll bar, telescopic dampers; rear: rigid axle, lower trailing radius arms, upper oblique torque arms, coil springs, telescopic dampers.

STEERING recirculating ball, servo; turns lock to lock: 3.30.

BRAKES front disc (diameter 10.80 in, 27.4 cm), front internal radial fins, rear drum, servo; swept area: total 359.54 sq in, 2,319 sq cm.

ELECTRICAL EQUIPMENT 12 V; 50 Ah battery; 37 A alternator; Motorcraft electronic distributor; 2 headlamps.

DIMENSIONS AND WEIGHT wheel base: 118 in, 300 cm - Coupé 114 in, 289 cm; tracks: 59.70 in, 152 cm front, 60.62 in, 154 cm rear; length: Coupé 209.90 in, 533 cm - Sedan 218.34 in, 554 cm; width: Coupé 77.40 in, 197 cm - Sedan 77.30 in, 196 cm; height: Coupé 51.60 in, 131 cm - Sedan 53.91 in, 137 cm; ground clearance: Coupé 4.88 in, 12.4 cm - Sedan 4.71 in, 12 cm; weight: Coupé 3,622 lb, 1,643 kg - Sedan 3,631 lb, 1,647 kg; turning circle (between walls): Coupé 41.4 ft, 12.6 m - Sedan 42.5 ft, 13 m; fuel tank: 20.9 imp gal, 25 US gal, 95 l.

OPTIONALS limited slip differential; FR78 x 14, GR78 x 15, H78 x 14 or HR78 x 14 tyres with 6'' wide rims; anti-roll bar on rear suspension; tilt of steering wheel; electric windows except for Coupé; heated rear window; heavy-duty battery; heavy-duty cooling system; air-conditioning.

140 hp power team

See 120 hp power team, except for:

ENGINE 8 cylinders; 360 cu in, 5,899 cc (4.08 x 3.44 in, 103.6 x 87.3 mm); compression ratio: 8.25:1; max power (DIN): 140 hp at 3,350 rpm; max torque (DIN): 278 lb ft, 38.3 kg m at 2,000 rpm; max engine rpm: 3,800; 23.7 hp/l; 5 crankshaft bearings; camshafts: 1, at centre of Vee; 1 Ford 2V 8RA2 (8RA2C for California only) downdraught twin barrel carburettor; cooling system: 25.9 imp pt, 31.1 US pt, 14.7 l - Coupé 29.2 imp pt, 35.1 US pt, 16.6 l.

TRANSMISSION gearbox: Torque-Command automatic transmission with max ratio of converter at stall 2; axle ratio: 2.870 (3.150 for California); width of rims: St. Wagon 6''; tyres: St. Wagon H78 x 14.

PERFORMANCE max speed: about 96 mph, 155 km/h; power-weight ratio: 27.3 lb/hp, 12.4 kg/hp - St. Wagon 30 lb/hp, 13.6 kg/hp; speed in direct drive at 1,000 rpm: 26 mph, 40.8 km/h; consumption: 16.8 m/imp gal, 14 m/US gal, 16.8 l x 100 km.

ELECTRICAL EQUIPMENT 60 Ah battery; 40 A alternator.

DIMENSIONS AND WEIGHT front track: St. Wagon 59.54 in, 151 cm; length: St. Wagon 219.28 in, 557 cm; width: St. Wagon 77.20 in, 196 cm; height: St. Wagon 56 in, 142 cm; ground clearance: St. Wagon 6.46 in, 16.4 cm; weight: St. Wagon 4,208 lb, 1,908 kg - Coupé and Sedan plus 204 lb, 92 kg; turning circle (between walls): St. Wagon 42.5 ft, 13 m; fuel tank: St. Wagon 17.6 imp gal, 21 US gal, 80 l.

OPTIONALS heated rear window not available for St. Wagon.

ANTIQUE-CLASSIC   USA

Frazer Nash

PRICES EX WORKS: $ 4,995 (body only)
                 $ 1,995 (kit only)

ENGINE Volkswagen, rear, 4 stroke; 4 cylinders, horizontally opposed; 96.7 cu in, 1,584 cc (3.37 x 2.72 in, 85.5 x 69 mm); compression ratio: 8.5:1; max power (DIN): 50 hp at 4,000 rpm; max torque (DIN): 78 lb ft, 10.8 kg m at 2,800 rpm; max engine rpm: 4,600; 31.6 hp/l; block with cast iron liners and light alloy fins, light alloy head; 4 crankshaft bearings; valves: overhead, push-rods and rockers; camshafts: 1, central, lower; lubrication: gear pump, filter in sump, oil cooler, 4.4 imp pt, 5.3 US pt, 2.5 l; 1 Solex 34 PICT 2 downdraught carburettor; fuel feed: mechanical pump; air-cooled.

TRANSMISSION driving wheels: rear; clutch: single dry plate; gearbox: mechanical; gears: 4, fully synchronized; ratios: I 3.780, II 2.060, III 1.260, IV 0.930, rev 4.010; lever: central; final drive: spiral bevel; axle ratio: 3.875; width of rims: 4''; tyres: 5.60 x 15.

PERFORMANCE max speed: 90 mph, 145 km/h; power-weight ratio: 32 lb/hp, 14.5 kg/hp; consumption: 30.7 m/imp gal, 25.6 m/US gal, 9.2 l x 100 km.

CHASSIS backbone platform; front suspension: independent, twin swinging longitudinal trailing arms, transverse laminated torsion bar, anti-roll bar, telescopic dampers; rear: independent, swinging semi-axles, swinging longitudinal trailing arms, transverse torsion bars, telescopic dampers.

STEERING worm and roller.

BRAKES drum; lining area: total 111 sq in, 716 sq cm.

ELECTRICAL EQUIPMENT 12 V; 36 Ah battery; alternator; Bosch distributor; 4 headlamps.

DIMENSIONS AND WEIGHT wheel base: 108.50 in, 276 cm; tracks: 51.50 in, 131 cm front, 53.10 in, 135 cm rear; length: 177.50 in, 451 cm; height: 58 in, 147 cm; ground clearance: 5.90 in, 15 cm; weight: 1,600 lb, 726 kg; weight distribution: 30% front, 70% rear; fuel tank: 8.8 imp gal, 10.6 US gal, 40 l.

BODY roadster; 2 doors; 2 seats.

OPTIONALS tonneau cover.

ANTIQUE-CLASSIC Frazer Nash

AUBURN   USA

Speedster

PRICE EX WORKS: $ 24,900

ENGINE Lincoln Continental, front, 4 stroke; 8 cylinders; 460 cu in, 7,539 cc (4.36 x 3.85 in, 110.7 x 97.8 mm); compression ratio: 8:1; max power (DIN): 208 hp at 4,000 rpm; max torque (DIN): 356 lb ft, 49.1 kg m at 2,000 rpm; max engine rpm: 4,400; 27.6 hp/l; cast iron block and head; 5 crankshafts bearings; valves: overhead, in line, push-rods and rockers, hydraulic tappets; camshafts: 1, at centre of Vee; lubrication: rotary pump, full flow filter, 8.3 imp pt, 9.9 US pt, 4.7 l; 1 Motorcraft 9510 D7VE-AA downdraught 4-barrel carburettor; cleaner air system; dual exhaust system with catalytic converter; fuel feed: mechanical pump; water-cooled, 30.8 imp pt, 37 US pt, 17.5 l.

TRANSMISSION driving wheels: rear; gearbox: Select-Shift Merc-O-Matic automatic transmission, hydraulic torque converter and planetary gears with 3 ratios, max ratio of converter at stall 2.03, possible manual selection; ratios: I 2.460, II 1.460, III 1, rev 2.180; lever: central; final drive: hypoid bevel, limited slip differential; axle ratio: 2.750; width of rims: 6''; tyres: JR78 x 15.

PERFORMANCE not declared.

CHASSIS box-type ladder frame; front suspension: independent, wishbones, lower trailing arms, coil springs, anti-roll bar, telescopic dampers; rear: rigid axle, lower trailing radius arms, upper torque arms, transverse linkage bar, coil springs, telescopic dampers.

STEERING recirculating ball, tilt of steering wheel, servo.

BRAKES front disc, front internal radial fins, rear drum.

ELECTRICAL EQUIPMENT 12 V; 68 Ah battery; 60 A alternator; Motorcraft transistorized ignition; 2 headlamps.

DIMENSIONS AND WEIGHT wheel base: 127 in, 323 cm; tracks: 63 in, 160 cm front, 65 in, 165 cm rear; length: 191 in, 485 cm; height: 58 in, 147 cm; ground clearance: 7 in, 17.8 cm; weight: 3,200 lb, 1,451 kg; weight distribution: 50% front, 50% rear; fuel tank: 15 imp gal, 18 US gal, 68 l.

BODY convertible in plastic material; 2 doors; 2 seats; leather interior.

OPTIONALS tonneau cover; wire wheels; air-conditioning.

Dual Cowl Phaeton

PRICE EX WORKS: $ 60,000

ENGINE Lincoln Continental, front, 4 stroke; 8 cylinders; 460 cu in, 7,539 cc (4.36 x 3.85 in, 110.7 x 97.8 mm); compression ratio: 8:1; max power (DIN): 208 hp at 4,000 rpm; max torque (DIN): 356 lb ft, 49.1 kg m at 2,000 rpm; max engine rpm: 4,400; 27.6 hp/l; cast iron block and head; 5 crankshaft bearings; valves: overhead, in line, push-rods and rockers, hydraulic tappets; camshafts: 1, at centre of Vee; lubrication: rotary pump, full flow filter, 8.3 imp pt, 9.9 US pt, 4.7 l; 1 Motorcraft 9510 D7VE-AA downdraught 4-barrel carburettor; cleaner air system; dual exhaust system with catalytic converter; fuel feed: mechanical pump; water-cooled, 30.8 imp pt, 37 US pt, 17.5 l.

TRANSMISSION driving wheels: rear; gearbox: Select-Shift Merc-O-Matic automatic transmission, hydraulic torque con-

---

AUBURN Dual Cowl Phaeton

AVANTI II Coupé

DUAL COWL PHAETON

verter and planetary gears with 3 ratios, max ratio of converter at stall 2.03, possible manual selection; ratios: I 2.460, II 1.460, III 1, rev 2.180; lever: central; final drive: hypoid bevel, limited slip differential; axle ratio: 2.750; width of rims: 6''; tyres: JR78 x 15.

PERFORMANCE not declared.

CHASSIS box-type ladder frame; front suspension: independent, wishbones, lower trailing arms, coil springs, anti-roll bar, telescopic dampers; rear: rigid axle, lower trailing radius arms, upper torque arms, transverse linkage bar, coil springs, telescopic dampers.

STEERING recirculating ball, tilt of steering wheel, servo.

BRAKES front disc, front internal radial fins, rear drum.

ELECTRICAL EQUIPMENT 12 V; 68 Ah battery; 60 A alternator; Motorcraft transistorized ignition; 2 headlamps.

DIMENSIONS AND WEIGHT wheel base: 140 in, 356 cm; tracks: 63 in, 160 cm front, 65 in, 165 cm rear; length: 204 in, 518 cm; height: 58 in, 147 cm; ground clearance: 7 in, 17.8 cm; weight: 4,100 lb, 1,860 kg; weight distribution: 50% front, 50% rear; fuel tank: 20.9 imp gal, 25 US gal, 95 l.

BODY convertible in plastic material; 4 doors; 4 seats, bench front seats; leather interior; tonneau cover; air-conditioning.

OPTIONALS wire wheels.

AVANTI   USA

Avanti II

PRICE EX WORKS: $ 15,970

ENGINE Chevrolet, front, 4 stroke; 8 cylinders; 350 cu in, 5,736 cc (4 x 3.48 in, 101.6 x 88.3 mm); compression ratio: 8.2:1; max power (DIN): 185 hp at 4,000 rpm; max torque (DIN): 280 lb ft, 38.6 kg m at 2,400 rpm; max engine rpm: 4,400; 32.3 hp/l; cast iron block and head; 5 crankshaft bearings; valves: overhead, in line, push-rods and rockers, hydraulic tappets; camshafts: 1, at centre of Vee; lubrication: gear pump, full flow filter, 8.3 imp pt, 9.9 US pt, 4.7 l; 1 Rochester 17058202 (17058502 for California only) downdraught 4-barrel carburettor; cleaner air system; dual exhaust system with catalytic converter; fuel feed: mechanical pump; water-cooled, 34.5 imp pt, 41.4 US pt, 19.6 l, viscous-coupling thermostatic fan.

TRANSMISSION driving wheels: rear; gearbox: Turbo-Hydramatic automatic transmission, hydraulic torque converter and planetary gears with 3 ratios, max ratio of converter at stall 2, possible manual selection; ratios: I 2.520, II 1.520, III 1, rev 1.940; lever: central; final drive: hypoid bevel; axle ratio: 3.070; width of rims: 6''; tyres: F78 x 15.

PERFORMANCE max speed: 120 mph, 193 km/h; power-weight ratio: 19.3 lb/hp, 8.7 kg/hp; speed in direct drive at 1,000 rpm: 28 mph, 45 km/h; consumption: 18 m/imp gal, 15 m/US gal, 15.6 l x 100 km.

CHASSIS box-type ladder frame, X cross members; front suspension: independent, wishbones, coil springs, anti-roll bar, telescopic dampers; rear: rigid axle, semi-elliptic leafsprings, upper torque arms, anti-roll bar, telescopic dampers.

STEERING cam and lever, tilt of steering wheel, servo.

BRAKES front disc with internal radial fins, rear drum, servo.

ELECTRICAL EQUIPMENT 12 V; 61 Ah battery; 37 A alternator; Delco-Remy high energy ignition system; 2 headlamps.

DIMENSIONS AND WEIGHT wheel base: 109 in, 277 cm; tracks: 57.37 in, 146 cm front, 56.56 in, 144 cm rear; length: 197.80 in, 502 cm; width: 70.40 in, 179 cm; height: 54.40 in, 138 cm; ground clearance: 6.19 in, 15.7 cm; weight: 3,570 lb, 1,619 kg; turning circle (between walls): 37.5 ft, 11.4 m; fuel tank: 15.8 imp gal, 19 US gal, 72 l.

BODY coupé, in plastic material; 2 doors; 4 seats, separate front seats, built-in headrests; heated rear window; tinted glass; air-conditioning.

OPTIONALS electric sunshine roof; electric windows; luxury equipment; leather upholstery; fog lamps; automatic speed control; reclining front seats; Borrani wire wheels; FR78 x 15 tyres.

BRADLEY   USA

GT I Coupé

PRICES EX WORKS: $ 3,995 (body only)
$ 2,995 (kit only)

ENGINE Volkswagen, rear, 4 stroke; 4 cylinders, horizontally opposed; 96.7 cu in, 1,584 cc (3.37 x 2.72 in, 85.5 x 69 mm); compression ratio: 7.5:1; max power (DIN): 50 hp at 4,000 rpm; max torque (DIN): 78 lb ft, 10.8 kg m at 2,800 rpm; max engine rpm: 4,600; 31.6 hp/l; block with cast iron liners and light alloy fins, light alloy head; 4 crankshaft bearings; valves: overhead, push-rods and rockers; camshafts: 1, central, lower; lubrication: gear pump, filter in sump, oil cooler, 5.3 imp pt, 6.3 US pt, 3 l; 2 Solex 32 PDSIT downdraught carburettors; fuel feed: mechanical pump; air-cooled, electric thermostatic fan.

TRANSMISSION driving wheels: rear; clutch: single dry plate; gearbox: mechanical; gears: 4 fully synchronized; ratios: I 3.800, II 2.060, III 1.260, IV 0.890, rev. 3.610; lever: central; final drive: spiral bevel; axle ratio: 4.125; width of rims: 6''; tyres: front 175 SR x 14, rear 185 SR x 14.

PERFORMANCE max speed: 103 mph, 165 km/h; power-weight ratio: 28.9 lb/hp, 13.1 kg/hp; speed in top at 1,000 rpm: 21.7 mph, 35 km/h; consumption: 87.7 m/imp gal, 31.4 m/US gal, 7.5 l x 100 km.

CHASSIS backbone platform; front suspension: independent, twin swinging longitudinal trailing arms, transverse torsion bars, anti-roll bar, telescopic dampers; rear: independent, semi-trailing arms, transverse torsion bars, telescopic dampers.

STEERING worm and roller, telescopic damper; turns lock to lock: 2.60.

BRAKES drum.

ELECTRICAL EQUIPMENT 12 V; 45 Ah battery; 280 W dynamo; Bosch distributor; 4 retractable iodine headlamps.

DIMENSIONS AND WEIGHT wheel base: 94.50 in, 240 cm; tracks: 57 in, 14 cm front, 56 in, 142 cm rear; length: 160 in, 406 cm; width: 68 in, 173 cm; height: 45 in, 114 cm; ground clearance: 6.50 in, 16.5 cm; weight: 1,450 lb, 657 kg; weight distribution: 45% front, 55% rear; turning circle (between walls): 34.2 ft, 10.4 m; fuel tank: 9.2 imp gal, 11 US gal, 42 l.

BODY coupé in plastic material; 2 doors; 2 seats; roll bar.

OPTIONALS semi-automatic transmission with 3 ratios; custom exhaust system; tuned engine; air-conditioning.

GT II Coupé

See GT I Coupé, except for:

PRICES EX WORKS: $ 6,000 (body only)
$ 5,000 (kit only)

ENGINE Volkswagen, rear, 4 stroke; 4 cylinders, horizontally opposed; 96.7 cu in, 1,584 cc (3.37 x 2.72 in, 85.5 x 69

BRADLEY GT II Coupé

mm); compression ratio: 7.5:1; max power (SAE): 63 hp at 4,000 rpm; max torque (SAE): 72 lb ft, 9.9 kg m at 2,800 rpm; 39.8 hp/l; 1 Solex 34 PICT 2 downdraught carburettor.

TRANSMISSION gearbox ratios: I 3.780, II 2.060, III 1.260, IV 0.930, rev 3.780; axle ratio: 4.120.

PERFORMANCE max speeds: about 100 mph, 161 km/h; power-weight ratio: 30.2 lb/hp, 13.7 kg/hp; consumption: 35.8 m/imp gal, 30 m/US gal, 7.9 l x 100 km.

ELECTRICAL EQUIPMENT 2 retractable headlamps.

DIMENSIONS AND WEIGHT length: 178 in, 452 cm; width: 69 in, 175 cm; height: 46 in, 117 cm; weight: 1,900 lb, 861 kg; fuel tank: 10.8 imp gal, 13 US gal, 49 l.

BODY coupé in plastic material with steel reinforced roof; 2 doors; 2 seats with built-in headrests; laminated windscreen; tinted glass.

OPTIONALS automatic transmission; light alloy wheels.

BUICK   USA

Skyhawk Series

PRICES EX WORKS:

Skyhawk S Hatchback Coupé	$ 4,103
Skyhawk Hatchback Coupé	$ 4,367

105 hp power team

ENGINE front, 4 stroke; 6 cylinders, Vee-slanted at 90°; 231 cu in, 3,785 cc (3.80 x 3.40 in, 96.5 x 86.4 mm); compression ratio: 8:1; max power (DIN): 105 hp at 3,400 rpm; max torque (DIN): 185 lb ft, 25.5 kg m at 2,000 rpm; max engine rpm: 4,200; 27.7 hp/l; cast iron block and head; 4 crankshaft bearings; valves: overhead, in line, push-rods and rockers, hydraulic tappets; camshafts: 1, at centre of Vee; lubrication: gear pump, full flow filter, 8.3 imp pt, 9.9 US pt, 4.7 l; 1 Rochester 2GE downdraught twin barrel carburettor; cleaner air system; exhaust system with catalytic converter; fuel feed: electric pump; water-cooled, 20.1 imp pt, 24.1 US pt, 11.4 l.

TRANSMISSION driving wheels: rear; clutch: single dry plate; gearbox: mechanical; gears: 4, fully synchronized; ratios: I 3.500, II 2.480, III 1.660, IV 1, rev 3.500; lever: central; final drive: hypoid bevel; axle ratio: 2.930; width of rims: 6'' - Skyhawk S 5''; tyres: BR78 x 13 - Skyhawk S B78 x 13.

PERFORMANCE max speed: about 109 mph, 175 km/h; power-weight ratio: Skyhawk 26.6 lb/hp, 12 kg/hp - Skyhawk S 26.3 lb/hp, 11.9 kg/hp; speed in direct drive at 1,000 rpm: 26.2 mph, 42.2 km/h; consumption: 22.8 m/imp gal° 18 m/US gal, 12.4 l x 100 km.

CHASSIS integral; front suspension: independent, wishbones (lower trailing links), coil springs, anti-roll bar, telescopic dampers; rear: rigid axle, lower trailing radius arms, upper torque arms, transverse linkage bar, coil springs, telescopic dampers.

STEERING recirculating ball; turns lock to lock: 4.40.

BRAKES front disc (diameter 9.74 in, 24.7 cm), front internal radial fins, rear drum; swept area: total 264.7 sq in, 1,707 sq cm.

ELECTRICAL EQUIPMENT 12 V; 2,500 W battery; 37 A alternator; Delco-Remy transistorized ignition; 4 headlamps.

DIMENSIONS AND WEIGHT wheel base: 97 in, 246 cm; tracks: 54.70 in, 139 cm front, 53.60 in, 136 cm rear; length: 179.30 in, 455 cm; width: 65.40 in, 166 cm; height: 50.20 in, 127 cm; ground clearance: 4.90 in, 12.4 cm; weight: Skyhawk 2,789 lb, 1,265 kg - Skyhawk S 2,760 lb, 1,252 kg; turning circle (between walls): 38.5 ft, 11.7 m; fuel tank: 15.4 imp gal, 18.5 US gal, 70 l.

BODY hatchback coupé; 2 + 1 doors; 2 + 2 seats, separate front seats; folding rear seat.

OPTIONALS Turbo-Hydramatic 350 automatic transmission with 3 ratios (I 2.520, II 1.520, III 1, rev 1.930), max ratio of converter at stall 2.25, possible manual selection, central lever, 2.560 or 2.930 axle ratio; 5-speed fully synchronized mechanical gearbox (I 3.400, II 2.080, III 1.390, IV 1, V 0.800, rev 3.360), central lever, 2.930 axle ratio; limited slip differential; BR70 x 13 tyres with 6'' wide rims; power steering; tilt of steering wheel; servo brake; heavy-duty radiator; heavy-duty battery; reclining backrests; tinted glass; heated rear window; air-conditioning; sunshine roof.

Skylark Series

PRICES EX WORKS:

Skylark S Coupé	$ 3,872
Skylark Coupé	$ 3,999
Skylark Hatchback Coupé	$ 4,181
Skylark Sedan	$ 4,074
Skylark Custom Coupé	$ 4,242
Skylark Custom Hatchback Coupé	$ 4,424
Skylark Custom Sedan	$ 4,317

For V8 engines add $ 150.

Power team:	Standard for:	Optional for:
105 hp	all	—
145 hp	—	all
170 hp	—	all

105 hp power team

(not available in California).

ENGINE front, 4 stroke; 6 cylinders, Vee-slanted at 90°; 231 cu in, 3,785 cc (3.80 x 3.40 in, 96.5 x 86.4 mm); compression ratio: 8:1; max power (DIN): 105 hp at 3,400 rpm; max torque (DIN): 185 lb ft, 25.5 kg m at 2,000 rpm; max engine rpm: 4,400; 27.7 hp/l; cast iron block and head; 4 crankshaft bearings; valves: overhead, in line, push-rods and rockers, hydraulic tappets; camshafts: 1, at centre

BUICK Skyhawk Hatchback Coupé

of Vee; lubrication: gear pump, full flow filter, 8.3 imp pt, 9.9 US pt, 4.7 l; 1 Rochester 2GE downdraught twin barrel carburettor; cleaner air system; exhaust system with catalytic converter; fuel feed: electric pump; water-cooled, 21.1 imp pt, 25.4 US pt, 12 l.

TRANSMISSION driving wheels: rear; clutch: single dry plate; gearbox: mechanical; gears: 3, fully synchronized; ratios: I 3.500, II 1.810, III 1, rev 3.620; lever: steering column; final drive: hypoid bevel; axle ratio: 3.080; width of rims: 5''; tyres: E78 x 14   Skylark Custom ER78 x 14.

PERFORMANCE max speed: about 96 mph, 155 km/h; power-weight ratio: Sedan 30.3 lb/hp, 13.8 kg/hp - Custom Sedan 30.6 lb/hp, 13.9 kg/hp; speed in direct drive at 1,000 rpm: 24.2 mph, 39 km/h; consumption: 22.8 m/imp gal, 19 m/US gal, 12.4 l x 100 km.

CHASSIS integral with separate partial front box-type frame; front suspension: independent, wishbones (lower trailing links), coil springs, anti-roll bar, telescopic dampers; rear: rigid axle, semi-elliptic leafsprings, telescopic dampers.

STEERING recirculating ball; turns lock to lock: 4.99.

BRAKES front disc (diameter 11 in, 27.9 cm), front internal radial fins, rear drum; swept area: total 344 sq in, 2,219 sq cm.

ELECTRICAL EQUIPMENT 12 V; 2,500 W battery; 37 A alternator; Delco-Remy transistorized ignition; 2 headlamps.

DIMENSIONS AND WEIGHT wheel base: 111 in, 282 cm; front track: 59.10 in, 150 cm; rear track: 59.70 in, 152 cm - sedans 59.60 in, 151 cm; length: 200.20 in, 508 cm; width: 72.70 in, 185 cm; height: 52.20 in, 133 cm - sedans 53.10 in, 135 cm; ground clearance: 5.20 in, 13.2 cm; weight: Skylark S Coupé 3,172 lb, 1,438 kg - Coupé 3,142 lb, 1,425 kg - Hatchback Coupé 3,234 lb, 1,466 kg - Sedan 3,188 lb, 1,446 kg - Skylark Custom Coupé 3,142 lb, 1,425 kg - Hatchback Coupé 3,263 lb, 1,480 kg - Sedan 3,216 lb, 1,458 kg; turning circle (between walls): 41.7 ft, 12.7 m; fuel tank: 17.6 imp gal, 21 US gal, 80 l.

OPTIONALS Turbo-Hydramatic 350 automatic transmission with 3 ratios (I 2.520, II 1.520, III 1, rev 1.930), max ratio of converter at stall 2.25, possible manual selection, 2.560 or 3.230 axle ratio; limited slip differential; ER78 x 14 tyres; FR78 x 14 tyres with 6'' wide rims; anti-roll bar on rear suspension; heavy-duty radiator; heavy-duty battery; power steering; tilt of steering wheel; servo brake; reclining backrests; electric windows; air-conditioning.

145 hp power team

(not available in California).

See 105 hp power team, except for:

ENGINE 8 cylinders; 305 cu in, 4,999 cc (3.80 x 3.40 in, 96.5 x 86.4 mm); compression ratio: 8.5:1; max power (DIN): 145 hp at 3,800 rpm; max torque (DIN): 245 lb ft, 33.8 kg m at 2,400 rpm; 29 hp/l; 5 crankshaft bearings.

TRANSMISSION gearbox: Turbo-Hydramatic 350 automatic transmission (standard), hydraulic torque converter and planetary gears with 3 ratios, max ratio of converter at

BUICK Skylark Custom Coupé

stall 2.25, possible manual selection; ratios: I 2.520, II 1.520, III 1, rev 1.930; axle ratio: 2.410.

PERFORMANCE max speed: about 106 mph, 170 km/h; power-weight ratio: Sedan 23 lb/hp, 10.4 kg/hp - Custom Sedan 23.2 lb/hp, 10.5 kg/hp; speed in direct drive at 1,000 rpm: 27.5 mph, 44.2 km/h.

DIMENSIONS AND WEIGHT weight: plus 150 lb, 68 kg - coupés plus 184 lb, 83 kg.

OPTIONALS 3.080 axle ratio.

170 hp power team

(for California only).

See 105 hp power team, except for:

ENGINE 8 cylinders; 350 cu in, 5,736 cc (4 x 3.48 in, 101.6 x 88.3 mm); compression ratio: 8.5:1; max power (DIN): 170 hp at 3,800 rpm; max torque (DIN): 270 lb ft, 37.2 kg m at 2,400 rpm; max engine rpm: 4,600; 29.6 hp/l; 5 crankshaft bearings; 1 Rochester 4M downdraught 4-barrel carburettor; cooling system: 24.8 imp pt, 29.8 US pt, 14.1 l.

TRANSMISSION gearbox: Turbo-Hydramatic 350 automatic transmission (standard), hydraulic torque converter and planetary gears with 3 ratios, max ratio of converter at stall 2.25, possible manual selection; ratios: I 2.520, II 1.520, III 1, rev 1.930; axle ratio: 2.410.

PERFORMANCE max speed: about 112 mph, 180 km/h; power-weight ratio: Sedan 19.8 lb/hp, 9 kg/hp - Custom Sedan 20 kg/hp; speed in direct drive at 1,000 rpm: 27.5 mph, 14.2 km/h; consumption: 18 m/imp gal, 15 m/US gal, 15.7 l x 100 km.

DIMENSIONS AND WEIGHT weight: plus 184 lb, 83 kg.

OPTIONALS 3.080 axle ratio.

Century Series

PRICES EX WORKS:

1 Century Special Sedan	$ 4,486
2 Century Special Coupé	$ 4,389
3 Century Special Station Wagon	$ 4,976
4 Century Custom Sedan	$ 4,733
5 Century Custom Coupé	$ 4,633
6 Century Custom Station Wagon	$ 5,276
7 Century Sport Coupé	$ 5,019
8 Century Limited Sedan	$ 5,091
9 Century Limited Coupé	$ 4,991

For V8 engines add $ 150 for 3 and 6; add $ 190 for 7; add $ 210 for 1,2,4,5,8 and 9.

Power team	Standard for:	Optional for:
90 hp	all except 3,6	—
105 hp	3,6	all except 3,6
145 hp	—	all
160 hp	—	all except 3,6

90 hp power team

(not available in California).

ENGINE front, 4 stroke; 6 cylinders, Vee-slanted at 90°; 196 cu in, 3,212 cc (3.50 x 3.40 in, 88.9 x 96.4 mm); compression ratio: 8:1; max power (DIN): 90 hp at 3,600 rpm; max torque (DIN): 165 lb ft, 22.8 kg m at 2,000 rpm; max engine rpm: 4,000; 28 hp/l; cast iron block and head; 4 crankshaft bearings; valves: overhead, in line, push-rods and rockers, hydraulic tappets; camshafts: 1, at centre of Vee; lubrication: gear pump, full flow filter, 8.3 imp pt, 9.9 US pt, 4.7 l; 1 Rochester 2GE downdraught twin barrel carburettor; cleaner air system; exhaust system with catalytic converter; fuel feed: mechanical pump; water-cooled, 21.8 imp pt, 26.2 US pt, 12.4 l.

TRANSMISSION driving wheels: rear; clutch: single dry plate; gearbox: mechanical; gears: 3, fully synchronized; ratios: I 3.504, II 1.895, III 1, rev 3.625; lever: central; final drive: hypoid bevel; axle ratio: 2.930; width of rims: 6''; tyres: P185/75 x 14.

PERFORMANCE max speed: about 90 mph, 145 km/h; power-weight ratio: Century Special Sedan 34.3 lb/hp, 15.5 kg/hp; speed in direct drive at 1,000 rpm: 25 mph, 40.3 km/h; consumption: 27.7 m/imp gal, 23 m/US gal, 10.2 l x 100 km.

CHASSIS perimeter box-type frame; front suspension: independent, wishbones (lower trailing links), coil springs, anti-roll bar, telescopic dampers; rear: rigid axle, lower

BUICK Century Limited Sedan

trailing radius arms, upper oblique torque arms, coil springs, telescopic dampers.

STEERING recirculating ball; turns lock to lock: 6.14.

BRAKES front disc (diameter 10.50 in, 26.7 cm), front internal radial fins, rear drum, rear compensator; swept area: total 312.68 sq in, 2,017 sq cm.

ELECTRICAL EQUIPMENT 12 V; 2,500 W battery; 42 A alternator; Delco-Remy transistorized ignition; 2 headlamps.

DIMENSIONS AND WEIGHT wheel base: 108.10 in, 274 cm; tracks: 58.50 in, 149 cm front, 57.80 in, 147 cm rear; length: 195.60 in, 497 cm; width: 72.20 in, 183 cm; height: coupés 53.30 in, 135 cm - sedans 54.20 in, 138 cm; ground clearance: 6.10 in, 15.4 cm; weight: Special Sedan 3,084 lb, 1,399 kg - Coupé 3,073 lb, 1,394 kg - Custom Sedan 3,108 lb, 1,410 kg - Coupé 3,080 lb, 1,397 kg - Sport Coupé 3,097 lb, 1,405 kg - Limited Sedan 3,110 lb, 1,411 kg - Coupé 3,108 lb, 1,410 kg; turning circle (between walls): 43.3 ft, 13.2 m - coupés 42.2 ft, 12.9 m; fuel tank: 15 imp gal, 18.1 US gal, 68 l.

OPTIONALS Turbo-Hydramatic 350 automatic transmission with 3 ratios (I 2.520, II 1.520, III 1, rev 1.930), max ratio of converter at stall 2.25, possible manual selection, steering column or central lever; 2.730 axle ratio; limited slip differential; P195/75 x 14 or P205/70 x 14 tyres; automatic levelling control; anti-roll bar on rear suspension; tilt of steering wheel; power steering; servo brake; heavy-duty cooling system; heavy-duty battery; heated rear window; reclining backrests; electric windows; air-conditioning; electric sunshine roof except for sedans.

105 hp power team

See 90 hp power team, except for:

ENGINE 231 cu in, 3,785 cc (3.80 x 3.40 in, 96.5 x 86.4 mm); max power (DIN): 105 hp at 3,400 rpm; max torque (DIN): 185 lb ft, 25.5 kg m at 2,000 rpm; 27.7 hp/l.

TRANSMISSION gearbox: Turbo-Hydramatic automatic transmission (standard), hydraulic torque converter and planetary gears with 3 ratios, max ratio of converter at stall 2.25, possible manual selection; ratios: I 2.520, II 1.520, III 1, rev 1.930; axle ratio: 2.730; tyres: st. wagons P195/75 x 14.

PERFORMANCE max speed: about 93 mph, 150 km/h; power-weight ratio: Century Special St. Wagon 30.8 lb/hp, 14 kg/hp - Century Custom St. Wagon 31.3 lb/hp, 14.2 kg/hp; speed in direct drive at 1,000 rpm: 25.3 mph, 40.7 km/h; consumption: 26.4 m/imp gal, 22 m/US gal, 10.7 l x 100 km.

DIMENSIONS AND WEIGHT length: st. wagons 194.90 in, 495 cm; height: st. wagons 54.50 in, 138 cm; weight: Century Special St. Wagon 3,232 lb, 1,466 kg - Century Custom St. Wagon 3,289 lb, 1,492 kg.

OPTIONALS 2.410 or 3.230 axle ratio.

145 hp power team

(for California only).

See 90 hp power team, except for:

ENGINE 8 cylinders; 305 cu in, 4,999 cc (3.80 x 3.40 in, 96.5 x 86.4 mm); compression ratio: 8.5:1; max power (DIN): 145 hp at 3,800 rpm; max torque (DIN): 245 lb ft, 33.8 kg m at 2,400 rpm; max engine rpm: 4,400; 29 hp/l; 5 crankshaft bearings.

TRANSMISSION gearbox: Turbo-Hydramatic automatic transmission (standard), hydraulic torque converter and planetary gears with 3 ratios, max ratio of converter at stall 2.25, possible manual selection; ratios: I 2.520, II 1.520, III 1, rev 1.930; axle ratio: 2.290 - st. wagons 2.410; tyres: st. wagons P195/75 x 14.

PERFORMANCE max speed: about 103 mph, 165 km/h; power-weight ratio: Century Special Sedan 21.9 lb/hp, 9.9 kg/hp; speed in direct drive at 1,000 rpm: 25.3 mph, 40.7 km/h; consumption: 20.5 m/imp gal, 17 m/US gal, 13.8 l x 100 km.

DIMENSIONS AND WEIGHT length: st. wagons 194.90 in, 495 cm; height: st. wagons 54.50 in, 138 cm; weight: sedans and coupés plus 98 lb, 44 kg - Century Special St. Wagon 3,232 lb, 1,466 kg - Century Custom St. Wagon 3,289 lb, 1,492 kg.

OPTIONALS 2.730 or 2.560 axle ratio.

160 hp power team

(not available in California).

See 90 hp power team, except for:

ENGINE 8 cylinders; 305 cu in, 4,999 cc (3.80 x 3.40 in, 96.5 x 86.4 mm); compression ratio: 8.5:1; max power (DIN): 160

BUICK Century Custom Station Wagon

hp at 4,000 rpm; max torque (DIN): 235 lb ft, 32.4 kg m at 2,400 rpm; max engine rpm: 4,400; 32 hp/l; 5 crankshaft bearings; 1 Rochester M4ME downdraught 4-barrel carburettor.

TRANSMISSION gearbox: Turbo-Hydramatic automatic transmission (standard), hydraulic torque converter and planetary gears with 3 ratios, max ratio of converter at stall 2.25, possible manual selection; ratios: I 2.520, II 1.520, III 1, rev 1.930; axle ratio: 2.290.

PERFORMANCE max speed: about 106 mph, 170 km/h; power-weight ratio: Century Special Sedan 19.9 lb/hp, 9 kg/hp; speed in direct drive at 1,000 rpm: 26.1 mph, 42 km/h; consumption: 25.2 m/imp gal, 21 m/US gal, 11.2 l x 100 km.

DIMENSIONS AND WEIGHT weight: plus 98 lb, 44 kg.

OPTIONALS 2.730 axle ratio.

Regal Series

PRICES EX WORKS:

1 Regal Coupé	$ 4,852
2 Regal Limited Coupé	$ 5,233
3 Regal Sport Coupé	$ 5,853

For V8 engines add $ 190.

Power team:	Standard for:	Optional for:
90 hp	1,2	—
105 hp	—	1,2
145 hp	—	1,2
150 hp	3	—
160 hp	—	1,2
165 hp	—	3

90 hp power team

(not available in California).

ENGINE front, 4 stroke; 6 cylinders, Vee-slanted at 90°; 196 cu in, 3,212 cc (3.50 x 3.40 in, 88.9 x 96.4 mm); compression ratio: 8:1; max power (DIN): 90 hp at 3,600 rpm; max torque (DIN): 165 lb ft, 22.8 kg m at 2,000 rpm; max engine rpm: 4,000; 28 hp/l; cast iron block and head; 4 crankshaft bearings; valves: overhead, in line, push-rods and rockers, hydraulic tappets; camshafts: 1, at centre of Vee; lubrication: gear pump, full flow filter, 8.3 imp pt, 9.9 US pt, 4.7 l; 1 Rochester 2GE downdraught twin barrel carburettor; cleaner air system; exhaust system with catalytic converter; fuel feed: mechanical pump; water-cooled, 21.8 imp pt, 26.2 US pt, 12.4 l.

TRANSMISSION driving wheels: rear; clutch: single dry plate; gearbox: mechanical; gears: 3, fully synchronized; ratios: I 3.504, II 1.895, III 1, rev 3.625; lever: central; final drive: hypoid bevel; axle ratio: 2.930; width of rims: 6''; tyres: P185/75 x 14.

PERFORMANCE max speed: about 90 mph, 145 km/h; power-weight ratio: 34 lb/hp, 15.4 kg/hp; speed in direct drive at 1,000 rpm: 25 mph, 40.3 km/h; consumption: 27.7 m/imp gal, 23 m/US gal, 10.2 l x 100 km.

CHASSIS perimeter box-type frame; front suspension: independent, wishbones (lower trailing links), coil springs,

anti-roll bar, telescopic dampers; rear: rigid axle, lower trailing radius arms, upper oblique torque arms, coil springs, telescopic dampers.

STEERING recirculating ball; turns lock to lock: 6.14.

BRAKES front disc (diameter 10.50 in, 26.7 cm), front internal radial fins, rear drum, rear compensator; swept area: total 312.68 sq in, 2,017 sq cm.

ELECTRICAL EQUIPMENT 12 V; 2,500 W battery; 42 A alternator; Delco-Remy transistorized ignition; 4 headlamps.

DIMENSIONS AND WEIGHT wheel base: 108.10 in, 274 cm; tracks: 58.50 in, 149 cm front, 57.80 in, 147 cm rear; length: 199.60 in, 507 cm; width: 72.20 in, 183 cm; height: 53.40 in, 136 cm; ground clearance: 6.10 in, 15.4 cm; weight: 3,062 lb, 1,389 kg; turning circle (between walls): 42.2 ft, 12.9 m; fuel tank: 15 imp gal, 18.1 US gal, 68 l.

BODY coupé; 2 doors; 6 seats, bench front seats.

OPTIONALS Turbo-Hydramatic 350 automatic transmission with 3 ratios (I 2.520, II 1.520, III 1, rev 1.930), max ratio of converter at stall 2.25, possible manual selection, steering column or central lever, 2.730 axle ratio; limited slip differential; P195/75 x 14 or P205/70 x 14 tyres; automatic levelling control; anti-roll bar on rear suspension; tilt of steering wheel; power steering; servo brake; heavy-duty cooling system; heavy-duty battery; heated rear window; reclining backrests; electric windows; air-conditioning; electric sunshine roof.

BUICK Regal Sport Coupé (turbocharged engine)

BUICK Regal Sport Coupé

105 hp power team

See 90 hp power team, except for:

ENGINE 231 cu in, 3,785 cc (3.80 x 3.40 in, 96.5 x 86.4 mm); max power (DIN): 105 hp at 3,400 rpm; max torque (DIN): 185 lb ft, 25.5 kg m at 2,000 rpm; 27.7 hp/l.

TRANSMISSION gearbox: mechanical (Turbo-Hydramatic 350 automatic transmission standard for California only); gears: 4, fully synchronized; ratios: I 3.504, II 2.480, III 1.655, IV 1, rev 3.504; axle ratio: 2.930 (2.730 for California only).

PERFORMANCE max speed: about 93 mph, 150 km/h; power-weight ratio: 29.1 lb/hp, 13.2 kg/hp; speed in direct drive at 1,000 rpm: 25.3 mph, 40.7 km/h; consumption: 22.8 m/imp gal, 19 m/US gal, 12.4 l x 100 km.

145 hp power team

(for California only).

See 90 hp power team, except for:

ENGINE 8 cylinders; 305 cu in, 4,999 cc (3.80 x 3.40 in, 96.5 x 86.4 mm); compression ratio: 8.5:1; max power (DIN): 145 hp at 3,800 rpm; max torque (DIN): 245 lb ft, 33.8 kg m at 2,400 rpm; max engine rpm: 4,400; 29 hp/l; 5 crankshaft bearings.

TRANSMISSION gearbox: Turbo-Hydramatic automatic transmission (standard), hydraulic torque converter and planetary gears with 3 ratios, max ratio of converter at stall 2.25, possible manual selection; ratios: I 2.520, II 1.520, III 1, rev 1.930; axle ratio: 2.290.

PERFORMANCE max speed: about 103 mph, 165 km/h; power-weight ratio: 21.8 lb/hp, 9.9 kg/hp; speed in direct drive at 1,000 rpm: 25.3 mph, 40.7 km/h; consumption: 20.5 m/imp gal, 17 m/US gal, 13.8 l x 100 km.

DIMENSIONS AND WEIGHT weight: plus 104 lb, 47 kg.

OPTIONALS 2.730 or 2.560 axle ratio.

150 hp power team

(not available in California).

See 90 hp power team, except for:

ENGINE turbocharged; 231 cu in, 3,785 cc (3.80 x 3.40 in, 96.5 x 86.4 mm); max power (DIN): 150 hp at 3,800 rpm; max torque (DIN): 245 lb, 33.8 kg m at 2,400 rpm; 39.6 hp/l; 1 RPD 17058192 downdraught twin barrel carburettor.

TRANSMISSION gearbox: Turbo-Hydramatic automatic transmission (standard), hydraulic torque converter and planetary gears with 3 ratios, max ratio of converter at stall 2.25, possible manual selection; ratios: I 2.520, II 1.520, III 1, rev 1.930; axle ratio: 2.730.

PERFORMANCE max speed: about 109 mph, 175 km/h; power-weight ratio: 21.1 lb/hp, 9.6 kg/hp; speed in direct drive at 1,000 rpm: 27.3 mph, 43.9 km/h; consumption: 26.4 m/imp gal, 22 m/US gal, 10.7 l x 100 km.

DIMENSIONS AND WEIGHT weight: 3,170 lb, 1,438 kg.

160 hp power team

(not available in California).

See 145 hp power team, except for:

ENGINE max power (DIN): 160 hp at 4,000 rpm; max torque (DIN): 235 lb ft, 32.4 kg m at 2,400 rpm; 32 hp/l; 1 Rochester M4ME downdraught 4-barrel carburettor.

PERFORMANCE max speed: about 106 mph, 170 km/h; power-weight ratio: 19.9 lb/hp, 9 kg/hp; consumption: 25.2 m/imp gal, 21 m/US gal, 11.2 l x 100 km.

DIMENSIONS AND WEIGHT (see 90 hp power team) weight: plus 118 lb, 53 kg.

165 hp power team

See 150 hp power team, except for:

ENGINE turbocharged; max power (DIN): 165 hp at 4,000 rpm; max torque (DIN): 265 lb ft, 36.6 kg m at 2,800 rpm; 43.6 hp/l; 1 RPD 17058240 (17058540 for California only) downdraught 4-barrel carburettor.

PERFORMANCE max speed: about 112 mph, 180 km/h; power-weight ratio: 19.2 lb/hp, 8.7 kg/hp; consumption: 26.4 m/imp gal, 22 m/US gal, 10.7 l x 100 km.

OPTIONALS 2.930 axle ratio.

Le Sabre Series

PRICES EX WORKS:

1 Le Sabre Coupé	$ 5,384
2 Le Sabre Sedan	$ 5,459
3 Le Sabre Custom Coupé	$ 6,657
4 Le Sabre Custom Sedan	$ 5,757
5 Le Sabre Sport Coupé	$ 6,213

For V8 engines add $ 198.

Power team:	Standard for:	Optional for:
105 hp	1 to 4	—
140 hp	—	1 to 4
145 hp	—	1 to 4
150 hp	5	—
155 hp	—	1 to 4
165 hp	—	5
170 hp	—	1 to 4
185 hp	—	1 to 4

105 hp power team

ENGINE front, 4 stroke; 6 cylinders, Vee-slanted at 90°; 231 cu in, 3,785 cc (3.80 x 3.40 in, 96.5 x 86.4 mm); compression ratio: 8:1; max power (DIN): 105 hp at 3,400 rpm; max torque (DIN): 185 lb ft, 25.5 kg m at 2,000 rpm; max engine rpm: 4,200; 27.7 hp/l; cast iron block and head; 4 crankshaft bearings; valves: overhead, in line, push-rods and rockers, hydraulic tappets; camshafts: 1, at centre of Vee; lubrication: gear pump, full flow filter, 8.3 imp pt, 9.9 US pt, 4.7 l; 1 Rochester 2GC downdraught twin barrel carburettor; cleaner air system; exhaust system with catalytic converter; fuel feed: mechanical pump; water-cooled, 21.1 imp pt, 25.4 US pt, 12 l.

TRANSMISSION driving wheels: rear; gearbox: Turbo-Hydramatic 350 automatic transmission, hydraulic torque converter and planetary gears with 3 ratios, max ratio of converter at stall 2.25, possible manual selection; ratios: I 2.520, II 1.520, III 1, rev 1.930; lever: steering column; final drive: hypoid bevel; axle ratio: 2.730; width of rims: 6''; tyres FR78 x 15.

PERFORMANCE max speed: about 96 mph, 155 km/h; power-weight ratio: Le Sabre Sedan 32.4 lb/hp, 14.7 kg/hp; speed in direct drive at 1,000 rpm: 28 mph, 45 km/h; consumption: 23.9 m/imp gal, 20 m/US gal, 11.8 l x 100 km.

CHASSIS perimeter box-type frame; front suspension: independent, wishbones (lower trailing links), coil springs, anti-roll bar, telescopic dampers; rear: rigid axle, lower trailing radius arms, upper oblique torque arms, coil springs, telescopic dampers.

STEERING recirculating ball, variable ratio servo; turns lock to lock: 3.37.

BRAKES front disc (diameter 11 in, 27.9 cm), front internal radial fins, rear drum, servo; swept area: total 344 sq in, 2,219 sq cm.

ELECTRICAL EQUIPMENT 12 V; 2,500 W battery; 42 A alternator; Delco-Remy transistorized ignition; 4 headlamps.

BUICK Le Sabre Sport Coupé

DIMENSIONS AND WEIGHT wheel base: 115.90 in, 294 cm; tracks: 61.80 in, 157 cm front, 60.70 in, 154 cm rear; length: 218.20 in, 554 cm; width: 77.20 in, 196 cm; height: 55 in, 140 cm - sedans 55.70 in, 141 cm; ground clearance: 6.70 in, 17 cm; weight: Le Sabre Coupé 3,386 lb, 1,536 kg - Sedan 3,399 lb, 1,542 kg - Le Sabre Custom Coupé 3,397 lb, 1,541 kg - Sedan 3,446 lb, 1,563 kg; turning circle (between walls): 43 ft, 13.1 m; fuel tank: 17.6 imp gal, 21 US gal, 80 l.

OPTIONALS limited slip differential; 3.230 axle ratio: anti-roll bar on rear suspension; automatic levelling control; GR78 x 15 tyres with 6'' or 7'' wide rims; GR70 x 15 tyres with 7'' wide rims; heavy-duty cooling system; tilt of steering wheel; heated rear window; electric windows; vinyl roof; sunshine roof; air-conditioning.

140 hp power team

(not available in California).

See 105 hp power team, except for:

ENGINE 8 cylinders; 301 cu in, 4,932 cc (4 x 3 in, 101.7 x 76.2 mm); compression ratio: 8.2:1; max power (DIN): 140 hp at 3,600 rpm; max torque (DIN): 235 lb ft, 32.4 kg m at 2,000 rpm; 28.4 hp/l; 5 crankshaft bearings.

TRANSMISSION axle ratio: 2.410.

BUICK Le Sabre Custom Sedan

PERFORMANCE max speed: about 99 mph, 160 km/h; power-weight ratio: Le Sabre Sedan 24.3 lb/hp, 11 kg/hp.

ELECTRICAL EQUIPMENT 3,200 W battery.

OPTIONALS 3.230 axle ratio not available.

145 hp power team

(for California only).

See 105 hp power team, except for:

ENGINE 8 cylinders; 305 cu in, 4,999 cc (3.80 x 3.40 in, 96.5 x 86.4 mm); compression ratio: 8.5:1; max power (DIN): 145 hp at 3,800 rpm; max torque (DIN): 245 lb ft, 33.8 kg m at 2,400 rpm; max engine rpm: 4,400; 29 hp/l; 5 crankshaft bearings.

TRANSMISSION axle ratio: 2.410.

PERFORMANCE max speed: about 103 mph, 165 km/h; power-weight ratio: Le Sabre Sedan 23.4 lb/hp, 10.6 kg/hp; consumption: 18 m/imp gal, 15 m/US gal, 15.7 l x 100 km.

ELECTRICAL EQUIPMENT 3,200 W battery.

OPTIONALS 3.230 axle ratio not available.

150 hp power team

(not available in California).

See 105 hp power team, except for:

ENGINE turbocharged; max power (DIN): 150 hp at 3,800 rpm; max torque (DIN): 245 lb ft, 33.8 kg m at 2,400 rpm; 39.6 hp/l; 1 RPD 17058192 downdraught twin barrel carburettor.

TRANSMISSION axle ratio: 2.560.

PERFORMANCE max speed: about 109 mph, 175 km/h; power-weight ratio: 23.6 lb/hp, 10.7 kg/hp.

DIMENSIONS AND WEIGHT weight: 3,545 lb, 1,608 kg.

OPTIONALS 3.080 axle ratio.

155 hp power team

(not available in California).

See 105 hp power team, except for:

ENGINE 8 cylinders; 350 cu in, 5,736 cc (4.06 x 3.38 in, 103.1 x 85.8 mm); compression ratio: 8:1; max power (DIN): 155 hp at 3,400 rpm; max torque (DIN): 280 lb ft, 38.6 kg m at 1,800 rpm; 27 hp/l; 5 crankshaft bearings; 1 Rochester M4MC downdraught 4-barrel carburettor; cooling system: 24.8 imp pt, 29.8 US pt, 14.1 l.

TRANSMISSION axle ratio: 2.410.

PERFORMANCE max speed: about 103 mph, 165 km/h; power-weight ratio: Le Sabre Sedan 22 lb/hp, 10 kg/hp; consumption: 21.6 m/imp gal, 18 m/US gal, 13.1 l x 100 km.

ELECTRICAL EQUIPMENT 3,200 W battery.

OPTIONALS 2.730 or 3.080 axle ratio.

165 hp power team

See 150 hp power team, except for:

ENGINE turbocharged; max power (DIN): 165 hp at 4,000 rpm; max torque (DIN): 265 lb ft, 36.6 kg m at 2,800 rpm; 43.6 hp/l; 1 RPD 17058240 (17058540 for California only) downdraught 4-barrel carburettor.

TRANSMISSION axle ratio: 3.080.

PERFORMANCE power-weight ratio: 21.5 lb/hp, 9.7 kg/hp.

OPTIONALS 3.230 axle ratio.

170 hp power team

(for California only).

See 105 hp power team, except for:

ENGINE 8 cylinders; 350 cu in, 5,736 cc (4.06 x 3.38 in, 103.1 x 85.8 mm); compression ratio: 7.9:1; max power (DIN): 170 hp at 3,800 rpm; max torque (DIN): 275 lb ft, 37.9 kg m at 2,000 rpm; max engine rpm: 4,600; 29.6 hp/l; 5 crankshaft bearings; 1 Rochester M4MC downdraught 4-barrel carburettor; cooling system: 24.8 imp pt, 29.8 US pt, 14.1 l.

TRANSMISSION axle ratio: 2.410.

PERFORMANCE max speed: about 109 mph, 175 km/h; power-weight ratio: Le Sabre Sedan 20 lb/hp, 9 kg/hp; consumption: 20.5 m/imp gal, 17 m/US gal, 13.8 l x 100 km.

ELECTRICAL EQUIPMENT 3,200 W battery.

OPTIONALS 3.230 axle ratio not available.

185 hp power team

See 105 hp power team, except for:

ENGINE 8 cylinders; 403 cu in, 6,604 cc (4.35 x 3.38 in, 100.5 x 86 mm); max power (DIN): 185 hp at 3,600 rpm; max torque (DIN): 320 lb ft, 44.1 kg m at 2,200 rpm; max engine rpm: 4,400; 28 hp/l; 5 crankshaft bearings; 1 Rochester M4MC downdraught 4-barrel carburettor; cooling system: 24.8 imp pt, 29.8 US pt, 14.1 l.

TRANSMISSION axle ratio: 2.410 (3.080 for California only); tyres: GR78 x 15 (standard).

PERFORMANCE max speed: about 118 mph, 190 km/h; power-weight ratio: Le Sabre Sedan 18.4 lb/hp, 8.3 kg/hp; speed in direct drive at 1,000 rpm: 29.8 mph, 48 km/h; consumption: 20.5 m/imp gal, 17 m/US gal, 13.8 l x 100 km.

ELECTRICAL EQUIPMENT 3,500 W battery.

OPTIONALS 3.230 or 2.560 axle ratio.

valves: overhead, in line, push-rods and rockers, hydraulic tappets; camshafts: 1, at centre of Vee; lubrication: gear pump, full flow filter, 8.3 imp pt, 9.9 US pt, 4.7 l; 1 Rochester M4MC downdraught 4-barrel carburettor; cleaner air system; exhaust system with catalytic converter; fuel feed: mechanical pump; water-cooled, 24.8 imp pt, 29.8 US pt, 14.1 l.

TRANSMISSION driving wheels: rear; gearbox: Turbo-Hydramatic 350 automatic transmission, hydraulic torque converter and planetary gears with 3 ratios, max ratio of converter at stall 2, possible manual selection; ratios: I 2.520, II 1.520, III 1, rev 1.930; lever: steering column; final drive: hypoid bevel; axle ratio: 2.410 - Estate Wagon 2.730; width of rims: 7'' - Riviera 6''; tyres: HR78 x 15 - Riviera GR78 x 15.

PERFORMANCE max speed: 106 mph, 170 km/h; power-weight ratio: Electra 225 Sedan 24.2 lb/hp, 11 kg/hp - Electra Limited Hardtop Sedan 25.5 lb/hp, 11.5 kg/hp; speed in direct drive at 1,000 rpm: 26.7 mph, 43 km/h; consumption: 21.6 m/imp gal, 18 m/US gal, 13.1 l x 100 km.

CHASSIS perimeter box-type frame; front suspension: independent, wishbones (lower trailing links), coil springs, anti-roll bar, telescopic dampers; rear: rigid axle, lower trailing radius arms, upper oblique torque arms, coil springs, telescopic dampers (Estate Wagon only rigid axle, semi-elliptic leafsprings, telescopic dampers).

STEERING recirculating ball, variable ratio servo; turns lock to lock: 3.37.

BRAKES front disc (diameter 11.86 in, 30 cm), front internal radial fins, rear drum, servo; swept area: total 384.18 sq in, 2,478 sq cm - Estate Wagon 396.58 sq in, 2,559 sq cm.

ELECTRICAL EQUIPMENT 12 V; 3,200 W battery; 42 A alternator; Delco-Remy transistorized ignition; 4 headlamps.

DIMENSIONS AND WEIGHT wheel base: 115.90 in, 294 cm - Electra 118.90 in, 302 cm; front track: 61.80 in, 157 cm - Estate Wagon 62.20 in, 158 cm; rear track: 60.70 in, 154 cm - Estate Wagon 64 in, 163 cm; length: Estate Wagon 216.70 in, 550 cm - Electra 222.10 in, 564 cm - Riviera 218.20 in, 554 cm; width: 77.20 in, 196 cm - Estate Wagon 79.90 in, 203 cm; height: Estate Wagon 56.50 in, 143 cm - coupés 55 in, 140 cm - sedans 55.90 in, 142 cm; ground clearance: Estate Wagon 6.50 in, 16.5 cm - Electra 6.90 in, 17.5 cm - Riviera 6.70 in, 17 cm; weight: Estate Wagon 4,032 lb, 1,829 kg - Electra 225 Sedan 3,750 lb, 1,701 kg - Coupé 3,688 lb, 1,673 kg - Electra Limited Sedan 3,781 lb, 1,715 kg - Coupé 3,704 lb, 1,680 kg - Electra Park Avenue Sedan 3,781 lb, 1,715 kg - Coupé 3,721 lb, 1,688 kg - Riviera 3,861 lb, 1,706 kg; turning circle (between walls): 44.1 ft, 13.4 m - Estate Wagon 42.8 ft, 13 m; fuel tank: 21.1 imp gal, 25.3 US gal, 96 l - Estate Wagon 18.7 imp gal, 22.5 US gal, 85 l.

OPTIONALS central lever only for Riviera; limited slip differential; 3.080 axle ratio; automatic levelling control; anti-roll bar on rear suspension only for Riviera; tilt of steering wheel; heated rear window; electric windows (except for Riviera); electric sunshine roof; vinyl roof; air-conditioning.

170 hp power team

(for California only).

See 155 hp power team, except for:

ENGINE max power (DIN): 170 hp at 3,800 rpm; max torque (DIN): 275 lb ft, 37.9 kg m at 2,000 rpm; max engine rpm: 4,600; 29.6 hp/l.

PERFORMANCE max speed: about 109 mph, 175 km/h; power-weight ratio: Electra 225 Sedan 22 lb/hp, 10 kg/hp; consumption: 20.5 m/imp gal, 17 m/US gal, 13.8 l x 100 km.

185 hp power team

See 155 hp power team, except for:

ENGINE 403 cu in, 6,604 cc (4.35 x 3.38 in, 100.5 x 86 mm); max power (DIN): 185 hp at 3,600 rpm; max torque (DIN): 320 lb ft, 44.1 kg m at 2,400 rpm; max engine rpm: 4,400; 28 hp/l; cooling system: 32.6 imp pt, 39.1 US pt, 18.5 l.

TRANSMISSION axle ratio: Estate Wagon 2.560.

PERFORMANCE max speed: about 112 mph, 180 km/h; power-weight ratio: Electra 225 Sedan 20.2 lb/hp, 9.2 kg/hp; speed in direct drive at 1,000 rpm: 29.8 mph, 48 km/h; consumption: 19.2 m/imp gal, 16 m/US gal, 14.7 l x 100 km.

CHASSIS (for st. wagons only) rear suspension: rigid axle, semi-elliptic leafsprings, telescopic dampers.

OPTIONALS 3.080 axle ratio.

BUICK Electra Limited Sedan

Estate Wagon - Electra 225 - Electra Limited - Electra Park Avenue - Riviera Series

PRICES EX WORKS:

Estate Wagon Station Wagon	$ 6,300
Electra 225 Sedan	$ 7,318
Electra 225 Coupé	$ 7,143
Electra Limited Sedan	$ 7,700
Electra Limited Coupé	$ 7,525
Electra Park Avenue Sedan	$ 8,087
Electra Park Avenue Coupé	$ 7,836
Riviera Coupé	$ 8,081

For GB prices, see price index.

Power team:	Standard for:	Optional for:
155 hp	all	—
170 hp	—	all
185 hp	—	all

155 hp power team

(not available in California).

ENGINE front, 4 stroke; 8 cylinders; 350 cu in, 5,736 cc (4.06 x 3.38 in, 103.1 x 85.8 mm); compression ratio: 8:1; max power (DIN): 155 hp at 3,400 rpm; max torque (DIN): 280 lb ft, 38.6 kg m at 1,800 rpm; max engine rpm: 4,200; 27 hp/l; cast iron block and head; 5 crankshaft bearings;

BUICK Riviera Coupé

CADILLAC   USA

Seville

PRICE IN GB: £ 15,865*
PRICE EX WORKS: $ 14,267

ENGINE front, 4 stroke; 8 cylinders; 350 cu in, 5,736 cc (4.06 x 3.38 in, 103 x 85.8 mm); compression ratio: 8:1; max power (DIN): 170 hp at 4,200 rpm; max torque (DIN): 270 lb ft, 37.2 kg m at 2,000 rpm; max engine rpm: 4,800; 29.6 hp/l; cast iron block and head; 5 crankshaft bearings; valves: overhead, in line, push-rods and rockers, hydraulic tappets; camshafts: 1, at centre of Vee; lubrication: gear pump, full flow filter, 8.3 imp pt, 9.9 US pt, 4.7 l; electronic injection; cleaner air system; exhaust system with catalytic converter; fuel feed: 2 electric pumps; water-cooled, 28.7 imp pt, 34.5 US pt, 16.3 l.

TRANSMISSION driving wheels: rear; gearbox: Turbo-Hydramatic 400 automatic transmission, hydraulic torque converter and planetary gears with 3 ratios, max ratio of converter at stall 2, possible manual selection; ratios: I 2.480, II 1.480, III 1, rev 2.070; lever: steering column; final drive: hypoid bevel; axle ratio: 2.560; width of rims: 6''; tyres: GR78 x 15.

PERFORMANCE max speed: about 115 mph, 185 km/h; power weight ratio: 24.6 lb/hp, 11.1 kg/hp; speed in direct drive at 1,000 rpm: 30.4 mph, 49 km/h; consumption: 19.2 m/imp gal, 16 m/US gal, 14.7 l x 100 km.

CHASSIS integral, front auxiliary frame; front suspension: independent, wishbones, coil springs, anti-roll bar, telescopic dampers; rear: rigid axle, semi-elliptic leafsprings, anti-roll bar, automatic levelling control, telescopic dampers.

STEERING recirculating ball, tilt of steering wheel, variable ratio, servo; turns lock to lock: 3.

BRAKES disc (front diameter 11.74 in, 29.8 cm, rear 11.14 in, 28.3 cm), internal radial fins, rear compensator, servo; swept area: front 236.80 sq in, 1,527 sq cm, rear 237.24 sq in, 1,530 sq cm, total 474.04 sq in, 3,057 sq cm.

ELECTRICAL EQUIPMENT 12 V; 3,500 W battery; 80 A alternator; high energy ignition system; 4 headlamps.

DIMENSIONS AND WEIGHT wheel base: 114.30 in, 290 cm; tracks: 61.30 in, 156 cm front, 59 in, 150 cm rear; length: 204 in, 518 cm; width: 71.80 in, 182 cm; height: 54.60 in, 139 cm; ground clearance: 5.40 in, 13.7 cm; weight: 4,179 lb, 1,895 kg; turning circle (between walls): 42.3 ft, 12.9 m; fuel tank: 17.4 imp gal, 21 US gal, 79 l.

BODY saloon/sedan; 4 doors; 5 seats, separate front seats, reclining backrests with built-in headrests; electric windows; air-conditioning.

OPTIONALS limited slip differential; 3.080 axle ratio: G78 x 15 tyres; sunshine roof; leather upholstery; heated rear window; heavy-duty cooling system.

De Ville - Fleetwood Series

PRICES EX WORKS:

1 De Ville Coupé	$ 10,444
2 De Ville Sedan	$ 10,668
3 Fleetwood Brougham	$ 12,292
4 Fleetwood Limousine	$ 19,642
5 Fleetwood Formal Limousine	$ 20,363

Power team:	Standard for:	Optional for:
180 hp	all	—
195 hp	—	1 to 3

180 hp power team

ENGINE front, 4 stroke; 8 cylinders; 425 cu in, 6,964 cc (4.08 x 4.06 in, 104 x 103 mm); compression ratio: 8.2:1; max power DIN: 180 hp at 4,000 rpm; max torque DIN): 320 lb ft, 44.2 kg m at 2,000 rpm; max engine rpm: 4,200; 25.8 hp/l; cast iron block and head; 5 crankshaft bearings; valves: overhead, in line, push-rods and rockers, hydraulic tappets; camshafts: 1, at centre of Vee; lubrication: gear pump, full flow filter, 8.3 imp pt, 9.9 US pt, 4.7 l; 1 Rochester M4ME downdraught 4-barrel carburettor; cleaner air system; exhaust system with catalytic converter; fuel feed: mechanical pump; water-cooled, 32.7 imp pt, 39.3 US pt, 18.6 l.

TRANSMISSION driving wheels: rear; gearbox: Turbo-Hydramatic 400 automatic transmission, hydraulic torque converter and planetary gears with 3 ratios, max ratio of converter at stall 2, possible manual selection; ratios: I 2.480, II 1.480, III 1, rev 2.070; lever: steering column; final drive: hypoid bevel; axle ratio: 2.280 (2.730 for California only); width of rims: 6''; tyres: GR78 x 15.

PERFORMANCE max speed: about 112 mph, 180 km/h; power-weight ratio: De Ville Sedan 23.5 lb/hp, 10.7 kg/hp; speed in direct drive at 1,000 rpm: 28 mph, 45 km/h; consumption: 18 m/imp gal, 15 m/US gal, 15.7 l x 100 km.

CHASSIS ladder frame with cross member; front suspension: independent, wishbones, coil springs, anti-roll bar, telescopic dampers; rear: rigid axle, lower trailing radius arms, upper oblique torque arms, coil springs, anti-roll bar, telescopic dampers.

STEERING recirculating ball, variable ratio servo; turns lock to lock: 3.20.

BRAKES front disc (diameter 11 in, 27.9 cm), front internal radial fins, rear drum, rear compensator, servo; lining/swept area: front 236.80 sq in, 1,528 sq cm, rear 237.34 sq in, 1,530 sq cm, total 474.12 sq in, 3,058 sq cm.

ELECTRICAL EQUIPMENT 12 V; 3,500 W battery; 63 A alternator; Delco-Remy electronic ignition; 4 headlamps.

DIMENSIONS AND WEIGHT wheel base: 121.50 in, 308 cm - Limousine and Formal Limousine 144.50 in, 367 cm; tracks: 61.70 in, 157 cm front, 60.70 in, 154 cm rear; length: 221.20 in, 562 cm - Limousine and Formal Limousine 244.20 in,

CADILLAC Seville

620 cm; width: 76.40 in, 194 cm; height: De Ville Coupé 54.40 in, 138 cm - Sedan 55.30 in, 140 cm - Brougham 56.70 in, 144 cm - Limousine and Formal Limousine 56.90 in, 145 cm; ground clearance: 5.70 in, 14.5 cm - Brougham 5.50 in, 14 cm - Limousine and Formal Limousine 6.10 in, 15.6 cm; weight: De Ville Coupé 4,164 lb, 1,888 kg - Sedan 4,236 lb, 1,921 kg - Brougham 4,314 lb, 1,957 kg - Limousine 4,772 lb, 2,165 kg - Formal Limousine 4,858 lb, 2,204 kg; turning circle (between walls): 44 ft, 13.4 m - Limousine and Formal Limousine 51.6 ft, 15.6 m; fuel tank: 21.1 imp gal, 25.3 US gal, 96 l.

BODY 4 doors (Coupé 2); bench front seats; electric windows; air-conditioning.

OPTIONALS limited slip differential; 3.080 axle ratio: HR78 x15 tyres; automatic levelling control; tilt of steering wheel; 80 A alternator; heated rear window; sunshine roof; vinyl roof; heavy-duty cooling system; leather upholstery; Brougham d'Elegance equipment.

195 hp power team

See 180 hp power team, except for:

ENGINE max power (DIN): 195 hp at 3,800 rpm; max torque (DIN): 320 lb ft, 44.2 kg m at 2,400 rpm; 28 hp/l; electronic fuel injection; fuel feed: 2 electric pumps.

PERFORMANCE max speed: about 115 mph, 185 km/h; power-weight ratio: De Ville Sedan 21.7 lb/hp, 9.8 kg/hp; consumption: 16.8 m/imp gal, 14 m/US gal, 16.8 l x 100 km.

CADILLAC Fleetwood Brougham d'Elegance

Fleetwood Eldorado

PRICE EX WORKS: $ 11,921

ENGINE front, 4 stroke; 8 cylinders; 425 cu in, 6,964 cc (4.08 x 4.06 in, 104 x 103 mm); compression ratio: 8.2:1; max power (DIN): 180 hp at 4,000 rpm; max torque (DIN): 320 lb ft, 44.2 kg m at 2,000 rpm; max engine rpm: 4,200; 25.8 hp/l; cast iron block and head; 5 crankshaft bearings; valves: overhead, in line, push-rods and rockers, hydraulic tappets; camshafts: 1, at centre of Vee; lubrication: gear pump, full flow filter, 10 imp pt, 12 US pt, 5.7 l; 1 Rochester M4ME downdraught 4-barrel carburettor; cleaner air system; exhaust system with catalytic converter; fuel feed: mechanical pump; water-cooled, 42.9 imp pt, 51.6 US pt, 24.4 l.

TRANSMISSION driving wheels: front; gearbox: Turbo-Hydramatic 425 automatic transmission, hydraulic torque converter and planetary gears (chain torque by engine-mounted converter) with 3 ratios, max ratio of converter at stall 2, possible manual selection; ratios: I 2.480, II 1.480, III 1, rev 2.070; lever: steering column; final drive: spiral bevel; axle ratio: 2.730; width of rims: 6''; tyres LR78 x 15.

PERFORMANCE max speed: about 118 mph, 190 km/h; power-weight ratio: 27.3 lb/hp, 12.4 kg/hp; speed in direct drive at 1,000 rpm: 30.4 mph, 49 km/h; consumption: 13.3 m/imp gal, 11 m/US gal, 21.3 l x 100 km.

CHASSIS ladder frame with cross members; front suspension: independent, wishbones, longitudinal torsion bars, anti-roll bar, telescopic dampers; rear: rigid axle, lower trailing arms, upper oblique torque arms, automatic levelling control, coil springs, telescopic dampers.

STEERING recirculating ball, variable ratio, servo; turns lock to lock: 3.75.

BRAKES disc (diameter 11 in, 27.9 cm), internal radial fins, servo; swept area: front 229.70 sq in, 1,481 sq cm, rear 229.70 sq in, 1,481 sq cm, total 459.40 sq in, 2,962 sq cm.

ELECTRICAL EQUIPMENT 12 V; 3,500 W battery; 63 A alternator; high energy ignition system; 4 headlamps.

DIMENSIONS AND WEIGHT wheel base: 126.30 in, 321 cm; tracks: 63.70 in, 162 cm front, 63.60 in, 161 cm rear; length: 224 in, 569 cm; width: 79.80 in, 203 cm; height: 52.20 in 138 cm; ground clearance: 5.70 in, 14.5 cm; weight: 4,906 lb, 2,225 kg; turning circle (between walls): 46.9 ft, 14.3 m; fuel tank: 22.4 imp gal, 27 US gal, 102 l.

BODY coupé; 2 doors; 5 seats, built-in headrests, electric windows; tinted glass; air-conditioning.

OPTIONALS heavy-duty cooling system; 3.070 axle ratio; L78 x 15 tyres; tilt of steering wheel; heated rear window; 80 A alternator; electric sunshine roof; vinyl roof; leather upholstery; Biarritz equipment; reclining front seats.

CHECKER   USA

Marathon Series

PRICES EX WORKS:

1 Marathon Sedan	$ 6,419
2 Marathon De Luxe Sedan	$ 7,472

Power team:	Standard for:	Optional for:
110 hp	1	—
90 hp	1	—
145 hp	2	1
170 hp	—	both

110 hp power team

(not available in California).

ENGINE front, 4 stroke; 6 cylinders, vertical, in line; 250 cu in, 4,097 cc (3.87 x 3.53 in, 98.2 x 89.6 mm); compression ratio: 8.1:1; max power (DIN): 110 hp at 3,800 rpm; max torque (DIN): 190 lb ft, 26.2 kg m at 1,600 rpm; max engine rpm: 4,400; 26.8 hp/l; cast iron block and head; 7 crankshaft bearings; valves: overhead, in line, push-rods and rockers; camshafts: 1, side; lubrication: gear pump, full flow filter, 8.3 imp pt, 9.9 US pt, 4.7 l; 1 Rochester 17058020 A downdraught single barrel carburettor; cleaner air system; exhaust system with catalytic converter; fuel feed: mechanical pump; water-cooled, 24.3 imp pt, 29.2 US pt, 13.8 l.

TRANSMISSION driving wheels: rear; gearbox: Turbo-Hydramatic 400 automatic transmission, hydraulic torque converter and planetary gears with 3 ratios, max ratio of converter at stall 2.2, possible manual selection; ratios: I 2.480, II 1.480, III 1, rev 2.070; lever: steering column; final drive: hypoid bevel; axle ratio: 3.070; width of rims: 6''; tyres: G78 x 15.

PERFORMANCE max speed: about 90 mph, 145 km/h; power-weight ratio: 34.2 lb/hp, 15.5 kg/hp; speed in direct drive at 1,000 rpm: 24.2 mph, 38.9 km/h; consumption: 22.8 m/imp gal, 19 m/US gal, 12.4 l x 100 km.

CHASSIS box-type ladder frame with X reinforcements; front suspension: independent, wishbones, coil springs, anti-roll bar, telescopic dampers; rear: rigid axle, semi-elliptic leafsprings, telescopic dampers.

STEERING recirculating ball, variable ratio servo; turns lock to lock: 3.46.

BRAKES front disc (diameter 11.75 in, 29.8 cm), front internal radial fins, rear drum, servo; swept area: total 374.7 sq in, 2,417 sq cm.

ELECTRICAL EQUIPMENT 12 V; 80 Ah battery; 63 A alternator; Delco-Remy high energy ignition system; 4 headlamps.

DIMENSIONS AND WEIGHT wheel base: 120 in, 305 cm; tracks: 64.45 in, 164 cm front, 63.31 in, 161 cm rear; length: 204.75 in, 520 cm; width: 76 in, 193 cm; height: 62.75 in, 159 cm; ground clearance: 7.50 in, 19 cm; weight: 3,765 lb, 1,707 kg; turning circle (between walls): 43.3 ft, 13.2 m; fuel tank: 17.9 imp gal, 21.6 US gal, 82 l.

OPTIONALS limited slip differential; HR78 x 15 tyres; auxiliary rear seats; air-conditioning; heavy-duty telescopic dampers; tinted glass.

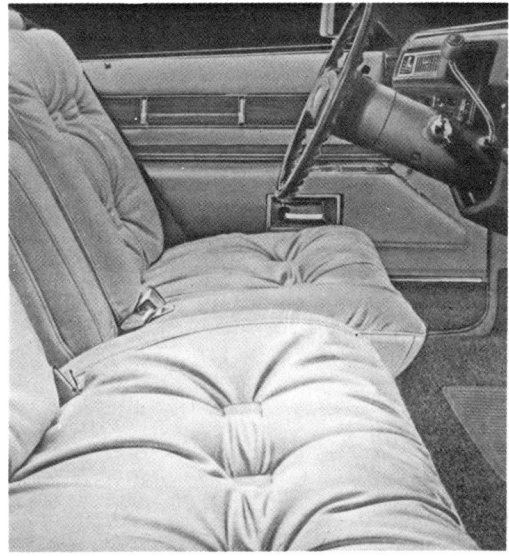

CADILLAC Fleetwood Eldorado Biarritz

90 hp power team

(for California only).

See 110 hp power team, except for:

ENGINE max power (DIN): 90 hp at 3,600 rpm; max torque (DIN): 175 lb ft, 24.1 kg m at 1,600 rpm; 22 hp/l; 1 Rochester 17058314 C downdraught single barrel carburettor.

PERFORMANCE power-weight ratio: 42.1 lb/hp, 19.1 kg/hp.

DIMENSIONS AND WEIGHT weight: 3,793 lb, 1,720 kg.

145 hp power team

See 110 hp power team, except for:

ENGINE 8 cylinders; 305 cu in, 4,998 cc (3.74 x 3.48 in, 94.9 x 88.3 mm); compression ratio: 8.4:1; max power (DIN): 145 hp at 3,800 rpm; max torque (DIN): 245 lb ft, 33.8 kg m at 2,400 rpm; 29 hp/l; 5 crankshaft bearings; camshafts: 1, at centre of Vee; 1 Rochester 17058108B downdraught twin barrel carburettor; cooling system: 28.7 imp pt, 34.5 US pt, 16.3 l.

TRANSMISSION axle ratio: 2.720.

PERFORMANCE max speed: about 103 mph, 165 km/h; power-weight ratio: Marathon 26.6 lb/hp, 12.1 kg/hp - Marathon De Luxe 28 lb/hp, 12.7 kg/hp; speed in direct drive at 1,000 rpm: 26.7 mph, 43 km/h; consumption: 20.5 m/imp gal, 17 m/US gal, 13.8 l x 100 km.

DIMENSIONS AND WEIGHT wheel base: Marathon De Luxe 129 in, 328 cm; length: Marathon De Luxe 213.75 in, 543 cm; weight: Marathon 3,862 lb, 1,751 kg - Marathon De Luxe 4,062 lb, 1,842 kg.

160 hp power team

See 110 hp power team, except for:

ENGINE 8 cylinders; 350 cu in, 5,736 cc (4 x 3.48 in, 101.6 x 88.3 mm); compression ratio: 8.2:1; max power (DIN): 160 hp at 3,800 rpm; max torque (DIN): 260 lb ft, 35.9 kg m at 2,400 rpm; 27.9 hp/l; 5 crankshaft bearings; camshafts: 1, at centre of Vee; 1 Rochester 17058504A downdraught 4-barrel carburettor; cooling system: 28.7 imp pt, 34.5 US pt, 16.3 l.

TRANSMISSION axle ratio: 2.720.

PERFORMANCE max speed: about 106 mph, 170 km/h; power-weight ratio: Marathon 24.2 lb/hp, 11 kg/hp - Marathon De Luxe 25.4 lb/hp, 11.5 kg/hp; speed in direct drive at 1,000 rpm: 26.7 mph, 43 km/h; consumption: 19.2 m/imp gal, 16 m/US gal, 14.7 l x 100 km.

DIMENSIONS AND WEIGHT (see 145 hp power team) weight: Marathon 3,865 lb, 1,753 kg - Marathon De Luxe 4,065 lb, 1,843 kg.

CHECKER Marathon Sedan

CHEVROLET   USA

Chevette Series

PRICES EX WORKS:

Chevette Scooter Hatchback Coupé	$ 2,999
Chevette Hatchback Coupé	$ 3,454
Chevette Hatchback Sedan	$ 3,574

Power team:	Standard for:	Optional for:
63 hp	all	—
68 hp	—	all

63 hp power team

ENGINE front, 4 stroke; 4 cylinders, vertical, in line; 97.6 cu in, 1,599 cc (3.23 x 2.98 in, 82 x 75.6 mm); compression ratio: 8.6:1; max power (DIN): 63 hp at 4,800 rpm; max torque (DIN): 82 lb ft, 11.3 kg m at 3,200 rpm; max engine rpm: 5,500; 39.4 hp/l; cast iron block and head; 5 crankshaft bearings; valves: overhead, hydraulic tappets; camshafts: 1, overhead, cogged belt; lubrication: gear pump, full flow filter, 8.3 imp pt, 9.9 US pt, 4.7 l; 1 Rochester 17058035 (17058335 for California only) downdraught single barrel carburettor; cleaner air system; exhaust system with catalytic converter; fuel feed: mechanical pump; water-cooled, 15 imp pt, 18 US pt, 8.5 l.

TRANSMISSION driving wheels: rear; clutch: single dry plate (diaphragm); gearbox: mechanical; gears: 4, fully synchronized; ratios: I 3.750, II 2.160, III 1.380, IV 1, rev 3.820; lever: central; final drive: hypoid bevel; axle ratio: 3.700; width of rims: 5''; tyres: 155/80 x 13.

PERFORMANCE max speed: about 87 mph, 140 km/h; power-weight ratio: Hatchback Sedan 32.4 lb/hp, 14.7 kg/hp; speed in direct drive at 1,000 rpm: 16.8 mph, 27 km/h; consumption: 40.9 m/imp gal, 34 m/US gal, 6.9 l x 100 km.

CHASSIS integral with cross member reinforcement; front suspension: independent, wishbones, coil springs, anti-roll bar, telescopic dampers; rear: rigid axle (torque tube), longitudinal trailing radius arms, coil springs, transverse linkage bar, anti-roll bar, telescopic dampers.

STEERING rack-and-pinion; turns lock to lock: 3.60.

BRAKES front disc (diameter 9.68 in, 24.6 cm), rear drum; swept area: total 297.7 sq in, 1,920 sq cm.

ELECTRICAL EQUIPMENT 12 V; 2,500 W battery; 32 A alternator; Delco-Remy high energy ignition system; 2 headlamps.

DIMENSIONS AND WEIGHT wheel base: 94.30 in, 239 cm - Hatchback Sedan 97.30 in, 247 cm; tracks: 51.20 in front, 51.20 in, 130 cm rear; length: 159.70 in, 406 cm - Hatchback Sedan 162.60 in, 413 cm; width: 61.80 in, 157 cm; height: 52.30 in, 133 cm; ground clearance: 5.30 in, 13.5 cm; weight: Chevette Scooter Hatchback Coupé 1,933 lb, 877 kg - Chevette Hatchback Coupé 1,969 lb, 893 kg - Hatchback Sedan 2,044 lb, 927 kg; turning circle (between walls): 34.3 ft, 10.5 m - Hatchback Sedan 34.9 ft, 10.6 m; fuel tank: 10.3 imp gal, 12.5 US gal, 47 l.

OPTIONALS Turbo-Hydramatic automatic transmission, hydraulic torque converter and planetary gears with 3 ratios (I 2.400, II 1.480, III 1, rev 1.920), max ratio of converter at stall 2.20, possible manual selection, central lever, 4.110 axle ratio; heavy-duty battery; servo brake; vinyl roof; heated rear window; air-conditioning.

68 hp power team

(not available in California).

See 63 hp power team, except for:

ENGINE max power (DIN): 68 hp at 5,000 rpm; max torque (DIN): 84 lb ft, 11.6 kg m at 3,200 rpm; 42.5 hp/l; 1 Rochester 17058039 downdraught single barrel carburettor.

PERFORMANCE max speed: about 93 mph, 150 km/h; power-weight ratio: Hatchback Sedan 30 lb/hp, 13.6 kg/hp.

Monza Series

PRICES EX WORKS:

1	Monza Coupé	$ 3,462
2	Monza Sport Coupé	$ 3,930
3	Monza Station Wagon	$ 3,698
4	Monza 2+2 Hatchback Coupé	$ 3,609
5	Monza 2+2 Sport Hatchback Coupé	$ 4,077

For V8 engines add $ 320.

Power team:	Standard for:	Optional for:
85 hp	all	—
90 hp	—	all
105 hp	—	all
135 hp	—	all
145 hp	—	all except 3

85 hp power team

ENGINE front, 4 stroke; 4 cylinders, vertical, in line; 151 cu in, 2,474 cc (4 x 3 in, 101.5 x 76.1 mm); compression ratio: 8.3:1; max power (DIN): 85 hp at 4,400 rpm; max torque (DIN): 123 lb ft, 17 kg m at 2,800 rpm; max engine rpm: 4,800; 34.4 hp/l; cast iron block and head; 5 crankshaft bearings; valves: overhead, in line, push-rods and rockers, hydraulic tappets; camshafts: 1, side; lubrication: gear pump, full flow filter, 7.6 imp pt, 9.1 US pt, 4.3 l; 1 Holley 10001049 downdraught twin barrel carburettor; cleaner air system; exhaust system with catalytic converter; fuel feed: mechanical pump; water-cooled, 18 imp pt, 21.6 US pt, 10.2 l.

TRANSMISSION driving wheels: rear; clutch: single dry plate (diaphragm); gearbox: mechanical; gears: 4, fully snchronized; ratios: I 3.500, II 2.480, III 1.660, IV 1, rev 3.500; lever: central; final drive: hypoid bevel; axle ratio: 2.730 - 2.930 (for California only); width of rims: 5'' - Sport models 6''; tyres: A78 x 13.

PERFORMANCE max speed: about 93 mph, 150 km/h; power-weight ratio: Monza Coupé 30.9 lb/hp, 14 kg/hp; speed in direct drive at 1,000 rpm: 20.1 mph, 32.3 km/h; consumption: 33.6 m/imp gal, 28 m/US gal, 8.4 l x 100 km.

CHASSIS integral; front suspension: independent, wishbones, coil springs, anti-roll bar, telescopic dampers; rear: rigid axle, lower trailing radius arms, upper oblique torque arms, coil springs, telescopic dampers.

STEERING recirculating ball; turns lock to lock: 4.40.

BRAKES front disc (diameter 9.74 in, 24.7 cm), rear drum; swept area; total 264.7 sq in, 1,707 sq cm.

ELECTRICAL EQUIPMENT 12 V; 3,200 W battery; 37 A alternator; Delco-Remy high energy ignition system; 2 headlamps.

DIMENSIONS AND WEIGHT wheel base: 97 in, 246 cm; tracks: 54.80 in, 139 cm front, 53.60 in, 136 cm rear; length: 179.20 in, 455 cm - Sport Hatchback Coupé 179.30 in, 455 cm - Sport Coupé 178.70 in, 454 cm - St. Wagon 178 in, 452 cm; width: 65.40 in, 166 cm; height: 50.20 in, 127 cm - Sport Hatchback Coupé and Sport Coupé 49.80 in, 126 cm - St. Wagon 51.80 in, 132 cm; ground clearance: 4.80 in, 12.2 cm; weight: Monza Coupé 2,625 lb, 1,190 kg - Sport Coupé 2,664 lb, 1,208 kg - St. Wagon 2,664 lb, 1,208 kg - 2 + 2 Hatchback Coupé 2,667 lb, 1,209 kg - Sport Hatchback Coupé 2,712 lb, 1,230 kg; turning circle (between walls): 38.4 ft, 11.7 m; fuel tank: 15.4 imp gal, 18.5 US gal, 70 l.

BODY 4 seats, separate front seats with built-in headrests.

OPTIONALS limited slip differential; 5-speed fully synchronized mechanical gearbox (I 3.400, II 2.080, III 1.390, IV 1, V 0.800, rev 3.360), 3.230 axle ratio; Turbo-Hydramatic automatic transmission with 3 ratios (I 2.400, II 1.480, III 1, rev 1.920), max ratio of converter at stall 2.20, possible manual selection, central lever, 2.730 or 3.080 axle ratio; BR78 x 13 tyres; power steering; adjustable tilt of steering wheel; servo brake; heavy-duty battery; reclining backrests; tinted glass; leather upholstery; heated rear window; anti-roll bar on rear suspension; « Spider » equipment (for 2 + 2 Sport Hatchback Coupé only); air-conditioning.

90 hp power team

(not available in California).

See 85 hp power team, except for:

ENGINE 6 cylinders, Vee-slanted at 90°; 196 cu in, 3,212 cc (3.50 x 3.40 in, 88.8 x 86.3 mm); compression ratio: 8:1; max power (DIN): 90 hp at 3,600 rpm; max torque (DIN): 165 lb ft, 22.8 kg m at 2,000 rpm; 28 hp/l; 4 crankshaft bearings; camshafts: 1, at centre of Vee; lubricating system: 8.3 imp pt, 9.9 US pt, 4.7 l; 1 Rochester 17058143 downdraught twin barrel carburettor; fuel feed: electric pump; cooling system: 19.4 imp pt, 23.3 US pt, 11 l.

TRANSMISSION axle ratio: 2.560; tyres: B78 x 13.

PERFORMANCE max speed: about 96 mph, 155 km/h; power-weight ratio: Monza Coupé 29.9 lb/hp, 13.6 kg/hp; consumption: 27.7 m/imp gal, 23 m/US gal, 10.2 l x 100 km.

ELECTRICAL EQUIPMENT 2,500 W battery; 42 A alternator.

DIMENSIONS AND WEIGHT weight: plus 71 lb, 32 kg.

OPTIONALS 5-speed fully synchronized mechanical gearbox with 2.730 axle ratio; Turbo-Hydramatic automatic transmission with 3 ratios (I 2.740, II 1.570, III 1, rev 2.070), max ratio of converter at stall 2, possible manual selection, 2.730, axle ratio.

105 hp power team

(for California only).

See 85 hp power team, except for:

ENGINE 6 cylinders, Vee-slanted at 90°; 231 cu in, 3,785 cc (3.080 x 3.40 in, 96.4 x 86.3 mm); compression ratio: 8:1; max power (DIN): 105 hp at 3,400 rpm; max torque (DIN): 185 lb ft, 25.5 kg m at 2,000 rpm; 27.7 hp/l; 4 crankshaft bearings; camshafts: 1, at centre of Vee; lubricating system: 8.3 imp pt, 9.9 US pt, 4.7 l; 1 Rochester 17058447 downdraught twin barrel carburettor; cooling system: 19.4 imp pt, 23.3 US pt, 11 l.

TRANSMISSION axle ratio: 2.930; tyres: B78 x 13.

PERFORMANCE max speed: about 99 mph, 160 km/h; power-weight ratio: Monza Coupé 25.7 lb/hp, 11.6 kg/hp; speed in direct drive at 1,000 rpm: 20.7 mph, 33.3 km/h; consumption: 24.1 m/imp gal, 20 m/US gal, 11.7 l x 100 km.

ELECTRICAL EQUIPMENT 2,500 W battery; 42 A alternator.

DIMENSIONS AND WEIGHT weight: plus 71 lb, 32 kg.

OPTIONALS 5-speed fully synchronized mechanical gearbox with 2.930 axle ratio; Turbo-Hydramatic automatic transmission with 3 ratios (I 2.740, II 1.570, III 1, rev 2.070), max ratio of converter at stall 2, possible manual selection, 2.560 or 2.930 axle ratio.

CHEVROLET Chevette Hatchback Sedan

CHEVROLET Monza Station Wagon

135 hp power team

(for California only).

See 85 hp power team, except for:

ENGINE 8 cylinders; 305 cu in, 4,998 cc (3.74 x 3.48 in, 94.9 x 88.3 mm); compression ratio: 8.5:1; max power (DIN): 135 hp at 3,800 rpm; max torque (DIN): 240 lb ft, 33.2 kg m at 2,000 rpm; 27 hp/l; camshafts: 1, at centre of Vee; lubrication: gear pump, full flow filter, 8.3 imp pt, 9.9 US pt, 4.7 l; 1 Rochester 17058404 downdraught twin barrel carburettor; fuel feed: electric pump; cooling system: 29.9 imp pt, 35.9 US pt, 17 l.

TRANSMISSION gearbox: Turbo-Hydramatic automatic transmission (standard), hydraulic torque converter and planetary gears with 3 ratios, max ratio of converter at stall 2.35, possible manual selection; ratios: I 2.520, II 1.520, III 1, rev 1.940; axle ratio: 2.930; tyres: BR70 x 13.

PERFORMANCE max speed: about 106 mph, 170 km/h; power-weight ratio: Monza Coupé 21.5 lb/hp, 9.7 kg/hp; speed in direct drive at 1,000 rpm: 27.8 mph, 44.7 km/h; consumption: 20.5 m/imp gal, 17 m/US gal, 13.8 l x 100 km.

ELECTRICAL EQUIPMENT 3,200 W battery.

DIMENSIONS AND WEIGHT weight: plus 275 lb, 125 kg.

OPTIONALS 5-speed fully synchronized mechanical gearbox not available.

CHEVROLET Monza Coupé

CHEVROLET Monza 2+2 Hatchback Coupé

145 hp power team

(not available in California).

See 85 hp power team, except for:

ENGINE 8 cylinders; 305 cu in, 4,998 cc (3.74 x 3.48 in, 94.9 x 88.3 mm); compression ratio: 8.4:1; max power (DIN): 145 hp at 3,800 rpm; max torque (DIN): 245 lb ft, 33.8 kg m at 2,400 rpm; 29 hp/l; camshafts: 1, at centre of Vee; lubrication: gear pump, full flow filter, 8.3 imp pt, 9.9 US pt, 4.7 l; 1 Rochester 17058107 downdraught twin barrel carburettor; fuel feed: electric pump; cooling system: 29.9 imp pt, 35.9 US pt, 17 l.

TRANSMISSION clutch: centrifugal; gearbox ratios: I 2.850, II 2.020, III 1.350, IV 1, rev 2.850; axle ratio: 3.080; tyres: BR70 x 13.

PERFORMANCE max speed: about 116 mph, 186 km/h; power-weight ratio: Monza Coupé 20 lb/hp, 9.1 kg/hp; speed in direct drive at 1,000 rpm: 24 mph, 38.7 km/h; consumption: 21.7 m/imp gal, 18 m/US gal, 13 l x 100 km.

ELECTRICAL EQUIPMENT 3,200 W battery.

DIMENSIONS AND WEIGHT weight: plus 275 lb, 125 kg.

OPTIONALS Turbo-Hydramatic automatic transmission with 3 ratios (I 2.520, II 1.520, III 1, rev 1.940), max ratio of converter at stall 2.35, 2.290 or 2.560 axle ratio; 5-speed fully synchronized mechanical gearbox not available.

Nova - Nova Custom Series

PRICES EX WORKS:

Nova Hatchback Coupé	$ 3,865
Nova Coupé	$ 3,702
Nova Sedan	$ 3,777
Nova Custom Coupé	$ 3,960
Nova Custom Sedan	$ 4,035

For V8 engines add $ 185.

Power team:	Standard for:	Optional for:
90 hp	all	—
110 hp	all	—
135 hp	—	all
145 hp	—	all
160 hp	—	all

90 hp power team

(for California only).

ENGINE front, 4 stroke; 6 cylinders, in line; 250 cu in, 4,097 cc (3.87 x 3.53 in, 98.2 x 89.6 mm); compression ratio: 8.1:1; max power (DIN): 90 hp at 3,600 rpm; max torque (DIN): 175 lb ft, 24.1 kg m at 1,600 rpm; max engine rpm: 4,400; 22 hp/l; cast iron block and head; 7 crankshaft bearings; valves: overhead, in line, push-rods and rockers, hydraulic tappets; camshafts: 1, side; lubrication: gear pump, full flow filter, 8.3 imp pt, 9.9 US pt, 4.7 l; 1 Rochester 17058314 downdraught single barrel carburettor; cleaner air system; exhaust system with catalytic converter; fuel feed: mechanical pump; water-cooled, 23.6 imp pt, 28.3 US pt, 13.4 l.

TRANSMISSION driving wheels: rear; gearbox: Turbo-Hydramatic automatic transmission, hydraulic torque converter and planetary gears with 3 ratios, max ratio of converter at stall 2, possible manual selection; ratios: I 2.520, II 1.520, III 1, rev 1.940; lever: steering column; final drive: hypoid bevel; axle ratio: 2.730; width of rims: 6''; tyres: E78 x 14.

PERFORMANCE max speed: about 93 mph, 150 km/h; power-weight ratio: Nova Sedan 35.3 lb/hp, 16 kg/hp; speed in direct drive at 1,000 rpm: 25.9 mph, 41.7 km/h; consumption: 20.5 m/imp gal, 17 m/US gal, 13.8 l x 100 km.

CHASSIS integral with separate partial front box-type frame; front suspension: independent, wishbones, coil springs, anti-roll bar, telescopic dampers; rear: rigid axle, semi-elliptic leafsprings, telescopic dampers.

STEERING recirculating ball; turns lock to lock: 4.99.

BRAKES front disc (diameter 11 in, 27.9 cm), front internal radial fins, rear drum; swept area: total 326.4 sq in, 2,105 sq cm.

ELECTRICAL EQUIPMENT 12 V; 2,500 W battery; 37 A alternator; Delco-Remy high energy ignition system; 2 headlamps.

DIMENSIONS AND WEIGHT wheel base: 111 in, 282 cm; tracks: 61.30 in, 156 cm front, 59 in, 150 cm rear; length: 196.70 in, 500 cm; width: 72.20 in, 183 cm; height: 52.70 in, 134 cm - sedans 53.60 in, 136 cm; clearance: 4.80 in, 12.2 cm; weight: Nova Hatchback Coupé 3,262 lb, 1,479 kg - Coupé 3,136 lb, 1,422 kg - Sedan 3,177 lb, 1,441 kg -

90 HP POWER TEAM

Nova Custom Coupé 3,209 lb, 1,455 kg - Sedan 3,246 lb, 1,472 kg; turning circle (between walls): 39.9 ft, 12.2 m; fuel tank: 17.6 imp gal, 21 US gal, 80 l.

OPTIONALS limited slip differential; heavy-duty radiator; central lever; heavy-duty suspension with rear anti-roll bar; power steering; tilt of steering wheel; servo brake; heavy-duty battery; air-conditioning; vinyl roof; electric windows.

110 hp power team

(not available in California).

See 90 hp power team, except for:

ENGINE max power (DIN): 110 hp at 3,800 rpm; max torque (DIN): 190 lb ft, 26.2 kg m at 1,600 rpm; 26.8 hp/l; 1 Rochester 17058013 downdraught single barrel carburettor.

TRANSMISSION clutch: single dry plate (diaphragm); gearbox: mechanical; gears: 3, fully synchronized; ratios: I 3.500, II 1.810, III 1, rev 3.620.

PERFORMANCE max speed: about 99 mph, 160 km/h; power-weight ratio: Nova Sedan 28.9 lb/hp, 13.1 kg/hp; speed in direct drive at 1,000 rpm: 22.6 mph, 36.4 km/h; consumption: 25.2 m/imp gal, 21 m/US gal, 11.2 l x 100 km.

OPTIONALS Turbo-Hydramatic automatic transmission with 3 ratios (I 2.520, II 1.520, III 1, rev 1.940), max ratio of converter at stall 2, possible manual selection, 2.730 axle ratio.

135 hp power team

(for California only).

See 90 hp power team, except for:

ENGINE 8 cylinders; 305 cu in, 4,998 cc (3.74 x 3.48 in, 94.8 x 88.3 mm); compression ratio: 8.4:1; max power (DIN): 135 hp at 3,800 rpm; max torque (DIN): 240 lb ft, 33.1 kg m at 2,000 rpm; 27 hp/l; 5 crankshaft bearings; camshafts: 1, at centre of Vee; 1 Rochester 17058408 downdraught twin barrel carburettor; cooling system: 28.7 imp pt, 34.5 US pt, 16.3 l.

TRANSMISSION axle ratio: 2.410.

PERFORMANCE max speed: about 103 mph, 165 km/h; power-weight ratio: Nova Sedan 24.6 lb/hp, 11.2 kg/hp; consumption: 18 m/imp gal, 15 m/US gal, 15.7 l x 100 km.

BRAKES servo (standard).

ELECTRICAL EQUIPMENT 3,200 W battery.

DIMENSIONS AND WEIGHT weight: Nova plus 145 lb, 66 kg - Nova Custom plus 135 lb, 61 kg.

CHEVROLET Nova Custom Coupé

145 hp power team

(not available in California).

See 90 hp power team, except for:

ENGINE 8 cylinders; 305 cu in, 4,998 cc (3.74 x 3.48 in, 94.9 x 88.3 mm); compression ratio: 8.4:1; max power (DIN): 145 hp at 3,800 rpm; max torque (DIN): 245 lb ft, 33.8 kg m at 2,400 rpm; 29 hp/l; 5 crankshaft bearings: 1, at centre of Vee; 1 Rochester 17058313 downdraught twin barrel carburettor; cooling system: 28.7 imp pt, 34.5 US pt, 16.3 l.

TRANSMISSION clutch: single dry plate (diaphragm), centrifugal; gearbox: mechanical; gears: 4, fully synchronized; ratios: I 2.850, II 2.020, III 1.350, IV 1, rev 2.850; axle ratio: 3.080.

PERFORMANCE max speed: about 106 mph, 170 km/h; power-weight ratio: Nova Sedan 22.9 lb/hp, 10.4 kg/hp; speed in direct drive at 1,000 rpm: 24 mph, 38.6 km/h; consumption: 20.5 m/imp gal, 17 m/US gal, 13.8 l x 100 km.

BRAKES servo (standard).

ELECTRICAL EQUIPMENT 3,200 W battery.

DIMENSIONS AND WEIGHT weight: Nova plus 145 lb, 66 kg - Nova Custom plus 135 lb, 61 kg.

OPTIONALS Turbo-Hydramatic automatic transmission with 3 ratios (I 2.520, II 1.520, III 1, rev 1.940), max ratio of converter at stall 2, possible manual selection, 2.410 or 3.080 axle ratio.

160 hp power team

See 90 hp power team, except for:

ENGINE 8 cylinders; 350 cu in, 5,736 cc (4 x 3.48 in, 101.6 x 88.3 mm); compression ratio: 8.2:1; max power (DIN): 160 hp at 3,800 rpm; max torque (DIN): 260 lb ft, 35.9 kg m at 2,400 rpm; 27.9 hp/l; 5 crankshaft bearings; camshafts: 1, at centre of Vee; 1 Rochester 17058202 (17058502 for California only) downdraught 4-barrel carburettor; cooling system: 28.9 imp pt, 34.7 US pt, 16.4 l.

TRANSMISSION axle ratio: 2.410.

PERFORMANCE max speed: about 106 mph, 170 km/h; power-weight ratio: Nova Sedan 20.8 lb/hp, 9.4 kg/hp; consumption: 20.5 m/imp gal, 17 m/US gal, 13.8 l x 100 km.

BRAKES servo (standard).

ELECTRICAL EQUIPMENT 3,200 W battery.

DIMENSIONS AND WEIGHT weight: Nova plus 144 lb, 65 kg - Nova Custom plus 133 lb, 60 kg.

OPTIONALS 3.080 axle ratio.

Camaro - Camaro LT Series

PRICES EX WORKS:

Camaro Sport Coupé	$ 4,414
Camaro LT Sport Coupé	$ 4,814

For V8 engines add $ 185.

Power team:	Standard for:	Optional for:
90 hp	both	—
110 hp	both	—
135 hp	—	both
145 hp	—	both
160 hp	—	both
170 hp	—	both
175 hp	—	both
185 hp	—	both

90 hp power team

(for California only).

ENGINE front, 4 stroke; 6 cylinders, vertical, in line; 250 cu in, 4,097 cc (3.87 x 3.53 in, 98.2 x 89.6 mm); compression ratio: 8.1:1; max power (DIN): 90 hp at 3,600 rpm; max torque (DIN): 175 lb ft, 24.1 kg m at 1,600 rpm; max engine rpm: 4,400; 22 hp/l; cast iron block and head; 7 crankshaft bearings; valves: overhead, in line, push-rods and rockers, hydraulic tappets; camshafts: 1, side; lubrication: gear pump, full flow filter, 8.3 imp pt, 9.9 US pt, 4.7 l; 1 Rochester 17058314 downdraught single barrel carburettor; cleaner air system; exhaust system with catalytic converter; fuel feed: mechanical pump; water-cooled, 24.3 imp pt, 29.2 US pt, 13.8 l.

CHEVROLET Nova Custom Sedan

TRANSMISSION driving wheels: rear; gearbox: Turbo-Hy-dramatic automatic transmission, hydraulic torque converter and planetary gears with 3 ratios, max ratio of converter at stall 2, possible manual selection; ratios: I 2.520, II 1.520, III 1, rev 1.940; lever: steering column; final drive: hypoid bevel; axle ratio: 2.730; width of rims: 6'' - Camaro LT 7''; tyres: FR78 x 14.

PERFORMANCE max speed: about 96 mph, 155 km/h; power-weight ratio: Camaro 37.7 lb/hp, 17.1 kg/hp - LT 37.2 lb/hp, 16.9 kg/hp; speed in direct drive at 1,000 rpm: 25.9 mph, 41.7 km/h; consumption: 20.5 m/imp gal, 17 m/US gal, 13.8 l x 100 km.

CHASSIS integral with separate partial front box-type frame; front suspension: independent, wishbones, coil springs, anti-roll bar, telescopic dampers; rear: rigid axle, semi-elliptic leafsprings, anti-roll bar, telescopic dampers.

STEERING recirculating ball, servo; turns lock to lock: 2.41.

BRAKES front disc (diameter 11 in, 27.9 cm), front internal radial fins, rear drum; swept area: total 326.4 sq in, 2,105 sq cm.

ELECTRICAL EQUIPMENT 12 V; 2,500 W battery; 37 A alternator; Delco-Remy high energy ignition system; 2 headlamps.

DIMENSIONS AND WEIGHT wheel base: 108 in, 274 cm; front track: Camaro 61.30 in, 156 cm - LT 61.60 in, 156 cm; rear track: Camaro 60 in, 152 cm - LT 60.30 in, 153 cm; length: 197.60 in, 502 cm; width: 74.40 in, 189 cm; height:

CHEVROLET Camaro Sport Coupé

49.20 in, 125 cm; ground clearance: 4.90 in, 12.4 cm; weight: Camaro 3,392 lb, 1,538 kg - LT 3,347 lb, 1,518 kg; turning circle (between walls): 41.1 ft, 12.5 m; fuel tank: 17.6 imp gal, 21 US gal, 80 l.

BODY coupé; 2 doors; 4 seats, separate front seats.

OPTIONALS limited slip differential; central lever E78 x 14 tyres with 6'' or 7'' wide rims; tilt of steering wheel; servo brake; electric windows; heavy-duty battery; heavy-duty radiator; reclining front seats; Rally Sport package; tinted glass; air-conditioning.

110 hp power team

(not available in California).

See 90 hp power team, except for:

ENGINE max power (DIN): 110 hp at 3,800 rpm; max torque (DIN): 190 lb ft, 26.2 kg m at 1,600 rpm; 26.8 hp/l; 1 Rochester 17058013 downdraught single barrel carburettor.

TRANSMISSION clutch: single dry plate (diaphragm); gearbox: mechanical; gears: 3, fully synchronized; ratios: I 3.500, II 1.810, III 1, rev 3.620; lever central.

PERFORMANCE max speed: about 99 mph, 160 km/h; power-weight ratio: Camaro 30.6 lb/hp, 13.9 kg/hp - LT 30.4 lb/hp, 13.8 kg/hp; speed in direct drive at 1,000 rpm: 24.2 mph, 30 km/h; consumption: 25.2 m/imp gal, 21 m/US gal, 11.2 l x 100 km.

DIMENSIONS AND WEIGHT weight: minus 23 lb, 10 kg.

OPTIONALS Turbo-Hydramatic automatic transmission with 3 ratios (I 2.520, II 1.520, III 1, rev 1.940), max ratio of converter at stall 2, possible manual selection, steering column lever, 2.730 axle ratio.

135 hp power team

(for California only).

See 90 hp power team, except for:

ENGINE 8 cylinders; 305 cu in, 4,998 cc (3.78 x 3.48 in, 94.9 x 88.3 mm); compression ratio: 8.4:1; max power (DIN): 135 hp at 3,800 rpm; max torque (DIN): 240 lb ft, 33.1 kg m at 2,000 rpm; 27 hp/l; 5 crankshaft bearings; camshafts: 1, at centre of Vee; 1 Rochester 17058412 downdraught twin barrel carburettor; cooling system: 28.7 imp pt, 34.5 US pt, 16.3 l.

TRANSMISSION axle ratio: 2.410.

PERFORMANCE max speed: about 109 mph, 175 km/h; power-weight ratio: Camaro 26 lb/hp, 11.8 kg/hp - LT 25.7 lb/hp, 11.7 kg/hp; consumption: 18 m/imp gal, 15 m/US gal, 15.7 l x 100 km.

BRAKES servo (standard).

ELECTRICAL EQUIPMENT 3,200 W battery.

DIMENSIONS AND WEIGHT weight: plus 125 lb, 57 kg.

145 hp power team

(not available in California).

See 90 hp power team, except for:

ENGINE 8 cylinders; 305 cu in, 4,998 cc (3.74 x 3.48 in, 94.9 x 88.3 mm); compression ratio: 8.4:1; max power (DIN): 145 hp at 3,800 rpm; max torque (DIN): 245 lb ft, 33.8 kg m at 2,400 rpm; 29 hp/l; 5 crankshaft bearings; camshafts: 1, at centre of Vee; 1 Rochester 17058020 downdraught twin barrel carburettor; cooling system: 28.7 imp pt, 34.5 US pt, 16.3 l.

TRANSMISSION clutch: single dry plate (diaphragm), centrifugal; gearbox: mechanical: gears: 4, fully synchronized; ratios: I 2.850, II 2.020, III 1.350, IV 1, rev 2.850; lever: central; axle ratio: 3.080.

PERFORMANCE max speed: about 112 mph, 180 km/h; power-weight ratio: Camaro 24.3 lb/hp, 11 kg/hp - LT 23.9 lb/hp, 10.9 kg/hp; speed in direct drive at 1,000 rpm: 25.5 mph, 41 km/h; consumption: 20.5 m/imp gal, 17 m/US gal, 13.8 l x 100 km.

BRAKES servo (standard).

ELECTRICAL EQUIPMENT 3,200 W battery.

DIMENSIONS AND WEIGHT weight: plus 125 lb, 57 kg.

OPTIONALS Turbo-Hydramatic automatic transmission with 3 ratios (I 2.520, II 1.520, III 1, rev 1.940), màx ratio of converter at stall 2, possible manual selection, steering column lever, 2.410 axle ratio.

160 hp power team

(for California only).

See 90 hp power team, except for:

ENGINE 8 cylinders; 350 cu in, 5,736 cc (4 x 3.48 in, 101.6 x 88.3 mm); compression ratio: 8.2:1; max power (DIN): 160 hp at 3,800 rpm; max torque (DIN): 260 lb ft, 35.9 kg m at 2,400 rpm; 27.0 hp/l; 5 crankshaft bearings; camshafts: 1, at centre of Vee; 1 Rochester 17058502 downdraught 4-barrel carburettor; cooling system: 28.9 imp pt, 34.7 US pt, 16.4 l.

TRANSMISSION axle ratio: 2.410.

PERFORMANCE max speed: about 115 mph, 185 km/h; power-weight ratio: Camaro 22 lb/hp, 10 kg/hp - LT 21.7 lb/hp, 9.9 kg/hp; speed in direct drive at 1,000 rpm: 26.7 mph, 43 km/h; consumption: 18 m/imp gal, 15 m/US gal, 15.7 l x 100 km.

BRAKES servo (standard).

ELECTRICAL EQUIPMENT 3,200 W battery.

DIMENSIONS AND WEIGHT weight: plus 132 lb, 60 kg.

OPTIONALS 3.080 axle ratio.

170 hp power team

(not available in California).

See 90 hp power team, except for:

ENGINE 8 cylinders; 350 cu in, 5,736 cc (4 x 3.48 in, 101.6 x 88.3 mm); compression ratio: 8.2:1; max power (DIN): 170 hp at 3,800 rpm; max torque (DIN): 270 lb ft, 37.2 kg m at 2,400 rpm; 29.6 hp/l; 5 crankshaft bearings; camshafts: 1, at centre of Vee; 1 Rochester 17058203 downdraught 4-barrel carburettor; cooling system: 28.9 imp pt, 34.7 US pt, 16.4 l.

TRANSMISSION clutch: single dry plate (diaphragm), centrifugal; gearbox: mechanical; gears: 4, fully synchronized; ratios: I 2.850, II 2.020, III 1.350, IV 1, rev 2.850; lever: central; axle ratio: 3.080.

PERFORMANCE max speed: about 118 mph, 190 km/h; power-weight ratio: Camaro 20.7 lb/hp, 9.4 kg/hp - LT 20.5 lb/hp, 9.3 kg/hp; speed in direct drive at 1,000 rpm: 26.8 mph, 43.2 km/h; consumption: 18 m/imp gal, 15 m/US gal, 15.7 l x 100 km.

BRAKES servo (standard).

ELECTRICAL EQUIPMENT 3,200 W battery.

DIMENSIONS AND WEIGHT weight: plus 132 lb, 60 kg.

OPTIONALS Turbo-Hydramatic automatic transmission with 3 ratios (I 2.520, II 1.520, III 1, rev 1.940), max ratio of converter at stall 2, possible manual selection, steering column lever, 2.410 or 3.080 axle ratio.

175 hp power team

(for California only).

See 160 hp power team, except for:

ENGINE max power (DIN): 175 hp at 3,800 rpm; max torque (DIN): 265 lb ft, 36.6 kg m at 2,400 rpm; 30.5 hp/l; dual exhaust system.

TRANSMISSION axle ratio: 3.420.

PERFORMANCE power-weight: Camaro 20.1 lb/hp, 9.1 kg/hp - LT 19.9 lb/hp, 9 kg/hp.

OPTIONALS 3.080 axle ratio not available.

185 hp power team

(not available in California).

See 170 hp power team, except for:

ENGINE max power (DIN): 185 hp at 4,000 rpm; max torque (DIN): 280 lb ft, 38.6 kg m at 2,400 rpm; max engine rpm: 4,400; 32.3 hp/l; dual exhaust system.

TRANSMISSION gearbox ratios: I 2.640, II 1.750, III 1.340, IV 1, rev 2.550; axle ratio: 3.730.

PERFORMANCE power-weight ratio: Camaro 19 lb/hp, 8.6 kg/hp - LT 18.8 lb/hp, 8.5 kg/hp.

OPTIONALS Turbo-Hydramatic automatic transmission with 3.420 axle ratio.

Chevelle Series

PRICES EX WORKS:

Malibu Coupé	$ 4,204
Malibu Sedan	$ 4,279
Malibu Station Wagon	$ 4,515
Malibu Classic Coupé	$ 4,461
Malibu Classic Landau Coupé	$ 4,684
Malibu Classic Sedan	$ 4,561
Malibu Classic Station Wagon	$ 4,713

For V8 engines add $ 190.

Power team:	Standard for:	Optional for:
95 hp	all	—
105 hp	all	—
135 hp	—	all
145 hp	—	all

95 hp power team

(not available in California).

ENGINE front, 4 stroke; 6 cylinders, Vee-slanted at 90°; 200 cu in, 3,277 cc (3.50 x 3.48 in, 88.9 x 88.4 mm); compression ratio: 8.2:1; max power (DIN): 95 hp at 3,800 rpm; max torque (DIN): 160 lb ft, 22.1 kg m at 2,000 rpm; max engine rpm: 4,200; 29 hp/l; cast iron block and head; 4 crankshaft bearings; valves: overhead, in line, push-rods and rockers, hydraulic tappets; camshafts: 1, at centre of Vee; lubrication: gear pump, full flow filter, 8.3 imp pt, 9.9 US pt, 4.7 l; 1 Rochester 17058131 downdraught twin barrel carburettor; cleaner air system; exhaust system with catalytic converter; fuel feed: mechanical pump; water-cooled, 24.3 imp pt, 29.2 US pt, 13.8 l.

TRANSMISSION driving wheels: rear; clutch: single dry plate (diaphragm); gearbox: mechanical; gears: 3, fully synchronized; ratios: I 3.500, II 1.810, III 1, rev 3.620; lever: central; final drive: hypoid bevel; axle ratio: 2.730; width of rims: 6''; tyres: P185/75R x 14 - st. wagons P195/75R x 14.

PERFORMANCE max speed: about 93 mph, 150 km/h; power-weight ratio: Malibu Sedan 31.8 lb/hp, 14.4 kg/hp; speed in direct drive at 1,000 rpm: 23.3 mph, 37.5 km/h; consumption: 28.8 m/imp gal, 24 m/US gal, 9.8 l x 100 km.

CHASSIS perimeter box-type with front and rear cross members; front suspension: independent, wishbones, coil springs, anti-roll bar, telescopic dampers; rear: rigid axle, lower trailing radius arms, upper oblique torque arms, coil springs, telescopic dampers.

STEERING recirculating ball; turns lock to lock: 5.30.

BRAKES front disc (diameter 10.30 in, 26.7 cm), front internal radial fins, rear drum; swept area: total 307.77 sq in, 1,986 sq cm.

ELECTRICAL EQUIPMENT 12 V; 3,200 W battery; 37 A alternator; Delco-Remy high energy ignition system; 4 headlamps.

DIMENSIONS AND WEIGHT wheel base: 108.10 in, 274 cm; tracks: 58.50 in, 149 cm front, 57.80 in, 147 cm rear; length: 192.70 in, 489 cm - st. wagons 193.40 in, 491 cm; width: 71.50 in, 182 cm - st. wagons 71.20 in, 181 cm; height: coupés 53.30 in, 135 cm - sedans 54.20 in, 138 cm - st. wagons 54.50 in, 138 cm; ground clearance: 5.40 in, 13.7 cm - st. wagons 5.70 in, 14.5 cm; weight: Malibu Coupé 3,014 lb, 1,367 kg - Sedan 3,022 lb, 1,371 kg - St. Wagon 3,175 lb, 1,440 kg - Malibu Classic Coupé 3,042 lb, 1,380 kg - Sedan 3,056 lb, 1,386 kg - St. Wagon 3,201 lb, 1,452 kg; turning circle (between walls): 40 ft, 12.2 m; fuel tank: 14.5 imp gal, 17.4 US gal, 66 l - st. wagons 15 imp gal, 18 US gal, 68 l.

OPTIONALS limited slip differential; Turbo-Hydramatic automatic transmission with 3 ratios (I 2.520, II 1.520, III 1, rev 1.940 or I 2.740, II 1.570, III 1, rev 2.070), max ratio of converter at stall 2 or 2.35, possible manual selection, 2.730 axle ratio; P195/75R x 14 tyres; anti-roll bar on rear suspension; power steering; tilt of steering wheel; servo brake; vinyl roof; heated rear window; electric windows; air-conditioning.

105 hp power team

(for California only).

See 95 hp power team, except for:

ENGINE 231 cu in, 3,785 cc (3.80 x 3.40 in, 96.4 x 86.3 mm); compression ratio: 8:1; max power (DIN): 105 hp at 3,400 rpm; max torque (DIN): 185 lb ft, 25.5 kg m at 2,000 rpm; 27.7 hp/l; 1 Rochester 17058448 downdraught twin barrel carburettor; cooling system: 26 imp pt, 31.3 US pt, 14.8 l.

TRANSMISSION gearbox: Turbo-Hydramatic automatic transmission (standard), hydraulic torque converter and planetary gears with 3 ratios, max ratio of converter at stall 2.35, possible manual selection: ratios: I 2.740, II 1.570, III 1, rev 2.070.

CHEVROLET Chevelle Malibu Sedan

PERFORMANCE max speed: about 96 mph, 155 km/h; power-weight ratio: Malibu Sedan 28.8 lb/hp, 13 kg/hp; speed in direct drive at 1,000 rpm: 28 mph, 45 km/h; consumption: 21.6 m/imp gal, 18 m/US gal, 13.1 l x 100 km.

ELECTRICAL EQUIPMENT 42 A alternator.

OPTIONALS Turbo-Hydramatic automatic transmission with 3 ratios (I 2.520, II 1.520, III 1, rev 1.940), max ratio of converter at stall 2.

135 hp power team

(for California only).

See 90 hp power team, except for:

ENGINE 8 cylinders; 305 cu in, 4,998 cc (3.74 x 3.48 in, 94.9 x 88.3 mm); compression ratio: 8.4:1; max power (DIN): 135 hp at 3,800 rpm; max torque (DIN): 240 lb ft, 33.1 kg m at 2,000 rpm; 27 hp/l; 5 crankshaft bearings; camshafts: 1, at centre of Vee; 1 Rochester 17058408 downdraught twin barrel carburettor; cooling system: 31.9 imp pt, 38.3 US pt, 18.1 l.

TRANSMISSION gearbox: Turbo-Hydramatic automatic transmission (standard), hydraulic torque converter and planetary gears with 3 ratios, max ratio of converter at stall 2, possible manual selection; ratios: I 2.520, II 1.520, III 1, rev 1.940; axle ratio: 2.290 - st. wagons 2.410.

CHEVROLET Chevelle Malibu Station Wagon

PERFORMANCE max speed: about 99 mph, 160 km/h; power-weight ratio: Malibu Sedan 23.4 lb/hp, 10.6 kg/hp; speed in direct drive at 1,000 rpm: 28 mph, 45 km/h; consumption: 20.5 m/imp gal, 17 m/US gal, 13.8 l x 100 km.

STEERING servo (standard); turns lock to lock: 3.30.

BRAKES servo (standard).

DIMENSIONS AND WEIGHT weight: plus 136 lb, 62 kg.

OPTIONALS 2.730 or 2.560 axle ratio.

145 hp power team

(not available in California).

See 135 hp power team, except for:

ENGINE max power (DIN): 145 hp at 3,800 rpm; max torque (DIN): 245 lb ft, 33.8 kg m at 2,400 rpm; 29 hp/l; 1 Rochester 17058108 downdraught twin barrel carburettor.

PERFORMANCE max speed: about 104 mph, 167 km/h; power-weight ratio: Malibu Sedan 21.8 lb/hp, 9.9 kg/hp; consumption: 21.6 m/imp gal, 18 m/US gal, 13.1 l x 100 km.

OPTIONALS 4-speed fully synchronized mechanical gearbox (I 2.850, II 2.020, III 1.350, IV 1, rev 2.850), 2.730 axle ratio.

Monte Carlo Series

PRICES EX WORKS:

Monte Carlo Coupé	$ 4,784
Monte Carlo Landau Coupé	$ 5,677

For V8 engines add $ 150.

Power team:	Standard for:	Optional for:
105 hp	both	—
135 hp	—	both
145 hp	—	both

105 hp power team

ENGINE front, 4 stroke; 6 cylinders, Vee-slanted at 90°; 231 cu in, 3,785 cc (3.80 x 3.40 in, 96.5 x 86.4 mm); compression ratio: 8:1; max power (DIN): 105 hp at 3,400 rpm; max torque (DIN): 185 lb ft, 25.5 kg m at 2,000 rpm; max engine rpm: 4,000; 27.7 hp/l; 4 crankshaft bearings; valves: overhead, in line, push-rods and rockers, hydraulic tappets; camshafts: 1, at centre of Vee; lubrication: gear pump, full flow filter, 8.3 imp pt, 9.9 US pt, 4.7 l; 1 Rochester 17058145 or 17058182 (17058448 for California only) downdraught twin barrel carburettor; cleaner air system; exhaust system with catalytic converter; fuel feed: mechanical pump; water-cooled, 26 imp pt, 31.3 US pt, 14.8 l.

TRANSMISSION driving wheels: rear; clutch: single dry plate (diaphragm), centrifugal; gearbox: mechanical (Turbo-Hydramatic automatic transmission standard on Landau Coupé); gears: 3, fully synchronized; ratios: I 3.500, II 1.810, III 1, rev 3.620; lever: central; final drive: hypoid bevel; axle ratio: 2.930 (2.730 for California only); width of rims: 6''; tyres: P205/70R x 14.

PERFORMANCE max speed: about 96 mph, 155 km/h; power-weight ratio: 29 lb/hp, 13.2 kg/hp; speed in direct drive at 1,000 rpm: 24 mph, 38.7 km/h; consumption: 22.8 m/imp gal, 19 m/US gal, 12.4 l x 100 km.

CHASSIS perimeter; front suspension: independent, wishbones, coil springs, anti-roll bar, telescopic dampers; rear: rigid axle, lower trailing radius arms, upper oblique torque arms, coil springs, anti-roll bar, telescopic dampers.

STEERING recirculating ball; turns lock to lock: 5.30.

BRAKES front disc (diameter 10.50 in, 26.7 cm), front internal radial fins, rear drum; swept area: total 307.77 sq in, 1,986 sq cm.

ELECTRICAL EQUIPMENT 12 V; 2,500 W battery; 42 A alternator; Delco-Remy high energy ignition system; 4 headlamps.

DIMENSIONS AND WEIGHT wheel base: 108.10 in, 274 cm; tracks: 58.50 in, 149 cm front, 57.80 in, 147 cm rear; length: 200.40 in, 509 cm; width: 71.50 in, 182 cm; height: 53.90 in, 137 cm; ground clearance: 4.80 in, 12.2 cm; weight: 3,051 lb, 1,384 kg; turning circle (between walls): 40.5 ft, 12.4 m; fuel tank: 14.5 imp gal, 17.4 US gal, 66 l.

BODY coupé; 2 doors; 6 seats, separate front seat, reclining backrests with built-in headrests.

OPTIONALS limited slip differential; Turbo-Hydramatic automatic transmission with 3 ratios (I 2.520, II 1.520, III 1, rev 1.940), max ratio of converter at stall 2, possible manual selection, steering column or central lever, 2.730 or 2.560 axle ratio; 4-speed fully synchronized mechanical gearbox (I 3.500, II 2.480, III 1.660, IV 1, rev 3.500), central lever, 2.930 axle ratio; power steering; tilt of steering wheel; servo brake; heated rear window; vinyl roof; electric windows; air-conditioning.

135 hp power team

(for California only).

See 105 hp power team, except for:

ENGINE 8 cylinders; 305 cu in, 4,998 cc (3.74 x 3.48 in, 94.9 x 88.3 mm); compression ratio: 8.4:1; max power (DIN): 135 hp at 3,800 rpm; max torque (DIN): 240 lb ft, 33.1 kg m at 2,000 rpm; max engine rpm: 4,400; 27 hp/l; 5 crankshaft bearings; 1 Rochester 17058408 downdraught twin barrel carburettor; cooling system: 31.9 imp pt, 38.3 US pt, 18.1 l.

TRANSMISSION gearbox: Turbo-Hydramatic automatic transmission (standard), hydraulic torque converter and planetary gears with 3 ratios, max ratio of converter at stall 2.35, possible manual selection: ratios: I 2.740, II 1.570, III 1, rev 2.070; axle ratio: 2.290.

PERFORMANCE max speed: about 106 mph, 170 km/h; power-weight ratio: 23.8 lb/hp, 10.8 kg/hp; speed in direct drive at 1,000 rpm: 26.4 mph, 42.5 km/h; consumption: 20.5 m/imp gal, 17 m/US gal, 13.8 l x 100 km.

STEERING servo (standard); turns lock to lock: 3.30.

BRAKES servo (standard).

ELECTRICAL EQUIPMENT 3,200 W battery; 37 A alternator.

DIMENSIONS AND WEIGHT weight: plus 164 lb, 74 kg.

OPTIONALS 2.730 or 2.560 axle ratio; 4-speed fully synchronized mechanical gearbox not available.

145 hp power team

(not available in California).

See 135 hp power team, except for:

ENGINE max power (DIN): 145 hp at 3,800 rpm; max torque (DIN): 245 lb ft, 33.8 kg m at 2,400 rpm; 29 hp/l; 1 Rochester 17058108 downdraught twin barrel carburettor.

PERFORMANCE power-weight ratio: 22.2 lb/hp, 10 kg/hp; consumption: 21.6 m/imp gal, 18 m/US gal, 13.1 l x 100 km.

OPTIONALS 2.730 or 2.560 axle ratio; 4-speed fully synchronized mechanical gearbox (I 2.850, II 2.020, III 1.350, IV 1, rev 2.850), 2.730 axle ratio.

Impala - Caprice Classic Series

PRICES EX WORKS:

1 Impala Coupé	$ 5,207
2 Impala Landau Coupé	$ 5,597
3 Impala Sedan	$ 5,282
4 Impala 6-pass. Station Wagon	$ 5,776
5 Impala 9-pass. Station Wagon	$ 5,903
6 Caprice Classic Coupé	$ 5,525
7 Caprice Classic Landau Coupé	$ 5,829
8 Caprice Classic Sedan	$ 5,625
9 Caprice Classic 6-pass. Station Wagon	$ 6,011
10 Caprice Classic 9-pass. Station Wagon	$ 6,150

For V8 engines add $ 185.

Power team:	Standard for:	Optional for:
90 hp	1,2,3,6,7,8	—
110 hp	1,2,3,6,7,8	—
135 hp	4,5,9,10	1,2,3,6,7,8
145 hp	4,5,9,10	1,2,3,6,7,8
160 hp	—	all
170 hp	—	all

90 hp power team

(for California only).

ENGINE front, 4 stroke; 6 cylinders, vertical, in line; 250 cu in, 4,097 cc (3.87 x 3.53 in, 98.2 x 89.6 mm); compression ratio: 8.1:1; max power (DIN): 90 hp at 3,600 rpm; max torque (DIN): 175 lb ft, 24.1 kg m at 1,600 rpm; max engine rpm: 4,400; 22 hp/l; cast iron block and head; 7 crankshaft bearings; valves: overhead, in line, push-rods and rockers, hydraulic tappets; camshafts: 1, side; lubrication: gear pump, full flow filter, 8.3 imp pt, 9.9 US pt, 4.7 l; 1 Rochester 17058314 downdraught single barrel carburettor; cleaner air system; exhaust system with catalytic converter; fuel feed: mechanical pump; water-cooled, 24.3 imp pt, 29.2 US pt, 13.8 l.

TRANSMISSION driving wheels: rear; gearbox: Turbo-Hydramatic automatic transmission, hydraulic torque converter and planetary gears with 3 ratios, max ratio of converter at stall 2, possible manual selection: ratios: I 2.520, II 1.520, III 1, rev 1.940; lever: steering column; final drive: hypoid bevel; axle ratio: 2.730; width of rims: 6''; tyres: FR78 x 15.

PERFORMANCE max speed: about 99 mph, 160 km/h; power-weight ratio: Impala Sedan 39.2 lb/hp, 17.8 kg/hp - Caprice

CHEVROLET Monte Carlo Coupé

CHEVROLET Caprice Classic Sedan

Classic Sedan 39.8 lb/hp, 18 kg/hp; speed in direct drive at 1,000 rpm: 24.9 mph, 40 km/h; consumption: 21.2 m/imp gal, 17 m/US gal, 13.8 l x 100 km.

CHASSIS perimeter box-type with cross members; front suspension: independent, wishbones, coil springs, anti-roll bar, telescopic dampers; rear: rigid axle, lower trailing radius arms, upper oblique torque arms, coil springs, anti-roll bar, telescopic dampers.

STEERING recirculating ball, servo; turns lock to lock: 3.16.

BRAKES front disc (diameter 11 in, 27.9 cm), front internal radial fins, rear drum, servo; swept area: total 329.8 sq in, 2,127 sq cm.

ELECTRICAL EQUIPMENT 12 V; 2,500 W battery; 37 A alternator; Delco-Remy high energy ignition system; 4 headlamps.

DIMENSIONS AND WEIGHT wheel base: 116 in, 295 cm; tracks: 61.80 in, 157 cm front, 60.80 in, 154 cm rear; length: 212.10 in, 538 cm; width: 76 in, 193 cm; height: sedans 56 in, 142 cm - coupés 55.30 in, 141 cm; ground clearance: 5.80 in, 14.7 cm; weight: Impala Coupé 3,510 lb, 1,592 kg - Impala Sedan 3,530 lb, 1,601 kg - Caprice Classic Coupé 3,548 lb, 1,609 kg - Sedan 3,578 lb, 1,622 kg; turning circle (between walls): 44.6 ft, 13.6 m; fuel tank: 17.6 imp gal, 21 US gal, 80 l.

OPTIONALS central lever; limited slip differential; electric windows; heavy-duty front suspension; GR78 x 15 or GR70 x 15 tyres with 7'' wide rims; speed control device; heated rear window; tilt of steering wheel; vinyl roof; heavy-duty suspension; air-conditioning.

110 hp power team

(not available in California).

See 90 hp power team, except for:

ENGINE max power (DIN): 110 hp at 3,800 rpm; max torque (DIN): 190 lb ft, 26.2 kg m at 1,600 rpm; 26.8 hp/l; 1 Rochester 17058014 downdraught single barrel carburettor.

PERFORMANCE power-weight ratio: Impala Sedan 35.3 lb/hp, 16 kg/hp - Caprice Classic Sedan 35.8 lb/hp, 16.2 kg/hp; consumption: 22.8 m/imp gal, 19 m/US gal, 12.4 l x 100 km.

135 hp power team

(for California only).

See 90 hp power team, except for:

ENGINE 8 cylinders; 305 cu in, 4,998 cc (3.74 x 3.48 in, 94.9 x 88.3 mm); compression ratio: 8.4:1; max power (DIN): 135 hp at 3,800 rpm; max torque (DIN): 240 lb ft, 33.1 kg m at 2,000 rpm; 27 hp/l; 5 crankshaft bearings; camshafts: 1, at centre of Vee; 1 Rochester 17058408 downdraught twin barrel carburettor; cooling system: 29.9 imp pt, 35.9 US pt, 17 l.

TRANSMISSION automatic transmission ratios: I 2.740, II 1.570, III 1, rev 2.070; max ratio of converter at stall 2.35; axle ratio: 2.410 - st. wagons 2.560; width of rims: st. wagons 7''; tyres: st. wagons HR78 x 15.

135 HP POWER TEAM

PERFORMANCE max speed: about 106 mph, 170 km/h; power-weight ratio: Impala 6-pass. St. Wagon 29.9 lb/hp, 13.6 kg/hp - Caprice Classic 6-pass. st. Wagon 30.2 lb/hp, 13.7 kg/hp; speed in direct drive at 1,000 rpm: 26.2 mph, 42 km/h; consumption: 18 m/imp gal, 15 m/US gal, 15.7 l x 100 km.

STEERING turns lock to lock: st. wagons 3.30.

BRAKES (for st. wagons only) front disc (diameter 11.86 in, 30.1 cm); swept area: total 375.14 sq in, 2,420 sq cm.

ELECTRICAL EQUIPMENT 3,200 W battery.

DIMENSIONS AND WEIGHT tracks: st. wagons 62.20 in, 158 cm front, 64.10 in, 163 cm rear; length: st. wagons 214.70 in, 545 cm; width: st. wagons 79.10 in, 201 cm; height: st. wagons 58 in, 147 cm; ground clearance: st. wagons 5.90 in, 15 cm; weight: Impala 6-pass. St. Wagon 4,037 lb, 1,831 kg - Caprice Classic 6-pass. St. Wagon 4,079 lb, 1,850 kg; turning circle (between walls): st. wagons 45.1 ft, 13.7 m; fuel tank: st. wagons 18.3 imp gal, 22 US gal, 83 l.

145 hp power team

(not available in California).

See 135 hp power team, except for:

ENGINE max power (DIN): 145 hp at 3,800 rpm; max torque (DIN): 245 lb ft, 33.8 kg m at 2,400 rpm; 29 hp/l; 1 Rochester 17058108 downdraught twin barrel carburettor.

PERFORMANCE power-weight ratio: Impala 6-pass. St. Wagon 27.8 lb/hp, 12.6 kg/hp - Caprice Classic 6-pass. St. Wagon 28.1 lb/hp, 12.7 kg/hp; consumption: 22.8 m/imp gal, 19 m/US gal, 12.4 l x 100 km.

160 hp power team

(for California only).

See 135 hp power team, except for:

ENGINE 350 cu in, 5,736 cc (4 x 3.48 in, 101.6 x 88.3 mm); compression ratio: 8.2:1; max power (DIN): 160 hp at 3,800 rpm; max torque (DIN): 260 lb ft, 35.9 kg m at 2,400 rpm; 27.9 hp/l; 1 Rochester 17058502 downdraught 4-barrel carburettor.

PERFORMANCE max speed: about 109 mph, 175 km/h; power-weight ratio: Impala Sedan 22.4 lb/hp, 10.1 kg/hp - Caprice Classic Sedan 22.7 lb/hp, 10.3 kg/hp.

DIMENSIONS AND WEIGHT weight: plus 53 lb, 24 kg.

OPTIONALS 3.080 axle ratio.

170 hp power team

(not available in California).

See 160 hp power team, except for:

ENGINE max power (DIN): 170 hp at 3,800 rpm; max torque (DIN): 270 lb ft, 37.2 kg m at 2,400 rpm; 29.6 hp/l; 1 Rochester 17058202 downdraught 4-barrel carburettor.

PERFORMANCE power-weight ratio: Impala Sedan 21.1 lb/hp, 9.6 kg/hp - Caprice Classic Sedan 21.4 lb/hp, 9.7 kg/hp; consumption: 20.5 m/imp gal, 17 m/US gal, 13.8 l x 100 km.

Corvette

PRICE EX WORKS: $ 9,351

185 hp power team

(standard).

ENGINE front, 4 stroke; 8 cylinders; 350 cu in, 5,736 cc (4 x 3.48 in, 101.6 x 88.3 mm); compression ratio: 8.2:1; max power (DIN): 185 hp at 4,000 rpm; max torque (DIN): 280 lb ft, 38.6 kg m at 2,400 rpm; max engine rpm: 4,400; 32.3 hp/l; cast iron block and head; 5 crankshaft bearings; valves: overhead, in line, push-rods and rockers, hydraulic tappets; camshafts: 1, at centre of Vee; lubrication: gear pump, full flow filter, 8.3 imp pt, 9.9 US pt, 4.7 l; 1 Rochester 17058203 (17058502 for California only) downdraught 4-barrel carburettor; cleaner air system; dual exhaust system with catalytic converter; fuel feed: mechanical pump; water-cooled, 34.5 imp pt, 41.4 US pt, 19.6 l, viscous-coupling thermostatic fan.

CHEVROLET Corvette Coupé

TRANSMISSION driving wheels: rear; clutch: single dry plate, semi-centrifugal; gearbox: mechanical (Turbo-Hydramatic automatic transmission standard for California only); gears: 4, fully synchronized; ratios: I 2.850, II 2.020, III 1.350, IV 1, rev 2.850; lever: central; final drive: hypoid bevel, limited slip differential; axle ratio: 3.360 (3.080 for California only); width of rims: 8''; tyres P225/70R x 15.

PERFORMANCE max speed: about 118 mph, 190 km/h; power-weight ratio: 18.6 lb/hp, 8.4 kg/hp; speed in direct drive at 1,000 rpm: 28 mph, 45 km/h; consumption: 19.2 m/imp gal, 16 m/US gal, 14.7 l x 100 km.

CHASSIS ladder frame with cross members; front suspension: independent, wishbones, coil springs, anti-roll bar, telescopic dampers; rear: independent, wishbones, semi-axles as upper arms, transverse semi-elliptic leafspring, trailing radius arms, telescopic dampers.

STEERING recirculating ball, servo; turns lock to lock: 2.92.

BRAKES disc (diameter 11.75 in, 30 cm), internal radial fins, servo; swept area: total 498.3 sq in, 3,214 sq cm.

ELECTRICAL EQUIPMENT 12 V; 3,500 W battery: 42 A alternator; Delco-Remy high energy ignition system; 4 retractable headlamps.

DIMENSIONS AND WEIGHT wheel base: 98 in, 249 cm; tracks: 58.70 in, 149 cm front, 59.50 in, 151 cm rear; length: 185.20 in, 470 cm; width: 69 in, 175 cm; height: 48 in, 122 cm; ground clearance: 4.30 in, 10.9 cm; weight: 3,444 lb, 1,562 kg; turning circle (between walls): 38.6 ft, 11.8 m; fuel tank: 20 imp gal, 24 US gal, 91 l.

BODY coupé, in plastic material; 2 doors; 2 seats, built-in headrests.

OPTIONALS Turbo-Hydramatic automatic transmission with 3 ratios (I 2.520, II 1.520, III 1, rev 1.940), max ratio of converter at stall 2, possible manual selection, 3.080 or 3.550 axle ratio; tilt of steering wheel; Gymkhana suspension; anti-roll bar on rear suspension; electric windows; heavy-duty battery; air-conditioning; light alloy wheels; heated rear window.

220 hp power team

(not available in California).

See 185 hp power team, except for:

ENGINE compression ratio: 8.9:1; max power (DIN): 220 hp at 5,200 rpm; max torque (DIN): 260 lb ft, 35.9 kg m at 3,600 rpm; max engine rpm: 5,600; 38.4 hp/l; 1 Rochester 17058211 downdraught 4-barrel carburettor.

TRANSMISSION gearbox ratios: I 2.640, II 1.750, III 1.340, IV 1, rev 2.550; axle ratio: 3.700.

PERFORMANCE max speed: about 131 mph, 211 km/h; power-weight ratio: 15.7 lb/hp, 7.1 kg/hp.

DIMENSIONS AND WEIGHT weight: plus 20 lb, 9 kg.

OPTIONALS 3.360 axle ratio; 4-speed fully synchronized mechanical gearbox (I 2.430, II 1.610, III 1.230, IV 1, rev 2.350), 3.700 axle ratio; Turbo-Hydramatic automatic transmission with 3.550 axle ratio.

CHRYSLER   USA

Le Baron Series

PRICES EX WORKS:

Le Baron Coupé	$ 5,114
Le Baron Sedan	$ 5,270
Le Baron Medallion Coupé	$ 5,484
Le Baron Medallion Sedan	$ 5,640
Le Baron Town and Country Station Wagon	$ 5,672

For V8 engines add $ 176.

Power team:	Standard for:	Optional for:
110 hp	all	—
90 hp	all	—
140 hp	—	all
155 hp (5,211 cc)	—	all
155 hp (5,900 cc)	—	all
170 hp	—	all

110 hp power team

(not available in California)

ENGINE front, 4 stroke; 6 cylinders, vertical, in line; 225 cu in, 3,687 cc (3.40 x 4.12 in, 86.4 x 104.6 mm); compression ratio: 8.4:1; max power (DIN): 110 hp at 3,600 rpm; max torque (DIN): 180 lb ft, 24.8 kg m at 2,000 rpm; max engine rpm: 4,000; 29.8 hp/l; cast iron block and head; 4 crankshaft bearings; valves: overhead, in line, push-rods and rockers; camshafts: 1, side; lubrication: rotary pump, full flow filter, 8.3 imp pt, 9.9 US pt, 4.7 l; 1 Carter BBD 8136S downdraught twin barrel carburettor; cleaner air system; exhaust system with catalytic converter; fuel feed: mechanical pump; water-cooled, 20.1 imp pt, 24.1 US pt, 11.4 l.

TRANSMISSION driving wheels: rear; clutch: single dry plate; gearbox: mechanical; gears: 4, fully synchronized with overdrive/top; ratios: I 3.090, II 1.670, III 1, IV 0.710, rev 3.000; lever: central; final drive: hypoid bevel; axle ratio: 3.230 - St. Wagon 3.210; width of rims: 5.5''; tyres: FR78 x 15.

PERFORMANCE max speed: about 93 mph, 150 km/h; power-weight ratio: Le Baron Sedan 31.5 lb/hp, 14.3 kg/hp; speed in top at 1,000 rpm: 24.2 mph, 39 km/h; consumption: 23.9 m/imp gal, 20 m/US gal, 11.8 l x 100 km.

CHASSIS integral, front auxiliary frame with cross members; front suspension: independent, wishbones, transverse torsion bars, anti-roll bar, telescopic dampers; rear: rigid axle, semi-elliptic leafsprings, telescopic dampers.

STEERING recirculating ball, servo; turns lock to lock: 3.50.

BRAKES front disc (diameter 10.82 in, 27.5 cm), front internal radial fins, rear drum; swept area: total 355.24 sq in, 2,291 sq cm.

ELECTRICAL EQUIPMENT 12 V; 375 A battery; 41 A alternator; Essex or Prestolite transistorized ignition; 4 headlamps.

DIMENSIONS AND WEIGHT wheel base: 112.70 in, 286 cm; tracks: 60 in, 152 cm front, 58.50 in, 149 cm rear; length: coupés 204.10 in, 518 cm - sedans 206.10 in, 523 cm - St. Wagon 202.80 in, 515 cm; width: 73.30 in, 186 cm - coupés 73.50 in, 187 cm; height: coupés 53.30 in, 135 cm - sedans 55.30 in, 140 cm - St. Wagon 55.70 in, 141 cm; ground clearance: 4.90 in, 12.4 cm - St. Wagon 5.40 in, 13.7 cm; weight: Lo Baron Coupé 3,421 lb, 1,551 kg - Sedan 3,466 lb, 1,572 kg - Le Baron Medallion Coupé 3,496 lb, 1,585 kg - Sedan 3,550 lb, 1,610 kg - Le Baron Town and Country St. Wagon 3,598 lb, 1,632 kg; turning circle (between walls): 43.5 ft, 13.3 m; fuel tank: 16.3 imp gal, 19.5 US gal, 74 l.

OPTIONALS limited slip differential; 3.210 axle ratio; Torqueflite automatic transmission with 3 ratios (I 2.450, II 1.450, III 1, rev 2.220), max ratio of converter at stall 2.01, possible manual selection, steering column or central lever, 2.760 or 2.710 axle ratio; heavy-duty suspension; tilt of steering wheel; servo brake (standard on Town and Country); electric windows; heated rear window; reclining front seats; speed control; Landau vinyl roof; air-conditioning.

90 hp power team

(for California only).

See 110 hp power team, except for:

ENGINE max power (DIN): 90 hp at 3,600 rpm; max torque (DIN): 160 lb ft, 22.1 kg m at 1,600 rpm; 24.4 hp/l; 1 Carter BBD8137S downdraught single barrel carburettor.

TRANSMISSION gearbox: Torqueflite automatic transmission (standard), hydraulic torque converter and planetary gears with 3 ratios, max ratio of converter at stall 2.01, possible manual selection; ratios: I 2.450, II 1.450, III 1, rev 2.220.

PERFORMANCE max speed: about 90 mph, 145 km/h; power-weight ratio: Le Baron Sedan 38.5 lb/hp, 17.5 kg/hp; speed in direct drive at 1,000 rpm: 25.5 mph, 41 km/h; consumption: 19.2 m/imp gal, 16 m/US gal, 14.7 l x 100 km.

ELECTRICAL EQUIPMENT 325 A battery.

140 hp power team

(not available in California).

See 110 hp power team, except for:

ENGINE 8 cylinders; 318 cu in, 5,211 cc (3.91 x 3.31 in, 99.2 x 84 mm); compression ratio: 8.5:1; max power (DIN): 140 hp at 4,000 rpm; max torque (DIN): 245 lb ft, 33.8 kg m at 1,600 rpm; max engine rpm: 4,400; 26.9 hp/l; 5 crankshaft bearings; valves: hydraulic tappets; camshafts: 1, at centre of Vee; 1 Carter BBD8175S downdraught twin barrel carburettor; cooling system: 26.6 imp pt, 31.9 US pt, 15.1 l.

TRANSMISSION gearbox: mechanical (Torqueflite automatic transmission standard for Town and Country); axle ratio: 2.940 - Town and Country 2.710.

CHRYSLER Le Baron Medallion Coupé

CHRYSLER Le Baron Town and Country Station Wagon

PERFORMANCE max speed: about 102 mph, 164 km/h; power-weight ratio: Le Baron Sedan 24.8 lb/hp, 11.2 kg/hp; consumption: 21.6 m/imp gal, 18 m/US gal, 13.1 l x 100 km.

ELECTRICAL EQUIPMENT 325 A battery; Lean-Burn electronic ignition.

OPTIONALS (except for Town and Country) Torqueflite automatic transmission with max ratio of converter at stall 1.90 and 2.470 or 2.450 axle ratio.

155 hp (5,211 cc) power team

(for California only).

See 140 hp power team, except for.

ENGINE max power (DIN): 155 hp at 4,000 rpm; max torque (DIN): 245 lb ft, 33.8 kg m at 1,600 rpm; 29.7 hp/l; 1 Carter TQ9147S downdraught 4-barrel carburettor.

TRANSMISSION gearbox: Torqueflite automatic transmission (standard), hydraulic torque converter and planetary gears with 3 ratios, max ratio of converter at stall 1.90, possible manual selection: ratios: I 2.450, II 1.450, III 1, rev 2.220; axle ratio: 2.760 - Town and Country 2.710.

PERFORMANCE max speed: about 103 mph, 165 km/h; power-weight ratio: Le Baron Sedan 22.4 lb/hp, 10.1 kg/hp; speed in direct drive at 1,000 rpm: 25.5 mph, 41 km/h; consumption: 19.2 m/imp gal, 16 m/US gal, 14.7 l x 100 km.

OPTIONALS 2.710 axle ratio (except for Town and Country).

155 hp (5,900 cc) power team

(not available in California).

See 110 hp power team, except for:

ENGINE 8 cylinders; 360 cu in, 5,900 cc (4 x 3.58 in, 101.6 x 89.6 mm); max power (DIN): 155 hp at 3,600 rpm; max torque (DIN): 270 lb ft, 37.2 kg m at 2,400 rpm; 26.3 hp/l; 5 crankshaft bearings; valves: hydraulic tappets; camshafts: 1, at centre of Vee; 1 Holley R7991A downdraught twin barrel carburettor; cooling system: 26.6 imp pt, 31.9 US pt, 15.1 l.

TRANSMISSION gearbox: Torqueflite automatic transmission (standard), hydraulic torque converter and planetary gears with 3 ratios, max ratio of converter at stall 1.90, possible manual selection; ratios: I 2.450, II 1.450, III 1, rev 2.220; axle ratio: 2.450.

PERFORMANCE max speed: about 106 mph, 170 km/h; power-weight ratio: Le Baron Sedan 22.4 lb/hp, 10.1 kg/hp; speed in direct drive at 1,000 rpm: 26.4 mph, 42.5 km/h; consumption: 20.5 m/imp gal, 17 m/US gal, 13.8 l x 100 km.

ELECTRICAL EQUIPMENT 440 A battery; Lean-Burn electronic ignition.

170 hp power team

(for California only).

See 155 hp (5,900 cc) power team, except for:

ENGINE max power (DIN): 170 hp at 4,000 rpm; max torque (DIN): 270 lb ft, 37.2 kg m at 1,600 rpm; max engine rpm: 4,400; 28.8 hp/l; 1 Carter TQ9134S downdraught 4-barrel carburettor.

TRANSMISSION axle ratio: 2.710.

PERFORMANCE max speed: about 109 mph, 175 km/h; power-weight ratio: Le Baron Sedan 20.4 lb/hp, 9.2 kg/hp; consumption: 16.8 m/imp gal, 14 m/US gal, 16.8 l x 100 km.

Cordoba

PRICE EX WORKS: $ 5,750

140 hp power team

(optional, not available in California).

ENGINE front, 4 stroke; 8 cylinders; 318 cu in, 5,211 cc (3.91 x 3.31 in, 99.2 x 84 mm); compression ratio: 8.5:1; max power (DIN): 140 hp at 4,000 rpm; max torque (DIN): 245 lb ft, 33.8 kg m at 1,600 rpm; max engine rpm: 4,400; 26.9 hp/l; cast iron block and head; 5 crankshaft bearings; valves: overhead, in line, push-rods and rockers, hydraulic tappets; camshafts: 1, at centre of Vee; lubrication: rotary pump, full flow filter, 8.3 imp pt, 9.9 US pt, 4.7 l; 1 Holley R7990A downdraught twin barrel carburettor; cleaner air system; exhaust system with catalytic converter; fuel feed: mechanical pump; water-cooled, 27.5 imp pt, 33 US pt, 15.6 l.

CHRYSLER Cordoba 2-door Hardtop

140 HP POWER TEAM

TRANSMISSION driving wheels: rear; gearbox: Torqueflite automatic transmission, hydraulic torque converter and planetary gears with 3 ratios, max ratio of converter at stall 1.90, possible manual selection; ratios: I 2.450, II 1.450, III 1, rev 2.220; lever: steering column or central; final drive: hypoid bevel; axle ratio: 2.710; width of rims: 5.5''; tyres: GR78 x 15.

PERFORMANCE max speed: about 103 mph, 165 km/h; power-weight ratio: 28.7 lb/hp, 13 kg/hp; speed in direct drive at 1,000 rpm: 25.5 mph, 41 km/h; consumption: 19.2 m/imp gal, 16 m/US gal, 14.7 l x 100 km.

CHASSIS integral, front auxiliary frame with cross members; front suspension: independent, wishbones, longitudinal torsion bars, anti-roll bar, telescopic dampers; rear: rigid axle, semi-elliptic leafsprings, anti-roll bar, telescopic dampers.

STEERING recirculating ball, servo; turns lock to lock: 3.50.

BRAKES front disc (diameter 11.58 in, 29.4 cm), front internal radial fins, rear drum, servo; swept area: total 375.29 sq in, 2,420 sq cm.

ELECTRICAL EQUIPMENT 12 V; 325 A battery; 60 A alternator; Lean-Burn electronic ignition; 4 headlamps.

DIMENSIONS AND WEIGHT wheel base: 115 in, 292 cm; tracks: 61.90 in, 157 cm front, 62 in, 157 cm rear; length: 215.80 in, 548 cm; width: 77.10 in, 196 cm; height: 53.10 in, 135 cm; ground clearance: 5.30 in, 13.5 cm; weight: 4,021 lb, 1,823 kg; turning circle (between walls): 44.9 ft, 13.7 m; fuel tank: 21.1 imp gal, 25.5 US gal, 96 l.

BODY hardtop; 2 doors; 6 seats, bench front seats with built-in headrests.

OPTIONALS limited slip differential; HR78 x 15 or FR78 x 15 tyres; GR60 x 15 tyres with 6.5'' wide rims; tilt of steering wheel; electric windows; electric sunshine roof; heated rear window; speed control device; air-conditioning; 100 A alternator.

155 hp (5,211 cc) power team

(optional, for California only).

See 140 hp power team, except for:

ENGINE max power (DIN): 155 hp at 4,000 rpm; max torque (DIN): 245 lb ft, 33.8 kg m at 1,600 rpm; 29.7 hp/l; 1 Carter TQ9147S downdraught 4-barrel carburettor.

PERFORMANCE power-weight ratio: 25.9 lb/hp, 11.8 kg/hp.

155 hp (5,900 cc) power team

(optional, not available in California).

See 140 hp power team, except for:

ENGINE 360 cu in, 5,900 cc (4 x 3.58 in, 101.6 x 89.6 mm); compression ratio: 8.4:1; max power (DIN): 155 hp at 3,600 rpm; max torque (DIN): 270 lb ft, 37.2 kg m at 2,400 rpm; 26.3 hp/l; 1 Holley R7991A downdraught twin barrel carburettor; cooling system: 26.6 imp pt, 31.9 US pt, 15.1 l.

TRANSMISSION axle ratio: 2.450.

PERFORMANCE max speed: about 109 mph, 175 km/h; power-weight ratio: 25.9 lb/hp, 11.8 kg/hp; consumption: 20.5 m/imp gal, 17 m/US gal, 13.8 l x 100 km.

ELECTRICAL EQUIPMENT 440 A battery.

170 hp power team

(standard, for California only).

See 140 hp power team, except for:

ENGINE 360 cu in, 5,900 cc (4 x 3.58 in, 101.6 x 89.6 mm); compression ratio: 8.4:1; max power (DIN): 170 hp at 3,600 rpm; max torque (DIN): 265 lb ft, 36.6 kg m at 1,600 rpm; 28.8 hp/l; 1 Carter TQ9134 downdraught 4-barrel carburettor; cooling system: 26.6 imp pt, 31.9 US pt, 15.1 l.

PERFORMANCE max speed: about 112 mph, 180 km/h; power-weight ratio: 23.7 lb/hp, 10.7 kg/hp; consumption: 16.8 m/imp gal, 14 m/US gal, 16.8 l x 100 km.

ELECTRICAL EQUIPMENT 440 A battery; Essex or Prestolite transistorized ignition.

190 hp power team

(standard, not available in California).

See 135 hp power team, except for:

ENGINE 400 cu in, 6,555 cc (4.34 x 3.38 in, 110.2 x 85.8 mm); compression ratio: 8.2:1; max power (DIN): 190 hp at 3,600 rpm; max torque (DIN): 305 lb ft, 42.1 kg m at 3,200 rpm; 29 hp/l; 1 Carter TQ9102S downdraught 4-barrel carburettor.

TRANSMISSION axle ratio: 2.450.

PERFORMANCE max speed: about 115 mph, 185 km/h; power-weight ratio: 21.2 lb/hp, 9.6 kg/hp; consumption: 18 m/imp gal, 15 m/US gal, 15.7 l x 100 km.

ELECTRICAL EQUIPMENT 440 A battery.

Newport - New Yorker Brougham Series

PRICES EX WORKS:

1 Newport 2-door Hardtop	$ 5,727
2 Newport 4-door Hardtop	$ 5,802
3 New Yorker Brougham 2-door Hardtop	$ 7,591
4 New Yorker Brougham 4-door Hardtop	$ 7,715

Power team:	Standard for:	Optional for:
155 hp	—	1,2
170 hp	all	—
185 hp	—	all
190 hp	all	—
195 hp	—	all

155 hp power team

(not available in California).

ENGINE front, 4 stroke; 8 cylinders; 360 cu in, 5,900 cc (4 x 3.58 in, 101.6 x 89.6 mm); compression ratio: 8.4:1; max power (DIN): 155 hp at 3,600 rpm; max torque (DIN): 270 lb ft, 37.2 kg m at 2,400 rpm; 26.3 hp/l; cast iron block and head; 5 crankshaft bearings; valves: overhead, in line, push-rods and rockers, hydraulic tappets; camshafts: 1, at centre of Vee; lubrication: rotary pump, full flow filter, 8.3 imp pt, 9.9 US pt, 4.7 l; 1 Holley R7991A downdraught twin barrel carburettor; cleaner air system; exhaust system with catalytic converter; fuel feed: mechanical pump; water-cooled, 26.6 imp pt, 31.9 US pt, 15.1 l.

TRANSMISSION driving wheels: rear; gearbox: Torqueflite automatic transmission, hydraulic torque converter and planetary gears with 3 ratios, max ratio of converter at stall 1.90, possible manual selection; ratios: I 2.450, II 1.450, III 1, rev 2.200; lever: steering column; final drive: hypoid bevel; axle ratio: 2.710; width of rims: 5.5''; tyres: HR78 x 15.

PERFORMANCE max speed: about 106 mph, 170 km/h; power-weight ratio: 4-dr. Hardtop 28.8 lb/hp, 13 kg/hp; speed in direct drive at 1,000 rpm: 28 mph, 45 km/h; consumption: 18 m/imp gal, 15 m/US gal, 15.7 l x 100 km.

CHASSIS integral with front auxiliary frame; front suspension: independent, wishbones (lower trailing links), longitudinal torsion bars, anti-roll bar, telescopic dampers; rear: rigid axle, semi-elliptic leafsprings, telescopic dampers.

STEERING recirculating ball, servo; turns lock to lock: 3.50.

BRAKES front disc (diameter 11.62 in, 29.5 cm), front internal radial fins, rear drum, servo; swept area: total 384.4 sq in, 2,479 sq cm.

ELECTRICAL EQUIPMENT 12 V; 440 A battery; 60 A alternator; Lean-Burn electronic ignition; 4 headlamps.

DIMENSIONS AND WEIGHT wheel base: 123.90 in, 315 cm; tracks: 64 in, 163 cm front, 63.40 in, 161 cm rear; length: 227.10 in, 577 cm; width: 2-dr. Hardtop 79.70 in, 202 cm - 4-dr. Hardtop 79.50 in, 202 cm; height: 54.70 in, 139 cm; ground clearance: 4.70 in, 12 cm; weight: 2-dr. Hardtop 4,394 lb, 1,993 kg - 4-dr. Hardtop 4,460 lb, 2,022 kg; turning circle (between walls): 48 ft, 14.6 m; fuel tank: 22 imp gal, 26.5 US gal, 100 l.

BODY hardtop; 6 seats, bench front seats with built-in headrests.

OPTIONALS limited slip differential; JR78 x 15 tyres with 6.5'' wide rims; tilt and telescopic steering wheel; reclining front seats; speed control device; heated rear window; electric windows; tinted glass; electric sunshine roof; vinyl roof; heavy-duty suspension; air-conditioning.

170 hp power team

(for California only).

See 155 hp power team, except for:

ENGINE max power (DIN): 170 hp at 4,000 rpm; max torque (DIN): 270 lb ft, 37.2 kg m at 1,600 rpm; max engine rpm: 4,400; 28.8 hp/l; 1 Carter TQ9134S downdraught 4-barrel carburettor.

PERFORMANCE power-weight ratio: Newport 4-dr. Hardtop 26.2 lb/hp, 11.9 kg/hp - New Yorker Brougham 4-dr. Hardtop 27.5 lb/hp, 12.4 kg/hp; consumption: 16.8 m/US gal, 16.8 l x 100 km.

ELECTRICAL EQUIPMENT Essex or Prestolite transistorized ignition.

DIMENSIONS AND WEIGHT length: New Yorker Broughams 231 in, 587 cm; weight: Newport 2-dr. Hardtop 4,394 lb, 1,993 kg - 4-dr. Hardtop 4,460 lb, 2,022 kg - New Yorker Brougham 2-dr. Hardtop 4,619 lb, 2,095 kg - 4-dr. Hardtop 4,669 lb, 2,117 kg.

185 hp power team

(for California only).

See 155 hp power team, except for:

ENGINE 440 cu in, 7,210 cc (4.32 x 3.75 in, 109.7 x 95.2 mm); compression ratio: 8.2:1; max power (DIN): 185 hp

CHRYSLER Newport 2-door Hardtop

CHRYSLER New Yorker Brougham 4-door Hardtop

at 3,600 rpm; max torque (DIN): 310 lb ft, 42.8 kg m at 2,400 rpm; 25.7 hp/l; 1 Carter TQ9101SN downdraught 4-barrel carburettor.

PERFORMANCE max speed: about 109 mph, 175 km/h; power-weight ratio: Newport 4-dr. Hardtop 24.4 lb/hp, 11.1 kg/hp - New Yorker Brougham 4-dr. Hardtop 25.5 lb/hp, 11.6 kg/hp; speed in direct drive at 1,000 rpm: 30.4 mph, 49 km/h; consumption: 13.3 m/imp gal, 11 m/US gal, 21.3 l x 100 km.

ELECTRICAL EQUIPMENT 500 A battery.

DIMENSIONS AND WEIGHT (see 170 hp power team) weight: Newports plus 57 lb, 26 kg - New Yorker Broughams plus 51 lb, 23 kg.

190 hp power team

(not available in California).

See 155 hp power team, except for:

ENGINE 400 cu in, 6,555 cc (4.34 x 3.38 in, 110.2 x 85.8 mm); compression ratio: 8.2:1; max power (DIN): 190 hp at 3,600 rpm; max torque (DIN): 305 lb ft, 42.1 kg m at 3,200 rpm; 29 hp/l; 1 Carter TQ9140S downdraught 4-barrel carburettor; cooling system: 27.5 imp pt, 33 US pt, 15.6 l.

PERFORMANCE max speed: about 112 mph, 180 km/h; power-weight ratio: Newport 4-dr. Hardtop 23.5 lb/hp, 10.6 kg/hp - New Yorker Brougham 4-dr. Hardtop 24.6 lb/hp, 11.1 kg/hp; speed in direct drive at 1,000 rpm: 30.4 mph, 49 km/h; consumption: 16.8 m/imp gal, 14 m/US gal, 16.8 l x 100 km.

DIMENSIONS AND WEIGHT (see 170 hp power team).

195 hp power team

(not available in California).

See 190 hp power team, except for:

ENGINE 440 cu in, 7,210 cc (4.32 x 3.75 in, 109.7 x 95.2 mm); max power (DIN): 195 hp at 3,600 rpm; max torque (DIN): 320 lb ft, 44.1 kg m at 2,000 rpm; 27 hp/l; 1 Carter TQ9109S downdraught 4-barrel carburettor; cooling system: 26.6 imp pt, 31.9 US pt, 15.1 l.

PERFORMANCE power-weight ratio: Newport 4-dr. Hardtop 23.2 lb/hp, 10.5 kg/hp - New Yorker Brougham 4-dr. Hardtop 24.2 lb/hp, 11 kg/hp; consumption: 14.4 m/imp gal, 12 m/US gal, 19.6 l x 100 km.

ELECTRICAL EQUIPMENT 500 A battery.

DIMENSIONS AND WEIGHT (see 170 hp power team) weight: Newports plus 57 lb, 27 kg - New Yorker Broughams plus 51 lb, 23 kg.

DODGE   USA

Omni

PRICE EX WORKS: $ 3,706

75 hp power team

(standard, not available in California).

ENGINE front, transverse, slanted 15° to front, 4 stroke; 4 cylinders, in line; 104.7 cu in, 1,714 cc (3.13 x 3.40 in, 79.5 x 86.4 mm); compression ratio: 8.2:1; max power (DIN): 75 hp at 5,600 rpm; max torque (DIN): 90 lb ft, 12.4 kg m at 3,200 rpm; max engine rpm: 6,500; 43.8 hp/l; cast iron block, light alloy head; 5 crankshaft bearings; valves: overhead, in line, thimble tappets; camshafts: 1, overhead, cogged belt; lubrication: gear pump, full flow filter, 6.7 imp pt, 8 US pt, 3.8 l; 1 Holley R8376A downdraught twin barrel carburettor; cleaner air system; exhaust system with catalytic converter; fuel feed: mechanical pump; water-cooled, 12.8 imp pt, 15.4 US pt, 7.3 l.

TRANSMISSION driving wheels: front; clutch: single dry plate (diaphragm); gearbox: mechanical; gears: 4, fully synchronized; ratios: I 3.450, II 1.940, III 1.290, IV 0.970, rev 3.170; lever: central; final drive: spiral bevel; axle ratio: 3.480; width of rims: 4.5''; tyres: P155/80R x 13.

PERFORMANCE max speed: about 91 mph, 146 km/h; power-weight ratio: 27.5 lb/hp, 12.5 kg/hp; speed in top at 1,000 rpm: 16.7 mph, 26.9 km/h; consumption: 24.6 m/imp gal, 20.5 m/US gal, 11.5 l x 100 km.

CHASSIS integral; front suspension: independent, by McPherson, lower wishbones, anti-roll bar, coil springs/telescopic struts; rear: independent, semi-trailing arms, coil springs, telescopic dampers.

STEERING rack-and-pinion; turns lock to lock: 4.

BRAKES front disc (diameter 5.04 in, 12.8 cm), front internal radial fins, rear drum; swept area: total 197.5 sq in, 1,274 sq cm.

ELECTRICAL EQUIPMENT 12 V; 325 A battery; 60 A alternator; Lean-Burn electronic ignition; 2 headlamps.

DIMENSIONS AND WEIGHT wheel base: 99.20 in, 252 cm; tracks: 55.50 in, 141 cm front, 55.10 in, 140 cm rear; length: 164.80 in, 419 cm; width: 66.20 in, 168 cm; height: 53.40 in, 136 cm; ground clearance: 5.10 in, 13 cm; weight: 2,059 lb, 934 kg; turning circle (between walls): 36.2 ft, 11 m; fuel tank: 10.8 imp gal, 13 US gal, 49 l.

BODY hatchback; 4 doors; 4 seats, separate front seats with built-in headrests.

OPTIONALS Torqueflite automatic transmission, hydraulic torque converter and planetary gears with 3 ratios (I 2.470, II 1.470, III 1, rev 2.100), max ratio of converter at stall 1.97, possible manual selection, central lever, 3.480 axle ratio; P165/75R x 13 tyres; power steering; servo brake; reclining backrests, heated rear window; rear window wiper-washer; vinyl roof; air-conditioning.

70 hp power team

(standard, for California only).

See 75 hp power team, except for:

ENGINE max power (DIN): 70 hp at 5,600 rpm; max torque (DIN): 85 lb ft, 11.7 kg m at 3,200 rpm; 40.8 hp/l; 1 Holley R8386A downdraught twin barrel carburettor.

TRANSMISSION axle ratio: 3.700.

PERFORMANCE power-weight ratio: 29.4 lb/hp, 13.3 kg/hp.

OPTIONALS Torqueflite automatic transmission with 3.740 axle ratio.

Aspen Series

PRICES EX WORKS:

1 Aspen 2-door Coupé	$ 3,747
2 Aspen 4-door Sedan	$ 3,865
3 Aspen Station Wagon	$ 4,207

For V8 engines add $ 169 for 1 and 2. For 3 add $ 129.

Power team:	Standard for:	Optional for:
90 hp	all	—
100 hp	1,2	—
110 hp	3	1,2
140 hp	—	all
155 hp (5,211 cc)	—	all
155 hp (5,900 cc)	—	all
160 hp	—	all
175 hp	—	1

DODGE Omni 4-door Hatchback

DODGE Aspen 4-door Sedan

90 hp power team

(for California only).

ENGINE front, 4 stroke; 6 cylinders, in line; 225 cu in, 3,687 cc (3.40 x 4.12 in, 86.4 x 104.6 mm); compression ratio: 8.4:1; max power (DIN): 90 hp at 3,600 rpm; max torque (DIN): 160 lb ft, 22.1 kg m at 1,600 rpm; max engine rpm: 4,000; 24.4 hp/l; cast iron block and head; 4 crankshaft bearings; valves: overhead, in line, push-rods and rockers; camshafts: 1, side; lubrication: rotary pump, full flow filter, 8.3 imp pt, 9.9 US pt, 4.7 l; 1 Holley R8010A downdraught single barrel carburettor; cleaner air system; exhaust system with catalytic converter; fuel feed: mechanical pump; water-cooled, 21.6 imp pt, 26 US pt, 12.3 l.

TRANSMISSION driving wheels: rear; clutch: single dry plate; gearbox: mechanical (Torqueflite automatic transmission standard for St. Wagon); gears: 4, fully synchronized with overdrive/top; ratios: I 3.090, II 1.670, III 1, IV 0.710, rev 3.000; lever: central; final drive: hypoid bevel; axle ratio: 3.230 - St. Wagon 3.210; width of rims: 5'' - St. Wagon 5.5''; tyres: D78 x 14 - St. Wagon F78 x 14.

PERFORMANCE max speed: about 93 mph, 150 km/h; power-weight ratio: Sedan 35.3 lb/hp, 16 kg/hp; speed in direct drive at 1,000 rpm: 24.2 mph, 39 km/h; consumption: 19.2 m/imp gal, 16 m/US gal, 14.7 l x 100 km.

CHASSIS integral, front auxiliary frame with cross members; front suspension: independent, wishbones, longitudinal torsion bars, anti-roll bar, telescopic dampers; rear: rigid axle, semi-elliptic leafsprings, telescopic dampers.

STEERING recirculating ball; turns lock to lock: 5.30.

BRAKES front disc (diameter 10.82 in, 27.5 cm), internal radial fins, rear drum; swept area: total 355.3 sq in, 2,291 sq cm.

ELECTRICAL EQUIPMENT 12 V; 325 A battery; 41 A alternator; Essex or Prestolite transistorized ignition; 2 headlamps.

DIMENSIONS AND WEIGHT wheel base: 112.70 in, 286 cm - Coupé 108.70 in, 276 cm; tracks: 60 in, 152 cm front, 58.50 in, 149 cm rear; length: 201.20 in, 511 cm - Coupé 197.20 in, 502 cm; width: 73.30 in, 186 cm; height: Coupé 53.30 in, 135 cm - Sedan 55.30 in, 140 cm - St. Wagon 55.70 in, 141 cm; ground clearance: Coupé 4.60 in, 11.7 cm - Sedan 5.10 in, 13 cm - St. Wagon 5.60 in, 14.2 cm; weight: Coupé 3,137 lb, 1,422 kg - Sedan 3,177 lb, 1,441 kg - St. Wagon 3,404 lb, 1,544 kg; turning circle (between walls): 43.4 ft, 13.2 m - Coupé 42.1 ft, 12.8 m; fuel tank: 15 imp gal, 18 US gal, 68 l - St. Wagon 16.3 imp gal, 19.5 US gal, 74 l.

OPTIONALS Torqueflite automatic transmission with 3 ratios (I 2.450, II 1.450, III 1, rev 2.220), max ratio of converter at stall 2.01, possible manual selection; 3.230 or 3.210 axle ratio; limited slip differential; E78 x 14 tyres; F78 x 14, ER78 x 14, FR78 x 14 tyres with 5.5'' wide rims; E70 x 14 tyres with 6'' wide rims; GR78 x 14 tyres with 6'' wide rims (for St. Wagon); power steering; tilt of steering wheel; servo brake (except for St. Wagon); reclining backrests; electric windows; speed control device; heated rear window; air-conditioning.

100 hp power team

(not available in California).

See 90 hp power team, except for:

ENGINE max power (DIN): 100 hp at 3,600 rpm; max torque (DIN): 170 lb ft, 23.4 kg m at 1,600 rpm; 27.1 hp/l; 1 Holley 7988A downdraught single barrel carburettor.

TRANSMISSION gears: 3, fully synchronized; ratios: I 3.080, II 1.700, III 1, rev 2.900.

PERFORMANCE max speed: about 96 mph, 155 km/h; power-weight ratio: Sedan 31.8 lb/hp, 14.4 kg/hp; consumption: 27.7 m/imp gal, 23 m/US gal, 10.2 l x 100 km.

OPTIONALS Torqueflite automatic transmission with 2.760 or 2.710 axle ratio.

110 hp power team

(not available in California).

See 100 hp power team, except for:

ENGINE max power (DIN): 110 hp at 3,600 rpm; max torque (DIN): 180 lb ft, 24.8 kg m at 2,000 rpm; 29.8 hp/l; 1 Carter BBD8136S downdraught twin barrel carburettor.

TRANSMISSION axle ratio: 3.210.

PERFORMANCE max speed: about 99 mph, 160 km/h; power-weight ratio: Sedan 28.9 lb/hp, 13.1 kg/hp; consumption: 25.2 m/imp gal, 21 m/US gal, 11.2 l x 100 km.

OPTIONALS Torqueflite automatic transmission with 2.940 axle ratio.

140 hp power team

(not available in California).

See 90 hp power team, except for:

ENGINE 8 cylinders; 318 cu in, 5,211 cc (3.91 x 3.31 in, 99.2 x 84 mm); compression ratio: 8.5:1; max power (DIN): 140 hp at 4,000 rpm; max torque (DIN): 245 lb ft, 33.8 kg m at 1,600 rpm; max engine rpm: 4,400; 26.9 hp/l; 5 crankshaft bearings; valves: hydraulic tappets; camshafts: 1, at centre of Vee; 1 Carter BBD8175S downdraught twin barrel carburettor; cooling system: 26.6 imp pt, 31.9 US pt, 15.1 l.

TRANSMISSION axle ratio: 2.940.

PERFORMANCE max speed: about 103 mph, 165 km/h; power-weight ratio: Sedan 22.7 lb/hp, 10.3 kg/hp; consumption: 21.6 m/imp gal, 18 m/US gal, 13.1 l x 100 km.

OPTIONALS Torqueflite automatic transmission with max ratio of converter at stall 1.90, 2.470 2.450 or 2.710 axle ratio.

155 hp (5,211 cc) power team

(for California only).

See 140 hp power team, except for:

ENGINE max power (DIN): 155 hp at 4,000 rpm; max torque (DIN): 245 lb ft, 33.8 kg m at 1,600 rpm; 29.7 hp/l; 1 Carter TQ9147S downdraught 4-barrel carburettor.

TRANSMISSION gearbox: Torqueflite automatic transmission (standard), hydraulic torque converter and planetary gears with 3 ratios, max ratio of converter at stall 1.90, possible manual selection; ratios: I 2.450, II 1.450, III 1, rev 2.220; axle ratio: 2.760 - St. Wagon 2.710.

PERFORMANCE max speed: about 106 mph, 170 km/h; power-weight ratio: Sedan 20.5 lb/hp, 9.3 kg/hp; speed in direct drive at 1,000 rpm: 26.4 mph, 42.5 km/h; consumption: 19.2 m/imp gal, 16 m/US gal, 14.7 l x 100 km.

OPTIONALS 2.710 axle ratio (except for St. Wagon).

155 hp (5,900 cc) power team

(not available in California).

See 140 hp power team, except for:

ENGINE 360 cu in, 5,900 cc (4 x 3.58 in, 101.6 x 89.6 mm); compression ratio: 8.4:1; max power (DIN): 155 hp at 3,600 rpm; max torque (DIN): 270 lb ft, 37.2 kg m at 2,400 rpm; 26.3 hp/l; 1 Holley 7991A downdraught twin barrel carburettor.

TRANSMISSION gearbox: Torqueflite automatic transmission (standard), hydraulic torque converter and planetary gears with 3 ratios, max ratio of converter at stall 1.90, possible manual selection; ratios: I 2.450, II 1.450, III 1, rev 2.220; axle ratio: 2.450.

PERFORMANCE max speed: about 106 mph, 170 km/h; power-weight ratio: Sedan 20.5 lb/hp, 9.3 kg/hp; speed in direct drive at 1,000 rpm: 26.4 mph, 42.5 km/h; consumption: 20.5 m/imp gal, 17 m/US gal, 13.8 l x 100 km.

ELECTRICAL EQUIPMENT 440 A battery.

160 hp power team

(for California only).

See 155 hp (5,900 cc) power team, except for:

ENGINE compression ratio: 8:1; max power (DIN): 160 hp at 3,600 rpm; max torque (DIN): 265 lb ft, 36.6 kg m at 1,600 rpm; 27.1 hp/l; 1 Carter TQ9134S downdraught 4-barrel carburettor.

TRANSMISSION axle ratio: 3.210.

PERFORMANCE power-weight ratio: Sedan 19.8 lb/hp, 9 kg/hp; consumption: 15.6 m/imp gal, 13 m/US gal, 18.1 l x 100 km.

OPTIONALS 2.710 axle ratio (except for St. Wagon).

DODGE Aspen Series (110 hp engine)

DODGE Diplomat Medallion Coupé

175 hp power team

(not available in California).

See 155 hp (5,900 cc) power team, except for:

ENGINE compression ratio: 8:1; max power (DIN): 175 hp at 4,000 rpm; max torque (DIN): 260 lb ft, 35.9 kg m at 2,400 rpm; max engine rpm: 4,400; 29.7 hp/l; 1 Carter TQ9104S downdraught 4-barrel carburettor.

TRANSMISSION axle ratio: 3.210.

PERFORMANCE max speed: about 109 mph, 175 km/h; power-weight ratio: Coupé 17.9 lb/hp, 8.1 kg/hp; consumption: 15.6 m/imp gal, 13 m/US gal, 18.1 l x 100 km.

OPTIONALS 2.710 axle ratio.

Diplomat Series

PRICES EX WORKS:

Diplomat Coupé	$ 4,991
Diplomat Sedan	$ 5,147
Diplomat Station Wagon	$ 5,486
Diplomat Medallion Coupé	$ 5,361
Diplomat Medallion Sedan	$ 5,517

For V8 engines add $ 176

Power team:	Standard for:	Optional for:
110 hp	all	—
90 hp	all	—
140 hp	—	all
155 hp (5,211 cc)	—	all
155 hp (5,900 cc)	—	all
170 hp	—	all

110 hp power team

(not available in California).

ENGINE front, 4 stroke; 6 cylinders, vertical, in line; 225 cu in, 3,687 cc (3.40 x 4.12 in, 86.4 x 104.6 mm); compression ratio: 8.4:1; max power (DIN): 110 hp at 3,600 rpm; max torque (DIN): 180 lb ft, 24.8 kg m at 2,000 rpm; max engine rpm: 4,000; 29.8 hp/l; cast iron block and head; 4 crankshaft bearings; valves: overhead, in line, push-rods and rockers; camshafts: 1, side; lubrication: rotary pump, full flow filter, 8.3 imp pt, 9.9 US pt, 4.7 l; 1 Carter BBD8136S downdraught twin barrel carburettor; cleaner air system; exhaust system with catalytic converter; fuel feed: mechanical pump; water-cooled, 20.1 imp pt, 24.1 US pt, 11.4 l.

TRANSMISSION driving wheels: rear; clutch: single dry plate; gearbox: mechanical; gears: 4, fully synchronized with overdrive/top; ratios: I 3.090, II 1.670, III 1, IV 0.710, rev 3.000; lever: central; final drive: hypoid bevel; axle ratio: 3.230 - St. Wagon 3.210; width of rims: 5.5''; tyres: FR78 x 15.

PERFORMANCE max speed: about 93 mph, 150 km/h; power-weight ratio: Diplomat Sedan 31.5 lb/hp, 14.3 kg/hp; speed in top at 1,000 rpm: 24.2 mph, 39 km/h; consumption: 23.9 m/imp gal, 20 m/US gal, 11.8 l x 100 km.

CHASSIS integral, front auxiliary frame with cross members; front suspension: independent, wishbones, transverse torsion

DODGE Diplomat Station Wagon

bars, anti-roll bar, telescopic dampers; rear: rigid axle, semi-elliptic leafsprings, telescopic dampers.

STEERING recirculating ball, servo; turns lock to lock: 3.50.

BRAKES front disc (diameter 10.82 in, 27.5 cm), front internal radial fins, rear drum; swept area: total 355.24 sq in, 2,291 sq cm.

ELECTRICAL EQUIPMENT 12 V; 375 A battery; 41 A alternator; Essex or Prestolite transistorized ignition; 4 headlamps.

DIMENSIONS AND WEIGHT wheel base: 112.70 in, 286 cm; tracks: 60 in, 152 cm front, 58.50 in, 149 cm rear; length: coupés 204.10 in, 518 cm - sedans 206.10 in, 523 cm - St. Wagon 202.80 in, 515 cm; width: 73.30 in, 186 cm - coupés 73.50 in, 187 cm; height: coupés 53.30 in, 135 cm - sedans 55.30 in, 140 cm - St. Wagon 55.70 in, 141 cm; ground clearance: 4.90 in, 12.4 cm - St. Wagon 5.40 in, 13.7 cm; weight: Diplomat Coupé 3,421 lb, 1,551 kg - Sedan 3,466 lb, 1,572 kg - St. Wagon 3,554 lb, 1,612 kg - Diplomat Medallion Coupé 3,496 lb, 1,585 kg - Sedan 3,550 lb, 1,610 kg; turning circle (between walls): 43.5 ft, 13.3 m; fuel tank: 16.3 imp gal, 19.5 US gal, 74 l.

OPTIONALS limited slip differential; 3.210 axle ratio; Torqueflite automatic transmission with 3 ratios (I 2.450, II 1.450, III 1, rev 2.220), max ratio of converter at stall 2.01, possible manual selection, steering column or central lever, 2.760 or 2.710 axle ratio; tilt of steering wheel; servo brake (standard for St. Wagon); heavy-duty suspension; heated rear window; reclining front seats; electric windows; speed control; Landau vinyl roof; air-conditioning.

90 hp power team

(for California only).

See 110 hp power team, except for:

ENGINE max power (DIN): 90 hp at 3,600 rpm; max torque (DIN): 160 lb ft, 22.1 kg m at 1,600 rpm; 24.4 hp/l; 1 Carter BBD0137C downdraught single barrel carburettor.

TRANSMISSION gearbox: Torqueflite automatic transmission (standard), hydraulic torque converter and planetary gears with 3 ratios, max ratio of converter at stall 2.01, possible manual selection; ratios: I 2.450, II 1.450, III 1, rev 2.220.

PERFORMANCE max speed: about 90 mph, 145 km/h; power-weight ratio: Diplomat Sedan 38.5 lb/hp, 17.5 kg/hp; speed in direct drive at 1,000 rpm: 25.5 mph, 41 km/h; consumption: 19.2 m/imp gal, 16 m/US gal, 14.7 l x 100 km.

ELECTRICAL EQUIPMENT 325 A battery.

140 hp power team

(not available in California).

See 110 hp power team, except for:

ENGINE 8 cylinders; 318 cu in, 5,211 cc (3.91 x 3.31 in, 99.2 x 84 mm); compression ratio: 8.5:1; max power (DIN): 140 hp at 4,000 rpm; max torque (DIN): 245 lb ft, 33.8 kg m at 1,600 rpm; max engine rpm: 4,400; 26.9 hp/l; 5 crankshaft bearings; valves: hydraulic tappets; camshafts: 1, at centre of Vee; 1 Carter BBD8175S downdraught twin barrel carburettor; cooling system: 26.6 imp pt, 31.9 US pt, 15.1 l.

TRANSMISSION gearbox: mechanical (Torqueflite automatic transmission standard for St. Wagon); axle ratio: 2.940 - St. Wagon 2.710.

PERFORMANCE max speed: about 102 mph, 164 km/h; power-weight ratio: Diplomat Sedan 24.8 lb/hp, 11.2 kg/hp; consumption: 21.6 m/imp gal, 18 m/US gal, 13.1 l x 100 km.

ELECTRICAL EQUIPMENT 325 A battery; Lean-Burn electronic ignition.

OPTIONALS (except for St. Wagon) Torqueflite automatic transmission with max ratio of converter at stall 1.90, 2.470 or 2.450 axle ratio.

155 hp (5,211 cc) power team

(for California only).

See 140 hp power team, except for:

ENGINE max power (DIN): 155 hp at 4,000 rpm; max torque (DIN): 245 lb ft, 33.8 kg m at 1,600 rpm; 29.7 hp/l; 1 Carter TQ9147S downdraught 4-barrel carburettor.

TRANSMISSION gearbox: Torqueflite automatic transmission (standard), hydraulic torque converter and planetary gears with 3 ratios, max ratio of converter at stall 1.90, possible manual selection; ratios: I 2.450, II 1.450, III 1, rev 2.220; axle ratio: 2.760 - St. Wagon 2.710.

PERFORMANCE max speed: about 103 mph, 165 km/h; power-weight ratio: Diplomat Sedan 22.4 lb/hp, 10.1 kg/hp; speed in direct drive at 1,000 rpm: 25.5 mph, 41 km/h; consumption: 19.2 m/imp gal, 16 m/US gal, 14.7 l x 100 km.

OPTIONALS 2.710 axle ratio (except for St. Wagon).

155 hp (5,900 cc) power team

(not available in California).

See 110 hp power team, except for:

ENGINE 8 cylinders; 360 cu in, 5,900 cc (4 x 3.58 in, 101.6 x 89.6 mm); max power (DIN): 155 hp at 3,600 rpm; max torque (DIN): 270 lb ft, 37.2 kg m at 2,400 rpm; 26.3 hp/l; 5 crankshaft: 1, at centre of Vee; 1 Holley R7991A downdraught twin barrel carburettor; cooling system: 26.6 imp pt, 31.9 US pt, 15.1 l.

TRANSMISSION gearbox: Torqueflite automatic transmission (standard), hydraulic torque converter and planetary gears with 3 ratios, max ratio of converter at stall 1.90, possible manual selection; ratios: I 2.450, II 1.450, III 1, rev 2.220; axle ratio: 2.450.

PERFORMANCE max speed: about 106 mph, 170 km/h; power-weight ratio: Diplomat Sedan 22.4 lb/hp, 10.1 kg/hp; speed in direct drive at 1,000 rpm: 26.4 mph, 42.5 km/h; consumption: 20.5 m/imp gal, 17 m/US gal, 13.8 l x 100 km.

ELECTRICAL EQUIPMENT 440 A battery; Lean-Burn electronic ignition.

170 hp power team

(for California only).

See 155 hp (5,900 cc) power team, except for:

ENGINE max power (DIN): 170 hp at 4,000 rpm; max torque (DIN): 270 lb ft, 37.2 kg m at 1,600 rpm; max engine rpm: 4,400; 28.8 hp/l; 1 Carter TQ9134S downdraught 4-barrel carburettor.

TRANSMISSION axle ratio: 2.710.

PERFORMANCE max speed: about 109 mph, 175 km/h; power-weight ratio: Diplomat Sedan 20.4 lb/hp, 9.2 kg/hp; consumption: 16.8 m/imp gal, 14 m/US gal, 16.8 l x 100 km.

Monaco Series

PRICES EX WORKS:

1 Monaco Hardtop	$	4,230
2 Monaco Sedan	$	4,310
3 Monaco 6-pass. Station Wagon	$	5,043
4 Monaco 9-pass. Station Wagon	$	5,186
5 Monaco Brougham Hardtop	$	4,476
6 Monaco Brougham Sedan	$	4,527
7 Monaco Crestwood 6-pass. Station Wagon	$	5,486
8 Monaco Crestwood 9-pass. Station Wagon	$	5,629

For V8 engines add $ 176.

Power team:	Standard for:	Optional for:
110 hp	1,2,5,6	—
140 hp	—	1,2,5,6
155 hp (5,211 cc)	1,2,5,6	—
155 hp (5,900 cc)	3,4,7,8	1,2,5,6
170 hp	3,7	1,2,5,6
190 hp	—	all

110 hp power team

(not available in California).

ENGINE front, 4 stroke; 6 cylinders, in line; 225 cu in, 3,687 cc (3.40 x 4.12 in, 86.4 x 104.6 mm); compression ratio: 8.4:1; max power (DIN): 110 hp at 3,600 rpm; max torque (DIN): 180 lb ft, 24.8 kg m at 2,000 rpm; max engine rpm: 4,000; 29.8 hp/l; cast iron block and head; 4 crankshaft bearings; valves: overhead, in line, push-rods and rockers; camshafts: 1, side; lubrication: rotary pump, full flow filter, 8.3 imp pt, 9.9 US pt, 4.7 l; 1 Carter BBD8136S downdraught twin barrel carburettor; cleaner air system; exhaust system with catalytic converter; fuel feed: mechanical pump; water-cooled, 21.6 imp pt, 26 US pt, 12.3 l.

TRANSMISSION driving wheels: rear; clutch: single dry plate; gearbox: mechanical; gears: 3, fully synchronized; ratios: I 3.080, II 1.700, III 1, rev 2.900; lever: steering column; final drive: hypoid bevel; axle ratio: 3.210; width of rims: 5.5''; tyres: F78 x 15.

PERFORMANCE max speed: about 96 mph, 155 km/h; power-weight ratio: Monaco Sedan 33 lb/hp, 15 kg/hp; speed in

DODGE Monaco Brougham Sedan

direct drive at 1,000 rpm: 24.2 mph, 39 km/h; consumption: 23.9 m/imp gal, 20 m/US gal, 11.8 l x 100 km.

CHASSIS integral with isolated front cross members; front suspension: independent, wishbones (lower trailing links), longitudinal torsion bars, anti-roll bar, telescopic dampers; rear: rigid axle, semi-elliptic leafsprings, telescopic dampers.

STEERING recirculating ball; turns lock to lock: 5.30.

BRAKES front disc (diameter 11.58 in, 29.4 cm), front internal radial fins, rear drum, servo; swept area: total 372 sq in, 2,400 sq cm.

ELECTRICAL EQUIPMENT 12 V; 375 A battery; 60 A alternator; Essex or Prestolite transistorized ignition; 4 headlamps.

DIMENSIONS AND WEIGHT wheel base: 114.90 in, 292 cm - sedans 117.40 in, 298 cm; tracks: 61.90 in, 157 cm front, 62 in, 157 cm rear; length: 213.20 in, 541 cm - sedans 218 in, 554 cm; width: 77.70 in, 197 cm; height: 52.90 in, 134 cm - sedans 54.30 in, 138 cm; ground clearance: 5.10 in, 12.9 cm; weight: Monaco Hardtop 3,610 lb, 1,637 kg - Sedan 3,634 lb, 1,648 kg - Monaco Brougham Hardtop 3,616 lb, 1,640 kg - Sedan 3,649 lb, 1,655 kg; turning circle (between walls): 45.5 ft, 13.9 m; fuel tank: 17.2 imp gal, 20.5 US gal, 78 l.

OPTIONALS limited slip differential; Torqueflite automatic transmission with 3 ratios (I 2.450, II 1.450, III 1, rev

2.200), max ratio of converter at stall 2.01, possible manual selection, steering column or central lever, 2.710 axle ratio; G78 x 15, GR78 x 15 or 215 x 15 tyres; power steering; tilt of steering wheel; anti-roll bar on rear suspension; electric windows; heated rear window; sunshine roof; air-conditioning; 100 A alternator.

140 hp power team

(not available in California).

See 110 hp power team, except for:

ENGINE 8 cylinders; 318 cu in, 5,211 cc (3.91 x 3.31 in, 99.2 x 84 mm); compression ratio: 8.5:1; max power (DIN): 140 hp at 4,000 rpm; max torque (DIN): 245 lb, 33.8 kg m at 1,600 rpm; max engine rpm: 4,400; 26.9 hp/l; 5 crankshaft bearings; valves: hydraulic tappets; camshafts: 1, at centre of Vee; 1 Holley R7990A downdraught twin barrel carburettor; cooling system: 27.5 imp pt, 33 US pt, 15.6 l.

TRANSMISSION gearbox: Torqueflite automatic transmission (standard), max ratio of converter at stall 1.90; axle ratio: 2.710.

PERFORMANCE max speed: about 103 mph, 165 km/h; power-weight ratio: Monaco Sedan 27.8 lb/hp, 12.6 kg/hp; speed in direct drive at 1,000 rpm: 25.5 mph, 41 km/h; consumption: 19.2 m/imp gal, 16 m/US gal, 14.7 l x 100 km.

STEERING servo (standard); turns lock to lock: 3.50.

ELECTRICAL EQUIPMENT 325 A battery; Lean-Burn electronic ignition.

DIMENSIONS AND WEIGHT weight: plus 253 lb, 115 kg; fuel tank: 21.1 imp gal, 25.5 US gal, 96 l.

155 hp (5,211 cc) power team

(for California only).

See 140 hp power team, except for:

ENGINE max power (DIN): 155 hp at 4,000 rpm; max torque (DIN): 245 lb ft, 33.8 kg m at 1,600 rpm; 29.7 hp/l; 1 Carter TQ9147S downdraught 4-barrel carburettor; max power (DIN): 145 hp at 4,000 rpm; max torque (DIN): 245 lb ft, 33.8 kg m at 1,600 rpm; max engine rpm: 4,400; 27.8 hp/l; 5 crankshaft bearings; valves: hydraulic tappets; camshafts: 1, at centre of Vee; 1 Carter BBD8093S downdraught twin barrel carburettor; cooling system: 27.5 imp pt, 33 US pt, 15.6 l.

TRANSMISSION axle ratio: 2.710.

PERFORMANCE max speed: about 106 mph, 170 km/h; power-weight ratio: Monaco Sedan 25.1 lb/hp, 11.4 kg/hp.

155 hp (5,900 cc) power team

(not available in California).

See 140 hp power team, except for:

ENGINE 8 cylinders; 360 cu in, 5,900 cc (4 x 3.58 in, 101.6 x 89.6 mm); max power (DIN): 155 hp at 3,600 rpm; max torque (DIN): 270 lb ft, 37.2 kg m at 2,400 rpm; 26.3 hp/l; 5 crankshaft bearings; valves: hydraulic tappets; camshafts: 1, at centre of Vee; 1 Holley R7990A downdraught twin barrel carburettor; cooling system: 26.6 imp pt, 31.9 US pt, 15.1 l.

TRANSMISSION gearbox: Torqueflite automatic transmission (standard), max ratio of converter at stall 1.90; axle ratio: 2.450 - st. wagons 2.710; width of rims: st. wagons 6.5''; tyres: st. wagons H78 x 15.

PERFORMANCE max speed: about 109 mph, 175 km/h; power-weight ratio: 6-pass. st. wagons 27.8 lb/hp, 12.6 kg/hp; speed in direct drive at 1,000 rpm: 25.5 mph, 41 km/h; consumption: 18 m/imp gal, 15 m/US gal, 15.7 l x 100 km.

STEERING servo (standard); turns lock to lock: 3.50.

BRAKES swept area: total 387.1 sq in, 2,497 sq cm.

ELECTRICAL EQUIPMENT 440 A battery; Learn-Burn electronic ignition.

DIMENSIONS AND WEIGHT wheel base: st. wagons 117.50 in, 298 cm; rear track: st. wagons 63.40 in, 161 cm; length: st. wagons 225.10 in, 572 cm; width: st. wagons 78.80 in, 198 cm; height: st. wagons 56.90 in, 144 cm; ground clearance: st. wagons 5.30 in, 13.5 cm; weight: Monaco Hardtop 3,905 lb, 1,771 kg - Sedan 3,929 lb, 1,781 kg - 6-pass. St. Wagon 4,311 lb, 1,955 kg - 9-pass. St. Wagon 4,375 lb, 1,984 kg - Monaco Brougham Hardtop 3,911 lb, 1,773 kg - Sedan 3,944 lb, 1,788 kg - Monaco Crestwood 6-pass. St. Wagon 4,305 lb, 1,952 kg - 9-pass. St. Wagon 4,379 lb, 1,986 kg; fuel tank: st. wagons 16.7 imp gal, 20 US gal, 76 l.

OPTIONALS anti-roll bar on rear suspension not available for st. wagons.

DODGE Monaco Brougham Hardtop

170 hp power team

(for California only).

See 155 hp (5,900 cc) power team, except for:

ENGINE max power (DIN): 170 hp at 4,000 rpm; max torque (DIN): 270 lb ft, 37.2 kg m at 1,600 rpm; 28.8 hp/l; 1 Carter TQ9134S downdraught 4-barrel carburettor.

TRANSMISSION axle ratio: 2.710.

PERFORMANCE max speed: about 112 mph, 180 km/h; power-weight ratio: 6-pass. st. wagons 25.4 lb/hp, 11.5 kg/hp; speed in direct drive at 1,000 rpm: 28 mph, 45 km/h; consumption: 16.8 m/imp gal, 14 m/US gal, 16.8 l x 100 km.

ELECTRICAL EQUIPMENT Essex or Prestolite transistorized ignition.

190 hp power team

(not available in California).

See 155 hp (5,900 cc) power team, except for:

ENGINE 400 cu in, 6,555 cc (4.34 x 3.38 in, 110.2 x 85.8 mm); compression ratio: 8.2:1; max power (DIN): 190 hp at 3,600 rpm; max torque (DIN): 305 lb ft, 42.1 kg m at 3,200 rpm;

DODGE Monaco Brougham Sedan

DODGE Charger Special Edition Hardtop

29 hp/l; 1 Carter TQ9140S downdraught 4-barrel carburettor; cooling system: 27.5 imp pt, 33 US pt, 15.6 l.

TRANSMISSION tyres: G78 x 15 - st. wagons H78 x 15

PERFORMANCE max speed: about 115 mph, 185 km/h; power-weight ratio: Monaco Sedan 21.6 lb/hp, 9.8 kg/hp; speed in direct drive at 1,000 rpm: 28 mph, 45 km/h; consumption: 18 m/imp gal, 15 m/US gal, 15.7 l x 100 km.

ELECTRICAL EQUIPMENT Lean-Burn electronic ignition.

DIMENSIONS AND WEIGHT weight: plus 178 lb, 81 kg - st. wagons plus 102 lb, 46 kg.

Charger Special Edition

PRICE EX WORKS: $ 5,307

140 hp power team

(standard, not available in California).

ENGINE front, 4 stroke; 8 cylinders; 318 cu in, 5,211 cc (3.91 x 3.31 in, 99.2 x 84 mm); compression ratio: 8.5:1; max power (DIN): 140 hp at 4,000 rpm; max torque (DIN): 245 lb ft, 33.8 kg m at 1,600 rpm; max engine rpm: 4,400; 26.9 hp/l; cast iron block and head; 5 crankshaft bearings; valves: overhead, in line, push-rods and rockers, hydraulic tappets; camshafts: 1, at centre of Vee; lubrication: rotary pump, full flow filter, 8.3 imp pt, 9.9 US pt, 4.7 l; 1

Holley R7990A downdraught twin barrel carburettor; cleaner air system; exhaust system with catalytic converter; fuel feed: mechanical pump; water-cooled, 27.5 imp pt, 33 US pt, 15.6 l.

TRANSMISSION driving wheels: rear; gearbox: Torqueflite automatic transmission, hydraulic torque converter and planetary gears with 3 ratios, max ratio of converter at stall 1.90, possible manual selection; ratios: I 2.450, II 1.450, III 1, rev 2.220; lever: steering column or central; final drive: hypoid bevel; axle ratio: 2.710; width of rims: 5.5''; tyres: FR78 x 15.

PERFORMANCE max speed: about 103 mph, 165 km/h; power-weight ratio: 27.8 lb/hp, 12.6 kg/hp; speed in direct drive at 1,000 rpm: 28.5 mph, 45.8 km/h; consumption: 19.2 m/imp gal, 16 m/US gal, 14.7 l x 100 km.

CHASSIS integral with isolated front cross members; front suspension: independent, wishbones (lower trailing links), longitudinal torsion bars, anti-roll bar, telescopic dampers; rear: rigid axle, semi-elliptic leafsprings, anti-roll bar, telescopic dampers.

STEERING recirculating ball, servo; turns lock to lock: 3.50.

BRAKES front disc (diameter 11.68 in, 29.7 cm), front internal radial fins, rear drum, servo; swept area: total 375.3 sq in, 2,420 sq cm.

ELECTRICAL EQUIPMENT 12 V; 325 A battery; 60 A alternator; Lean-Burn electronic Ignition; 4 headlamps.

DIMENSIONS AND WEIGHT wheel base: 114.90 in, 292 cm; tracks: 61.90 in, 157 cm front, 62 in, 157 cm rear; length:

215.30 in, 547 cm; width: 77.10 in, 196 cm; height: 52.90 in, 134 cm; ground clearance: 5.10 in, 13 cm; weight: 3,895 lb, 1,766 kg; turning circle (between walls): 44.9 ft, 13.7 m; fuel tank: 21.1 imp gal, 25.5 US gal, 96 l.

BODY hardtop; 2 doors; 6 seats.

OPTIONALS limited slip differential; HR78 x 15 or GR78 x 15 tyres; GR60 x 15 tyres with 6.5'' wide rims; tilt of steering wheel; electric windows; heated rear window; reclining front seats; 100 A alternator; electric sunshine roof; Landau vinyl roof; speed control; air-conditioning.

155 hp (5,211 cc) power team

(standard for California only).

See 140 hp poer tea,m except for:

ENGINE max power (DIN): 155 hp at 4,000 rpm; max torque (DIN): 245 lb ft, 33.8 kg m at 1,600 rpm; 29.7 hp/l; 1 Carter TQ9147S downdraught 4-barrel carburettor.

PERFORMANCE max speed: about 106 mph, 170 km/h; power-weight ratio: 25.1 lb/hp, 11.4 kg/hp.

155 hp (5,900 cc) power team

(optional, not available in California).

See 140 hp power team, except for:

ENGINE 360 cu in, 5,900 cc (4 x 3.58 in, 101.6 x 89.6 mm); compression ratio: 8.4:1; max power (DIN): 155 hp at 3,600 rpm; max torque (DIN): 270 lb ft, 37.2 kg m at 2,400 rpm; 26.3 hp/l; 1 Holley R7991A downdraught twin barrel carburettor; cooling system: 26.6 imp pt, 31.9 US pt, 15.1 l.

TRANSMISSION axle ratio: 2.450.

PERFORMANCE max speed: about 108 mph, 174 km/h; power-weight ratio: 25.3 lb/hp, 11.5 kg/hp; consumption: 20.5 m/imp gal, 17 m/US gal, 13.8 l x 100 km.

ELECTRICAL EQUIPMENT 440 A battery.

DIMENSIONS AND WEIGHT weight: plus 34 lb, 15 kg.

170 hp power team

(optional for California only).

See 155 hp (5,900 cc) power team, except for:

ENGINE max power (DIN): 170 hp at 3,600 rpm; max torque (DIN): 265 lb ft, 36.6 kg m at 1,600 rpm; 28.8 hp/l; 1 Carter TQ9134S downdraught 4-barrel carburettor.

TRANSMISSION axle ratio: 2.710.

PERFORMANCE max speed: about 112 mph, 180 km/h; power-weight ratio: 23.1 lb/hp, 10.5 kg/hp; consumption: 16.8 m/imp gal, 14 m/US gal, 16.8 l x 100 km.

ELECTRICAL EQUIPMENT Essex or Prestolite transistorized ignition.

190 hp power team

(optional, not available in California).

See 155 hp (5,900 cc) power team, except for:

ENGINE 400 cu in, 6,555 cc (4.34 x 3.38 in, 110.2 x 85.8 mm); compression ratio: 8.2:1; max power (DIN): 190 hp at 3,600 rpm; max torque (DIN): 305 lb ft, 42.1 kg m at 3,200 rpm; 29 hp/l; 1 Carter TQ9140S downdraught 4-barrel carburettor.

PERFORMANCE max speed: about 118 mph, 190 km/h; power-weight ratio: 21.3 lb/hp, 9.6 kg/hp; speed in direct drive at 1,000 rpm: 30.4 mph, 49 km/h; consumption: 18 m/imp gal, 15.7 l x 100 km.

DIMENSIONS AND WEIGHT weight: plus 149 lb, 68 kg.

Magnum XE

PRICE EX WORKS: $ 5,448

140 hp power team

(standard, not available in California).

ENGINE front, 4 stroke; 8 cylinders; 318 cu in, 5,211 cc (3.91 x 3.31 in, 99.2 x 84 mm); compression ratio: 8.5:1; max power (DIN): 140 hp at 4,000 rpm; max torque (DIN): 245 lb ft, 33.8 kg m at 1,600 rpm; max engine rpm: 4,400; 26.9 hp/l; cast iron block and head; 5 crankshaft bearings; valves: overhead, in line, push-rods and rockers, hydraulic tappets; camshafts: 1, at centre of Vee; lubrication: rotary pump, full flow filter, 8.3 imp pt, 9.9 US pt, 4.7 l; 1 Holley R7990A downdraught twin barrel carburettor; cleaner air system; exhaust system with catalytic converter; fuel feed: mechanical pump; water-cooled, 27.5 imp pt, 33 US pt, 15.6 l.

TRANSMISSION driving wheels: rear; gearbox: Torqueflite automatic transmission, hydraulic torque converter and planetary gears with 3 ratios, max ratio of converter at stall 1.90, possible manual selection; ratios: I 2.450, II 1.450, III 1, rev 2.220; lever: steering column or central; final drive: hypoid bevel; axle ratio: 2.710; width of rims: 5.5''; tyres: FR78 x 15.

PERFORMANCE max speed: about 103 mph, 165 km/h; power-weight ratio: 27.8 lb/hp, 12.6 kg/hp; speed in direct drive at 1,000 rpm: 28.5 mph, 45.8 km/h; consumption: 19.2 m/imp gal, 16 m/US gal, 14.7 l x 100 km.

CHASSIS integral with isolated front cross members; front suspension: independent, wishbones (lower trailing links), longitudinal torsion bars, anti-roll bar, telescopic dampers; rear: rigid axle, semi-elliptic leafsprings, anti-roll bar, telescopic dampers.

STEERING recirculating ball, servo; turns lock to lock: 3.50.

BRAKES front disc (diameter 11.68 in, 29.7 cm), front internal radial fins, rear drum, servo; swept area: total 375.3 sq in, 2,420 sq cm.

ELECTRICAL EQUIPMENT 12 V; 325 A battery; 60 A alternator; Lean-Burn electronic ignition; 4 headlamps.

DIMENSIONS AND WEIGHT wheel base: 114.90 in, 292 cm; tracks: 61.90 in, 157 cm front, 62 in, 157 cm rear; length: 215.80 in, 548 cm; width: 77.10 in, 196 cm; height: 53.10 in, 135 cm; ground clearance: 5.30 in, 13.4 cm; weight: 3,893 lb, 1,765 kg; turning circle (between walls): 44.9 ft, 13.7 m; fuel tank: 21.1 imp gal, 25.5 US gal, 96 l.

BODY hardtop; 2 doors; 6 seats.

OPTIONALS limited slip differential; GR78 x 15 or HR78 x 15 tyres; GR60 x 15 tyres with 6.5'' wide rims; tilt of steering wheel; 100 A alternator; speed control; reclining front seats; heated rear window; electric windows; electric sunshine roof; Landau vinyl roof; air-conditioning.

155 hp (5,211 cc) power team

(standard for California only).

See 140 hp power team, except for:

ENGINE max power (DIN): 155 hp at 4,000 rpm; max torque (DIN): 245 lb ft, 33.8 kg m at 1,600 rpm; 29.7 hp/l; 1 Carter TQ9147S downdraught 4-barrel carburettor.

PERFORMANCE max speed: about 106 mph, 170 km/h; power-weight ratio: 25.1 lb/hp, 11.4 kg/hp.

DODGE Magnum XE Hardtop

155 hp (5,900 cc) power team

(optional, not available in California).

See 140 hp power team, except for:

ENGINE 360 cu in, 5,900 cc (4 x 3.58 in, 101.6 x 89.6 mm); compression ratio: 8.4:1; max power (DIN): 155 hp at 3,600 rpm; max torque (DIN): 270 lb ft, 37.2 kg m at 2,400 rpm; 26.3 hp/l; 1 Holley R7991A downdraught twin barrel carburettor; cooling system: 26.6 imp pt, 31.9 US pt, 15.1 l.

TRANSMISSION axle ratio: 2.450.

PERFORMANCE max speed: about 108 mph, 174 km/h; power-weight ratio: 25.3 lb/hp, 11.5 kg/hp; consumption: 20.5 m/imp gal, 17 m/US gal, 13.8 l x 100 km.

ELECTRICAL EQUIPMENT 440 A battery.

DIMENSIONS AND WEIGHT weight: plus 34 lb, 15 kg.

170 hp power team

(optional for California only).

See 155 hp (5,900 cc) power team, except for:

ENGINE max power (DIN): 170 hp at 3,600 rpm; max torque (DIN): 265 lb ft, 36.6 kg m at 1,600 rpm; 28.8 hp/l; 1 Carter TQ 9134S downdraught 4-barrel carburettor.

TRANSMISSION axle ratio: 2.710.

PERFORMANCE max speed: about 112 mph, 180 km/h; power-weight ratio: 23.1 lb/hp, 10.5 kg/hp; consumption: 16.8 m/imp gal, 14 m/US gal, 16.8 l x 100 km.

ELECTRICAL EQUIPMENT Essex or Prestolite transistorized ignition.

190 hp power team

(optional, not available in California).

See 155 hp (5,900 cc) power team, except for:

ENGINE 400 cu in, 6,555 cc (4.34 x 3.38 in, 110.2 x 85.8 mm); compression ratio: 8.2:1; max power (DIN): 190 hp at 3,600 rpm; max torque (DIN): 305 lb ft, 42.1 kg m at 3,200 rpm; 29 hp/l; 1 Carter TQ9140S downdraught 4-barrel carburettor.

PERFORMANCE max speed: about 118 mph, 190 km/h; power-weight ratio: 21.3 lb/hp, 9.6 kg/hp; speed in direct drive at 1,000 rpm: 30.4 mph, 49 km/h; consumption: 18 m/imp gal, 15 m/US gal, 15.7 l x 100 km.

DIMENSIONS AND WEIGHT weight: plus 149 lb, 68 kg.

DUESENBERG   USA

SSJ

PRICE EX WORKS: $ 60,000

ENGINE Chrysler, front, 4 stroke; 8 cylinders; 440 cu in, 7,210 cc (4.32 x 3.75 in, 109.7 x 95.2 mm); compression ratio: 8.2:1; max power (DIN): 215 hp at 4,000 rpm; max torque (DIN): 330 lb ft, 45.5 kg m at 3,200 rpm; max engine rpm: 4,400; 29.8 hp/l; cast iron block and head; 5 crankshaft bearings; valves: overhead, in line, push-rods and rockers, hydraulic tappets; camshafts: 1, at centre of Vee; lubrication: rotary pump, full flow filter, 8.3 imp pt, 9.9 US pt, 4.7 l; 1 Carter TQ-9009S (TQ-9010S for California only) downdraught 4-barrel carburettor; cleaner air system; exhaust system with catalytic converter; fuel feed: mechanical pump; water-cooled, 28.3 imp pt, 34 US pt, 16.1 l.

TRANSMISSION driving wheels: rear; gearbox: Torqueflite automatic transmission, hydraulic torque converter and planetary gears with 3 ratios, max ratio of converter at stall 2.02, possible manual selection; ratios: I 2.450, II 1.450, III 1, rev 2.200; lever: central; final drive: hypoid bevel; axle ratio: 3.540; types: 7.00/7.50 x 18.

PERFORMANCE max speed: about 110 mph, 177 km/h; power-weight ratio: 16.7 lb/hp, 7.6 kg/hp; speed in direct drive at 1,000 rpm: 25 mph, 40.2 km/h; consumption: 12.3 m/imp gal, 10.2 m/US gal, 23 l x 100 km.

CHASSIS channel section ladder frame; front suspension: rigid axle, semi-elliptic leafsprings, friction dampers; rear: rigid axle, semi-elliptic leafsprings, telescopic dampers.

STEERING recirculating ball, servo.

BRAKES drum (diameter 12.50 in, 31.8 cm), servo.

DODGE Magnum XE Hardtop

DUESENBERG SSJ Roadster

full flow filter, oil cooler, 19 imp pt, 22.8 US pt, 10.8 l; Lucas Bosch electronic injection; fuel feed: electric pump; water-cooled, 36 imp pt, 43.3 US pt, 20.5 l, 1 viscous coupling thermostatic fan and 1 electric thermostatic fan.

TRANSMISSION driving wheels: rear; clutch: single dry plate (diaphragm), hydraulically controlled; gearbox: mechanical; gears: 4, fully synchronized; ratios: I 3.238, II 1.905, III 1.389, IV 1, rev 3.428; lever: central; final drive: hypoid bevel, limited slip differential; axle ratio: 3.070; width of rims: 6''; tyres: 205/70 VR x 15.

PERFORMANCE max speed: about 150 mph, 241 km/h; power-weight ratio: 10.4 lb/hp, 4.7 kg/hp; speed in direct drive at 1,000 rpm: 24.8 mph, 39.9 km/h; consumption: 14 m/imp gal, 11.6 m/US gal, 20.2 l x 100 km.

CHASSIS box-type ladder frame with cross members; front suspension: independent, wishbones, coil springs, anti-roll bar, telescopic dampers; rear: independent, wishbones, semi-axles as upper arms, transverse semi-elliptic leaf-springs, trailing radius arms, telescopic dampers.

STEERING recirculating ball, servo; turns lock to lock: 4.10.

BRAKES front disc, rear drum.

ELECTRICAL EQUIPMENT 12 V; 2 headlamps.

DIMENSIONS AND WEIGHT wheel base: 128 in, 325 cm; length: 203.94 in, 518 cm; height: 57.09 in, 145 cm; ground clearance: 10 in, 25.4 cm; weight: 3,000 lb, 1,360 kg; fuel tank: 16.7 imp gal, 20 US gal, 76 l.

ELECTRICAL EQUIPMENT 12 V; 500 A battery; 65 A alternator; Chrysler distributor; 4 headlamps.

DIMENSIONS AND WEIGHT wheel base: 128 in, 325 cm; tracks: 63.30 in, 161 cm front, 64.58 in, 164 cm rear; length: 166.50 in, 423 cm; width: 78.50 in, 199 cm; height: 60 in, 152 cm; weight: 3,600 lb. 1,633 kg; fuel tank: 17.6 imp gal, 21 US gal, 80 l.

BODY roadster; 2 doors; 2 seats.

OPTIONALS air-conditioning.

ELEGANT MOTORS   USA

898 Phaeton

PRICE EX WORKS: $ 40,000

ENGINE Jaguar, front, 4 stroke; 12 cylinders, Vee-slanted at 60°; 326 cu in, 5,343 cc (3.54 x 2.76 in, 90 x 70 mm); compression ratio: 8:1; max power (DIN): 288 hp at 5,750 rpm; max torque (DIN): 295 lb ft, 40.7 kg m at 3,500 rpm; max engine rpm: 6,500; 53.9 hp/l; light alloy block and head, wet liners, hemisperical combustion chambers; 7 crankshaft bearings; valves: overhead, in line, thimble tappets; camshafts: 1, per block, overhead; lubrication: rotary pump,

ELEGANT MOTORS 898 Phaeton

BODY phaeton in plastic material; 2 doors; 2 + 2 seats, separate front seats.

OPTIONALS leather upholstery; electric windows; tonneau cover; dual exhaust system; supercharger; air-conditioning.

856 Speedster

See 898 Phaeton, except for:

PRICE EX WORKS: $ 30,000

BODY roadster; 2 seats.

ELITE   USA

Laser 917

PRICES EX WORKS: $ 7,500 (body only)
                $ 4,595 (kit only)

ENGINE Volkswagen, rear, 4 stroke; 4 cylinders, horizontally opposed; 96.7 cu in, 1,584 cc (3.37 x 2.72 in, 85.5 x 69 mm); compression ratio: 8.5:1; max power (DIN): 50 hp at 4,000 rpm; max torque (DIN): 78 lb ft, 10.8 kg m at 2,800 rpm; max engine rpm: 4,600; 31.6 hp/l; block with cast iron liners and light alloy fins, light alloy head; 4 crankshaft bearings; valves: overhead, push-rods and rockers; camshafts: 1, central, lower; lubrication: gear pump, filter in sump, oil cooler, 4.4 imp pt, 5.3 US pt, 2.5 l; 1 Solex 34

ELITE Laser 917

LASER 917

PICT 2 downdraught carburettor; fuel feed: mechanical pump; air-cooled.

TRANSMISSION driving wheels: rear; clutch: single dry plate; gearbox: mechanical; gears: 4, fully synchronized; ratios: I 3.780, II 2.060, III 1.260, IV 0.930, rev 4.010; lever: central; final drive: spiral bevel; axle ratio: 3.875; width of rims: 4''; tyres: 5.60 x 15.

PERFORMANCE max speed: about 100 mph, 161 km/h; power-weight ratio: 39 lb/hp, 17.6 kg/hp; consumption: 30.7 m/imp gal, 25.6 m/US gal, 9.2 l x 100 km.

CHASSIS backbone platform; front suspension: independent, twin swinging longitudinal trailing arms, transverse laminated torsion bars, anti-roll bar, telescopic dampers; rear: independent, swinging semi-axles, swinging longitudinal trailing arms, transverse torsion bars, telescopic dampers.

STEERING worm and roller.

BRAKES front disc (diameter 10.91 in, 27.7 cm), rear drum; lining area: front 12.4 sq in, 80 sq cm, rear 55.5 sq in, 358 sq cm, total 67.9 sq in, 438 sq cm.

ELECTRICAL EQUIPMENT 12 V; 36 Ah battery; 50 A alternator; Bosch distributor; 4 headlamps.

DIMENSIONS AND WEIGHT wheel base: 94.50 in, 240 cm; tracks: 58 in, 147 cm front, 59 in, 150 cm rear; length: 174 in, 442 cm; height: 43.50 in, 110 cm; ground clearance: 6.50 in, 16.5 cm; weight: 1,950 lb, 884 kg; weight distribution: 40% front, 60% rear; fuel tank: 12.5 imp gal, 15 US gal, 57 l.

BODY sports in plastic material; 2 doors; 2 seats.

EXCALIBUR Series III SS Roadster

EXCALIBUR   USA

Series III

PRICES EX WORKS:

SS Roadster	$ 25,200*
SS Phaeton	$ 25,200*

215 hp power team

(not available in California).

ENGINE Chevrolet, front, 4 stroke; 8 cylinders; 454 cu in, 7,440 cc (4.25 x 4 in, 107.9 x 101.6 mm); compression ratio: 7.9:1; max power (DIN): 215 hp at 4,000 rpm; max torque (DIN): 350 lb ft, 48.3 kg m at 2,400 rpm; max engine rpm: 4,400; 28.9 hp/l; cast iron block and head; 5 crankshaft bearings; valves: overhead, in line, push-rods and rockers, hydraulic tappets; camshafts: 1, at centre of Vee; lubrication: gear pump, full flow filter, 8.3 imp pt, 9.9 US pt, 4.7 l; 1 Rochester 7045200 downdraught 4-barrel carburettor; cleaner air system; dual exhaust system; water-cooled, 52.8 imp pt, 63.4 US pt, 30 l.

TRANSMISSION driving wheels: rear; gearbox: Turbo-Hydramatic 400 automatic transmission, hydraulic torque converter and planetary gears with 3 ratios, max ratio of converter at stall 2.2, possible manual selection; ratios: I 2.480, II 1.480, III 1, rev 2.080; lever: steering column or central; final drive: hypoid bevel, limited slip differential; axle ratio: 2.730; width of rims: 7.5''; tyres: GR78 x 15.

PERFORMANCE max speed: 110 mph, 177 km/h; power-weight ratio: 20.2 lb/hp, 9.2 kg/hp; speed in direct drive at 1,000 rpm: 25 mph, 40.2 km/h; consumption: 12.3 m/imp gal, 10.2 m/US gal, 23 l x 100 km.

CHASSIS box-type ladder frame; front suspension: independent, wishbones, coil springs, anti-roll bar, telescopic dampers; rear: independent, semi-axle as upper pivoting arm and angular strut rod as lower pivoting arm, transverse semi-elliptic leafspring, trailing radius arms, anti-roll bar, telescopic dampers adjustable while running.

STEERING recirculating ball, variable ratio, tilt and telescopic, servo; turns lock to lock: 3.

BRAKES disc, internal radial fins, servo; swept area: total 461 sq in, 2,973 sq cm.

ELECTRICAL EQUIPMENT 12 V; 73 Ah battery; 61 A alternator; Delco-Remy high energy ignition system; 4 headlamps.

DIMENSIONS AND WEIGHT wheel base: 112 in, 284 cm; front and rear track: 62.50 in, 159 cm; length: 175 in, 444 cm; width: 72 in, 183 cm; height: 58 in, 147 cm; ground clearance: 5.70 in, 14.4 cm; weight: 4,350 lb, 1,973 kg; weight distribution: 48% front, 52% rear; turning circle (between walls): 35 ft, 10.7 m; fuel tank: 20.9 imp gal, 25 US gal, 95 l.

BODY 2 doors; 2 or 4 seats, separate front seats; leather upholstery; wire wheels; all-weather removable hardtop; tonneau cover; air-conditioning; heating system.

EXCALIBUR Series III SS Phaeton

FORD Pinto Station Wagon

FORD   USA

Pinto Series

PRICES EX WORKS:

Pinto Sedan	$ 3,336
Pinto Runabout	$ 3,451
Pinto Station Wagon	$ 3,794

In states of Alaska, Arizona, California, Hawaii, Idaho, Nevada, Oregon, Utah and Washington, prices are the following: Sedan, $ 3,214; Runabout, $ 3,329; Station Wagon, $ 3,671.
For V6 engine add $ 273.

Power team:	Standard for:	Optional for:
88 hp	all	—
90 hp	—	all

88 hp power team

ENGINE front, 4 stroke; 4 cylinders, in line; 140 cu in, 2,300 cc (3.78 x 3.13 in, 95.9 x 79.5 mm); compression ratio: 9:1; max power (DIN): 88 hp at 4,800 rpm; max torque (DIN): 118 lb ft, 16.3 kg m at 2,800 rpm; max engine rpm: 5,200; 38.3 hp/l; cast iron block and head; 5 crankshaft bearings; valves: overhead, Vee-slanted, rockers, hydraulic tappets; camshafts: 1, overhead, cogged belt; lubrication: gear pump, full flow filter, 7.6 imp pt, 9.1 US pt, 4.3 l; 1 Holley-Weber 9510 D8EE-DA (D8EE-JA for California only) downdraught twin barrel carburettor; cleaner air system; exhaust system with catalytic converter; fuel feed: mechanical pump; water-cooled, 14.4 imp pt, 17.3 US pt, 8.2 l.

TRANSMISSION driving wheels: rear; clutch: single dry plate; gearbox: mechanical; gears: 4, fully synchronized; ratios: I 3.980, II 2.140, III 1.420, IV 1, rev 3.990; lever: central; final drive: hypoid bevel; axle ratio: 2.730 (3.180 for St. Wagon in California); width of rims: 5''; tyres: A78 x 13.

PERFORMANCE max speed: about 96 mph, 155 km/h; power-weight ratio: Sedan 26.4 lb/hp, 12 kg/hp; speed in direct drive at 1,000 rpm: 19.3 mph, 31 km/h; consumption: 34.9 m/imp gal, 29 m/US gal, 8.1 l x 100 km.

CHASSIS integral; front suspension: independent, wishbones (lower leading arms), coil springs (anti-roll bar for St. Wagon only), telescopic dampers; rear: rigid axle, semi-elliptic leafsprings, telescopic dampers.

STEERING rack-and-pinion; turns lock to lock: 4.15.

BRAKES front disc (diameter 9.30 in, 23.6 cm), front internal radial fins, rear drum; swept area: front 145.5 sq in, 938 sq cm, rear 99 sq in, 639 sq cm, total 244.5 sq in, 1,577 sq cm.

ELECTRICAL EQUIPMENT 12 V; 45 Ah battery; 40 A alternator; Motorcraft transistorized ignition; 2 headlamps.

DIMENSIONS AND WEIGHT wheel base: 94.50 in, 240 cm - St. Wagon 94.80 in, 241 cm; tracks: 55 in, 140 cm front, 55.80 in, 141 cm rear; length: 169.30 in, 430 cm - St. Wagon

179.10 in, 455 cm; width: 69.40 in, 176 cm - St. Wagon 69.70 in, 177 cm; height: 50.60 in, 128 cm - St. Wagon 52.10 in, 132 cm; ground clearance: 4.58 in, 11.6 cm - St. Wagon 5.11 in, 13 cm; weight: Sedan 2,322 lb, 1,053 kg - Runabout 2,370 lb, 1,075 kg - St. Wagon 2,517 lb, 1,141 kg; turning circle (between walls): 35.9 ft, 10.9 m; fuel tank: 10.8 imp gal, 13 US gal, 49 l - St. Wagon 11.7 imp gal, 14 US gal, 53 l.

BODY 4 seats, separate front seats; folding rear seat (standard for Runabout and St. Wagon only).

OPTIONALS limited slip differential; Cruise-O-Matic automatic transmission with 3 ratios (I 2.470, II 1.470, III 1, rev 2.110), max ratio of converter at stall 2.9, possible manual selection, central lever, 3.180 axle ratio; BR78 x 13, BR70 x 13, B78 x 13 or A70 x 13 tyres; heavy-duty suspension with front anti-roll bar (except for St. Wagon); 53 Ah battery; power steering; servo brake; sunshine roof; aluminum wheels; vinyl roof (except for St. Wagon); tinted glass; heated rear window; air-conditioning; Pony equipment (for Sedan only); Squire or Cruising equipment (for St. Wagon).

90 hp power team

See 88 hp power team, except for:

ENGINE 6 cylinders, Vee-slanted at 60°; 170.8 cu in, 2,800 cc (3.66 x 2.70 in, 92.9 x 68.5 mm); compression ratio: 8.7:1; max power (DIN): 90 hp at 4,200 rpm; max torque (DIN): 143 lb ft, 19.7 kg m at 2,200 rpm; max engine rpm: 4,800; 32.1 hp/l; 4 crankshaft bearings; valves: overhead, in line, push-rods and rockers; camshafts: 1, at centre of Vee; lubricating system: 8.3 imp pt, 9.3 US pt, 4.7 l; 1 Motorcraft 9510 D8BE-MA (D8ZE-YB for California only) downdraught twin barrel carburettor; cooling system: 14.1 imp pt, 16.9 US pt, 8 l.

TRANSMISSION gearbox: Cruise-O-Matic automatic transmission (standard), max ratio of converter at stall 2.05 (2.9 for California only), possible manual selection; ratios: I 2.460, II 1.460, III 1, rev 2.190 or I 2.470, II 1.470, III 1, rev 2.110 (for California only); axle ratio: 3.400.

PERFORMANCE max speed: about 99 mph, 160 Km/h; power-weight ratio: Sedan 27.2 lb/hp, 12.3 kg/hp; speed in direct drive at 1,000 rpm: 23.5 mph, 37.9 km/h; consumption: 23.9 m/imp gal, 20 m/US gal, 11.8 l x 100 km.

DIMENSIONS AND WEIGHT weight: plus 128 lb, 58 kg.

Mustang II Series

PRICES IN GB AND EX WORKS:

	£	$
1 Mustang II Hardtop	—	3,555
2 Mustang II Hatchback	—	3,798
3 Mustang II Ghia Hardtop	6,350*	3,972
4 Mustang II Mach I Hatchback	6,300*	4,253

For V6 engines add $ 213 - For V8 engines add $ 361 (for Mach I add $ 148).

Power team:	Standard for:	Optional for:
88 hp	1 to 3	—
90 hp	4	1 to 3
133 hp	—	all
139 hp	—	all

88 hp power team

ENGINE front, 4 stroke; 4 cylinders, in line; 140 cu in, 2,300 cc (3.78 x 3.13 in, 95.9 x 79.5 mm); compression ratio: 9:1; max power (DIN): 88 hp at 4,800 rpm; max torque (DIN): 118 lb ft, 16.3 kg m at 2,800 rpm; max engine rpm: 5,200; 38.3 hp/l; cast iron block and head; 5 crankshaft bearings; valves: overhead, Vee-slanted, rockers, hydraulic tappets; camshafts: 1, overhead, cogged belt; lubrication: rotary pump, full flow filter, 8.3 imp pt, 9.9 US pt, 4.7 l; 1 Holley-Weber 9510 D8EE-DA or JA (D8BE-DA or CA for California only) downdraught twin barrel carburettor; cleaner air system; exhaust system with catalytic converter; fuel feed: mechanical pump; water-cooled, 14.1 imp pt, 16.9 US pt, 8 l.

TRANSMISSION driving wheels: rear; clutch: single dry plate; gearbox: mechanical; gears: 4, fully synchronized; ratios: I 3.500, II 2.210, III 1.430, IV 1, rev 3.390; lever: central; final drive: hypoid bevel; axle ratio: 3.180; width of rims: 5''; tyres: B78 x 13 - Ghia BR78 x 13.

PERFORMANCE max speed: about 96 mph, 155 km/h; power-weight ratio: Hardtop 29.6 lb/hp, 13.4 kg/hp; speed in direct drive at 1,000 rpm: 19.3 mph, 31 km/h; consumption: 31.4 m/imp gal, 26 m/US gal, 9 l x 100 km.

CHASSIS platform with front subframe; front suspension: independent, wishbones (lower trailing links), coil springs, anti-roll bar, telescopic dampers; rear: rigid axle, semi-elliptic leafsprings, anti-roll bar, telescopic dampers.

FORD Pinto Runabout

FORD Mustang II Series

STEERING rack-and-pinion; turns lock to lock: 4.15.

BRAKES front disc (diameter 9.30 in, 23.6 cm), front internal radial fins, rear drum; swept area: front 145.5 sq in, 938 sq cm, rear 99 sq in, 639 sq cm, total 244.5 sq in, 1,577 sq cm.

ELECTRICAL EQUIPMENT 12 V; 45 Ah battery; 40 A alternator; Motorcraft transistorized ignition; 2 headlamps.

DIMENSIONS AND WEIGHT wheel base: 96.20 in, 244 cm; tracks: 55.60 in, 141 cm front, 55.80 in, 142 cm rear; length: 175 in, 444 cm; width: 70.20 in, 178 cm; height: 50.30 in, 128 cm - Hatchback 50 in, 127 cm; ground clearance: 4.50 in, 11.4 cm; weight: Hardtop 2,608 lb, 1,182 kg - Hatchback 2,654 lb, 1,203 kg - Ghia 2,646 lb, 1,200 kg; turning circle (between walls): 33.7 ft, 10.3 m; fuel tank: 10.3 imp gal, 13 US gal, 49 l.

BODY 4 seats, separate front seats, reclining backrests with built-in headrests; folding rear seat (standard for Hatchback only).

OPTIONALS limited slip differential; Select-Shift Cruise-O-Matic automatic transmission with 3 ratios (I 2.470, II 1.470, III 1, rev 2.110), max ratio of converter at stall 2.9, possible manual selection, central lever, 3.180 axle ratio; BR70 x 13 tyres; 195/70R x 13 tyres with 5.5'' wide rims; power steering; servo brake; light alloy wheels; 53 Ah battery; folding rear seat; vinyl roof; sunshine roof; auxiliary fuel tank; heated rear window; air-conditioning; Cobra II and King Cobra equipment (for Hatchback only).

FORD Mustang II Cobra II Hatchback

285

90 hp power team

See 88 hp power team, except for:

ENGINE 6 cylinders, Vee-slanted at 60°; 170.8 cu in, 2,800 cc (3.66 x 2.70 in, 92.9 x 68.5 mm); compression ratio: 8.7:1; max power (DIN): 90 hp at 4,200 rpm; max torque (DIN): 143 lb ft, 19.7 kg m at 2,200 rpm; max engine rpm: 4,600; 32.1 hp/l; 4 crankshaft bearings; valves: overhead, in line, push-rods and rockers; camshafts: 1, at centre of Vee; 1 Ford 2150 9510 D8BE-DA (Motorcraft 2700 9510 D8ZE-DA with variable Venturi for California only) downdraught twin barrel carburettor; cooling system: 13.7 imp pt, 16.5 US pt, 7.8 l.

TRANSMISSION gearbox: mechanical (Select-Shift Cruise-O-Matic automatic transmission standard for California only); ratios: I 4.070, II 2.570, III 1.660, IV 1, rev 3.950; axle ratio: 3.000 (3.400 for California only); tyres: Mach I BR70 x 13.

PERFORMANCE max speed: about 99 mph, 160 km/h; power-weight ratio: Mach I 30.4 lb/hp, 13.8 kg/hp; consumption: 26.4 m/imp gal, 22 m/US gal, 10.7 l x 100 km.

DIMENSIONS AND WEIGHT weight: Mach I 2,733 lb, 1,240 kg.

OPTIONALS Select-Shift Cruise-O-Matic automatic transmission with 3.000 axle ratio.

FORD Mustang II Series

FORD Mustang II King Cobra Hatchback

FORD Fairmont 2-door Sedan

133 hp power team

(for California only).

See 88 hp power team, except for:

ENGINE 8 cylinders; 302 cu in, 4,950 cc (4 x 3 in, 101.6 x 76.2 mm); compression ratio: 8.1:1; max power (DIN): 133 hp at 3,600 rpm; max torque (DIN): 243 lb ft, 33.5 kg m at 1,600 rpm; max engine rpm: 4,000; 26.9 hp/l; valves: overhead, in line, push-rods and rockers, hydraulic tappets; camshafts: 1, at centre of Vee; 1 Motorcraft 2700 9510 D8ZE-HA downdraught twin barrel carburettor with variable Venturi; cooling system: 27.1 imp pt, 32.6 US pt, 15.4 l.

TRANSMISSION gearbox: Select-Shift Cruise-O-Matic automatic transmission (standard), max ratio of converter at stall 2.05, possible manual selection; ratios: I 2.460, II 1.460, II 1, rev 2.190; axle ratio: 2.790; tyres: Mach I BR70 x 13.

PERFORMANCE max speed: about 100 mph, 161 km/h; power-weight ratio: Hardtop 21.7 lb/hp, 9.9 kg/hp; speed in direct drive at 1,000 rpm: 26.4 mph, 42.5 km/h; consumption: 21.6 m/imp gal, 18 m/US gal, 13.1 l x 100 km.

DIMENSIONS AND WEIGHT weight: Hardtop 2,892 lb, 1,311 kg - Hatchback 2,930 lb, 1,329 kg - Ghia 2,938 lb, 1,332 kg - Mach I 2,733 lb, 1,240 kg; fuel tank: 13.6 imp gal, 16.5 US gal, 62 l.

139 hp power team

(not available in California)

See 133 hp power team, except for:

ENGINE compression ratio: 8.4:1; max power (DIN): 139 hp at 3,600 rpm; max torque (DIN): 250 lb ft, 34.5 kg m at 1,600 rpm; 28.1 hp/l; 1 Ford 2150 9510 D8BE-KA downdraught twin barrel carburettor.

TRANSMISSION gearbox: mechanical; gears: 4, fully synchronized; ratios: I 2.640, II 1.890, III 1.340, IV 1, rev 2.560; axle ratio: 3.000.

PERFORMANCE max speed: about 105 mph, 169 km/h; power-weight ratio: Hardtop 20.8 lb/hp, 9.4 kg/hp; speed in direct drive at 1,000 rpm: 26.2 mph, 42.2 km/h; consumption: 22.8 m/imp gal, 19 m/US gal, 12.4 l x 100 km.

Fairmont Series

PRICES EX WORKS:

1 Fairmont 2-door Sedan	$ 3,589
2 Fairmont 4-door Sedan	$ 3,663
3 Fairmont Sport Coupé	$ —
4 Fairmont Station Wagon	$ 4,031

For 6-cylinder engine add $ 120. For V8 add $ 319.

Power team:	Standard for:	Optional for:
88 hp	1 to 3	—
85 hp	4	1 to 3
133 hp	—	all
139 hp	—	all

88 hp power team

ENGINE front, 4 stroke; 4 cylinders, in line; 140 cu in, 2,300 cc (3.78 x 3,13 in, 95.9 x 79.5 mm); compression ratio: 9:1; max power (DIN): 88 hp at 4,800 rpm; max torque (DIN): 118 lb ft, 16.3 kg m at 2,800 rpm; max engine rpm: 5,200; 38.3 hp/l; cast iron block and head; 5 crankshaft bearings; valves: overhead, Vee-slanted, hydraulic tappets; camshafts: 1, overhead, cogged belt; lubrication: rotary pump, full flow filter, 8.3 imp pt, 9.9 US pt, 4.7 l; 1 Holley-Weber 5200 downdraught twin barrel carburettor; cleaner air system; exhaust system with catalytic converter; fuel feed: mechanical pump; water-cooled, 14.1 imp pt, 16.9 US pt, 8 l.

TRANSMISSION driving wheels: rear; clutch: single dry plate; gearbox: mechanical; gears: 4, fully synchronized; ratios: I 3.980, II 2.140, III 1.420, IV 1, rev 3.990; lever: central; final drive: hypoid bevel; axle ratio: 3.080; width of rims: 5''; tyres: B78 x 14.

PERFORMANCE max speed: about 96 mph, 155 km/h; power-weight ratio: 4-dr. Sedan 29.8 lb/hp, 13.5 kg/hp; speed in direct drive at 1,000 rpm: 19.3 mph, 31 km/h; consumption: 31.4 m/imp gal, 26 m/US gal, 9 l x 100 km.

CHASSIS integral with 2 cross members; front suspension: independent, by McPherson, wishbones (lower control arms), coil springs/telescopic damper struts, anti-roll bar; rear: rigid axle, lower trailing radius arms, upper oblique torque arms, transverse linkage bar, coil springs, telescopic dampers.

FORD Fairmont Station Wagon

STEERING rack-and-pinion; turns lock to lock: 4.10.

BRAKES front disc (diameter 10 in, 25.4 cm), front internal radial fins, rear drum; swept area: front 196.6 sq in, 1,268 sq cm, rear 99 sq in, 639 sq cm, total 295.6 sq in, 1,907 sq cm.

ELECTRICAL EQUIPMENT 12 V; 36 Ah battery; 40 A alternator; Motorcraft transistorized ignition; 4 headlamps.

DIMENSIONS AND WEIGHT wheel base 105.50 in, 268 cm; tracks 56.60 in, 144 cm front, 57 in, 145 cm rear; length: 193.80 in, 492 cm - Sport Coupé 195.80 in, 497 cm; width: 71 in, 180 cm; height: sedans 53.50 in, 136 cm - Sport Coupé 52.20 in, 133 cm; ground clearance: 4.61 in, 11.7 cm; weight: 2-dr. Sedan 2,585 lb, 1,172 kg - 4-dr. Sedan 2,627 lb, 1,191 kg - Sport Coupé 2,622 lb, 1,189 kg; fuel tank: 13.4 imp gal, 16 US gal, 61 l.

OPTIONALS Select-Shift Cruise-O-Matic automatic transmission with 3 ratios (I 2.470, II 1.470, III 1, rev 2.110), max ratio of converter at stall 2.9, possible manual selection, steering column lever, 3.080 axle ratio; BR78 x 14, C78 x 14, CR78 x 14 or DR78 x 14 tyres; heavy-duty suspension; power steering; servo brake; 45 Ah battery; 54 Ah battery; heated rear window; Sports equipment (only for sedans); Luxury equipment; air-conditioning.

85 hp power team

See 88 hp power team, except for:

ENGINE 6 cylinders, in line; 200 cu in, 3,277 cc (3.68 x 3.13 in, 95.3 x 79.5 mm); compression ratio: 8.5:1; max power (DIN): 85 hp at 3,600 rpm; max torque (DIN): 154 lb ft, 21.2 kg m at 1,600 rpm; max engine rpm: 4,000; 25.9 hp/l; 7 crankshaft bearings; valves: overhead, in line, push-rods and rockers, hydraulic tappets; camshafts: 1, side; 1 Carter YFA (Holley 1946 for California only) downdraught single barrel carburettor; cooling system: 15 imp pt, 18 US pt, 8.5 l.

TRANSMISSION gearbox: mechanical (Select-Shift Cruise-O-Matic automatic transmission standard for California only); gears: 3, fully synchronized; ratios: I 3.560, II 1.900, III 1, rev 3.780; axle ratio: 2.730 (3.080 for California only); tyres: St. Wagon CR78 x 14.

PERFORMANCE max speed: about 99 mph, 160 km/h; power-weight ratio: St. Wagon 30.3 lb/hp, 14.7 kg/hp; speed in direct drive at 1,000 rpm: 24.9 mph, 40 km/h; consumption: 28.8 m/imp gal, 24 m/US gal, 9.8 l x 100 km.

BRAKES (for St. Wagon) swept area: total 306.6 sq in, 1,977 sq cm.

ELECTRICAL EQUIPMENT 60 A alternator.

DIMENSIONS AND WEIGHT height: St. Wagon 54.80 in, 139 cm; weight: St. Wagon 2,754 lb, 1,249 kg.

OPTIONALS Select-Shift Cruise-O-Matic automatic transmission with 3 ratios (I 2.460, II 1.460, III 1, rev 2.190), max ratio of converter at stall 2, possible manual selection, steering column or central lever, 2.730 axle ratio.

FORD Fairmont Station Wagon (85 hp engine)

133 hp power team

(for California only).

See 88 hp power team, except for:

ENGINE 8 cylinders; 302 cu in, 4,950 cc (4 x 3 in, 101.6 x 76.2 mm); compression ratio: 8.1:1; max power (DIN): 133 hp at 3,600 rpm; max torque (DIN): 243 lb ft, 33.5 kg m at 1,600 rpm; max engine rpm: 4,000; 26.9 hp/l; valves: overhead, in line, push-rods and rockers, hydraulic tappets; camshafts: 1, at centre of Vee; 1 Ford 2700 downdraught twin barrel carburettor with variable Venturi; cooling system: 23.1 imp pt, 27.7 US pt, 13.1 l.

TRANSMISSION gearbox: Select-Shift Cruise-O-Matic automatic transmission (standard), hydraulic torque converter and planetary gears with 3 ratios, max ratio of converter at stall 2, possible manual selection; ratios: I 2.460, II 1.460, III 1, rev 2.190; lever: steering column; axle ratio: 2.730; tyres: St. Wagon CR78 x 14.

PERFORMANCE max speed: about 100 mph, 161 km/h; power-weight ratio: 4-dr. Sedan 21.7 lb/hp, 9.8 kg/hp; speed in direct drive at 1,000 rpm: 26.4 mph, 42.5 km/h; consumption: 21.6 m/imp gal, 18 m/US gal, 13.1 l x 100 km.

BRAKES (for St. Wagon) swept area: total 306.6 sq in, 1,977 sq cm.

DIMENSIONS AND WEIGHT height: St. Wagon 54.80 in, 139 cm; weight: 2-dr. Sedan 2,840 lb, 1,288 kg - 4-dr. Sedan 2,882 lb, 1,307 kg - Sport Coupé 2,877 lb, 1,304 kg - St. Wagon 2,967 lb, 1,345 kg.

OPTIONALS 2.470 axle ratio.

139 hp power team

(not available in California).

See 133 hp power team, except for:

ENGINE compression ratio: 8.4:1; max power (DIN): 139 hp at 3,600 rpm; max torque (DIN): 250 lb ft, 34.5 kg m at 1,600 rpm; 28.1 hp/l; 1 Ford 2150 downdraught twin barrel carburettor.

TRANSMISSION axle ratio: 2.470.

PERFORMANCE max speed: about 105 mph, 169 km/h; power-weight ratio: 4-dr. Sedan 20.7 lb/hp, 9.4 kg/hp; speed in direct drive at 1,000 rpm: 26.2 mph, 42.2 km/h; consumption: 22.8 m/imp gal, 19 m/US gal, 12.4 l x 100 km.

Granada Series

PRICES EX WORKS:

Granada 2-door Sedan	$ 4,264
Granada 4-door Sedan	$ 4,342
Granada Ghia 2-door Sedan	$ 4,649
Granada Ghia 4-door Sedan	$ 4,728
Granada ESS 2-door Sedan	$ 4,836
Granada ESS 4-door Sedan	$ 4,914

FORD Granada ESS 4-door Sedan

GRANADA SERIES

For V8 engines add $ 181.

Power team:	Standard for:	Optional for:
97 hp	all	—
133 hp	—	all
139 hp	—	all

97 hp power team

ENGINE front, 4 stroke; 6 cylinders, in line; 250 cu in, 4,097 cc (3.68 x 3.91 in, 93.5 x 99.3 mm); compression ratio: 8.5:1; max power (DIN): 97 hp at 3,200 rpm; max torque (DIN): 210 lb ft, 29 kg m at 1,400 rpm; max engine rpm: 3,800; 23.7 hp/l; cast iron block and head; 7 crankshaft bearings; valves: overhead, in line, push-rods and rockers, hydraulic tappets; camshafts: 1, side; lubrication: rotary pump, full flow filter, 8.3 imp pt, 9.9 US pt, 4.7 l; 1 Carter YFA 9510 D8DE-BB (D8DE-AA for California only) downdraught single barrel carburettor; cleaner air system; exhaust system with catalytic converter; fuel feed: mechanical pump; water-cooled, 17.4 imp pt, 21 US pt, 9.9 l.

TRANSMISSION driving wheels: rear; clutch: single dry plate, semi-centrifugal; gearbox: mechanical (Select-Shift Cruise-O-Matic automatic transmission standard for California only); gears: 4, fully synchronized with overdrive/top; ratios: I 3.290, II 1.840, III 1, IV 0.810, rev 3.290; lever: central; final drive: hypoid bevel; axle ratio: 3.000 (2.470 for California only); width of rims: 6''; tyres: DR78 x 14.

PERFORMANCE max speed: about 93 mph, 150 km/h; power-weight ratio: 4-dr. 32 lb/hp, 14.5 kg/hp; speed in direct drive at 1,000 rpm: 25.5 mph, 41 km/h; consumption: 25.2 m/imp gal, 21 m/US gal, 11.2 l x 100 km.

CHASSIS integral; front suspension: independent, wishbones (lower trailing links), coil springs, anti-roll bar, telescopic dampers; rear: rigid axle, semi-elliptic leafsprings, telescopic dampers.

STEERING recirculating ball; turns lock to lock: 5.18.

BRAKES front disc (diameter 11.03 in, 28 cm), rear drum; swept area: front 222.5 sq in, 1,435 sq cm, rear 125.6 sq in, 810 sq cm, total 348.1 sq in, 2,245 sq cm.

ELECTRICAL EQUIPMENT 12 V; 36 Ah battery; 40 A alternator; Motorcraft transistorized ignition; 2 headlamps.

DIMENSIONS AND WEIGHT wheel base: 109.90 in, 279 cm; tracks: 59 in, 150 cm front, 57.70 in, 146 cm rear; length: 197.70 in, 502 cm; width: 74 in, 188 cm; height: 53.20 in, 135 cm - 4-dr. 53.30 in, 135 cm; ground clearance: 4.84 in, 12.3 cm; weight: 2-dr. 3,070 lb, 1,392 kg - 4-dr. 3,105 lb, 1,408 kg; fuel tank: 15 imp gal, 18 US gal, 68 l.

BODY saloon/sedan; 4-5 seats, separate front seats, reclining backrests.

OPTIONALS limited slip differential; Selec-Shift Cruise-O-Matic automatic transmission with 3 ratios (I 2.460, II 1.460, III 1, rev 2.190), max ratio of converter at stall 2.29,

FORD Granada ESS 4-door Sedan

possible manual selection, steering column or central lever, 2.470 or 2.500 axle ratio: aluminum wheels; ER78 x 14 or FR78 x 14 tyres; tilt of steering wheels; power steering; servo brake; disc brakes (front diameter 11.03 in, 28 cm, rear 10.66 in, 27.1 cm), total swept area 433.7 sq in, 2,797 sq cm; 54 Ah battery; electric windows; heated rear window; tinted glass; vinyl roof; sunshine roof; air-conditioning.

133 hp power team

(for California only).

See 97 power team, except for:

ENGINE 8 cylinders; 302 cu in, 4,950 cc (4 x 3 in, 101.6 x 76.2 mm); compression ratio: 8.1:1; max power (DIN): 133 hp at 3,600 rpm; max torque (DIN): 243 lb ft, 33.5 kg m at 1,600 rpm; max engine rpm: 4,000; 26.9 hp/l; 5 crankshaft bearings; camshafts: 1, at centre of Vee; 1 Ford 2700 9510 D8BE-EA downdraught twin barrel carburettor with variable Venturi; cooling system: 24.3 imp pt, 29.2 US pt, 13.8 l.

TRANSMISSION gearbox: Select-Shift Cruise-O-Matic automatic transmission (standard), hydraulic torque converter and planetary gears with 3 ratios, max ratio of converter at stall 2.29, possible manual selection: ratios: I 2.460, II 1.460, III 1, rev 2.190; lever: steering column; axle ratio: 2.470.

PERFORMANCE max speed: about 96 mph, 155 km/h; power-weight ratio: 4-dr. 24 lb/hp, 10.9 kg/hp; speed in direct drive at 1,000 rpm: 25.6 mph, 41.2 km/h; consumption: 21.6 m/imp gal, 18 m/US gal, 13.1 l x 100 km.

DIMENSIONS AND WEIGHT weight: plus 93 lb, 42 kg.

OPTIONALS 2.500 axle ratio.

139 hp power team

(not available in California).

See 97 hp power team, except for:

ENGINE 8 cylinders; 302 cu in, 4,950 cc (4 x 3 in, 101.6 x 76.2 mm); compression ratio: 8.4:1; max power (DIN): 139 hp at 3,600 rpm; max torque (DIN): 250 lb ft, 34.5 kg m at 1,600 rpm; max engine rpm: 4,000; 28.1 hp/l; 5 crankshaft bearings; camshafts: 1, at centre of Vee; 1 Ford 2150A 9510 D8DE-HA downdraught twin barrel carburettor; cooling system: 24.3 imp pt, 29.2 US pt, 13.8 l.

PERFORMANCE max speed: about 103 mph, 165 km/h; power-weight ratio: 4-dr. 23 lb/hp, 10.4 kg/hp; consumption: 22.8 m/imp gal, 19 m/US gal, 12.4 l x 100 km.

DIMENSIONS AND WEIGHT weight: plus 90 lb, 41 kg.

LTD II Series

PRICES EX WORKS:

LTD II S 2-door Hardtop	$ 4,814
LTD II S 4-door Sedan	$ 4,889
LTD II 2-door Hardtop	$ 5,069
LTD II 4-door Sedan	$ 5,169
LTD II Brougham 2-door Hardtop	$ 5,405
LTD II Brougham 4-door Sedan	$ 5,505

Power team:	Standard for:	Optional for:
134 hp	all	—
144 hp	—	all
152 hp	—	all
166 hp	—	all

134 hp power team

(not available in California).

ENGINE front, 4 stroke; 8 cylinders; 302 cu in, 4,950 cc (4 x 3 in, 101.6 x 76.2 mm); compression ratio: 8.4:1; max power (DIN): 134 hp at 3,400 rpm; max torque (DIN): 248 lb ft, 34.2 kg m at 1,600 rpm; max engine rpm: 4,000; 27.1 hp/l; cast iron block and head; 5 crankshaft bearings; valves: overhead, in line, push-rods and rockers, hydraulic tappets; camshafts: 1, at centre of Vee; lubrication: rotary pump, full flow filter, 8.3 imp pt, 9.9 US pt, 4.7 l; 1 Ford 2150A D8OE-EA downdraught twin barrel carburettor; cleaner air system; exhaust system with catalytic converter; fuel feed: mechanical pump; water-cooled, 22.5 imp pt, 27.1 US pt, 12.8 l.

TRANSMISSION driving wheels: rear; gearbox: Select-Shift Cruise-O-Matic automatic transmission, hydraulic torque converter and planetary gears with 3 ratios, max ratio of converter at stall 2.14, possible manual selection: ratios: I 2.460, II 1.460, III 1, rev 2.220; lever: steering column or central; final drive: hypoid bevel; axle ratio: 2.750; width of rims: 5.5''; tyres: HR78 x 14.

PERFORMANCE max speed: about 96 mph, 155 km/h; power-weight ratio: LTD II S Sedan 31 lb/hp, 14.1 kg/hp; speed in direct drive at 1,000 rpm: 26.1 mph, 42 km/h; consumption: 20.5 m/imp gal, 17 m/US gal, 13.8 l x 100 km.

CHASSIS perimeter box-type; front suspension: independent, wishbones (lower trailing links), coil springs, anti-roll bar, telescopic dampers; rear: rigid axle, lower trailing radius arms, upper oblique torque arms, coil springs, anti-roll bar, telescopic dampers.

STEERING recirculating ball, servo; turns lock to lock: 3.99.

BRAKES front disc (diameter 10.72 in, 27.2 cm), front internal radial fins, rear drum, servo; swept area: front 212 sq in, 1,367 sq cm, rear 155.9 sq in, 1,005 sq cm, total 367.9 sq in, 2,372 sq cm.

ELECTRICAL EQUIPMENT 12 V; 36 Ah battery; 40 A alternator; Motorcraft transistorized ignition; 4 headlamps.

DIMENSIONS AND WEIGHT wheel base: 118 in, 300 cm - hardtops 114 in, 290 cm; tracks: 63.60 in, 162 cm front, 63.50 in, 162 cm rear; length: 219.50 in, 558 cm - hardtops 215.50 in, 547 cm; width: 78.60 in, 200 cm; height: 53.30 in, 135 cm - hardtops 52.60 in, 134 cm; ground clearance: 4.75 in, 12 cm; weight: LTD II S Hardtop 4,084 lb, 1,852 kg - Sedan 4,160 lb, 1,886 kg - LTD II Hardtop 4,107 lb, 1,862 kg - Sedan 4,184 lb, 1,897 kg; turning circle (bet-

FORD LTD II 2-door Hardtop

ween walls): 42.4 ft, 12.9 m; fuel tank: 17.6 imp gal, 21 US gal, 80 l.

OPTIONALS limited slip differential; H78 x 14 tyres; tilt of steering wheel; heated rear window; electric windows; vinyl roof; air-conditioning.

144 hp power team

(not available in California).

See 134 hp power team, except for:

ENGINE 351 cu in, 5,732 cc (4 x 3.50 in, 101.6 x 88.8 mm); compression ratio: 8.3:1; max power (DIN): 144 hp at 3,200 rpm; max torque (DIN): 277 lb ft, 38.2 kg m at 1,600 rpm; 25.1 hp/l; 1 Ford 2150 A D8WE-DA downdraught twin barrel carburettor; cooling system: 26.4 imp pt, 31.7 US pt, 15 l.

TRANSMISSION axle ratio: 2.500.

PERFORMANCE max speed: about 104 mph, 167 km/h; power-weight ratio: LTD II S Sedan 29.9 lb/hp, 13.5 kg/hp; consumption: 19.2 m/imp gal, 16 m/US gal, 14.7 l x 100 km.

ELECTRICAL EQUIPMENT 45 Ah battery.

DIMENSIONS AND WEIGHT weight: plus 144 lb, 65 kg.

FORD LTD II Series

FORD Thunderbird Diamond Jubilee Edition

152 hp power team

See 144 hp power team, except for:

ENGINE compression ratio: 8:1; max power (DIN): 152 hp at 3,600 rpm; max torque (DIN): 278 lb ft, 38.3 kg m at 1,800 rpm; 26.5 hp/l; 1 Ford 2150A TBD downdraught twin barrel carburettor; cooling system: 28.5 imp pt, 34.2 US pt, 16.2 l.

TRANSMISSION axle ratio: 2.500.

PERFORMANCE max speed: about 106 mph, 170 km/h; power-weight ratio: LTD II S Sedan 28.3 lb/hp, 12.8 kg/hp; speed in direct drive at 1,000 rpm: 26.4 mph, 42.5 km/h; consumption: 21.6 m/imp gal, 18 m/US gal, 13.1 l x 100 km.

OPTIONALS 2.750 axle ratio.

166 hp power team

See 152 hp power team, except for:

ENGINE 400 cu in, 6,555 cc (4 x 4 in, 101.6 x 101.6 mm); max power (DIN): 166 hp at 3,800 rpm; max torque (DIN): 319 lb ft, 44 kg m at 1,800 rpm; max engine rpm: 4,400; 25.3 hp/l.

TRANSMISSION automatic transmission ratios: I 2.460, II 1.460, III 1, rev 2.180; max ratio of converter at stall 2.05; axle ratio: 2.750.

FORD Thunderbird Series

PERFORMANCE max speed: about 109 mph, 175 km/h; power-weight ratio: LTD II S Sedan 25.4 lb/hp, 11.5 kg/hp; consumption: 18 m/imp gal, 15 m/US gal, 15.7 l x 100 km.

ELECTRICAL EQUIPMENT 54 Ah battery.

DIMENSIONS AND WEIGHT weight: plus 63 lb, 28 kg.

Thunderbird Series

PRICES EX WORKS:

Thunderbird	$ 5,411
Thunderbird Town Landau	$ 8,420
Thunderbird Diamond Jubilee Edition	$ 10,106

Power team:	Standard for:	Optional for:
134 hp	all	—
144 hp	—	all
152 hp	—	all
166 hp	—	all

134 hp power team

(not available in California).

ENGINE front, 4 stroke; 8 cylinders; 302 cu in, 4,950 cc (4 x 3 in, 101.6 x 76.2 mm); compression ratio: 8.4:1; max power (DIN): 134 hp at 3,400 rpm; max torque (DIN): 248 lb ft, 34.2 kg m at 1,600 rpm; max engine rpm: 4,000; 27.1 hp/l; cast iron and block; 5 crankshaft bearings; valves: overhead, in line, push-rods and rockers, hydraulic tappets; camshafts: 1, at centre of Vee; lubrication: rotary pump, full flow filter, 8.3 imp pt, 9.9 US pt, 4.7 l; 1 Ford 2150A D7DE-KA downdraught twin barrel carburettor; cleaner air system; exhaust system with catalytic converter; fuel feed: mechanical pump; water-cooled, 22.5 imp pt, 27.1 US pt, 12.8 l.

TRANSMISSION driving wheels: rear; gearbox: Select-Shift Cruise-O-Matic automatic transmission, hydraulic torque converter and planetary gears with 3 ratios, max ratio of converter at stall 1.92, possible manual selection; ratios: I 2.460, II 1.460, III 1, rev 2.220; lever: steering column or central; final drive: hypoid bevel; axle ratio: 2.750; width of rims: 6''; tyres: HR78 x 15.

PERFORMANCE max speed: about 103 mph, 165 km/h; power-weight ratio: 30.1 lb/hp, 13.7 kg/hp; speed in direct drive at 1,000 rpm: 26.1 mph, 41 km/h; consumption: 20.5 m/imp gal, 17 m/US gal, 13.8 l x 100 km.

CHASSIS perimeter box-type; front suspension: independent, wishbones (lower trailing links), coil springs, anti-roll bar, telescopic dampers; rear: rigid axle, lower trailing radius arms, upper torque arms, coil springs, anti-roll bar, telescopic dampers.

STEERING recirculating ball, servo; turns lock to lock: 3.99.

BRAKES front disc (diameter 10.72 in, 27.2 cm), front internal radial fins, rear drum, servo; swept area: front 212 sq in, 1,367 sq cm, rear 155.9 sq in, 1,005 sq cm, total 367.9 sq in, 2,372 sq cm.

ELECTRICAL EQUIPMENT 12 V; 36 Ah battery; 40 A alternator; Motorcraft transistorized ignition; 4 headlamps.

DIMENSIONS AND WEIGHT wheel base: 114 in, 290 cm; tracks: 63.20 in, 160 cm front, 63.10 in, 160 cm rear; length: 215.50 in, 547 cm; width: 78.50 in, 199 cm; height: 53 in, 135 cm; ground clearance: 4.90 in, 12.4 cm; weight: 4,040 lb, 1,832 kg; turning circle (between walls): 46.7 ft, 14.2 m; fuel tank: 17.6 imp gal, 21 US gal, 80 l.

BODY hardtop; 2 doors; 6 seats.

OPTIONALS limited slip differential; HR70 x 15 tyres with 6.5'' wide rims; heavy-duty suspension; aluminum wheels; tilt of steering wheel; speed control; heated rear window; electric windows; air-conditioning.

144 hp power team

(not available in California).

See 134 hp power team, except for:

ENGINE 351 cu in, 5,732 cc (4 x 3.50 in, 101.6 x 88.8 mm); compression ratio: 8.3:1; max power (DIN): 144 hp at 3,200 rpm; max torque (DIN): 277 lb ft, 38.2 kg m at 1,600 rpm; 25.1 hp/l; 1 Ford 2150A D70E-FA downdraught twin barrel carburettor; cooling system: 28.5 imp pt, 34.2 US pt, 16.2 l.

TRANSMISSION axle ratio: 2.500.

PERFORMANCE max speed: about 106 mph, 170 km/h; power-weight ratio: 29.1 lb/hp, 13.2 kg/hp; consumption: 19.2 m/imp gal, 16 m/US gal, 14.7 l x 100 km.

ELECTRICAL EQUIPMENT 45 Ah battery.

DIMENSIONS AND WEIGHT weight: 4,192 lb, 1,901 kg.

152 hp power team

See 144 hp power team, except for:

ENGINE compression ratio: 8:1; max power (DIN): 152 hp at 3,600 rpm; max torque (DIN): 278 lb ft, 38.3 kg m at 1,800 rpm; 26.5 hp/l; 1 Ford 2150 A downdraught twin barrel carburettor.

PERFORMANCE max speed: about 109 mph, 175 km/h; power-weight ratio: 25.6 lb/hp, 12.5 kg/hp; consumption: 21.6 m/imp gal, 18 m/US gal, 13.1 l x 100 km.

166 hp power team

See 152 hp power team, except for:

ENGINE 400 cu in, 6,555 cc (4 x 4 in, 101.6 x 101.6 mm); max power (DIN): 166 hp at 3,800 rpm; max torque (DIN): 319 lb ft, 44 kg m at 1,800 rpm; max engine rpm: 4,400; 25.3 hp/l; 1 Ford 2150A downdraught twin barrel carburettor.

TRANSMISSION automatic transmission ratios: I 2.460, II 1.460, III 1, rev 2.180; max ratio of converter at stall 2.05; axle ratio: 2.500.

PERFORMANCE max speed: about 112 mph, 180 km/h; power-weight ratio: 26.5 lb/hp, 12 kg/hp; speed in direct drive at 1,000 rpm: 26.1 mph, 41 km/h; consumption: 18 m/imp gal, 15 m/US gal, 15.7 l x 100 km.

ELECTRICAL EQUIPMENT 54 Ah battery.

DIMENSIONS AND WEIGHT weight: plus 260 lb, 93 kg.

LTD Series

PRICES EX WORKS:

1 LTD 2-door Hardtop	$ 5,335
2 LTD 4-door Hardtop	$ 5,410
3 LTD Station Wagon	$ 5,797
4 LTD Landau 2-door Hardtop	$ 5,898
5 LTD Landau 4-door Hardtop	$ 5,973
6 LTD Country Squire Station Wagon	$ 6,207

Power team:	Standard for:	Optional for:
134 hp	1,2,4,5	—
144 hp	—	1,2,4,5
145 hp	3,6	1,2,4,5
160 hp	—	all
202 hp	—	all

134 hp power team

(not available in California).

ENGINE front, 4 stroke; 8 cylinders; 302 cu in, 4,950 cc (4 x 3 in, 101.6 x 76.2 mm); compression ratio: 8.4:1; max power (DIN): 134 hp at 3,400 rpm; max torque (DIN): 248 lb ft, 34.2 kg m at 1,600 rpm; max engine rpm: 4,000; 27.1 hp/l; cast iron block and head; 5 crankshaft bearings; valves: overhead, in line, push-rods and rockers, hydraulic tappets; camshafts: 1, at centre of Vee; lubrication: rotary pump, full flow filter, 8.3 imp pt, 9.9 US pt, 4.7 l; 1 Ford 2150A DBOE-EA downdraught twin barrel carburettor; cleaner air system; exhaust system with catalytic converter; fuel feed: mechanical pump; water-cooled, 22.5 imp pt, 27.1 US pt, 12.8 l.

TRANSMISSION driving wheels: rear; gearbox: Select-Shift Cruise-O-Matic automatic transmission, hydraulic torque converter and planetary gears with 3 ratios, max ratio of converter at stall 2.14, possible manual selection; ratios: I 2.460, II 1.460, III 1, rev 2.220; lever: steering column; final drive: hypoid bevel; axle ratio: 2.750; width of rims: 6''; tyres: 2-dr. GR78 x 15 - 4-dr. HR78 x 15.

PERFORMANCE max speed: about 96 mph, 155 km/h; power-weight ratio: 4-dr. 31.8 lb/hp, 14.4 kg/hp - Landau 4-dr. 31.4 lb/hp, 14.2 kg/hp; speed in direct drive at 1,000 rpm: 25.4 mph, 40.8 km/h; consumption: 20.5 m/imp gal, 17 m/US gal, 13.8 l x 100 km.

CHASSIS perimeter box-type; front suspension: independent, wishbones (lower trailing links), coil springs, anti-roll bar, telescopic dampers; rear: rigid axle, lower trailing radius arms, upper oblique torque arms, transverse linkage bar, coil springs, telescopic dampers.

STEERING recirculating ball, servo; turns lock to lock: 3.99.

BRAKES front disc (diameter 11.80 in, 30 cm), front internal radial fins, rear drum, servo; swept area: front 242 sq in, 1,561 sq cm, rear 173.3 sq in, 1,117 sq cm, total 415.3 sq in, 2,678 sq cm.

ELECTRICAL EQUIPMENT 12 V; 36 Ah battery; 40 A alternator; Motorcraft transistorized ignition; 4 headlamps.

DIMENSIONS AND WEIGHT wheel base: 121 in, 307 cm; tracks: 64.10 in, 162 cm front, 64.30 in, 163 cm rear; length: 224.10 in, 569 cm - Landau 226.80 in, 576 cm; width: 79.50 in, 202 cm; height: 54.80 in, 139 cm - 2-dr. 53.80 in, 136 cm; ground clearance: 5.50 in, 14 cm; weight: 2-dr. Hardtop

FORD LTD 4-door Hardtop

FORD LTD 4-door Hardtop

FORD LTD Country Squire Station Wagon

4,221 lb, 1,914 kg - 4-dr. Hardtop 4,261 lb, 1,932 kg - Landau 2-dr. Hardtop 4,164 lb, 1,888 kg - 4-dr. Hardtop 4,212 lb, 1,910 kg; turning circle (between walls): 45.3 ft, 13.8 m; fuel tank: 20.2 imp gal, 24.2 US gal, 92 l.

OPTIONALS limited slip differential; JR78 x 15 tyres; LR78 x 15 tyres with 6.5'' wide rims; tilt of steering wheel; disc brakes, total swept area 365.9 sq in, 2,360 sq cm; heavy-duty battery; heated rear window; electric windows; electric sunshine roof; reclining front seats; speed control; air-conditioning.

144 hp power team

(not available in California).

See 134 hp power team, except for:

ENGINE 351 cu in, 5,732 cc (4 x 3.50 in, 101.6 x 88.8 mm); compression ratio: 8.3:1; max power (DIN): 144 hp at 3,200 rpm; max torque (DIN): 277 lb ft, 38.2 kg m at 1,600 rpm; 25.1 hp/l; 1 Ford 2150A D8WE-DA downdraught twin barrel carburettor; cooling system: 28.5 imp pt, 34.2 US pt, 16.2 l.

TRANSMISSION automatic transmission ratios: I 2.400, II 1.470, III 1, rev 2; max ratio of converter at stall 2; axle ratio: 2.470.

PERFORMANCE max speed: about 103 mph, 165 km/h; power-weight ratio: 4-dr. 29.6 lb/hp, 13.4 kg/hp - Landau 4-dr. 29.2 lb/hp, 13.3 kg/hp; speed in direct drive at 1,000 rpm: 28.5 mph, 45.8 km/h; consumption: 19.2 m/imp gal, 16 m/US gal, 14.7 l x 100 km.

ELECTRICAL EQUIPMENT 45 Ah battery.

OPTIONALS 2.500 axle ratio.

145 hp power team

(not available in California).

See 144 hp power team, except for:

ENGINE compression ratio: 8:1; max power (DIN): 145 hp at 3,400 rpm; max torque (DIN): 273 lb ft, 37.8 kg m at 1,800 rpm; 25.3 hp/l; 1 Ford 2150A TBD downdraught twin barrel carburettor.

TRANSMISSION width of rims: st. wagons 6.5''; tyres: st. wagons JR78 x 15.

PERFORMANCE max speed: about 99 mph, 160 km/h; power-weight ratio: st. wagons 31.5 lb/hp, 14.3 kg/hp.

DIMENSIONS AND WEIGHT length: st. wagons 225.70 in, 573 cm; width: st. wagons 79.70 in, 202 cm; height: st. wagons 56.70 in, 114 cm; weight: st. wagons 4,573 lb, 2,074 kg; fuel tank: st. wagons 17.6 imp gal, 21 US gal, 80 l.

160 hp power team

See 145 hp power team, except for:

ENGINE 400 cu in, 6,555 cc (4 x 4 in, 101.6 x 101.6 mm); compression ratio: 8:1; max power (DIN): 160 hp at 3,800 rpm; max torque (DIN): 314 lb ft, 43.3 kg m at 1,800 rpm;

max engine rpm: 4,400; 24.4 hp/l; cooling system: 28.5 imp pt, 34.2 US pt, 16.2 l.

TRANSMISSION automatic transmission ratios: I 2.460, II 1.460, III 1, rev 2.180; max ratio of converter at stall 2.18; axle ratio: 2.470 (2.750 for California only).

PERFORMANCE max speed: about 109 mph, 175 km/h; power-weight ratio: 4-dr. 26.6 lb/hp, 12 kg/hp - Landau 4-dr. 26.3 lb/hp, 11.9 kg/hp; speed in direct drive at 1,000 rpm: 24.7 mph, 39.8 km/h; consumption: 18 m/imp gal, 15 m/US gal, 15.7 l x 100 km.

ELECTRICAL EQUIPMENT 54 Ah battery.

202 hp power team

(not available in California).

See 160 hp power team, except for:

ENGINE 460 cu in, 7,539 cc (4.36 x 3.85 in, 110.7 x 97.8 mm); max power (DIN): 202 hp at 4,000 rpm; max torque (DIN): 348 lb ft, 48 kg m at 2,000 rpm; 26.8 hp/l; 1 Motorcraft TBD downdraught 4-barrel carburettor; cooling system: 32 imp pt, 38.5 US pt, 18.2 l.

TRANSMISSION automatic transmission ratios: I 2.460, II 1.460, III 1, rev 2.180; max ratio of converter at stall 1.87; axle ratio: 2.500.

INTERMECCANICA Speedster

PERFORMANCE max speed: about 112 mph, 180 km/h; power-weight ratio: 4-dr. 21.8 lb/hp, 9.9 kg/hp - Landau 4-dr. 21.5 lb/hp, 9.8 kg/hp; speed in direct drive at 1,000 rpm: 28 mph, 45 km/h; consumption: 16.8 m/imp gal, 14 m/US gal, 16.8 l x 100 km.

ELECTRICAL EQUIPMENT 68 Ah battery.

DIMENSIONS AND WEIGHT weight: plus 137 lb, 62 kg.

OPTIONALS 2.750 axle ratio.

INTERMECCANICA USA

Speedster

PRICE EX WORKS: $ 6,985

ENGINE Volkswagen, rear, 4 stroke; 4 cylinders, horizontally opposed; 96.7 cu in, 1,584 cc (3.37 x 2.72 in, 85.5 x 69 mm); compression ratio: 8.5:1; max power (DIN): 50 hp at 4,000 rpm; max torque (DIN): 78 lb ft, 10.8 kg m at 2,800 rpm; max engine rpm: 4,600; 31.6 hp/l; block with cast iron liners and light alloy fins, light alloy head; 4 crankshaft bearings; valves: overhead, push-rods and rockers; camshafts: 1, central, lower; lubrication: gear pump, filter in sump, oil cooler, 4.4 imp pt, 5.3 US pt, 2.5 l; 1 Solex 1661 downdraught single barrel carburettor; fuel feed: mechanical pump; air-cooled.

TRANSMISSION driving wheels: rear; clutch: single dry plate; gearbox: mechanical; gears: 4, fully synchronized; ratios: I 3.780, II 2.060, III 1.260, IV 0.930, rev 4.010; lever: central; final drive: spiral bevel; axle ratio: 3.875; width of rims: 4''; tyres: 5.60 x 15.

PERFORMANCE max speed: 110 mph, 176 km/h; power-weight ratio: 31.6 lb/hp, 14.3 kg/hp; consumption: 33.6 m/imp gal, 28 m/US gal, 8.4 l x 100 km.

CHASSIS box-section perimeter frame; front suspension: independent, twin swinging longitudinal trailing arms, transverse laminated torsion bars, anti-roll bar, telescopic dampers; rear: independent, swinging semi-axles, swinging longitudinal trailing arms, transverse torsion bars, telescopic dampers.

STEERING worm and roller.

BRAKES drum; lining area: total 111 sq in, 716 sq cm.

ELECTRICAL EQUIPMENT 12 V; 36 Ah battery; alternator; Bosch distributor; 2 headlamps.

DIMENSIONS AND WEIGHT wheel base: 82.70 in, 210 cm; tracks: 51.57 in, 131 cm front, 53.15 in, 135 cm rear; weight: 1,580 lb, 716 kg; weight distribution: 41% front, 59% rear; fuel tank: 5.9 imp gal, 7 US gal, 27 l.

BODY roadster in plastic material; 2 doors; 2 seats; tonneau cover.

OPTIONALS turbocharger.

INTERNATIONAL HARVESTER USA

Scout Series and SS II

PRICES EX WORKS:

1 Scout II Station Wagon 4 x 2	$	5,120
2 Scout II Station Wagon 4 x 4	$	6,080
3 Scout II Diesel Station Wagon 4 x 2	$	7,701
4 Scout II Diesel Station Wagon 4 x 4	$	8,717
5 Scout Traveler Station Wagon 4 x 2	$	5,510
6 Scout Traveler Station Wagon 4 x 4	$	6,473
7 Scout Traveler Diesel Station Wagon 4 x 2	$	8,091
8 Scout Traveler Diesel Station Wagon 4 x 4	$	9,114
9 SS II Station Wagon 4 x 4	$	5,387

For 140 hp V8 engines add $ 176

For 158 hp V8 engines add $ 234

Power team:	Standard for:	Optional for:
86 hp	1,2,5,6,9	—
81 hp	3,4,7,8	—
140 hp	—	1,2,5,6,9
158 hp	—	1,2,5,6,9

86 hp power team

ENGINE front, 4 stroke; 4 cylinders, in line; 196 cu in, 3,212 cc (4.13 x 3.66 in, 104.8 x 92.9 mm); compression ratio: 8.02:1; max power (DIN): 86 hp at 3,800 rpm; max torque (DIN): 157 lb ft, 21.6 kg m at 2,200 rpm; max engine rpm: 4,000; 26.8 hp/l; cast iron block and head; 5 crankshaft bearings; valves: overhead, in line, push-rods and rockers, hydraulic tappets; camshafts: 1, side; lubrication: gear pump, full flow filter, 11.6 imp pt, 14 US pt, 6.6 l; 1 Holley 1940 downdraught single barrel carburettor; cleaner air system; fuel feed: mechanical pump; water-cooled, 23.2 imp pt, 27.9 US pt, 13.2 l.

TRANSMISSION driving wheels: rear or front and rear; clutch: single dry plate; gearbox: mechanical; gears: 3, fully synchronized; ratios: I 2.997, II 1.550, III 1, rev 2.997; lever: central; final drive: hypoid bevel; axle ratio: 4.090; width of rims: 5.5''; tyres: H78 x 15.

PERFORMANCE max speed: 80 mph, 129 km/h; power-weight ratio: 41.8 lb/hp, 19 kg/hp; speed in direct drive at 1,000 rpm: 20.1 mph, 32.3 km/h; consumption: 18 m/imp gal, 15 m/US gal, 15.7 l x 100 km.

CHASSIS perimeter box-type frame; front and rear suspension: rigid axle, semi-elliptic leafsprings, telescopic dampers.

STEERING worm and roller.

INTERNATIONAL HARVESTER SS II Station Wagon 4 x 4

86 HP POWER TEAM

BRAKES front disc (diameter 11.75 in, 29.8 cm), rear drum; swept area: front 226 sq in, 1,458 sq cm, rear 101.8 sq in, 656 sq cm, total 327.8 sq in, 2,114 sq cm.

ELECTRICAL EQUIPMENT 12 V; 55 Ah battery; 37 A alternator; Holley electronic ignition; 2 headlamps.

DIMENSIONS AND WEIGHT wheel base: 100 in, 254 cm - Travelers 118 in, 300 cm; front and rear track: 57 in, 145 cm; length: 166.20 in, 422 cm - Travelers 184.20 in, 468 cm; width: 70 in, 178 cm; height: 65.70 in, 167 cm - Travelers 66 in, 168 cm; ground clearance: 7.60 in, 19.3 cm; weight: 3,598 lb, 1,632 kg - Travelers 3,601 lb, 1,633 kg; turning circle (between walls): 36.4 ft, 11.1 m - Travelers 40.5 ft, 12.3 m; fuel tank: 15.8 imp gal, 19 US gal, 72 l.

BODY 2 + 1 doors; 5 seats, separate front seats.

OPTIONAL ACCESSORIES 4-speed fully synchronized mechanical gearbox (I 4.020, II 2.410, III 1.410, IV 1, rev 4.730 or I 6.320, II 3.090, III 1.680, IV 1, rev 6.960); gearbox with transfer box; 3-speed automatic transmission; 3.540 axle ratio; HR78 x 15 tyres; limited slip differential; power steering; tilt of steering wheel; front bucket seats with console; folding rear seat; 61 A alternator; 72 Ah battery; heavy-duty front and rear suspension; air-conditioning; Rallye equipment.

INTERNATIONAL HARVESTER Scout II Series (Diesel engine)

81 hp power team

See 86 hp power team, except for:

ENGINE Diesel, 4 stroke; 6 cylinders, vertical, in line; 198 cu in, 3,245 cc (3.27 x 3.94 in, 83 x 100 mm); compression ratio: 22:1; max power (DIN): 81 hp at 4,000 rpm; max torque (DIN): 137 lb ft, 18.9 kg m at 2,000 rpm; max engine rpm: 4,400; 25 hp/l; 7 crankshaft bearings.

PERFORMANCE power-weight ratio: 44.3 lb/hp, 20.1 kg/hp.

PRACTICAL INSTRUCTIONS fuel: Diesel oil.

140 hp power team

See 86 hp power team, except for:

ENGINE 8 cylinders; 304 cu in, 4,982 cc (3.88 x 3.22 in, 98.5 x 81.7 mm); compression ratio: 8.19:1; max power (DIN): 140 hp at 3,800 rpm; max torque (DIN): 243 lb ft, 33.5 kg m at 2,400 rpm; 28.1 hp/l; camshafts: 1, at centre of Vee; dual exhaust system.

TRANSMISSION axle ratio: 3.540.

PERFORMANCE max speed: 90 mph, 145 km/h; power-weight ratio: 27.4 lb/hp, 12.4 kg/hp - Travelers 28.4 lb/hp, 12.9 kg/hp; speed in direct drive at 1,000 rpm: 20.3 mph, 36.2 km/h; consumption: 16.8 m/imp gal, 14 m/US gal, 16.8 l x 100 km.

DIMENSIONS AND WEIGHT weight: 3,843 lb, 1,743 kg - Travelers 3,981 lb, 1,805 kg.

158 hp power team

See 86 hp power team, except for:

ENGINE 8 cylinders; 345 cu in, 5,654 cc (3.88 x 3.66 in, 98.5 x 92.9 mm); compression ratio: 8.05:1; max power (DIN): 158 hp at 3,600 rpm; max torque (DIN): 288 lb ft, 39.7 kg m at 2,000 rpm; max engine rpm: 3,800; 28.2 hp/l; camshafts: 1, at centre of Vee; dual exhaust system; cooling system: 33.3 imp pt, 40 US pt, 18.9 l.

TRANSMISSION axle ratio: 3.540.

PERFORMANCE max speed: 90 mph, 145 km/h; power-weight ratio: 24.3 lb/hp, 11 kg/hp - Travelers 25.2 lb/hp, 11.4 kg/hp; speed in direct drive at 1,000 rpm: 25 mph, 40.3 km/h; consumption: 14.4 m/imp gal, 12 m/US gal, 19.6 l x 100 km.

DIMENSIONS AND WEIGHT weight: 3,843 lb, 1,743 kg - Travelers 3,981 lb, 1,805 kg.

Jeep CJ-5 - CJ-7 Series

PRICES IN GB AND EX WORKS:	£	$
Jeep CJ-5 Roadster	—	4,895
Jeep CJ-7 Roadster	5,049	4,995

For 98 hp engine add $ 77.
For V8 engine add $ 186.

Power team:	Standard for:	Optional for:
88 hp	both	—
98 hp	—	both
126 hp	—	both

88 hp power team

(not available in California).

ENGINE front, 4 stroke; 6 cylinders, in line; 232 cu in, 3,802 cc (3.75 x 3.50 in, 95.2 x 88.8 mm); compression ratio: 8:1; max power (DIN): 88 hp at 3,400 rpm; max torque (DIN): 164 lb ft, 22.6 kg m at 1,600 rpm; max engine rpm: 4,000; 23.1 hp/l; cast iron block and head; 7 crankshaft bearings; valves: overhead, in line, push-rods and rockers, hydraulic tappets; camshafts: 1, side; lubrication: gear pump, full flow filter, 10 imp pt, 12 US pt, 5.7 l; 1 Carter downdraught single barrel carburettor; fuel feed: mechanical pump; water-cooled, 17.4 imp pt, 21 US pt, 9.9 l.

TRANSMISSION driving wheels: front (automatically-engaged with transfer box low ratio) and rear; clutch: single dry plate; gearbox: mechanical; gears: 3, with high and low ratios, fully synchronized; ratios: I 2.990, II 1.750, III 1, rev 3.170; low ratios: I 2.030, II 1; lever: central; final drive: hypoid bevel; axle ratio: 3.540; width of rims 5.5''; tyres: F78 x 15.

PERFORMANCE max speed: about 78 mph, 125 km/h; power-weight ratio: 30 lb/hp, 13.6 kg/hp; speed in direct drive at 1,000 rpm: 23.6 mph, 38 km/h; consumption: 21.6 m/imp gal, 18 m/US gal, 13.1 l x 100 km.

CHASSIS perimeter box-type with cross members; front and rear suspension: rigid axle, semi-elliptic leafsprings, telescopic dampers.

STEERING recirculating ball.

BRAKES drum; swept area: front 138 sq in, 890 sq cm, rear 138 sq in, 890 sq cm, total 276 sq in, 1,780 sq cm.

ELECTRICAL EQUIPMENT 12 V; 50 Ah battery; 37 A alternator; electronic ignition; 2 headlamps.

DIMENSIONS AND WEIGHT wheel base: CJ-5 83.50 in, 212 cm - CJ-7 93.50 in, 237 cm; tracks: 51.50 in, 131 cm front, 50 in, 127 cm rear; length: CJ-5 138.40 in, 351 cm - CJ-7 147.90 in, 376 cm; width: 68.60 in, 174 cm; height: 67.60 in, 172 cm; ground clearance: 6.90 in, 17.5 cm; weight: CJ-5 2,641 lb, 1,198 kg - CJ-7 2,638 lb, 1,196 kg; turning circle (between walls): CJ-5 34.1 ft, 10.4 m - CJ-7 38 ft, 11.6 m; fuel tank: 12.5 imp gal, 15 US gal, 57 l.

OPTIONAL ACCESSORIES rear limited slip differential; 4.090 axle ratio; 4-speed fully synchronized mechanical gearbox (I 4.020, II 2.410, III 1.410, IV 1, rev 4.730); sports steering wheel; power steering; servo brake; all or half metal top; rear bench seats; heavy-duty cooling system; 70 Ah battery; 62 A alternator; heavy-duty suspension; light alloy wheels; Levi's interior; Renegade equipment with luxury interior, racing style roll bar, heavy-duty cooling system and H78 x 15 tyres; Turbo-Hydramatic automatic transmission with 4-wheel drive Quadra-Trac system and 3.090 axle ratio; full plastic top.

98 hp power team

(standard in California).

See 88 hp power team, except for:

ENGINE 258 cu in, 4,228 cc (3.75 x 3.90 in, 95.2 x 99 mm); max power (DIN): 98 hp at 3,200 rpm; max torque (DIN): 193 lb ft, 26.6 kg m at 1,600 rpm; 23.2 hp/l.

PERFORMANCE power-weight ratio: 26.9 lb/hp, 12.2 kg/hp.

126 hp power team

See 88 hp power team, except for:

ENGINE 8 cylinders; 304 cu in, 4,982 cc (3.75 x 3.44 in, 95.2 x 87.3 mm); compression ratio: 8.4:1; max power (DIN): 126 hp at 3,600 rpm; max torque (DIN): 219 lb ft, 30.2 kg m at 2,000 rpm; 25.3 hp/l; 5 crankshaft bearings;

JEEP CORPORATION Jeep CJ-5 Roadster

JEEP CORPORATION Cherokee 2-door S Station Wagon

camshafts: 1, at centre of Vee; lubrication: 8.3 imp pt, 9.9 US pt, 4.7 I; 1 downdraught twin barrel carburettor; exhaust system with catalytic converter; cooling system: 23.2 imp pt, 28 US pt, 13.2 I.

PERFORMANCE max speed: about 84 mph, 135 km/h; power-weight ratio: 21 lb/hp, 9.5 kg/hp; consumption: 19.2 m/imp gal, 16 m/US gal, 14.7 I x 100 km.

Cherokee Series

PRICES IN GB AND EX WORKS:	£	$
Cherokee 2-door Station Wagon	7,799	6,129
Cherokee Wide Wheel 2-door Station Wagon	—	—
Cherokee 4-door Station Wagon	7,899	6,235

For V8 engines add $ 250.

Power team:	Standard for:	Optional for:
114 hp	all	—
129 hp	—	all
165 hp	—	all
205 hp	—	all

114 hp power team

(not available in California).

ENGINE front, 4 stroke; 6 cylinders, in line; 258 cu in, 4,228 cc (3.75 x 3.90 in, 95.2 x 99 mm); compression ratio: 8:1; max power (DIN): 114 hp at 3,600 rpm; max torque (DIN): 192 lb ft, 26.5 kg m at 2,000 rpm; max engine rpm: 4,000; 27 hp/l; cast iron block and head; 7 crankshaft bearings; valves: overhead, in line, push-rods and rockers, hydraulic tappets; camshafts: 1, side; lubrication: gear pump, full flow filter, 10 imp pt, 12 US pt, 5.7 I; 1 Carter downdraught twin barrel carburettor; fuel feed: mechanical pump; water-cooled, 17.4 imp pt, 21 US pt, 9.9 I.

TRANSMISSION driving wheels: front (automatically engaged with transfer box low ratio) and rear; clutch: single dry plate; gearbox: mechanical; gears: 3, with high and low ratios, fully synchronized; ratios: I 3.000, II 1.830, III 1, rev 3.100; low ratios: I 2.030, II 1; lever: central; final drive: hypoid bevel; axle ratio: 3.070; width of rims: 5.5''; tyres: H78 x 15 - Wide Wheel 10 x 15.

PERFORMANCE max speed: about 90 mph, 145 km/h; power-weight ratio: 4-dr. 36 lb/hp, 16.3 kg/hp; speed in direct drive at 1,000 rpm: 22.5 mph, 36.2 km/h; consumption: 21.6 m/imp gal, 18 m/US gal, 13.1 I x 100 km.

CHASSIS perimeter box-type with cross members; front and rear suspension: rigid axle, semi-elliptic leafsprings, telescopic dampers.

STEERING recirculating ball.

BRAKES front disc, rear drum, servo.

ELECTRICAL EQUIPMENT 12 V; 50 Ah battery; 37 A alternator; electronic ignition; 2 headlamps.

DIMENSIONS AND WEIGHT wheel base: 108.70 in, 276 cm; front track: 59.40 in, 151 cm - Wide Wheel 65.40 in, 166 cm; rear track: 57.80 in, 147 cm - Wide Wheel 62.30 in,

158 cm; length: 183.50 in, 466 cm; width: 75.60 in, 192 cm - Wide Wheel 78.90 in, 200 cm; height: 66.90 in, 170 cm - Wide Wheel 67.60 in, 172 cm; ground clearance: 7.70 in, 19.6 cm - Wide Wheel 8.60 in, 21.8 cm; weight: 2-dr. 3,971 lb, 1,801 kg - Wide Wheel 3,991 lb, 1,810 kg - 4-dr. 4,106 lb, 1,862 kg; turning circle (between walls): 37.7 ft, 11.5 m - Wide Wheel 39.4 ft, 12 m; fuel tank: 17.8 imp gal, 21.5 US gal, 81 I.

OPTIONAL ACCESSORIES 4-speed fully synchronized mechanical gearbox; Turbo-Hydramatic automatic transmission with 4-wheel drive Quadra-Trac system and 3.540 or 4.090 axle ratio; rear limited slip differential; light alloy wheels; power steering with variable ratio; sports steering wheel; tilt of steering wheel; de luxe interior; heavy-duty cooling system; 70 Ah battery; 63 A alternator; anti-roll bar on front suspension; heavy-duty suspension; tinted glass; heated rear window; air-conditioning; S equipment, Chief equipment (for Wide Wheel only).

129 hp power team

(standard in California).

See 114 hp power team, except for:

ENGINE 8 cylinders; 360 cu in, 5,899 cc (4.08 x 3.44 in, 103.6 x 87.3 mm); compression ratio: 8.25:1; max power (DIN): 129 hp at 3,700 rpm; max torque (DIN): 245 lb ft, 33.8 kg m at 1,600 rpm; max engine rpm: 4,200; 21.9 hp/l; 5 crankshaft bearings; camshafts: 1, at centre of Vee; lubri-

cation: 8.3 imp pt, 9.9 US pt, 4.7 I; 1 downdraught twin barrel carburettor; cleaner air system; cooling system: 21.6 imp pt, 26 US pt, 12.3 I.

TRANSMISSION ratios: I 2.997, II 1.832, III 1, rev 2.997.

PERFORMANCE max speed: about 99 mph, 160 km/h; power-weight ratio: 4-dr. 31.8 lb/hp, 14.4 kg/hp; speed in direct drive at 1,000 rpm: 24.9 mph, 40 km/h; consumption: 16.8 m/imp gal, 14 m/US gal, 16.8 I x 100 km.

ELECTRICAL EQUIPMENT 60 Ah battery; 40 A alternator.

OPTIONAL ACCESSORIES 3.540 axle ratio; Turbo-Hydramatic automatic transmission with 4-wheel drive Quadra-Trac system and 3.070 or 3.540 axle ratio.

165 hp power team

(not available in California).

See 114 hp power team, except for:

ENGINE 8 cylinders; 360 cu in, 5,899 cc (4.08 x 3.44 in, 103.6 x 87.3 mm); compression ratio: 8.25:1; max power (DIN): 165 hp at 3,500 rpm; max torque (DIN): 280 lb ft, 38.6 kg m at 2,800 rpm; 28 hp/l; 5 crankshaft bearings; camshafts: 1, at centre of Vee; lubrication: 8.3 imp pt, 9.9 US pt, 4.7 I; 1 downdraught 4-barrel carburettor; cleaner air system; cooling system: 21.6 imp pt, 26 US pt, 12.3 I.

TRANSMISSION driving wheels: front and rear (Quadra-Trac system with central limited slip differential); gearbox: Turbo-Hydramatic automatic transmission, hydraulic torque converter and planetary gears with 3 ratios, max ratio of converter at stall 2.3, possible manual selection; ratios: I 2.480, II 1.480, III 1, rev 2.080.

PERFORMANCE max speed: about 103 mph, 165 km/h; power-weight ratio: 4-dr. 24.9 lb/hp, 11.3 kg/hp; speed in direct drive at 1,000 rpm: 26.4 mph, 42.5 km/h; consumption: 15.6 m/imp gal, 13 m/US gal, 18.1 I x 100 km.

ELECTRICAL EQUIPMENT 60 Ah battery; 40 A alternator.

OPTIONAL ACCESSORIES 3.540 axle ratio.

205 hp power team

(not available in California).

See 114 hp power team, except for:

ENGINE 8 cylinders; 401 cu in, 6,571 cc (4.17 x 3.68 in, 105.8 x 93.4 mm); compression ratio: 8.3:1; max power (DIN): 205 hp at 3,500 rpm; max torque (DIN): 317 lb ft, 43.7 kg m at 2,800 rpm; 31.2 hp/l; 5 crankshaft bearings; camshafts: 1, at centre of Vee; lubrication: 8.3 imp pt, 9.9 US pt, 4.7 I; 1 downdraught 4-barrel carburettor; cleaner air system; cooling system: 21.6 imp pt, 26 US pt, 12.3 I.

TRANSMISSION driving wheels: front and rear (Quadra-Trac system with central limited slip differential); gearbox: Turbo-Hydramatic automatic transmission, hydraulic

JEEP CORPORATION Cherokee 4-door S Station Wagon

205 HP POWER TEAM

torque converter and planetary gears with 3 ratios, max ratio of converter at stall 2.3, possible manual selection; ratios: I 2.480, II 1.480, III 1, rev 2.080.

PERFORMANCE max speed: about 106 mph, 170 km/h; power-weight ratio: 4-dr. 20 lb/hp, 9.1 kg/hp; speed in direct drive at 1,000 rpm: 26.4 mph, 42.5 km/h; consumption: 14.4 m/imp gal, 12 m/US gal, 19.6 l x 100 km.

ELECTRICAL EQUIPMENT 60 Ah battery; 55 A alternator.

OPTIONAL ACCESSORIES 3.540 axle ratio.

Wagoneer

PRICE EX WORKS: $ 7,595

For 165 hp engine add $ 50.
For 205 hp engine add $ 225.

129 hp power team

(standard).

ENGINE front, 4 stroke; 8 cylinders; 360 cu in, 5,899 cc (4.08 x 3.44 in, 103.6 x 87.3 mm); compression ratio: 8.25:1; max power (DIN): 129 hp at 3,700 rpm; max torque (DIN): 245 lb ft, 33.8 kg m at 1,600 rpm; max engine rpm: 4,200; 21.9 hp/l; cast iron block and head; 5 crankshaft bearings; valves: overhead, in line, push-rods and rockers, hydraulic tappets; camshafts: 1, at centre of Vee; lubrication: gear pump, full flow filter, 8.3 imp pt, 9.9 US pt, 4.7 l; 1 downdraught twin barrel carburettor; cleaner air system; fuel feed: mechanical pump; water-cooled, 21.6 imp pt, 26 US pt, 12.3 l.

TRANSMISSION driving wheels: front and rear (Quadra-Trac system with central limited slip differential); gearbox: Turbo-Hydramatic automatic transmission, hydraulic torque converter and planetary gears with 3 ratios, max ratio of converter at stall 2.3, possible manual selection; ratios: I 2.480, II 1.480, III 1, rev 2.080; lever: central; final drive: hypoid bevel; axle ratio: 3.070; width of rims: 5.5''; tyres: H78 x 15.

PERFORMANCE max speed: about 99 mph, 160 km/h; power-weight ratio: 33.7 lb/hp, 15.3 kg/hp; speed in direct drive at 1,000 rpm: 26.4 mph, 42.5 km/h; consumption: 16.8 m/imp gal, 14 m/US gal, 16.8 l x 100 km.

CHASSIS perimeter box-type with cross members; front and rear suspension: rigid axle, semi-elliptic leafsprings, telescopic dampers.

STEERING recirculating ball, variable ratio, servo.

BRAKES front disc (diameter 12 in, 30 cm), rear drum, servo.

ELECTRICAL EQUIPMENT 12 V; 60 Ah battery; 40 A alternator; electronic ignition; 2 headlamps.

JEEP CORPORATION Wagoneer

DIMENSIONS AND WEIGHT wheel base: 108.70 in, 276 cm; tracks: 59.40 in, 151 cm front, 57.80 in, 147 cm rear; length: 183.50 in, 466 cm; width: 75.60 in, 192 cm; height: 66.70 in, 169 cm; ground clearance: 7.70 in, 19.6 cm; weight: 4,345 lb, 1,970 kg; turning circle (between walls): 37.7 ft, 11.5 m; fuel tank: 17.8 imp gal, 21.5 US gal, 81 l.

BODY estate car/station wagon; 4 + 1 doors; 6 seats; bench front seats; folding rear seat.

OPTIONAL ACCESSORIES 3.540 axle ratio; anti-roll bar on front suspension; light alloy wheels; tilt of steering wheel; 70 Ah battery; 63 A alternator; heavy-duty cooling system; heavy-duty suspension; tinted glass; heated rear window; air-conditioning.

165 hp power team

(optional, not available in California).

See 129 hp power team, except for:

ENGINE max power (DIN): 165 hp at 3,500 rpm; max torque (DIN): 280 lb ft, 38.6 kg m at 2,800 rpm; 28 hp/l; 1 downdraught 4-barrel carburettor.

PERFORMANCE max speed: about 103 mph, 165 km/h; power-weight ratio: 26.3 lb/hp, 11.9 kg/hp; consumption: 15.6 m/imp gal, 13 m/US gal, 18.1 l x 100 km.

205 hp power team

(optional, not available in California).

See 129 hp power team, except for:

ENGINE 401 cu in, 6,571 cc (4.17 x 3.68 in, 105.8 x 93.4 mm); compression ratio: 8.3:1; max power (DIN): 205 hp at 3,500 rpm; max torque (DIN): 317 lb ft, 43.7 kg m at 2,800 rpm; 31.2 hp/l; 1 downdraught 4-barrel carburettor.

PERFORMANCE max speed: about 106 mph, 170 km/h; power-weight ratio: 21.2 lb/hp, 9.6 kg/hp; consumption: 14.4 m/imp gal, 12 m/US gal, 19.6 l x 100 km.

ELECTRICAL EQUIPMENT 55 A alternator.

LINCOLN   USA

Versailles

PRICE EX WORKS: $ 12,529

ENGINE front, 4 stroke; 8 cylinders; 302 cu in, 4,950 cc (4 x 3 in, 101.6 x 76.2 mm); compression ratio: 8.4:1 (8.1:1 for California only); max power (DIN): 133 hp at 3,600 rpm; max torque (DIN): 243 lb ft, 33.5 kg m at 1,600 rpm; max engine rpm: 4,000; 26.9 hp/l; cast iron block and head; 5 crankshaft bearings; valves: overhead, in line, push-rods and rockers, hydraulic tappets; camshafts: 1, at centre of Vee; lubrication: rotary pump, full flow filter, 8.3 imp pt, 9.9 US pt, 4.7 l; 1 Ford 2700 D84E-DB downdraught carburettor with variable Venturi cooling system; cleaner air system; exhaust system with catalytic converter; fuel feed: mechanical pump; water-cooled, 23.8 imp pt, 28.5 US pt, 13.5 l.

TRANSMISSION driving wheels: rear; gearbox: Select-Shift Cruise-O-Matic automatic transmission, hydraulic torque converter and planetary gears with 3 ratios, max ratio of converter at stall 2.04, possible manual selection; ratios: I 2.460, II 1.460, III 1, rev 2.190; lever: steering column; final drive: hypoid bevel; axle ratio: 2.500; width of rims: 6''; tyres: FR78 x 14.

PERFORMANCE max speed: about 108 mph, 174 km/h; power-weight ratio: 28.3 lb/hp, 12.8 kg/hp; speed in direct drive at 1,000 rpm: 30 mph, 48.3 km/h; consumption: 21.6 m/imp gal, 18 m/US gal, 13.1 l x 100 km.

CHASSIS integral; front suspension: independent, wishbones (lower trailing links), coil springs, anti-roll bar, telescopic dampers; rear: rigid axle, semi-elliptic leafsprings, telescopic dampers.

STEERING recirculating ball, servo; turns lock to lock: 3.70.

BRAKES disc (front diameter 11.03 in, 28 cm, rear 10.66 in, 27 cm), internal radial fins, rear compensator, servo; swept area: front 222.5 sq in, 1,435 sq cm, rear 221.2 sq in, 1,432 sq cm, total 443.7 sq in, 2,867 sq cm.

ELECTRICAL EQUIPMENT 12 V; 53 Ah battery; 60 A alternator; Motorcraft transistorized ignition; 4 headlamps.

DIMENSIONS AND WEIGHT wheel base: 109.90 in, 279 cm; tracks: 59 in, 150 cm front, 57.70 in, 146 cm rear; length: 200.90 in, 510 cm; width: 74.50 in, 189 cm; height: 54.10 in, 137 cm; ground clearance: 5.10 in, 13 cm; weight: 3,759 lb, 1,705 kg; fuel tank: 16.1 imp gal, 19.2 US gal, 73 l.

BODY saloon/sedan; 4 doors; 5 seats, bench front seats with built-in headrests; tinted glass; electric windows; air-conditioning.

OPTIONALS limited slip differential; central lever; tilt of steering wheel; reclining backrests; heated rear windows; leather upholstery; electric sunshine roof; vinyl roof.

Continental Series

PRICES EX WORKS:

Continental Sedan	$ 10,166
Continental Coupé	$ 9,974
Continental Town Sedan	$ 11,606
Continental Town Coupé	$ 11,414

Power team:	Standard for:	Optional for:
166 hp	all	—
210 hp	—	all

166 hp power team

ENGINE front, 4 stroke; 8 cylinders; 400 cu in, 6,555 cc (4 x 4 in, 101.6 x 101.6 mm); compression ratio: 8:1; max power (DIN): 166 hp at 3,800 rpm; max torque (DIN): 319 lb ft, 44 kg m at 1,800 rpm; max engine rpm: 4,600; 25.3 hp/l; cast iron block and head; 5 crankshaft bearings; valves: overhead, in line, push-rods and rockers, hydraulic

LINCOLN Versailles

LINCOLN Continental Town Sedan

tappets; camshafts: 1, at centre of Vee; lubrication: rotary pump, full flow filter, 8.3 imp pt, 9.9 US pt, 4.7 l; 1 Ford 2150A 9510 D80E-HA (DESE-EA for California only) downdraught twin barrel carburettor; cleaner air system; exhaust system with catalytic converter; fuel feed: mechanical pump; water-cooled, 28.5 imp pt, 34.2 US pt, 16.2 l.

TRANSMISSION driving wheels: rear; gearbox: Select-Shift Merc-O-Matic automatic transmission, hydraulic torque converter and planetary gears with 3 ratios, max ratio of converter at stall 1.87, possible manual selection; ratios: I 2.460, II 1.460, III 1, rev 2.180; lever: steering column; final drive: hypoid bevel; axle ratio: 2.750; width of rims: 6''; tyres: 225 x 15.

PERFORMANCE max speed: about 110 mph, 177 km/h; power-weight ratio: 28 lb/hp, 12.7 kg/hp; speed in direct drive at 1,000 rpm: 29 mph, 46.6 km/h; consumption: 18 m/imp gal, 15 m/US gal, 15.7 l x 100 km.

CHASSIS box-type ladder frame; front suspension: independent, wishbones (lower trailing links), coil springs, anti-roll bar, telescopic dampers; rear: rigid axle, lower trailing radius arms, upper oblique torque arms, transverse linkage bar, coil springs, telescopic dampers.

STEERING recirculating ball, servo; turns lock to lock: 4.08.

BRAKES front disc (diameter 11.80 in, 30 cm), front internal radial fins, rear drum, rear compensator, servo; swept area: front 242 sq in, 1,561 sq cm, rear 173.2 sq in, 1,117 sq cm, total 415.2 sq in, 2,678 sq cm.

LINCOLN Continental Series

ELECTRICAL EQUIPMENT 12 V; 63 Ah battery; 60 A alternator; Motorcraft transistorized ignition; 4 headlamps.

DIMENSIONS AND WEIGHT wheel base: 127.20 in, 323 cm; front and rear tracks: 64.30 in, 163 cm; length: 233 in, 592 cm; width: Sedan 80 in, 203 cm - Coupé 79.70 in, 202 cm; height: Sedan 55.20 in, 140 cm - Coupé 55 in, 140 cm; ground clearance: 5.20 in, 13.2 cm; weight: Sedan 4,642 lb, 2,105 kg - Coupé 4,650 lb, 2,109 kg; turning circle (between walls): 51.5 ft, 15.8 m; fuel tank: 20 imp gal, 24.2 US gal, 91 l.

BODY 6 seats, bench front seats; tinted glass; electric windows; air-conditioning.

OPTIONALS limited slip differential; JR78 x 15 or LR78 x 15 tyres; aluminium wheels; tilt of steering wheel; 4-wheel disc brakes, total swept area 465.9 sq in, 3,005 sq cm; anti-skid brakes; heated rear window; automatic speed control; reclining backrest with built-in headrest; sunshine roof; Williamsburg equipment (for Town Sedan only).

210 hp power team

(not available in California).

See 166 hp power team, except for:

ENGINE 460 cu in, 7,539 cc (4.36 x 3.85 in, 110.7 x 97.8 mm); max power (DIN): 210 hp at 4,200 rpm; max torque (DIN): 357 lb ft, 49.2 kg m at 2,200 rpm; 27.8 hp/l; 1 Motorcraft 9510 D8VE-FA downdraught 4-barrel carburettor; dual exhaust system; cooling system: 30.8 imp pt, 37 US pt, 17.5 l.

PERFORMANCE max speed: about 118 mph, 190 km/h; power-weight ratio: 22.6 lb/hp, 10.3 kg/hp; consumption: 15.6 m/imp gal, 13 m/US gal, 18.1 l x 100 km.

ELECTRICAL EQUIPMENT 68 Ah battery.

DIMENSIONS AND WEIGHT weight: plus 106 lb, 48 kg.

Continental Mark V

PRICE EX WORKS: $ 12,099

166 hp power team

(standard).

ENGINE front, 4 stroke; 8 cylinders; 400 cu in, 6,555 cc (4 x 4 in, 101.6 x 101.6 mm); compression ratio: 8:1; max power (DIN): 166 hp at 3,800 rpm; max torque (DIN): 319 lb ft, 44 kg m at 1,800 rpm; max engine rpm: 4,600; 25.3 hp/l; cast iron block and head; 5 crankshaft bearings; valves: overhead, in line, push-rods and rockers, hydraulic tappets; camshafts: 1, at centre of Vee; lubrication: rotary pump, full flow filter, 8.3 imp pt, 9.9 US pt, 4.7 l; 1 Ford 2150A 9510 D80E-HA (D8SE-EA for California only) downdraught twin barrel carburettor; cleaner air system; exhaust system with catalytic converter; fuel feed: mechanical pump; water-cooled, 28.5 imp pt, 34.2 US pt, 16.2 l.

TRANSMISSION driving wheels: rear; gearbox: Select-Shift Merc-O-Matic automatic transmission, hydraulic torque converter and planetary gears with 3 ratios, max ratio of converter at stall 1.87, possible manual selection; ratios: I 2.460, II 1.460, III 1, rev 2.180; lever: steering column; final drive: hypoid bevel; axle ratio: 2.750; width of rims: 6''; tyres: 225 x 15.

PERFORMANCE max speed: about 110 mph, 177 km/h; power-weight ratio: 27.4 lb/hp, 12.4 kg/hp; speed in direct drive at 1,000 rpm: 29 mph, 46.6 km/h; consumption: 18 m/imp gal, 15 m/US gal, 15.7 l x 100 km.

CHASSIS box-type perimeter frame; front suspension: independent, wishbones (lower trailing links), coil springs, anti-roll bar, telescopic dampers; rear: rigid axle, lower trailing radius arms, upper oblique torque arms, coil springs, anti-roll bar, telescopic dampers.

STEERING recirculating ball, servo; turns lock to lock: 3.99.

BRAKES disc (front diameter 11.80 in, 30 cm, rear 11.50 in, 29.2 cm), internal radial fins, rear compensator, servo; swept area: front 242 sq in, 1,561 sq cm, rear 223.9 sq in, 1,444 sq cm, total 465.9 sq in, 3,005 sq cm.

ELECTRICAL EQUIPMENT 12 V; 63 Ah battery; 60 A alternator; Motorcraft transistorized ignition; 4 headlamps.

DIMENSIONS AND WEIGHT wheel base: 120.40 in, 306 cm; tracks: 63.20 in, 160 cm front, 62.60 in, 159 cm rear; length: 230.30 in, 585 cm; width: 79.70 in, 202 cm; height: 52.90 in, 134 cm; ground clearance: 6.80 in, 173 cm; weight: 4,556 lb, 2,066 kg; turning circle (between walls): 46.7 ft, 14.2 m; fuel tank: 20.9 imp gal, 25 US gal, 95 l.

BODY hardtop; 2 doors; 6 seats; bench front seats with built-in headrest; electric windows; air-conditioning.

OPTIONALS limited slip differential; L78 x 15 tyres; aluminium wheels; reclining backrest; sunshine roof; anti-skid brakes; heated rear window; speed control device; Diamond Jubilee Edition version.

LINCOLN Continental Mk V Diamond Jubilee Edition

210 hp power team

(optional, not available in California).

See 166 hp power team, except for:

ENGINE 460 cu in, 7,539 cc (4.36 x 3.85 in, 110.7 x 97.8 mm); max power (DIN): 210 hp at 4,200 rpm; max torque (DIN): 357 lb ft, 49.2 kg m at 2,200 rpm; 27.8 hp/l; 1 Motorcraft 9510 D8VE-FA downdraught 4-barrel carburettor; cooling system: 30.8 imp pt, 37 US pt, 17.5 l.

TRANSMISSION axle ratio: 2.500.

PERFORMANCE max speed: about 118 mph, 190 km/h; power-weight ratio: 22.2 lb/hp, 10.1 kg/hp; consumption: 16.8 m/imp gal, 14 m/US gal, 16.8 l x 100 km.

ELECTRICAL EQUIPMENT 68 Ah battery.

DIMENSIONS AND WEIGHT weight: plus 109 lb, 49 kg.

OPTIONALS dual exhaust system; 2.750 axle ratio.

MERCURY   USA

Bobcat Series

PRICES EX WORKS:

Bobcat Runabout	$ 3,573
Bobcat Station Wagon	$ 3,878
Bobcat Villager Station Wagon	$ 4,010

For V6 engine add $ 273.

Power team:	Standard for:	Optional for:
88 hp	all	—
90 hp	—	all

88 hp power team

ENGINE front, 4 stroke; 4 cylinders, in line; 140 cu in, 2,300 cc (3.78 x 3.13 in, 95.9 x 79.5 mm); compression ratio: 9:1; max power (DIN): 88 hp at 4,800 rpm; max torque (DIN): 118 lb ft, 16.3 kg m at 2,800 rpm; max engine rpm: 5,200; 38.3 hp/l; cast iron block and head; 5 crankshaft bearings; valves: overhead, Vee-slanted, rockers, hydraulic tappets; camshafts: 1, overhead, cogged belt; lubrication: gear pump, full flow filter, 7.6 imp pt, 9.1 US pt, 4.3 l; 1 Holley-Weber 9510 D8EE-DA (D8EE-JA for California only) downdraught twin barrel carburettor; cleaner air system; exhaust system with catalytic converter; fuel feed: mechanical pump; water-cooled, 14.4 imp pt, 17.3 US pt, 8.2 l.

TRANSMISSION driving wheels: rear; clutch: single dry plate; gearbox: mechanical; gears: 4, fully synchronized; ratios: I 3.980, II 2.140, III 1.420, IV 1, rev 3.990; lever: central; final drive: hypoid bevel; axle ratio: 2.730; width of rims: 5''; tyres: A78 x 13.

PERFORMANCE max speed: about 93 mph, 150 km/h; power-weight ratio: Runabout 27.2 lb/hp, 12.3 kg/hp; speed in direct drive at 1,000 rpm: 19.3 mph, 31 km/h; consumption: 34.9 m/imp gal, 29 m/US gal, 8.1 l x 100 km.

CHASSIS integral; front suspension: independent, wishbones (lower leading arms), coil springs (anti-roll bar standard for st. wagons only), telescopic dampers; rear: rigid axle, semi-elliptic leafsprings, telescopic dampers.

STEERING rack-and-pinion; turns lock to lock: 4.15.

BRAKES front disc (diameter 9.30 in, 23.6 cm), front internal radial fins, rear drum, rear compensator; swept area: front 145.5 sq in, 938 sq cm, rear 99 sq in, 638 sq cm, total 244.5 sq in, 1,576 sq cm.

ELECTRICAL EQUIPMENT 12 V; 45 Ah battery; 40 A alternator; Motorcraft transistorized ignition; 2 headlamps.

DIMENSIONS AND WEIGHT wheel base: 94.50 in, 240 cm - st. wagons 94.80 in, 241 cm; tracks: 55 in, 140 cm front, 55.80 in, 142 cm rear; length: 169.30 in, 430 cm - st. wagons 179.10 in, 455 cm; width: 69.40 in, 176 cm - st. wagons 69.70 in, 177 cm; height: 50.60 in, 128 cm - st. wagons 52.10 in, 132 cm; ground clearance: 4.58 in, 11.6 cm - st. wagons 5.11 in, 13 cm; weight: Runabout 2,392 lb, 1,085 kg - st. wagons 2,522 lb, 1,143 kg; turning circle (between walls): 35.9 ft, 10.9 m; fuel tank: 10.8 imp gal, 13 US gal, 49 l (9.7 imp gal, 11.7 US gal, 44 l for California only) - st. wagons 11.7 imp gal, 14 US gal, 53 l.

BODY 2 + 1 doors; 4 seats; separate front seats; folding rear seat.

OPTIONALS limited slip differential; Select-Shift Cruise-O-Matic automatic transmission, hydraulic torque converter and planetary gears with 3 ratios (I 2.470, II 1.470, III 1, rev 2.110), max ratio of converter at stall 2.9, possible manual selection, central lever, 3.180 axle ratio; BR78 x 13, BR70 x 13, B78 x 13 or A70 x 13 tyres; aluminum wheels

MERCURY Bobcat Villager Station Wagon

with 5.5'' wide rims; heavy-duty suspension with front anti-roll bar; power steering; servo brake; 53 Ah battery; 70 A alternator; heated rear window; tinted glass; sunshine roof; vinyl roof; luxury interior: Sports equipment; air-conditioning.

90 hp power team

See 88 hp power team, except for:

ENGINE 6 cylinders, Vee-slanted at 60°; 170.8 cu in, 2,800 cc (3.66 x 2.70 in, 92.9 x 68.5 mm); compression ratio: 8.7:1; max power (DIN): 90 hp at 4,200 rpm; max torque (DIN): 143 lb ft, 19.7 kg m at 2,200 rpm; max engine rpm: 4,600; 32.1 hp/l; 4 crankshaft bearings; valves: overhead, in line, push-rods and rockers; camshafts: 1, at centre of Vee; lubricating system: 8.3 imp pt, 9.9 US pt, 4.7 l; 1 Motorcraft 9510 D8BE-MA (D8ZE-YB with variable Venturi cooling system for California only) downdraught twin barrel carburettor; cooling system: 14.1 imp pt, 16.9 US pt, 8 l.

TRANSMISSION gearbox: Select-Shift Cruise-O-Matic automatic transmission (standard), max ratio of converter at stall 2.9 (2.05 for California only); ratios: I 2.470, II 1.470, III 1, rev 2.110 (I 2.460, II 1.460, III 1, rev 2.190 for California only); axle ratio: 3.400.

PERFORMANCE max speed: about 96 mph, 155 km/h; power-weight ratio: Runabout 28 lb/hp, 12.7 kg/hp; speed in direct drive at 1,000 rpm: 21.6 mph, 34.7 km/h; consumption: 23.9 m/imp gal, 20 m/US gal, 11.8 l x 100 km.

DIMENSIONS AND WEIGHT weight: plus 128 lb, 58 kg.

Zephyr Series

PRICES EX WORKS:

Zephyr 2-door Sedan	$ 3,742
Zephyr 4-door Sedan	$ 3,816
Zephyr Sport Coupé	$ —
Zephyr Station Wagon	$ 4,184

For V6 engine add $ 120; for V8 add $ 319.

Power team:	Standard for:	Optional for:
88 hp	all	—
85 hp	—	all
133 hp	—	all
139 hp	—	all

88 hp power team

ENGINE front, 4 stroke; 4 cylinders, in line; 140 cu in, 2,300 cc (3.78 x 3.13 in, 95.9 x 79.5 mm); compression ratio: 9:1; max power (DIN): 88 hp at 4,800 rpm; max torque (DIN): 118 lb ft, 16.3 kg m at 2,800 rpm; max engine rpm: 5,200; 38.3 hp/l; cast iron block and head; 5 crankshaft bearings; valves: overhead, Vee-slanted, rockers, hydraulic tappets; camshafts: 1, overhead, cogged belt; lubrication: gear pump, full flow filter, 7.6 imp pt, 9.1 US pt, 4.3 l; 1 Holley-Weber 5200 downdraught twin barrel carburettor; cleaner air system; exhaust system with catalytic converter; fuel feed: mechanical pump; water-cooled, 14.3 imp pt, 17.1 US pt, 8.1 l.

TRANSMISSION driving wheels: rear; clutch: single dry plate; gearbox: mechanical; gears: 4, fully synchronized;

MERCURY Zephyr ES 2-door Sedan

ratios: I 3.980, II 2.140, III 1.420, IV 1, rev 3.990; lever: central: final drive: hypoid bevel; axle ratio: 3.080; width of rims: 5''; tyres: B78 x 14 - St. Wagon CR78 x 14.

PERFORMANCE max speed: about 95 mph, 153 km/h; power-weight ratio: 4-dr. Sedan 29.9 lb/hp, 13.5 kg/hp; speed in direct drive at 1,000 rpm: 19.8 mph, 31.9 km/h; consumption: 31.4 m/imp gal, 26 m/US gal, 9 l x 100 km.

CHASSIS integral with two cross members; front suspension: independent, by McPherson, coil springs/telescopic damper struts, lower wishbones, anti-roll bar; rear: rigid axle, lower trailing radius arms, upper oblique torque arms, coil springs, telescopic dampers.

STEERING rack-and-pinion; turns lock to lock: 4.10.

BRAKES front disc (diameter 10.06 in, 25.5 cm); front internal radial fins, rear drum, rear compensator; swept area: front 196.6 sq in, 1,268 sq cm, rear 99 sq in, 638 sq cm, total 295.6 sq in, 1,906 sq cm - St. Wagon rear 110 sq in, 710 sq cm, total 306.6 sq in, 1,978 sq cm.

ELECTRICAL EQUIPMENT 12 V; 36 Ah battery; 40 A alternator; Motorcraft transistorized ignition; 4 headlamps.

DIMENSIONS AND WEIGHT wheel base: 105.50 in, 268 cm; tracks: 56.60 in, 144 cm front, 57 in, 145 cm rear; length: 193.80 in, 492 cm - Sport Coupé 195.80 in, 497 cm; width: 71 in, 180 cm; height: sedans 53.50 in, 136 cm - Sport Coupé 52.20 in, 133 cm - St. Wagon 54.80 in, 139 cm; ground clearance: 4.60 in, 11.8 cm; weight: 2-dr. Sedan 2,585 lb, 1,172 kg - 4-dr. Sedan 2,627 lb, 1,191 kg - Sport Coupé 2,622 lb, 1,189 kg - St. Wagon 2,666 lb, 1,209 kg; fuel tank: 13.4 imp gal, 16 US gal, 61 l.

BODY 5 seats, bench front seats.

OPTIONALS Select-Shift Cruise-O-Matic automatic transmission, hydraulic torque converter and planetary gears with 3 ratios (I 2.470, II 1.470, III 1, rev 2.110), max ratio of converter at stall 2.9, possible manual selection, steering column lever, 3.080 axle ratio; aluminum wheels; BR78 x 14, C78 x 14, CR78 x 14 or DR78 x 14 tyres; 45 or 54 Ah battery; power steering; servo brake; heated rear window; heavy-duty suspension; rear window wiper-washer (for St. Wagon); tinted glass; vinyl roof; luxury interior; air-conditioning; ES equipment (except for St. Wagon); Villager equipment (for St. Wagon).

85 hp power team

See 88 hp power team, except for:

ENGINE 6 cylinders, in line; 200 cu in, 3,277 cc (3.68 x 3.13 in, 93.5 x 79.5 mm); compression ratio: 8.5:1; max power (DIN): 85 hp at 3,600 rpm; max torque (DIN): 154 lb ft, 21.3 kg m at 1,600 rpm; max engine rpm: 4,400; 25.9 hp/l; 7 crankshaft bearings; valves: overhead, in line, push-rods and rockers, hydraulic tappets; camshafts: 1, side; lubricating system: 8.3 imp pt, 9.9 US pt, 4.7 l; 1 Carter YFA (1 Holley 1946 for California only) downdraught single barrel carburettor; cooling system: 15 imp pt, 18 US pt, 8.5 l.

TRANSMISSION gearbox: mechanical (Select-Shift Cruise-O-Matic automatic transmission standard for California only); gears: 3, fully synchronized; ratios: I 3.560, II 1.000, III 1, rev 3.780; axle ratio: 2.730 (3.080 for California only).

PERFORMANCE power-weight ratio: 4-dr. Sedan 31.4 lb/hp, 14.3 kg/hp; consumption: 28.8 m/imp gal, 24 m/US gal, 9.8 l x 100 km.

ELECTRICAL EQUIPMENT 60 A alternator.

DIMENSIONS AND WEIGHT weight: plus 46 lb, 21 kg.

OPTIONALS Select-Shift Cruise-O-Matic automatic transmission with 2.730 or 3.080 axle ratio.

133 hp power team

(for California only).

See 88 hp power team, except for:

ENGINE 8 cylinders; 302 cu in, 4,950 cc (4 x 3 in, 101.6 x 76.2 mm); compression ratio: 8.1:1; max power (DIN): 133 hp at 3,600 rpm; max torque (DIN): 243 lb ft, 33.5 kg m at 1,600 rpm; 26.9 hp/l; valves: overhead, in line, push-rods and rockers, hydraulic tappets; camshafts: 1, at centre of Vee; lubricating system: 8.3 imp pt, 9.9 US pt, 4.7 l; 1 Ford 2700 with variable Venturi downdraught single barrel carburettor; cooling system: 23.1 imp pt, 27.7 US pt, 13.1 l.

TRANSMISSION gearbox: Select-Shift Cruise-O-Matic automatic transmission (standard), hydraulic torque converter and planetary gears with 3 ratios, max ratio of converter at stall 2, possible manual selection; ratios: I 2.460, II 1.460, III 1, rev 2.190; lever: steering column; axle ratio: 2.470.

PERFORMANCE max speed: about 100 mph, 161 km/h; power-weight ratio: 4-dr. Sedan 21.7 lb/hp, 9.8 kg/hp; speed in direct drive at 1,000 rpm: 27.8 mph, 44.7 km/h; consumption: 21.6 m/imp gal, 18 m/US gal, 13.1 l x 100 km.

DIMENSIONS AND WEIGHT weight: plus 255 lb, 115 kg.

139 hp power team

(not available in California).

See 133 hp power team, except for:

ENGINE compression ratio: 8.4:1; max power (DIN): 139 hp at 3,600 rpm; max torque (DIN): 250 lb ft, 34.5 kg m at 1,600 rpm; 28.1 hp/l; 1 Ford 2150 downdraught twin barrel carburettor.

PERFORMANCE max speed: about 105 mph, 169 km/h; power-weight ratio: 4-dr. Sedan 20.7 lb/hp, 9.4 kg/hp; consumption: 22.8 m/imp gal, 19 m/US gal, 12.4 l x 100 km.

Monarch Series

PRICES IN GB AND EX WORKS:	£	$
Monarch 2-door Sedan	—	4,330
Monarch 4-door Sedan	—	4,409
Monarch Ghia 2-door Sedan	7,165	4,756
Monarch Ghia 4-door Sedan	7,225	4,835
Monarch ESS 2-door Sedan	—	4,854
Monarch ESS 4-door Sedan	—	4,933

For V8 engine add $ 181.

Power team:	Standard for:	Optional for:
97 hp	all	—
133 hp	—	all
139 hp	—	all

MERCURY Monarch 2-door Sedan

97 hp power team

ENGINE front, 4 stroke; 6 cylinders, in line; 250 cu in, 4,097 cc (3.68 x 3.91 in, 93.5 x 99.3 mm); compression ratio: 8.5:1; max power (DIN): 97 hp at 3,200 rpm; max torque (DIN): 210 lb ft, 29 kg m at 1,400 rpm; max engine rpm: 4,000; 23.7 hp/l; cast iron block and head; 7 crankshaft bearings; valves: overhead, in line, push-rods and rockers, hydraulic tappets; camshafts: 1, side; lubrication: rotary pump, full flow filter, 8.3 imp pt, 9.9 US pt, 4.7 l; 1 Carter YFA 9510 D8DE-BA (D8KE-AA for California only) downdraught single barrel carburettor; cleaner air system; exhaust system with catalytic converter; fuel feed: mechanical pump; water-cooled, 17.4 imp pt, 21 US pt, 9.9 l.

TRANSMISSION driving wheels: rear; clutch: single dry plate, semi-centrifugal; gearbox: mechanical (Select-Shift Cruise-O-Matic automatic transmission standard for California only); gears: 4, fully synchronized with overdrive/top; ratios: I 3.290, II 1.840, III 1, IV 0.810, rev 3.290; lever: central; final drive: hypoid bevel; axle ratio: 3.000 (2.470 for California only); width of rims: 6''; tyres: DR78 x 14.

PERFORMANCE max speed: about 93 mph, 150 km/h; power-weight ratio: 4-dr. 32.1 lb/hp, 14.6 kg/hp; speed in top at 1,000 rpm: 29.1 mph, 46.9 km/h; consumption: 25.2 m/imp gal, 21 m/US gal, 11.2 l x 100 km.

CHASSIS integral; front suspension: independent, wishbones (lower trailing links), coil springs, anti-roll bar, telescopic dampers; rear: rigid axle, semi-elliptic leafsprings, telescopic dampers.

STEERING recirculating ball; turns lock to lock: 5.18.

BRAKES front disc (diameter 11.03 in, 28 cm), front internal radial fins, rear drum, rear compensator; swept area: front 222.5 sq in, 1,435 sq cm, rear 125.7 sq in, 811 sq cm, total 348.2 sq in, 2,246 sq cm.

ELECTRICAL EQUIPMENT 12 V; 36 Ah battery; 40 A alternator; Motorcraft transistorized ignition; 2 headlamps.

DIMENSIONS AND WEIGHT wheel base: 109.90 in, 279 cm; tracks: 59 in, 150 cm front, 57.70 in, 147 cm rear; length: 197.70 in, 502 cm; width: 74 in, 188 cm; height: 2-dr. 53.20 in, 135 cm - 4-dr. 53.30 in, 135 cm; ground clearance: 4.84 in, 12.3 cm; weight: 2-dr. 3,073 lb, 1,393 kg - 4-dr. 3,114 lb, 1,412 kg; fuel tank: 15 imp gal, 18 US gal, 68 l.

BODY saloon/sedan; 5 seats, separate front seats, reclining backrests with built-in headrests.

OPTIONALS limited slip differential; Select-Shift Cruise-O-Matic automatic transmission, hydraulic torque converter and planetary gears with 3 ratios (I 2.460, II 1.460, III 1, rev 2.900), max ratio of converter at stall 2.29, possible manual selection, steering column or central lever, 2.470 or 2.500 axle ratio; aluminum wheels; ER78 x 14 or FR78 x 14 tyres; power steering; tilt of steering wheel; servo brake; 4-wheel disc brakes, total swept area 433.7 sq in, 2,797 sq cm; 54 Ah battery; 70 A alternator; electric windows; tinted glass; heated rear window; speed control device; vinyl roof; sunshine roof; Sports equipment; air-conditioning.

MERCURY Monarch 4-door Sedan

133 hp power team

(for California only).

See 97 hp power team, except for:

ENGINE 8 cylinders; 302 cu in, 4,950 cc (4 x 3 in, 101.6 x 76.2 mm); compression ratio: 8.1:1; max power (DIN): 133 hp at 3,600 rpm; max torque (DIN): 243 lb ft, 33.5 kg m at 1,600 rpm; 26.9 hp/l; 5 crankshaft bearings; camshafts: 1, at centre of Vee; 1 Ford 2700 9510 TBD downdraught carburettor with variable Venturi; cooling system: 23.6 imp pt, 28.3 US pt, 13.4 l.

TRANSMISSION gearbox: Select-Shift Cruise-O-Matic automatic transmission (standard), hydraulic torque converter and planetary gears with 3 ratios, max ratio of converter at stall 2.29, possible manual selection; ratios: I 2.460, II 1.460, III 1, rev 2.900; lever: steering column; axle ratio: 2.470.

PERFORMANCE max speed: about 96 mph, 155 km/h; power-weight ratio: 4-dr. 24.1 lb/hp, 10.9 kg/hp; speed in direct drive at 1,000 rpm: 26.7 mph, 43 km/h; consumption: 21.6 m/imp gal, 18 m/US gal, 13.1 l x 100 km.

DIMENSIONS AND WEIGHT weight: plus 93 lb, 42 kg.

OPTIONALS central lever; 2.500 axle ratio.

139 hp power team

(not available in California).

See 97 hp power team, except for:

ENGINE 8 cylinders; 302 cu in, 4,950 cc (4 x 3 in, 101.6 x 76.2 mm); compression ratio: 8.4:1; max power (DIN): 139 hp at 3,600 rpm; max torque (DIN): 250 lb ft, 34.5 kg m at 1,600 rpm; 28.1 hp/l; 5 crankshaft bearings; camshafts: 1, at centre of Vee; 1 Ford 2150A 9510 TBD downdraught twin barrel carburettor; cooling system: 23.6 imp pt, 28.3 US pt, 13.4 l.

PERFORMANCE max speed: about 103 mph, 165 km/h; power-weight ratio: 4-dr. 23 lb/hp, 10.5 kg/hp; consumption: 22.8 m/imp gal, 19 m/US gal, 12.4 l x 100 km.

DIMENSIONS AND WEIGHT weight: plus 90 lb, 41 kg.

Cougar Series

PRICES EX WORKS:

Cougar 2-door Hardtop	$ 5,009
Cougar 4-door Hardtop	$ 5,126
Cougar XR-7 2-door Hardtop	$ 5,603

Power team:	Standard for:	Optional for:
134 hp	all	—
144 hp	—	all
152 hp	—	all
166 hp	—	all

134 hp power team

(not available in California).

ENGINE front, 4 stroke; 8 cylinders; 302 cu in, 4,950 cc (4 x 3 in, 101.6 x 76.2 mm); compression ratio: 8.4:1; max power (DIN): 134 hp at 3,400 rpm; max torque (DIN): 248 lb ft, 34.3 kg m at 1,600 rpm; max engine rpm: 4,000; 27.1 hp/l; cast iron block and head; 5 crankshaft bearings; valves: overhead, in line, push-rods and rockers, hydraulic tappets; camshafts: 1, at centre of Vee; lubrication: rotary pump, full flow filter, 8.3 imp pt, 9.9 US pt, 4.7 l; 1 Ford 2150A D80E-EA downdraught twin barrel carburettor; cleaner air system; exhaust system with catalytic converter; fuel feed: mechanical pump; water-cooled, 22.5 imp pt, 27.1 US pt, 12.8 l.

TRANSMISSION driving wheels: rear; gearbox: Select-Shift automatic transmission, hydraulic torque converter and planetary gears with 3 ratios, max ratio of converter at stall 1.92, possible manual selection; ratios: I 2.460, II 1.460, III 1, rev 2.200; lever: steering column; final drive: hypoid bevel; axle ratio: 2.750; width of rims: 5.5'' - XR-7 6''; tyres: HR78 x 14 - XR-7 HR78 x 15.

PERFORMANCE max speed: about 99 mph, 160 km/h; power-weight ratio: 4-dr. 30.1 lb/hp, 13.7 kg/hp; speed in direct drive at 1,000 rpm: 26.4 mph, 42.5 km/h; consumption: 20.5 m/imp gal, 17 m/US gal, 13.8 l x 100 km.

CHASSIS perimeter frame; front suspension: independent, wishbones (lower trailing links), coil springs, anti-roll bar,

MERCURY Cougar 2-door Hardtop

telescopic dampers; rear: rigid axle, lower trailing radius arms, upper oblique torque arms, coil springs, telescopic dampers.

STEERING recirculating ball, servo; turns lock to lock: 3.99.

BRAKES front disc (diameter 10.72 in, 27.2 cm), front internal radial fins, rear drum, rear compensator, servo; swept area: front 212 sq in, 1,367 sq cm, rear 155.9 sq in, 1,005 sq cm, total 367.9 sq in, 2,372 sq cm.

ELECTRICAL EQUIPMENT 12 V; 36 Ah battery; 40 A alternator; Motorcraft transistorized ignition; 4 headlamps.

DIMENSIONS AND WEIGHT wheel base: 118 in, 300 cm - 2-dr. 114 in, 289 cm; front track: 63.60 in, 162 cm - XR-7 63.20 in, 161 cm; rear track: 63.50 in, 161 cm - XR-7 63.10 in, 160 cm; length: 2-dr. 215.50 in, 547 cm - 4-dr. 219.50 in, 558 cm; width: 78.60 in, 200 cm; height: 52.60 in, 134 cm - 4-dr. 53.30 in, 135 cm - XR-7 52.90 in, 134 cm; ground clearance: 4.75 in, 12 cm; weight: 2-dr. 3,961 lb, 1,796 kg - 4-dr. 4,039 lb, 1,831 kg - XR-7 4,087 lb, 1,853 kg; turning circle (between walls): 42.4 ft, 12.9 m; fuel tank: 17.4 imp gal, 21 US gal, 79 l.

OPTIONALS limited slip differential; H78 x 14 tyres; HR70 x 15 tyres (for XR-7 only); anti-roll bar on rear suspension only with Cross Country equipment; tilt of steering wheel; electric windows; reclining backrests; heated rear window; tinted glass; vinyl roof; speed control device; air-conditioning.

144 hp power team

(not available in California).

See 134 hp power team, except for:

ENGINE 351 cu in, 5,732 cc (4 x 3.50 in, 101.6 x 88.8 mm); compression ratio: 8.3:1; max power (DIN): 144 hp at 3,200 rpm; max torque (DIN): 277 lb ft, 38.2 kg m at 1,600 rpm; 25.1 hp/l; 1 Ford 2150A D8WE-DA downdraught twin barrel carburettor; cooling system: 26.4 imp pt, 31.7 US pt, 15 l.

TRANSMISSION gearbox: Select-Shift automatic transmission with max ratio of converter at stall 2.17; ratios: I 2.400, II 1.470, III 1, rev 2; axle ratio: 2.500.

PERFORMANCE max speed: about 103 mph, 165 km/h; power-weight ratio: 4-dr. 29 lb/hp, 13.2 kg/hp; consumption: 19.2 m/imp gal, 16 m/US gal, 14.7 l x 100 km.

ELECTRICAL EQUIPMENT 45 Ah battery.

DIMENSIONS AND WEIGHT weight: plus 144 lb, 65 kg.

152 hp power team

See 144 hp power team, except for:

ENGINE compression ratio: 8:1; max power (DIN): 152 hp at 3,600 rpm; max torque (DIN): 278 lb ft, 38.3 kg m at 1,800 rpm; 26.5 hp/l; 1 Ford 2150A TBD downdraught twin barrel carburettor; cooling system: 28.5 imp pt, 34.2 US pt, 16.2 l.

PERFORMANCE max speed: about 106 mph, 170 km/h; power-weight ratio: 4-dr. 27.5 lb/hp, 12.5 kg/hp; consumption: 21.6 m/imp gal, 18 m/US gal, 13.1 l x 100 km.

OPTIONALS 2.750 axle ratio (except for California).

166 hp power team

See 152 hp power team, except for.

ENGINE 400 cu in, 6,555 cc (4 x 4 in, 101.6 x 101.6 mm); max power (DIN): 166 hp at 3,800 rpm; max torque (DIN): 319 lb ft, 44 kg m at 1,800 rpm; max engine rpm: 4,400; 25.3 hp/l; 1 Ford 2150A TBD downdraught twin barrel carburettor.

TRANSMISSION gearbox: Select-Shift automatic transmission with max ratio of converter at stall 2.05; ratios: I 2.460, II 1.460, III 1, rev 2.180; axle ratio: 2.500 (2.750 for California only).

PERFORMANCE max speed: about 109 mph, 175 km/h; power-weight ratio: 4-dr. 24.7 lb/hp, 11.2 kg/hp; consumption: 18 m/imp gal, 15 m/US gal, 15.7 l x 100 km.

ELECTRICAL EQUIPMENT 54 Ah battery.

DIMENSIONS AND WEIGHT weight: plus 63 lb, 28 kg.

OPTIONALS 2.750 or 3.000 axle ratio.

Marquis Series

PRICES EX WORKS:

Marquis 2-door Hardtop	$ 5,764
Marquis 4-door Hardtop	$ 5,806
Marquis Station Wagon	$ 5,958
Marquis Brougham 2-door Hardtop	$ 6,380
Marquis Brougham 4-door Hardtop	$ 6,480
Grand Marquis 2-door Hardtop	$ 7,132
Grand Marquis 4-door Hardtop	$ 7,232

Power team:	Standard for:	Optional for:
145 hp	all	—
160 hp	—	all
202 hp	—	all

145 hp power team

(not available in California).

ENGINE front, 4 stroke; 8 cylinders; 351 cu in, 5,732 cc (4 x 3.50 in, 101.6 x 88.8 mm); compression ratio: 8:1; max power (DIN): 145 hp at 3,400 rpm; max torque (DIN): 273 lb ft, 37.7 kg m at 1,800 rpm; max engine rpm: 4,400; 25.3 hp/l; cast iron block and head; 5 crankshaft bearings; valves: overhead, in line, push-rods and rockers, hydraulic tappets; camshafts: 1, at centre of Vee; lubrication: rotary pump, full flow filter, 8.3 imp pt, 9.9 US pt, 4.7 l; 1 Ford 2150A downdraught twin barrel carburettor; cleaner air system; exhaust system with catalytic converter; fuel feed: mechanical pump; water-cooled, 28.2 imp pt, 33.8 US pt, 16 l.

MERCURY Grand Marquis 4-door Hardtop

TRANSMISSION driving wheels: rear; gearbox: Select-Shift Merc-O-Matic automatic transmission, hydraulic torque converter and planetary gears with 3 ratios, max ratio of converter at stall 2.17, possible manual selection: ratios: I 2.400, II 1.470, III 1, rev 2; lever: steering column; final drive: hypoid bevel; axle ratio: 2.470; width of rims: 6'' - St. Wagon 6.5''; tyres: HR78 x 15 - St. Wagon JR78 x 15.

PERFORMANCE max speed: about 103 mph, 165 km/h; power-weight ratio: Marquis 4-dr. Hardtop 29.8 lb/hp, 13.5 kg/hp; speed in direct drive at 1,000 rpm: 30.1 mph, 48.5 km/h; consumption: 19.2 m/imp gal, 16 m/US gal, 14.7 l x 100 km.

CHASSIS perimeter box-type frame; front suspension: independent, wishbones (lower trailing links), coil springs, anti-roll bar, telescopic dampers; rear: rigid axle, lower trailing radius arms, upper torque arms, transverse linkage bar, coil springs, telescopic dampers.

STEERING recirculating ball, servo; turns lock to lock: 3.99.

BRAKES front disc (diameter 11.80 in, 30 cm), front internal radial fins, rear drum, rear compensator, servo; swept area: front 242 sq in, 1,561 sq cm, rear 173.2 sq in, 1,117 sq cm, total 415.2 sq in, 2,678 sq cm.

ELECTRICAL EQUIPMENT 12 V; 45 Ah battery; 40 A alternator; Motorcraft transistorized ignition; 4 headlamps.

DIMENSIONS AND WEIGHT wheel base: 124 in, 315 cm - St. Wagon 121 in, 307 cm; tracks: 64.10 in, 163 cm front, 64.30 in, 163 cm rear; length: 229 in, 582 cm - St. Wagon 227.10 in, 577 cm; width: 79.60 in, 202 cm - St. Wagon 79.70 in, 202 cm; height: 2-dr. 54.80 in, 139 cm - 4-dr. 53.80 in, 137 cm - St. Wagon 56.90 in, 144 cm; ground clearance: 5.50 in, 14 cm; weight: Marquis 2-dr. 4,296 lb, 1,948 kg - 4-dr. 4,328 lb, 1,963 kg - St. Wagon 4,578 lb, 2,076 kg - Brougham 2-dr. 4,317 lb, 1,958 kg - 4-dr. 4,346 lb, 1,971 kg - Grand Marquis 2-dr. 4,470 lb, 2,027 kg - 4-dr. 4,517 lb, 2,048 kg; turning circle (between walls): 46.5 ft, 14.2 m; fuel tank: 20.2 imp gal, 24.2 US gal, 92 l - St. Wagon 17.6 imp gal, 21 US gal, 80 l.

OPTIONALS limited slip differential; 2.500 axle ratio; automatic levelling control; JR78 x 15, J78 x 15 or LR78 x 15 tyres with 6.5'' wide rims; tilt of steering wheel; 4-wheel disc brakes, total swept area 465.9 sq in, 3,005 sq cm; anti-skid brakes; electric windows; reclining backrests; heated rear window; speed control device; heavy-duty battery; aluminum wheels; vinyl roof; air-conditioning; Colony Park equipment for St. Wagon.

160 hp power team

See 145 hp power team, except for:

ENGINE 400 cu in, 6,555 cc (4 x 4 in, 101.6 x 101.6 mm); max power (DIN): 160 hp at 3,800 rpm; max torque (DIN): 314 lb ft, 43.3 kg m at 1,800 rpm; 24.4 hp/l; 1 Ford 2150A downdraught twin barrel carburettor; cooling system: 31 imp pt, 37.2 US pt, 17.6 l.

TRANSMISSION gearbox: Select-Shift Merc-O-Matic automatic transmission with max ratio of converter at stall 1.94; ratios: I 2.460, II 1.460, III 1, rev 2.180; axle ratio: 2.470 (2.750 for California only).

PERFORMANCE max speed: about 106 mph, 170 km/h; power-weight ratio: Marquis 4-dr. Hardtop 27.1 lb/hp, 12.3 kg/hp; speed in direct drive at 1,000 rpm: 27.8 mph, 44.7 km/h; consumption: 18 m/imp gal, 15 m/US gal, 15.7 l x 100 km.

ELECTRICAL EQUIPMENT 54 Ah battery.

DIMENSIONS AND WEIGHT weight: plus 11 lb, 5 kg.

OPTIONALS 2.750 or 3.000 axle ratio.

202 hp power team

(not available in California).

See 145 hp power team, except for:

ENGINE 460 cu in, 7,539 cc (4.36 x 3.85 in, 110.7 x 97.8 mm); max power (DIN): 202 hp at 4,000 rpm; max torque (DIN): 348 lb ft, 48 kg m at 2,000 rpm; 26.8 hp/l; 1 Motorcraft downdraught 4-barrel carburettor; cooling system: 32.7 imp pt, 39.3 US pt, 18.6 l.

TRANSMISSION gearbox: Select-Shift Merc-O-Matic automatic transmission with max ratio of converter at stall 1.94; ratios: I 2.460, II 1.460, III 1, rev 2.180; axle ratio: 2.500.

PERFORMANCE max speed: about 109 mph, 175 km/h; power-weight ratio: Marquis 4-dr. Hardtop 22 lb/hp, 10 kg/hp; speed in direct drive at 1,000 rpm: 27.2 mph, 43.7 km/h; consumption: 16.8 m/imp gal, 14 m/US gal, 16.8 l x 100 km.

ELECTRICAL EQUIPMENT 68 Ah battery.

DIMENSIONS AND WEIGHT weight: plus 114 lb, 52 kg.

OPTIONALS 2.750 axle ratio.

MONOCOQUE Box

MONOCOQUE — USA

Box

PRICE EX WORKS: $ 8,800

ENGINE Honda, rear, transverse, 4 stroke; 4 cylinders, in line; 97.6 cu in, 1,599 cc (2.91 x 3.66 in, 74 x 93 mm); compression ratio: 8:1; max power (JIS): 80 hp at 5,300 rpm; max torque (JIS): 89 lb ft, 12.3 kg m at 3,000 rpm; max engine rpm: 5,800; 50 hp/l; cast iron block, light alloy head; 5 crankshaft bearings; valves: 3 per cylinder (intake in auxiliary combustion chamber, both intake and exhaust in main chamber), overhead, Vee-slanted, rockers; camshafts: 1, overhead, cogged belt; lubrication: rotary pump, full flow filter, 5.3 imp pt, 6.3 US pt, 3 l; 1 Keihin-Honda downdraught 3-barrel CVCC carburettor; fuel feed: electric pump; water-cooled, 8.8 imp pt, 10.6 US pt, 5 l.

TRANSMISSION driving wheels: front and rear; clutch: single dry plate (diaphragm), hydraulically controlled; gearbox: mechanical; gears: 5, fully synchronized; ratios: I 3.181, II 1.823, III 1.181, IV 0.846, V 0.714, rev 2.916; lever: central; final drive: hypoid bevel; axle ratio: 4.933; width of rims: 4''; tyres: 6.00 x 12.

PERFORMANCE max speeds: about 75 mph, 120 km/h; power-weight ratio: 12.5 lb/hp, 5.7 kg/hp; consumption: 56.5 m/imp gal, 47 m/US gal, 5 l x 100 km.

OLDSMOBILE Starfire Sport Coupé

CHASSIS box-type perimeter frame with cross members; front and rear suspension: independent, wishbones (swinging semi-axles), coil springs, telescopic dampers.

STEERING rack-and-pinion.

BRAKES disc.

ELECTRICAL EQUIPMENT 12 V; 30 Ah battery; 35 A alternator; Mitsubishi distributor; 4 headlamps.

DIMENSIONS AND WEIGHT wheel base: 77 in, 196 cm; tracks: 68 in, 173 cm front, 68 in, 173 cm rear; length: 124 in, 315 cm; height: 42 in, 107 cm; ground clearance: 10 in, 25.4 cm; weight: 1,000 lb, 454 kg; weight distribution: 50% front, 50% rear; fuel tank: 8.4 imp gal, 10 US gal, 38 l.

BODY in plastic material; 1 front opening door; 2 seats.

OPTIONALS aluminum wheels; amphibious drive gear; air-oil suspensions; larger fuel tank.

OLDSMOBILE — USA

Starfire Series

PRICES EX WORKS:

Starfire Sport Coupé	$ 3,925
Starfire SX Sport Coupé	$ 4,130

For V8 engine add $ 320.

Power team:	Standard for:	Optional for:
85 hp	both	—
105 hp	—	both
145 hp	—	both

85 hp power team

(not available in California).

ENGINE front, 4 stroke; 4 cylinders, in line; 151 cu in, 2,474 cc (4 x 3 in, 101.6 x 76.1 mm); compression ratio: 8.3:1; max power (DIN): 85 hp at 4,400 rpm; max torque (DIN): 123 lb ft, 17 kg m at 2,800 rpm; max engine rpm: 4,800; 34.4 hp/l; cast iron block and head; 5 crankshaft bearings; valves: overhead, in line, push-rods and rockers, hydraulic tappets; camshafts: 1, side; lubrication: gear pump, full flow filter, 8.3 imp pt, 9.9 US pt, 4.7 l; 1 Holley 5210 downdraught single barrel carburettor; cleaner air system; exhaust system with catalytic converter; fuel feed: mechanical pump; water-cooled, 18.3 imp pt, 22 US pt, 10.4 l.

TRANSMISSION driving wheels: rear; clutch: single dry plate; gearbox: mechanical; gears: 4, fully synchronized; ratios: I 3.500, II 2.200, III 1.470, IV 1, rev 3.110; lever: central; final drive: hypoid bevel; axle ratio: 2.730; width of rims: 5''; tyres: B78 x 13.

PERFORMANCE max speed: about 93 mph, 150 km/h; power-weight ratio: Starfire 31.9 lb/hp, 14.5 kg/hp; speed in direct drive at 1,000 rpm: 21.2 mph, 34.1 km/h; consumption: 33.6 m/imp gal, 28 m/US gal, 8.4 l x 100 km.

85 HP POWER TEAM

CHASSIS integral; front suspension: independent, wishbones (lower trailing links), coil springs, anti-roll bar, telescopic dampers; rear: rigid axle, lower trailing radius arms, upper oblique torque arms, transverse linkage bar, coil springs, anti-roll bar, telescopic dampers.

STEERING recirculating ball; turns lock to lock: 4.40.

BRAKES front disc (diameter 9.88 in, 25.1 cm), front internal radial fins, rear drum, rear compensator; swept area: total 264.7 sq in, 1,707 sq cm.

ELECTRICAL EQUIPMENT 12 V; 2,500 W battery; 37 A alternator; Delco-Remy transistorized ignition; 4 headlamps.

DIMENSIONS AND WEIGHT wheel base: 97 in, 246 cm; tracks: 54.70 in, 139 cm front, 53.60 in, 136 cm rear; length: 179.30 in, 455 cm; width: 65.40 in, 166 cm; height: 50.20 in, 127 cm; ground clearance: 4.90 in, 12.4 cm; weight: Starfire 2,711 lb, 1,229 kg - Starfire SX 2,716 lb, 1,231 kg; turning circle (between walls): 41 ft, 12.5 m; fuel tank: 15.4 imp gal, 18.5 US gal, 70 l.

BODY coupé; 2 doors; 4 seats, separate front seats; folding rear seat.

OPTIONALS limited slip differential; 3.080 axle ratio; 5-speed fully synchronized mechanical gearbox (I 3.400, II 2.080, III 1.390, IV 1, V 0.800, rev 3.360), 2.730 or 3.230 axle ratio; Turbo-Hydramatic 200 automatic transmission, hydraulic torque converter and planetary gears with 3 ratios (I 2.520, II 1.520, III 1, rev 1.940), max ratio of converter at stall 2.25, possible manual selection, 2.730 or 2.930 axle ratio; BR78 x 13 tyres with 6'' wide rims; power steering; servo brake; heated rear window; air-conditioning.

105 hp power team

See 85 hp power team, except for:

ENGINE 6 cylinders, Vee-slanted at 90°; 231 cu in, 3,785 cc (3.80 x 3.40 in, 96.5 x 86.4 mm); compression ratio: 8:1; max power (DIN): 105 hp at 3,400 rpm; max torque (DIN): 185 lb ft, 25.5 kg m at 2,000 rpm; max engine rpm: 4,000; 27.7 hp/l; 4 crankshaft bearings; camshafts: 1, at centre of Vee; 1 Rochester 17057145 downdraught twin barrel carburettor; cooling system: 20.1 imp pt, 24.2 US pt, 11.2 l.

TRANSMISSION clutch: semi-centrifugal; gearbox ratios: I 3.110, II 2.200, III 1.470, IV 1, rev 3.110; axle ratio: 2.930.

PERFORMANCE max speed: about 103 mph, 165 km/h; power-weight ratio: Starfire 25.8 lb/hp, 11.7 kg/hp; speed in direct drive at 1,000 rpm: 25.6 mph, 41.2 km/h; consumption: 22.8 m/imp gal, 19 m/US gal, 12.4 l x 100 km.

ELECTRICAL EQUIPMENT 3,200 W battery.

OPTIONALS 5-speed fully synchronized mechanical gearbox with 2.930 axle ratio; Turbo-Hydramatic 200 automatic transmission with 2.560 or 2.930 axle ratio.

145 hp power team

See 85 hp power team, except for:

ENGINE 8 cylinders; 305 cu in, 4,998 cc (3.74 x 3.48 in, 94.9 x 88.3 mm); compression ratio: 8.5:1; max power (DIN): 145 hp at 3,800 rpm; max torque (DIN): 245 lb ft, 33.8 kg m at 2,400 rpm; max engine rpm: 4,400; 39 hp/l; camshafts: 1, at centre of Vee; 1 Rochester 17057107 downdraught twin barrel carburettor; fuel feed: electric pump; cooling system: 27.5 imp pt, 33.1 US pt, 15.4 l.

TRANSMISSION clutch: semi-centrifugal; gearbox ratios: I 2.850, II 2.020, III 1.350, IV 1, rev 2.850; axle ratio: 3.080.

PERFORMANCE max speed: about 106 mph, 170 km/h; power-weight ratio: Starfire 18.7 lb/hp, 6.5 kg/hp; speed in direct drive at 1,000 rpm: 24 mph, 38.6 km/h; consumption: 21.6 m/imp gal, 18 m/US gal, 13.1 l x 100 km.

ELECTRICAL EQUIPMENT 3,200 W battery.

OPTIONALS 5-speed fully synchronized mechanical gearbox not available; Turbo-Hydramatic 200 automatic transmission with 2.290 or 2.560 axle ratio.

Omega Series

PRICES EX WORKS:

Omega Coupé	$ 3,973
Omega Sedan	$ 4,048
Omega Hatchback Coupé	$ 4,137
Omega Brougham Coupé	$ 4,179
Omega Brougham Sedan	$ 4,254

For V8 engines add $ 150.

Power team:	Standard for:	Optional for:
105 hp	all	—
145 hp	—	all
160 hp	—	all

105 hp power team

ENGINE front, 4 stroke; 6 cylinders, Vee-slanted at 90°; 231 cu in, 3,785 cc (3.80 x 3.40 in, 96.5 x 86.4 mm); compression ratio: 8:1; max power (DIN): 105 hp at 3,400 rpm; max torque (DIN): 185 lb ft, 25.5 kg m at 2,000 rpm; max engine rpm: 4,200; 27.7 hp/l; cast iron block and head; 4 crankshaft bearings; valves: overhead, in line, push-rods and rockers, hydraulic tappets; camshafts: 1, at centre of Vee; lubrication: gear pump, full flow filter, 8.3 imp pt, 9.9 US pt, 4.7 l; 1 Rochester 2GC downdraught twin barrel carburettor; cleaner air system; exhaust system with catalytic converter; fuel feed: mechanical pump; water-cooled, 21.3 imp pt, 25.6 US pt, 12.1 l.

TRANSMISSION driving wheels: rear; clutch: single dry plate; gearbox: mechanical; gears: 3, fully synchronized; ratios: I 3.110, II 1.840, III 1, rev 3.200; lever: central; final drive: hypoid bevel; axle ratio: 3.080; width of rims: 5''; tyres: E78 x 14.

PERFORMANCE max speed: about 96 mph, 155 km/h; power-weight ratio: Sedan 31 lb/hp, 14 kg/hp; speed in direct drive at 1,000 rpm: 24.2 mph, 38.9 km/h; consumption: 22.8 m/imp gal, 19 m/US gal, 12.4 l x 100 km.

CHASSIS integral with front separate partial frame; front suspension: independent, wishbones, coil springs, anti-roll bar, telescopic dampers; rear: rigid axle, semi-elliptic leafsprings, telescopic dampers.

STEERING recirculating ball; turns lock to lock: 6.11.

BRAKES front disc (diameter 10.88 in, 27.6 cm), front internal radial fins, rear drum, rear compensator; swept area: front 226.2 sq in, 1,459 sq cm, rear 119.4 sq in, 770 sq cm, total 345.6 sq in, 2,229 sq cm.

ELECTRICAL EQUIPMENT 12 V; 2,500 W battery; 37 A alternator; Delco-Remy transistorized ignition; 2 headlamps.

DIMENSIONS AND WEIGHT wheel base: 111 in, 282 cm; tracks: 61.90 in, 157 cm front, 59.60 in, 151 cm rear; length: 199.60 in, 507 cm; width: 72.90 in, 185 cm; height: 53.80 in, 137 cm - sedans 54.70 in, 139; ground clearance: 4.86 in, 12.3 cm; weight: Omega Coupé 3,215 lb, 1,458 kg - Sedan 3,252 lb, 1,475 kg - Hatchback Coupé 3,280 lb, 1,487 kg - Omega Brougham Coupé 3,279 lb, 1,487 kg - Sedan 3,276 lb, 1,485 kg; turning circle (between walls): 41.3 ft, 12.6 m; fuel tank: 17.6 imp gal, 21 US gal, 80 l.

OPTIONALS limited slip differential; 5-speed fully synchronized mechanical gearbox with 2.930 axle ratio; Turbo-Hydramatic 200 automatic transmission, hydraulic torque converter and planetary gears with 3 ratios (I 2.740, II 1.570, III 1, rev 2.070), max ratio of converter at stall 2.25, possible manual selection, 3.230 or 2.560 axle ratio; steering column or central lever; power steering; tilt of steering wheel; servo brake; electric windows; vinyl roof; air-conditioning.

145 hp power team

See 105 hp power team, except for:

ENGINE 8 cylinders; 305 cu in, 4,998 cc (3.74 x 3.48 in, 94.9 x 88.3 mm); compression ratio: 8.5:1; max power (DIN): 145 hp at 3,800 rpm; max torque (DIN): 245 lb ft, 33.8 kg m at 2,400 rpm; 29 hp/l; 5 crankshaft bearings; 1 Rochester 2GC downdraught twin barrel carburettor; cooling system: 26.2 imp pt, 31.5 US pt, 14.9 l.

PERFORMANCE max speed: about 103 mph, 165 km/h; power-weight ratio: Sedan 23.5 lb/hp, 10.7 kg/hp; consumption: 20.5 m/imp gal, 17 m/US gal, 13.8 l x 100 km.

ELECTRICAL EQUIPMENT 3,200 W battery; 37 A alternator; Delco-Remy high energy ignition system.

DIMENSIONS AND WEIGHT weight: plus 157 lb, 71 kg.

OPTIONALS Turbo-Hydramatic 350 automatic transmission, hydraulic torque converter and planetary gears with 3 ratios (I 2.520, II 1.520, III 1, rev 1.930), 3.080 or 2.410 axle ratio.

160 hp power team

(for California only).

See 145 hp power team, except for:

ENGINE 350 cu in, 5,736 cc (4.06 x 3.38 in, 103.1 x 85.8 mm); max power (DIN): 160 hp at 3,800 rpm; max torque (DIN):

OLDSMOBILE Omega Brougham Sedan

OLDSMOBILE Omega Coupé

OLDSMOBILE Cutlass Cruiser Station Wagon

260 lb ft, 35.9 kg m at 2,400 rpm; 32 hp/l; 1 Rochester 4GC downdraught 4-barrel carburettor; cooling system: 24.3 imp pt, 29.2 US pt, 13.8 l.

TRANSMISSION gearbox: Turbo-Hydramatic 350 automatic transmission (standard), hydraulic torque converter and planetary gears with 3 ratios, max ratio of converter at stall 2.25, possible manual selection; ratios: I 2.520, II 1.520, III 1, rev 1.930; axle ratio: 2.410.

PERFORMANCE max speed: 106 mph, 170 km/h; power-weight ratio: Sedan 20.5 lb/hp, 9.3 kg/hp; speed in direct drive at 1,000 rpm: 27.8 mph, 44.7 km/h; consumption: 22.8 m/imp gal, 19 m/US gal, 12.4 l x 100 km.

DIMENSIONS AND WEIGHT weight: plus 27 lb, 12 kg.

Cutlass Series

PRICES EX WORKS:

Cutlass Salon Coupé	$ 4,408
Cutlass Salon Sedan	$ 4,508
Cutlass Cruiser Station Wagon	$ 5,241
Cutlass Salon Brougham Coupé	$ 4,695
Cutlass Salon Brougham Sedan	$ 4,795
Cutlass Supreme Coupé	$ 4,841
Cutlass Calais Coupé	$ 5,195
Cutlass Supreme Brougham Coupé	$ 5,246

For V8 engines add $ 150.

Power team:	Standard for:	Optional for:
105 hp	all	—
110 hp	—	all
145 hp	—	all
160 hp	—	all

105 hp power team

ENGINE front, 4 stroke; 6 cylinders, Vee-slanted at 90°; 231 cu in, 3,785 cc (3.80 x 3.40 in, 96.5 x 86.4 mm); compression ratio: 8:1; max power (DIN): 105 hp at 3,400 rpm; max torque (DIN): 185 lb ft, 25.5 kg m at 2,000 rpm; max engine rpm: 4,200; 27.7 hp/l; cast iron block and head; 4 crankshaft bearings; valves: overhead, in line, push-rods and rockers, hydraulic tappets; camshafts: 1, at centre of Vee; lubrication: gear pump, full flow filter, 8.3 imp pt, 9.9 US pt, 4.7 l; 1 Rochester 2 GC downdraught twin barrel carburettor; cleaner air system; exhaust system with catalytic converter; fuel feed: mechanical pump; water-cooled, 21.3 imp pt, 25.6 US pt, 12.1 l.

TRANSMISSION driving wheels: rear; clutch: single dry plate (diaphragm), centrifugal; gearbox: mechanical (Turbo-Hydramatic 350 automatic transmission standard for St. Wagon); gears: 3, fully synchronized; ratios: I 3.500, II 1.895, III 1, rev 3.620; lever: central; final drive: hypoid bevel; axle ratio: 2.930 - St. Wagon 2.730; width of rims: 6''; tyres: P185/75R x 14 - St. Wagon P195/75R x 14.

PERFORMANCE max speed: about 96 mph, 155 km/h; power-weight ratio: Salon Sedan 29.2 lb/hp, 13.3 kg/hp; speed in direct drive at 1,000 rpm: 24.2 mph, 38.9 km/h; consumption: 23 m/imp gal, 19 m/US gal, 12.3 l x 100 km.

CHASSIS channel section perimeter type frame; front suspension: independent, wishbones, coil springs, anti-roll bar, telescopic dampers; rear: rigid axle, lower trailing radius arms, upper oblique torque arms, coil springs, telescopic dampers.

STEERING recirculating ball; turns lock to lock: 6.60.

BRAKES front disc (diameter 10.38 in, 26.4 cm), front internal radial fins, rear drum, rear compensator; swept area: total 312.7 sq in, 2,017 sq cm.

ELECTRICAL EQUIPMENT 12 V; 2,500 W battery; 42 A alternator; Delco-Remy transistorized ignition; 4 headlamps.

DIMENSIONS AND WEIGHT wheel base: 108.10 in, 274 cm; tracks: 58.50 in, 149 cm front, 57.80 in, 147 cm rear; length: 197.70 in, 502 cm - St. Wagon 196.60 in, 499 cm; width: 71.90 in, 183 cm - St. Wagon 71.70 in, 182 cm; height: 53.30 in, 135 cm - sedans 54.20 in, 138 cm - St. Wagon 54.50 in, 138 cm; ground clearance: 5.20 in, 13.1 cm - St. Wagon 7.42 in, 18.8 cm; weight: Cutlass Salon Coupé 3,058 lb, 1,378 kg - Sedan 3,070 lb, 1,393 kg - Salon Brougham Coupé 3,097 lb, 1,405 kg - Sedan 3,121 lb, 1,416 kg - Supreme Brougham Coupé 3,138 lb, 1,423 kg - Supreme Coupé 3,109 lb, 1,410 kg - Calais Coupé 3,146 lb, 1,427 kg - Cruiser St. Wagon 3,213 lb, 1,457 kg; turning circle (between walls): sedans 40.6 ft, 12.5 m - coupés 40.2 ft, 12.2 m - St. Wagon 40.5 ft, 12.3 m; fuel tank: 14.5 imp gal, 17.4 US gal, 66 l - St. Wagon 15.2 imp gal, 18.2 US gal, 69 l.

OPTIONALS limited slip differential; Turbo-Hydramatic 350 automatic transmission with 3 ratios (I 2.520, II 1.520, III

1, rev 1.930), max ratio of converter at stall 2.25, possible manual ratio, 2.730 or 3.230 axle ratio; 4-speed fully synchronized mechanical gearbox; 5-speed fully synchronized mechanical gearbox; P205/75R x 14 tyres with 6'' wide rims; aluminum wheels; power steering; tilt of steering wheel; servo brake; heavy-duty suspension; vinyl roof; electric windows; automatic levelling control; air-conditioning.

110 hp power team

See 105 hp power team, except for:

ENGINE 8 cylinders; 260 cu in, 4,261 cc (3.50 x 3.38 in, 88.8 x 85.8 mm); compression ratio: 7.5:1; max power (DIN): 110 hp at 3,400 rpm; max torque (DIN): 205 lb ft, 28.3 kg m at 1,800 rpm; 25.8 hp/l; 5 crankshaft bearings; cooling system: 28.2 imp pt, 33.8 US pt, 16 l.

TRANSMISSION axle ratio: 2.560 - St. Wagon 2.410.

PERFORMANCE max speed: about 99 mph, 160 km/h; power-weight ratio: Salon Sedan 28.9 lb/hp, 13.1 kg/hp; consumption: 27.7 m/imp gal, 23 m/US gal, 10.2 l x 100 km.

STEERING servo (standard); turns lock to lock: 3.60.

BRAKES servo (standard).

ELECTRICAL EQUIPMENT 61 A alternator.

DIMENSIONS AND WEIGHT weight: plus 110 lb, 50 kg - St. Wagon plus 171 lb, 78 kg.

OPTIONALS Turbo-Hydramatic 350 automatic transmission with 2.290 or 2.930 axle ratio.

145 hp power team

See 105 hp power team, except for:

ENGINE 8 cylinders; 305 cu in, 4,998 cc (3.74 x 3.48 in, 94.9 x 88.3 mm); compression ratio: 8.5:1; max power (DIN): 145 hp at 3,800 rpm; max torque (DIN): 245 lb ft, 33.8 kg m at 2,400 rpm; max engine rpm: 4,400; 39 hp/l; 5 crankshaft bearings; cooling system: 26 imp pt, 31.3 US pt, 14.8 l.

TRANSMISSION axle ratio: 2.730 - St. Wagon 2.560.

PERFORMANCE max speed: about 103 mph, 165 km/h; power-weight ratio: Salon Sedan 22 lb/hp, 10 kg/hp; speed in direct drive at 1,000 rpm: 27 mph, 43.4 km/h; consumption: 21.6 m/imp gal, 18 m/US gal, 13.1 l x 100 km.

STEERING servo (standard); turns lock to lock: 3.60

BRAKES servo (standard).

ELECTRICAL EQUIPMENT 3,200 W battery; 63 A alternator.

DIMENSIONS AND WEIGHT weight: plus 125 lb, 57 kg - St. Wagon plus 174 lb, 79 kg.

OPTIONALS Turbo-Hydramatic 350 automatic transmission with 2.560 or 2.730 axle ratio.

OLDSMOBILE Cutlass Salon Brougham Sedan

OLDSMOBILE Delta 88 Royale Towne Sedan

160 hp power team

See 145 hp power team, except for:

ENGINE max power (DIN): 160 hp at 4,000 rpm; max torque (DIN): 235 lb ft, 32.4 kg m at 2,400 rpm; 32 hp/l; 1 Rochester 4 GC downdraught 4-barrel carburettor.

TRANSMISSION gearbox: Turbo-Hydramatic 350 automatic transmission (standard), hydraulic torque converter and planetary gears with 3 ratios, max ratio of converter at stall 2.25, possible manual selection: ratios: I 2.520, II 1.520, III 1, rev 1.930; axle ratio: 2.560.

PERFORMANCE max speed: about 106 mph, 170 km/h; power-weight ratio: Saloon Sedan 20 lb/hp, 9.1 kg/hp; speed in direct drive at 1,000 rpm: 26.4 mph, 42.5 km/h; consumption: 25.2 m/imp gal, 21 m/US gal, 11.2 l x 100 km.

OPTIONALS 2.730 axle ratio.

Delta 88 - Delta 88 Royale - Ninety-Eight - Custom Cruiser Series

PRICES EX WORKS:

1 Delta 88 Hardtop Coupé	$ 5,482
2 Delta 88 Towne Sedan	$ 5,358
3 Delta 88 Royale Hardtop Coupé	$ 5,706
4 Delta 88 Royale Towne Sedan	$ 5,806
5 Ninety-Eight Luxury Coupé	$ 7,063
6 Ninety-Eight Luxury Sedan	$ 7,240
7 Ninety-Eight Regency Coupé	$ 7,426
8 Ninety-Eight Regency Sedan	$ 7,610
9 Custom Cruiser Station Wagon	$ 6,323

Power team:	Standard for:	Optional for:
105 hp	1 to 4	—
110 hp	—	1 to 4
170 hp	5 to 9	1 to 4
185 hp	—	all
120 hp	—	all

105 hp power team

ENGINE front, 4 stroke; 6 cylinders, Vee-slanted at 90°; 231 cu in, 3,785 cc (3.80 x 3.40 in, 96.5 x 86.4 mm); compression ratio: 8:1; max power (DIN): 105 hp at 3,400 rpm; max torque (DIN): 185 lb ft, 25.5 kg m at 2,000 rpm; max engine rpm: 4,200; 27.7 hp/l; cast iron block and head; 4 crankshaft bearings; valves: overhead, in line, push-rods and rockers, hydraulic tappets; camshafts: 1, at centre of Vee; lubrication: gear pump, full flow filter, 8.3 imp pt, 9.9 US pt, 4.7 l; 1 Rochester 2 downdraught twin barrel carburettor; cleaner air system; exhaust system with catalytic converter; fuel feed: mechanical pump; water-cooled, 21.3 imp pt, 25.6 US pt, 12.1 l.

TRANSMISSION driving wheels: rear; gearbox: Turbo-Hydramatic 350 automatic transmission, hydraulic torque converter and planetary gears with 3 ratios, max ratio of converter at stall 2.25, possible manual selection: ratios: I 2.520, II 1.520, III 1, rev 1.930; lever: steering column; final drive: hypoid bevel; axle ratio: 2.730; width of rims: 6''; tyres: FR78 x 15.

OLDSMOBILE Ninety-Eight Regency Sedan Diesel

PERFORMANCE max speed: about 93 mph, 150 km/h; power-weight ratio: 88 Towne Sedan 33.1 lb/hp, 15 kg/hp; speed in direct drive at 1,000 rpm: 27.4 mph, 44.1 km/h; consumption: 24.1 m/imp gal, 20 m/US gal, 11.7 l x 100 km.

CHASSIS channel section perimeter type frame; front suspension: independent, wishbones, coil springs, anti-roll bar, telescopic dampers; rear: rigid axle, lower trailing radius arms, upper oblique torque arms, coil springs, telescopic dampers.

STEERING recirculating ball, variable ratio servo; turns lock to lock: 3.50.

BRAKES front disc (diameter 11 in, 27.9 cm), front internal radial fins, rear drum, rear compensator, servo; swept area: total 384.2 sq in, 2,478 sq cm.

ELECTRICAL EQUIPMENT 12 V; 2,500 W battery; 42 A alternator; Delco-Remy transistorized ignition; 4 headlamps.

DIMENSIONS AND WEIGHT wheel base: 116 in, 295 cm; tracks: 61.70 in, 157 cm front, 60.70 in, 154 cm rear; length: 217.50 in, 552 cm; width: 76.80 in, 195 cm; height: coupés 54.50 in, 138 cm — sedans 55.20 in, 140 cm; ground clearance: 5.92 in, 15 cm; weight: 88 Hardtop Coupé 3,433 lb, 1,557 kg - Towne Sedan 3,477 lb, 1,577 kg - 88 Royale Hardtop Coupé 3,444 lb, 1,562 kg - Towne Sedan 3,506 lb, 1,590 kg; turning circle (between walls): 42.6 ft, 13 m; fuel tank: 17.6 imp gal, 21 US gal, 80 l.

OPTIONALS limited slip differential; Turbo-Hydramatic 200 automatic transmission with 3.230 axle ratio; GR78 x 15 or HR78 x 15 tyres; tilt of steering wheel; electric windows; heated rear window; vinyl roof; air-conditioning.

110 hp power team

See 105 hp power team, except for:

ENGINE 8 cylinders; 260 cu in, 4,261 cc (3.50 x 3.38 in, 88.8 x 85.8 mm); compression ratio: 7.5:1; max power (DIN): 110 hp at 3,400 rpm; max torque (DIN): 205 lb ft, 28.3 kg m at 1,800 rpm; 25.8 hp/l; 5 crankshaft bearings; cooling system: 28.2 imp pt, 33.8 US pt, 16 l.

TRANSMISSION axle ratio: 2.560.

PERFORMANCE max speed: about 96 mph, 155 km/h; power-weight ratio: 88 Towne Sedan 33 lb/hp, 15 kg/hp; consumption: 25.2 m/imp gal, 21 m/US gal, 11.2 l x 100 km.

ELECTRICAL EQUIPMENT 3,200 W battery; 61 A alternator.

DIMENSIONS AND WEIGHT weight: plus 161 lb, 73 kg.

170 hp power team

See 105 hp power team, except for:

ENGINE 8 cylinders; 350 cu in, 5,736 cc (4.06 x 3.38 in, 103.1 x 85.8 mm); max power (DIN): 170 hp at 3,800 rpm; max torque (DIN): 275 lb ft, 37.9 kg m at 2,000 rpm; 29.6 hp/l; 5 crankshaft bearings; 1 Rochester 4 downdraught 4-barrel carburettor; cooling system: 24.3 imp pt, 29.2 US pt, 13.8 l.

OLDSMOBILE 120 hp Diesel engine

TRANSMISSION axle ratio: 2.410 - Custom Cruiser 2.730.

PERFORMANCE max speed: about 103 mph, 165 km/h; power-weight ratio: Ninety-Eight Luxury Sedan 22.6 lb/hp, 10.2 kg/hp; consumption: 22.8 m/imp gal, 19 m/US gal, 12.4 l x 100 km.

ELECTRICAL EQUIPMENT 3,200 W battery; 63 A alternator.

DIMENSIONS AND WEIGHT wheel base: Ninety-Eights 119 in, 302 cm; tracks: Custom Cruiser 62.10 in, 158 cm front, 64.10 in, 163 cm rear; Ninety-Eights 220.40 in, 560 cm - Custom Cruiser 217.10 in, 551 cm; width: Custom Cruiser 79.80 in, 203 cm; height: Ninety-Eights 55.50 in, 141 cm - Custom Cruiser 57.20 in, 145 cm; ground clearance: Custom Cruiser 5.78 in, 14.7 cm; weight: Ninety-Eight Luxury Coupé 3,795 lb, 1,721 kg - Sedan 3,834 lb, 1,739 kg - Regency Coupé 3,795 lb, 1,721 kg - Sedan 3,865 lb, 1,753 kg - Custom Cruiser 4,068 lb, 1,845 kg.

185 hp power team

See 170 hp power team, except for:

ENGINE 403 cu in, 6,604 cc (4.35 x 3.38 in, 110.4 x 85.8 mm); max power (DIN): 185 hp at 3,600 rpm; max torque (DIN): 320 lb ft, 44.1 kg m at 2,200 rpm; 28 hp/l; cooling system: 26.2 imp pt, 31.4 US pt, 14.9 l.

TRANSMISSION axle ratio: 2.560.

PERFORMANCE max speed: about 109 mph, 175 km/h; power-weight ratio: Ninety-Eight Luxury Sedan 21.1 lb/hp, 9.6

OLDSMOBILE Toronado Brougham Coupé

kg/hp; consumption: 19.2 m/imp gal, 16 m/US gal, 14.7 l x 100 km.

ELECTRICAL EQUIPMENT 3,500 W battery.

DIMENSIONS AND WEIGHT weight: plus 70 lb, 32 kg.

120 hp power team

See 170 hp power team, except for:

ENGINE Diesel, 4 stroke; compression ratio: 22.5:1; max power (DIN): 120 hp at 3,600 rpm; max torque (DIN): 220 lb ft, 30.3 kg m at 1,600 rpm; 20.9 hp/l; lubrication system: 12.5 imp pt, 15 US pt, 7.1 l; cooling system: 29.9 imp pt, 35.9 US pt, 17 l.

PERFORMANCE max speed: about 96 mph, 155 km/h; power-weight ratio: Ninety-Eight Luxury Sedan 33.6 lb/hp, 15.2 kg/hp; speed in direct drive at 1,000 rpm: 26.7 mph, 43 km/h; consumption: 28.8 m/imp gal, 24 m/US gal, 9.8 l x 100 km.

DIMENSIONS AND WEIGHT weight plus 196 lb, 89 kg.

Toronado Series

PRICES EX WORKS:

Toronado Brougham Coupé	$ 8,899
Toronado XSR Coupé	$ —

190 hp power team

ENGINE 403 cu in, 6,604 cc (4.35 x 3.38 in, 110.4 x 85.8 mm); (4.35 x 3.38 in, 110.4 x 85.8 mm); compression ratio: 8:1; max power (DIN): 190 hp at 3,600 rpm; max torque (DIN): 325 lb ft, 44.8 kg m at 2,000 rpm; max engine rpm: 4,200; 28.8 hp/l; cast iron block and head; 5 crankshaft bearings; valves: overhead, in line, push-rods and rockers, hydraulic tappets; camshafts: 1, at centre of Vee; lubrication: gear pump, full flow filter, 8.3 imp pt, 9.9 US pt, 4.7 l; 1 Rochester 4MC downdraught 4-barrel carburettor; cleaner air system; dual exhaust system with catalytic converter; fuel feed: mechanical pump; water-cooled, 28.5 imp pt, 34.2 US pt, 16.2 l.

TRANSMISSION driving wheels: front; gearbox: Turbo-Hydramatic 425 automatic transmission, hydraulic torque converter and planetary gears (chain torque engine-mounted converter) with 3 ratios, possible manual selection: ratios: I 2.480, II 1.480, III 1, rev 2.080; lever: steering column; final drive: spiral bevel; axle ratio: 2.730; width of rims: 6''; tyres: JR78 x 15.

PERFORMANCE max speed: about 118 mph, 190 km/h; power-weight ratio: Brougham Coupé 24.4 lb/hp, 11.1 kg/hp; speed in direct drive at 1,000 rpm: 30.4 mph, 49 km/h; consumption: 18 m/imp gal, 15 m/US gal, 15.7 l x 100 km.

CHASSIS channel section perimeter type frame; front suspension: independent, wishbones, longitudinal torsion bars, telescopic dampers; rear: rigid axle, lower trailing radius arms, upper oblique arms, coil springs, telescopic dampers.

STEERING recirculating ball, servo; turns lock to lock: 3.24.

BRAKES front disc (diameter 10.88 in, 27.6 cm), front internal radial fins, rear drum, rear compensator, servo; swept area: front 226.2 sq in, 1,459 sq cm, rear 138.2 sq in, 891 sq cm, total 364.4 sq in, 2,350 sq cm.

ELECTRICAL EQUIPMENT 12 V; 3,500 W battery; 42 A alternator; Delco-Remy transistorized ignition; 4 headlamps.

DIMENSIONS AND WEIGHT wheel base: 122 in, 310 cm; tracks: 63.60 in, 162 cm front, 63.50 in, 161 cm rear; length: 227.50 in, 578 cm; width: 80 in, 203 cm; height: 53.20 in, 135 cm; ground clearance: 4.75 in, 12.1 cm; weight: 4,643 lb, 2,105 kg - XSR 4,627 lb, 2,098 kg; fuel tank: 21.6 imp gal, 26 US gal, 98 l.

BODY 2 doors; 6 seats; electric windows.

OPTIONALS L78 x 15 tyres; tilt of steering wheel; heated rear window; air-conditioning; heavy-duty cooling system.

PLYMOUTH   USA

Horizon

PRICE EX WORKS: $ 3,706

75 hp power team

(standard, not available in California).

ENGINE front, transverse, slanted 15° to front, 4 stroke; 4 cylinders, in line; 104.7 cu in, 1,714 cc (3.13 x 3.40 in, 79.5 x 86.4 mm); compression ratio: 8.2:1; max power (DIN): 75 hp at 5,600 rpm; max torque (DIN): 90 lb ft, 12.4 kg m at 3,200 rpm; max engine rpm: 6,500; 43.8 hp/l; cast iron block, light alloy head; 5 crankshaft bearings; valves: overhead, in line, thimble tappets; camshafts: 1, overhead, cogged belt; lubrication: gear pump, full flow filter, 6.7 imp pt, 8 US pt, 3.8 l; 1 Holley R8376A downdraught twin barrel carburettor; cleaner air system; exhaust system with catalytic converter; fuel feed: mechanical pump; water-cooled, 12.8 imp pt, 15.4 US pt, 7.3 l.

TRANSMISSION driving wheels: front; clutch: single dry plate (diaphragm); gearbox: mechanical; gears: 4, fully synchronized; ratios: I 3.450, II 1.940, III 1.290, IV 0.970, rev 3.170; lever: central; final drive: spiral bevel; axle ratio: 3.480; width of rims: 4.5''; tyres: P155/80R x 14.

PERFORMANCE max speed: about 91 mph, 146 km/h; power-weight ratio: 27.5 lb/hp, 12.5 kg/hp; speed in top at 1,000 rpm: 16.7 mph, 26.9 km/h; consumption: 24.6 m/imp gal, 20.5 m/US gal, 11.5 l x 100 km.

CHASSIS integral; front suspension: independent, by McPherson, lower wishbones, anti-roll bar, coil springs/telescopic dampers struts; rear: independent, semi-trailing arms, coil springs, telescopic dampers.

STEERING rack-and-pinion; turns lock to lock: 4.

BRAKES front disc (diameter 5.04 in, 12.8 cm), front internal radial fins, rear drum; swept area: total 197.5 sq in, 1,274 sq cm.

ELECTRICAL EQUIPMENT 12 V; 325 A battery; 60 A alternator; Lean-Burn electronic ignition; 2 headlamps.

DIMENSIONS AND WEIGHT wheel base: 99.20 in, 252 cm; tracks: 55.50 in, 141 cm front, 55.10 in, 140 cm rear; length: 164.80 in, 419 cm; width: 66.20 in, 168 cm; height: 53.40 in, 136 cm; ground clearance: 5.10 in, 13 cm; weight: 2,059 lb, 934 kg; turning circle (between walls): 36.2 ft, 11 m; fuel tank: 10.8 imp gal, 13 US gal, 49 l.

BODY hatchback; 4 doors; 4 seats, separate front seats with built-in headrests.

OPTIONALS Torqueflite automatic transmission, hydraulic torque converter and planetary gears with 3 ratios (I 2.470, II 1.470, III 1, rev 2.100), max ratio of converter at stall 1.97, possible manual selection, central lever, 3.480 axle ratio; P165/75R x 13 tyres; power steering; servo brake; reclining backrests; heated rear window; rear window wiper-washer; vinyl roof; air-conditioning.

70 hp power team

(standard, for California only).

See 75 hp power team, except for:

ENGINE max power (DIN): 70 hp at 5,600 rpm; max torque (DIN): 85 lb ft, 11.7 kg m at 3,200 rpm; 40.8 hp/l; 1 Holley R8386A downdraught twin barrel carburettor.

TRANSMISSION axle ratio: 3.700.

PERFORMANCE power-weight ratio: 29.4 lb/hp, 13.3 kg/hp.

OPTIONALS Torqueflite automatic transmission with 3.740 axle ratio.

PLYMOUTH Horizon 4-door Hatchback

Volaré Series

PRICES EX WORKS:

1 Volaré 2-door Coupé	$ 3,735
2 Volaré 4-door Sedan	$ 3,853
3 Volaré Station Wagon	$ 4,195

For V8 engines add $ 169.

Power team:	Standard for:	Optional for:
100 hp	1,2	—
90 hp	all	—
110 hp	3	1,2
140 hp	—	all
155 hp (5,211 cc)	—	all
155 hp (5,900 cc)	—	all
160 hp	—	all
175 hp	—	1

100 hp power team

(not available in California).

ENGINE front, 4 stroke; 6 cylinders, vertical, in line; 225 cu in, 3,687 cc (3.40 x 4.12 in, 86.4 x 104.6 mm); compression ratio: 8.4:1; max power (DIN): 100 hp at 3,600 rpm; max torque (DIN): 170 lb ft, 23.4 kg m at 1,600 rpm; max engine rpm: 4,400; 27.1 hp/l; cast iron block and head; 4 crankshaft bearings; valves: overhead, in line, push-rods and rockers; camshafts: 1, side; lubrication: rotary pump, full flow filter, 8.3 imp pt, 9.9 US pt, 4.7 l; 1 Holley R7988A downdraught single barrel carburettor; cleaner air system; exhaust system with catalytic converter; fuel feed: mechanical pump; water-cooled, 20.1 imp pt, 24.1 US pt, 11.4 l.

TRANSMISSION driving wheels: rear; clutch: single dry plate; gearbox: mechanical; gears: 3, fully synchronized; ratios: I 3.080, II 1.700, III 1, rev 2.900; lever: steering column or central; final drive: hypoid bevel; axle ratio: 3.230; width of rims: 5''; tyres: D78 x 14.

PERFORMANCE max speed: about 90 mph, 145 km/h; power-weight ratio: Sedan 31.8 lb/hp, 14.4 kg/hp; speed in direct drive at 1,000 rpm: 20.4 mph, 32.9 km/h; consumption: 27.7 m/imp gal, 23 m/US gal, 10.2 l x 100 km.

CHASSIS integral with front cross members; front suspension: independent, wishbones, transverse torsion bars, anti-roll bar, telescopic dampers; rear: rigid axle, semi-elliptic leafsprings, telescopic dampers.

STEERING recirculating ball; turns lock to lock: 5.30.

BRAKES front disc (diameter 10.82 in, 27.5 cm), front internal radial fins, rear drum, rear compensator; swept area: total 355.3 sq in, 2,291 sq cm.

ELECTRICAL EQUIPMENT 12 V; 325 A battery; 41 A alternator; Essex or Prestolite transistorized ignition; 4 headlamps.

DIMENSIONS AND WEIGHT wheel base: 112.70 in, 286 cm - Coupé 108.70 in, 276 cm; tracks: 60 in, 152 cm front, 58.50 in, 149 cm rear; length: 201.10 in, 511 cm - Coupé 197.20 in, 502 cm; width: 77.30 in, 196 cm; height: 55.30 in, 140 cm - Coupé 53.30 in, 135 cm; ground clearance: 5.10 in, 13 cm - Coupé 4.60 in, 11.7 cm; weight: Coupé 3,138 lb, 1,423 kg - Sedan 3,177 lb, 1,441 kg; turning circle (between walls): 43.4 ft, 13.2 m - Coupé 42.1 ft, 12.8 m; fuel tank: 15 imp gal, 18 US gal, 68 l.

OPTIONALS limited slip differential; 3.210 axle ratio; Torqueflite automatic transmission with 3 ratios (I 2.450, II 1.450, III 1, rev 2.220), max ratio of converter at stall 2.01, possible manual selection, steering column or central lever, 2.760 or 2.710 axle ratio; E78 x 14 tyres; DR78 x 14 tyres with 5.5''; FR70 x 14 tyres with 6'' wide rims; power steering; tilt of steering wheel; servo brake; electric windows; Premier equipment; Road Runner equipment (Coupé only); reclining backrests; heated rear window; vinyl roof; air-conditioning.

90 hp power team

(for California only).

See 100 hp power team, except for:

ENGINE max power (DIN): 90 hp at 3,600 rpm; max torque (DIN): 160 lb ft, 22.1 kg m at 1,600 rpm; 24.4 hp/l; 1 Holley R8010A downdraught single barrel carburettor.

TRANSMISSION gearbox: mechanical (Torqueflite automatic transmission standard for St. Wagon); gears: 4, fully synchronized with overdrive/top; ratios: I 3.090, II 1.670, III 1, IV 0.710, rev 3); axle ratio: 3.230 - St. Wagon 3.210; width of rims: 5.5''; tyres: St. Wagon F78 x 14.

PLYMOUTH Volaré Road Runner Coupé

PLYMOUTH Volaré Road Runner Coupé

PERFORMANCE power-weight ratio: Sedan 35.3 lb/hp, 16 kg/hp; consumption: 19.2 m/imp gal, 16 m/US gal, 14.7 l x 100 Km.

BRAKES St. Wagon servo (standard).

DIMENSIONS AND WEIGHT height: St. Wagon 55.70 in, 141 cm; ground clearance: St. Wagon 5.60 in, 14.2 cm; fuel tank: St. Wagon 16.3 imp gal, 19.5 US gal, 74 l.

OPTIONALS Torqueflite automatic transmission with 3.230 or 3.210 axle ratio.

110 hp power team

(not available in California).

See 100 hp power team, except for:

ENGINE max power (DIN): 110 hp at 3,600 rpm; max torque (DIN): 180 lb ft, 24.8 kg m at 2,000 rpm; 29.8 hp/l; 1 Carter BBD8136S downdraught twin barrel carburettor.

TRANSMISSION axle ratio: 3.230 - St. Wagon 3.210; width of rims: St. Wagon 5.5''; tyres: St. Wagon F78 x 14.

PERFORMANCE max speed: about 93 mph, 150 km/h; power-weight ratio: St. Wagon 30.9 lb/hp, 14 kg/hp; consumption: 22.8 m/imp gal, 19 m/US gal, 12.4 l x 100 km.

BRAKES St. Wagon servo (standard).

DIMENSIONS AND WEIGHT height: St. Wagon 55.70 in, 141 cm; ground clearance: St. Wagon 5.60 in, 14.2 cm; weight: St. Wagon 3,404 lb, 1,544 kg; fuel tank: St. Wagon 16.3 imp gal, 19.5 US gal, 74 l.

OPTIONALS Torqueflite automatic transmission with 2.940 axle ratio.

140 hp power team

(not available in California).

See 100 hp power team, except for:

ENGINE 8 cylinders; 318 cu in, 5,211 cc (3.91 x 3.31 in, 99.2 x 84 mm); compression ratio: 8.5:1; max power (DIN): 140 hp at 4,000 rpm; max torque (DIN): 245 lb ft, 33.8 kg m at 1,600 rpm; 26.9 hp/l; 5 crankshaft bearings; valves: hydraulic tappets; camshafts: 1, at centre of Vee; 1 Carter BBD8175S downdraught twin barrel carburettor; cooling system: 26.6 imp pt, 31.9 US pt, 15.1 l.

TRANSMISSION gears: 4, fully synchronized with overdrive/top; ratios: I 3.090, II 1.670, III 1, IV 0.710, rev 3; axle ratio: 2.940; width of rims: St. Wagon 5.5''; tyres: St. Wagon F78 x 14.

PERFORMANCE max speed: about 102 mph, 164 km/h; power-weight ratio: Sedan 23.5 lb/hp, 10.7 kg/hp; speed in top at 1,000 rpm: 25.5 mph, 41 km/h; consumption: 21.6 m/imp gal, 18 m/US gal, 13.1 l x 100 km.

BRAKES St. Wagon servo (standard).

ELECTRICAL EQUIPMENT Lean-Burn electronic ignition system.

DIMENSIONS AND WEIGHT height: St. Wagon 55.70 in, 141 cm; ground clearance: St. Wagon 5.60 in, 14.2 cm; weight: Sedan 3,294 lb, 1,494 kg - Coupé 3,255 lb, 1,476 kg - St. Wagon 3,492 lb, 1,583 kg; fuel tank: 16.3 imp gal, 19.5 US gal, 74 l.

OPTIONALS Torqueflite automatic transmission with max ratio of converter at stall 1.90 and 2.470 or 2.450 axle ratio (St. Wagon 2.710).

155 hp (5,211 cc) power team

(for California only).

See 140 hp power team, except for:

ENGINE max power (DIN): 155 hp at 4,000 rpm; max torque (DIN): 245 lb ft, 33.8 kg m at 1,600 rpm; 29.7 hp/l; 1 Carter TQ9147S downdraught 4-barrel carburettor.

TRANSMISSION gearbox: Torqueflite automatic transmission (standard), hydraulic torque converter and planetary gears with 3 ratios, max ratio of converter at stall 1.90, possible manual selection; ratios: I 2.450, II 1.450, III 1, rev 2.220; axle ratio: 2.760 - St. Wagon 2.710.

PERFORMANCE max speed: about 103 mph, 165 km/h; power-weight ratio: Sedan 21.2 lb/hp, 9.6 kg/hp; speed in direct drive at 1,000 rpm: 25.6 mph, 41.2 km/h; consumption: 19.2 m/imp gal, 16 m/US gal, 14.7 l x 100 km.

PLYMOUTH Volaré Premier Station Wagon

155 hp (5,900 cc) power team

(not available in California).

See 140 hp power team, except for:

ENGINE 360 cu in, 5,900 cc (4 x 3.58 in, 101.6 x 89.6 mm); compression ratio: 8.4:1; max power (DIN): 155 hp at 3,600 rpm; max torque (DIN): 270 lb ft, 37.2 kg m at 2,400 rpm; 26.3 hp/l; 1 Holley R7991A downdraught twin barrel carburettor.

TRANSMISSION gearbox: Torqueflite automatic transmission (standard), hydraulic torque converter and planetary gears with 3 ratios, max ratio of converter at stall 1.90, possible manual selection; ratios: I 2.450, II 1.450, III 1, rev 2.220; axle ratio: 2.450; tyres: Sedan E78 x 14.

PERFORMANCE max speed: about 106 mph, 170 km/h; power-weight ratio: Sedan 22.1 lb/hp, 10 kg/hp; speed in direct drive at 1,000 rpm: 29.3 mph, 47.2 km/h; consumption: 20.5 m/imp gal, 17 m/US gal, 13.8 l x 100 km.

ELECTRICAL EQUIPMENT 440 A battery.

DIMENSIONS AND WEIGHT weight: Coupé plus 85 lb, 38 kg - Sedan plus 129 lb, 58 kg - St. Wagon 39 lb, 17 kg.

160 hp power team

(for California only).

See 155 hp (5,900 cc) power team, except for:

ENGINE compression ratio: 8:1; max power (DIN): 160 hp at 3,600 rpm; max torque (DIN): 265 lb ft, 36.6 kg m at 1,600 rpm; 27.1 hp/l; 1 Carter TQ9134S downdraught 4-barrel carburettor.

TRANSMISSION axle ratio: 3.210 - St. Wagon 2.710.

PERFORMANCE max speed: about 106 mph, 170 km/h; power-weight ratio: Sedan 21.4 lb/hp, 9.7 kg/hp; consumption: 15.6 m/imp gal, 13 m/US gal, 18.1 l x 100 km.

ELECTRICAL EQUIPMENT Essex or Prestolite transistorized ignition.

175 hp power team

(not available in California).

See 155 hp (5,900 cc) power team, except for:

ENGINE compression ratio: 8:1; max power (DIN): 175 hp at 4,000 rpm; max torque (DIN): 260 lb ft, 35.9 kg m at 2,400 rpm; 29.7 hp/l; 1 Carter TQ9104S downdraught 4-barrel carburettor.

TRANSMISSION axle ratio: 3.210.

PERFORMANCE max speed: about 109 mph, 175 km/h; power-weight ratio: Coupé 19.3 lb/hp, 8.7 kg/hp; speed in direct

drive at 1,000 rpm: 27.2 mph, 43.7 km/h; consumption: 15.6 m/imp gal, 13 m/US gal, 18.1 l x 100 km.

DIMENSIONS AND WEIGHT weight: Coupé plus 116 lb, 53 kg.

OPTIONALS 2.710 axle ratio.

Fury Series

PRICES EX WORKS:

1 Fury 2-door Hardtop	$ 4,212
2 Fury 4-door Sedan	$ 4,292
3 Fury Sport 2-door Hardtop	$ 4,452
4 Fury Salon 4-door Sedan	$ 4,527
5 Fury Suburban 6-pass. Station Wagon	$ 4,024
6 Fury Suburban 9-pass. Station Wagon	$ 5,167
7 Fury Sport Suburban 6-pass. Station Wagon	$ 5,482
8 Fury Sport Suburban 9-pass. Station Wagon	$ 5,625

For V8 engines add $ 176.

Power team:	Standard for:	Optional for:
110 hp	1 to 4	—
140 hp	—	1 to 4
155 hp (5,211 cc)	1 to 4	—
155 hp (5,900 cc)	5 to 8	1 to 4
160 hp	5,7	1 to 4
170 hp	5,7	1 to 4
190 hp	—	all

PLYMOUTH Fury Sport 2-door Hardtop

110 hp power team

(not available in California).

ENGINE front, 4 stroke; 6 cylinders, vertical, in line; 225 cu in, 3,687 cc (3.40 x 4.12 in, 86.4 x 104.6 mm); compression ratio: 8.4:1; max power (DIN): 110 hp at 3,600 rpm; max torque (DIN): 180 lb ft, 24.8 kg m at 2,000 rpm; max engine rpm: 4,400; 29.8 hp/l; cast iron block and head; 4 crankshaft bearings; valves: overhead, in line, push-rods and rockers; camshafts: 1, side; lubrication: rotary pump, full flow filter, 8.3 imp pt, 9.9 US pt, 4.7 l; 1 Carter BBD8136S downdraught twin barrel carburettor; cleaner air system; exhaust system with catalytic converter; fuel feed: mechanical pump; water-cooled, 21.6 imp pt, 26 US pt, 12.3 l.

TRANSMISSION driving wheels: rear; clutch: single dry plate; gearbox: mechanical; gears: 3, fully synchronized; ratios: I 3.080, II 1.700, III 1, rev 2.900; lever: steering column; final drive: hypoid bevel; axle ratio: 3.210; width of rims: 5.5''; tyres: F78 x 15.

PERFORMANCE max speed: about 93 mph, 150 km/h; power-weight ratio: Fury Sedan 33 lb/hp, 15 kg/hp; speed in direct drive at 1,000 rpm: 25.9 mph, 41.7 km/h; consumption: 23.9 m/imp gal, 20 m/US gal, 11.8 l x 100 km.

CHASSIS integral with isolated front cross members; front suspension: independent, wishbones, longitudinal torsion bars, anti-roll bar, telescopic dampers; rear: rigid axle, semi-elliptic leafsprings, telescopic dampers.

STEERING recirculating ball; turns lock to lock: 5.30.

BRAKES front disc (diameter 11.58 in, 29.4 cm), front internal radial fins, rear drum, rear compensator, servo; swept area: total 372 sq in, 2,400 sq cm.

ELECTRICAL EQUIPMENT 12 V; 375 A battery; 60 A alternator; Essex or Prestolite transistorized ignition; 4 headlamps.

DIMENSIONS AND WEIGHT wheel base: 117.40 in, 298 cm - hardtops 114.90 in, 292 cm; tracks: 61.90 in, 157 cm front, 62 in, 157 cm rear; length: 218 in, 554 cm - hardtops 213.20 in, 541 cm; width: 77.70 in, 197 cm; height: 54.30 in, 138 cm - hardtops 52.90 in, 134 cm; ground clearance: 5.10 in, 13 cm; weight: Fury Hardtop 3,602 lb, 1,633 kg - Sedan 3,634 lb, 1,648 kg - Fury Sport 3,608 lb, 1,636 kg - Fury Salon 3,647 lb, 1,654 kg; turning circle (between walls): 45.5 ft, 13.8 m; fuel tank: 16.9 imp gal, 20.5 US gal, 77 l.

OPTIONALS limited slip differential; Torqueflite automatic transmission with 3 ratios (I 2.450, II 1.450, III 1, rev 2.220), max ratio of converter at stall 2.01, possible manual selection, steering column or central lever, 2.710 axle ratio; G78 x 14, GR78 x 14 or 215 x 15 tyres; GR60 x 15 tyres with 7'' wide rims; power steering tilt; tilt of steering wheel; anti-roll bar on rear suspension; electric windows; reclining backrests with built-in headrests; speed control device; heated rear window; air-conditioning.

140 hp power team

(not available in California).

See 110 hp power team, except for:

ENGINE 8 cylinders; 318 cu in, 5,211 cc (3.91 x 3.31 in, 99.2 x 84 mm); compression ratio: 8.5:1; max power (DIN): 140 hp at 4,000 rpm; max torque (DIN): 245 lb ft, 33.8 kg m at 1,600 rpm; 26.9 hp/l; 5 crankshaft bearings; valves: hydraulic tappets; camshafts: 1, at centre of Vee; 1 Holley R7990A downdraught twin barrel carburettor; cooling system: 27.5 imp pt, 33 US pt, 15.6 l.

TRANSMISSION gearbox: Torqueflite automatic transmission (standard), hydraulic torque converter and planetary gears with 3 ratios, max ratio of converter at stall 1.90, possible manual selection; ratios: I 2.450, II 1.450, III 1, rev 2.220; lever: steering column or central; axle ratio: 2.710.

PERFORMANCE max speed: about 96 mph, 155 km/h; power-weight ratio: Fury Sedan 27.8 lb/hp, 12.6 kg/hp; consumption: 19.2 m/imp gal, 16 m/US gal, 14.7 l x 100 km.

STEERING servo (standard).

BRAKES swept area: total 387.1 sq in, 2,497 sq cm.

ELECTRICAL EQUIPMENT 325 A battery; Lean-Burn electronic ignition system.

DIMENSIONS AND WEIGHT weight: plus 253 lb, 115 kg; fuel tank: 21.3 imp gal, 25.5 US gal, 97 l.

155 hp (5,211 cc) power team

(for California only).

See 140 hp power team, except for:

ENGINE max power (DIN): 155 hp at 4,000 rpm; max torque (DIN): 245 lb ft, 33.8 kg m at 1,600 rpm; 29.7 hp/l; 1 Carter TQ9147S downdraught 4-barrel carburettor.

PERFORMANCE max speed: about 99 mph, 160 km/h; power-weight ratio: Fury Sedan 25.1 lb/hp, 11.4 kg/hp.

155 hp (5,900 cc) power team

(not available in California).

See 140 hp power team, except for:

ENGINE 360 cu in, 5,900 cc (4 x 3.58 in, 101.6 x 89.6 mm); compression ratio: 8.4:1; max power (DIN): 155 hp at 3,600 rpm; max torque (DIN): 270 lb ft, 37.2 kg m at 2,400 rpm; 26.3 hp/l; 1 Holley R7991A downdraught twin barrel carburettor; cooling system: 26.6 imp pt, 31.9 US pt, 15.1 l.

TRANSMISSION axle ratio: 2.450 - st. wagons 2.710; width of rims: st. wagons 6.5''; tyres: st. wagons H78 x 15.

PERFORMANCE max speed: about 103 mph, 165 km/h; power-weight ratio: Suburban 6-pass. 27.8 lb/hp, 12.6 kg/hp;

PLYMOUTH Fury Salon 4-door Sedan

speed in direct drive at 1,000 rpm: 28.5 mph, 45.8 km/h; consumption: 18 m/imp gal, 15 m/US gal, 15.7 l x 100 km.

ELECTRICAL EQUIPMENT 440 A battery.

DIMENSIONS AND WEIGHT wheel base: st. wagons 117.50 in, 298 cm; rear track: st. wagons 63.40 in, 161 cm; length: st. wagons 225.10 in, 572 cm; width: st. wagons 78.80 in, 200 cm; height: st. wagons 56.90 in, 144 cm; ground clearance: st. wagons 5.30 in, 13.5 cm; weight: Fury Hardtop 3,897 lb, 1,767 kg - Sedan 3,929 lb, 1,782 kg - Fury Sport 3,903 lb, 1,770 kg - Fury Salon 3,942 lb, 1,787 kg - Suburban 6-pass. 4,311 lb, 1,955 kg - 9-pass. 4,370 lb, 1,982 kg - Sport Suburban 6-pass. 4,300 lb, 1,950 kg - 9-pass. 4,373 lb, 1,983 kg; fuel tank: st. wagons 16.7 imp gal, 20 US gal, 76 l.

160 hp power team

(for California only).

See 155 hp (5,900 cc) power team, except for:

ENGINE compression ratio: 8:1; max power (DIN): 160 hp at 3,600 rpm; max torque (DIN): 265 lb ft, 36.6 kg m at 1,600 rpm; 27.1 hp/l; 1 Carter TQ9104S downdraught 4-barrel carburettor.

TRANSMISSION axle ratio: 2.710.

PERFORMANCE power-weight ratio: Suburban 6-pass. 26.9 lb/hp; consumption: 16.8 m/imp gal, 14 m/US gal, 16.8 l x 100 km.

ELECTRICAL EQUIPMENT Essex or Prestolite transistorized ignition.

170 hp power team

(for California only).

See 160 hp power team, except for:

ENGINE compression ratio: 8.4:1; max power (DIN): 170 hp at 4,000 rpm; max torque (DIN): 270 lb ft, 37.2 kg m at 1,600 rpm; 28.8 hp/l.

PERFORMANCE max speed: about 106 mph, 170 km/h; power-weight ratio: Suburban 6-pass. 25.4 lb/hp, 11.5 kg/hp; speed in direct drive at 1,000 rpm: 26.4 mph, 42.5 km/h.

190 hp power team

(not available in California).

See 155 hp (5,900 cc) power team, except for:

ENGINE 400 cu in, 6,555 cc (4.34 x 3.38 in, 110.2 x 85.8 mm); compression ratio: 8.2:1; max power (DIN): 190 hp at 3,600 rpm; max torque (DIN): 305 lb ft, 42.1 kg m at 3,200 rpm; 29 hp/l; 1 Carter 9140S downdraught 4-barrel carburettor; cooling system: 27.5 imp pt, 33 US pt, 15.6 l.

TRANSMISSION tyres: G78 x 15 - st. wagons H78 x 15.

PERFORMANCE max speed: about 109 mph, 175 km/h; power-weight ratio: Fury Sedan 21.3 lb/hp, 9.6 kg/hp; speed in direct drive at 1,000 rpm: 30.2 mph, 48.6 km/h; consumption: 13.3 m/imp gal, 11 m/US gal, 21.3 l x 100 km.

ELECTRICAL EQUIPMENT Lean-Burn electronic ignition system.

DIMENSIONS AND WEIGHT weight: plus 115 lb, 52 kg - st. wagons plus 109 lb, 49 kg.

OPTIONALS H78 x 15 tyres with 5.5'' wide rims (except for st. wagons).

PONTIAC   USA

Sunbird Series

PRICES EX WORKS:

1 Sunbird Coupé	$ 3,540
2 Sunbird Sport Coupé	$ 3,773
3 Sunbird Sport Hatchback Coupé	$ 3,912
4 Sunbird Sport Safari Station Wagon	$ 3,741

For V6 engine add $ 170.

Power team:	Standard for:	Optional for:
85 hp	all	—
105 hp	—	all

85 hp power team

ENGINE front, 4 stroke; 4 cylinders, in line; 151 cu in, 2,475 cc (4 x 3 in, 101.6 x 76.2 mm); compression ratio: 8.3:1; max power (DIN): 85 hp at 4,400 rpm; max torque (DIN): 123 lb ft, 17 kg m at 2,800 rpm; max engine rpm: 5,200; 34.3 hp/l; cast iron block and head; 5 crankshaft bearings; valves: overhead, in line, push-rods and rockers, hydraulic tappets; camshafts: 1, side; lubrication: gear pump, full flow filter, 6.7 imp pt, 8 US pt, 3.8 l; 1 Holley 5210 downdraught twin barrel carburettor; cleaner air system; exhaust system with catalytic converter; fuel feed: mechanical pump; water-cooled, 17.8 imp pt, 21.4 US pt, 10.1 l.

TRANSMISSION driving wheels: rear; clutch: single dry plate; gearbox: mechanical; gears: 4, fully synchronized; ratios: I 3.500, II 2.480, III 1.660, IV 1, rev 3.500; lever: central; final drive: hypoid bevel; axle ratio: 2.730; width of rims: 5''; tyres: A78 x 13.

PERFORMANCE max speed: about 87 mph, 140 km/h; power-weight ratio: Sunbird Coupé 31.3 lb/hp, speed in direct drive at 1,000 rpm: 19.8 mph, 31.8 km/h; consumption: 33.6 m/imp gal, 28 m/US gal, 8.4 l x 100 km.

CHASSIS integral; front suspension: independent, wishbones, coil springs, anti-roll bar, telescopic dampers; rear: rigid

PONTIAC Sunbird Coupé

PONTIAC Sunbird Formula Sport Hatchabck Coupé

axle, lower trailing radius arms, upper oblique torque arms, coil springs, telescopic dampers.

STEERING recirculating ball; turns lock to lock: 4.40.

BRAKES front disc (diameter 9.74 in, 24.7 cm), rear drum; swept area: total 264.7 sq in, 1,707 sq cm.

ELECTRICAL EQUIPMENT 12 V; 3,200 W battery; 37 A alternator; Delco-Remy transistorized ignition; 4 headlamps.

DIMENSIONS AND WEIGHT wheel base: 97 in, 246 cm; tracks: 55.30 in, 140 cm front, 54.10 in, 137 cm rear; length: coupés 177.80 in, 452 cm - Hatchback 179.30 in, 455 cm - St. Wagon 177.60 in, 451 cm; width: 65.40 in, 166 cm; height: coupés 49.90 in, 127 cm - Hatchback 49.60 in, 126 cm - St. Wagon 51.80 in, 132 cm; ground clearance: 4.90 in, 12.4 cm - coupés 4.80 in, 12.2 cm; weight: Sunbird Coupé 2,662 lb, 1,207 kg - Sunbird Sport Coupé 2,662 lb, 1,207 kg - Hatchback 2,694 lb, 1,221 kg - St. Wagon 2,610 lb, 1,183 kg; turning circle (between walls): 38.4 ft, 11.7 m; fuel tank: 15.4 imp gal, 18.5 US gal, 70 l.

BODY 4 seats, separate front seats; folding rear seat.

OPTIONALS limited slip differential; 3.080 axle ratio; 5-speed fully synchronized mechanical gearbox (I 3.400, II 2.080, III 1.390, IV 1, V 0.800, rev 3.360), 3.230 or 2.730 axle ratio; Turbo-Hydramatic automatic transmission with 3 ratios (I 2.740, II 1.570, III 1, rev 2.070), max ratio of converter at stall 2.20, possible manual selection, central lever, 2.730 or 3.080 axle ratio; B78 x 13 tyres; BR78 x 13 or BR70 x 13 tyres with 6'' wide rims; heavy-duty suspension; power steering; tilt of steering wheel; servo brake; air-conditioning; Formula equipment for Hatchback only.

105 hp power team

See 85 hp power team, except for:

ENGINE 6 cylinders, Vee-slanted at 90°; 231 cu in, 3,785 cc (3.80 x 3.40 in, 96.5 x 86.4 mm); compression ratio: 8:1; max power (DIN): 105 hp at 3,400 rpm; max torque (DIN): 185 lb ft, 25.5 kg m at 2,000 rpm; max engine rpm: 4,000; 27.7 hp/l; 4 crankshaft bearings; camshafts: 1, at centre of Vee; lubricating system: 8.3 imp pt, 9.9 US pt, 4.7 l; 1 Rochester 2GE downdraught twin barrel carburettor; cooling system: 20.1 imp pt, 24.1 US pt, 12.4 l.

TRANSMISSION axle ratio: 2.930; tyres: B78 x 13 (standard).

PERFORMANCE max speed: about 99 mph, 160 km/h; power-weight ratio: Sunbird Coupé 26 lb/hp, 11.8 kg/hp; speed in direct drive at 1,000 rpm: 29.2 mph, 47 km/h; consumption: 22.8 m/imp gal, 19 m/US gal, 12.4 l x 100 km.

ELECTRICAL EQUIPMENT 2,500 W battery.

DIMENSIONS AND WEIGHT weight: plus 74 lb, 34 kg.

OPTIONALS 5-speed fully synchronized mechanical gearbox with 2.930 axle ratio; Turbo-Hydramatic automatic transmission with 3 ratios (I 2.520, II 1.520, III 1, rev 1.940), max ratio of converter at stall 2.25, possible manual selection, 2.560 or 2.930 axle ratio.

Phoenix Series

PRICES EX WORKS:

Phoenix Coupé	$ 3,872
Phoenix Hatchback Coupé	$ 4,068
Phoenix Sedan	$ 3,947
Phoenix LJ Coupé	$ 4,357
Phoenix LJ Sedan	$ 4,432

For V8 engines add $ 150.

Power team:	Standard for:	Optional for:
85 hp	—	all
105 hp	all	
145 hp	—	all
160 hp	—	all

85 hp power team

(not available in California).

ENGINE front, 4 stroke; 4 cylinders, in line; 151 cu in, 2,475 cc (4 x 3 in, 101.6 x 76.2 mm); compression ratio: 8.3:1; max power (DIN): 85 hp at 4,400 rpm; max torque (DIN): 123 lb ft, 17 kg m at 2,800 rpm; max engine rpm: 5,200; 34.3 hp/l; cast iron block and head; 5 crankshaft bearings; valves: overhead, in line, push-rods and rockers, hydraulic tappets; camshafts: 1, side; lubrication: gear pump, full flow filter, 6.7 imp pt, 8 US pt, 3.8 l; 1 Holley 5210 downdraught twin

PONTIAC Phoenix Sedan

barrel carburettor; cleaner air system; exhaust system with catalytic converter; fuel feed: mechanical pump; water-cooled, 20.4 imp pt, 24.5 US pt, 11.6 l.

TRANSMISSION driving wheels: rear; gearbox: Turbo-Hydramatic automatic transmission, hydraulic torque converter and planetary gears with 3 ratios, max ratio of converter at stall 2.2, possible manual selection; ratios: I 2.740, II 1.570, III 1, rev 2.070; lever: steering column; final drive: hypoid bevel; axle ratio: 3.420; width of rims: 5'' - Phoenix LJ 6''; tyres: E78 x 14.

PERFORMANCE max speed: about 87 mph, 140 km/h; power-weight ratio: Phoenix Sedan 37.3 lb/hp, 16.9 kg/hp; speed in direct drive at 1,000 rpm: 19.8 mph, 31.8 km/h; consumption: 27.7 m/imp gal, 23 m/US gal, 10.2 l x 100 km.

CHASSIS integral with separate partial frame; front suspension: independent, wishbones, coil springs, anti-roll bar, telescopic dampers; rear: rigid axle, semi-elliptic leafsprings, telescopic dampers.

STEERING recirculating ball; turns lock to lock: 4.99.

BRAKES front disc (diameter 11 in, 27.9 cm), front internal radial fins, rear drum; swept area: total 337.3 sq in, 2,175 sq cm.

ELECTRICAL EQUIPMENT 12 V; 3,200 W battery; 37 A alternator; Delco-Remy transistorized ignition; 2 headlamps.

DIMENSIONS AND WEIGHT wheel base: 111.10 in, 282 cm; tracks: 61.80 in, 157 cm front, 59.60 in, 151 cm rear; length: 203.40 in, 517 cm; width: 73.20 in, 186 cm; height: 52.30 in, 133 cm - sedans 53.20 in, 135 cm; ground clearance: 4.20 in, 10.7 cm; weight: Phoenix Coupé 3,119 lb, 1,414 kg - Hatchback 3,202 lb, 1,452 kg - Sedan 3,169 lb, 1,437 kg - LJ Coupé 3,228 lb, 1,464 kg - Sedan 3,277 lb, 1,486 kg; turning circle (between walls): 39.1 ft, 11.9 m; fuel tank: 17.6 imp gal, 21 US gal, 80 l.

BODY 6 seats, bench front seats.

OPTIONALS central lever; limited slip differential; F78 x 14 tyres; FR78 x 14 tyres with 7'' wide rims; heavy-duty suspension with rear anti-roll bar; power steering; tilt of steering wheel; servo brake; heavy-duty battery; electric windows; heated rear window except for Hatchback; separate front seats with reclining backrests; air-conditioning; speed control device.

105 hp power team

See 85 hp power team, except for:

ENGINE 6 cylinders, Vee-slanted at 90°; 231 cu in, 3,785 cc (3.80 x 3.40 in, 96.5 x 86.4 mm); compression ratio: 8:1; max power (DIN): 105 hp at 3,400 rpm; max torque (DIN): 185 lb ft, 25.5 kg m at 2,000 rpm; max engine rpm: 4,000; 27.7 hp/l; 4 crankshaft bearings; camshafts: 1, at centre of Vee; lubricating system: 8.3 imp pt, 9.9 US pt, 4.7 l; 1 Rochester 2GE downdraught twin barrel carburettor; cooling system: 22.9 imp pt, 27.5 US pt, 13 l.

TRANSMISSION clutch: single dry plate; gearbox: mechanical (Turbo-Hydramatic automatic transmission standard for California only); gears: 3, fully synchronized; ratios: 3.500, II 1.890, III 1, rev 3.500; axle ratio: 3.080.

PERFORMANCE max speed: about 93 mph, 150 km/h; power-weight ratio: Phoenix Sedan 30.2 lb/hp, 13.7 kg/hp; speed in direct drive at 1,000 rpm: 27.4 mph, 44.1 km/h; consumption: 22.8 m/imp gal, 19 m/US gal, 12.4 l x 100 km.

ELECTRICAL EQUIPMENT 2,500 W battery.

OPTIONALS Turbo-Hydramatic automatic transmission with 3 ratios (I 2.740, II 1.570, III 1, rev 2.070), max ratio of converter at stall 2.2, possible manual selection, 2.560 or 3.230 axle ratio.

145 hp power team

See 85 hp power team, except for:

ENGINE 8 cylinders; 305 cu in, 4,998 cc (3.74 x 3.48 in, 95 x 88.4 mm); compression ratio: 8.4:1; max power (DIN): 145 hp at 3,800 rpm; max torque (DIN): 245 lb ft, 33.8 kg m at 2,400 rpm; max engine rpm: 4,400; 29 hp/l; camshafts: 1, at centre of Vee; lubricating system: 8.3 imp pt, 9.9 US pt, 4.7 l; 1 Rochester 2GC downdraught twin barrel carburettor; cooling system: 27.6 imp pt, 33.2 US pt, 15.7 l.

TRANSMISSION clutch: single dry plate; gearbox: mechanical (Turbo-Hydramatic automatic transmission standard for California only); gears: 4, fully synchronized; ratios: I 2.850, II 2.020, III 1.350, IV 1, rev 2.850; lever: central; axle ratio: 3.080.

PERFORMANCE max speed: about 99 mph, 160 km/h; power-weight ratio: Phoenix Sedan 22.5 lb/hp, 10.2 kg/hp; speed in direct drive at 1,000 rpm: 26.2 mph, 42.1 km/h; consumption: 20.5 m/imp gal, 17 m/US gal, 13.8 l x 100 km.

145 HP POWER TEAM

BRAKES servo (standard).

DIMENSIONS AND WEIGHT weight: plus 96 lb, 44 kg.

OPTIONALS Turbo-Hydramatic automatic transmission with 3 ratios (I 2.520, II 1.520, III 1, rev 1.920), max ratio of converter at stall 2.5, possible manual selection, steering column lever, 2.410 or 3.080 axle ratio.

160 hp power team

See 145 hp power team, except for:

ENGINE 350 cu in, 5,736 cc (4 x 3.48 in, 101.6 x 88.3 mm); compression ratio: 8.2:1; max power (DIN): 160 hp at 3,800 rpm; max torque (DIN): 260 lb ft, 35.9 kg m at 2,400 rpm; 27.9 hp/l; 1 Rochester M4MC downdraught 4-barrel carburettor.

TRANSMISSION gearbox: Turbo-Hydramatic automatic transmission, hydraulic torque converter and planetary gears with 3 ratios, max ratio of converter at stall 2.5, possible manual selection; ratios: I 2.520, II 1.520, III 1, rev 1.920; axle ratio: 3.080.

PERFORMANCE max speed: about 103 mph, 165 km/h; power-weight ratio: Phoenix Sedan 19.9 lb/hp, 9 kg/hp; speed in direct drive at 1,000 rpm: 27 mph, 43.4 km/h; consumption: 18 m/imp gal, 15 m/US gal, 15.7 l x 100 km.

DIMENSIONS AND WEIGHT weight: plus 21 lb, 9 kg.

OPTIONALS 2.410 axle ratio.

Firebird Series

PRICES EX WORKS:

1 Firebird Hardtop Coupé	$	4,545
2 Firebird Esprit Hardtop Coupé	$	4,842
3 Firebird Formula Hardtop Coupé	$	5,448
4 Firebird Trans Am Hardtop Coupé	$	5,799

For V8 engines add $ 150.

Power team:	Standard for:	Optional for:
105 hp	1,2	—
135 hp	—	1,2
145 hp	3	1,2
160 hp	—	1 to 3
170 hp	—	1 to 3
180 hp	4	3
185 hp	—	3,4
220 hp	—	3,4

105 hp power team

ENGINE front, 4 stroke; 6 cylinders, Vee-slanted at 90°; 231 cu in, 3,785 cc (3.80 x 3.40 in, 96.5 x 86.4 mm); compression ratio: 8:1; max power (DIN): 105 hp at 3,400 rpm; max torque (DIN): 185 lb ft, 25.5 kg m at 2,000 rpm; max

PONTIAC Firebird Formula Hardtop Coupé

engine rpm: 4,000; 27.7 hp/l; cast iron block and head; 4 crankshaft bearings; valves: overhead, in line, push-rods and rockers, hydraulic tappets; camshafts: 1, at centre of Vee; lubrication: gear pump, full flow filter, 8.3 imp pt, 9.9 US pt, 4.7 l; 1 Rochester 2GE downdraught twin barrel carburettor; cleaner air system; exhaust system with catalytic converter; fuel feed: mechanical pump; water-cooled, 26.4 imp pt, 31.7 US pt, 15 l.

TRANSMISSION driving wheels: rear; clutch: single dry plate; gearbox: mechanical; gears: 3, fully synchronized; ratios: I 3.110, II 1.840, III 1, rev 3.220; lever: central; final drive: hypoid bevel; axle ratio: 3.080; width of rims: 6''; tyres: FR78 x 15.

PERFORMANCE max speed: about 93 mph, 150 km/h; power-weight ratio: Firebird 31 lb/hp, 14 kg/hp; speed in direct drive at 1,000 rpm: 27.4 mph, 44.1 km/h; consumption: 22.8 m/imp gal, 19 m/US gal, 12.4 l x 100 km.

CHASSIS integral with separate partial frame; front suspension: independent, wishbones (lower trailing links), coil springs, anti-roll bar, telescopic dampers; rear: rigid axle, semi-elliptic leafsprings, anti-roll bar, telescopic dampers.

STEERING recirculating ball, variable ratio servo; turns lock to lock: 2.41.

BRAKES front disc (diameter 11 in, 27.9 cm), front internal radial fins, rear drum; swept area: total 326.49 sq in, 2,106 sq cm.

ELECTRICAL EQUIPMENT 12 V; 2,500 W battery; 42 A alternator; Delco-Remy transistorized ignition; 4 headlamps.

DIMENSIONS AND WEIGHT wheel base: 108.20 in, 275 cm; tracks: 61.30 in, 156 cm front, 60 in, 152 cm rear; length: 196.80 in, 500 cm; width: 73.40 in, 186 cm; height: 49.30 in, 125 cm; ground clearance: 5.20 in, 13.2 cm; weight: Firebird 3,254 lb, 1,475 kg - Esprit 3,285 lb, 1,490 kg; turning circle (between walls): 41.3 ft, 12.6 m; fuel tank: 17.6 imp gal, 21 US gal, 80 l.

BODY hardtop coupé; 2 doors; 4 seats, separate front seats, built-in headrests.

OPTIONALS limited slip differential; Turbo-Hydramatic automatic transmission with 3 ratios (I 2.520, II 1.520, III 1, rev 1.920), max ratio of converter at stall 2.25, possible manual selection, steering column lever, 2.560 or 3.230 axle ratio; F78 x 14 or G78 x 14 tyres; tilt of steering wheel; servo brake; electric windows; removable roof panels; heated rear window; air-conditioning.

135 hp power team

(for California only).

See 105 hp power team, except for:

ENGINE 8 cylinders; 305 cu in, 4,998 cc (3.74 x 3.48 in, 95 x 88.3 mm); compression ratio: 8.4:1; max power (DIN): 135 hp at 3,800 rpm; max torque (DIN): 240 lb ft, 33.1 kg m at 2,000 rpm; max engine rpm: 4,400; 27 hp/l; 5 crankshaft bearings; 1 Rochester 2GC downdraught twin barrel carburettor; cooling system: 34.8 imp pt, 41.9 US pt, 19.8 l.

TRANSMISSION gearbox: Turbo-Hydramatic automatic transmission (standard), hydraulic torque converter and planetary gears with 3 ratios, max ratio of converter at stall 2, possible manual selection; ratios: I 2.520, II 1.520, III 1, rev 1.920; axle ratio: 2.410.

PERFORMANCE max speed: about 96 mph, 155 km/h; power-weight ratio: Firebird 25 lb/hp, 11.4 kg/hp - Esprit 25.3 lb/hp, 11.5 kg/hp; speed in direct drive at 1,000 rpm: 25.4 mph, 40.8 km/h; consumption: 18 m/imp gal, 15 m/US gal, 15.7 l x 100 km.

BRAKES servo (standard).

ELECTRICAL EQUIPMENT 3,200 W battery.

DIMENSIONS AND WEIGHT weight: plus 128 lb, 58 kg.

145 hp power team

(not available in California).

See 105 hp power team, except for:

ENGINE 8 cylinders; 305 cu in, 4,998 cc (3.74 x 3.48 in, 95 x 88.3 mm); compression ratio: 8.4:1; max power (DIN): 145 hp at 3,800 rpm; max torque (DIN): 245 lb ft, 33.8 kg m at 2,400 rpm; max engine rpm: 4,400; 29 hp/l; 5 crankshaft bearings; 1 Rochester 2GC downdraught twin barrel carburettor; cooling system: 34.8 imp pt, 41.9 US pt, 19.8 l.

TRANSMISSION gears: 4, fully synchronized; ratios: I 2.850, II 2.020, III 1.350, IV 1, rev 2.850; width of rims: Formula 7''; tyres: Formula GR70 x 15.

PERFORMANCE max speed: about 99 mph, 160 km/h; power-weight ratio: Formula 23.8 lb/hp, 10.8 kg/hp; speed in direct drive at 1,000 rpm: 26.2 mph, 42.1 km/h; consumption: 20.5 m/imp gal, 17 m/US gal, 13.8 l x 100 km.

BRAKES servo (standard).

ELECTRICAL EQUIPMENT 3,200 W battery.

DIMENSIONS AND WEIGHT tracks: Formula 61.60 in, 156 cm front, 60.30 in, 153 cm rear; height: Formula 49.50 in, 125 cm; ground clearance: Formula 5.30 in, 13.5 cm; weight: Firebird 3,382 lb, 1,534 kg - Esprit 3,413 lb, 1,457 kg - Formula 3,452 lb, 1,565 kg.

OPTIONALS Turbo-Hydramatic automatic transmission with max ratio of converter at stall 2 and 2.410 axle ratio.

160 hp power team

(for California only).

See 145 hp power team, except for:

ENGINE 350 cu in, 5,736 cc (3.88 x 3.75 in, 98.5 x 95.2 mm); compression ratio: 8.2:1; max power (DIN): 160 hp at 3,800 rpm; max torque (DIN): 260 lb ft, 35.9 kg m at 2,400 rpm; 27.9 hp/l; 1 Rochester M4MC downdraught 4-barrel carburettor; cooling system: 33.3 imp pt, 40 US pt, 18.9 l.

PONTIAC Firebird Trans Am Hardtop Coupé

PONTIAC Grand Le Mans Coupé

TRANSMISSION gearbox: Turbo-Hydramatic automatic transmission (standard), max ratio of converter at stall 2, possible manual selection; ratios: I 2.520, II 1.520, III 1, rev 1.920; axle ratio: 2.410.

PERFORMANCE power-weight ratio: Firebird 21.2 lb/hp, 9.6 kg/hp; consumption: 19.2 m/imp gal, 16 m/US gal, 14.7 l x 100 km.

DIMENSIONS AND WEIGHT weight: plus 17 lb, 8 kg.

170 hp power team

(not available in California).

See 160 hp power team, except for:

ENGINE max power (DIN): 170 hp at 3,800 rpm; max torque (DIN): 270 lb ft, 37.2 kg m at 2,400 rpm; 29.6 hp/l.

TRANSMISSION gears: 4, fully synchronized; ratios: I 2.850, II 2.020, III 1.350, IV 1, rev 2.850; axle ratio: 3.080.

PERFORMANCE max speed: about 103 mph, 165 km/h; power-weight ratio: Firebird 20 lb/hp, 9.1 kg/hp; speed in direct drive at 1,000 rpm: 27 mph, 43.4 km/h.

OPTIONALS Turbo-Hydramatic automatic transmission with max ratio of converter at stall 2 and 2.410 or 3.080 axle ratio.

180 hp power team

(not available in California).

See 170 hp power team, except for:

ENGINE 400 cu in, 6,555 cc (4.12 x 3.75 in, 104.6 x 95.2 mm); compression ratio: 7.7:1; max power (DIN): 180 hp at 3,600 rpm; max torque (DIN): 325 lb ft, 44.8 kg m at 1,600 rpm; 27.5 hp/l; cooling system: 30.6 imp pt, 36.8 US pt, 17.4 l.

TRANSMISSION gearbox: Turbo-Hydramatic automatic transmission (standard), max ratio of converter at stall 2.5, possible manual selection; ratios: I 2.520, II 1.520, III 1, rev 1.920; axle ratio: 2.560; width of rims: 7''; tyres: Trans Am GR70 x 15.

PERFORMANCE max speed: about 110 mph, 177 km/h; power-weight ratio: Trans Am 19.5 lb/hp, 8.8 kg/hp; speed in direct drive at 1,000 rpm: 30.6 mph, 49.2 km/h.

DIMENSIONS AND WEIGHT weight: Trans Am 3,511 lb, 1,592 kg - Formula 3,621 lb, 1,642 kg.

185 hp power team

(for California only).

See 180 hp power team, except for:

ENGINE 403 cu in, 6,604 cc (4.35 x 3.38 in, 110.4 x 85.8 mm); compression ratio: 7.9:1; max power (DIN): 185 hp at

PONTIAC Grand Am Sedan

3,600 rpm; max torque (DIN): 320 lb ft, 44.1 kg m at 2,200 rpm; 28 hp/l; cooling system: 34 imp pt, 40.8 US pt, 19.3 l.

PERFORMANCE max speed: about 112 mph, 180 km/h; power-weight ratio: Trans Am 19.7 lb/hp, 8.9 kg/hp.

ELECTRICAL EQUIPMENT 3,500 W battery.

DIMENSIONS AND WEIGHT weight: plus 139 lb, 63 kg.

OPTIONALS 3.230 axle ratio.

220 hp power team

(not available in California).

See 180 hp power team, except for:

ENGINE compression ratio: 8:1; max power (DIN): 220 hp at 4,000 rpm; max torque (DIN): 320 lb ft, 44.1 kg m at 2,800 rpm; max engine rpm: 4,400; 33.6 hp/l; duel exhaust system.

TRANSMISSION gears: 4, fully synchronized; ratios: I 2.430, II 1.610, III 1.230, IV 1, rev 2.350; axle ratio: 3.420.

PERFORMANCE max speed: about 118 mph, 190 km/h; power-weight ratio: Trans Am 16.6 lb/hp, 7.5 kg/hp; speed in direct drive at 1,000 rpm: 28 mph, 45 km/h.

OPTIONALS Turbo-Hydramatic automatic transmission with 3.230 axle ratio.

Le Mans - Grand Le Mans - Grand Am Series

PRICES EX WORKS:

1 Le Mans Coupé	$ 4,405
2 Le Mans Sedan	$ 4,480
3 Le Mans Safari Station Wagon	$ 4,937
4 Grand Le Mans Coupé	$ 4,777
5 Grand Le Mans Sedan	$ 4,881
6 Grand Le Mans Safari Station Wagon	$ 5,265
7 Grand Am Coupé	$ 5,464
8 Grand Am Sedan	$ 5,568

For V8 engines add $ 150.

Power team:	Standard for:	Optional for:
105 hp	1 to 6	—
135 hp	—	all except 3,6
140 hp	7,8	—
145 hp	—	1 to 6
150 hp	—	7,8

105 hp power team

ENGINE front, 4 stroke; 6 cylinders, Vee-slanted at 90°; 231 cu in, 3,785 cc (3.80 x 3.40 in, 96.5 x 86.4 mm); compression ratio: 8:1; max power (DIN): 105 hp at 3,400 rpm; max torque (DIN): 185 lb ft, 25.5 kg m at 2,000 rpm; max engine rpm: 4,000; 27.7 hp/l; cast iron block and head; 4 crankshaft bearings; valves: overhead, in line, push-rods and rockers, hydraulic tappets; camshafts: 1, at centre of Vee; lubrication: gear pump, full flow filter, 8.3 imp pt, 9.9 US pt, 4.7 l; 1 Rochester 2GE downdraught twin barrel carburettor; cleaner air system; exhaust system with catalytic converter; fuel feed: mechanical pump; water-cooled, 23.2 imp pt, 27.9 US pt, 13.2 l.

TRANSMISSION driving wheels: rear; clutch: single dry plate; gearbox: mechanical (Turbo-Hydramatic transmission standard for st. wagons); gears: 3, fully synchronized; ratios: I 3.500, II 1.890, III 1, rev 3.500; lever: steering column; final drive: hypoid bevel; axle ratio: 2.930 - st. wagons 2.730; width of rims: 6''; tyres: P185/75R x 14 - st. wagons P195/75R x 14.

PERFORMANCE max speed: about 93 mph, 150 km/h; power-weight ratio: Le Mans Sedan 29 lb/hp, 13.2 kg/hp; speed in direct drive at 1,000 rpm: 27.4 mph, 44.1 km/h; consumption: 22.8 m/imp gal, 19 m/US gal, 12.4 l x 100 km.

CHASSIS perimeter; front suspension: independent, wishbones (lower trailing links), coil springs, anti-roll bar, telescopic dampers; rear: rigid axle, lower trailing radius arms, upper oblique torque arms, coil springs, telescopic dampers.

STEERING recirculating ball (variable ratio servo standard for st. wagons); turns lock to lock: 5.60 - st. wagons 3.50.

BRAKES front disc (diameter 11 in, 27.9 cm), front internal radial fins, rear drum, rear compensator (servo standard for st. wagons); swept area: total 307.73 sq in, 1,984 sq cm.

ELECTRICAL EQUIPMENT 12 V; 3,200 W battery; 42 A alternator; Delco-Remy transistorized ignition; 2 headlamps.

DIMENSIONS AND WEIGHT wheel base: 108.07 in, 274 cm; tracks: 58.50 in, 149 cm front, 58.03 in, 147 cm rear; length: coupés 199.25 in, 506 cm - sedans 198.46 in, 504 cm - st. wagons 197.83 in, 502 cm; width: 72.36 in, 184 cm; height: coupés 53.46 in, 136 cm - sedans 54.37 in, 138 cm - st. wagons 54.84 in, 139 cm; ground clearance: 5.60 in, 14.2 cm - st. wagons 5.90 in, 15 cm; weight: Le Mans Coupé 3,038 lb, 1,378 kg - Sedan 3,047 lb, 1,382 kg - Safari 3,226 lb, 1,463 kg - Grand Le Mans Coupé 3,072 lb, 1,393 kg - Sedan 3,098 lb, 1,405 kg - Safari 3,241 lb, 1,470 kg; turning circle (between walls): 37.5 in, 11.4 m; fuel tank: 15.2 imp gal, 18.2 US gal, 69 l.

OPTIONALS limited slip differential; Turbo-Hydramatic automatic transmission with 3 ratios (I 2.740, II 1.570, III 1, rev 2.070), max ratio of converter at stall 2, possible manual selection, steering column lever, 2.730 or 3.230 axle ratio; 4-speed fully synchronized mechanical gearbox (I 3.500, II 2.480, III 1.660, IV 1, rev 3.500), steering column lever, 2.930 axle ratio; P205/70R x 14 tyres; tilt of steering wheel; power steering (except for st. wagons); servo brake (except for st. wagons); electric windows; speed control device; heated rear window; electric sunshine roof; air-conditioning.

135 hp power team

(for California only).

See 105 hp power team, except for:

ENGINE 8 cylinders; 305 cu in, 4,998 cc (3.74 x 3.48 in, 95 x 88.3 mm); compression ratio: 8.4:1; max power (DIN): 135 hp at 3,800 rpm; max torque (DIN): 240 lb ft, 33.1 kg m at 2,000 rpm; max engine rpm: 4,400; 27 hp/l; 5 crankshaft

135 HP POWER TEAM

bearings; 1 Rochester 2GC downdraught twin barrel carburettor; cooling system: 28.3 imp pt, 34 US pt, 16.1 l.

TRANSMISSION gearbox: Turbo-Hydramatic automatic transmission (standard), hydraulic torque converter and planetary gears with 3 ratios, max ratio of converter at stall 2.3, possible manual selection; ratios: I 2.740, II 1.570, III 1, rev 2.070; axle ratio: 2.290.

PERFORMANCE max speed: about 103 mph, 165 km/h; power-weight ratio: Le Mans Sedan 23.5 lb/hp, 10.6 kg/hp; speed in direct drive at 1,000 rpm: 25.4 mph, 40.8 km/h; consumption: 20.5 m/imp gal, 17 m/US gal, 13.8 l x 100 km.

STEERING servo (standard); turns lock to lock: 3.30.

DIMENSIONS AND WEIGHT weight: Le Mans and Grand Le Mans models plus 121 lb, 55 kg - Grand Am Coupé 3,208 lb, 1,455 kg - Sedan 3,239 lb, 1,469 kg.

OPTIONALS 4-speed fully synchronized mechanical gearbox not available.

140 hp power team

(not available in California).

See 135 hp power team, except for:

ENGINE 301 cu in, 4,932 cc (4 x 3 in, 101.6 x 76.2 mm); compression ratio: 8.2:1; max power (DIN): 140 hp at 3,600 rpm; max torque (DIN): 235 lb ft, 32.4 kg m at 2,000 rpm; 28.4 hp/l; 1 Rochester M2MC downdraught twin barrel carburettor; cooling system: 38.4 imp pt, 46.1 US pt, 21.8 l.

PERFORMANCE max speed: about 105 mph, 169 km/h; power-weight ratio: Grand Am Sedan 23.1 lb/hp, 11.8 kg/hp; consumption: 23.9 m/imp gal, 20 m/US gal, 11.8 l x 100 km.

145 hp power team

See 105 hp power team, except for:

ENGINE 8 cylinders; 305 cu in, 4,998 cc (3.74 x 3.48 in, 95 x 88.3 mm); compression ratio: 8.4:1; max power (DIN): 145 hp at 3,800 rpm; max torque (DIN): 245 lb ft, 33.8 kg m at 2,400 rpm; max engine rpm: 4,400; 29 hp/l; 5 crankshaft bearings; 1 Rochester 2GC downdraught twin barrel carburettor; cooling system: 28.3 imp pt, 34 US pt, 16.1 l.

TRANSMISSION gearbox: Turbo-Hydramatic automatic transmission (standard), hydraulic torque converter and planetary gears with 3 ratios, max ratio of converter at stall 2.3, possible manual selection; ratios: I 2.740, II 1.570, III 1, rev 2.070 (st. wagons I 2.520, II 1.520, III 1, rev 2.070); axle ratio: 2.290 - st. wagons 2.410.

PERFORMANCE max speed: about 105 mph, 169 km/h; power-weight ratio: Le Mans Sedan 21.8 lb/hp, 9.9 kg/hp; speed in direct drive at 1,000 rpm: 27.7 mph, 44.5 km/h; consumption: 23.9 m/imp gal, 20 m/US gal, 11.8 l x 100 km.

STEERING servo (standard); turns lock to lock: 3.30 - st. wagons 3.50.

DIMENSIONS AND WEIGHT weight: plus 121 lb, 55 kg.

OPTIONALS 2.730 axle ratio; 4-speed fully synchronized mechanical gearbox not available.

150 hp power team

(not available in California).

See 140 hp power team, except for:

ENGINE max power (DIN): 150 hp at 4,000 rpm; max torque (DIN): 240 lb ft, 33.1 kg m at 2,000 rpm; max engine rpm: 4,400; 30.4 hp/l; 1 Rochester M4MC downdraught 4-barrel carburettor.

TRANSMISSION axle ratio: 2.410.

PERFORMANCE max speed: about 109 mph, 175 km/h; power-weight ratio: Grand Am Sedan 21.6 lb/hp, 9.8 kg/hp; speed in direct drive at 1,000 rpm: 27.2 mph, 43.7 km/h.

OPTIONALS 2.730 axle ratio.

Grand Prix Series

PRICES EX WORKS:

1 Grand Prix Hardtop Coupé		$ 4,880
2 Grand Prix LJ Hardtop Coupé		$ 5,815
3 Grand Prix SJ Hardtop Coupé		$ 6,088

For V8 engines add $ 150.

Power team:	Standard for:	Optional for:
105 hp	1	—
135 hp	—	all
140 hp	2	1
150 hp	3	2

105 hp power team

ENGINE front, 4 stroke; 6 cylinders, Vee-slanted at 90°; 231 cu in, 3,785 cc (3.80 x 3.40 in, 96.5 x 86.4 mm); compression ratio: 8:1; max power (DIN): 105 hp at 3,400 rpm; max torque (DIN): 185 lb ft, 25.5 kg m at 2,000 rpm; max engine rpm: 4,000; 27.7 hp/l; cast iron block and head; 4 crankshaft bearings; valves: overhead, in line, push-rods and rockers, hydraulic tappets; camshafts: 1, at centre of Vee; lubrication: gear pump, full flow filter, 8.3 imp pt, 9.9 US pt, 4.7 l; 1 Rochester 2GE downdraught twin barrel carburettor; cleaner air system; exhaust system with catalytic converter; fuel feed: mechanical pump; water-cooled, 23.9 imp pt, 28.8 US pt, 13.6 l.

TRANSMISSION driving wheels: rear; clutch: single dry plate; gearbox: mechanical; gears: 3, fully synchronized; ratios: I 3.500, II 1.890, III 1, rev 3.500; lever: steering column; final drive: hypoid bevel; axle ratio: 2.930; width of rims: 6''; tyres: P195/75R x 14.

PERFORMANCE max speed: about 96 mph, 155 km/h; power-weight ratio: 29.5 lb/hp, 13.4 kg/hp; speed in direct drive at 1,000 rpm: 28.3 mph, 45.6 km/h; consumption: 22.8 m/imp gal, 19 m/US gal, 12.4 l x 100 km.

CHASSIS perimeter; front suspension: independent, wishbones, coil springs, anti-roll bar, telescopic dampers; rear: rigid axle, lower trailing radius arms, upper oblique torque arms, coil springs, telescopic dampers.

STEERING recirculating ball; turns lock to lock: 7.

BRAKES front disc (diameter 11 in, 27.9 cm), front internal radial fins, rear drum, rear compensator; swept area: total 362.6 sq in, 2,339 sq cm.

ELECTRICAL EQUIPMENT 12 V; 2,500 W battery, 42 A alternator; Delco-Remy transistorized ignition; 4 headlamps.

DIMENSIONS AND WEIGHT wheel base: 108.07 in, 274 cm; tracks: 58.50 in, 149 cm front, 58.03 in, 147 cm rear; length: 201.18 in, 511 cm; width: 72.76 in, 185 cm; height: 53.27 in, 135 cm; ground clearance: 5.24 in, 13.5 cm; weight: 3,100 lb, 1,406 kg; fuel tank: 15.2 imp gal, 18.2 US gal, 69 l.

BODY hardtop coupé; 2 doors; 6 seats, separate front seats with built-in headrests.

OPTIONALS limited slip differential; Turbo-Hydramatic automatic transmission with 3 ratios (I 2.520, II 1.520, III 1, rev 1.940), max ratio of converter at stall 2.3, possible manual selection, steering column lever, 2.730 or 3.230 axle ratio; P205/70R x 14 tyres; power steering; tilt of steering wheel; servo brake; electric windows; automatic levelling control speed control device; heated rear window; electric sunshine roof; reclining backrests; air-conditioning; leather upholstery.

135 hp power team

(for California only).

See 105 hp power team, except for:

ENGINE 8 cylinders; 305 cu in, 4,998 cc (3.74 x 3.48 in, 95 x 88.3 mm); compression ratio: 8.4:1; max power (DIN): 135 hp at 3,800 rpm; max torque (DIN): 240 lb ft, 33.1 kg m at 2,000 rpm; max engine rpm: 4,400; 27 hp/l; 5 crankshaft bearings; 1 Rochester 2GC downdraught twin barrel carburettor; cooling system: 28.3 imp pt, 34 US pt, 16.1 l.

TRANSMISSION gearbox: Turbo-Hydramatic transmission (standard), hydraulic torque converter and planetary gears with 3 ratios, max ratio of converter at stall 2, possible manual selection; ratios: I 2.740, II 1.570, III 1, rev 2.070; axle ratio: 2.290.

PERFORMANCE max speed: about 103 mph, 165 km/h; power-weight ratio: Grand Prix 23.8 lb/hp, 10.8 kg/hp; speed in direct drive at 1,000 rpm: 27 mph, 43.4 km/h; consumption: 20.5 m/imp gal, 17 m/US gal, 13.8 l x 100 km.

BRAKES servo (standard).

ELECTRICAL EQUIPMENT 3,200 W battery.

DIMENSIONS AND WEIGHT weight: Grand Prix 3,210 lb, 1,456 kg - SJ 3,230 lb, 1,465 kg - LJ 3,217 lb, 1,459 kg.

OPTIONALS 2.730 axle ratio.

140 hp power team

(not available in California).

See 135 hp power team, except for:

ENGINE 301 cu in, 4,932 cc (4 x 3 in, 101.6 x 76.2 mm); compression ratio: 8.2:1; max power (DIN): 140 hp at 3,600 rpm; max torque (DIN): 235 lb ft, 32.4 kg m at 2,000 rpm; 28.4 hp/l; 1 Rochester M2MC downdraught twin barrel carburettor; cooling system: 38.4 imp pt, 46.1 US pt, 21.8 l.

TRANSMISSION automatic transmission ratios: I 2.520, II 1.520, III 1, rev 1.940.

PERFORMANCE max speed: about 106 mph, 170 km/h; power-weight ratio: LJ 23.7 lb/hp, 10.7 kg/hp; consumption: 23.9 m/imp gal, 20 m/US gal, 11.8 l x 100 km.

DIMENSIONS AND WEIGHT weight: Grand Prix 3,219 lb, 1,460 kg - LJ 3,319 lb, 1,505 kg.

150 hp power team

(not available in California).

See 140 hp power team, except for:

ENGINE max power (DIN): 150 hp at 4,000 rpm; max torque (DIN): 240 lb ft, 33.1 kg m at 2,000 rpm; max engine rpm: 4,400; 30.4 hp/l; 1 Rochester M4MC downdraught 4-barrel carburettor.

PONTIAC Grand Prix Hardtop Coupé

TRANSMISSION automatic transmission ratios: I 2.740, II 1.570, III 1, rev 2.070; max ratio of converter at stall 2.3; axle ratio: 2.410.

PERFORMANCE max speed: about 109 mph, 175 km/h; power-weight ratio: SJ 21.5 lb/hp, 9.8 kg/hp; speed in direct drive at 1,000 rpm: 27.2 mph, 43.7 km/h.

DIMENSIONS AND WEIGHT weight: Grand Prix plus 101 lb, 46 kg - SJ 3,230 lb, 1,465 kg.

OPTIONALS 2.730 axle ratio.

Catalina - Bonneville - Grand Safari Series

PRICES EX WORKS:

1 Catalina Coupé	$ 5,375
2 Catalina Sedan	$ 5,410
3 Catalina Safari Station Wagon	$ 5,924
4 Bonneville Coupé	$ 5,831
5 Bonneville Sedan	$ 5,931
6 Bonneville Brougham Coupé	$ 6,577
7 Bonneville Brougham Sedan	$ 6,677
8 Grand Safari Station Wagon	$ 6,227

For V8 engines add $ 150.

Power team:	Standard for:	Optional for:
105 hp	1,2	—
140 hp	3 to 8	1,2
155 hp	—	all
170 hp	—	all
180 hp	—	all
185 hp	—	all

105 hp power team

ENGINE front, 4 stroke; 6 cylinders, Vee-slanted at 90°; 231 cu in, 3,785 cc (3.80 x 3.40 in, 96.5 x 86.4 mm); compression ratio: 8:1; max power (DIN): 105 hp at 3,200 rpm; max torque (DIN): 185 lb ft, 25.5 kg m at 2,000 rpm; max engine rpm: 4,000; 27.7 hp/l; 4 crankshaft bearings; valves: overhead, in line, push-rods and rockers, hydraulic tappets; camshafts: 1, at centre of Vee; lubrication: gear pump, full flow filter, 8.3 imp pt, 9.9 US pt, 4.7 l; 1 Rochester 2GE downdraught twin barrel carburettor; cleaner air system; exhaust system with catalytic converter; fuel feed: mechanical pump; water-cooled, 21.3 imp pt, 25.6 US pt, 12.1 l.

TRANSMISSION driving wheels: rear; gearbox: Turbo-Hydramatic transmission, hydraulic torque converter and planetary gears with 3 ratios, max ratio of converter at stall 2.3, possible manual selection; ratios: I 2.520, II 1.520, III 1, rev 1.940; lever: steering column; final drive: hypoid bevel; axle ratio: 2.730; width of rims: 6''; tyres: FR78 x 15.

PERFORMANCE max speed: about 93 mph, 150 km/h; power-weight ratio: Catalina Sedan 33.1 lb/hp, 15 kg/hp; speed in direct drive at 1,000 rpm: 23.3 mph, 37.5 km/h; consumption: 23.9 m/imp gal, 20 m/US gal, 11.8 l x 100 km.

PERFORMANCE max speed: about 93 mph, 150 km/h; power-weight ratio: Catalina Sedan 33.1 lb/hp, 15 kg/hp; speed in direct drive at 1,000 rpm: 23.3 mph, 37.5 km/h; consumption: 23.9 m/imp gal, 20 m/US gal, 11.8 l x 100 km.

PONTIAC Grand Prix SJ Hardtop Coupé

PONTIAC Catalina Series

PONTIAC Catalina Sedan

CHASSIS perimetr; front suspension: independent, wishbones, coil springs, anti-roll bar, telescopic dampers; rear: rigid axle, lower trailing radius arms, upper oblique torque arms, coil springs, telescopic dampers.

STEERING recirculating ball, variable ratio servo; turns lock to lock: 3.50.

BRAKES front disc (diameter 11 in, 27.9 cm), front internal radial fins, rear drum, servo; swept area: total 337.3 sq in, 2,175 sq cm.

ELECTRICAL EQUIPMENT 12 V; 2,500 W battery; 42 A alternator; Delco-Remy transistorized ignition; 4 headlamps.

DIMENSIONS AND WEIGHT wheel base: 115.90 in, 295 cm; tracks: 61.70 in, 157 cm front, 60.70 in, 154 cm rear; length: 214.30 in, 544 cm; width: 78 in, 198 cm; height: Coupé 53.90 in, 137 cm - Sedan 54.50 in, 138 cm; ground clearance: 5.60 in, 14.2 cm; weight: Coupé 3.438 lb, 1,559 kg - Sedan 3,471 lb, 1,574 kg; turning circle (between walls): 41.6 ft, 12.7 m; fuel tank: 17.6 imp gal, 21 US gal, 80 l.

OPTIONALS limited slip differential; 3.230 axle ratio; GR78 x 15 or HR78 x 15 tyres with 6'' wide rims; GR70 x 15 tyres with 7'' wide rims; tilt of steering wheel; automatic levelling control; electric windows; reclining backrests; speed control device; heated rear window; air-conditioning.

140 hp power team

(not available in California).

See 105 hp power team, except for:

ENGINE 8 cylinders; 301 cu in, 4,932 cc (4 x 3 in, 101.5 x 76.1 mm); compression ratio: 8.2:1; max power (DIN): 135 hp at 3,600 rpm; max torque (DIN): 235 lb ft, 32.4 kg m at 2,000 rpm; 28.4 hp/l; 5 crankshaft bearings; lubricating system: 10 imp pt, 12 US pt, 5.7 l; 1 Rochester M2MC downdraught twin barrel carburettor; cooling system: 34.8 imp pt, 41.9 US pt, 19.8 l.

TRANSMISSION gearbox: Turbo-Hydramatic automatic transmission, max ratio of converter at stall 2; axle ratio: 2.410 - st. wagons 2.560; tyres: st. wagons HR78 x 15.

PERFORMANCE max speed: about 99 mph, 160 km/h; power-weight ratio: Bonneville Sedan 26 lb/hp, 11.8 kg/hp; speed in direct drive at 1,000 rpm: 22.6 mph, 36.4 km/h.

BRAKES swept area: st. wagons total 362.58 sq in, 2,339 sq cm.

ELECTRICAL EQUIPMENT 3,200 W battery.

DIMENSIONS AND WEIGHT tracks: st. wagons 62.10 in, 158 cm front, 64.10 in, 163 cm rear; length: st. wagons 215.10 in, 546 cm; height: st. wagons 57.30 in, 146 cm; ground clearance: st. wagons 6 in, 15.2 cm; weight: Catalina Coupé 3,559 lb, 1,614 kg - Sedan 3,592 lb, 1,629 kg - Catalina Safari 3,976 lb, 1,803 kg - Bonneville Coupé 3,581 lb, 1,624 kg - Sedan 3,638 lb, 1,650 kg - Brougham Coupé 3,612 lb, 1,638 kg - Sedan 3,669 lb, 1,664 kg - Grand Safari 4,002 lb, 1,815 kg; turning circle (between walls): st. wagons 42.3 ft, 12.9 m.

155 hp power team

(not available in California).

See 140 hp power team, except for:

ENGINE 350 cu in, 5,736 cc (3.80 x 3.85 in, 96.5 x 97.8 mm); compression ratio: 8:1; max power (DIN): 155 hp at 3,400 rpm; max torque (DIN): 280 lb ft, 38.6 kg m at 1,800 rpm; 27 hp/l; 1 Rochester M4MC downdraught 4-barrel carburettor; cooling system: 25.2 imp pt, 30.2 US pt, 14.3 l.

TRANSMISSION axle ratio: 2.730.

PERFORMANCE max speed: about 103 mph, 165 km/h; power-weight ratio: Catalina Sedan 24.6 lb/hp, 11.1 kg/hp; speed in direct drive at 1,000 rpm: 30.1 mph, 48.5 km/h; consumption: 21.6 m/imp gal, 18 m/US gal, 13.1 l x 100 km.

DIMENSIONS AND WEIGHT weight: plus 93 lb, 42 kg - Catalina plus 218 lb, 99 kg.

OPTIONALS 3.080 axle ratio (for st. wagons).

170 hp power team

(for California only).

See 140 hp power team, except for:

ENGINE 350 cu in, 5,736 cc (4.06 x 3.38 in, 103.8 x 86 mm); compression ratio: 7.9:1; max power (DIN): 170 hp at 3,800 rpm; max torque (DIN): 275 lb ft, 37.9 kg m at 2,000 rpm; 29.6 hp/l; 1 Rochester M4MC downdraught 4-barrel carburettor; cooling system: 25.2 imp pt, 30.2 US pt, 14.3 l.

TRANSMISSION axle ratio: 2.410 - st. wagons 2.560.

170 HP POWER TEAM

PERFORMANCE max speed: about 106 mph, 170 km/h; power-weight ratio: Catalina Sedan 22.1 lb/hp, 10 kg/hp; speed in direct drive at 1,000 rpm: 27.8 mph, 44.7 km/h; consumption: 20.5 m/imp gal, 17 m/US gal, 13.8 l x 100 km.

DIMENSIONS AND WEIGHT weight: Catalina plus 172 lb, 78 kg - Bonnevilles and Bonneville Broughams plus 52 lb, 24 kg - st. wagons plus 50 lb, 23 kg.

180 hp power team

(not available in California).

See 140 hp power team, except for:

ENGINE 400 cu in, 6,555 cc (4.12 x 3.75 in, 104.6 x 95.2 mm); compression ratio: 7.7:1; max power (DIN): 180 hp at 3,600 rpm; max torque (DIN): 325 lb ft, 44.8 kg m at 1,600 rpm; 27.5 hp/l; 1 Rochester M4MC downdraught 4-barrel carburettor; cooling system: 27.1 imp pt, 32.6 US pt, 15.4 l.

PERFORMANCE max speed: about 109 mph, 175 km/h; power-weight ratio: Catalina Sedan 21.4 lb/hp, 9.7 kg/hp; speed in direct drive at 1,000 rpm: 30.2 mph, 48.6 km/h; consumption: 19.2 m/imp gal, 16 m/US gal, 14.7 l x 100 km.

DIMENSIONS AND WEIGHT weight: Catalina plus 265 lb, 120 kg - Bonnevilles and Bonneville Broughams plus 143 lb, 65 kg - st. wagons plus 137 lb, 62 kg.

185 hp power team

(for California only).

See 140 hp power team, except for:

ENGINE 403 cu in, 6,604 cc (4.35 x 3.38 in, 110.4 x 85.8 mm); compression ratio: 7.9:1; max power (DIN): 185 hp at 3,600 rpm; max torque (DIN): 320 lb ft, 44.1 kg m at 2,000 rpm; 28 hp/l; 1 Rochester M4MC downdraught 4-barrel carburettor; cooling system: 27.1 imp pt, 32.6 US pt, 15.4 l.

PERFORMANCE max speed: about 112 mph, 180 km/h; power-weight ratio: Catalina Sedan 20.6 lb/hp, 9.3 kg/hp; speed in direct drive at 1,000 rpm: 31.1 mph, 50 km/h; consumption: 19.2 m/imp gal, 16 m/US gal, 14.7 l x 100 km.

ELECTRICAL EQUIPMENT 3,500 W battery.

DIMENSIONS AND WEIGHT weight: Catalina plus 216 lb, 98 kg - Bonnevilles and Bonneville Broughams plus 95 lb, 43 kg - st. wagons plus 93 lb, 42 kg.

STUTZ   USA

Blackhawk VI

PRICE EX WORKS: $ 64,500

ENGINE front, 4 stroke; V8 cylinders; 403 cu in, 6,605 cc (4.35 x 3.38 in, 110.5 x 85.8 mm); compression ratio: 7.9:1; max power (DIN): 185 hp at 3,600 rpm; max torque (DIN): 320 lb ft, 44.1 kg m at 2,000 rpm; max engine rpm: 3,800; 28 hp/l; cast iron block and head; 5 crankshaft bearings; valves: overhead, in line, push-rods and rockers, hydraulic tappets; camshafts: 1, at centre of Vee; lubrication: gear pump, 8.3 imp pt, 9.9 US pt, 4.7 l; 1 4-barrel carburettor; fuel feed: mechanical pump; water-cooled, 31.7 imp pt, 38.1 US pt, 18 l.

TRANSMISSION driving wheels: rear; gearbox: Turbo-Hydramatic automatic transmission, hydraulic torque converter and planetary gears with 3 ratios.

PERFORMANCE power-weight ratio: 24 lb/hp, 10.9 kg/hp.

CHASSIS box-type perimeter frame; front suspension: independent, wishbones, coil springs, anti-roll bar, adjustable telescopic dampers; rear: rigid axle, lower trailing radius arms, upper oblique arms, coil springs, adjustable telescopic dampers.

STEERING recirculating ball, adjustable steering wheel, servo.

BRAKES front disc, rear drum.

ELECTRICAL EQUIPMENT 12 V; alternator; Delco-Remy distributor; electronic ignition; 2 headlamps.

DIMENSIONS AND WEIGHT wheel base: 116 in, 295 cm; tracks: 61.60 in, 156 cm front, 61.10 in, 155 cm rear; length:

PONTIAC Bonneville Coupé

STUTZ Blackhawk VI

227 in, 577 cm; height: 54 in, 137 cm; weight: 4,450 lb, 2,018 kg; fuel tank: 20.9 imp gal, 25 US gal, 95 l.

BODY coupé; 2 doors; 5-6 seats, bench or separate front seats.

OPTIONAL ACCESSORIES air-conditioning; tinted glass; electric sun roof; electric windows; electrically-controlled seats; leather upholstery.

TOTAL REPLICA   USA

Ford Phaeton

PRICE EX WORKS: $ 17,000

ENGINE Chevrolet, front, 4 stroke; 8 cylinders; 350 cu in, 5,736 cc (4 x 3.48 in, 101.6 x 88.3 mm); cast iron block and head; 5 crankshaft bearings; valves: overhead, in line, push-rods and rockers, hydraulic tappets; camshafts: 1, at centre of Vee; lubrication: gear pump, full flow filter, 8.3 imp pt, 9.9 US pt, 4.7 l; fuel feed: mechanical pump; water-cooled, 18.3 imp pt, 22 US pt, 10.4 l.

TRANSMISSION driving wheels: rear; gearbox: Turbo-Hydramatic automatic transmission, hydraulic torque converter

TOTAL REPLICA Ford Phaeton

and planetary gears with 3 ratios; lever: central; final drive: hypoid bevel.

PERFORMANCE max speed: about 100 mph, 161 km/h; consumption: not declared.

CHASSIS perimeter box-type with front and rear cross members; front suspension: rigid axle, semi-elliptic leafsprings, telescopic dampers; rear: rigid axle, lower trailing radius arms, upper oblique torque arms, coil springs, telescopic dampers.

STEERING recirculating ball.

BRAKES front disc, rear drum.

ELECTRICAL EQUIPMENT 12 V; alternator; Delco-Remy high energy ignition system; 2 headlamps.

DIMENSIONS AND WEIGHT wheel base: 103.50 in, 263 cm; tracks: 58 in, 147 cm front, 58.50 in, 149 cm rear; length: 153 in, 389 cm; height: 69 in, 175 cm; ground clearance: 5.50 in, 14 cm; weight: 2,360 lb, 1,070 kg; weight distribution: 55% front, 45% rear; fuel tank: 9.9 imp gal, 12 US gal, 45 l.

BODY phaeton in plastic material; 2 doors; 5 seats, separate front seats.

VOLKSWAGEN 1200

VOLKSWAGEN 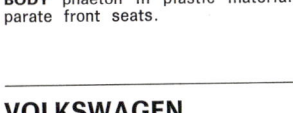 MEXICO

1200

ENGINE rear, 4 stroke; 4 cylinders, horizontally opposed; 72.7 cu in, 1,192 cc (3.03 x 2.52 in, 77 x 64 mm); compression ratio: 7.3:1; max power (DIN): 34 hp at 3,800 rpm; max torque (DIN): 55 lb ft, 7.6 kg m at 1,700 rpm; max engine rpm: 4,500; 28.5 hp/l; block with cast iron liners and light alloy fins, light alloy head; 4 crankshaft bearings; valves: overhead, push-rods and rockers; camshafts: 1, central, lower; lubrication: gear pump, filter in sump, oil cooler, 4.4 imp pt, 5.3 US pt, 2.5 l; 1 Solex 30 PICT downdraught single barrel carburettor; fuel feed: mechanical pump; air-cooled.

TRANSMISSION driving wheels: rear; clutch: single dry plate: gearbox: mechanical; gears: 4, fully synchronized; ratios: I 3.780, II 2.060, III 1.260, IV 0.890, rev 4.010; lever: central; final drive: spiral bevel; axle ratio: 4.375; width of rims: 4''; tyres: 5.60 x 15.

PERFORMANCE max speeds: (I) 18 mph, 31 km/h; (II) 35 mph, 57 km/h; (III) 58 mph, 94 km/h; (IV) 71 mph, 115 km/h; power-weight ratio: 49.2 lb/hp, 22.3 kg/hp; carrying capacity: 838 lb, 380 kg; acceleration: standing ¼ mile 23 sec, 0-50 mph (0-80 km/h) 18 sec; speed in top at 1,000 rpm: 18.6 mph, 30 km/h; consumption: 37.7 m/imp gal, 31.4 m/US gal, 7.5 l x 100 km.

CHASSIS backbone platform; front suspension: independent, twin swinging longitudinal trailing arms, transverse laminated torsion bars, anti-roll bar, telescopic dampers; rear: independent, swinging semi-axles, swinging longitu-

CHEVROLET Chevette Series

dinal trailing arms, transverse torsion bars, telescopic dampers.

STEERING worm and roller, telescopic damper; turns lock to lock: 2.60.

BRAKES drum; lining area: total 111 sq in, 716 sq cm.

ELECTRICAL EQUIPMENT 12 V; 36 Ah battery; 270 W dynamo; Bosch distributor; 2 headlamps.

DIMENSIONS AND WEIGHT wheel base: 94.49 in, 240 cm; tracks: 51.57 in, 131 cm front, 53.15 in, 135 cm rear; length: 159.84 in, 406 cm; width: 61.02 in, 155 cm; height: 59.06 in, 150 cm; ground clearance: 5.90 in, 15 cm; weight: 1,676 lb, 760 kg; weight distribution: 43% front, 57% rear; turning circle (between walls): 36.1 ft, 11 m; fuel tank: 8.8 imp gal, 10.6 US gal, 40 l.

BODY saloon/sedan; 2 doors; 5 seats, separate front seats, adjustable backrests.

CHEVROLET   BRAZIL

Chevette Series

PRICES EX WORKS:

2 door Sedan	73,495 cruzeiros
L 2-door Sedan	78,897 cruzeiros
SL 2-door Sedan	82,244 cruzeiros

60 hp power team

ENGINE front, 4 stroke; 4 cylinders, in line; 85.3 cu in, 1,398 cc (3.23 x 2.61 in, 82 x 66.2 mm); compression ratio: 7.8:1; max power (DIN): 60 hp at 5,400 rpm; max torque (DIN): 67 lb ft, 9.2 kg m at 3,600 rpm; max engine rpm: 6,000; 42.9 hp/l; cast iron block, light alloy head; 5 crankshaft bearings; valves: overhead, rockers; camshafts: 1, overhead, cogged belt; lubrication: gear pump, full flow filter, 6.2 imp pt, 7.4 US pt, 3.5 l; 1 Solex H 32/34 PDSI downdraught carburettor; fuel feed: mechanical pump; water-cooled, 12.3 imp pt, 14.8 US pt, 7 l.

TRANSMISSION driving wheels: rear; clutch: single dry plate (diaphragm); gearbox: mechanical; gears: 4, fully synchronized; ratios: I 3.746, II 2.157, III 1.378, IV 1, rev 3.815; lever: central; final drive: hypoid bevel; axle ratio: 4.100; width of rims: 5''; tyres: 165 x 13.

PERFORMANCE max speed: 87 mph, 140 km/h; power-weight ratio: 30.6 lb/hp, 13.9 kg/hp; carrying capacity: 915 lb, 415 kg; speed in direct drive at 1,000 rpm: 16 mph, 25.7 km/h; consumption: 37.7 m/imp gal, 31.4 m/US gal, 7.5 l x 100 km.

CHASSIS integral; front suspension: independent, wishbones, coil springs, anti-roll bar, telescopic dampers; rear: rigid axle, twin trailing radius arms, transverse linkage bar, coil springs, anti-roll bar, telescopic dampers.

STEERING rack-and-pinion; turns lock to lock: 3.25.

CHEVROLET Chevette SL 2-door Sedan

60 HP POWER TEAM

BRAKES front disc (diameter 9.37 in, 23.8 cm), rear drum, servo; lining area: front 17.1 sq in, 110 sq cm, rear 46.8 sq in, 302 sq cm, total 63.9 sq in, 412 sq cm.

ELECTRICAL EQUIPMENT 12 V; 36 Ah battery; 28 A alternator; Arno distributor; 2 headlamps.

DIMENSIONS AND WEIGHT wheel base: 94.09 in, 239 cm; front and rear track: 51.18 in, 130; length: 162.20 in, 412 cm; width: 61.81 in, 157 cm; height: 51.97 in, 132 cm; ground clearance: 5.51 in, 14 cm; weight: 1,843 lb, 836 kg; turning circle (between walls): 32.1 ft, 9.8 m; fuel tank: 9.9 imp gal, 11.9 US gal, 45 l.

BODY 2 doors; 5 seats, separate front seats; luxury equipment; reclining backrests with built-in headrests.

Opala Sedan/Coupé

PRICES EX WORKS: Sedan 100,207 cruzeiros
Coupé 100,916 cruzeiros

ENGINE front, 4 stroke; 4 cylinders, in line; 151 cu in, 2,474 cc (4 x 3 in, 101.6 x 76.2 mm); compression ratio: 7.5:1; max power (DIN): 80 hp at 4,400 rpm; max torque (DIN): 120 lb ft, 16.5 kg m at 2,400-2,800 rpm; max engine rpm: 5.200; 32.3 hp/l; cast iron block and head; 5 crankshaft bearings; valves: overhead, push-rods and rock-

CHEVROLET Opala Sedan

CHEVROLET Opala SS-4 Caravan

ers, hydraulic tappets; camshafts: 1, side; lubrication: gear pump, full flow filter, 6.2 imp pt, 7.4 US pt, 3.5 l; 1 DFV or Brosol-Sole H 40/44 EIS downdraught single barrel carburettor; fuel feed: mechanical pump; water-cooled, 15 imp pt, 18 US pt, 8.5 l.

TRANSMISSION driving wheels: rear; clutch: single dry plate; gearbox: mechanical; gears: 3, fully synchronized; ratios: I 3.070, II 1.680, III 1, rev 3.570; lever: steering column; final drive: hypoid bevel; axle ratio: 3.540; width of rims: 5''; tyres: 6.45 x 14.

PERFORMANCE max speed: 90 mph, 145 km/h; power-weight ratio: 29.8 lb/hp, 13.5 kg/hp; carrying capacity: 1,091 lb, 495 kg; speed in direct drive at 1,000 rpm: 22.6 mph, 36.4 km/h; consumption: 22.6 m/imp gal, 18.8 m/US gal, 12.5 l x 100 km.

CHASSIS integral; front suspension: independent, wishbones, coil springs, anti-roll bar, telescopic dampers; rear: rigid axle, longitudinal torsion bars, transverse linkage bar, coil springs, anti-roll bar, telescopic dampers.

STEERING screw and sector; turns lock to lock: 3.25.

BRAKES front disc, rear drum, servo.

ELECTRICAL EQUIPMENT 12 V; 45 Ah battery; 32 A alternator; Arno distributor; 2 headlamps.

DIMENSIONS AND WEIGHT wheel base: 105.12 in, 267 cm; tracks: 55.51 in, 141 front, 55.12 in, 140 cm rear; length: 183.86 in, 467 cm; width: 68.11 in, 173 cm; height: Sedan 54.72 in, 139 cm - Coupé 53.54 in, 136 cm; ground clearance:

5.79 in, 14.7 cm; weight: Sedan 2,384 lb, 1,081 kg - Coupé 2,379 lb, 1,079 kg; turning circle (between walls): 37.7 ft, 11.5 m; fuel tank: 11.9 imp gal, 14.3 US gal, 54 l.

BODY saloon/sedan, 4 doors - coupé, 2 doors; 6 seats, bench front seats - 5 seats, separate front seats.

VARIATIONS

ENGINE 6 cylinders, in line, 249.8 cu in, 4.093 cc (3.87 x 3.53 in, 98.4 x 89.6 mm), 8:1 compression ratio, max power (DIN) 153 hp at 4,600 rpm, max torque (DIN) 215 lb ft, 29.7 kg m at 2,400 rpm, 37.4 hp/l, 7 crankshaft bearings, lubrication 8.8 imp pt, 10.6 US pt, 5 l, 1 DFV 446052 downdraught twin barrel carburettor, cooling system 18 imp pt, 21.6 US pt, 10.2 l.
TRANSMISSION 3.080 axle ratio, 7.35 S x 14 tyres.
PERFORMANCE max speed about 118 mph, 190 km/h, power-weight ratio 15.6 lb/hp, 7.1 kg/hp, speed in direct drive at 1,000 rpm 23.6 mph, 38 km/h, fuel consumption 18.2 m/imp gal, 15.2 m/US gal, 15.5 l x 100 km.

OPTIONAL ACCESSORIES 4-speed fully synchronized mechanical gearbox (I 3.070, II 2.020, III 1.390, IV 1, rev 3.570), 3.080 axle ratio, central lever; "Automatic" automatic transmission, hydraulic torque converter and planetary gears with 3 ratios (I 2.310, II 1.460, III 1, rev 1.850), max ratio of converter at stall 2.4, possible manual selection, steering column or central lever; power-assisted steering (only with 6-cylinder engine); separate front seats with reclining backrests; air-conditioning (only with 6-cylinder engine); halogen headlamps; fog lamps; vinyl roof; tinted glass; metallic spray.

Opala Caravan

See Opala Sedan/Coupé, except for:

PRICE EX WORKS: 110,763 cruzeiros

TRANSMISSION tyres: 6.95 x 14.

PERFORMANCE power-weight ratio: 31.7 lb/hp, 14.4 kg/hp.

DIMENSIONS AND WEIGHT length: 182.28 in, 463 cm; height: 54.72 in, 139 cm; weight: 2,535 lb, 1,150 kg.

BODY estate car/station wagon; 2 + 1 doors; folding rear seat.

OPTIONAL ACCESSORIES 6.45 S x 14 tyres.

Opala SS-4 Coupé

See Opala Sedan/Coupé, except for:

PRICE EX WORKS: 116,193 cruzeiros

ENGINE max power (DIN): 88 hp at 4,600 rpm; max torque DIN): 135 lb ft, 18.6 kg m at 2,600 rpm; 35.6 hp/l; 1 Zenith WW4 downdraught twin barrel carburettor.

TRANSMISSION gears: 4, fully synchronized; ratios: I 3.070, II 2.020, III 1.390, IV 1, rev 3.570; lever: central; tyres: 7.35 S x 14.

PERFORMANCE max speed: 99 mph, 160 km/h; power-weight ratio: 27.3 lb/hp, 12.4 kg/hp; speed in direct drive at 1,000 rpm: 20.5 mph, 33 km/h.

DIMENSIONS AND WEIGHT height: 53.54 in, 136 cm; weight: 2,412 lb, 1,094 kg.

BODY coupé; 2 doors; 5 seats, separate front seats, reclining backrests.

Opala SS-4 Caravan

See Opala SS-4 Coupé, except for:

PRICE EX WORKS: 123,367 cruzeiros

TRANSMISSION tyres: 6.95 S x 14.

PERFORMANCE power-weight ratio: 29.1 lb/hp, 13.2 kg/hp.

DIMENSIONS AND WEIGHT length: 182.28 in, 463 cm; height: 54.72 in, 139 cm; weight: 2,569 lb, 1,165 kg.

BODY estate car/st. wagon; 2 + 1 doors.

Opala SS-6 Coupé

See Opala SS-4 Coupé, except for:

PRICE EX WORKS: 145,911 cruzeiros

ENGINE 6 cylinders; 250 cu in, 4,097 cc (3.87 x 3.53 in, 98.4 x 89.7 mm); compression ratio: 7.8:1; max power (DIN): 149 hp at 4,600 rpm; max torque (DIN): 209 lb ft, 28.8 kg m at 2,400 rpm; 36.4 hp/l; 7 crankshaft bearings; lubrication:

8.8 imp pt, 10.6 US pt, 5 l; cooling system: 17.2 imp pt. 20.7 US pt, 9.8 l.

TRANSMISSION axle ratio: 3.070; tyres: 7.35H x 14.

PERFORMANCE max speed: about 106 mph, 170 km/h; power-weight ratio: 17.2 lb/hp, 7.8 kg/hp; speed in direct drive at 1,000 rpm: 23.6 mph, 38 km/h; consumption: 18.2 m/imp gal, 15.2 m/US gal, 15.5 l x 100 km.

DIMENSIONS AND WEIGHT weight: 2,567 lb, 1,164 kg.

Opala SS-6 Caravan

See Opala SS-6 Coupé, except for:

PRICE EX WORKS: 139,184 cruzeiros

ENGINE lubrication: 7.9 imp pt, 9.5 US pt, 4.5 l; cooling system: 15 imp pt, 18 US pt, 8.5 l.

TRANSMISSION tyres: 6.95S x 14.

PERFORMANCE power-weight ratio: 18.3 lb/hp, 8.3 kg/hp.

DIMENSIONS AND WEIGHT length: 182.28 in, 463 cm; height: 54.72 in, 139 cm; weight: 2,723 lb, 1,235 kg.

BODY estate car/st. wagon; 2 + 1 doors.

Comodoro 4 Sedan/4 Coupé

PRICES EX WORKS: Comodoro 4 Sedan: 127,797 cruzeiros
Comodoro 4 Coupé: 127,234 cruzeiros

ENGINE front, 4 stroke; 4 cylinders, in line; 151 cu in, 2,474 cc (4 x 3 in, 101.6 x 76.2 mm); compression ratio: 7.5:1; max power (DIN): 88 hp at 4,600 rpm; max torque (DIN): 135 lb ft, 18.6 kg m at 2,600 rpm; max engine rpm: 5,000; 35.6 hp/l; cast iron block and head; 5 crankshaft bearings; valves: overhead in line, push-rods and rockers, hydraulic tappets; camshafts: 1, side; lubrication: gear pump, full flow filter, 6.2 imp pt, 7.4 US pt, 3.5 l; 1 Brosol - Solex H 40/41 DIS or DVF/Zenith 2285 downdraught twin barrel carburettor; fuel feed: mechanical pump; sealed circuit cooling, liquid, 15 imp pt, 18 US pt, 8.5 l.

TRANSMISSION driving wheels: rear; clutch: single dry plate; gearbox: mechanical; gears: 3, fully synchronized; ratios: I 3.070, II 1.680, III 1, rev 3.570; lever: steering column; final drive: hypoid bevel; axle ratio: 3.540; width of rims: 5''; tyres: 6.95 x 14.

PERFORMANCE max speeds: (I) 34 mph, 55 km/h; (II) 63 mph, 101 km/h; (III) 106 mph, 170 km/h; power-weight ratio: 28.2 lb/hp, 12.8 kg/hp; carrying capacity: 882 lb, 400 kg; speed in direct drive at 1,000 rpm: 23.6 mph, 38 km/h; consumption: 18.2 m/imp gal, 15.2 m/US gal, 15.5 l x 100 km.

CHASSIS integral; front suspension: independent, wishbones, coil springs, anti-roll bar, telescopic dampers; rear: rigid axle, longitudinal torsion bars, transverse linkage bar, coil springs, anti-roll bar, telescopic dampers.

STEERING screw and sector, servo.

BRAKES front disc, rear drum, servo.

ELECTRICAL EQUIPMENT 12 V; 45 Ah battery; 32 A alternator; Arno distributor; 2 headlamps.

DIMENSIONS AND WEIGHT wheel base: 105.12 in, 267 cm; tracks: 55.51 in, 141 cm front, 55.12 in, 140 cm rear; length: 185.12 in, 470 cm; width: 69.29 in, 176 cm; height: Sedan 54.72 in, 139 cm - Coupé 53.54 in, 136 cm; ground clearance: 5.79 in, 14.7 cm; weight: Sedan 2,481 lb, 1,125 kg - Coupé 2,487 lb, 1,128 kg, turning circle (between walls): 37.7 ft, 11.5 m; fuel tank: 11.9 imp gal, 14.3 US gal, 54 l.

BODY saloon/sedan, 4 doors - 4 coupé, 2 doors; 5 seats, separate front seats; vinyl roof.

OPTIONAL ACCESSORIES « Automatic » automatic transmission; reclining backrests; halogen headlamps; fog lamps; tinted glass; air-conditioning.

Comodoro 6 Sedan/6 Coupé

See Comodoro-4 Sedan/4 Coupé, except for:

PRICES EX WORKS: Sedan 154,614 cruzeiros
Coupé 152,978 cruzeiros

ENGINE 6 cylinders; 250 cu in, 4,097 cc (3.87 x 3.53 in, 98.4 x 89.7 mm); max power (DIN): 127 hp at 3,800 rpm; max torque (DIN): 201 lb ft, 27.8 kg m at 2,200 rpm; max engine rpm: 4,400; 31 hp/l; 7 crankshaft bearings; lubrication: 8.8 imp pt, 10.6 US pt, 5 l; cooling system: 17.2 imp pt, 20.7 US pt, 9.8 l.

TRANSMISSION gears: 4, fully synchronized; ratios: I 3.070, II 2.020, III 1.390, IV 1, rev 3.570; lever: central; axle ratio: 3.080; tyres: 7.35 S x 14.

CHEVROLET Comodoro Sedan

CHEVROLET Comodoro Coupé

PERFORMANCE max speeds: (I) 34 mph, 55 km/h; (II) 52 mph, 84 km/h; (III) 76 mph, 122 km/h; (IV) 106 mph, 170 km/h; power-weight ratio: 20.8 lb/hp, 9.4 kg/hp.

DIMENSIONS AND WEIGHT weight: 2,644 lb, 1,199 kg.

VARIATIONS

ENGINE 8:1 compression ratio, max power (DIN) 153 hp at 4,600 rpm, max torque (DIN) 215 lb ft, 29.7 kg m at 2,400 rpm, 37.4 hp/l, 1 DFV 44 6052 downdraught twin barrel carburettor.
PERFORMANCE max speed 118 mph, 190 km/h, power-weight ratio 17.2 lb/hp, 7.8 kg/hp.

Veraneio/Veraneio De Luxo

ENGINE front, 4 stroke; 6 cylinders, vertical in line; 261.2 cu in, 4,280 cc (3.75 x 3.94 in, 95.2 x 100.1 mm); compression ratio: 7.8:1; max power (SAE): 151 hp at 3,800 rpm; max torque (SAE): 233 lb ft, 32.1 kg m at 2,400 rpm; max engine rpm: 4,200; 35.3 hp/l; cast iron block and head; 3 crankshaft bearings; valves: overhead, in line, push-rods and rockers; camshafts: 1, side; lubrication: gear pump, full flow filter, 8.3 imp pt, 9.9 US pt, 4.7 l; 1 DFV-Zenith 228 downdraught single barrel carburettor; fuel feed: mechanical pump; water-cooled, 28.2 imp pt, 33.8 US pt, 16 l.

TRANSMISSION driving wheels: rear; clutch: single dry plate (diaphragm); gearbox: mechanical; gears: 3, fully synchronized; ratios: I 3.167, II 1.753, III 1, rev 3.761; lever: steering column; final drive: hypoid bevel, limited slip differential; axle ratio: 3.900; width of rims: 5.5''; tyres 7.10 x 15.

PERFORMANCE max speed: 90 mph, 145 km/h; power-weight ratio: 28.3 lb/hp, 12.8 kg/hp; carrying capacity: 1,058 lb, 480 kg; speed in direct drive at 1,000 rpm: 20.9 mph, 33.6 km/h; consumption: 17.7 m/imp gal, 14.7 m/US gal, 16 l x 100 km.

CHASSIS box-type ladder frame; front suspension: independent, wishbones, coil springs, telescopic dampers; rear: rigid axle, longitudinal trailing arms, coil springs, anti-roll bar, telescopic dampers.

STEERING worm and roller.

BRAKES drum; swept area: total 276.4 sq in, 1,783 sq cm.

ELECTRICAL EQUIPMENT 12 V; 45 Ah battery; 37 A alternator; Arno distributor; 2 headlamps.

DIMENSIONS AND WEIGHT wheel base: 114.96 in, 292 cm; tracks: 63.39 in, 161 cm front, 64.96 in, 155 cm rear; length: 203.15 in, 516 cm - De Luxo 207.87 in, 528 cm; width: 77.95 in, 198 cm; height: 68.11 in, 173 cm; ground clearance: 7.87 in, 20 cm; weight: 4,267 lb, 1,935 kg; turning circle (between walls): 42.6 ft, 13 m; fuel tank: 15.4 imp gal, 18.5 US gal, 70 l.

BODY estate car/st. wagon; 4 + 1 doors; 6 seats, bench front seats; folding rear seat - De Luxo, luxury equipment.

OPTIONAL ACCESSORIES power-assisted steering.

CHEVROLET Veraneio De Luxo

DODGE   BRAZIL

Polara/Polara Gran Luxo

PRICES EX WORKS: Polara   78,400 cruzeiros
               Gran Luxo   88,300 cruzeiros

ENGINE front, 4 stroke; 4 cylinders, vertical, in line; 109.8 cu in, 1,799 cc (3.39 x 3.04 in, 86 x 77.1 mm); compression ratio: 7.7:1; max power (SAE): 85 hp at 5,000 rpm; max torque (SAE): 103 lb ft, 14.2 kg m at 3,500 rpm; max engine rpm: 6,400; 47.2 hp/l; cast iron block and head; 5 crankshaft bearings; valves: overhead, in line, push-rods and rockers; camshafts: 1, side; lubrication: rotary pump, full flow filter, 7.2 imp pt, 8.7 US pt, 4 l; 1 SU HS-6 horizontal single barrel carburettor; fuel feed: mechanical pump; water-cooled, 10.6 imp pt, 12.7 US pt, 6 l.

TRANSMISSION driving wheels: rear; clutch: single dry plate (diaphragm); gearbox: mechanical; gears: 4, fully synchronized; ratios: I 3.538, II 2.165, III 1.387, IV 1, rev 3.680; lever: central; final drive: hypoid bevel; axle ratio: 3,890; width of rims: 5''; tyres: 6.45 x 13.

PERFORMANCE max speeds: (I) 30 mph, 49 km/h; (II) 50 mph, 81 km/h; (III) 78 mph, 120 km/h; (IV) 95 mph, 153 km/h; power-weight ratio: 24 lb/hp, 10.9 kg/hp - Gran Luxo 24.9 lb/hp, 11.3 kg/hp; carrying capacity: 882 lb, 400 kg; acceleration: standing ¼ mile 18.2 sec, 0-50 mph (0-80 km/h) 8.2 sec; speed in direct drive at 1,000 rpm: 17.4 mph, 28 km/h; consumption: 33.2 m/imp gal, 27.7 m/US gal, 8.5 l x 100 km.

CHASSIS integral; front suspension: independent, by McPherson, coil springs/telescopic damper struts, wishbones (lower trailing links), anti-roll bar; rear: rigid axle, swinging longitudinal trailing arms, upper oblique torque arms, coil springs, telescopic dampers.

STEERING rack-and-pinion; turns lock to lock: 3.60.

BRAKES front disc, rear drum, servo; swept area: front 22 sq in, 142 sq cm, rear 60.1 sq in, 387 sq cm, total 82.1 sq in, 529 sq cm.

ELECTRICAL EQUIPMENT 12 V; 40 Ah battery; 360 W alternator; Bosch or Wapsa distributor; 2 headlamps.

DIMENSIONS AND WEIGHT wheel base: 98 in, 249 cm; tracks: 52 in, 132 cm front, 52 in, 132 cm rear; length: 162.40 in, 412 cm; width: 62.50 in, 159 cm; height: 54.20 in, 138 cm; ground clearance: 5.50 in, 14 cm; dry weight: 2,051 lb, 930 kg - Gran Luxo 2,126 lb, 964 kg; turning circle (between walls): 30.8 ft, 9.4 m; fuel tank: 9.2 imp gal, 11.1 US gal, 42 l.

BODY coupé; 2 doors; 5 seats, separate front seats.

OPTIONAL ACCESSORIES 165 SR x 13 tyres.

DODGE Polara Gran Luxo

Dart De Luxo Sedan/Gran Sedan

PRICES EX WORKS: De Luxo Sedan 123,000 cruzeiros
                  Grand Sedan   159,000 cruzeiros

ENGINE front, 4 stroke; 8 cylinders, Vee-slanted at 90°; 318 cu in, 5,212 cc (3.91 x 3.31 in, 99.3 x 84.1 mm); compression ratio: 7.5:1; max power (SAE): 198 hp at 4,400 rpm; max torque (SAE): 301 lb ft, 41.5 kg m at 2,400 rpm; max engine rpm: 4,800; 38 hp/l; cast iron block and head; 5 crankshaft bearings; valves: overhead, in line, push-rods and rockers, hydraulic tappets; camshafts: 1, at centre of Vee; lubrication: rotary pump, full flow filter, 8.3 imp pt, 9.9 US pt, 4.7 l; 1 DFV downdraught twin barrel carburettor; fuel feed: mechanical pump; water-cooled, 31.7 imp pt, 38.1 US pt, 18 l.

TRANSMISSION driving wheels: rear; clutch: single dry plate; gearbox: mechanical; gears: 3, fully synchronized; ratios: I 2.670, II 1.600, III 1, rev 3.440; lever: steering column; final drive: hypoid bevel; axle ratio: 3.150; width of rims: 5.5''; tyres: 7.35 x 14.

PERFORMANCE max speeds: (I) 48 mph, 78 km/h; (II) 71 mph, 115 km/h; (III) 102 mph, 164 km/h; power-weight ratio: 16.7 lb/hp, 7.6 kg/hp - Gran Sedan 16.6 lb/hp, 7.5 kg/hp; carrying capacity: 882 lb, 400 kg; acceleration: standing ¼ mile 19 sec, 0-50 mph (0-80 km/h) 9.8 sec; speed in direct drive at 1,000 rpm: 23 mph, 37 km/h; consumption: 17.4 m/imp gal, 4.3 m/US gal, 16.5 l x 100 km.

CHASSIS integral; front suspension: independent, wishbones (lower trailing links), longitudinal torsion bars, anti-roll bar, telescopic dampers; rear: rigid axle, semi-elliptic leafsprings, telescopic dampers.

STEERING recirculating ball, servo; turns lock to lock: 6.50.

BRAKES front disc, rear drum, servo; swept area: front 156 sq in, 1,006 sq cm, rear 102.3 sq in, 660 sq cm, total 259.3 sq in, 1,672 sq cm.

ELECTRICAL EQUIPMENT 12 V; 45 Ah battery; 480 W alternator; Chrysler electronic distributor; 4 headlamps.

DIMENSIONS AND WEIGHT wheel base: 111 in, 282 cm; tracks: 58.27 in, 148 cm front, 56.30 in, 143 cm rear; length: 195.30 in, 496 cm; width: 71.30 in, 181 cm; height: 54.70 in, 139 cm; ground clearance: 6.30 in, 16 cm; weight: 3,301 lb, 1,497 kg - Gran Sedan 3,285 lb, 1,490 kg; turning circle (between walls): 40.3 ft, 12.3 m; fuel tank: 13.6 imp gal, 16.4 US gal, 62 l.

BODY saloon/sedan; 4 doors; 6 seats, bench front seats.

OPTIONAL ACCESSORIES Torqueflite automatic transmission with 3 ratios (I 2.540, II 1.450, III 1, rev 2.200), max ratio of converter at stall 2.4, possible manual selection; 3.070 axle ratio; dual exhaust system; metallic spray; air-conditioning.

Dart De Luxo Coupé

See Dart De Luxo Sedan/Gran Sedan, except for:

PRICE EX WORKS: 122,000 cruzeiros

PERFORMANCE power-weight ratio: 16.6 lb/hp, 7.5 kg/hp.

DIMENSIONS AND WEIGHT weight: 3,285 lb, 1,490 kg.

BODY coupé; 2 doors.

OPTIONAL ACCESSORIES 4-speed fully synchronized mechanical gearbox (I 2.670, II 1.860, III 1.300, IV 1, rev 3.140), central lever; Torqueflite automatic transmission not available.

Charger R/T

PRICE EX WORKS: 175,000 cruzeiros

ENGINE front, 4 stroke; 8 cylinders, Vee-slanted at 90°; 318 cu in, 5,212 cc (3.91 x 3.31 in, 99.3 x 84.1 mm); compression ratio: 7.5:1; max power (SAE): 205 hp at 4,400 rpm; max torque (SAE): 304 lb ft, 42 kg m at 2,400 rpm; max engine rpm: 4,800; 39.3 hp/l; cast iron block and head; 5 crankshaft bearings; valves: overhead, in line, push-rods and rockers, hydraulic tappets; camshafts: 1, at centre of Vee; lubrication: rotary pump, full flow filter, 8.3 imp pt, 9.9 US pt, 4.7 l; 1 DFV downdraught twin barrel carburettor; dual exhaust system; fuel feed: mechanical pump; water-cooled, 31.7 imp pt, 38.1 US pt, 18 l.

TRANSMISSION driving wheels: rear; clutch: single dry plate; gearbox: mechanical; gears: 4, fully synchronized; ratios: I 2.670, II 1.860, III 1.300, IV 1, rev 3.140; lever: central; final drive: hypoid bevel; axle ratio: 3.150; width of rims: 5.5''; tyres: 7.35 S x 14.

DODGE Dart De Luxo Coupé

PERFORMANCE max speeds: (I) 39 mph, 62 km/h; (II) 56 mph, 90 km/h; (III) 81 mph, 130 km/h; (IV) 112 mph, 180 km/h; power-weight ratio: 16.3 lb/hp, 7.4 kg/hp; carrying capacity: 882 lb, 400 kg; acceleration: standing ¼ mile 18.5 sec, 0-50 mph (0-80 km/h) 9 sec; speed in direct drive at 1,000 rpm: 23 mph, 37 km/h; consumption: 20.2 m/imp gal, 16.8 m/US gal, 14 l x 100 km.

CHASSIS integral; front suspension: independent, wishbones (lower trailing links), longitudinal torsion bars, anti-roll bar, telescopic dampers; rear: rigid axle, semi-elliptic leafsprings, telescopic dampers.

STEERING recirculating ball, servo; turns lock to lock: 6.50.

BRAKES front disc, rear drum, servo; swept area: front 156 sq in, 1,006 sq cm, rear 102.3 sq in, 660 sq cm, total 259.3 sq in, 1,672 sq cm.

ELECTRICAL EQUIPMENT 12 V; 45 Ah battery; 480 W alternator; Chrysler electronic distributor; 4 headlamps.

DIMENSIONS AND WEIGHT wheel base: 111 in, 282 cm; tracks: 58.27 in, 148 cm front, 56.30 in, 143 cm rear; length: 195.30 in, 496 cm; width: 71.30 in, 181 cm; height: 54.70 in, 139 cm; ground clearance: 6.30 in, 16 cm; weight: 3,341 lb, 1,515 kg; turning circle (between walls): 40.3 ft, 12.3 m; fuel tank: 13.6 imp gal, 16.4 US gal, 62 l.

BODY coupé; 2 doors; 5 seats, separate front seats.

OPTIONAL ACCESSORIES Torqueflite automatic transmission, hydraulic torque converter and planetary gears with 3 ratios (I 2.540, II 1.450, III 1, rev 2.200), max ratio of converter at stall 2.4, possible manual selection; 3.070 axle ratio; air-conditioning.

FIAT   BRAZIL

147 L

ENGINE front, 4 stroke; 4 cylinders, transverse; 64 cu in, 1,049 cc (2.99 x 2.23 in, 76 x 57.8 mm); compression ratio: 7.2:1; max power (SAE): 55 hp at 5,800 rpm; max torque (SAE): 57 lb ft, 7.8 kg m at 3,800 rpm; max engine rpm: 6,000; 52.4 hp/l; light alloy block; 5 crankshaft bearings; valves: overhead; camshafts: 1, overhead; lubrication: gear pump, full flow filter (cartridge), 7 imp pt, 8.5 US pt, 4 l; 1 downdraught carburettor; fuel feed: mechanical pump; water-cooled, 10.2 imp pt, 12.3 US pt, 5.8 l.

TRANSMISSION driving wheels: front; clutch: single dry plate (diaphragm); gearbox: mechanical; gears: 4, fully synchronized; ratios: I 4.091, II 2.235, III 1.455, IV 0.957, rev 3.714; lever: central; final drive: cylindrical gears; axle ratio: 4.417; width of rims: 4''; tyres: 145 SR x 13.

PERFORMANCE max speed: 84 mph, 135 km/h; power-weight ratio: 32.1 lb/hp, 14.5 kg/hp; carrying capacity: 882 lb, 400 kg; acceleration: standing ¼ mile 20.4 sec; consumption: 36.7 m/imp gal, 30.5 m/US gal, 7.7 l x 100 km.

DODGE Charger R/T

FIAT 147 L

CHASSIS integral; front suspension: independent, by McPherson, coil springs/telescopic damper struts, lower wishbones, anti-roll-bar; rear: independent, single wide-based wishbone, transverse anti-roll leafspring, telescopic dampers.

STEERING rack-and-pinion; turns lock to lock: 3.40.

BRAKES front disc, rear drum; lining area: front 12 sq in, 77 sq cm, rear 16.7 sq in, 108 sq cm, total 28.7 sq in, 185 sq cm.

ELECTRICAL EQUIPMENT 12 V; 36 Ah battery; 35 A alternator; 2 headlamps.

DIMENSIONS AND WEIGHT tracks: 50 in, 127 cm front, 50.79 in, 129 cm rear; length: 142.91 in, 363 cm; width: 60.83 in, 154 cm; height: 53.15 in, 135 cm; weight: 1,764 lb, 800 kg; weight distribution: 49.6% front, 50.4% rear; turning circle (between walls): 39 ft, 9.1 m; fuel tank: 8.4 imp gal, 10 US gal, 38 l.

BODY saloon/sedan; 2 + 1 doors; 5 seats, separate front seats; folding rear seat.

FNM   BRAZIL

Alfa Romeo 2300

ENGINE front, 4 stroke; 4 cylinders, vertical, in line; 141 cu in, 2,310 cc (3.46 x 3.74 in, 88 x 95 mm); compression ratio: 7.5:1; max power (SAE): 140 hp at 5,700 rpm; max torque (SAE): 152 lb ft, 21 kg m at 3,500 rpm; max engine rpm: 5,700; 60.6 hp/l; light alloy block and head; 5 crankshaft bearings; valves: overhead, Vee-slanted at 90°, thimble tappets; camshafts: 2, overhead; lubrication: gear pump, filter on by-pass, 12.3 imp pt, 14.8 US pt, 7 l; 1 Solex 35 APAIG downdraught twin barrel carburettor; fuel feed: mechanical pump; water-cooled, 16 imp pt, 19.2 US pt, 9.1 l, electric thermostatic fan.

TRANSMISSION driving wheels: rear; clutch: single dry plate (diaphragm), hydraulically controlled; gearbox: mechanical; gears: 5, fully synchronized; ratios: I 3.303, II 1.985, III 1.353, IV 1, V 0.790, rev 3.008; lever: central; final drive: hypoid bevel; axle ratio: 4.770; width of rims: 6''; tyres: 185 SR x 14.

PERFORMANCE max speeds: (I) 25 mph, 41 km/h; (II) 42 mph, 68 km/h; (III) 62 mph, 100 km/h; (IV) 84 mph, 135 km/h; (V) 106 mph, 170 km/h; power-weight ratio: 19 lb/hp, 8.6 kg/hp; carrying capacity: 1,180 lb, 535 kg; speed in top at 1,000 rpm: 19.3 mph, 31 km/h; consumption: 24.6 m/imp gal, 20.5 m/US gal, 11.5 l x 100 km.

CHASSIS integral; front suspension: independent, wishbones (lower trailing links), coil springs, anti-roll bar, telescopic dampers; rear: rigid axle, trailing lower radius arms, upper transverse Vee radius arm, coil springs/telescopic damper struts.

STEERING worm and roller; turns lock to lock: 4.50.

BRAKES disc (front diameter 11.02 in, 28 cm, rear 11.06 in, 28.1 cm), dual circuit, rear compensator, servo; swept area: front 207.1 sq in, 1,336 sq cm, rear 207.1 sq in, 1,336 sq cm, total 414.2 sq in, 2,672 sq cm.

ELECTRICAL EQUIPMENT 12 V; 54 Ah battery; 420 W alternator; Bosch distributor; 4 headlamps.

DIMENSIONS AND WEIGHT wheel base: 107.48 in, 273 cm; tracks: 55.12 in, 140 cm front, 55.12 in, 140 cm rear; length: 134.65 in, 469 cm; width: 66.54 in, 169 cm; height: 57.48 in, 146 cm; ground clearance: 5.91 in, 15 cm; weight: 2,668 lb, 1,210 kg; turning circle (between walls): 41 ft, 12.6 m; fuel tank: 22 imp gal, 26.4 US gal, 100 l.

BODY saloon/sedan; 4 doors; 5 seats, separate front seats, reclining backrests.

Alfa Romeo 2300 B

See Alfa Romeo 2300, except for:

ENGINE max power (SAE): 141 hp at 5,700 rpm; max torque (SAE): 156 lb ft, 21.5 kg m at 3,500 rpm; 61 hp/l; 1 Solex C-34 EIES downdraught twin barrel carburettor.

PERFORMANCE consumption: 27.6 m/imp gal, 23 m/US gal, 10.2 l x 100 km.

CHASSIS rear suspension: twin transverse linkage bar.

DIMENSIONS AND WEIGHT height: 59.69 in, 144 cm.

BODY built-in headrests.

OPTIONAL ACCESSORIES air-conditioning; tinted glass.

FNM Alfa Romeo 2300 B

Alfa Romeo 2300 TI

See Alfa Romeo 2300, except for:

ENGINE max power (SAE): 149 hp at 5,700 rpm; max torque (SAE): 167 lb ft, 23 kg m at 3,500 rpm; 64.5 hp/l; 2 Solex C-40 DHE downdraught twin barrel carburettor.

PERFORMANCE max speed 109 mph, 175 km/h; power-weight ratio: 18.2 lb/hp, 8.2 kg/hp; consumption: 25.4 m/imp gal, 21 m/US gal, 11.1 l x 100 km.

ELECTRICAL EQUIPMENT 540 W alternator; 4 Iodine headlamps.

DIMENSIONS AND WEIGHT length: 185.82 in, 472 cm; height: 59.69 in, 144 cm; weight: 2,712 lb, 1,230 kg.

BODY luxury equipment; built-in headrests on rear seats.

OPTIONAL ACCESSORIES air-conditioning; tinted glass.

FORD   BRAZIL

Corcel II Base/L/LDO

PRICES EX WORKS: Corcel II Base: 77,990 cruzeiros
Corcel II L: 85,649 cruzeiros
Corcel II LDO: 100,344 cruzeiros

ENGINE front, 4 stroke; 4 cylinders, vertical, in line; 83.7 cu in, 1,372 cc (2.96 x 3.03 in, 75.3 x 77 mm); compression ratio: 8:1; max power (DIN) 54 hp at 4,600 rpm; max torque (DIN): 75 lb ft, 10.4 kg m at 2,800 rpm; max engine rpm: 5,800; 39,6 hp/l; cast iron block, light alloy head; 5 crankshaft bearings; valves: overhead, push-rods and rockers; camshafts: 1, in crankcase; lubrication: gear pump, full flow filter, 5.3 imp pt, 6.3 US pt, 3 l; 1 DFV 228 downdraught carburettor; fuel feed: mechanical pump; sealed circuit cooling, water, 7.6 imp pt, 9.1 US pt, 4.3 l.

TRANSMISSION driving wheels: front; clutch: single dry plate; gearbox: mechanical; gears: 4, fully synchronized; ratios: I 3.620, II 2.210, III 1.420, IV 0.970, rev 3.080; lever: central; final drive: hypoid bevel; axle ratio: 4.125; width of rims: 4.5''; tyres: 4.50 x 13.

PERFORMANCE max speeds: (I) 25 mph, 40 km/h; (II) 41 mph, 66 km/h; (III) 63 mph, 101 km/h; (IV) 95 mph, 153 km/h; power-weight ratio: Base 35.2 lb/hp - L 35.5 lb/hp, 16.1 kg/hp - LDO 37.1 lb/hp, 16.8 kg/hp; carrying capacity: 873 lb, 396 kg; acceleration: 0-50 mph (0-80 km/h) 18.6 sec; speed in top at 1,000 rpm: 17 mph, 27 km/h; consumption: 31.3 m/imp gal, 26.2 m/US gal, 9 l x 100 km.

CHASSIS integral; front suspension: independent, wishbones, upper trailing arms, coil springs, anti-roll bar, telescopic dampers; rear: rigid axle, upper and lower trailing arms, coil springs, telescopic dampers.

STEERING rack-and-pinion; turns lock to lock: 3.39.

FORD Corcel II L

BRAKES front disc, rear drum; lining area: total 150 sq in, 968 sq cm.

ELECTRICAL EQUIPMENT 12 V; 42 Ah battery; alternator; Bosch distributor; 2 headlamps.

DIMENSIONS AND WEIGHT wheel base: 96.06 in, 244 cm; tracks: 53.50 in, 136 cm front, 53.14 in, 135 cm rear; length: 175.98 in, 447 cm - LDO 177.16 in, 450 cm; width: 65.35 in, 166 cm; height: 53.14 in, 135 cm; ground clearance: 5.50 in, 14 cm; weight: Base 1,900 lb, 862 kg - L 1,920 lb, 871 kg - LDO 2,002 lb, 908 kg; weight distribution: 59% front, 41% rear; turning circle (between walls): 37.4 ft, 11.4 m; fuel tank: 12.5 imp gal, 15 US gal, 57 l.

BODY saloon/sedan; 2 doors; 5 seats, separate front seats.

OPTIONAL ACCESSORIES servo brake; 5'' wide rims; 5.00 x 13 tyres.

Corcel II Belina Base/L/LDO

See Corcel II Base/L/LDO, except for:

PRICES EX WORKS: Corcel II Berlina Base: 87,260 cruzeiros
Corcel II Berlina L: 92,718 cruzeiros
Corcel II Berlina LDO: 103,737 cruzeiros

PERFORMANCE power-weight ratio: Base 36.4 lb/hp, 16.5 kg/hp - L 36.7 lb/hp, 16.7 kg/hp - LDO 37.4 lb/hp, 16.9

kg/hp; carrying capacity: 1,005 lb, 456 kg; acceleration: 0-50 mph (0-80 km/h) 20.6 sec; consumption: 30 m/imp gal, 25.1 US gal, 9.4 l x 100 km.

DIMENSIONS AND WEIGHT length: 176.77 in, 449 cm - LDO 177.95 in, 452 cm; height: 53.54 in, 136 cm; weight: Base 1,967 lb, 892 kg - L 1,986 lb, 901 kg - LDO 2,022 lb, 917 kg; fuel tank: 13.8 imp gal, 16.6 US gal, 63 l.

BODY estate car/st. wagon; 2+1 doors.

Corcel II GT

See Corcel II Base/L/LDO, except for:

PRICE EX WORKS: 97,031 cruzeiros

ENGINE max power (DIN): 57 hp at 4,800 rpm; max torque (DIN): 72 lb ft, 10 kg m at 2,800 rpm; 41,5 hp/l; 1 Solex 35 DDIS - 2V downdraught carburettor.

PERFORMANCE power-weight ratio: 34.3 lb/hp, 15.6 kg/hp.

DIMENSIONS AND WEIGHT weight: 1,958 lb, 888 kg.

Maverick Sedan Super/ Super Luxo/LDO

ENGINE front, 4 stroke; 4 cylinders, in line; 140.4 cu in, 2,301 cc (3.78 x 3.13 in, 96 x 79.4 mm); compression ratio: 7.8:1; max power (SAE): 99 hp at 5,400 rpm; max torque (SAE): 122 lb ft, 16.9 kg m at 3,200 rpm; max engine rpm: 5,700; 43 hp/l; cast iron block and head; 5 crankshaft bearings; valves: overhead, push-rods and rockers; camshafts: 1, overhead; lubrication: rotary pump, full flow filter, 8.3 imp pt, 9.9 US pt, 4.7 l; 1 Solex downdraught single barrel carburettor; fuel feed: mechanical pump; water-cooled, 13.4 imp pt, 16.1 US pt, 7.6 l.

TRANSMISSION driving wheels: rear; clutch: single dry plate; gearbox: mechanical; gears: 4, fully synchronized; ratios: I 3.569, II 2.378, III 1.531, IV 1, rev 4.229; lever: steering column; final drive: hypoid bevel; axle ratio: 3.920; width of rims: 5''; tyres: 6.95 S x 14 or D 70 S x 14.

PERFORMANCE max speed: 96 mph, 155 km/h; power-weight ratio: 29.1 lb/hp, 13.2 kg/hp; carrying capacity: 882 lb, 400 kg; speed in direct drive at 1,000 rpm: 18 mph, 29 km/h; consumption: 28.8 m/imp gal, 24 m/US gal, 9.8 l x 100 km.

CHASSIS integral; front suspension: independent, wishbones (lower trailing links), coil springs, anti-roll bar, telescopic dampers; rear: rigid axle, semi-elliptic leafsprings, telescopic dampers.

STEERING worm and roller; turns lock to lock: 6.50.

BRAKES front disc, internal radial fins, rear drum; lining area: total 91.6 sq in, 591 sq cm.

ELECTRICAL EQUIPMENT 12 V; 54 Ah battery; 30 A alternator; Motorcraft distributor; 2 headlamps.

DIMENSIONS AND WEIGHT wheel base: 103.15 in, 262 cm; front and rear track: 56.30 in, 143 cm; length: 186.22 in, 473 cm; width: 70.47 in, 179 cm; height: 53.54 in, 136 cm; ground clearance: 6.81 in, 17.3 cm; weight: 3,889 lb, 1,310 kg; turning circle (between walls): 37.4 ft, 11.4 m; fuel tank: 14.3 imp gal, 17.2 US gal, 65 l.

BODY saloon/sedan; 4 doors; 6 seats, bench front seats; (for Super Luxo only) luxury equipment.

VARIATIONS

ENGINE 8 cylinders, Vee-slanted at 90°, 302 cu in, 4,950 cc (4 x 3 in, 101.6 x 76.2 mm), 7.5:1 compression ratio, max power (SAE) 197 hp at 4,600 rpm, max torque (SAE) 286 lb ft, 39.5 kg m at 2,400 rpm, max engine rpm 4,900, 39.8 hp/l, 5 crankshaft bearings, overhead valves with hydraulic tappets, 1 camshaft at centre of Vee, 1 Motorcraft D20F-KB downdraught twin barrel carburettor, cooling system 20.1 imp pt, 24.1 US pt, 11.4 l.
PERFORMANCE max speed 112 mph, 180 km/h, power-weight ratio 15.4 lb/hp, 7 kg/hp, consumption 21.6 m/imp gal, 18 m/US gal, 13.1 l x 100 km.
STEERING recirculating ball, 5.80 turns lock to lock.
ELECTRICAL EQUIPMENT 40 A alternator.

OPTIONAL ACCESSORIES gearbox ratios (I 2.920, II 2.030, III 1.420, IV 1, rev 3.430), 3.070 axle ratio; Select-Shift Cruise-o-Matic automatic transmission, hydraulic torque converter and planetary gears with 3 ratios (I 2.460, II 1.460, III 1, rev 2.200), max ratio of converter at stall 2, possible manual selection, 3.070 axle ratio; 3-speed fully synchronized mechanical gearbox (I 2.920, II 1.750, III 1, rev 3.760), 3.070 axle ratio; recirculating ball steering gear; power-assisted steering; total swept area 338 sq in, 2,180 sq cm; separate front seats; vinyl roof; metallic spray; air-conditioning only with V8 engine.

FORD Maverick Coupé GT-4

FORD Galaxie Landau

Maverick Coupé Super/ Super Luxo/LDO/GT-4

See Maverick Sedan Super/Super Luxo/LDO, except for:

PERFORMANCE power-weight ratio: 28.7 lb/hp, 13 kg/hp.

DIMENSIONS AND WEIGHT length: 179.13 in, 455 cm; weight: 2,833 lb, 1,285 kg; weight distribution: 53.3% front, 44.7% rear; turning circle (between walls): 35.1 ft, 10.7 m.

BODY coupé; 2 doors; 5 seats; (for Super Luxo only) luxury equipment.

Maverick Coupé GT

See Maverick Sedan Super/Super Luxo/LDO, except for:

ENGINE 8 cylinders, Vee-slanted at 90°; 302 cu in, 4,950 cc (4 x 3 in, 101.6 x 76.2 mm); compression ratio: 7.5:1; max power (SAE): 197 hp at 4,600 rpm; max torque (SAE): 286 lb ft, 39.5 kg m at 2,400 rpm; max engine rpm: 4,900; 39.8 hp/l; valves: overhead, in line, push-rods and rockers, hydraulic tappets; camshafts: 1, at centre of Vee; 1 Motorcraft D20F-KB downdraught twin barrel carburettor; cooling system: 20.1 imp pt, 24.1 US pt, 11.4 l.

TRANSMISSION ratios: I 2.920, II 2.030, III 1.420, IV 1, rev 3.430; lever: central; axle ratio: 3.070; width of rims: 6''; tyres: D70 S x 14.

PERFORMANCE max speeds: (I) 39 mph, 62 km/h; (II) 56 mph, 90 km/h; (III) 81 mph, 130 km/h; (IV) 114 mph, 183 km/h; power-weight ratio: 15 lb/hp, 6.8 kg/hp; speed in direct drive at 1,000 rpm: 23.6 mph, 38 km/h; consumption: 21.6 m/imp gal, 18 m/US gal, 13.1 l x 100 km.

STEERING recirculating ball, servo; turns lock to lock: 5.80.

BRAKES swept area: total 338 sq in, 2,180 sq cm.

ELECTRICAL EQUIPMENT 40 A alternator.

DIMENSIONS AND WEIGHT length: 180.71 in, 459 cm; height: 53.94 in, 137 cm; weight: 2,955 lb, 1,340 kg; weight distribution: 53.3% front, 44.7% rear; turning circle (between walls): 35.1 ft, 10.7 m.

BODY coupé; 2 doors; 5 seats; separate front seats; air-conditioning.

VARIATIONS

None.

Galaxie 500/LTD/Landau

ENGINE front, 4 stroke; 8 cylinders, Vee-slanted at 90°; 302 cu in, 4,950 cc (4 x 3 in, 101.6 x 76.2 mm); compression ratio: 7.7:1; max power (SAE): 199 hp at 4,600 rpm; max torque (SAE): 288 lb ft, 39.8 kg m at 2,400 rpm; max engine rpm: 4,800; 40.2 hp/l; cast iron block and head; 5 crankshaft bearings; valves: overhead, push-rods and

rockers; camshafts: 1, at centre of Vee; lubrication: gear pump, full flow filter, 8.3 imp pt, 9.9 US pt, 4.7 l; 1 Motorcraft downdraught twin barrel carburettor; fuel feed: mechanical pump; water-cooled, 21.5 imp pt, 25.8 US pt, 12.2 l.

TRANSMISSION driving wheels: rear; clutch: single dry plate; gearbox: mechanical; gears: 3, fully synchronized; ratios: I 2.920, II 1.750, III 1, rev 3.760; lever: steering column; final drive: hypoid bevel; axle ratio: 3.540; width of rims: 5''; tyres: 7.75 x 15.

PERFORMANCE max speeds: (I) 35 mph, 56 km/h; (II) 58 mph, 94 km/h; (III) 103 mph, 165 km/h; power-weight ratio: 19.4 lb/hp, 8.6 kg/hp; carrying capacity: 1,069 lb, 485 kg; speed in direct drive at 1,000 rpm: 22.4 mph, 36 km/h; consumption: 19.6 m/imp gal, 16.3 m/US gal, 14.4 l x 100 km.

CHASSIS box-type ladder frame; front suspension: independent, wishbones, lower trailing arms, coil springs, anti-roll bar, telescopic dampers; rear: rigid axle, lower trailing arms, upper torque arms, coil springs, telescopic dampers.

STEERING recirculating ball, servo; turns lock to lock: 4.

BRAKES front disc, internal radial fins, rear drum, servo; lining area: total 110.2 sq in, 711 sq cm.

ELECTRICAL EQUIPMENT 12 V; 54 Ah battery; 50 A alternator; 4 headlamps.

DIMENSIONS AND WEIGHT wheel base: 119.02 in, 302 cm; front and rear track: 62.42 in, 158 cm; length: 212.99 in, 541 cm; width: 78.74 in, 200 cm; height: 55.51 in, 141 cm; ground clearance: 5.51 in, 14 cm; weight: 3,859 lb, 1,750 kg; turning circle (between walls): 45.3 ft, 13.8 m; fuel tank: 16.7 imp gal, 20.1 US gal, 76 l.

BODY saloon/sedan; 4 doors; 6 seats, bench front seats; (for LTD only) luxury equipment.

OPTIONAL ACCESSORIES Ford-o-Matic automatic transmission, hydraulic torque converter and planetary gears with 3 ratios (I 2.460, II 1.460, III 1, rev 2.200), max ratio of converter at stall 2.1, possible manual selection, 3.310 axle ratio; vinyl roof (only for Galaxie 500); air-conditioning.

GURGEL

BRAZIL

X-12/X-12 TR

PRICE EX WORKS: 63,180 cruzeiros

ENGINE Volkswagen, rear, 4 stroke; 4 cylinders, horizontally opposed; 96.7 cu in, 1,584 cc (3.37 x 2.72 in, 85.5 x 69 mm); compression ratio: 7.2:1; max power (DIN): 50 hp at 4,200 rpm; max torque (DIN): 80 lb ft, 11 kg m at 2,200 rpm; max engine rpm: 4,600; 31.6 hp/l; block with cast iron liners and light alloy fins, light alloy head; 4 crankshaft bearings; valves: overhead, push-rods and rockers; camshafts: 1, central, lower; lubrication: gear pump, oil cooler, 4.4 imp pt, 5.3 US pt, 2.5 l; 1 Solex H 30 Pic downdraught single barrel carburettor; fuel feed: mechanical pump; air-cooled.

TRANSMISSION driving wheels: rear; clutch: single dry plate; gearbox: mechanical; gears: 4, fully synchronized; ratios: I 3.800, II 2.060, III 1.320, IV 0.890, rev 3.880; lever: central; final drive: spiral bevel; axle ratio: 4.375; width of rims: 4.5''; tyres: 7.35 x 15.

PERFORMANCE max speeds: (I) 17 mph, 27 km/h; (II) 32 mph, 51 km/h; (III) 50 mph, 80 km/h; (IV) 73 mph, 118 km/h; power-weight ratio: 33.5 lb/hp, 15.2 kg/hp; carrying capacity: 772 lb, 350 kg; speed in top at 1,000 rpm: 19.3 mph, 31 km/h; consumption: 28.2 m/imp gal, 23.5 m/US gal, 10 l x 100 km.

CHASSIS backbone platform; front suspension: independent, twin swinging longitudinal trailing arms, transverse laminated torsion bars, telescopic dampers; rear: independent, swinging semi-axles, swinging longitudinal trailing arms, transverse torsion bars, telescopic dampers.

STEERING worm and roller; turns lock to lock: 2.50.

BRAKES drum; swept area: front 20.5 sq in, 132 sq cm, rear 20.8 sq in, 134 sq cm, total 41.2 sq in, 266 sq cm.

ELECTRICAL EQUIPMENT 12 V; 36 Ah battery; 350 W dynamo; Bosch distributor; 2 headlamps.

GURGEL X-12

319

X-12/X-12 TR

DIMENSIONS AND WEIGHT wheel base: 81.50 in, 207 cm; tracks: 52.36 in, 133 cm front, 52.76 in, 134 cm rear: length: 128.74 in, 328 cm; width: 62.99 in, 160 cm; height: 59.45 in, 151 cm; ground clearance: 9.84 in, 25 cm; weight: 1,676 lb, 760 kg; turning circle (between walls): 31.2 ft, 9.5 m; fuel tank: 8.8 imp gal, 10.6 US gal, 40 l.

BODY in plastic material; 2 doors; 4 seats, separate front seats (X-12 open in plastic material, no doors).

OPTIONAL ACCESSORIES limited slip differential; anti-roll bar on front and rear suspension.

X-20

PRICE EX WORKS: 81,940 cruzeiros

TRANSMISSION axle ratio: 4.125; tyres: 7.75 x 15.

PERFORMANCE max speeds: (I) 16 mph, 25 km/h; (II) 30 mph, 48 km/h; (III) 47 mph, 75 km/h; (IV) 62 mph, 100 km/h; power-weight ratio: 44.1 lb/hp, 20 kg/hp; consumption: 23.5 m/imp gal, 19.6 m/US gal, 12 l x 100 km.

DIMENSIONS AND WEIGHT wheel base: 88.19 in, 224 cm; front and rear track: 56.69 in, 144 cm; length: 144.88 in, 368 cm; width: 70.87 in, 180 cm; height: 74.80 in, 190 cm; ground clearance: 13.78 in, 35 cm; weight: 2,205 lb, 1,000 kg; fuel tank: 17.6 imp gal, 21.1 US gal, 80 l.

BODY 8 seats.

LAFER   BRAZIL

MP

PRICE EX WORKS: 85,100 cruzeiros

ENGINE Volkswagen, rear, 4 stroke; 4 cylinders, horizontally opposed; 96.7 cu in, 1,584 cc (3.37 x 2.72 in, 85.5 x 69 mm); compression ratio: 7.2:1; max power (DIN): 50 hp at 4,200 rpm; max torque (DIN): 80 lb ft, 11 kg m at 2,200 rpm; max engine rpm: 4,600; 31.6 hp/l; block with cast iron liners and light alloy fins, light alloy head; 4 crankshaft bearings; valves: overhead, in line, push-rods and rockers; camshafts: 1, central, lower; lubrication: gear pump, filter in sump, oil cooler, 4.4 imp pt, 5.3 US pt, 2.5 l; 2 Solex H 32 twin barrel carburettors; fuel feed: mechanical pump; air-cooled.

TRANSMISSION driving wheels: rear; clutch: single dry plate; gearbox: mechanical; gears: 4, fully synchronized; ratios: I 3.800, II 2.060, III 1.320, IV 0.890, rev 3.880; lever: central; final drive: spiral bevel; axle ratio: 4.125; width of rims: 5''; tyres: 5.60 x 15.

PERFORMANCE max speeds: (I) 22 mph, 35 km/h; (II) 39 mph, 62 km/h; (III) 62 mph, 100 km/h; (IV) 86 mph,

LAFER MP

138 km/h; power-weight ratio: 33.5 lb/hp, 15.2 kg/hp; carrying capacity: 353 lb, 160 kg; speed in top at 1,000 rpm: 19.3 mph, 31 km/h; consumption: 31 m/imp gal, 25.8 m/US gal, 9.1 l x 100 km.

CHASSIS backbone platform, rear auxiliary frame; front suspension: independent, twin swinging longitudinal trailing arms, transverse laminated torsion bars, anti-roll bar, telescopic dampers; rear: independent, semi-trailing arms, transverse compensating torsion bars, anti-roll bar, telescopic dampers.

STEERING worm and roller; turns lock to lock: 2.60.

BRAKES front disc (diameter 10.94 in, 27.8 cm), rear drum; swept area: front 12.4 sq in, 80 sq cm, rear 69.8 sq in, 450 sq cm, total 82.2 sq in, 530 sq cm.

ELECTRICAL EQUIPMENT 12 V; 36 Ah battery; 35 A alternator; Bosch distributor; 2 headlamps.

DIMENSIONS AND WEIGHT wheel base: 94.49 in, 240 cm; tracks: 51.97 in, 132 cm front, 53.54 in, 136 cm rear; length: 153.94 in, 391 cm; width: 61.81 in, 157 cm; height: 53.15 in, 135 cm; ground clearance: 5.70 in, 14 cm; weight: 1,676 lb, 760 kg; turning circle (between walls): 36.1 ft, 11 m; fuel tank: 10.1 imp gal, 12.1 US gal, 46 l.

BODY roadster; 2 doors; 2 seats.

OPTIONAL ACCESSORIES 175 SR x 14 tyres with light alloy wheels; hardtop.

LL

ENGINE front, 4 stroke; 6 cylinders, in line; 250 cu in, 4,097 cc (3.87 x 3.53 in, 98.4 x 89.6 mm); compression ratio: 8:1; max power (DIN): 169 hp at 4,800 rpm; max torque (DIN): 261 lb ft, 36 kg m at 2,400 rpm; max engine rpm: 5,400; 42.2 hp/l; cast iron block and head; 7 crankshaft bearings; valves: overhead, in line, push-rods and rockers; camshafts: 1, side; lubrication: gear pump, full flow filter, 7 imp pt, 8.5 US pt, 4 l; 1 Solex H 40 EIS downdraught single barrel carburettor; fuel feed: mechanical and electric pump; water-cooled, 33.4 imp pt, 40.2 US pt, 19 l.

TRANSMISSION driving wheels: rear; clutch: single dry plate; gearbox: mechanical; gears: 4, fully synchronized; ratios: I 2.790, II 2.020, III 1.390, IV 1, rev 3.570; lever: central; final drive: hypoid bevel; axle ratio: 3.080; width of rims: 8''; tyres: 70 HR x 14.

PERFORMANCE max speeds: (I) 45 mph, 73 km/h; (II) 63 mph, 101 km/h; (III) 91 mph, 147 km/h; (IV) 137 mph, 220 km/h; power-weight ratio: 17.6 lb/hp, 7.9 kg/hp; carrying capacity: 706 lb, 320 kg; acceleration: standing ¼ mile 16.2 sec, 0-50 mph (0-80 km/h) 7.5 sec; speed in direct drive at 1,000 rpm: 25 mph, 41 km/h; consumption: 19.5 m/imp gal, 16.2 m/US gal, 14.5 l x 100 km.

CHASSIS integral; front suspension: independent, wishbones, coil springs, anti-roll bar, telescopic dampers; rear: rigid axle, longitudinal trailing arms, coil springs, telescopic dampers.

STEERING recirculating ball, servo; turns lock to lock: 3.75.

BRAKES front disc, rear drum, servo; swept area: front 114.4 sq in, 738 sq cm, rear 58.9 sq in, 380 sq cm, total 173.3 sq in, 1,118 sq cm.

ELECTRICAL EQUIPMENT 12 V; 60 Ah battery; 55 A alternator; Bosch distributor; 4 headlamps.

DIMENSIONS AND WEIGHT wheel base: 105.12 in, 267 cm; tracks: 57.09 in, 145 cm front, 58.66 in, 149 cm rear; length: 177.95 in, 452 cm; width: 69.68 in, 177 cm; height: 50.79 in, 129 cm; ground clearance: 7.09 in, 18 cm; weight: 2,977 lb, 1,350 kg; weight distribution: 53% front, 47% rear; turning circle (between walls): 41 ft, 12.5 m; fuel tank: 18.9 imp gal, 22.7 US gal, 86 l.

BODY coupé; 2 doors; 2 + 2 seats, separate front seats.

OPTIONAL ACCESSORIES 0.930 gearbox ratio in IV, automatic transmission.

PUMA   BRAZIL

Mini

ENGINE front, 4 stroke; 2 cylinders, horizontally opposed; 46.4 cu in, 760 cc (3.27 x 2.72 in, 83 x 69 mm); compression ratio: 7.6:1; max power (SAE): 30 hp at 4,500 rpm; max torque (SAE): 43 lb ft, 6 kg m at 3,000 rpm; max engine rpm: 5,000; 39.5 hp/l; light alloy block and head; 3 crankshaft bearings; valves: overhead, Vee-slanted, push-rods and rockers; camshafts: 1, central; lubrication: gear pump, filter in sump, 3.5 imp pt, 4.2 US pt, 2 l; 1 Solex 28

LAFER LL

downdraught single barrel carburettor; fuel feed: mechanical pump; air-cooled.

TRANSMISSION driving wheels: front; clutch: single dry plate; gearbox: mechanical; gears: 4, fully synchronized; lever: central; final drive: spiral bevel; width of rims: 4.5''; tyres: 135 x 13.

PERFORMANCE max speed: 65 mph, 105 km/h; power-weight ratio: 36.8 lb/hp, 16.7 kg/hp; consumption: 56.5 m/imp gal, 47 m/US gal, 5 l x 100 km.

CHASSIS tubular; front suspension: independent, twin swinging longitudinal trailing arms, transverse laminated torsion bars, telescopic dampers; rear: independent, swinging longitudinal trailing arms, transverse torsion bars, telescopic dampers.

STEERING rack-and-pinion; turns lock to lock: 4.

BRAKES drum.

ELECTRICAL EQUIPMENT 12 V; 44 Ah battery; 35 A alternator; Bosch distributor; 2 headlamps.

DIMENSIONS AND WEIGHT wheel base: 70.47 in, 179 cm; length: 104.80 in, 266 cm; width: 58.27 in, 148 cm; height: 53.94 in, 137 cm; ground clearance: 6.69 in, 17 cm; weight: 1,103 lb, 500 kg; fuel tank: 6.6 imp gal, 7.9 US gal, 30 l.

BODY saloon/sedan, in plastic material; 2 doors; 2 seats.

PUMA GTS 1600

GTE 1600

PRICE EX WORKS: 134,000 cruzeiros

ENGINE Volkswagen, rear, 4 stroke; 4 cylinders, horizontally opposed; 96.7 cu in, 1,584 cc (3.37 x 2.72 in, 85.5 x 69 mm); compression ratio: 9:1; max power (SAE): 90 hp at 5,800 rpm; max torque (SAE): 96 lb ft, 13.2 kg m at 3,000 rpm; max engine rpm: 6,000; 56.8 hp/l; block with cast iron liners and light alloy fins, light alloy head; 4 crankshaft bearings; valves: overhead, push-rods and rockers; camshafts: 1, central, lower; lubrication: gear pump, filter in sump, oil cooler, 4.4 imp pt, 5.3 US pt, 2.5 l; 2 Solex-Brosol H40 EIS downdraught single barrel carburettors; fuel feed: mechanical pump; air-cooled.

TRANSMISSION driving wheels: rear; clutch: single dry plate; gearbox: mechanical; gears: 4, fully synchronized; ratios: I 3.800, II 2.060, III 1.320, IV 0.890, rev 3.880; lever: central; final drive: spiral bevel; axle ratio: 4.125; width of rims: 6''; tyres: front 185/70HR x 14, rear 195/70HR x 14.

PERFORMANCE max speeds: (I) 26 mph, 42 km/h; (II) 47 mph, 76 km/h; (III) 75 mph, 120 km/h; (IV) 113 mph, 182 km/h; power-weight ratio: 18.4 lb/hp, 8.3 kg/hp; carrying capacity: 507 lb, 230 kg; acceleration: 0-50 mph (0-80 km/h) 12.5 sec; speed in top at 1,000 rpm: 19.9 mph, 32 km/h; consumption: 35.3 m/imp gal, 29.4 m/US gal, 8 l x 100 km.

CHASSIS backbone, rear auxiliary frame; front suspension: independent, twin swinging longitudinal trailing arms, transverse torsion bars, anti-roll bar, telescopic dampers; rear: independent, semi-trailing arms, transverse linkage by oblique swinging trailing arms, transverse torsion bars, telescopic dampers.

STEERING worm and roller; turns lock to lock: 2.70.

BRAKES front disc (diameter 10.94 in, 27.8 cm), rear drum; lining area: front 11.2 sq in, 72 sq cm, rear 52.6 sq in, 339 sq cm, total 63.8 sq in, 441 sq cm.

ELECTRICAL EQUIPMENT 12 V; 36 Ah battery; 350 W alternator; Bosch distributor; 2 headlamps.

DIMENSIONS AND WEIGHT wheel base: 84.65 in, 215 cm; tracks: 54.33 in, 138 cm front, 55.11 in, 140 cm rear; length: 157.48 in, 400 cm; width: 65.55 in, 166 cm; height: 47.24 in, 120 cm; ground clearance: 5.98 in, 15.2 cm; weight: 1,654 lb, 750 kg; weight distribution: 40% front, 60% rear; turning circle (between walls): 32.5 ft, 9.9 m; fuel tank: 8.8 imp gal, 10.6 US gal, 40 l.

BODY coupé, in plastic material; 2 doors; 2 seats, reclining backrests, built-in headrests; light alloy wheels.

VARIATIONS

ENGINE 109.8 cu in, 1,800 cc; 115.9 cu in, 1,900 cc; 122 cu in, 2,000 cc; 128.1 cu in, 2,100 cc.

OPTIONAL ACCESSORIES 4-speed fully synchronized mechanical gearbox (I 2.570, II 1.610, III 1.240, IV 0.960, rev 3.880), 4.375 axle ratio; 4-speed fully synchronized mechanical gearbox (I 1.740, II 1.320, III 1.120, IV 0.960, rev 3.880), 3.880 axle ratio; ZF limited slip differential; anti-roll bar on rear suspension.

GTS 1600

See GTE 1600, except for:

PRICE EX WORKS: 140,000 cruzeiros

BODY sports.

OPTIONAL ACCESSORIES hardtop.

GTB

PRICE EX WORKS: 204,000 cruzeiros

ENGINE front, 4 stroke; 6 cylinders, in line; 250 cu in, 4,097 cc (3.87 x 3.52 in, 98.4 x 89.5 mm); compression ratio: 7.8:1; max power (SAE): 171 hp at 4,800 rpm; max torque (SAE): 236 lb ft, 32.5 kg m at 2,600 rpm; max engine rpm: 5,000; 41.7 hp/l; cast iron block and head; 7 crankshaft bearings; valves: overhead, in line, push-rods and rockers, hydraulic tappets; camshafts: 1, side; lubrication: gear pump, full flow filter, 7 imp pt, 8.5 US pt, 4 l; 1 DFV or Solex-Brosol 40 downdraught single barrel carburettor; fuel feed: mechanical pump; water-cooled, 18 imp pt, 21.6 US pt, 10.2 l.

TRANSMISSION driving wheels: rear; clutch: single dry plate (diaphragm), hydraulically controlled; gearbox: mechanical; gears: 4, fully synchronized; ratios: I 3.070, II 2.020, III 1.390, IV 1, rev 3.570; lever: central; final drive: hypoid bevel; axle ratio: 3.080; width of rims: front 7'', rear 8''; tyres: front 205/70HR x 14, rear 215/70HR x 14.

PERFORMANCE max speeds: (I) 40 mph, 64 km/h; (II) 61 mph, 98 km/h; (III) 88 mph, 142 km/h; (IV) 123 mph, 198 km/h; power-weight ratio: 12.6 lb/hp, 5.7 kg/hp; carrying capacity: 617 lb, 280 kg; speed in direct drive at 1,000 rpm: 24.6 mph, 39.6 km/h; consumption: 21.4 m/imp gal, 17.8 m/US gal, 13.2 l x 100 km.

CHASSIS box-type perimeter frame with cross members; front suspension: independent, wishbones (lower trailing links), coil springs, telescopic dampers; rear: rigid axle, twin upper longitudinal leading arms, lower transverse arms, telescopic dampers.

STEERING worm and roller.

BRAKES front disc, rear drum, servo.

ELECTRICAL EQUIPMENT 12 V; 44 Ah battery; 32 A alternator; Bosch distributor; 2 iodine headlamps.

DIMENSIONS AND WEIGHT wheel base: 95.28 in, 242 cm; front and rear track: 55.51 in, 141 cm; length: 169.29 in, 430 cm; width: 68.50 in, 174 cm; height: 49.61 in, 126 cm; ground clearance: 5.91 in, 15 cm; weight: 2,161 lb, 980 kg; turning circle (between walls): 33.8 ft, 10.3 m; fuel tank: 11.9 imp gal, 14.3 US gal, 54 l.

BODY coupé; 2 doors; 2 + 2 seats, separate front seats, reclining backrests; light alloy wheels; tinted glass; air-conditioning.

VOLKSWAGEN   BRAZIL

1300/1300 L Limousine

PRICES EX WORKS: 1300:   49,323 cruzeiros
1300 L: 51,511 cruzeiros

ENGINE rear, 4 stroke; 4 cylinders, horizontally opposed; 78.4 cu in, 1,285 cc (3.03 x 2.72 in, 77 x 69 mm); compression ratio: 6.8:1; max power (DIN): 38 hp at 4,000 rpm; max torque (DIN): 62 lb ft, 8.5 kg m at 2,000 rpm; max engine rpm: 4,600; 29.6 hp/l; cylinder block with cast iron liners and light alloy head; 4 crankshaft bearings; valves: overhead, push-rods and rockers; camshafts: 1, central, lower; lubrication: gear pump, filter in sump, oil cooler, 4.4 imp pt, 5.3 US pt, 2.5 l; 1 Solex H 30 PIC downdraught single barrel carburettor; fuel feed: mechanical pump; air-cooled.

TRANSMISSION driving wheels: rear; clutch: single dry plate; gearbox: mechanical; gears: 4, fully synchronized; ratios: I 3.800, II 2.060, III 1.320, IV 0.880, rev 3.880; lever: central; final drive: spiral bevel; axle ratio: 4.375; width of rims: 4.5''; tyres: 5.60 x 15.

PERFORMANCE max speeds: (I) 17.4 mph, 28 km/h; (II) 32 mph, 52 km/h; (III) 50 mph, 80 km/h; (IV) 75 mph, 120 km/h; power-weight ratio: 45.2 lb/hp, 20.5 kg/hp; carrying capacity: 838 lb, 380 kg; acceleration: 0-50 mph (0-80 km/h)

VOLKSWAGEN 1300 L Limousine

1300/1300 L LIMOUSINE

14.3 sec; speed in top at 1,000 rpm: 18.6 mph, 30 km/h; consumption: 39.8 m/imp gal, 33.1 m/US gal, 7.1 l x 100 km.

CHASSIS backbone platform; front suspension: independent, twin swinging longitudinal trailing arms, transverse laminated torsion bars, anti-roll bar, telescopic dampers; rear: independent, swinging semi-axles, swinging longitudinal trailing arms, transverse torsion bars, telescopic dampers.

STEERING worm and roller, telescopic damper; turns lock to lock: 2.60.

BRAKES drum; lining area: total 112.9 sq in, 728 sq cm.

ELECTRICAL EQUIPMENT 12 V; 36 Ah battery; 350 W dynamo; Bosch distributor; 2 headlamps.

DIMENSIONS AND WEIGHT wheel base: 94.49 in, 240 cm; tracks: 51.18 in, 130 cm front, 50.79 in, 129 cm rear; length: 158.66 in, 403 cm; width: 60.63 in, 154 cm; height: 59.06 in, 150 cm; ground clearance: 5.91 in, 15 cm; weight: 1,720 lb, 780 kg; turning circle (between walls): 36.1 ft, 11 m; fuel tank: 9 imp gal, 10.8 US gal, 41 l.

BODY saloon/sedan; 2 doors; 5 seats, separate front seats, adjustable backrests.

OPTIONAL ACCESSORIES heating.

1600 Limousine

See 1300 Limousine, except for:

PRICE EX WORKS: 52,232 cruzeiros

ENGINE 96.7 cu in, 1,584 cc (3.37 x 2.72 in, 85.5 x 69 mm); compression ratio: 7.2:1; max power (DIN): 56 hp at 4,200 rpm; max torque (DIN): 80 lb ft, 11 kg m at 3,000 rpm; 35.3 hp/l; 2 Solex 32 PDSIT downdraught single barrel carburettors.

TRANSMISSION axle ratio: 4.125; width of rims: 5''; tyres: 5.90-x 14.

PERFORMANCE max speed: 86 mph, 138 km/h; power-weight ratio: 31.4 lb/hp, 14.3 kg/hp; acceleration: 0-50 mph (0-80 km/h) 10.2 sec; consumption: 32.1 m/imp gal, 26.7 m/US gal, 8.8 l x 100 km.

BRAKES front disc (diameter 10.94 in, 27.8 cm); rear drum; lining area: front 11.8 sq in, 76 sq cm, rear 56.4 sq in, 364 sq cm, total 68.2 sq in, 440 sq cm.

DIMENSIONS AND WEIGHT tracks: 51.97 in, 132 cm front, 53.15 in, 135 cm rear.

BODY luxury equipment.

Passat Series

PRICES EX WORKS

1 Passat 2-door Limousine	76,194	cruzeiros
2 Passat 4-door Limousine	77,648	cruzeiros
3 Passat L 2-door Limousine	78,146	cruzeiros
4 Passat L 4-door Limousine	78,965	cruzeiros
5 Passat LS 2-door Limousine	84,571	cruzeiros
6 Passat TS 2-door Limousine	91,516	cruzeiros
7 Passat LSE 4-door Limousine	—	

Power team:	Standard for:	Optional for:
65 hp	from 1 to 5	—
80 hp	6,7	—

65 hp power team

ENGINE front, slanted 20° to right, 4 stroke; 4 cylinders, in line; 89.8 cu in, 1,471 cc (3.01 x 3.15 in, 76.5 x 80 mm); compression ratio: 7.4:1; max power (DIN): 65 hp at 5,600 rpm; max torque (DIN): 75 lb ft, 10.3 kg m at 3,000 rpm; max engine rpm: 6,500; 44.2 hp/l; cast iron block, light alloy head; 5 crankshaft bearings; valves: overhead, in line, thimble tappets; camshafts: 1, overhead, cogged belt; lubrication: gear pump, full flow filter, 5.3 imp pt, 6.3 US pt, 3 l; 1 Solex H 35 PDSI (T) downdraught single barrel carburettor; fuel feed: mechanical pump; water-cooled, 10.9 imp pt, 13.1 US pt, 6.2 l, electric thermostatic fan.

TRANSMISSION driving wheels: front; clutch: single dry plate (diaphragm); gearbox: mechanical; gears: 4, fully synchronized; ratios: I 3.454, II 1.940, III 1.290, IV 0.910, rev 3.170; lever: central; final drive: spiral bevel; axle ratio: 4.111; width of rims: 4.5''; tyres: 155 SR x 13.

VOLKSWAGEN Passat TS 2-door Limousine

PERFORMANCE max speed: 90 mph, 145 km/h; power-weight ratio: 29.2 lb/hp, 13.2 kg/hp - Passat 4-door/L 4-door 30 lb/hp, 13.6 kg/hp; carrying capacity: 992 lb, 450 kg - Passat 4-door/L 4-door 937 lb, 425 kg; speed in top at 1,000 rpm: 16.5 mph, 26.6 km/h; consumption: 34 m/imp gal, 28.3 m/US gal, 8.3 l x 100 km.

CHASSIS integral, front auxiliary subframe; front suspension: independent, by McPherson, lower wishbones, anti-roll bar, coil springs/telescopic damper struts; rear: rigid axle, trailing radius arms, transverse linkage bar, coil springs, anti-roll bar, telescopic dampers.

STEERING rack-and-pinion, telescopic damper.

BRAKES front disc (diameter 9.41 in, 23.9 cm), rear drum, servo.

ELECTRICAL EQUIPMENT 12 V; 36 Ah battery; 35 A alternator; Bosch distributor; 2 headlamps.

DIMENSIONS AND WEIGHT wheel base: 97.24 in, 247 cm; tracks: 52.76 in, 134 cm front, 52.36 in, 133 cm rear; length: 165.60 in, 421 cm; width: 62.99 in, 160 cm; height: 53.35 in, 135 cm; ground clearance: 5.12 in, 13 cm; weight: 1,896 lb, 860 kg - Passat 4-door/L 4-door 1,951 lb, 885 kg; turning circle (between walls): 33.8 ft, 10.3 m; fuel tank: 9.9 imp gal, 11.9 US gal, 45 l.

BODY saloon/sedan; 5 seats, separate front seats, reclining backrests; for L and LS luxury equipment.

80 hp power team

See 65 hp power team, except for:

ENGINE 96.9 cu in, 1,588 cc (3.13 x 3.15 in, 79.5 x 80 mm); compression ratio: 7.5:1; max power (DIN): 80 hp at 5,600 rpm; max torque (DIN): 87 lb ft, 12 kg m at 3,000 rpm; 50.4 hp/l; 1 Solex H 32/35 TDID (T) downdraught single barrel carburettor.

TRANSMISSION gearbox ratios: I 3.454, II 1.950, III 1.290 IV 0.910, rev 3.170; tyres: 175 SR x 13 or 175 HR x 13.

PERFORMANCE max speed: 99 mph, 160 km/h; power-weight ratio: 23.7 lb/hp, 10.7 kg/hp - LSE 24.4 lb/hp, 11.1 kg/hp; carrying capacity: LSE 937 lb, 425 kg; consumption: 34.9 m/imp gal, 28 m/US gal, 8.1 l x 100 km.

ELECTRICAL EQUIPMENT 42 Ah battery; TS 4 headlamps.

DIMENSIONS AND WEIGHT weight: LSE 1,951 lb, 885 kg.

BODY built-in headrests; LSE executive equipment.

OPTIONAL ACCESSORIES metallic spray; heating; air-conditioning; heated rear window.

Brasilia 2-door/4-door

PRICE EX WORKS: 63,674 cruzeiros

ENGINE rear, 4 stroke; 4 cylinders, horizontally opposed; 96.7 cu in, 1,584 cc (3.37 x 2.72 in, 85.5 x 69 mm); compression ratio: 7.2:1; max power (DIN): 54 hp at 4,200 rpm; max torque (DIN): 78 lb ft, 10.8 kg m at 3,000 rpm; max engine rpm: 4,600; 34.1 hp/l; cylinder block with cast iron liners and light alloy fins, light alloy head; 4 crankshaft bearings; valves: overhead, push-rods and rockers; camshafts: 1, central, lower; lubrication: gear pump, filter in sump, oil cooler, 4.4 imp pt, 5.3 US pt, 2.5 l; 2 Solex H 32 PDSI downdraught single barrel carburettors; fuel feed: mechanical pump; air-cooled.

TRANSMISSION driving wheels: rear; clutch: single dry plate; gearbox: mechanical; gears: 4, fully synchronized; ratios: I 3.800, II 2.060, III 1.320, IV 0.880, rev 3.880; lever: central; final drive: spiral bevel; axle ratio: 4.125; width of rims: 5''; tyres: 5.90 x 14.

PERFORMANCE max speeds: (I) 20 mph, 32 km/h; (II) 36 mph, 58 km/h; (III) 57 mph, 92 km/h; (IV) 86 mph, 138 km/h; power-weight ratio: 36.3 lb/hp, 16.5 kg/hp; carrying capacity: 926 lb, 420 kg; speed in top at 1,000 rpm: 19.3 mph, 31 km/h; consumption: 32.5 m/imp gal, 27 m/US gal, 8.7 l x 100 km.

CHASSIS backbone platform, rear auxiliary frame; front suspension: independent, twin swinging longitudinal trailing arms, transverse torsion bars, anti-roll bar, telescopic dampers; rear: independent, semi-trailing arms, transverse compensating torsion bar, anti-roll bar, telescopic dampers.

STEERING worm and roller, telescopic damper; turns lock to lock: 2.70.

BRAKES front disc (diameter 10.94 in, 27.8 cm), rear drum; lining area: total 38.4 sq in, 248 sq cm.

VOLKSWAGEN Brasilia 4-door

VOLKSWAGEN Variant II

ELECTRICAL EQUIPMENT 12 V; 36 Ah battery; 35 A alternator; Bosch distributor; 4 headlamps.

DIMENSIONS AND WEIGHT wheel base: 94.49 in, 240 cm; tracks: 51.97 in, 132 cm front, 53.54 in, 136 cm rear; length: 157.87 in, 401 cm; width 63.39 in, 161 cm; height: 56.30 in, 143 cm; weight: 1,962 lb, 890 kg; turning circle (between walls): 36.1 ft, 11 m; fuel tank: 10.1 imp gal, 12.1 US gal, 46 l.

BODY saloon/sedan; 2 doors; 4-door (only for export); 5 seats, separate front seats, adjustable backrests.

OPTIONAL ACCESSORIES heating; heated rear window; metallic spray.

Variant II

ENGINE rear, 4 stroke; 4 cylinders, horizontally opposed; 196.7 cu in, 1,584 cc (3.36 x 2.71 in, 85.5 x 69 mm); compression ratio: 7.2:1; max power (DIN): 56 hp at 4,200 rpm; max torque (DIN): 80 lb ft, 11 kg m at 2,800 rpm; max engine rpm: 4,600; 35.3 hp/l; cylinder block with cast iron liners and light alloy fins, light alloy head; 4 crankshaft bearings; valves: overhead, push-rods and rockers; camshafts: 1, central, lower; lubrication: gear pump, filter in sump, oil cooler, 4.4 imp pt, 5.3 US pt, 2.5 l; 2 Solex 32 PDSIT carburettors; fuel feed: mechanical pump; air-cooled.

TRANSMISSION driving wheels: rear; clutch: single dry plate; gearbox: mechanical; gears: 4, fully synchronized; ratios: I 3.800, II 2.060, III 1.320, IV 0.880, rev 3.880; lever: central; final drive: spiral bevel; axle ratio: 4.375; width of rims: 5''; tyres: 175 x 14.

PERFORMANCE max speeds: (I) 19 mph, 31 km/h; (II) 36 mph, 58 km/h; (III) 59 mph, 95 km/h; (IV) 86 mph, 138 km/h; power-weight ratio: 38.2 lb/hp, 17.3 kg/hp; carrying capacity: 1,102 lb, 500 kg; acceleration: 0-50 mph (0-80 km/h) 12.5 sec; speed in top at 1,000 rpm: 19.9 mph, 32 km/h; consumption: 30.4 m/imp gal, 25.3 m/US gal, 9.3 l x 100 km.

CHASSIS backbone platform, rear auxiliary frame; front suspension: independent, by McPherson, lower wishbones, anti-roll bar, coil springs/telescopic damper struts; rear: independent, transverse torsion bars, semi-axles with homokinetic joints, telescopic dampers.

STEERING rack-and-pinion; turns lock to lock: 3.94.

BRAKES front disc, rear drum; swept area: front 16.3 sq in, 105 sq cm, rear 70.1 sq in, 452 sq cm, total 86.4 sq in, 557 sq cm.

ELECTRICAL EQUIPMENT 12 V; 36 Ah battery; 490 W dynamo; Bosch distributor; 4 headlamps.

DIMENSIONS AND WEIGHT wheel base: 98.20 in, 249 cm; tracks: 53.74 in, 136 cm front, 55.20 in, 140 cm rear; length: 170.31 in, 433 cm; width: 64.17 in, 163 cm; height: 56.29 in, 143 cm; ground clearance: 5.90 in, 15 cm; weight: 2,138 lb, 970 kg; weight distribution: 36.4% front, 63.6% rear; turning circle (between walls): 34.4 ft, 10.5 m; fuel tank: 11 imp gal, 13.2 US gal, 50 l.

BODY estate car/st. wagon; 2 + 1 doors; 5 seats, separate front seats, adjustable backrests; folding rear seat.

OPTIONAL ACCESSORIES metallic spray; heating; built-in headrests; heated rear window; rear window wiper-washer.

CHEVROLET ARGENTINA

Chevy Standard/Super

PRICES EX WORKS: Chevy Standard: 5,089,000 pesos
Chevy Super: 5,585,000 pesos

ENGINE front, 4 stroke; 6 cylinders, vertical, in line; 230 cu in, 3,769 cc (3.87 x 3.25 in, 98.4 x 82.6 mm); compression ratio: 7.5:1; max power (DIN): 126 hp at 4,400 rpm; max torque (DIN): 199 lb ft, 27.4 kg m at 2,400 rpm; max engine rpm: 4,400; 33.4 hp/l; cast iron block and head; 7 crankshaft bearings; valves: overhead, in line, push-rods and rockers, hydraulic tappets; camshafts: 1, side; lubrication: gear pump, full flow filter, 7.7 imp pt, 9.3 US pt, 4.4 l; 1 Holley downdraught single barrel carburettor; fuel feed: mechanical pump; water-cooled, 22.4 imp pt, 26.8 US pt, 12.7 l.

TRANSMISSION driving wheels: rear; clutch: single dry plate; gearbox: mechanical; gears: 3, fully synchronized; ratios: I 2.850, II 1.680, III 1, rev 2.950; lever: steering column; final drive: hypoid bevel; axle ratio: 3.080; width of rims: 6''; tyres: 7.35 x 14.

PERFORMANCE max speeds: (I) 37 mph, 59 km/h; (II) 65 mph, 104 km/h; (III) 101 mph, 162 km/h; power-weight ratio: 25.8 lb/hp, 11.7 kg/hp; carrying capacity: 1,098 lb, 498 kg; acceleration: standing 1/4 mile 19.5 sec, 0-50 mph

(0-80 km/h) 9.5 sec; speed in direct drive/top at 1,000 rpm: 24.5 mph, 39.5 km/h; consumption: Standard 26.6 m/imp gal, 22.2 m/US gal, 10.6 l x 100 km at 50 mph, 80 km/h - Super 25.9 m/imp gal, 21.6 m/US gal, 10.9 l x 100 km at 50 mph, 80 km/h.

CHASSIS integral, front auxiliary frame; front suspension: independent, wishbones, coil springs, anti-roll bar, telescopic dampers; rear: rigid axle, semi-elliptic leafsprings, telescopic dampers.

STEERING recirculating ball; turns lock to lock: 5.

BRAKES front disc, rear drum, servo; swept area: front 223.9 sq in, 1,444 sq cm, rear 111.3 sq in, 718 sq cm, total 335.2 sq in, 2,162 sq cm.

ELECTRICAL EQUIPMENT 12 V; 55 Ah battery; 32 A alternator; Delco-Remy distributor; 2 headlamps.

DIMENSIONS AND WEIGHT wheel base: 110.98 in, 282 cm; front and rear track: 59.45 in, 151 cm; length: 191.34 in, 486 cm; width: 72.56 in, 184 cm; height: 54.33 in, 138 cm; ground clearance: 6.30 in, 16 cm; weight: 3,263 lb, 1,480 kg; weight distribution: 51.4% front, 48.6% rear; turning circle (between walls): 43.3 ft, 13.2 m; fuel tank: 15 imp gal, 18 US gal, 68 l.

BODY saloon/sedan; 4 doors; 6 seats, bench front seats; (for Super only) luxury interior.

OPTIONAL ACCESSORIES power-steering; tinted glass; heated rear window; air-conditioning; 3.360 or 3.310 axle ratio; 42 A alternator; 185 HR x 14 tubeless tyres; iodine headlamps; 250 cu in, 4,097 engine with 8.1:1 compression ratio; (for Super only) 2-speed automatic transmission.

Chevy Malibú

See Chevy Standard/Super, except for:

PRICE EX WORKS: 6,942,000 pesos

ENGINE 250 cu in, 4,097 cc (3.87 x 3.53 in, 98.4 x 89.7 mm); compression ratio: 8.1:1; max power (DIN): 138 hp at 4,400 rpm; max torque (DIN): 228 lb ft, 31.4 kg m at 1,800 rpm; 33.7 hp/l; 1 Bendix downdraught carburettor.

TRANSMISSION gears: 4, fully synchronized; ratios: I 2.850, II 2.020, III 1.350, IV 1, rev 2.850; lever: central.

PERFORMANCE max speeds: (I) 37 mph, 59 km/h; (II) 53 mph, 85 km/h; (III) 80 mph, 129 km/h; (IV) 104 mph, 168 km/h; power-weight ratio: 24 lb/hp, 10.9 kg/hp; acceleration: standing 1/4 mile 18.2 sec, 0-50 mph (0-80 km/h) 8 sec; consumption: 25.9 m/imp gal, 21.6 m/US gal, 10.9 l x 100 km at 50 mph, 80 km/h.

ELECTRICAL EQUIPMENT iodine headlamps.

BODY 5 seats, separate front seats, reclining backrests; heated rear window; tinted glass.

DIMENSIONS AND WEIGHT weight: 3,330 lb, 1,510 kg; weight distribution: 53.6% front, 46.4% rear.

OPTIONAL ACCESSORIES power-steering; air-conditioning; 3.360 or 3.310 axle ratio; 42 A alternator; 185 HR x 14 tubeless tyres; 2-speed automatic transmission.

CHEVROLET Chevy Super

Chevy Coupé Serie 2

See Chevy Standard/Super, except for:

PRICE EX WORKS: 8,571,000 pesos

ENGINE 250 cu in, 4,097 cc (3.87 x 3.53 in, 98.4 x 89.7 mm); compression ratio: 8.1:1; max power (DIN): 150 hp at 4,000 rpm; max torque (DIN): 234 lb ft, 32.3 kg m at 2,000 rpm; max engine rpm: 4,600; 36.6 hp/l; 1 Holley downdraught twin barrel carburettor.

TRANSMISSION gears: 4, fully synchronized; ratios: I 2.850, II 2.020, III 1.350, IV 1, rev 2.850; lever: central; tyres: 205/70 x 14.

PERFORMANCE max speeds: (I) 37 mph, 59 km/h; (II) 52 mph, 84 km/h; (III) 78 mph, 126 km/h; (IV) 107 mph, 172 km/h; power-weight ratio: 22 lb/hp, 10 kg/hp; acceleration: standing ¼ mile 17.7 sec, 0-50 mph (0-80 km/h) 7.4 sec; speed in direct drive at 1,000 rpm: 24 mph, 38.6 km/h; consunmption: 26.9 m/imp gal, 22.4 m/US gal, 10.5 l x 100 km at 50 mph, 80 km/h.

ELECTRICAL EQUIPMENT iodine headlamps.

BODY 2 doors; 5 seats, separate front seats, reclining backrests; heated rear window; tinted glass.

DIMENSIONS AND WEIGHT height: 53.54 in, 136 cm; ground clearance: 5.98 in, 15 cm; weight: 3,296 lb, 1,495 kg; distribution of weight: 53.6% front, 46.4% rear.

OPTIONAL ACCESSORIES power-steering; air-conditioning; 42 A alternator; 2-speed automatic transmission.

DODGE   ARGENTINA

1500

ENGINE front, 4 stroke; 4 cylinders, vertical, in line; 91.4 cu in, 1,498 cc (3.39 x 2.53 in, 86.1 x 64.3 mm); compression ratio: 8:1; max power (SAE): 72 hp at 5,400 rpm; max torque (SAE): 88 lb ft, 12.2 kg m at 3,200 rpm; max engine rpm: 5,400; 48.1 hp/l; cast iron block and head; 5 crankshaft bearings; valves: overhead, in line, push-rods and rockers; camshafts: 1, side; lubrication: rotary pump, full flow filter, 7 imp pt, 8.5 US pt, 4 l; 1 Holley A-RX-7034A single barrel carburettor; fuel feed: mechanical pump; water-cooled, 13 imp pt, 15.6 US pt, 7.4 l.

TRANSMISSION driving wheels: rear; clutch: single dry plate (diaphragm); gearbox: mechanical; gears: 4, fully synchronized; ratios: I 3.317, II 2.029, III 1.366, IV 1, rev 3.450; lever: central; final drive: hypoid bevel; axle ratio: 3.890; width of rims: 5''; tyres: 5.60 x 13.

PERFORMANCE max speeds: (I) 29 mph, 46 km/h; (II) 48 mph, 77 km/h; (III) 71 mph, 114 km/h; (IV) 90 mph, 145 km/h; power-weight ratio: 28.2 lb/hp, 12.8 kg/hp; carrying capacity: 882 lb, 400 kg; acceleration: 0-50 mph (0-80 km/h) 9.5 sec; speed in direct drive at 1,000 rpm: 18.6 mph, 30 km/h; consumption: 25.7 m/imp gal, 21.4 m/US gal, 11 l x 100 km.

CHASSIS integral; front suspension: independent, by McPherson, lower trailing links, coil springs, anti-roll bar, telescopic dampers; rear: rigid axle, lower trailing radius arms, upper oblique torque arms, coil springs, telescopic dampers.

STEERING rack-and-pinion; turns lock to lock: 3.66.

BRAKES front disc, rear drum; lining area: front 15.7 sq in, 100.1 sq cm, rear 53.5 sq in, 345 sq cm, total 69.2 sq in, 446 sq cm.

ELECTRICAL EQUIPMENT 12 V; 48 Ah battery; 32 A alternator; Chrysler-TRIA distributor; 2 headlamps.

DIMENSIONS AND WEIGHT wheel base: 97.99 in, 249 cm; tracks: 50.98 in, 129 cm front, 51.26 in, 130 cm rear; length: 162.99 in, 414 cm; width: 62.52 in, 159 cm; height: 53.15 in, 135 cm; ground clearance: 5.59 in, 14 cm; weight: 2,029 lb, 920 kg; weight distribution: 54.2% front, 45.8% rear; turning circle (between walls): 31.8 ft, 9.7 m; fuel tank: 9.9 imp gal, 11.9 US gal, 45 l.

BODY saloon/sedan; 4 doors; 5 seats, separate front seats, reclining backrests.

OPTIONAL ACCESSORIES Borg-Warner 45 automatic transmission.

1500 M 1.8

ENGINE front, 4 stroke; 4 cylinders, vertical, in line; 109.7 cu in, 1,798 cc (3.39 x 3.04 in, 86.1 x 77.2 mm); compression ratio: 8.6:1; max power (SAE): 92 hp at 4,900 rpm; max torque (SAE): 116 lb ft, 16 kg m at 3,400 rpm; max engine rpm: 5,800; 51.2 hp/l; cast iron block and head; 5 crankshaft bearings; valves: overhead, in line, push-rods and rockers; camshafts: 1, side; lubrication: rotary pump, full flow filter, 7 imp pt, 8.5 US pt, 4 l; 1 Holley A-RX-7035A single barrel carburettor; fuel feed: mechanical pump; water-cooled, 11.4 imp pt, 13.7 US pt, 6.5 l.

TRANSMISSION driving wheels: rear; clutch: single dry plate (diaphragm); gearbox: mechanical; gears: 4, fully synchronized; ratios: I 3.317, II 2.029, III 1.366, IV 1, rev 3.450; lever: central; final drive: hypoid bevel; axle ratio: 3.890; width of rims: 5''; tyres: 5.60 x 13.

PERFORMANCE max speeds: (I) 31 mph, 50 km/h; (II) 47 mph, 75 km/h; (III) 78 mph, 125 km/h; (IV) 93 mph, 150 km/h; power-weight ratio: 22.9 lb/hp, 10.4 kg/hp; carrying capacity: 882 lb, 400 kg; acceleration: 0-50 mph (0-80 km/h) 9.5 sec; speed in direct drive at 1,000 rpm: 21.7 mph, 35 km/h; consumption: 31.4 m/imp gal, 26.1 m/US gal, 9 l x 100 km.

CHASSIS integral; front suspension: independent, by McPherson, lower trailing links, coil springs, anti-roll bar, telescopic dampers; rear: rigid axle, lower trailing radius arms, upper oblique torque arms, coil springs, telescopic dampers.

STEERING rack-and-pinion; turns lock to lock: 3.66.

BRAKES front disc, rear drum, servo, dual circuit; lining area: front 15.7 sq in, 100.1 sq cm, rear 53.5 sq in, 345 sq cm, total 69.2 sq in, 446 sq cm.

CHEVROLET Chevy Malibú

ELECTRICAL EQUIPMENT 12 V; 48 Ah battery; 32 A alternator; Chrysler-TRIA distributor; 2 iodine headlamps.

DIMENSIONS AND WEIGHT wheel base: 97.99 in, 249 cm; tracks: 50.98 in, 129 cm front, 51.26 in, 130 cm rear; length: 162.99 in, 414 cm; width: 62.52 in, 159 cm; height: 53.15 in, 135 cm; ground clearance: 5.59 in, 14 cm; weight: 2,110 lb, 957 kg; weight distribution: 54.2% front, 45.8% rear; turning circle (between walls): 31.8 ft, 9.7 m; fuel tank: 9.9 imp gal, 11.9 US gal, 45 l.

BODY saloon/sedan; 4 doors; 5 seats, separate front seats, reclining backrests with built-in headrests.

OPTIONAL ACCESSORIES Borg-Warner 45 automatic transmission; 155 x 13 tyres; heated rear window.

1500 M 1.8 Rural

See 1500 M 1.8, except for:

PERFORMANCE power-weight ratio: 31.5 lb/hp, 14.3 kg/hp.

CHASSIS rear suspension: 4 swinging links.

DIMENSIONS AND WEIGHT length: 165.35 in, 420 cm; height: 53.54 in, 136 cm; weight: 2,910 lb, 1,320 kg; weight distribution: 45.8% front, 54.2% rear.

BODY estate car/station wagon; 4 + 1 doors.

Coronado

ENGINE front, 4 stroke; 6 cylinders, vertical, in line; 225 cu in, 3,688 cc (3.40 x 4.13 in, 86.4 x 104.8 mm); compression ratio: 8.4:1; max power (SAE): 145 hp at 4,400 rpm; max torque (SAE): 215 lb ft, 29.7 kg m at 2,400 rpm; max engine rpm: 4,600; 39.3 hp/l; cast iron block and head; 4 crankshaft bearings; valves: overhead, in line, push-rods and rockers; camshafts: 1, side; lubrication: rotary pump, full flow filter, 8.8 imp pt, 10.6 US pt, 5 l; 1 Holley R 2535A downdraught single barrel carburettor; fuel feed: mechanical pump; water-cooled, 21.6 imp pt, 2⁶ US pt, 12.3 l.

TRANSMISSION driving wheels: rear; clutch: single dry plate; gearbox: mechanical; gears: 3, fully synchronized ratios: I 2.830, II 1.560, III 1, rev 2.660; lever: steering column; final drive: hypoid bevel; axle ratio: 3.070; width of rims: 5.5''; tyres: 135 x 14.

PERFORMANCE max speeds: (I) 34 mph, 55 km/h; (II) 7¹ mph, 115 km/h; (III) 99 mph, 160 km/h; power-weight ratio: 21.4 lb/hp, 9.7 kg/hp; carrying capacity: 1,213 lb, 550 kg; acceleration: 0-50 mph (0-80 km/h) 9 sec; speed in direct drive at 1,000 rpm: 24.9 mph, 40 km/h; consumption: 21.7 m/imp gal, 18.1 m/US gal, 13 l x 100 km.

CHASSIS integral; front suspension: independent, wishbones, lower trailing links, longitudinal torsion bars, telescopic dampers; rear: rigid axle, semi-elliptic leaf-springs, telescopic dampers.

STEERING recirculating ball; turns lock to lock: 5.30.

BRAKES front disc, rear drum, servo, dual circuit; lining area: front 60.5 sq in, 390 sq cm, rear 32.4 sq in, 209 sq cm, total 92.9 sq in, 599 sq cm.

DODGE 1500 M 1.8

DODGE GTX

ELECTRICAL EQUIPMENT 12 V; 59 Ah battery; 40 A alternator; Chrysler electronic ignition; 2 iodine headlamps.

DIMENSIONS AND WEIGHT wheel base: 110.63 in, 281 cm; tracks: 56.30 in, 143 cm front, 57.48 in, 146 cm rear; length: 197.24 in, 501 cm; width: 70.87 in, 180 cm; height: 55.51 in, 141 cm; ground clearance: 6.38 in, 16 cm; weight: 3,109 lb, 1,410 kg; weight distribution: 55% front, 45% rear; turning circle (between walls): 38.7 ft, 11.8 m; fuel tank: 15 imp gal, 18 US gal, 68 l.

BODY saloon/sedan; 4 doors; 6 seats, bench front seats.

OPTIONAL ACCESSORIES power steering.

Coronado Automatic

See Coronado, except for:

TRANSMISSION gearbox: Torqueflite automatic transmission, hydraulic torque converter and planetary gears with 3 ratios + reverse, max ratio of converter at stall 2.1, possible manual selection; ratios: I 2.450, II 1.450, III 1, rev 2.200; tyres: 7.35 x 14.

PERFORMANCE max speeds: (I) 32 mph 52 km/h; (II) 68 mph, 110 km/h; (III) 96 mph, 155 km/h; acceleration: 0-50 mph (0-80 km/h) 10 sec; consumption: 20.2 m/imp gal, 16.8 m/US gal, 14 l x 100 km.

STEERING servo: turns lock to lock: 3.50.

CHASSIS front suspension: anti-roll bar.

BRAKES front disc with internal radial fins.

BODY vinyl roof.

GTX

See Coronado, except for:

ENGINE 8 cylinders, Vee-slanted at 90°; 317.9 cu in, 5,210 cc (3.91 x 3.31 in, 99.3 x 84 mm); compression ratio: 8.8:1; max power (SAE): 230 hp at 4,400 rpm; max torque (SAE): 345 lb ft, 47.6 kg m at 2,000 rpm; 5 crankshaft bearings; valves: hydraulic tappets; camshafts: 1, at centre of Vee; lubrication: 10.6 imp pt, 12.7 US pt, 6 l; 1 Holley A-RX-7224 downdraught twin barrel carburettor; cooling system: 24.6 imp pt, 29.6 US pt, 14 l.

TRANSMISSION gears: 4, fully synchronized; ratios: I 3.090, II 2.100, III 1.450, IV 1, rev 2.680; lever: central; axle ratio: 2.870; width of rims: 6''; tyres: 195 HR x 14.

PERFORMANCE max speeds: (I) 43 mph, 70 km/h; (II) 56 mph, 90 km/h; (III) 87 mph, 140 km/h; (IV) 121 mph, 195 km/h; power-weight ratio: 14.4 lb/hp, 6.4 kg/hp; acceleration: 0-50 mph (0-80 km/h) 7 sec; speed in direct drive

at 1,000 rpm: 28 mph, 45 km/h; consumption: 20.2 m/imp gal, 16.8 m/US gal, 14 l x 100 km.

CHASSIS front suspension: anti-roll bar.

BRAKES front disc with internal radial fins.

DIMENSIONS AND WEIGHT length: 197.64 in, 502 cm; width: 74.92 in, 190 cm; height: 53.54 in, 136 cm; ground clearance: 5.98 in, 15 cm; weight: 3,303 lb, 1,480 kg; weight distribution: 56% front, 44% rear.

BODY coupé; 2 doors; 5 seats, separate front seats, reclining backrests with built-in headrests; vinyl roof.

OPTIONAL ACCESSORIES limited slip differential; 2.850 axle ratio; power steering.

FIAT   ARGENTINA

600 R

ENGINE rear, 4 stroke; 4 cylinders, vertical, in line; 48.6 cu in, 797 cc (2.44 x 2.60 in, 62 x 66 mm); compression ratio: 7.7:1; max power (SAE): 36 hp at 5,000 rpm; max torque (SAE): 37 lb ft, 5.1 kg m at 2,500 rpm; max engine rpm: 45.2 hp/l; cast iron block, light alloy head; 3 crankshaft bearings; valves: overhead, in line, pushrods and rockers; camshafts: 1, side: lubrication: gear pump, centrifugal filter, 6.5 imp pt, 7.8 US pt, 3.7 l; 1 Weber 28 ICP 6 or Solex C 28 PIB 3 or Holley 28 ICP 6 downdraught single barrel carburettor; fuel feed: mechanical pump; sealed circuit cooling, liquid, 7.9 imp pt, 9.5 US pt, 4.5 l.

TRANSMISSION driving wheels: rear; clutch: single dry plate; gearbox: mechanical; gears: 4, II, III and IV synchronized; ratios: I 3.385, II 2.055, III 1.333, IV 0.896, rev 4.275; lever: central; final drive: spiral bevel; axle ratio: 4.875; width of rims: 4''; tyres: 5.20 x 12.

PERFORMANCE max speeds: (I) 19 mph, 30 km/h; (II) 28 mph, 45 km/h; (III) 43 mph, 70 km/h; (IV) 68 mph, 110 km/h; power-weight ratio: 37.7 lb/hp, 17.1 kg/hp; carrying capacity: 706 lb, 320 kg; acceleration: standing ¼ mile 26.7 sec, 0-50 mph (0-80 km/h) 24 sec; speed in top at 1,000 rpm: 14.1 mph, 22.7 km/h; consumption: 48.7 m/imp gal, 40.6 m/US gal, 5.8 l x 100 km.

CHASSIS integral; front suspension: independent, wishbones, transverse leafsprings lower arms, telescopic dampers; rear: independent, oblique semi-trailing arms, coil springs, telescopic dampers.

STEERING screw and sector; turns lock to lock: 2.12.

BRAKES drum; lining area: front 33.5 sq in, 216 sq cm, rear 33.5 sq in, 216 sq cm, total 67 sq in, 432 sq cm.

ELECTRICAL EQUIPMENT 12 V; 32 Ah battery; 230 W dynamo; Garef-Marelli distributor; 2 headlamps.

DIMENSIONS AND WEIGHT wheel base: 78.74 in, 200 cm; tracks: 45.28 in, 115 cm front, 45.67 in, 116 cm rear; length: 134.25 in, 341 cm; width: 54.33 in, 138 cm; height: 55.12 in, 140 cm; ground clearance: 5.71 in, 14.5 cm; weight: 1,356 lb, 615 kg; weight distribution: 46% front, 54% rear; turning circle (between walls): 28.5 ft, 8.7 m; fuel tank: 5.9 imp gal, 7.1 US gal, 27 l.

BODY saloon/sedan; 2 doors; 4 seats, separate front seats.

600 S

See 600 R, except for:

ENGINE 51.4 cu in, 843 cc (2.56 x 2.50 in, 65 x 63.5 mm); compression ratio: 7.4:1; max power (DIN): 32 hp at 4,800 rpm; 38 hp/l; 1 Weber 28 IGP 10 downdraught single barrel carburettor.

PERFORMANCE power-weight ratio: 42.3 lb/hp, 19.2 kg/hp.

ELECTRICAL EQUIPMENT 475 W dynamo.

133

ENGINE rear, longitudinal, 4 stroke; 4 cylinders, vertical, in line; 55.1 cu in, 903 cc (2.56 x 2.68 in, 65 x 68 mm); compression ratio: 8.4:1; max power (DIN): 40 hp at 5,600 rpm; max torque (DIN): 47 lb ft, 6.5 kg m at 3,000 rpm; max engine rpm: 6,200; 44.3 hp/l; cast iron block, light alloy head; 3 crankshaft bearings; valves: overhead, in line, pushrods and rockers; camshafts: 1, side; lubrication: gear pump, full flow filter (cartridge), 6 imp pt, 7.2 US pt, 3.4 l; 1 Weber 30 IGF 19 vertical single barrel carburettor; exhaust

FIAT 600 R

FIAT 133

133

gas recirculation; fuel feed: mechanical pump; water-cooled, 8.8 imp pt, 10.6 US pt, 5 l.

TRANSMISSION driving wheels: front; clutch: single dry plate (diaphragm); gearbox: mechanical; gears: 4, fully synchronized; ratios: I 3.636, II 2.055, III 1.409, IV 0.963, rev 3.615; lever: central; final drive: hypoid bevel; axle ratio: 4.625; width of rims: 4.5''; tyres: 145 R x 13.

PERFORMANCE max speed: 81 mph, 130 km/h; carrying capacity: 706 lb, 320 kg; consumption: 40.9 m/imp gal, 34.1 m/US gal, 6.9 l x 100 km.

CHASSIS integral; front suspension: independent, wishbones, transverse leafspring lower arms, transverse torsion bar, anti-roll bar, telescopic dampers; rear: independent, semi-trailing arms, coil springs, torsion bar, anti-roll bar, telescopic dampers.

STEERING screw and sector; turns lock to lock: 2.26.

BRAKES front disc, rear drum.

ELECTRICAL EQUIPMENT 12 V; 34 Ah batery; 475 W dynamo; 2 headlamps.

DIMENSIONS AND WEIGHT wheel base: 79.53 in, 202 cm; tracks: 45.28 in, 115 cm front, 47.64 in, 121 cm rear; length: 137.40 in, 349 cm; width: 55.91 in, 142 cm; height: 52.36 in, 133 cm; turning circle (between walls): 31.5 ft, 9.6 m; fuel tank: 6.6 imp gal, 7.9 US gal, 30 l.

BODY saloon/sedan; 2 doors; 4 seats, separate front seats.

128 Berlina

ENGINE front, transverse, 4 stroke; 4 cylinders, in line; 68.1 cu in, 1,116 cc (3.15 x 2.19 in, 80 x 55.5 mm); compression ratio: 8.8:1; max power (SAE): 63 hp at 6,000 rpm; max torque (DIN): 59 lb ft, 8.1 kg m at 3,000 rpm; max engine rpm: 6,500; 56.4 hp/l; cast iron block, light alloy head; 5 crankshaft bearings; valves: overhead, thimble tappets; camshafts: 1, overhead, cogged belt; lubrication: gear pump, full flow filter (cartridge), 7.9 imp pt, 9.5 US pt, 4.5 l; 1 Weber 32 ICEV 14 or Solex C 32 DISA 24 downdraught single barrel carburettor; fuel feed: mechanical pump; water-cooled, 11.4 imp pt, 13.7 US pt, 6.5 l, electric thermostatic fan.

TRANSMISSION driving wheels: front; clutch: single dry plate; gearbox: mechanical; gears: 4, fully synchronized; ratios: I 3.583, II 2.235, III 1.454, IV 1.042, rev 3.714; lever: central; final drive: cylindrical gears; axle ratio: 4.077; width of rims: 4.5''; tyres: 145 SR x 13.

PERFORMANCE max speeds: (I) 28 mph, 45 km/h; (II) 47 mph, 75 km/h; (III) 71 mph, 115 km/h; (IV) 87 mph, 140 km/h; power-weight ratio: 28.2 lb/hp, 12.8 kg/hp; carrying capacity: 882 lb, 400 kg; acceleration: standing ¼ mile 19.7 sec, 0-50 mph (0-80 km/h) 11.6 sec; speed in top at 1,000 rpm: 15.2 mph, 24.4 km/h; consumption: 35.3 m/imp gal, 29.4 m/US gal, 8 l x 100 km.

CHASSIS integral; front suspension: independent, by McPherson, coil springs/telescopic damper struts, lower wishbones, anti-roll bar; rear: independent, single wide-based wishbones, transverse anti-roll leafsprings, telescopic dampers.

STEERING rack-and-pinion; turns lock to lock: 3.40.

BRAKES front disc (diameter 8.94 in, 22.7 cm), rear drum, rear compensator, servo; lining area: front 19.2 sq in, 124 sq cm, rear 33.5 sq in, 216 sq cm, total 52.7 sq in, 340 sq cm.

ELECTRICAL EQUIPMENT 12 V; 34 Ah battery; 38 A alternator; Garef-Marelli distributor; 2 headlamps.

DIMENSIONS AND WEIGHT wheel base: 96.06 in, 244 cm; tracks: 51.57 in, 131 cm front, 51.57 in, 131 cm rear; length: 152.76 in, 388 cm; width: 62.60 in, 159 cm; height: 55.91 in, 142 cm; ground clearance: 7.60 in, 19.3 cm; weight: 1,775 lb, 805 kg; weight distribution: 61.5% front, 38.5% rear; turning circle (between walls): 33.8 ft, 10.3 m; fuel tank: 8.4 imp gal, 10 US gal, 38 l.

BODY saloon/sedan; 4 doors; 5 seats, separate front seats.

128 L Berlina

See 128 Berlina, except for:

ENGINE 78.7 cu in, 1,290 cc (3.39 x 2.19 in, 86 x 55.5 mm); compression ratio: 8.9:1; max power (SAE): 70 hp at 6,250 rpm; max torque (DIN): 67 lb ft, 9.2 kg m at 3,250 rpm; max engine rpm: 7,000; 54.3 hp/l; 1 Weber 32 ICEV 10 downdraught single barrel carburettor.

TRANSMISSION gearbox ratio: IV 1.030; tyres: 155 SR x 13.

PERFORMANCE max speeds: (I) 28 mph, 45 km/h; (II) 47 mph, 75 km/h; (III) 73 mph, 118 km/h; (IV) over 90 mph, 145 km/h; power-weight ratio: 26.1 lb/hp, 11.9 kg/hp; speed in top at 1,000 rpm: 15.5 mph, 25 km/h; consumption: 33.2 m/imp gal, 27.7 m/US gal, 8.5 l x 100 km.

STEERING turns lock to lock: 3.50.

DIMENSIONS AND WEIGHT weight: 1,841 lb, 835 kg; turning circle (between walls): 35.8 ft, 10.9 m.

BODY luxury equipment; reclining front seats.

1300 TV Iava

See 128 L Berlina, except for:

ENGINE compression ratio: 8.9:1; max power (SAE): 90 hp at 6,250 rpm; 69.8 hp/l; 1 Solex C 34 EIES downdraught twin barrel carburettor; exhaust gas recirculation.

TRANSMISSION width of rims: 5''.

PERFORMANCE max speed: over 99 mph, 160 km/h.

DIMENSIONS AND WEIGHT tracks: 52.76 in, 134 cm front, 53.15 in, 135 cm rear.

FIAT 128 L Berlina

FIAT 128 Familiar 5 Puertas

128 Familiar 5 Puertas

See 128 L Berlina, except for:

PERFORMANCE max speed: over 87 mph, 140 km/h; power-weight ratio: 26.9 lb/hp, 12.2 kg/hp; acceleration: standing ¼ mile 20 sec, 0-50 mph (0-80 km/h) 12 sec.

DIMENSIONS AND WEIGHT length: 153.15 in, 389 cm; weight: 1,885 lb, 855 kg; weight distribution: 60% front, 40% rear.

BODY estate car/station wagon; 4+1 doors; 5 seats. separate front seats, reclining backrests; folding rear seat.

125 Berlina

ENGINE front, 4 stroke; 4 cylinders, vertical, in line; 98.1 cu in, 1,608 cc (3.15 x 3.15 in, 80 x 80 mm); compression ratio: 8.8:1; max power (DIN): 100 hp at 6,200 rpm; max torque (DIN): 96 lb ft, 13.3 kg m at 4,000 rpm; max engine rpm: 6,200; 62 hp/l; cast iron block, light alloy head; 5 crankshaft bearings; valves: overhead; camshafts: 2, overhead, cogged belt; lubrication: gear pump, full flow filter, 8.6 imp pt, 10.4 US pt, 4.9 l; 1 Weber 34 DCHE 20 or Solex C34 PAIA/33 downdraught twin barrel carburettor; exhaust gas recirculation; fuel feed: mechanical pump; water-cooled, 13.2 imp pt, 15.9 US pt, 7.5 l, electric thermostatic fan.

TRANSMISSION driving wheels: rear; clutch: single dry plate; gearbox: mechanical; gears: 4, fully synchronized; ratios: I 3.670, II 2.110, III 1.360, IV 1, rev 3.870; lever: central; final drive: hypoid bevel; axle ratio: 3.900; width of rims: 5''; tyres: 175 S x 13.

PERFORMANCE max speeds: (I) 28 mph, 45 km/h; (II) 50 mph, 80 km/h; (III) 78 mph, 125 km/h; (IV) 106 mph, 170 km/h; power-weight ratio: 23.1 lb/hp, 10.5 kg/hp; carrying capacity: 882 lb, 400 kg; acceleration: standing ¼ mile 18.6 sec, 0-50 mph (0-80 km/h) 9 sec; speed in direct drive at 1,000 rpm: 17.5 mph, 28.2 km/h; consumption: 28.5 m/imp gal, 23.8 m/US gal, 9.9 l x 100 km.

CHASSIS integral; front suspension: independent, wishbones, coil springs, anti-roll bar, telescopic dampers; rear: rigid axle, upper torque arms, semi-elliptic leafsprings, telescopic dampers.

STEERING worm and roller; turns lock to lock: 3.

BRAKES front disc, rear drum, servo.

ELECTRICAL EQUIPMENT 12 V; 48 Ah battery; 38 A alternator; Garef Marelli distributor; 4 headlamps.

DIMENSIONS AND WEIGHT wheel base: 98.82 in, 251 cm; tracks: 51.57 in, 131 cm front, 50.79 in, 129 cm rear; length: 167.32 in, 425 cm; width: 63.39 in, 161 cm; height: 56.69 in, 144 cm; ground clearance: 7.28 in, 18.5 cm; weight: 2,326 lb, 1,055 kg; turning circle (between walls): 35.4 ft, 10.8 m; fuel tank: 9.9 imp gal, 11.9 US gal, 45 l.

BODY saloon/sedan; 4 doors; 5 seats, separate front seats, reclining backrests.

OPTIONAL ACCESSORIES 175 SR x 13 tyres with 5.5'' wide rims.

FIAT 125 Sport

125 Familiar

See 125 Berlina, except for:

PERFORMANCE max speed: 103 mph, 165 km/h; power-weight ratio: 24 lb/hp, 10.9 kg/hp; acceleration: standing ¼ mile 19 sec, 0-50 mph (0-80 km/h) 9.5 sec.

DIMENSIONS AND WEIGHT length: 168.11 in, 427 cm; weight: 2,043 lb, 1,090 kg; weight distribution: 50% front, 50% rear.

BODY estate car/station wagon; 4 + 1 doors; 5 seats, separate front seats, reclining backrests; folding rear seat.

125 Sport

See 125 Berlina, except for:

TRANSMISSION width of rims: 5.5''; tyres: 175 SR x 13.

PERFORMANCE max speed: over 109 mph, 175 km/h; carrying capacity: 728 lb, 330 kg.

ELECTRICAL EQUIPMENT 2 halogen headlamps.

DIMENSIONS AND WEIGHT tracks: 52.36 in, 133 cm front, 51.18 in, 130 cm rear; length: 166.14 in, 422 cm; width: 60.24 in, 153 cm; height: 54.33 in, 138 cm; ground clearance: 5.91 in, 15 cm; weight: 2,315 lb, 1,050 kg; weight distribution: 55% front, 45% rear.

BODY coupé; 2 doors; 4 seats, separate front seats, reclining backrests.

FORD — ARGENTINA

Taunus L 2000 Sedan/GXL Sedan

ENGINE front, 4 stroke; 4 cylinders, in line; 121.4 cu in, 1,990 cc (3.52 x 3.13 in, 89.3 x 79.4 mm); compression ratio: 8:1; max power (SAE): 92 hp at 5,500 rpm; max torque (SAE): 109 lb ft, 15.1 kg m at 3,000 rpm; max engine rpm: 6,000; 46.2 hp/l; cast iron block and head; 5 crankshaft bearings; valves: overhead, push-rods and rockers; camshafts: 1, overhead, cogged belt; lubrication: gear pump, full flow filter, 7.9 imp pt, 9.5 US pt, 4.5 l; 1 Zenith downdraught single barrel carburettor; fuel feed: mechanical pump; water-cooled, 13.9 imp pt, 16.7 US pt, 7.9 l.

TRANSMISSION driving wheels: rear; clutch: single dry plate; gearbox: mechanical; gears: 4, fully synchronized; ratios: I 3.360, II 1.810, III 1.260, IV 1, rev 3.360; lever: central; final drive: hypoid bevel; axle ratio: 3.540; width of rims: 5.5''; tyres: 6.95 S x 13.

PERFORMANCE max speed: 95 mph, 153 km/h; power-weight ratio: 27.1 lb/hp, 12.3 kg/hp; speed in direct drive at 1,000 rpm: 18.5 mph, 29.7 km/h; consumption: 26.6 m/imp gal, 22.2 m/US gal, 10.6 l x 100 km.

CHASSIS integral; front suspension: independent, wishbones, coil springs/telescopic dampers, anti-roll bar; rear: rigid axle, lower trailing arms, upper oblique trailing arms, coil springs, telescopic dampers.

STEERING rack-and-pinion.

BRAKES front disc (diameter 9.75 in, 24.8 cm), rear drum; lining area: front 28.5 sq in, 184 sq cm, rear 59.8 sq in, 386 sq cm, total 88.3 sq in, 570 sq cm.

ELECTRICAL EQUIPMENT 12 V; 45 Ah battery; 540 W alternator; 2 headlamps.

DIMENSIONS AND WEIGHT wheel base: 101.57 in, 258 cm; front and rear track: 55.91 in, 142 cm; length: 171.26 in, 435 cm; width: 66.93 in, 170 cm; height: 52.76 in, 134 cm; ground clearance: 4.61 in, 11.7 cm; weight: 2,496 lb, 1,132 kg; turning circle (between walls): 35.1 ft, 10.7 m; fuel tank: 11.9 imp gal, 14.3 US gal, 54 l.

BODY saloon/sedan; 4 doors; 5 seats - GXL, luxury equipment.

OPTIONAL ACCESSORIES servo brake; 175 SR x 13 tyres; anti-roll bar on rear suspension.

Taunus GXL 2300 Sedan/GT Coupé

See Taunus L 2000 Sedan GXL Sedan, except for:

ENGINE 140.3 cu in, 2,299 cc (3.78 x 3.13 in, 96 x 79.4 mm); compression ratio: 9:1; max power (SAE): 122 hp at 5,000 rpm; max torque (SAE): 142 lb ft, 19.6 kg m at 3,500 rpm; max engine rpm: 5,500; 53 hp/l; 1 Solex downdraught twin barrel carburettor; cooling system: 13.7 imp pt, 16.5 US pt, 7.8 l.

PERFORMANCE max speed: 106 mph, 170 km/h; power-weight ratio: 20.5 lb/hp, 9.3 kg/hp; consumption: 28.5 m/imp gal, 23.8 m/US gal, 9.9 l x 100 km.

ELECTRICAL EQUIPMENT 38 A alternator.

DIMENSIONS AND WEIGHT height: coupé 51.97 in, 132 cm.

BODY coupé; 2 doors.

FORD Taunus L 2000 Sedan

IKA-RENAULT Torino Grand Routier

IKA-RENAULT ARGENTINA

Torino Grand Routier

ENGINE front, 4 stroke; 6 cylinders, in line; 230 cu in, 3,770 cc (3.34 x 4.37 in, 84.9 x 111.1 mm); compression ratio: 8:1; max power (SAE): 180 hp at 4,700 rpm; max torque (SAE): 225 lb ft, 31 kg m at 2,500 rpm; max engine rpm: 5,000; 47.7 hp/l; 7 crankshaft bearings; valves: overhead; camshafts: 1, overhead; lubrication: gear pump, full flow filter, 7.9 imp pt, 9.5 US pt, 4.5 l; 1 Carter ABD downdraught twin barrel carburettor; fuel feed: mechanical pump; water-cooled, 20.4 imp pt, 24.5 US pt, 11.6 l.

TRANSMISSION driving wheels: rear; clutch: single dry plate; gearbox: mechanical; gears: 4, fully synchronized; ratios: I 2.830, II 1.850, III 1.380, IV 1, rev 3.150; lever: central; final drive: hypoid bevel; axle ratio: 3.310; width of rims: 6''; tyres: 185 HR x 15.

PERFORMANCE max speed: 115 mph, 185 km/h; power-weight ratio: 17.4 lb/hp, 7.9 kg/hp; consumption: 21.7 m/imp gal, 18.1 m/US gal, 13 l x 100 km.

CHASSIS integral; front suspension: independent, wishbones, anti-roll bar, coil springs, telescopic dampers; rear: rigid axle, semi-elliptic leafsprings, telescopic dampers.

STEERING recirculating ball; turns lock to lock: 6.25.

OPEL K - 180 Luxo

OPEL K-180 Rally

BRAKES front disc, rear drum, dual circuit, servo; swept area: total 202.8 sq in, 1,308 sq cm.

ELECTRICAL EQUIPMENT 12 V; 55 Ah battery; 40 A alternator; 4 headlamps.

DIMENSIONS AND WEIGHT wheel base: 107.09 in, 272 cm; tracks: 57.48 in, 146 cm front, 55.91 in, 142 cm rear; length: 186.61 in, 474 cm; width: 70.87 in, 180 cm; height: 56.69 in, 144 cm; ground clearance: 6.69 in, 17 cm; weight: 3,138 lb, 1,423 kg; fuel tank: 14.1 imp gal, 16.9 US gal, 64 l.

BODY saloon/sedan; 4 doors; 5/6 seats.

Torino TSX

See Torino Grand Routier, except for:

ENGINE compression ratio: 8.2:1; max power (SAE): 200 hp at 4,500 rpm; max torque (SAE): 239 lb ft, 33 kg m at 3,000 rpm; 53 hp/l; 1 Carter ABD 2053-6 downdraught twin barrel carburettor; cooling system: 21.6 imp pt, 26 US pt, 12.3 l.

TRANSMISSION ratios: I 3.540, II 2.310, III 1.500, IV 1, rev 3.150.

PERFORMANCE max speed: 124 mph, 200 km/h; power-weight ratio: 15.3 lb/hp, 6.9 kg/hp; consumption: 18.8 m/imp gal, 15.7 m/US gal, 15 l x 100 km.

ELECTRICAL EQUIPMENT 42 A alternator.

DIMENSIONS AND WEIGHT height: 55.91 in, 142 cm; ground clearance: 6.30 in, 16 cm; weight: 3,076 lb, 1,395 kg.

BODY hardtop; 2 doors; 5 seats.

OPEL ARGENTINA

K - 180/K - 180 Luxo/K - 180 Rally

PRICES EX WORKS: K-180: 3,558,000 pesos
K-180 Luxo: 4,198,000 pesos
K-180 Rally: 4,262,000 pesos

ENGINE front, 4 stroke; 4 cylinders, in line; 110 cu in, 1,802 cc (3.56 x 2.75 in, 90.4 x 69.8 mm); compression ratio: 8.2:1, max power (DIN): 73.8 hp at 5,200 rpm; max torque (DIN): 96 lb ft, 13.3 kg m at 2,400 rpm; max engine rpm: 5,200; 41 hp/l; cast iron block and head; 5 crankshaft bearings; valves: overhead, push-rods and rockers, hydraulic tappets; camshafts: 1, side, cogged belt; lubrication: gear pump, full flow filter, 6.9 imp pt, 8.2 US pt, 3.9 l; 1 Bendix C311-A1 downdraught single barrel carburettor; fuel feed: mechanical pump; water-cooled, 15.7 imp pt, 18.8 US pt, 8.9 l.

TRANSMISSION driving wheels: rear; clutch: single dry plate (diaphragm); gearbox: mechanical; gears: 4, fully synchronized; ratios: I 3.404, II 2.157, III 1.378, IV 1, rev 3.815; lever: central; final drive: hypoid bevel; axle ratio: 3.730; width of rims: 5''; tyres: 5.60 S x 13.

PERFORMANCE max speeds: (I) 27 mph, 44 km/h; (II) 43 mph, 70 km/h; (III) 69 mph, 111 km/h; (IV) 93 mph, 149 km/h; power-weight ratio: 28.9 lb/hp, 13.1 kg/hp; carrying capacity: 860 lb, 390 kg; acceleration: standing ¼ mile 20.8 sec, 0-50 mph (0-80 km/h) 12.1 sec; speed in direct drive at 1,000 rpm: 18 mph, 28.9 km/h; consumption: 37.2 m/imp gal, 30.9 m/US gal, 7.6 l x 100 km at 50 mph, 80 km/h.

CHASSIS integral; front suspension: independent, wishbones, coil springs, anti-roll bar, telescopic dampers; rear: rigid axle (torque tube), longitudinal trailing radius arms, coil springs, transverse linkage bar, telescopic dampers.

STEERING rack-and-pinion; turns lock to lock: 3.50.

BRAKES front disc, rear drum; swept area: front 182.9 sq in, 1,180 sq cm, rear 111.9 sq in, 722 sq cm, total 294.8 sq in, 1,902 sq cm.

ELECTRICAL EQUIPMENT 12 V; 44 Ah battery; 32 A alternator; Bosch distributor; 2 headlamps.

DIMENSIONS AND WEIGHT wheel base: 94.09 in, 239 cm; front and rear track: 51.18 in, 130 cm; length: 162.20 in, 412 cm; width: 61.81 in, 157 cm; height: 51.97 in, 132 cm; ground clearance: 6.69 in, 17 cm; weight: 2,126 lb, 964 kg; weight distribution: 54.6% front, 45.4% rear; turning circle (between walls): 32.5 ft, 9.9 m; fuel tank: 9.9 imp gal, 11.9 US gal, 45 l.

BODY saloon/sedan; 4 doors; 5 seats, separate front seats, reclining backrests.

OPTIONAL ACCESSORIES servo brake; iodine headlamps; heated rear window; 165 SR x 13 tyres; tinted glass.

Middle East
Africa
Asia
Australasia

Models now in production

Illustrations and technical information

OTOSAN   TURKEY

Anadol A1

PRICE EX WORKS: 50,000 liras

ENGINE Ford, front, 4 stroke; 4 cylinders, vertical, in line; 79.1 cu in, 1,298 cc (3.19 x 2.48 in, 81 x 63 mm); compression ratio: 8:1; max power (DIN): 54 hp at 5,500 rpm; max torque (DIN): 63 lb ft, 8.7 kg m at 3,000 rpm; max engine rpm: 5,700; 41.6 hp/l; cast iron block and head; 5 crankshaft bearings; valves: overhead, in line, push-rods and rockers; camshafts: 1, side; lubrication: rotary or vane-type pump, full flow filter, 6.3 imp pt, 7.6 US pt, 3.6 l; 1 Ford GPD downdraught single barrel carburettor; fuel feed: mechanical pump; water-cooled, 10 imp pt, 12 US pt, 5.7 l.

TRANSMISSION driving wheels: rear; clutch: single dry plate (diaphragm); gearbox: mechanical; gears: 4, fully synchronized; ratios: I 3.543, II 2.396, III 1.412, IV 1, rev 3.963; lever: central; final drive: hypoid bevel; axle ratio: 4.125; width of rims: 4.5''; tyres: 5.60/5.90 x 13.

PERFORMANCE max speeds: (I) 22 mph, 35 km/h; (II) 36 mph, 58 km/h; (III) 56 mph, 90 km/h; (IV) 87 mph, 140 km/h; power-weight ratio: 37.6 lb/hp, 17 kg/hp; carrying capacity: 970 lb, 440 kg; speed in direct drive at 1,000 rpm: 16.3 mph, 26.3 km/h; consumption: 33.2 m/imp gal, 27.7 m/US gal, 8.5 l x 100 km.

CHASSIS box-type perimeter frame with cross members; front suspension: independent, wishbones, coil springs, anti-roll bar, telescopic dampers; rear: rigid axle, semi-elliptic leafsprings, telescopic dampers.

STEERING rack-and-pinion; turns lock to lock: 3.90.

BRAKES front disc (diameter 9.13 in, 23.2 cm), rear drum; lining area: front 15.7 sq in, 101 sq cm, rear 46 sq in, 297 sq cm, total 61.7 sq in, 398 sq cm.

ELECTRICAL EQUIPMENT 12 V; 45 Ah battery; 42 A alternator; Ford distributor; 2 headlamps.

DIMENSIONS AND WEIGHT wheel base: 100.98 in, 256 cm; tracks: 51.97 in, 132 cm front, 50.39 in, 128 cm rear; length: 174.80 in, 444 cm; width: 64.76 in, 164 cm; height: 55.91 in, 142 cm; ground clearance: 6.30 in, 16 cm; weight: 2,029 lb, 920 kg; weight distribution: 52% front, 48% rear; turning circle (between walls): 31.5 ft, 9.6 m; fuel tank: 8.6 imp gal, 10.3 US gal, 39 l.

BODY saloon/sedan, in reinforced plastic material; 2 doors; 5 seats, separate front seats; vinyl roof.

OPTIONAL ACCESSORIES 4-speed fully synchronized mechanical gearbox (I 3.580, II 2.010, III 1.397, IV 1, rev 3.324).

Anadol A2

See Anadol A1, except for:

PRICE EX WORKS: 75,000 liras

PERFORMANCE power-weight ratio: 38.6 lb/hp, 17.5 kg/hp; carrying capacity: 1,103 lb, 500 kg.

DIMENSIONS AND WEIGHT weight: 2,084 lb, 945 kg.

BODY 4 doors; bench front seats.

Anadol SL

See Anadol A2, except for:

BRAKES lining area: front 15.5 sq in, 100 sq cm, rear 38.8 sq in, 250 sq cm, total 54.3 sq in, 350 sq cm.

Anadol STC - 16

PRICE EX WORKS: 71,400 liras

ENGINE Ford, front, 4 stroke; 4 cylinders, vertical, in line; 97.6 cu in, 1,599 cc (3.19 x 3.06 in, 81 x 77.6 mm); compression ratio: 9:1; max power (DIN): 68 hp at 5,200 rpm; max torque (DIN): 86 lb ft, 11.8 kg m at 2,600 rpm; max engine rpm: 5,700; 42.5 hp/l; cast iron block and head; 5 crankshaft bearings; valves: overhead, in line, push-rods and rockers; camshafts: 1, side; lubrication: rotary or vane-type pump, full flow filter, 7.2 imp pt, 8.7 US pt, 4.1 l; 1 Ford GPD downdraught single barrel carburettor; fuel feed: mechanical pump; water-cooled, 13.7 imp pt, 16.5 US pt, 7.8 l.

TRANSMISSION driving wheels: rear; clutch: single dry plate (diaphragm); gearbox: mechanical; gears: 4, fully synchronized; ratios: I 2.972, II 2.010, III 1.397, IV 1, rev 3.324; lever: central; final drive: hypoid bevel; axle ratio: 4.125; width of rims: 5''; tyres: 165 SR x 13.

OTOSAN Anadol STC - 16

OTOSAN Böcek

PERFORMANCE max speeds: (I) 37 mph, 60 km/h; (II) 56 mph, 90 km/h; (III) 81 mph, 130 km/h; (IV) 99 mph, 160 km/h; power-weight ratio: 29.8 lb/hp, 13.5 kg/hp; carrying capacity: 441 lb, 200 kg; speed in direct drive at 1,000 rpm: 19.6 mph, 31.6 km/h; consumption: 21.6 m/imp gal, 18 m/US gal, 13.1 l x 100 km.

CHASSIS box-type perimeter frame with cross members; front suspension: independent, wishbones, coil springs, anti-roll bar, telescopic dampers; rear: rigid axle, semi-elliptic leafsprings, telescopic dampers.

STEERING rack-and-pinion; turns lock to lock: 3.34.

BRAKES front disc (diameter 9.13 in, 23.2 cm), rear drum, servo; lining area: front 15.7 sq in, 101 sq cm, rear 46 sq in, 297 sq cm, total 61.7 sq in, 398 sq cm.

ELECTRICAL EQUIPMENT 12 V; 45 Ah battery; 42 A alternator; Autolite distributor; 2 headlamps.

DIMENSIONS AND WEIGHT wheel base: 89.76 in, 228 cm; tracks: 51.97 in, 132 cm front, 50.39 in, 128 cm rear; length: 156.69 in, 398 cm; width: 64.57 in, 164 cm; height: 50.39 in, 128 cm; ground clearance: 6.38 in, 16.2 cm; weight: 2,029 lb, 920 kg; weight distribution: 49.4% front, 50.6% rear; turning circle (between walls): 29.5 ft, 9 m; fuel tank: 8.6 imp gal, 10.3 US gal, 39 l.

BODY coupé, in reinforced plastic material; 2 doors; 2 seats, reclining backrests, built-in headrests.

OPTIONAL ACCESSORIES 4-speed fully synchronized mechanical gearbox (I 3.580, II 2.010, III 1.397, IV 1, rev 3.324)

Anadol SV - 1600

See Anadol STC - 16, except for:

PRICE EX WORKS: 84,850 liras

ENGINE compression ratio: 8:1; max power (DIN): 65 hp at 5,200 rpm; max torque (DIN): 81 lb ft, 11.2 kg m at 2,600 rpm; 40.6 hp/l.

TRANSMISSION ratios: I 3.543, II 2.396, III 1.412, IV 1, rev 3.963; width of rims: 5.5''.

PERFORMANCE max speed: 90 mph, 145 km/h; power-weight ratio: 31.9 lb/hp, 14.5 kg/hp; carrying capacity: 1,433 lb, 650 kg.

DIMENSIONS AND WEIGHT wheel base: 100.79 in, 256 cm; length: 174.80 in, 444 cm; height: 55.51 in, 141 cm; ground clearance: 6.69 in, 17 cm; weight: 2,073 lb, 940 kg; turning circle (between walls): 35.1 ft, 10.7 m.

BODY estate car/st. wagon, in reinforced plastic material; 4 + 1 doors; 5 seats, separate front seats; folding rear seat.

PRACTICAL INSTRUCTIONS fuel: 94 oct petrol; tyre pressure: front 25-26 psi, 1.7-1.8 atm, rear 24-36 psi, 1.7-2.5 atm.

Böcek

ENGINE Ford, front, 4 stroke; 4 cylinders, vertical, in line; 79.1 cu in, 1,298 cc (3.19 x 2.48 in, 81 x 63 mm); compression ratio: 8:1; max power (DIN): 54 hp at 5,500 rpm; max torque (DIN): 63 lb ft, 8.7 kg m at 3,000 rpm; max engine rpm: 5,700; 41.6 hp/l; cast iron block and head; 5 crankshaft bearings; valves: overhead, in line, push-rods and rockers; camshafts: 1, side; lubrication: rotary or vane-type pump, full flow filter 6.3 imp pt, 7.6 US pt, 3.6 l; 1 Ford GPD downdraught single barrel carburettor; fuel feed: mechanical pump; water-cooled, 10 imp pt, 12 US pt, 5.7 l.

TRANSMISSION driving wheels: rear; clutch: single dry plate (diaphragm); gearbox: mechanical; gears: 4, fully synchronized; ratios: I 2.972, II 2.010, III 1.397, IV 1, rev 3.324; lever: central; final drive: hypoid bevel; axle ratio: 4.444; width of rims: 5.5''; tyres: 5.90 x 13.

PERFORMANCE max speed: not declared; power-weight ratio: 27.2 lb/hp, 12.3 kg/hp; carrying capacity: 827 lb, 375 kg; consumption: not declared.

CHASSIS box-type perimeter frame with cross members; front suspension: independent, wishbones, coil springs, anti-roll bar, telescopic dampers; rear: rigid axle, trailing arms, coil springs, telescopic dampers.

STEERING rack-and-pinion; turns lock to lock: 3.90.

BRAKES front disc (diameter 9.13 in, 23.2 cm), rear drum, servo; lining area: front 15.7 sq in, 101 sq cm, rear 46 sq in, 297 sq cm, total 61.7 sq in, 398 sq cm.

ELECTRICAL EQUIPMENT 12 V; 45 Ah battery; 42 A alternator; Ford distributor; 2 headlamps.

DIMENSIONS AND WEIGHT wheel base: 81.89 in, 208 cm; tracks: 52.05 in, 132 cm front, 50.71 in, 129 cm rear;

length: 125.98 in, 320 cm; width: 61.42 in, 148 cm; height: 55 in, 146 cm; ground clearance: 6.38 in, 16.2 cm; weight: 1,469 lb, 666 kg; fuel tank: 8.8 imp gal, 10.6 US gal, 40 l.

BODY open, in reinforced plastic material; no doors; 4-5 seats, separate front seats.

OPTIONAL ACCESSORIES 4-speed fully synchronized mechanical gearbox (I 3.580, II 2.010, III 1.397, IV 1, rev 3.324); 6.25 x 13 tyres with 6'' wide rims; 225 x 13 tyres with 6.5'' wide rims; 50GT x 13 tyres with 7.5'' wide rims.

TOFAS   TURKEY

Murat 131

ENGINE Fiat, front, 4 stroke; 4 cylinders, vertical, in line; 79.1 cu in, 1,297 cc (2.99 x 2.81 in, 76 x 71.5 mm); compression ratio: 7.8:1; max power (SAE): 70 hp at 5,250 rpm; max torque (SAE): 72 lb ft, 10 kg m at 3,400 rpm; max engine rpm: 5,750; 54 hp/l; cast iron block, light alloy head; 5 crankshaft bearings; valves: overhead, in line, slanted at 10°, push-rods and rockers; camshafts: 1, side, in crankcase, cogged belt; lubrication: gear pump, full flow filter (cartridge), 7.4 imp pt, 8.9 US pt, 4.2 l; 1 Solex 32 TEIE 42 downdraught twin barrel carburettor; fuel feed: mechanical pump; water-cooled, 13.4 imp pt, 16.1 US pt, 7.6 l, electric thermostatic fan.

TRANSMISSION driving wheels: rear; clutch: single dry plate (diaphragm); gearbox: mechanical; gears: 4, fully synchronized; ratios: I 3.667, II 2.100, III 1.361, IV 1, rev 3.526; lever: central; final drive: hypoid bevel; axle ratio: 4.100; width of rims: 4.5''; tyres: 165 SR x 13.

PERFORMANCE max speed: 93 mph, 150 km/h; power-weight ratio: 31 lb/hp, 14.1 kg/hp; carrying capacity: 882 lb, 400 kg; acceleration: standing ¼ mile 19.2 sec; speed in direct drive at 1,000 rpm: 15.7 mph, 25.3 km/h; consumption: 31.7 m/imp gal, 26.4 m/US gal, 8.9 l x 100 km.

CHASSIS integral; front suspension: independent, by McPherson, coil springs/telescopic damper struts, lower wishbones, anti-roll bar; rear: rigid axle, twin trailing lower radius arms, transverse linkage bar, coil springs, telescopic dampers.

STEERING rack-and-pinion; turns lock to lock: 3.40.

BRAKES front disc (diameter 8.94 in, 22.7 cm), rear drum (diameter 8.97 in, 22.8 cm), rear compensator, servo; lining area: front 19.2 sq in, 124 sq cm, rear 36.9 sq in, 238 sq cm, total 56.1 sq in, 362 sq cm.

ELECTRICAL EQUIPMENT 12 V; 45 Ah battery; 44 A alternator; Marelli distributor; 2 headlamps.

DIMENSIONS AND WEIGHT wheel base: 98.03 in, 249 cm; tracks: 53.94 in, 137 cm front, 51.57 in, 131 cm rear; length: 166.93 in, 424 cm; width: 64.17 in, 163 cm; height: 55.12 in, 140 cm; ground clearance: 5.51 in, 14 cm; weight: 2,172 lb, 985 kg; weight distribution: 53% front, 47% rear; turning circle (between walls): 34.8 ft, 10.6 m; fuel tank: 11 imp gal, 13.2 US gal, 50 l.

BODY saloon/sedan; 4 doors; 5 seats, separate front seats.

ROM CARMEL   ISRAEL

Rom 1300

ENGINE front, 4 stroke, 4 cylinders, in line; 79.2 cu in, 1,297 cc (3.19 x 2.48 in, 81 x 63 mm); compression ratio: 8:1; max power (DIN): 54 hp at 5,500 rpm; max torque (DIN): 63 lb ft, 8.7 kg m at 3,000 rpm; max engine rpm: 5,800; 41.6 hp/l; cast iron block and head; 5 crankshaft bearings; valves: 8, overhead, roller chain; camshafts: 1, overhead; lubrication: rotary pump, full flow filter, 5.8 imp pt, 7 US pt, 3.3 l; 1 Solex downdraught carburettor; fuel feed: mechanical pump; water-cooled, 8.8 imp pt, 10.6 US pt, 5 l.

TRANSMISSION driving wheels: rear; clutch: single dry plate (diaphragm); gearbox: mechanical; gears: 4, fully synchronized; ratios: I 3.660, II 2.190, III 1.430, IV 1, rev 4.240; lever: central; final drive: hypoid bevel; axle ratio: 4.110; width of rims: 4.5''; tyres: 5.60 x 13.

PERFORMANCE max speeds: (I) 24 mph, 38 km/h; (II) 40 mph, 64 km/h; (III) 61 mph, 98 km/h; (IV) 87 mph, 140 km/h; power-weight ratio: 36.8 lb/hp, 16.6 kg/hp; carrying capacity: 882 lb, 400 kg; speed in direct drive at 1,000 rpm: 14.5 mph, 23.3 km/h; consumption: 34.4 m/imp gal, 28.7 m/US gal, 8.2 l x 100 m.

CHASSIS separate steel frame, boxed side-members, arc welded; front suspension: independent, wishbones, coil springs, anti-roll bar, telescopic dampers; rear: rigid axle, semi-elliptic leafsprings, telescopic dampers.

STEERING rack-and-pinion; turns lock to lock: 3.

BRAKES front disc, rear drum, servo; swept area: front 142.2 sq in, 917 sq cm, rear 62.8 sq in, 405 sq cm, total 205 sq in, 1,322 sq cm.

ELECTRICAL EQUIPMENT 12 V; 40 Ah battery; 336 W alternator; Motorcraft distributor; 2 headlamps.

DIMENSIONS AND WEIGHT wheel base: 98.43 in, 250 cm; front and rear track: 49.21 in, 125 cm; length: 162.99 in, 414 cm; width: 61.42 in, 156 cm; height: 59.06 in, 150 cm; ground clearance: 6.50 in, 16.5 cm; weight: 1,985 lb, 900 kg; turning circle (between walls): 31.8 ft, 9.7 m; fuel tank: 9.2 imp gal, 11.1 US gal, 42 l.

BODY saloon/sedan, in plastic material; 4 doors; 5 seats, separate front seats.

PRACTICAL INSTRUCTIONS fuel: 94 oct petrol; oil: engine 5.6 imp pt, 6.8 US pt, 3.2 l, SAE 20/50, change every 6,200 miles, 10,000 km - gearbox 1.6 imp pt, 1.9 US pt, 0.9 l, SAE 80, change every 12,400 miles, 20,000 km - final drive 1.5 imp pt, 1.8 US pt, 0.8 l, SAE 90 HYP, change every 12,400 miles, 20,000 km; greasing: 4 points, every 6,200 miles, 10,000 km.

TOFAS Murat 131

TOFAS Murat 131

ROM CARMEL Rom 1300

EL NASR   EGYPT

Nasr 128

ENGINE front, transverse, 4 stroke; 4 cylinders, in line; 68.1 cu in, 1,116 cc (3.15 x 2.19 in, 80 x 55.5 mm); compression ratio: 7.8:1; max power (DIN): 51 hp at 6,000 rpm; max torque (DIN): 55 lb ft, 7.6 kg m at 3,500 rpm; max engine rpm: 6.500; 45.7 hp/l; cast iron block, light alloy head; 5 crankshaft bearings; valves: overhead, thimble tappets; camshafts: 1, overhead; lubrication: gear pump, full flow filter (cartridge), 8.8 imp pt, 10.6 US pt, 5 l; 1 Weber 32 ICEV 17 downdraught carburettor; fuel feed: mechanical pump; water-cooled, 11.4 imp pt, 13.7 US pt, 6.5 l, electric thermostatic fan.

TRANSMISSION driving wheels: front; clutch: single dry plate; gearbox: mechanical; gears: 4, fully synchronized; ratios: I 3.583, II 2.235, III 1.454, IV 1.042, rev 3.714; lever: central; final drive: cylindrical gears; axle ratio: 3.765; width of rims: 4.5''; tyres: 145 SR x 13.

PERFORMANCE max speeds: (I) 30 mph, 48 km/h; (II) 50 mph, 80 km/h; (III) 75 mph, 120 km/h; (IV) 84 mph, 135 km/h; power-weight ratio: 34.8 lb/hp, 15.8 kg/hp; carrying capacity: 882 lb, 400 kg; acceleration: standing ¼ mile 21 sec, 0-50 mph (0-80 km/h) 15.8 sec; speed in top at 1,000 rpm: 14.9 mph, 24 km/h; consumption: 35.3 m/imp gal, 29.4 m/US gal, 8 l x 100 km.

CHASSIS integral; front suspension: independent, by McPherson, coil springs, telescopic damper struts, lower wishbones, anti-roll bar; rear: independent, single wide-based wishbone, transverse leafspring, telescopic dampers.

STEERING rack-and-pinion; turns lock to lock: 3.50.

BRAKES front disc (diameter 8.94 in, 22.7 cm), rear drum, rear compensator, servo; lining area: front 19.2 sq in, 124 sq cm, rear 33.5 sq in, 216 sq cm, total 52.7 sq in, 340 sq cm.

ELECTRICAL EQUIPMENT 12 V; 34 Ah battery; 33 A alternator; Marelli distributor; 2 headlamps.

DIMENSIONS AND WEIGHT wheel base: 96.38 in, 245 cm; tracks: 51.50 in, 131 cm front, 51.69 in, 131 cm rear; length: 151.18 in, 384 cm; width: 62.60 in, 159 cm; height: 55.91 in, 142 cm; ground clearance: 5.71 in, 14.5 cm; weight: 1,775 lb, 805 kg; weight distribution: 61.5% front, 38.5% rear; turning circle (between walls): 35.8 ft, 10.9 m; fuel tank: 8.4 imp gal, 10 US gal, 38 l.

BODY saloon/sedan; 4 doors; 5 seats, separate front seats.

PRACTICAL INSTRUCTIONS fuel: 86 oct petrol; oil: engine 7.4 imp pt, 8.9 US pt, 4.2 l, SAE 30W (winter) 40 (summer), change every 6,200 miles, 10,000 km - gearbox' and final drive 5.5 imp pt, 6.6 US pt, 3.1 l, SAE 90 EP, change every 18,600 miles, 30,000 km; greasing: every 18,600 miles, 30,000 km, 1 point; sparking plug: 240°; tappet clearances: inlet 0.012 in, 0.30 mm, exhaust 0.016 in, 0.40 mm; valve timing: 12° 52° 52° 12°; tyre pressure: front 26 psi, 1.8 atm, rear 24 psi, 1.7 atm.

Nasr 125

ENGINE front, 4 stroke; 4 cylinders, vertical, in line; 90.4 cu in, 1,481 cc (3.03 x 3.13 in, 77 x 79.5 mm); compression ratio: 9:1; max power (DIN): 70 hp at 5,400 rpm; max torque (DIN): 83 lb ft, 11.5 kg m at 3,200 rpm; max engine rpm: 5,500; 45.2 hp/l; cast iron block, light alloy head; 3 crankshaft bearings; valves: overhead, in line, push-rods and rockers; camshafts: 1, side; lubrication: gear pump, centrifugal filter, cartridge on by-pass, 7.5 imp pt, 9 US pt, 4.3 l; 1 Weber 34 DCHD 1 downdraught twin barrel carburettor; fuel feed: mechanical pump; water-cooled, 11.8 imp pt, 14.2 US pt, 6.7 l.

TRANSMISSION driving wheels: rear; clutch: single dry plate, hydraulically controlled; gearbox: mechanical; gears: 4, fully synchronized; ratios: I 3.750, II 2.300, III 1.490, IV 1, rev 3.870; lever: central; final drive: hypoid bevel; axle ratio: 4.100; width of rims: 4.5''; tyres: 5.60 S x 13.

PERFORMANCE max speeds: (I) 25 mph, 40 km/h; (II) 40 mph, 65 km/h; (III) 62 mph, 100 km/h; (IV) 93 mph, 150 km/h; power-weight ratio: 31.1 lb/hp, 14.1 kg/hp; carrying capacity: 882 lb, 400 kg; acceleration: 0-50 mph (0-80 km/h) 13 sec; speed in direct drive at 1,000 rpm: 16.1 mph, 25.9 km/h; consumption: 29.7 m/imp gal, 24.8 m/US gal, 9.5 l x 100 km.

CHASSIS integral; front suspension: independent, wishbones, lower trailing links, coil springs, anti-roll bar, telescopic dampers; rear: rigid axle, semi-elliptic leaf-springs, telescopic dampers.

STEERING worm and roller; turns lock to lock: 3.

BRAKES disc, servo.

ELECTRICAL EQUIPMENT 12 V; 53 Ah battery; 770 W alternator; Marelli distributor; 4 headlamps.

DIMENSIONS AND WEIGHT wheel base: 98.43 in, 250 cm; tracks: 51.18 in, 130 cm front, 51.18 in, 130 cm rear; length: 166.65 in, 423 cm; width: 63.98 in, 162 cm; height: 56.69 in, 144 cm; ground clearance: 5.51 in, 14 cm; weight: 2,183 lb, 990 kg; turning circle (between walls): 36.1 ft, 11 m; fuel tank: 9.9 imp gal, 11.9 US gal, 45 l.

BODY saloon/sedan; 4 doors; 5 seats, separate front seats, reclining backrests.

PRACTICAL INSTRUCTIONS fuel: 86 oct petrol; oil: engine 6.2 imp pt, 7.4 US pt, 3.5 l, SAE 20W-30, change every 6,200 miles, 10,000 km - gearbox 2.3 imp pt, 2.7 US pt, 1.3 l, SAE 90, change every 18,600 miles, 30,000 km - final drive 1.6 imp pt, 1.9 US pt, 0.9 l, SAE 90, change every 18,600 miles, 30,000 km; greasing: every 1,600 miles, 2,500 km, 3 points; sparking plug: 240°; tappet clearances: inlet 0.008 in, 0.20 mm, exhaust 0.008 in, 0.25 mm; valve timing: 25° 51° 64° 12°; tyre pressure: front 21 psi, 1.5 atm, rear 24 psi, 1.7 atm.

EL NASR Nasr 128

VOLKSWAGEN   NIGERIA

1200

ENGINE rear, 4 stroke; 4 cylinders, horizontally opposed; 72.7 cu in, 1,192 cc (3.03 x 2.52 in, 77 x 64 mm); compression ratio: 7.3:1; max power (DIN): 34 hp at 3,800 rpm; max torque (DIN): 55 lb ft, 7.6 kg m at 1,700 rpm; max engine rpm: 4,500; 28.5 hp/l; block with cast iron liners and light alloy fins, light alloy head; 4 crankshaft bearings; valves: overhead, push-rods and rockers; camshafts: 1, central, lower; lubrication: gear pump, filter in sump, oil cooler, 4.4 imp pt, 5.3 US pt, 2.5 l; 1 Solex 30 PICT downdraught single barrel carburettor; fuel feed: mechanical pump; air-cooled.

TRANSMISSION driving wheels: rear; clutch: single dry plate; gearbox: mechanical; gears: 4, fully synchronized; ratios: I 3.780, II 2.060, III 1.260, IV 0.890, rev 4.010; lever: central; final drive: spiral bevel; axle ratio: 4.375; width of rims: 4''; tyres: 5.60 x 15.

PERFORMANCE max speeds: (I) 19 mph, 31 km/h; (II) 35 mph, 57 km/h; (III) 58 mph, 94 km/h; (IV) 71 mph, 115 km/h; power-weight ratio: 49.2 lb/hp, 22.3 kg/hp; carrying capacity: 838 lb, 380 kg; acceleration: standing ¼ mile 23

VOLKSWAGEN 1200

CHEVROLET 1900

sec, 0-50 mph (0-80 km/h) 18 sec; speed in top at 1,000 rpm: 18.6 mph, 30 km/h; consumption: 37.7 m/imp gal, 31.4 m/US gal, 7.5 l x 100 km.

CHASSIS backbone platform; front suspension: independent, twin swinging longitudinal trailing arms, transverse laminated torsion bars, anti-roll bar, telescopic dampers; rear: independent, swinging semi-axles, swinging longitudinal trailing arms, transverse torsion bars, telescopic dampers.

STEERING worm and roller telescopic damper; turns lock to lock: 2.60.

BRAKES drum; lining area: total 111 sq in, 716 sq cm.

ELECTRICAL EQUIPMENT 12 V; 36 Ah battery; 270 W dynamo; Bosch distributor; 2 headlamps.

DIMENSIONS AND WEIGHT wheel base: 94.49 in, 240 cm; tracks: 51.57 in, 131 cm front, 53.15 in, 135 cm rear; length: 159.84 in, 406 cm; width: 61.02 in, 155 cm; height: 59.06 in, 150 cm; ground clearance: 5.90 in, 15 cm; weight: 1,676 lb, 760 kg; weight distribution: 43% front, 57% rear; turning circle (between walls): 36.1 ft, 11 m; fuel tank: 8.8 imp gal, 10.6 US gal, 40 l.

BODY saloon/sedan; 2 doors; 5 seats, separate front seats, adjustable backrests.

PRACTICAL INSTRUCTIONS fuel: 87 oct petrol; oil: engine 4.4 imp pt, 5.3 US pt, 2.5 l, SAE 10W-20 (winter) 20W-30 (summer), change every 3,100 miles, 5,000 km - gearbox and final drive 5.3 imp pt, 6.3 US pt, 3 l, SAE 90 change every 31,000 miles, 50,000 km; greasing: every 6,200 miles, 10,000 km, 4 points; sparking plug: 175°; tappet clearances: inlet 0.004 in, 0.10 mm, exhaust 0.004 in, 0.10 mm; valve timing: 6° 35°5' 42°5' 3°; tyre pressure: front 16 psi, 1.1 atm, rear 24 psi, 1.7 atm.

CHEVROLET SOUTH AFRICA

1300/1300 LS

PRICE EX WORKS: 1300 LS: 3,284 rand

ENGINE front, 4 stroke; 4 cylinders, vertical, in line; 76.6 cu in, 1,256 cc (3.18 x 2.40 in, 81 x 61 mm); compression ratio: 9.2:1; max power (SAE): 79 hp at 5,400 rpm; max torque (SAE): 78 lb ft, 10.7 kg m at 3,400 rpm; max engine rpm: 5,800; 62.9 hp/l; cast iron block and head; 3 crankshaft bearings; valves: overhead, in line, push-rods and rockers; camshafts: 1, side; lubrication: gear pump, full flow filter, 5.1 imp pt, 6.1 US pt, 2.9 l; 1 Stromberg CDS 1.50 downdraught carburettor; fuel feed: mechanical pump; water-cooled, 10.2 imp pt, 12.3 US pt, 5.8 l.

TRANSMISSION driving wheels: rear; clutch: single dry plate (diaphragm); gearbox: mechanical; gears: 4, fully syn-

chronized; ratios: I 3.460, II 2.213, III 1.404, IV 1, rev 3.707; lever: central; final drive: hypoid bevel; axle ratio: 4.110; width of rims: 5''; tyres: 155 SR x 13.

PERFORMANCE max speed: about 87 mph, 140 km/h; power-weight ratio: 24 lb/hp, 10.9 kg/hp; carrying capacity: 882 lb, 400 kg; consumption: 40.4 m/imp gal, 33.6 m/US gal, 7 l x 100 km.

CHASSIS integral; front suspension: independent, wishbones, coil springs, anti-roll bar, telescopic dampers; rear: rigid axle, wishbones, coil springs, telescopic dampers.

STEERING rack-and-pinion; turns lock to lock: 3.16.

BRAKES front disc, rear drum, servo.

ELECTRICAL EQUIPMENT 12 V; 32 Ah battery; generator; 2 headlamps.

DIMENSIONS AND WEIGHT wheel base: 96.85 in, 246 cm; front and rear track: 51.57 in, 131 cm; length: 162.99 in, 414 cm; width: 64.56 in, 164 cm; height: 53.15 in, 135 cm; weight: 1,896 lb, 860 kg; fuel tank: 13.2 imp gal, 15.8 US gal, 60 l.

BODY saloon/sedan; 4 doors; 5 seats, separate front seats (for LS only reclining backrests and tinted glass).

OPTIONAL ACCESSORIES vinyl roof; metallic spray.

1900/1900 LS

See 1300/1300 LS, except for:

PRICE EX WORKS: 1900 LS: 3,471 rand

ENGINE 119.6 cu in, 1,960 cc (3.56 x 3 in, 90.5 x 76.2 mm); compression ratio: 9.1:1; max power (SAE): 109 hp at 5,000 rpm; max torque (SAE): 118 lb ft, 16.3 kg m at 3,600 rpm; max engine rpm: 5,400; 55.6 hp/l; 1 Weber 28/36 DCD downdraught carburettor.

TRANSMISSION gearbox ratios: I 3.430, II 2.160, III 1.370, IV 1, rev 3.320; axle ratio: 3.700; tyres: 165 SR x 13.

PERFORMANCE max speed: about 99 mph, 160 km/h; power-weight ratio: 19.6 lb/hp, 8.9 kg/hp.

DIMENSIONS AND WEIGHT weight: 2,117 lb, 960 kg.

OPTIONAL ACCESSORIES Tri-Matic automatic transmission, hydraulic torque converter and planetary gears with 3 ratios (I 2.310, II 1.460, III 1, rev 1.860).

Hatch Series

PRICES EX WORKS:

1 1300 De Luxe 3-door Hatchback	3,224	rand
2 1300 LS 3-door Hatchback	3,399	rand
3 1900 De Luxe 3-door Hatchback	3,395	rand
4 1900 LS 3-door Hatchback	3,569	rand

Power team:	Standard for:	Optional for:
79 hp	1,2	—
109 hp	3,4	—

---

79 hp power team

ENGINE front, 4 stroke; 4 cylinders, vertical, in line; 76.6 cu in, 1,256 cc (3.18 x 2.40 in, 81 x 61 mm); compression ratio: 9.2:1; max power (SAE): 79 hp at 5,400 rpm; max torque (SAE): 78 lb ft, 10.7 kg m at 3,400 rpm; max engine rpm: 5,800; 62.9 hp/l; cast iron block and head; 3 crankshaft bearings; valves: overhead, in line, push-rods and rockers; camshafts: 1, side; lubrication: gear pump, full flow filter, 5.1 imp pt, 6.1 US pt, 2.9 l; 1 Stromberg CDS 1.50 downdraught carburettor; fuel feed: mechanical pump; water-cooled, 10.2 imp pt, 12.3 US pt, 5.8 l.

TRANSMISSION driving wheels: rear; clutch: single dry plate (diaphragm); gearbox: mechanical; gears: 4, fully synchronized; ratios: I 3.460, II 2.213, III 1.404, IV 1, rev 3.707; lever: central; final drive: hypoid bevel; axle ratio: 4.110; width of rims: 5''; tyres: 155 SR x 13.

PERFORMANCE max speed: about 85 mph, 137 km/h; carrying capacity: 882 lb, 400 kg; speed in direct drive at 1,000

CHEVROLET 1300 LS 3-door Hatchback

79 HP POWER TEAM

rpm: 15.8 mph, 25.5 km/h; consumption: 40.4 m/imp gal, 33.6 m/US gal, 7 l x 100 km.

CHASSIS integral; front suspension: independent, wishbones, coil springs, telescopic dampers; rear: rigid axle, trailing lower radius arms, upper oblique radius arms, coil springs, telescopic dampers.

STEERING rack-and-pinion; turns lock to lock: 3.16.

BRAKES front disc (diameter 8.54 in, 21.7 cm), rear drum; swept area: total 193.6 sq in, 1,266 sq cm.

ELECTRICAL EQUIPMENT 12 V; 32 Ah battery; generator; 2 headlamps.

DIMENSIONS AND WEIGHT wheel base: 96.89 in, 246 cm; tracks: 51.42 in, 131 cm front, 51.50 in, 131 cm rear; length: 152.99 in, 389 cm; width: 64.68 in, 164 cm; height: 53.94 in, 137 cm; ground clearance: 5 in, 12.7 cm; turning circle (between walls): 31.5 ft, 9.6 m; fuel tank: 13.2 imp gal, 15.8 US gal, 60 l.

BODY 5 seats, separate front seats; reclining backrests and tinted glass (standard for LS only).

OPTIONAL ACCESSORIES metallic spray; vinyl roof; (for De Luxe only) reclining backrests and tinted glass.

CHEVROLET Chevair 1900 De Luxe
4-door Sedan

CHEVROLET SII 2500 Station Wagon

109 hp power team

See 79 hp power team, except for:

ENGINE 119.6 cu in, 1,960 cc (3.56 x 3 in, 90.5 x 76.2 mm); compression ratio: 9:1; max power (SAE): 109 hp at 5,000 rpm; max torque (SAE): 118 lb ft, 16.3 kg m at 3,600 rpm; max engine rpm: 5,400; 55.6 hp/l; 1 Weber 28/36 DCD downdraught carburettor.

TRANSMISSION gearbox ratios: I 3.430, II 2.160, III 1.370, IV 1, rev 3.320; axle ratio: 3.700; tyres: 165 SR x 13.

PERFORMANCE max speed: about 99 mph, 160 km/h; consumption: 35.8 m/imp gal, 29.8 m/US gal, 7.9 l x 100 km.

ELECTRICAL EQUIPMENT 336 W alternator.

OPTIONAL ACCESSORIES automatic transmission.

Chevair Series

PRICES EX WORKS:

1 1900 De Luxe 4-door Sedan		3,941	rand
2 2300 GL 4-door Sedan		4,206	rand

Power team:	Standard for:	Optional for:
91 hp	1	—
105 hp	2	—

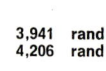

CHEVROLET Chevair 2300 GL 4-door Sedan

91 hp power team

ENGINE front, 4 stroke; 4 cylinders, vertical in line; 119.6 cu in, 1,960 cc (3.56 x 3 in, 90.5 x 76.2 mm); compression ratio: 9:1; max power (SAE): 91 hp at 5,200 rpm; max torque (SAE): 114 lb ft, 15.7 kg m at 2,400 rpm; max engine rpm: 5,500; 46.4 hp/l; cast iron block and head; 5 crankshaft bearings; valves: overhead; 1 Rochester/Monojet carburettor.

TRANSMISSION driving wheels: rear: clutch: single dry plate; gearbox: mechanical; gears: 4, fully synchronized; ratios: I 3.428, II 2.156, III 1.366, IV 1, rev 3.317; lever: central; final drive: hypoid bevel; axle ratio: 3.700; width of rims: 5.5''; tyres: 165 SR x 13.

PERFORMANCE acceleration: 0-50 mph (0-80 km/h) 9.2 sec; speed in direct drive at 1,000 rpm: 21 mph, 34.5 km/h; consumption: 36.7 m/imp gal, 30.5 m/US gal, 7.7 l x 100 km.

CHASSIS integral; front suspension: independent, wishbones, coil springs, telescopic dampers; rear: rigid axle, trailing lower radius arms, coil springs, telescopic dampers.

STEERING rack-and-pinion; turns lock to lock: 4.

BRAKES front disc, rear drum.

ELECTRICAL EQUIPMENT 12 V; 32 Ah battery; 37 A alternator; 2 headlamps.

DIMENSIONS AND WEIGHT wheel base: 99.13 in, 252 cm; front and rear track: 54.13 in, 137 cm; length: 175.47 in, 446 cm; width: 64.96 in, 165 cm; height: 51.97 in, 132 cm; ground clearance: 5 in, 12.7 cm; turning circle (between walls): 31.2 ft, 9.5 m; fuel tank: 12.3 imp gal, 14.8 US gal, 56 l.

BODY 5 seats, separate front seats, reclining backrests.

OPTIONAL ACCESSORIES Tri-Matic automatic transmission, hydraulic torque converter and planetary gears with 3 ratios (I 2.310, II 1.460, III 1, rev 1.860), max ratio of converter at stall 2.33, possible manual selection; metallic spray; vinyl roof; tinted glass.

105 hp power team

See 91 hp power team, except for:

ENGINE 141.6 cu in, 2,320 cc (3.87 x 3 in, 98.4 x 76.2 mm); max power (SAE): 105 hp at 5,100 rpm; max torque (SAE): 136 lb ft, 18.7 kg m at 3,300 rpm; 45.3 hp/l.

TRANSMISSION axle ratio: 3.420.

PERFORMANCE acceleration: 0-50 mph (0-80 km/h) 8.4 sec; speed in direct drive at 1,000 rpm: 20 mph, 32 km/h; consumption: 37.2 m/imp gal, 30.9 m/US gal, 7.6 l x 100 km.

DIMENSIONS AND WEIGHT length: 177.17 in, 450 cm.

BODY built-in headrests.

SII Series

PRICES EX WORKS:

1 2500 4-door Sedan	4,397	rand
2 2500 5-door Station Wagon	4,625	rand
3 3800 4-door Sedan	—	
4 3800 5-door Station Wagon	4,911	rand
5 4100 4-door Sedan	—	
6 4100 GA 4-door Sedan	5,757	rand

Power team:	Standard for:	Optional for:
120 hp	1,2	—
142 hp	3,4	—
157 hp	5,6	—

120 hp power team

ENGINE front, 4 stroke; 4 cylinders, vertical, in line; 153.3 cu in, 2,512 cc (3.87 x 3.25 in, 98.4 x 82.5 mm); compression ratio: 8.5:1; max power (SAE): 120 hp at 4,600 rpm; max torque (SAE): 144 lb ft, 19.9 kg m at 3,600 rpm; max engine rpm: 4,800; 47.8 hp/l; cast iron block and head; 5 crankshaft bearings; valves: overhead, in line, push-rods and rockers, hydraulic tappets; camshafts: 1, side; lubrication: gear pump, full flow filter, 6.7 imp pt, 8 US pt, 3.8 l; 1 Weber 36 DCD 7 downdraught twin barrel carburettor; fuel feed: mechanical pump; water-cooled, 14.8 imp pt, 17.8 US pt, 8.4 l.

TRANSMISSION driving wheels: rear; clutch: single dry plate (diaphragm), hydraulically controlled; gearbox: mechanical; gears: 4, fully synchronized; ratios: I 3.428, II 2.156, III 1.366, IV 1, rev 3.317; lever: central; final drive: hypoid bevel; axle ratio: 3.230; width of rims: 5''; tyres: 175 SR x 14.

CHEVROLET Kommando LS 4-door Sedan

PERFORMANCE max speed: about 96 mph, 155 km/h; power-weight ratio: Sedan 20.9 lb/hp, 9.5 kg/hp; carrying capacity: Sedan 882 lb, 400 kg - Station Wagon 1,213 lb, 550 kg; speed in direct drive at 1,000 rpm: 22.1 mph, 35.5 km/h; consumption: 23.5 m/imp gal, 19.6 m/US gal, 12 l x 100 km.

CHASSIS integral; front suspension: independent, wishbones (lower trailing links), coil springs, anti-roll bar, telescopic dampers; rear: rigid axle, twin trailing lower radius arms, upper torque arms, transverse linkage bar, coil springs, anti-roll bar, telescopic dampers.

STEERING rack-and-pinion; turns lock to lock: 4.

BRAKES front disc (diameter 10.67 in, 27.1 cm), rear drum, rear compensator, servo; lining area: front 24.7 sq in, 159 sq cm, rear 62.8 sq in, 405 sq cm, total 87.5 sq in, 564 sq cm.

ELECTRICAL EQUIPMENT 12 V; 48 Ah battery; 37 A alternator; 2 headlamps.

DIMENSIONS AND WEIGHT wheel base: 105.12 in, 267 cm; tracks: 56.30 in, 143 cm front, 55.51 in, 141 cm rear; length: Sedan 179.90 in, 457 cm - Station Wagon 180.87 in, 459 cm; width: 68.11 in, 173 cm; height: Sedan 55.12 in, 140 cm - Station Wagon 54.80 in, 139 cm; ground clearance: 5.04 in, 12.8 cm; weight: Sedan 2,518 lb, 1,142 kg - Station Wagon 2,725 lb, 1,236 kg; turning circle (between walls): 36.7 ft, 11.2 m; fuel tank: 15.4 imp gal, 18.5 US gal, 70 l.

BODY 5 seats, separate front seats, reclining backrests.

OPTIONAL ACCESSORIES 2.920 axle ratio; Tri-Matic automatic transmission with 3 ratios (I 2.310, II 1.460, III 1, rev 1.860), max ratio of converter at stall 2.33, possible manual selection; headrests; metallic spray; tinted glass; sunshine roof, vinyl roof and heated rear window (except for Station Wagon).

142 hp power team

See 120 hp power team, except for:

ENGINE 6 cylinders, vertical, in line; 230 cu in, 3,769 cc (3.87 x 3.26 in, 98.4 x 82.5 mm); max power (SAE): 142 hp at 4,400 rpm; max torque (SAE): 206 lb ft, 28.4 kg m at 1,600 rpm; max engine rpm: 4,600; 37.7 hp/l; 7 crankshaft bearings; lubrication: 7.6 imp pt, 9.1 US pt, 4.3 l; 1 Rochester Monojet carburettor; cooling system: 21.6 imp pt, 26 US pt, 12.3 l.

TRANSMISSION gearbox: Tri-Matic automatic transmission with 3 ratios, max ratio of converter at stall 2, possible manual selection; ratios: I 2.520, II 1.520, III 1, rev 1.940; width of rims: 6''; tyres: 185 SR x 14.

PERFORMANCE max speed: about 103 mph, 165 km/h; power-weight ratio: 19.8 lb/tp, 9 kg/hp; speed in direct drive at 1,000 rpm: 22.7 mph, 36.5 km/h; consumption: 23.7 m/imp gal, 19.8 m/US gal, 11.9 l x 100 km.

ELECTRICAL EQUIPMENT 4 halogen headlamps.

DIMENSIONS AND WEIGHT weight: 2,814 lb, 1,276 kg.

OPTIONAL ACCESSORIES (for Station Wagon only) mechanical gearbox with 4 ratios (I 3.110, II 2.200, III 1.470, IV 1, rev 3.110); air-conditioning; heated rear window; power-steering; vinyl roof.

157 hp power team

See 120 hp power team, except for:

ENGINE 6 cylinders, vertical, in line; 249.7 cu in, 4,093 cc (3.87 x 3.53 in, 98.4 x 89.7 mm); max power (SAE): 157 hp at 4,200 rpm; max torque (SAE): 227 lb ft, 31.4 kg m at 1,600 rpm; max engine rpm: 4,600; 38.4 hp/l; 7 crankshaft bearings; lubrication: 7.6 imp pt, 9.1 US pt, 4.3 l; 1 Rochester Monojet carburettor; cooling system: 21.6 imp pt, 26 US pt, 12.3 l.

TRANSMISSION gearbox: Tri-Matic automatic transmission with 3 ratios, max ratio of converter at stall 2, possible manual selection; ratios: I 2.520, II 1.520, III 1, rev 1.940; width of rims: 6''; tyres: 185 SR x 14.

PERFORMANCE max speed: over 103 mph, 165 km/h; power-weight ratio: 17.9 lb/hp, 8.1 kg/hp; speed in direct drive at 1,000 rpm: 25.1 mph, 40.4 km/h; consumption: 20.2 m/imp gal, 16.8 m/US gal, 14 l x 100 km.

ELECTRICAL EQUIPMENT 4 halogen headlamps.

DIMENSIONS AND WEIGHT weight: 2,814 lb, 1,276 kg.

BODY tinted glass; headrests; metallic spray; vinyl roof; (for GA only) power-steering.

OPTIONAL ACCESSORIES power-steering; air-conditioning.

Kommando Series

PRICES EX WORKS:

Kommando 4-door Sedan	—
Kommando LS 4-door Sedan	**5,503** rand

134 hp power team

ENGINE front, 4 stroke; 6 cylinders, vertical, in line; 249.9 cu in, 4,095 cc (3.87 x 3.53 in, 98.4 x 89.7 mm); compression ratio: 9:1; max power (SAE): 134 hp at 4,200 rpm; max torque (SAE): 210 lb ft, 29 kg m at 1,600 rpm; max engine rpm: 5,000; 32.8 hp/l; cast iron block and head; 7 crankshaft bearings; valves: overhead in line, push-rods and rockers, hydraulic tappets; camshafts: 1, side; lubrication: gear pump, full flow filter, 8.3 imp pt, 9.9 US pt, 4.7 l; 1 Rochester Monojet carburettor; fuel feed: mechanical pump; water-cooled, 21.6 imp pt, 26 US pt, 12.3 l.

TRANSMISSION driving wheels: rear; clutch: single dry plate (diaphragm); gearbox: mechanical (Tri-Matic automatic transmission standard for LS only); gears: 3, fully synchronized; ratios: I 3.070, II 1.680, III 1, rev 3.590; lever: steering column; final drive: hypoid bevel; axle ratio: 3.230 - LS 2.920; tyres: 7.35 x 14 or 185 SR x 14.

PERFORMANCE max speed: about 103 mph, 165 km/h; power-weight ratio: 22.1 lb/hp, 10.7 kg/hp; carrying capacity: 1,058 lb, 480 kg; speed in direct drive at 1,000 rpm: 22.8 mph, 36.7 km/h; consumption: 17.4 m/imp gal, 14.5 m/US gal, 16.2 l x 100 km.

CHASSIS integral; front suspension: independent, wishbones, coil springs, anti-roll bar, telescopic dampers; rear: rigid axle, twin trailing lower radius arms, upper torque

arms, transverse linkage bar, coil springs, anti-roll bar, telescopic dampers.

STEERING recirculating ball; turns lock to lock: 3.68.

BRAKES front disc (diameter 10.87 in, 27.6 cm), internal radial fins, rear drum, servo.

ELECTRICAL EQUIPMENT 12 V; 45 Ah battery; 37 A alternator; 2 headlamps.

DIMENSIONS AND WEIGHT wheel base: 110.90 in, 282 cm; tracks: 59.49 in, 151 cm front, 60.20 in, 153 cm rear; length: 190.47 in, 484 cm - LS 190.98 in, 485 cm; width: 73.78 in, 187 cm - LS 74.09 in, 188 cm; height: 54.29 in, 138 cm - LS 54.37 in, 138 cm; ground clearance: 5.79 in, 14.7 cm - LS 5.98 in, 15.2 cm; weight: 2,956 lb, 1,345 kg; turning circle (between walls): 39.7 ft, 12.1 m; fuel tank: 17.6 imp gal, 21 US gal, 80 l.

BODY 5 seats, bench front seats.

OPTIONAL ACCESSORIES Tri-Matic automatic transmission with 3 ratios (I 2.520, II 1.520, III 1, rev 1.940), max ratio of converter at stall 2, possible manual selection, 2.920 axle ratio; heated rear window; metallic spray; automatic speed control; (for LS only) vinyl roof; reclining backrests; headrests; power-steering; air-conditioning.

Constantia - Caprice Classic Series

PRICES EX WORKS:

1 Constantia 4-door Sedan	6,126	rand
2 Constantia 5-door Station Wagon	—	
3 Caprice Classic 4-door Sedan	11,530	rand

Power team:	Standard for:	Optional for:
134 hp	1,2	—
167 hp	3	1

134 hp power team

ENGINE front, 4 stroke; 6 cylinders, vertical, in line; 249.9 cu in, 4,095 cc (3.87 x 3.53 in, 98.4 x 89.7 mm); compression ratio: 9:1; max power (SAE): 134 hp at 4,200 rpm; max torque (SAE): 210 lb ft, 29 kg m at 1,600 rpm; max engine rpm: 5,000; 32.8 hp/l; cast iron block and head; 7 crankshaft bearings; valves: overhead, in line, push-rods and rockers, hydraulic tappets; camshafts: 1, side; lubrication: gear pump, full flow filter, 8.3 imp pt, 9.9 US pt, 4.7 l; 1 Rochester Monojet carburettor; fuel feed: mechanical pump; water-cooled, 21.6 imp pt, 26 US pt, 12.3 l.

TRANSMISSION driving wheels: rear; clutch, single dry plate (diaphragm); gearbox: mechanical (Tri-Matic automatic transmission standard for Sedan only); gears: 3, fully synchronized; ratios: I 3.070, II 1.680, III 1, rev 3.590; lever: steering column; final drive: hypoid bevel; axle ratio: Sedan 2.920 - Station Wagon 3.230; tyres: 7.35 x 14 or 185 SR x 14.

PERFORMANCE max speed: about 109 mph, 175 km/h; power-weight ratio: 22.1 lb/hp, 10.7 kg/hp; carrying capacity: 1,058 lb, 480 kg - Station Wagon 1,213 lb, 550 kg; speed

CHEVROLET Caprice Classic 4-door Sedan

134 HP POWER TEAM

in direct drive at 1,000 rpm: 22.8 mph, 36.7 km/h; consumption: 17.3 m/imp gal, 14.4 m/US gal, 16.3 l x 100 km.

CHASSIS integral; front suspension: independent, wishbones, coil springs, anti-roll bar, telescopic dampers; rear: rigid axle, twin trailing lower radius arms, upper torque arms, transverse linkage bar, coil springs, anti-roll bar, telescopic dampers.

STEERING recirculating ball, variable ratio servo (standard for Sedan only); turns lock to lock: Sedan 2.60 - Station Wagon 3.68.

BRAKES front disc (diameter 10.87 in, 27.6 cm), front internal radial fins, rear drum, servo.

ELECTRICAL EQUIPMENT 12 V; 45 Ah battery; 37 A alternator; 4 headlamps.

DIMENSIONS AND WEIGHT wheel base: 113.98 in, 289 cm; tracks: 59.49 in, 151 cm front, 60.20 in, 153 cm rear; length: Sedan 203.07 in, 516 cm - Station Wagon 192.48 in, 489 cm; width: 74.09 in, 188 cm; height: Sedan 54.57 in, 139 cm - Station Wagon 55.28 in, 140 cm; ground clearance: Sedan 6.10 in, 15.5 cm - Station Wagon 6.30 in, 16 cm; weight: 2,956 lb, 1,345 kg; turning circle (between walls): 40.3 ft, 12.3 m; fuel tank: 18.3 imp gal, 21.9 US gal, 83 l.

BODY 6 seats, bench front seats.

OPTIONAL ACCESSORIES Tri-Matic automatic transmission with 3 ratios (Sedan I 2.520, II 1.520, III 1, rev 1.940 - Station Wagon I 2.480, II 1.480, III 1, rev 2), max ratio of converter at stall 2, possible manual selection; 2.780 axle ratio; power-steering; automatic speed control; headrests; metallic spray; tinted glass; heated rear window; separate front seats with reclining backrests; air-conditioning; (for Sedan only) vinyl roof; electric windows.

167 hp power team

See 134 hp power team, except for:

ENGINE 8 cylinders, Vee-slanted at 90°; 307.7 cu in, 5,042 cc (4 x 3.07 in, 101.6 x 77.8 mm); compression ratio: 9.7:1; max power (SAE): 167 hp at 3,900 rpm; max torque (SAE): 290 lb ft, 40 kg m at 3,300 rpm; max engine rpm: 4,200; 33.1 hp/l; 5 crankshaft bearings; camshafts: 1, at centre of Vee; 1 Rochester downdraught twin barrel carburettor; cooling system: 23.6 imp pt, 28.3 US pt, 13.4 l.

TRANSMISSION gearbox: Tri-Matic automatic transmission, hydraulic torque converter and planetary gears with 3 ratios, max ratio of converter at stall 2, possible manual selection; ratios: I 2.480, II 1.480, III 1, rev 2; axle ratio: 2.780; tyres: ER70 H x 14.

PERFORMANCE max speed: about 115 mph, 185 km/h; power-weight ratio: 21.7 lb/hp, 9.8 kg/hp; speed in direct drive at 1,000 rpm: 24.9 mph, 40 km/h; consumption: 16 m/imp gal, 13.3 m/US gal, 17.7 l x 100 km.

STEERING variable ratio servo; turns lock to lock: 2.60.

ELECTRICAL EQUIPMENT 53 Ah battery.

DIMENSIONS AND WEIGHT length: Caprice Classic 204.09 in, 518 cm; ground clearance: Caprice Classic 6.42 in, 16.3 cm; weight: 3,627 lb, 1,645 kg.

BODY tinted glass; electric windows; headrests; (standard for Caprice Classic only) air-conditioning, automatic speed control, separate front seats with reclining backrests, heated rear window and vinyl roof.

Nomad

ENGINE front, 4 stroke; 4 cylinders, vertical, in line; 153 cu in, 2,507 cc (3.87 x 3.25 in, 98.4 x 82.5 mm); compression ratio: 8.5:1; max power (SAE): 87 hp at 4,300 rpm; max torque (SAE): 162 lb ft, 22.3 kg m at 3,200 rpm; max engine rpm: 4,600; 34.7 hp/l; 5 crankshaft bearings; valves: overhead, hydraulic tappets; camshafts: 1, side; lubrication: gear pump, full flow filter, 5.8 imp pt, 7 US pt, 3.3 l; 1 Rochester Monojet downdraught twin barrel carburettor; fuel feed: mechanical pump; water-cooled, 13 imp pt, 15.6 US pt, 7.4 l.

TRANSMISSION driving wheels: rear; clutch: single dry plate (diaphragm), hydraulically controlled; gearbox: mechanical; gears: 4, fully synchronized; ratios: I 4.258, II 2.567, III 1.531, IV 1, rev 4.121; lever: central; final drive: hypoid bevel; axle ratio: 4.000; width of rims: 5''; tyres: 6.95 x 14.

PERFORMANCE max speed: about 74 mph, 120 km/h; power-weight ratio: 26 lb/hp, 11.8 kg/hp; carrying capacity: 1,235

CHEVROLET Constantia 5-door Station Wagon

lb, 560 kg; speed in direct drive at 1,000 rpm: 17.8 mph, 28.7 km/h; consumption: 23.5 m/imp gal, 19.6 m/US gal, 12 l x 100 km.

CHASSIS integral; front suspension: wishbones, coil springs, heavy-duty double-acting telescopic dampers; rear: rigid axle, twin longitudinal trailing arms, leafspring, heavy-duty double-acting telescopic dampers.

STEERING rack-and-pinion.

BRAKES front disc, rear drum, dual circuit, servo; lining area: front 24.6 sq in, 159 sq cm, rear 77.5 sq in, 500 sq cm, total 102.1 sq in, 659 sq cm.

ELECTRICAL EQUIPMENT 12 V; 55 Ah battery; 37 A alternator; 2 headlamps.

DIMENSIONS AND WEIGHT wheel base: 81.89 in, 208 cm; front and rear track: 51.57 in, 131 cm; length: 137.01 in, 348 cm; width: 61.81 in, 157 cm; height: 60.23 in, 153 cm; weight: 2,260 lb, 1,025 kg; turning circle (between walls): 38.7 ft, 11.8 m; fuel tank: 13.2 imp gal, 15.8 US gal, 60 l.

BODY estate car/st. wagon; 2 doors; 3-7 seats; separate front seats.

OPTIONAL ACCESSORIES nylon roof with perspex windows; fibreglass canopy; removable door windows; 175SR x 14 tyres.

CHEVROLET Nomad

Escort 1300 L 2-door/4-door Sedan

ENGINE front, 4 stroke; 4 cylinders, vertical, in line; 79.1 cu in, 1,297 cc (3.19 x 2.48 in, 81 x 63 mm); compression ratio: 9.2:1; max power (DIN): 57 hp at 5,500 rpm; max torque (DIN): 67 lb ft, 9.3 kg m at 3,000 rpm; max engine rpm: 5,700; 43.9 hp/l; cast iron block and head; 5 crankshaft bearings; valves: overhead, in line, push-rods and rockers; camshafts: 1, side, chain driven; lubrication: rotary or vane-type pump, full flow filter, 6.5 imp pt, 7.8 US pt, 3.7 l; 1 Ford GPD downdraught single barrel carburettor; fuel feed: mechanical pump; water-cooled, 8.8 imp pt, 10.6 US pt, 5 l.

TRANSMISSION driving wheels: rear; clutch: single dry plate (diaphragm); gearbox: mechanical; gears: 4, fully synchronized; ratios: I 3.656, II 2.185, III 1.425, IV 1, rev 4.235; lever: central; final drive: hypoid bevel; axle ratio: 4.110; width of rims: 4.5''; tyres: 155 SR x 13.

PERFORMANCE max speed: 88 mph, 142 km/h; power-weight ratio: 2-door saloon 34.2 lb/hp, 15.5 kg/hp - 4-door saloon 35.4 lb/hp, 16 kg/hp; carrying capacity: 939 lb, 426 kg; acceleration: 0-50 mph (0-80 km/h) 12.5 sec; speed in direct drive at 1,000 rpm: 15.5 mph, 24.9 km/h; consumption: 42.2 m/imp gal, 35.1 m/US gal, 6.7 l x 100 km at 50 mph, 80 km/h.

CHASSIS integral; front suspension: independent, by McPherson, coil springs/telescopic damper struts, anti-roll bar; rear: rigid axle, semi-elliptic leafsprings, telescopic dampers.

STEERING rack-and-pinion; turns lock to lock: 3.50.

BRAKES front disc, rear drum, servo.

ELECTRICAL EQUIPMENT 12 V; 44 Ah battery; 35 A alternator; Motorcraft distributor; 2 headlamps.

DIMENSIONS AND WEIGHT wheel base: 94.76 in, 241 cm; tracks: 49.72 in, 126 cm front, 50.75 in, 129 cm rear; length: 157.40 in, 400 cm; width: 62.83 in, 160 cm; height: 55.04 in, 140 cm; ground clearance: 3.94 in, 10 cm; weight: 2-door saloon 1,951 lb, 885 kg - 4-door saloon 2,018 lb, 915 kg; turning circle (between walls): 29.2 ft, 8.9 m; fuel tank: 9 imp gal, 10.8 US gal, 41 l.

BODY saloon/sedan; 2 or 4 doors; 5 seats, separate front seats, reclining backrests.

Escort 1600 GL 4-door Sedan

See Escort 1300 L 2-door Sedan/4-door Sedan, except for:

ENGINE 97.5 cu in, 1,598 cc (3.19 x 3.06 in, 81 x 77.6 mm); compression ratio: 9:1; max power (DIN): 84 hp at 5,500 rpm; max torque (DIN): 92 lb ft, 12.7 kg m at 3,500 rpm; 52.6 hp/l; lubrication: 6.7 imp pt, 8 US pt, 3.8 l; 1 Weber 32/32 DGV downdraught twin barrel carburettor; cooling system: 9.5 imp pt, 11.4 US pt, 5.4 l.

FORD Escort 1300 L 2-door Sedan

TRANSMISSION gearbox ratios: I 3.337, II 1.995, III 1.418, IV 1, rev 3.867; axle ratio: 3.890.

PERFORMANCE max speed: 100 mph, 161 km/h; power-weight ratio: 24 lb/hp, 10.9 kg/hp; acceleration: 0-50 mph (0-80 km/h) 8.4 sec; speed in direct drive at 1,000 rpm: 18.5 mph, 29.8 km/h; consumption: 46.3 m/imp gal, 38.6 m/US gal, 6.1 l x 100 km at 50 mph, 80 km/h.

ELECTRICAL EQUIPMENT 45 A alternator; halogen headlamps.

DIMENSIONS AND WEIGHT weight: 2,018 lb, 915 kg.

BODY 4 doors; vinyl roof.

OPTIONAL ACCESSORIES Bordeaux C 3 automatic transmission, hydraulic torque converter and planetary gears with 3 ratios (I 2.474, II 1.474, III 1, rev 2.111), max ratio of converter at stall 2, possible manual selection, max speed 98 mph, 157 km/h, acceleration 0-50 mph (0-80 km/h) 9.9 sec, consumption 41.5 m/imp gal, 34.6 m/US gal, 6.8 l x 100 km at 50 mph, 80 km/h, 55 Ah battery.

Cortina 1600 L Sedan

PRICE EX WORKS: 4,600 rand

ENGINE front, 4 stroke; 4 cylinders, vertical, in line; 97.5 cu in, 1,598 cc (3.19 x 3.06 in, 81 x 77.6 mm); compression ratio: 9:1; max power (DIN): 84 hp at 5,500 rpm; max torque (DIN): 92 lb ft, 12.7 kg m at 3,500 rpm; max engine rpm: 6,300; 52.5 hp/l; cast iron block and head; 5 crankshaft bearings; valves: overhead, in line, push-rods and rockers; camshafts: 1, overhead; lubrication: rotary pump, full flow filter, 7.6 imp pt, 9.1 US pt, 4.3 l; 1 Weber downdraught twin barrel carburettor; fuel feed: mechanical pump; water-cooled, 11.4 imp pt, 13.7 US pt, 6.5 l.

TRANSMISSION driving wheels: rear; clutch: single dry plate, semi-centrifugal; gearbox: mechanical; gears: 4, fully synchronized; ratios: I 3.580, II 2.010, III 1.397, IV 1, rev 3.320; lever: central; final drive: hypoid bevel; axle ratio: 3.890; width of rims: 5.5''; tyres 165 SR x 13.

PERFORMANCE max speeds: (I) 31 mph, 50 km/h; (II) 53 mph, 86 km/h; (III) 74 mph, 119 km/h; (IV) 99 mph, 159 km/h; power-weight ratio: 26 lb/hp, 11.8 kg/hp; carrying capacity: 948 lb, 430 kg; acceleration: standing ¼ mile 19.2 sec, 0-50 mph (0-80 km/h) 9.1 sec; speed in direct drive at 1,000 rpm: 17 mph, 27.8 km/h; consumption: 37 m/imp gal, 31 m/US gal, 7.6 l x 100 km.

CHASSIS integral, front auxiliary frame; front suspension: independent, coil springs, telescopic dampers; rear: rigid axle, trailing radius arms, 4 linkage bars, coil springs, telescopic dampers.

STEERING rack-and-pinion; turns lock to lock: 4.40.

BRAKES front disc, rear drum, servo; swept area: front 194.6 sq in, 1,255 sq cm, rear 96.1 sq in, 620 sq cm, total 290.7 sq in, 1,875 sq cm.

ELECTRICAL EQUIPMENT 12 V; 40 Ah battery; 45 A alternator; 2 headlamps.

DIMENSIONS AND WEIGHT wheel base: 101.57 in, 258 cm; tracks: 56.69 in, 144 cm front, 55.90 in, 142 cm rear; length: 172.44 in, 438 cm; width: 66.90 in, 170 cm; height: 53.93 in, 137 cm; ground clearance: 6.69 in, 17 cm; weight: 2,194 lb, 995 kg; weight distribution: 53% front, 47% rear; turning circle (between walls): 32 ft, 9.9 m; fuel tank: 14.3 imp gal, 17.1 US gal, 65 l.

BODY saloon/sedan; 4 doors; 5 seats, separate front seats, reclining backrests.

OPTIONAL ACCESSORIES metallic spray; tinted glass.

Cortina 1600 L Station Wagon

See Cortina 1600 L Sedan, except for:

PRICE EX WORKS: 4,873 rand

PERFORMANCE power-weight ratio: 27.3 lb/hp, 12.4 kg/hp.

DIMENSIONS AND WEIGHT length: 174.80 in, 444 cm; weight: 2,293 lb, 1,040 kg.

BODY st. wagon/estate car; 4 + 1 doors; folding rear seat.

Cortina 2000 GL Sedan

See Cortina 1600 L Sedan, except for:

PRICE EX WORKS: 4,976 rand

ENGINE 121.6 cu in, 1,993 cc (3.58 x 3.03 in, 91 x 77 mm); compression ratio: 9.2:1; max power (DIN): 98 hp at 5,200 rpm; max torque (DIN): 112 lb ft, 15.4 kg m at 3,500 rpm; max engine rpm: 5,800; 49 hp/l; lubrication: 6.5 imp pt, 7.8 US pt, 3.7 l.

TRANSMISSION gearbox ratios: I 3.650, II 1.970, III 1.370, IV 1, rev 3.660; axle ratio: 3.700.

PERFORMANCE max speeds: (I) 30 mph, 48 km/h; (II) 55 mph, 89 km/h; (III) 75 mph, 121 km/h; (IV) 104 mph, 168 km/h; power-weight ratio: 23.3 lb/hp, 10.6 kg/hp; acceleration: standing ¼ mile 18.2 sec, 0-50 mph (0-80 km/h) 7.8 sec; speed in direct drive at 1,000 rpm: 18 mph, 29 km/h; consumption: 36 m/imp gal, 30 m/US gal, 7.9 l x 100 km.

DIMENSIONS AND WEIGHT weight: 2,282 lb, 1,035 kg.

OPTIONAL ACCESSORIES Ford C3 automatic transmission, hydraulic torque converter and planetary gears with 3 ratios (I 2.474, II 1.474, III 1, rev 2.111), max ratio of converter at stall 2, possible manual selection, max speed 101 mph, 162 km/h, consumption 35 m/imp gal, 29 m/US gal, 8.1 l x 100 km.

Cortina 2000 GL Station Wagon

See Cortina 2000 GL Sedan, except for:

PRICE EX WORKS: 5,249 rand

PERFORMANCE power-weight ratio: 24.3 lb/hp, 11 kg/hp.

DIMENSIONS AND WEIGHT length: 174.80 in, 444 cm; weight: 2,381 lb, 1,080 kg.

BODY st. wagon/estate car; 4 + 1 doors; folding rear seat.

Cortina 3000 S Sedan

See Cortina 1600 L Sedan, except for:

PRICE EX WORKS: 5,633 rand

ENGINE 6 cylinders, Vee-slanted at 60°; 182.7 cu in, 2,994 cc (3.69 x 2.83 in, 93.7 x 72 mm); compression ratio: 8.6:1; max power (DIN): 138 hp at 5,000 rpm; max torque (DIN): 174 lb ft, 24 kg m at 3,000 rpm; max engine rpm: 5,700; 46 hp/l; 4 crankshaft bearings; lubrication: 9.8 imp pt, 11.8 US pt, 5.6 l; cooling system: 18.8 imp pt, 22.6 US pt, 10.7 l.

TRANSMISSION gearbox ratios: I 3.160, II 1.950, III 1.410, IV 1, rev 3.350; axle ratio: 3.080; tyres: 185/70 SR x 13.

PERFORMANCE max speeds: (I) 41 mph, 66 km/h; (II) 65 mph, 105 km/h; (III) 87 mph, 140 km/h; (IV) 88 mph, 117 km/h; power-weight ratio: 18.3 lb/hp, 8.3 kg/hp; acceleration: standing ¼ mile 16.9 sec, 0-50 mph (0-80 km/h) 6.4 sec; speed in direct drive at 1,000 rpm: 22.6 mph, 36.4 km/h; consumption: 32.8 m/imp gal, 27.3 m/US gal, 8.6 l x 100 km.

FORD Cortina 3000 Ghia Sedan

CORTINA 3000 S SEDAN

BRAKES swept area: front 194.6 sq in, 1,255 sq cm, rear 122.8 sq in, 792 sq cm, total 317.4 sq in, 2,047 sq cm.

DIMENSIONS AND WEIGHT height: 53.15 in, 135 cm; ground clearance: 5.90 in, 15 cm; weight: 2,522 lb, 1,144 kg; weight distribution: 56% front, 44% rear.

Cortina 3000 Ghia Sedan

See Cortina 3000 S Sedan, except for:

PRICE EX WORKS: 6,670 rand

TRANSMISSION gearbox: Ford C3 automatic transmission, hydraulic torque converter and planetary gears; ratios: I 2.474, II 1.474, III 1, rev 2.110; tyres: 175 SR x 13.

PERFORMANCE max speed: (I) 48 mph, 78 km/h; (II) 81 mph, 131 km/h; (III) 114 mph, 184 km/h; acceleration: standing ¼ mile 17.8 sec, 0-50 mph (0-80 km/h) 7.2 sec; speed in direct drive at 1,000 rpm: 21.7 mph, 35 km/h.

DIMENSIONS AND WEIGHT height: 53.93 in, 137 cm; ground clearance: 6.69 in, 17 cm.

Cortina 3000 Ghia Station Wagon

See Cortina 3000 Ghia Sedan, except for:

PRICE EX WORKS: 6,952 rand

PERFORMANCE power-weight ratio: 18.8 lb/hp, 8.5 kg/hp.

DIMENSIONS AND WEIGHT length: 176.38 in, 448 cm; weight: 2,602 lb, 1,180 kg.

BODY st. wagon/estate car; 4 + 1 doors; folding rear seat.

Granada 3000 GL Sedan

ENGINE front, 4 stroke; 6 cylinders, Vee-slanted at 60°; 182.7 cu in, 2,994 cc (3.69 x 2.85 in, 93.7 x 72.4 mm); compression ratio: 8.9:1; max power (SAE): 159 hp at 5,200 rpm; max torque (SAE): 191 lb ft, 26.4 kg m at 3,000 rpm; max engine rpm: 5,500; 53.1 hp/l; cast iron block and head; 4 crankshaft bearings; valves: overhead, push-rods and rockers; camshafts: 1, at centre of Vee; lubrication: rotary pump, full flow filter, 9.9 imp pt, 11.8 US pt, 5.6 l; 1 Weber 38/38 EGAS downdraught twin barrel carburettor; fuel feed: mechanical pump; water-cooled, 20.1 imp pt, 24.1 US pt, 11.4 l.

TRANSMISSION driving wheels: rear; clutch: single dry plate (diaphragm); gearbox: mechanical; gears: 4, fully synchronized; ratios: I 3.160, II 1.940, III 1.410, IV 1, rev 3.346; lever: central; final drive: hypoid bevel; axle ratio: 3.450; width of rims: 5''; tyres: 175 SR x 14.

PERFORMANCE max speed: about 114 mph, 184 km/h; power-weight ratio: 18 lb/hp, 8.2 kg/hp; speed in direct drive at 1,000 rpm: 20.8 mph, 33.4 km/h; consumption: 24 m/imp gal, 20.1 m/US gal, 11.7 l x 100 km.

CHASSIS integral, front and rear auxiliary frames; front suspension: independent, wishbones (lower trailing links), coil springs, anti-roll bar, telescopic dampers; rear: independent, semi-trailing arms, coil springs, telescopic dampers.

STEERING rack-and-pinion, servo; turns lock to lock: 3.50.

BRAKES front disc (diameter 10.31 in, 26.2 cm), front internal radial fins, rear drum, servo; swept area: total 334.3 sq in, 2,156 sq cm.

ELECTRICAL EQUIPMENT 12 V; 45 Ah battery; 45 A alternator; Motorcraft distributor; 2 headlamps.

DIMENSIONS AND WEIGHT wheel base: 109.05 in, 277 cm; tracks: 59.45 in, 151 cm front, 60.63 in, 154 cm rear; length: 179.92 in, 457 cm; width: 70.47 in, 179 cm; height: 53.94 in, 137 cm; ground clearance: 5.12 in, 13 cm; weight: 2,867 lb, 1,300 kg; turning circle (between walls): 33.8 ft, 10.8 m; fuel tank: 14.3 imp gal, 17.2 US gal, 65 l.

BODY saloon/sedan; 4 doors; 5 seats, separate front seats, reclining backrests.

OPTIONAL ACCESSORIES Ford C3 automatic transmission, hydraulic torque converter and planetary gears with 3 ratios (I 2.474, II 1.474, III 1, rev 2.111), max ratio of converter at stall 2.34, possible manual selection, max speed 110 mph, 177 km/h, consumption 22.8 m/imp gal, 19 m/US gal, 12.4 l x 100 km; air-conditioning; halogen headlamps; vinyl roof; tinted glass; laminated windscreen; metallic spray.

FORD Granada 3000 Ghia Sedan

Granada 3000 Ghia Sedan

See Granada 3000 GL Sedan, except for:

ELECTRICAL EQUIPMENT halogen headlamps (standard).

BODY luxury equipment; reclining backrests with adjustable built-in headrests; tinted glass (standard); air-conditioning (standard).

LEYLAND   SOUTH AFRICA

Mini De Luxe

PRICE EX WORKS: 2,855 rand

ENGINE front, transverse, 4 stroke; 4 cylinders, in line; 67 cu in, 1,098 cc (2.75 x 2.78 in, 69.8 x 70.6 mm); compression ratio: 8:1; max power (DIN): 48.7 hp at 5,400 rpm; max torque (DIN): 58 lb ft, 8 kg m at 2,200 rpm; max engine rpm: 5,800; 44.4 hp/l; cast iron block and head; 3 crankshaft bearings; valves: overhead, in line, push-rods and rockers; camshafts: 1, side; lubrication: eccentric pump, full flow filter (cartridge), 8.4 imp pt, 10.1 US pt, 4.8 l; 1 SU type HS4 semi-downdraught carburettor; fuel feed: mechanical pump; water-cooled, 7.4 imp pt, 8.9 US pt, 4.2 l.

TRANSMISSION driving wheels: front; clutch: single dry plate (diaphragm); gearbox: mechanical; gears: 4, fully synchronized; ratios: I 3.525, II 2.218, III 1.433, IV 1, rev 3.544; lever: central; final drive: hypoid bevel; axle ratio: 3.760; width of rims: 3.5''; tyres: 5.20 x 10, tubeless.

PERFORMANCE max speed: 82 mph, 132 km/h; speed in direct drive at 1,000 rpm: 16.5 mph, 26.5 km/h; consumption: 40.4 m/imp gal, 33.6 m/US gal, 7 l x 100 km.

CHASSIS integral, front and rear auxiliary frames; front and rear suspension: independent, rubber cone springs, telescopic dampers.

STEERING rack-and-pinion; turns lock to lock: 2.70.

BRAKES drum; swept area: front 66 sq in, 426 sq cm, rear 55 sq in, 355 sq cm, total 121 sq in, 781 sq cm.

ELECTRICAL EQUIPMENT 12 V; 40 Ah battery; 35 A alternator; 420 W alternator; Lucas distributor; 2 headlamps.

DIMENSIONS AND WEIGHT wheel base: 79.92 in, 203 cm; tracks: 47.24 in, 120 cm front, 45.67 in, 116 cm rear; length: 118.11 in, 300 cm; width: 55.12 in, 140 cm; height: 51.18 in, 130 cm; ground clearance: 6.30 in, 16 cm; fuel tank: 7.5 imp gal, 8.9 US gal, 34 l.

LEYLAND Mini GTS

BODY saloon/sedan; 2 doors; 4 seats, separate front seats; heated rear window.

PRACTICAL INSTRUCTIONS fuel: 94 oct petrol; oil: engine, gearbox and final drive 9 imp pt, 10.8 US pt, 5 l, SAE 20W-50, change every 6,000 miles, 9,700 km; greasing: every 6,000 miles, 9,700 km , 8 points; sparking plug: Champion N9Y; tappet clearances: inlet 0.012 in, 0.30 mm, exhaust 0.012 in, 0.30 mm.

Mini Clubman

See Mini De Luxe, except for:

PRICE EX WORKS: 3,070 rand

TRANSMISSION axle ratio: 3.440.

BRAKES single circuit.

DIMENSIONS AND WEIGHT length: 124.41 in, 316 cm.

Mini GTS

See Mini De Luxe, except for:

PRICE EX WORKS: 3,250 rand

ENGINE 77.8 cu in, 1,275 cc (3.20 x 2.78 in, 81.3 x 70.6 mm); compression ratio: 9.75:1; max power (DIN): 66.9 hp at 5,750 rpm; max torque (DIN): 76 lb ft, 10.5 kg m at 3,250 rpm; max engine rpm: 6,000; 62.5 hp/l; 1 SU type HS 2 semi-downdraught carburettor; fuel feed: electric pump.

TRANSMISSION ratios: I 3.330, II 2.090, III 1.350, IV 1, rev 3.350; axle ratio: 3.440; width of rims: 4.5''; tyres: 145/70 SR x 12.

PERFORMANCE max speed: 87 mph, 140 km/h; speed in direct drive at 1,000 rpm: 16.8 mph, 27 km/h.

BRAKES front disc, internal radial fins, rear drum.

Marina 1300

PRICE EX WORKS: 3,559 rand

ENGINE front, 4 stroke; 4 cylinders, in line; 77.8 cu in, 1,275 cc (2.78 x 3.20 in, 70.6 x 81.3 mm); compression ratio: 8.8:1; max power (DIN): 59.8 hp at 5,250 rpm; max torque (DIN): 69 lb ft, 9.6 kg m at 2,500 rpm; max engine rpm: 5,500; 46.9 hp/l; cast iron block and head; 3 crankshaft bearings; valves: overhead, push-rods; camshafts: 1, side; lubrication: eccentric pump, full flow filter, 6.5 imp pt, 7.8 US pt, 3.7 l; 1 SU type HS4 semi-downdraught carburettor; fuel feed: electric pump; water-cooled, 9.3 imp pt, 11.2 US pt, 5.3 l.

TRANSMISSION driving wheels: rear; clutch: single dry plate (diaphragm), hydraulically controlled; gearbox: mechanical; gears: 4, fully synchronized; ratios: I 3.430, II 2.110, III 1.430, IV 1, rev 3.750; lever: central; final drive: hypoid bevel; axle ratio: 4.110; width of rims: 4.5''; tyres: 155 SR x 13.

PERFORMANCE max speeds: (I) 26 mph, 42 km/h; (II) 42 mph, 68 km/h; (III) 62 mph, 99 km/h; (IV) 88 mph, 142 km/h; power-weight ratio: 36.1 lb/hp, 16.4 kg/hp; carrying capacity: 873 lb, 396 kg; acceleration: 0-50 mph (0-80 km/h) 15.3 sec; speed in direct drive at 1,000 rpm: 16 mph, 25.8 km/h; consumption: 37.2 m/imp gal, 30.9 m/US gal, 7.6 l x 100 km.

CHASSIS integral; front suspension: independent, wishbones, lower trailing links, longitudinal torsion bars, lever dampers as upper arms, telscopic dampers; rear: rigid axle; semi-elliptic leafsprings, telescopic dampers.

STEERING rack-and-pinion; turns lock to lock: 4.

BRAKES front disc, rear drum; swept area: front 219.9 sq in, 1,418 sq cm, rear 87.5 sq in, 564 sq cm, total 307.4 sq in, 1,982 sq cm.

ELECTRICAL EQUIPMENT 12 V; 40 Ah battery; 17 A alternator; Lucas distributor; 2 headlamps.

DIMENSIONS AND WEIGHT wheel base: 96 in, 244 cm; front and rear track: 51.97 in, 132 cm; length: 166.12 in, 422 cm; width: 64.81 in, 165 cm; height: 56.12 in, 142 cm; ground clearance: 5.9 in, 15 cm; weight: 2,161 lb, 980 kg; turning circle (between walls): 31 ft, 9.4 m; fuel tank: 11.2 imp gal, 13.5 US gal, 51 l.

BODY saloon/sedan; 4 doors; 5 seats, separate front seats, reclining backrests.

PRACTICAL INSTRUCTIONS fuel: 98 oct petrol; oil: engine 6.5 imp pt, 7.8 US pt, 3.7 l, SAE 10W-30 (winter) 20W-50 (summer), change every 6,000 miles, 9,700 km - gearbox 1.5 imp pt, 1.8 US pt, 0.8 l, change every 6,000 miles, 9,700 km - final drive 1.8 imp pt, 2.1 US pt, 1 l, change every 6,000 miles, 9,700 km; greasing: every 3,000 miles,

LEYLAND Marina 1300

4,800 km, 4 points; sparking plug: 225°; tappet clearances: inlet 0.012 in, 0.30 mm, exhaust 0.012 in, 0.30 mm.

OPTIONAL ACCESSORIES metallic spray; vinyl roof.

Marina 1750

See Marina 1300, except for:

PRICE EX WORKS: 4,270 rand

ENGINE 106.7 cu in, 1,748 cc (3 x 3.77 in, 76.2 x 95.8 mm); compression ratio: 8.6:1; max power (DIN): 79 hp at 4,800 rpm; max torque (DIN): 99 lb ft, 13.7 kg m at 3,100 rpm; max engine rpm: 5,800; 45.2 hp/l; 5 crankshaft bearings; valves: overhead, in line, push-rods; camshafts: 1, overhead; lubrication: rotary pump, 6.9 imp pt, 8.2 US pt, 3.9 l; 1 SU type HS6 semi-downdraught carburettor; fuel feed: mechanical pump; water-cooled, expansion tank, 10.6 imp pt, 12.7 US pt, 6 l.

TRANSMISSION ratios: I 3.110, II 1.920, III 1.310, IV 1, rev 3.420; axle ratio: 3.890.

PERFORMANCE max speeds: (I) 33 mph, 53 km/h; (II) 53 mph, 85 km/h; (III) 78 mph, 125 km/h; (IV) 95 mph, 153 km/h; power-weight ratio: 28.9 lb/hp, 13.1 kg/hp; carrying capacity: 882 lb, 400 kg; speed in direct drive at 1,000 rpm: 18.1 mph, 29.2 km/h; consumption: 23.7 m/imp gal, 19.8 m/US gal, 11.9 l x 100 km.

DIMENSIONS AND WEIGHT front track: 52.38 in, 133 cm; ground clearance: 5.75 in, 14.6 cm; weight: 2,284 lb, 1,036 kg.

PRACTICAL INSTRUCTIONS oil: engine 6 imp pt, 7.2 US pt, 3.4 l - gearbox 1.9 imp pt, 2.3 US pt, 1.1 l; valve timing: 5° 45° 51° 21°.

OPTIONAL ACCESSORIES Borg-Warner 65 automatic transmission with 3 ratios (I 2.930, II 1.450, III 1, rev 2.090), possible manual selection, power-weight ratio 29.4 lb/hp. 13.4 kg/hp, weight 2,326 lb, 1,055 kg.

Marina 2600

See Marina 1750, except for:

PRICE EX WORKS: 4,975 rand

ENGINE 6 cylinders; 160.1 cu in, 2,623 cc (3 x 3.77 in, 76.2 x 95.8 mm); compression ratio: 9:1; max power (DIN): 111.5 hp at 4,500 rpm; max torque (DIN): 145 lb ft, 20 kg m at 2,000 rpm; max engine rpm: 5,500; 42.5 hp/l; 7 crankshaft bearings; lubrication: 9.2 imp pt, 11 US pt, 5.2 l; cooling system: 15.8 imp pt, 19 US pt, 9 l.

TRANSMISSION gearbox: Borg-Warner 65 automatic transmission (standard), hydraulic torque converter and planetary gears with 3 ratios; ratios: I 2.390, II 1.450, III 1, rev 2.090; axle ratio: 3.700.

LEYLAND Marina 2600

MARINA 2600

PERFORMANCE max speed: 103 mph, 165 km/h; power-weight ratio: 21.9 lb/hp, 9.9 kg/hp; speed in direct drive at 1,000 rpm: 18.6 mph, 30 km/h; consumption: 20.5 m/imp gal, 17 m/US gal, 13.8 l x 100 km.

DIMENSIONS AND WEIGHT front and rear track: 52.36 in, 133 cm; width: 64.57 in, 164 cm; height: 54.72 in, 139 cm; ground clearance: 6.50 in, 16.5 cm; weight: 2,447 lb, 1,110 kg; turning circle (between walls): 32.8 ft, 10 m.

PRACTICAL INSTRUCTIONS oil: engine 8.3 imp pt, 9.9 US pt, 4.7 l - automatic transmission 5.6 imp pt, 6.8 US pt, 3.2 l.

Triumph Chicane

PRICE EX WORKS: 5,685 rand

ENGINE front, 4 stroke; 6 cylinders, vertical, in line; 152.4 cu in, 2,498 cc (2.94 x 3.74 in, 74.7 x 95 mm); compression ratio: 9.5:1; max power (DIN): 101 hp at 4,750 rpm; max torque (DIN): 136 lb ft, 18.7 kg m at 2,200 rpm; max engine rpm: 5,500; 40.4 hp/l; cast iron block and head; 4 crankshaft bearings; valves: overhead, in line, push-rods and rockers; camshafts: 1, side; lubrication: eccentric pump, full flow filter, 9 imp pt, 10.8 US pt, 5.1 l; 2 SU type HS4 carburettors; fuel feed: mechanical pump; water-cooled, 13.6 imp pt, 16.3 US pt, 7.7 l.

TRANSMISSION driving wheels: rear; gearbox: Borg-Warner 65 automatic transmission, hydraulic torque converter and planetary gears with 3 ratios, max ratio of converter at stall 2, possible manual selection; ratios: I 2.390, II 1.450, III 1, rev 2.090; lever: central; final drive: hypoid bevel; axle ratio: 3.700; width of rims: 5''; tyres: 185 SR x 13.

PERFORMANCE max speeds: (I) 64 mph, 104 km/h; (II) 70 mph, 112 km/h; (III) 103 mph, 165 km/h; power-weight ratio: 25.3 lb/hp, 11.5 kg/hp; carrying capacity: 882 lb, 400 kg; speed in direct drive at 1,000 rpm: 19 mph, 30 km/h; consumption: 22.9 m/imp gal, 19 m/US gal, 12.4 l x 100 km.

CHASSIS integral, rear auxiliary frame; front suspension: independent, by McPherson, coil springs/telescopic damper struts, lower wishbones (trailing links); rear: independent, semi-trailing arms, coil springs, telescopic dampers.

STEERING rack-and-pinion, servo; turns lock to lock: 4.

BRAKES front disc (diameter 9.75 in, 24.8 cm), rear drum, servo; swept area: front 200 sq in, 1,290 sq cm, rear 99.1 sq in, 639 sq cm, total 299.1 sq in, 1,929 sq cm.

ELECTRICAL EQUIPMENT 12 V; 40 Ah battery; 36 A alternator; Lucas distributor; 4 headlamps.

DIMENSIONS AND WEIGHT wheel base: 105.91 in, 269 cm; tracks: 52.44 in, 133 cm front, 52.83 in, 134 cm rear;

length: 182.20 in, 463 cm; width: 64.96 in, 165 cm; height: 55.91 in, 142 cm; ground clearance: 5.91 in, 15 cm; weight: 2,560 lb, 1,161 kg; turning circle (between walls): 34.1 ft. 10.4 m; fuel tank: 14 imp gal, 16.9 US gal, 64 l.

BODY saloon/sedan; 4-doors; 5 seats, separate front seats. reclining backrests.

PRACTICAL INSTRUCTIONS fuel: 98-100 oct petrol; oil: engine 8 imp pt, 9.5 US pt, 4.5 l, SAE 20W-30, change every 6,000 miles, 9,700 km - automatic transmission 2.5 imp pt, 3 US pt, 1.4 l, SAE 90, no change recommended - final drive 2.3 imp pt, 2.7 US pt, 1.3 l, no change recommended; greasing: every 6,000 miles, 9,700 km, 4 points; sparking plug: 225º; tappet clearances: inlet 0.010 in, 0.25 mm, exhaust 0.010 in, 0.25 mm; tyre pressure: front 26 psi, 1.8 atm, rear 30 psi, 2.1 atm.

OPTIONAL ACCESSORIES 4-speed fully synchronized mechanical gearbox with Laycock-de-Normanville overdrive on III and IV [I 3.281, II 2.100, III 1.386 (overdrive 1.137), IV 1 (overdrive 0.820), rev 3.369], 3.450 axle ratio; metallic spray; vinyl roof.

Jaguar XJ6 Executive

PRICE EX WORKS: 16,600 rand

ENGINE front, 4 stroke; 6 cylinders, vertical, in line; 258.4 cu in, 4,235 cc (3.63 x 4.17 in, 92 x 106 mm); compression ratio: 7.8:1; max power (DIN): 172 hp at 4,500 rpm; max torque (DIN): 231 lb ft, 31.9 kg m at 3,000 rpm; max engine rpm: 5,300; 40.6 hp/l; cast iron block, light alloy head, hemispherical combustion chambers, dry liners; 7 crankshaft bearings; valves: overhead, Vee-slanted, thimble tappets; camshafts: 2, overhead; lubrication: eccentric pump, full flow filter, oil cooler, 14.5 imp pt, 17.3 US pt, 8.2 l; 2 SU type HS8 horizontal carburettors; fuel feed: 2 electrical pumps; water-cooled, 35.5 imp pt, 38.9 US pt, 18.4 l, viscous coupling thermostatic fan.

TRANSMISSION driving wheels: rear; gearbox: Borg-Warner 65 automatic transmission, hydraulic torque converter and planetary gears with 3 ratios; ratios: I 2.390, II 1.450, III 1, rev 2.090; lever: central; final drive: hypoid bevel; axle ratio: 3.070; width of rims: 6''; tyres: E 70 VR x 15, tubeless.

PERFORMANCE max speed: 121 mph, 195 km/h; power-weight ratio: 22 lb/hp, 10 kg/hp; speed in direct drive at 1,000 rpm: 23.1 mph, 37.2 km/h; consumption: 16 m/imp gal, 13.4 m/US gal, 17.6 l x 100 km.

CHASSIS integral, front and rear auxiliary frames; front suspension: independent, wishbones, lower trailing links, coil springs, anti-roll bar, telescopic dampers; rear: independent, wishbones, semi-axles as upper arms, trailing lower radius arms, 4 coil springs, 4 telescopic dampers.

STEERING rack-and-pinion, adjustable steering wheel, servo; turns lock to lock: 3.31.

BRAKES disc (front diameter 11.18 in, 28.4 cm, rear 10.36 in, 26.4 cm), front internal radial fins, servo; swept area: front 234.5 sq in, 1,512 sq cm, rear 213.7 sq in, 1,378 sq cm, total 448.2 sq in, 2,890 sq cm.

ELECTRICAL EQUIPMENT 12 V; 66 Ah battery; 66 A alternator; Lucas distributor; 4 halogen headlamps.

DIMENSIONS AND WEIGHT wheel base: 112.79 in, 286 cm; tracks: 57.87 in, 147 cm front, 58.66 in, 149 cm rear; length: 194.68 in, 494 cm; width: 69.29 in, 176 cm; height: 53.94 in, 137 cm; ground clearance: 7.01 in, 17.8 cm; weight: 3,790 lb, 1,719 kg; turning circle (between walls): 38 ft, 11.6 m; fuel tank: 23.1 imp gal, 27.7 US gal, 105 l (2 separate tanks).

BODY saloon/sedan; 4 doors; 5 seats, separate front seats, reclining backrests; heated rear window; electric windows; air-conditioning; chrome sculptured wheels.

PRACTICAL INSTRUCTIONS fuel: 97 oct petrol; oil: engine 14.5 imp pt, 17.3 US pt, 8.2 l, SAE 20W-50, change every 6,000 miles, 9,700 km - gearbox SAE 90 EP, change every 12,000 miles, 19,400 km; greasing: every 6,000 miles, 9,700 km, 17 points; sparking plug: Champion N 11 Y; tappet clearances: inlet 0.012-0.014 in, 0.30-0.35 mm, exhaust 0.012-0.014 in, 0.30-0.35 mm.

Rover 2600 SD/SDX

PRICE EX WORKS: 7,800 rand

ENGINE front, 4 stroke; 6 cylinders, in line; 160.1 cu in, 2,623 cc (3 x 3.77 in, 76.2 x 95.8 mm); compression ratio: 8.7:1; max power (DIN): 111.5 hp at 4,500 rpm; max torque (DIN): 145 lb ft, 20 kg m at 2,000 rpm; max engine rpm: 5,500; 42.5 hp/l; 7 crankshaft bearings; valves: overhead, in line; camshafts: 1, overhead; lubrication: rotary pump, full flow filter, 8.3 imp pt, 9.9 US pt, 4.7 l; 2 SU type HIF6 semi-downdraught carburettors; fuel feed: electric pump; water-cooled 16.2 imp pt, 19.5 US pt, 9.2 l.

LEYLAND Triumph Chicane

LEYLAND Jaguar XJ6 Executive

LEYLAND Rover 3500 SDE

TRANSMISSION driving wheels: rear; clutch: single dry plate (diaphragm), hydraulically controlled; gearbox: mechanical; gears: 5, fully synchronized; ratios: I 3.321, II 2.087, III 1.396, IV 1, V 0.833, rev 3.428; lever: central; final drive: hypoid bevel; width of rims: 6''; tyres: 185 SR x 14, tubeless.

PERFORMANCE max speed: about 110 mph, 177 km/h; power-weight ratio: 25.7 lb/hp, 11.7 kg/hp.

CHASSIS integral, front cross members; front suspension: independent, by McPherson, wishbones (lower trailing links), coil spring/telescopic damper struts, anti-roll bar; rear: rigid axle (torque tube), coil springs with combined telescopic dampers, transverse Watt linkage.

STEERING rack-and-pinion, servo; turns lock to lock: 2.70.

BRAKES front disc, rear drum, servo; swept area: front 208.2 sq in, 1,343 sq cm, rear 127.3 sq in, 821 sq cm, total 335.5 sq in, 2,164 sq cm.

ELECTRICAL EQUIPMENT 12 V; 55 Ah battery; alternator; 4 headlamps, 2 halogen.

DIMENSIONS AND WEIGHT wheel base: 111 in, 282 cm; front and rear track: 59 in, 150 cm; length: 185 in, 470 cm; width: 69.70 in, 177 cm; height: 53.10 in, 135 cm; ground clearance: 6.10 in, 15.5 cm; weight: 2,866 lb, 1,300 kg; turning circle (between walls): 34.1 ft, 10.4 m; fuel tank: 14.5 imp gal, 17.4 US gal, 66 l.

BODY saloon/sedan; 4 doors; 5 seats, separate front seats; luxury equipment.

PRACTICAL INSTRUCTIONS fuel: 100 oct petrol; oil: engine 8.3 imp pt, 9.9 US pt, 4.7 l, SAE 20W-30, change every 6,000 miles, 9,700 km - gearbox 2.6 imp pt, 3.2 US pt, 1.5 l, SAE 90 EP, change every 6,000 miles, 9,700 km.

OPTIONAL ACCESSORIES Borg-Warner 65 automatic transmission, hydraulic torque converter and planetary gears with 3 ratios (I 2.390, II 1.450, III 1, rev 2.090).

Rover 3500 SDE

See 2600 SD/SDX, except for:

PRICE EX WORKS: 13,500 rand

ENGINE front, 4 stroke; 8 cylinders, Vee-slanted at 90°; 315 cu in, 3,528 cc (3.50 x 2.80 in, 88.9 x 71.1 mm); compression ratio: 9.35:1; max power (DIN): 157.7 hp at 5,250 rpm; max torque (DIN): 198 lb ft, 27.3 kg m at 2,500 rpm; max engine rpm: 6,000; 44.7 hp/l; light alloy block and head, dry liners; 5 crankshaft bearings; valves: overhead, in line, push-rods and rockers, hydraulic tappets; camshafts: 1, at centre of Vee; lubrication: 9.5 imp pt, 11.4 US pt, 5.4 l; water cooled, 19.5 imp pt, 23.5 US pt, 11.1 l.

TRANSMISSION gearbox: Borg-Warner 65 automatic trans-

mission, hydraulic torque converter and planetary gears with 3 ratios: I 2.390, II 1.450, III 1, rev 2.090.

PERFORMANCE max speed: 126 mph, 203 km/h; power-weight ratio: 18.3 lb/hp, 8.3 kg/hp; carrying capacity: 1,235 lb, 560 kg; acceleration: 0-50 mph (0-80 km/h) 6.4 sec; speed in direct drive at 1,000 rpm: 28.8 mph, 46.4 km/h; consumption: 26 m/imp gal, 21.6 m/US gal, 10.9 l x 100 km.

STEERING adjustable steering column; turns lock to lock: 2.75.

ELECTRICAL EQUIPMENT 68 Ah battery; 55 A alternator; Lucas electronic ignition.

DIMENSIONS AND WEIGHT weight: 2,895 lb, 1,313 kg.

BODY laminated windscreen with tinted glass; heated rear window; metallic spray; folding rear seat.

PRACTICAL INSTRUCTIONS final drive 1.6 imp pt, 1.9 US pt, 0.9 l, change every 6,000 miles, 9,700 km; valve timing: 10° 75° 68° 37°; tyre pressure: front 26 psi, 1.8 atm, rear 26 psi, 1.8 atm.

OPTIONAL ACCESSORIES Dunlop Denovo wheels and tyres; 195/HR x 14 tyres with light alloy wheels; electric windows.

PERANA-FORD   SOUTH AFRICA

Granada V8 Series

PRICES EX WORKS:

Granada 4-door Saloon	R —
Granada 2-door Coupé	R 7,365
Granada 4-door XL Saloon	R 7,255
Granada 4-door GXL Saloon	R —
Granada Ghia 4-door Saloon	R 8,595

258 hp power team

ENGINE Ford, front, 4 stroke; 8 cylinders, Vee-slanted; 302 cu in, 4,950 cc (4 x 3 in, 101.6 x 76.2 mm); compression ratio: 9.3:1; max power (SAE): 258 hp at 4,800 rpm; max torque (SAE): 299 lb ft, 41.3 kg m at 2,600 rpm; max engine rpm: 5,000; 52.1 hp/l; cast iron block and head; 5 crankshaft bearings; valves: overhead, push-rods and rockers, hydraulic tappets; camshafts: 1, overhead, lubrication: rotary pump, full flow filter, 8.8 imp pt, 10.6 US pt, 5 l; 1 Holley 600 CFM downdraught 4-barrel carburettors, cleaner air system; fuel feed: mechanical pump; cooling system, 21.1 imp pt, 25.4 US pt, 12 l.

TRANSMISSION driving wheels: rear; gearbox: Select-Shift Cruise-O-Matic C4, automatic transmission, hydraulic torque converter and planetary gears with 3 ratios: I 2.460, II 1.460, III 1, rev 2.200; lever: central; final drive: hypoid bevel; axle ratio: 2.920; width of rims: 6''; tyres: 185 HR x 14.

PERFORMANCE max speeds: (I) 53 mph, 85 km/h; (II) 95 mph, 153 km/h; (III) 129 mph, 207 km/h; power-weight ratio: 11.1 lb/hp, 5 kg/hp; carrying capacity: 1,014 lb, 460 kg; acceleration: standing ¼ mile 15.6 sec, 0-50 mph (0-80 km/h) 6 sec; speed in direct drive at 1,000 rpm: 25.8 mph, 41.6 km/h; consumption: 23 m/imp gal, 19.1 m/US gal, 12.3 l x 100 km.

CHASSIS integral, front and rear auxiliary frames; front suspension: independent, wishbones (lower trailing links), coil springs, anti-roll bar, telescopic dampers; rear: independent, semi-trailing arms, coil springs, telescopic dampers.

STEERING rack-and-pinion, servo; turns lock to lock: 3.60.

BRAKES front disc, internal radial fins, rear drum, servo.

ELECTRICAL EQUIPMENT 12 V; 44 Ah battery; 35 A alternator; 2 headlamps.

DIMENSIONS AND WEIGHT wheel base: 109.05 in, 277 cm; tracks: 59.45 in, 151 cm front, 60.24 in, 153 cm rear; length: 179.92 in, 457 cm; width: 70.47 in, 179 cm; height: saloons 53.94 in, 137 cm - Coupé 52.76 in, 134 cm; ground clearance: 5.12 in, 13 cm; weight: 2,867 lb, 1,300 kg; turning circle (between walls): 33.8 ft, 10.3 m; fuel tank: 14.3 imp gal, 17.2 US gal, 65 l.

BODY 5 seats, separate front seats.

PRACTICAL INSTRUCTIONS fuel: 90 oct petrol; oil: engine 8.8 imp pt, 10.6 US pt, 5 l, SAE 10W40, change every 6,200 miles, 10,000 km - gearbox 14.1 imp pt, 16.9 US pt, 8 l, SAE 80; greasing: none; sparking plug: Champion UF9Y; tyre pressure: front 26 psi, 1.8 atm, rear 28 psi, 2 atm.

PERANA-FORD Granada 4-door GXL Sedan

PAYKAN   IRAN

Saloon

ENGINE front, 4 stroke; 4 cylinders, slanted 10°, in line; 105.3 cu in, 1,725 cc (3.21 x 3.25 in, 81.5 x 82.5 mm); compression ratio: 7.5:1; max power (DIN): 64 hp at 4,500 rpm; max torque (DIN): 90 lb ft, 12.4 kg m at 2,500 rpm; max engine rpm: 5,600; 37.1 hp/l; cast iron block, light alloy head; 5 crankshaft bearings; valves: overhead, in line, push-rods and rockers; camshafts: 1, side; lubrication: rotary pump, full flow filter, 7.5 imp pt, 8.9 US pt, 4.2 l; 1 Zenith-Stromberg 150 CDS horizontal carburettor; fuel feed: mechanical pump; water-cooled, 12.3 imp pt, 14.8 US pt, 7 l.

TRANSMISSION driving wheels: rear; clutch: single dry plate (diaphragm), hydraulically controlled; gearbox: mechanical; gears: 4, fully synchronized; ratios: I 3.353, II 2.141, III 1.392, IV 1, rev 3.569; lever: central; final drive: hypoid bevel; axle ratio: 3.890; width of rims: 4.5''; tyres: 5.60 x 13.

PERFORMANCE max speed: 87 mph, 140 km/h; power-weight ratio: 32 lb/hp, 14.5 kg/hp; carrying capacity: 882 lb, 400 kg; speed in direct drive at 1,000 rpm: 17.4 mph, 28 km/h; consumption: 28.2 m/imp gal, 23.5 m/US gal, 10 l x 100 km.

CHASSIS integral; front suspension: independent, by McPherson, coil springs/telescopic damper struts, anti-roll bar; rear: rigid axle, semi-elliptic leafsprings, telescopic dampers.

STEERING recirculating ball; turns lock to lock: 3.75.

BRAKES front disc (diameter 9.61 in, 24.4 cm), rear drum, servo; swept area: total 278 sq in, 1,793 sq cm.

ELECTRICAL EQUIPMENT 12 V; 54 Ah battery; 24 A alternator; Lucas distributor; 2 headlamps.

DIMENSIONS AND WEIGHT wheel base: 98.43 in, 250 cm; front and rear track: 51.97 in, 132 cm; length: 169.29 in, 430 cm; width: 63.39 in, 161 cm; height: 55.51 in, 141 cm; ground clearance: 6.69 in, 17 cm; weight: 2,051 lb, 930 kg; turning circle (between walls): 33.5 ft, 10.2 m; fuel tank: 9.9 imp gal, 11.9 US gal, 45 l.

BODY saloon/sedan; 4 doors; 5 seats, separate front seats.

OPTIONAL ACCESSORIES Laycock overdrive on III and IV (0.803 ratio), 4.220 or 3.890 axle ratio; Borg-Warner 35 automatic transmission, hydraulic torque converter and planetary gears with 3 ratios (I 2.393, II 1.450, III 1, rev 2.094), max ratio of converter at stall 2, possible manual selection, steering column lever, 3.890 or 4.220 axle ratio.

Saloon GT

See Saloon, except for:

ENGINE compression ratio: 9.2:1; max power (DIN): 79 hp at 5,200 rpm; max torque (DIN): 91 lb ft, 12.6 kg m at 4,000 rpm; max engine rpm: 6,400; 45.8 hp/l; 2 Stromberg semi-downdraught carburettors.

TRANSMISSION gearbox ratios: I 3.120, II 1.990, III 1.295, IV 1, rev 3.320; axle ratio: 3.700; tyres: 165 SR x 13.

PERFORMANCE max speed: 96 mph, 155 km/h; power-weight ratio: 28 lb/hp, 12.7 kg/hp; speed in direct drive at 1,000 rpm: 18.3 mph, 29.5 km/h; consumption: 25.7 m/imp gal, 21.4 m/US gal, 11 l x 100 km.

ELECTRICAL EQUIPMENT 30 A alternator.

DIMENSIONS AND WEIGHT weight: 2,205 lb, 1,000 kg.

OPTIONAL ACCESSORIES Laycock overdrive on III and IV (0.803 ratio), 3.890 axle ratio; Borg-Warner 35 automatic transmission with 3.700 axle ratio.

HINDUSTAN   INDIA

Ambassador Mark 3

ENGINE front, 4 stroke; 4 cylinders, vertical, in line; 90.88 cu in, 1,489 cc (2.87 x 3.50 in, 73 x 88.9 mm); compression ratio: 7.2:1; max power (SAE): 50 hp at 4,200 rpm; max torque (SAE): 74 lb ft, 10.2 kg m at 3,000 rpm; max engine rpm: 4,800; 33.6 hp/l; cast iron block and head; 3 crankshaft bearings; valves: overhead, in line, push-rods and rockers; camshafts: 1, side; lubrication: gear pump, full flow filter, 8 imp pt, 9.6 US pt, 4.5 l; 1 SU type HS 2

PAYKAN Saloon GT

semi-downdraught carburettor; fuel feed: electric pump; water-cooled, 14.1 imp pt, 16.9 US pt, 8 l.

TRANSMISSION driving wheels: rear; clutch: single dry plate; gearbox: mechanical; gears: 4, II, III and IV synchronized; ratios: I 3.807, II 2.253, III 1.506, IV 1, rev 3.807; lever: steering column; final drive: hypoid bevel; axle ratio: 4.875; width of rims: 4''; tyres: 5.90 x 15.

PERFORMANCE max speeds: (I) 20 mph, 32 km/h; (II) 33 mph, 53 km/h; (III) 49 mph, 79 km/h; (IV) 74 mph, 119 km/h; power-weight ratio: 49.1 lb/hp, 22.3 kg/hp; carrying capacity: 850 lb, 386 kg; acceleration: standing ¼ mile 25 sec, 0-50 mph (0-80 km/h) 19.8 sec; speed in direct drive at 1,000 rpm: 15.5 mph, 25 km/h; consumption: 26.9 m/imp gal, 22.4 m/US gal, 10.5 l x 100 km.

CHASSIS integral; front suspension: independent, wishbones, longitudinal torsion bars, telescopic dampers; rear: rigid axle, semi-elliptic leafsprings, telescopic dampers.

STEERING rack-and-pinion; turns lock to lock: 3.75.

BRAKES drum, rear compensator; lining area: front 48.1 sq in, 310 sq cm, rear 48.1 sq in, 310 sq cm, total 96.2 sq in, 620 sq cm.

ELECTRICAL EQUIPMENT 12 V; 60 Ah battery; 20 A dynamo; Lucas distributor; 2 headlamps.

DIMENSIONS AND WEIGHT wheel base: 97 in, 246 cm; tracks: 53.50 in, 136 cm front, 53 in, 135 cm rear; length:

170.87 in, 434 cm; width: 65 in, 165 cm; height: 63 in, 160 cm; ground clearance: 7.87 in, 20 cm; weight: 2,456 lb, 1,114 kg; turning circle (between walls): 35.4 ft, 10.8 m; fuel tank: 12 imp gal, 14.4 US gal, 55 l.

BODY saloon/sedan; 4 doors; 5 seats, bench front seats.

PRACTICAL INSTRUCTIONS fuel: 83 oct petrol; oil: engine 7.9 imp pt, 9.5 US pt, 4.5 l, SAE 30, change every 3,000 miles, 4,800 km - gearbox 1.9 imp pt, 2.3 US pt, 1.1 l, SAE 90, change every 6,000 miles, 9,600 km - final drive 1.9 imp pt, 2.3 US pt, 1.1 l, SAE 90, change every 6,000 miles, 9,600 km; tappet clearances (hot): inlet 0.015 in, 0.38 mm, exhaust 0.015 in, 0.38 mm; valve timing: 0° 50° 35° 15°; tyre pressure: front 24 psi, 1.7 atm, rear 24 psi, 1.7 atm.

PREMIER   INDIA

Padmini

ENGINE front, 4 stroke; 4 cylinders, vertical, in line; 66.5 cu in, 1,089 cc (2.68 x 2.95 in, 68 x 75 mm); compression ratio: 7.3:1; max power (SAE): 40 hp at 4,800 rpm; max torque (SAE): 58 lb ft, 8 kg m at 2,400 rpm; max engine rpm: 4,800; 36.7 hp/l; cast iron block, light alloy head; 3 crankshaft bearings; valves: overhead, in line, push-rods and rockers; camshafts: 1, side; lubrication: 5.3 imp pt, 6.3 US pt, 3 l; 32 BIC type IBX downdraught single barrel carburettor; fuel feed: mechanical pump; water-cooled, 8.8 imp pt, 10.6 US pt, 5 l.

TRANSMISSION driving wheels: rear; clutch: single dry plate; gearbox: mechanical; gears: 4, II, III and IV synchronized; ratios: I 3.860, II 2.380, III 1.570, V 1, rev 3.860; lever: steering column; final drive: hypoid bevel; axle ratio: 4.300; width of rims: 3.5''; tyres: 5.20 x 14.

PERFORMANCE max speeds: (I) 19 mph, 30 km/h; (II) 31 mph, 50 km/h; (III) 47 mph, 75 km/h; (IV) 75 mph, 120 km/h; power-weight ratio: 49.3 lb/hp, 22.4 kg/hp; carrying capacity: 882 lb, 400 kg; acceleration: standing ¼ mile 26.9 sec, 0-50 mph, (0-80 km/h) 20.3 sec; speed in direct drive at 1,000 rpm: 15.6 mph, 25 km/h; consumption: 42.2 m/imp gal, 35.1 m/US gal, 6.7 l x 100 km.

CHASSIS integral; front suspension: independent, wishbones anti-roll bar, coil springs, telescopic dampers; rear: rigid axle, anti-roll bar, semi-elliptic leafsprings, telescopic dampers.

STEERING worm and roller; turns lock to lock: 4.80.

BRAKES drum; lining area: front 76.9 sq in, 496 sq cm, rear 76.9 sq in, 496 sq cm, total 153.8 sq in, 992 sq cm.

ELECTRICAL EQUIPMENT 12 V; 45 Ah battery; 22 A dynamo; Lucas distributor; 2 headlamps.

DIMENSIONS AND WEIGHT wheel base: 92.13 in, 234 cm; tracks: 48.50 in, 123 cm front, 47.83 in, 121 cm rear; length: 155.12 in, 394 cm; width: 57.40 in, 146 cm; height: 57.40 in, 146 cm; ground clearance: 5.04 in, 13 cm; weight: 1,973

HINDUSTAN Ambassador Mk 3

PREMIER Padmini De Luxe

lb, 895 kg; turning circle (between walls): 34.7 ft, 10.9 m; fuel tank: 8.4 imp gal, 10 US gal, 38 l.

BODY saloon/sedan; 4 doors; 4 seats, bench front seats.

PRACTICAL INSTRUCTIONS fuel: 83 oct petrol; oil: engine 5.3 imp pt, 6.3 US pt, 3 l, SAE 30-50, change every 5,600 miles, 9,000 km - gearbox 1.9 imp pt, 2.3 US pt, 1.1 l, SAE 90 EP, change every 18,600 miles, 30,000 km - final drive 1.1 imp pt, 1.3 US pt, 0.6 l, change every 18,600 miles, 30,000 km; tappet clearances: inlet 0.004 in, 0.10 mm, exhaust 0.004 in, 0.10 mm; valve timing: 16° 56° 56° 16°; tyre pressure: front 22 psi, 1.5 atm, rear 26 psi, 1.8 atm.

Padmini De Luxe

See Padmini, except for:

ENGINE compression ratio: 8:1; max power (SAE): 47 hp at 5,000 rpm; max torque (SAE): 58 lb ft, 8 kg m at 3,000 rpm; max engine rpm: 5,000; 43.6 hp/l.

TRANSMISSION lever: central.

PERFORMANCE max speeds: (I) 21 mph, 33 km/h; (II) 34 mph, 54 km/h; (III) 51 mph, 81 km/h; (IV) 80 mph, 128 km/h; power-weight ratio: 42 lb/hp, 19 kg/hp.

BODY separate front seats.

PRACTICAL INSTRUCTIONS fuel: 93 oct petrol.

STANDARD INDIA

Gazel

ENGINE front, 4 stroke; 4 cylinders, vertical, in line; 57.85 cu in, 948 cc (2.48 x 2.99 in, 63 x 76 mm); compression ratio: 7.2:1; max power (DIN): 35 hp at 4,800 rpm; max torque (DIN): 48 lb ft, 6.6 kg m at 2,400 rpm; max engine rpm: 4,800: 36.9 hp/l; cast iron block and head; 3 crankshaft bearings; valves: overhead, push-rods and rockers; camshafts: 1, side; lubrication: full flow filter, 7 imp pt, 8.4 US pt, 4 l; 1 Solex B30 PSEI downdraught single barrel carburettor; fuel feed: mechanical pump; water-cooled, 8.4 imp pt, 10.1 US pt, 4.8 l.

TRANSMISSION driving wheels: rear; clutch: single dry plate; gearbox: mechanical; gears: 4, fully synchronized; ratios: I 4.271, II 2.460, III 1.454, IV 1, rev 4.271; lever: central; final drive: hypoid bevel; axle ratio: 4.870; tyres: 5.20 x 13.

PERFORMANCE max speed: 71 mph, 115 km/h; power-weight ratio: 57.3 lb/hp, 26 kg/hp; consumption: 28.2 m/imp gal, 23.5 m/US gal, 10 l x 100 km.

CHASSIS central steel backbone, box-type ladder frame; front suspension: independent, wishbones, anti-roll bar, coil springs, telescopic dampers; rear: trailing radius arms, anti-roll bar, coil springs, telescopic dampers.

STANDARD Gazel

STEERING rack-and-pinion.

ELECTRICAL EQUIPMENT 12 V; 40 Ah battery; 264 W dynamo; 2 headlamps.

DIMENSIONS AND WEIGHT wheel base: 91.33 in, 232 cm; front and rear track: 48.03 in, 122 cm; length: 156.29 in, 397 cm; width: 59.84 in, 152 cm; height: 57.87 in, 147 cm; ground clearance: 6.30 in, 16 cm; weight: 2,006 lb, 910 kg; turning circle (between walls): 26.9 ft, 8.2 m.

BODY saloon/sedan; 4 doors; 5 seats, separate front seats.

HONGKI CHINA (People's Republic)

Limousine

ENGINE front, 4 stroke; 8 cylinders, Vee-slanted at 90°; 344.9 cu in, 5,652 cc (3.94 x 3.54 in, 100 x 90 mm); compression ratio: 8.1:1; max power (SAE): 210 hp at 4,400 rpm; max torque (SAE): 312 lb ft, 43 kg m at 3,000 rpm; max engine rpm: 4,400; 37.1 hp/l; cast iron block and head; 5 crankshaft bearings; valves: overhead, in line, push-rods and rockers; camshafts: 1, at centre of Vee; lubrication: gear pump, full flow filter, 8.1 imp pt, 9.7 US pt, 4.6 l; 1 downdraught twin barrel carburettor; fuel feed: mechanical pump; water-cooled, 19.4 imp pt, 23.3 US pt, 11 l.

HONGKI Limousine

LIMOUSINE

TRANSMISSION driving wheels: rear; gearbox: automatic transmission, hydraulic torque converter and planetary gears with 2 ratios, max ratio of converter at stall 2.1; ratios: I 1.950, II 1, rev 1.950; lever: steering column; final drive: hypoid bevel; axle ratio: 2.800; tyres: 8.20 x 15.

PERFORMANCE max speeds: (I) 61 mph, 98 km/h; (II) 118 mph, 190 km/h; power-weight ratio: 28.6 lb/hp, 13 kg/hp; carrying capacity: 1,147 lb, 520 kg; speed in direct drive at 1,000 rpm: 27 mph, 43.4 km/h; consumption: 17.1 m/imp gal, 14.3 m/US gal, 16.5 l x 100 km.

CHASSIS box-type ladder frame; front suspension: independent, wishbones, coil springs, telescopic dampers; rear: rigid axle, semi-elliptic leafsprings, telescopic dampers.

STEERING recirculating ball, servo.

BRAKES drum.

ELECTRICAL EQUIPMENT 12 V; 2 x 54 Ah batteries; dynamo: 2 headlamps.

DIMENSIONS AND WEIGHT wheel base: 133.86 in, 340 cm; front and rear track: 61.09 in, 155 cm; length: 225.59 in, 573 cm; width: 79.13 in, 201 cm; height: 65.75 in, 167 cm; ground clearance: 6.30 in, 16 cm; weight: 6,015 lb, 2,728 kg; turning circle (between walls): 47.2 ft, 14.4 m; fuel tank: 20.9 imp gal, 25.1 US gal, 95 l.

BODY limousine; 4 doors; 6 seats, bench front seats; electrically-controlled rear seat and windows; air-conditioning.

PRACTICAL INSTRUCTIONS fuel: 86 oct petrol; oil: engine 7.4 imp pt, 8.9 US pt, 4.2 l, SAE 5W-20 (winter) 20W-40 (summer), change every 1,900 miles, 3,000 km - automatic transmission 15.8 imp pt, 19 US pt, 9 l, SAE 80 - final drive 3.7 imp pt, 4.4 US pt, 2.1 l, SAE 90; tyre pressure: front 24 psi, 1.7 atm, rear 26 psi, 1.8 atm.

PEKING   CHINA (People's Republic)

BJ 212

ENGINE front, 4 stroke; 4 cylinders, vertical, in line; 149.2 cu in, 2,445 cc (3.62 x 3.62 in, 92 x 92 mm); compression ratio: 6.7:1; max power (SAE): 75 hp at 3,500 rpm; max torque (SAE): 127 lb ft, 17.5 kg m at 2,500 rpm; max engine rpm: 4,000; 30.7 hp/l; cast iron block, light alloy head; valves: overhead, Vee-slanted, push-rods and rockers; camshafts: 1, side; lubrication: gear-pump, full flow filter, 9.7 imp pt, 11.6 US pt, 5.5 l; 1 K-22D downdraught single barrel carburettor; fuel feed: mechanical pump; water-cooled, 21.1 imp pt, 25.4 US pt, 12 l.

TRANSMISSION driving wheels: front (automatically engaged with transfer box low ratio) and rear; clutch: single dry plate; gearbox: mechanical; gears: 3, II and III synchronized; ratios: I 3.115, II 1.772, III 1, rev 3.738; transfer box ratios: I 1.150, II 2.780; lever: central; final drive: spiral bevel; axle ratio: 5.125; width of rims: 4.5''; tyres: 6.50 x 16.

PERFORMANCE max speeds: (I) 20 mph, 32 km/h; (II) 35 mph, 56 km/h; (III) 59 mph, 95 km/h; power-weight ratio: 41 lb/hp, 18.6 kg/hp; carrying capacity: 882 lb, 400 kg; speed in direct drive at 1,000 rpm: 13.9 mph, 22.3 km/h; consumption: 20.2 m/imp gal, 16.8 m/US gal, 14 l x 100 km.

CHASSIS box-type ladder frame; front and rear suspension: rigid axle, semi-elliptic leafsprings, telescopic dampers.

STEERING worm and double roller.

BRAKES drum; lining area: total 153.5 sq in, 990 sq cm.

ELECTRICAL EQUIPMENT 12 V; 54 Ah battery; 220 W dynamo; 2 headlamps.

DIMENSIONS AND WEIGHT wheel base: 90.55 in, 230 cm; front and rear track: 56.69 in, 144 cm; length: 151.57 in, 385 cm; width: 68.90 in, 175 cm; ground clearance: 8.27 in, 21 cm; weight: 3,076 lb, 1,395 kg; turning circle (between walls): 42.6 ft, 13 m; fuel tank: 13.2 imp gal, 15.8 US gal, 60 l.

BODY open; 4 doors; 5 seats, separate front seats.

PRACTICAL INSTRUCTIONS fuel: 72 oct petrol; oil: engine 9 imp pt, 10.8 US pt, 5.1 l, SAE 20W-30, change every 1,900 miles, 3,000 km - gearbox 1.4 imp pt, 1.7 US pt, 0.8 l, change every 7,400 miles, 12,000 km - final drive 1.4 imp pt, 1.7 US pt, 0.8 l, SAE 80-90, change every 7,400 miles, 12,000 km; greasing: every 1,200 miles, 2,000 km, 20 points; sparking plug: 145°; tappet clearances: inlet 0.009 in, 0.23 mm, exhaust 0.011 in, 0.28 mm; valve timing: 9° 51' 47° 13°; tyre pressure: front 28 psi, 2 atm, rear 31 psi, 2.2 atm.

PEKING BJ 212

HYUNDAI   SOUTH KOREA

Pony Saloon

ENGINE Mitsubishi, front, 4 stroke; 4 cylinders, vertical, in line; 75.5 cu in, 1,238 cc (2.87 x 2.91 in, 73 x 74 mm); compression ratio: 9:1; max power (DIN): 80 hp at 6,300 rpm; max torque (DIN): 78.3 lb ft, 10.8 kg m at 4,000 rpm; 64.6 hp/l; light alloy head; 5 crankshaft bearings; valves: overhead, rockers; camshafts: 1, overhead; lubrication: filter, 7 imp pt, 8.4 US pt, 4 l; 1 Stromberg downdraught twin barrel carburettor; water-cooled, 10.5 imp pt, 12.7 US pt, 6 l.

TRANSMISSION driving wheels: rear; clutch: single dry plate (diaphragm), hydraulically controlled; gearbox: mechanical; gears: 4, fully synchronized; ratios: I 3.523, II 2.193, III 1.492, IV 1, rev 3.367; lever: central; final drive: hypoid bevel; axle ratio: 3.889.

PERFORMANCE max speed: about 90 mph, 145 km/h; power-weight ratio: 23.9 lb/hp, 10.8 kg/hp; carrying capacity: 882 lb, 400 kg; speed in direct drive at 1,000 rpm: 15.3 mph, 24.6 km/h; consumption: 28.2 m/imp gal, 23.5 m/US gal, 10 l x 100 km.

CHASSIS integral; front suspension: independent, by McPherson, coil springs/telescopic damper struts, lower wish-

---

bones (trailing links), anti-roll bar; rear: rigid axle, semi-elliptic leafsprings, telescopic dampers.

STEERING recirculating ball.

BRAKES front disc (diameter 9.7 in, 24.7 cm), rear drum.

ELECTRICAL EQUIPMENT 12 V; 32 Ah battery; 40 A alternator; Mitsubishi distributor; 4 headlamps.

DIMENSIONS AND WEIGHT wheel base: 92.13 in, 234 cm; tracks: 50 in, 127 cm front, 49.21 in, 125 cm rear; length: 156.69 in, 398 cm; width: 61.42 in, 156 cm; height: 53.54 in, 136 cm; ground clearance: 6.89 in, 17.5 cm; weight: 1,918 lb, 870 kg; turning circle: 30.2 ft, 9.2 m; fuel tank: 9.9 imp gal, 11.9 US gal, 45 l.

BODY saloon/sedan; 4 doors; 5 seats, separate front seats, reclining backrests.

Pony Coupé

See Pony Saloon, except for:

PERFORMANCE: power-weight ratio: 22.9 lb/hp, 10.4 kg/hp.

DIMENSIONS AND WEIGHT weight: 1,830 lb, 830 kg.

BODY coupé; 2 doors; 4 seats.

KIA   SOUTH KOREA

Brisa 1100

ENGINE front, 4 stroke; 4 cylinders, in line; 60.1 cu in, 985 cc (2.76 x 2.52 in, 70 x 64 mm); compression ratio: 8.8:1; max power (SAE): 62 hp (45.5 kW) at 6,000 rpm; max torque (SAE): 59 lb ft, 8.1 kg m (79.5 Nm) at 3,500 rpm; max engine rpm: 6,200; 62.9 hp/l (46.2 kW/l); cast iron block, light alloy head; 5 crankshaft bearings; valves: overhead, rockers; camshafts: 1, overhead; lubrication: rotary pump, full flow filter, 6.5 imp pt, 7.8 US pt, 3.7 l; 1 Hitachi DTB downdraught twin barrel carburettor; fuel feed: mechanical pump; water-cooled, 10.4 imp pt, 12.5 US pt, 5.9 l.

TRANSMISSION driving wheels: rear; clutch: single dry plate (diaphragm); gearbox: mechanical; gears: 4, fully synchronized; ratios: I 3.655, II 2.185, III 1.425, IV 1, rev 3.655; lever: central; final drive: hypoid bevel; axle ratio: 4.375; tyres: 6.00 x 12.

PERFORMANCE max speeds: (I) 25 mph, 40 km/h; (II) 40 mph, 65 km/h; (III) 65 mph, 105 km/h; (V) 87 mph, 140 km/h; power-weight ratio: 29 lb/hp, 12.7 kg/hp; carrying capacity: 882 lb, 400 kg; speed in direct drive at 1,000 rpm: 14.9 mph, 24 km/h; consumption: 35.3 m/imp gal, 29.4 m/US gal, 8 l x 100 km.

CHASSIS integral; front suspension: independent, by McPherson, coil springs/telescopic damper struts, lower wish-

HYUNDAI Pony Coupé

bones (trailing links), anti-roll bar; rear: rigid axle, semi-elliptic leafsprings, telescopic dampers.

STEERING recirculating ball; turns lock to lock: 3.80.

BRAKES front disc, rear drum, dual circuit; lining area: front 39.7 sq in, 256 sq cm, rear 39.7 sq in, 256 sq cm, total 79.4 sq in, 512 sq cm.

ELECTRICAL EQUIPMENT 12 V; 35 Ah battery; alternator; Mitsubishi distributor; 2 headlamps.

DIMENSIONS AND WEIGHT wheel base: 88.98 in, 226 cm; tracks: 49.61 in, 126 cm front, 48.82 in, 124 cm rear; length: 151.57 in, 385 cm; width: 60.63 in, 154 cm; height: 54.72 in, 139 cm; ground clearance: 6.30 in, 16 cm; weight: 1,742 lb, 790 kg; weight distribution: 56% front, 44% rear; turning circle (between walls): 27.6 ft, 8.4 m; fuel tank: 8.8 imp gal, 10.6 US gal, 40 l.

BODY saloon/sedan; 4 doors; 5 seats, separate front seats.

PRACTICAL INSTRUCTIONS fuel: 85-90 oct petrol; oil: engine 6.5 imp pt, 7.8 US pt, 3.7 l, SAE 20W-30, change every 3,700 miles, 6,000 km - gearbox 2.3 imp pt, 2.7 US pt, 1.3 l, SAE 80, change every 12,400 miles, 20,000 km - final drive 2.1 imp pt, 2.5 US pt, 1.2 l, change every 12,400 miles, 20,000 km; greasing: none; tappet clearances: inlet 0.010 in, 0.25 mm, exhaust 0.012 in, 0.30 mm; valve timing: 13° 50° 57° 6°; tyre pressure: front 26 psi, 1.8 atm, rear 26 psi, 1.8 atm.

Brisa 1300

See Brisa 1100, except for:

ENGINE 77.6 cu in, 1,272 cc (2.87 x 2.99 in, 73 x 76 mm); compression ratio: 9.2:1; max power (SAE): 87 hp at 6,000 rpm; max torque (SAE): 80 lb ft, 11 kg m at 3,500 rpm; 68.4 hp/l.

TRANSMISSION axle ratio: 4.111.

PERFORMANCE max speed: 93 mph, 150 km/h; power-weight ratio: 20.7 lb/hp, 9.4 kg/hp; acceleration: standing ¼ mile 18.1 sec; speed in direct drive at 1,000 rpm: 15.8 mph, 25.5 km/h.

DIMENSIONS AND WEIGHT weight: 1,797 lb, 815 kg.

YLN   TAIWAN

707 De Luxe

ENGINE front, 4 stroke; 4 cylinders, vertical, in line; 95.6 cu in, 1,567 cc (3.07 x 3.23 in, 78 x 82 mm); compression ratio: 8.3:1; max power (SAE): 80 hp at 5,200 rpm; max torque (SAE): 91 lb ft, 12.6 kg m at 3,000 rpm; max engine rpm: 5,200; 51 hp/l; cast iron block and head; 3 crankshaft bearings; valves: overhead, in line, push-rods and rockers; camshafts: 1, side; lubrication: rotary pump, full flow filter (cartridge), 4.6 imp pt, 5.5 US pt, 2.6˙ l; 1 Nikki 214282-171 downdraught twin barrel carburettor; fuel feed: mechanical pump; water-cooled, 8.8 imp pt, 10.6 US pt, 5 l.

TRANSMISSION driving wheels: rear; clutch: single dry plate (diaphragm); gearbox: mechanical; gears: 4, fully synchronized; ratios: I 3.657, II 2.177, III 1.419, IV 1, rev 3.638; lever: central; final drive: hypoid bevel; axle ratio: 4.111; width of rims: 4.5''; tyres: 5.60 x 13.

PERFORMANCE max speeds: (I) 25 mph, 40 km/h; (II) 43 mph, 70 km/h; (III) 63 mph, 102 km/h; (IV) 90 mph, 145 km/h; power-weight ratio: 25.8 lb/hp, 11.7 kg/hp; carrying capacity: 606 lb, 275 kg; speed in direct drive at 1,000 rpm: 16.3 mph, 26.2 km/h; consumption: 36.7 m/imp gal, 30.5 m/US gal, 7.7 l x 100 km.

CHASSIS integral; front suspension: independent, wishbones, coil springs/telescopic damper struts, anti-roll bar; rear: rigid axle, semi-elliptic leafsprings, telescopic dampers.

STEERING recirculating ball.

BRAKES drum, 2 front leading shoes; swept area: front 89.1 sq in, 575 sq cm, rear 89.1 sq in, 575 sq cm, total 178.2 sq in, 1,150 sq cm.

ELECTRICAL EQUIPMENT 12 V; 50 Ah battery; 35 A alternator; Shin-lin D411-91 distributor; 4 headlamps.

DIMENSIONS AND WEIGHT wheel base: 96.46 in, 245 cm; tracks: 50.79 in, 129 cm front, 51.57 in, 131 cm rear; length: 162.20 in, 412 cm; width: 62.20 in, 158 cm; height: 55.12 in, 140 cm; ground clearance: 6.69 in, 17 cm; weight: 2,062 lb, 935 kg; turning circle (between walls): 31.5 ft, 9.6 m; fuel tank: 11 imp gal, 13.2 US gal, 50 l.

KIA Brisa 1100 - 1300

YLN 707 De Luxe

BODY saloon/sedan; 4 doors; 5 seats, separate front seats, reclining backrests, built-in headrests.

PRACTICAL INSTRUCTIONS fuel: 85 oct petrol; oil: engine 4.6 imp pt, 5.5 US pt, 2.6 l, SAE 30 (winter), 40 (summer), change every 3,100 miles, 5,000 km - gearbox 2.6 imp pt, 3.2 US pt, 1.5 l, SAE 90, change every 31,100 miles, 50,000 km - final drive 1.6 imp pt, 1.9 US pt, 0.9 l, SAE 90, change every 31,100 miles, 50,000 km; greasing: every 31,100 miles, 50,000 km, 14 points; tappet clearances: inlet 0.014 in, 0.35 mm, exhaust 0.014 in, 0.35 mm; valve timing: 18° 54° 56° 16°; tyre pressure: front 23 psi, 1.6 atm, rear 23 psi, 1.6 atm.

803 DL

ENGINE Diesel, front, 4 stroke; 4 cylinders, vertical, in line; 132 cu in, 2,164 cc (3.26 x 3.93 in, 83 x 100 mm); compression ratio: 20:1; max power (SAE): 66 hp at 4,000 rpm; max torque (SAE): 104.3 lb ft, 14.4 kg m at 1,800 rpm; max engine rpm: 30.5 hp/l; cast iron block and head; 3 crankshaft bearings; valves: overhead, push-rods and rockers; camshafts: 1, side; lubrication: gear pump, full flow filter, 10.4 imp pt, 12.5 US pt, 5.9 l; fuel injection system; fuel feed: mechanical pump; water-cooled, 14.1 imp pt, 16.9 US pt, 8 l.

TRANSMISSION driving wheels: rear; clutch: single dry plate (diaphragm); gearbox: mechanical; gears: 4, fully synchronized; ratios: I 3.592, II 2.246, III 1.415, IV 1, rev

YLN 803 DL

803 DL

3.657; lever: steering column; final drive: hypoid bevel; axle ratio: 4.100; width of rims: 5''; tyres: 175 SR x 14.

PERFORMANCE max speed: 78 mph, 125 km/h; power-weight ratio: 21.1 lb/hp, 46.6 kg/hp.

CHASSIS integral; front suspension: independent, double wishbones, coil springs, anti-roll bar, telescopic double acting dampers; rear: rigid axle, semi-elliptic leafspring, telescopic double acting dampers.

STEERING recirculating ball.

BRAKES front disc, rear drum; swept area: front 227 sq in, 1,464 sq cm, rear 117.4 sq in, 757 sq cm, total 344.3 sq in, 2,221 sq cm.

ELECTRICAL EQUIPMENT 12 V; 70 Ah battery; 40 A alternator; 4 headlamps.

DIMENSIONS AND WEIGHT wheel base: 105.90 in, 269 cm; tracks: 54.53 in, 139 cm front, 54.33 in, 138 cm rear; length: 184.64 in, 469 cm; width: 66.53 in, 169 cm; height: 56.89 in, 144 cm; ground clearance: 7.48 in, 19 cm; weight: 3,076 lb, 1,395 kg; turning circle (between walls): 36.1 ft, 11 m; fuel tank: 14.7 imp gal, 17.7 US gal, 67 l.

BODY saloon/sedan; 4 doors; 6 seats, bench front seats.

PRACTICAL INSTRUCTIONS oil: engine 8.8 imp pt, 10.6 US pt, 5 l, gearbox 2.8 imp pt, 3.4 US pt, 1.6 l, change every 31,000 miles, 50,000 km - final drive 1.6 imp pt, 1.9 US pt, 0.9 l, change every 31,000 miles, 50,000 km; valve timing: 28° 67° 67° 28°; tyre pressure: front and rear 21 psi, 1.5 atm.

DAIHATSU   JAPAN

Max Cuore Series

PRICES (Tokyo):

Standard 2-door Sedan	**547,000 yen**
De Luxe 4-door Sedan	**618,000 yen**
Custom 2-door Sedan	**611,000 yen**
Custom 4-door Sedan	**645,000 yen**
Custom EX 2-door Sedan	**637,000 yen**
Custom EX 4-door Sedan	**671,000 yen**
Hi-Custom 4-door Sedan	**671,000 yen**
Hi-Custom EX 4-door Sedan	**697,000 yen**

28 hp power team

ENGINE front, transverse, 4 stroke; 2 cylinders, in line; 33.4 cu in, 547 cc (2.82 x 2.68 in, 71.6 x 68 mm); compression ratio: 8.7:1; max power (JIS): 28 hp at 6,000 rpm; max torque (JIS): 28 lb ft, 3.9 kg m at 3,500 rpm; max engine rpm: 7,800; 51.2 hp/l; cast iron block, light alloy head; 3 crankshaft bearings; valves: overhead, rockers; camshafts: 1 overhead, cogged belt; lubrication: rotary pump, full flow filter, 5.1 imp pt, 6.1 US pt, 2.9 l; 1 Aisan downdraught twin barrel carburettor; fuel feed: mechanical pump; emission control by Daihatsu lean-burn system with turbulence generating pot in each combustion chamber and catalytic converter; water-cooled, 5.3 imp pt, 6.3 US pt, 3 l.

TRANSMISSION driving wheels: front; clutch: single dry plate (diaphragm); gearbox: mechanical; gears: 4, fully synchronized; ratios: I 4.727, II 2.823, III 1.809, IV 1.269, rev 4.865; lever: central; final drive: hypoid bevel; axle ratio: 3.955; width of rims: 3.5''; tyres: 5.20 x 10.

PERFORMANCE max speeds: (I) 18 mph, 29 km/h; (II) 31 mph, 50 km/h; (III) 47 mph, 75 km/h; (IV) 68 mph, 110 km/h; power-weight ratio: 2-dr. sedans 42.6 lb/hp, 19.3 kg/hp - 4-dr. sedans 44.1 lb/hp, 20 kg/hp; carrying capacity: 706 lb, 320 kg; acceleration: standing ¼ mile 21.8 sec; speed in top at 1,000 rpm: 8.8 mph, 14.2 km/h; fuel consumption: 52.3 m/imp gal, 43.6 m/US gal, 5.4 l x 100 km at 37 mph, 60 km/h.

CHASSIS integral; front suspension: independent, by McPherson, coil springs/telescopic damper struts, lower wishbones (trailing links); rear: independent, semi-trailing arms, coil springs, telescopic dampers.

STEERING rack-and-pinion; turns lock to lock: 3.30.

BRAKES drum, single circuit; lining area: front 18.6 sq in, 120 sq cm, rear 18.6 sq in, 120 sq cm, total 37.2 sq in, 240 sq cm.

ELECTRICAL EQUIPMENT 12 V; 26 Ah battery; 35 A alternator; 2 headlamps.

DIMENSIONS AND WEIGHT wheel base: 82.28 in, 209 cm; front and rear tracks: 48.03 in, 122 cm; length: 124.40 in, 316 cm; width: 54.72 in, 139 cm; height: 51.97 in, 132 cm; ground clearance: 7.09 in, 18 cm; weight: 2-dr. sedans 1,191 lb, 540 kg - 4-dr. sedans 1,235 lb, 560 kg; weight distribution: 64% front, 36% rear; turning circle (between walls): 30.2 ft, 9.2 m; fuel tank: 5.7 imp gal, 6.9 US gal, 26 l.

BODY saloon/sedan; 4 seats, separate front seats.

PRACTICAL INSTRUCTIONS fuel: 85-90 oct mixture; oil: engine 5.3 imp pt, 6.3 US pt, 3 l, oil in separate tank - gearbox and final drive 2.6 imp pt, 3.2 US pt, 1.5 l, SAE 90, change every 12,400 miles, 20,000 km; valve timing 21° 59° 59° 21°; front and rear tyre pressure: 26 psi, 1.8 atm.

OPTIONALS tyres 145 SR x 10.

Charade Series

PRICES (Tokyo):

Charade XO	**653,000 yen**
Charade XG	**692,000 yen**
Charade XT	**748,000 yen**
Charade XTE	**799,000 yen**
Charade XGE	**798,000 yen**

55 hp power team

ENGINE front, transverse, 4 stroke; 3 cylinders, in line; 60.6 cu in, 993 cc (2.99 x 2.87 in, 76 x 73 mm); compression ratio: 8.7:1; max power (JIS): 55 hp at 5,500 rpm; max torque (JIS): 57 lb ft, 7.8 kg m at 2,800 rpm; max engine rpm: 6,000; 55.4 hp/l; cast iron block, light alloy head; 4 crankshaft bearings; valves: overhead, push-rods and rockers; camshafts: 1, overhead; lubrication: rotary pump, full flow filter, 5.1 imp pt, 6.1 US pt, 2.9 l; 1 Aisan-Stromberg downdraught twin barrel carburettor; fuel feed: mechanical pump; water-cooled, 7 imp pt, 8.5 US pt, 4 l.

TRANSMISSION driving wheels: front; clutch: single dry plate (diaphragm); gearbox: mechanical; gears: 4, fully synchronized; ratios: I 3.666, II 2.150, III 1.464, IV 0.971, rev 3.529; lever: central; final drive: helical spur gears; axle ratio: 4.588; width of rims: 5''; tyres: 6.00 x 12 (XT XTE 155 SR x 12).

PERFORMANCE max speeds: (I) 25 mph, 40 km/h; (II) 40 mph, 64 km/h; (III) 58 mph, 94 km/h; (IV) 84 mph, 135 km/h; power-weight ratio: XO 25.4 lb/hp, 11.5 kg/hp; carrying capacity: 882 lb, 400 kg; consumption: 53.3 m/imp gal, 44.4 m/US gal, 5.3 l x 100 km at 37 mph, 60 km/h.

CHASSIS integral; front suspension: independent, by McPherson, coil springs/telescopic dampers struts; rear: independent, upper and lower trailing links, Panhard rod, coil spring, telescopic dampers.

DAIHATSU Max Cuore Custom 2-door Sedan

DAIHATSU Charade XGE

STEERING rack-and-pinion; turns lock to lock: 3.40.

BRAKES drum (front disc on XTE, XTG and XT); lining area: front 47.1 sq in, 304 sq cm (disc 16.7 sq in, 108 sq cm), rear 37.2 sq in, 240 sq cm, total 84.3 sq in, 544 sq cm.

ELECTRICAL EQUIPMENT 12 V; 30 Ah battery; 40 A alternator; 2 headlamps.

DIMENSIONS AND WEIGHT wheel base: 90.55 in, 230 cm; tracks: 51.18 in, 130 cm front, 50.39 in, 128 cm rear; length: 136.22 in, 346 cm; width: 59.45 in, 151 cm; height: 53.54 in, 136 cm; ground clearance: 7.09 in, 18 cm; weight: XO 1,389 lb, 630 kg - XG 1,411 lb, 640 kg - XT 1,433 lb, 650 kg - XGE 1,444 lb, 655 kg - XTE 1,455 lb, 660 kg; weight distribution: 63% front, 37% rear; turning circle (between walls): 32.8 ft, 10 m; fuel tank: 7.5 imp gal, 9 US gal, 34 l.

BODY saloon/sedan; 4 + 1 doors; 5 seats; separate front seats, reclining backrests, headrests.

PRACTICAL INSTRUCTIONS fuel: 85-90 oct petrol; oil: engine 5.1 imp pt, 6.1 US pt, 2.9 l, SAE 20W-30, change every 3,100 miles, 5,000 km - gearbox and final drive 2.5 imp pt, 3 US pt, 1.4 l, SAE 80, change every 18,600 miles, 30,000 km; tappet clearances: inlet 0.008 in, 0.20 mm, exhaust 0.008 in, 0.20 mm; valve timing: 21° 49° 49° 21°; tyre pressure: front 24.2 psi, 1.7 atm, rear 24.2 psi, 1.7 atm.

OPTIONALS 5-speed mechanical gearbox; V 0.971; max speed 87 mph, 140 km/h.

DAIHATSU Max Cuore Series

Charmant 1200 De Luxe 4-door Sedan

PRICE (Tokyo): 766,000 yen

ENGINE front, 4 stroke; 4 cylinders, vertical, in line; 71.1 cu in, 1,166 cc (2.95 x 2.60 in, 75 x 66 mm); compression ratio: 9:1; max power (JIS): 64 hp at 5,800 rpm; max torque (JIS): 67 lb ft, 9.2 kg m at 3,600 rpm; max engine rpm: 6,300; 54.9 hp/l; cast iron cylinder block, light alloy head; 5 crankshaft bearings; valves: overhead, push-rods and rockers; camshafts: 1, side; lubrication: rotary pump, full flow filter, 6.2 imp pt, 7.4 US pt, 3.5 l; 1 Aisan 3K-U downdraught twin barrel carburettor; catalytic converter, secondary air injection and exhaust gas recirculation; fuel feed: mechanical pump; water-cooled, 10.8 imp pt, 12.7 US pt, 6 l.

TRANSMISSION driving wheels: rear; clutch: single dry plate (diaphragm); gearbox: mechanical; gears: 4, fully synchronized; ratios: I 3.789, II 2.220, III 1.435, IV 1, rev 4.100; width of rims: 4.5''; tyres: 6.00 x 12.

PERFORMANCE max speeds: (I) 25 mph, 40 km/h; (II) 43 mph, 70 km/h; (III) 67 mph, 108 km/h; (IV) 93 mph, 150 km/h; power-weight ratio: 28.1 lb/hp, 12.7 kg/hp; carrying capacity: 882 lb, 400 kg; speed in direct drive at 1,000 rpm: 14.5 mph, 23.3 km/h; fuel consumption: 56.5 m/imp gal, 47 m/US gal, 5 l x 100 km at 37 mph, 60 km/h.

CHASSIS integral; front suspension: independent, by McPherson, coil springs/telescopic dampers struts, lower wishbones (trailing links), anti-roll bar; rear: rigid axle, semi-elliptic leafsprings, telescopic dampers.

DAIHATSU Charade XTE

STEERING recirculating ball; turns lock to lock: 3.40.

BRAKES front disc, rear drum, servo.

ELECTRICAL EQUIPMENT 12 V; 32 Ah battery; 40 A alternator; Denso distributor; 4 headlamps.

DIMENSIONS AND WEIGHT wheel base: 91.73 in, 233 cm; tracks: 49.21 in, 125 cm front, 48.82 in, 124 cm rear; length: 157.09 in, 399 cm; width: 59.84 in, 152 cm; height: 53.94 in, 137 cm; ground clearance: 6.69 in, 17 cm; dry weight: 1,797 lb, 815 kg; distribution of weight: 55.7% front, 44.3% rear; turning circle (between walls): 32.8 ft, 10 m; fuel tank: 9.5 imp gal, 11.4 US gal, 43 l.

BODY saloon/sedan; 4 doors; 5 seats, separate front seats.

PRACTICAL INSTRUCTIONS fuel: 85-90 oct petrol; oil: engine 6.2 imp pt, 7.4 US pt, 3.5 l - gearbox 3 imp pt, 3.6 US pt, 1.7 l, SAE 90 - final drive 1.8 imp pt, 2.1 US pt, 1 l; tappet clearances (hot): inlet 0.008 in, 0.20 mm, exhaust 0.012 in, 0.30 mm; valve timing: 16° 50° 50° 16°; tyre pressure: front 21 psi, 1.5 atm, rear 21 psi, 1.5 atm.

Charmant 1200 Custom 4-door Sedan

See Charmant 1200 De Luxe 4-door Sedan, except for:

PRICE (Tokyo): 800,000 yen

PERFORMANCE power-weight ratio: 28.4 lb/hp, 12.9 kg/hp.

DIMENSIONS AND WEIGHT dry weight: 1,819 lb, 825 kg.

OPTIONAL ACCESSORIES 5-speed fully synchronized mechanical gearbox (I 3.587, II 2.022, III 1.384, IV 1, V 0.861, rev 3.484); automatic transmission with 2 ratios (I 1.820, II 1, rev 1.820), 4.300 axle ratio.

Charmant 1200 Hi-Custom 4-door Sedan

See Charmant 1200 Custom 4-door Sedan, except for:

PRICE (Tokyo): 830,000 yen

PERFORMANCE power-weight ratio: 28.6 lb/hp, 13 kg/hp.

DIMENSIONS AND WEIGHT length: 157.48 in, 400 cm; dry weight: 1,830 lb, 830 kg.

Charmant 1400 Custom 4-door Sedan

See Charmant 1200 De Luxe 4-door Sedan, except for:

PRICE (Tokyo): 858,000 yen

ENGINE 85,9 cu in, 1,407 cc (3.15 x 2.76 in, 80 x 70 mm); compression ratio: 9:1; max power (JIS): 82 hp at 5,800 rpm; max torque (JIS): 84 lb ft, 11.6 kg m at 3,400 rpm; max engine rpm: 6,600; 58.3 hp/l; lubricating system capacity: 7.7 imp pt, 9.3 US pt, 4.4 l; cooling system: 12.3 imp pt, 14.8 US pt, 7 l.

TRANSMISSION gearbox ratios: I 3.587, II 2.022, III 1.384, IV 1, rev 3.484; axle ratio: 3.727; tyres: 6.15 x 13.

PERFORMANCE max speeds: (I) 31 mph, 50 km/h; (II) 53 mph, 86 km/h; (III) 78 mph, 125 km/h; (IV) 103 mph, 165 km/h; power-weight ratio: 23.3 lb/hp, 11 kg/hp; speed in direct drive at 1,000 rpm: 15.7 mph, 25.2 km/h; consumption: 34 m/imp gal, 28.3 m/US gal, 8.3 l x 100 km.

ELECTRICAL EQUIPMENT 35 Ah battery.

DIMENSIONS AND WEIGHT tracks: 49.61 in, 126 cm front, 48.82 in, 124 cm rear; ground clearance: 6.10 in, 15.5 cm; weight: 1,996 lb, 905 kg.

PRACTICAL INSTRUCTIONS oil: engine 6.5 imp pt, 7.8 US pt, 3.7 l - gearbox 2.6 imp pt, 3.2 US pt, 1.5 l - final drive 1.8 imp pt, 2.1 US pt, 1 l; tappet clearances (hot): inlet 0.008 in, 0.20 mm, exhaust 0.013 in, 0.33 mm; valve timing: 22° 42° 63° 7°.

Charmant 1400 Hi-Custom 4-door Sedan

See Charmant 1400 Custom 4-door Sedan, except for:

PRICE (Tokyo): 888,000 yen

PERFORMANCE power-weight ratio: 24.5 lb/hp, 11.1 kg/hp.

DIMENSIONS AND WEIGHT weight: 2,007 lb, 910 kg.

OPTIONAL ACCESSORIES 5-speed fully synchronized mechanical gearbox (I 3.587, II 2.022, III 1.384, IV 1, V 0.861, rev 3.484) with 4.300 axle ratio; automatic transmission with 2 ratios (I 1.820, II 1, rev 1.820) and 3.909 axle ratio.

DAIHATSU Charmant 1400 4-door Sedan

Charmant 1400 Grand Custom 4-door Sedan

See Charmant 1400 HI-Custom 4-door Sedan, except for:

PRICE (Tokyo): 923,000 yen

Charmant 1400 Sporty Custom 4-door Sedan

See Charmant 1400 HI-Custom 4-door Sedan, except for:

PRICE (Tokyo): 898,000 yen

TRANSMISSION axle ratio: 3.909; tyres: 155 SR x 13.

OPTIONAL ACCESSORIES 5-speed mechanical gearbox with 4.100 axle ratio.

Delta Wagon Series

PRICES (Tokyo):

Delta Wagon Standard	914,000 yen
Delta Wagon De Luxe	969,000 yen
Delta Wagon Custom	1,064,000 yen

85 hp power team

ENGINE front, 4 stroke; 4 cylinders, in line; 96.9 cu in, 1,588 cc (3.35 x 2.76 in, 85 x 70 mm); compression ratio: 8.5:1; max power (JIS): 85 hp at 5,400 rpm; max torque (JIS): 91 lb ft, 12.5 kg m at 3,400 rpm; max engine rpm: 6,000; 53.5 hp/l; cast iron block, light alloy head; 5 crankshaft bearings; valves: overhead, push-rods and rockers; camshafts: 1, side; lubrication: rotary pump, full flow filter, 7.7 imp pt, 9.3 US pt, 4.4 l; 1 Aisan 12T downdraught twin barrel carburettor; fuel feed: mechanical pump; water-cooled, 8.8 imp pt, 10.6 US pt, 5 l.

TRANSMISSION driving wheels: rear; clutch: single dry plate (diaphragm); gearbox: mechanical; gears: 4, fully synchronized; ratios: I 4.400, II 2.750, III 1.681, IV 1, rev 5.009; lever: steering column; final drive: hypoid bevel; axle ratio: 1.556; width of rims: 4'' - Custom 4.5''; tyres: 5.50 x 13 - Custom 165 SR x 14.

PERFORMANCE max speeds: (I) 22 mph, 35 km/h; (II) 33 mph, 53 km/h; (III) 53 mph, 86 km/h; (IV) 93 mph, 150 km/h; power-weight ratio: 27.9 lb/hp, 12.6 kg/hp; consumption: 39.8 m/imp gal, 33.1 m/US gal, 7.1 l x 100 km at 37 mph, 60 km/h.

CHASSIS integral; front suspension: independent; double wishbones, coil springs, telescopic dampers; rear: rigid axle, semi-elliptic leafsprings, telescopic dampers.

STEERING recirculating ball.

BRAKES drum, servo - Custom front disc; swept area: front 67.6 sq in, 436 sq cm, rear 54.6 sq in, 353 sq cm, total 122.2 sq in, 788 sq cm.

ELECTRICAL EQUIPMENT 12 V; 33 Ah battery; 40 A alternator; Denso distributor; 2 headlamps.

DIMENSIONS AND WEIGHT wheel base: 86.42 in, 219 cm; tracks: 56.30 in, 143 cm front, 52.95 in, 134 cm rear; length: 157.09 in, 399 cm; width: 64.96 in, 165 cm; height: 68.70 in, 174 cm; ground clearance: 6.89 in, 17.5 cm; weight: 2,370 lb, 1,075 kg; weight distribution: 57.8% front, 42.2% rear; fuel tank: 12.1 imp gal, 14.5 US gal, 55 l.

BODY estate car/station wagon; 3 doors; 8 seats, separate front seats; De Luxe, luxury interior.

PRACTICAL INSTRUCTIONS fuel: 90 oct petrol; oil: engine 7.7 imp pt, 9.3 US pt, 4.4 l, gearbox 3.2 imp pt, 3.8 US pt, 1.8 l - final drive 2.1 imp pt, 2.5 US pt, 1.2 l; tappet clearances: inlet 0.008 in, 0.20 mm, exhaust 0.012 in, 0.30 mm; valve timing: 8° 50° 55° 3°; tyre pressure: front 23 psi, 1.6 atm, rear 23 psi, 1.6 atm.

Taft Series

PRICES (Tokyo):

1 Taft	960,000 yen
2 Taft 6-seater Long Body	995,000 yen
3 Taft Gran	1,045,000 yen
4 Taft Gran 6-seater Long Body	1,080,000 yen

For GB prices, see price index.

Power team:	Standard for:	Optional for:
55 hp	1,2	—
80 hp	3,4	—

55 hp power team

ENGINE front, 4 stroke; 4 cylinders, vertical, in line; 58.5 cu in, 958 cc (2.68 x 2.60 in, 68 x 66 mm); compression ratio: 9:1; max power (JIS): 55 hp at 5,500 rpm; max torque (JIS): 58 lb ft, 8 kg m at 4,000 rpm; max engine rpm: 6,000; 60.5 hp/l; cast iron block, light alloy head; 3 crankshaft bearings; valves: overhead, push-rods and rockers; camshafts: 1, side; lubrication: rotary pump, full flow filter, 6.2 imp pt, 7.4 US pt, 3.5 l; 1 Aisan-Stromberg downdraught twin barrel carburettor; fuel feed: mechanical pump; water-cooled, 6.7 imp pt, 8 US pt, 3.8 l.

TRANSMISSION driving wheels: front and rear; clutch: single dry plate (diaphragm); gearbox: mechanical; gears: 4, fully synchronized and 2-ratio transfer box; ratios: I 3.707, II 2.167, III 1.513, IV 1, rev 3.434 transfer box ratios: high 1.307, low 2.361; lever: central; final drive: hypoid bevel; axle ratio: 5.571; width of rims: 4.5''; tyres: 6.00 x 16.

PERFORMANCE max speeds (rear wheel drive only): (I) 17 mph, 27 km/h; (II) 31 mph, 50 km/h; (III) 47 mph, 76 km/h; (IV) 62 mph, 100 km/h; power-weight ratio: 37.3 lb/hp, 16.9 kg/hp - Long Body 38 lb/hp 17.2 kg/hp; carrying capacity: 882 lb, 400 kg - Long Body 1,058 lb, 480 kg; speed in direct drive at 1,000 rpm: 10.3 mph, 16.6 km/h; consumption: 28.2 m/imp gal, 23.5 m/US gal, 10 l x 100 km at 37 mph, 60 km/h.

CHASSIS box-type ladder frame; front and rear suspension: rigid axle, semi-elliptic leafsprings, telescopic dampers.

STEERING recirculating ball; turns lock to lock: 2.70.

BRAKES drum; lining area: front 72.6 sq in, 468 sq cm, rear 72.6 sq in, 468 sq cm, total 145.2 sq in, 936 sq cm.

ELECTRICAL EQUIPMENT 12 V; 35 Ah battery; 35 A alternator; Nihon Denso distributor; 2 headlamps.

DIMENSIONS AND WEIGHT wheel base: 79.53 in, 202 cm; front and rear tracks: 47.24 in, 120 cm; length: 130.71 in, 332 cm - Long Body 137.01 in, 348 cm; width: 57.48 in, 146 cm; height: 73.23 in, 186 cm - Long Body 72.83 in, 185 cm; ground clearance: 8.46 in, 21.5 cm; weight: 2,172 lb, 985 kg - Long Body 2,216 lb, 1,005 kg; weight distribution: 55% front, 45% rear; turning circle (between walls): 35.4 ft, 10.8 m; fuel tank: 8.8 imp gal, 10.6 US gal, 40 l.

BODY open with folding top; 4 seats, separate front seats - Long Body 6 seats.

PRACTICAL INSTRUCTIONS fuel: 85-90 oct petrol; oil: engine 6.2 imp pt, 7.4 US pt, 3.5 l, SAE 20W-30, change every 3,100 miles, 5,000 km - gearbox 3.9 imp pt, 4.7 US pt, 2.2 l, SAE 90, change every 18,600 miles, 30,000 km - final drive 2.6 imp pt, 3.2 US pt, 1.5 l, SAE 90, change every 18,600 miles, 30,000 km; greasing: none; tappet clearances (hot): inlet 0.010 in, 0.25 mm, exhaust 0.010 in, 0.25 mm; valve timing: 15° 55° 55° 15°; tyre pressure: front 21 psi, 1.5 atm, rear 28 psi, 2 atm.

OPTIONAL ACCESSORIES power take-off and winch system.

80 hp power team

See 55 hp power team, except for:

ENGINE 96.8 cu in, 1,587 cc (3.17 x 3.07 in, 80.5 x 78 mm); compression ratio: 8.1; max power (JIS): 80 hp at 5,200 rpm; max torque (JIS): 91 lb ft, 12.5 kg m at 3,000 rpm; max engine rpm: 6,000; 50.4 hp/l; lubrication: 7.4 imp pt, 8.9 US pt, 4.2 l; 1 Aisan downdraught twin barrel carburettor; cooling system, 12.3 imp pt, 14.8 US pt, 7 l.

TRANSMISSION axle ratio: 4.770.

PERFORMANCE max speeds: (I) 21 mph, 33 km/h; (II) 35 mph, 57 km/h; (III) 50 mph, 80 km/h; (IV) 71 mph, 115 km/h; power-weight ratio: 29.2 lb/hp, 13.2 kg/hp - Long Body 29.8 lb/hp, 13.5 kg/hp; consumption: 19.8 m/imp gal, 16.4 m/US gal, 14.3 l x 100 km at 37 mph, 60 km/h.

ELECTRICAL EQUIPMENT 30 A alternator.

DIMENSIONS AND WEIGHT weight: 2,337 lb, 1,060 kg - Long Body 2,381 lb, 1,080 kg.

PRACTICAL INSTRUCTIONS valve timing: 20° 50° 60° 10°.

OPTIONALS hardtop; steel doors.

HONDA   JAPAN

Civic CVCC Series

PRICES (Tokyo):

1 1200 Standard 2-door Sedan	656,000	yen
2 1200 De Luxe 3-door Sedan	711,000	yen
3 1200 De Luxe 4-door Sedan	729,000	yen
4 1200 Hi-De Luxe 3-door Sedan	760,000	yen
5 1200 Hi-De Luxe 4-door Sedan	778,000	yen
6 1200 GL 3-door Sedan	787,000	yen
7 1200 GL II-5 3-door Sedan	822,000	yen
8 1200 GF 4-door Sedan	805,000	yen
9 1200 GF-5 4-door Sedan	825,000	yen
10 1500 RSL 3-door Sedan	911,000	yen
11 1500 GTL 3-door Sedan	862,000	yen
12 1500 GF-5E 4-door Sedan	872,000	yen
13 1500 GF 5-door Sedan	872,000	yen
14 1500 GF-5 5-door Sedan	892,000	yen

For GB and USA prices, see price index.

Power team:	Standard for:	Optional for:
65 hp	1 to 9	—
75 hp	10 to 14	—

65 hp power team

ENGINE front, transverse, 4 stroke, stratified charge; 4 cylinders, vertical, in line; 75.5 cu in, 1,238 cc (2.83 x 2.99 in, 72 x 76 mm); compression ratio: 7.9:1; max power

DAIHATSU Taft Gran

HONDA Civic CVCC 1500 GF-5 5-door Sedan

HONDA Civic 1500 Van Custom

(JIS): 65 hp at 5,500 rpm; max torque (JIS): 70 lb ft, 9.6 kg m at 3,500 rpm; max engine rpm: 6,000; 52.5 hp/l; light alloy cylinder block with cast iron liners, light alloy head; 5 crankshaft bearings; valves: 3 per cylinder (one intake and one exhaust in main combustion chamber, one intake in auxiliary chamber), overhead, Vee-slanted, rockers; camshafts: 1, overhead, cogged belt; lubrication: rotary pump, full flow filter, 5.3 imp pt, 6.3 US pt, 3 l; 1 Keihin-Honda downdraught 3-barrel CVCC carburettor; fuel feed: mechanical pump; water-cooled, 7 imp pt, 8.5 US pt, 4 l.

TRANSMISSION driving wheels: front; clutch: single dry plate (diaphragm); gearbox: mechanical; gears: 4 (5 for GL II-5 and GF-5 only), fully synchronized; ratios: I 3.181, II 1.823, III 1.181, IV 0.846, rev 2.916 (for GL II-5 and GF-5 V 0.714); lever: central; final drive: hypoid bevel; axle ratio: 4.624; width of rims: 4''; tyres: 6.00 x 12 - GL II-5 155 SR x 12.

PERFORMANCE max speeds: (I) 26 mph, 42 km/h; (II) 45 mph, 72 km/h; (III) 70 mph, 112 km/h; (IV) 93 mph, 150 km/h; power-weight ratio: Standard 2-dr. Sedan 22.7 lb/hp, 10.3 kg/hp; carrying capacity: 882 lb, 400 kg; consumption: 36.7 m/imp gal, 30.5 m/US gal, 7.7 l x 100 km.

CHASSIS integral, front auxiliary frame; front suspension: independent, by McPherson, coil springs/telescopic damper struts, lower wishbones (trailing links), anti-roll bar; rear: independent, by McPherson, coil springs/telescopic damper struts, lower wishbones (torque arms).

STEERING rack-and-pinion; turns lock to lock: 3.10 2-dr. Sedan, 3.50 4-dr. Sedan.

BRAKES front disc, rear drum; lining area: front 15.2 sq in, 98 sq cm, rear 34.7 sq in, 224 sq cm, total 49.9 sq in, 322 sq cm.

ELECTRICAL EQUIPMENT 12 V; 30 Ah battery; 35 A alternator; Mitsubishi distributor; 2 headlamps.

DIMENSIONS AND WEIGHT wheel base: 2-and 3-dr. models 86.61 in, 220 cm, 4-dr. models 89.76 in, 228 cm; tracks: 51.18 in, 130 cm front, 50.39 in, 128 cm rear; length: 2-and 3-dr. models 140.16 in, 356 cm, GL II-5 143.50 in, 364 cm, 4-dr. models 143.90 in, 366 cm; width: 59.25 in, 150 cm; height: 52.17 in, 132 cm; ground clearance: 6.69 in, 17 cm; weight: Standard 2-dr. 1,477 lb, 670 kg - De Luxe and Hi-De Luxe 3-dr. 1,510 lb, 685 kg - GL 3-dr. 1,521 lb, 690 kg - GL II-5 3-dr. 1,532 lb, 695 kg - De Luxe and Hi-De Luxe 4-dr. 1,588 lb, 720 kg - GF and GF-5 4-dr. 1,599 lb, 725 kg; weight distribution: Standard 63% front, 37% rear; turning circle (between walls): 33.8 ft, 10.3 m (4-dr. models 35.1 ft, 10.7 m); fuel tank: 8.4 imp gal, 10 US gal, 38 l (4-dr. models 8.8 imp gal, 10.6 US gal, 40 l).

PRACTICAL INSTRUCTIONS fuel: 85-90 oct petrol; oil: engine 5.3 imp pt, 6.3 US pt, 3 l, SAE 10W-30, change every 3,100 miles, 5,000 km - gearbox and final drive 4.4 imp pt, 5.3 US pt, 2.5 l, SAE 10W-40; tappet clearances: inlet 0.006 in, 0.15 mm, exhaust 0.008 in, 0.20 mm; valve timing: 10° 35° 40° 10° (auxiliary combustion chamber opens 40° before tdc, closes 0° after bdc); tyre pressure: front 21 psi, 1.5 atm, rear 21 psi, 1.5 atm.

OPTIONAL ACCESSORIES semi-automatic transmission with 2 ratios (I 1.636, II 1.034, rev 2.045), 4.117 axle ratio; air-conditioning.

75 hp power team

See 65 hp power team, except for:

ENGINE 90.8 cu in, 1,488 cc (2.91 x 3.41, 74 x 86.5 mm); max power (JIS): 75 hp at 5,500 rpm; max torque (JIS): 80.4 lb ft, 11.1 kg m at 3,000 rpm; 50.4 hp/l.

TRANSMISSION gears: 4 for GF 5-dr. only (5 for RSL, GTL, GF-5E and GF-5); axle ratio: RSL 4.642 - GF-5E 4.066 - GTL and 5-dr. models 4.428; tyres: 6.005 x 12 - RSL 155 SR x 13.

PERFORMANCE max speeds: RSL (I) 26 mph, 42 km/h, (II) 45 mph, 73 km/h, (III) 70 mph, 113 km/h, (IV) 98 mph, 158 km/h, (V) 99 mph, 160 km/h - GF-5E (I) 29 mph, 46 km/h, (II) 51 mph, 82 km/h, (III) 78 mph, 126 km/h, (IV) 93 mph, 150 km/h, (V) 93 mph, 150 km/h - GF-5 (I) 27 mph, 43 km/h, (II) 47 mph, 76 km/h, (III) 73 mph, 118 km/h, (IV) 93 mph, 150 km/h, (V) 93 mph, 150 km/h; power-weight ratio: RSL 3-dr. Sedan 22.5 lb/hp, 10.2 kg/hp; consumption: 40.9 m/imp gal, 34.1 m/US gal, 6.9 l x 100 km.

DIMENSIONS AND WEIGHT length: GTL 143.50 in, 364 cm, RSL and 4/5 dr. models 146.85 in, 373 cm; height: RSL 59.65 in, 151 cm, other models 59.06 in, 150 cm; weight: RSL and GF-5E 1,687 lb, 765 kg - GTL 1,643 lb, 745 kg - GF and GF-5 1,731 lb, 785 kg; fuel tank: 8.8 imp gal, 10.6 US gal, 40 l.

PRACTICAL INSTRUCTIONS tyre pressure: front 23 psi, 1.6 atm, rear 23 psi, 1.6 atm.

OPTIONAL ACCESSORIES semi-automatic transmission with 2 ratios (I 1.565, II 0.966, rev 2.045), 4.117 axle ratio, max speed 90 mph, 145 km/h (except for RSL and GF-5E).

Civic Wagon Series

PRICES IN USA AND IN TOKYO:	$	yen
1 Civic CVCC 1500 Station Wagon	3,859	—
2 Civic 1500 Van Custom	—	—

Power team:	Standard for:	Optional for:
70 hp	1	—
75 hp	2	—

70 hp power team

(for USA only)

ENGINE front, transverse, 4 stroke, stratified charge; 4 cylinders, vertical, in line; 90.8 cu in, 1,488 cc (2.91 x 3.41 in, 74 x 86.5 mm); compression ratio: 7.9:1; max power (JIS): 70 hp at 5,500 rpm; max torque (JIS): 78 lb ft, 10.7 kg m at 3,000 rpm; max engine rpm: 6,000; 47 hp/l; cast iron cylinder block, light alloy head; 5 crankshaft bearings; valves: 3 per cylinder (intake in auxiliary combustion chamber, intake and exhaust in main chamber), overhead, Vee-slanted, rockers; camshafts: 1, overhead, cogged belt; lubrication: rotary pump, full flow filter, 5.3 imp pt, 6.3 US pt, 3 l; 1 Keihin-Honda downdraught 3-barrel CVCC carburettor; fuel feed: electric pump; water-cooled, 7 imp pt, 8.5 US pt, 4 l.

TRANSMISSION driving wheels: front; clutch: single dry plate (diaphragm); gearbox: mechanical; gears: 4, fully synchronized; ratios: I 3.181, II 1.823, III 1.181, IV 0.846, rev 2.916; lever: central; final drive: helical spur gears; axle ratio: 4.642; width of rims: 4''; tyres: 6.00S x 12.

PERFORMANCE max speeds: (I) 25 mph, 41 km/h; (II) 45 mph, 72 km/h; (III) 68 mph, 110 km/h; (IV) 93 mph, 150 km/h; power-weight ratio: 28.3 lb/hp, 12.8 kg/hp; carrying capacity: 882 lb, 400 kg; speed in top at 1,000 rpm: 15 mph, 24.1 km/h; fuel consumption: 58.8 m/imp gal, 49 m/US gal, 4.8 l x 100 km at 37 mph, 60 km/h.

CHASSIS integral, front auxiliary frame; front suspension: independent, by McPherson, coil springs/telescopic damper struts, lower wishbones (trailing links), anti-roll bar; rear: rigid axle, semi-elliptic leafsprings, telescopic dampers.

STEERING rack-and-pinion; turns lock to lock: 3.10.

BRAKES front disc, rear drum, servo; lining area: front 15.2 sq in, 98 sq cm, rear 34.7 sq in, 224 sq cm, total 49.9 sq in, 322 sq cm.

ELECTRICAL EQUIPMENT 12 V; 30 Ah battery; 35 A alternator; CVCC distributor; 2 headlamps.

DIMENSIONS AND WEIGHT wheel base: 89.76 in, 228 cm; tracks: 51.18 in, 130 cm front, 50.39 in, 128 cm rear; length: 159.72 in, 406 cm; width: 59.06 in, 150 cm; height: 54.09 in, 137 cm; ground clearance: 6.69 in, 17 cm; dry weight: 1,985 lb, 900 kg; distribution of weight: 63.7% front, 36.3% rear; turning circle (between walls): 32.1 ft, 9.8 m; fuel tank: 9.7 imp gal, 11.6 US gal, 44 l.

BODY estate car/station wagon; 4+1 doors; 5 seats, separate front seats, built-in headrests.

70 HP POWER TEAM

PRACTICAL INSTRUCTIONS fuel: 85-90 oct petrol; oil: engine 5.3 imp pt, 6.3 US pt, 3 l, SAE 10W-30, change every 3,100 miles, 5,000 km - gearbox and final drive 4.4 imp pt, 5.3 US pt, 2.5 l, SAE 10W-40, change every 24,800 miles, 40,000 km; valve timing: 15° 30° 30° 15° (auxiliary combustion chamber opens 30° before tdc, closes 10° after bdc); tyre pressure: front 23 psi, 1.6 atm, rear 23 psi, 1.6 atm.

OPTIONAL ACCESSORIES semi-automatic transmission with 2 ratios (I 1.565, II 0.966, rev 2.045), 4.117 axle ratio, max speed 90 mph, 145 km/h; air-conditioning.

75 hp power team

(domestic version).

See 70 hp power team, except for:

ENGINE max power (JIS): 75 hp at 5,500 rpm; max torque (JIS): 80.4 lb ft, 11.1 kg m at 3,300 rpm; valves: 2 per cylinder.

TRANSMISSION axle ratio: 4.428; tyres: 5.00 x 12.

PERFORMANCE max speeds: (I) 27 mph, 43 km/h, (II) 47 mph, 75 km/h, (III) 71 mph, 115 km/h, (IV) 90 mph, 145 km/h; power-weight ratio: 26.5 lb/hp, 12 kg/hp; fuel consumption: 53.3 m/imp gal, 44.4 m/US gal, 5.3 l x 100 km at 37 mph, 60 km/h.

DIMENSIONS AND WEIGHT length: 151.97 in, 386 cm.

PRACTICAL INSTRUCTIONS valve timing: 10° 40° 40° 10°.

Accord Series

PRICES (Tokyo):

1 Accord SL 3-door Hatchback	921,000	yen
2 Accord GL 3-door Hatchback	981,000	yen
3 Accord LX 3-door Hatchback	1,041,000	yen
4 Accord EX 3-door Hatchback	1,140,000	yen
5 Accord EX-L 3-door Hatchback	1,230,000	yen
6 Accord SL 4-door Sedan	941,000	yen
7 Accord GF 4-door Sedan	1,036,000	yen
8 Accord EX 4-door Sedan	1,160,000	yen
9 Accord EX L-4-door Sedan	1,260,000	yen

For GB and USA prices, see price index.

Power team:	Standard for:	Optional for:
82 hp	all	—
68 hp	USA versions	—

82 hp power team

ENGINE front, transverse, 4 stroke, stratified charge; 4 cylinders, in line; 97.6 cu in, 1,599 cc (2.91 x 3.66 in, 74 x 93 mm); compression ratio: 8:1; max power (JIS): 82 hp at 5,300 rpm; max torque (JIS): 89 lb ft, 12.3 kg m at 3,000 rpm; max engine rpm: 5,800; 51.3 hp/l; cast iron block, light alloy head; 5 crankshaft bearings; valves: 3 per cylinder (one intake and one exhaust in main combustion chamber, one intake in auxiliary chamber), overhead rockers; camshafts: 1, overhead, cogged belt; lubrication: rotary pump, full flow filter, 5.3 imp pt, 6.3 US pt, 3 l; 1 Keihin-Honda downdraught 3-barrel CVCC carburettor; fuel feed: electric pump; water-cooled, 8.8 imp pt, 10.6 US pt, 5 l.

TRANSMISSION driving wheels: front; clutch: single dry plate (diaphragm), hydraulically controlled; gearbox: mechanical; gears: 4 (5 for LX and EX only), fully synchronized; ratios: I 3.181, II 1.823, III 1.181, IV 0.846, rev 2.916 (for LX and EX V 0.714); lever: central; final drive: hypoid bevel; axle ratio: 4.428; width of rims: 4.5''; tyres: 6.15 x 13 - LX and EX 155 SR x 13.

PERFORMANCE max speeds: (I) 27 mph, 43 km/h; (II) 45 mph, 73 km/h; (III) 71 mph, 115 km/h; (IV) 90 mph, 145 km/h - LX and EX (I) 21 mph, 33 km/h; (II) 35 mph, 57 m/h; (III) 55 mph, 88 km/h; (IV) 76 mph, 122 km/h; (V) 90 mph, 145 km/h; power-weight ratio: SL 3-dr. 22.6 lb/hp, 10.2 kg/hp; consumption: 35.3 m/imp gal, 29.4 m/US gal, 8 l x 100 km.

CHASSIS integral, front auxiliary frame; front suspension: independent, by McPherson, coil springs/telescopic damper struts, lower transverse arms, diagonal links, anti-roll bar; rear: independent, by McPherson, coil springs/telescopic damper struts, lower transverse arms, radius rods.

STEERING rack-and-pinion - EX servo, turns lock to lock: 3.20, 3.10 EX.

BRAKES front disc, rear drum, servo, rear pressure control valve; lining area: front 19.4 sq in, 125 sq cm, rear 34.7 sq in, 224 sq cm, total 54.1 sq in, 349 sq cm.

HONDA Accord EX-L Hatchback

ELECTRICAL EQUIPMENT 12 V; 35 Ah battery; 50 A alternator; 4 headlamps.

DIMENSIONS AND WEIGHT wheel base: 93.70 in, 238 cm; tracks: 55.12 in, 140 cm front, 54.72 in, 139 cm rear; length: SL 3-dr. 161.60 in, 410 cm - GL, LX, EX 3-dr. 162.40 in, 412 cm - EX-L 3-dr. 166.54 in, 423 cm - SL 4-dr. 170.28 in, 432 cm - GF, EX 4-dr. 171.06 in, 434 cm - EX-L 4-dr. 175.20 in, 445 cm; width: 63.78 in, 162 cm; height: 3-dr. models 52.76 in, 134 cm, 4-dr. models 53.54 in, 136 cm; ground clearance: 6.50 in, 16.5 cm; weight: SL 3-dr. 1,852 lb, 840 kg - GL 3-dr. 1,874 lb, 850 kg - LX 3-dr. 1,918 lb, 870 kg - EX 3-dr. 1,940 lb, 880 kg - EX-L 3-dr. 1,962 lb, 890 kg - SL 4-dr. 1,973, 895 kg - GF 4-dr. 1,996 lb, 905 kg - EX 4-dr. 2,029 lb, 920 kg - EX-L 4-dr. 2,073 lb, 940 kg; weight distribution: 61% front, 39% rear; turning circle (between walls): 36.1 ft, 11 m; fuel tank: 11 imp gal, 13.2 US gal, 50 l.

PRACTICAL INSTRUCTIONS fuel: 85-90 oct petrol; oil: engine 5.3 imp pt, 6.3 US pt, 3 l, SAE 10W/40, change every 3,100 miles, 5,000 km - gearbox and final drive 4.4 imp pt, 5.3 US pt, 2.5 l, SAE 10W/40, change every 24,800 miles, 40,000 km; sparking plug type: NGK B5 ES; tappet clearances: inlet 0.006 in, 0.15 mm, exhaust 0.006 in, 0.15 mm; valve timing: 10° 35° 40° 10° (auxiliary combustion chamber opens 40° before tdc, closes 0° after bdc); tyre pressure: front 24 psi, 1.7 atm, rear 24 psi, 1.7 atm.

OPTIONAL ACCESSORIES semi-automatic transmission, hydraulic torque converter and constant mesh with 2 ratios: (I 1.565, II 0.903, rev 2.045), possible manual selection 4.117 axle ratio.

68 hp power team

(only for USA).

See 82 hp power team, except for:

ENGINE max power (JIS): 68 hp at 5,000 rpm; max torque (JIS): 85 lb ft, 11.7 kg m at 3,000 rpm; 42.5 hp/l.

TRANSMISSION ratios: I 3.181, II 1.823, III 1.181, IV 0.846. V 0.714; axle ratio 4.260.

PERFORMANCE power-weight ratio: 29.7 lb/hp, 13.5 kg/hp.

DIMENSIONS AND WEIGHT length: 162.99 in, 414 cm; weight: 2,018 lb, 915 kg.

OPTIONAL ACCESSORIES Hondamatic 2-speed semi-automatic transmission.

ISUZU   JAPAN

Gemini Series

PRICES (Tokyo):

1 1600 LD 4-door Sedan	894,000	yen
2 1600 LD 2-door Coupé	924,000	yen
3 1600 LT 4-door Sedan	933,000	yen
4 1600 LT 2-door Coupé	963,000	yen
5 1600 LS 4-door Sedan	1,001,000	yen
6 1600 LS 2-door Coupé	1,063,000	yen
7 Minx 4-door Sedan	1,013,000	yen
8 Minx 2-door Coupé	1,043,000	yen
9 1800 LT 4-door Sedan	963,000	yen
10 1800 LT 2-door Coupé	993,000	yen
11 1800 LS 4-door Sedan	1,046,000	yen
12 1800 LS 2-door Coupé	1,093,000	yen
13 1800 LS/G 2-door Coupé	1,168,000	yen

Power team:	Standard for:	Optional for:
100 hp	1 to 8	—
110 hp	9 to 13	—

100 hp power team

ENGINE front, 4 stroke; 4 cylinders, in line; 97.6 cu in, 1,584 cc (3.23 x 2.95 in, 82 x 75 mm); compression ratio: 8.7:1; max power (JIS): 100 hp at 6,000 rpm; max torque (JIS): 101 lb ft, 14 kg m at 4,000 rpm; max engine rpm: 6,500; 63.1 hp/l; cast iron block, light alloy head; 5 crankshaft bearings; valves: overhead, rockers; camshafts: 1, overhead; lubrication: rotary pump, full flow filter, 8.8 imp pt, 10.6 US pt, 5 l; 1 Nikki-Stromberg downdraught twin barrel carburettor, catalytic converter, secondary air injection and exhaust gas recirculation; fuel feed: electric pump; water-cooled, 10.8 imp pt, 12.7 US pt, 6 l.

HONDA Accord EX 4-door Sedan

TRANSMISSION driving wheels: rear; clutch: single dry plate (diaphragm); gearbox: mechanical; gears: 4, fully synchronized - for LS moleds 5; ratios: I 3.506, II 2.174, III 1.417, IV 1, rev 3.826 (for LS models I 3.506, II 2.174, III 1.471, IV 1, V 0.855, rev 3.759); lever: central; final drive: hypoid bevel; axle ratio: 3.909; width of rims: 5''; tyres: 6.15 x 13 - 1600 LS 4-door Sedan Z78 x 13 - 1600 LS Coupé SR x 13.

PERFORMANCE max speeds: (I) 29 mph, 47 km/h; (II) 48 mph, 78 km/h; (III) 73 mph, 117 km/h; (IV) 103 mph, 165 km/h; power-weight ratio: 1600 LD 4-door Sedan 20.3 lb/hp, 9.2 kg/hp; carrying capacity: 882 lb, 400 kg; speed in direct drive at 1,000 rpm: 16.2 mph, 26.1 km/h; consumption: 39.8 m/imp gal, 33.1 m/US gal, 7.1 l x 100 km.

CHASSIS integral; front suspension: independent, wishbones, coil springs, anti-roll bar, telescopic dampers; rear: rigid axle, lower radius arms, torque tube, Panhard rod, coil springs, telescopic dampers.

STEERING rack-and-pinion; turns lock to lock: 4.20.

BRAKES front disc, rear drum, servo; lining area: front 17.4 sq in, 112 sq cm, rear 49 sq in, 316 sq cm, total 66.4 sq in, 428 sq cm.

ELECTRICAL EQUIPMENT 12 V; 35 Ah battery; alternator; Hitachi distributor; 2 headlamps.

DIMENSIONS AND WEIGHT wheel base: 94.49 in, 240 cm; tracks: 51.18 in, 130 cm front, 51.38 in, 130 cm rear; length: 162.60 in, 413 cm; width: 61.81 in, 157 cm; height: 53.54 in, 136 cm - coupés 52.36 in, 133 cm; ground clearance: 5.71 in, 14.5 cm; weight: 1600 LD 4-door Sedan 2,040 lb, 925 kg - 1600 LD 2-door Coupé 1,996 lb, 905 kg - 1600 LT, LS and Minx sedans 2,051 lb, 930 kg - 1600, LT, LS and Minx coupés 2,007 lb, 910 kg; weight distribution: 54.5% front, 45.5% rear; turning circle (between walls): 32.8 ft, 10 m; fuel tank: 11.4 imp gal, 13.7 US gal, 52 l.

BODY 5 seats, separate front seats.

PRACTICAL INSTRUCTIONS fuel: 85-90 oct lead-free petrol; oil: engine 8.8 imp pt, 10.6 US pt, 5 l, SAE 20W-30, change every 3,100 miles, 5,000 km - gearbox 2.1 imp pt, 2.5 US pt, 1.2 l, SAE 20W-30, change every 24,900 miles, 40,000 km - final drive 1.8 imp pt, 2.1 US pt, 1 l, SAE 90, change every 24,900 miles, 40,000 km; greasing: none; tappet clearances: inlet 0.006 in, 0.15 mm, exhaust 0.010 in, 0.25 mm; valve timing: 21° 65° 55° 20°; tyre pressure: front 23 psi, 1.6 atm, rear 23 psi, 1.6 atm.

OPTIONAL ACCESSORIES 5-speed mechanical gearbox (V 0.855); Borg-Warner automatic transmission, hydraulic torque converter and planetary gears with 3 ratios (I 2.450, II 1.450, III 1, rev 2.222), with max power (DIN) 94 hp at 5,400 rpm, max torque (DIN) 99 lb ft, 13.6 kg m at 3,800 rpm, 59.3 hp/l, power-weight ratio 22.5 lb/hp, 10.2 kg/hp, max speed 99 mph, 160 km/h; for 1600 LS Coupé air-conditioning.

110 hp power team

See 100 hp power team, except for:

ENGINE 110.9 cu in, 1,817 cc (3.31 x 3.23 in, 84 x 82 mm); compression ratio: 8.5:1; max power (JIS): 110 hp at 5,600 rpm; max torque (JIS): 112 lb ft, 15.5 kg m at 4,000 rpm; 60.5 hp/l.

TRANSMISSION gears: 4, fully synchronized; ratios: I 3.207, II 1.989, III 1.356, IV 1, V 0.855, rev 3.438; axle ratio: 3.909; tyres: LS models 155 SR x 13 - 1800 LS/G 2-door Coupé 175/70 SR x 13.

PERFORMANCE max speed: 106 mph, 170 km/h; power-weight ratio: sedans 19.2 lb/hp, 8.7 kg/hp.

DIMENSIONS AND WEIGHT weight: sedans 2,106 lb, 955 kg - coupés 2,062 lb, 935 kg.

OPTIONAL ACCESSORIES with 3-speed automatic transmission engine max power (JIS) 105 hp at 5,400 rpm, 57.8 hp/l, power-weight ratio sedans 20.1 lb/hp, 9.1 kg/hp.

Florian SII Series

PRICES (Tokyo):

1 1800 De Luxe 4-door Sedan	1,211,000	yen
2 1800 Super De Luxe 4-door Sedan	1,383,000	yen
3 Diesel 2000 Semi-De Luxe 4-door Sedan	1,253,000	yen
4 Diesel 2000 De Luxe 4-door Sedan	1,298,000	yen
5 Diesel 2000 Super De Luxe 4-door Sedan	1,470,000	yen

Power team:	Standard for:	Optional for:
105 hp	1,2	—
62 hp	3 to 5	—

ISUZU Florian SII Diesel 2000 Series

ISUZU Gemini 1600 LT 4-door Sedan

105 hp power team

ENGINE front, 4 stroke; 4 cylinders, vertical, in line; 110.9 cu in, 1,817 cc (3.31 x 3.23 in, 84 x 82 mm); compression ratio: 8.7:1; max power (JIS): 105 hp at 5,400 rpm; max torque (JIS): 109 lb ft, 15 kg m at 3,800 rpm; max engine rpm: 6,300; 57.8 hp/l; cast iron block, light alloy head; 5 crankshaft bearings; valves: overhead, Vee-slanted, rockers; camshafts: 1, overhead; lubrication: rotary pump, full flow filter, 6.3 imp pt, 7.6 US pt, 3.6 l; 1 Stromberg downdraught twin barrel carburettor, catalytic converter, secondary air injection and exhaust gas recirculation; fuel feed: mechanical pump; water-cooled, 10.6 imp pt, 12.7 US pt, 6 l.

TRANSMISSION driving wheels: rear; clutch: single dry plate (diaphragm); gearbox: mechanical; gears: 5, fully synchronized; ratios: I 3.207, II 1.989, III 1.356, IV 1, V 0.855, rev 3.438; lever: central; final drive: hypoid bevel; axle ratio: 3.727; width of rims: 4.5''; tyres: 6.45 x 13.

PERFORMANCE max speed: 99 mph, 160 km/h; power-weight ratio: 21.6 lb/hp, 9.8 kg/hp; consumption: not declared.

CHASSIS integral; front suspension: independent, wishbones, coil springs, anti-roll bar, telescopic dampers; rear: rigid axle, semi-elliptic leafsprings, telescopic dampers.

STEERING worm and roller; turns lock to lock: 3.50.

BRAKES front disc, rear drum, servo; lining area: front 16.7 sq in, 108 sq cm, rear 57.5 sq in, 371 sq cm, total 74.2 sq in, 479 sq cm.

ELECTRICAL EQUIPMENT 12 V; 35 Ah battery; 40 A alternator; Hitachi distributor; 4 headlamps.

DIMENSIONS AND WEIGHT wheel base: 98.43 in, 250 cm; tracks: 52.56 in, 133 cm front, 51.77 in, 131 cm rear; length: 174.41 in, 443 cm; width: 63.78 in, 162 cm; height: 56.89 in, 144 cm; ground clearance: 6.69 in, 17 cm; weight: 2,260 lb, 1,025 kg; weight distribution: 55% front, 45% rear; turning circle (between walls): 34.1 ft, 10.4 m; fuel tank: 9.7 imp gal, 11.6 US gal, 44 l.

BODY 5 seats, separate front seats.

PRACTICAL INSTRUCTIONS fuel: 85-90 oct lead-free petrol; oil: engine 6.3 imp pt, 7.6 US pt, 3.6 l, SAE 20W-30, change every 3,100 miles, 5,000 km - gearbox 2.1 imp pt, 2.5 US pt, 1.2 l, SAE 30, change every 24,900 miles, 40,000 km - final drive 1.8 imp pt, 2.1 US pt, 1 l, SAE 90-140, change every 24,900 miles, 40,000 km; greasing: none; tappet clearances: inlet 0.006 in, 0.15 mm, exhaust 0.010 in, 0.25 mm; valve timing: 21° 65° 55º 20°; tyre pressure: front 20 psi, 1.4 atm, rear 20 psi, 1.4 atm.

62 hp power team

See 105 hp power team, except for:

ENGINE Diesel, 119.1 cu in, 1,951 cc (3.39 x 3.31 in, 86 x 84 mm); compression ratio: 20:1; max power (JIS): 62 hp at 4,400 rpm; max torque (JIS): 91 lb ft, 12.5 kg m at 2,200 rpm; valves: overhead, Vee-slanted, push-rods and rockers;

ISUZU Gemini 1600 LT 4-door Sedan

lubrication; 11.4 imp pt, 13.7 US pt, 6.5 l; Bosch fuel injection; cooling system: 13.2 imp pt, 15.9 US pt, 7.5 l.

TRANSMISSION gears: 5 (Semi-De Luxe 4), fully synchronized; ratios: I 3.467, II 1.989, III 1.356, IV 1, V 0.855, rev 3.438 (Semi-De Luxe I 3.467, II 1.989, III 1.356, IV 1, rev 3.499); axle ratio: 4.100.

PERFORMANCE max speeds: (I) 22 mph, 35 km/h; (II) 39 mph, 62 km/h; (III) 59 mph, 95 km/h; (IV) 75 mph, 120 km/h; (V) 81 mph, 131 km/h; power-weight ratio: Semi-De Luxe 39 lb/hp, 17.7 kg/hp; consumption: 58.8 m/imp gal, 49 m/US gal, 4.8 l x 100 km at 37 mph, 60 km/h.

DIMENSIONS AND WEIGHT weight: Semi-De Luxe 2,426 lb, 1,100 kg - De Luxe and Super De Luxe 2,492 lb, 1,130 kg.

117 XE Coupé/117 XG Coupé

PRICES (Tokyo): 117 XE Coupé: 2,205,000 yen
117 XG Coupé: 1,920,000 yen

ENGINE front, 4 stroke; 4 cylinders, vertical, in line; 110.9 cu in, 1,817 cc (3.31 x 3.23 in, 84 x 82 mm); compression ratio: 9:1; max power (JIS): 130 hp at 6,400 rpm; max torque (JIS): 120 lb ft, 16.5 kg m at 5,000 rpm; max engine rpm: 7,000; 71.5 hp/l; cast iron block, light alloy head; 5 crankshaft bearings; valves: overhead, thimble tappets; camshafts: 2, overhead; lubrication: rotary pump, full flow filter, 8.8 imp pt, 10.6 US pt, 5 l; Bosch electronic fuel injection system, catalytic converter, secondary air injection and exhaust gas recirculation; fuel feed: mechanical pump; water-cooled, 15.8 imp pt, 19 US pt, 9 l.

TRANSMISSION driving wheels: rear; clutch: single dry plate (diaphragm); gearbox: mechanical; gears: 5, fully synchronized; ratios: I 3.207, II 1.989, III 1.355, IV 1, V 0.855, rev 3.438; lever: central; final drive: hypoid bevel; axle ratio: 4.100; tyres: 185/70 HR x 13.

PERFORMANCE max speed: 115 mph, 185 km/h; power-weight ratio: 19.2 lb/hp, 8.7 kg/hp; consumption: not declared.

CHASSIS integral with platform; front suspension: independent, wishbones, coil springs, anti-roll bar, telescopic dampers; rear: rigid axle, semi-elliptic leafsprings, torque arms, anti-roll bar, telescopic dampers.

STEERING recirculating ball; turns lock to lock: 3.50.

BRAKES front disc, rear drum, servo; lining area: front 16.7 sq in, 108 sq cm, rear 57.5 sq in, 371 sq cm, total 74.2 sq in, 479 sq cm.

ELECTRICAL EQUIPMENT 12 V; 35 Ah battery; 40 A alternator; Hitachi D408-53 alternator; 4 headlamps.

DIMENSIONS AND WEIGHT wheel base: 98.43 in, 250 cm; tracks: 53.15 in, 135 cm front, 51.57 in, 131 cm rear; length: 170.08 in, 432 cm; width: 62.99 in, 160 cm; height: 51.97 in, 132 cm; ground clearance: 70.87 in, 18 cm; weight: 2,481 lb, 1,125 kg; weight distribution: 55% front, 45% rear; turning circle (between walls): 37.4 ft, 11.4 m; fuel tank: 12.3 imp gal, 14.8 US gal, 56 l.

BODY coupé; 2 doors; 4 seats, separate front seats, reclining backrests, built-in headrests.

PRACTICAL INSTRUCTIONS fuel: 90 oct lead-free petrol; oil: engine 8.8 imp pt, 10.6 US pt, 5 l, SAE 20W-50, change every 3,100 miles, 5,000 km - gearbox 2.1 imp pt, 2.5 US pt, 1.2 l, SAE 30, change every 24,900 miles, 40,000 km - final drive 1.8 imp pt, 2.1 US pt, 1 l, SAE 90, change every 24,900 miles, 40,000 km; tappet clearances: inlet 0.005 in, 0.13 mm, exhaust 0.009 in, 0.23 mm; valve timing: 28° 55° 65° 7°; tyre pressure: front 23 psi, 1.6 atm, rear 23 psi, 1.6 atm.

OPTIONAL ACCESSORIES Borg-Warner automatic transmission, hydraulic torque converter and planetary gears with 3 ratios (I 2.450, II 1.450, III 1, rev 2.222); air-conditioning.

117 XC Coupé/117 XC-J Coupé

See 117 XE Coupé/117 XG Coupé, except for:

PRICES (Tokyo): 117 XC Coupé: 1,677,000 yen
117 XC-J Coupé: 1,754,000 yen

ENGINE max power (JIS): 115 hp at 5,800 rpm; max torque (JIS): 116 lb ft, 16 kg m at 3,800 rpm; max engine rpm: 6,600; 63.3 hp/l; valves: overhead, rockers; camshafts: 1, overhead; lubrication: 14.1 imp pt, 16.9 US pt, 8 l.

TRANSMISSION tyres: for 117 XC Coupé only 165 SR x 13.

PERFORMANCE max speed: 112 mph, 180 km/h; power-weight ratio: 20.7 lb/hp, 9.4 kg/hp.

ISUZU Florian SII Diesel 2000 Series

ISUZU 117 XC-J Coupé

DIMENSIONS AND WEIGHT weight: 2,381 lb, 1,080 kg.

PRACTICAL INSTRUCTIONS oil: engine 7 imp pt, 8.5 US pt, 4 l; valve timing: 21° 65° 55° 20°.

117 XT Coupé

See 117 XE Coupé/117 XG Coupé, except for:

PRICE (Tokyo): 1,475,000 yen

ENGINE compression ratio: 8.7:1; max power (JIS) 105 hp at 5,400 rpm; max torque (JIS): 109 lb ft, 15 kg m at 3,800 rpm; max engine rpm: 6,600; 57.8 hp/l; valves: overhead, rockers; camshafts: 1, overhead; lubrication: 14.1 imp pt, 16.9 US pt, 8 l; 1 Stromberg downdraught twin barrel carburettor.

TRANSMISSION tyres: 6.45 x 13.

PERFORMANCE max speed: 106 mph, 170 km/h; power-weight ratio: 20.7 lb/hp, 9.4 kg/hp.

CHASSIS rear suspension: rigid axle, semi-elliptic leafsprings, telescopic dampers.

DIMENSIONS AND WEIGHT weight: 2,381 lb, 1,080 kg.

PRACTICAL INSTRUCTIONS oil: engine 7 imp pt, 8.5 US pt, 4 l; valve timing: 21° 65° 55° 20°.

OPTIONAL ACCESSORIES automatic transmission, hydraulic torque converter and planetary gears with 3 ratios (I 2.450, II 1.450, III 1, rev 2.222).

MAZDA   JAPAN

Familia AP Series

PRICES (Tokyo):

Standard 3-door Sedan	640,000 yen
Standard 5-door Sedan	675,000 yen
De Luxe 3-door Sedan	710,000 yen
De Luxe 5-door Sedan	745,000 yen
GF 3-door Sedan	760,000 yen
GF 5-door Sedan	790,000 yen
Super Custom 3-door Sedan	800,000 yen
Super Custom 5-door Sedan	835,000 yen
Super Custom 1978 emission 3-door Sedan	823,000 yen
Super Custom 1978 emission 5-door Sedan	850,000 yen

72 hp power team

ENGINE front, 4 stroke, Mazda low emission lean-burn engine with secondary air induction, exhaust gas recirculation and catalytic converter (1978 emission models, Mazda controlled combustion engine with secondary air induction, exhaust gas recirculation and three elements catalyst); 4 cylinders, in line; 77.6 cu in, 1,272 cc (2.87 x 2.99 in, 73 x 76 mm); compression ratio: 9.2:1; max power (JIS): 72 hp at 5,700 rpm; max torque (JIS): 76 lb ft, 10.5 kg m at 3,500 rpm; max engine rpm: 6,000; 56.6 hp/l; cast iron block, light alloy head; 5 crankshaft bearings; valves: overhead, rockers; camshafts: 1, overhead; lubrication: rotary pump, full flow filter, 5.3 imp pt, 6.3 US pt, 3 l; 1 2-stage downdraught twin barrel carburettor; fuel feed: mechanical pump; water-cooled, 9.7 imp pt, 11.6 US pt, 5.5 l.

TRANSMISSION driving wheels: rear; clutch: single dry plate (diaphragm); gearbox: mechanical; gears: 4, fully synchronized (Super Custom models 5); ratios: I 3.337, II 1.995, III 1.301, IV 1 (Super Custom V 0.831), rev 3.337; lever: central; final drive: hypoid bevel; axle ratio: 3.909; width of rims: 4.5''; tyres: 6.00 x 12.

PERFORMANCE max speeds: (I) 28 mph, 45 km/h; (II) 47 mph, 76 km/h; (III) 72 mph, 116 km/h; (IV) 90 mph, 145 km/h; power-weight ratio: Standard 3-dr. Sedan 23.8 lb/hp, 10.8 kg/hp; acceleration: standing 1/4 mile 20.2 sec, 0-50 mph (0-80 km/h) 11 sec; speed in direct drive at 1,000 rpm: 15.3 mph, 24.6 km/h; consumption: 40.9 m/imp gal, 34.1 m/US gal, 6.9 l x 100 km (1978 emission models 39.8 m/imp gal, 33.1 m/US gal, 7.1 l x 100 km).

CHASSIS integral; front suspension: independent, by McPherson, coil springs/telescopic damper struts, lower wishbones (trailing links), anti-roll bar; rear: rigid axle, lower trailing arms, upper torque rods, Panhard coil springs, telescopic dampers.

STEERING recirculating ball; turns lock to lock: 3.50.

BRAKES front drum, rear disc (Super Custom models disc, servo); lining area: front 39.7 sq in, 256 sq cm, rear 39.7 sq in, 256 sq cm, total 79.4 sq in, 512 sq cm (Super Custom models front 18 sq in, 116 sq cm, rear 39.7 sq in, 256 sq cm, total 57.7 sq in, 372 sq cm).

ELECTRICAL EQUIPMENT 12 V; 32 Ah battery; 35 A alternator; 2 headlamps.

DIMENSIONS AND WEIGHT wheel base: 91.14 in, 231 cm; tracks: 50.98 in, 129 cm front, 51.57 in, 131 cm rear; length: 150.39 in, 382 cm - Super Custom models 150.79 in, 383 cm; width: 63.19 in, 160 cm; height: 53.94 in, 137 cm; ground clearance: 6.30 in, 16 cm; weight: Standard and De Luxe 3-dr. sedans 1,720 lb, 780 kg - GF Super Custom 3-dr. Sedan 1,742 lb, 790 kg - Super Custom 3-dr. sedans 1,764 lb, 800 kg - Standard and De Luxe 5-dr. sedans 1,753 lb, 795 kg - GF Super Custom 5-dr. sedans 1,775 lb, 805 kg - weight distribution: 56% front, 44% rear; fuel tank: 8.8 imp gal, 10.6 US gal, 40 l.

BODY 4 seats, separate front seats, built-in headrests, reclining front and rear seats.

PRACTICAL INSTRUCTIONS fuel: 85-90 oct, lead-free petrol; oil: engine 5.3 imp pt, 6.3 US pt, 3 l, SAE 20W-30, change every 3,700 miles, 6,000 km - gearbox 1.6 imp pt, 1.9 US pt, 0.9 l, SAE 80, change every 12,400 miles, 20,000 km - final drive 1.1 imp pt, 1.3 US pt, 0.6 l, SAE 90, change every 12,400 miles, 20,000 km; greasing: none; tappet clearances: inlet 0.010 in, 0.25 mm, exhaust 0.012 in, 0.30 mm; valve timing: 22° 37° 53° 6°; tyre pressure: front 26 psi, 1.8 atm, rear 26 psi, 1.8 atm.

OPTIONAL ACCESSORIES 5-speed fully synchronized mechanical gearbox (I 3.337, II 1.995, III 1.301, IV 1, V 0.831, rev 3.337); JATCO 3N 71B automatic transmission, hydraulic torque converter and planetary gears with 3 ratios (I 2.458, II 1.458, III 1, rev 2.181), 4.100 axle ratio; 155 SR x 13 tyres; air-conditioning.

Familia (USA) Series

PRICES IN USA:

GLC Regular 3-door Sedan	$ 3,199*
GLC De Luxe 3-door Sedan	$ 3,499*
GLC De Luxe 5-door Sedan	$ 3,649*

52 hp power team

See Familia AP Series, 72 hp power team, except for:

ENGINE catalytic converter air induction, EGR (catalytic converter air injection, EGR for California only); max power (SAE): 52 hp (49 hp for California only) at 5,000 rpm; max torque (SAE): 64 lb ft, 8.8 kg m (63 lb ft, 8.7 kg m for California only) at 3,000 rpm; 40.9 hp/l (38.5 hp/l for California only).

TRANSMISSION gearbox ratios: I 3.655, II 2.185, III 1.425, IV 1, rev 3.655; axle ratio: 3.727; tyres: 6.15 x 13.

PERFORMANCE max speed: 86 mph, 138 km/h; power-weight ratio: 37.8 lb/hp, 17.1 kg/hp (40.4 lb/hp, 17.3 kg/hp for California only).

BRAKES front disc, rear drum.

ELECTRICAL EQUIPMENT 45 Ah battery (35 Ah for California only).

DIMENSIONS AND WEIGHT length: 154.33 in, 392 cm; weight: 1,965 lb, 891 kg (1,980 lb, 898 kg for California only).

OPTIONAL ACCESSORIES 5-speed fully synchronized mechanical gearbox (I 3.655, II 2.185, III 1.425, IV 1, V 0.827); JATCO 3N 71B automatic transmission, hydraulic torque converter and planetary gears with 3 ratios (I 2.458, II 1.458, III 1, rev 2.181), 4.100 axle ratio; 155 SR x 13 tyres; air-conditioning.

Grand Familia Series

PRICES (Tokyo):

1	1300 AP De Luxe 4-door Sedan	738,000 yen
2	1300 AP LX 4-door Sedan	783,000 yen
3	1300 AP FX 2-door Coupé	793,000 yen
4	1300 AP GL 4-door Sedan	828,000 yen
5	1300 AP GF 2-door Coupé	858,000 yen
6	1600 AP LX 4-door Sedan	813,000 yen
7	1600 AP GL 4-door Sedan	873,000 yen
8	1600 AP GL II 4-door Sedan	923,000 yen
9	1600 AP FX 2-door Coupé	833,000 yen
10	1600 AP GF 2-door Coupé	893,000 yen
11	1600 AP GF II 2-door Coupé	923,000 yen

Power team:	Standard for:	Optional for:
72 hp	1 to 5	—
90 hp	6 to 11	—

72 hp power team

ENGINE front, lean-burn type, 4 stroke; 4 cylinders, in line; 77.6 cu in, 1,272 cc (2.87 x 2.99 in, 73 x 76 mm); compression ratio: 9.2:1; max power (JIS): 72 hp at 5,700 rpm; max torque (JIS): 76 lb ft, 10.5 kg m at 3,500 rpm; max engine rpm: 5,700; 56.6 hp/l; cast iron cylinder block, light alloy head; 5 crankshaft bearings; valves: overhead, rockers; camshafts: 1, overhead; lubrication: rotary pump, full flow filter, 6.5 imp pt, 7.8 US pt, 3.7 l; 1 Hitachi DCG306 downdraught twin barrel carburettor; catalytic converter, secondary air injection and exhaust gas recirculation; fuel feed: mechanical pump; sealed circuit cooling, liquid, 8.8 imp pt, 10.6 US pt, 5 l.

TRANSMISSION driving wheels: rear; clutch: single dry plate (diaphragm); gearbox: mechanical; gears: 4, fully synchronized; ratios: I 3.337, II 1.995, III 1.301, IV 1, rev 3.337; lever: central; final drive: hypoid bevel; axle ratio: 4.100; width of rims: 4''; tyres: 6.00 x 12 - FX and GF Coupé 6.15 x 13.

PERFORMANCE max speeds: (I) 25 mph, 41 km/h; (II) 45 mph, 72 km/h; (III) 68 mph, 110 km/h; (IV) 87 mph, 140 km/h; power-weight ratio: De Luxe Sedan 25.3 lb/hp, 11.4 kg/hp; carrying capacity: 882 lb, 400 kg; speed in direct drive at 1,000 rpm: 15.3 mph, 24.6 km/h; consumption: 56.5 m/imp gal, 47 m/US gal, 5 l x 100 km at 37 mph, 60 km/h.

CHASSIS integral; front suspension: independent, by McPherson, coil springs/telescopic damper struts, lower wish-

MAZDA Familia AP GF 3-door Sedan

MAZDA Familia AP Super Custom 5-door Sedan

72 HP POWER TEAM

bones (trailing links), anti-roll bar; rear: rigid axle, semi-elliptic leafsprings, telescopic dampers.

STEERING recirculating ball, variable ratio; turns lock to lock: 3.50.

BRAKES drum (front disc for coupés only); lining area: front 39.7 sq in, 256 sq cm (coupés 19.8 sq in, 128 sq cm), rear 39.7 sq in, 256 sq cm, total 79.4 sq in, 512 sq cm (coupés 59.5 sq in, 384 sq cm).

ELECTRICAL EQUIPMENT 12 V; 45 Ah battery; 35 A alternator; Mitsubishi distributor; 2 headlamps.

DIMENSIONS AND WEIGHT wheel base: 90.94 in, 231 cm; front and rear track: 50.39 in, 128 cm - coupés 50.79 in, 129 cm; length: 156.30 in, 397 cm - coupés 160.43 in, 407 cm; width: 62.60 in, 159 cm; height: 54.33 in, 138 cm - coupés 53.15 in, 135 cm; ground clearance: 6.30 in, 16 cm; weight: De Luxe Sedan 1,819 lb, 825 kg - LX Sedan 1,830 lb, 830 kg - FX Coupé 1,841 lb, 835 kg - GF Coupé 1,852 lb, 840 kg; turning circle (between walls): 30.8 ft, 9.4 m; fuel tank: 9.9 imp gal, 11.9 US gal, 45 l.

BODY 5 seats, separate front seats, reclining backrests, built-in headrests.

PRACTICAL INSTRUCTIONS fuel: 85-90 oct, lead-free petrol; oil: engine 6.5 imp pt, 7.8 US pt, 3.7 l, SAE 10W-30, change every 3,700 miles, 6,000 km - gearbox 2.3 imp pt, 2.7 US pt, 1.3 l, SAE 90, change every 31,100 miles, 50,000 km - final drive 1.8 imp pt, 2.1 US pt, 1 l, SAE 90, change every 31,100 miles, 50.000 km; valve timing: 22° 37° 53° 6°.

90 hp power team

See 72 hp power team, except for:

ENGINE 96.8 cu in, 1,586 cc (3.07 x 3.27 in, 78 x 83 mm); compression ratio: 8.6:1; max power (JIS): 90 hp at 6,000 rpm; max torque (JIS): 94 lb ft, 13 kg m at 3,500 rpm; 56.7 hp/l.

TRANSMISSION gearbox ratios: I 3.403, II 2.005, III 1.373, IV 1, rev 3.665; axle ratio: 3.909; tyres: 6.15 x 13 - GF II Coupé Z28 x 13.

PERFORMANCE max speed: 99 mph, 160 km/h; power-weight ratio: LX Sedan 22.3 lb/hp, 10.1 kg/hp; acceleration: standing ¼ mile 18.8 sec - coupés 18.1 sec.

BRAKES front disc, rear drum, servo.

DIMENSIONS AND WEIGHT height: sedans 53.94 in, 137 cm; ground clearance: 6.50 in, 16.5 cm; weight: LX Sedan 2,007 lb, 910 kg - GL Sedan 2,029 lb, 920 kg - GL II Sedan 2,051 lb, 930 kg - FX Coupé 1,973 lb, 895 kg - GF Coupé 1,996 lb, 905 kg - GF II Coupé 2,018 lb, 915 kg.

OPTIONAL ACCESSORIES (for GL II Sedan and GF II Coupé only) 5-speed fully synchronized mechanical gearbox (I 3.380, II 2.077, III 1.390, IV 1, V 0.841, rev 3.389).

Capella AP Series

1 1600 AP De Luxe Sedan		913,000 yen
2 1600 AP GL Sedan		983,000 yen
3 1800 AP GL Sedan		1,043,000 yen
4 1800 AP De Luxe Coupé		988,000 yen
5 1800 AP GF Coupé		1,073,000 yen
6 RE-AP GR Sedan		1,104,000 yen
7 RE-AP GR II Sedan		1,194,000 yen
8 RE-AP GS Coupé		1,134,000 yen
9 RE-AP GS II Coupé		1,124,000 yen

Power team:	Standard for:	Optional for:
90 hp	1,2	—
100 hp	3 to 5	—
125 hp	6 to 9	—

90 hp power team

ENGINE front, 4 stroke; 4 cylinders, vertical, in line; 96.8 cu in, 1,586 cc (3.07 x 3.27 in, 78 x 83 mm); compression ratio: 8.6:1; max power (JIS): 90 hp at 6,000 rpm; max torque (JIS): 94 lb ft, 13 kg m at 3,500 rpm; max engine rpm: 6,300; 56.7 hp/l; cast iron block, light alloy head; 5 crankshaft bearings; valves: overhead, rockers; camshafts: 1, overhead; lubrication: rotary pump, full flow filter, 6.3 imp pt, 7.6 US pt, 3.6 l; 1 Nikki-Stromberg downdraught twin barrel carburettor; emission control with secondary air induction, exhaust gas recirculation and

catalytic converter; fuel feed: electric pump; water-cooled, 12.3 imp pt, 14.8 US pt, 7 l.

TRANSMISSION driving wheels: rear; clutch: single dry plate (diaphragm); gearbox: mechanical; gears: 4, fully synchronized; ratios: I 3.403, II 2.005, III 1.373, IV 1, rev 3.665; lever: central; final drive: hypoid bevel; axle ratio: 3.909; width of rims: 4.5''; tyres: 6.15 x 13.

PERFORMANCE max speeds: (I) 29 mph, 47 km/h; (II) 50 mph, 80 km/h; (III) 73 mph, 117 km/h; (IV) 96 mph, 155 km/h; power-weight ratio: GL Sedan 23.9 lb/hp, 10.8 kg/hp; carrying capacity: 882 lb, 400 kg; acceleration: standing ¼ mile 17.8 sec; speed in direct drive at 1,000 rpm: 16.6 mph, 26.7 km/h; consumption: not declared.

CHASSIS integral; front suspension: independent, by Mc-Pherson, coil springs/telescopic damper struts, lower wishbones (trailing links), anti-roll bar; rear: rigid axle, lower trailing arms, upper torque arms, transverse linkage bar, coil springs, telescopic dampers.

STEERING recirculating ball, variable ratio; turns lock to lock: 3.30.

BRAKES front disc, rear drum; lining area: front 24.8 sq in, 160 sq cm, rear 39.7 sq in, 256 sq cm, total 64.5 sq in, 416 sq cm.

ELECTRICAL EQUIPMENT 12 V; 35 Ah battery; 40 A alternator; Mitsubishi distributor; 4 headlamps.

MAZDA Capella 1800 AP GF Coupé

MAZDA Capella 1800 AP GF Coupé

DIMENSIONS AND WEIGHT wheel base: 97.24 in, 247 cm; front and rear track: 50.79 in, 129 cm; length: 167.72 in, 426 cm; width: 62.20 in, 158 cm; height: 55.91 in, 142 cm; ground clearance: 6.30 in, 16 cm; weight: De Luxe Sedan 2,040 lb, 925 kg - GL Sedan 2,150 lb, 975 kg; weight distribution: 56.4% front, 43.6% rear; turning circle (between walls): 33.5 ft, 10.2 m; fuel tank: 11 imp gal, 13.2 US gal, 50 l.

BODY 5 seats, separate front seats, reclining backrests, built-in headrests.

PRACTICAL INSTRUCTIONS fuel: 85-90 oct, lead-free petrol; oil: engine 6.3 imp pt, 7.6 US pt, 3.6 l, SAE 10W-20, change every 3,700 miles, 6,000 km - gearbox 2.5 imp pt, 3 US pt, 1.4 l, SAE 90, change every 29,800 miles, 48,000 km - final drive 2.1 imp pt, 2.5 US pt, 1.2 l, SAE 90, change every 29,800 miles, 48,000 km; tappet clearances (hot): inlet 0.012 in, 0.30 mm, exhaust 0.012 in, 0.30 mm; tyre pressure: front 24 psi, 1.7 atm, rear 24 psi, 1.7 atm.

100 hp power team

See 90 hp power team, except for:

ENGINE 107.9 cu in, 1,769 cc (3.15 x 3.46 in, 80 x 88 mm); max power (JIS): 100 hp at 6,000 rpm; max torque (JIS): 110 lb ft, 15.2 kg m at 4,000 rpm; max engine rpm: 6,500; 56.5 hp/l.

TRANSMISSION gears: 5, fully synchronized; ratios: I 3.380, II 2.077, III 1.390, IV 1, V 0.841, rev 3.389; tyres: 6.45 x 13 or 165 SR x 13.

PERFORMANCE max speed: 103 mph, 165 km/h; power-weight ratio: GL Sedan 21.8 lb/hp, 9.9 kg/hp.

DIMENSIONS AND WEIGHT height: 56.50 in, 143 cm - coupés 55.31 in 140 cm; weight: GL Sedan 2,183 lb, 990 kg - De Luxe Coupé 2,128 lb, 965 kg - GF Coupé 2,161 lb, 980 kg.

125 hp power team

See 90 hp power team, except for:

ENGINE front, 4 stroke, Wankel type; 2 co-axial 3-lobe rotors; 35 x 2 cu in, 573 x 2 cc; compression ratio: 9.4:1; max power (JIS): 125 hp at 6,500 rpm; max torque (JIS): 120 lb ft, 16.5 kg m at 4,000 rpm; max engine rpm: 7,000; light alloy engine block, dual ignition, cast iron rotors; 2 crankshaft bearings; lubrication: rotary pump, full flow filter, oil cooler, 9.7 imp pt, 11.6 US pt, 5.5 l; 1 Nikki-Stromberg downdraught 4-barrel carburettor; cooling system: 14.1 imp pt, 16.9 US pt, 8 l.

TRANSMISSION gearbox ratios: I 3.683, II 2.263, III 1.397, IV 1, rev 3.692; axle ratio: 4.111; tyres: GR II Sedan 6.45 x 13 - GS II Coupé 165 SR x 13.

PERFORMANCE max speed: 115 mph, 185 km/h; power-weight ratio: GR Sedan 18.2 lb/hp, 8.2 kg/hp; standing ¼ mile 15.6 sec; speed in direct drive at 1,000 rpm: 16.5 mph, 26.5 km/h; consumption: 25.7 m/imp gal, 21.4 m/US gal, 11 l x 100 km.

ELECTRICAL EQUIPMENT 45 Ah battery; 2 Mitsubishi distributors.

DIMENSIONS AND WEIGHT height: coupés 54.13 in, 137 cm; weight: GR Sedan 2,271 lb, 1,030 kg - SR II Sedan 2,282 lb, 1,035 kg - GS Coupé 2,260 lb, 1,025 kg - GS II Coupé 2,271 lb, 1,030 kg; fuel tank: 14.3 imp gal, 17.2 US gal, 65 l.

PRACTICAL INSTRUCTIONS oil: engine 9.7 imp pt, 11.6 US pt, 5.5 l, SAE 10W-30 - gearbox 4.4 imp pt, 5.3 US pt, 2.5 l, change every 31,100 miles, 50,000 km.

OPTIONAL ACCESSORIES (for GR II Sedan and GS II Coupé only) 5-speed fully synchronized mechanical gearbox (I 3.683, II 2.263, III 1.397, IV 1, V 0.862, rev 3.692); JATCO automatic transmission with 3 ratios (I 2.458, II 1.458, III 1, rev 2.181), 165 SR x 13 tyres, max speed 112 mph, 180 km/h.

Luce Series

PRICES (Tokyo):

1 1800 Custom Special 4-door Sedan	996,000	yen
2 2000 Custom 4-door Sedan	1,165,000	yen
3 2000 Custom 4-door Hardtop	1,230,000	yen
4 2000 Super Custom 4-door Sedan	1,280,000	yen
5 2000 Super Custom 4-door Hardtop	1,345,000	yen
6 2000 Custom Special 4-door Hardtop	1,105,000	yen
7 RE Custom 4-door Sedan	1,260,000	yen
8 RE Custom 4-door Hardtop	1,325,000	yen
9 RE Super Custom 4-door Sedan	1,500,000	yen
10 RE Super Custom 4-door Hardtop	1,565,000	yen
11 RE Custom Special 4-door Sedan	1,130,000	yen
12 RE Custom Special 4-door Hardtop	1,195,000	yen
13 RE Limited 4-door Sedan	1,915,000	yen
14 RE Limited 4-door Hardtop	1,980,000	yen

For GB price, see price index.

Power team:	Standard for:	Optional for:
100 hp	1	—
110 hp	2 to 6	—
125 hp	7 to 12	—
135 hp	13,14	—

100 hp power team

ENGINE front, 4 stroke; 4 cylinders, vertical, in line; 107.9 cu in, 1,769 cc (3.15 x 3.46 in, 80 x 88 mm); compression ratio: 8.6:1; max power (JIS): 100 hp at 6,000 rpm; max torque (JIS): 110 lb ft, 15.2 kg m at 4,000 rpm; max engine rpm: 6,500; 56.5 hp/l; cast iron block, light alloy head; 5 crankshaft bearings; valves: overhead, rockers; camshafts: 1, overhead; lubrication: rotary pump, full flow filter, 6.3 imp pt, 7.6 US pt, 3.6 l; 1 downdraught twin barrel carburettor; fuel feed: electric pump; water-cooled, 12.3 imp pt, 14.8 US pt, 7 l.

TRANSMISSION driving wheels: rear; clutch: single dry plate (diaphragm); gearbox: mechanical; gears: 4, fully synchronized; ratios: I 3.403, II 2.005, III 1.373, IV 1, rev 3.900; lever: central; final drive: hypoid bevel; axle ratio: 3.909; width of rims: 4.5''; tyres: 6.45 x 13.

PERFORMANCE max speeds: (I) 30 mph, 48 km/h; (II) 52 mph, 83 km/h; (III) 75 mph, 120 km/h; (IV) 103 mph, 165 km/h; power-weight ratio: 23.5 lb/hp, 10.6 kg/hp; carrying capacity: 882 lb, 400 kg; acceleration: standing ¼ mile 17.1 sec; speed in direct drive at 1,000 rpm: 19.5 mph, 31.4 km/h; consumption: not declared.

CHASSIS integral; front suspension: independent, by McPherson, coil springs/telescopic damper struts, lower wishbones (trailing links), anti-roll bar; rear: rigid axle, semi-elliptic leafsprings, telescopic dampers.

STEERING recirculating ball, variable ratio; turns lock to lock: 3.40.

BRAKES front disc, rear drum, servo.

ELECTRICAL EQUIPMENT 12 V; 35 Ah battery; 60 A alternator; Mitsubishi distributor; 4 headlamps.

DIMENSIONS AND WEIGHT wheel base: 98.82 in, 251 cm; tracks: 54.33 in, 138 cm front, 53.94 in, 137 cm rear; length: 173.23 in, 440 cm; width: 65.35 in, 166 cm; height:

55.51 in, 141 cm; ground clearance: 6.89 in, 17.5 cm; weight: 2,348 lb, 1,065 kg; fuel tank: 14.3 imp gal, 17.2 US gal, 65 l.

BODY 5 seats, separate front seats, reclining backrests, built-in headrests.

PRACTICAL INSTRUCTIONS fuel: 85-90 oct petrol; oil: engine 6.3 imp pt, 7.6 US pt, 3.6 l, SAE 20W-30, change every 3,700 miles, 6,000 km - gearbox 3 imp pt, 3.6 US pt, 1.7 l, SAE 90, change every 29,800 miles, 48,000 km - final drive 2.5 imp pt, 3 US pt, 1.4 l, SAE 90, change every 29,800 miles, 48,000 km; tappet clearances: inlet 0.012 in, 0.30 mm, exhaust 0.012 in, 0.30 mm; valve timing: 10° 57° 54° 13°.

OPTIONAL ACCESSORIES automatic transmission, hydraulic torque converter and planetary gears with 3 ratios.

110 hp power team

See 100 hp power team, except for:

ENGINE 120.2 cu in, 1,970 cc (3.15 x 3.86 in, 80 x 98 mm); max power (JIS): 110 hp at 5,300 rpm; max torque (JIS): 123 lb ft, 17 kg m at 3,000 rpm; max engine rpm: 5,600; 55.8 hp/l; lubrication: 7.7 imp pt, 9.3 US pt, 4.4 l.

TRANSMISSION gears: 5, fully synchronized (for Custom Special 4-dr. Hardtop 4); ratios: I 3.403, II 1.925, III 1.373, IV 1, V 0.854, rev 3.665; (for Super Custom 4-dr. Hardtop only width of rims: 5.5''; tyres: 175 SR x 14).

PERFORMANCE max speed: 99 mph, 160 km/h; power-weight ratio: Custom 4-dr. Sedan 22.1 lb/hp, 10 kg/hp; consumption: 29.7 m/imp gal, 24.7 m/US gal, 9.5 l x 100 km.

DIMENSIONS AND WEIGHT length: 179.92 in, 457 cm; height: hardtops 54.72 in, 139 cm; weight: Custom 4-dr. Sedan and Custom Special 4-dr. Hardtop 2,436 lb, 1,105 kg - Custom 4-dr. Hardtop 2,448 lb, 1,110 kg - Super Custom 4-dr. Sedan 2,458 lb, 1,115 kg - Super Custom 4-dr. Hardtop 2,470 lb, 1,120 kg.

BODY adjustable headrests.

125 hp power team

See 100 hp power team, except for:

ENGINE front, 4 stroke, Wankel rotary type with Mazda REAPS emission control system (thermal reactor, air injection and ignition control); 2 co-axial 3-lobe rotors; 35 x 2 cu in, 573 x 2 cc; compression ratio: 9.4:1; max power (JIS): 125 hp at 6,500 rpm; max torque (JIS): 120 lb ft, 16.5 kg m at 4,000 rpm; max engine rpm: 7,000; light alloy engine block, dual ignition, cast iron rotors; 2 crankshaft bearings; lubrication: 9.2 imp pt, 11 US pt, 5.2 l; 1 Nikki 210284 downdraught 4-barrel carburettor; cooling system: 15.8 imp pt, 19 US pt, 9 l.

TRANSMISSION gears: 5, fully synchronized; ratios: I 3.674, II 2.217, III 1.432, IV 1, V 0.825, rev 3.542; axle ratio: 4.100; width of rims: 5'' - Super Custom models 5.5''; tyres: 6.45 x 14 - Super Custom models 175 SR x 14.

PERFORMANCE max speeds: (I) 32 mph, 52 km/h; (II) 53 mph, 86 km/h; (III) 76 mph, 123 km/h; (IV) 108 mph, 175 km/h; (V) 108 mph, 175 km/h; power-weight ratio: Custom 4-dr. Sedan 19.9 lb/hp, 9 kg/hp; consumption: 19.2 m/imp gal, 16 m/US gal, 14.7 l x 100 km.

STEERING (for Super Custom models only) servo; turns lock to lock: 4.

ELECTRICAL EQUIPMENT 63 A alternator.

DIMENSIONS AND WEIGHT length: 179.92 in, 457 cm - Custom Special models 179.13 in, 455 cm; height: hardtops 54.72 in, 139 cm; weight: Custom 4-dr. Sedan and Custom Special 4-dr. Hardtop 2,470 lb, 1,120 kg - Custom 4-dr. Hardtop 2,481 lb, 1,125 kg - Super Custom 4-dr. Sedan 2,492 lb, 1,130 kg - Super Custom 4-dr. Hardtop 2,514 lb, 1,140 kg - Custom Special 4-dr. Sedan 2,459 lb, 1,115 kg.

PRACTICAL INSTRUCTIONS oil: engine 9.2 imp pt, 11 US pt, 5.2 l, SAE 10W-30, change every 3,700 miles, 6,000 km; valve timing: 32° 40° 71° 48°.

OPTIONAL ACCESSORIES (for Super Custom models only) JATCO automatic transmission, hydraulic torque converter and planetary gears with 3 ratios (I 2.458, II 1.458, III 1, rev 2.181).

135 hp power team

See 125 hp power team, except for:

ENGINE 39.9 cu in, 654 x 2 cc; max power (JIS): 135 hp at 6,000 rpm; max torque (JIS): 138 lb ft, 19 kg m at 4,000 rpm; lubrication: 11 imp pt, 13.3 US pt, 6.3 l; cooling system: 17.6 imp pt, 21.1 US pt, 10 l.

TRANSMISSION gearbox: mechanical with hydraulic fluid coupling; gears: 5, fully synchronized; ratios: I 3.380, II 2.077, III 1.390, IV 1, V 0.841, rev 3.389; axle ratio: 3.727; width of rims: 5.5''; tyres: 175 SR x 14.

PERFORMANCE max speeds: (I) 36 mph, 58 km/h; (II) 59 mph, 95 km/h; (III) 90 mph, 145 km/h; (IV) 109 mph, 175 km/h; (V) 109 mph, 175 km/h; power-weight ratio: 20 lb/hp, 9.1 kg/hp; consumption: 17.8 m/imp gal, 14.9 m/US gal, 15.8 l x 100 km.

STEERING servo; turns lock to lock: 4.

DIMENSIONS AND WEIGHT length: 181.89 in, 462 cm; height: sedan 55.51 in, 141 cm - hardtop 54.33 in, 138 cm; weight: sedan 2,712 lb, 1,230 kg - hardtop 2,723 lb, 1,235 kg.

OPTIONAL ACCESSORIES with JATCO automatic transmission max speed 106 mph, 170 km/h.

MAZDA Luce 2000 Super Custom 4-door Hardtop

Cosmo Series

PRICES (Tokyo):

1 1800 AP Custom Special Coupé	**1,055,000**	yen
2 1800 AP Custom Coupé	**1,190,000**	yen
3 1800 AP Super Custom Coupé	**1,355,000**	yen
4 2000 AP Custom Coupé	**1,255,000**	yen
5 2000 AP Super Custom Coupé	**1,395,000**	yen
6 L 2000 AP Custom Special Coupé	**1,205,000**	yen
7 L 2000 AP Custom Coupé	**1,340,000**	yen
8 L 2000 AP Super Custom Coupé	**1,480,000**	yen
9 AP Custom Special Coupé	**1,200,000**	yen
10 AP Custom Coupé	**1,330,000**	yen
11 AP Super Custom Coupé	**1,538,000**	yen
12 L RE Custom Special Coupé	**1,285,000**	yen
13 L RE Custom Coupé	**1,415,000**	yen
14 L RE Super Custom Coupé	**1,590,000**	yen
15 AP Limited Coupé	**1,795,000**	yen
16 L RE Limited Coupé	**1,855,000**	yen

For USA price, see price index.

Power team:	Standard for:	Optional for:
100 hp	1 to 3	—
110 hp	4 to 8	—
125 hp	9 to 14	—
135 hp	15,16	—

100 hp power team

ENGINE front, 4 stroke, Mazda low emission system with secondary air induction, exhaust gas recirculation and three-elements catalyst; 4 cylinders, vertical, in line; 107.9 cu in, 1,769 cc (3.15 x 3.46 in, 80 x 88 mm); compression ratio: 8.6:1; max power (JIS): 100 hp at 6,000 rpm; max torque (JIS): 110 lb ft, 15.2 kg m at 4,000 rpm; max engine rpm: 6,000; 56.5 hp/l; cast iron block, light alloy head; 5 crankshaft bearings; valves: overhead, rockers; camshafts: 1, overhead; lubrication: rotary pump, full flow filter, 6.3 imp pt, 7.6 US pt, 3.6 l; 1 Nikki downdraught twin barrel carburettor; fuel feed: electric pump; water-cooled, 12.3 imp pt, 14.8 US pt, 7 l.

TRANSMISSION driving wheels: rear; clutch: single dry plate (diaphragm); gearbox: mechanical; gears: 4, fully synchronized; ratios I 3.403, II 2.005, III 1.373, IV 1, rev 3.665; lever: central; final drive: hypoid bevel; axle ratio: 4.100; width of rims: 5.5''; tyres: Z28 x 14.

PERFORMANCE max speeds: (I) 31 mph, 50 km/h; (II) 50 mph, 80 km/h; (III) 75 mph, 120 km/h; (IV) 103 mph, 165 km/h; power-weight ratio: 24.7 lb/hp, 11.2 kg/hp; carrying capacity: 882 lb, 400 kg; acceleration: standing ¼ mile 18.8 sec, 0-50 mph (0-80 km/h) 9.2 sec; speed in direct drive at 1,000 rpm: 17.1 mph, 27.5 km/h; consumption: 40.4 m/imp gal, 33.6 m/US gal, 7 l x 100 km.

CHASSIS integral with front and rear auxiliary frames; front suspension: independent, by McPherson, coil springs/telescopic damper struts, lower wishbones (trailing links), anti-roll bar; rear: rigid axle, lower trailing arms, upper oblique torque arms, Panhard rod, coil springs, telescopic dampers.

STEERING recirculating ball, variable ratio; turns lock to lock: 4.30.

BRAKES front disc, rear drum, servo; lining area: front 26.7 sq in, 172 sq cm, rear 18.6 sq in, 120 sq cm, total 45.3 sq in, 292 sq cm.

ELECTRICAL EQUIPMENT 12 V; 35 Ah battery; 50 A alternator; Mitsubishi distributor; 4 headlamps.

DIMENSIONS AND WEIGHT wheel base: 98.82 in, 251 cm; tracks: 54.33 in, 138 cm front, 53.94 in, 137 cm rear; length: 176.18 in, 447 cm; width: 66.34 in, 168 cm; height: 52.36 in, 133 cm; ground clearance: 6.50 in, 16.5 cm; weight: 2,470 lb, 1,120 kg; weight distribution: 56.7% front, 43.3% rear; turning circle (between walls): 36.7 ft, 11.2 m; fuel tank: 14.3 imp gal, 17.2 US gal, 65 l.

BODY coupé; 2 doors; 5 seats, separate front seats.

PRACTICAL INSTRUCTIONS fuel: 85-90 oct, lead-free petrol; oil: engine 6.3 imp pt, 7.6 US pt, 3.6 l, SAE 10W-40, change every 3,700 miles, 6,000 km - gearbox 2.5 imp pt, 3 US pt, 1.4 l, SAE 90, change every 29,800 miles, 48,000 km - final drive 2.1 imp pt, 2.5 US pt, 1.2 l, SAE 90, change every 29,800 miles, 48,000 km; greasing: none; tappet clearances (hot): inlet 0.012 in, 0.30 mm, exhaust 0.012 in, 0.30 mm; valve timing: 10° 57° 54° 13°; tyre pressure: front 26 psi, 1.8 atm, rear 26 psi, 1.8 atm.

OPTIONAL ACCESSORIES 5-speed fully synchronized mechanical gearbox; automatic transmission, hydraulic torque converter and planetary gears with 3 ratios.

110 hp power team

See 100 hp power team, except for:

ENGINE 120.2 cu in, 1,970 cc (3.15 x 3.86 in, 80 x 98 mm); max power (JIS): 110 hp at 5,300 rpm; max torque (JIS): 123 lb ft, 17 kg m at 3,000 rpm; 55.8 hp/l; lubrication: 7.7 imp pt, 9.3 US pt, 4.4 l.

TRANSMISSION gears: 5, fully synchronized; ratios: I 3.403, II 1.925, III 1.373, IV 1, V 0.854, rev 3.665; axle ratio: 3.909; tyres: L models 6.45 x 14 - Super Custom Coupé 185/70 SR x 14.

PERFORMANCE power-weight ratio: Custom Coupé 22.4 lb/hp, 10.2 kg/hp; consumption: 28.2 m/imp gal, 23.5 m/US gal, 10 l x 100 km.

DIMENSIONS AND WEIGHT length: L models 177.16 in, 450 cm; height: L models 52.75 in, 134 cm; weight: Custom Coupé 2,470 lb, 1,120 kg - Super Custom Coupé 2,481 lb, 1,125 kg - L Custom and Custom Special coupés 2,547 lb, 1,155 kg - L Super Custom Coupé 2,558 lb, 1,160 kg.

125 hp power team

See 100 hp power team, except for:

ENGINE front, 4 stroke, Wankel type with Mazda REAPS emission control system (thermal reactor and air injection); 2 co-axial 3-lobe rotors; 35 x 2 cu in, 573 x 2 cc; compression ratio: 9.4:1; max power (JIS): 125 hp at 6,500 rpm; max torque (JIS): 120 lb ft, 16.5 kg m at 4,000 rpm; max engine rpm: 7,000; light alloy engine block, dual ignition, cast iron rotors; 2 crankshaft bearings; lubrication: rotary pump, full flow filter, oil cooler, 9.2 imp pt, 11 US pt, 5.2 l; 1 Nikki 2-10284 downdraught 4-barrel carburettor; cooling system: 15.8 imp pt, 19 US pt, 9 l.

TRANSMISSION gears: 4, fully synchronized - L models 5; ratios: I 3.683, II 2.263, III 1.397, IV 1 - L models V 0.862, rev 3.692; axle ratio: 3.909.

PERFORMANCE max speeds: (I) 35 mph, 56 km/h; (II) 56 mph, 90 km/h; (III) 89 mph, 144 km/h; (IV) 115 mph, 185 km/h; power-weight ratio: Custom Special Coupé 20.5 lb/hp, 9.3 kg/hp; acceleration: standing ¼ mile 16.3 sec, 0-50 mph (0-80 km/h) 6.4 sec; speed in direct drive at 1,000 rpm: 16.4 mph, 26.4 km/h; consumption: 36.7 m/imp gal, 30.5 m/US gal, 7.7 l x 100 km.

ELECTRICAL EQUIPMENT 63 A alternator.

DIMENSIONS AND WEIGHT weight: 2,558 lb, 1,160 kg - Custom Coupé and L Custom Special Coupé 2,547 lb, 1,155 kg; weight distribution: 57.3% front, 42.7% rear.

PRACTICAL INSTRUCTIONS oil: engine 9.2 imp pt, 11 US pt, 5.2 l, SAE 10W-40, change every 3,700 miles, 6,000 km - gearbox 3 imp pt, 3.6 US pt, 1.7 l, SAE 90, change every 29,800 miles, 48,000 km.

OPTIONAL ACCESSORIES 5-speed fully synchronized mechanical gearbox (I 3.683, II 2.263, III 1.397, IV 1, V 0.862, rev 3.692); automatic transmission with 3 ratios (only for Super Custom Coupé); 185/70 SR x 14 tyres.

135 hp power team

See 125 hp power team, except for:

ENGINE 39.9 x 2 cu in, 654 x 2 cc; max power (JIS): 135 hp at 6,000 rpm; max torque (JIS): 138 lb ft, 19 kg m at 4,000 rpm; lubrication: 11.1 imp pt, 13.3 US pt, 6.3 l; 1 Hitachi KCH 348 downdraught 4-barrel carburettor.

TRANSMISSION gearbox: mechanical with hydraulic fluid coupling; gears: 5, fully synchronized; ratios: I 3.380, II 2.077, III 1.390, IV 1, V 0.841, rev 3.389; axle ratio: 3.636; tyres: 185/70 SR x 14.

PERFORMANCE max speeds: (I) 39 mph, 63 km/h; (II) 65 mph, 104 km/h; (III) 96 mph, 155 km/h; (IV) 121 mph, 195 km/h; (V) 118 mph, 190 km/h; power-weight ratio: AP Limited Coupé 19.9 lb/hp, 9 kg/hp; acceleration: standing ¼ mile 15.9 sec, 0-50 mph (0-80 km/h) 6.2 sec; speed in top at 1,000 rpm: 17.3 mph, 27.9 km/h.

CHASSIS rear suspension: anti-roll bar.

STEERING servo; turns lock to lock: 3.50.

ELECTRICAL EQUIPMENT 45 Ah battery.

DIMENSIONS AND WEIGHT length: AP Limited Coupé 178.94 in, 454 cm - L RE Limited Coupé 177.16 in, 450 cm; weight: AP Limited Coupé 2,690 lb, 1,220 kg - L RE Limited Coupé 2,646 lb, 1,200 kg; weight distribution: 57.8% front, 42.2% rear.

PRACTICAL INSTRUCTIONS oil: engine 11.1 imp pt, 13.3 US pt, 6.3 l, SAE 10W-40, change every 3,100 miles, 5,000 km - gearbox 4.4 imp pt, 5.3 US pt, 2.5 l, change every 25,000 miles, 40,000 km.

OPTIONAL ACCESSORIES automatic transmission with 3 ratios (I 2.458, II 1.458, III 1, rev 2.181), max ratio of converter at stall 2, max speeds (I) 53 mph, 85 km/h, (II) 90 mph, 145 km/h, (III) 118 mph, 190 km/h, acceleration standing ¼ mile 17.7 sec, consumption 31 m/imp gal, 25.8 m/US gal, 9.1 l x 100 km; air-conditioning.

Roadpacer Sedan

PRICE (Tokyo): 3,835,000 yen

ENGINE front, 4 stroke, Wankel type with emission control system (thermal reactor, air injection and exhaust gas recirculation); 2 co-axial 3-lobe rotors; 39.9 x 2 cu in, 654 x 2 cc; compression ratio: 9.4:1; max power (JIS): 135 hp at 6,000 rpm; max torque (JIS): 138 lb ft, 19 kg m at 4,000 rpm; max engine rpm: 6,000; light alloy engine block, dual ignition, cast iron rotors; 2 crankshaft bearings; lubrication: rotary pump, full flow filter, oil cooler, 11.1 imp pt, 13.3 US pt, 6.3 l; 1 Hitachi downdraught 4-barrel carburettor; fuel feed: electric pump; water-cooled, 15.8 imp pt, 19 US pt, 9 l.

TRANSMISSION driving wheels: rear; gearbox: JATCO automatic transmission, hydraulic torque converter and planetary gears with 3 ratios, max ratio of converter at stall 2, possible manual selection; ratios: I 2.458, II 1.458, III 1, rev 2.181; lever: steering column; final drive:

MAZDA Cosmo 2000 AP Super Custom Coupé

hypoid bevel; axle ratio: 4.444; width of rims: 5''; tyres: 7.50 x 14.

PERFORMANCE max speed: 103 mph, 165 kmh; power-weight ratio: 25.7 lb/hp, 11.7 kg/hp; carrying capacity: 1,058 lb, 480 kg; speed in direct drive at 1,000 rpm: 17.1 mph, 27.5 km/h; consumption: not declared.

CHASSIS integral, front auxiliary frame; front suspension: independent, wishbones, coil springs, anti-roll bar, telescopic dampers; rear: rigid axle, lower trailing arms, upper oblique torque arms, coil springs, telescopic dampers.

STEERING worm and roller, variable ratio, servo; turns lock to lock: 2.60.

BRAKES front disc, internal radial fins, rear drum, servo.

ELECTRICAL EQUIPMENT 12 V; 45 Ah battery; 63 A alternator; 4 headlamps.

DIMENSIONS AND WEIGHT wheel base: 111.42 in, 283 cm; front and rear track: 60.24 in, 153 cm; height: 190.94 in, 485 cm; width: 74.21 in, 188 cm; height: 57.68 in, 146 cm; ground clearance: 6.30 in, 16 cm; weight: 3,473 lb, 1,575 kg; turning circle (between walls): 41.3 ft, 12.6 m; fuel tank: 16.5 imp gal, 19.8 US gal, 75 l.

BODY saloon/sedan; 4 doors; 5-6 seats, bench front seats.

PRACTICAL INSTRUCTIONS fuel: 85-90 oct, lead-free petrol; oil: engine 11.1 imp pt, 13.3 US pt, 6.3 l, SAE 10W-40, change every 3,100 miles, 5,000 km - automatic transmission 10.9 imp pt, 13.1 US pt, 6.2 l.

OPTIONAL ACCESSORIES separate front seats.

MITSUBISHI   JAPAN

Minica Ami 55 Series

PRICES (Tokyo):

Hi Standard Sedan	545,000	yen
Super De Luxe Sedan	611,000	yen
GL Sedan	635,000	yen
XL Sedan	658,000	yen

31 hp power team

ENGINE front, 4 stroke; 2 cylinders, in line; 33.3 cu in, 546 cc (2.75 x 2.79 in, 70 x 71 mm); compression ratio: 9:1; max power (JIS): 31 hp at 6,000 rpm; max torque (JIS): 30 lb ft, 4.1 kg m at 3,000 rpm; max engine rpm: 6,500; 56.7 hp/l; cast iron block, light alloy head; 3 crankshaft bearings; valves: overhead, rockers; camshafts: 1, overhead; lubrication: rotary pump, full flow filter, 5.1 imp pt, 6.1 US pt, 2.9 l; 1 Mikuni 24-30 DIDS downdraught twin barrel carburettor; fuel feed: electric pump; emission control catalytic converter, secondary air injection, exhaust gas recirculation; water-cooled, 5.3 imp pt, 6.3 US pt, 3 l.

TRANSMISSION driving wheels: rear; clutch: single dry plate (diaphragm); gearbox: mechanical; gears: 4, fully synchronized; ratios: I 3.882, II 2.265, III 1.473, IV 1, rev 4.271; lever: central; final drive: hypoid bevel; axle ratio: 4.625; width of rims: 3.5''; tyres: 5.20 x 10.

PERFORMANCE max speeds: (I) 20 mph, 32 km/h; (II) 34 mph, 55 km/h; (III) 53 mph, 85 km/h; (IV) 68 mph, 110 km/h; power-weight ratio: Hi Standard and GL 39.8 lb/hp, 18 kg/hp - Super De Luxe and XL 40.2 lb/hp, 18.2 kg/hp; consumption: 54 m/imp gal, 45 m/US gal, 5.2 l x 100 km.

CHASSIS integral; front suspension: independent, by McPherson, coil springs/telescopic damper struts, anti-roll bar, lower wishbones (trailing links); rear: rigid axle, twin longitudinal trailing radius arms, transverse linkage bar, coil springs, telescopic dampers.

STEERING recirculating ball.

BRAKES drum, dual circuit; lining area: total 67 sq in, 432 sq cm.

ELECTRICAL EQUIPMENT 12 V; 24 Ah battery; 25 A alternator; Mitsubishi distributor; 2 headlamps.

DIMENSIONS AND WEIGHT wheel base: 78.84 in, 200 cm; tracks: 48.03 in, 122 cm front, 46.85 in, 119 cm rear; length: Hi Standard and GL 124.41 in, 316 cm - Super De Luxe and XL 125.19 in, 318 cm - width: 55.12 in, 140 cm; height: 51.96 in, 132 cm; ground clearance: 5.51 in, 14 cm; weight: Hi Standard and GL 1,235 lb, 560 kg - Super De Luxe and XL 1,245 lb, 565 kg; fuel tank: 6.6 imp gal, 7.9 US gal, 30 l.

BODY 2 doors; 4 seats, separate front seats, reclining backrests, built-in headrests; folding rear seat.

PRACTICAL INSTRUCTIONS fuel: 85-90 oct petrol; oil: engine 4.8 imp pt, 5.7 US pt, 2.7 l, SAE 30, change every 3,100 miles, 5,000 km - gearbox 1.1 imp pt, 1.3 US pt, 0.6 l, SAE 80, change every 24,900 miles, 40,000 km - final drive 1.1 imp pt, 1.3 US pt, 0.6 l, SAE 80, change every 24,900 miles, 40,000 km; tyre pressure: front and rear 25.6 psi, 1.8 atm.

Lancer Series

PRICES (Tokyo):

1 1200 Populaire 2-door Sedan	778,000	yen
2 1200 Populaire 4-door Sedan	800,000	yen
3 1200 GL 2-door Sedan	817,000	yen
4 1200 GL 4-door Sedan	839,000	yen
5 1200 SL-5 2-door Sedan	863,000	yen
6 1200 SL-5 4-door Sedan	885,000	yen
7 1400 GL 2-door Sedan	875,000	yen
8 1400 GL 4-door Sedan	900,000	yen
9 1400 SL-5 2-door Sedan	934,000	yen
10 1400 SL-5 4-door Sedan	956,000	yen
11 1600 GSL 4-door Sedan	1,004,000	yen
12 1600 GSR 2-door Sedan	1,078,000	yen

For GB prices, see price index.

Power team:	Standard for:	Optional for:
70 hp	1 to 6	—
82 hp	7 to 10	—
86 hp	11	—
100 hp	12	—

MAZDA Roadpacer Sedan

---

70 hp power team

ENGINE front, 4 stroke; 4 cylinders, vertical, in line; 75.91 cu in, 1,244 cc (2.74 x 3.23 in, 69.5 x 82 mm); compression ratio: 9:1; max power (JIS): 70 hp at 5,500 rpm; max torque (JIS): 77 lb ft, 10.7 kg m at 3,000 rpm; max engine rpm: 6,000; 56.3 hp/l; cast iron block, light alloy head; 5 crankshaft bearings; valves: overhead, Vee-slanted, rockers; camshafts: 1, overhead; lubrication: rotary pump, full flow filter, 6.2 imp pt, 7.4 US pt, 3.5 l; 1 Stromberg 28-32 DIDTA downdraught twin barrel carburettor; Mitsubishi MCA-Jet super lean-burn low emission engine with third air inlet valve, exhaust gas recirculation and small capacity catalyst in exhaust manifold; fuel feed: mechanical pump; water-cooled, 10.6 imp pt, 12.7 US pt, 6 l.

TRANSMISSION driving wheels: rear; clutch: single dry plate (diaphragm); gearbox: mechanical; gears: 4 (5 for SL-5 models only), fully synchronized; ratios: I 3.525, II 2.193, III 1.442, IV 1, rev 3.867 - SL-5 models I 3.215, II 2, III 1.316, IV 1, V 0.853, rev 3.667; lever: central; final drive: hypoid bevel; axle ratio: 4.222; tyres: 6.15 x 13.

PERFORMANCE max speeds: (I) 26 mph, 42 km/h; (II) 42 mph, 68 km/h; (III) 65 mph, 105 km/h; (IV) 93 mph, 150 km/h; power-weight ratio: 1200 Populaire 2-dr. Sedan 26.1 lb/hp, 11.8 kg/hp; consumption: 39.8 m/imp gal, 33.1 m/US gal, 7.1 l x 100 km.

CHASSIS integral; front suspension: independent, by McPherson, coil springs/telescopic damper struts, lower wishbones, anti-roll bar; rear: rigid axle, semi-elliptic leafsprings, telescopic dampers.

STEERING recirculating ball, variable ratio.

BRAKES drum (front disc for GL and SL-5 models only); lining area: front 60.3 sq in, 389 sq cm, rear 47.8 sq in, 308 sq cm, total 108.1 sq in, 697 sq cm.

ELECTRICAL EQUIPMENT 12 V; 32 Ah battery; 35 A alternator; Mitsubishi distributor; 2 headlamps.

DIMENSIONS AND WEIGHT wheel base: 92.13 in, 234 cm; tracks: Populaire models 50 in, 127 cm - GL and SL-5 models 50.59 in, 128 cm front, 49.21 in, 125 cm rear; length: 157.28 in, 399 cm; width: 60.43 in, 153 cm; height: 53.74 in, 136 cm; ground clearance: 6.50 in, 16.5 cm; weight: Populaire 2-dr. 1,830 lb, 830 kg - Populaire 4-dr. 1,885 lb, 855 kg - GL 2-dr. 1,841 lb, 835 kg - GL 4-dr. 1,896 lb, 860 kg - SL-5 2-dr. 1,852 lb, 840 kg - SL-5 4-dr. 1,907 lb, 865 kg; weight distribution: 56% front, 44% rear; turning circle (between walls): 31.5 ft, 9.6 m; fuel tank: 11 imp gal, 13.2 US gal, 50 l.

BODY 5 seats, separate front seats, reclining backrests, built-in headrests.

PRACTICAL INSTRUCTIONS fuel: 85-90 oct petrol; oil: engine 6.2 imp pt, 7.4 US pt, 3.5 l, SAE 20W-30, change every 3,100 miles, 5,000 km - gearbox 3 imp pt, 3.6 US pt, 1.7 l, SAE 90, change every 24,900 miles, 40,000 km - final drive 1.9 imp pt, 2.3 US pt, 1.1 l, SAE 90, change every 24,000 miles, 40,000 km.

MITSUBISHI Minica Ami 55 XL Sedan

82 hp power team

See 70 hp power team, except for:

ENGINE 87.8 cu in, 1,439 cc (2.87 x 3.39 in, 73 x 86 mm); max power (JIS): 82 hp at 5,400 rpm; max torque (JIS): 89 lb ft, 12.3 kg m at 3,000 rpm; 57 hp/l; 1 Stromberg 28-32 DIDSA downdraught twin barrel carburettor.

TRANSMISSION axle ratio: 3.909 - SL-5 models 4.222.

PERFORMANCE max speed: 96 mph, 155 km/h; power-weight ratio: GL 2-dr. 22.9 lb/hp, 10.4 kg/hp; consumption: SL-5 models 36.6 m/imp gal, 30.5 m/US gal, 7.7 l x 100 km.

BRAKES front disc, rear drum; lining area: front 19.8 sq in, 128 sq cm, rear 47.8 sq in, 308 sq cm, total 67.6 sq in, 436 sq cm.

DIMENSIONS AND WEIGHT front track: 50.59 in, 128 cm; weight: GL 2-dr. and SL-5 2-dr. 1,885 lb, 855 kg - GL 4-dr. and SL-5 4-dr. 1,940 lb, 880 kg.

OPTIONAL ACCESSORIES (for GL 4-dr. Sedan only) Borg-Warner 35 automatic transmission with 3 ratios (I 2.450, II 1.450, III 1, rev 2.222).

86 hp power team

See 70 hp power team, except for:

ENGINE 97.4 cu in, 1,597 cc (3.03 x 3.39 in, 76.9 x 86 mm); compression ratio: 8.5:1; max power (JIS): 86 hp at 5,000 rpm; max torque (JIS): 98 lb ft, 13.5 kg m at 3,000 rpm; Mitsubishi twin contra-rotating omni-phase balancing shafts; 1 Stromberg 28-32 DIDSA downdraught twin barrel carburettor.

TRANSMISSION gears: 5, fully synchronized; ratios: I 3.215, II 2, III 1.316, IV 1, V 0.853, rev 3.667; axle ratio: 3.909.

PERFORMANCE max speed: 96 mph, 155 km/h; power-weight ratio: 22.9 lb/hp, 10.4 kg/hp; speed in top at 1,000 rpm: 14.8 mph, 23.8 km/h; consumption: 38.1 m/imp gal, 31.8 m/US gal, 7.4 l x 100 km.

BRAKES front disc, rear drum; lining area: front 19.8 sq in, 128 sq cm, rear 47.8 sq in, 308 sq cm, total 67.6 sq in, 436 sq cm.

DIMENSIONS AND WEIGHT front track: 50.59 in, 128 cm; weight: 1,973 lb, 895 kg.

100 hp power team

See 70 hp power team, except for:

ENGINE 97.4 cu in, 1,597 cc (3.03 x 3.39 in, 76.9 x 86 mm); compression ratio: 9.5:1; max power (JIS): 100 hp at 6,300 rpm; max torque (JIS): 98 lb ft, 13.5 kg m at 4,000 rpm; max engine rpm: 7,000; 62.6 hp/l; Mitsubishi twin contra-rotating balancing shafts incorporated with crankshaft; camshafts: cogged belt; 2 Stromberg 28-32 DISDA downdraught twin barrel carburettors; emission control thermal

MITSUBISHI Lancer 1200 SL-5 2-door Sedan

reactor, secondary air injection and exhaust gas recirculation.

TRANSMISSION gears: 5, fully synchronized; ratios: I 3.215, II 2, III 1.316, IV 1, V 0.853, rev 3.667; final drive: limited slip differential; tyres: 155 SR x 13.

PERFORMANCE max speed: 103 mph, 165 km/h; power-weight ratio: 19.6 lb/hp, 8.9 kg/hp.

BRAKES front disc, rear drum; lining area: front 19.8 sq in, 128 sq cm, rear 47.8 sq in, 308 sq cm, total 67.6 sq in, 436 sq cm.

DIMENSIONS AND WEIGHT tracks: 51.18 in, 130 cm front, 50 in, 127 cm rear; weight: 1,962 lb, 890 kg.

PRACTICAL INSTRUCTIONS fuel: 98-100 oct petrol; valve timing: 24° 64° 67° 21°.

Celeste Series

PRICES (Tokyo):

1 1400 SR Coupé	917,000	yen
2 1400 GL Coupé	957,000	yen
3 1400 SL Coupé	1,013,000	yen
4 1600 GL Coupé	1,099,000	yen
5 1600 XL Coupé	1,097,000	yen
6 1600 GT Coupé	1,149,000	yen
7 1600 GSR Coupé	1,122,000	yen

Power team:	Standard for:	Optional for:
82 hp	1 to 3	—
86 hp	4 to 6	—
100 hp	7	—

82 hp power team

ENGINE front, 4 stroke; 4 cylinders, vertical, in line; 87.8 cu in, 1,439 cc (2.87 x 3.39 in, 73 x 86 mm); compression ratio: 9:1; max power (JIS): 82 hp at 5,400 rpm; max torque (JIS): 89 lb ft, 12.3 kg m at 3,000 rpm; max engine rpm: 6,000; 56.9 hp/l; cast iron block, light alloy head; 5 crankshaft bearings; valves: overhead, Vee-slanted, rockers; camshafts: 1, overhead; lubrication: rotary pump, full flow filter, 7 imp pt, 8.5 US pt, 4 l, 1 Stromberg 28-32 DIDTA downdraught twin barrel carburettor; Mitsubishi MCA-Jet super lean-burn low emission engine with third air inlet valve, exhaust gas recirculation and small capacity catalyst in exhaust manifold; fuel feed: mechanical pump; water-cooled, 10.6 imp pt, 12.7 US pt, 6 l.

TRANSMISSION driving wheels: rear; clutch: single dry plate (diaphragm); gearbox: mechanical; gears: 4 (5 for GSL only), fully synchronized; ratios: I 3.525, II 2.193, III 1.442, IV 1, rev 3.867 - GSL I 3.215, II 2, III 1.316, IV 1, V 0.853, rev 3.667; lever: central; final drive: hypoid bevel; axle ratio: 3.909 - GSL 4.222; width of rims: 4.5''; tyres 155 SR x 13.

PERFORMANCE max speeds: (I) 28 mph, 45 km/h; (II) 45 mph, 72 km/h; (III) 67 mph, 108 km/h; (IV) 96 mph, 155 km/h; power-weight ratio: 32.1 lb/hp, 14.5 kg/hp; carrying capacity: 882 lb, 400 kg; consumption: 36.6 m/imp gal, 30.5 m/US gal, 7.7 l x 100 km.

CHASSIS integral; front suspension: independent, by McPherson, coil springs/telescopic damper struts, lower wishbones (trailing links), anti-roll bar; rear: rigid axle, semi-elliptic leafsprings, telescopic dampers.

STEERING recirculating ball, variable ratio.

BRAKES front disc, rear drum, rear compensator.

ELECTRICAL EQUIPMENT 12 V; 32 Ah battery; 35 A alternator; Mitsubishi distributor; 2 headlamps.

DIMENSIONS AND WEIGHT wheel base: 92.13 in, 234 cm; tracks: 52.17 in, 132 cm front, 50.98 in, 129 cm rear; length: 162.01 in, 411 cm; width: 63.39 in, 161 cm; height: 52.17 in, 132 cm; ground clearance: 6.30 in, 16 cm; weight: 2,635 lb, 1,195 kg; weight distribution: 55.4% front, 44.6% rear; fuel tank: 11 imp gal, 13.2 US gal, 50 l.

BODY 2 + 1 doors; 5 seats, separate front seats.

PRACTICAL INSTRUCTIONS fuel: 85-90 oct petrol; oil: engine 7 imp pt, 8.5 US pt, 4 l, SAE 20W-30, change every 3,100 miles, 5,000 km - gearbox 3 imp pt, 3.6 US pt, 1.7 l, SAE 90, change every 24,900 miles, 40,000 km - final drive 1.9 imp pt, 2.3 US pt, 1.1 l, SAE 90, change every 24,900 miles, 40,000 km; tappet clearances (hot): inlet 0.006 in, 0.15 mm, exhaust 0.010 in, 0.25 mm; valve timing: 20° 48° 51° 17°.

OPTIONAL ACCESSORIES (for GL only) Borg-Warner 35 automatic transmission with 3 ratios (I 2.680, II 1.508, III 1, rev 2.310).

MITSUBISHI Celeste 1400 SR Coupé

86 hp power team

See 82 hp power team, except for:

ENGINE 97.4 cu in, 1,597 cc (3.03 x 3.39 in, 76.9 x 86 mm); compression ratio: 8.5:1; max power (JIS): 86 hp at 5,000 rpm; max torque (JIS): 98 lb ft, 13.5 kg m at 3,000 rpm; 57.6 hp/l; Mitsubishi twin contra-rotating balancing shafts incorporated with crankshaft; camshafts: cogged belt.

TRANSMISSION gearbox: GL automatic transmission, hydraulic torque converter and planetary gears with 3 ratios - XL and GT 5-speed fully synchronized mechanical gearbox; ratios: GL I 2.680, II 1.508, III 1, rev 2.310 - XL and GT I 3.215, II 2, III 1.316, IV 1, V 0.853, rev 3.667; axle ratio: 3.909; tyres: GT 175/70 HR x 13.

PERFORMANCE max speed: GL 93 mph, 150 km/h - XL and GT 99 mph, 160 km/h; power-weight ratio: GL and GT 24.4 lb/hp, 11 kg/hp - XL 24 lb/hp, 10.9 kg/hp; consumption: 38.2 m/imp gal, 31.8 m/US gal, 7.4 l x 100 km.

DIMENSIONS AND WEIGHT length: GT 166.54 in, 423 cm; weight: GL and GT 2,095 lb, 950 kg - XL 2,062 lb, 935 kg.

100 hp power team

See 82 hp power team, except for:

ENGINE 97.4 cu in, 1,597 cc (3.03 x 3.39 in, 76.9 x 86 mm); compression ratio: 9.5:1; max power (JIS): 100 hp at 6,300 rpm; max torque (JIS): 98 lb ft, 13.5 kg m at 4,000 rpm; 62.6 hp/l; 2 Stromberg 28-32 DIDTA downdraught twin barrel carburettors; emission control thermal reactor, secondary air injection and exhaust gas recirculation.

TRANSMISSION gears: 5, fully synchronized; ratios: I 3.215, II 2, III 1.316, IV 1, V 0.853, rev 3.667; axle ratio: 4.222; tyres: 175/70 HR x 13.

PERFORMANCE max speeds: (I) 31 mph, 50 km/h; (II) 51 mph, 82 km/h; (III) 79 mph, 127 km/h; (IV) 103 mph, 165 km/h; (V) 103 mph, 165 km/h; power-weight ratio: 28.8 lb/hp, 9.4 kg/hp.

DIMENSIONS AND WEIGHT weight: 2,084 lb, 945 kg.

PRACTICAL INSTRUCTIONS fuel: 98 oct petrol; valve timing: 24° 64° 67° 21°.

Galant Sigma Series

PRICES (Tokyo):

1 1600 Custom 4-door Sedan	997,000	yen
2 1600 GL 4-door Sedan	1,062,000	yen
3 1600 SL 4-door Sedan	1,107,000	yen
4 1600 SL Super 4-door Sedan	1,187,000	yen
5 1850 GL 4-door Sedan	1,149,000	yen
6 1850 SL 4-door Sedan	1,184,000	yen
7 2000 GLX 4-door Sedan	1,234,000	yen
8 2000 Super 4-door Sedan	1,447,000	yen
9 2000 GSL 4-door Sedan	1,294,000	yen
10 2000 GSR 4-door Sedan	1,335,000	yen

For GB prices, see price index.

Power team:	Standard for:	Optional for:
86 hp	1 to 4	—
97 hp	5,6	—
105 hp	7 to 9	—
115 hp	10	—

86 hp power team

ENGINE front, 4 stroke; 4 cylinders, in line; 97.4 cu in, 1,597 cc (3.03 x 3.39 in, 76.9 x 86 mm); compression ratio: 8.5:1; max power (JIS): 86 hp at 5,000 rpm; max torque (JIS): 98 lb ft, 13.5 kg m at 3,000 rpm; max engine rpm: 5,700; 53.8 hp/l; cast iron block, light alloy head; 5 crankshaft bearings; Mitsubishi Saturn 80 omni-phase balancing shafts; valves: overhead, Vee-slanted, rockers; camshafts: 1, overhead; lubrication: rotar pump, full flow filter, 7 imp pt, 8.5 US pt, 4 l; 1 Stromberg 28-32 DIDTA downdraught twin barrel carburettor; Mitsubishi MCA-Jet super lean-burn low emission engine, with third air inlet valve, exhaust gas recirculation and catalyst in exhaust manifold; fuel feed: mechanical pump; water-cooled, 10.6 imp pt, 12.7 US pt, 6 l.

TRANSMISSION driving wheels: rear; clutch: single dry plate (diaphragm); gearbox: mechanical; gears: 4 (5 for SL only), fully synchronized; ratios: I 3.525, II 2.193, III 1.442, IV 1, rev 3.867 - SL I 3.215, II 2, III 1.316, IV 1, V 0.853, rev 3.667; lever: central; final drive: hypoid bevel; axle ratio: 3.909 - SL 4.222; width of rims: 4.5'' (5'' for SL only); tyres: 6.45 x 13 - SL 165 SR x 13.

PERFORMANCE max speeds: (I) 28 mph, 45 km/h; (II) 45 mph, 72 km/h; (III) 68 mph, 110 km/h; (IV) 96 mph, 155 km/h - SL (V) 96 mph, 155 km/h; power-weight ratio: Custom and GL 25.2 lb/hp, 11.4 kg/hp - SL 25.5 lb/hp, 11.5 kg/hp - SL Super 25.7 lb/hp, 11.7 kg/hp; consumption: not declared.

CHASSIS integral; front suspension: independent, by McPherson, coil springs/telescopic damper struts, lower wishbones (trailing links), anti-roll bar; rear: rigid axle, semi-elliptic leafsprings, telescopic dampers.

STEERING recirculating ball, variable ratio.

BRAKES front disc, rear drum, servo; lining area: front 19.2 sq in, 124 sq cm, rear 47.8 sq in, 308 sq cm, total 67 sq in, 432 sq cm.

ELECTRICAL EQUIPMENT 12 V; 35 Ah battery; 40 A alternator; Mitsubishi distributor; 4 headlamps.

DIMENSIONS AND WEIGHT wheel base: 99.02 in, 251 cm; tracks: 53.15 in, 135 cm front, 52.76 in, 134 cm rear; length: 169.29 in, 430 cm; width: 65.16 in, 165 cm; height: 53.54 in, 136 cm; ground clearance: 6.30 in, 16 cm; weight: Custom and GL 2,172 lb, 985 kg - SL 2,194 lb, 995 kg - SL Super 2,216 lb, 1,005 kg; turning circle (between walls): 36.1 ft, 11 m; fuel tank: 13.2 imp gal, 15.8 US gal, 60 l.

BODY 4 doors; 5 seats, separate front seats.

MITSUBISHI Galant Sigma 1600 SL 4-door Sedan

PRACTICAL INSTRUCTIONS fuel: 85-90 oct petrol; oil: engine 7 imp pt, 8.5 US pt, 4 l, SAE 20W-30, change every 3,100 miles, 5,000 km - gearbox 3 imp pt, 3.6 US pt, 1.7 l - SL 3.5 imp pt, 4.2 US pt, 2 l, SAE 80, change every 24,900 miles, 40,000 km - final drive 1.9 imp pt, 2.3 US pt, 1.1 l, SAE 90, change every 24,000 miles, 40,000 km; tappet clearances (hot): inlet 0.006 in, 0.15 mm, exhaust 0.010 in, 0.25 mm; valve timing: 20° 48° 51° 17°.

OPTIONAL ACCESSORIES (for GL only) Borg-Warner 35 automatic transmission with 3 ratios (I 2.450, II 1.450, III 1, rev 2.222).

97 hp power team

See 86 hp power team, except for:

ENGINE 113.2 cu in, 1,855 cc (3.19 x 3.54 in, 81 x 90 mm); max power (JIS): 97 hp at 5,700 rpm; max torque (JIS): 107 lb ft, 14.7 kg m at 3,800 rpm; max engine rpm: 6,200; 52.3 hp/l; Mitsubishi Astron 80 twin contra-rotating balancing shafts incorporated with crankshaft; lubrication: gear pump, full flow filter, 7.6 imp pt, 9.1 US pt, 4.3 l; 1 Stromberg 30-32 DIDTA downdraught twin barrel carburettor; cooling system: 13.6 imp pt, 16.3 US pt, 7.7 l.

TRANSMISSION gears: (for SL only) 5, fully synchronized; ratios: I 3.369, II 2.035, III 1.360, IV 1, V 0.856, rev 3.635; axle ratio: GL 3.545 - SL 3.909; width of rims: 5''; tyres: 165 SR x 13.

PERFORMANCE max speeds: GL (I) 29 mph, 47 km/h; (II) 47 mph, 75 km/h; (III) 70 mph, 113 km/h; (IV) 99 mph, 160 km/h - SL (I) 28 mph, 45 km/h; (II) 45 mph, 73 km/h; (III) 68 mph, 110 km/h; (IV) 93 mph, 150 km/h; (V) 103 mph, 165 km/h; power-weight ratio: GL 23.7 lb/hp, 10.7 kg/hp - SL 23.9 lb/hp, 10.9 kg/hp.

DIMENSIONS AND WEIGHT weight: GL 2,304 lb, 1,045 kg - SL 2,326 lb, 1,055 kg.

PRACTICAL INSTRUCTIONS oil: engine 7.6 imp pt, 9.1 US pt, 4.3 l; valve timing: 25° 55° 62° 14°.

105 hp power team

See 86 hp power team, except for:

ENGINE 121.7 cu in, 1,995 cc (3.31 x 3.54 in, 84 x 90 mm); max power (JIS): 105 hp at 5,400 rpm; max torque (JIS): 119 lb ft, 16.5 kg m at 3,500 rpm; 52.6 hp/l; Mitsubishi Astron 80 twin contra-rotating balancing shafts incorporated with crankshaft; lubrication: gear pump, full flow filter, 7.6 imp pt, 9.1 US pt, 4.3 l; 1 Stromberg 30-32 DIDTA downdraught twin barrel carburettor; cooling system: 13.6 imp pt, 16.3 US pt, 7.7 l.

TRANSMISSION gears: 5, fully synchronized; ratios: I 3.369, II 2.035, III 1.360, IV 1, V 0.856, rev 3.635; width of rims: 5''; tyres: GLX 6.45 x 13 - Super 165 SR x 14 - GSL 185/70 HR x 13.

PERFORMANCE max speeds: (I) 28 mph, 45 km/h; (II) 45 mph, 73 km/h; (III) 68 mph, 110 km/h; (IV) 92 mph, 148

MITSUBISHI Galant Sigma 1600 SL 4-door Sedan

105 HP POWER TEAM

km/h; (V) 102 mph, 165 km/h; power-weight ratio: GLX and GSL 22.3 lb/hp, 10.1 kg/hp - Super 23.4 lb/hp, 10.6 kg/hp; consumption: 32.4 m/imp gal, 27 m/US gal, 8.7 l x 100 km.

BRAKES disc (for Super only).

DIMENSIONS AND WEIGHT length: 170.47 in, 433 cm; weight: GLX and GLS 2,348 lb, 1,065 kg - Super 2,459 lb, 1,115 kg.

PRACTICAL INSTRUCTIONS oil: engine 7.6 imp pt, 9.1 US pt, 4.3 l; valve timing: 25° 55° 62° 14°.

OPTIONAL ACCESSORIES (for GLX and Super only) Borg-Warner 35 automatic transmission with 3 ratios (I 2.450, II 1.450, III 1, rev 2.222), 3.545 axle ratio; (for Super only) power-steering.

115 hp power team

See 105 hp power team, except for:

ENGINE compression ratio: 9.5:1; max power (JIS): 115 hp at 6,000 rpm; max torque (JIS): 120 lb ft, 16.5 kg m at 4,000 rpm; 57.6 hp/l; 2 Stromberg 28-32 DIDSA downdraught twin barrel carburettors; emission control system with thermal reactor, air injection and exhaust gas recirculation.

TRANSMISSION tyres: 185/70 HR x 13.

PERFORMANCE max speed: 109 mph, 175 km/h; power-weight ratio: 20.7 lb/hp, 9.4 kg/hp; speed in top at 1,000 rpm: 17.8 mph, 28.6 km/h.

BRAKES disc.

ELECTRICAL EQUIPMENT electronic ignition.

DIMENSIONS AND WEIGHT weight: 2,381 lb, 1,080 kg.

PRACTICAL INSTRUCTIONS fuel: 98-100 oct petrol; oil: gearbox 4 imp pt, 4.9 US pt, 2.3 l; valve timing: 24° 64° 59° 25°.

Galant Lambda Series

PRICES (Tokyo):

1 1600 SL 2-door Coupé	**1,195,000**	yen
2 1600 GS 2-door Coupé	**1,240,000**	yen
3 2000 GSL 2-door Coupé	**1,370,000**	yen
4 2000 Super Touring 2-door Coupé	**1,626,000**	yen
5 2000 Super Touring Automatic 2-door Coupé	**1,666,000**	yen
6 2000 GSR 2-door Coupé	**1,519,000**	yen

Power team:	Standard for:	Optional for:
86 hp	1	—
100 hp	2	—
105 hp	3 to 5	—
115 hp	6	—

86 hp power team

ENGINE front, 4 stroke; 4 cylinders, in line; 97.45 cu in, 1,597 cc (3.03 x 3.38 in, 77 x 86 mm); compression ratio: 8.5:1; max power (JIS): 86 hp at 5,000 rpm; max torque (JIS): 98 lb ft, 13.5 kg m at 3,000 rpm; max engine rpm: 5,700; 53.9 hp/l; cast iron block, light alloy head; Mitsubishi twin contra-rotating balancing shafts incorporated with crankshaft; valves: overhead, rockers; camshafts: 1, overhead; lubrication: rotary pump, full flow filter, 7 imp pt, 8.4 US pt, 4 l; 1 Stromberg 30-32 DIDTA downdraught twin barrel carburettor; Mitsubishi MCA-Jet super lean-burn low emission engine with third air inlet valve, exhaust gas recirculation and small capacity catalyst in exhaust manifold; fuel feed: mechanical pump; water-cooled, 10.6 imp pt, 12.7 US pt, 6 l.

TRANSMISSION driving wheels: rear; clutch: single dry plate (diaphragm); gearbox: mechanical; gears: 5, fully synchronized; ratios: I 3.215, II 2, III 1.316, IV 1, V 0.853, rev 3.667; lever: central; final drive: hypoid bevel; axle ratio: 4.222; width of rims: 5''; tyres: 165 SR x 13.

PERFORMANCE max speed: 96 mph, 155 km/h; power-weight ratio: 26.5 lb/hp, 12 kg/hp; consumption: 32.4 m/imp gal, 27 m/US gal, 8.7 l x 100 km.

CHASSIS integral; front suspension: independent, by McPherson, coil springs/telescopic damper struts, anti-roll bar, lower wishbones; rear: rigid axle, semi-elliptic leaf-springs, telescopic dampers.

STEERING recirculating ball, variable ratio.

BRAKES front disc, rear drum.

ELECTRICAL EQUIPMENT 12 V; 35 Ah battery; 45 A alternator; Mitsubishi distributor; 4 headlamps.

DIMENSIONS AND WEIGHT wheel base: 99.02 in, 251 cm; tracks: 53.94 in, 137 cm front, 53.54 in, 136 cm rear; length: 174.41 in, 443 cm; width: 65.94 in, 167 cm; height: 52.36 in, 133 cm; ground clearance: 6.30 in, 16 cm; weight: 2,282 lb, 1,035 kg; turning circle (between walls): 36.1 ft, 11 m; fuel tank: 13.2 imp gal, 15.8 US gal, 60 l.

BODY 5 seats, separate front seats.

PRACTICAL INSTRUCTIONS fuel: 85-90 oct petrol; oil: engine 7 imp pt, 8.4 US pt, 4 l, SAE 20W-30, change every 3,100 miles, 5,000 km - gearbox 4 imp pt, 4.9 US pt, 2.3 l, SAE 80, change every 24,900 miles, 40,000 km - final drive 1.9 imp pt, 2.3 US pt, 1.1 l, SAE 80, change every 24,900 miles, 40,000 km; tappet clearances: inlet 0.006 in, 0.15 mm, exhaust 0.010 in, 0.25 mm; valve timing: 25° 55° 62° 14°; tyre pressure: front and rear 24 psi, 1.7 atm.

OPTIONAL ACCESSORIES Borg-Warner 35 automatic transmission with 3 ratios (I 2.450, II 1.450, III 1, rev 2.222).

100 hp power team

See 86 hp power team, except for:

ENGINE compression ratio: 9.5:1; max power (JIS): 100 hp at 6,000 rpm; max torque (JIS): 98 lb ft, 13.5 kg m

MITSUBISHI Galant Lambda 2000 Super Touring 2-door Coupé

MITSUBISHI Galant Sigma 2000 Super 4-door Sedan

at 3,000 rpm; 62.6 hp/l; 2 Stromberg 28-32 DIDSA downdraught twin barrel carburettors; emission control thermal reactor, exhaust gas recirculation.

TRANSMISSION tyres: 185/70 HR x 13.

PERFORMANCE max speed: 103 mph, 165 km/h; power-weight ratio: 23.4 lb/hp, 10.6 kg/hp.

DIMENSIONS AND WEIGHT weight: 2,337 lb, 1,060 kg.

105 hp power team

See 86 hp power team, except for:

ENGINE 121.7 cu in, 1,995 cc (3.31 x 3.54 in, 84 x 90 mm); max power (JIS): 105 hp at 5,400 rpm; max torque (JIS): 120 lb ft, 16.5 kg m at 3,500 rpm; lubrication: 7.6 imp pt, 9.1 US pt, 4.3 l; cooling system: 12.3 imp pt, 14.8 US pt, 7 l.

TRANSMISSION gearbox: mechanical - Super Touring Automatic automatic transmission, hydraulic torque converter and planetary gears with 3 ratios; ratios: I 3.369, II 2.035, III 1.360, IV 1, V 0.856, rev 3.650 - Super Touring Automatic I 2.450, II 1.450, III 1, rev 2.220; axle ratio: 3.889 - Super Touring Automatic 3.545; tyres: 165 SR x 14 - Super Touring models 195/70 HR x 14.

MITSUBISHI Galant Lambda 1600 SL 2-door Coupé

PERFORMANCE max speeds: (I) 30 mph, 48 km/h; (II) 48 mph, 77 km/h; (III) 73 mph, 117 km/h; (IV) 98 mph, 158 km/h; (V) 103 mph, 165 km/h; power-weight ratio: GSL 23.3 lb/hp, 10.6 kg/hp - Super Touring models 24.4 lb/hp, 11.1 kg/hp.

STEERING Super Touring Automatic servo.

BRAKES disc, servo; lining area: front 32.9 sq in, 219 sq cm, rear 19.8 sq in, 128 sq cm, total 52.7 sq in, 340 sq cm.

DIMENSIONS AND WEIGHT length: Super Touring models 177.56 in, 451 cm; weight: GSL 2,447 lb, 1,110 kg - Super Touring models 2,569 lb, 1,165 kg.

115 hp power team

See 105 hp power team, except for:

ENGINE compression ratio: 9.5:1; max power (JIS): 115 hp at 6,000 rpm; max engine rpm: 6,500; 57.6 hp/l; 2 Stromberg 28-32 DIDSA downdraught twin barrel carburettors; emission control with thermal reactor, secondary air injection and exhaust gas recirculation.

TRANSMISSION width of rims: 5.5''; tyres: 195/70 HR x 14.

PERFORMANCE max speeds: (I) 34 mph, 54 km/h; (II) 56 mph, 90 km/h; (III) 83 mph, 133 km/h; (IV) 103 mph, 165

MITSUBISHI Debonair Executive SE 4-door Sedan

MITSUBISHI Debonair Executive SE 4-door Sedan

km/h; (V) 109 mph, 175 km/h; power weight ratio: 21.6 lb/hp, 9.8 kg/hp.

DIMENSIONS AND WEIGHT weight: 2,480 lb, 1,125 kg.

PRACTICAL INSTRUCTIONS valve timing: 24° 64° 59° 25°; tyre pressure: front and rear 28 psi, 2 atm.

Debonair Series

PRICES (Tokyo):

Executive SE 4-door Sedan	**2,340,000 yen**
Executive SE 6-passenger 4-door Sedan	**2,280,000 yen**

120 hp power team

ENGINE front, 4 stroke; 4 cylinders, in line; 155.9 cu in, 2,555 cc (3.59 x 3.86 in, 91.1 x 98 mm); compression ratio: 8.2:1; max power (JIS): 120 hp at 5,000 rpm; max torque (JIS): 152 lb ft, 21 kg m at 3,000 rpm; max engine rpm: 5,500; 47 hp/l; cast iron block, light alloy head; Mitsubishi twin contra-rotating balancing shafts; 5 crankshaft bearings; valves: overhead, rockers; camshafts: 1, overhead; lubrication: rotary pump, full flow filter, 8.8 imp pt, 10.6 US pt, 5 l; 1 Stromberg 30-32 DIDTA downdraught twin barrel carburettor; emission control with thermal reactor and exhaust gas recirculation; fuel feed: mechanical pump; water-cooled, 13.2 imp pt, 15.9 US pt, 7.5 l.

TRANSMISSION driving wheels: rear; gearbox: automatic transmission, hydraulic torque converter and planetary gears with 3 ratios; ratios: I 2.680, II 1.508, III 1, rev 2.310; lever: steering column; final drive: hypoid bevel; axle ratio: 3.889; tyres: 175 SR x 14.

PERFORMANCE max speeds: (I) 35 mph, 57 km/h; (II) 65 mph, 105 km/h; (III) 96 mph, 155 km/h; power-weight ratio: 25.5 lb/hp, 11.6 kg/hp; consumption: not declared.

CHASSIS integral; front suspension: independent, double wishbones, coil springs/telescopic dampers, anti-roll bar; rear: rigid axle, semi-elliptic leafsprings, telescopic dampers.

STEERING recirculating ball, servo.

BRAKES front disc, rear drum, servo.

ELECTRICAL EQUIPMENT 12 V; 60 Ah battery; 55 A alternator; Mitsubishi distributor; 4 headlamps.

DIMENSIONS AND WEIGHT wheel base: 105.91 in, 269 cm; front and rear track: 54.72 in, 139 cm; length: 183.86 in, 467 cm; width: 66.54 in, 169 cm; height: 57.48 in, 146 cm; ground clearance: 6.69 in, 17 cm; weight: 3,065 lb, 1,390 kg; weight distribution: 56% front, 44% rear; fuel tank: 15.4 imp gal, 18.5 US gal, 70 l.

BODY 5 seats, separate front seats - Executive 6-passenger, 6 seats, bench front seat.

PRACTICAL INSTRUCTIONS fuel: 85-90 oct petrol; oil: en-

gine 8.8 imp pt, 10.6 US pt, 5 l, SAE 20W-30, change every 3,100 miles, 5,000 km - gearbox automatic transmission fluid change every 24,000 miles, 40,000 km - final drive 1.9 imp pt, 2.3 US pt, 1.1 l, SAE 90, change every 24,000 miles, 40,000 km; tappet clearances: inlet 0.006 in, 0.15 mm, exhaust 0.010 in, 0.25 mm; valve timing: 25° 59° 64° 20°.

Jeep H-J58

PRICE (Tokyo): 1,208,000 yen

ENGINE front, 4 stroke; 4 cylinders, vertical, in line; 121.7 cu in, 1,995 cc (3.31 x 3.54 in, 84 x 90 mm); compression ratio: 8.5:1; max power (JIS): 100 hp at 5,000 rpm; max torque (JIS): 123 lb ft, 17 kg m at 3,000 rpm; max engine rpm: 5,400; 50.1 hp/l; cast iron block, light alloy head; 5 crankshaft bearings; valves: overhead, Vee-slanted, rockers; camshafts: 1, overhead; lubrication: rotary pump, full flow filter, 7.6 imp pt, 9.1 US pt, 4.3 l; 1 Stromberg 30-32 DIDTA downdraught twin barrel carburettor; fuel feed: mechanical pump; water-cooled, 14 imp pt, 17 US pt, 8 l.

TRANSMISSION driving wheels: front (automatically-engaged with transfer box) and rear; clutch: single dry plate (diaphragm), hydraulically controlled; gearbox: mechanical; gears: 4, fully synchronized; ratios: I 2.971, II 1.795, III 1.345, IV 1, rev 3.157; transfer box: high 1, low 2.465; lever: central; final drive: hypoid bevel; axle ratio: 5.375; width of rims: 4.5''; tyres: 6.00 x 16.

PERFORMANCE max speeds: (I) 27 mph, 43 km/h; (II) 47 mph, 75 km/h; (III) 58 mph, 94 km/h; (IV) 75 mph, 120 km/h; power-weight ratio: 23.8 lb/hp, 10.8 kg/hp; carrying capacity: 551 lb, 250 kg; speed in direct drive at 1,000 rpm: 13.8 mph, 22.2 km/h; consumption: not declared.

CHASSIS ladder frame; front and rear suspension: rigid axle, semi-elliptic leafsprings, telescopic dampers.

STEERING cam and lever, variable ratio.

BRAKES drum.

ELECTRICAL EQUIPMENT 12 V; 35 Ah battery; 35 A alternator; Mitsubishi distributor; 2 headlamps.

DIMENSIONS AND WEIGHT wheel base: 79.92 in, 203 cm; front and rear track: 48.62 in, 123 cm; length: 133.46 in, 339 cm; width: 65.55 in, 166 cm; height: 75 in, 190 cm; ground clearance: 8.27 in, 21 cm; weight: 2,381 lb, 1,080 kg; weight distribution: 55% front, 45% rear; turning circle (between walls): 40 ft, 12.2 m; fuel tank: 9.7 imp gal, 11.6 US gal, 44 l.

BODY open; 2 detachable doors; 4 seats, separate front seats.

PRACTICAL INSTRUCTIONS fuel: 85-90 oct petrol; tyre pressure: front 21 psi, 1.5 atm, rear 36 psi, 2.5 atm.

Jeep H-J56

See Jeep H-J58, except for:

PRICE (Tokyo): 1,248,000 yen

ENGINE 145.5 cu in, 2,384 cc (3.46 x 3.86 in, 88 x 98 mm); compression ratio: 8:1; max power (JIS): 110 hp at 5,000 rpm; max torque (JIS): 145 lb ft, 20 kg m at 3,000 rpm; 46.1 hp/l.

PERFORMANCE power-weight ratio: 21.7 lb/hp, 9.9 kg/hp.

ELECTRICAL EQUIPMENT 50 Ah battery.

DIMENSIONS AND WEIGHT weight: 2,392 lb, 1,085 kg.

Jeep J54

See Jeep H-J58, except for:

PRICE (Tokyo): 1,343,000 yen

ENGINE Diesel, 4 stroke; 162.3 cu in, 2,659 cc (3.62 x 3.94 in, 92 x 100 mm); compression ratio: 20:1; max power (JIS): 80 hp at 3,700 rpm; max torque (JIS): 130 lb ft, 18 kg m at 2,200 rpm; 30.1 hp/l.

TRANSMISSION transfer box ratio: high 0.933, low 2.384.

PERFORMANCE power-weight ratio: 29.9 lb/hp, 13.6 kg/hp.

ELECTRICAL EQUIPMENT 24 V; 70 Ah x 2 batteries.

DIMENSIONS AND WEIGHT weight: 2,392 lb, 1,085 kg; fuel tank: 9.9 imp gal, 11.9 US gal, 45 l.

PRACTICAL INSTRUCTIONS fuel: Diesel oil.

Jeep H-J26

See Jeep H-J58, except for:

PRICE (Tokyo): 1,332,000 yen.

ENGINE 145.5 cu in, 2,384 cc (3.46 x 3.86 in, 88 x 98 mm); compression ratio: 8:1; max power (JIS): 110 hp at 5,000 rpm; max torque (JIS): 145 lb ft, 20 kg m at 3,000 rpm; 46.1 hp/l.

TRANSMISSION lever: steering column.

PERFORMANCE power-weight ratio: 25.8 lb/hp, 11.7 kg/hp.

STEERING recirculating ball.

ELECTRICAL EQUIPMENT 50 Ah battery.

DIMENSIONS AND WEIGHT wheel base: 87.60 in, 222 cm; front and rear track: 50.79 in, 129 cm; length: 145.08 in, 368 cm; width: 65.75 in, 167 cm; height: 76.77 in, 195 cm; weight: 2,844 lb, 1,290 kg.

BODY 7 seats.

Jeep J24

See Jeep H-J26, except for:

PRICE (Tokyo): 1,427,000 yen

ENGINE Diesel, 4 stroke; 162.3 cu in, 2,659 cc (3.62 x 3.94 in, 92 x 100 mm); compression ratio: 20:1; max power (JIS): 80 hp at 3,700 rpm; max torque (JIS): 130 lb ft, 18 kg m at 2,200 rpm; 30.1 hp/l.

TRANSMISSION transfer box ratios: high 0.933, low 2.348; lever: steering column.

PERFORMANCE power-weight ratio: 35.5 lb/hp, 16.1 kg/hp.

PRACTICAL INSTRUCTIONS fuel: Diesel oil.

NISSAN   JAPAN

Cherry F II Series

PRICES (Tokyo):

1	1200 Standard 2-door Sedan	658,000 yen
2	1200 De Luxe 2-door Sedan	702,000 yen
3	1200 De Luxe 4-door Sedan	729,000 yen
4	1200 De Luxe Coupé	752,000 yen
5	1200 GL 2-door Sedan	760,000 yen
6	1200 GL 4-door Sedan	787,000 yen
7	1200 GL Coupé	810,000 yen
8	1200 GL-L Coupé	840,000 yen
9	1400 GL 4-door Sedan	833,000 yen
10	1400 GL Coupé	856,000 yen
11	1400 GL-L 4-door Sedan	863,000 yen
12	1400 GL-L Coupé	886,000 yen
13	1400 GX 4-door Sedan	873,000 yen
14	1400 GX Coupé	896,000 yen
15	Datsun F10 Coupé	—
16	Datsun F10 Station Wagon	—
17	1400 Twin GX 4-door Sedan	938,000 yen
18	1400 Twin GX Coupé	936,000 yen
19	1400 Twin GX-L 4-door Sedan	968,000 yen
20	1400 Twin GX-L Coupé	966,000 yen

Ford GB and USA prices, see price index.

Power team:	Standard for:	Optional for:
68 hp	1 to 8	—
80 hp	9 to 14	—
80 hp	15,16	—
92 hp	17 to 20	—

68 hp power team

ENGINE front, transverse, 4 stroke; 4 cylinders, in line; 71.5 cu in, 1,171 cc (2.87 x 2.76 in, 73 x 70 mm); compression ratio: 9:1; max power (JIS): 68 hp at 6,000 rpm; max torque (JIS): 70 lb ft, 9.7 kg m at 3,600 rpm; max engine rpm: 6,300; 58.1 hp/l; cast iron cylinder block, light alloy head; 3 crankshaft bearings; valves: overhead, push-rods and rockers; camshafts: 1, side; lubrication: rotary pump, full flow filter, 6 imp pt, 7.2 US pt, 3.4 l; 1 Hitachi DCG 306-26 downdraught twin barrel carburettor; emission control with catalytic converter, secondary air injection and exhaust gas recirculation; fuel feed: mechanical pump; water-cooled, 9.5 imp pt, 11.4 US pt, 5.4 l.

TRANSMISSION driving wheels: front; clutch: single dry plate (diaphragm); gearbox: mechanical; gears: 4, fully synchronized; ratios: I 3.673, II 2.217, III 1.448, IV 1,

MITSUBISHI Jeep H-J58

rev 4.093; lever: central; final drive: helical spur gears; axle ratio: 4.067; width of rims: 4''; tyres: 6.00 x 12.

PERFORMANCE max speeds: (I) 26 mph, 42 km/h; (II) 42 mph, 67 km/h; (III) 64 mph, 103 km/h; (IV) 93 mph, 150 km/h; power-weight ratio: Standard 2-dr. Sedan 24 lb/hp, 10.9 kg/hp; carrying capacity: 882 lb, 400 kg; acceleration: standing ¼ mile 19.2 sec; speed in direct drive at 1,000 rpm: 14 mph, 22.7 km/h; consumption: 38.2 m/imp gal, 31.8 m/US gal, 7.4 l x 100 km.

CHASSIS integral, front auxiliary frame; front suspension: independent, by McPherson, coil springs/telescopic damper struts, lower wishbones (trailing links); rear: independent, longitudinal trailing arms, coil springs, telescopic dampers.

STEERING rack-and-pinion; turns lock to lock: 3.20.

BRAKES drum (for GL models only front disc, rear drum); lining area: front 42.2 sq in, 272 sq cm, rear 32.2 sq in, 208 sq cm, total 74.4 sq in, 480 sq cm.

ELECTRICAL EQUIPMENT 12 V; 32 Ah battery; 35 A alternator; Hitachi distributor; 2 headlamps.

DIMENSIONS AND WEIGHT wheel base: 94.29 in, 239 cm; tracks: 50 in, 127 cm front, 48.62 in, 123 cm rear; length: 151.18 in, 384 cm; width: 59.06 in, 150 cm; height: sedans 52.95 in, 134 cm - coupés 51.77 in, 131 cm; ground clearance: 6.69 in, 17 cm; dry weight: Standard 2-dr. Sedan, 1,632 lb, 740 kg - De Luxe 2-dr. Sedan 1,643 lb, 745 kg -

4-dr. Sedan 1,676 lb, 760 kg - Coupé 1,687 lb, 765 kg - GL 2-dr. Sedan 1,676 lb, 760 kg - 4-dr. Sedan 1,709 lb, 775 kg - Coupé 1,720 lb, 780 kg; distribution of weight: 64% front, 36% rear; turning circle (between walls): 34.1 ft, 10.4 m; fuel tank: 8.8 imp gal, 10.6 US gal, 40 l.

BODY 5 seats, separate front seats, reclining backrests, built-in headrests.

PRACTICAL INSTRUCTIONS fuel: 90 oct lead-free petrol; oil: engine 6 imp pt, 7.2 Us pt, 3.4 l, SAE 20W-30, change every 3,100 miles, 5,000 km - gearbox and final drive 4 imp pt, 4.9 US pt, 2.3 l, SAE 90, change every 31,000 miles, 50,000 km; tappet clearances (hot): inlet 0.014 in, 0.35 mm, exhaust 0.014 in, 0.35 mm; valve timing: 14° 54° 56° 12°; tyre pressure: front 26 psi, 1.8 atm, rear 24 psi, 1.7 atm.

80 hp power team

See 68 hp power team, except for:

ENGINE 85.2 cu in, 1,397 cc (2.99 x 3.03 in, 76 x 77 mm); compression ratio: 8.5:1; max power (JIS): 80 hp at 6,000 rpm; max torque (JIS): 83 lb ft, 11.5 kg m at 3,600 rpm; 57.3 hp/l; 1 Hitachi DCH306 downdraught twin barrel carburettor.

TRANSMISSION gearbox ratios: I 3.275, II 1.977, III 1.383, IV 1, rev 3.649; axle ratio: 3.933; width: 4.5''; tyres: 6.15 S x 13 - GX Sedan and Coupé 165/70 HR x 13.

NISSAN Cherry F II 1200 Standard 2-door Sedan

PERFORMANCE max speed: 99 mph, 160 km/h; power-weight ratio: GL 4-dr. Sedan 22 lb/hp, 10 kg/hp; consumption: 35.3 m/imp gal, 29.4 m/US gal, 8 l x 100 km.

CHASSIS front suspension: anti-roll bar.

BRAKES front disc, rear drum, servo; lining area: front 14.6 sq in, 94 sq cm, rear 32.2 sq in, 208 sq cm, total 46.8 sq in, 302 sq cm.

DIMENSIONS AND WEIGHT tracks: 50.39 in, 128 cm front, 49.02 in, 124 cm rear; dry weight: GL 4-dr. Sedan 1,764 lb, 800 kg - Coupé 1,775 lb, 805 kg - GX 4-dr. Sedan 1,775 lb, 805 kg - Coupé 1,786 lb, 810 kg.

OPTIONAL ACCESSORIES 5-speed fully synchronized mechanical gearbox (I 4.108, II 2.475, III 1.720, IV 1.254, V1, rev 4.093), 3.471 axle ratio; for GX and GL models only Nissan Sportsmatic semi-automatic transmission hydraulic torque converter, solenoid operated clutch, with 3 ratios (I 1.603, II 1, III 0.726, rev 1.846), 4.692 axle ratio; air-conditioning.

80 hp power team

(for USA only).

See 80 hp power team, except for:

ENGINE emission control with catalytic converter and exhaust gas recirculation, 49 States air injection (for California only), exhaust gas recirculation air injection.

TRANSMISSION gears: 5 (4 for Station Wagon), fully synchronized; ratios: I 4.020, II 2.480 (2.660 for California only), III 1.720, IV 1.250, V 1, rev 4.090 - Station Wagon I 3.280, II 1.980, III 1.380, IV 1, rev 3.650; axle ratio: 3.470; tyres: 165 HR x 13 - Station Wagon 6.15 x 13.

PERFORMANCE power-weight ratio: Coupé 24.7 lb/hp, 11.2 kg/hp - Station Wagon 24.3 lb/hp, 11 kg/hp.

CHASSIS (for Station Wagon only) rear suspension: rigid axle, semi-elliptic leafsprings, telescopic dampers.

DIMENSIONS AND WEIGHT rear track: Station Wagon 50.20 in, 127 cm; length: 155.50 in, 395 cm; height: Station Wagon 53.70 in, 136 cm; weight: Coupé 1,970 lb, 893 kg - Station Wagon 1,950 lb, 884 kg.

92 hp power team

See 80 hp power team, except for:

ENGINE max power (JIS): 92 hp at 6,400 rpm; max torque (JIS): 85 lb ft, 11.7 kg m at 4,400 rpm; max engine rpm: 7,300; 65.8 hp/l; 2 Hitachi HJC 38 W-1 horizontal carburettors.

TRANSMISSION tyres: 165/70 HR x 13.

PERFORMANCE max speed: 103 mph, 165 km/h; power-weight ratio: Twin GX 4-dr. Sedan 19.2 lb/hp, 8.7 kg/hp.

DIMENSIONS AND WEIGHT weight: Twin GX 4-dr. Sedan 1,775 lb, 805 kg - Twin GX Coupé 1,786 lb, 810 kg - Twin GX-L 4-dr. Sedan 1,775 lb, 805 kg - Twin GX-L Coupé 1,786 lb, 810 kg.

PRACTICAL INSTRUCTIONS valve timing: 20° 56° 58° 18°.

Sunny Series

PRICES (Tokyo):

1 1200 Semi De Luxe 2-door Sedan	737,000	yen
2 1200 Semi De Luxe 4-door Sedan	757,000	yen
3 1200 De Luxe 2-door Sedan	788,000	yen
4 1200 De Luxe 4-door Sedan	808,000	yen
5 1200 De Luxe Coupé	838,000	yen
6 1200 GL 2-door Sedan	850,000	yen
7 1200 GL 4-door Sedan	870,000	yen
8 1200 GL Coupé	910,000	yen
9 1400 De Luxe 2-door Sedan	833,000	yen
10 1400 De Luxe 4-door Sedan	853,000	yen
11 1400 De Luxe Coupé	883,000	yen
12 1400 GL 2-door Sedan	902,000	yen
13 1400 GL 4-door Sedan	917,000	yen
14 1400 GL Coupé	947,000	yen
15 1400 SGL 4-door Sedan	975,000	yen
16 1400 SGL Coupé	1,010,000	yen
17 1400 GX 4-door Sedan	962,000	yen
18 1400 GX Coupé	1,001,000	yen
19 1400 SGX 4-door Sedan	1,020,000	yen
20 1400 SGX Coupé	1,064,000	yen

For USA prices, see price index.

Power team:	Standard for:	Optional for:
70 hp	1 to 8	—
80 hp	9 to 20	—

NISSAN Sunny 1200 De Luxe 2-door Sedan

70 hp power team

ENGINE front, 4 stroke; 4 cylinders, vertical, in line; 75.48 cu in, 1,237 cc (2.95 x 2.76 in, 75 x 70 mm); compression ratio: 9:1; max power (JIS): 70 hp at 6,000 rpm; max torque (JIS): 73.9 lb ft, 10.2 kg m at 3,600 rpm; max engine rpm: 6,250; 56.6 hp/l; cast iron cylinder block, light alloy head; 5 crankshaft bearings; valves: overhead, push-rods and rockers; camshafts: 1, side; lubrication: rotary pump, full flow filter, 6 imp pt, 7.2 US pt, 3.4 l; 1 Hitachi DCH 306-41 downdraught twin barrel carburettor; emission control with catalytic converter, secondary air injection and exhaust gas recirculation; fuel feed: mechanical pump; water-cooled, 7 imp pt, 8.4 US pt, 4 l.

TRANSMISSION driving wheels: rear; clutch: single dry plate (diaphragm); gearbox: mechanical; gears: 4, fully synchronized; ratios: I 3.757, II 2.169, III 1.404, IV 1, rev 3.640; lever: central; final drive: hypoid bevel; axle ratio: 3.889; width of rims: 4''; tyres: 6.00 x 12.

PERFORMANCE max speeds: (I) 25 mph, 40 km/h; (II) 44 mph, 70 km/h; (III) 70 mph, 112 km/h; (IV) 90 mph, 145 km/h; power-weight ratio: Semi De Luxe 2-dr. Sedan 24.9 lb/hp, 11.3 kg/hp; speed in direct drive at 1,000 rpm: 16.4 mph, 26.4 km/h; consumption: 40.9 m/imp gal, 34.1 m/US gal, 6.9 l x 100 km.

CHASSIS integral; front suspension: independent by McPherson, coil springs/telescopic damper struts, lower wishbones (trailing links); rear: rigid axle, lower trailing rods, upper torque rods, coil springs, telescopic dampers.

STEERING recirculating ball; turns lock to lock: 3.50.

BRAKES drum (front disc for GL Coupé only); lining area: front 42.2 sq in, 272 sq cm, rear 42.2 sq in, 272 sq cm, total 84.4 sq in, 544 sq cm - GL Coupé front 13.3 sq in, 85.6 sq cm, total 55.5 sq in, 357.6 sq cm.

ELECTRICAL EQUIPMENT 12 V; 32 Ah battery; alternator; Hitachi distributor; 2 headlamps.

DIMENSIONS AND WEIGHT wheel base: 92.13 in, 234 cm; tracks: 51.18 in, 130 cm front, 51.18 in, 130 cm rear; length: Semi De Luxe and De Luxe models 155.12 in, 394 cm - GL models 157.28 in, 399 cm; width: 62.20 in, 158 cm; height: 53.94 in, 137 cm - coupés 52.76 in, 134 cm; ground clearance: 6.50 in, 16 cm; weight: Semi De Luxe 2-dr. 1,742 lb, 790 kg - Semi De Luxe 4-dr. 1,764 lb, 800 kg - De Luxe 2-dr. 1,753 lb, 795 kg - De Luxe 4-dr., coupé and GL 2-dr. 1,775 lb, 805 kg - GL 4-dr. and coupé 1,797 lb, 815 kg; turning circle (between walls): 31.5 ft, 9.6 m; fuel tank: 11 imp gal, 13.2 US gal, 50 l.

PRACTICAL INSTRUCTIONS fuel: 90 oct lead-free petrol; oil: engine 6 imp pt, 7.2 US pt, 3.4 l, SAE 20W-30, change every 3.100 miles, 5,000 km - gearbox 2.1 imp pt, 2.5 US pt, 1.2 l, SAE 90, change every 31,000 miles, 50,000 km - final drive 1.6 imp pt, 1.9 US pt, 0.9 l, SAE 90, change every 31,000 miles, 50,000 km; tappet clearances: inlet 0.014 in, 0.35 mm, exhaust 0.014 in, 0.35 mm; valve timing: 14° 54° 56° 12°; tyre pressure: front 21 psi, 1.5 atm, rear 21 psi, 1.5 atm.

NISSAN Sunny 1400 SGX Coupé

80 hp power team

See 70 hp power team, except for:

ENGINE 85.2 cu in, 1,397 cc (2.99 x 3.03 in, 76 x 77 mm); max power (JIS): 80 hp at 6,000 rpm; max torque (JIS): 83 lb ft, 11.5 kg m at 3,600 rpm; max engine rpm: 6,600; 57.3 hp/l; 1 Hitachi DCH 306-51 or 52 downdraught twin barrel carburettor.

TRANSMISSION gearbox ratios: I 3.513, II 2.170, III 1.378, IV 1, rev 3.764; tyres: GX and SGX Sedan 155 SR x 13 - GX and SGX Coupé 165/70 HR x 13.

PERFORMANCE max speeds: (I) 27 mph, 44 km/h; (II) 45 mph, 72 km/h; (III) 70 mph, 112 km/h; (IV) 93 mph, 150 km/h; power-weight ratio: De Luxe Sedan 22.60 lb/hp, 10.25 kg/hp; consumption: 38.1 m/imp gal, 31.8 m/US gal, 7.4 l x 100 km.

BRAKES front disc, rear drum; lining area: front 13.3 sq in, 85.6 sq cm, rear 42.2 sq in, 272 sq cm, total 55.5 sq in, 357.6 sq cm.

DIMENSIONS AND WEIGHT tracks: 52.36 in, 133 cm front; width: 62.60 in, 159 cm (except De Luxe); weight: De Luxe Sedan and Coupé 1,808 lb, 820 kg - GL, SGL Sedan and Coupé 1,852 lb, 840 kg - GX, SGX Sedan and Coupé 1,895 lb, 865 kg.

PRACTICAL INSTRUCTIONS valve timing: 14° 54° 56° 20°.

OPTIONAL ACCESSORIES 5-speed fully synchronized mechanical gearbox (I 3.513, II 2.170, III 1.378, IV 1, V 0.846, rev 3.464); JATCO automatic transmission with 3 ratios (I 2.458, II 1.458, III 1, rev 2.182).

Violet - Auster - Stanza Series

PRICES (Tokyo):

1 Violet 1400 Standard Sedan	838,000	yen
2 Violet 1400 De Luxe Sedan	901,000	yen
3 Violet 1400 De Luxe Hatchback Coupé	936,000	yen
4 Auster 1400 De Luxe Sedan	901,000	yen
5 Auster 1400 De Luxe Hatchback Coupé	936,000	yen
6 Violet 1400 GL Sedan	942,000	yen
7 Violet 1400 GL Hatchback Coupé	977,000	yen
8 Violet 1600 De Luxe Sedan	921,000	yen
9 Auster 1600 De Luxe Sedan	921,000	yen
10 Violet 1600 GL Sedan	962,000	yen
11 Violet 1600 GL Hatchback Coupé	997,000	yen
12 Violet 1600 GL-L Sedan	997,000	yen
13 Auster 1600 CS Sedan	995,000	yen
14 Auster 1600 CS Hatchback Coupé	1,030,000	yen
15 Violet 1600 G1-L Hatchback Coupé	1,032,000	yen
16 Stanza Luxury Sedan	946,000	yen
17 Stanza Extra Sedan	992,000	yen
18 Stanza TS Sedan	1,002,000	yen
19 Violet GL-EL Sedan	1,079,000	yen
20 Violet GL-EL Hatchback Coupé	1,114,000	yen
21 Auster CS-E Sedan	1,062,000	yen
22 Auster CS-E Hatchback Coupé	1,097,000	yen
23 Auster CS-LE Sedan	1,116,000	yen
24 Auster CS-LE Hatchback Coupé	1,151,000	yen
25 Stanza Extra-E Sedan	1,062,000	yen
26 Stanza TS-E Sedan	1,072,000	yen
27 Stanza GT-E Sedan	1,127,000	yen
28 Stanza Maxima GT-E Sedan	1,177,000	yen

For USA prices, see price index.

Power team:	Standard for:	Optional for:
80 hp	1 to 7	—
100 hp	8 to 18	—
97 hp	USA version	—
110 hp	19 to 28	—

80 hp power team

ENGINE front, 4 stroke; 4 cylinders, vertical, in line; 85.2 cu in, 1,397 cc (2.99 x 3.03 in, 76 x 77 mm); compression ratio: 9:1; max power (JIS): 80 hp at 6,000 rpm; max torque (JIS): 83.3 lb ft, 11.5 kg m at 3,600 rpm; max engine rpm: 6,250; 57.3 hp/l; cast iron cylinder block; light alloy head; 5 crankshaft bearings; valves: overhead, in line, push-rods and rockers; camshafts: 1, side; lubrication: rotary pump, full flow filter, 6 imp pt, 7.2 US pt, 3.4 l; 1 Hitachi DCH 306-32 downdraught twin barrel carburettor; emission control with catalytic converter, secondary air injection and exhaust gas recirculation; fuel feed: mechanical pump; water-cooled, 7 imp pt, 8.4 US pt, 4 l.

TRANSMISSION driving wheels: rear; clutch: single dry plate (diaphragm); gearbox: mechanical; gears: 4, fully synchronized; ratios: I 3.513, II 2.170, III 1.378, IV 1, rev 3.764; lever: central; final drive: hypoid bevel; axle ratio: 3.889; width of rims: 4.5''; tyres: 5.60 x 13.

NISSAN Auster CS-E Hatchback Coupé

PERFORMANCE max speeds: (I) 28 mph, 45 km/h; (II) 47 mph, 75 km/h; (III) 75 mph, 120 km/h; (IV) 93 mph, 150 km/h; power-weight ratio: De Luxe Sedan 24.1 lb/hp, 10.9 kg/hp; consumption: 35.3 m/imp gal, 29.4 m/US gal, 8 l x 100 km.

CHASSIS integral; front suspension: independent, by McPherson, coil springs/telescopic dampers struts, lower wishbones (trailing links), anti-roll bar; rear: rigid axle, lower trailing rods, upper torque rods, coil springs, telescopic dampers.

STEERING recirculating ball; turns lock to lock: 3.70.

BRAKES front disc, rear drum; lining area: front 17.4 sq in, 112 sq cm, rear 54 sq cm, 348 sq cm, total 71.4 sq in, 460 sq cm.

ELECTRICAL EQUIPMENT 12 V; 32 Ah battery; 50 A alternator; Hitachi distributor; 4 headlamps.

DIMENSIONS AND WEIGHT wheel base: 94.49 in, 240 cm; tracks: 52.36 in, 133 cm; length: Sedan 160.63 in, 408 cm - Coupé 167.72 in, 426 cm; width: 62.99 in, 160 cm; height: Sedan 54.72 in, 139 cm - Coupé 53.15 in, 135 cm; ground clearance: 6.30 in, 16 cm; weight: De Luxe Sedan 1,929 lb, 875 kg - De Luxe Coupé 1,985 lb, 900 kg - Violet 1400 GL Coupé 1,996 lb, 905 kg; weight distribution: 55% front, 45% rear; turning circle (between walls): 32.8 ft, 10 m; fuel tank: 11 imp gal, 13.2 US gal, 50 l.

PRACTICAL INSTRUCTIONS fuel: 85-90 oct petrol; oil: engine 7 imp pt, 8.4 US pt, 4 l, SAE 20W-30, change every

3,100 miles, 5,000 km - gearbox 2.3 imp pt, 2.7 US pt, 1.3 l, SAE 90, change every 31,000 miles, 50,000 km - final drive 1.6 imp pt, 1.9 US pt, 0.9 l, change every 31,000 miles, 50,000 km; tappet clearances (warm): inlet 0.014 in, 0.35 mm, exhaust 0.014 in, 0.35 mm; valve timing: 14° 54° 56° 20°; tyre pressure: front 23 psi, 1.6 atm, rear 23 psi, 1.6 atm.

100 hp power team

See 80 hp power team, except for:

ENGINE 97.3 cu in, 1,595 cc (3.27 x 2.90 in, 83 x 73.7 mm). compression ratio: 8.5:1; max power (JIS): 100 hp at 6,000 rpm; max torque (JIS): 98 lb ft, 13.5 kg m at 4,000 rpm; 62.7 hp/l; valves: overhead, rockers; camshafts: 1, overhead.

TRANSMISSION gears: 4; ratios: I 3.657, II 2.177, III 1.419, IV 1, rev 3.638; axle ratio: 3.700; tyres: Auster 1600 CS models 165 SR x 13 - Stanza Extra and Maxima 6.45 x 13.

PERFORMANCE max speeds: (I) 27 mph, 43 km/h, (II) 60 mph, 80 km/h, (III) 78 mph, 126 km/h, (IV) 93 mph, 150 km/h; power-weight ratio: De Luxe Sedan 20.3 lb/hp, 9.2 kg/hp; consumption: Stanza models 34 m/imp gal, 28.3 m/US gal, 8.3 l.

CHASSIS rear suspension: Auster CS models anti-roll bar.

DIMENSIONS AND WEIGHT length: Stanza Maxima 163.39 in, 41.5 cm; weight: De Luxe Sedan 2,029 lb, 920 kg - GL and CS Sedan 2,040 lb, 925 kg - Stanza models 2,062 lb, 935 kg - GL, GL-L and CS Coupé 2,095 lb, 950 kg.

PRACTICAL INSTRUCTIONS valve timing: 12° 48° 54° 14°.

OPTIONAL ACCESSORIES 5-speed fully synchronized mechanical gearbox (I 3.657, II 2.177, III 1.419, IV 1, V 0.852, rev 3.860), max speed 99 mph, 160 km/h; automatic transmission with 3 ratios (I 2.458, II 1.458, III 1, rev 2.182), 3.889 axle ratio, max speed 93 mph, 150 km/h.

97 hp power team

(for USA only).

See 100 hp power team, except for:

ENGINE 119.1 cu in, 1,952 cc (3.35 x 3.39 in, 85 x 86 mm); max power (SAE): 97 hp at 5,600 rpm; max torque (SAE): 102 lb ft, 14.1 kg m at 3,200 rpm; 49.7 hp/l.

TRANSMISSION tyres: 165 SR x 13.

110 hp power team

See 80 hp power team, except for:

ENGINE 97.3 cu in, 1,595 cc (3.27 x 2.90 in, 83 x 73.7 mm); max power (JIS): 110 hp at 6,200 rpm; max torque (JIS):

NISSAN Auster CS-E Hatchback Coupé

100 lb ft, 13.8 kg m at 4,000 rpm; 69 hp/l; Bosch electronically-controlled injection system; fuel feed: electric pump.

TRANSMISSION axle ratio: 3.700; tyres: Auster Coupé and Stanza TS-E, GT-E, Maxima GT-E 165 SR x 13 - Stanza Extra-E 6.45 x 13.

PERFORMANCE max speed: 103 mph, 165 km/h; power-weight ratio: Sedan 18.9 lb/hp, 8.6 kg/hp.

CHASSIS rear suspension: anti-roll bar.

DIMENSIONS AND WEIGHT length: Stanza models 163.39 in, 415 cm; weight: Auster and Violet Sedan 2,034 lb, 945 kg - Auster and Violet Coupé 2,139 lb, 970 kg - Stanza E models 2,106 lb, 955 kg.

OPTIONAL ACCESSORIES 5-speed fully synchronized mechanical gearbox (I 3.657, II 2.117, III 1.419, IV 1, V 0.852, rev 3.860).

Datsun Bluebird Series

PRICES (Tokyo):

1 1600 De Luxe Sedan	969,000 yen
2 1600 GL Sedan	1,035,000 yen
3 1600 GL Hardtop	1,070,000 yen
4 1600 GL-L Sedan	1,064,000 yen
5 1600 GL-L Hardtop	1,099,000 yen
6 1800 De Luxe Sedan	977,000 yen
7 1800 GL Sedan	1,077,000 yen
8 1800 GL Hardtop	1,112,000 yen
9 1800 SSS Sedan	1,130,000 yen
10 1800 SSS Hardtop	1,165,000 yen
11 1800 SSS (Z 18) Sedan	1,185,000 yen
12 1800 SSS (Z 18) Hardtop	1,220,000 yen
13 1800 GL-E Sedan	1,157,000 yen
14 1800 GL-E Hardtop	1,192,000 yen
15 1800 SSS-E Sedan	1,213,000 yen
16 1800 SSS-E Hardtop	1,248,000 yen
17 1800 SSS-ES Sedan	1,182,000 yen
18 1800 SSS-ES Hardtop	1,217,000 yen
19 2000 G6 Sedan	1,220,000 yen
20 2000 G6 Hardtop	1,256,000 yen
21 2000 G6L Sedan	1,310,000 yen
22 2000 G6L Hardtop	1,310,000 yen
23 2000 G6E Sedan	1,415,000 yen
24 2000 G6E Hardtop	1,415,000 yen
25 2000 G6EL Sedan	1,503,000 yen
26 2000 G6EL Hardtop	1,539,000 yen

For USA price, see price index.

Power team:	Standard for:	Optional for:
100 hp	1 to 5	—
105 hp	6 to 10	—
105 hp (Z 18)	11 to 12	—
115 hp	13 to 18	—
115 hp (1,998 cc)	19 to 22	—
130 hp	23 to 26	—
130 hp (2,393 cc)	USA versions	—

NISSAN Stanza Maxima GT-E Sedan

100 hp power team

ENGINE front, 4 stroke; 4 cylinders, in line; 97.3 cu in, 1,595 cc (3.27 x 2.90 in, 83 x 73.7 mm); compression ratio: 8.5:1; max power (JIS): 100 hp at 6,000 rpm; max torque (JIS): 98 lb ft, 13.5 kg m at 4,000 rpm; 62.7 hp/l; cast iron cylinder block, light alloy head; 5 crankshaft bearings; valves: overhead, in line, rockers; camshafts: 1, overhead; lubrication: rotary pump, full flow filter, 8.1 imp pt, 9.7 US pt, 4.6 l; 1 Nikki downdraught twin barrel carburettor; emission control with catalytic converter, secondary air injection and exhaust gas recirculation; fuel feed: mechanical pump; water-cooled, 10.6 imp pt, 12.7 US pt, 6 l.

TRANSMISSION driving wheels: rear; clutch: single dry plate (diaphragm); gearbox: mechanical; gears: 4, fully synchronized; ratios: I 3.657, II 2.177, III 1.419, IV 1, rev 3.638; lever: central; final drive: hypoid bevel; axle ratio: 3.900; width of rims: 4.5''; tyres: 6.45 x 14.

PERFORMANCE max speeds: (I) 28 mph, 45 km/h; (II) 49 mph, 79 km/h; (III) 75 mph, 120 km/h; (IV) 103 mph, 165 km/h; power-weight ratio: De Luxe Sedan 22 lb/hp, 10 kg/hp - GL Sedan and Hardtop 22.2 lb/hp, 10.1 kg/hp; carrying capacity: 882 lb, 400 kg; consumption: 32.5 m/imp gal, 27 m/US gal, 8.7 l x 100 km.

CHASSIS integral; front suspension: independent, by McPherson, coil springs/telescopic damper struts, lower wishbones (trailing links), anti-roll bar; rear: rigid axle, lower trailing arms, upper torque rods, coil springs, telescopic dampers.

STEERING recirculating ball; turns lock to lock: 3.40.

BRAKES front disc, rear drum, servo; lining area: front 15.5 sq in, 100 sq cm, rear 54 sq in, 348 sq cm, total 69.5 sq in, 448 sq cm.

ELECTRICAL EQUIPMENT 12 V; 35 Ah battery; 50 A alternator; Hitachi distributor; 4 headlamps.

DIMENSIONS AND WEIGHT wheel base: 98.43 in, 250 cm; tracks: 52.76 in, 134 cm front, 53.15 in, 135 cm rear; length: De Luxe Sedan 171.46 in, 435 cm - GL Sedan and Hardtop 172.64 in, 438 cm; width: 64.17 in, 163 cm; height: sedans 54.72 in, 139 cm - GL Hardtop 54.33 in, 138 cm; ground clearance: 6.89 in, 17.5 cm; weight: De Luxe Sedan 2,205 lb, 1,000 kg - GL Sedan and Hardtop 2,216 lb, 1,005 kg; weight distribution: 55.5% front, 44.5% rear; turning circle (between walls): 36.1 ft, 11 m; fuel tank: 13.2 imp gal, 15.8 US gal, 60 l.

BODY 5 seats, separate front seats, reclining backrests, built-in headrests.

PRACTICAL INSTRUCTIONS fuel: 85-90 lead-free oct petrol; oil: engine 8.1 imp pt, 9.7 US pt, 4.6 l, change every 3,100 miles, 5,000 km - gearbox 3.5 imp pt, 4.2 US pt, 2 l, SAE 90, change every 31,000 miles, 50,000 km - final drive 1.4 imp pt, 1.7 US pt, 0.8 l, SAE 90, change every 31,000 miles, 50,000 km; tappet clearances: inlet 0.010 in, 0.25 mm, exhaust 0.012 in, 0.030 mm; valve timing: 12° 48° 54° 14°; tyre pressure: front 23 psi, 1.6 atm, rear 23 psi, 1.6 atm.

105 hp power team

See 100 hp power team, except for:

ENGINE 108 cu in, 1,770 cc (3.35 x 3.07 in, 85 x 78 mm); max power (JIS): 105 hp at 6,000 rpm; max torque (JIS): 109 lb ft, 15 kg m at 6,000 rpm; 59.3 hp/l.

TRANSMISSION gearbox ratios: I 3.382, II 2.013, III 1.312, IV 1, rev 3.365; axle ratio: 3.889 - SSS models 4.111; tyres: SSS models 165 SR x 14.

PERFORMANCE power-weight ratio: De Luxe Sedan 21.1 lb/hp, 9.7 kg/hp - GL models 21.6 lb/hp, 9.8 kg/hp - SSS models 22.3 lb/hp, 10.1 kg/hp.

CHASSIS SSS models rear suspension: independent; semi-trailing arms, coil springs, telescopic dampers.

DIMENSIONS AND WEIGHT tracks: SSS models 53.15 in, 135 cm front, 52.95 in, 134 cm rear; weight: De Luxe Sedan 2,216 lb, 1,025 kg - GL models 2,271 lb, 1,030 kg - SSS models 2,337 lb, 1,060 kg.

OPTIONAL ACCESSORIES 3-speed automatic transmission; 5-speed fully synchronized mechanical gearbox (I 3.382, II 2.013, III 1.312, IV 1, V 0.854, rev 3.570).

105 hp power team (Z18)

See 105 hp power team, except for:

ENGINE Nissan NAPS-Z fast-burn low emission engine with twin sparking plugs per cylinder; valves: overhead, in inverted Vee.

TRANSMISSION gears: 5, fully synchronized; axle ratio: 4.111; tyres: 165 SR x 14.

PERFORMANCE consumption: 36.7 m/imp gal, 30.5 m/US gal, 7.7 l x 100 km.

CHASSIS rear suspension: independent, semi-trailing arms, coil springs, telescopic dampers.

DIMENSIONS AND WEIGHT weight: SSS Sedan and Hardtop 2,348 lb, 1,065 kg.

PRACTICAL INSTRUCTIONS valve timing: 16° 52° 54° 14°.

115 hp power team

See 100 hp power team, except for:

ENGINE max power (JIS): 115 hp at 6,200 rpm; max torque (JIS): 112 lb ft, 15.5 kg m at 3,600 rpm; 65 hp/l; lubrication: Bosch electronic fuel injection; fuel feed: electric pump.

TRANSMISSION gears: 5, for SSS-ES models, fully synchronized; ratios: I 3.382, II 2.013, III 1.312, IV 1, V 0.854, rev 3.570; axle ratio: 4.111; width of rims: 5'' for SSS-ES models; tyres: SSS-ES models 185/70 HR x 14.

PERFORMANCE power-weight ratio: GL-E Sedan 20 lb/hp, 9 kg/hp - SSS-E models 20.4 lb/hp, 9.3 kg/hp - SSS-ES models 20.6 lb/hp, 9.4 kg/hp; consumption: 28.2 m/imp gal, 23.5 m/Us gal, 10 l x 100 km.

NISSAN Stanza Maxima GT-E Sedan

115 HP POWER TEAM

CHASSIS rear suspension: independent, semi-trailing arms, coil springs, telescopic dampers (SSS-ES models anti-roll bar - GL-E Sedan rigid axle, semi-elliptic leafsprings, telescopic dampers).

BRAKES SSS-ES models rear disc; lining area: front 15.5 sq in, 100 sq cm, rear 14.3 sq in, 92 sq cm, total 29.8 sq in, 192 sq cm.

DIMENSIONS AND WEIGHT weight: GL-E Sedan 2,293 lb, 1,040 kg - SSS-E models 2,348 lb, 1,065 kg - SSS-ES models 2,370 lb, 1,075 kg.

PRACTICAL INSTRUCTIONS valve timing: 16° 52° 54° 14°.

115 hp power team (1,998 cc)

See 100 hp power team, except for:

ENGINE 6 cylinders, vertical, in line; 121.9 cu in, 1,998 cc (3.07 x 2.74 in, 78 x 69.7 mm); compression ratio: 8.6:1; max power (JIS): 115 hp at 5,600 rpm; max torque (JIS): 120 lb ft, 16.5 kg m at 3,600 rpm; max engine rpm: 6,000; 57.6 hp/l; 7 crankshaft bearings: lubricating system capacity: 10 imp pt, 12 US pt, 5.7 l; 1 downdraught twin barrel carburettor; cooling system capacity: 15.8 imp pt, 19 US pt, 9 l.

TRANSMISSION gearbox ratios: I 3.321, II 2.077, III 1.308, IV 1, rev 3.382; axle ratio: 4.111; width of rims: 5''; tyres: 6.45 S x 14.

PERFORMANCE max speeds: (I) 30 mph, 48 km/h; (II) 45 mph, 73 km/h; (III) 75 mph, 120 km/h; (IV) 103 mph, 165 km/h; power-weight ratio: 22 lb/hp, 99 kg/hp; consumption: 24.4 m/imp gal, 20.3 m/US gal, 11.6 l x 100 km.

CHASSIS rear suspension: independent, semi-trailing arms, coil springs, telescopic dampers.

STEERING recirculating ball, variable ratio; turns lock to lock: 3.90.

BRAKES lining area: front 22.3 sq in, 144 sq cm, rear 54 sq in, 348 sq cm, total 76.3 sq in, 492 sq cm.

DIMENSIONS AND WEIGHT wheel base: 104.33 in, 265 cm; tracks: 53.15 in, 135 cm front, 52.95 in, 134 cm rear; length: 175.39 in, 445 cm; width: 64.17 in, 163 cm; height: sedans 54.53 in, 138 cm - hardtops 54.13 in, 137 cm; ground clearance: 66.93 in, 17 cm; weight: 2,525 lb, 1,145 kg; weight distribution: 57% front, 43% rear; turning circle (between walls): 38 ft, 11.6 m.

PRACTICAL INSTRUCTIONS oil: engine 10 imp pt, 12 US pt, 5.7 l - gearbox 2.8 imp pt, 3.4 US pt, 1.6 l - final drive 1.9 imp pt, 2.3 US pt, 1.1 l; valve timing: 8° 44° 50° 10°.

OPTIONAL ACCESSORIES automatic transmission with 3 ratios (I 2.458, II 1.458, III 1, rev 2.182); 5-speed fully synchronized mechanical gearbox (I 3.321, II 2.077, III 1.308, IV 1, V 0.864, rev 3.382), max speed 109 mph, 175 km/h; power-steering.

130 hp power team

See 100 hp power team, except for:

ENGINE 6 cylinders, vertical, in line; 121.9 cu in, 1,998 cc (3.07 x 2.74 in, 78 x 69.7 mm); compression ratio: 8.6:1; max power (JIS): 130 hp at 6,000 rpm; max torque (JIS): 123 lb ft, 17 kg m at 4,400 rpm; max engine rpm: 6,000; 65.1 hp/l; 7 crankshaft bearings; lubricating system capacity: 10 imp pt, 12 US pt, 5.7 l; Bosch L-Jetronic electronic fuel injection; emission control with catalytic converter, exhaust gas recirculation; fuel feed: electric pump; cooling system capacity: 15.8 imp pt, 19 US pt, 9 l.

TRANSMISSION gears: 5, fully synchronized; ratios: I 3.321, II 2.077, III 1.308, IV 1, V 0.864, rev 3.382; tyres: 6.45 S x 14.

PERFORMANCE max speed: 112 mph, 180 km/h; power-weight ratio: Sedan 19.8 lb/hp, 9 kg/hp - Hardtop 20.1 lb/hp, 9.1 kg/hp.

STEERING recirculating ball, variable ratio; turns lock to lock: 3.90.

BRAKES Hardtop disc; lining area: front 22.3 sq in, 144 sq cm, rear 15.2 sq in, 98 sq cm, total 76.3 sq in, 492 sq cm.

DIMENSIONS AND WEIGHT wheel base: 104.33 in, 2.65 cm; tracks: 53.15 in, 135 cm front, 52.76 in, 134 cm rear; length: 175 in, 445 cm; width: 64.57 in, 164 cm; height:

NISSAN Datsun Bluebird 1800 SSS (105 hp Z18 engine)

NISSAN Datsun Bluebird 1800 SSS Sedan

Sedan 54.33 in, 138 cm - Hardtop 53.90 in, 137 cm; ground clearance: 7.09 in, 18 cm; weight: Sedan 2,569 lb, 1,165 kg - Hardtop 2,602 lb, 1,180 kg; weight distribution: 58% front, 42% rear; turning circle (between walls): 38 ft, 11.6 m.

PRACTICAL INSTRUCTIONS oil: engine 10 imp pt, 12 US pt, 5.7 l - gearbox 2.8 imp pt, 3.4 US pt, 1.6 l - final drive 1.9 imp pt, 2.3 US pt, 1.1 l; valve timing: 12° 48° 54° 14°.

OPTIONAL ACCESSORIES automatic transmission with 3 ratios (I 2.458, II 1.458, III 1, rev 2.182), 5½'' x 14 alloy wheels 185/70 HR x 14 tyres, 165/SR x 14 tyres, 195/HR x 14 tyres; power steering: turns lock to lock 3.2.

130 hp power team (2,393)

(for USA only).

See 130 hp power team, except for:

ENGINE 146 cu in, 2,393 cc (3.27 x 2.90 in, 83 x 73.7 mm); max power (DIN): 130 hp at 6,000 rpm; max torque (DIN): 123 lb ft, 17 kg m at 4,400 rpm; 54.3 hp/l.

Skyline Series

PRICES (Tokyo):

1	1600 TI Sedan	996,000 yen
2	1600 TI-L Sedan	1,080,000 yen
3	1600 TI-L Hardtop	1,115,000 yen
4	1800 TI Sedan	1,046,000 yen
5	1800 TI-L Sedan	1,111,000 yen
6	1800 TI-L Hardtop	1,185,000 yen
7	1800 TI-EL Sedan	1,215,000 yen
8	1800 TI-EL Hardtop	1,296,000 yen
9	1800 TI-ES Sedan	1,345,000 yen
10	1800 TI-ES Hardtop	1,380,000 yen
11	2000 GT Sedan	1,214,000 yen
12	2000 GT Hardtop	1,259,000 yen
13	2000 GT-L Sedan	1,274,000 yen
14	2000 GT-L Hardtop	1,319,000 yen
15	2000 GT-E Sedan	1,319,000 yen
16	2000 GT-E Hardtop	1,392,000 yen
17	2000 GT-EL Sedan	1,379,000 yen
18	2000 GT-EL Hardtop	1,452,000 yen
19	2000 GT-EX Sedan	1,510,000 yen
20	2000 GT-EX Hardtop	1,584,000 yen
21	2000 GT-ES Sedan	1,560,000 yen
22	2000 GT-ES Hardtop	1,605,000 yen

Power team:	Standard for:	Optional for:
100 hp	1 to 3	—
105 hp	4 to 6	—
115 hp	7 to 10	—
115 hp (1,998 cc)	11 to 14	—
130 hp	15 to 22	—

100 hp power team

ENGINE front, 4 stroke; 4 cylinders, in line; 97.3 cu in, 1,595 cc (3.27 x 2.90 in, 83 x 73.7 mm); compression ratio: 8.5:1; max power (JIS): 100 hp at 6,000 rpm; max torque (JIS): 98 lb ft, 13.5 kg m at 4,000 rpm; max engine

NISSAN Datsun Bluebird 2000 G6L Sedan

rpm: 6,300; 62.7 hp/l; cast iron cylinder block, light alloy head; 5 crankshaft bearings; valves: overhead, in line, rockers; camshafts: 1, overhead; lubrication: rotary pump, full flow filter, 8.1 imp pt, 9.7 US pt, 4.6 l; 1 Nikki 21A 304-05 downdraught twin barrel carburettor; emission control with catalytic converter, secondary air injection and exhaust gas recirculation; fuel feed: mechanical pump; water-cooled, 12.3 imp pt, 14.8 US pt, 7 l.

TRANSMISSION driving wheels: rear; clutch: single dry plate (diaphragm); gearbox: mechanical; gears: 4, fully synchronized; ratios: I 3.657, II 2.177, III 1.419, IV 1, rev 3.638; lever: central; final drive: hypoid bevel; axle ratio: 4.111; width of rims: 4.5''; tyres 6.45 x 13.

PERFORMANCE max speeds: (I) 25 mph, 40 km/h; (II) 47 mph, 75 km/h; (III) 68 mph, 110 km/h; (IV) 96 mph, 155 km/h; power-weight ratio: TI Sedan 22.7 lb/hp, 10.3 kg/hp; consumption: 32.4 m/imp gal, 27 m/US gal, 8.7 l x 100 km.

CHASSIS integral; front suspension: independent, by McPherson, coil springs/telescopic damper struts, lower wishbones (trailing links), anti-roll bar; rear: rigid axle, lower trailing links, upper torque rods, coil springs, telescopic dampers.

STEERING recirculating ball; turns lock to lock: 3.60.

BRAKES front disc, rear drum, servo; lining area: front 15.5 sq in, 100 sq cm, rear 54 sq in, 348 sq cm, total 69.5 sq in, 448 sq cm.

ELECTRICAL EQUIPMENT 12 V; 35 Ah battery; 50 A alternator; Hitachi distributor; 4 headlamps.

DIMENSIONS AND WEIGHT wheel base: 98.82 in, 251 cm; tracks: 53.54 in, 136 cm front, 53.15 in, 135 cm rear; length: 173.23 in, 440 cm; width: 63.78 in, 162 cm; height: Sedan 54.72 in, 139 cm - Hardtop 54.13 in, 137 cm; ground clearance: 6.30 in, 16 cm; weight: TI Sedan 2,271 lb, 1,030 kg - TI-L Sedan 2,304 lb, 1,045 kg - TI-L Hardtop 2,315 lb, 1,050 kg; turning circle (between walls): 36.1 ft, 11 m; fuel tank: 13.2 imp gal, 15.8 US gal, 60 l.

PRACTICAL INSTRUCTIONS fuel: 85-90 oct lead-free petrol; oil: engine 8.1 imp pt, 9.7 US pt, 4.6 l, SAE 20W-30, change every 3,100 miles, 5,000 km - gearbox 3 imp pt, 3.6 US pt, 1.7 l, SAE 90, change every 31,000 miles, 50,000 km - final drive 1.8 imp pt, 2.1 US pt, 1 l, SAE 90, change every 31,000 miles, 50,000 km; tappet clearances (hot): inlet 0.010 in, 0.25 mm, exhaust 0.012 in, 0.30 mm; valve timing: 12° 48° 54° 14°; tyre pressure: front 23 psi, 1.6 atm, rear 23 psi, 1.6 atm.

105 hp power team

See 100 hp power team, except for:

ENGINE 108 cu in, 1,770 cc (3.35 x 3.07 in, 85 x 78 mm); max power (JIS): 105 hp at 6,000 rpm; max torque (JIS): 109 lb ft, 15 kg m at 3,600 rpm; 59.3 hp/l.

TRANSMISSION gearbox ratios: I 3.382, II 2.013, III 1.312, IV 1, rev 3.365; axle ratio: 3.889.

PERFORMANCE max speeds: (I) 27 mph, 44 km/h; (II) 45 mph, 73 km/h; (III) 68 mph, 110 km/h; (IV) 103 mph, 165 km/h; power-weight ratio: TI Sedan 21.9 lb/hp, 9.9 kg/hp; consumption: 29.7 m/imp gal, 24.7 m/US gal, 9.5 l x 100 km.

DIMENSIONS AND WEIGHT weight: TI Sedan 2,304 lb, 1,045 kg - TI-L Sedan 2,326 lb, 1,055 kg - TI-L Hardtop 2,337 lb, 1,060 kg.

OPTIONAL ACCESSORIES 5-speed mechanical gearbox, ratio V 0.854, rev 3.570; automatic transmission with 3 ratios (I 2.458, II 1.458, III 1, rev 2.182).

115 hp power team

See 105 hp power team, except for:

ENGINE max power (JIS): 115 hp at 6,200 rpm; max torque (JIS): 112.3 lb ft, 15.5 kg m at 3,600 rpm; Bosch L-Jetronic electronic fuel injection.

TRANSMISSION axle ratio: 4.111; tyres: TI-EL Sedan 6.45 x 14 - TI-EL Hardtop and TI-ES Sedan 165 SR x 14.

PERFORMANCE max speed: 103 mph, 165 km/h; power-weight ratio: TI-EL Sedan 20.3 lb/hp, 9.2 kg/hp; consumption: 28.2 m/imp gal, 23.5 m/US gal, 10 l x 100 km.

CHASSIS rear suspension: ES anti-roll bar.

BRAKES ES rear disc.

DIMENSIONS AND WEIGHT height: EL and ES Sedan 55.31 in, 140 cm - EL and ES Hardtop 54.92 in, 139 cm; weight: EL Sedan 2,337 lb, 1,060 kg - EL Hardtop 2,348 lb, 1,065 kg - ES Sedan 2,381 lb, 1,080 kg - ES Hardtop 2,392 lb, 1,085 kg.

PRACTICAL INSTRUCTIONS valve timing 16° 52° 54° 14°.

NISSAN Skyline 1800 TI-EL

NISSAN Skyline 2000 GT Sedan

115 hp power team (1,998 cc)

See 100 hp power team, except for:

ENGINE 6 cylinders, in line; 121.9 cu in, 1,998 cc (3.07 x 2.74 in, 78 x 69.7 mm); compression ratio: 8.6:1; max power (JIS): 115 hp at 5,600 rpm; max torque (JIS): 120 lb ft, 16.5 kg m at 3,600 rpm; 57.6 hp/l; 7 crankshaft bearings; lubrication: rotary pump, full flow filter, 10 imp pt, 12 US pt, 5.7 l; 1 Hitachi downdraught twin barrel carburettor; water-cooled, 15.8 imp pt, 19 US pt, 9 l.

TRANSMISSION gearbox ratios: I 3.592, III 2.246, III 1.415, IV 1, rev 3.657; tyres: 6.45 S x 14.

PERFORMANCE max speeds: (I) 26 mph, 42 km/h; (II) 43 mph, 70 km/h; (III) 58 mph, 110 km/h; (IV) 99 mph, 160 km/h; power-weight ratio: GT and GT-L Sedan 22.8 lb/hp, 10.3 kg/hp - GT and GT-L Hardtop 23 lb/hp, 10.4 kg/hp; consumption: 24.5 m/imp gal, 20.4 m/US gal, 11.5 l x 100 km.

CHASSIS rear suspension: independent, semi-trailing arms, coil springs, telescopic dampers.

STEERING recirculating ball, variable ratio; turns lock to lock: 4.

BRAKES rear compensator; lining area: front 22.3 sq in, 144 sq cm, rear 54 sq in, 348 sq cm, total 89.3 sq in, 576 sq cm.

DIMENSIONS AND WEIGHT wheel base: 102.76 in, 261 cm; tracks: 53.94 i,n 137 cm front; length: 181.10 in, 460 cm; weight: GT and GT-L Sedan 2,624 lb, 1,190 kg - GT and GT-L Hardtop 2,646 lb, 1,200 kg; turning circle (between walls): 38 ft, 11.6 m.

PRACTICAL INSTRUCTIONS fuel: 98-100 oct lead-free petrol; oil: engine 10 imp pt, 12 US pt, 5.7 l - gearbox 2.8 imp pt, 3.4 US pt, 1.6 l; tappet clearances: exhaust 0.012 in, 0.30 mm; valve timing: 8° 44° 50° 10°; tyre pressure: front 21 psi, 1.5 atm, rear 24 psi, 1.7 atm.

OPTIONAL ACCESSORIES 5-speed fully synchronized mechanical gearbox (I 3.321, II 2.077, III 1.308, IV 1, V 0.864, rev 3.382), 4.111 axle ratio, max speed V 106 mph, 170 km/h; automatic transmission with 3 ratios (I 2.458, II 1.458, III 1, rev 2.182); power steering, turns lock to lock 3.60.

130 hp power team

See 100 hp power team, except for:

ENGINE 6 cylinders, in line; 121.9 cu in, 1,998 cc (3.07 x 2.74 in, 78 x 69.7 mm); compression ratio: 8.6:1; max power (JIS): 130 hp at 6,000 rpm; max torque (JIS): 123 lb ft, 17 kg m at 4,000 rpm; 65.1 hp/l; 7 crankshaft bearings; lubricating system capacity: 10 imp pt, 12 US pt, 5.7 l; Bosch L-Jetronic electronic fuel injection; emission control with catalytic converter exhaust gas recirculation; fuel feed: electric pump: water-cooled, 15.8 imp pt, 19 US pt, 9 l.

TRANSMISSION gears: 5, fully synchronized; ratios: I 3.321, II 2.077, III 1.308, IV 1, V 0.864, rev 3.382; axle ratio: 4.111; width of rims: 5''; tyres: 6.45S x 14 - GT-EX and GT-ES 185/70HR x 14.

NISSAN Skyline 1800 TI-EL Sedan

130 HP POWER TEAM

PERFORMANCE max speeds: (I) 31 mph, 50 km/h; (II) 50 mph, 80 km/h; (III) 78 mph, 126 km/h; (IV) 104 mph, 168 km/h; (V) 109 mph, 175 km/h; power-weight ratio: GT-E Sedan 19.8 lb/hp, 9 kg/hp; consumption: 24.3 m/imp gal, 20.3 m/US gal, 11.6 l x 100 km.

CHASSIS rear suspension: independent, semi-trailing arms, coil springs, telescopic dampers - GT-EX and GT-ES models anti-roll bar.

STEERING recirculating ball, variable ratio; turns lock to lock: 4.

BRAKES rear compensator; lining area: front 22.3 sq in, 144 sq cm; rear 54 sq in, 348 sq cm, total 89.3 sq in, 576 sq cm (GT-EX and GT-ES models rear disc; rear lining area: 14.3 sq in, 92 sq cm).

DIMENSIONS AND WEIGHT wheel base: 102.76 in, 261 cm; tracks: 53.94 in, 137 cm front, 53.15 in, 135 cm rear; length: 181.10 in, 460 cm; width: EX 64.37 in, 163 cm; weight: GT-E, GT-EL Sedan and Hardtop 2,591 lb, 1,175 kg - GT-EX Sedan 2,624 lb, 1,190 kg - GT-EX Hardtop and GT-ES Sedan 2,635 lb, 1,195 kg - GT-ES Hardtop 2,646 lb, 1,200 kg; turning circle (between walls): 38 ft, 11.6 m.

PRACTICAL INSTRUCTIONS fuel: 98-100 oct petrol; oil: engine 10 imp pt, 12 US pt, 5.7 l - gearbox 2.8 imp pt, 3.4 US pt, 1.6 l; tappet clearances: exhaust 0.012 in, 0.30 mm; valve timing: 12° 48° 54° 14°; tyre pressure: front 21 psi, 1.5 atm, rear 24 psi, 1.7 atm.

OPTIONAL ACCESSORIES automatic transmission with 3 ratios (I 2.458, II 1.458, III 1, rev 2.182), 4.111 axle ratio, max speed 106 mph, 170 km/h; power steering; 3.60 turns lock to lock; 5.5'' cast alloy wheels.

Laurel Series

PRICES (Tokyo):

1 1800 De Luxe 4-door Sedan	1,089,000	yen
2 1800 Custom 4-door Sedan	1,118,000	yen
3 1800 Custom 2-door Hardtop	1,146,000	yen
4 1800 GL 4-door Sedan	1,168,000	yen
5 1800 GL 2-door Hardtop	1,211,000	yen
6 2000 Custom 6 4-door Sedan	1,224,000	yen
7 2000 Custom 6 2-door Hardtop	1,303,000	yen
8 2000 Custom 6 4-door Hardtop	1,357,000	yen
9 2000 GL6 4-door Sedan	1,286,000	yen
10 2000 GL6 2-door Hardtop	1,359,000	yen
11 2000 GL6 4-door Hardtop	1,411,000	yen
12 2000 SGL 4-door Sedan	1,430,000	yen
13 2000 SGL 2-door Hardtop	1,500,000	yen
14 2000 SGL 4-door Hardtop	1,558,000	yen
15 2000 GL6-E 4-door Sedan	1,391,000	yen
16 2000 GL6-E 2-door Hardtop	1,464,000	yen
17 2000 GL6-E 4-door Hardtop	1,523,000	yen
18 2000 SGL-E 4-door Sedan	1,535,000	yen
19 2000 SGL-E 2-door Hardtop	1,605,000	yen
20 2000 SGL-E 4-door Hardtop	1,663,000	yen
21 2800 SGL 4-door Sedan	1,865,000	yen
22 2800 SGL 2-door Hardtop	1,908,000	yen
23 2800 SGL 4-door Hardtop	1,976,000	yen

Power team:	Standard for:	Optional for:
105 hp	1 to 5	—
115 hp	6 to 14	—
130 hp	15 to 20	—
140 hp	21 to 23	—

105 hp power team

ENGINE front, 4 stroke; 4 cylinders, in line; 108 cu in, 1,770 cc (3.35 x 3.07 in; 85 x 78 mm); compression ratio: 8.5:1; max power (JIS): 105 hp at 6,000 rpm; max torque (JIS): 109 lb ft, 15 kg m at 3,600 rpm; max engine rpm: 6,400; 59.3 hp/l; cast iron cylinder block, light alloy head; 5 crankshaft bearings; valves: overhead, in line, rockers; camshafts: 1, overhead; lubrication: rotary pump, full flow filter, 7.5 imp pt, 9 US pt, 4.3 l; 1 Hitachi DCH340 downdraught twin barrel carburettor; emission control with catalytic converter, secondary air injection and exhaust gas recirculation; fuel feed: mechanical pump; water-cooled, 14 imp pt, 16.9 US pt, 8 l.

TRANSMISSION driving wheels: rear; clutch: single dry plate (diaphragm); gearbox: mechanical; gears: 4, fully synchronized; ratios: I 3.382, II 2.013, III 1.312, IV 1, rev 3.365; lever: central; final drive: hypoid bevel; axle ratio: 4.111; width of rims: 5''; tyres: 6.45 x 14.

PERFORMANCE max speeds: (I) 30 mph, 48 km/h; (II) 52 mph, 83 km/h; (III) 77 mph, 124 km/h; (IV) 99 mph, 160 km/h; power-weight ratio: De Luxe Sedan 23.3 lb/hp, 10.6 kg/hp; consumption: 28.2 m/imp gal, 23.5 m/US gal, 10 l x 100 km.

NISSAN Skyline 2000 GT-ES Hardtop

CHASSIS integral; front suspension: independent, by McPherson, coil springs/telescopic damper struts, lower wishbones (trailing links), anti-roll bar; rear: rigid axle, lower trailing links, upper torque rods, coil springs, telescopic dampers.

STEERING recirculating ball; turns lock to lock: 4.

BRAKES front disc, rear drum, servo; lining area: front 22.3 sq in, 144 sq cm, rear 54 sq in, 348 sq cm, total 76.3 sq in, 492 sq cm.

ELECTRICAL EQUIPMENT 12 V; 35 Ah battery; 50 A alternator; Hitachi distributor; 4 headlamps.

DIMENSIONS AND WEIGHT wheel base, 105.12 in, 267 cm; tracks: 54.33 in, 138 cm front, 53.94 in, 137 cm rear; length: 177.17 in, 450 cm; width: 63.75 in, 167 cm; height: Sedan 55.31 in, 140 cm - Hardtop 54.92 in, 139 cm; ground clearance: 6.69 in, 17 cm; weight: De Luxe and Custom Sedan 2,448 lb, 1,110 kg - GL Sedan and Custom Hardtop 2,470 lb, 1,120 kg - GL Hardtop 2,492 lb, 1,130 kg; turning circle (between walls): 38 ft, 11.6 m; fuel tank: 13.2 imp gal, 15.8 US gal, 60 l.

PRACTICAL INSTRUCTIONS fuel: 85-90 oct petrol; oil: engine 7.5 imp pt, 9 US pt, 4.3 l, SAE 20W-30, change every 3,100 miles, 5,000 km - gearbox 3 imp pt, 3.6 US pt, 1.7 l, SAE 90, change every 31,100 miles, 50,000 km - final drive 1.8 imp pt, 2.1 US pt, 1 l, SAE 90, change every 31,100 miles, 50,000 km; greasing: none; tappet clearances (hot): inlet 0.010 in, 0.25 mm, exhaust 0.012

in, 0.30 mm; valve timing: 12° 48° 54° 14°; tyre pressure: front 21 psi, 1.5 atm, rear 21 psi, 1.5 atm.

OPTIONAL ACCESSORIES 5-speed mechanical gearbox, V 0.854; automatic transmission with 3 ratios (I 2.458, II 1.458, III 1, rev 2.182) with central lever; 5.5'' light alloy wheels with 185/70HR x 14 tyres.

115 hp power team

See 105 hp power team, except for:

ENGINE 6 cylinders, in line; 121.9 cu in, 1,998 cc (3.07 x 2.74 in, 78 x 69.7 mm); compression ratio: 8.6:1; max power (JIS): 115 hp at 5,600 rpm; max torque (JIS): 120 lb ft, 16.5 kg m at 3,600 rpm; max engine rpm: 6,000; 60 hp/l; 7 crankshaft bearings; lubricating system capacity: 10 imp pt, 12 US pt, 5.7 l; water-cooled, 15.8 imp pt, 19 US pt, 9 l.

TRANSMISSION gearbox ratios: I 3.592, II 2.246, III 1.415, IV 1, rev 3.657; axle ratio: Sedan 3.889 - Hardtop 3.900; tyres: Custom 6, GL6 Sedan and Hardtop 6.45 x 14 - SGL Sedan C70H x 14 - SGL Hardtop 185/70 HR x 14.

PERFORMANCE max speed: 106 mph, 170 km/h; power-weight ratio: Custom 6 Sedan 22.4 lb/hp, 10.2 kg/hp.

CHASSIS rear suspension: Hardtop independent, semi-trailing arms, coil springs, telescopic dampers.

NISSAN Laurel 1800 GL Sedan

STEERING SGL models servo; turns lock to lock: 3.60

BRAKES rear compensator.

DIMENSIONS AND WEIGHT rear track: Hardtop 53.54 in, 136 cm; length: 178.15 in, 452 cm; width: 66.34 in, 168 cm; weight: Custom 6 Sedan 2,580 lb, 1,170 kg - Custom 6 2-dr. Hardtop 2,657 lb, 1,205 kg - Custom 6 4-dr. Hardtop 2,690 lb, 1,220 kg - GL6 Sedan 2,602 lb, 1,180 kg - GL6 2-dr. Hardtop 2,668 lb, 1,210 kg - GL6 4-dr. Hardtop 2,701 lb, 1,225 kg - SGL Sedan 2,624 lb, 1,190 kg - SGL 2-dr. Hardtop 2,690 lb, 1,220 kg - SGL 4-dr. Hardtop 2,723 lb, 1,235 kg; distribution of weight: 55.7% front, 44.3% rear.

PRACTICAL INSTRUCTIONS oil: engine 10 imp pt, 12 US pt, 5.7 l - gearbox 2.8 imp pt, 3.4 US pt, 1.6 l; valve timing: 8° 44° 50° 10°; tyre pressure: front 23 psi, 1.6 atm. rear 23 psi, 1.6 atm.

130 hp power team

See 105 hp power team, except for:

ENGINE 6 cylinders, in line; 121.9 cu in, 1,998 cc (3.07 x 2.74 in, 78 x 69.7 mm); compression ratio: 8.6:1; max power (JIS): 130 hp at 6,000 rpm; max torque (JIS): 123 lb ft, 17 kg m at 4,400 rpm; max engine rpm: 6,000; 65.1 hp/l; 7 crankshaft bearings; lubricating system capacity: 10 imp pt, 12 US pt, 5.7 l; Bosch L-Jetronic electronic fuel injection; fuel feed: electric pump; water-cooled, 15.8 imp pt, 19 US pt, 9 l.

TRANSMISSION gears: 5, fully synchronized; ratios: I 3.592, II 2.246, III 1.415, IV 1, V 0.882; axle ratio: 4.111; tyres: GL6-E Sedan and Hardtop 6.45 x 14 - SGL-E Sedan C70H x 14 - SGL-E Hardtop 185/70 HR x 14.

PERFORMANCE max speed: 109 mph, 175 km/h; power-weight ratio: GL6-E Sedan 20 lb/hp, 9 kg/hp; consumption: 23.1 m/imp gal, 19.3 m/US gal, 12.2 l x 100 km.

CHASSIS rear suspension: Hardtop independent, semi-trailing arms, coil spring, telescopic dampers.

STEERING SGL-E models servo; turns lock to lock: 3.60.

BRAKES rear compensator.

DIMENSIONS AND WEIGHT tracks: Hardtop 53.54 in, 136 cm rear; length: 178.15 in, 452 cm; width: 66.34 in, 168 cm; weight: GL6-E Sedan 2,602 lb, 1,180 kg - GL6-E 2-dr. Hardtop 2,668 lb, 1,210 kg - GL6-E 4-dr. Hardtop 2,701 lb, 1,225 kg - SGL-E Sedan, 2,624 lb, 1,190 kg - SGL-E 2-dr. Hardtop 2,701 lb, 1,225 kg - SGL-E 4-dr. Hardtop 2,723 lb, 1,235 kg.

PRACTICAL INSTRUCTIONS oil: engine 10 imp pt, 12 US pt, 5.7 l - gearbox 2.8 imp pt, 3.4 US pt, 1.6 l; tyre pressure: front 23 psi, 1.6 atm, rear 23 psi, 1.6 atm.

OPTIONAL ACCESSORIES 3-speed automatic transmission; 5.5'' light alloy wheels with 185/70HR x 14 tyres.

140 hp power team

See 105 hp power team, except for:

ENGINE 6 cylinders, in line; 168 cu in, 2,753 cc (3.39 x 3.11 in, 86 x 79 mm); compression ratio: 8.6:1; max power (JIS): 140 hp at 5,200 rpm; max torque (JIS): 163 lb ft, 22.5 kg m at 3,600 rpm; max engine rpm: 6,200; 50.1 hp/l; 7 crankshaft bearings; lubricating system capacity: 10 imp pt, 12 US pt, 5.7 l; 1 downdraught twin barrel carburettor; water-cooled, 17.6 imp pt, 21.1 US pt, 10 l.

TRANSMISSION gears: 5, fully synchronized; ratios: I 3.321, II 2.077, III 1.308, IV 1, V 0.864, rev 3.382; axle ratio: 3.700; tyres: Sedan C70H x 14 - Hardtop 185/70HR x 14.

PERFORMANCE max speeds: (I) 36 mph, 58 km/h; (II) 52 mph, 83 km/h; (III) 89 mph, 144 km/h; IV 104 mph, 168 km/h; V 112 mph, 180 km/h; power-weight ratio: SGL Sedan 20.3 lb/hp, 8.8 kg/hp.

CHASSIS rear suspension: Hardtop independent, semi-trailing arms, coil springs, telescopic dampers.

STEERING servo; turns lock to lock: 3.60.

BRAKES front disc, rear drum, rear compensator, servo; lining area: front 20.5 sq in, 132 sq cm.

DIMENSIONS AND WEIGHT tracks: Hardtop 53.54 in, 136 cm rear; length: 178.15 in, 452 cm; width: 66.34 in, 168 cm; weight: SGL Sedan 2,723 lb, 1,235 kg - SGL 2-dr. Hardtop 2,811 lb, 1,275 kg - SGL 4-dr. Hardtop 2,844 lb, 1,290 kg.

PRACTICAL INSTRUCTIONS oil: engine 10 imp pt, 12 US pt, 5.7 l - gearbox 2.8 imp pt, 3.4 US pt, 1.6 l; tyre pressure: front 23 psi, 1.6 atm, rear 23 psi, 1.6 atm.

OPTIONAL ACCESSORIES 3-speed automatic transmission; 185/70HR x 14 tyres.

NISSAN Laurel 2800 SGL 4-door Hardtop

NISSAN Silvia LS Coupé

Silvia Series

PRICES (Tokyo):

1 LS Coupé	1,075,000	yen
2 LS Type S Coupé	1,125,000	yen
3 LS Type L Coupé	1,114,000	yen
4 LS Type X Coupé	1,205,000	yen
5 LS Type G Coupé	1,305,000	yen
6 LS-E Type S Coupé	1,209,000	yen
7 LS-E Type L Coupé	1,225,000	yen
8 LS-E Type X Coupé	1,283,000	yen
9 LS-E Type G Coupé	1,383,000	yen

For USA price, see price index.

Power team:	Standard for:	Optional for:
105 hp	1 to 5	—
115 hp	6 to 9	—

105 hp power team

ENGINE front, 4 stroke; 4 cylinders, in line; 108 cu in, 1,770 cc (3.35 x 3.07 in, 85 x 78 mm); compression ratio: 8.5:1; max power (JIS): 105 hp at 6,000 rpm; max torque (JIS): 109 lb ft, 15 kg m at 3,600 rpm; max engine rpm: 6,000; 59.3 hp/l; cast iron cylinder block, light alloy head; 5 crankshaft bearings; valves: overhead, in line, rockers; camshafts: 1, overhead; lubrication: rotary pump, full flow filter, 8.1 imp pt, 9.7 US pt, 4.6 l; 1 Hitachi DCH340 downdraught twin barrel carburettor; emission control with

NISSAN Silvia LS-E Type S Coupé

369

105 HP POWER TEAM

catalytic converter, secondary air injection and exhaust gas recirculation; fuel feed: mechanical pump; water-cooled, 10.6 imp pt, 12.7 US pt, 6 l.

TRANSMISSION driving wheels: rear; clutch: single dry plate (diaphragm); gearbox: mechanical; gears: 4, fully synchronized; ratios: I 3.382, II 2.013, III 1.312, IV 1, rev 3.365; lever: central; final drive: hypoid bevel, axle ratio: 3.700; width of rims: 4.5''; tyres: LS and LS-L Z78 x 13 - LS-S, LS-X and LS-G 175/70 HR x 13.

PERFORMANCE max speeds: (I) 31 mph, 50 km/h; (II) 51 mph, 82 km/h; (III) 81 mph, 130 km/h; (IV) 106 mph, 170 km/h; power-weight ratio: 20.8 lb/hp, 9.4 kg/hp; carrying capacity: 882 lb, 400 kg; speed in direct drive at 1,000 rpm: 17.6 mph, 28.3 km/h; consumption: 26.4 m/imp gal, 22 m/US gal, 10.7 l x 100 km.

CHASSIS integral; front suspension: independent, by McPherson, coil springs/telescopic damper struts, lower wishbones (trailing links), anti-roll bar; rear: rigid axle, semi-elliptic leafsprings, telescopic dampers.

STEERING recirculating ball; turns lock to lock: 2.90.

BRAKES front disc, rear drum, servo; lining area: front 15.5 sq in, 100 sq cm, rear 54 sq in, 348 sq cm, total 69.5 sq in, 448 sq cm.

ELECTRICAL EQUIPMENT 12 V; 35 Ah battery; 50 A alternator; Hitachi distributor; 2 headlamps.

DIMENSIONS AND WEIGHT wheel base: 92.13 in, 234 cm; tracks: 50.39 in, 128 cm front, 49.80 in, 126 cm rear; length: 162.79 in, 413 cm; width: 62.99 in, 160 cm; height: 51.18 in, 130 cm; ground clearance: 6.50 in, 16.5 cm; dry weight: 2,183 lb, 990 kg; distribution of weight: 55% front, 45% rear; turning circle (between walls): 35.4 ft, 10.8 m; fuel tank: 13.2 imp gal, 15.8 US gal, 60 l.

BODY coupé; 2 doors; 5 seats, separate front seats.

PRACTICAL INSTRUCTIONS fuel: 85-90 oct lead-free petrol; oil: engine 8.1 imp pt, 9.7 US pt, 4.6 l, SAE 20W-30, change every 3,100 miles, 5,000 km - gearbox 3 imp pt, 3.6 US pt, 1.7 l, SAE 90, change every 31,000 miles, 50,000 km - final drive 2.3 imp pt, 2.7 US pt, 1.3 l, SAE 90, change every 31,000 miles, 50,000 km; tappet clearances (hot): inlet 0.010 in, 0.25 mm, exhaust 0.012 in, 0.30 mm; valve timing: 12° 48° 54° 14°; tyre pressure: front 23 psi, 1.6 atm, rear 23 psi, 1.6 atm.

OPTIONAL ACCESSORIES 5-speed fully synchronized mechanical gearbox (I 3.382, II 2.013, III 1.312, IV 1, V 0.854, rev 3.570), 3.889 axle ratio, max speed 109 mph, 175 km/h; JATCO automatic transmission with 3 ratios (I 2.458, II 1.458, III 1, rev 2.182), max speed 103 mph, 165 km/h.

115 hp power team

See 105 hp power team, except for:

ENGINE max power (JIS): 115 hp at 6,200 rpm; max torque (JIS): 112 lb ft, 15.5 kg m at 3,600 rpm; max engine rpm: 6,200; 65 hp/l; Bosch L-Jetronic electronic fuel injection, exhaust gas recirculation.

TRANSMISSION tyres: 175/HR x 13.

PERFORMANCE max speed: 109 mph, 175 km/h; power-weight ratio: 19.2 lb/hp, 8.7 kg/hp; consumption: 29.7 m/imp gal, 24.8 m/US gal, 9.5 l x 100 km.

DIMENSIONS AND WEIGHT weight: 2,205 lb, 1,000 kg.

PRACTICAL INSTRUCTIONS valve timing: 16° 52° 54° 14°.

OPTIONAL ACCESSORIES only 5-speed fully synchronized mechanical gearbox.

Cedric - Gloria Series

PRICES (Tokyo):

1 Cedric 2000 Standard Sedan	1,202,000	yen
2 Cedric 2000 De Luxe Sedan	1,309,000	yen
3 Cedric 2000 Custom De Luxe Sedan	1,473,000	yen
4 Cedric 2000 Custom De Luxe 4-dr Hardtop	1,614,000	yen
5 Cedric 2000 GL Sedan	1,654,000	yen
6 Cedric 2000 GL 4-door Hardtop	1,824,000	yen
7 Cedric 2000 GL-E Sedan	1,734,000	yen
8 Cedric 2000 GL-E 2-door Hardtop	1,872,000	yen
9 Cedric 2000 GL-E 4-door Hardtop	1,929,000	yen
10 Cedric 2000 SGL-E Sedan	2,096,000	yen
11 Cedric 2000 SGL-E 2-door Hardtop	2,244,000	yen
12 Cedric 2000 SGL-E 4-door Hardtop	2,299,000	yen
13 Cedric 2000 F Type SGL-E 4-door Hardtop	2,319,000	yen
14 Gloria 2000 Diesel Standard Sedan	1,282,000	yen
15 Gloria 2200 Diesel Standard Sedan	1,354,000	yen
16 Gloria 2200 Diesel De Luxe Sedan	1,451,000	yen
17 Gloria 2200 Diesel GL Sedan	1,686,000	yen
18 Gloria 2800 SGL Sedan	2,404,000	yen
19 Gloria 2800 SGL 4-door Hardtop	2,576,000	yen
20 Gloria 2800 Brougham Sedan	2,643,000	yen
21 Gloria 2800 Brougham 2-door Hardtop	2,527,000	yen
22 Gloria 2800 Brougham 4-door Hardtop	2,770,000	yen

NISSAN Gloria 2200 (Diesel engine)

Power team:	Standard for:	Optional for:
115 hp	1 to 6	—
130 hp	7 to 13	—
80 hp	—	1 to 6
60 hp	14	—
65 hp	15 to 17	—
140 hp	18,19	—
145 hp	20 to 22	—

115 hp power team

ENGINE front, 4 stroke; 6 cylinders, in line; 121.9 cu in, 1,998 cc (3.07 x 2.74 in, 78 x 69.7 mm); compression ratio: 8.6:1; max power (JIS): 115 hp at 5,600 rpm; max torque (JIS): 120 lb ft, 16.5 kg m at 3,600 rpm; 57.6 hp/l; cast iron cylinder block, light alloy head; 7 crankshaft bearings; valves: overhead, in line, rockers; camshafts: 1, overhead; lubrication: rotary pump, full flow filter, 8.3 imp pt, 9.9 US pt, 4.7 l; 1 Hitachi DCH340 downdraught twin barrel carburettor; emission control with catalytic converter, secondary air injection and exhaust gas recirculation; fuel feed: mechanical pump; water-cooled, 17.6 imp pt, 21.1 US pt, 10 l.

TRANSMISSION driving wheels: rear; clutch: single dry plate (diaphragm); gearbox: mechanical; gears: 4, fully synchronized; ratios: I 3.592, II 2.246, III 1.415, IV 1, rev 3.657; lever: central; final drive: hypoid bevel; axle ratio: 4.375; width of rims: 5''; tyres: 6.95 x 14.

PERFORMANCE max speeds: (I) 25 mph, 40 km/h; (II) 53 mph, 85 km/h; (III) 87 mph, 140 km/h; (IV) 96 mph, 155 km/h; power-weight ratio: Standard Sedan 25.9 lb/hp, 11.7 kg/hp; carrying capacity: 882 lb, 400 kg; consumption: 38.2 m/imp gal, 31.8 m/US gal, 7.4 l x 100 km at 37 mph, 60 km/h.

CHASSIS integral; front suspension: independent, wishbones, coil springs, anti-roll bar, telescopic dampers; rear: rigid axle, semi-elliptic leafsprings, telescopic dampers.

STEERING recirculating ball, servo; turns lock to lock: 4.70 (GL and SGL models 3.80).

BRAKES front disc, rear drum, servo: lining area: front 23.6 sq in, 152 sq cm, rear 71.9 sq in, 464 sq cm, total 95.5 sq in, 616 sq cm.

ELECTRICAL EQUIPMENT 12 V; 35 Ah battery; 50 A alternator; 4 headlamps.

DIMENSIONS AND WEIGHT wheel base: 105.91 in, 269 cm; front and rear tracks: 54.33 in, 138 cm; length: 184.65 in, 469 cm; width: 66.54 in, 169 cm; height: sedans 56.69 in, 144 cm - 4-dr. hardtops 56.30 in, 143 cm; ground clearance: 7.09 in, 18 cm; weight: Standard Sedan 2,977 lb, 1,350 kg - De Luxe Sedan 3,021 lb, 1,370 kg - Custom De Luxe Sedan 3,043 lb, 1,380 kg - Custom De Luxe 4-dr. Hardtop 3,087 lb, 1,400 kg - Gl Sedan 3,120 lb, 1,415 kg - GL 4-dr. Hardtop 3,164 lb, 1,435 kg - SGL Sedan 3,120 lb, 1415 kg - SGL 4-dr. Hardtop 3,164 lb, 1,435 kg; turning circle (between walls): 39.4 ft, 12 m; fuel tank: 14.7 imp gal, 17.7 US gal, 67 l.

BODY 5 seats, separate front seats, reclining backrests, built-in headrests.

PRACTICAL INSTRUCTIONS fuel: 90 oct lead-free petrol; oil: engine 8.3 imp pt, 9.9 US pt, 4.7 l, SAE 20W-30, change every 3,100 miles, 5,000 km - gearbox 2.6 imp pt, 3.2 US pt, 1.5 l, SAE 90, change every 31,000 miles, 50,000 km - final drive 1.6 imp pt, 1.9 US pt, 0.9 l, SAE 90, change every 31,000 miles, 50,000 km; tappet clearances: inlet 0.010 in, 0.25 mm, exhaust 0.012 in, 0.30 mm; valve timing: 8° 44° 50° 10°; tyre pressure: front 21 psi, 1.5 atm, rear 21 psi, 1.5 atm.

OPTIONAL ACCESSORIES 4-speed fully synchronized mechanical gearbox (I 3.143, II 1.641, III 1, IV 0.784, rev 3.657), steering column lever, 4.625 axle ratio; Nissan automatic transmission with 3 ratios (I 2.458, II 1.458, III 1, rev 2.182), steering column lever, 4.625 axle ratio.

130 hp power team

See 115 hp power team, except for:

ENGINE max power (JIS): 130 hp at 6,000 rpm; max torque (JIS): 123 lb ft, 17 kg m at 4,400 rpm; 65.1 hp/l; Bosch electronic fuel injection; emission control with catalytic converter; fuel feed: electric pump.

PERFORMANCE max speed: 106 mph, 170 km/h; power-weight ratio: sedans 24 lb/hp, 10.9 kg/hp.

STEERING turns lock to lock: 3.80.

NISSAN Gloria 2200 Diesel GL Sedan

DIMENSIONS AND WEIGHT weight: sedans 3,120 lb, 1,415 kg - 2-dr. hardtops 3,098 lb, 1,405 kg - 4-dr. hardtops 3,164 lb, 1,435 kg.

PRACTICAL INSTRUCTIONS valve timing: 12° 48° 54° 14°.

80 hp power team

See 115 hp power team, except for:

ENGINE 4 cylinders, in line; 120.9 cu in, 1,982 cc (3.43 x 3.27 in, 87.2 x 83 mm); compression ratio: 9:1; max power (JIS): 80 hp at 4,800 rpm; max torque (JIS): 109 lb ft, 15 kg m at 2,800 rpm; 40.4 hp/l; 3 crankshaft bearings; valves: overhead, in line, push-rods and rockers; camshafts: 1, side; 1 245304 LPG carburettor; emission control with catalytic converter; cooling system capacity: 12.3 imp pt, 14.8 US pt, 7 l.

TRANSMISSION gears: 3, fully synchronized; ratios: I 3.143, II 1.641, III 1, rev 3.657; lever: steering column; tyres: 6.40 x 14.

PERFORMANCE max speed: 81 mph, 130 km/h; power-weight ratio: 38 lb/hp, 17.2 kg/hp.

BRAKES drum, servo.

DIMENSIONS AND WEIGHT dry weight: 3,043 lb, 1,380 kg.

PRACTICAL INSTRUCTIONS fuel: liquid petroleum gas; tappet clearances (hot): inlet 0.015 in, 0.38 mm, exhaust 0.015 in, 0.38 mm; valve timing: 16° 52° 54° 14°.

60 hp power team

See 80 hp power team, except for:

ENGINE Diesel, 4 cylinders, in line; 121.5 cu in, 1,991 cc (3.27 x 3.62 in, 83 x 92 mm); compression ratio: 20:1; max power (JIS): 60 hp at 4,000 rpm; max torque (JIS): 94 lb ft, 13 kg m at 1,800 rpm; 30.1 hp/l; lubricating system capacity: 9.9 imp pt, 11.8 US pt, 5.6 l; fuel injection, Ricardo Commet pre-combustion chamber type.

PERFORMANCE max speed: 68 mph, 110 km/h; power-weight ratio: 50.7 lb/hp, 23 kg/hp; fuel consumption: 52.3 m/imp gal, 43.6 m/US gal, 5.4 l x 100 km at 37 mph, 60 km/h.

DIMENSIONS AND WEIGHT dry weight: 3,043 lb, 1,380 kg.

PRACTICAL INSTRUCTIONS fuel: Diesel oil; oil: engine 9.9 imp pt, 11.8 US pt, 5.6 l; valve timing: 28° 67° 67° 28°.

OPTIONAL ACCESSORIES 4-speed fully synchronized mechanical gearbox with steering column lever.

65 hp power team

See 60 hp power team, except for:

ENGINE Diesel; 132 cu in, 2,164 cc (3.27 x 3.94 in, 83 x 100 mm); compression ratio: 20.8:1; max power (JIS): 65 hp at 4,000 rpm; max torque (JIS): 105 lb ft, 14.5 kg m at 1,800 rpm; 30 hp/l.

TRANSMISSION tyres: Standard 6.40 x 14 - De Luxe and GL 6.95 x 14.

PERFORMANCE max speed: 81 mph, 130 km/h; power-weight ratio: Standard 46.3 lb/hp, 21 kg/hp.

STEERING GL servo; turns lock to lock: 3.80.

BRAKES GL front disc.

DIMENSIONS AND WEIGHT weight: Standard 3,010 lb, 1,365 kg - De Luxe 3,021 lb, 1,370 kg - GL 3,120 lb, 1,415 kg.

OPTIONAL ACCESSORIES 4-speed mechanical gearbox with steering column lever and overdrive IV ratio (I 3.143, II 1.641, III 1, IV 0.784), axle ratio 4.625; 5-speed mechanical gearbox (I 3.592, II 2.246, III 1.415, IV 1, V 0.882), axle ratio 4.111.

140 hp power team

See 115 hp power team, except for:

ENGINE 168 cu in, 2,753 cc (3.39 x 3.11 in, 86 x 79 mm); compression ratio: 8.3:1; max power (JIS): 140 hp at 5,200 rpm; max torque (JIS): 163 lb ft, 22.5 kg m at 3,600 rpm: 50.9 hp/l; 1 Hitachi DAH342 downdraught twin barrel carburettor; fuel feed: electric pump.

TRANSMISSION gears: 5; ratios: I 3.321, II 2.077, III 1.308, IV 1, V 0.864, rev 3.382; axle ratio: 3.889; tyres: 7.35 S x 14.

PERFORMANCE max speed: 112 mph, 180 km/h; power-weight ratio: SGL Sedan 22.4 lb/hp, 10.2 kg/hp.

NISSAN Fairlady Z 2+2 Sports

STEERING turns lock to lock: 3.80.

DIMENSIONS AND WEIGHT weight: SGL Sedan 3,142 lb, 1,425 kg - SGL 2-dr. Hardtop 3,120 lb, 1,415 kg - 4-dr. hardtops 3,208 lb, 1,455 kg.

PRACTICAL INSTRUCTIONS valve timing: 12° 48° 54° 14°.

OPTIONAL ACCESSORIES 4-speed fully synchronized mechanical gearbox with 4.375 axle ratio; JATCO automatic transmission with 3 ratios (I 2.458, II 1.458, III 1, rev 2.182), max speed 96 mph, 155 km/h, axle ratio 4.111.

145 hp power team

See 140 hp power team, except for:

ENGINE max power (JIS): 145 hp at 5,200 rpm; max torque (JIS): 166.7 lb ft, 23 kg m at 4,000 rpm; 52.7 hp/l; Bosch L-Jetronic fuel injection.

PERFORMANCE power-weight ratio: Brougham Sedan 22.6 lb/hp, 10.2 kg/hp; consumption: 20.3 m/imp gal, 16.9 m/US gal, 13.9 l x 100 km.

DIMENSIONS AND WEIGHT length: 188.38 in, 478 cm; weight: Brougham Sedan 3,274 lb, 1,485 kg - Brougham 2-dr. Hardtop 3,175 lb, 1,440 kg - Brougham 4-dr. Hardtop 3,330 lb, 1,510 kg.

NISSAN Fairlady Z 2+2 Sports

Fairlady - Datsun 280 Z Series

PRICES (Tokyo):

1 Fairlady Z Sports	1,370,000	yen
2 Fairlady ZL Sports	1,565,000	yen
3 Fairlady ZT Sports	1,715,000	yen
4 Fairlady Z 2 + 2 Sports	1,552,000	yen
5 Fairlady ZL 2 + 2 Sports	1,747,000	yen
6 Fairlady ZT 2 + 2 Sports	1,897,000	yen
7 Datsun 280 Z Sports	—	
8 Datsun 280 Z 2 + 2 Sports	—	

For USA prices, see price index.

Power team:	Standard for:	Optional for:
130 hp	1 to 6	—
149 hp	7,8	—

130 hp power team

ENGINE front, 4 stroke; 6 cylinders, in line; 121.9 cu in, 1,998 cc (3.07 x 2.74 in, 78 x 69.7 mm); compression ratio: 8.6:1; max power (JIS): 130 hp at 6,000 rpm; max torque (JIS): 123 lb ft, 17 kg m at 4,400 rpm; max engine rpm: 7,500; 65.1 hp/l; cast iron cylinder block, light alloy head; 7 crankshaft bearings; valves: overhead, in line, rockers; camshafts: 1, overhead; lubrication: rotary pump, full flow filter, 7 imp pt, 8.5 US pt, 4 l; Bosch electronic fuel injection; emission control, exhaust gas recirculation; fuel feed: electric pump; water-cooled, 16.5 imp pt, 19.9 US pt, 9.4 l.

TRANSMISSION driving wheels: rear; clutch: single dry plate; gearbox: mechanical; gears: 4 (5 for ZL and ZL 2+2 only), fully synchronized; ratios: I 3.592, II 2.246, III 1.415, IV 1, rev 3.164 - ZL and ZL 2+2 I 3.321, II 2.077, III 1.308, IV 1, V 0.864, rev 3.382; lever: central; final drive: hypoid bevel; axle ratio: 3.900 - ZL and ZL 2+2 4.110; width of rims: 5'' - ZT models 5.5''; tyres: 6.45 H x 14 - ZT models 195/70 HR x 14.

PERFORMANCE max speeds: 112 mph, 180 km/h; power-weight ratio: Z 19 lb/hp, 8.6 kg/hp; carrying capacity: 397 lb, 180 kg; acceleration: standing ¼ mile 17 sec; speed in direct drive at 1,000 rpm: 15.8 mph, 25.3 km/h; consumption: 42.2 m/imp gal, 35.1 m/US gal, 6.7 l x 100 km at 37 mph, 60 km/h.

CHASSIS integral, front auxiliary frame; front suspension: independent, by McPherson, coil springs/telescopic damper struts, lower wishbones (trailing links), anti-roll bar; rear: independent, semi-trailing arms, coil springs, telescopic dampers - ZL and ZT 2+2 anti-roll bar.

STEERING rack-and-pinion; turns lock to lock: 2.60 - 2+2 models 3.10.

BRAKES front disc, rear drum, servo; lining area: front 24.8 sq in, 160 sq cm, 54 sq in, 348 sq cm, total 78.8 sq in, 508 sq cm.

ELECTRICAL EQUIPMENT 12 V; 35 Ah battery; 500 W alternator; Mitsubishi distributor; 2 headlamps.

DIMENSIONS AND WEIGHT wheel base: 90.55 in, 230 cm - Z 2+2 and ZL 2+2 102.56 in, 260 cm; tracks: 53.15 in, 135 cm front, 52.76 in, 134 cm rear; length: 161.81 in, 411 cm - Z 2+2 and ZL 2+2 174.21 in, 442 cm; width: 64.17 in, 163 cm - Z 2+2 and ZL 2+2 64.96 in, 165 cm; height: 50.79 in, 129 cm; ground clearance: 5.91 in, 15 cm; weight:

130 HP POWER TEAM

Z 2,459 lb, 1,115 kg - 2L and ZT 2,503 lb, 1,135 kg - Z 2 + 2 2,613 lb, 1,185 kg - ZL 2 + 2 and ZT 2 + 2 2,657 lb, 1,205 kg; turning circle (between walls): 31.5 ft, 9.6 m; fuel tank: 13.2 imp gal, 15.8 US gal, 60 l.

BODY coupé; 2 doors; 2 seats (4 for Z 2 + 2, ZL 2 + 2 and ZT 2 + 2), reclining backrests, built-in headrests.

PRACTICAL INSTRUCTIONS fuel: 98-100 oct lead-free petrol; oil: engine 7 imp pt, 8.5 US pt, 4 l, SAE 20W-30, change every 3,100 miles, 5,000 km - gearbox 2.6 imp pt, 3.2 US pt, 1.5 l, SAE 90, change every 31,100 miles, 50,000 km - final drive 2.3 imp pt, 2.7 US pt, 1.3 l, SAE 90, change every 31,100 miles, 50,000 km; greasing: every 31,100 miles, 50,000 km, 5 points; tappet clearances (hot): inlet 0.010 in, 0.25 mm, exhaust 0.012 in, 0.30 mm; valve timing: 12° 48° 54° 14°; tyre pressure: front 33 psi, 2.3 atm, rear 33 psi, 2.3 atm.

OPTIONAL ACCESSORIES (for ZL and ZL 2+2 only) automatic transmission with 3 ratios (I 2.458, II 1.458, III 1, rev 2.182).

149 hp power team

See 130 hp power team, except for:

ENGINE 168 cu in, 2,754 cc (3.39 x 3.11 in, 86.1 x 79 mm); compression ratio: 8.3:1; max power (SAE): 149 hp at 5,600 rpm; max torque (SAE): 163 lb ft, 22.5 kg m at 4,400 rpm; max engine rpm: 6,000; 54.1 hp/l; lubricating system capacity: 7.2 imp pt, 8.7 US pt, 4.1 l; 2 Hitachi HJG46W horizontal twin barrel carburettors; fuel feed: mechanical pump; cooling system capacity: 10.6 imp pt, 12.7 US pt, 6 l.

TRANSMISSION gearbox ratios: I 3.321, II 2.080, III 1.310, IV 1, rev 3.382; axle ratio: 3.550; width of rims: 5''; tyres: 195/70 x 14.

PERFORMANCE max speeds: (I) 37 mph, 59 km/h; (II) 60 mph, 96 km/h; (III) 96 mph, 154 km/h; (IV) 115 mph, 185 km/h; power-weight ratio: 19.3 lb/hp, 8.7 kg/hp.

ELECTRICAL EQUIPMENT 40 Ah battery; Hitachi distributor.

DIMENSIONS AND WEIGHT length: 280Z 173.20 in, 440 cm; width: 64.20 in, 163 cm; height: 51 in, 129 cm; dry weight: 2,875 lb, 1,304 kg.

President Series

PRICES (Tokyo):

President C Sedan	3,846,000 yen
President D Sedan	4,238,000 yen
President Sovereign Sedan	4,627,000 yen

200 hp power team

ENGINE front, 4 stroke; 8 cylinders, Vee-slanted at 90°; 269.3 cu in, 4,414 cc (3.62 x 3.27 in, 92 x 83 mm); compression ratio: 8.6:1; max power (JIS): 200 hp at 4,800 rpm; max torque (JIS): 250 lb ft, 34.5 kg m at 3,200 rpm; max engine rpm: 5,200; 45.1 hp/l; cast iron cylinder block, light alloy head; 5 crankshaft bearings; valves: overhead, Vee-slanted, push-rods and rockers, hydraulic tappets; camshafts: 1, at centre of Vee; lubrication: gear pump, full flow filter, 8.3 imp pt, 9.9 US pt, 4.7 l; Bosch L-Jetronic fuel injection; emission control with 2 catalytic converters and exhaust gas recirculation; fuel feed: electric pump; water-cooled, 28.2 imp pt, 33.8 US pt, 16 l.

TRANSMISSION driving wheels: rear; gearbox: automatic transmission, hydraulic torque converter and planetary gears with 3 ratios; ratios: I 2.458, II 1.458, III 1, rev 2.182; lever: steering column; final drive: hypoid bevel; axle ratio: 3.364; width of rims: 5''; tyres: 7.75S x 14.

PERFORMANCE max speeds: (I) 42 mph, 68 km/h; (II) 65 mph, 115 km/h; (III) 112 mph, 180 km/h; power-weight ratio: C Sedan 20.3 lb/hp, 9.2 kg/hp; consumption: 14.7 m/imp gal, 12.2 m/US gal, 19.2 l x 100 km.

CHASSIS integral; front suspension: independent, wishbones, coil springs, anti-roll bar, telescopic dampers; rear: rigid axle, semi-elliptic leafsprings, telescopic dampers.

STEERING recirculating ball, servo; turns lock to lock: 4.10.

BRAKES front disc, rear drum, servo; lining area: front 26.7 sq in, 172 sq cm, rear 71.9 sq in, 464 sq cm, total 98.6 sq in, 636 sq cm.

ELECTRICAL EQUIPMENT 12 V; 60 Ah battery; 600 W alternator; Hitachi distributor; 4 headlamps.

DIMENSIONS AND WEIGHT wheel base: 112.20 in, 285 cm; front and rear tracks: 58.66 in, 149 cm; length: 206.69 in, 525 cm - D and Sovereign 207.87 in, 528 cm; width: 72.05 in, 183 cm; height: 58.27 in, 148 cm; ground clearance: 7.28 in, 18 cm; weight: C Sedan 4,057 lb, 1,850 kg - D Sedan 4,123 lb, 1,870 kg - Sovereign 4,134 lb, 1,875 kg; weight distribution: 54% front, 46% rear; turning circle (between walls): 42 ft, 12.8 m; fuel tank: 16.5 imp gal, 19.8 US gal, 7.5 l.

NISSAN President Sovereign Sedan

BODY saloon/sedan; 4 doors; 6 seats, bench front seats, reclining backrests, built-in headrests; electrically-controlled windows.

PRACTICAL INSTRUCTIONS fuel: 90 oct lead-free petrol; oil: engine 8.3 imp pt, 9.9 US pt, 4.7 l, SAE 10W-30, change every 3,100 miles, 5,000 km - automatic transmission 13.6 imp pt, 16.3 US pt, 7.7 l - final drive 2.6 imp pt, 3.2 US pt, 1.5 l, SAE 90, change every 24,900 miles, 40,000 km; greasing: every 12,400 miles, 20,000 km, 19 points; valve timing: 22° 62° 60° 16°; tyre pressure: front 24 psi, 1.7 atm, rear 24 psi, 1.7 atm.

OPTIONAL ACCESSORIES air-conditioning; separate front seats.

Patrol 4WD

PRICE (Tokyo): 1,302,000 yen

ENGINE front, 4 stroke; 6 cylinders, vertical, in line; 241.4 cu in, 3,956 cc (3.37 x 4.50 in, 85.7 x 114.3 mm); compression ratio: 7.6:1; max power (JIS): 130 hp at 3,600 rpm; max torque (JIS): 217 lb ft, 30 kg m at 1,600 rpm; max engine rpm: 3,600; 32.9 hp/l; cast iron cylinder block and head; 7 crankshaft bearings; valves: overhead, in line, push-rods and rockers; camshafts: 1, side; lubrication: gear pump, full flow filter, oil cooler; 9.3 imp pt, 11.2 US pt, 5.3 l; 1 Hitachi VC 42-4A downdraught carburettor; fuel feed: mechanical pump; water-cooled, 32.2 imp pt, 38.7 US pt, 18.3 l.

TRANSMISSION driving wheels: front (automatically engaged with transfer box low ratio) and rear; clutch: single dry plate; gearbox: mechanical; gears: 3, with high and low ratios, II and III synchronized; ratios: I 2.900, II 1.562, III 1, rev 4.015; low ratios: I 6.565, II 3.536, III 2.264, rev 9.089; levers: 3, central; final drive: hypoid bevel; axle ratio: 4.100; tyres: 6.50 x 16.

PERFORMANCE max speed: 78 mph, 125 km/h; power-weight ratio: 28.2 lb/hp, 12.8 kg/hp; carrying capacity: 1,654 lb, 750 kg; speed in direct drive at 1,000 rpm: 21.6 mph, 34.7 km/h; fuel consumption: not declared.

CHASSIS ladder frame; front and rear suspension: rigid axle, semi-elliptic leafsprings, telescopic dampers.

STEERING worm and roller.

BRAKES drum, servo.

ELECTRICAL EQUIPMENT 12 V; 60 Ah battery; 35 A alternator; Hitachi distributor; 2 headlamps.

DIMENSIONS AND WEIGHT wheel base: 98.43 in, 250 cm; tracks: 54.57 in, 139 cm front, 55.28 in, 140 cm rear; length: 160.24 in, 407 cm; width: 67.52 in, 171 cm; height: 79.33 in, 201 cm; ground clearance: 8.46 in, 21.5 cm; dry weight: 3,660 lb, 1,660 kg; turning circle (between walls): 38.7 ft, 11.9 m; fuel tank: 14.3 imp gal, 17.2 US gal, 65 l.

BODY open; 2 doors; 3 seats, bench front seats.

PRACTICAL INSTRUCTIONS fuel: 85-90 oct petrol.

NISSAN Patrol 4WD

24,900 miles, 40,000 km or 2 years; tappet clearances: inlet 0.006 in, 0.15 mm, exhaust 0.010 in, 0.25 mm; valve timing: 24° 64° 64° 24°; tyre pressure: front 13 psi, 0.9 atm, rear 28 psi, 2 atm.

Leone SEEC-T Series

PRICES (Tokyo):

1 1400 Standard 2-door Sedan	749,000	yen
2 1400 De Luxe 2-door Sedan	836,000	yen
3 1400 De Luxe 4-door Sedan	861,000	yen
4 1400 GL 2-door Sedan	900,000	yen
5 1400 GL 4-door Sedan	925,000	yen
6 1600 De Luxe 4-door Sedan	886,000	yen
7 1600 GL 4-door Sedan	950,000	yen
8 1600 Custom 4-door Sedan	986,000	yen
9 1600 Super Custom 4-door Sedan	1,096,000	yen
10 1600 GL Coupé	997,000	yen
11 1600 GF Hardtop	1,017,000	yen
12 1600 Grand Am 4-door Sedan	1,096,000	yen
13 1600 Grand Am Hardtop	1,164,000	yen
14 1600 Super Touring 4-door Sedan	1,099,000	yen
15 1600 RX Coupé	1,089,000	yen
16 1600 GFT Hardtop	1,114,000	yen
17 1600 Grand Am T Hardtop	1,286,000	yen
18 1600 4WD 4-door Sedan	1,320,000	yen
19 1600 4WD Station Wagon	1,124,000	yen

For GB and USA prices, see price index.

Power team:	Standard for:	Optional for:
72 hp	1 to 5	—
82 hp	6 to 13	—
95 hp	14 to 17	—
80 hp	18	—
85 hp	19	—

SUBARU Rex 550 SEEC-T A II Sedan

SUBARU   JAPAN

Rex 550 SEEC-T Series

PRICES (Tokyo):

Standard 2-door Sedan	551,000	yen
A I 2-door Sedan	618,000	yen
A I 4-door Sedan	643,000	yen
A II 2-door Sedan	657,000	yen
A II 4-door Sedan	682,000	yen
A II G 4-door Sedan	709,000	yen

31 hp power team

ENGINE rear, low emission SEEC-T type, transverse, 4 stroke; 2 cylinders, in line; 33.2 cu in, 544 cc (2.99 x 2.36 in, 76 x 60 mm); compression ratio: 8.5:1; max power (JIS): 31 hp at 6,200 rpm; max torque (JIS): 30.4 lb ft, 4.2 kg m at 3,500 rpm; max engine rpm: 7,000; 56.9 hp/l; cast iron block, light alloy head; 3 crankshaft bearings; valves: overhead, Vee-slanted, rockers; camshafts: 1, overhead; lubrication: rotary pump, full flow filter, 4.4 imp pt, 5.3 US pt, 2.5 l; 1 Hitachi DCG306 downdraught twin barrel carburettor; fuel feed: mechanical pump; water-cooled, 10.6 imp pt, 12.7 US pt, 6 l.

TRANSMISSION driving wheels: rear; clutch: single dry plate (diaphragm); gearbox: mechanical; gears: 4, fully synchronized; ratios: I 4.363, II 2.625, III 1.809, IV 1.269, rev 4.272; lever: central; final drive: helical spur gears; axle ratio: 4.315; width of rims: 3.5''; tyres: 5.20 x 10.

PERFORMANCE max speeds: (I) 21 mph, 34 km/h; (II) 34 mph, 55 km/h; (III) 50 mph, 80 km/h; (IV) 65 mph, 105 km/h; power-weight ratio: Standard 2-dr. Sedan 38 lb/hp, 17.3 kg/hp; carrying capacity: 706 lb, 320 kg; consumption: 58.8 m/imp gal, 48 m/US gal, 4.8 l x 100 km.

CHASSIS integral; front and rear suspension: independent, semi-trailing arms, torsion bars, telescopic dampers.

STEERING rack-and-pinion; turns lock to lock: 3.20.

BRAKES drum (for AII and AIIG, front disc brakes); lining area: front 37.2 sq in, 240 sq cm, rear 33.5 sq in, 216 sq cm, total 70.7 sq in, 456 sq cm.

ELECTRICAL EQUIPMENT 12 V; 30 Ah battery; 35 A alternator; Hitachi distributor; 2 headlamps.

DIMENSIONS AND WEIGHT wheel base: 75.59 in, 192 cm; tracks: 48.43 in, 123 cm front, 47.83 in, 121 cm rear; length: 125.39 in, 318 cm; height: 52.17 in, 132 cm; width: 54.92 in, 139 cm; ground clearance: 6.89 in, 17.5 cm; weight: Standard 2-dr. 1,180 lb, 535 kg - AI 2-dr. 1,202 lb, 545 kg - AI 4-dr. 1,246 lb, 565 kg - AII 2-dr. 1,213 lb, 550 kg - AII 4-dr. 1,257 lb, 570 kg - AIIG 4-dr. 1,257 lb, 570 kg; weight distribution: 37% front, 63% rear; turning circle (between walls): 30.2 ft, 9.2 m; fuel tank: 5.5 imp gal, 6.6 US gal, 25 l.

BODY saloon/sedan; 4 seats, separate front seats, reclining backrests, built-in headrests.

PRACTICAL INSTRUCTIONS fuel: 85-90 oct petrol; oil: engine 4.4 imp pt, 5.3 US pt, 2.5 l, SAE 10W-30 or 10W-40, change every 3,100 miles, 5,000 km - gearbox and final drive 1.6 imp pt, 1.9 US pt, 0.9 l, SAE 80, change every

SUBARU Rex 550 SEEC-T (31 hp engine)

72 hp power team

ENGINE front, SEEC-T type, low emission system with secondary air injection by suction valve, 4 stroke; 4 cylinders, horizontally opposed; 83 cu in, 1,361 cc (3.35 x 2.36 in, 85 x 60 mm); compression ratio: 8.5:1; max power (JIS): 72 hp at 6,000 rpm; max torque (JIS): 74 lb ft, 10.2 kg m at 3,600 rpm; max engine rpm: 6,400; 52.9 hp/l; light alloy cylinder block and head; 3 crankshaft bearings; valves: overhead, push-rods and rockers; camshafts: 1, side; lubrication: rotary pump, full flow filter, 5.8 imp pt, 7 US pt, 3.3 l; 1 Hitachi-Zenith-Stromberg DCJ306 downdraught twin barrel carburettor; fuel feed electric pump; water-cooled, 10.6 imp pt, 12.7 US pt, 6 l.

TRANSMISSION driving wheels: front; clutch: single dry plate (diaphragm); gearbox: mechanical; gears: 4, fully synchronized; ratios: I 3.666, II 2.157, III 1.464, IV 1.029, rev 4.100; lever: central; final drive: hypoid bevel; axle ratio: 4.125; width of rims: 4.5''; tyres: 6.15 x 13.

PERFORMANCE max speeds: (I) 27 mph, 44 km/h; (II) 45 mph, 73 km/h; (III) 67 mph, 108 km/h; (IV) 93 mph, 150 km/h; power-weight ratio: Standard 2-dr. Sedan 24.6 lb/hp, 11.2 kg/hp; carrying capacity: 882 lb, 400 kg; consumption: 34 m/imp gal, 28.3 m/US gal, 8.3 l x 100 km.

CHASSIS integral; front suspension: independent, by McPherson, coil springs/telescopic damper struts, lower wishbones (trailing links), anti-roll bar; rear: independent, semi-trailing arms, torsion bars, telescopic dampers.

SUBARU Leone SEEC-T 1600 Grand Am T Hardtop

72 HP POWER TEAM

STEERING rack-and-pinion; turns lock to lock: 3.80.

BRAKES drum (for GL front disc brakes); lining area: front 65.1 sq in, 420 sq cm - GL 24.2 sq in, 156 sq cm, rear 26 sq in, 168 sq cm, total 91.1 sq in, 588 sq cm - GL 50.2 sq in, 324 sq cm.

ELECTRICAL EQUIPMENT 12 V; 35 Ah battery; 50 A alternator; Hitachi distributor; 2 headlamps.

DIMENSIONS AND WEIGHT wheel base: 96.85 in, 246 cm; tracks: 49.80 in, 126.5 cm front, 49.60 in, 126 cm rear; length: 157.09 in, 399 cm; width: 61.02 in, 155 cm; height: 54.92 in, 139 cm; ground clearance: 6.69 in, 17 cm; weight: Standard 2-dr. Sedan 1,775 lb, 805 kg - De Luxe 2-dr. Sedan 1,797 lb, 815 kg - De Luxe 4-dr. Sedan 1,852 lb, 840 kg - GL 2-dr. Sedan 1,819 lb, 825 kg - GL 4-dr. Sedan 1,874 lb, 850 kg; turning circle (between walls): 35.4 ft, 10.8 m; fuel tank: 11 imp gal, 13.2 US gal, 50 l.

BODY 5 seats, separate front seats, reclining backrests, built-in headrests.

PRACTICAL INSTRUCTIONS fuel: 85-90 oct petrol; oil: engine 5.8 imp pt, 7 US pt, 3.3 l, SAE 10W-30, change every 3,100 miles, 5,000 km - gearbox and final drive 4.4 imp pt, 5.3 US pt, 2.5 l, SAE 90, change every 24,900 miles, 40,000 km; tappet clearances: inlet 0.010 in, 0.25 mm, exhaust 0.012 in, 0.30 mm; valve timing: 20° 60° 60° 20°; tyre pressure: front 24 psi, 1.7 atm, rear 20 psi, 1.4 atm.

82 hp power team

See 72 hp power team, except for:

ENGINE 97.3 cu in, 1,595 cc (3.62 x 2.36 in, 92 x 60 mm); max power (JIS): 82 hp at 5,600 rpm; max torque (JIS): 87 lb ft, 12 kg m at 3,600 rpm; 51.4 hp/l; 1 Hitachi DCG 306 downdraught twin barrel carburettor.

TRANSMISSION gears: Custom, Super Custom and Grand Am models 5 fully synchronized; ratios: V 0.789; axle ratio: 3.700; tyres: Grand Am models 155 SR x 13.

PERFORMANCE max speeds: (I) 31 mph, 50 km/h; (II) 50 mph, 80 km/h; (III) 75 mph, 120 km/h; (IV) 99 mph, 160 km/h; power-weight ratio: De Luxe 4-dr. Sedan 22.6 lb/hp, 10.2 kg/hp; consumption: 31 m/imp gal, 25.8 m/US, 9.1 l x 100 km.

BRAKES front disc, rear drum; lining area: front 24.2 sq in, 156 sq cm, rear 26 sq in, 168 sq cm, total 50.2 sq in, 324 sq cm.

ELECTRICAL EQUIPMENT (for GL and Custom sedans, and GF Hardtop) 4 headlamps.

DIMENSIONS AND WEIGHT length: GL Coupé and Super Custom Sedan 158.07 in, 401 cm - Grand Am models 164.17 in, 417 cm; height: Coupé 53.35 in, 135 cm - Hardtop 53.54 in, 136 cm; weight: De Luxe 4-dr. Sedan 1,852 lb, 840 kg - GL 4-dr. Sedan 1,874 lb, 850 kg - Custom 4-dr. Sedan 1,885 lb, 855 kg - Super Custom 4-dr. Sedan 1,896 lb, 860 kg - GL Coupé 1,819 lb, 825 kg - GF Hardtop 1,874 lb, 850 kg - Grand Am 4-dr. Sedan 1,940 lb, 880 kg - Grand Am Hardtop 1,951 lb, 885 kg.

OPTIONAL ACCESSORIES automatic transmission with 3 ratios (I 2.600, II 1.505, III 1, rev 2.167) 3.811 axle ratio.

95 hp power team

See 82 hp power team, except for:

ENGINE compression ratio: 9.5:1; max power (JIS): 95 hp at 6,400 rpm; max torque (JIS): 89 lb ft, 12.3 kg m at 4,000 rpm; 59.6 hp/l; 2 Hitachi DCG306 downdraught twin barrel carburettors.

TRANSMISSION gears: 5, fully synchronized; ratios: I 3.666, II 2.157, III 1.518, IV 1.156, V 0.942, rev 4.110; axle ratio: 3.700; tyres: 155 SR x 13 - RX Coupé 165/70 HR x 13.

PERFORMANCE max speeds: (I) 34 mph, 55 km/h; (II) 55 mph, 88 km/h; (III) 79 mph, 127 km/h; (IV) 102 mph, 165 km/h; (V) 105 mph, 170 km/h; power-weight ratio: Super Touring Sedan 20.4 lb/hp, 9.1 kg/hp; consumption: 29.7 m/imp gal, 24.7 m/US gal, 9.5 l x 100 km.

STEERING turns lock to lock: 2.90.

BRAKES front disc, rear drum, servo; lining area: front 24.2 sq in, 156 sq cm, rear 26 sq in, 168 sq cm, total 50.2 sq in, 324 sq cm (Super Touring Sedan and RX Coupé rear disc brake).

SUBARU Leone SEEC-T 1600 Super Custom Sedan

ELECTRICAL EQUIPMENT Super Touring Sedan and GFT Hardtop 4 headlamps.

DIMENSIONS AND WEIGHT front track: RX Coupé 50.39 in, 128 cm - Grand Am T 50.98 in, 129.5 cm; rear track: RX Coupé 50.19 in, 127.5 cm - Grand Am T 50.78 in, 129 cm; length: Grand Am T Hardtop 164.17 in, 417 cm; height: RX Coupé 53.35 in, 135.5 cm - GTF and Grand Am T Hardtop 53.54 in, 136 cm; weight: Super Touring Sedan 1,938 lb, 870 kg - RX Coupé 1,863 lb, 845 kg - GFT Hardtop 1,885 lb, 855 kg - Grand Am T Hardtop 1,951 lb, 885 kg.

PRACTICAL INSTRUCTIONS tappet clearances: inlet 0.010 in, 0.25 mm, exhaust 0.014 in, 0.30 mm; valve timing: 30° 66° 70° 26°.

80 hp power team

See 72 hp power team, except for:

ENGINE 97.3 cu in, 1,595 cc (3.62 x 2.36 in, 92 x 60 mm); max power (JIS): 80 hp at 5,600 rpm; max torque (JIS): 86 lb ft, 11.9 kg m at 3,600 rpm; 50.1 hp/l.

TRANSMISSION driving wheels: front and rear with transfer box; ratios: I 4.090, II 2.312, III 1.464, IV 1.029, rev 4.100; axle ratios: front 3.889, rear 3.900; tyres: 155SR x 13.

PERFORMANCE max speeds: (I) 25 mph, 40 km/h; (II) 45 mph, 72 km/h; (III) 72 mph, 116 km/h; (IV) 93 mph, 150 km/h.

BRAKES front disc, rear drum; lining area: front 24.2 sq in, 156 sq cm, rear 26 sq in, 168 sq cm, total 50.2 sq in, 324 sq cm.

DIMENSIONS AND WEIGHT tracks: 49.61 in, 126 cm front, 49.41 in, 125.5 cm rear; height: 56.10 in, 142.5 cm; ground clearance: 7.68 in, 19.5 cm; fuel tank: 9.9 imp gal, 11.9 US gal, 45 l.

BODY saloon/sedan; 4 doors.

PRACTICAL INSTRUCTIONS oil: gearbox and final drive 5.3 imp pt, 6.3 US pt, 3 l - rear final drive 1.4 imp pt, 1.7 US pt, 0.8 l, SAE 90, change every 24,900 miles, 40,000 km; valve timing: 20° 60° 60° 20°; tyre pressure: front 23 psi, 1.6 atm, rear 23 psi, 1.6 atm.

85 hp power team

See 80 hp power team, except for:

ENGINE no SEEC-T type; max power (JIS): 85 hp at 5,600 rpm; max torque (JIS): 88 lb ft, 12.2 kg m at 3,600 rpm; 53.3 hp/l; 1 Hitachi DCG306 downdraught twin barrel carburettor.

PERFORMANCE power-weight ratio: 24.6 lb/hp, 11.2 kg/hp; consumption: 29.7 m/imp pt, 24.7 m/US pt, 9.5 l x 100 km.

DIMENSIONS AND WEIGHT wheel base: 96.06 in, 244 cm; tracks: 49.41 in, 125 cm front, 47.44 in, 120 cm rear; length: 158.46 in, 402.5 cm; height: 57.48 in, 146 cm; ground clearance: 8.27 in, 21 cm; dry weight: 2,095 lb, 950 kg; turning circle (between walls): 40 ft, 12.2 m.

BODY estate car/station wagon; 4+1 doors.

PRACTICAL INSTRUCTIONS valve timing: 24° 64° 70° 18°.

SUBARU Leone SEEC-T 1600 4WD Sedan

SUZUKI   JAPAN

Fronte 7-S Series

PRICES (Tokyo) yen:	2-stroke	4-stroke
1 Standard 2-door Sedan	527,000	556,000
2 De Luxe 2-door Sedan	576,000	604,000
3 De Luxe 4-door Sedan	599,000	627,000
4 Super De Luxe 4-door Sedan	662,000	662,000
5 Custom 2-door Sedan	658,000	658,000
6 Custom 4-door Sedan	698,000	698,000
7 Cervo Coupé CX	608,000	—
8 Cervo Coupé CXG	698,000	—

Power team:	Standard for:	Optional for:
28 hp (2-stroke)	1 to 8	—
28 hp (4-stroke)	1 to 6	—

28 hp power team

(2-stroke engine)

ENGINE rear, transverse, 2 stroke; 3 cylinders, in line; 32.9 cu in, 539 cc (2.40 x 2.42 in, 61 x 61.5 mm); compression ratio: 7; max power (JIS): 28 hp at 5,000 rpm; max torque (JIS): 38.4 lb ft, 5.3 kg m at 3,000 rpm; max engine rpm: 6,400; 51.9 hp/l; cast iron block, light alloy head; 4 crankshaft bearings on ball bearings; lubrication: mechanical pump, injection to cylinders and crankshaft bearings, total loss system, 7 imp pt, 8.5 US pt, 4 l; 1 Mikuni-Solex downdraught carburettor; fuel feed: mechanical pump emission control 2 stage catalyst to meet 1978 Japanese emission standards; water-cooled, 9.5 imp pt, 11.4 US pt, 5.4 l.

TRANSMISSION driving wheels: rear; clutch: single dry plate (diaphragm); gearbox: mechanical; engine-gearbox ratio: 1.471; gears: 4, fully synchronized; ratios: I 3.182, II 1.875, III 1.238, IV 0.880, rev 2.727; lever: central; final drive: helical spur gears; axle ratio: 4.385; width of rims: 3.5''; tyres: 5.20 x 10 (Cervo Coupé CXG 145 SR x 10).

PERFORMANCE max speeds: (I) 18 mph, 30 km/h; (II) 32 mph, 52 km/h; (III) 49 mph, 79 km/h; (IV) 65 mph, 105 km/h; power-weight ratio: Standard 2-dr. Sedan 41.7 lb/hp, 18.9 kg/hp; consumption: 49.5 m/imp gal, 41.3 m/US gal, 5.7 l x 100 km.

CHASSIS integral; front suspension: independent, wishbones, coil springs, anti-roll bar, telescopic dampers; rear: independent, semi-trailing arms, coil springs, telescopic dampers.

STEERING rack-and-pinion; turns lock to lock: 2.75.

BRAKES drum (front disc on Cervo Coupé CXG); lining area: front 31.6 sq in, 204 sq cm, rear 31.6 sq in, 204 sq cm, total 63.2 sq in, 408 sq cm.

ELECTRICAL EQUIPMENT 12 V; 24 Ah battery; 35 A alternator; 2 headlamps.

SUZUKI Fronte 7-S Super De Luxe 4-door Sedan

DIMENSIONS AND WEIGHT wheel base: 79.92 in, 203 cm; tracks: 47.64 in, 121 cm front (Cervo Coupé 48.03 in, 122 cm), 46.65 in, 118 cm rear (Cervo Coupé 46.85 in, 119 cm); length: 125.59 in, 319 cm; width: 54.92 in, 139 cm; height: 51.18 in, 130 cm (Cervo Coupé 47.64 in, 121 cm); weight: Standard and De Luxe 2-dr. sedans 1,169 lb, 530 kg - Cervo Coupé CX 1,180 lb, 535 kg - Custom 2-dr. Sedan 1,191 lb, 540 kg - De Luxe 4-dr. Sedan 1,202 lb, 545 kg - Cervo Coupé CXG 1,212 lb, 550 kg - Super De Luxe and Custom 4-dr. sedans 1,224 lb, 555 kg; turning circle (between walls): 26.9 ft, 8.2 m; fuel tank: 5.7 imp gal, 6.9 US gal, 26 l.

BODY 4 seats, separate front seats, reclining backrests, built-in headrests.

PRACTICAL INSTRUCTIONS fuel: 85-90 oct mixture; oil: engine 7 imp pt, 8.5 US pt, 4 l, oil in separate tank - gearbox and final drive 2.1 imp pt, 2.5 US pt, 1.2 l, SAE 80; tyre pressure: front 16 psi, 1.1 atm, rear 33 psi, 2.3 atm.

28 hp power team

(4-stroke engine)

See 28 hp power team (2 stroke engine), except for:

ENGINE rear, transverse, 4 stroke; 2 cylinders, in line; 33.4 cu in, 547 cc (2.82 x 2.68 in, 71.6 x 68 mm); compression ratio: 8.7; max power (JIS): 28 hp at 6,000 rpm; max torque (JIS): 28.3 lb ft, 3.9 kg m at 3,500 rpm; max engine rpm: 6,300; 51.2 hp/l; 3 crankshaft bearings; valves: 2, overhead, rocker arms; camshafts: 1, overhead; lubrication: rotary pump, full flow filter, 5.1 imp pt, 6.1 US pt, 2.9 l; 1 downdraught twin barrel carburettor; emission control by Daihatsu lean-burn system with turbulence generating pot in the combustion chamber and catalytic converter.

TRANSMISSION engine - gearbox ratio: direct; ratios: I 3.583, II 2.176, III 1.375, IV 0.965, rev 3.363; axle ratio: 5.285.

PERFORMANCE max speeds: (I) 18 mph, 30 km/h; (II) 31 mph, 50 km/h; (III) 50 mph, 80 km/h; (IV) 68 mph, 110 km/h; power-weight ratio: Standard 2-dr. Sedan 43.2 lb/hp, 19.6 kg/hp.

DIMENSIONS AND WEIGHT weight: Standard 2-dr. Sedan 1,212 lb, 550 kg - De Luxe and Custom 2-dr. sedans 1,224 lb, 555 kg - De Luxe and Custom 4-dr. sedans 1,257 lb, 570 kg.

PRACTICAL INSTRUCTION fuel: 85-90 oct lead-free petrol; oil: engine 5.1 imp pt, 6.1 US pt, 2.9 l.

Fronte Hatch 55 Series

PRICES (Tokyo):

Hatch 55B Station Wagon	507,000 yen
Hatch 55D Station Wagon	537,000 yen
Hatch 55T Station Wagon	567,000 yen

25 hp power team

ENGINE front, 2 stroke; 3 cylinders, in line; 32.8 cu in, 539 cc (2.40 x 2.42 in, 61 x 61.5 mm); compression ratio: 6.4:1; max power (JIS): 25 hp at 4,500 rpm; max torque (JIS): 37 lb ft, 5.1 kg m at 3,000 rpm; max engine rpm: 6,000; 46.4 hp/l; cast iron block, light alloy head; 4 crankshaft bearings; lubrication: mechanical pump, injection to cylinders and crankshaft bearings, total loss system, 6.2 imp pt, 7.4 US pt, 3.5 l; 1 Solex downdraught carburettor; fuel feed: mechanical pump; water-cooled, 7.2 imp pt, 8.7 US pt, 4.1 l.

TRANSMISSION driving wheels: rear; clutch: single dry plate (diaphragm); gearbox: mechanical; engine-gearbox ratio 1.600; gears: 4, fully synchronized; ratios: I 3.428, II 2.109, III 1.307, IV 1, rev 3.600; lever: central; final drive: hypoid bevel; axle ratio: 5.125; tyres: 5.00 x 10.

PERFORMANCE max speeds: (I) 21 mph, 33 km/h; (II) 32 mph, 52 km/h; (III) 48 mph, 77 km/h; (IV) 67 mph, 108 km/h; power-weight ratio: 55 B 48.5 lb/hp, 22 kg/hp - 55 D and 55 49 T lb/hp, 22.2 kg/hp; carrying capacity: 662 lb, 300 kg; consumption: 70.6 m/imp gal, 58.8 m/US gal, 4 l x 100 km at 37 mph, 60 km/h.

CHASSIS integral; front suspension: independent, by McPherson, coil springs/telescopic damper struts, anti-roll bar, lower wishbones; rear: rigid axle, semi-elliptic leafsprings, telescopic dampers.

SUZUKI Cervo Coupé CXG

25 HP POWER TEAM

STEERING recirculating ball.

BRAKES drum.

ELECTRICAL EQUIPMENT 12 V; 24 Ah battery; 35 Ah alternator; 2 headlamps.

DIMENSIONS AND WEIGHT wheel base: 82.68 in, 210 cm; tracks: 46.46 in, 118 cm front, 42.52 in, 108 cm rear; length: 123.59 in, 319 cm; width: 53.74 in, 136 cm; height: 54.13 in, 137 cm; ground clearance: 5.91 in, 15 cm; weight: 55 B 1,213 lb, 550 kg - 55D and 55 T 1,224 lb, 555 kg; turning circle (between walls): 28.2 ft, 8.6 m; fuel tank: 5.7 imp gal, 6.9 US gal, 26 l.

BODY estate car/station wagon; 2 + 1 doors; 2 + 2 seats, separate front seats, reclining backrests; built-in headrests; back seat folding down to luggage table.

PRACTICAL INSTRUCTIONS fuel: 85-90 oct, mixture; oil: engine 6.2 imp pt, 7.4 US pt, 3.5 l - gearbox 2.1 imp pt, 2.5 US pt, 1.2 l, SAE 80 - final drive 1.6 imp pt, 1.9 US pt, 0.9 l, SAE 90; tyre pressure: front 17 psi, 1.2 atm, rear 38 psi, 2.7 atm.

Jimny 55 - Jimny 8 Series

PRICE (Tokyo):

1 Jimny 55 Softtop	748,000	yen
2 Jimny 55 Steelbody Wagon	797,000	yen
3 Jimny 8 Softtop	859,000	yen
4 Jimny 8 Steelbody Wagon	908,000	yen

Power team:	Standard for:	Optional for:
26 hp	1,2	—
41 hp	3,4	—

26 hp power team

ENGINE front, 2 stroke; 3 cylinders, in line; 32.8 cu in, 539 cc (2.40 x 2.42 in, 61 x 61.5 mm); compression ratio: 6.2:1; max power (JIS): 26 hp at 4,500 rpm; max torque (JIS): 38 lb ft, 5.3 kg m at 3,000 rpm; max engine rpm: 6,000; 48.2 hp/l; cast iron block, light alloy head; 4 crankshaft bearings, on ball bearings; lubrication: mechanical pump, injection to cylinders and crankshaft bearings, total system, 4.9 imp pt, 5.9 US pt, 2.8 l; 1 Solex downdraught carburettor; fuel feed: mechanical pump; water-cooled, 7.2 imp pt, 8.7 US pt, 4.1 l.

TRANSMISSION driving wheels: front and rear; clutch: single dry plate; gearbox: mechanical; gears: 4, fully synchronized and 2-ratio transfer box; ratios: I 3.855, II 2.359, III 1.543, IV 1, rev 4.026; transfer box ratios: Softtop I 3.012, II 1.714 - Steelbody I 2.571, II 1.562; levers: central; final drive: hypoid bevel; axle ratio: 4.875; width of rims: 4.5''; tyres: 6.00 x 16 - Steelbody 5.60 x 15.

PERFORMANCE max speeds: (I) 15 mph, 24 km/h; (II) 20 mph, 38 km/h; (III) 37 mph, 60 km/h; (IV) 55 mph, 88 km/h; power-weight ratio: Softtop 57.2 lb/hp, 26 kg/hp - Steelbody 60.2 lb/hp, 27.3 kg/hp; carrying capacity: Softtop 551 lb, 250 kg - Steelbody 441 lb, 200 kg; consumption: 47.9 m/imp gal, 39.9 m/US gal, 5.9 l x 100 km at 37 mph, 60 km/h.

CHASSIS box-type ladder frame; front suspension: rigid axle, semi-elliptic leafsprings, telescopic dampers; rear: rigid axle, semi-elliptic leafspring, telescopic dampers.

STEERING recirculating ball; turns lock to lock: 3.20.

BRAKES drum.

ELECTRICAL EQUIPMENT 12 V; 24 Ah battery; 35 A alternator; Nihon Denso distributor; 2 headlamps.

DIMENSIONS AND WEIGHT wheel base: 75.98 in, 193 cm; tracks: 42.91 in, 109 cm front, 43.31 in, 110 cm rear; length: 124.80 in, 317 cm; width: 50.98 in, 129 cm; height: Softtop 72.64 in, 184 cm - Steelbody 64.96 in, 165 cm; ground clearance: Softtop 9.45 in, 24 cm - Steelbody 8.07 in, 20.5 cm; weight: Softtop 1,488 lb, 675 kg - Steelbody 1,566 lb, 710 kg; turning circle (between walls): 28.9 ft, 8.8 m; fuel tank: 5.7 imp gal, 6.9 US gal, 26 l.

PRACTICAL INSTRUCTIONS fuel: 85-90 oct, mixture; oil: engine 6 imp pt, 7.2 US pt, 3.4 l, oil in separate tank - gearbox 1.4 imp pt, 1.7 US pt, 0.8 l, SAE 90, change every 6 months - transfer box 1.2 imp pt, 1.5 US pt, 0.7 l, SAE 90, change every 6 months - final drive 1.4 imp pt, 1.7 US pt,

SUZUKI Fronte Hatch 55T Station Wagon

SUZUKI Jimny (4-stroke 4-cylinder engine)

0.8 l, SAE 90, change every 6 months; tyre pressure: front 16 psi, 1.1 atm, rear 16 psi, 1.1 atm.

OPTIONAL ACCESSORIES (for Steelbody only) 2-ratio transfer box (I 1.714, II 3.012) with 6.000 x 16 tyres.

41 hp power team

See 26 hp power team, except for:

ENGINE front, 4 stroke; 4 cylinders, in line; 48.6 cu in, 797 cc (2.44 x 2.60 in, 62 x 66 mm); compression ratio: 8.7; max power (JIS): 41 hp at 5,500 rpm; max torque (JIS): 44 lb ft, 6.1 kg m at 3,500 rpm; 51.4 hp/l; valves: 2, overhead, rocker arms; camshafts: 1, overhead; lubrication: gear pump, full flow filter, 6.2 imp pt, 7.4 US pt, 3.5 l; 1 Mikuni-Solex sidedraught carburettor; water-cooled 6.7 imp pt, 8 US pt, 3.8 l.

TRANSMISSION final drive: 4.556.

PERFORMANCE max speeds: (I) 17 mph, 28 km/h; (II) 26 mph, 42 km/h; (III) 26 mph, 64 km/h; (IV) 60 mph, 97 km/h; power-weight ratio: Softtop 38.4 lb/hp, 17.4 kg/hp; consumption: 45.5 m/imp gal, 37.9 m/US gal, 6.2 l x 100 km at 37 mph, 60 km/h.

DIMENSIONS AND WEIGHT weight: Softtop 1,576 lb, 715 kg - Steelbody 1,676 lb, 760 kg.

PRACTICAL INSTRUCTION fuel: 85-90 oct lead-free petrol; oil: engine 6.2 imp pt, 7.4 US pt, 3.5 l.

SUZUKI Jimny 8 Steelbody Wagon

TOYOTA Publica Hi-De Luxe 2-door Sedan

TOYOTA   JAPAN

Publica - Starlet Series

PRICES EX WORKS:

1 Publica Standard 2-door Sedan	609,000	yen
2 Publica De Luxe 2-door Sedan	642,000	yen
3 Publica Hi-De Luxe 2-door Sedan	686,000	yen
4 Publica XL 2-door Sedan	719,000	yen
5 Starlet Standard 4-door Sedan	655,000	yen
6 Starlet De Luxe 4-door Sedan	685,000	yen
7 Starlet De Luxe Coupé	680,000	yen
8 Starlet Hi-De Luxe 4-door Sedan	727,000	yen
9 Starlet Hi-De Luxe Coupé	724,000	yen
10 Starlet XL 4-door Sedan	780,000	yen
11 Starlet XL Coupé	772,000	yen
12 Starlet ST Coupé	827,000	yen

64 hp power team

ENGINE front, 4 stroke; 4 cylinders, in line; 71.1 cu in, 1,166 cc (2.87 x 2.60 in, 75 x 66 mm); compression ratio: 9:1; max power (JIS): 64 hp at 5,800 rpm; max torque (JIS): 67 lb ft, 9.2 kg m at 3,600 rpm; max engine rpm: 6,300; 54.9 hp/l; cast iron block, light alloy head; 5 crankshaft bearings; valves: overhead, push-rods and rockers; camshafts: 1, side; lubrication: rotary pump, full flow filter, 6.2 imp pt, 7.4 US pt, 3.5 l; 1 Aisan 3K-U downdraught twin barrel carburettor; emission control with catalytic converter, secondary air injection and exhaust gas recirculation; fuel feed: mechanical pump; water-cooled, 10.9 imp pt, 13.1 US pt, 6.2 l.

TRANSMISSION driving wheels: rear; clutch: single dry plate (diaphragm); gearbox: mechanical; gears: 4, fully synchronized - Starlet ST Coupé 5, fully synchronized; ratios: I 3.789, II 2.220, III 1.435, IV 1, rev 4.316 - for Starlet ST Coupé V 0.865; lever: central; final drive: hypoid bevel; axle ratio: 3.909 - Starlet ST Coupé 4.100; width of rims: 4''; tyres: 6.00 x 12 - Starlet ST Coupé 155SR x 12.

PERFORMANCE max speeds: (I) 26 mph, 42 km/h; (II) 45 mph, 73 km/h; (III) 70 mph, 113 km/h; (IV) 96 mph, 155 km/h; power-weight ratio: Publica Standard 2-dr. Sedan 24.5 lb/hp, 11 kg/hp - Starlet Standard 4-dr. Sedan 26.5 lb/hp, 12 kg/hp; carrying capacity: 882 lb, 400 kg; consumption: 62.8 m/imp gal, 52.3 m/US gal, 4.5 l x 100 km at 37 mph, 60 km/h.

CHASSIS integral; front suspension: independent, by McPherson, coil springs/telescopic damper struts, lower wishbones (trailing links), anti-roll bar; rear: rigid axle, semi-elliptic leafsprings, telescopic dampers.

STEERING recirculating ball; turns lock to lock: 3.10.

BRAKES drum (for Hi-De Luxe and XL models front disc brakes); lining area: front 35.7 sq in, 230 sq cm - Hi-De Luxe and XL models 16.7 sq in, 108 sq cm, rear 35.7 sq in, 230 sq cm, total 71.4 sq in, 460 sq cm - Hi-De Luxe and XL models 52.4 sq in, 338 sq cm.

ELECTRICAL EQUIPMENT 12 V; 32 Ah battery; 30 A alternator; Denso distributor; 2 headlamps.

DIMENSIONS AND WEIGHT wheel base: 85.04 in, 216 cm - Starlets 88.98 in, 226 cm; front track: 48.43 in, 123 cm - Starlets 49.61 in, 126 cm; rear track: 47.24 in, 120 cm - Starlets 48.82 in, 124 cm; length: 145.28 in, 369 cm - Starlets 149.21 in, 379 cm; width: 57.09 in, 145 cm - Starlets 60.24 in, 153 cm; height: 54.33 in, 138 cm - Starlet coupés 51.97 in, 132 cm - Starlet sedans 52.76 in, 134 cm; ground clearance: 6.69 in, 17 cm; weight: Publica Standard 2-dr. Sedan 1,566 lb, 710 kg - De Luxe 2-dr. Sedan 1,588 lb, 720 kg - Hi-De Luxe 2-dr. Sedan 1,599 lb, 725 kg - XL 2-dr. Sedan 1,610 lb, 730 kg - Starlet Standard 4-dr. Sedan and XL Coupé 1,698 lb, 770 kg - De Luxe 4-dr. Sedan 1,720 lb, 780 kg - Hi-De Luxe 4-dr. Sedan and ST Coupé 1,731 lb, 785 kg - XL 4-dr. Sedan 1,742 lb, 790 kg - De Luxe Coupé 1,665 lb, 755 kg; turning circle (between walls): 31.5 ft, 9.6 m; fuel tank: 8.8 imp gal, 10.6 US gal, 40 l - Starlets 8.1 imp gal, 9.8 US gal, 37 l.

BODY 5 seats, separate front seats, reclining backrests, built-in headrests.

PRACTICAL INSTRUCTIONS fuel: 85-90 lead-free oct petrol; oil: engine 6.2 imp pt, 7.4 US pt, 3.5 l, SAE 20W-30, change every 3,100 miles, 5,000 km - gearbox 3 imp pt, 3.6 US pt, 1.7 l, SAE 80, change every 18,600 miles, 30,000 km - final drive 1.1 imp pt, 1.3 US pt, 0.6 l, SAE 90, change every 18,600 miles, 30,000 km; greasing: none; tappet clearances (hot): inlet 0.008 in, 0.20 mm, exhaust 0.012 in, 0.30 mm; valve timing: 16° 50° 50° 16°; tyre pressure: front 20 psi, 1.4 atm, rear 20 psi, 1.4 atm.

OPTIONAL ACCESSORIES automatic transmission, hydraulic torque converter and planetary gears with 2 ratios (I 1.820, II 1, rev 1.820), 4.100 axle ratio; 5-speed fully synchronized mechanical gearbox (I 3.587, II 2.022, III 1.384, IV 1, V 0.861, rev 3.484).

Corolla Series

PRICES (Tokyo):

1 1300 Standard 2-door Sedan	698,000	yen
2 1300 Standard 4-door Sedan	723,000	yen
3 1300 De Luxe 2-door Sedan	743,000	yen
4 1300 De Luxe 4-door Sedan	768,000	yen
5 1300 De Luxe 2-door Hardtop	798,000	yen
6 1300 De Luxe 2-door Coupé	811,000	yen
7 1300 De Luxe 3-door Liftback	836,000	yen
8 1300 HI-De Luxe 2-door Sedan	800,000	yen
9 1300 Hi-De Luxe 4-door Sedan	825,000	yen
10 1300 Hi-De Luxe 2-door Hardtop	851,000	yen
11 1300 Hi-De Luxe 2-door Coupé	863,000	yen
12 1300 Hi-De Luxe 3-door Liftback	892,000	yen
13 1300 SL 4-door Sedan	856,000	yen
14 1300 SL 2-door Hardtop	888,000	yen
15 1300 SL 2-door Coupé	892,000	yen
16 1300 SL 3-door Liftback	935,000	yen
17 1300 SR 2-door Coupé	898,000	yen
18 1400 De Luxe 2-door Sedan	779,000	yen
19 1400 De Luxe 4-door Sedan	804,000	yen
20 1400 De Luxe 2-door Hardtop	834,000	yen
21 1400 De Luxe 2-door Coupé	848,000	yen
22 1400 De Luxe 3-door Liftback	873,000	yen
23 1400 Hi-De Luxe 2-door Sedan	824,000	yen
24 1400 Hi-De Luxe 4-door Sedan	849,000	yen
25 1400 Hi-De Luxe 2-door Hardtop	875,000	yen
26 1400 Hi-De Luxe 2-door Coupé	886,000	yen
27 1400 Hi-De Luxe 3-door Liftback	924,000	yen
28 1400 SL 4-door Sedan	894,000	yen
29 1400 SL 2-door Hardtop	925,000	yen
30 1400 SL 2-door Coupé	929,000	yen
31 1400 SL 3-door Liftback	961,000	yen
32 1600 Hi-De Luxe 4-door Sedan	884,000	yen
33 1600 Hi-De Luxe Automatic 4-door Sedan	884,000	yen
34 1600 Hi-De Luxe 2-door Hardtop	910,000	yen
35 1600 Hi-De Luxe Automatic 2-door Hardtop	910,000	yen
36 1600 Hi-De Luxe 2-door Coupé	919,000	yen
37 1600 Hi-De Luxe Automatic 2-door Coupé	919,000	yen
38 1600 Hi-De Luxe 3-door Liftback	978,000	yen
39 1600 Hi-De Luxe Automatic 3-door Liftback	978,000	yen
40 1600 GSL 4-door Sedan	970,000	yen
41 1600 GSL Automatic 4-door Sedan	970,000	yen
42 1600 GSL 2-door Hardtop	1,003,000	yen
43 1600 GSL Automatic 2-door Hardtop	1,003,000	yen
44 1600 GSL 2-door Coupé	1,003,000	yen
45 1600 GSL Automatic 2-door Coupé	1,003,000	yen
46 1600 GSL 3-door Liftback	1,058,000	yen
47 1600 GSL Automatic 3-door Liftback	1,058,000	yen
48 1600 SR 2-door Coupé	1,011,000	yen
49 1600 Levin 2-door Coupé	1,227,000	yen
50 1600 Levin GT 2-door Coupé	1,282,000	yen
51 1600 GT 3-door Liftback	1,332,000	yen

For GB price, see price index.

Power team:	Standard for:	Optional for:
72 hp	1 to 17	—
82 hp	18 to 31	—
88 hp	32,34,36,38,40,42,44,46,48	—
90 hp	33,35,37,39,41,43,45,47	—
110 hp	49 to 51	—

TOYOTA Starlet ST Coupé

72 hp power team

ENGINE front, 4 stroke; 4 cylinders, in line; 78.72 cu in, 1,290 cc (2.95 x 2.87 in, 75 x 73 mm); compression ratio: 9:1; max power (JIS): 72 hp at 5,600 rpm; max torque (JIS): 76 lb ft, 10.5 kg m at 3,600 rpm; max engine rpm: 6,000; 55.8 hp/l; cast iron block, light alloy head; 5 crankshaft bearings; valves: overhead, push-rods and rockers; camshafts: 1, side; lubrication: rotary pump, full flow filter, 6.2 impt pt, 7.4 US pt, 3.5 l; 1 Aisan 4K-U downdraught twin barrel carburettor; emission control with catalytic converter, secondary air injection and exhaust gas recirculation; fuel feed: mechanical pump; water-cooled, 10.6 imp pt, 12.7 US pt, 6 l.

TRANSMISSION driving wheels: rear; clutch: single dry plate (diaphragm); gearbox: mechanical; gears: 4, fully synchronized; ratios: I 3.789, II 2.220, III 1.435, IV 1, rev 4.316; lever: central; final drive: hypoid bevel; axle ratio: 3.909; width of rims: 4''; tyres: 6.00 x 12 - Hi-De Luxe and SL models 6.15 x 13 - SR Coupé 155 SR x 13.

PERFORMANCE max speeds: (I) 25 mph, 40 km/h; (II) 46 mph, 74 km/h; (III) 67 mph, 108 km/h; (IV) 93 mph, 150 km/h; power-weight ratio: Standard 2-dr. Sedan 24.5 lb/hp, 11.1 kg/hp; consumption: 40 m/imp gal, 33 m/US gal, 7.1 l x 100 km.

CHASSIS integral; front suspension: independent, by McPherson, coil springs/telescopic damper struts, lower wish-

TOYOTA Corolla 1600 GSL 4-door Sedan

TOYOTA Corolla 1600 Hi-De Luxe Hardtop

bones (trailing links), anti-roll bar; rear: rigid axle, semi-elliptic leafsprings, telescopic dampers.

STEERING recirculating ball, variable ratio; turns lock to lock: 3.60.

BRAKES drum (for Hi-De Luxe and SL models front disc); lining area: front 47.1 sq in, 304 sq cm, rear 41.6 sq in, 268 sq cm, total 88.7 sq in, 572 sq cm.

ELECTRICAL EQUIPMENT 12 V; 32 Ah battery; 40 A alternator; Nihon-Denso distributor; 2 headlamps.

DIMENSIONS AND WEIGHT wheel base: 93.31 in, 237 cm; tracks: 50.98 in, 129 cm front, 50.59 in, 128 cm rear; length: 157.09 in, 339 cm - coupés 160.24 in, 407 cm - liftbacks 162.20 in, 412 cm; width: 61.81 in, 157 cm - coupés and liftbacks 62.99 in, 160 cm; height: sedans 54.33 in, 138 cm - hardtops 53.54 in, 136 cm - coupés and liftbacks 51.97 in, 132 cm - SR Coupé 51.57 in, 131 cm; ground clearance: 6.30 in, 16 cm; weight: Standard and De Luxe 2-dr. sedans 1,764 lb, 800 kg - Standard and De Luxe 4-dr. sedans and Hi-De Luxe 2-dr. Sedan 1,797 lb, 875 kg - De Luxe Hardtop and Coupé 1,808 lb, 820 kg - Hi-De Luxe 4-dr. Sedan, Hardtop and Coupé 1,830 lb, 830 kg - SL 4-dr. Sedan, Hardtop and Coupé 1,852 lb, 840 kg - De Luxe Liftback 1,863 lb, 845 kg - SR Coupé 1,874 lb, 850 kg - Hi-De Luxe Liftback 1,885 lb, 855 kg - SL Liftback 1,896 lb, 860 kg; turning circle (between walls): 33.5 ft, 10.2 m; fuel tank: 11 imp gal, 13.2 US gal, 50 l.

BODY 5 seats, separate front seats, reclining backrests, built-in headrests.

TOYOTA Corolla 1600 Hi-De Luxe Hardtop

PRACTICAL INSTRUCTIONS fuel: 90 oct lead-free petrol; oil: engine 6.2 imp pt, 7.4 US pt, 3.5 l, SAE 20W-30, change every 3,100 miles, 5,000 km - gearbox 1.8 imp pt, 2.1 US pt, 1 l, SAE 90, change every 18,600 miles, 30,000 km - final drive 1.4 imp pt, 1.7 US pt, 0.8 l, SAE 90, change every 18,600 miles, 30,000 km; greasing: none; tappet clearances (hot): inlet 0.008 in, 0.20 mm, exhaust 0.012 in, 0.30 mm; valve timing: 16° 50° 50° 16°; tyre pressure: front 20 psi, 1.4 atm, rear 20 psi, 1.4 atm.

OPTIONAL ACCESSORIES (for Hi-De Luxe and SL models and SR Coupé) 5-speed fully synchronized mechanical gearbox (I 3.789, II 2.220, III 1.435, IV 1, V 0.865, rev 4.316).

82 hp power team

See 72 hp power team, except for:

ENGINE 85.9 cu in, 1,407 cc (3.15 x 2.76 in, 80 x 70 mm); compression ratio: 8.5:1; max power (JIS): 82 hp at 5,800 rpm; max torque (JIS): 84 lb ft, 11.6 kg m at 3,400 rpm; max engine rpm: 6,300; 58.3 hp/l; valves: overhead, Vee-slanted, push-rods and rockers; lubrication: 7.9 imp pt, 9.5 US pt, 4.5 l; 1 Aisan T-U downdraught twin barrel carburettor; cooling system: 14.1 imp pt, 16.9 US pt, 8 l.

TRANSMISSION gearbox ratios: I 3.587, II 2.022, III 1.384, IV 1, rev 3.484; axle ratio: 3.727 - SL models 3.909; tyres: 6.15 x 13 - SL models 155 SR x 13.

PERFORMANCE max speeds: (I) 29 mph, 47 km/h; (II) 51 mph, 82 km/h; (III) 75 mph, 120 km/h; (IV) 99 mph, 160 km/h; power-weight ratio: De Luxe 2-dr. Sedan 24 lb/hp, 10.9 kg/hp; consumption: 35 m/imp gal, 29 m/US gal, 8 l x 100 km.

BRAKES lining area: total 114.8 sq in, 740 sq cm (for Hi-De Luxe and SL models front disc brakes, rear drum, total lining area 78.2 sq in, 504 sq cm).

ELECTRICAL EQUIPMENT 35 Ah battery.

DIMENSIONS AND WEIGHT front track: 51.18 in, 130 cm; weight: 2-dr. Sedan 1,962 lb, 890 kg - Hi-De Luxe 2-dr. Sedan 1,973 lb, 895 kg - De Luxe 4-dr. Sedan 1,984 lb, 900 kg - De Luxe 2-dr. Hardtop, Hi-De Luxe 4-dr. Sedan and 2-door Hardtop, coupés 1,995 lb, 905 kg - SL 4-dr. Sedan and 2-dr. Hardtop 2,006 lb, 910 kg - De Luxe 3-dr. Liftback 2,050 lb, 930 kg - Hi-De Luxe 3-dr. Liftback 2,073 lb, 940 kg - SL 3-dr. Liftback 2,083 lb, 945 kg.

PRACTICAL INSTRUCTIONS oil: engine 7.9 imp pt, 9.5 US pt, 4.5 l; tappet clearances: inlet 0.008 in, 0.20 mm, exhaust 0.013 in, 0.33 mm; valve timing: 22° 42° 63° 7°.

OPTIONAL ACCESSORIES 5-speed fully synchronized mechanical gearbox (I 3.587, II 2.022, III 1.384, IV 1, V 0.861, rev 3.484), 3.909 axle ratio (SL models 4.100).

88 hp power team

See 82 hp power team, except for:

ENGINE 96.9 cu in, 1,588 cc (3.35 x 2.76 in, 85 x 70 mm); compression ratio: 9:1; max power (JIS): 88 hp at 5,600 rpm; max torque (JIS): 96 lb ft, 13.3 kg m at 3,400 rpm; 55.4

hp/l; 1 Aisan 12 T-U downdraught twin barrel carburettor; low emission control TGP lean-burn type with auxiliary combustion chambers, secondary air injection, exhaust gas recirculation and catalytic converter.

TRANSMISSION axle ratio: Hi-De Luxe models 3.727 - GSL models 3.909; tyres: Hi-De Luxe models 6.15 x 13 - GSL models 155 SR x 13 (for SR only 5 gears, V ratio 0.861, axle ratio 4.100, tyres 175/70 HR x 13).

PERFORMANCE max speed: 99 mph, 160 km/h; power-weight ratio: Hi-De Luxe 4-dr. Sedan 22.4 lb/hp, 10.2 kg/hp; consumption: 34 m/imp gal, 28 m/US gal, 8.3 l x 100 km.

DIMENSIONS AND WEIGHT weight: Hi-De Luxe Sedan, Hardtop and Coupé 1,973 lb, 895 kg - GSL and SR coupés 2,007 lb, 910 kg - GSL Sedan and Hardtop 2,018 lb, 915 kg - Hi-De Luxe Liftback 2,051 lb, 930 kg - GSL Liftback 2,073 lb, 940 kg.

90 hp power team

See 82 hp power team, except for:

ENGINE 96.9 cu in, 1,588 cc (3.35 x 2.76 in, 85 x 70 mm); compression ratio: 9:1; max power (JIS): 90 hp at 6,000 rpm; max torque (JIS): 94 lb ft, 13 kg m at 3,800 rpm; 56.7 hp/l; 1 Aisan 2T-U downdraught twin barrel carburettor.

TRANSMISSION Toyoglide automatic transmission, hydraulic torque converter; gears: 3; ratios: I 2.450, II 1.450, III 1, rev 2.222; axle ratio: 3.909; tyres: 6.15 x 13 - GSL models 155 SR x 13.

PERFORMANCE max speed: 103 mph, 165 km/h; power-weight ratio: Hi-De Luxe Automatic 4-dr. Sedan 22.5 lb/hp, 10.2 kg/hp.

DIMENSIONS AND WEIGHT weight: Hi-De Luxe Sedan, Hardtop and Coupé 2,029 lb, 920 kg - GSL Coupé 2,062 lb, 935 kg - GSL Sedan and Hardtop 2,073 lb, 940 kg - Hi-De Luxe Liftback 2,095 lb, 950 kg - GSL Liftback 2,117 lb, 960 kg.

110 hp power team

See 82 hp power team, except for:

ENGINE 96.9 cu in, 1,588 cc (3.35 x 2.76 in, 85 x 70 mm); compression ratio: 8.4:1; max power (JIS): 110 hp at 6,000 rpm; max torque (JIS): 105 lb ft, 14.5 kg m at 4,800 rpm; max engine rpm: 6,400; 69.3 hp/l; camshafts: 2, overhead; Bosch-Denso L-jetronic electronic fuel jniection.

TRANSMISSION gears: 5; fully synchronized; ratios: I 3.587, II 2.022, III 1.384, IV 1, V 0.861, rev 3.484; axle ratio: 4.300; width of rims: 5''; tyres: 175/70 HR x 13.

PERFORMANCE power-weight ratio: Levin Coupé 19 lb/hp, 8.6 kg/hp.

DIMENSIONS AND WEIGHT width: 62.99 in, 160 cm; height: 51.57 in, 131 cm; weight: Levin Coupé 2,095 lb, 950 kg - Levin GT Coupé 2,106 lb, 955 kg - Levin GT Liftback 2,150 lb, 975 kg.

PRACTICAL INSTRUCTIONS valve timing: 16° 48° 48° 16°.

Corolla (USA) Series

PRICES IN USA:

Corolla De Luxe 2-door Sedan	$ 3,688*
Corolla De Luxe 4-door Sedan	$ 3,798*
Corolla De Luxe 5-door Station Wagon	$ 4,118*
Corolla 2-door Sport Coupé	$ 4,083*
Corolla 2-door Liftback	$ 4,123*
Corolla SR-5 2-door Sport Coupé	$ 4,498*
Corolla SR-5 2-door Liftback	$ 4,638*

75 hp power team

ENGINE front, 4 stroke; 4 cylinders, in line; 96.9 cu in, 1,588 cc (3.35 x 2.76 in, 85 x 70 mm); compression ratio: 8.5:1; max power (SAE): 75 hp at 5,800 rpm; max torque (SAE): 83 lb ft, 11.4 kg m at 3,800 rpm; max engine rpm: 6,300; 47.2 hp/l; cast iron block and head; 5 crankshaft bearings; valves: overhead, push-rods and rockers; camshafts: 1, side; lubrication: rotary pump, full flow filter, 7.7 imp pt, 9.3 US pt, 4.4 l; 1 Aisan downdraught twin barrel carburettor; fuel feed: mechanical pump; water-cooled, 13.7 imp pt, 16.5 US pt, 7.8 l.

TRANSMISSION driving wheels: rear; clutch: single dry plate (diaphragm); gearbox: mechanical; gears: 4 (5 for SR-5 only), fully synchronized; ratios: I 3.587, II 2.022, III 1.384, IV 1, rev 3.484 (SR-5 I 3.587, II 2.022, III 1.384, IV 1, V 0.861, rev 3.484); lever: central; final drive: hypoid bevel; axle ratio: 4.100 - SR-5 4.300; width of rims: 4.5''; tyres: 6.45S x 13 - Hardtop 165SR x 13 - SR-5 180/70HR x 13.

TOYOTA Corolla 1600 Levin GT 2-door Coupé

TOYOTA Corolla 1600 GSL 3-door Liftback

TOYOTA Corolla 1600 GSL Liftback

PERFORMANCE max speed: 99 mph, 160 km/h; power-weight ratio: 4-dr. Sedan 30.3 lb/hp, 13.7 kg/hp; consumption: not declared.

CHASSIS integral; front suspension: independent, by McPherson, coil springs/telescopic damper struts, lower wishbones (trailing links), anti-roll bar; rear: rigid axle, semi-elliptic leafsprings, telescopic dampers.

STEERING recirculating ball, variable ratio; turns lock to lock: 3.60 - SR-5 3.

BRAKES front disc, rear drum, servo; lining area: total 60.2 sq in, 388 sq cm.

ELECTRICAL EQUIPMENT 12 V; 35 Ah battery; 40 A alternator; Nihon-Denso distributor; 2 headlamps.

DIMENSIONS AND WEIGHT wheel base: 93.31 in, 237 cm; front track: 50.98 in, 129 cm - SR-5 52 in, 132 cm; rear track: 50.59 in, 128 cm - SR-5 52.60 in, 134 cm; length: 165.20 in, 420 cm - station wagons 167.70 in, 426 cm; width: 61.80 in, 157 cm - SR-5 65 in, 165 cm; height: 53.94 in, 137 cm - hardtops 53.15 in, 135 cm; ground clearance: 6.69 in, 17 cm; weight: 4-dr. Sedan 2,270 lb, 1,029 kg - Hardtop 2,280 lb, 1,034 kg - SR-5 Hardtop 2,360 lb, 1,070 kg - 5-dr. Station Wagon 2,325 lb, 1,054 kg; turning circle (between walls): 33.5 ft, 10.2 m; fuel tank: 11 imp gal, 13.2 US gal, 50 l.

BODY 5 seats, separate front seats, reclining backrests, built-in headrests.

75 HP POWER TEAM

PRACTICAL INSTRUCTIONS fuel: 90, oct petrol; oil: engine 7.7 imp pt, 9.3 US pt, 4.4 l, SAE 20W-30, change every 3,100 miles, 5,000 km - gearbox 1.8 imp pt, 2.1 US pt, 1 l, SAE 90, change every 18,600 miles, 30,000 km - final drive 1.4 imp pt, 1.7 US pt, 0.8 l, SAE 90, change every 18,600 miles, 30,000 km; greasing: none; tappet clearances: inlet 0.008 in, 0.20 mm, exhaust 0.013 in, 0.33 mm; valve timing: 16° 54° 58° 12°; tyre pressure: front 20 psi, 1.4 atm, rear 20 psi, 1.4 atm.

OPTIONAL ACCESSORIES 5-speed fully synchronized mechanical gearbox (I 3.587, II 2.022, III 1.384, IV 1, V 0.861, rev 3.484), 4.300 axle ratio; automatic transmission with 3 ratios (I 2.450, II 1.450, III 1, rev 2.222).

Sprinter Series

PRICES (Tokyo):

1 1300 DX 4-door Sedan	785,000	yen
2 1300 DX Hardtop	819,000	yen
3 1300 DX Coupé	831,000	yen
4 1300 DX Liftback	857,000	yen
5 1300 XL 4-door Sedan	842,000	yen
6 1300 XL Hardtop	867,000	yen
7 1300 XL Coupé	879,000	yen
8 1300 XL Liftback	916,000	yen
9 1300 ST 4-door Sedan	873,000	yen
10 1300 ST Hardtop	904,000	yen
11 1300 ST Coupé	908,000	yen
12 1300 ST Liftback	956,000	yen
13 1400 DX 4-door Sedan	830,000	yen
14 1400 DX Hardtop	859,000	yen
15 1400 DX Coupé	864,000	yen
16 1400 DX Liftback	891,000	yen
17 1400 XL 4-door Sedan	861,000	yen
18 1400 XL Hardtop	891,000	yen
19 1400 XL Coupé	904,000	yen
20 1400 XL Liftback	943,000	yen
21 1400 ST 4-door Sedan	909,000	yen
22 1400 ST Hardtop	939,000	yen
23 1400 ST Coupé	943,000	yen
24 1400 ST Liftback	982,000	yen
25 1600 XL 4-door Sedan	900,000	yen
26 1600 XL Automatic 4-door Sedan	900,000	yen
27 1600 XL Hardtop	930,000	yen
28 1600 XL Automatic Hardtop	930,000	yen
29 1600 XL Coupé	941,000	yen
30 1600 XL Automatic Coupé	941,000	yen
31 1600 XL Liftback	992,000	yen
32 1600 XL Automatic Liftback	992,000	yen
33 1600 GS 4-door Sedan	991,000	yen
34 1600 GS Automatic 4-door Sedan	991,000	yen
35 1600 GS Hardtop	1,023,000	yen
36 1600 GS Automatic Hardtop	1,023,000	yen
37 1600 GS Coupé	1,023,000	yen
38 1600 GS Automatic Coupé	1,023,000	yen
39 1600 GS Liftback	1,078,000	yen
40 1600 GS Automatic Liftback	1,078,000	yen
41 1600 SR Coupé	1,033,000	yen
42 1600 Trueno GT	1,302,000	yen
43 1600 Liftback GT	1,352,000	yen

Power team:	Standard for:	Optional for:
72 hp	1 to 12	—
82 hp	13 to 24	—
88 hp	25,27,29,31,33,35,37,39,41	—
90 hp	26,28,30,32,34,36,38,40	—
110 hp	42,43	—

72 hp power team

ENGINE front, 4 stroke; 4 cylinders, in line; 78.7 cu in, 1,290 cc (2.95 x 2.87 in, 75 x 73 mm); compression ratio: 9:1; max power (JIS): 72 hp at 5,600 rpm; max torque (JIS): 76 lb ft, 10.5 kg m at 3,600 rpm; max engine rpm: 6,000; 55.8 hp/l; cast iron block, light alloy head; 5 crankshaft bearings; valves: overhead, push-rods and rockers; camshafts: 1, side; lubrication: rotary pump, full flow filter, 6.2 imp pt, 7.4 US pt, 3.5 l; 1 Aisan 4K-U downdraught twin barrel carburettor; emission control with catalytic converter, secondary air injection and exhaust gas recirculation; fuel feed: mechanical pump; water-cooled, 10.6 imp pt, 12.7 US pt, 6 l.

TRANSMISSION driving wheels: rear; clutch: single dry plate (diaphragm); gearbox: mechanical; gears: 4, fully synchronized; ratios: I 3.789, II 2.220, III 1.435, IV 1, rev 4.316; lever: central; final drive: hypoid bevel; axle ratio: 3.909; width of rims: 4'' - ST models 4.5''; tyres: 6.00 x 12 - XL and ST models 6.15 x 13.

PERFORMANCE max speeds: (I) 25 mph, 40 km/h; (II) 46 mph, 74 km/h; (II) 67 mph, 108 km/h; (IV) 93 mph, 150 km/h; power-weight ratio: DX 4-dr. Sedan 25 lb/hp, 11.4 kg/hp; consumption: 40 m/imp gal, 33 m/US gal, 7.1 l x 100 km.

CHASSIS integral; front suspension: independent, by McPherson, coil springs/telescopic damper struts, lower wish-

TOYOTA Sprinter 1400 ST 4-door Sedan

TOYOTA Sprinter 1600 GS Hardtop

TOYOTA Sprinter 1600 GS Hardtop

bones (trailing links), anti-roll bar; rear: rigid axle, semi-elliptic leafsprings, telescopic dampers.

STEERING recirculating ball, variable ratio; turns lock to lock: 3.60.

BRAKES drum (for XL and ST models front disc); lining area: front 47.1 sq in, 304 sq cm, rear 41.6 sq in, 268 sq cm, total 88.7 sq in, 572 sq cm.

ELECTRICAL EQUIPMENT 12 V; 32 Ah battery; 40 A alternator; Nihon-Denso distributor; 2 headlamps.

DIMENSIONS AND WEIGHT wheel base: 93.31 in, 237 cm; tracks: 50.98 in, 129 cm front, 50.59 in, 128 cm rear; length: sedans and hardtops 157.09 in, 399 cm - coupés 160.24 in, 407 cm - liftbacks 162.20 in, 412 cm; width: 62.99 in, 160 cm - sedans and hardtops 61.81 in, 157 cm; height: 51.97 in, 132 cm - sedans and hardtops 53.54 in, 136 cm; ground clearance: 6.30 in, 16 cm - sedans 6.69 in, 17 cm; weight: DX 4-dr. Sedan 1,808 lb, 820 kg - DX and XL coupés 1,830 lb, 830 kg - XL 4-dr. Sedan 1,841 lb, 835 kg - ST Sedan and Coupé 1,852 lb, 840 kg - DX and XL Liftbacks 1,885 lb, 855 kg - ST Liftback 1,896 lb, 860 kg - DX and XL hardtops 1,995 lb, 905 kg - ST Hardtop 2,007 lb, 910 kg; turning circle (between walls): 33.5 ft, 10.2 m; fuel tank: 11 imp gal, 13.2 US gal, 50 l.

BODY 5 seats, separate front seats, reclining backrests, built-in headrests.

PRACTICAL INSTRUCTIONS fuel: 90 oct lead-free petrol; oil: engine 6.2 imp pt, 7.4 US pt, 3.5 l, SAE 20W-30, change every 3,100 miles, 5.000 km - gearbox 1.8 imp pt, 2.1 US pt, 1 l, SAE 90, change every 18,600 miles, 30,000 km - final drive 1.4 imp pt, 1.7 US pt, 0.8 l, SAE 90, change every 18,600 miles, 30,000 km; greasing: none; tappet clearances (hot): inlet 0.008 in, 0.20 mm, exhaust 0.012 in, 0.30 mm; valve timing: 16° 50° 50° 16°; tyre pressure: front 20 psi, 1.4 atm, rear 20 psi, 1.4 atm.

OPTIONAL ACCESSORIES 5-speed fully synchronized mechanical gearbox (I 3.789, II 2.220, III 1.453, IV 1, V 0.865, rev 4.316), 3.909 axle ratio.

82 hp power team

See 72 hp power team, except for:

ENGINE 85.9 cu in, 1,407 cc (3.15 x 2.76 in, 80 x 70 mm); compression ratio: 8.5:1; max power (JIS): 82 hp at 5,800 rpm; max torque (JIS): 84 lb ft, 11.6 kg m at 3,400 rpm; max engine rpm: 6,300; 58.3 hp/l; valves: overhead, Vee-slanted, push-rods and rockers; 1 Aisan T-U downdraught twin barrel carburettor; cooling system: 14.1 imp pt, 16.8 US pt, 8 l.

TRANSMISSION gearbox ratios: I 3.587, II 2.022, III 1.384, IV 1, rev 3.484; axle ratio: 3.727 - ST models 3.909; width of rims: 4.5''; tyres: 6.15 x 13 - ST models 155 SR x 13.

PERFORMANCE max speeds: (I) 29 mph, 47 km/h; (II) 51 mph, 82 km/h; (III) 75 mph, 120 km/h; (IV) 99 mph, 160 km/h; power-weight ratio: DX 4-dr. Sedan 24.3 lb/hp, 11 kg/hp; consumption: 32 m/imp gal, 29 m/US gal, 8 l x 100 km.

BRAKES front disc, rear drum; lining area: total 78.2 sq in, 504 sq cm.

ELECTRICAL EQUIPMENT 35 Ah battery.

DIMENSIONS AND WEIGHT front track: 51.18 in, 130 cm; weight: DX and XL sedans and hardtops, DX, XL and ST coupés 1,996 lb, 905 kg - ST Hardtop 2,007 lb, 910 kg - ST 4-dr. Sedan 2,018 lb, 915 kg - DX Liftback 2,051 lb, 930 kg - XL Liftback 2,073 lb, 940 kg - ST Liftback 2,084 lb, 945 kg.

OPTIONAL ACCESSORIES 5-speed fully synchronized mechanical gearbox (I 3.587, II 2.022, III 1.384, IV 1, V 0.861, rev 3.484), 3.909 axle ratio (for SL models only 4.100).

88 hp power team

See 82 hp power team, except for:

ENGINE TTC-L low emission lean-burn type with auxiliary combustion chambers; 96.9 cu in, 1,588 cc (3.35 x 2.76 in, 85 x 70 mm); compression ratio: 9:1; max power (JIS): 88 hp at 5,600 rpm; max torque (JIS): 96 lb ft, 13.3 kg m at 3,400 rpm; 55.4 hp/l; 1 Aisan 12T-U downdraught twin barrel carburettor; emission control turbulence generating pot auxiliary combustion chambers, exhaust gas recirculation, secondary air injection and catalytic converter.

TRANSMISSION axle ratio: XL models 3.727 - GS models and SR Coupé 3.909; tyres: SR Coupé 175/70 HR x 14.

PERFORMANCE max speed: 99 mph, 160 km/h; power-weight ratio: XL-4-dr. Sedan 22.4 lb/hp, 10.2 kg/hp; consumption: 34 m/imp gal, 28 m/US gal, 8.3 l x 100 km.

DIMENSIONS AND WEIGHT weight: XL Sedan, Hardtop and Coupé 1,973 lb, 895 kg - GS Sedan and Hardtop 2,029 lb, 920 kg - GS and SR coupés 2,007 lb, 910 kg - XL Liftback 2,051 lb, 930 kg - GS Liftback 2,073 lb, 940 kg.

PRACTICAL INSTRUCTIONS valve timing: 22° 42° 63° 7°.

90 hp power team

See 82 hp power team, except for:

ENGINE 96.9 cu in, 1,588 cc (3.35 x 2.76 in, 85 x 70 mm); compression ratio: 9:1; max power (JIS): 90 hp at 6,000 rpm; max torque (JIS): 94 lb ft, 13 kg m at 3,800 rpm; 56.7 hp/l; 1 Aisan 2T-U downdraught twin barrel carburettor.

TRANSMISSION Toyoglide automatic transmission, hydraulic torque converter; gears: 3; ratios: I 2.450, II 1.450, III 1, rev 2.222; axle ratio: 3.909; tyres: 6.15 x 13 - GS models 115 SR x 13.

PERFORMANCE max speed: 96 mph, 155 km/h; power-weight ratio: XL 4-dr. Sedan 24.7 lb/hp, 11.2 kg/hp.

DIMENSIONS AND WEIGHT weight: XL Sedan, Hardtop and Coupé 2,029 lb, 920 kg - GS Coupé 2,062 lb, 935 kg - GS Hardtop 2,073 lb, 940 kg - GS Sedan 2,084 lb, 945 kg - XL Liftback 2,095 lb, 950 kg - GS Liftback 2,117 lb, 960 kg.

110 hp power team

See 82 hp power team, except for:

ENGINE 96.9 cu in, 1,588 cc (3.35 x 2.76 in, 85 x 70 mm); compression ratio: 8.4:1; max power (JIS): 110 hp at 6,000 rpm; max torque (JIS): 105 lb ft, 14.5 kg m at 4,800 rpm; max engine rpm: 6,400; 69.3 hp/l; camshafts: 2, overhead; Bosch-Denso L-jetronic electronic fuel jniection.

TRANSMISSION gears: 5, fully synchronized; ratios: I 3.587, II 2.022, III 1.384, IV 1, V 0.861, rev 3.484; axle ratio: 4.300; width of rims: 5''; tyres 175/70 HR x 13.

PERFORMANCE power-weight ratio: Trueno GT 19.1 lb/hp, 8.7 kg/hp - Liftback GT 19.5 lb/hp, 8.9 kg/hp.

DIMENSIONS AND WEIGHT height: 51.57 in, 131 cm; weight: Trueno GT 2,106 lb, 955 kg - Liftback GT 2,150 lb, 975 kg.

PRACTICAL INSTRUCTIONS valve timing: 16° 48° 48° 16°.

Carina Series

PRICES (Tokyo):

1 1600 Standard 2-door Sedan	845,000	yen
2 1600 Standard 4-door Sedan	865,000	yen
3 1600 De Luxe 2-door Sedan	903,000	yen
4 1600 De Luxe 4-door Sedan	924,000	yen
5 1600 De Luxe 2-door Hardtop	958,000	yen
6 1600 Super De Luxe 2-door Sedan	941,000	yen
7 1600 Super De Luxe 4-door Sedan	961,000	yen
8 1600 Super De Luxe 2-door Hardtop	996,000	yen
9 1600 ST 4-door Sedan	1,026,000	yen
10 1600 ST 2-door Hardtop	1,061,000	yen
11 1600 SR 2-door Hardtop	1,061,000	yen
12 1800 De Luxe 4-door Sedan	989,000	yen
13 1800 De Luxe 2-door Hardtop	1,024,000	yen
14 1800 Super De Luxe 4-door Sedan	1,052,000	yen
15 1800 Super De Luxe 2-door Hardtop	1,087,000	yen
16 1800 ST 4-door Sedan	1,117,000	yen
17 1800 ST 2-door Hardtop	1,152,000	yen
18 1800 SR 2-door Hardtop	1,152,000	yen
19 1800 SE 4-door Sedan	1,171,000	yen
20 1800 SE 2-door Hardtop	1,206,000	yen
21 1800 De Luxe Automatic 4-door Sedan	1,018,000	yen
22 1800 De Luxe Automatic 2-door Hardtop	1,053,000	yen
23 1800 Super De Luxe Automatic 4-door Sedan	1,081,000	yen
24 1800 Super De Luxe Automatic 2-door Hardtop	1,116,000	yen
25 1800 ST Automatic 4-door Sedan	1,123,000	yen
26 1800 ST Automatic 2-door Hardtop	1,158,000	yen
27 1800 SE Automatic 4-door Sedan	1,200,000	yen
28 1800 SE Automatic 2-door Hardtop	1,235,000	yen
29 2000 Super De Luxe 4-door Sedan	1,049,000	yen
30 2000 Super De Luxe 2-door Hardtop	1,084,000	yen
31 2000 ST 4-door Sedan	1,114,000	yen
32 2000 ST 2-door Hardtop	1,149,000	yen
33 2000 SE 4-door Sedan	1,168,000	yen
34 2000 SE 2-door Hardtop	1,203,000	yen
35 2000 GT 4-door Sedan	1,472,000	yen
36 2000 GT 2-door Hardtop	1,507,000	yen

For GB price, see price index.

Power team:	Standard for:	Optional for:
88 hp	1 to 11	—
95 hp	12 to 20	—
98 hp	21 to 28	—
100 hp	29 to 34	—
110 hp	35,36	—
130 hp	35,36	—

TOYOTA Sprinter 1600 Liftback GT

TOYOTA Sprinter 1600 Trueno GT

88 hp power team

ENGINE TTC-L lean-burn low emission type with turbulence generating pot auxiliary combustion chambers; front, 4 stroke; 4 cylinders, in line; 96.9 cu in, 1,588 cc (3.35 x 2.76 in, 85 x 70 mm); compression ratio: 9:1; max power (JIS): 88 hp at 5,600 rpm; max torque (JIS): 96 lb ft, 13.3 kg m at 3,400 rpm; max engine rpm: 6,000; 55.4 hp/l; cast iron block, light alloy head; 5 crankshaft bearings; valves: overhead, Vee-slanted, push-rods and rockers; camshafts: 1, side; lubrication: rotary pump, full flow filter, 7.4 imp pt, 8.9 US pt, 4.2 l; 1 Aisan 12T-U downdraught twin barrel carburettor; emission control with catalytic converter, secondary air injection and exhaust gas recirculation; fuel feed: mechanical pump; water-cooled, 14.1 imp pt, 16.9 US pt, 8 l.

TRANSMISSION driving wheels: rear; clutch: single dry plate (diaphragm); gearbox: mechanical; gears: 4, fully synchronized; ratios: I 3.587, II 2.022, III 1.384, IV 1, rev 3.484; lever: central; final drive: hypoid bevel; axle ratio: 3.909; width of rims: Standard models 4'' - De Luxe, Super De Luxe and ST models and SR Hardtop 4.5''; tyres: Standard models 5.60 x 13 - De Luxe and Super De Luxe models 6.45 x 13 - ST models and SR Hardtop 165 SR x 13.

PERFORMANCE max speeds: (I) 29 mph, 46 km/h; (II) 52 mph, 83 km/h; (III) 75 mph, 120 km/h; (IV) 102 mph, 165 km/h; power-weight ratio: Standard 2-dr. Sedan 22.9 lb/hp, 10.4 kg/hp; consumption: 34 m/imp gal, 28 m/US gal, 8.3 l x 100 km.

CHASSIS integral; front suspension: independent, by McPherson, coil springs/telescopic damper struts, lower wishbones (trailing links), anti-roll bar; rear: rigid axle, twin trailing radius arms, transverse linkage bar, coil springs, telescopic dampers.

STEERING recirculating ball; turns lock to lock: 3.80 - SR Hardtop 3.50.

BRAKES drum (for Super De Luxe and ST models and SR Hardtop front disc): lining area: front 60.8 sq in, 392 sq cm, rear 54 sq in, 384 sq cm, total 114.8 sq in, 740 sq cm.

ELECTRICAL EQUIPMENT 12 V; 35 Ah battery: 45 A alternator; Nihon-Denso distributor; 4 headlamps.

DIMENSIONS AND WEIGHT wheel base: 98.42 in, 250 cm; tracks: 52.56 in, 133 cm front; 53.15 in, 135 cm rear; length: Standard models 162.20 in, 420 cm - De Luxe and Super De Luxe models 165.75 in, 421 cm - ST models and SR Hardtop 166.54 in, 423 cm; width: 64.17 in, 163 cm; height: sedans 54.72 in, 139 cm - De Luxe, Super De Luxe and ST hardtops 52.76 in, 134 cm - SR Hardtop 52.36 in, 133 cm; ground clearance: 6.30 in, 16 cm - SR Hardtop 6.10 in, 15.5 cm; weight: Standard 2-dr. Sedan 2,018 lb, 915 kg - De Luxe 2-dr. Sedan 2,029 lb, 920 kg - Standard 4-dr. and Super De Luxe 2-dr. sedans 2,040 lb, 925 kg - De Luxe 4-dr. Sedan 2,050 lb, 930 kg - De Luxe 2-dr. Hardtop and Super De Luxe and ST 4-dr. sedans 2,062 lb, 935 kg - Super De Luxe and ST hardtops 2,073 lb, 940 kg - SR Hardtop 2,084 lb, 945 kg; weight distribution: 57.3% front, 42.7% rear; turning circle (between walls): 35.4 ft, 10.8 m; fuel tank: 13.4 imp gal, 16.1 US gal, 61 l.

BODY 5 seats, separate front seats, reclining backrests, built-in headrests.

TOYOTA Carina 1600 Standard 2-door Sedan

TOYOTA Carina 1600 Super De Luxe Hardtop

OPTIONAL ACCESSORIES 5-speed fully synchronized mechanical gearbox (I 3.587, II 2.022, III 1.384, IV 1, V 0.861, rev 3.484), 4.100 axle ratio.

95 hp power team

See 88 hp power team, except for:

ENGINE 108 cu in, 1,770 cc (3.35 x 3.01 in, 85 x 78 mm); max power (JIS): 95 hp at 5,400 rpm; max torque (JIS): 109 lb ft, 15 kg m at 3,400 rpm; 53.7 hp/l; 1 13T-U downdraught twin barrel carburettor.

TRANSMISSION (for models and SR Hardtop only gears: 5, fully synchronized; ratios: I 3.587, II 2.022, III 1.384, IV 1, V 0.861, rev 3.484; axle ratio: 3.909) axle ratio: 3.727; width of rims: (for SR Hardtop only) 5''; tyres: De Luxe and Super De Luxe models 6.45 x 13 - SE and ST models 165 SR x 13 - SR Hardtop 185/70 HR x 13.

PERFORMANCE max speed: 106 mph, 170 km/h; power-weight ratio: De Luxe 4-dr. Sedan 22.1 lb/hp, 10 kg/hp; consumption: 32 m/imp gal, 27 m/US gal, 8.7 l x 100 km.

DIMENSIONS AND WEIGHT weight: De Luxe Sedan 2,095 lb, 950 kg - De Luxe Hardtop and Super De Luxe and ST sedans 2,106 lb, 955 kg - SE Sedan, Super De Luxe and ST hardtops 2,117 lb, 960 kg - SR and SE hardtops 2,139 lb, 970 kg.

OPTIONAL ACCESSORIES 5-speed mechanical gearbox (except ST models and SR Hardtop), 3.909 axle ratio.

98 hp power team

See 88 hp power team, except for:

ENGINE hemispherical combustion chambers; 108 cu in, 1,770 cc (3.35 x 3.01 in, 85 x 78 mm); max power (JIS): 98 hp at 5,700 rpm; max torque (JIS): 110 lb ft, 15.2 kg m at 3,400 rpm; 1 3T-U downdraught twin barrel carburettor.

TRANSMISSION Toyoglide automatic transmission with hydraulic torque converter and planetary gears; ratios: I 2.450, II 1.450, III 1, rev 2.222; axle ratio: 3.909; tyres: De Luxe and Super De Luxe models 6.45 x 13 - SE and ST models 165 SR x 13.

PERFORMANCE max speed: 106 mph, 170 km/h; power-weight ratio: De Luxe Sedan 21.5 lb/hp, 9.7 kg/hp; consumption: 32 m/imp gal, 27 m/US gal, 8.7 l x 100 km.

DIMENSIONS AND WEIGHT weight: De Luxe Sedan 2,106 lb, 955 kg - De Luxe Hardtop and Super De Luxe and ST sedans 2,117 lb, 960 kg - SE Sedan and Super De Luxe and ST hardtops 2,128 lb, 965 kg - SE Hardtop 2,139 lb, 970 kg.

100 hp power team

See 88 hp power team, except for:

ENGINE 120.1 cu in, 1,968 cc (3.48 x 3.15 in, 88.5 x 80 mm); compression ratio: 8.5:1; max power (JIS): 100 hp at 5,500

TOYOTA Carina 1600 Super De Luxe Hardtop

rpm; max torque (JIS): 112 lb ft, 15.5 kg m at 3,600 rpm; max engine rpm: 6,300; 50.8 hp/l; valves: overhead, rockers; camshafts: 1, overhead; lubrication: 8.8 imp pt, 10.6 US pt, 5 l; 1 Aisan 18R-U downdraught twin barrel carburettor.

TRANSMISSION gears: 4, fully synchronized (5 for ST models only); ratios: I 3.579, II 2.081, III 1.397, IV 1, rev 4.399 - ST models I 3.287, II 2.043, III 1.394, IV 1, V 0.853, rev 4.039; axle ratio: 3.727 - ST models 3.909; width of rims: 4.5''; tyres: 6.45 x 13 - ST models 165 SR x 13.

PERFORMANCE max speeds: (I) 29 mph, 47 km/h; (II) 51 mph, 82 km/h; (III) 76 mph, 122 km/h; (IV) 106 mph, 170 km/h; power-weight ratio: Super De Luxe Sedan 21.7 lb/hp, 9.8 kg/hp; consumption: 28 m/imp gal, 23 m/US gal, 10 l x 100 km.

STEERING variable ratio, servo; turns lock to lock: 3.80.

BRAKES front disc, rear drum, servo.

DIMENSIONS AND WEIGHT weight: Super De Luxe Sedan 2,172 lb, 985 kg - Super De Luxe Hardtop and ST and SE Sedans 2,183 lb, 990 kg - ST and SE hardtops 2,194 lb, 995 kg.

PRACTICAL INSTRUCTIONS tappet clearances: inlet 0.007 in, 0.18 mm; valve timing: 20° 48° 56° 12°.

OPTIONAL ACCESSORIES (except ST models) 5-speed fully synchronized mechanical gearbox (I 3.287, II 2.043, III 1.394, IV 1, V 0.853, rev 4.039), 3.909 axle ratio; Toyoglide automatic transmission, hydraulic torque converter with 3 ratios (I 2.450, II 1.450, III 1, rev 2.222), 3.909 axle ratio.

110 hp power team

See 88 hp power team, except for:

ENGINE compression ratio: 8.4:1; max power (JIS): 110 hp at 6,000 rpm; max torque (JIS): 105 lb ft, 14.5 kg m at 4,800 rpm; max engine rpm: 6,400; 69.3 hp/l; camshafts: 2, overhead; Bosch-Denso L-jetronic electronic injection.

TRANSMISSION gears: 5, fully synchronized; ratios: I 3.587, II 2.022, III 1.384 IV 1, V 0.861, rev 3.484; axle ratio: 4.100; width of rims: 5''; tyres: 185/70 HR x 13.

PERFORMANCE max speeds: (I) 29 mph, 47 km/h; (II) 52 mph, 83 km/h; (III) 76 mph, 122 km/h; (IV) 106 mph, 170 km/h; (V) 106 mph, 170 km/h; power-weight ratio: Sedan 19.6 lb/hp, 8.9 kg/hp; consumption: 29.7 m/imp gal, 24.8 m/US gal, 9.5 l x 100 km.

STEERING turns lock to lock: 3.50.

BRAKES rear disc.

CHASSIS rear suspension: anti-roll bar.

DIMENSIONS AND WEIGHT height: Sedan 54.33 in, 138 cm - Hardtop 52.36 in, 133 cm; tracks: 53.15 in, 135 cm front, 53.54 in, 136 cm rear; ground clearance: 6.10 in, 15.5 cm; weight: Sedan 2,161 lb, 980 kg - Hardtop 2,172 lb, 985 kg.

TOYOTA Carina 2000 SE 4-door Sedan

TOYOTA Celica 1600 XT Coupé

TOYOTA Carina 2000 SE 4-door Sedan

130 hp power team

See 88 hp power team, except for:

ENGINE 120.1 cu in, 1,968 cc (3.48 x 3.15 in, 88.5 x 80 mm); compression ratio: 8.3:1; max power (JIS): 130 hp at 6,000 rpm; max torque (JIS): 120 lb ft, 16.5 kg m at 4,800 rpm; max engine rpm: 6,300; 66 hp/l; valves: overhead, Vee-slanted, thimble tappets; camshafts: 2, overhead; lubrication: 8.8 imp pt, 10.6 US pt, 5 l; 2 Solex 18R-GU horizontal twin barrel carburettors; cooling system: 16 imp pt, 19.2 US pt, 9.1 l.

TRANSMISSION gears: 5, fully synchronized; ratios: I 3.525, II 2.054, III 1.396, IV 1, V 0.858, rev 3.755; axle ratio: 3.909; width of rims: 5''; tyres: 185/70 HR x 13.

PERFORMANCE max speed: 112 mph, 180 km/h; power-weight ratio: Sedan 17.5 lb/hp, 7.9 kg/hp; consumption: 28 m/imp gal, 23 m/US gal, 10 l x 100 km.

CHASSIS rear suspension: anti-roll bar.

STEERING variable ratio, servo; turns lock to lock: 3.80.

BRAKES front disc, rear drum, servo.

ELECTRICAL EQUIPMENT transistorized ignition.

DIMENSIONS AND WEIGHT tracks: 53.15 in, 135 cm front, 53.54 in, 136 cm rear; height: Sedan 54.33 in, 138 cm - Hardtop 52.36 in, 133 cm; ground clearance: 5.91 in, 15 cm; weight: Sedan 2,271 lb, 1,030 kg - Hardtop 2,282 lb, 1,035 kg.

Celica Series

PRICES EX WORKS:

1	1600 ET	Coupé	985,000 yen
2	1600 LT	Coupé	1,045,000 yen
3	1600 LT	Liftback	1,125,000 yen
4	1600 ST	Coupé	1,080,000 yen
5	1600 ST	Liftback	1,160,000 yen
6	1600 XT	Coupé	1,130,000 yen
7	1600 XT	Liftback	1,226,000 yen
8	1600 GTV	Coupé	1,419,000 yen
9	1600 GTV	Liftback	1,515,000 yen
10	1600 GT	Coupé	1,467,000 yen
11	1600 GT	Liftback	1,563,000 yen
12	1800 LT	Coupé	1,075,000 yen
13	1800 LT	Liftback	1,155,000 yen
14	1800 ST	Coupé	1,110,000 yen
15	1800 ST	Liftback	1,190,000 yen
16	1800 XT	Coupé	1,160,000 yen
17	1800 XT	Liftback	1,256,000 yen
18	1800 SE	Coupé	1,251,000 yen
19	1800 SE	Liftback	1,347,000 yen
20	2000 ST	Coupé	1,107,000 yen
21	2000 ST	Liftback	1,187,000 yen
22	2000 XT	Coupé	1,157,000 yen
23	2000 XT	Liftback	1,253,000 yen
24	2000 SE	Coupé	1,248,000 yen
25	2000 SE	Liftback	1,344,000 yen
26	2000 GTV	Coupé	1,529,000 yen
27	2000 GTV	Liftback	1,625,000 yen
28	2000 GT	Coupé	1,577,000 yen
29	2000 GT	Liftback	1,673,000 yen

For GB and USA prices, see price index.

Power team:	Standard for:	Optional for:
88 hp	1 to 7	—
110 hp	8 to 11	—
95 hp	12 to 19	—
98 hp	12 to 19	—
100 hp	20 to 25	—
130 hp	26 to 29	—

88 hp power team

ENGINE Toyota TTC-L lean-burn low emissione engine with turbulence generating pot auxiliary combustion chamber; front, 4 stroke; 4 cylinders, in line; 96.9 cu in, 1,588 cc (3.35 x 2.76 in, 85 x 70 mm); compression ratio: 9:1; max power (JIS): 88 hp at 5,600 rpm; max torque (JIS): 96 lb ft, 13.3 kg m at 3,400 rpm; max engine rpm: 6,000; 55 hp/l; cast iron block, light alloy head; 5 crankshaft bearings; valves: overhead, Vee-slanted, push-rods and rockers; camshafts: 1, side; lubrication: rotary pump, full flow filter, 7.4 imp pt, 8.9 US pt, 4.2 l; 1 Aisan 12T-U downdraught twin barrel carburettor; emission control with catalytic converter, secondary air injection and exhaust gas recirculation; fuel feed: mechanical pump; water-cooled, 14.1 imp pt, 16.9 US pt, 8 l.

TRANSMISSION driving wheels: rear; clutch: single dry plate (diaphragm); gearbox: mechanical; gears: 4, fully synchronized; ratios: I 3.587, II 2.022, III 1.384, IV 1, rev 3.484; lever: central; final drive: hypoid bevel; axle ratio: 3.909; width of rims: 4.5''; tyres: 6.45 x 13 - ST and XT models 165 SR x 13.

88 HP POWER TEAM

PERFORMANCE max speeds: (I) 29 mph, 46 km/h; (II) 52 mph, 83 km/h; (III) 75 mph, 120 km/h; (IV) 103 mph, 165 km/h; power-weight ratio: ET and LT coupés 23 lb/hp, 10.5 kg/hp; consumption: 34 m/imp gal, 28.3 m/US gal, 8.3 l x 100 km.

CHASSIS integral; front suspension: independent, by McPherson, coil springs/telescopic damper struts, lower wishbones (trailing links), anti-roll bar; rear: rigid axle, twin trailing radius arms, transverse linkage bar, coil springs, telescopic dampers.

STEERING recirculating ball; turns lock to lock; 3.80.

BRAKES front disc, rear drum; lining area: front 24.2 sq in, 156 sq cm, rear 54 sq in, 348 sq cm, total 78.2 sq in, 504 sq cm.

ELECTRICAL EQUIPMENT 12 V; 35 Ah battery; 45 A alternator; Nihon-Denso distributor; 4 headlamps.

DIMENSIONS AND WEIGHT wheel base: 98.43 in, 250 cm; tracks: 52.56 in, 133 cm front, 53.15 in, 135 cm rear; length: ET Coupé and LT models 169.69 in, 431 cm - ST and XT models 170.47 in, 433 cm; width: 64.17 in, 163 cm; height: coupés 51.57 in, 131 cm - liftbacks 50.98 in, 129 cm; ground clearance: ET Coupé and LT models 6.30 in, 16 cm - ST and XT models 5.90 in, 15 cm; weight: ET and LT coupés 2,040 lb, 925 kg - LT Liftback and ST Coupé 2,051 lb, 930 kg - ST Liftback and XT Coupé 2,062 lb, 935 kg - XT Liftback 2,073 lb, 940 kg; weight distribution: 56.7% front, 43.3% rear; turning circle (between walls): 36.1 ft, 11 m; fuel tank: 13.4 imp gal, 16.1 US gal, 61 l.

BODY 5 seats, separate front seats, reclining backrests, built-in headrests.

OPTIONAL ACCESSORIES 5-speed fully synchronized mechanical gearbox (I 3.587, II 2.022, III 1.384, IV 1, V 0.861, rev 3.484), 4.100 axle ratio, max speed 106 mph, 170 km/h.

110 hp power team

See 88 hp power team, except for:

ENGINE compression ratio: 8.4:1; max power (JIS): 110 hp at 6,000 rpm; max torque (JIS): 105 lb ft, 14.5 kg m at 4,800 rpm; max engine rpm: 6,400; 69 hp/l; camshafts: 2, overhead; lubrication: 6.7 imp pt, 8 US pt, 3.8 l; Bosch-Denso L-jetronic electronic injection.

TRANSMISSION gears: 5, fully synchronized; ratios: I 3.587, II 2.022, III 1.384, IV 1, 0.861, rev 3.484; axle ratio: 4.100; width of rims: 5''; tyres: 185/70 HR x 13.

PERFORMANCE max speeds: (I) 29 mph, 47 km/h; (II) 51 mph, 83 km/h; (III) 76 mph, 122 km/h; (IV) 106 mph, 170

TOYOTA Celica 1600 XT Coupé

km/h; (V) 109 mph, 175 km/h; power-weight ratio: GTV Coupé 20 lb/hp 9 kg/hp.

CHASSIS rear suspension: anti-roll bar.

STEERING turns lock to lock: 3.50.

BRAKES rear disc.

DIMENSIONS AND WEIGHT tracks: 53.15 in, 135 cm front, 53.54 in, 136 cm rear; width: 64.57 in, 164 cm; weight: GTV Coupé 2,194 lb, 995 kg - GTV Liftback and GT Coupé 2,205 lb, 1,000 kg - GT Liftback 2,216 lb, 1,005 kg.

95 hp power team

See 88 hp power team, except for:

ENGINE 108 cu in, 1,770 cc (3.35 x 3.07 in, 85 x 78 mm); max power (JIS): 95 hp at 5,400 rpm; max torque (JIS): 109 lb ft, 15 kg m at 3,400 rpm; 54 hp/l; 1 Aisan 13T-U downdraught twin barrel carburettor.

TRANSMISSION axle ratio: 3.727.

PERFORMANCE max speed: 106 mph, 170 km/h; power-weight ratio: LT Coupé 22 lb/hp, 10 kg/hp; consumption: 32.4 m/imp gal, 27 m/US gal, 8.7 l x 100 km.

DIMENSIONS AND WEIGHT width: SE models 64.57 in, 164 cm; weight: LT Coupé 2,084 lb, 945 kg - LT Liftback and ST Coupé 2,095 lb, 950 kg - ST Liftback and XT Coupé 2,106 lb, 955 kg - XT Liftback and SE Coupé 2,117 lb, 960 kg - SE Liftback 2,128 lb, 965 kg.

98 hp power team

See 88 hp power team, except for:

ENGINE hemispherical combustion chamber; 108 cu in, 1,770 cc (3.35 x 3.07 in, 85 x 78 mm); max power (JIS): 98 hp at 5,700 rpm; max torque (JIS): 110 lb ft, 15.2 kg m at 3,400 rpm; 55 hp/l; 1 Aisan 3T-U downdraught twin barrel carburettor.

TRANSMISSION Toyoglide automatic transmission, hydraulic torque converter and planetary gears; ratios: I 2.450, II 1.450, III 1, rev 2.222; axle ratio: 3.909.

PERFORMANCE max speed: 106 mph, 170 km/h; power-weight ratio: LT Coupé 21.2 lb/hp, 9.6 kg/hp; consumption: 32.4 m/imp gal, 27 m/US gal, 8.7 l x 100 km.

DIMENSIONS AND WEIGHT width: SE models 64.57 in, 164 cm; weight: LT Coupé 2,084 lb, 945 kg - LT Liftback and ST Coupé 2,095 lb, 950 kg - ST Liftback and XT Coupé 2,106 lb, 955 kg - XT Liftback and SE Coupé 2,117 lb, 960 kg - SE Liftback 2,128 lb, 965 kg.

100 hp power team

See 88 hp power team, except for:

ENGINE 120.1 cu in, 1,968 cc (3.48 x 3.15 in, 88.5 x 80 mm); compression ratio: 8.5:1; max power (JIS): 100 hp at 5,500 rpm; max torque (JIS): 112 lb ft, 15.5 kg m at 3,600 rpm; 50.8 hp/l; cast iron block and head; valves: overhead, in line, rockers; camshafts: 1, overhead; 1 Aisan 18R-U downdraught twin barrel carburettor.

TRANSMISSION gearbox ratios: I 3.579, II 2.081, III 1.397, IV 1, rev 4.399; axle ratio: 3.727; tyres: 165 SR x 13.

PERFORMANCE max speed: 106 mph, 170 km/h; power-weight ratio: ST Coupé 21.6 lb/hp, 9.8 kg/hp; consumption: 28.2 m/imp gal, 23.5 m/US gal, 10 l x 100 km.

STEERING variable ratio, servo.

BRAKES servo.

DIMENSIONS AND WEIGHT width: SE models 64.57 in, 164 cm; weight: ST Coupé 2,161 lb, 980 kg - ST Liftback and XT Coupés 2,172 lb, 98,5 kg - XT Liftback and SE Coupé 2,183 lb, 990 kg - SE Liftback 2,194 lb, 995 kg.

OPTIONAL ACCESSORIES 5-speed fully synchronized mechanical gearbox (I 3.287, II 2.043, III 1.394, IV 1, V 0.853, rev 4.039), 3.909 axle ratio, max speed 109 mph, 175 km/h; Toyoglide automatic transmission, hydraulic torque converter with 3 ratios (I 2.400, II 1.479, III 1, rev 1.920), 3.909 axle ratio, max speed 103 mph, 165 km/h.

TOYOTA Celica 2000 GT Liftback

130 hp power team

See 88 hp power team, except for:

ENGINE 120.1 cu in, 1,968 cc (3.48 x 3.15 in, 88.5 x 80 mm); compression ratio: 8.3:1; max power (JIS): 130 hp at 6,000 rpm; max torque (JIS): 120 lb ft, 16.5 kg m at 4,800 rpm; 66 hp/l; cast iron block and head; valves: thimble tappets; camshafts: 2, overhead; 2 Solex 18R-GU horizontal twin barrel carburettors.

TRANSMISSION gears: 5, fully synchronized; ratios: I 3.525, II 2.054, III 1.396, IV 1, V 0.858, rev 3.755; axle ratio: 3.909; width of rims: 5''; tyres: 185/70HR x 13.

PERFORMANCE max speed: 112 mph, 180 km/h; power-weight ratio: GTV Coupé 18 lb/hp, 8 kg/hp; consumption: 28.2 m/imp gal, 23.5 m/US gal, 10 l x 100 km.

CHASSIS rear suspension: anti-roll bar.

STEERING variable ratio, servo; turns lock to lock: 3.50.

BRAKES rear disc, servo.

DIMENSIONS AND WEIGHT tracks: 53.13 in, 135 cm front, 53.54 in, 136 cm rear; ground clearance: 5.91 in, 15 cm; weight: GTV Coupé 2,304 lb, 1,045 kg - GT Coupé and GTV Liftback 2,315 lb, 1,050 kg - GT Liftback 2,326 lb, 1,055 kg.

TOYOTA Corona 1600 Series

TOYOTA Corona 1600 De Luxe 2-door Sedan

TOYOTA Corona 1600 SL Hardtop

Celica (USA) Series

PRICES IN USA:

ST Hardtop	$ 4,719*
GT Hardtop	$ 5,119*
GT Liftback	$ 5,339*

96 hp power team

ENGINE front, 4 stroke; 4 cylinders, vertical, in line; 139.7 cu in, 2,289 cc; compression ratio: 8.4:1; max power (SAE): 96 hp at 4,800 rpm; max torque (SAE): 120 lb ft, 16.5 kg m at 2,800 rpm; max engine rpm: 5,600; 41.9 hp/l; cast iron block, light alloy head; 5 crankshaft bearings; valves: overhead, Vee-slanted, rockers; camshafts: 1, overhead; lubrication: rotary pump, full flow filter, 6.5 imp pt, 7.8 US pt, 3.7 l; 1 Aisan downdraught twin barrel carburettor; fuel feed: mechanical pump; water-coodel, 11.4 imp pt, 13.7 US pt, 6.5 l.

TRANSMISSION driving wheels: rear; clutch: single dry plate (diaphragm); gearbox: mechanical; gears: 4 (5 for GT models only), fully synchronized; ratios: I 3.579, II 2.081, III 1.397, IV 1, rev 4.399 - GT models I 3.287, II 2.043, III 1.394, IV 1, V 0.853, rev 4.039; lever: central; final drive: hypoid bevel; axle ratio: 3.727 - GT models 3.909; width of rims: 5''; tyres: ST 175SR x 14 - GT models 185/70HR x 14.

PERFORMANCE max speed: 109 mph, 175 km/h; consumption: not declared.

CHASSIS integral; front suspension: independent, by Mc-Pherson, coil springs/telescopic damper struts, lower wishbones (trailing links), anti-roll bar; rear: rigid axle, twin trailing radius arms, transverse linkage bar, coil springs, telescopic dampers.

STEERING recirculating ball; turns lock to lock: 3.50.

BRAKES front disc, rear drum, servo; lining area: front 24.2 sq in, 156 sq cm, rear 54 sq in, 348 sq cm, total 78.2 sq in, 504 sq cm.

ELECTRICAL EQUIPMENT 12 V; 35 Ah battery; 40 A alternator; Nihon-Denso distributor; 4 headlamps.

BODY 5 seats, separate front seats, reclining backrests, built-in headrests.

OPTIONAL ACCESSORIES Toyoglide automatic transmission, hydraulic torque converter with 3 ratios (I 2.400, II 1.479, III 1, rev 1.920), 3.900 axle ratio, max speed 103 mph, 165 km/h, acceleration standing ¼ mile 19 sec.

Corona Series

PRICES (Tokyo):

1	1600 Standard 4-door Sedan	817,000	yen
2	1600 De Luxe 2-door Sedan	934,000	yen
3	1600 De Luxe 4-door Sedan	954,000	yen
4	1600 De Luxe Automatic 4-door Sedan	986,000	yen
5	1600 De Luxe 2-door Hardtop	961,000	yen
6	1600 De Luxe Automatic 2-door Hardtop	1,021,000	yen
7	1600 GL 2-door Sedan	986,000	yen
8	1600 GL 4-door Sedan	1,006,000	yen
9	1600 GL Automatic 4-door Sedan	1,038,000	yen
10	1600 GL 2-door Hardtop	1,013,000	yen
11	1600 GL Automatic 2-door Hardtop	1,073,000	yen
12	1600 SL 4-door Sedan	1,042,000	yen
13	1600 SL 2-door Hardtop	1,077,000	yen
14	1800 De Luxe 4-door Sedan	1,004,000	yen
15	1800 De Luxe 2-door Hardtop	1,039,000	yen
16	1800 GL 4-door Sedan	1,078,000	yen
17	1800 GL 2-door Hardtop	1,113,000	yen
18	1800 GL 4-door Sedan	1,132,000	yen
19	1800 SL 2-door Hardtop	1,167,000	yen
20	1800 De Luxe Automatic 4-door Sedan	1,036,000	yen
21	1800 De Luxe Automatic 2-door Hardtop	1,071,000	yen
22	1800 GL Automatic 4-door Sedan	1,110,000	yen
23	1800 GL Automatic 2-door Hardtop	1,145,000	yen
24	1800 SL Automatic 4-door Sedan	1,141,000	yen
25	1800 SL Automatic 2-door Hardtop	1,176,000	yen
26	2000 DE Luxe 4-door Sedan	946,000	yen
27	2000 GL 4-door Sedan	1,025,000	yen
28	2000 GL 2-door Hardtop	1,060,000	yen
29	2000 GT 4-door Sedan	1,433,000	yen
30	2000 GT 2-door Hardtop	1,468,000	yen

Power team:	Standard for:	Optional for:
88 hp	2,3,5,7,8,10	—
90 hp	1,4,6,9,11,12,13	—
95 hp	14 to 19	—
98 hp	20 to 25	—
88 hp (stratified charge)	26 to 28	—
130 hp	29,30	—

88 hp power team

ENGINE TTC-L lean-burn system with turbulence generating pot auxiliary combustion chambers; front, 4-stroke; 4 cylinders, vertical, in line; 96.9 cu in, 1,588 cc (3.35 x 2.76 in, 85 x 70 mm); compression ratio: 9:1; max power (JIS): 88 hp at 5,600 rpm; max torque (JIS): 96 lb ft, 13.3 kg m at 3,400 rpm; max engine rpm: 6,000; 55 hp/l; cast iron block, light alloy head; 5 crankshaft bearings; valves: overhead, push-rods and rockers; camshafts: 1, side; lubrication: rotary pump, full flow filter, 7.4 imp pt, 8.9 US pt, 4.2 l; 1 Aisan 12T-U downdraught twin barrel carburettor; emission control with catalytic converter, secondary air injection and exhaust gas recirculation; fuel feed: mechanical pump; water-cooled, 14.1 imp pt, 16.9 US pt, 8 l.

TRANSMISSION driving wheels: rear; clutch: single dry plate (diaphragm); gearbox: mechanical; gears: 4, fully synchronized; ratios: I 3.587, II 2.022, III 1.384, IV 1, rev 3.484; lever: central; final drive: hypoid bevel; axle ratio: 3.909; width of rims: 4.5''; tyres: 6.45 x 13.

PERFORMANCE max speeds: (I) 20 mph, 46 km/h; (II) 52 mph, 83 km/h; (III) 75 mph, 120 km/h; (IV) 99 mph, 160 km/h; power-weight ratio: De Luxe 2-dr. Sedan 24.8 lb/hp, 11.2 kg/hp; consumption: 49.6 m/imp gal, 41.3 m/US gal, 5.7 l x 100 km at 37 mph, 60 km/h.

CHASSIS integral; front suspension: independent, wishbones, coil springs, anti-roll bar, telescopic dampers; rear: rigid axle, semi-elliptic leafsprings, telescopic dampers.

STEERING recirculating ball · GL models variable ratio; turns lock to lock: 3.80.

BRAKES front disc, rear drum; lining area: front 23.6 sq in, 152 sq cm, rear 54.6 sq in, 352 sq cm, total 78.2 sq in, 504 sq cm.

ELECTRICAL EQUIPMENT 12 V; 35 Ah battery; 45 A alternator; 4 headlamps.

DIMENSIONS AND WEIGHT wheel base: 98.42 in, 250 cm; tracks: 53.15 in, 135 cm front, 51.97 in, 132 cm rear; length: De Luxe models 167.72 in, 426 cm · GL models 169.29 in, 430 cm; width: De Luxe models 63.39 in, 161 cm · GL models 63.38 in, 162 cm; height: sedans 54.72 in, 139 cm · hardtops 53.54 in, 136 cm; ground clearance: 6.50 in, 16.5 cm; weight: De Luxe 2-dr. Sedan 2,183 lb, 990 kg · De Luxe Sedan 2,194 lb, 995 kg · De Luxe 4-dr. Sedan 2,205 lb, 1,000 kg · GL 4-dr. Sedan and De Luxe Hardtop 2,216 lb, 1,005 kg · GL Hardtop 2,227 lb, 1,010 kg; weight distribution: 56.6% front, 43.4% rear; turning circle (between walls): 36.1 ft, 11 m; fuel tank: 13.2 imp gal, 15.8 US gal, 60 l.

BODY 5 seats, separate front seats, reclining backrests, built-in headrests.

OPTIONAL ACCESSORIES 5-speed mechanical gearbox (I 3.587, II 2.022, III 1.384, IV 1, V 0.861, rev 3.484).

95 hp power team

See 88 hp power team, except for:

ENGINE 108 cu in, 1,770 cc (3.35 x 3.07 in, 85 x 78 mm); max power (JIS): 90 hp at 5,400 rpm; max torque (JIS): 109 lb ft, 15 kg m at 3,400 rpm; 54 hp/l; 1 Aisan 13T-U downdraught twin barrel carburettor.

TRANSMISSION gears: (for SL models only) 5, fully synchronized; ratios: I 3.587, III 2.022, III 1.384, IV 1, V 0.861, rev 0.861; axle ratio: 3.727 - SL models 4.100; tyres: SL models 165 SR x 14.

PERFORMANCE power-weight ratio: De Luxe 4-dr. Sedan 23.4 lb/hp, 10.6 kg/hp.

STEERING variable ratio; turns lock to lock: 3.90.

DIMENSIONS AND WEIGHT length: SL models 174.40 in, 443 cm; weight: De Luxe Hardtop 2,216 lb, 1,005 kg - De Luxe 4-dr. Sedan and GL Hardtop 2,227 lb, 1,010 kg - GL 4-dr. Sedan 2,238 lb, 1,015 kg - SL Hardtop 2,315 lb, 1,050 kg - SL 4-dr. Sedan 2,359 lb, 1,070 kg.

OPTIONAL ACCESSORIES (except SL models) 5-speed mechanical gearbox, 3.727 axle ratio.

98 hp power team

See 88 hp power team, except for:

ENGINE hemispherical combustion chambers without TTC-L lean-burn system; 108 cu in, 1,770 cc (3.35 x 3.07 in, 85 x 78 mm); max power (JIS): 98 hp at 5,700 rpm; max torque (JIS): 110 lb ft, 15.2 kg m at 3,400 rpm; 35.3 hp/l; 1 Aisan 3T-U downdraught twin barrel carburettor.

TOYOTA Corona 1800 SL Hardtop

TOYOTA Corona 2000 GT Hardtop

TOYOTA Corona 2000 GT Sedan

TRANSMISSION Toyoglide automatic transmission, hydraulic torque converter and planetary gears; ratios: I 2.450, II 1.450, III 1, rev 2.222; axle-ratio: 3.909; tyres: SL models 165 SR x 14.

PERFORMANCE power-weight ratio: De Luxe models 22.7 lb/hp, 10.3 kg/hp.

STEERING variable ratio; turns lock to lock: 3.90.

DIMENSIONS AND WEIGHT weight: De Luxe models 2,227 lb, 1,010 kg - GL models 2,238 lb, 1,015 kg.

90 hp power team

See 88 hp power team, except for:

ENGINE hemispherical combustion chambers without TTC-L lean-burn system; max power (JIS): 90 hp at 6,000 rpm; max torque (JIS): 94 lb ft, 13 kg m at 3,800 rpm; 56.7 hp/l; 1 Aisan 2T-U downdraught twin barrel carburettor.

TRANSMISSION Toyoglide automatic transmission, hydraulic torque converter and planetary gears - SL models 5-speed mechanical gearbox; ratios: I 2.450, II 1.450, III 1, rev 2.222 - SL models I 3.587, II 2.022, III 1.384, IV 1, V 0.861, rev 3.484; axle ratio: SL models 4.300; tyres: 165 SR x 14.

PERFORMANCE power-weight ratio: De Luxe 4-dr. Sedan 24.6 lb/hp, 11.2 kg/hp.

DIMENSIONS AND WEIGHT weight: De Luxe 4-dr. Sedan 2,216 lb, 1,005 kg - GL 4-dr. Sedan and De Luxe Hardtop 2,227 lb, 1,010 kg - GL Hardtop 2,238 lb, 1,015 kg - SL 4-dr. Sedan 2,304 lb, 1,045 kg - SL Hardtop 2,315 lb, 1,050 kg.

88 hp power team (stratified charge)

See 88 hp power team, except for:

ENGINE low emission Compound Vortex type (stratified charge) with auxiliary combustion chambers; 120.1 cu in, 1,968 cc (3.48 x 3.15 in, 88.5 x 80 mm); compression ratio: 8:1; max power (JIS): 88 hp at 5,000 rpm; max torque (JIS): 101 lb ft, 14 kg m at 3,400 rpm; 44.7 hp/l; valves: 3 per cylinder (intake in auxiliary chamber, intake and exhaust in main chamber), rockers; 1 Aisan 19 R downdraught 3-barrel (one barrel for auxiliary chamber, two for main chamber) carburettor; cooling system: 13.9 imp pt, 16.7 US pt, 7.9 l.

TRANSMISSION axle ratio: 4.100.

PERFORMANCE max speed: 87 mph, 140 km/h; power-weight ratio: 26.3 lb/hp, 11.9 kg/hp; consumption: 42.2 m/imp gal, 35.1 m/US gal, 6.7 l x 100 km at 37 mph, 60 km/h.

DIMENSIONS AND WEIGHT weight: 2,315 lb, 1,050 kg.

OPTIONAL ACCESSORIES 5-speed fully synchronized mechanical gearbox.

130 hp power team

See 88 hp power team, except for:

ENGINE hemispherical combustion chambers without TTC-L lean-burn system; 120.1 cu in, 1,968 cc (3.48 x 3.15 in, 88.5 x 80 mm); compression ratio: 8.3:1; max power (JIS): 130 hp at 6,000 rpm; max torque (JIS): 120 lb ft, 16.5 kg m at 4,800 rpm; max engine rpm: 6,600; 66 hp/l; valves: overhead, Vee-slanted, thimble tappets; camshafts: 2, overhead; 2 Solex 18R-GU horizontal twin barrel carburettors; cooling system: 14.4 imp pt, 17.3 US pt, 8.2 l.

TRANSMISSION gears: 5, fully synchronized; ratios: I 3.525, II 2.054, III 1.396, IV 1, V 0.858, rev 3.755; axle ratio: 4.100; width of rims: 5''; tyres: 185/70HR x 14.

PERFORMANCE max speed: 112 mph, 180 km/h; power-weight ratio: Sedan 19.2 lb/hp, 8.6 kg/hp - Hardtop 19.3 lb/hp, 8.7 kg/hp.

CHASSIS rear suspension: twin torque arms.

STEERING variable ratio; turns lock to lock: 3.90.

BRAKES servo.

DIMENSIONS AND WEIGHT length: 167.32 in, 425 cm; weight: Sedan 2,492 lb, 1,130 kg - Hardtop 2,514 lb, 1,140 kg.

OPTIONAL ACCESSORIES limited slip differential.

TOYOTA Corona 1800 GL 4-door Sedan

Corona (USA) Series

PRICES IN USA:

Corona Custom 2-door Sedan	$ 4,134*
Corona De Luxe 4-door Sedan	$ 4,449*
Corona Hardtop	—
Corona De Luxe Station Wagon	$ 4,779*
Corona SR-5 Hardtop	—

96 hp power team

ENGINE front, 4 stroke; 4 cylinders, vertical, in line; 133.6 cu in, 2,189 cc; compression ratio: 9:1; max power (SAE): 96 hp at 4,800 rpm; max torque (SAE): 120 lb ft, 16.5 kg m at 2,800 rpm; max engine rpm: 5,600; 43.8 hp/l; cast iron block, light alloy head; 5 crankshaft bearings; valves: overhead, Vee-slanted, rockers; camshafts: 1, overhead; lubrication: rotary pump, full flow filter, 6.5 imp pt, 7.8 US pt, 3.7 l; 1 Aisan downdraught twin barrel carburettor; fuel feed: mechanical pump; water-cooled, 14.4 imp pt, 17.3 US pt, 8.2 l.

TRANSMISSION driving wheels: rear; clutch: single dry plate (diaphragm); gearbox: mechanical; gears: 4 (5 for SR-5 only), fully synchronized; ratios: I 3.579, II 2.081, III 1.397, IV 1, rev 4.399 (SR-5 I 3.287, II 2.043, III 1.394, IV 1, V 0.853, rev 4.039); lever: central; final drive: hypoid

bevel; axle ratio: 3.727; width of rims: 5''; tyres: B78 x 14 - Hardtop 175 SR x 14 - SR-5 185/70 HR x 14.

PERFORMANCE max speed: 112 mph, 180 km/h; consumption: not declared.

CHASSIS integral; front suspension: independent, wishbones, coil springs, anti-roll bar, telescopic dampers; rear: rigid axle, semi-elliptic leafsprings, anti-roll bar, telescopic dampers.

STEERING recirculating ball, variable ratio; turns lock to lock: 3.90.

BRAKES front disc, rear drum, servo; lining area: front 23.6 sq in, 152 sq cm, rear 54.6 sq in, 352 sq cm, total 78.2 sq in, 504 sq cm.

ELECTRICAL EQUIPMENT 12 V; 35 Ah battery; 55 A alternator; Denso distributor; 4 headlamps.

DIMENSIONS AND WEIGHT wheel base: 98.43 in, 250 cm; front track: 53 in, 135 cm; rear track: 52 in, 132 cm - Station Wagon 53.20 in, 135 cm; length: 173.20 in, 440 cm - Station Wagon 176.40 in, 448 cm; width: 63.80 in, 162 cm; height: 55.10 in, 140 cm - hardtops 54.10 in, 137 cm - Station Wagon 56.30 in, 143 cm; ground clearance: 6.69 in, 17 cm; turning circle (between walls): 36.1 ft, 11 m; fuel tank: 12.1 imp gal, 14.5 US gal, 55 l.

BODY 5 seats, separate front seats, reclining backrests, built-in headrests.

OPTIONAL ACCESSORIES (except SR-5) 5-speed fully synchronized mechanical gearbox (I 3.287, II 2.043, III 1.394, IV 1, V 0.853, rev 4.039); automatic transmission with 3 ratios (I 2.450, II 1.450, III 1, rev 2.222), 3.909 axle ratio.

Mark II - Chaser Series

PRICES (Tokyo):

1 Mark II 1800 De Luxe 4-dr Sedan	1,053,000 yen
2 Mark II 1800 De Luxe 2-dr Hardtop	1,090,000 yen
3 Chaser 1800 De Luxe 4-dr Sedan	1,059,000 yen
4 Chaser 1800 De Luxe 2-dr Hardtop	1,096,000 yen
5 Mark II 1800 GL 4-dr Sedan	1,101,000 yen
6 Mark II 1800 GL 2-dr Hardtop	1,138,000 yen
7 Chaser 1800 XL 4-dr Sedan	1,107,000 yen
8 Chaser 1800 XL 2-dr Hardtop	1,144,000 yen
9 Mark II 1800 De Luxe Automatic 4-dr Sedan	1,085,000 yen
10 Mark II 1800 De Luxe Automatic 2-dr Hardtop	1,122,000 yen
11 Chaser 1800 De Luxe Automatic 4-dr Sedan	1,091,000 yen
12 Chaser 1800 De Luxe Automatic 2-dr Hardtop	1,128,000 yen
13 Mark II 1800 GL Automatic 4-dr Sedan	1,133,000 yen
14 Mark II 1800 GL Automatic 2-dr Hardtop	1,170,000 yen
15 Chaser 1800 XL Automatic 4-dr Sedan	1,139,000 yen
16 Chaser 1800 XL Automatic 2-dr Hardtop	1,176,000 yen
17 Mark II 2000 Standard 4-dr Sedan	982,000 yen
18 Mark II 2000 De Luxe 4-dr Sedan	1,050,000 yen
19 Mark II 2000 De Luxe 2-dr Hardtop	1,087,000 yen
20 Chaser 2000 De Luxe 4-dr Sedan	1,056,000 yen
21 Chaser 2000 De Luxe 2-dr Hardtop	1,093,000 yen
22 Mark II 2000 GL 4-dr Sedan	1,098,000 yen
23 Mark II 2000 GL 2-dr Hardtop	1,135,000 yen
24 Chaser 2000 XL 4-dr Sedan	1,104,000 yen
25 Chaser 2000 XL 2-dr Hardtop	1,141,000 yen
26 Chaser 2000 GS 4-dr Sedan	1,204,000 yen
27 Chaser 2000 GS 2-dr Hardtop	1,291,000 yen
28 Mark II 2000 GSL 4-dr Sedan	1,218,000 yen
29 Mark II 2000 GSL 2-dr Hardtop	1,285,000 yen
30 Mark II 2000 L 4-dr Sedan	1,198,000 yen
31 Mark II 2000 L 2-dr Hardtop	1,265,000 yen
32 Mark II 2000 LG 4-dr Sedan	1,303,000 yen
33 Mark II 2000 LG 2-dr Hardtop	1,370,000 yen
34 Chaser 2000 SXL 4-dr Sedan	1,204,000 yen
35 Chaser 2000 SXL 2-dr Hardtop	1,271,000 yen
36 Mark II 2000 EFI L 4-door Sedan	1,324,000 yen
37 Mark II 2000 EFI L 2-dr Hardtop	1,391,000 yen
38 Mark II 2000 EFI LG 4-dr Sedan	1,429,000 yen
39 Mark II 2000 EFI LG 2-dr Hardtop	1,496,000 yen
40 Chaser 2000 EFI SXL 4-dr Sedan	1,333,000 yen
41 Chaser 2000 EFI SXL 2-dr Hardtop	1,397,000 yen
42 Chaser 2000 EFI SGS 4-dr Sedan	1,448,000 yen
43 Chaser 2000 EFI SGS 2-dr Hardtop	1,515,000 yen
44 Mark II 2000 EFI LG Touring 4-dr Sedan	1,486,000 yen
45 Mark II 2000 EFI LG Touring 2-dr Hardtop	1,553,000 yen
46 Chaser 2000 SG Touring 4-dr Sedan	1,564,000 yen
47 Chaser 2000 SG Touring 2-dr Hardtop	1,601,000 yen
48 Mark II 2000 EFI Grande 4-dr Sedan	1,796,000 yen
49 Mark II 2000 EFI Grande 2-dr Hardtop	1,833,000 yen
50 Mark II 2600 Grande Automatic 4-dr Sedan	1,913,000 yen
51 Mark II 2600 Grande Automatic 2-dr Hardtop	1,952,000 yen

For GB and USA prices, see price index.

TOYOTA Mark II 2600 Grande Sedan

Power team:	Standard for:	Optional for:
95 hp	1 to 8	—
98 hp	9 to 16	—
100 hp	17 to 29	—
110 hp	30 to 35	—
125 hp	36 to 49	—
135 hp	50, 51	—

95 hp power team

ENGINE TTC-L lean-burn low emission engine with turbulence generating pot auxiliary combustion chamber; front, 4 stroke; 4 cylinders, in line; 108 cu in, 1,770 c (3.35 x 3.07 in, 85 x 78 mm); compression ratio: 9:1; max power (JIS): 95 hp at 5,700 rpm; max torque (JIS): 109 lb ft, 15 kg m at 3,400 rpm; max engine rpm: 6,000; 53.7 hp/l; cast iron block, light alloy head; 5 crankshaft bearings; valves: overhead, rockers; camshafts: 1, overhead; lubrication: rotary pump, full flow filter, 7.4 imp pt, 8.9 US pt, 4.2 l; 1 Aisan 13T-U downdraught twin barrel carburettor; emission control with catalytic converter, secondary air injection and exhaust gas recirculation; fuel feed: mechanical pump; water-cooled, 14.1 imp pt, 16.9 US pt, 8 l.

TRANSMISSION driving wheels: rear; clutch: single dry plate (diaphragm); gearbox: mechanical; gears: 4, fully synchronized; ratios: I 3.579, II 2.081, III 1.397, IV 1, rev 4.399; lever: central; final drive: hypoid bevel; axle ratio: 3.909; width of rims: 5''; tyres: 6.45 x 14.

PERFORMANCE max speeds: (I) 29 mph, 47 km/h; (II) 52 mph, 83 km/h; (III) 76 mph, 123 km/h; (IV) 103 mph, 165 km/h; power-weight ratio: De Luxe sedans 24.3 lb/hp, 11 kg/hp; consumption: 31.4 m/imp gal, 26.1 m/US gal, 9 l x 100 km.

CHASSIS integral; front suspension: independent, by McPherson, lower transverse arms, diagonal trailing locating rods, anti-roll bar, coil springs, telescopic damper struts; rear: rigid axle, lower trailing links, upper torque rods, coil springs, telescopic dampers.

STEERING recirculating ball, variable ratio; turns lock to lock: 4.30.

BRAKES front disc, rear drum, servo; lining area: front 22.3 sq in, 144 sq cm, rear 54.6 sq in, 352 sq cm, total 76.9 sq in, 496 sq cm.

ELECTRICAL EQUIPMENT 12 V; 35 Ah battery; 55 A alternator; Nihon Denso distributor; 2 headlamps.

DIMENSIONS AND WEIGHT wheel base: 103.94 in, 264 cm; tracks: 53.94 in, 137 cm front, 53.15 in, 135 cm rear; length: De Luxe models 177.17 in, 450 cm - GL and XL models 178.35 in, 453 cm; width: 65.75 in, 167 cm; height: sedans 55.51 in, 141 cm - hardtops 54.72 in, 139 cm; ground clearance: 6.69 in, 17 cm; weight: De Luxe 4-dr. sedans 2,304 lb, 1,045 kg - De Luxe hardtops 2,315 lb, 1,050 kg - GL and XL 4-dr. sedans 2,326 lb, 1,055 kg - GL and XL hardtops 2,337 lb, 1,060 kg; weight distribution: 54% front, 46% rear; turning circle (between walls): 37 ft, 11.4 m.

BODY 5 seats, separate front seats, reclining backrests, built-in headrests.

OPTIONAL ACCESSORIES 5-speed fully synchronized mechanical gearbox (I 3.287, II 2.043, II 1.394, IV 1, V 0.853).

TOYOTA Mark II 2600 Grande Hardtop

TOYOTA Mark II 2600 Grande Hardtop

98 hp power team

See 95 hp power team, except for:

ENGINE hemispherical combustion chambers without TTC-L lean-burn engine; max power (JIS): 98 hp at 5,700 rpm; max torque (JIS): 110 lb ft, 15.2 kg m at 3,400 rpm; 1 Aisan 3T-U downdraught twin barrel carburettor.

TRANSMISSION Toyoglide automatic transmission, hydraulic torque converter and planetary gears; ratios: I 2.450, II 1.450, I rev 2.222; axle ratio: 4.100.

PERFORMANCE power-weight ratio: De Luxe sedans 23.5 lb/hp, 10.7 kg/hp.

100 hp power team

See 95 hp power team, except for:

ENGINE 120.1 cu in, 1,968 cc (3.48 x 3.15 in, 88.5 x 80 mm); compression ratio: 8.5:1; max power (JIS): 100 hp at 5,500 rpm; max torque (JIS): 112 lb ft, 15.5 kg m at 3,600 rpm; 50.8 hp/l; cast iron block and head; lubrication 8.8 imp pt, 10.6 US pt, 5 l; 1 Aisan 18R-U downdraught twin barrel carburettor.

TRANSMISSION gears: 4 (5 for GSL and GS models), fully synchronized; ratios: Standard (I 3.368, II 1.644, III 1, IV 0.813, rev 4.079) - De Luxe, GL and XL models (I 3.579, II 2.081, III 1.397, IV 1, rev 4.399) - GSL and GS models (I 3.287, II 2.043, III 1.394, IV 1, V 0.853, rev 4.039); lever: central - Standard steering column; axle ratio: 3.909 - GSL and GS models 4.100; tyres: 6.45 x 14 - GSL and GS models 175 SR x 14.

PERFORMANCE max speeds: (I) 31 mph, 50 km/h; (II) 53 mph, 86 km/h; (III) 78 mph, 126 km/h; (IV) 103 mph, 165 km/h; power-weight ratio: Standard Sedan 23.5 lb/hp, 10.6 kg/hp - De Luxe sedans 23.6 lb/hp, 10.7 kg/hp; consumption: 39.2 m/imp gal, 32.7 m/US gal, 7.2 l x 100 km.

BRAKES (for GSL and GS models only) disc; lining area: front 22.3 sq in, 144 sq cm, rear 18 sq in, 116 sq cm, total 40.3 sq in, 260 sq cm.

ELECTRICAL EQUIPMENT 50 A alternator.

DIMENSIONS AND WEIGHT rear track: GSL and GS models 54.33 in, 138 cm; length: Standard Sedan and De Luxe models 177.17 in, 450 cm - GL, GSL and GS models 178.35 in, 453 cm; height: sedans 55.71 in, 141 cm - hardtops 54.72 in, 139 cm; weight: Standard Sedan 2,348 lb, 1,065 kg - De Luxe sedans 2,359 lb, 1,070 kg - De Luxe hardtops 2,370 lb, 1,075 kg - GL and XL sedans 2,381 lb, 1,080 kg - GL and XL hardtops 2,392 lb, 1,085 kg - GSL and GS sedans 2,492 lb, 1,130 kg - GSL and GS hardtops 2,503 lb, 1,135 kg.

BODY (for Standard only) 6 seats, bench front seats.

OPTIONAL ACCESSORIES steering column lever; Toyoglide automatic transmission, hydraulic torque converter and planetary gears with 3 ratios (I 2.450, II 1.450, III 1, rev 2.222).

TOYOTA Chaser 2000 SXL 4-door Sedan

TOYOTA Chaser 2000 SG Touring 2-door Hardtop

DIMENSIONS AND WEIGHT tracks: Grande and SG Touring 54.72 in, 139 cm front, Grande and SG Touring 54.72 in, 139 cm rear - SGS models 54.33 in, 138 cm; width: 66.14 in, 168 cm; weight: SXL Sedan 2,459 lb, 1,115 kg - SXL Hardtop 2,470 lb, 1,120 kg - SGS Sedan 2,536 lb, 1,150 kg - SGS Hardtop 2,547 lb, 1,155 kg - SG Touring Sedan 2,569 lb, 1,165 kg - LG Touring models and SG Touring Hardtop 2,580 lb, 1,170 kg - Grande Sedan 2,679 lb, 1,215 kg - Grande Hardtop 2,690 lb, 1,220 kg.

OPTIONAL ACCESSORIES automatic transmission with 3 ratios (I 2.400, II 1.479, III 1, rev 1.920), 3.909 axle ratio.

135 hp power team

See 100 hp power team, except for:

ENGINE 6 cylinders, in line; 156.4 cu in, 2,563 cc (3.15 x 3.35 in, 80 x 85 mm); max power (JIS): 135 hp at 5,400 rpm; max torque (JIS): 149 lb ft, 20.5 kg m at 3,600 rpm; 52.7 hp/l; cast iron block, light alloy head; 7 crankshaft bearings; valves; overhead, Vee-slanted, rockers; lubrication: 9.2 imp pt, 11 US pt, 5.2 l; 1 Aisan M-U downdraught twin barrel carburettor; cooling system: 19.4 imp pt, 23.3 US pt, 11 l.

TRANSMISSION automatic transmission, hydraulic torque converter and planetary gears; ratios: I 2.400, II 1.479, III 1, rev 1.920; axle ratio: 3.909; tyres: 185/70 HR x 14.

PERFORMANCE power-weight ratio: Grande Sedan 19.8 lb/hp, 9 kg/hp; consumption: 36.7 m/imp gal, 30.5 m/US gal, 7.7 l x 100 km.

CHASSIS rear suspension: independent, semi-trailing arms, coil springs, telescopic dampers, anti-roll bar.

STEERING servo.

BRAKES rear disc.

DIMENSIONS AND WEIGHT front and rear track: 54.72 in, 139 cm; length: 181.69 in, 461 cm; width: 66.14 in, 168 cm; weight: Grande Sedan 2,679 lb, 1,215 kg - Grande Hardtop 2,690 lb, 1,220 kg.

110 hp power team

See 100 hp power team, except for:

ENGINE 6 cylinders, in line; 121.3 cu in, 1,988 cc (2.95 x 2.95 in, 75 x 75 mm); max power (JIS): 110 hp at 5,600 rpm; max torque (JIS): 116 lb ft, 16 kg m at 3,800 rpm; 55.3 hp/l; cast iron block, light alloy head; 7 crankshaft bearings; valves: overhead, Vee-slanted, rockers; lubrication: 9.2 imp pt, 11 US pt, 5.2 l; 1 Aisan M-U downdraught twin barrel carburettor; cooling system: 19.4 imp pt, 23.3 US pt, 11 l.

PERFORMANCE max speeds: (I) 28 mph, 45 km/h; (II) 48 mph, 78 km/h; (III) 73 mph, 117 km/h; (IV) 103 mph, 165 km/h; power-weight ratio: L Sedan 22.1 lb/hp, 10 kg/hp; consumption: 40.9 m/imp gal, 34.1 m/US gal, 6.9 l x 100 km.

STEERING LG models, servo; turns lock to lock: 3.40.

ELECTRICAL EQUIPMENT 55 Ah battery.

DIMENSIONS AND WEIGHT width: LG models 66.14 in, 168 cm; height: Station Wagon 56.10 in, 142 cm; weight: L Sedan 2,437 lb, 1,105 kg - L Hardtop 2,448 lb, 1,100 kg - LG Sedan 2,470 lb, 1,120 kg - LG Hardtop 2,481 lb, 1,125 kg - SXL Sedan 2,437 lb, 1,105 kg - SXL Hardtop 2,448 lb, 1,110 kg.

OPTIONAL ACCESSORIES automatic transmission with 3 ratios (I 2.400, II 1.479, III 1, rev 1.920); 5-speed mechanical gearbox (I 3.287, II 2.043, III 1.394, IV 1, V 0.853, rev 4.039).

125 hp power team

See 100 hp power team, except for:

ENGINE 6 cylinders, in line; 121.3 cu in, 1,988 cc (2.95 x 2.95 in, 75 x 75 mm); max power (JIS): 125 hp at 6,000 rpm; max torque (JIS): 123 lb ft, 17 kg m at 4,400 rpm; 62.9 hp/l; cast iron block light alloy head; 7 crankshaft bearings; valves: overhead, Vee-slanted, rockers; lubrication: 9.2 imp pt, 11 US pt, 5.2 l; 1 Aisan M-U downdraught twin barrel carburettor; three element catalytic converter with oxygen sensor; cooling system: 19.4 imp pt, 23.3 US pt, 11 l.

TRANSMISSION gears: 5, fully synchronized; ratios: I 3.287, II 2.043, III 1.394, IV 1, V 0.853, rev 4.039; tyres: 175 SR x 14 - SXL models 6.45 x 14 - Grande and SG Touring models 185/70 HR x 14.

PERFORMANCE max speeds: (I) 32 mph, 52 km/h; (II) 52 mph, 83 km/h; (III) 76 mph, 123 km/h; (IV) 109 mph, 175 km/h; (V) 109 mph, 175 km/h; power-weight ratio: SXL Sedan 19.6 lb/hp, 8.9 kg/hp; consumption: 25.4 m/imp gal, 21.2 m/US gal, 11.1 l x 100 km.

CHASSIS rear suspension: (except for SXL models) independent, semi-trailing arms, coil springs, telescopic dampers, anti-roll bar.

STEERING (except for SXL and SGS models) servo; turns lock to lock: 3.40.

BRAKES rear disc.

Crown Series

PRICES (Tokyo):

1 2000 De Luxe-A Sedan	1,360,000	yen
2 2000 De Luxe Sedan	1,498,000	yen
3 2000 De Luxe 2-door Hardtop	1,444,000	yen
4 2000 De Luxe 4-door Hardtop	1,479,000	yen
5 2000 Super De Luxe Sedan	1,680,000	yen
6 2000 Super De Luxe 2-door Hardtop	1,773,000	yen
7 2000 Super De Luxe 4-door Hardtop	1,790,000	yen
8 2000 Super Saloon Sedan	1,803,000	yen
9 2000 Super Saloon 4-door Hardtop	1,948,000	yen
10 2000 EFI De Luxe-A Sedan	1,453,000	yen
11 2000 EFI De Luxe Sedan	1,644,000	yen
12 2000 EFI De Luxe 2-door Hardtop	1,590,000	yen
13 2000 EFI De Luxe 4-door Hardtop	1,577,000	yen
14 2000 EFI Super De Luxe Sedan	1,773,000	yen
15 2000 EFI Super De Luxe 2-door Hardtop	1,896,000	yen
16 2000 EFI Super De Luxe 4-door Hardtop	1,936,000	yen
17 2000 EFI Super Saloon Sedan	1,896,000	yen
18 2000 EFI Super Saloon 2-door Hardtop	2,074,000	yen
19 2000 EFI Super Saloon 4-door Hardtop	2,006,000	yen
20 2200 Diesel Standard Sedan	1,342,000	yen
21 2200 Diesel De Luxe-A Sedan	1,447,000	yen
22 2200 Diesel De Luxe Sedan	1,585,000	yen
23 2600 Super Saloon Sedan	2,052,000	yen
24 2600 Super Saloon 2-door Hardtop	2,166,000	yen
25 2600 Super Saloon 4-door Hardtop	2,147,000	yen
26 2600 Royal Saloon Sedan	2,497,000	yen
27 2600 Royal Saloon 4-door Hardtop	2,526,000	yen

For GB price, see price index.

Power team:	Standard for:	Optional for:
110 hp	1 to 9	—
125 hp	10 to 19	—
72 hp	20 to 22	—
135 hp	23 to 27	—

110 hp power team

ENGINE front, 4 stroke; 6 cylinders, vertical, in line; 121.3 cu in, 1,988 cc (2.95 x 2.95 in, 75 x 75 mm); compression ratio: 8.6:1; max power (JIS): 110 hp at 5,600 rpm; max torque (JIS): 116 lb ft, 16 kg m at 3,800 rpm; max engine rpm: 6,200; 55.3 hp/l; cast iron block, light alloy head; 7 crankshaft bearings; valves: overhead, Vee-slanted, rockers; camshafts: 1, overhead; lubrication: rotary pump, full flow filter, 9.9 imp pt, 11.8 US pt, 5.6 l; 1 Aisan M-U type downdraught twin barrel carburettor; emission control with catalytic converter, secondary air injection and exhaust gas recirculation; fuel feed: mechanical pump; water-cooled, 19.4 imp pt, 23.3 US pt, 11 l

TOYOTA Crown 2000 EFI Super Saloon 2-door Hardtop

110 HP POWER TEAM

TRANSMISSION driving wheels: rear; clutch: single dry plate (diaphragm), hydraulically controlled; gearbox: mechanical; gears: 4, fully synchronized (5 for Super De Luxe 2-dr. Hardtop only); ratios: I 3.579, II 2.081, III 1.397, IV 1, rev 4.399 - Super De Luxe 2-dr. Hardtop I 3.287, II 2.043, III 1.394, IV 1, V 0.853, rev 4.039; lever: central; final drive: hypoid bevel; axle ratio: 4.556; width of rims: 5''; tyres: 6.95 x 14.

PERFORMANCE max speeds: (I) 27 mph, 44 km/h; (II) 47 mph, 76 km/h; (III) 70 mph, 112 km/h; (IV) 99 mph, 160 km/h; power-weight ratio: De Luxe-A Sedan 27.7 lb/hp, 12.5 kg/hp; carrying capacity: 882 lb, 400 kg; speed in direct drive at 1,000 rpm: 15.5 mph, 25 km/h; consumption: 36.7 m/imp gal, 30.5 m/US gal, 7.7 l x 100 km.

CHASSIS box-type perimeter frame; front suspension: independent, double wishbones, coil springs, anti-roll bar, telescopic dampers; rear: rigid axle, lower radius arms, upper torque arm, coil springs, telescopic dampers.

STEERING recirculating ball; turns lock to lock: 4.60.

BRAKES front disc, rear drum, servo; lining area: front 22.8 sq in, 147.6 sq cm, rear 75.7 sq in, 488 sq cm, total 98.5 sq in, 635.6 sq cm.

ELECTRICAL EQUIPMENT 12 V; 45 Ah battery; 50 A alternator; Denso distributor; 4 headlamps.

DIMENSIONS AND WEIGHT wheel base: 105.91 in, 269 cm; tracks: 55.51 in, 141 cm front, 54.33 in, 138 cm rear; length: 183.07 in, 465 cm - sedans 184.65 in, 469 cm; width: 66.49 in, 169 cm; height: sedans 56.69 in, 144 cm - De Luxe 2-dr. Hardtop 55.51 in, 141 cm - 4-dr. hardtops 55.91 in, 142 cm; ground clearance: 6.89 in, 17.5 cm; weight: sedans 3,043 lb, 1,380 kg - 2-dr. hardtops 3,032 lb, 1,375 kg - De Luxe and Super De Luxe 4-dr. hardtops 3,164 lb, 1,435 kg - Super Saloon 4-dr. Hardtop 3,164 lb, 1,435 kg; turning circle (between walls): 40 ft, 12.2 m; fuel tank: 13.2 imp gal, 15.8 US gal, 60 l.

BODY 5 seats, separate front seats, reclining backrests, built-in headrests.

OPTIONAL ACCESSORIES 5-speed fully synchronized mechanical gearbox (I 3.287, II 2.043, III 1.394, IV 1, V 0.853, rev 4.039), 4.778 axle ratio (except for Super De Luxe 2-dr. Hardtop); automatic transmission with 3 ratios (I 2.400, II 1.479, III 1, rev 1.920), 4.556 axle ratio; power steering with 3.90 turns lock to lock; air-conditioning.

125 hp power team

See 110 hp power team, except for:

ENGINE max power (JIS): 125 hp at 6,000 rpm; max torque (JIS): 123 lb ft, 17 kg m at 4,400 rpm; 62.9 hp/l; Toyota EFI electronically-controlled injection system; emission control with three element catalytic converter with oxygen sensor and exhaust gas recirculation; fuel feed: electric pump.

TRANSMISSION gears: (for De Luxe Sedan and 2-dr. Hardtop, Super De Luxe hardtops and Super Saloon 2-dr. Hardtop only) 5, fully synchronized; ratios: I 3.287, II 2.043, III 1.394, IV 1, V 0.853, rev 4.039; axle ratio: 4.778; tyres: sedans 6.95 x 14 - hardtops D78 x 14.

PERFORMANCE max speed: 106 mph, 170 km/h; power-weight ratio: De Luxe-A Sedan 25.2 lb/hp, 11.4 kg/hp; consumption: 38.2 m/imp gal, 31.8 m/US gal, 7.4 l x 100 km.

STEERING servo; turns lock to lock: 3.90.

DIMENSIONS AND WEIGHT weight: sedans and 2-dr. hardtops 3,153 lb, 1,430 kg - 4-dr. hardtops 3,19E lb, 1,450 kg.

OPTIONAL ACCESSORIES automatic transmission with 3 ratios (I 2.400, II 1.479, III 1, rev 1.920), 4.556 axle ratio.

72 hp power team

See 110 hp power team, except for:

ENGINE front, Diesel, 4 stroke; 4 cylinders, vertical, in line; 133.5 cu in, 2,188 cc (3.54 x 3.39 in, 90 x 86 mm); compression ratio: 21.5:1; max power (JIS): 72 hp at 4,200 rpm; max torque (JIS): 105 lb ft, 14.5 kg m at 2,000 rpm; max engine rpm: 4,500; 32.9 hp/l; Ricardo Comet pre-combustion chamber type Diesel; camshafts: 1, overhead, cogged belt; lubrication: 11.4 imp pt, 13.7 US pt, 6.5 l; cooling system: 14.1 imp pt, 16.9 US pt, 8 l.

TOYOTA Crown 2200 Diesel De Luxe Sedan

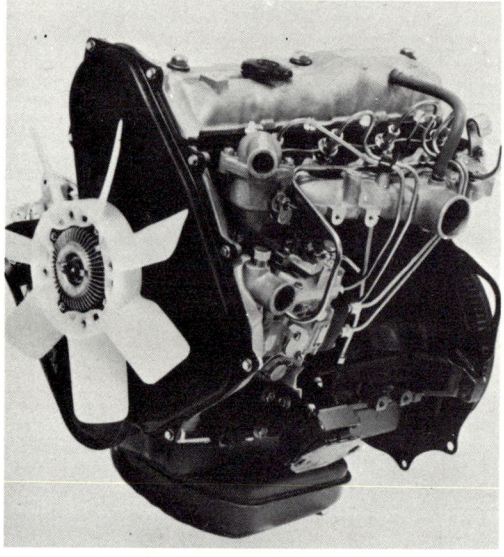

TOYOTA Crown 2200 Diesel De Luxe Sedan

TRANSMISSION lever: steering column; axle ratio: 3.909; width of rims: 4.5''; tyres: Standard 6.40 x 14 - De Luxe-A and De Luxe 6.95 x 14.

PERFORMANCE max speeds: (I) 23 mph, 37 km/h; (II) 42 mph, 67 km/h; (III) 60 mph, 96 km/h; (IV) 81 mph, 130 km/h; power-weight ratio: Standard 41 lb/hp, 18.6 kg/hp; consumption: 55.4 m/imp gal, 46.1 m/US gal, 5.1 l x 100 km at 37 mph, 60 km/h.

BRAKES (for Standard only) drum.

DIMENSIONS AND WEIGHT length: Standard 184.25 in, 468 cm - De Luxe-A and De Luxe 184.65 in, 469 cm; weight: Standard 2,955 lb, 1,340 kg - De Luxe-A 3,010 lb, 1,365 kg - De Luxe 3,043 lb, 1,380 kg.

135 hp power team

See 110 hp power team, except for:

ENGINE 156.4 cu in, 2,563 cc (3.15 x 3.35 in, 80 x 85 mm); compression ratio: 8.5:1; max power (JIS): 135 hp at 5,400 rpm; max torque (JIS): 149 lb ft, 20.5 kg m at 3,600 rpm; 52.7 hp/l; 1 Aisan 4M-U downdraught twin barrel carburettor.

TRANSMISSION gearbox: mechanical; gears: 4, fully synchronized (5 for Super Saloon 2-dr. Hardtop and Royal

TOYOTA Crown 2600 Royal Saloon

Saloon 4-dr. Hardtop); ratios: I 3.368, II 1.644, III 1, IV 0.813, rev 4.079 - Super Saloon 2-dr. Hardtop and Royal Saloon 4-dr. Hardtop I 3.287, II 2.043, III 1.394, IV 1, V 0.853, rev 4.039; (for Royal Saloon and Super Saloon sedans only automatic transmission, hydraulic torque converter and planetary gears; ratios: I 2.450, II 1.450, III 1, rev 2.222); axle ratio: 4.100; width of rims: 5.5''; tyres: D78 x 14.

PERFORMANCE max speed: 109 mph, 175 km/h - Sedan 99 mph, 160 km/h; power-weight ratio: Sedan 23.3 hp/l, 10.6 kg/hp.

STEERING servo; turns lock to lock: 3.90.

BRAKES (for Sedan only) disc, front internal radial fins, servo; lining area: front 28.2 sq in, 182 sq cm, rear 18.1 sq in, 117.2 sq cm, total 46.3 sq in, 299.2 sq cm.

DIMENSIONS AND WEIGHT tracks: 56.30 in, 143 cm front, 55.12 in, 140 cm rear; length: Sedan 187.40 in, 476 cm - Hardtop 188.61 in, 474 cm; ground clearance: 7.09 in, 18 cm; weight: Sedan 3,153 lb, 1,430 kg - Hardtop 3,197 lb, 1,450 kg.

OPTIONAL ACCESSORIES 5-speed mechanical gearbox (I 3.287, II 2.043, III 1.394, IV 1, V 0.853, rev 4.039) (except for Super Saloon 2-dr. Hardtop and Royal Saloon 4-dr. Hardtop); 3-speed automatic transmission, hydraulic torque converter and planetary gears with 3 ratios (I 2.450, II 1.450, III 1, rev 2.222) (except for Royal Saloon and Super Saloon sedans); electronic skid control brakes.

Century Series

170 hp power team

ENGINE front, 4 stroke; 8 cylinders, Vee-slanted at 90°; 206 cu in, 3,376 cc (3.27 x 3.07 in, 83 x 78 mm); compression ratio: 8.5:1; max power (JIS): 170 hp at 5,400 rpm; max torque (JIS): 192 lb ft, 26.5 kg m at 3,600 rpm; max engine rpm: 6,000; 50.3 hp/l; light alloy block and head; 5 crankshaft bearings; valves: overhead, push-rods and rockers; camshafts: 1, at centre of Vee; lubrication: gear pump, full flow filter, 8.8 imp pt, 10.6 US pt, 5 l; 1 Aisan 4-V-U downdraught 4-barrel carburettor; emission control with 2 catalytic converters, secondary air injection and exhaust gas recirculation; fuel feed: electric pump; water-cooled, 23.6 imp pt, 28.3 US pt, 13.4 l.

TRANSMISSION driving wheels: rear; gearbox: Toyoglide automatic transmission, hydraulic torque converter and planetary gears with 3 ratios, max ratio of converter at stall 2; ratios: I 2.400, II 1.479, III 1, rev 1.920; lever: steering column; final drive: hypoid bevel; axle ratio: 3.727; tyres: 7.35 x 14.

TOYOTA Crown 2600 Royal Saloon

TOYOTA Crown 2600 Super Saloon 4-door Hardtop

PERFORMANCE max speed: 99 mph, 160 km/h; power-weight ratio: Century D 24.3 lb/hp, 11 kg/hp - Century C 23.7 lb/hp, 10.7 kg/hp; carrying capacity: 1,058 lb, 480 kg.

CHASSIS integral; front suspension: independent, by McPherson, air bellows/telescopic damper struts, lower wishbones (trailing links), anti-roll bar; rear: rigid axle, lower radius arms, upper torque arm, transverse linkage bar, coil springs, telescopic dampers.

STEERING recirculating ball, servo.

BRAKES front disc, rear drum, servo; swept area: front 92.7 sq in, 598 sq cm, rear 75 sq in, 484 sq cm, total 167.7 sq in, 1,082 sq cm.

ELECTRICAL EQUIPMENT 12 V; 45 Ah battery; 780 W alternator; Nihon Denso distributor; 2 iodine headlamps.

DIMENSIONS AND WEIGHT wheel base: 112.60 in, 286 cm; tracks: 60.24 in, 153 cm front, 60.63 in, 154 cm rear; length: 196.06 in, 498 cm; width: 74.41 in, 189 cm; height: 57.48 in, 146 cm; ground clearance: 6.89 in, 17 cm; weight: Century D 4,134 lb, 1,875 kg - Century C 4,024 lb, 1,825 kg; weight distribution: 53.9% front, 46.1% rear; turning circle (between walls): 37.4 ft, 11.4 m; fuel tank: 19.8 imp gal, 23.6 US gal, 90 l.

BODY saloon/sedan; 4 doors; 6 seats, bench front seats.

OPTIONAL ACCESSORIES limited slip differential; separate front seats; semi-separate front seats.

TOYOTA Century D Sedan

TOYOTA Landcruiser F156V-K

Landcruiser FJ56V-K

PRICE IN USA: $ 7,348*

ENGINE front, 4 stroke; 6 cylinders, vertical, in line; 258.1 cu in, 4,230 cc (3.70 x 4 in, 94 x 101.6 mm); compression ratio: 7.8:1; max power (SAE): 140 hp at 3,600 rpm; max torque (SAE): 217 lb ft, 30 kg m at 1,800 rpm; max engine rpm: 4,000; 33.1 hp/l; cast iron block and head; 7 crankshaft bearings; valves: overhead, in line, push-rods and rockers; camshafts: 1, side; lubrication: rotary pump, filter on by-pass, oil cooler, 15 imp pt, 18 US pt, 8.5 l; 1 Aisan downdraught twin barrel carburettor; fuel feed: mechanical pump; water-cooled, 26.8 imp pt, 32.1 US pt, 15.2 l.

TRANSMISSION driving wheels: front (automatically engaged with transfer box low ratio) and rear; clutch: single dry plate (diaphragm); gearbox: mechanical; gears: 4, with high and low ratios, fully synchronized; ratios: I 4.925, II 2.643, III 1.519, IV 1, rev 4.925; low ratios: high 1, low 1.992; lever: central; final drive: hypoid bevel; axle ratio: 3.700; tyres: 7.00 x 15.

PERFORMANCE max speed: 87 mph, 140 km/h; power-weight ratio: 30.4 lb/hp, 13.8 kg/hp; carrying capacity: 1,103 lb, 500 kg; speed in direct drive at 1,000 rpm: 21.7 mph, 35 km/h; consumption: not declared.

CHASSIS ladder frame; front and rear suspension: rigid axle, semi-elliptic leafsprings, telescopic dampers.

STEERING recirculating ball and nut.

BRAKES drum.

ELECTRICAL EQUIPMENT 12 V; 50 Ah battery; 40 A alternator; Nihon Denso distributor; 2 headlamps.

DIMENSIONS AND WEIGHT wheel base: 106.30 in, 270 cm; tracks: 55.71 in, 141 cm front, 55.12 in, 140 cm rear; length: 184.05 in, 467 cm; width: 68.31 in, 173 cm; height: 73.43 in, 186 cm; ground clearance: 8.27 in, 21 cm; weight: 4,256 lb, 1,930 kg; turning circle (between walls): 40.7 ft, 12.4 m; fuel tank: 18 imp gal, 21.6 US gal, 82 l.

BODY estate car/station wagon; 4+1 doors; 2 or 5 seats.

Landcruiser BJ40-KC

See Landcruiser FJ56V-K, except for:

PRICE IN USA: $ 6,328*

ENGINE Diesel, 4 stroke; 4 cylinders, vertical, in line; 181.7 cu in, 2,977 cc (3.74 x 4.13 in, 95 x 105 mm); compression ratio: 20:1; max power (SAE): 85 hp at 3,600 rpm; max torque (SAE): 145 lb ft, 20 kg m at 2,200 rpm; 28.6 hp/l; 5 crankshaft bearings; fuel injection pump.

TRANSMISSION axle ratio: 4.111.

PERFORMANCE max speed: 75 mph, 120 km/h; power-weight ratio: 42.1 lb/hp, 19.1 kg/hp; speed in direct drive at 1,000 rpm: 18.6 mph, 30 km/h.

DIMENSIONS AND WEIGHT wheel base: 89.96 in, 228 cm; length: 152.36 in, 387 cm; width: 65.55 in, 166 cm; height: 77.17 in, 196 cm; weight: 3,583 lb, 1,625 kg.

BODY open, fully opening canvas sunshine roof; 2 or 6 seats.

TOYOTA Landcruiser FJ56V-K

GENERAL MOTORS   MALAYSIA

Harimau/Amigo

PRICE EX WORKS: SM 3,900

ENGINE Vauxhall Viva, front, 4 stroke; 4 cylinders, vertical, in line; 76.6 cu in, 1,256 cc (3.19 x 2.40 in, 81 x 61 mm); compression ratio: 7.3:1; max power (SAE): 59 hp at 5,400 rpm; max torque (SAE): 64 lb ft, 8.8 kg m at 3,200 rpm; max engine rpm: 5,800; 47 hp/l; cast iron block and head; 3 crankshaft bearings; valves: overhead, in line, push-rods and rockers; camshafts: 1, side; lubrication: gear pump, full flow filter, 5.5 imp pt, 6.6 US pt, 3.1 l; 1 Zenith 150 CDS downdraught carburettor; fuel feed: mechanical pump; water-cooled, 10.2 imp pt, 12.3 US pt, 5.8 l.

TRANSMISSION driving wheels: rear; clutch: single dry plate (diaphragm); gearbox: mechanical; gears: 4, fully synchronized; ratios: I 3.460, II 2.213, III 1.404, IV 1, rev 3.707; lever: central; final drive: hypoid bevel; axle ratio: 4.125; width of rims: 4.5''; tyres: 6.15 x 13.

PERFORMANCE max speed: 75 mph, 120 km/h; power-weight ratio: 23.1 lb/hp, 10.5 kg/hp; carrying capacity: 1,521 lb, 690 kg; speed in direct drive at 1,000 rpm: 12.9 mph, 20.7 km/h; consumption: 33 m/imp gal, 27.7 m/US gal, 8.5 l x 100 km.

CHASSIS perimeter box-type with cross members; front suspension: independent, wishbones, transverse anti-roll bar leafsprings, telescopic dampers; rear: rigid axle, semi-elliptic leafspring, telescopic dampers.

STEERING rack-and-pinion.

BRAKES drum, dual circuit.

ELECTRICAL EQUIPMENT 12 V; 32 Ah battery; 336 W alternator; AC Delco distributor; 2 headlamps.

DIMENSIONS AND WEIGHT wheel base: 91.50 in, 232 cm; front and rear track: 51.18 in, 130 cm; length: 141.42 in, 359 cm; width: 63.39 in, 161 cm; height: 67.72 in, 172 cm; ground clearance: 6.69 in, 17 cm; weight: 1,367 lb, 620 kg; turning circle (between walls): 29.8 ft, 9.1 m; fuel tank: 9.9 imp gal, 11.9 US gal, 45 l.

BODY open; 2 doors; 2-10 seats.

PRACTICAL INSTRUCTIONS fuel: 90 oct petrol; oil: engine 4.9 imp pt, 5.9 US pt, 2.8 l, SAE 10W-30, change every 6,000 miles, 9,700 km - gearbox 0.9 imp pt, 1.1 US pt, 0.5 l, SAE 90, change every 6 months - final drive 1.2 imp pt, 1.5 US pt, 0.7 l, no change recommended; tappet clearances: inlet 0.008 in, 0.20 mm, exhaust 0.008 in, 0.20 mm; valve timing: 39° 73° 71° 41.

Opel Kadett City

PRICE EX WORKS: SM 10,836

ENGINE front, 4 stroke; 4 cylinders, in line; 60.6 cu in, 993 cc (2.83 x 2.40 in, 72 x 61 mm); compression ratio: 9.2:1; max power (DIN): 45 hp at 5,600 rpm; 45.3 hp/l.

GENERAL MOTORS Amigo

GENERAL MOTORS Opel Kadett City

Opel Gemini 1.6 Coupé

See Opel Gemini 1.6 Sedan, except for:

PRICE EX WORKS: SM 12,268

DIMENSIONS AND WEIGHT height: 53 in, 133 cm; weight: 1,918 lb, 870 kg.

BODY coupé; 2 doors.

Opel Rekord Berlina

PRICE EX WORKS: SM 18,408

ENGINE front, 4 stroke; 4 cylinders; 115.7 cu in, 1,897 cc (3.66 x 2.75 in, 93 x 69.8 mm); compression ratio: 9.8:1; max power (DIN): 107 hp at 5,200 rpm; 56.4 hp/l; cast iron block; water-cooled.

TRANSMISSION driving wheels: rear; gearbox: mechanical; gears: 4, fully synchronized; width of rims: 5.5''; tyres: 175 SR x 14.

PERFORMANCE max speed: 100 mph, 161 km/h; power-weight ratio: 22.5 lb/hp, 10.2 kg/hp; carrying capacity: 1,003 lb, 455 kg.

CHASSIS front suspension: independent, coil springs; rear: rigid axle, damper struts.

PERFORMANCE max speed: 76 mph, 122 km/h; power-weight ratio: 38.9 lb/hp, 17.6 kg/hp; carrying capacity: 904 lb, 410 kg.

BRAKES front disc, rear drum; dual circuit.

DIMENSIONS AND WEIGHT wheel base: 94.09 in, 239 cm; length: 153.15 in, 389 cm; weight: 1,753 lb, 795 kg.

BODY saloon/sedan; 3 doors; 4 seats, separate front seats.

Opel Kadett 1.2 Standard

PRICE EX WORKS: SM 10,935

ENGINE front, 4 stroke; 4 cylinders, in line; 72.98 cu in, 1,196 cc; compression ratio: 7.8:1; max power (DIN): 61 hp at 5,800 rpm; max torque (DIN): 65 lb ft, 8.9 kg m at 3,800 rpm; 51 hp/l; valves: overhead, in line; lubrication: full flow filter; 1 downdraught carburettor.

TRANSMISSION driving wheels: rear; clutch: single dry plate (diaphragm); gearbox: mechanical; gears: 4, fully synchronized; lever: central; width of rims: 5''; tyres: 6.15 x 13.

PERFORMANCE power-weight ratio: 28.5 lb/hp, 12.9 kg/hp.

CHASSIS independent; front suspension: wishbones, coil springs, torsion bar, telescopic dampers; rear: rigid axle, trailing arms, coil springs, telescopic dampers.

STEERING rack-and-pinion.

BRAKES front disc, rear drum, dual circuit, servo.

ELECTRICAL EQUIPMENT 12 V; 45 A alternator.

DIMENSIONS AND WEIGHT wheel base: 94.30 in, 239 cm; tracks: 51.20 in, 130 cm front, 51.10 in, 130 cm rear; length: 162.30 in, 412 cm; width: 62.20 in, 158 cm; height: 53.90 in, 137 cm; weight: 1,742 lb, 790 kg.

BODY saloon/sedan; 4 doors; 5 seats, separate front seats.

Opel Kadett 1.2 De Luxe

See Opel Kadett 1.2 Standard, except for:

PRICE EX WORKS: SM 11,810

ENGINE compression ratio: 9.2:1; max power (DIN): 65 hp at 5,600 rpm; max torque (DIN): 70 lb ft, 9,7 kg m at 3,800 rpm; 54.3 hp/l.

PERFORMANCE power-weight ratio: 26.8 lb/hp, 12.1 kg/hp.

Opel Gemini 1.6 Sedan

PRICE EX WORKS: SM 12,430

ENGINE front, 4 stroke; 4 cylinders; 97 cu in, 1,584 cc (3.20 x 3 in, 82 x 75 mm); compression ratio: 8.7:1; max torque (DIN): 101 lb ft, 14 kg m at 4,000 rpm; camshafts: 1, overhead, in line; lubrication: full flow filter, 8.8 imp pt, 10.6 US pt, 5 l; 1 Nikki-Stromberg downdraught twin barrel car-

GENERAL MOTORS Opel Rekord Berlina

burettor; fuel feed: mechanical pump; water-cooled, 11.4 imp pt, 13.7 US pt, 6.5 l.

TRANSMISSION driving wheels: rear; clutch: single dry plate (diaphragm); gearbox: mechanical; gears: 4, fully synchronized; ratios: I 3.057, II 2.175, III 1.418, IV 1, rev 3.826; axle ratio: 3.889; width of rims: 5''; tyres: 155 SR x 13.

PERFORMANCE max speed: 106 mph, 170 km/h.

CHASSIS front suspension: independent, wishbones, coil spring, anti-roll bar, telescopic dampers; rear: torque tube, coil springs, telescopic dampers.

STEERING rack-and-pinion.

BRAKES front disc, rear drum, dual circuit, servo.

ELECTRICAL EQUIPMENT 12 V; 35 Ah battery.

DIMENSIONS AND WEIGHT wheel base: 95 in, 240 cm; tracks: 51.20 in, 130 cm front, 51.40 in, 130 cm rear: 163 in, 413 cm; width: 62 in, 157 cm; height: 54 in, 136 cm; ground clearance: 5.7 in, 14 cm; weight: 1,962 lb, 890 kg; turning circle (between walls): 30.2 ft, 9.2 m; fuel tank: 11.4 imp gal, 14 US gal, 52 l.

BODY saloon/sedan; 4 doors; 5 seats, separate front seats.

PRACTICAL INSTRUCTIONS fuel: 90 oct petrol; oil: engine 8.8 imp pt, 10.6 US pt, 5 l, change every 3,100 miles, 5,000 km - gearbox 2.1 imp pt, 2.5 US pt, 1.2 l, change every 24,900 miles, 40,000 km; tappet clearances: inlet 0.006 in, 0.15 mm, exhaust 0.010 in, 0.25 mm.

STEERING recirculating ball.

BRAKES front disc, rear drum; dual circuit, servo.

DIMENSIONS AND WEIGHT wheel base: 105.12 in, 267 cm; length: 181.50 in, 461 cm; weight: 2,403 lb, 1,090 kg.

BODY saloon/sedan; 4 doors; 5 seats, separate front seats; vinyl roof.

OPTIONAL ACCESSORIES automatic gearbox.

Opel Rekord 2100 D

PRICE EX WORKS: SM 21,229

ENGINE Diesel; 4 cylinders; 126.19 cu in, 2,068 cc (3.46 x 3.34 in, 88 x 85 mm); compression ratio: 22:1; max power (DIN): 60 hp; 29 hp/l.

TRANSMISSION width of rims: 5.5''; tyres: 175 SR x 14.

PERFORMANCE max speed: 84 mph, 135 km/h; power-weight ratio: 61.9 lb/hp, 28.1 kg/hp; consumption: 39.2 m/imp gal, 32.5 m/US gal, 7.2 l x 100 km.

DIMENSIONS AND WEIGHT wheel base: 115.10 in, 267 cm; length: 179.90 in, 457 cm; width: 67.70 in, 172 cm; height: 55.50 in, 141 cm; weight: 3,715 lb, 1,685 kg.

BODY saloon/sedan; 4 doors; 5 seats, separate front seats.

TORO   PHILIPPINES

1300

ENGINE Volkswagen, rear, 4 stroke; 4 cylinders, horizontally opposed; 74.8 cu in, 1,285 cc (3.03 x 2.72 in, 77 x 69 mm); compression ratio: 7.5:1; max power (DIN): 44 hp at 4,100 rpm; max torque (DIN): 64 lb ft, 8.8 kg m at 3,000 rpm; max engine rpm: 4,600; 34.2 hp/l; block with cast iron liners and light alloy fins, light alloy head; 4 crankshaft bearings; valves: overhead, push-rods and rockers; camshafts: 1, central, lower; lubrication: gear pump, filter in sump, oil cooler, 4.4 imp pt, 5.3 US pt, 2.5 l; 1 Solex 31 PICT downdraught single barrel carburettor; fuel feed: mechanical pump; air-cooled.

TRANSMISSION driving wheels: rear; clutch: single dry plate; gearbox: mechanical; gears: 4, fully synchronized; ratios: I 3.780, II 2.060, III 1.260, IV 0.890, rev 4.010; lever: central; final drive: spiral bevel; axle ratio: 4.375; width of rims: 4''; tyres: 5.60 x 15.

PERFORMANCE max speeds: (I) 25 mph, 41 km/h; (II) 47 mph, 75 km/h; (III) 76 mph, 123 km/h; (IV) 96 mph, 155 km/h; power-weight ratio: 44.6 lb/hp, 20.2 kg/hp; carrying capacity: 882 lb, 400 kg; speed in top at 1,000 rpm: 18.6 mph, 29.9 km/h; consumption: 32.1 m/imp gal, 26.7 m/US gal, 8.8 l x 100 km.

CHASSIS backbone platform; front suspension: independent, twin swinging longitudinal trailing arms, transverse laminated torsion bars, anti-roll bar, telescopic dampers; rear: independent, swinging semi-axles, swinging longitudinal trailing arms, transverse torsion bars, telescopic dampers.

STEERING worm and roller, telescopic damper.

BRAKES drum; lining area: total 125.3 sq in, 808 sq cm.

ELECTRICAL EQUIPMENT 12 V; 36 Ah battery; 260 W dynamo; Bosch distributor; 2 headlamps.

DIMENSIONS AND WEIGHT wheel base: 94.49 in, 240 cm; tracks: 51.97 in, 132 cm front, 53.15 in, 135 cm rear; length: 169.29 in, 430 cm; width: 64.37 in, 163 cm; height: 52.95 in, 134 cm; weight: 1,962 lb, 890 kg; turning circle (between walls): 37.1 ft, 11.3 m; fuel tank: 9 imp gal, 10.8 US gal, 41 l.

BODY coupé, in plastic material; 2 doors; 2+2 seats, separate front seats.

PRACTICAL INSTRUCTIONS fuel: 91 oct petrol; oil: engine 4.4 imp pt, 5.3 US pt, 2.5 l, SAE 10W-20 (winter) 20W-30 (summer), change every 3,100 miles, 5,000 km - gearbox and final drive 5.3 imp pt, 6.3 US pt, 3 l, SAE 90, change every 31,000 miles, 50,000 km; greasing: every 6,200 miles, 10,000 km, 4 points; sparking plug: 175°; tappet clearances: inlet 0.004 in, 0.10 mm, exhaust 0.004 in, 0.10 mm; valve timing: 7°30' 37° 44°30' 4°.

CHRYSLER   AUSTRALIA

Centura Series

PRICES EX WORKS: (Australian $):

1 Centura GL 4-door Sedan	$ 6,058
2 Centura GLX 4-door Sedan	$ 6,467

Power team:	Standard for:	Optional for:
123 hp	both	—

123 hp power team

ENGINE 6 cylinders; 245 cu in, 4,015 cc (3.76 x 3.68 in, 95.5 x 93.5 mm); compression ratio: 7.6:1; max power (SAE): 123 hp at 4,400 rpm; max torque (SAE): 178 lb ft, 24.5 kg m at 1,800 rpm; max engine rpm: 4,800; 30.6 hp/l; cast iron block and head, hemispherical combustion chambers; 7 crankshaft bearings; valves: overhead, in line, push-rods and rockers, hydraulic tappets; camshafts: 1, side; lubrication: gear pump, full flow filter, 8.3 imp pt, 9.9 US pt, 4.7 l; 1 Carter RBS downdraught single barrel carburettor; cleaner air system; fuel feed: mechanical pump; cooling system: 32.2 imp pt, 27.9 US pt, 13.2 l.

TRANSMISSION driving wheels: rear; clutch: single dry plate (diaphragm); gearbox: mechanical; gears: 4, fully synchronized; ratios: I 3.320, II 2, III 1.430, IV 1, rev 3; lever: central; final drive: hypoid bevel; axle ratio: 2.920; width of rims: 5.5''; tyres: 175 SR x 14

PERFORMANCE max speed: 107 mph, 173 km/h; power-weight ratio: 21.9 lb/hp, 9.9 kg/hp; carrying capacity: 937 lb, 425 kg; speed in direct drive at 1,000 rpm: 23 mph, 37 km/h; consumption: 20.5 m/imp gal, 17 m/US gal, 13.8 l x 100 km.

TORO 1300

CHASSIS integral; front suspension: independent, by McPerson, coil springs/telescopic damper struts, lower wishbones, anti-roll bar; rear: rigid axle, lower longitudinal trailing arms, upper torque arms, transverse linkage bar, coil springs, telescopic dampers.

STEERING rack-and-pinion; turns lock to lock: 4.50.

BRAKES front disc (diameter 10.80 in, 27.4 cm), rear drum, rear compensator, internal radial fins, servo; swept area: total 295.2 sq in, 1,904 sq cm.

ELECTRICAL EQUIPMENT 12 V; 45 Ah battery; 490 W alternator; Ducellier distributor; electronic injection; 4 headlamps.

DIMENSIONS AND WEIGHT wheel base: 105.12 in, 267 cm; tracks: 55.39 in, 141 cm front, 55 in, 140 cm rear; length: 180.51 in, 458 cm; width: 67.99 in, 173 cm; height: 56.30 in, 143 cm; ground clearance: 4.72 in, 12 cm; weight: 2,700 lb, 1,225 kg; weight distribution: 53.8% front, 46.2% rear; turning circle (between walls): 36.1 ft, 11 m; fuel tank: 13.5 imp gal, 16.1 US gal, 61 l.

BODY saloon/sedan; 4 doors; 5 seats, separate front seats, reclining backrests, built-in headrests.

OPTIONAL ACCESSORIES Torqueflite automatic transmission with 3 ratios (I 2.390, II 1.450, III 1, rev 2.090); tinted glass; heated rear window; air-conditioning.

Valiant Series

PRICES EX WORKS (Australian $):

1 Valiant Sedan		$ 6,210
2 Valiant Station Wagon		$ 6,620
3 Valiant Regal Sedan		$ 7,903
4 Valiant Regal Station Wagon		$ 8,713
5 Valiant Regal SE		$ 11,221
6 Valiant Charger 770 Hardtop		$ 6,839

Power team:	Standard for:	Optional for:
138 hp	1,2,3,6	—
146 hp	—	1,2,3,6
143 hp	4,5	all

138 hp power team

ENGINE front, 4 stroke; 6 cylinders, vertical, in line; 245 cu in, 4,015 cc (3.76 x 3.68 in, 95.4 x 93.4 mm); compression ratio: 9:1; max power (SAE): 138 hp at 4,400 rpm; max torque (SAE): 201 lb ft, 27.7 kg m at 1,800 rpm; max engine rpm: 4,800; 34.4 hp/l; cast iron block and head, hemispherical combustion chambers; 7 crankshaft bearings; valves: overhead, in line, push-rods and rockers, hydraulic tappets; camshafts: 1, side; lubrication: gear pump, full flow filter, 8.3 imp pt, 9.9 US pt, 4.7 l; 1 downdraught single barrel carburettor; cleaner air system; fuel feed:

CHRYSLER Centura GL 4-door Sedan

mechanical pump; water-cooled, 23.2 imp pt, 27.9 US pt, 13.2 l.

TRANSMISSION driving wheels: rear; clutch: single dry plate (diaphragm); gearbox: mechanical; gears: 3, fully synchronized; ratios: I 2.950, II 1.690, III 1, rev 3.670; lever: central; final drive: hypoid bevel; axle ratio: 2.920; width of rims: 5.5''; tyres: 6.95 x 14 - Station Wagon 7.35 x 14.

PERFORMANCE max speed: about 109 mph, 175 km/h; power-weight ratio: Sedan 22.7 lb/hp, 10.3 kg/hp; speed in direct drive at 1,000 rpm: 23 mph, 37 km/h; consumption: not declared.

CHASSIS integral; front suspension: independent, wishbones, longitudinal torsion bars, telescopic dampers, anti-roll bar; rear: rigid axle, semi-elliptic leafsprings, telescopic dampers.

STEERING recirculating ball.

BRAKES front disc (diameter 11 in, 27.9 cm), front internal radial fins, rear drum, servo; swept area: total 327 sq in, 2,113 sq cm.

ELECTRICAL EQUIPMENT 12 V; 45 Ah battery; 35 A alternator; Chrysler electronic ignition; 2 headlamps.

DIMENSIONS AND WEIGHT wheel base: 115 in, 292 cm; tracks: 58.32 in, 148 cm front, 58.72 in, 149 cm rear; length: 198.40 in, 504 cm; width: 74.20 in, 188 cm; height: 55.80 in, 142 cm; weight: Sedan 3,127 lb, 1,418 kg - St. Wagon 3,367 lb, 1,527 kg - Regal Sedan 3,158 lb, 1,432 kg - Charger 770 Hardtop 3,162 lb, 1,434 kg; turning circle (between walls): 38.6 ft, 11.8 m; fuel tank: 17.5 imp gal, 20.9 US gal, 79 l.

BODY reclining backrests.

OPTIONAL ACCESSORIES Torqueflite automatic transmission, hydraulic torque converter and planetary gears with 3 ratios (I 2.390, II 1.450, III 1, rev 2.090), max ratio of converter at stall 2, possible manual selection, steering column; 4-speed fully synchronized mechanical gearbox (I 3.320, II 2.600, III 1.430, IV 1, rev 3), central lever; limited slip differential; light alloy wheels; F78S x 14 tyres; 185SR x 14 or ER70H x 14 tyres with 6.5'' wide rims; heavy-duty suspension; vinyl roof; heated rear window; Sports equipment; anti-roll bar on front suspension; power steering only with automatic transmission; electric windows; air-conditioning; tinted glass; 3.230 axle ratio.

146 hp power team

See 138 hp power team, except for:

ENGINE 265.1 cu in, 4,345 cc (3.91 x 3.68 in, 99.2 x 93.4 mm); max power (SAE): 146 hp at 4,800 rpm; max torque (SAE): 212 lb ft, 29.2 kg m at 2,000 rpm; max engine rpm: 5,200; 33.6 hp/l; 1 downdraught twin barrel carburettor.

TRANSMISSION (standard for Charger 770 only) gears: 4, fully synchronized; ratios: I 3.320, II 2.600, III 1.430, IV 1, rev 3; width of rims: 6.5''; tyres: 185 SR x 14.

PERFORMANCE max speed: about 112 mph, 180 km/h; power-weight ratio: Sedan 21.4 lb/hp, 9.7 kg/hp.

DIMENSIONS AND WEIGHT (for Charger 770 only) tracks: 59.32 in, 151 cm front, 59.72 in, 152 cm rear.

OPTIONAL ACCESSORIES 3.230 axle ratio.

143 hp power team

See 138 hp power team, except for:

ENGINE 8 cylinders, Vee-slanted at 90°; 318 cu in, 5,211 cc (3.91 x 3.31 in, 99.2 x 84 mm); compression ratio: 8.2:1; max power (SAE): 143 hp at 4,400 rpm; max torque (SAE): 253 lb ft, 35 kg m at 2,400 rpm; 27.4 hp/l; 5 crankshaft bearings; camshafts: 1, at centre of Vee; 1 downdraught twin barrel carburettor; cooling system: 26 imp pt, 31.3 US pt, 14.8 l.

TRANSMISSION gearbox: Torqueflite automatic transmission, hydraulic torque converter and planetary gears with 3 ratios, max ratio of converter at stall 2, possible manual selection; ratios: I 2.450, II 1.450, III 1, rev 2.200; axle ratio: 2.920; width of rims: Charger 770 6.5''; tyres: Charger 770 185 SR x 14.

PERFORMANCE max speed: about 115 mph, 185 km/h; power-weight ratio: Sedan 21.8 lb/hp, 9.9 kg/hp; speed in direct drive at 1,000 rpm: 26.7 mph, 43 km/h.

ELECTRICAL EQUIPMENT 50 Ah battery.

DIMENSIONS AND WEIGHT tracks: Charger 770 59.32 in, 151 cm front, 59.72 in, 152 cm rear; weight: Regal St. Wagon 3,535 lb, 1,603 kg - Regal SE Sedan 3,592 lb, 1,629 kg.

CHRYSLER Valiant Regal

FORD   AUSTRALIA

Escort Series

PRICES EX WORKS (Australian $):

1 Escort L 2-door Sedan	$ 4,492
2 Escort GL 2-door Sedan	$ 4,885
3 Escort GL 4-door Sedan	$ 5,011
4 Escort Ghia 4-door Sedan	$ 5,828

Power team:	Standard for:	Optional for:
98 hp	1 to 3	—
112 hp	4	—

98 hp power team

ENGINE front, 4 stroke; 4 cylinders, vertical in line; 97.5 cu in, 1,598 cc (3.19 x 3.06 in, 87 x 77.6 mm); compression ratio: 9:1; max power (SAE): 98 hp at 6,000 rpm; max torque (SAE): 101 lb ft, 14 kg m at 4,000 rpm; max engine rpm: 6,500; 61.3 hp/l; cast iron block and head; 5 crankshaft bearings; valves: overhead, in line, push-rods and rockers; camshafts: 1, side, chain driven; lubrication: rotary or vane type pump, full flow filter, 5.7 imp pt, 6.8 US pt, 3.2 l; 1 Weber 32/32 DGV downdraught twin barrel carburettor; fuel feed: mechanical pump; water-cooled, 9.5 imp pt, 11.4 US pt, 5.4 l.

TRANSMISSION driving wheels: rear; clutch: single dry plate (diaphragm); gearbox: mechanical; gears: 4, fully synchronized; ratios: I 3.337, II 1.995, III 1.418, IV 1, rev 3.876; lever: central; final drive: hypoid bevel; axle ratio: 4.125; width of rims: 4.5''; tyres: 155 SR x 13.

PERFORMANCE max speed: 101 mph, 162 km/h; power-weight ratio: L 2-dr. 19.7 lb/hp, 8.9 kg/hp - GL 2-dr. 20 lb/hp, 9 kg/hp - GL 4-dr. 20.4 lb/hp, 9.3 kg/hp; carrying capacity: 939 lb, 426 kg; acceleration: 0-50 mph (0-80 km/h) 16.5 sec; speed in direct drive at 1,000 rpm: 16 mph, 25.8 km/h; consumption: 37.8 m/imp gal, 31.4 m/US gal, 7.5 l x 100 km.

CHASSIS integral; front suspension: independent, by McPherson, coil springs/telescopic dampers struts, anti-roll bar; rear: rigid axle, semi-elliptic leafsprings, anti-roll bar, telescopic dampers.

STEERING rack-and-pinion; turns lock to lock: 3.50.

BRAKES front disc (diameter 9.60 in, 24.4 cm), rear drum, servo.

ELECTRICAL EQUIPMENT 12 V; 38 Ah battery; 35 A alternator; Motorcraft distributor; 2 headlamps.

FORD Escort Ghia 4-door Sedan

98 HP POWER TEAM

DIMENSIONS AND WEIGHT wheel base: 94.50 in, 240 cm; tracks: 49.50 in, 126 cm front, 50.60 in, 128 cm rear; length: 156.80 in, 398 cm; width: 62.80 in, 159 cm; height: 54.50 in, 138 cm; ground clearance: 4.92 in, 12.5 cm; weight: L 2-dr. 1,936 lb, 878 kg - GL 2-dr. 1,959 lb, 884 kg - GL 4-dr. 2,004 lb, 909 kg; turning circle (between walls): 29.5 ft, 9 m; fuel tank: 9 imp gal, 10.8 US gal, 41 l.

BODY 5 seats, separate front seats.

PRACTICAL INSTRUCTIONS fuel: 97 oct petrol; oil: engine 5.8 imp pt, 7 US pt, 3.3 l, SAE 10W-30, change every 6,000 miles, 9,700 km - gearbox 1.6 imp pt, 1.9 US pt, 0.9 l, SAE 80, no change recommended - final drive 1.7 imp pt, 2.1 US pt, 1 l, SAE 90, no change recommended; greasing: none; tappet clearances: inlet 0.010 in, 0.25 mm, exhaust 0.017 in, 0.43 mm; valve timing: 21° 55° 70° 22°; tyre pressure: front 24 psi, 1.7 atm, rear 24 psi, 1.7 atm.

OPTIONAL ACCESSORIES Ford C3 automatic transmission, hydraulic torque converter and planetary gears with 3 ratios (I 2.474, II 1.474, III 1, rev 2.111), max ratio of converter at stall 2.3, possible manual selection.

112 hp power team

See 98 hp power team, except for:

ENGINE 121.9 cu in, 1,998 cc (3.56 x 3.02 in, 90.4 x 76.7 mm); compression ratio: 9.2:1; max power (SAE): 112 hp at 6,000 rpm; max torque (SAE): 122 lb ft, 16.8 kg m at 3,500 rpm; 56 hp/l; valves: overhead, Vee-slanted, rockers; camshafts: 1, overhead, cogged belt; lubrication: 6.2 imp pt, 7.4 US pt, 3.5 l; 1 Autolite downdraught twin barrel carburettor; cooling system: 12.5 imp pt, 15 US pt, 7.1 l.

TRANSMISSION axle ratio: 3.540; width of rims: 5''; tyres: YR 78S x 13.

PERFORMANCE max speed: about 110 mph, 177 km/h; power-weight ratio: 18.7 lb/hp, 8.5 kg/hp; speed in direct drive at 1,000 rpm: 18.5 mph, 29.7 km/h; consumption: 36.7 m/imp gal, 30.5 m/US gal, 7.7 l x 100 km.

DIMENSIONS AND WEIGHT weight: 2,095 lb, 950 kg.

PRACTICAL INSTRUCTIONS valve timing: 29° 63° 71° 21°.

Cortina TE Series

PRICES EX WORKS (Australian $):

1 Cortina TE L Sedan	$ 5,225
2 Cortina TE L Station Wagon	$ 5,682
3 Cortina TE GL Sedan	$ 5,641
4 Cortina TE GL Station Wagon	$ 6,154
5 Cortina TE Ghia Sedan	$ 6,178

Power team:	Standard for:	Optional for:
112 hp	all	—
130 hp	—	1 to 4
155 hp	—	all

112 hp power team

ENGINE front, 4 stroke; 4 cylinders, vertical, in line; 121.9 cu in, 1,998 cc (3.56 x 3.02 in, 90.4 x 76.7 mm); compression ratio: 9.2:1; max power (SAE): 112 hp at 6,000 rpm; max torque (SAE): 122 lb ft, 16.8 kg m at 3,500 rpm; max engine rpm: 6,500; 56 hp/l; cast iron cylinder block and head; 5 crankshaft bearings; valves: overhead, Vee-slanted, rockers; camshafts: 1, overhead, cogged belt; lubrication: rotary pump, full flow filter, 6.2 imp pt, 7.4 US pt, 3.5 l; 1 Autolite downdraught twin barrel carburettor; fuel feed: mechanical pump; water-cooled, 12.5 imp pt, 15 US pt, 7.1 l.

TRANSMISSION driving wheels: rear; clutch: single dry plate (diaphragm); gearbox: mechanical; gears: 4, fully synchronized; ratios: I 3.650, II 1.970, III 1.370, IV 1, rev 3.660; lever: central; final drive: hypoid bevel; axle ratio: 3.700; width of rims: 4.5'' - Cortina TE Ghia 5.5''; tyres: 165 SR x 13 - Cortina TE Ghia 175 SR x 13 (standard).

PERFORMANCE max speed: about 103 mph, 165 km/h; power-weight ratio: sedans 22.4 lb/hp, 10.2 kg/hp; carrying capacity: 882 lb, 400 kg; speed in direct drive at 1,000 rpm: 18.3 mph, 29.5 km/h; consumption: 29.7 m/imp gal, 24.8 m/US gal, 9.5 l x 100 km.

CHASSIS integral, front auxiliary frame; front suspension: independent, wishbones, coil springs, anti-roll bar, telescopic dampers; rear: rigid axle, lower longitudinal trailing

FORD Cortina TE GL Sedan

radius arms, upper oblique torque arms, coil springs, anti-roll bar, telescopic dampers.

STEERING rack-and-pinion; turns lock to lock: 3.70.

BRAKES front disc (diameter 9.80 in, 24.9 cm), rear drum, servo.

ELECTRICAL EQUIPMENT 12 V; 55 Ah battery; 22 A alternator; Autolite distributor; 4 headlamps.

DIMENSIONS AND WEIGHT wheel base: 101.50 in, 258 cm; front and rear track: 56 in, 142 cm; length: sedans 167.70 in, 426 cm - station wagons 171.70 in, 436 cm; width: 67.20 in, 171 cm; height: sedans 51.80 in, 131 cm - station wagons 52.60 in, 134 cm; ground clearance: sedans 5.80 in, 14.7 cm - station wagons 5.90 in, 14.8 cm; dry weight: sedans 2,510 lb, 1,138 kg - station wagons 2,640 lb, 1,197 kg; turning circle (between walls): 31.8 ft, 9.7 m; fuel tank: 12 imp gal, 14.3 US gal, 54 l.

BODY 5 seats, separate front seats, reclining backrests; heated rear window (standard for Cortina TE Ghia only).

OPTIONAL ACCESSORIES automatic transmission with 3 ratios (I 2.393, II 1.450, III 1, rev 2.094), 3.500 axle ratio; 175 SR x 13 tyres with 5.5'' wide rims; BR 704 x 13 tyres; Rally equipment; sports steering wheel; sports road wheels; vinyl roof, heated rear window and sunshine roof (except for station wagons).

FORD Falcon 500 4-door Sedan

130 hp power team

See 112 hp power team, except for:

ENGINE 6 cylinders, vertical, in line; 200 cu in, 3,277 cc (3.68 x 3.13 in, 93.4 x 79.4 mm); compression ratio: 9.1:1; max power (SAE): 130 hp at 4,600 rpm; max torque (SAE): 190 lb ft, 26.2 kg m at 2,000 rpm; max engine rpm: 4,800; 39.7 hp/l; 7 crankshaft bearings; valves: overhead, in line, push-rods and rockers and rockers, hydraulic tappets; camshafts: 1, side; lubrication: 7 imp pt, 8.5 US pt, 4 l; 1 Autolite downdraught single barrel carburettor; cooling system: 15.5 imp pt, 18.6 US pt, 8.8 l.

TRANSMISSION gears: 3, fully synchronized; ratios: I 2.950, II 1.690, III 1, rev 3.670; axle ratio: 2.920.

PERFORMANCE max speed: about 106 mph, 170 km/h; power-weight ratio: sedans 19.3 lb/hp, 8.7 kg/hp; speed in direct drive at 1,000 rpm: 22 mph, 35.4 km/h; consumption: 23.5 m/imp gal, 19.6 m/US gal, 12 l x 100 km.

ELECTRICAL EQUIPMENT 38 A alternator.

OPTIONAL ACCESSORIES 4-speed fully synchronized mechanical gearbox (I 2.820, II 1.840, III 1.320, IV 1, rev 2.560), 2.920 axle ratio; automatic transmission with 3 ratios (I 2.393, II 1.450, III 1, rev 2.094), 2.920 axle ratio.

155 hp power team

See 130 hp power team, except for:

ENGINE 250 cu in, 4,097 cc (3.68 x 3.91 in, 93.4 x 99.2 mm); compression ratio: 9.3:1; max power (SAE): 155 hp at 4,000 rpm; max torque (SAE): 240 lb ft, 33.1 kg m at 1,600 rpm; max engine rpm: 4,600; 37.8 hp/l.

TRANSMISSION axle ratio: 2.770.

PERFORMANCE max speed: about 109 mph, 175 km/h; power-weight ratio: sedans 16.1 lb/hp, 7.3 kg/hp; speed in direct drive at 1,000 rpm: 23.6 mph, 38 km/h; consumption: 22.6 m/imp gal, 18.8 m/US gal, 12.5 l x 100 km.

OPTIONAL ACCESSORIES 4-speed fully synchronized mechanical gearbox with 2.770 axle ratio; automatic transmission with 2.770 axle ratio.

Falcon - Falcon 500 - Fairmont Series

PRICES EX WORKS (Australian $):

1 Falcon 4-door Sedan	$ 5,614
2 Falcon Station Wagon	$ 5,978
3 Falcon 500 4-door Sedan	$ 6,079
4 Falcon 500 2-door Hardtop	$ 6,867
5 Fairmont 4-door Sedan	$ 7,681
6 Fairmont 2-door Coupé	$ 7,816
7 Fairmont Station Wagon	$ 8,114
8 Fairmont GXL Sedan	$ 8,887

Power team:	Standard for:	Optional for:
130 hp	1 to 3	—
155 hp	4,5	3
240 hp	6 to 8	3 to 5
260 hp	—	3,4

130 hp power team

ENGINE front, 4 stroke; 6 cylinders, in line; 200 cu in, 3,277 cc (3.68 x 3.13 in, 93.4 x 79.4 mm); compression ratio: 8.8:1; max power (SAE): 130 hp at 4,600 rpm; max torque (SAE): 190 lb ft, 26.2 kg m at 2,000 rpm; max engine rpm: 4,800; 39.7 hp/l; cast iron cylinder block and head; 7 crankshaft bearings; valves: overhead, push-rods and rockers, hydraulic tappets; camshafts: 1, side; lubrication: gear pump, full flow filter, 7 imp pt, 8.5 US pt, 4 l; 1 Autolite downdraught single barrel carburettor; fuel feed: mechanical pump; water-cooled, 15.5 imp pt, 18.6 US pt, 8.8 l.

TRANSMISSION driving wheels: rear; clutch: single dry plate (diaphragm), hydraulically controlled; gearbox: mechanical; gears: 3, fully synchronized; ratios: I 2.950, II 1.690, III 1, rev 3.670; lever: steering column; final drive: hypoid bevel; axle ratio: 3.230; width of rims: 5''; tyres: 6.95 L x 14 - Station Wagon 7.35 x 14.

PERFORMANCE max speed: about 96 mph, 154 km/h; speed in direct drive at 1,000 rpm: 20.5 mph, 33 km/h; consumption: 19.9 m/imp gal, 16.6 m/US gal, 14.2 l x 100 km.

CHASSIS integral; front suspension: independent, wishbones, lower trailing links, coil springs, anti-roll bar, telescopic dampers; rear: rigid axle, semi-elliptic leafsprings, telescopic dampers.

STEERING recirculating ball.

BRAKES front disc (diameter 11.25 in, 28.6 cm), rear drum; swept area: total 297.2 sq in, 1,917 sq cm.

ELECTRICAL EQUIPMENT 12 V; 45 Ah battery; 38 A alternator; Autolite distributor; 2 headlamps.

DIMENSIONS AND WEIGHT wheel base: 116 in, 295 cm - sedans 110 in, 279 cm; tracks: 60.50 in, 154 cm front, 60 in, 152 cm rear; length: 189.30 in, 481 cm - Station Wagon 198.90 in, 505 cm; width: 74.80 in, 190 cm; height: 53.90 in, 137 cm - Station Wagon 55.40 in, 141 cm; ground clearance: 5.40 in, 13.7 cm - Station Wagon 6.40 in, 16.2 cm; turning circle (between walls): 39.4 ft, 12 m - Station Wagon 41.2 ft, 12.6 m; fuel tank: 14.5 imp gal, 17.4 US gal, 66 l - Station Wagon 16 imp gal, 19.3 US gal, 73 l.

OPTIONAL ACCESSORIES Select-Shift Cruise-o-matic automatic transmission with 3 ratios (I 2.390, II 1.450, III 1, rev 2.090), max ratio of converter at stall 2, possible manual selection; 7.35 L x 14, 7.35 S x 14, 185 SR x 14 or ER 70H x 14 tyres with 6'' wide rims; power steering; servo brake; 4-wheel disc brakes; heated rear window; tinted glass; vinyl roof; GS Rally equipment; reclining backrests; sunshine roof (not available for Station Wagon).

155 hp power team

See 130 hp power team, except for:

ENGINE 250 cu in, 4,097 cc (3.68 x 3.91 in, 93.4 x 99.2 mm); compression ratio: 9.1:1; max power (SAE): 155 hp at 4,000 rpm; max torque (SAE): 240 lb ft, 33.1 kg m at 1,600 rpm; max engine rpm: 4,600; 37.8 hp/l.

PERFORMANCE max speed: about 99 mph, 159 km/h; speed in direct drive at 1,000 rpm: 22 mph, 35.4 km/h; consumption: 19.5 m/imp gal, 16.2 m/US gal, 14.5 l x 100 km.

BRAKES front disc with internal radial fins, servo.

OPTIONAL ACCESSORIES Select-Shift Cruise-o-Matic automatic transmission with steering column or central lever and 2.920 axle ratio; 4-speed fully synchronized mechanical gearbox (I 2.820, II 1.840, III 1.320, IV 1, rev 2.560), with central lever and 3.230 axle ratio; air-conditioning; electric windows.

240 hp power team

See 130 hp power team, except for:

ENGINE 8 cylinders, Vee-slanted at 90°; 302 cu in, 4,950 cc (4 x 3 in, 101.6 x 76.1 mm); compression ratio: 9.4:1; max power (SAE): 240 hp at 5,000 rpm; max torque (SAE): 305 lb ft, 42.1 kg m at 2,600 rpm; max engine rpm: 5,200; 48.5 hp/l; 5 crankshaft bearings; camshafts: 1, at centre of Vee; 1 Autolite downdraught twin barrel carburettor; cooling system: 22.5 imp pt, 27.1 US pt, 12.8 l.

TRANSMISSION gearbox ratios: I 2.710, II 1.690, III 1, rev 3.370; axle ratio: 2.920; width of rims: 6''; tyres: 7.35 S x 14.

PERFORMANCE max speed: about 112 mph, 180 km/h; speed in direct drive at 1,000 rpm: 25 mph, 40 km/h; consumption: 17.2 m/imp gal, 14.3 m/US gal, 16.4 l x 100 km.

BRAKES front disc with internal radial fins, servo.

FORD Fairlane 500 4-door Sedan

DIMENSIONS AND WEIGHT (for Fairmont Coupé only) wheel base: 111 in, 282 cm; rear track: 60.50 in, 154 cm; width: 77.50 in, 197 cm; height: 51.90 in, 132 cm; fuel tank: 17.5 imp gal, 20.9 US gal, 79 l.

OPTIONAL ACCESSORIES Select-Shift Cruise-o-Matic automatic transmission with 3 ratios (I 2.460, II 1.460, III 1, rev 2.200), max ratio of converter at stall 2, steering column or central lever, 2.920 axle ratio; 4-speed fully synchronized mechanical gearbox (I 2.820, II 1.840, III 1.320, IV 1, rev 2.560), with central lever and 2.920 axle ratio; dual exhaust system; air-conditioning; electric windows.

260 hp power team

See 130 hp power team, except for:

ENGINE 8 cylinders, Vee-slanted at 90°; 351 cu in, 5,752 cc (4 x 3.50 in, 101.6 x 88.8 mm); compression ratio: 9.1:1; max power (SAE): 260 hp at 4,600 rpm; max torque (SAE): 355 lb ft, 49 kg m at 2,600 rpm; max engine rpm: 4,900; 45.2 hp/l; 5 crankshaft bearings; camshafts: 1, at centre of Vee; 1 Autolite downdraught twin barrel carburettor; cooling system: 24.6 imp pt, 29.6 US pt, 14 l.

TRANSMISSION clutch: 2 dry plates (diaphragm), hydraulically controlled; gears: 4, fully synchronized; ratios: I 2.820, II 1.840, III 1.320, IV 1, rev 2.560; lever: central; axle ratio: 3.000; width of rims: 6''; tyres: 7.35 H x 14.

PERFORMANCE max speed: about 118 mph, 190 km/h; speed in direct drive at 1,000 rpm: 25 mph, 40 km/h; consumption: 16.6 m/imp gal, 13.8 m/US gal, 17 l x 100 km.

BRAKES front disc with internal radial fins, servo.

OPTIONAL ACCESSORIES Select-Shift Cruise-o-Matic automatic transmission with 3 ratios (I 2.460, II 1.460, III 1, rev 2.200), max ratio of converter at stall 2, steering column or central lever, 2.750 axle ratio; limited slip differential; dual exhaust system; air-conditioning; electric windows.

Fairlane Series

PRICES EX WORKS (Australian $):

1 Fairlane 500 4-door Sedan	$ 10,270
2 Fairlane Marquis 4-door Sedan	$ 12,307

Power team:	Standard for:	Optional for:
240 hp	1	—
260 hp	2	1

240 hp power team

ENGINE front, 4 stroke; 8 cylinders, Vee-slanted at 90°; 302 cu in, 4,950 cc (4 x 3 in, 101.6 x 76.1 mm); compression ratio: 9.4:1; max power (SAE): 240 hp at 5,000 rpm; max torque (SAE): 305 lb ft, 42.1 kg m at 2,600 rpm; max engine rpm: 5,200; 48.5 hp/l; cast iron block and head; 5 crankshaft bearings; valves: overhead, push-rods and rockers, hydraulic tappets; camshafts: 1, at centre of Vee; lubrication: gear pump, full flow filter, 7.6 imp pt, 9.1 US pt, 4.3 l; 1 Stromberg downdraught twin barrel carburettor; fuel feed: mechanical pump; water-cooled, 22.5 imp pt, 27.1 US pt, 12.8 l.

TRANSMISSION driving wheels: rear; clutch: single dry plate (diaphragm), hydraulically controlled; gearbox: mechanical; gears: 3, fully synchronized; ratios: I 2.710, II 1.690, II 1, rev 3.370; lever: steering column; final drive: hypoid bevel; axle ratio: 2.920; width of rims: 5''; tyres: 7.35 l x 14.

PERFORMANCE max speed: about 102 mph, 164 km/h; power-weight ratio: 14.3 lb/hp, 6.5 kg/hp; speed in direct drive at 1,000 rpm: 22 mph, 35.4 km/h; consumption: 16.8 m/imp gal, 14 m/US gal, 16.8 l x 100 km.

CHASSIS integral; front suspension: independent, wishbones, lower trailing links, coil springs, anti-roll bar, telescopic dampers; rear: rigid axle, semi-elliptic leafsprings, telescopic dampers.

STEERING recirculating ball, servo.

BRAKES front disc (diameter 11.25 in, 28.6 cm), internal radial fins, rear drum, servo; swept area: total 296.9 sq in, 1,915 sq cm.

ELECTRICAL EQUIPMENT 12 V; 45 Ah battery; 38 A alternator; Autolite distributor; 4 headlamps.

FORD Falcon 500 Hardtop - Fairmont Coupé

240 HP POWER TEAM

DIMENSIONS AND WEIGHT wheel base: 116 in, 295 cm; tracks: 60.50 in, 154 cm front, 60 in, 152 cm rear; length: 198.90 in, 505 cm; width: 74.60 in, 189 cm; height: 53.90 in, 137 cm; ground clearance: 5.40 in, 13.7 cm; weight: 3,415 lb, 1,549 kg; turning circle (between walls): 41.2 ft, 12.6 m; fuel tank: 17.5 imp gal, 20.9 US gal, 79 l.

BODY saloon/sedan; 4 doors; 5-6 seats, separate front seats.

OPTIONAL ACCESSORIES Select-Shift Cruise-o-Matic automatic transmission with 3 ratios (I 2.460, II 1.460, III 1, rev 2.200), max ratio of converter af stall 2, possible manual selection, central or steering column lever; 185 x 14 or ER 70 HR x 14 tyres with 6'' wide rims; bench front seats; sunshine roof; air-conditioning.

260 hp power team

See 240 hp power team, except for:

ENGINE 351 cu in, 5,752 cc (4 x 3.50 in, 101.6 x 88.8 mm); max power (SAE): 260 hp at 4,600 rpm; max torque (SAE): 335 lb ft, 49 kg m at 2,600 rpm; max engine rpm: 4,900; 45.2 hp/l; cooling system: 24.6 imp pt, 29.6 US pt, 14 l.

TRANSMISSION (standard) gearbox: Select-Shift Cruise-o-Matic automatic transmission, hydraulic torque converter and planetary gears with 3 ratios, max ratio of converter at stall 2.40, possible manual selection: ratios: I 2.460, II 1.460, III 1, rev 2.200; lever: central; axle ratio: 2.750.

PERFORMANCE max speed: about 106 mph, 171 km/h; power-weight ratio: 13.2 lb/hp, 6 kg/hp; consumption: 16 m/imp gal, 13.3 m/US gal, 17.7 l x 100 km.

OPTIONAL ACCESSORIES limited slip differential.

LTD 4-door Sedan

PRICE EX WORKS: Australian $ 15,192

ENGINE front, 4 stroke; 8 cylinders, Vee-slanted at 90°; 351 cu in, 5,752 cc (4 x 3.50 in, 101.6 x 88.8 mm); compression ratio: 11:1; max power (SAE): 290 hp at 5,000 rpm; max torque (SAE): 380 lb ft, 52.4 kg m at 3,200 rpm; max engine rpm: 5,400; 50.4 hp/l; cast iron cylinder block and head; 5 crankshaft bearings; valves: overhead, in line, push-rods and rockers, hydraulic tappets; camshafts: 1, at centre of Vee; lubrication: gear pump, full flow filter, 8.3 imp pt, 9.9 US pt, 4.7 l; 1 Autolite downdraught 4-barrel carburettor; fuel feed: mechanical pump; water-cooled, 24.6 imp pt, 29.6 US pt, 14 l.

TRANSMISSION driving wheels: rear; gearbox: Select-Shift Cruise-o-Matic automatic transmission, hydraulic torque converter and planetary gears with 3 ratios, max ratio of converter at stall 2, possible manual selection: ratios: I 2.400, II 1.470, III 1, rev 2; lever: central; final drive: hypoid bevel, limited slip differential; axle ratio: 2.750; width of rims: 6''; tyres: ER 70 H x 15.

PERFORMANCE max speed: 124 mph, 200 km/h; power-weight ratio: 13.7 lb/hp, 6.2 kg/hp; carrying capacity: 1,103 lb, 500 kg; speed in direct drive at 1,000 rpm: 23.6 mph, 38 km/h; consumption: 14.9 m/imp gal, 12.4 m/US gal, 19 l x 100 km.

CHASSIS perimeter box-type with cross members; front suspension: independent, wishbones (lower trailing links), coil springs, anti-roll bar, telescopic dampers; rear: rigid axle, semi-elliptic leafsprings, telescopic dampers.

STEERING recirculating ball, variable ratio, servo.

BRAKES disc (diameter 11.25 in, 28.6 cm), internal radial fins, rear compensator, servo.

ELECTRICAL EQUIPMENT 12 V; 55 Ah battery; 42 alternator Autolite distributor; 4 headlamps.

DIMENSIONS AND WEIGHT wheel base: 121 in, 307 cm; tracks: 60.50 in, 154 cm front, 60 in, 152 cm rear; length: 203.80 in, 518 cm; width: 74.80 in, 190 cm; height: 54.30 in, 138 cm; ground clearance: 6.50 in, 16.5 cm; weight: 3,950 lb, 1,971 kg; turning circle (between walls): 42.2 ft, 12.9 m; fuel tank: 17.5 imp gal, 20.9 US gal, 79 l.

BODY 6 seats, separate front seats, reclining backrests; tinted glass; vinyl roof; heated rear window; air-conditioning; electric windows.

OPTIONAL ACCESSORIES leather upholstery.

FORD LTD 4-door Sedan

HOLDEN   AUSTRALIA

Gemini Series

PRICES EX WORKS (Australian $):

Gemini TC 4-door Sedan	$ 4,482
Gemini TC SL 4-door Sedan	$ 4,851
Gemini TC SL Coupé	$ 4,995

100 hp power team

ENGINE front, 4 stroke; 4 cylinders, in line; 96.7 cu in, 1,584 cc (3.23 x 2.95 in, 82 x 75 mm); compression ratio: 8.7:1; max power (DIN): 100 hp at 6,000 rpm; max torque (DIN): 101 lb ft, 14 kg m at 4,000 rpm; max engine rpm: 6,500; 62.7 hp/l; cast iron block, light alloy head; 5 crankshaft bearings; valves: overhead, rockers; camshafts: 1, overhead; lubrication: rotary pump, full flow filter, 8.8 imp pt, 10.6 US pt, 5 l; 1 Nikki-Stromberg downdraught twin barrel carburettor; fuel feed: electric pump; water-cooled, 10.8 imp pt, 12.7 US pt, 6 l.

TRANSMISSION driving wheels: rear; clutch: single dry plate (diaphragm); gearbox: mechanical; gears: 4, fully synchronized; ratios: I 3.507, II 2.157, III 1.418, IV 1, rev 3.927; lever: central; final drive: hypoid bevel; axle ratio: 3.889; width of rims: 4.5''; tyres: Y78L x 13 - 155 SR x 13.

HOLDEN Gemini TC SL 4-door Sedan

PERFORMANCE max speeds: (I) 29 mph, 47 km/h; (II) 48 mph, 78 km/h; (III) 73 mph, 117 km/h; (IV) 106 mph, 170 km/h; power-weight ratio: sedans 20.2 lb/hp, 9.2 kg/hp - Coupé 19.9 lb/hp, 9 kg/hp; carrying capacity: 882 lb, 400 kg; speed in direct drive at 1,000 rpm: 16.2 mph, 26.1 km/h; consumption: 29.4 m/imp gal, 24.5 m/US gal, 9.6 l x 100 km.

CHASSIS integral; front suspension: independent, wishbones, coil springs, anti-roll bar, telescopic dampers; rear: rigid axle, lower radius arms, torque tube, Panhard rod, coil springs, telescopic dampers.

STEERING rack-and-pinion; turns lock to lock: 3.

BRAKES front disc (diameter 9.41 in, 23.9 cm), rear drum, servo; lining area: front 17.4 sq in, 112 sq cm, rear 49 sq in, 316 sq cm, total 66.4 sq in, 428 sq cm.

ELECTRICAL EQUIPMENT 12 V; 35 Ah battery; 40 A alternator; Hitachi distributor; 2 headlamps.

DIMENSIONS AND WEIGHT wheel base: 94.49 in, 240 cm; tracks: 51.18 in, 130 cm front, 51.57 in, 131 cm rear; length: 162.60 in, 413 cm; width: 61.81 in, 157 cm; height: 51.90 in, 131 cm; ground clearance: 5.71 in, 14.5 cm; weight: Sedan 2,022 lb, 918 kg - SL Sedan 2,034 lb, 923 kg - SL Coupé 1,991 lb, 903 kg; turning circle (between walls): 32.8 ft, 10 m; fuel tank: 11.4 imp gal, 13.7 US gal, 52 l.

BODY 5 seats, separate front seats.

OPTIONAL ACCESSORIES Trimatic automatic transmission with 3 ratios (I 2.310, II 1.460, III 1) with central lever and 3.890 axle ratio; air-conditioning.

Sunbird

PRICE EX WORKS (Australian $): $ 5,460

ENGINE front, 4 stroke; 4 cylinders, vertical, in line; 115.8 cu in, 1,897 cc (3.66 x 2.75 in, 93 x 69.8 mm); compression ratio: 8.8:1; max power (SAE): 96 hp at 5,200 rpm; max torque (SAE): 116 lb ft, 16 kg m at 3,600 rpm; max engine rpm: 6,000; 48.5 hp/l; cast iron block and head; 5 crankshaft bearings; valves: overhead, thimble tappets; camshafts: 1, overhead; lubrication: gear pump, full flow filter, 6.7 imp pt, 8 US pt, 3.8 l; 1 Solex 32 DIDTA-4 downdraught twin barrel carburettor; fuel feed: mechanical pump; water-cooled, 15 imp pt, 18 US pt, 8.5 l.

TRANSMISSION driving wheels: rear; clutch: single dry plate (diaphragm); gearbox: mechanical; gears: 4, fully synchronized; ratios: I 3.400, II 2.160, III 1.370, IV 1, rev 3.810; lever: central; final drive: hypoid bevel; axle ratio: 3.900; width of rims: 5.5''; tyres: AR 78S x 13.

PERFORMANCE max speed: about 93 mph, 150 km/h; power-weight ratio: 26.7 lb/hp, 12.1 kg/hp; carrying capacity: 1,091 lb, 495 kg; speed in direct drive at 1,000 rpm: 15.5 mph, 25 km/h; consumption: not declared.

CHASSIS integral; front suspension: independent, wishbones, coil springs, telescopic dampers, anti-roll bar; rear: rigid axle, trailing lower radius arms, upper oblique radius arms, coil springs, telescopic dampers, anti-roll bar.

STEERING rack-and-pinion; turns lock to lock: 3.60.

BRAKES front disc (diameter 10 in, 25.4 cm), rear drum.

HOLDEN Sunbird

HOLDEN Torana LX 4150 SS Hatchback

ELECTRICAL EQUIPMENT 12 V; 48 Ah battery; 250 W alternator; AC Delco or Bosch distributor; 2 headlamps.

DIMENSIONS AND WEIGHT wheel base: 101.80 in, 249 cm; tracks: 55.30 in, 140 cm front, 54.40 in, 138 cm rear; length: 176.90 in, 449 cm; weight: 67.10 in, 170 cm; height: 52.10 in, 132 cm; ground clearance: 4.80 in, 12.2 cm; weight: 2,559 lb, 1,161 kg; turning circle (between walls): 36 ft, 11 m; fuel tank: 11.6 imp gal, 13.8 US gal, 52 l.

BODY saloon/sedan; 4 doors; 4 seats; separate front seats, reclining backrests.

OPTIONAL ACCESSORIES Trimatic automatic transmission with 3 ratios (I 2.310, II 1.460, III 1, rev 1.850); heated rear window.

Torana LX Series

PRICES EX WORKS (Australian $):

1 Torana LX 2850 S 4-door Sedan	$	5,480
2 Torana LX 3300 S 4-door Sedan	$	5,593
3 Torana LX 4150 S 4-door Sedan	$	5,758
4 Torana LX 2850 SL 4-door Sedan	$	6,037
5 Torana LX 3300 SL 4-door Sedan	$	6,150
6 Torana LX 3300 SL Hatchback	$	6,398
7 Torana LX 4150 SL 4-door Sedan	$	6,315
8 Torana LX 4150 SL Hatchback	$	6,666
9 Torana LX 3300 SL/R 4-door Sedan	$	6,560
10 Torana LX 4150 SL/R 4-door Sedan	$	6,828
11 Torana LX 5000 SL/R 4-door Sedan	$	6,960
12 Torana LX 3300 SS Hatchback	$	6,796
13 Torana LX 4150 SS Hatchback	$	7,064
14 Torana LX 5000 SS Hatchback	$	7,196

Power team:	Standard for:	Optional for:
105 hp	1,4	—
110 hp	2,5,6,9,12	1,4
175 hp	3,7,8,10,13	—
250 hp	11,14	—

105 hp power team

ENGINE 6 cylinders, in line; 173 cu in, 2,834 cc (3.50 x 3 in, 88.9 x 76.2 mm); compression ratio: 9.4:1; max power (SAE): 105 hp at 4,000 rpm; max torque (SAE): 165 lb ft, 22.8 kg m at 2,400 rpm; max engine rpm: 6,000; 37 hp/l; 7 crankshaft bearings; valves: overhead, push-rods and rockers; camshafts: 1, side; lubrication: gear pump, full flow filter, 7.5 imp pt, 8.9 US pt, 4.2 l; 1 Stromberg BXUV-3 downdraught single barrel carburettor; fuel feed: mechanical pump; water-cooled, 15 imp pt, 18 US pt, 8.5 l.

TRANSMISSION driving wheels: rear; clutch: single dry plate (diaphragm); gearbox: mechanical; gears: 3, fully synchronized; ratios: I 3.070, II 1.680, III 1, rev 3.590; lever: steering column; final drive: hypoid bevel; axle ratio: 3.360; width of rims: 4.5''; tyres: A78L x 13.

PERFORMANCE max speed: about 103 mph, 165 km/h; power-weight ratio: S 24 lb/hp, 10.9 kg/hp - SL 24.7 lb/hp, 11.2 kg/hp; carrying capacity: S 1,080 lb, 490 kg - SL 900 lb, 408 kg; speed in direct drive at 1,000 rpm: 20.1 mph, 32.3 km/h; consumption: not declared.

CHASSIS integral; front suspension: independent, wishbones, coil springs, telescopic dampers; rear: rigid axle, trailing

lower radius arms, upper oblique radius arms, coil springs, telescopic dampers.

STEERING rack-and-pinion; turns lock to lock: 3.30.

BRAKES front disc, rear drum, servo; swept area: front 99 sq in, 638 sq cm, rear 99 sq in, 638 sq cm, total 198 sq in, 1,276 sq cm - SL total 275.4 sq in, 1,776 sq cm.

ELECTRICAL EQUIPMENT 12 V; 48 Ah battery; 520 W alternator; AC Delco or Bosch distributor; 2 headlamps.

DIMENSIONS AND WEIGHT wheel base: 101.80 in, 259 cm; tracks: 54.90 in, 139 cm front, 54 in, 137 cm rear; length: S 176.90 in, 449 cm - SL 177.50 in, 451 cm; width: 67.10 in, 170 cm; height: 52.40 in, 133 cm; ground clearance: 4.80 in, 12.2 cm; weight: S 2,520 lb, 1,143 kg - SL 2,951 lb, 1,175 kg; turning circle (between walls): 36 ft, 11 m; fuel tank: 12 imp gal, 14.3 US gal, 54 l.

BODY saloon/sedan; 4 doors; 4 seats, separate front seats; reclining backrests.

OPTIONAL ACCESSORIES Trimatic automatic transmission with 3 ratios (I 2.310, II 1.460, III 1, rev 1.850); 4-speed fully synchronized mechanical gearbox (I 3.050, II 2.190, III 1.510, IV 1, rev 3.050); 3.080 or 2.780 axle ratio; limited slip differential; dual exhaust system; vinyl roof; air-conditioning.

110 hp power team

See 105 hp power team, except for:

ENGINE 201.2 cu in, 3,298 cc (3.62 x 3.25 in, 92.1 x 82.5 mm); max power (SAE): 110 hp at 4,000 rpm; max torque (SAE): 191 lb ft, 26.4 kg m at 1,600 rpm; 33.3 hp/l.

TRANSMISSION gears: 4, fully synchronized; gearbox ratios: I 3.050, II 2.190, III 1.510, IV 1, rev 3.050; axle ratio: 3.080; width of rims: 5.5''; tyres: 175 SR x 13.

PERFORMANCE max speed: about 109 mph, 175 km/h; power-weight ratio: SL Hatchback 24.1 lb/hp, 10.9 kg/hp; speed in direct drive at 1,000 rpm: 22.1 mph, 35.6 km/h.

CHASSIS front and rear suspension: anti-roll bar.

BRAKES swept area: front 99 sq in, 638 sq cm, rear 176.4 sq in, 1,138 sq cm, 275.4 sq in, 1,776 sq cm.

DIMENSIONS AND WEIGHT length: 177.50 in, 451 cm; height: SL Sedan 52.50 in, 133 cm - SL/R and SL Hatchback 52.20 in, 133 cm - SS 52 in, 132 cm; ground clearance: 4.90 in, 12.4 cm; weight: SL Sedan 2,590 lb, 1,175 kg - SL/R 2,610 lb, 1,183 kg - SL Hatchback 2,654 lb, 1,204 kg - SS 2,674 lb, 1,213 kg.

OPTIONAL ACCESSORIES Trimatic automatic transmission with 2.780 axle ratio.

175 hp power team

See 110 hp power team, except for:

ENGINE 8 cylinders; 253 cu in, 4,146 cc (3.62 x 3.06 in, 91.9 x 77.6 mm); compression ratio: 9:1; max power (SAE): 175 hp at 4,800 rpm; max torque (SAE): 240 lb ft, 33.1 kg m at 3,000 rpm; 42.2 hp/l; 5 crankshaft bearings; camshafts: 1, at centre of Vee; lubrication: 8.5 imp pt, 10.1 US pt, 4.8 l; 1 Bendix-Stromberg BXV-2 downdraught twin barrel carburettor; cooling system: 21 imp pt, 25.2 US pt, 11.9 l.

PERFORMANCE max speed: about 112 mph, 180 km/h; power-weight ratio: SL Hatchback 15.2 lb/hp, 6.9 kg/hp.

250 hp power team

See 110 hp power team, except for:

ENGINE 8 cylinders; 308 cu in, 5,047 cc (4 x 3.06 in, 101.5 x 77.6 mm); compression ratio: 9.7:1; max power (SAE): 250 hp at 5,000 rpm; max torque (SAE): 320 lb ft, 44.1 kg m at 3,400 rpm; 49.5 hp/l; 5 crankshaft bearings; camshafts: 1, at centre of Vee; lubrication: 8.5 imp pt, 10.1 US pt, 4.8 l; 1 Rochester 4MV downdraught 4-barrel carburettor; cooling system: 20 imp pt, 23.9 US pt, 11.3 l.

TRANSMISSION gearbox ratios: I 2.540, II 1.830, III 1.380, IV 1, rev 2.540; limited slip differential; axle ratio: 2.780; tyres: BR70H x 13.

PERFORMANCE max speed: about 115 mph, 185 km/h; power-weight ratio: 11.3 lb/hp, 5.1 kg/hp; speed in direct drive at 1,000 rpm: 24.3 mph, 39.1 km/h.

DIMENSIONS AND WEIGHT weight: 2,829 lb, 1,283 kg.

OPTIONAL ACCESSORIES 3.080 axle ratio; Trimatic automatic transmission not available.

HOLDEN HZ Premier 4-door Sedan

HZ Kingswood - HZ Premier - HZ GTS - HZ Statesman De Ville - HZ Statesman Caprice Series

PRICES EX WORKS: (Australian $):

1 HZ Kingswood SL 4-door Sedan	$ 6,377
2 HZ Kingswood SL Station Wagon	$ 6,727
3 HZ Premier 4-door Sedan	$ 7,783
4 HZ Premier Station Wagon	$ 8,089
5 HZ GTS 4-door Sedan	$ 8,482
6 HZ Statesman De Ville 4-door Sedan	$ 9,993
7 HZ Statesman Caprice 4-door Sedan	$ 14,729

Power team:	Standard for:	Optional for:
110 hp	1 to 4	—
161 hp	5	1 to 4
216 hp	6,7	1 to 5

110 hp power team

ENGINE front, 4 stroke; 6 cylinders, vertical, in line; 201.2 cu in, 3,298 cc (3.62 x 3.25 in, 91.9 x 82.5 mm); compression ratio: 9.4:1; max power (SAE): 110 hp at 4,000 rpm; max torque (SAE): 190 lb ft, 26.2 kg m at 1,600 rpm; max engine rpm: 5,000; 33.3 hp/l; cast iron block and head; 7 crankshaft bearings; valves: overhead, in line, push-rods and rockers, hydraulic tappets; camshafts: 1, side; lubrication: gear pump, full flow filter, 7.5 imp pt, 8.9 US pt, 4.2 l; 1 Bendix-Stromberg BXV-2 downdraught single barrel carburettor; fuel feed: mechanical pump; water-cooled, 14 imp pt, 16.7 US pt, 7.9 l.

TRANSMISSION driving wheels: rear; clutch: single dry plate (diaphragm); gearbox: mechanical (Trimatic automatic transmission standard for Premier models); gears: 3, fully synchronized; ratios: I 3.070, II 1.680, III 1, rev 3.590 (Premier models I 2.310, II 1.460, III 1, rev 1.850); lever: steering column; final drive: hypoid bevel; axle ratio: 3.550 - Premier models 3.080 or 3.360; width of rims: 5''; tyres: Kingswood models C78L x 14 - Premier models E78L x 14.

PERFORMANCE max speed: about 96 mph, 155 km/h; power-weight ratio: Kingswood SL 4-dr. Sedan 26.9 lb/hp, 12.2 kg/hp - Premier 4-dr. Sedan 27.8 lb/hp, 12.6 kg/hp; carrying capacity: 882 lb, 400 kg; speed in direct drive at 1,000 rpm: 20 mph, 32.2 km/h.

CHASSIS integral, front auxiliary box-type frame; front suspension: independent, wishbones, coil springs, anti-roll bar, telescopic dampers; rear: rigid axle, trailing lower radius arms, upper oblique radius arms, coil springs, telescopic dampers.

STEERING recirculating ball; turns lock to lock: 3.68.

BRAKES front disc, internal radial fins (diameter 10.8 in, 27.6 cm), rear drum.

ELECTRICAL EQUIPMENT 12 V; 48 Ah battery; 35 A alternator; Bosch or Lucas distributor; 4 headlamps.

DIMENSIONS AND WEIGHT wheel base: sedans 111 in, 282 cm - station wagons 114 in, 289 cm; tracks: 59.50 in, 151 cm front, 60.20 in, 153 cm rear; length: Kingswood SL 4-dr. Sedan 190.30 in, 483 cm - Station Wagon 192.30 in, 488 cm - Premier 4-dr. Sedan 190.80 in, 485 cm - Station Wagon 192.80 in, 490 cm; width: 74.30 in, 189 cm; height: Kingswood SL 4-dr. Sedan 54.10 in, 137 cm - Station Wagon 55.30 in, 140 cm - Premier 4-dr. Sedan 54.40 in, 138 cm - Station Wagon 55.10 in, 140 cm; ground clearance: 5.60 in, 14.2 cm; weight: Kingswood SL 4-dr. Sedan 2,960 lb, 1,342 kg - Station Wagon 3,145 lb, 1,426 kg - Premier 4-dr. Sedan 3,062 lb, 1,389 kg - Station Wagon 3,242 lb, 1,470 kg; turning circle (between walls): sedans 39.7 ft, 12.1 m - station wagons 40.5 ft, 12.3 m; fuel tank: 16.5 imp gal, 19.8 US gal, 75 l.

BODY 5 seats, separate front seats.

OPTIONAL ACCESSORIES Trimatic automatic transmission with 3 ratios (I 2.310, II 1.460, III 1, rev 1.850), 3.360 axle ratio; 4-speed fully synchronized mechanical gearbox (I 3.740, II 2.190, III 1.510, IV 1, rev 3.050); limited slip differential; 3.900 or 3.360 axle ratio; central lever; power steering; front disc brakes with servo; electric windows; tinted glass; sunshine roof; vinyl roof; air-conditioning.

161 hp power team

See 110 hp power team, except for:

ENGINE 8 cylinders; 253 cu in, 4,146 cc (3.62 x 3.06 in, 91.9 x 77.6 mm); max power (SAE): 161 hp at 4,550 rpm; max torque (SAE): 240 lb ft, 33.1 kg m at 2,600 rpm; 38.8 hp/l; 5 crankshaft bearings; camshafts: 1, at centre of Vee; lubrication: 8.5 imp pt, 10.1 US pt, 4.8 l; 1 Bendix-Stromberg BXV-2 downdraught twin barrel carburettor; cooling system: 21 imp pt, 25.2 US pt, 11.9 l.

TRANSMISSION gears: 4, fully synchronized; ratios: I 3.050, II 2.190, III 1.510, IV 1, rev 3.050; width of rims: 6''; tyres: ER 70H x 14.

PERFORMANCE max speed: about 109 mph, 175 km/h; power-weight ratio: 20.2 lb/hp, 9.2 kg/hp.

STEERING turns lock to lock: 3.07.

ELECTRICAL EQUIPMENT Bosch distributor.

DIMENSIONS AND WEIGHT tracks: 59.80 in, 152 cm front, 60.50 in, 154 cm rear; length: 190.30 in, 483 cm; width: 73.90 in, 188 cm; height: 53.70 in, 136 cm; weight: 3,253 lb, 1,475 kg.

OPTIONAL ACCESSORIES Trimatic automatic transmission with 2.780 axle ratio; 4-speed fully synchronized mechanical gearbox (I 2.540, II 1.830, III 1.380, IV 1, rev 2.540), central lever, 3.360 axle ratio.

216 hp power team

See 110 hp power team, except for:

ENGINE 8 cylinders; 307.8 cu in, 5,044 cc (4 x 3.06 in, 101.6 x 77.7 mm); compression ratio: 9.7:1; max power (SAE): 216 hp at 4,800 rpm; max torque (SAE): 295 lb ft, 40.7 kg m at 3,100 rpm; max engine rpm: 5,400; 42.8 hp/l; 5 crankshaft bearings; camshafts: 1, at centre of Vee; lubrication: 8.5 imp pt, 10.1 US pt, 4.8 l; 1 Rochester 4MV downdraught 4-barrel carburettor; cooling system: 20 imp pt, 23.9 US pt, 11.3 l.

TRANSMISSION gearbox: Turbo-Hydramatic automatic transmission; ratios: I 2.480, II 1.480, III 1, rev 2.080; lever: central; axle ratio: 3.360; width of rims: 6''; tyres: De Ville E78S x 14 - Caprice FR78S x 14.

PERFORMANCE max speed: about 115 mph, 185 km/h; power-weight ratio: De Ville 15.7 lb/hp, 7.1 kg/hp - Caprice 16.8 lb/hp, 7.6 kg/hp.

STEERING servo; turns lock to lock: 3.07.

BRAKES servo.

ELECTRICAL EQUIPMENT 55 A alternator; Bosch distributor.

DIMENSIONS AND WEIGHT length: De Ville 203.10 in, 516 cm - Caprice 904.10 in, 518 cm; width: 74.30 in, 189 cm; height: De Ville 54.60 in, 139 cm - Caprice 54.80 in, 139 cm; weight: De Ville 3,406 lb, 1,545 kg - Caprice 3,635 lb, 1,649 kg.

OPTIONAL ACCESSORIES 4-speed fully synchronized mechanical gearbox (I 2.540, II 1.830, III 1.380, IV 1, rev 2.540).

HOLDEN HZ GTS 4-door Sedan

Car manufacturers
and coachbuilders

An outline of their history, structure and activities

CAR MANUFACTURERS

A.C. CARS Ltd — Great Britain

Founded in 1900 by Portwine & Weller, assumed title Auto-carriers (A.C.) Ltd in 1907, moved from London to Thames Ditton in 1911. Present title since 1930. Chairman: W.D. Hurlock. Managing Director: A.D. Turner. Works Director: R. Alsop. Secretary/Financial Director: A. Wilson. Head office press office and works: The High Street, Thames Ditton, Surrey. 170 employees. Models: ACE Bristol 2 l Le Mans (1959); ACE Cobra Le Mans (1963). Entries and wins in numerous competitions (Monte Carlo Rally, Le Mans, etc.).

ADAM OPEL AG — Germany (Federal Republic)

Founded in 1862. Owned by General Motors Corp. USA since 1929. Chairman: J.F. Waters jr. Members of the board: W. Schlotfeldt, G.W. Roberts, K. Kartzke, F. Beickler, E. Rohde, F. Schwenger, J.E. Rhame, J.M. Fleming. Head office and press office: 6090 Rüsselsheim/Main. Works: Bochum, Kaiserslautern, Rüsselsheim. 58,421 employees. 921,696 cars produced in 1976. Car production begun in 1898. Most important models: 10/18 (1908); 4/8 (1909); 6/16 (1910); 8/25 (1920); 4/12 (1924); 4/14 (1925-29); Olympia (1936); Super Six, Admiral (1938); Kapitän (1939); Rekord (1961); Kadett (1962); Admiral, Diplomat, Commodore (1968); GT (1969); Ascona, Manta (1970).

ASSEMBLY IN OTHER COUNTRIES — **Belgium:** GM Continental S.A. (associated company), Noorderlaan 75, Antwerp (assem. Kadett, Rekord, Commodore, Ascona, Manta). **Korea:** V.P. GM Overseas Corp. (concessionaire), Shinjn Motor Co. Ltd., 62-10, 2-ka Choong Moo Ro, Coong-ku, Seoul (assem. Rekord). **Malaysia:** Capital Motor Assembly Corp. Sdn, P.O.B. 204, Yohore Bahru (assem. Kadett, Rekord). **Morocco:** Société Marocaine de Mécanique Industrielle et Automobile, Blod Moulay Ismael 22, Casablanca (assem. Rekord). **Portugal:** GM de Portugal Ltda (associated company), Rua Particular n. 1 de Rafinaria Colonial 26, Lisbon (assem. Kadett, Rekord). **South Africa:** GM South Africa Pty Ltd (associated company), Kempston Rd, Port Elizabeth (assem. Ascona, Rekord). **Thailand:** GM Thailand Ltd, Catlay Trust Bldg, 4th Fl. 1016 Rama IV Rd, Bangkok (assem. Rekord). **Uruguay:** GM Uruguaya S.A. (associated company), C.C. 234, Montevideo (assem. Kadett, Rekord). **Zaire:** GM Zaire (associated company), Boulevard Patrice Lumumba, Masina 1, Kinshasa (assem. Kadett, Commodore). 315,123 cars produced outside Federal Republic in 1976.

ALFA ROMEO S.p.A. — Italy

Founded in 1910 as Anonima Lombarda Fabbrica Automobili, became Accomandita Semplice Ing. Nicola Romeo in 1915, Società Anonima Italiana Ing. Nicola Romeo & C. in 1918, S.A. Alfa Romeo in 1930. Became part of IRI group in 1933 and assumed name of S.A. Alfa Romeo Milano-Napoli in 1939. Present title since 1946. For volume of production it holds second place in Italian motor industry. President: G. Cortesi. Vice-Presidents: E. Peracchi, F. Viezzoli. General Manager: V. Moro. Head office and press office: Arese (Milan), Works: Arese (Milan), Pomigliano d'Arco (Naples). 44,000 employees. 201,200 vehicles produced in 1976 at home and abroad. Most important models: 24 hp (1910); 40-60 hp (1913); RL Targa Florio (1923); P2 (1924); 6C-1500 (1926); 6C-1750 (1929); 8C-2300 (1930); P3 (1932); 8C-2600 (1933); 8C-2900 (1935); 158 (1938); 6C-2500 SS (1939); 2500 Freccia d'Oro (1947); 1900 (1950); Giulietta Sprint (1954); Giulietta Berlina (1955); Giulietta Spider (1956); Giulietta TI (1957); 2000 (1958); Giulia TI, Giulia Sprint, Giulia Spider, 2600 (1962); Giulia SprInT, Giulia TZ (1963); Giulia 1300, Giulia Spider Veloce (1964); Giulia 1300 TI, Giulia Super, GTA (1965); Junior (1966); 1750, 1300 Spider Junior, GTA 1300 Junior, "33" Coupé (1968); Giulia 1600 S, 1300 Junior Z (1969); Giulia 1300 Super, Montreal (1970); 2000 Berlina, 2000 GT Veloce, 2000 Spider Veloce (1971); Alfasud (1972); Alfetta (1973), Giulietta (1977). Entries and wins in numerous competitions. European Mountain Championship and European Touring Challenge Cup in 1967, in 1968 the 33/2 I was classified first at Daytona, in Targa Florio and Nürburgring 1000 km. In 1969 Alfa Romeo won European Touring Challenge Cup, National Championship for Makes in Brazil, three American National Drivers Championships and numerous national championships. In 1970, first place in European Championship for Touring Cars and many national championships. In 1971, in Makers' International Championship, a 33-3 was placed outright first in Brands Hatch 1000 km, in Targa Florio and Watkins Glen 6 Hour. It won European Touring Car Makers' Championship, coming first and second in final classification. In 1971 it also won a series of international championships, including Austrian Mountain Championship and Belgian Touring Drivers' Championship, Dutch Touring Championship for Touring Cars up to 1300 cc, Italian Absolute Championship for Special Touring Cars, American National Championship for SCCA Drivers, class C Sedan and Class C Sports Racing, and finally Venezuelan National Championship outright. In 1973 2000 GTV won Coupe du Roi and in 1974 2000 GTV won Coupe du Roi and 33 TT 12 finished 1, 2 and 3 in Monza 1000 km. 1975 holders of World Championship for Makes and 1977 of World Sports Car Championship.

MANUFACTURE AND ASSEMBLY IN OTHER COUNTRIES — **Indonesia:** P.T. Caryasatrya Ltd (concessionaire), Jalon P. Arena Pekan Raya J kt., Djacarta - P.O. Box 2126, Djacarta (assem. Giulia Super, Alfetta, Alfasud). **Malaysia:** City Motors SDN BHD (concessionaire), Foo yet Kai Building 270 Hugh how Street, Ipoh Perak (assem. Giulia Super, Alfasud, 2000 Berlina); Swedish Motor Assemblies (concessionaire), Kuala Lumpur (assem. Alfasud, Alfetta). **Portugal:** Mocar Ltda (concessionaire), rua Tenente Espeana 31-I, Lisbon (assem. GT Junior, 2000 Berlina, 2000 GTV). **South Africa:** Alfa Romeo Sudafrica (Pty) Ltd (associated company), P.O.B. 78438, Johannesburg (manuf. Giulia Super, Alfetta, GT Junior, 2000 Berlina, Alfetta GT, 2000 GT, 2000 Spider Veloce, Alfasud). **Thailand:** Bangkok International Motors Ltd (concessionaire), 647/2 Sukhumvit Rd., Bangkok (assem. Giulia Super, 2000 Berlina, Alfasud).

ALPINE - see AUTOMOBILES ALPINE S.A.

AMERICAN MOTORS CORPORATION — USA

(Makes: Gremlin, Pacer, Concord, Matador, Jeep vehicles)

Established in 1954 as result of merger between Nash-Kelvinator Corp. and Hudson Motor Car Co.; acquired Jeep Corp., Feb. 1970. Chairman: R.D. Chapin Jr. President and Chief Executive Officer: G.C. Meyers. Central office and press office: American Center Building, P.O. Box 442, Southfield, Mich. 48034. Technical center: 14250 Plymouth Rd., Detroit, Mich. 48232. Passenger car works: 5626, 25th Ave. Kenosha, Wisc. 53140; 3880 N. Richards, Milwaukee, Wisc. 53201. Jeep plant: Toledo, Ohio. Plastics operations: Windsor Plastics, Inc., 601 N. Congress Ave, Evansville, Ind., 47711; Mercury Plastics Co., Inc., 34501 Harper, Mt Clemens, Mich. 48043; Evart Products Co., Evart, Mich. 49631 (subsidiaries-injection moulding); AM General Corp., 32500 Van Born Rd., Wayne, Mich. 48184 (subsidiary). Works: 701 W. Chippewa Ave, South Bend, Ind., 46623; 13200 E. McKinley Hwy, Mishawaka, Ind., 46544; 1428 West Henry St, Indianapolis, Ind. 46221 (military trucks, post-office delivery trucks and transit buses). 29,100 employees. 213,606 cars and 126,742 Jeep vehicles produced in 1976.

MANUFACTURE AND ASSEMBLY IN OTHER COUNTRIES — **Argentina:** Ika-Renault S.A., Sarmiento 1230, Buenos Aires (assem. Classic, Torino, Jeep CJ-5 and trucks). **Australia:** Australian Motor Industries Ltd (associated company), G.P.O.B. 2006S, 155 Bertie St, Port Melbourne (Matador). **Canada:** American Motors (Canada) Ltd (subsidiary), Brampton, Ont. (Concord, Gremlin). **Costa Rica:** Motorizada de Costa Rica S.A., San José (assem. Jeep CJ-5, Wagoneer). **India:** Mahindra & Mahindra Ltd, Gateway Bldg, Apollo Bunder, Bombay (assem. Jeep CJ-4 and Wagoneer). **Indonesia:** N.V. Indonesian Service Co. Ltd, P.O.B. 121, Djakarta-Kota (assem. Jeep CJ-5). **Iran:** Sherkate Sahami Jeep, Ekbatan Ave, Jeep Bldg, Teheran (assem. Arya, Shahin, Jeep CJ-5 and Wagoneer). **Israel:** Matmar Industries Ltd. P.O.B. 1007, Haifa (assem. Jeep CJ-5). **Japan:** Mitsubishi Heavy-Industries Ltd, No. 10, 2-chome, Marunouchi, Chiyoda-ku, Tokyo (manuf. Jeep CJ-5). **Korea:** Shinjin Jeep Co., 62-7 Ika Choong Mu-Ro Choong Ku, Seoul (assem. Jeep CJ-5). **Mexico:** Vehiculos Automotores Mexicanos S.A., Poniente 150, num. 837, Industrial Vallejo, Mexico City 16, D.F. (assem. American, Pacer, Jeep CJ-5 and Wagoneer). **Morocco:** Société d'Importation & Distribution Automobile, 84 av. Lalla Yacoute, Casablanca (assem. Jeep CJ-5). **Pakistan:** Naya Daur Motors Ltd., State Life Building, Dr. Ziauddin Ahmed Rd, Karachi 3 (assem. Jeep trucks, Jeep station wagons and CJ-5). **Philippines:** Jeep Philippines, Guevent Bldg, 49 Libertad St., Mandaluyong, Rizal (assem. Jeep CJ-5, CJ-6). **South Africa:** Jeep South Africa, P.O.B. 80, Uitenhage (assem. Jeep CJ-5, CJ-7). **Spain:** Construcciones y Auxiliar de Ferrocarriles S.A., V.I.A.S.A. Division, Apdo 279, Zaragoza (manuf. Jeep CJ-5). **Taiwan:** Yue Loong Motor Co. Ltd, 150 Nanking East Rd, Sec. II, Taipei (assem. Jeep CJ-5). **Thailand:** Thai Yarnyon Co. Ltd, 388/3 Petchburi Rd, Bangkok (assem. Jeep CJ-5). **Turkey:** Genoto General Otomotive Sanyi, ve Ticaret AS, Takisim la Martin Cad. No. 8/1, Istanbul (assem. CJ-6, trucks). **Venezuela:** Constructora Venezolana de Vehiculos C.A., P.O.B. 61033, Caracas (assem. Hornet); Jeep de Venezuela S.A., Apdo 41-42, Tejerias, Edo Uragua (assem. Jeep CJ-5 and Wagoneer). 28,529 passengers cars and 2,642 Jeep vehicles produced outside USA in 1976.

ANTHONY STEVENS AUTOMOBILES Ltd. — Great Britain

Directors: S. Stevens, G. McBride. Head office and works: 7 Old Square, Warwick.

ANTIQUE & CLASSIC AUTOMOTIVE Inc. — USA

Established in 1973 as Antique & Classic Cars, Inc. Present title since 1977. Chairman: S.J. Wilson, President: K.L. Malick. Directors: R. Paulus, Nancy Wilson, S. Wilson. Head office: 100 Sonwil Industrial Park, Buffalo, N.Y. 14225. Press office and works: 8000 Rein Rd, Buffalo, N.Y. 14225. 15 employees. 1200 cars produced.

● *The information given in these descriptions refers specifically to cars and therefore does not cover the activities in which any of the car manufacturers are engaged in other fields of industry.*

ARGYLL TURBO CARS Ltd **Great Britain**

Founded in 1977. Directors: R.M. Henderson, A. Smith, H. Crow, J. Hughes. Head office and works: Minnow House, Lochgilphead, Argyll, Scotland.

ARKLEY - see JOHN BRITTEN GARAGES Ltd.

ARO DACIA **Rumania**
INTREPRINDEREA MECANICA MUSCEL

Head office, press office and works: Str. Vasile Roaità 173. Cimpulung Jud. Arges. 53,600 cars produced in 1974.

ASTON MARTIN LAGONDA (1975) Ltd **Great Britain**

Founded in 1913 as Bamford & Martin is one of greatest names in the world of touring and competition cars. The name "Aston Martin" was evolved between the wars as a result of many successes at Aston Clinton Hill Climb. The title Aston Martin Lagonda Ltd has been used since 1947 when it was taken over by D. Brown. Went into voluntary liquidation in January 1975. Since 27-6-1975 owned by a consortium headed by P. Sprague and G. Minden. Directors: P. Sprague (USA), G. Minden (Canada), A.G. Curtis, D.G. Flather (U.K.). Works: Tickford St. Newport Pagnell, Bucks MK16 Pan. 350 employees. 232 cars produced in 1976. Most important models: Lionel Martin series (1921-25); first 1.5 l series (1927-32); second 1.5 l series (1932-34); third 1.5 l series (1934-36); 2 l series with single overhead camshaft (1936-40); 2 l DB1 series (1948-50); 2.6 l DB2 series (1950-1953); 2.6 and 2.9 l DB3 series (1952-53); 2.6 and 2.9 l DB2/4 series (1953-55); 2.9 l DB3S series (1955-56); 2.9 l DB2/4 Mk II series (1955-57); 2.6 l, 2.9 l Lagonda Saloon, Convertible (1949-1956); 2.9 l DB Mk III series (1957-59); 3.7 l DB4 series (1959-63); 3.7 l DB4 GT series (1959-63); 4 l Lagonda Rapide (1961-63); 4 l DB5 series (1963-65); 4 l DB6 Saloon and Volante Convertible (1965-69); DB6 Mk 2 Saloon with electronic fuel injection or carburettor induction (1969-70); DBS 4 l Saloon (1967); DBS V8 Saloon 5.35 l 4 O.H.C. fuel injection engine (1969); V8 (1973); Lagonda 4-door (1974). Entries in numerous competitions (Le Mans, Spa, Tourist Trophy, Nürburgring, Aintree). Won Le Mans and World Sports Car Championship in 1959.

AUBURN-CORD-DUESENBERG Co. **USA**

President: G.A. Pray. Head office, press office and works: 122 South Elm Place, Broken Arrow, Oklahoma 74012.

AUDI NSU AUTO UNION AG **Germany (Federal Republic)**

Established in 1969 as result of merger between Auto Union GmbH (founded in Zwickau in 1932 and transferred to Ingolstadt in 1948 when Zwickau company was nationalized) and NSU Motorenwerke AG (founded in 1873 at Riedlingen, moved to Neckarsulm in 1880; changed its name to Neckarsulmer Fahrzeugwerke AG in 1919 and became NSU Motorenwerke AG in 1960). Board of Directors: G.M. Strobl, WR. Habbel, F. Piëch, H. Kialka, W. Neuwald. Head office and press office: Postfach 220, D-8070 Ingolstadt. Works: as above, Necharsulm. 25,363 employees. 246,175 cars produced in 1976. Most important models: NSU Ro 80 (1967); Audi 100 and 100 LS (1969); Audi 100 Coupé S (1970); Audi 100 GL (1971); Audi 80, 80 L, 80 S, 80 LS, 80 GL (1972).

ASSEMBLY IN OTHER COUNTRIES — **South Africa:** VW of South Africa Ltd (associated company), P.O.B. 80, Uitenhage (assem. Audi 100 range). 116.249 cars produced outside Federal Republic in 1976.

AUSTIN - see BRITISH LEYLAND Ltd

AUTOBIANCHI **Italy**

Created in 1955 in collaboration between Edoardo Bianchi firm and Fiat and Pirelli. Incorporated into Fiat in 1968 as Autobianchi Company, retaining, however, own maker's marks, sales organisation and maintenance services. Office: Lancia, v. V. Lancia 27, 10141 Turin. About 4,000 employees. 88,653 cars produced in 1976. For further information see Lancia S.p.A.

AUTOMOBILES ALPINE S.A. **France**

Founded in 1955. President: J. Rédélé. Head office and press office: 3 bd. Foch, Epinay s/Seine. Works: 40 av. Pasteur, Dieppe. 563 employees. 1,047 cars produced in 1976. Most important models: Mille Miles (1955); Coupé Sport and Sport Convertible (1959-60); Berlinette Tour de France (1961); A110 956 and 1108 cc series (1962); M. 63 (1963); M. 64 and F2 (1964); A 310 (1971). Entries and wins in numerous competitions (rallies, Le Mans, Montecarlo, etc.).

MANUFACTURE IN OTHER COUNTRIES — **Brazil:** Willys Overland do Brasil (associated company), São Paulo (manuf. Interlagos). **Bulgaria:** Bullet (associated company), Sofia. **Mexico:** Diesel Nacional (associated company), Mexico City. **Spain:** Fasa (associated company), Vallaloid.

AUTOMOBILES MONTEVERDI Ltd **Switzerland**

Founded in 1967. Chairman and Managing Director: P. Monteverdi. Vice-Chairman: R. Jenzer. General Manager: P. Berger. Head office, press office and works: Oberwilerstr. 14-20, 4102 Binningen/Basel. 170 employees. 1300 cars produced in 1976. Most important models: 2-seater (1968); High Speed 375 L 2+2 (1969); Hal 450 SS (1970); High Speed 375/4 Limousine (1971); Berlinetta (1972); Hai 450 GTS (1973); Palm Beach (1975).

AUTOMOBILES PEUGEOT S.A. **France**

Founded in 1890 as Les Fils Peugeot Fres. Present title since 1966. In December 1974 acquired 38.2% of Citroën stock and in May 1976 take over full control of Citroën. Directorate: J. Boilot, J. Baratte, X. Karcher. F. Perrin-Pelletier. Head office and press office: 75 av. de la Grande-Armée, Paris. Works: Dijon, Lille, Montbéliard, Mulhouse, Sochaux, St. Etienne, Vesoul. About 70,000 employees. About 760,000 cars produced in 1976. Most important models: Bebé Peugeot (1911); 201, 301, 302, 402, 203 (1929-60); 403 (1955); 404 (1960); 204 (1965); 504 (1968); 304 (1969); 604 (1975). First place in ACF (1912-13, 1923-24).

MANUFACTURE AND ASSEMBLY IN OTHER COUNTRIES — **Argentina:** Safrar (subsidiary), Buenos Aires (manuf. 404, 504). **Chile:** Automotores San Cristobal S.A.I.C., Santiago (assem. 404). **Madagascar:** Somacoa, Tananarive (assem. 304, 404). **Malaysia:** Asia Automobiles Industries, Petaling-Jaya (assem. 204, 504). **Nigeria:** Scoa, Lagos (assem. 404). **Paraguay:** Automotores y Maquinaria, C.C. 1160, Asuncion (assem. 404, 504). **Portugal:** Movauto, Setubal (assem. 204, 304, 404, 504). **South Africa:** National Motors Assemblies (subsidiary), Johannesburg (assem. 404, 504). **Uruguay:** S.A.D.A.R., Montevideo (assem. 404).

AUTOMOBILI FERRUCCIO LAMBORGHINI S.p.A. **Italy**

Founded in 1962 as Automobili Ferruccio Lamborghini Sas. Present title since 1965. President and General Manager: R. Leimer. Head office, press office and works: v. Modena 1b, 40019 S. Agata Bolognese (Bologna). 240 employees. 213 cars produced in 1976. Models: 350 GT (1963); 400 GT (1966); Miura (1967); Espada, Islero (1968); Jarama (1970); Urraco (1971); Countach (1974).

AUTOMOBILI INTERMECCANICA **USA**

President: F. Reisner. Vice President and General Manager: A.E.T. Baumgartner. Head office, press office and works: 2421 S. Susan St, Santa Ana, California.

AVANTI MOTOR CORPORATION **USA**

Founded in 1965. President: A.D. Altman. Vice-Presidents: F. Bear, E. Harding. Secretary and Tresurer: F. Bear, L. Newman. Head office and works: 765 S. Lafayette Blvd, South Bend, Ind. 46634. 100 employees. 175 cars produced in 1976.

AZLK - AVTOMOBILNY ZAVOD IMENI LENINSKOGO KOMSOMOLA **USSR**

Press office: Avtoexport, Ul. Volkhonka 14, Moscow G. 19. Works: Moscow, Izhevsk. 27,000 employees. About 390,000 cars produced in 1976.

BASIL GREEN MOTORS (Tvl) (Pty) Ltd **South Africa**

(Make: Perana-Ford)

Founded in 1967. Chairmen and Managing Directors: B. Green, R. Rosen. Head office, press office and works: 48 Plantation Rd, Eastleigh, Edenvale, Johannesburg. 38 employees. 350 cars produced in 1975. Models: Cortina Mk II V6 Perana (1967-70); Escort Perana 2000, Capri V8 Perana (1971-72); Granada V8 Perana (1973).

BAYERISCHE MOTOREN WERKE AG **Germany (Federal Republic)**

Established in 1916 as Bayerische Flugzeugwerke AG. Present title since 1918. Chairman: E. von Kuenheim. Members of the board: H. Koch, H. Schäfer, K. Radermacher, H.E. Schönbeck, E. Sarfert. Head office and press office: P.O.B. 400240 8 Munich 40. Works: Munich, Berlin, Landshut, Dingolfing. 30,192 employees. 275,022 cars produced in 1975. Most important models: 3/15 hp Saloon (1928); 326, 327, 328 (1936); 501 6 cyl. (1951); V8 (1954); 503 and 507 Sport (1955); 700 (1959); 1500 (1962); 1800 (1963); 2000 (1966); 2002, 2500, 2800 (1968); 3,0, CS (1971; 520, 520 i (1972). Entries and wins in numerous competitions (Mille Miglia, Monza 12 hour, Hockenheim, Nürburgring, Friburg Mountain Record, Brands Hatch, European Mountain Championship, Salzburgring, Rally TAP; winner 1968, 1969 and 1973 European Cup for Touring Cars, Francorchamps 24 hour, Formula 2).

ASSEMBLY IN OTHER COUNTRIES — **South Africa:** BMW (South Africa) (Pty) Ltd, 6 Frans de Toit St, Rosslyn, Pretoria (assem. 520, 528). 6,500 cars assembled outside Federal Republic in 1976.

BENTLEY MOTORS Ltd **Great Britain**

A wholly owned subsidiary of Rolls-Royce Motors Ltd, specializing in high-class vehicles. Head office: Pym's Lane, Crewe, Ches. Press office: 14-15 Conduit St., London W1. Works: Pym's Lane, Crewe, Ches, 99 cars produced in 1975. Most important models: first Bentley 3.5 l manufactured by Rolls-Royce (1933); 4-5 l MK VI (1946); Continental (1951); "R" Type (1952); S1 (1955); S2 (1959); S3 (1962); "T" series (1965); Corniche (1971).

BRADLEY - AUTOMOTIVE DIVISION THOR CORP. **USA**

Founded in 1971. President: G. Bradley. Vice-President R. & D: D. Fuller. Director of Marketing: J.E. Meegan. Head office, 495 Shehard Plaza, Minneapolis, Minn. 55426. 110 employees. Over 2.600 cars in kit form produced in 1976.

BRISTOL CARS Partnership **Great Britain**

Established in 1946 as Car Division of Bristol Aeroplane Co., became affiliated company of Bristol Aeroplane Co. in 1955, and subsidiary of Bristol Siddeley Engines in 1959. Became privately owned company in 1960 and owned by partnership from 1966. Partners: T.A.D. Crook, F.S. Derham. Head office, press office and works: Filton, Bristol. Most important models: 400 (1947); 401 and 402 (1949); 403 and 404 (1953-55); 405 (1954-58); 406 (1958); 407 (1961); 408 (1963); 409 (1965); 410 (1967); 411 (1969); 412 (1975); 603 (1976). Entries and first places in numerous competitions with Bristol cars or Bristol-engined cars (Monte Carlo Rally, Targa Florio, Mille Miglia) with F1 and F2 (British GP, GP of Europe, Sebring, Reims, Montlhéry, Le Mans, etc.), from 1946 until 1955.

BRITISH LEYLAND Ltd **Great Britain**

(Makes: Austin, Daimler, Jaguar, MG, Mini, Morris, Princess, Rover, Triumph, Vanden Plas).

British Leyland, 95% of whose shares are now held by British Government, is Britain's largest producer of motor vehicles. Formed in May 1968, following merger between British Motor Holdings (BMC and Jaguar) and Leyland Motor Corporation (Leyland Motors, Rover and Triumph), it employs 181,000 throughout the world and current annual sales exceed £ 2,892 million. Head office British Leyland 174 Marylebone Rd, London NW1 5AA. Hon. President: Lord Stokes. Chairman: M. Edwardes. Deputy chairman: J. MacGregor. The new Company is divided into four Groups: Leyland Cars, Leyland Truck and Bus, Leyland Special Products and Leyland International. 180,000 employees. In 1976. 981,000 passenger cars were produced, and a total of 769,354 vehicles at home and abroad.

MANUFACTURE AND ASSEMBLY IN OTHER COUNTRIES — The Company sells its vehicles in 175 countries. The major manufacturing and assembly plants are at Seneffe in Belgium (cars), Madras in India (commercial vehicles), Sydney in Australia (mainly commercial vehicles but also Minis and Mini-Mokes), and Cape-Town and Durban in South Africa (cars and commercial vehicles). There are many smaller factories in other parts of the world, including Turkey, Zaire, Zambia, Malaysia, New Zealand and Hong Kong. For specific details apply to Leyland International, 174 Marylebone Rd, London NW1 5AA.

BUICK - see GENERAL MOTORS CORPORATION

CADILLAC - see GENERAL MOTORS CORPORATION

CATERHAM CAR Sales Ltd **Great Britain**

(Make: Seven)

In 1973 took over manufacture of Lotus Seven Series III introduced by Lotus Cars Ltd in 1957. Managing Director:

G.B. Nearn. Director: D.S. Wakefield. Head office, press office and works: 36/40 Town End, Caterham Hill, Surrey GR3 5UG. 18 employees. 159 cars produced in 1976. Models: Super Seven Series III powered by Lotus big valve twin cam engine.

CHECKER MOTORS CORPORATION USA

Founded in 1922. Chairman and President: D. Markin. Executive Vice-President: R.E. Oakland. Head office, press office and works: 2016 N. Pitcher St, Kalamazoo, Mich. 49007. 1,000 employees. 4,800 cars produced in 1976.

CHEVROLET - see GENERAL MOTORS CORPORATION GENERAL MOTORS OF CANADA Ltd and GENERAL MOTORS SOUTH AFRICA (Pty) Ltd

CHRYSLER AUSTRALIA Ltd Australia

Founded in 1951. Affiliated with Chrysler Corporation USA. Chairman: T.D. Anderson. Directors: I. Webber, R. Smith, W. Bivens, D.B. Coleman, J.M. Hill, J.W. Wiley. Head office, press office and works: South Rd, Clovelly Park, South Australia. 6,250 employees. 54,000 cars produced in 1976.

CHRYSLER CORPORATION USA

(Makes: Chrysler, Dodge, Plymouth)

Founded in 1925 as successor to Maxwell Motors Corp. It holds third place in world's motor industry. Chrysler Corp. American operations are made up of a U.S. Automotive Sales Division selling Chrysler, Dodge, Plymouth cars and trucks. Chairman: J.J. Riccardo. President: E.A. Cafiero. Vice President South America, Far East and Asia: E.H. Doyle. Executive Vice President Europe: D.H. Lander. Head office and press office Chrysler Corp.: 1200 Lynn Townsend Dr., Mich. 48288. Mailing address: Chrysler Corp., P.O. Box 1919, Detroit, Mich. 48231. Works: eight vehicle assembly plants and 35 supporting manufacturing plants throughout the U.S. Over 262,700 employees. 2,595,214 cars produced in 1976. Most important models: Chrysler (1924); Plymouth and Dodge (1928). In 1958 Chrysler Corp. acquired 25% of Chrysler France shares; in 1963 it increased its holding to 64%, in 1965 to 69%, in 1966 to 77% of Chrysler United Kingdom Ltd shares, in 1971 85% of voting shares. Chrysler acquired 88.4% total equity and 93.7% voting equity in Chrysler United Kingdom Ltd in 1972. At present Chrysler holds 100% of all Chrysler United Kingdom shares and 99.3% of Chrysler France. In 1969, acquired 86% of Chrysler España S.A. shares and in 1972 97.5%.

MANUFACTURE AND ASSEMBLY IN OTHER COUNTRIES — **Australia:** Chrysler Australia Ltd (subsidiary), South Rd, Clovelly Park, South Australia (manuf. Valiant, Charger, Ranger, Galant). **Colombia:** Chrysler Colmotores (subsidiary), Apdo Aéreo 7329, Bogotà (assem. Simca, Dodge, Dodge Dart, Dart). **Peru:** Chrysler Peru S.A. (subsidiary), Apdo 5037, Lima (assem. Dodge Coronet, Hillman Minx De Luxe). South Africa: Sigma Motor Corp. Ltd (associated company), P.O.B. 411, Pretoria (manuf. Valiant, Hillman, Chrysler, Colt Fastback). **Spain:** Chrysler España S.A. (subsidiary), Apdo 140 Villaverde, Madrid 21 (manuf. Dodge, Simca). **Venezuela:** Chrysler de Venezuela S.A. (subsidiary), Apdo 62362, Caracas 106 (assem. Dodge Dart, Hillman Coronet). 1,067,331 cars produced outside USA and Canada in 1976.

CHRYSLER CORPORATION DO BRASIL Brazil

(Make: Dodge)

Founded in 1967 as Chrysler do Brasil S.A. Ind. e Comércio, it began producing Dodge trucks and Dodge Dart in May 1969. In 1971 it became Chrysler Corporation do Brasil and started production of Dodge 1800 in November 1972. Managing Director: D.W. Dancey. Head office, press office and works: Av. Dr. José Fornari 715, B. Ferrazopolis, São Bernardo do Campo, São Paulo 3.762 employees. 17,380 cars produced in 1976. At present it produces Dodge trucks and Dodge, Polara, Dart and Charger models.

CHRYSLER ESPANA S.A. Spain

(Makes: Dodge, Simca)

General Manager: W.J. Storen. Head office, press office and works: Apdo 140, Villaverde, Madrid 21.

CHRYSLER FEVRE ARGENTINA S.A.I.C. Argentina

(Make: Dodge)

Founded in 1959 as Fevre y Basset Ltda. Present title since 1965. Chairman: J. Watson. Head office and press office: Florencio Varela 1903, San Justo, Buenos Aires. Works: as above; Charcas 4200, Monte Chingolo, Lanús, Buenos Aires. 5,000 employees. 13,500 cars produced in 1976. Most important models: Valiant I (1962); Valiant II (1963); Valiant III (1964-65); Valiant IV (1966); Valiant V (1967-68); Dodge Polara, Coronado, GT (1969); Dodge Polara, Coronado, GT, GTX (1970); Polara, Coronado, GTX, Polara Coupé, 1500 (1971-72); Polara, Coronado, GTX, Polara Coupé, 1500, GT90 (1972-73); GTX, Polara, Polara RT, Coronado, 1500, GT90 (1974); Polara, Coronado, Polara RT, GTX, 1500, 1500 1.8 engine, 1500 Automatic (1975); Polara, Coronado, Polara RT, GTX, 1500, 1500 Automatic, 1500 1.8 engine (1977).

CHRYSLER FRANCE France

(Makes: Chrysler, Simca)

Founded in 1934 as Sté Industrielle de Mécanique et de Carrosserie Automobile. Assumed title Société Simca Automobiles in 1960. In 1971 controlling interest passed to Chrysler Motors Corp. Present title since 1970. President and General Manager: J.W. Day. Vice-President: J. Forgeot. Joint General Manager: G. Roy. Members of the board: L.B. Warren, P. Grezel, P.A. Heinen, D.H. Lander, F.M. Rogers, G.H. Gillespie, G. Héreil, G.A. Hunt, F. Monahan, J. Terray. Head office and press office: 136 av. des Champs Elysées, 75008, Paris. Works: Poissy; La Rochelle-Perigny; Sully-sur-Loire; Sept Fons; Vieux Condé; Bondy; Valenciennes. 38,226 employees. 579,942 cars produced in 1976. Most important models: Simca 5 (1936); Simca 8-1100 (1938); Simca 6, 8-1100 (1948); Simca 8-1200, 8 Sport (1949); 9 Aronde (1951); Aronde, Coupé de Ville (1953); Aronde Week-End, Vedette (1955); Aronde 1300, Ocean, Plein Ciel (1956); Ariane 4 (1957); Aronde Montlhéry, Ariane 8, Vedette (1958); Aronde 6, 7, P.60 (1959); Aronde Etoile 6 and 7, P.60, Ocean, Plein Ciel (1960); Ariane (1961); Aronde Montlhéry and Monaco Spéciale, Simca 1000 (1962); Simca 900, 1300, 1500 (1963); Simca 1000 and 1500 A (1966); Simca 1301, 1501, 1200 S (1967); Simca 1100 (1968); Simca 4 CV, 1000 Special, 1100 5 CV, 1501 Special (1969); Simca 1301 Special, 1000 Rallye (1970); Chrysler 160, 160 GT, 180, Simca 1100 Special (1971); Simca 1000, 1000 Rallye 1 (1972); Simca 1000 Rallye 2, 1100 VF2, Chrysler 2 litres (1973); Simca 1100 S, 1501 S, 1100 TI, 1100 LX (1974); Simca 1100 GLX, 1000 SR, 1307 GLS, 1307 S, 1308 GT (1975), Simca 1000 Extra, 100 SLS, 1005 GLS, 1100 AS (1976).

CHRYSLER UNITED KINGDOM Ltd Great Britain

(Make: Chrysler, Hillman, Sunbeam)

Founded in 1917 as Rootes Motors Ltd. In 1967 became a member of Chrysler Group. Present title since 1970. Chairman: G.A. Hunt. Managing Director: G.A. Lacy. Directors: G. Héreil, C.A. Parsons, Sir Eric Roll, L.B. Warren, G. Gillespie, P. Griffiths, G. Kennedy, C.C. Birch, T.J. Daly, D.H. Lander, R. Grantham, Head office and press office: Bowater House, 68 Knightsbridge, London SW1 7LH. Works: Chrysler Scotland Ltd, Linwood, nr. Paisley, Renfrewshire, Scotland; Ryton on Dunsmore, Stoke, nr. Coventry, Warwick.; Dunstable, Luton, Beds. 21,900 employees. 153,515 cars produced in 1976.

MANUFACTURE AND ASSEMBLY IN OTHER COUNTRIES — **Colombia:** Chrysler Colmotores S.A. (subsidiary). Apdo Aereo 7329, Bogotà I (assem. Avenger, Estate). **Eire:** Chrysler Ireland Ltd (subsidiary), Shanowen Rd, Whitehall, Dublin 9 (assem. Hunter). **Indonesia:** N.V. Jakarta Motor C. (Concessionaire), DJL Tijkini Raya 58, Tromol Pos 251, Djakarta (assem. Avenger). **Iran:** I.N.I.M., P.O.B. 14/1637 km 18, Industrial Manufacturing Co. Ltd (associated company), Karadj Rd, Teheran (manuf. and assem. Hunter, Paykan, Avenger). **Malaysia:** Associated Motor Industries (concessionaire), P.O.B. 763, Kuala Lumpur (assem. Avenger). **Malta:** Industrial Motor Co. Ltd (concessionaire), National Rd, Blata 1-Bajda (assem. Hunter, Estate). **New Zealand:** Todd Motors Ltd LMVD (concessionaire), P.O.B. 50-349 « Todd Park », Heriot Drive, Porirua (assem. Hunter, Estate, Avenger). **Peru:** Chrysler Perú S.A. (associated company), Apdo 5037, Carretera Pau Norte, km 6.5, Lima (assem. Hunter). **Portugal:** Representateos Automoveis Chrysler Sarl (associated company), Avda de Roma 15B, Apdo 1208, Lisbon I (assem. Avenger). **Thailand:** Han Co (concessionaire), 98 Soi Aree, Sukhumvit 26, Bangkok (assem. Hunter, Avenger). **Trinidad:** H.E. Robinson Co. (concessionaire), B.O.B. 641, 82/84 Queen St, Port of Spain (assem. Hunter, Estate, Avenger). 89,234 cars produced outside U.K. in 1976.

CITROËN S.A. France

Founded in 1919 by André Citroën, became S.A. André Citroën in 1927. Present title since 1968. December 1974 38.2% of stock acquired by Automobiles Peugeot S.A. Since May 1976 Citroën S.A. is owned by the Peugeot S.A. group (to which Automobiles Peugeot S.A. belongs also). The first car launched since the merger of the two firms is the Citroën LM, presented in the summer of 1976. Directorate: G. Taylor, R. Ravenel, Y. Lombard. Head office and press office: 133 quai André Citroën, Paris 15e. Works: as above, Issy-les-Moulineaux, Puteaux, Levallois-Perret, Clichy, Saint-Ouen, Asnières, Aubervilliers, Gennevillieres, Saint-Denis, Nanterre, Rennes-La-Barre-Thomas, Rennes-La-Janais, Strasbourg, Caen, Froncle, Saint-Etienne, Mulhouse, Reims, Metz, Venissieux et Bourg (Berliet). About 53,000 employees. 741,363 cars produced in 1976. Most important models: Torpedo A Type (1919); B2 10 CV (1921); 5 CV (1922); B12 10 CV (1925); B14 (1926); C6 (1928); 7A 7 and 11 CV (1934); 15 Six (1938); 2 CV (1948); 2 CV 425 cc (1954); DS 19 (1955); ID 19 (1957); 2 CV 4 x 4 (1958); Ami 6 3 CV (1961); Ami 6 Break DS Pallas (1964); DS 21 (1965); Dyane (1967); Mehari (1968); Ami 8 (1969); SM and GS (1970); CX (1974); LM (1976). Entries and first places in numerous competitions: World distance and speed record at Montlhéry (1932-33), 28th Monte Carlo Rally and Constructors' Cup (1959), Liège-Sofia-Liège Road Marathon (1961), Norwegian Snow and Ice Winter Rally, Lyon-Charbonnière-Solitude, Alpine Trophy, Thousand Lakes Rally, Constructors' Cup, Trophy of Nations (1962), Finnish Snow Rally, Northern Roads, Lyon-Charbonnière-Solitude, Norwegian Winter Rally, International Alpine Criterium, Constructors' Cup in Monte Carlo Rally and Liège-Sofia-Liège Marathon, Tour of Corsica (1963), Spa-Sofia Liège Marathon (1964), Rallie Neige et Glace, Mobil Economy Run, Coupe des Alpes, Monte Carlo (1966), Contructors' Cup (1967), Neige et Glace, Mobil Economy Run (1968), Morocco Rally (1969, 1970 and 1971).

MANUFACTURE AND ASSEMBLY IN OTHER COUNTRIES — **Argentina:** Citroën Argentine (subsidiary), Zepita 3220, Buenos Aires (assem. 2 CV). **Belgium:** Sté Belge de Automobiles Citroën S.A. (subsidiary), 7 Place de l'Yser, Brussels (assem. 2 CV, Mehari, Dyane). **Chile:** Sociedad Importadora e Industrial J. Lhorente y Cia. Ltda. (subsidiary), Arica Lote 26, Chinthorre (manuf. 2 CV). **Dahomey:** Cotonou (assem. 2 CV, Ami 8). **Iran:** Teheran (assem. Dyane). **Madagascar:** Enterprise de Construction Auto-Malgache (concessionaire), Route de Majunga, Tananarive (assem. 2 CV, Dyane, Ami 8). **Portugal:** Sociedad Citroën Lusitania Sarl (subsidiary), Estrada de Nelas, Beira Alta, Mangualde (Dyane 6, Ami 8, GS, DS). **South Africa:** Stanley Motors Ltd (concessionaire), Natalspruit, Johannesburg (assem. ID 19). **Spain:** Citroën Hispania (subsidiary), free zone of Vigo (manuf. 2 CV, Ami 6, Dyane, Mehari, GS). **Yugoslavia:** Tovarna Motornih Vozil (Tomos) (concessionaire), Koper (manuf. 2 CV, Ami 8, DS).

CONCEPT CARS Ltd Great Britain

Founded in 1974. Chairman and Managing Director: P.W. Timpson, Head office, press office and works: 27 Main St, Middleton, Market Harborough, Leics. 4 employees. 10 cars produced in 1976.

CUSTOCA Austria

Proprietor: G. Höller. Head office and works: 8714 Kraubath/Mur 55.

DACIA - see RÉGIE NATIONALE DES USINES RENAULT

DAIHATSU KOGYO COMPANY Ltd Japan

Established in 1907 as Hatsudoki Seizo Kabushiki Kaisha, assumed title of Daihatsu Kogyo Co. Ltd in 1951. Now consists of Daihatsu Motor Co. Ltd and Daihatsu Motor Sales Co. Ltd, and belongs to Toyota Group. Chairman: M. Yamamoto. President: S. Ohhara. Senior Managing. Directors: T. Eguchi, A. Makino, Y. Tsuboi, J. Ono. Head office and works: 1-1 Daihatsu-cho, Ikeda-shi, Osaka. Press office: Daihatsu Motor Sales Co. Ltd, 2-7 Ninonbashi-Honcho, Chuoku, Tokyo. 8,800 employees. 141,891 vehicles produced in 1976. Production of 4-wheeled vehicles begun in 1958. Most important models: Compagno Station Wagon (1963); Comgno 800 Sedan (1964); Compagno Spider and Sedan (1965); Fellow 360 (1966); Consorte Berlina (1969); Fellow Max (1970); Charmant (1974).

MANUFACTURE IN OTHER COUNTRIES — **Indonesia:** P.T. Astra International Inc., Jl. Ir. H. Jaunda No. 22, Djakarta. **Portugal:** Assistauto Sociedade de Assistencia Tecnica de Automoveis Ltda, Avda. de Igreja, Lote 1278, 1.º-D Lisboa-5. **South Africa:** Leyland South Africa Ltd, P.O. Box 6226, Johannesburg 2000.

DAIMLER - see LEYLAND CARS JAGUAR

DAIMLER-BENZ AG Germany (Federal Republic)

(Make: Mercedes-Benz)

Established in 1926 as a result of merger between Daimler-Motorengesellschaft and Benz & Cie, it is the best-known German manufacturer of highclass cars. Board of Directors: J. Zahn (chairman); G. Prinz, W. Langheck, H. Scherenberg, H. Schmidt, W. Niefer, R. Osswald, H.C. Hoppe, E. Reuter (members). Head office and press office: Mercedes-Strasse 136, 7 Stuttgart. Works: as above, Sindelfingen, Mannheim, Gaggenau, Berlin-Marienfelde, Düsseldorf, Bad Homburg, Wörth/Rhein. 126,652 employees. 378,241 cars produced in 1975. Most important models: Stuttgart 200, Mannheim (1926); Stuttgart 260, Mannheim 350 and Sport-Wagen SSK (1928); Grosser Mercedes (1930); Nürburg 500 (1931); 170 V (1935); 260 D, first Diesel car (1935); Grosser Mercedes (1938); 170 V (1946); 300 SL (1954); 190 SL (1955); 180 b/Db and 220 Sb (1959); 190 c/Dc and 300 Se (1961); 230 SL and 600 (1963); 250 (1966); 200, 220, 230, 250, 280 S, 280 SE, 300 SEL 6.3, 250 C, 250 SE (1968); 280 SE 3.5, 300 SEL 3.5 (1969); 350 SL, 450 SL (1971); 280 SE, 350 SE, 450 SE (1972); 240 D, 230/4 (1973); 240 D 3.0 (1974); 450 SEL 6.9 (1975); 200 D, 280 E(1976); 230 - 280 C, 280 CE (1977); 300 SD, 450 SLC, 240 - 300 TD, 230 - 250 T, 280 TE (1978). First places in numerous international competitions (1894-1955).

ASSEMBLY IN OTHER COUNTRIES — **Malaysia:** The Cycle & Carriage Industries Sdn Bhd (concessionaire), Lot 9, Jalan Pudu 219, Federal Highway, Petaling Jaya. **Philippines:** Universal Motors Corp. (concessionaire), 2232 Pasong Tamo Ave, P.O.B. 3250, Manila, Makati Rizal. **Portugal:** Movauto, Montagem de Vehiculos Automoveis Ltd, Setúbal. **Singapore:** Cycle & Carriage Co. (Industries) Ltd (concessionaire), 164-168 Hill View Ave, P.O.B. 12, Singapore 23.

DAVRIAN Ltd — **Great Britain**

Founded in 1968 to produce Imp-based cars. From body-chassis units to take all Chrysler Imp mechanical parts. It now produces chassis with common suspension to take Imp, Mini, Ford and VW engines. Managing Director: A.R.B. Evans. Head office and works: Glanteify Garage, Pontrhydfendigaid, Ystrad Meurig, Dyfed, Wales. 10 employees. 60 units from bodies to complete cars produced in 1976. Outright winner Modified Sports Championship in 1974.

DE TOMASO MODENA S.p.A. AUTOMOBILI — **Italy**

Founded in 1959. President: A. de Tomaso. General Manager: A. Bertocchi. Head office, press office and works: v. Emilia Ovest 1250, Modena. 60 employees. 1,100 cars produced in 1976. Most important models: OSCA 1500 monocoque, Sport with OSCA 1100 engine, Berlinetta Vallelunga with Ford Cortina 1500 engine (two-seater), Sport Prototype 5 litre (1965); Mangusta with V8 4700 engine (1966); Pantera with V8 5700 engine, 310 hp (1970); Deauville 4-door with 5700 engine (1971); Longchamp 2 + 2 with V8 5700 engine (1973).

DIM MOTOR — **Greece**

Founded in 1977. Head office and works: George E. Dimitriadis & Co., 23 Lekka St., Athens.

DODGE - see CHRYSLER CORPORATION, CHRYSLER CORPORATION DO BRASIL, CHRYSLER ESPANA, CHRYSLER FEVRE ARGENTINA SAIC

Dr. Ing. h.c. F. PORSCHE A.G. — **Germany (Federal Republic)**

Founded in 1948. Owned by Porsche Holding Co. (co-chairmen: F. Porsche, L. Piëch). Managing Directors: E. Fuhrmann, H. Branitzki, L.R. Schmidt, H. Bott, K. Kalkbrenner, H. Kurtz. Head office and press office: Porschestr. 42, 7 Stuttgart-Zuffenhausen. Works: Schwieberdingerstr., 7 Stuttgart-Zuffenhausen. About 4,500 employees. 32,954 cars produced in 1975. Most important models: type 356/1100, 1300, 1300 S, 1500 S (1950-1955); 356 A/1300, 1300 S, 1600, 1600 S, Carrera (1955-1959); 356 B/1600, 1600 S, 1600 S-90, Carrera (1959-1963); 356 C/1600 C, 1600 SC (1963-1965); 911, 912 (1965-1966); 911, 911 S, 912 (1967); 911 T, S, 912 (1968); 911 T, E, S, Carrera (1969-1976). 924, Turbo (1975); 928 (1977). First places in numerous international competitions: Le Mans 24 hour with 1100 Coupé (1951), Sebring (1958-59), European Mountain Championship (1960-68), Targa Florio and Nürburgring (1959-1967-68-69-70-73), Constructors' Cup for F2 cars (1960), European Rally Championship with Carrera (1961). GT World Championship up to 2000 cc (1962-63-64-65), World Cup for speed and endurance European Touring Car Trophy, 32 national championships. Overall wins in Le Mans 24 hours (1970-71-76-77), Rallye Monte Carlo winners (1968-69-70), International Rallye Championship (1968-69-70), International Grand Touring Car Championship and International Manufacturers Championship (1969-70-71-76-77).

DUESENBERG — **USA**

The company started building cars in 1970. After extensive reorganization in 1972-73 under the direction and ownership of E.W. Rose the company started a program of increased production. Head office, press office and works: 604 1/2 Manchester Terrace, Inglewood, Cal. 90301. 25 employees. 25 cars produced in 1976.

DUTTON SPORTS Ltd — **Great Britain**

First Dutton built in 1968. Chairman and Managing Director: T. Dutton-Woolley. Head office, press office and works: Newcroft Tangmere, Sussex. 8 employees. 76 cars produced in 1976. Most important models: B plus (1974); Malaga and Cantera (1975).

ELEGANT MOTORS Inc. — **USA**

Founded in 1971. Owners: D.O. Amy, H. Passwater. Head office, press office and works 829 Broad Ripple Ave, Indianapolis, Ind. 46220. 10 employees.

ELITE ENTERPRISES Inc. — **USA**

Established in 1969. President: G.W. Knapp. Head office, works: 690 E. 3rd St., Cokato, Minn. 55321. Press office: 210 E. 3rd St, Cokato, Minn. 55321.

EL-KG BUGATTIBAU — **Germany (Federal Republic)**

Head office and works: Hanauer Str. 51, 6360 Friedberg (Hessen) 1.

EL-NASR AUTOMOTIVE MANUFACTURING COMPANY — **Egypt**

Founded in 1959. Directors: A. Gazarin, A. Shawky, O. Amin. Head office and works: Wadi-Hof, Helwan. Press office: 1081 Cornish El-Nil St, Cairo. 7,400 employees. 7,500 cars produced in 1974.

ENNEZETA S.d.f. — **Italy**

Proprietors: R. Negri, M. Zanisi. Head office, press office and works: v. Einaudi 1, 20037 Paderno Dugnano, Milan.

EXCALIBUR AUTOMOBILE CORPORATION — **USA**

Founded in 1969 as SS Automobiles Inc. Present title since 1976. President: D.B. Stevens. Executive Vice-President: W.C. Stevens. Head office and works: 1735 South 106th St, Milwaukee, Wisc. 53214. 75 employees. 250 cars produced in 1976. Models: Roadster SS, Phaeton SS.

FABRYKA SAMOCHODÓW MALOLITRAZOWYCH — **Poland**

(Make: Syrena)

Director: R. Podolak. Head office and press office: Ul. Partyzantow 44, Bielsko-Biala. About 40,000 cars produced in 1975.

FABRYKA SAMOCHODÓW OSOBOWYCH — **Poland**

(Make: Polski-Fiat)

Founded in 1949. State-owned Company. Chairman: J. Bielecki. Vice-Presidents: M. Karwas, S. Tyminski, Z. Sokalski, W. Komendarck, J. Burchard, Z. Chorazy, E. Pietrzak. Head office, press office and works: ul. Stalingradzka 50, Warsaw. 22,000 employees. 25,000 employees. About 127,000 cars produced in 1976. Most important models: Warszawa 223 and 224 (1964), Syrena 104 (1958); Polski-Fiat 125 P (1968). Entries in Rallies (Monte Carlo, Acropolis, Jadransky, Semperit, Peace and Friendship, etc.).

FAIRTHORPE Ltd — **Great Britain**

Founded in 1957. Proprietor: D.C.T. Bennett. General Manager: T. Bennett. Head office: Deepwood House, Farnham Royal, Bucks. Press office and works: Denham Green Lane, Denham, Bucks. Most important models: Electron, Zeta, Mk VI EM, TXI, TX-GT, TX-S, TX-SS.

FASA-RENAULT — **Spain**

Founded in 1951. President: J.L. Rodriguez-Pomatta. Vice President: B. Hanon. Managing Director: M.H. Bougler. Head office: Avda de Burgos, km 5.5, Apdo. 262, Madrid 34. Works: Valladolid, Sevilla. 18,424 employees. 212.691 cars produced in 1976.

FELBER - see HAUTE PERFORMANCE MORGES

FERRARI S.p.A. — **Italy**

Founded in 1929 as Scuderia Ferrari, became Società Auto-Avio Costruzioni Ferrari in 1940 and Ferrari S.p.A.-SEFAC in 1960. Since 1-7-1969, Fiat has been associated on joint venture basis and company has used its present title. Its name is bound up with superb technical achievements in field of racing and GT cars. President: E. Ferrari. Managing Director: G. Sguazzini. General Manager: P. Fusaro. Directors: N. Tufarelli, L. Montezemolo, C. Pelloni, S. Pininfarina, P. Lardi. Head office: vl. Trento e Trieste 31, 41100 Modena. Press office and works: v. Abetone Inferiore 2, 41053 Maranello (Modena). 1200 employees (including Scaglietti, Modena). 1,500 cars produced in 1976. Most important GT models: 125 (1947); 166 Inter (1949); 340 America (1952); 250 GT, V12 250 GT, Superfast (1961); 275 GTB 4 Berlinetta (1963); Dino 206 GT Berlinetta, 365 Coupé GT 2+2 (1967); 365 GTB 4 Berlinetta, 246 GT Dino (1969); 308 GTB (1975). Entries and wins in various world competitions and championships. 22 times world champion.

FIAT (Brazil) - see FIAT S.p.A.

FIAT CONCORD S.A.I.C. — **Argentina**

Head office: Cerrito 740, Buenos Aires. Press office: as above; División Automoviles, Juramento 750, Buenos Aires. Works: Humberto I - 1001, Palomar - Pcia Buenos Aires. About 12,000 employees. 73,200 cars produced in 1974.

FIAT S.p.A. — **Italy**

Founded in July 1899 as Società Anonima Fabbrica Italiana di Automobili Torino. With the statutari modification of the shareholders' meeting in 1918, it assumed the title Fiat written either with capital or small letters. In 1968, FIAT incorporated Autobianchi and OM which are still produced as separate makes. In 1969 it took over Lancia and acquired 50% of Ferrari shares and in 1971 took over Abarth. In 1976, the reorganisation of the Fiat Group was practically completed. The new Fiat Holding is a structure in which all the sectors are now organized with their own design, production and marketing responsibilities, some of them as individual legal entities and other with Fiat S.p.A. but with similar management autonomy. Among these are: Settore Fiat Automobili. Head office: c.so Agnelli 200, Turin. Press office: c.so Matteotti 26, 10121 Turin. Works: Mirafiori, Rivalta, Lingotto (Turin), Vado Ligure, Termoli, Villar Perosa, Cassino, Florence, Bari. Fiat Veicoli Industriali S.p.A. Head office: v. Puglia 35, Turin. In 1975 it was merged into I.VE.CO. which brings together activities carried by Fiat, OM, Lancia and Magirus Deutz. Works: 15 in Europe (8 in Italy). President: G. Agnelli. Vice-President: U. Agnelli. Managing Director: C. Romiti. About 180,000 employees. 1,098,182 cars produced in 1976. Most important models: Fiat 3½ HP (1899-1900); 6 HP and 8 HP, 12 HP, 24-32 HP (1900-04); 16-24 HP (1903-04); Brevetti e 60 HP (1905-09); 18-24 (1908); Fiacre mod. 1 (1908-10); Fiat 1,2,3,4,5, (1910-18); Zero e 3 ter (1912-15); 2B e 3A (1912-21); 70 (1915-20); 501 (1919-26); 505 and 510 (1919-25); Superflat (1921-22); 519 (1922-24); 502 (1923-26); 509 (1925-27); 503 and 507 (1926-27); 512 (1926-28); 520 (1927-29); 521 (1928-31); 525 (1928-29); 525 S (1929-31); 514 and 514 MM (1929-32); 515, 522 C and 524 C (1931-34); 508 Balilla and 508 S Balilla Sport (1932-37); 518 Ardita (1933-38); 527 Ardita 2500 (1934-36); 1500 (1935-48); 500 (1936-48); 508 C Balilla 1100 (1937-39); 2800 (1938-44); 1100 (1939-48); 500 B and Giardiniera (1948-49); 1100 B and 1500 D (1948-49); 1500 E (1949-50); 1100 E (1949-53); 500 C (1949-54); 500 C Giardiniera (1949-52); 1100 ES (1950-51); 1400, 1400 A and 1400 B (1950-58); 500 C Belvedere (1951-55); 1900 A and 1900 B (1952-58); 8V (1952-54); Nuova 1100 and Nuova 1100 Familiare (1953-56); 1100 TV (1953-56); 600 (1955-60); 1100/103 E (1956-57); Nuova 500 Trasformabile (1957-60); 1100/103 D (1957-60); Nuova 500 Sport (1958-60); 1200 Gran Luce (1957-60); 1200 Trasformabile (1958-59); 1100/103 H (1959-60); 1800 and 1800 Familiare (1959-61); 1100 Special (1960-62); 500 D (1960-65); 600 D Multipla, 500 Giardiniera (1960-68); 1300, 1500, 1300 Familiare, 2300 Coupé, 2300 S Coupé (1961-68); 1600 S Cabriolet (1962-66); 850 (1964-71); 124 and 124 Sport Spider (1966); Dino Spider (1966); 125, Dino Coupé, 124 Sport Coupé, 850 Idroconvert (1967); 850 Special, Sport Coupé, Sport Spider, 500 L, 124 Special, 125 Special (1968); 128, 128 Familiare, 124 Sport Coupé 1600, 124 Sport Spider 1600, Dino Coupé 2400, Dino Spider 2400, 130 (1969); 124 Special T (1970); 127, 128 Rally, 128 Coupé, 130 3200, 130 Coupé (1971); 126, 127 3 Porte, X 1/9, 124 Spider Rally, 124 Coupé e Spider 1600 e 1800, 132 (1972); 126 Tetto Apribile, 132 GLS, 128 Special, 127 Special, 131 Mirafiori (1974); 128 3P (1975); 126 Personal (1976); 132 1600-2000, 127 900-1050 CL (1972). It has been entering competitions since 1900, when true racing car was not yet born. First national wins, followed by many others, in Automobile Tour of Italy with 6-8 HP, a car with two horizontal rear cylinders. Since 1904 numerous first places in international field. In 1927 officially retired from motor racing. Since 1970 works competition in rallies. In 1977 World Rally Championship with Fiat 131 Abarth.

MANUFACTURE AND ASSEMBLY IN OTHER COUNTRIES — **Argentina:** Fiat Concord S.A.I.C. (affiliated company) Cerrito 740, Buenos Aires (manuf. 600, 128, 125). **Brazil:** Fiat Automoveis (affiliated company), Avda São Luiz 50, 28º Andar, São Paulo (manuf. 147). **Chile:** Fiat Chile S.A. (affiliated company), Carmen 8, Santiago (assem. 600, 125). **Colombia:** Compania Colombiana Automotriz

S.A. (associated company), Calle 13 n. 38-54, Bogotà (asem. 128, 125). **Costa Rica:** S.A.V.A. (licensee company), Apdo 10042, San José (assem. 131, 127). **Egypt:** El-Nasr Automotive Mfg Co. Ltd (licensee company), Wadi-Hof, Helwan, Cairo (assem. 128). **Eire:** Fiat Ireland Ltd (affiliated company), Industrial Garden Estate, Chapelizod, Dublin (assem. 127, 128). **Indonesia:** Daha Motors (licensee company), Medan Merkeda Selatan 2, Djakarta (assem. 131, 127, 132 S). **Korea:** Asia Motors Co. Inc. (licensee company), Samwha Bldg, 21 Sokong-Dong, Chung-Ku, Seoul. **Malaysia:** Sharikat Fiat Distributors (licensee company), Tanglin Rd. 99/101, Singapore (assem. 127, 128, 131, 132). **Morocco:** Somaca (associated company), km 12 Autoroute de Rabat, Casablanca (assem. 127, 131, 132). **New Zealand:** Torino Motors Ltd (licensee company), 19/29 Nelson St, Auckland (assem. 128). **Poland:** Pol-Mot (licensee company), Stalingradzka 23, Warszawa (manuf. 126, 125 P). **Portugal:** Fiat Portuguesa Sarl (affiliated company), Av. Eng. Duarte Pacheco 15, Lisbon (assem. 127, 128, 131). **South Africa:** Fiat South Africa Pty Ltd, 2 Bosworth St. Alrode Extension, Alberton (assem. 128, 131, 132). **Spain:** Seat (associated company), av. del Generalisimo 146, Madrid (manuf. 127, 128 3P, 131 132). **Thailand:** Karnasuta General Assembly Co. (licensee company), P.O.B. 1421, Bangkok (assem. 128, 131, 132 S). **Turkey:** Tofas (associated company), K 57 Mecidiyekoy, Istanbul (manuf. 131). **Uruguay:** Ayax S.A. (licensee company), Av. Rondeau 1751, Montevideo (assem. 125, 600, 128); Mar y Sierra (concessionaire), 8 de Octubre 3381, Montevideo (assem. 125). **Venezuela:** Fiav (associated company), Alcabala de Candelaria à Urapal 8, Caracas (assem. 131, 132). **Yugoslavia:** Zavodi Crvena Zastava (associated company), Span, Boraca 2, Kragujevac (manuf. Zastava 750, 128, 1300). **Zambia:** Livingstone Motor Assemblers Ltd (associated company), P.O.B. 2718, Lusaka (assem. 127, 128, 131, 132 S). 700,000 cars produced outside Italy in 1976.

FIBERFAB - KAROSSERIE — **Germany (Federal Republic)**

Proprietor: J. Kuhnle. Head office, press office and works: 7141 Auenstein b. Heilbronn. About 120 cars produced in 1976.

FNM - FABRICA NACIONAL DE MOTORES S.A. — **Brazil**

Established in 1942. Is oldest motor manufacturing company in Brazil. Has been manufacturing Alfa Romeo industrial vehicles under licence since 1953. In October 1968 Alfa Romeo acquired 85% of the shares, thus gaining control of company. Since 1973, the stock has been heid by Alfa Romeo 51%, Fiat 43%, Federal Union and third parties 6%. In 1976 Fiat became the mayor shareholder. Alfa Romeo, which had previously been the major shareholder, now holds 6% of the stock and the Brazilian government 2.5%. President: H. do Nascimento e Silva. Superintendent: T. Dalpadullo. General Manager: M. Remida. Head office and press office: Avda Presidente Vargas 542, 20°, Rio de Janeiro. Works: Rodaria Washington Luiz, km 23, Duque de Caxias, Estado do Rio de Janeiro.

FORD BRASIL S.A. — **Brazil**

Established in 1967 as a result of merger between Ford Motor do Brasil S.A. and Willys Overland do Brasil. President and General Manager: J.W. O'Neill. Director Vice-President: R.C. Graham. Directors: V.J. Trivison, J.P. Dias, N. Chiaparini, W.F. Paul, R.B. Stevenson. M. Borghetti. Head office and press office: Av. Rudge Ramos 1501, São Bernardo do Campo. Works: Av. Henry Ford 1787, São Paulo; Av. do Taboão 899, São Bernardo do Campo, Parque das Indústrias, Tambaté, SP; Av. Henry Ford 17, Osasco, SP. 21,000 employees. About 200,000 vehicles produced in 1976. Most important models: Ford T (1924); Willys Jeep (1954); Rural Jeep (1958); Renault Dauphine (1959); Aero Willys (1960); Itamaraty (1965); Ford Galaxie 500 (1967); Corcel Sedan and Ford LTD Landau (1968); Corcel Coupé (1969); Corcel Belina Station Wagon (1970); Maverick (1973); Corcel II, Corcel II Belina (1977). Entries in numerous competitions from 1962 to 1968. Brazilian Makers Championship in 1972-73 with Corcel. Brazilian Touring Car Championship (Group 1) in 1973-74 with Maverick. Brazilian Makers Championship with Avallone-Ford in 1974 and with Hollywood-Berta-Ford in 1975. Formula Ford-Corcel main sponsor in 1974-75-76-77.

FORD MOTOR ARGENTINA S.A. — **Argentina**

Incorporated 1959. President: J.M. Courad. Head office and press office: cc Central 696, Buenos Aires. Works: Pacheco.

FORD MOTOR COMPANY — **USA**

(Makes: Ford, Lincoln, Mercury)

Founded in 1903, is the second largest of the American motor manufacturers. Chairman and Chief Executive Officer: Henry Ford II. Vice-Chairman: P. Caldwell. President and Chief Operating Officier: L.A. Iacocca. Executive Vice-President International Automotive Operations: D.E. Petersen. Executive Vice-President North American Automotive Operations: W.O. Bourke. Components include Ford Division (Rotunda Drive at Southfield Rd. Dearborn, Mich., Vice-President and General Manager W.P. Benton) and Lincoln-Mercury Division (3000 Schaefer Rd, Dearborn, Mich., Vice-President and General Manager W.S. Walla). World headquarters: The American Rd, Dearborn, Mich. Assembly plants: Atlanta, Ga.; Chicago, Ill.; Dearborn Wayne (2) and Wixom, Mich.; Kansas City and St. Louis, Mo.; Lorain and Avon Lake, Ohio; Los Angeles and San José, Calif.; Louisville, Ky. (2); Mahwah and Metuchen, N.J.; Norfolk, Va.; St. Paul Minn. 219,700 employees. 2,228,023 cars produced in 1976.

MANUFACTURE AND ASSEMBLY IN OTHER COUNTRIES (excluding models of Ford Motor Company Ltd, Great Britain, of Ford Motor Company of Canada Ltd, Canada, of Ford Werke AG, Germany, of Ford Brasil S.A., Brazil and of Ford Motor Company of Australia Ltd, Australia) — **Argentina:** Ford Motor Argentina S.A. (subsidiary), C.C. Central 696, Buenos Aires 32/1 (manuf. and assem. Fairlane, Falcon, Taunus). **Ireland:** Henry Ford & Sons Ltd (subsidiary), Marina Cork (assem. Cortina, Escort). **Mexico:** Ford Motor Co. Branch S.A. (subsidiary), Apdo 39 bis, Mexico City (manuf. and assem. Ford, Fairmont, LTD, Maverick, Mustang). **Netherlands:** Ford Nederland N.V. (subsidiary), Hemweg 201, Postbus 795, Amsterdam (assem. Cortina, Escort). **New Zealand:** Ford Motor Co. of New Zealand Ltd (subsidiary), P.O.B. 12, Lower Hutt (assem. Falcon). **Portugal:** Ford Lusitana Sarl (subsidiary), Apdo 2248 R. Rosa/Aranjo 2, Lisbon (assem. Capri, Cortina, Escort, Consul, Granada). **Singapore:** Ford Motor Co. Private Ltd (subsidiary), P.O.B. 4047, Bukit Timah, Singapore (assem. Falcon). **Spain:** Ford Espana S.A. (subsidiary), Edificio Cuzco III/Avda Generalisimo 59, Madrid 16 (manuf. and assem. Fiesta). **South Africa:** Ford Motor Co. of South Africa (Pty) Ltd (subsidiary), P.O.B. 788, Port Elizabeth (assem. Granada, Cortina). **Taiwan:** Ford Lio Ho Motor Co. Ltd (subsidiary), Taipei (assem. Escort, Cortina, Granada). **Uruguay:** Ford (Uruguay) S.A. (subsidiary), C.C. 296, Montevideo (assem. Falcon, Escort). **Venezuela:** Ford Motor de Venezuela S.A. (subsidiary), Apdo 61131 del Este, Caracas (assem. Fairlane, Ford), 1,252,071 cars produced outside USA in 1976.

FORD MOTOR COMPANY Ltd — **Great Britain**

Founded in 1911, owned by Ford Motor Company USA, it had its first head office at Trafford Park (Manchester). In 1925, construction of Dagenham works was begun where production was started in 1931. Chairman and Managing Director: T.N. Beckett, Head office and press office: Eagle Way, Warley Brentwood, Essex. Works: Dagenham, Essex; Halewood, nr. Liverpool, and others. 70,000 employees. 383,220 cars produced in 1976. Most important models: 8 hp "Y", 10 hp "C", 14.9 hp "B.F.", 24 hp "B", 30 hp "V8" (all prior to 2nd World War); Prefect (1938); Anglia (1939); Pilot (1947); Consul, Zephyr (1951); Anglia 100E, Popular, Zodiac (1953); Mk II Consul, Zephyr, Zodiac 1956); Anglia 105E (1959); Consul Classic 315, Capri (1961); Mk III Zephyr, Zodiac, Cortina (1962); Corsair (1963); Mk IV Zephyr, Zodiac (1966); Mk II Cortina (1966); Escort (1968); Capri (1969); Mk III Cortina (1970); Granada (1972). Entries and wins in numerous competitions.

ASSEMBLY IN OTHER COUNTRIES — **Costa Rica:** Anglofores Ltda. (concessionaire), Apdo 1768, San José (assem. Escort). **Eire:** Henry Ford and Son Ltd (associated company), Cork (assem. Cortina). **Holland:** N.V. Nederlandsche Ford Automobiel Fabriek (associated company), P.O.B. 795, Amsterdam (assem. Cortina). **Israel:** Palestina Automobile Corp. Ltd (concessionaire), P.O.B. 975, Tel Aviv (assem. Escort). **Korea:** Hyundal Motor Co. (concessionaire), 55 Chrongro 3KA, Seoul (assem. Cortina). **Malaysia:** Associated Motor Industries, Malaysian Sdn Bhd (concessionaire), 109 Jalan Pudu, Kuala Lumpur (assem. Cortina, Escort). **New Zealand:** Ford Motor Co. of New Zealand Ltd (associated company), P.O.B. 30012, Lower Hutt (assem. Escort, Cortina, Zephyr, Zodiac). **Pakistan:** Ali Autos Ltd (concessionaire), P.O.B. 4206, Karachi (assem. Cortina). **Peru:** Ford Motor Co. Perú S.A. (associated company), Apdo 4130, Lima (assem. Escort). **Philippines:** Ford Philipp. Inc. (associated company), P.O.B. 415, Makati Commercial Centre, Makati Rizal (assem. Cortina, Escort). **Portugal:** Ford Lusitana (associated company), Apdo 2248, R. Rosa Arajo 2, Lisbon (assem. Escort, Cortina). **Singapore:** Ford Motor Co. Private Ltd (associated company), P.O.B. 4047, Bukit Timah, Singapore (assem. Cortina, Escort, Capri). **South Africa:** Ford Motor Co. of South Africa (Pty) Ltd (associated company), P.O.B. 788, Port Elizabeth (assem. Escort, Cortina, Capri). **Venezuela:** Ford Motor Co. Venezuela S.A. (associated company), Apdo 61131 Del Este, Caracas (assem. Cortina). 82,220 cars produced outside U.K. in 1976.

FORD MOTOR COMPANY OF AUSTRALIA Ltd — **Australia**

Founded in 1925. Directors: B.S. Inglis, R.F. Bennett, B.L. Burton, W.L. Dise, F.A. Erdman, E.T. Gardner, W.F. Grandsden, K.A. Horner, D.C. Jacobi, R.M. Lamb, R.J. Marshall, J. Sagovac, E.A. Witts. Head office and press office: Private Bag, 6 Campbellfield, Victoria 3061 Works: Broadmeadows, Campbellfield, Geelong, Victoria. 14,600 employees. 130,228 cars produced in 1976.

FORD MOTOR COMPANY OF CANADA Ltd — **Canada**

(Makes: Ford, Mercury)

Founded in 1904 in Windsor, Ont. Has always built a large percentage of all cars and trucks produced by Canadian automotive industry. President and Chief Executive Officer: R.F. Bennett. Vice-Presidents: K. Hallsworth, W. Mitchell, W.L. Hawkins, D.W. Scott. Head office and press office: The Canadian Road, Oakville, Ont. 16J 5E4. Works: Oakville, St. Thomas. Windsor, Niagara Falls, Ont. 19,981 employees. 371,303 cars produced in 1976.

FORD MOTOR COMPANY OF SOUTH AFRICA — **South Africa**

Established in 1924. Now leader in South African motor industry. Managing Director: D.B. Pitt. Directors: N.G. Cohen, J.C. Dill, F.H. Ferreira, D.M. Morris, B.S. Rayner, C.J. Roberts. Head office and press office: 187 Main St, Port Elizabeth, Cape Province. Works: Neave Township, Struandale, Deal Party (Port Elizabeth). 4,860 employees. 28,117 cars produced in 1976. Company competes in rallying and the « works » Escorts were champions in 1976.

FORD WERKE AG — **Germany (Federal Republic)**

Founded in 1925. Owned by Ford Motor Company USA. Chairman and Managing Director: P. Weiher. Directors: F.J. Bohr, P.A. Guckel, H. Dederichs, H.W. Gäb, H. Bergemann, H.J. Lehmann, W. Inden, W. Ebers, A. Langer. Head office and press office: Ottoplatz 2, Köln-Deutz. Works: Henry Ford-Strasse 1, Köln-Niehl, Saarlouis. 52,929 employees. 312,798 cars produced in 1976. Most important models: Köln 1 l, Rheinland 3 l (1933); Eifel 1.2 l (1935); Taunus (1938); Taunus (since 1948); 12M (1952); 15M (1955); 17M (1960); 12M (1962); 17M and 20M (1964); 12M and 15M (1966); 17M, 20M and 20M 2.3 l (1967); Escort (1968); Capri (1969); Taunus (1970); Consul Granada (1972); Capri II (1974); Escort (1975); Fiesta (1976). Winner of East African Safari in 1969. European Saloon Car Championship 1971, 1972, 1974.

MANUFACTURE AND ASSEMBLY IN OTHER COUNTRIES — **Belgium:** Ford Werke AG Fabrieken (subsidiary), Genk. **Portugal:** Ford Lusitana Sarl (associated company), Apdo 2248, Lisbon 2 (assem. Consul, Granada). **South Africa:** Ford Motor Co. of South Africa Pty Ltd (associated company), P.O.B. 788, Port Elizabeth (assem. Consul, Granada).

FUJI HEAVY INDUSTRIES Ltd — **Japan**

(Make: Subaru)

A part of former Nakajima Aircraft Co. Reorganized after the end of World War II and named Fuji Sangyo Co. in August 1945. Disbanded and divided into 12 smaller companies by order of occupying Allied Forces in 1950. Five of smaller companies reunited as Fuji Heavy Industries Ltd in 1953. Manufacturer of cars and commercial vehicles, aircraft and industrial power units. Joined Nissan Group in 1968. Member of Nissan Group. President: E. Ohhara. Senior Managing Directors: N. Sakata, S. Irie. Managing Directors: K. Kawabata, S. Nagashima, I. Shibuya, Y. Suzuki, H. Yamamoto. Head office and press office: 1-7-2 Subaru Bldg, Nishi-Shinjuku, Shinjukuku, Tokyo. Works: Gumma, 10-1 Higashi Hon-cho, Ohta City; Mitaka, 3-9-6 Oshawa, Mitakashi. 13,638 employees. 138,190 cars produced in 1975. Most important models: 360 Sedan (1958); 1000 (1966); 1000 Sport (1967); 1300 G, R2 (1970); Leone (1971).

MANUFACTURE AND ASSEMBLY IN OTHER COUNTRIES — **Portugal:** Sociedad General de Importacao Ltda (associated company).

GAZ - GORKOVSKI AVTOMOBILNY ZAVOD — **USSR**

Press office: Avtoexport, Ul. Volkhonka 14, Moscow G 19. Works: Gorki. About 70,000 cars produced in 1976.

GENERAL MOTORS ARGENTINA, S.A. — **Argentina**

(Makes: Chevrolet, Opel)

Subsidiary of GM Corporation. Managing Director: A.V. Michelena. Head office and Barracas works: Osvaldo Cruz 2900 (1293), Buenos Aires. Press office and San Martin works: Avda A 85, No. 645 (1650), San Martin PCIA de Buenos Aires. 4,912 employees. 8,658 cars produced in 1976.

GENERAL MOTORS CORPORATION — **USA**

(Makes: Buick, Cadillac, Chevrolet, Oldsmobile, Pontiac)

Founded in 1908, is largest motor manufacturer in world with production range extending from the most economical and popular cars to the most costly. Chairman: T.A. Murphy. President: E.M. Estes. Vice-Chairman:: R.L.

Terrel. Executive Vice-Presidents: J.F. McDonald, R.R. Jensen, H.L. Kehrl, R.B. Smith. GM has brought together five American motor manufacturing factories, transforming them into following divisions: Buick Motor Division (902 East Hamilton Ave, Flint, Mich. 48550), General Manager D.C. Collier, 19,250 employees, 817,669 cars produced in 1976; Cadillac Motor Car Division (2860 Clark Ave, Detroit, Mich. 48232), General Manager E.C. Kennard, 11,000 employees, 304,485 cars produced in 1976; Chevrolet Motor Division (3044 West Grand Blvd, Detroit, Mich. 48202), General Manager R.D. Lund, 97,500 employees, 2.012,000 cars produced in 1976; Oldsmobile Division (920 Townsend St. Lansing, Mich. 48921), General Manager R.J. Cook, 17,000 employees, 983,697 cars produced in 1976; Pontiac Motor Division (One Pontiac Plaza, Pontiac, Mich. 48053), General Manager A.C. Mair, 17,400 employees. 784,631 cars produced in 1975. The GM also owns General Motors - Holden's Pty Ltd (Australia), Adam Opel AG (Germany) and Vauxhall Motors Ltd (Great Britain). Head office: 3044 West Grand Blvd, Detroit, Mich. 48202.

MANUFACTURE AND ASSEMBLY IN OTHER COUNTRIES (excluding: non-American GM makes) — **Argentina:** GM Argentina S.A. (subsidiary), Rio Limay 1725 (33/8), Buenos Aires (manuf. Chevrolet products). **Belgium:** GM Continental (subsidiary), 75 Norderlaan, Antwerp (assem. imported vehicles). **Brazil:** GM do Brasil S.A. (subsidiary), Avda Goias 1805, Rio de Janeiro (manuf. Chevrolet Chevette, Opala). **Chile:** GM Chile S.A. (subsidiary), Piloto Lazo 99, P.O.B. 14370, Santiago (assem. imported vehicles). **Iran:** GM Joran Ltd. (associated company), P.O. Box 8-6173, Teheran (manuf. Chevrolet Royale). **Malaysia:** GM Malaysia SDN.BHD (subsidiary), Batu Dua. Jalan Tampoi. P.O. Box 204, Johone Bahru (manuf. Harimau). **Mexico:** GM de Mexico S.A. de C.V. (subsidiary), Av. Ejercito Nacional 843, Mexico 59F (manuf. Chevrolet). **New Zealand:** GM New Zealand, Ltd (subsidiary), Trentham Assembly Plant, Alexander Rd, Upper Hutt (assem. imported vehicles). **Philippines:** GM Philippines Inc. (subsidiary), P.O. Box 1497 MCC, Makati, Rizal 3117 (manuf. BTV vehicles). **Portugal:** GM de Portugal Ltda (subsidiary), Av. Marechal Gomes da Costa 3, Lisbon 6 (assem. imported vehicles). **South Africa:** GM South African (Pty) Ltd (subsidiary, Kempston Rd, P.O.B. 1137, Port Elizabeth (manuf. Chevrolet; assem. imported vehicles). **Switzerland:** GM Suisse S.A. (subsidiary), Salzhausstr. 21 Bienne (assem. imported vehicles). **Uruguay:** GM Uruguaya S.A. (subsidiary), Av. Sayago 1385, Montevideo (assem. imported vehicles). **Venezuela:** GM de Venezuela C.A. (subsidiary), Carapa, Carretera de Antimano, Caracas (assem. imported vehicles). **Zaire:** GM Zaire S.E.R.L. (subsidiary), Boulevard Patrice Lumumba, Kinshasa (assem. imported vehicles). Cars produced outside USA in 1976 1,634,655.

GENERAL MOTORS DO BRASIL — **Brazil**

(Make: Chevrolet)

Subsidiary of GM Corporation. Managing Director: J.J. Sanchez. Head office, press office and works: Avda Goias 1805, Rio de Janeiro. 17,044 employees. 181,144 cars produced in 1976.

GENERAL MOTORS - HOLDEN'S Pty Ltd — **Australia**

Established in 1931 as result of merger between General Motors (Australia) Pty Ltd and Holden's Motor Body Builder Ltd. Affiliate of GM Corp. USA. Managing Director: C. Chapman. Head office and press office: 241 Salmon St, Fishermans Bend, Melbourne, Victoria. Works: as above; Dandenong, Victoria; Woodville, Elizabeth, S. Australia; Pagewood, N.S.W., Acacia Ridge, Queensland. 22,579 employees. 157,656 cars produced in 1976.

ASSEMBLY IN OTHER COUNTRIES — **New Zealand:** GM New Zealand Ltd, Trentham Plant No. 1, Private Bag, Upper Hutt (assem. Sedan, Premier). **South Africa:** GM South African (Pty) Ltd, Kempston Rd, Port Elizabeth (assem. Sedan).

GENERAL MOTORS (Malaysia) - see GENERAL MOTORS CORPORATION

GENERAL MOTORS OF CANADA Ltd — **Canada**

(Make: Chevrolet, Pontiac)

Established in 1918 as result of merger between McLaughlin Motor Car Company and Chevrolet Motor Car Company. It is a wholly owned subsidiary of General Motors Corp. President and General Manager: D.H. McPherson. Vice-President and General Manufacturing Manager: R.C. Walter. Vice-President and General Sales Manager: R.M. Colcomb. Vice-President and Finance Manager: W.R. Waugh. Vice-President and General Manager, Diesel Division: A. Grant Warner. Head office and press office: 215 William St, Oshawa, Ontario L1G1KZ. Works: as above, Ste. Therese, P.Q., St. Catharines, Windsor and Scarborough. 39,345 employees. 477,092 cars produced in 1976.

GENERAL MOTORS SOUTH AFRICAN (Pty) Ltd — **South Africa**

(Make: Chevrolet)

Founded in 1926. Managing Director: L.H. Wilking. Directors: K.P. Klayton, J.L. Fry, W.F. Kohl, C.R. von zur Gathen, J.B. Watson, R.J. Ironside. Head office and press office: Main St, Port Elizabeth. Works: Kempston Rd; Aloes Engine Plant, Port Elizabeth, 4,860 employees. 28,117 cars produced in 1976.

GIANNINI AUTOMOBILI S.p.A. — **Italy**

Founded in 1920 as F.lli Giannini A. & D., it later became Giannini Automobili S.p.A. President and Managing Director: V. Polverelli. Head office, press office and works: v. Idrovore della Magliana 57, Rome. 35 employees. 1,500 cars produced in 1976. Most important models: 750 Berlinetta San Remo (1949); Fiat 750 TV and 850 GT (1963); 850 Coupé Gazzella, Fiat 500 TV and TVS, 590 GT and GTS (1964); Fiat Berlina 850 S, 850 SL and 950, Fiat Coupé 850 and 1000, Fiat 1300 Super and 1500 GL, Fiat 500 TVS Montecarlo (1965); Fiat 650 NP, 128 NPS (1970); 650 NPL, 650 NP Modena, 128 NP-S, 128 NP Rally (1971). It is engaged above all in producing variations of Fiat cars. Entries in various competitions and first places in category in various Italian championships.

GINETTA CARS Ltd — **Great Britain**

Founded in 1958. Chairman and Managing Director: K.R. Walklett. Directors: T.G. Walklett, D.J. Walklett, I.A. Walklett. Head office, press office and works: West End Works, Witham, Essex CM8 1BE. 20 employees. 65 cars produced in 1976. Most important model: G 21.

G.P. CONCESSIONAIRES Ltd — **Great Britain**

Head office, press office and works: Worton Hall, Worton Rd, Isleworth, Middlesex.

GROUP LOTUS CARS COMPANIES Ltd — **Great Britain**

Founded in 1952. Chairman: A.C.B. Chapman. Group Board: A.C.B. Chapman, F.R. Bushell, P.R. Kirwan-Taylor. Managing Director: M.J. Kimberley. Head office, press office and works: Norwich, NR14 8EZ. 550 employees. 1,500 cars produced in 1976. Most important models: Mk Six (1952); Mk Eight, Mk Nine, Mk Ten, Elite (1957); Eleven (1960); Elan (1962); Cortina (1963); Elan + 2 (1967); Europa (1968); Elan Sprint, Elan + 2 'S' 130, Europa Twin Cam (1971); Europa Special (1972). Entries and first places in numerous international competitions with F1, F2, F3, F5 cars; six F1 World Champion Constructors victories in last 10 years (Indianapolis, Le Mans, Monte Carlo GP, Pacific GP at Laguna Seca, etc.). May 1975 Elite design won European Don Safety Trophy.

GURGEL S.A
INDUSTRIA E COMERCIO DE VEHICULOS — **Brazil**

Chairman and Managing Director: J.A.C. do Amaral Gurgel. 300 employees. Head office and works: Rod. Washington Luiz, km 171, Rio Claro 13500, S.P. Press office: Avda do Masino 2518. Jardim de Saude, São Paulo.

HAUTE PERFORMANCE MORGES — **Switzerland**

(Make: Felber)

Founded in 1975. Head office, press office and works: route Suisse, Morges.

HINDUSTAN MOTORS Ltd — **India**

Founded in 1942. Chairman: B.M. Birla. Vice-Chairman: G.P. Birla. Directors: R.N. Mafatlal, B.P. Khaitan, G.D. Kothari, M.R. Damle, N.L. Hingorani, S.M. Ghosh, M.V. Arunachalam. Head office and press office: Birla Bldg, 9/1 R.N. Mukherjee Rd, Calcutta 1. Works: P.O. Hind Motor, Hooghly, West Bengal. Car production begun in 1951. About 16,000 employees. 28,000 cars produced in 1976. Most important models: Hindustan 10, Hindustan 14, Baby Hindustan, Landmaster (1954); Ambassador (1957); Ambassador Mk II (1963); Ambassador Mark III (1975).

HOLDEN - see GENERAL MOTORS - HOLDEN'S Pty Ltd

HONDA MOTOR COMPANY Ltd — **Japan**

Founded in 1949 as Honda Giyitsu Kenkunjo. Present title since 1948. Manufacturer and exporter of motorcycles from 50 to 750 cc, automobiles, trucks, portable generators, general-purpose engines, power tillers, water pumps and outboard motors. President: K. Kawashima. Executive Vice-Presidents: K. Kawashima, M. Nishida. Senior Managing Directors: H. Sugiura, S. Shinomiya, N. Okamura, M. Suzuki. Directors: S. Honda, T. Fujisana. Directors and advisors: S. Honda (founder), T. Fujisawa (co-founder). Head office and press office: 6-27-8 Jingumae, Shibuyaku, Tokyo, Japan 150. Works: Saitama, 8-1 Honcho, Wako-shi, Saitama-ken; Suzuka, 1907 Mirata-cho, Suzuka-shi, Mie-ken; Hamamatsu, 34 Oi-machi, Hamamatsu-shi, Shizuoka-ken; Sayama, 1-10 Shinsayama, Sayama-shi, Saitama-ken. 20,200 employees including Honda R & D Co. 485,406 vehicles produced in 1976. Models: Sports 500 (1962); Sports 600 (1964); L 700, L 800 (1966); N360, LN360 (1967); N600 (1968); 1300 (1969); 1300 Coupé, NIII Sedan, Z Coupé (1970); Life (1971); Civic (1972); Civic CVCC 4-dr. Sedan (1973). Wins in F1 racings: Mexican GP (1965), Italian GP (1967). French GP and GP USA (1968) and entries in F1, F2, GP Racings.

HONGKI — **China (People's Republic)**

Public Relations office: China National Machinery Import & Export Corp., P.O.B. 49, Peking. Works: Chang-Chun, Kirin.

HYUNDAI MOTOR Co. — **South Korea**

Head office: Bae Jae Bldg, 55-4 Seosomoon-Dong, Seodaemoon-ku, Seoul. Press office: 178 Brompton Rd, London SW3 (Great Britain). Cars produced in 1976: 30,000.

IKA-RENAULT S.A.I.C. y F. — **Argentina**

Founded in 1955 under the name of Industrias Kaiser Argentina. Present title since 1968. Head office and press office: Sarmiento 1230, Buenos Aires. Works: Barrio Santa Isabel, P. Cordoba. About 9,000 employees.

INTERMECCANICA - see AUTOMOBILI INTERMECCANICA

INTERNATIONAL HARVESTER
INTERNATIONAL TRUCKS — **USA**

Founded in 1902. Principal products trucks, agricultural equipment, construction equipment and gas turbine engines sold in 168 countries. Chairman and Chief Executive Officer: Brooks McCormick. President and Chief Operating Officer: A.R. McCardell. President Truck Group: J.P. Kaine. World Headquarters: 401 North Michigan Avenue, Chicago, Illinois 60611. 97,000 employees worldwide. 126,276 trucks produced in 1976.

MANUFACTURE IN OTHER COUNTRIES — **Australia:** International Harvester Australia (subsidiary), Melbourne, Victoria (Scout). **Canada:** International Harvester Canada (subsidiary), Hamilton, Ontario (Scout). **Mexico:** International Harvester Mexico (subsidiary), Mexico City (Scout). **Philippines:** International Harvester MacLeod (subsidiary), Manila (Scout). **Turkey:** Turk Otomotiv Endustrileri A.S. (joint venture), Istanbul (Scout). **Venezuela:** Industria Venezolana de Maquinarias C.A. (joint venture), Caracas (Scout). Trucks produced outside USA 25,000.

IRAN NATIONAL INDUSTRIAL
MANUFACTURING Co. Ltd — **Iran**

(Make: Paykan)

General Manager: M. Khayyami. Head office, press office and works: Karay Rd., Teheran. 5,700 employees. About 90,000 cars produced in 1974.

ISUZU MOTORS Ltd — **Japan**

Established in 1937 as result of merger between Ishika-Wajima motor manufacturing factory, which held Wolseley manufacturing licence from 1918 to 1927, and Tokyo Gas & Electric, which began the manufacture of military trucks in 1916. Present title since 1949. In 1971, it became a joint venture company with G.M. Corp. with capital participation of 34.2% by the latter. Chairman: T. Aramaki. President: T. Okamoto. Executive Vice-Presidents: I. Uesugi, Y. Shimizu, H.V. Leonard Jr. Senior Managing Directors: T. Tsunoka, I. Iseki, T. Okubo, S. Beppu, K. Sano. Head office and press office: 22-10 Minami-oi, 6-chome, Shinagawa-ku, Tokyo. Works: Kawasaki, 25-1 Tonomachi 3-chome, Kawasaki City; Fujisawa, 8 Tsuchitana, Fujisawa City. 12,455 employees. 93,029 cars produced in 1976. Most important models: Bellett (1962); Bellett, Bellett Standard (1963); Florian (1967); 117 Coupé (1968); Bellett Gemini (1974).

JAGUAR - see LEYLAND CARS JAGUAR and LEYLAND SOUTH AFRICA Ltd

JEEP - see AMERICAN MOTORS CORP.

JOHN BRITTEN GARAGES Ltd **Great Britain**

(Make: Arkley)

Founded in 1971. Proprietor: J. Britten. Head office, press office and works: Barnet Rd, Arkley, Barnet, Herts. 15 employees. 60 cars produced in 1976.

JOHNARD VINTAGE CAR REPAIRS Ltd **Great Britain**

Specializes in the repair of vintage cars. Car production on limited scale started in January 1976. Directors: J.R. Guppy, D.S. Beck, A.C.A. Head cffice, press office and works: Blandford Heights, Shaftesbury Lane, Blandford Forum, Dorset. 6 employees. 10 cars produced in 1976.

KIA INDUSTRIAL Co. Ltd **South Korea**

Head office, press office and works: 8 Yang Dong, Seoul.

K.M.B. Autosports Ltd **Great Britain**

Directors: M.R. Smith, M.A. Fenton, P.W. Telley. Head office: Finedon Sidings, Finedon, Northants. Press office and works: 228-230 Mill Rd, Wellingborough, Northants.

LAFER S.A. INDUSTRIA E COMERCIO **Brazil**

Lafer S.A. Industria e Comercio is a Brazilian corporation controlled by the Lafer brothers, Samuel, Oscar and Percival. In October of 1972 entered the replicar field with the classic 1952 MG TD. A prototype appeared at the 1972 Brazilian Auto Show and the fibreglass car was shown at the 1974 Brazilian Auto Show. Head office Rua Lavapés 6, São Paulo. Press office and works: Av. Marginal, 1700 São Bernardo do Campo, São Paulo. 350 cars produced in 1975.

LAMBORGHINI - see AUTOMOBILI FERRUCCIO LAMBORGHINI S.p.A.

LANCIA & C. - FABBRICA AUTOMOBILI S.p.A. **Italy**

Founded in 1906, noted for production of extremely well-finished prestige cars. President: C. Righini. Managing Director and General Manager: G.M. Rossignolo. Head office and press office: v. Vincenzo Lancia 27, Turin. Works: as above; v. Caluso 50, Chivasso (Turin); Strada comunale, Verone (Vercelli). 11,000 employees. About 65,000 cars produced in 1976. Most important models: first car 14 hp (1907); Alfa, Dialfa (1908); Beta (1909); Gamma (1910); Delta, Didelta, Epsilon, Eta (1911); Theta (1913); Kappa (1919); Dikappa (1921); Trikappa (1922); Lambda (1923); Dilambda (1928); Artena, Astura (1931); Augusta (1933); Aprilia (1937); Ardea (1939); Aurelia (1950); Aurelia B20 (1951); Appia (1953); Flaminia (1957); Flavia (1960); Flavia Coupé and Convertible (1962); Flavia Sport, Fulvia (1963); Fulvia Coupé, Fulvia Sport (1965); Fulvia Coupé 1.3 HF (1966); Flavia 819 (1967); Fulvia Coupé 1.6 HF (1968); Flavia 2000 (1970); 2000 Berlina, 2000 Coupé (1971); Beta Berlina (1972); Beta Coupé (1973); Stratos (1974); Beta Spider, Beta HPE, Beta Monte Carlo (1975); Gamma, Coupé 1300, Gamma Coupé 1300 (1976).

ASSEMBLY IN OTHER COUNTRIES — **South Africa:** Trans-African Continental Motors Co. Pty Ltd (concessionaire), 174 Anderson St, Johannesburg (assem. Beta Berlina, Beta Coupé). **Thailand:** Yontrakit Motor Co., 12-14 Rong Huand Soi 5 Rd, Bangkok (Beta Berlina, Beta Coupé).

LAWIL S.p.A. **Italy**

Founded in 1969. President and Managing Director: C. Lavezzarl. Head office, press office and works: v. Maretti 29, Varzi (Pavia). 50 employees. About 1200 cars produced in 1976.

LEYLAND CARS JAGUAR **Great Britain**

(Makes: Daimler, Jaguar)

Founded in 1922 by Sir William Lyons as Swallow Sidecar Co., became SS. Cars Ltd and then Jaguar Cars Ltd in 1945. In 1960 it acquired Daimler Co., founded in 1896, in 1961 Guy Motors Ltd, in 1963 Coventry Climax Engines Ltd. In 1968 it became part of BLMC Ltd. Present title since 1976. Head office and works: Browns Lane, Allesley, Coventry, CV5 9DR. Most important models: SS I, SS II (1931-36); SS Jaguar (1935-49); SS Jaguar 100 (1935-40); Jaguar Mk V (1948-51); XK 120 (1948-54); Mk VII (1950-56); C-Type (1951-53); D-Type (1954-57); 2.4 (240) (1955); E-Type (1961-75); Mk 10 (1961-66); 420 G (1966); XJ6 (1968); XJ12 (1972) XJ-S (1975). Victories in various competitions (Liège-Rome-Liège, Alpine Rally, Monte Carlo Rally, Tour de France, Sebring Reims). First place at Le Mans (1951-1953-55-56-57), in German Touring Car Championship and in European Touring Challenge Cup (1963). Car of the year awards for XJ6 (1969) and XJ12 (1972).

ASSEMBLY IN OTHER COUNTRIES — **South Africa:** British Leyland Factory, Blackheath, Capetown. About 1,500 cars assembled in 1976.

LEYLAND CARS ROVER **Great Britain**

Founded in 1877 by J. Starley, became J.K. Starley and Co. Ltd in 1888 and The Rover Cycle Company in 1896. The Rover Company Ltd since 1906. Is now part of Leyland Cars Ltd. Present title since 1976. Works: Meteor Works, Lode Lane, Solihull, Warwicks. 14,500 employees. About 45,000 cars produced in 1976. Motor manufacturing begun in 1904. Most important models: 8 hp (1904-10); 6 hp (1906-10); 12 hp (1910-23); 8 hp Twin Air-cooled (1920-24); 10, 12, 14 and 16 hp range (1934-47); P3 models 60 and 75 (1948-49); P4 models 60, 75 80, 90, 95, 100, 105, 110 (1950-64); 3 l (1958); Rover 2000 (1963); 3.5 l Saloon and Coupé (1967); Rover 3500 (1968); Range Rover (1970). Car of the year award for Rover 3500 in 1976.

MANUFACTURE AND ASSEMBLY IN OTHER COUNTRIES — **Australia:** BLMC of Australia, Rover Division (associated company), P.O.B. 893-931 South Dowling St, Waterloo (manuf. Land Rover). **Costa Rica:** Ensambladora Automotriz S.A. (concessionaire), P.O.B. 10306, San José (assem. Land Rover and Range Rover). **Eire:** British Leyland Ireland (Jaguar, Rover, Triumph) Ltd (associated company), Cashel Rd, Dublin 12 (assem. Land Rover). **Ethiopia:** Amce-Share Company (concessionaire), P.O.B. 461, Addis Abeba (assem. Land Rover). **Ghana:** VAC Motors Ltd (concessionaire), P.O.B. 1642, Accra (assem. Land Rover, 109" Regular and 88" Estate Car). **Indonesia:** Java Motor Import. Corp. N.V. (concessionaire), P.O.B. 161, 17 Djalah Raya Kramat, Djakarta (assem. Land Rover). **Iran:** Sherkat Sahami Khass Sanaati Towlidi Morratab (concessionaire), P.O.B. 1508, Teheran (manuf. Land Rover). **Kenya:** Leyland Albion (E. Africa) Ltd (associated company), P.O.B. 18502, Nairobi (assem. Land Rover and Range Rover). **Morocco:** Aetoo-Lever Moroc (concessionaire), B.P. 519, Casablanca (assem. Land Rover). **Mozambique:** Compania Distribuidora de Automotive Sarl (concessionaire), C.P. 2510, Lorenco Marques (assem. Land Rover). **New Zealand:** The British Leyland Motor Corp. of New Zealand Ltd (associated company), P.O.B. 2179, Auckland (manuf. Land Rover and Rover cars). **Nigeria:** Bewac Ltd (concessionaire), Trans Amadi Industrial Estate, Port Harcourt (assem. Land Rover, 88" and 109" Regular and Etate Car). **Philippines:** Amalgamated Motors Inc. (concessionaire), P.O.B. P.A., 413 Port Area, Manila (manuf. Land Rover). **Portugal:** Sociedad Electro Mecanica de Automoveis Ltda (concessionaire), rua Nova de S. Mamede 30, Lisbon (assem. Land Rover). **Singapore:** Champion Motors Singapore Ltd (concessionaire), P.O.B. 627, Singapore 9 (assem. Land Rover). **South Africa:** Leyland Motor Corp. of South Africa Ltd (associated company), P.O.B. 1, Blackheat, Cape Town (manuf. Land Rover and Rover cars). **Spain:** Metalurgica de Santa Ana S.A. (concessionaire), Apdo 13170, Madrid (manuf. Land Rover). **Tanzania:** The Cooper Motor Corp. Ltd (associated company), P.O.B. 1852, Dar-es-Salam (assem. Land Rover). **Thailand:** Butler & Webster Ltd (concessionaire), 1539 New Petchbury Rd, P.O.B. 13, Bangkok (assem. Land Rover). **Trinidad:** Amalgamated Industries Ltd (concessionaire), Tumpuna Rd, Arima (assem. Land Rover and Rover cars). **Turkey:** BMC Sanayi Ve Ticaret A.S., P.O.B. 260, Izmir (assem. Land Rover and Range Rover). **Venezuela:** Mack de Venezuela C.A. (concessionaire), Apdo 168, Caracas (manuf. Land Rover and Range Rover). **Zambia:** Rover Zambia Ltd (associated company), P.O.B. SK 6, Skyways, Ndola (assem. Land Rover and Range Rover).

LEYLAND CARS TRIUMPH **Great Britain**

Founded in 1903 under name of Standard Motor Co.; incorporated Triumph Motor Co., in 1945; in 1968 became part of Specialist Car Division of British Leyland Motor Corp. Ltd. Present title since 1976. Head office and works: Canley, Coventry CV4 9DB. 10,000 employees. 109,000 cars produced in 1976. Most important models: 6 hp (1903); 24/30 hp (1906); 11.4 hp (1920); Eight (1939); Eight, Twelve, Fourteen (1945); Triumph 1800 Saloon and Roadster (1946); Vanguard (1947); Mayflower (1951); Standard 8, TR2 (1953); Herald (1958); TR4, Spitfire, Vitesse (1962); Triumph 2000 (1963); 1300, TR4A (1965); TR5 PI (1967) Herald 13/60, 2.5 P.I. (1968); TR6 (1969); Stag, Toledo, 1500 (1970); Dolomite (1972); Dolomite Sprint, 1500 TC (1973); 2500 TC (1974); Dolomite 1300, Dolomite 1500 e 1500 HL, Dolomite 1850 HL (1976).

ASSEMBLY IN OTHER COUNTRIES — **Australia:** Australian Motor Industries Ltd, G.P.O.B. 2006S Port Melbourne, Victoria (assem. 2000, 2500 TC). **Belgium:** N.V. Leyland Industries Belgium S.A. (associated company), Chaussee De Mons, Seneffe (assem. Spitfire Mk IV, TR6). **Eire:** British Leyland Ireland (Jaguar, Rover, Triumph) Ltd (subsidiary), Cashel Rd, Dublin (assem. 2000, 1500 TC Toledo, Spitfire). **New Zealand:** New Zealand Motor Corporation Ltd (associated company), P.O.B. 2599, Wellington (assem. 2500 TC, Toledo). **Portugal:** British Leyland de Portugal-Automoveis Ltda. (associated company), Apdo 5090, Lisbon 5 (assem. Spitfire and Dolomite). **South Africa:** British Leyland Motor Corporation of South Africa Ltd (associated company), P.O.B. 1, Blackheath, Cape Province (assem. 2500 TC).

LEYLAND SOUTH AFRICA Ltd **South Africa**

(Makes: Jaguar, Marina, Mini, Rover, Trimph).

Founded in 1896 as Lancashire Steam Motor Co., it became Leyland Motor Co. in 1911 and Leyland Motor Corporation of South Africa Limited in 1964. It incorporated Austin Motor Co. and B.M.C. and in 1972 became Leyland South Africa Ltd. Chairman: A. Park. Deputy Chairman: F.P. Jacobsz. Managing Director: T.P. Murrough. Directors: R.J. Ott, J.A. Visser, R.J. Broadley, R. du P. Hamman. Head office and press office: P.O Box 6226, Johannesburg 2000. Works: P.O. Box 190, Goodwood, Cape Town 7460. 4,600 employees. 9,846 cars produced in 1976.

LINCOLN - see FORD MOTOR COMPANY

LOTUS - see GROUP LOTUS CARS COMPANIES Ltd

(THE) LYNX COMPANY **Great Britain**

It is a company formed to produced prototypes and low volume specialist performance cars. It offers a unique service since it has a direct involvment in all aspects of motor car design and development by working alongside its associated company, Lynx Engineering, which specializes in the restoration and development of performance cars concentrating mainly on Jaguars. Head office, press office and works: Station Rd, Northiam, Nr. Rye, Sussex. 10 employees. 15 cars produced in 1976.

MALLORCA **Spain**

Head office, press office and works: Madrid.

MASERATI - see OFFICINE ALFIERI MASERATI S.p.A.

MATRA SPORTS **France**

Founded in 1932 as Deutch-Bonnet became René Bonnet in 1961. Present title since 1977. In 1968 a merger was decided with Engins Matra S.A. as "Motoring Division" of latter. President and Managing Director: J.L. Lagardère. Vice-President: S. Floirat. Head office: 4, rue de Presbourg, Paris 75008. Press office: av. Louis Bréguet, B.P.1, 78140 Velizy. Works: 1, av. Saint-Exupéry, 41000 Romorantin; 21 rue Paul Dauthier, 78140 Velizy. About 1,300 employees. 7,376 cars produced in 1976. Models: Deutch-Bonnet (1932-40); René Bonnet (1961-64); Matra-Bonnet (1965); Matra M530 (1966); Matra Simca " Bagheera " (1972); Bagheera Courrèges (1974); Bagheera S (1975); Bagheera X, Rancho (1977). Entries and wins in numerous competitions with F2 and F3 cars (Reims, Albi, Magny-Cours in 1965, Monaco, Rouen, GP de Monaco, Palmarès in 1966-67-68, Le Mans in 1972-73). World Champion F1 in 1969. Manufacturers world championship (3-litres Sport prototype) in 1972-73-74.

MAZDA - see TOYO KOGYO COMPANY Ltd

MERCEDES-BENZ - see DAIMLER-BENZ AG

MERCURY - see FORD MOTOR COMPANY and FORD MOTOR COMPANY OF CANADA Ltd

MG - see BRITISH LEYLAND Ltd

MINI - see BRITISH LEYLAND Ltd and LEYLAND SOUTH AFRICA Ltd

MITSUBISHI MOTOR CORPORATION **Japan**

Established in October 1917 as Mitsubishi Shipbuilding & Engineering Co. Ltd, later changed its name to Mitsubishi Heavy Industries Ltd. After the Second World War it split into three companies under Enterprise Reorganization Law, but these again reunited in June 1964 as Mitsubishi Heavy Industries Ltd. Products include ships and other vessels, railway vehicles, aircraft, space equipment, missiles, atomic equipment, heavy machinery. The Automobile Division became an independent company in June 1970 under name of Mitsubishi Motor Corp. In May 1971 it became a joint venture company with Chrysler Corp. (USA), with Mitsubishi holding 65% and Chrysler 35% of shares. President: T. Kubo. Executive Vice Presidents: Y. Sone, K. Sugiura, Y. Mochida. Senior Managing Directors: H. Sugiura, S. Watanabe, R.A. Perkins, M. Tanji, C.A. Polker, N. Ichikawa, S. Asai, M. Miguno, K. Kobayashi, S. Kobayashi, I. Nishina, K. Samejima. Head office and press office: No. 33-8 Shiba 5-chome, Minatoku, Tokyo. Works: Mizushima, No. 1, 1-chome, Mizushima, Kaigandori, Kurashiki, Okoyama-Pref.; Nagoya, No. 2, Oyecho, Minato-ku. Nagoya. 23,000 employees. 462,562 cars produced in 1976.

MANUFACTURE AND ASSEMBLY IN OTHER COUNTRIES — **Philippines;** Chrysler Philippines Corp., Cainta, Rizal Province. **Thailand:** United Development Motor Industries Co. Ltd, 28 Sukswadi Rd, Bangkuru Propradaeng, Samutprakan.

MONOCOQUE ENGINEERING — USA

Established in 1968 as Design Co. Present title since 1970. President: D.E. Hanebrink. Head office, press office and works: 1725 B-Z Monrovia St, Costa Mesa, Cal. 92627.

MONTEVERDI - see AUTOMOBILES MONTEVERDI Ltd

MORGAN MOTOR COMPANY Ltd — Great Britain

Founded in 1910. Managing Director: P.H.G. Morgan. Head office, press office and works: Pickersleigh Rd, Malvern Link, Worcs. WR14 2LL. Production of 4-wheeled vehicles begun in 1936. 105 emploees. 454 cars produced in 1976. Most important models: Morgan 4/4, Morgan Plus 8. Entries and wins in numerous competitions since 1911.

MORRIS - see BRITISH LEYLAND Ltd

NISSAN MOTOR Co. Ltd — Japan

Founded in 1933 under the name of Jidosha Seizo Co. Ltd. Present title since 1934. In 1966 it took over Price Motors Ltd. Chairman: K. Kawamata. Vice-Chairman: T. Iwakoshi. President: T. Ishihara. Executive Vice-Presidents: S. Sasaki, M. Ohkuma, M. Komaki. Senior Managing Directors: R. Nakagawa, F. Honda, R. Yamazaki, K. Tanaka, H. Takahashi, K. Kanao. Head office and press office: Ginza, Chuo-ku, Tokyo. Works: Mitaka, 8-1, 5-chome, Shimo-Renjaku, Mitaka, Tokyo; Murayama, 6000 Nakafuji, Musashi-Murayama, Kitatama-gun, Tokyo; Agikubo, 5-1, 3-chome, Momoi, Suginami-ku, Tokyo; Oppama, 1, Natsushima-Cho, Yokosuka; Tochigi, 2500, Kaminokawa, Tochigi-ken; Yokohama 2, Takara-cho, Kanagawaku, Yokohama; Yoshiwara, 1-1, Takara-cho, Yoshiwara Fuji, Shizuoka-ken; Zama, 5070, Nakagubo, Zama, Kanagawa-Ken. 52,577 employees. 1,803,872 cars produced in 1976. Most important models: Cedric (1960); Sunny, Gloria (1962); President (1965); Datsun, Nissan Prince Royal (1966); Datsun Bluebird 510 (1967); Laurel (1968); Datsun 240-Z, Nissan Skyline (1969); Cherry (1970); Datsun Bluebird U (1972). First places in Round Australia Rally (1958); East African Safari Rally and Kenya Rally (1966); Shell 4000 Canada Rally (1967-68); South Africa's Moonlight Rally and Beira Rally (1967); Zacateca Race, Malaysian Race, Aussie Race, Southern Cross Rally (1968); South African Castrol 2000 Rally, East African Safari Rally (1969-71).

MANUFACTURE AND ASSEMBLY IN OTHER COUNTRIES — **Australia:** Nissan Motor Co. (Australia) Pty Ltd (subsidiary), 210-218 Victoria St, Carlton, 3053 Melbourne. **Chile:** Industrias Nissan Motor Chile S.A. (associated company), Alameda B. O'Higgins 1460, Casilla 144-D, Santiago. **Malaysia:** Tan Chong & Sons Motor Co. (associated company), Kuala Lumpur. **Mexico:** Nissan Mexicana S.A. de C.V. (subsidiary), Avda. Insurgentes Sur No. 1457, Mexico City 19. **New Zealand:** Nissan Motor Distributors (New Zealand) Ltd (associated company), P.O.B. 1072, Auckland. **Peru:** Nissan Motor del Perú S.A. (subsidiary), P.O.B. 6107, Lima **Philippines:** Universal Motors Corp. (associated company), 2232-34, Pasong Tamo Ave., Makati, Rizal. **Portugal:** Entreposto Commercial de Automóveis (associated company), Lisbon. **South Africa:** Datsun Motor Vehicle Distributors Pty Ltd (associated company), P.O.B. 10, Rosslyn, Pretoria, Transvaal. **Taiwan:** Yue Loong Motor Co. Ltd (associated company), 16 Sing Yang St, Taipei. **Thailand:** Siam Motors and Nissan Co. Ltd (associated company), 865, Rama 1 Rd, Bangkok.

NUOVA INNOCENTI S.p.A. — Italy

Founded in 1933 as Società Anonima Fratelli Innocenti became Innocenti Anonima per Applicazioni Tubolari Acciaio and Innocenti Società Generale per l'Industria Metallurgica e Meccanica S.p.A. and Innocenti S.p.A. in 1961. Taken over by BLMC in 1972 and in 1976 by GEPI and de Tomaso assuming present title. British Leyland holds 5% of Nuova Innocenti. Innocenti Commerciale S.p.A. was founded to take care of distribution, with 20% of stock held by British Leyland. Nuova Innocenti holds 20% of the stock of British Leyland Italia. Production begun in May 1976. President: R. Spera. Managing Director: A. de Tomaso. General Manager: T. Pirondini. Head office and press office: v. Rubattino 37, Milan. Works: v. Pitteri 84, Milan. 2,113 employees. 35,000 cars produced in 1976. Most important models: Innocenti Austin A40 (1960); Innocenti Morris IM-3S (1963); Innocenti Austin J4 (1964); Innocenti Mini Minor (1965); Innocenti S. Spider (1966); Innocenti Mini Cooper Mk 2 (1968); Innocenti Mini Minor Mk 3, Mini Cooper Mk 3 and J5 (1970); Innocenti Mini 1000, Mini Cooper 1300 Mk 3 Austin J5 (1972); Innocenti Mini 90, Mini 120 and Regent (1974).

OFFICINE ALFIERI MASERATI S.p.A. — Italy

Founded in 1926, it is famous for its GT and racing cars. Managing Director: A. de Tomaso. Head office, press office and works: v. Ciro Menotti 322, Modena. About 500 employees. About 300 cars produced in 1976. Most important models: A 6/1500 (1948); A6G/2000 (1954); 3500 GT (1956); 5000 GT (1958); 3500 GTI, 5000 GTI (1960); Mistral, Quattroporte (1964); Mexico, Ghibli (1966); Indy (1969); Bora (1971); Merak (1972); Khamsin (1974); Merak SS (1975); Kyalami, Merak 2000, Quattroporte (1976). Victories up to 1957 in all types of motor racing: Targa Florio (1926), Indianapolis 500 Miles (1939-40), European Mountain Championship (1956-57), World Drivers' Championship with J.M. Fangio.

OLDSMOBILE - see GENERAL MOTORS CORPORATION

OPEL - see ADAM OPEL AG and GENERAL MOTORS ARGENTINA S.A.

OTOSAN A.S. — Turkey

Founded in 1959. It is part of Koç Group-Koç Holding and produces cars with fibreglass bodywork and Ford engines. General Maganer: E. Gönül. Head office and press office: P.K. 102, Kadiköy, Istanbul. Works: Otosan Otomobil Sanayii A.S. P.K. 102 Kadiköy, Istanbul. 2,630 employees. 11,000 cars produced in 1975.

PANTHER WESTWINDS Ltd — Great Britain

Founded in 1971. Managing Director: R. Jankel. Deputy Managing Director: L. Jankel. Head office, press office and works: Canada Rd, Byfleet, Surrey. 165 employees. 390 cars produced in 1977. Most important models: J 72.4.2 litre (1972); Lazer, FF (1973); De Ville Saloon (1974); Rio (1975); Lima, De Ville Convertible (1976).

PAYAN - see IRAN NATIONAL INDUSTRIAL MANUFACTURING Co. Ltd

PEKING — China (People's Republic)

Works: Dong Fang Hong, Peking. Public Relations office: China National Machinery Import & Export Corp., P.O.B. 49, Peking.

PERANA-FORD - see BASIL GREEN MOTORS (Tvl) (Pty) Ltd

PEUGEOT - see AUTOMOBILES PEUGEOT S.A.

PLYMOUTH - see CHRYSLER CORPORATION

POLSKI-FIAT - see FABRYKA SAMOCHODÓW OSOBOWYCH

PONTIAC - see GENERAL MOTORS CORPORATION and GENERAL MOTORS OF CANADA Ltd

PORSCHE - see Dr. Ing. h.c. F. PORSCHE A.G.

(THE) PREMIER AUTOMOBILES Ltd — India

Founded in 1944. Chairman: L. Hirachand. Managing Director: P.N. Vencatesan. Head office and press office: Construction House, Wlachand Hirachand Marg, Ballard Estate, Bombay-400 038. Works: L.B. Shastri Marg, Kurla, Bombay-400 038. About 9,000 employees. 17,481 cars produced in 1977.

PRINCESS - see BRITISH LEYLAND Ltd

PUMA INDÚSTRIA DE VEICULOS S.A. — Brazil

Founded in 1964 under name of Sociedade de Automóveis Luminari Ltda. Present title since 1975. Directors: L.R. Alves da Costa, M. Masteguim. J.M. Hellmeister. Head office, press office and works: Av. Presidente Wilson 4385, C.P. 42649, São Paulo. 630 employees. 1,911 cars produced in 1977. Models: Malzoni GT with DKW engine (1964-65); Puma GT with DKW engine (1966-67); Puma 1500 GT with VW engine (1968-69); Puma 1600 GTE with VW engine (1970); Puma 1600 GTE and GTS with VW engine (1971); Puma GTB 4100 with GM engine (1974).

RÉGIE NATIONALE DES USINES RENAULT — France

Founded in 1898 under the name of Société Anonyme des Usines Renault. Present title since 1945 when it was nationalized. It is today the largest motor manufacturer in France. President and General Manager: B. Vernier-Palliez. Head office and press office: 34 quai du Point du Jour, Boulogne Billancourt 92200. Works: Pierre Lefaucheux, Flins; Usine de Cléon, Cléon: Usine du Mans, Pierre-Piffault; Usine de Choisy, Choisy-le-Roy; Usine d'Orlèans, St. Jean-de-la-Ruelle; Usine du Havre, Sandouville; Usine de Dreux, Dreux; Usine de Doual, Doual. 106,753 employees. 1,659,973 cars produced in 1976. Most important models: 1.75 CV (1898); 2 cylinder (1904); 35 CV (1912); Marne Taxi, Type AG, Type TT (1923); 45 hp (1923-27); Celtaquatre (1934); Viva Grand Sport (1938); 4 CV (1947); Fregate (1951); Dauphine (1957); Floride (1959); Floride S, Caravelle, 8 (1962); Caravelle 1100 (1963); 8 Major (1964); 16 (1965); 4 Parisienne (1966); 16 TE, 6 (1968); 12 (1969); R 5, R 15, R 17 (1971); R 16 TX (1973); R 30, R 20 (1975); R 14 (1976). Entries and wins in numerous competitions (Monte Carlo Rally, Alpine Rally, Tour de Corse, Liège-Rome-Liège, Sebring, Reims, Nürburgring, Mobil Economy Run, etc.).

MANUFACTURE AND ASSEMBLY IN OTHER COUNTRIES — **Argentina:** Renault Argentine S.A. (subsidiary), Avda. Santa Maria, C.C. 8, Cordoba (manuf. 4, 6, 12). **Australia:** Renault Australia Pty Ltd (subsidiary), Dougharty Road, P.O. Box 60, West Heidelberg, Victoria (assem. 8, 10, 12, 16, 16 TS). **Belgium:** Rnur (subsidiary), 499 Schaarbeeklei, Vilvoorde 1 (assem. 4, 6, 8, 10). **Chile:** Automotores Franco Chilena (subsidiary), Casilla 10173, Los Andes (assem. 4); Corme Canica (concessionaire), Casilla 10173, Los Andes (assem. 4). **Colombia:** Sofasa (associated company), Apartado Aereo 4529, Medellin (assem. 4, 6); Socofam (associated company), Duitama, Boyaca (assem. 4, 6). **Eire:** Smith Engineering Ltd (subsidiary), Trinity Street, Wexford (assem. 4, 6, 8, 10, 12, 16). **Greece:** Soheca (concessionaire), Athene 126. **Indonesia:** Gaya Motors (concessionaire), Jalan'c Aphd, P.O. Box 2126 DKT, Djakarta Fair, Djakarta. **Iran:** Saipa (concessionaire), 553 av. Eisenhower, Teheran. **Ivory Coast:** Safar (subsidiary), B.P. 2764, Abidjan (assem. 4, 5, 6, 10, 12, 16, 16 TS). **Madagascar:** Somacoa (associated company), Route de Majunga, B.P. 796, Tananarive (assem. 4, 6, 12, 16, 16 TS). **Malaysia:** Champion Motors Sdn Bhd, Jalan Usaha, Shah Alam Selangor, P.O. Box 814, Kuala Lumpur (assem. 10, 16). **Mexico:** Diesel Association (concessionaire), Ciudad Sahagun, Hidalgo (assem. 4, 5, 10). **Morocco:** Somaca, km 12 Autoroute de Rabat, Casablanca (assem. 4, 6, 8, 12, 16, 16 TS). **New Zealand:** Campbell Industries Ltd (concessionaire), Jellicoe Crescent, P.O. Box 84, Thames (assem. 10, 12). **Philippines:** Renault Philippines (subsidiary), P.O. Box 1011, Makati, Rizal (assem. 4, 6, 8, 10, 12, 16, 16 TS). **Portugal:** Industrias Lusitanas Renault (associated company), Fabrica de Guarda, Guarda Gare (assem. 4, 6, 8, 10, 12, 16, 16 TS). **Rumania:** Interprendera de Autoturisme de Pitesti (concessionaire), Casuta Postala I.A.P., Ju de tul Argès, Colibasi (assem. 8, Dacia 1300). **Singapore:** Associated Motors Industries (concessionaire), Taman Jurong, P.O.B. 19, Singapore 22 (assem. 10, 12). **South Africa:** Motors Assemblies Ltd (associated company), P.O. Box 12030, Jacobs, Durban (assem. 4, 6, 10, 12, 16 TS). **Spain:** Fasa-Renault S.A. (subsidiary), Apartado 262, Autopista de Francia, Madrid (assem. 4, 6, 8, 12). **Trinidad:** Amalgamated Industries Ltd, Tumpuna Road, Arima Trinidad, Port of Spain (assem. 10, 12, 16). **Tunisia:** Stia (associated company), Route de Monastir, Sousse (assem. 4). **Turkey:** Oyak Renault (associated company), Zone Industrielle, P.K. 255, Bursa (assem. 12). **Uruguay:** Automotores, Cerro Largo 888, Santa Rosa, Montevideo (assem. 10, 12, 16). **Venezuela:** Cvvca (associated company), Edificio Gran Avenida Piso 4, Apartado del Este 61033, Caracas (assem. 10, 12, 16); Cvvca (associated company), Edo Carabobo, Mariara (assem. 10, 12, 16). **Yugoslavia:** Industrija Motornih Vozil (concessionaire), B.P. 60, Nuovo Mesto (assem. 4, 6, 8, 10, 12, 16).

(THE) RELIANT MOTOR COMPANY Ltd — Great Britain

Founded in 1934 under the name of Reliant Engineering Co. (Tamworth) Ltd. Present title since 1962. Acquired Bond Cars Ltd in 1969. Chairman: J.F. Nash. Managing Director: R.W. Wiggin. Directors: R.F.C. Musgrave, C. Burton, B.G. Wills, K.F. Fieldsend, M.E. Smith, R.L. Spencer. Head office and works: Two Gates, Tamworth, Staffs. Public Relations Argents: Adrian Ball & Associates Ltd, 20 Tudor Street, London EC4Y OHU. 1,800 employees. About 15,000 cars produced in 1976. Most important models: first sports car Sabre (1960); Sabre 6 (1961); Regal 3/25 (1962); Scimitar GT, Rebel 700 (1964); Rebel 700 Estate (1967); Scimitar GTE (1968); Scimitar GTE Automatic, Kitten (Saloon/Estate (1975); New Scimitar GTE Overdrive/Automatic (1976), Bond Bug (1970); Robin Saloon/Estate and Van (1973), all with glass fibre bodywork. Entries from 1962-64 in numerous competitions (Tulip Rally, RAC Rally of Great Britain, Monte Carlo Rally, Circuit of Ireland, Alpine Rally, Spa-Sofia-Liége Rally; winners of class in Total Economy Run in 1976 and 1977 with 55.5 mpg and 57.5 mpg respectively.

MANUFACTURE IN OTHER COUNTRIES — **Greece:** Mebea SA, 58-60 Aristotelous St, Athens 103 (manuf. TW9, Robin). **Turkey:** Otosan A.S., P.O.B. 102, Kadikoy, Istanbul (manuf. Anadol).

RENAULT (France) - see RÉGIE NATIONALE DES USINES RENAULT

ROLLS-ROYCE MOTORS Ltd — Great Britain

Rolls-Royce Motors Ltd was formed in April 1971 to take over the assets of the original Rolls-Royce Ltd in the automotive field. The first Rolls-Royce car ran in 1904 and they have always specialised in the production of high class cars of great quality. Chairman: I.J. Fraser, CBE, MC. Managing Director: D.A.S. Plastow. Directors: L.W. Harris, G.R. Fenn, T. Neville, C.S. Aston, H. Wuttke, H.P.N. Benson. Head office and works: Pym's Lane, Crewe, Ches.

Press office: 14 Conduit St, London W1. 9,500 employees. 3,162 cars produced in 1976. Most important models: first Rolls-Royce in 1904; Silver Ghost (1906-25); Twenty (1911); Phantom I (1925-29); Phantom II (1929-36); Phantom III (1936); Silver Wraith (1946); Phantom IV (1950); Silver Cloud I (1955); Silver Cloud II, Phantom V (1959); Silver Cloud III (1962); Silver Shadow (1965); Phantom VI (1968); Corniche (1971); Camargue (1975).

ROM CARMEL INDUSTRIES Ltd   Israel

Founded in 1958 as private company by L. Schneller and Y. Shubinski. From 1966 to 1971 in partnership with Standard Triumph Motor Co. England. Now Rom Carmel Industries Ltd, member of Clal Group. General Manager: N. Nemirowski. Head office, press office and works: P.O.B. 444, Haifa, Tirat Carmel. 650 employees. 1,800 cars produced in 1976. Most important models: Sussita, Carmel, Bilboa, Rom 1300. All with bodywork in fibreglass reinforced polyester.

ROVER - see LEYLAND CARS ROVER and LEYLAND SOUTH AFRICA Ltd

R.V. ALFONSO DMG Inc.   Philippines

(Make: Toro)

Head office, press office and works: Guevent Bldg., P.O. Box 1263, Manila.

SAAB-SCANIA AB   Sweden

The first Saab car was made in 1950 by the former Svenska Aeroplan Aktiebolaget. Saab cars are currently manufactured by the Saab Car Division of Saab-Scania AB which was formed in 1968 through the merger of Saab Aktiebolag and Scania-Vabis. Other Saab-Scania products include Scania commercial vehicles, aircraft, missiles, avionics, electronic equipment, computers, electromedical equipment, industrial valves, measuring systems, etc. Chairman: M. Wallenberg. President: C. Mileikowsky. Chief Executive Saab Car Division: S. Wennlo. Group head office: 8-581 88 Linköping. Head office and press office Saab Car Division: S-611 01 Nyköping. Works: Trollhättan, Nyköping, Kristineham, Arlöv. 37,000 employees. 95,927 cars produced in 1976. Most important models: 92, 93 (1950-60); 95 Estate (1959); 96 (1960); 96 V4 (1966); 99 (1968); Sonett III (1969); 99 Combi Coupé (1973). Numerous wins in international rallies including Monte Carlo (twice), RAC (5 times), Tulip Rally, Baja 1000, Swedish KAK, Arctic and 1000 Lakes in Finland, etc.

MANUFACTURE IN OTHER COUNTRIES — Finland: Oy Saab-Valmet Ab, Uusikaupunki (manuf. 95, 96, 99). Belgium: Saab Production S.A., Mechelen (manuf. 99). About 30,000 cars produced outside Sweden in 1975.

SBARRO - see SOCIÉTÉ DE FABRICATION D'AUTOMOBILES SBARRO S.a.r.l.

SCORA   France

President: M.J. Durand. Head office and works: route d'Egletons, 19550 Lapleau.

SEAT - SOCIEDAD ESPAÑOLA DE AUTOMOVILES DE TURISMO S.A.   Spain

Founded in 1950. President: J.M. Antoñanzas. Managing Directors: P. Vidal, J. Pañella. Head office and press office: Avda. Generalisimo 146, Madrid 16. Works: Zona Franca, Martorell, Barcellona, Landaben, Pamplona. 32,000 employees. 347,048 cars produced in 1976. Most important models: 133, 133 L, 133 Especial L, 127, 127 3P, 127 4P, 127 Comercial, 1200 Sport, 124 D, 124 D LS, 124 D Especial, 131 (1430), 131. (1600), 132 (1600), 132 (1800), 132 Mercedes Diesel, 128 3P (1200-1600), 124 Especial (1600-1800), 131 Automatico, 132 Automatico, Sport 1430.

SEVEN - see CATERHAM CAR Sales Ltd

SIMCA - see CHRYSLER ESPANA and CHRYSLER FRANCE

ŠKODA - AUTOMOBILOVÉ ZÁVODY NÁRODNI PODNIK   Czechoslovakia

Founded in 1894 by Laurin and Klement for the construction of velocipedes, assumed title of Laurin & Klement Co. Ltd in 1907. Škoda in 1925, and in 1945 became national corporation (AZNP). Director: M. Zapadlo. Commercial Deputy Director: Z. Rubin. Head office, press office and works:

410

Trída Rudé armady, Mladá Boleslav. 15,000 employees. Abouth 60,000 cars produced in 1976. Car production begun in 1905 (2-cylinder cars). Most important models: Laurin & Klement (1905); E 4-cyl. (1907); "S" Type (1911); 100, 105, 110, 120 Type (1923); 4R, 6R (1924); 420, 422 (1934); Popular, Rapid (1935-39); 1101, 1102 (1945-51); 440 (1956); Octavia, Felicia (1959); Octavia Combi, 1202 (1962); 1000 MB (1964); 100 L, 110 L, 1203 (1969); 110R Coupé (1970), 105, 120 (1977).

SOCIÉTÉ DE FABRICATION D'AUTOMOBILES SBARRO S.a.r.l.   Switzerland

Founded in 1973. Proprietor: F. Sbarro. Head office, press office and works: ACA Atelier, 1411 Les Tuileries de Grandson, Yverdon, Lausanne.

SPARTAN CAR COMPANY   Great Britain

Specializes in major accident repairs to sports and specialist cars. Designer: J. McIntyre. Head office and press office: 437 Westdale Lane, Mapperley, Nottingham. Works: Podder Lane, Mapperley Plains, Nottingham. 10 employees. 250 cars produced in 1976.

STANDARD MOTOR PRODUCTS OF INDIA Ltd   India

Head office, press office and works: 29 Mount Rd, Madras-600 002.

STEVENS - see ANTHONY STEVENS AUTOMOBILES Ltd.

STUTZ MOTOR CAR OF AMERICA Inc.   USA

Established in 1968. President: J.D. O'Donnell. Secretary and Treasurer: R.L. Curotto. Head office: Time-Life Bldg., Rockefeller Center, New York, N.Y. 10020. Press office: Bill Doll, Shannon & Co. Inc., 150 West 52nd St, New York, N.Y. 10019. 55 cars produced in 1976.

SUBARU - see FUJI HEAVY INDUSTRIES Ltd

SUZUKI MOTOR COMPANY Ltd   Japan

Founded in 1909 under the name of Suzuki Shokkuki Seisakusho. Present title since 1954. President: J. Suzuki. Executive Managing Director: O. Suzuki. Senior Managing Directors: A. Kinoshita, T. Okano. Head office and press office: 300 Kamimura, Hamagun, Shizouka-ken. Works: Kosai, Shirasuka 4520, Kosaishi, Suzuoka-ken; Iwata, Iwai 500, Iwata-shi, Shizouka-ken; Ohsuka, Ombuchi 6333, Omsuka-cho, Ogesagun, Shizouka-ken. 8,607 employees. 69,424 cars produced in 1976. Most important models: Suzulight 360 (1955); Suzuki Fronte 360 LC10 (1967); Fronte 500 (1968); Fronte Coupé (1971).

SYD LAWRENCE SPECIAL CARS Ltd   Great Britain

Founded in 1977. Managing Director: S.J. Lawrence. Directors: V.L.P. Davis, I. Ferguson. Head office and works: 37 High St., Southgate, London N14 6LD.

SYRENA - see FABRYKA SAMOCHODÓW MALOLITRAZOWYCH

TATRA Národní Podnik   Czechoslovakia

Tatra is one of oldest European motor manufacturers. In second half of 19th century de luxe coaches were being built in Nesselsdorf. Production of railway carriages was begun in 1882 and first motor-car, called the "President", was produced in 1897. General Director: M. Kopec. Head office and press office: Koprivnice. Works: Tatra Koprivnice okres Novy Jičin, 1,500 cars produced in 1976. Most important models: President (1897); B Type (1902); E Type 12 hp (1905); K Type (1906); T 14/15 (1914); Tatra 4/12, Tatra 11 (1923); 17/31 (1926-30); Tatra 30 (1927-29); Tatra 24/30 (1930-34); Tatra 52 (1930-38); Tatra 57 (1932); Tatra 75 (1933-37); Tatra 77 (1934); Tatra 87 (1936-38); Tatraplan (1949); Tatra 603 (1957); Tatra 2-603 (1964); Tatra 613 (1975). Has been entering competitions since 1900 (Targa Florio, Leningrad-Moscow-Tbilisso-Moscow, Alpine Rally, Polsky Rally, Vltava Rally, Marathon de la Route, etc.).

TECHNICAL EXPONENTS Ltd   Great Britain

Founded in 1965. Proprietor and General Manager: T.P. Bennett. Head office and press office: 74 Waterford Rd, London SW6. Works: Denham Green Lane, Denham, Bucks.

Most important models: TX Tripper, 1500 and 2000 Dolomite Sprint.

TOFAS - see FIAT S p.A.

TORO - see R.V. ALFONSO DMG Inc.

TOYO KOGYO COMPANY Ltd   Japan

(Make: Mazda)

Founded in 1920 under the name of Toyo Cork Kogyo Co. Ltd. Present title since 1927. President: K. Matsuda. Executive Vice-President: T. Murai. Senior Managing Directors: M. Kawano, Y. Yamazaki, H. Mineoka, S. Inomata, T. Hasegawa, K. Roppyakuda, T. Ishibashi. Head office, press office and works: 6047, Fuchumachi, Aki-gun, Hiroshima. 30,000 employees. 487,675 vehicles produced in 1976. Car production begun in 1930 with Mazda (3-speed). Most important models: 360 Coupé (1960); 360 and 600 (1962); 800 Sedan (1964); 1000 (1965); 1500 Sedan (1966); 1500 SS, 110 S (1967); R110 Coupé, R100 Coupé, 1800 Sedan (1968); RX-2, 616 Coupé and Sedan (1970). Entries in numerous competitions: Singapore GP (1966); Macao GP (1966-67); 84 hour Marathon (1968); Singapore GP, Francorchamps (1969); Francorchamps and Shell Springbok Series (1970).

ASSEMBLY IN OTHER COUNTRIES — Ghana: Mark Cofie Engineering Ltd (associated company). Ireland: Motor Distributors Ltd. (associated company), Nass Road, Dublin 12 (assem. 818). Korea: Kia Industrial Co. Ltd. (associated company), 8 Yang Dong, Choong Ku, Seoul. Malaysia: Asia Automobile Industries Sdn Bhd (affiliate), No. 11 Road 219 Federal Highway, Petaling Jaya, Selangor (assem. 1300 Sedan, 1500 Sedan). New Zealand: Mazda Motors of New Zealand (joint venture). Portugal: Sociedade Commercial Tasso de Sousa Ltda (associated company). South Africa: Illings (Pty) Ltd (associated company), P.O.B. 196, Isando (assem. 1300 Sedan). Thailand: Kamol Sukosol Co. Ltd. (associated company), 857 Makachai Road, Bangkok (assem. 818, Luce). Trinidad Tobago: Southern Sales & Service Co. Ltd, Port of Spain (associated company).

TOTAL PERFORMANCE Inc.   USA

Established in 1971. President: M.V. Lauria. Vice President: G.C. Gallicchio. Head office, press office and works: 406 S. Orchard St, Rt. 5, Wallingford, CT 06492. 20 employees. 40 cars produced in 1976.

TOYOTA MOTOR COMPANY Ltd   Japan

Founded in 1937. Chairman of the Board: S. Saito. President: E. Toyoda. Executive Vice-Presidents: S. Toyoda, T. Ohno, M. Hanai. Senior Managing Directors: M. Noguchi, S. Yamamoto, S. Matsuo, H. Mori. Head office and press office: 1, Toyota-cho, Toyota City. Works: Housha, 1, Toyote-cho, Toyota City; Motomachi, 1 Motomachi, Toyota City; Tokaoka, 1 Honda, Toyota City; Tsutsumi, 1 Tsutsumi-cho, Toyota City; Hiyoshi, 1 Miyoshimachi, Nishikamo-gun. 43,020 employees. 2,006,722 cars produced in 1976. Most important models: Toyo Ace (1954); Toyopet Crown (1955); Toyopet Corona (1957); Toyopet Crown Deluxe (1958); Toyopet Crown Diesel (1959); Toyopet New Corona and Publica (1960); Toyopet New Crown (1962); Crown Eight (1963); Toyota Corolla 1100 (1966); Toyota Century (1967); Toyota Corona Mk II, Toyota 1000 (1968); Celica, Carina (1970); Sprinter (1971).

ASSEMBLY IN OTHER COUNTRIES - Australia: Australian Motor Industries Ltd (associated company), 155 Bertie Street, Port Melbourne, 3207 Victoria (assem. Corolla, Corona, Crown). Brazil: Toyota do Brasil S.A. (subsidiary), Industria e Comercio Estrada de Piraporinha km 23, São Bernardo do Campo, São Paulo (assem. Land Cruiser). Canada: Canadian Motor Industries Ltd. (subsidiary), 1291 Bellamy Road, North Scouborough, Ontario. Costa Rica: Ensembladora Centroamericana de Costa Rica S.A. (associated company), Apartado 10085, San Jose. Ghana: Fattal Brothers Ltd (concessionaire), Ring Road, West Industrial Area, Ghana (assem. Corona). Malaysia: Champion Motors (Malaysia) Sdn Bhd (concessionaire), P.O.B. 814, Kuala Lumpur (assem. Corolla, Corona, Crown). Peru: Toyota del Peru S.A. (subsidiary), Zona Industrial 1-2, Ventanilla Puente de Piedra, Lima (assem. Corona, Land Cruiser, Stout). Philippines: Delta Motor Corp. (concessionaire), 2285 Pasong Tamo, Makati, Rizal (assem. Corolla, Corona, Crown). Portugal: Salvador Caetano Industrias Metallurgicas e Veiculos de Transporte Sarl (concessionaire), Vila Nova de Gaia (assem. Corolla, Dyna). Thailand: Toyota Motor Thailand Co. Ltd. (subsidiary), 180 Suriwongse Rd, Bangkok (assem. Corolla, Corona). Venezuela: Compañia Anónima Tocars (concessionaire), Edificio Tocars-Chacao, Av. Francisco de Miranda, Caracas (assem. Land Cruiser). Other assembly factories are in Eire, Indonesia, Pakistan, Trinidad Tobago.

TRABANT - see VEB SACHSENRING AUTOMOBILWERKE ZWICKAU

TRIDENT MOTOR COMPANY Ltd   **Great Britain**

Directors: E. Stern, L. Baker, W.J. Last. Head office, press office and works: Turrett Lane, Ipswich, Suffolk.

TRIUMPH - see LEYLAND CARS TRIUMPH and LEYLAND SOUTH AFRICA Ltd

TVR ENGINEERING Ltd   **Great Britain**

Established in 1954 as Grantura Engineering Ltd. Present title since 1966. Chairman: A. Lilley. Managing Director: M.A. Lilley. Director: S. Halsread. Head office, press office and works: Bristol Ave, Blackpool, Lancs. 84 employees. About 400 cars produced in 1976. Most important models: Mk I (1954-60); Mk II (1960); Mk II A (1962); Mk III (1963-64); Mk III 1800 (1963); Griffith series 200 (1964); Griffith 400 (1965); 200 V8 (1966); Tuscan SE, Vixen 1600 (1967); Vixen S2 (1968); Tuscan V6 (1969); 1600 M (1972-73); 2500 (1970-73); 2500 M, 3000 M (1972); Turbo (1975); Taimar (1976). Entries and wins in numerous competitions. Outright winners of 1970, 1971 and 1972 Modsports Championships. 1976 win in class B production sports cars.

UAZ - ULIANOVSKY AVTOMOBILNY ZAVOD   **USSR**

Press office: Avtoexport, Ul. Volkhonka 14, Moscow G. 19. Works: Ulianovsk.

VANDEN PLAS - see BRITISH LEYLAND Ltd

VAUXHALL MOTORS Ltd   **Great Britain**

Founded in 1903. Transferred from Vauxhall district of London to Luton in 1905. Present title since 1907. Taken over by General Motors Corp. in 1925. Chairman and Managing Director: W.R. Price. Directors: H.A. Carpenter, R.A. White, G.E. Moore, J.P. McCormack, D. Savage, P.E. Hitch, E.D. Fountain, P.G.H. Newton. Head office, press office and works: Kimpton Rd, Luton, Beds. 29,000 employees. 142,692 cars produced in 1976. Most important models: Velox (1949); Cresta (1954); Victor (1957); Viva (1963). Entries in various competitions from 1909 to 1924.

ASSEMBLY IN OTHER COUNTRIES — **Belgium:** General Motors Continental S.A. (associated company), P.B. 549, Antwerp. **Denmark:** General Motors International A.S. (associated company), Aldersrogade 20, Copenhagen. **Eire:** McCairns Motors (concessionaire), Alexandra Rd, East Wall, Dublin. **Malaysia:** Champion Motors (M) Sdn Bhd (concessionaire), P.O.B. 814, Kuala Lumpur. **New Zealand:** General Motors New Zealand Ltd (associated company), Wellington. **Pakistan:** National Motors (concessionaire), Karachi 28. **Philippines:** General Motors Philippines (concessionaire), Manila. **Portugal:** General Motors de Portugal Ltda (associated company), C.P. 2484, Av. Marechal Gomes de Costa, Lisbon 6. **Singapore:** Associated Motors Industries Ltd (concessionaire), P.O.B. 19, Tamar Jurong, Singapore 22. **South Africa:** General Motors South Africa (associated company), P.O.B. 1137, Kempston Rd, Port Elizabeth. **Trinidad:** Neal & Massy Industries Ltd (concessionaire), P.O.B. 1298, Port of Spain.

VAZ - VOLZHSKY AVTOMOBILNY ZAVOD   **USSR**

Press office: Avtoexport, Ul. Volkhonka 14, Moscow G. 19. Works: Togliatti. 75,000 employees. 685,000 cars produced in 1976.

VEB AUTOMOBILWERK EISENACH   **Germany (Democratic Republic)**

(Make: Wartburg)

Head office and press office: Heinrich-Heine-Str. 1, 59 Eisenach.

VEB SACHSENRING AUTOMOBILWERKE ZWICKAU   **Germany (Democratic Republic)**

(Make: Trabant)

Founded in 1904 under the name of A. Horch Motorwagenwerke AG Zwickau, became Audi-Mobilwagenwerke AG Zwickau in 1909, merged with Auto Union in 1932, nationalized in 1946. Present title since 1958. Head office and press office: W. Rathenau Strasse, Zwickau 95. 9,000 employees. Over 100,000 cars produced in 1976. Most important models: world record 500 hp 16-cyl-rear-engined car (1937-38); DKW 3.5-5 I, F2, F3, F4, F5, F6, F7, F8 (two stroke front drive engine up to 1945); F8 (1949-55); F9 (1949-52); P70, S 240 (1955-59); Trabant P50 (1958-62); 600 (1962-63); 601 (1964). Entries in numerous competitions (Munich-

Vienna-Budapest, Semperit, Thousand Lakes, Tulip, Monte Carlo, Vltava, Pneumat (D.D.R.) Rallies, Tour de Belgique).

VOLKSWAGENWERK AG   **Germany (Federal Republic)**

Founded in 1937 under name of Gesellschaft zur Vorbereitung des Deutschen Volkswagen mbH, became Volkswagenwerk GmbH in 1938. Present title since 1960. For volume of production is foremost German motor manufacturer. President: T. Schmücker. Directors: H. Backsmann, G.M. Strobl, G. Hartwich, H. Münzner, F. Thomée, P. Frerk, E. Fiala, W.P. Schmidt. Head office and press office: 3180 Wolfsburg. Works: as above, Braunschweig, Emden, Hannover, Kassel, Salzgitter. 93,026 employees. 1,316,034 cars produced in 1976. Most important models: Limousine 1200 (1945); 1200 Convertible (1959); 1200 Karmann-Ghia Coupé (1955); 1200 Karmann-Ghia Convertible (1957); 1500 and 1500 Karmann-Ghia Coupé (1961); 1500 N Limousine, 1500 S Limousine, 1500 S Karmann-Ghia Coupé (1963); 1600 TL (1965); 411 (1968); 411 E, 411 LE (1969); 1302, 1302 S, K 70 (1970); 1303 (1972). Passat, Passat Variant (1973); Golf, Scirocco (1974); Polo (1975); Derby (1977).

MANUFACTURE AND ASSEMBLY IN OTHER COUNTRIES — **Mexico:** Volkswagen de México S.A. de C.V. (associated company), Mexico City (1200, 181, Brasilia). **Nigeria:** Volkswagen of Nigeria (associated company), Lagos-Badagry Highway, km 18, Lagos (manuf. 1200). **South Africa:** Volkswagen of South Africa Ltd (associated company), Uitenhage (assem. 1200, Passat). 730,205 cars produced outside Federal Republic in 1976, including VW do Brasil.

VOLKSWAGEN DO BRASIL S.A.   **Brazil**

Founded in 1953. Chairman: W. Sauer. Head office, press office and works: v. Anchieta km 23.5, São Bernardo do Campo, São Paulo. CEP 09700. 472,420 cars produced in 1976.

VOLVO AB   **Sweden**

Founded in 1926. President and General Manager: P.G. Gyllenhammar. Head office, press office and works: S-405 08, Göteborg. 62,441 employees. 251,311 cars produced in 1976. Most important models: P4 (1927); 53-56 (1939); PV 50 (1944); PV 444 (1947); P 1900 (1954-57); 122S Amazon (1956); P 544 (1958-62); P 1800 (1961); 144 (1966); 164 (1968); 240 (1975); 343 (1976).

ASSEMBLY IN OTHER COUNTRIES — **Australia:** Volvo Australia Pty Ltd, Melbourne (Liverpool). **Belgium:** Volvo Europa N.V. (subsidiary), P.B. 237, Ghent. **Canada:** Volvo (Canada) Ltd, Willowdale. **Holland:** Volvo Car B.V., Lucas Gasselstraat 7, Eindhoven. **Malaysia:** Swedish Motor Assemblies Sdn Bhd (subsidiary), Batu Tiga, Industrial Estate, Selangor. About 129,000 cars assembled outside Sweden in 1975.

VOLVO CAR B.V.   **Holland**

Founded in 1928 by Hub and Wim van Doorne, assumed title Van Doorne's Automobielfarbieken in 1958. In 1975 A.B. Volvo obtained a controlling interest of 75% in Van Doorne's Automobielfabrieken B.V. which became Volvo Car B.V. a member of the Volvo Group. The Company designes and manufactures the compact medium-sized Volvo cars. Managing Directors: A. van der Padt, A. de Bruin, O. Wibaut. Head office and press office: Steenovenweg, Helmond. About 6,000 employees. 74,300 cars produced in 1976.

WARTBURG - see VEB AUTOMOBILWERK EISENACH

YLN - YUE LOONG MOTOR COMPANY Ltd   **Taiwan**

Founded in 1953 as Yue Loong Engineering Co. Ltd. Present title since 1960. President: T.L. Yen. Executive Vice-President: V. Wu. Special Assistant to Chairman and President: C.C. Yen. Managing Director: V.Z. Faung. Head office and press office: 150 Nanking East Road, Sec II, Taipei. Works: Hsin Tien Taipei. 1,800 employees. 16,018 cars produced in 1976. Under licence of Nissan Motor Co. and American Motors Corp. manufactures various types of sedans and jeeps, including YL-1 and YL-2. Models: 707, 803, 301.

ZAZ - ZAPOROZHSKY AVTOMOBILNY ZAVOD   **USSR**

Press office: Avtoexport, Ul. Volkhonka 14, Moscow G. 19. Works: Zaporozhje. About 190,000 cars produced in 1974.

ZIL   **USSR**

Press office: Avtoexport, Ul. Volkhonka 14, Moscow G. 19. Works: Moscow.

COACHBUILDERS

ARCADIPANE DESIGN STUDIO   **Australia**

Proprietor: P. Arcadipane. Head office, press office and works: 148 Northern Rd, West Heidelberg, Victoria.

BERTONE (Carrozzeria) S.p.A.   **Italy**

Founded in 1912. Produces small and medium series of car bodies; bespoke production for car manufacturing firms and construction of prototypes. President and Managing Director: N. Bertone. Head office: c.so Canonico Allamano 40-46, 10095 Grugliasco, Turin.

BITTER-AUTOMOBILE   **Germany (Federal Republic)**

Head office and press office: Stefanstr. 1, Klashammer, 5820 Gevelsberg.

CARROZZERIA FISSORE S.p.A.   **Italy**

Founded in 1919. President: E. Fissore. Managing Director: F. De Florian. Head office, press office and works: v. Torino 183, 12308 Savigliano, Cuneo.

CHRIS HUMBERSTONE DESIGN   **Great Britain**

Head office and press office: 47 Brewery Rd, Woking, Surrey GU21 4LL.

CLYDE CASSADY BUILDER Inc.   **USA**

President: C.R. Cassady. Head office, press office and works: 839-4 Winding Way, Fair Oaks, California 95628.

COGGIOLA Carrozziere   **Italy**

Proprietor: P. Coggiola. Head office, press office and works: strada S. Luigi 19, 10043 Orbassano, Turin.

COLEMAN MILNE Ltd   **Great Britain**

Founded in 1953. Specialist in the manufacture of Grosvenor, Dorchester and Minster limousines. Chairman and Joint Managing Director: R.S.C. Milne. Joint Managing Director: D.H. Hackett. Head office: Colmil Works, Wigan Rd, Hart Common, Westhoughton, Bolton, Lancs. 95 employees. 280 cars produced in 1976.

CRAYFORD AUTO DEVELOPMENT Ltd   **Great Britain**

Founded in 1960, specialising in convertibles, estate cars and cross country vehicles. Directors: G.D. McMullan, J.J. Smith. Head office: High Street, Westerham, Kent. 62 employees. 342 cars produced in 1976.

DeLOREAN MOTOR Co.   **USA**

Head office and press office: 100 West Long Lake Rd, Bloomfield Hills, Mich. 48013.

FRUA   **Italy**

Head office, press office and works: v. Papa Giovanni XXIII 13, Borgo San Pietro - Moncalieri, Turin.

GHIA S.p.A.   **Italy**

Founded in 1915. Produces car bodies. President and Managing Director: J.D. Head. Members of Board: V. Bonica, S. Cerulli Irelli. Head office: v. A. da Montefeltro 5, 10134 Turin.

GLENFROME CARS Ltd   **Great Britain**

Directors: G.K. Evans, V.D.J.R. Hunt. Head office and works: 115 Glenfrome Rd, Bristol BS2 9UY.

ITAL DESIGN SIRP S.p.A.   **Italy**

Founded in 1968. Styling and design of cars in small, medium and large series; construction of models and prototypes. Directors: L. Bosio, G. Giugiaro, A. Mantovani. Head office and press office: v. A. Grandi 11, 10024 Moncalieri, Turin.

MAGRAW ENGINEERING Ltd Great Britain

Directors: G.J.L. Magraw, M.I. Mech, V.M. Magraw. Head office, press office and works: 135 Widmore Rd, Bromley, Kent BR1 3BA.

MICHELOTTI Carrozzeria Italy

Coachbuilding engineering studio for custom-made cars. Proprietor: Giovanni Michelotti. Head office, press office and works: strada dei Boschi 8, 10092 Beinasco, Turin.

MINICARS Inc. USA

Head office and press office: 35 La Patera Lane, Goleta, California 93017.

PHAETON COACH CORPORATION USA

Founded in 1969 as Eagle Coach Company. Present title since 1974. President and General Manager: R.J. Harris. Products include custom limousines, sport cars and utility vehicles. General offices and showroom: 119 World Trade Center, P.O.B. 58353, Dallas, Texas 75258. Works: 5424 Gregg St., Dallas, Texas 75235.

PININFARINA (Carrozzeria) S.p.A. Italy

Founded in 1930. Produces special and de luxe bodies. President: S. Pininfarina. Managing Director: R. Carli, Member of Board: E. Carbonato. Head office: c. Stati Uniti 61, Turin. Works: v. Lesna 78-80, 10095 Grugliasco, Turin.

TAFOYA USA

Designer: Baron Samuel Tafoya, 2640 Woodside Drive, Dearborn, Michigan 48124.

TREBRON DESIGN Inc. Canada

Head office and press office: 2830 Sabourin, St. Laurent, Quebec. President: N. Hamy.

VEHICLE DESIGN FORCE USA

Founded in 1976. President: G. Wiegert. Head office and press office: 1623 West Washington Blvd, Venice, Cal. 90291.

WILHELM KARMANN GmbH Germany (Federal Republic)

Founded in 1874 as Klages became Wilhelm Karmann in 1902. Proprietor: W. Karman. Head office and press office: Karmannstr. 1, 45 Osnabrück. Works: as above, Rheine.

ZAGATO (Carrozzeria) S.p.A. Italy

Founded in 1919. Produces car bodies. President: E. Zagato. Managing Director: G. Zagato. Head office: v. Arese, 20017 Terrazzano di Rho, Milan.

ELECTRIC VEHICLE BUILDERS

AMERICAN MOTORS CORPORATION USA

Address: American Center Bldg, P.O.B. 442, Detroit, Mich. 48232.

AM GENERAL CORPORATION USA

Address: 32500 Van Born Road, Wayne, Michigan 48184.

BATTRONIC TRUCK CORPORATION USA

Address: Third and Walnut Sts., Boyertown, Pennsylvania 19512.

B&Z ELECTRIC CAR USA

Address: 3346 Olive Ave, Signal Hill, Cal. 90806.

BILLINGS ENERGY CORPORATION USA

Address: 2000 East Billings Ave, Provo, Utah 84601.

CHW - C.H. WATERMAN INDUSTRIES Inc. USA

Address: White Pond Road, Athol, Massachusetts 01331.

COPPER DEVELOPMENT ASSOCIATION Inc. USA

Address: 405 Lexington Avenue, New York, New York 10017.

DAIHATSU KOGYO COMPANY Ltd Japan

Address: 1-1 Daihatsu-cho, Ikeda-shi, Osaka.

DIE MESH CORPORATION USA

Address: 629 Fifth Avenue, Pelham, New York 10803.

EFP - ELECTRIC FUEL PROPULSION CORPORATION USA

Address: Robbins Executive Park East, 2237 Elliott Avenue, Troy, Michigan 48084.

ELECTRACTION Ltd Great Britain

Address: Heybridge Basin, Maldon, Essex.

ELECTRIC AUTO CORPORATION USA

Address: P.O.B. 11414, Caparra, Puerto Rico 00922.

EPC - ELECTRIC PASSENGER CARS Inc. USA

Address: 5127 Galt Way, San Diego, California 92117.

EVA - ELECTRIC VEHICLE ASSOCIATES USA

Address: P.O. Box 9803, Brook Park, Ohio 44142.

EXXON ENTERPRISES Inc. USA

Address: P.O.B. 192, Florham Park, New Jersey 07932.

FIAT Italy

Address: c.so Agnelli 200, Turin.

FLINDERS UNIVERSITY Australia

Address: Stuart Rd, Bedford Park, Adelaide, SA.

FSM - FABRYKA SAMOCHODÓW MALOLITRAZOWYCH Poland

Address: Ul. Partyzantow 44, Bielsko-Biala.

THE GARRETT CORPORATION USA

Address: 9851-9951 Sepulveda Blvd, Los Angeles, Cal. 90009.

GENERAL MOTORS CORPORATION USA

Address: Advance Product Engineering, Warren, Michigan.

GLOBE-UNION Inc. USA

Address: 5757 North Green Bay, Ave., Milwaukee, Wisconsin 53201.

JET INDUSTRIES Inc. USA

Address: 4201 South Congress, Austin, Texas.

LUCAS INDUSTRIES Ltd Great Britain

Address: Special Projects, 17 Evelyn Rd, Sparkhill, Birmingham B11 3JR.

MARATHON ELECTRIC VEHICLES Ltd Canada

Address: 8305 Le Creusot Street, Montreal, Quebec, HIP 2A2.

MAZDA - TOYO KOGYO COMPANY Ltd Japan

Address: 6047, Fuchumachi, Aki-gun, Hiroshima.

McKEE ENGINEERING CORPORATION USA

Address: 411 West Colfax Street, Palatine, Illinois 60067.

MELEX Poland

Address: Pol-Mot, ul. Stalingradzka 23, Warsaw.

MERCEDES-BENZ Germany (FR)

Address: Daimler-Benz AG, 7 Stuttgart 60.

NISSAN Japan

Address: Ginza, Chuo-ku, Tokyo.

P.G.E. - PROGETTI GESTIONI ECOLOGICHE Italy

Address: via Rosellino 1, Milan.

PIAGGIO S.p.A. Italy

Address: v. A. Cecchi 6, Genova.

PILCAR Switzerland

Address: rue François-Perréard 22, 1225 Chêne-Bourg, Geneve.

RAF USSR

Address: Avtoexport, Ul. Volkhonka 14, Moscow G. 19.

SAAB-SCANIA Sweden

Address: Saab Car Division, Fack, S-61101 Nyköping.

SEBRING VANGUARD Inc. (Electrics) USA

Address: Works: Sebring Industrial Park, P.O.B. 1479, Sebring, Flo. 33870; press office: 9130, Red Branch Rd, Oakland Ridge Industrial Center, Columbia, Maryland 21044.

SRF Israel

Address: P.O.B. 3745, Jerusalem.

TEILHOL VOITURE ELECTRIQUE France

Address: Zone Industrielle, 63600 Ambert.

VOLKSWAGENWERK AG Germany (Federal Republic)

Address: 3180 Wolfsburg.

VOLVO AB Sweden

Address: S-405 08 Göteborg.

ZAGATO S.p.A. Italy

Address: v. Arese, 20017 Terrazzano di Rho, Milan.

Indexes

Name of car

Maximum speed

Makes, models and prices

NAME OF CAR

Cars called by names (in alphabetical order)

Model	Make
ACADIAN	PONTIAC (CDN)
ACCORD	HONDA
ALFA ROMEO	FNM
ALFASUD	ALFA ROMEO
ALFETTA	ALFA ROMEO
ALLEGRO	AUSTIN
ALPINE	CHRYSLER (GB), FASA-RENAULT
AMBASSADOR	HINDUSTAN
AMI	CITROËN
ANADOL	OTOSAN
ASCONA	OPEL
ASPEN	DODGE (USA)
AUSTER	NISSAN
AVENGER	CHRYSLER (GB)
BEL AIR	CHEVROLET (CDN)
BENTLEY DONINGTON	JOHNARD VINTAGE CAR
BERLINETTA	MONTEVERDI
BETA	LANCIA
BLACKHAWK	STUTZ
BOBCAT	MERCURY (USA)
BOCEK	OTOSAN
BONITO	FIBERFAB
BONNEVILLE	PONTIAC (USA)
BORA	MASERATI
BOX	MONOCOQUE
BRASILIA	VOLKSWAGEN (BR)
BRISA	KIA
BUGATTI	EL-KG
CAMARGUE	ROLLS-ROYCE
CAMARO	CHEVROLET (USA)
CAMPAGNOLA	FIAT (I)
CAPELLA	MAZDA
CAPRI	FORD (D, GB)
CAPRICE	CHEVROLET (USA, ZA)
CARINA	TOYOTA
CATALINA	PONTIAC (USA)
CAVALIER	VAUXHALL
CEDRIC	NISSAN
CELESTE	MITSUBISHI
CELICA	TOYOTA
CENTAUR	CONCEPT
CENTRON	G.P.
CENTURY	BUICK, TOYOTA
CHAIKA	GAZ
CHARADE	DAIHATSU
CHARGER	DODGE (BR, USA)
CHARMANT	DAIHATSU
CHASER	TOYOTA
CHEROKEE	JEEP CORPORATION
CHERRY	NISSAN
CHEVAIR	CHEVROLET (ZA)
CHEVELLE	CHEVROLET (USA)
CHEVETTE	CHEVROLET (BR, USA), VAUXHALL
CHEVY	CHEVROLET (RA, USA)
CITY	OPEL (D)
CIVIC	HONDA
CLIPPER	TRIDENT
CLUBMAN	MINI (BRITISH LEYLAND)
COMODORO	CHEVROLET (BR)
CONCORD	AMERICAN MOTORS
CONSTANTIA	CHEVROLET (ZA)
CONTINENTAL	LINCOLN
CORDOBA	CHRYSLER (USA)
CORNICHE	BENTLEY, ROLLS-ROYCE
COROLLA	TOYOTA
CORONA	TOYOTA
CORONADO	DODGE (RA)
CORTINA	FORD (AUS, GB, ZA)
CORVETTE	CHEVROLET (USA)
COSMO	MAZDA

Model	Make
COUGAR	MERCURY (USA)
COUNTACH	LAMBORGHINI
COUPÉ	LANCIA, SCORA
CROWN	TOYOTA
CUSTOM	FORD (CDN, USA)
CUSTOM CRUISER	OLDSMOBILE
CUTLASS	OLDSMOBILE
DART	DODGE (BR)
DATSUN	NISSAN
DEAUVILLE	DE TOMASO
DEBONAIR	MITSUBISHI
DELTA	OLDSMOBILE
DELTA WAGON	DAIHATSU
DERBY	VOLKSWAGEN (D)
DE VILLE	CADILLAC, PANTHER
DINO	FERRARI
DIPLOMAT	DODGE (USA)
DOLOMITE	TRIUMPH
DOUBLE-SIX	DAIMLER
DUAL COWL	AUBURN
DYANE	CITROËN
ECLAT	LOTUS
ELECTRA	BUICK
ELITE	FORD (USA), LOTUS
ESCORT	FORD (AUS, D, GB, ZA)
ESPADA	LAMBORGHINI
ESPRIT	LOTUS
ESTATE WAGON	BUICK
FAIRLADY	NISSAN
FAIRLANE	FORD (AUS)
FAIRMONT	FORD (AUS, USA)
FALCON	FORD (AUS)
FAMILIA	MAZDA
FERRARI	PANTHER
FIESTA	FORD (D, GB)
FIREBIRD	PONTIAC (USA)
FLEETWOOD	CADILLAC
FLORIAN	ISUZU
FRAZER NASH	ANTIQUE-CLASSIC
FRONTE	SUZUKI
FURY	PLYMOUTH
GALANT	MITSUBISHI
GAMMA	LANCIA
GAZEL	STANDARD
GEMINI	ISUZU
GIULIETTA	ALFA ROMEO
GLORIA	NISSAN
GOLF	VOLKSWAGEN (D)
GRANADA	FORD (CDN, D, GB, USA, ZA), PERANA-FORD
GRAND AM	PONTIAC (USA)
GRAND FAMILIA	MAZDA
GRAND LE MANS	PONTIAC (USA)
GRAND PRIX	PONTIAC (USA)
GRAND SAFARI	PONTIAC (USA)
GREMLIN	AMERICAN MOTORS
HAI	MONTEVERDI
HATCH	CHEVROLET (ZA)
HIGH SPEED	MONTEVERDI
HORIZON	PLYMOUTH
HUNTER	CHRYSLER (GB)
HURRYCANE	CUSTOCA
IMP	DAVRIAN
IMPALA	CHEVROLET (USA)
JAGUAR	LEYLAND (ZA)
JEEP	JEEP CORP., MITSUBISHI
JIMNY	SUZUKI
KADETT	OPEL
KHAMSIN	MASERATI
KITTEN	RELIANT
KOMMANDO	CHEVROLET (ZA)
KYALAMI	MASERATI
LADA	VAZ
LAGONDA	ASTON MARTIN

Model	Make
LANCER	MITSUBISHI
LANDCRUISER	TOYOTA
LAND ROVER	ROVER
LASER	ELITE
LAUREL	NISSAN
LAURENTIAN	PONTIAC (CDN)
LE BARON	CHRYSLER (USA)
LE MANS	PONTIAC (USA)
LEONE	SUBARU
LE SABRE	BUICK
LIMA	PANTHER
LIMOUSINE	DAIMLER, HONGKI
LONGCHAMP	DE TOMASO
LUCE	MAZDA
MAGNUM	DODGE (USA), VAUXHALL
MALAGA	DUTTON
MANTA	OPEL
MARATHON	CHECKER
MARINA	LEYLAND (ZA), MORRIS
MARK II	TOYOTA
MARQUIS	MERCURY (CDN, USA)
MATADOR	AMERICAN MOTORS
MAX CUORE	DAIHATSU
MAXI	AUSTIN
MEHARI	CITROËN
MERAK	MASERATI
MIDGET	MG
MINI	LEYLAND (ZA), NUOVA INNOCENTI, PUMA
MINICA	MITSUBISHI
MONACO	DODGE (USA)
MONARCH	MERCURY (USA)
MONTE CARLO	CHEVROLET (USA)
MONZA	CHEVROLET (USA)
MOSKVICH	AZLK
MURAT	TOFAS
MUSTANG	FORD (USA)
NASR	EL NASR
NEWPORT	CHRYSLER (USA)
NEW YORKER	CHRYSLER (USA)
NINETY-EIGHT	OLDSMOBILE
NOMAD	CHEVROLET (ZA)
NOVA	CHEVROLET (USA)
NUOVA LELE	ENNEZETA
OMEGA	OLDSMOBILE
OMNI	DODGE (USA)
OPALA	CHEVROLET (BR)
PACER	AMERICAN MOTORS
PADMINI	PREMIER
PALM BEACH	MONTEVERDI
PANTERA	DE TOMASO
PARISIENNE	PONTIAC (CDN)
PASSAT	VOLKSWAGEN (D, BR)
PATROL	NISSAN
PHANTOM	ROLLS-ROYCE
PHOENIX	PONTIAC (USA)
PINTO	FORD (USA)
POLARA	DODGE (BR, USA)
POLO	VOLKSWAGEN (D)
PONY	HYUNDAI
PRESIDENT	NISSAN
PUBLICA	TOYOTA
QUATTROPORTE	MASERATI
RALLYE	OPEL (D)
RANGE ROVER	ROVER
REGAL	BUICK
REKORD	OPEL
REPLICA BMW	SBARRO
REX	SUBARU
RIO	PANTHER
RIVIERA	BUICK
ROADPACER	MAZDA
ROBIN	RELIANT
ROM	ROM CARMEL
ROVER	LEYLAND (ZA)

Model	Make
SAFARI	MONTEVERDI
SALOON	PAYKAN
SCIMITAR	RELIANT
SCIROCCO	VOLKSWAGEN (D)
SCOUT	INTERNATIONAL HARVESTER
SEVILLE	CADILLAC
SERIES III	SEVEN, EXCALIBUR
SHERPA	FIBERFAB
SHOPPER	AWS
SIENNA	STEVENS
SIERRA	MONTEVERDI
SIETE	FASA-RENAULT
SILVER SHADOW	ROLLS-ROYCE
SILVER WRAITH	ROLLS-ROYCE
SILVIA	NISSAN
SIMCA	CHRYSLER (E), CHRYSLER FRANCE (F)
SIMCA BAGHEERA	MATRA
SIMCA RANCHO	MATRA
SKYHAWK	BUICK
SKYLARK	BUICK
SKYLINE	NISSAN
SOVEREIGN	DAIMLER
SPEEDSTER	AUBURN, INTERMECCANICA
SPIDER JUNIOR	ALFA ROMEO
SPITFIRE	TRIUMPH
SPORTS	SPARTAN CARS
SPRINTER	TOYOTA
STANZA	NISSAN
STARFIRE	OLDSMOBILE
STARLET	TOYOTA
STRATO	CUSTOCA
STRATOS	LANCIA
SUNBEAM	CHRYSLER (GB)
SUNBIRD	PONTIAC (USA)
SUNNY	NISSAN
SUPER ROBIN	RELIANT
TAFT	DAIHATSU
TAIMAR	TVR
TAUNUS	FORD (D, RA)
THUNDERBIRD	FORD (USA)
TORINO	IKA-RENAULT
TORONADO	OLDSMOBILE
TRIUMPH CHICANE	LEYLAND (ZA)
TURBO	ARGYLL, PORSCHE, SAAB, TVR
URRACO	LAMBORGHINI
VANDEN PLAS	DAIMLER
VARIANT	VOLKSWAGEN (BR)
VENTURER	TRIDENT
VERANEIO	CHEVROLET (BR)
VERSAILLES	LINCOLN
VIOLET	NISSAN
VIVA	VAUXHALL
VOLARÉ	PLYMOUTH
VOLGA	GAZ
WAGONEER	JEEP CORPORATION
ZASTAVA	ZCZ
ZEPHYR	MERCURY (USA)

Cars called by letters (in alphabetical order)

Model	Make
A4 CITY	LAWIL
A 112	AUTOBIANCHI
A 310	ALPINE
AMX	AMERICAN MOTORS
BB	FERRARI
BJ 212	PEKING
B PLUS	DUTTON
CX	CITROËN

Model	Make
D TYPE	LYNX
FF	FELBER
G21	GINETTA
GS	CITROËN
GT	BRADLEY
GTB	PUMA
GTE	PUMA
GTM	K.M.B.
GTS	PUMA
GTX	DODGE (RA)
J 72	PANTHER
K-180	OPEL (RA)
LL	LAFER
LN	CITROËN
LTD	FORD (AUS, USA)
M-461-C	ARO DACIA
ME 3000	AC
MGB	MG
MK 2	SYD LAWRENCE
MP	LAFER
PLUS 8	MORGAN
S11	CHEVROLET (ZA)
S3 VARZINA	LAWIL
SS	ARKLEY, INTERNATIONAL HARVESTER, DUESENBERG
SSJ	DUESENBERG
T2	BENTLEY
T 613	TATRA
TR 7	TRIUMPH
TX	FAIRTHORPE
TX TRIPPER	TECHNICAL EXPONENTS
V8	ASTON MARTIN
VX	VAUXHALL
X 1/9	FIAT (I)
X-12	GURGEL
X-20	GURGEL
XJ	JAGUAR
XJ-S	JAGUAR

Cars called by numbers (in numerical order)

Model	Make
2 CV	CITROËN
4	FASA-RENAULT, RENAULT
4/4 1600	MORGAN
5	FASA-RENAULT, RENAULT
6	FASA-RENAULT, PANTHER, RENAULT
12	FASA-RENAULT, RENAULT
14	RENAULT
15	RENAULT
16	RENAULT
17	RENAULT
20	RENAULT
30	RENAULT
66	VOLVO (NL)
95	SAAB
96	SAAB
99	SAAB
104	PEUGEOT
105	ŠKODA, SYRENA
110	ŠKODA
114	ZIL
117	ISUZU, ZIL
120	ŠKODA
124	FIAT (I), SEAT
125	FIAT (RA)
125 P	POLSKI-FIAT
126	FIAT (I), GIANNINI
126 P	POLSKI-FIAT
127	FIAT (I), GIANNINI, SEAT
128	FIAT (I, RA), GIANNINI
131	FIAT (I), SEAT
132	FIAT (I), SEAT

Model	Make
133	FIAT (RA), SEAT
147	FIAT (BR)
181	VOLKSWAGEN (D)
200	MERCEDES-BENZ
220	MERCEDES-BENZ
230	MERCEDES-BENZ
240	ARO DACIA, MERCEDES-BENZ
242	VOLVO (S)
244	ARO DACIA, VOLVO (S)
245	VOLVO (S)
250	MERCEDES-BENZ
262	VOLVO (S)
264	VOLVO (S)
265	VOLVO (S)
280	MERCEDES-BENZ
300	MERCEDES-BENZ
304	PEUGEOT
305	PEUGEOT
308	FERRARI
316	BMW
318	BMW
320	BMW
323	BMW
343	VOLVO (NL)
350	MERCEDES-BENZ
353	WARTBURG
400	FERRARI
412	BRISTOL
450	MERCEDES-BENZ
469 B	UAZ
504	PEUGEOT
518	BMW
520	BMW
525	BMW
528	BMW
530	BMW
600	MERCEDES-BENZ
600 R	FIAT (RA)
600 S	FIAT (RA)
601	TRABANT
603	BRISTOL
604	PEUGEOT
630	BMW
633	BMW
707	YLN
728	BMW
730	BMW
733	BMW
803	YLN
850	MINI (BRITISH LEYLAND)
856	ELEGANT MOTORS
898	ELEGANT MOTORS
911	PORSCHE
924	PORSCHE
928	PORSCHE
968-A	ZAZ
1000	MINI (BRITISH LEYLAND)
1200	SEAT, VOLKSWAGEN (MEX, NIGERIA)
1275	MINI (BRITISH LEYLAND)
1300	CHEVROLET (RA, ZA), DACIA, FIAT (RA), FORD, VOLKSWAGEN (BR)
1303	VOLKSWAGEN (D)
1430	SEAT
1500	DODGE (RA), VANDEN PLAS
1600	TVR, VOLKSWAGEN (BR)
1800	MALLORCA, PRINCESS
1900	CHEVROLET (ZA)
2000	ALFA ROMEO
2200	PRINCESS
2300	ROVER
2600	ROVER
3000	TVR
3500	ROVER
3700	DODGE (E)

MAXIMUM SPEED

Up to 65 mph

	mph
LAWIL S3 Varzina	39
LAWIL A4 City	39
SUZUKI Jimny 55 - Jimny 8 Series (26 hp)	55
PEKING BJ 212	59
CITROËN Mehari 2 + 2	62
DAIHATSU Taft Series (55 hp)	62
GURGEL X-20	62
TRABANT 601 Limousine	62
CITROËN 2 CV Spécial	63
DIM Dim	65
FIAT (I) 126 Berlina Base	65
PUMA Mini	65
SUBARU Rex 550 SEEC-T Series	65

From 66 mph to 100 mph

	mph
ROVER Land Rover 88'' Regular	66
ARO DACIA 240/244	68
CITROËN 2 CV 6	68
DAIHATSU Max Cuore Series	68
FIAT (RA) 600 L	68
MITSUBISHI Minica Ami 55 Series	68
NISSAN Cedric - Gloria Series (60 hp)	68
POLSKI-FIAT 126 P	68
RENAULT 4	68
SUZUKI Fronte 7-S Series (4-stroke)	68
ZCZ Zastava 750 M	68
DAIHATSU Taft Series (80 hp)	71
FASA-RENAULT 4	71
FIAT (I) Campagnola	71
STANDARD Gazel	71
UAZ 469 B	71
VOLKSWAGEN (D) 181	71
VOLKSWAGEN (MEX-NIGERIA) 1200	71
GURGEL X-12 TR	73
MINI (BRITISH LEYLAND) 850 Saloon	73
RENAULT 6	73
CHEVROLET (ZA) Nomad	74
AZLK Moskvich 2138	75
CITROËN Dyane 6	75
CITROËN Ami 8 Break Confort	75
CITROËN LN	75
GIANNINI Fiat Giannini 126 Series (30 hp)	75
MITSUBISHI Jeep H-J58 Series	75
MONOCOQUE Box	75
PREMIER Padmini	75
SEAT 133	75
SYRENA 105	75
TOYOTA Landcruiser BJ40-KC	75
FORD (GB) Escort Series (41 hp)	76
OPEL (D) City-Kadett Series (40 hp)	76
RENAULT 5	76
MINI (BRITISH LEYLAND) 1000 Saloon	77
JEEP CORPORATION Jeep CJ-5 - CJ-7 Series (88-98 hp)	78
NISSAN Patrol 4WD	78
WARTBURG 353 W Tourist	78
YLN 803 DL	78
ZAZ 968-A	78
ARO DACIA M-461-C	79
AUSTIN Allegro Series (45 hp)	80
CHRYSLER (GB) Sunbeam Series (42 hp)	80
INTERNATIONAL HARVESTER Scout Series and SS II (86 hp)	80
PREMIER Padmini De Luxe	80
STEVENS Sienna	80
CHRYSLER (E) Chrysler Diesel	81
FASA-RENAULT 6	81
FIAT (RA) 133	81
FORD (D-GB) Fiesta Series (40 hp)	81
ISUZU Florian SII Series (62 hp)	81
MERCEDES-BENZ 200 D	81
MINI (BRITISH LEYLAND) Clubman Saloon	81
PEUGEOT 304 GLD Berline	81
RENAULT 6 Rodeo	81
ŠKODA 105 S	81

	mph
TOYOTA Crown Series (72 hp)	81
WARTBURG 353 W	81
FORD (GB) Cortina Series (50 hp)	82
MORRIS Marina (57 hp)	82
VAUXHALL Viva Series (57.7 hp)	82
VAZ Lada Series (80 hp)	82
VOLKSWAGEN (D) Polo-Derby Series (40 hp)	82
CHRYSLER FRANCE (F) Simca 1000 (40 hp)	83
FASA-RENAULT Siete	83
AUTOBIANCHI A 112 Normale	84
AZLK Moskvich 2137	84
DAIHATSU Charade Series	84
EL NASR Nasr 128	84
FASA-RENAULT 5 Series (44 hp)	84
FIAT (BR) 147 L	84
FIAT (I) 127 Series (45 hp)	84
GAZ Volga 25 Indenor Diesel	84
JEEP CORPORATION Jeep CJ-5 - CJ-7 (126 hp)	84
MERCEDES-BENZ 220 D	84
OPEL (D) Rekord Series (60 hp Diesel)	84
PEUGEOT 104	84
SEAT 133 Especial	84
SEAT 127 2 Puertas	84
SEAT 127 3-Puertas	84
TRIUMPH Dolomite 1300	84
ZCZ Zastava 101	84
AMERICAN MOTORS Gremlin (80 hp)	85
AMERICAN MOTORS Pacer Series (90 hp)	85
AMERICAN MOTORS Concord Series (90 hp)	85
CHEVROLET (ZA) Hatch Series (79 hp)	85
FORD (D-GB) Fiesta Series (45 hp)	85
FORD (D) Taunus Series (55 hp)	85
FORD (GB) Capri II Series (50 hp)	85
RENAULT 5 TL	85
VOLVO (NL) 66 DL 2-door	85
CHRYSLER (E) Simca 1200 Series (52 hp)	86
LAFER MP	86
MAZDA Familia (USA) Series	86
MERCEDES-BENZ 240 D	86
OPEL (D) Ascona Series (55 hp)	86
VOLKSWAGEN (BR) 1600 Limousine	86
VOLKSWAGEN (BR) Brasilia 2-door	86
VOLKSWAGEN (BR) Variant II	86
AUSTIN Allegro Series (54 hp)	87
AUTOBIANCHI A 112 Elegant	87
CHEVROLET (BR) Chevette Series (60 hp)	87
CHEVROLET (USA) Chevette Series (63 hp)	87
CHEVROLET (ZA) 1300	87
CHRYSLER FRANCE (F) Simca 1100 (50 hp)	87
FASA-RENAULT 12 Series (57 hp)	87
FIAT (I) 128 Series (55 hp)	87
KIA Brisa 1100	87
MAZDA Grand Familia Series (72 hp)	87
MINI (BRITISH LEYLAND) 1275 GT	87
NUOVA INNOCENTI Mini 90N	87
OTOSAN Anadol	87
PAYKAN Saloon	87
PEUGEOT 304 GL Break	87
PONTIAC (CDN) Acadian Series (63 hp)	87
PONTIAC (USA) Sunbird Series (85 hp)	87
PONTIAC (USA) Phoenix Series (85 hp)	87
RENAULT 12	87
RENAULT 16 TL (55 hp)	87
ROM CARMEL Rom 1300	87
SEAT 127	87
SEAT 132 Diesel	87
ŠKODA 120 L	87
TOYOTA Corona Series (88 hp)	87
TOYOTA Landcruiser FJ56V-k	87
VAZ Lada Series (60 hp)	87
VOLKSWAGEN (D) Golf Series (50 hp)	87
ZCZ Zastava 1300	87
AUDI NSU Audi 50	88
FORD (GB) Cortina Series (59 hp)	88
FORD (ZA) Escort 1300	88
FORD (ZA) Cortina 3000 S Sedan	88
LEYLAND Marina 1300	88
OPEL (D) Kadett-Ascona Series (60 hp)	88

	mph
VOLKSWAGEN (D) Polo-Derby Series (50 hp)	88
CHRYSLER (GB) Avenger Series (59 hp)	89
CHRYSLER (GB) Hunter Series (61 hp)	89
CHRYSLER (GB) Sunbeam Series (59 hp)	89
CITROËN CX 2000 Break Confort Diesel	89
FORD (D) Granada Series (70 hp)	89
OPEL (D) Manta Series (55 hp)	89
RENAULT 12	89
RENAULT 14	89
RENAULT 15 GTL Automatic	89
VOLKSWAGEN (D) Scirocco Series (50 hp)	89
AMERICAN MOTORS Gremlin (90 hp)	90
AMERICAN MOTORS Pacer Series (100 hp)	90
AMERICAN MOTORS Concord Series (100 hp)	90
AMERICAN MOTORS AMX (100 hp)	90
AMERICAN MOTORS Matador Series (120 hp)	90
ANTIQUE-CLASSIC Frazer Nash	90
AUDI NSU Audi 80 Series (55 hp)	90
AUSTIN Maxi Series (68 hp)	90
BUICK Century-Regal Series (90 hp)	90
CHECKER Marathon Series (90 hp)	90
CHEVROLET (BR) Opala	90
CHEVROLET (BR) Veraneio De Luxo	90
CHRYSLER (USA) Le Baron Series (90 hp)	90
DACIA 1300	90
DODGE (RA) 1500	90
DODGE (USA) Diplomat Series (90 hp)	90
FIAT (I) 128 Series (60 hp)	90
GAZ Volga	90
G.P. Centron II	90
HONDA Civic Wagon Series (75 hp)	90
HONDA Accord Series (68-82 hp)	90
HYUNDAI Pony	90
INTERNATIONAL HARVESTER Scout Series and SS II (140-158 hp)	90
JEEP CORPORATION Cherokee Series (114 hp)	90
MATRA Simca Rancho	90
MAZDA Familia AP Series	90
NISSAN Sunny Series (70 hp)	90
OPEL (D) Ascona Series (60 hp, 1,584 cc)	90
OTOSAN Anadol SV-1600	90
PEUGEOT 104	90
PLYMOUTH Volaré Series (90 hp)	90
POLSKI-FIAT 125 P	90
RENAULT 16 TL Automatic	90
SAAB 95 GL	90
ŠKODA 110 R Coupé	90
VOLKSWAGEN (BR) Passat Series (65 hp)	90
VOLVO (NL) 66 GL	90
VOLVO (NL) 343	90
VOLVO (S) 245	90
YLN 707 De Luxe	90
CHRYSLER FRANCE (F) Simca 1100 (58 hp)	91
CITROËN GSpecial Break	91
CITROËN CX 2200 Diesel	91
DODGE (USA) Omni (70 hp)	91
FORD (D) Taunus Series (68 hp)	91
OPEL (D) Manta-Rekord Series (60 hp)	91
PEUGEOT 504 L Break	91
PEUGEOT 305	91
PLYMOUTH Horizon (70-75 hp)	91
TRIUMPH Dolomite 1500	91
VAUXHALL Chevette-Cavalier Series (57.7 hp)	91
AUSTIN Allegro Series (68 hp)	92
AUSTIN Maxi Series (72 hp)	92
CHRLSER FRANCE (F) Simca Horizon (60 hp)	92
FASA-RENAULT 12 Series (70 hp)	92
FORD (D) Granada Series (73 hp)	92
MERCEDES-BENZ 300 D	92
RENAULT 12 TS	92
RENAULT 15 TL	92
RENAULT 16 TL (66 hp)	92
VANDEN PLAS 1500	92
VAZ Lada Series (68 hp)	92
ALFA ROMEO Alfasud Series (63 hp)	93
AZLK Moskvich 2140	93
BUICK Century-Regal Series (105 hp)	93

	mph
CHEVROLET (USA) Monza Series (85 hp)	93
CHEVROLET (USA) Nova - Nova Custom Series (90 hp)	93
CHEVROLET (USA) Chevelle Series (95 hp)	93
CHRYSLER (E) Simca 1200 Series (65 hp)	93
CHRYSLER (GB) Hunter Series (74 hp)	93
CHRYSLER FRANCE (F) Simca 1000 (60 hp)	93
CITROËN GSpecial Berline	93
CITROËN GS X	93
DAIHATSU Charmant 1200 De Luxe	93
DAIHATSU Delta Wagon Series	93
DODGE (RA) 1500 M 1.8	93
DODGE (USA) Aspen Series (90 hp)	93
DODGE (USA) Diplomat Series (110 hp)	93
EL NASR Nasr 125	93
FIAT (I) 128 3P 1100	93
FIAT (I) 131 Mirafiori Series (65 hp)	93
FORD (USA) Granada Series (97 hp)	93
GIANNINI Fiat Giannini 127 Series (58 hp)	93
HONDA Civic CVCC Series (65 hp)	93
HONDA Civic Wagon Series (70 hp)	93
KIA Brisa 1300	93
MERCURY (USA) Bobcat Series (88 hp)	93
MERCURY (USA) Monarch Series (97 hp)	93
MITSUBISHI Lancer Series (70 hp)	93
MITSUBISHI Celeste Series (86 hp)	93
MONTEVERDI Safari	93
NISSAN Cherry F II Series (68 hp)	93
NISSAN Sunny Series (80 hp)	93
NISSAN Violet - Auster - Stanza Series (80 hp)	93
OLDSMOBILE Starfire Series (85 hp)	93
OLDSMOBILE Delta 8 - Delta 88 Royale - Ninety-Eight Custom Cruiser Series (105 hp)	98
OPEL (RA) K-180	93
PEUGEOT 304	93
PLYMOUTH Volaré-Fury Series (110 hp)	93
PONTIAC (CDN) Acadian Series (68 hp)	93
PONTIAC (USA) Phoenix Series (105 hp)	93
PONTIAC (USA) Firebird Series (105 hp)	93
PONTIAC (USA) Le Mans - Grand Le Mans - Grand Am Series (105 hp)	93
PONTIAC (USA) Catalina - Bonneville - Grand Safari Series (105 hp)	93
RELIANT Kitten DL	93
SAAB 96 GL	93
SEAT 124-D	93
SEAT 131-L 5 Puertas	93
ŠKODA 120 LS	93
SUBARU Leone SEEC-T Series (72 hp)	93
TOFAS Murat 131	93
TOYOTA Corolla-Sprinter Series (72 hp)	93
VAUXHALL Viva Series (88 hp)	93
VAZ Lada Series (75 hp)	93
VOLKSWAGEN (D) Passat Series (55 hp)	93
AUSTIN Allegro Series (90 hp)	94
CHRYSLER (GB) Alpine GL	94
CHRYSLER FRANCE (F) Simca 1307 GLS	94
CITROËN GS	94
RENAULT 5 TS	94
VAUXHALL Magnum Series (88 hp)	94
VOLKSWAGEN (D) Polo-Derby Series (60 hp)	94
VOLVO (S) 242	94
VOLVO (S) 244	94
CHRYSLER (GB) Avenger Series (69 hp)	95
CHRYSLER (GB) Sunbeam Series (69 hp)	95
DAVRIAN Imp	95
DODGE (BR) Polara	95
FORD (D) Capri II Series (68 hp)	95
FORD (RA) Taunus	95
LEYLAND Marina 1750	95
MERCURY (USA) Zephyr Series (85 hp)	95
MG Midget	95
MORRIS Marina Series (72 hp)	95
PEUGEOT 305 SR	95
ALFA ROMEO Alfasud Series (68 hp)	96
AMERICAN MOTORS Matador Series (140 hp)	96
BUICK Skylark-Le Sabre Series (105 hp)	96

	mph
CHEVROLET (USA) Monza Series (90 hp)	96
CHEVROLET (USA) Camaro - Camaro LT Series (90 hp)	96
CHEVROLET (USA) Monte Carlo Series (105 hp)	96
CHEVROLET (ZA) SII Series (120 hp)	96
CUSTOCA Hurrycane-Strato ES	96
DODGE (RA) Coronado Automatic	96
DODGE (USA) Aspen-Monaco Series (100 hp)	96
FORD (AUS) Falcon - Falcon 500 - Fairmont Series (130 hp)	96
FORD (CDN) Custom 500 Series (134 hp)	96
FORD (USA) Pinto-Mustang II - Fairmont Series (88 hp)	96
FORD (USA) LTD Series (134 hp)	96
MAZDA Capella AP Series (90 hp)	96
MERCURY (USA) Bobcat Series (90 hp)	96
MERCURY (USA) Monarch Series (133 hp)	96
MITSUBISHI Lancer-Celeste Series (82 hp)	96
MITSUBISHI Galant Sigma Series (86 hp)	96
MITSUBISHI Galant Lambda Series (86 hp)	96
MITSUBISHI Debonair Series	96
NISSAN Skyline Series (100 hp)	96
NISSAN Cedric - Gloria Series (115 hp)	96
NUOVA INNOCENTI Mini 120	96
OLDSMOBILE Omega Series (105 hp)	96
OPEL (D) Rekord Series (75 hp)	96
PAYKAN Saloon GT	96
PEUGEOT 104 2S Coupé	96
PEUGEOT 504 L Berline	96
POLSKI-FIAT 125 P 1500	96
PONTIAC (USA) Firebird Series (135 hp)	96
PONTIAC (USA) Grand Prix Series (105 hp)	96
RELIANT Robin 850	96
ROVER Range Rover	96
SEAT 124-D Especial	96
SEAT 131-L	96
TOYOTA Publica - Starlet Series (64 hp)	96
TOYOTA Sprinter Series (90 hp)	96
VAZ Lada Series (78 hp)	96
OPEL (D) City Series (75 hp)	97
AUSTIN Maxi Series (91 hp)	98
CITROËN GS X 2	98
FORD (D) Fiesta Series (66 hp)	98
FORD (D) Granada Series (90 hp)	98
FORD (GB) Capri II Series (72 hp)	98
OPEL (D) Kadett-Ascona Series (75 hp)	98
PRINCESS 1800 - 2200 Series (82 hp)	98
RENAULT 20	98
VAUXHALL Cavalier Series (75 hp)	98
VOLKSWAGEN (D) Golf Series (70 hp)	98
ALFA ROMEO Alfasud Series (76 hp)	99
AUDI NSU Audi 80 Series (75 hp)	99
AUDI NSU Audi 100-100 Avant Series (85 hp)	99
AUTOBIANCHI A 112 Abarth	99
BMW 316	99
BMW 518	99
BUICK Le Sabre Series (140 hp)	99
CHEVROLET (BR) Opala	99
CHEVROLET (CDN) Bel Air Series (110 hp)	99
CHEVROLET (ZA) 1900	99
CHEVROLET (ZA) Hatch Series (109 hp)	99
DODGE (RA) Coronado	99
DODGE (USA) Aspen (110 hp)	99
FIAT (I) 128 3P 1300	99
FIAT (I) 131 Mirafiori Series (75 hp)	99
FIAT (RA) 1300 TV Iava	99
FORD (AUS) Falcon - Falcon 500 - Fairmont Series (155 hp)	99
FORD (CDN) Custom 500 Series (145 hp)	99
FORD (USA) Pinto-Mustang II Series (90 hp)	99
FORD (USA) Fairmont Series (85 hp)	99
FORD (USA) LTD Series (145 hp)	99
FORD (Z) Cortina 1600 L	99
HONDA Civic CVCC Series (75 hp)	99
ISUZU Florian SII Series (105 hp)	99
JEEP CORPORATION Cherokee Series Wagoneer (129 hp)	99

	mph
LANCIA Beta Berlina 1300	99
MAZDA Grand Familia Series (90 hp)	99
MAZDA Luce Series (110 hp)	99
MERCEDES-BENZ 200	99
MERCURY (USA) Cougar Series (134 hp)	99
MITSUBISHI Galant Sigma Series (97 hp)	99
NISSAN Cherry F II Series (80 hp)	99
NISSAN Skyline Series (115 hp, 1,998 cc)	99
NISSAN Laurel Series (105 hp)	99
NUOVA INNOCENTI Mini De Tomaso	99
OLDSMOBILE Cutlass Series (110 hp)	99
OPEL (D) Rallye Series (75 hp)	99
OTOSAN Anadol STC - 16	99
PEUGEOT 304 SLS Berline	99
PONTIAC (CDN) Laurentian - Parisienne Series (110 hp)	99
SEAT 128/3P	99
SEAT 131-E 5 Puertas	99
SUBARU Leone SEEC-T Series (82 hp)	99
TOYOTA Corolla Series (82-88 hp)	99
TOYOTA Corolla (USA) Series (75 hp)	99
TOYOTA Sprinter Series (82-88 hp)	99
TOYOTA Corona Series (88-90-95-98 hp)	99
TOYOTA Crown Series (110 hp)	99
TOYOTA Century Series (170 hp)	99
VOLKSWAGEN (BR) Passat Series (80 hp)	99
BRADLEY GT II Coupé	100
CHRYSLER (GB) Avenger Series (80 hp)	100
ELITE Laser 917	100
EL-KG Bugatti 35 B	100
FORD (USA) Fairmont-Mustang II Series (133 hp)	100
FORD (ZA) Escort 1600 GL 4-door Sedan	100
MERCURY (USA) Zephyr Series (133 hp)	100
MORRIS Marina Series (85 hp)	100
PANTHER Rio	100
TOTAL REPLICA Ford Phaeton	100
TRIUMPH Dolomite 1850 HL	100
TRIUMPH Spitfire 1500	100
VAUXHALL VX Series (88 hp)	100

From 101 mph to 120 mph

	mph
CHEVROLET (RA) Chevy	101
CHRYSLER FRANCE (F) Simca 1307 S	101
FORD (AUS) Escort Series (98 hp)	101
FORD (D-GB) Escort Series (84 hp)	101
FORD (D) Taunus Series (90 hp)	101
FORD (GB) Cortina Series (88 hp)	101
OPEL (D) Manta Series (75 hp)	101
PEUGEOT 504	101
VOLKSWAGEN (D) Scirocco Series (70 hp)	101
CHRYSLER (GB) Alpine	102
CHRYSLER (USA) Le Baron Series (140 hp)	102
CHRYSLER FRANCE (F) Simca 1308 GT	102
DODGE (BR) Dart	102
DODGE (USA) Diplomat Series (140 hp)	102
FORD (AUS) Fairlane Custom - Fairlane 500 Series (240 hp)	102
MATRA Simca Bagheera	102
MITSUBISHI Galant Sigma Series (105 hp)	102
PEUGEOT 504 GL Berline	102
PLYMOUTH Volaré Series (140 hp)	102
RENAULT 20 TL	102
SAAB 99	102
SEAT Sport 1430	102
TOYOTA Carina Series (88 hp)	102
VOLKSWAGEN (D) Passat Series (75 hp)	102
ALFA ROMEO Giulietta 1.3	103
BMW 318	103
BRADLEY GT I Coupé	103
BUICK Century-Regal Series (145 hp)	103
BUICK Le Sabre Series (145-165 hp)	103
CHECKER Marathon Series (145 hp)	103
CHEVROLET (USA) Nova - Nova Custom Series (135 hp)	103

	mph
CHEVROLET (ZA) SII Series (142-167 hp)	103
CHEVROLET (ZA) Kommando Series	103
CHRYSLER (USA) Le Baron Series (155 hp, 5,211 cc)	103
CHRYSLER (USA) Cordoba (140 hp)	103
CHRYSLER FRANCE (F) Simca 1100 (82 hp)	103
DAIHATSU Charmant 1400	103
DODGE (USA) Aspen-Monaco-Magnum XE Series (140 hp)	103
DODGE (USA) Diplomat Series (155 hp, 5,211 cc)	103
DODGE (USA) Charger Special Edition (140 hp)	103
FIAT (I) 132 1600 Berlina	103
FIAT (RA) 125 Familiar	103
FORD (AUS) Cortina TE Series (112 hp)	103
FORD (CDN) Custom 500 Series (144 hp)	103
FORD (GB) Cortina-Granada Series (98 hp)	103
FORD (USA) Granada Series (139 hp)	103
FORD (USA) Thunderbird Series (134 hp)	103
FORD (USA) LTD Series (144 hp)	103
GIANNINI Fiat Giannini 128 Series (80 hp)	103
ISUZU Gemini Series (100 hp)	103
JEEP CORPORATION Cherokee Series Wagoneer (165 hp)	103
LANCIA Coupé 1300	103
LEYLAND Marina 2600	103
LEYLAND Triumph Chicane	103
MAZDA Capella AP Series (100 hp)	103
MAZDA Luce Series (100 hp)	103
MAZDA Cosmo Series (100-110 hp)	103
MAZDA Roadpacer Sedan	103
MERCEDES-BENZ 300 SD	103
MERCURY (CDN) Marquis Meteor Series (145 hp)	103
MERCURY (USA) Monarch Series (139 hp)	103
MERCURY (USA) Cougar Series (144 hp)	103
MERCURY (USA) Marquis Series (145 hp)	103
MITSUBISHI Lancer-Celeste Series (100 hp)	103
MITSUBISHI Galant Lambda Series (100 hp)	103
NISSAN Cherry F II Series (92 hp)	103
NISSAN Violet - Auster - Stanza Series (110 hp)	103
NISSAN Datsun Bluebird Series (100 hp)	103
NISSAN Skyline Series (105-115 hp)	103
OLDSMOBILE Starfire Series (105 hp)	103
OLDSMOBILE Omega-Cutlass Series (145 hp)	103
OLDSMOBILE Delta 88 - Delta 88 Royale - Ninety - Eight - Custom Cruiser Series (170 hp)	103
OPEL (D) Rekord Series (90 hp)	103
PLYMOUTH Volaré Series (155 hp, 5,211 cc)	103
PLYMOUTH Fury Series (155 hp, 5,900 cc)	103
PONTIAC (USA) Phoenix Series (160 hp)	103
PONTIAC (USA) Le Mans - Grand Le Mans - Grand Am - Grand Prix Series (135 hp)	103
PONTIAC (USA) Catalina - Bonneville - Grand Safari Series (155 hp)	103
RENAULT 16 TX Automatic	103
RENAULT 17 TS Cabriolet Automatic	103
RENAULT 20 TS Automatic	103
SAAB 99 GL Combi Coupé 3-door	103
SEAT 131-E	103
SEAT 132	103
TOYOTA Corolla Series (90 hp)	103
TOYOTA Celica Series (88 hp)	103
TOYOTA Mark II - Chaser Series (95 hp)	103
VAUXHALL Magnum-VX Series (108 hp)	103
CHEVROLET (RA) Chevy Malibù	104
FORD (D) Taunus Series (98 hp)	104
FORD (D) Capri II Series (90 hp)	104
FORD (D) Granada Series (108 hp)	104
FORD (ZA) Cortina 2000 GL	104
OPEL (D) Ascona Series (90 hp)	104
VAUXHALL Cavalier Series (90 hp)	104
FAIRTHORPE TX 1500	105
FORD (GB) Granada Series (108 hp)	105
MORGAN 4/4 1600	105
PONTIAC (USA) Le Mans - Grand Le Mans - Grand Am Series (140-145 hp)	105
ALFA ROMEO Spider Junior 1300	106
AUDI NSU Audi 80 Series (85 hp)	106
BUICK Skylark Series (145 hp)	106
BUICK Century-Regal Series (160 hp)	106
BUICK Estate Wagon - Electra 225 - Electra Limited - Electra Park Avenue - Riviera Series (155 hp)	106
CHECKER Marathon Series (160 hp)	106
CHEVROLET (BR) Opala SS-6 Coupé	106
CHEVROLET (BR) Comodoro 4	106
CHEVROLET (CDN) Bel Air Series (145 hp)	106
CHEVROLET (USA) Monza Series (135 hp)	106
CHEVROLET (USA) Nova - Nova Custom Series (145-180 hp)	106
CHEVROLET (USA) Monte Carlo Series (135-145 hp)	106
CHEVROLET (USA) Impala - Caprice Classic Series (135-145 hp)	106
CHRYSLER (E) Simca 1200 Series (85 hp)	106
CHRYSLER (USA) Le Baron Series (155 hp, 5,900 cc)	106
CHRYSLER (USA) Newport - New Yorker Brougham Series (155-170 hp)	106
CHRYSLER FRANCE (F) Simca 1000 (86 hp)	106
CHRYSLER FRANCE (F) Chrysler Simca 1610	106
CHRYSLER FRANCE (F) Chrysler Simca 2 L Automatic	106
CITROËN CX 2000-2400	106
DODGE (USA) Aspen Series (155 hp, 5,211-5,900 cc)	106
DODGE (USA) Diplomat Series (155 hp, 5,900 cc)	106
DODGE (USA) Monaco-Charger Special Edition-Magnum XE Series (155 hp 5,211 cc)	106
FASA-RENAULT 5 Series (93 hp)	106
FIAT (I) X 1/9	106
FIAT (I) 132 2000 Berlina	106
FIAT (RA) 125 Berlina	106
FNM Alfa Romeo 2300	106
FORD (AUS) Cortina TE Series (130 hp)	106
FORD (AUS) Fairlane Custom - Fairlane 500 Series (260 hp)	106
FORD (D) Capri II Series (90 hp)	106
FORD (GB) Escort Series (95 hp)	106
FORD (GB) Cortina Series (108 hp)	106
FORD (GB) Capri II Series (88 hp)	106
FORD (RA) Taunus GXL 2300 Sedan	106
FORD (USA) Thunderbird Series (144 hp)	106
FORD (USA) LTD II Series (152 hp)	106
ISUZU Gemini Series (110 hp)	106
ISUZU 117 XT Coupé	106
JEEP CORPORATION Cherokee Series Wagoneer (205 hp)	106
LANCIA Beta Berlina 1600	106
MALLORCA 1800	106
MERCEDES-BENZ 230	106
MERCURY (CDN) Marquis Meteor Series (160 hp)	106
MERCURY (USA) Cougar Series (152 hp)	106
MERCURY (USA) Marquis Series (160 hp)	106
NISSAN Laurel Series (115 hp)	106
NISSAN Silvia Series (105 hp)	106
NISSAN Cedric - Gloria Series (130 hp)	106
OLDSMOBILE Starfire Series (145 hp)	106
OLDSMOBILE Omega-Cutlass Series (160 hp)	106
PLYMOUTH Volaré Series (155 hp, 5,900 cc)	106
PLYMOUTH Fury Series (170 hp)	106
PONTIAC (CDN) Laurentian - Parisienne Series (145 hp)	106
PONTIAC (USA) Grand Prix Series (140 hp)	106
PONTIAC (USA) Catalina - Bonneville - Grand Safari Series (170 hp)	106
PRINCESS 1800 - 2200 Series (110 hp)	106
RENAULT 16 TX	106
RENAULT 17 TS Cabriolet	106
RENAULT 20 TS	106
SAAB 99	106
SUBARU Leone SEEC-T Series (95 hp)	106
TOYOTA Carina (95-98-100-110 hp)	106
TOYOTA Celica Series (95-98-100 hp)	106
TOYOTA Crown Series (125 hp)	106
VAUXHALL VX Series (116 hp)	106
VOLVO (S) 245 DLE	106
CHEVROLET (RA) Chevy Coupé Series 2	107
FORD (D) Taunus Series (108 hp)	107
MG MGB	107
OPEL (D) Manta Series (90 hp)	107
OPEL (D) Rekord Series (100 hp)	107
PEUGEOT 504 TI Berline	107
VOLKSWAGEN (D) Passat Series (85 hp)	107
CITROËN CX 2000	108
DODGE (USA) Magnum XE (155 hp, 5,900 cc)	108
LANCIA Beta HPE 1600	108
LINCOLN Versailles	108
MAZDA Luce Series (125 hp)	108
SAAB 99 GL Injection	108
SAAB 99 EMS	108
SPARTAN CARS 2-seater Sports	108
TECHNICAL EXPONENTS TX Tripper 1500	108
ALFA ROMEO Spider Junior 1600	109
ALFA ROMEO Alfetta-Giulietta 1.6	109
BUICK Skyhawk-Regal Series (105 hp)	109
BUICK Le Sabre Series (150-165-170 hp)	109
CHEVROLET (CDN) Bel Air Series (170 hp)	109
CHEVROLET (USA) Camaro - Camaro LT Series (135 hp)	109
CHEVROLET (USA) Impala - Caprice Classic Series (160-170 hp)	109
CHEVROLET (ZA) Constantia - Caprice Classic Series (134 hp)	109
DODGE (USA) Aspen Series (175 hp)	109
DODGE (USA) Diplomat Series (170 hp)	109
DODGE (USA) Monaco Series (155 hp, 5,900 cc)	109
FIAT (RA) 125 Sport	109
FNM Alfa Romeo 2300 TI	109
FORD (AUS) Cortina TE Series (155 hp)	109
FORD (CDN) Custom 500 Series (160 hp)	109
FORD (USA) Thunderbird Series (152 hp)	109
MAZDA Luce Series (135 hp)	109
MITSUBISHI Galant Sigma Series (115 hp)	109
MITSUBISHI Galant Lambda Series (115 hp)	109
NISSAN Skyline-Laurel Series (130 hp)	109
NISSAN Silvia Series (115 hp)	109
OLDSMOBILE Delta 88 - Delta 88 Royale - Ninety Eight - Custom Cruiser Series (185 hp)	109
OPEL (D) Ascona Series (100 hp)	109
PLYMOUTH Volaré Series (175 hp)	109
PLYMOUTH Fury Series (190 hp)	109
PONTIAC (CDN) Laurentian - Parisienne Series (170 hp)	109
PONTIAC (USA) Le Mans - Grand Le Mans - Grand Am Series (150 hp)	109
PONTIAC (USA) Grand Prix Series (150 hp)	109
PONTIAC (USA) Catalina - Bonneville - Grand Safari Series (180 hp)	109
RENAULT 5 Alpine	109
TOYOTA Celica Series (110 hp)	109
TOYOTA Celica (USA) Series (96 hp)	109
TOYOTA Mark II - Chaser Series (125 hp)	109
TOYOTA Crown Series (135 hp)	109
TRIUMPH TR 7	109
VOLVO (S) 242 GT	109
VOLVO (S) 244 GL	109
ARKLEY SS	110
CONCEPT Centaur Mk II	110
DUESENBERG SSJ	110
EXCALIBUR Series III	110
FORD (AUS) Escort Series (112 hp)	110
FORD (GB) Escort Series (110 hp)	110

	mph
INTERMECCANICA Speedster	110
LINCOLN Continental Series (166-210 hp)	110
LINCOLN Continental Mark V (166 hp)	110
PANTHER Lima	110
PONTIAC (USA) Firebird Series (180 hp)	110
RENAULT 30 TS Automatic	110
AUDI NSU Audi 100 Series (115 hp)	111
AUDI NSU Audi 100 Avant Series (115 hp)	111
DODGE (E) 3700	111
FORD (D) Capri II Series (108 hp)	111
LANCIA Beta 1600	111
OPEL (D) Rekord Series (110 hp)	111
PEUGEOT 504	111
ALFA ROMEO Alfetta GT 1.6 - Alfetta 1.8	112
AUDI NSU Audi 80 Series (110 hp)	112
BMW 320	112
BMW 520	112
CADILLAC De Ville - Fleetwood Series (180 hp)	112
CHRYSLER (USA) Cordoba (170 hp)	112
CITROËN CX 2400	112
DODGE (BR) Charger R/T	112
DODGE (USA) Monaco-Charger Special Edition - Magnum XE Series (170 hp)	112
FORD (AUS) Falcon - Falcon 500 - Fairmont Series (240 hp)	112
FORD (CDN) Custom 500 Series (202 hp)	112
FORD (D) Escort Series (110 hp)	112
FORD (USA) Thunderbird Series (166 hp)	112
GAZ Chaika	112
ISUZU 117 XC	112
LANCIA Beta 2000	112
MERCEDES-BENZ 250	112
NISSAN Datsun Bluebird Series (130 hp)	112
NISSAN Laurel Series (140 hp)	112
NISSAN Cedric - Gloria Series (140-146 hp)	112
NISSAN Fairlady - Datsun 280 Z Series (130 hp)	112
NISSAN President Series	112
OPEL (D) Manta Series (100 hp)	112
ROLLS-ROYCE Phantom VI	112
SBARRO Replica BMW 328 Standard	112
TOYOTA Carina-Celica-Corona Series (130 hp)	112
TOYOTA Corona (USA) Series (96 hp)	112
FORD (GB) Granada Series (135 hp)	113
PEUGEOT 604 SL	113
PUMA 1600	113
TRIUMPH Dolomite Sprint	113
VOLKSWAGEN (D) Golf Series (110 hp)	113
FORD (D) Granada Series (135 hp)	114
FORD (ZA) Cortina 3000 Ghia	114
FORD (ZA) Granada 3000	114
PANTHER J 72 4.2-Litre	114
RENAULT 30 TS	114
ROVER 2300	114
SEVEN Series III	114
ALFA ROMEO Alfetta 2000	115
CADILLAC Seville	115
CADILLAC De Ville - Fleetwood Series (195 hp)	115
CHEVROLET (USA) Camaro - Camaro LT Series (160-175 hp)	115
CHRYSLER (USA) Cordoba (190 hp)	115
CHEVROLET (ZA) Constantia - Caprice Classic Series (167 hp)	115
DAIMLER Limousine	115
DODGE (USA) Monaco Series (190 hp)	115
FASA-RENAULT Alpine A 110	115
FIAT (I) 124 Sport Spider 1800	115
FORD (GB) Escort Series (115 hp)	115
IKA-RENAULT Torino Grand Routier	115
ISUZU 117	115
LANCIA Gamma 2000	115
MATRA Simca Bagheera	115
MAZDA Capella AP-Cosmo Series (125 hp)	115
NISSAN Fairlady - Datsun 280 Z Series (149 hp)	115

	mph
PEUGEOT 604 TI	115
VOLKSWAGEN (D) Scirocco Series (110 hp)	115
CHEVROLET (USA) Monza Series (145 hp)	116
LANCIA Beta Spider 2000	116
OPEL (D) Manta Series (110 hp)	116
TATRA T 613	116
CITROËN CX 2400 GTI	117
DAIMLER Sovereign 3.4	117
JAGUAR XJ 3.4	117
LANCIA Beta 2000 Coupé	117
OPEL (D) Rallye Series (110 hp)	117
PEUGEOT 504 V6 Coupé	117
ROVER 2600	117
VOLVO (S) 264	117
VOLVO (S) 262	117
VOLVO (S) 265	117
VOLVO (S) 265 GLE	117
AUDI NSU Audi 100 Series (136 hp)	118
AUDI NSU Audi 100 Avant Series (136 hp)	118
BENTLEY T2 Saloon-Corniche	118
BMW 323 i	118
BRISTOL 603	118
BUICK Le Sabre Series (185 hp)	118
CADILLAC Fleetwood Eldorado	118
CITROËN CX Prestige	118
DAIMLER Vanden Plas 4.2	118
DODGE (USA) Charger Special Edition (190 hp)	118
DODGE (USA) Magnum XE (190 hp)	118
FAIRTHORPE TX 2000	118
FELBER FF Lancia Michelotti	118
FIAT (I) 131 Fiat-Abarth Rally	118
FORD (AUS) Falcon - Falcon 500 - Fairmont Series (260 hp)	118
HONGKI Limousine	118
LANCIA Beta Montecarlo	118
LINCOLN Continental Mark V (210 hp)	118
MAZDA Cosmo Series (135 hp)	118
MERCEDES-BENZ 280	118
OLDSMOBILE Toronado Series (190 hp)	118
OPEL (D) Kadett Series (115 hp)	118
PANTHER Rio Especial	118
PONTIAC (USA) Firebird Series (220 hp)	118
ROLLS-ROYCE Silver Shadow II	118
ROLLS-ROYCE Silver Wraith II	118
ROLLS-ROYCE Corniche	118
ROLLS-ROYCE Camargue	118
BMW 728	119
AVANTI Avanti II	120
BMW 525	120
FORD (D-GB) Granada Series (160 hp)	120
K.M.B. GTM Mk 1-3	120
RELIANT Scimitar GTE	120
SYD LAWRENCE Mk 2 Sports	120

Over 120 mph

	mph
ALFA ROMEO Alfetta GTV 2000	121
ALFA ROMEO 2000 Spider Veloce	121
DAIMLER Sovereign 4.2	121
DODGE (RA) GTX	121
FELBER FF Lancia 2000 Roadster	121
FORD (D) Capri II Series (138 hp)	121
JAGUAR XJ 4.2	121
LANCIA Gamma 2500	121
FORD (D-GB) Capri II Series (138 hp)	122
PUMA GTB	123
SAAB Turbo	123
BMW 530 i	124
BMW 730	124
FORD (AUS) LTD 4-door Sedan	124
IKA-RENAULT Torino TSX	124
MERCEDES-BENZ 280	124
MONTEVERDI Sierra	124
ZIL 114-117	124
PORSCHE 924	125

	mph
TECHNICAL EXPONENTS TX Tripper 2000 Sprint	125
TRIDENT Venturer V6	125
ROVER 3500	126
BMW 733 i	127
LAMBORGHINI Urraco P 200	127
MERCEDES-BENZ 350	127
MERCEDES-BENZ 600	127
GINETTA G21	128
LOTUS Elite	128
PANTHER De Ville	128
BMW 528 i	129
PERANA-FORD Granada V8 Series	129
BMW 630 CS	130
LOTUS Eclat 520	130
MERCEDES-BENZ 350 SLC	130
MERCEDES-BENZ 450	130
TVR 3000 M	130
CHEVROLET (USA) Corvette (220 hp)	131
LOTUS Eclat	132
SBARRO Replica BMW 328 America	132
BMW 633 CSi	134
AC ME 3000	135
PORSCHE 911 SC	136
ALPINE A 310 V6	137
LAFER LL	137
MASERATI Merak 2000	137
FERRARI Dino 208 GT 4	138
LOTUS Esprit	138
BRISTOL 412 Convertible-Saloon	140
DAIMLER Double-Six	140
JAGUAR XJ 5.3	140
JOHNARD VINTAGE CAR Bentley Donington	140
MERCEDES-BENZ 450	140
MONTEVERDI High Speed 375/4 Limousine	140
TRIDENT Clipper V8	140
TVR Turbo	140
TVR Taimar	140
LANCIA Stratos	143
MASERATI Quattroporte	143
PORSCHE 928	143
DE TOMASO Longchamp 2+2	149
ENNEZETA Nuova Lele Iso Rivolta	149
FERRARI 400 Automatic	149
LAMBORGHINI Urraco P 250	149
MONTEVERDI High Speed 375 L	149
MONTEVERDI Palm Beach	149
ARGYLL Turbo GT	150
DE TOMASO Deauville	150
ELEGANT MOTORS Speedster-Phaeton	150
JAGUAR XJ-S	150
LYNX D Type	150
MASERATI Kyalami	150
MORGAN Plus 8	150
FELBER FF Ferrari	152
ASTON MARTIN Lagonda	155
FERRARI Dino 308 GT 4	155
LAMBORGHINI Urraco Silhouette P 300	155
LAMBORGHINI Espada 400 GT	155
MASERATI Merak SS	155
FERRARI 308 GTB	157
FERRARI 308 GTS	157
DE TOMASO Pantera L	158
ASTON MARTIN V8	160
PANTHER Ferrari F.F.	160
PORSCHE Turbo Coupé	162
LAMBORGHINI Urraco P 300	165
ASTON MARTINI V8 Vantage	170
MASERATI Khamsin	171
DE TOMASO Pantera GTS	174
LAMBORGHINI Countach LP 400 S	174
MASERATI Bora 4900	174
MONTEVERDI Berlinetta	174
MONTEVERDI Hai 450 GTS	180
FERRARI BB 512	188
LAMBORGHINI Countach LP 400	196
PANTHER 6	200

MAKES, MODELS AND PRICES

Page	MAKE AND MODEL	Price in GB £	Price in USA $	Price ex Works
	AC (Great Britain)			
145	ME 3000			—
	ALFA ROMEO (Italy)			
200	Alfasud 4-door Berlina			3,764,000*
200	Alfasud Super 4-door Berlina	2,900*		4,378,000*
200	Alfasud Super 1.3 4-door Berlina			4,484,000*
200	Alfasud Giardinetta 1.3 3-door S.W.			4,944,000*
200	Alfasud ti 1.3 2-door Berlina	3,199*		4,788,000*
200	Alfasud Sprint 2-door Coupé	4,000*		6,401,000*
201	Spider Junior 1300			6,596,000*
202	Spider Junior 1600			6,809,000*
202	Giulietta 1.3			6,549,000*
202	Giulietta 1.6			6,844,000*
203	Alfetta 1.6			7,133,000*
203	Alfetta GT 1.6	5,000*		7,682,000*
203	Alfetta 1.8			7,357,000*
203	Alfetta 2000		7,235*	8,490,000*
204	Alfetta GTV 2000	5,799*	8,515*	9,086,000*
204	2000 Spider Veloce	5,799*	8,895*	8,661,000*
	ALPINE (France)			
76	A 310 V6			79,600*
	AMERICAN MOTORS (USA)			
255	Gremlin		3,299	
256	Pacer Sedan		3,998	
256	Pacer Station Wagon		4,143	
257	Concord 2-door Sedan		3,699	
257	Concord 4-door Sedan		3,799	
257	Concord Hatchback		3,799	
257	Concord Station Wagon		3,999	
258	AMX		4,599	
258	Matador Coupé		4,799	
258	Matador Sedan		4,849	
258	Matador Station Wagon		5,299	
	ANTIQUE-CLASSIC (USA)			
259	Frazer Nash		4,995	
	ARGYLL (Great Britain)			
145	Turbo GT			9,500*
	ARKLEY (Great Britain)			
145	SS			2,658*
	ARO DACIA (Rumania)			
227	M-461-C			—
227	240			—
227	244			—
	ASTON MARTIN (Great Britain)			
146	V8	37,680*	19,999*	
146	V8 Vantage		22,999*	
147	Lagonda		32,620*	

Page	MAKE AND MODEL	Price in GB £	Price in USA $	Price ex Works
	AUBURN (USA)			
259	Speedster			24,900
259	Dual Cowl Phaeton			60,000
	AUDI NSU (Germany FR)			
104	Audi 50 LS			9,915*
105	Audi 50 GLS			10,405*
105	Audi 80 2-door Limousine			11,580*
105	Audi 80 4-door Limousine			12,130*
105	Audi 80 L 2-door Limousine			12,385*
105	Audi 80 L 4-door Limousine	4,097*		12,935*
105	Audi 80 GLS 2-door Limousine		5,895*	13,695*
105	Audi 80 GLS 4-door Limousine	4,490*	6,045*	14,245*
105	Audi 80 GTE 2-door Limousine			15,815*
105	Audi 80 GTE 4-door Limousine			16,365*
106	Audi 100 2-door Limousine			14,955*
106	Audi 100 4-door Limousine			15,535*
106	Audi 100 L 2-door Limousine			15,820*
106	Audi 100 L 4-door Limousine			16,400*
106	Audi 100 GL 4-door Limousine	6,020*	8,450*	17,710*
107	Audi 100 Avant L 5-door Limousine	5,099*		16,995*
107	Audi 100 Avant GL 5-door Limousine	5,145*		18,305*
	AUSTIN (Great Britain)			
147	Allegro 1100 De Luxe 2-door Saloon			2,394*
147	Allegro 1100 De Luxe 4-door Saloon			2,489*
147	Allegro 1300 Super 2-door Saloon			2,655*
147	Allegro 1300 Super 4-door Saloon			2,750*
147	Allegro 1300 Super Estate Car			2,930*
147	Allegro 1500 Super 4-door Saloon			2,831*
147	Allegro 1500 Super Estate Car			3,042*
147	Allegro 1500 Special 4-door Saloon			3,101*
147	Allegro 1750 HL 4-door Saloon			3,290*
149	Maxi 1500 Saloon			3,143*
149	Maxi 1750 Saloon			3,288*
149	Maxi 1750 HL Saloon			3,574*
	AUTOBIANCHI (Italy)			
204	A 112 Normale			3,328,000*
205	A 112 Elegant			3,670,000*
205	A 112 Abarth			4,036,000*
	AVANTI (USA)			
260	Avanti II			15,970
	AZLK (USSR)			
246	Moskvich 2138			—
246	Moskvich 2136			—
246	Moskvich 2140			—
246	Moskvich 2140 IZh			—
246	Moskvich 2137			—
246	Moskvich 2140 Combi IZh			—
	BENTLEY (Great Britain)			
149	T2 Saloon			26,740*
150	Corniche Saloon			38,879*
150	Corniche Convertible			41,289*

The prices refer to all the models listed in the volume. The first column shows the prices of cars imported into the United Kingdom; the second, the prices of cars imported into the United States of America; and the third, the prices of cars in the country of origin. An asterisk signifies: prices including VAT and its equivalent in European countries and also SCT (special car tax) in Great Britain; prices ex showroom in the United States of America. Prices in the USA do not include US transportation fees, state and local taxes; prices of cars imported into the United States (East Coast) include ocean freight, US excise tax and import duty. Due to the international monetary situation all prices shown are subject to confirmation.

Page	MAKE AND MODEL	Price in GB £	Price in USA $	Price ex Works
	BMW (Germany FR)			
108	316	3,999*		15,115*
108	318			16,124*
109	320	4,999*		18,142*
109	323 i			20,533*
109	518	5,249*		18,142*
109	520	6,099*		20,382*
110	525	6,999*		23,005*
110	528 i	8,128*		27,092*
110	530 i		13,620*	
110	728	8,950*		29,564*
111	730	10,540*		33,903*
111	733 i	11,550*		38,948*
111	630 CS			42,681*
111	633 CSi	14,799*		45,304*
	BRADLEY (USA)			
260	GT I Coupé			3,995
260	GT II Coupé			6,000
	BRISTOL (Great Britain)			
150	603 E			25,992*
151	603 S2			27,995*
151	412 S2 Convertible-Saloon			24,874*
	BUICK (USA)			
261	Skyhawk S Hatchback Coupé			4,103
261	Skyhawk Hatchback Coupé			4,367
261	Skylark S Coupé			3,872
261	Skylark Coupé			3,999
261	Skylark Hatchback Coupé			4,181
261	Skylark Sedan			4,074
261	Skylark Custom Coupé			4,242
261	Skylark Custom Hatchback Coupé			4,424
261	Skylark Custom Sedan			4,317
262	Century Special Sedan	7,447*		4,486
262	Century Special Coupé			4,389
262	Century Special Station Wagon			4,976
262	Century Custom Sedan			4,733
262	Century Custom Coupé			4,633
262	Century Custom Station Wagon			5,276
262	Century Sport Coupé			5,019
262	Century Limited Sedan			5,091
262	Century Limited Coupé			4,991
263	Regal Coupé	7,769*		4,852
263	Regal Limited Coupé			5,233
263	Regal Sport Coupé			5,853
264	Le Sabre Coupé			5,384
264	Le Sabre Sedan			5,459
264	Le Sabre Custom Coupé			6,657
264	Le Sabre Custom Sedan			5,757
264	Le Sabre Sport Coupé			6,213
265	Estate Wagon Station Wagon			6,300
265	Electra 225 Sedan			7,318
265	Electra 225 Coupé			7,143
265	Electra Limited Sedan			7,700
265	Electra Limited Coupé			7,525
265	Electra Park Avenue Sedan			8,087
265	Electra Park Avenue Coupé			7,836
265	Riviera Coupé			8,081
	CADILLAC (USA)			
266	Seville	14,110*		14,267
266	De Ville Coupé			10,444
266	De Ville Sedan			10,668
266	Fleetwood Brougham	13,718*		12,292
266	Fleetwood Limousine			19,642
266	Fleetwood Formal Limousine			20,363
267	Fleetwood Eldorado			11,921

Page	MAKE AND MODEL	Price in GB £	Price in USA $	Price ex Works
	CHECKER (USA)			
267	Marathon Sedan			6,419
267	Marathon De Luxe Sedan			7,472
	CHEVROLET (Argentina)			
323	Chevy Standard			5,089,000
323	Chevy Super			5,585,000
323	Chevy Malibú			6,942,000
324	Chevy Coupé Series 2			8,571,000
	CHEVROLET (Brazil)			
313	Chevette 2-door Sedan			73,000
313	Chevette L 2-door Sedan			79,000
313	Chevette SL 2-door Sedan			82,000
314	Opala Sedan			100,000
314	Opala Coupé			101,000
314	Opala Caravan			111,000
314	Opala SS-4 Coupé			116,000
314	Opala SS-4 Caravan			123,000
314	Opala SS-6 Coupé			146,000
315	Opala SS-6 Caravan			139,000
315	Comodoro 4 Sedan			128,000
315	Comodoro 4 Coupé			127,000
315	Comodoro 6 Sedan			155,000
315	Comodoro 6 Coupé			153,000
315	Veraneio			—
	CHEVROLET (Canada)			
252	Bel Air 2-door Sport Coupé			5,912
252	Bel Air 4-door Sedan			5,980
252	Bel Air 6-pass. Station Wagon			6,578
252	Bel Air 9-pass. Station Wagon			6,723
	CHEVROLET (South Africa)			
333	1300			—
333	1300 LS			3,284
333	1900			—
333	1900 LS			3,471
333	1300 De Luxe 3-door Hatchback			3,224
333	1300 LS 3-door Hatchback			3,399
333	1900 De Luxe 3-door Hatchback			3,395
333	1900 LS 3-door Hatchback			3,570
334	Chevair 1900 De Luxe 4-door Sedan			3,941
334	Chevair 2300 GL 4-door Sedan			4,206
334	SII 2500 4-door Sedan			4,397
334	SII 2500 5-door Station Wagon			4,625
334	SII 3800 4-door Sedan			—
334	SII 3800 5-door Station Wagon			4,911
334	SII 4100 4-door Sedan			—
334	SII 4100 GA 4-door Sedan			5,757
335	Kommando 4-door Sedan			—
335	Kommando LS 4-door Sedan			5,503
335	Constantia 4-door Sedan			6,126
335	Constantia 5-door Station Wagon			5,625
335	Caprice Classic 4-door Sedan			11,530
336	Nomad			—
	CHEVROLET (USA)			
268	Chevette Scooter Hatchback Coupé			2,999
268	Chevette Hatchback Coupé			3,454
268	Chevette Hatchback Sedan			3,574
268	Monza Coupé			3,462
268	Monza Sport Coupé			3,930
268	Monza Station Wagon			3,698
268	Monza 2+2 Hatchback Coupé			3,609
268	Monza 2+2 Sport Hatchback Coupé			4,077
269	Nova Hatchback Coupé			3,865

Page	MAKE AND MODEL	Price in GB £	Price in USA $	Price ex Works
269	Nova Coupé			3,702
269	Nova Sedan			3,777
269	Nova Custom Coupé			3,960
269	Nova Custom Sedan			4,035
270	Camaro Sport Coupé			4,414
270	Camaro LT Sport Coupé			4,814
272	Chevelle Malibu Coupé			4,204
272	Chevelle Malibu Sedan			4,279
272	Chevelle Malibu Station Wagon			4,515
272	Chevelle Malibu Classic Coupé			4,461
272	Chevelle Malibu Classic Landau Coupé			4,684
272	Chevelle Malibu Classic Sedan			4,561
272	Chevelle Malibu Classic Station Wagon			4,713
272	Monte Carlo Coupé	7,467*		4,784
272	Monte Carlo Landau Coupé			5,677
273	Impala Coupé			5,207
273	Impala Landau Coupé			5,597
273	Impala Sedan			5,282
273	Impala 6-pass. Station Wagon			5,776
273	Impala 9-pass. Station Wagon			5,903
273	Caprice Classic Coupé			5,525
273	Caprice Classic Landau Coupé			5,829
273	Caprice Classic Sedan	7,956*		5,625
273	Caprice Classic 6-pass. Station Wagon	8,515*		6,011
273	Caprice Classic 9-pass. Station Wagon			6,150
274	Corvette	10,105*		9,351
	CHRYSLER (Australia)			
394	Centura GL 4-door Sedan			6,058
394	Centura GLX 4-door Sedan			6,467
394	Valiant Sedan			6,210
394	Valiant Station Wagon			6,620
394	Valiant Regal Sedan			7,903
394	Valiant Regal Station Wagon			8,713
394	Valiant Regal SE			11,221
394	Valiant Charger 770 Hardtop			6,839
	CHRYSLER (Great Britain)			
151	Alpine GL			3,072*
152	Alpine S			3,477*
152	Alpine GLS			3,984*
152	Avenger LS 1.3 2-door Saloon			2,437*
152	Avenger LS 1.3 4-door Saloon			2,559*
152	Avenger LS 1.3 Estate Car			2,857*
152	Avenger GL 1.3 2-door Saloon			2,790*
152	Avenger GL 1.3 4-door Saloon			2,914*
152	Avenger GL 1.3 Estate Car			3,232*
152	Avenger LS 1.6 4-door Saloon			2,663*
152	Avenger LS 1.6 Estate Car			2,961*
152	Avenger GL 1.6 4-door Saloon			3,019*
152	Avenger GL 1.6 Estate Car			3,336*
152	Avenger GLS 1.6 4-door Saloon			3,416*
153	Hunter De Luxe			2,940*
153	Hunter Super			3,448*
154	Sunbeam LS Hatchback Saloon			2,324*
154	Sunbeam GL Hatchback Saloon			2,512*
154	Sunbeam S Hatchback Saloon			2,985*
	CHRYSLER (Spain)			
228	Simca 1200 L			251,000
228	Simca 1200 LS			263,000
228	Simca 1200 LS Break			298,000
228	Simca 1200 LX			275,000
228	Simca 1200 GLS			285,000
228	Simca 1200 GLS Confort			296,000
228	Simca 1200 Special TI			320,000
228	Simca 1200 Special TI Break			334,000

Page	MAKE AND MODEL	Price in GB £	Price in USA $	Price ex Works
229	Chrysler Diesel			429,000
229	Chrysler Diesel De Lujo			556,000
	CHRYSLER (USA)			
274	Le Baron Coupé			5,114
274	Le Baron Sedan			5,270
274	Le Baron Medallion Coupé			5,484
274	Le Baron Medallion Sedan			5,640
274	Le Baron Town and Country Station Wagon			5,672
275	Cordoba			5,750
276	Newport 2-door Hardtop			5,727
276	Newport 4-door Hardtop			5,802
276	New Yorker Brougham 2-door Hardtop			7,591
276	New Yorker Brougham 4-door Hardtop			7,715
	CHRYSLER FRANCE (France)			
76	Simca 1005 LS	1,906*		15,490*
76	Simca 1006 GLS	2,091*		18,300*
76	Simca Rallye 1			18,900*
76	Simca Rallye 2			23,800*
77	Simca 1100 LE 2-door Berline	2,326*		18,980*
77	Simca 1100 LE 4-door Berline	2,396*		20,400*
77	Simca 1100 LE Break			22,650*
77	Simca 1100 GLX 4-door Berline	2,569*		23,300*
77	Simca 1100 GLS Break	2,803*		24,300*
77	Simca 1100 ES 4-door Berline			24,230*
77	Simca 1100 TI 4-door Berline			27,500*
78	Simca Horizon LS			24,400*
78	Simca Horizon GL			25,500*
78	Simca Horizon GLS			27,500*
79	Simca 1307 GLS			26,990*
79	Simca 1307 S			29,950*
79	Simca 1308 GT			32,100*
79	Chrysler Simca 1610			30,500*
80	Chrysler Simca 2 L Automatic			33,400*
	CITROËN (France)			
80	2 CV Spécial			13,220*
80	2 CV 4			14,320*
80	2 CV 6	1,647*		15,320*
80	Mehari 2+2			18,750*
81	Dyane 6	1,799*		16,350*
81	Ami 8 Berline Confort	1,859*		18,060*
81	Ami 8 Break Confort	1,964*		19,060*
82	LN			18,960*
82	GSpecial Berline	2,579*		23,160*
83	GS X			24,360*
83	GSpecial Break	2,789*		23,400*
83	GS Club Berline	2,895*		25,460*
83	GS Club Break	3,098*		27,060*
83	GS Pallas	3,194*		27,460*
83	GS X 2	3,046*		26,360*
83	CX 2000 Confort	4,637*		34,860*
84	CX 2000 Break Confort			40,560*
84	CX 2000 Super	4,895*		38,160*
84	CX 2200 Diesel	5,469*		41,460*
84	CX 2200 Break Confort Diesel	5,848*		46,160*
85	CX 2400 Super	5,428*		40,460*
85	CX 2400 Break Super	5,575*		45,160*
85	CX 2400 Familiale Super	5,678*		49,760*
85	CX 2400 Pallas	5,979*		42,760*
85	CX 2400 GTI	6,580*		49,200*
85	CX Prestige	8,189*		60,150*
	CONCEPT (Great Britain)			
155	Centaur Mk II			1,990*

Page	MAKE AND MODEL	Price in GB £	Price in USA $	Price ex Works
	CUSTOCA (Austria)			
74	Hurrycane			29,000*
74	Strato ES			30,000*
	DACIA (Rumania)			
228	1300 Saloon			—
228	1300 Break			—
	DAIHATSU (Japan)			
346	Max Cuore Standard 2-door Sedan			547,000
346	Max Cuore De Luxe 4-door Sedan			618,000
346	Max Cuore Custom 2-door Sedan			611,000
346	Max Cuore Custom 4-door Sedan			645,000
346	Max Cuore Custom EX 2-door Sedan			637,000
346	Max Cuore Custom EX 4-door Sedan			671,000
346	Max Cuore Hi-Custom 4-door Sedan			671,000
346	Max Cuore Hi-Custom EX 4-door Sedan			697,000
346	Charade XO			653,000
346	Charade XG			692,000
346	Charade XT			748,000
346	Charade XTE			799,000
346	Charade XGE			798,000
347	Charmant 1200 De Luxe 4-door Sedan			766,000
347	Charmant 1200 Custom 4-door Sedan			800,000
347	Charmant 1200 Hi-Custom 4-door Sedan			830,000
347	Charmant 1400 Custom 4-door Sedan			858,000
347	Charmant 1400 Hi-Custom 4-door Sedan			888,000
348	Charmant 1400 Grand Custom 4-door Sedan			923,000
348	Charmant 1400 Sporty Custom 4-door Sedan			898,000
348	Delta Wagon Standard			914,000
348	Delta Wagon De Luxe			969,000
348	Delta Wagon Custom			1,064,000
348	Taft	3,599*		960,000
348	Taft 6-seater Long Body			995,000
348	Taft Gran	3,749*		1,045,000
348	Taft Gran 6-seater Long Body			1,080,000
	DAIMLER (Great Britain)			
156	Sovereign 3.4			8,830*
156	Sovereign 4.2			10,254*
156	Vanden Plas 4.2			13,662*
156	Double-Six			12,411
157	Double-Six - Vanden Plas			16,041*
157	Limousine			14,929*
	DAVRIAN (Great Britain)			
158	Imp			—
	DE TOMASO (Italy)			
205	Pantera L	14,450*		20,800,000*
206	Pantera GTS	14,918*		21,450,000*
206	Deauville	18,112*		27,300,000*
206	Longchamp 2+2	17,878*		25,650,000*
	DIM (Greece)			
198	Dim 2-door Sedan			—

Page	MAKE AND MODEL	Price in GB £	Price in USA $	Price ex Works
	DODGE (Argentina)			
324	1500			—
324	1500 M 1.8			—
324	1500 M 1.8 Rural			—
324	Coronado			—
325	Coronado Automatic			—
325	GTX			—
	DODGE (Brazil)			
316	Polara			78,000
316	Polara Gran Luxo			88,000
316	Dart De Luxo Sedan			123,000
316	Dart De Luxo Gran Sedan			159,000
316	Dart De Luxo Coupé			122,000
316	Charger R/T			175,000
	DODGE (Spain)			
229	3700 Nuevo			506,000
229	3700 GT			453,000
	DODGE (USA)			
277	Omni			3,706
277	Aspen 2-door Coupé			3,747
277	Aspen 4-door Sedan			3,865
277	Aspen Station Wagon			4,207
279	Diplomat Coupé			4,991
279	Diplomat Sedan			5,147
279	Diplomat Station Wagon			5,486
279	Diplomat Medallion Coupé			5,361
279	Diplomat Medallion Sedan			5,517
280	Monaco Hardtop			4,230
280	Monaco Sedan			4,310
280	Monaco 6-pass. Station Wagon			5,043
280	Monaco 9-pass. Station Wagon			5,186
280	Monaco Brougham Hardtop			4,476
280	Monaco Brougham Sedan			4,527
280	Monaco Crestwood 6-pass. Station Wagon			5,486
280	Monaco Crestwood 9-pass. Station Wagon			5,629
281	Charger Special Edition			5,307
282	Magnum XE			5,448
	DUESENBERG (USA)			
282	SSJ			60,000
	DUTTON (Great Britain)			
158	Malaga			295*
159	B Plus			295*
	ELEGANT MOTORS (USA)			
283	898 Phaeton			40,000
283	856 Speedster			30,000
	ELITE (USA)			
283	Laser 917			7,500
	EL-KG (Germany FR)			
112	Bugatti 35 B			10,650*
	EL NASR (Egypt)			
332	Nasr 128			—
332	Nasr 125			—

Page	MAKE AND MODEL	Price in GB £	Price in USA $	Price ex Works
	ENNEZETA (Italy)			
206	Nuova Lele Iso Rivolta			15,000,000*
	EXCALIBUR (USA)			
284	Series III SS Roadster			25,200*
284	Series III SS Phaeton			25,200*
	FAIRTHORPE (Great Britain)			
159	TX 1500			2,754*
159	TX 2000			3,453*
	FASA-RENAULT (Spain)			
230	4			172,000
230	4 TL			191,000
230	5			—
230	5 TL			235,000
230	5 GTL			249,000
230	5 TS			273,000
230	5 Copa			387,000
231	6			—
231	6 TL			241,000
231	Siete			—
231	Siete TL			246,000
231	12			281,000
231	12 Familiar			301,000
231	12 TL			299,000
231	12 TL Familiar			317,000
231	12 TS			330,000
231	12 TS Familiar			346,000
	FELBER (Switzerland)			
242	FF Lancia 1600 Roadster			43,000*
242	FF Lancia 2000 Roadster			45,000*
242	FF Lancia Michelotti			36,000*
242	FF Ferrari			92,000*
	FERRARI (Italy)			
207	Dino 208 GT 4			18,526,000*
207	Dino 308 GT 4	13,499*	27,650*	22,275,000*
207	308 GTB	14,500*	30,920*	24,030,000*
208	308 GTS	15,499*		24,975,000*
208	400 Automatic	23,999*		38,745,000*
208	BB 512	26,000*		41,715,000*
	FIAT (Argentina)			
325	600 R			—
325	600 S			—
325	133			—
326	128 Berlina			—
326	128 L Berlina			—
326	1300 TV lava			—
327	128 Familiar 5 Puertas			—
327	125 Berlina			—
327	125 Familiar			—
327	125 Sport			—
	FIAT (Brazil)			
317	147 L			—
	FIAT (Italy)			
208	126 Berlina Base	1,496*		2,319,000*
209	126 Personal	1,675*		2,484,000*
209	127 L 2-door Berlina	1,921*		3,392,000*

Page	MAKE AND MODEL	Price in GB £	Price in USA $	Price ex Works
209	127 L 3-door Berlina			3,510,000*
209	127 C 2-door Berlina			3,610,000*
209	127 C 3-door Berlina	2,084*		3,729,000*
209	127 CL 2-door Berlina			3,800,000*
209	127 CL 3-door Berlina	2,307*		3,918,000*
209	128 1100 Base 2-door Berlina	2,110*		3,746,000*
209	128 1100 Base 4-door Berlina		3,149*	3,959,000*
209	128 1100 Base Panorama			4,095,000*
209	128 1100 Confort 4-door Berlina	2,294*		4,165,000*
209	128 1100 CL 2-door Berlina			4,083,000*
209	128 1100 CL 4-door Berlina			4,295,000*
209	128 1100 CL Panorama			4,431,000*
209	128 1300 Base 4-door Berlina			4,089,000*
209	128 1300 Confort 4-door Berlina			4,301,000*
209	128 1300 CL 4-door Berlina	2,462*		4,431,000*
210	128 3P 1100			4,183,000*
211	128 3P 1300	2,890*	3,828*	4,331,000*
211	X 1/9	3,627*	5,195*	5,752,000*
211	131 Mirafiori 1300 2-door Berlina	2,457*		4,242,000*
211	131 Mirafiori 1300 4-door Berlina	2,613*		4,484,000*
211	131 Mirafiori 1300 5-door Familiare			4,861,000*
211	131 Mirafiori 1300 Special 2-door Berlina			4,725,000*
211	131 Mirafiori 1300 Special 4-door Berlina			4,968,000*
211	131 Mirafiori 1600 5-door Familiare			5,003,000*
211	131 Mirafiori 1600 Special 4-door Berlina	3,049*	4,640*	5,109,000*
211	131 Mirafiori Special 4-door Familiare	3,196*	4,998*	5,487,000*
212	131 Fiat-Abarth Rally			—
212	132 1600 Berlina			6,567,000*
213	132 2000 Berlina	4,226*		7,546,000*
213	124 Sport Spider 1800		6,299*	
214	Campagnola			8,767,000*
	FIBERFAB (Germany FR)			
112	Bonito			
112	Sherpa			—
	FNM (Brazil)			
317	Alfa Romeo 2300			—
317	Alfa Romeo 2300 B			—
318	Alfa Romeo 2300 TI			—
	FORD (Argentina)			
327	Taunus L 2000 Sedan			3,039,000
327	Taunus GXL Sedan			—
327	Taunus GXL 2300 Sedan			3,437,000
327	Taunus GT Coupé			4,526,000
	FORD (Australia)			
395	Escort L 2-door Sedan			4,492
395	Escort GL 2-door Sedan			4,885
395	Escort GL 4-door Sedan			5,011
395	Escort Ghia 4-door Sedan			5,828
396	Cortina TE L Sedan			5,225
396	Cortina TE L Station Wagon			5,682
396	Cortina TE GL Sedan			5,641
396	Cortina TE GL Station Wagon			6,154
396	Cortina TE Ghia Sedan			6,178
396	Falcon 4-door Sedan			5,614
396	Falcon Station Wagon			5,978
396	Falcon 500 4-door Sedan			6,079
396	Falcon 500 2-door Hardtop			6,867
396	Fairmont 4-door Sedan			7,681
396	Fairmont 2-door Coupé			7,816
396	Fairmont Station Wagon	7,350*		8,114
396	Fairmont GXL Sedan	7,575*		8,887

Page	MAKE AND MODEL	Price in GB £	Price in USA $	Price ex Works
397	Fairlane 500 4-door Sedan			10,270
397	Fairlane Marquis 4-door Sedan			12,307
398	LTD 4-door Sedan			15,192
	FORD (Brazil)			
318	Corcel II Base			78,000
318	Corcel II L			86,000
318	Corcel II LDO			100,000
318	Corcel II Belina Base			87,000
318	Corcel II Belina L			93,000
318	Corcel II Belina LDO			104,000
318	Corcel II GT			97,000
318	Maverick Sedan Super			—
318	Maverick Sedan Super Luxo			90,000
318	Maverick Sedan LDO			—
319	Maverick Coupé Super			—
319	Maverick Coupé Super Luxo			90,000
319	Maverick Coupé LDO			—
319	Maverick Coupé GT-4			101,000
319	Maverick Coupé GT			—
319	Galaxie 500			170,000
319	Galaxie LTD			183,000
319	Galaxie Landau			198,000
	FORD (Canada)			
252	Granada Special Edition 2-door Sedan			4,657
252	Granada Special Edition 4-door Sedan			4,776
253	Custom 500 2-door Pillared Hardtop			5,970
253	Custom 500 4-door Pillared Hardtop			6,038
253	Custom 500 Station Wagon			6,442
	FORD (Germany FR)			
113	Fiesta 3-door Limousine	3,958		8,735*
113	Fiesta L 3-door Limousine			9,340*
113	Fiesta S 3-door Limousine			10,510*
113	Fiesta Ghia 3-door Limousine			11,220*
113	Escort 2-door Limousine			9,240*
113	Escort 4-door Limousine			9,760*
113	Escort Turnier			9,995*
113	Escort L 2-door Limousine			9,865*
113	Escort L 4-door Limousine			10,385*
113	Escort L Turnier			10,620*
113	Escort GL 2-door Limousine			10,865*
113	Escort GL 4-door Limousine			11,385*
113	Escort GL Turnier			11,620*
113	Escort Ghia 2-door Limousine			12,825*
113	Escort Ghia 4-door Limousine			13,345*
113	Escort Sport 2-door Limousine			11,280*
113	Escort Sport 4-door Limousine			11,800*
113	Escort RS 2000 2-door Limousine			14,400*
115	Taunus 2-door Limousine			10,945*
115	Taunus 4-door Limousine			11,490*
115	Taunus Turnier			12,095*
115	Taunus L 2-door Limousine			11,555*
115	Taunus L 4-door Limousine			12,100*
115	Taunus L Turnier			12,705*
115	Taunus GL 2-door Limousine			13,395*
115	Taunus GL 4-door Limousine			13,940*
115	Taunus GL Turnier			14,545*
115	Taunus Ghia 2-door Limousine			15,775*
115	Taunus Ghia 4-door Limousine			16,320*
115	Taunus S 2-door Limousine			14,660*
115	Taunus S 4-door Limousine			15,205*
116	Capri II L Coupé			11,690*
116	Capri II GL Coupé			13,545*
116	Capri II S Coupé			15,305*
116	Capri II Ghia Coupé			18,280*
118	Granada 2-door Limousine			13,875*

Page	MAKE AND MODEL	Price in GB £	Price in USA $	Price ex Works
118	Granada 4-door Limousine			14,445*
118	Granada Turnier			14,995*
118	Granada L 2-door Limousine			14,620*
118	Granada L 4-door Limousine			15,100*
118	Granada L Turnier			15,990*
118	Granada GL 2-door Limousine			18,635*
118	Granada GL 4-door Limousine			19,205*
118	Granada GL Turnier			20,220*
118	Granada Ghia 4-door Limousine			23,250*
	FORD (Great Britain)			
160	Fiesta 3-door Saloon			2,196*
160	Fiesta L 3-door Saloon			2,420*
160	Fiesta S 3-door Saloon			2,785*
160	Fiesta Ghia 3-door Saloon			3,228*
160	Escort Popular 1100 2-door Saloon			2,123*
160	Escort Popular 110 Plus 2-door Saloon			2,254*
160	Escort Popular 1100 Plus 4-door Saloon			2,353*
160	Escort 1100 Estate Car			2,425*
160	Escort 1100 L 2-door Saloon			2,457*
160	Escort 1100 L 4-door Saloon			2,556*
160	Escort Popular 1300 2-door Saloon			2,225*
160	Escort Popular 1300 Plus 2-door Saloon			2,338*
160	Escort Popular 1300 Plus 4-door Saloon			2,437*
160	Escort 1300 Estate Car			2,553*
160	Escort 1300 L 2-door Saloon			2,528*
160	Escort 1300 L 4-door Saloon			2,627*
160	Escort 1300 L Estate Car			2,836*
160	Escort 1300 GL 2-door Saloon			2,765*
160	Escort 1300 GL 4-door Saloon			2,864*
160	Escort 1300 GL Estate Car			3,128*
160	Escort 1300 Sport 2-door Saloon			2,935*
160	Escort 1300 Ghia 2-door Saloon			3,338*
160	Escort 1300 Ghia 4-door Saloon			3,437*
160	Escort 1600 Sport 2-door Saloon			3,024*
160	Escort 1600 Ghia 4-door Saloon			3,526*
160	Escort RS Mexico 2-door Saloon			3,496*
160	Escort RS 1800 2-door Saloon			4,275*
160	Escort RS 2000 2-door Saloon			4,168*
163	Cortina 1300 2-door Saloon			2,647*
163	Cortina 1300 4-door Saloon			2,754*
163	Cortina 1300 L 2-door Saloon			2,849*
163	Cortina 1300 L 4-door Saloon			2,956*
163	Cortina 1600 4-door Saloon			2,919*
163	Cortina 1600 Estate Car			3,255*
163	Cortina 1600 L 4-door Saloon			3,121*
163	Cortina 1600 L Estate Car			3,488*
163	Cortina 1600 GL 4-door Saloon			3,423*
163	Cortina 1600 GL Estate Car			3,791*
163	Cortina 1600 Ghia 4-door Saloon			4,074*
163	Cortina 1600 Ghia Estate Car			4,442*
163	Cortina 2000 GL 4-door Saloon			3,621*
163	Cortina 2000 GL Estate Car			3,989*
163	Cortina 2000 S 4-door Saloon			3,858*
163	Cortina 2000 Ghia 4-door Saloon			4,192*
163	Cortina 2000 Ghia Estate Car			4,560*
163	Cortina 2300 GL 4-door Saloon			4,091*
163	Cortina 2300 GL Estate Car			4,459*
163	Cortina 2300 S 4-door Saloon			4,328*
163	Cortina 2300 Ghia 4-door Saloon			4,662*
163	Cortina 2300 Ghia Estate Car			5,030*
164	Capri II 1300 Coupé			2,792*
164	Capri II 1300 L Coupé			2,928*
164	Capri II 1600 L Coupé			3,101*
164	Capri II 1600 GL Coupé			3,362*
164	Capri II 1600 S Coupé			3,822*
164	Capri II 2000 GL Coupé			3,560*
164	Capri II 2000 S Coupé			3,940*

Page	MAKE AND MODEL	Price in GB £	Price in USA $	Price ex Works
164	Capri II 2000 Ghia Coupé			4,697*
164	Capri II 3000 S Coupé			4,327*
164	Capri II 3000 Ghia Coupé			5,337*
166	Granada 2000 L Saloon			4,347*
166	Granada 2000 L Estate Car			5,087*
166	Granada 2300 GL Saloon			5,519*
166	Granada 2800 S Saloon			6,200*
166	Granada 2800 GL Saloon			6,150*
166	Granada 2800 GL Estate Car			6,612*
166	Granada 2800 Ghia Saloon			7,078*
	FORD (South Africa)			
336	Escort 1300 L 2-door Sedan			—
336	Escort 1300 L 4-door Sedan			—
336	Escort 1600 GL 4-door Sedan			—
337	Cortina 1600 L Sedan			4,600
337	Cortina 1600 L Station Wagon			4,873
337	Cortina 2000 GL Sedan			4,976
337	Cortina 2000 GL Station Wagon			5,249
337	Cortina 3000 S Sedan			5,633
338	Cortina 3000 Ghia Sedan			6,670
338	Cortina 3000 Ghia Station Wagon			6,952
338	Granada 3000 GL Sedan			—
338	Granada 3000 Ghia Sedan			—
	FORD (USA)			
284	Pinto Sedan			3,471
284	Pinto Runabout			3,587
284	Pinto Station Wagon			3,870
285	Mustang II Hardtop			3,614
285	Mustang II Hatchback			3,857
285	Mustang II Ghia Hardtop	6,350*		4,031
285	Mustang II Mach I Hatchback	6,300*		4,312
286	Fairmont 2-door Sedan			3,589
286	Fairmont 4-door Sedan			3,663
286	Fairmont Sport Coupé			—
286	Fairmont Station Wagon			4,031
287	Granada 2-door Sedan			4,264
287	Granada 4-door Sedan			4,342
287	Granada Ghia 2-door Sedan			4,649
287	Granada Ghia 4-door Sedan			4,728
287	Granada ESS 2-door Sedan			4,836
287	Granada ESS 4-door Sedan			4,914
288	LTD II S 2-door Hardtop			4,814
288	LTD II S 4-door Sedan			4,889
288	LTD II 2-door Hardtop			5,069
288	LTD II 4-door Sedan			5,169
288	LTD II Brougham 2-door Hardtop			5,405
288	LTD II Brougham 4-door Sedan			5,505
289	Thunderbird			5,411
289	Thunderbird Town Landau			8,420
289	Thunderbird Diamond Jubilee Edition			10,106
290	LTD 2-door Hardtop			5,335
290	LTD 4-door Hardtop			5,410
290	LTD Station Wagon			5,797
290	LTD Landau 2-door Hardtop			5,898
290	LTD Landau 4-door Hardtop			5,973
290	LTD Country Squire Station Wagon			6,207
	GAZ (USSR)			
247	Volga 24			—
247	Volga 24-02			—
247	Volga 24 Indenor Diesel			—
247	Chaika			—
	GENERAL MOTORS (Malaysia)			
392	Harimau			3,900
392	Amigo			3,900

Page	MAKE AND MODEL	Price in GB £	Price in USA $	Price ex Works
392	Opel Kadett City			10,836
393	Opel Kadett 1.2 Standard			10,935
393	Opel Kadett 1.2 De Luxe			11,810
393	Opel Gemini 1.6 Sedan			12,430
393	Opel Gemini 1.6 Coupé			12,268
393	Opel Rekord Berlina			18,408
393	Opel Rekord 2100 D			21,229
	GIANNINI (Italy)			
214	Fiat 126 GP Base			2,470,000*
214	Fiat 126 GP Personal			2,625,000*
214	Fiat 126 GP S Base			2,615,000*
214	Fiat 126 GP S Personal			2,765,000*
214	Fiat 126 Sport Base DC			2,800,000*
215	Fiat 127 NP 2-dr			3,515,000*
215	Fiat 127 NP 2-dr Berlina Base			3,515,000*
215	Fiat 127 NP 3-dr Berlina Base			3,640,000*
215	Fiat 127 NP 2-dr Berlina Confort			3,710,000*
215	Fiat 127 NP 3-dr Berlina Confort			3,835,000*
215	Fiat 128 NP 2-dr Berlina Base			3,835,000*
215	Fiat 128 NP 4-dr Berlina Base			4,055,000*
215	Fiat 128 NP 2-dr Berlina Confort L			4,115,000*
215	Fiat 128 NP 4-dr Berlina Confort L			4,335,000*
215	Fiat 128 NP S 2-dr Berlina Base			4,055,000*
215	Fiat 128 NP S 4-dr Berlina Base			4,275,000*
215	Fiat 128 NP S 2-dr Berlina Confort L			4,335,000*
215	Fiat 128 NP S 4-dr Berlina Confort L			4,555,000*
215	Fiat 128 5M 2-dr Autostrada Base			4,525,000*
215	Fiat 128 5M 4-dr Autostrada Base			4,745,000*
215	Fiat 128 5M 2-dr Autostrada Confort L			4,835,000*
215	Fiat 128 5M 4-dr Autostrada Confort L			5,035,000*
	GINETTA (Great Britain)			
167	G21			4,500*
	G.P. (Great Britain)			
168	Centron II			950*
	GURGEL (Brazil)			
319	X-12			63,000
319	X-12 TR			63,000
320	X-20			82,000
	HINDUSTAN (India)			
342	Ambassador Mark 3			—
	HOLDEN (Australia)			
398	Gemini TC 4-door Sedan			4,482
398	Gemini TC SL 4-door Sedan			4,851
398	Gemini TC SL Coupé			4,995
398	Sunbird			5,460
399	Torana LX 2800 S 4-door Sedan			5,480
399	Torana LX 3300 S 4-door Sedan			5,593
399	Torana LX 4150 S 4-door Sedan			5,758
399	Torana LX 2850 SL 4-door Sedan			6,037
399	Torana LX 3300 SL 4-door Sedan			6,150
399	Torana LX 3300 SL Hatchback			6,398
399	Torana LX 4150 SL 4-door Sedan			6,315
399	Torana LX 4150 SL Hatchback			6,666
399	Torana LX 3300 SL/R 4-door Sedan			6,560
399	Torana LX 4150 SL/R 4-door Sedan			6,828
399	Torana LX 5000 SL/R 4-door Sedan			6,960
399	Torana LX 3300 SS Hatchback			6,796
399	Torana LX 4150 SS Hatchback			7,064

Page	MAKE AND MODEL	Price in GB £	Price in USA $	Price ex Works
399	Torana LX 5000 SS Hatchback			7,196
400	HZ Kingswood SL 4-door Sedan			6,377
400	HZ Kingswood SL Station Wagon			6,727
400	HZ Premier 4-door Sedan			7,783
400	HZ Premier Station Wagon			8,089
400	HZ GTS 4-door Sedan			8,482
400	HZ Statesman De Ville 4-door Sedan			9,993
400	HZ Statesman Caprice 4-door Sedan			14,729
	HONDA (Japan)			
348	Civic CVCC 1200 Standard 2-door Sedan		2,969*	656,000
348	Civic CVCC 1200 De Luxe 3-door Sedan	2,446*	3,319*	711,000
348	Civic CVCC 1200 De Luxe 4-door Sedan			729,000
348	Civic CVCC 1200 Hi-De Luxe 3-door Sedan		3,639*	760,000
348	Civic CVCC 1200 Hi-De Luxe 4-door Sedan			778,000
348	Civic CVCC 1200 GL 3-door Sedan			787,000
348	Civic CVCC 1200 GL II-5 3-door Sedan			822,000
348	Civic CVCC 1200 GF 4-door Sedan			805,000
348	Civic CVCC 1200 GF-5 4-door Sedan			825,000
348	Civic CVCC 1500 RSL 3-door Sedan		3,979*	911,000
348	Civic CVCC 1500 GTL 3-door Sedan			862,000
348	Civic CVCC 1500 GF-5E 4-door Sedan			872,000
348	Civic CVCC 1500 GF 5-door Sedan	2,616*		872,000
348	Civic CVCC 1500 GF-5 5-door Sedan		3,859*	892,000
349	Civic CVCC 1500 Station Wagon			—
349	Civic Wagon 1500 Van Custom			921,000
350	Accord SL 3-door Hatchback			981,000
350	Accord GL 3-door Hatchback	3,355*	4,645*	1,041,000
350	Accord LX 3-door Hatchback		5,465*	1,140,000
350	Accord EX 3-door Hatchback			1,230,000
350	Accord EX-L 3-door Hatchback			941,000
350	Accord SL 4-door Sedan			1,036,000
350	Accord GF 4-door Sedan			1,160,000
350	Accord EX 4-door Sedan			1,260,000
350	Accord EX-L 4-door Sedan			
	HONGKI (China People's Republic)			
343	Limousine			—
	HYUNDAI (South Korea)			
344	Pony Saloon			—
344	Pony Coupé			—
	IKA-RENAULT (Argentina)			
328	Torino Grand Routier			—
328	Torino TSX			—
	INTERMECCANICA (USA)			
291	Speedster			6,985
	INTERNATIONAL HARVESTER (USA)			
291	Scout II Station Wagon 4 x 2			5,120
291	Scout II Station Wagon 4 x 4			6,080
291	Scout II Diesel Station Wagon 4 x 2			7,701
291	Scout II Diesel Station Wagon 4 x 4			8,717
291	Scout Traveler Station Wagon 4 x 2			5,510
291	Scout Traveler Station Wagon 4 x 4			6,473
291	Scout Traveler Diesel S.W. 4 x 2			8,091
291	Scout Traveler Diesel S.W. 4 x 4			9,114
291	SS II Station Wagon 4 x 4			5,387

Page	MAKE AND MODEL	Price in GB £	Price in USA $	Price ex Works
	ISUZU (Japan)			
350	Gemini 1600 LD 4-door Sedan			894,000
350	Gemini 1600 LD 2-door Coupé			924,000
350	Gemini 1600 LT 4-door Sedan			933,000
350	Gemini 1600 LT 2-door Coupé			963,000
350	Gemini 1600 LS 4-door Sedan			1,001,000
350	Gemini 1600 LS 2-door Coupé			1,063,000
350	Gemini Minx 4-door Sedan			1,013,000
350	Gemini Minx 2-door Coupé			1,043,000
350	Gemini 1800 LT 4-door Sedan			963,000
350	Gemini 1800 LT 2-door Coupé			993,000
350	Gemini 1800 LS 4-door Sedan			1,046,000
350	Gemini 1800 LS 2-door Coupé			1,093,000
350	Gemini 1800 LS/G 2-door Coupé			1,168,000
351	Florian SII 1800 De Luxe 4-dr Sedan			1,211,000
351	Florian SII 1800 Super De Luxe 4-door Sedan			1,383,000
351	Florian SII Diesel 2000 Semi-De Luxe 4-door Sedan			1,253,000
351	Florian SII Diesel 2000 De Luxe 4-door Sedan			1,298,000
351	Florian SII Diesel 2000 Super De Luxe 4-door Sedan			1,470,000
352	117 XE Coupé			2,205,000
352	117 XG Coupé			1,920,000
352	117 XC Coupé			1,677,000
352	117 XC-J Coupé			1,754,000
352	117 XT Coupé			1,475,000
	JAGUAR (Great Britain)			
169	XJ 3.4			9,230*
169	XJ 4.2	16,500*		9,753*
169	XJ 5.3	17,750*		11,880*
170	XJ-S	21,700*		14,472*
	JEEP CORPORATION (USA)			
292	Jeep CJ-5 Roadster			4,895
292	Jeep CJ-7 Roadster		5,049*	4,995
293	Cherokee 2-door Station Wagon		7,799*	6,129
293	Cherokee Wide Wheel 2-door Station Wagon			—
293	Cherokee 4-door Station Wagon		7,899*	6,235
294	Wagoneer			7,595
	JOHNARD VINTAGE CAR (Great Britain)			
170	Bentley Donington			15,500*
	KIA (South Korea)			
344	Brisa 1100			—
345	Brisa 1300			—
	K.M.B. (Great Britain)			
171	GTM Mk 1-3			2,800*
	LAFER (Brazil)			
320	MP			85,000
320	LL			—
	LAMBORGHINI (Italy)			
216	Urraco P 200			19,352,000*
216	Urraco P 250			22,140,000*
216	Urraco P 300	14,560*		24,300,000*
216	Urraco Silhouette P 300	17,798*		29,700,000*

LAMBORGHINI (Italy)

Page	MAKE AND MODEL	Price in GB £	Price in USA $	Price ex Works
217	Espada 400 GT	22,990*		38,475,000*
217	Countach LP 400 S	25,960*		35,000,000*
218	Countach LP 400			49,950,000*
	LANCIA (Italy)			
218	Beta Berlina 1300	3,292*		6,767,000*
218	Coupé 1300	3,760*		7,050,000*
219	Beta Berlina 1600	3,825*	6,995*	7,033,000*
219	Beta Coupé 1600	4,376*	7,930*	7,522,000*
219	Beta HPE 1600	5,025*	8,995*	7,735,000*
219	Beta 1600 Spider	4,960*		8,112,000*
219	Beta Berlina 2000	4,081*		7,505,000*
219	Beta 2000 Coupé	4,789*		7,935,000*
220	Beta HPE 2000	5,438*		8,207,000*
220	Beta Spider 2000	5,128*		8,525,000*
220	Beta ES 2000	4,457*		—
220	Beta Montecarlo	5,927*	9,995*	9,281,000*
220	Gamma Berlina 2000			10,638,000*
221	Gamma Coupé 2000			13,599,000*
221	Gamma Berlina 2500			12,737,000*
221	Gamma Coupé 2500			16,126,000*
221	Stratos			16,200,000*
	LAWIL (Italy)			
222	S3 Varzina			1,853,000*
222	A4 City			1,829,000*
	LEYLAND (South Africa)			
338	Mini De Luxe			2,855
339	Mini Clubman			3,070
339	Mini GTS			3,250
339	Marina 1300			3,559
339	Marina 1750			4,270
339	Marina 2600			4,975
340	Triumph Chicane			5,685
340	Jaguar XJ6 Executive			16,600
340	Rover 2600 SD			7,800
340	Rover 2600 SDX			—
341	Rover 3500 SDE			13,500
	LINCOLN (USA)			
294	Versailles			12,529
294	Continental Sedan			10,166
294	Continental Coupé			9,974
294	Continental Town Sedan			11,606
294	Continental Town Coupé			11,414
295	Continental Mark V			12,099
	LOTUS (Great Britain)			
172	Esprit	17,440*	9,516*	
172	Eclat 520	15,350*	8,901*	
172	Eclat 521	16,698*	9,641*	
173	Eclat 522	17,688*	10,536*	
173	Eclat 523	18,250*	10,852*	
173	Eclat 524	18,775*	11,024*	
173	Elite 501		9,923*	
173	Elite 502		10,869*	
173	Elite 503	19,090*	11,188*	
173	Elite 504	19,615*	11,361*	
	LYNX (Great Britain)			
174	D Type			15,000*
	MALLORCA (Spain)			
232	1800			650,000

Page	MAKE AND MODEL	Price in GB £	Price in USA $	Price ex Works
	MASERATI (Italy)			
222	Merak 2000			16,520,000*
223	Merak SS	14,888*	25,800*	20,500,000*
223	Quattroporte			—
223	Kyalami	20,978*		27,890,000*
223	Bora 4900	22,991*	33,775*	30,780,000*
224	Khamsin	21,996*	35,945*	30,780,000*
	MATRA (France)			
86	Simca Rancho			35,995*
86	Simca Bagheera			39,300*
87	Simca Bagheera S	5,370*		43,100*
87	Simca Bagheera X			46,930*
	MAZDA (Japan)			
352	Familia AP Standard 3-door Sedan			640,000
352	Familia AP Standard 5-door Sedan			675,000
352	Familia AP De Luxe 3-door Sedan			710,000
352	Familia AP De Luxe 5-door Sedan			745,000
352	Familia AP GF 3-door Sedan			760,000
352	Familia AP GF 5-door Sedan			790,000
352	Familia AP Super Custom 3-door Sedan			800,000
352	Familia AP Super Custom 5-door Sedan			835,000
352	Familia AP Super Custom 1978 emission 3-door Sedan			823,000
352	Familia AP Super Custom 1978 emission 5-door Sedan			850,000
353	Familia GLC Regular 3-door Sedan		3,199*	
353	Familia GLC De Luxe 3-door Sedan		3,499*	
353	Familia GLC De Luxe 5-door Sedan		3,649*	
353	Grand Familia 1300 AP De Luxe 4-door Sedan			738,000
353	Grand Familia 1300 AP LX 4-door Sedan			783,000
353	Grand Familia 1300 AP FX 2-door Coupé			793,000
353	Grand Familia 1300 AP GL 4-door Sedan			828,000
353	Grand Familia 1300 AP GF 2-door Coupé			858,000
353	Grand Familia 1600 AP LX 4-door Sedan			813,000
353	Grand Familia 1600 AP GL 4-door Sedan			873,000
353	Grand Familia 1600 AP GL II 4-door Sedan			923,000
353	Grand Familia 1600 AP FX 2-door Coupé			833,000
353	Grand Familia 1600 AP GF 2-door Coupé			893,000
353	Grand Familia 1600 AP GF II 2-door Coupé			923,000
354	Capella 1600 AP De Luxe Sedan			913,000
354	Capella 1600 AP GL Sedan			983,000
354	Capella 1800 AP GL Sedan			1,043,000
354	Capella 1800 AP De Luxe Coupé			988,000
354	Capella 1800 AP GF Coupé			1,073,000
354	Capella RE-AP GR Sedan			1,104,000
354	Capella RE-AP GR II Sedan			1,194,000
354	Capella RE-AP GS Coupé			1,134,000
354	Capella RE-AP GS II Coupé			1,124,000
355	Luce 1800 Custom Special 4-door Sedan	3,399*		996,000
355	Luce 2000 Custom 4-door Sedan			1,165,000
355	Luce 2000 Custom 4-door Hardtop			1,230,000
355	Luce 2000 Super Custom 4-door Sedan			1,280,000
355	Luce 2000 Super Custom 4-door Hardtop			1,345,000

Page	MAKE AND MODEL	Price in GB £	Price in USA $	Price ex Works
355	Luce 2000 Custom Special 4-door Hardtop			1,105,000
355	Luce RE Custom 4-door Sedan			1,260,000
355	Luce RE Custom 4-door Hardtop			1,325,000
355	Luce RE Super Custom 4-door Sedan			1,500,000
355	Luce RE Super Custom 4-door Hardtop			1,565,000
355	Luce RE Custom Special 4-door Sedan			1,130,000
355	Luce RE Custom Special 4-door Hardtop			1,195,000
355	Luce RE Limited 4-door Sedan			1,915,000
355	Luce RE Limited 4-door Hardtop			1,980,000
356	Cosmo 1800 AP Custom Special Coupé			1,055,000
356	Cosmo 1800 AP Custom Coupé			1,190,000
356	Cosmo 1800 AP Super Custom Coupé			1,355,000
356	Cosmo 2000 AP Custom Coupé			1,255,000
356	Cosmo 2000 AP Super Custom Coupé	6,195*		1,395,000
356	Cosmo L 2000 AP Custom Special Coupé			1,205,000
356	Cosmo L 2000 AP Custom Coupé			1,340,000
356	Cosmo L 2000 AP Super Custom Coupé			1,480,000
355	Cosmo AP Custom Special Coupé			1,200,000
356	Cosmo AP Custom Coupé			1,330,000
356	Cosmo AP Super Custom Coupé			1,538,000
356	Cosmo L RE Custom Special Coupé			1,285,000
356	Cosmo L RE Custom Coupé			1,415,000
356	Cosmo L RE Super Custom Coupé			1,590,000
356	Cosmo AP Limited Coupé			1,795,000
356	Cosmo L RE Limited Coupé			1,855,000
356	Roadpacer Sedan			3,835,000
	MERCEDES-BENZ (Germany FR)			
120	200	5,995*		19,197*
120	230	7,594*	12,880*	20,160*
120	230 C	8,951*		25,290*
120	230 T			24,192*
120	250	8,395*		22,960*
121	250 Long Wheelbase			35,112*
121	250 T			26,992*
121	200 D	6,250*		19,712*
121	220 D			20,530*
121	240 D	7,594*	11,920*	21,246*
121	240 D Long Wheelbase			33,398*
121	240 TD			25,278*
121	300 D	8,995*	16,590*	23,531*
122	300 D Long Wheelbase			35,011*
122	300 TD			27,563*
122	300 SD			—
122	280			26,365*
123	280 C			30,117*
123	280 E	9,695*	17,114*	28,370*
123	280 CE	10,990*		32,122*
123	280 TE			32,346*
123	280 S			30,430*
123	280 SE	11,795*	19,993*	32,581*
123	280 SEL			35,168*
124	280 SL			35,941*
124	280 SLC			41,541*
124	350 SE	13,499*		36,758*
124	350 SEL			38,898*
124	350 SL	12,500*		39,715*
125	350 SLC			45,315*
125	450 SE	14,750*		41,294*
125	450 SEL	15,751*	25,241*	46,211*
125	450 SL	13,450*	22,601*	44,251*
125	450 SLC	15,995*	27,903*	49,851*

Page	MAKE AND MODEL	Price in GB £	Price in USA $	Price ex Works
125	450 SLC 5.0			59,371*
126	450 SEL 6.9	23,851*	39,377*	73,752*
126	600			134,624*
127	600 Pullman			154,560*
	MERCURY (Canada)			
254	Marquis Meteor 2-door Hardtop			6,511
254	Marquis Meteor 4-door Hardtop			6,586
254	Marquis Meteor Station Wagon			6,805
	MERCURY (USA)			
296	Bobcat Runabout			3,672
296	Bobcat Station Wagon			3,955
296	Bobcat Villager Station Wagon			4,010
296	Zephyr 2-door Sedan			3,742
296	Zephyr 4-door Sedan			3,816
296	Zephyr Sport Coupé			—
296	Zephyr Station Wagon			4,184
297	Monarch 2-door Sedan			4,330
297	Monarch 4-door Sedan			4,409
297	Monarch Ghia 2-door Sedan	7,165*		4,756
297	Monarch Ghia 4-door Sedan	7,225*		4,835
297	Monarch ESS 2-door Sedan			4,854
297	Monarch ESS 4-door Sedan			4,933
298	Cougar 2-door Hardtop			5,009
298	Cougar 4-door Hardtop			5,126
298	Cougar XR-7 2-door Hardtop			5,603
298	Marquis 2-door Hardtop			5,764
298	Marquis 4-door Hardtop			5,806
298	Marquis Station Wagon			5,958
298	Marquis Brougham 2-door Hardtop			6,380
298	Marquis Brougham 4-door Hardtop			6,480
298	Grand Marquis 2-door Hardtop			7,132
298	Grand Marquis 4-door Hardtop			7,232
	MG (Great Britain)			
174	Midget		4,150*	2,441*
175	MGB GT			4,037*
175	MGB Sports		5,150*	3,324*
	MINI (BRITISH LEYLAND) (Great Britain)			
175	850 Saloon			1,990*
176	1000 Saloon			2,094*
176	Clubman Saloon			2,321*
176	Clubman Estate Car			2,487*
176	1275 GT			2,589*
	MITSUBISHI (Japan)			
357	Minica Ami 55 Hi Standard Sedan			545,000
357	Minica Ami 55 Super De Luxe Sedan			611,000
357	Minica Ami 55 GL Sedan			635,000
357	Minica Ami 55 XL Sedan			658,000
357	Lancer 1200 Populaire 2-door Sedan			778,000
357	Lancer 1200 Populaire 4-door Sedan			800,000
357	Lancer 1200 GL 2-door Sedan			817,000
357	Lancer 1200 GL 4-door Sedan			839,000
357	Lancer 1200 SL-5 2-door Sedan			863,000
357	Lancer 1200 SL-5 4-door Sedan			885,000
357	Lancer 1400 GL 2-door Sedan	2,920*		875,000
357	Lancer 1400 GL 4-door Sedan	3,070*		900,000
357	Lancer 1400 SL-5 2-door Sedan			934,000
357	Lancer 1400 SL-5 4-door Sedan			956,000
357	Lancer 1600 GSL 4-door Sedan			1,004,000
357	Lancer 1600 GSR 2-door Sedan	3,340*		1,078,000

Page	MAKE AND MODEL	Price in GB £	Price in USA $	Price ex Works
358	Celeste 1400 SR Coupé			917,000
358	Celeste 1400 GL Coupé			957,000
358	Celeste 1400 SL Coupé			1,013,000
358	Celeste 1600 GL Coupé			1,099,000
358	Celeste 1600 XL Coupé			1,097,000
358	Celeste 1600 GT Coupé			1,149,000
358	Celeste 1600 GSR Coupé			1,122,000
359	Galant Sigma 1600 Custom 4-door Sedan			997,000
359	Galant Sigma 1600 GL 4-door Sedan	3,700*		1,062,000
359	Galant Sigma 1600 SL 4-door Sedan			1,107,000
359	Galant Sigma 1600 SL Super 4-door Sedan			1,187,000
359	Galant Sigma 1850 GL 4-door Sedan			1,149,000
359	Galant Sigma 1850 SL 4-door Sedan			1,184,000
359	Galant Sigma 2000 GLX 4-door Sedan	4,220*		1,234,000
359	Galant Sigma 2000 Super 4-door Sedan			1,447,000
359	Galant Sigma 2000 GSL 4-door Sedan			1,294,000
359	Galant Sigma 2000 GSR 4-door Sedan			1,335,000
360	Galant Lambda 1600 SL 2-door Coupé			1,195,000
360	Galant Lambda 1600 GS 2-door Coupé			1,240,000
360	Galant Lambda 2000 GSL 2-door Coupé			1,370,000
360	Galant Lambda 2000 Super Touring 2-door Coupé			1,626,000
360	Galant Lambda 2000 Super Touring Automatic 2-door Coupé			1,666,000
360	Galant Lambda 2000 GSR 2-door Coupé			1,519,000
361	Debonair Executive SE 4-door Sedan			2,340,000
361	Debonair Executive SE 6-passenger 4-door Sedan			2,280,000
361	Jeep H-J58			1,208,000
361	Jeep H-J56			1,248,000
361	Jeep J54			1,343,000
362	Jeep H-J26			1,332,000
362	Jeep J24			1,427,000

MONOCOQUE (USA)

Page	MAKE AND MODEL	Price in GB £	Price in USA $	Price ex Works
299	Box			8,800

MONTEVERDI (Switzerland)

Page	MAKE AND MODEL	Price in GB £	Price in USA $	Price ex Works
243	Sierra			69,000*
243	High Speed 375 L			98,000*
244	High Speed 375/4 Limousine			114,000*
244	Palm Beach			124,000*
244	Hai 450 GTS			140,000*
244	Safari			39,000*

MORGAN (Great Britain)

Page	MAKE AND MODEL	Price in GB £	Price in USA $	Price ex Works
177	4/4 1600 2-seater			3,990*
177	4/4 1600 4-seater			4,388*
177	Plus 8			5,961*

MORRIS (Great Britain)

Page	MAKE AND MODEL	Price in GB £	Price in USA $	Price ex Works
178	Marina 1.3 De Luxe 2-door Saloon			2,538*
178	Marina 1.3 De Luxe 4-door Saloon			2,647*
178	Marina 1.3 De Luxe Estate Car			3,044*
178	Marina 1.3 Super 2-door Saloon			2,668*
178	Marina 1.3 Super 4-door Saloon			2,776*
178	Marina 1.8 Super 2-door Saloon			2,904*
178	Marina 1.8 Super 4-door Saloon			3,013*
178	Marina 1.8 Super Estate Car			3,411*
178	Marina 1.8 Special 2-door Saloon			3,205*
178	Marina 1.8 Special 4-door Saloon			3,313*
178	Marina 1.8 GT 2-door Saloon			3,423*
178	Marina 1.8 HL 4-door Saloon			3,532*

NISSAN (Japan)

Page	MAKE AND MODEL	Price in GB £	Price in USA $	Price ex Works
362	Cherry F II 1200 Standard 2-door Sedan			658,000
362	Cherry F II 1200 De Luxe 2-door Sedan			702,000
362	Cherry F II 1200 De Luxe 4-door Sedan			729,000
362	Cherry F II 1200 De Luxe Coupé			752,000
362	Cherry F II 1200 GL 2-door Sedan			760,000
362	Cherry F II 1200 GL 4-door Sedan			787,000
362	Cherry F II 1200 GL Coupé	2,418*		810,000
362	Cherry F II 1200 GL-L Coupé			840,000
362	Cherry F II 1400 GL 4-door Sedan			833,000
362	Cherry F II 1400 GL Coupé			856,000
362	Cherry F II 1400 GL-L 4-door Sedan			863,000
362	Cherry F II 1400 GL-L Coupé			886,000
362	Cherry F II 1400 GX 4-door Sedan			873,000
362	Cherry F II 1400 GX Coupé			896,000
362	Cherry F II Datsun F10 Coupé		4,178*	
362	Cherry F II Datsun F10 Station Wagon		3,898*	
362	Cherry F II 1400 Twin GX 4-door Sedan			938,000
362	Cherry F II 1400 Twin GX Coupé			936,000
362	Cherry F II 1400 Twin GX-L 4-door Sedan			968,000
362	Cherry F II 1400 Twin GX-L Coupé			966,000
363	Sunny 1200 Semi De Luxe 2-door Sedan			737,000
363	Sunny 1200 Semi De Luxe 4-door Sedan			757,000
363	Sunny 1200 De Luxe 2-door Sedan			788,000
363	Sunny 1200 De Luxe 4-door Sedan			808,000
363	Sunny 1200 De Luxe Coupé			838,000
363	Sunny 1200 GL 2-door Sedan			850,000
363	Sunny 1200 GL 4-door Sedan			870,000
363	Sunny 1200 GL Coupé			910,000
363	Sunny 1400 De Luxe 2-door Sedan			833,000
363	Sunny 1400 De Luxe 4-door Sedan			853,000
363	Sunny 1400 De Luxe Coupé			883,000
363	Sunny 1400 GL 2-door Sedan		3,198*	902,000
363	Sunny 1400 GL 4-door Sedan			917,000
363	Sunny 1400 GL Coupé			947,000
363	Sunny 1400 SGL 4-door Sedan			975,000
363	Sunny 1400 SGL Coupé			1,010,000
363	Sunny 1400 GX 4-door Sedan		3,798*	962,000
363	Sunny 1400 GX Coupé		4,018*	1,001,000
363	Sunny 1400 SGX 4-door Sedan			1,020,000
363	Sunny 1400 SGX Coupé			1,064,000
364	Violet 1400 Standard Sedan			838,000
364	Violet 1400 De Luxe Sedan			901,000
364	Violet 1400 De Luxe Hatchback Coupé			936,000
364	Auster 1400 De Luxe Sedan			901,000
364	Auster 1400 De Luxe Hatchback Coupé			936,000
364	Violet 1400 GL Sedan			942,000
364	Violet 1400 GL Hatchback Coupé			977,000
364	Violet 1600 De Luxe Sedan			921,000
364	Auster 1600 De Luxe Sedan			921,000
364	Violet 1600 GL Sedan			962,000
364	Violet 1600 GL Hatchback Coupé			997,000
364	Violet 1600 GL-L Sedan			997,000

Page	MAKE AND MODEL	Price in GB £	Price in USA $	Price ex Works
364	Auster 1600 CS Sedan			995,000
364	Auster 1600 CS Hatchback Coupé			1,030,000
364	Violet 1600 G1-L Hatchback Coupé			1,032,000
364	Stanza Luxury Sedan			946,000
364	Stanza Extra Sedan			992,000
364	Stanza TS Sedan			1,002,000
364	Violet GL-EL Sedan	4,258*		1,079,000
364	Violet GL-EL Hatchback Coupé	4,498*		1,114,000
364	Auster CS-E Sedan			1,062,000
364	Auster CS-E Hatchback Coupé			1,097,000
364	Auster CS-LE Sedan			1,116,000
364	Auster CS-LE Hatchback Coupé			1,151,000
364	Stanza Extra-E Sedan			1,062,000
364	Stanza TS-E Sedan			1,072,000
364	Stanza GT-E Sedan			1,127,000
364	Stanza Maxima GT-E Sedan			1,177,000
365	Datsun Bluebird 1600 De Luxe Sedan			969,000
365	Datsun Bluebird 1600 GL Sedan			1,035,000
365	Datsun Bluebird 1600 GL Hardtop			1,070,000
365	Datsun Bluebird 1600 GL-L Sedan			1,064,000
365	Datsun Bluebird 1600 GL-L Hardtop			1,099,000
365	Datsun Bluebird 1800 De Luxe Sedan			977,000
365	Datsun Bluebird 1800 GL Sedan			1,077,000
365	Datsun Bluebird 1800 GL Hardtop			1,112,000
365	Datsun Bluebird 1800 SSS Sedan			1,130,000
365	Datsun Bluebird 1800 SSS Hardtop			1,165,000
365	Datsun Bluebird 1800 SSS (Z 18) Sedan			1,185,000
365	Datsun Bluebird 1800 SSS (Z 18) Hardtop			1,220,000
365	Datsun Bluebird 1800 GL-E Sedan			1,157,000
365	Datsun Bluebird 1800 GL-E Hardtop			1,192,000
365	Datsun Bluebird 1800 SSS-E Sedan			1,213,000
365	Datsun Bluebird 1800 SSS-E Hardtop			1,248,000
365	Datsun Bluebird 1800 SSS-ES Sedan			1,182,000
365	Datsun Bluebird 1800 SSS-ES Hardtop			1,217,000
365	Datsun Bluebird 2000 G6 Sedan			1,220,000
365	Datsun Bluebird 2000 G6 Hardtop			1,256,000
365	Datsun Bluebird 2000 G6L Sedan			1,310,000
365	Datsun Bluebird 2000 G6L Hardtop			1,310,000
365	Datsun Bluebird 2000 G6E Sedan	6,208*		1,415,000
365	Datsun Bluebird 2000 G6E Hardtop			1,415,000
365	Datsun Bluebird 2000 G6EL Sedan			1,503,000
365	Datsun Bluebird 2000 G6EL Hardtop			1,539,000
366	Skyline 1600 TI Sedan			996,000
366	Skyline 1600 TI-L Sedan			1,080,000
366	Skyline 1600 TI-L Hardtop			1,115,000
366	Skyline 1800 TI Sedan			1,046,000
366	Skyline 1800 TI-L Sedan			1,111,000
366	Skyline 1800 TI-L Hardtop			1,185,000
366	Skyline 1800 TI-EL Sedan			1,215,000
366	Skyline 1800 TI-EL Hardtop			1,296,000
366	Skyline 1800 TI-ES Sedan			1,345,000
366	Skyline 1800 TI-ES Hardtop			1,380,000
366	Skyline 2000 GT Sedan			1,214,000
366	Skyline 2000 GT Hardtop			1,259,000
366	Skyline 2000 GT-L Sedan			1,274,000
366	Skyline 2000 GT-L Hardtop			1,319,000
366	Skyline 2000 GT-E Sedan			1,319,000
366	Skyline 2000 GT-E Hardtop			1,392,000
366	Skyline 2000 GT-EL Sedan			1,379,000
366	Skyline 2000 GT-EL Hardtop			1,452,000
366	Skyline 2000 GT-EX Sedan			1,510,000
366	Skyline 2000 GT-EX Hardtop			1,584,000
366	Skyline 2000 GT-ES Sedan			1,560,000
366	Skyline 2000 GT-ES Hardtop			1,605,000
368	Laurel 1800 De Luxe 4-door Sedan			1,089,000
368	Laurel 1800 Custom 4-door Sedan			1,118,000
368	Laurel 1800 Custom 2-door Hardtop			1,146,000
368	Laurel 1800 GL 4-door Sedan			1,168,000
368	Laurel 1800 GL 2-door Hardtop			1,211,000
368	Laurel 2000 Custom 6 4-door Sedan			1,224,000
368	Laurel 2000 Custom 6 2-door Hardtop			1,303,000
368	Laurel 2000 Custom 6 4-door Hardtop			1,357,000
368	Laurel 2000 GL6 4-door Sedan			1,286,000
368	Laurel 2000 GL6 2-door Hardtop			1,359,000
368	Laurel 2000 GL6 4-door Hardtop			1,411,000
368	Laurel 2000 SGL 4-door Sedan			1,430,000
368	Laurel 2000 SGL 2-door Hardtop			1,500,000
368	Laurel 2000 SGL 4-door Hardtop			1,558,000
368	Laurel 2000 GL6-E 4-door Sedan			1,391,000
368	Laurel 2000 GL6-E 2-door Hardtop			1,464,000
368	Laurel 2000 GL6-E 4-door Hardtop			1,523,000
368	Laurel 2000 SGL-E 4-door Sedan			1,535,000
368	Laurel 2000 SGL-E 2-door Hardtop			1,605,000
368	Laurel 2000 SGL-E 4-door Hardtop			1,663,000
368	Laurel 2800 SGL 4-door Sedan			1,865,000
368	Laurel 2800 SGL 2-door Hardtop			1,908,000
368	Laurel 2800 SGL 4-door Hardtop			1,976,000
369	Silvia LS Coupé			1,075,000
369	Silvia LS Type S Coupé			1,125,000
369	Silvia LS Type L Coupé			1,114,000
369	Silvia LS Type X Coupé		4,988*	1,205,000
369	Silvia LS Type G Coupé			1,305,000
369	Silvia LS-E Type S Coupé			1,209,000
369	Silvia LS-E Type L Coupé			1,225,000
369	Silvia LS-E Type X Coupé			1,283,000
369	Silvia LS-E Type G Coupé			1,383,000
370	Cedric 2000 Standard Sedan			1,202,000
370	Cedric 2000 De Luxe Sedan			1,309,000
370	Cedric 2000 Custom De Luxe Sedan			1,473,000
370	Cedric 2000 Custom De Luxe 4-door Hardtop			1,614,000
370	Cedric 2000 GL Sedan			1,654,000
370	Cedric 2000 GL 4-door Hardtop			1,824,000
370	Cedric 2000 GL-E Sedan			1,734,000
370	Cedric 2000 GL-E 2-door Hardtop			1,872,000
370	Cedric 2000 GL-E 4-door Hardtop			1,929,000
370	Cedric 2000 SGL-E Sedan			2,096,000
370	Cedric 2000 SGL-E 2-door Hardtop			2,244,000
370	Cedric 2000 SGL-E 4-door Hardtop			2,299,000
370	Cedric 2000 F Type SGL-E 4-door Hardtop			2,319,000
370	Gloria 2000 Diesel Standard Sedan			2,282,000
370	Gloria 2200 Diesel Standard Sedan			1,354,000
370	Gloria 2200 Diesel De Luxe Sedan			1,451,000
370	Gloria 2200 Diesel GL Sedan			1,686,000
370	Gloria 2800 SGL Sedan			2,404,000
370	Gloria 2800 SGL 4-door Hardtop			2,576,000
370	Gloria 2800 Brougham Sedan			2,643,000
370	Gloria 2800 Brougham 2-door Hardtop			2,527,000
370	Gloria 2800 Brougham 4-door Hardtop			2,770,000
371	Fairlady Z Sports			1,370,000
371	Fairlady ZL Sports			1,565,000
371	Fairlady ZT Sports			1,715,000
371	Fairlady Z 2+2 Sports			1,552,000
371	Fairlady ZL 2+2 Sports			1,747,000
371	Fairlady ZT 2+2 Sports			1,897,000
371	Datsun 280 Z Sports		7,968*	
371	Datsun 280 Z 2+2 Sports		9,278*	
372	President C Sedan			3,846,000
372	President D Sedan			4,238,000
372	President Sovereign Sedan			4,627,000
372	Patrol 4WD			1,302,000
	NUOVA INNOCENTI (Italy)			
225	Mini 90N			3,037,000*
225	Mini 90L			3,167,000*

Page	MAKE AND MODEL	Price in GB £	Price in USA $	Price ex Works
225	Mini 90SL			3,410,000*
225	Mini 120L			3,485,000*
225	Mini 120 SL			3,680,000*
225	Mini De Tomaso			3,992,000*
	OLDSMOBILE (USA)			
299	Starfire Sport Coupé		3,925	
299	Starfire SX Sport Coupé		4,130	
300	Omega Coupé		3,973	
300	Omega Sedan		4,048	
300	Omega Hatchback Coupé		4,137	
300	Omega Brougham Coupé		4,179	
300	Omega Brougham Sedan		4,254	
301	Cutlass Salon Coupé		4,408	
301	Cutlass Salon Sedan		4,508	
301	Cutlass Cruiser Station Wagon		5,241	
301	Cutlass Salon Brougham Coupé		4,695	
301	Cutlass Salon Brougham Sedan		4,795	
301	Cutlass Supreme Coupé		4,841	
301	Cutlass Calais Coupé		5,195	
301	Cutlass Supreme Brougham Coupé		5,246	
302	Delta 88 Hardtop Coupé		5,482	
302	Delta 88 Towne Sedan		5,358	
302	Delta 88 Royale Hardtop Coupé		5,706	
302	Delta 88 Royale Towne Sedan		5,806	
302	Ninety-Eight Luxury Coupé		7,063	
302	Ninety-Eight Luxury Sedan		7,240	
302	Ninety-Eight Regency Coupé		7,426	
302	Ninety-Eight Regency Sedan		7,610	
302	Custom Cruiser Station Wagon		6,323	
303	Toronado Brougham Coupé		8,899	
303	Toronado XSR Coupé		—	
	OPEL (Argentina)			
328	K-180			3,558,000
328	K-180 Luxo			4,198,000
328	K-180 Rally			4,262,000
	OPEL (Germany FR)			
127	City Hatchback Coupé			9,586*
127	City L Hatchback Coupé	2,429*		10,135*
127	City « Berlina » Hatchback Coupé	2,703*		10,817*
128	Kadett 2-door Limousine	2,172*		9,480*
128	Kadett 4-door Limousine			10,004*
128	Kadett Caravan			10,246*
128	Kadett L 2-door Limousine	2,372*		10,030*
128	Kadett L 4-door Limousine	2,572*		10,554*
128	Kadett L Coupé	2,861*		10,393*
128	Kadett L Caravan	2,890*		10,796*
128	Kadett « Berlina » 2-door Limousine	2,599*		10,711*
128	Kadett « Berlina » 4-door Limousine	2,696*		11,144*
128	Kadett « Berlina » Caravan			11,387*
128	Kadett Aero Cabriolet			14,631*
128	Kadett GT/E Coupé			16,850*
130	Rallye 1.6 Coupé			12,007*
130	Rallye E Coupé			13,596*
130	Ascona 1.2 2-door Limousine			11,044*
130	Ascona 1.2 4-door Limousine			11,578*
130	Ascona 1.2 L 2-door Limousine			11,876*
130	Ascona 1.2 L 4-door Limousine			12,411*
130	Ascona 1.2 « Berlina » 2-door Limousine			12,665*
130	Ascona 1.2 « Berlina » 4-door Limousine			13,057*
130	Ascona 1.6 2-door Limousine	2,984*		11,467*
130	Ascona 1.6 4-door Limousine	3,086*		12,002*
130	Ascona 1.6 L 2-door Limousine	3,337*		12,300*
130	Ascona 1.6 L 4-door Limousine	3,437*		12,835*
130	Ascona 1.6 « Berlina » 2-door Limousine			13,089*

Page	MAKE AND MODEL	Price in GB £	Price in USA $	Price ex Works
130	Ascona 1.6 « Berlina » 4-door Limousine			13,480*
132	Manta 1.2 Coupé			12,169*
132	Manta 1.2 L Coupé			12,991*
132	Manta 1.2 « Berlinetta » Coupé			13,780*
132	Manta 1.6 Coupé	3,735*		12,592*
132	Manta 1.6 L Coupé			13,415*
132	Manta 1.6 « Berlinetta » Coupé	4,272*		14,204*
132	Manta E Coupé			15,660*
132	Manta E « Berlinetta » Coupé			16,418*
132	Manta GT/E Coupé			15,660*
134	Rekord 2-door Limousine	4,265*		13,763*
134	Rekord 4-door Limousine	4,390*		14,333*
134	Rekord 3-door Caravan			14,323*
134	Rekord 5-door Caravan			14,893*
134	Rekord L 2-door Limousine	5,150*		14,580*
134	Rekord L 4-door Limousine			14,999*
134	Rekord L 5-door Caravan	4,790*		15,705*
134	Rekord « Berlina » 2-door Limousine			15,312*
134	Rekord « Berlina » 4-door Limousine			15,730*
	OTOSAN (Turkey)			
330	Anadol A1			50,000
330	Anadol A2			75,000
330	Anadol SL			—
330	Anadol STC - 16			71,000
330	Anadol SV - 1600			85,000
330	Böcek			—
	PANTHER (Great Britain)			
179	Rio			8,397*
179	Rio Especial			9,445*
180	Lima			5,564*
180	J 72 4.2-litre			14,918*
180	De Ville Saloon			39,049*
181	De Ville Convertible			44,321*
181	Ferrari F.F.			—
182	6			39,950*
	PAYKAN (Iran)			
342	Saloon			—
342	Saloon GT			—
	PEKING (China People's Republic)			
344	BJ 212			—
	PERANA-FORD (South Africa)			
341	Granada V8 4-door Saloon			—
341	Granada V8 2-door Coupé			7,365
341	Granada V8 4-door XL Saloon			7,255
341	Granada V8 4-door GXL Saloon			—
341	Granada V8 Ghia 4-door Saloon			8,595
	PEUGEOT (France)			
87	104 GL Berline	2,287*		21,100*
87	104 GL6 Berline			22,650*
87	104 SL Berline	2,600*		23,700*
87	104 ZL Coupé			21,350*
88	104 ZS Coupé	2,704*		24,400*
88	304 GL Berline	2,810*		24,450*
88	304 GL Break	2,827*		24,500*
89	304 GLD Berline			28,700*
89	304 GLD Break			28,750*
89	304 SL Berline			25,800*
89	304 SL Break			26,550*
89	304 SLS Berline	3,051*		26,950*
		3,151*		

Page	MAKE AND MODEL	Price in GB £	Price in USA $	Price ex Works
89	305 GL			26,300*
89	305 GR			27,900*
89	305 SR			29,600*
90	504 L Berline	3,730*	7,490*	28,800*
90	504 L Break	4,107*	7,990*	30,650*
90	504 GL Berline	4,210*	8,790*	31,800*
90	504 GL Break	4,578*	9,290*	34,450*
91	504 Break Familial	4,610*		35,100*
91	504 TI Berline	4,623*		36,550*
91	504 Cabriolet			50,500*
92	504 Coupé			50,500*
92	504 V6 Coupé			61,500*
92	604 SL	6,695*	10,990*	46,500*
92	604 TI			52,500*
	PLYMOUTH (USA)			
303	Horizon			3,706
304	Volaré 2-door Coupé			3,735
304	Volaré 4-door Sedan			3,853
304	Volaré Station Wagon			4,195
305	Fury 2-door Hardtop			4,212
305	Fury 4-door Sedan			4,292
305	Fury Sport 2-door Hardtop			4,452
305	Fury Salon 4-door Sedan			4,527
305	Fury Suburban 6-pass. Station Wagon			4,024
305	Fury Suburban 9-pass. Station Wagon			5,167
305	Fury Sport Suburban 6-pass. Station Wagon			5,482
305	Fury Sport Suburban 9-pass. Station Wagon			5,625
	POLSKI-FIAT (Poland)			
226	126 P			—
226	125 P 1300			—
226	125 P 1300 Combi			—
227	125 P 1500	1,949*		—
227	125 P 1500 Combi	2,159*		—
	PONTIAC (Canada)			
254	Acadian S Hatchback Coupé			3,458
254	Acadian Hatchback Coupé			3,836
254	Acadian Hatchback Sedan			3,962
254	Laurentian Coupé			6,090
254	Laurentian Sedan			6,129
254	Laurentian Safari Station Wagon			6,722
254	Parisienne Coupé			6,660
254	Parisienne Sedan			6,776
	PONTIAC (USA)			
306	Sunbird Coupé			3,540
306	Sunbird Sport Coupé			3,773
306	Sunbird Sport Hatchback Coupé			3,912
306	Sunbird Sport Safari Station Wagon			3,741
307	Phoenix Coupé			3,872
307	Phoenix Hatchback Coupé			4,068
307	Phoenix Sedan			3,947
307	Phoenix LJ Coupé			4,357
307	Phoenix LJ Sedan			4,432
308	Firebird Hardtop Coupé			4,545
308	Firebird Esprit Hardtop Coupé			4,842
308	Firebird Formula Hardtop Coupé	7,917*		5,448
308	Firebird Trans Am Hardtop Coupé	7,917*		5,799
309	Le Mans Coupé			4,405
309	Le Mans Sedan			4,480
309	Le Mans Safari Station Wagon			4,937
309	Grand Le Mans Coupé			4,777

Page	MAKE AND MODEL	Price in GB £	Price in USA $	Price ex Works
309	Grand Le Mans Sedan			4,881
309	Grand Le Mans Safari Station Wagon			5,265
309	Grand Am Coupé			5,464
309	Grand Am Sedan			5,568
310	Grand Prix Hardtop Coupé			4,880
310	Grand Prix LJ Hardtop Coupé			5,815
310	Grand Prix SJ Hardtop Coupé			6,088
311	Catalina Coupé			5,375
311	Catalina Sedan			5,410
311	Catalina Safari Station Wagon			5,924
311	Bonneville Coupé			5,831
311	Bonneville Sedan			5,931
311	Bonneville Brougham Coupé			6,577
311	Bonneville Brougham Sedan			6,677
311	Grand Safari Station Wagon			6,227
	PORSCHE (Germany FR)			
136	924	7,350*	11,325*	25,960*
137	911 SC Coupé	12,600*	17,950*	41,850*
137	911 SC Targa	12,600*	19,050*	44,790*
137	Turbo Coupé	23,200*	34,000*	79,900*
138	928			58,800*
	PREMIER (India)			
342	Padmini			—
343	Padmini De Luxe			—
	PRINCESS (Great Britain)			
182	1800 Saloon			3,429*
182	1800 HL Saloon			3,707*
182	2200 HL Saloon			3,999*
182	2200 HLS Saloon			4,493*
	PUMA (Brazil)			
320	Mini			—
321	GTE 1600			134,000
321	GTS 1600			140,000
321	GTB			204,000
	RELIANT (Great Britain)			
183	Kitten DL Saloon			2,139*
183	Kitten DL Estate Car			2,251*
183	Robin 850 Saloon			1,719*
184	Robin 850 Estate Car			1,845*
184	Super Robin 850 Saloon			1,968*
184	Super Robin 850 Estate Car			2,043*
184	Robin 850 GBS Saloon			1,983*
184	Scimitar GTE			6,332*
	RENAULT (France)			
93	4	2,022*		15,800*
93	4 TL	2,190*		18,100*
93	4 Safari			17,100*
93	4 Rodeo (2 seats)			19,845*
93	4 Rodeo (4 seats)			22,100*
94	6 Rodeo			23,667*
94	5	2,127*		18,800*
94	5 TL	2,404*		21,100*
95	5 GTL	2,594*	3,495*	23,300*
95	5 TS	2,899*		25,200*
95	5 Alpine			34,600*
95	6			19,800*
96	6 TL	2,647*		21,300*
96	14	2,696*		25,400*

RENAULT (France)

Page	MAKE AND MODEL	Price in GB £	Price in USA $	Price ex Works
96	14 TL	2,871*		27,000*
96	12 Berline	2,548*		24,600*
97	12 Break			26,000*
97	12 TL Berline	2,822*		26,200*
97	12 Break TL	3,173*		27,500*
97	12 TS Berline	3,089*		27,700*
98	12 Break TS			29,500*
98	12 Berline Automatic	3,299*		29,700*
98	12 Break Automatic			30,700*
98	15 TL			29,000*
98	15 GTL	3,601*		31,100*
98	15 GTL Automatic	3,896*		35,690*
99	16 TL (55 hp)	3,419*		28,400*
99	16 TL (66 hp)			29,680*
99	16 TL Automatic	3,714*		32,200*
100	16 TX	4,170*		33,800*
100	16 TX Automatic	4,465*		36,900*
100	17 TS Cabriolet	4,484*		39,400*
101	17 TS Cabriolet Automatic	4,779*		42,500*
101	20 TL	4,138*		34,800*
101	20 TL Automatic	4,468*		37,900*
101	20 GTL			38,300*
101	20 GTL Automatic			41,400*
102	20 TS	4,724*		39,700*
102	20 TS Automatic	5,054*		32,000*
102	30 TS	6,125*		44,000*
103	30 TS Automatic	6,476*		47,200*
	ROLLS-ROYCE (Great Britain)			
184	Silver Shadow II		48,600*	26,740*
185	Silver Wraith II		55,400*	31,485*
185	Silver Wraith II with division			32,842*
185	Corniche Saloon		79,200*	38,879*
185	Corniche Convertible		84,500*	41,289*
185	Phantom VI			—
186	Camargue		104,000*	47,367*
	ROM CARMEL (Israel)			
331	Rom 1300			—
	ROVER (Great Britain)			
186	3500			7,174*
187	2600			5,992*
187	2300			5,645*
187	Land Rover 88" Regular			3,606*
187	Land Rover 109" Estate Car			4,229*
188	Range Rover			8,528*
	SAAB (Sweden)			
236	96 GL			—
237	95 GL			—
237	99 GL 2-door	4,275*		—
237	99 L 2-door	4,150*		—
237	99 GL 4-door	4,575*		—
237	99 GLE	6,595*	7,298*	—
238	99 GL Combi Coupé 3-door	4,785*		—
238	99 GL Super 2-door			—
238	99 GL Super 4-door	4,575*		—
238	99 GL Super Combi Coupé 3-door	5,175*		—
238	99 GL Super Combi Coupé 5-door	5,155*		—
238	99 GL Injection 2-door		6,698*	
238	99 GL Injection 4-door		6,898*	
238	99 GL Injection Combi Coupé 3-door		6,848*	
239	99 GL Injection Combi Coupé 5-door		7,248*	
239	99 EMS 2-door	6,275*	7,198*	—
239	99 EMS Combi Coupé 3-door			—
239	Turbo			—

Page	MAKE AND MODEL	Price in GB £	Price in USA $	Price ex Works
	SBARRO (Switzerland)			
245	Replica BMW 328 Standard			33,000*
246	Replica BMW 328 America			42,000*
	SCORA (France)			
103	Coupé			—
	SEAT (Spain)			
232	133			172,000*
232	133 Lujo			188,000*
232	133 Especial			154,000*
232	133 Especial Lujo			194,000*
232	127 2 Puertas			226,000*
233	127 2 Puertas Confort Lujo			247,000*
233	127 3 Puertas			235,000*
233	127 3 Puertas Confort Lujo			266,000*
233	127 4 Puertas			241,000*
233	127 4 Puertas Confort Lujo			272,000*
233	128/3P 1200			325,000*
233	Sport 1200			345,000*
233	128/3P 1430			340,000*
234	Sport 1430			360,000*
234	124-D			275,000*
234	124-D LS			305,000*
234	124-D Especial			325,000*
234	131-L			346,000*
235	131-L 5 Puertas			382,000*
235	131-E			392,000*
235	131-E 5 Puertas			419,000*
235	132-L			501,000*
236	132 Automatic			541,000*
236	132 Diesel			586,000*
	SEVEN (Great Britain)			
188	Series III			3,711*
	ŠKODA (Czechoslovakia)			
74	105 S	1,549*		—
75	105 L	1,625*		—
75	120 L	1,699*		—
75	120 LS	1,799*		—
75	110 R Coupé	1,599*		—
	SPARTAN CARS (Great Britain)			
189	2-seater Sports			3,391*
189	2+2-seater Sports			3,649*
	STANDARD (India)			
343	Gazel			—
	STEVENS (Great Britain)			
189	Sienna			2,700*
	STUTZ (USA)			
312	Blackhawk VI			64,500
	SUBARU (Japan)			
373	Rex 550 SEEC-T Standard 2-door Sedan			551,000
373	Rex 550 SEEC-T A I 2-door Sedan			618,000

Page	MAKE AND MODEL	Price in GB £	Price in USA $	Price ex Works
373	Rex 550 SEEC-T A I 4-door Sedan			643,000
373	Rex 550 SEEC-T A II 2-door Sedan			657,000
373	Rex 550 SEEC-T A II 4-door Sedan			682,000
373	Rex 550 SEEC-T A II G 4-door Sedan			709,000
373	Leone SEEC-T 1400 Standard 2-door Sedan		2,999*	749,000
373	Leone SEEC-T 1400 De Luxe 2-door Sedan		3,499*	836,000
373	Leone SEEC-T 1400 De Luxe 4-door Sedan		3,699*	861,000
373	Leone SEEC-T 1400 GL 2-door Sedan			900,000
373	Leone SEEC-T 1400 GL 4-door Sedan			925,000
373	Leone SEEC-T 1600 De Luxe 4-door Sedan	2,597*		886,000
373	Leone SEEC-T 1600 GL 4-door Sedan	2,714*		950,000
373	Leone SEEC-T 1600 Custom 4-door Sedan			986,000
373	Leone SEEC-T 1600 Super Custom 4-door Sedan			1,096,000
373	Leone SEEC-T 1600 GL Coupé	2,726*	3,699*	997,000
373	Leone SEEC-T 1600 GF Hardtop			1,017,000
373	Leone SEEC-T 1600 Grand Am 4-door Sedan			1,096,000
373	Leone SEEC-T 1600 Grand Am Hardtop			1,164,000
373	Leone SEEC-T 1600 Super Touring 4-door Sedan			1,099,000
373	Leone SEEC-T 1600 RX Coupé			1,089,000
373	Leone SEEC-T 1600 GFT Hardtop	3,101*	4,149*	1,114,000
373	Leone SEEC-T 1600 Grand Am T Hardtop			1,286,000
373	Leone SEEC-T 1600 4WD 4-door Sedan		3,949*	1,320,000
373	Leone SEEC-T 1600 4WD Station Wagon	3,697*	4,449*	1,124,000

SUZUKI (Japan)

Page	MAKE AND MODEL	Price in GB £	Price in USA $	Price ex Works
375	Fronte 7-S Standard 2-door Sedan (2-stroke)			527,000
375	Fronte 7-S Standard 2-door Sedan (4-stroke)			556,000
375	Fronte 7-S De Luxe 2-door Sedan (2-stroke)			576,000
375	Fronte 7-S De Luxe 2-door Sedan (4-stroke)			604,000
375	Fronte 7-S De Luxe 4-door Sedan (2-stroke)			599,000
375	Fronte 7-S De Luxe 4-door Sedan (4-stroke)			627,000
375	Fronte 7-S Super De Luxe 4-door Sedan (2- and 4-stroke)			662,000
375	Fronte 7-S Custom 2-door Sedan (2- and 4-stroke)			658,000
375	Front 7-S Custom 4-door Sedan (2- and 4-stroke)			698,000
375	Fronte 7-S Cervo Coupé CX (2-stroke)			608,000
375	Fronte 7-S Cervo Coupé CXG (2-stroke)			698,000
375	Fronte Hatch 55B Station Wagon			507,000
375	Fronte Hatch 55D Station Wagon			537,000
375	Fronte Hatch 55T Station Wagon			567,000
376	Jimny 55 Softtop			748,000
376	Jimny 55 Steelbody Wagon			797,000
376	Jimny 8 Softtop			859,000
376	Jimny 8 Steelbody Wagon			908,000

SYD LAWRENCE (Great Britain)

Page	MAKE AND MODEL	Price in GB £	Price in USA $	Price ex Works
189	Mk 2 Sports			15,000*

SYRENA (Poland)

Page	MAKE AND MODEL	Price in GB £	Price in USA $	Price ex Works
227	105			—

TATRA (Czechoslovakia)

Page	MAKE AND MODEL	Price in GB £	Price in USA $	Price ex Works
75	T 613			—

TECHNICAL EXPONENTS (Great Britain)

Page	MAKE AND MODEL	Price in GB £	Price in USA $	Price ex Works
190	TX Tripper 1500			2,923*
190	TX Tripper 1500 De Luxe			3,122*
190	TX Tripper 2000 Sprint			3,800*

TOFAS (Turkey)

Page	MAKE AND MODEL	Price in GB £	Price in USA $	Price ex Works
331	Murat 131			—

TORO (Philippines)

Page	MAKE AND MODEL	Price in GB £	Price in USA $	Price ex Works
394	1300			—

TOTAL REPLICA (USA)

Page	MAKE AND MODEL	Price in GB £	Price in USA $	Price ex Works
312	Ford Phaeton			17,000

TOYOTA (Japan)

Page	MAKE AND MODEL	Price in GB £	Price in USA $	Price ex Works
377	Publica Standard 2-door Sedan			609,000
377	Publica De Luxe 2-door Sedan			642,000
377	Publica Hi-De Luxe 2-door Sedan			686,000
377	Publica XL 2-door Sedan			719,000
377	Starlet Standard 4-door Sedan			655,000
377	Starlet De Luxe 4-door Sedan			685,000
377	Starlet De Luxe Coupé			680,000
377	Starlet Hi-De Luxe 4-door Sedan			727,000
377	Starlet Hi-De Luxe Coupé			724,000
377	Starlet XL 4-door Sedan			780,000
377	Starlet XL Coupé			772,000
377	Starlet ST Coupé			827,000
377	Corolla 1300 Standard 2-door Sedan			698,000
377	Corolla 1300 Standard 4-door Sedan			723,000
377	Corolla 1300 De Luxe 2-door Sedan			743,000
377	Corolla 1300 De Luxe 4-door Sedan			768,000
377	Corolla 1300 De Luxe 2-door Hardtop			798,000
377	Corolla 1300 De Luxe 2-door Coupé			811,000
377	Corolla 1300 De Luxe 3-door Liftback			836,000
377	Corolla 1300 Hi-De Luxe 2-door Sedan			800,000
377	Corolla 1300 Hi-De Luxe 4-door Sedan			825,000
377	Corolla 1300 Hi-De Luxe 2-door Hardtop			851,000
377	Corolla 1300 Hi-De Luxe 2-door Coupé			863,000
377	Corolla 1300 Hi-De Luxe 3-door Liftback			892,000
377	Corolla 1300 SL 4-door Sedan			856,000
377	Corolla 1300 SL 2-door Hardtop			888,000
377	Corolla 1300 SL 2-door Coupé			892,000
377	Corolla 1300 SL 3-door Liftback			935,000
377	Corolla 1300 SR 2-door Coupé			898,000
377	Corolla 1400 De Luxe 2-door Sedan			779,000
377	Corolla 1400 De Luxe 4-door Sedan			804,000
377	Corolla 1400 De Luxe 2-door Hardtop			834,000
377	Corolla 1400 De Luxe 2-door Coupé			848,000

Page	MAKE AND MODEL	Price in GB £	Price in USA $	Price ex Works
377	Corolla 1400 De Luxe 3-door Liftback			873,000
377	Corolla 1400 Hi-De Luxe 2-door Sedan			824,000
377	Corolla 1400 Hi-De Luxe 4-door Sedan			849,000
377	Corolla 1400 Hi-De Luxe 2-door Hardtop			875,000
377	Corolla 1400 Hi-De Luxe 2-door Coupé			886,000
377	Corolla 1400 Hi-De Luxe 3-door Liftback			924,000
377	Corolla 1400 SL 4-door Sedan			894,000
377	Corolla 1400 SL 2-door Hardtop			925,000
377	Corolla 1400 SL 2-door Coupé			929,000
377	Corolla 1400 SL 3-door Liftback	3,157*		961,000
377	Corolla 1600 Hi-De Luxe 4-door Sedan			884,000
377	Corolla 1600 Hi-De Luxe Automatic 4-door Sedan			884,000
377	Corolla 1600 Hi-De Luxe 2-door Hardtop			910,000
377	Corolla 1600 Hi-De Luxe Automatic 2-door Hardtop			910,000
377	Corolla 1600 Hi-De Luxe 2-door Coupé			919,000
377	Corolla 1600 Hi-De Luxe Automatic 2-door Coupé			919,000
377	Corolla 1600 Hi-De Luxe 3-door Liftback			978,000
377	Corolla 1600 Hi-De Luxe Automatic 3-door Liftback			978,000
377	Corolla 1600 GSL 4-door Sedan			970,000
377	Corolla GSL Automatic 4-door Sedan			970,000
377	Corolla 1600 GSL 2-door Hardtop			1,003,000
377	Corolla 1600 GSL Automatic 2-door Hardtop			1,003,000
377	Corolla 1600 GSL 2-door Coupé			1,003,000
377	Corolla 1600 GSL Automatic 2-door Coupé			1,003,000
377	Corolla 1600 GSL 3-door Liftback			1,058,000
377	Corolla 1600 GSL Automatic 3-door Liftback			1,058,000
377	Corolla 1600 SR 2-door Coupé			1,011,000
377	Corolla 1600 Levin 2-door Coupé			1,227,000
377	Corolla 1600 Levin GT 2-door Coupé			1,282,000
377	Corolla 1600 GT 3-door Liftback			1,332,000
379	Corolla De Luxe 2-door Sedan	3,688*		
379	Corolla De Luxe 4-door Sedan	3,798*		
379	Corolla De Luxe 5-door Station Wagon	4,118*		
379	Corolla 2-door Sport Coupé	4,083*		
379	Corolla 2-door Liftback	4,123*		
379	Corolla SR-5 2-door Sport Coupé	4,498*		
379	Corolla SR-5 2-door Liftback	4,638*		
380	Sprinter 1300 DX 4-door Sedan			785,000
380	Sprinter 1300 DX Hardtop			819,000
380	Sprinter 1300 DX Coupé			831,000
380	Sprinter 1300 DX Liftback			857,000
380	Sprinter 1300 XL 4-door Sedan			842,000
380	Sprinter 1300 XL Hardtop			867,000
380	Sprinter 1300 XL Coupé			879,000
380	Sprinter 1300 XL Liftback			916,000
380	Sprinter 1300 ST 4-door Sedan			873,000
380	Sprinter 1300 ST Hardtop			904,000
380	Sprinter 1300 ST Coupé			908,000
380	Sprinter 1300 ST Liftback			956,000
380	Sprinter 1400 DX 4-door Sedan			830,000
380	Sprinter 1400 DX Hardtop			859,000
380	Sprinter 1400 DX Coupé			864,000
380	Sprinter 1400 DX Liftback			891,000
380	Sprinter 1400 XL 4-door Sedan			861,000
380	Sprinter 1400 XL Hardtop			891,000

Page	MAKE AND MODEL	Price in GB £	Price in USA $	Price ex Works
380	Sprinter 1400 XL Coupé			904,000
380	Sprinter 1400 XL Liftback			943,000
380	Sprinter 1400 ST 4-door Sedan			909,000
380	Sprinter 1400 ST Hardtop			939,000
380	Sprinter 1400 ST Coupé			943,000
380	Sprinter 1400 ST Liftback			982,000
380	Sprinter 1600 XL 4-door Sedan			900,000
380	Sprinter 1600 XL Automatic 4-door Sedan			900,000
380	Sprinter 1600 XL Hardtop			930,000
380	Sprinter 1600 XL Automatic Hardtop			930,000
380	Sprinter 1600 XL Coupé			941,000
380	Sprinter 1600 XL Automatic Coupé			941,000
380	Sprinter 1600 XL Liftback			992,000
380	Sprinter 1600 XL Automatic Liftback			992,000
380	Sprinter 1600 GS 4-door Sedan			991,000
380	Sprinter 1600 GS Automatic 4-door Sedan			991,000
380	Sprinter 1600 GS Hardtop			1,023,000
380	Sprinter 1600 GS Automatic Hardtop			1,023,000
380	Sprinter 1600 GS Coupé			1,023,000
380	Sprinter 1600 GS Automatic Coupé			1,023,000
380	Sprinter 1600 GS Liftback			1,078,000
380	Sprinter 1600 GS Automatic Liftback			1,078,000
380	Sprinter 1600 SR Coupé			1,033,000
380	Sprinter 1600 Trueno GT			1,302,000
380	Sprinter 1600 Liftback GT			1,352,000
381	Carina 1600 Standard 2-door Sedan	3,180*		845,000
381	Carina 1600 Standard 4-door Sedan			865,000
381	Carina 1600 De Luxe 2-door Sedan			903,000
381	Carina 1600 De Luxe 4-door Sedan			924,000
381	Carina 1600 De Luxe 2-door Hardtop			958,000
381	Carina 1600 Super De Luxe 2-door Sedan			941,000
381	Carina 1600 Super De Luxe 4-door Sedan			961,000
381	Carina 1600 Super De Luxe 2-door Hardtop			996,000
381	Carina 1600 ST 4-door Sedan			1,026,000
381	Carina 1600 ST 2-door Hardtop			1,061,000
381	Carina 1600 SR 2-door Hardtop			1,061,000
381	Carina 1800 De Luxe 4-door Sedan			989,000
381	Carina 1800 De Luxe 2-door Hardtop			1,024,000
381	Carina 1800 Super De Luxe 4-door Sedan			1,052,000
381	Carina 1800 Super De Luxe 2-door Hardtop			1,087,000
381	Carina 1800 ST 4-door Sedan			1,117,000
381	Carina 1800 ST 2-door Hardtop			1,152,000
381	Carina 1800 SR 2-door Hardtop			1,152,000
381	Carina 1800 SE 4-door Sedan			1,171,000
381	Carina 1800 SE 2-door Hardtop			1,206,000
381	Carina 1800 De Luxe Automatic 4-door Sedan			1,018,000
381	Carina 1800 De Luxe Automatic 2-door Hardtop			1,053,000
381	Carina 1800 Super De Luxe Automatic 4-door Sedan			1,081,000
381	Carina 1800 Super De Luxe Automatic 2-door Hardtop			1,116,000
381	Carina 1800 ST Automatic 4-door Sedan			1,123,000
381	Carina 1800 ST Automatic 2-door Hardtop			1,158,000
381	Carina 1800 SE Automatic 4-door Sedan			1,200,000
381	Carina 1800 SE Automatic 2-door Hardtop			1,235,000
381	Carina 2000 Super De Luxe 4-door Sedan			1,049,000
381	Carina 2000 Super De Luxe 2-door Hardtop			1,084,000

Page	MAKE AND MODEL	Price in GB £	Price in USA $	Price ex Works
381	Carina 2000 ST 4-door Sedan			1,114,000
381	Carina 2000 ST 2-door Hardtop			1,149,000
381	Carina 2000 SE 4-door Sedan			1,168,000
381	Carina 2000 SE 2-door Hardtop			1,203,000
381	Carina 2000 GT 4-door Sedan			1,472,000
381	Carina 2000 GT 2-door Hardtop			1,507,000
383	Celica 1600 ET Coupé			985,000
383	Celica 1600 LT Coupé			1,045,000
383	Celica 1600 LT Liftback			1,125,000
383	Celica 1600 ST Coupé	3,586*	4,899*	1,080,000
383	Celica 1600 ST Liftback			1,160,000
383	Celica 1600 XT Coupé			1,130,000
383	Celica 1600 XT Liftback			1,226,000
383	Celica 1600 GTV Coupé			1,419,000
383	Celica 1600 GTV Liftback			1,515,000
383	Celica 1600 GT Coupé		5,309*	1,467,000
383	Celica 1600 GT Liftback		5,529*	1,563,000
383	Celica 1800 LT Coupé			1,075,000
383	Celica 1800 LT Liftback			1,155,000
383	Celica 1800 ST Coupé			1,110,000
383	Celica 1800 ST Liftback			1,190,000
383	Celica 1800 XT Coupé			1,160,000
383	Celica 1800 XT Liftback			1,256,000
383	Celica 1800 SE Coupé			1,251,000
383	Celica 1800 SE Liftback			1,347,000
383	Celica 2000 ST Coupé			1,107,000
383	Celica 2000 ST Liftback	3,909*		1,187,000
383	Celica 2000 XT Coupé	4,521*		1,157,000
383	Celica 2000 XT Liftback			1,253,000
383	Celica 2000 SE Coupé			1,248,000
383	Celica 2000 SE Liftback			1,344,000
383	Celica 2000 GTV Coupé			1,529,000
383	Celica 2000 GTV Liftback			1,625,000
283	Celica 2000 GT Coupé	4,775*		1,577,000
383	Celica 2000 GT Liftback			1,673,000
385	Celica ST Hardtop		4,719*	
385	Celica GT Hardtop		5,119*	
385	Celica GT Liftback		5,339*	
385	Corona 1600 Standard 4-door Sedan			817,000
385	Corona 1600 De Luxe 2-door Sedan			934,000
385	Corona 1600 De Luxe 4-door Sedan			954,000
385	Corona 1600 De Luxe Automatic 4-door Sedan			986,000
385	Corona 1600 De Luxe 2-door Hardtop			961,000
385	Corona 1600 De Luxe Automatic 2-door Hardtop			1,021,000
385	Corona 1600 GL 2-door Sedan			986,000
385	Corona 1600 GL 4-door Sedan			1,006,000
385	Corona 1600 GL Automatic 4-door Sedan			1,038,000
385	Corona 1600 GL 2-door Hardtop			1,013,000
385	Corona 1600 GL Automatic 2-door Hardtop			1,073,000
385	Corona 1600 SL 4-door Sedan			1,042,000
385	Corona 1600 SL 2-door Hardtop			1,077,000
385	Corona 1800 De Luxe 4-door Sedan			1,004,000
385	Corona 1800 De Luxe 2-door Hardtop			1,039,000
385	Corona 1800 GL 4-door Sedan			1,078,000
385	Corona 1800 GL 2-door Hardtop			1,113,000
385	Corona 1800 SL 4-door Sedan			1,132,000
385	Corona 1800 SL 2-door Hardtop			1,167,000
385	Corona 1800 De Luxe Automatic 4-door Sedan			1,036,000
385	Corona 1800 De Luxe Automatic 2-door Hardtop			1,071,000
385	Corona 1800 GL Automatic 4-door Sedan			1,110,000
385	Corona 1800 GL Automatic 2-door Hardtop			1,145,000
385	Corona 1800 SL Automatic 4-door Sedan			1,141,000
385	Corona 1800 SL Automatic 2-door Hardtop			1,176,000
385	Corona 2000 De Luxe 4-door Sedan			946,000
385	Corona 2000 GL 4-door Sedan			1,025,000
385	Corona 2000 GL 2-door Hardtop			1,060,000
385	Corona 2000 GT 4-door Sedan			1,433,000
385	Corona 2000 GT 2-door Hardtop			1,468,000
387	Corona Custom 2-door Sedan		4,254*	
387	Corona De Luxe 4-door Sedan		4,589*	
387	Corona Hardtop		—	
387	Corona De Luxe Station Wagon		4,929*	
387	Corona SR-5 Hardtop		—	
387	Mark II 1800 De Luxe 4-door Sedan			1,053,000
387	Mark II 1800 De Luxe 2-door Hardtop			1,090,000
387	Chaser 1800 De Luxe 4-door Sedan			1,059,000
387	Chaser 1800 De Luxe 2-door Hardtop			1,096,000
387	Mark II 1800 GL 4-door Sedan			1,101,000
387	Mark II 1800 GL 2-door Hardtop			1,138,000
387	Chaser 1800 XL 4-door Sedan			1,107,000
387	Chaser 1800 XL 2-door Hardtop			1,144,000
387	Mark II 1800 De Luxe Automatic 4-door Sedan			1,085,000
387	Mark II 1800 De Luxe Automatic 2-door Hardtop			1,122,000
387	Chaser 1800 De Luxe Automatic 4-door Sedan			1,091,000
387	Chaser 1800 De Luxe Automatic 2-door Hardtop			1,128,000
387	Mark II 1800 GL Automatic 4-door Sedan			1,133,000
387	Mark II 1800 GL Automatic 2-door Hardtop			1,170,000
387	Chaser 1800 XL Automatic 4-door Sedan			1,139,000
387	Chaser 1800 XL Automatic 2-door Hardtop			1,176,000
387	Mark II 2000 Standard 4-door Sedan	3,646*		982,000
387	Mark II 2000 De Luxe 4-door Sedan			1,050,000
387	Mark II 2000 De Luxe 2-door Hardtop			1,087,000
387	Chaser 2000 De Luxe 4-door Sedan			1,056,000
387	Chaser 2000 De Luxe 2-door Hardtop			1,093,000
387	Mark II 2000 GL 4-door Sedan			1,098,000
387	Mark II 2000 GL 2-door Hardtop			1,135,000
387	Chaser 2000 XL 4-door Sedan			1,104,000
387	Chaser 2000 XL 2-door Hardtop			1,141,000
387	Chaser 2000 GS 4-door Sedan			1,204,000
387	Chaser 2000 GS 2-door Hardtop			1,291,000
387	Mark II 2000 GSL 4-door Sedan			1,218,000
387	Mark II 2000 GSL 2-door Hardtop			1,285,000
387	Mark II 2000 L 4-door Sedan			1,198,000
387	Mark II 2000 L 2-door Hardtop			1,265,000
387	Mark II 2000 LG 4-door Sedan			1,303,000
387	Mark II 2000 LG 2-door Hardtop			1,370,000
387	Chaser 2000 SXL 4-door Sedan			1,204,000
387	Chaser 2000 SXL 2-door Hardtop			1,271,000
387	Mark II 2000 EFI L 4-door Sedan			1,324,000
387	Mark II 2000 EFI L 2-door Hardtop			1,391,000
387	Mark II 2000 EFI LG 4-door Sedan			1,429,000
387	Mark II 2000 EFI LG 2-door Hardtop			1,496,000
387	Chaser 2000 EFI SXL 4-door Sedan			1,333,000
387	Chaser 2000 EFI SXL 2-door Hardtop			1,397,000
387	Chaser 2000 EFI SGS 4-door Sedan			1,448,000
387	Chaser 2000 EFI SGS 2-door Hardtop			1,515,000
387	Mark II 2000 EFI LG Touring 4-door Sedan			1,486,000
387	Mark II 2000 EFI LG Touring 2-door Hardtop			1,553,000

Page	MAKE AND MODEL	Price in GB £	Price in USA $	Price ex Works
387	Chaser 2000 SG Touring 4-door Sedan			1,564,000
387	Chaser 2000 SG Touring 2-door Hardtop			1,601,000
387	Mark II 2000 EFI Grande 4-door Sedan			1,796,000
387	Mark II 2000 EFI Grande 2-door Hardtop			1,833,000
387	Mark II 2600 Grande Automatic 4-door Sedan		6,989*	1,913,000
387	Mark II 2600 Grande Automatic 2-door Hardtop			1,952,000
389	Crown 2000 De Luxe-A Sedan			1,360,000
389	Crown 2000 De Luxe Sedan			1,498,000
389	Crown 2000 De Luxe 2-door Hardtop			1,444,000
389	Crown 2000 De Luxe 4-door Hardtop			1,479,000
389	Crown 2000 Super De Luxe Sedan			1,680,000
389	Crown 2000 Super De Luxe 2-door Hardtop			1,773,000
389	Crown 2000 Super De Luxe 4-door Hardtop			1,790,000
389	Crown 2000 Super Saloon Sedan			1,803,000
389	Crown 2000 Super Saloon 4-door Hardtop			1,948,000
389	Crown 2000 EFI De Luxe-A Sedan			1,453,000
389	Crown 2000 EFI De Luxe Sedan			1,644,000
389	Crown 2000 EFI De Luxe 2-door Hardtop			1,590,000
389	Crown 2000 EFI De Luxe 4-door Hardtop			1,577,000
389	Crown 2000 EFI Super De Luxe Sedan			1,773,000
389	Crown 2000 EFI Super De Luxe 2-door Hardtop			1,896,000
389	Crown 2000 EFI Super De Luxe 4-door Hardtop			1,936,000
389	Crown 2000 EFI Super Saloon Sedan			1,896,000
389	Crown 2000 EFI Super Saloon 2-door Hardtop			2,074,000
389	Crown 2000 EFI Super Saloon 4-door Hardtop			2,006,000
389	Crown 2200 Diesel Standard Sedan			1,342,000
389	Crown 2200 Diesel De Luxe-A Sedan			1,447,000
389	Crown 2200 Diesel De Luxe Sedan			1,585,000
389	Crown 2600 Super Saloon Sedan		6,589*	2,052,000
389	Crown 2600 Super Saloon 2-door Hardtop			2,166,000
389	Crown 2600 Super Saloon 4-door Hardtop			2,147,000
389	Crown 2600 Royal Saloon Sedan			2,497,000
389	Crown 2600 Royal Saloon 4-door Hardtop			2,526,000
391	Century D Sedan			3,940,000
391	Century C Sedan			3,646,000
392	Landcruiser FJ56V-K	7,598*		—
392	Landcruiser BJ40-KC	6,548*		—
	TRABANT (Germany DDR)			
103	601 Limousine			—
104	601 Universal			—
	TRIDENT (Great Britain)			
190	Venturer V6			5,616*
191	Clipper V8			8,371*
	TRIUMPH (Great Britain)			
191	Dolomite 1300			2,953*
191	Dolomite 1500			3,178*
192	Dolomite 1500 HL			3,602*
192	Dolomite 1850 HL			4,018*
192	Dolomite Sprint			4,898*
192	Spitfire 1500		4,500*	2,776*
193	TR 7		5,849*	3,877*
	TVR (Great Britain)			
193	3000 M			5,716*
194	Turbo			8,618*
194	Taimar			6,223*
194	Taimar Turbo			9,242*
	UAZ (USSR)			
248	469 B			—
	VANDEN PLAS (Great Britain)			
194	1500			3,733*
	VAUXHALL (Great Britain)			
195	Chevette E 2-door Saloon			2,252*
195	Chevette E 4-door Saloon			2,351*
195	Chevette E 3-door Hatchback			2,291*
195	Chevette L 2-door Saloon			2,477*
195	Chevette L 4-door Saloon			2,575*
195	Chevette L 3-door Hatchback			2,516*
195	Chevette L Estate Car			2,773*
195	Chevette GL 3-door Hatchback			2,652*
195	Chevette GLS 4-door Saloon			2,920*
195	Chevette GLS 3-door Hatchback			2,861*
195	Viva E 2-door Saloon			2,307*
195	Viva E 4-door Saloon			2,406*
195	Viva 1300 L 2-door Saloon			2,532*
195	Viva 1300 L 4-door Saloon			2,630*
195	Viva 1300 L Estate Car			2,828*
195	Viva 1300 GLS 2-door Saloon			2,877*
195	Viva 1300 GLS 4-door Saloon			2,975*
195	Viva 1300 GLS Estate Car			3,173*
195	Viva 1800 L 2-door Saloon			2,693*
195	Viva 1800 L 4-door Saloon			2,792*
195	Viva 1800 L Estate Car			2,989*
196	Magnum 1800 2-door Saloon			3,038*
196	Magnum 1800 4-door Saloon			3,138*
196	Magnum 1800 Estate Car			3,335*
196	Magnum 2300 2-door Saloon			3,200*
196	Magnum 2300 4-door Saloon			3,298*
196	Magnum 2300 Estate Car			3,496*
197	Cavalier 1300 L 2-door Saloon			2,897*
197	Cavalier 1300 L 4-door Saloon			2,995*
197	Cavalier 1600 L 2-door Saloon			3,058*
197	Cavalier 1600 L 4-door Saloon			3,157*
197	Cavalier 1600 GL 4-door Saloon			3,469*
197	Cavalier 1900 GL 4-door Saloon			3,631*
197	Cavalier 1900 GLS Coupé			4,295*
197	VX 1800 Saloon			3,605*
197	VX 1800 Estate Car			3,901*
197	VX 2300 Saloon			3,766*
197	VX 2300 Estate Car			4,062*
197	VX 2300 GLS Saloon			4,792*
197	VX 4/90 Saloon			4,474*
	VAZ (USSR)			
248	Lada 1200 4-door Sedan	1,955*		—
248	Lada 1200 5-door Combi	2,230*		—
248	Lada 1300 ES 4-door Sedan	2,271*		—
248	Lada 1500 4-door Sedan	2,515*		—
248	Lada 1500 5-door Combi	2,353*		—
248	Lada 1500 ES 5-door Combi	2,657*		—

Page	MAKE AND MODEL	Price in GB £	Price in USA $	Price ex Works
248	Lada 1600 4-door Sedan			—
248	Niva 2121 3-door Combi			—
	VOLKSWAGEN (Brazil)			
321	1300			49,000
321	1300 L Limousine			52,000
322	1600 Limousine			52,000
322	Passat 2-door Limousine			76,000
322	Passat 4-door Limousine			78,000
322	Passat L 2-door Limousine			78,000
322	Passat L 4-door Limousine			79,000
322	Passat LS 2-door Limousine			85,000
322	Passat TS 2-door Limousine			92,000
322	Passat LSE 4-door Limousine			—
322	Brasilia 2-door			64,000
322	Brasilia 4-door			64,000
323	Variant II			—
	VOLKSWAGEN (Germany FR)			
138	Polo 2-door Limousine	2,410*		8,620*
138	Polo L 2-door Limousine	2,665*		9,255*
138	Polo S 2-door Limousine			8,925*
138	Polo LS 2-door Limousine	2,895*		9,560*
138	Polo GLS 2-door Limousine			10,255*
139	Derby 2-door Limousine			9,055*
139	Derby L 2-door Limousine			9,690*
139	Derby S 2-door Limousine			9,360*
139	Derby LS 2-door Limousine			9,995*
139	Derby GLS 2-door Limousine			10,535*
140	Golf 2-door Limousine	2,650*	4,030*	9,540*
140	Golf 4-door Limousine			10,075*
140	Golf L 2-door Limousine		4,509*	10,250*
140	Golf L 4-door Limousine	3,065*	4,649*	10,785*
140	Golf GL 2-door Limousine		4,845*	11,030*
140	Golf GL 4-door Limousine		4,985*	11,565*
140	Golf S 2-door Limousine			10,360*
140	Golf S 4-door Limousine			10,895*
140	Golf LS 2-door Limousine	3,215*		11,070*
140	Golf LS 4-door Limousine			11,605*
140	Golf GLS 2-door Limousine			11,850*
140	Golf GLS 4-door Limousine	3,500*		12,385*
140	Golf GTI 2-door Limousine	4,192*		14,435*
141	Golf D 2-door Limousine			10,950*
141	Golf D 4-door Limousine			11,485*
141	Golf LD 2-door Limousine		4,704*	11,660*
141	Golf LD 4-door Limousine		4,844*	12,195*
141	Golf GL D 2-door Limousine		5,040*	12,440*
141	Golf GL D 4-door Limousine		5,180*	12,975*
141	Scirocco Coupé			12,460*
141	Scirocco L Coupé			13,430*
141	Scirocco S Coupé			12,990*
141	Scirocco LS Coupé			13,960*
141	Scirocco GT Coupé			14,460*
141	Scirocco GL Coupé	4,395*	5,875*	15,160*
141	Scirocco GTI Coupé	4,858*		16,780*
141	Scirocco GLI Coupé			17,480*
143	Passat 2-door Limousine			11,195*
143	Passat 4-door Limousine			11,745*
143	Passat Variant			12,105*
143	Passat L 2-door Limousine			11,945*
143	Passat L 4-door Limousine			12,495*
143	Passat L Variant			12,855*
143	Passat GL 2-door Limousine			12,855*
143	Passat GL 4-door Limousine			13,405*
143	Passat GL Variant			13,765*
143	Passat S 2-door Limousine			11,675*
143	Passat S 4-door Limousine			12,225*
143	Passat S Variant			12,585*
143	Passat LS 2-door Limousine		5,749*	12,425*
143	Passat LS 4-door Limousine	3,920*	5,849*	12,975*

Page	MAKE AND MODEL	Price in GB £	Price in USA $	Price ex Works
143	Passat LS Variant	4,065*	6,149*	13,335*
143	Passat GLS 2-door Limousine			13,335*
143	Passat GLS 4-door Limousine	4,190*		13,885*
143	Passat GLS Variant			14,245*
144	1303 Cabriolet		5,495*	—
144	181			13,730*
	VOLKSWAGEN (Mexico)			
313	1200			—
	VOLKSWAGEN (Nigeria)			
332	1200			—
	VOLVO (Holland)			
199	66 DL 2-door			13,480*
199	66 DL 3-door			14,480*
199	66 GL 2-door	2,757*		14,180*
199	66 GL 3-door	2,890*		15,180*
200	343 L			16,900*
200	343 DL	3,550*		17,900*
	VOLVO (Sweden)			
239	242 L			—
239	244 L			—
240	242 DL		6,645*	—
240	244 DL	4,769*	7,145*	—
240	244 GL	6,231*		—
240	242 GT		8,071*	—
240	245 L			—
241	245 DL	5,357*	7,495*	—
241	245 DLE	6,251*		—
241	264 DL	6,270*		—
241	264 GL	6,799*	10,245*	—
241	264 GLE	7,598*		—
241	264 TE			—
241	262 C		14,776*	—
241	265 DL	7,066*		—
241	265 GL	6,898*	10,495*	—
242	265 GLE	7,398*		—
	WARTBURG (Germany DDR)			
104	353 W			—
104	353 W Tourist			—
	YLN (Taiwan)			
345	707 De Luxe			—
345	803 DL			—
	ZAZ (USSR)			
249	968-A			—
	ZCZ (Yugoslavia)			
250	Zastava 750 M			—
250	Zastava 750 Luxe			—
250	Zastava 101			—
250	Zastava 1300			—
250	Zastava 1300 Luxe			—
	ZIL (USSR)			
249	114 Limousine			—
250	117 Limousine			—